THE *Life Recovery*™ BIBLE

Tyndale House
Publishers, Inc.
Wheaton, Illinois

Recovery™ BIBLE

The Living Bible

Library of Congress Cataloging-in-Publication Data

Bible. English. Living Bible. 1992.
The Life Recovery Bible : The Living Bible.
p. cm.
Includes indexes.
ISBN 0-8423-2827-0 (hardcover, deluxe) ISBN 0-8423-2083-0 (hardcover)
ISBN 0-8423-2809-2 (softcover)
1. Twelve-step programs—Religious aspects—Christianity—Meditations.
2. Bible—Meditations. I. Tyndale House Publishers.
II. Title.
BS550.2.T38 1992
220.5'208—dc20 92-11333

Printed in the United States of America
99 98 97 96 95 94 93 92
10 9 8 7 6 5 4 3 2

THE TWELVE STEPS

1. We admitted that we were powerless over our dependencies—that our life had become unmanageable.
2. We came to believe that a Power greater than ourselves could restore us to sanity.
3. We made a decision to turn our will and our life over to the care of God as we understood him.
4. We made a searching and fearless moral inventory of ourselves.
5. We admitted to God, to ourselves, and to another human being the exact nature of our wrongs.
6. We were entirely ready to have God remove all these defects of character.
7. We humbly asked him to remove our shortcomings.
8. We made a list of all persons we had harmed and became willing to make amends to them all.
9. We made direct amends to such people wherever possible, except when to do so would injure them or others.
10. We continued to take personal inventory and when we were wrong promptly admitted it.
11. We sought through prayer and meditation to improve our conscious contact with God, as we understood him, praying only for knowledge of his will for us and the power to carry it out.
12. Having had a spiritual awakening as the result of these steps, we tried to carry this message to others, and to practice these principles in all our affairs.

The Twelve Steps used in the Twelve Steps devotional reading plan in this Bible have been adapted from the Twelve Steps of Alcoholics Anonymous.

THE TWELVE STEPS OF ALCOHOLICS ANONYMOUS

1. We admitted we were powerless over alcohol—that our lives had become unmanageable.
2. Came to believe that a Power greater than ourselves could restore us to sanity.
3. Made a decision to turn our will and our lives over to the care of God *as we understood Him.*
4. Made a searching and fearless moral inventory of ourselves.
5. Admitted to God, to ourselves and to another human being the exact nature of our wrongs.
6. Were entirely ready to have God remove all these defects of character.
7. Humbly asked Him to remove our shortcomings.
8. Made a list of all persons we had harmed, and became willing to make amends to them all.
9. Made direct amends to such people wherever possible, except when to do so would injure them or others.
10. Continued to take personal inventory and when we were wrong promptly admitted it.
11. Sought through prayer and meditation to improve our conscious contact with God, *as we understood Him,* praying only for knowledge of His will for us and the power to carry that out.
12. Having had a spiritual awakening as the result of these steps, we tried to carry this message to alcoholics, and to practice these principles in all our affairs.

CONTENTS

THE BOOKS OF THE BIBLE

ALPHABETICAL BOOK LISTING

CONTRIBUTORS

Executive Editors
David A. Stoop
Stephen F. Arterburn

Associate Editors
A. Boyd Luter
Connie Neal

Managing Editor
Mark R. Norton

Editorial Staff
Derrick Blanchette
Meg Diehl
Diane Eble
Betsy Elliott
Dietrich Gruen
Lucille Leonard
Phyllis LePeau
Daryl Lucas
Judith Morse
Kathy Stinnette
Ramona Tucker
Sally van der Graaff
Esther Waldrop
Karen Walker
Wightman Weese

Production Staff
Dan Beery
Linda Oswald
Lois Rusch
Julee Schwarzburg

Graphic Designer
Timothy R. Botts

Writers
Donald E. Anderson
Shelley M. Chapin
R. Tony Cothren
Shelly O. Cunningham
Barry C. Davis
Harold Dollar
Joseph M. Espinoza
Thomas J. Finley
William J. Gaultiere
Ronald N. Glass
Daniel M. Hahn
Eric Hoey
Mark W. Hoffman
John C. Hutchison
Tommy A. Jarrett
Stephen M. Johnson
G. Ted Martinez
Kathy McReynolds
V. Eric Nachtrieb
Connie Neal
Stephen L. Newman
T. Ken Oberholtzer
Scott B. Rae
Richard O. Rigsby
Jane E. Rodgers
Walter B. Russell
Richard F. Travis

USER'S GUIDE

The Holy Bible is a book about recovery. It records how the world began and how God created it to be good. Then it tells us about the beginning of sin—about the first time people decided to reject God's plan. It spells out the fatal consequences that result from rejecting God's program. But the Bible doesn't leave us in despair. It reveals a plan for recovery and the source of the power to accomplish it. It provides us with the only pathway to wholeness—God's program for reconciliation and healing.

Each feature in *The Life Recovery Bible* leads its readers to the powerful resources for recovery found in the Holy Scriptures:

DEVOTIONAL READING PLANS

Each devotional is set near the Scripture it comments on and directs the reader to the next devotional in the reading chain. To get a bird's-eye view of each of these reading plans, turn to the indexes at the back of this Bible.

* The **Twelve Step Devotional Reading Plan** includes eighty-four Bible-based devotionals built around the Twelve Steps.

To begin this reading plan, turn to page 17.

* The **Recovery Principle Devotional Reading Plan** is composed of fifty-six Bible-based devotionals shaped around principles important in the recovery process.

To begin this reading plan, turn to page 3.

* The **Serenity Prayer Devotional Reading Plan** is made up of thirty Bible-based devotionals related to the Serenity Prayer.

To begin this reading plan, turn to page 21.

RECOVERY PROFILES

In this feature over sixty individuals and relationships are profiled and important recovery lessons are drawn from their lives. For a quick view of the profiles included, see the Index to Recovery Profiles on page 1527.

INTRODUCTORY MATERIAL FOR BIBLE BOOKS

Each book of the Bible is preceded by a number of helpful features.

* **Book Introductions** present the content and themes from the standpoint of recovery.
* **The Big Picture** gives a panoramic view of the book in outline form.
* **The Bottom Line** provides vital historical information for the book.
* **Recovery Themes** presents and discusses important themes for people in recovery.

RECOVERY COMMENTARY NOTES

The Bible text is supported by numerous **Recovery Notes** that pinpoint passages and thoughts important to recovery. The notes are indexed in the Life Recovery Topical Index beginning on page 1473.

* Additional commentary material is provided in the **Recovery Reflections** that follow many of the Bible books. Here, notes are topically arranged and reflect back on the preceding book. The topics discussed in this feature are indexed in the Index to Recovery Reflections on page 1535.

INDEXES

The **Life Recovery Topical Index** guides the reader to the important notes, profiles, devotionals, and recovery themes related to more than a hundred terms important to issues in the recovery process.

* The **Index to Recovery Profiles** alphabetically lists and locates the sixty Relationship Profiles that appear in this Bible.
* The **Index to Twelve Step Devotionals** lists and locates the eighty-four Twelve Step devotionals.
* The **Index to Recovery Principle Devotionals** lists and locates the fifty-six recovery principle devotionals.
* The **Index to Serenity Prayer Devotionals** lists and locates the thirty Serenity Prayer devotionals.
* The **Index to Recovery Reflections** lists and locates the various topics discussed in the Reflections feature of this Bible.

PREFACE

THE BIBLE is the greatest book on recovery ever written. In its pages, we watch as God sets out a plan for the recovery of his broken people and creation. We meet numerous individuals whose hurting lives are mended through the wisdom and power of God. We meet the God who is waiting with arms outstretched for all of us to turn back to him, seek after his ways, and recover the wonderful plan he has for us.

Many of us are just waking up to the fact that recovery is an essential part of life for everyone. It is the simple but challenging process of daily seeking God's will for our life instead of demanding to go our own way. It is allowing God to do for us what we cannot do for ourselves, while also taking the steps necessary to draw closer to our Creator and Redeemer. It is a process of allowing God to heal our wounded soul so we can help others in the process of healing. All of us need to take part in this process; it is an inherent part of being human.

Let us set out together on a journey toward healing and newfound strength. Not strength found within ourselves, but strength found through trusting God and allowing him to direct our decisions and plans. This journey will take us through the Twelve Steps and other materials designed to help us focus on the powerful provisions God offers for recovery. *The Life Recovery Bible* will enrich our experience and expand our understanding of the God who loves us and sent his Son to die that we might be made whole.

Without God, there is no recovery, only disappointing substitutions and repeated failure. We pray that the resources within these pages will help us all better understand who God is and how he wants to heal our brokenness and set us on the path toward wholeness.

THE OLD TESTAMENT

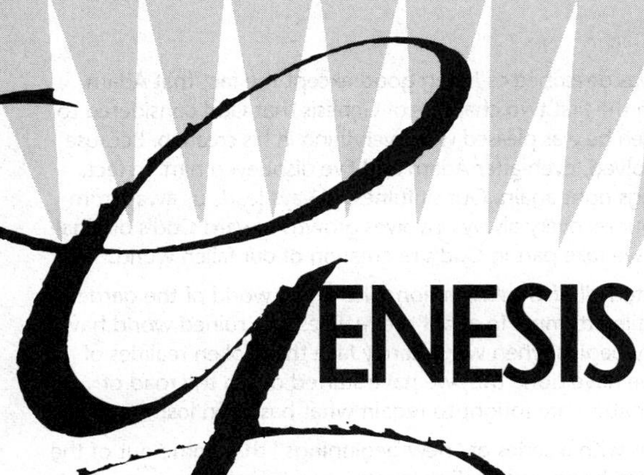

GENESIS

THE BIG PICTURE

A. GOD SETS THE STAGE (1:1–11:32)
1. Formation of the Universe (1:1–2:25)
   a. God creates matter, energy, and the natural order (1:1–2:3)
   b. God prepares pristine surroundings for the first family (2:4-25)
2. Fall of the Human Race (3:1–3:24)
   a. Commission of sin (3:1-8)
   b. Curse on sin (3:9-24)
3. Failure of Society (4:1–9:29)
   a. Failure of humankind (4:1–6:22)
   b. Flood of judgment (7:1–9:29)
4. Folly of Rebellion (10:1–11:32)
   a. Dispersal of the people (10:1-32)
   b. Disobedience of the people (11:1-32)

B. GOD CHOOSES THE PLAYERS (12:1–50:26)
1. Abraham (12:1–25:18)
2. Isaac (25:19–27:46)
3. Jacob (28:1–36:43)
4. Joseph (37:1–50:26)

The book of Genesis is a book of beginnings. It records how the world began and how God created it to be good. It tells us about the first people and how God made them to be excellent. But then it tells us about the beginning of sin—about the first time people decided to reject the program God had laid out for them. It records the first days of shame and of covering up. It records the beginning of our separation from God, each other, and the world God gave us.

We will see how people with perfect health, living in a perfect environment, rebelled against God. And we will see the consequences of their rebellion. We are given intimate glimpses of individuals dominated by hatred, drunkenness, lust, unhealthy family relationships, money, cheating, irresponsibility, dishonesty, jealousy, violence, and other difficulties.

But the book of Genesis doesn't leave us in despair. It tells us of yet another beginning. It records how God chose a man named Abraham to father a special nation. And through this nation would come the solution for our separation from God, each other, and the world God gave us. Genesis begins the story of how God began his work of healing broken humanity—a healing to be expressed in the laws he would give his people, and culminating in the coming of Jesus, the promised Messiah.

The book of Genesis reminds us of where all our problems began. It spells out the fatal consequences of rejecting God's program. But it also begins the agelong story of God's unstoppable love for the human race. Through this book we will discover that the only pathway to spiritual wholeness is in following God's program.

THE BOTTOM LINE

PURPOSE: To tell us about the beginning of things, including human opportunities and difficulties, and to demonstrate that God's solutions are the only ones that work. AUTHOR: Moses. AUDIENCE: The people of Israel. DATE WRITTEN: Chapters 1–11 deal with the undateable past; the events of chapters 12–50 are to be dated between about 2000 and 1800 B.C. The book was probably written shortly after 1445 B.C. SETTING: Mesopotamia, then Canaan, finally Egypt. KEY VERSE: "And Abram believed God; then God considered him righteous on account of his faith" (15:6). KEY EVENTS: Creation, the Fall, the Flood, the Tower of Babel. KEY PEOPLE: Abraham, Isaac, Jacob, Joseph.

RECOVERY THEMES

A Good Creation: Everything about God's creation was described as being good except the fact that Adam was alone. In fact, Adam's isolation is the only thing in the first two chapters of Genesis that God considered to be a problem. When God created a partner for man, then he was pleased with everything in his creation. Because God was pleased with what he created, he stayed involved, even after Adam and Eve disobeyed him. In fact, ever since the Fall God has been seeking to make things right again. Our sinfulness always leads us away from God and distorts the way God created us to be. But our recovery always involves growth toward God's original ideal for the human race. As we progress in recovery, we take part in God's re-creation of our fallen world.

A Ruined World: Adam and Eve's disobedience affected all of God's creation. The idyllic world of the garden was gone forever, and life became a struggle. Our futile attempts to avoid the realities of a ruined world have led us into all kinds of destructive behaviors. Recovery begins when we squarely face the broken realities of our world—its daily struggles and hardships. Once we have done this, we have started down the road of recovery. We have entered the spiritual arena where battles are fought to regain what has been lost.

Promises of Healing: The book of Genesis presents us with a series of "new beginnings" that come out of the ruin of our sinfulness. In the original Fall, God promised hope and healing for us when he told the serpent that the offspring of the woman would crush his head. When people generally continued to disobey, God sent the Flood as judgment for their sinfulness. After the Flood, God again promised victory and represented that promise with a rainbow. Then the human race rejected God again, building a great tower as a memorial of their pride. In response, God confused their languages, further fragmenting society. Then God chose a man named Abram and promised to bless all nations of the world through his offspring. Each time that human sin brought ruin, God promised victory and recovery in the face of it.

Hope for Reconciliation: As people began to experience the terrible consequences of their disobedience, God didn't leave them to figure out a plan for recovery all alone. He didn't leave a long list of principles or rules to follow that would repair their damaged relationships. Instead, God always worked with people on a very personal level in the recovery process. As we enter into the recovery process, we find it to be relational in character. It requires us to seek reconciliation with people close to us; and this includes God. In Genesis, God modeled this pattern for us time and again. He chose certain individuals and worked patiently in their lives, reconciling them with the people around them.

CHAPTER 1

God Creates a Good World

When God began creating the heavens and
the earth, 2the earth was a shapeless, chaotic
mass, with the Spirit of God brooding over
the dark vapors.
3Then God said, "Let there be light." And
light appeared. 4,5And God was pleased with it
and divided the light from the darkness. He
called the light "daytime," and the darkness
"nighttime." Together they formed the first
day.
6And God said, "Let the vapors separate to
form the sky above and the oceans below."
7,8So God made the sky, dividing the vapor
above from the water below. This all happened on the second day.
9,10Then God said, "Let the water beneath
the sky be gathered into oceans so that the
dry land will emerge." And so it was. Then
God named the dry land "earth," and the
water "seas." And God was pleased. 11,12And he
said, "Let the earth burst forth with every sort
of grass and seed-bearing plant, and fruit trees
with seeds inside the fruit, so that these seeds
will produce the kinds of plants and fruits
they came from." And so it was, and God was
pleased. 13This all occurred on the third day.

1:4 God was pleased with his creation. He declared that it was good. God stopped now and then to approve of what he designed and created (1:4-5, 9-10, 11-12, 18, 21-22, 25, 31). Many of our problems and dependencies result from the misuse of God's good creation. Our recovery may involve discovering the good things that we have misused and learning how to enjoy them in the way God intended.

1:24 The phrase "And so it was" (also in 1:9-12, 14-15) shows us that God's creative activity was done in complete conformity to the specifications he had originally intended. God accomplishes his will with certainty and precision. It should reassure us to know that God's good desires for us can be accomplished with the same certainty.

2:2-3 This is the first mention of Sabbath rest—one day of rest in seven. By his example God encourages us to designate a portion of our life to rest and spiritual rejuvenation. Without proper rest, it is very difficult to deal with the other matters in our life, especially our progress in recovery.

14,15Then God said, "Let bright lights appear
in the sky to give light to the earth and to
identify the day and the night; they shall
bring about the seasons on the earth, and
mark the days and years." And so it was. 16For
God had made two huge lights, the sun and
moon, to shine down upon the earth—the
larger one, the sun, to preside over the day
and the smaller one, the moon, to preside
through the night; he had also made the stars.
17And God set them in the sky to light the
earth, 18and to preside over the day and night,
and to divide the light from the darkness. And
God was pleased. 19This all happened on the
fourth day.

20Then God said, "Let the waters teem with
fish and other life, and let the skies be filled
with birds of every kind." 21,22So God created
great sea animals, and every sort of fish and
every kind of bird. And God looked at them
with pleasure, and blessed them all. "Multiply
and stock the oceans," he told them, and to
the birds he said, "Let your numbers increase.
Fill the earth!" 23That ended the fifth day.

24And God said, "Let the earth bring forth
every kind of animal—cattle and reptiles and
wildlife of every kind." And so it was. 25God
made all sorts of wild animals and cattle and
reptiles. And God was pleased with what he
had done.

26Then God said, "Let us make a man—
someone like ourselves, to be the master of all
life upon the earth and in the skies and in the
seas."

27So God made man like his Maker.
Like God did God make man;
Man and maid did he make them.

28And God blessed them and told them, "Multiply and fill the earth and subdue it; you are
masters of the fish and birds and all the animals. 29And look! I have given you the seed-
bearing plants throughout the earth and all
the fruit trees for your food. 30And I've given
all the grass and plants to the animals and
birds for their food." 31Then God looked over
all that he had made, and it was excellent in
every way. This ended the sixth day.

CHAPTER 2

Now at last the heavens and earth were successfully completed, with all that they contained. 2So on the seventh day, having
finished his task, God ceased from this work
he had been doing, 3and God blessed the
seventh day and declared it holy, because it

▸ The recovery principle devotional reading plan begins here.

Self-perception

READ GENESIS 1:26-31

If we have lived in bondage to our compulsive behaviors for a while, we probably see more bad inside us than good. Many of us tend to see life in terms of all or nothing. As a result, we probably think of ourself as being all bad. But in recovery, we need a balanced understanding of ourself. We need to see that along with our bad points we have also been gifted with strengths. It's not an either/or proposition. A balanced view of ourself will help us better understand our shortcomings while also giving us greater hope in our potential.

At the end of the fifth day of creation God had made everything except for the first man and woman. The Bible tells us that when he had finished, "God was pleased with what he had done." Then God created the first man and woman. "So God made man like his Maker. Like God did God make man. . . . And God blessed them and told them, 'Multiply and fill the earth and subdue it; you are masters of the fish and birds and all the animals.' . . . Then God looked over all that he had made, and it was excellent in every way" (Genesis 1:25, 27-31).

God made a distinction between his estimation of the human race and the rest of creation. God made us in his very image, with capacities far beyond those of mere animals. God was (and is) excited about us! He gave us abilities and responsibilities to reflect his own nature in all of creation. When he created us, he was proud of what he made!

Although we have a sinful nature which came after the Fall, we also must remember that we were created in the likeness of God. There's an excellence and dignity inherent in being human that should cause us to ponder our potential for good as well as bad. ***Turn to page 25, Genesis 22.***

was the day when he ceased this work of creation.

[4]Here is a summary of the events in the creation of the heavens and earth when the Lord God made them.

[5]There were no plants or grain sprouting up across the earth at first, for the Lord God hadn't sent any rain; nor was there anyone to farm the soil. [6](However, water welled up from the ground at certain places and flowed across the land.)

God Creates Adam and Eve

[7]The time came when the Lord God formed a man's body from the dust of the ground and breathed into it the breath of life. And man became a living person.

[8]Then the Lord God planted a garden in Eden, to the east, and placed in the garden the man he had formed. [9]The Lord God planted all sorts of beautiful trees there in the garden, trees producing the choicest of fruit. At the center of the garden he placed the Tree of Life, and also the Tree of Conscience, giving knowledge of Good and Bad. [10]A river from the land of Eden flowed through the garden to water it; afterwards the river divided into four branches. [11,12]One of these was named the Pishon; it winds across the entire length of the land of Havilah, where nuggets of pure gold are found, also beautiful bdellium and even lapis lazuli. [13]The second branch is called the Gihon, crossing the entire length of the land of Cush. [14]The third branch is the Tigris, which flows to the east of the city of Asher. And the fourth is the Euphrates.

[15]The Lord God placed the man in the Garden of Eden as its gardener, to tend and care for it. [16,17]But the Lord God gave the man this warning: "You may eat any fruit in the garden except fruit from the Tree of Conscience—for its fruit will open your eyes to make you aware of right and wrong, good and bad. If you eat its fruit, you will be doomed to die."

[18]And the Lord God said, "It isn't good for man to be alone; I will make a companion for him, a helper suited to his needs." [19,20]So the Lord God formed from the soil every kind of animal and bird, and brought them to the man to see what he would call them; and whatever he called them, that was their name. But still there was no proper helper for the man. [21]Then the Lord God caused the man to fall into a deep sleep, and took one of his ribs and closed up the place from which he had removed it, [22]and made the rib into a woman, and brought her to the man.

[23]"This is it!" Adam exclaimed. "She is part of my own bone and flesh! Her name is 'woman' because she was taken out of a man." [24]This explains why a man leaves his father and mother and is joined to his wife in such a way that the two become one person. [25]Now although the man and his wife were both naked, neither of them was embarrassed or ashamed.

CHAPTER 3

Adam and Eve Sin

The serpent was the craftiest of all the creatures the Lord God had made. So the serpent came to the woman. "Really?" he asked. "*None* of the fruit in the garden? God says you mustn't eat *any* of it?"

[2,3]"Of course we may eat it," the woman told him. "It's only the fruit from the tree at the *center* of the garden that we are not to eat. God says we mustn't eat it or even touch it, or we will die."

[4]"That's a lie!" the serpent hissed. "You'll not die! [5]God knows very well that the instant

---

2:8-14 God provided a perfect environment for the first people. We often blame our outward circumstances for our difficulties. It is important to note here that in spite of their ideal surroundings, our first parents fell—they failed. Although the environment we live in can certainly add to our problems, it is never entirely at fault. We need to take responsibility for our own mistakes and failures.

3:1-5 The account here pictures for us the process of temptation. The serpent offered something that had been forbidden by God as a very attractive option. The serpent also caused Eve to doubt God and the truth of his Word. During the debate, Eve offered some halfhearted opposition, but her growing doubt in God weakened her resolve. In the end she gave in. Satan strengthened his temptation by weakening Eve's faith in God. Staying close to God and maintaining our faith in him will weaken the power of temptation in our life.

3:12-13 When Adam was questioned, notice that he blamed the woman for his problem. He even backhandedly blamed God by reminding God that he was the one who gave him the woman in the first place. Then Eve blamed the serpent for the problem. Passing the buck is a standard human response to guilt. But our recovery requires that we take a thorough inventory of our life, accepting responsibility for everything we have done or failed to do.

ADAM & EVE

It was an ideal situation: a man and his wife living harmoniously together in a lush, beautiful garden that God had created for their pleasure. They enjoyed perfect relationships with God and with each other. But when Eve submitted to temptation, they overstepped their God-given boundaries and plunged the human race into sin. Harmony was broken. Shame and guilt penetrated their lives and created an invisible barrier between them and God. The consequences of their disobedience and lack of self-control are with us to this day.

Adam and Eve knew that they had gone against God's plan—a plan that was created with their best interests in mind. And the consequences of their sin followed immediately. Right away they became afraid of the God who loved them so much, and they hid from his presence. They also became ashamed of their nakedness and set out to cover themselves. The relationship between the man and his wife began to show cracks and strains. Accusations were made. Blame was shifted. Neither of them wanted to be held accountable. They refused to admit that they were wrong. Needless to say, their relationship was damaged. Their sin had separated them from each other and from God.

But the story doesn't end there. Adam and Eve stayed together in spite of the shame and guilt they felt. Their lives were marred by sin and scarred by wounds inflicted on one another. However, they faced the reality that life had to go on and began to build a new life together. And by love, commitment, and the grace of God, they persevered through life's trials.

The story of Adam and Eve is found in the opening chapters of Genesis. Adam and/or Eve are also mentioned in 1 Chronicles 1:1; Romans 5:12-21; 1 Corinthians 15:22, 45-47; 2 Corinthians 11:3; and 1 Timothy 2:13-15.

STRENGTHS AND ACCOMPLISHMENTS:
- They were the parents of the entire human race.
- They were committed to each other through the trials they faced.
- Their story provides us with the first illustration of God's grace.

WEAKNESSES AND MISTAKES:
- They were disobedient to the plan that God had revealed to them.
- They were not willing to take responsibility for their sin.
- They made excuses rather than admitting the truth.
- They brought sin into the world and passed it on to their descendants.

LESSONS FROM THEIR LIVES:
- A good marriage requires love and commitment even through the tough times.
- Relationships that accept God's grace and forgiveness persevere through life's difficulties.
- Complacency is a breeding ground for temptation—be on guard against Satan's schemes.
- The mistakes of parents are often passed on to their descendants.

KEY VERSE:
"Then God said, 'Let us make a man—someone like ourselves, to be the master of all life upon the earth and in the skies and in the seas.' So God made man like his Maker. Like God did God make man; man and maid did he make them" (Genesis 1:26-27).

---

you eat it you will become like him, for your eyes will be opened—you will be able to distinguish good from evil!"

6The woman was convinced. How lovely and fresh looking it was! And it would make her so wise! So she ate some of the fruit and gave some to her husband, and he ate it too.
7And as they ate it, suddenly they became aware of their nakedness, and were embarrassed. So they strung fig leaves together to cover themselves around the hips.

8That evening they heard the sound of the Lord God walking in the garden; and they hid themselves among the trees. 9The Lord God called to Adam, "Why are you hiding?"

10And Adam replied, "I heard you coming and didn't want you to see me naked. So I hid."

11"Who told you you were naked?" the Lord God asked. "Have you eaten fruit from the tree I warned you about?"

12"Yes," Adam admitted, "but it was the woman you gave me who brought me some, and I ate it."

13Then the Lord God asked the woman, "How could you do such a thing?"

"The serpent tricked me," she replied.

14So the Lord God said to the serpent, "This is your punishment: You are singled out from among all the domestic and wild animals of the whole earth—to be cursed. You shall grovel in the dust as long as you live, crawling
along on your belly. 15From now on you and the woman will be enemies, as will your offspring and hers. You will strike his heel, but he will crush your head."

16Then God said to the woman, "You shall
bear children in intense pain and suffering; yet
even so, you shall welcome your husband's
affections, and he shall be your master."
17And to Adam, God said, "Because you
listened to your wife and ate the fruit when I
told you not to, I have placed a curse upon the
soil. All your life you will struggle to extract a
living from it. 18It will grow thorns and thistles for you, and you shall eat its grasses. 19All
your life you will sweat to master it, until your
dying day. Then you will return to the ground
from which you came. For you were made
from the ground, and to the ground you will
return."
20The man named his wife Eve (meaning
"The life-giving one"), for he said, "She shall
become the mother of all mankind"; 21and the
Lord God clothed Adam and his wife with
garments made from skins of animals.
22Then the Lord said, "Now that the man
has become as we are, knowing good from
bad, what if he eats the fruit of the Tree of Life
and lives forever?" 23So the Lord God banished
him forever from the Garden of Eden, and sent
him out to farm the ground from which he
had been taken. 24Thus God expelled him, and
placed mighty angels at the east of the Garden
of Eden, with a flaming sword to guard the
entrance to the Tree of Life.

CHAPTER 4

Cain Murders Abel

Then Adam had sexual intercourse with Eve
his wife, and she conceived and gave birth to
a son, Cain (meaning "I have created"). For,
as she said, "With God's help, I have created
a man!" 2Her next child was his brother, Abel.
Abel became a shepherd, while Cain was a
farmer. 3At harvest time Cain brought the
Lord a gift of his farm produce, 4and Abel
brought the fatty cuts of meat from his best
lambs, and presented them to the Lord. And
the Lord accepted Abel's offering, 5but not
Cain's. This made Cain both dejected and
very angry, and his face grew dark with fury.
6"Why are you angry?" the Lord asked him.
"Why is your face so dark with rage? 7It can be
bright with joy if you will do what you
should! But if you refuse to obey, watch out.
Sin is waiting to attack you, longing to destroy you. But you can conquer it!"
8One day Cain suggested to his brother,
"Let's go out into the fields." And while they
were together there, Cain attacked and killed
his brother.
9But afterwards the Lord asked Cain,
"Where is your brother? Where is Abel?"
"How should I know?" Cain retorted. "Am
I supposed to keep track of him wherever he
goes?"
10But the Lord said, "Your brother's blood
calls to me from the ground. What have you
done? 11You are hereby banished from this
ground which you have defiled with your
brother's blood. 12No longer will it yield crops
for you, even if you toil on it forever! From
now on you will be a fugitive and a tramp
upon the earth, wandering from place to
place."

3:21 The first death did occur on the day of Adam's sin, but it was the death of an animal to provide a covering for Adam and Eve's nakedness. God's immediate provision for sin was the slaying of an innocent substitute to provide skins to clothe the guilty couple. The clothing they wore must have served as a reminder—engraving the sight of the dying animal in their minds—a picture of the terrible consequences of their sin. As we recognize the suffering we may have caused others, we also are reminded of the consequences of rejecting God's program for our life.

4:6-7 When God rejected Cain's offering, Cain reacted first with disappointment, but then with anger. God did not reject Cain for his strong feelings, but offered him an opportunity for a new start. How sad that Cain refused this second chance and went out instead to kill his brother. We need to be careful when we face obstacles to our recovery. We need to carefully weigh the strong feelings we encounter before acting on them. If we don't, we may be passing up an excellent opportunity for a fresh start. God is not put off by our strong feelings. Our recovery is based on God's grace, which always offers us an opportunity to begin again.

4:15 The "mark of Cain" was not, as some have taught, a badge of guilt. It was a sign that God gave to Cain for his protection. Even after Cain's great failure, God desired to protect him from harm. Many of us look back and marvel at how God protected us before we began our recovery. He wants us to be restored and often protects us in the midst of evil so that we are not destroyed. Even after our greatest failures, our gracious God desires only our healing and recovery.

4:19-24 Some people insist that the human race is developing and becoming better and better. When we compare Lamech with his ancestor Cain, it is obvious that the trend usually goes in the opposite direction. Without God's help, we only get worse. It is only by following God's program and receiving his grace that we can hope to escape the natural slide toward pain and destruction.

13Cain replied to the Lord, "My punishment is greater than I can bear. 14For you have
banished me from my farm and from you,
and made me a fugitive and a tramp; and
everyone who sees me will try to kill me."
15The Lord replied, "They won't kill you, for
I will give seven times your punishment to
anyone who does." Then the Lord put an
identifying mark on Cain as a warning not to
kill him. 16So Cain went out from the presence
of the Lord and settled in the land of Nod, east
of Eden.

Cain's Family

17Then Cain's wife conceived and presented
him with a baby son named Enoch; so when
Cain founded a city, he named it Enoch, after
his son.
18Enoch was the father of Irad; Irad was the
father of Mehujael; Mehujael was the father
of Methusael; Methusael was the father of
Lamech;
19Lamech married two wives—Adah and
Zillah. 20To Adah was born a baby named
Jabal. He became the first of the cattlemen
and those living in tents. 21His brother's name
was Jubal, the first musician—the inventor of
the harp and flute. 22To Lamech's other wife,
Zillah, was born Tubal-cain. He opened the
first foundry forging instruments of bronze
and iron.
23One day Lamech said to Adah and Zillah,
"Listen to me, my wives. I have killed a youth
who attacked and wounded me. 24If anyone
who kills Cain will be punished seven times,
anyone taking revenge against me for killing
that youth should be punished seventy-seven
times!"

Adam's Family

25Later on Eve gave birth to another son and
named him Seth (meaning "Granted"); for, as
Eve put it, "God has granted me another son
for the one Cain killed." 26When Seth grew up,
he had a son and named him Enosh. It was
during his lifetime that men first began to call
themselves "the Lord's people."

CHAPTER 5

Here is a list of some of the descendants of
Adam—the man who was like God from the
day of his creation. 2God created man and
woman and blessed them, and called them
Man from the start.
3-5*Adam:* Adam was 130 years old when his
son Seth was born, the very image of his
father in every way. After Seth was born,

Coming out of Hiding

BIBLE READING: Genesis 3:6-13

We made a searching and fearless moral inventory of ourselves.

Many of us have spent our life in a state of hiding, ashamed of who we are inside. We may hide by living a double life, using our drug of choice to make us feel like someone else, or by self-righteously setting ourselves above others. Step Four involves uncovering the things we have been hiding, even from ourselves.

After Adam and Eve disobeyed God, "suddenly they became aware of their nakedness, and were embarrassed. So they strung fig leaves together to cover themselves around the hips. . . . The Lord God called to Adam, 'Why are you hiding?' And Adam replied, 'I heard you coming and didn't want you to see me naked. So I hid'" (Genesis 3:7-10). Human beings have been covering up and hiding ever since!

Jesus consistently confronted the religious leaders for their hypocrisy. The word *hypocrite* describes a person who pretends to have virtues or qualities that he really doesn't have. One time Jesus said to them, "Hypocrites! You are so careful to polish the outside of the cup, but the inside is foul with extortion and greed. . . . First cleanse the inside of the cup, and then the whole cup will be clean" (Matthew 23:25-26).

When the real person inside comes out of hiding, we will have to deal with some dirt! Making this inventory is a good way to "cleanse the inside"; and some of that cleansing may involve bathing our life with tears. It is only by uncovering the hidden parts of ourselves that we will be able to change the outer person, including our addictive/compulsive behaviors. ***Turn to page 541, Nehemiah 8.***

Adam lived another 800 years, producing sons and daughters, and died at the age of 930.

6-8*Seth:* Seth was 105 years old when his son Enosh was born. Afterwards he lived another 807 years, producing sons and daughters, and died at the age of 912.

9-11*Enosh:* Enosh was ninety years old when his son Kenan was born. Afterwards he lived another 815 years, producing sons and daughters, and died at the age of 905.

12-14*Kenan:* Kenan was seventy years old when his son Mahalalel was born. Afterwards he lived another 840 years, producing sons and daughters, and died at the age of 910.

15-17*Mahalalel:* Mahalalel was sixty-five years old when his son Jared was born. Afterwards he lived 830 years, producing sons and daughters, and died at the age of 895.

18-20*Jared:* Jared was 162 years old when his son Enoch was born. Afterwards he lived another 800 years, producing sons and daughters, and died at the age of 962.

21-24*Enoch:* Enoch was sixty-five years old when his son Methuselah was born. Afterwards he lived another 300 years in fellowship with God, and produced sons and daughters; then, when he was 365, and in constant touch with God, he disappeared, for God took him!

25-27*Methuselah:* Methuselah was 187 years old when his son Lamech was born; afterwards he lived another 782 years, producing sons and daughters, and died at the age of 969.

28-31*Lamech:* Lamech was 182 years old when his son Noah was born. Lamech named him Noah (meaning "Relief") because he said, "He will bring us relief from the hard work of farming this ground which God has cursed." Afterwards Lamech lived 595 years, producing sons and daughters, and died at the age of 777.

32*Noah:* Noah was 500 years old and had three sons, Shem, Ham, and Japheth.

CHAPTER 6

The People Turn from God

Now a population explosion took place upon the earth. It was at this time that beings from the spirit world looked upon the beautiful earth women and took any they desired to be their wives. 3Then Jehovah said, "My Spirit must not forever be disgraced in man, wholly evil as he is. I will give him 120 years to mend his ways."

4In those days, and even afterwards, when the evil beings from the spirit world were sexually involved with human women, their children became giants, of whom so many legends are told. 5When the Lord God saw the extent of human wickedness, and that the trend and direction of men's lives were only towards evil, 6he was sorry he had made them. It broke his heart.

7And he said, "I will blot out from the face of the earth all mankind that I created. Yes, and the animals too, and the reptiles and the birds. For I am sorry I made them."

Noah Obeys God

8But Noah was a pleasure to the Lord. Here is the story of Noah:9,10He was the only truly righteous man living on the earth at that

5:1-32 This chapter has often been called the obituary column. Its recurring refrain is "and [he] died . . . and [he] died . . . and [he] died." Although physical death did not occur on the day Adam sinned, it did eventually come. Adam had reestablished his relationship with God, but the physical consequences of his sin could not be avoided forever. We may hope that after reestablishing our relationship with God, our troubles will be over. But a relationship with God rarely frees us from the consequences of past sin. The consequences usually catch up with us sooner or later. But if we suffer for past mistakes, we can know that God will be with us each step of the way.

5:21-24 Little is said about the spiritual state of these patriarchs of the human race. But the account of Enoch's life provides us with a bright spot in this otherwise dismal chapter. Enoch was said to be "in constant touch with God." His life should give us hope. He wasn't trapped by the mistakes or apathy of his peers and ancestors. Instead, he made a new start. And he did it by constantly walking with God.

6:3 In spite of the sinfulness of the human race, God still acted graciously toward them. He gave them 120 years to mend their ways and turn to him. God always gives ample warning before he sends judgment. He does this to give us time to change our ways. He wants us to experience the advantages of a life lived according to his plans and purposes. He never desires our destruction.

6:8-10 God did not destroy the righteous with the wicked. These verses are another statement of God's grace. God extended grace to Noah and his family. Noah knew Enoch's secret. He lived his life in constant fellowship with God. He broke the mold set by his ancestors and neighbors by drawing close to God. As a result, Noah lived through the flood and became the second father of the human race.

CAIN & ABEL

How often parents of two children have been heard to exclaim, "There have *never* been two children who were more different!" Adam and Eve could well have been the originators of that comment. Cain apparently felt himself to be in direct competition with Abel. This led to a rivalry that was never resolved, resulting in a major tragedy.

Cain became a farmer and Abel a shepherd. It was their offerings, however, not their occupations, that revealed the true nature of their character. Abel did things God's way, following his requirements. He is called "righteous" in Matthew 23:35, and Hebrews 11:4 says his offering was made by faith. Cain, on the other hand, did things his own way. Jude suggests that his "way" was that of rebellion (Jude 1:11). Cain brought an offering of produce from his gardens, while Abel brought the fatty cuts of meat from his best lambs.

Abel's altar was ugly; every sense was assaulted by the bloody carcass lying across it. But the blood was a part of God's plan according to Hebrews 12:24. Cain's offering had the potential of being beautiful. Picture fresh produce, just out of the garden—fruits, vegetables, flowers, and grain—probably lovingly and artistically arranged. Perhaps Cain wanted to be accepted by God on the basis of his own merits. He may not have been willing to have a relationship with God based on a bloody sacrifice. When God accepted Abel's offering and rejected Cain's, Cain became angry. But God did not reject him for his anger. Even at that point, God reasoned with him. He offered Cain another opportunity to change his mind and accept divine grace; but still Cain refused. Jealous of Abel whose offering had been accepted and raging because God had rejected his own, Cain murdered his brother.

Cain tried to hide his terrible deed, but God was not fooled. God confronted Cain with the murder and assigned the consequence of lifelong exile. Cain spent the rest of his life as an alien, wandering in lands far from his family. But even in exile God protected him; God placed his mark upon Cain to protect him from being killed.

STRENGTHS AND ACCOMPLISHMENTS:
- Abel was obedient to God.
- Abel is the first hero mentioned in the "Gallery of Faith" in Hebrews 11.
- Both sons developed skills and worked hard in the occupations they chose.

WEAKNESSES AND MISTAKES:
- Cain insisted on doing things his own way.
- When rejected, Cain reacted with rage.
- Cain allowed his rage to lead him to commit the first murder.

LESSONS FROM THEIR LIVES:
- Our righteousness is based on our willingness to follow God's program by faith.
- Feeling anger does not separate us from God unless we express it in destructive ways.
- Though we may try to hide our sins for a time, God's justice will prevail.

KEY VERSE:
"It was by faith that Abel obeyed God and brought an offering that pleased God more than Cain's offering did. God accepted Abel and proved it by accepting his gift; and though Abel is long dead, we can still learn lessons from him about trusting God" (Hebrews 11:4).

The account of Cain and Abel is given in Genesis 4. Both also are mentioned in Hebrews 11:4 and 1 John 3:12. Cain alone is referred to in Jude 1:11; Abel is spoken of in Matthew 23:35; Luke 11:51; and Hebrews 12:24.

---

time. He tried always to conduct his affairs according to God's will. And he had three sons—Shem, Ham, and Japheth.

11Meanwhile, the crime rate was rising rapidly across the earth, and, as seen by God, the world was rotten to the core.

12,13As God observed how bad it was, and saw that all mankind was vicious and depraved, he said to Noah, "I have decided to destroy all mankind; for the earth is filled with crime because of man. Yes, I will destroy mankind from the earth. 14Make a boat from resinous wood, sealing it with tar; and construct decks and stalls throughout the ship. 15Make it 450 feet long, 75 feet wide, and 45 feet high. 16Construct a skylight all the way around the ship, eighteen inches below the roof; and make three decks inside the boat—a bottom, middle, and upper deck—and put a door in the side.

17"Look! I am going to cover the earth with a flood and destroy every living being—everything in which there is the breath of life. All will die. 18But I promise to keep you safe in the ship, with your wife and your sons and their wives. [19,20]Bring a pair of every animal—a male and a female—into the boat with you, to keep them alive through the flood. Bring in a pair of each kind of bird and animal and reptile. [21]Store away in the boat all the food that they and you will need." [22]And Noah did everything as God commanded him.

CHAPTER 7
Finally the day came when the Lord said to Noah, "Go into the boat with all your family, for among all the people of the earth, I consider you alone to be righteous. [2]Bring in the animals, too—a pair of each, except those kinds I have chosen for eating and for sacrifice: take seven pairs of each of them, [3]and seven pairs of every kind of bird. Thus there will be every kind of life reproducing again after the flood has ended. [4]One week from today I will begin forty days and nights of rain; and all the animals and birds and reptiles I have made will die."

[5]So Noah did everything the Lord commanded him. [6]He was 600 years old when the flood came. [7]He boarded the boat with his wife and sons and their wives, to escape the flood. [8,9]With him were all the various kinds of animals—those for eating and sacrifice, and those that were not, and the birds and reptiles. They came into the boat in pairs, male and female, just as God commanded Noah.

God Sends a Great Flood

[10-12]One week later, when Noah was 600 years, two months, and seventeen days old, the rain came down in mighty torrents from the sky, and the subterranean waters burst forth upon the earth for forty days and nights. [13]But Noah had gone into the boat that very day with his wife and his sons, Shem, Ham, and Japheth, and their wives. [14,15]With them in the boat were pairs of every kind of animal—domestic and wild—and reptiles and birds of every sort. [16]Two by two they came, male and female, just as God had commanded. Then the Lord God closed the door and shut them in.

[17]For forty days the roaring floods prevailed, covering the ground and lifting the boat high above the earth. [18]As the water rose higher and higher above the ground, the boat floated safely upon it; [19]until finally the water covered all the high mountains under the whole heaven, [20]standing twenty-two feet and more above the highest peaks. [21]And all living things upon the earth perished—birds, domestic and wild animals, and reptiles and all mankind—[22]everything that breathed and lived upon dry land. [23]All existence on the earth was blotted out—man and animals alike, and reptiles and birds. God destroyed them all, leaving only Noah alive, and those with him in the boat. [24]And the water covered the earth 150 days.

CHAPTER 8
God didn't forget about Noah and all the animals in the boat! He sent a wind to blow across the waters, and the floods began to disappear, [2]for the subterranean water sources ceased their gushing, and the torrential rains subsided. [3,4]So the flood gradually receded until, 150 days after it began, the boat came to rest upon the mountains of Ararat. [5]Three months later, as the waters continued to go down, other mountain peaks appeared.

[6]After another forty days, Noah opened a porthole [7]and released a raven that flew back and forth until the earth was dry. [8]Meanwhile he sent out a dove to see if it could find dry ground, [9]but the dove found no place to light, and returned to Noah, for the water was still too high. So Noah held out his hand and drew the dove back into the boat.

6:22 One has to wonder whether God's instructions made any sense to Noah. God told him to build a gigantic boat far from the nearest body of navigable water. But here we see that Noah was obedient even though God's instructions were hard to understand. This is one of the secrets of success in any recovery program. We may not understand how everything works, but we do what God tells us is necessary for our recovery. When we step out in faith as Noah did, God will give us the success we seek.

8:1 Noah had listened to God and obeyed all his requests. But now the ark was floating over the earth on the flood waters—not an ideal situation to be in. But God didn't forget about Noah. It is comforting to know that when we obey God, he will not forget us. He will stand by us until his plans for us are complete.

9:1-17 Noah and his family were the only people left after the Flood. The comforts of civilization had been washed away. They had to start all over again. God gave Noah his special blessing and instituted a program that, if followed, would result in a healthy society. God has given us his Word, which contains the ultimate blueprint for healthy living. And just as God gave the human race a new start with Noah, he can give each of us a new start, too.

NOAH & SONS

Parents often wonder if they can have a positive effect on their children in our corrupt world. Noah leaves us with a good model of what a godly parent should be like. Noah was the only righteous man left in a generation of corrupt individuals. He led his family by example in a world that looked upon Noah as being "out of touch." Society mocked him for his belief in and obedience to God.

The principles of obedience to God, consistency, and patience were taught to Noah's sons and their wives. When judgment came upon the world, Noah, his wife, his sons, and their wives were spared. Later in life, after the Flood, the Bible tells us that Noah became drunk on the wine of his vineyard. Two of his sons (Shem and Japheth) responded to the situation in a godly manner while one (Ham) did not. Noah's drunkenness and Ham's subsequent indiscretion resulted in the suffering of some of Ham's descendants.

As we look at Noah's life, we are reminded that our children learn from our example. They often receive great blessings from the good things we do, but also suffer from our mistakes. All of us, like Noah, have made mistakes. But those mistakes can become insignificant through our repentance and obedience to God's Word. We must remember that children become like the adults who surround them.

STRENGTHS AND ACCOMPLISHMENTS:
- Noah was the only follower of God left in his generation.
- Noah was the second father of the human race.
- Noah taught his sons patience, consistency, and obedience to God.

WEAKNESSES AND MISTAKES:
- Noah embarrassed himself by getting drunk in front of his sons.
- Ham acted in an ungodly manner resulting in a curse upon some of his descendants.

LESSONS FROM THEIR LIVES:
- God is faithful to those who trust and obey him.
- Obedience to God is a lifelong commitment.
- Good parents teach their children by example.

KEY VERSE:
"And Noah did everything as God commanded him" (Genesis 6:22).

The story of Noah and his sons is told in Genesis 5:29–10:32. Noah is referred to in 1 Chronicles 1:4; Isaiah 54:9; Ezekiel 14:14, 20; Matthew 24:37-38; Luke 3:36; 17:26-27; Hebrews 11:7; 1 Peter 3:20; and 2 Peter 2:5.

---

[10]Seven days later Noah released the dove
again, [11]and this time, toward evening, the
bird returned to him with an olive leaf in her
beak. So Noah knew that the water was almost gone. [12]A week later he released the dove
again, and this time she didn't come back.
[13]Twenty-nine days after that, Noah
opened the door to look, and the water was
gone. [14]Eight more weeks went by. Then at
last the earth was dry. [15,16]Then God told
Noah, "You may all go out. [17]Release all the
animals, birds, and reptiles, so that they will
breed abundantly and reproduce in great
numbers." [18,19]So the boat was soon empty.
Noah, his wife, and his sons and their wives
all disembarked, along with all the animals,
reptiles, and birds—all left the ark in pairs
and groups.
[20]Then Noah built an altar and sacrificed
on it some of the animals and birds God had
designated for that purpose. [21]And Jehovah
was pleased with the sacrifice and said to
himself, "I will never do it again—I will never
again curse the earth, destroying all living
things, even though man's bent is always
toward evil from his earliest youth, and even
though he does such wicked things. [22]As long
as the earth remains, there will be springtime
and harvest, cold and heat, winter and summer, day and night."

CHAPTER 9

God blessed Noah and his sons and told them
to have many children and to repopulate the
earth.
[2,3]"All wild animals and birds and fish will
be afraid of you," God told him; "for I have
placed them in your power, and they are
yours to use for food, in addition to grain and
vegetables. [4]But never eat animals unless their
life-blood has been drained off. [5,6]And murder
is forbidden. Man-killing animals must die,
and any man who murders shall be killed; for
to kill a man is to kill one made like God. [7]Yes,
have many children and repopulate the earth
and subdue it."
[8]Then God told Noah and his sons, [9-11]"I
solemnly promise you and your children and

the animals you brought with you—all these birds and cattle and wild animals—that I will never again send another flood to destroy the earth. [12]And I seal this promise with this sign: [13]I have placed my rainbow in the clouds as a sign of my promise until the end of time, to you and to all the earth. [14]When I send clouds over the earth, the rainbow will be seen in the clouds, [15]and I will remember my promise to you and to every being, that never again will the floods come and destroy all life. [16,17]For I will see the rainbow in the cloud and remember my eternal promise to every living being on the earth."

Noah's Family

[18]The names of Noah's three sons were Shem, Ham, and Japheth. (Ham is the ancestor of the Canaanites.) [19]From these three sons of Noah came all the nations of the earth.

[20,21]Noah became a farmer and planted a vineyard, and he made wine. One day as he was drunk and lay naked in his tent, [22]Ham, the father of Canaan, saw his father's nakedness and went outside and told his two brothers.

[23]Then Shem and Japheth took a robe and held it over their shoulders and, walking backwards into the tent, let it fall across their father to cover his nakedness as they looked the other way. [24,25]When Noah awoke from his drunken stupor, and learned what had happened and what Ham, his younger son, had done, he cursed Ham's descendants:

"A curse upon the Canaanites," he swore.
"May they be the lowest of slaves
To the descendants of Shem and Japheth."

[26,27]Then he said,

"God bless Shem,
And may Canaan be his slave.
God bless Japheth,
And let him share the prosperity of Shem,
And let Canaan be his slave."

[28]Noah lived another 350 years after the flood [29]and was 950 years old at his death.

CHAPTER 10

These are the families of Shem, Ham, and Japheth, who were the three sons of Noah; for sons were born to them after the flood.

[2]The sons of Japheth were: Gomer, Magog, Madai, Javan, Tubal, Meshech, Tiras.

[3]The sons of Gomer: Ashkenaz, Riphath, Togarmah.

[4]The sons of Javan: Elishah, Tarshish, Kittim, Dodanim.

[5]Their descendants became the maritime nations in various lands, each with a separate language.

[6]The sons of Ham were: Cush, Mizraim, Put, Canaan.

[7]The sons of Cush were: Seba, Havilah, Sabtah, Raamah, Sabteca.

The sons of Raamah were: Sheba, Dedan.

[8]One of the descendants of Cush was Nimrod, who became the first of the kings.[9]He was a mighty hunter, blessed of God, and his name became proverbial. People would speak of someone as being "like Nimrod—a mighty hunter, blessed of God." [10]The heart of his empire included Babel, Erech, Accad, and Calneh in the land of Shinar. [11,12]From there he extended his reign to Assyria. He built Nineveh, Rehoboth-Ir, Calah, and Resen (which is located between Nineveh and Calah), the main city of the empire.

[13,14]Mizraim was the ancestor of the people inhabiting these areas: Ludim, Anamim, Lehabim, Naphtuhim, Pathrusim, Casluhim (from whom came the Philistines), and Caphtorim.

[15-19]Canaan's oldest son was Sidon, and he was also the father of Heth; from Canaan descended these nations: Jebusites, Amorites, Girgashites, Hivites, Arkites, Sinites, Arvadites, Zemarites, Hamathites. Eventually the descendants of Canaan spread from Sidon all the way to Gerar, in the Gaza strip; and to Sodom, Gomorrah, Admah, and Zeboiim, near Lasha.

[20]These, then, were the descendants of Ham, spread abroad in many lands and nations, with many languages.

[21]Eber descended from Shem, the oldest brother of Japheth. [22]Here is a list of Shem's other descendants: Elam, Asshur, Arpachshad, Lud, Aram.

9:20-21 With all the talk of Noah's righteousness and his fellowship with God, it is surprising to read that, by his choice, he fell prey to the excesses of alcohol. The account of Noah's drunkenness and shame comes as a shock to the reader, but it is a reminder that even in ideal conditions it is easy for us to slip and fall. We can never relax and feel as if we have it made, for that is when we become most vulnerable to failure.

10:1-32 This chapter is often called the Table of Nations. It is refreshing to realize that the God we worship is not a local deity. He is sovereign over all ethnic and language groups, nations, and political entities. The God who holds kings and empires in his hands surely has the power to hold us, too.

ABRAHAM & SARAH

Many give lip service to walking by faith; Abraham and Sarah modeled it. They were imperfect but willing instruments used by God to implement his perfect plan.

Abram, with Sarai, departed by faith from a pagan world for a new life of God's choosing. God promised a land and a nation of descendants, including One through whom all the peoples of the world would be blessed. The covenant defied human logic: Abram was seventy-five; Sarai was ten years younger and infertile. Their hopes of children had long vanished. Yet Abram believed God's promises.

During their pilgrimage, the pair often strayed from God's will. They succumbed to fear and dishonesty in dealings with Pharaoh and Abimelech. Difficulty in persevering led them to second-guess God. Abram's resulting union with Hagar resulted in domestic strife. Jealousy naturally erupted, and family relationships became strained. Abram behaved irresponsibly and Sarai acted with deliberate cruelty. Years later a wiser Abraham would listen to God's instructions for handling the handmaid and her son.

Abram's and Sarai's failures neither diminished God's love for them nor altered his commitment to his promises. Through turmoil and temptation, the couple's mutual affection and respect survived. Eventually God changed their names. Sarah's faith grew, and a quarter-century after God's promises were first given, she bore a son. They named him Isaac. The delayed gratification must have been sweet! Sarah enjoyed Isaac for many years, and after her death she was tenderly mourned by both husband and son.

Worship and obedience were such a part of Abraham's life that when God tested Abraham's faith, he willingly surrendered his son, Isaac, for a sacrifice. Then, God provided a lamb as a burnt offering to take Isaac's place on the altar. God's provision in Abraham's life can bring hope to us even today.

STRENGTHS AND ACCOMPLISHMENTS:
- They voluntarily left comfortable, familiar surroundings to pursue God's will.
- Both are heralded in Scripture as examples of faithful obedience.
- Abraham's physical descendants include the Jewish nation, from which came Jesus the Messiah.
- Abraham's spiritual descendants include all who have trusted Jesus for salvation.

WEAKNESSES AND MISTAKES:
- They at times presumed to know God's plans before he revealed them and attempted foolishly to assist him.
- When victimized by fear, Abraham was not above protecting himself at the expense of his wife's safety and integrity.
- Both acted intolerably toward Hagar and her son.

LESSONS FROM THEIR LIVES:
- A fresh start is possible at any stage of life.
- The fulfillment of God's promises does not depend upon our performance, but upon his grace.
- It is dangerous to move ahead without first seeking God's direction.

KEY VERSE:
"Then God did as he had promised, and Sarah became pregnant and gave Abraham a baby son in his old age, at the time God had said" (Genesis 21:1-2).

The story of Abraham and Sarah is found in Genesis 11–25. Among the many other references to Abraham are Romans 4:1-24; 9:7-9; Galatians 3:6-9, 14, 18; James 2:21-23; Hebrews 6:13-15; 7:1-2, 4-6; 11:8-12, 17-19. Sarah is mentioned in Romans 4:19; 9:9; Hebrews 11:11; and 1 Peter 3:6.

23Aram's sons were: Uz, Hul, Gether, Mash.
24Arpachshad's son was Shelah, and Shelah's son was Eber.
25Two sons were born to Eber: Peleg (meaning "Division," for during his lifetime the people of the world were separated and dispersed), and Joktan (Peleg's brother).
26-30Joktan was the father of Almodad, Sheleph, Hazarmaveth, Jerah, Hadoram, Uzal, Diklah, Obal, Abima-el, Sheba, Ophir, Havilah, Jobab.
These descendants of Joktan lived all the way from Mesha to the eastern hills of Sephar.
31These, then, were the descendants of Shem, classified according to their political groupings, languages, and geographical locations.
32All of the men listed above descended from Noah, through many generations, living in the various nations that developed after the flood.

CHAPTER 11

The Tower of Babel

At that time all mankind spoke a single language. 2As the population grew and spread
eastward, a plain was discovered in the land

of Babylon and was soon thickly populated. [3,4]The people who lived there began to talk about building a great city, with a temple-tower reaching to the skies—a proud, eternal monument to themselves.

"This will weld us together," they said, "and keep us from scattering all over the world." So they made great piles of hardburned brick, and collected bitumen to use as mortar.

[5]But when God came down to see the city and the tower mankind was making, [6]he said, "Look! If they are able to accomplish all this when they have just *begun* to exploit their linguistic and political unity, just think of what they will do later! Nothing will be unattainable for them! [7]Come, let us go down and give them different languages, so that they won't understand each other's words!"

[8]So, in that way, God scattered them all over the earth; and that ended the building of the city. [9]That is why the city was called Babel (meaning "confusion"), because it was there that Jehovah confused them by giving them many languages, thus widely scattering them across the face of the earth.

Shem's Family

[10,11]Shem's line of descendants included Arpachshad, born two years after the flood when Shem was 100 years old; after that he lived another 500 years and had many sons and daughters.

[12,13]When Arpachshad was thirty-five years old, his son Shelah was born, and after that he lived another 403 years and had many sons and daughters.

[14,15]Shelah was thirty years old when his son Eber was born, living 403 years after that, and had many sons and daughters.

[16,17]Eber was thirty-four years old when his son Peleg was born. He lived another 430 years afterwards and had many sons and daughters.

[18,19]Peleg was thirty years old when his son Reu was born. He lived another 209 years afterwards and had many sons and daughters.

[20,21]Reu was thirty-two years old when Serug was born. He lived 207 years after that, with many sons and daughters.

[22,23]Serug was thirty years old when his son Nahor was born. He lived 200 years afterwards, with many sons and daughters.

[24,25]Nahor was twenty-nine years old at the birth of his son Terah. He lived 119 years afterwards and had sons and daughters.

[26]By the time Terah was seventy years old, he had three sons, Abram, Nahor, and Haran.

[27]And Haran had a son named Lot. [28]But Haran died young, in the land where he was born (in Ur of the Chaldeans), and was survived by his father.

[29]Meanwhile, Abram married his half sister Sarai, while his brother Nahor married their orphaned niece, Milcah, who was the daughter of their brother Haran; and she had a sister named Iscah. [30]But Sarai was barren; she had no children. [31]Then Terah took his son Abram, his grandson Lot (his son Haran's child), and his daughter-in-law Sarai, and left Ur of the Chaldeans to go to the land of Canaan; but they stopped instead at the city of Haran and settled there. [32]And there Terah died at the age of 205.

11:3-4 Whatever else the Tower of Babel might have represented, it was a mighty monument to human pride. It was a symbol of man's rebellion against the revealed will of God. This type of pride is always destructive to human community and to the process of recovery.

11:5-9 The Tower of Babel incident records the progression of broken communication that began back in the Garden of Eden. After sin entered the world, Adam and Eve began to hide the truth. They tried to blame each other and God for their mistakes, resulting in separation from God and barriers between that first couple. The sinful pride of the people of Babel caused another great rift in human communication. Numerous languages now divided them into various groups making their cooperation difficult, if not impossible. But the story doesn't end there. God is in the business of restoring broken communication. He chose the nation of Israel and spoke to them, giving them his laws. His Son was born through this nation, so he could speak to us and walk among us. And when the Holy Spirit came, the diversity of language was no longer a barrier to communication (Acts 2:5-12). God's program is designed to enhance our communication with him and the people around us.

12:1 A relationship with God is a two-way street. He is there to help us, but he also expects us to follow his plan. When God called Abram to leave his country and his people and to go to a land that God would show him, God promised to guide him. But Abram had to step out in faith. God has promised to be with us as we seek his help in recovery, but he may also ask something of us. As with Abraham, God may call us away from the familiar world that drags us down. And if we want to progress, we will need to follow his plan.

LOT & FAMILY

Many people in this world live for wealth, comfort, and the easy life. And they want to get it as quickly as possible! To make this happen, they often sacrifice the really important things in life. This was true in the life of Abraham's nephew Lot. Looking for the easy road to wealth and comfort, he made decisions that ended up destroying everything he had lived for.

Lot always thought of himself first. He demonstrated this when he chose the rich pastureland of the valleys, leaving Abraham with the rugged hill country. Embracing the easy comforts of the valley's cities and the physical prosperity they offered, he grew blind to the legacy he was leaving his descendants. When the men of Sodom demanded that Lot send his angelic guests out to take part in their sexual practices, Lot offered his daughters as an alternative. His desire to be accepted by the sinful people of his adopted homeland led him to fail to treat his daughters with the respect and protection they deserved.

The result of Lot's selfishness and greed was the loss of his fortune and the ruin of his family. He sacrificed all he had worked for and his family to the gods of comfort and wealth. He witnessed his wife's death as a result of her disobedience to God—something he had modeled for her. His daughters followed Lot's example, too. They used the quickest and easiest means available to overcome their lonely and childless state—drunkenness, seduction, and incest.

Our society places great value on wealth, comfort, and success, calling us all to join the mad rush to get them. This focus is so pervasive that it may be hard for us to see it as being bad. But though living for wealth may not seem such a terrible sin, its destructive effects upon people in our world are widespread. We must learn to put God first. If we put wealth first, we will lose all the really important things in life—our family and our relationship with God.

STRENGTHS AND ACCOMPLISHMENTS:
- Lot was successful at generating wealth.
- The apostle Peter referred to him as a just and righteous man.

WEAKNESSES AND MISTAKES:
- Lot often chose the easiest course of action, and usually at the expense of doing what was right.
- When faced with making a decision, Lot thought of himself first.
- Lot's daughters used sinful means to meet their needs instead of seeking God's provision.

LESSONS FROM THEIR LIVES:
- If we live for comfort and wealth, they will come between us and our family.
- We need to take care of our responsibilities to God and people first if we want our life to be successful.
- Mistakes made by parents usually lead to mistakes made by their children.
- When we put wealth and comfort before obedience to God, the result will be destructive.

KEY VERSE:
"Come, let's fill him [Lot] with wine and then we will sleep with him, so that our clan will not come to an end" (Genesis 19:32).

The story of Lot and his family is told in Genesis 13 and 19. Lot is also mentioned in Deuteronomy 2:9; Luke 17:28-32; and 2 Peter 2:7-8.

CHAPTER 12

Abram Begins a New Life

God had told Abram, "Leave your own country behind you, and your own people, and go
to the land I will guide you to. 2If you do, I will
cause you to become the father of a great nation; I will bless you and make your name famous, and you will be a blessing to many
others. 3I will bless those who bless you and
curse those who curse you; and the entire world will be blessed because of you."

4So Abram departed as the Lord had instructed him, and Lot went too; Abram was
seventy-five years old at that time. 5He took
his wife Sarai, his nephew Lot, and all his wealth—the cattle and slaves he had gotten in
Haran—and finally arrived in Canaan. 6Traveling through Canaan, they came to a place near Shechem, and set up camp beside the oak at Moreh. (This area was inhabited by Canaanites at that time.)

7Then Jehovah appeared to Abram and said, "I am going to give this land to your descendants." And Abram built an altar there
to commemorate Jehovah's visit. 8Afterwards
Abram left that place and traveled southward to the hilly country between Bethel on the west and Ai on the east. There he made camp,

and made an altar to the Lord and prayed to
him. 9Thus he continued slowly southward to
the Negeb, pausing frequently.

Abram Deceives Pharaoh

10There was at that time a terrible famine in
the land: and so Abram went on down to
Egypt to live. 11-13But as he was approaching
the borders of Egypt, he asked Sarai his wife
to tell everyone that she was his sister! "You
are very beautiful," he told her, "and when
the Egyptians see you they will say, 'This is his
wife. Let's kill him and then we can have her!'
But if you say you are my sister, then the
Egyptians will treat me well because of you,
and spare my life!" 14And sure enough, when
they arrived in Egypt everyone spoke of her
beauty. 15When the palace aides saw her, they
praised her to their king, the Pharaoh, and she
was taken into his harem. 16Then Pharaoh
gave Abram many gifts because of her—
sheep, oxen, donkeys, men and women
slaves, and camels.

17But the Lord sent a terrible plague upon
Pharaoh's household on account of her being
there. 18Then Pharaoh called Abram before
him and accused him sharply. "What is this
you have done to me?" he demanded. "Why
didn't you tell me she was your wife? 19Why
were you willing to let me marry her, saying
she was your sister? Here, take her and be
gone!" 20And Pharaoh sent them out of the
country under armed escort—Abram, his
wife, and all his household and possessions.

CHAPTER 13

Lot Leaves Abram

So they left Egypt and traveled north into the
Negeb—Abram with his wife, and Lot, and all
that they owned, for Abram was very rich in
livestock, silver, and gold. 3,4Then they continued northward toward Bethel where he
had camped before, between Bethel and Ai—
to the place where he had built the altar. And
there he again worshiped the Lord.

5Lot too was very wealthy, with sheep and
cattle and many servants. 6But the land could
not support both Abram and Lot with all their
flocks and herds. There were too many animals for the available pasture. 7So fights broke
out between the herdsmen of Abram and Lot,
despite the danger they all faced from the
tribes of Canaanites and Perizzites present in
the land. 8Then Abram talked it over with Lot.
"This fighting between our men has got to
stop," he said. "We can't afford to let a rift
develop between our clans. Close relatives
such as we are must present a united front!
9I'll tell you what we'll do. Take your choice of
any section of the land you want, and we will
separate. If you want that part over there to
the east, then I'll stay here in the western
section. Or, if you want the west, then I'll go
over there to the east."

10Lot took a long look at the fertile plains of
the Jordan River, well watered everywhere
(this was before Jehovah destroyed Sodom
and Gomorrah); the whole section was like
the Garden of Eden, or like the beautiful
countryside around Zoar in Egypt. 11So that is
what Lot chose—the Jordan valley to the east
of them. He went there with his flocks and
servants, and thus he and Abram parted company. 12For Abram stayed in the land of Canaan, while Lot lived among the cities of the
plain, settling at a place near the city of
Sodom. 13The men of this area were unusually
wicked, and sinned greatly against Jehovah.

14After Lot was gone, the Lord said to
Abram, "Look as far as you can see in every

12:11-20 As Abram and Sarai approached Egypt, Abram began to fear that the Egyptians would kill him to take his beautiful wife. So Abram and Sarai spun a lie to "protect" their relationship. They spread a story that they were brother and sister. This was a half-truth—they were half siblings. But it should be recognized that a half-truth is a whole lie. And like most lies, this one backfired, almost destroying Abram and Sarai's marriage. Total honesty is an essential part of our recovery. We need to be careful to avoid doing what Abram and Sarai did, even though they did it with the best of intentions. Dishonesty never pays—never try to rationalize it.

13:5-11 A conflict developed between the families of Abram and Lot over pastureland for their flocks. To strengthen the strained family relationship, Abram offered Lot first choice of the land. Abram realized that people were more important than possessions, so he sacrificed his right to the best land to maintain harmony between their families. In recovery, we need to learn this important lesson: our relationships are more important than the things we own.

13:11-13 One bad choice often leads to another. The choices Lot made here and in the following chapters led him toward his later fall. Here, he selfishly chose the best land and the easy life-style that would accompany it. In 13:12-13, he chose to move closer to the wicked city of Sodom. In 19:1-18, he chose to become an important man in a wicked place. In 19:30-38, his fall reached its final depths as he had incestuous relations with his daughters. We need to think ahead, reflecting upon the probable consequences of our present decisions.

direction, 15for I am going to give it all to you
and your descendants. 16And I am going to
give you so many descendants that, like dust,
they can't be counted! 17Hike in all directions
and explore the new possessions I am giving
you." 18Then Abram moved his tent to the
oaks of Mamre, near Hebron, and built an
altar to Jehovah there.

CHAPTER 14

Abram Rescues Lot

Now war filled the land—Amraphel, king of
Shinar, Arioch, king of Ellasar, Ched-or-laomer, king of Elam, and Tidal, king of Goiim
2fought against: Bera, king of Sodom, Birsha,
king of Gomorrah, Shinab, king of Admah,
Shemeber, king of Zeboiim, and the king of
Bela (later called Zoar).

3These kings (of Sodom, Gomorrah, Admah, Zeboiim, and Bela) mobilized their armies in Siddim Valley (that is, the valley of the
Dead Sea). 4For twelve years they had all been
subject to King Ched-or-laomer, but now in
the thirteenth year, they rebelled.

5,6One year later, Ched-or-laomer and his
allies arrived and the slaughter began. For
they were victorious over the following tribes
at the places indicated: the Rephaim in Ash-
teroth-karnaim; the Zuzim in Ham; the Emim
in the plain of Kiriathaim; the Horites in
Mount Seir, as far as El-paran at the edge of
the desert.

7Then they swung around to Enmishpat
(later called Kadesh) and destroyed the
Amalekites, and also the Amorites living in
Hazazan-tamar.

8,9But now the other army, that of the kings
of Sodom, Gomorrah, Admah, Zeboiim, and
Bela (Zoar), unsuccessfully attacked Ched-or-
laomer and his allies as they were in the Dead
Sea Valley (four kings against five). 10As it
happened, the valley was full of asphalt pits.
And as the army of the kings of Sodom and
Gomorrah fled, some slipped into the pits,
and the remainder fled to the mountains.
11Then the victors plundered Sodom and Gomorrah and carried off all their wealth and
food, and went on their homeward way, 12tak-
ing with them Lot—Abram's nephew who
lived in Sodom—and all he owned. 13One of
the men who escaped came and told Abram
the Hebrew, who was camping among the
oaks belonging to Mamre the Amorite
(brother of Eshcol and Aner, Abram's allies).

14When Abram learned that Lot had been
captured, he called together the men born
into his household, 318 of them in all, and

▶ **The Twelve Step devotional reading plan begins here.**

No-Win Situations

BIBLE READING: Genesis 16:1-15

We admitted that we were powerless over our dependencies—that our life had become unmanageable.

Sometimes we are powerless because of our station in life. We may be in a situation where other people have power over us. We may feel that we are trapped by the demands of others, and that there's no way to please them all. It's a double bind: to please one is to disappoint another. Sometimes when we feel stuck and frustrated with our relationships, we look for a measure of control by escaping through our addictive behaviors.

Hagar is a picture of powerlessness. She had no rights. As a girl, she was a slave to Sarai and Abram. When they were upset because Sarai could not bear children, Hagar was given to Abram as a surrogate. When she did become pregnant, as they had wanted, Sarai was so jealous that she beat the girl and she ran away. All alone, out in the wilderness, she was met by an Angel who told her, "Return to your mistress and act as you should, for I will make you into a great nation. Yes, you are pregnant and your baby will be a son, and you are to name him Ishmael ('God hears'), because God has heard your woes" (Genesis 16:9-11).

When we are caught in no-win situations, it's tempting to run away through our addictive/compulsive escape hatches. At times like these God is there, and he is listening to our woes. We need to learn to express our pain to God instead of just trying to escape. He hears our cries and is willing to give us hope for the future. ***Turn to page 283, Judges 16.***

chased after the retiring army as far as Dan.
15He divided his men and attacked during the
night from several directions, and pursued
the fleeing army to Hobah, north of Damascus, 16and recovered everything—the loot that
had been taken, his relative Lot, and all of
Lot's possessions, including the women and
other captives.
17As Abram returned from his strike against
Ched-or-laomer and the other kings at the
Valley of Shaveh (later called King's Valley),
the king of Sodom came out to meet him,
18and Melchizedek, the king of Salem (Jerusalem), who was a priest of the God of Highest
Heaven, brought him bread and wine.
19,20Then Melchizedek blessed Abram with this
blessing:

> "The blessing of the supreme God, Creator
> of heaven and earth, be upon you,
> Abram; and blessed be God, who has
> delivered your enemies over to you."

Then Abram gave Melchizedek a tenth of all
the loot.
21The king of Sodom told him, "Just give me
back my people who were captured; keep for
yourself the booty stolen from my city."
22But Abram replied, "I have solemnly
promised Jehovah, the supreme God, Creator
of heaven and earth, 23that I will not take so
much as a single thread from you, lest you say,
'Abram is rich because of what I gave him!'
24All I'll accept is what these young men of
mine have eaten; but give a share of the loot
to Aner, Eshcol, and Mamre, my allies."

CHAPTER 15

God Gives Abram a Promise

Afterwards Jehovah spoke to Abram in a vision, and this is what he told him: "Don't be
fearful, Abram, for I will defend you. And I
will give you great blessings."
2,3But Abram replied, "O Lord Jehovah,
what good are all your blessings when I have
no son? For without a son, some other member of my household will inherit all my
wealth."
4Then Jehovah told him, "No, no one else
will be your heir, for you will have a son to
inherit everything you own."
5Then God brought Abram outside beneath
the nighttime sky and told him, "Look up
into the heavens and count the stars if you
can. Your descendants will be like that—too
many to count!" 6And Abram believed God;
then God considered him righteous on account of his faith.
7And he told him, "I am Jehovah who
brought you out of the city of Ur of the
Chaldeans, to give you this land."
8But Abram replied, "O Lord Jehovah, how
can I be sure that you will give it to me?"
9Then Jehovah told him to take a three-year-
old heifer, a three-year-old female goat, a
three-year-old ram, a turtledove and a young
pigeon, 10and to slay them and to cut them
apart down the middle, and to separate the
halves, but not to divide the birds. 11And
when the vultures came down upon the carcasses, Abram shooed them away.
12That evening as the sun was going down,

14:14-16 A number of important character traits emerge as we examine Abram's prompt military action. He proved himself to be a man of courage, always ready to act when the situation demanded it. He was willing to give up certain luxuries in order to follow the program God had laid out for him. These are important characteristics for us to emulate as we continue in our recovery.

15:4-5 Because of the frustration of seventy-five childless years, God's promise of numerous children must have stretched Abram's faith to the very limit. God's plan for Abram seemed an impossibility—thousands of descendants from an old man and a barren woman. But God's promise did actually come about. God's plans for us may be beyond belief—even impossible. We may think we are beyond hope. But with God, nothing is impossible!

15:6 This is one of the most important verses in the Old Testament. Abram believed God, and God considered him righteous. In other words, it was Abram's faith, not his works, that made him righteous before God. For us to continue in recovery, we need to trust God more and trust our works less. We are powerless over the pressures of sin, but God will help us through the toughest temptations if we trust him. He will count us righteous because of our trust in him, not because we are perfect.

16:1-4 Since God's promise of a child had been given, about two years had passed without anything happening. Sometimes the hardest part of our recovery is the waiting. Here Abram and Sarai show us what not to do when things don't progress as quickly as we might hope. Rather than accepting God's timing, they took matters into their own hands. They assigned a servant girl, Hagar, to be a surrogate mother for Abram's son. This "solution" has been a source of conflict to this day. Abram's descendants through Hagar are the Arab nations whose conflict with the Jews keeps the Middle East in constant turmoil.

HAGAR & ISHMAEL

Hagar is often overshadowed by the two prominent people in her life—Abraham and Sarah. Her story is woven into the fabric of great events that make up Abraham's life. Yet God chose this "insignificant" woman to bear the son who was destined to be the father of the Arab nations.

When Hagar became pregnant, she gave in to her motherly pride and looked down on her mistress, Sarah, who had been unable to bear children. This prompted a great deal of strife in Abraham's family and much suffering for Hagar. The pain and alienation she suffered because of the baby could have put considerable strain on the mother-child relationship from the beginning. But Hagar showed no regrets about having her son. She joyfully received him and accepted him despite the complicated and emotionally charged circumstances surrounding his birth.

Hagar and her son, Ishmael, had much in common. They were both rejected by Abraham's household. Together they experienced the torture of the hot, barren desert after Sarah demanded that Abraham send them away. They became nameless outcasts, discarded by those who had once valued them. Under such circumstances, it must have been difficult to maintain a positive self-assessment.

Yet this mother and son persevered through these trials because they had faith in God, who had appeared to them in the wilderness. They knew that they were of great worth in his sight, and they rebuilt their identity upon his promises. To this day their story is used to illustrate God's deep concern for all who have been discarded and rejected. It also shows us that God's assessment of our life is far more important that what other people think.

STRENGTHS AND ACCOMPLISHMENTS:
- Hagar was willing to humbly return to Sarah even though she had been badly mistreated.
- Hagar stood by her son even though he was the source of many of her trials.

WEAKNESSES AND MISTAKES:
- When Hagar became pregnant, she pridefully looked down on Sarah, prompting much of the strife that followed.
- Hagar momentarily abandoned her son under a tree at the time of his greatest need.

LESSONS FROM THEIR LIVES:
- A loving mother/son relationship is a precious gift from God.
- God is deeply concerned about those who have been abused and rejected.
- God is able to restore a sense of self-worth even in the most trying times.

KEY VERSES:
"Return to your mistress and act as you should, for I will make you into a great nation. Yes, you are pregnant and your baby will be a son, and you are to name him Ishmael ('God hears'), because God has heard your woes" (Genesis 16:9-11).

The story of Hagar and Ishmael is told in Genesis 16–21. The apostle Paul briefly discusses them in Galatians 4:21-31.

---

a deep sleep fell upon Abram, and a vision of terrible foreboding, darkness, and horror.

13Then Jehovah told Abram, "Your descendants will be oppressed as slaves in a foreign land for 400 years. 14But I will punish the nation that enslaves them, and at the end they will come away with great wealth. 15(But you will die in peace, at a ripe old age.) 16After four generations they will return here to this land; for the wickedness of the Amorite nations living here now will not be ready for punishment until then."

17As the sun went down and it was dark, Abram saw a smoking firepot and a flaming torch that passed between the halves of the carcasses. 18So that day Jehovah made this covenant with Abram: "I have given this land to your descendants from the Wadi-el-Arish to the Euphrates River. 19-21And I give to them these nations: Kenites, Kenizzites, Kadmonites, Hittites, Perizzites, Rephaim, Amorites, Canaanites, Girgashites, Jebusites."

CHAPTER 16

Sarai Becomes Jealous of Hagar

But Sarai and Abram had no children. So Sarai took her maid, an Egyptian girl named Hagar, 2,3and gave her to Abram to be his second wife.

"Since the Lord has given me no children," Sarai said, "you may sleep with my servant girl, and her children shall be mine."

And Abram agreed. (This took place ten years after Abram had first arrived in the land of Canaan.) 4So he slept with Hagar, and she conceived; and when she realized she was

pregnant, she became very proud and arrogant toward her mistress Sarai.
5Then Sarai said to Abram, "It's all your fault. For now this servant girl of mine despises me, though I myself gave her the privilege of being your wife. May the Lord judge you for doing this to me!"
6"You have my permission to punish the girl as you see fit," Abram replied. So Sarai beat her and she ran away.
7The Angel of the Lord found her beside a desert spring along the road to Shur.

8*The Angel:* "Hagar, Sarai's maid, where have you come from, and where are you going?"

Hagar: "I am running away from my mistress."

9-12*The Angel:* "Return to your mistress and act as you should, for I will make you into a great nation. Yes, you are pregnant and your baby will be a son, and you are to name him Ishmael ('God hears'), because God has heard your woes. This son of yours will be a wild one—free and untamed as a wild ass! He will be against everyone, and everyone will feel the same toward him. But he will live near the rest of his kin."

13Thereafter Hagar spoke of Jehovah—for it was he who appeared to her—as "the God who looked upon me," for she thought, "I saw God and lived to tell it."
14Later that well was named "The Well of the Living One Who Sees Me." It lies between Kadesh and Bered.
15So Hagar gave Abram a son, and Abram named him Ishmael. 16(Abram was eighty-six years old at this time.)

CHAPTER 17

God and Abram Make an Agreement

When Abram was ninety-nine years old, God appeared to him and told him, "I am the Almighty; obey me and live as you should. 2-4I will prepare a contract between us, guaranteeing to make you into a mighty nation. In fact you shall be the father of not only one nation, but a multitude of nations!" Abram fell face downward in the dust as God talked with him.
5"What's more," God told him, "I am changing your name. It is no longer 'Abram' ('Exalted Father'), but 'Abraham' ('Father of Nations')—for that is what you will be. I have declared it. 6I will give you millions of descendants who will form many nations! Kings shall be among your descendants! 7,8And I will continue this agreement between us generation after generation, forever, for it shall be between me and your children as well. It is a contract that I shall be your God and the God of your posterity. And I will give all this land of Canaan to you and them, forever. And I will be your God.
9,10"Your part of the contract," God told him, "is to obey its terms. You personally and all your posterity have this continual responsibility: that every male among you shall be circumcised; 11the foreskin of his penis shall be cut off. This will be the proof that you and they accept this covenant. 12Every male shall be circumcised on the eighth day after birth. This applies to every foreign-born slave as well as to everyone born in your household. This is a permanent part of this contract, and it applies to all your posterity. 13All must be circumcised. Your bodies will thus be marked as participants in my everlasting covenant.

16:7-13 When Hagar was helpless to help herself, and when she recognized her powerlessness over her situation, the Angel of the Lord came and ministered to her. Until we recognize that our situation is unmanageable without outside help, God waits and does not enter the situation to help us. But when we are ready to admit our need and cry out, he is ready to step in.
17:5-6 Since Abram was childless, his name (meaning, "Exalted Father") must have been a source of embarrassment to him. Here it is changed to "Abraham," which means "Father of Nations." Abraham's name, in a real sense, became his promise from God. It would have been a continual reminder and source of hope that God would come through for him in the end.
17:9-10, 24-27 Most of our significant relationships are symbolized by an outward sign. For example, married people wear rings as a sign of their marriage commitment. Circumcision was a sign of the agreement or covenant between God and Abraham. It was a mark by which Abraham's descendants were set apart as God's special people. Inner changes need to be accompanied by outer signs; beliefs need to be proven by actions. In recovery, as changes begin to take place inside, we need to express these changes outwardly in our actions and life-style.
18:1-6 Hebrews 13:2 urges the practice of hospitality since some have "entertained angels without realizing it." Abraham's treatment of the three strangers here may have been the background for this verse in Hebrews. Surely this is an example to be followed. As we progress in recovery, one of our goals is to help others to discover the new way of life that we have found. What better way than to be hospitable toward others?

READ GENESIS 18:20-33

▶ **The Serenity Prayer devotional reading plan begins here.**

GOD grant me the serenity to accept the things I cannot change the courage to change the things I can and the wisdom to know the difference

AMEN

We all face difficult situations that involve the people we love. In some of these situations the wise course of action may not be clear. We may feel a heavy burden to act, but have no idea what to do.

Abraham found himself in such a situation. The Lord had told Abraham that he intended to destroy the people of Sodom and Gomorrah for their wickedness. Since Abraham's nephew, Lot, lived among the people of these cities, Abraham was concerned for their welfare. So Abraham approached God and said, "'Will you kill good and bad alike? Suppose you find fifty godly people there within the city—will you destroy it, and not spare it for their sakes? That wouldn't be right! Surely you wouldn't do such a thing, to kill the godly with the wicked! . . . Should not the Judge of all the earth be fair?' And God replied, 'If I find fifty godly people there, I will spare the entire city for their sake'" (Genesis 18:23-26). The bargaining went on: Suppose there are only forty-five . . . forty . . . thirty . . . twenty . . . ten? And God said, "Then, for the sake of the ten, I won't destroy it" (18:32).

Abraham wasn't sure what he could do in the situation he faced; he wasn't even sure what was right in this situation. He talked it over with God, reasoning it out, trying to do whatever he could. When we don't know how much of a change we can or even should make, we can start by talking it over with God. Then we can try to do as much as we feel confident doing. ***Turn to page 47, Genesis 37.***

---

14 Anyone who refuses these terms shall be cut
off from his people; for he has violated my
contract."
15 Then God added, "Regarding Sarai your
wife—her name is no longer 'Sarai' but 'Sarah'
('Princess'). 16 And I will bless her and give you
a son from her! Yes, I will bless her richly, and
make her the mother of nations! Many kings
shall be among your posterity."
17 Then Abraham threw himself down in
worship before the Lord, but inside he was
laughing in disbelief! "Me, be a father?" he
said in amusement. "Me—100 years old? And
Sarah, to have a baby at 90?"
18 And Abraham said to God, "Yes, do bless
Ishmael!"
19 "No," God replied, "that isn't what I said.
Sarah shall bear you a son; and you are to
name him Isaac ('Laughter'), and I will sign
my covenant with him forever, and with his
descendants. 20 As for Ishmael, all right, I will
bless him also, just as you have asked me to. I
will cause him to multiply and become a great
nation. Twelve princes shall be among his
posterity. 21 But my contract is with Isaac, who
will be born to you and Sarah next year at
about this time."
22 That ended the conversation and God
left. 23 Then, that very day, Abraham took Ishmael
his son and every other male—born in
his household or bought from outside—and
cut off their foreskins, just as God had told
him to. 24-27 Abraham was ninety-nine years old
at that time, and Ishmael was thirteen. Both
were circumcised the same day, along with all
the other men and boys of the household,
whether born there or bought as slaves.

CHAPTER 18

Angels Visit with Abraham

The Lord appeared again to Abraham while he was living in the oak grove at Mamre. This is the way it happened: One hot summer afternoon as he was sitting in the opening of his tent, [2]he suddenly noticed three men coming toward him. He sprang up and ran to meet them and welcomed them.

[3,4]"Sirs," he said, "please don't go any farther. Stop awhile and rest here in the shade of this tree while I get water to refresh your feet, [5]and a bite to eat to strengthen you. Do stay awhile before continuing your journey."

"All right," they said, "do as you have said."

[6]Then Abraham ran back to the tent and said to Sarah, "Quick! Mix up some pancakes! Use your best flour, and make enough for the three of them!" [7]Then he ran out to the herd and selected a fat calf and told a servant to hurry and butcher it. [8]Soon, taking them cheese and milk and the roast veal, he set it before the men and stood beneath the trees beside them as they ate.

[9]"Where is Sarah, your wife?" they asked him.

"In the tent," Abraham replied.

[10]Then the Lord said, "Next year I will give you and Sarah a son!" (Sarah was listening from the tent door behind him.) [11]Now Abraham and Sarah were both very old, and Sarah was long since past the time when she could have a baby.

[12]So Sarah laughed silently. "A woman my age have a baby?" she scoffed to herself. "And with a husband as old as mine?"

[13]Then God said to Abraham, "Why did Sarah laugh? Why did she say 'Can an old woman like me have a baby?' [14]Is anything too hard for God? Next year, just as I told you, I will certainly see to it that Sarah has a son."

[15]But Sarah denied it. "I didn't laugh," she lied, for she was afraid.

Abraham Intervenes for Sodom

[16]Then the men stood up from their meal and started on toward Sodom; and Abraham went with them part of the way.

[17]"Should I hide my plan from Abraham?" God asked. [18]"For Abraham shall become a mighty nation, and he will be a source of blessing for all the nations of the earth. [19]And I have picked him out to have godly descendants and a godly household—men who are just and good—so that I can do for him all I have promised."

[20]So the Lord told Abraham, "I have heard that the people of Sodom and Gomorrah are utterly evil, and that everything they do is wicked. [21]I am going down to see whether these reports are true or not. Then I will know."

[22,23]So the other two went on toward Sodom, but the Lord remained with Abraham a while. Then Abraham approached him and said, "Will you kill good and bad alike? [24]Suppose you find fifty godly people there within the city—will you destroy it, and not spare it for their sakes? [25]That wouldn't be right! Surely you wouldn't do such a thing, to kill the godly with the wicked! Why, you would be treating godly and wicked exactly the same! Surely you wouldn't do that! Should not the Judge of all the earth be fair?"

[26]And God replied, "If I find fifty godly people there, I will spare the entire city for their sake."

[27]Then Abraham spoke again. "Since I have begun, let me go on and speak further to the Lord, though I am but dust and ashes. [28]*Suppose there are only forty-five?* Will you destroy the city for lack of five?"

And God said, "I will not destroy it if I find forty-five."

[29]Then Abraham went further with his request. *"Suppose there are only forty?"*

And God replied, "I won't destroy it if there are forty."

[30]"Please don't be angry," Abraham pleaded. "Let me speak: *suppose only thirty are found there?"*

And God replied, "I won't do it if there are thirty there."

[31]Then Abraham said, "Since I have dared to speak to God, let me continue—*suppose there are only twenty?"*

And God said, "Then I won't destroy it for the sake of the twenty."

[32]Finally, Abraham said, "Oh, let not the

18:17-19 Many people wonder why God chose one man and his family out of all others. Was this fair? These verses show us that God had an important purpose for choosing this one family. God picked Abraham so he could teach his descendants God's ways, for through his ancestral line would come Jesus the Messiah, a source of blessing for all the nations of the earth. God never planned to bless only one family. God chose one family to bring blessings and a means of recovery to all of us.

18:22-32 Often, we are urged to pray for others who have problems and difficulties. In these verses, we hear Abraham as he entreats God on behalf of Lot and his family. He is deeply concerned for their welfare and intercedes for them as he speaks with God. This is similar to what we are asked to do in the twelfth step of our recovery. We are to reach out and help others who are in need. Prayer is a powerful means of doing this.

Lord be angry; I will speak but this once more!
Suppose only ten are found?"
And God said, "Then, for the sake of the
ten, I won't destroy it."
33And the Lord went on his way when he
had finished his conversation with Abraham.
And Abraham returned to his tent.

CHAPTER 19

God Destroys Sodom

That evening the two angels came to the
entrance of the city of Sodom, and Lot was
sitting there as they arrived. When he saw
them he stood up to meet them, and welcomed them.
2"Sirs," he said, "come to my home as my
guests for the night; you can get up as early as
you like and be on your way again."
"Oh, no thanks," they said, "we'll just
stretch out here along the street."
3But he was very urgent, until at last they
went home with him, and he set a great feast
before them, complete with freshly baked unleavened bread. After the meal, 4as they were
preparing to retire for the night, the men of
the city—yes, Sodomites, young and old from
all over the city—surrounded the house 5and
shouted to Lot, "Bring out those men to us so
we can rape them."
6Lot stepped outside to talk to them, shutting the door behind him. 7"Please, fellows,"
he begged, "don't do such a wicked thing.
8Look—I have two virgin daughters, and I'll
surrender them to you to do with as you wish.
But leave these men alone, for they are under
my protection."
9"Stand back," they yelled. "Who do you
think you are? We let this fellow settle among
us and now he tries to tell us what to do! We'll
deal with you far worse than with those other
men." And they lunged at Lot and began
breaking down the door.
10But the two men reached out and pulled
Lot in and bolted the door 11and temporarily
blinded the men of Sodom so that they
couldn't find the door.
12"What relatives do you have here in the
city?" the men asked. "Get them out of this
place—sons-in-law, sons, daughters, or anyone else. 13For we will destroy the city completely. The stench of the place has reached to
heaven and God has sent us to destroy it."
14So Lot rushed out to tell his daughters'
fiancés, "Quick, get out of the city, for the
Lord is going to destroy it." But the young
men looked at him as though he had lost his
senses.
15At dawn the next morning the angels
became urgent. "Hurry," they said to Lot,
"take your wife and your two daughters who
are here and get out while you can, or you will
be caught in the destruction of the city."
16When Lot still hesitated, the angels seized
his hand and the hands of his wife and two
daughters and rushed them to safety, outside
the city, for the Lord was merciful.
17"Flee for your lives," the angels told him.
"And don't look back. Escape to the mountains.
Don't stay down here on the plain or you will
die."
18-20"Oh no, sirs, please," Lot begged, "since
you've been so kind to me and saved my life,
and you've granted me such mercy, let me flee
to that little village over there instead of into
the mountains, for I fear disaster in the mountain. See, the village is close by and it is just a
small one. Please, please, let me go there instead. Don't you see how small it is? And my
life will be saved."
21"All right," the angel said, "I accept your
proposition and won't destroy that little city.
22But hurry! For I can do nothing until you are
there." (From that time on that village was
named Zoar, meaning "Little City.")
23The sun was rising as Lot reached the
village. 24Then the Lord rained down fire and
flaming tar from heaven upon Sodom and
Gomorrah, 25and utterly destroyed them,
along with the other cities and villages of the
plain, eliminating all life—people, plants, and
animals alike. 26But Lot's wife looked back as

19:16 Even after Lot became aware of the impending doom of Sodom, he and his family continued to linger there. The angels had to force them to leave. Sometimes, even when we know what course of action is required, we need a push to get us moving. Let us thank God for the "angels" he has provided to help us through times of crisis. Sometimes, as the twelfth step suggests, we may be needed to push others out of a situations that are dangerous for them.

19:17-26 As we seek recovery from our problems and dependencies there is no looking back, no lingering. Doing so will only result in our destruction. Lot's wife failed to follow the program that the angels had set out for her family. They were to run from Sodom, never to look back. Lot's wife did look back, and it spelled her destruction. As we leave the destructive situations in our life it will be tempting to look back. But this final episode in the life of Lot's wife demonstrates the fatal consequences. We need to run, without looking back.

she was following along behind him and became a pillar of salt.

[27]That morning Abraham was up early and hurried out to the place where he had stood before the Lord. [28]He looked out across the plain to Sodom and Gomorrah and saw columns of smoke and fumes, as from a furnace, rising from the cities there. [29]So God heeded Abraham's plea and kept Lot safe, removing him from the maelstrom of death that engulfed the cities.

The Sin of Lot's Daughters

[30]Afterwards Lot left Zoar, fearful of the people there, and went to live in a cave in the mountains with his two daughters. [31]One day the older girl said to her sister, "There isn't a man anywhere in this entire area that our father would let us marry. And our father will soon be too old for having children. [32]Come, let's fill him with wine and then we will sleep with him, so that our clan will not come to an end." [33]So they got him drunk that night, and the older girl went in and had sexual intercourse with her father; but he was unaware of her lying down or getting up again.

[34]The next morning she said to her younger sister, "I slept with my father last night. Let's fill him with wine again tonight, and you go in and lie with him, so that our family line will continue." [35]So they got him drunk again that night, and the younger girl went in and lay with him, and, as before, he didn't know that anyone was there. [36]And so it was that both girls became pregnant from their father. [37]The older girl's baby was named Moab; he became the ancestor of the nation of the Moabites. [38]The name of the younger girl's baby was Benammi; he became the ancestor of the nation of the Ammonites.

CHAPTER 20

Abraham Deceives Abimelech

Now Abraham moved south to the Negeb and settled between Kadesh and Shur. One day, when visiting the city of Gerar, [2]he declared that Sarah was his sister! Then King Abimelech sent for her, and had her brought to him at his palace.

[3]But that night God came to him in a dream and told him, "You are a dead man, for that woman you took is married."

[4]But Abimelech hadn't slept with her yet, so he said, "Lord, will you slay an innocent man? [5]He told me, 'She is my sister,' and she herself said, 'Yes, he is my brother.' I hadn't the slightest intention of doing anything wrong."

[6]"Yes, I know," the Lord replied. "That is why I held you back from sinning against me; that is why I didn't let you touch her. [7]Now restore her to her husband, and he will pray for you (for he is a prophet) and you shall live. But if you don't return her to him, you are doomed to death along with all your household."

[8]The king was up early the next morning, and hastily called a meeting of all the palace personnel and told them what had happened. And great fear swept through the crowd.

[9,10]Then the king called for Abraham. "What is this you've done to us?" he demanded. "What have I done that deserves treatment like this, to make me and my kingdom guilty of this great sin? Who would suspect that you would do a thing like this to me? Whatever made you think of this vile deed?"

[11,12]"Well," Abraham said, "I figured this to be a godless place. 'They will want my wife and will kill me to get her,' I thought. And besides, she *is* my sister—or at least a half sister (we both have the same father)—and I

19:30-38 The incest in Lot's family was a direct consequence of Lot's irresponsible decisions in the past. He had spent his years in a wicked city and had failed to find suitable husbands for his daughters. Their desire for children led to deceit and incest. But there is hope beyond the shocking details of this story. Even though Lot failed in so many ways, many centuries later the apostle Peter used him as a clear example of one whose righteousness came by grace through faith (2 Peter 2:7-8). Lot was an extremely flawed person; but God is a gracious God. There is hope available for each of us, no matter how sordid our past.

20:1-18 Why is it so difficult to learn life's most important lessons? To protect himself, Abraham lied, telling Abimelech that his wife, Sarah, was his sister. The sad truth is, Abraham had made this mistake before (12:10-20). He had fallen into a pattern of using lies and deceit to protect himself. But this practice only caused pain to everyone involved. It also displayed how weak Abraham's faith in God was when confronted with difficult situations. The truth is crucial to building healthy relationships. And if we stand by the truth, we can trust God to stand by us when things get tough.

21:1-2 God keeps his word. When we claim his promises, we know that our sovereign God is able to fulfill them. Under normal circumstances there was no way that Sarah could have become a mother. But God gave her a child anyway. Sometimes we may feel our recovery is just as impossible; but with God, it can be a reality. With him, anything is possible.

married her. 13And when God sent me traveling far from my childhood home, I told her,
'Have the kindness to mention, wherever we
come, that you are my sister.'"
14Then King Abimelech took sheep and
oxen and servants—both men and women—
and gave them to Abraham, and returned
Sarah his wife to him.
15"Look my kingdom over, and choose the
place where you want to live," the king told
him. 16Then he turned to Sarah. "Look," he
said, "I am giving your 'brother' a thousand
silver pieces as damages for what I did, to
compensate for any embarrassment and to
settle any claim against me regarding this
matter. Now justice has been done."
17Then Abraham prayed, asking God to
cure the king and queen and the other
women of the household, so that they could
have children; 18for God had stricken all the
women with barrenness to punish Abimelech
for taking Abraham's wife.

CHAPTER 21

Isaac Is Born

Then God did as he had promised, and Sarah
became pregnant and gave Abraham a baby
son in his old age, at the time God had said;
3and Abraham named him Isaac (meaning
"Laughter!"). 4,5Eight days after he was born,
Abraham circumcised him, as God required.
(Abraham was 100 years old at that time.)
6And Sarah declared, "God has brought me
laughter! All who hear about this shall rejoice
with me. 7For who would have dreamed that
I would ever have a baby? Yet I have given
Abraham a child in his old age!"
8Time went by and the child grew and was
weaned; and Abraham gave a party to celebrate the happy occasion. 9But when Sarah
noticed Ishmael—the son of Abraham and
the Egyptian girl Hagar—teasing Isaac, 10she
turned upon Abraham and demanded, "Get
rid of that slave girl and her son. He is not
going to share your property with my son. I
won't have it."
11This upset Abraham very much, for after
all, Ishmael too was his son.
12But God told Abraham, "Don't be upset
over the boy or your slave-girl wife; do as
Sarah says, for Isaac is the son through whom
my promise will be fulfilled. 13And I will make
a nation of the descendants of the slave-girl's
son, too, because he also is yours."
14So Abraham got up early the next morning,
prepared food for the journey, and strapped a
canteen of water to Hagar's shoulders and sent

Faith

READ GENESIS 22:1-19

We demonstrate faith just by the fact that we are involved in a recovery program. If we didn't have faith in the promise of a better future for ourself and our family, we wouldn't put ourself through the hard work and pain involved in recovery. But as time passes, we may grow discouraged at the length of the process. We may have our spirits dampened by the ups and downs along the road, feeling our faith ebb more often than flow. Some people report instant release from their addictions, but for most of us it will take faith and patience to inherit the promise of a new life.

The writer of Hebrews wrote, "You will be anxious to follow the example of those who receive all that God has promised them because of their strong faith and patience. For instance, there was God's promise to Abraham: God took an oath in his own name, . . . that he would bless Abraham again and again, and give him a son and make him the father of a great nation of people. Then Abraham waited patiently until finally God gave him a son, Isaac, just as he had promised" (Hebrews 6:12-15). The entire story of Abraham's life can be found in Genesis 11–25.

The key point to consider here is that Abraham waited twenty-five years to see the promise fulfilled. As he waited, there were times when he showed impatience. At one point he took matters into his own hands, having a son by means of a surrogate wife. At times he probably wondered if he had ever really received the promise at all. He even laughed in disbelief when he was told the promise was soon to come about. But in the end he received the promise and "God blessed him in every way" (Genesis 24:1). Let's keep holding on! The fact that recovery usually takes time doesn't mean that our faith is in vain. ***Turn to page 91, Exodus 20.***

her away with their son. She walked out into
the wilderness of Beersheba, wandering aim-
lessly.
15When the water was gone she left the
youth in the shade of a bush 16and went off
and sat down a hundred yards or so away. "I
don't want to watch him die," she said, and
burst into tears, sobbing wildly.
17Then God heard the boy crying, and the
Angel of God called to Hagar from the sky,
"Hagar, what's wrong? Don't be afraid! For
God has heard the lad's cries as he is lying
there. 18Go and get him and comfort him, for
I will make a great nation from his descendants."
19Then God opened her eyes and she saw a
well; so she refilled the canteen and gave the
lad a drink. 20,21And God blessed the boy and he
grew up in the wilderness of Paran, and became
an expert archer. And his mother arranged a
marriage for him with a girl from Egypt.

Abraham and Abimelech Agree

22About this time King Abimelech and Phicol,
commander of his troops, came to Abraham
and said to him, "It is evident that God helps
you in everything you do; 23swear to me by
God's name that you won't defraud me or my
son or my grandson, but that you will be on
friendly terms with my country, as I have
been toward you."
24Abraham replied, "All right, I swear to it!"
25Then Abraham complained to the king
about a well the king's servants had taken
violently away from Abraham's servants.
26"This is the first I've heard of it," the king
exclaimed, "and I have no idea who is responsible. Why didn't you tell me before?"
27Then Abraham gave sheep and oxen to
the king, as sacrifices to seal their pact.
28,29But when he took seven ewe lambs and
set them off by themselves, the king inquired,
"Why are you doing that?"
30And Abraham replied, "They are my gift
to you as a public confirmation that this well
is mine."
31So from that time on the well was called
Beer-sheba ("Well of the Oath"), because that
was the place where they made their covenant. 32Then King Abimelech and Phicol,
commander of his army, returned home
again. 33And Abraham planted a tamarisk tree
beside the well and prayed there to the Lord,
calling upon the Eternal God. 34And Abraham
lived in the Philistine country for a long time.

CHAPTER 22

Abraham Offers His Only Son

Later on, God tested Abraham's [faith and
obedience].
"Abraham!" God called.
"Yes, Lord?" he replied.
2"Take with you your only son—yes, Isaac
whom you love so much—and go to the land
of Moriah and sacrifice him there as a burnt
offering upon one of the mountains which I'll
point out to you!"
3The next morning Abraham got up early,
chopped wood for a fire upon the altar, saddled his donkey, and took with him his son
Isaac and two young men who were his servants, and started off to the place where God
had told him to go. 4On the third day of the
journey Abraham saw the place in the distance.
5"Stay here with the donkey," Abraham
told the young men, "and the lad and I will
travel yonder and worship, and then come
right back."
6Abraham placed the wood for the burnt

22:1-2 God's request that Abraham sacrifice his son was a great test of faith, perhaps the greatest such test in history. Abraham's lifelong dreams were being realized in his beloved son Isaac. Wasn't God's promise of numerous descendants to be fulfilled through this child? But Abraham believed that God had his best in mind—and Abraham was right! He believed that no matter what God required of him, his obedience to God's plan was most important. He trusted that God would still make his promises come true, even without Isaac. Our faith in God's program may be confronted by similar tests. Are we ready to follow through with obedience?

22:16-18 The love Abraham must have felt for this long-awaited son! How his heart must have ached at the thought of killing him! How could this have been right? At the end of the story we see that God spared Isaac by providing a ram as his substitute. God has provided a substitute for all of us—Jesus Christ. God did not spare himself the pain of seeing his Son suffer and die. He suffered so that we might be spared suffering and have a means for recovery from sin and its destructive effects.

23:1 In this chapter we see Abraham mourning for his precious wife, Sarah. His grief was genuine, and he wanted to make proper preparations for paying his last respects. Grief comes into each of our lives, and proper channels for its expression must be found. If we fail to grieve over our personal losses properly, it will be easy to fall into addictions and dependencies to try and hide the pain. If we express our pain constructively, it will be less likely to destroy us.

offering upon Isaac's shoulders, while he himself carried the knife and the flint for striking
a fire. So the two of them went on together.
7"Father," Isaac asked, "we have the wood
and the flint to make the fire, but where is the
lamb for the sacrifice?"
8"God will see to it, my son," Abraham
replied. And they went on.
9When they arrived at the place where God
had told Abraham to go, he built an altar and
placed the wood in order, ready for the fire, and
then tied Isaac and laid him on the altar over
the wood. 10And Abraham took the knife and
lifted it up to plunge it into his son, to slay him.
11At that moment the Angel of God shouted
to him from heaven, "Abraham! Abraham!"
"Yes, Lord!" he answered.
12"Lay down the knife; don't hurt the lad in
any way," the Angel said, "for I know that
God is first in your life—you have not withheld even your beloved son from me."
13Then Abraham noticed a ram caught by
its horns in a bush. So he took the ram and
sacrificed it, instead of his son, as a burnt
offering on the altar. 14Abraham named the
place "Jehovah provides"—and it still goes by
that name to this day.
15Then the Angel of God called again to
Abraham from heaven. 16"I, the Lord, have
sworn by myself that because you have
obeyed me and have not withheld even your
beloved son from me, 17I will bless you with
incredible blessings and multiply your descendants into countless thousands and millions, like the stars above you in the sky, and
like the sands along the seashore. They will
conquer their enemies, 18and your offspring
will be a blessing to all the nations of the
earth—all because you have obeyed me."
19So they returned to his young men and
traveled home again to Beer-sheba.

Nahor's Family

20-23After this, a message arrived that Milcah,
the wife of Abraham's brother Nahor, had
borne him eight sons. Their names were: Uz,
the oldest, Buz, the next oldest, Kemuel
(father of Aram), Chesed, Hazo, Pildash, Jid-
laph, Bethuel (father of Rebekah).
24He also had four other children from his
concubine, Reumah: Tebah, Gaham, Tahash,
Maacah.

CHAPTER 23

Sarah Dies

When Sarah was 127 years old, she died in
Hebron in the land of Canaan; there Abraham

Taking Time to Grieve

BIBLE READING: Genesis 23:1-4; 35:19-21

We were entirely ready for God to remove all these defects of character.

The pathway to recovery and finding new life also involves the death process. The different means we used to cope were "defective," but still, they did give us comfort or companionship. Giving them up is often like suffering the death of a loved one.

Abraham and his grandson, Jacob, both lost loved ones as they traveled to the Promised Land. "Sarah . . . died in Hebron in the land of Canaan; there Abraham mourned and wept for her. Then, standing beside her body, he said . . . 'Here I am, a visitor in a foreign land, with no place to bury my wife. Please sell me a piece of ground for this purpose.' . . . So Abraham buried Sarah there" (Genesis 23:1-4, 19). A generation later, Jacob was given a new name, Israel, and the promise of a great heritage in the Promised Land. On his way there, he, too, lost his beloved wife. She died while giving birth to their son Benjamin. "So Rachel died, and was buried near the road to Ephrath (also called Bethlehem). And Jacob set up a monument of stones upon her grave, and it is there to this day. Then Israel journeyed on" (Genesis 35:19-21).

As we journey on in our new life, we will necessarily lose some of our defective ways of coping. When this happens, we need to stop and take time to give our losses a proper burial. We need to put them away, cover the shame, and allow ourselves to grieve the loss of something very familiar to us. When the time of grieving is over, we, too, can journey on. ***Turn to page 623, Psalm 51.***

mourned and wept for her. 3Then, standing beside her body, he said to the men of Heth:

4"Here I am, a visitor in a foreign land, with no place to bury my wife. Please sell me a piece of ground for this purpose."

5,6"Certainly," the men replied, "for you are an honored prince of God among us; it will be a privilege to have you choose the finest of our sepulchres, so that you can bury her there."

7Then Abraham bowed low before them and said, 8"Since this is your feeling in the matter, be so kind as to ask Ephron, Zohar's son, 9to sell me the cave of Mach-pelah, down at the end of his field. I will of course pay the full price for it, whatever is publicly agreed upon, and it will become a permanent cemetery for my family."

10Ephron was sitting there among the others, and now he spoke up, answering Abraham as the others listened, speaking publicly before all the citizens of the town: 11"Sir," he said to Abraham, "please listen to me. I will give you the cave and the field without any charge. Here in the presence of my people, I give it to you free. Go and bury your dead."

12Abraham bowed again to the men of Heth, 13and replied to Ephron, as all listened: "No, let me buy it from you. Let me pay the full price of the field, and then I will bury my dead."

14,15"Well, the land is worth 400 pieces of silver," Ephron said, "but what is that between friends? Go ahead and bury your dead."

16So Abraham paid Ephron the price he had suggested—400 pieces of silver, as publicly agreed. 17,18This is the land he bought: Ephron's field at Mach-pelah, near Mamre, and the cave at the end of the field, and all the trees in the field. They became his permanent possession, by agreement in the presence of the men of Heth at the city gate. 19,20So Abraham buried Sarah there, in the field and cave deeded to him by the men of Heth as a burial plot.

CHAPTER 24

Isaac Gets Married

Abraham was now a very old man, and God blessed him in every way. 2One day Abraham said to his household administrator, who was his oldest servant,

3"Swear by Jehovah, the God of heaven and earth, that you will not let my son marry one of these local girls, these Canaanites. 4Go instead to my homeland, to my relatives, and find a wife for him there."

5"But suppose I can't find a girl who will come so far from home?" the servant asked. "Then shall I take Isaac there, to live among your relatives?"

6"No!" Abraham warned. "Be careful that you don't do that under any circumstance. 7For the Lord God of heaven told me to leave that land and my people, and promised to give me and my children this land. He will send his angel on ahead of you, and he will see to it that you find a girl from there to be my son's wife. 8But if you don't succeed, then you are free from this oath; but under no circumstances are you to take my son there."

9So the servant vowed to follow Abraham's instructions.

10He took with him ten of Abraham's camels loaded with samples of the best of everything his master owned and journeyed to Iraq, to Nahor's village. 11There he made the camels kneel down outside the town, beside a spring. It was evening, and the women of the village were coming to draw water.

12"O Jehovah, the God of my master," he prayed, "show kindness to my master Abraham and help me to accomplish the purpose of my journey. 13See, here I am, standing beside this spring, and the girls of the village are coming out to draw water. 14This is my request: When I ask one of them for a drink and she says, 'Yes, certainly, and I will water your camels too!'—let her be the one you have appointed as Isaac's wife. That is how I will know."

15,16As he was still speaking to the Lord about this, a beautiful young girl named Rebekah arrived with a water jug on her shoulder and filled it at the spring. (Her father was Bethuel the son of Nahor and his wife Milcah.) 17Running over to her, the servant asked her for a drink.

18"Certainly, sir," she said, and quickly lowered the jug for him to drink. 19Then she said, "I'll draw water for your camels, too, until they have enough!"

20So she emptied the jug into the watering trough and ran down to the spring again and kept carrying water to the camels until they had enough. 21The servant said no more, but watched her carefully to see if she would finish the job, so that he would know whether she was the one. 22Then at last, when the camels had finished drinking, he produced a quarter-ounce gold earring and two five-ounce gold bracelets for her wrists.

ISAAC & REBEKAH

Deception is extremely harmful in any relationship but even more so in the relationship of a husband and wife. Isaac and Rebekah started out with a marriage in which each loved and honored the other. However, as the marriage progressed, so did the deception on both sides. The end result was a family torn apart by strife.

As his father, Abraham, had done with Sarah, Isaac lied to Abimelech, claiming that Rebekah was not his wife. He did this to protect himself, fearing that Abimelech would kill him to take his wife. Deception based on the idea that "the end justifies the means" may at times seem a necessary evil within some families. But, in fact, it often starts a string of hurtful lies between marriage partners and other family members.

Isaac and Rebekah were blessed with twin sons, Esau and Jacob. Isaac liked Esau the best, while Rebekah preferred Jacob. This playing of favorites split the family in two and set the stage for further conflict and deception. When the time came for Isaac to give Esau his blessing, Jacob willingly took part in Rebekah's plan to deceive her husband. Deception had become a natural practice in this dysfunctional family.

This story of deception in a marriage is sad, but hardly uncommon. What started out as a loving marriage based on honesty and a desire to serve God soon became filled with deception and distance. It is important to notice, however, that God remained faithful to his promises to Isaac and Rebekah despite their failures.

Isaac and Rebekah's story is told in Genesis 24-28. Both are mentioned in Romans 9:10. Isaac is also referred to in Romans 9:7-8; Hebrews 11:17-20; and James 2:21-24.

STRENGTHS AND ACCOMPLISHMENTS:
- They had a caring and loving marriage—at least until their sons were born.
- They were the recipients of God's promises to Abraham.

WEAKNESSES AND MISTAKES:
- Isaac and Rebekah often allowed the end to justify the means.
- In facing difficult situations, Isaac and Rebekah often lied to avoid the problems they faced.
- Both of them alienated each other by playing favorites with their sons.

LESSONS FROM THEIR LIVES:
- God keeps his promises and remains faithful even when we are faithless.
- God's promises and plans are bigger than we are.
- Playing favorites is harmful in a family.
- Deception is destructive in marriage and other significant relationships.

KEY VERSE:
"And Isaac brought Rebekah into his mother's tent, and she became his wife. He loved her very much, and she was a special comfort to him after the loss of his mother" (Genesis 24:67).

23"Whose daughter are you, miss?" he
asked. "Would your father have any room to
put us up for the night?"
24"My father is Bethuel," she replied. "My
grandparents are Milcah and Nahor. 25Yes, we
have plenty of straw and food for the camels,
and a guest room."
26The man stood there a moment with head
bowed, worshiping Jehovah. 27"Thank you,
Lord God of my master Abraham," he prayed;
"thank you for being so kind and true to him,
and for leading me straight to the family of
my master's relatives."
28The girl ran home to tell her folks,
29,30and when her brother Laban saw the
ring, and the bracelets on his sister's wrists,
and heard her story, he rushed out to the
spring where the man was still standing
beside his camels, and said to him, 31"Come
and stay with us, friend; why stand here
outside the city when we have a room all
ready for you, and a place prepared for the
camels!"
32So the man went home with Laban, and
Laban gave him straw to bed down the camels, and feed for them, and water for the camel
drivers to wash their feet. 33Then supper was
served. But the old man said, "I don't want to
eat until I have told you why I am here."
"All right," Laban said, "tell us your errand."
34"I am Abraham's servant," he explained.
35"And Jehovah has overwhelmed my master
with blessings so that he is a great man among
the people of his land. God has given him
flocks of sheep and herds of cattle, and a
fortune in silver and gold, and many slaves
and camels and donkeys.
36"Now when Sarah, my master's wife, was
very old, she gave birth to my master's son, and
my master has given him everything he owns.
37And my master made me promise not to let

Isaac marry one of the local girls, [38]but to come to his relatives here in this far-off land, to his brother's family, and to bring back a girl from here to marry his son. [39]'But suppose I can't find a girl who will come?' I asked him. [40]'She will,' he told me—'for my Lord, in whose presence I have walked, will send his angel with you and make your mission successful. Yes, find a girl from among my relatives, from my brother's family. [41]You are under oath to go and ask. If they won't send anyone, then you are freed from your promise.'

[42]"Well, this afternoon when I came to the spring I prayed this prayer: 'O Jehovah, the God of my master Abraham, if you are planning to make my mission a success, please guide me in this way: [43]Here I am, standing beside this spring. I will say to some girl who comes out to draw water, "Please give me a drink of water!" [44]And she will reply, "Certainly! And I'll water your camels too!" Let that girl be the one you have selected to be the wife of my master's son.'

[45]"Well, while I was still speaking these words, Rebekah was coming along with her water jug upon her shoulder; and she went down to the spring and drew water and filled the jug. I said to her, 'Please give me a drink.' [46]She quickly lifted the jug down from her shoulder so that I could drink, and told me, 'Certainly, sir, and I will water your camels too!' So she did! [47]Then I asked her, 'Whose family are you from?' And she told me, 'Nahor's. My father is Bethuel, the son of Nahor and his wife Milcah.' So I gave her the ring and the bracelets. [48]Then I bowed my head and worshiped and blessed Jehovah, the God of my master Abraham, because he had led me along just the right path to find a girl from the family of my master's brother. [49]So tell me, yes or no. Will you or won't you be kind to my master and do what is right? When you tell me, then I'll know what my next step should be, whether to move this way or that."

[50]Then Laban and Bethuel replied, "The Lord has obviously brought you here, so what can we say? [51]Take her and go! Yes, let her be the wife of your master's son, as Jehovah has directed."

[52]At this reply, Abraham's servant fell to his knees before Jehovah. [53]Then he brought out jewels set in solid gold and silver for Rebekah, and lovely clothing; and he gave many valuable presents to her mother and brother. [54]Then they had supper, and the servant and the men with him stayed there overnight. But early the next morning he said, "Send me back to my master!"

[55]"But we want Rebekah here at least another ten days or so!" her mother and brother exclaimed. "Then she can go."

[56]But he pleaded, "Don't hinder my return; the Lord has made my mission successful, and I want to report back to my master."

[57]"Well," they said, "we'll call the girl and ask her what she thinks."

[58]So they called Rebekah. "Are you willing to go with this man?" they asked her.

And she replied, "Yes, I will go."

[59]So they told her good-bye, sending along the woman who had been her childhood nurse, [60]and blessed her with this blessing as they parted:

"Our sister,
May you become
The mother of many millions!
May your descendants
Overcome all your enemies."

[61]So Rebekah and her servant girls mounted the camels and went with him.

[62]Meanwhile, Isaac, whose home was in the Negeb, had returned to Beer-lahai-roi. [63]One evening as he was taking a walk out in the fields, meditating, he looked up and saw the camels coming. [64]Rebekah noticed him and quickly dismounted.

[65]"Who is that man walking through the fields to meet us?" she asked the servant.

And he replied, "It is my master's son!" So she covered her face with her veil. [66]Then the servant told Isaac the whole story.

[67]And Isaac brought Rebekah into his mother's tent, and she became his wife. He loved her very much, and she was a special comfort to him after the loss of his mother.

CHAPTER 25

Abraham Dies

Now Abraham married again. Keturah was his new wife, and she bore him several children: Zimran, Jokshan, Medan, Midian, Ishbak, Shuah. [3]Jokshan's two sons were Sheba and Dedan. Dedan's sons were Asshurim, Letu-

24:67 When we lose someone close to us, it is important that we take some time for rebuilding. It is encouraging to notice that, after losing one major family relationship, Isaac found comfort in a new one. As people are taken away from us, God will provide others to give us the support we need to live a healthy and productive life.

ESAU & JACOB

Sibling rivalry is a natural, though sometimes difficult, aspect of family relationships. Brothers, especially those close in age, often don't get along well as children or young adults. But the twins, Esau and Jacob, took this natural conflict to another level of intensity altogether. Fortunately there was reconciliation later in life, though it required considerable emotional and spiritual growth on the part of both.

Actually, the intense rivalry was predicted by God even before the twins were born. And the situation wasn't helped any by the parents playing favorites with their sons. Isaac clearly preferred Esau, while Rebekah favored Jacob. Relationships in this family went from bad to worse when Esau sold Jacob his birthright for the momentary gratification of his hungry stomach.

One event finally shattered the already fragile relationship between these brothers. Jacob deceived his almost blind father into giving him the final blessing that was intended for the firstborn, Esau. Jacob's elaborate scheme, masterminded by his mother, so enraged Esau that he vowed to kill his brother after his father's death. The victim of his own lack of honesty, Jacob fled for his life. He settled with his uncle Laban and soon married his two daughters, Leah and Rachel.

While living with Laban's family, Jacob became the object of his uncle's own deceitful practices. Through this experience, Jacob learned painful lessons regarding the importance of love and honesty. God had been working in Jacob's life, drawing him progressively closer to himself. So with a sure knowledge of God's presence, Jacob became willing to face his past. He set out on the long journey home and, despite his fears, found forgiveness and reconciliation in the waiting embrace of his brother.

STRENGTHS AND ACCOMPLISHMENTS:

- Both were willing to let go of past failures to find a better future.
- Esau grew to the point of being able to forgive after feeling significant disappointment and anger.
- Jacob matured to the point where he could be honest and humbly seek forgiveness.

WEAKNESSES AND MISTAKES:

- Both were intent on having their own way with little thought of how it might affect others.
- Esau sought instant gratification and suffered great losses as a result.
- Jacob was often dishonest and deceitful in his dealings.

LESSONS FROM THEIR LIVES:

- Parents should never play favorites with their children.
- Forgiveness can take place even when deep hurts have been suffered.
- Even habitually deceitful people can face the past and recover their relationships.

KEY VERSE:

"And then Esau ran to meet him [Jacob] and embraced him affectionately and kissed him; and both of them were in tears!" (Genesis 33:4).

The story of Esau and Jacob is told in Genesis 25–33. Both are also mentioned in Malachi 1:2-3; Acts 3:13; Romans 9:10-13; and Hebrews 11:9, 20-21. Esau is referred to in Hebrews 12:16-17, while Jacob is mentioned in Hosea 12:3-5 and Matthew 1:2; 22:32.

---

shim, and Leummim. 4Midian's sons were
Ephah, Epher, Hanoch, Abida, and Eldaah.
5Abraham deeded everything he owned to
Isaac; 6however, he gave gifts to the sons of his
concubines and sent them off into the east,
away from Isaac.
7,8Then Abraham died, at the ripe old age of
175, 9,10and his sons Isaac and Ishmael buried
him in the cave of Mach-pelah near Mamre,
in the field Abraham had purchased from
Ephron the son of Zohar, the Hethite, where
Sarah, Abraham's wife, was buried.
11After Abraham's death, God poured out
rich blessings upon Isaac. (Isaac had now
moved south to Beer-lahai-roi in the Negeb.)
12-15Here is a list, in the order of their births,
of the descendants of Ishmael, who was the
son of Abraham and Hagar the Egyptian,
Sarah's slave girl: Nebaioth, Kedar, Abdeel,
Mibsam, Mishma, Dumah, Massa, Hadad,
Tema, Jetur, Naphish, Kedemah. 16These
twelve sons of his became the founders of
twelve tribes that bore their names. 17Ishmael
finally died at the age of 137, and joined his
ancestors. 18These descendants of Ishmael
were scattered across the country from Havilah to Shur (which is a little way to the northeast of the Egyptian border in the direction of
Assyria). And they were constantly at war
with one another.

Jacob and Esau Are Born

19This is the story of Isaac's children: 20Isaac
was forty years old when he married Rebekah,

the daughter of Bethuel the Aramean from Paddam-aram. Rebekah was the sister of Laban. 21Isaac pleaded with Jehovah to give Rebekah a child, for even after many years of marriage she had no children. Then at last she became pregnant. 22And it seemed as though children were fighting each other inside her!

"I can't endure this," she exclaimed. So she asked the Lord about it.

23And he told her, "The sons in your womb shall become two rival nations. One will be stronger than the other; and the older shall be a servant of the younger!"

24And sure enough, she had twins. 25The first was born so covered with reddish hair that one would think he was wearing a fur coat! So they called him "Esau." 26Then the other twin was born with his hand on Esau's heel! So they called him Jacob (meaning "Grabber"). Isaac was sixty years old when the twins were born.

Esau Sells His Birthright

27As the boys grew, Esau became a skillful hunter, while Jacob was a quiet sort who liked to stay at home. 28Isaac's favorite was Esau, because of the venison he brought home, and Rebekah's favorite was Jacob.

29One day Jacob was cooking stew when Esau arrived home exhausted from the hunt.

30*Esau:* "Boy, am I starved! Give me a bite of that red stuff there!" (From this came his nickname "Edom," which means "Red Stuff.")

31*Jacob:* "All right, trade me your birthright for it!"

32*Esau:* "When a man is dying of starvation, what good is his birthright?"

33*Jacob:* "Well then, vow to God that it is mine!"

And Esau vowed, thereby selling all his eldest-son rights to his younger brother. 34Then Jacob gave Esau bread, peas, and stew; so he ate and drank and went on about his business, indifferent to the loss of the rights he had thrown away.

CHAPTER 26

Isaac Deceives Abimelech

Now a severe famine overshadowed the land, as had happened before, in Abraham's time, and so Isaac moved to the city of Gerar where Abimelech, king of the Philistines, lived.

2Jehovah appeared to him there and told him, "Don't go to Egypt. 3Do as I say and stay here in this land. If you do, I will be with you and bless you, and I will give all this land to you and to your descendants, just as I promised Abraham your father. 4And I will cause your descendants to become as numerous as the stars! And I will give them all of these lands; and they shall be a blessing to all the nations of the earth. 5I will do this because Abraham obeyed my commandments and laws."

6So Isaac stayed in Gerar. 7And when the men there asked him about Rebekah, he said, "She is my sister!" For he feared for his life if he told them she was his wife; he was afraid they would kill him to get her, for she was very attractive. 8But sometime later, King Abimelech, king of the Philistines, looked out of a window and saw Isaac and Rebekah making love.

9Abimelech called for Isaac and exclaimed,

25:23 This prenatal prophecy concerning Jacob and Esau portends conflict between the brothers—and it goes beyond just normal sibling rivalry! Unfortunately, the subsequent family history amply bears this out. Sibling rivalry is often very destructive to family relationships and can easily get out of control. Siblings often separate for life, carrying with them years of hard feelings that taint all their other relationships. Reconciliation with those we have hurt is one of the goals of recovery. Let us take steps toward recovering our important relationships.

25:34 Esau traded his rights as a firstborn son for a bowl of stew to fill his empty stomach. He was indifferent to the things in life that were really important. His primary concern was his physical satisfaction, with no thought at all for his future. He hadn't learned how to delay gratification. The lesson Esau needed to learn is very important for all of us in recovery. We need to see things in the long view. If we can picture the positive results of life in recovery, we will be able to give up the momentary pleasures that keep us from getting there.

26:6-11 Children learn from their parents. Unfortunately, they are not selective about what they learn. They don't learn the good things and ignore the bad. These verses demonstrate what Isaac learned from his father, Abraham. Doubtless, he had heard how Abraham had passed Sarah off as his sister to protect himself (12:10-20; 20:1-18). It is amazing how the sinful patterns of our parents are often repeated in our own life. How often our family dysfunctions repeat themselves generation after generation! Isaac would have been wise to tell the truth and trust God to protect him. Trust in God is one weapon we have to fight against destructive family patterns.

"She is your wife! Why did you say she is your
sister?"
"Because I was afraid I would be murdered," Isaac replied. "I thought someone
would kill me to get her from me."
10"How could you treat us this way?" Abimelech exclaimed. "Someone might carelessly
have raped her, and we would be doomed."
11Then Abimelech made a public proclamation: "Anyone harming this man or his wife
shall die."

Isaac Has a Dispute with Abimelech

12That year Isaac's crops were tremendous—
100 times the grain he sowed. For Jehovah
blessed him. 13He was soon a man of great
wealth and became richer and richer. 14He had
large flocks of sheep and goats, great herds of
cattle, and many servants. And the Philistines
became jealous of him. 15So they filled up his
wells with earth—all those dug by the servants of his father Abraham.
16And King Abimelech asked Isaac to leave
the country. "Go somewhere else," he said,
"for you have become too rich and powerful
for us."
17So Isaac moved to Gerar Valley and lived
there instead. 18And Isaac redug the wells of
his father Abraham, the ones the Philistines
had filled after his father's death, and gave
them the same names they had had before,
when his father had named them. 19His shepherds also dug a new well in Gerar Valley, and
found a gushing underground spring.
20Then the local shepherds came and
claimed it. "This is our land and our well,"
they said, and argued over it with Isaac's herdsmen. So he named the well, "The Well of
Argument!" 21Isaac's men then dug another
well, but again there was a fight over it. So he
called it, "The Well of Anger." 22Abandoning
that one, he dug again, and the local residents
finally left him alone. So he called it, "The Well
of Room Enough for Us at Last!" "For now at
last," he said, "the Lord has made room for us
and we shall thrive."

Isaac and Abimelech Are Reconciled

23When he went to Beer-sheba, 24Jehovah appeared to him on the night of his arrival. "I
am the God of Abraham your father," he said.
"Fear not, for I am with you and will bless
you, and will give you so many descendants
that they will become a great nation—because
of my promise to Abraham, who obeyed me."
25Then Isaac built an altar and worshiped
Jehovah; and he settled there, and his servants dug a well.
26One day Isaac had visitors from Gerar.
King Abimelech arrived with his advisor,
Ahuzzath, and also Phicol, his army commander.
27"Why have you come?" Isaac asked them.
"This is obviously no friendly visit, since you
kicked me out in a most uncivil way."
28"Well," they said, "we can plainly see that
Jehovah is blessing you. We've decided to ask
for a treaty between us. 29Promise that you
will not harm us, just as we have not harmed
you, and in fact, have done only good to you
and have sent you away in peace; we bless you
in the name of the Lord."
30So Isaac prepared a great feast for them,
and they ate and drank in preparation for the
treaty ceremonies. 31In the morning, as soon
as they were up, they each took solemn oaths
to seal a nonaggression pact. Then Isaac sent
them happily home again.
32That very same day Isaac's servants came
to tell him, "We have found water"—in the
well they had been digging. 33So he named the
well, "The Well of the Oath," and the city that
grew up there was named "Oath," and is
called that to this day.
34Esau, at the age of forty, married a girl
named Judith, daughter of Be-eri the Hethite;
and he also married Basemath, daughter of
Elon the Hethite. 35But Isaac and Rebekah
were bitter about his marrying them.

CHAPTER 27

Jacob Deceives Isaac

One day, in Isaac's old age when he was almost blind, he called for Esau his oldest son.

Isaac: "My son?"
Esau: "Yes, father?"
2-4*Isaac:* "I am an old man now, and expect
every day to be my last. Take your bow
and arrows out into the fields and get me
some venison, and prepare it just the way

26:23-24 Isaac was afraid, and he had good reason to be. He was surrounded by hostile neighbors who greatly outnumbered his household. He didn't have a place to call his own, except the burial site of his parents. He lived in Gerar "by permission," as it were. At this time, God came to Isaac with this soothing message, "Fear not." We may feel as if we don't belong anywhere. We may have forfeited our place in society. It may seem as though there are enemies all around us. But even when things are at their worst, we need to be aware that God is with us, whispering, "Fear not."

I like it—savory and good—and bring it here for me to eat, and I will give you the blessings that belong to you, my first-born son, before I die."

5But Rebekah overheard the conversation. So when Esau left for the field to hunt for the venison, 6,7she called her son Jacob and told him what his father had said to his brother.

8-10*Rebekah:* "Now do exactly as I tell you. Go out to the flocks and bring me two young goats, and I'll prepare your father's favorite dish from them. Then take it to your father, and after he has enjoyed it he will bless *you* before his death, instead of Esau!"

11,12*Jacob:* "But mother! He won't be fooled that easily. Think how hairy Esau is, and how smooth my skin is! What if my father feels me? He'll think I'm making a fool of him and curse me instead of blessing me!"

13*Rebekah:* "Let his curses be on me, dear son. Just do what I tell you. Go out and get the goats."

14So Jacob followed his mother's instructions, bringing the dressed kids, which she
prepared in his father's favorite way. 15Then
she took Esau's best clothes—they were there
in the house—and instructed Jacob to put
them on. 16 And she made him a pair of gloves
from the hairy skin of the young goats, and
fastened a strip of the hide around his neck;
17then she gave him the meat, with its rich
aroma, and some fresh-baked bread.

18Jacob carried the platter of food into the room where his father was lying.

Jacob: "Father?"

Isaac: "Yes? Who is it, my son—Esau or Jacob?"

19*Jacob:* "It's Esau, your oldest son. I've done as you told me to. Here is the delicious venison you wanted. Sit up and eat it, so that you will bless me with all your heart!"

20*Isaac:* "How were you able to find it so quickly, my son?"

Jacob: "Because Jehovah your God put it in my path!"

21*Isaac:* "Come over here. I want to feel you and be sure it really is Esau!"

22(Jacob goes over to his father. He feels him!)

Isaac: (to himself) "The voice is Jacob's, but the hands are Esau's!"

23(The ruse convinces Isaac and he gives Jacob his blessings):

24*Isaac:* "Are you really Esau?"

Jacob: "Yes, of course."

25*Isaac:* "Then bring me the venison, and I will eat it and bless you with all my heart."

(Jacob takes it over to him and Isaac eats; he also drinks the wine Jacob brings him.)

26*Isaac:* "Come here and kiss me, my son!"

(Jacob goes over and kisses him on the cheek. Isaac sniffs his clothes, and finally seems convinced.)

27-29*Isaac:* "The smell of my son is the good smell of the earth and fields that Jehovah has blessed. May God always give you plenty of rain for your crops, and good harvests and grapes. May many nations be your slaves. Be the master of your brothers. May all your relatives bow low before you. Cursed are all who curse you, and blessed are all who bless you."

30(As soon as Isaac has blessed Jacob, and
almost before Jacob leaves the room, Esau
arrives, coming in from his hunting. 31He also
has prepared his father's favorite dish and
brings it to him.)

Esau: "Here I am, father, with the venison. Sit up and eat it so that you can give me your finest blessings!"

27:1-29 It is heartbreaking to watch Rebekah and Jacob conspire to deceive Isaac. Notice the great lengths to which they go to fool the old man. They knew that Jacob was the heir to God's promises through Abraham (see 25:23, 29-33), but through their deceit they were trying to make God's program happen. That never works without causing pain or added trouble somewhere else. God is in charge of the timetable of our recovery program. We need to stick with the truth and move at his pace.

27:33 At this point Isaac realized he had blessed Jacob instead of Esau, but he could not take his blessing back. Jacob would receive the inheritance and blessing of the firstborn son. It became clear that it was God's plan that Jacob should be the recipient of God's promises to Abraham, so Isaac acquiesced to God's will. There are often times when God, through circumstances, will veto our plans. Through grace, he often delivers us from making bad choices and protects us from the terrible consequences. As the third step reminds us, we must surrender our will to God if we are to progress in recovery.

32 *Isaac:* "Who is it?"
Esau: "Why, it's me, of course! Esau, your
oldest son!"

33 (Isaac begins to tremble noticeably.)

Isaac: "Then who is it who was just here
with venison, and I have already eaten it
and blessed him with irrevocable blessing?"

34 (Esau begins to sob with deep and bitter
sobs.)

Esau: "O my father, bless me, bless me too!"
35 *Isaac:* "Your brother was here and tricked
me and has carried away your blessing."
36 *Esau:* (bitterly) "No wonder they call him
'The Cheater.' For he took my birthright,
and now he has stolen my blessing. Oh,
haven't you saved even one blessing for
me?"
37 *Isaac:* "I have made him your master, and
have given him yourself and all of his relatives as his servants. I have guaranteed
him abundance of grain and wine—what
is there left to give?"
38 *Esau:* "Not one blessing left for me? O my
father, bless me too."

(Isaac says nothing as Esau weeps.)

39,40 *Isaac:* "Yours will be no life of ease and
luxury, but you shall hew your way with
your sword. For a time you will serve
your brother, but you will finally shake
loose from him and be free."

41 So Esau hated Jacob because of what he
had done to him. He said to himself, "My
father will soon be gone, and then I will kill
Jacob." 42 But someone got wind of what he
was planning and reported it to Rebekah. She
sent for Jacob and told him that his life was
being threatened by Esau.

43 "This is what to do," she said. "Flee to
your Uncle Laban in Haran. 44 Stay there with
him awhile until your brother's fury is spent,
45 and he forgets what you have done. Then I
will send for you. For why should I be be-
reaved of both of you in one day?"

46 Then Rebekah said to Isaac, "I'm sick and
tired of these local girls. I'd rather die than see
Jacob marry one of them."

CHAPTER 28

Jacob Is Sent to Find a Wife

So Isaac called for Jacob and blessed him and
said to him, "Don't marry one of these Canaanite girls. 2 Instead, go at once to Paddan-
aram, to the house of your grandfather
Bethuel, and marry one of your cousins—
your Uncle Laban's daughters. 3 God Almighty
bless you and give you many children; may
you become a great nation of many tribes!
4 May God pass on to you and to your descendants the mighty blessings promised to Abraham. May you own this land where we now
are foreigners, for God has given it to Abraham."

5 So Isaac sent Jacob away, and he went to
Paddan-aram to visit his Uncle Laban, his
mother's brother—the son of Bethuel the Aramean.

6-8 Esau realized that his father despised the
local girls, and that his father and mother had
sent Jacob to Paddan-aram, with his father's
blessing, to get a wife from there, and that
they had strictly warned him against marrying a Canaanite girl, and that Jacob had
agreed and had left for Paddan-aram. 9 So Esau
went to his Uncle Ishmael's family and married another wife from there, besides the
wives he already had. Her name was Mahalath, the sister of Nebaioth, and daughter of
Ishmael, Abraham's son.

Jacob's Dream and God's Promise

10 So Jacob left Beer-sheba and journeyed toward Haran. 11 That night, when he stopped to
camp at sundown, he found a rock for a
headrest and lay down to sleep, 12 and
dreamed that a staircase reached from earth to
heaven, and he saw the angels of God going
up and down upon it.

13 At the top of the stairs stood the Lord. "I
am Jehovah," he said, "the God of Abraham,
and of your father, Isaac. The ground you are
lying on is yours! I will give it to you and to
your descendants. 14 For you will have descendants as many as dust! They will cover the
land from east to west and from north to
south; and all the nations of the earth will be
blessed through you and your descendants.
15 What's more, I am with you, and will protect

27:34-40 Here, Esau demonstrates tearful remorse, but according to Hebrews 12:16-17, it was too late. As a young man he had sold his future for instant gratification. Now he had to suffer the consequences for not waiting to fill his hungry stomach. Those of us in recovery know what this is like. Time and again we have chosen to sell our future for immediate satisfaction or for something that will dull the pain we are hiding inside. But even though time has been lost, there is hope for those who are willing to take steps toward recovery.

you wherever you go, and will bring you back safely to this land; I will be with you constantly until I have finished giving you all I am promising."

[16,17]Then Jacob woke up. "God lives here!" he exclaimed in terror. "I've stumbled into his home! This is the awesome entrance to heaven!" [18]The next morning he got up very early and set his stone headrest upright as a memorial pillar, and poured olive oil over it. [19]He named the place Bethel ("House of God"), though the previous name of the nearest village was Luz.

[20]And Jacob vowed this vow to God: "If God will help and protect me on this journey and give me food and clothes, [21]and will bring me back safely to my father, then I will choose Jehovah as my God! [22]And this memorial pillar shall become a place for worship; and I will give you back a tenth of everything you give me!"

CHAPTER 29

Jacob Meets Rachel

Jacob traveled on, finally arriving in the land of the East. [2]He saw in the distance three flocks of sheep lying beside a well in an open field, waiting to be watered. But a heavy stone covered the mouth of the well. [3](The custom was that the stone was not removed until all the flocks were there. After watering them, the stone was rolled back over the mouth of the well again.) [4]Jacob went over to the shepherds and asked them where they lived.

"At Haran," they said.

[5]"Do you know a fellow there named Laban, the son of Nahor?"

"We sure do."

[6]"How is he?"

"He's well and prosperous. Look, there comes his daughter Rachel with the sheep."

[7]"Why don't you water the flocks so they can get back to grazing?" Jacob asked. "They'll be hungry if you stop so early in the day!"

[8]"We don't roll away the stone and begin the watering until all the flocks and shepherds are here," they replied.

[9]As this conversation was going on, Rachel arrived with her father's sheep, for she was a shepherdess. [10]And because she was his cousin—the daughter of his mother's brother—and because the sheep were his uncle's, Jacob went over to the well and rolled away the stone and watered his uncle's flock. [11]Then Jacob kissed Rachel and started crying! [12,13]He explained about being her cousin on her father's side, and that he was her Aunt Rebekah's son. She quickly ran and told her father, Laban, and as soon as he heard of Jacob's arrival, he rushed out to meet him and greeted him warmly and brought him home. Then Jacob told him his story.

[14]"Just think, my very own flesh and blood," Laban exclaimed.

Jacob Marries Rachel and Leah

After Jacob had been there about a month, [15]Laban said to him one day, "Just because we are relatives is no reason for you to work for me without pay. How much do you want?" [16]Now Laban had two daughters, Leah, the older, and her younger sister, Rachel. [17]Leah had lovely eyes, but Rachel was shapely, and in every way a beauty. [18]Well, Jacob was in love with Rachel. So he told her father, "I'll work for you seven years if you'll give me Rachel as my wife."

[19]"Agreed!" Laban replied. "I'd rather give her to you than to someone outside the family."

[20]So Jacob spent the next seven years working to pay for Rachel. But they seemed to him but a few days, he was so much in love. [21]Finally the time came for him to marry her.

"I have fulfilled my contract," Jacob said to Laban. "Now give me my wife, so that I can sleep with her."

[22]So Laban invited all the men of the settlement to celebrate with Jacob at a big party. [23]Afterwards, that night, when it was dark, Laban took Leah to Jacob, and he slept with her. [24](And Laban gave to Leah a servant girl, Zilpah, to be her maid.) [25]But in the morning—it was Leah!

"What sort of trick is this?" Jacob raged at

28:20-22 Jacob's vow to God here is possibly just another of his schemes—something like a "foxhole" prayer. But even though Jacob was probably trying to "con" God—give him "an offer he couldn't refuse"—God honored and blessed Jacob. God's dealings with Jacob should give us some idea of how gracious he really is. Jacob wasn't exemplary or wise; he didn't know the God of his fathers as he should have. Yet God still was willing to work with him and bless him.

29:25 Jacob's response to Laban's trickery reveals an interesting principle. Nobody resents being cheated more than a cheater. If there is a characteristic in others that we find particularly annoying, we would be wise to examine ourselves. It is probably one of our own.

Laban. "I worked for seven years for Rachel. What do you mean by this trickery?"

26"It's not our custom to marry off a younger daughter ahead of her sister," Laban replied smoothly. 27"Wait until the bridal week is over and you can have Rachel too—if you promise to work for me another seven years!"

28So Jacob agreed to work seven more years. Then Laban gave him Rachel, too. 29And Laban gave to Rachel a servant girl, Bilhah, to be her maid. 30So Jacob slept with Rachel, too, and he loved her more than Leah, and stayed and worked the additional seven years.

Jacob Has Many Children

31But because Jacob was slighting Leah, Jehovah let her have a child, while Rachel was barren. 32So Leah became pregnant and had a son, Reuben (meaning "God has noticed my trouble"), for she said, "Jehovah has noticed my trouble—now my husband will love me." 33She soon became pregnant again and had another son and named him Simeon (meaning "Jehovah heard"), for she said, "Jehovah heard that I was unloved, and so he has given me another son." 34Again she became pregnant and had a son, and named him Levi (meaning "Attachment") for she said, "Surely now my husband will feel affection for me, since I have given him three sons!" 35Once again she was pregnant and had a son and named him Judah (meaning "Praise"), for she said, "Now I will praise Jehovah!" And then she stopped having children.

CHAPTER 30

Rachel, realizing she was barren, became envious of her sister. "Give me children or I'll die," she exclaimed to Jacob.

2Jacob flew into a rage. "Am I God?" he flared. "He is the one who is responsible for your barrenness."

3Then Rachel told him, "Sleep with my servant-girl Bilhah, and her children will be mine." 4So she gave him Bilhah to be his wife, and he slept with her, 5and she became pregnant and presented him with a son. 6Rachel named him Dan (meaning "Justice"), for she said, "God has given me justice, and heard my plea and given me a son." 7Then Bilhah, Rachel's servant-girl, became pregnant again and gave Jacob a second son. 8Rachel named him Naphtali (meaning "Wrestling"), for she said, "I am in a fierce contest with my sister and I am winning!"

9Meanwhile, when Leah realized that she wasn't getting pregnant anymore, she gave her servant-girl Zilpah to Jacob, to be his wife, 10and soon Zilpah presented him with a son. 11Leah named him Gad (meaning "My luck has turned!").

12Then Zilpah produced a second son, 13and Leah named him Asher (meaning "Happy"), for she said, "What joy is mine! The other women will think me blessed indeed!"

14One day during the wheat harvest, Reuben found some mandrakes growing in a field and brought them to his mother Leah. Rachel begged Leah to give some of them to her.

15But Leah angrily replied, "Wasn't it enough to steal my husband? And now will you steal my son's mandrakes too?"

Rachel said sadly, "He will sleep with you tonight because of the mandrakes."

16That evening as Jacob was coming home from the fields, Leah went out to meet him. "You must sleep with me tonight!" she said; "for I am hiring you with some mandrakes my son has found!" So he did. 17And God answered her prayers and she became pregnant again, and gave birth to her fifth son. 18She named him Issachar (meaning "Wages"), for she said, "God has repaid me for giving my slave-girl to my husband." 19Then once again she became pregnant, with a sixth son. 20She named him Zebulun (meaning "Gifts"), for she said, "God has given me good gifts for my husband. Now he will honor me, for I have given him six sons." 21Afterwards she gave birth to a daughter and named her Dinah.

22Then God remembered about Rachel's plight, and answered her prayers by giving her a child. 23,24For she became pregnant and gave birth to a son. "God has removed the dark slur against my name," she said. And she named him Joseph (meaning "May I also have another!"), for she said, "May Jehovah give me another son."

Jacob Becomes Wealthy

25Soon after the birth of Joseph to Rachel, Jacob said to Laban, "I want to go back home. 26Let me take my wives and children—for I earned them from you—and be gone, for you

30:25-43 God always treated Jacob in ways far better than he deserved. God blessed him in spite of his trickery and deceit. God works that way with us, too. He is willing to bless us with healing even when we don't really deserve it. None of us really deserves God's love; all of us have failed in many ways. But God still reaches out to help us when we look to him in faith.

know how fully I have paid for them with my
service to you.”
27“Please don’t leave me,” Laban replied,
“for a fortune-teller that I consulted told me
that the many blessings I’ve been enjoying
are all because of your being here. 28How
much of a raise do you need to get you to
stay? Whatever it is, I’ll pay it.”
29Jacob replied, “You know how faithfully
I’ve served you through these many years,
and how your flocks and herds have grown.
30For it was little indeed you had before I
came, and your wealth has increased enor-
mously; Jehovah has blessed you from everything I do! But now, what about me? When
should I provide for my own family?”
31,32“What wages do you want?” Laban
asked again.
Jacob replied, “If you will do one thing, I’ll
go back to work for you. Let me go out among
your flocks today and remove all the goats
that are speckled or spotted, and all the black
sheep. Give them to me as my wages. 33Then
if you ever find any white goats or sheep in
my flock, you will know that I have stolen
them from you!”
34“All right!” Laban replied. “It shall be as
you have said!”
35,36So that very day Laban went out and
formed a flock for Jacob of all the male goats
that were ringed and spotted, and the females
that were speckled and spotted with any white
patches, and all of the black sheep. He gave
them to Jacob’s sons to take them three days’
distance, and Jacob stayed and cared for Laban’s flock. 37Then Jacob took fresh shoots
from poplar, almond, and sycamore trees, and
peeled white streaks in them, 38and placed
these rods beside the watering troughs so that
Laban’s flocks would see them when they
came to drink; for that is when they mated.
39,40So the flocks mated before the white-
streaked rods, and their offspring were
streaked and spotted, and Jacob added them to
his flock. Then he divided out the ewes from
Laban’s flock and segregated them from the
rams, and let them mate only with Jacob’s
black rams. Thus he built his flocks from Laban’s. 41Moreover, he watched for the stronger
animals to mate, and placed the peeled
branches before them, 42but didn’t with the
feebler ones. So the less healthy lambs were
Laban’s and the stronger ones were Jacob’s!
43As a result, Jacob’s flocks increased rapidly
and he became very wealthy, with many servants, camels, and donkeys.

CHAPTER 31

Jacob Leaves Laban

But Jacob learned that Laban’s sons were
grumbling, “He owes everything he owns to
our father. All his wealth is at our father’s
expense.” 2Soon Jacob noticed a considerable
cooling in Laban’s attitude toward him.
3Jehovah now spoke to Jacob and told him,
“Return to the land of your fathers, and to
your relatives there; and I will be with you.”
4So one day Jacob sent for Rachel and Leah
to come out to the field where he was with the
flocks, 5to talk things over with them.
“Your father has turned against me,” he told
them, “and now the God of my fathers has
come and spoken to me. 6You know how hard
I’ve worked for your father, 7but he has been
completely unscrupulous and has broken his
wage contract with me again and again and
again. But God has not permitted him to do me
any harm! 8For if he said the speckled animals
would be mine, then all the flock produced
speckled; and when he changed and said I
could have the streaked ones, then all the
lambs were streaked! 9In this way God has
made me wealthy at your father’s expense.
10“And at the mating season, I had a dream,

31:3 Moving can be a time of major crisis. It is interesting to note that during all the major change points of Jacob’s life, God always reestablished contact with him. Here, as Jacob faced a crisis with Laban’s family, God gave Jacob instructions concerning his next move. God revealed to Jacob the next step in his divine program as it was needed. God is always there to help us during our crisis moments. During these times we need to learn to stop and listen to what he has to say.

31:14-15 Leah and Rachel left their father’s home willingly. This is not surprising. We have enough evidence to know that Laban’s family was highly dysfunctional. At this point, Jacob’s family needed to move on if they were to become the family God intended them to be. Sometimes our home of origin is a source of much pain and confusion. In such cases, it is important for us to leave that dysfunctional context in order to build a new life in a more healthy atmosphere.

31:17-20 Even though God was very active in Jacob’s life, the old patterns still persisted. Jacob’s recovery from his deceitful youth was an ongoing process. This time he deceived Laban. Most of us are in recovery for a lifetime. Jacob’s habits and tendencies certainly didn’t go away overnight. Neither will ours. We need to be aware of our weaknesses and look to God for his help at each step along the way.

and saw that the he-goats mating with the
flock were streaked, speckled, and mottled.
11Then, in my dream, the Angel of God called
to me 12and told me that I should mate the
white female goats with streaked, speckled,
and mottled male goats. 'For I have seen all
that Laban has done to you,' the Angel said. 13'I
am the God you met at Bethel,' he continued,
'the place where you anointed the pillar and
made a vow to serve me. Now leave this country and return to the land of your birth.'"
14Rachel and Leah replied, "That's fine with
us! There's nothing for us here—none of our
father's wealth will come to us anyway! 15He
has reduced our rights to those of foreign
women; he sold us, and what he received for
us has disappeared. 16The riches God has
given you from our father were legally ours
and our children's to begin with! So go ahead
and do whatever God has told you to."

Laban Chases after Jacob

17-20So one day while Laban was out shearing
sheep, Jacob set his wives and sons on camels,
and fled without telling Laban his intentions.
He drove the flocks before him—Jacob's
flocks he had gotten there at Paddan-aram—
and took everything he owned and started
out to return to his father Isaac in the land of
Canaan. 21So he fled with all of his possessions
(and Rachel stole her father's household gods
and took them with her) and crossed the
Euphrates River and headed for the territory
of Gilead.
22Laban didn't learn of their flight for three
days. 23Then, taking several men with him, he
set out in hot pursuit and caught up with
them seven days later, at Mount Gilead. 24That
night God appeared to Laban in a dream.
"Watch out what you say to Jacob," he was
told. "Don't give him your blessing and don't
curse him." 25Laban finally caught up with
Jacob as he was camped at the top of a ridge;
Laban, meanwhile, camped below him in the
mountains.
26"What do you mean by sneaking off like
this?" Laban demanded. "Are my daughters
prisoners, captured in a battle, that you have
rushed them away like this? 27Why didn't you
give me a chance to have a farewell party,
with singing and orchestra and harp? 28Why
didn't you let me kiss my grandchildren and
tell them good-bye? This is a strange way to
act. 29I could crush you, but the God of your
father appeared to me last night and told me,
'Be careful not to be too hard on Jacob!' 30But
see here—though you feel you must go, and

Personal Boundaries

BIBLE READING: Genesis 31:45-55

We continued to take personal inventory and when we were wrong promptly admitted it.

We all have particular weaknesses, and it is often helpful to establish personal boundary lines to support these weaker areas. We may need to clearly define our commitments to others; we may need to agree on certain limitations in order to maintain peace. Once the boundaries have been established, honesty is needed to maintain them. An assessment of our honesty in keeping our commitments needs to be part of our regular inventory.

Jacob and his father-in-law, Laban, had some conflicts. As they were working them out, they entered into an agreement by drawing a clearly defined boundary line and setting up a monument to remind them of that commitment. "'May the Lord see to it that we keep this bargain when we are out of each other's sight. . . . This heap [of stones],' Laban continued, 'stands between us as a witness of our vows. . . .' So Jacob took oath before the mighty God of his father, Isaac, to respect the boundary line" (Genesis 31:49, 51-53).

Restoring trust in our relationships is part of recovery. To do this we should define our expectations and cautiously enter into commitments. We are not merely responsible for what the other person knows about. We are personally responsible for our own honesty before the watchful eyes of God. These relational commitments are not to be entered into lightly. But when we make them, they must be vigilantly maintained.

Turn to page 1239, Romans 5.

long so intensely for your childhood home—
why have you stolen my idols?"
31"I sneaked away because I was afraid,"
Jacob answered. "I said to myself, 'He'll take
his daughters from me by force.' 32But as for
your household idols, a curse upon anyone
who took them. Let him die! If you find a
single thing we've stolen from you, I swear
before all these men, I'll give it back without
question." For Jacob didn't know that Rachel
had taken them.
33Laban went first into Jacob's tent to search
there, then into Leah's, and then searched the
two tents of the concubines, but didn't find
them. Finally he went into Rachel's tent. 34Ra-
chel, remember, was the one who had stolen
the idols; she had stuffed them into her camel
saddle and now was sitting on them! So although Laban searched the tents thoroughly,
he didn't find them.
35"Forgive my not getting up, father," Rachel explained, "but I'm having my monthly
period." So Laban didn't find them.
36,37Now Jacob got mad. "What did you
find?" he demanded of Laban. "What is my
crime? You have come rushing after me as
though you were chasing a criminal and have
searched through everything. Now put everything I stole out here in front of us, before your
men and mine, for all to see and to decide
whose it is! 38Twenty years I've been with you,
and all that time I cared for your ewes and
goats so that they produced healthy offspring,
and I never touched one ram of yours for food.
39If any were attacked and killed by wild animals, did I show them to you and ask you to
reduce the count of your flock? No, I took the
loss. You made me pay for every animal stolen
from the flocks, whether I could help it or not.
40I worked for you through the scorching heat
of the day, and through the cold and sleepless
nights. 41Yes, twenty years—fourteen of them
earning your two daughters, and six years to
get the flock! And you have reduced my wages
ten times! 42In fact, except for the grace of
God—the God of my grandfather Abraham,
even the glorious God of Isaac, my father—
you would have sent me off without a penny
to my name. But God has seen your cruelty
and my hard work, and that is why he appeared to you last night."
43Laban replied, "These women are my
daughters, and these children are mine, and
these flocks and all that you have—all are
mine. So how could I harm my own daughters and grandchildren? 44Come now and we
will sign a peace pact, you and I, and will live
by its terms."
45So Jacob took a stone and set it up as a
monument, 46and told his men to gather
stones and make a heap, and Jacob and Laban
ate together beside the pile of rocks. 47,48They
named it "The Witness Pile"—"Jegar-
sahadutha," in Laban's language, and "Gal-
eed" in Jacob's.
"This pile of stones will stand as a witness
against us [if either of us trespasses across this
line]," Laban said. 49So it was also called "The
Watchtower" (Mizpah). For Laban said, "May
the Lord see to it that we keep this bargain
when we are out of each other's sight. 50And if
you are harsh to my daughters, or take other
wives, I won't know, but God will see it.
51,52This heap," Laban continued, "stands between us as a witness of our vows that I will
not cross this line to attack you and you will
not cross it to attack me. 53I call upon the God
of Abraham and Nahor, and of their father, to
destroy either one of us who does."
So Jacob took oath before the mighty God
of his father, Isaac, to respect the boundary
line. 54Then Jacob presented a sacrifice to God
there at the top of the mountain, and invited
his companions to a feast, and afterwards
spent the night with them on the mountain.
55Laban was up early the next morning and
kissed his daughters and grandchildren, and
blessed them, and returned home.

CHAPTER 32

Jacob Reconciles with Esau

So Jacob and his household started on again.
And the angels of God came to meet him.
When he saw them he exclaimed, "God lives
here!" So he named the place "God's territory!"

31:49 This verse is often quoted as a sweet benediction, but, in actuality, it is a very negative wish that becomes almost a threat. It's as if Laban were saying, "I can't watch you anymore, so when you're out of my sight, I pray that God will keep his eye on you, you rascal!"

32:3 Twenty years prior to these events Jacob had run away from Esau afraid for his life. Jacob had no way of knowing whether his brother, Esau, had experienced healing from the old wounds and resentments. Since he did not know, he had to make elaborate preparations for reestablishing contact. Jacob's example in this chapter gives many helpful hints to those of us seeking reconciliation with people we have hurt in the past.

3Jacob now sent messengers to his brother,
Esau, in Edom, in the land of Seir, 4with this
message: "Hello from Jacob! I have been living with Uncle Laban until recently, 5and now
I own oxen, donkeys, sheep, goats, and many
servants, both men and women. I have sent
these messengers to inform you of my coming, hoping that you will be friendly to us."
6The messengers returned with the news
that Esau was on the way to meet Jacob—with
an army of 400 men! 7Jacob was frantic with
fear. He divided his household, along with the
flocks and herds and camels, into two groups;
8for he said, "If Esau attacks one group, perhaps the other can escape."
9Then Jacob prayed, "O God of Abraham
my grandfather, and of my father Isaac—O
Jehovah who told me to return to the land of
my relatives, and said that you would do me
good— 10I am not worthy of the least of all
your loving-kindnesses shown me again and
again just as you promised me. For when I left
home I owned nothing except a walking stick!
And now I am two armies! 11O Lord, please
deliver me from destruction at the hand of
my brother Esau, for I am frightened—terribly
afraid that he is coming to kill me and these
mothers and my children. 12But you promised
to do me good, and to multiply my descendants until they become as the sands along
the shores—too many to count."
13-15Jacob stayed where he was for the night,
and prepared a present for his brother Esau:
200 female goats, 20 male goats, 200 ewes, 20
rams, 30 milk camels, with their colts, 40
cows, 10 bulls, 20 female donkeys, 10 male
donkeys.
16He instructed his servants to drive them on
ahead, each group of animals by itself, separated by a distance between. 17He told the men
driving the first group that when they met Esau
and he asked, "Where are you going? Whose
servants are you? Whose animals are these?"—
18they should reply: "These belong to your servant Jacob. They are a present for his master
Esau! He is coming right behind us!"
19Jacob gave the same instructions to each
driver, with the same message. 20Jacob's strategy was to appease Esau with the presents
before meeting him face to face! "Perhaps,"
Jacob hoped, "he will be friendly to us." 21So
the presents were sent on ahead, and Jacob
spent that night in the camp.
22-24But during the night he got up and
wakened his two wives and his two concubines and eleven sons, and sent them across
the Jordan River at the Jabbok ford with all his

Long-Awaited Healing

BIBLE READING: Genesis 33:1-11

We made direct amends to such people wherever possible, except when to do so would injure them or others.

Returning to someone we have hurt is a scary thing. The passing years, lack of communication, and memories of anger and hateful emotional exchanges can all create tremendous anxiety. Even though we may make some contact through a third party, there will still be tension until we see that person face to face.

This was the case for Jacob upon returning to see Esau. "Then, far in the distance, Jacob saw Esau coming with his 400 men. . . . Then Jacob went on ahead. . . . And then Esau ran to meet him and embraced him affectionately and kissed him; and both of them were in tears!" After being introduced to Jacob's family, Esau asked, "'And what were all the flocks and herds I met as I came?' . . Jacob replied, 'They are my gifts, to curry your favor!' 'Brother, I have plenty,' Esau laughed. 'Keep what you have.' 'No, but please accept them,' Jacob said, 'for what a relief it is to see your friendly smile! I was as frightened of you as though approaching God! Please take my gifts. For God has been very generous to me and I have enough.' So Jacob insisted, and finally Esau accepted them" (Genesis 33:1, 3-4, 8-11).

Jacob's tremendous fear gave way to relief. The last time Jacob had seen Esau, Jacob was in fear for his life. With the passing of time, both of them had changed. When Jacob faced his brother, he found that there was still affection, even though they both remembered the pain. ***Turn to page 353, 2 Samuel 9.***

possessions, then returned again to the camp and was there alone; and a Man wrestled with him until dawn. 25And when the Man saw that he couldn't win the match, he struck Jacob's hip and knocked it out of joint at the socket.

26Then the Man said, "Let me go, for it is dawn."

But Jacob panted, "I will not let you go until you bless me."

27"What is your name?" the Man asked.

"Jacob," was the reply.

28"It isn't anymore!" the Man told him. "It is Israel—one who has power with God. Because you have been strong with God, you shall prevail with men."

29"What is *your* name?" Jacob asked him.

"No, you mustn't ask," the Man told him. And he blessed him there.

30Jacob named the place "Peniel" ("The Face of God"), for he said, "I have seen God face to face, and yet my life is spared." 31The sun rose as he started on, and he was limping because of his hip. 32(That is why even today the people of Israel don't eat meat from near the hip, in memory of what happened that night.)

CHAPTER 33

Then, far in the distance, Jacob saw Esau coming with his 400 men. 2Jacob now arranged his family into a column, with his two concubines and their children at the head, Leah and her children next, and Rachel and Joseph last. 3Then Jacob went on ahead. As he approached his brother he bowed low seven times before him. 4And then Esau ran to meet him and embraced him affectionately and kissed him; and both of them were in tears!

5Then Esau looked at the women and children and asked, "Who are these people with you?"

"My children," Jacob replied. 6Then the concubines came forward with their children, and bowed low before him. 7Next came Leah with her children, and bowed, and finally Rachel and Joseph came and made their bows.

8"And what were all the flocks and herds I met as I came?" Esau asked.

And Jacob replied, "They are my gifts, to curry your favor!"

9"Brother, I have plenty," Esau laughed. "Keep what you have."

10"No, but please accept them," Jacob said, "for what a relief it is to see your friendly smile! I was as frightened of you as though approaching God! 11Please take my gifts. For God has been very generous to me and I have enough." So Jacob insisted, and finally Esau accepted them.

12"Well, let's be going," Esau said. "My men and I will stay with you and lead the way."

13But Jacob replied, "As you can see, some of the children are small, and the flocks and herds have their young, and if they are driven too hard, they will die. 14So you go on ahead of us and we'll follow at our own pace and meet you at Seir."

15"Well," Esau said, "at least let me leave you some of my men to assist you and be your guides."

"No," Jacob insisted, "we'll get along just fine. Please do as I suggest."

16So Esau started back to Seir that same day. 17Meanwhile Jacob and his household went as far as Succoth. There he built himself a camp, with pens for his flocks and herds. (That is why the place is called Succoth, meaning "huts.") 18Then they arrived safely at Shechem, in Canaan, and camped outside the city. 19(He bought the land he camped on from the family of Hamor, Shechem's father, for 100 pieces of silver. 20And there he erected an altar and called it "El-Elohe-Israel," "The Altar to the God of Israel.")

CHAPTER 34

Jacob's Sons Take Revenge

One day Dinah, Leah's daughter, went out to visit some of the neighborhood girls, 2but when Shechem, son of King Hamor the Hivite, saw her, he took her and raped her. 3He fell

33:4 Although Esau does seem genuinely delighted to see his long-lost brother, we can only speculate about his true feelings. This happy reunion certainly didn't signal the end of the brothers' feud. Conflict between their families continued throughout Old Testament times. The book of Obadiah records the joy that Esau's descendants, the Edomites, expressed over the Israelites' defeat. Obadiah, an Israelite, also joyfully announced the doom of Edom. Even in the New Testament, the hated family of Herod traced its lineage back to Esau. Some conflicts are not easily resolved but if they are left unresolved, they can become a burden to generations far into the future.

34:2 The act of rape is always hideous in itself, but the consequences are usually just as heartbreaking. In this occurrence, rape led to deception and ultimately to murder. Dysfunctional patterns, and the acts that follow out of them, feed cycles of deepening destruction and hurt. Someone has to choose to break the cycle and begin the process of recovery and healing.

JACOB & SONS

While not the first dysfunctional family in the Bible, Jacob's brood was certainly among the most controversial. Like father, like son, the saying goes. Jacob's own lack of discretion, honesty, patience, and unconditional love negatively impacted his clan.

Jacob had never been his father's favorite, and he tragically played favorites with his own sons. Joseph was obviously preferred; Benjamin ran a close second. The rest were far back in the pack and understandably jealous.

The deceptions that Jacob had put over on his father and brother many years earlier were mirrored in the lies of his sons about the fate of Joseph. As the brutal massacre of Shechem brutally illustrated, openness and honesty didn't characterize the sons' relationships with outsiders either. Jacob's silence at Dinah's rape perhaps spurred Simeon and Levi to seek vengeance on their own. Certainly their father set no clear boundaries on their behavior until it was much too late.

Jacob's polygamy influenced his sons also. Reuben even slept with his father's concubine Bilhah. Why not? He had grown up watching a marital triangle expand to include two servant concubines. He had even been a party to his mother's and Rachel's rivalry for Jacob's favors. He was not the only one to sin sexually. Judah, too, succumbed to temptation with his disguised daughter-in-law, Tamar.

Jacob and his sons did mature significantly over the years. When famine forced them to visit Egypt, they were no longer the selfish, jealous, deceitful band of earlier years. Instead, they were genuinely concerned for their aging father, protective of young Benjamin, and remorseful when confronted with the truth of what they had done to Joseph. The past reconciled, they could begin an exciting new life in Egypt with the brother they had abandoned. They were, to a great extent, worthy to become the forefathers of Israel's twelve tribes. Judah would even head the royal line, with its most famous descendant the King of kings, Jesus Christ.

STRENGTHS AND ACCOMPLISHMENTS:
- In later years the brothers honestly cared about their father.
- They were the forefathers of the twelve tribes of Israel.
- They eventually learned the value of loyalty and honesty.

WEAKNESSES AND MISTAKES:
- Jacob modeled favoritism, impatience, and sexual indiscretion for his sons.
- Unbridled passion and intense jealousy motivated the boys, who found it difficult to establish boundaries for their behavior.
- Honesty was a learned response, acquired rather late in life for Jacob and several of his sons.

LESSONS FROM THEIR LIVES:
- The sins of the parents are often reflected in their children.
- Parental favoritism has devastating consequences.
- God can take the evil in our life and use it to accomplish great good.

KEY VERSE:
"Hurry, return to my father and tell him, 'Your son Joseph says, "God has made me chief of all the land of Egypt. Come down to me right away!"'" (Genesis 45:9).

The story of Jacob and his sons is found in Genesis 34–50. Jacob is also mentioned in Hosea 12:3-5; Matthew 1:2; 22:32; Acts 3:13; 7:46; Romans 9:11-13; and Hebrews 11:9, 20-21.

---

deeply in love with her, and tried to win her affection.

4Then he spoke to his father about it. "Get this girl for me," he demanded. "I want to marry her."

5Word soon reached Jacob of what had happened, but his sons were out in the fields herding cattle, so he did nothing until their return. 6,7Meanwhile King Hamor, Shechem's father, went to talk with Jacob, arriving just as Jacob's sons came in from the fields, too shocked and angry to overlook the insult, for it was an outrage against all of them.

8Hamor told Jacob, "My son Shechem is truly in love with your daughter, and longs for her to be his wife. Please let him marry her. 9,10Moreover, we invite you folks to live here among us and to let your daughters marry our sons, and we will give our daughters as wives for your young men. And you shall live among us wherever you wish and carry on your business among us and become rich!"

11Then Shechem addressed Dinah's father and brothers. "Please be kind to me and let me have her as my wife," he begged. "I will give whatever you require. 12No matter what dowry or gift you demand, I will pay it—only give me the girl as my wife."

13Her brothers then lied to Shechem and Hamor, acting dishonorably because of what Shechem had done to their sister. 14They said, "We couldn't possibly. For you are not circumcised. It would be a disgrace for her to marry such a man. 15I'll tell you what we'll do—if every man of you will be circumcised, 16then we will intermarry with you and live here and unite with you to become one people. 17Otherwise we will take her and be on our way."

18,19Hamor and Shechem gladly agreed, and lost no time in acting upon this request, for Shechem was very much in love with Dinah, and could, he felt sure, sell the idea to the other men of the city—for he was highly respected and very popular. 20So Hamor and Shechem appeared before the city council and presented their request.

21"Those men are our friends," they said. "Let's invite them to live here among us and ply their trade. For the land is large enough to hold them, and we can intermarry with them. 22But they will only consider staying here on one condition—that every one of us men be circumcised, the same as they are. 23But if we do this, then all they have will become ours and the land will be enriched. Come on, let's agree to this so that they will settle here among us."

24So all the men agreed, and all were circumcised. 25But three days later, when their wounds were sore and sensitive to every move they made, two of Dinah's brothers, Simeon and Levi, took their swords, entered the city without opposition, and slaughtered every man there, 26including Hamor and Shechem. They rescued Dinah from Shechem's house and returned to their camp again. 27Then all of Jacob's sons went over and plundered the city because their sister had been dishonored there. 28They confiscated all the flocks and herds and donkeys—everything they could lay their hands on, both inside the city and outside in the fields, 29and took all the women and children, and wealth of every kind.

30Then Jacob said to Levi and Simeon, "You have made me stink among all the people of this land—all the Canaanites and Perizzites. We are so few that they will come and crush us, and we will all be killed."

31"Should he treat our sister like a prostitute?" they retorted.

CHAPTER 35

Rachel and Isaac Die

"Move on to Bethel now, and settle there," God said to Jacob, "and build an altar to worship me—the God who appeared to you when you fled from your brother Esau."

2So Jacob instructed all those in his household to destroy the idols they had brought with them, and to wash themselves and to put on fresh clothing. 3"For we are going to Bethel," he told them, "and I will build an altar there to the God who answered my prayers in the day of my distress, and was with me on my journey."

4So they gave Jacob all their idols and their earrings, and he buried them beneath the oak tree near Shechem. 5Then they started on again. And the terror of God was upon all the cities they journeyed through, so that they were not attacked. 6Finally they arrived at Luz (also called Bethel), in Canaan. 7And Jacob erected an altar there and named it "The altar to the God who met me here at Bethel" because it was there at Bethel that God appeared to him when he was fleeing from Esau.

8Soon after this Rebekah's old nurse, Deborah, died and was buried beneath the oak tree in the valley below Bethel. And ever after it was called "The Oak of Weeping."

9Upon Jacob's arrival at Bethel, en route from Paddan-aram, God appeared to him once again and blessed him. 10And God said to him, "You shall no longer be called Jacob ('Grabber'), but Israel ('One who prevails with God'). 11I am God Almighty," the Lord said to him, "and I will cause you to be fertile and to multiply and to become a great nation, yes, many nations; many kings shall be among your descendants. 12And I will pass on to you the land I gave to Abraham and Isaac. Yes, I will give it to you and to your descendants."

13,14Afterwards Jacob built a stone pillar at the place where God had appeared to him; and he poured wine over it as an offering to God and then anointed the pillar with olive

34:20-31 Vengeance belongs to God and when an individual takes revenge—no matter how just the cause may be—there usually are serious consequences. Because of their deception and slaughter of the Hivites, Jacob and his family became extremely unpopular with their neighbors. Because they were a small clan at this point, such a situation presented them with grave danger. In recovery, revenge is extremely counterproductive. It only breaks down the reconciliation process that is necessary for personal growth and healthy relationships.

oil. [15]Jacob named the spot Bethel ("House of God"), because God had spoken to him there.

[16]Leaving Bethel, he and his household traveled on toward Ephrath (Bethlehem). But Rachel's pains of childbirth began while they were still a long way away. [17]After a very hard delivery, the midwife finally exclaimed, "Wonderful—another boy!" [18]And with Rachel's last breath (for she died) she named him "Ben-oni" ("Son of my sorrow"); but his father called him "Benjamin" ("Son of my right hand").

[19]So Rachel died, and was buried near the road to Ephrath (also called Bethlehem). [20]And Jacob set up a monument of stones upon her grave, and it is there to this day.

[21]Then Israel journeyed on and camped beyond the Tower of Eder. [22]It was while he was there that Reuben slept with Bilhah, his father's concubine, and someone told Israel about it.

Here are the names of the twelve sons of Jacob:

[23]The sons of Leah: Reuben, Jacob's oldest child, Simeon, Levi, Judah, Issachar, Zebulun.

[24]The sons of Rachel: Joseph, Benjamin.

[25]The sons of Bilhah, Rachel's servant-girl: Dan, Naphtali.

[26]The sons of Zilpah, Leah's servant-girl: Gad, Asher.

All these were born to him at Paddan-aram.

[27]So Jacob came at last to Isaac his father at Mamre in Kiriath-arba (now called Hebron), where Abraham too had lived. [28,29]Isaac died soon afterwards, at the ripe old age of 180. And his sons Esau and Jacob buried him.

CHAPTER 36

Esau's Family

Here is a list of the descendants of Esau (also called Edom): [2,3]Esau married three local girls from Canaan: Adah (daughter of Elon the Hethite), Oholibamah (daughter of Anah and granddaughter of Zibeon the Hivite), Basemath (his cousin—she was a daughter of Ishmael—the sister of Nebaioth).

[4]Esau and Adah had a son named Eliphaz. Esau and Basemath had a son named Reuel.

[5]Esau and Oholibamah had sons named Jeush, Jalam, and Korah. All these sons were born to Esau in the land of Canaan.

[6-8]Then Esau took his wives, children, household servants, cattle and flocks—all the wealth he had gained in the land of Canaan—and moved away from his brother Jacob to Mount Seir. (For there was not land enough to support them both because of all their cattle.)

[9]Here are the names of Esau's descendants, the Edomites, born to him in Mount Seir:

[10-12]Descended from his wife Adah, born to her son Eliphaz were: Teman, Omar, Zepho, Gatam, Kenaz, Amalek (born to Timna, Eliphaz' concubine).

[13,14]Esau also had grandchildren from his wife Basemath. Born to her son Reuel were: Nahath, Zerah, Shammah, Mizzah.

[15,16]Esau's grandchildren became the heads of clans, as listed here: the clan of Teman, the clan of Omar, the clan of Zepho, the clan of Kenaz, the clan of Korah, the clan of Gatam, the clan of Amalek.

The above clans were the descendants of Eliphaz, the oldest son of Esau and Adah.

[17]The following clans were the descendants of Reuel, born to Esau and his wife Basemath while they lived in Canaan: the clan of Nahath, the clan of Zerah, the clan of Shammah, the clan of Mizzah.

[18,19]And these are the clans named after the sons of Esau and his wife Oholibamah (daughter of Anah): the clan of Jeush, the clan of Jalam, the clan of Korah.

[20,21]These are the names of the tribes that descended from Seir, the Horite—one of the native families of the land of Seir: the tribe of Lotan, the tribe of Shobal, the tribe of Zibeon, the tribe of Anah, the tribe of Dishon, the tribe of Ezer, the tribe of Dishan.

[22]The children of Lotan (the son of Seir) were Hori and Heman. (Lotan had a sister, Timna.)

35:22 The families in the book of Genesis seem to be inordinately dysfunctional. Deceit and lies are often used for the sake of convenience. Communication between family members is poor. The incidence of incest is high. Here we see that Reuben slept with one of his father's wives. This kind of sexual sin reaps a bitter harvest. Reuben's blessing and inheritance as the firstborn son was forfeited because of this single act of sexual gratification (49:4). Reuben needed to keep the long view in focus. If he had thought about what he might lose, he might have withstood the temptation.

36:6-8 Esau and his family could not live in the same area as Jacob and his family. The excuse they gave for moving was the lack of land available. For some families, no amount of room is enough for them to live together. The reconciliation of these brothers was started, but it seems never to have been completed. We need to expect reconciliation to take time. It doesn't happen with one happy reunion. It needs to be worked out over a period of time, in the everyday situations of life.

[23]The children of Shobal: Alvan, Manahath, Ebal, Shepho, Onam.
[24]The children of Zibeon: Aiah, Anah. (This is the boy who discovered a hot springs in the wasteland while he was grazing his father's donkeys.)
[25]The children of Anah: Dishon, Oholibamah.
[26]The children of Dishon: Hemdan, Eshban, Ithran, Cheran.
[27]The children of Ezer: Bilhan, Zaavan, Akan.
[28-30] The children of Dishan: Uz, Aran.
[31-39]These are the names of the kings of Edom (before Israel had her first king):

King Bela (son of Beor), from Dinhabah in Edom.
Succeeded by: King Jobab (son of BoZerah), from the city of Bozrah.
Succeeded by: King Husham, from the land of the Temanites.
Succeeded by: King Hadad (son of Bedad), the leader of the forces that defeated the army of Midian when it invaded Moab. His city was Avith.
Succeeded by: King Samlah, from Masrekah.
Succeeded by: King Shaul, from Rehoboth-by-the-River.
Succeeded by: King Baal-hanan (son of Achbor).
Succeeded by: King Hadad, from the city of Pau.

King Hadad's wife was Mehetabel, daughter of Matred and granddaughter of Mezahab.
[40-43]Here are the names of the sub-tribes of Esau, living in the localities named after themselves: the clan of Timna, the clan of Alvah, the clan of Jetheth, the clan of Oholibamah, the clan of Elah, the clan of Pinon, the clan of Kenaz, the clan of Teman, the clan of Mibzar, the clan of Magdiel, the clan of Iram.
These, then, are the names of the subtribes of Edom, each giving its name to the area it occupied. (All were Edomites, descendants of Esau.)

CHAPTER 37

Joseph's Dreams

So Jacob settled again in the land of Canaan, where his father had lived.
[2]Jacob's son Joseph was now seventeen years old. His job, along with his half brothers, the sons of his father's wives Bilhah and Zilpah, was to shepherd his father's flocks. But Joseph reported to his father some of the bad things they were doing. [3]Now as it happened, Israel
loved Joseph more than any of his other children, because Joseph was born to him in his old age. So one day Jacob gave him a special gift—a brightly colored coat. [4]His brothers of course
noticed their father's partiality, and consequently hated Joseph; they couldn't say a kind word to him. [5]One night Joseph had a dream
and promptly reported the details to his brothers, causing even deeper hatred.
[6]"Listen to this," he proudly announced.
[7]"We were out in the field binding sheaves, and my sheaf stood up, and your sheaves all gathered around it and bowed low before it!"
[8]"So you want to be our king, do you?" his brothers derided. And they hated him both for the dream and for his cocky attitude.
[9]Then he had another dream and told it to his brothers. "Listen to my latest dream," he boasted. "The sun, moon, and eleven stars bowed low before me!" [10]This time he told his
father as well as his brothers; but his father rebuked him. "What is this?" he asked. "Shall I indeed, and your mother and brothers come and bow before you?" [11]His brothers were fit
to be tied concerning this affair, but his father gave it quite a bit of thought and wondered what it all meant.

Joseph Is Sold into Egypt

[12]One day Joseph's brothers took their father's flocks to Shechem to graze them there. [13,14]A
few days later Israel called for Joseph, and told

37:3 The biblical account does not hide the fact that Joseph was Jacob's favorite son. Joseph had no choice but to accept the blessings of his distinction, along with its accompanying sufferings. It is interesting to note that the pattern of parental favoritism did not start with the life Joseph. It had been played out in the lives of his father Jacob and his grandfather Isaac as well. It is never healthy for parents to play favorites among their children, but it is a common pattern in dysfunctional families. It is a pattern that causes untold suffering many generations down the road.
37:19-20 The terrible impact of jealousy is portrayed in this passage. The brothers are now at the point of planning Joseph's murder. They almost followed through on their plan, but cooler heads prevailed. They ended up selling Joseph into slavery and then lying to their father, Jacob. Here we see the tragic, cumulative effects of the dysfunctional patterns of deceit and favoritism in the family context.

READ GENESIS 37:19-29

GOD grant me the serenity to accept the things I cannot change the courage to change the things I can and the wisdom to know the difference AMEN

There are times when life just treats us unfairly. We may protest the injustices, fall victim to self-pity, give in to a "poor me" kind of attitude, or sink into depression. During these times when life is unfair, we really need serenity.

If anyone in history could claim to have been treated unfairly, it was Joseph. He was one of twelve brothers, the favorite of his father. In their jealousy, the ten older brothers staged his death to fool their father and sold Joseph into slavery in Egypt. Once a slave, Joseph devoted himself to serving his master well and was quickly promoted. He was then propositioned by his master's wife, and when Joseph refused her, he was falsely accused of rape. Thrown into prison, and with no hope of release, he again did his best to serve. He was soon running the administration of the prison. In the end, after many long years, Joseph was freed. He was promoted to the position of prime minister of Egypt. From this position Joseph was able to confront and forgive his brothers who had sold him into slavery many years before (Genesis 37–45).

It takes serenity, courage, and wisdom to maintain a healthy attitude when life isn't fair. We can't change the fact that our world is imperfect and things are far from the way they should be, but we can choose the attitude we will take. We need serenity from God to help us change our response to the injustices of life. We need courage to face with optimism the days when we are treated unfairly. We need wisdom to know whether to fight injustice or to make the best of a bad situation. ***Turn to page 231, Joshua 1.***

---

him, "Your brothers are over in Shechem
grazing the flocks. Go and see how they are
getting along, and how it is with the flocks,
and bring me word."
"Very good," Joseph replied. So he traveled
to Shechem from his home at Hebron Valley.
15 A man noticed him wandering in the fields.
"Who are you looking for?" he asked.
16 "For my brothers and their flocks," Joseph
replied. "Have you seen them?"
17 "Yes," the man told him, "they are no
longer here. I heard your brothers say they
were going to Dothan." So Joseph followed
them to Dothan and found them there. 18 But
when they saw him coming, recognizing him
in the distance, they decided to kill him!
19,20 "Here comes that master dreamer," they
exclaimed. "Come on, let's kill him and toss
him into a well and tell Father that a wild
animal has eaten him. Then we'll see what
will become of all his dreams!"
21,22 But Reuben hoped to spare Joseph's life.
"Let's not kill him," he said; "we'll shed no
blood—let's throw him alive into this well
here; that way he'll die without our touching
him!" (Reuben was planning to get him out
later and return him to his father.) 23 So when
Joseph got there, they pulled off his brightly
colored robe, 24 and threw him into an empty
well—there was no water in it. 25 Then they sat
down for supper. Suddenly they noticed a
string of camels coming towards them in the
distance, probably Ishmaelite traders who
were taking gum, spices, and herbs from
Gilead to Egypt.
26,27 "Look there," Judah said to the others.
"Here come some Ishmaelites. Let's sell Joseph
to them! Why kill him and have a guilty conscience? Let's not be responsible for his death,
for, after all, he is our brother!" And his brothers agreed. 28 So when the traders came by, his
brothers pulled Joseph out of the well and sold

him to them for twenty pieces of silver, and they took him along to Egypt. [29]Some time later, Reuben (who was away when the traders came by) returned to get Joseph out of the well. When Joseph wasn't there, he ripped at his clothes in anguish and frustration.

[30]"The child is gone; and I, where shall I go now?" he wept to his brothers. [31]Then the brothers killed a goat and spattered its blood on Joseph's coat, [32]and took the coat to their father and asked him to identify it.

"We found this in the field," they told him. "Is it Joseph's coat or not?" [33]Their father recognized it at once.

"Yes," he sobbed, "it is my son's coat. A wild animal has eaten him. Joseph is without doubt torn in pieces."

[34]Then Israel tore his garments and put on sackcloth and mourned for his son in deepest mourning for many weeks. [35]His family all tried to comfort him, but it was no use.

"I will die in mourning for my son," he would say, and then break down and cry.

[36]Meanwhile, in Egypt, the traders sold Joseph to Potiphar, an officer of the Pharaoh—the king of Egypt. Potiphar was captain of the palace guard, the chief executioner.

CHAPTER 38

Judah and Tamar

About this time, Judah left home and moved to Adullam and lived there with a man named Hirah. [2]There he met and married a Canaanite girl—the daughter of Shua. [3-5]They lived at Chezib and had three sons, Er, Onan, and Shelah. These names were given to them by their mother, except for Er, who was named by his father.

[6]When his oldest son, Er, grew up, Judah arranged for him to marry a girl named Tamar. [7]But Er was a wicked man, and so the Lord killed him.

[8]Then Judah said to Er's brother, Onan, "You must marry Tamar, as our law requires of a dead man's brother; so that her sons from you will be your brother's heirs."

[9]But Onan was not willing to have a child who would not be counted as his own, and so, although he married her, whenever he went in to sleep with her, he spilled the sperm on the bed to prevent her from having a baby which would be his brother's. [10]So far as the Lord was concerned, it was very wrong of him [to deny a child to his deceased brother], so he killed him, too. [11]Then Judah told Tamar, his daughter-in-law, not to marry again at that time, but to return to her childhood home and to her parents, and to remain a widow there until his youngest son, Shelah, was old enough to marry her. (But he didn't really intend for Shelah to do this, for fear God would kill him, too, just as he had his two brothers.) So Tamar went home to her parents.

[12]In the process of time Judah's wife died. After the time of mourning was over, Judah

---

37:31-35 All Jacob's life he had manipulated people and circumstances to serve his own purposes. He was a schemer and a trickster. Here we see the trickster being tricked once again—by his sons. Again we see a destructive family pattern being passed on to the next generation.

38:1-5 We are told that Judah moved from his family home, married a Canaanite girl, and settled down among them. Some of Judah's unsavory activities in this chapter seem out of sync with what we might expect of one of Israel's patriarchs. We cannot help but wonder whether some of his behavior was not influenced by the people he was living with. The Canaanites were known for their immoral life-style. For us to progress in recovery we need to spend time with people who will encourage us to develop a wholesome life-style. We may also need to give up the relationships that lead us into destructive activities.

38:1-30 Judah's more sensational sin of propositioning a prostitute often blinds readers to his primary failure. According to the laws practiced at the time, if a husband died before fathering a son, his family was responsible for providing his widow with a husband. This was Judah's responsibility, but when his second son died soon after marrying Tamar, Judah was understandably shaken and delayed giving her his third son. It seems that Judah was hoping he would never be called upon to carry out his duty. His attitude didn't solve the problem, but only led to the sordid events that followed. It is easy for us to act like Judah, ignoring our problems or blaming them on our environment or other people. But the first step in solving any problem is admitting we have it. Then we can take responsible steps to solve it.

38:12-26 When Judah failed to deal with Tamar in a responsible way, Tamar decided to take action. And though not everything she did was exemplary, she wisely confronted Judah in a way that caught his attention without alienating him. Very often direct confrontation with people who have wronged us will only deepen the conflict. In such cases, a less direct means of communication may prove helpful.

JUDAH & TAMAR

Judah was the fourth and last son of Leah, Jacob's first wife. Among the patriarch's twelve sons, Judah evidently occupied a position of prominence. Early on in the biblical story, he persuaded his brothers not to kill Joseph. And when they went to Egypt for food, Judah spoke and acted on his brothers' behalf. Later the royal line would come through the descendants of Judah. Tamar was a girl of Canaanite descent, chosen by Judah to be the wife of Er, his oldest son.

As the story of Judah begins, we are told he left his childhood home and moved some distance away from his brothers. He settled in a Canaanite community and married a Canaanite girl. Judah's wife gave birth to three sons: Er, Onan, and Shelah. Er was said to be evil in God's sight and after marrying Tamar, God punished him with death. Onan, as Tamar's brother-in-law, was expected to give her a son who could carry on Er's name and receive his inheritance. But Onan refused to fulfill his responsibility and suffered the same fate as his older brother.

Now it was left to young Shelah to raise up offspring for Er and Onan. But Judah was afraid that his last son would also die. So he told Tamar to return to her father's house until Shelah was older. Judah's intent seemed clear: Shelah would eventually fulfill his duty as a brother-in-law and have a son with Tamar. Time passed and Tamar's expectations were not fulfilled. So she took matters into her own hands, assumed the guise of a prostitute, and tricked Judah into getting her pregnant.

When Judah heard Tamar was pregnant, he demanded her punishment as any self-respecting father-in-law would do. But she showed Judah the items he had given as a pledge, proving that he was the father of the child. So Judah acknowledged that he was in the wrong. Tamar later gave birth to two sons, one of whom is named in the kingly lineage of David, and of Jesus the Messiah.

STRENGTHS AND ACCOMPLISHMENTS:
- After being confronted, Judah admitted his failures and took responsibility for them.

WEAKNESSES AND MISTAKES:
- Judah lost close contact with the patriarchal family, perhaps weakening his resolve to do right.
- Judah failed to fulfill his paternal responsibilities toward Tamar.
- Judah let fear dictate his actions, perhaps indicating his lack of faith.
- Tamar failed to confront Judah directly, resorting to indirect manipulation.

LESSONS FROM THEIR LIVES:
- A shallow walk with God can lead to trouble in family relationships.
- Commitments made to others, whether stated or implied, must be kept.
- God's grace can bring future blessings out of our biggest mistakes.
- Tactful confrontation is needed when legitimate expectations have not been fulfilled.

KEY VERSE:
"Judah . . . said, 'She [Tamar] is more in the right than I am, because I refused to keep my promise to give her to my son Shelah.' But he did not marry her" (Genesis 38:26).

The story of Judah and Tamar is told in Genesis 38. Judah is mentioned in Genesis 29–50 and throughout the Old Testament as one of the fathers of the twelve tribes. Judah and Tamar are both mentioned in Jesus' family tree in Matthew 1.

---

and his friend Hirah, the Adullamite, went to
Timnah to supervise the shearing of his
sheep. 13When someone told Tamar that her
father-in-law had left for the sheep shearing
at Timnah, 14and realizing by now that she
was not going to be permitted to marry Shelah, though he was fully grown, she laid aside
her widow's clothing and covered herself with
a veil to disguise herself, and sat beside the
road at the entrance to the village of Enaim,
which is on the way to Timnah. 15Judah noticed her as he went by and thought she was
a prostitute, since her face was veiled. 16So he
stopped and propositioned her to sleep with
him, not realizing of course that she was his
own daughter-in-law.

"How much will you pay me?" she asked.

17"I'll send you a young goat from my
flock," he promised.

"What pledge will you give me, so that I can be sure you will send it?" she asked.

18"Well, what do you want?" he inquired.

"Your identification seal and your walking stick," she replied. So he gave them to
her and she let him come and sleep with
her; and she became pregnant as a result.
19Afterwards she resumed wearing her widow's clothing as usual. 20Judah asked his

friend Hirah the Adullamite to take the young goat back to her, and to pick up the pledges he had given her, but Hirah couldn't find her!

[21]So he asked around of the men of the city, "Where does the prostitute live who was soliciting out beside the road at the entrance of the village?"

"But we've never had a public prostitute here," they replied. [22]So he returned to Judah and told him he couldn't find her anywhere, and what the men of the place had told him.

[23]"Then let her keep them!" Judah exclaimed. "We tried our best. We'd be the laughingstock of the town to go back again."

[24]About three months later word reached Judah that Tamar, his daughter-in-law, was pregnant, obviously as a result of prostitution.

"Bring her out and burn her," Judah shouted.

[25]But as they were taking her out to kill her she sent this message to her father-in-law: "The man who owns this identification seal and walking stick is the father of my child. Do you recognize them?"

[26]Judah admitted that they were his and said, "She is more in the right than I am, because I refused to keep my promise to give her to my son Shelah." But he did not marry her.

[27]In due season the time of her delivery arrived and she had twin sons. [28]As they were being born, the midwife tied a scarlet thread around the wrist of the child who appeared first, [29]but he drew back his hand and the other baby was actually the first to be born. "Where did *you* come from!" she exclaimed. And ever after he was called Perez (meaning "Bursting Out"). [30]Then, soon afterwards, the baby with the scarlet thread on his wrist was born, and he was named Zerah.

CHAPTER 39

Joseph Serves Potiphar

When Joseph arrived in Egypt as a captive of the Ishmaelite traders, he was purchased from them by Potiphar, a member of the personal staff of Pharaoh, the king of Egypt. Now this man Potiphar was the captain of the king's bodyguard and his chief executioner. [2]The Lord greatly blessed Joseph there in the home of his master, so that everything he did succeeded. [3]Potiphar noticed this and realized that the Lord was with Joseph in a very special way. [4]So Joseph naturally became quite a favorite with him. Soon he was put in charge of the administration of Potiphar's household, and all of his business affairs. [5]At once the Lord began blessing Potiphar for Joseph's sake. All his household affairs began to run smoothly, his crops flourished and his flocks multiplied. [6]So Potiphar gave Joseph the complete administrative responsibility over everything he owned. He hadn't a worry in the world with Joseph there, except to decide what he wanted to eat! Joseph, by the way, was a very handsome young man.

[7]One day at about this time Potiphar's wife

39:2 God blessed Joseph even in the worst of circumstances. Even as a slave in a strange household and in a foreign land, God made Joseph a success. It should not be inferred that God will also make us successful. Rather, our chief goal should be to follow Joseph's example of being faithful to God's program, no matter what the consequences.

39:7-18 Joseph withstood the temptation of Potiphar's wife even though he was far from home and the temptation continued day after day. This was not a one-time crisis, but a constant, wearing temptation. How did he stand up to it? Two things seem to have helped: Joseph's respect for his master; and even more important, Joseph's respect for God. As we draw closer to God, we will begin to sense his presence in our life. Doing something that runs counter to his program will cause us pain. Walking close to God will provide us with added protection against the temptations we face.

39:19-20 It seems as if the good guys often finish last—the innocent seem to suffer. It looks as though Joseph's faithfulness to God was rewarded with years in prison. This may have discouraged Joseph, but it didn't stop him. Even in prison he continued living according to God's program. In the end, after a number of setbacks, he was rewarded. We may need to look past difficult present circumstances to see that God may have a purpose in our suffering. It may be an important part of our education for future success.

40:1-8 Here we see how Joseph's consistency gained the respect and trust of his jailer and his fellow prisoners. One can imagine that the normal prisoner then, as now, was a pretty sullen character. This makes Joseph's acceptance by them even more significant. His behavior in prison clearly exemplifies the first three steps in recovery. Joseph recognized his powerlessness over the situation he was in and committed his situation to God.

began making eyes at Joseph, and suggested
that he come and sleep with her.
8Joseph refused. "Look," he told her, "my
master trusts me with everything in the entire
household; 9he himself has no more authority
here than I have! He has held back nothing
from me except you yourself because you are
his wife. How can I do such a wicked thing as
this? It would be a great sin against God."
10But she kept on with her suggestions day
after day, even though he refused to listen,
and kept out of her way as much as possible.
11Then one day as he was in the house going
about his work—as it happened, no one else
was around at the time—12she came and
grabbed him by the sleeve demanding, "Sleep
with me." He tore himself away, but as he did,
his jacket slipped off and she was left holding
it as he fled from the house. 13When she saw
that she had his jacket, and that he had fled,
14,15she began screaming; and when the other
men around the place came running in to see
what had happened, she was crying hysterically. "My husband had to bring in this Hebrew slave to insult us!" she sobbed. "He tried
to rape me, but when I screamed, he ran, and
forgot to take his jacket."
16She kept the jacket, and when her husband came home that night, 17she told him
her story.
"That Hebrew slave you've had around
here tried to rape me, 18and I was only saved
by my screams. He fled, leaving his jacket
behind!"
19Well, when her husband heard his wife's
story, he was furious. 20He threw Joseph into
prison, where the king's prisoners were kept
in chains. 21But the Lord was with Joseph
there, too, and was kind to him by granting
him favor with the chief jailer. 22In fact, the
jailer soon handed over the entire prison administration to Joseph, so that all the other
prisoners were responsible to him. 23The chief
jailer had no more worries after that, for Joseph took care of everything, and the Lord
was with him so that everything ran
smoothly and well.

CHAPTER 40

Joseph Interprets Two Dreams

Some time later it so happened that the king
of Egypt became angry with both his chief
baker and his chief butler, so he jailed them
both in the prison where Joseph was, in the
castle of Potiphar, the captain of the guard,
who was the chief executioner. 4They remained under arrest there for quite some

Overcoming Denial

BIBLE READING: Genesis 38:1-30

We admitted to God, to ourselves, and to another human being the exact nature of our wrongs.

Admitting our wrongs to ourself can be the most difficult part of Step Five. Denial can be blinding! How can we be expected to admit to ourself those things we are blind to? Here's a clue that can help us. We will often condemn in others the wrongs most deeply hidden within ourself.

According to ancient Jewish law, a widow was entitled to marry the surviving brother of her husband in order to produce children. Tamar had been married successively to two brothers who died without giving her children. Her father-in-law, Judah, promised to give her his youngest son also, but he never did. This left her alone and destitute. In an effort to protect herself, she disguised herself as a prostitute and became pregnant by Judah himself. And she kept his identification seal, which he had given her as a pledge for payment (Genesis 38:1-23).

When Judah heard that Tamar was pregnant and unmarried, he demanded her execution. "But as they were taking her out to kill her she sent this message to her father-in-law: 'The man who owns this identification . . . is the father of my child. Do you recognize them?' Judah admitted that they were his and said, 'She is more in the right than I am'" (Genesis 38:25-26).

It won't be easy to be honest with ourself. "The heart is the most deceitful thing there is, and desperately wicked" (Jeremiah 17:9). However, we can look at those things we condemn in others as a clue to what may be lurking within ourself. ***Turn to page 927, Hosea 11.***

time, and Potiphar assigned Joseph to wait on them. 5One night each of them had a dream. 6The next morning Joseph noticed that they looked dejected and sad.

7"What in the world is the matter?" he asked.

8And they replied, "We both had dreams last night, but there is no one here to tell us what they mean."

"Interpreting dreams is God's business," Joseph replied. "Tell me what you saw."

9,10The butler told his dream first. "In my dream," he said, "I saw a vine with three branches that began to bud and blossom, and soon there were clusters of ripe grapes. 11I was holding Pharaoh's wine cup in my hand, so I took the grapes and squeezed the juice into it, and gave it to him to drink."

12"I know what the dream means," Joseph said. "The three branches mean three days! 13Within three days Pharaoh is going to take you out of prison and give you back your job again as his chief butler. 14And please have some pity on me when you are back in his favor, and mention me to Pharaoh, and ask him to let me out of here. 15For I was kidnapped from my homeland among the Hebrews, and now this—here I am in jail when I did nothing to deserve it."

16When the chief baker saw that the first dream had such a good meaning, he told his dream to Joseph, too.

"In my dream," he said, "there were three baskets of pastries on my head. 17In the top basket were all kinds of bakery goods for Pharaoh, but the birds came and ate them."

18,19"The three baskets mean three days," Joseph told him. "Three days from now Pharaoh will take off your head and impale your body on a pole, and the birds will come and pick off your flesh!"

20Pharaoh's birthday came three days later, and he held a party for all of his officials and household staff. He sent for his chief butler and chief baker, and they were brought to him from the prison. 21Then he restored the chief butler to his former position; 22but he sentenced the chief baker to be impaled, just as Joseph had predicted. 23Pharaoh's wine taster, however, promptly forgot all about Joseph, never giving him a thought.

CHAPTER 41

Joseph Becomes Ruler of Egypt

One night two years later, Pharaoh dreamed that he was standing on the bank of the Nile River, 2when suddenly, seven sleek, fat cows came up out of the river and began grazing in the grass. 3Then seven other cows came up from the river, but they were very skinny and all their ribs stood out. They went over and stood beside the fat cows. 4Then the skinny cows ate the fat ones! At which point, Pharaoh woke up!

5Soon he fell asleep again and had a second dream. This time he saw seven heads of grain on one stalk, with every kernel well formed and plump. 6Then, suddenly, seven more heads appeared on the stalk, but these were shriveled and withered by the east wind. 7And these thin heads swallowed up the seven plump, well-formed heads! Then Pharaoh woke up again and realized it was all a dream. 8Next morning, as he thought about it, he became very concerned as to what the dreams might mean; he called for all the magicians and sages of Egypt and told them about it, but not one of them could suggest what his dreams meant.9Then the king's wine taster spoke up. "Today I remember my sin!" he said. 10"Some time ago when you were angry with a couple of us and put me and the chief baker in jail in the castle of the captain of the guard, 11the chief baker and I each had a dream one night. 12We told the dreams to a young Hebrew fellow there who was a slave of the captain of the guard, and he told us what our dreams meant. 13And everything happened just as he said: I was restored to my position of wine taster, and the chief baker was executed, and impaled on a pole."

14Pharaoh sent at once for Joseph. He was brought hastily from the dungeon, and after

40:23 After prophesying the wine taster's release, Joseph must have felt disappointed when he was forgotten. But here again, Joseph refused to play the victim. He didn't poison his life by complaining and assigning blame. He didn't give up and grow bitter. Instead, he continued to live a life that was faithful to God and his plan.

41:14 At last Joseph was given the opportunity for freedom. God's perfect timing had come. We may get discouraged by our slow progress, but we need to faithfully follow God the best we can. Someday we may find we are truly free of the things that bind us. If we experience such deliverance, we can then rejoice. For many of us, however, our dependencies will haunt us throughout this life. If we find ourselves in this situation, we can still rejoice, knowing that through it all we are building a deeper relationship with God.

JOSEPH & BROTHERS

Overconfidence is usually viewed as a negative personality trait. The youthful boasting that Joseph displayed with his brothers was no exception to the rule. His claims that the others would someday bow down to him coupled with his father's favoritism led to jealousy and broken family relationships. In the end, his brothers sold him into slavery, cutting him off from his family altogether.

Through years of difficulties and suffering, Joseph's overconfidence was developed by God into a mature self-assurance. In times of personal struggle, this self-assurance, along with his personal knowledge of God, enabled Joseph to ask, "What shall I do now?" instead of "Why me God?"

Joseph's self-assurance made him capable of tackling and succeeding at jobs that most other people would have run away from. His high personal integrity, refined throughout his life, took him from the bottom of the social ladder to the top. Because of this, Joseph was in a position to save the young nation of Israel during a time of terrible famine.

Overconfidence without God's perspective will invariably lead us down the pathway to many other personal problems and mistakes. On the other hand, self-assurance linked with a strong faith in God will enable us to overcome the many obstacles we face in life.

STRENGTHS AND ACCOMPLISHMENTS:
- Joseph was elevated from slavery to the position of prime minister.
- He had high personal integrity.
- He was a man of great spiritual sensitivity.
- He enabled a nation to prepare for a seven-year famine.

WEAKNESSES AND MISTAKES:
- When he was a young man, his overconfidence severely damaged his family relationships.

LESSONS FROM HIS LIFE:
- Our responses to the circumstances we face are more important than the circumstances themselves.
- God can mold our weaknesses into strengths.
- God can cause situations that others intended for evil to be used for good.

KEY VERSE:
"Turning to Joseph, Pharaoh said to him, 'Since God has revealed the meaning of the dreams to you, you are the wisest man in the country!'" (Genesis 41:39).

Joseph's story is told in Genesis 37–50. Joseph is also mentioned in Acts 7:9-18 and Hebrews 11:22.

---

a quick shave and change of clothes, came in
before Pharaoh.
15"I had a dream last night," Pharaoh told
him, "and none of these men can tell me
what it means. But I have heard that you can
interpret dreams, and that is why I have called
for you."
16"I can't do it by myself," Joseph replied,
"but God will tell you what it means!"
17So Pharaoh told him the dream. "I was
standing upon the bank of the Nile River," he
said, 18"when suddenly, seven fat, healthy-
looking cows came up out of the river and
began grazing along the river bank. 19But then
seven other cows came up from the river, very
skinny and bony—in fact, I've never seen
such poor-looking specimens in all the land
of Egypt. 20And these skinny cattle ate up the
seven fat ones that had come out first, 21and
afterwards they were still as skinny as before!
Then I woke up.
22"A little later I had another dream. This
time there were seven heads of grain on one
stalk, and all seven heads were plump and
full. 23Then, out of the same stalk, came seven
withered, thin heads. 24And the thin heads
swallowed up the fat ones! I told all this to my
magicians, but not one of them could tell me
the meaning."
25"Both dreams mean the same thing," Joseph told Pharaoh. "God was telling you what
he is going to do here in the land of Egypt.
26The seven fat cows (and also the seven fat,
well-formed heads of grain) mean that there
are seven years of prosperity ahead. 27The
seven skinny cows (and also the seven thin
and withered heads of grain) indicate that
there will be seven years of famine following
the seven years of prosperity.
28"So God has showed you what he is about
to do: 29The next seven years will be a period
of great prosperity throughout all the land of
Egypt; 30but afterwards there will be seven
years of famine so great that all the prosperity
will be forgotten and wiped out; famine will
consume the land. 31The famine will be so
terrible that even the memory of the good
years will be erased. 32The double dream gives
double impact, showing that what I have told
you is certainly going to happen, for God has

decreed it, and it is going to happen soon. 33My suggestion is that you find the wisest man in Egypt and put him in charge of administering a nationwide farm program. 34,35Let Pharaoh divide Egypt into five administrative districts, and let the officials of these districts gather into the royal storehouses all the excess crops of the next seven years, 36so that there will be enough to eat when the seven years of famine come. Otherwise, disaster will surely strike."

37Joseph's suggestions were well received by Pharaoh and his assistants. 38As they discussed who should be appointed for the job, Pharaoh said, "Who could do it better than Joseph? For he is a man who is obviously filled with the Spirit of God." 39Turning to Joseph, Pharaoh said to him, "Since God has revealed the meaning of the dreams to you, you are the wisest man in the country! 40I am hereby appointing you to be in charge of this entire project. What you say goes, throughout all the land of Egypt. I alone will outrank you."

41,42Then Pharaoh placed his own signet ring on Joseph's finger as a token of his authority, and dressed him in beautiful clothing and placed the royal gold chain about his neck and declared, "See, I have placed you in charge of all the land of Egypt."

43Pharaoh also gave Joseph the chariot of his second-in-command, and wherever he went the shout arose, "Kneel down!" 44And Pharaoh declared to Joseph, "I, the king of Egypt, swear that you shall have complete charge over all the land of Egypt."

45Pharaoh gave him a name meaning "He has the godlike power of life and death!" And he gave him a wife, a girl named Asenath, daughter of Potiphera, priest of Heliopolis. So Joseph became famous throughout the land of Egypt. 46He was thirty years old as he entered the service of the king. Joseph went out from the presence of Pharaoh and began traveling all across the land.

47And sure enough, for the next seven years there were bumper crops everywhere. 48During those years, Joseph requisitioned for the government a portion of all the crops grown throughout Egypt, storing them in nearby cities. 49After seven years of this, the granaries were full to overflowing, and there was so much that no one kept track of the amount.

50During this time before the arrival of the first of the famine years, two sons were born to Joseph by Asenath, the daughter of Potiphera, priest of the sun god Re of Heliopolis. 51Joseph named his oldest son Manasseh (meaning "Made to Forget"—what he meant was that God had made up to him for all the anguish of his youth, and for the loss of his father's home). 52The second boy was named Ephraim (meaning "Fruitful"—"For God has made me fruitful in this land of my slavery," he said).

53So at last the seven years of plenty came to an end. 54Then the seven years of famine began, just as Joseph had predicted. There were crop failures in all the surrounding countries, too, but in Egypt there was plenty of grain in the storehouses. 55The people began to starve. They pleaded with Pharaoh for food, and he sent them to Joseph. "Do whatever he tells you to," he instructed them.

56,57So now, with severe famine all over the world, Joseph opened up the storehouses and sold grain to the Egyptians and to those from other lands who came to Egypt to buy grain from Joseph.

CHAPTER 42

Joseph's Brothers Buy Grain

When Jacob heard that there was grain available in Egypt he said to his sons, "Why are you standing around looking at one another? 2I have heard that there is grain available in Egypt. Go down and buy some for us before we all starve to death."

3So Joseph's ten older brothers went down to Egypt to buy grain. 4However, Jacob wouldn't let Joseph's younger brother Benjamin go with them, for fear some harm might happen to him [as it had to his brother Joseph]. 5So it was that Israel's sons arrived in Egypt along with many others from many lands to buy food, for the famine was as severe in Canaan as it was everywhere else.

6Since Joseph was governor of all Egypt, and in charge of the sale of the grain, it was to

---

41:38-40 The primary quality that Pharaoh mentioned about Joseph was his dependence on God. He ignored the fact that Joseph had a questionable past, colored by rumors and a long prison term. Pharaoh could see that God's Spirit was in Joseph, making him a very wise young man. This more than made up for any questions Pharaoh might have had about his past. So Pharaoh promoted Joseph to be the prime minister of Egypt! Some of us may believe that our past has destroyed any hope of a prosperous future. But when we give ourselves to God, asking for his help, no past is too terrible or dark to overcome.

him that his brothers came, and bowed low before him, with their faces to the earth. 7Joseph recognized them instantly, but pretended he didn't.

"Where are you from?" he demanded roughly.

"From the land of Canaan," they replied. "We have come to buy grain."

8,9Then Joseph remembered the dreams of long ago! But he said to them, "You are spies. You have come to see how destitute the famine has made our land."

10"No, no," they exclaimed. "We have come to buy food. 11We are all brothers and honest men, sir! We are not spies!"

12"Yes, you are," he insisted. "You have come to see how weak we are."

13"Sir," they said, "there are twelve of us brothers, and our father is in the land of Canaan. Our youngest brother is there with our father, and one of our brothers is dead."

14"So?" Joseph asked. "What does that prove? You are spies. 15This is the way I will test your story: I swear by the life of Pharaoh that you are not going to leave Egypt until this youngest brother comes here. 16One of you go and get your brother! I'll keep the rest of you here, bound in prison. Then we'll find out whether your story is true or not. If it turns out that you don't have a younger brother, then I'll know you are spies."

17So he threw them all into jail for three days.

18The third day Joseph said to them, "I am a God-fearing man and I'm going to give you an opportunity to prove yourselves. 19I'm going to take a chance that you are honorable; only one of you shall remain in chains in jail, and the rest of you may go on home with grain for your families; 20but bring your youngest brother back to me. In this way I will know whether you are telling me the truth; and if you are, I will spare you." To this they agreed.

21Speaking among themselves, they said, "This has all happened because of what we did to Joseph long ago. We saw his terror and anguish and heard his pleadings, but we wouldn't listen."

22"Didn't I tell you not to do it?" Reuben asked. "But you wouldn't listen. And now we are going to die because we murdered him."

23Of course they didn't know that Joseph understood them as he was standing there, for he had been speaking to them through an interpreter. 24Now he left the room and found a place where he could weep. Returning, he selected Simeon from among them and had him bound before their eyes. 25Joseph then ordered his servants to fill the men's sacks with grain, but also gave secret instructions to put each brother's payment at the top of his sack! He also gave them provisions for their journey. 26So they loaded up their donkeys with the grain and started for home.27But when they stopped for the night and one of them opened his sack to get some grain to feed the donkeys, there was his money in the mouth of the sack!

28"Look," he exclaimed to his brothers, "my money is here in my sack." They were filled with terror. Trembling, they exclaimed to each other. "What is this that God has done to us?" 29So they came to their father, Jacob, in the land of Canaan and told him all that had happened.

30"The king's chief assistant spoke very roughly to us," they told him, "and took us for spies. 31'No, no,' we said, 'we are honest men, not spies. 32We are twelve brothers, sons of one father; one is dead, and the youngest is with our father in the land of Canaan.' 33Then the man told us, 'This is the way I will find out if you are what you claim to be. Leave one of your brothers here with me and take grain for your families and go on home, 34but bring your youngest brother back to me. Then I shall know whether you are spies or honest men; if you prove to be what you say, then I

42:7-20 When Joseph recognized his brothers, he took some time to test them. He wanted to discover something of their attitudes before he revealed himself to them. In recovery we are told to work toward reconciliation with the important people in our life. We need wisdom from God to do this in a way that will bring healing to both ourselves and the people close to us. Joseph didn't instantly jump back into a relationship with his brothers. He took the time he needed to do it in a wise way.

42:21-22 After many years Joseph's brothers were still haunted by their guilty conscience. They had sold their brother into Egypt with no plans of ever seeing him again—and no hope of reconciliation or forgiveness. We may wonder how many times during those years Reuben said, "I told you so." It is clear that this period had been one of misery for the brothers. A necessary step in our recovery is seeking reconciliation with others we have wronged. Only then can we experience the healing we need to live a healthy and peaceful life.

will give you back your brother and you can
come as often as you like to purchase grain.'"
35As they emptied out the sacks, there at the
top of each was the money paid for the grain!
Terror gripped them, as it did their father.
36Then Jacob exclaimed, "You have be-
reaved me of my children—Joseph didn't
come back, Simeon is gone, and now you
want to take Benjamin too! Everything has
been against me."
37Then Reuben said to his father, "Kill my
two sons if I don't bring Benjamin back to
you. I'll be responsible for him."
38But Jacob replied, "My son shall not go
down with you, for his brother Joseph is dead
and he alone is left of his mother's children.
If anything should happen to him, I would
die."

CHAPTER 43

Joseph's Brothers Return to Egypt

But there was no relief from the terrible famine throughout the land. 2When the grain
they had brought from Egypt was almost
gone, their father said to them, "Go again and
buy us a little food."
3-5But Judah told him, "The man wasn't
fooling one bit when he said, 'Don't ever
come back again unless your brother is with
you.' We cannot go unless you let Benjamin
go with us."
6"Why did you ever tell him you had another brother?" Israel moaned. "Why did you
have to treat me like that?"
7"But the man specifically asked us about
our family," they told him. "He wanted to
know whether our father was still living and
he asked us if we had another brother, so we
told him. How could we know that he was
going to say, 'Bring me your brother'?"
8Judah said to his father, "Send the lad with
me and we will be on our way; otherwise we
will all die of starvation—and not only we,
but you and all our little ones. 9I guarantee his
safety. If I don't bring him back to you, then
let me bear the blame forever. 10For we could
have gone and returned by this time if you
had let him come."
11So their father Israel finally said to them,
"If it can't be avoided, then at least do this.
Load your donkeys with the best products of
the land. Take them to the man as gifts—
balm, honey, spices, myrrh, pistachio nuts,
and almonds. 12Take double money so that
you can pay back what was in the mouths of
your sacks, as it was probably someone's mistake, 13and take your brother and go. 14May
God Almighty give you mercy before the
man, so that he will release Simeon and return Benjamin. And if I must bear the anguish
of their deaths, then so be it."
15So they took the gifts and double money
and went to Egypt, and stood before Joseph.
16When Joseph saw that Benjamin was with
them, he said to the manager of his household, "These men will eat with me this noon.
Take them home and prepare a big feast." 17So
the man did as he was told and took them to
Joseph's palace. 18They were badly frightened
when they saw where they were being taken.
"It's because of the money returned to us in
our sacks," they said. "He wants to pretend we
stole it and seize us as slaves, with our donkeys."
19As they arrived at the entrance to the
palace, they went over to Joseph's household
manager, 20and said to him, "O sir, after our
first trip to Egypt to buy food, 21as we were
returning home, we stopped for the night and
opened our sacks, and the money was there
that we had paid for the grain. Here it is; we
have brought it back again, 22along with additional money to buy more grain. We have no
idea how the money got into our sacks."
23"Don't worry about it," the household
manager told them; "your God, even the God
of your fathers, must have put it there, for we
collected your money all right."
Then he released Simeon and brought him
out to them. 24They were then conducted into
the palace and given water to refresh their
feet; and their donkeys were fed. 25Then they
got their presents ready for Joseph's arrival at
noon, for they were told that they would be
eating there. 26When Joseph came home they
gave him their presents, bowing low before
him.
27He asked how they had been getting
along. "And how is your father—the old man
you spoke about? Is he still alive?"

42:36 How bitter with grief had Jacob become! He had harbored years of resentment and sadness. His relationship with his sons was built on dishonesty. Walls of lies had been built up—layer upon layer. This separated Jacob from close fellowship with his family. He was all alone in his grief, trapped by the fear that he might lose yet another son. Yet even though Jacob was alone and helpless in his pain, God had a plan for his deliverance. He would soon be set free from many years of bitterness and grief.

28“Yes,” they replied. “He is alive and well.”
Then again they bowed before him.
29Looking at his brother Benjamin, he
asked, “Is this your youngest brother, the one
you told me about? How are you, my son?
God be gracious to you.” 30Then Joseph made
a hasty exit, for he was overcome with love for
his brother and had to go out and cry. Going
into his bedroom, he wept there. 31Then he
washed his face and came out, keeping himself under control. “Let’s eat,” he said.
32Joseph ate by himself, his brothers were
served at a separate table, and the Egyptians
at still another; for Egyptians despise Hebrews
and never eat with them. 33He told each of
them where to sit, and seated them in the
order of their ages, from the oldest to the
youngest, much to their amazement! 34Their
food was served to them from his own table.
He gave the largest serving to Benjamin—five
times as much as to any of the others! They
had a wonderful time bantering back and
forth, and the wine flowed freely!

CHAPTER 44

Joseph Tests His Brothers

When his brothers were ready to leave, Joseph
ordered his household manager to fill each of
their sacks with as much grain as they could
carry—and to put into the mouth of each
man’s sack the money he had paid! 2He was
also told to put Joseph’s own silver cup at the
top of Benjamin’s sack, along with the grain
money. So the household manager did as he
was told. 3The brothers were up at dawn and
on their way with their loaded donkeys.
4But when they were barely out of the city,
Joseph said to his household manager, “Chase
after them and stop them and ask them why
they are acting like this when their benefactor
has been so kind to them? 5Ask them, ‘What
do you mean by stealing my lord’s personal
silver drinking cup, which he uses for fortune
telling? What a wicked thing you have
done!’” 6So he caught up with them and
spoke to them along the lines he had been
instructed.
7“What in the world are you talking
about?” they demanded. “What kind of
people do you think we are, that you accuse
us of such a terrible thing as that? 8Didn’t we
bring back the money we found in the mouth
of our sacks? Why would we steal silver or
gold from your master’s house? 9If you find
his cup with any one of us, let that one die.
And all the rest of us will be slaves forever to
your master.”
10“Fair enough,” the man replied, “except
that only the one who stole it will be a slave,
and the rest of you can go free.”
11They quickly took down their sacks from
the backs of their donkeys and opened them.
12He began searching the oldest brother’s sack,
going on down the line to the youngest. And
the cup was found in Benjamin’s! 13They
ripped their clothing in despair, loaded the
donkeys again, and returned to the city.14Jo-
seph was still home when Judah and his
brothers arrived, and they fell to the ground
before him.
15“What were you trying to do?” Joseph
demanded. “Didn’t you know such a man as
I would know who stole it?”
16And Judah said, “Oh, what shall we say to
my lord? How can we plead? How can we
prove our innocence? God is punishing us for
our sins. Sir, we have all returned to be your
slaves, both we and he in whose sack the cup
was found.”
17“No,” Joseph said. “Only the man who
stole the cup, he shall be my slave. The rest of
you can go on home to your father.”
18Then Judah stepped forward and said, “O
sir, let me say just this one word to you. Be
patient with me for a moment, for I know you
can doom me in an instant, as though you
were Pharaoh himself.
19“Sir, you asked us if we had a father or a
brother, 20and we said, ‘Yes, we have a father,
an old man, and a child of his old age, a little
one. And his brother is dead, and he alone is
left of his mother’s children, and his father
loves him very much.’ 21And you said to us,
‘Bring him here so that I can see him.’ 22But
we said to you, ‘Sir, the lad cannot leave his
father, for his father would die.’ 23But you told
us, ‘Don’t come back here unless your youngest brother is with you.’ 24So we returned to
our father and told him what you had said.
25And when he said, ‘Go back again and buy

44:18-34 Judah stepped forward to plead for Benjamin’s freedom, fearing what his enslavement would do to Jacob, their father. Many years earlier, the brothers had chosen to sell Joseph into slavery, just for reasons of personal hatred. This had caused their father deep pain. But here, Judah was willing to put himself on the line for his grieving father. Judah and his brothers had grown up a great deal over the years. They had learned from their past mistakes and proved to Joseph that they were ready for reconciliation with their long lost brother.

us a little food,' 26we replied, 'We can't, unless you let our youngest brother go with us. Only then may we come.'

27"Then my father said to us, 'You know that my wife had two sons, 28and that one of them went away and never returned—doubtless torn to pieces by some wild animal; I have never seen him since. 29And if you take away his brother from me also, and any harm befalls him, I shall die with sorrow.' 30 And now, sir, if I go back to my father and the lad is not with us—seeing that our father's life is bound up in the lad's life— 31when he sees that the boy is not with us, our father will die; and we will be responsible for bringing down his gray hairs with sorrow to the grave. 32Sir, I pledged my father that I would take care of the lad. I told him, 'If I don't bring him back to you, I shall bear the blame forever.' 33Please sir, let me stay here as a slave instead of the lad, and let the lad return with his brothers. 34For how shall I return to my father if the lad is not with me? I cannot bear to see what this would do to him."

CHAPTER 45

Joseph Forgives His Brothers

Joseph could stand it no longer.

"Out, all of you," he cried out to his attendants, and he was left alone with his brothers. 2Then he wept aloud. His sobs could be heard throughout the palace, and the news was quickly carried to Pharaoh's palace.

3"I am Joseph!" he said to his brothers. "Is my father still alive?" But his brothers couldn't say a word, they were so stunned with surprise.

4"Come over here," he said. So they came closer. And he said again, "I am Joseph, your brother whom you sold into Egypt! 5But don't be angry with yourselves that you did this to me, for God did it! He sent me here ahead of you to preserve your lives. 6These two years of famine will grow to seven, during which there will be neither plowing nor harvest. 7God has sent me here to keep you and your families alive, so that you will become a great nation. 8Yes, it was God who sent me here, not you! And he has made me a counselor to Pharaoh, and manager of this entire nation, ruler of all the land of Egypt.

9"Hurry, return to my father and tell him, 'Your son Joseph says, "God has made me chief of all the land of Egypt. Come down to me right away! 10You shall live in the land of Goshen so that you can be near me with all your children, your grandchildren, your flocks and herds, and all that you have. 11,12I will take care of you there'" (you men are witnesses of my promise, and my brother Benjamin has heard me say it) "'for there are still five years of famine ahead of us. Otherwise you will come to utter poverty along with all your household.'" 13Tell our father about all my power here in Egypt, and how everyone obeys me. And bring him to me quickly."

14Then, weeping with joy, he embraced Benjamin and Benjamin began weeping too. 15And he did the same with each of his brothers, who finally found their tongues! 16The news soon reached Pharaoh—"Joseph's brothers have come"; and Pharaoh was very happy to hear it, as were his officials.

17Then Pharaoh said to Joseph, "Tell your brothers to load their pack animals and return quickly to their homes in Canaan, 18and to bring your father and all of your families and come here to Egypt to live. Tell them, 'Pharaoh will assign to you the very best territory in the land of Egypt. You shall live off the fat of the land!' 19And tell your brothers to take wagons from Egypt to carry their wives and little ones, and to bring your father here. 20Don't worry about your property, for the best of all the land of Egypt is yours."

21So Joseph gave them wagons, as Pharaoh had commanded, and provisions for the journey, 22and he gave each of them new clothes—but to Benjamin he gave five changes of clothes and three hundred pieces of silver! 23He sent his father ten donkey-loads of the

45:1-3 Joseph finally revealed himself to his brothers. For him it was a beautiful reunion, because he had experienced healing by walking with God. But for his brothers, excluding Benjamin, hidden guilt had burdened them for a long time. They were terrified when they recognized Joseph. It is terrifying to open long-hidden guilt to the light, but this is the only road to reconciliation and peace.

45:4-7 Joseph told his brothers not to be angry at themselves for the mistakes they had made in the past. It was now time to rejoice in the present! This was true forgiveness. Joseph was able to see how God had used their mistake to save thousands of lives, including their own. God often turns past disasters into opportunities for great success. When we begin to see that God is working in our life, we will be better able to forgive the people who have wronged us in the past. And if we can see how God has turned around the lives of people we have wronged, we will begin to understand how much God wants our guilt removed and our relationships reconciled.

good things of Egypt, and ten donkeys loaded
with grain and all kinds of other food, to eat
on his journey. 24So he sent his brothers off.

"Don't quarrel along the way!" was his
parting shot! 25And leaving, they returned to
the land of Canaan, to Jacob their father.

26"Joseph is alive," they shouted to him.
"And he is ruler over all the land of Egypt!"
But Jacob's heart was like a stone; he couldn't
take it in. 27But when they had given him
Joseph's messages, and when he saw the wagons filled with food that Joseph had sent him,
his spirit revived.

28And he said, "It must be true! Joseph my
son is alive! I will go and see him before I die."

CHAPTER 46

Jacob Moves to Egypt

So Israel set out with all his possessions, and
came to Beer-sheba, and offered sacrifices
there to the God of his father, Isaac. 2During
the night God spoke to him in a vision.

"Jacob! Jacob!" he called.

"Yes?" Jacob answered.

3,4"I am God," the voice replied, "the God
of your father. Don't be afraid to go down to
Egypt, for I will see to it that you become a
great nation there. And I will go down with
you into Egypt and I will bring your descendants back again; but you shall die in Egypt
with Joseph at your side."

5So Jacob left Beer-sheba, and his sons
brought him to Egypt, along with their little
ones and their wives, in the wagons Pharaoh
had provided for them. 6They brought their
livestock, too, and all their belongings accumulated in the land of Canaan, and came to
Egypt—Jacob and all his children, 7sons and
daughters, grandsons and granddaughters—
all his loved ones.

8-14Here are the names of his sons and
grandchildren who went with him into
Egypt:

Reuben, his oldest son;
Reuben's sons: Hanoch, Pallu, Hezron, and Carmi.
Simeon and his sons: Jemuel, Jamin, Ohad, Jachin, Zohar, and Shaul (Shaul's mother was a girl from Canaan).
Levi and his sons: Gershon, Kohath, Merari.
Judah and his sons: Er, Onan, Shelah, Perez, Zerah (however, Er and Onan died while still in Canaan, before Israel went to Egypt).
The sons of Perez were Hezron and Hamul.
Issachar and his sons: Tola, Puvah, Iob, Shimron.
Zebulun and his sons: Sered, Elon, Jahleel.

15So these descendants of Jacob and Leah,
not including their daughter Dinah, born to
Jacob in Paddan-aram, were thirty-three in
all.

16,17Also accompanying him were:

Gad and his sons: Ziphion, Haggi, Shuni, Ezbon, Eri, Arodi, and Areli.
Asher and his sons: Imnah, Ishvah, Ishvi, Beriah, and a sister, Serah.
Beriah's sons were Heber and Malchiel.

18These sixteen persons were the sons of
Jacob and Zilpah, the slave-girl given to Leah
by her father, Laban.

19-22Also in the total of Jacob's household
were these fourteen sons and descendants of
Jacob and Rachel:

Joseph and Benjamin;
Joseph's sons, born in the land of Egypt, were Manasseh and Ephraim (their mother was Asenath, the daughter of Potiphera, priest of Heliopolis);
Benjamin's sons: Bela, Becher, Ashbel, Gera, Naaman, Ehi, Rosh, Muppim, Huppim, and Ard.

23-25Also in the group were these seven sons
and descendants of Jacob and Bilhah, the
slave-girl given to Rachel by her father, Laban:

Dan and his son: Hushim.
Naphtali and his sons: Jahzeel, Guni, Jezer, and Shillem.

45:24 Joseph knew his brothers so well; he knew they were inclined to argue. Even though Joseph's brothers had matured a great deal since he had last seen them, they still had a long way to go. Deeply ingrained attitudes and habits are hard to get rid of. It all takes time. Joseph's parting shot here shows that he had a sense of humor. But it also reveals that he accepted his brothers as they were, arguments and all.

46:1-4 Some might think it was wrong for the Hebrews to leave the Promised Land, but God's promise to Jacob here shows that God approved of this family reunion in Egypt. When our life is subject to God's authority, where and when we go are up to him. God often uses surprising means to work his will. Notice that God brought Jacob and his family to Egypt for their preservation and growth.

26So the total number of those going to Egypt, of his own descendants, not counting the wives of Jacob's sons, was sixty-six. 27With Joseph and his two sons included, this total of Jacob's household there in Egypt totaled seventy.

28Jacob sent Judah on ahead to tell Joseph that they were on the way, and would soon arrive in Goshen—which they did. 29Joseph jumped into his chariot and journeyed to Goshen to meet his father and they fell into each other's arms and wept a long while.

30Then Israel said to Joseph, "Now let me die, for I have seen you again and know you are alive."

31And Joseph said to his brothers and to all their households, "I'll go and tell Pharaoh that you are here, and that you have come from the land of Canaan to join me. 32And I will tell him, 'These men are shepherds. They have brought with them their flocks and herds and everything they own.' 33So when Pharaoh calls for you and asks you about your occupation, 34tell him, 'We have been shepherds from our youth, as our fathers have been for many generations.' When you tell him this, he will let you live here in the land of Goshen." For shepherds were despised and hated in other parts of Egypt.

CHAPTER 47

Upon their arrival, Joseph went in to see Pharaoh.

"My father and my brothers are here from Canaan," he reported, "with all their flocks and herds and possessions. They wish to settle in the land of Goshen."

2He took five of his brothers with him, and presented them to Pharaoh.

3Pharaoh asked them, "What is your occupation?"

And they replied, "We are shepherds like our ancestors. 4We have come to live here in Egypt, for there is no pasture for our flocks in Canaan—the famine is very bitter there. We request permission to live in the land of Goshen."

5,6And Pharaoh said to Joseph, "Choose anywhere you like for them to live. Give them the best land of Egypt. The land of Goshen will be fine. And if any of them are capable, put them in charge of my flocks, too."

7Then Joseph brought his father Jacob to Pharaoh. And Jacob blessed Pharaoh.

8"How old are you?" Pharaoh asked him.

9Jacob replied, "I have lived 130 long, hard years, and I am not nearly as old as many of my ancestors." 10Then Jacob blessed Pharaoh again before he left.

11So Joseph assigned the best land of Egypt—the land of Rameses—to his father and brothers, just as Pharaoh had commanded. 12And Joseph furnished food to them in accordance with the number of their dependents.

The Famine Gets Worse

13The famine became worse and worse, so that all the land of Egypt and Canaan was starving. 14Joseph collected all the money in Egypt and Canaan in exchange for grain, and he brought the money to Pharaoh's treasure-houses. 15When the people were out of money, they came to Joseph crying again for food.

"Our money is gone," they said, "but give us bread; for why should we die?"

16"Well then," Joseph replied, "give me your livestock. I will trade you food in exchange."

17So they brought their cattle to Joseph in exchange for food. Soon all the horses, flocks, herds, and donkeys of Egypt were in Pharaoh's possession.

18The next year they came again and said, "Our money is gone, and our cattle are yours, and there is nothing left but our bodies and land. 19Why should we die? Buy us and our land and we will be serfs to Pharaoh. We will trade ourselves for food, then we will live, and the land won't be abandoned."

20So Joseph bought all the land of Egypt for Pharaoh; all the Egyptians sold him their fields because the famine was so severe. And the land became Pharaoh's. 21Thus all the people of Egypt became Pharaoh's serfs. 22The only land he didn't buy was that belonging to the priests, for they were assigned food from Pharaoh and didn't need to sell.

23Then Joseph said to the people, "See, I have bought you and your land for Pharaoh.

46:29 God approves of the outward expression of emotion. It is an honest display of feelings that draws us closer to others. To hide our feelings is a form of dishonesty. We need to learn to show our feelings in wise and loving ways. Our culture urges people to hide their feelings; we are expected to be stoic, even in times of extreme sorrow or joy. Jacob and Joseph embraced and wept a long while, openly displaying their emotions for all to see.

Here is grain. Go and sow the land. 24And
when you harvest it, a fifth of everything you
get belongs to Pharaoh. Keep four parts for
yourselves to be used for next year's seed, and
as food for yourselves and for your households and little ones."

25"You have saved our lives," they said. "We
will gladly be the serfs of Pharaoh."

26So Joseph made it a law throughout the
land of Egypt—and it is still the law—that
Pharaoh should have as his tax 20 percent of
all the crops except those produced on the
land owned by the temples.

Jacob Blesses Joseph's Sons

27So Israel lived in the land of Goshen in
Egypt, and soon the people of Israel began to
prosper, and there was a veritable population
explosion among them. 28Jacob lived seventeen years after his arrival, so that he was 147
years old at the time of his death. 29As the time
drew near for him to die, he called for his son
Joseph and said to him, "Swear to me most
solemnly that you will honor this, my last
request: do not bury me in Egypt. 30But when
I am dead, take me out of Egypt and bury me
beside my ancestors." And Joseph promised.
31"Swear that you will do it," Jacob insisted.
And Joseph did. Soon afterwards Jacob took
to his bed.

CHAPTER 48

One day not long after this, word came to
Joseph that his father was failing rapidly. So,
taking with him his two sons, Manasseh and
Ephraim, he went to visit him. 2When Jacob
heard that Joseph had arrived, he gathered his
strength and sat up in the bed to greet him,
3and said to him,

"God Almighty appeared to me at Luz in
the land of Canaan and blessed me, 4and said
to me, 'I will make you a great nation and I
will give this land of Canaan to you and to
your children's children, for an everlasting
possession.' 5And now, as to these two sons of
yours, Ephraim and Manasseh, born here in
the land of Egypt before I arrived, I am adopting them as my own, and they will inherit
from me just as Reuben and Simeon will. 6But
any other children born to you shall be your
own, and shall inherit Ephraim's and Manasseh's portion from you. 7For your mother,
Rachel, died after only two children when I
came from Paddan-aram, as we were just a
short distance from Ephrath, and I buried her
beside the road to Bethlehem." 8Then Israel
looked over at the two boys. "Are these the
ones?" he asked.

9"Yes," Joseph told him, "these are my sons
whom God has given me here in Egypt."

And Israel said, "Bring them over to me and
I will bless them."

10Israel was half blind with age, so that he
could hardly see. So Joseph brought the boys
close to him and he kissed and embraced
them.

11And Israel said to Joseph, "I never thought
that I would see you again, but now God has
let me see your children too."

12,13Joseph took the boys by the hand,
bowed deeply to him, and led the boys to
their grandfather's knees—Ephraim at Israel's
left hand and Manasseh at his right. 14But
Israel crossed his arms as he stretched them
out to lay his hands upon the boys' heads, so
that his right hand was upon the head of
Ephraim, the younger boy, and his left hand
was upon the head of Manasseh, the older. He
did this purposely.

15Then he blessed Joseph with this blessing:
"May God, the God of my fathers Abraham
and Isaac, the God who has shepherded me
all my life, wonderfully bless these boys. 16He
is the Angel who has kept me from all harm.
May these boys be an honor to my name and
to the names of my fathers Abraham and
Isaac; and may they become a mighty nation."

17But Joseph was upset and displeased when
he saw that his father had laid his right hand
on Ephraim's head; so he lifted it to place it
on Manasseh's head instead.

18"No, Father," he said. "You've got your
right hand on the wrong head! This one over
here is the older. Put your right hand on him!"

19But his father refused. "I know what I'm
doing, my son," he said. "Manasseh too shall

48:1-9 Before blessing his grandsons, Ephraim and Manasseh, Jacob recalled the blessings that God had bestowed upon him. We know that the sins and failures of parents are often passed on to succeeding generations. But here we see that blessings are passed on as well. Abraham had established a relationship with God that he modeled before Isaac, which he then passed on to Jacob, and then to the succeeding generation. Let us establish the kind of relationship with God that will endure in the generations that follow. That way we will be able to bless our children with the blessings God has given us.

become a great nation, but his younger
brother shall become even greater."
20So Jacob blessed the boys that day with
this blessing: "May the people of Israel bless
each other by saying, 'God make you as prosperous as Ephraim and Manasseh.'" (Note
that he put Ephraim before Manasseh.)
21Then Israel said to Joseph, "I am about to
die, but God will be with you and will bring
you again to Canaan, the land of your fathers.
22And I have given the choice land of Shekem
to you instead of to your brothers, as your
portion of that land which I took from the
Amorites with my sword and with my bow."

CHAPTER 49

Jacob Blesses His Sons

Then Jacob called together all his sons and
said, "Gather around me and I will tell you
what is going to happen to you in the days to
come. 2Listen to me, O sons of Jacob; listen to
Israel your father.
3"Reuben, you are my oldest son, the child
of my vigorous youth. You are the head of the
list in rank and in honor. 4But you are unruly
as the wild waves of the sea, and you shall be
first no longer. I am demoting you, for you
slept with one of my wives and thus dishonored me.
5"Simeon and Levi are two of a kind. They
are men of violence and injustice. 6O my soul,
stay away from them. May I never be a party
to their wicked plans. For in their anger they
murdered a man, and maimed oxen just for
fun. 7Cursed be their anger, for it is fierce and
cruel. Therefore, I will scatter their descendants throughout Israel.
8"Judah, your brothers shall praise you. You
shall destroy your enemies. Your father's sons
shall bow before you. 9Judah is a young lion
that has finished eating its prey. He has settled
down as a lion—who will dare to rouse him?
10The scepter shall not depart from Judah until Shiloh comes, whom all people shall obey.
11He has chained his steed to the choicest vine
and washed his clothes in wine. 12His eyes are
darker than wine and his teeth are whiter
than milk.
13"Zebulun shall dwell on the shores of the
sea and shall be a harbor for ships, with his
borders extending to Sidon.
14"Issachar is a strong beast of burden resting among the saddlebags. 15When he saw
how good the countryside was, how pleasant
the land, he willingly bent his shoulder to the
task and served his masters with vigor.
16"Dan shall govern his people like any
other tribe in Israel. 17He shall be a serpent in
the path that bites the horses' heels, so that
the rider falls off. 18I trust in your salvation,
Lord.
19"A marauding band shall stamp upon
Gad, but he shall rob and pursue them!
20"Asher shall produce rich foods, fit for
kings!
21"Naphtali is a deer let loose, producing
lovely fawns.
22"Joseph is a fruitful tree beside a fountain.
His branches shade the wall. 23He has been
severely injured by those who shot at him and
persecuted him, 24but their weapons were
shattered by the Mighty One of Jacob, the
Shepherd, the Rock of Israel. 25May the God of
your fathers, the Almighty, bless you with
blessings of heaven above and of the earth
beneath—blessings of the breasts and of the
womb, 26blessings of the grain and flowers,
blessings reaching to the utmost bounds of
the everlasting hills. These shall be the blessings upon the head of Joseph who was exiled
from his brothers.
27"Benjamin is a wolf that prowls. He devours his enemies in the morning, and in the
evening divides the loot."
28So these are the blessings that Israel, their
father, blessed his twelve sons with.

Jacob Dies and Is Buried

29,30Then he told them, "Soon I will die. You
must bury me with my fathers in the land of

49:5-7 Simeon and Levi were characterized by violent tempers, and the history of these brothers in Genesis corroborates Jacob's assessment. After their sister Dinah was raped, they took revenge by deceiving and slaughtering all the men of the city (34:1-31). This tendency needed to be curbed. Many years later, however, when God called out for people to stand on his side, the Levites stood forth and vigorously defended God's cause (see Exodus 32:25-29). As a result, they were chosen as God's priests in Israel. Let us look to God to transform our weaknesses into strengths, just as he did with the descendants of Levi.

49:13-27 The remarks by Jacob concerning each of his sons seem very harsh, but the information he shared, including a confession of his own failure as a father, should have given helpful direction to each of them. We have a lot to learn from our parents, but often they aren't willing to be honest with us. Or if they are, we aren't really ready to listen. We need to learn both to speak honestly and to listen with respect.

Canaan, in the cave in the field of Mach-pelah, facing Mamre—the field Abraham bought from Ephron the Hethite for a burial ground. 31There they buried Abraham and Sarah, his wife; there they buried Isaac and Rebekah, his wife; and there I buried Leah. 32It is the cave which my grandfather Abraham purchased from the sons of Heth." 33Then, when Jacob had finished his prophecies to his sons, he lay back in the bed, breathed his last, and died.

CHAPTER 50

Joseph threw himself upon his father's body and wept over him and kissed him. 2Afterwards he commanded his morticians to embalm the body. 3The embalming process required forty days, with a period of national mourning of seventy days. 4Then, when at last the mourning was over, Joseph approached Pharaoh's staff and requested them to speak to Pharaoh on his behalf.

5"Tell His Majesty," he requested them, "that Joseph's father made Joseph swear to take his body back to the land of Canaan, to bury him there. Ask His Majesty to permit me to go and bury my father; assure him that I will return promptly."

6Pharaoh agreed. "Go and bury your father, as you promised," he said.

7So Joseph went, and a great number of Pharaoh's counselors and assistants—all the senior officers of the land, 8as well as all of Joseph's people—his brothers and their families. But they left their little children and flocks and herds in the land of Goshen. 9So a very great number of chariots, cavalry, and people accompanied Joseph.

10When they arrived at Atad (meaning "Threshing Place of Brambles"), beyond the Jordan River, they held a very great and solemn funeral service, with a seven-day period of lamentation for Joseph's father. 11The local residents, the Canaanites, renamed the place Abel-mizraim (meaning "Egyptian Mourners") for they said, "It is a place of very deep mourning by these Egyptians." 12,13So his sons did as Israel commanded them, and carried his body into the land of Canaan and buried it there in the cave of Mach-pelah—the cave Abraham had bought in the field of Ephron the Hethite, close to Mamre.

14Then Joseph returned to Egypt with his brothers and all who had accompanied him to the funeral of his father.

Joseph Reassures His Brothers

15But now that their father was dead, Joseph's brothers were frightened.

"Now Joseph will pay us back for all the evil we did to him," they said. 16,17So they sent him this message: "Before he died, your father instructed us to tell you to forgive us for the great evil we did to you. We servants of the God of your father beg you to forgive us." When Joseph read the message, he broke down and cried.

18Then his brothers came and fell down before him and said, "We are your slaves."

19But Joseph told them, "Don't be afraid of me. Am I God, to judge and punish you? 20As far as I am concerned, God turned into good what you meant for evil, for he brought me to this high position I have today so that I could save the lives of many people. 21No, don't be afraid. Indeed, I myself will take care of you and your families." And he spoke very kindly to them, reassuring them.

22So Joseph and his brothers and their families continued to live in Egypt. Joseph was 110 years old when he died. 23He lived to see the birth of his son Ephraim's children, and the children of Machir, Manasseh's son, who played at his feet.

24"Soon I will die," Joseph told his brothers, "but God will surely come and get you, and bring you out of this land of Egypt and take you back to the land he promised to the descendants of Abraham, Isaac and Jacob." 25Then Joseph made his brothers promise with an oath that they would take his body back with them when they returned to Canaan. 26So Joseph died at the age of 110, and they embalmed him, and his body was placed in a coffin in Egypt.

50:15-21 When Jacob died, Joseph's brothers feared that he would take revenge for their past differences. They thought Joseph had spared them only for the sake of their father. Here they discovered that Joseph's forgiveness was complete, with no ulterior motives. Joseph had already granted his brothers complete forgiveness; his brothers couldn't believe it and thus had not yet received it. They had needlessly lived in fear of a coming punishment. God hands us forgiveness that is just as complete, but we need to believe it, and then receive it. Only then can we experience the freedom he offers.

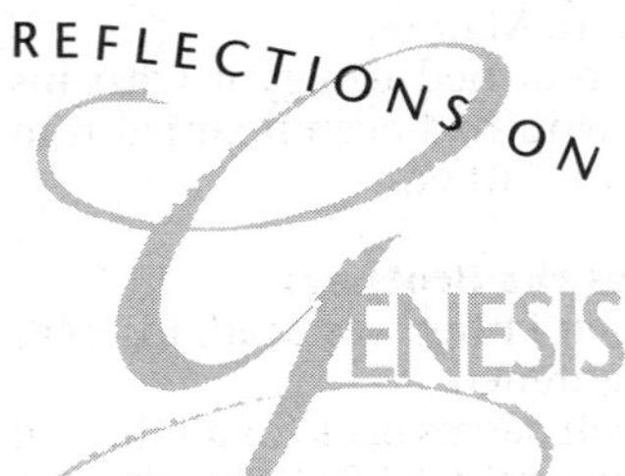
REFLECTIONS ON
GENESIS

insights FROM THE NAMES OF GOD

The Hebrew name for God used in **Genesis 1:1** (*Elohim*) demonstrates the enormity of God's power to transform lives. This name for God is in the plural form, signifying his strength and might. It also hints that God is in some sense plural—a community unto himself (see also 1:26; 3:22; 11:7). But though this name is plural, it is treated grammatically as singular, revealing God's unified and personal nature. He is omnipotent in power, but personal in his touch. He is able and willing to provide the help we need.

In **Genesis 2:4** a new Hebrew name for God is introduced: "Lord" (*Yahweh* or *Jehovah*). This is the personal name for God; it is his relationship name. It describes the God who chose Abraham and established a covenant with him. It describes the God who chose to relate to the Israelites and make them his people. It is the name that reminds us that God wants to have a relationship with us.

insights FROM GOD'S CREATION

As the source of all things, God is always able to meet our needs. The Hebrew verb translated "create" in **Genesis 1:1** describes an act that only God can do; and it is used to describe three things that science cannot explain: the creation of something from nothing (1:1), the creation of living things from inanimate matter (1:21-22), and the creation of man (1:27). A God who can create people and the world we live in can certainly empower a person in the process of recovery.

Genesis 1:2 describes the earth before it was shaped by God's creative hand. It was shapeless, chaotic, and dark. These three characteristics forebode nothing but trouble. But then we are told that "the Spirit of God [was] brooding over the dark vapors." This fourth characteristic is a source of hope and promises recovery. The presence of the Holy Spirit was a necessary element in the events of all six days of creation. In the same way, his presence in our life is necessary before any rebuilding and recovery can take place.

In **Genesis 1:3** God said, "Let there be light." The word *Let* in this verse is used to introduce one of God's purposes for his creation—that there should be light in the world. This word is used repeatedly in this chapter to introduce the various things that God intended for his creation (see 1:6, 9, 11, 14-15, 20, 24, 26). He had a purpose and plan for everything. He also has a plan for each of us. And his plan is designed to bring about the best for his creation. We need only be willing to turn our recovery over to his design and plan.

In **Genesis 1:26-27** we see that the first people were created to be like God. Oceans of ink have been spilled attempting to explain what this means. One characteristic that all the writers agree upon is the ability of people to make moral decisions. We have the power of choice, and we are accountable to God and to others for the choices we make. To continue in recovery we must take responsibility for this aspect of God's nature that is alive and well in each of us.

insights ABOUT TEMPTATION

In **Genesis 2:16-17** God forbade Adam and Eve to eat from a single tree. Why did he do this? Why didn't God create a world where people couldn't sin? Or why didn't he make people so they couldn't disobey his commands? The answer lies in the very nature of God. God is love and desires to have a loving relationship with his creatures. He wants us to respond to him with love in return. But a loving response is only possible when we have the choice to do otherwise. He wants us to obey because we love him, not because we have no other choice.

In **Genesis 1:1-3** Satan began his temptation of Eve by planting doubt in her mind concerning what God had said. Notice that Eve wasn't very clear on the details of God's command. God had told them not to *eat* fruit from a certain tree (2:17). Eve claimed that God had said they were not even to *touch* the tree. She was making God's requirements more difficult than God himself had done! Her own confusion about what God had said made her even more susceptible to the serpent's wiles. We will need a proper understanding of God's truth if we hope to stand against Satan's temptations.

In **Genesis 3:6** notice that Eve quickly succumbed to a visual temptation. Until Eve really *saw* the tree, she was not influenced by the three common elements of all temptation. She saw that the tree was good for food ("the lust of the flesh"), it looked lovely and fresh ("the lust of the eyes"), and it was a tree that would make her wise ("the pride of life"). These are still important weapons in Satan's arsenal of temptation (see 1 John 2:16).

insights ABOUT SIN AND ITS CONSEQUENCES

In **Genesis 3:7** Adam and Eve became aware of their nakedness. With their act of disobedience came embarrassment and shame. They did their best to cover themselves; they didn't like what they saw when they looked at themselves. This happens to all of us when we sin and when we become dependent on cruel addictions. We don't like what we see, so we cover it up with lies and half-truths. And we do it to preserve our relationships. But in the end, our intimacy with others is destroyed. We need to be honest with ourselves and others and work at reestablishing our relationships. This is a significant part of our recovery.

In **Genesis 3:10** Adam admitted that he was hiding from God. One of the terrible consequences of our sin is the isolation that results. We want to hide from other people; we want to hide from God. Our failures will always make us want to hide. But recovery means that we must bring our sin out into the open; this will then bring us back into our relationships—with others and with God.

In **Genesis 3:15** it becomes obvious that Adam and Eve are powerless in the face of the sin question. Alone, they cannot overwhelm Satan and escape the temptations he offers. In his grace, God promised that the offspring of the woman would defeat Satan. He promised that he would take charge of the recovery process and overcome the enemy. This is good news—the first mention of the gospel of grace that would eventually be fulfilled by the coming of Jesus, the Messiah.

In **Genesis 3:18-19** we see that after the Fall, even the earth responded differently to its human masters. In the beginning it was their constant ally, yielding its fruits easily to their hands. But now, it brought forth thorns and thistles and weeds. Work became an arduous task, frustrating and unfulfilling.

There was no reason for Adam and Eve to expect to live on after their failure. God had clearly stated that the consequences of their sin would be death (see 2:17). Yet in **Genesis 3:20** Adam displayed his faith in our gracious God by naming his wife Eve, which means "the life-giving one." He believed that she would live to be the mother of the human race. Adam's faith in God gave him hope for the future, even when his past gave him little to hope for.

insights FROM CAIN AND ABEL

In **Genesis 4:4** Abel slew an innocent substitute as his offering, and God accepted him. Abel was obedient to God's instructions. Our relationship with God can be established by accepting God's gracious forgiveness and allowing the innocent sacrifice of his Son to stand in our place. Abel's sacrifice of one of his lambs was the second death mentioned in the Bible.

In **Genesis 4:5** we see that God rejected Cain's offering. We may wonder why this was so. We don't have all the details, but we do know that his offering was given in rebellion (see Jude 1:11). Apparently Cain wanted to do things his way; he didn't want to follow the program that God had mapped out for this first human family. Notice that Cain responded first with disappointment. He wanted to be accepted by God, but he wanted to earn divine approval by his hard work in the fields. God could not accept his gift of farm produce. Acceptance by God cannot be bought with hard work; we need to admit our need and humbly allow a sacrifice to stand in our place. God has provided us with the perfect sacrifice in the person of Jesus Christ. He stands in our place, paying for all our failures and sins, freeing us to start again.

insights FROM NOAH'S LIFE

After years of waiting, God saw that the human race still refused to live according to his plan. In **Genesis 6:5-6** we see that things were getting worse, not better. This broke God's heart because of the great love he had for his creation. It should encourage us to know that God doesn't punish us in anger. He does it for our good because he loves us.

In **Genesis 6:7** God promises to judge his fallen and sinful creation. Even though God is patient with us and gives us many chances to change our ways, we cannot act with impunity. Because he is righteous, God must act to protect innocent people who are hurt by sin.

God had assigned Noah the monumental task of rebuilding human society on earth. But God didn't just hand Noah the task and walk away. In **Genesis 9:9-13** God promises to support Noah's work and sets a rainbow in the sky as a seal of his promise. Many of us are rebuilding, too. We can be sure that God will support our recovery with his presence and promises. And we should keep an eye out for the "rainbows" along the way. God often leaves us signs to remind us of his loving presence and care.

✲*insights* FROM ABRAHAM'S LIFE

In **Genesis 12:2-3** God gave Abram some special promises. He would make Abram a great nation; he would bless him and make him famous; and he would make Abram a blessing to others. God promised to bless those who blessed Abram and to curse those who cursed him. Notice that God's promises to Abram illustrate Step Twelve in recovery. After receiving God's blessing, Abram was to turn around and share it with others.

Initially Abram responded with half-obedience to God's call, moving with his family from Ur to Haran (11:31-32). **Genesis 12:4,** however, indicates the beginning of Abram's radical obedience to God. Having discovered God's will, Abram became willing to do what God's plan required of him. Our recovery begins when we learn to seek God's will and become willing to follow it without reservation.

We may wonder what Abram expected the Promised Land to be like. In **Genesis 12:10** we see that he arrived to find the land ravaged by famine. It probably wasn't what he had expected or hoped for, but it was the place that God had intended for him and his descendants. There will be times in recovery when things are difficult. Sometimes we may need to do things that we are not comfortable doing. But we need to follow God—even when his program doesn't lead us down the paths we had expected or hoped for.

The lie that Abram told in **Genesis 12:11-13** showed that he lacked faith in God. He didn't believe that God would protect him, so he took things into his own hands. We may feel that a little lie is justified if it is intended to protect something important to us. We may even succeed in getting away with it for a while, but all lies reap long-term consequences. It is best to trust God to protect us as we tell the truth. The God of truth will stand with us as we step out in faith.

In **Genesis 22:8-13** we find Abraham about to sacrifice his son Isaac. Much to the relief of Abraham and Isaac, however, God provided a substitute. We do not know what Abraham had in mind when he told his son that God would provide a sacrifice, but we do know that God has provided a sacrifice for us—not simply a ram caught in a thicket, but his only Son. Anyone who believes in him will have the means for discovering a new life now, and through eternity as well.

✲*insights* FROM JOSEPH'S LIFE

Many commentators have noted that nothing bad is ever said about Joseph. That may be true of his adult life, but as a boy he was irritatingly overconfident. In **Genesis 37:2** we see that he was also a tattletale. Joseph's arrogant behavior as a youth, along with his father's favoritism, planted seeds of hatred in his brothers' hearts. Joseph consequently suffered years of slavery in Egypt. Joseph was certainly more worthy of praise than his brothers, but he can hardly be given perfect marks.

In **Genesis 39:19-23** we see that God was with Joseph even in prison. We are told that he prospered in everything he did. And through all his trials, Joseph remained faithful to God. It would have been easy for him to start playing the victim and just give up. When we play the victim, we start to blame others and lose our ability to act. We need to stop blaming and start acting, doing our best in the situations in which God places us.

In **Genesis 50:15-21** a clear message comes across: man proposes but God disposes. Joseph's brothers intended their actions toward Joseph for evil, but God turned those actions into good. It is wonderful that God can veto our foolish plans, transforming our mistakes and failures into the means for his gracious purposes.

THE BIG PICTURE

A. THE EXODUS: PAINFUL PATHWAY TO FREEDOM (1:1–18:27)
1. Need: Going from Bad to Worse (1:1–2:25)
2. Provision: God Restores a Fallen Leader (3:1–4:31)
3. Intervention: Tough Love, Escalating Consequences (5:1–12:36)
4. Freedom: The Thrill of Victory, the Agony of Defeat (12:37–18:27)

B. THE LAW: ESTABLISHING ACCOUNTABILITY AND BOUNDARIES (19:1–40:38)
1. Covenant: Faithful Relationship between God and Man (19:1–24:18)
2. Closeness: Understanding and Drawing Near to God (25:1–31:18)
3. Covenant Renewal: Blowing It and Being Restored (32:1–34:35)
4. Construction: Choosing to Glorify God (35:1–40:38)

Exit . . . Leave . . . Escape—these words tell us what the Exodus was all about. At the end of Genesis the sons of Jacob (Israel) had gone to Egypt to avoid famine and had enjoyed favored status there. But as time passed, their comfortable dream turned to a nightmare. A Pharaoh enslaved the Israelites, forcing them to do back-breaking tasks in his building projects. So the Israelites, hopelessly enslaved, turned their faces heavenward and begged for help.

The Exodus from Egypt was God's answer to his people's cries. He acted by calling a man named Moses—an ordinary man—to lead his people out of bondage to a new life. Moses had already made an exodus from Egypt, fleeing for his life after murdering an Egyptian. God found him in the wilderness near Mount Sinai and called him to deliver his people.

Moses was not exactly an eager leader—he initially balked at God's call. But God used Moses greatly despite his weaknesses. Moses did amazing miracles in Egypt to bring about Israel's deliverance. He also spoke with God face to face, receiving God's instructions for healthy, responsible living in the community of Israel. Moses was living proof that God can use anyone who is available to him.

The Exodus is also part of a much bigger deliverance story. It began with Abraham, whom God chose to father a nation that would carry God's healing touch to our world. God preserved this nation through slavery in Egypt and led them through the wilderness to the Promised Land. Centuries later, one of its descendants, Jesus the Messiah, gave his life to deliver the human race from sin's destructive grip. Through him, each of us can add a chapter to this story.

THE BOTTOM LINE

PURPOSE: To trace the deliverance of an enslaved people and their growth as a nation related to God. AUTHOR: Moses. AUDIENCE: The people of Israel. DATE WRITTEN: Sometime between 1445 and 1410 B.C., probably shortly after the writing of Genesis. SETTING: Egypt, then the wilderness of Sinai. KEY VERSES: "Then the Lord told him, 'I have seen the deep sorrows of my people in Egypt, and have heard their pleas for freedom. . . . Now I am going to send you to Pharaoh, to demand that he let you lead my people out of Egypt'" (3:7, 10). KEY PEOPLE AND RELATIONSHIPS: Moses with Pharaoh, Aaron and Miriam, Zipporah and Jethro, Joshua. KEY PLACES: Egypt, Midian, the Red Sea, the Wilderness of Sinai.

RECOVERY THEMES

Deliverance Starts with Slavery: We can never really leave problems behind if we deny they exist. Our denial will only cause our problems to live on inside us. If we are to be delivered from slavery, we need to begin by recognizing that we are slaves. As the book of Exodus begins, the Israelites have just begun to realize that they are helplessly enslaved to the Egyptians. Gradually over the years, the glorious days of Joseph's leadership had faded and disappeared. For decades people probably denied the truth of their situation by remembering the "good old days." But here, there could be no denial; the people of Israel were slaves. And that recognition was the first step toward their deliverance, just as it is with us. We need to acknowledge our own slavery in order to start the process toward deliverance.

God Hears the Helpless: It is likely that the Israelite slaves in Egypt felt like God was deaf to their cries for help. But the book of Exodus shows us that God listens to the heart-cries of the helpless. After their deliverance from Egypt, the Israelites were instructed to teach their children about the faithfulness of God by reminding them of how God heard their cries for help (see Deuteronomy 6:20-25). This would encourage them during the tough situations they would soon face. This should also bring us encouragement today—God still hears the cries of the helpless.

God Uses Broken People: God responded to the cries of his people by choosing a man to lead them. He chose someone who had great skills and training, but who also had greatly failed. For forty years Moses was a fugitive shepherd, hiding because he had murdered an Egyptian. He was also a shy, reticent man who resisted God's calling in his life. He resisted to the point that God became angry and appointed Moses' brother, Aaron, to act as his spokesman to the people. God allows us to see all sides of Moses—the good and the bad—to show us that he can do great things through imperfect people. All we need to do is open ourselves to his plan for our life.

God's Program: The story of Moses and the deliverance of the Israelites from Egypt is a continuation of God's recovery program that began in Genesis. Once again God used a relationship with a chosen individual, Moses, to work his program. And he gave Moses and the Israelites instructions for living healthy and holy lives in their traveling community. God's recovery program is designed to release us from the bondage of our sinful dependencies—our personal slavery.

CHAPTER 1

The Hebrews Are Enslaved

This is the list of the sons of Jacob who accompanied him to Egypt, with their families:
Reuben, Simeon, Levi, Judah, Issachar, Zebulun, Benjamin, Dan, Naphtali, Gad, Asher.
[5]So the total number who went with him
was seventy (for Joseph was already there). [6]In
due season Joseph and each of his brothers
died, ending that generation. [7]Meanwhile,
their descendants were very fertile, increasing
rapidly in numbers; there was a veritable population explosion so that they soon became a
large nation, and they filled the land of Goshen.
[8]Then, eventually, a new king came to the
throne of Egypt who felt no obligation to the
descendants of Joseph.
[9]He told his people, "These Israelis are becoming dangerous to us because there are so
many of them. [10]Let's figure out a way to put
an end to this. If we don't, and war breaks out,
they will join our enemies and fight against us
and escape out of the country."
[11]So the Egyptians made slaves of them and
put brutal taskmasters over them to wear
them down under heavy burdens while building the cities of Pithom and Rameses as supply centers for the king. [12]But the more the
Egyptians mistreated and oppressed them,
the more the Israelis seemed to multiply! The
Egyptians became alarmed [13,14]and made the
Hebrew slavery more bitter still, forcing them
to toil long and hard in the fields and to carry
heavy loads of mortar and brick.
[15,16]Then Pharaoh, the king of Egypt, in-

1:8-11 The Israelites had not yet come to the point of admitting their helplessness. Even though they were being oppressed with increasing severity, they continued to rise to the occasion. This did not please the persecuting Egyptians. They feared that Israel would rise up against them and in the event of war, they might join Egypt's enemies or even leave the country (Exodus 1:9-12). It was not until the Israelites discovered their powerlessness and asked God for help that he responded with deliverance.

structed the Hebrew midwives (their names were Shiphrah and Puah) to kill all Hebrew boys as soon as they were born, but to let the girls live. 17But the midwives feared God and didn't obey the king—they let the boys live too.

18The king summoned them before him and demanded, "Why have you disobeyed my command and let the baby boys live?"

19"Sir," they told him, "the Hebrew women have their babies so quickly that we can't get there in time! They are not slow like the Egyptian women!"

20And God blessed the midwives [because they were God-fearing women]. So the people of Israel continued to multiply and to become a mighty nation. 21And because the midwives revered God, he gave them children of their own. 22Then Pharaoh commanded all of his people to throw the newborn Hebrew boys into the Nile River. But the girls, he said, could live.

CHAPTER 2

Moses Is Born

There were at this time a Hebrew fellow and girl of the tribe of Levi who married and had a family, and a baby son was born to them. When the baby's mother saw that he was an unusually beautiful baby, she hid him at home for three months. 3Then, when she could no longer hide him, she made a little boat from papyrus reeds, waterproofed it with tar, put the baby in it, and laid it among the reeds along the river's edge. 4The baby's sister watched from a distance to see what would happen to him.

5Well, this is what happened: A princess, one of Pharaoh's daughters, came down to bathe in the river, and as she and her maids were walking along the riverbank, she spied the little boat among the reeds and sent one of the maids to bring it to her. 6When she opened it, there was a baby! And he was crying. This touched her heart. "He must be one of the Hebrew children!" she said.

7Then the baby's sister approached the princess and asked her, "Shall I go and find one of the Hebrew women to nurse the baby for you?"

8"Yes, do!" the princess replied. So the little girl rushed home and called her mother!

9"Take this child home and nurse him for me," the princess instructed the baby's mother, "and I will pay you well!" So she took him home and nursed him.

10Later, when he was older, she brought him back to the princess and he became her son. She named him Moses (meaning "to draw out") because she had drawn him out of the water.

Moses Escapes from Egypt

11One day, many years later when Moses had grown up and become a man, he went out to visit his fellow Hebrews and saw the terrible conditions they were under. During his visit he saw an Egyptian knock a Hebrew to the ground—one of his own Hebrew brothers! 12Moses looked this way and that to be sure no one was watching, then killed the Egyptian and hid his body in the sand.

13The next day as he was out visiting among the Hebrews again, he saw two of them fighting. "What are you doing, hitting your own Hebrew brother like that?" he said to the one in the wrong.

14"And who are you?" the man demanded. "I suppose you think you are *our* prince and judge! And do you plan to kill me as you did

---

1:18-21 In the short term, the Hebrew midwives had to overcome their fears of the Egyptian king. It must have been terrifying to face such a cruel and powerful person, not knowing how he would respond. Their wisdom not only allowed Israel to continue growing (1:20), but the midwives were also blessed by God with families of their own. They had put off any hope of reward from the king, but God's reward for their patience was worth waiting for.

1:22–2:8 Moses' mother had a problem: she knew that she couldn't hide her beloved baby from the Egyptians indefinitely. So she displayed remarkable wisdom and faith by literally obeying Pharaoh's command to put her son into the Nile River (1:22; 2:3). But she did it in a way that preserved his life, trusting God to look after him. We don't know whether Moses' mother hoped that Pharaoh's daughter would find the baby. But after doing all she could for her son, she was willing to leave him in God's hands.

2:11-14 Moses undoubtedly thought that he was helping his fellow Hebrew when he killed this Egyptian taskmaster. However, covering up his violent deed did not help the situation. He couldn't bury his mistake in the sand, or in the past, so as to keep it from being known and rising to haunt him. He needed to responsibly and honestly face what he had done. When we hide our mistakes, they have a way of coming back to haunt us. It is best to face them right away so we can put them to rest, once and for all.

that Egyptian yesterday?" When Moses realized that his deed was known, he was frightened. 15And sure enough, when Pharaoh
heard about it he ordered Moses arrested and
executed. But Moses ran away into the land
of Midian. As he was sitting there beside a
well, 16seven girls who were daughters of the
priest of Midian came to draw water and fill
the water troughs for their father's flocks.
17But the shepherds chased the girls away.
Moses then came to their aid and rescued
them from the shepherds and watered their
flocks.

18When they returned to their father, Reuel,
he asked, "How did you get the flocks watered
so quickly today?"

19"An Egyptian defended us against the
shepherds," they told him; "he drew water for
us and watered the flocks."

20"Well, where is he?" their father demanded. "Did you just leave him there? Invite him home for supper."

21Moses eventually decided to accept Reuel's invitation to live with them, and Reuel
gave him one of the girls, Zipporah, as his
wife. 22They had a baby named Gershom
(meaning "foreigner"), for he said, "I am a
stranger in a foreign land."

The Burning Bush

23Several years later the king of Egypt died.
The Israelis were groaning beneath their burdens, in deep trouble because of their slavery,
and weeping bitterly before the Lord. He
heard their cries from heaven, 24and remembered his promise to Abraham, Isaac, and
Jacob [to bring their descendants back into
the land of Canaan]. 25Looking down upon
them, he knew that the time had come for
their rescue.

CHAPTER 3

One day as Moses was tending the flock of his
father-in-law, Jethro, the priest of Midian, out
at the edge of the desert near Horeb, the
mountain of God, 2suddenly the Angel of
Jehovah appeared to him as a flame of fire in
a bush. When Moses saw that the bush was on
fire and that it didn't burn up, 3,4he went over
to investigate. Then God called out to him,

"Moses! Moses!"

"Who is it?" Moses asked.

5"Don't come any closer," God told him.
"Take off your shoes, for you are standing on
holy ground. 6I am the God of your fathers—
the God of Abraham, Isaac, and Jacob." (Moses covered his face with his hands, for he was
afraid to look at God.)

7Then the Lord told him, "I have seen the
deep sorrows of my people in Egypt and have
heard their pleas for freedom from their harsh
taskmasters. 8I have come to deliver them
from the Egyptians and to take them out of
Egypt into a good land, a large land, a land
'flowing with milk and honey'—the land
where the Canaanites, Hittites, Amorites, Perizzites, Hivites, and Jebusites live. 9Yes, the
wail of the people of Israel has risen to me in
heaven, and I have seen the heavy tasks the
Egyptians have oppressed them with. 10Now I
am going to send you to Pharaoh, to demand
that he let you lead my people out of Egypt."

11"But I'm not the person for a job like
that!" Moses exclaimed.

12Then God told him, "I will certainly be
with you, and this is the proof that I am the
one who is sending you: When you have led
the people out of Egypt, you shall worship
God here upon this mountain!"

13But Moses asked, "If I go to the people of
Israel and tell them that their fathers' God has
sent me, they will ask, 'Which God are you
talking about?' What shall I tell them?"

14"'The Sovereign God,'" was the reply.
"Just say, 'I Am has sent me!' 15Yes, tell them,
'Jehovah, the God of your ancestors Abra-
ham, Isaac, and Jacob, has sent me to you.'

2:23-25 Israel finally hit bottom, and admitted to themselves that they were powerless over the circumstances they faced. They turned to God and begged him to deliver them from their slavery. But as we see, God's deliverance didn't come right away. They had to wait patiently for God to change their dismal situation. We need to see that we are helpless and give our situation over to God. But in doing so, we must recognize that we are also giving up our control. We need to be willing to let God do things his way and according to his timing.

3:10-11 Moses felt totally unqualified to fill the role God was commanding him to assume. He was well educated; he knew the ways of the royal court of Egypt (2:10); he also had great leadership ability, which he would demonstrate for the next forty years. These qualities made him the best man for the job. But Moses was unable to see or accept this reality. He didn't have an accurate sense of who he was. Perhaps he saw himself as a fugitive murderer, worthy of no task greater than shepherding his father-in-law's livestock. Often our past mistakes blind us to our present gifts. We need to see ourselves as God sees us and then respond accordingly.

MOSES

The flaw in an old coin will usually enhance its value; the flaw in a gem will cause its value to significantly decrease. The flaws in Moses' life worked both ways. In light of his many flaws, Moses' greatness as a person and leader is truly remarkable. He struggled constantly with besetting weaknesses. His self-doubt plagued him and almost caused him to refuse God's initial call.

He often reacted impulsively to the situations around him without thinking or listening to God first. He killed an Egyptian supervisor to protect a Hebrew slave; he jumped in to referee a fight between two Hebrews, and in order to protect a few shepherd girls, he sent a group of rough shepherds packing. Moses was impulsive, and it often got him into trouble. Moses also had to learn to set personal boundaries, sharing his leadership role with the people under him. At one point he worked from dawn till dusk just solving the people's disputes.

But weaknesses are just one side of the coin; the other side is stamped with strengths. Moses' self-doubt and personal fears gave God a chance to show his power. God turned a fugitive shepherd into a great national leader. God called him into his very presence! God could never have used a proud, strong person in this way.

God also used Moses' impulsive tendencies for good. Moses killed an Egyptian to protect a Hebrew slave. This led Moses to flee to the wilderness on his own personal exodus from Egypt. But through this, God was preparing Moses to lead a nation out of that land. Moses' skill at reacting to crises undoubtedly strengthened him as the leader of a great traveling nation. He was decisive in dealing with conflicts; he knew how to get things done. The positive side of Moses' failure to set personal boundaries was his sacrificial leadership over a period of many years.

Moses persevered through numerous ups and downs. He climbed to many mountaintop experiences—periods of faith and commitment to God that resulted in extraordinary spiritual growth. However, he also had times when his lack of patience and faith or his self-doubt caused him problems. Moses is acclaimed by Scripture and God himself to be one of the greatest people who ever lived. Despite Moses' emotional ups and downs and periods of self-doubt, God was able to use him to do great things. This should give all of us hope that we, too, can be used in amazing ways by God.

STRENGTHS AND ACCOMPLISHMENTS:

- He was one of the greatest leaders in the entire Old Testament.
- He was a man of great faith and courage in following God.
- He was an example of self-giving and humility.
- He was willing to accept wise counsel from God and others.

WEAKNESSES AND MISTAKES:

- He often acted impulsively, without looking to God for advice.
- At times he became almost frozen with self-doubt.
- At one point he was driven to the brink of a breakdown by overwork.
- He displayed a lack of adequate personal boundaries.

LESSONS FROM HIS LIFE:

- The way to handle the ups and downs of life is to face them with faith in God and commitment to his plan.
- We don't have to be perfect to be greatly used by God; we can still be "in process."
- We need personal boundaries to avoid workaholism, depression, and burnout.

KEY VERSE:
"And it was because he [Moses] trusted God that he left the land of Egypt and wasn't afraid of the king's anger. Moses kept right on going; it seemed as though he could see God right there with him" (Hebrews 11:27).

Moses' story spans the books of Exodus, Leviticus, Numbers, and Deuteronomy. The name Moses, often associated with the law, is found throughout the rest of the Bible. Moses is also referred to at some length in Acts 7:20-40, 44; and Hebrews 11:23-29.

(This is my eternal name, to be used throughout all generations.)
16"Call together all the elders of Israel," God
instructed him, "and tell them about Jehovah appearing to you here in this burning bush and that he said to you, 'I have visited my people and have seen what is happening to
them there in Egypt. 17I promise to rescue
them from the drudgery and humiliation they are undergoing, and to take them to the land now occupied by the Canaanites, Hittites, Amorites, Perizzites, Hivites, and Jebu-

sites, a land "flowing with milk and honey.'" 18The elders of the people of Israel will accept your message. They must go with you to the king of Egypt and tell him, 'Jehovah, the God of the Hebrews, has met with us and instructed us to go three days' journey into the desert to sacrifice to him. Give us your permission.'

19"But I know that the king of Egypt will not let you go except under heavy pressure. 20So I will give him all the pressure he needs! I will destroy Egypt with my miracles, and then at last he will let you go. 21And I will see to it that the Egyptians load you down with gifts when you leave, so that you will by no means go out empty-handed! 22Every woman will ask for jewels, silver, gold, and the finest of clothes from her Egyptian master's wife and neighbors. You will clothe your sons and daughters with the best of Egypt!"

CHAPTER 4

But Moses said, "They won't believe me! They won't do what *I* tell them to. They'll say, 'Jehovah never appeared to you!'"

2"What do you have there in your hand?" the Lord asked him.

And he replied, "A shepherd's rod."

3"Throw it down on the ground," the Lord told him. So he threw it down—and it became a serpent, and Moses ran from it!

4Then the Lord told him, "Grab it by the tail!" He did, and it became a rod in his hand again!

5"Do that and they will believe you!" the Lord told him. "Then they will realize that Jehovah, the God of their ancestors Abraham, Isaac, and Jacob, has really appeared to you. 6Now reach your hand inside your robe, next to your chest." And when he did, and took it out again, it was white with leprosy! 7"Now put it in again," Jehovah said. And when he did, and took it out again, it was normal, just as before!

8"If they don't believe the first miracle, they will the second," the Lord said, 9"and if they don't accept you after these two signs, then take water from the Nile River and pour it upon the dry land, and it will turn to blood."

10But Moses pleaded, "O Lord, I'm just not a good speaker. I never have been, and I'm not now, even after you have spoken to me, for I have a speech impediment."

11"Who makes mouths?" Jehovah asked him. "Isn't it I, the Lord? Who makes a man so that he can speak or not speak, see or not see, hear or not hear? 12Now go ahead and do as I tell you, for I will help you to speak well, and I will tell you what to say."

13But Moses said, "Lord, please! Send someone else."

14Then the Lord became angry. "All right," he said, "your brother, Aaron, is a good speaker. And he is coming here to look for you and will be very happy when he finds you. 15So I will tell you what to tell him, and I will help both of you to speak well, and I will tell you what to do. 16He will be your spokesman to the people. And you will be as God to him, telling him what to say. 17And be sure to take your rod along so that you can perform the miracles I have shown you."

18Moses returned home and talked it over with Jethro, his father-in-law. "With your per-

3:16-22 God called Moses to speak to the elders of Israel regarding the new life awaiting them in the Promised Land (Genesis 15:18-21). Along with the hope of entering such wonderful new territory, however, was the reality of dealing with the king of Egypt. The promise was wonderful, but the difficulty of the process could not be underestimated. They had a powerful Egyptian king to confront; they had years of ingrained attitudes of domination to overcome. The process we may face in recovery may also be difficult. But no matter what the pain, it will be worth it if we reach the promise of freedom and blessing.

4:10-12 Moses may have had a speech impediment, but that wasn't a legitimate excuse for not following God's plan. He didn't have an accurate perception of who he could become with God's help. While Moses was engaging in a kind of self-examination, he was doing so with a negative, fearful attitude. He was not yet at the point of letting God change him. Our weaknesses should never be an excuse to avoid recovery. With God's help, anything is possible. We need to realize that God can capitalize on our strengths, helping us reach our full potential.

4:18-28 Before Moses could take the mantle of Israel's leadership, there were two unresolved issues he needed to face. First, Moses had not circumcised his son, which was his responsibility under the covenant God had given to Abraham and his descendants (Genesis 17:9-14). So here God forced the issue so Moses could legitimately lead God's covenant people. Second, Moses needed to reintroduce himself to Aaron, his brother, a family member whose relationship had been buried in the past. We often need to deal with unresolved issues in our past before progressing with God's program for our life.

mission," Moses said, "I will go back to Egypt
and visit my relatives. I don't even know
whether they are still alive."
"Go with my blessing," Jethro replied.
[19]Before Moses left Midian, Jehovah said to
him, "Don't be afraid to return to Egypt, for
all those who wanted to kill you are dead."
[20]So Moses took his wife and sons and put
them on a donkey, and returned to the land
of Egypt, holding tightly to the "rod of God"!

Moses Returns to Egypt

[21]Jehovah told him, "When you arrive back in
Egypt you are to go to Pharaoh and do the
miracles I have shown you, but I will make
him stubborn so that he will not let the
people go. [22]Then you are to tell him,
'Jehovah says, "Israel is my eldest son, [23]and I
have commanded you to let him go away and
worship me, but you have refused: and now
see, I will slay your eldest son."'"
[24]As Moses and his family were traveling
along and had stopped for the night, Jehovah
appeared to Moses and threatened to kill him.
[25,26]Then Zipporah his wife took a flint knife
and cut off the foreskin of her young son's
penis, and threw it against Moses' feet, remarking disgustedly, "What a blood-smeared
husband you've turned out to be!"
Then God let him alone.
[27]Now Jehovah said to Aaron, "Go into the
wilderness to meet Moses." So Aaron traveled
to Mount Horeb, the mountain of God, and
met Moses there, and they greeted each other
warmly. [28]Moses told Aaron what God had
said they must do, and what they were to say,
and told him about the miracles they must do
before Pharaoh.
[29]So Moses and Aaron returned to Egypt
and summoned the elders of the people of
Israel to a council meeting. [30]Aaron told them
what Jehovah had said to Moses, and Moses
performed the miracles as they watched.
[31]Then the elders believed that God had sent
them, and when they heard that Jehovah had
visited them and had seen their sorrows, and
had decided to rescue them, they all rejoiced
and bowed their heads and worshiped.

CHAPTER 5

Israel's Bondage Worsens

After this presentation to the elders, Moses
and Aaron went to see Pharaoh. They told
him, "We bring you a message from Jehovah,
the God of Israel. He says, 'Let my people go,
for they must make a holy pilgrimage out into
the wilderness, for a religious feast, to worship
me there.'"
[2]"Is that so?" retorted Pharaoh. "And who
is Jehovah, that I should listen to him, and let
Israel go? I don't know Jehovah and I will not
let Israel go."
[3]But Aaron and Moses persisted. "The God
of the Hebrews has met with us," they declared. "We must take a three days' trip into
the wilderness and sacrifice there to Jehovah
our God; if we don't obey him, we face death
by plague or sword."
[4,5]"Who do you think you are," Pharaoh
shouted, "distracting the people from their
work? Get back to your jobs!" [6]That same day
Pharaoh sent this order to the taskmasters
and officers he had set over the people of
Israel: [7,8]"Don't give the people any more
straw for making bricks! However, don't reduce their production quotas by a single
brick, for they obviously don't have enough
to do or else they wouldn't be talking about
going out into the wilderness and sacrificing
to their God. [9]Load them with work and make
them sweat; that will teach them to listen to
Moses' and Aaron's lies!"
[10,11]So the taskmasters and officers informed
the people: "Pharaoh has given orders to furnish you with no more straw. Go and find it
wherever you can; but you must produce just
as many bricks as before!" [12]So the people
scattered everywhere to gather straw.
[13]The taskmasters were brutal. "Fulfill your
daily quota just as before," they kept demanding. [14]Then they whipped the Israeli work-
crew bosses. "Why haven't you fulfilled your
quotas either yesterday or today?" they
roared.
[15]These foremen went to Pharaoh and
pleaded with him. "Don't treat us like this,"
they begged. [16]"We are given no straw and
told to make as many bricks as before, and we

5:10-21 The Israelite foremen needed to understand how difficult the process toward their freedom would be. They were deeply discouraged by Pharaoh's additional demands because they had unrealistic hopes of an immediate and painless deliverance. They also became disillusioned about the leadership ability of Moses and Aaron. They needed wisdom to see their troubles with the long view in mind. These were only the first steps on the road to freedom. We need to be aware that the recovery road is long and difficult. There are few, if any, immediate and painless cures. If we realize this, we will find the difficulties we face less discouraging.

are beaten for something that isn't our fault—it is the fault of your taskmasters for making such unreasonable demands."

[17]But Pharaoh replied, "You don't have enough work, or else you wouldn't be saying, 'Let us go and sacrifice to Jehovah.' [18]Get back to work. No straw will be given you, and you must deliver the regular quota of bricks."

[19]Then the foremen saw that they were indeed in a bad situation. [20]When they met Moses and Aaron waiting for them outside the palace, as they came out from their meeting with Pharaoh, [21]they swore at them. "May God judge you for making us stink before Pharaoh and his people," they said, "and for giving them an excuse to kill us."

[22]Then Moses went back to the Lord. "Lord," he protested, "how can you mistreat your own people like this? Why did you ever send me if you were going to do this to them? [23]Ever since I gave Pharaoh your message, he has only been more and more brutal to them, and you have not delivered them at all!"

CHAPTER 6

"Now you will see what I shall do to Pharaoh," the Lord told Moses. "For he must be forced to let my people go; he will not only let them go, but will *drive them out of his land!* [2,3]I am Jehovah, the Almighty God who appeared to Abraham, Isaac, and Jacob—though I did not reveal my name, Jehovah, to them. [4]And I entered into a solemn covenant with them; under its terms I promised to give them and their descendants the land of Canaan where they were living. [5]And now I have heard the groanings of the people of Israel, in slavery now to the Egyptians, and I remember my promise.

[6]"Therefore tell the descendants of Israel that I will use my mighty power and perform great miracles to deliver them from slavery and make them free. [7]And I will accept them as my people and be their God. And they shall know that I am Jehovah their God who has rescued them from the Egyptians. [8,9]I will bring them into the land I promised to give to Abraham, Isaac, and Jacob. It shall belong to my people."

The Hebrews Become Discouraged

So Moses told the people what God had said, but they wouldn't listen any more because they were too dispirited after the tragic consequence of what he had said before.

[10]Now the Lord spoke to Moses again and told him, [11]"Go back again to Pharaoh and tell him that he *must* let the people of Israel go."

[12]"But look," Moses objected, "my own people won't even listen to me any more; how can I expect Pharaoh to? I'm no orator!"

[13]Then the Lord ordered Moses and Aaron to return to the people of Israel and to Pharaoh, king of Egypt, demanding that the people be permitted to leave.

Moses' Family History

[14]These are the names of the heads of the clans of the various tribes of Israel:

The sons of Reuben, Israel's oldest son: Hanoch, Pallu, Hezron, Carmi.

[15]The heads of the clans of the tribe of Simeon: Jemuel, Jamin, Ohad, Jachin, Zohar, Shaul (whose mother was a Canaanite).

[16]These are the names of the heads of the clans of the tribe of Levi, in the order of their ages: Gershon, Kohath, Merari. (Levi lived 137 years.)

[17]The sons of Gershon were: Libni, Shimei (and their clans).

5:22-23 Moses prayed to God with perplexed honesty. He faced a real problem. In following God's program for freeing Israel, the people were encountering increased suffering. Moses, however, did not yet realize that God was preparing to force Pharaoh to let Israel go. God had not failed the test of trustworthiness. Freedom is often a lengthy process. We need to recognize this as we seek our recovery. If we do, we will be less likely to be discouraged by the obstacles we face along the way.

6:8-13 When we fail to realize how difficult the process toward freedom can be, it is all too easy to become discouraged and give up. After suffering a number of setbacks, the Israelites were ready to give up. At such times, patience and perseverance are absolutely essential. We also need to remember that difficulties and failures are often the back door to ultimate success.

6:14-27 To a great extent, Moses and Aaron were the product of their family heritage, sketched briefly in the genealogy included here (6:14-25). Now they faced difficult opposition to their goal of freeing the Israelites. But out of their past came signs of hope, strengthening their courage to continue their quest for freedom. For example, God had promised Abraham and his descendants a land of their own, free from oppression. God's promises from the past gave Moses and Aaron the encouragement they needed to continue their fight for freedom. God's promises can do the same for us today.

18The sons of Kohath: Amram, Izhar, Hebron, Uzziel. (Kohath lived 133 years.)
19The sons of Merari: Mahli, Mushi.
The above are the families of the Levites,
listed according to their ages.
20And Amram married Jochebed, his
father's sister; and Aaron and Moses were
their sons.
Amram lived to the age of 137.
21The sons of Izhar: Korah, Nepheg, Zichri.
22The sons of Uzziel: Misha-el, Elzaphan,
Sithri.
23Aaron married Elisheba, the daughter of
Amminadab and sister of Nahshon. Their children were: Nadab, Abihu, Eleazar, Ithamar.
24The sons of Korah: Assir, Elkanah, Abia-
saph.
These are the families within the clan of
Korah.
25Aaron's son Eleazar married one of the
daughters of Puti-el, and Phinehas was one of
his children. These are all the names of the
heads of the clans of the Levites and the
families within the clans.
26Aaron and Moses, included in that list, are
the same Aaron and Moses to whom Jehovah
said, "Lead all the people of Israel out of the
land of Egypt," 27and who went to Pharaoh to
ask permission to lead the people from the
land, 28,29and to whom the Lord said, "I am
Jehovah. Go in and give Pharaoh the message
I have given you."
30This is that Moses who argued with the
Lord, "I can't do it; I'm no speaker—why
should Pharaoh listen to *me?"*

CHAPTER 7

Moses' Rod Becomes a Snake

Then the Lord said to Moses, "See, I have
appointed you as my ambassador to Pharaoh,
and your brother, Aaron, shall be your spokesman. 2Tell Aaron everything I say to you, and
he will announce it to Pharaoh, demanding
that the people of Israel be allowed to leave
Egypt. 3But I will cause Pharaoh to stubbornly
refuse, and I will multiply my miracles in the
land of Egypt. 4Yet even then Pharaoh won't
listen to you; so I will crush Egypt with a final
major disaster and then lead my people out.
5The Egyptians will find out that I am indeed
God when I show them my power and force
them to let my people go."
6So Moses and Aaron did as the Lord commanded them. 7Moses was eighty years old
and Aaron eighty-three at this time of their
confrontation with Pharaoh.

The Water Turns to Blood

8Then the Lord said to Moses and Aaron,
9"Pharaoh will demand that you show him a
miracle to prove that God has sent you; when
he does, Aaron is to throw down his rod, and
it will become a serpent."
10So Moses and Aaron went in to see Pharaoh, and performed the miracle, as Jehovah
had instructed them—Aaron threw down his
rod before Pharaoh and his court, and it became a serpent. 11Then Pharaoh called in his
sorcerers—the magicians of Egypt—and they
were able to do the same thing with their
magical arts! 12Their rods became serpents,

6:28-30 Once again we are reminded of God's insistence that Moses respond in faith, despite his fears and his perceived speech problem (6:30; see 4:10; 6:12). In the process of the Exodus, God repeatedly challenged Moses' personal insecurities and his negative, self-defeating attitudes. Faith in a trustworthy God was the solution to this problem. Trusting God with our problems and insecurities is a key step in our recovery as well.

7:1-5 Nowhere is the stubbornness of Pharaoh's heart sketched more vividly. Moses and Aaron were fully involved in the process of confronting this unyielding persecutor. And at this point, their task of freeing the people must have seemed impossible. But God had assured them that their goal of freedom would be reached by his sovereign power. We may be battling with a powerful, unreasonable enemy, internally or externally. But when God desires something to happen, it will happen, no matter what the opposition.

7:7 Notice that Aaron is the older son, but God called Moses to be the primary leader. This cut across the grain of cultural expectation. The firstborn was always considered the first in line for a position of power or influence. But God often chose unlikely people to accomplish his plans. Consider also Isaac, Jacob, Judah, Joseph, Gideon, and David. None of them was a firstborn son, but all were given a significant part to play in God's plan. God often does things that surprise us; he uses unlikely people. No matter what our past, each of us has a special place in his plan.

7:8-13 When we decide to commit ourself to God, we can be assured of God's power within, which is greater than any other. Here God shows his power to Pharaoh by turning Aaron's rod into a serpent. But in this case, as is often true in life, victory through God's power is not always immediate. Notice that Pharaoh's magicians also performed this same sign. But then the "rod of God" turned and devoured the others, showing that if we depend on God's power, we will find victory.

too! But Aaron's serpent swallowed their serpents! 13 Pharaoh's heart was still hard and
stubborn, and he wouldn't listen, just as the
Lord had predicted. 14 The Lord pointed this
out to Moses, that Pharaoh's heart had been
unmoved, and that he would continue to
refuse to let the people go.
15 "Nevertheless," the Lord said, "go back to
Pharaoh in the morning, to be there as he
goes down to the river. Stand beside the riverbank and meet him there, holding in your
hand the rod that turned into a serpent. 16 Say
to him, 'Jehovah, the God of the Hebrews, has
sent me back to demand that you let his
people go to worship him in the wilderness.
You wouldn't listen before, 17 and now the
Lord says this: "You are going to find out that
I am God. For I have instructed Moses to hit
the water of the Nile with his rod, and the
river will turn to blood! 18 The fish will die and
the river will stink, so that the Egyptians will
be unwilling to drink it."'"
19 Then the Lord instructed Moses: "Tell
Aaron to point his rod toward the waters of
Egypt: all its rivers, canals, marshes, and reservoirs, and even the water stored in bowls
and pots in the homes will turn to blood."
20 So Moses and Aaron did as the Lord commanded them. As Pharaoh and all of his
officials watched, Aaron hit the surface of the
Nile with the rod, and the river turned to
blood. 21 The fish died and the water became
so foul that the Egyptians couldn't drink it;
and there was blood throughout the land of
Egypt. 22 But then the magicians of Egypt used
their secret arts and they, too, turned water
into blood; so Pharaoh's heart remained hard
and stubborn, and he wouldn't listen to Moses and Aaron, just as the Lord had predicted,
23 and he returned to his palace, unimpressed.
24 Then the Egyptians dug wells along the
riverbank to get drinking water, for they
couldn't drink from the river.
25 A week went by.

CHAPTER 8

Frogs Cover the Land

Then the Lord said to Moses, "Go in again to
Pharaoh and tell him, 'Jehovah says, "Let my
people go and worship me. 2 If you refuse, I
will send vast hordes of frogs across your land
from one border to the other. 3,4 The Nile River
will swarm with them, and they will come out
into your houses, even into your bedrooms
and right into your beds! Every home in Egypt
will be filled with them. They will fill your
ovens and your kneading bowls; you and your
people will be immersed in them!"'"
5 Then the Lord said to Moses, "Instruct
Aaron to point the rod toward all the rivers,
streams, and pools of Egypt, so that there will
be frogs in every corner of the land." 6 Aaron
did, and frogs covered the nation. 7 But the
magicians did the same with their secret arts,
and they, too, caused frogs to come up upon
the land.
8 Then Pharaoh summoned Moses and
Aaron and begged, "Plead with God to take
the frogs away, and I will let the people go and
sacrifice to him."
9 "Be so kind as to tell me when you want
them to go," Moses said, "and I will pray that
the frogs will die at the time you specify,
everywhere except in the river."
10 "Do it tomorrow," Pharaoh said.
"All right," Moses replied, "it shall be as
you have said; then you will know that there
is no one like the Lord our God. 11 All the frogs
will be destroyed, except those in the river."
12 So Moses and Aaron went out from the
presence of Pharaoh, and Moses pleaded with
the Lord concerning the frogs he had sent.
13 And the Lord did as Moses promised—dead
frogs covered the countryside and filled the
nation's homes. 14 They were piled into great
heaps, making a terrible stench throughout
the land. 15 But when Pharaoh saw that the
frogs were gone, he hardened his heart and
refused to let the people go, just as the Lord
had predicted.

The Dust Becomes Lice

16 Then the Lord said to Moses, "Tell Aaron to
strike the dust with his rod, and it will become
lice, throughout all the land of Egypt." 17 So
Moses and Aaron did as God commanded,
and suddenly lice infested the entire nation,
covering the Egyptians and their animals.

7:14–8:19 The first cycle of three plagues—blood (7:14-24), frogs (8:1-15), and lice (8:16-19)—as intense as it was, did not turn Pharaoh from his cruel behavior. He still continued in his denial. At the height of the frog plague, he nearly relented, asking Moses and Aaron to pray to God on his behalf (8:8-13). However, when things let up momentarily, he hardened his heart again (8:15). We must be careful to persevere to the end, not getting overconfident when things start to go well. We must realize our constant need for God even when things are going well, or we are doomed to failure in the long-term process toward freedom.

18Then the magicians tried to do the same thing with their secret arts, but this time they failed.

19"This is the finger of God," they exclaimed to Pharaoh. But Pharaoh's heart was hard and stubborn, and he wouldn't listen to them, just as the Lord had predicted.

Flies Swarm the People

20Next the Lord told Moses, "Get up early in the morning and meet Pharaoh as he comes out to the river to bathe, and say to him, 'Jehovah says, "Let my people go and worship me. 21If you refuse I will send swarms of flies throughout Egypt. Your homes will be filled with them and the ground will be covered with them. 22But it will be very different in the land of Goshen where the Israelis live. No flies will be there; thus you will know that I am the Lord God of all the earth, 23for I will make a distinction between your people and my people. All this will happen tomorrow."'"

24And Jehovah did as he had said, so that there were terrible swarms of flies in Pharaoh's palace and in every home in Egypt.

25Pharaoh hastily summoned Moses and Aaron and said, "All right, go ahead and sacrifice to your God, but do it here in the land. Don't go out into the wilderness."

26But Moses replied, "That won't do! Our sacrifices to God are hated by the Egyptians, and if we do this right here before their eyes, they will kill us. 27We must take a three-day trip into the wilderness and sacrifice there to Jehovah our God, as he commanded us."

28"All right, go ahead," Pharaoh replied, "but don't go too far away. Now, hurry and plead with God for me."

29"Yes," Moses said, "I will ask him to cause the swarms of flies to disappear. But I am warning you that you must never again lie to us by promising to let the people go and then changing your mind."

30So Moses went out from Pharaoh and asked the Lord to get rid of the flies. 31,32And the Lord did as Moses asked and caused the swarms to disappear, so that not one remained. But Pharaoh hardened his heart again and did not let the people go!

CHAPTER 9

The Egyptian Animals Die

"Go back to Pharaoh," the Lord commanded Moses, "and tell him, 'Jehovah, the God of the Hebrews, demands that you let his people go to sacrifice to him. 2If you refuse, 3the power of God will send a deadly plague to destroy your cattle, horses, donkeys, camels, flocks, and herds. 4But the plague will affect only the cattle of Egypt; none of the Israeli herds and flocks will even be touched!'"

5The Lord announced that the plague would begin the very next day, 6and it did. The next morning all the cattle of the Egyptians began dying, but not one of the Israeli herds was even sick. 7Pharaoh sent to see whether it was true that none of the Israeli cattle were dead, yet when he found out that it was so, even then his mind remained unchanged and he refused to let the people go.

Boils Cover the People

8Then Jehovah said to Moses and Aaron, "Take ashes from the kiln and have Moses toss them into the sky as Pharaoh watches. 9They will spread like fine dust over all the land of Egypt and cause boils to break out upon people and animals alike, throughout the land."

10So they took ashes from the kiln and went to Pharaoh; as he watched, Moses tossed them toward the sky, and they became boils that broke out on men and animals alike throughout all Egypt. 11And the magicians couldn't stand before Moses because of the boils, for the boils appeared upon them too. 12But Jehovah hardened Pharaoh in his stubbornness, so that he refused to listen, just as the Lord had predicted to Moses.

Hail Destroys the Crops

13Then the Lord said to Moses, "Get up early in the morning and stand before Pharaoh and tell him, 'Jehovah the God of the Hebrews

8:20–9:12 The second cycle of three plagues—flies (8:20-32), death of Egyptian lifestock (9:1-7), and boils (9:8-12)—is similarly resisted by Pharaoh. However, during the detestable onslaught of flies, Pharaoh tried to bargain with Moses and God. He agreed to allow Israel to offer sacrifices to God, first in Egypt and then a short distance away in the wilderness. But he made this concession on the grounds that Moses pray to God on his behalf to stop the plague (8:25-28). Moses did pray, but Pharaoh went back on his word, hardening his heart (8:29-32). Pharaoh failed on two counts. First, he tried to bargain with God to get what he wanted. God is more than willing to give us what is best for us, but we must accept his terms, not ours. Second, Pharaoh failed to keep his word with God. This could only lead to continued disaster.

says, "Let my people go to worship me. [14]This
time I am going to send a plague that will
really speak to you and to your servants and
to all the Egyptian people, and prove to you
there is no other God in all the earth. [15]I could
have killed you all by now, [16]but I didn't, for I
wanted to demonstrate my power to you and
to all the earth. [17]So you still think you are so
great, do you, and defy my power, and refuse
to let my people go? [18]Well, tomorrow about
this time I will send a hailstorm across the
nation such as there has never been since
Egypt was founded! [19]Quick! Bring in your
cattle from the fields, for every man and animal left out in the fields will die beneath the
hail!"'"
[20]Some of the Egyptians, terrified by this
threat, brought their cattle and slaves in from
the fields; [21]but those who had no regard for
the word of Jehovah left them out in the
storm.
[22]Then Jehovah said to Moses, "Point your
hand toward heaven and cause the hail to fall
throughout all Egypt, upon the people, animals, and trees."
[23]So Moses held out his hand, and the Lord
sent thunder and hail and lightning. [24]It was
terrible beyond description. Never in all the
history of Egypt had there been a storm like
that. [25]All Egypt lay in ruins. Everything left in
the fields, men and animals alike, was killed,
and the trees were shattered and the crops
were destroyed. [26]The only spot in all Egypt
without hail that day was the land of Goshen
where the people of Israel lived.
[27]Then Pharaoh sent for Moses and Aaron.
"I finally see my fault," he confessed.
"Jehovah is right, and I and my people have
been wrong all along. [28]Beg God to end this
terrifying thunder and hail, and I will let you
go at once."
[29]"All right," Moses replied, "as soon as I
have left the city I will spread out my hands
to the Lord, and the thunder and hail will
stop. This will prove to you that the earth is
controlled by Jehovah. [30]But as for you and
your officials, I know that even yet you will
not obey him." [31]All the flax and barley were
knocked down and destroyed (for the barley
was ripe, and the flax was in bloom), [32]but the
wheat and the emmer were not destroyed, for
they were not yet out of the ground.
[33]So Moses left Pharaoh and went out of the
city and lifted his hands to heaven to the
Lord, and the thunder and hail stopped, and
the rain ceased pouring down. [34]When Pharaoh saw this, he and his officials sinned yet
more by their stubborn refusal to do what
they had promised; [35]so Pharaoh refused to let
the people leave, just as the Lord had predicted to Moses.

CHAPTER 10

Locusts Cover the Land

Then the Lord said to Moses, "Go back again
and make your demand upon Pharaoh; but I
have hardened him and his officials, so that I
can do more miracles demonstrating my
power.[2]What stories you can tell your children and grandchildren about the incredible
things I am doing in Egypt! Tell them what
fools I made of the Egyptians, and how I
proved to you that I am Jehovah."
[3]So Moses and Aaron requested another

9:13-35 During the devastating plague of hail, Pharaoh went so far as to admit that he and his people had sinned and that God was righteous (9:27-28). But after Moses prayed to God and the plagues had halted, Pharaoh and the Egyptian officials again hardened their hearts. Pharaoh still was not willing to face the reality of God's sovereign power, even though he had been clearly convicted of his shortcomings. When we started our recovery, we may have recognized that we were powerless in our circumstances. But then as we saw improvement, we failed to take the second and third steps, giving our life over to God's helping power. If we fail to depend wholeheartedly on God's power, we will be sure to fail once again.

10:2 Not only are sins and dysfunctional qualities passed on from one generation to the next (see 20:5); so are positive patterns and memories (see 20:6). God's power over the Egyptians was to be celebrated by each successive generation of Israelites. The faith and spirit of God's people who experienced the Exodus would bolster the faith of their descendants, giving them the courage to conquer enemies in the future. God's powerful acts for his people can also give us hope as we face dependencies and problems too big for us. And remember, the victories we win with God's help will influence and strengthen our descendants far into the future.

10:1-20 During the plague of locusts, Pharaoh again attempted to bargain with God. He first consented to let only the men go out from Egypt to worship God (10:10-11), retaining the women and children as hostages. But the severity of the locust plague caused him to admit his sin and ask Moses to intercede before God (10:12-19). In the end, however, Pharaoh's heart was again hardened (10:20), and he still refused to let them leave. His continued denial led him further and further away from obedience to God's will.

audience with Pharaoh and told him: "Jehovah, the God of the Hebrews, asks, 'How long will you refuse to submit to me? Let my people go so they can worship me. [4,5]If you refuse, tomorrow I will cover the entire nation with a thick layer of locusts so that you won't even be able to see the ground, and they will finish destroying everything that escaped the hail. [6]They will fill your palace, and the homes of your officials, and all the houses of Egypt. Never in the history of Egypt has there been a plague like this will be!'" Then Moses stalked out.

[7]The court officials now came to Pharaoh and asked him, "Are you going to destroy us completely? Don't you know even yet that all Egypt lies in ruins? Let the *men* go and serve Jehovah their God!"

[8]So Moses and Aaron were brought back to Pharaoh. "All right, go and serve Jehovah your God!" he said. "But just who is it you want to go?"

[9]"We will go with our sons and daughters, flocks and herds," Moses replied. "We will take everything with us; for we must all join in the holy pilgrimage."

[10]"In the name of God I will not let you take your little ones!" Pharaoh retorted. "I can see your plot! [11]Never! You that are men, go and serve Jehovah, for that is what you asked for." And they were driven out from Pharaoh's presence.

[12]Then the Lord said to Moses, "Hold out your hand over the land of Egypt to bring locusts—they will cover the land and eat everything the hail has left."

[13]So Moses lifted his rod and Jehovah caused an east wind to blow all that day and night; and when it was morning, the east wind had brought the locusts. [14]And the locusts covered the land of Egypt from border to border; it was the worst locust plague in all Egyptian history; and there will never again be another like it. [15]For the locusts covered the face of the earth and blotted out the sun so that the land was darkened; and they ate every bit of vegetation the hail had left; there remained not one green thing—not a tree, not a plant throughout all the land of Egypt.

[16]Then Pharaoh sent an urgent call for Moses and Aaron and said to them, "I confess my sin against Jehovah your God and against you. [17]Forgive my sin only this once, and beg Jehovah your God to take away this deadly plague. I solemnly promise that I will let you go as soon as the locusts are gone."

[18]So Moses went out from Pharaoh and entreated the Lord, [19]and he sent a very strong west wind that blew the locusts out into the Red Sea, so that there remained not one locust in all the land of Egypt! [20]But the Lord hardened Pharaoh's heart and he did not let the people go.

Darkness Covers Egypt

[21]Then Jehovah said to Moses, "Lift your hands to heaven, and darkness without a ray of light will descend upon the land of Egypt." [22]So Moses did, and there was thick darkness over all the land for three days. [23]During all that time the people scarcely moved—but all the people of Israel had light as usual.

[24]Then Pharaoh called for Moses and said, "Go and worship Jehovah—but let your flocks and herds stay here; you can even take your children with you."

[25]"No," Moses said, "we must take our flocks and herds for sacrifices and burnt offerings to Jehovah our God. [26]Not a hoof shall be left behind; for we must have sacrifices for the Lord our God, and we do not know what he will choose until we get there."

[27]So the Lord hardened Pharaoh's heart and he would not let them go.

[28]"Get out of here and don't let me ever see you again," Pharaoh shouted at Moses. "The day you do, you shall die."

[29]"Very well," Moses replied. "I will never see you again."

CHAPTER 11

Egypt's Firstborn Will Die

Then the Lord said to Moses, "I will send just one more disaster on Pharaoh and his land, and after that he will let you go; in fact, he will be so anxious to get rid of you that he will practically throw you out of the country. [2]Tell all the men and women of Israel to ask their Egyptian neighbors for gold and silver jewelry."

10:21-29 After three days of darkness, Pharaoh agreed to let all the Israelites leave Egypt to worship God, but he refused to let them take their livestock (10:24). While this was a further concession on Pharaoh's part, it still was far from wholehearted repentance. Further perseverance by Moses only incited Pharaoh to escalate the confrontation with dangerous threats (10:24-28). Our recovery is dependent on our admitting the reality of our problems and sin. If we cannot admit the problems we face, we can hardly ask God to help us with them.

3(For God caused the Egyptians to be very
favorable to the people of Israel, and Moses
was a very great man in the land of Egypt and
was revered by Pharaoh's officials and the
Egyptian people alike.)
4Now Moses announced to Pharaoh,
"Jehovah says, 'About midnight I will pass
through Egypt. 5And all the oldest sons shall
die in every family in Egypt, from the oldest
child of Pharaoh, heir to his throne, to the
oldest child of his lowliest slave; and even the
firstborn of the animals. 6The wail of death
will resound throughout the entire land of
Egypt; never before has there been such anguish, and it will never be again.
7"'But not a dog shall move his tongue
against any of the people of Israel, nor shall
any of their animals die. Then you will know
that Jehovah makes a distinction between
Egyptians and Israelis.' 8All these officials of
yours will come running to me, bowing low
and begging, 'Please leave at once, and take all
your people with you.' Only then will I go!"
Then, red-faced with anger, Moses stomped
from the palace.
9The Lord had told Moses, "Pharaoh won't
listen, and this will give me the opportunity
of doing mighty miracles to demonstrate my
power." 10So, although Moses and Aaron did
these miracles right before Pharaoh's eyes, the
Lord hardened his heart so that he wouldn't
let the people leave the land.

CHAPTER 12

The First Passover

Then the Lord said to Moses and Aaron,
2"From now on, this month will be the first
and most important of the entire year. 3,4An-
nually, on the tenth day of this month (announce this to all the people of Israel) each
family shall get a lamb (or, if a family is small,
let it share the lamb with another small family in the neighborhood; whether to share in
this way depends on the size of the families).
5This animal shall be a year-old male, either a
sheep or a goat, without any defects.
6"On the evening of the fourteenth day of
this month, all these lambs shall be killed,
7and their blood shall be placed on the two
side-frames of the door of every home and on
the panel above the door. Use the blood of the
lamb eaten in that home. 8Everyone shall eat
roast lamb that night, with unleavened bread
and bitter herbs. 9The meat must not be eaten
raw or boiled, but roasted, including the head,
legs, heart, and liver. 10Don't eat any of it the
next day; if all is not eaten that night, burn
what is left.
11"Eat it with your traveling clothes on,
prepared for a long journey, wearing your
walking shoes and carrying your walking
sticks in your hands; eat it hurriedly. This
observance shall be called the Lord's Passover.
12For I will pass through the land of Egypt
tonight and kill all the oldest sons and firstborn male animals in all the land of Egypt,
and execute judgment upon all the gods of
Egypt—for I am Jehovah. 13The blood you
have placed on the doorposts will be proof
that you obey me, and when I see the blood I
will pass over you and I will not destroy your
firstborn children when I smite the land of
Egypt.
14"You shall celebrate this event each year
(this is a permanent law) to remind you of this
fatal night. 15The celebration shall last seven
days. For that entire period you are to eat only
bread made without yeast. Anyone who dis-

11:1-3 People who are not directly involved in a dysfunctional or abusive relationship often evaluate things quite differently from those who are. While Pharaoh obviously hated and feared Moses and the Israelites, the majority of Egypt's leaders and populace did not share his feelings (11:2-3). A crucial step in accurately understanding the realities we face is to realize that not everyone has it in for us. Some will regard our progress toward recovery quite favorably; some will even cheer us on!

11:9-10 God gave Pharaoh numerous chances to soften his heart. The tough love he displayed in this progression of plagues eventually did lead the king to hit bottom emotionally (see 12:29-32). God often intervenes in our life in similar ways. When difficult times come, many of us become angry with God. It may be wise, however, to start listening. God may be giving us a chance to find a new life. He will use the difficulties we face to show us our errors and lead us to correct our ways. Let's not, like Pharaoh, refuse God's interventions until it is too late. Let us learn God's hard lessons, realizing that God is with us through all the difficulties and pain.

12:14-16 The Passover was to become an occasion of celebration for future generations of Israel. It would be a time to remember their deliverance from slavery. Part of building a new life involves replacing old unhealthy thoughts and actions with healthy new ones. This may include taking on new traditions that celebrate our recovery from past problems. These should emphasize the positive differences between our old dysfunctional existence and the healthy freedom we experience in our new life.

obeys this rule at any time during the seven days of the celebration shall be excommunicated from Israel. [16]On the first day of the celebration, and again on the seventh day, there will be special religious services for the entire congregation, and no work of any kind may be done on those days except the preparation of food.

[17]"This annual 'Celebration with Unleavened Bread' will cause you always to remember today as the day when I brought you out of the land of Egypt; so it is a law that you must celebrate this day annually, generation after generation. [18]Only bread without yeast may be eaten from the evening of the fourteenth day of the month until the evening of the twenty-first day of the month. [19]For these seven days there must be no trace of yeast in your homes; during that time anyone who eats anything that has yeast in it shall be excommunicated from the congregation of Israel. These same rules apply to foreigners who are living among you just as much as to those born in the land. [20]Again I repeat, during those days you must not eat anything made with yeast; serve only yeastless bread."

[21]Then Moses called for all the elders of Israel and said to them, "Go and get lambs from your flocks, a lamb for one or more families depending upon the number of persons in the families, and kill the lamb so that God will pass over you and not destroy you. [22]Drain the lamb's blood into a basin, and then take a cluster of hyssop branches and dip them into the lamb's blood, and strike the hyssop against the lintel above the door and against the two side panels, so that there will be blood upon them, and none of you shall go outside all night.

[23]"For Jehovah will pass through the land and kill the Egyptians; but when he sees the blood upon the panel at the top of the door and on the two side pieces, he will pass over that home and not permit the Destroyer to enter and kill your firstborn. [24]And remember, this is a permanent law for you and your posterity. [25]And when you come into the land that the Lord will give you, just as he promised, and when you are celebrating the Passover, [26]and your children ask, 'What does all this mean? What is this ceremony about?' [27]you will reply, 'It is the celebration of Jehovah's passing over us, for he passed over the homes of the people of Israel, though he killed the Egyptians; he passed over our houses and did not come in to destroy us.'" And all the people bowed their heads and worshiped.

[28]So the people of Israel did as Moses and Aaron had commanded. [29]And that night, at midnight, Jehovah killed all the firstborn sons in the land of Egypt, from Pharaoh's oldest son to the oldest son of the captive in the dungeon; also all the firstborn of the cattle. [30]Then Pharaoh and his officials and all the people of Egypt got up in the night; and there was bitter crying throughout all the land of Egypt, for there was not a house where there was not one dead.

[31]And Pharaoh summoned Moses and Aaron during the night and said, "Leave us; please go away, all of you; go and serve Jehovah as you said. [32]Take your flocks and herds and be gone; and oh, give me a blessing as you go." [33]And the Egyptians were urgent upon the people of Israel, to get them out of the land as quickly as possible. For they said, "We are as good as dead."

[34]The Israelis took with them their bread dough without yeast, and bound their kneading troughs into their spare clothes, and carried them on their shoulders. [35]And the people of Israel did as Moses said and asked the Egyptians for silver and gold jewelry and for clothing. [36]And the Lord gave the Israelis favor with the Egyptians, so that they gave them whatever they wanted. And the Egyptians were practically stripped of everything they owned!

12:24-27 Children are usually curious as to why their parents believe and do what they do. They are quick to pick up on halfhearted or hypocritical actions. But they are also quick to learn when positive lessons and values are modeled and taught. The Israelites were to teach their children important lessons from the past, recalling God's great victories for their ancestors. This would then provide the groundwork for their faith in God, enabling them to step forward into life with a healthy confidence. We should remember that much of the present and future grows out of the past. Let us capitalize on the good things in the past to strengthen our prospects for the future.

12:28-51 After this final plague, the Israelites were not just allowed to leave; they were commanded to get out! In the pain and shock of his son's death, Pharaoh didn't attach any conditions to the Israelites' Exodus. He only asked for Moses' blessing (12:32). God had worked out the timing and all the details necessary for the Exodus to take place. Similarly, the all-knowing and all-powerful God lays out the recovery process of those committed to his program.

The Exodus

[37]That night the people of Israel left Rameses
and started for Succoth; there were six hundred thousand of them, besides all the
women and children, going on foot. [38]People
of various sorts went with them; and there
were flocks and herds—a vast exodus of cattle.
[39]When they stopped to eat, they baked bread
from the yeastless dough they had brought
along. It was yeastless because the people
were pushed out of Egypt and didn't have
time to wait for bread to rise to take with them
on the trip.

[40,41]The sons of Jacob and their descendants
had lived in Egypt 430 years, and it was on the
last day of the 430th year that all of Jehovah's
people left the land. [42]This night was selected
by the Lord to bring his people out from the
land of Egypt; so the same night was selected
as the date of the annual celebration of God's
deliverance.

[43]Then Jehovah said to Moses and Aaron,
"These are the rules concerning the observance of the Passover. No foreigners shall eat
the lamb, [44]but any slave who has been purchased may eat it if he has been circumcised.
[45]A hired servant or a visiting foreigner may
not eat of it. [46]You shall, all of you who eat
each lamb, eat it together in one house, and
not carry it outside; and you shall not break
any of its bones. [47]All the congregation of
Israel shall observe this memorial at the same
time.

[48]"As to foreigners, if they are living with
you and want to observe the Passover with
you, let all the males be circumcised, and then
they may come and celebrate with you—then
they shall be just as though they had been
born among you; but no uncircumcised person shall ever eat the lamb. [49]The same law
applies to those born in Israel and to foreigners living among you."

[50]So the people of Israel followed all of
Jehovah's instructions to Moses and Aaron.
[51]That very day the Lord brought out the
people of Israel from the land of Egypt, wave
after wave of them crossing the border.

CHAPTER 13

Firstborn Dedicated to God

The Lord instructed Moses, "Dedicate to me
all of the firstborn sons of Israel, and every
firstborn male animal; they are mine!"

[3]Then Moses said to the people, "This is a
day to remember forever—the day of leaving
Egypt and your slavery; for the Lord has
brought you out with mighty miracles. Now
remember, during the annual celebration of
this event you are to use no yeast; don't even
have any in your homes. [4,5]Celebrate this day
of your exodus, at the end of March each year,
when Jehovah brings you into the land of the
Canaanites, Hittites, Amorites, Hivites, and
Jebusites—the land he promised your fathers,
a land 'flowing with milk and honey.' [6,7]For
seven days you shall eat only bread without
yeast, and there must be no yeast in your
homes or anywhere within the borders of
your land! Then, on the seventh day, a great
feast to the Lord shall be held.

[8]"During those celebration days each year
you must explain to your children why you
are celebrating—it is a celebration of what the
Lord did for you when you left Egypt. [9]This
annual memorial week will brand you as his
own unique people, just as though he had
branded his mark of ownership upon your
hands or your forehead.

[10]"So celebrate the event annually in late
March. [11]And remember, when the Lord
brings you into the land he promised to your
ancestors long ago, where the Canaanites are
now living, [12]all firstborn sons and firstborn
male animals belong to the Lord, and you
shall give them to him. [13]A firstborn donkey
may be purchased back from the Lord in
exchange for a lamb or baby goat; but if you
decide not to trade, the donkey shall be killed.
However, you *must* buy back your firstborn
sons.

[14]"And in the future, when your children ask
you, 'What is this all about?' you shall tell
them, 'With mighty miracles Jehovah brought
us out of Egypt from our slavery. [15]Pharaoh
wouldn't let us go, so Jehovah killed all the
firstborn males throughout the land of Egypt,
both of men and animals; that is why we now

13:1-2, 11-16 The consecration of the firstborn sons of Israel points to the important position of the firstborn in family dynamics (see also 22:29-30). Since God had spared the lives of the firstborn of Israel during the Passover, in a very real sense they all belonged to him. As a result, the Israelites had to sacrifice a lamb to buy their firstborn sons back from God. All of our children should be viewed as being "on loan" from God. The public dedication of our children to God is a helpful tradition reminding us of this fact. When parents recognize this truth, they are well on the way toward raising children with a healthy and accurate self-understanding.

give all the firstborn males to the Lord—except that all the eldest sons are always bought back.' [16]Again I say, this celebration shall identify you as God's people, just as much as if his brand of ownership were placed upon your foreheads. It is a reminder that the Lord brought us out of Egypt with great power."

A Pillar of Cloud and Fire

[17,18]So at last Pharaoh let the people go.

God did not lead them through the land of the Philistines, although that was the most direct route from Egypt to the Promised Land. The reason was that God felt the people might become discouraged by having to fight their way through, even though they had left Egypt armed; he thought they might return to Egypt. Instead, God led them along a route through the Red Sea wilderness.

[19]Moses took the bones of Joseph with them, for Joseph had made the sons of Israel vow before God that they would take his bones with them when God led them out of Egypt—as he was sure God would.

[20]Leaving Succoth, they camped in Etham at the edge of the wilderness. [21]The Lord guided them by a pillar of cloud during the daytime and by a pillar of fire at night. So they could travel either by day or night. [22]The cloud and fire were never out of sight.

CHAPTER 14

Crossing the Red Sea

Jehovah now instructed Moses, [2]"Tell the people to turn toward Piha-hiroth between Migdol and the sea, opposite Baal-zephon, and to camp there along the shore. [3]For Pharaoh will think, 'Those Israelites are trapped now, between the desert and the sea!' [4]And once again I will harden Pharaoh's heart and he will chase after you. I have planned this to gain great honor and glory over Pharaoh and all his armies, and the Egyptians shall know that I am the Lord."

So they camped where they were told.

[5]When word reached the king of Egypt that the Israelis were not planning to return to Egypt after three days, but to keep on going, Pharaoh and his staff became bold again. "What is this we have done, letting all these slaves get away?" they asked. [6]So Pharaoh led the chase in his chariot, [7]followed by the pick of Egypt's chariot corps—600 chariots in all—and other chariots driven by Egyptian officers. [8]He pursued the people of Israel, for they had taken much of the wealth of Egypt with them. [9]Pharaoh's entire cavalry—horses, chariots, and charioteers—was used in the chase; and the Egyptian army overtook the people of Israel as they were camped beside the shore near Piha-hiroth, across from Baal-zephon.

[10]As the Egyptian army approached, the people of Israel saw them far in the distance, speeding after them, and they were terribly frightened and cried out to the Lord to help them.

[11]And they turned against Moses, whining, "Have you brought us out here to die in the desert because there were not enough graves

13:17-18 Swinging southeast to the Red Sea was not the fastest route from Egypt to the Promised Land, but it was the route that God chose for the Israelites to follow. The shortest route between two points is not always the best. God's will often calls us to take the more scenic routes. These, though longer and sometimes harder, are often God's means for accomplishing our recovery. In the Israelites' case, they were given the opportunity to see God overcome a huge obstacle—the Red Sea. This gave them additional fuel for their faith, building their courage for the journey ahead. It also helped them avoid dangers in the land of the Philistines that they were not yet prepared to face.

13:21-22 God guided his people out of slavery to a new life of freedom and responsibility by his visible presence in the pillar of cloud and fire. He led them to recover the promises he had given their ancestor, Abraham, centuries earlier. When we are committed to God, we, too, can count on his leading. He has sent his Holy Spirit to lead us (Galatians 5:18) and has promised to never leave or forsake us (Hebrews 13:5).

14:1-9 The Israelites were between a rock and a hard place—the Red Sea on one side and the Egyptian army on the other. And though the Israelites had already seen God do great miracles in Egypt (7:1–12:51), it must have been hard for them to wait and see how God would save them from this ominous situation. Our situations may seem just as hopeless, but nothing is a hopeless dead end for God. He will always provide a door leading to the next step in his plan.

14:10-12 In all their fear the Israelites cried out to God for help. Their terrified complaints show that their faith in God was limited. But at least they took the right first steps—they admitted their powerlessness in the situation and then looked to God for help. They were honest about what they were feeling. As a result, their discouragement and fear were soon turned into amazement and rejoicing (14:21–15:21).

for us in Egypt? Why did you make us leave Egypt? 12Isn't this what we told you, while we were slaves, to leave us alone? We said it would be better to be slaves to the Egyptians than dead in the wilderness."

13But Moses told the people, "Don't be afraid. Just stand where you are and watch, and you will see the wonderful way the Lord will rescue you today. The Egyptians you are looking at—you will never see them again. 14The Lord will fight for you, and you won't need to lift a finger!"

15Then the Lord said to Moses, "Quit praying and get the people moving! Forward, march! 16Use your rod—hold it out over the water, and the sea will open up a path before you, and all the people of Israel shall walk through on dry ground! 17I will harden the hearts of the Egyptians, and they will go in after you and you will see the honor I will get in defeating Pharaoh and all his armies, chariots, and horsemen. 18And all Egypt shall know that I am Jehovah."

19Then the Angel of God, who was leading the people of Israel, moved the cloud around behind them, 20and it stood between the people of Israel and the Egyptians. And that night, as it changed to a pillar of fire, it gave darkness to the Egyptians but light to the people of Israel! So the Egyptians couldn't find the Israelis!

21Meanwhile, Moses stretched his rod over the sea, and the Lord opened up a path through the sea, with walls of water on each side; and a strong east wind blew all that night, drying the sea bottom. 22So the people of Israel walked through the sea on dry ground! 23Then the Egyptians followed them between the walls of water along the bottom of the sea—all of Pharaoh's horses, chariots, and horsemen. 24But in the early morning Jehovah looked down from the cloud of fire upon the array of the Egyptians, and began to harass them. 25Their chariot wheels began coming off, so that their chariots scraped along the dry ground. "Let's get out of here," the Egyptians yelled. "Jehovah is fighting for them and against us."

26When all the Israelites were on the other side, the Lord said to Moses, "Stretch out your hand again over the sea, so that the waters will come back over the Egyptians and their chariots and horsemen." 27Moses did, and the sea returned to normal beneath the morning light. The Egyptians tried to flee, but the Lord drowned them in the sea. 28The water covered the path and the chariots and horsemen. And of all the army of Pharaoh that chased after Israel through the sea, not one remained alive.

29The people of Israel had walked through on dry land, and the waters had been walled up on either side of them. 30Thus Jehovah saved Israel that day from the Egyptians; and the people of Israel saw the Egyptians dead, washed up on the seashore. 31When the people of Israel saw the mighty miracle the Lord had done for them against the Egyptians, they were afraid and revered the Lord, and believed in him and in his servant Moses.

CHAPTER 15

Songs to the Lord

Then Moses and the people of Israel sang this song to the Lord:

I will sing to the Lord, for he has
triumphed gloriously;
He has thrown both horse and rider into
the sea.
2The Lord is my strength, my song, and
my salvation.
He is my God, and I will praise him.
He is my father's God—I will exalt him.
3The Lord is a warrior—
Yes, Jehovah is his name.
4He has overthrown Pharaoh's chariots
and armies,
Drowning them in the sea.
The famous Egyptian captains are dead
beneath the waves.
5The water covers them.
They went down into the depths like a
stone.
6Your right hand, O Lord, is glorious in
power;
It dashes the enemy to pieces.
7In the greatness of your majesty
You overthrew all those who rose against
you.
You sent forth your anger, and it
consumed them as fire consumes straw.
8At the blast of your breath
The waters divided!

15:1-21 Israel's escape through the Red Sea took a mighty miracle from God and an act of faith by the Israelites. Often the road to victory is not easy, but it is still worth it. There will be something to rejoice about in the end if we depend on God to help us through. And when we have gained the victory, we need to stand up, sing, and rejoice, remembering God's miracles on our behalf.

They stood as solid walls to hold the seas
apart.
9The enemy said, "I will chase after them,
Catch up with them, destroy them.
I will cut them apart with my sword
And divide the captured booty."
10But God blew with his wind, and the sea
covered them.
They sank as lead in the mighty waters.
11Who else is like the Lord among the
gods?
Who is glorious in holiness like him?
Who is so awesome in splendor,
A wonder-working God?
12You reached out your hand and the
earth swallowed them.
13You have led the people you redeemed.
But in your loving-kindness
You have guided them wonderfully
To your holy land.
14The nations heard what happened, and
they trembled.
Fear has gripped the people of Philistia.
15The leaders of Edom are appalled,
The mighty men of Moab tremble;
All the people of Canaan melt with fear.
16Terror and dread have overcome them.
O Lord, because of your great power they
won't attack us!
Your people whom you purchased
Will pass by them in safety.
17You will bring them in and plant them
on your mountain,
Your own homeland, Lord—
The sanctuary you made for them to live in.
18Jehovah shall reign forever and forever.
19The horses of Pharaoh, his horsemen,
and his chariots
Tried to follow through the sea;
But the Lord let down the walls of water
on them
While the people of Israel walked through
on dry land.

20Then Miriam the prophetess, the sister of
Aaron, took a tambourine and led the women
in dances.
21And Miriam sang this song:

Sing to the Lord, for he has triumphed
gloriously.
The horse and rider have been drowned
in the sea.

Bitter Water at Marah

22Then Moses led the people of Israel on from
the Red Sea, and they moved out into the
wilderness of Shur and were there three days
without water. 23Arriving at Marah, they
couldn't drink the water because it was bitter
(that is why the place was called Marah,
meaning "bitter").
24Then the people turned against Moses.
"Must we die of thirst?" they demanded.
25Moses pleaded with the Lord to help
them, and the Lord showed him a tree to
throw into the water, and the water became
sweet.
It was there at Marah that the Lord laid
before them the following conditions, to test
their commitment to him: 26"If you will listen
to the voice of the Lord your God, and obey
it, and do what is right, then I will not make
you suffer the diseases I sent on the Egyptians,
for I am the Lord who heals you." 27And they
came to Elim where there were twelve springs
and seventy palm trees; and they camped
there beside the springs.

CHAPTER 16

God Sends Manna and Quail

Now they left Elim and journeyed on into the
Sihn Wilderness, between Elim and Mt. Sinai,
arriving there on the fifteenth day of the
second month after leaving Egypt. 2There,
too, the people spoke bitterly against Moses
and Aaron.
3"Oh, that we were back in Egypt," they
moaned, "and that the Lord had killed us
there! For there we had plenty to eat. But now

15:22-27 Those of us just beginning the recovery process often have a short memory. We quickly forget the important victories that have brought us to our present state of freedom. We also may tend to fall back into reacting to crises as we did in the painful past. Despite God's recent victories on the Israelites' behalf, they still became desperate when their water ran out. And this happened only a few days after the miracle at the Red Sea! They were still unwilling, or unable, to exercise faith in God. But even so, God came through with an immediate, abundant provision of their need (see Ephesians 3:20).

16:1-36 Next to our need for water (15:22-27), our need for food is the most critical. Again, the Israelites failed to believe that God would meet their needs. They lacked faith in God's power and still didn't understand their privileges as God's people. But God faithfully provided for them anyway, and the people's faith was given further reason to grow. This example of God's gracious provision should encourage us to seek help during the wilderness periods of our own life.

you have brought us into this wilderness to kill us with starvation."

4 Then the Lord said to Moses, "Look, I'm going to rain down food from heaven for them. Everyone can go out each day and gather as much food as he needs. And I will test them in this, to see whether they will follow my instructions or not. 5 Tell them to gather twice as much as usual on the sixth day of each week."

6 Then Moses and Aaron called a meeting of all the people of Israel and told them, "This evening you will realize that it was the Lord who brought you out of the land of Egypt. 7-9 In the morning you will see more of his glory; for he has heard your complaints against him (for you aren't really complaining against *us*—who are *we?*). The Lord will give you meat to eat in the evening, and bread in the morning. Come now before Jehovah and hear his reply to your complaints."

10 So Aaron called them together and suddenly, out toward the wilderness, from within the guiding cloud, there appeared the awesome glory of Jehovah.

11,12 And Jehovah said to Moses, "I have heard their complaints. Tell them, 'In the evening you will have meat and in the morning you will be stuffed with bread, and you shall know that I am Jehovah your God.'"

13 That evening vast numbers of quail arrived and covered the camp, and in the morning the desert all around the camp was wet with dew; 14 and when the dew disappeared later in the morning it left thin white flakes that covered the ground like frost. 15 When the people of Israel saw it they asked each other, "What is it?"

And Moses told them, "It is the food Jehovah has given you. 16 Jehovah has said for everyone to gather as much as is needed for his household—about two quarts for each person."

17 So the people of Israel went out and gathered it—some getting more and some less before it melted on the ground, 18 and there was just enough for everyone. Those who gathered more had nothing left over and those who gathered little had no lack! Each home had just enough.

19 And Moses told them, "Don't leave it overnight."

20 But of course some of them wouldn't listen, and left it until morning; and when they looked, it was full of maggots and had a terrible odor; and Moses was very angry with them. 21 So they gathered the food morning by morning, each home according to its need; and when the sun became hot upon the ground, the food melted and disappeared. 22 On the sixth day there was twice as much as usual on the ground—four quarts instead of two; the leaders of the people came and asked Moses why this had happened.

23 And he told them, "Because the Lord has appointed tomorrow as a day of seriousness and rest, a holy Sabbath to the Lord when we must refrain from doing our daily tasks. So cook as much as you want to today, and keep what is left for tomorrow."

24 And the next morning the food was wholesome and good, without maggots or odor. 25 Moses said, "This is your food for today, for today is the Sabbath to Jehovah and there will be no food on the ground today. 26 Gather the food for six days, but the seventh is a Sabbath, and there will be none there for you on that day."

27 But some of the people went out anyway to gather food, even though it was the Sabbath, but there wasn't any.

28,29 "How long will these people refuse to obey?" the Lord asked Moses. "Don't they realize that I am giving them twice as much on the sixth day, so that there will be enough for two days? For the Lord has given you the seventh day as a day of Sabbath rest; stay in your tents and don't go out to pick up food from the ground that day." 30 So the people rested on the seventh day.

31 And the food became known as "manna" (meaning "What is it?"); it was white, like coriander seed, and flat, and tasted like honey bread.

32 Then Moses gave them this further instruction from the Lord: they were to take two quarts of it to be kept as a museum specimen forever, so that later generations could see the bread the Lord had fed them with in the wilderness, when he brought them from Egypt. 33 Moses told Aaron to get a container and put two quarts of manna in it and to keep it in a sacred place from generation to generation. 34 Aaron did this, just as the Lord had instructed Moses, and eventually it was kept in the Ark in the Tabernacle.

35 So the people of Israel ate the manna forty years until they arrived in the land of Canaan, where there were crops to eat. 36 The omer—the container used to measure the manna—held about two quarts; it is approximately a tenth of a bushel.

CHAPTER 17

God Provides Water

Now, at God's command, the people of Israel
left the Sihn desert, going by easy stages to
Rephidim. But upon arrival, there was no
water!
2So once more the people growled and
complained to Moses. "Give us water!" they
wailed.
"Quiet!" Moses commanded. "Are you trying to test God's patience with you?"
3But, tormented by thirst, they cried out,
"Why did you ever take us out of Egypt? Why
did you bring us here to die, with our children
and cattle too?"
4Then Moses pleaded with Jehovah. "What
shall I do? For they are almost ready to stone
me."
5,6Then Jehovah said to Moses, "Take the
elders of Israel with you and lead the people
out to Mt. Horeb. I will meet you there at the
rock. Strike it with your rod—the same one
you struck the Nile with—and water will
come pouring out, enough for everyone!"
Moses did as he was told, and the water
gushed out! 7Moses named the place Massah
(meaning "tempting Jehovah to slay us"), and
sometimes they referred to it as Meribah
(meaning "argument" and "strife!")—for it
was there that the people of Israel argued
against God and tempted him to slay them by
saying, "Is Jehovah going to take care of us or
not?"

Aaron and Hur Support Moses

8But now the warriors of Amalek came to fight
against the people of Israel at Rephidim. 9Mo-
ses instructed Joshua to issue a call to arms to
the Israelites, to fight the army of Amalek.
"Tomorrow," Moses told him, "I will stand
at the top of the hill, with the rod of God in
my hand!"
10So Joshua and his men went out to fight
the army of Amalek. Meanwhile Moses,
Aaron, and Hur went to the top of the hill.
11And as long as Moses held up the rod in his
hands, Israel was winning; but whenever he
rested his arms at his sides, the soldiers of
Amalek were winning. 12Moses' arms finally
became too tired to hold up the rod any
longer; so Aaron and Hur rolled a stone for
him to sit on, and they stood on each side,
holding up his hands until sunset. 13As a result, Joshua and his troops crushed the army
of Amalek, putting them to the sword.
14Then the Lord instructed Moses, "Write
this into a permanent record, to be remembered forever, and announce to Joshua that I
will utterly blot out every trace of Amalek."
15,16Moses built an altar there and called it
"Jehovah-nissi" (meaning "Jehovah is my
flag").
"Raise the banner of the Lord!" Moses said.
"For the Lord will be at war with Amalek
generation after generation."

CHAPTER 18

Jethro Visits Moses

Word soon reached Jethro, Moses' father-in-
law, the priest of Midian, about all the wonderful things God had done for his people and
for Moses, and how the Lord had brought
them out of Egypt.
2Then Jethro took Moses' wife, Zipporah, to
him (for he had sent her home), 3along with

17:1-7 As we begin the recovery process, we are often hindered repeatedly by the same old mistakes. We have certain weaknesses that haunt us time and again. The Israelites displayed this same tendency. They rebelled against Moses' leadership just because of a short-term lack of water (see 15:22-27). To make this place a monument to the people's lack of faith, Moses named it Massah (meaning "tempting Jehovah to slay us") and Meribah (meaning "argument" and "strife"). By these names, the people would be reminded of their past mistakes, hopefully encouraging them to be wiser the next time. We need to be reminded of our past mistakes from time to time in order to avoid them in the future.

17:8-16 The people had just put God on trial, testing him and wondering whether he was with them (17:7). In response, God overwhelmed the Amalekite forces in battle. In so doing he employed an instructive visual aid. Moses stood upon a hill in full view of the people and the battlefield. When his hands were raised, the Israelite army prevailed. The raised hands did not speak of Moses' power, but rather of God's empowering. Through such incidents, Israel was to learn that their freedom was dependent on their faith in God, not on their own strength.

18:1-12 Relationships between married children and their parents, especially with in-laws, can often be difficult. It is crucial for married children to leave their parents (Genesis 2:24), physically and emotionally. This includes relating to our parents and in-laws on an adult level. It is also necessary to "honor" our parents (Exodus 20:12). The relationship between Moses and Jethro, characterized by honesty and mutual respect, is a good example for us to follow.

Moses' two sons, Gershom (meaning "foreigner," for Moses said when he was born, "I
have been wandering in a foreign land") 4and
Eliezer (meaning "God is my help," for Moses
said at his birth, "The God of my fathers was
my helper and delivered me from the sword
of Pharaoh"). 5,6They arrived while Moses and
the people were camped at Mt. Sinai.
"Jethro, your father-in-law, has come to
visit you," Moses was told, "and he has
brought your wife and your two sons."
7Moses went out to meet his father-in-law
and greeted him warmly; they asked about
each other's health and then went into Moses'
tent to talk further. 8Moses related to his
father-in-law all that had been happening
and what the Lord had done to Pharaoh and
the Egyptians in order to deliver Israel, and all
the problems there had been along the way,
and how the Lord had delivered his people
from all of them. 9Jethro was very happy
about everything the Lord had done for Israel,
and about his bringing them out of Egypt.
10"Bless the Lord," Jethro said, "for he has
saved you from the Egyptians and from Pharaoh, and has rescued Israel. 11I know now
that the Lord is greater than any other god
because he delivered his people from the
proud and cruel Egyptians."
12Jethro offered sacrifices to God, and afterwards Aaron and the leaders of Israel came to
meet Jethro, and they all ate the sacrificial
meal together before the Lord.

Jethro Advises Moses

13The next day Moses sat as usual to hear the
people's complaints against each other, from
morning to evening.
14When Moses' father-in-law saw how
much time this was taking, he said, "Why are
you trying to do all this alone, with people
standing here all day long to get your help?"
15,16"Well, because the people come to me
with their disputes, to ask for God's decisions," Moses told him. "I am their judge,
deciding who is right and who is wrong, and
instructing them in God's ways. I apply the
laws of God to their particular disputes."
17"It's not right!" his father-in-law exclaimed. 18"You're going to wear yourself
out—and if you do, what will happen to the
people? Moses, this job is too heavy a burden
for you to try to handle all by yourself.
19,20Now listen, and let me give you a word of
advice, and God will bless you: Be these
people's lawyer—their representative before
God—bringing him their questions to decide;
you will tell them his decisions, teaching
them God's laws, and showing them the principles of godly living.
21"Find some capable, godly, honest men
who hate bribes, and appoint them as judges,
one judge for each 1000 people; he in turn
will have ten judges under him, each in
charge of a hundred; and under each of them
will be two judges, each responsible for the
affairs of fifty people; and each of these will
have five judges beneath him, each counsel-
ing ten persons. 22Let these men be responsible to serve the people with justice at all
times. Anything that is too important or complicated can be brought to you. But the
smaller matters they can take care of themselves. That way it will be easier for you because you will share the burden with them.
23If you follow this advice, and if the Lord
agrees, you will be able to endure the pressures, and there will be peace and harmony in
the camp."
24Moses listened to his father-in-law's advice and followed this suggestion. 25He chose
able men from all over Israel and made them
judges over the people—thousands, hundreds, fifties, and tens. 26They were constantly
available to administer justice. They brought
the hard cases to Moses but judged the
smaller matters themselves.
27Soon afterwards Moses let his father-in-
law return to his own land.

CHAPTER 19

God Speaks to Moses

The Israelis arrived in the Sinai peninsula
three months after the night of their departure from Egypt. 2,3After breaking camp at
Rephidim, they came to the base of Mt. Sinai

18:13-26 This episode reveals that Moses had a difficult time setting boundaries in his life. Jethro gave Moses some wise and creative advice, helping him to protect himself from the extensive demands of the people. But even this good advice did not solve this problem for Moses once and for all. His tendency to assume that God expected him to do everything (18:13-16) shows up later on in a slightly different way (Numbers 11:10-17). There Moses appears near emotional burnout, just as Jethro had predicted (Exodus 18:17-18). We need to set appropriate boundaries in our own life, maximizing the use of the time and energy that we have, while also protecting ourselves from burnout.

and set up camp there. Moses climbed the rugged mountain to meet with God, and from somewhere in the mountain God called to him and said,

"Give these instructions to the people of Israel. Tell them, 4'You have seen what I did to the Egyptians, and how I brought you to myself as though on eagle's wings. 5Now if you will obey me and keep your part of my contract with you, you shall be my own little flock from among all the nations of the earth; for all the earth is mine. 6And you shall be a kingdom of priests to God, a holy nation.'"

7Moses returned from the mountain and called together the leaders of the people and told them what the Lord had said.

8They all responded in unison, "We will certainly do everything he asks of us." Moses reported the words of the people to the Lord.

9Then he said to Moses, "I am going to come to you in the form of a dark cloud, so that the people themselves can hear me when I talk with you, and then they will always believe you. 10Go down now and see that the people are ready for my visit. Sanctify them today and tomorrow, and have them wash their clothes. 11Then, the day after tomorrow, I will come down upon Mt. Sinai as all the people watch. 12Set boundary lines the people may not pass, and tell them, 'Beware! Do not go up into the mountain or even touch its boundaries; whoever does shall die— 13no hand shall touch him, but he shall be stoned or shot to death with arrows, whether man or animal.' Stay away from the mountain entirely until you hear a ram's horn sounding one long blast; then gather at the foot of the mountain!"

14So Moses went down to the people and sanctified them and they washed their clothing.

15He told them, "Get ready for God's appearance two days from now, and do not have sexual intercourse with your wives."

16On the morning of the third day there was a terrific thunder and lightning storm, and a huge cloud came down upon the mountain, and there was a long, loud blast as from a ram's horn; and all the people trembled. 17Moses led them out from the camp to meet God, and they stood at the foot of the mountain. 18All Mt. Sinai was covered with smoke because Jehovah descended upon it in the form of fire; the smoke billowed into the sky as from a furnace, and the whole mountain shook with a violent earthquake. 19As the trumpet blast grew louder and louder, Moses spoke and God thundered his reply. 20So the Lord came down upon the top of Mt. Sinai and called Moses up to the top of the mountain, and Moses ascended to God.

21But the Lord told Moses, "Go back down and warn the people not to cross the boundaries. They must not come up here to try to see God, for if they do, many of them will die. 22Even the priests on duty must sanctify themselves, or else I will destroy them."

23"But the people won't come up into the mountain!" Moses protested. "You told them not to! You told me to set boundaries around the mountain and to declare it off limits because it is reserved for God."

24But Jehovah said, "Go down and bring Aaron back with you, and don't let the priests and the people break across the boundaries to try to come up here, or I will punish them."

25So Moses went down to the people and told them what God had said.

CHAPTER 20

The Ten Commandments

Then God issued this edict:

2"I am Jehovah your God who liberated you from your slavery in Egypt.

3"You may worship no other god than me.

4"You shall not make yourselves any idols: no images of animals, birds, or fish. 5You must never bow or worship it in any way; for I, the

---

19:2-6 Israel's new sense of identity and ability was to be founded upon her relationship with God. The Israelites had suffered under Egyptian bondage. Their sense of identity had been defined by that terrible experience. Now God had graciously delivered them and had brought them to himself. The people of Israel needed to see themselves as a kingdom of priests and a holy nation (19:6). They were no longer a nation of slaves. As we progress in recovery, we also need to see ourselves as people loved and blessed by God, not as slaves to our compulsions and dependencies.

19:7-8 When Moses returned from God's presence and asked for the people's response, they gave the right answer: "We will certainly do everything he [God] asks of us" (19:8). But had they really counted the cost before giving their response (Luke 14:28)? It is difficult for people needing recovery to be completely honest with others, even with themselves. This rapid-fire answer was probably motivated by a fearful desire to appease their terrifying God. It was not properly motivated by a wholehearted love for him.

Lord your God, am very possessive. I will not
share your affection with any other god!
"And when I punish people for their sins,
the punishment continues upon the children,
grandchildren, and great-grandchildren of
those who hate me; 6but I lavish my love
upon thousands of those who love me and
obey my commandments.
7"You shall not use the name of Jehovah
your God irreverently, nor use it to swear to a
falsehood. You will not escape punishment if
you do.
8"Remember to observe the Sabbath as a
holy day. 9Six days a week are for your daily
duties and your regular work, 10but the seventh day is a day of Sabbath rest before the
Lord your God. On that day you are to do no
work of any kind, nor shall your son, daughter, or slaves—whether men or women—or
your cattle or your house guests. 11For in six
days the Lord made the heaven, earth, and
sea, and everything in them, and rested the
seventh day; so he blessed the Sabbath day
and set it aside for rest.
12"Honor your father and mother, that you
may have a long, good life in the land the
Lord your God will give you.
13"You must not murder.
14"You must not commit adultery.
15"You must not steal.
16"You must not lie.
17"You must not be envious of your neighbor's house, or want to sleep with his wife, or
want to own his slaves, oxen, donkeys, or
anything else he has."
18All the people saw the lightning and the
smoke billowing from the mountain, and
heard the thunder and the long, frightening
trumpet blast; and they stood at a distance,
shaking with fear.
19They said to Moses, "You tell us what God
says and we will obey, but don't let God speak
directly to us, or it will kill us."
20"Don't be afraid," Moses told them, "for
God has come in this way to show you his
awesome power, so that from now on you will
be afraid to sin against him!"
21As the people stood in the distance, Moses
entered into the deep darkness where God
was.
22And the Lord told Moses to be his spokesman to the people of Israel. "You are witnesses
to the fact that I have made known my will to
you from heaven. 23Remember, you must not
make or worship idols made of silver or gold
or of anything else!
24"The altars you make for me must be
simple altars of earth. Offer upon them your
sacrifices to me—your burnt offerings and
peace offerings of sheep and oxen. Build altars
only where I tell you to, and I will come and
bless you there. 25You may also build altars
from stone, but if you do, then use only uncut
stones and boulders. Don't chip or shape the
stones with a tool, for that would make them
unfit for my altar. 26And don't make steps for
the altar, or someone might look up beneath
the skirts of your clothing and see your nakedness.

CHAPTER 21

Laws Concerning Relationships

"Here are other laws you must obey:
2"If you buy a Hebrew slave, he shall serve
only six years and be freed in the seventh

20:1-11 The first four of the Ten Commandments provided the Israelites with a few foundational principles to govern their relationship with God. They were not to worship any other gods (20:3), make idols of any kind (20:4-6), misuse God's name (20:7), or violate God's Sabbath day of rest (20:8-11). Each of these principles represent boundaries that God had set to define his relationship with his people. Jesus later summed up this vertical relationship as the greatest commandment: "Love the Lord your God with all your heart, soul, and mind" (Matthew 22:36-38). Loving God includes living out a consistent faith and commitment to him.
20:12-17 The final six of the Ten Commandments deal with principles that define boundaries for healthy human relationships. Only the command to honor our parents (20:12; see also Ephesians 6:1-3) is stated positively. The other five are negative: do not murder (Exodus 20:13), commit adultery (20:14), steal (20:15), lie (20:16), or covet anything belonging to your neighbor (20:17). Jesus summed up these human relational boundaries like this: "Love your neighbor as much as you love yourself" (Matthew 22:39). This great commandment assumes that we have cultivated a healthy self-respect and follow it up with loving actions that respect the boundaries of others.
21:12-27 These laws deal with the consequences of inappropriate, abusive behavior. Notice that compensation for wrong behavior is emphasized, making it clear that God holds us accountable for our actions. These laws reveal God's instructions for maintaining an orderly, healthy society when proper boundaries have been overstepped. They safeguard human relationships and personal identities while also recognizing the worth of life and property.

year, and need pay nothing to regain his freedom.
3"If he sold himself as a slave before he
married, then if he married afterwards, only
he shall be freed; but if he was married before
he became a slave, then his wife shall be freed
with him at the same time. 4But if his master
gave him a wife while he was a slave, and they
have sons or daughters, the wife and children
shall still belong to the master, and he shall go
out by himself free.
5"But if the man shall plainly declare, 'I
prefer my master, my wife, and my children,
and I would rather not go free,' 6then his
master shall bring him before the judges and
shall publicly bore his ear with an awl, and
after that he will be a slave forever.
7"If a man sells his daughter as a slave, she
shall not be freed at the end of six years as the
men are. 8If she does not please the man who
bought her, then he shall let her be bought
back again; but he has no power to sell her to
foreigners, since he has wronged her by no
longer wanting her after marrying her. 9And if
he arranges an engagement between a Hebrew slave-girl and his son, then he may no
longer treat her as a slave-girl, but must treat
her as a daughter. 10If he himself marries her
and then takes another wife, he may not
reduce her food or clothing, or fail to sleep
with her as his wife. 11If he fails in any of these
three things, then she may leave freely without any payment.
12"Anyone who hits a man so hard that he
dies shall surely be put to death. 13But if it is
accidental—an act of God—and not intentional, then I will appoint a place where he
can run and get protection. 14However, if a
man deliberately attacks another, intending
to kill him, drag him even from my altar, and
kill him.
15"Anyone who strikes his father or mother
shall surely be put to death.
16"A kidnapper must be killed, whether he
is caught in possession of his victim or has
already sold him as a slave.
17"Anyone who reviles or curses his mother
or father shall surely be put to death.
18"If two men are fighting, and one hits the
other with a stone or with his fist and injures
him so that he must be confined to bed, but
doesn't die, 19if later he is able to walk again,
even with a limp, the man who hit him will
be innocent except that he must pay for the
loss of his time until he is thoroughly healed,
and pay any medical expenses.
20"If a man beats his slave to death—

Self-protection

READ EXODUS 20:8-11

When we are in recovery we need to be especially careful to have all our faculties about us. If we allow ourselves to get overtired, we will be less able to cope with the demands of life. It will be harder for us to maintain our sobriety, and we will be more susceptible to a relapse.

Rest is essential to the maintenance of any kind of balanced life. The Bible recognizes the importance of rest for people, for farmland, for animals, and even for God himself. Weekly rest was even included as one of the Ten Commandments. God declared, "Six days a week are for your daily duties and your regular work, but the seventh day is a day of Sabbath rest before the Lord your God. On that day you are to do no work of any kind. . . . For in six days the Lord made the heaven, earth, and sea, and everything in them, and rested the seventh day; so he blessed the Sabbath day and set it aside for rest" (Exodus 20:9-11). "The Lord then gave these further instructions to Moses: 'Tell the people of Israel to rest on my Sabbath day, for the Sabbath is a reminder of the covenant between me and you forever; it helps you to remember that I am Jehovah [God] who makes you holy'" (Exodus 31:12-13).

God wants us to have the rest we need for a balanced life. As a part of our recovery program we should include a weekly Sabbath or intermission. This should be a time to relax from our regular duties and allow our body to rest. It should also be a time of spiritual refreshment, a time to reflect on God's promises and remember that it is God who sustains us in our recovery. ***Turn to page 297, Ruth 2.***

whether the slave is male or female—that
man shall surely be punished. 21However, if
the slave does not die for a couple of days,
then the man shall not be punished—for the
slave is his property.
22"If two men are fighting, and in the process hurt a pregnant woman so that she has a
miscarriage, but she lives, then the man who
injured her shall be fined whatever amount
the woman's husband shall demand, and as
the judges approve. 23But if any harm comes
to the woman and she dies, he shall be executed.
24"If her eye is injured, injure his; if her
tooth is knocked out, knock out his; and so
on—hand for hand, foot for foot, 25burn for
burn, wound for wound, lash for lash.
26"If a man hits his slave in the eye, whether
man or woman, and the eye is blinded, then
the slave shall go free because of his eye. 27And
if a master knocks out his slave's tooth, he
shall let him go free to pay for the tooth.
28"If an ox gores a man or woman to death,
the ox shall be stoned and its flesh not eaten,
but the owner shall not be held—29unless the
ox was known to gore people in the past, and
the owner had been notified and still the ox
was not kept under control; in that case, if it
kills someone, the ox shall be stoned and the
owner also shall be killed. 30But the dead
man's relatives may accept a fine instead, if
they wish. The judges will determine the
amount.
31"The same law holds if the ox gores a boy
or a girl. 32But if the ox gores a slave, whether
male or female, the slave's master shall be
given thirty pieces of silver, and the ox shall
be stoned.

Laws about Property

33"If a man digs a well and doesn't cover it,
and an ox or a donkey falls into it, 34the owner
of the well shall pay full damages to the
owner of the animal, and the dead animal
shall belong to him.
35"If a man's ox injures another, and it dies,
then the two owners shall sell the live ox and
divide the price between them—and each
shall also own half of the dead ox. 36But if the
ox was known from past experience to gore,
and its owner has not kept it under control,
then there will not be a division of the income; but the owner of the living ox shall pay
in full for the dead ox, and the dead one shall
be his.

CHAPTER 22

"If a man steals an ox or sheep and then kills
or sells it, he shall pay a fine of five to one—
five oxen shall be returned for each stolen ox.
For sheep, the fine shall be four to one—four
sheep returned for each sheep stolen.
2"If a thief is caught in the act of breaking
into a house and is killed, the one who killed
him is not guilty. 3But if it happens in the
daylight, it must be presumed to be murder
and the man who kills him is guilty.
"If a thief is captured, he must make full
restitution; if he can't, then he must be sold
as a slave for his debt.
4"If he is caught in the act of stealing a live
ox or donkey or sheep or whatever it is, he
shall pay double value as his fine.
5"If someone deliberately lets his animal
loose and it gets into another man's vineyard;
or if he turns it into another man's field to
graze, he must pay for all damages by giving
the owner of the field or vineyard an equal
amount of the best of his own crop.
6"If the field is being burned off and the fire
gets out of control and goes into another field
so that the shocks of grain, or the standing
grain, are destroyed, the one who started the
fire shall make full restitution.
7"If someone gives money or goods to anyone to keep for him, and it is stolen, the thief
shall pay double if he is found. 8But if no thief
is found, then the man to whom the valuables
were entrusted shall be brought before God to

21:32 Thirty pieces of silver was likely the standard or average price for a slave in the ancient Near East. Yet as much as this may have been worth, it could not compare to the true value of a human life created in God's image (Genesis 1:26-27). Oppressed people are often bound by a poor self-image. It would have been of interest to all slaves at this ancient time to learn that the Son of God would someday be betrayed for thirty pieces of silver (Matthew 26:15). He submitted to such humiliation so that he could heal us from our sinful past, breaking the bonds of our sin. He came to set us free, buying us back with his very life.

22:1-15 These regulations concerning restitution for property losses are related to the recovery issues of personal boundaries and accountability. We should be able to expect that our personal boundaries and property will be respected by others in society. We should also be able to expect appropriate restitution when such boundaries are violated or our property destroyed. Accountability for actions that violate others is an important part of God's program for a healthy society.

determine whether or not he himself has
stolen his neighbor's property.
9"In every case in which an ox, donkey,
sheep, clothing, or anything else is lost, and
the owner believes he has found it in the
possession of someone else who denies it,
both parties to the dispute shall come before
God for a decision, and the one whom God
declares guilty shall pay double to the other.
10"If a man asks his neighbor to keep a
donkey, ox, sheep, or any other animal for
him, and it dies, or is hurt, or gets away, and
there is no eyewitness to report just what
happened to it, 11then the neighbor must take
an oath that he has not stolen it, and the
owner must accept his word, and no restitution shall be made for it. 12But if the animal or
property has been stolen, the neighbor caring
for it must repay the owner. 13If it was attacked
by some wild animal, he shall bring the torn
carcass to confirm the fact, and shall not be
required to make restitution.
14"If a man borrows an animal (or anything
else) from a neighbor, and it is injured or
killed, and the owner is not there at the time,
then the man who borrowed it must pay for
it. 15But if the owner is there, he need not pay;
and if it was rented, then he need not pay,
because this possibility was included in the
original rental fee.

Some General Laws

16"If a man seduces a girl who is not engaged
to anyone and sleeps with her, he must pay
the usual dowry and accept her as his wife.
17But if her father utterly refuses to let her
marry him, then he shall pay the money
anyway.
18"A sorceress shall be put to death.
19"Anyone having sexual relations with an
animal shall certainly be executed.
20"Anyone sacrificing to any other god than
Jehovah shall be executed.
21"You must not oppress a stranger in any
way; remember, you yourselves were foreigners in the land of Egypt.
22"You must not exploit widows or orphans; 23if you do so in any way, and they cry
to me for my help, I will surely give it. 24And
my anger shall flame out against you, and I
will kill you with enemy armies, so that your
wives will be widows and your children fatherless.
25"If you lend money to a needy fellow-
Hebrew, you are not to handle the transaction
in an ordinary way, with interest. 26If you take
his clothing as a pledge of his repayment, you

Making Restitution

BIBLE READING: Exodus 22:10-15

We made a list of all persons we had harmed and became willing to make amends to them all.

Dysfunctional family systems tend to affect people in a number of different ways. Some of us come to see ourselves as irresponsible and continually condemn ourselves. Others of us tend to admit that we are irresponsible, but excuse ourselves because of all the things we have suffered. Still others of us may not even notice our irresponsible behavior, but have recurrent problems with other people because we fail to respect their property.

The Bible clearly states, "If a man borrows an animal (or anything else) from a neighbor, and it is injured or killed, and the owner is not there at the time, then the man who borrowed it must pay for it" (Exodus 22:14). David once wrote, "Evil men borrow and 'cannot pay it back'! But the good man returns what he owes with some extra besides" (Psalm 37:21).

The Bible does tell us that it's important to take responsibility for the things we borrow. We may feel like we are being condemned as chronically evil if we have had a problem with irresponsibility. The word translated "evil men" really means one who is morally wrong or a person who acts badly. God sees irresponsible behavior as a bad action that can be corrected. He doesn't see us as hopelessly bad. Regardless of what we have been through, we are still held responsible to respect the property of others. We need to consider those we have harmed by being negligent or irresponsible with the use of their property. ***Turn to page 119, Leviticus 4.***

must let him have it back at night. 27For it is
probably his only warmth; how can he sleep
without it? If you don't return it, and he cries
to me for help, I will hear and be very gracious
to him [at your expense], for I am very compassionate.
28"You shall not blaspheme God, nor curse
government officials—your judges and your
rulers.
29"You must be prompt in giving me the
tithe of your crops and your wine, and the
redemption payment for your oldest son.
30"As to the firstborn of the oxen and the
sheep, give it to me on the eighth day, after
leaving it with its mother for seven days.
31"And since you yourselves are holy—my
special people—do not eat any animal that
has been attacked and killed by a wild animal.
Leave its carcass for the dogs to eat.

CHAPTER 23
"Do not pass along untrue reports. Do not
cooperate with an evil man by affirming on
the witness stand something you know is
false.
2,3"Don't join mobs intent on evil. When
on the witness stand, don't be swayed in your
testimony by the mood of the majority present, and do not slant your testimony in favor
of a man just because he is poor.
4"If you come upon an enemy's ox or donkey that has strayed away, you must take it
back to its owner. 5If you see your enemy
trying to get his donkey onto its feet beneath
a heavy load, you must not go on by but must
help him.
6"A man's poverty is no excuse for twisting
justice against him.
7"Keep far away from falsely charging anyone with evil; never let an innocent person be
put to death. I will not stand for this.
8"Take no bribes, for a bribe makes you
unaware of what you clearly see! A bribe hurts
the cause of the person who is right.
9"Do not oppress foreigners; you know
what it's like to be a foreigner; remember your
own experience in the land of Egypt.
10"Sow and reap your crops for six years,
11but let the land rest and lie fallow during the
seventh year, and let the poor among the
people harvest any volunteer crop that may
come up; leave the rest for the animals to
enjoy. The same rule applies to your vineyards
and your olive groves.
12"Work six days only, and rest the seventh;
this is to give your oxen and donkeys a rest,
as well as the people of your household—your
slaves and visitors.
13"Be sure to obey all of these instructions;
and remember—never mention the name of
any other god.

Three Special Festivals
14"There are three annual religious pilgrimages you must make.
15"The first is the Pilgrimage of Unleavened
Bread, when for seven days you are not to eat
bread with yeast, just as I commanded you
before. This celebration is to be an annual
event at the regular time in March, the month
you left Egypt; everyone must bring me a
sacrifice at that time. 16Then there is the Harvest Pilgrimage, when you must bring to me
the first of your crops. And, finally, the Pilgrimage of Ingathering at the end of the harvest season. 17At these three times each year,
every man in Israel shall appear before the
Lord God.
18"No sacrificial blood shall be offered with
leavened bread; no sacrificial fat shall be left
unoffered until the next morning.
19"As you reap each of your crops, bring me

22:16-28 There are certain kinds of behavior that are abominable to God and others that are brutally inhumane. God has set clear boundaries in such cases and demands our accountability to them. The apostle Paul implied that such behavior, which is totally devoid of faith and commitment to God, is not only self-destructive, but also erodes the very fabric of society (Romans 1:18-32). Our recovery demands that we refrain from irresponsible behavior and seek reconciliation with those we have wronged.

23:1-8 This section is basically an expansion of 20:16, which prohibits false testimony. The truth eventually comes out (see 1 Timothy 5:24-25), so honesty is not only the right policy, but also the smart one. Even if someone seems to be getting away with lies for a time, that person must still answer to God (Exodus 23:7). In the end he will be held accountable.

23:10-19 God gave instructions concerning Sabbath regulations (see 20:8-11) and annual festivals for several reasons. First, these events were a time for worship, faith, and renewed commitment to God. Second, they were object lessons that pictured important spiritual truths for God's people. Third, they were times for rest; they protected God's people from overwork and imbalance. These events were designed to encourage the people's health—spiritually, emotionally, physically. We also need regular times of worship, reflection, and rest.

the choicest sample of the first day's harvest;
it shall be offered to the Lord your God.
"Do not boil a young goat in its mother's
milk.

Serve God Alone

20"See, I am sending an Angel before you to
lead you safely to the land I have prepared for
you. 21Reverence him and obey all of his instructions; do not rebel against him, for he
will not pardon your transgression; he is my
representative—he bears my name. 22But if
you are careful to obey him, following all my
instructions, then I will be an enemy to your
enemies. 23For my Angel shall go before you
and bring you into the land of the Amorites,
Hittites, Perizzites, Canaanites, Hivites, and
Jebusites, to live there. And I will destroy
those people before you.
24"You must not worship the gods of these
other nations, nor sacrifice to them in any
way, and you must not follow the evil example of these heathen people; you must utterly
conquer them and break down their shameful
idols.
25"You shall serve the Lord your God only;
then I will bless you with food and with water,
and I will take away sickness from among
you. 26There will be no miscarriages nor barrenness throughout your land, and you will
live out the full quota of the days of your life.
27"The terror of the Lord shall fall upon all
the people whose land you invade, and they
will flee before you; 28and I will send hornets
to drive out the Hivites, Canaanites, and Hittites from before you. 29I will not do it all in
one year, for the land would become a wilderness, and the wild animals would become too
many to control. 30But I will drive them out a
little at a time, until your population has
increased enough to fill the land. 31And I will
set your enlarged boundaries from the Red Sea
to the Philistine coast, and from the southern
deserts as far as the Euphrates River; and I will
cause you to defeat the people now living in
the land, and you will drive them out ahead
of you.
32"You must make no covenant with them,
nor have anything to do with their gods.
33Don't let them live among you! For I know
that they will infect you with their sin of
worshiping false gods, and that would be an
utter disaster to you."

CHAPTER 24

The People Promise to Obey

The Lord now instructed Moses, "Come up
here with Aaron, Nadab, Abihu, and seventy
of the elders of Israel. All of you except Moses
are to worship at a distance. 2Moses alone
shall come near to the Lord; and remember,
none of the ordinary people are permitted to
come up into the mountain at all."
3Then Moses announced to the people all
the laws and regulations God had given him;
and the people answered in unison, "We will
obey them all."
4Moses wrote down the laws; and early the
next morning he built an altar at the foot of
the mountain, with twelve pillars around the
altar because there were twelve tribes of Israel.
5Then he sent some of the young men to
sacrifice the burnt offerings and peace offerings to the Lord. 6Moses took half of the blood
of these animals and drew it off into basins.
The other half he splashed against the altar.
7And he read to the people the Book he had
written—the Book of the Covenant—containing God's directions and laws. And the
people said again, "We solemnly promise to
obey every one of these rules."
8Then Moses threw the blood from the basins toward the people and said, "This blood
confirms and seals the covenant the Lord has
made with you in giving you these laws."
9Then Moses, Aaron, Nadab, Abihu, and

23:32-33 The temptations of life within the Promised Land serve as a vivid illustration of how proper standards and boundaries can be tragically forgotten. The Israelites were warned about our tendency to make a good, clean start, but then to compromise our values and goals. They were warned not to make treaties with the people of the land. They were to push them right out, replacing them with communities of their own. In recovery it is easy to make a good start, but then to compromise, allowing certain "little" practices to go on unchecked. In the end, these things will spell disaster, eroding the new life we have started to build.

24:1-8 Although Israel's response to God's covenant was the same as before (see 19:8), they were now beginning to "count the cost" of their commitment to God. At this point they were called upon to make sacrifices to him. As they saw the animals slaughtered and heard their cries, surely they were reminded of how costly their redemption from Egypt had been. It was a clear reminder of God's gracious forgiveness, for God allowed these animals to die as payment for the people's infractions of the law. We should feel similar gratitude as we think of Jesus on the cross and realize that we are the ones who should have been there.

seventy of the elders of Israel went up into the
mountain. [10]And they saw the God of Israel;
under his feet there seemed to be a pavement
of brilliant sapphire stones, as clear as the
heavens.

[11]Yet, even though the elders saw God, he
did not destroy them; and they had a meal
together before the Lord.

Moses Climbs Mount Sinai

[12]And the Lord said to Moses, "Come up to me
into the mountain, and remain until I give
you the laws and commandments I have written on tablets of stone, so that you can teach
the people from them." [13]So Moses and
Joshua, his assistant, went up into the mountain of God.

[14]He told the elders, "Stay here and wait for
us until we come back; if there are any problems while I am gone, consult with Aaron and
Hur."

[15]Then Moses went up the mountain and
disappeared into the cloud at the top. [16]And
the glory of the Lord rested upon Mt. Sinai,
and the cloud covered it six days; the seventh
day he called to Moses from the cloud.
[17]Those at the bottom of the mountain saw
the awesome sight: the glory of the Lord on
the mountaintop looked like a raging fire.
[18]And Moses disappeared into the cloud-
covered mountaintop, and was there for forty
days and forty nights.

CHAPTER 25

Instructions for the Tabernacle

Jehovah said to Moses, "Tell the people of
Israel that everyone who wants to may bring
me an offering from this list: gold, silver,
bronze, blue cloth, purple cloth, scarlet cloth,
fine linen, goats' hair, red-dyed rams' skins,
goatskins, acacia wood, olive oil for the
lamps, spices for the anointing oil and for the
fragrant incense, onyx stones, stones to be set
in the ephod and in the breastplate.

[8]"For I want the people of Israel to make me
a sacred Temple where I can live among them.

[9]"This home of mine shall be a tent pavil-
ion—a Tabernacle. I will give you a drawing of
the construction plan and the details of each
furnishing.

Instructions for the Ark

[10]"Using acacia wood, make an Ark $3\frac{3}{4}$ feet
long, $2\frac{1}{4}$ feet wide, and $2\frac{1}{4}$ feet high. [11]Over-
lay it inside and outside with pure gold, with
a molding of gold all around it. [12]Cast four
rings of gold for it and attach them to the four
lower corners, two rings on each side.
[13,14]Make poles from acacia wood overlaid
with gold, and fit the poles into the rings at
the sides of the Ark to carry it. [15]These carrying
poles shall never be taken from the rings, but
are to be left there permanently. [16]When the
Ark is finished, place inside it the tablets of
stone I will give you, with the Ten Commandments engraved on them.

[17]"And make a lid of pure gold, $3\frac{3}{4}$ feet long
and $2\frac{1}{4}$ feet wide. This is the place of mercy
for your sins. [18]Then make two statues of
Guardian Angels using beaten gold, and place
them at the two ends of the lid of the Ark.
[19]They shall be one piece with the mercy
place, one at each end. [20]The Guardian Angels
shall be facing each other, looking down
upon the place of mercy, and shall have wings
spread out above the gold lid. [21]Install the lid
upon the Ark, and place within the Ark the
tablets of stone I shall give you. [22]And I will
meet with you there and talk with you from
above the place of mercy between the Guardian Angels; and the Ark will contain the laws
of my covenant. There I will tell you my
commandments for the people of Israel.

24:9-11 One of the best ways for us to see ourselves as we actually are is to gain a clear view of God and his glorious person. The person who tends to glorify himself will quickly change his ways if he gets even a glimpse of God's awesome glory. On the other hand, the person who is self-deprecating needs to understand that he is made in God's image (Genesis 1:26-27) and that he is destined to be in God's glorious presence forever (Revelation 21–22). One glimpse of God in his glory will heal both our pride and our self-deprecation, giving us a healthy and balanced self-assessment.

25:8-9 When Adam and Eve sinned in the garden, they created a terrible rift in the relationship between God and the human race. But God has spent the centuries since reaching out to us, seeking to heal the relationship. God's declaration that he would dwell among the Israelites in a Tabernacle was a step in this process of reconciliation. God wanted to live among his people. The details of the pattern he laid out also show that God clearly sets boundaries within which he relates to his people. Later, when Jesus Christ became a man, God's personal presence among the human race represented an even more personal relationship with us (John 1:14). God is in the business of reconciliation.

Instructions for the Table

[23]"Then make a table of acacia wood 3 feet long, $1\frac{1}{2}$ feet wide, and $2\frac{1}{4}$ feet high. [24]Overlay it with pure gold, and run a rib of gold around it. [25]Put a molding four inches wide around the edge of the top, and a gold ridge along the molding, all around. [26,27]Make four gold rings and put the rings at the outside corner of the four legs, close to the top; these are rings for the poles that will be used to carry the table. [28]Make the poles from acacia wood overlaid with gold. [29]And make gold dishes, spoons, pitchers, and flagons; [30]and always keep the special Bread of the Presence on the table before me.

Instructions for the Lampstand

[31]"Make a lampstand of pure, beaten gold. The entire lampstand and its decorations shall be one piece—the base, shaft, lamps, and blossoms. [32,33]It will have three branches going out from each side of the center shaft, each branch decorated with three almond flowers. [34,35]The central shaft itself will be decorated with four almond flowers—one placed between each set of branches; also, there will be one flower above the top set of branches and one below the bottom set. [36]These decorations and branches and the shaft are all to be one piece of pure, beaten gold. [37]Then make seven lamps for the lampstand, and set them so that they reflect their light forward. [38]The snuffers and trays are to be made of pure gold. [39]You will need about 107 pounds of pure gold for the lampstand and its accessories.

[40]"Be sure that everything you make follows the pattern I am showing you here on the mountain.

CHAPTER 26

Instructions for the Tent

"Make the tabernacle-tent from ten colored sheets of fine linen, 42 feet long and 6 feet wide, dyed blue, purple, and scarlet, with figures of Guardian Angels embroidered on them. [3]Join five sheets end to end for each side of the tent, forming two long pieces, one for each side. [4,5]Use loops at the edges to join these two long pieces together side by side. There are to be fifty loops on each side, opposite each other. [6]Then make fifty gold clasps to fasten the loops together, so that the Tabernacle, the dwelling place of God, becomes a single unit.

[7,8]"The roof of the Tabernacle is made of goats' hair tarpaulins. There are to be eleven of these tarpaulins, each 45 feet across and 6 feet wide. [9]Connect five of these tarpaulins into one wide section; and use the other six for another wide section. (The sixth tarpaulin will hang down to form a curtain across the front of the sacred tent.) [10,11]Use fifty loops along the edges of each of these two wide pieces, to join them together with fifty bronze clasps. Thus the two widths become one. [12]There will be a $1\frac{1}{2}$-foot length of this roof-covering hanging down from the back of the tent, [13]and a $1\frac{1}{2}$-foot length at the front. [14]On top of these blankets is placed a layer of rams' skins, dyed red, and over them a top layer of goatskins. This completes the roof-covering.

[15,16]"The framework of the sacred tent shall be made from acacia wood, each frame-piece being 15 feet high and $2\frac{1}{4}$ feet wide, standing upright, [17]with grooves on each side to mortise into the next upright piece. [18,19]Twenty of these frames will form the south side of the sacred tent, with forty silver bases for the frames to fit into—two bases under each piece of the frame. [20]On the north side there will also be twenty of these frames, [21]with their forty silver bases, two bases for each frame, one under each edge. [22]On the west side there will be six frames, [23]and two frames at each corner. [24]These corner frames will be connected at the bottom and top with clasps. [25]So, in all, there will be eight frames on that end of the building with sixteen silver bases for the frames—two bases under each frame.

[26,27]"Make bars of acacia wood to run across the frames, five bars on each side of the Tabernacle. Also five bars for the rear of the building, facing westward. [28]The middle bar, halfway up the frames, runs all the way from end to end of the Tabernacle. [29]Overlay the frames with gold, and make gold rings to hold the bars; and also overlay the bars with gold. [30]Set up this Tabernacle-tent in the manner I showed you on the mountain.

Instructions for the Curtains

[31]"[Inside the Tabernacle], make a curtain from fine linen, with blue, purple, and scarlet Guardian Angels embroidered into the cloth.

26:31-33 The curtain between the Holy Place and the Most Holy Place was a boundary between the perfect holiness of God and the sinfulness of humankind. Violation of this boundary had dire, even fatal, consequences. It would seem to be a valid implication that people, made in the image of God (Genesis 1:26-27), can also set realistic boundaries that should be respected.

32Hang this curtain on gold hooks set into
four pillars made from acacia wood overlaid
with gold. The pillars are to be set in silver
bases. 33Behind this curtain place the Ark containing the stone tablets engraved with God's
laws. The curtain will separate the Holy Place
and the Most Holy Place.
34"Now install the mercy place—the golden
lid of the Ark—in the Most Holy Place. 35Place
the table and lampstand across the room from
each other on the outer side of the veil, the
lampstand on the south and the table on the
north.
36"As a screen for the door of the sacred
tent, make another curtain from fine linen,
skillfully embroidered in blue, purple, and
scarlet. 37Hang this curtain on gold hooks set
into posts made from acacia wood overlaid
with gold. The posts are to rest on bronze
bases.

CHAPTER 27

Instructions for the Altar

"Using acacia wood, make a square altar 7½
feet wide, and 4½ feet high. 2Make horns for
the four corners of the altar, attach them
firmly, and overlay everything with bronze.
3The ash buckets, shovels, basins, carcass-
hooks, and fire pans are all to be made of
bronze. 4Make a bronze grating, with a metal
ring at each corner, 5and fit the grating halfway down into the firebox, resting it upon the
ledge built there. 6For moving the altar, make
poles from acacia wood overlaid with bronze.
7To carry it, put the poles into the rings at each
side of the altar. 8The altar is to be hollow,
made from planks, just as was shown you on
the mountain.

Instructions for the Courtyard

9,10"Then make a courtyard for the Tabernacle,
enclosed with curtains made from fine-
twined linen. On the south side the curtains
will stretch for 150 feet, and be held up by
twenty posts, fitting into twenty bronze post
holders. The curtains will be held up with
silver hooks attached to silver rods, attached
to the posts. 11It will be the same on the north
side of the court—150 feet of curtains held up
by twenty posts fitted into bronze sockets,
with silver hooks and rods. 12The west side of
the court will be 75 feet wide, with ten posts
and ten sockets. 13The east side will also be 75
feet. 14,15On each side of the entrance there
will be 22½ feet of curtain, held up by three
posts imbedded in three sockets.
16"The entrance to the court will be a 30-
foot-wide curtain, made of beautifully embroidered blue, purple, and scarlet fine-
twined linen, and attached to four posts imbedded in their four sockets. 17All the posts
around the court are to be connected by silver
rods, using silver hooks, the posts being imbedded in solid bronze bases. 18So the entire
court will be 150 feet long and 75 feet wide,
with curtain walls 7½ feet high, made from
fine-twined linen.
19"All utensils used in the work of the Tabernacle, including all the pins and pegs for
hanging the utensils on the walls, will be
made of bronze.
20"Instruct the people of Israel to bring you
pure olive oil to use in the lamps of the
Tabernacle, to burn there continually. 21Aaron
and his sons shall place this eternal flame in
the outer holy room, tending it day and night
before the Lord, so that it never goes out. This
is a permanent rule for the people of Israel.

CHAPTER 28

Clothing for the Priests

"Consecrate Aaron your brother, and his sons
Nadab, Abihu, Eleazar, and Ithamar, to be
priests, to minister to me. 2Make special
clothes for Aaron, to indicate his separation
to God—beautiful garments that will lend
dignity to his work. 3Instruct those to whom
I have given special skill as tailors to make the
garments that will set him apart from others,
so that he may minister to me in the priest's
office. 4This is the wardrobe they shall make:
a chestpiece, an ephod, a robe, an embroidered shirt, a turban, and a sash. They shall
also make special garments for Aaron's sons.
5,6"The ephod shall be made by the most
skilled of the workmen, using gold, blue, purple, and scarlet threads of fine linen. 7It will
consist of two pieces, front and back, joined
at the shoulders. 8And the sash shall be made
of the same material—threads of gold, blue,
purple, and scarlet fine-twined linen. 9Take
two onyx stones and engrave on them the

27:20-21 God's command to keep the lamps burning throughout the hours of darkness indicates that God is a God of light (see 1 John 1:5). Under cover of darkness, it is difficult to judge reality and easier to hide the truth. God is not a God of darkness. He wants his people to be transparent, having integrity and faith. He wants them to be obedient to his program for living. That is what it means to live in the light of God's presence as Christ does (1 John 1:7).

names of the tribes of Israel. 10Six names shall
be on each stone, so that all the tribes are
named in the order of their births. 11When
engraving these names, use the same technique as in making a seal; and mount the
stones in gold settings. 12Fasten the two stones
upon the shoulders of the ephod, as memorial
stones for the people of Israel: Aaron will
carry their names before the Lord as a constant reminder. 13,14Two chains of pure,
twisted gold shall be made and attached to
gold clasps on the shoulder of the ephod.
15"Then, using the most careful workmanship, make a chestpiece to be used as God's
oracle; use the same gold, blue, purple, and
scarlet threads of fine-twined linen as you did
in the ephod. 16This chestpiece is to be of two
folds of cloth, forming a pouch nine inches
square. 17Attach to it four rows of stones: A
ruby, a topaz, and an emerald shall be in the
first row. 18The second row will be carbuncle,
a sapphire, and a diamond. 19The third row
will be an amber, an agate, and an amethyst.
20The fourth row will be an onyx, a beryl, and
a jasper—all set in gold settings. 21Each stone
will represent one of the tribes of Israel and
the name of that tribe will be engraved upon
it like a seal.
22-24"Attach the top of the chestpiece to the
ephod by means of two twisted cords of pure
gold. One end of each cord is attached to gold
rings placed at the outer top edge of the
chestpiece. 25The other ends of the two cords
are attached to the front edges of the two
settings of the onyx stones on the shoulder of
the ephod. 26Then make two more gold rings
and place them on the two lower, inside edges
of the chestpiece; 27also make two other gold
rings for the bottom front edge of the ephod
at the sash. 28Now attach the bottom of the
chestpiece to the bottom rings of the ephod
by means of blue ribbons; this will prevent
the chestpiece from coming loose from the
ephod. 29In this way Aaron shall carry the
names of the tribes of Israel on the chestpiece
over his heart (it is God's oracle) when he goes
into the Holy Place; thus Jehovah will be
reminded of them continually. 30,31Insert into
the pocket of the chestpiece the Urim and
Thummim, to be carried over Aaron's heart
when he goes in before Jehovah. Thus Aaron
shall always be carrying the oracle over his
heart when he goes in before the Lord.
"The ephod shall be made of blue cloth,
32with an opening for Aaron's head. It shall
have a woven band around this opening, just
as on the neck of a coat of mail, so that it will
not fray. 33,34The bottom edge of the ephod
shall be embroidered with blue, purple, and
scarlet pomegranates, alternated with gold
bells. 35Aaron shall wear the ephod whenever
he goes in to minister to the Lord; the bells
will tinkle as he goes in and out of the presence of the Lord in the Holy Place, so that he
will not die.
36"Next, make a plate of pure gold and
engrave on it, just as you would upon a seal,
'Consecrated to Jehovah.' 37,38This plate is to
be attached by means of a blue ribbon to the
front of Aaron's turban. In this way Aaron will
be wearing it upon his forehead, and thus
bear the guilt connected with any errors regarding the offerings of the people of Israel. It
shall always be worn when he goes into the
presence of the Lord, so that the people will
be accepted and forgiven.
39"Weave Aaron's embroidered shirt from
fine-twined linen, using a checkerboard pattern; make the turban, too, of this linen; and
make him an embroidered sash.
40"Then, for Aaron's sons, make robes,
sashes, and turbans to give them honor and
respect. 41Clothe Aaron and his sons with
these garments, and then dedicate these men
to their ministry by anointing their heads
with olive oil, thus sanctifying them as the
priests, my ministers. 42Also make linen un-
dershorts for them, to be worn beneath their
robes next to their bodies, reaching from hips
to knees. 43These are to be worn whenever
Aaron and his sons go into the Tabernacle or
to the altar in the Holy Place, lest they be
guilty and die. This is a permanent ordinance
for Aaron and his sons.

CHAPTER 29

Dedicating the Priests

"This is the ceremony for the dedication of
Aaron and his sons as priests: get a young bull
and two rams with no defects, 2and bread
made without yeast, and thin sheets of sweet-
ened bread mingled with oil, and unleavened

28:29-32 The priest's breastplate was inscribed with the names of Israel's tribes. This showed that he represented the nation and was spiritually responsible for the people. The Urim and Thummim were a means to determine the will of God in key decisions. Similarly, those in positions of responsibility must seriously and consistently seek God's will as they make decisions, or be accountable for acting otherwise.

wafers with oil poured over them. (The various kinds of bread shall be made with finely ground wheat flour.) [3,4]Place the bread in a basket and bring it to the entrance of the Tabernacle, along with the young bull and the two rams.

"Bathe Aaron and his sons there at the entrance. [5]Then put Aaron's robe on him, and the embroidered shirt, ephod, chestpiece, and sash, [6]and place on his head the turban with the gold plate. [7]Then take the anointing oil and pour it upon his head. [8]Next, dress his sons in their robes, [9]with their woven sashes, and place caps on their heads. They will then be priests forever; thus you shall consecrate Aaron and his sons.

[10]"Then bring the young bull to the Tabernacle, and Aaron and his sons shall lay their hands upon its head; [11]and you shall kill it before the Lord, at the entrance of the Tabernacle. [12]Place its blood upon the horns of the altar, smearing it on with your finger, and pour the rest at the base of the altar. [13]Then take all the fat that covers the inner parts, also the gall bladder and two kidneys, and the fat on them, and burn them upon the altar. [14]Then take the body, including the skin and the dung, outside the camp and burn it as a sin offering.

[15,16]"Next, Aaron and his sons shall lay their hands upon the head of one of the rams as it is killed. Its blood shall also be collected and sprinkled upon the altar. [17]Cut up the ram and wash off the entrails and the legs; place them with the head and the other pieces of the body, [18]and burn it all upon the altar; it is a burnt offering to the Lord, and very pleasant to him.

[19,20]"Now take the other ram, and Aaron and his sons shall lay their hands upon its head as it is killed. Collect the blood and place some of it upon the tip of the right ear of Aaron and his sons, and upon their right thumbs and the big toes of their right feet; sprinkle the rest of the blood over the altar. [21]Then scrape off some of the blood from the altar and mix it with some of the anointing oil and sprinkle it upon Aaron and his sons and upon their clothes; and they and their clothing shall be sanctified to the Lord.

[22]"Then take the fat of the ram, including the fat tail and the fat that covers the insides, also the gall bladder and the two kidneys and the fat surrounding them, and the right thigh—for this is the ram for ordination of Aaron and his sons— [23]and one loaf of bread, one cake of shortening bread, and one wafer from the basket of unleavened bread that was placed before the Lord: [24]Place these in the hands of Aaron and his sons, to wave them in a gesture of offering to the Lord. [25]Afterwards, take them from their hands and burn them on the altar as a fragrant burnt offering to him. [26]Then take the breast of Aaron's ordination ram and wave it before the Lord in a gesture of offering; afterwards, keep it for yourself.

[27]"Give the breast and thigh of the consecration ram [28]to Aaron and his sons. The people of Israel must always contribute this portion of their sacrifices—whether peace offerings or thanksgiving offerings—as their contribution to the Lord.

[29]"These sacred garments of Aaron shall be preserved for the consecration of his son who succeeds him, from generation to generation, for his anointing ceremony. [30]Whoever is the next High Priest after Aaron shall wear these clothes for seven days before beginning to minister in the Tabernacle and the Holy Place.

[31]"Take the ram of consecration—the ram used in the ordination ceremony—and boil its meat in a sacred area. [32]Aaron and his sons shall eat the meat, also the bread in the basket, at the door of the Tabernacle. [33]They alone shall eat those items used in their atonement (that is, in their consecration ceremony). The ordinary people shall not eat them, for these things are set apart and holy. [34]If any of the meat or bread remains until the morning, burn it; it shall not be eaten, for it is holy.

[35]"This, then, is the way you shall ordain Aaron and his sons to their offices. This ordination shall go on for seven days. [36]Every day you shall sacrifice a young bull as a sin offering for atonement; afterwards, purge the altar by making atonement for it; pour olive oil upon it to sanctify it. [37]Make atonement for the altar and consecrate it to God every day for seven days. After this the altar shall be exceedingly holy, so that whatever touches it shall be set apart for God.

29:1-46 This chapter constantly reiterates the need for consecration in a number of ways. To consecrate means "to set apart," whether it be a person or an object. It is only when there is proper consecration that the closest relationship between our holy God and sinful people is possible. In the New Testament those who have faith in Christ are called *saints*. This means that they are "set apart"; they are "holy ones." All of us have been set apart by God to live a healthy and holy life.

The Daily Sacrifices
38“Each day offer two yearling lambs upon the
altar, 39one in the morning and the other in
the evening. 40With one of them offer 3 quarts
of finely ground flour mixed with 2½ pints
of oil, pressed from olives; also 2½ pints of
wine, as an offering.
41Offer the other lamb in the evening, along
with the flour and the wine as in the morning,
for a fragrant offering to the Lord, an offering
made to the Lord by fire.
42“This shall be a perpetual daily offering at
the door of the Tabernacle before the Lord,
where I will meet with you and speak with
you. 43And I will meet with the people of Israel
there, and the Tabernacle shall be sanctified
by my glory. 44 Yes, I will sanctify the Tabernacle and the altar and Aaron and his sons who
are my ministers, the priests. 45And I will live
among the people of Israel and be their God,
46and they shall know that I am the Lord their
God. I brought them out of Egypt so that I
could live among them. I am Jehovah their
God.

CHAPTER 30
Preparing for Worship
“Then make a small altar for burning incense.
It shall be made from acacia wood. 2It is to be
eighteen inches square and three feet high,
with horns carved from the wood of the altar—they are not to be merely separate parts
that are attached. 3Overlay the top, sides, and
horns of the altar with pure gold, and run a
gold molding around the entire altar. 4Be-
neath the molding, on each of two sides,
construct two gold rings to hold the carrying
poles. 5The poles are to be made of acacia
wood overlaid with gold. 6Place the altar just
outside the veil, near the place of mercy that
is above the Ark containing the Ten Commandments. I will meet with you there.
7“Every morning when Aaron trims the
lamps, he shall burn sweet spices on the altar,
8and each evening when he lights the lamps
he shall burn the incense before the Lord, and
this shall go on from generation to generation. 9Offer no unauthorized incense, burnt
offerings, meal offerings, or wine offerings.
10“Once a year Aaron must sanctify the
altar, placing upon its horns the blood of the
sin offering for atonement. This shall be a
regular, annual event from generation to generation, for this is the Lord’s supremely holy
altar.”
11,12And Jehovah said to Moses, “Whenever
you take a census of the people of Israel, each
man who is numbered shall give a ransom to
the Lord for his soul, so that there will be no
plague among the people when you number
them. 13His payment shall be half a dollar.
14All who have reached their twentieth birthday shall give this offering. 15The rich shall
not give more and the poor shall not give less,
for it is an offering to the Lord to make atonement for yourselves. 16Use this money for the
care of the Tabernacle; it is to bring you, the
people of Israel, to the Lord’s attention, and
to make atonement for you.”
17,18And the Lord said to Moses, “Make a
bronze basin with a bronze pedestal. Put it
between the Tabernacle and the altar, and fill
it with water. 19Aaron and his sons shall wash
their hands and feet there, 20when they go
into the Tabernacle to appear before the Lord,
or when they approach the altar to burn offerings to the Lord. They must always wash
before doing so, or they will die. 21These are
instructions to Aaron and his sons from generation to generation.”
22,23Then the Lord told Moses to collect the
choicest of spices—eighteen pounds of pure
myrrh; half as much of cinnamon and of
sweet cane; 24the same amount of cassia as of
myrrh; and 1½ gallons of olive oil. 25The Lord
instructed skilled perfumemakers to compound all this into a holy anointing oil.
26,27“Use this,” he said, “to anoint the Tabernacle, the Ark, the table and all its instruments, the lampstand and all its utensils, the
incense altar, 28the burnt offering altar with
all its instruments, and the washbasin and its
pedestal. 29Sanctify them, to make them
holy; whatever touches them shall become
holy. 30Use it to anoint Aaron and his sons,
sanctifying them so that they can minister to
me as priests. 31And say to the people of
Israel, ‘This shall always be my holy anointing oil. 32It must never be poured upon an
ordinary person, and you shall never make
any of it yourselves, for it is holy, and it shall
be treated by you as holy. 33Anyone who
compounds any incense like it or puts any of

30:1-10 As graphic and compelling as the sacrificial system was, it still could only provide temporary atonement and forgiveness. While these sacrifices and offerings served as beautiful pictures of the final sacrifice of Christ (John 1:29), they could not provide permanent forgiveness. Only through faith in Christ is such forgiveness possible.

it upon someone who is not a priest shall be
excommunicated.'"
34These were the Lord's directions to Moses
concerning the incense: "Use sweet spices—
stacte, onycha, galbanum, and pure frankincense, weighing out the same amounts of
each, 35using the usual techniques of the in-
censemaker, and seasoning it with salt; it shall
be a pure and holy incense. 36Beat some of it
very fine and put some of it in front of the Ark
where I meet with you in the Tabernacle; this
incense is most holy. 37Never make it for yourselves, for it is reserved for the Lord and you
must treat it as holy. 38Anyone making it for
himself shall be excommunicated."

CHAPTER 31
Workmen with Special Skills
The Lord also said to Moses, "See, I have
appointed Bezalel (son of Uri, and grandson
of Hur, of the tribe of Judah), 3and have filled
him with the Spirit of God, giving him great
wisdom, ability, and skill in constructing the
Tabernacle and everything it contains. 4He is
highly capable as an artistic designer of objects made of gold, silver, and bronze. 5He is
skilled, too, as a jeweler and in carving wood.
6"And I have appointed Oholiab (son of
Ahisamach of the tribe of Dan) to be his
assistant; moreover, I have given special skill
to all who are known as experts, so that they
can make all the things I have instructed you
to make: 7the Tabernacle; the Ark with the
place of mercy upon it; all the furnishings of
the Tabernacle; 8the table and its instruments;
the pure gold lampstand with its instruments;
the altar of incense; 9the burnt offering altar
with its instruments; the laver and its pedestal; 10the beautifully made, holy garments for
Aaron the priest, and the garments for his
sons, so that they can minister as priests; 11the
anointing oil; and the sweet-spice incense for
the Holy Place. They are to follow exactly the
directions I gave you."

Resting on the Sabbath
12,13The Lord then gave these further instructions to Moses: "Tell the people of Israel to
rest on my Sabbath day, for the Sabbath is a
reminder of the covenant between me and
you forever; it helps you to remember that I
am Jehovah who makes you holy. 14,15Yes, rest
on the Sabbath, for it is holy. Anyone who
does not obey this command must die; anyone who does any work on that day shall be
killed. 16,17Work six days only, for the seventh
day is a special day to remind you of my
covenant—a weekly reminder forever of my
promises to the people of Israel. For in six
days the Lord made heaven and earth, and
rested on the seventh day, and was refreshed."
18Then, as God finished speaking with Moses on Mount Sinai, he gave him the two
tablets of stone on which the Ten Commandments were written with the finger of God.

CHAPTER 32
The Golden Calf
When Moses didn't come back down the
mountain right away, the people went to
Aaron. "Look," they said, "make us a god to
lead us, for this fellow Moses who brought us
here from Egypt has disappeared; something
must have happened to him."
2,3"Give me your gold earrings," Aaron replied.
So they all did—men and women, boys and
girls. 4Aaron melted the gold, then molded
and tooled it into the form of a calf. The
people exclaimed, "O Israel, this is the god
that brought you out of Egypt!"
5When Aaron saw how happy the people
were about it, he built an altar before the calf
and announced, "Tomorrow there will be a
feast to Jehovah!"
6So they were up early the next morning
and began offering burnt offerings and peace
offerings to the calf-idol; afterwards they sat
down to feast and drink at a wild party, followed by sexual immorality.
7Then the Lord told Moses, "Quick! Go on

31:12-17 Keeping the weekly Sabbath was to become a regular rhythm in the lives of the Israelites. This day was set apart for God as a day of special worship, and for the people as a day of rest. In modern society the weekend is often considered a time to get away from our work. But we often fail to set aside a day for God as he intended. As we look forward to Sunday, let us look for ways to make it holy unto God as well as spiritually refreshing for us.

32:1-20 Israel shattered the second commandment by making the golden calf. God had clearly said, "You shall not make yourselves any idols" (20:4-6). Weak-kneed Aaron tried to put a good face on this blasphemy, but to no avail. The people's behavior represented a wholesale turning from their previously professed faith and commitment to God. This incident contains a warning to those who believe they have progressed so far in recovery that they are immune to failure (see 1 John 5:21). No matter how far we have come, we are never safe from the danger of a relapse.

down, for your people that you brought from
Egypt have defiled themselves, 8and have
quickly abandoned all my laws. They have
molded themselves a calf, and worshiped it,
and sacrificed to it, and said, 'This is your god,
O Israel, that brought you out of Egypt.'"
9Then the Lord said, "I have seen what a
stubborn, rebellious lot these people are.
10Now let me alone and my anger shall blaze
out against them and destroy them all; and I
will make you, Moses, into a great nation
instead of them."
11But Moses begged God not to do it.
"Lord," he pleaded, "why is your anger so hot
against your own people whom you brought
from the land of Egypt with such great power
and mighty miracles? 12Do you want the
Egyptians to say, 'God tricked them into coming to the mountains so that he could slay
them, destroying them from off the face of
the earth'? Turn back from your fierce wrath.
Turn away from this terrible evil you are planning against your people! 13Remember your
promise to your servants—to Abraham, Isaac,
and Israel. For you swore by your own self, 'I
will multiply your posterity as the stars of
heaven, and I will give them all of this land I
have promised to your descendants, and they
shall inherit it forever.'"
14So the Lord changed his mind and spared
them.
15Then Moses went down the mountain,
holding in his hands the Ten Commandments written on both sides of two stone
tablets. 16(God himself had written the commandments on the tablets.)
17When Joshua heard the noise below
them, of all the people shouting, he exclaimed to Moses, "It sounds as if they are
preparing for war!"
18But Moses replied, "No, it's not a cry of
victory or defeat, but singing."
19When they came near the camp, Moses
saw the calf and the dancing, and in terrible
anger he threw the tablets to the ground, and
they lay broken at the foot of the mountain.
20He took the calf and melted it in the fire, and
when the metal cooled, he ground it into
powder and spread it upon the water and
made the people drink it.
21Then he turned to Aaron. "What in the
world did the people do to you," he demanded, "to make you bring such a terrible
sin upon them?"
22"Don't get so upset," Aaron replied. "You
know these people and what a wicked bunch
they are. 23They said to me, 'Make us a god to
lead us, for something has happened to this
fellow Moses who led us out of Egypt.' 24Well,
I told them, 'Bring me your gold earrings.' So
they brought them to me and I threw them
into the fire, and . . . well . . . this calf came
out!"
25When Moses saw that the people had
been committing adultery—at Aaron's encouragement, and much to the amusement of
their enemies— 26he stood at the camp entrance and shouted, "All of you who are on
the Lord's side, come over here and join me."
And all the Levites came.
27He told them, "Jehovah the God of Israel
says, 'Get your swords and go back and forth
from one end of the camp to the other and
kill even your brothers, friends, and neighbors.'" 28So they did, and about three thousand men died that day.
29Then Moses told the Levites, "Today you
have ordained yourselves for the service of
the Lord, for you obeyed him even though it
meant killing your own sons and brothers;
now he will give you a great blessing."
30The next day Moses said to the people,
"You have sinned a great sin, but I will return
to the Lord on the mountain—perhaps I will
be able to obtain his forgiveness for you."
31So Moses returned to the Lord and said,
"Oh, these people have sinned a great sin and
have made themselves gods of gold. 32Yet now

32:21-29 Aaron reveals himself to be a "people-pleaser." He caved in to the idolatrous desires of the Israelites to avoid confronting them with the sin in their lives. He also displayed a lack of honesty and an unwillingness to face the reality of his actions. To avoid his accountability to God and Moses he made a farfetched excuse for his behavior (32:22-24). The consequences of Aaron's failure were terrible, reaching far beyond his personal reprimand. Let us learn from Aaron's mistakes. We must defend and live out God's program, even when it is unpopular with the crowd. If we don't, the consequences for both us and the people around us could be terrible.

32:30-35 In the wake of their horrible idolatry, Moses took on the role of a loving father toward Israel. In seeking atonement and forgiveness for the people's sins, Moses asked God to hold back the terrible consequences; he even suggested that he take the punishment upon himself. It is difficult for many parents and leaders to see that some under their charge must learn responsibility by facing the full consequences of their wrong choices. In this case, God required that these disobedient people suffer the ultimate consequence—death.

if you will only forgive their sin—and if not, then blot *me* out of the book you have written."

33And the Lord replied to Moses, "Whoever has sinned against me will be blotted out of my book. 34And now go, lead the people to the place I told you about, and I assure you that my Angel shall travel on ahead of you; however, when I come to visit these people, I will punish them for their sins."

35And the Lord sent a great plague upon the people because they had worshiped Aaron's calf.

CHAPTER 33

The People Repent

The Lord said to Moses, "Lead these people you brought from Egypt to the land I promised Abraham, Isaac, and Jacob; for I said, 'I will give this land to your descendants.' 2I will send an Angel before you to drive out the Canaanites, Amorites, Hittites, Perizzites, Hivites, and Jebusites. 3It is a land 'flowing with milk and honey'; but I will not travel among you, for you are a stubborn, unruly people, and I would be tempted to destroy you along the way."

4When the people heard these stern words, they went into mourning and stripped themselves of their jewelry and ornaments.

5For the Lord had told Moses to tell them, "You are an unruly, stubborn people. If I were there among you for even a moment, I would exterminate you. Remove your jewelry and ornaments until I decide what to do with you." 6So, after that, they wore no jewelry.

The Tent of Meeting

7Moses always erected the sacred tent (the "Tent for Meeting with God," he called it) far outside the camp, and everyone who wanted to consult with Jehovah went out there.

8Whenever Moses went to the Tabernacle, all the people, when they saw it, stood and would rise and stand in their tent doors. 9As he entered, the pillar of cloud would come down and stand at the door while the Lord spoke with Moses. 10Then all the people worshiped from their tent doors, bowing low to the pillar of cloud. 11Inside the tent the Lord spoke to Moses face to face, as a man speaks to his friend. Afterwards Moses would return to the camp, but the young man who assisted him, Joshua (son of Nun), stayed behind in the Tabernacle.

Moses Asks to See God

12Moses talked there with the Lord and said to him, "You have been telling me, 'Take these people to the Promised Land,' but you haven't told me whom you will send with me. You say you are my friend, and that I have found favor before you; 13please, if this is really so, guide me clearly along the way you want me to travel so that I will understand you and walk acceptably before you. For don't forget that this nation is your people."

14And the Lord replied, "I myself will go with you and give you success."

15For Moses had said, "If you aren't going with us, don't let us move a step from this place. 16If you don't go with us, who will ever know that I and my people have found favor with you, and that we are different from any other people upon the face of the earth?"

17And the Lord had replied to Moses, "Yes, I will do what you have asked, for you have certainly found favor with me, and you are my friend."

18Then Moses asked to see God's glory.

19The Lord replied, "I will make my goodness pass before you, and I will announce to you the meaning of my name Jehovah, the Lord. I show kindness and mercy to anyone I want to. 20But you may not see the glory of my face, for man may not see me and live. 21However, stand here on this rock beside me. 22And when my glory goes by, I will put you in the

33:1-6 This display of emotion by God and the people's response is instructive. God reassured Israel that he would stand by his covenant commitments. He would give them the Promised Land and protect them through the time of its recovery. However, God became so angry with Israel due to their stubborn disobedience that he was forced to back away. After God had expressed his anger with self-control, the people underwent a heart-wrenching self-examination, truly mourning their sins and repenting before God. Even when we have failed miserably, we can be assured that God's promises of reconciliation will stand. All we need to do is go to God openly with our sins, seeking his help to find a new way of life.

33:12-23 When Moses asked to experience more of God's comforting presence and see his glory, he was not seeking to glorify himself. A clear vision of God is important for all of us to have. As we see him more clearly, we better understand who we are—strengths and limitations. This scene shows Moses growing spiritually in a remarkable way. All of us should seek to know God better and to experience his presence in our life.

cleft of the rock and cover you with my hand until I have passed. [23]Then I will remove my hand, and you shall see my back but not my face."

CHAPTER 34

Moses Speaks with God

The Lord told Moses, "Prepare two stone tablets like the first ones, and I will write upon them the same commands that were on the tablets you broke. [2]Be ready in the morning to come up into Mount Sinai and present yourself to me on the top of the mountain. [3]No one shall come with you and no one must be anywhere on the mountain. Do not let the flocks or herds feed close to the mountain."

[4]So Moses took two tablets of stone like the first ones, and was up early and climbed Mount Sinai, as the Lord had told him to, taking the two stone tablets in his hands.

[5,6]Then the Lord descended in the form of a pillar of cloud and stood there with him, and passed in front of him and announced the meaning of his name. "I am Jehovah, the merciful and gracious God," he said, "slow to anger and rich in steadfast love and truth. [7]I, Jehovah, show this steadfast love to many thousands by forgiving their sins; or else I refuse to clear the guilty, and require that a father's sins be punished in the sons and grandsons, and even later generations."

[8]Moses fell down before the Lord and worshiped. [9]And he said, "If it is true that I have found favor in your sight, O Lord, then please go with us to the Promised Land; yes, it is an unruly, stubborn people, but pardon our iniquity and our sins, and accept us as your own."

[10]The Lord replied, "All right, this is the contract I am going to make with you. I will do miracles such as have never been done before anywhere in all the earth, and all the people of Israel shall see the power of the Lord—the terrible power I will display through you.[11]Your part of the agreement is to obey all of my commandments; then I will drive out from before you the Amorites, Canaanites, Hittites, Perizzites, Hivites, and Jebusites.

[12]"Be very, very careful never to compromise with the people there in the land where you are going, for if you do, you will soon be following their evil ways. [13]Instead, you must break down their heathen altars, smash the obelisks they worship, and cut down their shameful idols. [14]For you must worship no other gods, but only Jehovah, for he is a God who claims absolute loyalty and exclusive devotion.

[15]"No, do not make a peace treaty of any kind with the people living in the land, for they are spiritual prostitutes, committing adultery against me by sacrificing to their gods. If you become friendly with them and one of them invites you to go with him and worship his idol, you are apt to do it. [16]And you would accept their daughters, who worship other gods, as wives for your sons—and then your sons would commit adultery against me by worshiping their wives' gods. [17]You must have nothing to do with idols.

[18]"Be sure to celebrate the Feast of Unleavened Bread for seven days, just as I instructed you, at the dates appointed each year in March; that was the month you left Egypt.

[19]"Every firstborn male is mine—cattle, sheep, and goats. [20]The firstborn colt of a donkey may be redeemed by giving a lamb in its place. If you decide not to redeem it, then its neck must be broken. But your sons must all be redeemed. And no one shall appear before me without a gift.

[21]"Even during plowing and harvest times, work only six days, and rest on the seventh.

[22]"And you must remember to celebrate these three annual religious festivals: the Festival of Weeks, the Festival of the First Wheat, and the Harvest Festival. [23]On each of these three occasions all the men and boys of Israel shall appear before the Lord. [24]No one will attack and conquer your land when you go up

---

34:1-4 In spite of the horrible sin that the people of Israel had committed in building the golden calf (see 32:1-35), God was willing to give them another chance to commit themselves to him and obey his covenant. When Moses came down from Mount Sinai the first time, he smashed the tablets inscribed with the Ten Commandments (32:19). Now God displayed his great and undeserved grace (34:6) by rewriting the tablets for his people. Our failures can never be so great that God's forgiveness becomes impossible.

34:5-7 When God anounced the meaning of his name to Moses, he was explaining who he was. In ancient cultures the meaning of a person's name was understood to be a window into his character, not just a surface title. As we commit ourselves to God and let him change us, it is important that we get to know God's character. He is compassionate, gracious, patient, loving, trustworthy, forgiving, and just.

to appear before the Lord your God those
three times each year. For I will drive out the
nations from before you and enlarge your
boundaries.
25“You must not use leavened bread with
your sacrifices to me, and none of the meat of
the Passover lamb may be kept over until the
following morning. 26And you must bring the
best of the first of each year’s crop to the
Tabernacle of the Lord your God. You must
not cook a young goat in its mother’s milk.”
27And the Lord said to Moses, “Write down
these laws that I have given you, for they
represent the terms of my covenant with you
and with Israel.”
28Moses was up on the mountain with the
Lord for forty days and forty nights, and in all
that time he neither ate nor drank. At that
time God wrote out the Covenant—the Ten
Commandments—on the stone tablets.
29Moses didn’t realize as he came back
down the mountain with the tablets that his
face glowed from being in the presence of
God. 30Because of this radiance upon his face,
Aaron and the people of Israel were afraid to
come near him.
31But Moses called them over to him, and
Aaron and the leaders of the congregation
came and talked with him. 32Afterwards, all
the people came to him, and he gave them
the commandments the Lord had given him
upon the mountain. 33When Moses had finished speaking with them, he put a veil over
his face; 34but whenever he went into the
Tabernacle to speak with the Lord, he removed the veil until he came out again; then
he would pass on to the people whatever
instructions God had given him, 35and the
people would see his face aglow. Afterwards
he would put the veil on again until he returned to speak with God.

CHAPTER 35
Gifts for the Tabernacle
Now Moses called a meeting of all the people
and told them, “These are the laws of Jehovah
you must obey.
2“Work six days only; the seventh day is a
day of solemn rest, a holy day to be used to
worship Jehovah; anyone working on that
day must die. 3Don’t even light the fires in
your homes that day.”
4Then Moses said to all the people, “This is
what the Lord has commanded: 5-9All of you
who wish to, all those with generous hearts,
may bring these offerings to Jehovah:

Gold, silver, and bronze;
Blue, purple, and scarlet cloth, made of fine-twined linen or of goats’ hair;
Tanned rams’ skins and specially treated goatskins;
Acacia wood;
Olive oil for the lamps;
Spices for the anointing oil and for the incense;
Onyx stones and stones to be used for the ephod and chestpiece.

10-19“Come, all of you who are skilled craftsmen having special talents, and construct
what God has commanded us:

The Tabernacle tent, and its coverings, clasps, frames, bars, pillars, and bases;
The Ark and its poles;
The place of mercy;
The curtain to enclose the Holy Place;
The table, its carrying poles, and all of its utensils;
The Bread of the Presence;
Lamp holders, with lamps and oil;
The incense altar and its carrying poles;
The anointing oil and sweet incense;
The curtain for the door of the Tabernacle;
The altar for the burnt offerings;
The bronze grating of the altar, and its carrying poles and utensils;
The basin with its pedestal;
The drapes for the walls of the court;
The pillars and their bases;
Drapes for the entrance to the court;
The posts of the Tabernacle court, and their cords;
The beautiful clothing for the priests, to

34:29-35 Moses’ experience in God’s presence was a transforming one. God’s holy presence was so radiant that it caused Moses’ face to glow. The physical glow on his face was only part of the result of drawing so close to God. This experience gave Moses the faith he needed to continue leading the Israelites through the wilderness. Drawing close to God should also provide us with the strength we need to make it through our wilderness experiences.
35:4-9, 20-29 This freewill offering was given by the Israelites to show their commitment to God. Many of the other sacrifices and offerings in the laws of Moses were mandatory. They were required, almost like paying taxes. The freewill offering was completely voluntary and was to be used to build and finance the Tabernacle. All the people joyfully gave and in so doing, selflessly served God and each other.

be used when ministering in the Holy
Place;
The holy garments for Aaron the priest,
and for his sons."

20 So all the people went to their tents to
prepare their gifts. 21 Those whose hearts were
stirred by God's Spirit returned with their
offerings of materials for the Tabernacle, its
equipment, and for the holy garments. 22 Both
men and women came, all who were willing-
hearted. They brought to the Lord their offerings of gold, jewelry—earrings, rings from
their fingers, necklaces—and gold objects of
every kind. 23 Others brought blue, purple, and
scarlet cloth made from the fine-twined linen
or goats' hair; and rams' skins dyed red, and
specially treated goatskins. 24 Others brought
silver and bronze as their offering to the Lord;
and some brought the acacia wood needed in
the construction.

25 The women skilled in sewing and spinning prepared blue, purple, and scarlet thread
and cloth, and fine-twined linen, and
brought them in. 26 Some other women gladly
used their special skill to spin the goats' hair
into cloth. 27 The leaders brought onyx stones
to be used for the ephod and the chestpiece;
28 and spices, and oil—for the light, and for
compounding the anointing oil and the sweet
incense. 29 So the people of Israel—every man
and woman who wanted to assist in the work
given to them by the Lord's command to
Moses—brought their freewill offerings to
him.

30,31 And Moses told them, "Jehovah has specifically appointed Bezalel (the son of Uri and
grandson of Hur of the tribe of Judah) as
general superintendent of the project. 32 He
will be able to create beautiful workmanship
from gold, silver, and bronze; 33 he can cut and
set stones like a jeweler and can do beautiful
carving; in fact, he has every needed skill.
34 And God has made him and Oholiab gifted
teachers of their skills to others. (Oholiab is
the son of Ahisamach, of the tribe of Dan.)
35 God has filled them both with unusual skills
as jewelers, carpenters, embroidery designers
in blue, purple, and scarlet on linen backgrounds, and as weavers—they excel in all the
crafts we will be needing in the work.

CHAPTER 36
"All the other craftsmen with God-given abilities are to assist Bezalel and Oholiab in constructing and furnishing the Tabernacle." So
Moses told Bezalel and Oholiab and all others
who felt called to the work to begin. 3 Moses
gave them the materials donated by the
people and additional gifts were received each
morning.

4-7 But finally the workmen all left their task
to meet with Moses and told him, "We have
more than enough materials on hand now to
complete the job!" So Moses sent a message
throughout the camp announcing that no
more donations were needed. Then at last the
people were restrained from bringing more!

Preparation for Building

8,9 The skilled weavers first made ten sheets
from fine linen, then embroidered into them
blue, purple, and scarlet Guardian Angels.
Each sheet was 42 feet long and 6 feet wide.
10 Five of these sheets were attached end to
end, then five others similarly attached, forming two long roofsheets. 11,12 Fifty blue ribbons
were looped along the edges of these two long
sheets, each loop being opposite its mate on
the other long sheet. 13 Then fifty clasps of gold
were made to connect the loops, thus tying
the two long sheets together to form the ceiling of the Tabernacle.

14,15 Above the ceiling was a second layer
formed by eleven draperies made of goats'
hair (uniformly 45 feet long and 6 feet wide).
16 Bezalel coupled five of these draperies together to make one long piece, and six others
to make another long piece. 17 Then he made
fifty loops along the end of each 18 and fifty
small bronze clasps to couple the loops so that
the draperies were firmly attached to each
other.

19 The top layer of the roof was made of
rams' skins, dyed red, and tanned goatskins.

20 For the sides of the Tabernacle he used
frames of acacia wood standing on end. 21 The
height of each frame was 15 feet and the
width 2 1/4 feet. 22 Each frame had two clasps
joining it to the next. 23 There were twenty
frames on the south side, 24 with the bottoms
fitting into forty silver bases. Each frame was
connected to its base by two clasps. 25,26 There

35:30–36:3 People who are greatly gifted need to have a clear sense of their identity. Often such people can be described as either self-glorifying or self-deprecating. Neither is a healthy or accurate self-assessment, and neither is pleasing to God. There should be no sense of superiority or inferiority among God's people, since every member plays a unique and important role (1 Corinthians 12:12-27).

were also twenty frames on the north side of the Tabernacle, with forty silver bases, two for each frame. 27The west side of the Tabernacle, which was its rear, was made from six frames, 28plus another at each corner. 29These frames, including those at the corners, were linked to each other at both top and bottom by rings. 30So, on the west side, there were a total of eight frames with sixteen silver bases beneath them, two for each frame.

31,32Then he made five sets of bars from acacia wood to tie the frames together along the sides, five for each side of the Tabernacle. 33The middle bar of the five was halfway up the frames, along each side, running from one end to the other. 34The frames and bars were all overlaid with gold, and the rings were pure gold.

35The blue, purple, and scarlet inner curtain was made from woven linen, with Guardian Angels skillfully embroidered into it. 36The curtain was then attached to four gold hooks set into four posts of acacia wood, overlaid with gold and set into four silver bases.

37Then he made a drapery for the entrance to the Tabernacle; it was woven from finespun linen, embroidered with blue, purple, and scarlet. 38This drapery was connected by five hooks to five posts. The posts and their capitals and rods were overlaid with gold; their five bases were molded from bronze.

CHAPTER 37

Making the Ark

Next Bezalel made the Ark. This was constructed of acacia wood and was $3\frac{3}{4}$ feet long, $2\frac{1}{4}$ feet wide, and $2\frac{1}{4}$ feet high. 2It was plated with pure gold inside and out, and had a molding of gold all the way around the sides. 3There were four gold rings fastened into its four feet, two rings at each end. 4Then he made poles from acacia wood, and overlaid them with gold, 5and put the poles into the rings at the sides of the Ark, to carry it.

6Then, from pure gold, he made a lid called "the place of mercy"; it was $3\frac{3}{4}$ feet long and $2\frac{1}{4}$ feet wide. 7He made two statues of Guardian Angels of beaten gold and placed them at the two ends of the gold lid. 8They were molded so that they were actually a part of the gold lid—it was all one piece. 9The Guardian Angels faced each other, with outstretched wings that overshadowed the place of mercy, looking down upon it.

10Then he made a table, using acacia wood, 3 feet long, $1\frac{1}{2}$ feet wide, and $2\frac{1}{4}$ feet high. 11It was overlaid with pure gold, with a gold molding all around the edge. 12A rim 4 inches high was constructed around the edges of the table, with a gold molding along the rim. 13Then he cast four rings of gold and placed them into the four table legs, 14close to the molding, to hold the carrying poles in place. 15He made the carrying poles of acacia wood covered with gold. 16Next, using pure gold, he made the bowls, flagons, dishes, and spoons to be placed upon this table.

Making the Lampstand

17Then he made the lampstand, again using pure, beaten gold. Its base, shaft, lamp-holders, and decorations of almond flowers were all of one piece. 18The lampstand had six branches, three from each side. 19Each of the branches was decorated with identical carvings of blossoms. 20,21The main stem of the lampstand was similarly decorated with almond blossoms, a flower on the stem beneath each pair of branches; also a flower below the bottom pair and above the top pair, four in all. 22The decorations and branches were all one piece of pure, beaten gold. 23,24Then he made the seven lamps at the ends of the branches, the snuffers, and the ashtrays, all of pure gold. The entire lampstand weighed 107 pounds, all pure gold.

Making the Incense Altar

25The incense altar was made of acacia wood. It was 18 inches square and 3 feet high, with its corner-horns made as part of the altar so that it was all one piece. 26He overlaid it all with pure gold and ran a gold molding around the edge. 27Two gold rings were placed on each side, beneath this molding, to hold the carrying poles. 28The carrying poles were gold-plated acacia wood.

29Then, from sweet spices, he made the sacred oil for anointing the priests, and the

37:1-9 High expectations are difficult for anyone to cope with, even for people with a great deal of ability. It is quite common for supremely gifted people to never approach their potential because they fear failure. The craftsman Bezalel did not allow the high expectations laid upon him to hinder his work. Because God had filled him with his Spirit and given him unusual skills, he willingly used his gifts to glorify God, not only in building the Tabernacle, but also in teaching others. Bezalel's life is a good example for us to live by today.

pure incense, using the techniques of the
most skilled perfumers.

CHAPTER 38
Making the Burnt Offering Altar
The burnt-offering altar was also constructed
of acacia wood; it was 7 1/2 feet square at the
top, and 4 1/2 feet high. 2There were four horns
at the four corners, all of one piece with the
rest. This altar was overlaid with bronze.
3Then he made bronze utensils to be used
with the altar—the pots, shovels, basins, meat
hooks, and fire pans. 4Next he made a bronze
grating that rested upon a ledge about halfway up [in the firebox]. 5Four rings were cast
for each side of the grating, to insert the
carrying poles. 6The carrying poles themselves
were made of acacia wood, overlaid with
bronze. 7The carrying poles were inserted into
the rings at the side of the altar. The altar was
hollow, with plank siding.
8The bronze washbasin and its bronze pedestal were cast from the solid bronze mirrors
donated by the women who assembled at the
entrance to the Tabernacle.

Building the Courtyard
9Then he constructed the courtyard. The
south wall was 150 feet long; it consisted of
drapes woven from fine-twined linen thread.
10There were twenty posts to hold drapes,
with bases of bronze and with silver hooks
and rods. 11The north wall was also 150 feet
long, with twenty bronze posts and bases and
with silver hooks and rods. 12The west side
was 75 feet wide; the walls were made from
drapes supported by ten posts and bases, and
with silver hooks and rods. 13The east side was
also 75 feet wide.
14,15The drapes at either side of the entrance
were 22 1/2 feet wide, each with three posts and
three bases. 16All the drapes making up the
walls of the court were woven of fine-twined
linen. 17Each post had a bronze base, and all
the hooks and rods were silver; the tops of the
posts were overlaid with silver, and the rods
to hold up the drapes were solid silver.
18The drapery covering the entrance to the
court was made of fine-twined linen, beautifully embroidered with blue, purple, and scarlet thread.
It was 30 feet long and 7 1/2 feet wide, just
the same as the drapes composing the walls of
the court. 19It was supported by four posts,
with four bronze bases and with silver hooks
and rods; the tops of the posts were also silver.
20All the nails used in constructing the Tabernacle and court were bronze.
21This summarizes the various steps in
building the Tabernacle to house the Ark, so
that the Levites could carry on their ministry.
All was done in the order designated by Moses
and was supervised by Ithamar, son of Aaron
the priest. 22Bezalel (son of Uri and grandson
of Hur, of the tribe of Judah) was the master
craftsman, 23assisted by Oholiab (son of Ahisamach of the tribe of Dan); he too was a
skilled craftsman and also an expert at engraving, weaving, and at embroidering blue,
purple, and scarlet threads into fine linen
cloth.

The Materials Used
24The people brought gifts of 3,140 pounds of
gold, all of which was used throughout the
Tabernacle.
25,26The amount of silver used was 9,575
pounds, which came from the fifty-cent head
tax collected from all those registered in the
census who were twenty years old or older, a
total of 603,550 men. 27The bases for the
frames of the sanctuary walls and for the posts
supporting the veil required 9,500 pounds of
silver, 95 pounds for each socket. 28The silver
left over was used for the posts and to overlay
their tops, and for the rods and hooks.
29-31The people brought 7,540 pounds of
bronze, which was used for casting the bases
for the posts at the entrance to the Tabernacle, and for the bronze altar, the bronze grating, the altar utensils, the bases for the posts
supporting the drapes enclosing the court,
and for all the nails used in the construction
of the Tabernacle and the court.

CHAPTER 39
Making the Priest's Clothing
Then, for the priests, the people made beautiful garments of blue, purple, and scarlet
cloth—garments to be used while ministering
in the Holy Place. This same cloth was used
for Aaron's sacred garments, in accordance

38:21-31 The dollar value of the gold, silver, bronze, and other materials used to build the Tabernacle would be mind-boggling. But the value of the materials used does not reflect empty extravagance or showiness. It only illustrates how precious and invaluable the presence of God really is. We can see here that the people's faith had surpassed the point of hanging on to material things. They were beginning to learn to trust God as they shared the wealth that insured their future security.

with the Lord's instructions to Moses. 2The
ephod was made from this cloth too, woven
from fine-twined linen thread. 3Bezalel beat
gold into thin plates and cut it into wire
threads, to work into the blue, purple, and
scarlet linen; it was a skillful and beautiful
piece of workmanship when finished.

4,5The ephod was held together by shoulder
straps at the top and was tied down by an
elaborate one-piece woven sash made of the
same gold, blue, purple, and scarlet cloth cut
from fine-twined linen thread, just as God
had directed Moses. 6,7The [two] onyx stones,
attached to the [two] shoulder straps of the
ephod, were set in gold, and the stones were
engraved with the names of the tribes of Israel, just as initials are engraved upon a ring.
These stones were reminders to Jehovah concerning the people of Israel; all this was done
in accordance with the Lord's instructions to
Moses.

8The chestpiece was a beautiful piece of
work, just like the ephod, made from the
finest gold, blue, purple, and scarlet linen. 9It
was a piece nine inches square, doubled over
to form a pouch; 10there were four rows of
stones across it. In the first row were a sardius,
a topaz, and a carbuncle; 11in the second row
were an emerald, a sapphire, and a diamond.
12In the third row were a jacinth, an agate, and
an amethyst. 13In the fourth row, a beryl, an
onyx, and a jasper—all set in gold filigree.
14The stones were engraved like a seal, with
the names of the twelve tribes of Israel.

15-18[To attach the chestpiece to the ephod],
a gold ring was placed at the top of each
shoulder strap of the ephod, and from these
gold rings, two strands of twined gold attached to gold clasps on the top corners of the
chestpiece. 19Two gold rings were also set at
the lower edge of the chestpiece, on the under
side, next to the ephod. 20Two other gold rings
were placed low on the shoulder straps of the
ephod, close to where the ephod joined its
beautifully woven sash. 21The chestpiece was
held securely above the beautifully woven
sash of the ephod by tying the rings of the
chestpiece to the rings of the ephod with a
blue ribbon.

All this was commanded to Moses by the
Lord.

22The main part of the ephod was woven,
all of blue, 23and there was a hole at the center,
just as in a coat of mail, for the head to go
through, reinforced around the edge so that it
would not tear. 24Pomegranates were attached
to the bottom edge of the robe; these were
made of linen cloth, embroidered with blue,
purple, and scarlet. 25,26Bells of pure gold were
placed between the pomegranates along the
bottom edge of the skirt, with bells and pomegranates alternating all around the edge. This
robe was worn when Aaron ministered to the
Lord, just as the Lord had commanded Moses.

27Robes were now made for Aaron and his
sons from fine-twined linen thread. 28,29The
chestpiece, the beautiful turbans, and the
caps and the underclothes were all made of
this linen, and the linen belt was beautifully
embroidered with blue, purple, and scarlet
threads, just as Jehovah had commanded Moses. 30Finally, they made the holy plate of pure
gold to wear on the front of the turban, engraved with the words, "Consecrated to
Jehovah." 31It was tied to the turban with a
blue cord, just as the Lord had instructed.

32And so at last the Tabernacle was finished,
following all of the Lord's instructions to Moses.

Moses Inspects the Work

33-40Then they brought the entire Tabernacle
to Moses:

Furniture; clasps; frames; bars;
Posts; bases; layers of covering for the
roof and sides—the rams' skins dyed
red, the specially tanned goatskins, and
the entrance drape; the Ark with the
Ten Commandments in it;
The carrying poles;
The place of mercy;
The table and all its utensils;
The Bread of the Presence;
The pure [gold] lampstand with its lamps,
utensils, and oil;
The gold altar;
The anointing oil;
The sweet incense;
The curtain-door of the Tabernacle;
The bronze altar;
The bronze grating;
The poles and the utensils;

39:1-31 The priestly garments were ornate and detailed, in accordance with God's instructions to Moses. The intricate details point to the fact that the priest was to be holy—set apart for God (39:30). The death of Christ made it possible for all believers to be priests (1 Peter 2:9), for we are to be holy and pure, committed to God in everything we do. Like the priestly garments, our actions need to reflect externally what we are on the inside through Christ—holy and set apart.

The washbasin and its base;
The drapes for the walls of the court and the posts holding them up;
The bases and the drapes at the gate of the court;
The cords and nails;
All the utensils used there in the work of the Tabernacle.

41They also brought for his inspection the beautifully tailored garments to be worn while ministering in the Holy Place and the holy garments for Aaron the priest, and those for his sons, to be worn when on duty.

42So the people of Israel followed all the Lord's instructions to Moses. 43And Moses inspected all their work and blessed them because it was all as the Lord had instructed him.

CHAPTER 40

The Tabernacle Is Built

The Lord now said to Moses, 2"Put together the Tabernacle on the first day of the first month. 3In it place the Ark containing the Ten Commandments; and install the veil to enclose the Ark within the Holy of Holies. 4Then bring in the table and place the utensils on it, and bring in the lampstand and light the lamps.

5"Place the gold altar for the incense in front of the Ark. Set up the drapes at the entrance of the Tabernacle, 6and place the altar for burnt offerings in front of the entrance. 7Set the washbasin between the Tabernacle-tent and the altar, and fill it with water. 8Then make the courtyard around the outside of the tent, and hang the curtain-door at the entrance to the courtyard.

9"Take the anointing oil and sprinkle it here and there upon the Tabernacle and everything in it, upon all of its utensils and parts, and all the furniture, to hallow it; and it shall become holy. 10Sprinkle the anointing oil upon the altar of burnt offering and its utensils, sanctifying it; for the altar shall then become most holy. 11Then anoint the washbasin and its pedestal, sanctifying it.

12"Now bring Aaron and his sons to the entrance of the Tabernacle and wash them with water; 13and clothe Aaron with the holy garments and anoint him, sanctifying him to minister to me as a priest. 14Then bring his sons and put their robes upon them, 15and anoint them as you did their father, that they may minister to me as priests; their anointing shall be permanent from generation to generation: all their children and children's children shall forever be my priests."

16So Moses proceeded to do all as the Lord had commanded him. 17On the first day of the first month, in the second year, the Tabernacle was put together. 18Moses erected it by setting its frames into their bases and attaching the bars. 19Then he spread the coverings over the framework and put on the top layers, just as the Lord had commanded him.

20Inside the Ark he placed the stones with the Ten Commandments engraved on them, and attached the carrying poles to the Ark and installed the gold lid, the place of mercy. 21Then he brought the Ark into the Tabernacle and set up the curtain to screen it, just as the Lord had commanded.

22Next he placed the table at the north side of the room outside the curtain 23and set the Bread of the Presence upon the table before the Lord, just as the Lord had commanded.

24And he placed the lampstand next to the table, on the south side of the Tabernacle. 25Then he lighted the lamps before the Lord, following all the instructions, 26and placed the gold altar in the Tabernacle next to the curtain, 27and burned upon it the incense made from sweet spices, just as the Lord had commanded.

28He attached the curtain at the entrance of the Tabernacle, 29and placed the outside altar for the burnt offerings near the entrance, and offered upon it a burnt offering and a meal offering, just as the Lord had commanded him.

30Next he placed the washbasin between

39:33-43 The Tabernacle was completed, following all of God's instructions (39:32, 42-43). It had required a great deal of tedious work, but it all had been done God's way. This was not self-defeating perfectionism, or a substandard "good-enough-for-God" mentality. Rather, here was the melding of faith, commitment to God, and perseverance. Their successful building of the Tabernacle was dependent on their following God's program. A successful recovery is built upon the same principle.
40:1-33 Setting up the Tabernacle began a new life of worship for the Israelites. Undoubtedly, as with any large task, it took a great deal of patience and self-control to finish the job. This required that the Israelites delay their gratification, but it also made the victory celebration and worship all the more joyous. Sometimes recovery takes many years of delayed gratification, but in the end the joyous freedom we experience will be worth it.

the tent and the altar and filled it with water
so that the priests could use it for washing.
[31]Moses and Aaron and Aaron's sons washed
their hands and feet there. [32]Whenever they
walked past the altar to enter the Tabernacle,
they stopped and washed, just as the Lord had
commanded Moses.
[33]Then he erected the enclosure surrounding the tent and the altar, and set up the
curtain-door at the entrance of the enclosure.
So at last Moses finished the work.
[34]Then the cloud covered the Tabernacle
and the glory of the Lord filled it. [35]Moses was
not able to enter because the cloud was standing there, and the glory of the Lord filled the
Tabernacle. [36]Whenever the cloud lifted and
moved, the people of Israel journeyed onward, following it. [37]But if the cloud stayed,
they stayed until it moved. [38]The cloud rested
upon the Tabernacle during the daytime, and
at night there was fire in the cloud so that all
the people of Israel could see it.

This continued throughout all their journeys.

40:34-38 Israel could count on God's guiding presence in the Tabernacle all the way to the Promised Land. This new relationship to God provided the Israelites with the consistent challenge of self-examination and spiritual growth. Believers today follow Christ by faith, but those same challenges are present. God's guiding presence in our life should provide us with the strength and direction we need to progress in our recovery and spiritual growth.

insights FROM MOSES' LIFE

As we see in **Exodus 2:8-10,** God graciously allowed Moses to be raised by his real mother. Not only did that allow for his normal, healthy development, but it also gave Moses a true understanding of who he was—a Hebrew. Apparently the education he received in the Egyptian royal court never altered Moses' sense of identity with his people. As he grew to manhood, his desire to promote their freedom figured prominently.

In **Exodus 4:1-9** we see the series of miracles that God gave to Moses and the Israelites to bolster their faith in Moses' message and mission. God does not normally use such wondrous signs to strengthen our faith, but he has performed one miracle that should give us all the encouragement we need. He raised Jesus Christ from the dead, showing that he is no slave to the destruction of sin and death (1 Corinthians 15:1-6). This miracle should give us all faith in God's promises and hope in the Good News he offers.

In **Exodus 4:13-17** we see Moses as he tried desperately to escape God's call for his life. He didn't want to go back to Egypt as God's spokesman. He was apparently afraid to face the huge responsibility that this entailed. But God held Moses accountable to his divine plan. He laid out for Moses exactly how the mission in Egypt would be accomplished, despite Moses' presumed handicap. God has a special plan for each of us. If we let him, he will bring it to pass no matter what our weaknesses.

In **Exodus 4:29–5:3** Moses and Aaron approached the elders of Israel with God's message. This alone took a great deal of courage, but by taking the chance, they were able to encourage the elders to seek freedom from the Egyptians. In an even greater step of courage, they confronted Pharaoh, demanding that things be set straight. God's word to Moses and Aaron gave them the courage to act on behalf of others. Their courage also sparked courage in others, which, in turn, helped them take another step. Courage begets courage. Our own recovery, if properly shared, will inspire others to move forward as well. This, in turn, will strengthen us to move ahead even further.

In **Exodus 7:6-7** we are told that Moses was eighty years old and that Aaron was eighty-three at the time they confronted Pharaoh. The courage and faith demonstrated by Moses and Aaron despite the difficulties before them is doubly amazing when their age is considered. During this later season of life, most people try to avoid confrontations and other difficult challenges. But Moses and Aaron knowingly faced their trials head-on. Similar courage in the face of trials late in life is seen in the life of Daniel (see Daniel 6).

insights FROM PHARAOH'S LIFE

Egypt's pharaoh exemplified perfectly the persecutor-type personality. In **Exodus 5:3-9** we watch him as he bulldozed the legitimate boundaries of others to get his way. Then he failed to respond properly when he was honestly confronted about the way he was treating the Israelites. He became upset when Moses sought to set appropriate boundaries. Instead of examining himself, Pharaoh then accused the Israelites of being lazy and demanded even more of them. This kind of person is tough to deal with, but God proves here that people like this are no match for him.

In **Exodus 11:4-8** Moses warned Pharaoh of the final plague—the death of the firstborn. This plague would touch people from all levels of Egyptian society and their livestock as well. In ancient Egypt the role of the firstborn son was very important. And the firstborn sons affected by this plague included Pharaoh's son, who was heir to the Egyptian throne. It was this plague that finally helped Pharaoh to hit bottom—at least temporarily. It took this severe loss to get the attention of his hard heart. Let us learn from Pharaoh's mistake and face our problems while our losses are still recoverable. Continued denial can only lead to terrible suffering.

insights FROM ISRAEL'S EXODUS

In **Exodus 12:1-2** we watch as Israel began its escape from Egypt. The event of Israel's exodus from Egypt marked a turning point for Israel. God's people were giving up their life of slavery and turning to a new life of responsibility and freedom. It is possible to build a new life that is so markedly different that we can declare a new phase or season of life. Such a "declaration of newness" can provide a new sense of identity and can be a healthy boundary line, setting us apart from our past failures. At this point in their history the Israelites were declaring such a boundary line—a turning point. We may find it helpful to do the same thing, reinforcing the process of recovery in our life.

In **Exodus 12:3-13** we see that those who trusted God's promise and put the sacrificial blood over their doors were spared the loss of their firstborn sons. Similarly, we who have faith in the sacrifice of Jesus Christ, the ultimate Passover Lamb (1 Corinthians 5:5), are spared from eternal death (John 3:16). We also become brand new people in Christ (2 Corinthians 5:17). God initiates and maintains the necessary spiritual and emotional recovery processes in our life if we are willing to trust him to do it.

In **Exodus 13:19** we see that Joseph's bones made the journey to the Promised Land. Many years earlier Joseph had made his descendants promise that they would bring his body with them (Genesis 50:24-26). Joseph believed God's promise to Abraham that someday Canaan would belong to his descendants. Joseph was a godly example to his descendants, and here we see that he was remembered four hundred years after his death. Not everything in anyone's family history is negative. The good things should be remembered and treasured, even as the bad ones must be faced and dealt with.

In **Exodus 14:13-31** we see a great miracle take place! God opened up a dry path through the Red Sea for the people to cross. Notice that even with this amazing miracle the Israelites still had to respond in faith. They still had to walk between the massive walls of water that could have become a tidal wave at any moment. These steps of faith required commitment to God, and they surely resulted in the growth of the Israelites' faith. The miracles that God works in our life also require that we respond in faith, stepping out to receive all the blessings he desires for us.

insights DISCOVERED AT MOUNT SINAI

In **Exodus 19:12-23** we see that God set limits or boundaries beyond which the people of Israel, or even their livestock, were not to step. There was mortal danger for those who overstepped God's boundaries. The unauthorized approach into God's holy presence meant certain death. For us, the boundaries are not usually this clear. It is not so immediately obvious when one person violates the boundaries of another. But the consequences of violating these God-given boundaries can also be destructive. It is crucial for us to set personal boundaries as clearly and firmly as possible. We also need to respect the boundaries of others.

In **Exodus 20:18-20** we see the people of Israel as they shook with fear before God's holy presence. Fear is an emotion that can be either healthy or unhealthy. When we fear danger or the consequences of inappropriate actions, it is a helpful guide. But when fear is constant or overwhelming and not connected to reality, it is unhealthy. The fear of God can be defined as thoughtful reverence for God; it is certainly a healthy emotion, based on the reality of God's holiness. Fear of God should result in a vibrant faith and motivate us to act according to God's program for our life.

insights FROM GOD'S LAWS

In **Exodus 21:2-11** God showed concern for people in bondage and granted them a means of gaining their freedom. But as with any recovery situation involving a network of relationships, there were possible complications. Some people may have been affected adversely by the freeing of a slave and set out to stop the process. And when slaves were freed, they needed to learn some difficult lessons about living responsibly without a master to direct their thinking. In the recovery process, these same truths apply. Some of the people close to us may stand against our recovery because they benefit somehow from our bondage. Such obstacles must be overcome. We also need to learn to live responsibly and unselfishly as we begin our life of freedom.

In **Exodus 21:5-6** God offered each slave the option of becoming a slave for life. This idea of a "bond servant for life" by personal choice was used in the New Testament to illustrate the commitment we should have to Jesus Christ (Philippians 1:1). Being a slave to a loving and gracious master is a wonderful thing. It has been said that we are all slaves to something—material things, alcohol, drugs, or any number of things. But none of these masters is kind; they all sell us out to destruction. Only God truly loves his servants. He is the only Master worthy of our voluntary, lifelong devotion and service.

According to **Exodus 21:28-36,** we are not only accountable for our own actions, but also for everything we own. For example, the Israelites were required to control their animals so they couldn't damage the property of others. Even if the owners were not directly involved in an incident, they were still held accountable for the actions of their livestock or members of their household. This kind of mature accountability serves as the basis for a just and responsible society.

In **Exodus 23:20-26** God promised the Israelites the protection of his angel and the instructions necessary for living wisely as they journeyed toward the Promised Land. As we face recovery, God does the same for us. He is able to lead and protect us in ways we will never know about. And he has given us his Word, which contains instructions for living according to his program. If we do as he says and look to him for help, we will experience the fulfillment of his promises.

LEVITICUS

THE BIG PICTURE

A. A PROPER PERSPECTIVE THROUGH A TRUE UNDERSTANDING OF GOD (1:1–16:34).
  1. Worship through the Offerings (1:1–7:38)
     a. Contentment found through gratitude to God (1:1–3:17)
     b. Contentment found through complete cleansing by God (4:1–5:13)
     c. Restitution for wrongs committed against others (5:14–6:7)
     d. Other instructions for the offerings (6:8–7:38)
  2. The Roles of Leaders and People in the Offerings (8:1–15:33)
  3. The Completeness of God's Forgiveness—Day of Atonement (16:1-34)

B. A PROPER PERSPECTIVE THROUGH OBEDIENCE AND ACCOUNTABILITY TO GOD (17:1–27:34)

Rules . . . regulations . . . strange sacrifices—what could the God who requires such things be like? What relevance could these foreign laws possibly have for us? As we look closely at this lengthy list of rules and regulations, some comforting truths about our God and how he relates to us come through.

The book of Leviticus portrays a God who is awesome and holy; he is pure, clean, sinless, perfect. The numerous regulations given to the Israelites confirm this truth. The people needed to humbly obey God if they wanted to live in close fellowship with him. But despite God's holiness, he reaches out to broken, sinful people. He provided a way—even though a difficult one—for the Israelites to recover from their past failures through a system of laws and sacrifices.

We all know that "a picture is worth a thousand words." Leviticus is filled with powerful images—pictures that show us both God's gracious character and the terrible consequences of sin. Could there be a more striking reminder of God's grace than the realization that God allowed a suffering, sacrificial animal to take our place? Could there be a more powerful way for us to visualize the consequences of sin than to watch the bloody death of that animal, suffering on our behalf?

The laws and sacrifices in Leviticus help us to understand who God is—holy, but gracious and forgiving. They also foreshadow God's later provision of the perfect sacrifice—Jesus Christ. God calls us to obedience, but he knows that we are far from perfect. He provides the means for our recovery and cleansing through the sacrificial death of Jesus Christ. Victory comes as we regularly confess sin, worship God, and thank him for his forgiveness.

THE BOTTOM LINE

PURPOSE: To show that God desires to have personal fellowship with those who turn to him. Only through the channels of worship and personal obedience to God can we fully experience the cleansing and freedom he offers. AUTHOR: Moses. AUDIENCE: The people of Israel. DATE WRITTEN: Shortly after the events the book records, between 1445–1407 B.C. SETTING: Camped at Mount Sinai, the people of Israel are given God's special instructions. KEY VERSE: "For I am the Lord who brought you out of the land of Egypt to be your God. You must therefore be holy, for I am holy" (11:45). KEY PLACE: Mount Sinai. KEY PEOPLE: Moses and Aaron.

RECOVERY THEMES

God's Holy Character: When we focus on God's gracious character, it is easy to forget that he is also terrifying, holy, and awesome in power. He is far above us in his majesty and power, as well as in his actions and his thoughts. As the book of Leviticus reminds us of God's holy power, we should be comforted by the fact that there is nothing he cannot do. But God's holy distance never stops him from relating closely to his people. Though high above us, he is still intimately concerned with each one of us and our recovery.

God's Loving Character: Even the sacrifices, which are so graphically detailed in this book, are an extension of God's love toward each of us. Over and over we encounter the sinfulness of human individuals. We are also repeatedly reminded of the holiness of God's character. Because of the great chasm between God's holiness and our sinfulness, something was needed to bridge the gap so that we could relate to God. He graciously provided the sacrifices to bridge that gap, thus revealing his love for all people. This love was ultimately expressed when he sent his Son as a sacrifice to pay for our sins, making it possible for us to draw near to our holy God.

The Power of Symbolism: For thousands of years God had been working to draw his chosen people back into a relationship with himself. A few followed the true God, but the majority were drawn to false gods. With the sacrifices, God's people had a graphic symbol not only of the costly consequences of their sin, but also of how they were to relate to God. We all need symbols to remind us of important truths from God's Word.

Our Need for Grace: When we see the power and majesty of God in Leviticus, we are confronted with our powerlessness to do anything about our problem of sin. Just as the Israelites were powerless as slaves in Egypt, we are slaves to our human tendency toward sin and its destructive consequences. We need grace. We need help. So God, in his grace, set up a system of sacrifices that provided a means for our debts of sin to be paid.

CHAPTER 1

The Burnt Offering

The Lord now spoke to Moses from the Tabernacle, [2,3]and commanded him to give the following instructions to the people of Israel: "When you sacrifice to the Lord, use animals from your herds and flocks.

"If your sacrifice is to be an ox given as a burnt offering, use only a bull with no physical defects. Bring the animal to the entrance of the Tabernacle where the priests will accept your gift for the Lord. [4]The person bringing it is to lay his hand upon its head, and it then becomes his substitute: the death of the animal will be accepted by God instead of the death of the man who brings it, as the penalty for his sins. [5]The man shall then kill the animal there before the Lord, and Aaron's sons, the priests, will present the blood before the Lord, sprinkling it upon all sides of the altar at the entrance of the Tabernacle. [6,7]Then the priests will skin the animal and quarter it, and build a wood fire upon the altar, [8]and put the sections of the animal and its head and fat upon the wood. [9]The internal organs and the legs are to be washed, then the priests will burn them upon the altar, and they will be an acceptable burnt offering with which the Lord is pleased.

[10]"If the animal used as a burnt offering is a sheep or a goat, it too must be a male, and without any blemishes. [11]The man who brings it will kill it before the Lord on the north side of the altar, and Aaron's sons, the priests, will sprinkle its blood back and forth upon the altar. [12]Then the man will quarter it, and the priests will lay the pieces, with the head and the fat, on top of the wood on the altar. [13]But

---

1:1 The very first words of this book, "The Lord now spoke," reveal a God who seeks out and initiates relationships with people. Similar words are found in Genesis 3:9 (the same Hebrew word is used), where it says "the Lord God called" to Adam and Eve after they had disobeyed him and offered them a way of recovery from their sin. Through God's instructions in Exodus and Leviticus, God provided Israel with more elaborate "object lessons" to remind them of how much he had done for them. God is still calling to us today, offering forgiveness, hope, and restored fellowship with him.

1:2-3 The offerings in Leviticus 1–3 are voluntary acts of worship, involving the free will of the individual. While God emphasizes the importance of committing our life to him and provides ways for us to do that, we must choose to act; he does not violate our free will. By actively refusing or passively ignoring a relationship with God, we are choosing life without God's help and hope. The choice is ours!

the internal organs and the legs shall first be washed with water. Then the priests shall burn it all upon the altar as an offering to the Lord; for burnt offerings give much pleasure to the Lord.

14"If anyone wishes to use a bird as his burnt offering, he may choose either turtledoves or young pigeons. 15-17A priest will take the bird to the altar and wring off its head, and the blood shall be drained out at the side of the altar. Then the priest will remove the crop and the feathers and throw them on the east side of the altar with the ashes. Then, grasping it by the wings, he shall tear it apart, but not completely. And the priest shall burn it upon the altar, and the Lord will have pleasure in this sacrifice.

CHAPTER 2

The Grain Offering

"Anyone who wishes to sacrifice a grain offering to the Lord is to bring fine flour and is to pour olive oil and incense upon it. 2Then he is to take a handful, representing the entire amount, to one of the priests to burn, and the Lord will be fully pleased. 3The remainder of the flour is to be given to Aaron and his sons as their food; but all of it is counted as a holy burnt offering to the Lord.

4"If bread baked in the oven is brought as an offering to the Lord, it must be made from finely ground flour, baked with olive oil but without yeast. Wafers made without yeast and spread with olive oil may also be used as an offering. 5If the offering is something from the griddle, it shall be made of finely ground flour without yeast, and mingled with olive oil. 6Break it into pieces and pour oil upon it—it is a form of grain offering. 7If your offering is cooked in a pan, it too shall be made of fine flour mixed with olive oil.

8"However it is prepared—whether baked, fried, or grilled—you are to bring this grain offering to the priest and he shall take it to the altar to present it to the Lord.

9"The priests are to burn only a representative portion of the offering, but all of it will be fully appreciated by the Lord. 10The remainder belongs to the priests for their own use, but it is all counted as a holy burnt offering to the Lord.

11"Use no yeast with your offerings of flour; for no yeast or honey is permitted in burnt offerings to the Lord. 12You may offer yeast bread and honey as thanksgiving offerings at harvest time, but not as burnt offerings.

13"Every offering must be seasoned with salt, because the salt is a reminder of God's covenant.

14"If you are offering from the first of your harvest, remove the kernels from a fresh ear, crush and roast them, then offer them to the Lord. 15Put olive oil and incense on the offering, for it is a grain offering. 16Then the priests shall burn part of the bruised grain mixed with oil and all of the incense as a representative portion before the Lord.

CHAPTER 3

The Offering of Thanksgiving

"When anyone wants to give an offering of thanksgiving to the Lord, he may use either a bull or a cow, but the animal must be entirely without defect if it is to be offered to the Lord! 2The man who brings the animal shall lay his hand upon its head and kill it at the door of the Tabernacle. Then Aaron's sons shall throw the blood against the sides of the altar 3-5and shall burn before the Lord the fat that covers

---

2:1, 4, 14 The grain offering was to consist of *fine* flour or the *first* of the grain harvest. As an animal without defect was required for the other offerings, so the best of one's produce was to be offered here. God was reminding his people that he was worthy of more than just the leftovers; he deserved the best they could offer. God wanted their undivided devotion. In recovery, we cannot entrust ourselves to God halfheartedly. We need to give ourselves wholeheartedly over to him and his plan.

2:1-16 The grain offering (sometimes called the cereal or meal offering) is the only offering described here that does not involve a blood sacrifice. This offering was made up of the most common of daily foods. It symbolized that the offerer had surrendered his whole life to God in recognition of all that God had provided. The recovery process often involves moving from an unhealthy overdependence on some substance or person to a healthy dependence upon God. That commitment involves not only the giving of ourselves to God (the burnt offering), but also giving him the things of everyday life (the grain offering).

3:3-5 In ancient times the fat portions of the animal were considered the very best parts (Genesis 4:4; 45:18). As with the other offerings, God asked that the choice parts be reserved for him. This is a clear reminder that we need to bring our best to God, committing our life to him completely, no matter what the cost.

the inward parts, the two kidneys and the loin-fat on them, and the gall bladder. And it will give the Lord much pleasure.

6“If a goat or sheep is used as a thank-offering to the Lord, it must have no defect and may be either a male or female.

7,8“If it is a lamb, the man who brings it shall lay his hand upon its head and kill it at the entrance of the Tabernacle; the priests shall throw the blood against the sides of the altar, 9-11and shall offer upon the altar the fat, the tail removed close to the backbone, the fat covering the internal organs, the two kidneys with the loin-fat on them, and the gall bladder, as a burnt offering to the Lord.

12“If anyone brings a goat as his offering to the Lord, 13he shall lay his hand upon its head and kill it at the entrance of the Tabernacle. The priest shall throw its blood against the sides of the altar, 14and shall offer upon the altar, as a burnt offering to the Lord, the fat that covers the insides, 15,16the two kidneys and the loin-fat on them, and the gall bladder. This burnt offering is very pleasing to the Lord. All the fat is Jehovah's. 17This is a permanent law throughout your land, that you shall eat neither fat nor blood.”

CHAPTER 4

The Sin Offering

Then the Lord gave these further instructions to Moses:

2“Tell the people of Israel that these are the laws concerning anyone who unintentionally breaks any of my commandments. 3If a priest sins unintentionally and so brings guilt upon the people, he must offer a young bull without defect as a sin offering to the Lord. 4He shall bring it to the door of the Tabernacle, and shall lay his hand upon its head and kill it there before Jehovah. 5Then the priest shall take the animal's blood into the Tabernacle, 6and shall dip his finger in the blood and sprinkle it seven times before the Lord in front of the veil that bars the way to the Holy of Holies. 7Then the priest shall put some of the blood upon the horns of the incense altar before the Lord in the Tabernacle; the remainder of the blood shall be poured out at the base of the altar for burnt offerings, at the entrance to the Tabernacle. 8Then he shall take all the fat on the entrails, 9the two kidneys and the loin-fat on them, and the gall bladder, 10and shall burn them on the altar of burnt offering, just as in the case of a bull or cow sacrificed as a thank-offering. 11,12But the remainder of the young bull—the skin, meat, head, legs, internal organs, and intestines—shall be carried to a ceremonially clean place outside the camp—a place where the ashes are brought from the altar—and burned there on a wood fire.

13“If the entire nation of Israel sins without realizing it and does something that Jehovah has said not to do, all the people are guilty. 14When they realize it, they shall offer a young bull for a sin offering, bringing it to the Tabernacle 15where the leaders of the nation shall

---

3:3-5 We are told that the offering of thanksgiving would “give the Lord much pleasure.” God graciously established a way for the people to show their thanks, to give back some of the blessings he had bestowed upon them. Sometimes the way we live brings God a great deal of pain and causes separation from him. Our offerings of thanks to God are a special step toward reconciliation with him—they give him much joy. Reconciliation with God is an important step in our recovery and toward a life filled with joy.

3:1-17 The offering of thanksgiving (sometimes called the fellowship offering or peace offering) was brought to God as an expression of thanks for his blessings, healing, or help in difficult times. The Hebrew word for “peace” (*shalom*) is a rich term that includes the ideas of physical health, emotional well-being, spiritual wholeness, and material prosperity. The person bringing the offering of thanksgiving was expressing faith and thanks that God had provided what was lacking in his life. It was an act of praise that God had restored him to completeness and harmony with both God and other people. How can we thank God for the peace he has brought into our life?

4:2 The meaning of the word for *sin* here is “to miss the mark.” Romans 3:23 states that all of us have sinned and fallen short of God's glory. The Old and New Testament words for *sin* both emphasize the fact that it keeps us from experiencing the fullness of life that God wants us to enjoy. All of us have failed in some way, so God has provided a means for our healing and reconciliation. It is available to us through repentance and obedience to God's program for healthy living.

4:3 The sin offering was not only for the average Israelite; it was for the priests as well. Even Israel's High Priest was not exempt from sin and its consequences. The writer of Hebrews tells us that we have a sinless High Priest, Jesus, who is able to sympathize with our weaknesses (Hebrews 4:14-16). So we are to boldly approach God in prayer, that we may find mercy and grace to help us in our times of need.

lay their hands upon the animal's head and kill it before the Lord. 16Then the priest shall bring its blood into the Tabernacle, 17and shall dip his finger in the blood and sprinkle it seven times before the Lord, in front of the veil. 18Then he shall put blood upon the horns of the altar there in the Tabernacle before the Lord, and all the remainder of the blood shall be poured out at the base of the burnt offering altar, at the entrance to the Tabernacle. 19All the fat shall be removed and burned upon the altar. 20He shall follow the same procedure as for a sin offering; in this way the priest shall make atonement for the nation, and everyone will be forgiven. 21The priest shall then cart the young bull outside the camp and burn it there, just as though it were a sin offering for an individual, only this time it is a sin offering for the entire nation.

22"If one of the leaders sins without realizing it and is guilty of disobeying one of God's laws, 23as soon as it is called to his attention he must bring as his sacrifice a male goat without any physical defect. 24He shall lay his hand upon its head and kill it at the place where the burnt offerings are killed, and present it to the Lord. This is his sin offering. 25Then the priest shall take some of the blood of this sin offering and place it with his finger upon the horns of the altar of burnt offerings, and the rest of the blood shall be poured out at the base of the altar. 26All the fat shall be burned upon the altar, just as if it were the fat of the sacrifice of a thank-offering; thus the priest shall make atonement for the leader concerning his sin, and he shall be forgiven.

27"If any one of the common people sins and doesn't realize it, he is guilty. 28But as soon as he does realize it, he is to bring as his sacrifice a female goat without defect to atone for his sin. 29He shall bring it to the place where the animals for burnt offerings are killed, and there lay his hand upon the head of the sin offering and kill it. 30And the priest shall take some of the blood with his finger and smear it upon the horns of the burnt offering altar. Then the priest shall pour out the remainder of the blood at the base of the altar. 31All the fat shall be taken off, just as in the procedure for the thank-offering sacrifice, and the priest shall burn it upon the altar; and the Lord will appreciate it. Thus the priest shall make atonement for that man, and he shall be forgiven.

32"However, if he chooses to bring a lamb as his sin offering, it must be a female without physical defect. 33He shall bring it to the place

Unintentional Sins

BIBLE READING: Leviticus 4:1-28

We made a list of all persons we had harmed and became willing to make amends to them all.

As we allowed our life to get out of control, we probably hurt people without even realizing it. In fact, much of the pain we have caused has probably been unintentional. There are those we didn't even remember hurting until someone else pointed it out to us. Nevertheless, we still need to take responsibility for our actions by making amends.

When God gave the commandments, he included instructions for handling mistakes as well as intentional sins. He said, "These are the laws concerning anyone who unintentionally breaks any of my commandments. . . . If any one of the common people sins and doesn't realize it, he is guilty. But as soon as he does realize it, he is to bring as his sacrifice a female goat without defect to atone for his sin" (Leviticus 4:2, 27-28). "If by mistake you or future generations fail to carry out all of these regulations which the Lord has given you . . . then when the people realize their error, they must offer one young bull for a burnt offering. . . . And they shall be forgiven; for it was an error, and they have corrected it with their sacrifice" (Numbers 15:22-25).

We are responsible for the way our behavior has affected others. This is true even when we didn't realize we were hurting them. These unintentional sins need to be acknowledged and corrected as soon as we discover them. God forgives all our sins. In the recovery process, however, the unintentional sins need to be accounted for along with the more glaring ones. ***Turn to page 133, Leviticus 16.***

where the burnt offerings are killed, and lay his hand upon its head and kill it there as a sin offering. [34]The priest shall take some of the blood with his finger and smear it upon the horns of the burnt offering altar, and all the rest of the blood shall be poured out at the base of the altar. [35]The fat shall be used just as in the case of a thank-offering lamb—the priest shall burn the fat on the altar as in any other sacrifice made to Jehovah by fire; and the priest shall make atonement for the man, and his sin shall be forgiven.

CHAPTER 5

"Anyone refusing to give testimony concerning what he knows about a crime is guilty.

[2]"Anyone touching anything ceremonially unclean—such as the dead body of an animal forbidden for food, wild or domesticated, or the dead body of some forbidden insect—is guilty, even though he wasn't aware of touching it. [3]Or if he touches human discharge of any kind, he becomes guilty as soon as he realizes that he has touched it.

[4]"If anyone makes a rash vow, whether the vow is good or bad, when he realizes what a foolish vow he has taken, he is guilty.

[5]"In any of these cases, he shall confess his sin [6]and bring his guilt offering to the Lord, a female lamb or goat, and the priest shall make atonement for him, and he shall be freed from his sin, and need not fulfill the vow.

Exceptions for the Poor

[7]"If he is too poor to bring a lamb to the Lord, then he shall bring two turtledoves or two young pigeons as his guilt offering; one of the birds shall be his sin offering and the other his burnt offering. [8]The priest shall offer as the sin sacrifice whichever bird is handed to him first, breaking its neck, but not severing its head from its body. [9]Then he shall sprinkle some of the blood at the side of the altar and the rest shall be drained out at the base of the altar; this is the sin offering. [10]He shall offer the second bird as a burnt offering, following the customary procedures that have been set forth; so the priest shall make atonement for him concerning his sin, and he shall be forgiven.

[11]"If he is too poor to bring turtledoves or young pigeons as his sin offering, then he shall bring a tenth of a bushel of fine flour. He must not mix it with olive oil or put any incense on it because it is a sin offering. [12]He shall bring it to the priest, and the priest shall take out a handful as a representative portion and burn it on the altar just as any other offering to Jehovah made by fire; this shall be his sin offering. [13]In this way the priest shall make atonement for him for any sin of this kind, and he shall be forgiven. The rest of the flour shall belong to the priest, just as was the case with the grain offering."

The Guilt Offering

[14]And the Lord said to Moses, [15]"If anyone sins by unintentionally defiling what is holy, then he shall bring a ram without defect, worth whatever fine you charge against him, as his guilt offering to the Lord. [16]And he shall make restitution for the holy thing he has defiled, or the tithe omitted, by paying for the loss, plus a 20 percent penalty; he shall bring it to the priest, and the priest shall make atonement for him with the ram of the guilt offering, and he shall be forgiven.

[17,18]"Anyone who disobeys some law of God without realizing it is guilty anyway, and must bring his sacrifice of a value determined by Moses. This sacrifice shall be a ram without blemish taken to the priest as a guilt offering; with it the priest shall make atonement for

---

4:1–5:13 The sin offering brought atonement and provided forgiveness for an individual's sin in relation to God. In contrast, the guilt offering (5:14–6:7) brought atonement for acts perpetrated against others. As we seek to recover from past sins and failures, it is clear that we must start by admitting our helplessness before God. We must begin by seeing that all sin is first of all committed against God, who created and loves those we have wronged. We need to echo David's prayer, "It is against you, and you alone I sinned, and did this terrible thing" (Psalm 51:4). The consequences of our sins, however, usually fall upon us or the people around us. Ultimately we must seek reconciliation with the people we have wronged and make any necessary restitution.

5:14–6:7 The guilt offering was a special kind of sin offering. It was offered by a wrongdoer that he might receive forgiveness from God, while also making restitution for the pain or loss he had caused someone else. This offering held the wrongdoer acountable for his actions and paved the path toward his reconciliation with the wronged party. We, too, must consider the effects of our sins on others. Our recovery demands that we seek reconciliation with God by asking for his forgiveness and making amends with the people we have wronged, wherever possible.

him, so that he will be forgiven for whatever it is he has done without realizing it. 19It must be offered as a guilt offering, for he is certainly guilty before the Lord."

CHAPTER 6
And the Lord said to Moses, 2"If anyone sins against me by refusing to return a deposit on something borrowed or rented, or by refusing to return something entrusted to him, or by robbery, or by oppressing his neighbor, 3or by finding a lost article and lying about it, swearing that he doesn't have it— 4,5on the day he is found guilty of any such sin, he shall restore what he took, adding a 20 percent fine, and give it to the one he has harmed; and on the same day he shall bring his guilt offering to the Tabernacle. 6His guilt offering shall be a ram without defect, and must be worth whatever value you demand. He shall bring it to the priest, 7and the priest shall make atonement for him before the Lord, and he shall be forgiven."

Rules for the Burnt Offering
8Then the Lord said to Moses, 9*"Give Aaron and his sons these regulations concerning the burnt offering:*

"The burnt offering shall be left upon the hearth of the altar all night, with the altar fire kept burning. 10(The next morning) the priest shall put on his linen undergarments and his linen outer garments, and clean out the ashes of the burnt offering, and put them beside the altar. 11Then he shall change his clothes and carry the ashes outside the camp to a place that is ceremonially clean. 12Meanwhile, the fire on the altar must be kept burning—it must not go out. The priest shall put on fresh wood each morning, and lay the daily burnt offering on it, and burn the fat of the daily peace offering. 13The fire must be kept burning upon the altar continually. It must never go out.

Rules for the Grain Offering
14*"These are the regulations concerning the grain offering:*

"Aaron's sons shall stand in front of the altar to offer it before the Lord. 15The priest shall then take out a handful of the finely ground flour, with the olive oil and the incense mixed into it, and burn it upon the altar as a representative portion for the Lord; and it will be received with pleasure by the Lord. 16After taking out this handful, the remainder of the flour will belong to Aaron and his sons for their food; it shall be eaten without yeast in the courtyard of the Tabernacle. 17(Stress this instruction, that if it is baked, it must be without yeast.) I have given to the priests this part of the burnt offerings made to me. However, all of it is most holy, just as is the entire sin offering and the entire guilt offering. 18It may be eaten by any male descendant of Aaron, any priest, generation after generation. But only the priests may eat these offerings made by fire to the Lord."

19,20And Jehovah said to Moses, "On the day Aaron and his sons are anointed and inducted into the priesthood, they shall bring to the Lord a regular grain offering—a tenth of a bushel of fine flour, half to be offered in the morning and half in the evening. 21It shall be cooked on a griddle, using olive oil, and should be well cooked, then brought to the Lord as an offering that pleases him very much. 22,23As the sons of the priests replace their fathers, they shall be inducted into office by offering this same sacrifice on the day of their anointing. This is a perpetual law. These offerings shall be entirely burned up before the Lord; none of it shall be eaten."

Rules for the Sin Offering
24Then the Lord said to Moses, 25*"Tell Aaron and his sons that these are the instructions concerning the sin offering:*

"This sacrifice is most holy, and shall be killed before the Lord at the place where the burnt offerings are killed. 26The priest who performs the ceremony shall eat it in the courtyard of the Tabernacle. 27Only those who are sanctified—the priests—may touch this meat; if any blood sprinkles onto their clothing, it must be washed in a holy place. 28Then the clay pot in which the clothing is boiled shall be broken; or if a bronze kettle is used, it must be scoured and rinsed out thoroughly. 29Every male among the priests may eat this offering, but only they, for it is most holy. 30No sin offering may be eaten by the priests if any of its blood is taken into the Tabernacle to make atonement in the Holy Place. That carcass must be entirely burned with fire before the Lord.

CHAPTER 7
Rules for the Guilt Offering
"Here are the instructions concerning the most holy offering for guilt:

2"The sacrificial animal shall be killed at the place where the burnt offering sacrifices are slain, and its blood shall be sprinkled back and forth upon the altar. [3]The priest will offer upon the altar all its fat, including the tail, the fat that covers the insides, [4]the two kidneys and the loin-fat, and the gall bladder—all shall be set aside for sacrificing. [5]The priests will burn them upon the altar as a guilt offering to the Lord. [6]Only males among the priests may then eat the carcass, and it must be eaten in a holy place, for this is a most holy sacrifice.

[7]"The same instructions apply to both the sin offering and the guilt offering—the carcass shall be given to the priest who is in charge of the atonement ceremony, for his food. [8](When the offering is a burnt sacrifice, the priest who is in charge shall also be given the animal's hide.) [9]The priests who present the people's grain offerings to the Lord shall be given whatever remains of the sacrifice after the ceremony is completed. This rule applies whether the sacrifice is baked, fried, or grilled. [10]All other grain offerings, whether mixed with olive oil or dry, are the common property of all sons of Aaron.

Rules for the Offering of Thanksgiving

[11]*"Here are the instructions concerning the sacrifices given to the Lord as special peace offerings:*

[12]"If it is an offering of thanksgiving, unleavened short bread shall be included with the sacrifice, along with unleavened wafers spread with olive oil and loaves from a batter of flour mixed with olive oil. [13]This thanksgiving peace offering shall be accompanied with loaves of leavened bread. [14]Part of this sacrifice shall be presented to the Lord by a gesture of waving it before the altar, then it shall be given to the assisting priest, the one who sprinkles the blood of the animal presented for the sacrifice. [15]After the animal has been sacrificed and presented to the Lord as a peace offering to show special appreciation and thanksgiving to him, its meat is to be eaten that same day, and none left to be eaten the next day.

[16]"However, if someone brings a sacrifice that is not for thanksgiving, but is because of a vow or is simply a voluntary offering to the Lord, any portion of the sacrifice that is not eaten the day it is sacrificed may be eaten the next day. [17,18]But anything left over until the third day shall be burned. For if any of it is eaten on the third day, the Lord will not accept it; it will have no value as a sacrifice, and there will be no credit to the one who brought it to be offered; and the priest who eats it shall be guilty, for it is detestable to the Lord, and the person who eats it must answer for his sin.

[19]"Any meat that comes into contact with anything that is ceremonially unclean shall not be eaten, but burned; and as for the meat that may be eaten, it may be eaten only by a person who is ceremonially clean. [20]Any priest who is ceremonially unclean but eats the thanksgiving offering anyway, shall be cut off from his people, for he has defiled what is sacred. [21]Anyone who touches anything that is ceremonially unclean, whether it is uncleanness from man or beast, and then eats the peace offering, shall be cut off from his people, for he has defiled what is holy."

[22]Then the Lord said to Moses, [23]"Tell the people of Israel never to eat fat, whether from oxen, sheep, or goats. [24]The fat of an animal that dies of disease, or is attacked and killed by wild animals, may be used for other purposes, but never eaten. [25]Anyone who eats fat from an offering sacrificed by fire to the Lord shall be outlawed from his people.

[26,27]"Never eat blood, whether of birds or animals. Anyone who does shall be excommunicated from his people."

[28]And the Lord said to Moses, [29]"Tell the people of Israel that anyone bringing a thanksgiving offering to the Lord must bring it personally with his own hands. [30]He shall bring the offering of the fat and breast, which is to be presented to the Lord by waving it before the altar. [31]Then the priest shall burn the fat upon the altar, but the breast shall belong to Aaron and his sons, [32,33]while the right thigh shall be given to the officiating priest. [34]For I have designated the breast and thigh as donations from the people of Israel to the sons of Aaron. Aaron and his sons must always be given this portion of the sacrifice. [35]This is their pay! It is to be set apart from the burnt offerings, and given to all who have been appointed to minister to the Lord as

7:12-13 The most common type of peace offering was the offering of thanksgiving. It involved the presentation of various kinds of unleavened and leavened cakes, part of which were sacrificed and part eaten in a communal meal. The Israelite believer learned from this the importance of a public expression of thanks to God. God wants us, as well, to praise him before others, especially when he has given us a victory over sin. This public expression of gratitude to God will not only enhance our spiritual growth, but be a first step toward helping others.

priests—to Aaron and to his sons. 36For on the day the Lord anointed them, he commanded that the people of Israel give these portions to them; it is their right forever throughout all their generations."

37These were the instructions concerning the burnt offering, grain offering, sin offering, and guilt offering, and concerning the consecration offering and the peace offering; 38these instructions were given to Moses by the Lord on Mount Sinai, to be passed on to the people of Israel so that they would know how to offer their sacrifices to God in the Sinai desert.

CHAPTER 8

Aaron and His Sons Are Dedicated

The Lord said to Moses, "Now bring Aaron and his sons to the entrance of the Tabernacle, together with their garments, the anointing oil, the young bull for the sin offering, the two rams, and the basket of bread made without yeast; and summon all Israel to a meeting there."

4So all the people assembled, 5and Moses said to them, "What I am now going to do has been commanded by Jehovah."

6Then he took Aaron and his sons and washed them with water, 7and he clothed Aaron with the special coat, sash, robe, and the ephod-jacket with its beautifully woven belt. 8Then he put on him the chestpiece and deposited the Urim and the Thummim inside its pouch; 9and placed on Aaron's head the turban with the sacred gold plate at its front—the holy crown—as the Lord had commanded Moses.

10Then Moses took the anointing oil and sprinkled it upon the Tabernacle itself and on each item in it, sanctifying them. 11When he came to the altar he sprinkled it seven times, and also sprinkled the utensils of the altar and the washbasin and its pedestal, to sanctify them. 12Then he poured the anointing oil upon Aaron's head, thus setting him apart for his work. 13Next Moses placed the robes on Aaron's sons, with the belts and caps, as the Lord had commanded him.

14Then he took the young bull for the sin offering, and Aaron and his sons laid their hands upon its head 15,16as Moses killed it. He smeared some of the blood with his finger upon the four horns of the altar and upon the altar itself, to sanctify it, and poured out the rest of the blood at the base of the altar; thus he sanctified the altar, making atonement for it. He took all the fat covering the entrails, the fatty mass above the liver, and the two kidneys and their fat, and burned them all on the altar. 17The carcass of the young bull, with its hide and dung, was burned outside the camp, as the Lord had commanded Moses.

18Then he presented to the Lord the ram for the burnt offering. Aaron and his sons laid their hands upon its head, 19and Moses killed it and sprinkled the blood back and forth upon the altar. 20Next he quartered the ram and burned the pieces, the head and the fat. 21He then washed the insides and the legs with water, and burned them upon the altar, so that the entire ram was consumed before the Lord; it was a burnt offering that pleased the Lord very much, for Jehovah's directions to Moses were followed in every detail.

22Then Moses presented the other ram, the ram of consecration; Aaron and his sons laid their hands upon its head. 23Moses killed it and took some of its blood and smeared it upon the lobe of Aaron's right ear and the thumb of his right hand and upon the big toe of his right foot. 24Next he smeared some of the blood upon Aaron's sons—upon the lobes of their right ears, upon their right thumbs, and upon the big toes of their right feet. The rest of the blood he sprinkled back and forth upon the altar.

25Then he took the fat, the tail, the fat upon the inner organs, the gall bladder, the two kidneys with their fat, and the right shoulder, 26and placed on top of these one unleavened wafer, one wafer spread with olive oil, and a slice of bread, all taken from the basket that had been placed there before the Lord. 27All this was placed in the hands of Aaron and his sons to present to the Lord by a gesture of waving them before the altar. 28Moses then took it all back from them and burned it upon the altar, along with the burnt offering to the Lord; and Jehovah was pleased by the offering. 29Now Moses took the breast and pre-

8:1-4 Among the Israelites, the priest entered God's holy presence with the people's requests; he was the mediator between God and the people. God instituted the priesthood because he desired to have fellowship with his people. But the mediation of the priesthood was also a stern reminder that God is an awesome and holy God, who cannot be approached lightly. Since we as believers are called "holy priests" (1 Peter 2:5), we may come boldly before God, offering him our life as a spiritual sacrifice. But we must be careful to approach him as a holy God and not take sin lightly.

sented it to the Lord by waving it before the
altar; this was Moses' portion of the ram of
consecration, just as the Lord had instructed
him.
30Next he took some of the anointing oil
and some of the blood that had been sprinkled upon the altar, and sprinkled it upon
Aaron and upon his clothes and upon his
sons and upon their clothes, thus consecrating to the Lord's use Aaron and his sons and
their clothes.
31Then Moses said to Aaron and his sons,
"Boil the meat at the entrance of the Tabernacle, and eat it along with the bread that is in
the basket of consecration, just as I instructed
you to do. 32Anything left of the meat and
bread must be burned."
33Next he told them not to leave the Tabernacle entrance for seven days, after which
time their consecration would be completed—for it takes seven days. 34Then Moses
stated again that all he had done that day had
been commanded by the Lord in order to
make atonement for them. 35And again he
warned Aaron and his sons to stay at the
entrance of the Tabernacle day and night for
seven days. "If you leave," he told them, "you
will die—this is what the Lord has said."
36So Aaron and his sons did all that the Lord
had commanded Moses.

CHAPTER 9

The Priests Begin Their Work

On the eighth day (of the consecration ceremonies), Moses summoned Aaron and Aaron's sons and the elders of Israel, 2and told
Aaron to take a bull calf from the herd for a
sin offering, and a ram without bodily defect
for a burnt offering, and to offer them before
the Lord.
3"And tell the people of Israel," Moses instructed, "to select a male goat for their sin
offering, also a yearling calf and a yearling
lamb, all without bodily defect, for their
burnt offering. 4In addition, the people are to
bring to the Lord a peace offering sacrifice—
an ox and a ram, and a grain offering—flour
mingled with olive oil. For today," Moses said,
"Jehovah will appear to them."
5So they brought all these things to the
entrance of the Tabernacle, as Moses had
commanded, and the people came and stood
there before the Lord.
6Moses told them, "When you have followed the Lord's instructions, his glory will
appear to you."
7Moses then told Aaron to proceed to the
altar and to offer the sin offering and the
burnt offering, making atonement for himself
first, and then for the people, as the Lord had
commanded. 8So Aaron went up to the altar
and killed the calf as a sacrifice for his own
sin; 9his sons caught the blood for him, and
he dipped his finger in it and smeared it upon
the horns of the altar, and poured out the rest
at the base of the altar. 10Then he burned upon
the altar the fat, kidneys, and gall bladder
from this sin offering, as the Lord had commanded Moses, 11but he burned the meat and
hide outside the camp.
12Next he killed the burnt offering animal,
and his sons caught the blood, and he sprinkled it back and forth upon the altar; 13they
brought the animal to him piece by piece,

8:30-36 The priests were sprinkled with blood from the sacrifices. This symbolized their cleansing and reconciliation to God through the sacrificial death of the animal offering. The high price for their sin, the death of a living animal, would have been a pungent reminder of how important obedience was. The apostle Peter described believers as those cleansed "with the blood of Jesus Christ" (1 Peter 1:2). Because of the high price paid for our sins—the sacrificial death of Christ on the cross—we ought to be living a life of obedience to his Word.

9:7 Because Aaron was the High Priest, he offered sacrifices to make atonement for his sins and those of the people. But Jesus Christ, our High Priest, does more than offer sacrifices for us; he actually became our sin offering. He made all animal sacrifices obsolete by offering himself on the cross as the perfect sacrifice. And by giving himself sacrificially for others, he set a clear example for us to live by. His example should lead us to give ourselves to others as a means to their healing and enrichment.

9:8-24 This account of Aaron's sacrifices reflects the actual order in which the various sacrifices were offered by an individual. The sin offering was first, showing the priority of confession and cleansing from sin before God. The following burnt or grain offering represented the worshiper's obedience in giving his life over to God. Then the peace offering was an expression of gratitude for his continuing walk with God. Similarly, the first step for us in our recovery from sin and failure must be the admission that we are hopeless on our own. The next step is the commitment of our life to God through Jesus Christ, our sacrifice. This is then followed by ongoing fellowship with God, accountability for sin, and spiritual growth.

including the head, and he burned each part upon the altar. 14Then he washed the insides and the legs, and offered these also upon the altar as a burnt offering.

15Next he sacrificed the people's offering; he killed the goat and offered it in just the same way as he had the sin offering for himself. 16Thus he sacrificed their burnt offering to the Lord, in accordance with the instructions God had given.

17Then he presented the grain offering, taking a handful and burning it upon the altar in addition to the regular morning offering.

18Next he killed the ox and ram—the people's peace offering sacrifice; and Aaron's sons brought the blood to him, and he sprinkled it back and forth upon the altar. 19Then he collected the fat of the ox and the ram—the fat from their tails and the fat covering the inner organs—and the kidneys and gall bladders. 20The fat was placed upon the breasts of these animals, and Aaron burned it upon the altar; 21but he waved the breasts and right shoulders slowly before the Lord as a gesture of offering it to him, just as Moses had commanded.

22Then, with hands spread out toward the people, Aaron blessed them and came down from the altar. 23Moses and Aaron went into the Tabernacle, and when they came out again they blessed the people; and the glory of the Lord appeared to the whole assembly. 24Then fire came from the Lord and consumed the burnt offering and fat on the altar; and when the people saw it, they all shouted and fell flat upon the ground before the Lord.

CHAPTER 10

Nadab and Abihu Are Punished

But Nadab and Abihu, the sons of Aaron, placed unholy fire in their censers, laid incense on the fire, and offered the incense before the Lord—contrary to what the Lord had just commanded them! 2So fire blazed forth from the presence of the Lord and destroyed them.

3Then Moses said to Aaron, "This is what the Lord meant when he said, 'I will show myself holy among those who approach me, and I will be glorified before all the people.'" And Aaron was speechless.

4Then Moses called for Mishael and Elzaphon, Aaron's cousins, the sons of Uzziel, and told them, "Go and get the charred bodies from before the Tabernacle, and carry them outside the camp."

5So they went over and got them, and carried them out in their coats as Moses had told them to.

6Then Moses said to Aaron and his sons Eleazar and Ithamar, "Do not mourn—do not let your hair hang loose as a sign of your mourning, and do not tear your clothes. If you do, God will strike you dead too, and his wrath will come upon all the people of Israel. But the rest of the people of Israel may lament the death of Nadab and Abihu, and mourn because of the terrible fire the Lord has sent. 7But you are not to leave the Tabernacle under penalty of death, for the anointing oil of Jehovah is upon you." And they did as Moses commanded.

8,9Now the Lord instructed Aaron, "Never drink wine or strong drink when you go into the Tabernacle, lest you die; and this rule applies to your sons and to all your descendants from generation to generation. 10 Your duties will be to arbitrate for the people, to teach them the difference between what is holy and what is ordinary, what is pure and what is impure; 11and to teach them all the laws Jehovah has given through Moses."

10:1-3 The sin and swift judgment of Aaron's two eldest sons indicates the greater responsibility of those who occupy positions of leadership and authority. Although the specifics of their sin are not explained in Scripture, it is likely that their wrong actions proceeded from wrong attitudes. Perhaps they believed that as leaders they were exempt from the moral law. While God's grace and long-suffering may often spare us from immediate judgment, we should be aware that we are accountable to him. When we become irresponsible and disobedient to God's program, the consequences will be grave.

10:8-9 This passage about the use of wine or other intoxicating beverages illustrates the importance of self-control on the part of the priests. Because of the importance of their work and example, God required certain boundaries and evidence of self-control. Alcohol would affect their ability to carry out the task God had called them to do. This illustrates our need for self-control and boundaries as we seek to carry an effective and positive testimony of God's love to others.

10:8-11 First, Aaron was told how to act (10:8-9); then he was told what to teach (10:10-11). This illustrates an important principle: actions speak louder than words. God calls us to live in a way that will, by example, reinforce what we teach others. If we fail to live by what we teach, we may as well have never spoken.

12 Then Moses said to Aaron and to his sons who were left, Eleazar and Ithamar, "Take the grain offering—the food that remains after the handful has been offered to the Lord by burning it on the altar—make sure there is no leaven in it, and eat it beside the altar. The offering is most holy; 13 therefore, you must eat it in the sanctuary, in a holy place. It belongs to you and to your sons, from the offerings to Jehovah made by fire; for so I am commanded. 14 But the breast and the thigh, which have been offered to the Lord by the gesture of waving it before him, may be eaten in any holy place. It belongs to you and to your sons and daughters for your food. It is your portion of the peace offering sacrifices of the people of Israel.

15 The people are to bring the thigh that was set aside, along with the breast that was offered when the fat was burned, and they shall be presented before the Lord by the gesture of waving them. And afterwards they shall belong to you and your family, for the Lord has commanded this."

16 Then Moses searched everywhere for the goat of the sin offering and discovered that it had been burned! He was very angry about this with Eleazar and Ithamar, the remaining sons of Aaron.

17 "Why haven't you eaten the sin offering in the sanctuary, since it is most holy, and God has given it to you to take away the iniquity and guilt of the people, to make atonement for them before the Lord?" he demanded. 18 "Since its blood was not taken inside the sanctuary, you should certainly have eaten it there, as I ordered you."

19 But Aaron interceded with Moses. "They offered their sin offering and burnt offering before the Lord," he said, "but if I had eaten the sin offering on such a day as this, would it have pleased the Lord?" 20 And when Moses heard that, he was satisfied.

CHAPTER 11

Clean and Unclean Animals

Then the Lord said to Moses and Aaron,

2,3 "Tell the people of Israel that the animals which may be used for food include any animal with cloven hooves which chews its cud. 4-7 This means that the following may *not* be eaten:

The camel (it chews the cud but does not have cloven hooves);
The coney, or rock badger (because although it chews the cud, it does not have cloven hooves);
The hare (because although it chews the cud, it does not have cloven hooves);
The swine (because although it has cloven hooves, it does not chew the cud).

8 You may not eat their meat or even touch their dead bodies; they are forbidden foods for you.

9 "As to fish, you may eat whatever has fins and scales, whether taken from rivers or from the sea; 10 but all other water creatures are strictly forbidden to you. 11 You mustn't eat their meat or even touch their dead bodies. 12 I'll repeat it again—any water creature that does not have fins or scales is forbidden to you.

13-19 "Among the birds, these are the ones you may *not* eat: the eagle, the metire, the osprey, the falcon (all kinds), the kite, the raven (all kinds), the ostrich, the nighthawk, the seagull, the hawk (all kinds), the owl, the cormorant, the ibis, the marsh hen, the pelican, the vulture, the stork, the heron (all kinds), the hoopoe, the bat.

20 "No insects may be eaten, 21,22 with the exception of those that jump; locusts of all varieties—ordinary locusts, bald locusts, crickets, and grasshoppers—may be eaten. 23 All insects that fly and walk or crawl are forbidden to you.

24 "Anyone touching their dead bodies shall be defiled until the evening 25 and must wash his clothes immediately. He must also quarantine himself until nightfall, as being ceremonially defiled.

26 "You are also defiled by touching any animal with only semiparted hoofs, or any animal that does not chew the cud. 27 Any animal that walks on paws is forbidden to you as food. Anyone touching the dead body of such an animal shall be defiled until evening. 28 Anyone carrying away the carcass shall wash his clothes and be ceremonially defiled until evening; for it is forbidden to you.

11:1-47 The elaborate dietary laws of this section illustrate the fact that God's relationship with his people extends even to the practical areas of everyday living. While we are not bound by the specifics of these dietary standards, we know that God is just as interested in the details of our life. If our eating or drinking leads to excess, abuse, or poor health, God is interested. He also holds us accountable to deal with the problem. Personal holiness relates even to the mundane areas of life.

29,30"These are the forbidden small animals
which scurry about your feet or crawl upon
the ground: the mole, the rat, the great lizard,
the gecko, the mouse, the lizard, the snail, the
chameleon.
31Anyone touching their dead bodies shall
be defiled until evening, 32and anything upon
which the carcass falls shall be defiled—any
article of wood, or of clothing, a rug, or a sack;
anything it touches must be put into water
and is defiled until evening. After that it may
be used again. 33If it falls into a pottery bowl,
anything in the bowl is defiled, and you shall
smash the bowl. 34If the water used to cleanse
the defiled article touches any food, all of it is
defiled. Any drink which is in the defiled bowl
is also contaminated.
35"If the dead body of such an animal
touches any clay oven, it is defiled and must
be smashed. 36If the body falls into a spring or
cistern where there is water, that water is not
defiled; yet anyone who pulls out the carcass
is defiled. 37And if the carcass touches grain to
be sown in the field, it is not contaminated;
38but if the seeds are wet and the carcass falls
upon it, the seed is defiled.
39"If an animal which you are permitted to
eat dies of disease, anyone touching the carcass shall be defiled until evening. 40Also, anyone eating its meat or carrying away its
carcass shall wash his clothes and be defiled
until evening.
41,42"Animals that crawl shall not be eaten.
This includes all reptiles that slither along
upon their bellies as well as those that have
legs. No crawling thing with many feet may
be eaten, for it is defiled. 43Do not defile yourselves by touching it.
44"I am the Lord your God. Keep yourselves
pure concerning these things, and be holy, for
I am holy; therefore do not defile yourselves
by touching any of these things that crawl
upon the earth. 45For I am the Lord who
brought you out of the land of Egypt to be
your God. You must therefore be holy, for I
am holy." 46These are the laws concerning
animals, birds, and whatever swims in the
water or crawls upon the ground. 47These are
the distinctions between what is ceremonially
clean and may be eaten, and what is ceremonially defiled and may not be eaten, among
all animal life upon the earth.

CHAPTER 12

Mothers and Childbirth

The Lord told Moses to give these instructions
to the people of Israel:
2"When a baby boy is born, the mother
shall be ceremonially defiled for seven days,
and under the same restrictions as during her
monthly menstrual periods. 3On the eighth
day, her son must be circumcised. 4Then, for
the next thirty-three days, while she is recovering from her ceremonial impurity, she must
not touch anything sacred nor enter the Tabernacle.
5"When a baby girl is born, the mother's
ceremonial impurity shall last two weeks, during which time she will be under the same
restrictions as during menstruation. Then for
a further sixty-six days she shall continue her
recovery.
6"When these days of purification are
ended (the following instructions are applicable whether her baby is a boy or girl), she
must bring a yearling lamb as a burnt offering, and a young pigeon or a turtledove for a
sin offering.
She must take them to the door of the
Tabernacle to the priest; 7and the priest will
offer them before the Lord and make atonement for her; then she will be ceremonially
clean again after her bleeding at childbirth.
"These then, are the procedures after childbirth. 8But if she is too poor to bring a lamb,
then she must bring two turtledoves or two
young pigeons. One will be for a burnt offering and the other for a sin offering. The priest
will make atonement for her with these, so
that she will be ceremonially pure again."

CHAPTER 13

Laws Concerning Leprosy

The Lord said to Moses and Aaron, "If anyone
notices a swelling in his skin, or a scab or boil
or pimple with transparent skin, leprosy is to
be suspected. He must be brought to Aaron
the priest or to one of his sons 3for the spot to
be examined. If the hair in this spot turns
white, and if the spot looks to be more than

11:44 What does it mean to be holy? It doesn't mean just to have a pious attitude toward God. The Hebrew word literally means "to be set apart," both unto God and from sin. This chapter emphasizes the aspect of being set apart unto God. These dietary laws and other guidelines for daily living gave the Israelites a unique identity as God's people. God also calls us to a life of holiness, a life that clearly reflects God's standards.

skin-deep, it is leprosy, and the priest must
declare him a leper.
4"But if the white spot in the skin does not
seem to be deeper than the skin and the hair
in the spot has not turned white, the priest
shall quarantine him for seven days. 5At the
end of that time, on the seventh day, the
priest will examine him again, and if the spot
has not changed and has not spread in the
skin, then the priest must quarantine him
seven days more. 6Again on the seventh day
the priest will examine him, and if the marks
of the disease have become fainter and have
not spread, then the priest shall pronounce
him cured; it was only a scab, and the man
need only wash his clothes and everything
will be normal again. 7But if the spot spreads
in the skin after he has come to the priest to
be examined, he must come back to the priest
again, 8and the priest shall look again, and if
the spot has spread, then the priest must
pronounce him a leper.
9,10"When anyone suspected of having leprosy is brought to the priest, the priest is to
look to see if there is a white swelling in the
skin with white hairs in the spot, and an ulcer
developing. 11If he finds these symptoms, it is
an established case of leprosy, and the priest
must pronounce him defiled. The man is not
to be quarantined for further observation, for
he is definitely diseased. 12But if the priest sees
that the leprosy has erupted and spread all
over his body from head to foot wherever he
looks, 13then the priest shall pronounce him
cured of leprosy, for it has all turned white; he
is cured. 14,15But if there is raw flesh anywhere,
the man shall be declared a leper. It is proved
by the raw flesh. 16,17But if the raw flesh later
changes to white, the leper will return to the
priest to be examined again. If the spot has
indeed turned completely white, then the
priest will pronounce him cured.
18"In the case of a man who has a boil in his
skin which heals, 19but which leaves a white
swelling or a bright spot, sort of reddish
white, the man must go to the priest for
examination. 20If the priest sees that the
trouble seems to be down under the skin, and
if the hair at the spot has turned white, then
the priest shall declare him defiled, for leprosy
has broken out from the boil. 21But if the
priest sees that there are no white hairs in this
spot, and the spot does not appear to be
deeper than the skin, and if the color is gray,
then the priest shall quarantine him for seven
days. 22If during that time the spot spreads,
the priest must declare him a leper. 23But if the
bright spot grows no larger and does not
spread, it is merely the scar from the boil, and
the priest shall declare that all is well.
24"If a man is burned in some way, and the
burned place becomes bright reddish white or
white, 25then the priest must examine the
spot. If the hair in the bright spot turns white
and the problem seems to be more than skin-
deep, it is leprosy that has broken out from
the burn, and the priest must pronounce him
a leper. 26But if the priest sees that there are no
white hairs in the bright spot and the brightness appears to be no deeper than the skin
and is fading, the priest shall quarantine him
for seven days 27and examine him again the
seventh day. If the spot spreads in the skin,
the priest must pronounce him a leper. 28But
if the bright spot does not move or spread in
the skin, and is fading, it is simply a scar from
the burn, and the priest shall declare that he
does not have leprosy.
29,30"If a man or woman has a sore on the
head or chin, the priest must examine him;
if the infection seems to be below the skin
and yellow hair is found in the sore, the
priest must pronounce him a leper. 31But if
the priest's examination reveals that the
spot seems to be only in the skin but there
is healthy hair in it, then he shall be quarantined for seven days, 32and examined
again on the seventh day. If the spot has not
spread and no yellow hair has appeared,
and if the infection does not seem to be
deeper than the skin, 33he shall shave off all
the hair around the spot (but not on the
spot itself) and the priest shall quarantine
him for another seven days. 34He shall be
examined again on the seventh day, and if
the spot has not spread, and it appears to be
no deeper than the skin, the priest shall
pronounce him well, and after washing his

13:1–15:33 These detailed health regulations excluded many Israelites from the larger society. They were banned from fellowship with others for being "ceremonially unclean." Lepers and prostitutes were automatically unclean, according to the law, and were thus ostracized. This fact should help us appreciate even more the compassionate heart of Jesus Christ. He healed lepers and the woman who had been slowly bleeding for years; he talked with prostitutes and other outcasts. He cared most about the needy, the unclean. He considered it his work to show them the road to recovery and forgiveness.

clothes, he is free. 35But if, later on, this spot begins to spread, 36then the priest must examine him again and, without waiting to see if any yellow hair develops, declare him a leper. 37But if it appears that the spreading has stopped and black hairs are found in the spot, then he is healed and is not a leper, and the priest shall declare him healed.

38"If a man or a woman has white, transparent areas in the skin, 39but these spots are growing dimmer, this is not leprosy, but an ordinary infection that has broken out in the skin.

40"If a man's hair is gone, this does not make him a leper even though he is bald! 41If the hair is gone from the front part of his head, he simply has a bald forehead, but this is not leprosy. 42However, if in the baldness there is a reddish white spot, it may be leprosy breaking out. 43In that case the priest shall examine him, and if there is a reddish white lump that looks like leprosy, 44then he is a leper, and the priest must pronounce him such.

45"Anyone who is discovered to have leprosy must tear his clothes and let his hair grow in wild disarray, and cover his upper lip and call out as he goes, "I am a leper, I am a leper." 46As long as the disease lasts, he is defiled and must live outside the camp.

47,48"If leprosy is suspected in a woolen or linen garment or fabric, or in a piece of leather or leather-work, 49and there is a greenish or a reddish spot in it, it is probably leprosy, and must be taken to the priest to be examined. 50The priest will put it away for seven days 51and look at it again on the seventh day. If the spot has spread, it is a contagious leprosy, 52and he must burn the clothing, fabric, linen or woolen covering, or leather article, for it is contagious and must be destroyed by fire.

53"But if when he examines it again on the seventh day the spot has not spread, 54the priest shall order the suspected article to be washed, then isolated for seven more days. 55If after that time the spot has not changed its color, even though it has not spread, it is leprosy and shall be burned, for the article is infected through and through. 56But if the priest sees that the spot has faded after the washing, then he shall cut it out from the garment or leather goods or whatever it is in. 57However, if it then reappears, it is leprosy and he must burn it. 58But if after washing it there is no further trouble, it can be put back into service after another washing."

59These are the regulations concerning leprosy in a garment or anything made of skin or leather, indicating whether to pronounce it leprous or not.

CHAPTER 14

Reinstating Healed Members

And the Lord gave Moses these regulations concerning a person whose leprosy disappears:

3"The priest shall go out of the camp to examine him. If the priest sees that the leprosy is gone, 4he shall require two living birds of a kind permitted for food, and shall take some cedar wood, a scarlet string, and some hyssop branches, to be used for the purification ceremony of the one who is healed. 5The priest shall then order one of the birds killed in an earthenware pot held above running water. 6The other bird, still living, shall be dipped in the blood, along with the cedar wood, the scarlet thread, and the hyssop branch. 7Then the priest shall sprinkle the blood seven times upon the man cured of his leprosy, and the priest shall pronounce him cured, and shall let the living bird fly into the open field.

8"Then the man who is cured shall wash his clothes, shave off all his hair, and bathe himself, and return to live inside the camp; however, he must stay outside his tent for seven days. 9The seventh day he shall again shave all the hair from his head, beard, and eyebrows, and wash his clothes and bathe, and shall then be declared fully cured of his leprosy.

10"The next day, the eighth day, he shall take two male lambs without physical defect, one yearling ewe-lamb without physical defect, ten quarts of finely ground flour mixed with olive oil, and a pint of olive oil; 11then the priest who examines him shall place the man and his offerings before the Lord at the entrance of the Tabernacle. 12The priest shall take one of the lambs and the pint of olive oil and offer them to the Lord as a guilt offering by the gesture of waving them before the altar. 13Then he shall kill the lamb at the place where sin offerings and burnt offerings are killed, there at the Tabernacle; this guilt offering shall then be given to the priest for food, as in the case of a sin offering. It is a most holy offering. 14The priest shall take the blood from this guilt offering and smear some of it upon the tip of the right ear of the man being cleansed, and upon the thumb of his right hand, and upon the big toe of his right foot.

15"Then the priest shall take the olive oil

and pour it into the palm of his left hand,
16and dip his right finger into it, and sprinkle
it with his finger seven times before the Lord.
17Some of the oil remaining in his left hand
shall then be placed by the priest upon the tip
of the man's right ear and the thumb of his
right hand and the big toe of his right foot—
just as he did with the blood of the guilt
offering. 18The remainder of the oil in his
hand shall be used to anoint the man's head.
Thus the priest shall make atonement for him
before the Lord.

19"Then the priest must offer the sin offering and again perform the rite of atonement
for the person being cleansed from his leprosy; and afterwards the priest shall kill the
burnt offering, 20and offer it along with the
grain offering upon the altar, making atonement for the man, who shall then be pronounced finally cleansed.

21"If he is so poor that he cannot afford two
lambs, then he shall bring only one, a male
lamb for the guilt offering, to be presented to
the Lord in the rite of atonement by waving
it before the altar; and only three quarts of
fine white flour, mixed with olive oil, for a
grain offering, and a pint of olive oil.

22"He shall also bring two turtledoves or
two young pigeons—whichever he is able to
afford—and use one of the pair for a sin offering and the other for a burnt offering. 23He
shall bring them to the priest at the entrance
of the Tabernacle on the eighth day, for his
ceremony of cleansing before the Lord. 24The
priest shall take the lamb for the guilt offering, and the pint of oil, and wave them before
the altar as a gesture of offering to the Lord.
25Then he shall kill the lamb for the guilt
offering and smear some of its blood upon the
tip of the man's right ear—the man on whose
behalf the ceremony is being performed—and
upon the thumb of his right hand and upon
the big toe of his right foot.

26"The priest shall then pour the olive oil
into the palm of his own left hand, 27and with
his right finger he is to sprinkle some of it
seven times before the Lord. 28Then he must
put some of the olive oil from his hand upon
the tip of the man's right ear, and upon the
thumb of his right hand, and upon the big toe
of his right foot, just as he did with the blood
of the guilt offering. 29The remaining oil in his
hand shall be placed upon the head of the
man being cleansed, to make atonement for
him before the Lord.

30"Then he must offer the two turtledoves
or two young pigeons (whichever pair he is
able to afford). 31One of the pair is for a sin
offering and the other for a burnt offering, to
be sacrificed along with the grain offering;
and the priest shall make atonement for the
man before the Lord."

32These, then, are the laws concerning
those who are cleansed of leprosy but are not
able to bring the sacrifices normally required
for the ceremony of cleansing.

33,34Then the Lord said to Moses and Aaron,
"When you arrive in the land of Canaan
which I have given you, and I place leprosy in
some house there, 35then the owner of the
house shall come and report to the priest, 'It
seems to me that there may be leprosy in my
house!'

36"The priest shall order the house to be
emptied before he examines it, so that everything in the house will not be declared contaminated if he decides that there is leprosy
there. 37If he finds greenish or reddish streaks
in the walls of the house which seem to be
beneath the surface of the wall, 38he shall
close up the house for seven days, 39and return
the seventh day to look at it again. If the spots
have spread in the wall, 40then the priest shall
order the removal of the spotted section of
wall, and the material must be thrown into a
defiled place outside the city. 41Then he shall
order the inside walls of the house scraped
thoroughly and the scrapings dumped in a
defiled place outside the city. 42Other stones
shall be brought to replace those that have
been removed, new mortar used, and the
house replastered.

43"But if the spots appear again, 44the priest
shall come again and look, and if he sees that
the spots have spread, it is leprosy, and the
house is defiled. 45Then he shall order the
destruction of the house—all its stones, timbers, and mortar shall be carried out of the
city to a defiled place. 46Anyone entering the
house while it is closed shall be defiled until
evening. 47Anyone who lies down or eats in
the house shall wash his clothing.

48"But if, when the priest comes again to
look, the spots have not reappeared after the
fresh plastering, then he will pronounce the
house cleansed and declare the leprosy gone.
49He shall also perform the ceremony of
cleansing, using two birds, cedar wood, scarlet thread, and hyssop branches. 50He shall kill
one of the birds over fresh water in an earthenware bowl, 51,52and dip the cedar wood, hyssop branch, and scarlet thread, as well as the
living bird, into the blood of the bird that was
killed over the fresh water, and shall sprinkle

the house seven times. In this way the house shall be cleansed. 53Then he shall let the live bird fly away into an open field outside the city. This is the method for making atonement for the house and cleansing it."

54These, then, are the laws concerning the various places where leprosy may appear: 55in a garment or in a house, 56or in any swelling in one's skin, or a scab from a burn, or a bright spot. 57In this way you will know whether or not it is actually leprosy. That is why these laws are given.

CHAPTER 15

Health Concerns for Men

The Lord told Moses and Aaron to give the people of Israel these further instructions:

"Any man who has a genital discharge is ceremonially defiled. 3This applies not only while the discharge is active, but also for a time after it heals. 4Any bed he lies on and anything he sits on is contaminated: 5so anyone touching the man's bed is ceremonially defiled until evening, and must wash his clothes and bathe himself. 6Anyone sitting on a seat the man has sat upon while defiled is himself ceremonially impure until evening, and must wash his clothes and bathe himself. 7The same instructions apply to anyone touching him. 8Anyone he spits on is ceremonially impure until evening, and must wash his clothes and bathe himself. 9Any saddle he rides on is defiled. 10Anyone touching or carrying anything else that was beneath him shall be defiled until evening, and must wash his clothes and bathe himself. 11If the defiled man touches anyone without first rinsing his hands, that person must wash his clothes and bathe himself and be defiled until evening. 12Any earthen pot touched by the defiled man must be broken, and every wooden utensil must be rinsed in water.

13"When the discharge stops, he shall begin a seven-day cleansing ceremony by washing his clothes and bathing in running water. 14On the eighth day he shall take two turtledoves or two young pigeons and come before the Lord at the entrance of the Tabernacle, and give them to the priest. 15The priest shall sacrifice them there, one for a sin offering and the other for a burnt offering; thus the priest shall make atonement before the Lord for the man because of his discharge.

16"Whenever a man's semen goes out from him, he shall take a complete bath and be ceremonially impure until the evening. 17Any clothing or bedding the semen spills on must be washed and remain ceremonially defiled until evening. 18After sexual intercourse, the woman as well as the man must bathe, and they are ceremonially defiled until the next evening.

Health Concerns for Women

19"Whenever a woman menstruates, she shall be in a state of ceremonial defilement for seven days afterwards, and during that time anyone touching her shall be defiled until evening. 20Anything she lies on or sits on during that time shall be defiled. 21-23Anyone touching her bed or anything she sits upon shall wash his clothes and bathe himself and be ceremonially defiled until evening. 24A man having sexual intercourse with her during this time is ceremonially defiled for seven days, and every bed he lies upon shall be defiled.

25"If the menstrual flow continues after the normal time, or at some irregular time during the month, the same rules apply as indicated above, 26so that anything she lies upon during that time is defiled, just as it would be during her normal menstrual period, and everything she sits on is in a similar state of defilement. 27Anyone touching her bed or anything she sits on shall be defiled, and shall wash his clothes and bathe and be defiled until evening. 28Seven days after the menstruating stops, she is no longer ceremonially defiled.

29"On the eighth day, she shall take two turtledoves or two young pigeons and bring them to the priest at the entrance of the Tabernacle, 30and the priest shall offer one for a sin offering and the other for a burnt offering, and make atonement for her before the Lord for her menstrual defilement. 31In this way you shall cleanse the people of Israel from their defilement, lest they die because of defiling my Tabernacle that is among them."

32This, then, is the law for the man who is defiled by a genital disease or by a seminal emission; 33and for a woman's menstrual period; and for anyone who has sexual intercourse with her while she is in her period of defilement afterwards.

CHAPTER 16

The Day of Atonement

After Aaron's two sons died before the Lord, the Lord said to Moses, "Warn your brother Aaron not to enter into the Holy Place behind the veil, where the Ark and the place of mercy are, just whenever he chooses. The penalty for intrusion is death. For I myself am present in the cloud above the place of mercy.

3"Here are the conditions for his entering there: He must bring a young bull for a sin offering, and a ram for a burnt offering. 4He must bathe himself and put on the sacred linen coat, shorts, belt, and turban. 5The people of Israel shall then bring him two male goats for their sin offering, and a ram for their burnt offering. 6First he shall present to the Lord the young bull as a sin offering for himself, making atonement for himself and his family. 7Then he shall bring the two goats before the Lord at the entrance of the Tabernacle,8and cast lots to determine which is the Lord's and which is to be sent away. 9The goat allotted to the Lord shall then be sacrificed by Aaron as a sin offering. 10The other goat shall be kept alive and placed before the Lord. The rite of atonement shall be performed over it, and it shall then be sent out into the desert as a scapegoat.

11"After Aaron has sacrificed the young bull as a sin offering for himself and his family, 12he shall take a censer full of live coals from the altar of the Lord, and fill his hands with sweet incense beaten into fine powder, and bring it inside the veil. 13There before the Lord he shall put the incense upon the coals, so that a cloud of incense will cover the mercy place above the Ark (containing the stone tablets of the Ten Commandments); thus he will not die. 14And he shall bring some of the blood of the young bull and sprinkle it with his finger upon the east side of the mercy place, and then seven times in front of it.

15"Then he must go out and sacrifice the people's sin offering goat, and bring its blood within the veil, and sprinkle it upon the place of mercy and in front of it, just as he did with the blood of the young bull. 16Thus he shall make atonement for the holy place because it is defiled by the sins of the people of Israel, and for the Tabernacle, located right among them and surrounded by their defilement. 17Not another soul shall be inside the Tabernacle when Aaron enters to make atonement in the Holy Place—not until after he comes out again and has made atonement for himself and his household and for all the people of Israel. 18Then he shall go out to the altar before the Lord and make atonement for it. He must smear the blood of the young bull and the goat on the horns of the altar, 19and sprinkle blood upon the altar seven times with his finger, thus cleansing it from the sinfulness of Israel and making it holy.

20"When he has completed the rite of atonement for the Holy Place, the entire Tabernacle, and the altar, he shall bring the live goat and, 21laying both hands upon its head, confess over it all the sins of the people of Israel. He shall lay all their sins upon the head of the goat and send it into the desert, led by a man appointed for the task. 22So the goat shall carry all the sins of the people into a land where no one lives, and the man shall let it loose in the wilderness.

23"Then Aaron shall go into the Tabernacle again and take off the linen garments he wore when he went behind the veil, and leave them there in the Tabernacle. 24Then he shall bathe in a sacred place, put on his clothes again, and go out and sacrifice his own burnt offering for the people, making atonement for himself and for them. 25He shall also burn upon the altar the fat for the sin offering.

26"(The man who took the goat out into the desert shall afterwards wash his clothes and bathe himself and then come back into the

---

16:1-22 The Day of Atonement is a thematic pivot point for the book of Leviticus. For the Israelites who participated in the ceremony with hearts of faith, this solemn day provided assurance that their past sins had been completely dealt with. Today, through the sacrificial work of Christ, we also can find assurance of forgiveness and a right standing before God. We can leave our past failures behind to build a new life governed by God's program.

16:15-19 The goat for the people's sin offering was slaughtered, and its blood was sprinkled on the lid of the Ark of the Covenant, sometimes called the "place of mercy." This yearly sacrifice atoned for the sins of the people, but it had to be offered again the following year. Hebrews 10:1-4 makes it clear that these sacrifices were not a permanent solution to the problem of sin; they were only a temporary measure. Jesus Christ has now provided a perfect and permanent sacrifice for our sins. Through faith, we can be assured of complete forgiveness—permanently!

16:22 The innocent scapegoat was sent away, carrying with it the guilt of the entire Israelite nation. A dysfunctional family will often choose its own scapegoat from among its members. This person is loaded down with the guilt of the whole family and then ostracized. This frees the other members from their feelings of failure and gives them someone to blame. For those of us who have experienced this, it should encourage us to know that God has sent his Son to be a Scapegoat for us. Though innocent, he has chosen to carry away the guilt of the entire human race. We need not shoulder it any longer; no human being should be expected to. We can hand it over to him.

camp.) 27And the young bull and the goat
used for the sin offering (their blood was
taken into the Holy Place by Aaron, to make
atonement) shall be carried outside the camp
and burned, including the hides and internal
organs. 28Afterwards, the person doing the
burning shall wash his clothes and bathe
himself and then return to camp.
29,30"This is a permanent law: You must do
no work on the twenty-fifth day of September, but must spend the day in self-examination and humility. This applies whether you
are born in the land or are a foreigner living
among the people of Israel; for this is the day
commemorating the atonement, cleansing
you in the Lord's eyes from all of your sins. 31It
is a Sabbath of solemn rest for you, and you
shall spend the day in quiet humility; this is a
permanent law. 32This ceremony, in later generations, shall be performed by the anointed
High Priest, consecrated in place of his ancestor Aaron; he shall be the one to put on the
holy linen garments, 33and make atonement
for the holy sanctuary, the Tabernacle, the
altar, the priests, and the people. 34This shall
be an everlasting law for you, to make atonement for the people of Israel once each year,
because of their sins."

And Aaron followed all these instructions that the Lord gave to Moses.

CHAPTER 17

Improper Sacrifices

The Lord gave to Moses these additional instructions for Aaron and the priests and for all the people of Israel:

3,4"Any Israelite who sacrifices an ox, lamb,
or goat anywhere except at the Tabernacle is
guilty of murder and shall be excommunicated from his nation. 5The purpose of this
law is to stop the people of Israel from sacrificing in the open fields, and to cause them to
bring their sacrifices to the priest at the entrance of the Tabernacle, and to burn the fat
as a savor the Lord will appreciate and enjoy— 6for in this way the priest will be able to
sprinkle the blood upon the altar of the Lord
at the entrance of the Tabernacle, and to burn
the fat as a savor the Lord will appreciate and
enjoy— 7instead of the people's sacrificing to
evil spirits out in the fields. This shall be a
permanent law for you, from generation to
generation. 8,9I repeat: Anyone, whether an
Israelite or a foreigner living among you who
offers a burnt offering or a sacrifice anywhere
other than at the entrance of the Tabernacle,

Scapegoats

BIBLE READING: Leviticus 16:20-22

We made a list of all persons we had harmed and became willing to make amends to them all.

It is natural to hope that the people we have hurt will think better of us once we have sought to make amends. We may fear that there are some who will never upgrade their opinions about us, no matter what we do. In reality they may not, especially if they have chosen to use us as a scapegoat.

Before the coming of Jesus, the Jews were instructed to select a live goat that would carry away their sins. (Jesus became our scapegoat when he took our sins upon himself.) The priest was to place his hands on this goat and confess over it all the sins of the people. "He [the priest] shall lay all their sins upon the head of the goat and send it into the desert, led by a man appointed for the task. So the goat shall carry all the sins of the people into a land where no one lives" (Leviticus 16:21-22).

Some of the people we have hurt will use us as their scapegoat. Since we have hurt them, they feel justified in sending us away with more than our share of the burden. They unconsciously place the blame for their pain on us, so we can carry it away. As their scapegoat, we play the role of removing something they were unable to deal with in any other way. Because of this, they may never welcome us back. We should prepare for this kind of response and realize that their behavior says more about them than it says about us. ***Turn to page 709, Ecclesiastes 4.***

where it will be sacrificed to the Lord, shall be excommunicated.

10“And I will turn my face against anyone, whether an Israelite or a foreigner living among you, who eats blood in any form. I will excommunicate him from his people. 11For the life of the flesh is in the blood, and I have given you the blood to sprinkle upon the altar as an atonement for your souls; it is the blood that makes atonement because it is the life. 12That is the reasoning behind my decree to the people of Israel, that neither they, nor any foreigner living among them, may eat blood. 13Anyone, whether an Israelite or a foreigner living among you, who goes hunting and kills an animal or bird of a kind permitted for food, must pour out the blood and cover it with dust, 14for the blood is the life. That is why I told the people of Israel never to eat it, for the life of every bird and animal is its blood. Therefore, anyone who eats blood must be excommunicated.

15“And anyone—native born or foreigner—who eats the dead body of an animal that dies a natural death, or is killed by wild animals, must wash his clothes and bathe himself and be defiled until evening; after that he shall be declared cleansed. 16But if he does not wash his clothes and bathe, he shall suffer the consequence.”

CHAPTER 18

Forbidden Sexual Relationships

The Lord then told Moses to tell the people of Israel,

“I am Jehovah your God, 3so don’t act like heathen—like the people of Egypt where you lived so long, or the people of Canaan where I am going to take you. 4,5You must obey only my laws, and you must carry them out in detail, for I am the Lord your God. If you obey them, you shall live. I am the Lord.

6“None of you shall marry a near relative, for I am the Lord. 7Do not disgrace your father by having intercourse with your mother, 8nor any other of your father’s wives. 9Do not have intercourse with your sister or half sister, whether the daughter of your father or your mother, whether brought up in the same household or elsewhere.

10“You shall not have intercourse with your granddaughter—the daughter of either your son or your daughter—for she is a close relative. 11You may not have intercourse with a half sister—your father’s wife’s daughter; 12nor your aunt—your father’s sister—because she is so closely related to your father; 13nor your aunt—your mother’s sister—because she is a close relative of your mother; 14nor your aunt—the wife of your father’s brother.

15“You may not marry your daughter-in-law—your son’s wife; 16nor your brother’s wife, for she is your brother’s. 17You may not marry both a woman and her daughter or granddaughter, for they are near relatives, and to do so is horrible wickedness. 18You shall not marry two sisters, for they will be rivals. However, if your wife dies, then it is all right to marry her sister.

19“There must be no sexual relationship with a woman who is menstruating; 20nor with anyone else’s wife, to defile yourself with her.

21“You shall not give any of your children to Molech, burning them upon his altar; never profane the name of your God, for I am Jehovah.

22“Homosexuality is absolutely forbidden, for it is an enormous sin. 23A man shall have no sexual intercourse with any female ani-

18:4-5 God promises life to all those who live according to his program. The Hebrew expression “to live” does not just mean “to exist.” It refers to finding contentment and enjoyment in life—living life to its fullest. While the personal moral standards in this section of Leviticus are quite restrictive, God’s plan offers freedom beyond our wildest dreams. It is the paths of sin that are truly restrictive. When we obey God’s standards we are free to discover life as God intended it to be. His plan leads to peace and contentment through mature and satisfying relationships.

18:6-18 God instituted marriage as a foundational human relationship and forbade anything that might destroy it—incest included. Some societies in history have endorsed incestuous relationships, but they have suffered the tragic consequences. The people in such societies have suffered physical and mental abnormalities, leading eventually to societal decline. God’s purpose in setting boundaries for both personal and family life has always been to protect us from destruction. He desires to build families that promote healing and wholeness among their members.

18:20 Fidelity in marriage is central to God’s plan for society and family; it is one of the Ten Commandments (Exodus 20:14). Since the bond of marriage is a foundational building block of society, adultery is a blatant violation of a community’s trust. Healthy relationships require self-control and the acceptance of self-imposed boundaries, but God didn’t intend to deprive us of anything in marriage. God wants the marriage relationship to bring us the ultimate in joy and fulfillment.

mal, thus defiling himself; and a woman must never give herself to a male animal, to mate with it; this is a terrible perversion.

24"Do not defile yourselves in any of these ways, for these are the things the heathen do; and because they do them, I am going to cast them out from the land into which you are going. 25That entire country is defiled with this kind of activity; that is why I am punishing the people living there, and will throw them out of the land. 26You must strictly obey all of my laws and ordinances, and you must not do any of these abominable things; these laws apply both to you who are born in the nation of Israel and to foreigners living among you.

27"Yes, all these abominations have been done continually by the people of the land where I am taking you, and the land is defiled. 28Do not do these things or I will throw you out of the land, just as I will throw out the nations that live there now. 29,30Whoever does any of these terrible deeds shall be excommunicated from this nation. So be very sure to obey my laws, and do not practice any of these horrible customs. Do not defile yourselves with the evil deeds of those living in the land where you are going. For I am Jehovah your God."

CHAPTER 19

Commands for Daily Life

The Lord also told Moses to tell the people of Israel, "You must be holy because I, the Lord your God, am holy. You must respect your mothers and fathers, and obey my Sabbath law, for I am the Lord your God. 3,4Do not make or worship idols, for I am Jehovah your God.

5"When you sacrifice a peace offering to the Lord, offer it correctly so that it will be accepted: 6Eat it the same day you offer it, or the next day at the latest; any remaining until the third day must be burned. 7For any of it eaten on the third day is repulsive to me and will not be accepted. 8If you eat it on the third day, you are guilty, for you profane the holiness of Jehovah, and you shall be excommunicated from Jehovah's people.

9"When you harvest your crops, don't reap the corners of your fields, and don't pick up stray grains of wheat from the ground. 10It is the same with your grape crop—don't strip every last piece of fruit from the vines, and don't pick up the grapes that fall to the ground. Leave them for the poor and for those traveling through, for I am Jehovah your God.

11"You must not steal nor lie nor defraud. 12You must not swear to a falsehood, thus bringing reproach upon the name of your God, for I am Jehovah.

13"You shall not rob nor oppress anyone, and you shall pay your hired workers promptly. If something is due them, don't even keep it overnight.

14"You must not curse the deaf nor trip up a blind man as he walks. Fear your God; I am Jehovah!

15"Judges must always be just in their sentences, not noticing whether a person is poor or rich; they must always be perfectly fair.

16"Don't gossip. Don't falsely accuse your neighbor of some crime, for I am Jehovah.

17"Don't hate your brother. Rebuke anyone who sins; don't let him get away with it, or you will be equally guilty. 18Don't seek vengeance. Don't bear a grudge; but love your neighbor as yourself, for I am Jehovah.

19"Obey my laws: Do not mate your cattle with a different kind; don't sow your field with two kinds of seed; don't wear clothes made of half wool and half linen.

19:1-4 Holiness begins at home, and respect for parents is given a prominent place here as it is in the Ten Commandments (Exodus 20:12). Strained family relationships, resulting in dysfunctional families, can become one of the greatest barriers to the life of fulfillment and contentment God desires for us. If God places a priority on respect within family relationships, we should do the same.

19:9-10 The laws given here (illustrated in the story of Ruth) show that God is concerned about poor people. There was a sense of community among the Israelites that went beyond the immediate family. The Israelites were called to consider poor or underprivileged people as their brothers or sisters. With so many needs among God's people today—physical, emotional, spiritual—we should be quick to respond. Only in an atmosphere of acceptance and love can the needs of others be discerned and truly met.

19:11-13, 35-37 God's program for successful living demands honesty in both word and deed. Dishonesty and misrepresentation lead to suspicion, mistrust, and hatred, ultimately destroying our relationships. Human relationships can only grow and thrive if we are willing to tell the truth, the only real basis for trust between people. When there is honesty in our relationships, we can confidently look to others in times of need.

20"If a man seduces a slave girl who is engaged to be married, they shall be tried in a
court but not put to death, because she is not
free. 21The man involved shall bring his guilt
offering to the Lord at the entrance of the
Tabernacle; the offering shall be a ram. 22The
priest shall make atonement with the ram for
the sin the man has committed, and it shall
be forgiven him.
23"When you enter the land and have
planted all kinds of fruit trees, do not eat
the first three crops, for they are considered
ceremonially defiled. 24And the fourth year
the entire crop shall be devoted to the Lord,
and shall be given to the Lord in praise to
him. 25Finally, in the fifth year, the crop is
yours.
26"I am Jehovah your God! You must not
eat meat with undrained blood nor use fortune-telling or witchcraft.
27"You must not trim off your hair on your
temples or clip the edges of your beard, as the
heathen do. 28You shall not cut yourselves nor
put tattoo marks upon yourselves in connection with funeral rites; I am the Lord.
29"Do not violate your daughter's sanctity
by making her a prostitute, lest the land become full of enormous wickedness.
30"Keep my Sabbath laws and reverence my
Tabernacle, for I am the Lord.
31"Do not defile yourselves by consulting
mediums and wizards, for I am Jehovah your
God.
32"You shall give due honor and respect to
the elderly, in the fear of God. I am Jehovah.
33"Do not take advantage of foreigners in
your land; do not wrong them. 34They must
be treated like any other citizen; love them as
yourself, for remember that you too were foreigners in the land of Egypt. I am Jehovah
your God.
35,36"You must be impartial in judgment.
Use accurate measurements—lengths,
weights, and volumes—and give full measure, for I am Jehovah your God who
brought you from the land of Egypt. 37You
must heed all of my commandments and
ordinances, carefully obeying them, for I
am Jehovah."

CHAPTER 20

Punishments for Sin

The Lord gave Moses these further instructions for the people of Israel:
"Anyone—whether an Israelite or a foreigner living among you—who sacrifices his
child as a burnt offering to Molech shall without fail be stoned by his peers. 3And I myself
will turn against that man and cut him off
from all his people, because he has given his
child to Molech, thus making my Tabernacle
unfit for me to live in, and insulting my holy
name. 4And if the people of the land pretend
they do not know what the man has done and
refuse to put him to death, 5then I myself will
set my face against that man and his family
and cut him off, along with all others who
turn to other gods than me.
6"I will set my face against anyone who
consults mediums and wizards instead of me
and I will cut that person off from his people.
7So sanctify yourselves and be holy, for I am
the Lord your God. 8You must obey all of my
commandments, for I am the Lord who sanctifies you.
9"Anyone who curses his father or mother
shall surely be put to death—for he has cursed
his own flesh and blood.
10"If a man commits adultery with another
man's wife, both the man and woman shall be
put to death. 11If a man sleeps with his father's
wife, he has defiled what is his father's; both
the man and the woman must die, for it is
their own fault. 12And if a man has sexual
intercourse with his daughter-in-law, both
shall be executed: they have brought it upon
themselves by defiling each other. 13The penalty for homosexual acts is death to both
parties. They have brought it upon themselves. 14If a man has sexual intercourse with
a woman and with her mother, it is a great
evil. All three shall be burned alive to wipe out
wickedness from among you.
15"If a man has sexual intercourse with an
animal, he shall be executed and the animal
killed. 16If a woman has sexual intercourse
with an animal, kill the woman and the animal, for they deserve their punishment.
17"If a man has sexual intercourse with his

20:1-5 The earlier prohibition against worshiping Molech (18:21) is given again here in even stronger language. Most of the Israelites probably doubted they could ever participate in this type of pagan worship, which included sacrificing children to this god. Yet Israel's history records that several centuries later, King Manasseh sacrificed some of his sons to this god and no one even objected (2 Chronicles 33:6). Our life can also be greatly tainted by the behavior of the people around us. Given enough time, their values may become ours. With God's help we need to stand by our commitment to the moral boundaries he has set up.

sister, whether the daughter of his father or of his mother, it is a shameful thing, and they shall publicly be cut off from the people of Israel. He shall bear his guilt. 18If a man has sexual intercourse with a woman during her period of menstruation, both shall be excommunicated, for he has uncovered the source of her flow, and she has permitted it.

19"Sexual intercourse is outlawed between a man and his maiden aunt—whether the sister of his mother or of his father—for they are near of kin; they shall bear their guilt. 20If a man has intercourse with his uncle's wife, he has taken what belongs to his uncle; their punishment is that they shall bear their sin and die childless. 21If a man marries his brother's wife, this is impurity; for he has taken what belongs to his brother, and they shall be childless.

22"You must obey all of my laws and ordinances so that I will not throw you out of your new land. 23You must not follow the customs of the nations I cast out before you, for they do all these things I have warned you against; that is the reason I abhor them. 24I have promised you their land; I will give it to you to possess it. It is a land 'flowing with milk and honey.' I am the Lord your God who has made a distinction between you and the people of other nations.

25"You shall therefore make a distinction between the birds and animals I have given you permission to eat and those you may not eat. You shall not contaminate yourselves and make yourselves hateful to me by eating any animal or bird which I have forbidden, though the land teem with them. 26You shall be holy to me, for I the Lord am holy, and I have set you apart from all other peoples to be mine.

27"A medium or a wizard—whether man or woman—shall surely be stoned to death. They have caused their own doom."

CHAPTER 21

Rules for the Priests

The Lord said to Moses: "Tell the priests never to defile themselves by touching a dead person, 2,3unless it is a near relative—a mother, father, son, daughter, brother, or unmarried sister for whom he has special responsibility since she has no husband. 4For the priest is a leader among his people, and he may not ceremonially defile himself as an ordinary person can.

5"The priests shall not clip bald spots in their hair or beards, nor cut their flesh. 6They shall be holy unto their God and shall not dishonor and profane his name; otherwise they will be unfit to make food offerings by fire to the Lord their God. 7A priest shall not marry a prostitute, nor a woman of another tribe, and he shall not marry a divorced woman, for he is a holy man of God. 8The priest is set apart to offer the sacrifices of your God; he is holy, for I, the Lord who sanctifies you, am holy. 9The daughter of any priest who becomes a prostitute, thus violating her father's holiness as well as her own, shall be burned alive.

10"The High Priest—anointed with the special anointing oil and wearing the special garments—must not let his hair hang loose in mourning, nor tear his clothing, 11nor be in the presence of any dead person—not even his father or mother. 12He shall not leave the sanctuary [when on duty], nor treat my Tabernacle like an ordinary house, for the consecration of the anointing oil of his God is upon him; I am Jehovah. 13He must marry a virgin. 14,15He may not marry a widow, nor a woman who is divorced, nor a prostitute. She must be a virgin from his own tribe, for he must not be the father of children of mixed blood—half priestly and half ordinary."

16,17And the Lord said to Moses, "Tell Aaron that any of his descendants from generation to generation who have any bodily defect may not offer the sacrifices to God. 18For instance, if a man is blind or lame, or has a broken nose or any extra fingers or toes, 19or has a broken foot or hand, 20or has a humped back, or is a dwarf, or has a defect in his eye, or has pimples or scabby skin, or has imperfect testicles—21although he is a descendant of Aaron—he is not permitted to offer the fire sacrifices to the Lord because of his physical defect. 22However, he shall be fed with the food of the priests from the offerings sacrificed to God, both from the holy and most holy offerings. 23But he shall not go in behind the veil, nor come near the altar, because of the physical defect; this would defile my sanctuary, for it is Jehovah who sanctifies it."

21:7-8 The priest's personal life, including the area of his marriage, was to be holy, reflecting his commitment to God. As believers, each of us is a part of Christ and our body is the home of the Holy Spirit (1 Corinthians 6:15-20). Being holy includes setting healthy boundaries that will lead to purity in sexual relationships.

[24]So Moses gave these instructions to Aaron and his sons and to all the people of Israel.

CHAPTER 22

The Lord told Moses, "Instruct Aaron and his sons to be very careful not to defile my holy name by desecrating the people's sacred gifts; for I am Jehovah. [3]From now on and forever, if a priest who is ceremonially defiled sacrifices the animals brought by the people or handles the gifts dedicated to Jehovah, he shall be discharged from the priesthood. For I am Jehovah!

[4]"No priest who is a leper or who has a running sore may eat the holy sacrifices until healed. And any priest who touches a dead person, or who is defiled by a seminal emission, [5]or who touches any reptile or other forbidden thing, or who touches anyone who is ceremonially defiled for any reason—[6]that priest shall be defiled until evening and shall not eat of the holy sacrifices until after he has bathed that evening. [7]When the sun is down, then he shall be purified again and may eat the holy food, for it is his source of life. [8]He may not eat any animal that dies of itself or is torn by wild animals, for this will defile him. I am Jehovah. [9]Warn the priests to follow these instructions carefully, lest they be declared guilty and die for violating these rules. I am the Lord who sanctifies them.

[10]"No one may eat of the holy sacrifices unless he is a priest; no one visiting the priest, for instance, nor a hired servant, may eat this food. [11]However, there is one exception—if the priest buys a slave with his own money, that slave may eat it, and any slave children born in his household may eat it. [12]If a priest's daughter is married outside the tribe, she may not eat the sacred offerings. [13]But if she is a widow or divorced and has no son to support her, and has returned home to her father's household, she may eat of her father's food again. But otherwise, no one who is not in the priestly families may eat this food.

[14]"If someone should eat of the holy sacrifices without realizing it, he shall return to the priest the amount he has used, with 20 percent added; [15]for the holy sacrifices brought by the people of Israel must not be defiled by being eaten by unauthorized persons, for these sacrifices have been offered to the Lord. [16]Anyone who violates this law is guilty and is in great danger because he has eaten the sacred offerings; for I am Jehovah who sanctifies the offerings."

Acceptable Animal Offerings

[17,18]And the Lord said to Moses, "Tell Aaron and his sons and all the people of Israel that if an Israelite or other person living among you offers a burnt offering sacrifice to the Lord—whether it is to fulfill a promise or is a spontaneous free will offering—[19]it will only be acceptable to the Lord if it is a male animal without defect; it must be a young bull or a sheep or a goat. [20]Anything that has a defect must not be offered, for it will not be accepted.

[21]"Anyone sacrificing a peace offering to the Lord from the herd or flock, whether to fulfill a vow or as a voluntary offering, must sacrifice an animal that has no defect, or it will not be accepted: [22]An animal that is blind or disabled or mutilated, or which has sores or itch or any other skin disease, must not be offered to the Lord; it is not a fit burnt offering for the altar of the Lord. [23]If the young bull or lamb presented to the Lord has anything superfluous or lacking in its body parts, it may be offered as a free will offering, but not for a vow. [24]An animal that has injured genitals—crushed or castrated—shall not be offered to the Lord at any time. [25]This restriction applies to the sacrifices made by foreigners among you as well as those made by yourselves, for no defective animal is acceptable for this sacrifice."

[26,27]And the Lord said to Moses, "When a bullock, sheep, or goat is born, it shall be left with its mother for seven days, but from the eighth day onward it is acceptable as a sacrifice by fire to the Lord. [28]You shall not slaughter a mother animal and her offspring the same day, whether she is a cow or ewe. [29,30]When you offer the Lord a sacrifice of thanksgiving, you must do it in the right way, eating the sacrificial animal the same day it is slain. Leave none of it for the following day. I am the Lord.

[31]"You must keep all of my commandments, for I am the Lord. [32,33]You must not

22:31-33 God calls us to remember his deliverance in the past in order to find strength to live for him in the present. He has graciously made it possible for us to be free from the power of the sin in our past. He has rescued us from Satan's kingdom and delivered us from our slavery to sin. He wants us to remember all he has done in the past so we can find courage to face the challenges ahead.

treat me as common and ordinary. Revere me and hallow me, for I, the Lord, made you holy to myself and rescued you from Egypt to be my own people! I am Jehovah!"

CHAPTER 23

Special Days of Celebration

The Lord said to Moses, "Announce to the people of Israel that they are to celebrate several annual festivals of the Lord—times when all Israel will assemble and worship me. [3](These are in addition to your Sabbaths—the seventh day of every week—which are always days of rest in every home, times for assembling to worship, and for resting from the normal business of the week.)

[4]These are the holy festivals which are to be observed each year:

The Passover

[5]"*The Passover of the Lord:* This is to be celebrated on the first day of April, beginning at sundown.

The Festival of Unleavened Bread

[6]"*The Festival of Unleavened Bread:* This is to be celebrated beginning the day following the Passover, and for seven days you must not eat any bread made with yeast. [7]On the first day of this festival, you shall gather the people for worship, and all ordinary work shall cease. [8]You shall do the same on the seventh day of the festival. On each of the intervening days you shall make an offering by fire to the Lord.

The Festival of First Fruits

[9-11]"*The Festival of First Fruits:* When you arrive in the land I will give you and you reap your first harvest, bring the first sheaf of the harvest to the priest on the day after the Sabbath. He shall wave it before the Lord in a gesture of offering, and it will be accepted by the Lord as your gift. [12]That same day you shall sacrifice to the Lord a male yearling lamb without defect as a burnt offering. [13]A grain offering shall accompany it, consisting of a fifth of a bushel of finely ground flour mixed with olive oil, to be offered by fire to the Lord; this will be very pleasant to him. Also offer a drink offering consisting of three pints of wine. [14]Until this is done you must not eat any of the harvest for yourselves—neither fresh kernels nor bread nor parched grain. This is a permanent law throughout your nation.

The Harvest Festival

[15,16]"*The Harvest Festival (Festival of Pentecost):* Fifty days later you shall bring to the Lord an offering of a sample of the new grain of your later crops. [17]This shall consist of two loaves of bread from your homes to be waved before the Lord in a gesture of offering. Bake this bread from a fifth of a bushel of fine flour containing yeast. It is an offering to the Lord of the first sampling of your later crops. [18]Along with the bread and the wine, you shall sacrifice as burnt offerings to the Lord seven yearling lambs without defects, one young bull, and two rams. All are fire offerings, very acceptable to Jehovah. [19]And you shall offer one male goat for a sin offering and two male yearling lambs for a peace offering.

[20]"The priests shall wave these offerings before the Lord along with the loaves representing the first sampling of your later crops. They are holy to the Lord and will be given to the priests as food. [21]That day shall be announced as a time of sacred convocation of all the people; don't do any work that day. This is a law to be honored from generation to generation. [22](When you reap your harvests, you must not thoroughly reap all the corners of the fields, nor pick up the fallen grain; leave it for the poor and for foreigners living among you who have no land of their own; I am Jehovah your God!)

The Festival of Trumpets

[23,24]"*The Festival of Trumpets:* Mid-September is a time for all the people to meet together for worship; it is a time of remembrance, and is to be announced by loud blowing of trumpets. [25]Don't do any hard work on that day, but offer a sacrifice by fire to the Lord.

The Day of Atonement

[26,27]"*The Day of Atonement* follows nine days later: All the people are to come together before the Lord, saddened by their sin; and they shall offer sacrifices by fire to the Lord.

23:4-8 The yearly festivals of Passover and Unleavened Bread reminded the Israelites how God had delivered them from Egyptian bondage. Leviticus 1–7 contains specific instructions on how the Israelites were to worship God. In order for us to experience a true relationship with God, we must first acknowledge that Christ is our Passover Lamb. John the Baptist introduced him as "the Lamb of God who takes away the world's sin" (John 1:29). This initial step will enable us to worship God in spirit and in truth.

[28]Don't do any work that day, for it is a special day for making atonement before the Lord your God. [29]Anyone who does not spend the day in repentance and sorrow for sin shall be excommunicated from his people. [30,31]And I will put to death anyone who does any kind of work that day. This is a law of Israel from generation to generation. [32]For this is a Sabbath of rest, and in it you shall go without food and be filled with sorrow; this time for atonement begins in the evening and continues through the next day.

The Festival of Shelters

[33,34]"*The Festival of Shelters:* Five days later, on the last day of September, is the Festival of Shelters to be celebrated before the Lord for seven days. [35]On the first day there will be a sacred assembly of all the people; don't do any hard work that day. [36]On each of the seven days of the festival you are to sacrifice an offering by fire to the Lord. The eighth day requires another sacred convocation of all the people, at which time there will again be an offering by fire to the Lord. It is the closing assembly, and no regular work is permitted.

[37]"(These, then, are the regular annual festivals—sacred convocations of all people—when offerings to the Lord are to be made by fire. [38]These annual festivals are in addition to your regular Sabbaths—the weekly days of holy rest. The sacrifices made during the festivals are to be in addition to your regular giving and normal fulfillment of your vows.)

[39]"This last day of September, at the end of your harvesting, is the time to begin to celebrate this seven-day festival before the Lord. Remember that the first and last days of the festival are special days of rest. [40]On the first day, take boughs of fruit trees laden with fruit, and palm fronds, and the boughs of leafy trees—such as willows that grow by the brooks—and [build shelters with them], rejoicing before the Lord your God for seven days. [41]This seven-day annual feast is a law from generation to generation. [42]During those seven days, all of you who are native Israelites are to live in these shelters. [43]The purpose of this is to remind the people of Israel, generation after generation, that I rescued you from Egypt, and caused you to live in shelters. I am Jehovah your God."

[44]So Moses announced these annual festivals of the Lord to the people of Israel.

CHAPTER 24

The Memorial Offering

The Lord said to Moses, "Tell the people of Israel to bring you pure olive oil for an eternal flame [3,4]in the lampstand of pure gold which stands outside the veil that secludes the Holy of Holies. Each morning and evening Aaron shall supply it with fresh oil and trim the wicks. It will be an eternal flame before the Lord from generation to generation.

[5-8]"Every Sabbath day the High Priest shall place twelve loaves of bread in two rows upon the gold table that stands before the Lord. These loaves shall be baked from finely ground flour, using a fifth of a bushel for each. Pure frankincense shall be sprinkled along each row. This will be a memorial offering made by fire to the Lord, in memory of his everlasting covenant with the people of Israel. [9]The bread shall be eaten by Aaron and his sons, in a place set apart for the purpose. For these are offerings made by fire to the Lord under a permanent law of God and are most holy."

Punished for Cursing God

[10]Out in the camp one day, a young man whose mother was an Israelite and whose father was an Egyptian, got into a fight with one of the men of Israel. [11]During the fight the Egyptian man's son cursed God, and was brought to Moses for judgment. (His mother's name was Shelomith, daughter of Dibri of the tribe of Dan.) [12]He was put in jail until the Lord would indicate what to do with him.

[13,14]And the Lord said to Moses, "Take him outside the camp and tell all who heard him to lay their hands upon his head; then all the people are to execute him by stoning. [15,16]And tell the people of Israel that anyone who curses his God must pay the penalty: he must die. All the congregation shall stone him; this law applies to the foreigner as well as to the

23:33-43 The Festival of Shelters, like Israel's other yearly feasts, was to remind the people of a crucial event in their history. Required for all Israelite males, the festival celebrated God's protective care of his people during their forty-year sojourn in the wilderness. It pictured the tremendous grace of God in this "recovery period," from slavery in Egypt to victory in Canaan. This same God is faithful to us in our times of recovery from sin, and he extends his grace to us. We may not have a formal week of feasting to remember those times, but we should set aside one day each week to remember them and praise God for our spiritual growth.

Israelite who blasphemes the name of
Jehovah. He must die.
17"Also, all murderers must be executed.
18Anyone who kills an animal [that isn't his]
shall replace it. 19The penalty for injuring anyone is to be injured in exactly the same way:
20fracture for fracture, eye for eye, tooth for
tooth. Whatever anyone does to another shall
be done to him.
21"To repeat, whoever kills an animal must
replace it, and whoever kills a man must die.
22You shall have the same law for the foreigner
as for the home-born citizen, for I am Jehovah
your God."
23So they took the youth out of the camp
and stoned him until he died, as Jehovah had
commanded Moses.

CHAPTER 25

Sabbath Rest for the Land

While Moses was on Mount Sinai, the Lord
gave him these instructions for the people of
Israel:
"When you come into the land I am going
to give you, you must let the land rest before
the Lord every seventh year. 3For six years you
may sow your field and prune your vineyards
and harvest your crops, 4but during the seventh year the land is to lie fallow before the
Lord, uncultivated. Don't sow your crops and
don't prune your vineyards during that entire
year. 5Don't even reap for yourself the volunteer crops that come up, and don't gather the
grapes for yourself; for it is a year of rest for
the land. 6,7Any crops that do grow that year
shall be free to all—for you, your servants,
your slaves, and any foreigners living among
you. Cattle and wild animals alike shall be
allowed to graze there.

The Year of Jubilee

8"Every fiftieth year, 9on the Day of Atonement, let the trumpets blow loud and long
throughout the land. 10For the fiftieth year
shall be holy, a time to proclaim liberty
throughout the land to all enslaved debtors,
and a time for the canceling of all public and
private debts. It shall be a year when all the
family estates sold to others shall be returned
to the original owners or their heirs.
11"What a happy year it will be! In it you
shall not sow, nor gather crops nor grapes;
12for it is a holy Year of Jubilee for you. That
year your food shall be the volunteer crops
that grow wild in the fields. 13Yes, during the
Year of Jubilee everyone shall return home to
his original family possession; if he has sold
it, it shall be his again! 14-16Because of this, if
the land is sold or bought during the preceding forty-nine years, a fair price shall be arrived at by counting the number of years until
the Jubilee. If the Jubilee is many years away,
the price will be high; if few years, the price
will be low; for what you are really doing is
selling the number of crops the new owner
will get from the land before it is returned to
you.
17,18"You must fear your God and not over-
charge! For I am Jehovah. Obey my laws if you
want to live safely in the land. 19When you
obey, the land will yield bumper crops and
you can eat your fill in safety. 20But you will
ask, 'What shall we eat the seventh year, since
we are not allowed to plant or harvest crops
that year?' 21,22The answer is, 'I will bless you
with bumper crops the sixth year that will last
you until the crops of the eighth year are
harvested!' 23And remember, the land is mine,
so you may not sell it permanently. You are
merely my tenants and sharecroppers!

Laws for Property Owners

24"In every contract of sale there must be a
stipulation that the land can be redeemed at
any time by the seller. 25If anyone becomes
poor and sells some of his land, then his
nearest relatives may redeem it. 26If there is no
one else to redeem it, and he himself gets
together enough money, 27then he may always buy it back at a price proportionate to
the number of harvests until the Jubilee, and
the owner must accept the money and return
the land to him. 28But if the original owner is
not able to redeem it, then it shall belong to
the new owner until the Year of Jubilee; but at
the Jubilee year it must be returned again.
29"If a man sells a house in the city, he has

25:1-7 The sabbatical year, like the weekly Sabbath day, was instituted by God as a special period of rest for the Israelites. Every seventh year was a time of rest for the land, animals, and people. Their rest from work was in itself an act of faith, proving that they believed God would provide for the coming year. It also gave them time to reflect on the fact that God was the true provider: everything they owned ultimately came from his generous hand. When we realize this truth, we will be better able to commit ourselves into God's hands. He is more than able to provide for our needs and help us in our recovery.

up to one year to redeem it, with full right of redemption during that time. 30But if it is not redeemed within the year, then it will belong permanently to the new owner—it does not return to the original owner in the Year of Jubilee. 31But village houses—a village is a settlement without fortifying walls around it—are like farmland, redeemable at any time, and are always returned to the original owner in the Year of Jubilee.

32"There is one exception: The homes of the Levites, even though in walled cities, may be redeemed at any time, 33and must be returned to the original owners in the Year of Jubilee; for the Levites will not be given farmland like the other tribes, but will receive only houses in their cities, and the surrounding fields. 34The Levites are not permitted to sell the fields of common land surrounding their cities, for these are their permanent possession, and they must belong to no one else.

35"If your brother becomes poor, you are responsible to help him; invite him to live with you as a guest in your home. 36Fear your God and let your brother live with you; and don't charge him interest on the money you lend him. 37Remember—no interest; and give him what he needs, at your cost: don't try to make a profit! 38For I, the Lord your God, brought you out of the land of Egypt to *give* you the land of Canaan, and to be your God.

Laws for Israelite Slaves

39"If a fellow Israelite becomes poor and sells himself to you, you must not treat him as an ordinary slave, 40but rather as a hired servant or as a guest; and he shall serve you only until the Year of Jubilee. 41At that time he can leave with his children and return to his own family and possessions. 42For I brought you from the land of Egypt, and you are my servants; so you may not be sold as ordinary slaves 43or treated harshly; fear your God.

44"However, you may purchase slaves from the foreign nations living around you, 45and you may purchase the children of the foreigners living among you, even though they have been born in your land. 46They will be permanent slaves for you to pass on to your children after you; but your brothers, the people of Israel, shall not be treated so.

47"If a foreigner living among you becomes rich, and an Israelite becomes poor and sells himself to the foreigner or to the foreigner's family, 48he may be redeemed by one of his brothers, 49his uncle, nephew, or anyone else who is a near relative. He may also redeem himself if he can find the money. 50The price of his freedom shall be in proportion to the number of years left before the Year of Jubilee—whatever it would cost to hire a servant for that number of years. 51If there are still many years until the Jubilee, he shall pay almost the amount he received when he sold himself; 52if the years have passed and only a few remain until the Jubilee, then he will repay only a small part of the amount he received when he sold himself. 53If he sells himself to a foreigner, the foreigner must treat him as a hired servant rather than as a slave or as property. 54If he has not been redeemed by the time the Year of Jubilee arrives, then he and his children shall be freed at that time. 55For the people of Israel are *my* servants; I brought them from the land of Egypt; I am the Lord your God.

CHAPTER 26

Rewards for Obedience

"You must have no idols; you must never worship carved images, obelisks, or shaped stones, for I am the Lord your God. 2You must obey my Sabbath laws of rest, and reverence my Tabernacle, for I am the Lord.

3"If you obey all of my commandments, 4,5I will give you regular rains, and the land will yield bumper crops, and the trees will be loaded with fruit long after the normal time!

25:8-55 The Year of Jubilee took place every fifty years. At this time all the lands and possessions that had passed from one family to another during the previous forty-nine years were returned to the original owners. This reminded the Israelites that God was really the owner of all their possessions. They were only the managers. This would have curbed their tendency toward materialism. It would also provide families that had lost everything during the previous fifty years a chance for recovery. True contentment in life comes only when we see our material possessions as gifts from the hand of God. Jesus taught that we should give God first place in our life and live as he wants us to; then God will provide everything we need to live in this world (Matthew 6:33).

25:35-38 God's call to love our neighbors was extended here to those who had fallen into poverty. The fellowship of God's people was always intended to be redemptive; those in need were to be cared for by those with plenty. This was true not only for physical needs, but for emotional and spiritual needs as well. Recovery and rebuilding in our life will rarely happen if we have to do it all alone. It takes the support and encouragement of those in God's family who are closest to us.

And grapes will still be ripening when sowing
time comes again. You shall eat your fill, and
live safely in the land, 6for I will give you
peace, and you will go to sleep without fear. I
will chase away the dangerous animals. 7You
will chase your enemies; they will die beneath
your swords. 8Five of you will chase a hundred, and a hundred of you, ten thousand!
You will defeat all of your enemies. 9I will look
after you, and multiply you, and fulfill my
covenant with you. 10You will have such a
surplus of crops that you won't know what to
do with them when the new harvest is ready!
11And I will live among you and not despise
you. 12I will walk among you and be your God,
and you shall be my people. 13For I am the
Lord your God who brought you out of the
land of Egypt, so that you would be slaves no
longer; I have broken your chains so that you
can walk with dignity.

Consequences of Disobedience

14"But if you will not listen to me or obey me,
15but reject my laws, 16this is what I will do to
you: I will punish you with sudden terrors
and panic, and with tuberculosis and burning
fever; your eyes shall be consumed and your
life shall ebb away; you will sow your crops in
vain, for your enemies will eat them. 17I will
set my face against you and you will flee
before your attackers; those who hate you will
rule you; you will even run when no one is
chasing you!

18"And if you still disobey me, I will punish
you seven times more severely for your sins.
19I will break your proud power and make
your heavens as iron and your earth as
bronze. 20Your strength shall be spent in vain;
for your land shall not yield its crops, nor
your trees their fruit.

21"And if even then you will not obey me
and listen to me, I will send you seven times
more plagues because of your sins. 22I will
send wild animals to kill your children and
destroy your cattle and reduce your numbers
so that your roads will be deserted.

23"And if even this will not reform you, but
you continue to walk against my wishes,
24then I will walk against your wishes, and I,
even I, will personally smite you seven times
for your sin. 25I will revenge the breaking of
my covenant by bringing war against you.
You will flee to your cities, and I will send a
plague among you there; and you will be
conquered by your enemies. 26I will destroy
your food supply so that one oven will be
large enough to bake all the bread available
for ten entire families; and you will still be
hungry after your pittance has been doled out
to you.

27"And if you still won't listen to me or obey
me, 28then I will let loose my great anger and
send you seven times greater punishment for
your sins. 29You shall eat your own sons and
daughters, 30and I will destroy the altars on
the hills where you worship your idols, and I
will cut down your incense altars, leaving
your dead bodies to rot among your idols; and
I will abhor you. 31I will make your cities
desolate, and destroy your places of worship,
and will not respond to your incense offerings. 32Yes, I will desolate your land; your
enemies shall live in it, utterly amazed at what
I have done to you.

33"I will scatter you out among the nations,
destroying you with war as you go. Your land
shall be desolate and your cities destroyed.
34,35Then at last the land will rest and make up
for the many years you refused to let it lie idle;
for it will lie desolate all the years that you are
captives in enemy lands. Yes, then the land
will rest and enjoy its Sabbaths! It will make
up for the rest you didn't give it every seventh
year when you lived upon it.

36"And for those who are left alive, I will
cause them to be dragged away to distant

26:11-13 God's promises of rewards for Israel's obedience are culminated in this powerful affirmation of his love for his people. Again, the Exodus is used as a reminder that God took them from bondage and humiliation and lifted them up to become a people of dignity. As we learn to obey him, God offers us the same hope of recovery. His deliverance can provide us with a new life of moral and spiritual dignity. God assures us of this by offering to bring Christ's personal presence into each Christian's life (Matthew 28:20).

26:14-39 Here God warns his people about what will happen to those who are disobedient to God's laws. After reading this, some might get the idea that God is harsh and unloving. It might seem that he delights in punishing those who refuse to do things his way. But this long list of warnings about the consequences of sin is really an extended love letter from God. God doesn't want us to suffer; he doesn't want to punish us. But God does understand the destructive consequences of sin. He knows that certain activities will cause suffering to us and to those around us. So he warns us away from them, giving us a program to follow that will lead to healthy and joyful living. God's program, though viewed by some as restrictive, is actually the shortest path to a life of fulfillment.

lands as prisoners of war and slaves. There they will live in constant fear. The sound of a leaf driven in the wind will send them fleeing as though chased by a man with a sword; they shall fall when no one is pursuing them. [37]Yes, though none pursue they shall stumble over each other in flight, as though fleeing in battle, with no power to stand before their enemies. [38]You shall perish among the nations and be destroyed among your enemies. [39]Those left shall pine away in enemy lands because of their sins, the same sins as those of their fathers.

Results of Confessed Sin

[40,41]"But at last they shall confess their sins and their fathers' sins of treachery against me. (Because they were against me, I was against them, and brought them into the land of their enemies.) When at last their evil hearts are humbled and they accept the punishment I send them for their sins, [42]then I will remember again my promises to Abraham, Isaac, and Jacob, and I will remember the land (and its desolation). [43]For the land shall enjoy its Sabbaths as it lies desolate. But then at last they shall accept their punishment for rejecting my laws and for despising my rule. [44]But despite all they have done, I will not utterly destroy them and my covenant with them, for I am Jehovah their God. [45]For their sakes I will remember my promises to their ancestors to be their God. For I brought their forefathers out of Egypt as all the nations watched in wonder. I am Jehovah."

[46]These were the laws, ordinances, and instructions that Jehovah gave to the people of Israel, through Moses, on Mount Sinai.

CHAPTER 27

Payments to the Lord

The Lord said to Moses, "Tell the people of Israel that when a person makes a special vow to give himself to the Lord, he shall give these payments instead: [3]A man from the age of twenty to sixty shall pay twenty-five dollars; [4]a woman from the age of twenty to sixty shall pay fifteen dollars; [5]a boy from five to twenty shall pay ten dollars; a girl, five dollars. [6]A boy one month to five years old shall have paid for him two and a half dollars; a girl, one and a half dollars. [7]A man over sixty shall pay seven and a half dollars; a woman, five dollars. [8]But if the person is too poor to pay this amount, he shall be brought to the priest, and the priest shall talk it over with him, and he shall pay as the priest shall decide.

[9]"But if it is an animal that is vowed to be given to the Lord as a sacrifice, it must be given. [10]The vow may not be changed; the donor may neither change his mind about giving it to the Lord, nor substitute good for bad or bad for good; if he does, both the first and the second shall belong to the Lord! [11,12]But if the animal given to the Lord is not a kind that is permitted as a sacrifice, the owner shall bring it to the priest to value it, and he shall be told how much to pay instead. [13]If the animal is a kind that may be offered as a sacrifice, but the man wants to redeem it, then he shall pay 20 percent more than the value set by the priest.

[14,15]"If someone donates his home to the Lord and then wishes to redeem it, the priest will decide its value, and the man shall pay that amount plus 20 percent, and the house will be his again.

[16]"If a man dedicates any part of his field to the Lord, value it in proportion to its size, as indicated by the amount of seed required to sow it. A section of land that requires ten bushels of barley seed for sowing is valued at twenty-five dollars. [17]If a man dedicates his field in the Year of Jubilee, then the whole estimate shall stand; [18]but if it is after the Year of Jubilee, then the value shall be in proportion to the number of years remaining until the next Year of Jubilee. [19]If the man decides to redeem the field, he shall pay 20 percent in addition to the priest's valuation, and the field will be his again. [20]But if he decides not to redeem the field, or if he has sold the field to someone else [and has given to the Lord his rights to it at the Year of Jubilee], it shall not be returned to him again. [21]When it is freed in the Year of Jubilee, it shall belong to the Lord as a field devoted to him, and it shall be given to the priests.

[22]"If a man dedicates to the Lord a field he has bought, but which is not part of his family possession, [23]the priest shall estimate the value until the Year of Jubilee, and he shall immediately give that estimated value to the

26:40-42 Even after a harsh warning for those disobedient to his laws (26:14-39), God shows great love for his people in this promise of restoration. God delights in restoring those who repent. The parable of the Prodigal Son (Luke 15) also tells of a loving father who delights in finding his lost son. Even if we have fallen away from him, God still waits with open arms for us to return.

Lord, [24]and in the Year of Jubilee the field shall
return to the original owner from whom it
was bought. [25]All the valuations shall be
stated in standard money.
[26]"You may not dedicate to the Lord the
firstborn of any ox or sheep, for it is already
his. [27]But if it is the firstborn of an animal that
cannot be sacrificed because it is not on the
list of those acceptable to the Lord, then the
owner shall pay the priest's estimate of its
worth, plus 20 percent; or if the owner does
not redeem it, the priest may sell it to someone else. [28]However, anything utterly devoted
to the Lord—people, animals, or inherited
fields—shall not be sold or redeemed, for they
are most holy to the Lord. [29]No one sentenced
by the courts to die may pay a fine instead;
he shall surely be put to death.
[30]"A tenth of the produce of the land,
whether grain or fruit, is the Lord's, and is
holy. [31]If anyone wants to buy back this fruit
or grain, he must add a fifth to its value. [32]And
the Lord owns every tenth animal of your
herds and flocks and other domestic animals,
as they pass by for counting. [33]The tenth given
to the Lord shall not be selected on the basis
of whether it is good or bad, and there shall
be no substitutions; for if there is any change
made, then both the original and the substitution shall belong to the Lord, and may not
be bought back!"
[34]These are the commandments the Lord
gave to Moses for the people of Israel on
Mount Sinai.

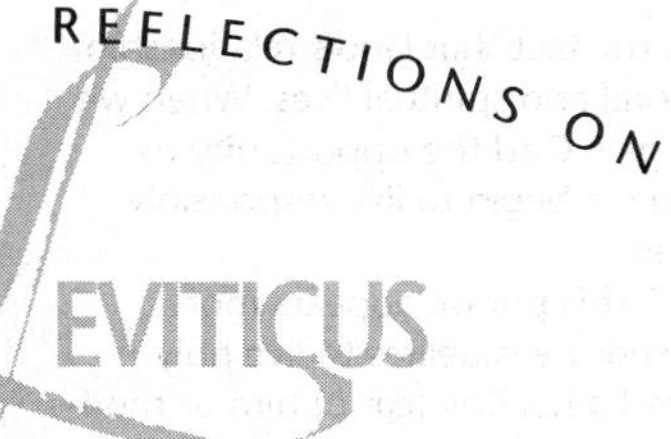

REFLECTIONS ON LEVITICUS

insights FROM THE OFFERINGS

In **Leviticus 1:3-13** we see the first object lesson given to God's people—the burnt offering. By identifying himself with the offering, the person bringing the offering was committing his life to God in a fresh way. In Romans 12:1-2 Paul similarly spoke of presenting our body as a living sacrifice to God. This is an essential step in recovery and a step toward positive growth for anyone. Only when we place our life in God's hands will he be able to change us through his power.

Not every Israelite was financially able to bring a large animal sacrifice to God. In **Leviticus 1:10-14** we see that God allowed worshipers to bring smaller offerings (a sheep, goat, dove, or pigeon), as they were able. Joseph and Mary, the parents of Jesus, were evidently quite poor because they offered the smallest of the sacrifices (see Luke 2:24). We may feel we have very little to offer to God compared to other people, but he doesn't compare us with others. He asks that our worship and commitment to him simply reflect what he has given to us.

The sin offering, introduced in **Leviticus 4:1-2**, was not a voluntary act of worship, but a required response to sin. God takes sin very seriously and holds us accountable for dealing with it through confession. Confession of sin is not just a voluntary activity; it is demanded by God and is a basic requirement for healthy living.

The sin offering was not just for blatant, intentional sins. As we see in **Leviticus 4:2-3, 13, 22, 27**, it was primarily designed to deal with unintentional sins. God takes sin seriously—even the sins we aren't aware of! God recognizes that even unintentional sins have grave consequences. We sometimes sin unintentionally against our children in ways that our parents have sinned against us. Family sins pass on down the line. We need to carefully examine ourselves before God on a regular basis and repent of all known sin in our life—with no excuses or denials. We can be thankful that God understands our human frailty and graciously provides ways for us to deal with it.

insights FROM THE ATONEMENT CEREMONY

The word *atonement* means "to cover"; it appears in **Leviticus 16:10** and in fifty-one other places in the book. The covering of sin brought reconciliation between the Israelites and God, thus the term *at-one-ment*. God intends this for our life as well. He wants us to find forgiveness for our sins and to be reconciled to him. God is in the business of restoring broken relationships. By means of forgiveness, he provides a way for the restoration of relationships broken by sin.

In **Leviticus 16:7-22** we see two goats set apart for the atonement ceremony. The first was associated with the people's sin and was sacrificed to God as a sin offering. The second goat, also associated with the sins of the people, was led into the wilderness and then released. This "scapegoat" took the sins of the people and carried them away. This illustrated the truth of Psalm 103:12, that God removes "our sins as far away from us as the east is from the west." God has done this through the ultimate Scapegoat, Jesus Christ, who has taken all our sins upon himself. One of the most important steps in our recovery from sin and failure is learning to let it go. The fact that God himself has taken it away should help us as we do this.

insights FROM GOD'S LAWS

In **Leviticus 11:44-45** God forbade the Israelites to touch crawling creatures. God may have given this law for logical reasons, such as a concern for his people's health. It seems, however, that many of these laws were given for theological reasons—so the Israelites might be different from the surrounding nations—"set apart" or "holy" unto God. While God may sometimes show us logical reasons for obeying him, this should not be our primary motivation for obedience. We are to obey him because he calls us to be different—"set apart" or "holy"—just as he is holy. And we can trust that his program will lead us to discover the best life has to offer, whether what he asks seems logical to us or not.

Leviticus 18:1-5 sets the tone for the rest of the book. It affirms the fact that God's relationship with his people was intended to affect the practical areas of their moral and spiritual lives. When we commit our life to God through a relationship with Jesus Christ, we give God the opportunity to transform us. Spiritual growth can only come about, however, when we begin to live responsibly before God, handing over all our moral decisions to his wise direction.

In **Leviticus 18:4-5** we see the refrain "I am the Lord your God." This phrase appears more often in Leviticus than in any other book of the Bible. When God asked the Israelites to live holy lives, he knew that this would be difficult. God knew they would need a healthy fear of him to motivate them to obedience. So he continually reminded them of his identity as the Lord their God—the God who had revealed himself with terrifying power at Mount Sinai. Fear or respect for God is a good starting point if we want to live according to his plan. And it should encourage us to know that this terrifying God sent his Son to help us to live according to that plan.

Incest (18:6-18), adultery (18:20), child sacrifice (18:21), homosexuality (18:22), and bestiality (18:23) were all practiced by godless societies in the ancient Near East. In **Leviticus 18:24-30** God tells us that these lead to the deterioration and destruction of society. It is only through a relationship with God that people are able to be morally pure and recover from the destructive effects of their sin. God's standards are given for our good.

In **Leviticus 19:1-2** God's call to holiness is repeated (see 11:44). God's holiness is the model and motivation for God's people to lead holy lives. God knows our weaknesses and our failures, yet he places before us the goal of his righteousness. It is only with Christ's help that we can reach this goal. Through his death we have cleansing from our failures and sins, and through his life (lived in us by the power of the Holy Spirit) we have the power to live a morally pure and holy life.

As we compare **Leviticus 19:18** and **19:33-34** we see that the call to love one's neighbor was extended not only to fellow Israelites, but to foreigners as well. This was a radical concept among the people of ancient times just as it is for us today. Jesus quoted this commandment as the second great commandment of the law (Matthew 22:39; Mark 12:31; Luke 10:27). It should be easier for us to have compassion on others if we remember that God had compassion on us and freed us from our slavery to sin.

NUMBERS

THE BIG PICTURE

A. PREPARATIONS (IN SINAI) FOR A LIFE OF FAITH IN THE PROMISED LAND (1:1–10:10)
   1. Taking the Census (1:1–4:49)
   2. Cleansing the Camp (5:1–7:89)
   3. Dedicating the Priests (8:1-26)
   4. Celebrating the Passover (9:1–10:10)

B. BARRIERS TO A LIFE OF FAITH IN THE WILDERNESS WANDERINGS (10:11–21:35)
   1. From Sinai to Kadesh (10:11–14:45)
   2. In the Wilderness Wanderings near Kadesh (15:1–19:22)
   3. From Kadesh to Moab (20:1–21:35)

C. PREPARATIONS (IN MOAB) FOR A LIFE OF FAITH IN THE PROMISED LAND (22:1–36:13)
   1. God's Sovereignty over Balaam and Balak (22:1–25:18)
   2. A Final Census (26:1-65)
   3. Preparations to Enter Canaan (27:1–36:13)

This book has long been known as Numbers because it begins and ends with a census of Israel. However, the Hebrew name for the book, "In the Wilderness," better describes what the book is about. While in the wilderness, God's people experienced not only God's kindness and patience, but also his holy discipline. They learned that their new freedom from Egyptian bondage included the responsibility to serve and obey God.

After their exodus from Egypt, the Israelites moved quickly through the wilderness to the edge of the Promised Land. But when they saw the strength of the people living there, they became afraid and refused to conquer it. As a result, they were sent back into the wilderness to wander for almost forty years—just because they refused to act upon God's promises! Numbers ends with the Israelites again poised at the border of the Promised Land. Forty years of wilderness lessons had taught them that God's power was available to all who trusted and obeyed him.

The Israelites' experiences illustrate the importance of a practical faith in God. They show us the blessed fruits of obedience and the disastrous consequences of sin. We see how God's love is shown not only by his gracious forgiveness, but also through his wise discipline and call to accountability.

It is usually in our wilderness experiences that we discover the true meaning of life, faith, and a personal relationship with God. God graciously offers us deliverance and cleansing, but our newfound freedom carries with it personal responsibility. We need to act on God's promises and follow the program he sets out for us. If we do, he will lead us through the wilderness; he will never allow us to wander forever.

THE BOTTOM LINE

PURPOSE: To demonstrate historically that God's great mercy and forgiveness toward his people are consistent with the firm, loving discipline he shows when they disobey. AUTHOR: Moses. AUDIENCE: The people of Israel. DATE WRITTEN: During and shortly after Israel's wilderness experience, between 1445–1406 B.C. SETTING: Beginning with a census at the Sinai encampment, Numbers follows the people of Israel during thirty-eight years of wilderness wandering near Kadesh Barnea to the plains of Moab, just east of the Promised Land. KEY VERSES: "Oh, please, show the great power [of your patience] by forgiving our sins and showing us your steadfast love" (14:17-18). KEY PLACES: Mount Sinai, Kadesh Barnea, Moab. KEY PEOPLE: Moses, Aaron, Caleb, Joshua.

RECOVERY THEMES

Experiencing the Wilderness: All of us wish that our recovery would involve a dramatic escape from slavery and an immediate entrance into the Promised Land. We would love to leave out the wilderness experience in between. But growth and recovery occur within the wilderness. It's in the wilderness that we come to terms with who we really are. We discover faith and the reality of God's faithfulness and patience. It's in the wilderness that we discover that we cannot make it alone, that we need to turn our life over to God and depend on him. Numbers reveals the value of our own wilderness experiences as we progress in our recovery.

The Importance of Faith: Faith is the opposite of self-sufficiency. The Israelites were confronted daily with the fact that left to their own abilities, they would die in the wilderness. They were forced to live one day at a time, acting on their faith that God would provide what they needed each day. They needed a practical faith—one that looked to God for safety, food, and even health. When we enter the wilderness experiences of our own recovery, we need the same practical faith that allows us to live one day at a time.

Personal Accountability: The Israelites wandered for forty years in the wilderness because they believed the report of the ten faithless spies instead of God's promises to deliver them from their enemies. Each wilderness step they took should have reminded them that they were responsible for their predicament. Most of them, however, chose to blame God and Moses instead. They refused to admit the truth—that they were wandering because of the choices they had made. We also are in our present circumstances because of choices we have made. We need to take personal responsibility for our life if we desire to progress in our recovery.

CHAPTER 1

The People Are Counted

It was on the fifteenth day of April of the
second year after the Israelis left Egypt that
the Lord issued the following instructions to
Moses. (He was in the Tabernacle at the camp
of Israel on the Sinai peninsula at the time.)
2-15"Take a census of all the men twenty
years old and older who are able to go to war,
indicating their tribe and family. You and
Aaron are to direct the project, assisted by
these leaders from each tribe:"

Tribe	*Leader*
Reuben	Elizur (son of Shedeur)
Simeon	Shelumiel (son of Zurishaddai)
Judah	Nahshon (son of Amminadab)
Issachar	Nethanel (son of Zuar)
Zebulun	Eliab (son of Helon)
Ephraim (son of Joseph)	Elishama (son of Ammihud)
Manasseh (son of Joseph)	Gamaliel (son of Pedahzur)
Benjamin	Abidan (son of Gideoni)
Dan	Ahiezer (son of Ammishaddai)
Asher	Pagiel (son of Ochran)
Gad	Eliasaph (son of Deuel)
Naphtali	Ahira (son of Enan)

16These were the tribal leaders elected from
among the people.
17-19 On the same day Moses and Aaron and
the above-named leaders summoned all the
men of Israel who were twenty years old or
older to come and register, each man indicating his tribe and family, as the Lord had
commanded Moses. 20-46Here is the final tabu-
lation:

Tribe	*Total*
Reuben (the oldest son of Jacob)	46,500
Simeon	59,300
Gad	45,650
Judah	74,600
Issachar	54,400
Zebulun	57,400
Joseph: Ephraim (son of Joseph)	40,500
Joseph: Manasseh (son of Joseph)	32,200
Benjamin	35,400
Dan	62,700
Asher	41,500
Naphtali	53,400
Grand Total:	603,550

47-49This total does not include the Levites,
for the Lord had said to Moses, "Exempt the
entire tribe of Levi from the draft, and do
not include their number in the census.
50For the Levites are assigned for the work
connected with the Tabernacle and its
transportation. They are to live near the
Tabernacle, 51and whenever the Tabernacle
is moved, the Levites are to take it down and
set it up again; anyone else touching it shall
be executed. 52Each tribe of Israel shall have
a separate camping area with its own flag.
53The Levites' tents shall be clustered
around the Tabernacle as a wall between the
people of Israel and God's wrath—to protect

1:1 The opening expression, "the Lord issued the following instructions," is similar to that found in Leviticus and indicates God's personal interest in the lives of his people. He communicated clearly with his people, giving them instructions for healthy living. He was interested in the way they worshiped (Leviticus) as well as in the events of their daily lives (Numbers). He was interested in delivering and directing his people. This should remind us of his commitment to us today.

them from his fierce anger against their sins."
[54]So all these instructions of the Lord to Moses were put into effect.

CHAPTER 2
Tribal Arrangement in the Camp
The Lord gave these further instructions to Moses and Aaron: "Each tribe will have its own tent area, with its flagpole and tribal banner; and at the center of these tribal compounds will be the Tabernacle." [3-31]Here are the tribal locations:

Tribe:	*Leader:*	*Location:*	*Census:*
Judah	Nahshon (son of Amminadab)	East side of Tabernacle	74,600
Issachar	Nethanel (son of Zuar)	Next to Judah	54,400
Zebulun	Eliab (son of Helon)	Next to Issachar	57,400

So the total of all those on Judah's side of the camp was 186,400. These three tribes led the way whenever the Israelites traveled to a new campsite.

Reuben	Elizur (son of Shedeur)	South side of Tabernacle	46,500
Simeon	Shelumiel (son of Zurishaddai)	Next to Reuben	59,300
Gad	Eliasaph (son of Reuel)	Next to Simeon	45,650

So the total of the Reuben side of the camp was 151,450. These three tribes were next in line whenever the Israelis traveled.

Next in the line of march was the Tabernacle, with the Levites. When traveling, each tribe stayed together under its own flag, just as each was separate from the others in camp.

Ephraim	Elishama (son of Ammihud)	West side of Tabernacle	40,500
Manasseh	Gamaliel (son of Pedahzur)	Next to Ephraim	32,200
Benjamin	Abidan (son of Gideoni)	Next to Manasseh	35,400

So the total on the Ephraim side of the camp was 108,100, and they were next in the line of march.

Dan	Ahiezer (son of Ammishaddai)	North side of Tabernacle	62,700
Asher	Pagiel (son of Ochran)	Next to Dan	41,500
Naphtali	Ahira (son of Enan)	Next to Asher	53,400

So the total on Dan's side of the camp was 157,600. They brought up the rear whenever Israel traveled. [32,33]In summary, the armies of Israel totaled 603,550 (not including the Levites, who were exempted by Jehovah's commandment to Moses). [34]So the people of Israel set up their camps, each tribe under its own banner, in the locations indicated by the Lord to Moses.

CHAPTER 3
The Levites' Work
At the time when the Lord spoke to Moses on Mount Sinai, [2]Aaron's sons were: Nadab (his oldest), Abihu, Eleazar, Ithamar. [3]All were anointed as priests and set apart to minister at the Tabernacle. [4]But Nadab and Abihu died before the Lord in the wilderness of Sinai when they used unholy fire. And since they had no children, this left only Eleazar and Ithamar to assist their father, Aaron.
[5]Then the Lord said to Moses, [6]"Summon the tribe of Levi and present them to Aaron as his assistants. [7-9]They will follow his instructions and perform the sacred duties at the Tabernacle on behalf of all the people of Israel. For they are assigned to him as representatives of all the people of Israel. They are

1:2-46 Taking a census of the Israelites prior to their journey to the Promised Land not only had organizational and military significance (1:3), but also served an important psychological purpose. As each individual identified his tribal and family background (1:18), it was a powerful reminder to the Israelites of their unity and common family heritage. This sense of unity would become essential as they faced the enemies and challenges ahead. Similarly, the assurance of support and unity within the family of Christ is a critical need for those who face wilderness periods in their lives today (Philippians 2:1-3).
2:1-34 As they traveled and camped, the Israelites were to arrange themselves by tribe around the Tabernacle. God wanted the Israelites to keep him in constant focus, making him the center of all their thoughts and actions. Many of us try to face the challenges of life alone, but find the battle overwhelming. It is only through the power of God, as we keep him constantly before us, that true victory and recovery can be realized.
3:1–4:49 The detailed organization of the Levites and priests in these chapters illustrates the principle that God's calling is accompanied by responsibility and accountability. Out of Israel, God sovereignly chose one tribe (Levi), and out of that tribe he chose specific families who were to lead in Israel's worship. With great privilege comes great responsibility. When God places us in a position of influence, we must not take it lightly. We need to recognize our responsibility to obey God and our accountability before him.

in charge of all the furnishings and maintenance of the Tabernacle. [10]However, only Aaron and his sons may carry out the duties of the priesthood; anyone else who presumes to assume this office shall be executed."

[11,12]And the Lord said to Moses, "I have accepted the Levites in substitution for all the oldest sons of the people of Israel. The Levites are mine [13]in exchange for all the oldest sons. From the day I killed all the oldest sons of the Egyptians, I took for myself all the firstborn in Israel of both men and animals! They are mine; I am Jehovah."

[14,15]The Lord now spoke again to Moses at the Sinai peninsula, telling him, "Take a census of the tribe of Levi, indicating each person's clan; count every male down to one month old." [16-24]So Moses did:

Levi's son	*Levi's grandsons (clan names)*	*Census*	*Leader*	*Camp Location*
Gershon	Libni Shimei	7,500	Elisaph (son of Lael)	West side of Tabernacle

[25-30]*Responsibilities:*

The responsibility of these two clans of Levites was the care of the Tabernacle: its coverings, its entry drapes, the drapes covering the fence surrounding the courtyard, the screen at the entrance of the courtyard surrounding the Tabernacle, the altar, and all the ropes used in tying the Tabernacle together.

Levi's son	*Levi's grandsons (clan names)*	*Census*	*Leader*	*Camp Location*
Kohath	Amran Izhar Hebron Uzziel	8,600	Elizaphan (son of Uzziel)	South side of Tabernacle

[31-35]*Responsibilities:*

The responsibility of these four clans of Levites was the care of the Ark, the table, the lampstand, the altars, the various utensils used in the Tabernacle, the veil, and any repairs needed on any of these items. (Note: Eleazar, Aaron's son, shall be the chief administrator over the leaders of the Levites, with special responsibility for the oversight of the sanctuary.)

Levi's son	*Levi's grandsons (clan names)*	*Census*	*Leader*	*Camp Location*
Merari	Mahli Mushi	6,200	Zuriel (son of Abihail)	North side of Tabernacle

[36,37]*Responsibilities:*

The responsibility of these two clans was the care of the frames of the Tabernacle building; the posts; the bases for the posts, and all of the equipment needed for their use; the posts around the courtyard and their bases, pegs, and ropes.

[38]The area east of the Tabernacle was reserved for the tents of Moses and of Aaron and his sons, who had the final responsibility for the Tabernacle on behalf of the people of Israel. (Anyone who was not a priest or Levite, but came into the Tabernacle, was to be executed.)

[39]So all the Levites, as numbered by Moses and Aaron at the command of the Lord, were 22,000 males one month old and older.

The Firstborn Are Counted

[40]Then the Lord said to Moses, "Now take a census of all the eldest sons in Israel who are one month old and older, and register each name. [41]The Levites shall be mine (I am Jehovah) as substitutes for the eldest sons of Israel; and the Levites' cattle are mine as substitutes for the firstborn cattle of the whole nation."

[42]So Moses took a census of the eldest sons of the people of Israel, as the Lord had commanded, [43]and found the total number of eldest sons one month old and older to be 22,273.

[44]Now the Lord said to Moses, [45]"Give me the Levites instead of the eldest sons of the people of Israel; and give me the cattle of the Levites instead of the firstborn cattle of the people of Israel; yes, the Levites shall be mine; I am Jehovah. [46]To redeem the 273 eldest sons in excess of the number of Levites, [47,48]pay five dollars for each one to Aaron and his sons."

[49]So Moses received redemption money for the 273 eldest sons of Israel who were in excess of the number of Levites. (All the others were redeemed because the Levites had been given to the Lord in their place.) [50]The money collected came to a total of $1,365. [51]And Moses gave it to Aaron and his sons as the Lord had commanded.

CHAPTER 4

Work for the Clan of Kohath

Then the Lord said to Moses and Aaron, "Take a census of the Kohath division of the Levite tribe. [3]This census will be of all males from ages thirty to fifty who are able to work in the Tabernacle. [4]These are their sacred duties:

[5]"When the camp moves, Aaron and his sons will enter the Tabernacle first and take down the veil and cover the Ark with it. [6]Then they will cover the veil with goatskin leather, cover the goatskins with a blue cloth, and place the carrying poles of the Ark in their rings.

7"Next they must spread a blue cloth over
the table where the Bread of the Presence is
displayed, and place the dishes, spoons,
bowls, cups, and the Bread upon the cloth.
8They will spread a scarlet cloth over that, and
finally a covering of goatskin leather on top
of the scarlet cloth. Then they shall insert the
carrying poles into the table.
9"Next they must cover with a blue cloth
the lampstand, the lamps, snuffers, trays, and
the reservoir of olive oil. 10This entire group of
objects shall then be covered with goatskin
leather, and the bundle shall be placed upon
a carrying frame.
11"They must then spread a blue cloth over
the gold altar, cover it with a covering of
goatskin leather, and insert the carrying poles
into the altar. 12All of the remaining utensils
of the Tabernacle are to be wrapped in a blue
cloth, covered with goatskin leather, and
placed on the carrying frame.
13"The ashes are to be removed from the
altar, and the altar shall be covered with a
purple cloth. 14All of the altar utensils are to
be placed upon the cloth—the firepans,
hooks, shovels, basins, and other containers—and a cover of goatskin leather will be
spread over them. Finally, the carrying poles
are to be put in place. 15When Aaron and his
sons have finished packing the sanctuary and
all the utensils, the clan of Kohath shall come
and carry the units to wherever the camp is
traveling; but they must not touch the holy
items, lest they die. This, then, is the sacred
work of the sons of Kohath.
16"Aaron's son Eleazar shall be responsible
for the oil for the light, the sweet incense, the
daily grain offering, and the anointing oil—
in fact, the supervision of the entire Tabernacle and everything in it will be his
responsibility."
17-19Then the Lord said to Moses and Aaron,
"Don't let the families of Kohath destroy
themselves! This is what you must do so that
they will not die when they carry the most
holy things: Aaron and his sons shall go in
with them and point out what each is to carry.
20Otherwise they must never enter the sanctuary for even a moment, lest they look at the
sacred objects there and die."

Work for the Clan of Gershon

21-23And the Lord said to Moses, "Take a census
of the Gershonite division of the tribe of Levi,
all of the men between the ages of thirty and
fifty who are eligible for the sacred work of
the Tabernacle. 24These will be their duties:
25"They will carry the curtains of the Tabernacle, the Tabernacle itself with its coverings,
the goatskin leather roof, and the curtain for
the Tabernacle entrance. 26They are also to
carry the drapes covering the courtyard fence,
and the curtain across the entrance to the
courtyard that surrounds the altar and the
Tabernacle. They will also carry the altar, the
ropes, and all of the accessories. They are fully
responsible for the transportation of these
items. 27Aaron or any of his sons may assign
the Gershonites' tasks to them, 28but the Gershonites will be directly responsible to Aaron's son Ithamar.

Work for the Clan of Merari

29"Now take a census of the Merari division of
the Levite tribe, all of the men from thirty to
fifty who are eligible for the Tabernacle service. 30,31When the Tabernacle is moved, they
are to carry the frames of the Tabernacle, the
bars, the bases, 32the frames for the courtyard
fence with their bases, pegs, cords, and everything else connected with their use and repair.
"Assign duties to each man by name. 33The
Merari division will also report to Aaron's son
Ithamar."

Counting the Able-bodied Levites

34So Moses and Aaron and the other leaders
took a census of the Kohath division, 35includ-
ing all of the men thirty to fifty years of age
who were eligible for the Tabernacle service,
36and found that the total number was 2,750.
37All this was done to carry out the Lord's
instructions to Moses. 38-41A similar census of
the Gershon division totaled 2,630. 42-45And of
the Merari division, 3,200. 46-48Thus Moses
and Aaron and the leaders of Israel found that
the total of all the Levites who were thirty to
fifty years old and who were eligible for the
Tabernacle service and transportation was
8,580. 49This census was taken in response to
the Lord's instructions to Moses.

4:1-49 The efficient operation of the Israelite camp (especially the moving process) required detailed organization and cooperation. When each person cooperated and did his unique task, results were achieved. The ministry of the church today, especially in meeting some of the greatest human needs, requires a cooperative effort of people using their unique spiritual gifts to help others (1 Corinthians 12:24-27). Only then will we be able to reach those in need and provide the necessary environment for recovery and growth.

CHAPTER 5

Dealing with Leprosy

These are further instructions from the Lord to Moses: "Inform the people of Israel that they must expel all lepers from the camp, and all who have open sores, or who have been defiled by touching a dead person. [3]This applies to men and women alike. Remove them so that they will not defile the camp where I live among you." [4]These instructions were put into effect.

Consequences of Stealing

[5,6]Then the Lord said to Moses, "Tell the people of Israel that when anyone, man or woman, betrays the Lord by betraying a trust, it is sin. [7]He must confess his sin and make full repayment for what he has stolen, adding 20 percent and returning it to the person he took it from. [8]But if the person he wronged is dead, and there is no near relative to whom the payment can be made, it must be given to the priest, along with a lamb for atonement. [9,10]When the people of Israel bring a gift to the Lord it shall go to the priests."

A Test for an Unfaithful Wife

[11,12]And the Lord said to Moses, "Tell the people of Israel that if a man's wife commits adultery, [13]but there is no proof, there being no witness, [14]and he is jealous and suspicious, [15]the man shall bring his wife to the priest with an offering for her of a tenth of a bushel of barley meal without oil or frankincense mingled with it—for it is a suspicion offering—to bring out the truth as to whether or not she is guilty.

[16]"The priest shall bring her before the Lord, [17]and take holy water in a clay jar and mix into it dust from the floor of the Tabernacle. [18]He shall unbind her hair and place the suspicion offering in her hands to determine whether or not her husband's suspicions are justified. The priest shall stand before her holding the jar of bitter water that brings a curse. [19]He shall require her to swear that she is innocent, and then he shall say to her, 'If no man has slept with you except your husband, be free from the effects of this bitter water that causes the curse. [20]But if you have committed adultery, [21,22]then Jehovah shall make you a curse among your people, for he will make your thigh rot away and your body swell.' And the woman shall be required to say, 'Yes, let it be so.' [23]Then the priest shall write these curses in a book and wash them off into the bitter water. [24](When he requires the woman to drink the water, it becomes bitter within her [if she is guilty].)

[25]"Then the priest shall take the suspicion offering from the woman's hand and wave it before Jehovah, and carry it to the altar. [26]He shall take a handful, representing all of it, and burn the handful upon the altar, and then require the woman to drink the water. [27]If she has been defiled, having committed adultery against her husband, the water will become bitter within her, and her body will swell and her thigh will rot, and she shall be a curse among her people. [28]But if she is pure and has not committed adultery, she shall be unharmed and will soon become pregnant.

[29]"This, then, is the law concerning a wayward wife—or a husband's suspicions against his wife—[30]to determine whether or not she has been unfaithful to him. He shall bring her before the Lord and the priest shall handle the situation as outlined above. [31]Her husband shall not be brought to trial for causing her horrible disease, for she is responsible."

CHAPTER 6

The Nazirite Vow

The Lord gave Moses these further instructions for the people of Israel: "When either a man or a woman takes the special vow of a Nazirite, consecrating himself to the Lord in a special way, [3,4]he must not thereafter, during the entire period of his special consecration to the Lord, taste strong drink or wine or even

---

5:5-7 This command for dealing with sin emphasizes the same principles as do the sin and guilt offerings of Leviticus 4–5. God has provided clear steps for those who have violated others. These steps include admitting the wrong things we have done and providing restitution wherever possible. If we follow these simple steps, we will have made significant progress in our recovery.

5:11-15 The seriousness of adultery is underscored in this passage. Marriage was intended to be a picture of God's covenant relationship with his people. The ritual described in 5:16-31 was used to demonstrate guilt and was not simply a magic spell. God will forgive all sins, even adultery, as was shown by Christ's words to the adulterous woman (John 8:2-11). But his charge to her, "Go and sin no more," emphasizes the fact that forgiveness carries with it a responsibility to live by God's standards. God's priorities for his people have always emphasized pure relationships, especially in marriage.

fresh wine, grape juice, grapes, or raisins! He
may eat nothing that comes from grape vines,
not even the seeds or skins!
5"Throughout that time he must never
cut his hair, for he is holy and consecrated
to the Lord; that is why he must let his hair
grow. 6,7"And he may not go near any dead
body during the entire period of his vow,
even if it is the body of his father, mother,
brother, or sister; for his vow of consecration remains in effect, 8and he is consecrated to the Lord throughout the entire
period. 9"If he is defiled by having someone
fall dead beside him, then seven days later
he shall shave his defiled head; he will then
be cleansed from the contamination of being in the presence of death. 10The next day,
the eighth day, he must bring two turtledoves or two young pigeons to the priest at
the entrance of the Tabernacle. 11The priest
shall offer one of the birds for a sin offering,
and the other for a burnt offering, and make
atonement for his defilement. And he must
renew his vows that day and let his hair
begin to grow again. 12The days of his vow
that were fulfilled before his defilement no
longer count. He must begin all over again
with a new vow, and must bring a male
lamb a year old for a guilt offering.
13"At the conclusion of the period of his
vow of separation to the Lord, he must go to
the entrance of the Tabernacle 14and offer a
burnt sacrifice to the Lord, a year-old lamb
without defect. He must also offer a sin offering, a yearling ewe lamb without defect; a
peace offering, a ram without defect; 15a basket of bread made without yeast; pancakes
made of fine flour mixed with olive oil; unleavened wafers spread with oil; and the accompanying grain offering and drink
offerings. 16The priest shall present these offerings before the Lord: first the sin offering
and the burnt offering; 17then the ram for a
peace offering, along with the basket of
bread made without yeast; and finally the
grain offering along with the drink offering.
18"Then the Nazirite shall shave his long
hair—the sign of his vow of separation. This
shall be done at the entrance of the Tabernacle, after which the hair shall be put in the
fire under the peace offering sacrifice. 19After
the man's head has been shaved, the priest
shall take the roasted shoulder of the lamb,
one of the pancakes (made without yeast),
and one of the wafers (also made without
yeast), and put them all into the man's
hands. 20The priest shall then wave it all back
and forth before the Lord in a gesture of
offering; all of it is a holy portion for the
priest, as are the rib piece and shoulder that
were waved before the Lord. After that the
Nazirite may again drink wine, for he is freed
from his vow.
21"These are the regulations concerning a
Nazirite and his sacrifices at the conclusion of
his period of special dedication. In addition to
these sacrifices he must bring any further offering he promised at the time he took his
vow to become a Nazirite."

The Priestly Blessing

22,23Now the Lord said to Moses, "Tell Aaron
and his sons that they are to give this special
blessing to the people of Israel: 24-26'May the
Lord bless and protect you; may the Lord's
face radiate with joy because of you; may he
be gracious to you, show you his favor, and
give you his peace.' 27This is how Aaron and
his sons shall call down my blessings upon
the people of Israel; and I myself will personally bless them."

6:3-4 The name *Nazirite* comes from a Hebrew word meaning "to separate." One aspect of this vow was separation from various activities and attitudes, symbolizing a person's willingness to set personal standards for himself during the time of the vow. This principle of personal accountability is always necessary for anyone seeking to live a life pleasing to God. Self-discipline and self-examination both play key roles in our relationship with God as we continue the process of recovery.
6:5-8 An important aspect of the Nazirite vow was the separation *unto* God, dedicating one's life for his use. Romans 12:1 commands us to present our body as a living sacrifice to God. The Nazirite vow provided opportunities to do this on special occasions, but we are to give ourselves to God regularly. Even in the most hopeless human situations, God gives hope. But that hope cannot come without us committing ourselves to God through Jesus Christ.
6:24-26 The simple words of this blessing reflect God's desire for all his people. He is the source of all blessings, grace, and peace in life; only through a relationship with this God can we hope to experience the fullness of life described here. The blessing seems to build to its final word—peace. The beautiful Hebrew word *shalom* used here means much more than an absence of conflict. It implies a complete sense of well-being, health, and contentment. God offers this to anyone who is willing to follow him, and especially to those whose lives have been bruised and broken.

CHAPTER 7

Gifts for the Tabernacle

Moses anointed and sanctified each part of the Tabernacle, including the altar and its utensils, on the day he finished setting it up. [2]Then the leaders of Israel—the chiefs of the tribes, the men who had organized the census—brought their offerings. [3]They brought six covered wagons, each drawn by two oxen—a wagon for every two leaders and an ox for each one; and they presented them to the Lord in front of the Tabernacle.

[4,5]"Accept their gifts," the Lord told Moses, "and use these wagons for the work of the Tabernacle. Give them to the Levites for whatever needs they may have."

[6]So Moses presented the wagons and the oxen to the Levites. [7]Two wagons and four oxen were given to the Gershon division for their use, [8]and four wagons and eight oxen were given to the Merari division, which was under the leadership of Ithamar, Aaron's son. [9]None of the wagons or teams was given to the Kohath division, for they were required to carry their portion of the Tabernacle upon their shoulders.

[10]The leaders also presented dedication gifts on the day the altar was anointed, placing them before the altar. [11]The Lord said to Moses, "Let each of them bring his gift on a different day for the dedication of the altar."

[12]So Nahshon, the son of Amminadab of the tribe of Judah, brought his gift the first day. [13]It consisted of a silver platter weighing three pounds and a silver bowl of about two pounds, both filled with grain offerings of fine flour mixed with oil.[14]He also brought a tiny gold box of incense which weighed only about four ounces. [15]He brought a young bull, a ram, and a male yearling lamb as burnt offerings; [16]a male goat for a sin offering; [17]and for the peace offerings two oxen, five rams, five male goats, and five male yearling lambs.

[18-23]The next day Nethanel, the son of Zuar, chief of the tribe of Issachar, brought his gifts and offerings. They were exactly the same as Nahshon had presented on the previous day.

[24-29]On the third day Eliab, the son of Helon, chief of the tribe of Zebulun, came with his offerings—the same as those presented on the previous days.

[30-35]On the fourth day the gifts were presented by Elizur, son of Shedeur, chief of the tribe of Reuben; his gifts and offerings were the same as those given on the previous days.

[36-41]On the fifth day came Shelumiel, the son of Zurishaddai, chief of the tribe of Simeon, with the same gifts.

[42-47]The next day it was Eliasaph's turn, son of Deuel, chief of the tribe of Gad. He, too, offered the same gifts and sacrifices.

[48-53]On the seventh day, Elishama, the son of Ammihud, chief of the tribe of Ephraim, brought his gifts, the same as those presented on the previous days.

[54-59]Gamaliel, son of Pedahzur, prince of the tribe of Manasseh, came the eighth day with the same offerings.

[60-65] On the ninth day it was Abidan the son of Gideoni, chief of the tribe of Benjamin, with his gifts, the same as those offered by the others.

[66-71]Ahiezer, the son of Ammishaddai, brought his gifts on the tenth day. He was the chief of the tribe of Dan and his offerings were the same as those on the previous days.

[72-77]Pagiel, son of Ochran, chief of the tribe of Asher, brought his gifts on the eleventh day—the same gifts and offerings as the others.

[78-83]On the twelfth day came Ahira, son of Enan, chief of the tribe of Naphtali, with his offerings; they were identical to those brought by the others.

[84-86]So, beginning the day the altar was anointed, it was dedicated by these gifts from the chiefs of the tribes of Israel. Their combined offerings were as follows:

12 silver platters (each weighing about three pounds);

12 silver bowls (each weighing about two pounds); (so the total weight of the silver was about sixty pounds);

12 gold trays (the trays weighing about four ounces apiece); (so the total weight of gold was about three pounds).

[87]For the burnt offerings they brought:

7:1-88 The way we use our possessions is an important part of our accountability to God. This passage shows how God's ministry among his people often depends upon the personal gifts of individuals and families. An attitude of sacrifice and generosity is needed among us if we hope to meet the needs of others. Sometimes this sacrifice may involve our giving physical gifts, as did each of the tribal leaders. Sometimes it may involve giving some of our time, as did the Levites. God does ask that we bring an offering to him (7:11); the nature and amount of the offering is to be voluntary and from the heart.

12 bulls, 12 rams,
12 yearling male goats (with the grain offerings that accompanied them).

For sin offerings they brought:

12 male goats.

[88]For the peace offerings they brought:

24 young bulls,
60 rams, 60 male goats,
60 male lambs one year old.

[89]When Moses went into the Tabernacle to speak with God, he heard the Voice speaking to him from above the place of mercy over the Ark, between the statues of the two Guardian Angels.

CHAPTER 8

Setting Up the Lamps

The Lord said to Moses, [2]"Tell Aaron that when he lights the seven lamps in the lampstand, he is to set them so that they will throw their light forward."

[3]So Aaron did this. [4]The lampstand, including the floral decorations on the base and branches, was made entirely of beaten gold. It was constructed according to the exact design the Lord had shown Moses.

The Levites Are Dedicated

[5,6]Then the Lord said to Moses, "Now set apart the Levites from the other people of Israel.
[7]Do this by sprinkling water of purification upon them, then having them shave their entire bodies and wash their clothing and themselves. [8]Have them bring a young bull and a grain offering of fine flour mingled with oil, along with another young bull for a sin offering. [9]Then bring the Levites to the door of the Tabernacle as all the people watch.
[10]There the leaders of the tribes shall lay their hands upon them, [11]and Aaron, with a gesture of offering, shall present them to the Lord as a gift from the entire nation of Israel. The Levites will represent all the people in serving the Lord.

[12]"Next, the Levite leaders shall lay their hands upon the heads of the young bulls and offer them before the Lord; one for a sin offering and the other for a burnt offering, to make atonement for the Levites. [13]Then the Levites are to be presented to Aaron and his sons, just as any other gift to the Lord is given to the priests! [14]In this way you will dedicate the Levites from among the rest of the people of Israel, and the Levites shall be mine. [15]After you have sanctified them and presented them in this way, they shall go in and out of the Tabernacle to do their work.

[16]"They are mine from among all the people of Israel, and I have accepted them in place of all the firstborn children of the Israelites: I have taken the Levites as their substitutes. [17]For all the firstborn among the people of Israel are mine, both men and animals; I claimed them for myself the night I killed all the firstborn Egyptians. [18]Yes, I have accepted the Levites in place of all the eldest sons of Israel. [19]And I will give the Levites as a gift to Aaron and his sons. The Levites will carry out the sacred duties required of the people of Israel in the Tabernacle, and will offer the people's sacrifices, making atonement for them. There will be no plague among the Israelites—as there would be if the ordinary people entered the Tabernacle."

[20]So Moses and Aaron and all the people of Israel dedicated the Levites, carefully following Jehovah's instructions to Moses. [21]The Levites purified themselves and washed their clothes, and Aaron presented them to the Lord in a gesture of offering. He then performed the rite of atonement over them to purify them. [22]After that they went into the Tabernacle as assistants to Aaron and his sons; everything was done just as the Lord had commanded Moses.

[23,24]The Lord also instructed Moses, "The Levites are to begin serving in the Tabernacle at the age of twenty-five, and are to retire at

---

8:5-8, 12 This section focuses upon the Levitical priests, noting several important aspects of their preparation for service. They were to be cleansed prior to service. The sin offering made on their behalf showed that even they, Israel's spiritual leaders, needed to be cleansed of sin. Only our Great High Priest, Jesus Christ, serves in the priestly role without sin. And even though he is sinless, he can fully sympathize with our weaknesses, so that we need not fear approaching him in any time of need (Hebrews 4:14-16).

8:9-11, 13-16 The Levitical priests not only offered sacrifices and offerings to God, but were to consider themselves "living sacrifices." Their lives were to be given completely over to God. The New Testament also teaches that we are to consider ourselves as holy priests, giving our life as a "living sacrifice" unto God (Romans 12:1-2; 1 Peter 2:5). A life founded on commitment to God contains the essential ingredients of a life filled with contentment and purpose.

the age of fifty. [25,26]After retirement they can assist with various light duties in the Tabernacle, but will have no regular responsibilities."

CHAPTER 9

The Passover Comes Again

Jehovah gave these instructions to Moses while he and the rest of the Israelis were on the Sinai peninsula, during the first month of the second year after leaving Egypt:

[2,3]"The people of Israel must celebrate the Passover annually on April first, beginning in the evening. Be sure to follow all of my instructions concerning this celebration."

[4,5]So Moses announced that the Passover celebration would begin on the evening of April first, there in the Sinai peninsula, just as the Lord had commanded. [6,7]But as it happened, some of the men had just attended a funeral and were ceremonially defiled by having touched the dead, so they couldn't eat the Passover lamb that night. They came to Moses and Aaron and explained their problem and protested at being forbidden from offering their sacrifice to the Lord at the time he had appointed.

[8]Moses said he would ask the Lord about it, [9]and this was God's reply:

[10]"If any of the people of Israel, now or in the generations to come, are defiled at Passover time because of touching a dead body, or if they are on a journey and cannot be present, they may still celebrate the Passover, but one month later, [11]on May first, beginning in the evening. They are to eat the lamb at that time, with unleavened bread and bitter herbs. [12]They must not leave any of it until the next morning, and must not break a bone of it, and must follow all the regular instructions concerning the Passover.

[13]"But anyone who is not defiled, and anyone who is not away on a trip, and yet refuses to celebrate the Passover at the regular time, shall be excommunicated from the people of Israel for refusing to sacrifice to Jehovah at the proper time; he must bear his guilt. [14]And if a foreigner is living among you and wants to celebrate the Passover to the Lord, he shall follow all these same instructions. There is one law for all."

The Pillar of Cloud and Fire

[15]On the day the Tabernacle was raised the Cloud covered it; and that evening the Cloud changed to the appearance of fire, and stayed that way throughout the night. [16]It was always so—the daytime Cloud changing to the appearance of fire at night. [17]When the Cloud lifted, the people of Israel moved on to wherever it stopped, and camped there. [18]In this way they journeyed at the command of the Lord and stopped where he told them to, then remained there as long as the Cloud stayed. [19]If it stayed a long time, then they stayed a long time. But if it stayed only a few days, then they remained only a few days; for so the Lord had instructed them. [20,21]Sometimes the fire-cloud stayed only during the night and moved on the next morning. But day or night, when it moved, the people broke camp and followed. [22]If the Cloud stayed above the Tabernacle two days, a month, or a year, that is how long the people of Israel stayed; but as soon as it moved, they moved. [23]So it was that they camped or traveled at the commandment of the Lord; and whatever the Lord told Moses they should do, they did.

CHAPTER 10

The Silver Trumpets

Now the Lord said to Moses, "Make two trumpets of beaten silver to be used for summoning the people to assemble and for signaling the breaking of camp. [3]When both trumpets are blown, the people will know that they are to gather at the entrance of the Tabernacle. [4]But if only one is blown, then only the chiefs of the tribes of Israel shall come to you.

9:1-14 The Passover was to be an annual feast for all the Israelites, a celebration of their deliverance from bondage in Egypt (Exodus 12:1-51). A problem arose, however, for those who were ceremonially unclean at the time of Passover. According to the strict standards of the law, they were not allowed to join in the celebration even though it was required of them. So Moses brought this problem to God, who graciously instituted a second date of celebration for those who couldn't participate at the regular time. God also wants all of us to participate in a relationship with him. We should not allow our failures and sins to keep us from coming to God. He has provided a means for us to come, no matter how "unclean" we may be. Our Passover Lamb, Jesus Christ, has taken away all the sins of the world (John 1:29; 1 Corinthians 5:7).

9:15-23 As the cloud moved, so did the Israelites. They had to stay alert, watching each day for God's guidance. It was essential for the people to trust God rather than to make their own plans. This object lesson of obedience is to be the description of our day-by-day walk with God—to trust in him completely and not to trust in ourselves (Proverbs 3:5-6).

5-7"Different trumpet blasts will be necessary to distinguish between the summons to
assemble and the signal to break camp and
move onward. When the travel signal is
blown, the tribes camped on the east side of
the Tabernacle shall leave first; at the second
signal, the tribes on the south shall go. 8Only
the priests are permitted to blow the trumpets. This is a permanent instruction to be
followed from generation to generation.
9"When you arrive in the Promised Land
and go to war against your enemies, God will
hear you and save you from your enemies
when you sound the alarm with these trumpets. 10Use the trumpets in times of gladness,
too, blowing them at your annual festivals
and at the beginning of each month to rejoice
over your burnt offerings and peace offerings.
And God will be reminded of his covenant
with you. For I am Jehovah, your God."

Moving the Tabernacle

11The Cloud lifted from the Tabernacle on the
twentieth day of the second month of the
second year of Israel's leaving Egypt; 12so the
Israelites left the Sinai wilderness, and followed the Cloud until it stopped in the wilderness of Paran. 13This was their first journey
after having received the Lord's travel instructions to Moses.
14At the head of the march was the tribe of
Judah grouped behind its flag and led by
Nahshon, the son of Amminadab. 15Next
came the tribe of Issachar, led by Nethanel,
the son of Zuar, 16and the tribe of Zebulun, led
by Eliab, the son of Helon.
17The Tabernacle was taken down and the
men of the Gershon and Merari divisions of
the tribe of Levi were next in the line of
march, carrying the Tabernacle upon their
shoulders. 18Then came the flag of the camp
of Reuben, with Elizur the son of Shedeur
leading his people. 19Next was the tribe of
Simeon headed by Shelumiel, the son of Zurishaddai; 20and the tribe of Gad led by Eliasaph, the son of Deuel.
21Next came the Kohathites carrying the
items from the inner sanctuary. (The Tabernacle was already erected in its new location by
the time they arrived.) 22Next in line was the
tribe of Ephraim behind its flag, led by Elishama, the son of Ammihud; 23and the tribe
of Manasseh led by Gamaliel the son of Pedahzur; 24and the tribe of Benjamin, led by
Abidan the son of Gideoni. 25Last of all were
the tribes headed by the flag of the tribe of
Dan under the leadership of Ahiezer, the son
of Ammishaddai; 26the tribe of Asher, led by
Pagiel, the son of Ochran; 27and the tribe of
Naphtali, led by Ahira, the son of Enan. 28That
was the order in which the tribes traveled.
29One day Moses said to his brother-in-law,
Hobab (son of Reuel, the Midianite), "At last
we are on our way to the Promised Land.
Come with us and we will do you good; for
the Lord has given wonderful promises to
Israel!"
30But his brother-in-law replied, "No, I must
return to my own land and kinfolk."
31"Stay with us," Moses pleaded, "for you
know the ways of the wilderness and will be a
great help to us. 32If you come, you will share
in all the good things the Lord does for us."
33They traveled for three days after leaving
Mount Sinai, with the Ark at the front of the
column to choose a place for them to stop. 34It
was daytime when they left, with the Cloud
moving along ahead of them as they began
their march. 35As the Ark was carried forward,
Moses cried out, "Arise, O Lord, and scatter
your enemies; let them flee before you." 36And
when the Ark was set down he said, "Return,
O Lord, to the millions of Israel."

CHAPTER 11

The Israelites Complain

The people were soon complaining about all
their misfortunes, and the Lord heard them.
His anger flared out against them because of

10:11-36 This section begins the account of Israel's journey through the wilderness on the way to the Promised Land. They were entering new territory, on their way to building a new life, but the immediate results were not encouraging. As they set out for the Promised Land, they were not willing to trust God to lead and protect them. Their weak faith showed up in their impatience with God, which resulted in thirty-eight years of wilderness wandering. Often building a new life involves entering uncharted territory. It takes great patience to let God guide us each step of the way. Let us learn from the mistakes of the Israelites (1 Corinthians 10; Hebrews 3–4).

10:35-36 Even though the presence of God was with Israel, evidenced by the cloud and the Ark of the Covenant (10:33-34), Moses continually prayed for the well-being of his people. He was their intercessor and knew the importance of the ministry of prayer. Praying for others, especially for those who are in the process of recovery, is a resource often overlooked. But it may be our most effective means of laying hold of the awesome power of God.

their complaints, so the fire of the Lord began
destroying those at the far end of the camp.
2They screamed to Moses for help, and when
he prayed for them the fire stopped. 3Ever
after, the area was known as "The Place of
Burning," because the fire from the Lord
burned among them there.
4,5Then the Egyptians who had come with
them began to long for the good things of
Egypt. This added to the discontent of the
people of Israel and they wept, "Oh, for a few
bites of meat! Oh, that we had some of the
delicious fish we enjoyed so much in Egypt,
and the wonderful cucumbers and melons,
leeks, onions, and garlic! 6But now our
strength is gone, and day after day we have to
face this manna!"
7The manna was the size of small seeds,
whitish yellow in color. 8The people gathered
it from the ground and pounded it into flour,
then boiled it, and then made pancakes from
it—they tasted like pancakes fried in vegeta-
ble oil. 9The manna fell with the dew during
the night.
10Moses heard all the families standing
around their tent doors weeping, and the
anger of the Lord grew hot; Moses too was
highly displeased.
11Moses said to the Lord, "Why pick on me,
to give me the burden of a people like this?
12Are they *my* children? Am I their father? Is
that why you have given me the job of nursing them along like babies until we get to the
land you promised their ancestors? 13Where
am I supposed to get meat for all these
people? For they weep to me saying, 'Give us
meat!' 14I can't carry this nation by myself!
The load is far too heavy! 15If you are going to
treat me like this, please kill me right now; it
will be a kindness! Let me out of this impossible situation!"
16Then the Lord said to Moses, "Summon
before me seventy of the leaders of Israel;
bring them to the Tabernacle, to stand there
with you. 17I will come down and talk with
you there, and I will take of the Spirit which
is on you and will put it upon them also; they
shall bear the burden of the people along with
you, so that you will not have the task alone.
18"And tell the people to purify themselves,
for tomorrow they shall have meat to eat. Tell
them, 'The Lord has heard your tearful complaints about all you left behind in Egypt, and
he is going to give you meat. You shall eat it,
19,20not for just a day or two, or five or ten or
even twenty! For one whole month you will
have meat until you vomit it from your noses;
for you have rejected the Lord who is here
among you, and you have wept for Egypt.'"
21But Moses said, "There are 600,000 men
alone [besides all the women and children],
and yet you promise them meat for a whole
month! 22If we butcher all our flocks and
herds it won't be enough! We would have to
catch every fish in the ocean to fulfill your
promise!"
23Then the Lord said to Moses, "When did
I become weak? Now you shall see whether
my word comes true or not!"
24So Moses left the Tabernacle and reported
Jehovah's words to the people; and he gathered the seventy elders and placed them
around the Tabernacle. 25And the Lord came
down in the Cloud and talked with Moses,
and the Lord took of the Spirit that was upon
Moses and put it upon the seventy elders; and
when the Spirit rested upon them, they
prophesied for some time.
26But two of the seventy—Eldad and Me-

11:1-3 Instead of trusting God to take care of them, the people started to complain. This first complaint against God is just one of many during their wilderness travels. God reacted quickly and harshly to their murmuring because it was seriously undermining the program of recovery God had set forth for them. Their complaining indicated their ingratitude, impatience, and lack of faith. The difficult process of going from Egyptian bondage to God's promised home in Canaan could only be accomplished if the people patiently trusted God to get them through. The same is true of our own recovery process.

11:4-5 We are told here that a group of Egyptians traveling with Israel began complaining. Notice that the complaints were then spread by the Israelites. This illustrates the importance of supportive company in our recovery process. One of Satan's strategies to undermine our faith may be the negative attitudes and comments of those around us. We need to avoid spending time with those who drag us down and seek out people who build us up and strengthen us in our recovery.

11:10-15 When Moses complained angrily to God about his unpleasant circumstances, God didn't rebuke him; he evidently sympathized with his problem. God's response toward Moses stands in stark contrast to the severe judgment brought upon the Israelites for their complaints. God evidently saw that Moses' motives were pure and his faith, genuine; thus, he responded to Moses' honest cry for help. God is never afraid of the anger we may feel about the situations we face. He expects honesty in our prayers.

AARON & MIRIAM

The pecking order in most families is established by order of birth—oldest to youngest. The family of Aaron, Miriam, and Moses started out this way, too. But with time it became clear that God had special plans for Moses. At the time of Moses' birth, his sister, Miriam, was given a special part in preserving him from Pharaoh's decree demanding the death of all the Hebrew baby boys. Miriam continued to watch Moses from a distance as he grew up in Pharaoh's palace as the adopted son of Pharaoh's daughter. Still later, Miriam watched God raise up Moses to lead the Israelites out of their slavery in Egypt. Brother Aaron was also called to play a special role in the life of Moses. At one point Aaron was assigned to be his brother's spokesman. Later God called Aaron to be Israel's high priest.

Moses' older siblings became disturbed that God had chosen Moses and raised him to a level above them. At a number of points during Moses' life they criticized him openly. This displeased God greatly, for it undermined the leadership of the man he had chosen to lead his people. Aaron and Miriam had both been given important roles in the nation of Israel. Their jealousy of Moses made them blind to the importance of their own gifts. God judged Miriam's criticism of Moses suddenly and harshly—with leprosy. People with this disease were not only doomed to a long and painful death, but to banishment from society. It was only because of the intercessory prayer of brother Moses that Miriam was later healed by God (Numbers 12).

We must be careful not to confuse constructive criticism with sibling jealousy. Sibling jealousy left unaddressed can lead to the destruction of the family, and in some cases, a much greater community. But when these problems are brought before God, he can restore even these relationships, just as he did for Aaron, Miriam, and Moses.

The story of Aaron and Miriam is told throughout the book of Exodus. Aaron is also referred to in Leviticus, Numbers, Deuteronomy, and Hebrews 7:11. Miriam is mentioned in Numbers 12; 20; and Deuteronomy 24:9. Both are mentioned in 1 Chronicles 6:3 and Micah 6:4.

STRENGTHS AND ACCOMPLISHMENTS:

- Both were gifted to help the Israelites.
- Aaron was called by God to be Israel's first High Priest.
- Miriam was an able leader and prophetess.

WEAKNESSES AND MISTAKES:

- Both were jealous of Moses' authority.
- Miriam openly criticized Moses' leadership.
- Both complained about Moses' marriage.
- Aaron allowed himself to be manipulated by the people.

LESSONS FROM THEIR LIVES:

- Order of birth doesn't necessarily define a person's level of success.
- God chooses his leaders according to his own set of criteria, not ours.
- The motives behind the criticism, not just the criticism itself, need to be dealt with.
- God gives us all special gifts, and he uses them to fulfill his plans.
- Jealousy of others can easily blind us to our own special gifts.

KEY VERSES:

"One day Miriam and Aaron were criticizing Moses because his wife was a Cushite woman, and they said, 'Has the Lord spoken only through Moses? Hasn't he spoken through us, too?' But the Lord heard them" (Numbers 12:1-2).

---

dad—were still in the camp, and when the
Spirit rested upon them, they prophesied
there. 27Some young men ran and told Moses
what was happening, 28and Joshua (the son of
Nun), one of Moses' personally chosen assistants, protested, "Sir, make them stop!"
29But Moses replied, "Are you jealous for
my sake? I only wish that all of the Lord's
people were prophets, and that the Lord
would put his Spirit upon them all!" 30Then
Moses returned to the camp with the elders of Israel.
31The Lord sent a wind that brought quail
from the sea and let them fall into the camp
and all around it! As far as one could walk in
a day in any direction, there were quail flying
three or four feet above the ground. 32So the
people caught and killed quail all that day and
through the night and all the next day too!
The least anyone gathered was 100 bushels!
Quail were spread out all around the camp.
33But as everyone began eating the meat, the
anger of the Lord rose against the people and
he killed large numbers of them with a

plague. 34So the name of that place was called, "The Place of the Graves Caused by Lust," because they buried the people there who had lusted for meat and for Egypt. 35And from that place they journeyed to Hazeroth, where they stayed awhile.

CHAPTER 12
Miriam and Aaron Criticize Moses

One day Miriam and Aaron were criticizing Moses because his wife was a Cushite woman, 2and they said, "Has the Lord spoken only through Moses? Hasn't he spoken through us, too?"

But the Lord heard them. 3,4Immediately he summoned Moses, Aaron, and Miriam to the Tabernacle: "Come here, you three," he commanded. So they stood before the Lord. (Now Moses was the humblest man on earth.)

5Then the Lord descended in the Cloud and stood at the entrance of the Tabernacle. "Aaron and Miriam, step forward," he commanded; and they did. 6And the Lord said to them, "Even with a prophet, I would communicate by visions and dreams; 7,8but that is not how I communicate with my servant Moses. He is completely at home in my house! With him I speak face to face! And he shall see the very form of God! Why then were you not afraid to criticize him?"

9Then the anger of the Lord grew hot against them, and he departed. 10As the Cloud moved from above the Tabernacle, Miriam suddenly became white with leprosy. When Aaron saw what had happened, 11he cried out to Moses, "Oh, sir, do not punish us for this sin; we were fools to do such a thing. 12Don't let her be as one dead, whose body is half rotted away at birth."

13And Moses cried out to the Lord, "Heal her, O God, I beg you!"

14And the Lord said to Moses, "If her father had but spit in her face she would be defiled seven days. Let her be banished from the camp for seven days, and after that she can come back again."

15So Miriam was excluded from the camp for seven days, and the people waited until she was brought back in before they traveled again. 16Afterwards they left Hazeroth and camped in the wilderness of Paran.

CHAPTER 13
Twelve Spies Are Sent

Jehovah now instructed Moses, 2"Send spies into the land of Canaan—the land I am giving to Israel; send one leader from each tribe."

3-15(The Israelis were camped in the wilderness of Paran at the time.) Moses did as the Lord had commanded and sent these twelve tribal leaders:

Shammua, son of Zaccur, from the tribe of Reuben;
Shaphat, son of Hori, from the tribe of Simeon;
Caleb, son of Jephunneh, from the tribe of Judah;
Igal, son of Joseph, from the tribe of Issachar;
Hoshea, son of Nun, from the half-tribe of Ephraim;
Palti, son of Raphu, from the tribe of Benjamin;
Gaddiel, son of Sodi, from the tribe of Zebulun;
Gaddi, son of Susi, from the tribe of Joseph (actually, the half-tribe of Manasseh);
Ammiel, son of Gemalli, from the tribe of Dan;
Sethur, son of Michael, from the tribe of Asher;
Nahbi, son of Vophsi, from the tribe of Naphtali;
Geuel, son of Machi, from the tribe of Gad.

16It was at this time that Moses changed Hoshea's name to Joshua.

17Moses sent them out with these instructions: "Go northward into the hill country of the Negeb, 18and see what the land is like; see also what the people are like who live there, whether they are strong or weak, many or few; 19and whether the land is fertile or not; and what cities there are, and whether they are villages or are fortified; 20whether the land is rich or poor, and whether there are many trees. Don't be

12:3-4 This parenthetical statement about Moses' humility is one of the most revealing evaluations of his character found in Scripture. He is described as the most humble man in the world. This is essentially the same quality commended by the first beatitude: "Humble men are very fortunate!" (Matthew 5:3). Evidence of Moses' humility is found in his great patience and perseverance as he leads Israel through the wilderness. Our own humility is extremely important as we give our life into God's hands for recovery.

CALEB

Many of us seek the acceptance of others when we make decisions. We try not to admit it, but a careful examination of past decisions will probably show that we are like so many others—as we pursue the approval of others, we often side with the majority viewpoint. Unfortunately, in our world system, the majority viewpoint seldom gives God and his Word any consideration.

Caleb was an individual who saw things from God's perspective and stood against the majority opinion. Ten of the twelve spies who had entered Canaan, a clear majority, believed that the Promised Land couldn't be conquered. They came back with stories of impregnable walled cities, defended by terrible giants. They told the people that the task was hopeless, letting their fears and the majority opinion decide the course of action. But Caleb, along with Joshua, differed with the majority, embracing a godly, minority opinion. Caleb agreed that Canaan was well fortified and the task formidable. But he also believed that even the greatest of enemies was no match for the mighty God of Israel. Caleb spoke out, calling the people to believe in God's promises. Caleb knew that with God's help, they could conquer all the obstacles and difficulties that the majority had reported.

Sadly, the people of Israel didn't listen to Caleb. They followed the majority opinion and refused to take the land God had promised them. As a direct result, the entire nation of Israel was left to wander in the wilderness for nearly forty years. Of all the adult Israelites who left Egypt, only Caleb and Joshua would enter the Promised Land.

It is so easy for us to focus on the obstacles in our own life—all those things that make change seem impossible. We can learn from Caleb, who believed God's word despite the obstacles before him. When the situation appeared hopeless, he knew that victory could come by turning his life and will over to the God who had promised him and his people the victory. Caleb knew that self-worth could not be found in the approval of other people, but only in the loving eyes of God. He had learned to live for God's approval, not the approval of others.

STRENGTHS AND ACCOMPLISHMENTS:

- He was one of the twelve handpicked spies sent into Canaan.
- He was able to express his faith in God even in the face of opposition.
- Despite overwhelming opposition he remained faithful to God and his promises.
- He remained faithful to Joshua and Moses throughout the wilderness wanderings.
- He based his self-worth on God's opinion, not the opinions of others.

LESSONS FROM HIS LIFE:

- Right and wrong can never be based solely on the majority opinion.
- Boldness in a God-centered life is appropriate.
- An effective faith should have both words and actions behind it.
- Our self-worth should not be based upon our acceptance by the majority.

KEY VERSE:

"But my servant Caleb is a different kind of man—he has obeyed me fully. I will bring him into the land he entered as a spy, and his descendants shall have their full share in it" (Numbers 14:24).

Caleb's story is told in Numbers 13–14 and Joshua 14–15. He is also mentioned in Judges 1 and 1 Chronicles 4:15.

---

afraid, and bring back some samples of the crops you see." (The first of the grapes were being harvested at that time.)

21So they spied out the land all the way from the wilderness of Zin to Rehob near Hamath. 22Going northward, they passed first through the Negeb and arrived at Hebron. There they saw the Ahimanites, Sheshites, and Talmites, all families descended from Anak. (By the way, Hebron was very ancient, having been founded seven years before Tanis in Egypt.) 23Then they came to what is now known as the Valley of Eshcol where they cut down a single cluster of grapes so large that it took two of them to carry it on a pole between them! They also took some samples of the pomegranates and figs. 24The Israelis named the valley "Eshcol" at that time (meaning "Cluster") because of the cluster of grapes they found!

The Spies Incite Rebellion

[25]After forty days of exploration they returned from their tour. [26]They made their report to Moses, Aaron, and all the people of Israel in the wilderness of Paran at Kadesh, and they showed the fruit they had brought with them.

[27]This was their report: "We arrived in the land you sent us to see, and it is indeed a magnificent country—a land 'flowing with milk and honey.' Here is some fruit we have brought as proof. [28]But the people living there are powerful, and their cities are fortified and very large; and what's more, we saw Anakim giants there! [29]The Amalekites live in the south, while in the hill country there are the Hittites, Jebusites, and Amorites; down along the coast of the Mediterranean Sea and in the Jordan River valley are the Canaanites."

[30]But Caleb reassured the people as they stood before Moses. "Let us go up at once and possess it," he said, "for we are well able to conquer it!"

[31]"Not against people as strong as they are!" the other spies said. "They would crush us!"

[32]So the majority report of the spies was negative: "The land is full of warriors, the people are powerfully built, [33]and we saw some of the Anakim there, descendants of the ancient race of giants. We felt like grasshoppers before them, they were so tall!"

CHAPTER 14

Then all the people began weeping aloud, and they carried on all night. [2]Their voices rose in a great chorus of complaint against Moses and Aaron.

"We wish we had died in Egypt," they wailed, "or even here in the wilderness, [3]rather than be taken into this country ahead of us. Jehovah will kill us there, and our wives and little ones will become slaves. Let's get out of here and return to Egypt!"[4]The idea swept the camp. "Let's elect a leader to take us back to Egypt!" they shouted.

Moses Intercedes for the People

[5]Then Moses and Aaron fell face downward on the ground before the people of Israel. [6]Two of the spies, Joshua (the son of Nun), and Caleb (the son of Jephunneh), ripped their clothing [7]and said to all the people, "It is a wonderful country ahead, [8]and the Lord loves us. He will bring us safely into the land and give it to us. It is *very* fertile, a land 'flowing with milk and honey'! [9]Oh, do not rebel against the Lord, and do not fear the people of the land. For they are but bread for us to eat! The Lord is with us and he has removed his protection from them! Don't be afraid of them!"

[10,11]But the only response of the people was to talk of stoning them. Then the glory of the Lord appeared, and the Lord said to Moses, "How long will these people despise me? Will they *never* believe me, even after all the miracles I have done among them? [12]I will disinherit them and destroy them with a plague, and I will make you into a nation far greater and mightier than they are!"

[13]"But what will the Egyptians think when they hear about it?" Moses pleaded with the Lord. "They know full well the power you displayed in rescuing your people. [14]They have told this to the inhabitants of this land, who are well aware that you are with Israel and that you talk with her face to face. They see the pillar of cloud and fire standing above us, and they know that you lead and protect

---

13:30 The minority report of Caleb, and later Joshua (14:6-9), emphasized God's power to overcome even the greatest of problems. Their faith enabled them to see problems not as obstacles, but as opportunities for God to prove himself. The basis for their faith was God's promise to save his people from their enemies (10:9). When we have an active faith in God, our view of life and its challenges will emphasize the positive rather than the negative.

13:33 The words of the ten spies in this verse reveal their perception of themselves: "We felt like grasshoppers before them, they were so tall!" The Israelites failed to perceive themselves as God saw them. They were his chosen people, backed by the promises of the Creator of the universe. God had promised to give them the land of Canaan. As we face life's greatest challenges, our self-perception needs to come from our faith in God, not the difficult problems we face. We need to realize that God loves us and has promised to help us overcome the adversity and sin in our life.

14:24 In contrast to the unbelief of the other Israelites, Caleb trusted God and obeyed him fully. The positive consequence of his faith was his entrance into the Promised Land, though he had to wait nearly forty years to arrive there. All the other adults except Joshua died as they wandered on their forty-year wilderness trek. If we seek recovery in our own strength, we also will wander in the wilderness, never experiencing the wholeness God desires for us. But if we step out, trusting God to lead and protect us, we will discover a new life. Notice that even Caleb and Joshua had to wander in the wilderness on their way, but through perseverance and faith in God they did finally arrive.

us day and night. [15]Now if you kill all your people, the nations that have heard your fame will say, [16]'The Lord had to kill them because he wasn't able to take care of them in the wilderness. He wasn't strong enough to bring them into the land he swore he would give them.'

[17,18]"Oh, please, show the great power [of your patience] by forgiving our sins and showing us your steadfast love. Forgive us, even though you have said that you don't let sin go unpunished, and that you punish the father's fault in the children to the third and fourth generation. [19]Oh, I plead with you, pardon the sins of this people because of your magnificent, steadfast love, just as you have forgiven them all the time from when we left Egypt until now."

Forty Years in the Wilderness

[20,21]Then the Lord said, "All right, I will pardon them as you have requested. But I vow by my own name that just as it is true that all the earth shall be filled with the glory of the Lord, [22]so it is true that not one of the men who has seen my glory and the miracles I did both in Egypt and in the wilderness—and ten times refused to trust me and obey me— [23]shall even see the land I promised to this people's ancestors. [24]But my servant Caleb is a different kind of man—he has obeyed me fully. I will bring him into the land he entered as a spy, and his descendants shall have their full share in it. [25]But now, since the people of Israel are so afraid of the Amalekites and the Canaanites living in the valleys, tomorrow you must turn back into the wilderness in the direction of the Red Sea."

[26,27]Then the Lord said to Moses and to Aaron, "How long will this wicked nation complain about me? For I have heard all that they have been saying. [28]Tell them, 'The Lord vows to do to you what you feared: [29]You will all die here in this wilderness! Not a single one of you twenty years old and older, who has complained against me, [30]shall enter the Promised Land. Only Caleb (son of Jephunneh) and Joshua (son of Nun) are permitted to enter it.

[31]"'You said your children would become slaves of the people of the land. Well, instead I will bring *them* safely into the land and they shall inherit what you have despised. [32]But as for you, your dead bodies shall fall in this wilderness. [33]You must wander in the desert like nomads for forty years. In this way you will pay for your faithlessness, until the last of you lies dead in the desert.

[34,35]"'Since the spies were in the land for forty days, you must wander in the wilderness for forty years—a year for each day, bearing the burden of your sins. I will teach you what it means to reject me. I, Jehovah, have spoken. Every one of you who has conspired against me shall die here in this wilderness.'"

[36-38]Then the ten spies who had incited the rebellion against Jehovah by striking fear into the hearts of the people were struck dead before the Lord. Of all the spies, only Joshua and Caleb remained alive. [39]What sorrow there was throughout the camp when Moses reported God's words to the people!

[40]They were up early the next morning and started toward the Promised Land.

"Here we are!" they said. "We realize that we have sinned, but now we are ready to go on into the land the Lord has promised us."

[41]But Moses said, "It's too late. Now you are disobeying the Lord's orders to return to the wilderness. [42]Don't go ahead with your plan or you will be crushed by your enemies, for the Lord is not with you. [43]Don't you remember? The Amalekites and the Canaanites are there! You have deserted the Lord, and now he will desert you."

[44]But they went ahead into the hill country, despite the fact that neither the Ark nor Moses left the camp. [45]Then the Amalekites and the Canaanites who lived in the hills came down and attacked them and chased them to Hormah.

CHAPTER 15

More Rules about Offerings

The Lord told Moses to give these instructions to the people of Israel: "When your children finally live in the land I am going to give them, [3,4]and they want to please the Lord with a burnt offering or any other offering by fire, their sacrifice must be an animal from their flocks of sheep and goats, or from their herds of cattle. Each sacrifice—whether an ordinary

---

14:34-45 After Moses announced God's judgment, the Israelites showed superficial attitudes of repentance. Then they tried to conquer parts of Canaan in their own strength, but their mission was unsuccessful. As we seek to overcome our dependencies and compulsions, we need to do it in God's way, with God's timing, and with God's help. The obstacles we face are too great to be tackled alone, but with God's help, nothing is impossible.

one, or a sacrifice to fulfill a vow, or a free-will offering, or a special sacrifice at any of the annual festivals—must be accompanied by a grain offering. If a lamb is being sacrificed, use three quarts of fine flour mixed with three pints of oil, 5accompanied by three pints of wine for a drink offering.

6"If the sacrifice is a ram, use six quarts of fine flour mixed with four pints of oil,7and four pints of wine for a drink offering. This will be a sacrifice that is a pleasing fragrance to the Lord.

8,9"If the sacrifice is a young bull, then the grain offering accompanying it must consist of nine quarts of fine flour mixed with three quarts of oil, 10plus three quarts of wine for the drink offering. This shall be offered by fire as a pleasing fragrance to the Lord.

11,12"These are the instructions for what is to accompany each sacrificial bull, ram, lamb, or young goat. 13,14These instructions apply both to native-born Israelis and to foreigners living among you who want to please the Lord with sacrifices offered by fire; 15,16for there is the same law for all, native-born or foreigner, and this shall be true forever from generation to generation; all are the same before the Lord. Yes, one law for all!"

17,18The Lord also said to Moses at this time, "Instruct the people of Israel that when they arrive in the land that I am going to give them, 19-21they must present to the Lord a sample of each year's new crops by making a loaf, using coarse flour from the first grain that is cut each year. This loaf must be waved back and forth before the altar in a gesture of offering to the Lord. It is an annual offering from your threshing floor and must be observed from generation to generation.

22"If by mistake you or future generations fail to carry out all of these regulations that the Lord has given you over the years through Moses, 23,24then when the people realize their error, they must offer one young bull for a burnt offering. It will be a pleasant odor before the Lord, and must be offered along with the usual grain offering and drink offering, and one male goat for a sin offering. 25And the priest shall make atonement for all of the people of Israel and they shall be forgiven; for it was an error, and they have corrected it with their sacrifice made by fire before the Lord, and by their sin offering. 26All the people shall be forgiven, including the foreigners living among them, for the entire population is involved in such error and forgiveness.

27"If the error is made by a single individual, then he shall sacrifice a one-year-old female goat for a sin offering, 28and the priest shall make atonement for him before the Lord, and he shall be forgiven. 29This same law applies to individual foreigners who are living among you.

30"But anyone who deliberately makes the 'mistake,' whether he is a native Israeli or a foreigner, is blaspheming Jehovah, and shall be cut off from among his people. 31For he has despised the commandment of the Lord and deliberately failed to obey his law; he must be executed and die in his sin."

Rules Concerning the Sabbath

32One day while the people of Israel were in the wilderness, one of them was caught gathering wood on the Sabbath day. 33He was arrested and taken before Moses and Aaron and the other judges. 34They jailed him until they could find out the Lord's mind concerning him.

35Then the Lord said to Moses, "The man must die—all the people shall stone him to death outside the camp."

36So they took him outside the camp and killed him as the Lord had commanded.

Rules Concerning Clothing

37,38The Lord said to Moses, "Tell the people of Israel to make tassels for the hems of their clothes (this is a permanent regulation from generation to generation) and to attach the

15:1-36 This restatement of many of the Levitical laws was intended to train the new generation concerning their accountability to God. They would be allowed to enter the Promised Land and enjoy God's blessings. But they needed to realize that in their new life there, they would be accountable to God. Privilege always brings with it responsibility, and God was affirming this principle with a new generation of Israelites.

15:37-41 The Israelites were required to wear tassels on the corners of their clothing. This would remind them constantly of their covenant relationship with God and that they were to obey him. It would be a visual reminder that their commitment to obey God was important in every realm of life. Although the New Testament does not command such a ritual for us today, the principle behind it is helpful. As we commit our life to God, we need to realize that obedience is important in all areas of life.

tassels to their clothes with a blue cord. 39The purpose of this regulation is to remind you, whenever you notice the tassels, of the commandments of the Lord, and that you are to obey his laws instead of following your own desires and going your own ways, as you used to do in serving other gods. 40It will remind you to be holy to your God. 41For I am Jehovah your God who brought you out of the land of Egypt; yes, I am the Lord, your God."

CHAPTER 16

Korah Incites Rebellion

One day Korah (son of Izhar, grandson of Kohath, and a descendant of Levi) conspired with Dathan and Abiram (the sons of Eliab) and On (the son of Peleth), all three from the tribe of Reuben, 2to incite a rebellion against Moses. Two hundred and fifty popular leaders, all members of the Assembly, were involved.

3They went to Moses and Aaron and said, "We have had enough of your presumption; you are no better than anyone else; everyone in Israel has been chosen of the Lord, and he is with all of us. What right do you have to put yourselves forward, claiming that we must obey you, and acting as though you were greater than anyone else among all these people of the Lord?"

4When Moses heard what they were saying he fell face downward to the ground. 5Then he said to Korah and to those who were with him, "In the morning the Lord will show you who are his, and who is holy, and whom he has chosen as his priest. 6,7Do this: You, Korah, and all those with you, take censers tomorrow and light them, and put incense upon them before the Lord, and we will find out whom the Lord has chosen. You are the presumptuous ones, you sons of Levi."

8,9Then Moses spoke again to Korah: "Does it seem a small thing to you that the God of Israel has chosen you from among all the people of Israel to be near to himself as you work in the Tabernacle of Jehovah, and to stand before the people to minister to them? 10Is it nothing to you that he has given this task to only you Levites? And now are you demanding the priesthood also? 11,12That is what you are really after! That is why you are revolting against Jehovah. And what has Aaron done, that you are dissatisfied with him?" Then Moses summoned Dathan and Abiram (the sons of Eliab), but they refused to come.

13"Is it a small thing," they mimicked, "that you brought us out of lovely Egypt to kill us here in this terrible wilderness, and that now you want to make yourself our king? 14What's more, you haven't brought us into the wonderful country you promised, nor given us fields and vineyards. Whom are you trying to fool? We refuse to come."

15Then Moses was very angry and said to the Lord, "Do not accept their sacrifices! I have never stolen so much as a donkey from them and have not hurt one of them."

16And Moses said to Korah, "Come here tomorrow before the Lord with all your friends; Aaron will be here too. 17Be sure to bring your censers with incense on them; a censer for each man, 250 in all; and Aaron will also be here with his."

18So they did. They came with their censers and lit them and placed the incense on them, and stood at the entrance of the Tabernacle with Moses and Aaron. 19Meanwhile, Korah had stirred up the entire nation against Moses and Aaron, and they all assembled to watch. Then the glory of Jehovah appeared to all the people, 20and Jehovah said to Moses and Aaron, 21"Get away from these people so that I may instantly destroy them."

22But Moses and Aaron fell face downward to the ground before the Lord. "O God, the God of all mankind," they pleaded, "must you be angry with all the people when one man sins?"

The Rebels Are Punished

23,24And the Lord said to Moses, "Then tell the people to get away from the tents of Korah, Dathan, and Abiram."

25So Moses rushed over to the tents of

16:1–17:13 The three stories in this section illustrate the priority of Aaron's priesthood in God's leadership of his people, Israel. God made it clear that Aaron was his chosen spiritual leader. Proper worship of God could come only through his high priesthood. The writer of Hebrews shows us that Jesus Christ is a High Priest superior in every way to Aaron (Hebrews 4:1–10:39). As Aaron's budding rod demonstrated that he was chosen by God, so Christ's resurrection proved that he was to be the only mediator between God and the human race (1 Timothy 2:5). For us today, cleansing from sin and a proper approach to God can come only through a relationship with Christ (John 14:6). He makes it possible for us to be reconciled to God.

Dathan and Abiram, followed closely by the 250 Israeli leaders. 26"Quick!" he told the people, "get away from the tents of these wicked men, and don't touch anything that belongs to them, lest you be included in their sins [and be destroyed with them]."

27So all the people stood back from the tents of Korah, Dathan, and Abiram. And Dathan and Abiram came out and stood at the entrances of their tents with their wives and sons and little ones.

28And Moses said, "By this you shall know that Jehovah has sent me to do all these things that I have done—for I have not done them on my own. 29If these men die a natural death or from some ordinary accident or disease, then Jehovah has not sent me. 30But if the Lord does a miracle and the ground opens up and swallows them and everything that belongs to them, and they go down alive into Sheol, then you will know that these men have despised the Lord."

31He had hardly finished speaking the words when the ground suddenly split open beneath them, 32and a great fissure swallowed them up, along with their tents and families and the friends who were standing with them, and everything they owned. 33So they went down alive into Sheol and the earth closed upon them, and they perished. 34All of the people of Israel fled at their screams, fearing that the earth would swallow them too. 35Then fire came from Jehovah and burned up the 250 men who were offering incense.

36,37And the Lord said to Moses, "Tell Eleazar the son of Aaron the priest to pull those censers from the fire; for they are holy, dedicated to the Lord. He must also scatter the burning incense 38from the censers of these men who have sinned at the cost of their lives. He shall then beat the metal into a sheet as a covering for the altar, for these censers are holy because they were used before the Lord; and the altar sheet shall be a reminder to the people of Israel."

39So Eleazar the priest took the 250 bronze censers and beat them out into a sheet of metal to cover the altar, 40to be a reminder to the people of Israel that no unauthorized person—no one who is not a descendant of Aaron—may come before the Lord to burn incense, lest the same thing happen to him as happened to Korah and his associates. Thus the Lord's directions to Moses were carried out.

41But the very next morning all the people began muttering again against Moses and Aaron, saying, "You have killed the Lord's people."

42Soon a great, sullen mob formed; suddenly, as they looked toward the Tabernacle, the Cloud appeared and the awesome glory of the Lord was seen. 43,44Moses and Aaron came and stood at the entrance of the Tabernacle, and the Lord said to Moses,

45"Get away from these people so that I can instantly destroy them." But Moses and Aaron fell face downward to the earth before the Lord.

46And Moses said to Aaron, "Quick, take a censer and place fire in it from the altar; lay incense on it, and carry it quickly among the people and make atonement for them; for God's anger has gone out among them—the plague has already begun."

47Aaron did as Moses had told him to, and ran among the people, for the plague had indeed already begun; and he put on the incense and made atonement for them. 48And he stood between the living and the dead, and the plague was stopped, 49but not before 14,700 people had died (in addition to those who had died the previous day with Korah). 50Then Aaron returned to Moses at the entrance of the Tabernacle; and so the plague was stopped.

CHAPTER 17

Aaron's Authority Is Vindicated

Then the Lord said to Moses, "Tell the people of Israel that each of their tribal chiefs is to bring you a wooden rod with his name inscribed upon it. Aaron's name is to be on the rod of the tribe of Levi. 4Put these rods in the inner room of the Tabernacle where I meet with you, in front of the Ark. 5I will use these rods to identify the man I have chosen: for buds will grow on his rod! Then at last this murmuring and complaining against you will stop!"

6So Moses gave the instructions to the people, and each of the twelve chiefs (including Aaron) brought him a rod. 7He put them before the Lord in the inner room of the Tabernacle, 8and when he went in the next day, he found that Aaron's rod, representing the tribe of Levi, had budded and was blossoming, and had ripe almonds hanging from it!

9When Moses brought them out to show the others, they stared in disbelief! Then each man except Aaron claimed his rod. 10The Lord told Moses to place Aaron's rod permanently beside the Ark as a reminder of this rebellion.

He was to [bring it out and show it to the people again] if there were any further complaints about Aaron's authority; this would ward off further catastrophe to the people. [11]So Moses did as the Lord commanded him.

[12,13]But the people of Israel only grumbled the more. "We are as good as dead," they whined. "Everyone who even comes close to the Tabernacle dies. Must we all perish?"

CHAPTER 18

The Duties Are Divided

The Lord now spoke to Aaron: "You and your sons and your family are responsible for any desecration of the sanctuary," he said, "and will be held liable for any impropriety in your priestly work.

[2,3]"Your kinsmen, the tribe of Levi, are your assistants; but only you and your sons may perform the sacred duties in the Tabernacle itself. The Levites must be careful not to touch any of the sacred articles or the altar, lest I destroy both them and you. [4]No one who is not a member of the tribe of Levi shall assist you in any way. [5]Remember, only the priests are to perform the sacred duties within the sanctuary and at the altar. If you follow these instructions, the wrath of God will never again fall upon any of the people of Israel for violating this law. [6]I say it again—your kinsmen the Levites are your assistants for the work of the Tabernacle. They are a gift to you from the Lord. [7]But you and your sons, the priests, shall personally handle all the sacred service, including the altar and all that is within the veil, for the priesthood is your special gift of service. Anyone else who attempts to perform these duties shall die."

[8]The Lord gave these further instructions to Aaron: "I have given the priests all the gifts which are brought to the Lord by the people; all these offerings presented to the Lord by the gesture of waving them before the altar belong to you and your sons, by permanent law. [9]The grain offerings, the sin offerings, and the guilt offerings are yours, except for the sample presented to the Lord by burning upon the altar. All these are most holy offerings. [10]They are to be eaten only in a most holy place, and only by males. [11]All other gifts presented to me by the gesture of waving them before the altar are for you and your families, sons and daughters alike. For all the members of your families may eat these unless anyone is ceremonially impure at the time.

[12]"Yours also are the first-of-the-harvest gifts the people bring as offerings to the Lord—the best of the olive oil, wine, grain, [13]and every other crop. Your families may eat these unless they are ceremonially defiled at the time. [14,15]So everything that is dedicated to the Lord shall be yours, including the firstborn sons of the people of Israel, and the firstborn of their animals. [16]However, you may never accept the firstborn sons, nor the firstborn of any animals that I do not permit for food. Instead, there must be a payment of two and a half dollars made for each firstborn child. It is to be brought when he is one month old.

[17]"However, the firstborn of cows, sheep, or goats may not be bought back; they must be sacrificed to the Lord. Their blood is to be sprinkled upon the altar, and their fat shall be burned as a fire offering; it is very pleasant to the Lord. [18]The meat of these animals shall be yours, including the breast and right thigh that are presented to the Lord by the gesture of waving before the altar. [19]Yes, I have given to you all of these 'wave offerings' brought by the people of Israel to the Lord; they are for you and your families as food; this is a permanent contract between the Lord and you and your descendants.

[20]"You priests may own no property nor have any other income, for I am all that you need.

[21]As for the tribe of Levi, your relatives, they shall be paid for their service with the tithes from the entire land of Israel.

[22]"From now on, Israelites other than the priests and Levites shall not enter the sanctuary lest they be judged guilty and die. [23]Only the Levites shall do the work there, and they shall be guilty if they fail. This is a permanent law among you, that the Levites shall own no property in Israel, [24]for the people's tithes, offered to the Lord by the gesture of waving before the altar, shall belong to the Levites; these are their inheritance, and so they have no need for property."

[25,26]The Lord also said to Moses, "Tell the Levites to give to the Lord a tenth of the tithes they receive—a tithe of the tithe, to be presented to the Lord by the gesture of waving before the altar. [27]The Lord will consider this as your first-of-the-harvest offering to him of grain and wine, as though it were from your own property. [28,29]This tithe of the tithe shall be selected from the choicest part of the tithes you receive as the Lord's portion, and shall be given to Aaron the priest. [30]It shall be credited to you just as though it were from your own

threshing floor and wine press. 31Aaron and his sons and their families may eat it in their homes or anywhere they wish, for it is their compensation for their service in the Tabernacle. 32You Levites will not be held guilty for accepting the Lord's tithes if you then give the best tenth to the priests. But beware that you do not treat the holy gifts of the people of Israel as though they were common, lest you die."

CHAPTER 19

Purification after Defilement

The Lord said to Moses and Aaron, "Here is another of my laws:

"Tell the people of Israel to bring you a red heifer without defect, one that has never been yoked. Give her to Eleazar the priest and he shall take her outside the camp and someone shall kill her as he watches. 4Eleazar shall take some of her blood upon his finger and sprinkle it seven times toward the front of the Tabernacle. 5Then someone shall burn the heifer as he watches—her hide, meat, blood, and dung. 6Eleazar shall take cedar wood and hyssop branches and scarlet thread, and throw them into the burning pile.

7"Then he must wash his clothes, and bathe, and afterwards return to the camp and be ceremonially defiled until the evening. 8And the one who burns the animal must wash his clothes and bathe, and he too shall be defiled until evening. 9Then someone who is not ceremonially defiled shall gather up the ashes of the heifer and place them in some purified place outside the camp, where they shall be kept for the people of Israel as a source of water for the purification ceremonies, for removal of sin. 10And the one who gathers up the ashes of the heifer must wash his clothes and be defiled until evening; this is a permanent law for the benefit of the people of Israel and any foreigners living among them.

11"Anyone who touches a dead human body shall be defiled for seven days, 12and must purify himself the third and seventh days with water [run through the ashes of the red heifer]; then he will be purified; but if he does not do this on the third day, he will continue to be defiled even after the seventh day. 13Anyone who touches a dead person and does not purify himself in the manner specified has defiled the Tabernacle of the Lord, and shall be excommunicated from Israel. The cleansing water was not sprinkled upon him, so the defilement continues.

14"When a man dies in a tent, these are the various regulations: Everyone who enters the tent, and those who are in it at the time, shall be defiled seven days. 15Any container in the tent without a lid over it is defiled.

16"If someone out in a field touches the corpse of someone who has been killed in battle or who has died in any other way, or if he even touches a bone or a grave, he shall be defiled seven days. 17To become purified again, ashes from the red heifer sin offering are to be added to spring water in a kettle. 18Then a person who is not defiled shall take hyssop branches and dip them into the water and sprinkle the water upon the tent and upon all the pots and pans in the tent, and upon anyone who has been defiled by being in the tent, or by touching a bone, or touching someone who has been killed or is otherwise dead, or has touched a grave. 19This shall take place on the third and seventh days; then the defiled person must wash his clothes and bathe himself, and that evening he will be out from under the defilement.

20"But anyone who is defiled and doesn't purify himself shall be excommunicated, for he has defiled the sanctuary of the Lord, and the water to cleanse him has not been sprinkled upon him; so he remains defiled. 21This is a permanent law. The man who sprinkles the water must afterwards wash his clothes; and anyone touching the water shall be defiled until evening. 22And anything a defiled person touches shall be defiled until evening."

CHAPTER 20

Moses Strikes the Rock

The people of Israel arrived in the wilderness of Zin in April and camped at Kadesh, where Miriam died and was buried. 2There was not enough water to drink at that place, so the people again rebelled against Moses and Aaron. A great mob formed, 3and they held a protest meeting.

"Would that we too had died with our dear brothers the Lord killed!" they shouted at Moses. 4"You have deliberately brought us into this wilderness to get rid of us, along with our flocks and herds. 5Why did you ever make us leave Egypt and bring us here to this evil place? Where is the fertile land of wonderful crops—the figs, vines, and pomegranates you told us about? Why, there isn't even water enough to drink!"

6Moses and Aaron turned away and went to the entrance of the Tabernacle, where they

fell face downward before the Lord; and the
glory of Jehovah appeared to them.
7And he said to Moses, 8"Get Aaron's rod;
then you and Aaron must summon the
people. As they watch, speak to that rock over
there and tell it to pour out its water! You will
give them water from a rock, enough for all
the people and all their cattle!"
9So Moses did as instructed. He took the rod
from the place where it was kept before the
Lord; 10then Moses and Aaron summoned the
people to come and gather at the rock; and he
said to them, "Listen, you rebels! Must we
bring you water from this rock?"
11Then Moses lifted the rod and struck the
rock twice, and water gushed out; and the
people and their cattle drank.
12But the Lord said to Moses and Aaron,
"Because you did not believe me and did not
sanctify me in the eyes of the people of Israel,
you shall not bring them into the land I have
promised them!"
13This place was named Meribah (meaning
"Rebel Waters"), because it was where the
people of Israel fought against Jehovah, and
where he showed himself to be holy before
them.

Edom Refuses to Let Israel Pass

14While Moses was at Kadesh he sent messengers to the king of Edom: "We are the descendants of your brother, Israel," he declared.
"You know our sad history, 15how our ancestors went down to visit Egypt and stayed
there so long, and became slaves of the Egyptians. 16But when we cried to the Lord he
heard us and sent an Angel who brought us
out of Egypt, and now we are here at Kadesh,
encamped on the borders of your land.
17Please let us pass through your country. We
will be careful not to go through your
planted fields, nor through your vineyards;
we won't even drink water from your wells,
but will stay on the main road and not leave
it until we have crossed your border on the
other side."
18But the king of Edom said, "Stay out! If
you attempt to enter my land, I will meet you
with an army!"
19"But, sir," protested the Israeli ambassadors, "we will stay on the main road and will
not even drink your water unless we pay
whatever you demand for it. We only want to
pass through and nothing else."
20But the king of Edom was adamant. "Stay
out!" he warned, and, mobilizing his army, he
marched to the frontier with a great
force.21,22Because Edom refused to allow Israel
to pass through their country, Israel turned
back and journeyed from Kadesh to Mount
Hor.

Aaron Dies

23Then the Lord said to Moses and Aaron at
the border of the land of Edom, 24"The time
has come for Aaron to die—for he shall not
enter the land I have given the people of
Israel, for the two of you rebelled against my
instructions concerning the water at Meribah.
25Now take Aaron and his son Eleazar and lead
them up onto Mount Hor. 26There you shall
remove Aaron's priestly garments from him
and put them on Eleazar his son; and Aaron
shall die there."
27So Moses did as the Lord commanded
him. The three of them went up together into
Mount Hor as all the people watched. 28When
they reached the summit, Moses removed the
priestly garments from Aaron and put them
on his son Eleazar; and Aaron died on the top
of the mountain. Moses and Eleazar returned,
29and when the people were informed of Aaron's death, they mourned for him for thirty
days.

20:2-13 After a water shortage, the Israelites started their murmuring again. The focus of this incident, however, was upon the failure of Moses and Aaron. Moses was severely judged by God for not following God's instructions specifically and for using his own method to produce water. Aaron was also judged because he evidently had a part in it. While the judgment seems severe, it illustrates the importance of obedience to God's Word, especially if we are in a leadership position. Moses and Aaron, by disobeying God's specific instructions, exhibited attitudes of personal rebellion against God. Commitment to God's program cannot be a partway proposition. Despite Moses' great success in the past, this failure kept him out of the Promised Land.

20:23-29 The death of Aaron, Israel's first high priest, was mourned by the people (20:29), but this wouldn't be the last of Israel's priestly funerals. The writer of Hebrews used this point to contrast the ministry of Jesus Christ with the ministry of other human priests: "Under the old arrangement there had to be many priests, so that when the older ones died off, the system could still be carried on by others who took their places. But Jesus lives forever and continues to be a Priest so that no one else is needed" (Hebrews 7:23-24). Our great High Priest will always be available to provide help for any problems we may have.

CHAPTER 21

Israel Defeats the King of Arad

When the king of Arad heard that the Israelis
were approaching (for they were traveling the
same route as the spies), he mobilized his
army and attacked Israel, taking some of the
men as prisoners. [2]Then the people of Israel
vowed to the Lord that if he would help them
conquer the king of Arad and his people, they
would completely annihilate all the cities of
that area. [3]The Lord heeded their request and
defeated the Canaanites; and the Israelis completely destroyed them and their cities. The
name of the region was thereafter called Hormah (meaning "Utterly Destroyed").

The Bronze Snake

[4]Then the people of Israel returned to Mount
Hor, and from there continued southward
along the road to the Red Sea in order to go
around the land of Edom. The people were
very discouraged; [5]they began to murmur
against God and to complain against Moses.
"Why have you brought us out of Egypt to die
here in the wilderness?" they whined. "There
is nothing to eat here, and nothing to drink,
and we hate this insipid manna."

[6]So the Lord sent poisonous snakes among
them to punish them, and many of them
were bitten and died.

[7]Then the people came to Moses and cried
out, "We have sinned, for we have spoken
against Jehovah and against you. Pray to him
to take away the snakes." So Moses prayed for
the people.

[8]Then the Lord told him, "Make a bronze
replica of one of these snakes and attach it to
the top of a pole; anyone who is bitten shall
live if he simply looks at it!"

[9]So Moses made the replica, and whenever
anyone who had been bitten looked at the
bronze snake, he recovered!

[10]Israel journeyed next to Oboth and
camped there. [11]Then they went on to
Iyeabarim, in the wilderness, a short distance
east of Moab, [12]and from there they traveled
to the valley of the brook Zared and set up
camp. [13]Then they moved to the far side of the
Arnon River, near the borders of the Amorites.
(The Arnon River is the boundary line between the Moabites and the Amorites. [14]This
fact is mentioned in *The Book of the Wars of
Jehovah,* where it is stated that the valley of
the Arnon River and the city of Waheb [15]lie
between the Amorites and the people of
Moab.)

[16]Then Israel traveled to Beer (meaning "A
Well"). This is the place where the Lord told
Moses, "Summon the people, and I will give
them water." [17,18]What happened is described
in this song the people sang:

Spring up, O well!
Sing of the water!
This is a well
The leaders dug.
It was hollowed
With their staves
And shovels.

Then they left the desert and proceeded on
through Mattanah, [19]Nahaliel, and Bamoth;
[20]then to the valley in the plateau of Moab,

21:1-3 Victory! This first great success was the result of complete obedience to God's will. This victory, along with others to follow, began an important era in Israel's history. They were able to see the truth of Joshua and Caleb's advice—faith would bring victory over any enemy or obstacle. God delights in proving himself in the lives of those who trust in his power to overcome life's obstacles. Our powerlessness over any problem can be covered by God's unlimited power to act on our behalf.

21:4-9 This incident was used by the apostle John in the New Testament as an illustration of what Christ did on our behalf. "As Moses in the wilderness lifted up the bronze image of a serpent on a pole, even so I must be lifted up upon a pole" (John 3:14). Evident in both passages is God's saving grace, which provides salvation and healing for anyone who responds in faith. Healing did not come to everyone in Israel, but only to those who by faith looked at the brass serpent on the pole. The apostle John makes it clear that personal forgiveness and victory over sin can come only to those who look to Christ on the cross. God provides the powerful means of recovery from sin and failure; we need to receive it in faith.

21:7 Notice here that Moses resumed his role as Israel's leader and mediator even after he was judged for his sin at Meribah. His failure undoubtedly brought him a great deal of personal pain and disappointment. He would lead several million Israelites to the Promised Land, but would never enter it himself. In spite of this, Moses showed no bitter feelings toward God; neither did he neglect his responsibilities. His recovery from this personal failure and his continued faithful service is evidence of Moses' great faith and dependence upon God. Our mistakes don't disqualify us from future success; they provide opportunities for learning, growth, and dependence on God.

which overlooks the desert with Mount Pisgah in the distance.

Israel Defeats King Sihon

[21]Israel now sent ambassadors to King Sihon
of the Amorites.

[22]"Let us travel through your land," they
requested. "We will not leave the road until
we have passed beyond your borders. We
won't trample your fields or touch your vineyards or drink your water."

[23]But King Sihon refused. Instead he mobilized his army and attacked Israel in the wilderness, battling them at Jahaz. [24]But Israel
slaughtered them and occupied their land
from the Arnon River to the Jabbok River, as
far as the borders of the Ammonites; but they
were stopped there by the rugged terrain.

[25,26]So Israel captured all the cities of the
Amorites and lived in them, including the
city of Heshbon, which had been King Sihon's
capital. [27-30]The ancient poets had referred to
King Sihon in this poem:

Come to Heshbon,
King Sihon's capital,
For a fire has flamed forth
And devoured
The city of Ar in Moab,
On the heights of the Arnon River.
Woe to Moab!
You are finished,
O people of Chemosh;
Your sons have fled,
And your daughters are captured
By King Sihon of the Amorites.
He has destroyed
The little children
And the men and women
As far as Dibon, Nophah, and Medeba.

The Israelites Defeat King Og

[31,32]While Israel was there in the Amorite
country, Moses sent spies to look over the
Jazer area; he followed up with an armed
attack, capturing all of the towns and driving
out the Amorites. [33]They next turned their
attention to the city of Bashan, but King Og
of Bashan met them with his army at Edrei.
[34]The Lord told Moses not to fear—that the
enemy was already conquered! "The same
thing will happen to King Og as happened to
King Sihon at Heshbon," the Lord assured
him. [35]And sure enough, Israel was victorious
and killed King Og, his sons, and his subjects,
so that not a single survivor remained; and
Israel occupied the land.

CHAPTER 22

Balaam Asked to Curse Israel

The people of Israel now traveled to the plains
of Moab and camped east of the Jordan River
opposite Jericho. [2,3]When King Balak of Moab
(the son of Zippor) realized how many of
them there were, and when he learned what
they had done to the Amorites, he and his
people were terrified. [4]They quickly consulted
with the leaders of Midian.

"This mob will eat us like an ox eats grass,"
they exclaimed.

So King Balak [5,6]sent messengers to Balaam
(son of Beor) who was living in his native land
of Pethor, near the Euphrates River. He begged
Balaam to come and help him.

"A vast horde of people has arrived from
Egypt, and they cover the face of the earth
and are headed toward me," he frantically
explained. "Please come and curse them for
me, so that I can drive them out of my land;
for I know what fantastic blessings fall on
those whom you bless, and I also know that
those whom you curse are doomed."

[7]The messengers he sent were some of the
top leaders of Moab and Midian. They went
to Balaam with money in hand and urgently
explained to him what Balak wanted.

[8]"Stay here overnight," Balaam said, "and
I'll tell you in the morning whatever the Lord
directs me to say." So they did.

[9]That night God came to Balaam and asked
him, "Who are these men?"

[10]"They have come from King Balak of
Moab," he replied. [11]"The king says that a vast
horde of people from Egypt has arrived at his
border, and he wants me to go at once and
curse them, in the hope that he can battle
them successfully."

[12]"Don't do it!" God told him. "You are not
to curse them, for I have blessed them!"

22:1-20 Balaam is a Mesopotamian *baru* (priest, diviner) who was hired by Balak, king of Moab, to place a curse upon Israel. King Balak wanted to prevent the Israelites from conquering Moab and other surrounding lands. Balaam, a man of great spiritual stature, openly admitted that he had no power to go beyond the will of God. He could not place a curse upon the people whom God desired to bless. This should help us realize that when it seems everyone is against us, we can be sure that God is able to protect us and provide us with the wisdom to survive the toughest of situations (James 1:2-5).

13 The next morning Balaam told the men,
"Go on home! The Lord won't let me do it."
14 So King Balak's ambassadors returned
without him and reported his refusal. 15 Balak
tried again. This time he sent a larger number
of even more distinguished ambassadors than
the former group. 16,17 They came to Balaam
with this message:

"King Balak pleads with you to come. He
promises you great honors plus any payment
you ask. Name your own figure! Only come
and curse these people for us."

18 But Balaam replied, "If he were to give me
a palace filled with silver and gold, I could do
nothing contrary to the command of the Lord
my God. 19 However, stay here tonight so that
I can find out whether the Lord will add
anything to what he said before."

20 That night God told Balaam, "You may
get up and go with these men, but be sure to
say only what I tell you to."

21 So the next morning he saddled his donkey and started off with them.

Balaam's Donkey Speaks

22,23 But God was angry about Balaam's eager
attitude, so he sent an angel to stand in the
road to kill him. As Balaam and two servants
were riding along, Balaam's donkey suddenly
saw the angel of the Lord standing in the road
with a drawn sword. She bolted off the road
into a field, but Balaam beat her back onto the
road. 24 Now the angel of the Lord stood at a
place where the road went between two vineyard walls. 25 When the donkey saw him
standing there, she squirmed past by pressing
against the wall, crushing Balaam's foot in the
process. So he beat her again. 26 Then the angel
of the Lord moved farther down the road and
stood in a place so narrow that the donkey
couldn't get by at all.

27 So she lay down in the road! In a great fit
of temper Balaam beat her again with his
staff.

28 Then the Lord caused the donkey to
speak! "What have I done that deserves your
beating me these three times?" she asked.

29 "Because you have made me look like a
fool!" Balaam shouted. "I wish I had a sword
with me, for I would kill you."

30 "Have I ever done anything like this before in my entire life?" the donkey asked.

"No," he admitted.

31 Then the Lord opened Balaam's eyes and
he saw the angel standing in the roadway
with drawn sword, and he fell flat on the
ground before him.

32 "Why did you beat your donkey those
three times?" the angel demanded. "I have
come to stop you because you are headed for
destruction. 33 Three times the donkey saw me
and shied away from me; otherwise I would
certainly have killed you by now and spared
her."

34 Then Balaam confessed, "I have sinned. I
didn't realize you were there. I will go back
home if you don't want me to go on."

35 But the angel told him, "Go with the men,
but say only what I tell you to say." So Balaam
went on with them. 36 When King Balak heard
that Balaam was on the way, he left the capital
and went out to meet him at the Arnon River,
at the border of his land.

37 "Why did you delay so long?" he asked
Balaam. "Didn't you believe me when I said I
would give you great honors?"

38 Balaam replied, "I have come, but I have
no power to say anything except what God
tells me to say; and that is what I shall speak."
39 Balaam accompanied the king to
Kiriathhuzoth, 40 where King Balak sacrificed
oxen and sheep, and gave animals to Balaam
and the ambassadors for their sacrifices. 41 The
next morning Balak took Balaam to the top of
Mount Bamoth-baal, from which he could see
the people of Israel spread out before him.

CHAPTER 23

Balaam Blesses Israel

Balaam said to the king, "Build seven altars
here, and prepare seven young bulls and
seven rams for sacrifice."

2 Balak followed his instructions, and a
young bull and a ram were sacrificed on each
altar.

3,4 Then Balaam said to the king, "Stand here
by your burnt offerings and I will see if the
Lord will meet me; and I will tell you what he
says to me." So he went up to a barren height,
and God met him there. Balaam told the

22:22-35 The humorous story about Balaam and his donkey illustrates Balaam's spiritual blindness with respect to the true God. As a specialist in divination, Balaam often relied upon signs from animals and nature to determine the future. In this situation, however, he had less spiritual perception than his donkey and was prevented from carrying out a diabolical plot against Israel. From Balaam we learn that the greatest of human wisdom often leads to spiritual blindness. True wisdom to face life's situations only comes from the sovereign, all-knowing God.

Lord, "I have prepared seven altars and have
sacrificed a young bull and a ram on each."
5Then the Lord gave Balaam a message for
King Balak.
6When Balaam returned, the king was
standing beside the burnt offerings with all
the princes of Moab. 7-10This was Balaam's
message:

"King Balak, king of Moab, has brought
me
From the land of Aram,
From the eastern mountains.
'Come,' he told me, 'curse Jacob for me!
Let your anger rise on Israel.'
But how can I curse
What God has not cursed?
How can I denounce
A people God has not denounced?
I see them from the cliff tops,
I watch them from the hills.
They live alone,
And prefer to remain distinct
From every other nation.
They are as numerous as dust!
They are beyond numbering.
If only I could die as happy as an Israelite!
Oh, that my end might be like theirs!"

11"What have you done to me?" demanded
King Balak. "I told you to curse my enemies,
and now you have blessed them!"
12But Balaam replied, "Can I say anything
except what Jehovah tells me to?"

Balaam's Second Blessing

13Then Balak told him, "Come with me to
another place; there you will see only a portion of the nation of Israel. Curse at least that
many!"
14So King Balak took Balaam into the fields
of Zophim at the top of Mount Pisgah, and
built seven altars there; and he offered up a
young bull and a ram on each altar.
15Then Balaam said to the king, "Stand here
by your burnt offering while I go to meet the
Lord." 16And the Lord met Balaam and told
him what to say. 17So he returned to where the
king and the princes of Moab were standing
beside their burnt offerings.
"What has Jehovah said?" the king eagerly
inquired.
18-24And he replied,

"Rise up, Balak, and hear:
Listen to me, you son of Zippor.
God is not a man, that he should lie;
He doesn't change his mind like humans
do.

STEP 3

Trusting God

BIBLE READING: Numbers 23:18-24

We made a decision to turn our will and our life over to the care of God as we understood him.

It is not uncommon to link our perceptions about God to our childhood experiences with people who played powerful roles in our life. If we have been victimized in the past by people who were capricious, abusive, distant, uncaring, or incompetent, we may now anticipate these qualities in God.

Just because God is a power greater than we are, and the people who victimized us represented a power greater than we were, we must not conclude that God will harm us if we entrust our life to him. Even Jesus tells us that he didn't entrust himself to men because he knew what was in their hearts. Nevertheless, he voluntarily turned his life over to the will of God the Father. "It is better to trust the Lord than to put confidence in men" (Psalm 118:8).

We may have learned in the past that putting confidence in people only brings pain and disappointment. We can't let this keep us from ever trusting again. In working through Step Three we can make a healthy decision to turn our will and our life over to the only one who is worthy of being trusted. The Bible tells us, "God is not a man, that he should lie; he doesn't change his mind like humans do" (Numbers 23:19). And God has said, "I will never, *never* fail you nor forsake you" (Hebrews 13:5).

We know that we can't make it all alone. But now we can stop being the victim. We can turn our life over to someone who is really able to care for our needs. ***Turn to page 219, Deuteronomy 30.***

Has he ever promised,
Without doing what he said?
Look! I have received a command to bless them,
For God has blessed them,
And I cannot reverse it!
He has not seen sin in Jacob.
He will not trouble Israel!
Jehovah their God is with them.
He is their king!
God has brought them out of Egypt.
Israel has the strength of a wild ox.
No curse can be placed on Jacob,
And no magic shall be done against him.
For now it shall be said of Israel,
'What wonders God has done for them!'
These people rise up as a lion;
They shall not lie down
Until they have eaten what they capture
And have drunk the blood of the slain!"

25"If you aren't going to curse them, at least
don't *bless* them!" the king exclaimed to Balaam.
26But Balaam replied, "Didn't I tell you that
I must say whatever Jehovah tells me to?"

Balaam's Third Blessing

27Then the king said to Balaam, "I will take
you to yet another place. Perhaps it will please
God to let you curse them from there."
28So King Balak took Balaam to the top of
Mount Peor, overlooking the desert. 29Balaam
again told the king to build seven altars, and
to prepare seven young bulls and seven rams
for the sacrifice. 30The king did as Balaam said,
and offered a young bull and ram on every
altar.

CHAPTER 24
Balaam realized by now that Jehovah planned
to bless Israel, so he didn't even go to meet the
Lord as he had earlier. Instead, he went at
once and looked out toward the camp of
Israel 2which stretched away across the plains,
divided by tribal areas.
Then the Spirit of God came upon him,
3-9and he spoke this prophecy concerning
them:

"Balaam the son of Beor says—
The man whose eyes are open says—
'I have listened to the word of God,
I have seen what God Almighty showed me;
I fell, and my eyes were opened:
Oh, the joys awaiting Israel,
Joys in the homes of Jacob.
I see them spread before me as green valleys,
And fruitful gardens by the riverside;
As aloes planted by the Lord himself;
As cedar trees beside the waters.
They shall be blessed with an abundance of water,
And they shall live in many places.
Their king will be greater than Agag;
Their kingdom is exalted.
God has brought them from Egypt.
Israel has the strength of a wild ox,
And shall eat up the nations that oppose him;
He shall break their bones in pieces,
And shall shoot them with many arrows.
Israel sleeps as a lion or a lioness—
Who dares arouse him?
Blessed is everyone who blesses you, O Israel,
And curses shall fall upon everyone who curses you.'"

10King Balak was livid with rage by now.
Striking his hands together in anger and disgust he shouted, "I called you to curse my
enemies and instead you have blessed them
three times. 11Get out of here! Go back home!
I had planned to promote you to great honor,
but Jehovah has kept you from it!"
12Balaam replied, "Didn't I tell your messengers 13that even if you gave me a palace filled
with silver and gold, I could not go beyond the
words of Jehovah, and could not say a word of
my own? I said that I would say only what
Jehovah says! 14Yes, I shall return now to my
own people. But first, let me tell you what the
Israelites are going to do to your people!"

23:18-24 Through the words of Balaam's second oracle, God affirmed not only his sovereignty, but also his truthful character: "God is not a man that he should lie; he doesn't change his mind like humans do." The future of Israel was secure because a sovereign God had chosen her for his glory and promised to bless her. The New Testament tells us that we were chosen by God before the world was made and he has blessed us with every spiritual blessing in Christ (Ephesians 1:3-14). Worldly wisdom, as illustrated by Balaam, cannot compare with the wisdom of God.

23:18-24 Israel's wilderness experience demonstrates not only the faithlessness of the exodus generation, but also the loving care of our sovereign God. Though the Israelites made numerous mistakes, God graciously led them to the Promised Land. Our life is also riddled with failures and sin, but God is still able and willing to lead us in our recovery.

Balaam's Fourth Blessing

[15-19]So he spoke this prophecy to him:

"Balaam the son of Beor is the man
Whose eyes are open!
He hears the words of God
And has knowledge from the Most High;
He sees what Almighty God has shown
him;
He fell, and his eyes were opened:
I see in the future of Israel,
Far down the distant trail,
That there shall come a star from Jacob!
This ruler of Israel
Shall smite the people of Moab,
And destroy the sons of Sheth.
Israel shall possess all Edom and Seir.
They shall overcome their enemies.
Jacob shall arise in power
And shall destroy many cities."

[20]Then Balaam looked over at the homes of
the people of Amalek and prophesied:

"Amalek was the first of the nations,
But its destiny is destruction!"

[21,22]Then he looked over at the Kenites:

"Yes, you are strongly situated,
Your nest is set in the rocks!
But the Kenites shall be destroyed,
And the mighty army of the king of
Assyria shall deport you from this land!"

[23,24]He concluded his prophecies by saying:

"Alas, who can live when God does this?
Ships shall come from the coasts of
Cyprus,
And shall oppress both Eber and Assyria.
They too must be destroyed."

[25]So Balaam and Balak returned to their
homes.

CHAPTER 25

The Israelites Worship Baal

While Israel was camped at Acacia, some of
the young men began going to wild parties
with the local Moabite girls. [2]These girls also
invited them to attend the sacrifices to their
gods, and soon the men were not only attending the feasts, but also bowing down and
worshiping the idols. [3]Before long all Israel
was joining freely in the worship of Baal, the
god of Moab; and the anger of the Lord was
hot against his people.
[4]He issued the following command to Moses:

"Execute all the tribal leaders of Israel.
Hang them up before the Lord in broad daylight, so that his fierce anger will turn away
from the people."
[5]So Moses ordered the judges to execute all
who had worshiped Baal.
[6]But one of the Israeli men insolently
brought a Midianite girl into the camp, right
before the eyes of Moses and all the people, as
they were weeping at the door of the Tabernacle. [7]When Phinehas (son of Eleazar and
grandson of Aaron the priest) saw this, he
jumped up, grabbed a spear, [8]and rushed after
the man into his tent, where he had taken the
girl. He thrust the spear all the way through
the man's body and into her stomach. So the
plague was stopped, [9]but only after 24,000
people had already died.
[10,11]Then the Lord said to Moses, "Phinehas
(son of Eleazar and grandson of Aaron the
priest) has turned away my anger for he was
angry with my anger, and would not tolerate
the worship of any God but me. So I have
stopped destroying all Israel as I had intended.
[12,13]Now because of what he has done—because of his zeal for his God, and because he
has made atonement for the people of Israel
by what he did—I promise that he and his
descendants shall be priests forever."
[14]The name of the man who was killed with
the Midianite girl was Zimri, son of Salu, a
leader of the tribe of Simeon. [15]The girl's name
was Cozbi, daughter of Zur, a Midianite
prince.
[16,17]Then the Lord said to Moses, "Destroy
the Midianites, [18]for they are destroying you
with their wiles. They are causing you to worship Baal, and they are leading you astray, as
you have just seen by the death of Cozbi."

CHAPTER 26

The People Are Counted Again

After the plague had ended, Jehovah said to
Moses and to Eleazar (son of Aaron the priest),
[2]"Take a census of all the men of Israel who
are twenty years old or older, to find out how

25:1-18 After God's victory over the false gods of Balaam, the Israelites were quickly seduced into Canaanite worship. Through this story we can see how clever and diverse Satan's strategies are. When unsuccessful in his attack from the outside (22:1–24:25), he succeeded in bringing decay from within. Israelite participation in immoral Canaanite worship practices resulted in the judgment of 24,000 of God's people. This shows how important our personal morality is to God.

many of each tribe and clan are able to go to war."

3,4So Moses and Eleazar issued census instructions to the leaders of Israel. (The entire nation was camped in the plains of Moab beside the Jordan River, opposite Jericho.) Here are the results of the census:

5-11*The tribe of Reuben:* 43,730.

(Reuben was Israel's oldest son.) In this tribe were the following clans, named after Reuben's sons:

The Hanochites, named after their ancestor Hanoch.
The Palluites, named after their ancestor Pallu. (In the subclan of Eliab—who was one of the sons of Pallu—were the families of Nemuel, Abiram, and Dathan. This Dathan and Abiram were the two leaders who conspired with Korah against Moses and Aaron, and in fact challenged the very authority of God! But the earth opened and swallowed them; and 250 men were destroyed by fire from the Lord that day, as a warning to the entire nation.)
The Hezronites, named after their ancestor Hezron.
The Carmites, named after their ancestor Carmi.

12-14*The tribe of Simeon:* 22,200.

In this tribe were the following clans, founded by Simeon's sons:

The Nemuelites, named after their ancestor Nemuel.
The Jaminites, named after their ancestor Jamin.
The Jachinites, named after their ancestor Jachin.
The Zerahites, named after their ancestor Zerah.
The Shaulites, named after their ancestor Shaul.

15-18*The tribe of Gad:* 40,500

In this tribe were the following clans founded by the sons of Gad:

The Zephonites, named after their ancestor Zephon.
The Haggites, named after their ancestor Haggi.
The Shunites, named after their ancestor Shuni.
The Oznites, named after their ancestor Ozni.
The Erites, named after their ancestor Eri.
The Arodites, named after their ancestor Arod.
The Arelites, named after their ancestor Areli.

19-22*The tribe of Judah:* 76,500

In this tribe were the following clans named after the sons of Judah—but not including Er and Onan who died in the land of Canaan:

The Shelanites, named after their ancestor Shelah.
The Perezites, named after their ancestor Perez.
The Zerahites, named after their ancestor Zerah.
This census also included the subclans of Perez:
The Hezronites, named after their ancestor Hezron.
The Hamulites, named after their ancestor Hamul.

23-25*The tribe of Issachar:* 64,300.

In this tribe were the following clans named after the sons of Issachar:

The Tolaites, named after their ancestor Tola.
The Punites, named after their ancestor Puvah.
The Jashubites, named after their ancestor Jashub.
The Shimronites, named after their ancestor Shimron.

26,27*The tribe of Zebulun:* 60,500.

In this tribe were the following clans named after the sons of Zebulun:

The Seredites, named after their ancestor Sered.
The Elonites, named after their ancestor Elon.
The Jahleelites, named after their ancestor Jahleel.

28-37*The tribe of Joseph:* 32,500 *in the half-tribe of Ephraim; and* 52,700 *in the half-tribe of Manasseh.*

In the half-tribe of Manasseh was the clan

26:1-65 The census in chapter 1 was taken primarily for organizational purposes. This later census was intended to prepare Israel for the conquest of the Promised Land and the later division of property. The decrease in numbers from the census taken forty years earlier was primarily due to the judgments suffered by Israel in the wilderness.

their ancestor Ma-
chir. ...irites was the Gil-
...their ancestor Gilead.
The subclan of ...dites:
...eadites, named after their ancestor
...amed after their ancestor
Je...named after their ancestor
...nites, named after their
Shechem.
...idaites, named after their
...or Shemida.
...herites, named after their
...tor Hepher. (Hepher's son,
...phehad, had no sons. Here are the
...mes of his daughters: Mahlah, Noah,
...oglah, Milcah, Tirzah.

...he 32,500 registered in the half-tribe of ...hraim included the following clans, named ...fter the sons of Ephraim:

The Shuthelahites, named after their ancestor Shuthelah. (A subclan of the Shuthelahites was the Eranites, named after their ancestor Eran, a son of Shuthelah.)
The Becherites, named after their ancestor Becher.
The Tahanites, named after their ancestor Tahan.

38-41 *The tribe of Benjamin:* 45,600.
In this tribe were the following clans named after the sons of Benjamin:

The Belaites, named after their ancestor Bela.
Subclans named after sons of Bela were:
The Ardites, named after their ancestor Ard.
The Naamites, named after their ancestor Naaman.
The Ashbelites, named after their ancestor Ashbel.
The Ahiramites, named after their ancestor Ahiram.
The Shuphamites, named after their ancestor Shephupham.
The Huphamites, named after their ancestor Hupham.

42,43 *The tribe of Dan:* 64,400.
In this tribe was the clan of the Shuhamites, named after Shuham, the son of Dan.

44-47 *The tribe of Asher:* 53,400.
In this tribe were the following clans named after the sons of Asher:

The Imnites, named after their ancestor Imnah.
The Ishvites, named after their ancestor Ishvi.
The Beriites, named after their ancestor Beriah.
Subclans named after the sons of Beriah were:
The Heberites, named after their ancestor Heber.
The Malchielites, named after their ancestor Malchiel.

Asher also had a daughter named Serah.

48-50 *The tribe of Naphtali:* 45,400.
In this tribe were the following clans, named after the sons of Naphtali:

The Jahzeelites, named after their ancestor Jahzeel.
The Gunites, named after their ancestor Guni.
The Jezerites, named after their ancestor Jezer.
The Shillemites, named after their ancestor Shillem.

51 So the total number of the men of draft age throughout Israel was 601,730.
52,53 Then the Lord told Moses to divide the land among the tribes in proportion to their population, as indicated by the census—54 the larger tribes to be given more land, the smaller tribes less land.
55,56 "Let the representatives of the larger tribes have a lottery, drawing for the larger sections," the Lord instructed, "and let the smaller tribes draw for the smaller sections."
57 These are the clans of the Levites numbered in the census:

The Gershonites, named after their ancestor Gershon.
The Kohathites, named after their ancestor Kohath.
The Merarites, named after their ancestor Merari.

58,59 These are the families of the tribe of Levi: the Libnites, the Hebronites, the Mahlites, the Mushites, the Korahites.
While Levi was in Egypt, a daughter, Jochebed, was born to him and she became the wife of Amram, son of Kohath. They were the
parents of Aaron, Moses, and Miriam. 60 To
Aaron were born Nadab, Abihu, Eleazar, and
Ithamar. 61 But Nadab and Abihu died when

they offered unauthorized incense before the Lord.

62*The total number of Levites in the census* was 23,000, counting all the males a month old and upward. But the Levites were not included in the total census figure of the people of Israel, for the Levites were given no land when it was divided among the tribes.

63So these are the census figures as prepared by Moses and Eleazar the priest, in the plains of Moab beside the Jordan River, across from Jericho. 64,65Not one person in this entire census had been counted in the previous census taken in the wilderness of Sinai! For all who had been counted then had died, as the Lord had decreed when he said of them, "They shall die in the wilderness." The only exceptions were Caleb (son of Jephunneh) and Joshua (son of Nun).

CHAPTER 27

Zelophehad's Daughters

One day the daughters of Zelophehad came to the entrance of the Tabernacle to give a petition to Moses, Eleazar the priest, the tribal leaders, and others who were there. The names of these women were Mahlah, Noah, Hoglah, Milcah, and Tirzah. They were members of the half-tribe of Manasseh (a son of Joseph). Their ancestor was Machir, son of Manasseh. Manasseh's son Gilead was their great-grandfather, his son Hepher was their grandfather, and his son Zelophehad was their father.

3,4"Our father died in the wilderness," they said, "and he was not one of those who perished in Korah's revolt against the Lord—it was a natural death, but he had no sons. Why should the name of our father disappear just because he had no son? We feel that we should be given property along with our father's brothers."

5So Moses brought their case before the Lord.

6,7And the Lord replied to Moses, "The daughters of Zelophehad are correct. Give them land along with their uncles; give them the property that would have been given to
their father if he ha
a general law among
and has no sons, then h 8Moreover, this is
passed on to his daughter if a man dies
daughter, it shall belong to nce shall be
if he has no brother, then
uncles. 11But if he has no unc has no
go to the nearest relative." 10And
is

Moses Appoints Joshua to Lead

12One day the Lord said to Moses, "Go
Mount Abarim and look across the river
land I have given to the people of Is
13After you have seen it, you shall die as Aa
your brother did, 14for you rebelled agai
my instructions in the wilderness of Zi
When the people of Israel rebelled, you di
not glorify me before them by following my
instructions to order water to come out of the
rock." He was referring to the incident at the
waters of Meribah ("Place of Strife") in Kadesh, in the wilderness of Zin.

15Then Moses said to the Lord, 16"O
Jehovah, the God of the spirits of all mankind, [before I am taken away] please appoint
a new leader for the people, 17a man who will
lead them into battle and care for them, so that the people of the Lord will not be as sheep without a shepherd."

18The Lord replied, "Go and get Joshua (son of Nun), who has the Spirit in him,
19and take him to Eleazar the priest, and as all the people watch, charge him with the responsibility of leading the people. 20Pub-
licly give him your authority so that all the people of Israel will obey him. 21He shall be
the one to consult with Eleazar the priest in order to get directions from the Lord. The Lord will speak to Eleazar through the use of the Urim, and Eleazar will pass on these instructions to Joshua and the people. In this way the Lord will continue to give them guidance."

22So Moses did as Jehovah commanded and took Joshua to Eleazar the priest. As the
people watched, 23Moses laid his hands upon
him and dedicated him to his responsibilities, as the Lord had commanded.

27:12-23 The torch of Israel's leadership was passed from Moses to Joshua. Moses was able to view the land of Canaan (27:12-14), but was not allowed to enter it because of his earlier failure. Rather than being self-centered and overcome with disappointment, his greatest concern was still for his people. The attitude reflected in his words reveal his godly character: "Please appoint a new leader for the people, a man who will lead them into battle and care for them, so that the people of the Lord will not be as sheep without a shepherd." Moses was content with God's plan for him. We, like Moses, must learn to be content with God's plan for us, even when it brings us temporary disappointments along the way. God always desires what is best for us.

CHAPTER 28

Daily Offerings

The Lord gave Moses these instructions to give to the people of Israel: "The offerings which you burn on the altar for me are my food, and are a pleasure to me; so see to it that they are brought regularly and are offered as I have instructed you.

3"When you make offerings by fire, you shall use yearling male lambs—each without defect. Two of them shall be offered each day as a regular burnt offering. 4One lamb shall be sacrificed in the morning, the other in the evening. 5 With them shall be offered a grain offering of three quarts of finely ground flour mixed with three pints of oil. 6This is the burnt offering ordained at Mount Sinai, to be regularly offered as a fragrant odor, an offering made by fire to the Lord. 7Along with it shall be the drink offering, consisting of three pints of strong wine with each lamb, poured out in the holy place before the Lord. 8Offer the second lamb in the evening with the same grain offering and drink offering. It too is a fragrant odor to the Lord, an offering made by fire.

Sabbath Offerings

9,10"On the Sabbath day, sacrifice two yearling male lambs—both without defect—in addition to the regular offerings. They are to be accompanied by a grain offering of six quarts of fine flour mixed with oil, and the usual drink offering.

Monthly Offerings

11"Also, on the first day of each month there shall be an extra burnt offering to the Lord of two young bulls, one ram, and seven male yearling lambs—all without defect. 12Accompany them with nine quarts of finely ground flour mixed with oil as a grain offering with each bull; and six quarts of finely ground flour mixed with oil as a grain offering for the ram; 13and for each lamb, three quarts of finely ground flour mixed with oil for a grain offering. This burnt offering shall be presented by fire and will please the Lord very much. 14Along with each sacrifice shall be a drink offering—six pints of wine with each bull, four pints for a ram, and three pints for a lamb. This, then, will be the burnt offering each month throughout the year.

15"Also on the first day of each month you shall offer one male goat for a sin offering to the Lord. This is in addition to the regular daily burnt offering and its drink offering.

Passover Offerings

16"On April first you shall celebrate the Passover—[when the death angel passed over the oldest sons of the Israelites in Egypt, leaving them unharmed]. 17On the following day a great, joyous seven-day festival will begin, but no leavened bread shall be served. 18On the first day of the festival all the people shall be called together before the Lord. No hard work shall be done on that day. 19You shall offer as burnt sacrifices to the Lord two young bulls, one ram, and seven yearling male lambs—all without defect. 20,21With each bull there shall be a grain offering of nine quarts of fine flour mixed with oil; with the ram there shall be six quarts; and with each of the seven lambs there shall be three quarts of fine flour. 22You must also offer a male goat as a sin offering, to make atonement for yourselves. 23These offerings shall be in addition to the usual daily sacrifices. 24This same sacrifice shall be offered on each of the seven days of the feast; they will be very pleasant to the Lord. 25On the seventh day there shall again be a holy and solemn assembly of all the people, and during that day you may do no hard work.

Harvest Festival Offerings

26"On the first day of the Harvest Festival all the people must come before the Lord for a special, solemn assembly to celebrate the new harvest. On that day you are to present the

---

28:1-2 Just as the offerings were to be brought regularly, so our fellowship with God is not to be irregular and compulsive. It should be a continual, moment-by-moment experience for believers. God desires more than ritual in our worship; he invites us to have a day-by-day relationship with him.

28:1-8 Only through continual fellowship with God could God's people expect to have victory as they entered the Promised Land. This is probably the reason for repeating the instructions for the burnt offering here. It was a reaffirmation of its significance for the new generation. By bringing the offering a person was committing his life to God in a fresh way. In a similar way, the apostle Paul called us to present our body as a living sacrifice to God (Romans 12:1-2). This is an essential step for our spiritual growth. Only when we place our life in God's hands will he be able to change us through his power.

first of the new crop of grain as a grain offering to the Lord; there is to be no regular work by anyone on that day. [27]A special burnt offering, very pleasant to the Lord, shall be offered that day. It shall consist of two young bulls, one ram, and seven yearling male lambs. [28,29]These shall be accompanied by your grain offering of nine quarts of fine flour mixed with oil with each bull, six quarts with the ram, and three quarts with each of the seven lambs. [30]Also offer one male goat to make atonement for yourselves. [31]These special offerings are in addition to the regular daily burnt offerings and grain offerings and drink offerings. Make sure that the animals you sacrifice are without defect.

CHAPTER 29

Trumpet Festival Offerings

"The Festival of Trumpets shall be celebrated on the fifteenth day of September each year; there shall be a solemn assembly of all the people on that day, and no hard work may be done. [2]On that day you shall offer a burnt sacrifice consisting of one young bull, one ram, and seven yearling male lambs—all without defect. These are sacrifices which the Lord will appreciate and enjoy. [3,4]A grain offering of nine quarts of fine flour mingled with oil shall be offered with the bull, six quarts with the ram, and three quarts with each of the seven lambs. [5]In addition, there shall be a male goat sacrificed as a sin offering, to make atonement for you. [6]These special sacrifices are in addition to the regular monthly burnt offering for that day, and also in addition to the regular daily burnt sacrifices, which are to be offered with the respective grain offerings and drink offerings, as specified by the ordinances governing them.

Day of Atonement Offerings

[7]"Ten days later another convocation of all the people shall be held. This will be a day of solemn humility before the Lord, and no work of any kind may be done. [8]On that day you shall offer a burnt sacrifice to the Lord—it will be very pleasant to him—of one young bull, one ram, seven yearling male lambs—each without defect—[9,10]and their accompanying grain offerings. Nine quarts of fine flour mixed with oil are to be offered with the bull, six with the ram, and three with each of the seven lambs. [11]You are also to sacrifice one male goat for a sin offering. This is in addition to the sin offering of the Day of Atonement [offered annually on that day], and in addition to the regular daily burnt sacrifices, grain offerings, and drink offerings.

Shelter Festival Offerings

[12]"Five days later there shall be yet another assembly of all the people, and on that day no hard work shall be done; it is the beginning of a seven-day festival before the Lord. [13]Your special burnt sacrifice that day, which will give much pleasure to the Lord, shall be thirteen young bulls, two rams, and fourteen male yearling lambs—each without defect—[14]accompanied by the usual grain offerings—nine quarts of fine flour mingled with oil for each of the thirteen young bulls; six quarts for each of the two rams; [15]and three quarts for each of the fourteen lambs. [16]There must also be a male goat sacrificed for a sin offering, in addition to the regular daily burnt sacrifice with its accompanying grain offerings and drink offerings.

[17]"On the second day of this seven-day festival you shall sacrifice twelve young bulls, two rams, and fourteen male yearling lambs—each without defect—[18]accompanied by the usual grain offerings and drink offerings. [19]Also, in addition to the regular daily burnt sacrifice, you are to sacrifice a male goat with its accompanying grain offering and drink offering for a sin offering.

[20]"On the third day of the festival, offer eleven young bulls, two rams, fourteen male yearling lambs—each without defect—[21]and the usual grain offering and drink offering with each sacrifice. [22]And in addition to the regular daily burnt sacrifices, sacrifice a male goat for a sin offering, with its accompanying grain offering and drink offering.

[23]"On the fourth day of the festival, you are to sacrifice ten young bulls, two rams, and fourteen male yearling lambs—each without defect—[24]each with its accompanying grain offering and drink offering; [25]also a male goat as a sin offering (along with the usual grain and drink offerings) in addition to the regular daily sacrifices.

[26,27]"On the fifth day of the festival, sacrifice nine young bulls, two rams, and fourteen male yearling lambs—each without defect—accompanied by the usual grain offerings and drink offerings; [28]also sacrifice a male goat with the usual grain and drink offerings, as a special sin offering, in addition to the usual daily sacrifices.

[29]"On the sixth day of the festival, you must sacrifice eight young bulls, two rams, and fourteen male yearling lambs—each without

defect—30along with their usual grain and drink offerings. 31In addition to the usual daily sacrifices, sacrifice a male goat and the usual grain and drink offerings as a sin offering.

32"On the seventh day of the festival, sacrifice seven young bulls, two rams, and fourteen male yearling lambs—each without defect—33each with its customary grain and drink offerings; 34also sacrifice an extra sin offering of one male goat, with the usual grain and drink offerings, in addition to the regular daily sacrifices.

35"On the eighth day summon the people to another solemn assembly; you must do no hard work that day. 36Sacrifice a burnt offering—they are very pleasant to the Lord—of one young bull, one ram, seven male yearling lambs—each without defect—37and the customary grain and drink offerings. 38Sacrifice also one male goat with the usual grain and drink offerings for a sin offering, in addition to the regular daily sacrifices. 39These offerings are compulsory at the times of your annual feasts, and are in addition to sacrifices and offerings you present in connection with vows, or as free-will offerings, burnt sacrifices, grain offerings, drink offerings, or peace offerings."

40So Moses gave all of these instructions to the people of Israel.

CHAPTER 30

Rules about Vows

Now Moses summoned the leaders of the tribes and told them, "The Lord has commanded that when anyone makes a promise to the Lord, either to do something or to quit doing something, that vow must not be broken: the person making the vow must do exactly as he has promised.

3"If a woman promises the Lord to do or not do something, and she is still a girl at home in her father's home, 4and her father hears that she has made a vow with penalties, but says nothing, then her vow shall stand. 5But if her father refuses to let her make the vow, or feels that the penalties she has agreed to are too harsh, then her promise will automatically become invalid. Her father must state his disagreement on the first day he hears about it; and then Jehovah will forgive her because her father would not let her do it.

6"If she takes a vow or makes a foolish pledge, and later marries, 7and her husband learns of her vow and says nothing on the day he hears of it, her vow shall stand. 8But if her husband refuses to accept her vow or foolish pledge, his disagreement makes it void, and Jehovah will forgive her.

9"But if the woman is a widow or is divorced, she must fulfill her vow.

10"If she is married and living in her husband's home when she makes the vow, 11and her husband hears of it and does nothing, the vow shall stand; 12but if he refuses to allow it on the first day he hears of it, her vow is void and Jehovah will forgive her. 13So her husband may either confirm or nullify her vow, 14but if he says nothing for a day, then he has already agreed to it. 15If he waits more than a day and then refuses to permit the vow, whatever penalties to which she agreed shall come upon him—he shall be responsible."

16These, then, are the commandments the Lord gave Moses concerning relationships between a man and his wife and between a father and his daughter who is living at home.

CHAPTER 31

War against Midian

Then the Lord said to Moses, "Take vengeance on the Midianites for leading you into idolatry, and then you must die."

3Moses said to the people, "Some of you must take arms to wage Jehovah's war against Midian. 4,5Conscript 1,000 men from each tribe." So this was done; and out of the many thousands of Israel, 12,000 armed men were sent to battle by Moses. 6Phinehas (son of Eleazar the priest) led them into battle, accompanied by the Ark, with trumpets blaring. 7And every man of Midian was killed. 8Among those killed were all five of the Midianite kings—Evi, Rekem, Zur, Hur, and Reba. Balaam, the son of Beor, was also killed.

9-11Then the Israeli army took as captives all the women and children, and seized the cattle and flocks and a lot of miscellaneous booty. All of the cities, towns, and villages of Midian were then burned. 12The captives and other war loot were brought to Moses and Eleazar the priest, and to the rest of the people of Israel who were camped on the plains of Moab beside the Jordan River, across from Jericho. 13Moses and Eleazar the priest and all the leaders of the people went out to meet the victorious army, 14but Moses was very angry with the army officers and battalion leaders.

15"Why have you let all the women live?" he demanded. 16"These are the very ones who followed Balaam's advice and caused the people of Israel to worship idols on Mount Peor, and they are the cause of the plague that destroyed us. 17Now kill all the boys and all the women who have had sexual intercourse. 18Only the little girls may live; you may keep them for yourselves. 19Now stay outside of the camp for seven days, all of you who have killed anyone or touched a dead body. Then purify yourselves and your captives on the third and seventh days. 20Remember also to purify all your garments and everything made of leather, goat's hair, or wood."

21Then Eleazar the priest said to the men who were in the battle, "This is the commandment Jehovah has given Moses: 22'Anything that will stand heat—such as gold, silver, bronze, iron, tin, or lead—23shall be passed through fire in order to be made ceremonially pure; it must then be further purified with the purification water. But anything that won't stand heat shall be purified by the water alone.' 24On the seventh day you must wash your clothes and be purified, and then you may come back into the camp."

25And the Lord said to Moses, 26"You and Eleazar the priest and the leaders of the tribes are to make a list of all the loot, including the people and animals; 27then divide it into two parts. Half of it is for the men who were in the battle, and the other half is to be given to the people of Israel. 28But first, the Lord gets a share of all the captives, oxen, donkeys, and flocks kept by the army. His share is one out of every five hundred. 29Give this share to Eleazar the priest to be presented to the Lord by the gesture of waving before the altar. 30Also levy a 2 percent tribute of all the captives, flocks, and cattle that are given to the people of Israel. Present this to the Levites in charge of the Tabernacle, for it is the Lord's portion."

31So Moses and Eleazar the priest did as the Lord commanded. 32-35The total booty (besides the jewelry, clothing, etc., which the soldiers kept for themselves) was 675,000 sheep; 72,000 oxen; 61,000 donkeys; and 32,000 young girls.

36-40So the half given to the army totaled: 337,500 sheep (of which 675 were given to the Lord); 36,000 oxen (of which 72 were given to the Lord); 30,500 donkeys (of which 61 were given to the Lord); 16,000 girls (of whom 32 went to the Levites).

41All of the Lord's portion was given to Eleazar the priest, as the Lord had directed Moses.

42-46The half of the booty assigned to the people of Israel—Moses had separated it from the half belonging to the warriors—amounted to: 337,500 sheep, 36,000 oxen, 30,500 donkeys, and 16,000 girls.

47In accordance with the Lord's directions, Moses gave 2 percent of these to the Levites.

48,49Then the officers and battalion leaders came to Moses and said, "We have accounted for all the men who went out to battle, and not one of us is missing! 50So we have brought a special thank-offering to the Lord from our loot—gold jewelry, bracelets, anklets, rings, earrings, and necklaces. This is to make atonement for our souls before the Lord."

51,52Moses and Eleazar the priest received this special offering from the captains and battalion leaders and company commanders, and found its total value to be more than $300,000. 53(The soldiers had also kept personal loot for themselves.) 54The offering was taken into the Tabernacle and kept there before the Lord as a memorial of the people of Israel.

CHAPTER 32

The Transjordan Is Divided

When Israel arrived in the land of Jazar and Gilead, the tribes of Reuben and Gad (who had large flocks of sheep) noticed what wonderful sheep country it was. 2So they came to Moses and Eleazar the priest and the other tribal leaders and said, 3,4"The Lord has used Israel to destroy the population of this whole countryside—Ataroth, Dibon, Jazer, Nimrah, Heshbon, Elealeh, Sebam, Nebo, and Beon. And it is all wonderful sheep country, ideal for our flocks. 5Please let us have this land as our portion instead of the land on the other side of the Jordan River."

6"You mean you want to sit here while your brothers go across and do all the fighting?" Moses demanded. 7"Are you trying to discourage the rest of the people from going across to the land that the Lord has given them? 8This is the same kind of thing your fathers did! I sent them from Kadesh-barnea to spy out the land, 9but when they finished their survey and returned from the valley of Eshcol, they discouraged the people from going on into the Promised Land. 10,11And the Lord's anger was hot against them, and he swore that of all those he had rescued from Egypt, no one over twenty years of age would ever see the land he promised Abraham, Isaac, and Jacob, for they had refused to do what he wanted them to.

12"The only exceptions were Caleb (son of Jephunneh the Kenizzite) and Joshua (son of Nun)—for they wholeheartedly followed the

Lord and urged the people to go on into the Promised Land.

[13]"The Lord made us wander back and forth in the wilderness for forty years until all that evil generation died. [14]But here you are, a brood of sinners doing exactly the same thing! Only there are more of you, so Jehovah's anger against Israel will be even fiercer this time. [15]If you turn away from God like this, he will make the people stay even longer in the wilderness, and you will be responsible for destroying his people and bringing disaster to this entire nation!"

[16]"Not at all!" they explained. "We will build sheepfolds for our flocks and cities for our little ones, [17]but we ourselves will go over armed, ahead of the rest of the people of Israel, until we have brought them safely to their inheritance. But first we will need to build walled cities here for our families, to keep them safe from attack by the local inhabitants. [18]We will not settle down here until all the people of Israel have received their inheritance. [19]We don't want land on the other side of the Jordan; we would rather have it on this side, on the east."

[20]Then Moses said, "All right, if you will do what you have said and arm yourselves for Jehovah's war, [21]and keep your troops across the Jordan until the Lord has driven out his enemies, [22]then, when the land is finally subdued before the Lord, you may return. Then you will have discharged your duty to the Lord and to the rest of the people of Israel. And the land on the eastern side shall be your possession from the Lord. [23]But if you don't do as you have said, then you will have sinned against the Lord, and you may be sure that your sin will catch up with you. [24]Go ahead and build cities for your families and sheepfolds for your sheep, and do all you have said."

[25]"We will follow your instructions exactly," the people of Gad and Reuben replied. [26]"Our children, wives, flocks, and cattle shall stay here in the cities of Gilead. [27]But all of us who are conscripted will go over to battle for the Lord, just as you have said."

[28]So Moses gave his approval by saying to Eleazar, Joshua, and the tribal leaders of Israel, [29]"If all the men of the tribes of Gad and Reuben who are conscripted for the Lord's battles go with you over Jordan, then, when the land is conquered, you must give them the land of Gilead; [30]but if they refuse, then they must accept land among the rest of you in the land of Canaan."

[31]The tribes of Gad and Reuben said again, "As the Lord has commanded, so we will do—[32]we will follow the Lord fully armed into Canaan, but our own land shall be here on this side of the Jordan."

[33]So Moses assigned the territory of King Sihon of the Amorites, and of King Og of Bashan—all the land and cities—to the tribes of Gad, Reuben, and the half-tribe of Manasseh (son of Joseph).

[34-36]The people of Gad built these cities: Dibon, Ataroth, Aroer, Atroth-shophan, Jazer, Jogbehah, Beth-nimrah, Beth-haran. They were all fortified cities with sheepfolds.

[37,38]The children of Reuben built the following cities: Heshbon, Elealeh, Kiriathaim, Nebo, Baal-meon, Sibmah. (The Israelites later changed the names of some of these cities they had conquered and rebuilt.)

[39]Then the clan of Machir of the tribe of Manasseh went to Gilead and conquered it, and drove out the Amorites who were living there. [40]So Moses gave Gilead to the Machirites, and they lived there. [41]The men of Jair, another clan of the tribe of Manasseh, occupied many of the towns in Gilead, and changed the name of their area to Havroth-jair. [42]Meanwhile, a man named Nobah led an army to Kenath and its surrounding villages, and occupied them, and he called the area Nobah, after his own name.

CHAPTER 33

Camped on the Plains of Moab

This is the itinerary of the nation of Israel from the time Moses and Aaron led them out of Egypt. [2]Moses had written down their movements as the Lord had instructed him. [3,4]They left the city of Rameses, Egypt, on the first day of April, the day after the night of the Passover. They left proudly, hurried along by

33:1-49 Moses sketched out Israel's wilderness itinerary to remind the new generation of how God had graciously protected them since their exodus from Egyptian bondage. It was important to reaffirm these truths in order to spiritually prepare for the challenge ahead of conquering the Promised Land. This procedure of reviewing God's past acts of faithfulness was often used by Israel's leaders to prepare the people for future challenges. In a similar way, praising God for past victories and blessings (answered prayer, a helping hand, progress in recovery) is an excellent way for us to prepare for future challenges.

the Egyptians who were burying all their eldest sons, killed by the Lord the night before. The Lord had certainly defeated all the gods of Egypt that night!

5,6After leaving Rameses, they stayed in Succoth, Etham (at the edge of the wilderness), and 7Pihahiroth (near Baal-zephon, where they camped at the foot of Mount Migdol).8From there they went through the middle of the Red Sea and on for three days into the Etham wilderness, camping at Marah.

9Leaving Marah, they came to Elim, where there are twelve springs of water and seventy palm trees; they stayed there for quite a long time.

10Leaving Elim, they camped beside the Red Sea, 11and then in the wilderness of Sihn.

12Next was Dophkah, 13and then Alush; 14then on to Rephidim (where there was no water for the people to drink).

15-37From Rephidim they went to the wilderness of Sinai; from the wilderness of Sinai to Kibroth-hattaavah;

From Kibroth-hattaavah to Hazeroth;
From Hazeroth to Rithmah;
From Rithmah to Rimmon-parez;
From Rimmon-parez to Libnah;
From Libnah to Rissah;
From Rissah to Kehelathah;
From Kehelathah to Mount Shepher;
From Mount Shepher to Haradah;
From Haradah to Makheloth;
From Makheloth to Tahath;
From Tahath to Terah;
From Terah to Mithkah;
From Mithkah to Hashmonah;
From Hashmonah to Moseroth;
From Moseroth to Bene-jaakan;
From Bene-jaakan to Hor-haggidgad;
From Hor-haggidgad to Jotbathah;
From Jotbathah to Abronah;
From Abronah to Ezion-geber;
From Ezion-geber to Kadesh (in the wilderness of Zin);
From Kadesh to Mount Hor (at the edge of the land of Edom).

38,39While they were at the foot of Mount Hor, Aaron the priest was directed by the Lord to go up into the mountain, and there he died. This occurred during the fortieth year after the people of Israel had left Egypt. The date of his death was July 15, when he was 123 years old.

40It was then that the Canaanite king of Arad, who lived in the Negeb, in the land of Canaan, heard that the people of Israel were approaching his land. 41After dealing with him, the Israelis journeyed from Mount Hor and camped in Zalmonah, 42then at Punon, 43then at Oboth, 44then Iyeabarim (at the border of Moab). 45From there they went to Dibon-gad, 46and then to Almon-diblathaim, 47and on into the mountains of Abarim, near Mount Nebo, 48and finally to the plains of Moab beside the river Jordan, opposite Jericho. 49While in that area they camped at various places along the Jordan River, from Bethjeshimoth as far as Abel-shittim, on the plains of Moab.

Instructions for Land Settlement

50,51It was while they were camped there that the Lord told Moses to tell the people of Israel, "When you pass across the Jordan River into the land of Canaan, 52you must drive out all the people living there and destroy all their idols—their carved stones, molten images, and the open-air sanctuaries in the hills where they worship their idols. 53I have given the land to you; take it and live there. 54You will be given land in proportion to the size of your tribes. The larger sections of land will be divided by lot among the larger tribes, and the smaller sections will be allotted to the smaller tribes. 55But if you refuse to drive out the people living there, those who remain will be as cinders in your eyes and thorns in your sides. 56And I will destroy you as I had planned for you to destroy them."

CHAPTER 34

The Land's Boundaries

The Lord told Moses to tell the people of Israel, "When you come into the land of Canaan (I am giving you the entire land as your homeland), 3the southern portion of the country will be the wilderness of Zin, along

33:55-56 Here God sternly warned his people to completely cleanse the Promised Land of ungodly nations. This will become a major theme in the book of Joshua. The Israelites failed to completely push out their Canaanite neighbors and as a result became like them. The New Testament writers also warned of the dangers of associating too closely with people who might draw us away from God and his program for living (1 Corinthians 10:1-33; Hebrews 3:1–4:16). We all are susceptible to being led astray by others. If we don't use wisdom in choosing our relationships, we may find ourselves falling back into our old way of life.

the edge of Edom. The southern boundary
will begin at the Dead Sea, [4]and will continue
south past Scorpion Pass in the direction of
Zin. Its southernmost point will be Kadesh-
barnea, from which it will go to Hazaraddar,
and on to Azmon. [5]From Azmon the boundary will follow the Brook of Egypt down to the
Mediterranean Sea.

[6]"Your western boundary will be the coastline of the Mediterranean Sea.

[7-9]"Your northern border will begin at the
Mediterranean Sea and will proceed eastward
to Mount Hor, then to Lebo-Hamath, and on
through Zedad and Ziphron to Hazar-enan.

[10,11]"The eastern border will be from Hazar-
enan south to Shepham, then on to Riblah at
the east side of Ain. From there it will make a
large half-circle, first going south and then
westward until it touches the southernmost
tip of the Sea of Galilee, [12]and then along the
Jordan River, ending at the Dead Sea."

[13]"This is the territory you are to apportion
among yourselves by lot," Moses said. "It is to
be divided up among the nine and one-half
tribes, [14,15]for the tribes of Reuben and Gad
and the half-tribe of Manasseh have already
been assigned land on the east side of the
Jordan, opposite Jericho."

[16-28]And the Lord said to Moses, "These are
the names of the men I have appointed to
handle the dividing up of the land: Eleazar
the priest, Joshua (son of Nun), and one
leader from each tribe, as listed below:

Tribe	*Leader*
Judah	Caleb (son of Jephunneh)
Simeon	Shemuel (son of Ammihud)
Benjamin	Elidad (son of Chislon)
Dan	Bukki (son of Jogli)
Manasseh	Hanniel (son of Ephod)
Ephraim	Kemuel (son of Shiphtan)
Zebulun	Elizaphan (son of Parnach)
Issachar	Paltiel (son of Azzan)
Asher	Ahihud (son of Shelomi)
Naphtali	Pedahel (son of Ammihud)

[29]These are the names of the men I have
appointed to oversee the dividing of the land
among the tribes."

CHAPTER 35

Cities for the Levites

While Israel was camped beside the Jordan on
the plains of Moab, opposite Jericho, the Lord
said to Moses,

[2]"Instruct the people of Israel to give to the
Levites as their inheritance certain cities and
surrounding pasture lands. [3]These cities are
for their homes, and the surrounding lands
for their cattle, flocks, and other livestock.
[4,5]Their gardens and vineyards shall extend
1500 feet out from the city walls in each
direction, with an additional 1500 feet beyond that for pastureland.

[6]"You shall give the Levites the six Cities of
Refuge, where a person who has accidentally
killed someone can run and be safe, and forty-
two other cities besides. [7]In all, there shall be
forty-eight cities with the surrounding pastureland given to the Levites. [8]These cities
shall be in various parts of the nation; the
larger tribes with many cities will give several
to the Levites, while the smaller tribes will
give fewer."

Cities of Refuge

[9,10]And the Lord said to Moses, "Tell the
people that when they arrive in the land,
[11]Cities of Refuge shall be designated for anyone to flee into if he has killed someone
accidentally. [12]These cities will be places of
protection from the dead man's relatives who
want to avenge his death; for the slayer must
not be killed unless a fair trial establishes his
guilt. [13,14]Three of these six Cities of Refuge are
to be located in the land of Canaan, and three
on the east side of the Jordan River. [15]These are
not only for the protection of Israelites, but
also for foreigners and travelers.

[16]"But if someone is struck and killed by a
piece of iron, it must be presumed to be

34:1-29 The boundaries given here were based upon faith in God. The Israelites had to trust that God would help them conquer the Promised Land. This great chapter of anticipation recalls God's promise to Abraham: "I will give all this land of Canaan to you and them, forever. And I will be your God" (Genesis 17:8). Those who were obedient to God would see the fulfillment of this promise that had been made hundreds of years earlier. God fulfills his promises, even though it sometimes takes longer than we expect. We must learn to trust him, following his plan with patience and humility.

35:9-34 The cities of refuge were provided by God as places where a person who had caused an accidental death could get a fair hearing. According to the law, murderers were subject to the death penalty. Even those guilty of manslaughter could be avenged by a near relative. The cities of refuge provided a place of safety for those who had accidently killed someone. This system demanded strict moral accountability of every Israelite, but it also provided a way of escape for those who had sinned unintentionally. Although God is just, he is also gracious.

murder, and the murderer must be executed.
17Or if the slain man was struck down with a
large stone, it is murder, and the murderer
shall die. 18The same is true if he is killed with
a wooden weapon. 19The avenger of his death
shall personally kill the murderer when he
meets him. 20So if anyone kills another out of
hatred by throwing something at him, or
ambushing him, 21or angrily striking him
with his fist so that he dies, he is a murderer;
and the murderer shall be executed by the
avenger.

22,23"But if it is an accident—a case in which
something is thrown unintentionally, or in
which a stone is thrown without anger, without realizing it will hit anyone, and without
wanting to harm an enemy—yet the man
dies, 24then the people shall judge whether or
not it was an accident, and whether or not to
hand the killer over to the avenger of the dead
man. 25If it is decided that it was accidental,
then the people shall save the killer from the
avenger; the killer shall be permitted to stay
in the City of Refuge; and he must live there
until the death of the High Priest.

26"If the slayer leaves the city, 27and the
avenger finds him outside and kills him, it is
not murder, 28for the man should have stayed
inside the city until the death of the High
Priest. But after the death of the High Priest,
the man may return to his own land and
home. 29These are permanent laws for all Israel from generation to generation.

30"All murderers must be executed, but only
if there is more than one witness; no man
shall die with only one person testifying
against him. 31Whenever anyone is judged
guilty of murder, he must die—no ransom
may be accepted for him. 32Nor may a payment be accepted from a refugee in a City of
Refuge, permitting him to return to his home
before the death of the High Priest. 33In this
way the land will not be polluted, for murder
pollutes the land, and no atonement can be
made for murder except by the execution of
the murderer. 34You shall not defile the land
where you are going to live, for I, Jehovah,
will be living there."

CHAPTER 36

A Secure Inheritance

Then the heads of the subclan of Gilead (of
the clan of Machir, of the tribe of Manasseh,
one of the sons of Joseph) came to Moses and
the leaders of Israel with a petition: "The Lord
instructed you to divide the land by lot
among the people of Israel," they reminded
Moses, "and to give the inheritance of our
brother Zelophehad to his daughters. 3But if
they marry into another tribe, their land will
go with them to the tribe into which they
marry. In this way the total area of our tribe
will be reduced 4and will not be returned at
the Year of Jubilee."

5Then Moses replied publicly, giving them
these instructions from the Lord: "The men of
the tribe of Joseph have a proper complaint.
6This is what the Lord has further commanded concerning the daughters of Zelophehad: 'Let them be married to anyone they
like, so long as it is within their own tribe. 7In
this way none of the land of the tribe will shift
to any other tribe, for the inheritance of every
tribe is to remain permanently as it was first
allotted. 8The girls throughout the tribes of
Israel who are heiresses must marry within
their own tribe, so that their land won't leave
the tribe. 9In this way no inheritance shall
move from one tribe to another.'"

10The daughters of Zelophehad did as the
Lord commanded Moses. 11,12These girls,
Mahlah, Tirzah, Hoglah, Milcah, and Noah,
were married to men in their own tribe of
Manasseh (son of Joseph); so their inheri-
tance remained in their tribe.

13These are the commandments and ordinances that the Lord gave to the people of
Israel through Moses, while they were
camped on the plains of Moab beside the
Jordan River, across from Jericho.

REFLECTIONS ON
NUMBERS

***insights** FROM THE TABERNACLE

In **Numbers 1:1** we see that Moses met God in the Tabernacle. This tent provided a place for the people to worship and illustrated God's presence among them. God's permanent presence in our life today can be found through a personal relationship with Jesus Christ. The apostle John recorded the ultimate fulfillment of the Old Testament Tabernacle: "Christ became a human being and lived here ['tabernacled'] on earth among us" (John 1:14). Since Christ is in our life, we have a tangible means of "meeting with God" each and every day. God's tangible presence will provide us with the help we need as we progress in recovery.

The priest's ultimate purpose was to serve God through his responsibilities in the Tabernacle. In **Numbers 8:15, 21** we see that he was "sanctified" (set apart) and accountable to God for active service. This accountability is an essential part of our salvation as well. We will be held accountable to God for the way we use our time, talents, and treasures as we serve him.

***insights** FROM THE NAZIRITE VOW

In **Numbers 6:1-21** the Nazirite vow is explained. This was a special commitment or promise made to God, through which a person could prove his personal devotion to God and demonstrate his seriousness in following him. Vows, in general, were voluntary, including the Nazirite vow mentioned here. God's endorsement of this voluntary practice emphasizes how much he delights in obedience that flows from the heart, as opposed to more legalistic compliance to a set of rules.

***insights** FROM THE WILDERNESS

When things got tough in the wilderness, the people wanted to go back to their life of bondage in Egypt. In **Numbers 11:4-6** the people seemed to think that a life of slavery was better than what they had there in the wilderness. They had stopped seeing with the eyes of faith. They had lost sight of their goal and of God's guiding presence. The recovery journey is much like Israel's experience in the wilderness. As things get tough, it is easy to look back at our old life with longing. We need to keep our eyes on God and his promises for us. If we do, we will eventually discover a new and better life.

We often fail to see our greatest blessings. God had supplied the people of Israel with miraculous provisions—manna from heaven. But in **Numbers 11:4-6** they revealed their discontent by complaining to God. They were blind to the fact that supplying millions of people in a desert with ample provisions was an awesome miracle. We may find ourselves complaining about our circumstances in life, especially as we seek recovery. We need to stop and examine all the wonderful blessings we have. Then we can continue our recovery with the positive attitudes of faith and thanksgiving toward God, our Great Provider.

The spy mission was undoubtedly planned to encourage Israel. They would see for themselves the richness of the land God had promised them. The spies' report in **Numbers 13:25-29** began with a glorious description of the Promised Land. But the mood abruptly changed as they began to focus on the "giants" that stood between them and their new life there. They failed to recognize God's power to overcome obstacles, no matter how great. Because of their lack of faith, they had to wander nearly forty more years in the wilderness. In our recovery we need to take our eyes off the obstacles and keep our eyes on God, whose power is sufficient for any "giants" we might face.

In **Numbers 14:5-11** the strong faith of four men is contrasted to the faithlessness of the entire nation. Moses and Aaron fell down before God (probably in intercessory prayer for the people). Joshua and Caleb reaffirmed their belief in God's ability to miraculously overcome the giants of

Canaan. The entire congregation, however, refused to listen and even discussed stoning them. These four men wanted to follow God's plan. The majority forced them to do otherwise. The result of not trusting God was a prolonged wilderness experience.

Numbers 33:50-53 beautifully illustrates the relationship between God's sovereignty and man's responsibility. God gave to the Israelites specific instructions about what they were to do in order to conquer Canaan. Yet he also affirmed that he had already given them the land. God promises us victory over many adversaries, but his victory cannot be claimed without active participation on our part. We need to take responsibility for our own recovery, but we should also look to God for help and guidance as we go about it.

DEUTERONOMY

THE BIG PICTURE

A. LOOKING TOWARD THE PAST: LESSONS FROM HISTORY (1:1–4:43)
   1. Commencing a Life of Defeat (1:1-46)
   2. Continuing a Life of Defeat (2:1-37)
   3. Concluding a Life of Defeat (3:1–4:43)

B. LOOKING AT THE PRESENT: LESSONS FROM LAW (4:44–26:19)
   1. The Decalogue and Its Explanation (4:44–11:32)
   2. The Directions for Israel (12:1–26:19)
      a. Ceremonial laws (12:1–16:17)
      b. Civil laws (16:18–20:20)
      c. Cultural laws (21:1–26:19)

C. LOOKING TOWARD THE PROMISE: LESSONS FROM PROPHECY (27:1–34:12)
   1. Reward or Rejection (27:1–28:68)
   2. Removal or Repentance (29:1–30:20)
   3. Reminders and Remembrances (31:1–34:12)

What might we do after failing persistently for almost forty years? How might we set out a new pattern for living? In this book, the Israelites were about to enter the Promised Land. But they had been there before—forty years earlier. They had failed to believe in God's promise to give them the land of Canaan. So God had allowed them to wander in the wilderness for almost forty years.

The Israelites were rebuilding. They were trying to make sense of forty wasted years. They were looking for ways to overcome the fear that had caused them to fail once before. They needed a controlling purpose, some practical steps, a few guidelines for action. In the book of Deuteronomy, Moses gave them the guidelines they needed.

Moses began by calling the people to learn from their history. He reminded them not only of their past failures, but also of God's mighty acts on their behalf. He encouraged them to use their past experiences—both good and bad—to set their faith on fire. Next, Moses directed the people to think about their present circumstances. He reviewed God's laws, giving them detailed instructions on how to respond to the challenges of life. Finally, Moses called the people to look toward the future. What would be the results of obeying God? What would be the consequences of disobeying him?

Rebuilding a broken life is serious business. In Deuteronomy, God gives that subject his full attention. He gives us some essential guidelines for God's program of victory. He shows how we can gain direction from the past, guidance for the present, and hope for the future. Deuteronomy is a handbook for rebuilders.

THE BOTTOM LINE

PURPOSE: To assist God's people as they live in the present, by reviewing what God has done in the past and considering what God has promised to do in the future. AUTHOR: Moses. AUDIENCE: The people of Israel. DATE WRITTEN: Just before Israel's entrance into the Promised Land, about 1406 or 1405 B.C. SETTING: The plains of Moab. KEY VERSE: "He brought us out of Egypt so that he could give us this land he had promised to our ancestors" (6:23). KEY EVENTS: Three sermons by Moses. KEY PERSON: Moses.

RECOVERY THEMES

Learning from the Past: For forty years the Israelites had lived out the consequences of their weak faith and disobedience. But instead of hiding their past mistakes, Moses brought them out into the open. The past holds many lessons for us. Our recovery demands that we learn from past failures, but we must also remember God's mighty acts on our behalf. Remembering that God will walk with us in our recovery should provide hope for the future and strength for the present.

A Program for the Present: One of our fears in looking at the past is that we will continue to live out our past mistakes. Moses made it clear that we need to learn from the past in order to live successfully in the present. He also reviewed the laws that God had given the Israelites to help them relate to each other in healthy and responsible ways. In our recovery, these clear guidelines, or steps, can help us to learn how to live responsibly and healthily. God does not leave us clueless—he provides a program to guide us as we live one day at a time.

Hope for the Future: In many ways our future is based on what we have learned from our past and on how we live in the present. Our success or failure may well depend upon whether or not we choose to follow God's program for recovery and wholeness in the present. But our future is also based on God's faithfulness to us. He is a God who loves us, forgives us, and redeems us from our slavery to sin. As we live each day in our recovery, we can be assured that God's love and grace are a present reality, providing hope for our future.

Rebuilding: How exciting to be able to start over again. This should be our attitude whenever we fail—anticipating a new start! The air must have been filled with excitement as the Israelites listened to Moses, anticipating their entrance into the Promised Land. There is hope! We can begin again! What an encouragement to our starting over again when we have failed! And God's grace in that process is limitless. The Israelites had failed repeatedly and miserably for over forty years, but God had now brought them to the edge of the Promised Land! They had yet another chance to begin again.

CHAPTER 1

Moses Speaks to Israel

This book records Moses' address to the people of Israel when they were camped in the valley of the Arabah in the wilderness of Moab, east of the Jordan River. (Cities in the area included Suph, Paran, Tophel, Laban, Hazeroth, and Dizahab.) The speech was given on February 15, forty years after the people of Israel left Mount Horeb—though it takes only eleven days to travel by foot from Mount Horeb to Kadesh-barnea, going by way of Mount Seir! At the time of this address, King Sihon of the Amorites had already been defeated at Heshbon, and King Og of Bashan had been defeated at Ashtaroth, near Edrei. Here, then, is Moses' address to Israel, stating all the laws God had commanded him to pass on to them:

6"It was forty years ago, at Mount Horeb,
that Jehovah our God told us, 'You have
stayed here long enough. 7Now go and occupy the hill country of the Amorites, the
valley of the Arabah, and the Negeb, and all
the land of Canaan and Lebanon—the entire
area from the shores of the Mediterranean
Sea to the Euphrates River. 8I am giving all of
it to you! Go in and possess it, for it is the
land the Lord promised to your ancestors
Abraham, Isaac, and Jacob, and all of their
descendants.'

9"At that time I told the people, 'I need
help! You are a great burden for me to carry
all by myself, 10for the Lord has multiplied
you to become as many as the stars! 11And
may he multiply you a thousand times more
and bless you as he promised, 12but what can
one man do to settle all your quarrels and
problems? 13So choose some men from each
tribe who are wise, experienced, and under-

1:1-5 This is a book of new hope; it is all about making a fresh start. The Israelites' failures were behind them. Opportunities for rebuilding their lives, their communities, and their nation lay ahead. At last Israel stood on the threshold of the Promised Land. It had taken them forty years to accomplish an eleven-day journey because of their willful disobedience and lack of faith. Moses took time to give them principles for rebuilding their lives in the Israelite community and in relationship with their God.

1:6 "You have stayed here long enough." In every life there are moments when it is essential to move on. There come times when action is necessary. When we stay too long at one place, we stagnate. In rebuilding a life, we must be careful to advance according to God's schedule—neither lagging behind nor running ahead.

standing, and I will appoint them as your leaders.'

[14]"They agreed to this; [15]I took the men they selected, some from every tribe, and appointed them as administrative assistants in charge of thousands, hundreds, fifties, and tens to decide their quarrels and assist them in every way. [16]I instructed them to be perfectly fair at all times, even to foreigners. [17]'When giving your decisions,' I told them, 'never favor a man because he is rich; be fair to great and small alike. Don't fear their displeasure, for you are judging in the place of God. Bring me any cases too difficult for you, and I will handle them.' [18]And I gave them other instructions at that time also.

[19-21]"Then we left Mount Horeb and traveled through the great and terrible desert, finally arriving among the Amorite hills to which the Lord our God had directed us. We were then at Kadesh-barnea [on the border of the Promised Land] and I said to the people, 'The Lord God has given us this land. Go and possess it as he told us to. Don't be afraid! Don't even doubt!'

[22]"But they replied, 'First let's send out spies to discover the best route of entry, and to decide which cities we should capture first.'

[23]"This seemed like a good idea, so I chose twelve spies, one from each tribe. [24,25]They crossed into the hills and came to the Valley of Eshcol, and returned with samples of the local fruit. One look was enough to convince us that it was indeed a good land the Lord our God had given us. [26]But the people refused to go in and rebelled against the Lord's command.

[27]"They murmured and complained in their tents and said, 'The Lord must hate us, bringing us here from Egypt to be slaughtered by these Amorites. [28]What are we getting into? Our brothers who spied out the land have frightened us with their report. They say that the people of the land are tall and powerful, and that the walls of their cities rise high into the sky! They have even seen giants there—the descendants of the Anakim!'

[29]"But I said to them, 'Don't be afraid! [30]The Lord God is your leader, and he will fight for you with his mighty miracles, just as you saw him do in Egypt. [31]And you know how he has cared for you again and again here in the wilderness, just as a father cares for his child!' [32]But nothing I said did any good.

"They refused to believe the Lord our God [33]who had led them all the way, and had selected the best places for them to camp, and had guided them by a pillar of fire at night and a pillar of cloud during the day.

[34,35]"Well, the Lord heard their complaining and was very angry. He vowed that not one person in that entire generation would live to see the good land he had promised their fathers, [36]except Caleb (the son of Jephunneh), who, because he had wholly followed the Lord, would receive as his personal inheritance some of the land he had walked over.

[37]"And the Lord was even angry with me because of them and said to me, 'You shall not enter the Promised Land! [38]Instead, your assistant, Joshua (the son of Nun), shall lead the people. Encourage him as he prepares to take over the leadership. [39]I will give the land to the children they said would die in the wilderness. [40]But as for you of the older generation, turn around now and go on back across the desert toward the Red Sea.'

[41]"Then they confessed, 'We have sinned! We will go into the land and fight for it as the Lord our God has told us to.' So they strapped on their weapons and thought it would be easy to conquer the whole area.

[42]"But the Lord said to me, 'Tell them not to do it, for I will not go with them; they will be struck down before their enemies.'

[43]"I told them, but they wouldn't listen. Instead, they rebelled again against the Lord's commandment and went on up into the hill country to fight. [44]But the Amorites who lived there came out against them and chased them like bees and killed them from Seir to Hormah. [45]Then they returned and wept before the Lord, but he wouldn't listen. [46]So they stayed there at Kadesh for a long time.

CHAPTER 2

Remembering Israel's Wanderings

"Then we turned back across the wilderness toward the Red Sea, for so the Lord had instructed me. For many years we wandered around in the area of Mount Seir. [2]Then at last the Lord said,

1:19-21 "Don't be afraid! Don't even doubt!" The expression "Fear not" and its variations is the most common command in Scripture. There are so many things to be afraid of. In challenging his people to a new course of action, God was insisting that they cast away their fears. God was really asking his people to trust in him. If we can learn to turn our focus away from our circumstances, toward God and his power, our helplessness and fears will soon melt away.

3"'You have stayed here long enough. Turn northward. 4Inform the people that they will be passing through the country belonging to their brothers the Edomites, the descendants of Esau who live in Seir; the Edomites will be nervous, so be careful. 5Don't start a fight! For I have given them all the Mount Seir hill country as their permanent possession, and I will not give you even a tiny piece of their land. 6Pay them for whatever food or water you use. 7The Lord your God has watched over you and blessed you every step of the way for all these forty years as you have wandered around in this great wilderness; and you have lacked nothing in all that time.'

8"So we passed through Edom where our brothers lived, crossing the Arabah Road that goes south to Elath and Ezion-geber, and traveling northward toward the Moab desert.

9"Then the Lord warned us, 'Don't attack the Moabites either, for I will not give you any of their land; I have given it to the descendants of Lot.'

10"(The Emim used to live in that area, a very large tribe, tall as the giants of Anakim; 11both the Emim and the Anakim are often referred to as the Rephaim, but the Moabites call them Emim. 12In earlier days the Horites lived in Seir, but they were driven out and displaced by the Edomites, the descendants of Esau, just as Israel would displace the peoples of Canaan, whose land had been assigned to Israel by the Lord.)

13"'Now cross Zered Brook,' the Lord said; and we did.

14,15"So it took us thirty-eight years to finally get across Zered Brook from Kadesh! For the Lord had decreed that this could not happen until all the men, who thirty-eight years earlier were old enough to bear arms, had died. Yes, the hand of the Lord was against them until finally all were dead.

16,17"Then at last the Lord said to me,

18"'Today Israel shall cross the borders of Moab at Ar, 19into the land of the Ammonites. But do not attack them, for I will not give you any of their land. I have given it to the descendants of Lot.'

20"(That area, too, used to be inhabited by the Rephaim, called 'Zamzummim' by the Ammonites. 21They were a large and powerful tribe, as tall as the Anakim; but Jehovah destroyed them as the Ammonites came in, and the Ammonites lived there in their place. 22The Lord had similarly helped the descendants of Esau at Mount Seir, for he destroyed the Horites who were living there before them. 23Another similar situation occurred when the people of Caphtor invaded and destroyed the tribe of Avvim living in villages scattered across the countryside as far away as Gaza.)

Moses Reviews the Battles

24"Then the Lord said, 'Cross the Arnon River into the land of King Sihon the Amorite, king of Heshbon. War against him and begin to take possession of his land. 25Beginning today I will make people throughout the whole earth tremble with fear because of you, and dread your arrival.'

26"Then from the wilderness of Kedemoth I sent ambassadors to King Sihon of Heshbon with a proposal of peace. 27'Let us pass through your land,' we said. 'We will stay on the main road and won't turn off into the fields on either side. 28We will not steal food as we go, but will purchase every bite we eat and everything we drink; all we want is permission to pass through. 29The Edomites at Seir allowed us to go through their country, and so did the Moabites, whose capital is at Ar. We are on our way across the Jordan into the land the Lord our God has given us.'

30"But King Sihon refused because Jehovah your God made him obstinate, so that he could destroy Sihon by the hands of Israel, as has now been done.

2:7 God was not rejecting his people when he consigned them to forty years of wilderness wanderings. He was lovingly guiding them in a way that would bring them some much needed discipline. It is comforting to remember that even after we have failed, God continues to shower his loving care upon us. He may lead us through a time of difficult discipline, but he never leaves us during the hard times. He often allows the hard times for our own good. God protected Israel in the wilderness even though they had rejected him. Even after our worst failures, when terrible consequences are bearing down on us, God is there.

2:14-17 Timing is often an essential element in God's plan. It is sometimes necessary for us to "hit bottom" before we can begin to rebuild our life. It was necessary for the Israelites to experience what seemed total defeat in the wilderness before they could learn how to trust God's plan and do things his way. We should be careful to learn from Israel's mistakes. Let us learn to give up our plans for life before we discover that the consequences are disastrous. We would be wise to accept God's program for healthy living.

31"Then the Lord said to me, 'I have begun to give you the land of King Sihon; when you possess it, it shall belong to Israel forever.'

32"King Sihon then declared war on us and mobilized his forces at Jahaz. 33,34 But the Lord our God crushed him, and we conquered all his cities and utterly destroyed everything, including the women and babies. We left nothing alive 35,36except the cattle, which we took as our reward, along with the booty gained from ransacking the cities we had taken. We conquered everything from Aroer to Gilead—from the edge of the Arnon River valley, and including all the cities in the valley. Not one city was too strong for us, for the Lord our God gave all of them to us. 37However, we stayed away from the people of Ammon and from the Jabbok River and the hill country cities, the places Jehovah our God had forbidden us to enter.

CHAPTER 3

"Next we turned toward King Og's land of Bashan. He immediately mobilized his army and attacked us at Edrei. But the Lord told me not to be afraid of him. 'All his people and his land are yours,' the Lord told me. 'You will do to him as you did to King Sihon of the Amorites at Heshbon.' 3So the Lord helped us fight against King Og and his people, and we killed them all. 4We conquered all sixty of his cities, the entire Argob region of Bashan. 5These were well-fortified cities with high walls and barred gates. Of course we also took all of the unwalled towns. 6We utterly destroyed the kingdom of Bashan just as we had destroyed King Sihon's kingdom at Heshbon, killing the entire population—men, women, and children alike. 7But we kept the cattle and loot for ourselves.

8"We now possessed all the land of the two kings of the Amorites east of the Jordan River—all the land from the valley of the Arnon to Mount Hermon. 9(The Sidonians called Mount Hermon 'Sirion,' while the Amorites called it 'Senir.') 10We had now conquered all the cities on the plateau, and all of Gilead and Bashan as far as the cities of Salecah and Edrei.

11"Incidentally, King Og of Bashan was the last of the giant Rephaim. His iron bedstead is kept in a museum at Rabbah, one of the cities of the Ammonites, and measures thirteen and a half feet long by six feet wide.

Review of Land Division

12"At that time I gave the conquered land to the tribes of Reuben, Gad, and the half-tribe of Manasseh. To the tribes of Reuben and Gad I gave the area beginning at Aroer on the Arnon River, plus half of Mount Gilead, including its cities. 13The half-tribe of Manasseh received the remainder of Gilead and all of the former kingdom of King Og, the Argob region. (Bashan is sometimes called 'The Land of the Rephaim.') 14The clan of Jair, of the tribe of Manasseh, took over the whole Argob region (Bashan) to the borders of the Geshurites and Maacathites. They renamed their country after themselves, calling it Havvoth-jair (meaning 'Jair's Villages') as it is still known today. 15Then I gave Gilead to the clan of Machir. 16The tribes of Reuben and Gad received the area extending from the Jabbok River in Gilead (which was the Ammonite frontier) to the middle of the valley of the Arnon River. 17They also received the Arabah (or wasteland), bounded by the Jordan River on the west, from Chinnereth to Mount Pisgah and the Dead Sea (also called the Sea of the Arabah).

18"At that time I reminded the tribes of Reuben and Gad and the half-tribe of Manasseh that, although the Lord had given them the land, they could not begin settling down until their armed men led the other tribes across the Jordan to the land the Lord was giving them.

19"'But your wives and children,' I told them, 'may live here in the cities the Lord has given you, caring for your many cattle 20until you return after the Lord has given victory to

3:1-2 Israel's resources were pitifully limited, but God gave them victory. It was not by their military strength but by God's power that they overcame the nation of Bashan. As we fit the pieces of our life back together, it is God's resources, not ours, that will bring success. Our powerlessness in life provides wonderful opportunities for God to prove his power.

3:12-20 Three of the Israelite tribes, Reuben, Gad, and half of Manasseh, wanted land on the east side of the Jordan River, just outside the Promised Land. God allowed them to do this, but he also demanded that they follow through on their promises to fight in the conquest of Canaan. The other tribes had counted on their support, and their failure to help in the conquest might have created deep divisions within God's chosen nation. An important step in recovery is learning to take responsibility for our promises and decisions. This is important as we seek to build, reconcile, and maintain our relationships with others.

the other tribes too. When they conquer the
land the Lord your God has given them across
the Jordan River, then you may return here to
your own land.'

Moses Recounts His Failure

21"Then I said to Joshua, 'You have seen what
the Lord your God has done to those two
kings. You will do the same to all the kingdoms on the other side of the Jordan. 22Don't
be afraid of the nations there, for the Lord
your God will fight for you.'

23-25"At that time I made this plea to God:
'O Lord God, please let me cross over into the
Promised Land—the good land beyond the
Jordan River with its rolling hills—and Lebanon. I want to see the result of all the greatness and power you have been showing us;
for what God in all of heaven or earth can do
what you have done for us?'

26"But the Lord was angry with me because
of you and would not let me cross over. 'Speak
of it no more,' he ordered, 27'but go to the top
of Mount Pisgah where you can look out in
every direction, and there you will see the
land in the distance. But you shall not cross
the Jordan River. 28Commission Joshua to replace you, and then encourage him, for he
shall lead the people across to conquer the
land you will see from the mountaintop.'

29"So we remained in the valley near Beth-
peor.

CHAPTER 4

Moses Urges the People to Obey

"And now, O Israel, listen carefully to these
laws I teach you, and obey them if you want
to live and enter into and possess the land
given you by the Lord God of your ancestors.
2Do not add other laws or subtract from these;
just obey them, for they are from the Lord
your God. 3You have seen what the Lord did
to you at Baalpeor, where he destroyed many
people for worshiping idols. 4But all of you
who were faithful to the Lord your God are
still alive today.

5"These are the laws for you to obey when
you arrive in the land where you will live.
They are from the Lord our God. He has given
them to me to pass on to you. 6If you obey
them, they will give you a reputation for
wisdom and intelligence. When the surrounding nations hear these laws, they will
exclaim, 'What other nation is as wise and
prudent as Israel!' 7For what other nation,
great or small, has God among them, as the
Lord our God is here among us whenever we
call upon him? 8And what nation, no matter
how great, has laws as fair as these I am giving
you today?

9"But watch out! Be very careful never to
forget what you have seen God doing for you.
May his miracles have a deep and permanent
effect upon your lives! Tell your children and
your grandchildren about the glorious
miracles he did. 10Tell them especially about
the day you stood before the Lord at Mount
Horeb, and he told me, 'Summon the people
before me and I will instruct them, so that
they will learn always to reverence me, and so
that they can teach my laws to their children.'
11You stood at the foot of the mountain, and
the mountain burned with fire; flames shot
far into the sky, surrounded by black clouds
and deep darkness. 12And the Lord spoke to
you from the fire; you heard his words but
didn't see him. 13He proclaimed the laws you
must obey—the Ten Commandments—and
wrote them on two stone tablets. 14Yes, it was
at that time that the Lord commanded me to
issue the laws you must obey when you arrive
in the Promised Land.

3:23-29 Even Moses was not exempt from God's requirements. As great as he was, God's commands still applied to him. We must never presume to be a "special case." We must not rationalize and excuse ourselves from God's program for healthy and holy living. Rather, we should seek out and then joyfully accept God's program for us. His plans are always in our best intrest.

4:2 God's directions are not to be tampered with. It is tempting to add to God's provisions or to take away from them. But if we are to have victory, we must accept God's way—as it is, not as we might wish it to be. These requirements were offered for Israel's guidance; they were a gracious provision of God's love. God, through his Word and loving presence in our life, also provides us with all we need to live a life of fulfillment and contentment.

4:15-19 God warned the Israelites time and again about the dangers of idolatry. Most of us aren't tempted to worship a carved figure or statue, but in our busy world, a multitude of other matters clamor for our attention and affection. It is sometimes difficult to remember that we owe our primary allegiance to God. He requires absolute faithfulness of his people; he will not be satisfied with second place in our life. If we desire to have victory over our dependencies or compulsions, we will need to put God in his rightful place—first.

A Warning against Idols

15"But beware! You didn't see the form of God
that day as he spoke to you from the fire at
Mount Horeb, 16,17so do not defile yourselves
by trying to make a statue of God—an idol in
any form, whether of a man, woman, animal,
bird, 18a small animal that runs along the
ground, or a fish. 19And do not look up into
the sky to worship the sun, moon, or stars.
The Lord may permit other nations to get
away with this, but not you.20The Lord has
rescued you from prison—Egypt—to be his
special people, his own inheritance; this is
what you are today. 21,22But he was angry with
me because of you; he vowed that I could not
go over the Jordan River into the good land
he has given you as your inheritance. I must
die here on this side of the river. 23Beware lest
you break the contract the Lord your God has
made with you! You will break it if you make
any idols, for the Lord your God has utterly
forbidden this. 24He is a devouring fire, a jealous God.

25"In the future, when your children and
grandchildren are born and you have been in
the land a long time, and you have defiled
yourselves by making idols, and the Lord your
God is very angry because of your sin,
26heaven and earth are witnesses that you
shall be quickly destroyed from the land.
Soon now you will cross the Jordan River and
conquer that land. But your days there will be
brief; you will then be utterly destroyed. 27For
the Lord will scatter you among the nations,
and you will be but few in number. 28There,
far away, you will worship idols made from
wood and stone, idols that neither see nor
hear nor eat nor smell.

29"But you will also begin to search again
for Jehovah your God, and you will find him
when you search for him with all your heart
and soul. 30When those bitter days have come
upon you in the latter times, you will finally
return to the Lord your God and listen to
what he tells you. 31For the Lord your God is
merciful—he will not abandon you nor destroy you nor forget the promises he has made
to your ancestors.

32"In all history, going back to the time
when God created man upon the earth,
search from one end of the heavens to the
other to see if you can find anything like this:
33An entire nation heard the voice of God
speaking to it from fire, as you did, and lived!
34Where else will you ever find another example of God's removing a nation from its slavery by sending terrible plagues, mighty
miracles, war, and terror? Yet that is what the
Lord your God did for you in Egypt, right
before your very eyes. 35He did these things so
you would realize that Jehovah is God, and
that there is no one else like him. 36He let you
hear his voice instructing you from heaven,
and he let you see his great pillar of fire upon
the earth; you even heard his words from the
center of the fire.

37"It was because he loved your ancestors
and chose to bless their descendants that he
personally brought you out from Egypt with
a great display of power. 38He drove away
other nations greater by far than you and gave
you their land as an inheritance, as it is today.
39This is your wonderful thought for the day:
Jehovah is God both in heaven and down
here upon the earth; and there is no God
other than him! 40You must obey these laws
that I will tell you today, so that all will be well
with you and your children, and so that you
will live forever in the land the Lord your God
is giving you."

Cities of Refuge

41Then Moses instructed the people of Israel to
set apart three cities east of the Jordan River,
42where anyone who accidentally killed someone could flee for safety. 43These cities were
Bezer, on the plateau in the wilderness, for the
tribe of Reuben; Ramoth, in Gilead, for the
tribe of Gad; and Golan, in Bashan, for the
tribe of Manasseh.

A Review of God's Laws

44-46Listed below are the laws Moses issued to
the people of Israel when they left Egypt, and
as they were camped east of the Jordan River
near the city of Beth-peor. (This was the land
formerly occupied by the Amorites under
King Sihon, whose capital was Heshbon; he
and his people were destroyed by Moses and
the Israelis. 47Israel conquered his land and

4:29-31 Here God reaffirms his compassion toward victims of painful circumstances. He proves his compassion by promising to come through for his people, even when they have failed him. He only asks that his people listen to him and follow his instructions for healthy and holy living. Our relationship with God is certain because it is based upon God's compassion for us, even when we don't necessarily deserve it. He has provided a means for our relationship to be reconciled—the work of Jesus Christ. God is faithful; we can be sure he will come through for us.

that of King Og of Bashan—they were two Amorite kings east of the Jordan. [48]Israel also conquered all the area from Aroer at the edge of the Arnon River valley to Mount Sirion, or Mount Hermon, as it is sometimes called; [49]and all the Arabah east of the Jordan River over to the Dead Sea, below the slopes of Mount Pisgah.)

CHAPTER 5

The Ten Commandments

Moses continued speaking to the people of Israel and said, "Listen carefully now to all these laws God has given you; learn them, and be sure to obey them!

[2,3]"The Lord our God made a contract with you at Mount Horeb—*not with your ancestors, but with you who are here alive today.* [4]He spoke with you face to face from the center of the fire, there at the mountain. [5]I stood as an intermediary between you and Jehovah, for you were afraid of the fire and did not go up to him on the mountain. He spoke to me and I passed on his laws to you. This is what he said:

[6]"'I am Jehovah your God who rescued you from slavery in Egypt.

[7]"'Never worship any god but me.

[8]"'Never make idols; don't worship images, whether of birds, animals, or fish. [9,10]You shall not bow down to any images nor worship them in any way, for I am the Lord your God. I am a jealous God, and I will bring the curse of a father's sins upon even the third and fourth generation of the children of those who hate me; but I will show kindness to a thousand generations of those who love me and keep my commandments.

[11]"'You must never use my name to make a vow you don't intend to keep. I will not overlook that.

[12]"'Keep the Sabbath day holy. This is my command. [13]Work the other six days, [14]but the seventh day is the Sabbath of the Lord your God; no work shall be done that day by you or by any of your household—your sons, daughters, servants, oxen, donkeys, or cattle; even foreigners living among you must obey this law. Everybody must rest as you do. [15]Why should you keep the Sabbath? It is because you were slaves in Egypt, and the Lord your God brought you out with a great display of miracles.

[16]"'Honor your father and mother (remember, this is a commandment of the Lord your God); if you do so, you shall have a long, prosperous life in the land he is giving you.

[17]"'You must not murder.

[18]"'You must not commit adultery.

[19]"'You must not steal.

[20]"'You must not tell lies.

[21]"'You must not burn with desire for another man's wife, nor envy him for his home, land, servants, oxen, donkeys, nor anything else he owns.'

[22]"The Lord has given these laws to each one of you from the heart of the fire, surrounded by the clouds and thick darkness that engulfed Mount Sinai. Those were the only commandments he gave you at that time, and he wrote them out on two stone tablets and gave them to me. [23]But when you heard the loud voice from the darkness and saw the terrible fire at the top of the mountain, all your tribal leaders came to me [24]and pleaded, 'Today the Lord our God has shown us his glory and greatness; we have even heard his voice from the heart of the fire. Now we know that a man may speak to God and not die; [25]but we will surely die if he speaks to us again. This awesome fire will consume us. [26,27]What man can hear, as we have, the voice

5:6-21 God gave his people the Ten Commandments after reminding them that he had redeemed them from slavery in Egypt. These laws stated how God's redeemed people were expected to act and contained a godly pattern of living for people of all ages. But they are not so much a collection of rules as a "job description," a set of ideal goals. We are all gripped by the powerful effects of sin; God's laws describe the goals of our recovery process. We will be working on these our whole life. With discipline and God's gracious help, we will find that these commandments naturally become part of our life.

5:9-10 God is jealous of our affections, and when we fail to give him the proper place in our life, negative consequences always result. And we are not the only ones who will suffer; so will our children and grandchildren. God created us to live according to his program. By following it, we can have hope for our future and the future of our children and grandchildren, too. We need to start by putting God first in our life.

5:20 Honesty must be characteristic of everyone in recovery. Healthy living before God demands that we are honest *with* others and *about* others. Being honest in our relationships is a necessary requirement for reconciliation with the people we have wronged, as well as with those who have wronged us.

of the living God speaking from the heart of the fire, and live? You go and listen to all that God says, then come and tell us, and we will listen and obey.'

[28]"And the Lord agreed to your request and said to me, 'I have heard what the people have said to you, and I agree. [29]Oh, that they would always have such a heart for me, wanting to obey my commandments. Then all would go well with them in the future, and with their children throughout all generations! [30]Go and tell them to return to their tents. [31]Then you come back and stand here beside me, and I will give you all my commandments, and you shall teach them to the people; and they will obey them in the land I am giving to them.'"

[32]So Moses told the people, "You must obey all the commandments of the Lord your God, following his directions in every detail, going the whole way he has laid out for you; [33]only then will you live long and prosperous lives in the land you are to enter and possess.

CHAPTER 6

A Call to Love God

"The Lord your God told me to give you all these commandments which you are to obey in the land you will soon be entering, where you will live. [2]The purpose of these laws is to cause you, your sons, and your grandsons to reverence the Lord your God by obeying all of his instructions as long as you live; if you do, you will have long, prosperous years ahead of you. [3]Therefore, O Israel, listen closely to each command and be careful to obey it, so that all will go well with you, and so that you will have many children. If you obey these commands, you will become a great nation in a glorious land 'flowing with milk and honey,' even as the God of your fathers promised you.

[4]"O Israel, listen: Jehovah is our God, Jehovah alone. [5]You must love him with *all* your heart, soul, and might. [6]And you must think constantly about these commandments I am giving you today. [7]You must teach them to your children and talk about them when you are at home or out for a walk; at bedtime and the first thing in the morning. [8]Tie them on your finger, wear them on your forehead, [9]and write them on the doorposts of your house!

[10-12]"When the Lord your God has brought you into the land he promised your ancestors, Abraham, Isaac, and Jacob, and when he has given you great cities full of good things—cities you didn't build, wells you didn't dig, and vineyards and olive trees you didn't plant—and when you have eaten until you can hold no more, then beware lest you forget the Lord who brought you out of the land of Egypt, the land of slavery. [13]When you are full, don't forget to be reverent to him and to serve him and to use *his* name alone to endorse your promises.

[14]"You must not worship the gods of the neighboring nations, [15]for Jehovah your God who lives among you is a jealous God, and his anger may rise quickly against you, and wipe you off the face of the earth. [16]You must not provoke him and try his patience as you did when you complained against him at Massah. [17]You must actively obey him in everything he commands. [18]Only then will you be doing what is right and good in the Lord's eyes. If you obey him, all will go well for you, and you will be able to go in and possess the good land that the Lord promised your ancestors. [19]You will also be able to throw out all the enemies living in your land, as the Lord agreed to help you do.

6:5 Here the Israelites were told to love God with all their heart, soul, and might. Jesus called this the most important commandment in the Bible. If we love God, we will naturally do everything else God wants us to do. The nature of the love commanded here, however, is often misunderstood. In the Bible, love is not primarily an emotion. It is a decision that shows itself in appropriate action. Thus, loving God entails the decision to follow God's program, looking to him constantly for help and forgiveness.
6:7 God's Word should be foremost in our thoughts when we get up in the morning, at bedtime, when we are at home, or when we are outdoors. In other words, it should be a matter of constant and primary concern. We know that recovery is an all-day, every-day process. Following God's prescriptions for healthy living should help us as we progress in our recovery, one day at a time.
6:18 This is one of the biblical formulas for success: "If you obey him [God], all will go well for you." It seems simple, but anyone who has tried it knows how hard it can be. God laid out a plan for successful and healthy living in the Israelite community. Most of these laws and principles apply to us as well. God has given us instructions for living a healthy and joy-filled life. It is clear that he desires our best. This should encourage us as we seek to follow his program, as difficult as it may be. And we can know for certain that when God's instructions become too difficult for us, he is right there to help us along.

20"In the years to come when your son asks
you, 'What is the purpose of these laws which
the Lord our God has given us?' 21you must
tell him, 'We were Pharaoh's slaves in Egypt,
and the Lord brought us out of Egypt with
great power 22and mighty miracles—with terrible blows against Egypt and Pharaoh and all
his people. We saw it all with our own eyes.
23He brought us out of Egypt so that he could
give us this land he had promised to our
ancestors. 24And he has commanded us to
obey all of these laws and to reverence him so
that he can preserve us alive as he has until
now. 25For it always goes well with us when we
obey all the laws of the Lord our God.'

CHAPTER 7

A Promise of Conquest

"When the Lord brings you into the Promised
Land, as he soon will, he will destroy the
following seven nations, all greater and
mightier than you are: the Hittites, the Girgashites, the Amorites, the Canaanites, the
Perizzites, the Hivites, the Jebusites.
2"When the Lord your God delivers them
over to you to be destroyed, do a complete job
of it—don't make any treaties or show them
mercy; utterly wipe them out. 3Do not intermarry with them, nor let your sons and
daughters marry their sons and daughters.
4That would surely result in your young
people's beginning to worship their gods.
Then the anger of the Lord would be hot
against you, and he would surely destroy you.
5"You must break down the heathen altars
and shatter the obelisks and cut up the
shameful images and burn the idols.
6"For you are a holy people, dedicated to
the Lord your God. He has chosen you from
all the people on the face of the whole earth
to be his own chosen ones. 7He didn't choose
you and pour out his love upon you because
you were a larger nation than any other, for
you were the smallest of all! 8It was just because he loves you, and because he kept his
promise to your ancestors. That is why he
brought you out of slavery in Egypt with such
amazing power and mighty miracles.
9"Understand, therefore, that the Lord your
God is the faithful God who for a thousand
generations keeps his promises and constantly loves those who love him and who
obey his commands. 10But those who hate
him shall be punished publicly and destroyed. He will deal with them personally.
11Therefore, obey all these commandments I
am giving you today. 12Because of your obedience, the Lord your God will keep his part of
the contract which, in his tender love, he
made with your fathers. 13And he will love
you and bless you and make you into a great
nation. He will make you fertile and give
fertility to your ground and to your animals,
so that you will have large crops of grain,
grapes, and olives, and great flocks of cattle,
sheep, and goats when you arrive in the land
he promised your fathers to give you. 14You
will be blessed above all the nations of the
earth; not one of you, whether male or
female, shall be barren, not even your cattle.
15 And the Lord will take away all your sickness
and will not let you suffer any of the diseases
of Egypt you remember so well; he will give
them all to your enemies!
16"You must destroy all the nations the Lord
your God delivers into your hands. Have no
pity, and do not worship their gods; if you do,
it will be a sad day for you. 17Perhaps you will
think to yourself, 'How can we ever conquer
these nations that are so much more powerful
than we are?' 18But don't be afraid of them!
Just remember what the Lord your God did to
Pharaoh and to all the land of Egypt. 19 Do you
remember the terrors the Lord sent upon
them—your parents saw it with their own
eyes—and the mighty miracles and wonders,
and the power and strength of Almighty God
that he used to bring you out of Egypt? Well,
the Lord your God will use this same might
against the people you fear. 20Moreover, the
Lord your God will send hornets to drive out
those who hide from you!
21"No, do not be afraid of those nations, for

7:6 The people that God chooses have the responsibility to live a holy life. This has a negative aspect; it means that the believer is separated from the defilement of the world. Probably of greater importance is the positive aspect; it means that we are separated to God, set aside for his purposes. We are set apart for wholeness and balance, characteristics we all work toward in recovery.

7:7-8 Why did God choose to treat the Israelites in a special way? Was it because they deserved it? No! In fact, in some respects they deserved it less than others. He chose them as his own because he had promised his loving care to their ancestor Abraham and his descendants. He treated them kindly because he is a gracious God. God wants us all to be free from bondage, whether we are "good enough" or not. If there are any chains binding us, God's loving hands are ready to set us on the road toward freedom.

the Lord your God is among you, and he is a great and awesome God. [22]He will cast them out a little at a time; he will not do it all at once, for if he did, the wild animals would multiply too quickly and become dangerous. [23]He will do it gradually, and you will move in against those nations and destroy them. [24]He will deliver their kings into your hands, and you will erase their names from the face of the earth. No one will be able to stand against you.

[25]"Burn their idols and do not touch the silver or gold they are made of. Do not take it or it will be a snare to you, for it is horrible to the Lord your God. [26]Do not bring an idol into your home and worship it, for then your doom is sealed. Utterly detest it, for it is a cursed thing.

CHAPTER 8

A Call to Remember God

"You must obey all the commandments I give you today. If you do, you will not only live, you will multiply and will go in and take over the land promised to your fathers by the Lord. [2]Do you remember how the Lord led you through the wilderness for all those forty years, humbling you and testing you to find out how you would respond, and whether or not you would really obey him? [3]Yes, he humbled you by letting you go hungry and then feeding you with manna, a food previously unknown to both you and your ancestors. He did it to help you realize that food isn't everything, and that real life comes by obeying every command of God. [4]For all these forty years your clothes haven't grown old, and your feet haven't been blistered or swollen. [5]So you should realize that, as a man punishes his son, the Lord punishes you to help you.

[6]"Obey the laws of the Lord your God. Walk in his ways and fear him. [7]For the Lord your God is bringing you into a good land of brooks, pools, gushing springs, valleys, and hills; [8]it is a land of wheat and barley, of grape vines, fig trees, pomegranates, olives, and honey; [9]it is a land where food is plentiful, and nothing is lacking; it is a land where iron is as common as stone, and copper is abundant in the hills. [10]When you have eaten your fill, bless the Lord your God for the good land he has given you.

[11]"But that is the time to be careful! Beware that in your plenty you don't forget the Lord your God and begin to disobey him. [12,13]For when you have become full and prosperous and have built fine homes to live in, and when your flocks and herds have become very large, and your silver and gold have multiplied, [14]that is the time to watch out that you don't become proud and forget the Lord your God who brought you out of your slavery in the land of Egypt. [15]Beware that you don't forget the God who led you through the great and terrible wilderness with the dangerous snakes and scorpions, where it was so hot and dry. He gave you water from the rock! [16]He fed you with manna in the wilderness (it was a kind of bread unknown before) so that you would become humble and so that your trust in him would grow, and he could do you good. [17]He did it so that you would never feel that it was your own power and might that made you wealthy. [18]Always remember that it is the Lord your God who gives you power to become rich, and he does it to fulfill his promise to your ancestors.

[19]"But if you forget about the Lord your God and worship other gods instead, and follow evil ways, you shall certainly perish, [20]just as the Lord has caused other nations in the past to perish. That will be your fate, too, if you don't obey the Lord your God.

7:22 Notice that the conquest was to take place a little at a time. God recognized that throwing enemies out of the land had to be followed by immediate rebuilding. He would give his people new territory only when they were ready to move in and take advantage of the conquest. We need to recognize that recovery also is a long-term process. We should not expect immediate perfection; instead, we should look for steady progress. God gives us victories as we are ready to take advantage of them and build on them. We need to trust him to move us forward according to his timing.

8:2 God often uses the hard times in life to teach us important lessons. Here we see that he had a twofold purpose in Israel's forty years of wandering. First, the trials were brought upon Israel to teach them humility. God wanted them to learn who they really were in relationship with their God. Second, the trials were given to test Israel—to demonstrate what was really in their hearts. Sometimes God tests us in similar ways, pushing us to examine ourselves. We need to take advantage of the difficult times, using them as stepping-stones toward progress.

8:16-18 As we begin to experience some success in rebuilding our life, we need to remember to give credit where credit is due. We must be careful to give God the glory. We must not selfishly claim what belongs to God alone, for this leads us to a proud self-sufficiency that invariably leads to a fall.

CHAPTER 9

A Reminder of God's Mercy

"O Israel, listen! Today you are to cross the Jordan River and begin to dispossess the nations on the other side. Those nations are much greater and more powerful than you are! They live in high walled cities. Among them are the famed Anak giants, against whom none can stand! [3]But the Lord your God will go before you as a devouring fire to destroy them, so that you will quickly conquer them and drive them out.

[4]"Then, when the Lord has done this for you, don't say to yourselves, 'The Lord has helped us because we are so good!' No, it is because of the wickedness of the other nations that he is doing it. [5]It is not at all because you are such fine, upright people that the Lord will drive them out from before you! I say it again, it is only because of the wickedness of the other nations, and because of his promises to your ancestors, Abraham, Isaac, and Jacob, that he will do it. [6]I say it yet again: *Jehovah your God is not giving you this good land because you are good, for you are not*—you are a wicked, stubborn people.

[7]"Don't you remember (oh, never forget it!) how continually angry you made the Lord your God out in the wilderness, from the day you left Egypt until now? For all this time you have constantly rebelled against him.

[8]"Don't you remember how angry you made him at Mount Horeb? He was ready to destroy you. [9]I was on the mountain at the time, receiving the contract which Jehovah had made with you—the stone tablets with the laws inscribed upon them. I was there for forty days and forty nights, and all that time I ate nothing. I didn't even take a drink of water. [10,11]At the end of those forty days and nights the Lord gave me the contract, the tablets on which he had written the commandments he had spoken from the fire-covered mountain while the people had watched below. [12]He told me to go down quickly because the people I had led out of Egypt had defiled themselves, quickly turning away from the laws of God, and had made an idol from molten metal.

[13,14]"'Let me alone that I may destroy this evil, stubborn people!' the Lord told me, 'and I will blot out their name from under heaven, and I will make a mighty nation of you, mightier and greater than they are.'

[15]"I came down from the burning mountain, holding in my hands the two tablets inscribed with the laws of God. [16]There below me I could see the calf you had made in your terrible sin against the Lord your God. How quickly you turned away from him! [17]I lifted the tablets high above my head and dashed them to the ground! I smashed them before your eyes! [18]Then, for another forty days and nights I lay before the Lord, neither eating bread nor drinking water, for you had done what the Lord hated most, thus provoking him to great anger. [19]How I feared for you—for the Lord was ready to destroy you. But that time, too, he listened to me. [20]Aaron was in great danger because the Lord was so angry with him; but I prayed, and the Lord spared him. [21]I took your sin—the calf you had made—and burned it and ground it into fine dust, and threw it into the stream that cascaded out of the mountain.

[22]"Again at Taberah and once again at Massah you angered the Lord, and yet again at Kibroth-hattaavah. [23]At Kadesh-barnea, when the Lord told you to enter the land he had given you, you rebelled and wouldn't believe that he would help you; you refused to obey him. [24]Yes, you have been rebellious against the Lord from the first day I knew you. [25]That is why I fell down before him for forty days and nights when the Lord was ready to destroy you.

[26]"I prayed to him, 'O Lord God, don't destroy your own people. They are your inheritance saved from Egypt by your mighty power and glorious strength. [27]Don't notice the rebellion and stubbornness of these people, but remember instead your promises to your servants Abraham, Isaac, and Jacob. Oh, please overlook the awful wickedness and sin of these people. [28]For if you destroy them, the Egyptians will say, "It is because the Lord wasn't able to bring them to the land he promised them," or "He destroyed them be-

---

9:3 This verse reminds us that if God is for us, who can be against us? God went ahead of his people to guide them and prepare the way for them. Israel's national enemies were destroyed by God. Is it too much to ask that God will vanquish the enemies in our life?

9:18-29 Moses prayed to God, interceding for his people. In the process of recovery we will experience times of temporary failure. It is at these times that the intercession of God's people is vital to our continued success. We need to build relationships of support that will result in this kind of intercession on our behalf.

cause he hated them: he brought them into the wilderness to slay them." [29]They are your people and your inheritance that you brought from Egypt by your great power and your mighty arm.'

CHAPTER 10

The Ten Commandments Reviewed

"At that time the Lord told me to cut two more stone tablets like the first ones, and to make a wooden Ark to keep them in, and to return to God on the mountain. [2]He said he would rewrite on the tablets the same commandments that were on the tablets I had smashed, and that I should place them in the Ark. [3]So I made an Ark of acacia wood and hewed out two stone tablets like the first two, and took the tablets up on the mountain to God. [4]He again wrote the Ten Commandments on them and gave them to me. (They were the same commandments he had given you from the heart of the fire on the mountain as you all watched below.) [5]Then I came down and placed the tablets in the Ark I had made, where they are to this day, just as the Lord commanded me.

[6]"The people of Israel then journeyed from Be-eroth of Bene-jaakan to Moserah, where Aaron died and was buried. His son Eleazar became the next priest.

[7]"Then they journeyed to Gudgodah, and from there to Jotbathah, a land of brooks and water. [8]It was there that Jehovah set apart the tribe of Levi to carry the Ark containing the Ten Commandments of Jehovah, and to stand before the Lord and to do his work and to bless his name, just as is done today. [9](That is why the tribe of Levi does not have a portion of land reserved for it in the Promised Land, as their brother tribes do; for as the Lord told them, he himself is their inheritance.)

[10]"As I said before, I stayed on the mountain before the Lord for forty days and nights the second time, just as I had the first, and the Lord again yielded to my pleas and didn't destroy you.

[11]"But he said to me, 'Arise and lead the people to the land I promised their fathers. It is time to go in and possess it.'

A Call to Obedience

[12,13]"And now, Israel, what does the Lord your God require of you except to listen carefully to all he says to you, and to obey for your own good the commandments I am giving you today, and to love him, and to worship him with all your hearts and souls? [14]Earth and highest heaven belong to the Lord your God. [15]And yet he rejoiced in your fathers and loved them so much that he chose you, their children, to be above every other nation, as is evident today. [16]Therefore, cleanse your sinful hearts and stop your stubbornness.

[17]"Jehovah your God is God of gods and Lord of lords. He is the great and mighty God, the God of terror who shows no partiality and takes no bribes. [18]He gives justice to the fatherless and widows. He loves foreigners and gives them food and clothing. [19](You too must love foreigners, for you yourselves were foreigners in the land of Egypt.) [20]You must fear the Lord your God and worship him and cling to him, and take oaths by his name alone. [21]He is your praise and he is your God, the one who has done mighty miracles you yourselves have seen. [22] When your ancestors went down into Egypt there were only seventy of them, but now the Lord your God has made you as many as the stars in the sky!

CHAPTER 11

"You must love the Lord your God and obey every one of his commands. [2]Listen! I am not talking now to your children who have never

10:1 The first stone tablets containing the law had been completely destroyed because of the people's failure. How encouraging to see that God instructed Moses to bring new ones so he could rewrite his instructions to the people. No matter how great our failures, God still seeks to reach out to us. God always gives humble people a chance to start again. But remember: this is a characteristic of God that should be appreciated, not presumed upon.

10:12-13 God's pattern for godly living begins with a proper relationship with him ("listen carefully to all he says"). Growing out of that relationship, defined by humble listening, is a proper lifestyle ("obey . . . the commandments"). Notice that obedience to God's laws is for the good of the person who obeys. As a result of that obedience we should have right attitudes and responses toward God ("love him . . . worship him"). Since God's pattern for living is in our best intrest, we would be wise to follow it.

10:16 It is so easy to become hardened by circumstances; it's natural for us to respond to difficulties with stubbornness and rebellion. But here we are asked to keep our heart soft and our ears open to God. God desires to communicate with us; we need to be willing to listen and then follow through.

experienced the Lord's punishments or seen
his greatness and his awesome power. 3They
weren't there to see the miracles he did in
Egypt against Pharaoh and all his land. 4They
didn't see what God did to the armies of Egypt
and to their horses and chariots—how he
drowned them in the Red Sea as they were
chasing you, and how the Lord has kept them
powerless against you until this very day!
5They didn't see how the Lord cared for you
time and again through all the years you were
wandering in the wilderness, until your arrival here. 6They weren't there when Dathan
and Abiram (the sons of Eliab, descendants of
Reuben) sinned, and the earth opened up and
swallowed them, with their households and
tents and all their belongings, as all Israel
watched!

Blessings or Curses

7"But *you* have seen these mighty miracles!
8How carefully, then, you should obey these
commandments I am going to give you today,
so that you may have the strength to go in
and possess the land you are about to enter.
9If you obey the commandments, you will
have a long and good life in the land the Lord
promised to your ancestors and to you, their
descendants—a wonderful land 'flowing with
milk and honey'! 10For the land you are about
to enter and possess is not like the land of
Egypt where you have come from, where irrigation is necessary. 11It is a land of hills and
valleys with plenty of rain— 12a land that the
Lord your God personally cares for! His eyes
are always upon it, day after day throughout
the year!

13"And if you will carefully obey all of his
commandments that I am going to give you
today, and if you will love the Lord your God
with all your hearts and souls and will worship him, 14then he will continue to send both
the early and late rains that will produce wonderful crops of grain, grapes for your wine,
and olive oil. 15He will give you lush pastureland for your cattle to graze in, and you yourselves shall have plenty to eat and be fully
content.

16"But beware that your hearts do not turn
from God to worship other gods. 17For if you
do, the anger of the Lord will be hot against
you, and he will shut the heavens—there will
be no rain and no harvest, and you will
quickly perish from the good land the Lord
has given you.18So keep these commandments carefully in mind. Tie them to your
hand to remind you to obey them, and tie
them to your forehead between your eyes!
19Teach them to your children. Talk about
them when you are sitting at home, when
you are out walking, at bedtime, and before
breakfast! 20Write them upon the doors of
your houses and upon your gates, 21so that as
long as there is sky above the earth, you and
your children will enjoy the good life awaiting you in the land the Lord has promised
you.

22"If you carefully obey all the commandments I give you, loving the Lord your God,
walking in all his ways, and clinging to him,
23then the Lord will drive out all the nations
in your land, no matter how much greater
and stronger than you they might be. 24Wher-
ever you go, the land is yours. Your frontiers
will stretch from the southern Negeb to Lebanon, and from the Euphrates River to the
Mediterranean Sea. 25No one will be able to
stand against you, for the Lord your God will
send fear and dread ahead of you wherever
you go, just as he has promised.

26"I am giving you the choice today between God's blessing or God's curse! 27There
will be blessing if you obey the commandments of the Lord your God that I am giving
you today, 28and a curse if you refuse them
and worship the gods of these other nations.
29When the Lord your God brings you into
the land to possess it, a blessing shall be proclaimed from Mount Gerizim and a curse
from Mount Ebal! 30(Gerizim and Ebal are
mountains west of the Jordan River, where
the Canaanites live, in the wasteland near
Gilgal, where the oaks of Moreh are.) 31For
you are to cross the Jordan and live in the land
the Lord is giving you. 32But you must obey all
the laws I am giving you today.

11:1 Obedience to God's instructions comes after the growth of our love-relationship with him. Love for God is a major motivating force in our obedience to the civil, ceremonial, and moral obligations he requests of us. Our love and obedience should be a natural response to the love he has shown to us.

11:16-17 If we are nurturing sinful thoughts and practices, we should expect God's anger. These verses should challenge us to take careful inventory of our life. We need to determine those areas in us that need restructuring and renewal. God's wrath is not a thing to be taken lightly. But if we are willing to change with his help, his grace is more than sufficient to help us overcome our problems.

CHAPTER 12

One Altar for Sacrifices

"These are the laws you must obey when you arrive in the land that Jehovah, the God of your fathers, has given you forever:

[2]"You must destroy all the heathen altars wherever you find them—high in the mountains, up in the hills, or under the trees. [3]Break the altars, smash the obelisks, burn the shameful images, cut down the metal idols, and leave nothing even to remind you of them!

[4,5]"You must not make sacrifices to your God just anywhere, as the heathen sacrifice to their gods. Rather, you must build a sanctuary for him at a place he himself will select as his home. [6]There you shall bring to the Lord your burnt offerings and other sacrifices—your tithes, your offerings presented by the gesture of waving before the altar, your offerings to fulfill your vows, your free-will offerings, and your offerings of the firstborn animals of your flocks and herds. [7]There you and your families shall feast before the Lord your God and shall rejoice in all he has done for you.

[8]"You will no longer go your own way as you do now, everyone doing whatever he thinks is right; [9](for these laws don't go into effect until you arrive in the place of rest the Lord will give to you). [10]But when you cross the Jordan River and live in the Promised Land, and the Lord gives you rest and keeps you safe from all your enemies, [11]then you must bring all your burnt sacrifices and other offerings to his sanctuary, the place he will choose as his home. [12]You shall rejoice there before the Lord with your sons and daughters and servants; and remember to invite the Levites to feast with you, for they have no land of their own.

[13]"You are not to sacrifice your burnt offerings just anywhere; [14]you may only do so in the place the Lord will choose. He will pick a place in the territory allotted to one of the tribes. Only there may you offer your sacrifices and bring your offerings. [15]However, the meat you eat may be butchered anywhere, just as you do now with gazelle and deer. Eat as much of this meat as you wish and as often as you are able to obtain it, because the Lord has prospered you. Those who are ceremonially defiled may eat it too. [16]The only restriction is that you are not to eat the blood—pour it out on the ground, like water.

[17]"But none of the offerings may be eaten at home. Neither the tithe of your grain and new wine and olive oil, nor the firstborn of your flocks and herds, nor anything you have vowed to give the Lord, nor your freewill offerings, nor the offerings to be presented to the Lord by waving them before his altar. [18]All these must be brought to the central altar where you, your children, and the Levites shall eat them before the Lord your God. He will tell you where this altar must be located. Rejoice before the Lord your God in everything you do. [19](By the way, be very careful not to forget about the Levites. Share with them.)

[20-23]"If, when the Lord enlarges your borders, the central altar is too far away from you, then your flocks and herds may be butchered on your own farms, just as you do now with gazelle and deer. And even persons who are ceremonially defiled may eat them. The only restriction is never to eat the blood, for the blood is the life, and you shall not eat the life with the meat. [24,25]Instead, pour the blood out upon the earth. If you do, all will be well with you and your children. [26,27]Only your gifts to the Lord, and the offerings you have promised in your vows, and your burnt offerings need be taken to the central altar. These may only be sacrificed upon the altar of the Lord your God. The blood will be poured out upon the altar, and you will eat the meat.

[28]"Be careful to obey all of these commandments. If you do what is right in the eyes of the Lord your God, all will go well with you and your children forever. [29]When he destroys the nations in the land where you will live, [30]don't follow their example in worshiping their gods. Do not ask, 'How do these nations worship their gods?' and then go and worship as they do! [31]You must not insult the Lord

---

12:4-5 A place of worship was essential to the well-being of God's Old Testament people. The Tabernacle and the Jerusalem Temple of later times provided that place. It is important for God's people of all ages to have a place where they can worship God properly. The encouragement that can be found by meeting with other believers to worship God is a helpful ingredient to any successful recovery.

12:12 Joy is one of the important ingredients of a healthy and godly life. It is often looked upon as something nice to have, but not absolutely necessary. This is never the perspective of the Bible. God's Word calls us to live a joy-filled life. As we approach God in worship, it is possible to have joy even when experiencing the pain of recovery.

your God like that! These nations have done horrible things that he hates, all in the name of their religion. They have even roasted their sons and daughters in front of their gods. [32]Obey all the commandments I give you. Do not add to or subtract from them.

CHAPTER 13

Beware of False Prophets

"If there is a prophet among you, or one who claims to foretell the future by dreams, [2]and if his predictions come true but he says, 'Come, let us worship the gods of the other nations,' [3]don't listen to him. For the Lord is testing you to find out whether or not you really love him with all your heart and soul. [4]You must *never* worship any God but Jehovah; obey only his commands and cling to him.

[5]"The prophet who tries to lead you astray must be executed, for he has attempted to foment rebellion against the Lord your God who brought you out of slavery in the land of Egypt. By executing him you will clear out the evil from among you.

[6,7]If your nearest relative or closest friend, even a brother, son, daughter, or beloved wife whispers to you to come and worship these foreign gods, [8]do not consent or listen, and have no pity: Do not spare that person from the penalty; don't conceal his horrible suggestion. [9]Execute him! Your own hand shall be the first upon him to put him to death, then the hands of all the people. [10]Stone him to death because he has tried to draw you away from the Lord your God who brought you from the land of Egypt, the place of slavery. [11]Then all Israel will hear about his evil deed and will fear such wickedness as this among you.

Worship Only the True God

[12-14]"If you ever hear it said about one of the cities of Israel that some worthless rabble have led their fellow citizens astray with the suggestion that they worship foreign gods, first check the facts to see if the rumor is true. If you find that it is, that it is certain that such a horrible thing is happening among you in one of the cities the Lord has given you, [15]you must without fail declare war against that city and utterly destroy all of its inhabitants, and even all of the cattle. [16]Afterwards you must pile all the booty into the middle of the street and burn it, then put the entire city to the torch, as a burnt offering to Jehovah your God. That city shall forever remain a lifeless mound and may never be rebuilt. [17]Keep none of the booty! Then the Lord will turn from his fierce anger and be merciful to you, and have compassion upon you, and make you a great nation just as he promised your ancestors.

[18]"Of course, the Lord your God will be merciful only if you have been obedient to him and to his commandments that I am giving you today, and if you have been doing that which is right in the eyes of the Lord.

CHAPTER 14

Clean and Unclean Foods

"Since you are the people of God, never cut yourselves [as the heathen do when they worship their idols] nor shave the front halves of your heads for funerals. [2]You belong exclusively to the Lord your God, and he has chosen you to be his own possession, more so than any other nation on the face of the earth.

[3-5]"You are not to eat any animal I have declared to be ceremonially defiled. These are the animals you may eat: the ox, the sheep, the goat, the deer, the gazelle, the roebuck, the wild goat, the ibex, the antelope, and the mountain sheep.

[6]"Any animal that has cloven hooves and chews the cud may be eaten, [7]but if the animal doesn't have both, it may not be eaten.

12:32 When all else fails, follow the directions. So often we attempt to accomplish God's work our own way and in our own strength. It is quite possible to do the right thing in the wrong way. We are to follow God's directions, all of God's directions, and nothing but God's directions. Do it God's way. That is the divine prescription for physical, emotional, and spiritual recovery.

13:1-5 This warning about false prophets is as important today as it was in ancient times. We all know of individuals who have gained a wide following, but their teachings do not measure up to the truth of God's Word. As we seek recovery, we need to measure the teachings we choose to live by against God's truth. We must make certain that we are following God's standards and strategies for recovery and wholeness.

14:1-2 As children of God, we need to stand out; we need to be different. We need to begin by realizing that nothing in our life is beneath God's interest. And because God is holy, our life should be characterized by holiness in all things. Those of us in recovery need to take a constant personal inventory, seeking to follow God's plans for achieving wholeness. This is an important part of following God's call to holy living.

So you may not eat the camel, the hare, or the
coney. They chew the cud but do not have
cloven hooves. 8Pigs may not be eaten because, although they have cloven hooves,
they don't chew the cud. You may not even
touch the dead bodies of such animals.
9"Only sea animals with fins and scales may
be eaten; 10all other kinds are ceremonially
defiled.
11-18"You may eat any bird except the following: the eagle, the vulture, the osprey, the
buzzard, the falcon (any variety), the raven
(any variety), the ostrich, the nighthawk, the
sea gull, the hawk (any variety), the screech
owl, the great owl, the horned owl, the pelican, the vulture, the cormorant, the stork, the
heron (any variety), the hoopoe, the bat.
19,20"With certain exceptions, insects are a
defilement to you and may not be eaten.
21"Don't eat anything that has died a natural death. However, a foreigner among you
may eat it. You may give it or sell it to him,
but don't eat it yourself, for you are holy to
the Lord your God.
"You must not boil a young goat in its
mother's milk.

Giving a Tithe to God

22"You must tithe all of your crops every year.
23Bring this tithe to eat before the Lord your
God at the place he shall choose as his sanctuary; this applies to your tithes of grain, new
wine, olive oil, and the firstborn of your flocks
and herds. The purpose of tithing is to teach
you always to put God first in your lives. 24If
the place the Lord chooses for his sanctuary is
so far away that it isn't convenient to carry
your tithes to that place, 25then you may sell
the tithe portion of your crops and herds and
take the money to the Lord's sanctuary.
26When you arrive, use the money to buy an
ox, a sheep, some wine, or beer, to feast there
before the Lord your God, and to rejoice with
your household.
27"Don't forget to share your income with
the Levites in your community, for they have
no property or crops as you do.
28"Every third year you are to use your entire tithe for local welfare programs: 29Give it
to the Levites who have no inheritance
among you, or to foreigners, or to widows and
orphans within your city, so that they can eat
and be satisfied; and then Jehovah your God
will bless you and your work.

CHAPTER 15

Rules about Lending Money

"At the end of every seventh year there is to
be a canceling of all debts! 2Every creditor
shall write 'Paid in full' on any promissory
note he holds against a fellow Israelite, for the
Lord has released everyone from his obligation. 3(This release does not apply to foreigners.) 4,5No one will become poor because of
this, for the Lord will greatly bless you in the
land he is giving you if you obey this command. The only prerequisite for his blessing is
that you carefully heed all the commands of
the Lord your God that I am giving you today.
6He will bless you as he has promised. You
shall lend money to many nations but will
never need to borrow! You shall rule many
nations, but they shall not rule over you!
7"But if, when you arrive in the land the
Lord will give you, there are any among you
who are poor, you must not shut your heart
or hand against them; 8you must lend them
as much as they need. 9Beware! Don't refuse a
loan because the year of debt cancellation is
close at hand! If you refuse to make the loan
and the needy man cries out to the Lord, it
will be counted against you as a sin. 10You
must lend him what he needs, and don't
moan about it either! For the Lord will prosper you in everything you do because of this!
11There will always be some among you who
are poor; that is why this commandment is
necessary. You must lend to them liberally.

Rules Concerning Hebrew Slaves

12"If you buy a Hebrew slave, whether a man
or woman, you must free him at the end of
the sixth year you have owned him, 13 and
don't send him away empty-handed! 14Give
him a large farewell present from your flock,
your olive press, and your wine press. Share
with him in proportion as the Lord your God
has blessed you. 15Remember that you were
slaves in the land of Egypt and the Lord your
God rescued you! That is why I am giving you
this command.
16"But if your Hebrew slave doesn't want to
leave—if he says he loves you and enjoys your
pleasant home and gets along well with you—
17then take an awl and pierce his ear into the
door, and after that he shall be your slave
forever. Do the same with your women slaves.
18But when you free a slave you must not feel
bad, for remember that for six years he has
cost you less than half the price of a hired
hand! And the Lord your God will prosper all
you do because you have released him!

Rules Concerning Firstborn Animals
19"You shall set aside for God all the firstborn
males from your flocks and herds. Do not use
the firstborn of your herds to work your fields,
and do not shear the firstborn of your flocks
of sheep and goats. 20Instead, you and your
family shall eat these animals before the Lord
your God each year at his sanctuary. 21How-
ever, if this firstborn animal has any defect
such as being lame or blind, or if anything
else is wrong with it, you shall not sacrifice it.
22Instead, use it for food for your family at
home. Anyone, even if ceremonially defiled
at the time, may eat it, just as anyone may eat
a gazelle or deer. 23But don't eat the blood;
pour it out upon the ground like water.

CHAPTER 16
A Review of the Festivals
"Always remember to celebrate the Passover
during the month of April, for that was when
Jehovah your God brought you out of Egypt
by night. 2Your Passover sacrifice shall be either a lamb or an ox, sacrificed to the Lord
your God at his sanctuary. 3Eat the sacrifice
with unleavened bread. Eat unleavened bread
for seven days as a reminder of the bread you
ate as you escaped from Egypt. This is to
remind you that you left Egypt in such a
hurry that there was no time for the bread to
rise. Remember that day all the rest of your
lives! 4For seven days no trace of yeast shall be
in your homes, and none of the Passover
lamb shall be left until the next morning.
5"The Passover is not to be eaten in your
homes. 6It must be eaten at the place the Lord
shall choose as his sanctuary. Sacrifice it there
on the anniversary evening just as the sun
goes down. 7Roast the lamb and eat it, then
start back to your homes the next morning.
8For the following six days you shall eat no
bread made with yeast. On the seventh day
there shall be a quiet gathering of the people
of each city before the Lord your God. Don't
do any work that day.
9"Seven weeks after the harvest begins,
10there shall be another festival before the
Lord your God called the Festival of Weeks. At
that time bring to him a free-will offering
proportionate in size to his blessing upon you
as judged by the amount of your harvest. 11It
is a time to rejoice before the Lord with your
family and household. And don't forget to
include the local Levites, foreigners, widows,
and orphans. Invite them to accompany you
to the celebration at the sanctuary. 12Remem-
ber! You were a slave in Egypt, so be sure to
carry out this command.
13"Another celebration, the Festival of Shelters, must be observed for seven days at the
end of the harvest season, after the grain is
threshed and the grapes have been pressed.
14This will be a happy time of rejoicing together with your family and servants. And

15:16-18 At first glance, these verses seem to have little to do with us. But the servant who serves first out of necessity and then out of devotion is similar to us and the way we relate to God, our Master. As new believers, our obedience is often given simply because it is required. But as we mature in our walk with God, our obedience grows out of our love for him. We soon come to realize that everything that God requires of us is for our own good. Perhaps we need to consider the vow of the perpetual slave—the bond servant of the New Testament (Romans 6:15-23).

15:19 The Israelites were to give the first of any profit they received to God. This is an important step for anyone seeking wholeness. It demands that we put God first in the area of our resources, which includes both time and money. This shows that we are aware that God is the source of our future provision and that we are willing to trust him with it. It is healthy to give up some of our wealth and any security it promises. Only when we trust God with our life can we begin to conquer the problems that are too big for us to face alone. This is where recovery starts.

16:1-8 When God delivered the Israelites from Egypt, he brought them out with signs and other wonders. The final plague resulted in the death of all of Egypt's firstborn sons. But God "passed over" the homes of the Israelites, sparing their firstborn sons. From then on God required that the Israelites give a sacrifice in place of all their firstborn sons. This was a constant reminder of how God had spared their children. This should also remind us that we have been "passed over" because of God's love for us. God gave the sacrifice of his firstborn Son, Jesus Christ, so we could be free of sin and its terrible consequences.

16:9-12 The Festival of Weeks or Pentecost was a season of great joy among God's people. It came near the beginning of the harvest season, and was a time of commemoration and rejoicing; a time to celebrate the gifts that God had given. It was also a time of fellowship, feasting, and sharing God's gifts with those in need. God ordained festivals so people would be brought together for mutual encouragement. As we seek to rebuild our life, we also need the fellowship of God's people to gain the strength that makes the rebuilding process possible. We need to learn to join with others for mutual encouragement and celebration.

don't forget to include the Levites, foreigners, orphans, and widows of your town.
[15]"This feast will be held at the sanctuary, which will be located at the place the Lord will designate. It is a time of deep thanksgiving to the Lord for blessing you with a good harvest and in so many other ways; it shall be a time of great joy.
[16]"Every man in Israel shall appear before the Lord your God three times a year at the sanctuary for these festivals:

The Festival of Unleavened Bread,
The Festival of Weeks,
The Festival of Shelters.

"On each of these occasions bring a gift to the Lord. [17]Give as you are able, according as the Lord has blessed you.

Judges for the People
[18]"Appoint judges and administrative officials for all the cities the Lord your God is giving you. They will administer justice in every part of the land. [19]Never twist justice to benefit a rich man, and never accept bribes. For bribes blind the eyes of the wisest and corrupt their decisions. [20]Justice must prevail.

"That is the only way you will be successful in the land that the Lord your God is giving you.

[21]"Never, under any circumstances, are you to erect shameful images beside the altar of the Lord your God. [22]And never set up stone pillars to worship them, for the Lord hates them!

CHAPTER 17
"Never sacrifice a sick or defective ox or sheep to the Lord your God. He doesn't feel honored by such gifts!
[2,3]"If anyone, whether man or woman, in any village throughout your land violates your covenant with God by worshiping other gods, the sun, moon, or stars—which I have strictly forbidden— [4]first check the rumor very carefully; if there is no doubt it is true, [5]then that man or woman shall be taken outside the city and shall be stoned to death. [6]However, never put a man to death on the testimony of only one witness; there must be at least two or three. [7]The witnesses shall throw the first stones, and then all the people shall join in. In this way you will purge all evil from among you.

[8]"If a case arises that is too hard for you to decide—for instance, whether someone is guilty of murder when there is insufficient evidence, or whether someone's rights have been violated—you shall take the case to the sanctuary of the Lord your God, [9]to the priests and Levites, and the chief judge on duty at the time will make the decision. [10]His decision is without appeal and is to be followed to the letter. [11]The sentence he imposes is to be fully executed. [12]If the defendant refuses to accept the decision of the priest or judge appointed by God for this purpose, the penalty is death. Such sinners must be purged from Israel. [13]Then everyone will hear about what happened to the man who refused God's verdict, and they will be afraid to defy a court's judgment.

Guidelines for the King
[14]"When you arrive in the land the Lord your God will give you, and have conquered it, and begin to think, 'We ought to have a king like the other nations around us'—[15]be sure that you select as king the man the Lord your God shall choose. He must be an Israelite, not a foreigner. [16]Be sure that he doesn't build up a large stable of horses for himself, nor send his

---

16:1-15 The times and seasons of Israel's religious life were spelled out in specific detail. And as Israel became a more settled agricultural nation, their lives were even further defined by the year's weather patterns. The people were given specific times to work and rest. They knew when to transact business and when to abstain. God had prescribed a regular and healthy rhythm of rest and work for his people. We also need to take regular rest periods if we want our life to progress toward wholeness.
17:1 God should get the best we have. For the ancient Israelites, this was important with respect to their material sacrifices. How much more does the principle apply in terms of us offering our life to God as a living sacrifice (see Romans 12:1). We need to do our best to preserve ourselves for God's service. Our recovery is an important part of this task.
17:8-13 Submission to authority is a concept that is largely lost in our culture, but it is consistent with biblical teaching. God is our supreme authority. The Bible also mentions other authority structures that will support healthy relationships and an orderly community. All of us are to be submissive to God. Wives and husbands are to be submissive to each other; children to parents; employees to employers; church members to elders, etc. When we learn to submit to one another in the proper manner, rebuilding can take place in a healthy and orderly way.

men to Egypt to raise horses for him there, for the Lord has told you, 'Never return to Egypt again.' 17He must not have too many wives, lest his heart be turned away from the Lord, neither shall he be excessively rich.

18"And when he has been crowned and sits upon his throne as king, then he must copy these laws from the book kept by the Levite-priests. 19That copy of the laws shall be his constant companion. He must read from it every day of his life so that he will learn to respect the Lord his God by obeying all of his commands. 20This regular reading of God's laws will prevent him from feeling that he is better than his fellow citizens. It will also prevent him from turning away from God's laws in the slightest respect and will ensure his having a long, good reign. His sons will then follow him upon the throne.

CHAPTER 18

Gifts for the Priests and Levites

"Remember that the priests and all the other members of the Levite tribe will not be given property like the other tribes. So the priests and Levites are to be supported by the sacrifices brought to the altar of the Lord and by the other offerings the people bring to him. 2They don't need to own property, for the Lord is their property! That is what he promised them! 3The shoulder, the cheeks, and the stomach of every ox or sheep brought for sacrifice must be given to the priests. 4In addition, the priests shall receive the harvest samples brought in thanksgiving to the Lord—the first of the grain, the new wine, the olive oil, and of the fleece at shearing time. 5For the Lord your God has chosen the tribe of Levi, of all the tribes, to minister to the Lord from generation to generation.

6,7"Any Levite, no matter where he lives in the land of Israel, has the right to come to the sanctuary at any time and minister in the name of the Lord, just like his brother Levites who work there regularly. 8He shall be given his share of the sacrifices and offerings as his right, not just if he is in need.

A Call to Holy Living

9"When you arrive in the Promised Land you must be very careful lest you be corrupted by the horrible customs of the nations now living there. 10For example, any Israeli who presents his child to be burned to death as a sacrifice to heathen gods must be killed. No Israeli may practice black magic, or call on the evil spirits for aid, or be a fortune teller, 11or be a serpent charmer, medium, or wizard, or call forth the spirits of the dead. 12Anyone doing these things is an object of horror and disgust to the Lord, and it is because the nations do these things that the Lord your God will displace them. 13You must walk blamelessly before the Lord your God. 14The nations you replace all do these evil things, but the Lord your God will not permit you to do such things.

Advice Concerning Prophets

15"Instead, he will raise up for you a Prophet like me, an Israeli, a man to whom you must listen and whom you must obey. 16For this is what you yourselves begged of God at Mount Horeb. There at the foot of the mountain you begged that you might not have to listen to the terrifying voice of God again, or see the awesome fire on the mountain, lest you die.

17"'All right,' the Lord said to me, 'I will do as they have requested. 18I will raise up from among them a Prophet, an Israeli like you. I will tell him what to say, and he shall be my spokesman to the people. 19I will personally deal with anyone who will not listen to him and heed his messages from me. 20But any prophet who falsely claims that his message is from me, shall die. And any prophet who claims to give a message from other gods must die.' 21If you wonder, 'How shall we know whether the prophecy is from the Lord or not?' 22this is the way to know: If the thing he prophesies doesn't happen, it is not the Lord who has given him the message; he has made it up himself. You have nothing to fear from him.

CHAPTER 19

Cities of Refuge

"When the Lord your God has destroyed the nations you will displace, and when you are living in their cities and homes, 2,3you must set apart three Cities of Refuge so that anyone who accidentally kills someone may flee to safety. Divide the country into three districts,

---

18:9-12 Beware of the occult. There is a resurgence of demonic activity in the world today. Many people think they can dabble in the occult without doing any harm, least of all to themselves. The Bible, however, condemns these activities in no uncertain terms. Mark this well: meaningful spiritual or emotional growth is impossible for anyone who is taking part in occult activities.

with one of these cities in each district; and
keep the roads to these cities in good repair.
4"Here is an example of the purpose of
these cities: 5If a man goes into the forest with
his neighbor to chop wood, and the axe head
flies off the handle and kills the man's neighbor, he may flee to one of those cities and be
safe. 6,7Anyone seeking to avenge the death
will not be able to. These cities must be scattered so that one of them will be reasonably
close to everyone; otherwise the angry
avenger might catch and kill the innocent
slayer, even though he should not have died
since he had not killed deliberately.
8"If the Lord enlarges your boundaries as he
promised your ancestors, and gives you all the
land he promised 9(whether he does this depends on your obedience to all these commandments I am giving you today—loving
the Lord your God and walking his paths),
then you must designate three additional Cities of Refuge. 10In this way you will be able to
avoid the death of innocent people, and you
will not be held responsible for unjustified
bloodshed.
11"But if anyone hates his neighbor and
springs out of hiding and kills him, and then
flees into one of the Cities of Refuge, 12the
elders of his hometown shall send for him
and shall bring him home and deliver him
over to the dead man's avenger, to kill him.
13Don't pity him! Purge all murderers from
Israel! Only then will all go well with you.
14"When you arrive in the land the Lord
your God is giving you, remember that you
must never steal a man's land by moving the
boundary marker.
15"Never convict anyone on the testimony
of one witness. There must be at least two,
and three is even better. 16If anyone gives false
witness, claiming he has seen someone do
wrong when he hasn't, 17both men shall be
brought before the priests and judges on duty
before the Lord at the time. 18They must be
closely questioned, and if the witness is lying,
19his penalty shall be the punishment he
thought the other man would get. In this way
you will purge out evil from among you.
20Then those who hear about it will be afraid
to tell lies on the witness stand. 21You shall not
show pity to a false witness. Life for life, eye
for eye, tooth for tooth, hand for hand, foot
for foot; this is your rule in such cases.

CHAPTER 20

Instructions for Soldiers

"When you go to war and see before you vast
numbers of horses and chariots, an army far
greater than yours, don't be frightened! The
Lord your God is with you—the same God
who brought you safely out of Egypt! 2Before
you begin the battle, a priest shall stand before the Israeli army and say,
3"'Listen to me, all you men of Israel! Don't
be afraid as you go out to fight today! 4For the
Lord your God is going with you! He will fight
for you against your enemies, and he will give
you the victory!'
5"Then the officers of the army shall address the men in this manner: 'Has anyone

19:1-7 In ancient Near Eastern societies, if a person killed someone, the deceased person's family had the right of vengeance, even if the killing was accidental. God's concern with justice in Israelite society led to his institution of cities of refuge. If a killing was accidental, the person guilty of manslaughter could run to one of these cities for safety from the avenging family. As we progress in our recovery, we also need places where we can escape the pressing demands of life, places where we can begin the task of rebuilding. Recovery groups or healing church fellowships often serve as places of refuge for those of us in recovery.

19:14 It is important to God that we respect the property of others. This verse forbids the moving of landmarks, specifically addressing the issue of real estate rights. Physical landmarks are an important kind of personal boundary. As we relate to others, we need to be sure that we respect the legitimate boundaries that they set up, physical or emotional. As we take inventory of our wrongs, we should pay close attention to this boundary issue. In what ways have we trespassed wrongly in other people's lives?

19:21 This is the famous *lex talionis:* "Life for life, eye for eye, tooth for tooth." It is the simplest form of the law of retribution. Given this kind of context, the task of recovery would be virtually impossible. All the wrongs we have ever committed would have to be leveled against us for our guilt to be satisfied. How wonderful that God has provided his Son to take the punishments on our behalf. Our recovery can only take place in the environment of grace that has been created by the work of Jesus Christ.

20:1 "Don't be frightened!" This great and encouraging imperative appears often in the Bible. It has occurred dozens of times in this book without receiving any special notice, but here in the context of enemies it seems particularly significant. Even as we face impossible odds in recovery, we should not fear. God is able to bring about our recovery against all odds.

just built a new house but not yet dedicated it? If so, go home! For you might be killed in the battle, and someone else would dedicate it! 6Has anyone just planted a vineyard but not yet eaten any of its fruit? If so, go home! You might die in battle and someone else would eat it! 7Has anyone just become engaged? Well, go home and get married! For you might die in the battle, and someone else would marry your fiancée. 8And now, is anyone afraid? If you are, go home before you frighten the rest of us!' 9When the officers have finished saying this to their men, they will announce the names of the battalion leaders.

10"As you approach a city to fight against it, first offer it a truce. 11If it accepts the truce and opens its gates to you, then all its people shall become your servants. 12But if it refuses and won't make peace with you, you must besiege it. 13When the Lord your God has given it to you, kill every male in the city; 14but you may keep for yourselves all the women, children, cattle, and booty. 15These instructions apply only to distant cities, not to those in the Promised Land itself.

16"For in the cities within the boundaries of the Promised Land you are to save no one; destroy every living thing. 17Utterly destroy the Hittites, the Amorites, the Canaanites, the Perizzites, the Hivites, and the Jebusites. This is the commandment of the Lord your God. 18The purpose of this command is to prevent the people of the land from luring you into idol worship and into participation in their loathsome customs, thus sinning deeply against the Lord your God.

19"When you besiege a city, don't destroy the fruit trees. Eat all the fruit you wish; just don't cut down the trees. They aren't enemies who need to be slaughtered! 20But you may cut down trees that aren't valuable for food. Use them for the siege [to make ladders, portable towers, and battering rams].

CHAPTER 21

Cleansing from Unsolved Murders

"If, when you arrive in the Promised Land, a murder victim is found lying in a field and no one has seen the murder, 2the elders and judges shall measure from the body to the nearest city. 3Then the elders of that city shall take a heifer that has never been yoked, 4and lead it to a valley where there is running water—a valley neither plowed nor sowed—and there break its neck.

5"Then the priests shall come (for the Lord your God has chosen them to minister before him and to pronounce his blessings and decide lawsuits and punishments), 6and shall wash their hands over the heifer, 7and say, 'Our hands have not shed this blood, neither have our eyes seen it. 8O Lord, forgive your people Israel whom you have redeemed, and do not charge them with murdering an innocent man. Forgive us the guilt of this man's blood.' 9In this way you will put away the guilt from among you by following the Lord's directions.

Marriage and Family Relationships

10"When you go to war and the Lord your God delivers your enemies to you, 11and you see among the captives a beautiful girl you want as your wife, 12take her home with you. She must shave her head and pare her nails 13and change her clothing, laying aside that which she was wearing when she was captured, then remain in your home in mourning for her father and mother for a full month. After that you may marry her. 14However, if after marrying her you decide you don't like her, you must let her go free—you may not sell her or treat her as a slave, for you have humiliated her.

15"If a man has two wives but loves one and not the other, and both have borne him children, and the mother of his oldest son is the wife he doesn't love, 16he may not give a larger inheritance to his younger son, the son of the wife he loves. 17He must give the customary double portion to his oldest son, who is the beginning of his strength and who owns the rights of a firstborn son, even though he is the son of the wife his father doesn't love.

18"If a man has a stubborn, rebellious son who will not obey his father or mother, even though they punish him, 19then his father

---

21:18-21 Rebellious children are one of the most heartbreaking products of a dysfunctional family. But sometimes, even when parents do the best they can, children still refuse to adhere to God's standards of conduct. In such cases, the Old Testament law offered this drastic measure. This law reveals how much God desires that we have healthy family relationships. He desires that the proper authority structures be established early in our family so such radical measures are not necessary. But if we have failed in the past, seeking reconciliation is an important step toward healing our family relationships.

and mother shall take him before the elders of the city [20]and declare, 'This son of ours is stubborn and rebellious and won't obey; he is a worthless drunkard.' [21]Then the men of the city shall stone him to death. In this way you shall put away this evil from among you, and all the young men of Israel will hear about what happened and will be afraid.

Burying Criminals

[22]"If a man has committed a crime worthy of death, and is executed and then hanged on a tree, [23]his body shall not remain on the tree overnight. You must bury him the same day, for anyone hanging on a tree is cursed of God. Don't defile the land the Lord your God has given you.

CHAPTER 22

Rules for a Healthy Community

"If you see someone's ox or sheep wandering away, don't pretend you didn't see it; take it back to its owner. [2]If you don't know who the owner is, take it to your farm and keep it there until the owner comes looking for it, and then give it to him. [3]The same applies to donkeys, clothing, or anything else you find. Keep it for its owner.

[4]"If you see someone trying to get an ox or donkey onto its feet when it has slipped beneath its load, don't look the other way. Go and help!

[5]"A woman must not wear men's clothing, and a man must not wear women's clothing. This is abhorrent to the Lord your God.

[6]"If a bird's nest is lying on the ground, or if you spy one in a tree, and there are young ones or eggs in it with the mother sitting in the nest, don't take the mother with the young. [7]Let her go, and take only the young. The Lord will bless you for it.

[8]"Every new house must have a guardrail around the edge of the flat rooftop to prevent anyone from falling off and bring guilt to both the house and its owner.

[9]"Do not sow other crops in the rows of your vineyard. If you do, both the crops and the grapes shall be confiscated by the priests.

[10]"Don't plow with an ox and a donkey harnessed together.

[11]"Don't wear clothing woven from two kinds of thread: for instance, wool and linen.

[12]"You must sew tassels on the four corners of your cloaks.

Dealing with Marriage Violations

[13,14]"If a man marries a girl, then after sleeping with her accuses her of having had premarital intercourse with another man, saying, 'She was not a virgin when I married her,' [15]then the girl's father and mother shall bring the proof of her virginity to the city judges.

[16]"Her father shall tell them, 'I gave my daughter to this man to be his wife, and now he despises her [17,18]and has accused her of shameful things, claiming that she was not a virgin when she married; yet here is the proof.' And they shall spread before the judges the blood-stained sheet from her marriage bed. The judges shall sentence the man to be whipped, [19]and fine him one hundred dollars to be given to the girl's father, for he has falsely accused a virgin of Israel. She shall remain his wife and he may never divorce her. [20]But if the man's accusations are true, and she was not a virgin, [21]the judges shall take the girl to the door of her father's home where the men of the city shall stone her to death. She has defiled Israel by flagrant crime, being a prostitute while living at home with her parents; and such evil must be cleansed from among you.

[22]"If a man is discovered committing adultery, both he and the other man's wife must be killed; in this way evil will be cleansed from Israel. [23,24]If a girl who is engaged is seduced within the walls of a city, both she and the man who seduced her shall be taken outside the gates and stoned to death—the girl because she didn't scream for help, and the man because he has violated the virginity of another man's fiancée. [25-27]In this way you will reduce crime among you. But if this deed

22:5 One of the ugliest results of the rebellion in our times is the confusion of sex roles. The Bible is unequivocal on this point: don't reverse sex roles. Men, rejoice in your maleness. Women, celebrate your femaleness. Be the sexual gender God intended you to be—in your appearance, in your clothing, and in your thinking. Outside of these parameters, meaningful recovery is impossible.

22:13-30 The home is of vital concern to God. He cares about marital faithfulness and purity. He spells out all of these regulations to demonstrate that the marriage relationship is of great and holy importance. Those of us recovering from a dysfunctional family need to understand God's pattern for marriage. Marital fidelity is the only means of establishing a healthy family with members characterized by maturity and wholeness.

takes place out in the country, only the man shall die. The girl is as innocent as a murder victim; for it must be assumed that she screamed, but there was no one to hear and rescue her out in the field. 28,29 If a man rapes a girl who is not engaged and is caught in the act, he must pay a fine to the girl's father and marry her; he may never divorce her. 30 A man shall not sleep with his father's widow since she belonged to his father.

CHAPTER 23

Rules Governing the Sanctuary

"If a man's testicles are crushed or his penis cut off, he shall not enter the sanctuary. 2 A bastard may not enter the sanctuary, nor any of his descendants for ten generations.

3 "No Ammonite or Moabite may ever enter the sanctuary, even after the tenth generation. 4 The reason for this law is that these nations did not welcome you with food and water when you came out of Egypt; they even tried to hire Balaam, the son of Beor from Pethor, Mesopotamia, to curse you. 5 But the Lord wouldn't listen to Balaam; instead, he turned the intended curse into a blessing for you because the Lord loves you. 6 You must never, as long as you live, try to help the Ammonites or the Moabites in any way. 7 But don't look down on the Edomites and the Egyptians; the Edomites are your brothers and you lived among the Egyptians. 8 The grandchildren of the Egyptians who came with you from Egypt may enter the sanctuary of the Lord.

Rules for Camp Hygiene

9,10 "When you are at war, the men in the camps must stay away from all evil. Any man who becomes ceremonially defiled because of a seminal emission during the night must leave the camp 11 and stay outside until the evening; then he shall bathe himself and return at sunset. 12 The toilet area shall be outside the camp. 13 Each man must have a spade as part of his equipment; after every bowel movement he must dig a hole with the spade and cover the excrement. 14 The camp must be holy, for the Lord walks among you to protect you and to cause your enemies to fall before you; and the Lord does not want to see anything indecent lest he turn away from you.

Rules for a Healthy Community

15,16 "If a slave escapes from his master, you must not force him to return; let him live among you in whatever town he shall choose, and do not oppress him.

17,18 "No prostitutes are permitted in Israel, either men or women; you must not bring to the Lord any offering from the earnings of a prostitute or a homosexual, for both are detestable to the Lord your God.

19 "Don't demand interest on loans you make to a brother Israelite, whether it is in the form of money, food, or anything else. 20 You may take interest from a foreigner, but not from an Israeli. For if you take interest from a brother, an Israeli, the Lord your God won't bless you when you arrive in the Promised Land.

21 "When you make a vow to the Lord, be prompt in doing whatever it is you promised him, for the Lord demands that you promptly fulfill your vows; it is a sin if you don't. 22 (But it is not a sin if you refrain from vowing!) 23 Once you make the vow, you must be careful to do as you have said, for it was your own choice, and you have vowed to the Lord your God.

24 "You may eat your fill of the grapes from another man's vineyard, but do not take any away in a container. 25 It is the same with someone else's grain—you may eat a few handfuls of it, but don't use a sickle.

CHAPTER 24

"If a man doesn't like something about his wife, he may write a letter stating that he has divorced her, give her the letter, and send her

23:17-18 In these verses prostitution is singled out for special condemnation. The bounds of marriage are the only valid context for sexual activity. In our society, sexual activity outside of marriage has become an accepted practice. Sexual purity now is something to be embarrassed about. Healthy marriages must be founded upon trust, which is based upon sexual purity. God's program for healthy relationships demands that our sexual activity be kept within the bounds of marriage. If we have failed in this area, there is hope for recovery, but the consequences of our failure will be far reaching.

23:21-23 Being trustworthy is an absolute necessity for anyone in recovery. All enduring relationships are built on trust. When we make promises, we must learn to keep them—even at great inconvenience to ourselves. Lying is a problem for many people. Lies break down relationships and eventually destroy us. We must realize that telling the truth is always best for us in the long run. The truth is one boundary we can never overstep without severe consequences.

away. [2]If she then remarries [3]and the second husband also divorces her or dies, [4]the former husband may not marry her again, for she has been defiled; this would bring guilt upon the land the Lord your God is giving you.

[5]"A newly married man is not to be drafted into the army nor given any other special responsibilities; for a year he shall be free to be at home, happy with his wife.

[6]"It is illegal to take a millstone as a pledge, for it is a tool by which its owner gains his livelihood. [7]If anyone kidnaps a brother Israelite and treats him as a slave or sells him, the kidnapper must die, in order to purge the evil from among you.

[8]"Be very careful to follow the instructions of the priest in cases of leprosy, for I have given him rules and guidelines you must obey to the letter: [9]Remember what the Lord your God did to Miriam as you were coming from Egypt.

[10]"If you lend anything to another man, you must not enter his house to get his security. [11]Stand outside! The owner will bring it out to you. [12,13]If the man is poor and gives you his cloak as security, you are not to sleep in it. Take it back to him at sundown so that he can use it through the night and bless you; and the Lord your God will count it as righteousness for you.

[14,15]"Never oppress a poor hired man, whether a fellow Israelite or a foreigner living in your town. Pay him his wage each day before sunset, for since he is poor he needs it right away; otherwise he may cry out to the Lord against you and it would be counted as a sin against you.

[16]"Fathers shall not be put to death for the sins of their sons nor the sons for the sins of their fathers; every man worthy of death shall be executed for his own crime.

[17]"Justice must be given to migrants and orphans, and you must never accept a widow's garment in pledge of her debt. [18]Always remember that you were slaves in Egypt and that the Lord your God rescued you; that is why I have given you this command. [19]If, when reaping your harvest, you forget to bring in a sheaf from the field, don't go back after it. Leave it for the migrants, orphans, and widows; then the Lord your God will bless and prosper all you do. [20]When you beat the olives from your olive trees, don't go over the boughs twice; leave anything remaining for the migrants, orphans, and widows. [21]It is the same for the grapes in your vineyard; don't glean the vines after they are picked, but leave what's left for those in need. [22]Remember that you were slaves in the land of Egypt—that is why I am giving you this command.

CHAPTER 25

"If a man is guilty of a crime and the penalty is a beating, the judge shall command him to lie down and be beaten in his presence with up to forty stripes in proportion to the seriousness of the crime; but no more than forty stripes may be given lest the punishment seem too severe, and your brother be degraded in your eyes.

[4]"Don't muzzle an ox as it treads out the grain.

[5]"If a man's brother dies without a son, his widow must not marry outside the family; instead, her husband's brother must marry her and sleep with her. [6]The first son she bears to him shall be counted as the son of the dead brother, so that his name will not be forgotten. [7]But if the dead man's brother refuses to do his duty in this matter, refusing to marry the widow, then she shall go to the city elders and say to them, 'My husband's brother refuses to let his brother's name continue—he refuses to marry me.' [8]The elders of the city will then summon him and talk it over with him, and if he still refuses, [9]the widow shall walk over to him in the presence of the elders, pull his sandal from his foot and spit in his face. She shall then say, 'This is what happens to a man who refuses to build his brother's house.' [10]And ever afterwards his house shall be referred to as 'the home of the man who had his sandal pulled off!'

[11]"If two men are fighting and the wife of one intervenes to help her husband by grabbing the testicles of the other man, [12]her hand shall be cut off without pity.

[13-15]"In all your transactions you must use accurate scales and honest measurements, so that you will have a long, good life in the land the Lord your God is giving you. [16]All who

24:1-4 Some might look at this regulation as proof that God supports divorce. On the contrary, God hates divorce (Malachi 2:16). Regulations like this were given to put controls on this unsatisfactory solution for disunity in marriage. Some of us may be recovering from a divorce situation. We can rest assured that God's grace is sufficient for our needs. We also need to set out to reconcile the broken relationships that have resulted, asking and granting forgiveness where necessary.

cheat with unjust weights and measurements are detestable to the Lord your God.

17"You must never forget what the people of Amalek did to you as you came from Egypt. 18Remember that they fought with you and struck down those who were faint and weary and lagging behind, with no respect or fear of God. 19Therefore, when the Lord your God has given you rest from all your enemies in the Promised Land, you are utterly to destroy the name of Amalek from under heaven. Never forget this.

CHAPTER 26

Giving God the First and Best

"When you arrive in the land and have conquered it and are living there, 2,3you must present to the Lord at his sanctuary the first sample from each annual harvest. Bring it in a basket and hand it to the priest on duty and say to him, 'This gift is my acknowledgment that the Lord my God has brought me to the land he promised our ancestors.' 4The priest will then take the basket from your hand and set it before the altar. 5You shall then say before the Lord your God, 'My ancestors were migrant Arameans who went to Egypt for refuge. They were few in number, but in Egypt they became a mighty nation. 6,7The Egyptians mistreated us and we cried to the Lord God. He heard us and saw our hardship, toil, and oppression, 8and brought us out of Egypt with mighty miracles and a powerful hand. He did great and awesome miracles before the Egyptians 9and has brought us to this place and given us this land "flowing with milk and honey!" 10And now, O Lord, see, I have brought you a token of the first of the crops from the ground you have given me.' Then place the samples before the Lord your God, and worship him. 11Afterwards, go and feast on all the good things he has given you. Celebrate with your family and with any Levites or migrants living among you.

12"Every third year is a year of special tithing. That year you are to give all your tithes to the Levites, migrants, orphans, and widows, so that they will be well fed. 13Then you shall declare before the Lord your God, 'I have given all of my tithes to the Levites, the migrants, the orphans, and the widows, just as you commanded me; I have not violated or forgotten any of your rules. 14I have not touched the tithe while I was ceremonially defiled (for instance, while I was in mourning), nor have I offered any of it to the dead. I have obeyed the Lord my God and have done everything you commanded me. 15Look down from your holy home in heaven and bless your people and the land you have given us, as you promised our ancestors; make it a land "flowing with milk and honey"!'

A Call to Wholehearted Obedience

16"You must wholeheartedly obey all of these commandments and ordinances that the Lord your God is giving you today. 17You have declared today that he is your God, and you have promised to obey and keep his laws and ordinances, and to heed all he tells you to do. 18And the Lord has declared today that you are his very own people, just as he promised, and that you must obey all of his laws. 19If you do, he will make you greater than any other nation, allowing you to receive praise, honor, and renown; but to attain this honor and renown you must be a holy people to the Lord your God, as he requires."

CHAPTER 27

A Monument for God's Laws

Then Moses and the elders of Israel gave the people these further instructions to obey:

2-4"When you cross the Jordan River and go into the Promised Land—a land 'flowing with milk and honey'—take out boulders from the river bottom and immediately pile them into a monument on the other side, at Mount Ebal. Face the stones with a coating of lime and then write the laws of God in the lime. 5,6And build an altar there to the Lord your God. Use uncut boulders, and on the altar offer burnt offerings to the Lord your God. 7Sacrifice peace offerings upon it also, and feast there with great joy before the Lord your God. 8Write all of these laws plainly [upon the monument]."

9Then Moses and the Levite-priests addressed all Israel as follows: "O Israel, listen! Today you have become the people of the Lord your God, 10so today you must begin to obey all of these commandments I have given you."

The Levites Shout Twelve Curses

11That same day Moses gave this charge to the people:

12"When you cross into the Promised Land, the tribes of Simeon, Levi, Judah, Issachar, Joseph, and Benjamin shall stand upon Mount Gerizim to proclaim a blessing, 13and the tribes of Reuben, Gad, Asher, Zebulun, Dan, and Naphtali shall stand upon Mount Ebal to proclaim a curse. 14Then the Levites standing between them shall shout to all Israel,

15“‘The curse of God be upon anyone who makes and worships an idol, even in secret, whether carved of wood or made from molten metal—for these handmade gods are hated by the Lord.’ And all the people shall reply, ‘Amen.’

16“‘Cursed is anyone who despises his father or mother.’ And all the people shall reply, ‘Amen.’

17“‘Cursed is he who moves the boundary marker between his land and his neighbor’s.’ And all the people shall reply, ‘Amen.’

18“‘Cursed is he who takes advantage of a blind man.’ And all the people shall reply, ‘Amen.’

19“‘Cursed is he who is unjust to the foreigner, the orphan, and the widow.’ And all the people shall reply, ‘Amen.’

20“‘Cursed is he who commits adultery with one of his father’s wives, for she belongs to his father.’ And all the people shall reply, ‘Amen.’

21“‘Cursed is he who has sexual intercourse with an animal.’ And all the people shall reply, ‘Amen.’

22“‘Cursed is he who has sexual intercourse with his sister, whether she be a full sister or a half sister.’ And all the people shall reply, ‘Amen.’

23“‘Cursed is he who has sexual intercourse with his widowed mother-in-law.’ And all the people shall reply, ‘Amen.’

24“‘Cursed is he who secretly slays another.’ And all the people shall reply, ‘Amen.’

25“‘Cursed is he who accepts a bribe to kill an innocent person.’ And all the people shall reply, ‘Amen.’

26“‘Cursed is anyone who does not obey these laws.’ And all the people shall reply, ‘Amen.’

CHAPTER 28

Obedience Brings Blessings

“If you fully obey all of these commandments of the Lord your God, the laws I am declaring to you today, God will transform you into the greatest nation in the world. 2-6These are the blessings that will come upon you:

Blessings in the city,
Blessings in the field;
Many children,
Ample crops,
Large flocks and herds;
Blessings of fruit and bread;
Blessings when you come in,
Blessings when you go out.

7“The Lord will defeat your enemies before you; they will march out together against you but scatter before you in seven directions! 8The Lord will bless you with good crops and healthy cattle, and prosper everything you do when you arrive in the land the Lord your God is giving you. 9He will change you into a holy people dedicated to himself; this he has promised to do if you will only obey him and walk in his ways. 10All the nations in the world shall see that you belong to the Lord, and they will stand in awe.

11“The Lord will give you an abundance of good things in the land, just as he promised: many children, many cattle, and abundant crops. 12He will open to you his wonderful treasury of rain in the heavens, to give you fine crops every season. He will bless everything you do; and you shall lend to many nations, but shall not borrow from them. 13If you will only listen and obey the commandments of the Lord your God that I am giving you today, he will make you the head and not the tail, and you shall always have the upper hand. 14But each of these blessings depends on your not turning aside in any way from the laws I have given you; and you must never worship other gods.

Disobedience Brings Punishment

15-19“If you won’t listen to the Lord your God and won’t obey these laws I am giving you today, then all of these curses shall come upon you:

Curses in the city,
Curses in the fields,

27:15-26 Sin never goes unpunished. God considers disobedience of such great importance that he even spells out its consequences. Like a loving father, he warns us of what will happen if we choose a sinful course of action. Even negative passages like this remind us that God only wants our best. He wants us to obey because disobedience can only bring us suffering. This should encourage us to follow God’s pattern for healthy living.

28:1-6 These verses reveal the one essential requirement for God’s blessings—obedience. We are to obey God and respond to his commandments. Notice that there are considerable rewards for obedience. Our recovery demands that we seek to know God’s will for us and then do it. Obedience to God’s Word, the Bible, is a good place to start.

Curses on your fruit and bread,
The curse of barren wombs,
Curses upon your crops,
Curses upon the fertility of your cattle
  and flocks,
Curses when you come in,
Curses when you go out.

20 "For the Lord himself will send his personal curse upon you. You will be confused and a failure in everything you do, until at last you are destroyed because of the sin of forsaking him. 21 He will send disease among you until you are destroyed from the face of the land you are about to enter and possess. 22 He will send tuberculosis, fever, infections, plague, and war. He will blight your crops, covering them with mildew. All these devastations shall pursue you until you perish.

23 "The heavens above you will be as unyielding as bronze, and the earth beneath will be as iron. 24 The land will become as dry as dust for lack of rain, and dust storms shall destroy you.

25 "The Lord will cause you to be defeated by your enemies. You will march out to battle gloriously, but flee before your enemies in utter confusion; and you will be tossed to and fro among all the nations of the earth. 26 Your dead bodies will be food to the birds and wild animals, and no one will be there to chase them away.

27 "He will send upon you Egyptian boils, tumors, scurvy, and itch, for none of which will there be a remedy. 28 He will send madness, blindness, fear, and panic upon you. 29 You shall grope in the bright sunlight just as the blind man gropes in darkness. You shall not prosper in anything you do; you will be oppressed and robbed continually, and nothing will save you.

30 "Someone else will marry your fiancée; someone else will live in the house you build; someone else will eat the fruit of the vineyard you plant. 31 Your oxen shall be butchered before your eyes, but you won't get a single bite of the meat. Your donkeys will be driven away as you watch and will never return to you again. Your sheep will be given to your enemies. And there will be no one to protect you. 32 You will watch as your sons and daughters are taken away as slaves. Your heart will break with longing for them, but you will not be able to help them. 33 A foreign nation you have not even heard of will eat the crops you will have worked so hard to grow. You will always be oppressed and crushed. 34 You will go mad because of all the tragedy you see around you. 35 The Lord will cover you with boils from head to foot.

36 "He will exile you and the king you will choose to a nation to whom neither you nor your ancestors gave a second thought; and while in exile you shall worship gods of wood and stone! 37 You will become an object of horror, a proverb and a byword among all the nations, for the Lord will thrust you away.

38 "You will sow much but reap little, for the locusts will eat your crops. 39 You will plant vineyards and care for them, but you won't eat the grapes or drink the wine, for worms will destroy the vines. 40 Olive trees will be growing everywhere, but there won't be enough olive oil to anoint yourselves! For the trees will drop their fruit before it is matured. 41 Your sons and daughters will be snatched away from you as slaves. 42 The locusts shall destroy your trees and vines. 43 Foreigners living among you shall become richer and richer while you become poorer and poorer. 44 They shall lend to you, not you to them! They shall be the head and you shall be the tail!

45 "All these curses shall pursue and overtake you until you are destroyed—all because you refuse to listen to the Lord your God. 46 These horrors shall befall you and your descendants as a warning: 47,48 You will become slaves to your enemies because of your failure to praise God for all that he has given you. The Lord will send your enemies against you, and you will be hungry, thirsty, naked, and in want of everything. A yoke of iron shall be placed around your neck until you are destroyed!

49 "The Lord will bring a distant nation against you, swooping down upon you like an eagle; a nation whose language you don't understand— 50 a nation of fierce and angry men who will have no mercy upon young or old. 51 They will eat you out of house and home until your cattle and crops are gone. Your grain, new wine, olive oil, calves, and lambs will all disappear. 52 That nation will lay siege to your cities and knock down your highest walls—the walls you will trust to pro-

---

28:15-68 Just as obedience results in God's blessing, disobedience brings God's curse. We need to discover what God's requirements are; then we must follow God's program in humble obedience. This passage outlines many of the negative consequences that follow from disobeying God's plan. We would be wise to take this warning to heart.

tect you. [53]You will even eat the flesh of your own sons and daughters in the terrible days of siege that lie ahead. [54]The most tenderhearted man among you will be utterly callous toward his own brother and his beloved wife and his children who are still alive. [55]He will refuse to give them a share of the flesh he is devouring—the flesh of his own children—because he is starving in the midst of the siege of your cities. [56,57]The most tender and delicate woman among you—the one who would not so much as touch her feet to the ground—will refuse to share with her beloved husband, son, and daughter. She will hide from them the afterbirth and the new baby she has borne, so that she herself can eat them: so terrible will be the hunger during the siege and the awful distress caused by your enemies at your gates.

[58,59]"If you refuse to obey all the laws written in this book, thus refusing reverence to the glorious and fearful name of Jehovah your God, then Jehovah will send perpetual plagues upon you and upon your children. [60]He will bring upon you all the diseases of Egypt that you feared so much, and they shall plague the land. [61]And that is not all! The Lord will bring upon you every sickness and plague there is, even those not mentioned in this book, until you are destroyed. [62]There will be few of you left, though before you were as numerous as stars. All this if you do not listen to the Lord your God.

[63]"Just as the Lord has rejoiced over you and has done such wonderful things for you and has multiplied you, so the Lord at that time will rejoice in destroying you; and you shall disappear from the land. [64]For the Lord will scatter you among all the nations from one end of the earth to the other. There you will worship heathen gods that neither you nor your ancestors have known, gods made of wood and stone! [65]There among those nations you shall find no rest, but the Lord will give you trembling hearts, darkness, and bodies wasted from sorrow and fear. [66]Your lives will hang in doubt. You will live night and day in fear, and will have no reason to believe that you will see the morning light. [67]In the morning you will say, 'Oh, that night were here!' And in the evening you will say, 'Oh, that morning were here!' You will say this because of the awesome horrors surrounding you. [68]Then the Lord will send you back to Egypt in ships, a journey I promised you would never need to make again; and there you will offer to sell yourselves to your enemies as slaves—but no one will even want to buy you."

CHAPTER 29

Moses Reviews God's Covenant

It was on the plains of Moab that Moses restated the covenant that the Lord had made with the people of Israel at Mount Horeb. [2,3]He summoned all Israel before him and told them,

"You have seen with your own eyes the great plagues and mighty miracles that the Lord brought upon Pharaoh and his people in the land of Egypt. [4]But even yet the Lord hasn't given you hearts that understand or eyes that see or ears that hear! [5]For forty years God has led you through the wilderness, yet your clothes haven't become old, and your shoes haven't worn out! [6]The reason he hasn't let you settle down to grow grain for bread or grapes for wine and strong drink is so that you would realize that it is the Lord your God who has been caring for you.

[7]"When we came here, King Sihon of Heshbon and King Og of Bashan came out against us in battle, but we destroyed them, [8]and took their land and gave it to the tribes of Reuben and Gad and to the half-tribe of Manasseh as their inheritance. [9]Therefore, obey the terms of this covenant so that you will prosper in everything you do. [10]All of you—your leaders, the people, your judges, and your administrative officers—are standing today before the Lord your God, [11]along with your little ones and your wives and the foreigners that are among you—those who chop your wood and carry your water. [12]You are standing here to enter into a contract with Jehovah your God, a contract he is making with you today. [13]He wants to confirm you today as his people, and to confirm that he is your God, just as he promised your ancestors, Abraham, Isaac, and Jacob. [14,15]This contract is not with you alone as you stand before him today, but with all future generations of Israel as well.

28:66-67 These verses graphically depict a life devoid of satisfaction. This person dreads both the night and the day. When it is dark, he wishes for light. When it is light, he wishes for dark. This is one of the inevitable consequences of rejecting God's plan for healthy living. There is no lasting satisfaction outside of a real relationship with God and obedience to his will. Seeking God's will and following it without reservation are essential parts of our recovery.

16"Surely you remember how we lived in
the land of Egypt, and how as we left, we
came safely through the territory of enemy
nations. 17And you have seen their heathen
idols made of wood, stone, silver, and gold.
18The day that any of you—man or woman,
family or tribe of Israel—begins to turn away
from the Lord our God and desires to worship
these gods of other nations, that day a root
will be planted that will grow bitter and poisonous fruit.

19"Let no one blithely think, when he hears
the warnings of this curse, 'I shall prosper
even though I walk in my own stubborn way!'
20For the Lord will not pardon! His anger and
jealousy will be hot against that man. And all
the curses written in this book shall lie heavily
upon him, and the Lord will blot out his
name from under heaven. 21The Lord will
separate that man from all the tribes of Israel,
to pour out upon him all the curses (which are
recorded in this book) that befall those who
break this contract. 22Then your children and
the generations to come and the foreigners
that pass by from distant lands shall see the
devastation of the land and the diseases the
Lord will have sent upon it. 23They will see
that the whole land is alkali and salt, a burned
over wasteland, unsown, without crops, without a shred of vegetation—just like Sodom
and Gomorrah and Admah and Zeboiim, destroyed by the Lord in his anger.

24"'Why has the Lord done this to his land?'
the nations will ask. 'Why was he so angry?'

25"And they will be told, 'Because the
people of the land broke the contract made
with them by Jehovah, the God of their ancestors, when he brought them out of the
land of Egypt. 26For they worshiped other
gods, violating his express command. 27That
is why the anger of the Lord was hot against
this land, so that all his curses (which are
recorded in this book) broke forth upon
them. 28In great anger the Lord rooted them
out of their land and threw them away into
another land, where they still live today!'

29"There are secrets the Lord your God has
not revealed to us, but these words that he has
revealed are for us and our children to obey
forever.

CHAPTER 30

A Call to Return to God

"When all these things have happened to
you—the blessings and the curses I have
listed—you will meditate upon them as you
are living among the nations where the Lord
your God will have driven you. 2If at that time
you want to return to the Lord your God, and
you and your children have begun wholeheartedly to obey all of the commandments I
have given you today, 3then the Lord your
God will rescue you from your captivity! He
will have mercy upon you and come and
gather you out of all the nations where he will
have scattered you. 4Though you are at the
ends of the earth, he will go and find you and
bring you back again 5to the land of your
ancestors. You shall possess the land again,
and he will do you good and bless you even

29:29 God does not hold us responsible for what we do not know, but he makes it clear that we are responsible for what we do know. And this is not to say that God condones ignorance of his revealed Word; rather, we are required to be aware of its instructions. Only by seeking out God's will in Scripture and then following it with his gracious help will we be able to rebuild our life.

30:1 The Israelites were commanded to meditate upon God's will for them. They were to recognize that both blessings and curses came from his hand as a response to their obedience or disobedience. We should do the same. If we don't, we are only hiding from the truth. This world runs according to God's sovereign program. If we refuse to go along, we are only insisting on our destruction.

30:19 Again God urged his people to choose life. We are reminded here of the claim of Jesus Christ: "I am the Way—yes, and the Truth and the Life. No one can get to the Father except by means of me" (John 14:6). We are urged to choose life. And the way to life is choosing God and his gracious forgiveness through Jesus Christ. Notice also that our decision is important not only for us, but for our children, too. Let's make the choice for life and pass the gift of abundant life on to our children as well.

31:3 The Israelites were on the verge of entering the Promised Land. They needed a fresh reminder of God's strength and a promise of victory. Some may have been putting their confidence in Joshua. Others may have been depending on the strength of their armies. But no matter how strong we or our leaders might be, victory comes from God alone. Some enemies are too great for us. Our personal resources or support groups, though helpful, will never be adequate to help us gain victory over our dependencies. We must learn to trust God alone, for he is greater than any of the enemies we might face.

more than he did your ancestors! [6]He will
cleanse your hearts and the hearts of your
children and of your children's children so
that you will love the Lord your God with all
your hearts and souls, and Israel shall come
alive again!
[7,8]"If you return to the Lord and obey all the
commandments that I command you today,
the Lord your God will take his curses and
turn them against your enemies—against
those who hate you and persecute you. [9]The
Lord your God will prosper everything you do
and give you many children and much cattle
and wonderful crops; for the Lord will again
rejoice over you as he did over your fathers.
[10]He will rejoice if you but obey the commandments written in this book of the law,
and if you turn to the Lord your God with all
your hearts and souls.

The Choice of Life or Death

[11]"Obeying these commandments is not
something beyond your strength and reach;
[12]for these laws are not in the far heavens, so
distant that you can't hear and obey them,
and with no one to bring them down to you;
[13]nor are they beyond the ocean, so far that no
one can bring you their message; [14]but they
are very close at hand—in your hearts and on
your lips—so obey them.
[15]"Look, today I have set before you life and
death, depending on whether you obey or
disobey. [16]I have commanded you today to
love the Lord your God and to follow his
paths and to keep his laws, so that you will
live and become a great nation, and so that
the Lord your God will bless you and the land
you are about to possess. [17]But if your hearts
turn away and you won't listen—if you are
drawn away to worship other gods— [18]then I
declare to you this day that you shall surely
perish; you will not have a long, good life in
the land you are going in to possess.
[19]"I call heaven and earth to witness against
you that today I have set before you life or
death, blessing or curse. Oh, that you would
choose life; that you and your children might
live![20]Choose to love the Lord your God and to
obey him and to cling to him, for he is your life
and the length of your days. You will then be
able to live safely in the land the Lord promised
your ancestors, Abraham, Isaac, and Jacob."

CHAPTER 31

Joshua Becomes Israel's Leader

After Moses had said all these things to the
people of Israel, [2]he told them, "I am now 120

Free to Choose

BIBLE READING: Deuteronomy 30:15-20

We made a decision to turn our will and our life over to the care of God as we understood him.

Everyone has a life-or-death decision to make. We have been created with the supreme privilege of free will, the ability to choose. Even when we are in the bondage of our addiction, we still have choices confronting us. When we are in recovery, we face the nagging lure of choosing to fall back into our addiction. The freedom to choose brings with it the burden of the results of our choices. And these choices affect our life and the lives of our children. Free will is our blessing and our responsibility!

God spoke through Moses, saying, "Look, today I have set before you life and death, depending on whether you obey or disobey. I have commanded you today to love the Lord your God and to follow his paths and to keep his laws, so that you will live . . . and so that the Lord your God will bless you . . . But if your hearts turn away and you won't listen . . . then I declare to you this day that you shall surely perish; . . . I call heaven and earth to witness against you that today I have set before you life or death, blessing or curse. Oh, that you would choose life; that you and your children might live! Choose to love the Lord your God and to obey him and to cling to him, for he is your life and the length of your days" (Deuteronomy 30:15-20).

Although we may feel out of control with respect to our addiction, we can choose to set our heart in the direction of life. We can choose to love God and begin to follow his paths. *Turn to page 627, Psalm 61.*

years old! I am no longer able to lead you, for
the Lord has told me that I shall not cross the
Jordan River. 3But the Lord himself will lead
you and will destroy the nations living there,
and you shall overcome them. Joshua is your
new commander, as the Lord has instructed.
4The Lord will destroy the nations living in
the land, just as he destroyed Sihon and Og,
the kings of the Amorites. 5The Lord will deliver over to you the people living there, and
you shall destroy them as I have commanded
you. 6Be strong! Be courageous! Do not be
afraid of them! For the Lord your God will be
with you. He will neither fail you nor forsake
you."

7Then Moses called for Joshua and said to
him, as all Israel watched, "Be strong! Be courageous! For you shall lead these people into
the land promised by the Lord to their ancestors; see to it that they conquer it. 8Don't be
afraid, for the Lord will go before you and will
be with you; he will not fail nor forsake you."

Moses Records God's Laws

9Then Moses wrote out the laws he had already delivered to the people and gave them
to the priests, the sons of Levi, who carried
the Ark containing the Ten Commandments
of the Lord. Moses also gave copies of the laws
to the elders of Israel. 10,11The Lord commanded that these laws be read to all the
people at the end of every seventh year—the
Year of Release—at the Festival of Tabernacles,
when all Israel would assemble before the
Lord at the sanctuary.

12"Call them all together," the Lord instructed, "—men, women, children, and foreigners living among you—to hear the laws of
God and to learn his will, so that you will
reverence the Lord your God and obey his
laws. 13Do this so that your little children who
have not known these laws will hear them
and learn how to revere the Lord your God as
long as you live in the Promised Land."

Israel's Disobedience Predicted

14Then the Lord said to Moses, "The time has
come when you must die. Summon Joshua
and come into the Tabernacle where I can
give him his instructions." So Moses and
Joshua came and stood before the Lord.

15He appeared to them in a great cloud at
the Tabernacle entrance, 16and said to Moses,
"You shall die and join your ancestors. After
you are gone, these people will begin worshiping foreign gods in the Promised Land.
They will forget about me and break the contract I have made with them. 17Then my anger
will flame out against them and I will abandon them, hiding my face from them, and
they shall be destroyed. Terrible trouble will
come upon them, so that they will say, 'God
is no longer among us!' 18I will turn away from
them because of their sins in worshiping
other gods.

19"Now write down the words of this song,
and teach it to the people of Israel as my
warning to them. 20When I have brought
them into the land I promised their ancestors—a land 'flowing with milk and honey'—
and when they have become fat and
prosperous, and worship other gods and despise me and break my contract, 21and great
disasters come upon them, then this song will
remind them of the reason for their woes. (For
this song will live from generation to generation.) I know now, even before they enter the
land, what these people are like."

22So, on that very day, Moses wrote down
the words of the song and taught it to the
Israelites. 23Then he charged Joshua (son of
Nun) to be strong and courageous and said to
him, "You must bring the people of Israel into
the land the Lord promised them; for the Lord
says, 'I will be with you.'"

24When Moses had finished writing down
all the laws that are recorded in this book, 25he
instructed the Levites who carried the Ark
containing the Ten Commandments 26to put
this book of the law beside the Ark, as a
solemn warning to the people of Israel.

27"For I know how rebellious and stubborn
you are," Moses told them. "If even today,
while I am still here with you, you are defiant
rebels against the Lord, how much more rebellious will you be after my death! 28Now
summon all the elders and officers of your
tribes so that I can speak to them, and call
heaven and earth to witness against them. 29I
know that after my death you will utterly
defile yourselves and turn away from God and
his commands; and in the days to come evil

31:23 This verse contains an important message for rebuilders. In spite of the difficulty of the task, we are told: "be strong and courageous." The basis for this strength and courage is the marvelous promise: "I will be with you." As we face the desperate challenges of recovery, we can find strength and courage in this message. Our God is a God who specializes in overcoming giant challenges (see 1 Samuel 17).

will crush you for you will do what the Lord says is evil, making him very angry."

Moses' Song

30So Moses recited this entire song to the whole assembly of Israel:

CHAPTER 32

"Listen, O heavens and earth!
Listen to what I say!
2My words shall fall upon you
Like the gentle rain and dew,
Like rain upon the tender grass,
Like showers on the hillside.
3I will proclaim the greatness of the Lord.
How glorious he is! 4He is the Rock. His work is perfect.
Everything he does is just and fair.
He is faithful, without sin.
5But Israel has become corrupt,
Smeared with sin. They are no longer his;
They are a stubborn, twisted generation.
6Is this the way you treat Jehovah?
O foolish people,
Is not God your Father?
Has he not created you?
Has he not established you and made you strong?
7Remember the days of long ago!
(Ask your father and the aged men;
They will tell you all about it.)
8When God divided up the world among the nations,
He gave each of them a supervising angel!
9But he appointed none for Israel;
For Israel was God's own personal possession!
10God protected them in the howling wilderness
As though they were the apple of his eye.
11He spreads his wings over them,
Even as an eagle overspreads her young.
She carries them upon her wings—
As does the Lord his people!
12When the Lord alone was leading them,
And they lived without foreign gods,
13God gave them fertile hilltops,
Rolling, fertile fields,
Honey from the rock,
And olive oil from stony ground!
14He gave them milk and meat—
Choice Bashan rams, and goats—
And the finest of the wheat;
They drank the sparkling wine.
15But Israel was soon overfed;
Yes, fat and bloated;
Then, in plenty, they forsook their God.
They shrugged away the Rock of their salvation.
16Israel began to follow foreign gods,
And Jehovah was very angry;
He was jealous of his people.
17They sacrificed to heathen gods,
To new gods never before worshiped.
18They spurned the Rock who had made them,
Forgetting it was God who had given them birth.
19God saw what they were doing,
And detested them!
His sons and daughters were insulting him.
20He said, 'I will abandon them;
See what happens to them then!
For they are a stubborn, faithless generation.
21They have made me very jealous of their idols,
Which are not gods at all.
Now I, in turn, will make them jealous
By giving my affections
To the foolish Gentile nations of the world.
22For my anger has kindled a fire
That burns to the depths of the underworld,
Consuming the earth and all of its crops,
And setting its mountains on fire.
23I will heap evils upon them
And shoot them down with my arrows.
24I will waste them with hunger,
Burning fever, and fatal disease.
I will devour them! I will set wild beasts upon them,

32:3-4 An important part of spiritual growth is learning to worship God. An important part of worship is praise. In these verses Moses takes the time to praise God for who he is—great, glorious, strong, perfect, just and fair, faithful, holy. We also need to take the time to rejoice in who God is and to praise him for his greatness. He is the Rock, our foundation for a stable life. His work in our life is perfect. We need to recognize God's ability to help and then allow him to do his mighty work on our behalf.

32:11-13 As we go about the rebuilding process, we need to be assured of God's protection and guidance. These precious verses from Moses' song should offer just the certainty we need. God will protect us as we seek recovery and guide us toward a life filled with joy and freedom.

To rip them apart with their teeth;
And deadly serpents
Crawling in the dust.
25Outside, the enemies' sword—
Inside, the plague—
Shall terrorize young men and girls alike;
The baby nursing at the breast,
And aged men.
26I had decided to scatter them to distant lands,
So that even the memory of them
Would disappear.
27But then I thought,
"My enemies will boast,
'Israel is destroyed by our own might;
It was not the Lord
Who did it!'"'
28Israel is a stupid nation;
Foolish, without understanding.
29Oh, that they were wise!
Oh, that they could understand!
Oh, that they would know what they are getting into!
30How could one single enemy chase a thousand of them,
And two put ten thousand to flight,
Unless their Rock had abandoned them,
Unless the Lord had destroyed them?
31But the rock of other nations
Is not like our Rock;
Prayers to their gods are valueless.
32They act like men of Sodom and Gomorrah:
Their deeds are bitter with poison;
33They drink the wine of serpent venom.
34But Israel is my special people,
Sealed as jewels within my treasury.
35Vengeance is mine,
And I decree the punishment of all her enemies:
Their doom is sealed.
36The Lord will see his people righted,
And will have compassion on them when they slip.
He will watch their power ebb away,
Both slave and free.
37Then God will ask,
'Where are their gods—
The rocks they claimed to be their refuge?
38Where are these gods now,
To whom they sacrificed their fat and wine?
Let those gods arise,
And help them!
39Don't you see that I alone am God?
I kill and make live.
I wound and heal—
No one delivers from my power.
40,41I raise my hand to heaven
And vow by my existence,
That I will whet the lightning of my sword!
And hurl my punishments upon my enemies!
42My arrows shall be drunk with blood!
My sword devours the flesh and blood
Of all the slain and captives.
The heads of the enemy
Are gory with blood.'
43Praise his people,
Gentile nations,
For he will avenge his people,
Taking vengeance on his enemies,
Purifying his land
And his people."

44,45When Moses and Joshua had recited all
the words of this song to the people, 46Moses
made these comments:

"Meditate upon all the laws I have given
you today, and pass them on to your children.
47These laws are not mere words—they are
your life! Through obeying them you will live
long, plentiful lives in the land you are going
to possess across the Jordan River."

Moses' Death Is Foretold

48That same day, the Lord said to Moses, 49"Go
to Mount Nebo in the Abarim mountains, in
the land of Moab across from Jericho. Climb
to its heights and look out across the land of
Canaan, the land I am giving to the people of
Israel. 50After you see the land, you must die
and join your ancestors, just as Aaron, your
brother, died in Mount Hor and joined them.
51For you dishonored me among the people of
Israel at the springs of Meribah-kadesh, in the
wilderness of Zin. 52You will see spread out
before you the land I am giving the people of
Israel, but you will not enter it."

CHAPTER 33

Moses Blesses the People

This is the blessing Moses, the man of God, gave to the people of Israel before his death:

2"The Lord came to us at Mount Sinai,
And dawned upon us from Mount Seir;
He shone from Mount Paran,
Surrounded by ten thousands of holy angels,
And with flaming fire at his right hand.
3How he loves his people—
His holy ones are in his hands.
They followed in your steps, O Lord.

They have received their directions from you.
4The laws I have given
Are your precious possession.
5The Lord became king in Jerusalem,
Elected by a convocation of the leaders of the tribes!
6Let Reuben live forever
And may his tribe increase!"

7And Moses said of Judah:

"O Lord, hear the cry of Judah
And unite him with Israel;
Fight for him against his enemies."

8Then Moses said concerning the tribe of Levi:

"Give to godly Levi
Your Urim and your Thummim.
You tested Levi at Massah and at Meribah;
9He obeyed your instructions
[and destroyed many sinners],
Even his own children, brothers, fathers, and mothers.
10The Levites shall teach God's laws to Israel
And shall work before you at the incense altar
And the altar of burnt offering.
11O Lord, prosper the Levites
And accept the work they do for you.
Crush those who are their enemies;
Don't let them rise again."

12Concerning the tribe of Benjamin, Moses said:

"He is beloved of God
And lives in safety beside him.
God surrounds him with his loving care,
And preserves him from every harm."

13Concerning the tribe of Joseph, he said:
"May his land be blessed by God
With the choicest gifts of heaven
And of the earth that lies below.
14May he be blessed
With the best of what the sun makes grow;
Growing richly month by month,
15With the finest of mountain crops
And of the everlasting hills.
16May he be blessed with the best gifts
Of the earth and its fullness,
And with the favor of God who appeared
In the burning bush.
Let all these blessings come upon Joseph,
The prince among his brothers.
17He is a young bull in strength and splendor,
With the strong horns of a wild ox
To push against the nations everywhere;
This is my blessing on the multitudes of Ephraim
And the thousands of Manasseh."

18Of the tribe of Zebulun, Moses said:

"Rejoice, O Zebulun, you outdoorsmen,
And Issachar, you lovers of your tents;
19They shall summon the people
To celebrate their sacrifices with them.
Lo, they taste the riches of the sea
And the treasures of the sand."
20Concerning the tribe of Gad, Moses said:

"A blessing upon those who help Gad.
He crouches like a lion,
With savage arm and face and head.
21He chose the best of the land for himself
Because it is reserved for a leader.
He led the people
Because he carried out God's penalties for Israel."

22Of the tribe of Dan, Moses said:

"Dan is like a lion's cub
Leaping out from Bashan."

23Of the tribe of Naphtali, Moses said:

"O Naphtali, you are satisfied
With all the blessings of the Lord;
The Mediterranean coast and the Negeb
Are your home."

24Of the tribe of Asher:

"Asher is a favorite son,
Esteemed above his brothers;
He bathes his feet in oil.
25May you be protected with strong bolts
Of iron and bronze,
And may your strength match the length of your days!
26There is none like the God of Jerusalem—
He descends from the heavens
In majestic splendor to help you.
27The eternal God is your Refuge,
And underneath are the everlasting arms.
He thrusts out your enemies before you;
It is he who cries, 'Destroy them!'
28So Israel dwells safely,
Prospering in a land of corn and wine,
While the gentle rains descend from heaven.
29What blessings are yours, O Israel!

Who else has been saved by the Lord?
He is your shield and your helper!
He is your excellent sword!
Your enemies shall bow low before you,
And you shall trample on their backs!"

CHAPTER 34
Moses Dies
Then Moses climbed from the plains of Moab
to Pisgah Peak in Mount Nebo, across from
Jericho. And the Lord pointed out to him the
Promised Land, as they gazed out across
Gilead as far as Dan:
2"There is Naphtali; and there is Ephraim
and Manasseh; and across there, Judah, extending to the Mediterranean Sea; 3there is
the Negeb; and the Jordan Valley; and Jericho,
the city of palm trees; and Zoar," the Lord told
him.
4"It is the Promised Land," the Lord told
Moses. "I promised Abraham, Isaac, and Jacob
that I would give it to their descendants. Now
you have seen it, but you will not enter it."
5So Moses, the disciple of the Lord, died in
the land of Moab as the Lord had said. 6The
Lord buried him in a valley near Beth-peor in
Moab, but no one knows the exact place.
7Moses was 120 years old when he died, yet
his eyesight was perfect and he was as strong
as a young man. 8The people of Israel
mourned for him for thirty days on the plains
of Moab.
9Joshua (son of Nun) was full of the spirit of
wisdom, for Moses had laid his hands upon
him; so the people of Israel obeyed him and
followed the commandments the Lord had
given to Moses.
10There has never been another prophet
like Moses, for the Lord talked to him face to
face. 11,12And at God's command he performed
amazing miracles that have never been
equaled.

33:29 Here is another promise of God's saving help. He provides defense for his people from their enemies and fights on their behalf. He assures them of ultimate victory. When our life is in disarray, it is comforting to know that God has genuine concern for our welfare. And as we seek recovery, we can be sure that God is on our side.

REFLECTIONS ON
DEUTERONOMY

insights FROM THE PAST

After a generation of consistent failure, Moses found it necessary to go back to the basics. As the Israelites were about to enter the Promised Land, **Deuteronomy 1:1-5** tells us they took time out to read God's laws once again. The name *Deuteronomy* actually means "second law" or "repetition of the law." It was necessary for Moses to share God's instructions with the new generation of Israelites as they faced new living conditions and the accompanying temptations. God's instructions for living are good for every generation. We need to take the time to regularly review them as we face the temptations and difficulties of recovery.

In **Deuteronomy 1:32** Moses reminded the Israelites of their refusal to believe what God had told them. There is no better formula for failure. When we refuse to trust in God, no program for recovery will be successful for long. In this verse we are told why the Israelites were forced to wander in the wilderness for forty years. They refused to trust in God! God had the power to deliver them from their powerless state, but the Israelites refused to take advantage of it. Believing God is essential for lasting success.

In **Deuteronomy 4:9** and at various other points in the following verses we see warning exclamations, such as "Watch out!" No matter how secure we may feel in our righteousness, if we are unwary, we are on the verge of a fall. Here Israel was charged to remember what God had done for them. Remembering the victories and failures of the past can help us keep on guard against sin and failure in the present. The Israelites were also instructed to pass their wisdom and experience on to the next generation. We also are responsible to pass on to our children the wisdom learned from our past. This will give them a chance, if they choose to listen, to avoid some of the mistakes we have made. God is concerned that godly attitudes and wisdom are passed on to each successive generation.

We see in **Deuteronomy 4:20** that God delivered Israel for a specific purpose. He forged Israel into a nation to be his chosen possession, and through this special nation God planned to bring salvation to the whole world. Why has God delivered us? God's purposes for us are quite specific. We need to ask these questions: What does God want from us? Why did God save us? He may intend to use us to bring his saving grace into the lives of many who suffer from problems similar to our own.

In **Deuteronomy 4:34-40** we see a glorious review of God's work on Israel's behalf. And in this account, Israel's many failures aren't even mentioned. They are forgotten in the amazing story of how God led his people from slavery in Egypt to the Promised Land. God's plans for Israel succeeded in the long run, despite Israel's tendency to rebel against God and his program. Since we all fail on our recovery journey, Israel's history should be a source of encouragement for us. God will continue to work with us, disciplining us when it is needed, comforting us when we are discouraged. If we trust him, our own history will be a glorious account of our journey from slavery to freedom—all the failures and mistakes graciously forgotten.

The Israelites were about to end forty difficult years of wilderness wandering. They were starting the task of beginning new lives and building a new nation. But when things start going well in life, it is easy to forget the help God has given us in the past. In **Deuteronomy 6:10-13** Moses gave the Israelites a special warning. He told the people to give God the respect and obedience he deserved. This was foundational for them to continue the rebuilding process. As we begin to make progress in recovery, it is easy to forget that it is only by God's grace that we have come this far. We need to realize that without God's help, we will quickly regress. Continued respect for and obedience to God are necessary for our progress in recovery.

In **Deuteronomy 6:23** Moses reminded the people that God's purpose was to bring them from bondage into a new life of freedom. He brought them out so that he could bring them into something much better. Most of us have suffered periods of bondage in our life. Maybe that is all we have known. We can be assured that when God leads us out of our slavery, he has a much better life in store for us. As we are freed from our dependencies, he will give us new things to live for—good and healthy things. God is reminding us here that his people are delivered for a purpose, and our recovery is part of that purpose.

insights FOR THE PRESENT

All relationships come with responsibilities. In **Deuteronomy 4:23-24** we are reminded that this is also true of our relationship with God. We cannot remake God as we would like him to be; we must relate to him as he is. And as the only true God, he demands that we give him our full devotion. As with any relationship, we need to be faithful to God if we wish our relationship to remain strong. This book calls the Israelites to follow through on their responsibilities to God. The consequences for ignoring responsibilities in any relationship are great. Failing in our relationship with God results in even deeper problems.

In **Deuteronomy 5:1** Moses reminded the people of the importance of obedience. God's laws gave the Israelites clear guidance as to what God expected of them, presenting them with God's standard of excellence. These guidelines supplied a pattern for healthy living in virtually every area of life. But sadly, none of us is fully able to live up to God's standards (see Romans 3:23). Because of this, God has extended his grace to us, accepting us on the basis of Jesus Christ and his work. God's presence with us will provide us with the help we need. God's grace makes it possible for us to rebuild our life according to God's standard.

In **Deuteronomy 5:5-6** Moses introduced the Ten Commandments by directing Israel's attention to the person of God, reminding the people that he was "the Lord" (*Yahweh* or *Jehovah*). This name is God's personal covenant name. It reminds us of his relationship with Abraham, Isaac, Jacob, and then with Moses and the nation of Israel. God is personal; he relates to us one-on-one. The Scriptures also state: "I am Jehovah your God." He is our God. Our personal relationship with God and our love for him should provide the motivation for our obedience to his laws.

In **Deuteronomy 6:6** it becomes clear that God's laws need more than our cursory attention.

Thinking about God's program for healthy living just once or twice a week isn't enough. We are to think about God's laws constantly, every day. In recovery we know the importance of living one day at a time. We need constant reminders if we are to overcome our dependencies and build a new life. God's plan for recovery must be reviewed constantly if we are to discover the freedom he promises.

In **Deuteronomy 7:9** we are reminded of God's steadfast faithfulness. He is a delivering and faithful God. He always keeps his promises. A major step in rebuilding our life is to take God at his word. His steadfast love is the reason behind every response God makes toward us. Notice, however, that he also asks something of us. We must believe, love, and obey him.

insights FROM THE TEN COMMANDMENTS

In **Deuteronomy 5:7-8** we are commanded to put God first in our life. It is easy to let our priorities get out of balance. The important things are forgotten; the urgent things claim our attention, affection, and resources. If we are to build our life according to God's specifications, then God has to be our highest priority. Anything that comes before God in our life becomes a false god. We need to stay clear of anything that might come between us and God.

Deuteronomy 5:11 prohibits the use of God's name in any way that brings it dishonor. This is often understood to refer to using God's name in an exclamation of anger or disgust. Actually this commandment refers not primarily to speech, but to life. As people who represent the name of God, we are responsible to act in ways that will bring him glory, not shame. Thus, when our actions and attitudes bring dishonor to God, this commandment is broken. We need to live with complete honesty in both word and deed, bringing honor rather than dishonor to God's name.

In **Deuteronomy 5:12-15** we are commanded to observe the Sabbath day of rest. God has placed a seven-day clock in our body. If we don't give it the rest it needs, the restructuring of our life will never be completely effective. Physical, emotional, and spiritual exhaustion will make it impossible for us to accomplish what our goals and plans call for. Although most of us do not celebrate the Old Testament Sabbath, our human makeup demands that we have at least one special day in seven—a day of rest.

In **Deuteronomy 5:16** we are commanded to honor our parents. This does not mean we should obey them blindly, never questioning their demands or actions. Some of us may have been abused by dysfunctional parents; obeying all their demands would only be destructive. Honoring our parents does, however, mean showing love toward them. This may mean that we must call them to account for their actions toward us when we are ready to take that step. It demands that we seek their best, bringing them honor. We should work to help them develop their honorable characteristics, while not enabling their dishonorable ones.

In **Deuteronomy 5:18** we are commanded to remain faithful in marriage. Dysfunctional families are often the result of unfaithfulness on the part of one or both of the marriage partners. Also, many of the sexual difficulties and problems with venereal disease and AIDS could be avoided if only this commandment were obeyed with consistency. A healthy marriage relationship requires 100 percent fidelity on the part of both partners. Recovery from a shattered marriage can come about only through the trust that develops out of this kind of loving commitment.

In **Deuteronomy 5:19** we are commanded not to steal. Healthy interpersonal relationships require that people have a healthy respect for one another. Such respect includes the recognition and protection of the personal property belonging to others. Stealing of all kinds is completely forbidden by this commandment. Theft of property is primarily in view, but theft of ideas and theft of reputation are included as well. "Honesty is the best policy" because it is God's policy.

The commandment in **Deuteronomy 5:21** is different from the others because it not only forbids certain actions, but certain attitudes as well. It insists that we carefully guard our thought life. Notice that when this commandment is broken, it usually leads to breaking others, too. As we work on our recovery, we must learn to keep our thought life in order. We need to live in the real world, not in worlds of fantasy and self-deception.

insights FOR THE FUTURE

In **Deuteronomy 6:7** we are told specifically to share God's wisdom with our children. In recovery we often focus on the suffering that has been passed down to us from past generations. Here we are reminded that the blessings of God's Word can also be passed on. Now is the time to break the cycle of suffering and pain! We can start by passing God's wisdom on to our children. Notice that this verse demands that we make God's Word an integral part of our life. We need to live it, not just speak it. We need to teach, not just with our words, but with our life-style as well.

The Israelites were about to enter the Promised Land and probably feared the powerful enemies they would face. But in **Deuteronomy 7:21** God made it clear that he was sufficient for the task, no matter how great it might be. As we take hold of the opportunity of building a new life, we also face great obstacles to our progress. We need to trust in God's sufficiency to help us in our own conquests. He is capable of overcoming any obstacles we might face.

In **Deuteronomy 30:2-3** God offered this gracious message to his people who were living in defeat: repent and be restored. Even though they had strayed away from God's requirements, all they needed to do was to return and obey. Our wholehearted repentance brings God's wholehearted forgiveness. With God, it is never too late to make a new start in life.

In **Deuteronomy 30:15** God laid out a clear choice for his people. On the one hand there was life and prosperity. On the other hand was death and adversity. Choosing God and his way leads to healthy living. Choosing against God leads to destruction and death. The choice we make here will lead either to recovery or destruction. The clear consequences should make the choice easy. It's up to us!

JOSHUA

THE BIG PICTURE

A. SECURING THE FRUITS OF VICTORY (1:1–12:24)
1. Inspiring the People (1:1–5:15)
2. Implementing the Plan (6:1–11:23)
3. Identifying the Progress (12:1-24)

B. SHARING THE FRUITS OF VICTORY (13:1–24:33)
1. Ensuring Fair Compensation (13:1–19:51)
2. Ensuring Full Cooperation (20:1–22:34)
3. Ensuring Faithful Continuance (23:1–24:33)

God had miraculously used Moses to lead the people of Israel out of bondage in Egypt and to the threshold of the Promised Land. But instead of conquering it, they had wandered in the wilderness for forty years. The book of Joshua records how God brought the next generation of Israelites to the borders of Canaan under Joshua's leadership.

Joshua was ideal for the job of leading Israel: he was a gifted leader and had served as Moses' assistant for many years. The primary reason for his success, however, was not his ability. It was his trust in God and his obedience to God's instructions. He constantly turned the attention of his people to the God who took care of them, who fought for them, who gave them the land. He recognized and declared that Israel's victories belonged to God alone.

The new generation of Israelites seemed to have recovered from their parents' lack of trust and tendency toward disobedience. Instead of resisting God's plan for conquest, they agreed to do everything that Joshua commanded. As a result, they witnessed miraculous victories, won in the face of impossible odds. As the Israelites continued to believe and obey God, incredible things were done on their behalf. They soon discovered that God was worthy of their trust.

It is hard for some of us to believe that God has a plan for our recovery or that he is able to bring it about. But such doubts are not grounded in the truth. God does care about us, and he is able to lead us to amazing victories over the most powerful of enemies. Remembering this truth should help us to step out in faith and follow God's program for victorious living.

THE BOTTOM LINE

PURPOSE: To reveal the importance of trusting and obeying God in the difficult process of achieving both physical and spiritual goals. AUTHOR: The book is anonymous, though tradition attributes much of it to Joshua. AUDIENCE: The people of Israel. DATE WRITTEN: Probably sometime between 1375 and 1300 B.C., soon after the events recorded. SETTING: Initially in the wilderness east of the Jordan River, but primarily in the Promised Land. KEY VERSES: "Be strong and brave, for you will be a successful leader of my people; . . . You need only to be strong and courageous and to obey to the letter every law Moses gave you" (1:6-7). KEY PLACES: Jordan River, Gilead, Jericho, Ai, Shiloh, Shechem. KEY PEOPLE: Joshua, Rahab, Caleb.

RECOVERY THEMES

Recovery Is Ongoing: How wonderful it would be to be completely recovered—to have arrived! That's one of our fantasies, and certainly one that the Israelites must have had. The first generation had not made it into the Promised Land. But this group had followed God's plan and conquered the land. What could possibly go wrong now? They may have said, "We're in the Promised Land at last—finally we can relax!" But the exact opposite was true. Their work had just begun! The same is true for us. When we think we have arrived, we have probably just begun our recovery. We need to recognize that recovery is a lifelong task.

The Conflict with Evil: God commanded his people to completely conquer the land of Canaan and its people. His concern was to purify the land from evil people and practices. The Israelites were the people of God's promise. They were to judge evil and to be a blessing to all nations. But to accomplish this, they had to be on guard against the evil around them. The ever-present fact of evil is one reason why our recovery can never be complete. We cannot eliminate it from our life. Many have tried, but if we escape the evil forces on the outside, we are confronted with the evil that lies within. We must be ever watchful of the old patterns in our life that could destroy our recovery.

Obedience Is Ongoing: God had given Israel instructions for every area of their lives. Joshua was obedient; the people sometimes wavered and were inconsistent. This brought trouble. But what was true in Joshua's day is still true for us. The more we trust and believe God, the more we will want to obey him. The more we obey him, the greater our joy, regardless of our circumstances. Obedience to God is not something to be resisted; it is the only pathway to a life filled with joy.

The Importance of Communication: Communication is extremely important in relationships characterized by stability and peace. The eastern tribes had built a large monument in Canaan before crossing the Jordan River. This act was misunderstood by the western tribes, who perceived it to be an act of rebellion against God. War between the tribes seemed inevitable, but fighting was averted by a simple conversation between the groups involved. After understanding was established, the reason for battle no longer existed. We often misinterpret the actions and words of others. Open and honest communication is a prerequisite for overcoming the resulting confusion and establishing peace.

CHAPTER 1

God's Charge to Joshua

After the death of Moses, the Lord's disciple,
God spoke to Moses' assistant, whose name
was Joshua (the son of Nun), and said to him,
[2]"Now that my disciple is dead, [you are
the new leader of Israel]. Lead my people
across the Jordan River into the Promised
Land. [3]I say to you what I said to Moses:
'Wherever you go will be part of the land of
Israel—[4]all the way from the Negeb desert in
the south to the Lebanon mountains in the
north, and from the Mediterranean Sea in
the west to the Euphrates River in the east,
including all the land of the Hittites.' [5]No
one will be able to oppose you as long as
you live, for I will be with you just as I was
with Moses; I will not abandon you or fail
to help you.
[6]"Be strong and brave, for you will be a
successful leader of my people; and they shall
conquer all the land I promised to their ancestors. [7]You need only to be strong and courageous and to obey to the letter every law
Moses gave you, for if you are careful to obey
every one of them, you will be successful in

1:1-9 Joshua may have been devastated by the death of Moses, a close friend, mentor, and father figure. But he was immediately thrust into a leadership role for which he undoubtedly felt unworthy and unprepared. How could Joshua ever fill the shoes of the man who had talked to God face to face? (Exodus 33:11). He dared not show fear before the people, or they would have lost confidence in his ability to lead them to victory. He needed to demonstrate a bold obedience to God's commands in order to ensure success. Joshua was able to do this because he was willing to turn his life and will over to God.

1:10-15 In his new role as commander-in-chief of Israel's armies, Joshua commanded his subordinates to prepare their people for the new and difficult venture that lay before them. He then reminded the Reubenites, Gadites, and the half-tribe of Manasseh of their promise to Moses to fight side by side with their fellow Israelites until all the land had been conquered (see Numbers 32:1-32). Joshua understandably was concerned to find out if they would stand with or defect from the main body of the people. If they defected, war might have broken out or, at the very least, discouragement might have set in among the people of Israel. We need to continue to guard ourself, evaluating, watching for seeds of discouragement.

READ JOSHUA 1:1-9

GOD grant me the serenity to accept the things I cannot change the courage to change the things I can and the wisdom to know the difference AMEN

There must have been a time when we had high hopes for a promising life—before those hopes were dashed. But then, through the crazy and chaotic circumstances of growing up, we learned to settle for a life that was far less than what we had once hoped for.

God led the nation of Israel out of bondage in Egypt, through the wilderness, and to the edge of the Promised Land. But as they stood on the border, looking into the fruitful and prosperous land of Canaan, they lacked the faith and courage to go in. Joshua was one of the few who had the faith to enter, but because of the others, he was held back. Forty years later the chance came again. Just before he entered the land, the Lord told him, "Yes, be bold and strong! Banish fear and doubt! For remember, the Lord your God is with you wherever you go" (Joshua 1:9).

We may have come to the conclusion that a sane, good life is reserved for people better or stronger than we are, but there is a Promised Land for each one of us. Jeremiah tells us, "For I know the plans I have for you, says the Lord. They are plans for good and not for evil, to give you a future and a hope" (Jeremiah 29:11). We need to be courageous. We need to believe that there can be good things in life for us. We, too, can be encouraged that regardless of the failures in our family and our past, we can start again. We can find our way out of the chaos of the wilderness, into the Promised Land of sane and healthy living. *Turn to page 269, Judges 5.*

---

everything you do. 8Constantly remind the
people about these laws, and you yourself
must think about them every day and every
night so that you will be sure to obey all of
them. For only then will you succeed. 9Yes, be
bold and strong! Banish fear and doubt! For
remember, the Lord your God is with you
wherever you go."

Joshua Encourages the People

10,11Then Joshua issued instructions to the
leaders of Israel to tell the people to get ready
to cross the Jordan River. "In three days we
will go across and conquer and live in the
land which God has given us!" he told them.
12,13Then he summoned the leaders of the
tribes of Reuben, Gad, and the half-tribe of
Manasseh and reminded them of their agreement with Moses: "The Lord your God has
given you a homeland here on the east side
of the Jordan River," Moses had told them,
14"so your wives and children and cattle may
remain here, but your troops, fully armed,
must lead the other tribes across the Jordan
River to help them conquer their territory on
the other side; 15stay with them until they
complete the conquest. Only then may you
settle down here on the east side of the Jordan."
16To this they fully agreed and pledged
themselves to obey Joshua as their commander-in-chief.
17,18"We will obey you just as we obeyed
Moses," they assured him, "and may the Lord
your God be with you as he was with Moses.
If anyone, no matter who, rebels against your
commands, he shall die. So lead on with courage and strength!"

CHAPTER 2

Rahab Protects the Spies

Then Joshua sent two spies from the Israeli camp at Acacia to cross the river and check out the situation on the other side, especially at Jericho. They arrived at an inn operated by a woman named Rahab, who was a prostitute. They were planning to spend the night there, 2but someone informed the king of Jericho that two Israelis who were suspected of being spies had arrived in the city that evening. 3He dispatched a police squadron to Rahab's home, demanding that she surrender them.

"They are spies," he explained. "They have been sent by the Israeli leaders to discover the best way to attack us."

4But she had hidden them, so she told the officer in charge, "The men were here earlier, but I didn't know they were spies. 5They left the city at dusk as the city gates were about to close, and I don't know where they went. If you hurry, you can probably catch up with them!"

6But actually she had taken them up to the roof and hidden them beneath piles of flax that were drying there. 7So the constable and his men went all the way to the Jordan River looking for them; meanwhile, the city gates were kept shut. 8Rahab went up to talk to the men before they retired for the night.

9"I know perfectly well that your God is going to give my country to you," she told them. "We are all afraid of you; everyone is terrified if the word *Israel* is even mentioned. 10For we have heard how the Lord made a path through the Red Sea for you when you left Egypt! And we know what you did to Sihon and Og, the two Amorite kings east of the Jordan, and how you ruined their land and completely destroyed their people. 11No wonder we are afraid of you! No one has any fight left in him after hearing things like that, for your God is the supreme God of heaven, not just an ordinary god. 12,13Now I beg for this one thing: Swear to me by the sacred name of your God that when Jericho is conquered you will let me live, along with my father and mother, my brothers and sisters, and all their families. This is only fair after the way I have helped you."

14The men agreed. "If you won't betray us, we'll see to it that you and your family aren't harmed," they promised. 15"We'll defend you with our lives." Then, since her house was on top of the city wall, she let them down by a rope from a window.

16"Escape to the mountains," she told them. "Hide there for three days until the men who are searching for you have returned; then go on your way."

17,18But before they left, the men had said to her, "We cannot be responsible for what happens to you unless this rope is hanging from this window and unless all your relatives—your father, mother, brothers, and anyone else—are here inside the house. 19If they go out into the street, we assume no responsibility whatsoever; but we swear that no one inside this house will be killed or injured. 20However, if you betray us, then this oath will no longer bind us in any way."

21"I accept your terms," she replied. And she left the scarlet rope hanging from the window.

2:1-7 Joshua wisely determined to discover the strength of his enemies, the people of the city of Jericho, before setting out to encounter them in battle (see Luke 14:31-32). Rahab, a prostitute and a citizen of Jericho, also made a wise decision when she took a stand for the God of Israel by assisting and protecting the spies sent by Joshua. Rahab displayed courage when she turned away from the security and praise of the world she knew and risked following the true God, of whom she knew little. It always takes courage to make changes in our life, especially when those changes take us into the unknown.

2:15-21 Rahab completed her chosen task of helping the spies by providing them with a rope, a window hidden from sight, and a plan (hide three days in the hills until it is safe) for their safe return to their people. The spies, in turn, established the ground rules of responsibility for Rahab and her family. They outlined the specific requirements of the relationship and the rewards for success or punishments for failure. Rahab is an excellent example of how God can use each of us, no matter how terrible our past or how unworthy we may feel.

3:1-6 These were anxious times for Joshua and the people. They set out on their trek to the Promised Land but then had to delay their entrance into that land for three full days while their leaders gave them instructions. Those instructions, moreover, dealt with both the physical and the spiritual realms. The people were commanded (1) to remain approximately a half mile behind the Ark of the Covenant when the priests carried it (i.e., they were not to try to run ahead of God but were to receive their direction from God) and (2) to dedicate themselves to God (i.e., they were to remain close to God in order to see what great things he would do). No doubt it was as difficult then as it is now to follow God's plan rather than to rebel and go our own way.

JOSHUA

We all have experienced the frustration of knowing the truth but having no one believe us. Few of us, however, have had to live with the consequences of this for almost forty years.

Joshua was one of the twelve Israelites chosen to spy out the land of Canaan. Tremendous responsibility came along with this job. Their report on what they saw would help over a million people make a decision about entering the Promised Land. When the twelve spies gave their report, ten said it would be impossible to conquer the land. Their understanding of God was limited by their weak faith; it was distorted. On the other hand, Joshua and Caleb agreed that the task would be difficult, but they urged the people to trust God to help them. They saw God as loving, powerful, and able to lead them safely into the Promised Land.

The people rebelled against God and sided with the majority report. In doing so, they ran from the responsibility of turning their wills and their lives over to God and following him. The result of their irresponsibility was tragic, as a whole generation—with the exception of Joshua and Caleb—died in the desert.

Three important principles are illustrated in Joshua's life. First, what we think about God has a powerful effect upon what we do. Second, ever since Adam's fall, human beings have had to endure pain whether they accept responsibility or decline it. Third, our decision to accept or run away from responsibility determines the type of pain we experience and the effect it will have on us. Joshua experienced significant pain despite putting God first in his life. But that pain did not bring his destruction. Rather, it was used by God to develop him into one of the most effective leaders in all of history.

Many of us think that we can escape pain by avoiding responsibility and its demands. What we fail to realize is that in running away from responsibility, we often experience a much deeper pain than we when we accept it.

STRENGTHS AND ACCOMPLISHMENTS:
- Joshua was a wise and gifted military strategist.
- When faced with life's challenges, he sought God's direction.
- He was not afraid to go against popular opinion.
- He led the Israelites into the Promised Land.
- He believed God's promises despite opposition.

LESSONS FROM HIS LIFE:
- Despite opposition, it is always best to follow God.
- Those we choose as mentors have a profound effect on us.
- Solid preparation and encouragement are keys to training a leader.

KEY VERSE:
"But if you are unwilling to obey the Lord, then decide today whom you will obey. Will it be the gods of your ancestors beyond the Euphrates or the gods of the Amorites here in this land? But as for me and my family, we will serve the Lord" (24:15).

Joshua's story is told in Exodus 17, 24, 32–33; Numbers 11, 13–14, 26–27, 32–34; Deuteronomy 1; 3; 31; 34; and the book of Joshua. He is also mentioned in Judges 1–2; 1 Kings 16:34; 1 Chronicles 7:27; and Hebrews 4:8.

22The spies went up into the mountains and stayed there three days, until the men who were chasing them had returned to the city after searching everywhere along the road without success. 23Then the two spies came down from the mountain and crossed the river and reported to Joshua all that had happened to them.

24"The Lord will certainly give us the entire land," they said, "for all the people over there are scared to death of us."

CHAPTER 3

Crossing the Jordan River

Early the next morning Joshua and all the people of Israel left Acacia and arrived that evening at the banks of the Jordan River, where they camped for a few days before crossing.

2-4On the third day officers went through the camp giving these instructions: "When you see the priests carrying the Ark of God, follow them. You have never before been

where we are going now, so they will guide
you. However, stay about a half mile behind,
with a clear space between you and the Ark;
be sure that you don't get any closer."
[5]Then Joshua told the people to purify
themselves. "For tomorrow," he said, "the
Lord will do a great miracle."
[6]In the morning Joshua ordered the priests,
"Take up the Ark and lead us across the river!"
And so they started out.
[7]"Today," the Lord told Joshua, "I will give
you great honor, so that all Israel will know
that I am with you just as I was with Moses.
[8]Instruct the priests who are carrying the Ark
to stop at the edge of the river."
[9]Then Joshua summoned all the people and
told them, "Come and listen to what the Lord
your God has said. [10]Today you are going to
know for sure that the living God is among
you and that he will, without fail, drive out
the Canaanites, Hittites, Hivites, Perizzites,
Girgashites, Amorites, and Jebusites—all the
people who now live in the land you will soon
occupy. [11]Think of it! The Ark of God, who is
Lord of the whole earth, will lead you across
the river!
[12]"Now select twelve men, one from each
tribe, for a special task. [13,14]When the priests
who are carrying the Ark touch the water with
their feet, the river will stop flowing as
though held back by a dam, and will pile up
as though against an invisible wall!" Now it
was the harvest season and the Jordan was
overflowing all its banks; but as the people set
out to cross the river and as the feet of the
priests who were carrying the Ark touched the
water at the river's edge, [15,16]suddenly, far up
the river at the city of Adam, near Zarethan,
the water began piling up as though against a
dam! And the water below that point flowed
on to the Dead Sea until the riverbed was
empty. Then all the people crossed at a spot
where the river was close to the city of Jericho,
[17]and the priests who were carrying the Ark
stood on dry ground in the middle of the
Jordan and waited as all the people passed by.

CHAPTER 4
The People Build a Monument

When all the people were safely across, the
Lord said to Joshua,
[2,3]"Tell the twelve men chosen for a special
task, one from each tribe, each to take a stone
from where the priests are standing in the
middle of the Jordan, and to carry them out
and pile them up as a monument at the place
where you camp tonight."
[4]So Joshua summoned the twelve men [5]and
told them, "Go out into the middle of the
Jordan where the Ark is. Each of you is to carry
out a stone on your shoulder—twelve stones
in all, one for each of the twelve tribes. [6]We
will use them to build a monument so that in
the future, when your children ask, 'What is
this monument for?' [7]you can tell them, 'It is
to remind us that the Jordan River stopped
flowing when the Ark of God went across!'
The monument will be a permanent reminder
to the people of Israel of this amazing
miracle."

3:7-14 God would drive out the enemies of Israel if the Israelites were obedient to him. Furthermore, in order for the people to see the power of God at work, the priests, acting by faith, had to carry the Ark of the Covenant and stand with their feet in the Jordan River. Would God leave Joshua looking foolish, or would God act in the way he had promised? Joshua did not doubt God but had the priests stand in the river. The Jordan River was at flood stage and hence extremely dangerous, if not impossible, to cross without God's help. Often God places us at a point where we must either stand for him or show that we don't really trust him. If we trust in God, we can be sure that he will never disappoint us.

4:1-7 The priests faithfully remained standing in the riverbed until the more than two million people had crossed into the Promised Land. Joshua, at the command of God, then sent twelve men back to the place where the priests were standing. Those men were to collect one stone per tribe to set up a memorial that would remind them, their children, and their children's children of what God had done on their behalf as they moved into the Promised Land. The stones would serve as a visible reminder of God's great power, should the people ever become discouraged when they faced powerful enemies in the future. If we take time to review our life, we also will find small reminders, monuments of God's presence with us.

4:8-14 Joshua took a direct interest in remembering the glory of God and in honoring the faith of the priests by personally erecting the permanent memorial in the middle of the river. And at the end of the crossing, God raised Joshua to a new status in the eyes of the people—he was honored in the same way that his predecessor Moses had been. Sometimes it helps to record the events where God provided a way when everything appeared hopeless. These entries can then become our monument to God's faithfulness and can be reviewed and celebrated in times of doubt.

8So the men did as Joshua told them. They took twelve stones from the middle of the Jordan river—one for each tribe, just as the Lord had commanded Joshua. They carried them to the place where they were camped for the night and constructed a monument there. 9Joshua also built another monument of twelve stones in the middle of the river, at the place where the priests were standing; and it is there to this day. 10The priests who were carrying the Ark stood in the middle of the river until all these instructions of the Lord, which had been given to Joshua by Moses, had been carried out. Meanwhile, the people had hurried across the riverbed, 11and when everyone was over, the people watched the priests carry the Ark up out of the riverbed.

12,13The troops of Reuben, Gad, and the half-tribe of Manasseh—fully armed as Moses had instructed, and forty thousand strong—led the other tribes of the Lord's army across to the plains of Jericho.

14It was a tremendous day for Joshua! The Lord made him great in the eyes of all the people of Israel, and they revered him as much as they had Moses and respected him deeply all the rest of his life. 15,16For it was Joshua who, at the Lord's command, issued the orders to the priests carrying the Ark.

"Come up from the riverbed," the Lord now told him to command them.

17So Joshua issued the order. 18And as soon as the priests came out, the water poured down again as usual and overflowed the banks of the river as before! 19This miracle occurred on the 25th of March. That day the entire nation crossed the Jordan River and camped in Gilgal at the eastern edge of the city of Jericho; 20and there the twelve stones from the Jordan were piled up as a monument.

21Then Joshua explained again the purpose of the stones: "In the future," he said, "when your children ask you why these stones are here and what they mean, 22you are to tell them that these stones are a reminder of this amazing miracle—that the nation of Israel crossed the Jordan River on dry ground! 23Tell them how the Lord our God dried up the river right before our eyes and then kept it dry until we were all across! It is the same thing the Lord did forty years ago at the Red Sea! 24He did this so that all the nations of the earth will realize that Jehovah is the mighty God, and so that all of you will worship him forever."

CHAPTER 5

The People Make a Commitment

When the nations west of the Jordan River—the Amorites and Canaanites who lived along the Mediterranean coast—heard that the Lord had dried up the Jordan River so the people of Israel could cross, their courage melted away completely and they were paralyzed with fear.

2,3The Lord then told Joshua to set aside a day to circumcise the entire male population of Israel. (It was the second time in Israel's history that this was done.) The Lord instructed them to manufacture flint knives for this purpose. The place where the circumcision rite took place was named "The Hill of the Foreskins." 4,5The reason for this second circumcision ceremony was that although when Israel left Egypt all of the men who had been old enough to bear arms had been circumcised, that entire generation had died during the years in the wilderness, and none of the boys born since that time had been circumcised. 6For the nation of Israel had traveled back and forth across the wilderness for forty years until all the men who had been old enough to bear arms when they left Egypt were dead; they had not obeyed the Lord, and he vowed that he wouldn't let them enter the land he had promised to Israel—a land that "flowed with milk and honey." 7So now Joshua circumcised their children—the men who had grown up to take their fathers' places.

8,9And the Lord said to Joshua, "Today I have ended your shame of not being circumcised." So the place where this was done was called Gilgal (meaning, "to end"), and is still called that today. After the ceremony the entire nation rested in camp until the raw flesh of their wounds had been healed.

5:1-9 Although the Amorites admitted they were helpless before the God of Israel, they did not turn to him for help. The people of Israel, however, took steps to ensure that their relationship with God was as it should be. In an act of obedience, they circumcised all the males among them. As a result, God took away their shame when they submitted to the painful act of circumcision. Fortunately, we do not have to go through a physical cutting to be rid of our shame. But we do have to go through the painful process of acknowledging our failures and allowing God to remove the shame from us. This process can be so painful that we are tempted to deny our shame rather than allow God to remove it.

10While they were camped at Gilgal on the plains of Jericho, they celebrated the Passover during the evening of April first. 11,12The next day they began to eat from the gardens and grain fields which they invaded, and they made unleavened bread. The following day no manna fell, and it was never seen again! So from that time on they lived on the crops of Canaan.

Battle Plans from God

13As Joshua was sizing up the city of Jericho, a man appeared nearby with a drawn sword. Joshua strode over to him and demanded, "Are you friend or foe?"

14"I am the Commander-in-Chief of the Lord's army," he replied.

Joshua fell to the ground before him and worshiped him and said, "Give me your commands."

15"Take off your shoes," the Commander told him, "for this is holy ground." And Joshua did.

CHAPTER 6

The gates of Jericho were kept tightly shut because the people were afraid of the Israelis; no one was allowed to go in or out.

2But the Lord said to Joshua, "Jericho and its king and all its mighty warriors are already defeated, for I have given them to you! 3,4Your entire army is to walk around the city once a day for six days, followed by seven priests walking ahead of the Ark, each carrying a trumpet made from a ram's horn. On the seventh day you are to walk around the city seven times, with the priests blowing their trumpets. 5Then, when they give one long, loud blast, all the people are to give a mighty shout, and the walls of the city will fall down; then move in upon the city from every direction."

The Battle for Jericho

6-9So Joshua summoned the priests and gave them their instructions: the armed men would lead the procession, followed by seven priests blowing continually on their trumpets. Behind them would come the priests carrying the Ark, followed by a rear guard.

10"Let there be complete silence except for the trumpets," Joshua commanded. "Not a single word from any of you until I tell you to shout; then *shout!*"

11The Ark was carried around the city once that day, after which everyone returned to the camp again and spent the night there. 12-14At dawn the next morning they went around again and returned again to the camp. They followed this pattern for six days.

15At dawn of the seventh day they started out again, but this time they went around the city not once, but seven times. 16The seventh time, as the priests blew a long, loud trumpet blast, Joshua yelled to the people, *"Shout!* The Lord has given us the city!"

17(He had told them previously, "Kill everyone except Rahab the prostitute and anyone in her house, for she protected our spies. 18Don't take any loot, for everything is to be

---

5:13-15 Note two important considerations regarding the identity of the Commander-in-Chief of the Lord's army: (1) He accepted worship when Joshua bowed down to him, and (2) the place where he stood was considered to be holy ground (compare Exodus 3:1-6). This "new" Commander, therefore, was more than a man and more than a mere angel; this Captain was none other than God himself. When Joshua recognized who the stranger was, he quickly deferred all claims of leadership to him. If each of us could acknowledge our powerlessness without God and relinquish control to God as Joshua did, we would avoid many of the self-inflicted wounds that hurt us. Fortunately, it is never too late to acknowledge God's lordship over us and to allow him to lead us in life's battles.

6:1-14 Israel was ready to attack, but God told them to wait. God required his people to do something that on the surface appeared to be very foolish. They were commanded to march around the city, day after day. The Israelites obeyed God and persisted in their faith, not fully understanding how God would destroy the walls of Jericho. If there are seemingly unbreakable barriers to our recovery, God can make those barriers come crumbling down, allowing us to be victorious. But we need to do things his way, even if we don't always understand why.

6:15-21 Once more Israel experienced delayed gratification. On the seventh day, on the verge of initiating the attack, the people of Israel were required to march seven times around the city. They were also prohibited from enjoying the spoils of victory, which were to be dedicated to God—they were not to steal from God. Finally Israel was given the go-ahead. In obedience to God, they pressed the attack and secured the victory, destroying their enemies completely. Learning to delay gratification is a major step toward maturity, both in our faith and in our recovery. God calls us to trust him, especially when every urge is to move ahead without delay.

RAHAB & FAMILY

It is amazing that a pagan prostitute would demonstrate even rudimentary trust in God. Because she believed, Joshua found an unlikely ally waiting within the city walls of Jericho. As the trumpets blared and the people thunderously marched, Rahab gathered her parents, brothers, and sisters about her in anticipation of rescue. A single scarlet cord tied to her window alerted the conquerors to spare the people within. Thanks to her surprising faith, her family was plucked from the ruins.

Given her line of work, Rahab surely wasn't accustomed to setting boundaries upon her behavior. She probably wasn't even aware of her personal sin. Her faith, like her job, was likely born of necessity. She was, above all, practical, and it made sense to believe in this powerful Hebrew God. She watched as fear paralyzed her people, and she recognized her own powerlessness in the situation. Jericho's fall was inevitable. The God who parted seas could surely topple walls. Her ability to see reality also prompted her to faith.

Aiding Joshua's men was a risky business, yet Rahab acted with courage and daring. She proved herself faithful by concealing the spies and giving them vital information. Her strategy of deceiving the king might be questioned, although nowhere in Scripture is she criticized for her methods. Instead, she is extolled as an example of righteousness and faith.

Following the rescue, God gave Rahab what she probably never dreamed possible in Jericho: the opportunity to break with the past and build a new life. Rahab and her relatives found a home among the Israelites, but there was more. She married Salmon and was blessed with a son, Boaz. Boaz would become the great-grandfather of King David, from whose line Jesus descended. Rahab's transformation proves once again that God is in the business of turning lives around. Rahab shines as a stellar example of a second chance, a forgiven past, and a recovered life. Though our recovery may not be as dramatic, God is able to pick up broken pieces and facilitate fresh beginnings.

STRENGTHS AND ACCOMPLISHMENTS:
- Rahab's faith in God was made visible by her actions.
- Rahab had a deep love and concern for her family.
- She recognized the hopeless reality of her situation.
- She sought help from the right source: God and his people.

WEAKNESSES AND MISTAKES:
- Rahab's initial trust in God seems to have been motivated by pragmatism and fear rather than loving gratitude.

LESSONS FROM HER LIFE:
- God is alive and available to facilitate fresh starts when we are willing to cooperate with his plans.
- Nothing is impossible with God.
- A proper view of God should convince us of his power and worth.

KEY VERSE:
"By faith—because she believed in God and his power—Rahab the harlot did not die with all the others in her city when they refused to obey God" (Hebrews 11:31).

Rahab's story is told in Joshua 2:1-21; 6:17-25. She is also mentioned in Matthew 1:5, Hebrews 11:31, and James 2:25.

---

destroyed. If it isn't, disaster will fall upon the
entire nation of Israel. [19]But all the silver and
gold and the utensils of bronze and iron will
be dedicated to the Lord and must be brought
into his treasury.")
[20]So when the people heard the trumpet
blast, they shouted as loud as they could. And
suddenly the walls of Jericho crumbled and
fell before them, and the people of Israel
poured into the city from every side and captured it! [21]They destroyed everything in it—
men and women, young and old; oxen;
sheep; donkeys—everything.
[22]Meanwhile Joshua had said to the two
spies, "Keep your promise. Go and rescue the
prostitute and everyone with her."
[23]The young men found her and rescued
her, along with her father, mother, brothers,
and other relatives who were with her. Arrangements were made for them to live outside the camp of Israel. [24]Then the Israelis
burned the city and everything in it except

that the silver and gold and the bronze and iron utensils were kept for the Lord's treasury. [25]Thus Joshua saved Rahab the prostitute and her relatives who were with her in the house, and they still live among the Israelites because she hid the spies sent to Jericho by Joshua.

[26]Then Joshua declared a terrible curse upon anyone who might rebuild Jericho, warning that when the foundation was laid, the builder's oldest son would die, and when the gates were set up, his youngest son would die.

[27]So the Lord was with Joshua, and his name became famous everywhere.

CHAPTER 7

Achan's Disobedience

But there was sin among the Israelis. God's command to destroy everything except that which was reserved for the Lord's treasury was disobeyed. For Achan (the son of Carmi, grandson of Zabdi, and great-grandson of Zerah, of the tribe of Judah) took some loot for himself, and the Lord was very angry with the entire nation of Israel because of this.

[2]Soon after Jericho's defeat, Joshua sent some of his men to spy on the city of Ai, east of Bethel.

[3]Upon their return they told Joshua, "It's a small city and it won't take more than two or three thousand of us to destroy it; there's no point in all of us going there."

[4]So approximately three thousand soldiers were sent—and they were soundly defeated. [5]About thirty-six of the Israelis were killed during the attack, and many others died while being chased by the men of Ai as far as the quarries. The Israeli army was paralyzed with fear at this turn of events. [6]Joshua and the elders of Israel tore their clothing and lay prostrate before the Ark of the Lord until evening, with dust on their heads.

[7]Joshua cried out to the Lord, "O Jehovah, why have you brought us over the Jordan River if you are going to let the Amorites kill us? Why weren't we content with what we had? Why didn't we stay on the other side? [8]O Lord, what am I to do now that Israel has fled from her enemies! [9]For when the Canaanites and the other nearby nations hear about it, they will surround us and attack us and wipe us out. And then what will happen to the honor of your great name?"

[10,11]But the Lord said to Joshua, "Get up off your face! Israel has sinned and disobeyed my commandment and has taken loot when I said it was not to be taken; and they have not only taken it, they have lied about it and have hidden it among their belongings. [12]That is why the people of Israel are being defeated. That is why your men are running from their enemies—for they are cursed. I will not stay with you any longer unless you completely rid yourselves of this sin.

[13]"Get up! Tell the people, 'Each of you must undergo purification rites in preparation for tomorrow, for the Lord your God of Israel says that someone has stolen from him, and you cannot defeat your enemies until you deal with this sin. [14]In the morning you must come by tribes, and the Lord will point out the tribe to which the guilty man belongs. And that tribe must come by its clans and the Lord will point out the guilty clan; and the clan must come by its families, and then each member of the guilty family must come one by one. [15]And the one who has stolen that which belongs to the Lord shall be burned with fire, along with everything he has, for he has violated the covenant of the Lord and has brought calamity upon all of Israel.'"

[16]So, early the next morning, Joshua brought the tribes of Israel before the Lord, and the tribe of Judah was indicated. [17]Then he brought the clans of Judah, and the clan of Zerah was singled out. Then the families of that clan were brought before the Lord and the family of Zabdi was indicated. [18]Zabdi's family was brought man by man, and his grandson Achan was found to be the guilty one.

Consequences for Achan's Sin

[19]Joshua said to Achan, "My son, give glory to the God of Israel and make your confession. Tell me what you have done."

[20]Achan replied, "I have sinned against the Lord, the God of Israel. [21]For I saw a beautiful

7:1-9 The Israelites grew overconfident from their victory over Jericho and proceeded to attack the small city of Ai without first consulting God. Their small force was soundly defeated because God was angry at Israel for the sin of Achan. Israel as a whole became utterly demoralized. Even Joshua became discouraged and complained to God, blaming him for their loss. We must be careful not to take back control of our life once we see what God can do when he is in control. On our own, we may allow some seemingly insignificant area of our life to lead us away from God's plan. Our call is to submit our whole life to his control.

robe imported from Babylon, and some silver worth $200, and a bar of gold worth $500. I wanted them so much that I took them, and they are hidden in the ground beneath my tent, with the silver buried deeper than the rest."

[22]So Joshua sent some men to search for the loot. They ran to the tent and found the stolen goods hidden there just as Achan had said, with the silver buried beneath the rest. [23]They brought it all to Joshua and laid it on the ground in front of him. [24]Then Joshua and all the Israelites took Achan, the silver, the robe, the wedge of gold, his sons, his daughters, his oxen, donkeys, sheep, his tent, and everything he had, and brought them to the valley of Achor.

[25]Then Joshua said to Achan, "Why have you brought calamity upon us? The Lord will now bring calamity upon you."

And the men of Israel stoned them to death and burned their bodies, [26]and piled a great heap of stones upon them. The stones are still there to this day, and even today that place is called "The Valley of Calamity." And so the fierce anger of the Lord was ended.

CHAPTER 8

The Israelites Destroy Ai

Then the Lord said to Joshua, "Don't be afraid or discouraged; take the entire army and go to Ai, for it is now yours to conquer. I have given the king of Ai and all of his people to you. [2]You shall do to them as you did to Jericho and her king; but this time you may keep the loot and the cattle for yourselves. Set an ambush behind the city."

[3,4]Before the main army left for Ai, Joshua sent thirty thousand of his bravest troops to hide in ambush close behind the city, alert for action.

[5]"This is the plan," he explained to them. "When our main army attacks, the men of Ai will come out to fight as they did before, and we will run away. [6]We will let them chase us until they have all left the city; for they will say, 'The Israelis are running away again just as they did before!' [7]Then you will jump up from your ambush and enter the city, for the Lord will give it to you. [8]Set the city on fire, as the Lord has commanded. You now have your instructions."

[9]So they left that night and lay in ambush between Bethel and the west side of Ai; but Joshua and the rest of the army remained in the camp at Jericho.[10]Early the next morning Joshua roused his men and started toward Ai, accompanied by the elders of Israel, [11-13]and stopped at the edge of a valley north of the city. That night Joshua sent another five thousand men to join the troops in ambush on the west side of the city. He himself spent the night in the valley.

[14]The King of Ai, seeing the Israelis across the valley, went out early the next morning and attacked at the Plain of Arabah. But of course he didn't realize that there was an ambush behind the city. [15]Joshua and the Israeli army fled across the wilderness as though badly beaten, [16]and all the soldiers in the city were called out to chase after them; so the city was left defenseless; [17]there was not a soldier left in Ai or Bethel, and the city gates were left wide open.

[18]Then the Lord said to Joshua, "Point your spear toward Ai, for I will give you the city." Joshua did. [19]And when the men in ambush saw his signal, they jumped up and poured into the city and set it on fire. [20,21]When the men of Ai looked behind them, smoke from the city was filling the sky, and they had nowhere to go. When Joshua and the troops

7:20-26 Once Achan was identified as the guilty party, he confessed his sin, but his confession came too late. Had he confessed earlier, he might have prevented the Israelite defeat and the death of his family members. After having Achan and his family stoned to death, Joshua erected another monument of stones (see 4:9, 20). This monument, however, was not to commemorate God's great power of deliverance, but to serve as a reminder that the sin of one person can impact negatively the well-being of many people. Perhaps each of us should take the time to write down when and where we rebelled against God and how that impacted our life and the lives of those around us. If we are to learn from our mistakes, we must not only remember the result, but we must also remember the steps that led to our turning away from God.

8:1-9 Once again, God gave Joshua detailed plans to follow. In line with this guidance, Joshua used his God-given reasoning to assess the situation and to develop a detailed strategy to defeat his enemies. For such a plan to be successful, the soldiers had to exercise discipline and self-control, attacking only when the enemy was most vulnerable. Thus, by using God's methods, Joshua and his people demonstrated that they had learned from their defeat and had grown spiritually. God's plans often require discipline and self-control. These character traits can only be attained through work and struggle. The ability to say no to our human urges places us in reach of God's divine plan.

who were with him saw the smoke, they knew that their men who had been in ambush were inside the city, so they turned upon their pursuers and began killing them. 22Then the Israelis who were inside the city came out and began destroying the enemy from the rear. So the men of Ai were caught in a trap and all of them died; not one man survived or escaped, 23except for the king of Ai, who was captured and brought to Joshua.

24When the army of Israel had finished slaughtering all the men outside the city, they went back and finished off everyone left inside. 25So the entire population of Ai, twelve thousand in all, was wiped out that day. 26For Joshua kept his spear pointed toward Ai until the last person was dead. 27Only the cattle and the loot were not destroyed, for the armies of Israel kept these for themselves. (The Lord had told Joshua they could.) 28So Ai became a desolate mound of refuse, as it still is today.

29Joshua hanged the king of Ai on a tree until evening, but as the sun was going down, he took down the body and threw it in front of the city gate. There he piled a great heap of stones over it, which can still be seen.

Joshua Reviews God's Laws

30Then Joshua built an altar to the Lord God of Israel at Mount Ebal, 31as Moses had commanded in the book of his laws: "Make me an altar of boulders that have neither been broken nor carved," the Lord had said concerning Mount Ebal. Then the priests offered burnt sacrifices and peace offerings to the Lord on the altar. 32And as the people of Israel watched, Joshua carved upon the stones of the altar each of the Ten Commandments.

33Then all the people of Israel—including the elders, officers, judges, and the foreigners living among them—divided into two groups, half of them standing at the foot of Mount Gerizim and half at the foot of Mount Ebal. Between them stood the priests with the Ark, ready to pronounce their blessing. (This was all done in accordance with the instructions given long before by Moses.) 34Joshua then read to them all of the statements of blessing and curses that Moses had written in the book of God's laws. 35Every commandment Moses had ever given was read before the entire assembly, including the women and children and the foreigners who lived among the Israelis.

CHAPTER 9

The Gibeonites Trick Joshua

When the kings of the surrounding area heard what had happened to Jericho, they quickly combined their armies to fight for their lives against Joshua and the Israelis. These were the kings of the nations west of the Jordan River, along the shores of the Mediterranean as far north as the Lebanon mountains—the Hittites, Amorites, Canaanites, Perizzites, Hivites, and Jebusites.

3-5But when the people of Gibeon heard what had happened to Jericho and Ai, they resorted to trickery to save themselves. They sent ambassadors to Joshua wearing worn-out clothing, as though from a long journey, with patched shoes, weatherworn saddlebags on their donkeys, old, patched wineskins and dry, moldy bread. 6When they arrived at the camp of Israel at Gilgal, they told Joshua and the men of Israel, "We have come from a distant land to ask for a peace treaty with you."

7The Israelis replied to these Hivites, "How do we know you don't live nearby? For if you do, we cannot make a treaty with you."

8They replied, "We will be your slaves."

"But who are you?" Joshua demanded. "Where do you come from?"

8:10-23 The Israelites executed God's plan exactly as he gave it to them. Joshua relied on God in the midst of the battle, and God gave the Israelites victory. When our desires, urges, and impulses lead us away from God, it may help to remember that Joshua's faith in God did not make life free from battles. The battles were to be fought and won through continued reliance on God. Like Joshua, we need to persevere with God's strength and resist the tendency to run from our own personal battles.

9:1-15 Frightened by the success of Israel over Jericho and Ai, the kings of the southern coastal regions formed a coalition to attack Israel. The Gibeonites, however, took a different tactic. Recognizing their helplessness before Israel, they wisely but deceptively sought peace. By establishing a peace treaty, they avoided becoming Israel's next victims. The Israelites, however, failed to investigate the Gibeonite situation thoroughly and to seek God's guidance in the matter. As a result, they entered into a covenant that was a violation of the command of God (see Exodus 23:31-33). We must always examine the agreements we make and the relationships we form. We must ask if God would approve of them at this particular time. A seemingly right relationship at the wrong time will always produce ungodly results.

9And they told him, "We are from a very
distant country; we have heard of the might
of the Lord your God and of all that he did in
Egypt, 10and what you did to the two kings of
the Amorites—Sihon, king of Heshbon, and
Og, king of Bashan. 11So our elders and our
people instructed us, 'Prepare for a long journey; go to the people of Israel and declare our
nation to be their servants, and ask for peace.'
12This bread was hot from the ovens when we
left, but now as you see, it is dry and moldy;
13these wineskins were new, but now they are
old and cracked; our clothing and shoes have
become worn out from our long, hard trip."

14,15Joshua and the other leaders finally believed them. They did not bother to ask the
Lord but went ahead and signed a peace
treaty. And the leaders of Israel ratified the
agreement with a binding oath.

16Three days later the facts came out—these
men were close neighbors. 17The Israeli army
set out at once to investigate and reached
their cities in three days. (The names of the
cities were Gibeon, Chephirah, Beeroth, and
Kiriath-jearim.) 18But the cities were not
harmed because of the vow which the leaders
of Israel had made before the Lord God. The
people of Israel were angry with their leaders
because of the peace treaty.

19But the leaders replied, "We have sworn
before the Lord God of Israel that we will not
touch them, and we won't. 20We must let
them live, for if we break our oath, the wrath
of Jehovah will be upon us."

21So they became servants of the Israelis,
chopping their wood and carrying their water.

22Joshua summoned their leaders and demanded, "Why have you lied to us by saying
that you lived in a distant land, when you
were actually living right here among us?
23Now a curse shall be upon you! From this
moment you must always furnish us with
servants to chop wood and carry water for the
service of our God."

24They replied, "We did it because we were
told that Jehovah instructed his disciple Moses to conquer this entire land and destroy all
the people living in it. So we feared for our
lives because of you; that is why we have done
it. 25But now we are in your hands; you may
do with us as you wish."

26So Joshua would not allow the people of
Israel to kill them, 27but they became wood-
choppers and water-carriers for the people of
Israel and for the altar of the Lord—wherever
it would be built (for the Lord hadn't yet told
them where to build it). This arrangement is
still in force at the time of this writing.

CHAPTER 10

The Sun Stands Still

When Adoni-zedek, the king of Jerusalem,
heard how Joshua had captured and destroyed Ai and had killed its king, the same as
he had done at Jericho, and how the people
of Gibeon had made peace with Israel and
were now their allies, 2he was very frightened.
For Gibeon was a great city—as great as the
royal cities and much larger than Ai—and its
men were known as hard fighters. 3So King
Adoni-zedek of Jerusalem sent messengers to
several other kings: King Hoham of Hebron,
King Piram of Jarmuth, King Japhia of Lachish, King Debir of Eglon.

4"Come and help me destroy Gibeon," he
urged them, "for they have made peace with
Joshua and the people of Israel."

5So these five Amorite kings combined
their armies for a united attack on Gib-
eon.6The men of Gibeon hurriedly sent messengers to Joshua at Gilgal.

"Come and help your servants!" they demanded. "Come quickly and save us! For all

---

9:16-27 The leaders of Israel accepted their mistake and honored God by adhering to the conditions of the treaty. Likewise, the Gibeonites, who had confessed their deception, willingly accepted the consequences of their actions and exchanged their freedom for their lives, becoming servants of Israel. We are all aware that some decisions last a lifetime. We have given up our freedom in order to save our own life. We need to remember that our decision to live in God's will offers more freedom than the "freedom" that often leads to addictive behaviors.

10:1-11 The troubles associated with the undesirable treaty with Gibeon were compounded—Israel now had to fight on behalf of the Gibeonites. Israel accepted its obligation, and God promised Israel victory over all five kings. Although Joshua achieved success, his real victory came from God. God killed more of the enemy with hailstones than the entire Israelite army did with their weapons. If we examine our accomplishments, we will find that while we were working so hard, God was preparing a way that allowed us to do more than we could have ever done alone. It is the fool who believes that all he is and has is due to his own effort and ability. Acknowledging God's hand in our past accomplishments allows us to hold onto God's hand more firmly in the face of future challenges.

the kings of the Amorites who live in the hills are here with their armies."

7So Joshua and the Israeli army left Gilgal and went to rescue Gibeon.

8"Don't be afraid of them," the Lord said to Joshua, "for they are already defeated! I have given them to you to destroy. Not a single one of them will be able to stand up to you."

9Joshua traveled all night from Gilgal and took the enemy armies by surprise. 10Then the Lord threw them into a panic so that the army of Israel slaughtered great numbers of them at Gibeon and chased the others all the way to Beth-horon and Azekah and Makkedah, killing them along the way. 11And as the enemy was racing down the hill to Beth-horon, the Lord destroyed them with a great hailstorm that continued all the way to Azekah; in fact, more men died from the hail than by the swords of the Israelis.

12As the men of Israel were pursuing and harassing the foe, Joshua prayed aloud, "Let the sun stand still over Gibeon, and let the moon stand in its place over the valley of Aijalon!"

13And the sun and the moon didn't move until the Israeli army had finished the destruction of its enemies! This is described in greater detail in *The Book of Jashar.* So the sun stopped in the heavens and stayed there for almost twenty-four hours! 14There had never been such a day before, and there has never been another since, when the Lord stopped the sun and moon—all because of the prayer of one man. But the Lord was fighting for Israel. 15(Afterwards Joshua and the Israeli army returned to Gilgal.)

Five Enemy Kings Are Captured

16During the battle the five kings escaped and hid in a cave at Makkedah. 17When the news was brought to Joshua that they had been found, 18he issued a command that a great stone be rolled against the mouth of the cave and that guards be placed there to keep the kings inside.

19Then Joshua commanded the rest of the army, "Go on chasing the enemy and cut them down from the rear. Don't let them get back to their cities, for the Lord will help you to completely destroy them."

20So Joshua and the Israeli army continued the slaughter and wiped out the five armies except for a tiny remnant that managed to reach their fortified cities. 21Then the Israelis returned to their camp at Makkedah without having lost a single man! And after that no one dared to attack Israel.

22,23Joshua now instructed his men to remove the stone from the mouth of the cave and to bring out the five kings—of Jerusalem, Hebron, Jarmuth, Lachish, and Eglon. 24Joshua told the captains of his army to put their feet on the kings' necks.

25"Don't ever be afraid or discouraged," Joshua said to his men. "Be strong and courageous, for the Lord is going to do this to all of your enemies."

26With that, Joshua plunged his sword into each of the five kings, killing them. He then hanged them on five trees until evening.

27As the sun was going down, Joshua instructed that their bodies be taken down and thrown into the cave where they had been hiding; and a great pile of stones was placed at the mouth of the cave. (The pile is still there today.)

Israel Destroys Southern Cities

28On that same day Joshua destroyed the city of Makkedah and killed its king and everyone in it. Not one person in the entire city was left alive. 29Then the Israelis went to Libnah. 30There, too, the Lord gave them the city and its king. Every last person was slaughtered, just as at Jericho.

31From Libnah they went to Lachish and attacked it. 32And the Lord gave it to them on the second day; here, too, the entire population was slaughtered, just as at Libnah.

33During the attack on Lachish, King Horam of Gezer arrived with his army to try to help defend the city, but Joshua's men killed him and destroyed his entire army.

34,35The Israeli army then captured Eglon on the first day and, as at Lachish, they killed

10:12-15 Joshua's faith was rewarded by God's action. Joshua prayed that God would supernaturally provide additional daylight hours to press the battle on to complete victory over the Amorite nation. God responded to Joshua's prayer by causing the sun and the moon to keep their respective positions in the sky until God himself claimed victory for Israel. For centuries, unbelievers have tried to explain away this miraculous example of God's divine intervention into the lives of his people. Our human nature drives us to find an explanation outside of God's power. We tend to explain away the times when God miraculously intervenes in our personal life. God does not call us to be ignorant, but we must be careful that we do not allow intellect to rob us of faith.

everyone in the city. 36After leaving Eglon
they went to Hebron 37and captured it and all
of its surrounding villages, slaughtering the
entire population. Not one person was left
alive. 38Then they turned back to Debir,
39which they quickly captured with all of its
outlying villages. And they killed everyone
just as they had at Libnah.

40So Joshua and his army conquered the
whole country—the nations and kings of the
hill country, the Negeb, the lowlands, and the
mountain slopes. They destroyed everyone in
the land, just as the Lord God of Israel had
commanded, 41slaughtering them from Kadesh-barnea to Gaza, and from Goshen to
Gibeon. 42This was all accomplished in one
campaign, for the Lord God of Israel was
fighting for his people. 43Then Joshua and his
army returned to their camp at Gilgal.

CHAPTER 11

Joshua Surprises Northern Kings

When King Jabin of Hazor heard what had
happened, he sent urgent messages to the
following kings:

King Jobab of Madon;
The king of Shimron;
The king of Achshaph;
All the kings of the northern hill country;
The kings in the Arabah, south of
Chinneroth;
Those in the lowland;
The kings in the mountain areas of Dor,
on the west;
The kings of Canaan, both east and west;
The kings of the Amorites;
The kings of the Hittites;
The kings of the Perizzites;
The kings in the Jebusite hill country;
The Hivite kings in the cities on the
slopes of Mount Hermon, in the land of
Mizpah.

4All these kings responded by mobilizing
their armies and uniting to crush Israel. Their
combined troops, along with a vast array of
horses and chariots, covered the landscape
around the Springs of Merom as far as one
could see; 5for they established their camp at
the Springs of Merom.

6But the Lord said to Joshua, "Don't be
afraid of them, for by this time tomorrow
they will all be dead! Hamstring their horses
and burn their chariots." 7Joshua and his
troops arrived suddenly at the Springs of Merom and attacked. 8And the Lord gave all that
vast army to the Israelis, who chased them as
far as Great Sidon and a place called the Salt
Pits, and eastward into the valley of Mizpah;
so not one enemy troop survived the battle.
9Then Joshua and his men did as the Lord had
instructed, for they hamstrung the horses and
burned all the chariots.

10On the way back, Joshua captured Hazor
and killed its king. (Hazor had at one time
been the capital of the federation of all those
kingdoms.) 11Every person there was killed
and the city was burned.

12Then he attacked and destroyed all the
other cities of those kings. All the people were
slaughtered, just as Moses had commanded
long before. 13(However, Joshua did not burn
any of the cities built on mounds except for
Hazor.) 14All the loot and cattle of the ravaged
cities were taken by the Israelis for themselves, but they killed all the people. 15For so
the Lord had commanded his disciple Moses;
and Moses had passed the commandment on
to Joshua, who did as he had been told: he
carefully obeyed all of the Lord's instructions
to Moses.

A Summary of Conquests

16So Joshua conquered the entire land—the
hill country, the Negeb, the land of Goshen,

11:1-9 Once again the situation looked hopelessly bleak for Joshua and Israel. Yet still one more time God reminded Joshua that he should act boldly because he, God, would accomplish the seemingly impossible. So Joshua and his troops obeyed God and courageously attacked when the enemy least expected it. God, as he promised, gave Israel the victory. When the situations we face seem hopeless, we can look back to the example of Joshua and his people. God prevailed even when the prospects for victory were bleak. God has not changed. His power to take what we have and do great things with it continues and far exceeds whatever we could do or imagine.

11:16-22 Entering new territories in the Promised Land was not easy. There were constant battles over a prolonged period of time that pitted the people of Israel against enemies who were entrenched in the land. Some of these enemies were the Anakim, the giants who had frightened the spies Moses sent into the land (see Numbers 13:25–14:25). By God's power, however, Israel conquered its worst fears. Whatever we fear the most today is easily handled by God's power. It is truly incredible that it takes so long for us to realize what is so obvious: God has the power to turn defeat into victory, producing maximum results from minimal faith and obedience.

the lowlands, the Arabah, and the hills and lowlands of Israel. 17The Israeli territory now extended all the way from Mount Halak, near Seir, to Baal-gad in the valley of Lebanon, at the foot of Mount Hermon. And Joshua killed all the kings of those territories. 18It took seven years of war to accomplish all of this. 19None of the cities was given a peace treaty except the Hivites of Gibeon; all of the others were destroyed. 20For the Lord made the enemy kings want to fight the Israelis instead of asking for peace; so they were mercilessly killed, as the Lord had commanded Moses.

21During this period Joshua routed all of the giants—the descendants of Anak who lived in the hill country in Hebron, Debir, Anab, Judah, and Israel; he killed them all and completely destroyed their cities. 22None was left in all the land of Israel, though some still remained in Gaza, Gath, and Ashdod.

23So Joshua took the entire land just as the Lord had instructed Moses; and he gave it to the people of Israel as their inheritance, dividing the land among the tribes. So the land finally rested from its war.

CHAPTER 12

A List of Conquered Kings

Here is the list of the kings on the east side of the Jordan River whose cities were destroyed by the Israelis: (The area involved stretched all the way from the valley of the Arnon River to Mount Hermon, including the cities of the eastern desert.)

2King Sihon of the Amorites, who lived in Heshbon. His kingdom extended from Aroer, on the edge of the Arnon Valley, and from the middle of the valley of the Arnon River to the Jabbok River, which is the boundary of the Ammonites. This includes half of the present area of Gilead, which lies north of the Jabbok River. 3Sihon also controlled the Jordan River valley as far north as the western shores of the Lake of Galilee; and as far south as the Dead Sea and the slopes of Mount Pisgah.

4King Og of Bashan, the last of the Rephaim, who lived at Ashtaroth and Edrei: 5He ruled a territory stretching from Mount Hermon in the north to Salecah on Mount Bashan in the east, and on the west, extending to the boundary of the kingdoms of Geshur and Maacah. His kingdom also stretched south to include the northern half of Gilead where the boundary touched the border of the kingdom of Sihon, king of Heshbon. 6Moses and the people of Israel had destroyed these people, and Moses gave the land to the tribes of Reuben and the half-tribe of Manasseh.

7Here is a list of the kings destroyed by Joshua and the armies of Israel on the west side of the Jordan. (This land which lay between Baal-gad in the Valley of Lebanon and Mount Halak, west of Mount Seir, was allotted by Joshua to the other tribes of Israel. 8-24The area included the hill country, the lowlands, the Arabah, the mountain slopes, the Judean Desert, and the Negeb.

The people who lived there were the Hittites, the Amorites, the Canaanites, the Perizzites, the Hivites, and the Jebusites): the king of Jericho; the king of Ai, near Bethel; the king of Jerusalem; the king of Hebron; the king of Jarmuth; the king of Lachish; the king of Eglon; the king of Gezer; the king of Debir; the king of Geder; the king of Hormah; the king of Arad; the king of Libnah; the king of Adullam; the king of Makkedah; the king of Bethel; the king of Tappuah; the king of Hepher; the king of Aphek; the king of Lasharon; the king of Madon; the king of Hazor; the king of Shimron-meron; the king of Achshaph; the king of Taanach; the king of Megiddo; the king of Kedesh; the king of Jokneam, in Carmel; the king of Dor in the city of Naphathdor; the king of Goiim in Gilgal; the king of Tirzah. So in all, thirty-one kings and their cities were destroyed.

CHAPTER 13

Joshua Divides the Land

Joshua was now an old man. "You are growing old," the Lord said to him, "and there are still many nations to be conquered. 2-7Here is a list of the areas still to be occupied:

All the land of the Philistines;
The land of the Geshurites;
The territory now belonging to the
  Canaanites from the brook of Egypt to
  the southern boundary of Ekron;

12:1-24 Recounting God's great works in the past was a constant practice of the Israelite people. In this instance, not only did they recall the victories of their present leader, Joshua, but also those of their previous leader, Moses. These recollections of victories served both as reminders of the great works God had done and as springboards for trusting God to act on Israel's behalf in future times of difficulty as well. We can become living reminders of the great things that can be realized through God's strength.

Five cities of the Philistines: Gaza,
Ashdod, Ashkelon, Gath, Ekron;
The land of the Avvim in the south;
In the north, all the land of the Canaanites, including Mearah (which belongs to the Sidonians), stretching northward to Aphek at the boundary of the Amorites;
The land of the Gebalites on the coast and all of the Lebanon mountain area from Baal-gad beneath Mount Hermon in the south to the entrance of Hamath in the north;
All the hill country from Lebanon to Misrephoth-maim, including all the land of the Sidonians.

I am ready to drive these people out from before the nation of Israel, so include all this territory when you divide the land among the nine tribes and the half-tribe of Manasseh as I have commanded you."

Land East of the Jordan

8 The other half of the tribe of Manasseh and
the tribes of Reuben and Gad had already
received their inheritance on the east side of
the Jordan, for Moses had previously assigned
this land to them. 9 Their territory ran from
Aroer, on the edge of the valley of the Arnon
River, included the city in the valley, and
crossed the tableland of Medeba to Dibon; 10 it
also included all the cities of King Sihon of the
Amorites, who reigned in Heshbon, and extended as far as the borders of Ammon. 11 It
included Gilead; the territory of the Geshurites and the Maacathites; all of Mount Hermon; Mount Bashan with its city of Salecah;
12 and all the territory of King Og of Bashan,
who had reigned in Ashtaroth and Edrei. (He
was the last of the Rephaim, for Moses had
attacked them and driven them out. 13 However, the people of Israel had not driven out
the Geshurites or the Maacathites, who still
live there among the Israelites to this day.)

Land for Reuben

14 The Territorial Assignments
The Land Given to the Tribe of Levi: Moses
hadn't assigned any land to the tribe of Levi:
instead, they were given the offerings brought
to the Lord.
15 *The Land Given to the Tribe of Reuben:* Fitting the size of its territory to its size of population, Moses had assigned the following area
to the tribe of Reuben: 16 Their land extended
from Aroer on the edge of the valley of the
Arnon River, past the city of Arnon in the
middle of the valley, to beyond the tableland
near Medeba. 17 It included Heshbon and the
other cities on the plain—Dibon, Bamoth-
baal, Beth-baal-meon, 18 Jahaz, Kedemoth,
Mephaath, 19 Kiriathaim, Sibmah, Zereth-
shahar on the mountain above the valley,
20 Beth-peor, Beth-jeshimoth, and the slopes of
Mount Pisgah.
21 The land of Reuben also included the cities of the tableland and the kingdom of Sihon. Sihon was the king who had lived in
Heshbon and was killed by Moses along with
the other chiefs of Midian—Evi, Rekem, Zur,
Hur, and Reba. 22 The people of Israel also
killed Balaam the magician, the son of Beor.
23 The Jordan River was the western boundary
of the tribe of Reuben.

Land for Gad

24 *The Land Given to the Tribe of Gad:* Moses also
assigned land to the tribe of Gad in proportion to its population. 25 This territory included Jazer, all the cities of Gilead, and half
of the land of Ammon as far as Aroer near
Rabbah. 26 It also extended from Heshbon to
Ramath-mizpeh and Betonim, and from Mahanaim to Lodebar. 27,28 In the valley were
Beth-haram, and Beth-nimrah, Succoth, Zaphon, and the rest of the kingdom of King
Sihon of Heshbon. The Jordan River was the
western border, extending as far as the Lake of

13:8-13 Moving from south to north on the east side of the Jordan River, representative cities of the inheritances promised by Moses to Reuben, Gad, and the half-tribe of Manasseh are listed. In the midst of this list, however, a lack of faithfulness is indicated: Israel failed to trust God sufficiently to drive out the Geshurites and the Maacathites. Even though we are tempted to blame God when things don't turn out, we should look first at where our faith has failed rather than at where we think God has failed.

13:15-32 So that no one could mistakenly believe that God did not give the tribes east of the Jordan an inheritance equal to that of tribes living in the Promised Land, a detailed listing of the territories granted to the tribes of Reuben, Gad, and the half-tribe of Manasseh is offered here. Even though these tribes were physically separated from their fellow Israelites west of the Jordan, they were not to be separated spiritually. In discouraging times when we only see problems, it can be helpful to make a detailed list of what God has provided for each of us. As we become aware of our many gifts from God, it becomes more and more difficult to be disheartened over temporary inconveniences. The God who provided the blessings of yesterday is there for us today.

Galilee; then the border turned east from the Jordan River.

Land for Manasseh

[29]*The Land Given to the Half-Tribe of Manasseh: Moses had assigned the following territory to the half-tribe of Manasseh in proportion to its needs:* [30]Their territory extended north from Mahanaim, included all of Bashan, the former kingdom of King Og, and the sixty cities of Jair in Bashan. [31]Half of Gilead and King Og's royal cities of Ashtaroth and Edrei were given to half of the clan Machir, who was Manasseh's son.

[32]That was how Moses divided the land east of the Jordan River where the people were camped at that time across from Jericho. [33]But Moses had given no land to the tribe of Levi for, as he had explained to them, the Lord God was their inheritance. He was all they needed. He would take care of them in other ways.

CHAPTER 14

Land West of the Jordan

The conquered lands of Canaan were allotted to the remaining nine and a half tribes of Israel. The decision as to which tribe would receive which area was decided by throwing dice before the Lord, and he caused them to turn up in the ways he wanted. Eleazar the priest, Joshua, and the tribal leaders supervised the lottery.

[3,4](Moses had already given land to the two and a half tribes on the east side of the Jordan River. The tribe of Joseph had become two separate tribes, Manasseh and Ephraim, and the Levites were given no land at all, except cities in which to live and the surrounding pasturelands for their cattle. [5]So the distribution of the land was in strict accordance with the Lord's directions to Moses.)

God Blesses Caleb

[6]*The Land Given to Caleb:* A delegation from the tribe of Judah, led by Caleb, came to Joshua in Gilgal.

"Remember what the Lord said to Moses about you and me when we were at Kadesh-barnea?" Caleb asked Joshua. [7]"I was forty years old at the time, and Moses had sent us from Kadesh-barnea to spy out the land of Canaan. I reported what I felt was the truth, [8]but our brothers who went with us frightened the people and discouraged them from entering the Promised Land. But since I had followed the Lord my God, [9]Moses told me, 'The section of Canaan you were just in shall belong to you and your descendants forever.'

[10]"Now, as you see, from that time until now the Lord has kept me alive and well for all these forty-five years since crisscrossing the wilderness, and today I am eighty-five years old. [11]I am as strong now as I was when Moses sent us on that journey, and I can still travel and fight as well as I could then! [12]So I'm asking that you give me the hill country that the Lord promised me. You will remember that as spies we found the Anakim living there in great, walled cities, but if the Lord is with me, I shall drive them out of the land."

[13,14]So Joshua blessed him and gave him Hebron as a permanent inheritance because he had followed the Lord God of Israel. [15](Before that time Hebron had been called Kiriath-arba, after a great hero of the Anakim.)

And there was no resistance from the local populations as the Israelis resettled the land.

CHAPTER 15

Land for Judah

The land given *to the Tribe of Judah* (as assigned by sacred lot): Judah's southern boundary began at the northern border of Edom, crossed the Wilderness of Zin, and

---

14:1-5 The leaders of Israel did not forget God's command given by Moses, but were obedient to it, resulting in the total and proper apportionment of the Promised Land. As it was for the Levites who settled on the east side of the Jordan, so it was also for those Levites who served God in the Promised Land—they received no specific territory for an inheritance—God himself was their inheritance. God, however, did not leave them homeless to roam the countryside, but he gave them cities in which to live and pasture lands to manage. What a great reminder to us as we compare ourselves to others. When we focus on what we have or don't have, we often forget that our greatest inheritance is God.

14:6-15 Advanced physical age did not deter Caleb from seeking the inheritance promised to him by God as a reward for his faith when he served under Moses as a spy in the Promised Land (see Numbers 14:24). Age alone does not make a person feel or act old. In fact, Caleb willingly sought to enter into battle against some of the more powerful armies that inhabited the land. Because he trusted God fully, Caleb succeeded in securing his promised inheritance. We need to continue to realize that in our own life, if God wants to grant us victory over any problem we encounter, that victory is already secured.

ended at the northern edge of the Negeb. 2-4More specifically, this boundary began at the south bay of the Dead Sea, ran along the road going south of Mount Akrabbim, on into the Wilderness of Zin to Hezron (south of Kadesh-barnea), and then up through Karka and Azmon, until it finally reached the Brook of Egypt, and along that to the Mediterranean Sea.

5The eastern boundary extended along the Dead Sea to the mouth of the Jordan River.

The northern boundary began at the bay where the Jordan River empties into the Salt Sea, 6crossed to Beth-hoglah, then proceeded north of Beth-arabah to the stone of Bohan (son of Reuben). 7From that point it went through the Valley of Achor to Debir, where it turned northwest toward Gilgal, opposite the slopes of Adummim on the south side of the valley. From there the border extended to the springs at En-shemesh and on to En-rogel. 8The boundary then passed through the Valley of Hinnom, along the southern shoulder of Jebus (where the city of Jerusalem is located), then west to the top of the mountain above the Valley of Hinnom, and on up to the northern end of the Valley of Rephaim. 9From there the border extended from the top of the mountain to the spring of Nephtoah, and from there to the cities of Mount Ephron before it turned northward to circle around Baalah (which is another name for Kiriath-jearim). 10,11Then the border circled west of Baalah to Mount Seir, passed along to the town of Chesalon on the northern shoulder of Mount Jearim, and went down to Beth-shemesh. Turning northwest again, the boundary line proceeded past the south of Timnah to the shoulder of the hill north of Ekron, where it bent to the left, passing south of Shikkeron and Mount Baalah. Turning again to the north, it passed Jabneel and ended at the Mediterranean Sea.

12The western border was the shoreline of the Mediterranean.

Land for Caleb

13*The Land Given to Caleb:* The Lord instructed Joshua to assign some of Judah's territory to Caleb (son of Jephunneh), so he was given the city of Arba (also called Hebron), which had been named after Anak's father. 14Caleb drove out the descendants of the three sons of Anak: Talmai, Sheshai, and Ahiman. 15Then he fought against the people living in the city of Debir (formerly called Kiriath-sepher).

16Caleb said that he would give his daughter Achsah to be the wife of anyone who would go and capture Kiriath-sepher. 17Othniel (son of Kenaz), Caleb's nephew, was the one who conquered it, so Achsah became Othniel's wife. 18,19As she was leaving with him, she urged him to ask her father for an additional field as a wedding present. She got off her donkey to speak to Caleb about this.

"What is it? What can I do for you?" he asked.

And she replied, "Give me another present! For the land you gave me is a desert. Give us some springs too!" Then he gave her the upper and lower springs.

20So this was the assignment of land to the tribe of Judah:

21-32The cities of Judah which were situated along the borders of Edom in the Negeb, namely: Kabzeel, Eder, Jagur, Kinah, Dimonah, Adadah, Kedesh, Hazor, Ithnan, Ziph, Telem, Bealoth, Hazor-hadattah, Kerioth-hezron (or, Hazor), Amam, Shema, Moladah, Hazar-gaddah, Heshmon, Beth-pelet, Hazar-

15:16-19 Caleb did not desire just any man to marry his daughter Achsah, but wanted as a son-in-law only that man who by faith would trust God for victory over the city of Debir. Othniel took up Caleb's challenge and defeated Debir. For his efforts, Othniel was doubly blessed. Not only was he honored by becoming part of Caleb's family (thus being related to a man of faith and a hero of Israel), but he also received a wife (Achsah) who demonstrated the characteristics of a godly woman. The challenge for our life and the lives of our children is to place faith in God as a number one priority. So many problem relationships would be avoided if we only sought out those strong in faith rather than those with prestige, power, or money.

15:20-63 Of all the tribes who received an inheritance, the greatest amount of information concerning any tribe's inheritance was recorded for Judah. The importance of the tribe of Judah may account for this phenomenon. Judah was chosen to be the son from whom future kings of Israel would arise and through whose lineage the Messiah would be born (see Genesis 49:10). Merely being part of such an important tribe, however, did not guarantee either faith or success. Despite God's promise of victory to those who obey him fully (see Deuteronomy 28:1-7), some of the tribe of Judah apparently lacked sufficient faith in God to oust the inhabitants of Jerusalem. Today, what areas of our life have habits, mistakes, and addictions taken over? If we put our full faith in God, he will give us victory.

shual, Beer-sheba, Biziothiah, Baalah, Iim, Ezem, Eltolad, Chesil, Hormah, Ziklag, Madmannah, Sansannah, Lebaoth, Shilhim, Ain, and Rimmon. In all, there were twenty-nine of these cities with their surrounding villages.

33-36 The following cities situated in the lowlands were also given to Judah: Eshtaol, Zorah, Ashnah, Zanoah, En-gannim, Tappuah, Enam, Jarmuth, Adullam, Socoh, Azekah, Shaaraim, Adithaim, Gederah, and Gederothaim. In all, there were fourteen of these cities with their surrounding villages.

37-44 The tribe of Judah also inherited twenty-five other cities with their villages: Zenan, Hadashah, Migdal-gad, Dilean, Mizpeh, Joktheel, Lachish, Bozkath, Eglon, Cabbon, Lahmam, Chitlish, Gederoth, Beth-dagon, Naamah, Makkedah, Libnah, Ether, Ashan, Iphtah, Ashnah, Nezib, Keilah, Achzib, and Mareshah.

45 The territory of the tribe of Judah also included all the towns and villages of Ekron. 46 From Ekron the boundary extended to the Mediterranean and included the cities along the borders of Ashdod with their nearby villages; 47 also the city of Ashdod with its villages, and Gaza with its villages as far as the Brook of Egypt; also the entire Mediterranean coast from the mouth of the Brook of Egypt on the south to Tyre on the north.

48-62 Judah also received these forty-four cities in the hill country with their surrounding villages: Shamir, Jattir, Socoh, Dannah, Kiriath-sannah (or Debir), Anab, Eshtemoh, Anim, Goshen, Holon, Giloh, Arab, Dumah, Eshan, Janim, Beth-tappuah, Aphekah, Humtah, Kiriath-arba (or, Hebron), Zior, Maon, Carmel, Ziph, Juttah, Jezreel, Jokdeam, Zanoah, Kain, Gibeah, Timnah, Halhul, Beth-zur, Gedor, Maarath, Beth-anoth, Eltekon, Kiriath-baal (also known as Kiriath-jearim), Rabbah, Beth-arabah, Middin, Secacah, Nibshan, The City of Salt, and En-gedi.

63 But the tribe of Judah could not drive out the Jebusites who lived in the city of Jerusalem, so the Jebusites live there among the people of Judah to this day.

CHAPTER 16

Land for Ephraim

The southern boundary *of the Tribes of Joseph* (Ephraim and the half-tribe of Manasseh): This boundary extended from the Jordan River at Jericho through the wilderness and the hill country to Bethel. It then went from Bethel to Luz, then on to Ataroth, in the territory of the Archites; and west to the border of the Japhletites as far as Lower Beth-horon, then to Gezer and on over to the Mediterranean.

5,6 *The Land Given to the Tribe of Ephraim:* The eastern boundary began at Ataroth-addar. From there it ran to Upper Beth-horon, then on to the Mediterranean Sea. The northern boundary began at the Sea, ran east past Michmethath, then continued on past Taanath-shiloh and Janoah. 7 From Janoah it turned southward to Ataroth and Naarah, touched Jericho, and ended at the Jordan River. 8 [The western half of the northern boundary] went from Tappuah and followed along Kanah Brook to the Mediterranean Sea. 9 Ephraim was also given some of the cities in the territory of the half-tribe of Manasseh. 10 The Canaanites living in Gezer were never driven out, so they still live as slaves among the people of Ephraim.

CHAPTER 17

Land for Manasseh

The land given *to the Half-tribe of Manasseh* (Joseph's oldest son): The clan of Machir (Manasseh's oldest son who was the father of

16:1-10 A godly person's descendants often reap numerous benefits from that person's life. Because Joseph had been used by God to deliver his father, Jacob, and his family from a famine that could have destroyed them, Jacob honored Joseph by "adopting" Joseph's two sons (Ephraim and Manasseh) and making them equal in status to Jacob's own sons (Genesis 48:1-5). Thus of the twelve sons of Jacob, Joseph's lineage was granted the privilege of being considered two tribes for the purpose of receiving an inheritance. Our faith and the life we develop around our faith will have ramifications for our family in many generations to come. There is no greater inheritance than to have lived a life of faith in prayerful submission to God.

17:1-6 The daughters of Zelophehad demonstrated true faith in God, believing that he would fulfill his promise of an inheritance to them. They based their confidence on an earlier ruling by Moses (which ultimately had come from God) that gave to them their father's inheritance in light of the fact that he had no sons to receive it (Numbers 27:1-7). The faith of Zelophehad's daughters thus was rewarded with land. God is the rewarder of faith. The reward may not always come in the form of land or possessions, but it will come in forms that far exceed the temporal values of material goods.

Gilead) had already been given the land of Gilead and Bashan [on the east side of the Jordan River], for they were great warriors. 2So now, land on the west side of the Jordan was given to the clans of Abiezer, Helek, Asriel, Shechem, Shemida, and Hepher.

3However, Hepher's son Zelophehad (grandson of Gilead, great-grandson of Machir, and great-great-grandson of Manasseh) had no sons. He had only five daughters whose names were Mahlah, Noah, Hoglah, Milcah, and Tirzah. 4These women came to Eleazar the priest and to Joshua and the Israeli leaders and reminded them,

"The Lord told Moses that we were to receive as much property as the men of our tribe."

5,6So, as the Lord had commanded through Moses, these five women were given an inheritance along with their five great-uncles, and the total inheritance came to ten sections of land (in addition to the land of Gilead and Bashan across the Jordan River).

7The northern boundary of the tribe of Manasseh extended southward from the border of Asher to Michmethath, which is east of Shechem. On the south the boundary went from Michmethath to the Spring of Tappuah. 8(The land of Tappuah belonged to Manasseh, but the city of Tappuah, on the border of Manasseh's land, belonged to the tribe of Ephraim.) 9From the spring of Tappuah the border of Manasseh followed the north bank of the Brook of Kanah to the Mediterranean Sea. (Several cities south of the brook belonged to the tribe of Ephraim, though they were located in Manasseh's territory.) 10The land south of the brook and as far west as the Mediterranean Sea was assigned to Ephraim, and the land north of the brook and east of the sea went to Manasseh. Manasseh's northern boundary was the territory of Asher, and the eastern boundary was the territory of Issachar.

11The half-tribe of Manasseh was also given the following cities, which were situated in the areas assigned to Issachar and Asher: Beth-shean, Ibleam, Dor, En-dor, Taanach, Megiddo (where there are the three cliffs), with their respective villages. 12But since the descendants of Manasseh could not drive out the people who lived in those cities, the Canaanites remained. 13Later on, however, when the Israelis became strong enough, they forced the Canaanites to work as slaves.

14Then the two tribes of Joseph came to Joshua and asked, "Why have you given us only one portion of land when the Lord has given us such large populations?"

15"If the hill country of Ephraim is not large enough for you," Joshua replied, "and if you are able to do it, you may clear out the forest land where the Perizzites and Rephaim live."

16-18"Fine," said the tribes of Joseph, "for the Canaanites in the lowlands around Beth-shean and the Valley of Jezreel have iron chariots and are too strong for us."

"Then you shall have the mountain forests," Joshua replied, "and since you are such a large, strong tribe you will surely be able to clear it all and live there. And I'm sure you can drive out the Canaanites from the valleys, too, even though they are strong and have iron chariots."

CHAPTER 18

Unconquered Territory

After the conquest—although seven of the tribes of Israel had not yet entered and conquered the land God had given them—all Israel gathered at Shiloh to set up the Tabernacle.

17:14-18 Even though they did not trust God enough to drive out all of their enemies and to secure all of the land of their inheritance (see 16:10; 17:12-13), the tribes of Ephraim and Manasseh complained that they did not have enough land in which to live. They also complained that the enemies living in the land of their inheritance were too strong for them to defeat. Joshua generously granted them their request for additional land but at the same time challenged them to fulfill their responsibility to drive out the Canaanites. The erosion of God's best always occurs when our will interferes with his. We come to believe we know so much and then recklessly destroy what God has provided. We must seek God, his will, and his power. If we do not, we may spend a lifetime compensating for mistakes made outside of his will.

18:1-10 Despite a general rest from war, the various tribes of Israel had not yet claimed their inheritance. Joshua chided them for their failure to recover that which God had apportioned to them. He then gave practical guidance as to how the remaining tribes should divide up the land. The tribes who earlier had not aggressively claimed their inheritance finally took action and followed Joshua's advice. Sometimes we need to be spurred to action by others. Maybe we don't have the courage to act—or perhaps we don't realize that we need to. But we should listen to the advice of wise leaders, recognizing that they can see our situation more objectively than we can.

[3]Then Joshua asked them, "How long are you going to wait before clearing out the people living in the land that the Lord your God has given to you? [4]Select three men from each tribe, and I will send them to scout the unconquered territory and bring back a report of its size and natural divisions so that I can divide it for you. [5,6]The scouts will map it into seven sections, and then I will throw the sacred dice to decide which section will be assigned to each tribe. [7]However, remember that the Levites won't receive any land; they are priests of the Lord. That is their wonderful heritage. And of course the tribes of Gad and Reuben and the half-tribe of Manasseh won't receive any more, for they already have land on the east side of the Jordan where Moses promised them that they could settle."

[8]So the scouts went out to map the country and to bring back their report to Joshua. Then the Lord could assign the sections of land to the tribes by the throw of the sacred dice. [9]The men did as they were told and divided the entire territory into seven sections, listing the cities in each section. Then they returned to Joshua and the camp at Shiloh. [10]There at the Tabernacle at Shiloh the Lord showed Joshua by the sacred lottery which tribe should have each section:

Land for Benjamin

[11]*The Land Given to the Tribe of Benjamin:*

The section of land assigned to the families of the tribe of Benjamin lay between the territory previously assigned to the tribes of Judah and Joseph.

[12]The northern boundary began at the Jordan River, went north of Jericho, then west through the hill country and the Wilderness of Beth-aven. [13]From there the boundary went south to Luz (also called Bethel) and proceeded down to Ataroth-addar in the hill country south of Lower Beth-horon. [14]There the border turned south, passing the mountain near Beth-horon and ending at the village of Kiriath-baal (sometimes called Kiriath-jearim), one of the cities of the tribe of Judah. This was the western boundary.

[15]The southern border ran from the edge of Kiriath-baal, over Mount Ephron to the spring of Naphtoah, [16]and down to the base of the mountain beside the valley of Hinnom, north of the valley of Rephaim. From there it continued across the valley of Hinnom, crossed south of the old city of Jerusalem where the Jebusites lived, and continued down to En-rogel. [17]From En-rogel the boundary proceeded northeast to En-shemesh and on to Geliloth (which is opposite the slope of Adummim). Then it went down to the Stone of Bohan (who was a son of Reuben), [18]where it passed along the north edge of the Arabah. The border then went down into the Arabah, [19]ran south past Beth-hoglah, and ended at the north bay of the Dead Sea—which is the southern end of the Jordan River.

[20]The eastern border was the Jordan River. This was the land assigned to the tribe of Benjamin. [21-28]These twenty-six cities were included in the land given to the tribe of Benjamin: Jericho, Beth-hoglah, Emek-keziz, Beth-arabah, Zimaraim, Bethel, Avvim, Parah, Ophrah, Chephar-ammoni, Ophni, Geba, Gibeon, Ramah, Beeroth, Mizpeh, Chephirah, Mozah, Rekem, Irpeel, Taralah, Zela, Haeleph, Jebus (or Jerusalem), Gibeah, and Kiriath-jearim. All of these cities and their surrounding villages were given to the tribe of Benjamin.

CHAPTER 19

Land for Simeon

The land given *to the Tribe of Simeon:* The tribe of Simeon received the next assignment of land—including part of the land previously

---

18:5-8 Rolling dice, or casting lots, to determine God's will was one means that God used to communicate with his Old Testament people (see Leviticus 16:8-10; Numbers 26:55-56; Jonah 1:7). Lots normally were either stones or sticks with identification marks that were placed into the fold of a garment or into a vessel and shaken until one fell out. The one that came out indicated God's will. It is sad to see some today continuing to make decisions as if they were rolling dice to discover God's will. We don't need to roll dice—we have God's Word to form the foundation of every decision we make.

19:1-16 Carved out from the southern sector of the boundaries of Judah, which previously had received more land than it required (see 15:1-62), the inheritance of the tribe of Simeon formed the southern border of the Promised Land. Although several cities were transferred from Judah to Simeon, none of those cities were taken away from Caleb and his family. By contrast, Zebulun's inheritance was in the northern region of the Promised Land, a region that one day would be the site of the hometown of the Messiah (i.e., Nazareth; see Matthew 2:23). There must have been tremendous temptation to compare each tribe's inheritance rather than to see each allotment as ordained by God. True faith frees us to accept God's provision as perfectly planned for us, whether it seems great or small.

assigned to Judah. 2-7Their inheritance included these seventeen cities with their respective villages: Beer-sheba, Sheba, Moladah, Hazar-shual, Balah, Ezem, Eltolad, Bethul, Hormah, Ziklag, Beth-marcaboth, Hazar-susah, Beth-lebaoth, Sharuhen, En-rimmon, Ether, and Ashan. 8The cities as far south as Baalath-beer (also known as Ramah-in-the-Negeb) were also given to the tribe of Simeon. 9So the Simeon tribe's inheritance came from what had earlier been given to Judah, for Judah's section had been too large for them.

Land for Zebulun

10*The Land Given to the Tribe of Zebulun:* The third tribe to receive its assignment of land was Zebulun. Its boundary started on the south side of Sarid. 11From there it circled to the west, going near Mareal and Dabbesheth until it reached the brook east of Jokneam. 12In the other direction, the boundary line went east to the border of Chisloth-tabor, and from there to Daberath and Japhia; 13then it continued east of Gath-hepher, Ethkazin, and Rimmon and turned toward Neah. 14The northern boundary of Zebulun passed Hannathon and ended at the Valley of Iphtahel. 15,16The cities in these areas, besides those already mentioned, included Kattath, Nahalal, Shimron, Idalah, Bethlehem, and each of their surrounding villages. Altogether there were twelve of these cities.

Land for Issachar

17-23*The Land Given to the Tribe of Issachar:* The fourth tribe to be assigned its land was Issachar. Its boundaries included the following cities: Jezreel, Chesulloth, Shunem, Hapharaim, Shion, Anaharath, Rabbith, Kishion, Ebez, Remeth, En-gannim, En-haddah, Beth-pazzez, Tabor, Shahazumah, and Beth-shemesh—sixteen cities in all, each with its surrounding villages. The boundary of Issachar ended at the Jordan River.

Land for Asher

24-26*The Land Given to the Tribe of Asher:* The fifth tribe to be assigned its land was Asher. The boundaries included these cities: Helkath, Hali, Beten, Achshaph, Allammelech, Amad, and Mishal.

The boundary on the west side went from Carmel to Shihor-libnath, 27turned east toward Beth-dagon, and ran as far as Zebulun in the Valley of Iphtahel, running north of Beth-emek and Neiel. It then passed to the east of Kabul, 28Ebron, Rehob, Hammon, Kanah, and Greater Sidon. 29Then the boundary turned toward Ramah and the fortified city of Tyre and came to the Mediterranean Sea at Hosah. The territory also included Mahalab, Achzib, 30,31Ummah, Aphek, and Rehob—an overall total of twenty-two cities and their surrounding villages.

Land for Naphtali

32*The Land Given to the Tribe of Naphtali:* The sixth tribe to receive its assignment was the tribe of Naphtali. 33Its boundary began at Judah, at the oak in Zaanannim, and extended across to Adami-nekeb, Jabneel, and Lakkum, ending at the Jordan River. 34The western boundary began near Heleph and ran past Aznoth-tabor, then to Hukkok, and coincided with the Zebulun boundary in the south, and with the boundary of Asher on the west, and with the Jordan River at the east. 35-39The fortified cities included in this territory were: Ziddim, Zer, Hammath, Rakkath, Chinnereth, Adamah, Ramah, Hazor, Kedesh, Edrei, Enhazor, Yiron, Migdal-el, Horem, Beth-anath, and Beth-shemesh.

So altogether the territory included nineteen cities with their surrounding villages.

Land for Dan

40*The Land Given to the Tribe of Dan:* The last tribe to be assigned its land was Dan. 41-46The cities within its area included: Zorah, Eshtaol, Ir-shemesh, Shaalabbin, Aijalon, Ithlah, Elon, Timnah, Ekron, Eltekeh, Gibbethon, Baalath, Jehud, Bene-berak, Gath-rimmon, Me-jarkon, and Rakkon, also the territory near Joppa. 47,48But some of this territory proved impossible to conquer, so the tribe of Dan captured the city of Leshem, slaughtered its people,

---

19:24-39 Neither Asher nor Naphtali was successful in driving out its enemies (see Judges 1:31-33). Failing to clear the land of all the nations dwelling in the Promised Land proved costly for the Israelite people. Rather than converting to God those whom they failed to destroy, the people of Israel were drawn away from God to serve the idols of those heathen nations. Those nations, in turn, would become like thorns in Israel's side (see Deuteronomy 31:16-20; Judges 2:1-3, 11-14). It is essential that we drive out the enemies of our family so future generations won't have to do battle with them. Whether they are alcoholism, sexual abuse, or other problems, we must resolve them rather than hand the legacy down to our children and their children.

and lived there; and they called the city "Dan," naming it after their ancestor.

Land for Joshua

49 So all the land was divided among the tribes, with the boundaries indicated; and the nation of Israel gave a special piece of land to Joshua, 50 for the Lord had said that he could have any city he wanted. He chose Timnath-serah in the hill country of Ephraim; he rebuilt it and lived there.

51 Eleazar the priest, Joshua, and the leaders of the tribes of Israel supervised the sacred lottery to divide the land among the tribes. This was done in the Lord's presence at the entrance of the Tabernacle at Shiloh.

CHAPTER 20

Cities of Refuge

The Lord said to Joshua,

2 "Tell the people of Israel to designate now the Cities of Refuge, as I instructed Moses. 3 If a man is guilty of killing someone unintentionally, he can run to one of these cities and be protected from the relatives of the dead man, who may try to kill him in revenge. 4 When the innocent killer reaches any of these cities, he will meet with the city council and explain what happened, and they must let him come in and must give him a place to live among them. 5 If a relative of the dead man comes to kill him in revenge, the innocent slayer must not be released to him for the death was accidental. 6 The man who caused the accidental death must stay in that city until he has been tried by the judges and found innocent, and must live there until the death of the High Priest who was in office at the time of the accident. But then he is free to return to his own city and home."

7 The cities chosen as Cities of Refuge were Kedesh of Galilee in the hill country of Naphtali; Shechem, in the hill country of Ephraim; and Kiriath-arba (also known as Hebron) in the hill country of Judah. 8 The Lord also instructed that three cities be set aside for this purpose on the east side of the Jordan River, across from Jericho. They were Bezer, in the wilderness of the land of the tribe of Reuben; Ramoth of Gilead, in the territory of the tribe of Gad; and Golan of Bashan, in the land of the tribe of Manasseh. 9 These Cities of Refuge were for foreigners living in Israel as well as for the Israelis themselves, so that anyone who accidentally killed another man could run to that place for a trial and not be killed in revenge.

CHAPTER 21

Towns for the Levites

Then the leaders of the tribe of Levi came to Shiloh to consult with Eleazar the priest and with Joshua and the leaders of the various tribes.

2 "The Lord instructed Moses to give cities to us Levites for our homes, and pastureland for our cattle," they said.

3 So they were given some of the recently conquered cities with their pasturelands. 4 Thirteen of these cities had been assigned originally to the tribes of Judah, Simeon, and Benjamin. These were given to some of the priests of the Kohath division (of the tribe of Levi, descendants of Aaron). 5 The other families of the Kohath division were given ten cities from the territories of Ephraim, Dan, and the half-tribe of Manasseh. 6 The Gershon division received thirteen cities, selected by sacred lot in the area of Bashan. These cities were given by the tribes of Issachar, Asher, Naphtali, and the half-tribe of Manasseh. 7 The Merari division received twelve cities from the tribes of Reuben, Gad, and Zebulun. 8 So the Lord's command to Moses was

20:1-6 The six cities of refuge show God's design to protect the innocent. Anyone who accidentally killed another (without hatred or intention) could escape to a city of refuge where his case would be tried by the leaders of that city. If proven innocent, the individual was required to remain as a protected person within the city until the current High Priest of Israel died. At the death of the High Priest, the protected person was free to leave without fear of retribution. If found guilty of intentional murder, however, he was put to death (see Numbers 35:16-21, 29-34). Many of us go through life with no place of refuge. We carry our burdens from problem to problem, repeating the sins of our past. There are churches and recovery groups that can be a refuge where we can come together and share our pain so that we no longer have to be victimized by it. God is a God of grace, and anyone seeking him will find refuge.

21:1-8 The Levites patiently waited for the other tribes to receive their inheritance before reminding Eleazar and Joshua of God's command that the tribes of Israel were to give to the Levites cities as an inheritance in which to live (see Numbers 35:1-8). Israel, in obedience to God's command, fulfilled its responsibility to God and to the tribe of Levi. Acting responsibly toward others brings honor not only to them and ourself, but to God as well.

obeyed, and the cities and pasturelands were assigned by the toss of the sacred dice.

9-16 First to receive their assignment were the priests—the descendants of Aaron, who was a member of the Kohath division of the Levites. The tribes of Judah and Simeon gave them the nine cities listed below, with their surrounding pasturelands:

Hebron, in the Judean hills, as a City of Refuge—it was also called Kiriath-arba (Arba was the father of Anak)—although the fields beyond the city and the surrounding villages were given to Caleb, the son of Jephunneh; Libnah, Jattir, Eshtemoa, Holon, Debir, Ain, Juttah, and Beth-shemesh.

17,18 The tribe of Benjamin gave them these four cities and their pasturelands: Gibeon, Gaba, Anathoth, and Almon. 19 So in all, thirteen cities were given to the priests—the descendants of Aaron.

20-22 The other families of the Kohath division received four cities and pasturelands from the tribe of Ephraim: Shechem (a City of Refuge), Gezer, Kibza-im, and Beth-horon.

23,24 The following four cities and pasturelands were given by the tribe of Dan: Elteke, Gibbethon, Aijalon, and Gath-rimmon.

25 The half-tribe of Manasseh gave the cities of Taanach and Gath-rimmon with their surrounding pasturelands. 26 So the total number of cities and pasturelands given to the remainder of the Kohath division was ten.

27 The descendants of Gershon, another division of the Levites, received two cities and pasturelands from the half-tribe of Manasseh: Golan, in Bashan (a City of Refuge), and Beeshterah.

28,29 The tribe of Issachar gave four cities: Kishion, Daberath, Jarmuth, and Engannim.

30,31 The tribe of Asher gave four cities and pasturelands: Mishal, Abdon, Helkath, and Rehob.

32 The tribe of Naphtali gave: Kedesh, in Galilee (a City of Refuge), Hammoth-dor, and Kartan.

33 So thirteen cities with their pasturelands were assigned to the division of Gershon.

34,35 The remainder of the Levites—the Merari division—were given four cities by the tribe of Zebulun: Jokneam, Kartah, Dimnah, and Nahalal.

36,37 Reuben gave them: Bezer, Jahaz, Kedemoth, and Mephaath. 38,39 Gad gave them four cities with pasturelands: Ramoth (a City of Refuge), Mahanaim, Heshbon, and Jazer.

40 So the Merari division of the Levites was given twelve cities in all.

41,42 The total number of cities and pasturelands given to the Levites came to forty-eight.

43 So in this way the Lord gave to Israel all the land he had promised to their ancestors, and they went in and conquered it and lived there. 44 And the Lord gave them peace, just as he had promised, and no one could stand against them; the Lord helped them destroy all their enemies. 45 Every good thing the Lord had promised them came true.

CHAPTER 22

An Altar for the Eastern Tribes

Joshua now called together the troops from the tribes of Reuben, Gad, and the half-tribe of Manasseh, 2,3 and addressed them as follows:

"You have done as the Lord's disciple Moses commanded you, and have obeyed every order I have given you—every order of the Lord your God. You have not deserted your brother tribes, even though the campaign has lasted for such a long time. 4 And now the Lord our God has given us success and rest as he promised he would. So go home now to the land given you by the Lord's servant Moses, on the other side of the Jordan River. 5 Be sure to continue to obey all of the commandments Moses gave you. Love the Lord and follow his plan for your lives. Cling to him and serve him enthusiastically."

6 So Joshua blessed them and sent them home. 7,8 (Moses had assigned the land of Bashan to the half-tribe of Manasseh, although the other half of the tribe was given land on the west side of the Jordan.) As Joshua sent away these troops, he blessed them and told them to share their great wealth with their relatives back home—their loot of cattle, silver, gold, bronze, iron, and clothing.

9 So the troops of Reuben, Gad, and the

21:43-45 God accomplished for the people of Israel all that he said he would do. The Israelites, for their part, had marched into and taken the land for their possession, so God gave them rest from their enemies. Furthermore, whenever the people served God faithfully and were obedient to his commands, he conquered even the most powerful of their enemies. Israel's problems arose only when they had committed acts of sin against God or had failed to act courageously in faith. Today, each of us faces the same challenge to remain faithful. The Israelites are profound examples of the need to continue to turn our life over to God.

half-tribe of Manasseh left the army of Israel
at Shiloh in Canaan and crossed the Jordan
River to their own homeland of Gilead. 10Be-
fore they went across, while they were still in
Canaan, they built a large monument for
everyone to see, in the shape of an altar.
11But when the rest of Israel heard about
what they had done, 12they mustered an army
at Shiloh and prepared to go to war against
their brother tribes. 13First, however, they sent
a delegation led by Phinehas, the son of Eleazar the priest. They crossed the river and
talked to the tribes of Reuben, Gad, and Manasseh. 14In this delegation were ten high
officials of Israel, one from each of the ten
tribes, and each a clan leader. 15When they
arrived in the land of Gilead they said to the
tribes of Reuben, Gad, and the half-tribe of
Manasseh,
16"The whole congregation of the Lord demands to know why you are sinning against
the God of Israel by turning away from him
and building an altar of rebellion against the
Lord. 17,18Was our guilt at Peor—from which
we have not even yet been cleansed despite
the plague that tormented us—so little that
you must rebel again? For you know that if
you rebel today the Lord will be angry with all
of us tomorrow. 19If you need the altar because
your land is defiled, then join us on our side
of the river where the Lord lives among us in
his Tabernacle, and we will share our land
with you. But do not rebel against the Lord by
building another altar in addition to the only
true altar of our God. 20Don't you remember
that when Achan, the son of Zerah, sinned
against the Lord, the entire nation was punished in addition to the one man who had
sinned?"
21This was the reply of the people of Reuben, Gad, and the half-tribe of Manasseh to
these high officials:
22,23"We swear by Jehovah, the God of gods,
that we have not built the altar in rebellion
against the Lord. He knows (and let all Israel
know it too) that we have not built the altar
to sacrifice burnt offerings or grain offerings
or peace offerings—may the curse of God be
on us if we did. 24,25We have done it because
we love the Lord and because we fear that in
the future your children will say to ours,
'What right do you have to worship the Lord
God of Israel? The Lord has placed the Jordan
River as a barrier between our people and your
people! You have no part in the Lord.' And
your children may make our children stop
worshiping him. 26,27So we decided to build
the altar as a symbol to show our children and
your children that we, too, may worship the
Lord with our burnt offerings and peace offerings and sacrifices, and your children will not
be able to say to ours, 'You have no part in the
Lord our God.' 28If they say this, our children
can reply, 'Look at the altar of the Lord that
our fathers made, patterned after the altar of
Jehovah. It is not for burnt offerings or sacrifices but is a symbol of the relationship with
God that both of us have.' 29Far be it from us
to turn away from the Lord or to rebel against
him by building our own altar for burnt offerings, grain offerings, or sacrifices. Only the
altar in front of the Tabernacle may be used
for that."
30When Phinehas the priest and the high
officials heard this from the tribes of Reuben,
Gad, and Manasseh, they were very happy.
31Phinehas replied to them, "Today we
know that the Lord is among us because you
have not sinned against the Lord as we
thought; instead, you have saved us from
destruction!"
32Then Phinehas and the ten ambassadors
went back to the people of Israel and told
them what had happened, 33and all Israel re-

22:10-20 Outraged that the tribes east of the Jordan had seemingly so quickly turned away from the God of their fathers and set up another altar of worship, the tribes living in the Promised Land prepared to go to war against their kinsmen. Before war broke out, however, wisdom prevailed, and a delegation was sent by the tribes living in the land to challenge the Transjordan tribes to return to God. The delegation boldly confronted their brothers, reminding them of the consequences of past rebellions against God (see Numbers 25:1-9; Joshua 7:1-26) and offering to let these tribes live with them in the Promised Land. Though it is often difficult and painful, we must confront others at times so that all of us can maintain faith. This is why recovery is never an individual process; others must be involved to both encourage and confront.

22:21-29 The Reubenites, the Gadites, and the half-tribe of Manasseh responded in amazement. They explained their actions in order to reestablish their immediate relationship with the rest of Israel. Their actions had been taken to ensure that future generations would know that the tribes east of the Jordan also worshiped the one true God of Israel. In this case, confrontation was effective. Even though it does not always bring the desired response, it is an important part of our recovery process.

joiced and praised God and spoke no more of
war against Reuben and Gad. [34]The people of
Reuben and Gad named the altar "The Altar
of Witness," for they said, "It is a witness
between us and them that Jehovah is our God
too."

CHAPTER 23
Joshua's Final Orders
Long after this, when the Lord had given
success to the people of Israel against their
enemies and when Joshua was very old, [2]he
called for the leaders of Israel—the elders,
judges, and officers—and said to them, "I am
an old man now, [3]and you have seen all that
the Lord your God has done for you during
my lifetime. He has fought for you against
your enemies and has given you their land.
[4,5]And I have divided to you the land of the
nations yet unconquered as well as the land
of those you have already destroyed. All the
land from the Jordan River to the Mediterranean Sea shall be yours, for the Lord your God
will drive out all the people living there now,
and you will live there instead, just as he has
promised you.

[6]"But be very sure to follow all the instructions written in the book of the laws of Moses;
do not deviate from them the least little bit.
[7]Be sure that you do not mix with the heathen
people still remaining in the land; do not
even mention the names of their gods, much
less swear by them or worship them. [8]But
follow the Lord your God just as you have
until now. [9]He has driven out great, strong
nations from before you, and no one has been
able to defeat you. [10]Each one of you has put
to flight a thousand of the enemy, for the
Lord your God fights for you, just as he has
promised. [11]So be very careful to keep on
loving him.

[12]"If you don't, and if you begin to intermarry with the nations around you, [13]then
know for a certainty that the Lord your God
will no longer chase those nations from your
land. Instead, they will be a snare and a trap
to you, a pain in your side and a thorn in your
eyes, and you will disappear from this good
land which the Lord your God has given you.

[14]"Soon I will be going the way of all the
earth—I am going to die.

"You know very well that God's promises to
you have all come true. [15,16]But as certainly as
the Lord has given you the good things he
promised, just as certainly he will bring evil
upon you if you disobey him. For if you worship other gods, he will completely wipe you
out from this good land that the Lord has
given you. His anger will rise hot against you,
and you will quickly perish."

CHAPTER 24
Joshua's Good-bye Speech
Then Joshua summoned all the people of
Israel to him at Shechem, along with their
leaders—the elders, officers, and judges. So

22:30-34 The leaders of the delegation of Israel listened carefully to the words of their brothers. As a result, the western leaders changed their attitude toward the tribes of Reuben, Gad, and the half-tribe of Manasseh from anger to reconciliation and joy. The leaders then praised God for the faithfulness of their eastern brothers and declared peace, thus averting the potential civil war. The east-bank altar thereafter was referred to as "The Altar of Witness" because it was a reminder to all of Israel that the Lord is God. The objective of confrontation always needs to be a loving reconciliation, even though that may not always be the outcome.

23:1-7 Joshua reminded the Israelites that the God of Israel was the one who had given them all their victories, that all of the Promised Land had been apportioned as God had said it would be, and that God would continue to defeat Israel's enemies so that his people would live at peace in the land. The people of Israel, therefore, were not to forsake God or ever to turn to the so-called gods of the nations living within the land. The Israelites' walk with God was an ongoing event, just like our own recovery.

23:14-16 Joshua spoke of reality: God had not failed Israel in the past. All that God said he would do, he did, and all of Israel knew that to be a fact. Joshua then issued a warning to the people. Just as God blessed them because of their acts of obedience, as he had promised, so too would he judge them harshly if they broke their covenant with him and worshiped other gods. In fact, if they were disobedient to God, he would not hesitate even to drive them from the Promised Land, the land he had fought to give them. In a loving relationship, others will hold us accountable for our actions, not because they want to "get" us, but because they want what is best for us.

24:1-13 Speaking on behalf of God, Joshua declared that everything of lasting value that had been done for Israel had been accomplished by God alone. What greater evidence do we need than this account of God's strength and the results that come from acting faithfully to achieve his will? Joshua's story is not unique. Each of us is a testimony either to what God can do when we are faithful or to the tragedy that occurs when we are not.

they came and presented themselves before God.

2Then Joshua addressed them as follows: "The Lord God of Israel says, 'Your ancestors, including Terah the father of Abraham and Nahor, lived east of the Euphrates River; and they worshiped other gods. 3But I took your father Abraham from that land across the river and led him into the land of Canaan and gave him many descendants through Isaac, his son. 4Isaac's children, whom I gave him, were Jacob and Esau. To Esau I gave the area around Mount Seir while Jacob and his children went into Egypt.

5"Then I sent Moses and Aaron to bring terrible plagues upon Egypt; and afterwards I brought my people out as free men. 6But when they arrived at the Red Sea, the Egyptians chased after them with chariots and cavalry. 7Then Israel cried out to me and I put darkness between them and the Egyptians; and I brought the sea crashing in upon the Egyptians, drowning them. You saw what I did. Then Israel lived in the wilderness for many years.

8"Finally I brought you into the land of the Amorites on the other side of the Jordan; and they fought against you, but I destroyed them and gave you their land. 9Then King Balak of Moab started a war against Israel, and he asked Balaam, the son of Beor, to curse you. 10But I wouldn't listen to him. Instead I made him bless you; and so I delivered Israel from him.

11"Then you crossed the Jordan River and came to Jericho. The men of Jericho fought against you, and so did many others—the Perizzites, the Canaanites, the Hittites, the Girgashites, the Hivites, and the Jebusites. Each in turn fought against you, but I destroyed them all. 12And I sent hornets ahead of you to drive out the two kings of the Amorites and their people. It was not your swords or bows that brought you victory! 13I gave you land you had not worked for and cities you did not build—these cities where you are now living. I gave you vineyards and olive groves for food, though you did not plant them.'

14"So revere Jehovah and serve him in sincerity and truth. Put away forever the idols your ancestors worshiped when they lived beyond the Euphrates River and in Egypt. Worship the Lord alone. 15But if you are unwilling to obey the Lord, then decide today whom you will obey. Will it be the gods of your ancestors beyond the Euphrates or the gods of the Amorites here in this land? But as for me and my family, we will serve the Lord."

The People Promise to Obey

16And the people replied, "We would never forsake the Lord and worship other gods! 17For the Lord our God is the one who rescued our fathers from their slavery in the land of Egypt. He is the God who did mighty miracles before the eyes of Israel, as we traveled through the wilderness, and preserved us from our enemies when we passed through their land. 18It was the Lord who drove out the Amorites and the other nations living here in the land. Yes, we choose the Lord, for he alone is our God."

19But Joshua replied to the people, "You can't worship the Lord God, for he is holy and jealous; he will not forgive your rebellion and sins. 20If you forsake him and worship other gods, he will turn upon you and destroy you, even though he has taken care of you for such a long time."

24:14-18 Joshua concluded by challenging the people to serve the true God and to reject the gods their ancestors foolishly served in the wilderness and in Egypt. He then mockingly suggested that if the people were so unwise as to not worship the God of Israel as the only true God, then they should choose to serve either the gods of the Euphrates region or the gods of those heathen nations living in the Promised Land. Joshua and his family, however, would serve the God of Israel. The people responded positively to Joshua's challenge and declared their undying commitment to the one true God. Each day we make a decision whom we will serve, either God or this world. What a wonderful experience to be able to firmly assert that you will only serve God, the Creator!

24:29-33 The great men of Israel had died—Moses, prior to Israel's entry into the Promised Land, and now, after the completion of the initial phase of Israel's conquest, Joshua and Eleazar the priest. How would the Israelites now react to the death of Joshua, who left them without an apparent successor? They responded by serving God. They also demonstrated their commitment to God by burying Joseph's bones in the Promised Land as a testimony to his faith and to God's faithfulness to his people (see Genesis 50:25; Exodus 13:19; Hebrews 11:22). We might ask ourselves this question: Would someone burying our bones do so as a testimony to our faith—or to our faithlessness? If it is faithlessness, we can change that testimony by turning to God today. If it is faith, we must persevere.

21But the people answered, "We choose the
Lord!"

22"You have heard yourselves say it," Joshua
said. "You have chosen to obey the Lord."

"Yes," they replied, "we are witnesses."

23"All right," he said, "then you must destroy all the idols you now own, and you must obey the Lord God of Israel."

24The people replied to Joshua, "Yes, we will worship and obey the Lord alone."

25So Joshua made a covenant with them
that day at Shechem, committing them to a
permanent and binding contract between
themselves and God. 26Joshua recorded the
people's reply in the book of the laws of God
and took a huge stone as a reminder and
rolled it beneath the oak tree that was beside
the Tabernacle.

27Then Joshua said to all the people, "This stone has heard everything the Lord said, so it will be a witness to testify against you if you go back on your word."

28Then Joshua sent the people away to their own sections of the country.

Joshua Dies

29Soon after this he died at the age of 110. 30He
was buried on his own estate at Timnath-serah, in the hill country of Ephraim, on the north side of the mountains of Gaash.

31Israel obeyed the Lord throughout the lifetimes of Joshua and the other old men who had personally witnessed the amazing deeds the Lord had done for Israel.

32The bones of Joseph, the people of Israel had brought them along when they left Egypt—were buried in Shechem, in the parcel of ground Jacob had bought from the sons of Hamor. (The land was located in the territory assigned to the tribes of Joseph.)

33Eleazar, the son of Aaron, also died; he was buried in the hill country of Ephraim, at Gibeah, the city that had been given to his son Phinehas.

REFLECTIONS ON

insights FROM RAHAB'S LIFE

In **Joshua 2:8-14** Rahab willingly admitted her hopeless condition before the God of Israel. She and her people saw no way of escape from the certain doom that would come from the hands of those who served God. Yet, instead of attempting to pursue a hopeless cause as did the others around her, Rahab sought mercy from the only source of help available. Moreover, she was able to secure an effective relationship with the spies on the basis of mutual trust.

In **Joshua 6:22-25** we see that Joshua remembered the promise his spies had made to Rahab the prostitute. He commanded his men to fulfill that promise and to provide safe passage for her and those with her. Following the total destruction of Jericho, Rahab and her relatives began a new life with Israel because they had served God by protecting the spies. God's provision for Rahab should be significant to each of us. God honored her faith and obedience. Since Rahab was a prostitute, he obviously wasn't honoring her perfection. Rahab is a bold reminder that we should come to God as we are rather than try to fix ourselves before we come.

insights FROM ISRAEL'S CEREMONIES OF REMEMBRANCE

Joshua 5:15-24 tells us that Israel's leaders set up a monument to God at Gilgal with the stones from the Jordan River. Joshua explained that this would serve as a reminder of the miracle God had done—the drying up of the flooded Jordan River. This miracle was reminiscent of the way God delivered Israel forty years earlier when he let the Jews cross the Red Sea on dry ground (see Exodus 14). We must remember that God is all-powerful and cares for us. Knowing that God has rescued us in the past can help us trust in his ability to save us today.

In **Joshua 5:10-12** we find the Israelites celebrating the Passover—a remembrance of God's deliverance of his people from Egypt forty years earlier. This undoubtedly bolstered the Israelites' faith as they faced the many battles ahead. We are told that God's miraculous provision of manna was stopped at this time. Now that the Israelites owned a productive land, they no longer needed food from heaven. This was a reminder that God would provide his people with what they needed in various ways, depending on the circumstances, and they would have to trust him to act in various ways in the future. We also find that God will work with us in different ways at varying stages of our recovery. All too often we resent God for not continuing to treat us as newborns in the faith. When life isn't easy, it is not a sign of abandonment by God. It is a sign that he is ready for us to grow in wisdom and faith. God often calls us to struggle in order to grow.

After the great victory recorded in **Joshua 8:24-35**, the people built a monument to God and erected an altar to him at Mount Ebal. At that time, Joshua had the words of the law, the blessings and curses (i.e., boundaries), read to the people to remind them of how God expected them to act in the Promised Land. In setting boundaries for our own behavior, we tend to either make them too rigid or not to develop healthy boundaries at all. Today, just as in Joshua's day, healthy boundaries are formed as we adhere to the teaching of God's Word.

In **Joshua 11:1-9**, Joshua declared that the tribes east of the Jordan had faithfully fulfilled their responsibilities. They had delayed the gratification of enjoying their own reward so that their brothers could receive what God had promised to them. Joshua then reminded them that they were always to love and obey God. Although there was much sorrow at leaving their kinsmen who lived west of the Jordan, there undoubtedly was also much joy for the Reubenites, Gadites, and the half-tribe of Manasseh since they were finally going home to their families. As they crossed the Jordan, the eastern tribes set up a monument to remind them of their kinship with the western tribes and of their loyalty to God.

Joshua understood the holiness of God, but he also was aware of the sinful tendencies of the Israelites. So in **Joshua 24:19-28,** he compelled the people to proclaim once again that they would follow God and that their words would be an eternal witness to their decision. To cement that commitment, Joshua, who had been a rock of faith before God throughout his life, recognized the importance of leaving one more permanent stone memorial as a reminder to the greatness and faithfulness of God. A record of our decision to follow God can be helpful to us in times of temptation. It can remind us that we were serious in our decision and that we are accountable for our actions.

insights FROM JOSHUA'S LIFE

In **Joshua 7:10-12,** God displayed his anger with Joshua, chastising him for complaining and for not having completely rid the people of their sin. The people needed to realize that victory was impossible for those who disobeyed God. We also must realize that our sins don't affect us alone. Our family, friends, and employers are all affected by our choices and our life-style. Rather than hide in shame, God wants us to confess our mistakes to each other. Only then will we be able to overcome the sin in our life.

In **Joshua 10:16-27,** after learning of the capture of the five kings, Joshua wisely commanded his troops not to rest on their laurels but to complete the mission God gave them. Later, while encouraging the Israelites for future battles, Joshua concluded his message by slaying the five kings and hanging them on five trees, so that all would see the victory that God had given. As we acknowledge God's work in our life in public ways, others can be reminded of God's presence in their life and of the victories God has promised.

In **Joshua 10:29-42** we are reminded that Joshua led the people from city to city and from victory to victory. With each day came new success as enemy after enemy was defeated. Each battle was fought in accordance with the commands of God. We see that no enemy will ever prove to be too strong for God to defeat. If God could handle these great armies, he will certainly be able to handle our personal problems. We can allow him to work by daily submitting to his plan. Often we do not experience victory over our struggles because after some initial progress, we stop the journey with God and go into battle alone, under our own power. We must never be satisfied with one victory when God has a lifetime of victories planned for us.

Despite Joshua's advanced age, **Joshua 13:1** tells us that God placed additional challenges before him. Retirement from doing God's will is not an option. We are called to follow God's will throughout our life, until God's time for us to "stop fighting and rest" finally arrives (2 Timothy 4:6-8).

In **Joshua 19:49-50,** Joshua was permitted to select a city for his inheritance. He could have chosen any city in the Promised Land, but he chose to live within the territory of Ephraim, the tribe from which he came (see Numbers 13:8, 16). Joshua remembered his roots and honored them with his decision. We lose our way when we forget where we've come from. Although our roots are not perfect, we can celebrate what is good about them and honor God in doing so.

In **Joshua 23:8-13,** Joshua continued to challenge the Israelites to maintain a strong faith in God, always remembering that God had accomplished a great work in defeating the powerful nations of the land on Israel's behalf. God gives more than enough courage and strength to succeed against all odds. In return, his people are to love him with full commitment, knowing that if they turn away from the true God to other so-called gods, God will no longer fight on their side. Each one of us will be tempted to turn our life over to a god that appears to immediately gratify our urges. God provides a way out of this temptation by clearly stating that failure is always preceded by faithless acts. If we want success, we must follow the true God.

JUDGES

THE BIG PICTURE

- A. PROLOGUE: A PATTERN OF UNFINISHED RECOVERY (1:1–3:6)
  1. Not Fully Dealing with the Issues (1:1–2:5)
  2. Making the Same Mistake Over and Over (2:6–3:6)
- B. CASE HISTORIES: THE UPS AND DOWNS OF INCOMPLETE RECOVERY (3:7–16:31)
  1. Rescued by Othniel, Ehud, and Shamgar (3:7-31)
  2. Rescued by Deborah and Barak (4:1–5:31)
  3. Rescued by Gideon (6:1–8:35)
  4. Rescued from Abimelech, the "In-house" Abuser (9:1-57)
  5. Rescued by Tola, Jair, Jephthah, Ibzan, Elon, and Abdon (10:1–12:15)
  6. Rescued by Samson (13:1–16:31)
- C. EPILOGUE: CLASSIC EXAMPLES OF GOING YOUR OWN WAY IN DENIAL (17:1–21:25)
  1. "Doing Your Own Thing" Religiously (17:1–18:31)
  2. "Doing Your Own Thing" Morally (19:1–21:25)

The conquest of the Promised Land under Joshua had been a miraculous success. It wasn't long, however, before the people forgot what had made it all possible—faith in God and obedience to his commands. They became trapped in a four-step spiritual cycle: (1) they fell into sin, (2) they were enslaved by an oppressor, (3) they cried out to God for help, and (4) God sent a leader (or judge) to deliver them. At the end of each painful round, there was a temporary period of faithfulness and stability. But soon, most of the people slipped back into the same vicious cycle of relapse.

The book of Judges shows what happens to a society when its citizens do whatever they choose (17:6). The people of Israel refused to learn from their past mistakes. They blinded themselves to the needs of others and to the commands of God. As a result, they became trapped by their individual delusions and brought suffering on themselves and the people around them. They refused to follow the path to freedom by obeying God's program for righteous and healthy living. Doing things our way still leads to enslavement and suffering; following God's program is the only path to freedom.

Let us learn from Israel's mistakes. We would be wise to notice that Israel's failures often came after great victories. Success is sometimes the first step toward a fall. We must humbly take inventory of our activities and relationships, keeping our eyes on God and obeying his will for us. But when we do fail, we can be sure that God is listening to our cries for help. He wants to deliver us once again.

THE BOTTOM LINE

PURPOSE: To see how tragic an incomplete recovery program can be and how dysfunctional patterns tend to continue from one generation to the next. And to see how God is ready to lift us up when we look to him for help. AUTHOR: Tradition attributes it to Samuel, though it could have been one of his contemporaries. AUDIENCE: The people of Israel. DATE WRITTEN: Probably between 1050–1000 B.C. SETTING: Various parts of the Promised Land of Israel. KEY VERSE: "For in those days Israel had no king, so everyone did whatever he wanted to—whatever seemed right in his own eyes" (17:6). KEY PLACES: Israel, Aram, Moab, Midian, Ammon, Philistia. KEY PEOPLE AND RELATIONSHIPS: Othniel, Ehud, Deborah and Barak, Gideon, Abimelech, Jephthah, Samson and Delilah.

RECOVERY THEMES

The Danger of Pride: It is so easy to begin to think we have "arrived." The Israelites had arrived in the Promised Land, their physical destination. What did they have to worry about now? After all, they were God's chosen people. They still had to learn, however, that "pride ends in a fall" (Proverbs 29:23). In the book of Judges, the Israelites discovered repeatedly that overconfidence leads to relapse. What was true back then is still true today. Recovery is an ongoing process that requires us to be vigilant in self-examination. To be sustained in recovery demands that we depend on God one day at a time.

The Cycle of Failure: Why do intelligent people fall repeatedly to the same tragic mistakes? One unhealthy marriage ends in divorce only to be followed by another. Recovery from an addiction only ends in a relapse. Again and again, God delivered the Israelites from their troubles. For short periods of time, the people gratefully guarded their faith and were consistent in their worship. But then their overconfidence set them up for additional failure. The frequency with which such cyclical failures occur almost makes one think such patterns are inevitable. They are not inevitable, but rather the result of failing to realize that recovery is a lifelong process and that we are continually in need of help.

Suffering the Consequences: God did not protect his people from the painful consequences of their actions. He allowed them to suffer the consequences so they could learn some valuable lessons. Facing the consequences of our actions can be a healthy part of our recovery. Whenever the Israelites finally "hit bottom" and admitted their helplessness, God moved in and delivered them. If they had continually depended on God and admitted their helplessness, they would have been able to break the cycle permanently. We never outgrow the early steps of our recovery. We are powerless to handle the chaos in our life, and we need to continually turn it over to God.

God Uses Flawed People: A number of the heroes of Judges were most notable for their flaws. Barak refused to fight for God without the help of the prophetess, Deborah. Gideon needed numerous affirmations before he would step out in faith for God. Samson's flaws are legendary, but God still used him to fight the enemies of Israel. We do not need to be whole in order to call upon God and receive help. We do not need to be whole to be used by God for his glory. We simply need to see and admit our need. We cannot earn God's blessing; we simply receive his gifts of grace.

CHAPTER 1

God Gives Victory

After Joshua died, the nation of Israel went to
the Lord to receive his instructions.
"Which of our tribes should be the first to
go to war against the Canaanites?" they inquired.
2God's answer came, "Judah. And I will give
them a great victory."
3The leaders of the tribe of Judah, however,
asked help from the tribe of Simeon. "Join us
in clearing out the people living in the territory allotted to us," they said, "and then we
will help you conquer yours." So the army of
Simeon went with the army of Judah. 4-6And
the Lord helped them defeat the Canaanites
and Perizzites, so that ten thousand of the
enemy were slain at Bezek. King Adoni-bezek
escaped, but the Israeli army soon captured
him and cut off his thumbs and big toes.
7"I have treated seventy kings in this same
manner and have fed them the scraps under
my table!" King Adoni-bezek said. "Now God
has paid me back." He was taken to Jerusalem
and died there.
8(Judah had conquered Jerusalem and massacred its people, setting the city on fire.)
9Afterward the army of Judah fought the Canaanites in the hill country and in the Negeb,
as well as on the coastal plains. 10Then Judah
marched against the Canaanites in Hebron
(formerly called Kiriath-arba), destroying the
cities of Sheshai, Ahiman, and Talmai. 11Later
they attacked the city of Debir (formerly
called Kiriath-sepher).

Caleb and His Daughter

12"Who will lead the attack against Debir?"
Caleb challenged them. "Whoever conquers
it shall have my daughter Achsah as his wife!"

1:1ff The book of Judges will give us an idea of the courage it takes to enter new territory in life. Even though much of the Promised Land (see Genesis 15:18-21) had already been taken under Joshua, it was still necessary to address the present reality of the enemies still living there. Only when the conquest was completed could Israel focus on building a new life in their new land. In the same way, it is important that we conquer and control our dependencies before we try to build a new life.

13Caleb's nephew, Othniel, son of his younger brother Kenaz, volunteered to lead the
attack; and he conquered the city and won
Achsah as his bride. 14As they were leaving for
their new home, she urged him to ask her
father for an additional piece of land. She
dismounted from her donkey to speak to Caleb about it.

"What do you wish?" he asked.

15And she replied, "You have been kind
enough to give me land in the Negeb, but
please give us springs of water too."

So Caleb gave her the upper and lower
springs.

An Incomplete Conquest

16When the tribe of Judah moved into its new
land in the Negeb wilderness south of Arad,
the descendants of Moses' father-in-law—
members of the Kenite tribe—accompanied
them. They left their homes in Jericho, "The
City of Palm Trees," and the two tribes lived
together after that. 17Afterwards the army of
Judah joined Simeon's, and they fought the
Canaanites at the city of Zephath and massacred all its people. So now the city is named
Hormah (meaning, "massacred"). 18The army
of Judah also conquered the cities of Gaza,
Ashkelon, and Ekron, with their surrounding
villages. 19The Lord helped the tribe of Judah
exterminate the people of the hill country,
though they failed in their attempt to conquer the people of the valley, who had iron
chariots.

20The city of Hebron was given to Caleb as
the Lord had promised; so Caleb drove out
the inhabitants of the city; they were descendants of the three sons of Anak.

21The tribe of Benjamin failed to exterminate the Jebusites living in their part of the
city of Jerusalem, so they still live there today,
mingled with the Israelis.

22,23As for the tribe of Joseph, they attacked
the city of Bethel, formerly known as Luz, and
the Lord was with them. First they sent
scouts, 24who captured a man coming out of
the city. They offered to spare his life and that
of his family if he would show them the
entrance passage through the wall. 25So he
showed them how to get in, and they massacred the entire population except for this man
and his family. 26Later the man moved to Syria
and founded a city there, naming it Luz, too,
as it is still known today.

27The tribe of Manasseh failed to drive out
the people living in Beth-shean, Taanach,
Dor, Ibleam, Megiddo, with their surrounding
towns; so the Canaanites stayed there. 28In
later years when the Israelis were stronger,
they put the Canaanites to work as slaves, but
never did force them to leave the country.
29This was also true of the Canaanites living
in Gezer; they still live among the tribe of
Ephraim.

30And the tribe of Zebulun did not massacre
the people of Kitron or Nahalol, but made
them their slaves; 31,32nor did the tribe of
Asher drive out the residents of Acco, Sidon,
Ahlab, Achzib, Helbah, Aphik, or Rehob; so
the Israelis still live among the Canaanites,
who were the original people of that land.
33And the tribe of Naphtali did not drive out
the people of Beth-shemesh or of Beth-anath,
so these people continue to live among them
as servants.

34As for the tribe of Dan, the Amorites
forced them into the hill country and
wouldn't let them come down into the valley;
35but when the Amorites later spread into
Mount Heres, Aijalon, and Shaalbim, the tribe
of Joseph conquered them and made them
their slaves. 36The boundary of the Amorites
begins at the ascent of Scorpion Pass, runs to
a spot called The Rock, and continues upward
from there.

CHAPTER 2

The Covenant Is Broken

One day the Angel of the Lord arrived at
Bochim, coming from Gilgal, and announced

1:19-36 The last half of this chapter shows how incomplete Israel's conquest of the Promised Land really was. God had promised to be with them and guide them in this difficult process. As they displayed courage and faith in God, God indeed brought them numerous victories. But lack of perseverance and faltering courage stopped God's people short of their goal. We must also persevere and place our faith in God if we desire to recover fully.

2:1-5 The Angel of the Lord stated in no uncertain terms that the foundational reason for Israel's half-completed conquest of the Promised Land was their halfhearted commitment to God. They allowed the altars of the various Canaanite peoples to remain, and those religious and moral temptations became repeated points of failure for God's people. To Israel's credit, they repented, attempting to set things right with God. No matter what we have done, we can turn to God. God will forgive us, but we must ask for that forgiveness.

to the people of Israel, "I brought you out of
Egypt into this land that I promised to your
ancestors, and I said that I would never break
my covenant with you, 2if you, on your part,
would make no peace treaties with the people
living in this land; I told you to destroy their
heathen altars. Why have you not obeyed?
3And now since you have broken the contract,
it is no longer in effect, and I no longer promise to destroy the nations living in your land;
rather, they shall be thorns in your sides, and
their gods will be a constant temptation to
you."
4The people broke into tears as the Angel
finished speaking; 5so the name of that place
was called "Bochim" (meaning, "the place
where people wept"). Then they offered sacrifices to the Lord.

Joshua Dies

6When Joshua finally disbanded the armies of
Israel, the tribes moved into their new territories and took possession of the land. 7-9Joshua,
the man of God, died at the age of 110 and
was buried at the edge of his property in
Timnath-heres, in the hill country of
Ephraim, north of Mount Gaash. The people
had remained true to the Lord throughout
Joshua's lifetime, and as long afterward as the
old men of his generation were still living—
those who had seen the mighty miracles the
Lord had done for Israel.

The People Abandon God

10But finally all that generation died; and the
next generation did not worship Jehovah as
their God and did not care about the mighty
miracles he had done for Israel. 11They did
many things that the Lord had expressly forbidden, including the worshiping of heathen
gods. 12-14They abandoned Jehovah, the God
loved and worshiped by their ancestors—the
God who had brought them out of Egypt.
Instead, they were worshiping and bowing
low before the idols of the neighboring nations. So the anger of the Lord flamed out
against all Israel. He left them to the mercy of
their enemies, for they had departed from
Jehovah and were worshiping Baal and the
Ashtaroth idols.

Judges for the People

15So now when the nation of Israel went out
to battle against its enemies, the Lord blocked
their path. He had warned them about this,
and in fact had vowed that he would do it. But
when the people were in this terrible plight,
16the Lord raised up judges to save them from
their enemies.
17Yet even then Israel would not listen to
the judges, but broke faith with Jehovah by
worshiping other gods instead. How quickly
they turned away from the true faith of their
ancestors, for they refused to obey God's commands. 18Each judge rescued the people of
Israel from their enemies throughout his lifetime, for the Lord was moved to pity by the
groaning of his people under their crushing
oppressions; so he helped them as long as that
judge lived. 19But when the judge died, the
people turned from doing right and behaved
even worse than their ancestors had. They
prayed to heathen gods again, throwing
themselves to the ground in humble worship.
They stubbornly returned to the evil customs
of the nations around them.
20Then the anger of the Lord would flame
out against Israel again. He declared, "Because
these people have violated the treaty I made
with their ancestors, 21I will no longer drive
out the nations left unconquered by Joshua
when he died. 22Instead, I will use these nations to test my people, to see whether or not

---

2:11-19 Here is seen the cycle of short-term recovery that is echoed throughout Judges. Because of prolonged denial of their sin, the people repeatedly ended up in spiritual and physical slavery to an oppressor. In their misery, they admitted their helplessness by praying to God. Then and only then did God provide the judges to free them from oppression. Tragically, it was only a matter of time before Israel committed the same mistakes over again. We cannot stand alone against our dependencies. We must also rely upon God, who will support our efforts, sustaining our recovery with his gracious power. If we fall, God is waiting for our cries, and he will respond with the help we need.

2:20–3:6 God used the wicked nations in the land to test the Israelites' obedience. God did not use these tests spitefully, in order to catch the Israelites and punish them. He only wanted to show them the painful consequences of living apart from his will. If we are experiencing pain and turmoil now, God may be testing us. Are we following his will? Are our addictions getting the better of us and keeping us from doing what we know is right? If so, we can turn to God and ask him to rescue us.

they will obey the Lord as their ancestors did."

23So the Lord left those nations in the land and did not drive them out, nor let Israel destroy them.

CHAPTER 3

Enemies in the Land

Here is a list of the nations the Lord left in the land to test the new generation of Israel who had not experienced the wars of Canaan. For God wanted to give opportunity to the youth of Israel to exercise faith and obedience in conquering their enemies: the Philistines (five cities), the Canaanites, the Sidonians, the Hivites living in Mount Lebanon, from Baal-hermon to the entrance of Hamath. 4These people were a test to the new generation of Israel, to see whether they would obey the commandments the Lord had given to them through Moses.

Othniel Delivers Israel

5So Israel lived among the Canaanites, Hittites, Hivites, Perizzites, Amorites, and Jebusites. 6But instead of destroying them, the people of Israel intermarried with them. The young men of Israel took their girls as wives, and the Israeli girls married their men. And soon Israel was worshiping their gods. 7So the people of Israel were very evil in God's sight, for they turned against Jehovah their God and worshiped Baal and the Asheroth idols.

8Then the anger of the Lord flamed out against Israel, and he let King Cushan-rishathaim of eastern Syria conquer them. They were under his rule for eight years. 9But when Israel cried out to the Lord, he gave them Caleb's nephew, Othniel (son of Kenaz, Caleb's younger brother) to save them. 10The Spirit of the Lord took control of him, and he reformed and purged Israel so that when he led the forces of Israel against the army of King Cushan-rishathaim, the Lord helped Israel conquer him completely.

11Then, for forty years under Othniel, there was peace in the land. But when Othniel died,12the people of Israel turned once again to their sinful ways, so God helped King Eglon of Moab to conquer part of Israel at that time. 13Allied with him were the armies of the Ammonites and the Amalekites. These forces defeated the Israelis and took possession of Jericho, often called "The City of Palm Trees." 14For the next eighteen years the people of Israel were required to pay crushing taxes to King Eglon.

Ehud Defeats Moab

15But when they cried to the Lord, he sent them a savior, Ehud (son of Gera, a Benjaminite), who was left-handed. Ehud was the man chosen to carry Israel's annual tax money to the Moabite capital. 16Before he went on this journey, he made himself a double-edged dagger eighteen inches long and hid it in his clothing, strapped against his right thigh. 17-19After delivering the money to King Eglon (who, by the way, was very fat!), he started home again. But outside the city, at the quarries of Gilgal, he sent his companions on and returned alone to the king.

"I have a secret message for you," he told him.

The king immediately dismissed all those who were with him so that he could have a private interview. 20Ehud walked over to him as he was sitting in a cool upstairs room and said to him, "It is a message from God!"

King Eglon stood up at once to receive it, 21whereupon Ehud reached beneath his robe with his strong left hand, pulled out the double-bladed dagger strapped against his right thigh, and plunged it deep into the king's belly. 22,23The hilt of the dagger disappeared beneath the flesh, and the fat closed over it as the entrails oozed out. Leaving the dagger there, Ehud locked the doors behind him and escaped across an upstairs porch.

24When the king's servants returned and saw that the doors were locked, they waited, thinking that perhaps he was using the bath-

---

3:7-10 Notice that the rescue of Israel by Othniel and the beginning of Israel's recovery from Syrian oppression was governed by the power of the Holy Spirit. As believers, we have the Holy Spirit living inside of us (1 Corinthians 6:19) and guiding us (Galatians 5:18). He is always there to give us direction, encouragement, and power as we face our problems.

3:11-30 It was Ehud's distinctiveness as a left-handed warrior that made possible his assassination of Eglon, the Moabite King. If he had been right-handed, his weapon would have been found. People often view their unique characteristics as liabilities rather than as positive attributes. God has made us the way we are for a purpose. We should not complain about our differences; we should use our unique abilities to help others and to serve God. God isn't running an assembly line; he custom-builds all of his people. (See 1 Corinthians 12 for a discussion of the differences among God's people.)

room. [25]But when, after a long time, he still didn't come out, they became concerned and got a key. And when they opened the door, they found their master dead on the floor.

[26]Meanwhile Ehud had escaped past the quarries to Seirah. [27]When he arrived in the hill country of Ephraim, he blew a trumpet as a call to arms and mustered an army under his own command.

[28]"Follow me," he told them, "for the Lord has put your enemies, the Moabites, at your mercy!"

The army then proceeded to seize the fords of the Jordan River near Moab, preventing anyone from crossing. [29]Then they attacked the Moabites and killed about ten thousand of the strongest and most skillful of their fighting men, letting not one escape. [30]So Moab was conquered by Israel that day, and the land was at peace for the next eighty years.

Shamgar

[31]The next judge after Ehud was Shamgar (son of Anath). He once killed six hundred Philistines with an ox goad, thereby saving Israel from disaster.

CHAPTER 4

Deborah and Barak

After Ehud's death the people of Israel again sinned against the Lord, [2,3]so the Lord let them be conquered by King Jabin of Hazor, in Canaan. The commander-in-chief of his army was Sisera, who lived in Harosheth-hagoiim. He had nine hundred iron chariots and made life unbearable for the Israelis for twenty years. But finally they begged the Lord for help.

[4]Israel's leader at that time, the one who was responsible for bringing the people back to God, was Deborah, a prophetess, the wife of Lappidoth. [5]She held court at a place now called "Deborah's Palm Tree," between Ramah and Bethel, in the hill country of Ephraim; and the Israelites came to her to decide their disputes.

[6]One day she summoned Barak (son of Abinoam), who lived in Kedesh, in the land of Naphtali, and said to him, "The Lord God of Israel has commanded you to mobilize ten thousand men from the tribes of Naphtali and Zebulun. Lead them to Mount Tabor [7]to fight King Jabin's mighty army with all his chariots, under General Sisera's command. The Lord says, 'I will draw them to the Kishon River, and you will defeat them there.'"

[8]"I'll go, but only if you go with me!" Barak told her.

[9]"All right," she replied, "I'll go with you; but I'm warning you now that the honor of conquering Sisera will go to a woman instead of to you!" So she went with him to Kedesh.

[10]When Barak summoned the men of Zebulun and Naphtali to mobilize at Kedesh, ten thousand men volunteered. And Deborah marched with them. [11](Heber, the Kenite—the Kenites were the descendants of Moses' father-in-law Hobab—had moved away from the rest of his clan, and had been living in various places as far away as the Oak of Zaanannim, near Kedesh.) [12]When General Sisera was told that Barak and his army were camped at Mount Tabor, [13]he mobilized his entire army, including the nine hundred iron chariots, and marched from Harosheth-hagoiim to the Kishon River.

[14]Then Deborah said to Barak, "Now is the time for action! The Lord leads on! He has already delivered Sisera into your hand!"

So Barak led his ten thousand men down the slopes of Mount Tabor into battle.

[15]Then the Lord threw the enemy into a panic, both the soldiers and the charioteers, and Sisera leaped from his chariot and escaped on foot. [16]Barak and his men chased the enemy and the chariots as far as Harosheth-hagoiim, until all of Sisera's army was destroyed; not one man was left alive. [17]Meanwhile, Sisera had escaped to the tent of Jael, the wife of Heber the Kenite, for there was a mutual-assistance agreement between King Jabin of Hazor and the clan of Heber.

[18]Jael went out to meet Sisera and said to him, "Come into my tent, sir. You will be safe here in our protection. Don't be afraid." So he went into her tent, and she covered him with a blanket.

4:4-9 Up until now, Deborah had served as a prophetess of God in Israel. Here she was called to take part in a military campaign to overthrow the Canaanite oppressors. Though this was new ground for her, she didn't hesitate for a minute. She trusted that God would care for and direct her. Barak, however, put more trust in Deborah than in God. Because of Barak's lack of faith, God had to accomplish his task through another. We have the potential to assist others recovering from situations that have plagued us in the past. But if we don't demonstrate the courage to lead, God may not be able to use us to help.

DEBORAH & BARAK

In a lawless, enemy-occupied country, a mother in Israel became a mother to Israel. Chosen by God, Deborah gained national prominence as a prophetess and judge during one of her country's blackest hours. Considering Israel's male-dominated culture, it was remarkable that a woman would be selected for such a task, but Deborah was a remarkable woman. She never hesitated to assume leadership, nor was she reluctant to later risk her life in a military campaign. She is seen as full of faith, courage, and confidence in God's power and promises. She turned her life over to God, making herself available to him and trusting him for the outcome.

Under God's direction, Deborah called Barak of Kedesh to assemble ten thousand men at Mount Tabor, in order to draw the enemy into battle. Barak was reluctant. This reluctance may have been prompted by insecurity, self-doubt, lack of faith, fear, concern over the reliability of Deborah's message, or even simple pragmatism in the face of terrible odds. Nonetheless, Barak did step out in faith, leading his outmanned and outclassed troops against a formidable foe. But the battle was God's. The Kenite woman, Jael, wrapped up the loose ends of the victory by killing Sisera in his sleep.

Barak's reticence had the expected repercussions. He was not only denied the honor of dispatching his enemy, but he saw the privilege go to a pagan female. Still, no mention of Barak's lapse is made in the epic song in chapter 5. It is also Barak, despite his timidity, who finds himself numbered among the heroes of faith in Hebrews 11. Just as for us, it was his final obedience, not his initial hesitance, that God found significant. God always commends our commitment while forgetting our failure. He did this with Barak and continues to do so with all those who trust him.

STRENGTHS AND ACCOMPLISHMENTS:
- Deborah's confidence in God gave her courage in difficult situations.
- Deborah proved to be a willing risk-taker for God.
- Despite initial reluctance, Barak demonstrated obedience to God.

WEAKNESSES AND MISTAKES:
- Barak hesitated before obeying God.

LESSONS FROM THEIR LIVES:
- Deborah's prominence demonstrates the value of women in God's sight.
- Lack of faith and obedience leads to oppression.
- God forgets the failures as he commends obedience and trust.
- A society's well-being depends on its faithfulness to God.

KEY VERSE:
"Praise the Lord! Israel's leaders bravely led; The people gladly followed! Yes, bless the Lord!" (Judges 5:2).

The story of Deborah and Barak is told in Judges 4–5. Barak is also mentioned in Hebrews 11:32.

19"Please give me some water," he said, "for I am very thirsty." So she gave him some milk and covered him again.

20"Stand in the door of the tent," he told her, "and if anyone comes by, looking for me, tell them that no one is here."

21Then Jael took a sharp tent peg and a hammer and, quietly creeping up to him as he slept, she drove the peg through his temples and into the ground; and so he died, for he was fast asleep from weariness.

22When Barak came by looking for Sisera, Jael went out to meet him and said, "Come, and I will show you the man you are looking for."

So he followed her into the tent and found Sisera lying there dead, with the tent peg through his temples.
23So that day the Lord used Israel to subdue King Jabin of Canaan.
24And from that time on Israel became stronger and stronger against King Jabin, until he and all his people were destroyed.

CHAPTER 5

Song of Deborah and Barak

Then Deborah and Barak sang this song about the wonderful victory:

2"Praise the Lord!
Israel's leaders bravely led;
The people gladly followed!

Yes, bless the Lord!
[3]Listen, O you kings and princes,
For I shall sing about the Lord,
The God of Israel.
[4]When you led us out from Seir,
Out across the fields of Edom,
The earth trembled
And the sky poured down its rain.
[5]Yes, even Mount Sinai quaked
At the presence of the God of Israel!
[6]In the days of Shamgar and of Jael,
The main roads were deserted.
Travelers used the narrow, crooked side
paths.
[7]Israel's population dwindled,
Until Deborah became a mother to Israel.
[8]When Israel chose new gods,
Everything collapsed.
Our masters would not let us have
A shield or spear.
Among forty thousand men of Israel,
Not a weapon could be found!
[9]How I rejoice
In the leaders of Israel
Who offered themselves so willingly!
Praise the Lord!
[10]Let all Israel, rich and poor,
Join in his praises—
Those who ride on white donkeys
And sit on rich carpets,
And those who are poor and must walk.
[11]The village musicians
Gather at the village well
To sing of the triumphs of the Lord.
Again and again they sing the ballad
Of how the Lord saved Israel
With an army of peasants!
The people of the Lord
Marched through the gates!
[12]Awake, O Deborah, and sing!
Arise, O Barak!
O son of Abinoam, lead away your
captives!
[13,14]Down from Mount Tabor marched the
noble remnant.
The people of the Lord
Marched down against great odds.
They came from Ephraim and Benjamin,
From Machir and from Zebulun.
[15]Down into the valley
Went the princes of Issachar
With Deborah and Barak.
At God's command they rushed into the
valley.
(But the tribe of Reuben didn't go.
[16]Why did you sit at home among the
sheepfolds,
Playing your shepherd pipes?
Yes, the tribe of Reuben has an uneasy
conscience.
[17]Why did Gilead remain across the
Jordan,
And why did Dan remain with his ships?
And why did Asher sit unmoved
Upon the seashore,
At ease beside his harbors?)
[18]But the tribes of Zebulun and Naphtali
Dared to die upon the fields of battle.
[19]The kings of Canaan fought in Taanach
By Megiddo's springs,
But did not win the victory.
[20]The very stars of heaven
Fought Sisera.
[21]The rushing Kishon River
Swept them away.
March on, my soul, with strength!
[22]Hear the stamping
Of the horsehoofs of the enemy!
See the prancing of his steeds!
[23]But the Angel of Jehovah
Put a curse on Meroz.
'Curse them bitterly,' he said,
'Because they did not come to help the
Lord
Against his enemies.'
[24]Blessed be Jael,
The wife of Heber the Kenite—

5:7, 12, 15 In this song of victory, the role of Deborah is emphasized. Women in ancient Israel rarely rose to positions of leadership. But Deborah's courage and faith in God made her an ideal prophetess. Then she was called to lead the forces of Israel against the oppressive Canaanites. What tremendous faith it must have taken for Deborah to assume this unlikely position! Victory can come even when God puts us in positions we are uncomfortable with. We must trust God's promises to us. "Is anything too hard for God?" (Genesis 18:14).

5:24-27 The other heroine of this beautiful song is Jael. Notice that Barak, who had faltered in regard to God's call, is barely mentioned. Again, it took amazing courage for Jael to do away with Sisera. She trusted God to direct and protect her as she did away with the commander of the oppressing army. This act of courage delivered many from bondage, giving them an opportunity to build a new life. If we expect any changes to take place in our life, we must take action against our oppressors.

READ JUDGES 5:1-12

GOD grant me the serenity to accept the things I cannot change the courage to change the things I can and the wisdom to know the difference AMEN

There are times when chaos reigns in our life because others are not willing or able to fulfill the role they should play. When this happens, we often suffer from the lack of leadership and protection. We may feel frustrated and angry.

The time of the judges was a time of confusion for Israel. Each person did what was right in his own eyes instead of obeying God's law. They were oppressed by tyrants, one of whom was General Sisera, who "made life unbearable for the Israelis for twenty years" (Judges 4:3). At this time God chose Deborah to be a judge. Her job was to decide the disputes of the people.

One day Deborah summoned a man named Barak and told him that God would use him to defeat the army of Sisera. "'I'll go, but only if you go with me!' Barak told her" (4:8). So Deborah agreed to go along, but she said, "I'm warning you now that the honor of conquering Sisera will go to a woman instead of to you!" (4:9). Barak lacked the faith to take on the responsibilities God had chosen him for. In the end, General Sisera did die at the hands of a woman. In the victory song, Deborah was honored. They sang, "Israel's population dwindled, until Deborah became a mother to Israel" (Judges 5:7).

When others don't fulfill their rightful duty and role, we have the option of finding a way to cope, with God's help. Deborah compensated for Barak's lack of faith. We don't have to endure the ongoing effects of other people's limitations. And we don't have to accept the painful circumstances that their weaknesses create. ***Turn to page 273, Judges 7.***

Yes, may she be blessed
Above all women who live in tents.
25He asked for water
And she gave him milk in a beautiful cup!
26Then she took a tent pin and a
  workman's hammer
And pierced Sisera's temples,
Crushing his head.
She pounded the tent pin through his
  head.
27He sank, he fell, he lay dead at her feet.
28The mother of Sisera watched through
  the window
For his return.
'Why is his chariot so long in coming?
Why don't we hear the sound of the
  wheels?'
29But her ladies-in-waiting—and she
  herself—replied,
30'There is much loot to be divided,
And it takes time.
Each man receives a girl or two;
And Sisera will get gorgeous robes,
And he will bring home
Many gifts for me.'
31O Lord, may all your enemies
Perish as Sisera did,
But may those who love the Lord
Shine as the sun!"

After that there was peace in the land for forty years.

CHAPTER 6

God Calls Gideon

Then the people of Israel began once again to
worship other gods, and once again the Lord
let their enemies harass them. This time it was
by the people of Midian, for seven years. 2The
Midianites were so cruel that the Israelis took
to the mountains, living in caves and dens.
3,4When they planted their seed, marauders

from Midian, Amalek, and other neighboring nations came and destroyed their crops and plundered the countryside as far away as Gaza, leaving nothing to eat and taking away all their sheep, oxen, and donkeys. [5]These
enemy hordes arrived on droves of camels too numerous to count and stayed until the land was completely stripped and devastated. [6,7]So
Israel was reduced to abject poverty because of the Midianites. Then at last the people of Israel began to cry out to the Lord for help.

[8]However, the Lord's reply through the prophet he sent to them was this: "The Lord God of Israel brought you out of slavery in Egypt, [9]and rescued you from the Egyptians
and from all who were cruel to you, and drove out your enemies before you, and gave you their land. [10]He told you he is the Lord your
God, and you must not worship the gods of the Amorites who live around you on every side. But you have not listened to him."

[11]But one day the Angel of the Lord came and sat beneath the oak tree at Ophrah, on the farm of Joash the Abiezrite. Joash's son, Gideon, had been threshing wheat by hand in the bottom of a grape press—a pit where grapes were pressed to make wine—for he was hiding from the Midianites.

[12]The Angel of the Lord appeared to him and said, "Mighty soldier, the Lord is with you!"

[13]"Stranger," Gideon replied, "if the Lord is with us, why has all this happened to us? And where are all the miracles our ancestors have told us about—such as when God brought them out of Egypt? Now the Lord has thrown us away and has let the Midianites completely ruin us."

[14]Then the Lord turned to him and said, "I will make you strong! Go and save Israel from the Midianites! I am sending you!"

[15]But Gideon replied, "Sir, how can *I* save Israel? My family is the poorest in the whole tribe of Manasseh, and I am the least thought of in the entire family!"

[16]Whereupon the Lord said to him, "But I, Jehovah, will be with you! And you shall quickly destroy the Midianite hordes!"

[17]Gideon replied, "If it is really true that you are going to help me like that, then do some miracle to prove it! Prove that it is really Jehovah who is talking to me! [18]But stay here
until I go and get a present for you."

"All right," the Angel agreed. "I'll stay here until you return."

[19]Gideon hurried home and roasted a young goat and baked some unleavened bread from a bushel of flour. Then, carrying the meat in a basket and broth in a pot, he took it out to the Angel, who was beneath the oak tree, and presented it to him.

[20]The Angel said to him, "Place the meat and the bread upon that rock over there, and pour the broth over it."

When Gideon had followed these instructions, [21]the Angel touched the meat and bread
with his staff, and fire flamed up from the rock and consumed them! And suddenly the Angel was gone!

[22]When Gideon realized that it had indeed been the Angel of the Lord, he cried out, "Alas, O Lord God, for I have seen the Angel of the Lord face to face!"

[23]"It's all right," the Lord replied. "Don't be afraid! You shall not die."

Gideon Tears Down Idols

[24]And Gideon built an altar there and named it "The Altar of Peace with Jehovah." (The altar is still there in Ophrah in the land of the Abiezrites.) [25]That night the Lord told Gideon
to hitch his father's best ox to the family altar of Baal and pull it down, and to cut down the

---

6:11-15 Gideon responded to the message of the Angel with little faith or hope. He was so used to the oppression of the Midianites that he had little confidence that things could ever be any different. Not only did Gideon view himself as weak and insignificant, he also viewed God with distrust, as being unfaithful to his covenant people. This is the typical response of a person trying to cope with terrible circumstances. We become so worn down by continual pain that we lose hope of ever breaking free. We are deeply aware of our own helplessness. But this is the starting point for recovery. Gideon had admitted that he was helpless; now he only needed to discover that God was able to deliver him.

6:22-40 Gideon's responses to God alternated between faith and fear. It took courage to build the altars to God, and even to tear down the altar to Baal, the false god. He also blew the trumpet of assembly for those who would fight for God. Yet, his fears limited him to destroying the place of idol worship in the middle of the night and questioning God's leadership (as seen in the fleece incident). Similarly many of us will use any excuse to not face what we fear. Fear is healthy; it can warn us of dangers and prompt us to be careful. But it should not stop us from doing what we know is right.

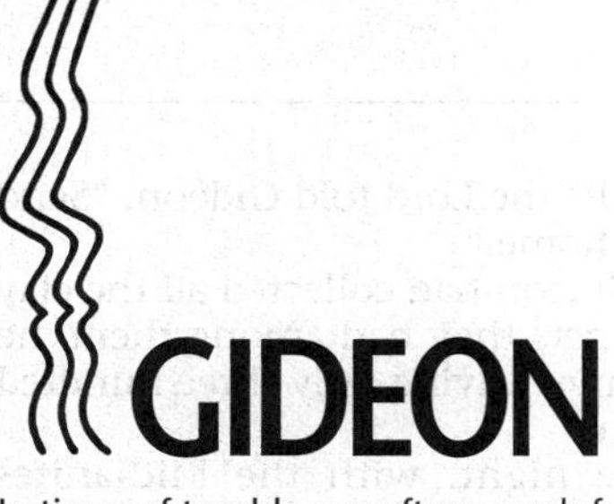

GIDEON

In times of trouble, we often search for the thunder and lightning of God's voice and direction. Mistakenly, we think that God will provide us with the solutions we seek in a spectacular way. The truth of the matter is that the answers often lie within us.

Gideon struggled in his commitment to God. Day in and day out he sought food and shelter for his family in a land constantly raided by hostile invaders. Gideon was under extreme pressure to remain resourceful in the face of his enemies. His deliverance came in an unexpected way.

God called Gideon to deliver the Israelites from the rule of their oppressors. Like many of us, Gideon felt inadequate in the face of a great task. He obeyed, but his doubts kept him dragging his feet. He waited time and again for confirmations of what God had already told him to do.

Many of us feel weak and think we are failures. We question God's interest in our life or our situation. Just as Gideon already had the talents, resourcefulness, and quickness that God needed, often we already have what God needs within us to overcome our obstacles. Even when our faith wavers, God empowers us as we act.

Gideon's story is told in Judges 6–8. Gideon is also mentioned in Hebrews 11:32.

STRENGTHS AND ACCOMPLISHMENTS:
- Gideon acted on his growing convictions, even when his faith wavered.
- He was responsible, even when times were difficult.

WEAKNESSES AND MISTAKES:
- Gideon was afraid to trust God because of his personal limitations.
- He failed to influence his family to follow after God's ways.
- He made a symbol from Midianite gold that was used for ungodly worship.

LESSONS FROM HIS LIFE:
- God gives us more responsibility as we are faithful.
- God uses each of us despite our personal limitations.
- Even in the wake of great victory, we are still capable of making mistakes.

KEY VERSE:
"Whereupon the Lord said to him, 'But I, Jehovah, will be with you! And you shall quickly destroy the Midianite hordes!'" (Judges 6:16).

---

wooden idol of the goddess Asherah that
stood nearby.
26"Replace it with an altar for the Lord your
God, built here on this hill, laying the stones
carefully. Then sacrifice the ox as a burnt
offering to the Lord, using the wooden idol as
wood for the fire on the altar."
27So Gideon took ten of his servants and did
as the Lord had commanded. But he did it at
night for fear of the other members of his
father's household, and for fear of the men of
the city; for he knew what would happen if
they found out who did it! 28Early the next
morning, as the city began to stir, someone
discovered that the altar of Baal was knocked
apart, the idol beside it was gone, and a new
altar had been built instead, with the remains
of a sacrifice on it.
29"Who did this?" everyone demanded. Finally they learned that it was Gideon, the son
of Joash.
30"Bring out your son," they shouted to
Joash. "He must die for insulting the altar of
Baal and for cutting down the Asherah idol."
31But Joash retorted to the whole mob,
"Does Baal need *your* help? What an insult to
a god! You are the ones who should die for
insulting Baal! If Baal is really a god, let him
take care of himself and destroy the one who
broke apart his altar!"
32From then on Gideon was called "Jerubbaal," a nickname meaning "Let Baal take
care of himself!"

Gideon Puts Out a Fleece

33Soon afterward the armies of Midian, Amalek, and other neighboring nations united in
one vast alliance against Israel. They crossed
the Jordan and camped in the valley of Jezreel. 34Then the Spirit of the Lord came upon
Gideon, and he blew a trumpet as a call to
arms, and the men of Abiezer came to him.
35He also sent messengers throughout Manasseh, Asher, Zebulun, and Naphtali, summoning their fighting forces, and all of them
responded.
36Then Gideon said to God, "If you are
really going to use me to save Israel as you
promised, 37prove it to me in this way: I'll put
some wool on the threshing floor tonight,

and if, in the morning, the fleece is wet and the ground is dry, I will know you are going to help me!"

38And it happened just that way! When he got up the next morning, he pressed the fleece together and wrung out a whole bowlful of water!

39Then Gideon said to the Lord, "Please don't be angry with me, but let me make one more test: this time let the fleece remain dry while the ground around it is wet!"

40So the Lord did as he asked; that night the fleece stayed dry, but the ground was covered with dew!

CHAPTER 7

Gideon's Army of Three Hundred

Jerubbaal (that is, Gideon—his other name) and his army got an early start and went as far as the spring of Harod. The armies of Midian were camped north of them, down in the valley beside the hill of Moreh.

2The Lord then said to Gideon, "There are too many of you! I can't let all of you fight the Midianites, for then the people of Israel will boast to me that they saved themselves by their own strength! 3Send home any of your men who are timid and frightened."

So twenty-two thousand of them left, and only ten thousand remained who were willing to fight.

4But the Lord told Gideon, "There are still too many! Bring them down to the spring and I'll show you which ones shall go with you and which ones shall not."

5,6So Gideon assembled them at the water. There the Lord told him, "Divide them into two groups decided by the way they drink. In Group 1 will be all the men who cup the water in their hands to get it to their mouths and lap it like dogs. In Group 2 will be those who kneel, with their mouths in the stream."

Only three hundred of the men drank from their hands; all the others drank with their mouths to the stream.

7"I'll conquer the Midianites with these three hundred!" the Lord told Gideon. "Send all the others home!"

8,9So after Gideon had collected all the clay jars and trumpets they had among them, he sent them home, leaving only three hundred men with him.

During the night, with the Midianites camped in the valley just below, the Lord said to Gideon, "Get up! Take your troops and attack the Midianites, for I will cause you to defeat them! 10But if you are afraid, first go down to the camp alone—take along your servant Purah if you like— 11and listen to what they are saying down there! You will be greatly encouraged and be eager to attack!"

So he took Purah and crept down through the darkness to the outposts of the enemy camp. 12,13The vast armies of Midian, Amalek, and the other nations of the Mideast were crowded across the valley like locusts—yes, like the sand upon the seashore—and there were too many camels even to count! Gideon crept up to one of the tents just as a man inside had wakened from a nightmare and was telling his tent-mate about it.

"I had this strange dream," he was saying, "and there was this huge loaf of barley bread that came tumbling down into our camp. It hit our tent and knocked it flat!"

14The other soldier replied, "Your dream can mean only one thing! Gideon, the son of Joash, the Israeli, is going to come and massacre all the allied forces of Midian!"

15When Gideon heard the dream and the interpretation, all he could do was just stand there worshiping God! Then he returned to his men and shouted, "Get up! For the Lord is going to use you to conquer all the vast armies of Midian!"

16He divided the three hundred men into three groups and gave each man a trumpet and a clay jar with a torch in it. 17Then he explained his plan.

"When we arrive at the outer guardposts of the camp," he told them, "do just as I do. 18As soon as I and the men in my group blow our

7:4-7 In further streamlining the fighting force from ten thousand to three hundred, God demonstrated to Gideon that he was looking for men who most consistently faced the reality of their present circumstances, keeping watch for the enemy while drinking. Facing the present reality is crucial to success in the recovery process. If we are constantly in touch with reality, we will not fall victim to sneak attacks—we will expect struggles with temptation. We can only combat our problems when we are alert.

7:24–8:3 Gideon's patient handling of the temperamental Ephraimites reflects a great deal of progress in overcoming his feelings of personal inadequacy (6:27). In contrast to the anger of Ephraim's leaders, Gideon displayed great self-control and wisdom as a leader. He was willing to go to great lengths to set things straight. Self-control and wisdom are important elements of the recovery process.

READ JUDGES 7:8-25

GOD grant me the serenity to accept the things I cannot change the courage to change the things I can and the wisdom to know the difference AMEN

For those of us who have lived in bondage to addictive/compulsive behaviors, loss of self-respect is a familiar feeling. It is easy to begin to see ourselves as chronically weak, small, even hopeless.

We may begin to believe that we are destined to bondage, poverty, and failure. When this view of our life persists, we give up the possibility of change. We settle for just trying to survive. We live in fear and shame, filling up with resentment as our life remains in the pit. We need to test these kinds of negative assumptions about ourself.

When we first meet Gideon, he is discouraged; he's a young man with little self-respect. His family was the poorest in a small tribe, and he was the least in his family. We first see him threshing wheat in a winepress, hiding the little food he has from his Midianite oppressors. An Angel appeared and called to him, "Mighty soldier, the Lord is with you!" (Judges 6:12). Gideon didn't look or feel like a mighty soldier, but God could see his potential. By the end of the story, Gideon had become the deliverer of his people (Judges 6–8). His first step toward success was to see himself as God saw him—as a "mighty warrior." Then he was able to hope in the possibility of freedom.

We, too, must begin by finding the courage to see ourself in a new light and to summon up the hope for a better life. Then as God gives us the strength, we can set about pursuing freedom from the bondage that surrounds us and our family. ***Turn to page 321, 1 Samuel 15.***

---

trumpets, you blow yours on all sides of the camp and shout, 'We fight for God and for Gideon!'"
19,20It was just after midnight and the
change of guards when Gideon and the hundred men with him crept to the outer edge of the camp of Midian.

Suddenly they blew their trumpets and broke their clay jars so that their torches blazed into the night. Then the other two hundred of his men did the same, blowing the trumpets in their right hands, and holding the flaming torches in their left hands, all shouting, "For the Lord and for Gideon!"

21Then they just stood and watched as the
whole vast enemy army began rushing
around in a panic, shouting and running
away. 22For in the confusion the Lord caused
the enemy troops to begin fighting and killing each other from one end of the camp to the other, and they fled into the night to places as far away as Beth-shittah near Zererah, and to the border of Abel-meholah near Tabbath.

23Then Gideon sent for the troops of Naphtali, Asher, and Manasseh and told them to come and chase and destroy the fleeing army
of Midian. 24Gideon also sent messengers
throughout the hill country of Ephraim summoning troops who seized the fords of the Jordan River at Beth-barah, thus preventing the Midianites from escaping by going across.
25Oreb and Zeeb, the two generals of Midian,
were captured. Oreb was killed at the rock now known by his name, and Zeeb at the winepress of Zeeb, as it is now called; and the Israelis took the heads of Oreb and Zeeb across the Jordan to Gideon.

CHAPTER 8

Gideon's Wise Answer

But the tribal leaders of Ephraim were violently angry with Gideon.

"Why didn't you send for us when you first

went out to fight the Midianites?" they demanded.

2,3But Gideon replied, "God let you capture Oreb and Zeeb, the generals of the army of Midian! What have I done in comparison with that? Your actions at the end of the battle were more important than ours at the beginning!" So they calmed down.

Zebah and Zalmunna Are Captured

4Gideon now crossed the Jordan River with his three hundred men. They were very tired, but still chasing the enemy. 5He asked the
men of Succoth for food. "We are weary from chasing after Zebah and Zalmunna, the kings of Midian," he said.

6But the leaders of Succoth replied, "You haven't caught them yet! If we feed you and you fail, they'll return and destroy us."

7Then Gideon warned them, "When the Lord has delivered them to us, I will return and tear your flesh with the thorns and briars of the wilderness."

8Then he went up to Penuel and asked for
food there, but got the same answer. 9And he
said to them also, "When this is all over, I will return and break down this tower."

10By this time King Zebah and King Zalmunna with a remnant of fifteen thousand troops were in Karkor. That was all that was left of the allied armies of the east; for one hundred twenty thousand had already been
killed. 11Then Gideon circled around by the caravan route east of Nobah and Jogbehah, striking at the Midianite army in surprise
raids. 12The two kings fled, but Gideon chased and captured them, routing their entire force.
13Later, Gideon returned by way of Heres Pass.
14There he captured a young fellow from Succoth and demanded that he write down the names of all the seventy-seven political and religious leaders of the city.

15He then returned to Succoth. "You taunted me that I would never catch King Zebah and King Zalmunna, and you refused to give us food when we were tired and hungry," he said. "Well, here they are!"

16Then he took the leaders of the city and scraped them to death with wild thorns and
briars. 17He also went to Penuel and knocked down the city tower and killed the entire male population.

18Then Gideon asked King Zebah and King Zalmunna, "The men you killed at Tabor—what were they like?"

They replied, "They were dressed just like you—like sons of kings!"

19"They must have been my brothers!" Gideon exclaimed. "I swear that if you hadn't killed them I wouldn't kill you."

20Then, turning to Jether, his oldest son, he instructed him to kill them. But the boy was only a lad and was afraid to.

21Then Zebah and Zalmunna said to Gideon, "You do it; we'd rather be killed by a man!" So Gideon killed them and took the ornaments from their camels' necks.

Gideon Refuses the Kingship

22Now the men of Israel said to Gideon, "Be our king! You and your sons and all your descendants shall be our rulers, for you have saved us from Midian."

23,24But Gideon replied, "I will not be your king, nor shall my son; the Lord is your King! However, I have one request. Give me all the earrings collected from your fallen foes"—for the troops of Midian, being Ishmaelites, all wore gold earrings.

25"Gladly!" they replied, and spread out a sheet for everyone to throw in the gold earrings he had gathered. 26Their value was estimated at $25,000, not including the crescents and pendants, or the royal clothing of the kings, or the chains around the camels' necks.
27Gideon made an ephod from the gold and put it in Ophrah, his hometown. But all Israel soon began worshiping it, so it became an evil deed that Gideon and his family did.

8:4-21 This pursuit and execution of the Midianite kings is a striking example of perseverance on the part of Gideon. In clear contrast to the tribes of Israel who failed to finish the job of driving out the Canaanites, Gideon continued until the Midianite forces were completely defeated. He changed the previous oppressive situation completely, opening the doorway to a new life of freedom for Israel. We should follow Gideon's example, doing all we can to escape oppression from our dependencies. God will help us to accomplish this; then he will help us go on to build a new life.

8:22-35 After Gideon's death, the Israelites again turned from the true God and began to worship idols. The ephod Gideon made to commemorate the defeat of the Midianites was soon worshiped by the people. And later, after Gideon's death, the Israelites went back to worshiping Baal and Baal-berith. The people still did not recognize the cycle of disobedience and oppression. We should, unlike Israel, learn from our past. When tempted to return to old addictions, we need to remember the consequences of those behaviors and persevere in recovery.

Gideon Dies

[28]That is the true account of how Midian was subdued by Israel. Midian never recovered, and the land was at peace for forty years—all during Gideon's lifetime. [29]He returned home [30]and eventually had seventy sons, for he married many wives. [31]He also had a concubine in Shechem, who presented him with a son named Abimelech. [32]Gideon finally died, an old, old man, and was buried in the sepulcher of his father, Joash, in Ophrah, in the land of the Abiezrites.

[33]But as soon as Gideon was dead, the Israelis began to worship the idols Baal and Baal-berith. [34]They no longer considered the Lord as their God, though he had rescued them from all their enemies on every side. [35]Nor did they show any kindness to the family of Gideon despite all he had done for them.

CHAPTER 9

Abimelech Tries to Become King

One day Gideon's son Abimelech visited his uncles—his mother's brothers—in Shechem.

[2]"Go and talk to the leaders of Shechem," he requested, "and ask them whether they want to be ruled by seventy kings—Gideon's seventy sons—or by one man—meaning me, your own flesh and blood!"

[3]So his uncles went to the leaders of the city and proposed Abimelech's scheme; and they decided that since his mother was a native of their town they would go along with it. [4]They gave him money from the temple offerings of the idol Baal-berith, which he used to hire some worthless loafers who agreed to do whatever he told them to. [5]He took them to his father's home at Ophrah and there, upon one stone, they slaughtered all seventy of his half brothers, except for the youngest, Jotham, who escaped and hid. [6]Then the citizens of Shechem and Beth-millo called a meeting under the oak beside the garrison at Shechem, and Abimelech was acclaimed king of Israel.

[7]When Jotham heard about this, he stood at the top of Mount Gerizim and shouted across to the men of Shechem, "If you want God's blessing, listen to me! [8]Once upon a time the trees decided to elect a king. First they asked the olive tree, [9]but it refused.

"'Should I quit producing the olive oil that blesses God and man, just to wave to and fro over the other trees?' it asked.

[10]"Then they said to the fig tree, 'You be our king!'

[11]"But the fig tree also refused. 'Should I quit producing sweetness and fruit just to lift my head above all the other trees?' it asked.

[12]"Then they said to the grapevine, 'You reign over us!'

[13]"But the grapevine replied, 'Shall I quit producing the wine that cheers both God and man, just to be mightier than all the other trees?'

[14]"Then all the trees finally turned to the thorn bush. 'You be our king!' they explained.

[15]"And the thorn bush replied, 'If you really want me, come and humble yourselves beneath my shade! If you refuse, let fire flame forth from me and burn down the great cedars of Lebanon!'

[16]"Now make sure that you have done the right thing in making Abimelech your king, that you have done right by Gideon and all of his descendants. [17]For my father fought for you and risked his life and delivered you from the Midianites, [18]yet you have revolted against him and killed his seventy sons upon one stone. And now you have chosen his slave girl's son, Abimelech, to be your king just because he is your relative. [19]If you are sure that you have done right by Gideon and his descendants, then may you and Abimelech have a long and happy life together. [20]But if you have not been fair to Gideon, then may Abimelech destroy the citizens of Shechem and Beth-millo; and may they destroy Abimelech!"

[21]Then Jotham escaped and lived in Beer for fear of his brother, Abimelech. [22,23]Three years later God stirred up trouble between King Abimelech and the citizens of Shechem, and they revolted. [24]In the events that followed, both Abimelech and the citizens of Shechem who aided him in butchering Gideon's seventy sons were given their just punishment

---

9:1-57 Abimelech, Gideon's son by a concubine, proved to be the virtual opposite of his father. Gideon rightly refused kingship over Israel, but Abimelech not only demanded it, he also attempted to kill anyone who stood in his way. And he died as violently as he lived. None of the faith, patience, and honesty that characterized Gideon is seen in Abimelech, perhaps indicating serious deficiencies in his childhood years (8:31). It is not enough to be a strong leader outside of the home environment; we must be a strong influence on our children. If our children do not spend time with a godly parental example, they may grow up with no positive role model to follow. If we don't teach our children how to walk in our ways, they may grow up to flout them, like Abimelech.

for these murders. 25For the men of Shechem set an ambush for Abimelech along the trail at the top of the mountain. (While they were waiting for him to come along, they robbed everyone else who passed that way.) But someone warned Abimelech about their plot.

26At that time Gaal (the son of Ebed) moved to Shechem with his brothers, and he became one of the leading citizens. 27During the harvest feast at Shechem that year, held in the temple of the local god, the wine flowed freely and everyone began cursing Abimelech.

28"Who is Abimelech," Gaal shouted, "and why should he be our king? Why should we be his servants? He and his friend Zebul should be *our* servants. Down with Abimelech! 29Make me your king and you'll soon see what happens to Abimelech! I'll tell Abimelech, 'Get up an army and come on out and fight!'"

30But when Zebul, the mayor of the city, heard what Gaal was saying, he was furious. 31He sent messengers to Abimelech in Arumah telling him, "Gaal, son of Ebed, and his relatives have come to live in Shechem, and now they are arousing the city to rebellion against you. 32Come by night with an army and hide out in the fields; 33and in the morning, as soon as it is daylight, storm the city. When he and those who are with him come out against you, you can do with them as you wish!"

34So Abimelech and his men marched through the night and split into four groups, stationing themselves around the city. 35The next morning as Gaal sat at the city gates, discussing various issues with the local leaders, Abimelech and his men began their march upon the city.

36When Gaal saw them, he exclaimed to Zebul, "Look over at that mountain! Doesn't it look like people coming down?"

"No!" Zebul said. "You're just seeing shadows that look like men!"

37"No, look over there," Gaal said. "I'm sure I see people coming toward us. And look! There are others coming along the road past the oak of Meonenim!"

38Then Zebul turned on him triumphantly. "Now where is that big mouth of yours?" he demanded. "Who was it who said, 'Who is Abimelech, and why should he be our king?' The men you taunted and cursed are right outside the city! Go on out and fight!"

39So Gaal led the men of Shechem into the battle and fought with Abimelech, 40but was defeated, and many of the men of Shechem were left wounded all the way to the city gate. 41Abimelech was living at Arumah at this time, and Zebul drove Gaal and his relatives out of Shechem and wouldn't let them live there any longer.

42The next day the men of Shechem went out to battle again. However, someone had told Abimelech about their plans, 43so he had divided his men into three groups hiding in the fields. And when the men of the city went out to attack, he and his men jumped up from their hiding places and began killing them. 44Abimelech stormed the city gate to keep the men of Shechem from getting back in, while his other two groups cut them down in the fields. 45The battle went on all day before Abimelech finally captured the city, killed its people, and leveled it to the ground. 46The people at the nearby town of Migdal saw what was happening and took refuge in the fort next to the temple of Baal-berith.

47,48When Abimelech learned of this, he led his forces to Mount Zalmon where he began chopping a bundle of firewood, and placed it upon his shoulder. "Do as I have done," he told his men. 49So each of them quickly cut a bundle and carried it back to the town where, following Abimelech's example, the bundles were piled against the walls of the fort and set on fire. So all the people inside died, about a thousand men and women.

50Abimelech next attacked the city of Thebez, and captured it. 51However, there was a fort inside the city and the entire population fled into it, barricaded the gates, and climbed to the top of the roof to watch. 52But as Abimelech was preparing to burn it, 53a woman on the roof threw down a millstone. It landed on Abimelech's head, crushing his skull.

54"Kill me!" he groaned to his youthful armor-bearer. "Never let it be said that a woman killed Abimelech!"

So the young man pierced him with his sword, and he died. 55When his men saw that he was dead, they disbanded and returned to their homes. 56,57Thus God punished both Abimelech and the men of Shechem for their sin of murdering Gideon's seventy sons. So the curse of Jotham, Gideon's son, came true.

CHAPTER 10

Tola and Jair

After Abimelech's death, the next judge of Israel was Tola (son of Puah and grandson of Dodo). He was from the tribe of Issachar, but lived in the city of Shamir in the hill country of Ephraim. 2He was Israel's judge for twenty-three years. When he died, he was buried in Shamir, [3]and was succeeded by Jair, a man from Gilead, who judged Israel for twenty-two years. [4]His thirty sons rode around together on thirty donkeys, and they owned thirty cities in the land of Gilead which are still called "The Cities of Jair." [5]When Jair died he was buried in Kamon.

Jephthah Defeats the Ammonites

[6]Then the people of Israel turned away from the Lord again and worshiped the heathen gods Baal and Ashtaroth, and the gods of Syria, Sidon, Moab, Ammon, and Philistia. Not only this, but they no longer worshiped Jehovah at all. [7,8]This made Jehovah very angry with his people, so he immediately permitted the Philistines and the Ammonites to begin tormenting them. These attacks took place east of the Jordan River in the land of the Amorites (that is, in Gilead), [9]and also in Judah, Benjamin, and Ephraim. For the Ammonites crossed the Jordan to attack the Israelis. This went on for eighteen years. [10]Finally the Israelis turned to Jehovah again and begged him to save them.

"We have sinned against you and have forsaken you as our God and have worshiped idols," they confessed.

[11]But the Lord replied, "Didn't I save you from the Egyptians, the Amorites, the Ammonites, the Philistines, [12]the Sidonians, the Amalekites, and the Maonites? Has there ever been a time when you cried out to me that I haven't rescued you? [13]Yet you continue to abandon me and to worship other gods. So go away; I won't save you any more. [14]Go and cry to the new gods you have chosen! Let them save you in your hour of distress!"

[15]But they pleaded with him again and said, "We have sinned. Punish us in any way you think best, only save us once more from our enemies."

[16]Then they destroyed their foreign gods and worshiped only the Lord; and he was grieved by their misery. [17]The armies of Ammon were mobilized in Gilead at that time, preparing to attack Israel's army at Mizpah.

[18]"Who will lead our forces against the Ammonites?" the leaders of Gilead asked each other. "Whoever volunteers shall be our king!"

CHAPTER 11

Now Jephthah was a great warrior from the land of Gilead, but his mother was a prostitute. His father (whose name was Gilead) had several other sons by his legitimate wife, and when these half brothers grew up, they chased Jephthah out of the country.

"You son of a whore!" they said. "You'll not get any of our father's estate."

[3]So Jephthah fled from his father's home and lived in the land of Tob. Soon he had quite a band of malcontents as his followers, living off the land as bandits. [4]It was about this time that the Ammonites began their war against Israel. [5]The leaders of Gilead sent for Jephthah, [6]begging him to come and lead their army against the Ammonites.

[7]But Jephthah said to them, "Why do you come to me when you hate me and have driven me out of my father's house? Why come now when you're in trouble?"

[8]"Because we need you," they replied. "If you will be our commander-in-chief against the Ammonites, we will make you the king of Gilead."

[9]"Sure!" Jephthah exclaimed. "Do you expect me to believe that?"

[10]"We swear it," they replied. "We promise with a solemn oath."

[11]So Jephthah accepted the commission and was made commander-in-chief and king. The contract was ratified before the Lord in Mizpah at a general assembly of all the people. [12]Then Jephthah sent messengers to the king of Ammon, demanding to know why

---

10:1-18 After suffering under Abimelech's leadership (Judges 9), Israel experienced forty-five stable years under the leadership of Tola and Jair. But Israel's spiritual recovery was still by no means complete. In fact, after Jair died, the Israelites' denial was so strong that it took them eighteen years to admit their helplessness and look to God for help. If we are honest, we will not have to suffer for eighteen years before realizing the consequences of our dependencies. It should be obvious when we start straying from God's will. If we keep our eyes open, we will be able to take immediate steps to get back on the right path.

11:12-28 Jephthah displayed great self-control by patiently confronting the Ammonite king about his attacks upon Israel. Considering the hunger for power that propels most oppressive people, it was unlikely that Jephthah would be able to persuade the Ammonites to stop their unprovoked attacks. Still, he argued his case well, though it was totally disregarded. We are called to try to make peace and speak the truth. It is not our responsibility, however, if others do not listen to us. We can only try to make them see our point of view.

Israel was being attacked. [13]The king of Ammon replied that the land belonged to the people of Ammon; it had been stolen from them, he said, when the Israelis came from Egypt; the whole territory from the Arnon River to the Jabbok and the Jordan was his, he claimed.

"Give us back our land peaceably," he demanded.

[14,15]Jephthah replied, "Israel did not steal the land. [16]What happened was this: When the people of Israel arrived at Kadesh, on their journey from Egypt after crossing the Red Sea, [17]they sent a message to the king of Edom asking permission to pass through his land. But their petition was denied. Then they asked the king of Moab for similar permission. It was the same story there, so the people of Israel stayed in Kadesh.

[18]"Finally they went around Edom and Moab through the wilderness, and traveled along the eastern border until at last they arrived beyond the boundary of Moab at the Arnon River; but they never once crossed into Moab. [19]Then Israel sent messengers to King Sihon of the Amorites, who lived in Heshbon, and asked permission to cross through his land to get to their destination.

[20]"But King Sihon didn't trust Israel, so he mobilized an army at Jahaz and attacked them. [21,22]But the Lord our God helped Israel defeat King Sihon and all your people, so Israel took over all of your land from the Arnon River to the Jabbok, and from the wilderness to the Jordan River.

[23]"So you see, it was the Lord God of Israel who took away the land from the Amorites and gave it to Israel. Why, then, should we return it to you? [24]You keep whatever your god Chemosh gives you, and we will keep whatever Jehovah our God gives us! [25]And besides, just who do you think you are? Are you better than King Balak, the king of Moab? Did he try to recover his land after Israel defeated him? No, of course not. [26]But now after three hundred years you make an issue of this! Israel has been living here for all that time, spread across the land from Heshbon to Aroer, and all along the Arnon River. Why have you made no effort to recover it before now? [27]No, I have not sinned against you; rather, you have wronged me by coming to war against me; but Jehovah the Judge will soon show which of us is right—Israel or Ammon."

[28]But the king of Ammon paid no attention to Jephthah's message.

[29]At that time the Spirit of the Lord came upon Jephthah, and he led his army across the land of Gilead and Manasseh, past Mizpah in Gilead, and attacked the army of Ammon. [30,31]Meanwhile Jephthah had vowed to the Lord that if God would help Israel conquer the Ammonites, then when he returned home in peace, the first person coming out of his house to meet him would be sacrificed as a burnt offering to the Lord!

[32]So Jephthah led his army against the Ammonites, and the Lord gave him the victory. [33]He destroyed the Ammonites with a terrible slaughter all the way from Aroer to Minnith, including twenty cities, and as far away as Vineyard Meadow. Thus the Ammonites were subdued by the people of Israel.

[34]When Jephthah returned home his daughter—his only child—ran out to meet him, playing on a tambourine and dancing for joy. [35]When he saw her, he tore his clothes in anguish.

"Alas, my daughter!" he cried out. "You have brought me to the dust. For I have made a vow to the Lord and I cannot take it back."

[36]And she said, "Father, you must do whatever you promised the Lord, for he has given you a great victory over your enemies, the Ammonites. [37]But first let me go up into the hills and roam with my girlfriends for two months, weeping because I'll never marry."

[38]"Yes," he said. "Go."

And so she did, bewailing her fate with her friends for two months. [39]Then she returned to her father, who did as he had vowed. So she was never married. And after that it became a custom in Israel [40]that the young girls went away for four days each year to lament the fate of Jephthah's daughter.

CHAPTER 12

Jephthah Attacks Ephraim

Then the tribe of Ephraim mobilized its army at Zaphon and sent this message to Jephthah:

11:29-40 Jephthah's recovery and leadership were guided by the Holy Spirit, but he still made a foolish mistake. His vow, which was an attempt to "make a deal" with God to ensure military victory, is a classic example of what it means to "smother the Holy Spirit" (1 Thessalonians 5:19). As with many who are in need of recovery, Jephthah lived to regret the vow made in the heat of the crisis. Often we do the same thing. We beg for God to fulfill some short-sighted goal, and in obtaining it, we miss God's best.

"Why didn't you call for us to help you fight against Ammon? We are going to burn down your house, with you in it!"

2"I summoned you, but you refused to come!" Jephthah retorted. "You failed to help us in our time of need, 3so I risked my life and went to battle without you, and the Lord helped me to conquer the enemy. Is that anything for you to fight us about?"

4Then Jephthah, furious at the taunt of Ephraim that the men of Gilead were mere outcasts and the scum of the earth, mobilized his army and attacked the army of Ephraim. 5He captured the fords of the Jordan behind the army of Ephraim, and whenever a fugitive from Ephraim tried to cross the river, the Gilead guards challenged him.

"Are you a member of the tribe of Ephraim?" they asked. If the man replied that he was not, 6then they demanded, "Say 'Shibboleth.'" But if he couldn't pronounce the *H* and said, "Sibboleth" instead of "Shibboleth," he was dragged away and killed. So forty-two thousand people of Ephraim died there at that time.

7Jephthah was Israel's judge for six years. At his death he was buried in one of the cities of Gilead.

Ibzan, Elon, and Abdon

8The next judge was Ibzan, who lived in Bethlehem. 9,10He had thirty sons and thirty daughters. He married his daughters to men outside his clan and brought in thirty girls to marry his sons. He judged Israel for seven years before he died, and was buried at Bethlehem.

11,12The next judge was Elon from Zebulun. He judged Israel for ten years and was buried at Aijalon in Zebulun.

13Next was Abdon (son of Hillel) from Pirathon. 14He had forty sons and thirty grandsons, who rode on seventy donkeys. He was Israel's judge for eight years. 15Then he died and was buried in Pirathon, in Ephraim, in the hill country of the Amalekites.

CHAPTER 13

Samson Is Born

Once again Israel sinned by worshiping other gods, so the Lord let them be conquered by the Philistines, who kept them in subjection for forty years.

2,3Then one day the Angel of the Lord appeared to the wife of Manoah, of the tribe of Dan, who lived in the city of Zorah. She had no children, but the Angel said to her, "Even though you have been barren so long, you will soon conceive and have a son! 4Don't drink any wine or beer and don't eat any food that isn't kosher. 5Your son's hair must never be cut, for he shall be a Nazirite, a special servant of God from the time of his birth; and he will begin to rescue Israel from the Philistines."

6The woman ran and told her husband, "A man from God appeared to me and I think he must be the Angel of the Lord, for he was almost too glorious to look at. I didn't ask where he was from, and he didn't tell me his name, 7but he told me, 'You are going to have a baby boy!' And he told me not to drink any wine or beer and not to eat food that isn't kosher, for the baby is going to be a Nazirite—he will be dedicated to God from the moment of his birth until the day of his death!"

8Then Manoah prayed, "O Lord, please let the man from God come back to us again and give us more instructions about the child you are going to give us." 9The Lord answered his prayer, and the Angel of God appeared once again to his wife as she was sitting in the field. But again she was alone—Manoah was not with her— 10so she quickly ran and found her

12:1-7 This tragic incident is in many ways a replay of Gideon's confrontation with the angry Ephraimites in Judges 8:1-3. The outcome, however, is very different because of the way in which Jephthah mishandled the situation. Instead of the humble self-control and patience shown by Gideon, Jephthah responded in angry pride. As a result, war erupted between Gilead and Ephraim, and the two tribes were unable to enjoy a relationship like the one forged with Ephraim by Gideon.

12:8-15 The brief mention of the leadership of Ibzan, Elon, and Abdon might be taken to mean that they were less significant judges. However, each of the three actually ruled longer than Jephthah: Ibzan, seven years; Elon, ten years; and Abdon, eight years. Apparently, events during their terms of leadership were not as tumultuous. The point here is that no one should base his or her self-worth or sense of accomplishment on whether or not he or she "makes the headlines."

13:1-14 The instructions given by the Angel to Manoah and his wife are similar to those given to Zacharias and Elizabeth, parents of John the Baptist (Luke 1:5-15). Both sets of parents were commanded to raise their children for special tasks for God. In fact, even their actions before their sons were born were very significant. All parents should be aware of how closely related their own actions and outlooks are to the sense of identity each child will have as an adult.

husband and told him, "The same man is here
again!"
[11]Manoah ran back with his wife and asked,
"Are you the man who talked to my wife the
other day?"
"Yes," he replied, "I am."
[12]So Manoah asked him, "Can you give us
any special instructions about how we should
raise the baby after he is born?"
[13,14]And the Angel replied, "Be sure that
your wife follows the instructions I gave her.
She must not eat grapes or raisins, or drink
any wine or beer, or eat anything that isn't
kosher."
[15]Then Manoah said to the Angel, "Please
stay here until we can get you something to
eat."
[16]"I'll stay," the Angel replied, "but I'll not
eat anything. However, if you wish to bring
something, bring an offering to sacrifice to
the Lord." (Manoah didn't yet realize that he
was the Angel of the Lord.)
[17]Then Manoah asked him for his name.
"When all this comes true and the baby is
born," he said to the Angel, "we will certainly
want to tell everyone that you predicted it!"
[18]"Don't even ask my name," the Angel
replied, "for it is a secret."
[19]Then Manoah took a young goat and a
grain offering and offered it as a sacrifice to
the Lord; and the Angel did a strange and
wonderful thing, [20]for as the flames from the
altar were leaping up toward the sky, and as
Manoah and his wife watched, the Angel ascended in the fire! Manoah and his wife fell
face downward to the ground, [21]and that was
the last they ever saw of him. It was then that
Manoah finally realized that it had been the
Angel of the Lord.
[22]"We will die," Manoah cried out to his
wife, "for we have seen God!"
[23]But his wife said, "If the Lord were going
to kill us, he wouldn't have accepted our
burnt offerings and wouldn't have appeared
to us and told us this wonderful thing and
done these miracles."
[24]When her son was born they named him
Samson, and the Lord blessed him as he grew
up. [25]And the Spirit of the Lord began to excite
him whenever he visited the parade grounds
of the army of the tribe of Dan, located between the cities of Zorah and Eshtaol.

CHAPTER 14

Samson Asks a Riddle

One day when Samson was in Timnah he
noticed a certain Philistine girl, [2]and when he
got home he told his father and mother that
he wanted to marry her. [3]They objected stren-
uously.
"Why don't you marry a Jewish girl?" they
asked. "Why must you go and get a wife from
these heathen Philistines? Isn't there one girl
among all the people of Israel you could
marry?"
But Samson told his father, "She is the one
I want. Get her for me."
[4]His father and mother didn't realize that
the Lord was behind the request, for God was
setting a trap for the Philistines, who at that
time were the rulers of Israel.
[5]As Samson and his parents were going to
Timnah, a young lion attacked Samson in the
vineyards on the outskirts of the town. [6]At
that moment the Spirit of the Lord came
mightily upon him and since he had no
weapon, he ripped the lion's jaws apart and
did it as easily as though it were a young goat!
But he didn't tell his father or mother about
it. [7]Upon arriving at Timnah, he talked with
the girl and found her to be just what he
wanted, so the arrangements were made.
[8]When he returned for the wedding, he
turned off the path to look at the carcass of

13:24–14:4 Samson was living proof that someone can grow up in a godly home under the blessing of God and still have major issues to face. Even the working of the Spirit of God in Samson's life did not protect him from his biggest blind spot: foreign women. Fortunately, as always, God used even Samson's weaknesses to bring glory to himself. Unfortunately, Samson did not understand his unhealthy attraction to be a point of weakness. Samson's problem with foreign women is symbolic of many who struggle today. God will provide an abundant life if we are willing to give up or avoid a "forbidden fruit." That fruit differs from one person to another. We should ask God to help us see what is a stumbling block to our recovery so we can reach our full potential.

14:10-20 During the prewedding feast, Samson foolishly bet that his guests could not solve his riddle. After being manipulated by his wife-to-be and losing the wager, Samson slaughtered other Philistines to get the garments he needed for payment. His volatile and dangerous personality was clearly evidenced by his actions. Samson possessed the maturity of a young boy stuffed inside an incredibly strong and gifted adult exterior. Often we aspire to be like people with great physical beauty, only to find that they are shallow of character. We must never forget how much God values who we are on the inside. God looks at people's hearts, not their appearances (1 Samuel 16:7).

SAMSON & DELILAH

The New Testament describes Samson as a man of faith. It mentions neither his failures nor his great strength. Though he possessed great physical strength, he was a moral weakling—following his own selfish desires and ignoring God. Samson spent most of his life pursuing his own goals, but in the end he finally admitted his need and cried out to God for help.

It seems that after the first three episodes of betrayal, Samson would have known not to trust Delilah. But like many of us, Samson thought that giving in to manipulation was an expression of love. He chose to please Delilah and to get what he wanted from her, rather than to obey God and deliver his people. Delilah chose to use her relationship with Samson for her own gain. It was clearly a dysfunctional relationship. Most of us have experienced the pain of being used, and we have undoubtedly used others. We have also known the searing agony of being betrayed.

It will accomplish nothing to look at Samson and think about what he did not accomplish. We are often victimized in our own life by thoughts of "what might have been." Samson shows us that as long as we have life, we have hope. It is never too late to turn our life over to God and allow him to redeem us and restore what has been lost. In spite of his failures, Samson is listed as a champion of faith in Hebrews 11. In spite of our failures, we, too, can be champions of faith as God continues to work out recovery in our life.

The story of Samson is found in Judges 13–16, and his relationship with Delilah is described in Judges 16. Samson is also mentioned in Hebrews 11:32.

STRENGTHS AND ACCOMPLISHMENTS:
- Samson was called by God before his birth.
- He is listed in the Hall of Faith (Hebrews 11).
- Samson believed God.
- He began to free his people from the Philistines.

WEAKNESSES AND MISTAKES:
- Samson abused the gift of strength God had given him.
- He was motivated by revenge rather than by righteousness.
- He allowed lust to cloud his thinking.
- Delilah valued riches over relationships.
- She betrayed Samson and lied to him.

LESSONS FROM THEIR LIVES:
- There is great danger in trusting our God-given abilities rather than trusting God himself.
- There is a price to be paid for sin.
- We must be careful to do what is right, not just what we want to do.
- God uses us in spite of our failures.

KEY VERSE:
"Then Samson prayed to the Lord and said, 'O Lord Jehovah, remember me again—please strengthen me one more time, so that I may pay back the Philistines for the loss of at least one of my eyes'" (Judges 16:28).

---

the lion. And he found a swarm of bees in it
and some honey! 9He took some of the honey
with him, eating as he went, and gave some
of it to his father and mother. But he didn't
tell them where he had gotten it.
10,11As his father was making final arrangements for the marriage, Samson threw a party
for thirty young men of the village, as was the
custom of the day. 12When Samson asked if
they would like to hear a riddle, they replied
that they would.

"If you solve my riddle during these seven days of the celebration," he said, "I'll give you thirty plain robes and thirty fancy robes. 13But if you can't solve it, then you must give the robes to me!"

"All right," they agreed, "let's hear it."

14This was his riddle: "Food came out of the
eater, and sweetness from the strong!" Three
days later they were still trying to figure it
out.
15On the fourth day they said to his new
wife, "Get the answer from your husband, or
we'll burn down your father's house with you
in it. Were we invited to this party just to
make us poor?"
16So Samson's wife broke down in tears before him and said, "You don't love me at all;
you hate me, for you have told a riddle to my
people and haven't told me the answer!"

"I haven't even told it to my father or mother; why should I tell you?" he replied.

17So she cried whenever she was with him
and kept it up for the remainder of the celebration. At last, on the seventh day, he told
her the answer and she, of course, gave the
answer to the young men. 18So before sunset
of the seventh day they gave him their reply.

"What is sweeter than honey?" they asked,
"and what is stronger than a lion?"
"If you hadn't plowed with my heifer, you
wouldn't have found the answer to my riddle!" he retorted.
19 Then the Spirit of the Lord came upon
him and he went to the city of Ashkelon,
killed thirty men, took their clothing, and
gave it to the young men who had told him
the answer to his riddle. But he was furious
about it and abandoned his wife and went
back home to live with his father and mother.
20 So his wife was married instead to the fellow
who had been best man at Samson's wedding.

CHAPTER 15

Samson Kills Many Enemies

Later on, during the wheat harvest, Samson
took a young goat as a present to his wife,
intending to sleep with her; but her father
wouldn't let him in.
2 "I really thought you hated her," he explained, "so I married her to your best man.
But look, her sister is prettier than she is.
Marry her instead."
3 Samson was furious. "You can't blame me
for whatever happens now," he shouted.
4 So he went out and caught three hundred
foxes and tied their tails together in pairs,
with a torch between each pair. 5 Then he lit
the torches and let the foxes run through the
fields of the Philistines, burning the grain to
the ground along with all the sheaves and
shocks of grain, and destroying the olive
trees.
6 "Who did this?" the Philistines demanded.
"Samson," was the reply, "because his
wife's father gave her to another man." So the
Philistines came and got the girl and her
father and burned them alive.
7 "Now my vengeance will strike again!"
Samson vowed. 8 So he attacked them with
great fury and killed many of them. Then he
went to live in a cave in the rock of Etam. 9 The
Philistines in turn sent a huge posse into
Judah and raided Lehi.
10 "Why have you come here?" the men of
Judah asked.
And the Philistines replied, "To capture
Samson and do to him as he has done to us."
11 So three thousand men of Judah went
down to get Samson at the cave in the rock of
Etam.
"What are you doing to us?" they demanded of him. "Don't you realize that the
Philistines are our rulers?"
But Samson replied, "I only paid them back
for what they did to me."
12,13 "We have come to capture you and take
you to the Philistines," the men of Judah told
him.
"All right," Samson said, "but promise me
that you won't kill me yourselves."
"No," they replied, "we won't do that."
So they tied him with two new ropes and
led him away. 14 As Samson and his captors
arrived at Lehi, the Philistines shouted with
glee; but then the strength of the Lord came
upon Samson, and the ropes with which he
was tied snapped like thread and fell from his
wrists! 15 Then he picked up a donkey's jawbone that was lying on the ground and killed
a thousand Philistines with it. 16,17 Tossing
away the jawbone, he remarked,

"Heaps upon heaps,
All with a donkey's jaw!

14:19–15:8 The motive of angry revenge came to dominate Samson's personality and actions more and more. Because of what the Philistines had done to him, he destroyed much of their wheat and other crops. Then he turned his rage on the Philistines themselves, killing many of them. There are many "rage-aholics" who, like Samson, desperately need recovery. Otherwise, they will destroy themselves, as Samson later did, and hurt the people they love. God calls us to take our hurts and give them to him while forgiving those who hurt us. Revenge never adequately repays the victimizer. In fact, it only causes the one who was hurt to be victimized again.

15:18-20 Samson was left emotionally drained after his victory over the Philistines. He now complained to God, perhaps exaggerating his situation ("Must I now die of thirst?"). After a major victory in our life, we may feel emotionally spent or physically pained. But we must not stop and have a "pity party." This will only lead to failure. We should rely on God's power to strengthen us and meet our needs. Then we can be ready to face the next battle in our recovery process.

16:4-17 The love affair between Samson and Delilah is one of the most pathetic examples of lust and manipulation in history. It should have been obvious to Samson that Delilah was working with the Philistines to destroy him. But to get the physical pleasures he craved, Samson led Delilah on, staying in a situation he should have run from. He blindly believed he was virtually indestructible. This left him open to utter humiliation and suffering. If we hope to succeed in recovery, we need to recognize our weaknesses and avoid situations where we are vulnerable.

I've killed a thousand men,
All with a donkey's jaw!"

(The place has been called "Jawbone Hill"
ever since.)
18But now he was very thirsty and he prayed
to the Lord and said, "You have given Israel
such a wonderful deliverance through me today! Must I now die of thirst and fall to the
mercy of these heathen?" 19So the Lord caused
water to gush out from a hollow in the
ground, and Samson's spirit was revived as he
drank. Then he named the place "The Spring
of the Man Who Prayed," and the spring is
still there today.
20Samson was Israel's leader for the next
twenty years, but the Philistines still controlled the land.

CHAPTER 16
Samson's Foolish Choices
One day Samson went to the Philistine city of
Gaza and spent the night with a prostitute.
2Word soon spread that he had been seen in
the city, so the police were alerted and many
men of the city lay in wait all night at the city
gate to capture him if he tried to leave.
"In the morning," they thought, "when
there is enough light, we'll find him and kill
him."
3Samson stayed in bed with the girl until
midnight, then went out to the city gates and
lifted them, with the two gateposts, right out
of the ground. He put them on his shoulders
and carried them to the top of the mountain
across from Hebron!
4Later on he fell in love with a girl named
Delilah over in the valley of Sorek. 5The five
heads of the Philistine nation went personally
to her and demanded that she find out from
Samson what made him so strong, so that
they would know how to overpower and subdue him and put him in chains.
"Each of us will give you a thousand dollars
for this job," they promised.
6So Delilah begged Samson to tell her his
secret. *"Please* tell me, Samson, why you are
so strong," she pleaded. "I don't think anyone
could ever capture you!"
7"Well," Samson replied, "if I were tied with
seven raw-leather bowstrings, I would become as weak as anyone else."
8So they brought her the seven bowstrings, and while he slept she tied him with
them. 9Some men were hiding in the next
room, so as soon as she had tied him up she
exclaimed,
"Samson! The Philistines are here!"

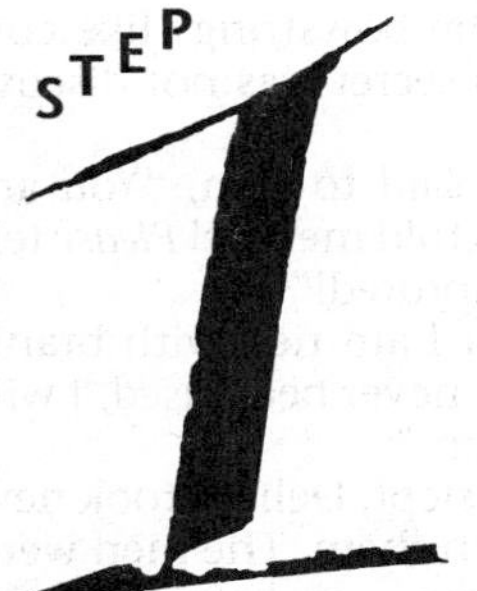

Dangerous Self-Deception

BIBLE READING: Judges 16:1-31

We admitted that we were powerless over our dependencies—that our life had become unmanageable.

When we refuse to admit our powerlessness we are only deceiving ourself. The lies we tell ourself and others are familiar: "I can stop any time I want to." "I'm in control; this *one* won't hurt anything." And all the while, we are inching closer to disaster.

Samson was one of Israel's judges. As a child, he had been dedicated to God, and God had gifted him with supernatural strength. But Samson had a lifelong weakness; it had to do with the way he related to women. Samson was especially blinded to the dangers he faced in his relationship with Delilah. His enemies were paying her to discover the secret of his strength. Three times she begged him to let her in on his secret. Each time she set him up and tried to hand him over to the enemy. Three times Samson lied to her and was able to escape. But each time he got closer to telling her the truth. In the end, Samson revealed his secret, was taken captive, and died a slave in enemy hands (Judges 14–16).

Samson's real problem can be found in the lies he told himself. By not admitting his powerlessness, he remained blind to the obvious danger his addiction was leading him into. This caused him to gradually inch his way toward an untimely death.

We need to be careful not to fall into the same trap. As we daily learn to acknowledge our powerlessness over our addictive/compulsive tendencies, we will become more aware of behavior that will likely lead to our downfall. ***Turn to page 417, 2 Kings 5.***

Then he snapped the bowstrings like cotton thread, and so his secret was not discovered.

[10]Afterward Delilah said to him, "You are making fun of me! You told me a lie! *Please* tell me how you can be captured!"

[11]"Well," he said, "if I am tied with brand new ropes which have never been used, I will be as weak as other men."

[12]So that time, as he slept, Delilah took new ropes and tied him with them. The men were hiding in the next room, as before. Again Delilah exclaimed,

"Samson! The Philistines have come to capture you!"

But he broke the ropes from his arms like spiderwebs!

[13]"You have mocked me again and told me more lies!" Delilah complained. "Now tell me how you can *really* be captured."

"Well," he said, "if you weave my hair into your loom . . . !"

[14]So while he slept, she did just that and then screamed, "The Philistines have come, Samson!" And he woke up and yanked his hair away, breaking the loom.

[15]"How can you say you love me when you don't confide in me?" she whined. "You've made fun of me three times now, and you still haven't told me what makes you so strong!"

[16,17]She nagged at him every day until he couldn't stand it any longer and finally told her his secret.

"My hair has never been cut," he confessed, "for I've been a Nazirite to God since before my birth. If my hair were cut, my strength would leave me, and I would become as weak as anyone else."

[18]Delilah realized that he had finally told her the truth, so she sent for the five Philistine leaders.

"Come just this once more," she said, "for this time he has told me everything."

So they brought the money with them.
[19]She lulled him to sleep with his head in her lap, and they brought in a barber and cut off his hair. Delilah began to hit him, but she could see that his strength was leaving him.

[20]Then she screamed, "The Philistines are here to capture you, Samson!" And he woke up and thought, "I will do as before; I'll just shake myself free." But he didn't realize that the Lord had left him. [21]So the Philistines captured him and gouged out his eyes and took him to Gaza, where he was bound with bronze chains and made to grind grain in the prison. [22]But before long his hair began to grow again.

Samson Pulls Down a Temple

[23,24]The Philistine leaders declared a great festival to celebrate the capture of Samson. The people made sacrifices to their god Dagon and excitedly praised him.

"Our god has delivered our enemy Samson to us!" they gloated as they saw him there in chains. "The scourge of our nation who killed so many of us is now in our power!" [25,26]Half drunk by now, the people demanded, "Bring out Samson so we can have some fun with him!"

So he was brought from the prison and made to stand at the center of the temple, between the two pillars supporting the roof. Samson said to the boy who was leading him by the hand, "Place my hands against the two pillars. I want to rest against them."

[27]By then the temple was completely filled with people. The five Philistine leaders were there as well as three thousand people in the balconies who were watching Samson and making fun of him.

[28]Then Samson prayed to the Lord and said, "O Lord Jehovah, remember me again—please strengthen me one more time, so that I may pay back the Philistines for the loss of at least one of my eyes."

[29]Then Samson pushed against the pillars with all his might.

[30]"Let me die with the Philistines," he prayed.

And the temple crashed down upon the Philistine leaders and all the people. So those he killed at the moment of his death were more than those he had killed during his entire lifetime. [31]Later, his brothers and other relatives came down to get his body, and they brought him back home and buried him be-

16:22-31 It took a lack of physical sight for Samson to gain personal and spiritual insight. But that was not the end of the story. In his prayer to God, Samson finally admitted his helplessness and committed himself into God's hands. Notice that Samson accomplished more in his God-appointed death than in his entire self-centered life. And despite Samson's serious flaws, he was remembered as a man of faith (see Hebrews 11:32). We can only imagine how Samson would have altered history had he been committed to God throughout his life. We need to examine our life for missed opportunities and then determine not to miss them when they arise again.

tween Zorah and Eshtaol, where his father, Manoah, was buried. He had led Israel for twenty years.

CHAPTER 17
Micah's Idol Collection

In the hill country of Ephraim lived a man named Micah.

[2]One day he said to his mother, "That thousand dollars you thought was stolen from you, and you were cursing about—well, I stole it!"

"God bless you for confessing it," his mother replied. [3]So he returned the money to her.

"I am going to give it to the Lord as a credit for your account," she declared. "I'll have an idol carved for you and plate it with the silver."

[4,5]So his mother took a fifth of it to a silversmith, and the idol he made from it was placed in Micah's shrine. Micah had many idols in his collection, also an ephod and some teraphim, and he installed one of his sons as the priest. [6](For in those days Israel had no king, so everyone did whatever he wanted to—whatever seemed right in his own eyes.)

[7,8]One day a young priest from the town of Bethlehem, in Judah, arrived in that area of Ephraim, looking for a good place to live. He happened to stop at Micah's house as he was traveling through.

[9]"Where are you from?" Micah asked him.

And he replied, "I am a priest from Bethlehem, in Judah, and I am looking for a place to live."

[10,11]"Well, stay here with me," Micah said, "and you can be my priest. I will give you one hundred dollars a year plus a new suit and your board and room." The young man agreed to this and became as one of Micah's sons. [12]So Micah consecrated him as his personal priest.

[13]"I know the Lord will really bless me now," Micah exclaimed, "because now I have a genuine priest working for me!"

CHAPTER 18
The Danites Steal Micah's Idols

As has already been stated, there was no king in Israel at that time. The tribe of Dan was trying to find a place to settle, for they had not yet driven out the people living in the land assigned to them. [2]So the men of Dan chose five army heroes from the cities of Zorah and Eshtaol as scouts to go and spy out the land they were supposed to settle in. Arriving in the hill country of Ephraim, they stayed at Micah's home. [3]Noticing the young Levite's accent, they took him aside and asked him, "What are you doing here? Why did you come?" [4]He told them about his contract with Micah, and that he was his personal priest.

[5]"Well, then," they said, "ask God whether or not our trip will be successful."

[6]"Yes," the priest replied, "all is well. The Lord is taking care of you."

[7]So the five men went on to the town of Laish and noticed how secure everyone felt. Their manner of life was Phoenician, and they were wealthy. They lived quietly and were unprepared for an attack, for there were no tribes in the area strong enough to try it. They

---

17:1-6 The slogan that summarizes all of the events of Judges 17–21 is first seen in 17:6: "In those days Israel had no king, so everyone did whatever he wanted to—whatever seemed right in his own eyes." This statement is rightly applied to the do-it-yourself idolatry of Micah. Without a king and well-defined enforcement of God's laws, there were almost no limits or boundaries placed upon the people. In this case, true worship was mocked by the making of idols (see Exodus 20:4) and the creation of a private priesthood. When we ignore God's commands for our life, we also mock God. Showing God proper respect entails following God's will for our life. If we do this, we will avoid self-destructive actions, like those of the Israelites in the following chapters.

17:7-13 The depth of the self-deception, or religious denial, in Israel during this time is clearly seen here. Not only was Micah not rebuked by the priest from Bethlehem for his open idolatry; the priest actually accepted Micah's job offer! This arrangement stood counter to God's clearly revealed will on the matter of worship in Israel. But Micah believed it would bring him great blessing anyway. He was either ignorant of God's laws or chose to ignore them. God has shown us in the Bible all that we need to know about healthy living. We are responsible to know what God desires of us and then to follow through on it.

18:2-6 The Danites were initially surprised, then intrigued, by Micah's arrangement of hiring a personal priest. Their first questions seem to indicate that they knew this arrangement was not right. But they liked the idea of having a personal hot line to God, especially after being told that their present mission would be successful. Sadly, it appears that Micah's priest spoke only for himself, not for God. The spiritual denial only increased on all sides. When confronted by something that is wrong or inappropriate, we must not compromise, even if there are apparent benefits.

lived a great distance from their relatives in Sidon, and had little or no contact with the nearby villages. [8]So the spies returned to their people in Zorah and Eshtaol.

"What about it?" they were asked. "What did you find?"

[9,10]And the men replied, "Let's attack! We have seen the land and it is ours for the taking—a broad, fertile, wonderful place—a real paradise. The people aren't even prepared to defend themselves! Come on, let's go! For God has given it to us!"

[11]So six hundred armed troops of the tribe of Dan set out from Zorah and Eshtaol. [12]They camped first at a place west of Kiriath-jearim in Judah (which is still called "The Camp of Dan"), [13]then they went on up into the hill country of Ephraim.

As they passed the home of Micah, [14]the five spies told the others. "There is a shrine in there with an ephod, some teraphim, and many plated idols. It's obvious what we ought to do!"

[15,16]So the five men went over to the house and with all of the armed men standing just outside the gate, they talked to the young priest and asked him how he was getting along. [17]Then the five spies entered the shrine and took the idols, the ephod, and the teraphim.

[18]"What are you doing?" the young priest demanded when he saw them carrying them out.

[19]"Be quiet and come with us," they said. "Be a priest to all of us. Isn't it better for you to be a priest to a whole tribe in Israel instead of just to one man in his private home?"

[20]The young priest was then quite happy to go with them, and he took along the ephod, the teraphim, and the idols.[21]They started on their way again, placing their children, cattle, and household goods at the front of the column. [22]When they were quite a distance from Micah's home, Micah and some of his neighbors came chasing after them, [23]yelling at them to stop.

"What do you want, chasing after us like this?" the men of Dan demanded.

[24]"What do you mean, 'What do I want'!" Micah retorted. "You've taken away all my gods and my priest, and I have nothing left!"

[25]"Be careful how you talk, mister," the men of Dan replied. "Somebody's apt to get angry and kill every one of you."

[26]So the men of Dan kept going. When Micah saw that there were too many of them for him to handle, he turned back home.

[27]Then, with Micah's idols and the priest, the men of Dan arrived at the city of Laish. There weren't even any guards, so they went in and slaughtered all the people and burned the city to the ground. [28]There was no one to help the inhabitants, for they were too far away from Sidon, and they had no local allies, for they had no dealings with anyone. This happened in the valley next to Beth-rehob. Then the people of the tribe of Dan rebuilt the city and lived there. [29]The city was named "Dan" after their ancestor, Israel's son, but it had originally been called Laish.

[30]Then they set up the idols and appointed a man named Jonathan (son of Gershom and grandson of Moses!) and his sons as their priests. This family continued as priests until the city was finally conquered by its enemies. [31]So Micah's idols were worshiped by the tribe of Dan as long as the Tabernacle remained at Shiloh.

CHAPTER 19

A Horrible Crime in Israel

At this time before Israel had a king, there was a man of the tribe of Levi living on the far side of the hill country of Ephraim, who brought home a girl from Bethlehem in Judah to be his concubine. [2]But she became angry with him

18:7-20 When the city of Laish appeared a promising solution to their problem, the Danites concluded that Micah's priest had spoken for God. Thus, when they came to Micah's house again, they stole his idols and hired his priest. Obviously, this priest felt no sense of accountability to God. After making the wrong decision to become Micah's priest, the young man had no problem becoming the priest to a whole tribe. We all know that the direction of our first step often affects the direction of the following steps. In order to remain free from our dependencies, we should make sure that each step is in the direction of recovery.

18:22-31 This episode is a classic example of an angry confrontation between two parties that both desperately need to change. Micah, the original idolater, asserted that he had been wronged because his idols and personal priest had been taken. The aggressive Danites responded with threats and intimidation. As a result, the Danites set up an elaborate long-term worship system as a rival to true worship in Israel. Micah's original "small mistake" had now spread and ensnared an entire tribe of Israel. We should be aware that small mistakes in our own life often spread into the lives of others around us.

and ran away, and returned to her father's
home in Bethlehem, and was there about four
months. [3]Then her husband, taking along a
servant and an extra donkey, went to see her
to try to win her back again. When he arrived
at her home, she let him in and introduced
him to her father, who was delighted to meet
him. [4]Her father urged him to stay awhile, so
he stayed three days, and they all had a very
pleasant time.

[5]On the fourth day they were up early,
ready to leave, but the girl's father insisted on
their having breakfast first. [6]Then he pleaded
with him to stay one more day, as they were
having such a good time. [7]At first the man
refused, but his father-in-law kept urging him
until finally he gave in. [8]The next morning
they were up early again, and again the girl's
father pleaded, "Stay just today and leave
sometime this evening." So they had another
day of feasting.

[9]That afternoon as he and his wife and
servant were preparing to leave, his father-in-
law said, "Look, it's getting late. Stay just
tonight, and we will have a pleasant evening
together and tomorrow you can get up early
and be on your way."

[10]But this time the man was adamant, so
they left, getting as far as Jerusalem (also
called Jebus) before dark.

[11]His servant said to him, "It's getting too
late to travel; let's stay here tonight."

[12,13]"No," his master said, "we can't stay in
this heathen city where there are no Israelites—we will go on to Gibeah, or possibly
Ramah."

[14]So they went on. The sun was setting just
as they came to Gibeah, a village of the tribe
of Benjamin, [15]so they went there for the
night. But as no one invited them in, they
camped in the village square.[16]Just then an
old man came by on his way home from his
work in the fields. (He was originally from
the hill country of Ephraim, but was living
now in Gibeah, even though it was in the
territory of Benjamin.) [17]When he saw the
travelers camped in the square, he asked
them where they were from and where they
were going.

[18]"We're on the way home from Bethlehem, in Judah," the man replied. "I live on
the far edge of the Ephraim hill country, near
Shiloh. But no one has taken us in for the
night, [19]even though we have fodder for our
donkeys and plenty of food and wine for
ourselves."

[20]"Don't worry," the old man said, "be my
guests; for you mustn't stay here in the
square. It's too dangerous."

[21]So he took them home with him. He fed
their donkeys while they rested, and afterward they had supper together.[22]Just as they
were beginning to warm to the occasion, a
gang of sex perverts gathered around the
house and began beating at the door and
yelling at the old man to bring out the man
who was staying with him, so they could rape
him. [23]The old man stepped outside to talk to
them.

"No, my brothers, don't do such a dastardly
act," he begged, "for he is my guest. [24]Here,
take my virgin daughter and this man's wife.
I'll bring them out and you can do whatever
you like to them—but don't do such a thing
to this man."

[25]But they wouldn't listen to him. Then the
girl's husband pushed her out to them, and
they abused her all night, taking turns raping
her until morning. Finally, just at dawn, they
let her go. [26]She fell down at the door of the
house and lay there until it was light. [27]When
her husband opened the door to be on his
way, he found her there, fallen down in front
of the door with her hands digging into the
threshold.

[28]"Well, come on," he said. "Let's get going."

But there was no answer, for she was dead;
so he threw her across the donkey's back and
took her home. [29]When he got there he took
a knife and cut her body into twelve parts and
sent one piece to each tribe of Israel. [30]Then
the entire nation was roused to action against
the men of Benjamin because of this awful
deed.

"There hasn't been such a horrible crime
since Israel left Egypt," everyone said. "We've
got to do something about it."

19:11-29 This tragic episode represents the moral low point of the book of Judges. This incident is even worse because the uncaring Levite gave up his concubine to save his own skin. Have we sacrificed the health and stability of our family so that we could engage in our selfish life-style? If so, we should accept responsibility for the consequences, unlike the Levite in these verses. He blamed the Benjamites and did not recognize his part in the tragedy. But if drugs, alcohol, or some other problem is harming our loved ones, we need to accept our part in the process. When we recognize that we are accountable, we can begin to get the help we need.

CHAPTER 20

Israel Attacks the Tribe of Benjamin

Then the entire nation of Israel sent their leaders and 450,000 troops to assemble with one mind before the Lord at Mizpah. They came from as far away as Dan and Beersheba, and everywhere between, and from across the Jordan in the land of Gilead. 3(Word of the mobilization of the Israeli forces at Mizpah soon reached the land of Benjamin.) The chiefs of Israel now called for the murdered woman's husband and asked him just what had happened.

4"We arrived one evening at Gibeah, a village in Benjamin," he began. 5"That night the men of Gibeah surrounded the house, planning to kill me, and they raped my wife until she was dead. 6So I cut her body into twelve pieces and sent the pieces throughout the land of Israel, for these men have committed a terrible crime. 7Now then, sons of Israel, express your mind and give me your counsel!"

8-10And as one man they replied, "Not one of us will return home until we have punished the village of Gibeah. A tenth of the army will be selected by lot as a supply line to bring us food, and the rest of us will destroy Gibeah for this horrible deed."

11So the whole nation united in this task.

12Then messengers were sent to the tribe of Benjamin, asking, "Did you know about the terrible thing that was done among you? 13Give up these evil men from the city of Gibeah so that we can execute them and purge Israel of her evil." But the people of Benjamin wouldn't listen. 14,15Instead, 26,000 of them arrived in Gibeah to join the 700 local men in their defense against the rest of Israel. 16 (Among all these there were 700 men who were left-handed sharpshooters. They could hit a target within a hair's breadth, never missing!) 17The army of Israel, not counting the men of Benjamin, numbered 400,000 men.

18Before the battle the Israeli army went to Bethel first to ask counsel from God. "Which tribe shall lead us against the people of Benjamin?" they asked.

And the Lord replied, "Judah shall go first."

19,20So the entire army left early the next morning to go to Gibeah, to attack the men of Benjamin. 21But the men defending the village stormed out and killed 22,000 Israelis that day. 22-24Then the Israeli army wept before the Lord until evening and asked him, "Shall we fight further against our brother Benjamin?"

And the Lord said, "Yes." So the men of Israel took courage and went out again the next day to fight at the same place. 25And that day they lost another 18,000 men, all experienced swordsmen.

26Then the entire army went up to Bethel and wept before the Lord and fasted until evening, offering burnt sacrifices and peace offerings. 27,28(The Ark of God was in Bethel in those days. Phinehas, the son of Eleazar and grandson of Aaron, was the priest.)

The men of Israel asked the Lord, "Shall we go out again and fight against our brother Benjamin, or shall we stop?"

And the Lord said, "Go, for tomorrow I will see to it that you defeat the men of Benjamin."

29So the Israeli army set an ambush all around the village, 30and went out again on the third day and set themselves in their usual battle formation. 31When the army of Benjamin came out of the town to attack, the Israeli forces retreated and Benjamin was drawn away from the town as they chased after Israel. And as they had done previously, Benjamin began to kill the men of Israel along the roadway running between Bethel and Gibeah, so that about thirty of them died.

32Then the army of Benjamin shouted,

20:8-25 We are often highly resistant to the fact that we are in need of recovery. The tribe of Benjamin foolishly denied the sins of Gibeah and self-righteously set out to defend its honor. They were unwilling to admit that there was sin in their midst. This story is a powerful illustration of denial and its consequences. We often hide our problems, denying our need for help until it is too late. We would be wise to humbly admit our sin and seek to make things right. If the Benjamites had been willing to discipline Gibeah, the rest of the tribe could have remained strong. But they let their pride keep them from confession and were, as a result, almost destroyed.

20:26-41 The rest of Israel was willing to be involved in serious self-examination and to commit themselves to God and his guidance. These steps of corporate recovery led to a painful yet decisive victory. God used the Benjamites' resistant pride to lead them into an ambush in which they lost almost all their troops (see 20:14-15). When we are confronted by others about our dependencies or wrong behaviors, we should acknowledge the problem and face reality before our denial of the situation destroys us.

"We're defeating them again!" But the armies
of Israel had agreed in advance to run away so
that the army of Benjamin would chase them
and be drawn away from the town. 33 But
when the main army of Israel reached Baal-
tamar, it turned and attacked, and the 10,000
men in ambush west of Geba jumped up from
where they were 34 and advanced against the
rear of the army of Benjamin, who still didn't
realize the impending disaster. 35-39 So the Lord
helped Israel defeat Benjamin, and the Israeli
army killed 25,100 men of Benjamin that day,
leaving but a tiny remnant of their forces.
Summary of the Battle: The army of Israel
retreated from the men of Benjamin in order
to give the ambush more room for maneuvering. When the men of Benjamin had killed
about thirty of the Israelis, they were confident of a massive slaughter just as on the
previous days. But then the men in ambush
rushed into the village and slaughtered everyone in it, and set it on fire. The great cloud of
smoke pouring into the sky was the signal for
the Israeli army to turn around and attack the
army of Benjamin, 40,41 who now looked behind them and were terrified to discover that
their city was on fire, and that they were in
serious trouble. 42 So they ran toward the wilderness, but the Israelis chased after them,
and the men who had set the ambush came
out and joined the slaughter from the rear.
43 They encircled the army of Benjamin east of
Gibeah, and killed most of them there. 44 Eighteen thousand of the Benjamin troops died in
that day's battle. 45 The rest of the army fled
into the wilderness toward the rock of Rimmon, but 5,000 were killed along the way, and
2,000 more near Gidom.
46,47 So the tribe of Benjamin lost 25,000
thousand brave warriors that day, leaving
only 600 men who escaped to the rock of
Rimmon, where they lived for four months.
48 Then the Israeli army returned and slaughtered the entire population of the tribe of
Benjamin—men, women, children, and cattle—and burned down every city and village
in the entire land.

CHAPTER 21
Wives for the Men of Benjamin

The leaders of Israel had vowed at Mizpah
never to let their daughters marry a man from
the tribe of Benjamin. 2 And now the Israeli
leaders met at Bethel and sat before God until
evening, weeping bitterly.
3 "O Lord God of Israel," they cried out,
"why has this happened, that now one of our
tribes is missing?"
4 The next morning they were up early and
built an altar, and offered sacrifices and peace
offerings on it. 5 And they said among themselves, "Was any tribe of Israel not represented when we held our council before the
Lord at Mizpah?" For at that time it was
agreed by solemn oath that anyone who refused to come must die. 6 There was deep sadness throughout all Israel for the loss of their
brother tribe, Benjamin.
"Gone," they kept saying to themselves,
"gone—an entire tribe of Israel has been cut
off and is gone. 7 And how shall we get wives
for the few who remain, since we have sworn
by the Lord that we will not give them our
daughters?"
8,9 Then they thought again of their oath to
kill anyone who refused to come to Mizpah
and discovered that no one had attended
from Jabesh-gilead. 10-12 So they sent 12,000 of
their best soldiers to destroy the people of
Jabesh-gilead. All the men, married women,
and children were slain, but the young virgins
of marriageable age were saved. There were
400 of these, and they were brought to the
camp at Shiloh.
13 Then Israel sent a peace delegation to the
little remnant of the men of Benjamin at
Rimmon Rock. 14 The 400 girls were given to
them as wives, and they returned to their
homes; but there were not enough of these
girls for all of them. 15 (What a sad time it was

21:1-12 In the heat of anger or emotions, many people needing recovery, or moving through the recovery process, make rash or unrealistic vows. In this passage Israel was forced to keep their vows because they were public and before God. They had not learned from Jephthah's tragic mistake of making a thoughtless vow (11:30-31, 34-39). This reveals a great lack of wisdom and self-control. Promises are made to be kept. We should not make a promise that we will regret or refuse to carry out later.

21:10-24 Frequently those needing recovery are willing to do whatever it takes to survive, without necessarily facing their root problems. There was no hint of repentance or commitment to God on the part of the Benjamites here, just the desire to survive. Also, in feeling sorry for the remnant of Benjamin, the rest of Israel used very questionable ways of "making it up to them." While it is a very commendable thing to help others, it should not be done wrongly or strictly out of guilt.

in Israel in those days because the Lord had
made a breach in the tribes of Israel.)
16"What shall we do for wives for the
others, since all the women of the tribe of
Benjamin are dead?" the leaders of Israel
asked. 17"There must be some way to get wives
for them, so that an entire tribe of Israel will
not be lost forever. 18 But we can't give them
our own daughters. We have sworn with a
solemn oath that anyone who does this shall
be cursed of God."
19Suddenly someone thought of the annual
religious festival held in the fields of Shiloh,
between Lebonah and Bethel, along the east
side of the road that goes from Bethel to
Shechem.
20They told the men of Benjamin who still
needed wives, "Go and hide in the vineyards, 21and when the girls of Shiloh come
out for their dances, rush out and catch
them and take them home with you to be
your wives! 22And when their fathers and
brothers come to us in protest, we will tell
them, 'Please be understanding and let
them have your daughters, for we didn't
find enough wives for them when we destroyed Jabesh-gilead, and you couldn't
have given your daughters to them without
being guilty.'"
23So the men of Benjamin did as they were
told and kidnapped the girls who took part in
the celebration, and carried them off to their
own land. Then they rebuilt their cities and
lived in them. 24So the people of Israel returned to their homes.
25(There was no king in Israel in those days,
and every man did whatever he thought was
right.)

REFLECTIONS ON JUDGES

✲insights FROM GIDEON'S LIFE

There are frequently background issues, such as the way people view themselves or their family's status, involved in recovery. Gideon's response to God in **Judges 6:15-16,** and his fear and hesitation later, were likely related to feelings of inadequacy. God offered his power (because of Gideon's commitment to him) as the means of dealing decisively with such issues. Our past and our family's status may seem like good excuses for doing nothing and hiding in comfortable (though detrimental) situations. But God says that he will be with us to help us carry out whatever tasks we have been assigned. All we need to do is trust in him.

In **Judges 7:1-7,** Gideon's forces were already outnumbered by the enemy, but God limited their numbers even more. In the end, only three hundred men would go to fight the Midianites. From a human standpoint, this put Israel at an impossible disadvantage. But God had limited their numbers for a reason: he wanted to show Israel that his power was sufficient no matter what the odds. Undoubtedly, Gideon became nervous as his army began to dwindle before his very eyes. But instead of walking out on God, he proceeded with an even stronger commitment to his plan. It is amazing how much can be accomplished with fewer resources and a stronger commitment to God's will. When we turn our life over to God each day, he can do more with us than with thousands of uncommitted soldiers.

The miraculous victory recorded in **Judges 7:8-23** illustrates some of the resources available to us in recovery. Certainly the person seeking recovery needs to know that it is possible to overcome great odds with God's power. Perhaps equally important is the realization that the oppressor or abuser in many situations will prove to be self-destructive. The abusive cycle, which may have seemed impossible to break, may actually prove to be surprisingly fragile as we face it with God's help.

✲insights FROM JEPHTHAH'S LIFE

We often suffer much ridicule because of our family background or for factors that are completely beyond our control. As we see in **Judges 11:1-11,** Jephthah apparently possessed considerable courage and natural leadership ability. But he was sensitive to having been rejected and sought to secure his position in Gilead even before the battle with the Ammonites. While Jephthah seemed confident in his ability as God's instrument to bring about freedom, he apparently still needed to forgive the people of Gilead and to gain a more balanced self-understanding. Like Jephthah, we may have been taunted by others due to our family background or for other problems beyond our control. We, too, need to forgive those people, put those events behind us, and then move on to the tasks to which God has called us.

insights FROM SAMSON'S LIFE

In **Judges 13:15-23,** the interaction between Samson's parents and the Angel demonstrates their balanced sense of self-esteem. They had been called for the high purpose of raising a child uniquely gifted to serve God. They also had been allowed to live even though they looked upon God. However, their giving of sacrifices indicated their proper sense of faith, humility, and thankfulness before God. Likewise, we may be called to do special things for God or his people. We should remember that we are serving God and that he is allowing us to do these things. Knowing this should temper any exaggerated sense of self-worth we may be tempted to feel.

As we see in **Judges 14:5-9,** even at an early point in life, Samson was insensitive to the vows that defined his relationship with God. Samson's Nazirite vow forbade his contact with anything dead (see Numbers 6), but Samson killed a lion and then revisited the carcass. It was indeed the Spirit of the Lord that strengthened him, but his God-given ability was very much capable of being abused. There is very little evidence of commitment to God at this point in Samson's life. Having been raised as a "special child," he was self-centered. This sinful self-obsession was the ruin of Samson as it is the ruin of too many people today.

As is evidenced by **Judges 15:1-17,** Samson was the most contradictory of Israel's judges. Called to be a Nazirite, he violently killed and destroyed, flaunting his previous "separation" before God (see Numbers 6). He would justify extreme actions based almost totally on angry vengeance. He also led a largely solitary, lonely existence for periods of time. Samson was far from ideal. Yet God still used him to begin the conquest of the neighboring Philistines, a task that would be finished much later by King David.

Unless we face and deal with our recovery issues, they will continue to reemerge throughout our life. Samson's flaw in regard to pagan women reasserted itself in **Judges 16:1-3.** Samson was known as a judge in Israel, a position of great respect and responsibility. Yet he exposed himself to both shame and danger by going to the prostitute in Gaza. Again, his strength and courage rescued him. But, as shall be seen, Samson's belief that he could handle his weakness was mistaken. None of us can fight our dependencies alone. We may get by for a while, even racking up some impressive victories, but eventually we will fall prey to temptation. We need to find a context where we can lean upon God and other people for the support we need.

It is a sad spectacle when a person in need of recovery finally hits bottom. For years Samson had steered around the potential disasters caused by his extreme behavior and anger. But in **Judges 16:18-21** Delilah used her knowledge about Samson to destroy him. Instead of facing the flaws in his life and then building a proper sense of identity and a new life, Samson was forced to admit his helplessness as a tortured Philistine slave. He had deserted God by his actions, and God's strength had left him. We don't need to hit bottom—we can face and defeat our problems before anything catastrophic happens.

insights FROM THE TRIBE OF DAN

In **Judges 18:1-2** the tribe of Dan was looking for the easy way out. This kind of behavior is typical of people in need of recovery. The Danites had been long unable to evict the Amorites from the land allotted to them under Joshua (Judges 1:34). So they gave up persevering toward that God-given goal. Instead, they sent scouts in search of an easier area to conquer that offered significant advantages to the Danites. There is no indication that the tribe ever considered the reasons for their previous defeat or that they had sought to learn from it. Instead, they looked for another easier solution which led them even further away from the God who could have given them victory.

RUTH

THE BIG PICTURE

A. THE BOTTOM DROPS OUT IN LIFE (1:1-5).
B. THE BEGINNING OF THE LONG ROAD TO RECOVERY (1:6-22).
C. THE SEEN PROCESS AND THE UNSEEN PROVISION IN RECOVERY (2:1-23).
D. THE FASHION OF REALITY IN AN OLD-FASHIONED LOVE STORY (3:1-18).
E. THE JOY OF FULFILLED RELATIONSHIPS (4:1-17).
F. THE LONG-TERM CONSEQUENCES OF SHORT-TERM CHOICES (4:18-22).

In the time of the judges, Naomi and her family moved to neighboring Moab to escape a severe famine in Israel. Naomi's husband died there, and her sons married Moabite women. In time, both of her sons also died, leaving Naomi destitute and alone, far from her relatives in Israel. One daughter-in-law, Orpah, returned to her own family; the other one, Ruth, stayed with Naomi to comfort her in her grief.

Grief is hard work; it is painful. People who are grieving need others to grieve with them and comfort them. Ruth's faithfulness to her mother-in-law during this time is, indeed, striking. She gave up the security of her family in Moab to face a future of probable loneliness and poverty in a foreign land. But her faithfulness yielded the fruits of God's blessing, and Naomi experienced God's comfort and love through her.

Together Ruth and Naomi trusted God to help them, and God came through in his own time. The circumstances through which their desperate needs were met reveal God's unseen hand at work. God led Naomi and Ruth back to Israel, where Ruth met Boaz, her future husband. In the end, not only did Ruth find security and love, but the sadness of Naomi's heart was replaced with joy.

We have all experienced some kind of loss. There are times when we may feel like the future is hopeless, even after we have given it over to God. As we grieve, we may feel abandoned and bitter toward God and the people around us. But we can rest in the fact that God is still with us—even when our emotions scream the opposite message—and that he is working on our behalf behind the scenes.

THE BOTTOM LINE

PURPOSE: To show that people who turn their lives over to God can make an extraordinary impact and can find peace and serenity in their own life. AUTHOR: Tradition names Samuel as the author, but it could have been a writer during the reign of David or Solomon. AUDIENCE: The people of Israel. DATE WRITTEN: Sometime between 1020–930 B.C. SETTING: During the period of the judges. KEY VERSE: "But Ruth replied, 'Don't make me leave you, for I want to go wherever you go and to live wherever you live; your people shall be my people, and your God shall be my God'" (1:16). KEY PLACES: Bethlehem, Moab. KEY PEOPLE AND RELATIONSHIPS: Naomi and Ruth, Ruth and Boaz, Naomi and Obed.

RECOVERY THEMES

Facing Our Losses: In the grief process, we face the agonizing reality of our losses. This takes time and a great deal of emotional energy. Because it is so hard, our tendency is to try to shut out the pain. We want to ignore what has happened, keep a stiff upper lip, smile at all costs. Avoiding the difficult process of grief does not produce growth and healing. Naomi felt embittered and abandoned by God. She faced her loss honestly and allowed herself to grieve. This was an important step toward her healing.

Comfort in Grief: The bottom fell out of Ruth's and Naomi's life. The easy way out for Ruth would have been to leave Naomi in her poverty and go back to the security of her own family. But Ruth trusted the God of Israel and chose to stay with Naomi. Naomi and Ruth received great comfort from each other. Those who are grieving need those who will mourn with them and help them carry their grief. During painful times, God often uses other people to bring us comfort.

God's Plan: This story relates an important link in God's plan for the redemption of our broken world. God used the faithfulness and integrity of Ruth, Naomi, and Boaz, first to bring about their own healing, but then to bring a child, Obed, into the world. This baby would become the grandfather of King David, and the ancestor of Jesus the Messiah, through whom we all find healing from the destructive forces of sin. The faithfulness of these three individuals has made possible the spiritual healing of the human race.

Difficult Times: It is easy to think that if circumstances were just a little better, our recovery would be more successful. But the test of any recovery process is how well it works when times are bad. The book of Ruth tells us about a family that suffered some extreme losses. First Naomi's husband died, then both of her sons. One daughter-in-law returned home to her family, but the other one stayed in this seemingly hopeless situation. Ruth refused to let difficult times determine the outcome of her future.

CHAPTER 1

Ruth Stays with Naomi

Long ago when judges ruled in Israel, a man
named Elimelech, from Bethlehem, left the
country because of a famine and moved to
the land of Moab. With him were his wife,
Naomi, and his two sons, Mahlon and Chilion. 3During the time of their residence there,
Elimelech died and Naomi was left with her
two sons.

4,5These young men, Mahlon and Chilion,
married girls of Moab, Orpah and Ruth. But
later, both men died, so that Naomi was left
alone, without her husband or sons. 6,7She decided to return to Israel with her daughters-in-
law, for she had heard that the Lord had blessed
his people by giving them good crops again.

8But after they had begun their homeward
journey, she changed her mind and said to
her two daughters-in-law, "Why don't you
return to your parents' homes instead of coming with me? And may the Lord reward you
for your faithfulness to your husbands and to
me. 9And may he bless you with another
happy marriage." Then she kissed them, and
they all broke down and cried.

10"No," they said. "We want to go with you
to your people."

11But Naomi replied, "It is better for you to
return to your own people. Do I have younger
sons who could grow up to be your husbands?
12No, my daughters, return to your parents'
homes, for I am too old to have a husband.
And even if that were possible, and I became

1:1-5 Elimelech and his family decided to move from Bethlehem to Moab to escape difficult circumstances. They fled political instability, economic problems, and famine. But there is a strange silence regarding their trust in God; nothing is said of their seeking God's guidance. The decision to move to Moab proved to have disastrous immediate and long-term consequences. Similar consequences often emerge when we attempt to escape difficult or painful circumstances without God's direction. In recovery it is important for us to face our painful circumstances and, with God's help, overcome them.

1:16-18 Ruth's desire to remain close to Naomi was actually a step of faith. Naomi had no financial security, no family members nearby for support or protection. By staying with Naomi, Ruth was cutting herself off from her own family, land, and culture. She was essentially committing her life into God's hands. After making her commitment to Naomi, Ruth stood by her, doing all she could to provide food and help for her mother-in-law. Committing ourselves to the process of recovery is not an easy road. We must realize this before we begin; otherwise we will be tempted to give up when things get tough. But, as with Ruth, sticking to our commitments will always yield great rewards in the long run.

RUTH, NAOMI, & BOAZ

What could be more emotionally devastating than to experience widowhood, the death of two children, and poverty all at one time? Any one of these shocking losses would be enough to overwhelm most of us. Together, however, these losses would likely cause any of us to break beneath the mountain of grief.

Naomi and her daughter-in-law Ruth dug out from under their mountain of despair hand in hand. Faced with a hopeless situation, Ruth chose to stay with Naomi even though Naomi had little to offer her. She also committed herself to Naomi's God. God saw Ruth through that difficult period of uncertainty to healing and brought her to the point where she was ready for marriage to Boaz.

As Naomi traveled through the grief process to recovery, she experienced anger, depression, and a sense that God had dealt her bitter blows and had abandoned her. She felt hopeless and initially could not understand Ruth's faith. But after Ruth's God-given success gleaning in Boaz's field, Naomi's outlook changed dramatically. She was able to see that God was at work rebuilding their lives. The marriage of Ruth and Boaz proved to be a time of joyful fulfillment for Naomi. And once again Naomi not only had a son, but also a grandson!

Boaz was wonderfully gentle and wise. Though strong and successful, he was sensitive and concerned about the needs of those around him. He was immediately interested in Ruth and Naomi's situation, while still carefully maintaining Ruth's dignity. Perhaps a widower himself, and likely some years older than Ruth, Boaz also displayed admirable self-control and respect for Ruth. He chose the path of delayed gratification in their relationship rather than a sexual compromise.

God led Naomi and Ruth to a new life filled with promise for the future. The son of Ruth and Boaz would become the grandfather of King David and the ancestor of Jesus the Messiah. They could never have known that their simple acts of faith would lead to the blessing of millions! God may have significant plans for us and our descendants, too. All we need to do is trust God and obey his will for us.

STRENGTHS AND ACCOMPLISHMENTS:
- Naomi and Ruth's relationship was centered on God.
- Ruth and Naomi were committed to each other.
- Ruth's actions were characterized by faith, loyalty, and boldness.
- Boaz was sensitive, generous, and full of integrity.

LESSONS FROM THEIR LIVES:
- Trust is the necessary foundation for a healthy relationship.
- Grief is the process that helps us to recover from losses.
- Those who are grieving need people to stand by them.
- God is intimately involved in our grief.

KEY VERSE:
"Don't make me leave you, for I want to go wherever you go and to live wherever you live; your people shall be my people, and your God shall be my God" (1:16).

The story of Ruth, Naomi, and Boaz is told in the book of Ruth. Boaz and Ruth are mentioned in Matthew 1:5, and Boaz is referred to in 1 Chronicles 2:11-12 and Luke 3:23-38.

---

pregnant tonight, and bore sons [13]would you
wait for them to grow up? No, of course not,
my daughters; oh, how I grieve for you that
the Lord has punished me in a way that injures you."

[14]And again they cried together, and Orpah
kissed her mother-in-law good-bye, and returned to her childhood home; but Ruth insisted on staying with Naomi.

[15]"See," Naomi said to her, "your sister-in-law has gone back to her people and to her
gods; you should do the same."

[16]But Ruth replied, "Don't make me leave
you, for I want to go wherever you go and to
live wherever you live; your people shall be
my people, and your God shall be my God; [17]I
want to die where you die and be buried
there. May the Lord do terrible things to me
if I allow anything but death to separate us."

[18]And when Naomi saw that Ruth had

made up her mind and could not be persuaded otherwise, she stopped urging her. 19So
they both came to Bethlehem, and the entire
village was stirred by their arrival.
"Is it really Naomi?" the women asked.
20But she told them, "Don't call me Naomi.
Call me Mara," (Naomi means "pleasant";
Mara means "bitter") "for Almighty God has
dealt me bitter blows. 21I went out full and the
Lord has brought me home empty; why
should you call me Naomi when the Lord has
turned his back on me and sent such calamity!"
22(Their return from Moab and arrival in
Bethlehem was at the beginning of the barley
harvest.)

CHAPTER 2
Ruth Gleans in the Fields
Now Naomi had an in-law there in Bethlehem who was a very wealthy man. His name
was Boaz.
2One day Ruth said to Naomi, "Perhaps I
can go out into the fields of some kind man
to glean the free grain behind his reapers."
And Naomi said, "All right, dear daughter.
Go ahead."
3So she did. And as it happened, the field
where she found herself belonged to Boaz,
this relative of Naomi's husband.
4,5Boaz arrived from the city while she was
there. After exchanging greetings with the
reapers he said to his foreman, "Hey, who's
that girl over there?"
6And the foreman replied, "It's that girl
from the land of Moab who came back with
Naomi. 7She asked me this morning if she
could pick up the grains dropped by the reapers, and she has been at it ever since except for
a few minutes' rest over there in the shade."
8,9Boaz went over and talked to her. "Listen,
my child," he said to her. "Stay right here with
us to glean; don't think of going to any other
fields. Stay right behind my women workers;
I have warned the young men not to bother
you; when you are thirsty, go and help yourself to the water."
10,11She thanked him warmly. "How can you
be so kind to me?" she asked. "You must know
I am only a foreigner."
"Yes, I know," Boaz replied, "and I also
know about all the love and kindness you
have shown your mother-in-law since the
death of your husband, and how you left your
father and mother in your own land and have
come here to live among strangers. 12May the
Lord God of Israel, under whose wings you
have come to take refuge, bless you for it."
13"Oh, thank you, sir," she replied. "You are
so good to me, and I'm not even one of your
workers!"
14At lunch time Boaz called to her, "Come
and eat with us."
So she sat with his reapers and he gave her
food, more than she could eat. 15And when
she went back to work again, Boaz told his
young men to let her glean right among the
sheaves without stopping her, 16and to snap
off some heads of barley and drop them on
purpose for her to glean, and not to make any
remarks. 17So she worked there all day, and in
the evening when she had beaten out the
barley she had gleaned, it came to a whole
bushel! 18She carried it back into the city and

2:1-3, 18-23 We must never forget that God is in charge of our recovery process. Ruth was guided by God into Boaz's field, though at the time she was unaware of it. Naomi recognized the fact of God's guidance later on. Throughout this story God was hard at work behind the scenes, whether the people involved recognized it or not. God often works the same way with us. He leads us to meet people and make decisions that make all the difference for us. It is only later that we begin to see how God has been leading us along. Knowing that God works in this way should encourage us as we face the challenges and unknowns in our own recovery.

2:4-17 This passage beautifully exhibits God's guidance in the ordinary decisions of life. Naomi and Ruth needed food, so Ruth went in search of it. As she stepped out in faith, persevering in her commitment to Naomi, God provided what she needed—a place to gather grain in an atmosphere of safety and respect (Philippians 4:19). God led her to the field of Boaz, a man of outstanding character—honest and willing to help others without demanding anything in return. When we experience such fortunate "coincidences" and helpful new relationships in life, we need to take the time to thank God for his provision.

3:6-14 This passage is one of the great biblical examples of how the truth, clear personal boundaries, and self-respect can protect people who are in a setting of temptation. Both Ruth and Boaz, though in a delicate and compromising situation, chose to do what was right. They avoided the sexual gratification that many couples would have embraced; they refused to yield to the "chemistry" of the moment. They considered the long-term consequences of sexual activity outside the bounds of marriage. Notice how Boaz showed an unselfish concern for Ruth's safety (3:13) and her reputation (3:14).

gave it to her mother-in-law, with what was left of her lunch.

[19]"So much!" Naomi exclaimed. "Where in the world did you glean today? Praise the Lord for whoever was so kind to you." So Ruth told her mother-in-law all about it and mentioned that the owner of the field was Boaz.

[20]"Praise the Lord for a man like that! God has continued his kindness to us as well as to your dead husband!" Naomi cried excitedly. "Why, that man is one of our closest relatives!"

[21]"Well," Ruth told her, "he said to come back and stay close behind his reapers until the entire field is harvested."

[22]"This is wonderful!" Naomi exclaimed. "Do as he has said. Stay with his girls right through the whole harvest; you will be safer there than in any other field!"

[23]So Ruth did and gleaned with them until the end of the barley harvest, and then the wheat harvest too.

CHAPTER 3

Ruth Marries Boaz

One day Naomi said to Ruth, "My dear, isn't it time that I try to find a husband for you and get you happily married again? [2]The man I'm thinking of is Boaz! He has been so kind to us and is a close relative. I happen to know that he will be winnowing barley tonight out on the threshing-floor. [3]Now do what I tell you—bathe and put on some perfume and some nice clothes and go on down to the threshing-floor, but don't let him see you until he has finished his supper. [4]Notice where he lies down to sleep; then go and lift the cover off his feet and lie down there, and he will tell you what to do concerning marriage."

[5]And Ruth replied, "All right. I'll do whatever you say."

[6,7]So she went down to the threshing-floor that night and followed her mother-in-law's instructions. After Boaz had finished a good meal, he lay down very contentedly beside a heap of grain and went to sleep. Then Ruth came quietly and lifted the covering off his feet and lay there. [8]Suddenly, around midnight, he wakened and sat up, startled. There was a woman lying at his feet!

[9]"Who are you?" he demanded.

"It's I, sir—Ruth," she replied. "Make me your wife according to God's law, for you are my close relative."

[10]"Thank God for a girl like you!" he exclaimed. "For you are being even kinder to Naomi now than before. Naturally you'd pre-

Love

READ RUTH 2:4-18

"Please love me!" Isn't this the whispered cry of our heart? We may be afraid to admit it for fear of rejection, but we all are hungry for love. Some of us are starving for affection because of previous losses. We find ourself gathering whatever crumbs we can find to fill that hunger deep inside.

Ruth was a young woman who had known loss and hunger. Her husband died, leaving her without any means of emotional or physical sustenance. She followed her mother-in-law, Naomi, to a foreign land and was forced to gather leftover grain from the harvested fields just to stay alive. The man who owned the fields was a relative who could, if he so chose, marry Ruth and fulfill her needs for love and protection. Naomi told her to go to the threshing floor where this man, Boaz, was sleeping and curl up at his feet. Culturally, this displayed a request to be taken care of. Boaz was quite happy to find Ruth there and later married her, providing the love and provision she had lost and now longed for (Ruth 1–4).

As we turn our life over to God, we need to venture toward developing healthy love relationships with people and with God. It's scary to say, "Please love me," but it's worth the risk. If we don't fill our hunger for love in a legitimate way, we will be driven back toward our addictive/compulsive behaviors. We can be sure that when we "curl up" at the feet of Jesus, he will be glad to find us there. He will provide for us, protect us, and love us. ***Turn to page 317, 1 Samuel 13.***

fer a younger man, even though poor. But you have put aside your personal desires. 11Now don't worry about a thing, my child; I'll handle all the details, for everyone knows what a wonderful person you are. 12But there is one problem. It's true that I am a close relative, but there is someone else who is more closely related to you than I am. 13Stay here tonight, and in the morning I'll talk to him, and if he will marry you, fine; let him do his duty; but if he won't, then I will, I swear by Jehovah; lie down until the morning."

14So she lay at his feet until the morning and was up early, before daybreak, for he had said to her, "Don't let it be known that a woman was here at the threshing-floor."

15-18"Bring your shawl," he told her. Then he tied up a bushel and a half of barley in it as a present for her mother-in-law and laid it on her back. Then she returned to the city.

"Well, what happened, dear?" Naomi asked her when she arrived home. She told Naomi everything and gave her the barley from Boaz, and mentioned his remark that she mustn't go home without a present.

Then Naomi said to her, "Just be patient until we hear what happens, for Boaz won't rest until he has followed through on this. He'll settle it today."

CHAPTER 4

So Boaz went down to the marketplace and found the relative he had mentioned.

"Say, come over here," he called to him. "I want to talk to you a minute."

So they sat down together. 2Then Boaz called for ten of the chief men of the village and asked them to sit as witnesses.

3Boaz said to his relative, "You know Naomi, who came back to us from Moab. She is selling our brother Elimelech's property. 4I felt that I should speak to you about it so that you can buy it if you wish, with these respected men as witnesses. If you want it, let me know right away, for if you don't take it, I will. You have the first right to purchase it and I am next."

The man replied, "All right, I'll buy it."

5Then Boaz told him, "Your purchase of the land from Naomi requires your marriage to Ruth so that she can have children to carry on her husband's name and to inherit the land."

6"Then I can't do it," the man replied. "For her son would become an heir to my property too; you buy it."

7In those days it was the custom in Israel for a man transferring a right of purchase to pull off his sandal and hand it to the other party; this publicly validated the transaction. 8So, as the man said to Boaz, "You buy it for yourself," he drew off his sandal.

9Then Boaz said to the witnesses and to the crowd standing around, "You have seen that today I have bought all the property of Elimelech, Chilion, and Mahlon, from Naomi, 10and that with it I have purchased Ruth the Moabitess, the widow of Mahlon, to be my wife, so that she can have a son to carry on the family name of her dead husband."

11And all the people standing there and the witnesses replied, "We are witnesses. May the Lord make this woman, who has now come into your home, as fertile as Rachel and Leah, from whom all the nation of Israel descended! May you be a great and successful man in Bethlehem, 12and may the descendants the Lord will give you from this young woman be as numerous and honorable as those of our ancestor Perez, the son of Tamar and Judah."

13So Boaz married Ruth, and when he slept with her, the Lord gave her a son.

14And the women of the city said to Na-

3:15-18 Earlier Boaz had provided abundantly for the short-term needs of Ruth and Naomi, but now that the harvest was over he gave them additional provisions. Naomi recognized in Boaz's generous gifts a willingness on his part to be responsible for Ruth (and Naomi) according to the stipulations of God's law (Deuteronomy 25:5-10). God provided for Naomi and Ruth through his wise laws and by sending a man who was willing to obey them. God also has given his Word to us for guidance. We need to follow through on his program if we hope to help others in their recovery or to progress in our own.

4:1-10 As we watch Boaz negotiate, it is clear that he was a wise and shrewd man. He did not lie or manipulate the circumstances, though he clearly sought a specific outcome. Boaz wisely anticipated the greedy response of Naomi's closer kinsman. This other man wanted the inheritance of Ruth's dead husband, but had no desire to care for Ruth or to father her children and care for them. When faced with the facts, he saw that the economic advantages of taking Ruth's case were limited, possibly even detrimental. He did not want to be held accountable to God's law and the economic loss it might entail. We must be careful not to seek only the advantages in our relationships; we must also accept the responsibilities. Like Boaz, we need to seek what is best for the people close to us.

omi, "Bless the Lord who has given you this
little grandson; may he be famous in Israel.
15May he restore your youth and take care of
you in your old age; for he is the son of your
daughter-in-law who loves you so much,
and who has been kinder to you than seven
sons!"
16,17Naomi took care of the baby, and the
neighbor women said, "Now at last Naomi
has a son again!"

And they named him Obed. He was the
father of Jesse and grandfather of King David.
18-22This is the family tree of Boaz, beginning with his ancestor Perez: Perez, Hezron,
Ram, Amminadab, Nashon, Salmon, Boaz,
Obed, Jesse, David.

4:18-22 Hidden in this family tree is powerful evidence that God uses fallible people to bring about his good will. Perez was the first of David's ancestors mentioned; he was the illegitimate son of Judah and his daughter-in-law, Tamar (Genesis 38:1-30). Boaz was the son of Salmon, whose wife was Rahab, the prostitute of Jericho (Joshua 2:1-24; Matthew 1:5). Then Ruth was a foreigner from Moab, not even one of God's chosen people. God used these people, far from ideal according to human standards, to bring about the birth of Israel's greatest king, David, and the world's only Savior, Jesus Christ. Knowing this truth should give us hope. No matter how sordid or painful our past, God can use us significantly if we are willing to put ourselves in his hands.

REFLECTIONS ON RUTH

insights FROM THE STORY OF RUTH

In **Ruth 1:6-22** we see the painful beginnings of the recovery process. In choosing to leave Moab, Naomi was admitting her powerlessness. She also displayed brutal honesty as she advised her daughters-in-law to return to their families of origin. Naomi knew that she would be unable to support them in the years ahead. But she also knew that in sending them away, she was dismissing her last vestige of support and security. As bleak as the situation was, Naomi was willing to summon the courage to build a new life. Too often our desire for short-term security prevents us from stepping out in faith. We cling to the people and things that help us feel secure. This, however, only keeps us from turning everything over to God. As a result, we often miss God's best for us.

Naomi's plan in **Ruth 3:1-7** to find a husband for her daughter-in-law may seem a little strange to us. Her plan, however, was based upon a scriptural provision for the protection of widows (Deuteronomy 25:5-10). God had assigned the responsibility of caring for a widow to the dead husband's brothers or near relatives. Since Boaz was a near relative to Ruth's dead husband, he was bound by the law to do something to help her. Ruth trusted Naomi's advice and took another courageous step of faith and obedience, following God's program for rebuilding her life. God often provides direction for our recovery in his Word, but this doesn't mean our recovery is automatic. We need to takes steps of faith and obedience, following his plan for recovery.

As we see in **Ruth 4:11-17,** the story of Ruth and Naomi's recovery from loneliness and destitution does have a happy ending. Naomi, who had lost her family (1:4-5), had a family once again. Ruth, who had lost her husband and all hope of a prosperous future (1:8-9), was given a husband, a son, and hope for the future. It is interesting to note that Ruth's sacrificial life-style not only brought recovery to herself and Naomi, but to all of us. Boaz and Ruth's son was named Obed, and he became the ancestor of Jesus Christ, who has provided the means for all of us to recover from the destructive effects of sin.

FIRST SAMUEL

THE BIG PICTURE

A. FINISHING WITH THE OLD—SAMUEL, THE LAST JUDGE (1:1–12:25).
   1. God's Man Is Brought on the Scene (1:1–3:21).
   2. The Problems Continue—War with the Philistines (4:1–7:17).
   3. A King Is Requested, Chosen, and Anointed (8:1–11:15)
   4. Samuel's Retirement (12:1-25).

B. STARTING WITH THE NEW—SAUL, THE FIRST KING (13:1–31:13).
   1. The Sudden Failure of Saul as Leader (13:1–15:35).
   2. A New Leader Appears—David (16:1–17:58).
   3. Saul's Obsession with David (18:1–30:31).
   4. The Death of Saul (31:1-13).

The book of 1 Samuel begins with the birth of the prophet Samuel and ends with the death of King Saul. It contains a catalog of lives for us to learn from—some exemplary, others not. Samuel was born in the time of the judges, when "everyone did whatever . . . seemed right in his own eyes" (Judges 17:6). The people were far from God. Eli was High Priest, but the flaws in his leadership can be seen in the dysfunctions of his own family. Since Israel lacked strong spiritual leadership, God chose Samuel and prepared him to lead the Israelites back to God.

Near the end of Samuel's ministry, the people demanded a king; they wanted to be like the surrounding nations. God was not pleased with Israel's demand, but he chose Saul to lead them anyway. Saul, though a man of great potential, was self-centered and disobedient; he never achieved what God had intended for him.

While Saul was still king, Samuel anointed David to the kingship. David became a national hero by killing Goliath, and he won numerous other great battles with God's help. But when Saul realized that David was in line for the throne, he was consumed by bitterness and tried to kill him. In the end, faced with defeat in battle, Saul took his own life.

This book exhibits portraits of some who moved toward God and toward wholeness, and others who moved away from God and toward disaster. Jealousy, bitterness, and disobedience destroyed the life of King Saul. But forgiveness, trust, and obedience brought David great success. This book clearly shows that the only way to wholeness is by following God's program through trust and obedience.

THE BOTTOM LINE

PURPOSE: To track Israel's transition from the period of the judges to the era of kingly rule. AUTHOR: Unknown, but probably most of it was written by Samuel. Nathan and Gad were also contributors. AUDIENCE: The people of Israel. DATE WRITTEN: The book was probably started during Samuel's lifetime and finished around 930 B.C. SETTING: The action takes place in Israel, between 1120 and 971 B.C. KEY VERSE: "Has the Lord as much pleasure in your burnt offerings and sacrifices as in your obedience? Obedience is far better than sacrifice" (15:22). KEY PLACES: Shiloh, Gibeah, Ramah, Bethlehem, Gath, Adullam, Hebron, the wilderness of Judah, Ziklag, Endor, Beth-shan. KEY PEOPLE AND RELATIONSHIPS: Samuel with Eli, with Saul, and then with David.

RECOVERY THEMES

Dependence on God: Of the three men prominent in the books of Samuel (Samuel, Saul, and David), only two truly depended on God. One of them, Saul, started with a flash, but his faith in God never matured. When God chose Saul as the first king, Saul clearly had the potential for greatness. But instead of obeying God and trusting him for success, Saul acted out of self-sufficiency and ended up a tragic failure. When we experience success in life, or when someone threatens our success, we need to keep our eyes on God. He is the giver of all success and is the only one who can help us continue in it.

Strength in Weakness: No matter how weak we may be, God is able to work through us to do mighty things. When young David killed the giant Goliath in God's name, his weakness became a funnel for God's power. Jonathan and his bodyguard virtually destroyed a vast Philistine army with God's help—a task impossible from a human perspective! There is only one way to begin our recovery: we must admit our powerlessness. Then God can step into our life and supply us with all the power we need to follow his will in recovery.

Necessity of Obedience: Over and over again, we are confronted by the importance of obedience for those who want to recover. To God, "obedience is far better than sacrifice" (15:22). In Saul's case, his lack of obedience led to his downfall. David, on the other hand, was a man after God's own heart. He trusted and obeyed God. Even when he could have killed Saul, he refused because Saul was God's anointed king. And though David failed and sinned, he repented and turned back to God. Be encouraged. No one can live a flawless life, but we do need to trust God and do our best to obey him.

Consequences of Disobedience: When Eli, Samuel, Saul, and David disobeyed God, they all faced tragic consequences. Their sin not only affected them, but also their children. Saul's disobedience destroyed not only himself but the majority of his family. Saul had various opportunities to get his life back on track, but his self-centered heart blocked him from looking to God for healing. Saul's lack of faith and obedience resulted in a bitter life and tragic death.

CHAPTER 1

God Gives Hannah a Son

This is the story of Elkanah, a man of the tribe of Ephraim who lived in Ramathaim-zophim, in the hills of Ephraim.

His father's name was Jeroham,
His grandfather was Elihu,
His great-grandfather was Tohu,
His great-great-grandfather was Zuph.

2He had two wives, Hannah and Peninnah. Peninnah had some children, but Hannah didn't.
3Each year Elkanah and his families journeyed to the Tabernacle at Shiloh to worship the Lord of the heavens and to sacrifice to him. (The priests on duty at that time were the two sons of Eli—Hophni and Phinehas.)
4On the day he presented his sacrifice, Elkanah would celebrate the happy occasion by giving presents to Peninnah and her children;
5but although he loved Hannah very much, he could give her only one present, for the Lord had sealed her womb; so she had no children to give presents to.
6Peninnah made matters worse by taunting Hannah because of her barrenness.
7Every year it was the same—Peninnah scoffing and laughing at her as they went to Shiloh, making her cry so much she couldn't eat.
8"What's the matter, Hannah?" Elkanah would exclaim. "Why aren't you eating? Why make such a fuss over having no children? Isn't having me better than having ten sons?"

1:9-11 In these verses Hannah breathed a beautiful prayer through her tears. She admitted her helplessness and acknowledged her need of a Power greater than herself. In faith she not only committed her infertility to God, but she also vowed to surrender to God's service the son he may choose to give her (1:11). All of us need to realize that without God's intervention we are helpless to overcome any of the problems or dependencies we might have. Learning to give up control and depend upon God is a step we all need to take.

1:12-18 Hannah's prayer was misunderstood by Eli the priest, who assumed she was drunk. In reality she was taking a vital step toward recovery by admitting her helplessness and committing her infertility to God. Sadly, attempts toward recovery are often misinterpreted, and the insensitive responses we experience can be disheartening. To her credit, Hannah persevered despite the criticism she experienced. Eli soon recognized Hannah's integrity and encouraged her in her prayer (1:17). No matter what discouragement we may face along the road to recovery, we must persevere. God will support us, even if the people around us do not.

HANNAH

Living in a dysfunctional family does not automatically mean that an individual will turn away from God. Neither does turning to God guarantee that the problems of a destructive family situation will go away. Reaching out to God, however, does ensure that we will have a far better chance of coping despite the devastating circumstances.

Hannah lived in a dysfunctional family situation. As was typical in the Israelite culture during the times of the judges, Elkanah, her husband, had a second wife named Peninnah. Such a relationship, although it may have met certain needs, almost inevitably was fraught with problems.

Elkanah foolishly played favorites—he loved Hannah more than Peninnah. He was apparently unaware of the negative impact his partiality was having on the relationship between his wives. Peninnah became jealous of Hannah and got back at her by flaunting the fact that she had children while Hannah did not. Bearing children in ancient Israel gave the mother both personal fulfillment and social status.

Hannah reacted with bitter anguish. No amount of comforting by her husband could relieve her pain—she wanted a child. In desperation, on a yearly pilgrimage to the Tabernacle, Hannah silently poured out her grief to God. She pleaded for a son and vowed to dedicate the child to God for his entire life. After admitting her helplessness and her need for utter dependence on God, Hannah returned home with a renewed spiritual confidence that God would fulfill her request. When God did give her a son, she named him Samuel, offered a prayer of praise to God, and fulfilled her vow by dedicating Samuel to God's service. God, in turn, blessed Hannah with additional children. Our only hope is to turn our life over to God, regardless of the circumstances, and then allow him to work recovery and healing within us.

STRENGTHS AND ACCOMPLISHMENTS:
- Hannah turned her life and her will over to God in her time of need.
- Hannah prayed from the heart.
- Hannah carried out her vow, even though it was costly.

WEAKNESSES AND MISTAKES:
- Hannah allowed the circumstances of her life to dictate her feelings and her sense of worth.

LESSONS FROM HER LIFE:
- We should turn our life over to God before our situation becomes unbearable.
- God ultimately is the only one who can fulfill our needs.
- Keeping our vows to God sustains our relationship with him, allowing him to shower us with his blessings.

KEY VERSE:
"She was in deep anguish and was crying bitterly as she prayed to the Lord" (1 Samuel 1:10).

Hannah's story is told in 1 Samuel 1:1–2:21.

---

9 One evening after supper, when they were
at Shiloh, Hannah went over to the Tabernacle. Eli the priest was sitting at his customary
place beside the entrance. 10 She was in deep
anguish and was crying bitterly as she prayed to the Lord.

11 And she made this vow: "O Lord of heaven, if you will look down upon my sorrow and answer my prayer and give me a son, then I will give him back to you, and he'll be yours for his entire lifetime, and his hair shall never be cut."

12,13 Eli noticed her mouth moving as she was praying silently and, hearing no sound, thought she had been drinking.

14 "Must you come here drunk?" he demanded. "Throw away your bottle."

15,16 "Oh no, sir!" she replied, "I'm not drunk! But I am very sad and I was pouring out my heart to the Lord. Please don't think that I am just some drunken bum!"

17 "In that case," Eli said, "cheer up! May the Lord of Israel grant you your petition, whatever it is!"

18 "Oh, thank you, sir!" she exclaimed, and went happily back, and began to take her meals again.

19,20 The entire family was up early the next morning and went to the Tabernacle to worship the Lord once more. Then they returned

home to Ramah, and when Elkanah slept
with Hannah, the Lord remembered her petition; in the process of time, a baby boy was
born to her. She named him Samuel (meaning
"asked of God") because, as she said, "I asked
the Lord for him."

Hannah Gives Samuel to God

21,22The next year Elkanah and Peninnah and
her children went on the annual trip to the
Tabernacle without Hannah, for she told her
husband, "Wait until the baby is weaned, and
then I will take him to the Tabernacle and
leave him there."
23"Well, whatever you think best," Elkanah
agreed. "May the Lord's will be done."
So she stayed home until the baby was
weaned. 24Then, though he was still so small,
they took him to the Tabernacle in Shiloh,
along with a three-year-old bull for the sacrifice, and a bushel of flour and some wine.
25After the sacrifice they took the child to Eli.
26"Sir, do you remember me?" Hannah
asked him. "I am the woman who stood here
that time praying to the Lord! 27I asked him to
give me this child, and he has given me my
request; 28and now I am giving him to the
Lord for as long as he lives." So she left him
there at the Tabernacle for the Lord to use.

CHAPTER 2

Hannah's Prayer of Thanks

This was Hannah's prayer:

"How I rejoice in the Lord!
How he has blessed me!
Now I have an answer for my enemies,
For the Lord has solved my problem.
How I rejoice!
2No one is as holy as the Lord!
There is no other God,
Nor any Rock like our God.
3Quit acting so proud and arrogant!
The Lord knows what you have done,
And he will judge your deeds.
4Those who were mighty are mighty no more!
Those who were weak are now strong.
5Those who were well are now starving;
Those who were starving are fed.
The barren woman now has seven children;
She with many children has no more!
6The Lord kills,
The Lord gives life.
7Some he causes to be poor
And others to be rich.
He cuts one down
And lifts another up.
8He lifts the poor from the dust—
Yes, from a pile of ashes—
And treats them as princes
Sitting in the seats of honor.
For all the earth is the Lord's
And he has set the world in order.
9He will protect his godly ones,
But the wicked shall be silenced in darkness.
No one shall succeed by strength alone.
10Those who fight against the Lord shall be broken;
He thunders against them from heaven.
He judges throughout the earth.
He gives mighty strength to his King,
And gives great glory to his anointed one."

11So they returned home to Ramah without
Samuel; and the child became the Lord's
helper, for he assisted Eli the priest.

Samuel Serves God

12Now the sons of Eli were evil men who didn't
love the Lord. 13,14It was their regular practice

2:1-3 Note the words in Hannah's prayer of rejoicing: "For the Lord has solved my problem. How I rejoice!" (2:1). She was praising the one responsible for her deliverance—God himself. He had delivered her from the trauma of infertility, giving her a son. And after Hannah gave Samuel into God's service, he blessed her with other children. This certainly would have lightened the burden of seeing her firstborn son only once a year. Obedience was surely difficult, even painful, but it was for the good of Hannah and Samuel, and ultimately for the good of all Israel. Our obedience to God, as painful as it might be at times, will ultimately bring us joy. It will also bring blessings to the people close to us.

2:12-17 Eli's sons sinned unspeakably by treating God's offerings with contempt. They failed to realize that the sacrifices were God's provision for the people's recovery from sin. They stole from the sacrifices as if these ceremonies had been instituted for their own personal pleasure rather than for their healing and purification. God has provided for our recovery by giving the ultimate sacrifice on our behalf. If we treat Christ with contempt, we are guilty of doing the same thing (Hebrews 10:26-29). Let us show proper respect for the compassion, love, and power that God has shown to us through Christ! Let us wholeheartedly embrace his provision for our healing.

SAMUEL

As soon as Samuel was weaned from Hannah, who had wept before God for a child, she gave him back to God. Samuel learned the various duties of the priesthood from Eli, Israel's High Priest. During his life, Samuel would serve as a priest, a prophet, and Israel's last judge. He was a godly man who transformed the office of judge from that of a crisis military leader to a stable position of leadership just short of kingship.

But Samuel was human and had his blind spots. When the people asked to have a king like the other countries, Samuel took this request as rejection of his own leadership. What Samuel didn't hear was the complaint of the people that his sons, whom he had appointed to be judges in his place, were "very corrupt in the administration of justice" (1 Samuel 8:3). The people hadn't rejected Samuel; they had rejected God's leadership and the leadership of Samuel's sons.

Perhaps Samuel was deaf to the people's complaints about his sons because he was blind to their corrupt ways. We often develop blind spots from dysfunctional situations within our family of origin. If Samuel had heard the people's complaints and corrected the problem, all might have been different. When we feel rejection, it should be a signal to evaluate carefully what is being said. In spite of his family issues, however, Samuel was one of the great men of faith and one of the great leaders in Israel's history.

STRENGTHS AND ACCOMPLISHMENTS:

- Samuel was sensitive to God's voice.
- He was the last and greatest judge in Israel.
- He commanded great respect from the people of Israel.

WEAKNESSES AND MISTAKES:

- He failed to lead his sons to a close relationship with God.

LESSONS FROM HIS LIFE:

- The feeling of rejection can blind us to God's truth.
- Who we are with God is more important than what we accomplish in life.

KEY VERSES:

"As Samuel grew, the Lord was with him and people listened carefully to his advice. And all Israel from one end of the land to the other knew that Samuel was going to be a prophet of the Lord" (1 Samuel 3:19-20).

Samuel's story is found in 1 Samuel 1:1–25:1; 28. He is mentioned in Psalm 99:6; Jeremiah 15:1; Acts 3:24; and Hebrews 11:32.

---

to send out a servant whenever anyone was offering a sacrifice, and while the flesh of the sacrificed animal was boiling, the servant would put a three-pronged fleshhook into the pot and demand that whatever it brought up be given to Eli's sons. They treated all of the Israelites in this way when they came to Shiloh
to worship. 15Sometimes the servant would come even before the rite of burning the fat on the altar had been performed, and he would demand raw meat before it was boiled, so that it could be used for roasting.

16If the man offering the sacrifice replied, "Take as much as you want, but the fat must first be burned" [as the law requires], then the servant would say,

"No, give it to me now or I'll take it by force."

17So the sin of these young men was very great in the eyes of the Lord; for they treated the people's offerings to the Lord with contempt.

18Samuel, though only a child, was the Lord's helper and wore a little linen robe just
like the priest's. 19Each year his mother made a little coat for him and brought it to him when she came with her husband for the
sacrifice. 20Before they returned home Eli would bless Elkanah and Hannah and ask God to give them other children to take the place of this one they had given to the Lord.
21 And the Lord gave Hannah three sons and two daughters. Meanwhile Samuel grew up in the service of the Lord.

22Eli was now very old, but he was aware of what was going on around him. He knew, for instance, that his sons were seducing the young women who assisted at the entrance of the Tabernacle.

23-25"I have been hearing terrible reports from the Lord's people about what you are doing," Eli told his sons. "It is an awful thing to make the Lord's people sin. Ordinary sin receives heavy punishment, but how much more this sin of yours that has been committed against the Lord!" But they wouldn't listen to their father, for the Lord was already planning to kill them.

[26]Little Samuel was growing in two ways—he was getting taller, and he was becoming everyone's favorite (and he was a favorite of the Lord's, too!).

A Prophet Speaks to Eli

[27]One day a prophet came to Eli and gave him this message from the Lord: "Didn't I demonstrate my power when the people of Israel were slaves in Egypt? [28]Didn't I choose your ancestor Levi from among all his brothers to be my priest, and to sacrifice upon my altar, and to burn incense, and to wear a priestly robe as he served me? And didn't I assign the sacrificial offerings to you priests? [29] Then why are you so greedy for all the other offerings which are brought to me? Why have you honored your sons more than me—for you and they have become fat from the best of the offerings of my people!

[30]"Therefore, I, the Lord God of Israel, declare that although I promised that your branch of the tribe of Levi could always be my priests, it is ridiculous to think that what you are doing can continue. I will honor only those who honor me, and I will despise those who despise me. [31]I will put an end to your family, so that it will no longer serve as priests. Every member will die before his time. None shall live to be old. [32]You will envy the prosperity I will give my people, but you and your family will be in distress and need. Not one of them will live out his days. [33]Those who are left alive will live in sadness and grief; and their children shall die by the sword. [34]And to prove that what I have said will come true, I will cause your two sons, Hophni and Phinehas, to die on the same day!

[35]"Then I will raise up a faithful priest who will serve me and do whatever I tell him to do. I will bless his descendants, and his family shall be priests to my kings forever. [36]Then all of your descendants shall bow before him, begging for money and food. 'Please,' they will say, 'give me a job among the priests so that I will have enough to eat.'"

CHAPTER 3

God Speaks to Samuel

Meanwhile little Samuel was helping the Lord by assisting Eli. Messages from the Lord were very rare in those days, [2,3]but one night after Eli had gone to bed (he was almost blind with age by now), and Samuel was sleeping in the Temple near the Ark, [4,5]the Lord called out, "Samuel! Samuel!"

"Yes?" Samuel replied. "What is it?" He jumped up and ran to Eli. "Here I am. What do you want?" he asked.

"I didn't call you," Eli said. "Go on back to bed." So he did. [6]Then the Lord called again, "Samuel!" And again Samuel jumped up and ran to Eli.

"Yes?" he asked. "What do you need?"

"No, I didn't call you, my son," Eli said. "Go on back to bed."

[7](Samuel had never had a message from Jehovah before.) [8]So now the Lord called the third time, and once more Samuel jumped up and ran to Eli.

"Yes?" he asked. "What do you need?"

Then Eli realized it was the Lord who had spoken to the child. [9]So he said to Samuel, "Go and lie down again, and if he calls again, say, 'Yes, Lord, I'm listening.'" So Samuel went back to bed.

[10]And the Lord came and called as before, "Samuel! Samuel!"

And Samuel replied, "Yes, I'm listening."

[11]Then the Lord said to Samuel, "I am going to do a shocking thing in Israel. [12]I am going to do all of the dreadful things I warned Eli about. [13]I have continually threatened him and his entire family with punishment because his sons are blaspheming God, and he doesn't stop them. [14]So I have vowed that the

---

3:1-10 Learning to listen to God's voice is an important part of our recovery (Isaiah 30:21; Hebrews 5:11). God spoke directly to young Samuel, but he also speaks to us vibrantly and relevantly through his Word (James 1:22). We need to take the time to understand God's truth in the Bible. There, we will find the wisdom and direction we need to progress in our recovery.

3:16-18 Samuel's honesty is obvious as he comes clean, telling Eli everything. He even told Eli the devastating truth about the priest's own family and the suffering they would endure. He confronted Eli with his failure, stating clearly the truth God had given him. Such forthrightness must be part and parcel of any recovery program. As we discover the truth about ourselves and others through knowledge of God's Word, we will need to speak that truth to others, confronting them in love for their encouragement and spiritual growth. This will never be easy, but it is an important part of any loving relationship.

sins of Eli and of his sons shall never be
forgiven by sacrifices and offerings."
15Samuel stayed in bed until morning, then
opened the doors of the Temple as usual, for
he was afraid to tell Eli what the Lord had said
to him. 16,17But Eli called him.
"My son," he said, "what did the Lord say
to you? Tell me everything. And may God
punish you if you hide anything from me!"
18So Samuel told him what the Lord had
said.
"It is the Lord's will," Eli replied; "let him
do what he thinks best."
19As Samuel grew, the Lord was with him
and people listened carefully to his advice.
20And all Israel from one end of the land to the
other knew that Samuel was going to be a
prophet of the Lord. 21,4:1Then the Lord began
to give messages to him there at the Tabernacle in Shiloh, and he passed them on to the
people of Israel.

CHAPTER 4

The Philistines Capture the Ark

At that time Israel was at war with the Philistines. The Israeli army was camped near Ebenezer, the Philistines at Aphek. 2And the
Philistines defeated Israel, killing four thousand of them. 3After the battle was over, the
army of Israel returned to their camp and
their leaders discussed why the Lord had let
them be defeated.
"Let's bring the Ark here from Shiloh," they
said. "If we carry it into battle with us, the
Lord will be among us and he will surely save
us from our enemies."
4So they sent for the Ark of the Lord of
heaven who is enthroned above the angels.
Hophni and Phinehas, the sons of Eli, accompanied it into the battle. 5When the Israelis
saw the Ark coming, their shout of joy was so
loud that it almost made the ground shake!
6"What's going on?" the Philistines asked.
"What's all the shouting about over in the
camp of the Hebrews?"
When they were told it was because the Ark
of the Lord had arrived, 7they panicked.
"God has come into their camp!" they cried
out. "Woe upon us, for we have never had to
face anything like this before! 8Who can save
us from these mighty gods of Israel? They are
the same gods who destroyed the Egyptians
with plagues when Israel was in the wilderness. 9Fight as you never have before, O Philistines, or we will become their slaves just as
they have been ours."
10So the Philistines fought desperately and
Israel was defeated again. Thirty thousand
men of Israel died that day, and the remainder
fled to their tents. 11And the Ark of God was
captured, and Hophni and Phinehas were
killed.
12A man from the tribe of Benjamin ran
from the battle and arrived at Shiloh the same
day with his clothes torn and dirt on his head.
13Eli was waiting beside the road to hear the
news of the battle, for his heart trembled for
the safety of the Ark of God. As the messenger
from the battlefront arrived and told what
had happened, a great cry arose throughout
the city.
14"What is all the noise about?" Eli asked.
And the messenger rushed over to Eli and told
him what had happened. 15(Eli was ninety-
eight years old and was blind.)
16"I have just come from the battle—I was
there today," he told Eli, 17"and Israel has been
defeated and thousands of the Israeli troops
are dead on the battlefield. Hophni and Phinehas were killed too, and the Ark has been
captured."
18When the messenger mentioned what
had happened to the Ark, Eli fell backward
from his seat beside the gate and his neck was
broken by the fall, and he died (for he was old
and fat). He had judged Israel for forty years.
19When Eli's daughter-in-law, Phinehas'
wife, who was pregnant, heard that the Ark
had been captured and that her husband and
father-in-law were dead, her labor pains suddenly began. 20Just before she died, the

---

4:16-22 Eli and his family, and indeed the entire nation of Israel, suffered the terrible consequences of disobedience. Eli and his sons died, and the Ark of the Covenant, the symbol of God's glorious presence with Israel, was captured by foreigners. We are reminded of how our refusal to abandon a selfish, addictive life-style brings suffering upon our family and the people close to us. The despair of such a family is illustrated by the final act of Eli's daughter-in-law, who used her final words to name her baby Ichabod. This name means "there is no glory" (4:21-22), for the glory of God had departed from Israel. In the hour of her death she acknowledged her hopelessness, but it was much too late for her and her family. The process of life recovery is far from easy. It involves surrender, loss, pain, and difficulty. Yet the solitary death of this young woman and the shattering of Eli's family should remind us of what is at stake if we do not persevere in our quest for recovery.

women who were attending her told her that
everything was all right and that the baby was
a boy. But she did not reply or respond in any
way. [21,22]Then she murmured, "Name the
child 'Ichabod,' for Israel's glory is gone."
(Ichabod means "there is no glory." She
named him this because the Ark of God had
been captured and because her husband and
her father-in-law were dead.)

CHAPTER 5
God Punishes the Philistines
The Philistines took the captured Ark of God
from the battleground at Ebenezer to the
temple of their idol Dagon in the city of
Ashdod. [3]But when the local citizens went to
see it the next morning, Dagon had fallen
with his face to the ground before the Ark of
Jehovah! They set him up again, [4]but the next
morning the same thing had happened—the
idol had fallen face down before the Ark of the
Lord again. This time his head and hands had
been cut off and were lying in the doorway;
only the trunk of his body was left intact.
[5](That is why to this day neither the priests of
Dagon nor his worshipers will walk on the
threshold of the temple of Dagon in Ashdod.)
[6]Then the Lord began to destroy the people
of Ashdod and the nearby villages with bubonic plague. [7]When the people realized what
was happening, they exclaimed, "We can't
keep the Ark of the God of Israel here any
longer. We will all perish along with our god
Dagon."
[8]So they called a conference of the mayors
of the five cities of the Philistines to decide
how to dispose of the Ark. The decision was
to take it to Gath. [9]But when the Ark arrived
at Gath, the Lord began destroying its people,
young and old, with the plague, and there was
a great panic. [10]So they sent the Ark to Ekron,
but when the people of Ekron saw it coming
they cried out, "They are bringing the Ark of
the God of Israel here to kill us too!"
[11]So they summoned the mayors again and
begged them to send the Ark back to its own
country, lest the entire city die. For the plague
had already begun, and great fear was sweeping across the city. [12]Those who didn't die
were deathly ill; and there was weeping everywhere.

CHAPTER 6
The Philistines Return the Ark
The Ark remained in the Philistine country
for seven months in all. [2]Then the Philistines
called for their priests and diviners and asked
them, "What shall we do about the Ark of
God? What sort of gift shall we send with it
when we return it to its own land?"
[3]"Yes, send it back with a gift," they were
told. "Send a guilt offering so that the plague
will stop. Then, if it doesn't, you will know
God didn't send the plague upon you after
all."
[4,5]"What guilt offering shall we send?" they
asked.
And they were told, "Send five gold models
of the tumor caused by the plague, and five
gold models of the rats that have ravaged the
whole land—the capital cities and villages
alike. If you send these gifts and then praise
the God of Israel, perhaps he will stop persecuting you and your god. [6]Don't be stubborn
and rebellious as Pharaoh and the Egyptians
were. They wouldn't let Israel go until God
had destroyed them with dreadful plagues.
[7]Now build a new cart and hitch to it two
cows that have just had calves—cows that
never before have been yoked—and shut their
calves away from them in the barn. [8]Place the
Ark of God on the cart beside a chest containing the gold models of the rats and tumors,
and let the cows go wherever they want to. [9]If

5:1-4 The ignoble fate of the Philistine idol Dagon illustrates that Israel's God is greater than all other gods (Jeremiah 32:27; 33:2; 1 John 4:4). Anything that controls us has become a "god" in our life, whether it is drugs, drink, sex, power, or money. We should be encouraged by the fact that God is stronger than any of the false idols we might serve. If we seek God in our recovery, our addictions will fall face down before him, setting us free to love the only God worthy of our affection.
5:6-12 Physical suffering (5:6, 9, 12) was a direct consequence of the disrespect the Philistines showed toward the true God (5:1-12). The parallels to today are unmistakable. By setting up addictions as false "gods" in our life, we show disrespect to the true God. We also violate God's laws by living selfishly and hurting the people close to us. Many—though not all—who violate God's standards experience physical repercussions. Often it is precisely this suffering that prompts us to seek help. So it was with the Philistines.
6:6 As the Philistine leaders looked for a way to get rid of the Ark, their priests reminded them of the high cost of Pharaoh's resistance to God years earlier in Egypt. This object lesson is for us as well. The refusal to move toward recovery is costly. Stubbornness and willfulness often carry the hefty price tags of wrecked lives, ruptured relationships, and unreconciled pasts.

they cross the border of our land and go into
Beth-shemesh, then you will know that it was
God who brought this great evil upon us; if
they don't [but return to their calves], then we
will know that the plague was simply a coin-
cidence and was not sent by God at all."
10So these instructions were carried out.
Two cows with newborn calves were hitched
to the cart and their calves were shut up in the
barn. 11Then the Ark of the Lord and the chest
containing the gold rats and tumors were
placed upon the cart. 12And sure enough, the
cows went straight along the road toward
Beth-shemesh, lowing as they went; and the
Philistine mayors followed them as far as the
border of Beth-shemesh. 13The people of Beth-
shemesh were reaping wheat in the valley,
and when they saw the Ark, they went wild
with joy!
14The cart came into the field of a man
named Joshua and stopped beside a large
rock. So the people broke up the wood of the
cart for a fire and killed the cows and sacrificed them to the Lord as a burnt offering.
15Several men of the tribe of Levi lifted the Ark
and the chest containing the gold rats and
tumors from the cart and laid them on the
rock. And many burnt offerings and sacrifices
were offered to the Lord that day by the men
of Beth-shemesh.
16After the five Philistine mayors had
watched for awhile, they returned to Ekron
that same day.17The five gold models of tumors which had been sent by the Philistines
as a guilt offering to the Lord were gifts from
the mayors of the capital cities, Ashdod, Gaza,
Ashkelon, Gath, and Ekron. 18The gold rats
were to placate God for the other Philistine
cities, both the fortified cities and the country
villages controlled by the five capitals. (By the
way, that large rock at Beth-shemesh can still
be seen in the field of Joshua.) 19But the Lord
killed seventy of the men of Beth-shemesh
because they looked into the Ark. And the
people mourned because of the many people
whom the Lord had killed.
20"Who is able to stand before Jehovah, this
holy God?" they cried out. "Where can we
send the Ark from here?"
21So they sent messengers to the people at
Kiriath-jearim and told them that the Philistines had brought back the Ark of the Lord.
"Come and get it!" they begged.

CHAPTER 7
So the men of Kiriath-jearim came and took
the Ark to the hillside home of Abinadab and
installed his son Eleazar to be in charge of it.
2The Ark remained there for twenty years, and
during that time all Israel was in sorrow because the Lord had seemingly abandoned
them.

Samuel Becomes Israel's Judge

3At that time Samuel said to them, "If you are
really serious about wanting to return to the
Lord, get rid of your foreign gods and your
Ashtaroth idols. Determine to obey only the
Lord; then he will rescue you from the Philistines."
4So they destroyed their idols of Baal and
Ashtaroth and worshiped only the Lord.
5Then Samuel told them, "Come to Mizpah, all of you, and I will pray to the Lord for
you."
6So they gathered there and, in a great ceremony, drew water from the well and poured
it out before the Lord. They also went without
food all day as a sign of sorrow for their sins.
So it was at Mizpah that Samuel became Israel's judge.
7When the Philistine leaders heard about
the great crowds at Mizpah, they mobilized
their army and advanced. The Israelis were
badly frightened when they learned that the
Philistines were approaching.
8"Plead with God to save us!" they begged
Samuel.

6:19 This seems a harsh judgment, but it carries with it a reminder of the high cost of disobedience. The Israelites in this passage were held accountable to the instructions God had given them regarding the treatment of the Ark. Either they were ignorant of these instructions or they chose to ignore them. God has given us instructions for healthy living in the Bible. When we fail to follow God's program, out of either ignorance or choice, the consequences will be devastating. Neglecting God's instructions on this occasion proved fatal for this group of Israelites. The same consequence may await us if we fail to listen to God and his Word.

7:7-11 The people of Israel were helpless as they faced the attacking Philistines. They didn't know what to do, so they turned to Samuel for help. Samuel then did the only thing possible: he asked God for help. God answered by giving Israel an overwhelming victory over the Philistines. This is how our own recovery begins. We realize that we are helpless against our enemies of addiction and dependency, so we turn to God for help. We can be sure that God will come through for us if we admit our helplessness and commit our life to him.

9So Samuel took a suckling lamb and offered it to the Lord as a whole burnt offering
and pleaded with him to help Israel. And the
Lord responded. 10Just as Samuel was sacrificing the burnt offering, the Philistines arrived
for battle, but the Lord spoke with a mighty
voice of thunder from heaven, and they were
thrown into confusion, and the Israelis
routed them 11and chased them from Mizpah
to Beth-car, killing them all along the way.
12Samuel then took a stone and placed it
between Mizpah and Jeshanah and named it
Ebenezer (meaning, "the Stone of Help"), for
he said, "The Lord has certainly helped us!"
13So the Philistines were subdued and didn't
invade Israel again at that time because the
Lord was against them throughout the remainder of Samuel's lifetime. 14The Israeli cities between Ekron and Gath, which had been
conquered by the Philistines, were now returned to Israel, for the Israeli army rescued
them from their Philistine captors. And there
was peace between Israel and the Amorites in
those days.

15Samuel continued as Israel's judge for the
remainder of his life. 16He rode circuit annually, setting up his court first at Bethel, then
Gilgal, and then Mizpah, and cases of dispute
were brought to him in each of those three
cities from all the surrounding territory.
17Then he would come back to Ramah, for his
home was there, and he would hear cases
there too. And he built an altar to the Lord at
Ramah.

CHAPTER 8

Israel Demands a King

In his old age, Samuel retired and appointed
his sons as judges in his place. 2Joel and Abijah, his oldest sons, held court in Beersheba;
3but they were not like their father, for they
were greedy for money. They accepted bribes
and were very corrupt in the administration
of justice. 4Finally the leaders of Israel met in
Ramah to discuss the matter with Samuel.
5They told him that since his retirement
things hadn't been the same, for his sons were
not good men.

"Give us a king like all the other nations
have," they pleaded. 6Samuel was terribly upset and went to the Lord for advice.

7"Do as they say," the Lord replied, "for I
am the one they are rejecting, not you—they
don't want me to be their king any longer.
8Ever since I brought them from Egypt they
have continually forsaken me and followed
other gods. And now they are giving you the
same treatment. 9Do as they ask, but warn
them about what it will be like to have a
king!"

7:12 The fact that Samuel set up a stone called Ebenezer, which means "the Stone of Help," should remind us of two principles. First, God's help in the past is a promise of help in the future. God offers much more than a onetime antidote or a quick fix. He is a continual remedy and source of strength as we go about rebuilding our life. Second, the fact that God's help is available on a daily basis should help us see that we need to look to him every day. The secret to recovery is to recognize that it happens one day at a time. If we depend upon God daily, we will find the strength and grace to endure and achieve the victory.

8:3-5 Not unlike the sons of Eli, Samuel's sons also failed to set boundaries on their behavior. They were greedy for money, taking bribes and perverting justice (8:3), actions for which they were held accountable. Their disobedience surely embarrassed their father, but also prompted a national outcry for governmental change (8:5). Because of failure in the leadership, the people rejected God's rule through the judges and demanded to have what all the surrounding nations had—a king. One wonders what might have happened if Samuel's sons had been able to handle delayed gratification and had acted more responsibly. It is clear that God will not allow sin to continue unpunished, especially among those he has put in positions of leadership.

8:18-20 The Israelites refused to listen to Samuel's God-given advice and soon were saddled with a less-than-satisfactory ruler, Saul. Wanting to be like the other nations, they clamored for a king and found out the hard way that what they wanted wasn't necessarily what they needed. God's dealings with his people suggest two lessons. First, the road to recovery is often lengthened when a deliberate choice is made to go against wise counsel (Psalm 106:15). Second, the constant pressure to be like everybody else makes it difficult to gain freedom and experience recovery. God may even allow us to have our own way in a situation so he can show us the ultimate folly of it.

9:2 Saul was certainly a man of impressive physical attributes, but in his case, his "gifts" became detrimental rather than helpful. People gifted with beauty, intelligence, size, or strength often fall into the trap of self-sufficiency. They begin to think they can go it alone. This attitude only stands in the way of achieving God's success. Our pride and notions of personal potential may prevent us from ever becoming humble enough to admit that we have needs. Saul looked good on paper, but he allowed his "strengths" to stand in the way of his only means of success—God's help. We must be careful to avoid this pitfall if we hope to succeed in our recovery.

SAUL

Saul's story is a tragic one. He was a man with great potential for leadership, but he failed miserably. He allowed his fearfulness, disobedience, and self-sufficiency to come between him and God's plan for his life.

At the beginning of his career, Saul was a shy and reluctant leader. He was found hiding in the baggage when Samuel called the people together to publicly anoint him as king. Saul's humble, restrained style worked well in the early days of his rule, but he came to a point where he had to decide to either follow or fight against God's authority in his life. Unfortunately, Saul made the wrong choice.

During his reign, Saul had his greatest successes when he obeyed God. His greatest failures resulted from acting on his own. Even his weaknesses, though, could have been used by God if Saul had recognized them and left them in God's hands.

Just like Saul, we are faced with the choice of turning our life and will over to God or continuing to fight his plan for us. As with Saul, our answer to that choice sets the course of our life.

Saul's story is told in 1 Samuel 9–31. He is also mentioned in Acts 13:21.

STRENGTHS AND ACCOMPLISHMENTS:
- Saul's family and troops were always loyal to him.
- When he was obeying God, his leadership and courage were great.
- He had a striking, charismatic appearance.

WEAKNESSES AND MISTAKES:
- He was driven by a fear that led to disobedience.
- He was a people pleaser.
- He disobeyed God in crucial situations.

LESSONS FROM HIS LIFE:
- God desires heartfelt obedience, not ritualistic, routine actions.
- Though costly, obedience to God is always best.

KEY VERSE:
"For rebellion is as bad as the sin of witchcraft, and stubbornness is as bad as worshiping idols. And now because you have rejected the word of Jehovah, he has rejected you from being king" (1 Samuel 15:23).

10So Samuel told the people what the Lord
had said:
11"If you insist on having a king, he will
conscript your sons and make them run before his chariots; 12some will be made to lead
his troops into battle, while others will be
slave laborers; they will be forced to plow in
the royal fields and harvest his crops without
pay, and make his weapons and chariot
equipment. 13He will take your daughters
from you and force them to cook and bake
and make perfumes for him. 14He will take
away the best of your fields and vineyards and
olive groves and give them to his friends. 15He
will take a tenth of your harvest and distribute
it to his favorites. 16He will demand your
slaves and the finest of your youth and will
use your animals for his personal gain. 17He
will demand a tenth of your flocks, and you
shall be his slaves. 18You will shed bitter tears
because of this king you are demanding, but
the Lord will not help you."
19But the people refused to listen to Samuel's warning.
"Even so, we still want a king," they said,
20"for we want to be like the nations around
us. He will govern us and lead us to battle."
21So Samuel told the Lord what the people
had said, 22and the Lord replied again, "Then
do as they say and give them a king."
So Samuel agreed and sent the men home
again.

CHAPTER 9
Saul Hunts His Father's Donkeys

Kish was a rich, influential man from the tribe
of Benjamin. He was the son of Abiel, grandson of Zeror, great-grandson of Becorath, and
great-great-grandson of Aphiah. 2His son Saul
was the most handsome man in Israel. And he
was head and shoulders taller than anyone
else in the land!
3One day Kish's donkeys strayed away, so
he sent Saul and a servant to look for them.
4They traveled all through the hill country of
Ephraim, the land of Shalisha, the Shaalim
area, and the entire land of Benjamin, but
couldn't find them anywhere. 5Finally, after
searching in the land of Zuph, Saul said to the
servant, "Let's go home; by now my father
will be more worried about us than about the
donkeys!"
6But the servant said, "I've just thought of
something! There is a prophet who lives here
in this city; he is held in high honor by all the
people because everything he says comes

true; let's go and find him, and perhaps he can
tell us where the donkeys are."
7"But we don't have anything to pay him
with," Saul replied. "Even our food is gone,
and we don't have a thing to give him."
8"Well," the servant said, "I have a dollar!
We can at least offer it to him and see what
happens!"
9-11"All right," Saul agreed, "let's try it!"
So they started into the city where the
prophet lived. As they were climbing a hill
toward the city, they saw some young girls
going out to draw water and asked them if
they knew whether the seer was in town. (In
those days prophets were called seers. "Let's
go and ask the seer," people would say, rather
than, "Let's go and ask the prophet," as we
would say now.)
12,13"Yes," they replied, "stay right on this
road. He lives just inside the city gates. He has
just arrived back from a trip to take part in a
public sacrifice up on the hill. So hurry, because he'll probably be leaving about the time
you get there; the guests can't eat until he
arrives and blesses the food."
14So they went into the city, and as they
were entering the gates they saw Samuel coming out toward them to go up the hill. 15The
Lord had told Samuel the previous day,
16"About this time tomorrow I will send
you a man from the land of Benjamin. You are
to anoint him as the leader of my people. He
will save them from the Philistines, for I have
looked down on them in mercy and have
heard their cry."
17When Samuel saw Saul the Lord said,
"That's the man I told you about! He will rule
my people."
18Just then Saul approached Samuel and
asked, "Can you please tell me where the
seer's house is?"
19"I am the seer!" Samuel replied. "Go on up
the hill ahead of me and we'll eat together; in
the morning I will tell you what you want to
know and send you on your way. 20And don't
worry about those donkeys that were lost
three days ago, for they have been found. And
anyway, you own all the wealth of Israel
now!"
21"Pardon me, sir," Saul replied. "I'm from
the tribe of Benjamin, the smallest in Israel,
and my family is the least important of all the
families of the tribe! You must have the wrong
man!"
22Then Samuel took Saul and his servant
into the great hall and placed them at the
head of the table, honoring them above the
thirty special guests. 23Samuel then instructed
the chef to bring Saul the choicest cut of meat,
the piece that had been set aside for the guest
of honor. 24So the chef brought it in and
placed it before Saul.
"Go ahead and eat it," Samuel said, "for I
was saving it for you, even before I invited
these others!"
So Saul ate with Samuel. 25After the feast,
when they had returned to the city, Samuel
took Saul up to the porch on the roof and
talked with him there. 26,27At daybreak the
next morning, Samuel called up to him, "Get
up; it's time you were on your way!"
So Saul got up, and Samuel accompanied
him to the edge of the city. When they
reached the city walls, Samuel told Saul to
send the servant on ahead. Then he told him,
"I have received a special message for you
from the Lord."

CHAPTER 10

Saul Is Anointed to Be King

Then Samuel took a flask of olive oil and
poured it over Saul's head, and kissed him on
the cheek and said,
"I am doing this because the Lord has appointed you to be the king of his people, Israel!
2When you leave me, you will see two men
beside Rachel's tomb at Zelzah, in the land of
Benjamin; they will tell you that the donkeys
have been found and that your father is worried about you and is asking, 'How am I to find

9:14-17 Notice that Samuel approached at the very moment Saul entered the town. This should remind us of how perfect God's timing is in the events of our own life! He often leads us to meet people or experience events that make our recovery possible. If we see this to be true as we look back on our life, we should take the time to thank God for his direction (Psalms 37:23-24; 138:8; Proverbs 3:5-6; Isaiah 48:17).

10:1 As Samuel anointed Saul to be king over Israel, he was also burying his personal dreams. Samuel was the last of the judges; his sons would never share his honor. But despite his disappointment, Samuel found the courage to follow God's will instead of his own. He was willing to change and even to assist in the process by helping Saul become king over Israel. Assisting others on the road to a new life sometimes means we must give up some personal dreams of our own. But if we are following God's will, helping others will turn out to be the surest way to discover a new life for ourself.

my son?' 3 And when you get to the oak of Tabor, you will see three men coming toward you who are on their way to worship God at the altar at Bethel; one will be bringing three young goats, another will have three loaves of bread, and the third will have a bottle of wine. 4 They will greet you and offer you two of the loaves, which you are to accept. 5 After that you will come to Gibeath-elohim, also known as "God's Hill," where the garrison of the Philistines is. As you arrive there you will meet a band of prophets coming down the hill playing a psaltery, a timbrel, a flute, and a harp, and prophesying as they come.

6 "At that time the Spirit of the Lord will come mightily upon you and you will prophesy with them, and you will feel and act like a different person. 7 From that time on your decisions should be based on whatever seems best under the circumstances, for the Lord will guide you. 8 Go to Gilgal and wait there seven days for me, for I will be coming to sacrifice burnt offerings and peace offerings. I will give you further instructions when I arrive."

9 As Saul said good-bye and started to go, God gave him a new attitude, and all of Samuel's prophecies came true that day. 10 When Saul and the servant arrived at the Hill of God, they saw the prophets coming toward them, and the Spirit of God came upon him, and he too began to prophesy.

11 When his friends heard about it, they exclaimed, "What? Saul a prophet?" 12 And one of the neighbors added, "With a father like his?" So that is the origin of the proverb, "Is Saul a prophet too?"

13 When Saul had finished prophesying he climbed the hill to the altar.

14 "Where in the world did you go?" Saul's uncle asked him.

And Saul replied, "We went to look for the donkeys, but we couldn't find them; so we went to the prophet Samuel to ask him where they were."

15 "Oh? And what did he say?" his uncle asked.

16 "He said the donkeys had been found!" Saul replied. (But he didn't tell him that he had been anointed as king!)

17 Samuel now called a convocation of all Israel at Mizpah 18,19 and gave them this message from the Lord God: "I brought you from Egypt and rescued you from the Egyptians and from all of the nations that were torturing you. But although I have done so much for you, you have rejected me and have said, 'We want a king instead!' All right, then, present yourselves before the Lord by tribes and clans."

20 So Samuel called the tribal leaders together before the Lord, and the tribe of Benjamin was chosen by sacred lot. 21 Then he brought each family of the tribe of Benjamin before the Lord, and the family of the Matrites was chosen. And finally the sacred lot selected Saul, the son of Kish. But when they looked for him, he had disappeared!

22 So they asked the Lord, "Where is he? Is he here among us?"

And the Lord replied, "He is hiding in the baggage."

23 So they found him and brought him out, and he stood head and shoulders above anyone else.

24 Then Samuel said to all the people, "This is the man the Lord has chosen as your king. There isn't his equal in all of Israel!"

And all the people shouted, "Long live the king!"

25 Then Samuel told the people again what the rights and duties of a king were; he wrote them in a book and put it in a special place before the Lord. Then Samuel sent the people home again.

26 When Saul returned to his home at Gibeah, a band of men whose hearts the Lord had touched became his constant companions. 27 There were, however, some bums and loafers who exclaimed, "How can this man save us?" And they despised him and refused to bring him presents, but he took no notice.

CHAPTER 11

Saul Defeats the Ammonites

At this time Nahash led the army of the Ammonites against the Israeli city of Jabesh-gilead. But the citizens of Jabesh asked for

---

10:26 The phrase "whose hearts the Lord had touched" spells out for us a critical phase in the recovery process. God touched Saul's life and then he touched a number of individuals to support Saul in his new life. These words recall a verse in the New Testament: "Jesus came over and touched them. 'Get up,' he said, 'don't be afraid'" (Matthew 17:7). The touch of God's healing hand enables us to deal with the past, persist in the present, and find direction for the future. Starting anew means we must first come to God for the salvation he offers in Jesus Christ (John 3:16); then we must depend on him for sustenance and strength (John 15:4-7).

peace. "Leave us alone and we will be your
servants," they pleaded.
2"All right," Nahash said, "but only on one
condition: I will gouge out the right eye of
every one of you as a disgrace upon all Israel!"
3"Give us seven days to see if we can get
some help!" replied the elders of Jabesh. "If
none of our brothers will come and save us,
we will agree to your terms."
4When a messenger came to Gibeah, Saul's
hometown, and told the people about their
plight, everyone broke into tears.
5Saul was plowing in the field, and when he
returned to town he asked, "What's the matter? Why is everyone crying?"
So they told him about the message from
Jabesh. 6Then the Spirit of God came strongly
upon Saul and he became very angry. 7He
took two oxen and cut them into pieces and
sent messengers to carry them throughout all
Israel.
"This is what will happen to the oxen of
anyone who refuses to follow Saul and Samuel to battle!" he announced. And God caused
the people to be afraid of Saul's anger, and
they came to him as one man. 8He counted
them in Bezek and found that there were
three hundred thousand of them in addition
to thirty thousand from Judah.
9So he sent the messengers back to Jabesh-
gilead to say, "We will rescue you before tomorrow noon!" What joy there was
throughout the city when that message arrived!
10The men of Jabesh then told their enemies, "We surrender. Tomorrow we will come
out to you and you can do to us as you wish."
11But early the next morning Saul arrived,
having divided his army into three detachments, and launched a surprise attack against
the Ammonites and slaughtered them all
morning. The remnant of their army was so
badly scattered that no two of them were left
together.
12Then the people exclaimed to Samuel,
"Where are those men who said that Saul
shouldn't be our king? Bring them here and
we will kill them!"
13But Saul replied, "No one will be executed
today; for today the Lord has rescued Israel!"
14Then Samuel said to the people, "Come,
let us all go to Gilgal and reconfirm Saul as our
king."
15So they went to Gilgal and in a solemn
ceremony before the Lord they crowned him
king. Then they offered peace offerings to the
Lord, and Saul and all Israel were very happy.

CHAPTER 12

God's Promises and Requirements

Then Samuel addressed the people again:
"Look," he said, "I have done as you asked.
I have given you a king. 2I have selected him
ahead of my own sons and now I stand here,
an old, gray-haired man who has been in
public service from the time he was a lad.
3Now tell me as I stand before the Lord and
before his anointed king—whose ox or donkey have I stolen? Have I ever defrauded you?
Have I ever oppressed you? Have I ever taken
a bribe? Tell me and I will make right whatever I have done wrong."
4"No," they replied, "you have never defrauded or oppressed us in any way and you
have never taken even one single bribe."
5"The Lord and his anointed king are my
witnesses," Samuel declared, "that you can
never accuse me of robbing you."
"Yes, it is true," they replied.
6"It was the Lord who appointed Moses and
Aaron," Samuel continued. "He brought your
ancestors out of the land of Egypt.
7"Now stand here quietly before the Lord as
I remind you of all the good things he has
done for you and for your ancestors:
8"When the Israelites were in Egypt and
cried out to the Lord, he sent Moses and
Aaron to bring them into this land. 9But they
soon forgot about the Lord their God, so he
let them be conquered by Sisera, the general
of King Hazor's army, and by the Philistines
and the king of Moab.
10"Then they cried to the Lord again and
confessed that they had sinned by turning
away from him and worshiping the Baal and
Ashtaroth idols. And they pleaded, 'We will
worship you and you alone if you will only
rescue us from our enemies.' 11Then the Lord
sent Gideon, Barak, Jephthah, and Samuel to
save you, and you lived in safety.

11:13-15 Saul proclaimed, "Today the Lord has rescued Israel!" (11:13). Following their victory over the Ammonites, Saul, Samuel, and the people confirmed Saul's kingship at Gilgal (11:14-15). Likewise, it is often a good idea for us to go public with our commitments so we will feel responsible for them and be held accountable by others. Platform speeches aren't usually necessary. Generally, confiding in a few trusted friends will do, as long as they will follow through and confront us when we slip up.

12"But when you were afraid of Nahash, the king of Ammon, you came to me and said that you wanted a king to reign over you. But the Lord your God was already your King, for he has always been your King. 13All right, here is the king you have chosen. Look him over. You have asked for him, and the Lord has answered your request.

14"Now if you will fear and worship the Lord, and listen to his commandments and not rebel against the Lord, and if both you and your king follow the Lord your God, then all will be well. 15But if you rebel against the Lord's commandments and refuse to listen to him, then his hand will be as heavy upon you as it was upon your ancestors.

16"Now watch as the Lord does great miracles. 17You know that it does not rain at this time of the year, during the wheat harvest; I will pray for the Lord to send thunder and rain today, so that you will realize the extent of your wickedness in asking for a king!"

18So Samuel called to the Lord, and the Lord sent thunder and rain; and all the people were very much afraid of the Lord and of Samuel.

19"Pray for us lest we die!" they cried out to Samuel. "For now we have added to all our other sins by asking for a king."

20"Don't be frightened," Samuel reassured them. "You have certainly done wrong, but make sure now that you worship the Lord with true enthusiasm, and that you don't turn your back on him in any way. 21Other gods can't help you. 22The Lord will not abandon his chosen people, for that would dishonor his great name. He made you a special nation for himself—just because he wanted to!

23"As for me, I will certainly not sin against the Lord by ending my prayers for you; and I will continue to teach you those things which are good and right.

24"Trust the Lord and sincerely worship him; think of all the tremendous things he has done for you. 25But if you continue to sin, you and your king will be destroyed."

CHAPTER 13

Saul Disobeys God

By this time Saul had reigned for one year. In the second year of his reign, 2he selected three thousand special troops and took two thousand of them with him to Michmash and Mount Bethel while the other thousand remained with Jonathan, Saul's son, in Gibeah in the land of Benjamin. The rest of the army was sent home. 3,4Then Jonathan attacked and destroyed the garrison of the Philistines at Geba. The news spread quickly throughout the land ofthe Philistines, and Saul sounded the call to arms throughout Israel. He announced that he had destroyed the Philistine garrison and warned his men that the army of Israel stank to high heaven as far as the Philistines were concerned. So the entire Israeli army mobilized again and joined at Gilgal. 5The Philistines recruited a mighty army of three thousand chariots, six thousand horsemen, and so many soldiers that they were as thick as sand along the seashore; and they camped at Michmash east of Beth-aven.

6When the men of Israel saw the vast mass of enemy troops, they lost their nerve entirely and tried to hide in caves, thickets, coverts, among the rocks, and even in tombs and cisterns. 7Some of them crossed the Jordan River and escaped to the land of Gad and Gilead. Meanwhile, Saul stayed at Gilgal, and those who were with him trembled with fear at what awaited them. 8Samuel had told Saul earlier to wait seven days for his arrival, but when he still didn't come, and Saul's troops were rapidly slipping away, 9he decided to sacrifice the burnt offering and the peace offerings himself. 10But just as he was finishing, Samuel arrived. Saul went out to meet him

---

12:14-15 Life is filled with choices, and the Bible is filled with clear direction on how to make decisions in line with God's program. A wise decision always takes into account whether or not we are showing proper respect for God, worshiping and serving him as we should, or obeying his commands (12:14). A poor decision will fail to keep God's desires and requirements in focus (12:15). Following God's program will reap positive long-term consequences, even though it may look difficult in the short run. Disobedience to God's revealed instructions will invariably lead us into bondage and the need for recovery.

12:20 Samuel exhorted the Israelites not to be afraid and to keep hanging in there. He was calling the people to persevere in their recovery from past failure. He didn't downplay their past sin; in fact, he reminded them of it. But he also called them to escape the mire of guilt and past failure. He emphasized the positive, saying, "Make sure now that you worship the Lord with true enthusiasm, and that you don't turn your back on him in any way." It is important to recognize the sin in our past, but it is even more important to look ahead to a positive future. And as the process continues, it is vital to remember that a new life is not built overnight.

and to receive his blessing, [11]but Samuel said, "What is this you have done?"

"Well," Saul replied, "when I saw that my men were scattering from me, and that you hadn't arrived by the time you said you would, and that the Philistines were at Michmash, ready for battle, [12]I said, 'The Philistines are ready to march against us and I haven't even asked for the Lord's help!' So I reluctantly offered the burnt offering without waiting for you to arrive."

[13]"You fool!" Samuel exclaimed. "You have disobeyed the commandment of the Lord your God. He was planning to make you and your descendants kings of Israel forever, [14]but now your dynasty must end; for the Lord wants a man who will obey him. And he has discovered the man he wants and has already appointed him as king over his people; for you have not obeyed the Lord's commandment."

An Army without Weapons

[15]Samuel then left Gilgal and went to Gibeah in the land of Benjamin.

When Saul counted the soldiers who were still with him, he found only six hundred left!
[16]Saul and Jonathan and these six hundred men set up their camp in Geba in the land of Benjamin; but the Philistines stayed at Michmash. [17]Three companies of raiders soon left the camp of the Philistines; one went toward Ophrah in the land of Shual, [18]another went to Beth-horon, and the third moved toward the border above the valley of Zeboim near the desert.

[19]There were no blacksmiths at all in the land of Israel in those days, for the Philistines wouldn't allow them for fear of their making swords and spears for the Hebrews. [20]So whenever the Israelites needed to sharpen their plowshares, discs, axes, or sickles, they had to take them to a Philistine blacksmith. [21]The schedule of charges was as follows:

For sharpening a plow point, 60¢
For sharpening a disc, 60¢
For sharpening an axe, 30¢
For sharpening a sickle, 30¢
For sharpening an ox goad, 30¢

[22]So there was not a single sword or spear in the entire "army" of Israel that day, except for Saul's and Jonathan's. [23]The mountain pass at Michmash had meanwhile been secured by a contingent of the Philistine army.

CHAPTER 14

Jonathan's Courageous Plan

A day or so later, Prince Jonathan said to his young bodyguard, "Come on, let's cross the valley to the garrison of the Philistines." But he didn't tell his father that he was leaving.

[2]Saul and his six hundred men were camped at the edge of Gibeah, around the pomegranate tree at Migron. [3]Among his men was Ahijah the priest (the son of Ahitub, Ichabod's brother; Ahitub was the son of

13:8-14 When we get our eyes off God and on the circumstances around us, we often develop an urge to act with impatience or indiscretion. Confronted by the seemingly insurmountable threat of the Philistine army and afraid that his men were about to desert him, Saul acted irresponsibly by offering a burnt sacrifice himself rather than waiting until a priest arrived. He failed to trust in God's timing and thus disobeyed one of God's commands. The consequences for taking things into his own hands were great: his descendants would be denied the right to rule in Israel. Being patient when things seem to be running behind schedule is sometimes the most difficult part of our recovery. We need to be true to God's program, even when it seems to be going too slowly. God's way is always the best way.

14:6-14 God is famous for giving people who trust him victory in impossible situations. Jonathan's confidence in God prompted him to step out in faith and tackle incredible odds. His faith and courage were rewarded with an amazing victory (14:13). It is sad that many of us never trust God enough to discover what he can do and the joy this brings. Notice that Jonathan did not take his step of faith alone, but was accompanied by a bodyguard. Similarly, recovery is not something we accomplish by ourselves. We need support—friends who like Jonathan's companion will exclaim, "Fine! . . . I'm with you heart and soul" (14:7). Significant relationships are not to be shunned "until we get better"; often God uses people to help us get there.

14:19-20 Saul's indecision as he heard the battle in the Philistine camp caused a great deal of confusion among his troops. He was waiting for a clear message from God about what to do. In the end, he found that he had no alternative but to attack, building upon Jonathan's victory (14:13-15). Saul's course of action should have been obvious. His rather insincere hesitation shows us that there is a time to pray and a time to act. We must avoid trying to be "spiritual" when it is time to take action. We don't need to pray about obvious things. We already know what people, places, and activities to avoid. Some things are obvious and must be pursued without delay.

Phinehas and the grandson of Eli, the priest
of the Lord in Shiloh).
No one realized that Jonathan had gone.
4 To reach the Philistine garrison, Jonathan
had to go over a narrow pass between two
rocky crags which had been named Bozez and
Seneh. 5 The crag on the north was in front of
Michmash and the southern one was in front
of Geba.
6 "Yes, let's go across to those heathen,"
Jonathan had said to his bodyguard. "Perhaps
the Lord will do a miracle for us. For it makes
no difference to him how many enemy troops
there are!"
7 "Fine!" the youth replied. "Do as you
think best; I'm with you heart and soul, whatever you decide."
8 "All right, then this is what we'll do," Jonathan told him. 9 "When they see us, if they
say, 'Stay where you are or we'll kill you!' then
we will stop and wait for them. 10 But if they
say, 'Come on up and fight!' then we will do
just that; for it will be God's signal that he will
help us defeat them!"
11 When the Philistines saw them coming
they shouted, "Look! The Israelis are crawling
out of their holes!" 12 Then they shouted to
Jonathan, "Come on up here and we'll show
you how to fight!"
"Come on, climb right behind me," Jonathan exclaimed to his bodyguard, "for the
Lord will help us defeat them!"
13 So they clambered up on their hands and
knees, and the Philistines fell back as Jonathan and the lad killed them right and left,
14 about twenty men in all, and their bodies
were scattered over about half an acre of land.
15 Suddenly panic broke out throughout the
entire Philistine army, and even among the
raiders. And just then there was a great earthquake, increasing the terror.
16 Saul's lookouts in Gibeah saw a strange
sight—the vast army of the Philistines began
to melt away in all directions.
17 "Find out who isn't here," Saul ordered.
And when they had checked, they found that
Jonathan and his bodyguard were gone.
18 "Bring the Ark of God," Saul shouted to
Ahijah. (For the Ark was among the people of
Israel at that time.) 19 But while Saul was talking to the priest, the shouting and the tumult
in the camp of the Philistines grew louder and
louder. "Quick! What does God say?" Saul
demanded.
20 Then Saul and his six hundred men
rushed out to the battle and found the Philistines killing each other, and there was terrible

Peer pressure

READ 1 SAMUEL 13:1-14

We are all susceptible to the negative influences of others. We get pushed into rushed decisions by peer pressure and find ourself in trouble as a result. This weakness should alert us to a defect in our life and our need for help.

Saul had this defect but refused God's help. Samuel had told Saul at his coronation that if he obeyed God's commands everything would be well with him (1 Samuel 12:14). But Saul allowed his men to pressure him into disobedience. Israel was at war. In the midst of battle it was customary to have a priest offer sacrifices, and Samuel promised Saul that he would come at an appointed time to do this. Saul waited for a while, but began to feel pressured because his troops were leaving him. He knew that it was against God's law for him to offer sacrifices, but he decided he could wait no longer and did it himself.

Just as Saul finished his sacrifice, Samuel arrived. "'You fool!' Samuel exclaimed. 'You have disobeyed the commandment of the Lord your God. He was planning to make you and your descendants kings of Israel forever, but now your dynasty must end; for the Lord wants a man who will obey him'" (1 Samuel 13:13-14). Saul would suffer the consequences for his disobedience.

If Saul had delayed his action just one more hour, he would have kept his kingdom. Our tendency to be unduly influenced by others needs to be replaced with strength from God and faith in his plan.
Turn to page 319, 1 Samuel 14.

confusion everywhere. [21]And now the Hebrews who had been drafted into the Philistine army revolted and joined with the
Israelis. [22]Finally even the men hiding in the
hills joined the chase when they saw that the
Philistines were running away. [23]So the Lord
saved Israel that day, and the battle continued
out beyond Beth-aven.

Saul's Foolish Order

[24,25]Saul had declared, "A curse upon anyone
who eats anything before evening—before I
have full revenge on my enemies." So no one
ate anything all day, even though they found
honeycomb on the ground in the forest, [26]for
they all feared Saul's curse. [27]Jonathan, however, had not heard his father's command; so
he dipped a stick into a honeycomb, and
when he had eaten the honey he felt much
better. [28]Then someone told him that his
father had laid a curse upon anyone who ate
food that day, and everyone was weary and
faint as a result.

[29]"That's ridiculous!" Jonathan exclaimed.
"A command like that only hurts us. See how
much better I feel now that I have eaten this
little bit of honey. [30]If the people had been
allowed to eat freely from the food they found
among our enemies, think how many more
we could have slaughtered!"

[31]But hungry as they were, they chased and
killed the Philistines all day from Michmash
to Aijalon, growing more and more faint.
[32]That evening they flew upon the battle loot
and butchered the sheep, oxen, and calves,
and ate the raw, bloody meat. [33]Someone reported to Saul what was happening, that the
people were sinning against the Lord by eating blood.

"That is very wrong," Saul said. "Roll a
great stone over here, [34]and go out among the
troops and tell them to bring the oxen and
sheep here to kill and drain them, and not to
sin against the Lord by eating the blood." So
that is what they did.

[35]And Saul built an altar to the Lord—his
first.

[36]Afterwards Saul said, "Let's chase the Philistines all night and destroy every last one of
them."

"Fine!" his men replied. "Do as you think
best."

But the priest said, "Let's ask God first."

[37]So Saul asked God, "Shall we go after the
Philistines? Will you help us defeat them?"
But the Lord made no reply all night.

[38]Then Saul said to the leaders, "Something's wrong! We must find out what sin was
committed today. [39]I vow by the name of the
God who saved Israel that though the sinner
be my own son Jonathan, he shall surely die!"
But no one would tell him what the trouble
was.

[40]Then Saul proposed, "Jonathan and I will
stand over here, and all of you stand over
there." And the people agreed.

[41]Then Saul said, "O Lord God of Israel,
why haven't you answered my question?
What is wrong? Are Jonathan and I guilty, or
is the sin among the others? O Lord God,
show us who is guilty." And Jonathan and
Saul were chosen by sacred lot as the guilty
ones, and the people were declared innocent.

[42]Then Saul said, "Now draw lots between
me and Jonathan." And Jonathan was chosen
as the guilty one.

[43]"Tell me what you've done," Saul demanded of Jonathan.

"I tasted a little honey," Jonathan admitted. "It was only a little bit on the end of a
stick; but now I must die."

[44]"Yes, Jonathan," Saul said, "you must die;
may God strike me dead if you are not executed for this."

[45]But the troops retorted, "Jonathan, who
saved Israel today, shall die? Far from it! We
vow by the life of God that not one hair on
his head will be touched, for he has been used
of God to do a mighty miracle today." So the
people rescued Jonathan.

[46]Then Saul called back the army, and the
Philistines returned home.

Saul's Military Successes

[47]And now, since he was securely in the saddle
as king of Israel, Saul sent the Israeli army out
in every direction against Moab, Ammon,
Edom, the kings of Zobah, and the Philistines.
And wherever he turned, he was successful.
[48]He did great deeds and conquered the
Amalekites and saved Israel from all those
who had been their conquerors.

[49]Saul had three sons, Jonathan, Ishvi, and
Malchishua; and two daughters, Merab and
Michal. [50,51]Saul's wife was Ahinoam, the
daughter of Ahimaaz. And the general-in-
chief of his army was his cousin Abner, his
uncle Ner's son. (Abner's father, Ner, and
Saul's father, Kish, were brothers; both were
the sons of Abiel.)

[52]The Israelis fought constantly with the
Philistines throughout Saul's lifetime. And
whenever Saul saw any brave, strong young
man, he conscripted him into his army.

CHAPTER 15

Saul Disobeys God

One day Samuel said to Saul, "I crowned you
king of Israel because God told me to. Now be
sure that you obey him. [2]Here is his commandment to you: 'I have decided to settle
accounts with the nation of Amalek for refusing to allow my people to cross their territory
when Israel came from Egypt. [3]Now go and
completely destroy the entire Amalek nation—men, women, babies, little children,
oxen, sheep, camels, and donkeys.'"

[4]So Saul mobilized his army at Telaim.
There were two hundred thousand troops in
addition to ten thousand men from Judah.
[5]The Amalekites were camped in the valley
below them. [6]Saul sent a message to the Kenites, telling them to get out from among the
Amalekites or else die with them. "For you
were kind to the people of Israel when they
came out of the land of Egypt," he explained.
So the Kenites packed up and left.

[7]Then Saul butchered the Amalekites from
Havilah all the way to Shur, east of Egypt. [8]He
captured Agag, the king of the Amalekites, but
killed everyone else. [9]However, Saul and his
men kept the best of the sheep and oxen and
the fattest of the lambs—everything, in fact,
that appealed to them. They destroyed only
what was worthless or of poor quality.

[10]Then the Lord said to Samuel, [11]"I am
sorry that I ever made Saul king, for he has
again refused to obey me."

Samuel was so deeply moved when he
heard what God was saying, that he cried to
the Lord all night. [12]Early the next morning
he went out to find Saul. Someone said that
he had gone to Mount Carmel to erect a
monument to himself and had then gone on
to Gilgal. [13]When Samuel finally found him,
Saul greeted him cheerfully.

"Hello there," he said. "Well, I have carried
out the Lord's command!"

[14]"Then what was all the bleating of sheep
and lowing of oxen I heard?" Samuel demanded.

[15]"It's true that the army spared the best of
the sheep and oxen," Saul admitted, "but
they are going to sacrifice them to the Lord
your God; and we have destroyed everything
else."

[16]Then Samuel said to Saul, "Stop! Listen to
what the Lord told me last night!"

"What was it?" Saul asked.

[17]And Samuel told him, "When you didn't
think much of yourself, God made you king
of Israel. [18]And he sent you on an errand and

Self-protection

READ 1 SAMUEL 14:1-12, 20-29

We once used our addictions to find comfort and to help us cope with life's daily battles. In recovery, we may have become so focused on the battle at hand that we have neglected our basic physical needs. We may have forgotten our need to enjoy some of the sweet things of life. Failure to take care of ourself can leave us weak and vulnerable.

During a difficult battle, King Saul had declared, "'A curse upon anyone who eats anything before evening—before I have full revenge on my enemies.' . . . Jonathan, however, had not heard his father's command; so he dipped a stick into a honeycomb, and when he had eaten the honey he felt much better. Then someone told him that his father had laid a curse upon anyone who ate food that day, and everyone was weary and faint as a result. 'That's ridiculous!' Jonathan exclaimed. 'A command like that only hurts us. See how much better I feel now'" (1 Samuel 14:24-29).

When we are in recovery, we already feel deprived. We need to make sure that we are being good to ourself in healthy ways, eating good food and tasting some of the sweet things that life naturally provides. Recovery isn't a time for unnecessary deprivation. If we allow ourself to become too hungry physically or emotionally, we'll find that we are weary and less able to fight the battles we face each day. ***Turn to page 357, 2 Samuel 13.***

told you, 'Go and completely destroy the sinners, the Amalekites, until they are all dead.' 19Then why didn't you obey the Lord? Why did you rush for the loot and do exactly what God said not to?"

20"But I *have* obeyed the Lord," Saul insisted. "I did what he told me to; and I brought King Agag but killed everyone else. 21And it was only when my troops demanded it that I let them keep the best of the sheep and oxen and loot to sacrifice to the Lord."

22Samuel replied, "Has the Lord as much pleasure in your burnt offerings and sacrifices as in your obedience? Obedience is far better than sacrifice. He is much more interested in your listening to him than in your offering the fat of rams to him. 23For rebellion is as bad as the sin of witchcraft, and stubbornness is as bad as worshiping idols. And now because you have rejected the word of Jehovah, he has rejected you from being king."

Saul Pleads for Forgiveness

24"I have sinned," Saul finally admitted. "Yes, I have disobeyed your instructions and the command of the Lord, for I was afraid of the people and did what they demanded. 25Oh, please pardon my sin now and go with me to worship the Lord."

26But Samuel replied, "It's no use! Since you have rejected the commandment of the Lord, he has rejected you from being the king of Israel."

27As Samuel turned to go, Saul grabbed at him to try to hold him back and tore his robe.

28And Samuel said to him, "See? The Lord has torn the kingdom of Israel from you today and has given it to a countryman of yours who is better than you are. 29And he who is the glory of Israel is not lying, nor will he change his mind, for he is not a man!"

30Then Saul pleaded again, "I have sinned; but oh, at least honor me before the leaders and before my people by going with me to worship the Lord your God."

31So Samuel finally agreed and went with him.

32Then Samuel said, "Bring King Agag to me." Agag arrived all full of smiles, for he thought, "Surely the worst is over and I have been spared!" 33But Samuel said, "As your sword has killed the sons of many mothers, now your mother shall be childless." And Samuel chopped him in pieces before the Lord at Gilgal. 34Then Samuel went home to Ramah, and Saul returned to Gibeah. 35Samuel never saw Saul again, but he mourned constantly for him; and the Lord was sorry that he had ever made Saul king of Israel.

CHAPTER 16

Samuel Anoints David to Be King

Finally the Lord said to Samuel, "You have mourned long enough for Saul, for I have rejected him as king of Israel. Now take a vial of olive oil and go to Bethlehem and find a man named Jesse, for I have selected one of his sons to be the new king."

2But Samuel asked, "How can I do that? If Saul hears about it, he will kill me."

"Take a heifer with you," the Lord replied, "and say that you have come to make a sacrifice to the Lord. 3Then call Jesse to the sacri-

---

15:16-21 Samuel confronted Saul in his denial, but it didn't help. Instead of admitting his failure to obey God's instructions, Saul continued the denial process, rationalizing his disobedience. Denial and rationalization are two of the biggest enemies to recovery. God places a premium on honesty. Notice that Saul sought to excuse himself by his intention to bring sacrifices to God. God does not want our pious prayers and religious activities unless they are accompanied by a humble and obedient heart. Hiding the sin in our life with pious words and deeds is no substitute for confessing our sins and allowing God to cleanse us.

15:22-30 Samuel's words pierced Saul's callous exterior like surgical steel (15:22-23). As we seek recovery, nothing can take the place of obedience to God. Everything hinges on the obedient heart, and this was the arena in which Saul had failed so miserably. He tried to cover his sins with religious activities, promising to offer sacrifices to God. But God was more interested in Saul's confession and obedience than in his sacrifice. Saul's obvious regret spurred him to grasp vainly at Samuel's robe (15:27). But reality proved painful; God's rejection of Saul after so many second chances was real. At this point, complete recovery for Saul had become virtually impossible (15:28-29).

16:1 Samuel was paralyzed by despair over Saul's failure, but God intervened and pointed Samuel toward a new venture. Saul had failed as king, but God had another man in mind for the job. It has been said that when the past is quarreling with the present there can be no future. We all need to quit living in the past after we have learned its lessons. There is a time for all of us to proceed to new assignments and goals. Recovery involves letting go of what was in the past so we can take hold of what is in the present and begin building a new life for the future.

READ 1 SAMUEL 15:10-23

GOD grant me the serenity
to accept the things I cannot change
the courage to change the things I can
and the wisdom to know the difference
AMEN

We need serenity to be able to accept the consequences of our actions. We may tend to feel wrongly accused and deny our wrongs or try to justify them. Unless we are willing to take responsibility for past failures, there is no hope for our recovery.

Saul was the first king of Israel. At his coronation the people were told, "Now if you will fear and worship the Lord and listen to his commandments and not rebel against the Lord, and if both you and your king follow the Lord your God, then all will be well" (1 Samuel 12:14). But Saul disobeyed God. "Then the Lord said to Samuel, 'I am sorry that I ever made Saul king, for he has again refused to obey me'" (15:10-11). When Samuel confronted Saul, he denied doing any wrong and put up his defenses. So Samuel replied, "Rebellion is as bad as the sin of witchcraft, and stubbornness is as bad as worshiping idols. And now because you have rejected the word of Jehovah, he has rejected you from being king" (15:23). Saul then led his entire family and country into years of civil war as he fought to remain king. He finally died at his own hand, surrounded by enemy troops. His three sons died with him.

There is no escaping the consequences of our actions. God can give us the serenity to accept this. When we face this with courage, we may well spare ourself and our loved ones many years of additional pain.
Turn to page 323, 1 Samuel 17.

---

fice, and I will show you which of his sons to anoint."

4So Samuel did as the Lord had told him to. When he arrived at Bethlehem, the elders of the city came trembling to meet him.

"What is wrong?" they asked. "Why have you come?"

5But he replied, "All is well. I have come to sacrifice to the Lord. Purify yourselves and come with me to the sacrifice."

And he performed the purification rite on Jesse and his sons, and invited them too.
6When they arrived, Samuel took one look at Eliab and thought, "Surely this is the man the Lord has chosen!"

7But the Lord said to Samuel, "Don't judge by a man's face or height, for this is not the one. I don't make decisions the way you do! Men judge by outward appearance, but I look at a man's thoughts and intentions."

8Then Jesse told his son Abinadab to step forward and walk in front of Samuel. But the Lord said, "This is not the right man either."

9Next Jesse summoned Shammah, but the Lord said, "No, this is not the one." In the same way all seven of his sons presented themselves to Samuel and were rejected.

10,11"The Lord has not chosen any of them," Samuel told Jesse. "Are these all there are?"

"Well, there is the youngest," Jesse replied. "But he's out in the fields watching the sheep."

"Send for him at once," Samuel said, "for we will not sit down to eat until he arrives."

12So Jesse sent for him. He was a fine looking boy, ruddy-faced, and with pleasant eyes. And the Lord said, "This is the one; anoint him."

13So as David stood there among his brothers, Samuel took the olive oil he had brought and poured it upon David's head; and the Spirit of Jehovah came upon him and gave him great power from that day onward. Then Samuel returned to Ramah.

David Plays Music for Saul

14But the Spirit of the Lord had left Saul, and instead, the Lord had sent a tormenting spirit that filled him with depression and fear. 15,16Some of Saul's aides suggested a cure.

"We'll find a good harpist to play for you whenever the tormenting spirit is bothering you," they said. "The harp music will quiet you and you'll soon be well again."

17"All right," Saul said. "Find me a harpist."

18One of them said he knew a young fellow in Bethlehem, the son of a man named Jesse, who was not only a talented harp player, but was handsome, brave, and strong, and had good, solid judgment. "What's more," he added, "the Lord is with him."

19So Saul sent messengers to Jesse, asking that he send his son David the shepherd. 20Jesse responded by sending not only David but a young goat and a donkey carrying a load of food and wine. 21From the instant he saw David, Saul admired and loved him; and David became his bodyguard.

22Then Saul wrote to Jesse, "Please let David join my staff, for I am very fond of him."

23And whenever the tormenting spirit from God troubled Saul, David would play the harp and Saul would feel better, and the evil spirit would go away.

CHAPTER 17

Goliath Challenges Israel

The Philistines now mustered their army for battle and camped between Socoh in Judah and Azekah in Ephes-dammim. 2Saul countered with a buildup of forces at Elah Valley. 3So the Philistines and Israelis faced each other on opposite hills, with the valley between them.

4-7Then Goliath, a Philistine champion from Gath, came out of the Philistine ranks to face the forces of Israel. He was a giant of a man, measuring over nine feet tall! He wore a bronze helmet, a two-hundred-pound coat of mail, bronze leggings, and carried a bronze javelin several inches thick, tipped with a twenty-five-pound iron spearhead, and his armor-bearer walked ahead of him with a huge shield.

8He stood and shouted across to the Israelis, "Do you need a whole army to settle this? I will represent the Philistines, and you choose someone to represent you, and we will settle this in single combat! 9If your man is able to kill me, then we will be your slaves. But if I kill him, then you must be our slaves! 10I defy the armies of Israel! Send me a man who will fight with me!"

11When Saul and the Israeli army heard this, they were dismayed and frightened.12David (the son of aging Jesse, a member of the tribe of Judah who lived in Bethlehem) had seven older brothers. 13The three oldest—Eliab, Abinadab, and Shammah—had already volunteered for Saul's army to fight the Philistines. 14,15David was the youngest son and was on Saul's staff on a part-time basis. He went back and forth to Bethlehem to help his father with the sheep. 16For forty days, twice a day, morning and evening the Philistine giant strutted before the armies of Israel.

17One day Jesse said to David, "Take this bushel of roasted grain and these ten loaves of bread to your brothers. 18Give this cheese to their captain and see how the boys are getting along; and bring us back a letter from them!"

19(Saul and the Israeli army were camped at the valley of Elah.)

20So David left the sheep with another shepherd and took off early the next morning with the gifts. He arrived at the outskirts of the camp just as the Israeli army was leaving for the battlefield with shouts and battle cries. 21Soon the Israeli and Philistine forces stood facing each other, army against army. 22David left his luggage with a baggage officer and hurried out to the ranks to find his brothers. 23As he was talking with them, he saw Goliath the giant step out from the Philistine troops and shout his challenge to the army of Israel. 24As soon as they saw him the Israeli army began to run away in fright.

25"Have you seen the giant?" the soldiers were asking. "He has insulted the entire army of Israel. And have you heard about the huge reward the king has offered to anyone who kills him? And the king will give him one of

16:6-13 God's choice of the man who would succeed Saul undoubtedly surprised Samuel. In this passage God tells us how he judges the value of individuals. It is not the physical gifts of strength or beauty that make them great. God judges people by their "thoughts and intentions." It is not what we see that is important; it is who a person is on the inside. Most of us are not models of physical perfection, so it might come as a relief that God does not judge us in this way. Saul had failed, despite his external attractiveness. God is concerned with our humility and obedience—requirements for anyone who hopes to succeed in recovery.

READ 1 SAMUEL 17:20-47

GOD grant me the serenity
to accept the things I cannot change
the courage to change the things I can
and the wisdom to know the difference
AMEN

There will be times in life when right and wrong stand in stark contrast. Even when we know what is right and how things should be changed, the power may seem to be on the wrong side.

We may feel powerless even though we know we are standing for what is right. But even when this is true, we still shouldn't give up. Sometimes situations where we feel powerless can prompt action that changes everything for the better.

David "saw Goliath the giant step out from the Philistine troops and shout his challenge to the army of Israel. As soon as they saw him the Israeli army began to run away in fright. 'Have you seen the giant?' the soldiers were asking. 'He has insulted the entire army of Israel.'" David convinced the king to let him fight the giant his own way. He shouted to Goliath, "You come to me with a sword and a spear, but I come to you in the name of the Lord of the armies of heaven and of Israel—the very God whom you have defied. Today the Lord will conquer you" (1 Samuel 17:23-25, 45-46).

The Israelite soldiers saw themselves as helpless victims. Their powerlessness paralyzed them, so they just stood there and took the abuse. David took courageous action to recover their dignity. There are times when we need courage and God's help to fight against the tendency to remain a victim. We need to stand up for our human dignity and respond in new ways if we are to claim our recovery. ***Turn to page 331, 1 Samuel 24.***

---

his daughters for a wife, and his whole family
will be exempted from paying taxes!"
26David talked to some others standing
there to verify the report. "What will a man
get for killing this Philistine and ending his
insults to Israel?" he asked them. "Who is this
heathen Philistine, anyway, that he is allowed
to defy the armies of the living God?" 27And
he received the same reply as before.
28But when David's oldest brother, Eliab,
heard David talking like that, he was angry.
"What are you doing around here, anyway?"
he demanded. "What about the sheep you're
supposed to be taking care of? I know what a
cocky brat you are; you just want to see the
battle!"
29"What have I done now?" David replied.
"I was only asking a question!"
30And he walked over to some others and
asked them the same thing and received the
same answer. 31When it was finally realized
what David meant, someone told King Saul,
and the king sent for him.

David Kills Goliath

32"Don't worry about a thing," David told
him. "I'll take care of this Philistine!"
33"Don't be ridiculous!" Saul replied. "How
can a kid like you fight with a man like him?
You are only a boy, and he has been in the
army *since* he was a boy!"
34But David persisted. "When I am taking
care of my father's sheep," he said, "and a lion
or a bear comes and grabs a lamb from the
flock, 35I go after it with a club and take the
lamb from its mouth. If it turns on me, I catch
it by the jaw and club it to death. 36I have done
this to both lions and bears, and I'll do it to
this heathen Philistine too, for he has defied
the armies of the living God! 37The Lord who

saved me from the claws and teeth of the lion and the bear will save me from this Philistine!"

Saul finally consented, "All right, go ahead," he said, "and may the Lord be with you!"

38,39 Then Saul gave David his own armor—a bronze helmet and a coat of mail. David put it on, strapped the sword over it, and took a step or two to see what it was like, for he had never worn such things before. "I can hardly move!" he exclaimed, and took them off again. 40 Then he picked up five smooth stones from a stream and put them in his shepherd's bag and, armed only with his shepherd's staff and sling, started across to Goliath. 41,42 Goliath walked out toward David with his shield-bearer ahead of him, sneering in contempt at this nice little red-cheeked boy!

43 "Am I a dog," he roared at David, "that you come at me with a stick?" And he cursed David by the names of his gods. 44 "Come over here and I'll give your flesh to the birds and wild animals," Goliath yelled.

45 David shouted in reply, "You come to me with a sword and a spear, but I come to you in the name of the Lord of the armies of heaven and of Israel—the very God whom you have defied. 46 Today the Lord will conquer you, and I will kill you and cut off your head; and then I will give the dead bodies of *your* men to the birds and wild animals, and the whole world will know that there is a God in Israel! 47 And Israel will learn that the Lord does not depend on weapons to fulfill his plans—he works without regard to human means! He will give you to us!"

48,49 As Goliath approached, David ran out to meet him and, reaching into his shepherd's bag, took out a stone, hurled it from his sling, and hit the Philistine in the forehead. The stone sank in, and the man fell on his face to the ground. 50,51 So David conquered the Philistine giant with a sling and a stone. Since he had no sword, he ran over and pulled Goliath's from its sheath and killed him with it, and then cut off his head. When the Philistines saw that their champion was dead, they turned and ran.

52 Then the Israelis gave a great shout of triumph and rushed after the Philistines, chasing them as far as Gath and the gates of Ekron. The bodies of the dead and wounded Philistines were strewn all along the road to Shaaraim. 53 Then the Israeli army returned and plundered the deserted Philistine camp.

54 (Later David took Goliath's head to Jerusalem, but stored his armor in his tent.)

55 As Saul was watching David go out to fight Goliath, he asked Abner, the general of his army, "Abner, what sort of family does this young fellow come from?"

"I really don't know," Abner said.

56 "Well, find out!" the king told him.

57 After David had killed Goliath, Abner brought him to Saul with the Philistine's head still in his hand.

58 "Tell me about your father, my boy," Saul said.

And David replied, "His name is Jesse and we live in Bethlehem."

CHAPTER 18

David and Jonathan Become Friends

After King Saul had finished his conversation with David, David met Jonathan, the king's son, and there was an immediate bond of love between them. Jonathan swore to be his blood brother, 4 and sealed the pact by giving him his robe, sword, bow, and belt.

King Saul now kept David with him and wouldn't let him return home any more. 5 He was Saul's special assistant, and he always carried out his assignments successfully. So Saul made him commander of his troops, an appointment that was applauded by the army

17:32-37 David was confident that God would deliver him from Goliath's wrath, no matter how improbable it may have seemed. David was a young shepherd boy, armed with sticks and stones. Goliath was a giant of a man, armed with a great sword and spear. In human terms, David didn't have a chance; but with God, he couldn't lose. God is able to provide the victory to all who are willing to trust him. We all face giants in our lives, problems that are too big for us to face alone. But even when the odds are stacked against us, we can't lose if God is on our side.

17:45-47 As David squared off against Goliath, he knew that in human terms, he didn't have a chance. His courage came from his recognition that the battle belonged to God. Like David, we are helpless in the battles we face without God's intervention. But with God, the victory is certain.

18:1-4 God graciously provided David with a close friend in the person of Jonathan. This friendship helped David survive Saul's various attempts on his life. God created us to be close to people and to need their companionship and help. The importance of a significant friend to whom one can be accountable during recovery cannot be overestimated. Recovery is not possible without accountability.

DAVID & JONATHAN

It is amazing that David and Jonathan formed one of the greatest friendships in history! There were vast differences between the two. The oldest son of King Saul, Jonathan was heir apparent to the throne of Israel. He was an experienced soldier, distinguished for his courage in battle. He was probably fifteen years older than David.

David, on the other hand, was the youngest son of Jesse and was a shepherd in the town of Bethlehem. When Jonathan first met him, David was probably a teenager and looked the part of the junior shepherd boy. And though he demonstrated the bold heart of a warrior when he defeated Goliath, he was primarily known as a talented musician in King Saul's court.

There seem to be two basic ingredients that shaped this unlikely relationship. They shared a common faith and commitment to God, and they loved each other unconditionally.

Their friendship was put to the test, however. David was anointed by Samuel, the prophet, to succeed Saul as king. As a result Saul tried repeatedly to kill David. This placed Jonathan at odds with his father. He risked himself to protect and encourage David, the one who would take his place as Israel's future king. No wonder David grieved so heavily at Jonathan's untimely death! It is a gift to have a friend who loves unconditionally. Building these relationships in our life is invaluable in recovery for ourselves and for others.

STRENGTHS AND ACCOMPLISHMENTS:
- David and Jonathan were men of faith and courage.
- They loved each other unconditionally.
- They demonstrated great perseverance in their friendship.
- Jonathan was one of the great encouragers in the Bible.

LESSONS FROM THEIR LIVES:
- Mutual commitment to God and unconditional love are vital ingredients in relationships.
- Difficulties can test and strengthen relationships.
- Encouragement vitalizes any relationship.

KEY VERSE:
"Prince Jonathan now went to find David; he met him at Horesh and encouraged him in his faith in God" (1 Samuel 23:16).

The story of David and Jonathan is told in 1 Samuel 18–31. It is remembered by David in 2 Samuel 1 and 9.

---

and general public alike. 6But something had
happened when the victorious Israeli army
was returning home after David had killed
Goliath. Women came out from all the towns
along the way to celebrate and to cheer for
King Saul, and were singing and dancing for
joy with tambourines and cymbals.
7However, this was their song: "Saul has
slain his thousands, and David his ten thousands!"

Saul Becomes Jealous of David

8Of course Saul was very angry. "What's this?"
he said to himself. "They credit David with
ten thousands and me with only thousands.
Next they'll be making him their king!"
9So from that time on King Saul kept a
jealous watch on David. 10The very next day,
in fact, a tormenting spirit from God overwhelmed
Saul, and he began to rave like a
madman. David began to soothe him by playing
the harp, as he did whenever this happened.
But Saul, who was fiddling with his
spear, 11,12suddenly hurled it at David, intending
to pin him to the wall. But David jumped
aside and escaped. This happened another
time, too, for Saul was afraid of him and
jealous because the Lord had left him and was
now with David. 13Finally Saul banned him
from his presence and demoted him to the
rank of captain. But the controversy put
David more than ever in the public eye.
14David continued to succeed in everything
he undertook, for the Lord was with him.
15,16When King Saul saw this, he became even
more afraid of him; but all Israel and Judah
loved him, for he was as one of them.

David Marries Michal

17One day Saul said to David, "I am ready to
give you my oldest daughter Merab as your
wife. But first you must prove yourself to be a
real soldier by fighting the Lord's battles." For
Saul thought to himself, "I'll send him out

against the Philistines and let them kill him rather than doing it myself."

18"Who am I that I should be the king's son-in-law?" David exclaimed. "My father's family is nothing!"

19But when the time arrived for the wedding, Saul married her to Adriel, a man from Meholath, instead. 20In the meantime Saul's daughter Michal had fallen in love with David, and Saul was delighted when he heard about it.

21"Here's another opportunity to see him killed by the Philistines!" Saul said to himself. But to David he said, "You can be my son-in-law after all, for I will give you my youngest daughter."

22Then Saul instructed his men to say confidentially to David that the king really liked him a lot, and that they all loved him and thought he should accept the king's proposition and become his son-in-law.

23But David replied, "How can a poor man like me from an unknown family find enough dowry to marry the daughter of a king?"

24When Saul's men reported this back to him, 25he told them, "Tell David that the only dowry I need is one hundred dead Philistines! Vengeance on my enemies is all I want." But what Saul had in mind was that David would be killed in the fight.

26David was delighted to accept the offer. So, before the time limit expired, 27he and his men went out and killed two hundred Philistines and presented their foreskins to King Saul. So Saul gave Michal to him.

28When the king realized how much the Lord was with David and how immensely popular he was with all the people, 29he became even more afraid of him and grew to hate him more with every passing day. 30Whenever the Philistine army attacked, David was more successful against them than all the rest of Saul's officers. So David's name became very famous throughout the land.

CHAPTER 19

Saul Tries to Kill David

Saul now urged his aides and his son Jonathan to assassinate David. But Jonathan, because of his close friendship with David, 2told him what his father was planning. "Tomorrow morning," he warned him, "you must find a hiding place out in the fields. 3I'll ask my father to go out there with me, and I'll talk to him about you; then I'll tell you everything I can find out."

4The next morning as Jonathan and his father were talking together, he spoke well of David and begged him not to be against David.

"He's never done anything to harm you," Jonathan pleaded. "He has always helped you in any way he could. 5Have you forgotten about the time he risked his life to kill Goliath, and how the Lord brought a great victory to Israel as a result? You were certainly happy about it then. Why should you now murder an innocent man? There is no reason for it at all!"

6Finally Saul agreed and vowed, "As the Lord lives, he shall not be killed."

7Afterwards Jonathan called David and told him what had happened. Then he took David to Saul and everything was as it had been before. 8War broke out shortly after that, and David led his troops against the Philistines and slaughtered many of them, and put to flight their entire army.

9,10But one day as Saul was sitting at home, listening to David playing the harp, suddenly the tormenting spirit from the Lord attacked him. He had his spear in his hand and hurled it at David in an attempt to kill him. But David dodged out of the way and fled into the night, leaving the spear imbedded in the timber of the wall.11Saul sent troops to watch David's house and kill him when he came out in the morning.

"If you don't get away tonight," Michal warned him, "you'll be dead by morning."

12So she helped him get down to the ground through a window. 13Then she took an idol and put it in his bed, and covered it with blankets, with its head on a pillow of goat's hair. 14When the soldiers came to arrest David and take him to Saul, she told them he was sick and couldn't get out of bed. 15Saul said to bring him in his bed, then, so that he could kill him. 16But when they came to carry him out, they discovered that it was only an idol!

17"Why have you deceived me and let my enemy escape?" Saul demanded of Michal.

19:1-2 Since David was a threat to Saul's dynasty, Jonathan could conceivably have felt threatened by David. Yet Jonathan displayed no such smallness or insecurity. He instead made himself available to help his friend, not only warning David of Saul's intentions, but also assisting in his escape. True friends are never swayed by self-interest; they are willing to help, even if they must make personal sacrifices to do so. A good friend will be there to help in a crisis.

"I had to," Michal replied. "He threatened
to kill me if I didn't help him."
18In that way David got away and went to
Ramah to see Samuel, and told him all that
Saul had done to him. So Samuel took David
with him to live at Naioth. 19When the report
reached Saul that David was at Naioth in
Ramah, 20he sent soldiers to capture him; but
when they arrived and saw Samuel and the
other prophets prophesying, the Spirit of God
came upon them and they also began to
prophesy. 21When Saul heard what had happened, he sent other soldiers, but they too
prophesied! The same thing happened a third
time! 22Then Saul himself went to Ramah and
arrived at the great well in Secu.

"Where are Samuel and David?" he demanded.

Someone told him they were at Naioth.
23But on the way to Naioth the Spirit of God
came upon Saul, and he too began to prophesy! 24He tore off his clothes and lay naked all
day and all night, prophesying with Samuel's
prophets. Saul's men were incredulous!

"What!" they exclaimed. "Is Saul a prophet
too?"

CHAPTER 20

Jonathan Saves David's Life

David now fled from Naioth in Ramah and
found Jonathan.

"What have I done?" he exclaimed. "Why
is your father so determined to kill me?"

2"That's not true!" Jonathan protested. "I'm
sure he's not planning any such thing, for he
always tells me everything he's going to do,
even little things, and I know he wouldn't
hide something like this from me. It just isn't
so."

3"Of course you don't know about it!"
David fumed. "Your father knows perfectly
well about our friendship, so he has said to
himself, 'I'll not tell Jonathan—why should I
hurt him?' But the truth is that I am only a
step away from death! I swear it by the Lord
and by your own soul!"

4"Tell me what I can do," Jonathan begged.

5And David replied, "Tomorrow is the beginning of the celebration of the new moon.
Always before, I've been with your father for
this occasion, but tomorrow I'll hide in the
field and stay there until the evening of the
third day. 6If your father asks where I am, tell
him that I asked permission to go home to
Bethlehem for an annual family reunion. 7If
he says, 'Fine!' then I'll know that all is well.
But if he is angry, then I'll know that he is
planning to kill me. 8Do this for me as my
sworn brother. Or else kill me yourself if I
have sinned against your father, but don't
betray me to him!"

9"Of course not!" Jonathan exclaimed.
"Look, wouldn't I say so if I knew that my
father was planning to kill you?"

10Then David asked, "How will I know
whether or not your father is angry?"

11"Come out to the field with me," Jonathan replied. And they went out there together.

12Then Jonathan told David, "I promise by
the Lord God of Israel that about this time
tomorrow, or the next day at the latest, I will
talk to my father about you and let you know
at once how he feels about you. 13If he is angry
and wants you killed, then may the Lord kill
me if I don't tell you, so you can escape and
live. May the Lord be with you as he used to
be with my father. 14And remember, you must
demonstrate the love and kindness of the
Lord not only to me during my own lifetime,
15but also to my children after the Lord has
destroyed all of your enemies."

16So Jonathan made a covenant with the
family of David, and David swore to it with a
terrible curse against himself and his descendants, should he be unfaithful to his promise.
17But Jonathan made David swear to it again,
this time by his love for him, for he loved him
as much as he loved himself.

18Then Jonathan said, "Yes, they will miss
you tomorrow when your place at the table is
empty. 19By the day after tomorrow, everyone
will be asking about you, so be at the hideout
where you were before, over by the stone pile.

19:18 In dire straits, David fled to his mentor, Samuel. Where we go when we are in trouble often reveals the kind of people we are. Samuel was one of the great spiritual leaders of Israel's history. David's decision to go to Samuel for help reveals his wisdom and his desire to rely on God. In the recovery process it is important that we find people who will help us to stay on track and lead us to depend on God for help.

20:4 David was exceedingly blessed to have a friend like Jonathan. After hearing of David's difficulties, he responded, "Tell me what I can do." Reliable and resourceful, Jonathan was ready to be supportive in helping David through this crisis. His willing response should challenge all of us who have loved ones in the process of recovery. We should be available to help others as they seek victory over their dependencies.

[20]I will come out and shoot three arrows in front of the pile as though I were shooting at a target. [21]Then I'll send a lad to bring the arrows back. If you hear me tell him, 'They're on this side,' then you will know that all is well and that there is no trouble. [22]But if I tell him, 'Go farther—the arrows are still ahead of you,' then it will mean that you must leave immediately. [23]And may the Lord make us keep our promises to each other, for he has witnessed them."

[24,25]So David hid himself in the field.

When the new moon celebration began, the king sat down to eat at his usual place against the wall. Jonathan sat opposite him and Abner was sitting beside Saul, but David's place was empty. [26]Saul didn't say anything about it that day, for he supposed that something had happened so that David was ceremonially impure. Yes, surely that must be it! [27]But when his place was still empty the next day, Saul asked Jonathan, "Why hasn't David been here for dinner either yesterday or today?"

[28,29]"He asked me if he could go to Bethlehem to take part in a family celebration," Jonathan replied. "His brother demanded that he be there, so I told him to go ahead."

[30]Saul boiled with rage. "You fool!" he yelled at him. "Do you think I don't know that you want this son of a nobody to be king in your place, shaming yourself and your mother? [31]As long as that fellow is alive, you'll never be king. Now go and get him so I can kill him!"

[32]"But what has he done?" Jonathan demanded. "Why should he be put to death?"

[33]Then Saul hurled his spear at Jonathan, intending to kill him; so at last Jonathan realized that his father really meant it when he said David must die. [34]Jonathan left the table in fierce anger and refused to eat all that day, for he was crushed by his father's shameful behavior toward David.

[35]The next morning, as agreed, Jonathan went out into the field and took a young boy with him to gather his arrows.

[36]"Start running," he told the boy, "so that you can find the arrows as I shoot them." So the boy ran and Jonathan shot an arrow beyond him. [37]When the boy had almost reached the arrow, Jonathan shouted, "The arrow is still ahead of you. [38]Hurry, hurry, don't wait." So the boy quickly gathered up the arrows and ran back to his master. [39]He, of course, didn't understand what Jonathan meant; only Jonathan and David knew. [40]Then Jonathan gave his bow and arrows to the boy and told him to take them back to the city.

[41]As soon as he was gone, David came out from where he had been hiding near the south edge of the field. Both of them were crying as they said goodbye, especially David. [42]At last Jonathan said to David, "Cheer up, for we have entrusted each other and each other's children into God's hands forever." So they parted, David going away and Jonathan returning to the city.

CHAPTER 21

Saul Pursues David

David went to the city of Nob to see Ahimelech, the priest. Ahimelech trembled when he saw him.

"Why are you alone?" he asked. "Why is no one with you?"

[2]"The king has sent me on a private matter," David lied. "He told me not to tell anybody why I am here. I have told my men where to meet me later. [3]Now, what is there to eat? Give me five loaves of bread or anything else you can."

[4]"We don't have any regular bread," the priest replied, "but there is the holy bread, which I guess you can have if only your young men have not slept with any women for awhile."

[5]"Rest assured," David replied. "I never let my men run wild when they are on an expedition, and since they stay clean even on ordinary trips, how much more so on this one!"

[6]So, since there was no other food available, the priest gave him the holy bread—the Bread of the Presence that was placed before the Lord in the Tabernacle. It had just been replaced that day with fresh bread.

21:1-2 The book of Proverbs tells us: "There are six things the Lord hates—no, seven: haughtiness, lying, murdering, plotting evil, eagerness to do wrong, a false witness, sowing discord among brothers" (Proverbs 6:16-19). In his encounter with Ahimelech, David revealed that he was capable of making wrong choices. He lied, and his single lie led to others (21:9-15). In the end this seemingly small falsehood, even though told for a good cause, proved costly—eighty-five innocent priests lost their lives (22:18-20). God values honesty. Even minor indiscretions can have devastating effects on the lives of others, especially the people close to us (Ephesians 4:25).

7(Incidentally, Doeg the Edomite, Saul's
chief herdsman, was there at that time for
ceremonial purification.)
8David asked Ahimelech if he had a spear or
sword he could use. "The king's business required such haste, and I left in such a rush
that I came away without a weapon!" David
explained.
9"Well," the priest replied, "I have the
sword of Goliath, the Philistine—the fellow
you killed in the valley of Elah. It is wrapped
in a cloth in the clothes closet. Take that if
you want it, for there is nothing else here."
"Just the thing!" David replied. "Give it to
me!"
10Then David hurried on, for he was fearful
of Saul, and went to King Achish of Gath.
11But Achish's officers weren't happy about
his being there. "Isn't he the top leader of
Israel?" they asked.
"Isn't he the one the people honor at their
dances, singing, 'Saul has slain his thousands
and David his ten thousands'?"
12David heard these comments and was
afraid of what King Achish might do to him,
13so he pretended to be insane! He scratched
on doors and let his spittle flow down his
beard, 14,15until finally King Achish said to his
men, "Must you bring me a madman? We
already have enough of them around here!
Should such a fellow as this be my guest?"

CHAPTER 22

Saul Executes the Priests

So David left Gath and escaped to the cave of
Adullam, where his brothers and other relatives soon joined him. 2Then others began
coming—those who were in any kind of
trouble, such as being in debt, or merely dis-
contented—until David was the leader of
about four hundred men.
3(Later David went to Mizpeh in Moab to
ask permission of the king for his father and
mother to live there under royal protection
until David knew what God was going to do
for him. 4They stayed in Moab during the
entire period when David was living in the
cave.)
5One day the prophet Gad told David to
leave the cave and return to the land of Judah.
So David went to the forest of Hereth.6The
news of his arrival in Judah soon reached
Saul. He was in Gibeah at the time, sitting
beneath an oak tree playing with his spear,
surrounded by his officers.
7"Listen here, you men of Benjamin!" Saul
exclaimed when he heard the news. "Has
David promised you fields and vineyards and
commissions in his army? 8Is that why you are
against me? For not one of you has ever told
me that my own son is on David's side. You're
not even sorry for me. Think of it! My own
son—encouraging David to come and kill
me!"
9,10Then Doeg the Edomite, who was standing there with Saul's men, spoke up. "When I
was at Nob," he said, "I saw David talking to
Ahimelech the priest. Ahimelech consulted
the Lord to find out what David should do,
and then gave him food and the sword of
Goliath the Philistine."
11,12King Saul immediately summoned Ahimelech and all his family and all the other
priests at Nob. When they arrived Saul
shouted at him, "Listen to me, you son of
Ahitub!"
"What is it?" quavered Ahimelech.
13"Why have you and David conspired
against me?" Saul demanded. "Why did you
give him food and a sword and talk to God for
him? Why did you encourage him to revolt
against me and to come here and attack me?"
14"But sir," Ahimelech replied, "is there
anyone among all your servants who is as
faithful as David your son-in-law? Why, he is
the captain of your bodyguard and a highly
honored member of your own household!
15This was certainly not the first time I had
consulted God for him! It's unfair for you to
accuse me and my family in this matter, for
we knew nothing of any plot against you."
16"You shall die, Ahimelech, along with
your entire family!" the king shouted. 17He

22:1 David's family joined him in the cave of Adullam. Likewise, recovery is a family project, involving our loved ones and a network of supportive friends and fellow strugglers. Companionship should not be shunned in a crisis. God never wants us to go it alone.

22:16-18 The priests in this passage are the innocent victims of Saul's mental illness, David's lie (21:2), and Doeg's desire to be accepted. David's apparently inconsequential lie became the catalyst for the sins of others. It gave Saul the opportunity to act in an unbalanced way. It gave Doeg the chance to try to get some attention. Sometimes the small lies we tell can be compounded by the failures of others to bring great suffering to innocent people. In such times, telling the truth will often put a stop to the sins of other people rather than perpetuating or compounding them. Honesty is always the best policy.

ordered his bodyguards, "Kill these priests, for
they are allies and conspirators with David;
they knew he was running away from me, but
they didn't tell me!"
But the soldiers refused to harm the clergy.
18Then the king said to Doeg, "You do it."
So Doeg turned on them and killed them,
eighty-five priests in all, all wearing their
priestly robes. 19Then he went to Nob, the city
of the priests, and killed the priests' families—
men, women, children, and babies, and also
all the oxen, donkeys, and sheep. 20Only Abiathar, one of the sons of Ahimelech, escaped
and fled to David.
21When he told him what Saul had done,
22David exclaimed, "I knew it! When I saw
Doeg there, I knew he would tell Saul. Now I
have caused the death of all of your father's
family. 23Stay here with me, and I'll protect
you with my own life. Any harm to you will
be over my dead body."

CHAPTER 23

David Protects the Town of Keilah

One day news came to David that the Philistines were at Keilah robbing the threshing
floors.
2David asked the Lord, "Shall I go and attack them?"
"Yes, go and save Keilah," the Lord told
him.
3But David's men said, "We're afraid even
here in Judah; we certainly don't want to go
to Keilah to fight the whole Philistine army!"
4David asked the Lord again, and the Lord
again replied, "Go down to Keilah, for I will
help you conquer the Philistines."
5They went to Keilah and slaughtered the
Philistines and confiscated their cattle, and so
the people of Keilah were saved. 6(Abiathar
the priest went to Keilah with David, taking
his ephod with him to get answers for David
from the Lord.) 7Saul soon learned that David
was at Keilah.
"Good!" he exclaimed. "We've got him
now! God has delivered him to me, for he has
trapped himself in a walled city!"
8So Saul mobilized his entire army to march
to Keilah and besiege David and his men. 9But
David learned of Saul's plan and told Abiathar
the priest to bring the ephod and to ask the
Lord what he should do.
10"O Lord God of Israel," David said, "I
have heard that Saul is planning to come and
destroy Keilah because I am here. 11Will the
men of Keilah surrender me to him? And will
Saul actually come, as I have heard? O Lord
God of Israel, please tell me."
And the Lord said, "He will come."
12"And will these men of Keilah betray me
to Saul?" David persisted.
And the Lord replied, "Yes, they will betray
you."
13So David and his men—about six hundred of them now—left Keilah and began
roaming the countryside. Word soon reached
Saul that David had escaped, so he didn't go
there after all. 14,15David now lived in the wilderness caves in the hill country of Ziph. One
day near Horesh he received the news that
Saul was on the way to Ziph to search for him
and kill him. Saul hunted him day after day,
but the Lord didn't let him find him.
16(Prince Jonathan now went to find David;
he met him at Horesh and encouraged him in
his faith in God.

23:14-15 The wonderful little phrase "but the Lord didn't let [Saul] find [David]" must not be overlooked. Saul pursued David, but God protected, provided for, and preserved David's life. During the difficult years of running from Saul, David must have often felt alone and abandoned by God. But here we are told that God was working to protect David throughout that time. Even when things look bad for us, God is with us, protecting us in ways we do not know. He is indeed worthy of our confidence and trust.

23:16-18 Once Jonathan located David, he encouraged him to find his strength in God. Jonathan was aware of the fearsome difficulties that David faced, but he also knew that God was equal to the task. We often face problems too big for us alone, but God is bigger than the worst of them. At times we may wonder what we have to offer our struggling friends. We can always do what Jonathan did for David. We can remind them that God is with them and that he is greater than any problem they might face.

24:4-6 David refused to follow the counsel of his men to kill Saul. Even the small act of cutting off a piece of Saul's robe troubled the younger man's conscience. Despite all that had happened, David's respect for the king and for his position remained intact. Despite the temptation of the situation and Saul's obvious vulnerability, David wisely restrained himself. David's intelligent response suggests two principles vital to the recovery process: (1) We need to be careful to assess the advice we get from the people around us, even from our close friends. (2) Our conscience must be tuned in to what God desires for a situation, not what may be an easy way out.

READ 1 SAMUEL 24:1-22

GOD grant me the serenity to accept the things I cannot change the courage to change the things I can and the wisdom to know the difference AMEN

When we are working to make changes in our life and relationships, we may not always be certain of what to do. When we face confusing situations, we need to rely on God's wisdom to help us make our decisions.

King Saul's jealousy and abuse made young David's life miserable. Saul knew that God had chosen David to be king instead of him. Although David was a loyal subject, Saul tried to kill him. Once, when David was hiding in a cave, King Saul came in without knowing David was there. "'Now's your time!' David's men whispered to him. 'Today is the day the Lord was talking about when he said, "I will certainly put Saul into your power, to do with as you wish"!' Then David crept forward and quietly slit off the bottom of Saul's robe! But then his conscience began bothering him. 'I shouldn't have done it,' he said to his men. 'It is a serious sin to attack God's chosen king in any way.' These words of David persuaded his men not to kill Saul" (1 Samuel 24:4-8).

David knew what God expected of him in this situation, and he chose to go along with God's will. In trying to give our will to God, it is important to know what his will is in a given situation. When we aren't sure what to do, we can look to see if the Bible gives us any guidance on similar situations. Then we will have a clear view of what it means to turn our will over to God. *Turn to page 333, 1 Samuel 25.*

17"Don't be afraid," Jonathan reassured
him. "My father will never find you! You are
going to be the king of Israel and I will be next
to you, as my father is well aware." 18So the
two of them renewed their pact of friendship;
and David stayed at Horesh while Jonathan
returned home.)

19But now the men of Ziph went to Saul in
Gibeah and betrayed David to him.

"We know where he is hiding," they said.
"He is in the caves of Horesh on Hachilah Hill,
down in the southern part of the wilderness.
20Come on down, sir, and we will catch him
for you and your fondest wish will be fulfilled!"

21"Well, praise the Lord!" Saul said. "At last
someone has had pity on me! 22Go and check
again to be sure of where he is staying and
who has seen him there, for I know that he is
very crafty. 23Discover his hiding places and
then come back and give me a more definite
report. Then I'll go with you. And if he is in
the area at all, I'll find him if I have to search
every inch of the entire land!"

24,25So the men of Ziph returned home. But
when David heard that Saul was on his way to
Ziph, he and his men went even further into
the wilderness of Maon in the south of the
desert. But Saul followed them there. 26He and
David were now on opposite sides of a mountain. As Saul and his men began to close in,
David tried his best to escape, but it was no
use. 27But just then a message reached Saul
that the Philistines were raiding Israel again,
28so Saul quit the chase and returned to fight
the Philistines. Ever since that time the place
where David was camped has been called,
"The Rock of Escape!" 29David then went to
live in the caves of Engedi.

CHAPTER 24

David Spares Saul's Life

After Saul's return from his battle with the
Philistines, he was told that David had gone

into the wilderness of Engedi; 2so he took three thousand special troops and went to search for him among the rocks and wild goats of the desert. 3At the place where the road passes some sheepfolds, Saul went into a cave to go to the bathroom, but as it happened, David and his men were hiding in the cave!

4"Now's your time!" David's men whispered to him. "Today is the day the Lord was talking about when he said, 'I will certainly put Saul into your power, to do with as you wish'!" Then David crept forward and quietly slit off the bottom of Saul's robe! 5But then his conscience began bothering him.

6"I shouldn't have done it," he said to his men. "It is a serious sin to attack God's chosen king in any way."

7,8These words of David persuaded his men not to kill Saul.

After Saul had left the cave and gone on his way, David came out and shouted after him, "My lord the king!" And when Saul looked around, David bowed low before him.

9,10Then he shouted to Saul, "Why do you listen to the people who say I am trying to harm you? This very day you have seen it isn't true. For the Lord placed you at my mercy back there in the cave, and some of my men told me to kill you, but I spared you. For I said, 'I will never harm him—he is the Lord's chosen king.' 11See what I have in my hand? It is the hem of your robe! I cut it off, but I didn't kill you! Doesn't this convince you that I am not trying to harm you and that I have not sinned against you, even though you have been hunting for my life?

12"The Lord will decide between us. Perhaps he will kill you for what you are trying to do to me, but I will never harm you. 13As that old proverb says, 'Wicked is as wicked does,' but despite your wickedness, I'll not touch you. 14And who is the king of Israel trying to catch, anyway? Should he spend his time chasing one who is as worthless as a dead dog or a flea? 15May the Lord judge as to which of us is right and punish whichever one of us is guilty. He is my lawyer and defender, and he will rescue me from your power!"

16Saul called back, "Is it really you, my son David?" Then he began to cry. 17And he said to David, "You are a better man than I am, for you have repaid me good for evil. 18Yes, you have been wonderfully kind to me today, for when the Lord delivered me into your hand, you didn't kill me. 19Who else in all the world would let his enemy get away when he had him in his power? May the Lord reward you well for the kindness you have shown me today. 20And now I realize that you are surely going to be king, and Israel shall be yours to rule. 21Oh, swear to me by the Lord that when that happens you will not kill my family and destroy my line of descendants!"

22So David promised, and Saul went home, but David and his men went back to their cave.

CHAPTER 25

Nabal Angers David

Shortly afterwards Samuel died, and all Israel gathered for his funeral and buried him in his family plot at Ramah.

Meanwhile David went down to the wilderness of Paran. 2A wealthy man from Maon owned a sheep ranch there, near the village of Carmel. He had three thousand sheep and a thousand goats, and was at his ranch at this time for the sheep shearing. 3His name was Nabal and his wife, a beautiful and very intelligent woman, was named Abigail. But the man, who was a descendant of Caleb, was uncouth, churlish, stubborn, and ill-mannered.

4When David heard that Nabal was shearing his sheep, 5he sent ten of his young men to Carmel to give him this message: 6"May God prosper you and your family and multiply everything you own. 7I am told that you are shearing your sheep and goats. While your shepherds have lived among us, we have never harmed them, nor stolen anything

---

25:36-38 The name *Nabal* means "fool," and in this passage Nabal demonstrated how appropriate his name was. His self-centered outlook kept him from fulfilling an act of common courtesy that was expected in ancient Israel. David and his band had protected Nabal and his herds from foreign marauders. It was expected that he would support them with some supplies. But Nabal lived for himself, satisfying his appetites, with little regard for others. His selfish bravado nearly resulted in the deaths of many innocent employees. It was only the intervention of his wife, Abigail, that prevented a disaster. Most of us have a little Nabal in us; we are a little foolish at times. Our dependencies drive us to make decisions that are destructive to us and to the people around us. An important part of recovery is taking inventory of the foolishness in our life. Nabal's end should encourage us to do so.

READ 1 SAMUEL 25:18-39

GOD grant me the serenity
to accept the things I cannot change
the courage to change the things I can
and the wisdom to know the difference
AMEN

When other people put us at risk or cause us pain, we may feel like there's nothing we can do.

We may be used to the role of victim. But there are ways to maintain our dignity and sanity even in the most oppressive circumstances.

Abigail is a good example of someone who didn't give in to helplessness but had the wisdom to know what she could and couldn't change. Her husband, Nabal (meaning "fool"), was "uncouth, churlish, stubborn, and ill-mannered" (1 Samuel 25:3). Before David became king, Nabal insulted his troops to the point that David and his men were on their way to kill him and anyone who got in their way. Through some fast thinking and some even faster talking, Abigail protected her family. She convinced David not to take vengeance into his own hands. A few weeks later Nabal was dead of natural, or perhaps supernatural, causes, and Abigail became David's wife.

We cannot always change other people. It takes wisdom and courage to accept this truth. But even when we can't change them, we can still change the situation to protect ourself from the effects of their behavior. Acceptance of another's addiction or personality does not mean that we have to accept being the victim of that person's wrongs. We can give up our crusade to change the other person without giving up our right to be treated with dignity. ***Turn to page 361, 2 Samuel 15.***

---

from them the whole time they have been in
Carmel. 8Ask your young men and they will
tell you whether or not this is true. Now I
have sent my men to ask for a little contribution from you, for we have come at a happy
time of holiday. Please give us a present of
whatever is at hand."
9The young men gave David's message to
Nabal and waited for his reply.
10"Who is this fellow David?" he sneered.
"Who does this son of Jesse think he is? There
are lots of servants these days who run away
from their masters. 11Should I take my bread
and my water and my meat that I've slaughtered for my shearers and give it to a gang
who comes from God knows where?"
12So David's messengers returned and told
him what Nabal had said.
13"Get your swords!" was David's reply as he
strapped on his own. Four hundred of them
started off with David and two hundred remained behind to guard their gear.
14Meanwhile, one of Nabal's men went and
told Abigail, "David sent men from the wilderness to talk to our master, but he insulted
them and railed at them. 15,16But David's men
were very good to us and we never suffered
any harm from them; in fact, day and night
they were like a wall of protection to us and
the sheep, and nothing was stolen from us the
whole time they were with us. 17You'd better
think fast, for there is going to be trouble for
our master and his whole family—he's such a
stubborn lout that no one can even talk to
him!"
18Then Abigail hurriedly took two hundred
loaves of bread, two barrels of wine, five
dressed sheep, two bushels of roasted grain,
one hundred raisin cakes, and two hundred
fig cakes, and packed them onto donkeys.
19"Go on ahead," she said to her young
men, "and I will follow." But she didn't tell
her husband what she was doing. 20As she was

riding down the trail on her donkey, she met
David coming toward her.
21David had been saying to himself, "A lot
of good it did us to help this fellow. We
protected his flocks in the wilderness so that
not one thing was lost or stolen, but he has
repaid me bad for good. All that I get for my
trouble is insults. 22May God curse me if even
one of his men remains alive by tomorrow
morning!"

Abigail Intercedes for Nabal

23When Abigail saw David, she quickly dismounted and bowed low before him.
24"I accept all blame in this matter, my
lord," she said. "Please listen to what I want
to say. 25Nabal is a bad-tempered boor, but
please don't pay any attention to what he
said. He is a fool—just like his name means.
But I didn't see the messengers you sent. 26Sir,
since the Lord has kept you from murdering
and taking vengeance into your own hands, I
pray by the life of God, and by your own life
too, that all your enemies shall be as cursed as
Nabal is. 27And now, here is a present I have
brought to you and your young men. 28For-
give me for my boldness in coming out here.
The Lord will surely reward you with eternal
royalty for your descendants, for you are
fighting his battles; and you will never do
wrong throughout your entire life. 29Even
when you are chased by those who seek your
life, you are safe in the care of the Lord your
God, just as though you were safe inside his
purse! But the lives of your enemies shall
disappear like stones from a sling! 30,31When
the Lord has done all the good things he
promised you and has made you king of Israel, you won't want the conscience of a murderer who took the law into his own hands!
And when the Lord has done these great
things for you, please remember me!"
32David replied to Abigail, "Bless the Lord
God of Israel who has sent you to meet me
today! 33Thank God for your good sense! Bless
you for keeping me from murdering the man
and carrying out vengeance with my own
hands. 34For I swear by the Lord, the God of
Israel who has kept me from hurting you, that
if you had not come out to meet me, not one
of Nabal's men would be alive tomorrow
morning."
35Then David accepted her gifts and told
her to return home without fear, for he would
not kill her husband. 36When she arrived
home she found that Nabal had thrown a big
party. He was roaring drunk, so she didn't tell
him anything about her meeting with David
until the next morning. 37,38By that time he
was sober, and when his wife told him what
had happened, he had a stroke and lay paralyzed for about ten days, then died, for the
Lord killed him.
39When David heard that Nabal was dead,
he said, "Praise the Lord! God has paid back
Nabal and kept me from doing it myself; he
has received his punishment for his sin."
Then David wasted no time in sending
messengers to Abigail to ask her to become his
wife. 40When the messengers arrived at Carmel and told her why they had come, 41she
readily agreed to his request. 42Quickly getting
ready, she took along five of her serving girls
as attendants, mounted her donkey, and followed the men back to David. So she became
his wife.
43David also married Ahinoam from Jezreel.
44King Saul, meanwhile, had forced David's
wife Michal, Saul's daughter, to marry a man
from Gallim named Palti (the son of Laish).

CHAPTER 26

David Again Spares Saul's Life

Now the men from Ziph came back to Saul at
Gibeah to tell him that David had returned to
the wilderness and was hiding on Hachilah
Hill. 2So Saul took his elite corps of three
thousand troops and went to hunt him down.
3,4Saul camped along the road at the edge of
the wilderness where David was hiding, but
David knew of Saul's arrival and sent out spies
to watch his movements.
5-7David slipped over to Saul's camp one
night to look around. King Saul and General

26:8-11 The advice of even loyal friends can sometimes get us into trouble. Abishai recommended the murder of Saul, but David was unwilling to accept the consequences of assassinating God's chosen king (26:9-11). He wisely placed boundaries on the behavior of his men and left Saul alone. David knew that Saul's judgment belonged in God's hands, and he wisely left it there. As we seek reconciliation with people, we may need to give our judgment of others back to God. This is an important step in the process of forgiveness and reconciliation.

26:17-21 Too little, too late. We hear from Saul's lips words that should have been uttered long before: (1) "I have done wrong"; (2) "I have been a fool"; (3) "I have been . . . very, very wrong." Such honest admissions reflect the concerns of a personal inventory, the basis for repentance, forgiveness, and reconciliation. This is an important part of our recovery process.

Abner were sleeping inside a ring formed by
the slumbering soldiers.
"Any volunteers to go down there with
me?" David asked Ahimelech (the Hittite) and
Abishai (Joab's brother and the son of Zeruiah).
"I'll go with you," Abishai replied. So David
and Abishai went to Saul's camp and found
him asleep, with his spear in the ground beside his head.
8"God has put your enemy within your
power this time for sure," Abishai whispered
to David. "Let me go and put that spear
through him. I'll pin him to the earth with
it—I'll not need to strike a second time!"
9"No," David said. "Don't kill him, for who
can remain innocent after attacking the
Lord's chosen king? 10Surely God will strike
him down some day, or he will die in battle or
of old age. 11But God forbid that I should kill
the man he has chosen to be king! But I'll tell
you what—we'll take his spear and his jug of
water and then get out of here!"
12So David took the spear and jug of water,
and they got away without anyone seeing
them or even waking up, because the Lord
had put them sound asleep. 13They climbed
the mountain slope opposite the camp until
they were at a safe distance.
14Then David shouted down to Abner and
Saul, "Wake up, Abner!"
"Who is it?" Abner demanded.
15"Well, Abner, you're a great fellow, aren't
you?" David taunted. "Where in all Israel is
there anyone as wonderf ul? So why haven't
you guarded your master the king when
someone came to kill him? 16This isn't good at
all! I swear by the Lord that you ought to die
for your carelessness. Where is the king's
spear and the jug of water that was beside his
head? Look and see!"
17,18Saul recognized David's voice and said,
"Is that you, my son David?"
And David replied, "Yes, sir, it is. Why are
you chasing me? What have I done? What is
my crime? 19If the Lord has stirred you up
against me, then let him accept my peace
offering. But if this is simply the scheme of a
man, then may he be cursed by God. For you
have driven me out of my home so that I can't
be with the Lord's people, and you have sent
me away to worship heathen gods. 20Must I
die on foreign soil, far from the presence of
Jehovah? Why should the king of Israel come
out to hunt my life like a partridge on the
mountains?"
21Then Saul confessed, "I have done wrong.
Come back home, my son, and I'll no longer
try to harm you; for you saved my life today.
I have been a fool, and very, very wrong."
22"Here is your spear, sir," David replied.
"Let one of your young men come over and
get it. 23The Lord gives his own reward for
doing good and for being loyal, and I refused
to kill you even when the Lord placed you in
my power. 24Now may the Lord save my life,
even as I have saved yours today. May he
rescue me from all my troubles."
25And Saul said to David, "Blessings on you,
my son David. You shall do heroic deeds and
be a great conqueror."
Then David went away and Saul returned
home.

CHAPTER 27

David Lives among the Philistines

But David kept thinking to himself, "Some
day Saul is going to get me. I'll try my luck
among the Philistines until Saul gives up and
quits hunting for me; then I will finally be safe
again."
2,3So David took his six hundred men and
their families to live at Gath under the protection of King Achish. He had his two wives
with him—Ahinoam of Jezreel and Abigail of
Carmel, Nabal's widow. 4Word soon reached
Saul that David had fled to Gath, so he quit
hunting for him.
5One day David said to Achish, "My lord, if
it is all right with you, we would rather live in
one of the country towns instead of here in
the royal city."
6So Achish gave him Ziklag (which still
belongs to the kings of Judah to this day),
7and they lived there among the Philistines
for a year and four months. 8He and his men

27:1 David's fearful thoughts were not consistent with God's promises. He knew that God had a special plan for his life, which included kingship over Israel. After years of running for his life, however, David seems to have become discouraged. Motivated by fear, he moved to the land of the Philistines where he ended up in some compromising situations (28:1-2; 29:1-7). David needed to persevere in his trust. God had protected him up until that point and was perfectly capable of continuing that protection. Recovery is never a short-term process, but after years of struggling it is sometimes tempting to step away from God's program. But if we desire God's help and success, we must persevere.

spent their time raiding the Geshurites, the Girzites, and the Amalekites—people who had lived near Shur along the road to Egypt ever since ancient times. [9]They didn't leave one person alive in the villages they hit and took for themselves the sheep, oxen, donkeys, camels, and clothing before returning to their homes.

[10]"Where did you make your raid today?" Achish would ask.

And David would reply, "Against the south of Judah and the people of Jerahmeel and the Kenites."

[11]No one was left alive to come to Gath and tell where he had really been. This happened again and again while he was living among the Philistines. [12]Achish believed David and thought that the people of Israel must hate him bitterly by now. "Now he will have to stay here and serve me forever!" the king thought.

CHAPTER 28

Saul Consults a Witch

About that time the Philistines mustered their armies for another war with Israel.

"Come and help us fight," King Achish said to David and his men.

[2]"Good," David agreed. "You will soon see what a help we can be to you."

"If you are, you shall be my personal bodyguard for life," Achish told him.

[3](Meanwhile, Samuel had died and all Israel had mourned for him. He was buried in Ramah, his hometown. King Saul had banned all mediums and wizards from the land of Israel.)

[4]The Philistines set up their camp at Shunem, and Saul and the armies of Israel were at Gilboa. [5,6]When Saul saw the vast army of the Philistines, he was frantic with fear and asked the Lord what he should do. But the Lord refused to answer him, either by dreams, or by Urim, or by the prophets.[7,8]Saul then instructed his aides to try to find a medium so that he could ask her what to do, and they found one at Endor. Saul disguised himself by wearing ordinary clothing instead of his royal robes. He went to the woman's home at night, accompanied by two of his men.

"I've got to talk to a dead man," he pleaded. "Will you bring his spirit up?"

[9]"Are you trying to get me killed?" the woman demanded. "You know that Saul has had all of the mediums and fortune-tellers executed. You are spying on me."

[10]But Saul took a solemn oath that he wouldn't betray her.

[11]Finally the woman said, "Well, whom do you want me to bring up?"

"Bring me Samuel," Saul replied.

[12]When the woman saw Samuel, she screamed, "You've deceived me! You are Saul!"

[13]"Don't be frightened!" the king told her. "What do you see?"

"I see a specter coming up out of the earth," she said.

[14]"What does he look like?"

"He is an old man wrapped in a robe."

Saul realized that it was Samuel and bowed low before him.

[15]"Why have you disturbed me by bringing me back?" Samuel asked Saul.

"Because I am in deep trouble," he replied. "The Philistines are at war with us, and God has left me and won't reply by prophets or dreams; so I have called for you to ask you what to do."

[16]But Samuel replied, "Why ask me if the Lord has left you and has become your enemy? [17]He has done just as he said he would and has taken the kingdom from you and given it to your rival, David. [18]All this has come upon you because you did not obey the Lord's instructions when he was so angry with Amalek. [19]What's more, the entire Israeli army will be routed and destroyed by the Philistines tomorrow, and you and your sons will be here with me."

[20]Saul now fell full length upon the ground, paralyzed with fright because of Samuel's words. He was also faint with hunger, for he had eaten nothing all day. [21]When the woman

28:1-2 Compromising our convictions often leaves us with hard choices. David had left Israel to hide among the Philistines and was now reaping the consequences. He was asked to join the Philistines in a battle against his own people. David had to deal with a difficult decision that God probably never intended him to face. When we make decisions without God and his Word in mind, we may end up in situations that could lead to our downfall. We need to keep God at the center of our decisions and carefully consider the likely consequences of our actions.

28:7-8 Saul's final act of rebellion involved witchcraft, which the Bible unequivocally condemns. In his desperation, Saul sought the guidance of spirits of the dead. Instead of finding help there, however, his destruction was only confirmed. The world of Satan worship and occult practices will never yield true recovery and must be avoided at all cost.

saw how distraught he was, she said, "Sir, I
obeyed your command at the risk of my life.
22Now do what I say, and let me give you
something to eat so you'll regain your
strength for the trip back."
23But he refused. The men who were with
him added their pleas to that of the woman
until he finally yielded and got up and sat on
the bed. 24The woman had been fattening a
calf, so she hurried out and killed it and
kneaded dough and baked unleavened bread.
25She brought the meal to the king and his
men, and they ate it. Then they went out into
the night.

CHAPTER 29
David Leaves the Philistines
The Philistine army now mobilized at Aphek,
and the Israelis camped at the springs in Jezreel. 2As the Philistine captains were leading
out their troops by battalions and companies,
David and his men marched at the rear with
King Achish.
3But the Philistine commanders demanded,
"What are these Israelis doing here?"
And King Achish told them, "This is David,
the runaway servant of King Saul of Israel.
He's been with me for years, and I've never
found one fault in him since he arrived."
4But the Philistine leaders were angry.
"Send them back!" they demanded. "They
aren't going into the battle with us—they'll
turn against us. Is there any better way for
him to reconcile himself with his master than
by turning against us in the battle? 5This is the
same man the women of Israel sang about in
their dances: 'Saul has slain his thousands and
David his ten thousands!'"
6So Achish finally summoned David and
his men.
"I swear by the Lord," he told them, "you
are some of the finest men I've ever met, and
I think you should go with us, but my commanders say no. 7Please don't upset them, but
go back quietly."
8"What have I done to deserve this treatment?" David demanded. "Why can't I fight
your enemies?"
9But Achish insisted, "As far as I'm concerned, you're as perfect as an angel of God.
But my commanders are afraid to have you
with them in the battle. 10Now get up early in
the morning and leave as soon as it is light."
11So David headed back into the land of the
Philistines while the Philistine army went on
to Jezreel.

CHAPTER 30
David Destroys the Amalekites
Three days later, when David and his men
arrived home at their city of Ziklag, they
found that the Amalekites had raided the city
and burned it to the ground, 2carrying off all
the women and children. 3As David and his
men looked at the ruins and realized what
had happened to their families, 4they wept
until they could weep no more. 5(David's two
wives, Ahinoam and Abigail, were among
those who had been captured.) 6David was
seriously worried, for in their bitter grief for
their children, his men began talking of killing him. But David took strength from the
Lord.
7Then he said to Abiathar the priest, "Bring
me the oracle!" So Abiathar brought it.
8David asked the Lord, "Shall I chase them?
Will I catch them?"
And the Lord told him, "Yes, go after them;
you will recover everything that was taken
from you!"
9,10So David and his six hundred men set
out after the Amalekites. When they reached
Besor Brook, two hundred of the men were
too exhausted to cross, but the other four
hundred kept going. 11,12Along the way they
found an Egyptian youth in a field and
brought him to David. He had not had anything to eat or drink for three days and nights,
so they gave him part of a fig cake, two clusters of raisins, and some water, and his
strength soon returned.
13"Who are you and where do you come
from?" David asked him.

29:1-10 David's move to Philistia was a compromising one. His safety there depended on his relationship with King Achish, who asked David to fight against the Israelites. Here Achish released David from his service. God delivered David from the consequences of his earlier decision. God's love is great! He often provides us with a way to escape difficult circumstances, even ones of our own making (see 1 Corinthians 10:13). But remember this: When God provides the way for us to escape a compromising situation, it is still our responsibility to take it.

30:1-6 During their time away from Ziklag, marauders had come and stolen the belongings and kidnapped the families of David and his men. In this crisis David shows us where to go for direction and hope: "David took strength from the Lord" (30:6). David knew where to go in a crisis. Entrusting our life to God, no matter how dire our circumstances, is an important step in our recovery.

"I am an Egyptian—the servant of an Amalekite," he replied. "My master left me behind three days ago because I was sick. [14]We were on our way back from raiding the Cherethites in the Negeb, and had raided the south of Judah and the land of Caleb, and had burned Ziklag."

[15]"Can you tell me where they went?" David asked.

The young man replied, "If you swear by God's name that you will not kill me or give me back to my master, then I will guide you to them."

[16]So he led them to the Amalekite encampment. They were spread out across the fields, eating and drinking and dancing with joy because of the vast amount of loot they had taken from the Philistines and from the men of Judah. [17]David and his men rushed in among them and slaughtered them all that night and the entire next day until evening. No one escaped except four hundred young men who fled on camels. [18,19]David got back everything they had taken. The men recovered their families and all of their belongings, and David rescued his two wives. [20]His troops rounded up all the flocks and herds and drove them on ahead of them. "These are all yours personally, as your reward!" they told David.

[21]When they reached Besor Brook and the two hundred men who had been too exhausted to go on, David greeted them joyfully. [22]But some of the ruffians among David's men declared, "They didn't go with us, so they can't have any of the loot. Give them their wives and their children and tell them to be gone."

[23]But David said, "No, my brothers! The Lord has kept us safe and helped us defeat the enemy. [24]Do you think that anyone will listen to you when you talk like this? We share and share alike—those who go to battle and those who guard the equipment."

[25]From then on David made this a law for all of Israel, and it is still followed.

[26]When he arrived at Ziklag, he sent part of the loot to the elders of Judah. "Here is a present for you, taken from the Lord's enemies," he wrote them. [27-31]The gifts were sent to the elders in the following cities where David and his men had been: Bethel, South Ramoth, Jattir, Aroer, Siphmoth, Eshtemoa, Racal, the cities of the Jerahmeelites, the cities of the Kenites, Hormah, Borashan, Athach, Hebron.

CHAPTER 31

Saul Dies in Battle

Meanwhile the Philistines had begun the battle against Israel, and the Israelis fled from them and were slaughtered wholesale on Mount Gilboa. [2]The Philistines closed in on Saul and killed his sons Jonathan, Abinidab, and Malchishua.

[3,4]Then the archers overtook Saul and wounded him badly. He groaned to his armor-bearer, "Kill me with your sword before these heathen Philistines capture me and torture me." But his armor-bearer was afraid to, so Saul took his own sword and fell upon the point of the blade, and it pierced him through. [5]When his armor-bearer saw that he was dead, he also fell upon his sword and died with him. [6]So Saul, his armor-bearer, his three sons, and his troops died together that same day.

[7]When the Israelis on the other side of the valley and beyond the Jordan heard that their comrades had fled and that Saul and his sons were dead, they abandoned their cities; and the Philistines lived in them.

[8]The next day when the Philistines went out to strip the dead, they found the bodies of Saul and his three sons on Mount Gilboa. [9]They cut off Saul's head and stripped off his armor and sent the wonderful news of Saul's death to their idols and to the people throughout their land.

[10]His armor was placed in the temple of Ashtaroth, and his body was fastened to the wall of Beth-shan.

[11]But when the people of Jabesh-gilead heard what the Philistines had done, [12]warriors from that town traveled all night to Beth-shan and took down the bodies of Saul and his sons from the wall and brought them to Jabesh, where they cremated them. [13]Then they buried their remains beneath the oak tree at Jabesh and fasted for seven days.

31:3-4 Suicide was the tragic end of a man who never learned to repent. Recovery would have been possible for Saul if he had admitted his helplessness, committed his life to God, and allowed God to change him. He never allowed anyone to assist him in matters of accountability and spiritual growth. He never learned to depend upon God. He never felt the courage or experienced an authentic desire to change. As a result, his life stands as a monument to squandered potential. Saul's tragic end should give us ample reason to embrace God's program for recovery.

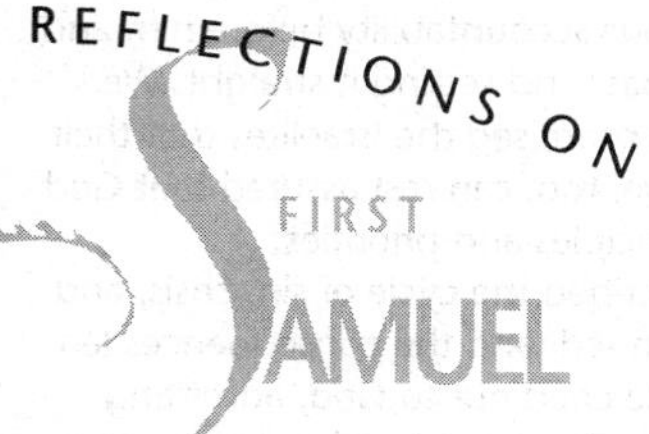
REFLECTIONS ON
FIRST
SAMUEL

insights FROM HANNAH'S LIFE

In ancient times, much of a woman's self-worth was built upon her ability to bear children. So, as is clear from **1 Samuel 1:1-8,** Hannah's childless state brought her a great deal of pain. And to make matters worse, Elkanah's second wife, Peninnah, ridiculed Hannah for her infertility. Certainly Hannah had tried everything humanly possible to become pregnant. She was at the end of her rope, helpless to change her situation. She was unable to see that a fulfilling life could be found without children. Her husband Elkanah tried to intervene, reminding Hannah of his unconditional love for her (1:8), but Hannah was unable to accept his comfort. Hannah had come to the point of acknowledging her helplessness, the first step toward her recovery.

Samuel's birth, mentioned in **1 Samuel 1:19-20,** shows us that God is a listening God. He solved Hannah's crisis by giving her a little son. The baby's name, Samuel, means "asked of God." This would have been a constant reminder that God heard Hannah's cries and then answered. We can be confident that when we petition God according to his will (1 John 5:14), he hears us, too. And no problem is ever too big for him to solve (Jeremiah 32:27).

In **1 Samuel 1:24-28** the time came for Hannah to fulfill her vow to God. The process of letting go of her little son certainly must have been painful. But Hannah recognized her accountability to God and unselfishly fulfilled her promise by releasing her much-loved son into his service. Her choice reflected her gratitude and her confidence in God, who had given Samuel to her in the first place. When we make commitments to God and others, we need to follow through on them. If we do, no matter how hard it may be, God will help us and bless our efforts. After Hannah gave up Samuel to God's service, God blessed her with additional children.

Hannah continued her prayer of praise in **1 Samuel 2:4-10,** thanking God for blessing her. She said, "Those who were weak are now strong" (2:4). God not only provided the deliverance, but also the strength for recovery. He gave Hannah the strength to persevere in the process, to seek freedom, to adopt new attitudes, to fulfill responsibilities, to set things straight, to build a new life. Such honest praise of God's power will naturally burst forth as we admit our helplessness and commit our life to God. As we surrender ourself, the Father is freed to do his good work in us.

In **1 Samuel 2:20-21** we see that Hannah was blessed with additional children. God is in the business of blessing his people beyond their requests and expectations (Ephesians 3:20).

insights FROM ELI'S LIFE

In **1 Samuel 2:23-34,** Eli exercised "tough love" as he confronted his sons about their blatant sin. He surely hoped they would make significant changes in their lives. Unfortunately, they didn't listen to their father. The young men refused to set boundaries on their behavior, and they displayed no desire to change. Their choice to go their own way brought dire consequences—ultimately, physical death (2:25, 34; see also 1 Corinthians 11:30-32). Eli, too, made a choice: he opted to ignore his sons' continued disobedience. Thus the High Priest failed in his responsibility to God and was eventually judged for it. Eli was told that his descendants would bring him tears of grief and would die in the prime of life. What a bitter harvest we reap when we refuse to turn from temptation and embrace God's power for change.

insights FROM SAMUEL'S LIFE

Samuel's exhortation to the Israelites in **1 Samuel 7:3-4** gives us a clear picture of what is involved in the recovery process. He tells them (1) to get rid of their foreign gods and idols, (2) to determine to obey God, and (3) to worship him only. Our recovery calls us to do the same. First we must get rid of all the idols in our life—anything that drives or controls us. This involves a deep self-examination, an honest assessment of motives and priorities, and a realization of our own helplessness and disobedience. Then we must commit ourself to God, recognizing our accountability before him and before the people close to us. This will necessitate reconciling the past and setting it straight. We must come clean, letting God wash away our filth and lies. Samuel promised the Israelites that their obedience would result in God's deliverance from the Philistines. We, too, can rest assured that God will facilitate our fresh start in life as we respond properly to his principles and priorities.

In **1 Samuel 12:8-11,** Samuel reviewed Israel's history and described the cycle of sin, crisis, and deliverance that was evident in the book of Judges. The Israelites sinned, and the consequences led them to enslavement. Helpless to shake their oppressors, the people cried out to God, admitting their sins of disobedience. By recognizing their helplessness, the Israelites were freed to turn to the only one who could help them, God himself. Then God provided a delivering judge to lead the people out of bondage. The crisis stage described by Samuel is similar to our experience of "hitting bottom." There we recognize our helplessness, and with God's help begin the process of recovery.

In **1 Samuel 12:23-25,** Samuel identified his failure to pray for the people as a sin against God. This shows the depth of his sense of accountability to God and his feelings of responsibility for the people. His spiritual maturity manifested itself in his desire to help others; he said, "I will continue to teach you those things which are good and right" (12:23). Indeed, Samuel went on to outline the people's program for recovery that they might gain freedom: (1) "trust the Lord," (2) "sincerely worship him," and (3) "think of all the tremendous things he has done for you" (12:24). Samuel concluded by warning the people of the dire consequences of refusing to obey God (12:25). We would all do well to heed Samuel's words.

insights FROM SAUL'S LIFE

Saul spoke in **1 Samuel 14:24-25,** saying, "before I have full revenge on my enemies." His comment here gives us a clue that Saul was on a downhill slide spiritually. Earlier he had declared, "Today the Lord has rescued Israel!" (11:13). But here he has changed his tune; no longer did he see God as the vital entity in the process of victory. The battle had become Saul's; the enemies were no longer God's enemies, but Saul's opponents. Thus the victory would belong to Saul and not to God. When we begin to take credit for our progress in recovery, we have already begun to regress toward failure. We must always remember that the enemies we face are too big for us unless we seek victory with the help of God.

In **1 Samuel 15:10-15,** God was grieved because Saul had followed his own inclinations rather than God's clear instructions. God's principles for healthy living call us to obey his instructions, to make a clean break with the past, and to refuse to compromise. Saul exhibited none of these qualities. He chose to spare King Agag and the finest animals instead of destroying everything as God had commanded (15:8-9). He even built a monument to himself rather than paying tribute to God for the miraculous victory (15:12). When confronted by Samuel, Saul tried to justify his actions (15:15), but making excuses has never paved the way to a new life. We must accept responsibility for our actions if we desire to grow. Until we do, there is no hope for recovery.

In **1 Samuel 15:32-33** we see that Saul was not willing to obey God completely; he spared King Agag against God's express orders. The execution of Agag by Samuel reminds us that a successful recovery demands a distinct break with the past and complete obedience to God's program. The past must be put to death if we hope to progress in our recovery.

insights FROM DAVID'S LIFE

Notice in **1 Samuel 17:32-37** that David's courage was, in part, a consequence of God's help in previous battles with lions and bears. David had learned how to trust God in his smaller battles, giving him the faith he needed to confront Goliath. It is easy to overlook our smaller victories and forget about the help God gave us during such times. We would be wise to take account of our victories, no matter how small, and allow them to build our courage and faith for the battles still ahead.

In **1 Samuel 23:1-9,** David repeatedly looked to God for direction in his life. He had grown accustomed to trusting God for direction during times of crisis. When God commanded David to lead his men against the Philistines at Keilah, David's men were afraid to act on that command. So David went to God a second time and when he did, God affirmed his first command but also added a reassuring message: "I will help you conquer the Philistines" (23:4). Like David and his men, we may respond with fear to God's direction in our life. But we can be sure that when God tells us to do something, he will stand by us each step of the way and help us gain the victory.

In **1 Samuel 23:24-28,** it appeared that Saul would finally capture David. But God intervened and Saul was forced to return home to defend against Philistine raids. After having an experience like this, it is no surprise that David wrote these words: "Jehovah himself is caring for you! He is your defender. He protects you day and night. He keeps you from all evil and preserves your life. He keeps his eye upon you as you come and go, and always guards you" (Psalm 121:5-8). God is in the business of protecting his own.

Though at times David appears a model of self-restraint, we see in **1 Samuel 25:12-13** that he was capable of giving in to impatience. In reacting to Nabal's poor manners, David failed to consult with God before taking action. He made a hasty decision while he was angry and upset. Such impulsiveness frequently results in mistakes with long-term consequences. Thankfully, God provided Abigail to prevent David from acting unwisely (25:32). When we are angry and tempted to act impulsively, we would be wise to calm down and listen to what God might have to say to us.

SECOND SAMUEL

THE BIG PICTURE

The book of 2 Samuel tells the story of King David, one of the most notable people in the Bible. In the opening verses, David received word that both Jonathan and Saul had been killed in battle. The Israelite army had fled in defeat, and thousands of the soldiers were dead or wounded on the battlefield. Samuel the prophet, David's mentor, was no longer around to give him comfort or advice. David had lost most of the people he had depended on. Yet in the wake of such losses, life for David was really just beginning.

In spite of his grief, David managed the kingdom affairs brilliantly after Saul's death. He demonstrated patience and kindness toward the northern tribes during the reign of Ish-bosheth. He wisely established the capital in Jerusalem, a neutral city. He brought the Ark of the Covenant back to Jerusalem. And his victories over the Philistines led to further consolidation of the kingdom.

Unfortunately, David did not do as well at managing the affairs of his heart. In the midst of his political success, he made some terrible mistakes. He fell into adultery and murder, which later resulted in incest and rebellion within his own family. This all led to the near destruction of his family and the kingdom he had so skillfully built.

But God did not allow David's mistakes to destroy the nation. He sent the prophet Nathan to initiate a recovery program for David, and Nathan's intervention brought the king to repentance. David was humble and willing to accept God's word of correction. He was willing to learn from his mistakes and for the rest of his life continued to look to God for strength and help.

THE BOTTOM LINE

PURPOSE: To record the history of King David, who, despite his personal failings, was a man who sought after God. AUTHOR: Unknown, though it includes writings from the prophets Nathan and Gad. AUDIENCE: The people of Israel. DATE WRITTEN: Sometime after David's death, around 930 B.C. SETTING: The land of Palestine. KEY VERSES: "Then David . . . prayed, 'O Lord God, why have you showered your blessings on such an insignificant person as I am? And now, in addition to everything else, you speak of giving me an eternal dynasty? Such generosity is far beyond any human standard!'" (7:18-19). KEY PLACES: Hebron, Jerusalem, Bahurim, Mahanaim. KEY PEOPLE AND RELATIONSHIPS: David with Joab, Abner, Michal, Bathsheba, Nathan, Amnon, Absalom, Mephibosheth.

RECOVERY THEMES

Recovery Follows Failure: There is life after failure; David's biography proves that fact. His list of sins included murder and adultery, not to mention neglect of his family. If anyone should have been written off in God's plan, it was David. But David's important place in history proves that God uses fallible people to work his will in history. God's grace is adequate for even the greatest of failures.

Justice with Mercy: David was a just king, and his justice was always tempered by mercy. He demonstrated this when he refused to strike back at Saul, even while being chased by him. He revealed it when he punished the murderers of Abner and Ish-bosheth, even though these men had been his enemies. He never rejoiced in wrongdoing—even when it brought him personal advantage. And when David himself sinned, he accepted God's judgment as right and just. David's attitudes and actions were grounded in his relationship with our just and merciful God. God had been fair with him, so David was fair with his people. God had been merciful toward him, so he dispensed mercy freely to others.

Accepting Reality: When Nathan confronted him about his sin, David accepted the truth. When reminded of the consequences of his sin, he repented with sorrow. Our recovery is based on our willingness to accept reality. When our life is out of control, we need to acknowledge God's reign and our great need for him. The secret to David's recovery was his dependence on God and his ability to accept the truth about his sin.

The Seriousness of Sin: David did not get away with his sin; it brought serious consequences. The baby born to David and Bathsheba died soon after its birth. Within his own family, incest was followed by murder. David's favorite son, Absalom, rebelled and was killed by David's own men. David had experienced the joy of God's blessing. But he also knew the depths of sorrow that followed from the bad choices he made.

CHAPTER 1

David Mourns for Saul and Jonathan

Saul was dead and David had returned to
Ziklag after slaughtering the Amalekites.
Three days later a man arrived from the Israeli
army with his clothes torn and with dirt on
his head as a sign of mourning. He fell to the
ground before David in deep respect.
3"Where do you come from?" David asked.
"From the Israeli army," he replied.
4"What happened?" David demanded.
"Tell me how the battle went."
And the man replied, "Our entire army
fled. Thousands of men are dead and
wounded on the field, and Saul and his son
Jonathan have been killed."
5"How do you know they are dead?"
6"Because I was on Mount Gilboa and saw
Saul leaning against his spear with the enemy
chariots closing in upon him. 7When he saw
me he cried out for me to come to him.
8"'Who are you?' he asked.
"'An Amalekite,' I replied.
9"'Come and put me out of my misery,' he
begged, 'for I am in terrible pain but life
lingers on.'
10"So I killed him, for I knew he couldn't
live. Then I took his crown and one of his
bracelets to bring to you, my lord."
11David and his men tore their clothes in
sorrow when they heard the news. 12They
mourned and wept and fasted all day for Saul
and his son Jonathan, and for the Lord's
people, and for the men of Israel who had
died that day.
13Then David said to the young man who
had brought the news, "Where are you
from?"
And he replied, "I am an Amalekite."
14"Why did you kill God's chosen king?"
David demanded.
15Then he said to one of his young men,
"Kill him!" So he ran him through with his
sword and he died.
16"You die self-condemned," David said,
"for you yourself confessed that you killed
God's appointed king."

David's Song for Saul and Jonathan

17,18Then David composed a dirge for Saul and
Jonathan and afterward commanded that it

1:8-10 The record of Saul's suicide in 1 Samuel 31:4 raises questions about the truth of the Amalekite's claims. More than likely, the man was lying in hopes of receiving a reward from David. He did receive his reward—death. Deceit is often a harbinger of disaster; honesty is always the best policy.
1:11-27 The honest outpouring of grief by David and his men over the deaths of Saul, Jonathan, and the other men of Israel was no sign of weakness. Instead, it indicated the love, respect, and sorrow they felt for their fallen countrymen. Sincere expressions of emotion are invaluable components of the healing process. We don't need to be afraid of displaying our emotions.

be sung throughout Israel. It is quoted here
from the book, *Heroic Ballads.*

19O Israel, your pride and joy lies dead
upon the hills;
Mighty heroes have fallen.
20Don't tell the Philistines, lest they
rejoice.
Hide it from the cities of Gath and
Ashkelon,
Lest the heathen nations laugh in triumph.
21O Mount Gilboa,
Let there be no dew nor rain upon you,
Let no crops of grain grow on your slopes.
For there the mighty Saul has died;
He is God's appointed king no more.
22Both Saul and Jonathan slew their
strongest foes,
And did not return from battle
empty-handed.
23How much they were loved, how
wonderful they were—
Both Saul and Jonathan!
They were together in life and in death.
They were swifter than eagles, stronger
than lions.
24But now, O women of Israel, weep for
Saul;
He enriched you
With fine clothing and gold ornaments.
25These mighty heroes have fallen in the
midst of the battle.
Jonathan is slain upon the hills.
26How I weep for you, my brother
Jonathan;
How much I loved you!
And your love for me was deeper
Than the love of women!
27The mighty ones have fallen,
Stripped of their weapons, and dead.

CHAPTER 2

Judah Crowns David King

David then asked the Lord, "Shall I move back
to Judah?"
And the Lord replied, "Yes."
"Which city shall I go to?"
And the Lord replied, "Hebron."
2So David and his wives—Ahinoam from
Jezreel and Abigail the widow of Nabal from
Carmel— 3and his men and their families all
moved to Hebron. 4Then the leaders of Judah
came to David and crowned him king of the
Judean confederacy.
When David heard that the men of Jabesh-
gilead had buried Saul, 5he sent them this
message: "May the Lord bless you for being so
loyal to your king and giving him a decent
burial. 6May the Lord be loyal to you in return
and reward you with many demonstrations of
his love! And I too will be kind to you because
of what you have done. 7And now I ask you to
be my strong and loyal subjects, now that
Saul is dead. Be like the tribe of Judah who
have appointed me as their new king."

Abner Crowns Ish-bosheth King

8But Abner, Saul's commander-in-chief, had
gone to Mahanaim to crown Saul's son Ish-
bosheth as king. 9His territory included
Gilead, Ashuri, Jezreel, Ephraim, the tribe of
Benjamin, and all the rest of Israel. 10,11Ish-
bosheth was forty years old at the time. He
reigned in Mahanaim for two years; meanwhile, David was reigning in Hebron and was
king of the Judean confederacy for seven and
one-half years.

Civil War in Israel

12One day General Abner led some of Ish-
bosheth's troops to Gibeon from Mahanaim,
13and General Joab (the son of Zeruiah) led
David's troops out to meet them. They met at
the pool of Gibeon, where they sat facing
each other on opposite sides of the pool.
14Then Abner suggested to Joab, "Let's watch
some sword play between our young men!"
Joab agreed, 15so twelve men were chosen
from each side to fight in mortal combat.
16Each one grabbed his opponent by the hair
and thrust his sword into the other's side, so
that all of them died. The place has been
known ever since as Sword Field.
17The two armies then began to fight each
other, and by the end of the day Abner and
the men of Israel had been defeated by Joab
and the forces of David.18Joab's brothers, Abishai and Asahel, were also in the battle. Asahel could run like a deer, 19and he began
chasing Abner. He wouldn't stop for anything, but kept on, singleminded, after Abner
alone.

2:1-11 We often make our greatest mistakes in situations where we are eager to act. After years as a fugitive, David must have burned with excitement at the thought of finally assuming Israel's throne. Yet he accepted a continued delay of his gratification and waited to take charge of the northern Israelite tribes at a later time. He listened to God's instructions and became king of only one tribe—Judah. We would be wise to learn from David's patience and trust in God.

20 When Abner looked behind and saw him coming, he called out to him, "Is that you, Asahel?"

"Yes," he called back, "it is."

21 "Go after someone else!" Abner warned. But Asahel refused and kept on coming. 22 Again Abner shouted to him, "Get away from here. I could never face your brother Joab if I have to kill you!"

23 But he refused to turn away, so Abner pierced him through the belly with the butt end of his spear. It went right through his body and came out his back. He stumbled to the ground and died there, and everyone stopped when they came to the place where he lay.

24 Now Joab and Abishai set out after Abner. The sun was just going down as they arrived at Ammah Hill near Giah, along the road into the Gibeon desert. 25 Abner's troops from the tribe of Benjamin regrouped there at the top of the hill, 26 and Abner shouted down to Joab, "Must our swords continue to kill each other forever? How long will it be before you call off your people from chasing their brothers?"

27 Joab shouted back, "I swear by God that even if you hadn't spoken, we would all have gone home tomorrow morning." 28 Then he blew his trumpet and his men stopped chasing the troops of Israel.

29 That night Abner and his men retreated across the Jordan Valley, crossed the river, and traveled all the next morning until they arrived at Mahanaim. 30 Joab and the men who were with him returned home, too, and when he counted his casualties, he learned that only nineteen men were missing, in addition to Asahel. 31 But three hundred and sixty of Abner's men (all from the tribe of Benjamin) were dead. 32 Joab and his men took Asahel's body to Bethlehem and buried him beside his father; then they traveled all night and reached Hebron at daybreak.

CHAPTER 3

David Becomes Stronger

That was the beginning of a long war between the followers of Saul and of David. David's position now became stronger and stronger, while Saul's dynasty became weaker and weaker.

2 Several sons were born to David while he was at Hebron. The oldest was Amnon, born to his wife Ahinoam. 3 His second son, Chileab, was born to Abigail, the widow of Nabal of Carmel. The third was Absalom, born to Maacah, the daughter of King Talmai of Geshur. 4 The fourth was Adonijah, who was born to Haggith. Then Shephatiah was born to Abital, and 5 Ithream was born to Eglah.

6 As the war went on, Abner became a very powerful political leader among the followers of Saul. 7 He took advantage of his position by sleeping with one of Saul's concubines, a girl named Rizpah. But when Ish-bosheth accused Abner of this, 8 Abner was furious.

"Am I a Judean dog to be kicked around like this?" he shouted. "After all I have done for you and for your father by not betraying you to David, is this my reward—to find fault with me about some woman? 9,10 May God curse me if I don't do everything I can to take away the entire kingdom from you, all the way from Dan to Beersheba, and give it to David, just as the Lord predicted."

11 Ish-bosheth made no reply, for he was afraid of Abner.

12 Then Abner sent messengers to David to discuss a deal—to surrender the kingdom of Israel to him in exchange for becoming commander-in-chief of the combined armies of Israel and Judah.

13 "All right," David replied, "but I will not negotiate with you unless you bring me my wife Michal, Saul's daughter." 14 David then sent this message to Ish-bosheth: "Give me back my wife Michal, for I bought her with the lives of one hundred Philistines."

15 So Ish-bosheth took her away from her

2:30-31 What a tragic picture! Hundreds died in a needless conflict between related tribes. This tragedy was the fruit of a divided nation and unwise leadership on the part of Joab. Often our families suffer in the same way. If past conflicts are not dealt with properly and family leaders make decisions driven by passion, suffering and pain are the sure result. This should be a warning for us to seek restoration early, before the consequences bring destruction that cannot be repaired.

3:17-18 Abner displayed the courage to take an unpopular stand and to make an important change in his life. He advised the elders of the northern tribes to take the necessary steps to make David their king. Good intentions are worthless until they are translated into actions, and Abner understood this. One of the major steps of recovery involves not only wanting change but taking active steps to pursue it. Abner's exhortation, "Now is the time!" (3:18) is a clarion call to all who want to progress toward a balanced life.

husband Palti. 16He followed along behind her
as far as Behurim, weeping as he went. Then
Abner told him, "Go on home now." So he
returned.
17Meanwhile, Abner consulted with the
leaders of Israel and reminded them that for a
long time they had wanted David as their
king.
18"Now is the time!" he told them. "For the
Lord has said, 'It is David by whom I will save
my people from the Philistines and from all
their other enemies.'"
19Abner also talked to the leaders of the
tribe of Benjamin; then he went to Hebron
and reported to David his progress with the
people of Israel and Benjamin. 20Twenty men
accompanied him, and David entertained
them with a feast.
21As Abner left, he promised David, "When
I get back I will call a convention of all the
people of Israel, and they will elect you as
their king, as you've so long desired." So
David let Abner return in safety.

Joab Kills Abner in Revenge

22But just after Abner left, Joab and some of
David's troops returned from a raid, bringing
much loot with them. 23When Joab was told
that Abner had just been there visiting the
king and had been sent away in peace, 24,25he
rushed to the king, demanding, "What have
you done? What do you mean by letting him
get away? You know perfectly well that he
came to spy on us and that he plans to return
and attack us!"
26Then Joab sent messengers to catch up
with Abner and tell him to come back. They
found him at the well of Sirah and he returned with them; but David knew nothing
about it. 27When Abner arrived at Hebron,
Joab took him aside at the city gate as if to
speak with him privately; but then he pulled
out a dagger and killed him in revenge for the
death of his brother Asahel.
28When David heard about it he declared, "I
vow by the Lord that I and my people are
innocent of this crime against Abner. 29Joab
and his family are the guilty ones. May each
of his children be victims of cancer, or be
lepers, or be sterile, or die of starvation, or be
killed by the sword!"
30So Joab and his brother, Abishai, killed
Abner because of the death of their brother,
Asahel, at the battle of Gibeon.
31Then David said to Joab and to all those
who were with him, "Go into deep mourning
for Abner." And King David accompanied the
bier to the cemetery. 32They buried Abner in
Hebron. And the king and all the people wept
at the graveside.
33,34"Should Abner have died like a fool?"
the king lamented.

"Your hands were not bound,
Your feet were not tied—
You were murdered—
The victim of a wicked plot."

And all the people wept again for him.
35,36David had refused to eat anything the day
of the funeral, and now everyone begged him
to take a bite of supper. But David vowed that
he would eat nothing until sundown. This
pleased his people, just as everything else he
did pleased them! 37Thus the whole nation,
both Judah and Israel, understood from
David's actions that he was in no way responsible for Abner's death.
38And David said to his people, "A great
leader and a great man has fallen today in
Israel; 39and even though I am God's chosen
king, I can do nothing with these two sons of
Zeruiah. May the Lord repay wicked men for
their wicked deeds."

CHAPTER 4

Ish-bosheth Is Murdered

When King Ish-bosheth heard about Abner's
death at Hebron, he was paralyzed with fear,
and his people too were badly frightened.
2,3The command of the Israeli troops then fell
to two brothers, Baanah and Rechab, who
were captains of King Ish-bosheth's raiding
bands. They were the sons of Rimmon, who
was from Beeroth in Benjamin. (People from
Beeroth are counted as Benjaminites even
though they fled to Gittaim, where they now
live.)
4(There was a little lame grandson of King

3:27 Joab chose to harbor a deep bitterness toward Abner and sought revenge rather than looking for a new start in life. It would have been better had Joab let go of painful past events; instead, he chose to avenge the death of his brother. His rash act of vengeance against Abner brought a curse upon his family and embarrassment and grief to his king. Our recovery requires that we seek release from our past, no matter how painful it may be. This can only be done as we learn to forgive the people who have wronged us. Forgiveness, though difficult, is the only sure path toward freedom from a painful past.

Saul's named Mephibosheth, who was the son of Prince Jonathan. He was five years old at the time Saul and Jonathan were killed at the battle of Jezreel. When the news of the outcome of the battle reached the capital, the child's nurse grabbed him and fled, but she fell and dropped him as she was running, and he became lame.)

[5]Rechab and Baanah arrived at King Ish-bosheth's home one noon as he was taking a nap. [6,7]They walked into the kitchen as though to get a sack of wheat, but then sneaked into his bedroom and murdered him and cut off his head. Taking his head with them, they fled across the desert that night and escaped. [8]They presented the head to David at Hebron.

"Look!" they exclaimed. "Here is the head of Ish-bosheth, the son of your enemy Saul who tried to kill you. Today the Lord has given you revenge upon Saul and upon his entire family!"

[9]But David replied, "I swear by the Lord who saved me from my enemies, [10]that when someone told me, 'Saul is dead,' thinking he was bringing me good news, I killed him; that is how I rewarded him for his 'glad tidings.' [11]And how much more shall I do to wicked men who kill a good man in his own house and on his bed! Shall I not demand your lives?"

[12]So David ordered his young men to kill them, and they did. They cut off their hands and feet and hanged their bodies beside the pool in Hebron. And they took Ish-bosheth's head and buried it in Abner's tomb in Hebron.

CHAPTER 5

David Becomes King of All Israel

Representatives of all the tribes of Israel now came to David at Hebron and gave him their pledge of loyalty.

"We are your blood brothers," they said. [2]"And even when Saul was our king you were our real leader. The Lord has said that you should be the shepherd and leader of his people."

[3]So David made a contract before the Lord with the leaders of Israel there at Hebron, and they crowned him king of Israel. [4,5](He had already been the king of Judah for seven years, since the age of thirty. He then ruled thirty-three years in Jerusalem as king of both Israel and Judah; so he reigned for forty years altogether.)

David Conquers Jerusalem

[6]David now led his troops to Jerusalem to fight against the Jebusites who lived there.

"You'll never come in here," they told him. "Even the blind and lame could keep you out!" For they thought they were safe. [7]But David and his troops defeated them and captured the stronghold of Zion, now called the City of David.

[8]When the insulting message from the defenders of the city reached David, he told his troops, "Go up through the water tunnel into the city and destroy those 'lame' and 'blind' Jebusites. How I hate them." (That is the origin of the saying, "Even the blind and the lame could conquer you!")

[9]So David made the stronghold of Zion (also called the City of David) his headquarters. Then, beginning at the old Millo section of the city, he built northward toward the present city center. [10]So David became greater and greater, for the Lord God of heaven was with him.

[11]Then King Hiram of Tyre sent cedar lumber, carpenters, and masons to build a palace for David. [12]David now realized why the Lord had made him the king and blessed his king-

4:9 David acknowledged God as the source of his deliverance. This is crucial in the process of our recovery. If we cannot give God the credit for our victories, it is obvious that we never really gave our life over to him in the first place. We need to give credit where credit is due. Praising God for our victories is a good way to show how much we depend on him and appreciate his help.

5:6-8 The arrogant Jebusites thought their city was invincible: They said, "You'll never come in here. . . . Even the blind and lame could keep you out!" As we progress in recovery, it is easy to assume that we are immune to a dramatic reversal. Then we are shocked when it happens, as were the Jebusites: "But David and his troops defeated them." We would be wise to be humble and keep our guard raised against a possible fall.

5:13 At the height of David's political progress, he began to build his harem. This was customary for kings in the ancient Near East, but his decision to be like other kings carried a price tag with it. In later years, conflict between David's many children almost destroyed both king and kingdom. Since polygamy was customary in Old Testament times, no moral judgment is cast here. But the consequence of family strife is attested numerous times in Scripture. Sometimes God's plan will lead us away from the norms of the society around us. If so, we can either seek God's ideal or suffer the consequences.

dom so greatly—it was because God wanted
to pour out his kindness on Israel, his chosen
people.
13After moving from Hebron to Jerusalem,
David married additional wives and concubines, and had many sons and daughters.
14-16These are his children who were born at
Jerusalem: Shammua, Shobab, Nathan, Solomon, Ibhar, Elishua, Nepheg, Japhia, Elishama, Eliada, Eliphelet.

David Defeats the Philistines

17When the Philistines heard that David had
been crowned king of Israel, they tried to
capture him; but David was told that they
were coming and went into the stronghold.
18The Philistines arrived and spread out across
the valley of Rephaim.
19Then David asked the Lord, "Shall I go out
and fight against them? Will you defeat them
for me?"

And the Lord replied, "Yes, go ahead, for I
will give them to you."
20So David went out and fought with them
at Baal-perazim and defeated them. "The Lord
did it!" he exclaimed. "He burst through my
enemies like a raging flood." So he named the
place "Bursting." 21At that time David and his
troops confiscated many idols that had been
abandoned by the Philistines. 22But the Philistines returned and again spread out across the
valley of Rephaim.
23When David asked the Lord what to do,
he replied, "Don't make a frontal attack. Go
behind them and come out by the balsam
trees. 24When you hear a sound like marching feet in the tops of the balsam trees,
attack! For it will signify that the Lord has
prepared the way for you and will destroy
them."
25So David did as the Lord had instructed
him and destroyed the Philistines all the way
from Geba to Gezer.

CHAPTER 6

David Brings the Ark to Jerusalem

Then David mobilized thirty thousand special
troops and led them to Baal-judah to bring
home the Ark of the Lord of heaven who is
enthroned above the Guardian Angels. 3The
Ark was placed upon a new cart and taken
from the hillside home of Abinadab. It was
driven by Abinadab's sons, Uzzah and Ahio.
4Ahio was walking in front 5and was followed
by David and the other leaders of Israel, who
were joyously waving branches of juniper
trees and playing every sort of musical instrument before the Lord—lyres, harps, tambourines, castanets, and cymbals.
6But when they arrived at the threshing
floor of Nacon, the oxen stumbled and Uzzah
put out his hand to steady the Ark. 7Then the
anger of the Lord flared out against Uzzah and
he killed him for doing this, so he died there
beside the Ark. 8David was angry at what the
Lord had done, and named the spot "The
Place of Wrath upon Uzzah" (which it is still
called to this day).
9David was now afraid of the Lord and
asked, "How can I ever bring the Ark home?"
10So he decided against taking it into the City
of David, but carried it instead to the home of
Obed-edom, who had come from Gath. 11It
remained there for three months, and the
Lord blessed Obed-edom and all his household.
12When David heard this, he brought the
Ark to the City of David with a great celebration. 13After the men who were carrying it had
gone six paces, they stopped and waited so
that he could sacrifice an ox and a fat lamb.
14And David danced before the Lord with all
his might and was wearing priests' clothing.
15So Israel brought home the Ark of the Lord
with much shouting and blowing of trumpets.
16(But as the procession came into the
city, Michal, Saul's daughter, watched from

6:1-8 David desired to bring the Ark of the Covenant, the symbol of God's presence, to Jerusalem. But he failed to follow God's specific instructions for transporting it. He probably hadn't ever read God's laws concerning the Ark, but God's Word was available to him. There are serious consequences for failing to honor God by not following his instructions. We are responsible to know what God desires of us; such knowledge will enable us to act according to his will. The Bible is our primary source for discovering God's program for healthy living.

6:16-23 Michal's anger was probably driven by far more than her embarrassment at David's conduct. Over the years, Michal had been a pawn on the chessboard of David's life. After Michal had been married to David for a short time, her father, King Saul, had given her to another man to spite David. In later kingdom negotiations David won her back, but then she found herself to be just one wife among many. Her life is a tragic example of how people can be used by others. Michal's anger at the injustice she had suffered affected her ability to enjoy the present. The same thing can happen to us; we need to take steps to uncover our pain, allowing God to free us from our past.

a window and saw King David leaping and dancing before the Lord; and she was filled with contempt for him.)

17The Ark was placed inside the tent that David had prepared for it; and he sacrificed burnt offerings and peace offerings to the Lord. 18Then he blessed the people in the name of the Lord of heaven 19and gave a present to everyone—men and women alike—of a loaf of bread, some wine, and a cake of raisins. When it was all over, and everyone had gone home, 20David returned to bless his family.

But Michal came out to meet him and exclaimed in disgust, "How glorious the king of Israel looked today! He exposed himself to the girls along the street like a common pervert!"

21David retorted, "I was dancing before the Lord who chose me above your father and his family and who appointed me as leader of Israel, the people of the Lord! So I am willing to act like a fool in order to show my joy in the Lord. 22Yes, and I am willing to look even more foolish than this, but I will be respected by the girls of whom you spoke!"

23So Michal was childless throughout her life.

CHAPTER 7

God Promises to Bless David

When the Lord finally sent peace upon the land, and Israel was no longer at war with the surrounding nations, 2David said to Nathan the prophet, "Look! Here I am living in this beautiful cedar palace while the Ark of God is out in a tent!"

3"Go ahead with what you have in mind," Nathan replied, "for the Lord is with you."

4But that night the Lord said to Nathan, 5"Tell my servant David not to do it! 6For I have never lived in a temple. My home has been a tent ever since the time I brought Israel out of Egypt. 7And I have never once complained to Israel's leaders, the shepherds of my people. Have I ever asked them, 'Why haven't you built me a beautiful cedar temple?'

8"Now go and give this message to David from the Lord of heaven: 'I chose you to be the leader of my people Israel when you were a mere shepherd, tending your sheep in the pastureland. 9I have been with you wherever you have gone and have destroyed your enemies. And I will make your name greater yet, so that you will be one of the most famous men in the world! 10,11I have selected a homeland for my people from which they will never have to move. It will be their own land where the heathen nations won't bother them as they did when the judges ruled my people. There will be no more wars against you; and your descendants shall rule this land for generations to come! 12For when you die, I will put one of your sons upon your throne, and I will make his kingdom strong. 13He is the one who shall build me a temple. And I will continue his kingdom into eternity. 14I will be his father and he shall be my son. If he sins, I will use other nations to punish him, 15but my love and kindness shall not leave him as I took it from Saul, your predecessor. 16Your family shall rule my kingdom forever.'"

17So Nathan went back to David and told him everything the Lord had said.

David Claims God's Promise

18Then David went into the Tabernacle and sat before the Lord and prayed, "O Lord God, why have you showered your blessings on such an insignificant person as I am? 19And now, in addition to everything else, you speak of giving me an eternal dynasty! Such generosity is far beyond any human standard! O Lord God! 20What can I say? For you know what I am like! 21You are doing all these things just because you promised to and because you want to! 22How great you are, Lord God! We have never heard of any other god like you.

7:9-13 God may have refused David's request to build the temple, but as we see here, God had an even better plan (Proverbs 3:4-6). God's plan involved establishing the Davidic covenant, which included the promise of an eternal kingdom with a descendant upon its throne forever. David was called upon to delay his desire to build a temple and to exercise patience and faith. There may be times when we have to wait patiently for our recovery to become a reality. But God has a special plan for each of us, and when it unfolds we can be sure it will be better than what we had hoped for.

7:18-29 A vital step in any successful recovery program involves recognizing God's authority in our life and allowing him to direct our plans. In this beautiful prayer, David called God "Lord" no fewer than six times. David realized that God was his master and that following his will was of utmost importance. By submitting to God's will and looking to him for help, we will discover the power we need to overcome our difficulties.

DAVID, MICHAL, & BATHSHEBA

David failed in many of his relationships. He tended to avoid conflict and therefore did not deal with some important issues in his life. David's first wife, Michal, was the daughter of King Saul. Their marriage was right out of a fairy tale. The king's beautiful daughter married the great war hero, who also happened to be the most talented musician of his day. Though early on their relationship appeared to be fine, over time their relationship developed difficulties. Michal was separated from David for a number of years when Saul gave her to another man to spite David. Years later David won her back but brought her into a house filled with other wives. Their relationship was never truly reestablished after Michal's return; they apparently kept the pain of their separation to themselves and from each other.

Michal exploded at David for dancing before the Ark as he celebrated its return to Jerusalem (6:16). It seems that her bitterness and frustration over the years of separation and neglect had built to the boiling point. Unfortunately, there is no indication that they ever tried to heal their damaged marriage relationship. Instead, they seem to have settled into a destructive silence.

David complicated his life further by his infatuation and adultery with Bathsheba (11:1-27). This sin led to a tangled web of deceit, Uriah's murder, and a rushed marriage to the pregnant Bathsheba. This string of self-induced tragedies left a cloud of shame that hung over David throughout the rest of his life. David's own children would repeat his mistakes, bringing further suffering to the royal family and the nation as a whole.

With all his mistakes, why was David considered more righteous than Saul, his predecessor? His heart was open before God, and he was willing to accept God's correction in his life. After each failure, he was willing to admit the truth, accept the consequences, and receive God's forgiveness. Even in the midst of his failures, pain, and grief, he remained a man whose primary desire was to know God. All of us, like David, have made mistakes. We have much to learn from him about recovering from the bad choices we have made.

STRENGTHS AND ACCOMPLISHMENTS:
- In the beginning, David and Michal had a strong marriage.
- David kept an open relationship with God.
- David was always willing to admit his failures and accept God's correction.

WEAKNESSES AND MISTAKES:
- David and Michal did not communicate effectively.
- David avoided family conflict and the resolution of problems.
- David allowed immediate gratification to lead him into sin.
- By hiding his sin of adultery, David was driven deeper into sin.

LESSONS FROM THEIR LIVES:
- A good marriage can be destroyed by unresolved issues.
- Communication must be a high priority in any relationship.
- One mistake usually leads to others.
- No matter how great our sin, God is willing to forgive us if we repent.

KEY VERSE:
"As the deer pants for water, so I long for you, O God. I thirst for God, the living God" (Psalm 42:1-2).

David and Michal's story is told in 1 Samuel 18–19, 25; 2 Samuel 3, 6; 1 Chronicles 15:29. David and Bathsheba's story is told in 2 Samuel 11–1 Kings 1.

And there is no other god. 23What other nation in all the earth has received such blessings as Israel, your people? For you have
rescued your chosen nation in order to bring
glory to your name. You have done great
miracles to destroy Egypt and its gods. 24You
chose Israel to be your people forever, and
you became our God.
25"And now, Lord God, do as you have
promised concerning me and my family.
26And may you be eternally honored when
you have established Israel as your people and
have established my dynasty before you. 27For
you have revealed to me, O Lord of heaven,
God of Israel, that I am the first of a dynasty
which will rule your people forever; that is
why I have been bold enough to pray this
prayer of acceptance. 28For you are indeed

God, and your words are truth; and you have
promised me these good things— [29]so do as
you have promised! Bless me and my family
forever! May our dynasty continue on and on
before you; for you, Lord God, have promised
it."

CHAPTER 8

David Strengthens His Kingdom

After this David subdued and humbled the
Philistines by conquering Gath, their largest
city. [2]He also devastated the land of Moab. He
divided his victims by making them lie down
side by side in rows. Two-thirds of each row,
as measured with a tape, were butchered, and
one-third were spared to become David's servants—they paid him tribute each year.

[3]He also destroyed the forces of King Hadadezer (son of Rehob) of Zobah in a battle at
the Euphrates River, for Hadadezer had attempted to regain his power. [4]David captured
seventeen hundred cavalry and twenty thousand infantry; then he lamed all of the chariot
horses except for one hundred teams. [5]He also
slaughtered twenty-two thousand Syrians
from Damascus when they came to help Hadadezer. [6]David placed several army garrisons
in Damascus, and the Syrians became David's
subjects and brought him annual tribute
money. So the Lord gave him victories wherever he turned. [7]David brought the gold
shields to Jerusalem which King Hadadezer's
officers had used. [8]He also carried back to
Jerusalem a very large amount of bronze from
Hadadezer's cities of Betah and Berothai.

[9]When King Toi of Hamath heard about
David's victory over the army of Hadadezer,
[10]he sent his son Joram to congratulate him,
for Hadadezer and Toi were enemies. He gave
David presents made from silver, gold, and
bronze. [11,12]David dedicated all of these to the
Lord, along with the silver and gold he had
taken from Syria, Moab, Ammon, the Philistines, Amalek, and King Hadadezer.

[13]So David became very famous. After his
return he destroyed eighteen thousand
Edomites at the Valley of Salt, [14]and then
placed garrisons throughout Edom, so that
the entire nation was forced to pay tribute to
Israel—another example of the way the Lord
made him victorious wherever he went.

[15]David reigned with justice over Israel and
was fair to everyone. [16]The general of his army
was Joab (son of Zeruiah), and his secretary of
state was Jehoshaphat (son of Ahilud). [17]Za-
dok (son of Ahitub) and Ahimelech (son of
Abiathar) were the High Priests, and Seraiah
was the king's private secretary. [18]Benaiah
(son of Jehoiada) was captain of his bodyguard, and David's sons were his assistants.

CHAPTER 9

David Is Kind to Mephibosheth

One day David began wondering if any of
Saul's family was still living, for he wanted to
be kind to them, as he had promised Prince
Jonathan. [2]He heard about a man named
Ziba, who had been one of Saul's servants,
and summoned him.

"Are you Ziba?" the king asked.

"Yes, sir, I am," he replied.

[3]The king then asked him, "Is anyone left
from Saul's family? If so, I want to fulfill a
sacred vow by being kind to him."

"Yes," Ziba replied, "Jonathan's lame son is
still alive."

[4]"Where is he?" the king asked.

"In Lo-debar," Ziba told him. "At the home
of Machir."

[5,6]So King David sent for Mephibosheth—
Jonathan's son and Saul's grandson. Mephibosheth arrived in great fear and greeted the
king in deep humility, bowing low before
him.

7:27-29 David took the time to review God's promises to him. God's Word is filled with promises for us, and God delights as we plead those promises before him in prayer. This can be especially helpful in the midst of a crisis. Not that God needs reminding, but our memory can usually stand some refreshing.

9:1-7 David had promised to treat Saul's family well for the sake of his friend Jonathan. And though many years had passed since the promise was given, David was true to it. He honored the memory of Jonathan by offering Mephibosheth a place in his household. David stood by his word and did what he could to set right a painful conflict from out of his past. Being responsible for our promises and dealing with past conflicts are important aspects of the recovery process.

10:1-5 Hanun was needlessly suspicious of the motives of David's men. As a result, he treated them shamefully and brought a great deal of needless bloodshed upon his people. Hanun's suspicions led him to distrust others and negated the attempts of David to forge a productive relationship. Allowing our fears to shape our conclusions can often lead to unnecessary conflict and a disruption of possible positive relationships. Much time, effort, and energy is wasted when we respond with suspicion and fear to the friendly overtures of other people.

[7]But David said, "Don't be afraid! I've asked
you to come so that I can be kind to you
because of my vow to your father Jonathan. I
will restore to you all the land of your grandfather Saul, and you shall live here at the
palace!"
[8]Mephibosheth fell to the ground before
the king. "Should the king show kindness to
a dead dog like me?" he exclaimed.
[9]Then the king summoned Saul's servant
Ziba. "I have given your master's grandson
everything that belonged to Saul and his family," he said. [10,11]"You and your sons and servants are to farm the land for him, to produce
food for his family; but he will live here with
me."
Ziba, who had fifteen sons and twenty servants, replied, "Sir, I will do all you have
commanded."
And from that time on, Mephibosheth ate
regularly with King David, as though he were
one of his own sons. [12]Mephibosheth had a
young son, Mica. All the household of Ziba
became Mephibosheth's servants, [13]but Mephibosheth (who was lame in both feet)
moved to Jerusalem to live at the palace.

CHAPTER 10

David Punishes the Ammonites

Some time after this the Ammonite king died
and his son Hanun replaced him.
[2]"I am going to show special respect for
him," David said, "because his father Nahash
was always so loyal and kind to me." So David
sent ambassadors to express regrets to Hanun
about his father's death.
[3]But Hanun's officers told him, "These men
aren't here to honor your father! David has
sent them to spy out the city before attacking
it!"
[4]So Hanun took David's men and shaved
off half their beards and cut their robes off at
the buttocks and sent them home half naked.
[5]When David heard what had happened he
told them to stay at Jericho until their beards
grew out; for the men were very embarrassed
over their appearance.
[6]Now the people of Ammon realized how
seriously they had angered David, so they
hired twenty thousand Syrian mercenaries
from the lands of Rehob and Zobah, one
thousand from the king of Maacah, and ten
thousand from the land of Tob. [7,8]When
David heard about this, he sent Joab and the
entire Israeli army to attack them. The
Ammonites defended the gates of their city
while the Syrians from Zobah, Rehob, Tob,

Keeping Promises

BIBLE READING: 2 Samuel 9:1-9

We made direct amends to such people wherever possible, except when to do so would injure them or others.

How many people are still living in the shadow of our unkept promises? Is it too late to go back now and try to make it up to them?

King David had made some promises to his friend Jonathan. "One day David began wondering if any of Saul's family was still living, for he wanted to be kind to them, as he had promised Prince Jonathan" (2 Samuel 9:1).

Jonathan's only living son, Mephibosheth, had lived a long time with the pain of David's unkept promise. It had shaped his life-style, his emotional condition, and the way he thought about himself. His grandfather, King Saul, had mistreated David before David became king. Perhaps Mephibosheth was afraid that David would mistreat him on account of his grandfather. Perhaps he had begun to take the guilt of his grandfather's sins upon himself. Generations of fear and guilt had been laid upon him—until David remembered and fulfilled his promise.

There are probably people in our life who have been affected by promises we have failed to keep. It is important that we try to fulfill whatever promises we can. When we can't, the least we can do is to ask what our neglect meant to those we disappointed. ***Turn to page 879, Ezekiel 33.***

and Maacah fought in the fields. 9When Joab
realized that he would have to fight on two
fronts, he selected the best fighters in his
army, placed them under his personal command, and took them out to fight the Syrians
in the fields. 10He left the rest of the army to
his brother Abishai, who was to attack the
city.
11"If I need assistance against the Syrians,
come out and help me," Joab instructed him.
"And if the Ammonites are too strong for you,
I will come and help you. 12Courage! We must
really act like men today if we are going to
save our people and the cities of our God. May
the Lord's will be done."
13And when Joab and his troops attacked,
the Syrians began to run away. 14Then, when
the Ammonites saw the Syrians running, they
ran too, and retreated into the city. Afterwards Joab returned to Jerusalem. 15,16The Syrians now realized that they were no match for
Israel. So when they regrouped, they were
joined by additional Syrian troops summoned by Hadadezer from the other side of
the Euphrates River. These troops arrived at
Helam under the command of Shobach, the
commander-in-chief of all of Hadadezer's
forces.
17When David heard what was happening,
he personally led the Israeli army to Helam,
where the Syrians attacked him. 18But again
the Syrians fled from the Israelis, this time
leaving seven hundred charioteers dead on
the field, also forty thousand cavalrymen, including General Shobach. 19When Hadadezer's allies saw that the Syrians had been
defeated, they surrendered to David and became his servants. And the Syrians were afraid
to help the Ammonites anymore after that.

CHAPTER 11

David and Bathsheba

In the spring of the following year, at the time
when wars begin, David sent Joab and the
Israeli army to destroy the Ammonites. They
began by laying siege to the city of Rabbah.
But David stayed in Jerusalem.
2One night he couldn't get to sleep and
went for a stroll on the roof of the palace. As
he looked out over the city, he noticed a
woman of unusual beauty taking her evening
bath. 3He sent to find out who she was and
was told that she was Bathsheba, the daughter
of Eliam and the wife of Uriah. 4Then David
sent for her and when she came he slept with
her. (She had just completed the purification
rites after menstruation.) Then she returned
home. 5When she found that he had gotten
her pregnant she sent a message to inform
him.
6So David dispatched a memo to Joab:
"Send me Uriah the Hittite." 7When he arrived, David asked him how Joab and the
army were getting along and how the war was
prospering. 8Then he told him to go home
and relax, and he sent a present to him at his
home. 9But Uriah didn't go there. He stayed
that night at the gateway of the palace with
the other servants of the king.
10When David heard what Uriah had done,
he summoned him and asked him, "What's
the matter with you? Why didn't you go
home to your wife last night after being away
for so long?"
11Uriah replied, "The Ark and the armies
and the general and his officers are camping
out in open fields, and should I go home to
wine and dine and sleep with my wife? I swear
that I will never be guilty of acting like that."

10:11-12 Joab gave wise counsel to Abishai before going to battle. First he devised a simple strategy of attack. Then he recognized God's role in the process. As we struggle with our adversaries, these principles can prove helpful. First we need a plan or program to follow; God's Word is filled with valuable insights for healthy living. We also need to recognize that no matter how good our plan, we still need God's help if we are going to succeed. God wants us to have victory—"May the Lord's will be done."

11:1-5 David chose to stay home and rest instead of leading his men into battle. That was his first mistake. Then, on a sleepless night, the king saw Bathsheba bathing on a nearby rooftop. David didn't have to watch her; he chose to do so. After indulging his visual lust, David gratified his sexual desire. He fell into the sin of adultery. It is the idle times in life that frequently get us into trouble (Proverbs 16:27). Staying busy with healthy activities can do much to protect us from temptation. We are also reminded to diligently guard what we allow ourself to watch or think about. Failure in our thought life will usually lead to a fall.

11:14-17 Since Uriah refused to sleep with his wife, which would have covered for Bathsheba's adulterous pregnancy, David engineered his death. One hidden sin almost always leads to another. Only when we confess our sins, bringing them out into the open, can we be free of the destructive cycle. In recovery we are called upon to admit our wrongs to God, ourself, and another person. This is an important step in breaking free from our past failures.

12"Well, stay here tonight," David told him, "and tomorrow you may return to the army."

So Uriah stayed around the palace. 13David invited him to dinner and got him drunk; but even so he didn't go home that night, but again he slept at the entry to the palace.

14Finally the next morning David wrote a letter to Joab and gave it to Uriah to deliver. 15The letter instructed Joab to put Uriah at the front of the hottest part of the battle—and then pull back and leave him there to die! 16So Joab assigned Uriah to a spot close to the besieged city where he knew that the enemies' best men were fighting; 17and Uriah was killed along with several other Israeli soldiers.

18When Joab sent a report to David of how the battle was going, 19-21he told his messenger, "If the king is angry and asks, 'Why did the troops go so close to the city? Didn't they know there would be shooting from the walls? Wasn't Abimelech killed at Thebez by a woman who threw down a millstone on him?'—then tell him, 'Uriah was killed too.'"

22So the messenger arrived at Jerusalem and gave the report to David.

23"The enemy came out against us," he said, "and as we chased them back to the city gates, 24the men on the wall attacked us; and some of our men were killed, and Uriah the Hittite is dead too."

25"Well, tell Joab not to be discouraged," David said. "The sword kills one as well as another! Fight harder next time, and conquer the city; tell him he is doing well."

26When Bathsheba heard that her husband was dead, she mourned for him; 27then, when the period of mourning was over, David sent for her and brought her to the palace and she became one of his wives; and she gave birth to his son. But the Lord was very displeased with what David had done.

CHAPTER 12

Nathan Confronts David

So the Lord sent the prophet Nathan to tell David this story:

"There were two men in a certain city, one very rich, owning many flocks of sheep and herds of goats; 3and the other very poor, owning nothing but a little lamb he had managed to buy. It was his children's pet, and he fed it from his own plate and let it drink from his own cup; he cuddled it in his arms like a baby daughter. 4Recently a guest arrived at the home of the rich man. But instead of killing a lamb from his own flocks for food for the traveler, he took the poor man's lamb and roasted it and served it."

5David was furious. "I swear by the living God," he vowed, "any man who would do a thing like that should be put to death; 6he shall repay four lambs to the poor man for the one he stole and for having no pity."

7Then Nathan said to David, "*You* are that rich man! The Lord God of Israel says, 'I made you king of Israel and saved you from the power of Saul. 8I gave you his palace and his wives and the kingdoms of Israel and Judah; and if that had not been enough, I would have given you much, much more. 9Why, then, have you despised the laws of God and done this horrible deed? For you have murdered Uriah and stolen his wife. 10Therefore murder shall be a constant threat in your family from this time on because you have insulted me by taking Uriah's wife. 11I vow that because of what you have done, I will cause your own household to rebel against you. I will give your wives to another man, and he will go to bed with them in public view. 12You did it secretly, but I will do this to you openly, in the sight of all Israel.'"

13"I have sinned against the Lord," David confessed to Nathan.

Then Nathan replied, "Yes, but the Lord has forgiven you, and you won't die for this sin. 14But you have given great opportunity to the enemies of the Lord to despise and blaspheme him, so your child shall die."

David and Bathsheba's Baby Dies

15Then Nathan returned to his home. And the Lord made Bathsheba's baby deathly sick. 16David begged him to spare the child and went without food, and lay all night before the Lord on the bare earth. 17The leaders of the nation pleaded with him to get up and eat with them, but he refused. 18Then, on the

---

12:1-7 God chose his prophet Nathan to intervene after David's failure. Notice how Nathan used a story to broach the topic with David. Then, when David had become emotionally involved, Nathan turned to direct confrontation: "*You* are that rich man!" Nathan hoped that this piercing declaration would help David realize the serious nature of his sin and bring him to repentance. Nathan's wise intervention should serve as a model for us. He confronted David with the terrible reality of his acts, but he did it in such a way that David would listen. Part of our recovery calls us to participate in the recovery of others; wise intervention is a part of this task.

seventh day, the baby died. David's aides were afraid to tell him.

"He was so broken up about the baby being sick," they said, "what will he do to himself when we tell him the child is dead?"

[19]But when David saw them whispering, he realized what had happened.

"Is the baby dead?" he asked.

"Yes," they replied, "he is." [20]Then David got up off the ground, washed himself, brushed his hair, changed his clothes, and went into the Tabernacle and worshiped the Lord. Then he returned to the palace and ate. [21]His aides were amazed.

"We don't understand you," they told him. "While the baby was still living, you wept and refused to eat; but now that the baby is dead, you have stopped your mourning and are eating again."

[22]David replied, "I fasted and wept while the child was alive, for I said, 'Perhaps the Lord will be gracious to me and let the child live.' [23]But why should I fast when he is dead? Can I bring him back again? I shall go to him, but he shall not return to me."

[24]Then David comforted Bathsheba; and when he slept with her, she conceived and gave birth to a son and named him Solomon. And the Lord loved the baby, [25]and sent congratulations and blessings through Nathan the prophet. David nicknamed the baby Jedidiah (meaning, "Beloved of Jehovah") because of the Lord's interest.

David Defeats the Ammonites

[26,27]Meanwhile Joab and the Israeli army were successfully ending their siege of Rabbah the capital of Ammon. Joab sent messengers to tell David, "Rabbah and its beautiful harbor are ours! [28]Now bring the rest of the army and finish the job, so that you will get the credit for the victory instead of me."

[29,30]So David led his army to Rabbah and captured it. Tremendous amounts of loot were carried back to Jerusalem, and David took the king of Rabbah's crown—a $50,000 treasure made from solid gold set with gems—and placed it on his own head. [31]He made slaves of the people of the city and made them labor with saws, picks, and axes and work in the brick kilns; that is the way he treated all of the cities of the Ammonites. Then David and the army returned to Jerusalem.

CHAPTER 13

Amnon Rapes Tamar

Prince Absalom, David's son, had a beautiful sister named Tamar. And Prince Amnon (her half brother) fell desperately in love with her. [2]Amnon became so tormented by his love for her that he became ill. He had no way of talking to her, for the girls and young men were kept strictly apart. [3]But Amnon had a very crafty friend—his cousin Jonadab (the son of David's brother Shimeah).

[4]One day Jonadab said to Amnon, "What's the trouble? Why should the son of a king look so haggard morning after morning?"

So Amnon told him, "I am in love with Tamar, my half sister."

[5]"Well," Jonadab said, "I'll tell you what to do. Go back to bed and pretend you are sick; when your father comes to see you, ask him to let Tamar come and prepare some food for you. Tell him you'll feel better if she feeds you."

[6]So Amnon did. And when the king came

12:29-31 After the death of Bathsheba's child, David returned to action. By leading the attack upon Rabbah, he had returned to his proper role. He should have been attacking this city at the time he sinned with Bathsheba (11:1). To David's credit, even though he had made some poor choices, he made a dramatic comeback. He went back to doing the things he should have been doing all along. After a relapse, we would be wise to follow David's example.

13:14-16 Amnon's selfish lust brought some terrible consequences. Tamar's future was destroyed, and her hopes for a good marriage were dashed. Amnon had to live with his guilt, and he soon would be murdered for his actions (13:29). Amnon also discovered the bitter taste of sexual activity driven by selfish desire. His self-centered "love" turned to hate within minutes. These contradictory feelings are often experienced by people in the throes of an addiction. Alternately we embrace and despise the activity or substance that controls us.

13:21-24 David was enraged when he first heard of Amnon's sin, but he never did anything about it. Perhaps he felt uncomfortable confronting Amnon, since he also had failed in this area. David's failure to intervene allowed the problem to fester, and eventually it exploded when Absalom murdered Amnon to avenge his sister's rape (13:29). When someone close to us acts irresponsibly, it is easy to allow our initial rage or concern to subside. Selective denial is often easier for us than confrontation. This was how David handled Amnon's sin, but the consequences to his family were devastating.

to see him, Amnon asked him for this favor—
that his sister Tamar be permitted to come
and cook a little something for him to eat.
7David agreed and sent word to Tamar to go
to Amnon's quarters and prepare some food
for him. 8So she did and went into his bedroom so that he could watch her mix some
dough; then she baked some special bread for
him. 9But when she set the serving tray before
him, he refused to eat!
"Everyone get out of here," he told his
servants; so they all left the apartment.
10Then he said to Tamar, "Now bring me the
food again here in my bedroom and feed it to
me." So Tamar took it to him. 11But as she was
standing there before him, he grabbed her
and demanded, "Come to bed with me, my
darling."
12"Oh, Amnon," she cried. "Don't be foolish! Don't do this to me! You know what a
serious crime it is in Israel. 13Where could I go
in my shame? And you would be called one
of the greatest fools in Israel. Please, just speak
to the king about it, for he will let you marry
me."
14But he wouldn't listen to her; and since he
was stronger than she, he forced her. 15Then
suddenly his love turned to hate, and now he
hated her more than he had loved her.
"Get out of here!" he snarled at her.
16"No, no!" she cried. "To reject me now is
a greater crime than the other you did to me."
But he wouldn't listen to her. 17,18He
shouted for his valet and demanded, "Throw
this woman out and lock the door behind
her."
So he put her out. She was wearing a long
robe with sleeves, as was the custom in those
days for virgin daughters of the king. 19Now
she tore the robe and put ashes on her head
and with her head in her hands went away
crying.

Absalom Murders Amnon

20Her brother Absalom asked her, "Is it true
that Amnon raped you? Don't be so upset,
since it's all in the family anyway. It's not
anything to worry about!"
So Tamar lived as a desolate woman in her
brother Absalom's quarters.
21-24When King David heard what had happened, he was very angry, but Absalom said
nothing one way or the other about this to
Amnon. However, he hated him with a deep
hatred because of what he had done to his
sister. Then, two years later, when Absalom's
sheep were being sheared at Baal-hazor in

Honesty

READ 2 SAMUEL 13:1-24

When the injustices experienced in the past cause us pain, we often seek to bury them in the deep recesses of our mind. Being dishonest with ourselves in this way, however, almost always allows pain from the past to translate into mistakes and suffering in the future. We often become powerless over the strength of our inner turmoil. We lose control of the very feelings we have tried to hide.

Absalom became powerless over his hatred and rage. It ultimately controlled his life to the point that he fought to overthrow his father's rule. He was outraged when his half brother raped his sister, Tamar. When King David did nothing to avenge his daughter, Absalom vowed revenge in his heart. He waited until the time was right and murdered the guilty brother. This sequence of abuse, family secrecy, denial, unprocessed feelings, and revenge destroyed Absalom's relationship with his father. He never forgave David and died in a military rebellion against him (2 Samuel 13:1–18:33).

We may use our addictive/compulsive behaviors to distract us from the unresolved pain within us. There may be so many strong emotions, which we don't know how to process appropriately, that we simply try to stuff them down inside. Eventually these feelings are expressed in some way. We need to be honest about our past hurts, express our feelings, convict the guilty, and work through forgiveness. If we try to ignore them, we will be controlled by our explosive hidden emotions. ***Turn to page 403, 1 Kings 19.***

Ephraim, Absalom invited his father and all
his brothers to come to a feast to celebrate the
occasion.
25The king replied, "No, my boy; if we all
came, we would be too much of a burden on
you."
Absalom pressed him, but he wouldn't
come, though he sent his thanks.
26"Well, then," Absalom said, "if you can't
come, how about sending my brother Amnon
instead?"
"Why Amnon?" the king asked.
27Absalom kept on urging the matter until
finally the king agreed and let all of his sons
attend, including Amnon.
28Absalom told his men, "Wait until Amnon gets drunk, then, at my signal, kill him!
Don't be afraid. I'm the one who gives the
orders around here, and this is a command.
Take courage and do it!"
29,30So they murdered Amnon. Then the
other sons of the king jumped on their mules
and fled. As they were on the way back to
Jerusalem, the report reached David: "Absalom has killed all of your sons, and not one is
left alive!"
31The king jumped up, ripped off his robe,
and fell prostrate to the ground. His aides also
tore their clothes in horror and sorrow.
32,33But just then Jonadab (the son of
David's brother Shimeah) arrived and said,
"No, not all have been killed! It was only
Amnon! Absalom has been plotting this ever
since Amnon raped Tamar. No, no! Your sons
aren't all dead! It was only Amnon."
34Meanwhile Absalom escaped. Now the
watchman on the Jerusalem wall saw a great
crowd coming toward the city along the road
at the side of the hill.
35"See!" Jonadab told the king. "There
they are now! Your sons are coming, just as
I said."
36They soon arrived, weeping and sobbing, and the king and his officials wept
with them. 37-39Absalom fled to King Talmai
of Geshur (the son of Ammihud) and stayed
there three years. Meanwhile David, now
reconciled to Amnon's death, longed day
after day for fellowship with his son Absalom.

CHAPTER 14

A Woman Intercedes for Absalom

When General Joab realized how much the
king was longing to see Absalom, 2,3 he sent for
a woman of Tekoa who had a reputation for
great wisdom and told her to ask for an appointment with the king. He told her what to
say to him.
"Pretend you are in mourning," Joab instructed her. "Wear mourning clothes, and
dishevel your hair as though you have been
in deep sorrow for a long time."
4When the woman approached the king,
she fell face downward on the floor in front
of him, and cried out, "O king! Help me!"
5,6"What's the trouble?" he asked.
"I am a widow," she replied, "and my two
sons had a fight out in the field, and since no
one was there to part them, one of them was
killed. 7Now the rest of the family is demanding that I surrender my other son to them to
be executed for murdering his brother. But if
I do that, I will have no one left, and my
husband's name will be destroyed from the
face of the earth."
8"Leave it with me," the king told her. "I'll
see to it that no one touches him."
9"Oh, thank you, my lord," she replied.
"And I'll take the responsibility if you are
criticized for helping me like this."
10"Don't worry about that!" the king replied. "If anyone objects, bring him to me; I
can assure you he will never complain again!"
11Then she said, "Please swear to me by God
that you won't let anyone harm my son. I
want no more bloodshed."
"I vow by God," he replied, "that not a hair
of your son's head shall be disturbed!"
12"Please let me ask one more thing of you!"
she said.
"Go ahead," he replied. "Speak!"
13"Why don't you do as much for all the
people of God as you have promised to do for
me?" she asked. "You have convicted yourself
in making this decision, because you have
refused to bring home your own banished son.
14All of us must die eventually; our lives are like
water that is poured out on the ground—it
can't be gathered up again. But God will bless
you with a longer life if you will find a way to

14:1-20 Joab, with the help of a woman from Tekoa, intervened in the conflict between David and Absalom. When we are living in denial, ignoring a festering problem in our life, God often uses other people to confront us with the real issues. The wise woman gently opened David's eyes to the situation and called him to restore his relationship with Absalom. David humbly listened and took steps to bring Absalom home from exile. When God provides wise counsel, we would be wise to humbly listen and then act accordingly.

AMNON & TAMAR

People can be destroyed emotionally by rape, incest, or any kind of sexual abuse. Breaking God's laws concerning sexual behavior always causes devastation in people's lives. One tragic example of this is the scandal between Amnon and Tamar.

Amnon was David's oldest son, and Tamar was Amnon's half sister. Amnon's sin began in his imagination. He chose to nurture his fantasy until he shared it with a cousin, who suggested a way to make this fantasy a reality. Then he chose to satisfy his desire, and he raped Tamar. He blinded himself to the consequences that were sure to follow.

Tamar felt violated, abandoned, and full of shame. Amnon's fleeting pleasure very likely cost Tamar the honorable future expected for a king's daughter. When Absalom, Tamar's full brother, was informed about what happened, he was filled with rage. Absalom plotted and then killed Amnon. Jonadab, the cousin, lost his integrity; Tamar lost her purity; Amnon lost his life; and David lost his son. These are just some of the consequences of Amnon's sin.

David headed a dysfunctional family. He failed to confront Amnon about his sin, perhaps because he had failed in a similar way with Bathsheba. Many of us know the painful consequences of being part of a family like this. Tamar's family responded to her crisis with silence, deception, rage, and denial. Amnon's sin had terrible consequences, and David's failure to deal directly with that sin only compounded the devastation.

STRENGTHS AND ACCOMPLISHMENTS:
- Though victimized, Tamar displayed strength of character.

WEAKNESSES AND MISTAKES:
- Amnon mistook lust for love, allowing temptation to overwhelm him.
- Amnon acted on some very unwise counsel.
- Amnon failed to take responsibility for his actions.
- King David was unwilling to confront the problem.

LESSONS FROM THEIR LIVES:
- All of our moral choices have long-term, even eternal, consequences.
- We must carefully consider whom to seek advice from.
- If we don't deal with sin immediately, its consequences will be compounded.
- The mistakes of parents are often repeated by their children.

KEY VERSE:
"'Oh, Amnon,' she cried. 'Don't be foolish! Don't do this to me! You know what a serious crime it is in Israel'" (2 Samuel 13:12).

The story of Amnon and Tamar is told in 2 Samuel 13. Amnon is also mentioned in 2 Samuel 3:2. Both are mentioned in David's family tree in 1 Chronicles 3.

---

bring your son back from his exile. 15,16 But I
have come to plead with you for my son
because my life and my son's life have been
threatened, and I said to myself, 'Perhaps the
king will listen to me and rescue us from those
who would end our existence in Israel. 17 Yes,
the king will give us peace again.' I know that
you are like the angel of God and can discern
good from evil. May God be with you."

18 "I want to know one thing," the king
replied.

"Yes, my lord?" she asked.

19 "Did Joab send you here?"

And the woman replied, "How can I deny
it? Yes, Joab sent me and told me what to say.
20 He did it in order to place the matter before
you in a different light. But you are as wise as
an angel of God, and you know everything
that happens!"

21 So the king sent for Joab and told him,
"All right, go and bring back Absalom."

22 Joab fell to the ground before the king and
blessed him and said, "At last I know that you
like me! For you have granted me this request!"

23 Then Joab went to Geshur and brought
Absalom back to Jerusalem.

24 "He may go to his own quarters," the king
ordered, "but he must never come here. I
refuse to see him."

Absalom Demands to See David

25 Now no one in Israel was such a handsome
specimen of manhood as Absalom, and no
one else received such praise. 26 He cut his hair
only once a year—and then only because it
weighed three pounds and was too much of a
load to carry around! 27 He had three sons and
one daughter, Tamar, who was a very beautiful girl.

28 After Absalom had been in Jerusalem for
two years and had not yet seen the king, 29 he

sent for Joab to ask him to intercede for him;
but Joab wouldn't come. Absalom sent for
him again, but again he refused to come.
30So Absalom said to his servants, "Go and
set fire to that barley field of Joab's next to
mine," and they did.
31Then Joab came to Absalom and demanded, "Why did your servants set my field
on fire?"
32And Absalom replied, "Because I wanted
you to ask the king why he brought me back
from Geshur if he didn't intend to see me. I
might as well have stayed there. Let me have
an interview with the king; then if he finds
that I am guilty of murder, let him execute
me."
33So Joab told the king what Absalom had
said. Then at last David summoned Absalom,
and he came and bowed low before the king,
and David kissed him.

CHAPTER 15
Absalom Rebels against David

Absalom then bought a magnificent chariot
and chariot horses, and hired fifty footmen to
run ahead of him. 2He got up early every
morning and went out to the gate of the city;
and when anyone came to bring a case to the
king for trial, Absalom called him over and
expressed interest in his problem.
3He would say, "I can see that you are right
in this matter; it's unfortunate that the king
doesn't have anyone to assist him in hearing
these cases. 4I surely wish I were the judge;
then anyone with a lawsuit could come to
me, and I would give him justice!"
5And when anyone came to bow to him,
Absalom wouldn't let him, but shook his
hand instead! 6So in this way Absalom stole
the hearts of all the people of Israel.
7,8After four years, Absalom said to the king,
"Let me go to Hebron to sacrifice to the Lord
in fulfillment of a vow I made to him while I
was at Geshur—that if he would bring me
back to Jerusalem, I would sacrifice to him."
9"All right," the king told him, "go and
fulfill your vow."
So Absalom went to Hebron. 10But while he
was there, he sent spies to every part of Israel
to incite rebellion against the king. "As soon
as you hear the trumpets," his message read,
"you will know that Absalom has been
crowned in Hebron." 11He took two hundred
men from Jerusalem with him as guests, but
they knew nothing of his intentions. 12While
he was offering the sacrifice, he sent for Ahithophel, one of David's counselors who lived
in Giloh. Ahithophel declared for Absalom, as
did more and more others. So the conspiracy
became very strong.
13A messenger soon arrived in Jerusalem to
tell King David, "All Israel has joined Absalom
in a conspiracy against you!"
14"Then we must flee at once or it will be
too late!" was David's instant response to his
men. "If we get out of the city before he
arrives, both we and the city of Jerusalem will
be saved."
15"We are with you," his aides replied. "Do
as you think best."
16So the king and his household set out at
once. He left no one behind except ten of his

14:28-33 Absalom had been in limbo for five years. He was exiled for three years in Geshur. Then he spent two years in Jerusalem without ever speaking to his father. Finally Absalom resorted to theatrics to force contact. He had waited long enough! Reunion with David, when it did come, was far too stilted and formal for genuine reconciliation. No tears were shed; no brokenness was evidenced; no effort was made to set things straight. The relationship between father and son was not restored. It seems that David gave Absalom only partial forgiveness. This led to bondage and bitterness and was probably worse than his giving no forgiveness at all. True forgiveness and reconciliation are an essential part of our recovery.

15:7-10 For Absalom, it had been eleven years since the rape of Tamar, nine years since his murder of Amnon, six years since his return to Jerusalem, and four years since his awkward reunion with David. He had given up hope of ever being truly reconciled with his father. Using religion as a cover, Absalom proceeded to lead an open rebellion against David. In recovery we are called to seek reconciliation with the people we have wronged. We must be careful not to delay; if we wait too long, we may suffer as David did.

15:19-22 As we face difficult trials in life, faithful friends can be our greatest asset. Ittai had led a foreign contingent of David's army for many years. As a foreigner, he could have returned to Jerusalem and declared his allegiance to Absalom. But instead, despite a probable tragic outcome, he stood by David. We need to seek out and cultivate true friends who will come alongside us, even when it would be to their advantage to leave. Sometimes the crucible of affliction helps us to see who our real friends are. It may also strengthen relationships that were not close previously, as in the case of David and Ittai.

READ 2 SAMUEL 15:1-26

GOD grant me the serenity to accept the things I cannot change the courage to change the things I can and the wisdom to know the difference AMEN

There are times in recovery when we're on top of the world; we feel as though our problem is licked for good. In such times, it is tempting to relax and stop living one day at a time. But then life surprises us with an unexpected problem.

King David had reached a pinnacle of success. He had killed giants, won battles, captured the hearts of his people, and overcome enemies on every side. While he was in this comfortable position, life surprised him with a rebellion led by his own son. Here's what happened: "A messenger soon arrived in Jerusalem to tell King David, 'All Israel has joined Absalom in a conspiracy against you!' 'Then we must flee at once or it will be too late!' was David's instant response to his men. 'If we get out of the city before he arrives, both we and the city of Jerusalem will be saved.' . . . 'If the Lord sees fit,' David said, 'he will bring me back to see the Ark and the Tabernacle again. But if he is through with me, well, let him do what seems best to him'" (2 Samuel 15:13-14, 25-26).

King David wisely accepted the reality at hand and responded to the situation as it was, not as he wished it to be. It seems that David was a little out of the habit of relying on God day by day, but he quickly placed his life back in God's hands. God did protect him and returned him to the throne in Jerusalem. When life hits us with unexpected threats, we, too, should be reminded that our life needs to be in God's hands. ***Turn to page 475, 1 Chronicles 28.***

---

young wives to keep the palace in order.
17,18 David paused at the edge of the city to let
his troops move past him to lead the way—six
hundred Gittites who had come with him
from Gath, and the Cherethites and Pelethites.
19,20 But suddenly the king turned to Ittai,
the captain of the six hundred Gittites, and
said to him, "What are you doing here? Go on
back with your men to Jerusalem, to your
king, for you are a guest in Israel, a foreigner
in exile. It seems but yesterday that you arrived, and now today should I force you to
wander with us, who knows where? Go on
back and take your troops with you, and may
the Lord be merciful to you."
21 But Ittai replied, "I vow by God and by
your own life that wherever you go, I will go,
no matter what happens—whether it means
life or death."
22 So David replied, "All right, come with
us." Then Ittai and his six hundred men and
their families went along.
23 There was deep sadness throughout the
city as the king and his retinue passed by,
crossed Kidron Brook, and went out into the
country. 24 Abiathar and Zadok and the Levites
took the Ark of the Covenant of God and set
it down beside the road until everyone had
passed. 25,26 Then, following David's instructions, Zadok took the Ark back into the city.
"If the Lord sees fit," David said, "he will bring
me back to see the Ark and the Tabernacle
again. But if he is through with me, well, let
him do what seems best to him."
27 Then the king told Zadok, "Look, here is
my plan. Return quietly to the city with your
son Ahimaaz and Abiathar's son Jonathan. 28 I
will stop at the ford of the Jordan River and
wait there for a message from you. Let me
know what happens in Jerusalem before I
disappear into the wilderness."
29 So Zadok and Abiathar carried the Ark of
God back into the city and stayed there.
30 David walked up the road that led to the
Mount of Olives, weeping as he went. His
head was covered and his feet were bare as a

sign of mourning. And the people who were with him covered their heads and wept as they climbed the mountain. 31When someone told David that Ahithophel, his advisor, was backing Absalom, David prayed, "O Lord, please make Ahithophel give Absalom foolish advice!" 32As they reached the spot at the top of the Mount of Olives where people worshiped God, David found Hushai the Archite waiting for him with torn clothing and earth upon his head.

33,34But David told him, "If you go with me, you will only be a burden; return to Jerusalem and tell Absalom, 'I will counsel you as I did your father.' Then you can frustrate and counter Ahithophel's advice. 35,36Zadok and Abiathar, the priests, are there. Tell them the plans that are being made to capture me, and they will send their sons Ahimaaz and Jonathan to find me and tell me what is going on."

37So David's friend Hushai returned to the city, getting there just as Absalom arrived.

CHAPTER 16

Ziba Joins David

David was just past the top of the hill when Ziba, the manager of Mephibosheth's household, caught up with him. He was leading two donkeys loaded with two hundred loaves of bread, one hundred clusters of raisins, one hundred bunches of grapes, and a small barrel of wine.

2"What are these for?" the king asked Ziba.

And Ziba replied, "The donkeys are for your people to ride on, and the bread and summer fruit are for the young men to eat; the wine is to be taken with you into the wilderness for any who become faint."

3"And where is Mephibosheth?" the king asked him.

"He stayed at Jerusalem," Ziba replied. "He said, 'Now I'll get to be king! Today I will get back the kingdom of my father, Saul.'"

4"In that case," the king told Ziba, "I give you everything he owns."

"Thank you, thank you, sir," Ziba replied.

Shimei Insults David

5As David and his party passed Bahurim, a man came out of the village cursing them. It was Shimei, the son of Gera, a member of Saul's family. 6He threw stones at the king and the king's officers and all the mighty warriors who surrounded them!

7,8"Get out of here, you murderer, you scoundrel!" he shouted at David. "The Lord is paying you back for murdering King Saul and his family; you stole his throne and now the Lord has given it to your son Absalom! At last you will taste some of your own medicine, you murderer!"

9"Why should this dead dog curse my lord the king?" Abishai demanded. "Let me go over and strike off his head!"

10"No!" the king said. "If the Lord has told him to curse me, who am I to say no? 11My own son is trying to kill me, and this Benjaminite is merely cursing me. Let him alone, for no doubt the Lord has told him to do it. 12And perhaps the Lord will see that I am being wronged and will bless me because of these curses."

13So David and his men continued on, and Shimei kept pace with them on a nearby hillside, cursing as he went and throwing stones at David and tossing dust into the air. 14The king and all those who were with him were weary by the time they reached Bahurim, so they stayed there awhile and rested.

Absalom Seizes the Throne

15Meanwhile, Absalom and his men arrived at Jerusalem, accompanied by Ahithophel. 16When David's friend, Hushai the Archite, arrived, he went immediately to see Absalom.

"Long live the king!" he exclaimed. "Long live the king!"

17"Is this the way to treat your friend David?" Absalom asked him. "Why aren't you with him?"

18"Because I work for the man who is chosen by the Lord and by Israel," Hushai replied. 19"And anyway, why shouldn't I? I helped your father and now I will help you!"

20Then Absalom turned to Ahithophel and asked him, "What shall I do next?"

21Ahithophel told him, "Go and sleep with your father's wives, for he has left them here to keep the house. Then all Israel will know that you have insulted him beyond the possi-

16:5-12 What did David get for thirty years of successful, sacrificial leadership? Stones and curses. Notice that David refused to seek revenge against Shimei. He was well aware of his own failures and was willing to accept Shimei's criticism. He was beyond the point of denial. At this point David put himself in God's hands, trusting that God would do what was right—whether it meant judgment or deliverance. As we experience failure in our life, we need to follow David's example. We must put ourselves in God's hands; he will always do what is best for us.

ABSALOM

Without true forgiveness, bitterness will inevitably tear our relationships apart. No relationship or family will hold together for long if the people involved are unable to grant a forgiveness characterized by both word and deed. Incomplete forgiveness can sometimes secure a semblance of peace within a family, but when that forgiveness is not evidenced by the way we live, true reconciliation will never result. Absalom, the third son of King David, suffered much and also caused much suffering because true forgiveness was not a part of his life.

Early in his life, Absalom discovered that his sister, Tamar, had been raped by his half brother Amnon. Absalom harbored hatred toward Amnon for a period of two years until he was able to kill him. Soon thereafter, Absalom fled to the protection of his grandfather Talmai, king of Geshur, in order to avoid the wrath of his father, David. After three years of separation, David relented and permitted Absalom to return to Jerusalem, but it wasn't until two years later that David finally spoke with Absalom. Apparently little was said between them, and David continued to ignore his son.

Although there was much weeping at the reunion of David and Absalom, the scars of isolation ran deep. Absalom was never able to regain the love he once had for his father, nor the relationship he longed for. In fact, Absalom spent the rest of his life scheming against his father; his life ended while he led a rebellion against King David. Absalom is an example of the wasted years and the broken hearts that can result when we fail to deal directly and decisively with major issues within our families.

WEAKNESSES AND MISTAKES:
- Absalom never once turned to God for guidance.
- Absalom took the law into his own hands.
- Absalom harbored hatred against those who crossed him.

LESSONS FROM HIS LIFE:
- Incomplete forgiveness destroys relationships.
- Words of forgiveness must be proven by action.
- Delaying forgiveness may render reconciliation almost impossible.
- The sins of parents are often repeated by their children.

KEY VERSE:
"However, [Absalom] hated [Amnon] with a deep hatred because of what he had done to his sister" (2 Samuel 13:21-24).

Absalom's story is told in 2 Samuel 13–19. He is also mentioned in 2 Samuel 3:3 and 1 Chronicles 3:2.

---

bility of reconciliation, and they will all close ranks behind you."
22So a tent was erected on the roof of the palace where everybody could see it, and Absalom went into the tent to lie with his father's wives. 23(Absalom did whatever Ahithophel told him to, just as David had; for every word Ahithophel spoke seemed as wise as though it had come directly from the mouth of God.)

CHAPTER 17
Absalom Follows Bad Advice
"Now," Ahithophel said, "give me twelve thousand men to start out after David tonight. 2,3I will come upon him while he is weary and discouraged, and he and his troops will be thrown into a panic and everyone will run away; and I will kill only the king and let all those who are with him live, and restore them to you."
4Absalom and all the elders of Israel approved of the plan, 5but Absalom said, "Ask Hushai the Archite what he thinks about this."
6When Hushai arrived, Absalom told him what Ahithophel had said.

"What is your opinion?" Absalom asked him. "Should we follow Ahithophel's advice? If not, speak up."
7"Well," Hushai replied, "this time I think Ahithophel has made a mistake. 8You know your father and his men; they are mighty warriors and are probably as upset as a mother bear who has been robbed of her cubs. And your father is an old soldier and isn't going to be spending the night among the troops; 9he has probably already hidden in some pit or

cave. And when he comes out and attacks and
a few of your men fall, there will be panic
among your troops and everyone will start
shouting that your men are being slaughtered. 10Then even the bravest of them,
though they have hearts of lions, will be paralyzed with fear; for all Israel knows what a
mighty man your father is and how courageous his soldiers are.
11"What I suggest is that you mobilize the
entire army of Israel, bringing them from as
far away as Dan and Beersheba, so that you
will have a huge force. And I think that you
should personally lead the troops. 12Then
when we find him we can destroy his entire
army so that not one of them is left alive.
13And if David has escaped into some city, you
will have the entire army of Israel there at
your command, and we can take ropes and
drag the walls of the city into the nearest
valley until every stone is torn down."
14Then Absalom and all the men of Israel
said, "Hushai's advice is better than Ahithophel's." For the Lord had arranged to defeat
the counsel of Ahithophel, which really was
the better plan, so that he could bring disaster
upon Absalom!15Then Hushai reported to Zadok and Abiathar, the priests, what Ahithophel had said and what he himself had
suggested instead.
16"Quick!" he told them. "Find David and
urge him not to stay at the ford of the Jordan
River tonight. He must go across at once into
the wilderness beyond; otherwise he will die,
and his entire army with him."
17Jonathan and Ahimaaz had been staying
at En-rogel so as not to be seen entering and
leaving the city. Arrangements had been
made for a servant girl to carry to them the
messages they were to take to King David.
18But a boy saw them leaving En-rogel to go to
David, and he told Absalom about it. Meanwhile, they escaped to Bahurim where a man
hid them inside a well in his backyard. 19The
man's wife put a cloth over the top of the well
with grain on it to dry in the sun; so no one
suspected they were there.
20When Absalom's men arrived and asked
her if she had seen Ahimaaz and Jonathan,
she said they had crossed the brook and were
gone. They looked for them without success
and returned to Jerusalem. 21Then the two
men crawled out of the well and hurried on
to King David. "Quick!" they told him, "cross
the Jordan tonight!" And they told him how
Ahithophel had advised that he be captured
and killed. 22So David and all the people with
him went across during the night and were all
on the other bank before dawn.
23Meanwhile, Ahithophel—publicly disgraced when Absalom refused his advice—
saddled his donkey, went to his hometown,
set his affairs in order, and hanged himself; so
he died and was buried beside his father.
24David soon arrived at Mahanaim. Meanwhile, Absalom had mobilized the entire
army of Israel and was leading the men across
the Jordan River. 25Absalom had appointed
Amasa as general of the army, replacing Joab.
(Amasa was Joab's second cousin; his father
was Ithra, an Ishmaelite, and his mother was
Abigail, the daughter of Nahash, who was the
sister of Joab's mother, Zeruiah.) 26Absalom
and the Israeli army now camped in the land
of Gilead.
27When David arrived at Mahanaim, he was
warmly greeted by Shobi (son of Nahash of
Rabbah, an Ammonite) and Machir (son of
Ammiel of Lodebar) and Barzillai (a Gileadite
of Rogelim). 28,29They brought him and those
who were with him mats to sleep on, cooking
pots, serving bowls, wheat and barley flour,
parched grain, beans, lentils, honey, butter,
and cheese. For they said, "You must be very
tired and hungry and thirsty after your long
march through the wilderness."

CHAPTER 18

Joab Kills Absalom

David now appointed regimental colonels
and company commanders over his troops.
2A third were placed under Joab's brother,
Abishai (the son of Zeruiah); and a third under Ittai, the Gittite. The king planned to lead
the army himself, but his men objected
strongly.
3"You mustn't do it," they said, "for if we
have to turn and run, and half of us die, it will
make no difference to them—they will be
looking only for you. You are worth ten thousand of us, and it is better that you stay here
in the city and send us help if we need it."

17:14 No matter how strong our enemies, they can never thwart God's plan. God used Hushai to lead Absalom toward disaster. God was working behind the scenes to protect David and give him a chance to recover his losses. As we continue in the recovery process, God will accomplish his purposes for us. And we can trust that he will work behind the scenes on our behalf, supporting our recovery in ways we'll never know.

4"Well, whatever you think best," the king
finally replied. So he stood at the gate of the
city as all the troops passed by.
5And the king commanded Joab, Abishai,
and Ittai, "For my sake, deal gently with
young Absalom." And all the troops heard the
king give them this charge.
6So the battle began in the forest of
Ephraim, 7and the Israeli troops were beaten
back by David's men. There was a great
slaughter and twenty thousand men laid
down their lives that day. 8The battle raged all
across the countryside, and more men disappeared in the forest than were killed. 9Dur-
ing the battle Absalom came upon some of
David's men and as he fled on his mule, it
went beneath the thick boughs of a great oak
tree, and his hair caught in the branches. His
mule went on, leaving him dangling in the
air. 10One of David's men saw him and told
Joab.
11"What? You saw him there and didn't kill
him?" Joab demanded. "I would have rewarded you handsomely and made you a
commissioned officer."
12"For a million dollars I wouldn't do it,"
the man replied. "We all heard the king say to
you and Abishai and Ittai, 'For my sake, please
don't harm young Absalom.' 13And if I had
betrayed the king by killing his son (and the
king would certainly find out who did it), you
yourself would be the first to accuse me."
14"Enough of this nonsense," Joab said.
Then he took three daggers and plunged
them into the heart of Absalom as he dangled
alive from the oak. 15Ten of Joab's young
armor-bearers then surrounded Absalom and
finished him off. 16Then Joab blew the trumpet, and his men returned from chasing the
army of Israel. 17They threw Absalom's body
into a deep pit in the forest and piled a great
heap of stones over it. And the army of Israel
fled to their homes.
18(Absalom had built a monument to himself in the King's Valley, for he said, "I have no
sons to carry on my name." He called it "Absalom's Monument," as it is still known today.)

David Mourns Absalom's Death

19Then Zadok's son Ahimaaz said, "Let me run
to King David with the good news that the
Lord has saved him from his enemy Absalom."
20"No," Joab told him, "it wouldn't be good
news to the king that his son is dead. You can
be my messenger some other time."
21Then Joab said to a man from Cush, "Go
tell the king what you have seen." The man
bowed and ran off.
22But Ahimaaz pleaded with Joab, "Please
let me go too."
"No, we don't need you now, my boy." Joab
replied. "There is no further news to send."
23"Yes, but let me go anyway," he begged.
And Joab finally said, "All right, go ahead."
Then Ahimaaz took a shortcut across the
plain and got there ahead of the man from
Cush. 24David was sitting at the gate of the
city. When the watchman climbed the stairs
to his post at the top of the wall, he saw a lone
man running toward them.
25He shouted the news down to David, and
the king replied, "If he is alone, he has news."
As the messenger came closer, 26the watchman saw another man running toward them.
He shouted down, "Here comes another one."
And the king replied, "He will have more
news."
27"The first man looks like Ahimaaz, the
son of Zadok," the watchman said.
"He is a good man and comes with good
news," the king replied.
28Then Ahimaaz cried out to the king, "All
is well!" He bowed low with his face to the
ground and said, "Blessed be the Lord your
God who has destroyed the rebels who dared
to stand against you."
29"What of young Absalom?" the king demanded. "Is he all right?"
"When Joab told me to come, there was a
lot of shouting; but I didn't know what was
happening," Ahimaaz answered.
30"Wait here," the king told him. So Ahimaaz stepped aside.
31Then the man from Cush arrived and
said, "I have good news for my lord the king.
Today Jehovah has rescued you from all those
who rebelled against you."

18:15 Absalom died a tragic death: a rebel and the victim of a broken relationship with his father. He was the product of an unreconciled past. If we are driven by painful emotions or events from the past, we also may end up fighting unnecessary battles and end up in an early grave. As with Absalom, we may not be completely to blame for our broken relationships. Yet we still are responsible to deal with the issues and to seek reconciliation. If we don't, we will probably destroy ourselves and bring all the people close to us down as well.

32“What about young Absalom? Is he all
right?” the king demanded.
And the man replied, “May all of your
enemies be as that young man is!”
33Then the king broke into tears, and went
up to his room over the gate, crying as he
went. “O my son Absalom, my son, my son
Absalom. If only I could have died for you! O
Absalom, my son, my son.”

CHAPTER 19

Joab Confronts David

Word soon reached Joab that the king was
weeping and mourning for Absalom. 2As the
people heard of the king’s deep grief for his
son, the joy of that day’s wonderful victory
was turned into deep sadness. 3The entire
army crept back into the city as though they
were ashamed and had been beaten in battle.
4The king covered his face with his hands
and kept on weeping, “O my son Absalom! O
Absalom my son, my son!”
5Then Joab went to the king’s room and
said to him, “We saved your life today and the
lives of your sons, your daughters, your wives,
and concubines; and yet you act like this,
making us feel ashamed, as though we had
done something wrong. 6You seem to love
those who hate you, and hate those who love
you. Apparently we don’t mean anything to
you; if Absalom had lived and all of us had
died, you would be happy. 7Now go out there
and congratulate the troops, for I swear by
Jehovah that if you don’t, not a single one of
them will remain here during the night; then
you will be worse off than you have ever been
in your entire life.”

David Returns to Jerusalem

8-10So the king went out and sat at the city
gates, and as the news spread throughout the
city that he was there, everyone went to him.
Meanwhile, there was much discussion and
argument going on all across the nation:
“Why aren’t we talking about bringing the
king back?” was the great topic everywhere.
“For he saved us from our enemies, the Philistines; and Absalom, whom we made our king
instead, chased him out of the country, but
now Absalom is dead. Let’s ask David to return and be our king again.”
11,12Then David sent Zadok and Abiathar the
priests to say to the elders of Judah, “Why are
you the last ones to reinstate the king? For all
Israel is ready, and only you are holding out.
Yet you are my own brothers, my own tribe,
my own flesh and blood!”
13And he told them to tell Amasa, “Since
you are my nephew, may God strike me dead
if I do not appoint you as commander-in-
chief of my army in place of Joab.” 14Then
Amasa convinced all the leaders of Judah, and
they responded as one man. They sent word
to the king, “Return to us and bring back all
those who are with you.”
15So the king started back to Jerusalem. And
when he arrived at the Jordan River, it seemed
as if everyone in Judah had come to Gilgal to
meet him and escort him across the river!
16Then Shimei (the son of Gera the Benjaminite), the man from Bahurim, hurried across
with the men of Judah to welcome King
David. 17A thousand men from the tribe of
Benjamin were with him, including Ziba, the
servant of Saul, and Ziba’s fifteen sons and
twenty servants; they rushed down to the
Jordan to arrive ahead of the king. 18They all
worked hard ferrying the king’s household
and troops across, and helped them in every
way they could.
As the king was crossing, Shimei fell down
before him, 19and pleaded, “My lord the king,
please forgive me and forget the terrible thing
I did when you left Jerusalem; 20for I know

18:32-33 David could have avoided this great sorrow had he been willing to forgive, to set things straight, and to restore his relationship with Absalom. David had failed to seek reconciliation, and now it was too late. He could never have Absalom back; he could never make things right with him. Once again, as earlier with Amnon, we see that the consequences of sin live long after the act itself. We also see the importance of reconciliation if we want to build a peaceful future.

19:5-7 Joab was courageous enough to confront David about his improper behavior. David had failed to thank his men for standing loyal to him throughout the civil war. They deserved grateful congratulations. Instead, David was mourning the loss of his son, who had also been his enemy. Joab’s intervention probably saved David’s still-shaky kingdom. The criticism of a friend is sometimes the right medicine to prompt us to proper action (Proverbs 27:6).

19:18-20 Shimei, trying to reconcile his relationship with King David, asked that David forgive and forget the stones and insults he had hurled during Absalom’s rebellion. Shimei wanted to be set free from the burden of his past mistakes, so he could build for a solid future. God offers us this kind of forgiveness when we come to his Son, Jesus. Through him our sins are forgiven and forgotten; we are given the opportunity to start over again with a clean slate.

very well how much I sinned. That is why I
have come here today, the very first person in
all the tribe of Joseph to greet you."
[21]Abishai asked, "Shall not Shimei die, for
he cursed the Lord's chosen king!"
[22]"Don't talk to me like that!" David exclaimed. "This is not a day for execution but
for celebration! I am once more king of Israel!"
[23]Then, turning to Shimei, he vowed, "Your
life is spared."
[24,25]Now Mephibosheth, Saul's grandson,
arrived from Jerusalem to meet the king. He
had not washed his feet or clothes nor
trimmed his beard since the day the king left
Jerusalem.
"Why didn't you come with me, Mephibosheth?" the king asked him.
[26]And he replied, "My lord, O king, my
servant Ziba deceived me. I told him, 'Saddle
my donkey so that I can go with the king.' For
as you know I am lame. [27]But Ziba has slandered me by saying that I refused to come. But
I know that you are as an angel of God, so do
what you think best. [28]I and all my relatives
could expect only death from you, but instead you have honored me among all those
who eat at your own table! So how can I
complain?"
[29]"All right," David replied. "My decision is
that you and Ziba will divide the land equally
between you."
[30]"Give him all of it," Mephibosheth said.
"I am content just to have you back again!"
[31,32]Barzillai, who had fed the king and his
army during their exile in Mahanaim, arrived
from Rogelim to conduct the king across the
river. He was very old now, about eighty, and
very wealthy.
[33]"Come across with me and live in Jerusalem," the king said to Barzillai. "I will take
care of you there."
[34]"No," he replied, "I am far too old for that.
[35]I am eighty years old today, and life has lost
its excitement. Food and wine are no longer
tasty, and entertainment is not much fun; I
would only be a burden to my lord the king.
[36]Just to go across the river with you is all the
honor I need! [37]Then let me return again to
die in my own city, where my father and
mother are buried. But here is Chimham. Let
him go with you and receive whatever good
things you want to give him."
[38]"Good," the king agreed. "Chimham shall
go with me, and I will do for him whatever I
would have done for you."
[39]So all the people crossed the Jordan with
the king; and after David had kissed and
blessed Barzillai, he returned home. [40]The
king then went on to Gilgal, taking Chimham
with him. And most of Judah and half of
Israel were there to greet him.[41]But the men of
Israel complained to the king because only
men from Judah had ferried him and his
household across the Jordan.
[42]"Why not?" the men of Judah replied.
"The king is one of our own tribe. Why
should this make you angry? We have
charged him nothing—he hasn't fed us or
given us gifts!"
[43]"But there are ten tribes in Israel," the
others replied, "so we have ten times as much
right in the king as you do; why didn't you
invite the rest of us? And, remember, we were
the first to speak of bringing him back to be
our king again."
The argument continued back and forth,
and the men of Judah were very rough in their
replies.

CHAPTER 20

Sheba Rebels against David

Then a hothead whose name was Sheba (son
of Bichri, a Benjaminite) blew a trumpet and
yelled, "We want nothing to do with David.
Come on, you men of Israel, let's get out of
here. He's not our king!"
[2]So all except Judah and Benjamin turned
around and deserted David and followed
Sheba! But the men of Judah stayed with their
king, accompanying him from the Jordan to
Jerusalem. [3]When he arrived at his palace in
Jerusalem, the king instructed that his ten
wives he had left to keep house should be
placed in seclusion. Their needs were to be
cared for, he said, but he would no longer
sleep with them as his wives. So they remained in virtual widowhood until their
deaths.
[4]Then the king instructed Amasa to mobilize the army of Judah within three days and
to report back at that time. [5]So Amasa went
out to notify the troops, but it took him
longer than the three days he had been given.
[6]Then David said to Abishai, "That fellow
Sheba is going to hurt us more than Absalom
did. Quick, take my bodyguard and chase
after him before he gets into a fortified city
where we can't reach him."
[7]So Abishai and Joab set out after Sheba
with an elite guard from Joab's army and the
king's own bodyguard. [8-10]As they arrived at
the great stone in Gibeon, they came face to
face with Amasa. Joab was wearing his uni-

form with a dagger strapped to his side. As he stepped forward to greet Amasa, he stealthily slipped the dagger from its sheath. "I'm glad to see you, my brother," Joab said, and took him by the beard with his right hand as though to kiss him. Amasa didn't notice the dagger in his left hand, and Joab stabbed him in the stomach with it, so that his bowels gushed out onto the ground. He did not need to strike again, and he died there. Joab and his brother, Abishai, left him lying there and continued after Sheba.

11One of Joab's young officers shouted to Amasa's troops, "If you are for David, come and follow Joab."

12But Amasa lay in his blood in the middle of the road, and when Joab's young officers saw that a crowd was gathering around to stare at him, they dragged him off the road into a field and threw a garment over him. 13With the body out of the way, everyone went on with Joab to capture Sheba.

14Meanwhile Sheba had traveled across Israel to mobilize his own clan of Bichri at the city of Abel in Beth-maacah. 15When Joab's forces arrived, they besieged Abel and built a mound to the top of the city wall and began battering it down.

16But a wise woman in the city called out to Joab, "Listen to me, Joab. Come over here so I can talk to you."

17As he approached, the woman asked, "Are you Joab?"

And he replied, "I am."

18So she told him, "There used to be a saying, 'If you want to settle an argument, ask advice at Abel.' For we always give wise counsel. 19You are destroying an ancient, peace-loving city, loyal to Israel. Should you destroy what is the Lord's?"

20And Joab replied, "That isn't it at all. 21All I want is a man named Sheba from the hill country of Ephraim, who has revolted against King David. If you will deliver him to me, we will leave the city in peace."

"All right," the woman replied, "we will throw his head over the wall to you."

22Then the woman went to the people with her wise advice, and they cut off Sheba's head and threw it out to Joab. And he blew the trumpet and called his troops back from the attack, and they returned to the king at Jerusalem.

23Joab was commander-in-chief of the army, and Benaiah was in charge of the king's bodyguard. 24Adoram was in charge of the forced labor battalions, and Jehoshaphat was the historian who kept the records. 25Sheva was the secretary, and Zadok and Abiathar were the chief priests. 26Ira the Jairite was David's personal chaplain.

CHAPTER 21

Saul's Sons Are Executed

There was a famine during David's reign that lasted year after year for three years, and David spent much time in prayer about it. Then the Lord said, "The famine is because of the guilt of Saul and his family, for they murdered the Gibeonites."

2So King David summoned the Gibeonites. They were not part of Israel but were what was left of the nation of the Amorites. Israel had sworn not to kill them; but Saul, in his nationalistic zeal, had tried to wipe them out.

3David asked them, "What can I do for you to rid ourselves of this guilt and to induce you to ask God to bless us?"

4"Well, money won't do it," the Gibeonites replied, "and we don't want to see Israelites executed in revenge."

"What can I do, then?" David asked. "Just tell me and I will do it for you."

5,6"Well, then," they replied, "give us seven of Saul's sons—the sons of the man who did his best to destroy us. We will hang them before the Lord in Gibeon, the city of King Saul."

"All right," the king said, "I will do it."

7He spared Jonathan's son Mephibosheth, who was Saul's grandson, because of the oath between himself and Jonathan. 8But he gave them Saul's two sons Armoni and Mephibosheth, whose mother was Rizpah, the daughter of Aiah. He also gave them the five adopted sons of Michal that she brought up for Saul's daughter Merab, the wife of Adriel. 9The men of Gibeon impaled them in the mountain before the Lord. So all seven of them died together at the beginning of the barley harvest.

10Then Rizpah, the mother of two of the men, spread sackcloth upon a rock and stayed there through the entire harvest season to

---

21:1-14 The land of Israel suffered a drought because King Saul had broken a treaty with the Gibeonites. The consequences of Saul's mistake lingered on, long after he had perpetrated it. Sometimes we allow things to remain hidden in our life that serve as barriers to God's blessings. We need to take steps to remove these barriers. When the Israelites did this, God answered prayers on behalf of the land and its people.

prevent the vultures from tearing at their bodies during the day and the wild animals from
eating them at night. 11When David learned
what she had done, 12-14he arranged for the
men's bones to be buried in the grave of Saul's
father, Kish. At the same time he sent a request to the men of Jabesh-gilead, asking
them to bring him the bones of Saul and
Jonathan. They had stolen their bodies from
the public square at Beth-shan where the Philistines had impaled them after they had died
in battle on Mount Gilboa. So their bones
were brought to him. Then at last God answered prayer and ended the famine.

Victories by David's Men

15Once when the Philistines were at war with
Israel, and David and his men were in the
thick of the battle, David became weak and
exhausted. 16Ishbi-benob, a giant whose
speartip weighed more than twelve pounds
and who was sporting a new suit of armor,
closed in on David and was about to kill him.
17But Abishai, the son of Zeruiah, came to his
rescue and killed the Philistine. After that
David's men declared, "You are not going out
to battle again! Why should we risk snuffing
out the light of Israel?"

18Later, during a war with the Philistines at
Gob, Sibbecai the Hushathite killed Saph, another giant. 19At still another time and at the
same place, Elhanan killed the brother of Goliath the Gittite, whose spearhandle was as
huge as a weaver's beam! 20,21And once when
the Philistines and the Israelis were fighting at
Gath, a giant with six fingers on each hand
and six toes on each foot defied Israel, and
David's nephew Jonathan—the son of David's
brother Shimei—killed him. 22These four were
from the tribe of giants in Gath and were
killed by David's troops.

CHAPTER 22

David's Song of Praise

David sang this song to the Lord after he had rescued him from Saul and from all his other enemies:

2"Jehovah is my rock,
My fortress and my Savior.
3I will hide in God,
Who is my rock and my refuge.
He is my shield
And my salvation,
My refuge and high tower.
Thank you, O my Savior,
For saving me from all my enemies.
4I will call upon the Lord,
Who is worthy to be praised;
He will save me from all my enemies.
5The waves of death surrounded me;
Floods of evil burst upon me;
6I was trapped and bound
By hell and death;
7But I called upon the Lord in my distress,
And he heard me from his Temple.
My cry reached his ears.
8Then the earth shook and trembled;
The foundations of the heavens quaked
Because of his wrath.
9Smoke poured from his nostrils;
Fire leaped from his mouth
And burned up all before him,
Setting fire to the world.
10He bent the heavens down and came to earth;
He walked upon dark clouds.
11He rode upon the glorious—
On the wings of the wind.
12Darkness surrounded him,
And clouds were thick around him;
13The earth was radiant with his brightness.
14The Lord thundered from heaven;
The God above all gods gave out a mighty shout.
15He shot forth his arrows of lightning
And routed his enemies.
16By the blast of his breath
Was the sea split in two.
The bottom of the sea appeared.
17From above, he rescued me.
He drew me out from the waters;
18He saved me from powerful enemies,

21:16-17 The acceptance of our limitations is a critical mark of maturity. David acknowledged his diminishing physical strength and agreed to stay away from battle. Sometimes our pride will not allow us to admit our limitations. As a result, we try to do things we are not capable of doing. We might think we are strong enough to sustain our recovery, even in unsafe contexts. Such an attitude will only lead to a fall. We would be wise to follow David and admit there are certain things we cannot and should not try to do.

22:1 Near the close of his life, David still had a song. You can't sing in a storm until you have surrendered to God's sovereignty. This chapter records lyrics that also appear in the Psalms (Psalm 18). David's song is a celebration of his deliverance. It is this sort of unabashed, authentic praise that puts the devil to flight.

From those who hated me
And from those who were too strong for
me.
19They came upon me
In the day of my calamity,
But the Lord was my salvation.
20He set me free and rescued me,
For I was his delight.
21The Lord rewarded me for my goodness,
For my hands were clean;
22And I have not departed from my God.
23I knew his laws,
And I obeyed them.
24I was perfect in obedience
And kept myself from sin.
25That is why the Lord has done so much
for me,
For he sees that I am clean.
26You are merciful to the merciful;
You show your perfections
To the blameless.
27To those who are pure,
You show yourself pure;
But you destroy those who are evil.
28You will save those in trouble,
But you bring down the haughty;
For you watch their every move.
29O Lord, you are my light!
You make my darkness bright.
30By your power I can crush an army;
By your strength I leap over a wall.
31As for God, his way is perfect;
The word of the Lord is true.
He shields all who hide behind him.
32Our Lord alone is God;
We have no other Savior.
33God is my strong fortress;
He has made me safe.
34He causes the good to walk a steady tread
Like mountain goats upon the rocks.
35He gives me skill in war
And strength to bend a bow of bronze.
36You have given me the shield of your
salvation;
Your gentleness has made me great.
37You have made wide steps for my feet,
To keep them from slipping.
38I have chased my enemies
And destroyed them.
I did not stop till all were gone.
39I have destroyed them
So that none can rise again.
They have fallen beneath my feet.
40For you have given me strength for the
battle
And have caused me to subdue
All those who rose against me.
41You have made my enemies
Turn and run away;
I have destroyed them all.
42They looked in vain for help;
They cried to God,
But he refused to answer.
43I beat them into dust;
I crushed and scattered them
Like dust along the streets.
44You have preserved me
From the rebels of my people;
You have preserved me
As the head of the nations.
Foreigners shall serve me
45And shall quickly submit to me
When they hear of my power.
46They shall lose heart
And come, trembling,
From their hiding places.
47The Lord lives.
Blessed be my Rock.
Praise to him—
The Rock of my salvation.
48Blessed be God
Who destroys those who oppose me
49And rescues me from my enemies.
Yes, you hold me safe above their heads.
You deliver me from violence.
50No wonder I give thanks to you, O Lord,
among the nations,
And sing praises to your name.
51He gives wonderful deliverance to his
king
And shows mercy to his anointed—
To David and his family,
Forever."

22:17-18 Through it all, David was able to recognize God's hand in his life. He knew that God had reached down, taken hold of him, and drawn him out of deep waters. Even at the end of his life he recognized his helplessness and God's sovereignty. Although this is one of the first requirements in recovery, it is a step we can never outgrow.

23:5 Through all of David's ups and downs God had stood by him. Early in life, God had promised that David would father a dynasty that would rule forever. There must have been times when David wondered if that would ever happen. He had seen his kingdom crumbling and his sons tearing each other apart, but he knew that God could sustain his promises. Here, near the end of his life, David's faith was still strong. Even now, David's God promises hope and forgiveness for us. We can be sure, no matter how bad things may seem at times, that he is faithful to his promises.

CHAPTER 23

David's Last Words

These are the last words of David:

"David, the son of Jesse, speaks.
David, the man to whom God gave such
wonderful success;
David, the anointed of the God of Jacob;
David, sweet psalmist of Israel:
2The Spirit of the Lord spoke by me,
And his word was on my tongue.
3The Rock of Israel said to me:
'One shall come who rules righteously,
Who rules in the fear of God.
4He shall be as the light of the morning;
A cloudless sunrise
When the tender grass
Springs forth upon the earth;
As sunshine after rain.'
5And it is my family
He has chosen!
Yes, God has made
An everlasting covenant with me;
His agreement is eternal, final, sealed.
He will constantly look after
My safety and success.
6But the godless are as thorns to be
thrown away,
For they tear the hand that touches them.
7One must be armed to chop them down;
They shall be burned."

David's Mighty Men

8These are the names of the Top Three—the most heroic men in David's army: the first was Josheb-basshebeth from Tah-chemon, known also as Adino, the Eznite. He once killed eight hundred men in one battle.

9Next in rank was Eleazar, the son of Dodo and grandson of Ahohi. He was one of the three men who, with David, held back the Philistines that time when the rest of the
Israeli army fled. 10He killed the Philistines until his hand was too tired to hold his sword; and the Lord gave him a great victory. (The rest of the army did not return until it was time to collect the loot!)

11,12After him was Shammah, the son of Agee from Harar. Once during a Philistine attack, when all his men deserted him and fled, he stood alone at the center of a field of lentils and beat back the Philistines; and God gave him a great victory.

13One time when David was living in the cave of Adullam and the invading Philistines were at the valley of Rephaim, three of The Thirty—the top-ranking officers of the Israeli army—went down at harvest time to visit

A New Hiding Place

BIBLE READING: 2 Samuel 22:1-33

We sought through prayer and meditation to improve our conscious contact with God, as we understood him, praying only for knowledge of his will for us and the power to carry that out.

In the past we used our addictions as a hiding place when life became overwhelming. Now that we are in recovery, life can at times feel even more overwhelming. We'll need a new place of refuge to escape the storms and find protection.

King David experienced many battles. He said of God, "Jehovah [God] is my rock, my fortress and my Savior. I will hide in God, who is my rock and my refuge. He is my shield and my salvation, my refuge and high tower. . . . I will call upon the Lord, who is worthy to be praised; he will save me from all my enemies. The waves of death surrounded me; floods of evil burst upon me; I was trapped and bound by hell and death; but I called upon the Lord in my distress, and he heard me from his Temple. My cry reached his ears. . . . He shields all who hide behind him. Our Lord alone is God; we have no other Savior. God is my strong fortress; he has made me safe" (2 Samuel 22:2-7, 31-33).

There will always be times when we feel the need for a safe place to run and hide. God can be that hiding place. When we were in distress, "trapped and bound by hell and death," we called to God, and he brought us to where we are today. He's always there, ready to shield and protect us whenever we call on him. ***Turn to page 609, Psalm 27.***

him. 14David was in the stronghold at the
time, for Philistine marauders had occupied
the nearby city of Bethlehem.
15David remarked, "How thirsty I am for
some of that good water in the city well!" (The
well was near the city gate.)
16So the three men broke through the Philistine ranks and drew water from the well
and brought it to David. But he refused to
drink it! Instead, he poured it out before the
Lord.
17"No, my God," he exclaimed, "I cannot
do it! This is the blood of these men who have
risked their lives."
18,19Of those three men, Abishai, the brother
of Joab (son of Zeruiah), was the greatest.
Once he took on three hundred of the enemy
single-handed and killed them all. It was by
such feats that he earned a reputation equal
to The Three, though he was not actually one
of them. But he was the greatest of The
Thirty—the top-ranking officers of the
army—and was their leader.
20There was also Benaiah (son of Jehoiada),
a heroic soldier from Kabzeel. Benaiah killed
two giants, sons of Ariel of Moab. Another
time he went down into a pit and, despite the
slippery snow on the ground, took on a lion
that was caught there and killed it. 21Another
time, armed only with a staff, he killed an
Egyptian warrior who was armed with a spear;
he wrenched the spear from the Egyptian's
hand and killed him with it. 22These were
some of the deeds that gave Benaiah almost
as much renown as the Top Three. 23He was
one of the greatest of The Thirty, but was not
actually one of the Top Three. And David
made him chief of his bodyguard.
24-39Asahel, the brother of Joab, was also one
of The Thirty. Others were:

Elhanan (son of Dodo) from Bethlehem;
Shammah from Harod;
Elika from Harod;
Helez from Palti;
Ira (son of Ikkesh) from Tekoa;
Abiezer from Anathoth;
Mebunnai from Hushath;
Zalmon from Ahoh;
Maharai from Netophah;
Heleb (son of Baanah) from Netophah;
Ittai (son of Ribai) from Gibeah, of the tribe of Benjamin;
Benaiah of Pirathon;
Hiddai from the brooks of Gaash;
Abi-albon from Arbath;
Azmaveth from Bahurim;
Eliahba from Shaalbon;
The sons of Jashen;
Jonathan;
Shammah from Harar;
Ahiam (the son of Sharar) from Harar;
Eliphelet (son of Ahasbai) from Maacah;
Eliam (the son of Ahithophel) from Gilo;
Hezro from Carmel;
Paarai from Arba;
Igal (son of Nathan) from Zobah;
Bani from Gad;
Zelek from Ammon;
Naharai from Beeroth, the armor-bearer of Joab (son of Zeruiah);
Ira from Ithra;
Gareb from Ithra;
Uriah the Hittite—thirty-seven in all.

CHAPTER 24

David Takes a Census

Once again the anger of the Lord flared
against Israel, and he caused David to harm
them by taking a national census. "Go and
count the people of Israel and Judah," the
Lord told him.
2So the king said to Joab, commander-in-
chief of his army, "Take a census of all the
people from one end of the nation to the
other, so that I will know how many of them
there are."
3But Joab replied, "God grant that you will
live to see the day when there will be a hundred times as many people in your kingdom
as there are now! But you have no right to
rejoice in their strength."
4But the king's command overcame Joab's
remonstrance; so Joab and the other army
officers went out to count the people of Israel.
5First they crossed the Jordan and camped at
Aroer, south of the city that lies in the middle
of the valley of Gad, near Jazer; 6then they
went to Gilead in the land of Tahtim-hodshi
and to Dan-jaan and around to Sidon; 7and
then to the stronghold of Tyre, and all the

24:10 Here again, David sinned. But notice how sensitive his conscience was: he quickly admitted his failure. Even near the end of his life, David was clearly less than perfect. Yet he was greatly used and deeply loved by God. This reality should encourage all of us; no one is perfect! God never requires perfection; he looks for a humble willingness to accept correction. God's grace is extended to everyone who comes to him without pretense.

cities of the Hivites and Canaanites, and south to Judah as far as Beersheba. 8Having gone through the entire land, they completed their task in nine months and twenty days. 9And Joab reported the number of the people to the king—800,000 men of conscription age in Israel and 500,000 in Judah.

David Submits to Judgment

10But after he had taken the census, David's conscience began to bother him, and he said to the Lord, "What I did was very wrong. Please forgive this foolish wickedness of mine."

11The next morning the word of the Lord came to the prophet Gad, who was David's contact with God.

The Lord said to Gad, 12"Tell David that I will give him three choices."

13So Gad came to David and asked him, "Will you choose seven years of famine across the land, or to flee for three months before your enemies, or to submit to three days of plague? Think this over and let me know what answer to give to God."

14"This is a hard decision," David replied, "but it is better to fall into the hand of the Lord (for his mercy is great) than into the hands of men."

15So the Lord sent a plague upon Israel that morning, and it lasted for three days; and seventy thousand men died throughout the nation. 16But as the death angel was preparing to destroy Jerusalem, the Lord was sorry for what was happening and told him to stop. He was by the threshing floor of Araunah the Jebusite at the time.

17When David saw the angel, he said to the Lord, "Look, I am the one who has sinned! What have these sheep done? Let your anger be only against me and my family."

18That day Gad came to David and said to him, "Go and build an altar to the Lord on the threshing floor of Araunah the Jebusite." 19So David went to do what the Lord had commanded him. 20When Araunah saw the king and his men coming toward him, he came forward and fell flat on the ground with his face in the dust.

21"Why have you come?" Araunah asked.

And David replied, "To buy your threshing floor, so that I can build an altar to the Lord, and he will stop the plague."

22"Use anything you like," Araunah told the king. "Here are oxen for the burnt offering, and you can use the threshing instruments and ox yokes for wood to build a fire on the altar. 23I will give it all to you, and may the Lord God accept your sacrifice."

24But the king said to Araunah, "No, I will not have it as a gift. I will buy it, for I don't want to offer to the Lord my God burnt offerings that have cost me nothing."

So David paid him for the threshing floor and the oxen. 25And David built an altar there to the Lord and offered burnt offerings and peace offerings. And the Lord answered his prayer, and the plague was stopped.

24:15-25 Once again, David's sin brought tremendous suffering upon innocent bystanders. Yet David responded properly and brought restitution. We leave him at his altar, his fellowship with God restored. We should be aware that the consequences of our sins and disobedience will touch the people around us. This is especially true when we are leaders, whether parents, teachers, pastors, or kings.

REFLECTIONS ON
SECOND
SAMUEL

insights FROM DAVID'S LIFE

David was anointed to be king of Israel years before his ascension to the throne. David's crowning in **2 Samuel 5:3-5** is a reminder that God is faithful to his promises. Notice that God's promises to David were not fulfilled right away. He had to wait for many difficult years. He spent much of that time as a fugitive, without a home or country. During that time, God supplied David with the help he needed to survive. The recovery process is never easy; it usually takes a lifetime. But God supplies his strength and protection as we continue in recovery.

In his initial attempt at retrieving the Ark, David had failed miserably. So in **2 Samuel 6:12-15,** David turned to the Scriptures to see what God had to say on the matter. Then he set everything straight, following implicitly God's instructions for moving the Ark. As he and the Israelites moved the Ark in the proper way, they discovered that the formerly terrifying task became an activity punctuated with joy. When we do things God's way, we will discover that even trying situations can become occasions for joy.

David's admission in **2 Samuel 12:9-13,** "I have sinned against the Lord," was the right response to his wrongdoing. Spurred on by Nathan's appeal, it was an acknowledgment of David's accountability before God. He had started the process leading to recovery, which involves confrontation, conviction, confession, and cleansing (Psalm 51). Notice, however, that despite David's humble confession, he would still have to face terrible consequences (12:10-12). Our confession only starts the process toward a new life; we still must face the consequences of our past actions. But we can be sure that as we build for a productive future, God will help us with the difficulties arising from our past.

insights FROM AMNON'S RAPE OF TAMAR

The consequences of our mistakes often remain long after they have been forgiven. David had pursued Bathsheba with no thought to the consequences. In **2 Samuel 13:1-2,** Amnon pursued an incestuous relationship with his half sister, Tamar. This was an indirect consequence of David's earlier failure. Amnon became obsessed with his quest to seduce the girl, and he satisfied his lusts, much as his father had done before him. We must remember that our children learn by watching what we do. Our actions for good or bad could have consequences for generations into the future.

As is true with all things given to us by God for pleasure, there is a right context for sexual gratification. God's Word gives us guidelines for having healthy sexual relationships. God calls us to a life of discipline, delayed gratification, and self-control. Lasting sexual satisfaction can only be found in the context of a committed marriage. In **2 Samuel 13:13** Tamar showed that she was aware of this truth as she tried to escape her attacker by appealing to his reason. Amnon, however, was too obsessed to stop and listen to her.

As we see from **2 Samuel 13:20,** Tamar was left a desolate woman and probably never married. Her situation should remind us of the price paid by people close to those who manifest addictive behavior. Sometimes we try to deny the pain we may have caused others. Our recovery demands that we take inventory of the wrongs we have committed and seek to restore our relationships and the lives of those we have wronged.

David had let two years pass and did nothing about Amnon's sin. David's failure to confront his son and restore family unity planted the seeds of vengeance and murder. As we see in **2 Samuel 13:37-39,** David also allowed three years to go by without communicating with Absalom, who had avenged his sister's rape by killing Amnon. The result was a broken relationship that flowered into a kingdom torn by rebellion. Forgiveness and the restoration of relationships are two primary concerns in recovery. David's disregard for these principles brought painful consequences upon both his family and his kingdom.

FIRST KINGS

THE BIG PICTURE

A. THE UNITED KINGDOM: PRIDE PRECEDES THE FALL (1:1–11:43)
   1. Fulfillment: Going from Good to Great (1:1–2:46)
   2. Greed: Serving Self before God (3:1–8:66)
   3. Denial: Running Away from Reality (9:1–11:43)

B. THE DIVIDED KINGDOM: A NATION SELF-DESTRUCTS (12:1–22:53)
   1. Rebellion: A Failure to "Let Go" (12:1–14:31)
   2. Indecision: An Attitude of Apathy (15:1–16:34)
   3. Recovery: God's Intervention (17:1–19:21)
   4. Refusal: God's Warning Ignored (20:1–22:53)

The book of 1 Kings was originally part of a larger book that also included 2 Kings. It recorded Israel's history from the last days of King David to the demise of both the northern and southern kingdoms. At the book's opening, Israel was still one nation under Solomon's rule, and the people were following God. Solomon led the nation to a position of world prominence, and his wisdom became legendary. Kings and queens from foreign lands traveled great distances just to meet him.

But like so many of us, the success of Solomon and the nation led them to self-sufficiency and pride. They turned their backs on the God who had blessed them so richly. This led to a divided kingdom that was ruled by a series of dysfunctional, corrupt kings. The people wandered from God and began to worship idols, ignoring the laws that God had given them.

Yet throughout this period of prideful rebellion, God continued to reach out to his people. Godly kings like Asa and prophets like Elijah called the people to turn their lives over to God, and some responded. Elijah's confrontation with Ahab and Jezebel was a dramatic example of how God called disobedient kings to account for their actions. Elijah, though a flawed human being, won many great victories for God through faith.

This book is filled with examples of people who trusted God and received his help. It is also filled with the accounts of people who disobeyed God and suffered the consequences for their rebellion. But even when the people disobeyed, God never gave up on them. He did everything he could to draw his people into a healthy, vibrant relationship with himself.

THE BOTTOM LINE

PURPOSE: To record the history of Solomon and the early kings of the divided kingdom and to illustrate the blessings of obeying God and the negative consequences of disobeying him. AUTHOR: Unknown, but possibly Jeremiah, Ezra, or Ezekiel. AUDIENCE: The people of Israel in Babylonian exile. DATE WRITTEN: Sometime between 560 and 538 B.C. SETTING: The united kingdom of Israel under Solomon; then the kingdoms of Israel and Judah. KEY VERSES: "And if you live in honesty and truth as your father David did, always obeying me, then I will cause your descendants to be the kings of Israel forever, just as I promised your father David" (9:4-5). KEY PEOPLE: David, Solomon, Rehoboam, Jeroboam, Elijah, Ahab, Jezebel.

RECOVERY THEMES

The Dangers of Success: Solomon achieved everything he could have ever desired—wealth, success, prestige, and power. His experience illustrates the fact that success often leads to failure, especially when we claim sole responsibility for our achievements. In recovery, when we think we have it made, we are probably on our way to a fall. Solomon, in his success, became proud and stubborn before God. He refused to hear the warnings God gave him and later suffered the consequences (see 11:9-11).

Dysfunction across Generations: David's weakness with women became a weakness in Solomon. Solomon set no boundaries on his sexual behavior. As dysfunctions cross over into the next generation, they are often intensified and become even more destructive. In David's case, his sin with Bathsheba led to painful consequences within his family. In Solomon's case, his lust for women resulted in his marrying many foreign wives who then led him into idolatry. This ultimately led his people away from God, affecting the whole nation of Israel.

Our Vulnerability to Relapse: We are often the most vulnerable to relapse when life is going well. Solomon's experience illustrates this truth. He was warned by God on several occasions, but because everything in his life was going so well, he didn't listen. He began to think he was beyond the point of needing to take a regular inventory of his life. Perhaps he believed he could do fine without God's help. One thing is guaranteed: "Pride goes before destruction and haughtiness before a fall" (Proverbs 16:18).

The Importance of Accountability: Recovery is impossible without God's help. And we need to be accountable to someone who will be honest with us. Such a person will confront us and help us see where our denial is lurking. When Solomon stopped listening to God, no one could get his attention. The same was true of the kings who followed him—they were accountable to no one. They were too proud to listen to God's word to them through the prophets. The result was sin and failure, which led to sin among their people. We would be wise to humble ourself and be open to wise counsel.

CHAPTER 1

Adonijah Tries to Become King

In his old age King David was confined to his bed; but no matter how many blankets were heaped upon him, he was always cold.

2"The cure for this," his aides told him, "is to find a young virgin to be your concubine and nurse. She will lie in your arms and keep you warm."

3,4So they searched the country from one end to the other to find the most beautiful girl in all the land. Abishag, from Shunam, was finally selected. They brought her to the king, and she lay in his arms to warm him (but he had no sexual relations with her).

5At about that time, David's son Adonijah (his mother was Haggith) decided to crown himself king in place of his aged father. So he hired chariots and drivers and recruited fifty men to run down the streets before him as royal footmen. 6Now his father, King David, had never disciplined him at any time—not so much as by a single scolding! He was a very handsome man and was Absalom's younger brother. 7He took General Joab and Abiathar the priest into his confidence, and they agreed to help him become king. 8But among those who remained loyal to King David and refused to endorse Adonijah were the priests Zadok and Benaiah, the prophet Nathan, Shimei, Rei, and David's army chiefs.

9Adonijah went to En-rogel where he sacrificed sheep, oxen, and fat young goats at the Serpent's Stone. Then he summoned all of his brothers—the other sons of King David—and all the royal officials of Judah, requesting that they come to his coronation. 10But he didn't invite Nathan the prophet, Benaiah, the loyal army officers, or his brother Solomon.

11Then Nathan the prophet went to Bathsheba, Solomon's mother, and asked her, "Do you realize that Haggith's son, Adonijah, is

---

1:5-6 This conflict between Adonijah and Solomon was one result of King David's earlier mistakes. We are told here that David had never disciplined his son Adonijah. His failure as a father led to conflict among his sons on a number of occasions. Notice also that Solomon was the son of David and Bathsheba, whose relationship began with adultery, deceit, and murder. Despite the painful start to their relationship, Bathsheba became David's favorite, and her son Solomon was promised the throne. It is interesting to see that God used David's many failures to work his divine will for Israel. Solomon became the wisest and most powerful of all of Israel's kings. We have all made mistakes. As we seek recovery, we can trust God to take our life—warts and all—and to make something good out of it.

now the king and that our lord David doesn't even know about it? 12If you want to save your own life and the life of your son Solomon—do exactly as I say! 13Go at once to King David and ask him, 'My lord, didn't you promise me that my son Solomon would be the next king and would sit upon your throne? Then why is Adonijah reigning?' 14And while you are still talking with him, I'll come and confirm everything you've said."

15So Bathsheba went into the king's bedroom. He was an old, old man now, and Abishag was caring for him. 16Bathsheba bowed low before him.

"What do you want?" he asked her.

17She replied, "My lord, you vowed to me by the Lord your God that my son Solomon would be the next king and would sit upon your throne. 18But instead, Adonijah is the new king, and you don't even know about it. 19He has celebrated his coronation by sacrificing oxen, fat goats, and many sheep and has invited all your sons and Abiathar the priest and General Joab. But he didn't invite Solomon. 20And now, my lord the king, all Israel is waiting for your decision as to whether Adonijah is the one you have chosen to succeed you. 21If you don't act, my son Solomon and I will be arrested and executed as criminals as soon as you are dead."

22,23While she was speaking, the king's aides told him, "Nathan the prophet is here to see you."

Nathan came in and bowed low before the king, 24and asked, "My lord, have you appointed Adonijah to be the next king? Is he the one you have selected to sit upon your throne? 25Today he celebrated his coronation by sacrificing oxen, fat goats, and many sheep, and has invited your sons to attend the festivities. He also invited General Joab and Abiathar the priest; and they are feasting and drinking with him and shouting, 'Long live King Adonijah!' 26But Zadok the priest and Benaiah and Solomon and I weren't invited. 27Has this been done with your knowledge? For you haven't said a word as to which of your sons you have chosen to be the next king."

David Declares Solomon King

28"Call Bathsheba," David said. So she came back in and stood before the king.

29And the king vowed, "As the Lord lives who has rescued me from every danger, 30I decree that your son Solomon shall be the next king and shall sit upon my throne, just as I swore to you before by the Lord God of Israel."

31Then Bathsheba bowed low before him again and exclaimed, "Oh, thank you, sir. May my lord the king live forever!"

32"Call Zadok the priest," the king ordered, "and Nathan the prophet, and Benaiah."

When they arrived, 33he said to them, "Take Solomon and my officers to Gihon. Solomon is to ride on my personal mule, 34and Zadok the priest and Nathan the prophet are to anoint him there as king of Israel. Then blow the trumpets and shout, 'Long live King Solomon!' 35When you bring him back here, place him upon my throne as the new king; for I have appointed him king of Israel and Judah."

36"Amen! Praise God!" replied Benaiah, and added, 37"May the Lord be with Solomon as he has been with you, and may God make Solomon's reign even greater than yours!"

38So Zadok the priest, Nathan the prophet, Benaiah, and David's bodyguard took Solomon to Gihon, riding on King David's own mule. 39At Gihon, Zadok took a flask of sacred oil from the Tabernacle and poured it over Solomon; and the trumpets were blown and all the people shouted, "Long live King Solomon!"

40Then they all returned with him to Jerusalem, making a joyous and noisy celebration all along the way.

41Adonijah and his guests heard the commotion and shouting just as they were finishing their banquet.

1:28-40 Nathan the prophet and Zadok the priest anointed Solomon king under the orders of King David. David realized that he was going to die soon and took care of his responsibility to secure the throne for Solomon. Unwisely, many of us put off the task of providing for our family's future. Planning for our death is not being morbid; it is part of what it means to be responsible.

1:41-53 Adonijah, as David's oldest living son, expected to take Israel's throne and, for a span of a few hours, apparently held the kingship. When Solomon finally gained control, he would have been expected to kill his rival. But Solomon showed great mercy and forgiveness to Adonijah. He gave Adonijah a chance to prove whether or not he was worthy of forgiveness. When we are attacked at a personal level, it is natural to seek revenge. Granting forgiveness demands great strength of character. We need to turn our revenge over to God; failing to forgive will only slow our recovery.

"What's going on?" Joab demanded. "Why is the city in such an uproar?"

42And while he was still speaking, Jonathan, the son of Abiathar the priest, rushed in.

"Come in," Adonijah said to him, "for you are a good man; you must have good news."

43"Our lord King David has declared Solomon as king!" Jonathan shouted. 44,45"The king sent him to Gihon with Zadok the priest and Nathan the prophet and Benaiah, protected by the king's own bodyguard; and he rode on the king's own mule. And Zadok and Nathan have anointed him as the new king! They have just returned, and the whole city is celebrating and rejoicing. That's what all the noise is. 46,47Solomon is sitting on the throne, and all the people are congratulating King David, saying, 'May God bless you even more through Solomon than he has blessed you personally! May God make Solomon's reign even greater than yours!' And the king is lying in bed, acknowledging their blessings. 48He is saying, 'Blessed be the Lord God of Israel who has selected one of my sons to sit upon my throne while I am still alive to see it.'"

49,50Then Adonijah and his guests jumped up from the banquet table and fled in panic; for they were fearful for their lives. Adonijah rushed into the Tabernacle and caught hold of the horns of the sacred altar. 51When word reached Solomon that Adonijah was claiming sanctuary in the Tabernacle, and pleading for clemency, 52Solomon replied, "If he behaves himself, he will not be harmed; but if he does not, he shall die." 53So King Solomon summoned him, and they brought him down from the altar. He came to bow low before the king; and then Solomon curtly dismissed him.

"Go on home," he said.

CHAPTER 2

David's Instructions for Solomon

As the time of King David's death approached, he gave this charge to his son Solomon:

2"I am going where every man on earth must some day go. I am counting on you to be a strong and worthy successor. 3Obey the laws of God and follow all his ways; keep each of his commands written in the law of Moses so that you will prosper in everything you do, wherever you turn. 4If you do this, then the Lord will fulfill the promise he gave me, that if my children and their descendants watch their step and are faithful to God, one of them shall always be the king of Israel—my dynasty will never end.

5"Now listen to my instructions. You know that Joab murdered my two generals, Abner and Amasa. He pretended that it was an act of war, but it was done in a time of peace. 6You are a wise man and will know what to do—don't let him die in peace. 7But be kind to the sons of Barzillai the Gileadite. Make them permanent guests of the king, for they took care of me when I fled from your brother Absalom. 8And do you remember Shimei, the son of Gera the Benjaminite from Bahurim? He cursed me with a terrible curse as I was going to Mahanaim; but when he came down to meet me at the Jordan River, I promised I wouldn't kill him. 9But that promise doesn't bind you! You are a wise man, and you will know how to arrange a bloody death for him."

10Then David died and was buried in Jerusalem. 11He had reigned over Israel for forty years, seven of them in Hebron and thirty-three in Jerusalem. 12And Solomon became the new king, replacing his father David; and his kingdom prospered.

Solomon's Enemies Are Killed

13One day Adonijah, the son of Haggith, came to see Solomon's mother, Bathsheba.

"Have you come to make trouble?" she asked him.

"No," he replied, "I come in peace. 14As a matter of fact, I have a favor to ask of you."

"What is it?" she asked.

15"Everything was going well for me," he

2:1-12 David instructed his son Solomon how to rule and whom to trust. David advised his son to keep his eyes on God. Solomon learned who his allies and enemies were. As parents, we need to sit down and talk with our children, just as David did with Solomon. This will increase our children's respect for us and equip them to face the challenges ahead.

2:13-25 Adonijah again plotted to take the throne by asking that Solomon allow him to marry David's nurse, Abishag. In ancient times, sleeping with one of the king's wives was tantamount to making a claim to the throne. Bathsheba was apparently unaware of Adonijah's plot and took him at his word. Solomon understood the true nature of Adonijah's request and ordered that he be executed, fulfilling his earlier promise (1:52-53). Solomon showed strength by living up to his previous promise. Likewise, we need to live up to any promises we make. This will help us maintain the boundaries we have set and protect our interests and the interests of the people we are responsible for.

SOLOMON

Our society and the "American dream" are built upon a strong work ethic. The harder we work, the greater our chance for success. But, if unchecked, the positive work ethic can deteriorate into workaholism—devoting all our time to the job, perhaps even becoming "addicted" to work. We sacrifice healthy family relationships, friendships, and our walk with God just so we can achieve more and advance in our profession.

Following the death of King David, Solomon became king of Israel. Solomon faced several revolts early in his reign, but he soon consolidated his power base and took firm control over his kingdom. Then God promised to give Solomon anything he desired, and Solomon chose wisdom so he could rule his people wisely. God was pleased with Solomon's selfless choice, and he gave this young king honor, wealth, and a long life, in addition to the wisdom he requested.

From this point on, Solomon became a workaholic. He started by building the Temple. Then he built his palace and fortified his country against intruders. All of these projects were done on an enormous scale, even by today's standards. In order to accomplish these tasks, Solomon sacrificed important relationships with his people, his family, and his God. He taxed his people heavily and required them to work hard on his building projects. He failed to teach his son Rehoboam how to use wisdom to rule the people. He also stopped listening to God and disobeyed him by marrying numerous pagan women and by worshiping their gods.

It is easy, in our busyness with work and achievements, to forget the source of our strength and success. We must remember that God and our family are the top priorities in life. Whenever anything else is placed above these, we have sacrificed everything and are headed for trouble.

STRENGTHS AND ACCOMPLISHMENTS:

- Solomon was the wisest man who ever lived.
- He passed his wisdom on by writing numerous proverbs and psalms.
- He built God's Temple in Jerusalem.
- He completed many difficult long-term projects.

WEAKNESSES AND MISTAKES:

- Solomon compromised his relationship with God by marrying foreign women.
- He worshiped the gods of his foreign wives.
- He placed loyalty to his work above his loyalty to God.
- He drained the people of their resources in order to achieve his goals.

LESSONS FROM HIS LIFE:

- If we reject God's plan, we will fail, no matter how much practical wisdom we have.
- Obedience to God is the beginning of personal success.
- We must seek to pass on the relationship we have with God to our children.

KEY VERSE:

"'Wasn't this exactly King Solomon's problem?' I demanded. 'There was no king who could compare with him, and God loved him and made him the king over all Israel; but even so he was led into idolatry by foreign women'" (Nehemiah 13:26).

Solomon's story is told in 2 Samuel 12:24; 1 Kings 1–11; 1 Chronicles 28—2 Chronicles 10. He is also mentioned in Nehemiah 13:26 and Matthew 6:29; 12:42.

---

said, "and the kingdom was mine: everyone
expected me to be the next king. But the
tables are turned, and everything went to my
brother instead; for that is the way the Lord
wanted it. 16But now I have just a small favor
to ask of you; please don't turn me down."

"What is it?" she asked.

17He replied, "Speak to King Solomon on
my behalf (for I know he will do anything you
request) and ask him to give me Abishag, the
Shunammite, as my wife."

18"All right," Bathsheba replied, "I'll ask
him."

19So she went to ask the favor of King
Solomon. The king stood up from his
throne as she entered and bowed low to her.
He ordered that a throne for his mother be
placed beside his; so she sat at his right
hand.

20"I have one small request to make of you,"
she said. "I hope you won't turn me down."

"What is it, my mother?" he asked. "You
know I won't refuse you."

21"Then let your brother Adonijah marry
Abishag," she replied.

22"Are you crazy?" he demanded. "If I were
to give him Abishag, I would be giving him
the kingdom too! For he is my older brother!
He and Abiathar the priest and General Joab
would take over!" 23,24Then King Solomon
swore with a great oath, "May God strike me
dead if Adonijah does not die this very day for
this plot against me! I swear it by the living
God who has given me the throne of my

father David and this kingdom he promised me."

25So King Solomon sent Benaiah to execute him, and he killed him with a sword.

26Then the king said to Abiathar the priest, "Go back to your home in Anathoth. You should be killed, too, but I won't do it now. For you carried the Ark of the Lord during my father's reign, and you suffered right along with him in all of his troubles."

27So Solomon forced Abiathar to give up his position as the priest of the Lord, thereby fulfilling the decree of Jehovah at Shiloh concerning the descendants of Eli.

28When Joab heard about Adonijah's death (Joab had joined Adonijah's revolt, though not Absalom's) he ran to the Tabernacle for sanctuary and caught hold of the horns of the altar. 29When news of this reached King Solomon, he sent Benaiah to execute him.

30Benaiah went into the Tabernacle and said to Joab, "The king says to come out!"

"No," he said, "I'll die here."

So Benaiah returned to the king for further instructions.

31"Do as he says," the king replied. "Kill him there beside the altar and bury him. This will remove the guilt of his senseless murders from me and from my father's family. 32Then Jehovah will hold him personally responsible for the murders of two men who were better than he. For my father was no party to the deaths of General Abner, commander-in-chief of the army of Israel, and General Amasa, commander-in-chief of the army of Judah. 33May Joab and his descendants be forever guilty of these murders, and may the Lord declare David and his descendants guiltless concerning their deaths."

34So Benaiah returned to the Tabernacle and killed Joab; and he was buried beside his house in the desert.

35Then the king appointed Benaiah as commander-in-chief, and Zadok as priest instead of Abiathar.

36,37The king now sent for Shimei and told him, "Build a house here in Jerusalem, and don't step outside the city on pain of death. The moment you go beyond Kidron Brook, you die; and it will be your own fault."

38"All right," Shimei replied, "whatever you say." So he lived in Jerusalem for a long time.

39But three years later two of Shimei's slaves escaped to King Achish of Gath. When Shimei learned where they were, 40he saddled a donkey and went to Gath to visit the king. And when he had found his slaves, he took them back to Jerusalem.

41When Solomon heard that Shimei had left Jerusalem and had gone to Gath and returned, 42he sent for him and demanded, "Didn't I command you in the name of God to stay in Jerusalem or die? You replied, 'Very well, I will do as you say.' 43Then why have you not kept your agreement and obeyed my commandment? 44And what about all the wicked things you did to my father, King David? May the Lord take revenge on you, 45but may I receive God's rich blessings, and may one of David's descendants always sit upon this throne."

46Then, at the king's command, Benaiah took Shimei outside and killed him.

So Solomon's grip upon the kingdom became secure.

CHAPTER 3

Solomon Asks for Wisdom

Solomon made an alliance with Pharaoh, the king of Egypt, and married one of his daughters. He brought her to Jerusalem to live in the City of David until he could finish building his palace and the Temple and the wall around the city.

2At that time the people of Israel sacrificed their offerings on altars in the hills, for the Temple of the Lord hadn't yet been built.

3(Solomon loved the Lord and followed all of his father David's instructions except that he continued to sacrifice in the hills and to offer incense there.) 4The most famous of the hilltop altars was at Gibeon, and now the king went there and sacrificed one thousand burnt offerings! 5The Lord appeared to him in a dream that night and told him to ask for anything he wanted, and it would be given to him!

6Solomon replied, "You were wonderfully kind to my father David because he was honest and true and faithful to you, and obeyed your commands. And you have continued

---

2:26-46 Solomon showed respect for his father's wisdom by having Joab and Shimei killed. Two things were accomplished by these acts. First, David's name was cleared of the wicked acts committed by these men. Second, Solomon cleared his kingdom of the enemies within. We all have enemies within our life—addictions, unforgiveness, guilt. These need to be completely removed if we want to recover and prosper.

your kindness to him by giving him a son to
succeed him. 7O Lord my God, now you have
made me the king instead of my father David,
but I am as a little child who doesn't know his
way around. 8And here I am among your own
chosen people, a nation so great that there are
almost too many people to count! 9Give me
an understanding mind so that I can govern
your people well and know the difference
between what is right and what is wrong. For
who by himself is able to carry such a heavy
responsibility?"
10The Lord was pleased with his reply and
was glad that Solomon had asked for wisdom.
11So he replied, "Because you have asked for
wisdom in governing my people and haven't
asked for a long life, or riches for yourself, or
the defeat of your enemies—12yes, I'll give you
what you asked for! I will give you a wiser
mind than anyone else has ever had or ever
will have! 13And I will also give you what you
didn't ask for—riches and honor! And no one
in all the world will be as rich and famous as
you for the rest of your life! 14And I will give
you a long life if you follow me and obey my
laws as your father David did."
15Then Solomon woke up and realized it
had been a dream. He returned to Jerusalem
and went into the Tabernacle. And as he stood
before the Ark of the Covenant of the Lord,
he sacrificed burnt offerings and peace offerings. Then he invited all of his officials to a
great banquet.

Solomon Proves His Wisdom

16Soon afterwards two young prostitutes came
to the king to have an argument settled.
17,18"Sir," one of them began, "we live in the
same house, just the two of us, and recently I
had a baby. When it was three days old, this
woman's baby was born too. 19But her baby
died during the night when she rolled over on
it in her sleep and smothered it. 20Then she
got up in the night and took my son from
beside me while I was asleep, and laid her
dead child in my arms and took mine to sleep
beside her. 21And in the morning when I tried
to feed my baby it was dead! But when it
became light outside, I saw that it wasn't my
son at all."
22Then the other woman interrupted, "It
certainly was her son, and the living child is
mine."
"No," the first woman said, "the dead one
is yours and the living one is mine." And so
they argued back and forth before the king.
23Then the king said, "Let's get the facts
straight: both of you claim the living child,
and each says that the dead child belongs to
the other. 24All right, bring me a sword." So a
sword was brought to the king. 25Then he said,
"Divide the living child in two and give half
to each of these women!"
26Then the woman who really was the
mother of the child, and who loved him very
much, cried out, "Oh no, sir! Give her the
child—don't kill him!"
But the other woman said, "All right, it will
be neither yours nor mine; divide it between
us!"
27Then the king said, "Give the baby to the
woman who wants him to live, for she is the
mother!"
28Word of the king's decision spread quickly
throughout the entire nation, and all the
people were awed as they realized the great
wisdom God had given him.

CHAPTER 4

Solomon's Cabinet Members

Here is a list of King Solomon's cabinet members:

Azariah (son of Zadok) was the High Priest;
Elihoreph and Ahijah (sons of Shisha) were secretaries;
Jehoshaphat (son of Ahilud) was the official historian and in charge of the archives;
Benaiah (son of Jehoiada) was commander-in-chief of the army;
Zadok and Abiathar were priests;

3:3-15 God approached Solomon in a dream and told him he could have anything he wanted. Solomon asked for wisdom and discernment so he could rule his people well. God was pleased with Solomon and granted him his wish, adding to it wealth and honor. Solomon put his concern for his people before the fulfillment of his own desires. And his selfless attitude brought him blessings beyond belief. Often the road to personal blessing is a life lived selflessly for others.

3:16-28 Solomon was put in a difficult situation. Two women claimed to be the mother of the same child. Obviously one of the women was lying, but which one? This was a major test for Solomon's wisdom. Solomon handled the situation wisely, and the child was returned to his real mother. Solomon had been given the special gift of wisdom to maintain peace in his kingdom. We all have gifts to offer others and need to use these gifts to the best of our ability.

Azariah (son of Nathan) was secretary of state;
Zabud (son of Nathan) was the king's personal priest and special friend;
Ahishar was manager of palace affairs;
Adoniram (son of Abda) was superintendent of public works.

[7]There were also twelve officials of Solomon's court—one man from each tribe—responsible for requisitioning food from the people for the king's household. Each of them arranged provisions for one month of the year.
[8-19]The names of these twelve officers were:

Ben-hur, whose area for this taxation was the hill country of Ephraim;
Ben-deker, whose area was Makaz, Shaalbim, Beth-shemesh, and Elon-beth-hanan;
Ben-hesed, whose area was Arubboth, including Socoh and all the land of Hepher;
Ben-abinadab (who married Solomon's daughter, the princess Taphath), whose area was the highlands of Dor;
Baana (son of Ahilud), whose area was Taanach and Megiddo, all of Beth-shean near Zarethan below Jezreel, and all the territory from Beth-shean to Abel-meholah and over to Jokmeam;
Ben-geber, whose area was Ramoth-gilead, including the villages of Jair (the son of Manasseh) in Gilead; and the region of Argob in Bashan, including sixty walled cities with bronze gates;
Ahinadab (the son of Iddo), whose area was Mahanaim;
Ahimaaz (who married Princess Basemath, another of Solomon's daughters), whose area was Naphtali;
Baana (son of Hushai), whose areas were Asher and Bealoth;
Jehoshaphat (son of Paruah), whose area was Issachar;
Shimei (son of Ela), whose area was Benjamin;
Geber (son of Uri), whose area was Gilead, including the territories of King Sihon of the Amorites and King Og of Bashan.

A general manager supervised these officials and their work.

Solomon's Kingdom

[20]Israel and Judah were a wealthy, populous,
contented nation at this time. [21]King Solomon ruled the whole area from the Euphrates
River to the land of the Philistines and down
to the borders of Egypt. The conquered
peoples of those lands sent taxes to Solomon
and continued to serve him throughout his
lifetime.
[22]The daily food requirements for the palace
were 195 bushels of fine flour, 390 bushels of
meal, [23]10 oxen from the fattening pens, 20
pasture-fed cattle, 100 sheep, and, from time to
time, deer, gazelles, roebucks, and plump fowl.
[24]His dominion extended over all the kingdoms west of the Euphrates River, from Tiph-
sah to Gaza. And there was peace throughout
the land.
[25]Throughout the lifetime of Solomon, all of
Judah and Israel lived in peace and safety; and
each family had its own home and garden.
[26]Solomon owned forty thousand chariot
horses and employed twelve thousand charioteers. [27]Each month the tax officials provided food for King Solomon and his court,
[28]also the barley and straw for the royal horses
in the stables.

Solomon's Legendary Wisdom

[29]God gave Solomon great wisdom and understanding, and a mind with broad interests.
[30]In fact, his wisdom excelled that of any of
the wise men of the East, including those in
Egypt. [31]He was wiser than Ethan the Ezrahite
and Heman, Calcol, and Darda, the sons of
Mahol; and he was famous among all the
surrounding nations. [32]He was the author of
3,000 proverbs and wrote 1,005 songs. [33]He
was a great naturalist, with interest in animals, birds, snakes, fish, and trees—from the
great cedars of Lebanon down to the tiny
hyssop which grows in cracks in the wall.
[34]And kings from many lands sent their ambassadors to him for his advice.

4:29-34 Teaching others what we know is one of the greatest gifts we can offer others. Solomon had been given wisdom by God (3:11-12). Instead of being "puffed up" at this point in his life, he chose to share his wealth of knowledge with others. People came from other countries to listen and learn from the wisdom with which God had gifted Solomon. All of us in recovery have been "gifted" with a special kind of knowledge. We know the guilt of failure, along with tidbits of wisdom for recovery. We can offer our experiences and victories to others, helping them to make the journey with us.

CHAPTER 5

Solomon Prepares to Build

King Hiram of Tyre had always been a great admirer of David, so when he learned that David's son Solomon was the new king of Israel, he sent ambassadors to extend congratulations and good wishes. 2,3Solomon replied with a proposal about the Temple of the Lord he wanted to build. His father David, Solomon pointed out to Hiram, had not been able to build it because of the numerous wars going on, and he had been waiting for the Lord to give him peace.

4"But now," Solomon said to Hiram, "the Lord my God has given Israel peace on every side; I have no foreign enemies or internal rebellions. 5So I am planning to build a Temple for the Lord my God, just as he instructed my father that I should do. For the Lord told him, 'Your son, whom I will place upon your throne, shall build me a Temple.' 6Now please assist me with this project. Send your woodsmen to the mountains of Lebanon to cut cedar timber for me, and I will send my men to work beside them, and I will pay your men whatever wages you ask; for as you know, no one in Israel can cut timber like you Sidonians!"

7Hiram was very pleased with the message from Solomon. "Praise God for giving David a wise son to be king of the great nation of Israel," he said. 8Then he sent this reply to Solomon: "I have received your message and I will do as you have asked concerning the timber. I can supply both cedar and cypress. 9My men will bring the logs from the Lebanon mountains to the Mediterranean Sea and build them into rafts. We will float them along the coast to wherever you need them; then we will break the rafts apart and deliver the timber to you. You can pay me with food for my household."

10So Hiram produced for Solomon as much cedar and cypress timber as he desired, 11and in return Solomon sent him an annual payment of 125,000 bushels of wheat for his household and 96 gallons of pure olive oil. 12So the Lord gave great wisdom to Solomon just as he had promised. And Hiram and Solomon made a formal alliance of peace.

13Then Solomon drafted thirty thousand laborers from all over Israel, 14and rotated them to Lebanon, ten thousand a month, so that each man was a month in Lebanon and two months at home. Adoniram was the general superintendent of this labor camp. 15Solomon also had seventy thousand additional laborers, eighty thousand stonecutters in the hill country, 16and thirty-three hundred foremen. 17The stonecutters quarried and shaped huge blocks of stone—a very expensive job—for the foundation of the Temple. 18Men from Gebal helped Solomon's and Hiram's builders in cutting the timber and making the boards, and in preparing the stone for the Temple.

CHAPTER 6

Solomon Builds the Temple

It was in the spring of the fourth year of Solomon's reign that he began the actual construction of the Temple. (This was 480 years after the people of Israel left their slavery in Egypt.) 2The Temple was ninety feet long, thirty feet wide, and forty-five feet high. 3All along the front of the Temple was a porch thirty feet long and fifteen feet deep. 4Narrow windows were used throughout.

5An annex of rooms was built along the full

5:1-12 The benefits of strong a relationship can reach even beyond death. King David had established a sound relationship with Hiram of Tyre. Solomon continued that relationship and enjoyed its numerous benefits. Solomon's great building projects could never have been achieved alone. Hiram was able to provide some of the expertise and many of the materials needed. God may have chosen people to encourage us and to provide us with resources we need for recovery. We need to allow God to use these people in our life.

5:13-14 It is necessary to set priorities in life. Solomon recognized this when he set up shifts of one month at work and two months at home (5:14). This schedule showed that Solomon placed great importance on the family. Whenever we set up schedules at work, home, and church, we need to examine the impact they have on our family. Too often we strive for material things and lose what is much more precious, such as wonderful memories and a warm relationship with our family.

6:1-10 Respect for God is of primary importance in our relationship with him. Solomon showed respect for God in the great amount of detail that was taken to design the Temple. No construction sounds were heard at the site of the Temple in order to show God respect (6:7). Solomon and the people went through a great deal of painstaking work to accomplish this task. How willing are we to show God the respect he deserves? We need to make God our first priority rather than putting him on a long list of obligations.

length of both sides of the Temple against the outer walls. [6]These rooms were three stories high, the lower floor being 7 1/2 feet wide, the second floor 9 feet wide, and the upper floor 10 1/2 feet wide. The rooms were connected to the walls of the Temple by beams resting on blocks built out from the wall—so the beams were not inserted into the walls themselves.

[7]The stones used in the construction of the Temple were prefinished at the quarry, so the entire structure was built without the sound of hammer, axe, or any other tool at the building site.

[8]The bottom floor of the side rooms was entered from the right side of the Temple, and there were winding stairs going up to the second floor; another flight of stairs led from the second to the third. [9]After completing the Temple, Solomon paneled it all, including the beams and pillars, with cedar. [10]As already stated, there was an annex on each side of the building, attached to the Temple walls by cedar timbers. Each story of the annex was 7 1/2 feet high.

[11,12]Then the Lord sent this message to Solomon concerning the Temple he was building: "If you do as I tell you to and follow all of my commandments and instructions, I will do what I told your father David I would do: [13]I will live among the people of Israel and never forsake them."

[14]At last the Temple was finished. [15]The entire inside, from floor to ceiling, was paneled with cedar, and the floors were made of cypress boards. [16]The thirty-foot inner room at the far end of the Temple—the Most Holy Place—was also paneled from the floor to the ceiling with cedar boards. [17]The remainder of the Temple—other than the Most Holy Place—was sixty feet long. [18]Throughout the Temple the cedar paneling laid over the stone walls was carved with designs of rosebuds and open flowers.

[19]The inner room was where the Ark of the Covenant of the Lord was placed. [20]This inner sanctuary was thirty feet long, thirty feet wide, and thirty feet high. Its walls and ceiling were overlaid with pure gold, and Solomon made a cedar-wood altar for this room. [21,22]Then he overlaid the interior of the remainder of the Temple—including the cedar altar—with pure gold; and he made gold chains to protect the entrance to the Most Holy Place.

[23-28]Within the inner sanctuary Solomon placed two statues of Guardian Angels made from olive wood, each fifteen feet high. They were placed so that their outspread wings reached from wall to wall, while their inner wings touched each other at the center of the room; each wing was 7 1/2 feet long, so each angel measured fifteen feet from wing tip to wing tip. The two angels were identical in all dimensions, and each was overlaid with gold.

[29]Figures of angels, palm trees, and open flowers were carved on all the walls of both rooms of the Temple, [30]and the floor of both rooms was overlaid with gold.

[31]The doorway to the inner sanctuary was a five-sided opening, [32]and its two olive-wood doors were carved with Guardian Angels, palm trees, and open flowers, all overlaid with gold.

[33]Then he made square doorposts of olive wood for the entrance to the Temple. [34]There were two folding doors of cypress wood, and each door was hinged to fold back upon itself. [35]Angels, palm trees, and open flowers were carved on these doors and carefully overlaid with gold.

[36]The wall of the inner court had three layers of hewn stone and one layer of cedar beams.

[37]The foundation of the Temple was laid in the month of May in the fourth year of Solomon's reign, [38]and the entire building was completed in every detail in November of the eleventh year of his reign. So it took seven years to build.

CHAPTER 7

Solomon Builds His Palace

Then Solomon built his own palace, which took thirteen years to construct.

[2]One of the rooms in the palace was called the Hall of the Forest of Lebanon. It was huge—measuring 150 feet long, 75 feet wide, and 45 feet high. The great cedar ceiling beams rested upon four rows of cedar pillars. [3,4]There were forty-five windows in the hall, set in three tiers, one tier above the other, five to a tier, facing each other from three walls.

6:11-13 God promised Solomon that he would be present with Israel as long as the people chose to obey his laws. Often we forget that obedience is the key to our inheritance of God's promises. We complain that God has failed us, but we do so from a position of disobedience. God, unlike man, is always faithful to his promises, including those promises that give us hope for recovery. We need to be faithful to God if we desire his promises to bear fruit in our life.

5 Each of the doorways and windows had a
square frame.
6 Another room was called the Hall of Pillars. It was seventy-five feet long and forty-
five feet wide, with a porch in front covered
by a canopy that was supported by pillars.
7 There was also the Throne Room or Judgment Hall, where Solomon sat to hear legal
matters; it was paneled with cedar from the
floor to the rafters.
8 His cedar-paneled living quarters surrounded a courtyard behind this hall. (He
designed similar living quarters, the same
size, in the palace that he built for Pharaoh's
daughter—one of his wives.) 9 These buildings
were constructed entirely from huge, expensive stones, cut to measure. 10 The foundation
stones were twelve to fifteen feet across. 11 The
huge stones in the walls were also cut to
measure and were topped with cedar beams.
12 The Great Court had three courses of hewn
stone in its walls, topped with cedar beams,
just like the inner court of the Temple and the
porch of the palace.

Equipment for the Temple

13 King Solomon then asked for a man named
Hiram to come from Tyre, for he was a skilled
craftsman in bronze work. 14 He was half Jewish, being the son of a widow of the tribe of
Naphtali, and his father had been a foundry
worker from Tyre. So he came to work for
King Solomon.
15 He cast two hollow bronze pillars, each
twenty-seven feet high and eighteen feet
around, with three-inch-thick walls. 16-22 At the
tops of the pillars he made two lily-shaped
capitals from molten bronze, each 7 1/2 feet
high. The upper part of each capital was
shaped like a lily, six feet high. Each capital
was decorated with seven sets of bronze,
chain-designed lattices and four hundred
pomegranates in two rows. Hiram set these
pillars at the entrance of the Temple. The one
on the south was named the Jachin Pillar, and
the one on the north, the Boaz Pillar.
23 Then Hiram cast a round bronze tank, 7 1/2
feet high and 15 feet from brim to brim; 45
feet in circumference. 24 On the underside of
the rim were two rows of ornaments an inch
or two apart, which were cast along with the
tank. 25 It rested on twelve bronze oxen standing tail to tail, three facing north, three west,
three south, and three east. 26 The sides of the
tank were four inches thick; its brim was
shaped like a goblet, and it had a twelve
thousand gallon capacity.
27-30 Then he made ten four-wheeled movable stands, each 6 feet square and 4 1/2 feet
high. They were constructed with undercar-
riages braced with square crosspieces. These
crosspieces were decorated with carved lions,
oxen, and angels. Above and below the lions
and oxen were wreath decorations. Each of
these movable stands had four bronze wheels
and bronze axles, and at each corner of the
stands were supporting posts made of bronze
and decorated with wreaths on each side.
31 The top of each stand was a round piece 1 1/2
feet high. Its center was concave, 2 1/4 feet
deep, decorated on the outside with wreaths.
Its panels were square, not round.
32 The stands rode on four wheels which
were connected to axles that had been cast as
part of the stands. The wheels were twenty-
seven inches high 33 and were similar to chariot wheels. All the parts of the stands were cast
from molten bronze, including the axles,
spokes, rims, and hubs. 34 There were supports
at each of the four corners of the stands, and
these, too, were cast with the stands. 35 A nine-
inch rim surrounded the tip of each stand,
banded with lugs. All was cast as one unit
with the stand. 36 Guardian Angels, lions, and
palm trees surrounded by wreaths were engraved on the borders of the band wherever
there was room. 37 All ten stands were the same
size and were made alike, for each was cast
from the same mold.
38 Then he made ten brass vats, and placed
them on the stands. Each vat was six feet
square and contained 240 gallons of water.
39 Five of these vats were arranged on the left
and five on the right-hand side of the room.
The tank was in the southeast corner, on the
right-hand side of the room. 40 Hiram also
made the necessary pots, shovels, and basins
and at last completed the work in the Temple
of the Lord that had been assigned to him by
King Solomon.
41-46 Here is a list of the items he made:

Two pillars;
A capital at the top of each pillar;
Latticework covering the bases of the
capitals of each pillar;
Four hundred pomegranates in two rows
on the latticework, to cover the bases of
the two capitals;
Ten movable stands holding ten vats;
One large tank and twelve oxen
supporting it;
Pots;
Shovels;
Basins.

All these items were made of burnished bronze and were cast at the plains of the Jordan River between Succoth and Zarethan. 47The total weight of these pieces was not known because they were too heavy to weigh!

48All the utensils and furniture used in the Temple were made of solid gold. This included the altar, the table where the Bread of the Presence of God was displayed, 49the lampstands (five on the right-hand side and five on the left, in front of the Most Holy Place), the flowers, lamps, tongs, 50cups, snuffers, basins, spoons, firepans, the hinges of the doors to the Most Holy Place, and the main entrance doors of the Temple. Each of these was made of solid gold.

51When the Temple was finally finished, Solomon took into the treasury of the Temple the silver, the gold, and all the vessels dedicated for that purpose by his father David.

CHAPTER 8

The Ark Is Set in Place

Then Solomon called a convocation at Jerusalem of all the leaders of Israel—the heads of the tribes and clans—to observe the transferring of the Ark of the Covenant of the Lord from the Tabernacle in Zion, the City of David, to the Temple. 2This celebration occurred at the time of the Tabernacle Festival in the month of October. 3,4During the festivities the priests carried the Ark to the Temple, along with all the sacred vessels that had previously been in the Tabernacle. 5King Solomon and all the people gathered before the Ark, sacrificing uncounted sheep and oxen.

6Then the priests took the Ark into the inner sanctuary of the Temple—the Most Holy Place—and placed it under the wings of the statues of the mighty angels. 7The angels had been constructed in such a manner that their wings spread out over the spot where the Ark would be placed; so now their wings overshadowed the Ark and its carrying poles. 8The poles were so long that they stuck out past the angels and could be seen from the next room, but not from the outer court; and they remain there to this day. 9There was nothing in the Ark at that time except the two stone tablets that Moses had placed there at Mount Horeb at the time the Lord made his covenant with the people of Israel after they left Egypt.

10*Look! As the priests are returning from the inner sanctuary, a bright cloud fills the Temple!* 11*The priests have to go outside because the glory of the Lord is filling the entire building!*

12,13Now King Solomon prayed this invocation:

"The Lord has said that he would live in
the thick darkness;
But, O Lord, I have built you a lovely
home on earth, a place for you to live
forever."

14Then the king turned around and faced the people as they stood before him, and blessed them.

15"Blessed be the Lord God of Israel," he said, "who has done today what he promised my father David: 16for he said to him, 'When I brought my people from Egypt, I didn't appoint a place for my Temple, but I appointed a man to be my people's leader.' 17This man was my father David. He wanted to build a Temple for the Lord God of Israel, 18but the Lord told him not to. 'I am glad you want to do it,' he said, 19'but your son is the one who shall build my Temple.' 20And now the Lord has done what he promised; for I have followed my father as king of Israel, and now this Temple has been built for the Lord God of Israel. 21And I have prepared a place in the Temple for the Ark that contains the covenant made by the Lord with our fathers, at the time that he brought them out of the land of Egypt."

Solomon Dedicates the Temple

22,23Then, as all the people watched, Solomon stood before the altar of the Lord with his hands spread out toward heaven and said, "O Lord God of Israel, there is no god like you in heaven or earth, for you are loving and kind and you keep your promises to your people if they do their best to do your will. 24Today you have fulfilled your promise to my father David, who was your servant; 25and now, O Lord God of Israel, fulfill your further promise to him: that if his descendants follow your ways and try to do your will as he did, one of them shall always sit upon the throne of Israel. 26Yes, O God of Israel, fulfill this promise too.

27"But is it possible that God would really live on earth? Why, even the skies and the highest heavens cannot contain you, much less this Temple I have built! 28And yet, O Lord my God, you have heard and answered my request: 29Please watch over this Temple night and day—this place you have promised to live in—and as I face toward the Temple and pray, whether by night or by day, please listen to me and answer my requests. 30Listen to every

plea of the people of Israel whenever they face
this place to pray; yes, hear in heaven where
you live, and when you hear, forgive.
31"If a man is accused of doing something
wrong and then, standing here before your
altar, swears that he didn't do it, 32hear him in
heaven and do what is right; judge whether or
not he did it.
33,34"And when your people sin and their
enemies defeat them, hear them from heaven
and forgive them if they turn to you again
and confess that you are their God. Bring
them back again to this land which you have
given to their fathers.
35,36"And when the skies are shut up and
there is no rain because of their sin, hear them
from heaven and forgive them when they
pray toward this place and confess your
name. And after you have punished them,
help them to follow the good ways in which
they should walk, and send rain upon the
land that you have given your people.
37"If there is a famine in the land caused by
plant disease or locusts or caterpillars, or if
Israel's enemies besiege one of her cities, or if
the people are struck by an epidemic or
plague—or whatever the problem is—38then
when the people realize their sin and pray
toward this Temple, 39hear them from heaven
and forgive and answer all who have made an
honest confession; for you know each heart.
40In this way they will always learn to reverence you as they continue to live in this land
that you have given their fathers.
41,42"And when foreigners hear of your great
name and come from distant lands to worship you (for they shall hear of your great
name and mighty miracles) and pray toward
this Temple, 43hear them from heaven and
answer their prayers. And all the nations of
the earth will know and fear your name just
as your own people Israel do; and all the earth
will know that this is your Temple.
44"When you send your people out to battle
against their enemies and they pray to you,
looking toward your chosen city of Jerusalem
and toward this Temple that I have built in
your name, 45hear their prayer and help them.
46"If they sin against you (and who
doesn't?) and you become angry with them
and let their enemies lead them away as captives to some foreign land, whether far or
near, 47and they come to their senses and turn
to you and cry to you saying, 'We have
sinned, we have done wrong'; 48if they honestly return to you and pray toward this land
that you have given their fathers, and toward
this city of Jerusalem that you have chosen,
and toward this Temple that I have built for
your name, 49hear their prayers and pleadings
from heaven where you live, and come to
their assistance.
50"Forgive your people for all of their evil
deeds, and make their captors merciful to
them; 51for they are your people—your inheritance that you brought out from the Egyptian furnace. 52May your eyes be open and
your ears listening to their pleas. O Lord, hear
and answer them whenever they cry out to
you, 53for when you brought our fathers out
of the land of Egypt, you told your servant
Moses that you had chosen Israel from among
all the nations of the earth to be your own
special people."
54,55Solomon had been kneeling with his
hands outstretched toward heaven. As he finished this prayer, he rose from before the altar
of Jehovah and cried out this blessing upon all
the people of Israel:
56"Blessed be the Lord who has fulfilled his
promise and given rest to his people Israel;
not one word has failed of all the wonderful
promises proclaimed by his servant Moses.
57May the Lord our God be with us as he was
with our fathers; may he never forsake us.
58May he give us the desire to do his will in
everything, and to obey all the commandments and instructions he has given our ancestors. 59And may these words of my prayer
be constantly before him day and night, so

8:46-53 Intercessory prayer is an important part of our relationship with God. Solomon showed that he understood this when he prayed for himself and the people. He asked God to have mercy on them before they had even made any mistakes (8:46-49). Intercessory prayer is important for us, too. When we feel that we can't resist temptation any longer, we can find strength from the prayers of others. We should ask at least one person to pray for our recovery. That person can also hold us accountable for our actions.

8:56-60 Solomon's prayer provides us with a good example to follow. It can be divided into six steps: (1) he began by praising God (8:56); (2) he requested God's presence (8:57); (3) he asked for help to do God's will (8:58); (4) he pledged to obey God in all things (8:58); (5) he asked God to remember his prayer (8:59); and (6) he prayed that all people would come to know God (8:60). These are all important aspects of a recovery program that reflects the truth of God's Word.

that he helps me and all of Israel in accordance with our daily needs. 60May people all over the earth know that the Lord is God and that there is no other god at all. 61O my people, may you live good and perfect lives before the Lord our God; may you always obey his laws and commandments, just as you are doing today."

62,63Then the king and all the people dedicated the Temple by sacrificing peace offerings to the Lord—a total of 22,000 oxen and 120,000 sheep and goats! 64As a temporary measure the king sanctified the court in front of the Temple for the burnt offerings, grain offerings, and the fat of the peace offerings: for the bronze altar was too small to handle so much. 65The celebration lasted for fourteen days, and a great crowd came from one end of the land to the other. 66Afterwards Solomon sent the people home, happy for all the goodness that the Lord had shown to his servant David and to his people Israel. And they blessed the king.

CHAPTER 9

Solomon Dedicates the Temple

When Solomon had finished building the Temple and the palace and all the other buildings he had always wanted, 2,3the Lord appeared to him the second time (the first time had been at Gibeon) and said to him,

"I have heard your prayer. I have hallowed this Temple that you have built and have put my name here forever. I will constantly watch over it and rejoice in it. 4And if you live in honesty and truth as your father David did, always obeying me, 5then I will cause your descendants to be the kings of Israel forever, just as I promised your father David when I told him, 'One of your sons shall always be upon the throne of Israel.'

6"However, if you or your children turn away from me and worship other gods and do not obey my laws, 7then I will take away the people of Israel from this land that I have given them. I will take them from this Temple which I have hallowed for my name, and I will cast them out of my sight; and Israel will become a joke to the nations and an example and proverb of sudden disaster. 8This Temple will become a heap of ruins, and everyone passing by will be amazed and will whistle with astonishment, asking, 'Why has the Lord done such things to this land and this Temple?' 9And the answer will be, 'The people of Israel abandoned the Lord their God who brought them out of the land of Egypt; they worshiped other gods instead. That is why the Lord has brought this evil upon them.'"

Solomon's Other Projects

10At the end of the twenty years during which Solomon built the Temple and the palace, 11,12he gave twenty cities in the land of Galilee to King Hiram of Tyre as payment for all the cedar and cypress lumber and gold he had furnished for the construction of the palace and Temple. Hiram came from Tyre to see the cities, but he wasn't at all pleased with them.

13"What sort of deal is this, my brother?" he asked. "These cities are a wasteland!" (And they are still known as "The Wasteland" today.) 14For Hiram had sent gold to Solomon valued at $3,500,000!

15Solomon had conscripted forced labor to build the Temple, his palace, Fort Millo, the wall of Jerusalem, and the cities of Hazor, Megiddo, and Gezer. 16Gezer was the city the king of Egypt conquered and burned, killing the Israeli population; later he had given the city to his daughter as a dowry—she was one of Solomon's wives. 17,18So now Solomon rebuilt Gezer along with Lower Beth-horon, Baalath, and Tamar, a desert city. 19He also built

9:1-9 God promised to extend to Solomon and his descendants the promises he had given to David. But with the promises came added responsibilities. God would not bless his people unless they chose to serve him and live according to his plan. If Israel worshiped other gods, then they would lose their position of blessing (9:4-7). We are often given warning signs before we commit sins. The Bible, friends, and our conscience all warn us of inappropriate behavior. Unfortunately, like Solomon and Israel, we often ignore the warnings and then must suffer the consequences.

9:10-28 Upon completing the Temple and the palace (9:10), Solomon did not take time out for God and family. He also failed to give his labor force a chance to rest. Instead, he went on a building spree. Solomon built the fortresses of Hazor, Megiddo, and Gezer and extended the fortified walls of Jerusalem to protect the Temple and palace (9:15). Solomon exhibited many of the characteristics of a workaholic. He sacrificed his relationships with God, his family, and his people to fulfill his compulsion to build. Many of the consequences of Solomon's driving personality were suffered by Rehoboam, his son. The people rebelled against Rehoboam because he promised to maintain the heavy burdens of labor and taxes initiated by Solomon (12:1-11).

cities for grain storage, cities in which to keep
his chariots, cities for homes for his cavalry
and chariot drivers, and resort cities near Jerusalem and in the Lebanon mountains and
elsewhere throughout the land.
20,21 Solomon conscripted his labor forces
from those who survived in the nations he
conquered—the Amorites, Hittites, Perizzites,
Hivites, and Jebusites. For the people of Israel
had not been able to wipe them out completely at the time of the invasion and conquest of Israel, and they continue as slaves
even today. 22 Solomon didn't conscript any
Israelis for this work, although they became
soldiers, officials, army officers, chariot commanders, and cavalrymen. 23 And there were
550 men of Israel who were overseers of the
labor forces.

Miscellaneous Notes:

24 King Solomon moved Pharaoh's daughter from the City of David—the old sector of
Jerusalem—to the new quarters he had built
for her in the palace. Then he built Fort
Millo.
25 After the Temple was completed, Solomon offered burnt offerings and peace offerings three times a year on the altar he
had built. And he also burned incense upon
it.
26 King Solomon had a shipyard in Ezion-
geber near Eloth on the Red Sea in the land of
Edom, where he built a fleet of ships.
27,28 King Hiram supplied experienced sailors
to accompany Solomon's crews. They used to
sail back and forth from Ophir, bringing gold
to King Solomon, the total value of which was
several million dollars each trip.

CHAPTER 10

The Queen of Sheba

When the queen of Sheba heard how wonderfully the Lord had blessed Solomon with wisdom, she decided to test him with some hard
questions. 2 She arrived in Jerusalem with a
long train of camels carrying spices, gold, and
jewels; and she told him all her problems.
3 Solomon answered all her questions; nothing was too difficult for him, for the Lord gave
him the right answers every time. 4 She soon
realized that everything she had ever heard
about his great wisdom was true. She also saw
the beautiful palace he had built, 5 and when
she saw the wonderful foods on his table, the
great number of servants and aides who stood
around in splendid uniforms, his cupbearers,
and the many offerings he sacrificed by fire to
the Lord—well, there was no more spirit in
her!
6 She exclaimed to him, "Everything I heard
in my own country about your wisdom and
about the wonderful things going on here is
all true. 7 I didn't believe it until I came, but
now I have seen it for myself! And really! The
half had not been told me! Your wisdom and
prosperity are far greater than anything I've
ever heard of! 8 Your people are happy and
your palace aides are content—but how could
it be otherwise, for they stand here day after
day listening to your wisdom! 9 Blessed be the
Lord your God who chose you and set you on
the throne of Israel. How the Lord must love
Israel—for he gave you to them as their king!
And you give your people a just, good government!"
10 Then she gave the king a gift of
$3,500,000 in gold, along with a huge quan-
tity of spices and precious gems; in fact, it was
the largest single gift of spices King Solomon
had ever received.
11 (And when King Hiram's ships brought
gold to Solomon from Ophir, they also
brought along a great supply of algum trees
and gems. 12 Solomon used the algum wood to
make pillars for the Temple and the palace,
and for harps and harpsichords for his choirs.
Never before or since has there been such a
supply of beautiful wood.)
13 In exchange for the gifts from the queen
of Sheba, King Solomon gave her everything
she asked him for, besides the presents he had
already planned. Then she and her servants
returned to their own land.

Solomon's Great Riches

14 Each year Solomon received gold worth a
quarter of a billion dollars, 15 besides sales
taxes and profits from trade with the kings of
Arabia and the other surrounding territories.
16,17 Solomon had some of the gold beaten into
two hundred pieces of armor (gold worth

10:1-13 When the Queen of Sheba visited Solomon, she wanted to confirm all of the rumors she had heard concerning his wealth and wisdom. She asked a series of "hard questions" and toured the palace. Upon verifying the reports of Solomon's greatness, she became an admirer of both Solomon and his God. Testing others is sometimes necessary, especially if reports of their achievements seem incredible or unbelievable. We should test their claims to see if (1) the reports are accurate and (2) they are from God. Often when something seems too good to be true, it is.

$6,000 went into each piece) and three hun-
dred shields ($1,800 worth of gold in each).
And he kept them in his palace in the Hall of
the Forest of Lebanon.
18He also made a huge ivory throne and
overlaid it with pure gold. 19It had six steps
and a rounded back, with arm rests; and a lion
standing on each side. 20And there were two
lions on each step—twelve in all. There was
no other throne in all the world so splendid
as that one.
21All of King Solomon's cups were of solid
gold, and in the Hall of the Forest of Lebanon
his entire dining service was made of solid
gold. (Silver wasn't used because it wasn't
considered to be of much value!)
22King Solomon's merchant fleet was in
partnership with King Hiram's, and once
every three years a great load of gold, silver,
ivory, apes, and peacocks arrived at the Israeli
ports.
23So King Solomon was richer and wiser
than all the kings of the earth. 24Great men
from many lands came to interview him and
listen to his God-given wisdom. 25They
brought him annual tribute of silver and gold
dishes, beautiful cloth, myrrh, spices, horses,
and mules.
26Solomon built up a great stable of horses
with a vast number of chariots and cavalry—
1,400 chariots in all and 12,000 cavalrymen,
who lived in the chariot cities and with the
king at Jerusalem. 27Silver was as common as
stones in Jerusalem in those days, and cedar
was of no greater value than the common
sycamore! 28Solomon's horses were brought to
him from Egypt and southern Turkey, where
his agents purchased them at wholesale
prices. 29An Egyptian chariot delivered to Jerusalem cost $400, and the horses were valued
at $150 each. Many of these were then resold
to the Hittite and Syrian kings.

CHAPTER 11

Solomon Turns from God

King Solomon married many other girls besides the Egyptian princess. Many of them
came from nations where idols were worshiped—Moab, Ammon, Edom, Sidon, and
from the Hittites—2even though the Lord had
clearly instructed his people not to marry into
those nations, because the women they married would get them started worshiping their
gods. Yet Solomon did it anyway. 3He had
seven hundred wives and three hundred concubines; and sure enough, they turned his
heart away from the Lord, 4especially in his
old age. They encouraged him to worship
their gods instead of trusting completely in
the Lord as his father David had done. 5Solo-
mon worshiped Ashtoreth, the goddess of the
Sidonians, and Milcom, the horrible god of
the Ammonites. 6Thus Solomon did what was
clearly wrong and refused to follow the Lord
as his father David did. 7He even built a
temple on the Mount of Olives, across the
valley from Jerusalem, for Chemosh, the depraved god of Moab, and another for Molech,
the unutterably vile god of the Ammonites.
8Solomon built temples for these foreign
wives to use for burning incense and sacrificing to their gods.
9,10Jehovah was very angry with Solomon
about this, for now Solomon was no longer
interested in the Lord God of Israel who had
appeared to him twice to warn him specifically against worshiping other gods. But he
hadn't listened, 11so now the Lord said to
him, "Since you have not kept our agreement
and have not obeyed my laws, I will tear the
kingdom away from you and your family and
give it to someone else. 12,13However, for the
sake of your father David, I won't do this
while you are still alive. I will take the kingdom away from your son. And even so I will

10:23 In the Old Testament a person's wealth often resulted from a good relationship with God. Throughout the earlier part of Solomon's life, this was the case. As Solomon grew older, however, his wealth led him to trust in himself rather than in God. We also have a tendency to allow our material wealth and pride to lead us away from God. We must remember that everything we have, even our life, is a gift from God. And as we begin to succeed in our recovery, we must remember to give God the credit he deserves. If we begin to think we did it alone, we are headed for trouble.

11:1-13 Solomon broke God's commands concerning marriage (Exodus 23:32-33) by marrying women from Moab, Edom, and other nations (11:1). God had prohibited marriage with the people of Canaan because he knew that they would lead the Israelites to worship other gods. Not only did Solomon begin to worship other gods, but he even built altars to them (11:7-8). God became angry and punished Solomon for his disobedience (11:9-13). It is tempting to go about things our own way, without looking to see what God has to say on any given matter. When we do this, however, we shouldn't be surprised when we face problems. God is calling attention to our mistakes, hoping we will turn back to him and his offer to rescue us.

let him be king of one tribe, for David's sake and for the sake of Jerusalem, my chosen city."

Solomon's Enemies

14So the Lord caused Hadad the Edomite to grow in power. And Solomon became apprehensive, for Hadad was a member of the royal family of Edom. 15Years before, when David had been in Edom with Joab to arrange for the burial of some Israeli soldiers who had died in battle, the Israeli army had killed nearly every male in the entire country. 16-18It took six months to accomplish this, but they finally killed all except Hadad and a few royal officials who took him to Egypt (he was a very small child at the time). They slipped out of Midian and went to Paran, where others joined them and accompanied them to Egypt, and Pharaoh had given them homes and food.

19Hadad became one of Pharaoh's closest friends, and he gave him a wife—the sister of Queen Tahpenes. 20She presented him with a son, Genubath, who was brought up in Pharaoh's palace among Pharaoh's own sons. 21When Hadad, there in Egypt, heard that David and Joab were both dead, he asked Pharaoh for permission to return to Edom.

22"Why?" Pharaoh asked him. "What do you lack here? How have we disappointed you?"

"Everything is wonderful," he replied "but even so, I'd like to go back home."

23Another of Solomon's enemies whom God raised to power was Rezon, one of the officials of King Hadadezer of Zobah who had deserted his post and fled the country. 24He had become the leader of a gang of bandits—men who fled with him to Damascus (where he later became king) when David destroyed Zobah. 25During Solomon's entire lifetime, Rezon and Hadad were his enemies, for they hated Israel intensely.

26Another rebel leader was Jeroboam (the son of Nebat), who came from the city of Zeredah in Ephraim; his mother was Zeruah, a widow. 27,28Here is the story back of his rebellion: Solomon was rebuilding Fort Millo, repairing the walls of this city his father had built. Jeroboam was very able, and when Solomon saw how industrious he was, he put him in charge of his labor battalions from the tribe of Joseph.

29One day as Jeroboam was leaving Jerusalem, the prophet Ahijah from Shiloh (who had put on a new robe for the occasion) met him and called him aside to talk to him. And as the two of them were alone in the field, 30Ahijah tore his new robe into twelve parts 31and said to Jeroboam, "Take ten of these pieces, for the Lord God of Israel says, 'I will tear the kingdom from the hand of Solomon and give ten of the tribes to you! 32But I will leave him one tribe for the sake of my servant David and for the sake of Jerusalem, which I have chosen above all the other cities of Israel. 33For Solomon has forsaken me and worships Ashtoreth, the goddess of the Sidonians; and Chemosh, the god of Moab; and Milcom, the god of the Ammonites. He has not followed my paths and has not done what I consider right; he has not kept my laws and instructions as his father David did. 34I will not take the kingdom from him now, however; for the sake of my servant David, my chosen one who obeyed my commandments, I will let Solomon reign for the rest of his life.

35"'But I will take away the kingdom from his son and give ten of the tribes to you. 36His son shall have the other one so that the descendants of David will continue to reign in Jerusalem, the city I have chosen to be the place for my name to be enshrined. 37And I will place you on the throne of Israel and give you absolute power. 38If you listen to what I tell you and walk in my path and do whatever I consider right, obeying my commandments

---

11:14-25 For years, God had allowed Solomon to rule in peace. He had put down the threat of hostile neighbors so "a man of peace" could build his Temple (1 Chronicles 28:2-3). But as Solomon turned his back on God, he was confronted with foreign enemies, such as Hadad (11:14) and Rezon (11:23). The problems we now face are often consequences of choices we have already made. Before blaming others for our situation, we should examine our past. We may find that we are the one responsible.

11:26-40 The greatest consequence for Solomon's sins was realized after his death—Israel was divided. God raised up Jeroboam as the first king of the northern kingdom of Israel. Solomon attempted to kill Jeroboam to try to prevent God's will from coming about (11:40). Solomon's decisions were obviously being driven by an inaccurate self-perception. He had begun to believe that his actions could rewrite the will of God. No matter how rich, popular, or important we might become, we will never be able to change what God has said will happen. How often do we fall prey to the sin of thinking we can outmaneuver God?

as my servant David did, then I will bless you; and your descendants shall rule Israel forever. (I once made this same promise to David.
[39]But because of Solomon's sin, I will punish the descendants of David—though not forever.)'"
[40]Solomon tried to kill Jeroboam, but he fled to King Shishak of Egypt and stayed there until the death of Solomon.

Solomon's Death

[41]The rest of what Solomon did and said is written in the book *The Acts of Solomon.* [42]He
ruled in Jerusalem for forty years, [43]and then died and was buried in the city of his father David; and his son Rehoboam reigned in his place.

CHAPTER 12

The Kingdom Is Divided

Rehoboam's inauguration was at Shechem, and all Israel came for the coronation ceremony. [2-4]Jeroboam, who was still in Egypt where he had fled from King Solomon, heard about the plans from his friends. They urged him to attend, so he joined the rest of Israel at Shechem and was the ringleader in getting the people to make certain demands upon Rehoboam.

"Your father was a hard master," they told Rehoboam. "We don't want you as our king unless you promise to treat us better than he did."

[5]"Give me three days to think this over," Rehoboam replied. "Come back then for my answer." So the people left.

[6]Rehoboam talked it over with the old men who had counseled his father Solomon.

"What do you think I should do?" he asked them.

[7]And they replied, "If you give them a pleasant reply and agree to be good to them and serve them well, you can be their king forever."

[8]But Rehoboam refused the old men's counsel and called in the young men with whom he had grown up.

[9]"What do you think I should do?" he asked them.

[10]And the young men replied, "Tell them, 'If you think my father was hard on you, well,
I'll be harder! [11]Yes, my father was harsh, but I'll be even harsher! My father used whips on you, but I'll use scorpions!'"

[12]So when Jeroboam and the people returned three days later, [13,14]the new king answered them roughly. He ignored the old men's advice and followed that of the young
men; [15]so the king refused the people's demands. (But the Lord's hand was in it—he caused the new king to do this in order to fulfill his promise to Jeroboam, made through Ahijah, the prophet from Shiloh.)

[16,17]When the people realized that the king meant what he said and was refusing to listen to them, they began shouting, "Down with David and all his relatives! Let's go home! Let Rehoboam be king of his own family!"

And they all deserted him except for the tribe of Judah, who remained loyal and accepted Rehoboam as their king. [18]When King
Rehoboam sent Adoram (who was in charge of the draft) to conscript men from the other tribes, a great mob stoned him to death. But King Rehoboam escaped by chariot and fled to Jerusalem. [19]And Israel has been in rebellion against the dynasty of David to this day.

11:41–12:1 Solomon's life ended (11:43), and his son Rehoboam inherited the throne (12:1). Before he died, David gave his son Solomon advice on how to run the kingdom (see 2:1-12). But Solomon failed to do this with his son. Rehoboam was left to rule without the counsel of his father. Fathers must never underestimate the value of helping their children in their new responsibilities. Fathers have valuable contributions to make, contributions that can save their children the pain of learning the lessons on their own.

12:6-14 Rehoboam was wise to ask for counsel (12:6). He made a mistake, however, in not evaluating the advice properly. Counsel should always be measured against the principles set forth in Scripture. Had Rehoboam done this, he would have seen that the advice of his peers (12:9-11) was unwise. We need to carefully weigh the counsel we receive, asking God for the wisdom to know what is right.

12:15-33 Both of the kings who followed Solomon, Jeroboam and Rehoboam, made foolish, self-serving decisions. Rehoboam followed his selfish inclinations, which led to the division of the kingdom (12:15). Jeroboam was so afraid of losing his kingdom (even though God appointed him king) that he broke God's laws. He made idols for the people to worship so they wouldn't have to go to Jerusalem to worship. The selfish attitudes of these two men led entire kingdoms on the path toward sin. We need to realize that our decisions always touch the lives of others. We should measure our decisions by God's truth and by how they will affect others.

[20]When the people of Israel learned of Jeroboam's return from Egypt, he was asked to
come before an open meeting of all the
people; and there he was made king of Israel.
Only the tribe of Judah continued under the
kingship of the family of David.
[21]When King Rehoboam arrived in Jerusalem, he summoned his army—all the able-
bodied men of Judah and Benjamin: 180,000
special troops—to force the rest of Israel to
acknowledge him as their king. [22]But God sent
this message to Shemaiah, the prophet:
[23,24]"Tell Rehoboam the son of Solomon,
king of Judah, and all the people of Judah and
Benjamin that they must not fight against
their brothers, the people of Israel. Tell them
to disband and go home, for what has happened to Rehoboam is according to my wish."
So the army went home as the Lord had
commanded.

Jeroboam Makes Golden Calves

[25]Jeroboam now built the city of Shechem in
the hill country of Ephraim, and it became his
capital. Later he built Penuel. [26]Jeroboam
thought, "Unless I'm careful, the people will
want a descendant of David as their king.
[27]When they go to Jerusalem to offer sacrifices
at the Temple, they will become friendly with
King Rehoboam; then they will kill me and
ask him to be their king instead."
[28]So on the advice of his counselors, the
king had two gold calf-idols made and told
the people, "It's too much trouble to go to
Jerusalem to worship; from now on these will
be your gods—they rescued you from your
captivity in Egypt!"
[29]One of these calf-idols was placed in
Bethel and the other in Dan. [30]This was of
course a great sin, for the people worshiped
them. [31]He also made shrines on the hills and
ordained priests from the rank and file of the
people—even those who were not from the
priest-tribe of Levi. [32,33]Jeroboam also announced that the annual Tabernacle Festival
would be held at Bethel on the first of November (a date he decided upon himself), similar
to the annual festival at Jerusalem; he himself
offered sacrifices upon the altar to the calves
at Bethel and burned incense to them. And it
was there at Bethel that he ordained priests
for the shrines on the hills.

CHAPTER 13

A Prophet Dies for Disobedience

As Jeroboam approached the altar to burn
incense to the gold calf-idol, a prophet of the
Lord from Judah walked up to him. [2]Then, at
the Lord's command, the prophet shouted,
"O altar, the Lord says that a child named
Josiah shall be born into the family line of
David, and he shall sacrifice upon you the
priests from the shrines on the hills who
come here to burn incense; and men's bones
shall be burned upon you."
[3]Then he gave this proof that his message
was from the Lord: "This altar will split apart,
and the ashes on it will spill to the ground."
[4]The king was very angry with the prophet
for saying this. He shouted to his guards,
"Arrest that man!" and shook his fist at him.
Instantly the king's arm became paralyzed in
that position; he couldn't pull it back again!
[5]At the same moment a wide crack appeared
in the altar and the ashes poured out, just as
the prophet had said would happen. For this
was the prophet's proof that God had been
speaking through him.
[6]"Oh, please, please," the king cried out to
the prophet, "beg the Lord your God to restore my arm again."
So he prayed to the Lord, and the king's
arm became normal again.
[7]Then the king said to the prophet, "Come
to the palace with me and rest awhile and
have some food; and I'll give you a reward
because you healed my arm."
[8]But the prophet said to the king, "Even if
you gave me half your palace, I wouldn't go
into it; nor would I eat or drink even water in
this place! [9]For the Lord has given me strict
orders not to eat anything or drink any water
while I'm here, and not to return to Judah by
the road I came on."
[10]So he went back another way.
[11]As it happened, there was an old prophet
living in Bethel, and his sons went home and
told him what the prophet from Judah had
done and what he had said to the king.
[12]"Which way did he go?" the old prophet
asked. So they told him.
[13]"Quick, saddle the donkey," the old man
said. And when they had saddled the donkey
for him, [14]he rode after the prophet and found
him sitting under an oak tree.
"Are you the prophet who came from
Judah?" he asked him.
"Yes," he replied, "I am."
[15]Then the old man said to the prophet,
"Come home with me and eat."
[16,17]"No," he replied, "I can't; for I am not
allowed to eat anything or to drink any water
at Bethel. The Lord strictly warned me against

it; and he also told me not to return home by the same road I came on."

[18]But the old man said, "I am a prophet too, just as you are; and an angel gave me a message from the Lord. I am to take you home with me and give you food and water."

But the old man was lying to him. [19]So they went back together, and the prophet ate some food and drank some water at the old man's home.

[20]Then, suddenly, while they were sitting at the table, a message from the Lord came to the old man, [21,22]and he shouted at the prophet from Judah, "The Lord says that because you have been disobedient to his clear command and have come here, and have eaten and drunk water in the place he told you not to, therefore your body shall not be buried in the grave of your fathers."

[23]After finishing the meal, the old man saddled the prophet's donkey, [24,25]and the prophet started off again. But as he was traveling along, a lion came out and killed him. His body lay there on the road, with the donkey and the lion standing beside it. Those who came by and saw the body lying in the road and the lion standing quietly beside it, reported it in Bethel where the old prophet lived.

[26]When he heard what had happened he exclaimed, "It is the prophet who disobeyed the Lord's command; the Lord fulfilled his warning by causing the lion to kill him."

[27]Then he said to his sons, "Saddle my donkey!" And they did.

[28]He found the prophet's body lying in the road; and the donkey and lion were still standing there beside it, for the lion had not eaten the body nor attacked the donkey. [29]So the prophet laid the body upon the donkey and took it back to the city to mourn over it and bury it.

[30]He laid the body in his own grave, exclaiming, "Alas, my brother!"

[31]Afterwards he said to his sons, "When I die, bury me in the grave where the prophet is buried. Lay my bones beside his bones. [32]For the Lord told him to shout against the altar in Bethel, and his curse against the shrines in the cities of Samaria shall surely be fulfilled."

[33]Despite the prophet's warning, Jeroboam did not turn away from his evil ways; instead, he made more priests than ever from the common people, to offer sacrifices to idols in the shrines on the hills. Anyone who wanted to could be a priest. [34]This was a great sin and resulted in the destruction of Jeroboam's kingdom and the death of all of his family.

CHAPTER 14

God Judges Jeroboam

Jeroboam's son Abijah now became very sick. [2]Jeroboam told his wife, "Disguise yourself so that no one will recognize you as the queen, and go to Ahijah the prophet at Shiloh—the man who told me that I would become king. [3]Take him a gift of ten loaves of bread, some fig bars, and a jar of honey, and ask him whether the boy will recover."

[4]So his wife went to Ahijah's home at Shiloh. He was an old man now and could no longer see. [5]But the Lord told him that the queen, pretending to be someone else, would come to ask about her son, for he was very sick. And the Lord told him what to tell her.

[6]So when Ahijah heard her at the door, he called out, "Come in, wife of Jeroboam! Why are you pretending to be someone else?" Then he told her, "I have sad news for you. [7]Give your husband this message from the Lord God of Israel: 'I promoted you from the ranks of the common people and made you king of Israel. [8]I ripped the kingdom away from the family of David and gave it to you, but you

---

13:33-34 Persistence in doing good is admirable. Persistence in doing wrong displays arrogance and is sure to result in great harm. Jeroboam's apostasy demonstrates just how harmful persistence can be when a person is doing the wrong thing. After he was warned of God's coming wrath (13:1-32), Jeroboam violated God's commands about the priesthood (Numbers 3:10) by making unqualified people priests. Without accountable relationships, all of us tend to start down the wrong track. We would be wise to find a trustworthy friend who will hold us accountable to the truth in God's Word.

14:1-11 Here we see a good example of the dangers of codependency. Jeroboam had made deceit a regular practice during his reign over Israel. As his son was lying on his deathbed, Jeroboam asked his codependent wife to deceive the prophet Abijah by disguising herself. The result of their combined sin was the destruction of their family. By consciously or unconsciously calling upon him or her to enable us in some way, we often cause our spouse to participate in our dependencies. Jeroboam's wife would have been wise to confront Jeroboam with his sinful ways. Instead, she enabled his sin, and the results were destructive. A spouse's confrontation, though difficult, can often initiate a person's recovery and deliver a family from great suffering.

have not obeyed my commandments as my
servant David did. His heart's desire was always to obey me and to do whatever I wanted
him to. 9But you have done more evil than all
the other kings before you; you have made
other gods and have made me furious with
your gold calves. And since you have refused
to acknowledge me, 10I will bring disaster
upon your home and will destroy all of your
sons—this boy who is sick and all those who
are well. I will sweep away your family as a
stable hand shovels out manure. 11I vow that
those of your family who die in the city shall
be eaten by dogs, and those who die in the
field shall be eaten by birds.'"

12Then Ahijah said to Jeroboam's wife, "Go
on home, and when you step into the city, the
child will die. 13All of Israel will mourn for
him and bury him, but he is the only member
of your family who will come to a quiet end.
For this child is the only good thing that the
Lord God of Israel sees in the entire family of
Jeroboam. 14And the Lord will raise up a king
over Israel who will destroy the family of
Jeroboam. 15Then the Lord will shake Israel
like a reed whipped about in a stream; he will
uproot the people of Israel from this good
land of their fathers and scatter them beyond
the Euphrates River, for they have angered the
Lord by worshiping idol-gods. 16He will abandon Israel because Jeroboam sinned and
made all of Israel sin along with him."

17So Jeroboam's wife returned to Tirzah;
and the child died just as she walked through
the door of her home. 18And there was mourning for him throughout the land, just as the
Lord had predicted through Ahijah.

19The rest of Jeroboam's activities—his wars
and the other events of his reign—are recorded in *The Annals of the Kings of Israel.*
20Jeroboam reigned twenty-two years, and
when he died, his son Nadab took the throne.

Rehoboam Rules Judah

21Meanwhile, Rehoboam the son of Solomon
was king in Judah. He was forty-one years old
when he began to reign, and he was on the
throne seventeen years in Jerusalem, the city
which, among all the cities of Israel, the Lord
had chosen to live in. (Rehoboam's mother
was Naamah, an Ammonite woman.) 22Dur-
ing his reign the people of Judah, like those in
Israel, did wrong and angered the Lord with
their sin, for it was even worse than that of
their ancestors. 23They built shrines and obelisks and idols on every high hill and under
every green tree. 24There was homosexuality
throughout the land, and the people of Judah
became as depraved as the heathen nations
which the Lord drove out to make room for
his people.

25In the fifth year of Rehoboam's reign,
King Shishak of Egypt attacked and conquered Jerusalem. 26He ransacked the Temple
and the palace and stole everything, including all the gold shields Solomon had made.
27Afterwards Rehoboam made bronze shields
as substitutes, and the palace guards used
these instead. 28Whenever the king went to
the Temple, the guards paraded before him
and then took the shields back to the guard
chamber.

29The other events in Rehoboam's reign are
written in *The Annals of the Kings of Judah.*
30There was constant war between Rehoboam
and Jeroboam. 31When Rehoboam died—his
mother was Naamah the Ammonitess—he
was buried among his ancestors in Jerusalem,
and his son Abijam took the throne.

CHAPTER 15

Abijam Rules Judah

Abijam began his three-year reign as king of
Judah in Jerusalem during the eighteenth year
of Jeroboam's reign in Israel. (Abijam's
mother was Maacah, the daughter of Absha-
lom.) 3He was as great a sinner as his father
was, and his heart was not right with God, as
King David's was. 4But despite Abijam's sin,
the Lord remembered David's love and did
not end the line of David's royal descendants.
5For David had obeyed God during his entire
life except for the affair concerning Uriah the
Hittite. 6During Abijam's reign there was constant war between Israel and Judah. 7The rest
of Abijam's history is recorded in *The Annals
of the Kings of Judah.* 8When he died he was
buried in Jerusalem, and his son Asa reigned
in his place.

14:22–15:3 Children learn from their parents. Rehoboam learned from Solomon that idol worship was all right. So when Rehoboam became king, idol worship flourished. When Rehoboam's son Abijam became king, he followed in the footsteps of his father, becoming "as great a sinner as his father was" (15:3). We may not realize how deeply our addictions affect others, but here we can see that Solomon's worship of idols led to the disobedience of his son and grandson. What are our children learning from our behavior and attitudes?

Asa Rules Judah
[9]Asa became king of Judah, in Jerusalem, in
the twentieth year of the reign of Jeroboam
over Israel, [10]and reigned forty-one years. (His
grandmother was Maacah, the daughter of
Abishalom.) [11]He pleased the Lord like his
ancestor King David. [12]He executed the male
prostitutes and removed all the idols his
father had made. [13]He deposed his grandmother Maacah as queen-mother because she
had made an idol—which he cut down and
burned at Kidron Brook. [14]However, the
shrines on the hills were not removed, for Asa
did not realize that these were wrong. [15]He
made permanent exhibits in the Temple of
the bronze shields his grandfather had dedicated, along with the silver and gold vessels
he himself had donated.
[16]There was lifelong war between King Asa
of Judah and King Baasha of Israel. [17]King
Baasha built the fortress city of Ramah in an
attempt to cut off all trade with Jerusalem.
[18]Then Asa took all the silver and gold left in
the Temple treasury and all the treasures of
the palace, and gave them to his officials to
take to Damascus, to King Ben-hadad of Syria,
with this message:
[19]"Let us be allies just as our fathers were. I
am sending you a present of gold and silver.
Now break your alliance with King Baasha of
Israel so that he will leave me alone."
[20]Ben-hadad agreed and sent his armies
against some of the cities of Israel; and he
destroyed Ijon, Dan, Abel-beth-maacah, all of
Chinneroth, and all the cities in the land of
Naphtali. [21]When Baasha received word of the
attack, he discontinued building the city of
Ramah and returned to Tirzah. [22]Then King
Asa made a proclamation to all Judah, asking
every able-bodied man to help demolish Ramah and haul away its stones and timbers.
And King Asa used these materials to build the
city of Geba in Benjamin and the city of
Mizpah.
[23]The rest of Asa's biography—his conquests and deeds and the names of the cities
he built—is found in *The Annals of the Kings of
Judah*. In his old age his feet became diseased,
[24]and when he died, he was buried in the royal
cemetery in Jerusalem. Then his son Jehoshaphat became the new king of Judah.

Nadab Rules Israel
[25]Meanwhile over in Israel, Nadab, the son of
Jeroboam, had become king. He reigned two
years, beginning in the second year of the
reign of King Asa of Judah. [26]But he was not a
good king; like his father, he worshiped many
idols and led all of Israel into sin.
[27]Then Baasha (the son of Ahijah, from the
tribe of Issachar) plotted against him and assassinated him while he was with the Israeli
army laying siege to the Philistine city of
Gibbethon. [28]So Baasha replaced Nadab as the
king of Israel in Tirzah during the third year
of the reign of King Asa of Judah. [29]He immediately killed all of the descendants of King
Jeroboam, so that not one of the royal family
was left, just as the Lord had said would happen when he spoke through Ahijah, the
prophet from Shiloh. [30]This was done because
Jeroboam had angered the Lord God of Israel
by sinning and leading the rest of Israel into
sin.

Baasha Rules Israel
[31]Further details of Baasha's reign are recorded
in *The Annals of the Kings of Israel*.
[32,33]There was continuous warfare between
King Asa of Judah and King Baasha of Israel.

15:9-13 Courage is needed to confront generations of corruption and dysfunctional behavior in any family. Asa showed courage when he confronted the sins of his forefathers by making the decision to serve God. Asa's changes included destroying idols and deposing his mother from her position as queen. The early years of Asa's reign leave us with a wonderful example of how to go about the rebuilding process.

15:25-31 Nadab continued to lead Israel into sin as his father, Jeroboam, had done before him. Leadership must be taken seriously because leaders are ultimately responsible for their followers. As a result of the irresponsible leadership of Jeroboam, God destroyed him and his descendants (15:30-31). Leadership and responsibility go hand in hand; so do recovery and responsibility. If we desire to succeed in recovery, we need to take responsibility for our actions. Then we need to make the appropriate changes in our life.

15:32-34 Baasha is a good example of a person in denial. Baasha ruled in Israel at the time of Asa's reign in Judah (15:32-33). Baasha surely was aware of Asa's reforms and the resultant blessings. He had also seen the sin of his forefathers and the trouble it had caused. But apparently he was blind to the facts, for he repeated the sins of his fathers (15:34). We need to search our life for areas where denial may keep us from making an accurate inventory. Otherwise we will never be able to deal with the problems in our life.

AHAB & JEZEBEL

In an odd way, bad role models can be as valuable to us as good ones. Their behavior provides clear guidance on how not to act. The consequences they suffer also provide a warning for any who might imitate them. Most of the time, we can observe the actions of dysfunctional people and plot a healthy course by doing exactly the opposite.

Ahab and Jezebel were classic examples of the bad role model. Ahab was an exceedingly evil and oppressive king, and Jezebel taught him things about evil that he never would have dreamed of alone. And it is not as if Ahab and Jezebel had no opportunities to understand and pursue recovery. The prophet Elijah was constantly confronting them. Again and again, Elijah intervened in their wicked dealings; again and again they rebutted his efforts to start them on the road to recovery.

Finally, though, Elijah's confrontation made a difference in Ahab's life. After Jezebel's outrageous scheme allowed Ahab to possess the vineyard of Naboth, Elijah predicted the violent death of Ahab. At that point, Ahab greatly humbled himself. He seemed to have hit bottom and to have begun moving toward recovery. There is, however, no record of further progress before Ahab's death in battle.

Jezebel, on the other hand, never made even the slightest move toward God and his ways. Whenever she was defeated by Elijah, she merely redoubled her efforts to maintain her idolatry and to get her own way. No wonder her name has become a byword for evil among God's people.

Like most people involved in evil, Ahab and Jezebel surrounded themselves with people of like mind. They avoided and punished people who held them accountable. When we are involved in destructive behavior, we also prefer the comforting darkness of sin and sinful friends. Recovery requires that we break with the past and our destructive relationships. We should listen to the people who love us and love God enough to hold us accountable for our actions.

WEAKNESSES AND MISTAKES:
- Ahab was the most evil king of Israel.
- Ahab married Jezebel, a pagan woman.
- Ahab allowed Jezebel to practice and promote idol worship in Israel.
- Ahab got depressed when he couldn't get what he wanted.
- Jezebel attempted to stamp out the worship of the true God.

LESSONS FROM THEIR LIVES:
- Human ability, wealth, power, and tenacity will lead us down a dead-end street if we ignore God's plan for us.
- Commitment to just "any god" will bring us little help; we must be committed to the true God through faith in Jesus Christ.

KEY VERSE:
"No one else was so completely sold out to the devil as Ahab, for his wife, Jezebel, encouraged him to do every sort of evil" (1 Kings 21:25).

Ahab and Jezebel's story is told in 1 Kings 16–22. Jezebel's story concludes in 2 Kings 9. Ahab is also mentioned in 2 Chronicles 18; 21–22; and Micah 6:16.

Baasha reigned for twenty-four years, 34but all
that time he continually disobeyed the Lord.
He followed the evil paths of Jeroboam, for he
led the people of Israel into the sin of worshiping idols.

CHAPTER 16

A message of condemnation from the Lord was delivered to King Baasha at this time by the prophet Jehu:

2"I lifted you out of the dust," the message
said, "to make you king of my people Israel;
but you have walked in the evil paths of
Jeroboam. You have made my people sin,
and I am angry! 3So now I will destroy you
and your family, just as I did the descendants
of Jeroboam. 4-7Those of your family who die
in the city will be eaten by dogs, and those
who die in the fields will be eaten by the
birds."

The message was sent to Baasha and his family because he had angered the Lord by all his evil deeds. He was as evil as Jeroboam despite the fact that the Lord had destroyed all of Jeroboam's descendants for their sins.

The rest of Baasha's biography—his deeds and conquests—are written in *The Annals of the Kings of Israel.*

Elah Rules Israel

[8]Elah, Baasha's son, began reigning during the twenty-sixth year of the reign of King Asa of Judah, but he reigned only two years. [9]Then General Zimri, who had charge of half the royal chariot troops, plotted against him. One day King Elah was half drunk at the home of Arza, the superintendent of the palace, in the capital city of Tirzah. [10]Zimri simply walked in and struck him down and killed him. (This occurred during the twenty-seventh year of the reign of King Asa of Judah.) Then Zimri declared himself to be the new king of Israel.

[11]He immediately killed the entire royal family—leaving not a single male child. He even destroyed distant relatives and friends. [12]This destruction of the descendants of Baasha was in line with what the Lord had predicted through the prophet Jehu. [13]The tragedy occurred because of the sins of Baasha and his son Elah; for they had led Israel into worshiping idols, and the Lord was very angry about it. [14]The rest of the history of Elah's reign is written in *The Annals of the Kings of Israel.*

Zimri Rules Israel

[15,16]But Zimri lasted only seven days; for when the army of Israel, which was then engaged in attacking the Philistine city of Gibbethon, heard that Zimri had assassinated the king, they decided on General Omri, commander-in-chief of the army, as their new ruler. [17]So Omri led the army of Gibbethon to besiege Tirzah, Israel's capital. [18]When Zimri saw that the city had been taken, he went into the palace and burned it over him and died in the flames. [19]For he, too, had sinned like Jeroboam; he had worshiped idols and had led the people of Israel to sin with him. [20]The rest of the story of Zimri and his treason are written in *The Annals of the Kings of Israel.*

Omri Rules Israel

[21]But now the kingdom of Israel was split in two; half the people were loyal to General Omri, and the other half followed Tibni, the son of Ginath. [22]But General Omri won and Tibni was killed; so Omri reigned without opposition.

[23]King Asa of Judah had been on the throne thirty-one years when Omri began his reign over Israel, which lasted twelve years, six of them in Tirzah. [24]Then Omri bought the hill now known as Samaria from its owner, Shemer, for $4,000 and built a city on it, calling it Samaria in honor of Shemer. [25]But Omri was worse than any of the kings before him; [26]he worshiped idols as Jeroboam had and led Israel into this same sin. So God was very angry. [27]The rest of Omri's history is recorded in *The Annals of the Kings of Israel.* [28]When Omri died he was buried in Samaria, and his son Ahab became king in his place.

Ahab Rules Israel

[29]King Asa of Judah had been on the throne thirty-eight years when Ahab became the king of Israel; and Ahab reigned for twenty-two years. [30]But he was even more wicked than his father Omri; he was worse than any other king of Israel! [31]And as though that were not enough, he married Jezebel, the daughter of King Ethbaal of the Sidonians, and then began worshiping Baal. [32]First he built a temple and an altar for Baal in Samaria. [33]Then he made other idols and did more to

16:8-10 Alcohol and drug abuse is often driven by the desire to escape the realities we face. Every year people die, families are torn apart, careers are ruined, and lives are shattered by unhealthy dependencies. God used Elah to demonstrate the dangers of alcoholism. Probably too intoxicated to defend himself, Elah was killed easily by Zimri (16:10). Alcohol affects our judgment and our reflexes. How many lives could be saved if we would all learn from Elah's mistake?

16:15-20 Zimri had the shortest reign (seven days) of all the kings of Israel. Omri led the army of Israel against Zimri at Tirzah, and seeing that his end was near, Zimri choose to commit suicide. Zimri, like those before him, was an evil king. But even at the end, he had time to call upon God to save him. Rather than submit to almighty God or face the judgment of his own people, Zimri took his own life. When it looks like there is no way out of our problems, we need not take drastic measures. We should always start by turning to God for help.

16:29-31 A descending spiral well illustrates how we tend to fall progressively deeper into trouble unless we take steps to turn things around. God uses the story of the kings of Israel to illuminate this principle to us. Ahab continued the downward spiral by being more wicked than anyone before him. Ahab and his forefathers serve as a reminder that problems left unresolved will continue, and even worsen, until confronted and resolved.

anger the Lord God of Israel than any of the other kings of Israel before him.

34(It was during his reign that Hiel, a man from Bethel, rebuilt Jericho. When he laid the foundations, his oldest son, Abiram, died; and when he finally completed it by setting up the gates, his youngest son, Segub, died. For this was the Lord's curse upon Jericho as declared by Joshua, the son of Nun.)

CHAPTER 17

Ravens Feed Elijah

Then Elijah, the prophet from Tishbe in Gilead, told King Ahab, "As surely as the Lord God of Israel lives—the God whom I worship and serve—there won't be any dew or rain for several years until I say the word!"

2Then the Lord said to Elijah, 3"Go to the east and hide by Cherith Brook at a place east of where it enters the Jordan River. 4Drink from the brook and eat what the ravens bring you, for I have commanded them to feed you."

5So he did as the Lord had told him to and camped beside the brook. 6The ravens brought him bread and meat each morning and evening, and he drank from the brook. 7But after awhile the brook dried up, for there was no rainfall anywhere in the land.

Elijah Helps a Poor Widow

8,9Then the Lord said to him, "Go and live in the village of Zarephath, near the city of Sidon. There is a widow there who will feed you. I have given her my instructions."

10So he went to Zarephath. As he arrived at the gates of the city he saw a widow gathering sticks; and he asked her for a cup of water.

11As she was going to get it, he called to her, "Bring me a bite of bread too."

12But she said, "I swear by the Lord your God that I haven't a single piece of bread in the house. And I have only a handful of flour left and a little cooking oil in the bottom of the jar. I was just gathering a few sticks to cook this last meal, and then my son and I must die of starvation."

13But Elijah said to her, "Don't be afraid! Go ahead and cook that 'last meal,' but bake me a little loaf of bread first; and afterwards there will still be enough food for you and your son. 14For the Lord God of Israel says that there will always be plenty of flour and oil left in your containers until the time when the Lord sends rain and the crops grow again!"

15So she did as Elijah said, and she and Elijah and her son continued to eat from her supply of flour and oil as long as it was needed. 16For no matter how much they used, there was always plenty left in the containers, just as the Lord had promised through Elijah!

17But one day the woman's son became sick and died.

18"O man of God," she cried, "what have you done to me? Have you come here to punish my sins by killing my son?"

19"Give him to me," Elijah replied. And he took the boy's body from her and carried it upstairs to the guest room where he lived, and laid the body on his bed, 20and then cried out to the Lord, "O Lord my God, why have you killed the son of this widow with whom I am staying?"

21And he stretched himself upon the child three times and cried out to the Lord, "O Lord my God, please let this child's spirit return to him."

22And the Lord heard Elijah's prayer; and the spirit of the child returned, and he became alive again! 23Then Elijah took him downstairs and gave him to his mother.

"See! He's alive!" he beamed.

24"Now I know for sure that you are a prophet," she told him afterward, "and that whatever you say is from the Lord!"

CHAPTER 18

Elijah Confronts King Ahab

It was three years later that the Lord said to Elijah, "Go and tell King Ahab that I will soon send rain again!"

2So Elijah went to tell him. Meanwhile the famine had become very severe in Samaria.

3,4The man in charge of Ahab's household

17:8-16 The widow of Zarephath demonstrated the delivering power of faith. She and her son faced starvation, but still she shared her last food with Elijah. She believed that God would come through, so she gave up her last resource for survival. The result was her deliverance. God provided for her need. When we are powerless—at the end of our rope—all we need to do is call out to God. He will take care of us and deliver us from our dependencies if we are willing to trust him.

17:17-24 As the widow encountered the tragedy of losing her son, her first impulse was to blame it on her own sin. God showed her that this was not the case by bringing her son back to life. Personal tragedy is not always the consequence of something we have done. We must be careful not to blame ourself without just cause. And we should never blame God either. Instead, we should look and see what we can learn from the situation.

affairs was Obadiah, who was a devoted follower of the Lord. Once when Queen Jezebel had tried to kill all of the Lord's prophets, Obadiah had hidden one hundred of them in two caves—fifty in each—and had fed them with bread and water.

5That same day, while Elijah was on the way to see King Ahab, the king said to Obadiah, "We must check every stream and brook to see if we can find enough grass to save at least some of my horses and mules. You go one way and I'll go the other, and we will search the entire land."

6So they did, each going alone. 7Suddenly
Obadiah saw Elijah coming toward him! Obadiah recognized him at once and fell to the ground before him.

"Is it really you, my lord Elijah?" he asked.

8"Yes, it is," Elijah replied. "Now go and tell the king I am here."

9"Oh, sir," Obadiah protested, "what harm have I done to you that you are sending me to
my death? 10For I swear by God that the king
has searched every nation and kingdom on earth from end to end to find you. And each time when he was told 'Elijah isn't here,' King Ahab forced the king of that nation to swear
to the truth of his claim. 11And now you say,
'Go and tell him Elijah is here'! 12 But as soon
as I leave you, the Spirit of the Lord will carry you away, who knows where, and when Ahab comes and can't find you, he will kill me; yet I have been a true servant of the Lord all my
life. 13Has no one told you about the time
when Queen Jezebel was trying to kill the Lord's prophets, and I hid a hundred of them in two caves and fed them with bread and
water? 14And now you say, 'Go tell the king
that Elijah is here'! Sir, if I do that, I'm dead!"

15But Elijah said, "I swear by the Lord God of the armies of heaven, in whose presence I stand, that I will present myself to Ahab today."

Elijah Defeats the Prophets of Baal

16So Obadiah went to tell Ahab that Elijah had come; and Ahab went out to meet him.

17"So it's you, is it?—the man who brought this disaster upon Israel!" Ahab exclaimed when he saw him.

18"You're talking about yourself," Elijah answered. "For you and your family have refused to obey the Lord and have worshiped
Baal instead. 19Now bring all the people of
Israel to Mount Carmel, with all 450 prophets of Baal and the 400 prophets of Asherah who are supported by Jezebel."

20So Ahab summoned all the people and the prophets to Mount Carmel.

21Then Elijah talked to them. "How long are you going to waver between two opinions?" he asked the people. "If the Lord is God, *follow* him! But if Baal is God, then follow *him!*"

22Then Elijah spoke again. "I am the only prophet of the Lord who is left," he told them,
"but Baal has 450 prophets. 23Now bring two
young bulls. The prophets of Baal may choose whichever one they wish and cut it into pieces and lay it on the wood of their altar, but without putting any fire under the wood; and I will prepare the other young bull and lay it on the wood on the Lord's altar, with no fire
under it. 24Then pray to your god, and I will
pray to the Lord; and the god who answers by sending fire to light the wood is the true God!" And all the people agreed to this test.

25Then Elijah turned to the prophets of Baal. "You first," he said, "for there are many of you; choose one of the bulls and prepare it and call to your god; but don't put any fire under the wood."

26So they prepared one of the young bulls and placed it on the altar; and they called to Baal all morning, shouting, "O Baal, hear us!" But there was no reply of any kind. Then they
began to dance around the altar. 27About
noontime, Elijah began mocking them.

"You'll have to shout louder than that," he scoffed, "to catch the attention of your god! Perhaps he is talking to someone, or is out sitting on the toilet, or maybe he is away on a trip, or is asleep and needs to be wakened!"

28So they shouted louder and, as was their custom, cut themselves with knives and
swords until the blood gushed out. 29They
raved all afternoon until the time of the evening sacrifice, but there was no reply, no voice, no answer.

30Then Elijah called to the people, "Come over here."

18:22-39 "The odds are against us" is a phrase that is commonly used in our society. Few enjoy being the underdog, the one that the odds are against. The underdog here was Elijah, who was greatly outnumbered by the prophets of Baal. Elijah trusted God to be with him in what has become one of the greatest spiritual victories of all time. When God is on our side, we are always a majority. No dependency or problem will ever be able to stop our progress. "If God is on our side, who can ever be against us?" (Romans 8:31).

And they all crowded around him as he
repaired the altar of the Lord that had been
torn down. 31He took twelve stones, one to
represent each of the tribes of Israel, 32and
used the stones to rebuild the Lord's altar.
Then he dug a trench about three feet wide
around the altar. 33He piled wood upon the
altar and cut the young bull into pieces and
laid the pieces on the wood.

"Fill four barrels with water," he said, "and
pour the water over the carcass and the
wood."

After they had done this he said, 34"Do it
again." And they did.

"Now, do it once more!" And they did;
35and the water ran off the altar and filled the
trench.

36At the customary time for offering the
evening sacrifice, Elijah walked up to the altar
and prayed, "O Lord God of Abraham, Isaac,
and Israel, prove today that you are the God
of Israel and that I am your servant; prove
that I have done all this at your command.
37O Lord, answer me! Answer me so these
people will know that you are God and that
you have brought them back to yourself."

38Then, suddenly, fire flashed down from
heaven and burned up the young bull, the
wood, the stones, the dust, and even evaporated all the water in the ditch!

39And when the people saw it, they fell to
their faces upon the ground shouting,
"Jehovah is God! Jehovah is God!"

40Then Elijah told them to grab the prophets of Baal. "Don't let a single one escape," he
commanded.

So they seized them all, and Elijah took
them to Kishon Brook and killed them there.

Elijah Prays for Rain

41Then Elijah said to Ahab, "Go and enjoy a
good meal! For I hear a mighty rainstorm
coming!"

42So Ahab prepared a feast. But Elijah
climbed to the top of Mount Carmel and got
down on his knees, with his face between his
knees, 43and said to his servant, "Go and look
out toward the sea."

He did, but returned to Elijah and told him,
"I didn't see anything."

Then Elijah told him, "Go again, and again,
and again, seven times!"

44Finally, the seventh time, his servant told
him, "I saw a little cloud about the size of a
man's hand rising from the sea."

Then Elijah shouted, "Hurry to Ahab and
tell him to get into his chariot and get down
the mountain, or he'll be stopped by the
rain!"

45And sure enough, the sky was soon black
with clouds, and a heavy wind brought a
terrific rainstorm. Ahab left hastily for Jezreel,
46and the Lord gave special strength to Elijah
so that he was able to run ahead of Ahab's
chariot to the entrance of the city!

CHAPTER 19

Elijah Runs for His Life

When Ahab told Queen Jezebel what Elijah
had done, and that he had slaughtered the
prophets of Baal, 2she sent this message to
Elijah: "You killed my prophets, and now I
swear by the gods that I am going to kill you
by this time tomorrow night."

3So Elijah fled for his life; he went to Beer-
sheba, a city of Judah, and left his servant
there.4Then he went on alone into the wilderness, traveling all day, and sat down under a
broom bush and prayed that he might die.

"I've had enough," he told the Lord. "Take
away my life. I've got to die sometime, and it
might as well be now."

5Then he lay down and slept beneath the
broom bush. But as he was sleeping, an angel
touched him and told him to get up and eat!
6He looked around and saw some bread bak-
ing on hot stones and a jar of water! So he ate
and drank and lay down again.

19:1-4 After our greatest victories, we are often the most vulnerable to a fall. Elijah had just won an amazing victory for God, but suddenly he was so discouraged he wanted to die. He had already forgotten the power that God had shown him on Mount Carmel. We often do the same thing. As we depend on God's power, we quickly progress in the recovery process. But then suddenly some kind of opposition comes our way or we are overcome by temptation. We begin to wish we could die. Let us learn from Elijah. We would be wise to consider our victories as warning signs, times when we should renew our dependence on God. This will help us to experience one success after another.

19:5-18 Self-doubt is a trait common to all of us. Elijah doubted himself when he was on the run from Jezebel. God dealt with Elijah in a loving, patient manner by reassuring him that he was not alone. Reassurance and rest are a solid prescription for someone afflicted with self-doubt. We need to build a community of support to help us through the difficult times of recovery. Without the help of others, it will be impossible for us to succeed.

[7]Then the angel of the Lord came again and touched him and said, "Get up and eat some more, for there is a long journey ahead of you."

[8]So he got up and ate and drank, and the food gave him enough strength to travel forty days and forty nights to Mount Horeb, the mountain of God, [9]where he lived in a cave.

God Speaks to Elijah

But the Lord said to him, "What are you doing here, Elijah?"

[10]He replied, "I have worked very hard for the Lord God of the heavens; but the people of Israel have broken their covenant with you and torn down your altars and killed your prophets, and only I am left; and now they are trying to kill me too."

[11]"Go out and stand before me on the mountain," the Lord told him. And as Elijah stood there the Lord passed by, and a mighty windstorm hit the mountain; it was such a terrible blast that the rocks were torn loose, but the Lord was not in the wind. After the wind, there was an earthquake, but the Lord was not in the earthquake. [12]And after the earthquake, there was a fire, but the Lord was not in the fire. And after the fire, there was the sound of a gentle whisper. [13]When Elijah heard it, he wrapped his face in his scarf and went out and stood at the entrance of the cave.

And a voice said, "Why are you here, Elijah?"

[14]He replied again, "I have been working very hard for the Lord God of the armies of heaven, but the people have broken their covenant and have torn down your altars; they have killed every one of your prophets except me; and now they are trying to kill me too."

[15]Then the Lord told him, "Go back by the desert road to Damascus, and when you arrive, anoint Hazael to be king of Syria. [16]Then anoint Jehu (son of Nimshi) to be king of Israel, and anoint Elisha (the son of Shaphat of Abel-meholah) to replace you as my prophet. [17]Anyone who escapes from Hazael shall be killed by Jehu, and those who escape Jehu shall be killed by Elisha! [18]And incidentally, there are 7,000 men in Israel who have never bowed to Baal nor kissed him!"

Elisha Follows Elijah

[19]So Elijah went and found Elisha who was plowing a field with eleven other teams ahead of him; he was at the end of the line with the last team. Elijah went over to him and threw his coat across his shoulders and walked away again.

[20]Elisha left the oxen standing there and ran after Elijah and said to him, "First let me go and say good-bye to my father and mother, and then I'll go with you!"

Elijah replied, "Go on back! Why all the excitement?"

[21]Elisha then returned to his oxen, killed them, and used wood from the plow to build a fire to roast their flesh. He passed around the meat to the other plowmen, and they all had a great feast. Then he went with Elijah, as his assistant.

CHAPTER 20

Victory over Syria

King Ben-hadad of Syria now mobilized his army and, with thirty-two allied nations and their hordes of chariots and horses, besieged Samaria, the Israeli capital. [2,3]He sent this message into the city to King Ahab of Israel: "Your silver and gold are mine, as are your prettiest wives and the best of your children!"

[4]"All right, my lord," Ahab replied. "All that I have is yours!"

[5,6]Soon Ben-hadad's messengers returned again with another message: "You must not only give me your silver, gold, wives, and children, but about this time tomorrow I will send my men to search your palace and the homes of your people, and they will take away whatever they like!"

[7]Then Ahab summoned his advisors. "Look what this man is doing," he complained to them. "He is stirring up trouble despite the fact that I have already told him he could have my wives and children and silver and gold, just as he demanded."

[8]"Don't give him anything more," the elders advised.

[9]So he told the messengers from Ben-hadad, "Tell my lord the king, 'I will give you

---

20:10-21 A common result of drug and alcohol abuse is impaired reasoning. This was demonstrated by Ben-hadad, who was drinking when Ahab's refusal to surrender arrived. Ben-hadad was soundly surprised by Ahab's attack in the middle of the day. He and the other kings of his coalition were drunk. While Ben-hadad survived, his men did not. Substance abuse does not mix with a victorious life.

everything you asked for the first time, but
your men may not search the palace and the
homes of the people.'" So the messengers
returned to Ben-hadad.
10Then the Syrian king sent this message to
Ahab: "May the gods do more to me than I am
going to do to you if I don't turn Samaria into
handfuls of dust!"
11The king of Israel retorted, "Don't count
your chickens before they hatch!"
12This reply of Ahab's reached Ben-hadad
and the other kings as they were drinking in
their tents.
"Prepare to attack!" Ben-hadad commanded his officers.
13Then a prophet came to see King Ahab
and gave him this message from the Lord:
"Do you see all these enemy forces? I will
deliver them all to you today. Then at last you
will know that I am the Lord."
14Ahab asked, "How will he do it?"
And the prophet replied, "The Lord says,
'By the troops from the provinces.'"
"Shall we attack first?" Ahab asked.
"Yes," the prophet answered.
15So he mustered the troops from the provinces, 232 of them, then the rest of his army
of 7,000 men.
16About noontime, as Ben-hadad and the thirty-two allied kings were
still drinking themselves drunk, the first of
Ahab's troops marched out of the city.
17As they approached, Ben-hadad's scouts
reported to him, "Some troops are coming!"
18"Take them alive," Ben-hadad commanded, "whether they have come for truce
or for war."
19By now Ahab's entire army had joined the
attack.
20Each one killed a Syrian soldier, and
suddenly the entire Syrian army panicked and
fled. The Israelis chased them, but King Ben-hadad and a few others escaped on horses.
21However, the great bulk of the horses and
chariots were captured, and most of the Syrian army was killed in a great slaughter.
22Then the prophet approached King Ahab
and said, "Get ready for another attack by the
king of Syria."
23For after their defeat, Ben-hadad's officers
said to him, "The Israeli God is a god of the
hills; that is why they won. But we can beat
them easily on the plains.
24Only this time
replace the kings with generals!
25Recruit another army like the one you lost; give us the
same number of horses, chariots, and men,
and we will fight against them in the plains;
there's not a shadow of a doubt that we will
beat them." So King Ben-hadad did as they

Tolerance vs. perfectionism

READ 1 KINGS 19:1-21

As perfectionists, we tend to see the world in black and white. We often feel like we're superhuman, able to take on anything—until we discover a flaw. Then we come crashing down and consider ourself to be completely worthless. This "all or nothing" way of thinking can be very dangerous to our recovery.

The prophet Elijah is one of the great heroes of the Bible. If anyone had reason to feel superhuman, it was he. His prayers brought a lengthy drought upon Israel—and then brought fire down from heaven, humiliating Queen Jezebel and her priests of Baal. But even Elijah could have a bad day. Let's consider his reaction after being threatened by Jezebel. "'I've had enough,' he told the Lord. 'Take away my life. . . . I have worked very hard for the Lord God of the heavens; but the people of Israel have broken their covenant with you and torn down your altars and killed your prophets, and only I am left; and now they are trying to kill me too'" (1 Kings 19:4, 10). The Lord replied, "Incidentally, there are 7,000 men in Israel who have never bowed to Baal" (19:18).

Like Elijah, if we're perfectionists, we may think that we are above everyone else. We work very hard to please God and other people, but we can grow dangerously discouraged if things don't seem to work. This tendency is something for us to watch for while working on Step Four. If we don't allow ourself to be less than perfect, we may find that we are at great risk during the times when life reminds us we are only human after all. ***Turn to page 579, Job 19.***

suggested. 26The following year he called up the Syrian army and marched out against Israel again, this time at Aphek. 27Israel then mustered its army, set up supply lines, and moved into the battle; but the Israeli army looked like two little flocks of baby goats in comparison to the vast Syrian forces that filled the countryside!

28Then a prophet went to the king of Israel with this message from the Lord: "Because the Syrians have declared, 'The Lord is a God of the hills and not of the plains,' I will help you defeat this vast army, and you shall know that I am indeed the Lord."

29The two armies camped opposite each other for seven days, and on the seventh day the battle began. And the Israelis killed 100,000 Syrian infantrymen that first day. 30The rest fled behind the walls of Aphek, but the wall fell on them and killed another 27,000. Ben-hadad fled into the city and hid in the inner room of one of the houses.

31"Sir," his officers said to him, "we have heard that the kings of Israel are very merciful. Let us wear sackcloth and put ropes on our heads and go out to King Ahab to see if he will let you live."

32So they went to the king of Israel and begged, "Your servant Ben-hadad pleads, 'Let me live!'"

"Oh, is he still alive?" the king of Israel asked. "He is my brother!"

33The men were quick to grab this straw of hope and hurried to clinch the matter by exclaiming, "Yes, your brother Ben-hadad!"

"Go and get him," the king of Israel told them. And when Ben-hadad arrived, he invited him up into his chariot!

34Ben-hadad told him, "I will restore the cities my father took from your father, and you may establish trading posts in Damascus, as my father did in Samaria."

35Meanwhile, the Lord instructed one of the prophets to say to another man, "Strike me with your sword!" But the man refused.

36Then the prophet told him, "Because you have not obeyed the voice of the Lord, a lion shall kill you as soon as you leave me." And sure enough, as he turned to go a lion attacked and killed him.

37Then the prophet turned to another man and said, "Strike me with your sword." And he did, wounding him.

38The prophet waited for the king beside the road, having placed a bandage over his eyes to disguise himself.

39As the king passed by, the prophet called out to him, "Sir, I was in the battle, and a man brought me a prisoner and said, 'Keep this man; if he gets away, you must die, or else pay me $2,000!' 40But while I was busy doing something else, the prisoner disappeared!"

"Well, it's your own fault," the king replied. "You'll have to pay."

41Then the prophet yanked off the bandage from his eyes, and the king recognized him as one of the prophets. 42Then the prophet told him, "The Lord says, 'Because you have spared the man I said must die, now you must die in his place, and your people shall perish instead of his.'"

43So the king of Israel went home to Samaria angry and sullen.

CHAPTER 21

Ahab Steals Naboth's Vineyard

Naboth, a man from Jezreel, had a vineyard on the outskirts of the city near King Ahab's palace. 2One day the king talked to him about selling him this land.

"I want it for a garden," the king explained, "because it's so convenient to the palace." He offered cash or, if Naboth preferred, a piece of better land in trade.

3But Naboth replied, "Not on your life! That land has been in my family for generations."

4So Ahab went back to the palace angry and sullen. He refused to eat and went to bed with his face to the wall!

5"What in the world is the matter?" his wife, Jezebel, asked him. "Why aren't you

20:35-43 When we reject God's will in favor of our own we are headed toward trouble. Ahab was commanded to execute Ben-hadad, but he allowed him to live. He saw Ben-hadad as a possible ally against Assyria. The result of Ahab's disobedience was eventually death. We must learn to obey God's Word in every detail. Only then will we be able to live a healthy life. If God calls us to remove certain things from our life, we must act immediately. Allowing them to remain will lead to our eventual destruction.

21:1-6 Ahab tried to use his power as king to force Naboth to sell him his vineyard, but Naboth refused his request. Even though Ahab was the king of Israel, he could not force Naboth to sell the land. He had to abide by God's laws. Ahab had been worshiping idols, but he still recognized God's authority in his life. If we are in positions of authority, we must remember that we will have to answer to God for our actions. Are we following his commands?

eating? What has made you so upset and angry?”

6“I asked Naboth to sell me his vineyard or to trade it, and he refused!” Ahab told her.

7“Are you the king of Israel or not?” Jezebel demanded. “Get up and eat and don’t worry about it. I’ll get you Naboth’s vineyard!”

8So she wrote letters in Ahab’s name, sealed them with his seal, and addressed them to the civic leaders of Jezreel, where Naboth lived. 9In her letter she commanded: “Call the citizens together for fasting and prayer. Then summon Naboth, 10and find two scoundrels who will accuse him of cursing God and the king. Then take him out and execute him.”

11The city fathers followed the queen’s instructions. 12They called the meeting and put Naboth on trial. 13Then two men who had no conscience accused him of cursing God and the king; and he was dragged outside the city and stoned to death. 14The city officials then sent word to Jezebel that Naboth was dead.

15When Jezebel heard the news, she said to Ahab, “You know the vineyard Naboth wouldn’t sell you? Well, you can have it now! He’s dead!”

16So Ahab went down to the vineyard to claim it.

17But the Lord said to Elijah, 18“Go to Samaria to meet King Ahab. He will be at Naboth’s vineyard, taking possession of it. 19Give him this message from me: ‘Isn’t killing Naboth bad enough? Must you rob him too? Because you have done this, dogs shall lick your blood outside the city just as they licked the blood of Naboth!’”

20“So my enemy has found me!” Ahab exclaimed to Elijah.

“Yes,” Elijah answered, “I have come to place God’s curse upon you because you have sold yourself to the devil. 21The Lord is going to bring great harm to you and sweep you away; he will not let a single one of your male descendants survive! 22He is going to destroy your family as he did the family of King Jeroboam and the family of King Baasha, for you have made him very angry and have led all of Israel into sin. 23The Lord has also told me that the dogs of Jezreel shall tear apart the body of your wife, Jezebel. 24The members of your family who die in the city shall be eaten by dogs, and those who die in the country shall be eaten by vultures.”

25No one else was so completely sold out to the devil as Ahab, for his wife, Jezebel, encouraged him to do every sort of evil. 26He was especially guilty because he worshiped idols just as the Amorites did—the people whom the Lord had chased out of the land to make room for the people of Israel.27When Ahab heard these prophecies, he tore his clothing, put on rags, fasted, slept in sackcloth, and went about in deep humility.

28Then another message came to Elijah: 29“Do you see how Ahab has humbled himself before me? Because he has done this, I will not do what I promised during his lifetime; it will happen to his sons; I will destroy his descendants.”

CHAPTER 22

Ahab Dies in Battle

For three years there was no war between Syria and Israel. 2But during the third year, while King Jehoshaphat of Judah was visiting King Ahab of Israel, 3Ahab said to his officials, “Do you realize that the Syrians are still occupying our city of Ramoth-gilead? And we’re sitting here without doing a thing about it!”

4Then he turned to Jehoshaphat and asked him, “Will you send your army with mine to recover Ramoth-gilead?”

And King Jehoshaphat of Judah replied, “Of course! You and I are brothers; my people are yours to command, and my horses are at your service. 5But,” he added, “we should ask the Lord first, to be sure of what he wants us to do.”

6So King Ahab summoned his 400 heathen prophets and asked them, “Shall I attack Ramoth-gilead, or not?”

And they all said, “Yes, go ahead, for God will help you conquer it.”

7But Jehoshaphat asked, “Isn’t there a prophet of the Lord here? I’d like to ask him too.”

8“Well, there’s one,” King Ahab replied, “but I hate him, for he never prophesies anything good. He always has something gloomy to say. His name is Micaiah, the son of Imlah.”

21:7-14 Jezebel’s need to “have it all” drove her to the point of plotting the death of an innocent man. An obsession, such as greed, can severely taint our sense of right and wrong. This is evident in the murder of Naboth. Many of us are enslaved to compulsive behaviors that lead to a multitude of other sins. We must begin our recovery by recognizing that these behaviors are a real problem. Then we can give our compulsions and dependencies over to God and seek to follow his program for healthy living.

"Oh, come now!" Jehoshaphat replied.
"Don't talk like that!"
[9]So King Ahab called to one of his aides,
"Go get Micaiah. Hurry!"
[10]Meanwhile, all the prophets continued
prophesying before the two kings, who were
dressed in their royal robes and were sitting
on thrones placed on the threshing floor near
the city gate. [11]One of the prophets, Zedekiah
(son of Chenaanah), made some iron horns
and declared, "The Lord promises that you
will push the Syrians around with these horns
until they are destroyed."
[12]And all the others agreed. "Go ahead and
attack Ramoth-gilead," they said, "for the
Lord will cause you to triumph!"
[13]The messenger who went to get Micaiah
told him what the other prophets were saying
and urged him to say the same thing.
[14]But Micaiah told him, "This I vow, that I
will say only what the Lord tells me to!"
[15]When he arrived, the king asked him,
"Micaiah, shall we attack Ramoth-gilead, or
not?"
"Why, of course! Go right ahead!" Micaiah
told him. "You will have a great victory, for
the Lord will cause you to conquer!"
[16]"How many times must I tell you to speak
only what the Lord tells you to?" the king
demanded.
[17]Then Micaiah told him, "I saw all Israel
scattered upon the mountains as sheep without a shepherd. And the Lord said, 'Their king
is dead; send them to their homes.'"
[18]Turning to Jehoshaphat, Ahab complained, "Didn't I tell you this would happen?
He *never* tells me anything good. It's *always*
bad."
[19]Then Micaiah said, "Listen to this further
word from the Lord. I saw the Lord sitting on
his throne, and the armies of heaven stood
around him.
[20]"Then the Lord said, 'Who will entice
Ahab to go and die at Ramoth-gilead?'
"Various suggestions were made, [21]until
one angel approached the Lord and said, 'I'll
do it!'
[22]"'How?' the Lord asked.
"And he replied, 'I will go as a lying spirit
in the mouths of all his prophets.'
"And the Lord said, 'That will do it; you will
succeed. Go ahead.'
[23]"Don't you see? The Lord has put a lying
spirit in the mouths of all these prophets, but
the fact of the matter is that the Lord has
decreed disaster upon you."
[24]Then Zedekiah (son of Chenaanah)
walked over and slapped Micaiah on the face.
"When did the Spirit of the Lord leave me
and speak to you?" he demanded.
[25]And Micaiah replied, "You will have the
answer to your question when you find yourself hiding in an inner room."
[26]Then King Ahab ordered Micaiah's arrest.
"Take him to Amon, the mayor of the city,
and to my son Joash. [27]Tell them, 'The king
says to put this fellow in jail and feed him
with bread and water—and only enough to
keep him alive—until I return in peace.'"
[28]"If you return in peace," Micaiah replied,
"it will prove that the Lord has not spoken
through me." Then he turned to the people
standing nearby and said, "Take note of what
I've said."
[29]So King Ahab of Israel and King Jehoshaphat of Judah led their armies to Ramoth-
gilead.
[30]Ahab said to Jehoshaphat, "You wear your
royal robes, but I'll not wear mine!"
So Ahab went into the battle disguised in
an ordinary soldier's uniform. [31]For the king
of Syria had commanded his thirty-two chariot captains to fight no one except King Ahab
himself. [32,33]When they saw King Jehoshaphat
in his royal robes, they thought, "That's the
man we're after." So they wheeled around to
attack him. But when Jehoshaphat shouted
out to identify himself, they turned back!
[34]However, someone shot an arrow at random
and it struck King Ahab between the joints of
his armor.
"Take me out of the battle, for I am badly
wounded," he groaned to his chariot driver.
[35]The battle became more and more intense
as the day wore on, and King Ahab went back
in, propped up in his chariot with the blood
from his wound running down onto the
floorboards. Finally, toward evening, he died.
[36,37]Just as the sun was going down the cry ran
through his troops. "It's all over—return
home! The king is dead!"

22:30-40 Whatever God says will happen, will happen. Ahab disguised himself in battle so he wouldn't be killed, but he was shot by a stray arrow. Notice that the prophecy in 21:21-24 came true here, three years after Elijah spoke it. Justice is served by God in his timing, not ours. People may seem to get away with sin and denial for awhile, but eventually their deeds will catch up with them.

And his body was taken to Samaria and buried there. [38]When his chariot and armor were washed beside the pool of Samaria, where the prostitutes bathed, dogs came and licked the king's blood just as the Lord had said would happen.

[39]The rest of Ahab's history—including the story of the ivory palace and the cities he built—is written in *The Annals of the Kings of Israel.* [40]So Ahab was buried among his ancestors, and Ahaziah, his son, became the new king of Israel.

Jehoshaphat Rules Judah

[41]Meanwhile, over in Judah, Jehoshaphat the son of Asa had become king during the fourth year of the reign of King Ahab of Israel. [42]Jehoshaphat was thirty-five years old when he ascended the throne, and he reigned in Jerusalem for twenty-five years. His mother was Azubah, the daughter of Shilhi. [43]He did as his father Asa had done, obeying the Lord in all but one thing: he did not destroy the shrines on the hills, so the people sacrificed and burned incense there. [44]He also made peace with Ahab, the king of Israel. [45]The rest of the deeds of Jehoshaphat and his heroic achievements and his wars are described in *The Annals of the Kings of Judah.*

[46]He also closed all the houses of male prostitution that still continued from the days of his father Asa. [47](There was no king in Edom at that time, only a deputy.)

[48]King Jehoshaphat built great freighters to sail to Ophir for gold; but they never arrived, for they were wrecked at Ezion-geber. [49]Ahaziah, King Ahab's son and successor, had proposed to Jehoshaphat that his men go, too, but Jehoshaphat had refused the offer.

[50]When King Jehoshaphat died he was buried with his ancestors in Jerusalem, the city of his forefather David; and his son Jehoram took the throne.

Ahaziah Rules Israel

[51]It was during the seventeenth year of the reign of King Jehoshaphat of Judah that Ahaziah, Ahab's son, began to reign over Israel in Samaria; and he reigned two years. [52,53]But he was not a good king, for he followed in the footsteps of his father and mother and of Jeroboam, who had led Israel into the sin of worshiping idols. So Ahaziah made the Lord God of Israel very angry.

22:41-43 Jehoshaphat was a good king who built on the positive steps of his father, Asa. Successful parenting involves modeling godly standards of conduct for our children. As our children watch us take steps toward recovery, they will learn about God's power of deliverance and the blessings that result from trust and obedience.

SECOND KINGS

The book of 2 Kings was originally part of a larger book that also included 1 Kings. It recorded Israel's history from the end of David's reign to the demise of both its kingdoms. The book of 2 Kings opens with Israel already divided into northern and southern kindgoms. It records a succession of kings, many of them ungodly, and the inevitable movement of both kingdoms toward destruction and exile. First the northern kingdom fell to Assyria. Then the southern kingdom fell to Babylon.

The progression of events in 2 Kings could easily be likened to the gathering darkness at nightfall. The people suffered from a progressive darkening of a spiritual nature—a denial and unbelief that led to spiritual darkness. Along the way, there were prophets like Elijah, Elisha, and Isaiah—and kings like Hezekiah and Josiah, who did their best to brighten the horizon by restoring God's way among the people. But eventually the influence of many godless kings brought destruction.

The writer of Kings wanted to make sure that the exiled Israelites learned from the mistakes of their parents. By narrating the events of their past, he showed how disobedience brought destruction and was the reason for their tragic plight. The people had disobeyed God, despite God's repeated attempts to get their attention through his prophets and a few godly kings.

The consequences for Israel's chronic sin were tragic and seemingly irreparable. The Temple was destroyed; David's royal line no longer ruled in Jerusalem; and the people were exiled from their homeland. Despite the gloomy ending of this book, however, the story of God's people will continue with rebuilding and restoration. There is always hope for the future.

THE BIG PICTURE

A. ISRAEL'S EXILE TO ASSYRIA: FROM DENIAL TO UTTER DEFEAT (1:1–17:41)
   1. Confrontation by Elijah and Elisha (1:1–13:25)
   2. Israel's Sin and Denial Leads to Defeat (14:1–17:41)

B. JUDAH'S EXILE TO BABYLON: REPEATED TRAGEDY FOR GOD'S PEOPLE (18:1–25:30)
   1. Fathers and Sons: Choices for Recovery or Oppression (18:1–23:30)
   2. The Last Stages of Denial and Defeat (23:31–25:30)

THE BOTTOM LINE

PURPOSE: To record the final years of the northern and southern kingdoms and to demonstrate that prolonged denial and disobedience to God's program are destructive. AUTHOR: Unknown, but possibly Jeremiah or another writer from the period of Babylonian exile (sixth century B.C.). AUDIENCE: The people of Israel in Babylonian exile. DATE WRITTEN: Sometime between 560 and 538 B.C. SETTING: The divided kingdoms of Israel and Judah, with concluding scenes in Babylonian exile. KEY VERSE: "But Israel wouldn't listen. The people were as stubborn as their ancestors and refused to believe in the Lord their God" (17:14). KEY PEOPLE AND RELATIONSHIPS: Elijah with Elisha, Hezekiah, Sennacherib, Isaiah, Manasseh, Josiah, and Nebuchadnezzar.

RECOVERY THEMES

The Power of Denial: Nothing is as frustrating as dealing with people in denial. No matter how well we may argue our point—no matter how good our evidence—it is impossible to penetrate their defenses. Of the thirty-nine kings that both Israel and Judah had after the death of Solomon, only eight of them responded to the truth of God. The others, in spite of all the evidence presented by the prophets, continued in denial and refused to admit the sin in their lives. As a result, the good kings spent most of their time undoing the evil of their predecessors.

A Model of Intervention: As we see how patient God was with Israel, it is important that we don't mistake his patience for indifference. God did confront these evil kings through his prophets, through miracles, and through his Word (see 22:8-13). God was active, confronting the sins of Israel and Judah, seeking to lovingly intervene with the truth. When we look back at the events in this book, it seems difficult to understand why the kings and the people were so rebellious. That is our warning. We also need to see that God was constantly and lovingly seeking to confront his people with the truth. That is our hope.

Hitting Bottom: Sometimes interventions don't work. That was the case with both Israel and Judah. Their denial continued to the bitter end, and even when the northern kingdom was conquered and its people exiled, the people of the southern kingdom failed to change their sinful ways. Hitting bottom is not only painful; it can also be dangerous. It has a profound effect on people's lives. If we want to avoid the pain and destruction of hitting bottom, we would be wise to heed the interventions of God and the people close to us.

God's Care for Us: The fact that God cares for his people is proven time and again in Israel's history and is especially emphasized in the book of Kings. Numerous times, God actively sought to stop Israel's slide toward destruction. He confronted wicked kings and punished their continued sin. But they failed to respond with repentance to God's acts of "tough love." God also gives us many chances to heed his message of hope and recovery. Sometimes we might be tempted to mistake his patience for indifference, but we can be sure that God is never indifferent toward his people. His love may sometimes be expressed in patience, but eventually it will be shown in judgment.

CHAPTER 1

Elijah Confronts King Ahaziah

After King Ahab's death the nation of Moab
declared its independence and refused to pay
tribute to Israel any longer.
2 Israel's new king, Ahaziah, had fallen off
the upstairs porch of his palace at Samaria and
was seriously injured. He sent messengers to
the temple of the god Baal-zebub at Ekron to
ask whether he would recover.
3 But an angel of the Lord told Elijah the
prophet, "Go and meet the messengers and
ask them, 'Is it true that there is no God in
Israel? Is that why you are going to Baal-
zebub, the god of Ekron, to ask whether the
king will get well? 4,5 Because King Ahaziah has
done this, the Lord says that he will never
leave the bed he is lying on; he will surely
die.'"
When Elijah told the messengers this, they
returned immediately to the king.
"Why have you returned so soon?" he
asked them.
6 "A man came up to us," they said, "and
told us to go back to the king and tell him,
'The Lord wants to know why you are asking
questions of Baal-zebub, the god of Ekron. Is
it because there is no God in Israel? Now,
since you have done this, you will not leave
the bed you are lying on; you will surely die.'"
7 "Who was this fellow?" the king demanded. "What did he look like?"
8 "He was a hairy man," they replied, "with
a wide leather belt."

1:2-5 Ahaziah sought guidance for recovery from the wrong spiritual source, and God made his error clear in no uncertain terms. Not everything passed off as spiritual guidance is "the real thing." God is far from pleased with those who know better, but still attempt recovery by means of "alternative resources," such as the New Age movement today. God is the only valid source of help for our recovery.

1:5-17 Ahaziah sought to silence Elijah and persisted in trying to capture the prophet even after his first two military detachments had been destroyed by God. Ahaziah's denial was amazingly powerful, and as it deepened, Ahaziah failed to see the innocent lives he was throwing away. We, like Ahaziah, often fail to notice the toll that our denial takes on the people around us. Admitting our dependencies will not only help us recover, but will also stop us from hurting the people close to us.

ELIJAH & ELISHA

Most of us know people whom we admire greatly. If we are fortunate, one or more of these people may be close enough to serve as a mentor for us in some way. Elisha had a relationship of this kind with Elijah. Elisha was the student; Elijah was the teacher. Both had a heart for God, though their ministries were very different.

Elijah's ministry was primarily confrontational—he had to reprove and prophesy against King Ahab. He prophesied a three-year drought; he destroyed the priests of Baal who were employed by Ahab; and he prophesied Ahab's death after Ahab killed Naboth for his vineyard. Elijah also served people—he miraculously provided food for a widow and later raised her son from the dead.

Elisha witnessed many of the events in Elijah's life and learned much about God's power. Elisha learned that God would soon be taking Elijah to heaven, so he determined to stay with Elijah for as long as possible. Because Elisha was present when Elijah was taken to heaven in a whirlwind, he received a double portion of Elijah's spirit, which he no doubt believed he would need if he was to follow in the same ministry as Elijah. But God had something else in mind.

Elisha's ministry was primarily one of comfort, not confrontation. He purified poisoned water, provided drinking water for King Jehoram, provided oil for a widow, cured a poisonous stew, multiplied food to feed a hundred people, cured a leper, prophesied the birth of a son to a Shunammite woman, and later raised that son from the dead.

Elisha did not get angry at God for directing his ministry to the common people, even though Elijah had dealt primarily with rulers. He accepted his mission and followed God in all he did. We can learn from Elisha and accept our calling without envying the greatness or importance our mentors seem to have achieved. All work is important to God, and we need to do everything we can to bring honor to him.

STRENGTHS AND ACCOMPLISHMENTS:
- Both men were bold in serving God in the face of formidable enemies.
- Elisha determined to secure God's blessing on his life and ministry.

WEAKNESSES AND MISTAKES:
- Elijah allowed victory to leave him isolated and vulnerable to despair.
- Elijah became fearful rather than turning to God when threatened by powerful enemies.

LESSONS FROM THEIR LIVES:
- We are to serve God with total commitment, without fear of the consequences.
- God is able to defeat all our enemies.
- We are vulnerable to failure after our greatest victories.

KEY VERSE:
"And Elisha replied, 'Please grant me twice as much prophetic power as you have had'" (2 Kings 2:9).

Elijah and Elisha's stories are told in 1 Kings 17–19; 21; 2 Kings 1–10; 13; and 2 Chronicles 21. Elijah is mentioned in Malachi 4:5; Matthew 11:14; 17:1-5; 27:47-49; Mark 6:15; 8:28; 9:2-13; 15:35-36; Luke 1:17; 4:25-26; 9:8, 19, 28-31; John 1:21, 24-25; Romans 11:2-3; and James 5:17. Elisha is mentioned in Luke 4:27.

"It was Elijah the prophet!" the king exclaimed. 9Then he sent an army captain with
fifty soldiers to arrest him. They found him sitting on top of a hill. The captain said to him, "O man of God, the king has commanded you to come along with us."
10But Elijah replied, "If I am a man of God, let fire come down from heaven and destroy you and your fifty men!" Then lightning struck them and killed them all!
11So the king sent another captain with fifty men to demand, "O man of God, the king says that you must come down right away."
12Elijah replied, "If I am a man of God, let fire come down from heaven and destroy you and your fifty men." And again the fire from God burned them up.
13Once more the king sent fifty men, but this time the captain fell to his knees before Elijah and pleaded with him, "O man of God, please spare my life and the lives of these, your fifty servants. 14Have mercy on us! Don't destroy us as you did the others."
15Then the angel of the Lord said to Elijah, "Don't be afraid. Go with him." So Elijah went to the king.
16"Why did you send messengers to Baal-zebub, the god of Ekron, to ask about your

sickness?" Elijah demanded. "Is it because
there is no God in Israel to ask? Because you
have done this, you shall not leave this bed;
you will surely die."
[17]So Ahaziah died as the Lord had predicted
through Elijah, and his brother Joram became
the new king—for Ahaziah did not have a son
to succeed him. This occurred in the second
year of the reign of King Jehoram (son of
Jehoshaphat) of Judah. [18]The rest of the history of Ahaziah's reign is recorded in *The
Annals of the Kings of Israel.*

CHAPTER 2

God Takes Elijah to Heaven

Now the time came for the Lord to take Elijah
to heaven—by means of a whirlwind! Elijah
said to Elisha as they left Gilgal, "Stay here, for
the Lord has told me to go to Bethel."
But Elisha replied, "I swear to God that I
won't leave you!"
So they went on together to Bethel. [3]There
the young prophets of Bethel Seminary came
out to meet them and asked Elisha, "Did you
know that the Lord is going to take Elijah
away from you today?"
"Quiet!" Elisha snapped. "Of course I know
it."
[4]Then Elijah said to Elisha, "Please stay here
in Bethel, for the Lord has sent me to Jericho."
But Elisha replied again, "I swear to God
that I won't leave you." So they went on
together to Jericho.
[5]Then the students at Jericho Seminary
came to Elisha and asked him, "Do you know
that the Lord is going to take away your master today?"
"Will you please be quiet?" he commanded. "Of course I know it!"
[6,7]Then Elijah said to Elisha, "Please stay
here, for the Lord has sent me to the Jordan
River."
But Elisha replied as before, "I swear to God
that I won't leave you."
So they went on together and stood beside
the Jordan River as fifty of the young prophets
watched from a distance. [8]Then Elijah folded
his cloak together and struck the water with
it; and the river divided and they went across
on dry ground!
[9]When they arrived on the other side Elijah
said to Elisha, "What wish shall I grant you
before I am taken away?"
And Elisha replied, "Please grant me twice
as much prophetic power as you have had."
[10]"You have asked a hard thing," Elijah replied. "If you see me when I am taken from
you, then you will get your request. But if not,
then you won't."
[11]As they were walking along, talking, suddenly a chariot of fire, drawn by horses of fire,
appeared and drove between them, separating them, and Elijah was carried by a whirlwind into heaven.
[12]Elisha saw it and cried out, "My father! My
father! The Chariot of Israel and the charioteers!"
As they disappeared from sight he tore his
robe. [13,14]Then he picked up Elijah's cloak and
returned to the bank of the Jordan River, and
struck the water with it.
"Where is the Lord God of Elijah?" he cried
out. And the water parted and Elisha went
across!
[15]When the young prophets of Jericho saw
what had happened, they exclaimed, "The
spirit of Elijah rests upon Elisha!" And they
went to meet him and greeted him respectfully.
[16]"Sir," they said, "just say the word and

2:1-7 Even mature believers can wrestle with denial. It was difficult for Elisha to face the truth about Elijah's departure. Elijah tried repeatedly to prepare him for this hard inevitability, but Elisha did not want to let go. Even the younger prophets were aware of this painful reality, but Elisha did not want to deal with the loss looming on the horizon. If we can admit that we may lose someone, we will be better able to cope with the loss when the time comes. Our ability to deal with the difficulties we face will be affected by our willingness to face the realities at hand.

2:8-14 It is difficult to get beyond the physical loss of a person we have been close to, especially when it's someone we have greatly admired. The trauma of such a loss, however, can be minimized through our faith in God. We can know that the departed is in God's hands and has only been "promoted" to eternal life in heaven. Facing this positive reality can help us to go on with life before God grants us our own heavenly promotion.

2:13-15 We all recognize the warping impact that a dysfunctional hero can have on us. But we should also realize that a godly mentor can make a significant impact for the better. Here, for example, Elisha took over where Elijah had left off. Elisha was recognized to have received the same spirit as Elijah. He lived his life with the same faith and commitment as his mentor. We need to seek out godly examples who will help us put God first in our life. By following a godly example, we will discover a pathway toward maturity and recovery.

fifty of our best athletes will search the wilderness for your master; perhaps the Spirit of the Lord has left him on some mountain or in some ravine."

"No," Elisha said, "don't bother."

17But they kept urging until he was embarrassed and finally said, "All right, go ahead." Then fifty men searched for three days, but didn't find him.

18Elisha was still at Jericho when they returned. "Didn't I tell you not to go?" he growled.

Elisha Purifies the Water

19Now a delegation of the city officials of Jericho visited Elisha. "We have a problem," they told him. "This city is located in beautiful natural surroundings, as you can see; but the water is bad and causes our women to have miscarriages."

20"Well," he said, "bring me a new bowl filled with salt." So they brought it to him.

21Then he went out to the city well and threw the salt in and declared, "The Lord has healed these waters. They shall no longer cause death or miscarriage."

22And sure enough! The water was purified, just as Elisha had said.

Elisha Is Mocked

23From Jericho he went to Bethel. As he was walking along the road, a gang of young men from the city began mocking and making fun of him because of his bald head. 24He turned around and cursed them in the name of the Lord; and two female bears came out of the woods and tore forty-two of them. 25Then he went to Mount Carmel and finally returned to Samaria.

CHAPTER 3

Elisha Predicts Israel's Victory

Ahab's son Joram began his reign over Israel during the eighteenth year of the reign of King Jehoshaphat of Judah; and he reigned twelve years. His capital was Samaria. 2He was a very evil man, but not as wicked as his father and mother had been, for he at least tore down the pillar to Baal that his father had made. 3Nevertheless he still clung to the great sin of Jeroboam (the son of Nebat), who had led the people of Israel into the worship of idols.

4King Mesha of Moab and his people were sheep ranchers. They paid Israel an annual tribute of 100,000 lambs and the wool of 100,000 rams; 5but after Ahab's death, the king of Moab rebelled against Israel. 6-8So King Joram mustered the Israeli army and sent this message to King Jehoshaphat of Judah:

"The king of Moab has rebelled against me. Will you help me fight him?"

"Of course I will," Jehoshaphat replied. "My people and horses are yours to command. What are your battle plans?"

"We'll attack from the wilderness of Edom," Jehoram replied.

9So their two armies, now joined also by troops from Edom, moved along a roundabout route through the wilderness for seven days; but there was no water for the men or their pack animals.

10"Oh, what shall we do?" the king of Israel cried out. "The Lord has brought us here to let the king of Moab defeat us."

11But Jehoshaphat, the king of Judah, asked, "Isn't there a prophet of the Lord with us? If so, we can find out what to do!"

"Elisha is here," one of the king of Israel's officers replied. Then he added, "He was Elijah's assistant."

12"Fine," Jehoshaphat said. "He's just the man we want." So the kings of Israel, Judah, and Edom went to consult Elisha.

13"I want no part of you," Elisha snarled at King Jehoram of Israel. "Go to the false prophets of your father and mother!"

But King Jehoram replied, "No! For it is the Lord who has called us here to be destroyed by the king of Moab!"

14"I swear by the Lord God that I wouldn't bother with you except for the presence of

---

3:1-3 Taking a first step toward recovery is not enough by itself. It was truly a positive move that Jehoram tore down the idolatrous pillar, but it did not constitute full spiritual recovery in any sense. Whatever motivated Jehoram to destroy the pillar was not heartfelt enough to bring about a complete break from idolatry. He had not come to the point of admitting his helplessness and turning to the true God in faith.

3:5-14 Even a flirtation with recovery will often result in further intervention by God. Here Jehoram's foray into the wilderness of Edom brought him and his thirsty troops near the point of helplessness. In their predicament, they consulted Elisha the prophet for insight. He challenged Jehoram's idolatry and urged the desperate king to be aware of the godly influence of King Jehoshaphat of Judah. We should not ignore the godly people God has placed in our life. They may be there to encourage us to take further steps toward recovery.

King Jehoshaphat of Judah," Elisha replied.
15"Now bring me someone to play the lute."
And as the lute was played, the message of the
Lord came to Elisha:

16"The Lord says to fill this dry valley with
trenches to hold the water he will send. 17You
won't see wind nor rain, but this valley will be
filled with water, and you will have plenty for
yourselves and for your animals! 18But this is
only the beginning, for the Lord will make
you victorious over the army of Moab! 19You
will conquer the best of their cities—even
those that are fortified—and ruin all the good
land with stones."

20And sure enough, the next day at about
the time when the morning sacrifice was offered—look! Water! It was flowing from the
direction of Edom, and soon there was water
everywhere.

21Meanwhile, when the people of Moab
heard about the three armies marching
against them, they mobilized every man who
could fight, old and young, and stationed
themselves along their frontier. 22But early the
next morning the sun looked red as it shone
across the water!

23"Blood!" they exclaimed. "The three armies have attacked and killed each other! Let's
go and collect the loot!"

24But when they arrived at the Israeli camp,
the army of Israel rushed out and began killing them; and the army of Moab fled. Then
the men of Israel moved forward into the land
of Moab, destroying everything as they went.
25They destroyed the cities, threw stones on
every good piece of land, stopped up the
wells, and felled the fruit trees; finally, only
Fort Kir-hareseth was left, but even that finally fell to them.

26When the king of Moab saw that the
battle had been lost, he led 700 of his swordsmen in a last desperate attempt to break
through to the king of Edom; but he failed.
27Then he took his oldest son, who was to
have been the next king, and to the horror of
the Israeli army, killed him and sacrificed him
as a burnt offering upon the wall. So the army
of Israel turned back in disgust to their own
land.

CHAPTER 4

Elisha Helps a Poor Widow

One day the wife of one of the seminary
students came to Elisha to tell him of her
husband's death. He was a man who had
loved God, she said. But he had owed some
money when he died, and now the creditor
was demanding it back. If she didn't pay, he
said he would take her two sons as his slaves.

2"What shall I do?" Elisha asked. "How
much food do you have in the house?"

"Nothing at all, except a jar of olive oil,"
she replied.

3"Then borrow many pots and pans from
your friends and neighbors!" he instructed.
4"Go into your house with your sons and shut
the door behind you. Then pour olive oil
from your jar into the pots and pans, setting
them aside as they are filled!"

5So she did. Her sons brought the pots and
pans to her, and she filled one after another!
6Soon every container was full to the brim!

"Bring me another jar," she said to her
sons.

"There aren't any more!" they told her. And
then the oil stopped flowing!

7When she told the prophet what had happened, he said to her, "Go and sell the oil and
pay your debt, and there will be enough
money left for you and your sons to live on!"

Elisha Restores a Child's Life

8One day Elisha went to Shunem. A prominent woman of the city invited him in to eat,

---

3:16-20 God had a battle plan devised for Jehoram. Jehoram had only to admit he needed help; God was there to ensure the victory. God always has a plan to rescue us; he provides the resources and guidance we need. We just need to admit that we are helpless and turn to him for help.

4:1-7 People willing to pursue recovery can count on the fact that when they are "at the end of their rope," God is holding on to them. He is the God of limitless resources, who can provide incredibly when we are in need. As was true with the widow and her sons, God sometimes waits to act until the last minute in order to stretch our faith. Then, when he comes through, our faith in his power is strengthened for the battles ahead.

4:8-37 Elisha did two amazing miracles in these verses. First, he promised that a woman unable to bear children would have a child. Then, after the child died, he brought him back to life. The God who performed these impossible miracles is also able to provide all the power we need for recovery. Notice that God often uses people, like Elijah, to bring about new or renewed life. We should be aware of this, accepting God's gifts through the people chosen to help us along the way. We must remember, too, that God may also use us to touch the lives of others in need.

and afterwards, whenever he passed that way,
he stopped for dinner.
9She said to her husband, "I'm sure this
man who stops in from time to time is a holy
prophet. 10Let's make a little room for him on
the roof; we can put in a bed, a table, a chair,
and a lamp, and he will have a place to stay
whenever he comes by."
11,12Once when he was resting in the room
he said to his servant Gehazi, "Tell the woman
I want to speak to her."

When she came, 13he said to Gehazi, "Tell
her that we appreciate her kindness to us.
Now ask her what we can do for her. Does she
want me to put in a good word for her to the
king or to the general of the army?"

"No," she replied, "I am perfectly content."
14"What can we do for her?" he asked Gehazi afterwards.

He suggested, "She doesn't have a son, and
her husband is an old man."
15,16"Call her back again," Elisha told him.

When she returned, he talked to her as she
stood in the doorway. "Next year at about this
time you shall have a son!"

"O man of God," she exclaimed, "don't lie
to me like that!"
17But it was true; the woman soon conceived and had a baby boy the following year,
just as Elisha had predicted.
18One day when her child was older, he
went out to visit his father, who was working
with the reapers. 19He complained about a
headache and soon was moaning in pain. His
father said to one of the servants, "Carry him
home to his mother."
20So he took him home, and his mother
held him on her lap; but around noontime he
died. 21She carried him up to the bed of the
prophet and shut the door; 22then she sent a
message to her husband: "Send one of the
servants and a donkey so that I can hurry to
the prophet and come right back."
23"Why today?" he asked. "This isn't a religious holiday."

But she said, "It's important. I must go."
24So she saddled the donkey and said to the
servant, "Hurry! Don't slow down for my
comfort unless I tell you to."
25As she approached Mount Carmel, Elisha
saw her in the distance and said to Gehazi,
"Look, that woman from Shunem is coming.
26Run and meet her and ask her what the
trouble is. See if her husband is all right and if
the child is well."

"Yes," she told Gehazi, "everything is fine."
27But when she came to Elisha at the mountain she fell to the ground before him and
caught hold of his feet. Gehazi began to push
her away, but the prophet said, "Let her alone;
something is deeply troubling her and the
Lord hasn't told me what it is."
28Then she said, "It was you who said I'd
have a son. And I begged you not to lie to me!"
29Then he said to Gehazi, "Quick, take my
staff! Don't talk to anyone along the way.
Hurry! Lay the staff upon the child's face."
30But the boy's mother said, "I swear to God
that I won't go home without you." So Elisha
returned with her.
31Gehazi went on ahead and laid the staff
upon the child's face, but nothing happened.
There was no sign of life. He returned to meet
Elisha and told him, "The child is still dead."
32When Elisha arrived, the child was indeed
dead, lying there upon the prophet's bed. 33He
went in and shut the door behind him and
prayed to the Lord. 34Then he lay upon the
child's body, placing his mouth upon the
child's mouth, and his eyes upon the child's
eyes, and his hands upon the child's hands.
And the child's body began to grow warm
again! 35Then the prophet went down and
walked back and forth in the house a few
times; returning upstairs, he stretched himself
again upon the child. This time the little boy
sneezed seven times and opened his eyes!
36Then the prophet summoned Gehazi.
"Call her!" he said. And when she came in, he
said, "Here's your son!"
37She fell to the floor at his feet and then
picked up her son and went out.

Poisonous Stew Made Edible

38Elisha now returned to Gilgal, but there was
a famine in the land. One day as he was
teaching the young prophets, he said to Gehazi, "Make some stew for supper for these
men."
39One of the young men went out into the
field to gather vegetables and came back with
some wild gourds. He shredded them and put
them into a kettle without realizing that they
were poisonous. 40But after the men had eaten
a bite or two they cried out, "Oh, sir, there's
poison in this stew!"
41"Bring me some meal," Elisha said. He
threw it into the kettle and said, "Now it's all
right! Go ahead and eat!" And then it didn't
harm them.

Elisha Multiplies Some Food

42One day a man from Baal-shalishah brought
Elisha a sack of fresh corn and twenty individ-

ual loaves of barley bread made from the first
grain of his harvest. Elisha told Gehazi to use
it to feed the young prophets.
43“What?” Gehazi exclaimed. “Feed one
hundred men with only this?”
But Elisha said, “Go ahead, for the Lord
says there will be plenty for all, and some will
even be left over!”
44And sure enough, there was, just as the
Lord had said!

CHAPTER 5

Naaman Is Healed of Leprosy

The king of Syria had high admiration for
Naaman, the commander-in-chief of his
army, for he had led his troops to many glorious victories. So he was a great hero, but he
was a leper. 2Bands of Syrians had invaded the
land of Israel, and among their captives was a
little girl who had been given to Naaman’s
wife as a maid.
3One day the little girl said to her mistress,
“I wish my master would go to see the
prophet in Samaria. He would heal him of his
leprosy!”
4Naaman told the king what the little girl
had said.
5“Go and visit the prophet,” the king told
him. “I will send a letter of introduction for
you to carry to the king of Israel.”
So Naaman started out, taking gifts of
$20,000 in silver, $60,000 in gold, and ten
suits of clothing. 6The letter to the king of
Israel said: “The man bringing this letter is my
servant Naaman; I want you to heal him of his
leprosy.”
7When the king of Israel read it, he tore his
clothes and said, “This man sends me a leper
to heal! Am I God, that I can kill and give life?
He is only trying to get an excuse to invade us
again.”
8But when Elisha the prophet heard about
the king of Israel’s plight, he sent this message
to him: “Why are you so upset? Send Naaman
to me, and he will learn that there is a true
prophet of God here in Israel.”
9So Naaman arrived with his horses and
chariots and stood at the door of Elisha’s
home. 10Elisha sent a messenger out to tell
him to go and wash in the Jordan River seven
times and he would be healed of every trace
of his leprosy! 11But Naaman was angry and
stalked away.
“Look,” he said, “I thought at least he
would come out and talk to me! I expected
him to wave his hand over the leprosy and
call upon the name of the Lord his God and
heal me! 12Aren’t the Abana River and Pharpar
River of Damascus better than all the rivers of
Israel put together? If it’s rivers I need, I’ll
wash at home and get rid of my leprosy.” So
he went away in a rage.
13But his officers tried to reason with him
and said, “If the prophet had told you to do
some great thing, wouldn’t you have done it?
So you should certainly obey him when he
says simply to go and wash and be cured!”
14So Naaman went down to the Jordan
River and dipped himself seven times, as the
prophet had told him to. And his flesh became as healthy as a little child’s, and he was
healed!15Then he and his entire party went
back to find the prophet; they stood humbly
before him and Naaman said, “I know at last
that there is no God in all the world except in
Israel; now please accept my gifts.”
16But Elisha replied, “I swear by Jehovah my
God that I will not accept them.”

5:1-8 People who are hurting deeply enough will try almost anything to find relief. For Naaman, a Syrian general, looking for help from a prophet in Israel was a desperate long shot. Naaman was willing to sacrifice prestige and wealth to find healing for his terrible disease. In the end, Naaman was healed of his leprosy, but not because he was willing to offer a reward. The real issue was not how much it cost; it was more important that he went to the only one really able to help him—the one true God.

5:20-27 The shameful example of Gehazi and the resulting consequences he faced should serve as a warning to us. For those of us pursuing recovery, we need to be aware that there are those who would try to take advantage of us as we experience the joy of recovery. For those working in the recovery field, we need to be careful not to take advantage of people as they experience the excitement of recovery. God is never pleased with this kind of exploitation.

6:1-7 By helping the prophet retrieve the borrowed axhead, God revealed his concern for the day-to-day needs of his people. He also showed how concerned he was for the maintenance of relationships. In ancient times, an axhead was extremely valuable, and losing such an item would have resulted in conflict between the borrower and lender. So Elisha’s miracle helped the young prophets not only with their building project, but also with the maintenance of their relationships. The maintenance of healthy relationships is essential to our recovery. God will support us in them if we are willing to look to him for help.

Naaman urged him to take them, but he absolutely refused.
17"Well," Naaman said, "all right. But please give me two muleloads of earth to take back with me, for from now on I will never again offer any burnt offerings or sacrifices to any other god except the Lord.
18However, may the Lord pardon me this one thing—when my master the king goes into the temple of the god Rimmon to worship there and leans on my arm, may the Lord pardon me when I bow too."
19"All right," Elisha said. So Naaman started home again.

Elisha's Greedy Servant

20But Gehazi, Elisha's servant, said to himself, "My master shouldn't have let this fellow get away without taking his gifts. I will chase after him and get something from him."
21So Gehazi caught up with him. When Naaman saw him coming, he jumped down from his chariot and ran to meet him.

"Is everything all right?" he asked.
22"Yes," he said, "but my master has sent me to tell you that two young prophets from the hills of Ephraim have just arrived, and he would like $2,000 in silver and two suits to give to them."
23"Take $4,000," Naaman insisted. He gave him two expensive robes, tied up the money in two bags, and gave them to two of his servants to carry back with Gehazi.
24But when they arrived at the hill where Elisha lived, Gehazi took the bags from the servants and sent the men back. Then he hid the money in his house.
25When he went in to his master, Elisha asked him, "Where have you been, Gehazi?"

"I haven't been anywhere," he replied.
26But Elisha asked him, "Don't you realize that I was there in thought when Naaman stepped down from his chariot to meet you? Is this the time to receive money and clothing and olive farms and vineyards and sheep and oxen and servants?
27Because you have done this, Naaman's leprosy shall be upon you and upon your children and your children's children forever."

And Gehazi walked from the room a leper, his skin as white as snow.

CHAPTER 6

Elisha Makes an Axhead Float

One day the seminary students came to Elisha and told him, "As you can see, our dormitory is too small. Tell us, as our president, whether

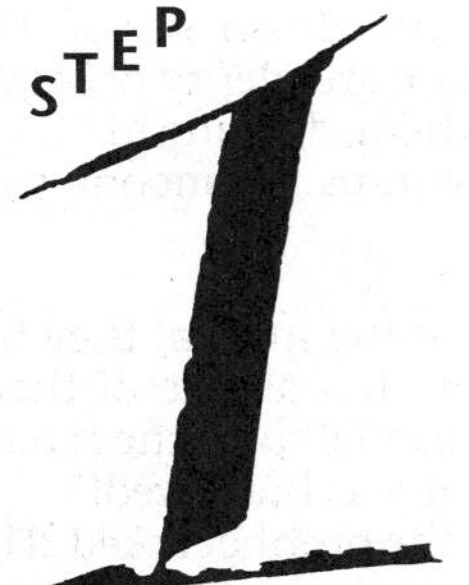

A Humble Beginning

BIBLE READING: 2 Kings 5:1-15

We admitted that we were powerless over our dependencies—that our life had become unmanageable.

It can be very humiliating to admit that we are powerless, especially if we are used to being in control. We may be powerful in some areas of our life, but out of control in terms of our addictive/compulsive behaviors. If we refuse to admit our powerlessness, we may lose everything. That one unmanageable part of our life may infect and destroy everything else.

The experiences of a man named Naaman illustrate how this is true (2 Kings 5:1-15). He was a powerful military and political figure, a man of wealth, position, and power. He also had leprosy, which promised to bring about the loss of everything he held dear. Lepers were made outcasts from their families and society. Ultimately, they faced a slow, painful, and disgraceful death.

Naaman heard that there was a prophet in Israel who could heal him. He found the prophet and was told that in order to be healed he needed to dip himself seven times in the Jordan River. He went away outraged, having expected his power to buy him an instant and easy cure. In the end, however, he acknowledged his powerlessness, followed the instructions, and recovered completely.

Our "disease" is as life threatening as the leprosy in Naaman's day. It slowly separates us from our family and leads toward the destruction of everything important to us. There is no instant or easy cure. The only answer is to admit our powerlessness, humble ourself, and submit to the process that will eventually bring recovery. ***Turn to page 569, Job 6.***

we can build a new one down beside the
Jordan River, where there are plenty of logs."
"All right," he told them, "go ahead."
3"Please, sir, come with us," someone suggested.
"I will," he said.
4When they arrived at the Jordan, they began cutting down trees; 5but as one of them
was chopping, his axhead fell into the river.
"Oh, sir," he cried, "it was borrowed!"
6"Where did it fall?" the prophet asked. The
youth showed him the place, and Elisha cut a
stick and threw it into the water; and the
axhead rose to the surface and floated! 7"Grab
it," Elisha said to him; and he did.

A Fiery Army Protects Elisha

8Once when the king of Syria was at war with
Israel, he said to his officers, "We will mobilize our forces at ____" (naming the place).
9Immediately Elisha warned the king of Israel, "Don't go near ____" (naming the same
place) "for the Syrians are planning to mobilize their troops there!"
10The king sent a scout to see if Elisha was
right, and sure enough, he had saved him
from disaster. This happened several times.
11The king of Syria was puzzled. He called
together his officers and demanded, "Which
of you is the traitor? Who has been informing
the king of Israel about my plans?"
12"It's not us, sir," one of the officers replied. "Elisha, the prophet, tells the king of
Israel even the words you speak in the privacy
of your bedroom!"
13"Go and find out where he is, and we'll
send troops to seize him," the king exclaimed.
And the report came back, "Elisha is at
Dothan."
14So one night the king of Syria sent a great
army with many chariots and horses to surround the city. 15When the prophet's servant
got up early the next morning and went outside, there were troops, horses, and chariots
everywhere.
"Alas, my master, what shall we do now?"
he cried out to Elisha.
16"Don't be afraid!" Elisha told him. "For
our army is bigger than theirs!"
17Then Elisha prayed, "Lord, open his eyes
and let him see!" And the Lord opened the
young man's eyes so that he could see horses
of fire and chariots of fire everywhere upon
the mountain!
18As the Syrian army advanced upon them,
Elisha prayed, "Lord, please make them
blind." And he did.
19Then Elisha went out and told them,
"You've come the wrong way! This isn't the
right city! Follow me and I will take you to the
man you're looking for." And he led them to
Samaria!
20As soon as they arrived Elisha prayed,
"Lord, now open their eyes and let them see."
And the Lord did, and they discovered that
they were in Samaria, the capital city of Israel!
21When the king of Israel saw them, he
shouted to Elisha, "Oh, sir, shall I kill them?
Shall I kill them?"
22"Of course not!" Elisha told him. "Do we
kill prisoners of war? Give them food and
drink and send them home again."
23So the king made a great feast for them
and then sent them home to their king. And
after that the Syrian raiders stayed away from
the land of Israel.

Elisha Predicts an Abundance of Food

24Later on, however, King Ben-hadad of Syria
mustered his entire army and besieged Samaria. 25As a result there was a great famine in
the city, and after a long while even a donkey's head sold for fifty dollars and a pint of
dove's dung brought three dollars!
26-30One day as the king of Israel was walking along the wall of the city, a woman called
to him, "Help, my lord the king!"
"If the Lord doesn't help you, what can I
do?" he retorted. "I have neither food nor
wine to give you. However, what's the matter?"
She replied, "This woman proposed that we
eat my son one day and her son the next. So
we boiled my son and ate him, but the next
day when I said, 'Kill your son so we can eat
him,' she hid him."
When the king heard this he tore his
clothes. (The people watching noticed

6:14-20 Elisha's servant was terrified by the awesome Syrian army because he couldn't see the help available to him. He was totally unaware of the great army of heavenly soldiers on his side. As we face the difficult task of recovery, we may be tempted to give up; our enemies may seem too powerful to overcome. But as we begin to see through the eyes of faith, we will discover the awesome power available to us. God's power is far greater than that of any of the enemies we might face. If we trust God for help and admit our powerlessness, we will find his power more than sufficient for our needs.

through the rip he tore in them that he was
wearing an inner robe made of sackcloth next
to his flesh.)
31“May God kill me if I don’t execute Elisha
this very day,” the king vowed.
32Elisha was sitting in his house at a meeting with the elders of Israel when the king
sent a messenger to summon him. But before
the messenger arrived Elisha said to the elders, “This murderer has sent a man to kill
me. When he arrives, shut the door and keep
him out, for his master will soon follow
him.”
33While Elisha was still saying this, the messenger arrived [followed by the king].

“The Lord has caused this mess,” the king
stormed. “Why should I expect any help from
him?”

CHAPTER 7

Elisha replied, “The Lord says that by this
time tomorrow two gallons of flour or four
gallons of barley grain will be sold in the
markets of Samaria for a dollar!”
2The officer assisting the king said, “That
couldn’t happen if the Lord made windows in
the sky!”

But Elisha replied, “You will see it happen,
but you won’t be able to buy any of it!”

Lepers Visit the Enemy Camp

3Now there were four lepers sitting outside the
city gates.

“Why sit here until we die?” they asked
each other. 4“We will starve if we stay here and
we will starve if we go back into the city; so
we might as well go out and surrender to the
Syrian army. If they let us live, so much the
better; but if they kill us, we would have died
anyway.”
5So that evening they went out to the camp
of the Syrians, but there was no one there!
6(For the Lord had made the whole Syrian
army hear the clatter of speeding chariots and
a loud galloping of horses and the sounds of
a great army approaching. “The king of Israel
has hired the Hittites and Egyptians to attack
us,” they cried out. 7So they panicked and fled
into the night, abandoning their tents,
horses, donkeys, and everything else.)
8When the lepers arrived at the edge of the
camp they went into one tent after another,
eating, drinking wine, and carrying out silver
and gold and clothing and hiding it. 9Finally
they said to each other, “This isn’t right. This
is wonderful news, and we aren’t sharing it
with anyone! Even if we wait until morning,
some terrible calamity will certainly fall upon
us; come on, let’s go back and tell the people
at the palace.”
10So they went back to the city and told the
watchmen what had happened—they had
gone out to the Syrian camp and no one was
there! The horses and donkeys were tethered
and the tents were all in order, but there was
not a soul around. 11Then the watchmen
shouted the news to those in the palace.
12The king got out of bed and told his officers, “I know what has happened. The Syrians
know we are starving, so they have left their
camp and have hidden in the fields, thinking
that we will be lured out of the city. Then they
will attack us and make slaves of us and get in.”
13One of his officers replied, “We’d better
send out scouts to see. Let them take five of
the remaining horses—if something happens
to the animals it won’t be any greater loss
than if they stay here and die with the rest of
us!”
14Four chariot-horses were found and the
king sent out two charioteers to see where the
Syrians had gone. 15They followed a trail of
clothing and equipment all the way to the
Jordan River—thrown away by the Syrians in
their haste. The scouts returned and told the
king, 16and the people of Samaria rushed out
and plundered the camp of the Syrians. So it
was true that two gallons of flour and four
gallons of barley were sold that day for one
dollar, just as the Lord had said!
17The king appointed his special assistant to
control the traffic at the gate, but he was
knocked down and trampled and killed as the
people rushed out. This is what Elisha had
predicted on the previous day when the king
had come to arrest him, 18and the prophet
had told the king that flour and barley would
sell for so little on the following day.
19The king’s officer had replied, “That

7:1-20 Many who stand on the brink of recovery never progress because as much as they desire victory, they believe it to be impossible. The officer of Israel tragically missed his opportunity for victory and freedom because of his unbelief. The obstacles to our recovery are never too great for God. But if we fail to believe this, we may be destroyed by the obstacles that God could easily have removed. By looking to God for help and placing our life in his hands, we can enjoy victorious blessings beyond our wildest dreams!

couldn't happen even if the Lord opened the
windows of heaven!"
And the prophet had said, "You will see it
happen, but you won't be able to buy any of
it!"
[20]And he couldn't, for the people trampled
him to death at the gate!

CHAPTER 8

A Woman's Land Is Returned

Elisha had told the woman whose son he had
brought back to life, "Take your family and
move to some other country, for the Lord has
called down a famine on Israel that will last
for seven years."
[2]So the woman took her family and lived in
the land of the Philistines for seven years.
[3]After the famine ended, she returned to the
land of Israel and went to see the king about
getting back her house and land. [4]Just as she
came in, the king was talking with Gehazi,
Elisha's servant, and saying, "Tell me some
stories of the great things Elisha has done."
[5]And Gehazi was telling the king about the
time when Elisha brought a little boy back to
life. At that very moment, the mother of the
boy walked in!
"Oh, sir!" Gehazi exclaimed. "Here is the
woman now, and this is her son—the very
one Elisha brought back to life!"
[6]"Is this true?" the king asked her. And she
told him that it was. So he directed one of his
officials to see to it that everything she had
owned was restored to her, plus the value of
any crops that had been harvested during her
absence.

Hazael Commits Murder

[7]Afterwards Elisha went to Damascus (the
capital of Syria), where King Ben-hadad lay
sick. Someone told the king that the prophet
had come.
[8,9]When the king heard the news, he said to
Hazael, "Take a present to the man of God and
tell him to ask the Lord whether I will get well
again."
So Hazael took forty camel-loads of the best
produce of the land as presents for Elisha and
said to him, "Your son Ben-hadad, the king of
Syria, has sent me to ask you whether he will
recover."
[10]And Elisha replied, "Tell him, 'Yes.' But
the Lord has shown me that he will surely
die!"
[11]Elisha stared at Hazael until he became
embarrassed, and then Elisha started crying.
[12]"What's the matter, sir?" Hazael asked him.
Elisha replied, "I know the terrible things
you will do to the people of Israel: you will
burn their forts, kill the young men, dash
their babies against the rocks, and rip open
the bellies of the pregnant women!"
[13]"Am I a dog?" Hazael asked him. "I would
never do that sort of thing."
But Elisha replied, "The Lord has shown me
that you are going to be the king of Syria."
[14]When Hazael went back, the king asked
him, "What did he tell you?"
And Hazael replied, "He told me that you
would recover."
[15]But the next day Hazael took a blanket
and dipped it in water and held it over the
king's face until he smothered to death. And
Hazael became king instead.

Jehoram Rules Judah

[16]King Jehoram, the son of King Jehoshaphat
of Judah, began his reign during the fifth year
of the reign of King Joram of Israel, the son of
Ahab. [17]Jehoram was thirty-two years old
when he became king, and he reigned in
Jerusalem for eight years. [18]But he was as
wicked as Ahab and the other kings of Israel;
he even married one of Ahab's daughters.
[19]Nevertheless, because God had promised his
servant David that he would watch over and
guide his descendants, he did not destroy
Judah.
[20]During Jehoram's reign, the people in

8:7-15 Recovery in the fullest sense cannot proceed when people refuse to handle things honestly. Elisha knew that King Ben-hadad could have come to physical "recovery" if he had been allowed to do so. However, Hazael would not let this happen because of his own desire to dominate and control. Likewise, many people working for recovery are hindered, even cruelly prevented, from doing so by those around them who prefer the opportunity to dominate. We need to surround ourselves with people who will honestly support our recovery process.

8:16-22 During King Jehoram's relatively brief rule over Judah, we see the actions and fruits of dysfunctional leadership. In spite of God's great patience with Jehoram (8:19), he continued to follow in the evil ways of his father-in-law, Ahab. When he found himself in dire straits, his army abandoned him. He was left alone to cope with his loss of Moab. If we resist God and oppress others, we can expect to be deserted by the people closest to us. We would be wise to learn from the sad consequences that resulted from Jehoram's wicked behavior.

Edom revolted from Judah and appointed their own king. [21]King Jehoram tried unsuccessfully to crush the rebellion: he crossed the Jordan River and attacked the city of Zair, but was quickly surrounded by the army of Edom. Under cover of night he broke through their ranks, but his army deserted him and fled. [22]So Edom has maintained its independence to this day. Libnah also rebelled at that time.

[23]The rest of the history of King Jehoram is written in *The Annals of the Kings of Judah.* [24,25]He died and was buried in the royal cemetery in the City of David—the old section of Jerusalem.

Ahaziah Rules Judah

Then his son Ahaziah became the new king during the twelfth year of the reign of King Jehoram of Israel, the son of Ahab. [26]Ahaziah was twenty-two years old when he began to reign, but he reigned only one year, in Jerusalem. His mother was Athaliah, the granddaughter of King Omri of Israel. [27]He was an evil king, just as all of King Ahab's descendants were—for he was related to Ahab by marriage.

[28]He joined King Joram of Israel (son of Ahab) in his war against Hazael, the king of Syria, at Ramoth-gilead. King Joram was wounded in the battle, [29]so he went to Jezreel to rest and recover from his wounds. While he was there, King Ahaziah of Judah (son of Jehoram) came to visit him.

CHAPTER 9

Jehu Is Anointed Israel's King

Meanwhile Elisha had summoned one of the young prophets.

"Get ready to go to Ramoth-gilead," he told him. "Take this vial of oil with you [2]and find Jehu (the son of Jehoshaphat, the son of Nimshi). Call him into a private room away from his friends, [3]and pour the oil over his head. Tell him that the Lord has anointed him to be the king of Israel; then run for your life!"

[4]So the young prophet did as he was told. When he arrived in Ramoth-gilead, [5]he found Jehu sitting around with the other army officers.

"I have a message for you, sir," he said.

"For which one of us?" Jehu asked.

"For you," he replied.

[6]So Jehu left the others and went into the house, and the young man poured the oil over his head and said, "The Lord God of Israel says, 'I anoint you king of the Lord's people, Israel. [7]You are to destroy the family of Ahab; you will avenge the murder of my prophets and of all my other people who were killed by Jezebel. [8]The entire family of Ahab must be wiped out—every male, no matter who. [9]I will destroy the family of Ahab as I destroyed the families of Jeroboam (son of Nebat) and of Baasha (son of Ahijah). [10]Dogs shall eat Ahab's wife Jezebel at Jezreel, and no one will bury her.'"

Then he opened the door and ran.

[11]Jehu went back to his friends and one of them asked him, "What did that crazy fellow want? Is everything all right?"

"You know very well who he was and what he wanted," Jehu replied.

[12]"No, we don't," they said. "Tell us."

So he told them what the man had said and that he had been anointed king of Israel!

[13]They quickly carpeted the bare steps with their coats and blew a trumpet, shouting, "Jehu is king!"

Jehu Kills Joram and Ahaziah

[14]That is how Jehu (son of Jehoshaphat, son of Nimshi) rebelled against King Joram. (King Joram had been with the army at Ramoth-gilead, defending Israel against the forces of King Hazael of Syria. [15]But he had returned to Jezreel to recover from his wounds.)

"Since you want me to be king," Jehu told

9:1-26 Joram was king of Israel, but he failed to command heartfelt loyalty from his troops. Instead, he manipulated them through fear. Jehu, however, had friends who risked their lives to be loyal servants of their friend and new king. When Joram's riders met Jehu, they allied with him, seeing an escape from their evil, oppressive master. If we are to expect loyalty from those around us, we need to be honest and fair with them. Loyalty is based on respect and admiration, not fear.

9:1–10:36 This extended account of the fulfillment of Elijah's earlier prophecy about the eventual destruction of evil King Ahab's family (see 1 Kings 21:19-29) should encourage those who have suffered under oppressive or abusive situations. When we have been victimized, we may wonder why God has allowed those who have hurt us to go unpunished. Here we see that eventually God does punish sin. No one will ever get away with it forever. God delays his judgment to give people more time to repent (see 2 Peter 3:9), but his patience does run out. After giving plenty of opportunities to repent, God always acts decisively to dish out just punishment upon perpetrators like Ahab's family.

the men who were with him, "don't let anyone escape to Jezreel to report what we have
done."
16Then Jehu jumped into a chariot and rode
to Jezreel himself to find King Joram, who was
lying there wounded. (King Ahaziah of Judah
was there too, for he had gone to visit him.)
17The watchman on the Tower of Jezreel saw
Jehu and his company approaching and
shouted, "Someone is coming."
"Send out a rider and find out if he is friend
or foe," King Joram shouted back. 18So a soldier rode out to meet Jehu.
"The king wants to know whether you are
friend or foe," he demanded. "Do you come
in peace?"
Jehu replied, "What do you know about
peace? Get behind me!"
The watchman called out to the king that
the messenger had met them but was not
returning. 19So the king sent out a second
rider. He rode up to them and demanded in
the name of the king to know whether their
intentions were friendly or not.
Jehu answered, "What do you know about
friendliness? Get behind me!"
20"He isn't returning either!" the watchman
exclaimed. "It must be Jehu, for he is driving
so furiously."
21"Quick! Get my chariot ready!" King Joram commanded.
Then he and King Ahaziah of Judah rode
out to meet Jehu. They met him at the field of
Naboth, 22and King Joram demanded, "Do
you come as a friend, Jehu?"
Jehu replied, "How can there be friendship
as long as the evils of your mother Jezebel are
all around us?"
23Then King Joram reined the chariot-
horses around and fled, shouting to King Ahaziah, "There is treachery, Ahaziah! Treason!"
24Then Jehu drew his bow with his full
strength and shot Joram between the shoulders; and the arrow pierced his heart, and he
sank down dead in his chariot.
25Jehu said to Bidkar, his assistant, "Throw
him into the field of Naboth, for once when
you and I were riding along behind his father
Ahab, the Lord revealed this prophecy to me:
26'I will repay him here on Naboth's property
for the murder of Naboth and his sons.' So
throw him out on Naboth's field, just as the
Lord said."
27Meanwhile, King Ahaziah of Judah had
fled along the road to Beth-haggan. Jehu rode
after him, shouting, "Shoot him too."
So they shot him in his chariot at the place
where the road climbs to Gur, near Ibleam. He
was able to go on as far as Megiddo, but died
there. 28His officials took him by chariot to
Jerusalem where they buried him in the royal
cemetery. 29(Ahaziah's reign over Judah had
begun in the twelfth year of the reign of King
Joram of Israel.)

Jezebel's Terrible Death

30When Jezebel heard that Jehu had come to
Jezreel, she painted her eyelids and fixed her
hair and sat at a window. 31When Jehu entered
the gate of the palace, she shouted at him,
"How are you today, you murderer! You son
of a Zimri who murdered his master!"
32He looked up and saw her at the window
and shouted, "Who is on my side?" And two
or three eunuchs looked out at him.
33"Throw her down!" he yelled.
So they threw her out the window, and her
blood spattered against the wall and on the
horses; and she was trampled by the horses'
hoofs.
34Then Jehu went into the palace for lunch.
Afterwards he said, "Someone go and bury
this cursed woman, for she is the daughter of
a king."
35But when they went out to bury her, they
found only her skull, her feet, and her hands.
36When they returned and told him, he remarked, "That is just what the Lord said would
happen. He told Elijah the prophet that dogs
would eat her flesh 37and that her body would
be scattered like manure upon the field, so that
no one could tell whose it was."

CHAPTER 10

Jehu Kills Ahab's Family

Then Jehu wrote a letter to the city council of
Samaria and to the guardians of Ahab's seventy sons—all of whom were living there.

10:1-12 As gory as this account is, it appears to have been motivated by commitment to God's will, as earlier expressed by the prophecy of Elijah about the destruction of Ahab's family (10:9-10; see 1 Kings 21:19-29). Although later events show that Jehu was probably not serious about spiritual recovery, he at least seems to be acting responsibly and with accountability toward both God and his people (10:9-10). However, he went too far in his killing spree (see Hosea 1:4-5). In our zeal to recover, we may go beyond what is necessary, being swept up in the emotion of the situation. Compulsive behavior can be devastating, even if we think we are doing it for the right reasons.

2,3"Upon receipt of this letter, select the best one of Ahab's sons to be your king, and prepare to fight for his throne. For you have chariots and horses and a fortified city and an armory."

4But they were too frightened to do it. "Two kings couldn't stand against this man! What can we do?" they said.

5So the manager of palace affairs and the city manager, together with the city council and the guardians of Ahab's sons, sent him this message:

"Jehu, we are your servants and will do anything you tell us to. We have decided that you should be our king instead of one of Ahab's sons."

6Jehu responded with this message: "If you are on my side and are going to obey me, bring the heads of your master's sons to me at Jezreel at about this time tomorrow."

(These seventy sons of King Ahab were living in the homes of the chief men of the city, where they had been raised since childhood.) 7When the letter arrived, all seventy of them were murdered, and their heads were packed into baskets and presented to Jehu at Jezreel. 8When a messenger told Jehu that the heads of the king's sons had arrived, he said to pile them in two heaps at the entrance of the city gate, and to leave them there until the next morning.

9,10In the morning he went out and spoke to the crowd that had gathered around them. "You aren't to blame," he told them. "I conspired against my master and killed him, but I didn't kill his sons! The Lord has done that, for everything he says comes true. He declared through his servant Elijah that this would happen to Ahab's descendants."

11Jehu then killed all the rest of the members of the family of Ahab who were in Jezreel, as well as all of his important officials, personal friends, and private chaplains. Finally, no one was left who had been close to him in any way. 12Then he set out for Samaria and stayed overnight at a shepherd's inn along the way. 13While he was there he met the brothers of King Ahaziah of Judah.

"Who are you?" he asked them.

And they replied, "We are brothers of King Ahaziah. We are going to Samaria to visit the sons of King Ahab and of the Queen Mother, Jezebel."

14"Grab them!" Jehu shouted to his men. And he took them out to the cistern and killed all forty-two of them.

15As he left the inn, he met Jehonadab, the son of Rechab, who was coming to meet him. After they had greeted each other, Jehu said to him, "Are you as loyal to me as I am to you?"

"Yes," Jehonadab replied.

"Then give me your hand," Jehu said, and he helped him into the royal chariot.

16"Now come along with me," Jehu said, "and see how much I have done for the Lord." So Jehonadab rode along with him. 17When he arrived in Samaria he butchered all of Ahab's friends and relatives, just as Elijah, speaking for the Lord, had predicted.

Jehu Kills the Priests of Baal

Then Jehu called a meeting of all the people of the city and said to them, "Ahab hardly worshiped Baal at all in comparison to the way I am going to! 18,19Summon all the prophets and priests of Baal, and call together all his worshipers. See to it that every one of them comes, for we worshipers of Baal are going to have a great celebration to praise him. Any of Baal's worshipers who don't come will be put to death."

But Jehu's plan was to exterminate them. 20,21He sent messengers throughout all Israel summoning those who worshiped Baal; and they all came and filled the temple of Baal from one end to the other. 22He instructed the head of the robing room, "Be sure that every worshiper wears one of the special robes."

23Then Jehu and Jehonadab (son of Rechab) went into the temple to address the people: "Check to be sure that only those who worship Baal are here; don't let anyone in who worships the Lord!"

24As the priests of Baal began offering sacrifices and burnt offerings, Jehu surrounded the building with eighty of his men and told them, "If you let anyone escape, you'll pay for it with your own life."

25As soon as he had finished sacrificing the burnt offering, Jehu went out and told his

---

10:17-29 Even in this crowning victory over Ahab's legacy of Baal worship, two troubling defects in Jehu's personality and actions are seen. First, Jehu was not honest about why he wanted the Baal worshipers to gather (10:17-25); he manipulated them with a lie. Second, he got rid of the Baal worship in the northern kingdom, but not all the false worship (10:26-29). The process of recovery can proceed only with honesty and wholehearted commitment to God. We will never recover if we tell only part of the truth or if we change only part of our life.

officers and men, "Go in and kill the whole
bunch of them. Don't let a single one escape."
So they slaughtered them all and dragged
their bodies outside. Then Jehu's men went
into the inner temple, [26]dragged out the pillar
used for the worship of Baal, and burned it.
[27]They wrecked the temple and converted it
into a public toilet, which it still is today.
[28]Thus Jehu destroyed every trace of Baal from
Israel. [29]However, he didn't destroy the gold
calves at Bethel and Dan—this was the great
sin of Jeroboam (son of Nebat), for it resulted
in all Israel sinning.
[30]Afterwards the Lord said to Jehu, "You
have done well in following my instructions
to destroy the dynasty of Ahab. Because of
this I will cause your son, your grandson, and
your great-grandson to be the kings of Israel."
[31]But Jehu didn't follow the Lord God of
Israel with all his heart, for he continued to
worship Jeroboam's gold calves that had been
the cause of such great sin in Israel.
[32,33]At about that time the Lord began to
whittle down the size of Israel. King Hazael
conquered several sections of the country
east of the Jordan River, as well as all of
Gilead, Gad, and Reuben; he also conquered
parts of Manasseh from the Aroer River in the
valley of the Arnon as far as Gilead and Bashan.
[34]The rest of Jehu's activities are recorded in
The Annals of the Kings of Israel. [35]When Jehu
died, he was buried in Samaria; and his son
Jehoahaz became the new king. [36]In all, Jehu
reigned as king of Israel, in Samaria, for
twenty-eight years.

CHAPTER 11

Athaliah Rules Judah

When Athaliah, the mother of King Ahaziah
of Judah, learned that her son was dead, she
killed all of his children, [2,3]except for his year-
old son Joash. Joash was rescued by his Aunt
Jehosheba, who was a sister of King Ahaziah
(for she was a daughter of King Jehoram,
Ahaziah's father). She stole him away from
among the rest of the king's children who
were waiting to be slain and hid him and his
nurse in a storeroom of the Temple. They
lived there for six years while Athaliah
reigned as queen.

Young Joash Becomes King

[4]In the seventh year of Queen Athaliah's
reign, Jehoiada the priest summoned the officers of the palace guard and the queen's bodyguard. He met them in the Temple, swore
them to secrecy, and showed them the king's
son.
[5]Then he gave them their instructions: "A
third of those who are on duty on the Sabbath
are to guard the palace. [6-8]The other two-thirds
shall stand guard at the Temple; surround the
king, weapons in hand, and kill anyone who
tries to break through. Stay with the king at
all times."
[9]So the officers followed Jehoiada's instructions. They brought to Jehoiada the men who
were going off duty on the Sabbath and those
who were coming on duty, [10]and he armed
them from the Temple's supply of spears and
shields that had belonged to King David.
[11]The guards, with weapons ready, stood
across the front of the sanctuary and sur-

10:30-33 It is entirely possible to please God in one part of our life and to displease him greatly in another. Jehu honored God by destroying Ahab's family, and he was blessed for it. However, his divided spiritual allegiance prevented the full recovery of the northern kingdom (10:31). Because there was no clean break from the sinful worship patterns established long before by King Jeroboam, God allowed Israel to move closer to hitting bottom (10:31-33). We, too, need to turn our entire life over to God's control. The areas we refuse to commit to God could very well be the root of our addiction or compulsion.

11:1-3 Recovery is a difficult, even terrifying, alternative for many who must live in close proximity to ruthless oppressors or abusive personalities. Such highly dysfunctional personalities will attempt to do whatever it takes to get their way and to solidify their rule by intimidation. The flaw in Athaliah's "reign of terror" was her failure to believe God's promises to David and his line (see 2 Samuel 7:12-16). The survival of young Joash was not only God's will; it was also a manifestation of God's ongoing care of his chosen people (see 2 Kings 12). We must trust in God's care for us and take the steps necessary for recovery.

11:4-21 Jehoiada's faith was the catalyst for Judah's move toward recovery. The process of anointing Joash and proclaiming him the rightful ruler was undergirded by his courage. Jehoiada desired to restore Judah to a right relationship with God. Under his leadership, the people and king made an agreement to worship God, follow his commands, and destroy the altars to false gods. Through the agreement they set up, all the people were responsible for the nation's recovery, and everyone was held accountable. Courage to change our situation and personal accountability to others are necessary parts of any successful recovery program.

rounded the altar, which was near Joash's hideaway.

[12]Then Jehoiada brought out the young prince and put the crown upon his head and gave him a copy of the Ten Commandments, and anointed him as king. Then everyone clapped and shouted, "Long live the king!"

[13,14]When Athaliah heard all the noise, she ran into the Temple and saw the new king standing beside the pillar, as was the custom at times of coronation, surrounded by her bodyguard and many trumpeters; and everyone was rejoicing and blowing trumpets.

"Treason! Treason!" she screamed, and began to tear her clothes.

[15]"Get her out of here," shouted Jehoiada to the officers of the guard. "Don't kill her here in the Temple. But kill anyone who tries to come to her rescue."

[16]So they dragged her to the palace stables and killed her there.

[17]Jehoiada made a treaty between the Lord, the king, and the people, that they would be the Lord's people. He also made a contract between the king and the people. [18]Everyone went over to the temple of Baal and tore it down, breaking the altars and images and killing Mattan, the priest of Baal, in front of the altar. And Jehoiada set guards at the Temple of the Lord. [19]Then he and the officers and the guard and all the people led the king from the Temple, past the guardhouse, and into the palace. And he sat upon the king's throne.

[20]So everyone was happy, and the city settled back into quietness after Athaliah's death. [21]Joash was seven years old when he became king.

CHAPTER 12

Joash Rules Judah

It was seven years after Jehu had become the king of Israel that Joash became king of Judah. He reigned in Jerusalem for forty years. (His mother was Zibiah, from Beersheba.) [2]All his life Joash did what was right because Jehoiada the High Priest instructed him. [3]Yet even so he didn't destroy the shrines on the hills—the people still sacrificed and burned incense there.

[4,5]One day King Joash said to Jehoiada, "The Temple building needs repairing. Whenever anyone brings a contribution to the Lord, whether it is a regular assessment or some special gift, use it to pay for whatever repairs are needed."

[6]But in the twenty-third year of his reign the Temple was still in disrepair. [7]So Joash called for Jehoiada and the other priests and asked them, "Why haven't you done anything about the Temple? Now don't use any more money for your own needs; from now on it must all be spent on getting the Temple into good condition."

[8]So the priests agreed to set up a special repair fund that would not go through their hands, lest it be diverted to care for their personal needs. [9]Jehoiada the priest bored a hole in the lid of a large chest and set it on the right-hand side of the altar at the Temple entrance. The doorkeepers put all of the people's contributions into it. [10]Whenever the chest became full, the king's financial secretary and the High Priest counted it, put it into bags, [11,12]and gave it to the construction superintendents to pay the carpenters, stonemasons, quarrymen, timber dealers, and stone merchants, and to buy the other materials needed to repair the Temple of the Lord. [13,14]It was not used to buy silver cups, gold snuffers, bowls, trumpets, or similar articles, but only for repairs to the building. [15]No accounting was required from the construction superintendents, for they were honest and faithful men. [16]However, the money that was contributed for guilt offerings and sin offerings was given to the priests for their own use. It was not put into the chest.

[17]About this time, King Hazael of Syria went to war against Gath and captured it; then he moved on toward Jerusalem to attack it. [18]King Joash took all the sacred objects that his ancestors—Jehoshaphat, Jehoram, and Ahaziah, the kings of Judah—had dedicated, along with what he himself had dedicated, and all the gold in the treasuries of the Temple

12:4-16 The difficult task of repairing the Temple was an important part of Judah's spiritual recovery. Yet raising the money to rebuild proved difficult. The priests and people were not willing to make the sacrifices necessary to get the job done. So Joash set up a system where the priests were accountable for the money they received. With this system of accountability the people of Judah were able to accomplish the renovation process. This should remind us that accountability and concrete planning are necessary for a successful rebuilding program. Without them, we will probably take the path of least resistance and make little progress in our recovery.

and the palace, and sent it to Hazael. So Hazael called off the attack.

[19]The rest of the history of Joash is recorded in *The Annals of the Kings of Judah.* [20]But his officers plotted against him and assassinated him in his royal residence at Millo on the road to Silla. [21]The assassins were Jozachar, the son of Shimeath, and Jehozabad, the son of Shomer—both trusted aides. He was buried in the royal cemetery in Jerusalem, and his son Amaziah became the new king.

CHAPTER 13

Jehoahaz Rules Israel

Jehoahaz (the son of Jehu) began a seventeen-year reign over Israel during the twenty-third year of the reign of King Joash of Judah. [2]But he was an evil king, and he followed the wicked paths of Jeroboam, who had caused Israel to sin. [3]So the Lord was very angry with Israel, and he continually allowed King Hazael of Syria and his son Ben-hadad to conquer them.

[4]But Jehoahaz prayed for the Lord's help, and the Lord listened to him; for the Lord saw how terribly the king of Syria was oppressing Israel. [5]So the Lord raised up leaders among the Israelis to rescue them from the tyranny of the Syrians; and then Israel lived in safety again as they had in former days. [6]But they continued to sin, following the evil ways of Jeroboam; and they continued to worship the goddess Asherah at Samaria. [7]Finally the Lord reduced Jehoahaz's army to fifty mounted troops, ten chariots, and ten thousand infantry; for the king of Syria had destroyed the others as though they were dust beneath his feet.

[8]The rest of the history of Jehoahaz is recorded in *The Annals of the Kings of Israel.*

Jehoash Rules Israel

[9,10]Jehoahaz died and was buried in Samaria, and his son Joash reigned in Samaria for sixteen years. He came to the throne in the thirty-seventh year of the reign of King Joash of Judah. [11]But he was an evil man, for, like Jeroboam, he encouraged the people to worship idols and led them into sin. [12]The rest of the history of the reign of Joash, including his wars against King Amaziah of Judah, are written in *The Annals of the Kings of Israel.* [13]Joash died and was buried in Samaria with the other kings of Israel; and Jeroboam II became the new king.

[14]When Elisha was in his last illness, King Joash visited him and wept over him.

"My father! My father! You are the strength of Israel!" he cried.

[15]Elisha told him, "Get a bow and some arrows," and he did.

[16,17]"Open that eastern window," he instructed.

Then he told the king to put his hand upon the bow, and Elisha laid his own hands upon the king's hands.

"Shoot!" Elisha commanded, and he did.

Then Elisha proclaimed, "This is the Lord's arrow, full of victory over Syria; for you will completely conquer the Syrians at Aphek. [18]Now pick up the other arrows and strike them against the floor."

12:17-18 Joash had made great strides toward leading Israel into spiritual recovery. But here we see that his faith wavered easily when he was put in a difficult situation. Under threat of Syrian attack, he gave away the Temple treasury to pay off King Hazael of Syria. He failed to turn to God, who was capable of delivering his people from the Syrians, and sought his own human solution. The consequences were great national losses and a perpetuation of faithless living. Even after great success, we are still susceptible to giving in to fear and denial. We need to trust God to defeat the "enemies" in our life. Trying to fight them on our own will only invest them with greater power.

13:1-7 The experience of King Jehoahaz of Israel is a solemn case study of what happens when you "play around" with recovery. Jehoahaz apparently was humbled by his consistent defeats at the hands of the Syrians. He admitted he was powerless and turned to God, the all-important first step of recovery. However, after God graciously granted a measure of relief and freedom, Jehoahaz fell back into his old dysfunctional patterns once again. The consequences of his actions then led to the near collapse of his rule. As we hit bottom, it is relatively easy to give things over to God—we have nothing worth holding on to. True recovery is only possible, however, when we leave our life in God's hands—even when things are going well.

13:9-19 King Joash of Israel (not Joash of Judah; see chapters 11–12) was another individual who started the recovery process, but didn't go far enough. Though he was an "evil man," Joash of Israel was greatly touched emotionally when the prophet Elisha was about to die. He expressed his great respect and his grief for Elisha. Thus, Elisha urged Joash to follow his instructions, which would lead him to victory. Joash followed the instructions halfheartedly and was thus limited in his progress. Anything less than complete commitment to our recovery will result in an incomplete recovery.

So the king picked them up and struck the floor three times. 19But the prophet was angry with him. "You should have struck the floor five or six times," he exclaimed, "for then you would have beaten Syria until they were entirely destroyed; now you will be victorious only three times."

20,21So Elisha died and was buried.

In those days bandit gangs of Moabites used to invade the land each spring. Once some men who were burying a friend spied these marauders so they hastily threw his body into the tomb of Elisha. And as soon as the body touched Elisha's bones, the dead man revived and jumped to his feet!

22King Hazael of Syria had oppressed Israel during the entire reign of King Jehoahaz. 23But the Lord was gracious to the people of Israel, and they were not totally destroyed. For God pitied them, and also he was honoring his contract with Abraham, Isaac, and Jacob. And this is still true. 24Then King Hazael of Syria died, and his son Ben-hadad reigned in his place.

25King Joash of Israel (the son of Jehoahaz) was successful on three occasions in reconquering the cities that his father had lost to Ben-hadad.

CHAPTER 14

Amaziah Rules Judah

During the second year of the reign of King Joash of Israel, King Amaziah began his reign over Judah. 2Amaziah was twenty-five years old at the time, and he reigned in Jerusalem for twenty-nine years. (His mother was Jehoaddin, a native of Jerusalem.) 3He was a good king in the Lord's sight, though not quite like his ancestor David; but he was as good a king as his father Joash. 4However, he didn't destroy the shrines on the hills, so the people still sacrificed and burned incense there.

5As soon as he had a firm grip on the kingdom, he killed the men who had assassinated his father; 6but he didn't kill their children, for the Lord had commanded through the law of Moses that fathers shall not be killed for their children, nor children for the sins of their fathers: everyone must pay the penalty for his own sins. 7Once Amaziah killed ten thousand Edomites in Salt Valley; he also conquered Sela and changed its name to Joktheel, as it is called to this day.

8One day he sent a message to King Joash of Israel (the son of Jehoahaz and the grandson of Jehu), daring him to mobilize his army and come out and fight.

9But King Joash replied, "The thistle of Lebanon demanded of the mighty cedar tree, 'Give your daughter to be a wife for my son.' But just then a wild animal passed by and stepped on the thistle and trod it into the ground! 10You have destroyed Edom and are very proud about it; but my advice to you is, be content with your glory and stay home! Why provoke disaster for both yourself and Judah?"

11But Amaziah refused to listen, so King Joash of Israel mustered his army. The battle began at Beth-shemesh, one of the cities of Judah, 12and Judah was defeated and the army fled home. 13King Amaziah was captured, and the army of Israel marched on Jerusalem and broke down its wall from the Gate of Ephraim to the Corner Gate, a distance of about six hundred feet. 14King Joash took many hostages and all the gold and silver from the Temple and palace treasury, also the gold cups. Then he returned to Samaria.

15The rest of the history of Joash and his war with King Amaziah of Judah are recorded in *The Annals of the Kings of Israel.* 16When Joash died, he was buried in Samaria with the other kings of Israel. And his son Jeroboam became the new king.

17Amaziah lived fifteen years longer than Joash, 18and the rest of his biography is recorded in *The Annals of the Kings of Judah.* 19There was a plot against his life in Jerusalem, and he fled to Lachish; but his enemies sent assassins and killed him there. 20His body was returned on horses, and he was buried in the royal cemetery, in the City of David section of Jerusalem.

21Then his son Azariah became the new

14:1-7 Amaziah of Judah demonstrated how a parent's behavior often has a significant impact on the behavior of his children. Amaziah was "as good a king as his father Joash." Joash's various strengths and weaknesses were evidenced in the behavior of his son Amaziah. Notable was their blind spot in regard to the shrines of false worship (14:4). Perhaps it is best to say that Amaziah's commitment to God was mostly defined by Joash's commitment. Likewise, we need to remember that our children are watching us and may well follow suit. Learning to trust God and obey his program for godly and healthy living is more than just a personal victory. It is an opportunity to leave a godly legacy for our children and grandchildren.

king at the age of sixteen. [22]After his father's death, he built Elath and restored it to Judah.

Jeroboam II Rules Israel

[23]Meanwhile, over in Israel, Jeroboam II had become king during the fifteenth year of the reign of King Amaziah of Judah. Jeroboam's reign lasted forty-one years. [24]But he was as evil as Jeroboam I (the son of Nebat), who had led Israel into the sin of worshiping idols. [25]Jeroboam II recovered the lost territories of Israel between Hamath and the Dead Sea, just as the Lord God of Israel had predicted through Jonah (son of Amittai) the prophet from Gathhepher. [26]For the Lord saw the bitter plight of Israel—she had no one to help her. [27]And he had not said that he would blot out the name of Israel, so he used King Jeroboam II to save her.

[28]The rest of Jeroboam's biography—all that he did, and his great power, and his wars, and how he recovered Damascus and Hamath (which had been captured by Judah)—is recorded in *The Annals of the Kings of Israel.* [29]When Jeroboam II, died he was buried with the other kings of Israel, and his son Zechariah became the new king of Israel.

CHAPTER 15

Azariah Rules Judah

New king of Judah: Azariah
Father's name: Amaziah, the former king
His age at the beginning of his reign: 16 years old
Length of reign: 52 years, in Jerusalem
Mother's name: Jecoliah of Jerusalem
Reigning in Israel at that time: King Jeroboam, who had been the king there for 27 years

[3]Azariah was a good king, and he pleased the Lord just as his father Amaziah had. [4]But like his predecessors, he didn't destroy the shrines on the hills where the people sacrificed and burned incense. [5]Because of this the Lord struck him with leprosy, which lasted until the day of his death; so he lived in a house by himself. And his son Jotham was the acting king. [6]The rest of the history of Azariah is recorded in *The Annals of the Kings of Judah.* [7]When Azariah died, he was buried with his ancestors in the City of David, and his son Jotham became king.

Zechariah Rules Israel

[8]New king of Israel: Zechariah
Father's name: Jeroboam
Length of reign: 6 months, in Samaria
Reigning in Judah at that time: King Azariah, who had been the king there for 38 years

[9]But Zechariah was an evil king in the Lord's sight, just like his ancestors. Like Jeroboam I (the son of Nebat), he encouraged Israel in the sin of worshiping idols. [10]Then Shallum (the son of Jabesh) conspired against him and assassinated him at Ibleam and took the crown himself. [11]The rest of the history of Zechariah's reign is found in *The Annals of the Kings of Israel.* [12](So the Lord's statement to Jehu came true, that Jehu's son, grandson, and great-grandson would be kings of Israel.)

Shallum Rules Israel

[13]New king of Israel: Shallum
Father's name: Jabesh
Length of reign: 1 month, in Samaria
Reigning in Judah at that time: King Uzziah, who had been the king there for 39 years

[14]One month after Shallum became king, Menahem (the son of Gadi) came to Samaria from Tirzah and assassinated him and took the throne. [15]Additional details about King Shallum and his conspiracy are recorded in *The Annals of the Kings of Israel.*

14:23-27 God, in his sovereignty, can use oppressive or abusive personalities as part of his wider plan. The evil reign of King Jeroboam II was allowed by God to last for forty-one years only because God had a special purpose for him (14:23-26). Even though Jeroboam II had no discernible faith or commitment toward God, God used him as his created instrument to maintain the independence of the northern kingdom for the time being. This perspective may help those in recovery understand why God does not always immediately punish an oppressive personality; God may have something special for this person to bring about.

15:8-12 The long, evil reign of Jeroboam II of the northern kingdom (14:23-29) could not guarantee stability or power for his equally evil son, Zechariah (15:9). God allowed Zechariah to survive for only six months before he was assassinated (15:10). God had kept the word of judgment he had made against Jehu generations before (15:12; see 10:30); this was the end of his primarily evil line of descendants. Jehu's failure had led to the failure of his descendants. Unless we seek recovery now, the results may be disastrous for our own children and grandchildren.

[16]Menahem destroyed the city of Tappuah and the surrounding countryside, for its citizens refused to accept him as their king; he killed the entire population and ripped open the pregnant women.

Menahem Rules Israel

[17]New king of Israel: Menahem
Length of reign: 10 years, in Samaria
Reigning in Judah at that time: King Azariah, who had been the king there for 39 years

[18]But Menahem was an evil king. He worshiped idols, as King Jeroboam I had done so long before, and he led the people of Israel into grievous sin. [19,20]Then King Pul of Assyria invaded the land; but King Menahem bought him off with a gift of $2,000,000, so he turned around and returned home. Menahem extorted the money from the rich, assessing each one $2,000 in the form of a special tax. [21]The rest of the history of King Menahem is written in *The Annals of the Kings of Israel.* [22]When he died, his son Pekahiah became the new king.

Pekahiah Rules Israel

[23]New king of Israel: Pekahiah
Father's name: King Menahem
Length of reign: 2 years, in Samaria
Reigning in Judah at that time: King Azariah, who had been the king there for 50 years

[24]But Pekahiah was an evil king, and he continued the idol-worship begun by Jeroboam I (son of Nebat) who led Israel down that evil trail.

[25]Then Pekah (son of Remaliah), the commanding general of his army, conspired against him with fifty men from Gilead and assassinated him in the palace at Samaria (Argob and Arieh were also slain in the revolt). So Pekah became the new king. [26]The rest of the history of King Pekahiah is recorded in *The Annals of the Kings of Israel.*

Pekah Rules Israel

[27]New king of Israel: Pekah
Father's name: Remaliah
Length of reign: 20 years, in Samaria
Reigning in Judah at that time: King Azariah, who had been the king there for 52 years

[28]Pekah, too, was an evil king, and he continued in the example of Jeroboam I (son of Nebat), who led all of Israel into the sin of worshiping idols. [29]It was during his reign that King Tiglath-pileser led an attack against Israel. He captured the cities of Ijon, Abel-beth-maacah, Janoah, Kedesh, Hazor, Gilead, Galilee, and all the land of Naphtali; and he took the people away to Assyria as captives. [30]Then Hoshea (the son of Elah) plotted against Pekah and assassinated him; and he took the throne for himself.

New king of Israel: Hoshea
Reigning in Judah at that time: King Jotham (son of Uzziah), who had been the king there for 20 years

[31]The rest of the history of Pekah's reign is recorded in *The Annals of the Kings of Israel.*

Jotham Rules Judah

[32,33]New king of Judah: Jotham
Father's name: King Uzziah
His age at the beginning of his reign: 25 years old
Length of reign: 16 years, in Jerusalem
Mother's name: Jerusha (daughter of Zadok)
Reigning in Israel at that time: King Pekah (son of Remaliah), who had been the king there for 2 years

[34,35]Generally speaking, Jotham was a good king. Like his father Uzziah, he followed the

---

15:13-14, 23-25 The reigns of kings Shallum and Pekahiah of the northern kingdom show us what normally happens to oppressive personalities who refuse to face their need for recovery. Both were assassinated after very brief reigns (15:14, 25). Shallum had been an assassin himself, so he died the same way he had risen to power (15:10). Pekahiah was killed by someone who was very close to him (15:25). If we tend to be oppressive in our relationships, we need to be careful—these people may tire of our abuse and either destroy us or abandon us to our misery.

15:32-38 The reign of King Jotham of Judah, first as coregent with his father (Azariah, 15:3-5; also known as Uzziah, 15:34-35) and then in his own right (15:32-33), was a "mixed bag." He exemplified faith and commitment to God up to a point, as had his predecessors. On the one hand, he gave attention to God's Temple. However, the ongoing presence of the hill shrines and false worship in Judah (15:34-35) prompted God to "turn up the heat." God allowed Syria and Israel to attack in order to shatter Jotham's denial (15:37). God will often bring trials into our life in order to alert us to our denial.

Lord. But he didn't destroy the shrines on the hills where the people sacrificed and burned incense. It was during King Jotham's reign that the upper gate of the Temple of the Lord was built. 36The rest of Jotham's history is written in *The Annals of the Kings of Judah.* 37In those days the Lord caused King Rezin of Syria and King Pekah of Israel to attack Judah. 38When Jotham died he was buried with the other kings of Judah in the royal cemetery, in the City of David section of Jerusalem. Then his son Ahaz became the new king.

CHAPTER 16

Ahaz Rules Judah

New king of Judah: Ahaz
- Father's name: Jotham
- His age at the beginning of his reign: 20 years old
- Length of reign: 16 years, in Jerusalem
- Character of his reign: evil
- Reigning in Israel at that time: King Pekah (son of Remaliah), who had been the king there for 17 years

2But he did not follow the Lord as his ancestor David had; 3he was as wicked as the kings of Israel. He even killed his own son by offering him as a burnt sacrifice to the gods, following the heathen customs of the nations around Judah—nations that the Lord destroyed when the people of Israel entered the land. 4He also sacrificed and burned incense at the shrines on the hills and at the numerous altars in the groves of trees.

5Then King Rezin of Syria and King Pekah (son of Remaliah) of Israel declared war on Ahaz and besieged Jerusalem; but they did not conquer it. 6However, at that time King Rezin of Syria recovered the city of Elath for Syria; he drove out the Jews and sent Syrians to live there, as they do to this day. 7King Ahaz sent a messenger to King Tiglath-pileser of Assyria, begging him to help him fight the attacking armies of Syria and Israel. 8Ahaz took the silver and gold from the Temple and from the royal vaults and sent it as a payment to the Assyrian king. 9So the Assyrians attacked Damascus, the capital of Syria. They took away the population of the city as captives, resettling them in Kir, and King Rezin of Syria was killed.

10King Ahaz now went to Damascus to meet with King Tiglath-pileser, and while he was there he noticed an unusual altar in a heathen temple. He jotted down its dimensions and made a sketch and sent it back to Uriah the priest with a detailed description. 11,12Uriah built one just like it by following these directions and had it ready for the king, who, upon his return from Damascus, inaugurated it with an offering. 13The king presented a burnt offering and a grain offering, poured a drink offering over it, and sprinkled the blood of peace offerings upon it. 14Then he removed the old bronze altar from the front of the Temple (it had stood between the Temple entrance and the new altar), and placed it on the north side of the new altar. 15He instructed Uriah the priest to use the new altar for the sacrifices of burnt offering, the evening grain offering, the king's burnt offering and grain offering, and the offerings of the people, including their drink offerings. The blood from the burnt offerings and sacrifices was also to be sprinkled over the new altar. So the old altar was used only for purposes of divination.

"The old bronze altar," he said, "will be only for my personal use."

16Uriah the priest did as King Ahaz instructed him. 17Then the king dismantled the wheeled stands in the Temple, removed their crosspieces and the water vats they sup-

---

16:1-4 It was only a matter of time before the halfhearted attempts at recovery by Judah's kings would cause great damage. Ahaz's reign wasn't even a "mixed bag." He completely denied his need for God and disobeyed God's laws (16:2-4), even sacrificing his own son to pagan gods. The partial recovery of many generations had a cumulative impact on the later generations. Children can quickly see through the hypocrisy of a halfhearted recovery. This may cause them to reject everything we stand for—especially the good things. What kind of example are we setting for our children?

16:5-9 King Ahaz paid tribute to the king of Assyria, placing his trust in the human resources at his disposal. In seeking human solutions to the conflict, however, he failed to trust God to help him. The peace that Ahaz established in Judah was dependent on the payment of money. When Ahaz's son Hezekiah refused to pay tribute money to Assyria, Assyria attacked (see 18:7, 13), but God protected Hezekiah and his kingdom. Had Ahaz turned to God for help, the peace he sought would have been unconditional—built upon the unchanging power and presence of God. We also need to look to God for help in our recovery. Looking for human help may be disappointing. People may help us only for what they get in return.

returned to Bethel and taught the colonists from Babylon how to worship the Lord.

[29]But these foreigners also worshiped their own gods. They placed them in the shrines on the hills near their cities. [30]Those from Babylon worshiped idols of their god Succoth-benoth; those from Cuth worshiped their god Nergal; and the men of Hamath worshiped Ashima. [31]The gods Nibhaz and Tartak were worshiped by the Avvites, and the people from Sephar even burned their own children on the altars of their gods Adrammelech and Anammelech.

[32]They also worshiped the Lord, and they appointed from among themselves priests to sacrifice to the Lord on the hilltop altars. [33]But they continued to follow the religious customs of the nations from which they came. [34]And this is still going on among them today—they follow their former practices instead of truly worshiping the Lord or obeying the laws he gave to the descendants of Jacob (whose name was later changed to Israel). [35,36]For the Lord had made a contract with them—that they were never to worship or make sacrifices to any heathen gods. They were to worship only the Lord who had brought them out of the land of Egypt with such tremendous miracles and power. [37]The descendants of Jacob were to obey all of God's laws and *never* worship other gods.

[38]For God had said, *"You must never forget the covenant I made with you; never worship other gods. [39]You must worship only the Lord; he will save you from all your enemies."*

[40]But Israel didn't listen, and the people continued to worship other gods. [41] These colonists from Babylon worshiped the Lord, yes—but they also worshiped their idols. And to this day their descendants do the same thing.

CHAPTER 18

Hezekiah Rules Judah

New king of Judah: Hezekiah

Father's name: Ahaz

His age at the beginning of his reign: 25 years old

Length of reign: 29 years, in Jerusalem

Mother's name: Abi (daughter of Zechariah)

Character of his reign: good (similar to that of his ancestor David)

Reigning in Israel at that time: King Hoshea (son of Elah), who had been the king there for 3 years

[4]He removed the shrines on the hills, broke down the obelisks, knocked down the shameful idols of Asherah, and broke up the bronze serpent that Moses had made, because the people of Israel had begun to worship it by burning incense to it; even though, as King Hezekiah pointed out to them, it was merely a piece of bronze. [5]He trusted very strongly in the Lord God of Israel. In fact, none of the kings before or after him were as close to God as he was. [6]For he followed the Lord in everything, and carefully obeyed all of God's commands to Moses. [7]So the Lord was with him and prospered everything he did. Then he rebelled against the king of Assyria and refused to pay tribute any longer. [8]He also conquered the Philistines as far distant as Gaza and its suburbs, destroying cities both large and small.

[9]It was during the fourth year of his reign (which was the seventh year of the reign of King Hoshea in Israel) that King Shalmaneser of Assyria attacked Israel and began a siege on the city of Samaria. [10]Three years later (during the sixth year of the reign of King Hezekiah and the ninth year of the reign of King Hoshea of Israel) Samaria fell. [11]It was at that time that the king of Assyria transported the Israelis to Assyria and put them in colonies in the city of Halath and along the banks of the Habor River in Gozan, and in the cities of the Medes. [12]For they had refused to listen to the Lord their God or to do what he wanted them

18:1-8 King Hezekiah made a radical break from the evil ways of his father, Ahaz. Hezekiah's stated faith and commitment gave him the courage to stand against Judah's sinful past and to take significant steps to rebuild his kingdom in God's way (18:5). His honesty in assessing the spiritual state of his kingdom and his willingness to break from sinful ways made him one of Judah's greatest kings (18:6-7). If we want to succeed in recovery, we also must honestly admit our failures and do all we can to rebuild our life in God's way.

18:9-16 Although Hezekiah was one of the best of Judah's kings, he responded exactly as his father had at the threat of the Assyrian invasion. Hezekiah trusted God with the smaller things, but at the threat of invasion, he looked for help elsewhere. Rather than trusting the God who gave him his kingdom, Hezekiah trusted the very enemy who was attacking him. Our addictions have the same effect on us. We choose to trust in the things that are ruining our life, rather than in the God who created us and desires our recovery. Putting our life into God's hands is the only way to experience true deliverance.

to do. Instead, they had transgressed his covenant and disobeyed all the laws given to them by Moses the servant of the Lord.

13 Later, during the fourteenth year of the reign of King Hezekiah, King Sennacherib of Assyria besieged and captured all the fortified cities of Judah. 14 King Hezekiah sued for peace and sent this message to the king of Assyria at Lachish: "I have done wrong. I will pay whatever tribute you demand if you will only go away." The king of Assyria then demanded a settlement of $1,500,000. 15 To gather this amount, King Hezekiah used all the silver stored in the Temple and in the palace treasury. 16 He even stripped off the gold from the Temple doors, and from the doorposts he had overlaid with gold, and gave it all to the Assyrian king.

Assyria Threatens Judah

17 Nevertheless the king of Assyria sent his field marshal, his chief treasurer, and his chief of staff from Lachish with a great army; and they camped along the highway beside the field where cloth was bleached, near the conduit of the upper pool. 18 They demanded that King Hezekiah come out to speak to them, but instead he sent a truce delegation of the following men: Eliakim, his business manager; Shebnah, his secretary; and Joah, his royal historian.

19 Then the Assyrian general sent this message to King Hezekiah: "The great king of Assyria says, 'No one can save you from my power! 20,21 You need more than mere promises of help before rebelling against me. But which of your allies will give you more than words? Egypt? If you lean on Egypt, you will find her to be a stick that breaks beneath your weight and pierces your hand. The Egyptian Pharaoh is totally unreliable! 22 And if you say, "We're trusting the Lord to rescue us"—just remember that he is the very one whose hilltop altars you've destroyed. For you require everyone to worship at the altar in Jerusalem!' 23 I'll tell you what: Make a bet with my master, the king of Assyria! If you have two thousand men left who can ride horses, we'll furnish the horses! 24 And with an army as small as yours, you are no threat to even the least lieutenant in charge of the smallest contingent in my master's army. Even if Egypt supplies you with horses and chariots, it will do no good. 25 And do you think we have come here on our own? No! The Lord sent us and told us, 'Go and destroy this nation!'"

26 Then Eliakim, Shebnah, and Joah said to them, "Please speak in Aramaic, for we understand it. Don't use Hebrew, for the people standing on the walls will hear you."

27 But the Assyrian general replied, "Has my master sent me to speak only to you and to your master? Hasn't he sent me to the people on the walls too? For they are doomed with you to eat their own excrement and drink their own urine!"

28 Then the Assyrian ambassador shouted in Hebrew to the people on the wall, "Listen to the great king of Assyria! 29 'Don't let King Hezekiah fool you. He will never be able to save you from my power. 30 Don't let him fool you into trusting in the Lord to rescue you. 31,32 Don't listen to King Hezekiah. Surrender! You can live in peace here in your own land until I take you to another land just like this one—with plentiful crops, grain, grapes, olive trees, and honey. All of this instead of death! Don't listen to King Hezekiah when he tries to persuade you that the Lord will deliver you. 33 Have any of the gods of the other nations ever delivered their people from the king of Assyria? 34 What happened to the gods of Hamath, Arpad, Sepharvaim, Hena, and Ivvah? Did they rescue Samaria? 35 What god has ever been able to save any nation from my power? So what makes you think the Lord can save Jerusalem?'"

36 But the people on the wall remained silent, for the king had instructed them to say nothing. 37 Then Eliakim (son of Hilkiah) the business manager, and Shebnah the king's secretary, and Joah (son of Asaph) the historian went to King Hezekiah with their clothes torn and told him what the Assyrian general had said.

CHAPTER 19

Isaiah Predicts Deliverance

When King Hezekiah heard their report, he tore his clothes and put on sackcloth and went into the Temple to pray. 2 Then he told Eliakim, Shebnah, and some of the older priests to clothe themselves in sackcloth and to go to Isaiah (son of Amoz), the prophet, with this message:

3 "King Hezekiah says, 'This is a day of trouble, insult, and dishonor. It is as when a child is ready to be born, but the mother has no strength to deliver it. 4 Yet perhaps the Lord your God has heard the Assyrian general defying the living God and will rebuke him. Oh, pray for the few of us who are left.'"

5,6 Isaiah replied, "The Lord says, 'Tell your master not to be troubled by the sneers these

Assyrians have made against me.' 7For the king of Assyria will receive bad news from home and will decide to return; and the Lord will see to it that he is killed when he arrives there."

8Then the Assyrian general returned to his king at Libnah (for he received word that he had left Lachish). 9Soon afterwards news reached the king that King Tirhakah of Ethiopia was coming to attack him. Before leaving to meet the attack, he sent back this message to King Hezekiah:

10"Don't be fooled by that god you trust in. Don't believe it when he says that I won't conquer Jerusalem. 11You know perfectly well what the kings of Assyria have done wherever they have gone; they have completely destroyed everything. Why would you be any different? 12Have the gods of the other nations delivered them—such nations as Gozan, Haran, Rezeph, and Eden in the land of Telassar? The former kings of Assyria destroyed them all! 13What happened to the king of Hamoth and the king of Arpad? What happened to the kings of Sepharvaim, Hena, and Ivvah?"

Hezekiah Asks God for Help

14Hezekiah took the letter from the messengers, read it, and went over to the Temple and spread it out before the Lord. 15Then he prayed this prayer:

"O Lord God of Israel, sitting on your throne high above the angels, you alone are the God of all the kingdoms of the earth. You created the heavens and the earth. 16Bend low, O Lord, and listen. Open your eyes, O Lord, and see. Listen to this man's defiance of the living God. 17Lord, it is true that the kings of Assyria have destroyed all those nations 18and have burned their idol-gods. But they weren't gods at all; they were destroyed because they were only things that men had made of wood and stone. 19O Lord our God, we plead with you to save us from his power; then all the kingdoms of the earth will know that you alone are God."

God Promises Safety for Jerusalem

20Then Isaiah sent this message to Hezekiah: "The Lord God of Israel says, 'I have heard you! 21And this is my reply to King Sennacherib: The virgin daughter of Zion isn't afraid of you! The daughter of Jerusalem scorns and mocks at you. 22Whom have you defied and blasphemed? And toward whom have you felt so cocky? It is the Holy One of Israel!

23"'You have boasted, "My chariots have conquered the highest mountains, yes, the peaks of Lebanon. I have cut down the tallest cedars and choicest cypress trees and have conquered the farthest borders. 24I have been refreshed at many conquered wells, and I destroyed the strength of Egypt just by walking by!"

25"'Why haven't you realized long before this that it is I, the Lord, who lets you do these things? I decreed your conquest of all those fortified cities! 26So of course the nations you conquered had no power against you! They were like grass shriveling beneath the hot sun, and like grain blighted before it is half grown. 27I know everything about you. I know all your plans and where you are going next; and I also know the evil things you have said about me. 28And because of your arrogance against me, I am going to put a hook in your nose and a bridle in your mouth and turn you back on the road by which you came. 29And this is the proof that I will do as I have promised: This year my people will eat the volunteer wheat and use it as seed for next year's crop; and in the third year they will have a bountiful harvest.

30"'O my people Judah, those of you who have escaped the ravages of the siege shall become a great nation again; you shall be rooted deeply in the soil and bear fruit for God. 31A remnant of my people shall become strong in Jerusalem. The Lord is eager to cause this to happen.

32"'And my command concerning the king of Assyria is that he shall not enter this city. He shall not stand before it with a shield, nor build a ramp against its wall, nor even shoot an arrow into it. 33He shall return by the road he came, 34for I will defend and save this city for the sake of my own name and for the sake of my servant David.'"

35That very night the angel of the Lord

19:2-34 As Hezekiah faced this impossible situation, he humbly turned to God for help. God answered Hezekiah's desperate plea and delivered his people from a formidable enemy. In this case, God didn't roar in with blaring trumpets or a terrifying earthquake. The enemy army was quietly lured from its siege of Jerusalem. We may wish for an instant, miraculous deliverance from our problem, but it doesn't usually happen that way. God most often uses quiet resources—the steady support of a friend, the encouragement of a support group, the quiet leading of the Holy Spirit—to strengthen us in our recovery.

killed 185,000 Assyrian troops, and dead bodies were seen all across the landscape in the morning.
[36]Then King Sennacherib returned to Nineveh; [37]and as he was worshiping in the temple of his god Nisroch, his sons Adrammelech and Sharezer killed him. They escaped into eastern Turkey—the land of Ararat—and his son Esarhaddon became the new king.

CHAPTER 20

Hezekiah's Illness

Hezekiah now became deathly sick, and Isaiah the prophet went to visit him.

"Set your affairs in order and prepare to die," Isaiah told him. "The Lord says you won't recover."

[2]Hezekiah turned his face to the wall.

[3]"O Lord," he pleaded, "remember how I've always tried to obey you and to please you in everything I do. . . . " Then he broke down and cried.

[4]So before Isaiah had left the courtyard, the Lord spoke to him again.

[5]"Go back to Hezekiah, the leader of my people, and tell him that the Lord God of his ancestor David has heard his prayer and seen his tears. I will heal him, and three days from now he will be out of bed and at the Temple!
[6]I will add fifteen years to his life and save him and this city from the king of Assyria. And it will all be done for the glory of my own name and for the sake of my servant David."

[7]Isaiah then instructed Hezekiah to boil some dried figs and to make a paste of them and spread it on the boil. And he recovered!
[8]Meanwhile, King Hezekiah had said to Isaiah, "Do a miracle to prove to me that the Lord will heal me and that I will be able to go to the Temple again three days from now."

[9]"All right, the Lord will give you a proof," Isaiah told him. "Do you want the shadow on the sundial to go forward ten points or backward ten points?"

[10]"The shadow always moves forward," Hezekiah replied; "make it go backward."

[11]So Isaiah asked the Lord to do this, and he caused the shadow to move ten points backward on the sundial of Ahaz!

Babylonians Visit Hezekiah

[12]At that time Merodach-baladan (the son of King Baladan of Babylon) sent ambassadors with greetings and a present to Hezekiah, for he had learned of his sickness. [13]Hezekiah
welcomed them and showed them all his treasures—the silver, gold, spices, aromatic oils, the armory—everything.

[14]Then Isaiah went to King Hezekiah and asked him, "What did these men want? Where are they from?"

"From far away in Babylon," Hezekiah replied.

[15]"What have they seen in your palace?" Isaiah asked.

And Hezekiah replied, "Everything. I showed them all my treasures."

[16]Then Isaiah said to Hezekiah, "Listen to the word of the Lord: [17]The time will come
when everything in this palace shall be carried to Babylon. All the treasures of your ancestors will be taken—nothing shall be left.
[18]Some of your own sons will be taken away and made into eunuchs who will serve in the palace of the king of Babylon."

[19]"All right," Hezekiah replied, "if this is what the Lord wants, it is good." But he was really thinking, "At least there will be peace and security during the remainder of my own life!"

19:35-37 All of the Assyrian general's boasting about his army's strength could not keep it from being destroyed by God (19:35). Those needing recovery are often terrified in the face of brutal human power, especially if they have been previously abused. Some of us feel powerless against the persistent enemies that lie within. But such oppressors or problems, no matter how great, stand no chance at all against God's power; he will ultimately overcome them.

20:1-11 Hezekiah pleaded with God to spare his life, reminding God of his previous consistent faith and commitment to God. So Hezekiah was granted another fifteen years of life. God also performed a great miracle as proof of his promise of life to Hezekiah, who seems to have been greatly troubled by doubt and possibly even depression at this point. Although God may not make the sun go backwards for us, we should never doubt that God will rescue us if we honestly cry out to him.

20:12-21 Hezekiah made a major mistake that seriously set back his recovery. When the delegation from the rising nation of Babylon came to Jerusalem, Hezekiah put on the most impressive show possible. Not only that, he took the credit for all his wealth instead of giving the glory to God (20:15). The unconsidered consequences of his prideful actions came to painful fruition in the Babylonian Exile (23:36–25:30). When we accept full honor for our accomplishments, we show that we have forgotten the true source of our success—God. We must remain humble if we want God to help us. He can't work in a life that isn't surrendered to him.

[20]The rest of the history of Hezekiah and his great deeds—including the pool and conduit he made and how he brought water into the city—are recorded in *The Annals of the Kings of Judah.* [21]When he died, his son Manasseh became the new king.

CHAPTER 21

Manasseh Rules Judah

New king of Judah: Manasseh
His age at the beginning of his reign: 12 years old
Length of reign: 55 years, in Jerusalem
Mother's name: Hephzibah
Character of his reign: evil; he did the same things the nations had done that were thrown out of the land to make room for the people of Israel

[3-5]He rebuilt the hilltop shrines that his father Hezekiah had destroyed. He built altars for Baal and made a shameful Asherah idol, just as Ahab the king of Israel had done. Heathen altars to the sun god, moon god, and the gods of the stars were placed even in the Temple of the Lord—in the very city and building that the Lord had selected to honor his own name. [6]And he sacrificed one of his sons as a burnt offering on a heathen altar. He practiced black magic and used fortune-telling, and patronized mediums and wizards. So the Lord was very angry, for Manasseh was an evil man, in God's sight. [7]Manasseh even set up a shameful Asherah-idol in the Temple—the very place that the Lord had spoken to David and Solomon about when he said, "I will place my name forever in this Temple, and in Jerusalem—the city I have chosen from among all the cities of the tribes of Israel. [8]If the people of Israel will only follow the instructions I gave them through Moses, I will never again expel them from this land of their fathers."

[9]But the people did not listen to the Lord, and Manasseh enticed them to do even more evil than the surrounding nations had done, even though Jehovah had destroyed those nations for their evil ways when the people of Israel entered the land.

[10]Then the Lord declared through the prophets,

[11]"Because King Manasseh has done these evil things and is even more wicked than the Amorites who were in this land long ago, and because he has led the people of Judah into idolatry: [12]I will bring such evil upon Jerusalem and Judah that the ears of those who hear about it will tingle with horror. [13]I will punish Jerusalem as I did Samaria, and as I did King Ahab of Israel and his descendants. I will wipe away the people of Jerusalem as a man wipes a dish and turns it upside down to dry. [14]Then I will reject even those few of my people who are left, and I will hand them over to their enemies. [15]For they have done great evil and have angered me ever since I brought their ancestors from Egypt."

[16]In addition to the idolatry which God hated and into which Manasseh led the people of Judah, he murdered great numbers of innocent people. And Jerusalem was filled from one end to the other with the bodies of his victims.

[17]The rest of the history of Manasseh's sinful reign is recorded in *The Annals of the Kings of Judah.* [18]When he died he was buried in the garden of his palace at Uzza, and his son Amon became the new king.

Amon Rules Judah

[19,20]New king of Judah: Amon
His age at the beginning of his reign: 22 years old
Length of reign: 2 years, in Jerusalem
Mother's name: Meshullemeth (daughter of Haruz, of Jotbah)
Character of his reign: evil

[21]He did all the evil things his father had done: he worshiped the same idols [22]and

21:1-17 Manasseh reversed all the positive steps instituted by Hezekiah for Judah's national recovery. His totally evil and oppressive reign brought God to declare an exile that would inevitably come upon Judah. Judah would follow the northern kingdom of Israel into exile just as they had followed them into sin. By the end of Manasseh's fifty-five-year reign, the possibility of meaningful recovery in Judah seemed very dim. This reminds us that those who submit to our leadership will often suffer consequences for our mistakes. This truth should cause us to think twice before abandoning our recovery.

21:19-26 King Amon of Judah was a virtual "carbon copy" of his father, Manasseh. God had allowed Manasseh's abusive oppression to continue for many years, but God did not do the same for Amon. God was lovingly anxious to promote one more cycle of recovery in Judah, as an offer of relief from their self-destructive unbelief and false worship. Josiah, Amon's young son, would be the initiator and primary instrument for a major cycle of recovery among God's people (22:1–23:30).

turned his back on the Lord God of his ancestors. He refused to listen to God's instructions. 23But his aides conspired against him and killed him in the palace. 24Then a posse of civilians killed all the assassins and placed Amon's son Josiah upon the throne. 25The rest of Amon's biography is recorded in *The Annals of the Kings of Judah.* 26He was buried in a crypt in the garden of Uzza, and his son Josiah became the new king.

CHAPTER 22

Josiah Rules Judah

New king of Judah: Josiah
- His age at the beginning of his reign: 8 years old
- Length of reign: 31 years, in Jerusalem
- Mother's name: Jedidah (daughter of Adaiah of Bozkath)
- Character of his reign: good; he followed in the steps of his ancestor King David, obeying the Lord completely

3,4In the eighteenth year of his reign, King Josiah sent his secretary Shaphan (son of Azaliah, son of Meshullam) to the Temple to give instruction to Hilkiah, the High Priest:

"Collect the money given to the priests at the door of the Temple when the people come to worship. 5,6Give this money to the building superintendents so that they can hire carpenters and masons to repair the Temple, and to buy lumber and stone."

7(The building superintendents were not required to keep account of their expenditures, for they were honest men.)

Josiah Discovers God's Law

8One day Hilkiah the High Priest went to Shaphan the secretary and exclaimed, "I have discovered a scroll in the Temple, with God's laws written on it!"

He gave the scroll to Shaphan to read. 9,10When Shaphan reported to the king about the progress of the repairs at the Temple, he also mentioned the scroll found by Hilkiah. Then Shaphan read it to the king. 11When the king heard what was written in it, he tore his clothes in terror. 12,13He commanded Hilkiah the priest, and Shaphan, and Asaiah, the king's assistant, and Ahikam (Shaphan's son), and Achbor (Michaiah's son) to ask the Lord, "What shall we do? For we have not been following the instructions of this book: you must be very angry with us, for neither we nor our ancestors have followed your commands."

14So Hilkiah the priest, and Ahikam, and Achbor, and Shaphan, and Asaiah went to the Mishneh section of Jerusalem to find Huldah the prophetess. (She was the wife of Shallum—son of Tikvah, son of Harhas—who was in charge of the palace tailor shop.) 15,16She gave them this message from the Lord God of Israel:

"Tell the man who sent you to me that I am going to destroy this city and its people, just as I stated in that book you read. 17For the people of Judah have thrown me aside and have worshiped other gods and have made me very angry; and my anger can't be stopped. 18,19But because you were sorry and concerned and humbled yourself before the Lord when you read the book and its warnings that this land would be cursed and become desolate, and because you have torn your clothing and wept before me in contrition, I will listen to your plea. 20The death of this nation will not occur until after you die—you will not see the evil that I will bring upon this place."

So they took the message to the king.

CHAPTER 23

Josiah Destroys Idol Worship

Then the king sent for the elders and other leaders of Judah and Jerusalem to go to the

---

22:1-7 Almost two hundred years before Josiah, King Joash of Judah had undertaken repairs of the Temple in a strikingly similar way (12:4-14). Josiah instituted Judah's last major cycle of recovery before its final demise. Recovery does often have its ups and downs, but the ultimate effect needs to be positive. In Judah, however, the net effect was negative. The great reforms and good intentions of the few good kings were negated by the activities of the bad. In recovery, we must persevere. We cannot have a victory now and then and then backslide for extended periods. Taking an uncommitted approach to recovery will ultimately lead us to destruction.

22:8-20 In spite of Josiah's heartfelt reforms in Judah, there would still be serious long-term consequences for the nation's sin. But Judah's destruction would be postponed significantly because of the humble faith and obedience of Josiah. While it may seem unfair for Judah to be held responsible for what they didn't know about God's laws, which had been lost, that's the way it often is in recovery. We may never have read the Bible and the wisdom it contains, but we are still accountable to its truth. God's program is clearly stated in his Word; all we have to do is read it. God's standards are absolute; there is no excuse for not following his ways.

Temple with him. So all the priests and prophets and the people, small and great, of Jerusalem and Judah gathered there at the Temple so that the king could read to them the entire book of God's laws which had been discovered in the Temple. 3He stood beside the pillar in front of the people, and he and they made a solemn promise to the Lord to obey him at all times and to do everything the book commanded.

4Then the king instructed Hilkiah the High Priest and the rest of the priests and the guards of the Temple to destroy all the equipment used in the worship of Baal, Asherah, and the sun, moon, and stars. The king had it all burned in the fields of the Kidron Valley outside Jerusalem, and he carried the ashes to Bethel. 5He killed the heathen priests who had been appointed by the previous kings of Judah, for they had burned incense in the shrines on the hills throughout Judah and even in Jerusalem. They had also offered incense to Baal and to the sun, moon, stars, and planets. 6He removed the shameful idol of Asherah from the Temple and took it outside Jerusalem to Kidron Brook; there he burned it and beat it to dust and threw the dust on the graves of the common people. 7He also tore down the houses of male prostitution around the Temple, where the women wove robes for the Asherah-idol.

8He brought back to Jerusalem the priests of the Lord, who were living in other cities of Judah, and tore down all the shrines on the hills where they had burned incense, even those as far away as Geba and Beersheba. He also destroyed the shrines at the entrance of the palace of Joshua, the former mayor of Jerusalem, located on the left side as one enters the city gate. 9However, these priests did not serve at the altar of the Lord in Jerusalem, even though they ate with the other priests.

10Then the king destroyed the altar of Topheth in the Valley of the Sons of Hinnom, so that no one could ever again use it to burn his son or daughter to death as a sacrifice to Molech. 11He tore down the statues of horses and chariots located near the entrance of the Temple, next to the quarters of Nathan-melech the eunuch. These had been dedicated by former kings of Judah to the sun god. 12Then he tore down the altars that the kings of Judah had built on the palace roof above the Ahaz Room. He also destroyed the altars that Manasseh had built in the two courts of the Temple; he smashed them to bits and scattered the pieces in Kidron Valley.

13Next he removed the shrines on the hills east of Jerusalem and south of Destruction Mountain. (Solomon had built these shrines for Ashtoreth, the evil goddess of the Sidonians; and for Chemosh, the evil god of Moab; and for Milcom, the evil god of the Ammonites.) 14He smashed the obelisks and cut down the shameful idols of Asherah; then he defiled these places by scattering human bones over them. 15He also tore down the altar and shrine at Bethel that Jeroboam I had made when he led Israel into sin. He crushed the stones to dust and burned the shameful idol of Asherah.

16As Josiah was looking around, he noticed several graves in the side of the mountain. He ordered his men to bring out the bones in them and to burn them there upon the altar at Bethel to defile it, just as the Lord's prophet had declared would happen to Jeroboam's altar.

17"What is that monument over there?" he asked.

And the men of the city told him, "It is the grave of the prophet who came from Judah and proclaimed that what you have just done would happen here at the altar at Bethel!"

18So King Josiah replied, "Leave it alone. Don't disturb his bones."

So they didn't burn his bones or those of the prophet from Samaria.

19Josiah demolished the shrines on the hills in all of Samaria. They had been built by the various kings of Israel and had made the Lord very angry. But now he crushed them into dust, just as he had done at Bethel. 20He executed the priests of the heathen shrines upon their own altars, and he burned human bones upon the altars to defile them. Finally he returned to Jerusalem.

21The king then issued orders for his people to observe the Passover ceremonies as recorded by the Lord their God in *The Book of*

23:1-20 The revival under Josiah was no halfhearted recovery. Unlike the moderate but incomplete process of recovery achieved by many of Judah's earlier kings, Josiah concluded that there could be no middle ground. As a strong statement of proper boundaries and limits, Josiah destroyed all aspects of the long-standing idol worship. He also went to great lengths to reinstitute proper worship of the true God, indicating his faith and commitment. Limits and boundaries are necessary if we want to recover. We have to know where the lines are if we are to stay within them.

the Covenant. [22]There had not been a Passover
celebration like that since the days of the
judges of Israel, and there was never another
like it in all the years of the kings of Israel and
Judah. [23]This Passover was in the eighteenth
year of the reign of King Josiah, and it was
celebrated in Jerusalem.
[24]Josiah also exterminated the mediums
and wizards, and every kind of idol worship,
both in Jerusalem and throughout the land.
For Josiah wanted to follow all the laws that
were written in the book that Hilkiah the
priest had found in the Temple. [25]There was
no other king who so completely turned to
the Lord and followed all the laws of Moses;
and no king since the time of Josiah has
approached his record of obedience.
[26]But the Lord still did not hold back his
great anger against Judah, caused by the evils
of King Manasseh. [27]For the Lord had said, "I
will destroy Judah just as I have destroyed
Israel; and I will discard my chosen city of
Jerusalem and the Temple that I said was
mine."
[28]The rest of the biography of Josiah is written in *The Annals of the Kings of Judah.* [29]In
those days King Neco of Egypt went out to
help the king of Assyria at the Euphrates
River. Then King Josiah went out with his
troops to fight King Neco; but King Neco
withstood him at Megiddo and killed him.
[30]His officers took his body back in a chariot
from Megiddo to Jerusalem and buried him in
the grave he had selected. And his son Jehoahaz was chosen by the nation as its new king.

Jehoahaz Rules Judah

[31,32]New king of Judah: Jehoahaz
His age at the beginning of his reign: 23 years old
Length of reign: 3 months, in Jerusalem
Mother's name: Hamutal (the daughter of Jeremiah of Libnah)
Character of his reign: evil, like the other kings who had preceded him

[33]Pharaoh-Neco jailed him at Riblah in Hamath to prevent his reigning in Jerusalem,
and he levied a tax against Judah totaling
$230,000. [34]The Egyptian king then chose Eli-
akim, another of Josiah's sons, to reign in
Jerusalem; and he changed his name to Jehoiakim. Then he took King Jehoahaz to Egypt,
where he died. [35]Jehoiakim taxed the people
to get the money that the Pharaoh had demanded.

Jehoiakim Rules Judah

[36,37]New king of Judah: Jehoiakim
His age at the beginning of his reign: 25 years old
Length of reign: 11 years, in Jerusalem
Mother's name: Zebidah (daughter of Pedaiah of Rumah)
Character of his reign: evil, like the other kings who had preceded him

CHAPTER 24

During the reign of King Jehoiakim, King
Nebuchadnezzar of Babylon attacked Jerusalem. Jehoiakim surrendered and paid him
tribute for three years, but then rebelled. [2]And
the Lord sent bands of Chaldeans, Syrians,
Moabites, and Ammonites against Judah in
order to destroy the nation, just as the Lord
had warned through his prophets that he
would. [3,4]It is clear that these disasters befell
Judah at the direct command of the Lord. He
had decided to wipe Judah out of his sight
because of the many sins of Manasseh, for he
had filled Jerusalem with blood, and the Lord
would not pardon it.
[5]The rest of the history of the life of Jehoi-

23:31-35 The character of King Jehoahaz, Josiah's son, may well imply a flaw in Josiah's life. The fact that Jehoahaz was evil (23:32), unlike his righteous father, may indicate that Josiah was not attentive or available to his children. Perhaps he was too busy initiating his reforms in Judah to "pass on" his faith and commitment to God to his children. While children may be able to see the godly things a parent does, they may follow evil ways if they are not loved and nurtured. We need to balance family time with the time we take for our recovery. If we don't, all our gains will probably be lost in the next generation. Our steps of self-improvement can easily become detrimental to our family's ultimate recovery.

23:36–24:4 The reign of King Jehoiakim of Judah was basically an eleven-year military and political nightmare. Rather than admitting his hopeless situation and turning to God, Jehoiakim continued to try to maneuver his way out of each successive crisis. As disaster after disaster befell Jehoiakim, his denial only deepened. He continued to trust in his own power and sank deeper into despair. There is no need to continue in our nightmare. If we stop our denial and accept the hopelessness of our situation, then we can turn to God for help. He will help us to break out of our downward spiral.

akim is recorded in *The Annals of the Kings of Judah*. [6]When he died, his son Jehoiachin became the new king. [7](The Egyptian pharaoh never returned after that, for the king of Babylon occupied the entire area claimed by Egypt—all of Judah from the Brook of Egypt to the Euphrates River.)

Jehoiachin Rules Judah

[8,9]New king of Judah: Jehoiachin
His age at the beginning of his reign: 18 years old
Length of reign: 3 months, in Jerusalem
Mother's name: Nehushta (daughter of Elnathan, a citizen of Jerusalem)

[10]During his reign the armies of King Nebuchadnezzar of Babylon besieged the city of Jerusalem. [11]Nebuchadnezzar himself arrived during the siege, [12]and King Jehoiachin, all of his officials, and the queen mother surrendered to him. The surrender was accepted, and Jehoiachin was imprisoned in Babylon during the eighth year of Nebuchadnezzar's reign.

[13]The Babylonians carried home all the treasures from the Temple and the royal palace; and they cut apart all the gold bowls which King Solomon of Israel had placed in the Temple at the Lord's directions. [14]King Nebuchadnezzar took ten thousand captives from Jerusalem, including all the princes and the best of the soldiers, craftsmen, and smiths. So only the poorest and least skilled people were left in the land. [15]Nebuchadnezzar took King Jehoiachin, his wives and officials, and the queen mother, to Babylon. [16]He also took seven thousand of the best troops and one thousand craftsmen and smiths, all of whom were strong and fit for war. [17]Then the king of Babylon appointed King Jehoiachin's great-uncle, Mattaniah, to be the next king; and he changed his name to Zedekiah.

Zedekiah Rules Judah

[18,19]New king of Judah: Zedekiah
His age at the beginning of his reign: 21 years old
Length of reign: 11 years, in Jerusalem
Mother's name: Hamutal (daughter of Jeremiah of Libnah)
Character of his reign: evil, like that of Jehoiakim

[20]So the Lord finally, in his anger, destroyed the people of Jerusalem and Judah. But now King Zedekiah rebelled against the king of Babylon.

CHAPTER 25

Then King Nebuchadnezzar of Babylon mobilized his entire army and laid siege to Jerusalem, arriving on March 25 of the ninth year of the reign of King Zedekiah of Judah. [2]The siege continued into the eleventh year of his reign.

[3]The last food in the city was eaten on July 24, [4,5]and that night the king and his troops made a hole in the inner wall and fled out toward the Arabah through a gate that lay between the double walls near the king's garden. The Babylonian troops surrounding the city took out after him and captured him in the plains of Jericho, and all his men scattered. [6]He was taken to Riblah, where he was tried and sentenced before the king of Babylon. [7]He was forced to watch as his sons were killed before his eyes; then his eyes were put out, and he was bound with chains and taken away to Babylon.

Jerusalem Is Demolished

[8]General Nebuzaradan, the captain of the royal bodyguard, arrived at Jerusalem from Babylon on July 22 of the nineteenth year of the reign of King Nebuchadnezzar. [9]He burned down the Temple, the palace, and all the other houses of any worth. [10]He then

---

24:18–25:7 It is sad to watch a person in the advanced stages of denial. It is sadder still to observe a large group of people who deny the painful reality of their situation. Even under the Babylonian puppet king Zedekiah, Judah attempted yet another rebellion against Babylon instead of turning to God. The continued denial of Zedekiah's true situation led to his cruel treatment by the Babylonians when he was finally exiled. Our continued denial will almost always lead us further into dark consequences. The sooner we admit our true predicament, the sooner we can recover.

25:8-26 Judah had now hit bottom in the most literal sense. King Nebuchadnezzar ordered Jerusalem, the once proud capital of Judah, to be destroyed. He plundered the city and Temple, carrying all its valuables off to Babylon. Realistically, corporate recovery for Judah was now indeed impossible. What was needed was a full-scale resurrection for God's people. If we have hit bottom, we may need to discover the new life offered by Jesus Christ. "When someone becomes a Christian, he becomes a brand new person inside. He is not the same anymore. A new life has begun" (2 Corinthians 5:17). For Christ to take away our sins and give us a new start, all we need to do is ask him into our life.

supervised the Babylonian army in tearing
down the walls of Jerusalem. 11The remainder
of the people in the city and the Jewish desert-
ers who had declared their allegiance to the
king of Babylon were all taken as exiles to
Babylon. 12But the poorest of the people were
left to farm the land.

13The Babylonians broke up the bronze pillars of the Temple and the bronze tank and its
bases and carried all the bronze to Babylon.
14,15They also took all the pots, shovels, firepans, snuffers, spoons, and other bronze instruments used for the sacrifices. The gold and
silver bowls, with all the rest of the gold and
silver, were melted down to bullion. 16It was
impossible to estimate the weight of the two
pillars and the great tank and its bases—all
made for the Temple by King Solomon—because they were so heavy. 17Each pillar was 27
feet high, with an intricate bronze network of
pomegranates decorating the 4½-foot capitals at the tops of the pillars.

18The general took Seraiah, the chief priest,
his assistant Zephaniah, and the three
Temple guards to Babylon as captives. 19A
commander of the army of Judah, the chief
recruiting officer, five of the king's counselors, and sixty farmers, all of whom were
discovered hiding in the city, 20were taken by
General Nebuzaradan to the king of Babylon
at Riblah, 21where they were put to the sword
and died.

So Judah was exiled from its land.

Judah's Last Hope

22Then King Nebuchadnezzar appointed Gedaliah (the son of Ahikam and grandson of
Shaphan) as governor over the people left in
Judah. 23When the Israeli guerrilla forces
learned that the king of Babylon had appointed Gedaliah as governor, some of these
underground leaders and their men joined
him at Mizpah. These included Ishmael, the
son of Nethaniah; Johanan, the son of Kareah; Seraiah, the son of Tanhumeth the Netophathite; and Jaazaniah, son of
Maachathite, and their men.

24Gedaliah vowed that if they would give
themselves up and submit to the Babylonians, they would be allowed to live in the land
and would not be exiled. 25But seven months
later, Ishmael, who was a member of the royal
line, went to Mizpah with ten men and killed
Gedaliah and his court—both the Jews and
the Babylonians.

26Then all the men of Judah and the guerrilla leaders fled in panic to Egypt, for they
were afraid of what the Babylonians would do
to them.

27King Jehoiachin was released from
prison on the twenty-seventh day of the last
month of the thirty-seventh year of his captivity.

This occurred during the first year of the
reign of King Evil-merodach of Babylon. 28He
treated Jehoiachin kindly and gave him pref-
erential treatment over all the other kings
who were being held as prisoners in Babylon.
29Jehoiachin was given civilian clothing to
replace his prison garb, and for as long as he
lived, he ate regularly at the king's table. 30The
king also gave him a daily cash allowance for
the rest of his life.

25:27-30 The kindness shown by Evil-merodach to captive King Jehoiachin decorates the tragic conclusion of Kings with a glimmer of hope. With the Babylonian Exile came the destruction of Jerusalem and an end to the rule of the Davidic kings. The exiled people lost all hope that God might still be with them. They probably thought that God's promises to his people through Abraham and David were no longer valid. When they heard that Jehoiachin, one of David's descendants, was being treated well in exile, however, hope must have stirred in their heavy hearts. Perhaps God's promises to them were still valid! The continued story of rebuilding after the exile shows us that this was true. God still planned for their restoration, and through this broken nation the King of kings, Jesus the Messiah, would be born. No matter how terrible the situation is that we face, there is hope for the future. Our sin has been paid for by the work of God's Son; God is still in the business of restoration.

REFLECTIONS ON
SECOND
KINGS

insights FROM THE MINISTRY OF ELISHA

Strong-willed people, especially leaders who are used to getting their way, have a hard time humbling themselves to enter recovery. What Elisha asked Naaman to do in **2 Kings 5:9-15** was simple, but it was hardly dignified. Elisha certainly didn't do things the way Naaman thought they should be done. Fortunately, Naaman was not so angry and resistant that he was unwilling to listen to the advice of his officers. By following Elisha's instructions, he found physical "recovery" and apparently entered the initial phase of spiritual recovery by recognizing the power of the only true God.

The power and patience of God in relation to recovery are both evident in **2 Kings 13:20-23.** The reviving power of God, found even in the dead body of Elisha (13:21), can empower a comeback in life even when a person thinks "it's all over." The patience of God is tied to his covenant made with Abraham and his successors (13:22-23). Except for God's great covenant loyalty, the northern kingdom would have been destroyed long before its fall to Assyria in 722 B.C. God offers us a covenant through Jesus Christ, through whom we are forgiven and empowered to become God's children. God will care for anyone who believes in his Son's name. We should accept that promise and let it guide us as we work toward recovery.

insights FROM THE LIVES OF JUDAH'S KINGS

The forty-year reign of King Joash of Judah was a time of substantial personal and national recovery. Yet, as much of a model of faith as Joash was, we see in **2 Kings 12:1-3** that he never completely destroyed the places of idol worship—the shrines on the hills. Since recovery is a lifelong process, we must not stop when we start to feel good. Our goal should be complete recovery, not just recovery in a few areas. We need to ask God to give us the strength and patience to gain back our entire life. Stopping too early will only lead to regression and failure.

The tragic incident related in **2 Kings 14:8-14** illustrates the dangers of overconfidence. After having defeated the Edomites, King Amaziah of Judah picked a fight with Israel—a fight that ended in disaster. It is easy to become overconfident in our own ability after winning a major victory—we feel invincible! But we must proceed with caution because we may be letting our emotions blind us to reality. Recovery is a long and difficult process, and we are setting ourself up for failure if we think the rest of the road will be effortless. We need to continually recognize our need for God's helping hand.

We see in **2 Kings 15:1-7** that King Azariah of Judah (also known as Uzziah) followed in the footsteps of his father, Amaziah (14:1-20), and his grandfather, Joash of Judah (12:1-21). Like them, he displayed a basic faith and commitment toward God (15:3). But, also like them, he tolerated false worship at the heathen hilltop shrines (15:4). As a result, even though his reign was fifty-two years long, it was mostly sad and solitary because God judged his halfhearted recovery by giving him leprosy (15:5). Partial commitment to recovery will never bring complete results. Only full devotion to the process will give us lasting healing.

In **2 Kings 18:17–19:1** we see that King Hezekiah of Judah bought off Assyrian invaders, but it was only a matter of time before the enemy would come back for more. The Assyrian spokesman, Rabshakeh, knew that Hezekiah had failed to trust in God in the earlier crisis. So he used that very point to intimidate the Judeans into surrendering. It was a terrible situation to face, but at least it led Hezekiah to a point of helplessness and surrender to God. He had no choice but to turn to God for help and to pursue recovery. Even if our situation looks hopeless, it is never too late to turn to God for help. God may have led us to this very place, just so we would turn to him for deliverance.

FIRST CHRONICLES

THE BIG PICTURE

A. ANTICIPATING DAVID'S REIGN (1:1–9:44)

B. THE REIGN OF DAVID (10:1–29:30)

1. The Passing of Saul (10:1-14)
2. The Accession of David (11:1–12:40)
3. David and the Ark of the Covenant (13:1–17:27)
4. The Account of David's Wars (18:1–20:8)
5. The Census Taken by David (21:1-30)
6. The Arrangements for the Temple (22:1–29:30)

The book of 1 Chronicles was originally part of a larger book that also included 2 Chronicles. It recorded Israel's history, starting with a genealogy of Adam's descendants and ending with Israel in Babylonian captivity. This condensed history of Israel was written to give Israel hope as they sought to rebuild their nation after the Exile.

The primary focus of 1 Chronicles was the reign of King David, who was presented as an ideal for the people to follow. The writer glosses quickly over David's faults, focusing on the positive aspects of his reign. We see David here as God saw him—a man after God's own heart.

The first nine chapters of 1 Chronicles record the ancestry of Israel from the dawn of history to the time of Israel's return from Babylon. The list emphasizes the royal line of David, which remained unbroken even through the terrible years of exile. This would have encouraged the Jews as they sought to rebuild their broken nation. While in exile, many had begun to think that God had abandoned them. The survival of David's descendants would have given them hope for the future.

The final half of 1 Chronicles records the events of David's reign, emphasizing his role in leading the people to worship God. And though David was never allowed to build God's Temple, God promised to build a royal "house" for him, pledging that David's descendants would reign forever. This promise was the basis for Israel's hope upon their return from exile. They could see that David's descendants were still among them. It was clear that despite Israel's past disobedience, God had not abandoned them completely. God was in the process of rebuilding his chosen people.

THE BOTTOM LINE

PURPOSE: To record the history of David's reign and to encourage and admonish the people of Israel as they sought to rebuild after the Babylonian exile. AUTHOR: Unknown, but ancient tradition suggests that Ezra was the author. AUDIENCE: The people of Israel after their return from exile in Babylon. DATE WRITTEN: Approximately 430 B.C. SETTING: The period of David's reign over Israel, the eleventh century B.C. KEY VERSES: "David now realized why the Lord had made him king and why he had made his kingdom so great; it was for a special reason—to give joy to God's people!" (14:2). KEY PEOPLE: David, Solomon.

RECOVERY THEMES

The Power of Grace: David's life story is filled with examples of God's grace. David was not a stranger to sin. In the books of Samuel we saw him commit adultery and murder in one fell swoop. And in this book David proved to be impulsive, even when his intentions were good. He failed to listen to God's plan for bringing the Ark to Jerusalem, and this led to the death of Uzza. The main theme of this book, however, is not David's failure, but his ability to learn from those failures. David had a heart that accepted God's correction and understood his loving forgiveness. It was his openness to God's grace that set David apart from the other kings of Israel. He knew the joy of forgiveness.

The Importance of Worship: David knew how to worship. The spiritual part of him was an open book before God. A life that ignores or neglects the spiritual is a life that is barren of purpose and weak in resolve. All recovery must include our spiritual side, or it will be anemic and unsuccessful. David shows us that spiritual issues and worship are central to our life. He also makes it very clear that worship is not only private; it involves our meeting together with others.

Recovery beyond Our Personal Recovery: David would never enjoy much of what he set up during his lifetime. He invested his time and possessions in things that would minister to others for centuries into the future. He collected materials for the Temple and organized the priests and Levites for their work there. He was able to see beyond himself to the needs of others. In our recovery, we need to look beyond ourself and see that when we experience healing and growth, we are not only affecting our own life, but the lives of those who follow us as well.

Learning to Accept No for an Answer: David had great plans for Israel. He was a dreamer; he could see great things ahead. But God had greater plans for David. While David assumed that he would build a Temple for Israel, God said no. So often, when God says no to us, we withdraw, argue, or feel rejection. Growth and recovery involve not only learning how to say no, but also how to accept the no that might come from God or from others. Notice also that when God denied David's desire to build the Temple, he promised in turn that he would build an eternal dynasty from David's lineage.

CHAPTER 1

Adam's Descendants

These are the earliest generations of mankind: Adam, Seth, Enosh, Kenan, Mahalalel, Jared, Enoch, Methuselah, Lamech, Noah, **Shem**, **Ham**, and **Japheth.**

[5-9]The sons of *Japheth* were: **Gomer,** Magog, Madai, **Javan**, Tubal, Meshech, and Tiras.

The sons of *Gomer:* Ashkenaz, Diphath, and Togarmah.

The sons of Javan: Elishah, Tarshish, Kittim, and Rodanim.

The sons of *Ham:* **Cush, Mizraim, Canaan,** and **Put.**

The sons of *Cush* were: Seba, Havilah, Sabta, Raama, and Sabteca.

The sons of Raama were Sheba and Dedan.

[10]Another of the sons of *Cush* was Nimrod, who became a great hero.

[11,12]The clans named after the sons of *Mizraim* were: the Ludim, the Anamim, the Lehabim, the Naphtuhim, the Pathrusim, the Caphtorim, and the Casluhim (the ancestors of the Philistines).

[13-16]Among *Canaan's* sons were: Sidon (his firstborn) and Heth.

Canaan was also the ancestor of the Jebusites, Amorites, Girgashites, Hivites, Arkites, Sinites, Arvadites, Zemarites, and Hamathites.

[17]The sons of *Shem:* Elam, Asshur, **Arpachshad,** Lud, Aram, Uz, Hul, Gether, and Meshech.

[18]*Arpachshad's* son was **Shelah**, and *Shelah's* son was **Eber.**

1:1 As the father of the human race, Adam is the "head of our family," so to speak. The account of his life in the perfect environment of Eden is given in Genesis 2. We often are prone to blame our environment or family background for the mistakes we make. Living in Eden, Adam couldn't use this as an excuse. He had no choice but to take responsibility for his actions. Blaming our environment or circumstances for the sins we commit will never lead us toward recovery. Each of us must accept responsibility for our past mistakes and take steps to correct them.

1:1 "Adam, Seth, Enosh . . ." Notice that neither Cain nor Abel followed Adam in the genealogy of Israel. The account in Genesis 4 records how Cain committed the first murder by killing his brother Abel. One of the consequences of Adam and Eve's first sin was their dysfunctional family. It is encouraging to notice, however, that despite Cain and Abel's failure to leave descendants in Israel's ancestry, God provided Adam's broken family with a new start. He gave them another son named Seth.

[19]*Eber* had two sons: Peleg (which means
"Divided," for it was during his lifetime that
the people of the earth were divided into
different language groups) and Joktan.
[20-23]The sons of Joktan: Almodad, Sheleph,
Hazarmaveth, Jerah, Hadoram, Uzal, Diklah,
Ebal, Abimael, Sheba, Ophir, Havilah, and
Jobab.
[24-27]So the son of *Shem* was Arpachshad, the
son of Arpachshad was Shelah, the son of
Shelah was Eber, the son of Eber was Peleg,
the son of Peleg was Reu, the son of Reu was
Serug, the son of Serug was Nahor, the son of
Nahor was Terah, the son of Terah was Abram
(later known as Abraham).
[28-31]Abraham's sons were Isaac and Ishmael.
The sons of *Ishmael:* Nebaioth (the oldest),
Kedar, Adbeel, Mibsam, Mishma, Dumah,
Massa, Hadad, Tema, Jetur, Naphish, and Kedemah.
[32]Abraham also had sons by his concubine
Keturah: Zimram, **Jokshan**, Medan, **Midian**,
Ishbak, and Shuah.
Jokshan's sons were Sheba and Dedan.
[33]The sons of *Midian:* Ephah, Epher, Hanoch, Abida, and Eldaah. These were the descendants of Abraham by his concubine
Keturah.
[34]Abraham's son *Isaac* had two sons, Esau
and Israel.
[35]The sons of *Esau:* **Eliphaz, Reuel**, Jeush,
Jalam, and Korah.
[36]The sons of *Eliphaz:* Teman, Omar, Zephi,
Gatam, Kenaz, Timna, and Amalek.
[37]The sons of *Reuel:* Nahath, Zerah, Shammah, and Mizzah.
[38,39]The sons of *Esau* also included **Lotan,**
Shobal, Zibeon, Anah, **Dishon, Ezer,** and
Dishan; and Esau's daughter was named
Timna. *Lotan's* sons: Hori and Homam.
[40]The sons of *Shobal:* Alian, Manahath,
Ebal, Shephi, and Onam. *Zibeon's* sons were
Aiah and **Anah.**
[41]*Anah's* son was **Dishon.** The sons of *Di-*
shon: Hamran, Eshban, Ithran, and Cheran.
[42]The sons of *Ezer:* Bilhan, Zaavan, and Jaa-
kan. *Dishan's* sons were Uz and Aran.
[43]Here is a list of the names of the kings of
Edom who reigned before the kingdom of
Israel began:
Bela (the son of Beor), who lived in the city
of Dinhabah.
[44]When Bela died, Jobab the son of Zerah
from Bozrah became the new king.
[45]When Jobab died, Husham from the
country of the Temanites became the king.
[46]When Husham died, Hadad the son of
Bedad—the one who destroyed the army of
Midian in the fields of Moab—became king
and ruled from the city of Avith.
[47]When Hadad died, Samlah from the city
of Masrekah came to the throne.
[48]When Samlah died, Shaul from the river
town of Rehoboth became the new king.
[49]When Shaul died, Baal-hanan the son of
Achbor became king.
[50]When Baal-hanan died, Hadad became
king and ruled from the city of Pai (his wife
was Mehetabel, the daughter of Matred and
granddaughter of Mezahab).
[51-54]At the time of Hadad's death, the kings
of Edom were: Chief Timna, Chief Aliah,
Chief Jetheth, Chief Oholibamah, Chief Elah,
Chief Pinon, Chief Kenaz, Chief Teman, Chief
Mibzar, Chief Magdiel, Chief Iram.

CHAPTER 2

Jacob's Descendants

The sons of Israel were:
Reuben, Simeon, Levi, Judah, Issachar, Zebulun, Dan, Joseph, Benjamin, Naphtali, Gad,
Asher.
[3]Judah had three sons by Bathshua, a girl
from Canaan: **Er,** Onan, and Shelah. But the
oldest son, *Er,* was so wicked that the Lord
killed him.
[4]Then Er's widow, Tamar, and her father-in-
law, Judah, became the parents of twin sons,
Perez and **Zerah.** So Judah had five sons.
[5]The sons of *Perez* were Hezron and Hamul.
[6]The sons of *Zerah* were: Zimri, **Ethan,** Heman, Calcol, and Dara.
[7](Achan, the son of Carmi, was the man
who robbed God and was such a troublemaker for his nation.)
[8]*Ethan's* son was Azariah.

2:3-15 For most of us, these verses contain a boring list of people in David's ancestry, the family line of the promised Messiah. Among these names, however, are hidden stories of God's grace. Notice that the Messiah's line comes through an illegitimate union between Judah and Tamar (2:4; see Genesis 38). Notice also that the line passes through Salma, who fathered Boaz through Rahab, a former Canaanite prostitute from Jericho (Joshua 1–2). And Boaz bore Obed through Ruth, a Moabite woman (Ruth 1–4). God used numerous people, some less than ideal or even unsavory, to bring his Messiah into the world. God can also use us significantly in his plan, no matter what our past.

9The sons of *Hezron* were Jerahmeel, Ram, and Chelubai.

10Ram was the father of Amminadab, and Amminadab was the father of Nahshon, a leader of Israel.

11Nahshon was the father of Salma, and Salma was the father of Boaz.

12Boaz was the father of Obed, and Obed was the father of Jesse.

13*Jesse's* first son was Eliab, his second was Abinadab, his third was Shimea, 14his fourth was Nethanel, his fifth was Raddai, 15his sixth was Ozem, and his seventh was David. 16He also had two girls (by the same wife) named **Zeruiah** and **Abigail.**

Zeruiah's sons were Abishai, Joab, and Asahel.

17*Abigail,* whose husband was Jether from the land of Ishmael, had a son named Amasa.

18Caleb (the son of **Hezron**) had two wives, **Azubah** and Jerioth. These are the children of *Azubah:* Jesher, Shobab, and Ardon.

19After Azubah's death, Caleb married Ephrath, who presented him with a son, **Hur.**

20*Hur's* son was **Uri,** and *Uri's* son was Bezalel.

21**Hezron** married Machir's daughter at the age of sixty, and she presented him with a son, **Segub.** (Machir was also the father of Gilead.)

22*Segub* was the father of Jair, who ruled twenty-three cities in the land of Gilead. 23But Geshur and Aram wrested these cities from him and also took Kenath and its sixty surrounding villages.

24Soon after his father *Hezron's* death, Caleb married Ephrathah, his father's widow, and she gave birth to Ashhur, the father of Tekoa.

25These are the sons of **Jerahmeel** (the oldest son of *Hezron*): **Ram** (the oldest), Bunah, Oren, Ozem, and Ahijah.

26*Jerahmeel's* second wife Atarah was the mother of **Onam.**

27The sons of *Ram:* Maaz, Jamin, and Eker.

28*Onam's* sons were **Shammai** and Jada. *Shammai's* sons were **Nadab** and **Abishur.**

29The sons of *Abishur* and his wife Abihail were Ahban and Molid.

30*Nadab's* sons were **Seled** and **Appaim.** *Seled* died without children, 31but *Appaim* had a son named **Ishi;** *Ishi's* son was **Sheshan;** and *Sheshan's* son was Ahlai.

32*Shammai's* brother Jada had two sons, **Jether** and **Jonathan.** *Jether* died without children, 33but *Jonathan* had two sons named Peleth and Zaza.

34,35*Sheshan* had no sons, although he had several daughters. He gave one of his daughters to be the wife of Jarha, his Egyptian servant. And they had a son whom they named **Attai.**

36Attai's son was Nathan; Nathan's son was Zabad; 37Zabad's son was Ephlal; Ephlal's son was Obed; 38Obed's son was Jehu; Jehu's son was Azariah; 39Azariah's son was Helez; Helez's son was Eleasah; 40Eleasah's son was Sismai; Sismai's son was Shallum; 41Shallum's son was Jekamiah; Jekamiah's son was Elishama.

42The oldest son of **Caleb** (Jerahmeel's brother) was Mesha; he was the father of Ziph, who was father of Mareshah, who was the father of **Hebron.**

43The sons of *Hebron:* Korah, Tappuah, **Rekem,** and **Shema.**

44*Shema* was the father of Raham, who was the father of Jorkeam. *Rekem* was the father of **Shammai.**

45*Shammai's* son was Maon, the father of Bethzur.

46*Caleb's* concubine Ephah bore him **Haran,** Moza, and Gazez; *Haran* had a son named Gazez.

47The sons of Jahdai: Regem, Jotham, Geshan, Pelet, Ephah, and Shaaph.

48,49Another of *Caleb's* concubines, Maacah, bore him Sheber, Tirhanah, Shaaph (the father of Madmannah), and Sheva (the father of Machbenah and of Gibea). *Caleb* also had a daughter, whose name was Achsah.

50The sons of Hur (who was the oldest son of *Caleb* and Ephrathah) were **Shobal** (the father of Kiriath-jearim), 51**Salma** (the father of Bethlehem), and Hareph (the father of Beth-gader).

52**Shobal**'s sons included **Kiriath-jearim** and Haroeh, the ancestor of half of the Menuhoth tribe.

53The families of *Kiriath-jearim* were the Ithrites, the Puthites, the Shumathites, and the

---

2:42-55 God rewards faith. This entire section is devoted to the family of Caleb, one of the twelve spies sent by Moses into Canaan. You will remember that Caleb, along with Joshua, brought a positive report based entirely upon his faith in God's provision. Caleb refused to be discouraged by difficult obstacles, believing that God could overcome anything he might face. We need not be stopped by the difficult circumstances we face in our recovery. Like Caleb, we should remember that God is able to overcome anything we might face. God is the source of true victory.

Mishraites (from whom descended the Zorathites and Eshtaolites).

[54]The descendants of Salma were his son Bethlehem, the Netophathites, Atrothbeth-joab, half the Manahathites, and the Zorites; [55]they also included the families of the writers living at Jabez—the Tirathites, Shimeathites, and Sucathites. All these are Kenites who descended from Hammath, the founder of the family of Rechab.

CHAPTER 3

David's Descendants

King David's oldest son was Amnon, who was born to his wife, Ahinoam of Jezreel.

The second was Daniel, whose mother was Abigail from Carmel.

[2]The third was Absalom, the son of his wife Maacah, who was the daughter of King Talmai of Geshur.

The fourth was Adonijah, the son of Haggith.

[3]The fifth was Shephatiah, the son of Abital.

The sixth was Ithream, the son of his wife Eglah.

[4]These six were born to him in Hebron, where he reigned seven and a half years. Then he moved the capital to Jerusalem, where he reigned another thirty-three years.

[5]While he was in Jerusalem, his wife Bathsheba (the daughter of Ammiel) became the mother of his sons Shimea, Shobab, Nathan, and **Solomon.**

[6-8]David also had nine other sons: Ibhar, Elishama, Eliphelet, Nogah, Nepheg, Japhia, Elishama, Eliada, and Eliphelet.

[9](This list does not include the sons of his concubines.) David also had a daughter Tamar.

[10-14]These are the descendants of King *Solomon:* Rehoboam, Abijah, Asa, Jehoshaphat, Joram, Ahaziah, Joash, Amaziah, Azariah, Jotham, Ahaz, Hezekiah, Manasseh, Amon, Josiah.

[15]The sons of *Josiah* were: Johanan, **Jehoiakim**, Zedekiah, Shallum.

[16]The sons of *Jehoiakim:* **Jeconiah**, Zedekiah.

[17,18]These are the sons who were born to King *Jeconiah* during the years that he was under house arrest: Shealtiel, Malchiram, **Pedaiah**, Shenazzar, Jekamiah, Hoshama, Nedabiah.

[19,20]*Pedaiah* was the father of **Zerubbabel** and Shimei.

Zerubbabel's children were: Meshullam, **Hananiah**, Hashubah, Ohel, Berechiah, Hasadiah, Jushab-hesed, Shelomith (a daughter).

[21,22]*Hananiah's* sons were Pelatiah and Jeshaiah; Jeshaiah's son was Rephaiah; Rephaiah's son was Arnan; Arnan's son was Obadiah; Obadiah's son was Shecaniah. Shecaniah's son was Shemaiah; Shemaiah had six sons, including Hattush, Igal, Bariah, **Neariah**, and Shaphat.

[23]*Neariah* had three sons: **Elioenai**, Hizkiah, Azrikam.

[24]*Elioenai* had seven sons: Hodaviah, Eliashib, Pelaiah, Akkub, Johanan, Delaiah, Anani.

CHAPTER 4

Judah's Descendants

These are the sons of Judah: Perez, Hezron, Carmi, Hur, **Shobal.**

[2]*Shobal's* son Reaiah was the father of Jahath, the ancestor of Ahumai and Lahad. These were known as the Zorathite clans.

[3,4]The descendants of Etam: Jezreel, Ishma, Idbash, Hazzelelponi (his daughter), Penuel (the ancestor of Gedor), Ezer (the ancestor of Hushah), the son of Hur, the oldest son of Ephrathah, who was the father of Bethlehem.

[5]Ashhur, the father of Tekoa, had two wives—**Helah**, and **Naarah.**

[6]*Naarah* bore him Ahuzzam, Hepher, Temeni, and Haahashtari; [7]and *Helah* bore him Zereth, Izhar, and Ethnan.

[8]Koz was the father of Anub and Zobebah; he was also the ancestor of the clan named after Aharhel, the son of Harum.

[9]Jabez was more distinguished than any of his brothers. His mother named him Jabez

---

3:1-24 This chapter is entirely devoted to the family of David. As such, it is the most important of the genealogies—the line of the promised Messiah. Many of these names are cited in the New Testament genealogies of Jesus in the books of Matthew and Luke. Just as the entire Old Testament looks forward to the Messiah, Jesus, we also must look to him if we hope to experience a meaningful recovery.

4:9-10 Jabez leaves us with another example of faith. In the midst of his difficulties and in spite of his name (meaning "distress" or "one who causes pain"), Jabez looked to God for the solution to his problems. He prayed that God would keep him from fulfilling the meaning of his name. This is a worthwhile prayer. People in recovery must be careful not to cause pain to others, but instead should try to be a blessing to them.

because she had such a hard time at his birth
(Jabez means "Distress").
10He was the one who prayed to the God of
Israel, "Oh, that you would wonderfully bless
me and help me in my work; please be with
me in all that I do, and keep me from all evil
and disaster!" And God granted him his request.
11,12The descendants of Recah were:

Chelub (the brother of Shuhah), whose son was Mahir, the father of **Eshton;**
Eshton was the father of Bethrapha, Paseah, and Tehinnah;
Tehinnah was the father of Irnahash.

13The sons of Kenaz were **Othniel** and **Seraiah.**

Othniel's sons were Hathath and **Meonothai;**

14*Meonothai* was the father of Ophrah;

Seraiah was the father of Joab, the ancestor of the inhabitants of Craftsman Valley (called that because many craftsmen lived there).

15The sons of Caleb (the son of Jephunneh):
Iru, **Elah**, Naam.
The sons of *Elah* included Kenaz.
16Jehallelel's sons were: Ziph, Ziphah, Tiria,
Asarel.
17Ezrah's sons were: Jether, **Mered**, Epher,
Jalon.
Mered married Bithiah, an Egyptian princess. She was the mother of Miriam, Shammai, and Ishbah—an ancestor of **Eshtemoa.**
18*Eshtemoa's* wife was a Jewess; she was the
mother of Jered, Heber, and Jekuthiel, who
were, respectively, the ancestors of the Gedor-
ites, Socoites, and Zanoahites.
19Hodiah's wife was the sister of Naham.
One of her sons was the father of Keilah the
Garmite, and another was the father of Eshtemoa the Maacathite.
20The sons of Shimon: Amnon, Rinnah,
Ben-hanan, Tilon.
The sons of Ishi: Zoheth, Ben-zoheth.
21,22The sons of Shelah (the son of Judah):

Er (the father of Lecah),
Laadah (the father of Mareshah),
The families of the linen workers who worked at Beth-ashbea,
Jokim,
The clans of Cozeba,
Joash,
Saraph (who was a ruler in Moab before he returned to Lehem).

These names all come from very ancient
records.
23These clans were noted for their pottery,
gardening, and planting; they all worked for
the king:

Simeon's Descendants

24The sons of Simeon: Nemuel, Jamin, Jarib,
Zerah, **Shaul.**
25*Shaul's* son was Shallum, his grandson was
Mibsam, and his great-grandson was
Mishma.
26*Mishma's* sons included Hammuel (the
father of Zaccur and grandfather of **Shimei**).
27*Shimei* had sixteen sons and six daughters,
but none of his brothers had large families—
they all had fewer children than was normal
in Judah.
28They lived at Beersheba, Moladah, Hazar-
shual, 29Bilhah, Ezem, Tolad, 30Bethuel, Hormah, Ziklag, 31Beth-marcaboth, Hazar-susim,
Beth-biri, and Shaaraim. These cities were under their control until the time of David.
32,33Their descendants also lived in or near
Etam, Ain, Rimmon, Tochen, and Ashan;
some were as far away as Baal. (These facts are
recorded in their genealogies.)
34-39These are the names of some of the
princes of wealthy clans who traveled to the
east side of Gedor Valley in search of pasture
for their flocks: Meshobab, Jamlech, Joshah,
Joel, Jehu, Elioenai, Jaakobah, Jeshohaiah,
Asaiah, Adiel, Jesimiel, Benaiah, Ziza (the son
of Shiphi, son of Allon, son of Jedaiah, son of
Shimri, son of Shemaiah).
40,41They found good pastures, and everything was quiet and peaceful; but the land
belonged to the descendants of Ham.
So during the reign of King Hezekiah of
Judah these princes invaded the land and
struck down the tents and houses of the descendants of Ham; they killed the inhabitants
of the land and took possession of it for themselves.
42Later, five hundred of these invaders from
the tribe of Simeon went to Mount Seir. (Their
leaders were Pelatiah, Neariah, Rephaiah, and
Uzziel—all sons of Ishi.)
43There they destroyed the few surviving
members of the tribe of Amalek. And they
have lived there ever since.

CHAPTER 5

Reuben's Descendants

The oldest son of Israel was Reuben, but since
he dishonored his father by sleeping with one
of his father's wives, his birthright was given

to his half brother, Joseph. So the official genealogy doesn't name Reuben as the oldest son.

[2]Although Joseph received the birthright, yet Judah was a powerful and influential tribe in Israel, and from Judah came a Prince.

[3]The sons of Reuben, Israel's son, were: Hanoch, Pallu, Hezron, Carmi.

[4]Joel's descendants were his son Shemaiah, his grandson Gog, and his great-grandson **Shimei.**

[5]*Shimei's* son was Micah; his grandson was Reaiah; and his great-grandson was **Baal.**

[6]*Baal's* son was Beerah. He was a prince of the tribe of Reuben and was taken into captivity by King Tilgath-pilneser of Assyria.

[7,8]His relatives became heads of clans and were included in the official genealogy: Jeiel, Zechariah, Bela (the son of Azaz, grandson of Shema, and great-grandson of **Joel**).

These Reubenites lived in Aroer and as far distant as Mount Nebo and Baal-meon.

[9]Joel was a cattleman, and he pastured his animals eastward to the edge of the desert and to the Euphrates River, for there were many cattle in the land of Gilead.

[10]During the reign of King Saul, the men of Reuben defeated the Hagrites in war and moved into their tents on the eastern edge of Gilead.

Gad's Descendants

[11]Across from them, in the land of Bashan, lived the descendants of Gad, who were spread as far as Salecah.

[12]Joel was the greatest and was followed by Shapham, also Janai and Shaphat. [13]Their relatives, the heads of the seven clans, were Michael, Meshullam, Sheba, Jorai, Jacan, Zia, and Eber.

[14]The descendants of Buz, in the order of their generations, were: Jahdo, Jeshishai, Michael, Gilead, Jaroah, Huri, Abihail.

[15]Ahi, the son of Abdiel and grandson of Guni, was the leader of the clan. [16]The clan lived in and around Gilead (in the land of Bashan) and throughout the entire pasture country of Sharon. [17]All were included in the official genealogy at the time of King Jotham of Judah and King Jeroboam of Israel.

[18]There were 44,760 armed, trained, and brave troops in the army of Reuben, Gad, and the half-tribe of Manasseh. [19]They declared war on the Hagrites, the Jeturites, the Naphishites, and the Nodabites. [20]They cried out to God to help them, and he did, for they trusted in him. So the Hagrites and all their allies were defeated. [21]The booty included 50,000 camels, 250,000 sheep, 2,000 donkeys, and 100,000 captives. [22]A great number of the enemy also died in the battle, for God was fighting against them. So the Reubenites lived in the territory of the Hagrites until the time of the exile.

Manasseh's Descendants

[23]The half-tribe of Manasseh spread through the land from Bashan to Baal-hermon, Senir, and Mount Hermon. They too were very numerous.

[24]The chiefs of their clans were the following: Epher, Ishi, Eliel, Azriel, Jeremiah, Hodaviah, Jahdiel.

Each of these men had a great reputation as a warrior and leader. [25]But they were not true to the God of their fathers; instead they worshiped the idols of the people whom God had destroyed. [26]So God caused King Pul of Assyria (also known as Tilgath-pilneser III) to invade the land and deport the men of Reuben, Gad, and the half-tribe of Manasseh. They took them to Halah, Habor, Hara, and the Gozan River, where they remain to this day.

CHAPTER 6

Levi's Descendants

These are the names of the sons of Levi:
Gershom, Kohath, Merari.

[2]*Kohath's* sons were: **Amram**, Izhar, Hebron, Uzziel.

[3]*Amram's* descendants included: **Aaron,** Moses, Miriam.

Aaron's sons were: Nadab, Abihu, Eleazar, Ithamar.

[4-15]The oldest sons of the successive generations of Aaron were as follows:

Eleazar, the father of
Phinehas, the father of
Abishua, the father of
Bukki, the father of

5:1 After plowing through all these names, people usually wonder, Why are these lists in the Bible? Each of these names represents an individual and, in some cases, a family. It is obvious from this that God values individuals and he uses them to work his plan. Most of these people never made a significant impact on history. Some of them were far from ideal. We don't have to look far to realize that God cares for us—no matter who we are or what we've done. This should be a comforting message for us as we seek to rebuild our life.

Uzzi, the father of
Zerahiah, the father of
Meraioth, the father of
Amariah, the father of
Ahitub, the father of
Zadok, the father of
Ahimaaz, the father of
Azariah, the father of
Johanan, the father of
Azariah (the High Priest in Solomon's Temple at Jerusalem), the father of
Amariah, the father of
Ahitub, the father of
Zadok, the father of
Shallum, the father of
Hilkiah, the father of
Azariah, the father of
Seraiah, the father of
Jehozadak (who went into exile when the Lord sent the people of Judah and Jerusalem into captivity under Nebuchadnezzar).

16 As previously stated, the sons of Levi
were: **Gershom, Kohath, Merari.**
17 The sons of *Gershom* were: Libni, Shimei.
18 The sons of *Kohath* were: Amram, Izhar,
Hebron, Uzziel.
19-21 The sons of *Merari* were: Mahli, Mushi.
The subclans of the Levites were:
In the Gershom clan: Libni, Jahath, Zimmah, Joah, Iddo, Zerah, Jeatherai.
22-24 In the Kohath clan: Amminadab, Korah,
Assir, **Elkanah**, Ebiasaph, Assir, Tahath, Uriel,
Uzziah, Shaul.
25-27 The subclan of *Elkanah* was further divided into the families of his sons: Amasai,
Ahimoth, Elkanah, Zophai, Nahath, Eliab, Jeroham, Elkanah.
28 The families of the subclan of Samuel
were headed by Samuel's sons: Joel, the oldest; Abijah, the second.
29,30 The subclans of the clan of Merari were
headed by his sons: Mahli, Libni, Shimei, Uzzah, Shimea, Haggiah, Asaiah.
31 King David appointed songleaders and
choirs to praise God in the Tabernacle after he
had placed the Ark in it. 32 Then, when Solomon built the Temple at Jerusalem, the choirs
carried on their work there.
33-38 These are the names and ancestries of
choir leaders: Heman the Cantor was from
the clan of Kohath; his genealogy was traced
back through: Joel, Samuel, Elkanah III, Jeroham, Eliel, Toah, Zuph, Elkanah II, Mahath,
Amasai, Elkanah I, Joel, Azariah, Zephaniah,
Tahath, Assir, Ebiasaph, Korah, Izhar, Kohath,
Levi, Israel.
39-43 Heman's assistant was his colleague Asaph, whose genealogy was traced back
through: Berechiah, Shimea, Michael,
Baaseiah, Malchijah, Ethni, Zerah, Adaiah,
Ethan, Zimmah, Shimei, Jahath, Gershom,
Levi.
44-47 Heman's second assistant was Ethan, a
representative from the clan of Merari, who
stood on his left. Merari's ancestry was traced
back through: Kishi, Abdi, Malluch, Hashabiah, Amaziah, Hilkiah, Amzi, Bani, Shemer,
Mahli, Mushi, Merari, Levi.
48 Their relatives—all the other Levites—
were appointed to various other tasks in the
Tabernacle. 49 But only Aaron and his descendants were the priests. Their duties included
sacrificing burnt offerings and incense, handling all the tasks relating to the inner sanctuary—the Holy of Holies—and the tasks
relating to the annual Day of Atonement for
Israel. They saw to it that all the details commanded by Moses the servant of God were
strictly followed.
50-53 The descendants of Aaron were: Eleazar,
Phinehas, Abishua, Bukki, Uzzi, Zerahiah,
Meraioth, Amariah, Ahitub, Zadok, Ahimaaz.
54 This is a record of the cities and land
assigned by lot to the descendants of Aaron,

6:1-30 This chapter contains the priestly genealogy. It is vital to have access to God. In the Old Testament, the priests represented the people before God. Whenever any breach in fellowship was committed, the priests had to serve as mediators to effect reconciliation. In the New Testament, Jesus Christ stands as our Mediator before God. This truth is where all recovery begins—Christ makes it possible for us to deal with our sin and draw close to God. But this is not where our recovery ends. We also need to be accountable to others who will support our recovery process. Without them, our growth will slow down and eventually stagnate.

6:31-48 These verses contain a genealogy of the family that led the people in worship. Music and singing were vital parts of serving God in the Temple, calling the people to express their thanks joyfully to God. Our worship of God needs to contain the element of joy. Joy is an aspect of worship that is often ignored during the recovery process. Worship must never become an arduous task—it should be a happy response to a good and loving God. It does not need to be an elaborate ceremony. It begins with simple thanks for God's grace, power, and rich blessings in our life.

all of whom were members of the Kohath clan:

[55-57]Hebron and its surrounding pasturelands in Judah (although the fields and suburbs were given to Caleb the son of Jephunneh), [58,59]and the following Cities of Refuge with their surrounding pasturelands: Libnah, Jattir, Eshtemoa, Hilen, Debir, Ashan, Beth-shemesh.

[60]Thirteen other cities with surrounding pastures—including Geba, Alemeth, and Anathoth—were given to the priests by the tribe of Benjamin. [61]Lots were then drawn to assign land to the remaining descendants of Kohath, and they received ten cities in the territory of the half-tribe of Manasseh.

[62]The subclans of the Gershom clan received by lot thirteen cities in the Bashan area from the tribes of Issachar, Asher, Naphtali, and Manasseh.

[63]The subclans of Merari received by lot twelve cities from the tribes of Reuben, Gad, and Zebulun.

[64,65]Cities and pasturelands were also assigned by lot to the Levites (and then renamed) from the tribes of Judah, Simeon, and Benjamin.

[66-69]The tribe of Ephraim gave these Cities of Refuge with the surrounding pasturelands to the subclans of Kohath: Shechem in Mount Ephraim, Gezer, Jokme-am, Beth-horon, Aijalon, Gath-rimmon.

[70]The following Cities of Refuge and their pasturelands were given to the subclans of the Kohathites by the half-tribe of Manasseh: Aner, Bileam.

[71]Cities of Refuge and pastureland given to the clan of Gershom by the half-tribe of Manasseh were: Golan, in Bashan; Ashtaroth.

[72]The tribe of Issachar gave them Kedesh, Daberath, [73]Ramoth, and Anem, and the surrounding pastureland of each.

[74]The tribe of Asher gave them Abdon, Mashal, [75]Hukok, and Rehob, with their pasturelands.

[76]The tribe of Naphtali gave them Kedesh in Galilee, Hammon, and Kiriathaim with pasturelands.

[77]The tribe of Zebulun gave Rimmono and Tabor to the Merari clan as Cities of Refuge.

[78,79]And across the Jordan River, opposite Jericho, the tribe of Reuben gave them Bezer (a desert town), Jahzah, Kedemoth and Mephaath, along with their pasturelands.

[80]The tribe of Gad gave them Ramoth in Gilead, Mahanaim, [81]Heshbon, and Jazer, each with their surrounding pasturelands.

CHAPTER 7

Issachar's Descendants

The sons of Issachar: **Tola,** Puah, Jashub, Shimron.

[2]The sons of *Tola,* each of whom was the head of a subclan: **Uzzi,** Rephaiah, Jeriel, Jahmai, Ibsam, Shemuel.

At the time of King David, the total number of men of war from these families totaled 22,600.

[3]*Uzzi's* son was Izrahiah among whose five sons were Michael, Obadiah, Joel, and Isshiah, all chiefs of subclans. [4]Their descendants, at the time of King David, numbered 36,000 troops; for all five of them had several wives and many sons. [5]The total number of men available for military service from all the clans of the tribe of Issachar numbered 87,000 stouthearted warriors, all included in the official genealogy.

Benjamin's Descendants

[6]The sons of Benjamin were: **Bela, Becher, Jediael.**

[7]The sons of *Bela:* Ezbon, Uzzi, Uzziel, Jerimoth, Iri.

These five mighty warriors were chiefs of subclans and were the leaders of 22,034 troops (all of whom were recorded in the official genealogies).

[8]The sons of *Becher* were: Zemirah, Joash, Eliezer, Elioenai, Omri, Jeremoth, Abijah, Anathoth, Alemeth.

[9]At the time of David there were 20,200 mighty warriors among their descendants; and they were led by their clan chiefs.

[10]The son of *Jediael* was **Bilhan.**

The sons of *Bilhan* were: Jeush, Benjamin, Ehud, Chenaanah, Zethan, Tarshish, Ahishahar.

[11]They were the chiefs of the subclans of *Jediael,* and their descendants included 17,200 warriors at the time of King David.

[12]The sons of Ir were Shuppim and Huppim. Hushim was one of the sons of Aher.

Naphtali's Descendants

[13]The sons of Naphtali (descendants of Jacob's wife Bilhah) were: Jahziel, Guni, Jezer, Shallum.

Manasseh's Descendants

[14]The sons of Manasseh, born to his Aramaean concubine, were Asriel and Machir (who became the father of Gilead).

[15]It was Machir who found wives for Huppim and Shuppim. Machir's sister was

Maacah. Another descendant was Zelophehad, who had only daughters.
16 Machir's wife, also named Maacah, bore
him a son whom she named Peresh; his
brother's name was Sheresh, and he had sons
named Ulam and Rakem.
17 Ulam's son was Bedan. So these were the
sons of Gilead, the grandsons of Machir, and
the great-grandsons of Manasseh.
18 Hammolecheth, Machir's sister, bore Ish-
hod, Abiezer, and Mahlah.
19 The sons of Shemida were Ahian, Shechem, Likhi, and Aniam.

Ephraim's Descendants

20,21 The sons of Ephraim: Shuthelah, Bered,
Tahath, Eleadah, Tahath, Zabad, Shuthelah,
Ezer, Elead.
Elead and *Ezer* attempted to rustle cattle at
Gath, but they were killed by the local farmers. 22 Their father Ephraim mourned for them
a long time, and his brothers tried to comfort
him. 23 Afterwards his wife conceived and bore
a son whom he called Beriah (meaning "a
tragedy") because of what had happened.
24 Ephraim's daughter's name was Sheerah.
She built Lower and Upper Beth-horon and
Uzzen-sheerah.
25-27 This is Ephraim's line of descent:

Rephah, the father of
Resheph, the father of
Telah, the father of
Tahan, the father of
Ladan, the father of
Ammihud, the father of
Elishama, the father of
Nun, the father of
Joshua.

28 They lived in an area bounded on one side
by Bethel and its surrounding towns, on the
east by Naaran, on the west by Gezer and its
villages, and finally by Shechem and its surrounding villages as far as Ayyah and its
towns.
29 The tribe of Manasseh, descendants of
Joseph the son of Israel, controlled the following cities and their surrounding areas: Beth-
shean, Taanach, Megiddo, and Dor.

Asher's Descendants

30 The children of Asher: Imnah, Ishvah, Ishvi,
Beriah, Serah (their sister).
31 The sons of *Beriah* were: **Heber**, Malchiel
(the father of Birzaith).
32 *Heber's* children were: **Japhlet, Shomer,
Hotham**, Shua (their sister).
33 *Japhlet's* sons were: Pasach, Bimhal, Ash-
vath.
34 His brother *Shomer's* sons were: Rohgah,
Jehubbah, Aram.
35 The sons of his brother *Hotham* were: Zophah, Imna, Shelesh, Amal.
36,37 The sons of *Zophah* were: Suah, Harne-
pher, Shual, Beri, Imrah, Bezer, Hod,
Shamma, Shilshah, **Ithran**, Beera.
38 The sons of *Ithran* were: Jephunneh,
Pispa, Ara.
39 The sons of Ulla were: Arah, Hanniel, Ri-
zia.
40 These descendants of Asher were heads of
subclans and were all skilled warriors and
chiefs. Their descendants in the official genealogy numbered 36,000 men of war.

CHAPTER 8

Benjamin's Descendants

The sons of Benjamin, according to age, were:
Bela, the first, Ashbel, the second, Aharah,
the third, Nohah, the fourth, Rapha, the fifth.
3-5 The sons of *Bela* were: Addar, Gera, Abi-
hud, Abishua, Naaman, Ahoah, Gera, She-
phuphan, Huram.
6,7 The sons of Ehud, chiefs of the subclans
living at Geba, were captured in war and exiled to Manahath. They were: Naaman, Ahijah, Gera (also called Heglam), the father of
Uzza and Ahihud.
8-10 Shaharaim divorced his wives **Hushim**
and Baara, but he had children in the land of
Moab by Hodesh, his new wife: Jobab, Zibia,
Mesha, Malcam, Jeuz, Sachia, Mirmah.
These sons all became chiefs of subclans.
11 His wife *Hushim* had borne him Abitub
and **Elpaal.**
12 The sons of *Elpaal* were: Eber, Misham,
Shemed (who built Ono and Lod and their
surrounding villages).
13 His other sons were **Beriah** and Shema,
chiefs of subclans living in Aijalon; they
chased out the inhabitants of Gath.

8:1-33 When the people demanded a king, God gave them Saul. These verses contain an account of his personal genealogy. Even though he was well received by the people, it soon became obvious that he was attempting to build Israel with only human resources. Any project, either on a personal or a national level, must have divine resources if anything lasting is to result. This is a lesson that we all need to apply to our recovery.

14*Elpaal's* sons also included: Ahio, **Shashak,** Jeremoth.
15,16The sons of *Beriah* were: Zebadiah, Arad, Eder, Michael, Ishpah, Joha.
17,18The sons of *Elpaal* also included: Zebadiah, Meshullam, Hizki, Heber, Ishmerai, Izliah, Jobab.
19-21The sons of Shimei were: Jakim, Zichri, Zabdi, Elienai, Zillethai, Eliel, Adaiah, Beraiah, Shimrath.
22-25The sons of *Shashak* were: Ishpan, Eber, Eliel, Abdon, Zichri, Hanan, Hananiah, Elam, Anthothijah, Iphdeiah, Penuel.
26,27The sons of Jeroham were: Shamsherai, Shehariah, Athaliah, Jaareshiah, Elijah, Zichri.
28These were the chiefs of the subclans living at Jerusalem.
29Jeiel, the father of Gibeon, lived at Gibeon; and his wife's name was Maacah. 30-32His
oldest son was named Abdon, followed by: Zur, Kish, Baal, Nadab, Gedor, Ahio, Zecher, Mikloth who was the father of Shimeah.

All of these families lived together near Jerusalem.
33Ner was the father of Kish, and Kish was the father of Saul;

Saul's sons included: **Jonathan,** Malchishua, Abinadab, Eshbaal.
34The son of *Jonathan* was Mephibosheth;
The son of Mephibosheth was Micah.
35The sons of Micah: Pithon, Melech, Tarea, Ahaz.
36Ahaz was the father of Jehoaddah, Jehoaddah was the father of: Alemeth, Azmaveth, Zimri. Zimri's son was Moza.
37Moza was the father of Binea, whose sons were: Raphah, Eleasah, Azel.
38Azel had six sons: Azrikam, Bocheru, Ishmael, Sheariah, Obadiah, Hanan.
39Azel's brother Eshek had three sons: **Ulam,** the first, Jeush, the second, Eliphelet, the third.
40*Ulam's* sons were prominent warriors who were expert marksmen with their bows. These men had 150 sons and grandsons, and they were all from the tribe of Benjamin.

CHAPTER 9

Returnees from Babylonian Exile

The family tree of every person in Israel was carefully recorded in *The Annals of the Kings of Israel.*

Judah was exiled to Babylon because the people worshiped idols.
2The first to return and live again in their former cities were families from the tribes of Israel and also the priests, the Levites, and the Temple assistants.
3Then some families from the tribes of Judah, Benjamin, Ephraim, and Manasseh arrived in Jerusalem:
4One family was that of Uthai (the son of Ammihud, son of Omri, son of Imri, son of Bani) of the clan of Perez (son of Judah).
5The Shilonites were another family to return, including Asaiah (Shilon's oldest son)
and his sons; 6there were also the sons of
Zerah, including Jeuel and his relatives: 690 in all.
7,8Among the members of the tribe of Benjamin who returned were these:

Sallu (the son of Meshullam, the son of Hodaviah, the son of Hassenuah);
Ibneiah (the son of Jeroham);
Elah (the son of Uzzi, the son of Michri);
Meshullam (the son of Shephatiah, the son of Reuel, the son of Ibnijah).

9These men were all chiefs of subclans. A total of 956 Benjaminites returned.
10,11The priests who returned were:

9:1-44 This chapter contains a record of the Jews who returned to Judah after the Babylonian Exile (539 B.C.). The books of Chronicles were written to encourage these people as they rebuilt their nation after their seventy-year exile. The Temple had been destroyed, and the Davidic line of kings had been discontinued. It must have been a great encouragement for them to see that they were still God's people. God had made promises to their ancestors, and though they had gone through hard times, God's promises were still valid for them. In Scripture, God gives numerous promises to his people. In Christ, God's promises are for all of us to embrace, no matter what we have done or suffered in the past. We, too, are the people of God.

9:1 We are reminded of the primary reason for Israel's punishment in exile—the people had turned from God and worshiped idols. The idols in our life often lead us into similar states of exile. As an addiction or compulsion takes over our life, our values get distorted. We forget about God, our family, and the other important things in life. As a result, we lose everything. But just as Israel was restored through their exile, we also can find restoration through the exiles we may experience. Even when our past is filled with sin and failure, God has the power to give us a new start. All we need to do is look to him.

Jedaiah, Jehoiarib, Jachin,
Azariah (the son of Hilkiah, son of
Meshullam, son of Zadok, son of
Meraioth, son of Ahitub). He was the
chief custodian of the Temple.

12 Another of the returning priests was Adaiah (son of Jeroham, son of Pashhur, son of
Malchijah).
Another priest was Maasai (son of Adiel,
son of Jahzerah, son of Meshullam, son of
Meshillemith, son of Immer).
13 In all, 1,760 priests returned.
14 Among the Levites who returned was Shemaiah (son of Hasshub, son of Azrikam, son
of Hashabiah, who was a descendant of Merari).
15,16 Other Levites who returned included:

Bakbakkar, Heresh, Galal,
Mattaniah (the son of Mica, who was the
son of Zichri, who was the son of
Asaph),
Obadiah (the son of Shemaiah, son of
Galal, son of Jeduthun),
Berechiah (the son of Asa, son of Elkanah,
who lived in the area of the Netopha-
thites).

17,18 The gatekeepers were Shallum (the chief
gatekeeper), Akkub, Talmon, and Ahiman—
all Levites. They are still responsible for the
eastern royal gate. 19 Shallum's ancestry went
back through Kore and Ebiasaph to Korah. He
and his close relatives the Korahites were in
charge of the sacrifices and the protection of
the sanctuary, just as their ancestors had supervised and guarded the Tabernacle. 20 Phinehas, the son of Eleazar, was the first director
of this division in ancient times. And the Lord
was with him.
21 At that time Zechariah, the son of Meshelemiah, had been responsible for the protection of the entrance to the Tabernacle. 22 There
were 212 doorkeepers in those days. They
were chosen from their villages on the basis of
their genealogies, and they were appointed by
David and Samuel because of their reliability.
23 They and their descendants were in charge
of the Lord's Tabernacle. 24 They were assigned
to each of the four sides: east, west, north, and
south. 25 And their relatives in the villages were
assigned to help them from time to time, for
seven days at a time.
26 The four head gatekeepers, all Levites,
were in an office of great trust, for they were
responsible for the rooms and treasuries in
the Tabernacle of God. 27 Because of their important positions, they lived near the Tabernacle, and they opened the gates each morning. 28 Some of them were assigned to care for
the various vessels used in the sacrifices and
worship; they checked them in and out to
avoid loss. 29 Others were responsible for the
furniture, the items in the sanctuary, and the
supplies such as fine flour, wine, incense, and
spices.
30 Other priests prepared the spices and incense.
31 And Mattithiah (a Levite and the oldest
son of Shallum the Korahite) was entrusted
with making the flat cakes for grain offerings.
32 Some members of the Kohath clan were in
charge of the preparation of the special bread
each Sabbath.
33,34 The cantors were all prominent Levites.
They lived in Jerusalem at the Temple and
were on duty at all hours. They were free from
other responsibilities and were selected by
their genealogies.

Saul's Family Tree

35-37 Jeiel (whose wife was Maacah) lived in
Gibeon. He had many sons, including: Gibeon, Abdon (the oldest), Zur, Kish, Baal, **Ner**,
Nadab, Gedor, Ahio, Zechariah, Mikloth.
38 Mikloth lived with his son Shimeam in
Jerusalem near his relatives.
39 Ner was the father of Kish, Kish was the
father of Saul, Saul was the father of Jonathan,
Malchi-shua, Abinadab, and Eshbaal.
40 Jonathan was the father of Mephibosheth;
Mephibosheth was the father of Micah;
41 Micah was the father of Pithon, Melech,
Tahrea, and Ahaz;
42 Ahaz was the father of Jarah;
Jarah was the father of Alemeth, Azmaveth,
and Zimri;
Zimri was the father of Moza.
43 Moza was the father of Binea, Rephaiah,
Eleasah, and Azel.
44 Azel had six sons: Azrikam, Bocheru, Ishmael, Sheariah, Obadiah, Hanan.

CHAPTER 10

The Death of King Saul

The Philistines attacked and defeated the Israeli troops, who turned and fled and were
slaughtered on the slopes of Mount Gilboa.
2 They caught up with Saul and his three sons,
Jonathan, Abinadab, and Malchi-shua, and
killed them all. 3 Saul had been hard pressed
with heavy fighting all around him, when the
Philistine archers shot and wounded him.
4 He cried out to his bodyguard, "Quick, kill

me with your sword before these uncircumcised heathen capture and torture me."

But the man was afraid to do it, so Saul took his own sword and fell against its point; and it pierced his body. 5Then his bodyguard, seeing that Saul was dead, killed himself in the same way. 6So Saul and his three sons died together; the entire family was wiped out in one day.

7When the Israelis in the valley below the mountain heard that their troops had been routed and that Saul and his sons were dead, they abandoned their cities and fled. And the Philistines came and lived in them. 8When the Philistines went back the next day to strip the bodies of the men killed in action and to gather the booty from the battlefield, they found the bodies of Saul and his sons. 9So they stripped off Saul's armor and cut off his head; then they displayed them throughout the nation and celebrated the wonderful news before their idols. 10They fastened his armor to the walls of the Temple of the Gods and nailed his head to the wall of Dagon's temple.

11But when the people of Jabesh-gilead heard what the Philistines had done to Saul, 12their heroic warriors went out to the battlefield and brought back his body and the bodies of his three sons. Then they buried them beneath the oak tree at Jabesh and mourned and fasted for seven days.

13Saul died for his disobedience to the Lord and because he had consulted a medium, 14and did not ask the Lord for guidance. So the Lord killed him and gave the kingdom to David, the son of Jesse.

CHAPTER 11

David Conquers Jerusalem

Then the leaders of Israel went to David at Hebron and told him, "We are your relatives, 2and even when Saul was king, you were the one who led our armies to battle and brought them safely back again. And the Lord your God has told you, 'You shall be the shepherd of my people Israel. You shall be their king.'"

3So David made a contract with them before the Lord, and they anointed him as king of Israel, just as the Lord had told Samuel. 4Then David and the leaders went to Jerusalem (or Jebus, as it used to be called) where the Jebusites—the original inhabitants of the land—lived. 5,6But the people of Jebus refused to let them enter the city. So David captured

10:1-10 Here is a horrifying account of personal defeat. Like many people in the process of recovery, Saul had started out well. At first, he was humble; he was willing to follow the leadership of the prophet Samuel. But then he began to take matters into his own hands. Once he started on the downward spiral, he added rebellion to rebellion. The final outcome was the defeat described in these verses. We need to be careful! We are capable of starting down this same pathway toward complete disaster. We must never forget to ask God to join us in our spiritual journey—each and every day.

10:11-12 In spite of Saul's failure and final downfall, the men of Jabesh-gilead remembered the kindness that Saul had shown toward them. They were loyal to his memory and, at great personal risk, rescued the bodies of Saul and his three sons. Even when a person is down and out, it should be remembered that he needs loyalty and encouragement. It is far easier to be loyal to those with power rather than to those who have fallen and been humbled.

10:13-14 As we face problems in life, we must be careful of where we go for help. God is the only true source of help. In many cases, looking elsewhere will prove fatal. This was true in Saul's case. Notice that Saul's sin, which cost him the throne, was not simply disobedience and rebellion. These verses affirm that Saul's primary mistake was his failure to seek God for help. Instead, he went to a source that stood against God. God is waiting to help us. All we need to do is recognize our helpless state and call out to him. Looking to the occult and other sources for help will always spell disaster.

11:1-3 With every God-given opportunity comes a God-given responsibility. This is clear in the career of David, the man after God's own heart. The people of Israel pledged themselves as subjects to him. In this relationship, the people had a perfect right to look to David for military leadership and personal protection. This is not an unhealthy state of dependency, but a proper definition of roles. When God gives us opportunities to help others, we need to realize that with the position of leadership comes a responsibility to "shepherd" God's people.

11:4-7 These verses recount David's capture of the city of Jerusalem, which would soon become the spiritual center of worship for Israel. This place remained the focal point for Israel's worship for centuries and is important in the thinking of Jews to this day. For all individuals facing the task of recovery, a spiritual center for corporate worship is extremely important. For proper healing, God has provided us with the worshiping community—the church. Through the church or other appropriate support groups God encourages us, giving us the strength we need to persevere in the process of recovery.

the fortress of Zion, later called the City of David, and said to his men, "The first man to kill a Jebusite shall be made commander-in-chief !" Joab, the son of Zeruiah, was the first, so he became the general of David's army. 7David lived in the fortress and that is why that area of Jerusalem is called the City of David. 8He extended the city out around the fortress while Joab rebuilt the rest of Jerusalem. 9And David became more and more famous and powerful, for the Lord of the heavens was with him.

David's Bravest Warriors

10These are the names of some of the bravest of David's warriors (who also encouraged the leaders of Israel to make David their king, as the Lord had said would happen):

11Jashobeam (the son of a man from Hachmon) was the leader of The Top Three—the three greatest heroes among David's men. He once killed 300 men with his spear.

12The second of The Top Three was Eleazar, the son of Dodo, a member of the subclan of Ahoh. 13He was with David in the battle against the Philistines at Pasdammim. The Israeli army was in a barley field and had begun to run away, 14but he held his ground in the middle of the field, and recovered it and slaughtered the Philistines; and the Lord saved them with a great victory.

15Another time, three of The Thirty went to David while he was hiding in the cave of Adullam. The Philistines were camped in the Valley of Rephaim, 16and David was in the stronghold at the time; an outpost of the Philistines had occupied Bethlehem. 17David wanted a drink from the Bethlehem well beside the gate, and when he mentioned this to his men, 18,19these three broke through to the Philistine camp, drew some water from the well, and brought it back to David. But he refused to drink it! Instead he poured it out as an offering to the Lord and said, "God forbid that I should drink it! It is the very blood of these men who risked their lives to get it."

20Abishai, Joab's brother, was commander of The Thirty. He had gained his place among The Thirty by killing 300 men at one time with his spear. 21He was the chief and the most famous of The Thirty, but he was not as great as The Three.

22Benaiah, whose father was a mighty warrior from Kabzeel, killed the two famous giants from Moab. He also killed a lion in a slippery pit when there was snow on the ground. 23Once he killed an Egyptian who was seven and a half feet tall, whose spear was as thick as a weaver's beam. But Benaiah went up to him with only a club in his hand, and pulled the spear away from him and used it to kill him. 24,25He was nearly as great as The Three, and he was very famous among The Thirty. David made him captain of his bodyguard.

26-47Other famous warriors among David's men were:

Asahel (Joab's brother);
Elhanan, the son of Dodo from Bethlehem;
Shammoth from Harod;
Helez from Pelon;
Ira (son of Ikkesh) from Tekoa;
Abiezer from Anathoth;
Sibbecai from Hushath;
Ilai from Ahoh;
Maharai from Netophah;
Heled (son of Baanah) from Netophah;
Ithai (son of Ribai) a Benjaminite from Gibeah;
Benaiah from Pirathon;
Hurai from near the brooks of Gaash;
Abiel from Arbath;
Azmaveth from Baharum;
Eliahba from Shaalbon;
The sons of Hashem from Gizon;
Jonathan (son of Shagee) from Harar;
Ahiam (son of Sacher) from Harar;
Eliphal (son of Ur);
Hepher from Mecherath;
Ahijah from Pelon;
Hezro from Carmel;
Naarai (son of Ezbai);
Joel (brother of Nathan);
Mibhar (son of Hagri);
Zelek from Ammon;
Naharai from Beeroth—he was General Joab's armorbearer;
Ira from Ithra;
Gareb from Ithra;

11:9 All of us desire success of one kind or another. When the Bible makes note of the success of any individual, it always attributes it to a strong relationship with God. True success is only possible when God is with the victorious individual. If we achieve personal greatness but are spiritually bankrupt, our efforts will have been in vain. True success in life can only be achieved when we put God first. Everything else in life is secondary.

Uriah the Hittite;
Zabad (son of Ahlai);
Adina (son of Shiza) from the tribe of Reuben—he was among the thirty-one leaders of the tribe of Reuben;
Hanan (son of Maacah);
Joshaphat from Mithna;
Uzzia from Ashterath;
Shama and Jeiel (sons of Hotham) from Aroer;
Jediael (son of Shimri);
Joha (his brother) from Tiza;
Eliel from Mahavi;
Jeribai and Joshaviah (sons of Elnaam);
Ithmah from Moab;
Eliel; Obed; Jaasiel from Mezoba.

CHAPTER 12

Warriors Join David

These are the names of the famous warriors
who joined David at Ziklag while he was hiding from King Saul. 2All of them were expert
archers and slingers, and they could use their
left hands as readily as their right! Like King
Saul, they were all of the tribe of Benjamin.
3-7Their chief was Ahiezer, son of Shemaah
from Gibeah. The others were:

His brother Joash; Jeziel and Pelet, sons of Azmaveth; Beracah; Jehu from Anathoth; Ishmaiah from Gibeon (a brave warrior rated as high or higher than The Thirty); Jeremiah; Jahaziel; Johanan; Jozabad from Gederah; Eluzai; Jerimoth; Bealiah; Shemariah; Shephatiah from Haruph; Elkanah, Isshiah, Azarel, Joezer, Jashobeam—all Korahites; Joelah and Zebadiah (sons of Jeroham from Gedor).

8-13Great and brave warriors from the tribe
of Gad also went to David in the wilderness.
They were experts with both shield and spear
and were "lion-faced men, swift as deer upon
the mountains."

Ezer was the chief;
Obadiah was second in command;
Eliab was third in command;
Mishmannah was fourth in command;
Jeremiah was fifth in command;
Attai was sixth in command;
Eliel was seventh in command;
Johanan was eighth in command;
Elzabad was ninth in command;
Jeremiah was tenth in command;
Machbannai was eleventh in command.

14These men were army officers; the weakest was worth a hundred normal troops, and
the greatest was worth a thousand! 15They
crossed the Jordan River during its seasonal
flooding and conquered the lowlands on
both the east and west banks.
16Others came to David from Benjamin and
Judah. 17David went out to meet them and
said, "If you have come to help me, we are
friends; but if you have come to betray me to
my enemies when I am innocent, then may
the God of our fathers see and judge you."
18Then the Holy Spirit came upon them,
and Amasai, a leader of The Thirty, replied,

"We are yours, David;
We are on your side, son of Jesse.
Peace, peace be unto you,
And peace to all who aid you;

12:1-7 All the warriors mentioned here were well prepared for conflict. Proper preparation for conflict is a necessary step for winning any battle. Any of us in the process of rebuilding our life will encounter episodes of such conflict. The example of David's warriors should encourage us to be prepared. We would be wise to draw close to God. When we are armed with God's armor, we will be prepared to fight life's battles (see Ephesians 6:10-18).

12:16-18 These verses record how a group of warriors came to David, wanting to submit to his leadership. During the period of anarchy experienced in Israel after Saul's death, many desperately sought direction for their lives. David gave this band of warriors the direction they needed. We all desire our life to be meaningful. Notice that the volunteers here were not only anxious to serve, but they were also empowered by the Holy Spirit. We often forget that spiritual empowerment is vital if we desire to accomplish anything significant in life, including recovery. It is "not by might, nor by power, but by my Spirit, says the Lord Almighty" (Zechariah 4:6). If we hope to move forward in recovery, we must do it with God's power.

12:18 In this passage, under spiritual direction, Amasai proclaimed peace to David. How can there be peace in the midst of conflict? The Hebrew word *shalom* conveys the idea of completeness. In a godly context it means "May you accept all that God has for you today." It is a peace based on the fact of God's presence, not on the surrounding circumstances. As such, this peace may be enjoyed even during warfare. No matter what personal conflicts we face, we can find some peace and comfort in acknowledging daily that God is in complete control of our life and world.

For your God is with you."

So David let them join him, and he made
them captains of his army.
19 Some men from Manasseh deserted the
Israeli army and joined David just as he was
going into battle with the Philistines against
King Saul. But as it turned out, the Philistine
generals refused to let David and his men go
with them. After much discussion they sent
them back, for they were afraid that David
and his men would imperil them by deserting
to King Saul.
20 Here is a list of the men from Manasseh
who deserted to David as he was en route to
Ziklag: Adnah, Jozabad, Jediael, Michael, Jozabad, Elihu, Zillethai.
Each was a high-ranking officer of Manasseh's troops.
21 They were brave and able warriors, and they assisted David when he fought
against the Amalek raiders at Ziklag.
22 More men joined David almost every day
until he had a tremendous army—the army of
God.
23 Here is the registry of recruits who
joined David at Hebron. They were all anxious to see David become king instead of Saul,
just as the Lord had said would happen.

24-37 From Judah, 6,800 troops armed with shields and spears.
From the tribe of Simeon, 7,100 outstanding warriors.
From the Levites, 4,600.
From the priests—descendants of Aaron—there were 3,700 troops under the command of Zadok, a young man of unusual courage, and Jehoiada. (He and twenty-two members of his family were officers of the fighting priests.)
From the tribe of Benjamin, the same tribe Saul was from, there were 3,000. (Most of that tribe retained its allegiance to Saul.)
From the tribe of Ephraim, 20,800 mighty warriors, each famous in his respective clan.
From the half-tribe of Manasseh, 18,000 were sent for the express purpose of helping David become king.
From the tribe of Issachar there were 200 leaders of the tribe with their relatives—all men who understood the temper of the times and knew the best course for Israel to take.
From the tribe of Zebulun there were 50,000 trained warriors; they were fully armed and totally loyal to David.
From Naphtali there were 1,000 officers and 37,000 troops equipped with shields and spears.
From the tribe of Dan there were 28,600 troops, all of them prepared for war.
From the tribe of Asher, there were 40,000 trained and ready troops.
From the other side of the Jordan River—where the tribes of Reuben and Gad and the half-tribe of Manasseh lived—there were 120,000 troops equipped with every kind of weapon.

38 All these men came in battle array to
Hebron with the single purpose of making
David the king of Israel. In fact, all of Israel
was ready for this change.
39 They feasted and
drank with David for three days, for preparations had been made for their arrival.
40 People
from nearby and from as far away as Issachar,
Zebulun, and Naphtali brought food on donkeys, camels, mules, and oxen. Vast supplies
of flour, fig cakes, raisins, wine, oil, cattle, and
sheep were brought to the celebration, for joy
had spread throughout the land.

CHAPTER 13

Uzza Touches the Ark and Dies

After David had consulted with all of his army
officers,
2 he addressed the assembled men of
Israel as follows:
"Since you think that I should be your king,
and since the Lord our God has given his
approval, let us send messages to our brothers
throughout the land of Israel, including the
priests and Levites, inviting them to come
and join us.
3 And let us bring back the Ark of
our God, for we have been neglecting it ever
since Saul became king."
4 There was unanimous consent, for everyone agreed with him.
5 So David summoned
the people of Israel from all across the nation
so that they could be present when the Ark of
God was brought from Kiriath-jearim.
6 Then David and all Israel went to Baalah

13:1-10 Here we see David doing a good thing, but in the wrong way. God had prescribed exactly the method of moving the Ark of the Covenant. David used the expedient way—and the results were catastrophic! God's clear guidelines were ignored. As we go about our recovery, we can fall into the same trap. We must be extremely careful of the means selected in our recovery process. Our recovery is clearly within God's will, but we need to go about it with God's plan in mind. If we don't, we will have to suffer the consequences.

(i.e., Kiriath-jearim) in Judah to bring back
the Ark of the Lord God enthroned above the
angels. 7It was taken from the house of Abinadab on a new cart. Uzza and Ahio drove the
oxen. 8Then David and all the people danced
before the Lord with great enthusiasm, accompanied by singing and by zithers, harps,
tambourines, cymbals, and trumpets. 9But as
they arrived at the threshing-floor of Chidon,
the oxen stumbled and Uzza reached out his
hand to steady the Ark. 10Then the anger of
the Lord blazed out against Uzza, and killed
him because he had touched the Ark. And so
he died there before God. 11David was angry
at the Lord for what he had done to Uzza and
he named the place "The Outbreak Against
Uzza." And it is still called that today.
12Now David was afraid of God and asked,
"How shall I ever get the Ark of God home?"
13Finally he decided to take it to the home
of Obed-edom the Gittite instead of bringing
it to the City of David. 14The Ark remained
there with the family of Obed-edom for three
months, and the Lord blessed him and his
family.

CHAPTER 14

God Blesses David

King Hiram of Tyre sent masons and carpenters to help build David's palace and he supplied him with much cedar lumber. 2David
now realized why the Lord had made him
king and why he had made his kingdom so
great; it was for a special reason—to give joy
to God's people!
3After David moved to Jerusalem, he married additional wives and became the father
of many sons and daughters.
4-7These are the names of the sons born to
him in Jerusalem: Shammua, Shobab, Nathan, Solomon, Ibhar, Elishua, Elpelet, Nogah, Nepheg, Japhia, Elishama, Beeliada,
Eliphelet.

David Conquers the Philistines

8When the Philistines heard that David was
Israel's new king, they mobilized their forces
to capture him. But David learned that they
were on the way, so he called together his
army. 9The Philistines were raiding the Valley
of Rephaim, 10 and David asked the Lord, "If I
go out and fight them, will you give me the
victory?"
And the Lord replied, "Yes, I will."
11So he attacked them at Baal-perazim and
wiped them out. He exulted, "God has used
me to sweep away my enemies like water
bursting through a dam!" That is why the
place has been known as Baal-perazim ever
since (meaning, "The Place of Breaking
Through").
12After the battle the Israelis picked up
many idols left by the Philistines, but David
ordered them burned.
13Later the Philistines raided the valley
again, 14and again David asked God what to
do.

13:9-11 We must take great care as we deal with obstacles in our path. We are prone to do the first thing that comes to us—almost a knee-jerk reaction. But some things are absolutely forbidden by God. Uzza discovered this basic principle too late. In dealing with barriers to recovery, we must be careful to do things God's way; otherwise, the results could be disastrous.

13:13-14 We often experience setbacks when we attempt to accomplish something good in our life. Such was the case in this passage. David wanted to bring the Ark to Jerusalem, but the death of Uzza brought his project to a standstill. The good thing went undone because God's requirements were not observed. We often experience similar setbacks to our recovery because we try to achieve them in our own way. We forget to seek God's will in the recovery process. God is concerned that we not only reach the goal but also go about it in the right way.

14:1-2 God gave great success to David. Everything he did had a positive outcome. Here we see one reason why God blessed him so much: God wanted to give joy to his people. By helping David, God was helping the whole nation of Israel. When God gives us success in recovery, he is probably doing it first of all because he loves us. But our success could also be the source of comfort and help to many others who suffer in similar ways. As Step Twelve advises, we need to reach out to help others as we become able. We may discover that God gave us victory so we could become a source of help and joy to others.

14:8 Enemies seem to gather against us as soon as we gain victory in any area of our life. When David became king, Israel's old enemies, the Philistines, began to attack. When we begin to be successful, we become the target of the devil's power, of our own fleshly desires, and even of the people close to us. Some of our loved ones may even become threatened by the changes taking place in our life. For this reason we must never forget our vulnerability. Each day we should look to God for protection against relapse.

The Lord replied, "Go around by the mulberry trees and attack from there. 15When you
hear a sound like marching in the tops of the
mulberry trees, that is your signal to attack,
for God will go before you and destroy the
enemy."
16So David did as the Lord commanded
him; and he cut down the army of the Philistines all the way from Gibeon to Gezer.
17David's fame spread everywhere, and the
Lord caused all the nations to fear him.

CHAPTER 15

The Ark Is Carried to Jerusalem

David now built several palaces for himself in
Jerusalem, and he also built a new Tabernacle
to house the Ark of God, 2and issued these
instructions: "[When we transfer the Ark to its
new home], no one except the Levites may
carry it, for God has chosen them for this
purpose; they are to minister to him forever."
3Then David summoned all Israel to Jerusalem to celebrate the bringing of the Ark into
the new Tabernacle. 4-10These were the priests
and Levites present:

120 from the clan of Kohath; with Uriel as their leader;
220 from the clan of Merari; with Asaiah as their leader;
130 from the clan of Gershom; with Joel as their leader;
200 from the subclan of Elizaphan; with Shemaiah as their leader;
80 from the subclan of Hebron; with Eliel as their leader;
112 from the subclan of Uzziel; with Amminadab as their leader.

11Then David called for Zadok and Abiathar, the High Priests, and for the Levite leaders: Uriel, Asaiah, Joel, Shemaiah, Eliel, and
Amminadab.
12"You are the leaders of the clans of the
Levites," he told them. "Now sanctify yourselves with all your brothers so that you may
bring the Ark of Jehovah, the God of Israel, to
the place I have prepared for it. 13The Lord
destroyed us before because we handled the
matter improperly—you were not carrying
it."
14So the priests and the Levites underwent
the ceremonies of sanctification in preparation for bringing home the Ark of Jehovah,
the God of Israel. 15Then the Levites carried
the Ark on their shoulders with its carrying
poles, just as the Lord had instructed Moses.
16King David also ordered the Levite leaders
to organize the singers into an orchestra, and
they played loudly and joyously upon psaltries, harps, and cymbals. 17Heman (son of
Joel), Asaph (son of Berechiah), and Ethan
(son of Kushaiah) from the clan of Merari
were the heads of the musicians.
18The following men were chosen as their
assistants: Zechariah, Jaaziel, Shemiramoth,
Jehiel, Unni, Eliab, Benaiah, Maaseiah, Mattithiah, Eliphelehu, Mikneiah, Obed-edom and
Jeiel, the doorkeepers.
19Heman, Asaph, and Ethan were chosen to
sound the bronze cymbals; 20and Zechariah,
Aziel, Shemiramoth, Jehiel, Unni, Eliab, Maaseiah, and Benaiah comprised an octet accompanied by harps. 21Mattithiah,
Eliphelehu, Mikneiah, Obed-edom, Jeiel, and
Azaziah were the harpists. 22The song leader
was Chenaniah, the chief of the Levites, who
was selected for his skill. 23Berechiah and Elkanah were guards for the Ark. 24Shebaniah,
Joshaphat, Nethanel, Amasai, Zechariah, Benaiah, and Eliezer—all of whom were
priests—formed a bugle corps to march at the
head of the procession. And Obed-edom and
Jehiah guarded the Ark.
25Then David and the elders of Israel and
the high officers of the army went with great
joy to the home of Obed-edom to take the Ark
to Jerusalem. 26And because God didn't destroy the Levites who were carrying the Ark,

---

14:16-17 David did as God commanded, and God granted him success. Simple obedience was certainly the key to David's victory. It is important here that we do not misunderstand and begin to see God as a "push-button" deity who will act or react based on a set formula. Some teach that if we have enough faith or if we follow certain instructions, we will experience an immediate cure. This is not always the case. Sometimes our obedience will be answered by new and difficult circumstances. When hard times fall repeatedly upon us, we need not fear that God has rejected us. Sometimes he uses such situations to work his will in us. We can be sure that God will always stand with us, even if he doesn't always give us an immediate cure.

15:25 What happens when victory is finally achieved? What are the emotions? What are the reactions? This verse says that these people did their work "with great joy." The joy of accomplishing God's will is one of the sweetest joys of all. Joy is an essential element in the life of the believer. Even as we go through the difficult and often painful process of recovery, we can experience great joy.

they sacrificed seven bulls and seven lambs.
27David, the Levites carrying the Ark, the singers, and Chenaniah the song leader were all
dressed in linen robes. David also wore a linen
ephod. 28So the leaders of Israel took the Ark
to Jerusalem with shouts of joy, the blowing
of horns and trumpets, the crashing of cymbals, and loud playing on the harps and zithers.
29(But as the Ark arrived in Jerusalem,
David's wife Michal, the daughter of King
Saul, felt a deep disgust for David as she
watched from the window and saw him dancing like a madman.)

CHAPTER 16

David Sings Praises to God

So they brought the Ark of God into the special tent that David had prepared for it, and the leaders of Israel sacrificed burnt offerings and peace offerings before God.
2At the
conclusion of these offerings David blessed
the people in the name of the Lord;
3then he
gave every person present (men and women
alike) a loaf of bread, some wine, and a cake
of raisins.
4He appointed certain of the Levites to minister before the Ark by giving constant praise
and thanks to the Lord God of Israel and by
asking for his blessings upon his people.
These are the names of those given this assignment:
5Asaph, the leader of this detail,
sounded the cymbals. His associates were Zechariah, Jeiel, Shemiramoth, Jehiel, Mattithiah,
Eliab, Benaiah, Obed-edom, and Jeiel; they
played the harps and zithers.
6The priests Be-
naiah and Jahaziel played their trumpets regularly before the Ark.
7At that time David began the custom of
using choirs in the Tabernacle to sing thanksgiving to the Lord. Asaph was the director of
this choral group of priests.

8"Oh, give thanks to the Lord and pray to
him," they sang.
"Tell the peoples of the world
About his mighty doings.
9Sing to him; yes, sing his praises
And tell of his marvelous works.
10Glory in his holy name;
Let all rejoice who seek the Lord.
11Seek the Lord; yes, seek his strength
And seek his face untiringly.
12,13O descendants of his servant Abraham,
O chosen sons of Jacob,
Remember his mighty miracles
And his marvelous miracles
And his authority:
14He is the Lord our God!
His authority is seen throughout the earth.

15:27-28 In modern America there seems to be the ingrained notion that people, especially men, should hide their true emotions. Many Christians support this idea, believing they should be stoic about their emotions. Contrary to this popular view, God's Word insists that we be honest about our feelings. In this passage, David responded with an intense emotional outburst that was commended, rather than condemned, by God. Tears of sorrow and joy should never be totally absent from our experience of life.

15:29 Even though God has given us emotions and encourages us to express them honestly, there are some who will always disapprove when feelings are demonstrated. When David's wife Michal saw him in the emotional celebration of his victory, she evidently found it disgusting. It is true that some expressions of emotion are inappropriate. But when we discover appropriate avenues of expression, we should not hesitate to express the feelings we have.

16:1-3 When God's will is accomplished, celebration should be an automatic response. We should celebrate each victory we have, no matter how small it may be. When David finally brought the Ark to Jerusalem, he threw a great celebration. The whole city enjoyed a happy time of worship, and David broke out refreshments for everyone. This kind of appropriate celebration will affirm our progress and encourage us to move forward once again.

16:8-13 In times of victory or defeat, recovery or stability, God remains the same. Our response to him in all circumstances should include the elements of thanksgiving and praise. There is never a time when it is inappropriate to seek God; indeed, 16:11 enjoins us to "seek his face untiringly." Surely these are imperatives that must be observed by each of us in recovery.

16:14-22 There are times when it is tempting for us to think that God has somehow lost control of things. We are not the only ones who have felt this way. There were times during Israel's history when God seemed far away. God's plan for his people must have seemed obscure and distant. But as time passed it became clear that God had been with Israel the whole time—even as they wandered in the wilderness. God used the difficult times to work out his plan. Sometimes crises and emergencies occur in our life that seem beyond God's sovereign control. We can be sure, however, that even in such times God is there and in control! During such times we must learn to rest in our knowledge of God's goodness and love.

[15]Remember his covenant forever—
The words he commanded
To a thousand generations:
[16]His agreement with Abraham,
And his oath to Isaac,
[17]And his confirmation to Jacob.
He promised Israel
With an everlasting promise:
[18]'I will give you the land of Canaan
As your inheritance.'
[19]When Israel was few in number—oh, so
few—
And merely strangers in the Promised
Land;
[20]When they wandered from country to
country,
From one kingdom to another—
[21]God didn't let anyone harm them.
Even kings were killed who sought to hurt
them.
[22]'Don't harm my chosen people,' he
declared.
'These are my prophets—touch them not.'
[23]Sing to the Lord, O earth,
Declare each day that he is the one who
saves!
[24]Show his glory to the nations!
Tell everyone about his miracles.
[25]For the Lord is great and should be
highly praised;
He is to be held in awe above all gods.
[26]The other so-called gods are demons,
But the Lord made the heavens.
[27]Majesty and honor march before him,
Strength and gladness walk beside him.
[28]O people of all nations of the earth,
Ascribe great strength and glory to his
name!
[29]Yes, ascribe to the Lord
The glory due his name!
Bring an offering and come before him;
Worship the Lord when clothed with
holiness!
[30]Tremble before him, all the earth!
The world stands unmoved.
[31]Let the heavens be glad, the earth rejoice;
Let all the nations say, 'It is the Lord who
reigns.'
[32]Let the vast seas roar,
Let the countryside and everything in it
rejoice!
[33]Let the trees in the woods sing for joy
before the Lord,
For he comes to judge the earth.
[34]Oh, give thanks to the Lord, for he is
good;
His love and his kindness go on forever.
[35]Cry out to him, 'Oh, save us, God of our
salvation;
Bring us safely back from among the
nations.
Then we will thank your holy name,
And triumph in your praise.'
[36]Blessed be Jehovah, God of Israel,
Forever and forevermore."

And all the people shouted "Amen!" and praised the Lord.

[37]David arranged for Asaph and his fellow
Levites to minister regularly at the Tabernacle,
doing each day whatever needed to be done.
[38]This group included Obed-edom (the son of
Jeduthun), Hosah and sixty-eight of their colleagues as guards.
[39]Meanwhile the old Tabernacle of the Lord
on the hill of Gibeon continued to be active.
David left Zadok the priest and his fellow-
priests to minister to the Lord there. [40]They
sacrificed burnt offerings to the Lord each
morning and evening upon the altar set aside
for that purpose, just as the Lord had commanded Israel. [41]David also appointed Heman, Jeduthun, and several others who were
chosen by name to give thanks to the Lord for
his constant love and mercy. [42]They used their
trumpets and cymbals to accompany the
singers with loud praises to God. And Jeduthun's sons were appointed as guards.
[43]At last the celebration ended and the
people returned to their homes, and David
returned to bless his own household.

CHAPTER 17

God Gives David a Promise

After David had been living in his new palace
for some time he said to Nathan the prophet,
"Look! I'm living here in a cedar-paneled
home while the Ark of the Covenant of God
is out there in a tent!"
[2]And Nathan replied, "Carry out your plan
in every detail, for it is the will of the Lord."
[3]But that same night God said to Nathan,

17:1-2 Have you ever had an idea that seemed ideal? In these verses, David had a wonderful idea: he wanted to build God a temple to house the Ark. David's idea to build the Temple was a good one, but, like all good ideas, it had to pass yet another test. It needed to conform to God's will and timing. Even our best ideas or plans will fail if we act counter to God's program for us. We must learn to seek God's will and submit to his plan if we desire to succeed in recovery.

[4]"Go and give my servant David this message: 'You are not to build my temple! [5]I've gone from tent to tent as my home from the time I brought Israel out of Egypt. [6]In all that time I never suggested to any of the leaders of Israel—the shepherds I appointed to care for my people—that they should build me a cedar-lined temple.'

[7]"Tell my servant David, 'The Lord of heaven says to you, I took you from being a shepherd and made you the king of my people. [8]And I have been with you everywhere you've gone; I have destroyed your enemies, and I will make your name as great as the greatest of the earth. [9]And I will give a permanent home to my people Israel and will plant them in their land. They will not be disturbed again; the wicked nations won't conquer them as they did before [10]when the judges ruled them. I will subdue all of your enemies. And I now declare that I will cause your descendants to be kings of Israel just as you are.

[11]"'When your time here on earth is over and you die, I will place one of your sons upon your throne; and I will make his kingdom strong. [12]He is the one who shall build me a temple, and I will establish his royal line of descent forever. [13]I will be his father, and he shall be my son; I will never remove my mercy and love from him as I did from Saul. [14]I will place him over my people and over the kingdom of Israel forever—and his descendants will always be kings.'"

[15]So Nathan told King David everything the Lord had said.

David Accepts God's Promise

[16]Then King David went in and sat before the Lord and said, "Who am I, O Lord God, and what is my family that you have given me all this? [17]For all the great things you have already done for me are nothing in comparison to what you have promised to do in the future! For now, O Lord God, you are speaking of future generations of my children being kings too! You speak as though I were someone very great. [18]What else can I say? You know that I am but a dog, yet you have decided to honor me! [19]O Lord, you have given me these wonderful promises just because you want to be kind to me, because of your own great heart. [20]O Lord, there is no one like you—there is no other God. In fact, we have never even heard of another god like you!

[21]"And what other nation in all the earth is like Israel? You have made a unique nation and have redeemed it from Egypt so that the people could be your people. And you made a great name for yourself when you did glorious miracles in driving out the nations from before your people. [22]You have declared that your people Israel belong to you forever, and you have become their God.

[23]"And now I accept your promise, Lord, that I and my children will always rule this nation. [24]And may this bring eternal honor to your name as everyone realizes that you always do what you say. They will exclaim, 'The Lord of heaven is indeed the God of Israel!' And Israel shall always be ruled by my children and their posterity! [25]Now I have the courage to pray to you, for you have revealed this to me. [26]God himself has promised this good thing to me! [27]May this blessing rest upon my children forever, for when you grant a blessing, Lord, it is an eternal blessing!"

CHAPTER 18

David Conquers Many Enemies

David finally subdued the Philistines and conquered Gath and its surrounding towns. [2]He also conquered Moab and required its people to send him a large sum of money every year. [3]He conquered the dominion of King Hadadezer of Zobah (as far as Hamath) at the time Hadadezer went to tighten his grip along the Euphrates River. [4]David captured a thousand of his chariots, seven thousand cavalry, and twenty thousand troops. He crippled

17:3-4 It is easy to become enamoured with the plans we make. We must remember, however, that God has veto power even over good ideas. Nathan, who had approved the idea of the Temple earlier, discovered that the timing was wrong. We tend to believe that if we desire a good thing, God's timing for it is now! Sometimes in recovery, progress may not come as quickly or smoothly as we would like it to. But we must learn that the only successful recovery program is the one submitted to God's control and timing.

17:9-10 As always, God had a better idea. David wanted to build God a house—and that was a good idea. But God assigned that job to Solomon, David's son. More important, God promised to build a "house" for David—a dynasty that would reign forever. From that dynasty came David's greater son, Jesus Christ, who provides salvation for all willing to receive it! This promise to David became a promise for all who need to recover from the powerful effects of sin.

all the chariot teams except a hundred that he
kept for his own use.
5When the Syrians arrived from Damascus
to help King Hadadezer, David killed twenty-
two thousand of them; 6then he placed a
garrison of his troops in Damascus, the Syrian
capital. So the Syrians, too, were forced to
send him large amounts of money every year.
And the Lord gave David victory everywhere
he went. 7He brought the gold shields of King
Hadadezer's officers to Jerusalem, 8as well as a
great amount of bronze from Hadadezer's cities of Tibhath and Cun. (King Solomon later
melted the bronze and used it for the Temple.
He molded it into the bronze tank, the pillars,
and the instruments used in offering sacrifices
on the altar.)
9When King Tou of Hamath learned that
King David had destroyed Hadadezer's army,
10he sent his son Hadoram to greet and congratulate King David on his success and to
present him with many gifts of gold, silver,
and bronze, seeking an alliance. For Hadadezer and Tou had been enemies and there had
been many wars between them. 11King David
dedicated these gifts to the Lord, as he did the
silver and gold he took from the nations of
Edom, Moab, Ammon, Amalek, and the Philistines.
12Abishai (son of Zeruiah) then destroyed
eighteen thousand Edomites in the Valley of
Salt. 13He put garrisons in Edom and forced
the Edomites to pay large sums of money
annually to David. This is just another example of how the Lord gave David victory after
victory. 14David reigned over all of Israel and
was a just ruler.
15Joab (son of Zeruiah) was commander-in-
chief of the army; Jehoshaphat (son of Ahilud) was the historian; 16Zadok (son of Ahitub)
and Ahimelech (son of Abiathar) were the
head priests; Shavsha was the king's special
assistant; 17Benaiah (son of Jehoiada) was in
charge of the king's bodyguard—the Cherethites and Pelethites—and David's sons were his
chief aides.

CHAPTER 19

David Defends Israel's Honor

When King Nahash of Ammon died, his son
Hanun became the new king.
2,3Then David declared, "I am going to
show friendship to Hanun because of all the
kind things his father did for me."

So David sent a message of sympathy to
Hanun for the death of his father. But when
David's ambassadors arrived, King Hanun's
counselors warned him, "Don't fool yourself
that David has sent these men to honor your
father! They are here to spy out the land so
that they can come in and conquer it!"
4So King Hanun insulted King David's ambassadors by shaving their beards and cutting
their robes off at the middle to expose their
buttocks; then he sent them back to David in
shame. 5When David heard what had happened, he sent a message to his embarrassed
emissaries, telling them to stay at Jericho until
their beards had grown out again. 6When
King Hanun realized his mistake he sent
$2,000,000 to enlist mercenary troops, chari-
ots, and cavalry from Mesopotamia, Aram-
maacah, and Zobah. 7He hired thirty-two
thousand chariots, as well as the support of
the king of Maacah and his entire army. These
forces camped at Medeba where they were
joined by the troops King Hanun had recruited from his cities.

18:4 Why did David cripple the horses? God had commanded that Israel's kings never build up large stables of horses (Deuteronomy 17:16). God wanted Israel to depend on him for protection, not on great armies of chariots and horses. This is an important principle for us to keep in mind. Only God can truly protect us and give us the power to overcome our dependencies and compulsions. We must be sure that as we build human means to support our recovery, we don't forget to seek God and lean on him. Our personal resources are never sufficient for success; we must learn to depend on God's power.

19:1-4 The distrust of Hanun's men caused them to misread David's friendly overtures. So instead of building a strong relationship with Israel, they created a destructive one. We often make the same mistake, especially if we have been disappointed by the people we love. If we are lied to, we learn to distrust others. This causes us to cut off even the healthy relationships offered to us. We must learn how to discern between the people we can trust and those we can't. Honest relationships are extremely important, and we cannot afford to alienate the people who will support our recovery.

19:5 In this very delicate situation, David showed deep sensitivity to the embarrassment of his ambassadors. He gave them time to recover their dignity before returning home. Surely there is a lesson here for all of us. Like David, we need to exhibit sensitivity to others as they deal with embarrassing issues. This is part of learning to support others in their recovery.

8 When David learned of this, he sent Joab
and the mightiest warriors of Israel. 9 The
army of Ammon went out to meet them and
began the battle at the gates of the city of
Medeba. Meanwhile, the mercenary forces
were out in the field. 10 When Joab realized
that the enemy forces were both in front and
behind him, he divided his army and sent one
group to engage the Syrians. 11 The other
group, under the command of his brother
Abishai, moved against the Ammonites.
12 "If the Syrians are too strong for me, come
and help me," Joab told his brother; "and if
the Ammonites are too strong for you, I'll
come and help you. 13 Be courageous and let
us act like men to save our people and the
cities of our God. And may the Lord do what
is best."
14 So Joab and his troops attacked the Syrians, and the Syrians turned and fled. 15 When
the Ammonites, under attack by Abishai's
troops, saw that the Syrians were retreating,
they fled into the city. Then Joab returned to
Jerusalem.
16 After their defeat, the Syrians summoned
additional troops from east of the Euphrates
River, led personally by Shophach, King Hadadezer's commander-in-chief. 17,18 When this
news reached David, he mobilized all Israel,
crossed the Jordan River, and engaged the enemy troops in battle. But the Syrians again fled
from David, and he killed seven thousand
charioteers and forty thousand of their troops.
He also killed Shophach, the commander-in-
chief of the Syrian army. 19 Then King Hadadezer's troops surrendered to King David and
became his subjects. And never again did the
Syrians aid the Ammonites in their battles.

CHAPTER 20

David Defeats the Ammonites

The following spring (spring was the season when wars usually began) Joab led the
Israeli army in successful attacks against
the cities and villages of the people of Ammon. After destroying them, he laid siege
to Rabbah and conquered it. Meanwhile,
David had stayed in Jerusalem. 2 When
David arrived on the scene, he removed the
crown from the head of King Milcom of
Rabbah and placed it upon his own head. It
was made of gold inlaid with gems and
weighed seventy-five pounds! David also
took great amounts of plunder from the
city. 3 He drove the people from the city and
set them to work with saws, iron picks, and
axes, as was his custom with all the conquered Ammonite peoples. Then David
and all his army returned to Jerusalem.

David Fights the Philistines

4 The next war was against the Philistines
again, at Gezer. But Sibbecai, a man from
Hushath, killed one of the sons of the giant,
Sippai, and so the Philistines surrendered.
5 During another war with the Philistines, Elhanan (the son of Jair) killed Lahmi, the
brother of Goliath the giant; the handle of his
spear was like a weaver's beam! 6,7 During another battle, at Gath, a giant with six fingers
on each hand and six toes on each foot (his
father was also a giant) defied and taunted
Israel; but he was killed by David's nephew
Jonathan, the son of David's brother Shimea.
8 These giants were descendants of the giants
of Gath, and they were killed by David and his
soldiers.

19:13 Joab's words here are worth remembering. He began by calling his men to act, but he also recognized that ultimately God was in control. In recovery we need to keep the same tension before us. We are responsible to act. We must strike out boldly to seek our recovery. Yet we are ultimately powerless and in desperate need of God's help. We need to continually leave things in God's hands and seek his will. As we face the trials of recovery, we can rest assured of God's powerful help, but we also need to take responsibility for our situation and act accordingly.

20:1-8 David knew who his enemies were, and he acted accordingly. With God's help he overcame each one in turn. We often make the mistake of allowing enemies into our life. We invite in people and activities dangerous to our health and treat them as our friends. David understood who his enemies were. In spiritual battle, we need to identify our enemies and act accordingly.

21:1 As we read the accounts of David's life, we would probably identify David's greatest sin as his episode of adultery, betrayal, and murder. However, God's evaluation of David's greatest sin seems to be somewhat different. Although God punished David for his acts of adultery and murder, the punishment suffered for David's census was far greater and more widespread. What was wrong with counting the people? David was counting the people to assess their human strength. He was putting his trust in Israel's numbers and the army it could muster. He had forgotten that with God's help, they needed no army at all to achieve victory. We often make the same mistake. We seek to do things in our own strength, rather than depending on God's. Seeking recovery through human strength alone will only end in disaster.

CHAPTER 21

Israel Suffers for David's Census

Then Satan brought disaster upon Israel, for he made David decide to take a census.

[2]"Take a complete census throughout the land and bring me the totals," he told Joab and the other leaders.

[3]But Joab objected. "If the Lord were to multiply his people a hundred times, would they not all be yours? So why are you asking us to do this? Why must you cause Israel to sin?"

[4]But the king won the argument, and Joab did as he was told; he traveled all through Israel and returned to Jerusalem. [5]The total population figure which he gave came to 1,100,000 men of military age in Israel and 470,000 in Judah. [6]But he didn't include the tribes of Levi and Benjamin in his figures because he was so distressed at what the king had made him do.

[7]And God, too, was displeased with the census and punished Israel for it.

[8]But David said to God, "I am the one who has sinned. Please forgive me, for I realize now how wrong I was to do this."

[9]Then the Lord said to Gad, David's personal prophet, [10,11]"Go and tell David, 'The Lord has offered you three choices. Which will you choose? [12]You may have three years of famine, or three months of destruction by the enemies of Israel, or three days of deadly plague as the angel of the Lord brings destruction to the land. Think it over and let me know what answer to return to the one who sent me.'"

[13]"This is a terrible decision to make," David replied, "but let me fall into the hands of the Lord rather than into the power of men, for God's mercies are very great."

[14]So the Lord sent a plague upon Israel and 70,000 men died as a result. [15]During the plague God sent an angel to destroy Jerusalem; but then he felt such compassion that he changed his mind and commanded the destroying angel, "Stop! It is enough!" (The angel of the Lord was standing at the time by the threshing-floor of Ornan the Jebusite.) [16]When David saw the angel of the Lord standing between heaven and earth with his sword drawn, pointing toward Jerusalem, he and the elders of Israel clothed themselves in sackcloth and fell to the ground before the Lord.

[17]And David said to God, "I am the one who sinned by ordering the census. But what have these sheep done? O Lord my God, destroy me and my family, but do not destroy your people."

[18]Then the angel of the Lord told Gad to instruct David to build an altar to the Lord at the threshing-floor of Ornan the Jebusite. [19,20]So David went to see Ornan, who was threshing wheat at the time. Ornan saw the angel as he turned, and his four sons ran and hid. [21]Then Ornan saw the king approaching. So he left the threshing-floor and bowed to the ground before King David.

[22]David said to Ornan, "Let me buy this threshing-floor from you at its full price; then I will build an altar to the Lord and the plague will stop."

[23]"Take it, my lord, and use it as you wish," Ornan said to David. "Take the oxen, too, for burnt offerings; use the threshing instruments for wood for the fire and use the wheat for the grain offering. I give it all to you."

[24]"No," the king replied, "I will buy it for the full price; I cannot take what is yours and give it to the Lord. I will not offer a burnt offering that has cost me nothing!"

[25]So David paid Ornan $4,300 in gold [26]and built an altar to the Lord there, and sacrificed burnt offerings and peace offerings upon it; and he called out to the Lord, who answered by sending down fire from heaven to burn up the offering on the altar. [27]Then the Lord commanded the angel to put back his sword into its sheath; [28]and when David saw that the Lord had answered his plea, he sacrificed to him again. [29]The Tabernacle and altar made by Moses in the wilderness were on the hill of

21:9-13 Have you ever been trapped by a dilemma? All the options open to you seem to be bad choices. Here David faced a dilemma where all three choices would bring terrible consequences. God offered him either (1) three years of famine, (2) three months of destruction by Israel's enemies, or (3) three days of a deadly plague. David chose the plague, and even though 70,000 men died as a result, he had made the best choice of the three. May God deliver us from situations where all of the options have severe consequences!

21:17 It is a terrible thing, but very often our personal sins have consequences in the lives of other people. David was aware that the people of his kingdom would suffer for his personal sin. It is heartrending to hear David's admission of guilt. He accepted full responsibility for his error. Then he prayed diligently for the rescue of his people. When people close to us suffer for our sins, we would be wise to pray that God would give them special grace to overcome the consequences of our failure.

Gibeon, [30]but David didn't have time to go there to plead before the Lord, for he was terrified by the drawn sword of the angel of Jehovah.

CHAPTER 22
David Prepares to Build the Temple

Then David said, "Right here at Ornan's threshing-floor is the place where I'll build the Temple of the Lord and construct the altar for Israel's burnt offering!"

[2]David now drafted all the resident aliens in Israel to prepare blocks of squared stone for the Temple. [3]They also manufactured iron into the great quantity of nails needed for the doors in the gates and for the clamps; and they smelted so much bronze that it was too much to weigh. [4]The men of Tyre and Sidon brought great rafts of cedar logs to David.

[5]"Solomon my son is young and tender," David said, "and the Temple of the Lord must be a marvelous structure, famous and glorious throughout the world; so I will begin the preparations for it now."

So David collected the construction materials before his death. [6]He now commanded his son Solomon to build a temple for the Lord God of Israel.

[7]"I wanted to build it myself," David told him, [8]"but the Lord said not to do it. 'You have killed too many men in great wars,' he told me. 'You have reddened the ground before me with blood: so you are not to build my Temple. [9]But I will give you a son,' he told me, 'who will be a man of peace, for I will give him peace with his enemies in the surrounding lands. His name shall be Solomon (meaning "Peaceful"), and I will give peace and quietness to Israel during his reign. [10]He shall build my Temple, and he shall be as my own son and I will be his father; and I will cause his sons and his descendants to reign over every generation of Israel.'

[11]"So now, my son, may the Lord be with you and prosper you as you do what he told you to do and build the Temple of the Lord. [12]And may the Lord give you the good judgment to follow all his laws when he makes you king of Israel. [13]For if you carefully obey the rules and regulations that he gave to Israel through Moses, you will prosper. Be strong and courageous, fearless and enthusiastic!

[14]"By hard work I have collected several billion dollars worth of gold bullion, millions in silver, and so much iron and bronze that I haven't even weighed it; I have also gathered timber and stone for the walls. This is at least a beginning, something with which to start. [15]And you have many skilled stonemasons and carpenters and craftsmen of every kind. [16]They are expert gold and silver smiths and bronze and iron workers. So get to work, and may the Lord be with you!"

[17]Then David ordered all the leaders of Israel to assist his son in this project.

[18]"The Lord your God is with you," he declared. "He has given you peace with the surrounding nations, for I have conquered them in the name of the Lord and for his people. [19]Now try with every fiber of your being to obey the Lord your God, and you will soon be bringing the Ark and the other holy articles of worship into the Temple of the Lord!"

CHAPTER 23
Duties of the Levites

By this time David was an old, old man, so he stepped down from the throne and appointed his son Solomon as the new king of Israel. [2]He summoned all the political and religious leaders of Israel for the coronation ceremony. [3]At this time a census was taken of the men of the

22:1-5 Although David would never build the Temple, he collected numerous materials for the project. A whole chapter is dedicated to David's preparations for building the Temple. What does this have to do with recovery? Any rebuilding project needs careful planning and the necessary materials and resources to get the job done. We need to assess our needs and seek the help and resources we need to support us in our recovery process.

22:6-19 In these verses, we are told of some of the spiritual preparations necessary for building the Temple. It is true that material preparations are essential for any building or rebuilding project, but the spiritual preparations are even more important. Even as David helped Solomon define the goals and procedures, so must we define these same elements for our recovery programs.

23:1-2 At a certain point in his life, David stepped down from his position of responsibility. Since many of us derive our self-worth from our activities, this is often a difficult thing to do. But none of us can take responsibility for everything. There are some matters that we are not capable of handling. We may need to relinquish some of our burdens to others. This is an important issue in recovery. We need to determine our limits and then stand by them. Being overly responsible can be just as destructive as being irresponsible.

tribe of Levi who were thirty years or older. The total came to 38,000.

[4,5]"Twenty-four thousand of them will supervise the work at the Temple," David instructed, "6,000 are to be bailiffs and judges, 4,000 will be temple guards, and 4,000 will praise the Lord with the musical instruments I have made."

[6]Then David divided them into three main divisions named after the sons of Levi—the Gershom division, the Kohath division, and the Merari division.

[7]Subdivisions of the *Gershom* corps were named after his sons Ladan and Shimei. [8,9]These subdivisions were still further divided into six groups named after the sons of *Ladan:* Jehiel the leader, Zetham, Joel; and the sons of *Shimei* — Shelomoth, Haziel, and Haran.

[10,11]The subclans of *Shimei* were named after his four sons: Jahath was greatest, Zizah was next, and Jeush and Beriah were combined into a single subclan because neither had many sons.

[12]The division of Kohath was subdivided into four groups named after his sons Amram, Izhar, Hebron, and Uzziel.

[13]*Amram* was the ancestor of Aaron and Moses. Aaron and his sons were set apart for the holy service of sacrificing the people's offerings to the Lord. He served the Lord constantly and pronounced blessings in his name at all times.

[14,15]As for Moses, the man of God, his sons, Gershom and Eliezer, were included with the tribe of Levi. [16]*Gershom's* sons were led by Shebuel, [17]and *Eliezer's* only son, Rehabiah, was the leader of his clan, for he had many children.

[18]The sons of *Izhar* were led by Shelomith.

[19]The sons of *Hebron* were led by Jeriah. Amariah was second in command, Jahaziel was third, and Jekameam was fourth.

[20]The sons of *Uzziel* were led by Micah, and Isshiah was the second in command.

[21]The sons of *Merari* were Mahli and Mushi. The sons of *Mahli* were Eleazar and Kish. [22]*Eleazar* died without any sons, and his daughters were married to their cousins, the sons of *Kish.* [23]*Mushi's* sons were Mahli, Eder, and Jeremoth.

[24]In the census, all the men of Levi who were twenty years old or older were classified under the names of these clans and subclans; and they were all assigned to the ministry at the Temple. [25]For David said, "The Lord God of Israel has given us peace, and he will always live in Jerusalem. [26]Now the Levites will no longer need to carry the Tabernacle and its instruments from place to place."

[27](This census of the tribe of Levi was one of the last things David did before his death.) [28]The work of the Levites was to assist the priests—the descendants of Aaron—in the sacrifices at the Temple; they also did the custodial work and helped perform the ceremonies of purification. [29]They provided the Bread of the Presence, the flour for the grain offerings, and the wafers made without yeast (either fried or mixed with olive oil); they also checked all the weights and measures. [30]Each morning and evening they stood before the Lord to sing thanks and praise to him. [31]They assisted in the special sacrifices of burnt offerings, the Sabbath sacrifices, the new moon celebrations, and at all the festivals. There were always as many Levites present as were required for the occasion. [32]And they took care of the Tabernacle and the Temple and assisted the priests in whatever way they were needed.

CHAPTER 24

Duties of the Priests

The priests (the descendants of Aaron) were placed into two divisions named after Aaron's sons, Eleazar and Ithamar.

Nadab and Abihu were also sons of Aaron, but they died before their father did and had

23:3-23 The Levites were called to serve in God's Temple, and here the program for their service is outlined. In order for the Levites to work effectively, a detailed system had to be set up. Duties had to be defined and assigned. In recovery we also need to define our relationships and responsibilities in ways that are workable and fair. When expectations are clear, our relationships will run more smoothly. Understanding our role in any family or organization is essential in order for our life to make sense.

23:24-31 These verses contain a new job description for Levites. Notice that some of the traditional levitical tasks were no longer necessary. They no longer needed to transport the Tabernacle. To deal with changes in the times, the role of the Levites was adjusted. Such changes were still under God's control. The role we play in our relationships also changes with time. We may have been dysfunctional in our marriage and family, but with our recovery we will experience some changes. We need to be willing to assess our former role in relationships and make the changes needed to function effectively in the places God puts us.

no children; so only Eleazar and Ithamar were left to carry on. 3David consulted with Zadok, who represented the Eleazar clan, and with Ahimelech, who represented the Ithamar clan; then he divided Aaron's descendants into many groups to serve at various times. 4*Eleazar's* descendants were divided into sixteen groups and *Ithamar's* into eight (for there was more leadership ability among the descendants of Eleazar).

5All tasks were assigned to the various groups by coin-toss so that there would be no preference, for there were many famous men and high officials of the Temple in each division. 6Shemaiah, a Levite and the son of Nethanel, acted as recording secretary and wrote down the names and assignments in the presence of the king and of these leaders: Zadok the priest, Ahimelech the son of Abiathar, and the heads of the priests and Levites. Two groups from the division of Eleazar and one from the division of Ithamar were assigned to each task.

7-18The work was assigned (by coin-toss) in this order:

First, the group led by Jehoiarib;
Second, the group led by Jedaiah;
Third, the group led by Harim;
Fourth, the group led by Seorim;
Fifth, the group led by Malchijah;
Sixth, the group led by Mijamin;
Seventh, the group led by Hakkoz;
Eighth, the group led by Ahijah;
Ninth, the group led by Jeshua;
Tenth, the group led by Shecaniah;
Eleventh, the group led by Eliashib;
Twelfth, the group led by Jakim;
Thirteenth, the group led by Huppah;
Fourteenth, the group led by Jeshebeab;
Fifteenth, the group led by Bilgah;
Sixteenth, the group led by Immer;
Seventeenth, the group led by Hezir;
Eighteenth, the group led by Happizzez;
Nineteenth, the group led by Pethahiah;
Twentieth, the group led by Jehezkel;
Twenty-first, the group led by Jachin;
Twenty-second, the group led by Gamul;
Twenty-third, the group led by Delaiah;
Twenty-fourth, the group led by Maaziah.

19Each group carried out the Temple duties as originally assigned by God through their ancestor Aaron.

20These were the other descendants of Levi: Amram; his descendant Shubael; and Shubael's descendant Jehdeiah; 21the Rehabiah group, led by his oldest son Isshiah; 22the Izhar group, consisting of Shelamoth and his descendant Jahath. 23The Hebron group: Jeriah, Hebron's oldest son; Amariah, his second son; Jahaziel, his third son; Jekameam, his fourth son.

24,25The Uzziel group was led by his son Micah and his grandsons Shamir and Isshiah, and by Isshiah's son Zechariah.

26,27The Merari group was led by his sons: Mahli and Mushi. (Jaaziah's group, led by his son Beno, included his brothers Shoham, Zaccur, and Ibri.) 28*Mahli's* descendants were Eleazar, who had no sons, 29and Kish, among whose sons was Jerahmeel. 30The sons of *Mushi* were Mahli, Eder, and Jerimoth.

These were the descendants of Levi in their various clans. 31Like the descendants of Aaron, they were assigned to their duties by coin-toss without distinction as to age or rank. It was done in the presence of King David, Zadok, Ahimelech, and the leaders of the priests and the Levites.

CHAPTER 25

Duties of the Musicians

David and the officials of the Tabernacle then appointed men to prophesy to the accompaniment of zithers, harps, and cymbals. These men were from the groups of Asaph, Heman, and Jeduthun. Here is a list of their names and their work:

2Under the leadership of Asaph, the king's private prophet, were his sons Zaccur, Joseph, Nethaniah, and Asharelah.

3Under Jeduthun, who led in giving thanks and praising the Lord (while accompanied by the zither), were his six sons: Gedaliah, Zeri, Jeshaiah, Shimei, Hashabiah, and Mattithiah.

4,5Under the direction of Heman, the king's private chaplain, were his sons: Bukkiah, Mattaniah, Uzziel, Shebuel, Jerimoth, Hananiah, Hanani, Eliathah, Geddalti, Romamti-ezer, Joshbekashah, Mallothi, Hothir, and Mahazioth. (For God had honored him with fourteen sons and three daughters.) 6,7Their music ministry included the playing of cymbals, harps, and zithers; all were under the direction of their father as they performed this ministry in the Tabernacle.

Asaph, Jeduthun, and Heman reported directly to the king. They and their families were all trained in singing praises to the Lord; each one—288 of them in all—was a master musician. 8The singers were appointed to their particular term of service by coin-toss, without regard to age or reputation.

[9-31]The first toss indicated Joseph of the Asaph clan;
The second, Gedaliah, along with twelve of his sons and brothers;
The third, Zaccur and twelve of his sons and brothers;
The fourth, Izri and twelve of his sons and brothers;
Fifth, Nethaniah and twelve of his sons and brothers;
Sixth, Bukkiah and twelve of his sons and brothers;
Seventh, Jesharelah and twelve of his sons and brothers;
Eighth, Jeshaiah and twelve of his sons and brothers;
Ninth, Mattaniah and twelve of his sons and brothers;
Tenth, Shimei and twelve of his sons and brothers;
Eleventh, Azarel and twelve of his sons and brothers;
Twelfth, Hashabiah and twelve of his sons and brothers;
Thirteenth, Shubael and twelve of his sons and brothers;
Fourteenth, Mattithiah and twelve of his sons and brothers;
Fifteenth, Jeremoth and twelve of his sons and brothers;
Sixteenth, Hananiah and twelve of his sons and brothers;
Seventeenth, Joshbekasha and twelve of his sons and brothers;
Eighteenth, Hanani and twelve of his sons and brothers;
Nineteenth, Mallothi and twelve of his sons and brothers;
Twentieth, Eliathah and twelve of his sons and brothers;
Twenty-first, Hothir and twelve of his sons and brothers;
Twenty-second, Giddalti and twelve of his sons and brothers;
Twenty-third, Mahazioth and twelve of his sons and brothers;
Twenty-fourth, Romamti-ezer and twelve of his sons and brothers.

CHAPTER 26

Duties of the Temple Guard

The temple guards were from the Asaph division of the Korah clan. The captain of the guard was Meshelemiah, the son of Kore.

[2,3]His sergeants were his sons: Zechariah (the oldest), Jediael (the second), Zebadiah (the third), Jathniel (the fourth), Elam (the fifth), Jehohanan (the sixth), Eliehoenai (the seventh).

[4,5]The sons of Obed-edom were also appointed as Temple guards: Shemaiah (the oldest), Jehozabad (the second), Joah (the third), Sacar (the fourth), Nethanel (the fifth), Ammiel (the sixth), Issachar (the seventh), Peullethai (the eighth).

What a blessing God gave him with all those sons!

[6,7]Shemaiah's sons were all outstanding men and had positions of great authority in their clan. Their names were: Othni, Rephael, Obed, Elzabad.

Their brave brothers, Elihu and Semachiah, were also very able men.

[8]All of these sons and grandsons of Obed-edom—all sixty-two of them—were outstanding men who were particularly well qualified for their work. [9]Meshelemiah's eighteen sons and brothers, too, were real leaders. [10]Hosah, one of the Merari group, appointed Shimri as the leader among his sons, though he was not the oldest. [11]The names of some of his other sons were: Hilkiah, the second; Tebaliah, the third; Zechariah, the fourth.

Hosah's sons and brothers numbered thirteen in all.

[12]The divisions of the Temple guards were named after the leaders. Like the other Levites, they were responsible to minister at the Temple. [13]They were assigned guard duty at the various gates without regard to the reputation of their families, for it was all done by coin-toss. [14,15]The responsibility of the east gate went to Shelemiah and his group; of the north gate to his son Zechariah, a man of unusual wisdom; of the south gate to Obed-edom and his group (his sons were given charge of the storehouses); [16]of the west gate and the Shallecheth Gate on the upper road, to Shuppim and Hosah. [17]Six guards were assigned daily to the east gate, four to the north

26:1-32 God wants all kinds of people to serve him. Not everyone is a musician or worship leader. Not everyone is gifted with a golden tongue. This chapter reminds us that gatekeepers, ushers, financial officers, and those essential to running the services are also valued by God. These duties, which we might consider mundane, are of great importance. God values our service even if few people ever become aware of it.

gate, four to the south gate, and two to each
of the storehouses. [18]Six guards were assigned
each day to the west gate, four to the upper
road, and two to the nearby areas. [19]The
Temple guards were chosen from the clans of
Korah and Merari.

Duties of Other Officials

[20-22]Other Levites, led by Ahijah, were given
the care of the gifts brought to the Lord and
placed in the Temple treasury. These men of
the Ladan subclan from the clan of Gershom
included Zetham and Joel, the sons of Jehieli.
[23,24]Shebuel, son of Gershom and grandson of
Moses, was the chief officer of the treasury. He
was in charge of the divisions named after
Amram, Izhar, Hebron, and Uzziel.

[25]The line of descendants from Eliezer went
through Rehabiah, Jeshaiah, Joram, Zichri,
and Shelomoth. [26]Shelomoth and his brothers
were appointed to care for the gifts given to
the Lord by King David and the other leaders
of the nation such as the officers and generals
of the army. [27]For these men dedicated their
war loot to support the operating expenses of
the Temple. [28]Shelomoth and his brothers
were also responsible for the care of the items
dedicated to the Lord by Samuel the prophet,
Saul the son of Kish, Abner the son of Ner,
Joab the son of Zeruiah, and anyone else of
distinction who brought gifts to the Lord.

[29]Chenaniah and his sons (from the subclan of Izhar) were appointed public administrators and judges. [30]Hashabiah and 1,700 of
his clansmen from Hebron, all outstanding
men, were placed in charge of the territory of
Israel west of the Jordan River; they were
responsible for the religious affairs and public
administration of that area. [31,32]Twenty-seven
hundred outstanding men of the clan of the
Hebronites, under the supervision of Jerijah,
were appointed to control the religious and
public affairs of the tribes of Reuben, Gad, and
the half-tribe of Manasseh. These men, all of
whom had excellent qualifications, were appointed on the basis of their ancestry and
ability at Jazer in Gilead in the fortieth year of
King David's reign.

CHAPTER 27

Commanders of the Army

The Israeli army was divided into twelve regiments, each with 24,000 troops, including
officers and administrative staff. These units
were called up for active duty one month
each year. Here is the list of the units and their
regimental commanders:

[2,3]The commander of the First Division was
Jashobeam. He had charge of 24,000 troops
who were on duty the first month of each
year.

[4]The commander of the Second Division
was Dodai (a descendant of Ahohi). He had
charge of 24,000 troops who were on duty the
second month of each year. Mikloth was his
executive officer.

[5,6]The commander of the Third Division
was Benaiah. His 24,000 men were on duty
the third month of each year. (He was the son
of Jehoiada the High Priest and was the chief
of the thirty highest-ranking officers in
David's army.) His son Ammizabad succeeded
him as division commander.

[7]The commander of the Fourth Division
was Asahel (the brother of Joab), who was
later replaced by his son Zebadiah. He had
24,000 men on duty the fourth month of
each year.

[8]The commander of the Fifth Division was
Shamuth from Izrah, with 24,000 men on
duty the fifth month of each year.

[9]The commander of the Sixth Division was
Ira, the son of Ikkesh from Tekoa; he had
24,000 men on duty the sixth month of each
year.

[10]The commander of the Seventh Division
was Helez from Pelona in Ephraim, with
24,000 men on duty the seventh month of
each year.

[11]The commander of the Eighth Division
was Sibbecai of the Hushite subclan from Zerah, who had 24,000 men on duty the eighth
month of each year.

[12]The commander of the Ninth Division
was Abiezer (from Anathoth in the tribe of
Benjamin), who commanded 24,000 troops
during the ninth month of each year.

[13]The commander of the Tenth Division
was Maharai from Netophah in Zerah, with
24,000 men on duty the tenth month of each
year.

[14]The commander of the Eleventh Division
was Benaiah from Pirathon in Ephraim, with

27:1-34 If we want to succeed in the rebuilding process, we need to submit to some kind of authority structure. Believers need to set themselves under the authority of a local church body. We need to be accountable to others. Here is a chapter that establishes the proper lines of authority for the people of Israel. This should remind us of the importance of accountability in the rebuilding process.

24,000 men on duty during the eleventh
month of each year.
15The commander of the Twelfth Division
was Heldai from Netophah in the area of
Othniel, who commanded 24,000 men on
duty during the twelfth month of each year.

Officers of the Tribes

16-22The top political officers of the tribes of
Israel were as follows:

Over Reuben, Eliezer (son of Zichri);
Over Simeon, Shephatiah (son of Maacah);
Over Levi, Hashabiah (son of Kemuel);
Over the descendants of Aaron, Zadok;
Over Judah, Elihu (a brother of King David);
Over Issachar, Omri (son of Michael);
Over Zebulun, Ishmaiah (son of Obadiah);
Over Naphtali, Jeremoth (son of Azriel);
Over Ephraim, Hoshea (son of Azaziah);
Over the half-tribe of Manasseh, Joel (son of Pedaiah);
Over the other half of Manasseh, in Gilead, Iddo (son of Zechariah);
Over Benjamin, Jaasiel (son of Abner);
Over Dan, Azarel (son of Jeroham).

23When David took his census, he didn't
include the twenty-year-olds or those younger, for the Lord had promised a population
explosion for his people. 24Joab began the
census, but he never finished it, for the anger
of God broke out upon Israel; the final total
was never put into the annals of King David.

Administrators of the Kingdom

25Azmaveth (son of Adiel) was the chief financial officer in charge of the palace treasuries,
and Jonathan (son of Uzziah) was chief of the
regional treasuries throughout the cities, villages, and fortresses of Israel.
26Ezri (son of Chelub) was manager of the
laborers on the king's estates. 27And Shimei
from Ramath had the oversight of the king's
vineyards; and Zabdi from Shiphma was responsible for his wine production and storage. 28Baal-hanan from Gedera was
responsible for the king's olive yards and sycamore trees in the lowlands bordering Philistine territory, while Joash had charge of the
supplies of olive oil.
29Shitrai from Sharon was in charge of the
cattle on the Plains of Sharon, and Shaphat
(son of Adlai) had charge of those in the
valleys. 30Obil, from the territory of Ishmael,
had charge of the camels, and Jehdeiah from
Meronoth had charge of the donkeys. 31The
sheep were under the care of Jaziz the Hagrite.
These men were King David's overseers.
32The attendant to the king's sons was Jonathan, David's uncle, a wise counselor and an
educated man. Jehiel (the son of Hachmoni)
was their tutor.
33Ahithophel was the king's official counselor, and Hushai the Archite was his personal
advisor. 34Ahithophel was assisted by Jehoiada
(the son of Benaiah) and by Abiathar. Joab
was commander-in-chief of the Israeli army.

CHAPTER 28

David Instructs Solomon

David now summoned all of his officials to
Jerusalem—the political leaders, the commanders of the twelve army divisions, the
other army officers, those in charge of his
property and livestock, and all the other men
of authority in his kingdom. 2He rose and
stood before them and addressed them as
follows:
"My brothers and my people! It was my
desire to build a temple in which the Ark of
the Covenant of the Lord could rest—a place
for our God to live in. I have now collected
everything that is necessary for the building,
3but God has told me, 'You are not to build my
temple, for you are a warrior and have shed
much blood.'
4"Nevertheless, the Lord God of Israel has
chosen me from among all my father's family
to begin a dynasty that will rule Israel forever;
he has chosen the tribe of Judah, and from
among the families of Judah, my father's family; and from among his sons, the Lord took
pleasure in me and has made me king over all
Israel. 5And from among my sons—the Lord
has given me many children—he has chosen
Solomon to succeed me on the throne of his
Kingdom of Israel. 6He has told me, 'Your son
Solomon shall build my Temple; for I have
chosen him as my son and I will be his father.

28:8-10 David took the time to pass God's wisdom on to Solomon. He began by acknowledging God's promise of a dynasty that would rule Israel forever. But David recognized that in order to receive the blessings of this great promise, he and his descendants were responsible to obey God's commands. Likewise, our obedience to God's will is the only pathway to blessing for us and for our descendants.

READ 1 CHRONICLES 28:1-21

GOD grant me the serenity
to accept the things I cannot change
the courage to change the things I can
and the wisdom to know the difference
AMEN

Full recovery doesn't stop when our broken parts are repaired. It includes building a new life that's free, full, and rich. Fear of failure, humiliation, or disappointment can keep us from seeking life in all its fullness. It takes courage to dream of the life we truly desire.

King David dreamed of building a magnificent temple, the likes of which the world had never seen. In commissioning his son Solomon to do the work he said, "Every part of this blueprint . . . was given to me in writing from the hand of the Lord. . . . Be strong and courageous and get to work. Don't be frightened by the size of the task, for the Lord my God is with you; he will not forsake you" (1 Chronicles 28:19-20). The apostle Paul said, "We who believe are carefully joined together with Christ as parts of a beautiful, constantly growing temple for God" (Ephesians 2:21).

Just as David dreamed of building a magnificent temple, we can dare to dream of building a magnificent new life. God has the blueprint already drawn up. It's natural to fear that if we allow ourself to hope we'll only be disappointed again, or that we might start and fail, suffering public humiliation. But we need only to "be strong and courageous and get to work." We need not be frightened by the size of the task, for "God who began the good work within you will keep right on helping you grow in his grace until his task within you is finally finished" (Philippians 1:6). ***Turn to page 493, 2 Chronicles 15.***

7And if he continues to obey my commandments and instructions as he has until now, I will make his kingdom last forever.'"

8Then David turned to Solomon and said:
"Here before the leaders of Israel, the people of God, and in the sight of our God, I am instructing you to search out every commandment of the Lord so that you may continue to rule this good land and leave it to
your children to rule forever. 9Solomon, my
son, get to know the God of your fathers. Worship and serve him with a clean heart and a willing mind, for the Lord sees every heart and understands and knows every thought. If you seek him, you will find him; but if you forsake him, he will permanently throw you
aside. 10So be very careful, for the Lord has
chosen you to build his holy Temple. Be strong and do as he commands."

11Then David gave Solomon the blueprint
of the Temple and its surroundings—the treasuries, the upstairs rooms, the inside rooms,
and the sanctuary for the place of mercy. 12He
also gave Solomon his plans for the outer court, the outside rooms, the Temple storage areas, and the treasuries for the gifts dedicated by famous persons. For the Holy Spirit had
given David all these plans. 13The king also
passed on to Solomon the instructions concerning the work of the various groups of priests and Levites; and he gave specifications for each item in the Temple which was to be used for worship and sacrifice.

14David weighed out enough gold and silver
to make these various items, 15as well as the
specific amount of gold needed for the lampstands and lamps. He also weighed out enough silver for the silver candlesticks and
lamps, each according to its use. 16He weighed
out the gold for the table on which the Bread of the Presence would be placed and for the other gold tables, and he weighed the silver

for the silver tables. 17Then he weighed out the gold for the solid gold hooks used in handling the sacrificial meat and for the basins, cups, and bowls of gold and silver. 18Finally, he weighed out the refined gold for the altar of incense and for the gold angels whose wings were stretched over the Ark of the Covenant of the Lord.

19"Every part of this blueprint," David told Solomon, "was given to me in writing from the hand of the Lord." 20Then he continued, "Be strong and courageous and get to work. Don't be frightened by the size of the task, for the Lord my God is with you; he will not forsake you. He will see to it that everything is finished correctly. 21And these various groups of priests and Levites will serve in the Temple. Others with skills of every kind will volunteer, and the army and the entire nation are at your command."

CHAPTER 29

The People Bring Gifts

Then King David turned to the entire assembly and said: "My son Solomon, whom God has chosen to be the next king of Israel, is still young and inexperienced, and the work ahead of him is enormous; for the temple he will build is not just another building—it is for the Lord God himself! 2Using every resource at my command, I have gathered as much as I could for building it—enough gold, silver, bronze, iron, wood, and great quantities of onyx, other precious stones, costly jewels, and marble. 3And now, because of my devotion to the Temple of God, I am giving all of my own private treasures to aid in the construction. This is in addition to the building materials I have already collected. 4,5These personal contributions consist of millions of dollars of gold from Ophir and huge amounts of silver to be used for overlaying the walls of the buildings. It will also be used for the articles made of gold and silver and for the artistic decorations. Now then, who will follow my example? Who will give himself and all that he has to the Lord?"

6,7Then the clan leaders, the heads of the tribes, the army officers, and the administrative officers of the king pledged huge sums of gold, silver and foreign currency, also 675 tons of bronze and 3,750 tons of iron. 8They also contributed great amounts of jewelry, which were deposited at the Temple treasury with Jehiel (a descendant of Gershom). 9Everyone was excited and happy for this opportunity of service, and King David was moved with deep joy.

David Praises God

10While still in the presence of the whole assembly, David expressed his praises to the Lord: "O Lord God of our father Israel, praise your name for ever and ever! 11Yours is the mighty power and glory and victory and majesty. Everything in the heavens and earth is yours, O Lord, and this is your kingdom. We adore you as being in control of everything. 12Riches and honor come from you alone, and you are the Ruler of all mankind; your hand controls power and might, and it is at your discretion that men are made great and given strength. 13O our God, we thank you and praise your glorious name, 14but who am I and who are my people that we should be permitted to give anything to you? Everything we have has come from you, and we only give you what is yours already! 15For we are here for but a moment, strangers in the land as our fathers were before us; our days on earth are like a shadow, gone so soon, without a trace. 16O Lord our God, all of this material that we have gathered to build a temple for your holy name comes from you! It all belongs to you!

28:19 God had a plan for building the Temple in Jerusalem. Here David passed it on to Solomon, who would complete the project. God also has a plan for each of us, and his blueprint includes our recovery. Each of us is a "Temple" for the Holy Spirit; God actually dwells inside all his people. We are responsible to rebuild our life in a way worthy of the one who dwells there. Let us seek God's plan for healthy living and then do everything we can to rebuild according to that plan.

29:3 Setting proper priorities is a necessary step in our recovery. We need to put God first in our thinking. We also need to help others. David gave out of his own personal wealth and energy. His personal treasures would help support the work of God in Israel. His giving would also contribute to the blessings received by people worshiping at the Temple for generations to come.

29:11-12 David's prayer of praise is filled with truths important for recovery. It recognizes that God is the source of all true success. It ascribes all greatness, power, glory, victory, and majesty to him. It recognizes that God is the source of all riches and honor; God is sovereign over peoples, tongues, and nations. These are essential truths. We must daily affirm the truth that God is our source of strength. We are helpless on our own, but God is more than able to help us overcome the problems that assail us.

[17]I know, my God, that you test men to see if
they are good; for you enjoy good men. I have
done all this with good motives, and I have
watched your people offer their gifts willingly
and joyously.
[18]"O Lord, God of our fathers Abraham,
Isaac, and Israel! Make your people always
want to obey you, and see to it that their love
for you never changes. [19]Give my son Solomon a good heart toward God, so that he will
want to obey you in the smallest detail and
will look forward eagerly to finishing the
building of your temple, for which I have
made all of these preparations."
[20]Then David said to all the people, "Give
praise to the Lord your God!" And they did,
bowing low before the Lord and the king.
[21]The next day they brought a thousand
young bulls, a thousand rams, and a thousand
lambs as burnt offerings to the Lord; they also
offered drink offerings and many other sacrifices on behalf of all Israel. [22]Then they feasted
and drank before the Lord with great joy.
And again they crowned King David's son
Solomon as their king. They anointed him
before the Lord as their leader, and they
anointed Zadok as their priest. [23]So God appointed Solomon to take the throne of his
father David; and he prospered greatly, and all
Israel obeyed him. [24]The national leaders, the
army officers, and his brothers all pledged
their allegiance to King Solomon. [25]And the
Lord gave him great popularity with all the
people of Israel, and he amassed even greater
wealth and honor than his father.

David Dies at an Old Age

[26,27]David was king of the land of Israel for
forty years; seven of them during his reign in
Hebron and thirty-three in Jerusalem. [28]He
died at an old age, wealthy and honored; and
his son Solomon reigned in his place. [29]De-
tailed biographies of King David have been
written in the history of Samuel the prophet,
the history written by Nathan the prophet,
and in the history written by the prophet
Gad. [30]These accounts tell of his reign and of
his might and all that happened to him and
to Israel and to the kings of the nearby nations.

SECOND CHRONICLES

THE BIG PICTURE

A. THE REIGN OF SOLOMON (1:1–9:31)
B. THE DOWNWARD SLIDE OF THE KINGS (10:1–36:4)
  1. Rehoboam (10:1–13:22)
  2. Asa (14:1–16:14)
  3. Jehoshaphat (17:1–20:37)
  4. Jehoram and Athaliah (21:1–22:12)
  5. Joash (23:1–24:27)
  6. Amaziah (25:1-28)
  7. Uzziah (26:1-23)
  8. Jotham (27:1-9)
  9. Ahaz (28:1-27)
  10. Hezekiah (29:1–32:33)
  11. Manasseh (33:1-25)
  12. Josiah (34:1–35:27)
  13. Sons of Josiah (36:1-14)
    a. Jehoahaz (36:1-4)
    b. Jehoiakim (36:5-8)
    c. Grandson, Jehoiachin (36:9-10)
    d. Zedekiah (36:11-14)
C. JUDAH EXILED TO BABYLON (36:5-21)
D. THE DECREE OF HOPE (36:22-23)

The book of 2 Chronicles was originally part of a larger book that also included 1 Chronicles. It recorded Israel's history starting with a genealogy of Adam's descendants and ending with Israel in Babylonian captivity. This condensed history was written to give Israel hope as they sought to rebuild their nation after the Babylonian exile.

Second Chronicles begins on a high note, recording Solomon's great success at building God's Temple in Jerusalem. But after his good start, Solomon made some mistakes that were intensified by his son Rehoboam, leading to the division of Israel into two kingdoms (931 B.C.). The succession of David's royal descendants in the southern kingdom exhibited varying degrees of success or failure. Some attempted to break from the dysfunctional patterns and lead the people to examine their lives and turn back to God. Through these kings, God brought revival and renewal to Israel. But the kings who set their hearts against God led the people back into sinful ways. As a result, the kingdom of Judah was conquered, and the people were taken captive by Babylonian armies.

The account then follows David's royal line on a slow but steady decline toward destruction and exile. But when things look their blackest, the final verses leave us with a message of hope. King Cyrus of Persia, stirred by the spirit of God, issued a decree allowing the Jerusalem temple to be rebuilt. This would have shown the Jews seeking to rebuild Israel that God had been working behind the scenes on their behalf. Despite their past failures and lack of faith, God was graciously working to bring about their recovery.

THE BOTTOM LINE

PURPOSE: To record the history of Judah's kings, both those who obeyed God and those who sinned against him. Their examples would encourage and admonish the people to rebuild their nation according to God's program. AUTHOR: Unknown, but Jewish tradition attributes it to Ezra. AUDIENCE: The people of Israel after their return from exile in Babylon. DATE WRITTEN: Approximately 430 B.C. SETTING: The kingdom of Judah between Solomon's reign (979 B.C.) and the decree of Cyrus (539 B.C.). KEY VERSE: "Then if my people will humble themselves and pray, and search for me, and turn from their wicked ways, I will hear them from heaven and forgive their sins and heal their land" (7:14). KEY EVENTS: The spiritual revivals that occurred under Asa, Jehoshaphat, Joash, Hezekiah, and Josiah.

RECOVERY THEMES

The Necessity of Faithfulness: When a king came along that was faithful to God, the people followed his lead and experienced recovery and restoration. But the victories of one day did not mean they would automatically win the trials of the next. They had to persevere in their faithfulness through each new day. When the path of faithfulness was forsaken, the people returned to their false gods and false worship. Their disobedience stood in sharp contrast with their faithfulness in earlier days. When the principles they learned were not incorporated into their daily lives on a continual basis, they experienced only a shallow recovery, which quickly eroded as temptations presented themselves.

God Must Be the Focus of Our Recovery: This book was written to encourage the Jews after their return from Babylonian exile. In their humiliating captivity, the people had hit bottom. As they returned to rebuild their Temple, land, and nation, God wanted them to learn that any successful rebuilding program centered around the true worship of God. A recovery program that does not begin and end with God's power becomes empty and weak. We need to learn the lesson that the Israelites struggled to grasp throughout their history—genuine recovery begins, survives, and continues through dependence on God.

The Ups and Downs of Recovery: We might think that God is pleased with us only when we make steady forward progress in our recovery. If we slip backward, even a little, it is easy to feel that everything is lost. But for all of us, recovery has its ups and downs. In this book we see the Israelites following a recovery pattern that will eventually lead to destruction. They take three steps backward and then only one step forward. But if we can make more steps forward than we do backward, we are on the right track. Our recovery will progress as we depend upon God for strength and guidance.

With God There Is Always Hope: Even when things seem blackest, God is at work. When we are overwhelmed by circumstances and feel God has forsaken us, it might help to remember that we are feeling what the people of Judah must have felt in Babylon—that all is lost! We might be encouraged as we look at the surprising reversal of their circumstances. In the midst of their despair, Cyrus granted a decree that allowed them to return to Jerusalem to rebuild their Temple. When our life is turned over to God, we can be confident that even in our darkest hour, God is at work—and there is hope!

CHAPTER 1

Solomon Asks God for Wisdom

King David's son Solomon was now the undisputed ruler of Israel, for the Lord his God had made him a powerful monarch. 2,3 He summoned all the army officers and judges to Gibeon as well as all the political and religious leaders of Israel. He led them up to the hill to the old Tabernacle constructed by Moses, the Lord's assistant, while he was in the wilderness. 4 (There was a later Tabernacle in Jerusalem, built by King David for the Ark of God when he removed it from Kiriath-jearim.) 5,6 The bronze altar made by Bezalel (son of Uri, son of Hur) still stood in front of the old Tabernacle, and now Solomon and those he had invited assembled themselves before it, as he sacrificed upon it 1,000 burnt offerings to the Lord.

7 That night God appeared to Solomon and told him, "Ask me for anything, and I will give it to you!"

8 Solomon replied, "O God, you have been so kind and good to my father David, and now you have given me the kingdom—9 this is all I want! For you have fulfilled your promise to David my father and have made me king over a nation as full of people as the

---

1:1 We all want to succeed, whether at escaping destructive patterns or at establishing positive habits. At the outset of this book, God gave Solomon unprecedented success in everything he did. But notice that Solomon's success depended on God's presence with him. Our success in recovery is impossible without God's helping presence in our life. We must recognize this if we hope to make progress.

1:7 What might we request if God gave us this offer? Solomon asked for wisdom, passing over the opportunity to ask for wealth or power. Solomon made a request that would serve the best interests of his people. God was pleased with his selfless attitude and rewarded him with more power and wealth than he ever could have wished for. In recovery, we also need to delay gratification in our decisions. We need to realize that short-term pleasure yields trouble in the long run. A wise decision demands our consideration of the long-term consequences and whether or not we are in agreement with God's will. Keeping God's will in focus always yields the greatest rewards.

earth is full of dust! 10Now give me wisdom and knowledge to rule them properly, for who is able to govern by himself such a great nation as this one of yours?"

11God replied, "Because your greatest desire is to help your people, and you haven't asked for personal wealth and honor, and you haven't asked me to curse your enemies, and you haven't asked for a long life, but for wisdom and knowledge to properly guide my people—12yes, I am giving you the wisdom and knowledge you asked for! And I am also giving you riches, wealth, and honor such as no other king has ever had before you! And there will never again be so great a king in all the world!"

13Solomon then left the Tabernacle, returned down the hill, and went back to Jerusalem to rule Israel. 14He built up a huge force of 1,400 chariots and recruited 12,000 cavalry to guard the cities where the chariots were garaged, though some, of course, were stationed at Jerusalem near the king. 15During Solomon's reign, silver and gold were as plentiful in Jerusalem as rocks on the road! And expensive cedar lumber was used like common sycamore! 16Solomon sent horse-traders to Egypt to purchase entire herds at wholesale prices. 17At that time Egyptian chariots sold for $400 each and horses for $100, delivered at Jerusalem. Many of these were then resold to the kings of the Hittites and Syria.

CHAPTER 2

Solomon Plans the Temple

Solomon now decided that the time had come to build a temple for the Lord and a palace for himself. 2This required a force of 70,000 laborers, 80,000 stonecutters in the hills, and 3,600 foremen. 3Solomon sent an ambassador to King Hiram at Tyre, requesting shipments of cedar lumber such as Hiram had supplied to David when he was building his palace.

4"I am about to build a temple for the Lord my God," Solomon told Hiram. "It will be a place where I can burn incense and sweet spices before God, and display the special sacrificial bread, and sacrifice burnt offerings each morning and evening, and on the Sabbaths, and at the new moon celebration and other regular festivals of the Lord our God. For God wants Israel always to celebrate these special occasions. 5It is going to be a wonderful temple because he is a great God, greater than any other. 6But who can ever build him a worthy home? Not even the highest heaven would be beautiful enough! And who am I to be allowed to build a temple for God? But it will be a place to worship him.

7"So send me skilled craftsmen—goldsmiths and silversmiths, brass and iron workers; and send me weavers to make purple, crimson, and blue cloth; and skilled engravers to work beside the craftsmen of Judah and Jerusalem who were selected by my father David. 8Also send me cedar trees, fir trees, and algum trees from the Forests of Lebanon, for your men are without equal as lumbermen, and I will send my men to help them. 9An immense amount of lumber will be needed, for the temple I am going to build will be large and incredibly beautiful. 10As to the financial arrangements, I will pay your men 20,000 sacks of crushed wheat, 20,000 barrels of barley, 20,000 barrels of wine, and 20,000 barrels of olive oil."

11King Hiram replied to King Solomon: "It is because the Lord loves his people that he has made you their king! 12Blessed be the Lord God of Israel who made the heavens and the earth and who has given to David such a wise, intelligent, and understanding son to build God's Temple and a royal palace for himself.

2:1 In order to continue on the path of successful recovery, we must begin with the proper resolve. Solomon was anxious to fulfill the plans God had for him. He began by building the Temple—a huge task—perhaps even an impossible one! God has certain tasks ordained for each of us. Our recovery may be the place we should start. Some of these tasks will be difficult; some may even be impossible! But with God's help, we will be able to accomplish them.

2:5 Solomon's achievements for God were great. Here we are told why: "It is going to be a wonderful temple because he is a great God." The deeper our relationship with God, the more we will realize how much he deserves our obedience and service. The realization of God's great power and love should give us courage as we face the difficult task of recovery. And as we seek to rebuild, we will discover that God's power is sufficient for the task.

2:6 This verse reminds us of how great God really is. He is far greater than we can even imagine or understand. Solomon's Temple was one of the great triumphs of the ancient world, but even it was not good enough for God. God's greatness may discourage some of us. Why would such a great God bother with us? We need to learn that though God is great, he is also loving and gracious. He reaches out to sinful, weak people like us to bring about our restoration. And as great as God is, he certainly does not lack the power we need to accomplish our recovery.

13“I am sending you a master craftsman—my famous Huramabi! He is a brilliant man, 14the son of a Jewish woman from Dan in Israel; his father is from here in Tyre. He is a skillful goldsmith and silversmith, and also does exquisite work with brass and iron and knows all about stonework, carpentry, and weaving; and he is an expert in the dyeing of purple and blue linen and crimson cloth. He is an engraver besides, and an inventor! He will work with your craftsmen and those appointed by my lord David, your father.15So send along the wheat, barley, olive oil, and wine you mentioned, 16and we will begin cutting wood from the Lebanon mountains, as much as you need, and bring it to you in log floats across the sea to Joppa, and from there you can take them inland to Jerusalem.”

17Solomon now took a census of all foreigners in the country (just as his father David had done) and found that there were 153,600 of them. 18He indentured 70,000 as common laborers, 80,000 as loggers, and 3,600 as foremen.

CHAPTER 3

Temple Construction Begins

Finally the actual construction of the Temple began. Its location was in Jerusalem at the top of Mount Moriah, where the Lord had appeared to Solomon’s father, King David, and where the threshing-floor of Ornan the Jebusite had been. David had selected it as the site for the Temple. 2The actual construction began on the seventeenth day of April in the fourth year of King Solomon’s reign.

3The foundation was ninety feet long and thirty feet wide. 4A covered porch ran along the entire thirty-foot width of the Temple, with the inner walls and ceiling overlaid with pure gold! The roof was 180 feet high.

5The main part of the Temple was paneled with cypress wood, plated with pure gold, and engraved with palm trees and chains. 6Beautiful jewels were inlaid into the walls to add to the beauty; the gold, by the way, was of the best, from Parvaim. 7All the walls, beams, doors, and thresholds throughout the Temple were plated with gold, with angels engraved on the walls.

8Within the Temple, at one end, was the most sacred room—the Holy of Holies—thirty feet square. This too was overlaid with the finest gold, valued at millions of dollars. 9Twenty-six-ounce gold nails were used. The upper rooms were also plated with pure gold.

10Within the innermost room, the Holy of Holies, Solomon placed two sculptured statues of angels and plated them with gold. 11-13They stood on the floor facing the outer room, with wings stretched wingtip to wingtip across the room, from wall to wall. 14Across the entrance to this room he placed a veil of blue and crimson finespun linen, decorated with angels.

15At the front of the Temple were two pillars 52 1/2 feet high, topped by a 7 1/2-foot capital flaring out to the roof. 16He made chains and placed them on top of the pillars, with 100 pomegranates attached to the chains.17Then he set up the pillars at the front of the Temple, one on the right and the other on the left. And he gave them names: Jachin (the one on the right), and Boaz (the one on the left).

CHAPTER 4

Huramabi’s Skillful Work

He also made a bronze altar 30 feet long, 30 feet wide, and 15 feet high. 2Then he forged a huge round tank 15 feet across from rim to rim. The rim stood 7 1/2 feet above the floor, and was 45 feet around. 3The tank was encir-

---

3:3-17 This begins a description of the Temple’s specifications. We are overwhelmed by the immense wealth required to build it. Large projects always require great resources. This is especially true in personal recovery projects. God is the only one with sufficient resources for the huge task of personal recovery. We need to learn to depend on his power.

4:1 Immediately upon entering the Temple area, worshipers were confronted by the great bronze altar. This object would remind them that each individual was in great need of forgiveness. Great numbers of animal sacrifices were offered in payment for the people’s sins. Before any approach to God was possible, forgiveness had to be achieved through sacrifice. God made it possible for us to approach him through the death and resurrection of his Son. Even as we approach God for forgiveness, we also need to seek restoration with the people we have wronged. Only by seeking forgiveness will we ever break free from the bondage of our past failures.

4:2 The bronze tank is the item of furniture corresponding to the Tabernacle’s laver. As they did God’s work, the priests became covered with the blood of the dead sacrificial animals. They were in need of immediate cleansing. Likewise, we often encounter pollution in our daily walk. How wonderful to remember that our daily sin can be forgiven through Christ!

cled at its base by two rows of gourd designs,
cast as part of the tank. 4The tank stood on
twelve metal oxen facing outward; three
faced north, three faced west, three faced
south, and three faced east. 5The walls of the
tank were five inches thick, flaring out like the
cup of a lily. It held 3,000 barrels of water.

6He also constructed ten vats for water to
wash the offerings, five to the right of the
huge tank and five to the left. The priests used
the tank, and not the vats, for their own
washing.

7Carefully following God's instructions, he
then cast ten gold lampstands and placed
them in the Temple, five against each wall;
8he also built ten tables and placed five
against each wall on the right and left. And he
molded 100 solid gold bowls. 9Then he constructed a court for the priests, also the public
court, and overlaid the doors of these courts
with bronze. 10The huge tank was in the
southeast corner of the outer room of the
Temple. 11Huramabi also made the necessary
pots, shovels, and basins for use in connection with the sacrifices.

So at last he completed the work assigned
to him by King Solomon:

12-16The construction of the two pillars,
The two flared capitals on the tops of the
pillars,
The two sets of chains on the capitals,
The 400 pomegranates hanging from the
two sets of chains on the capitals,
The bases for the vats and the vats
themselves,
The huge tank and the twelve oxen under
it,
The pots, shovels, and fleshhooks.

This skillful craftsman, Huramabi, made all
of the above-mentioned items for King Solomon using polished bronze. 17,18The king did
the casting at the claybanks of the Jordan
valley between Succoth and Zeredah. Great
quantities of bronze were used, too heavy to
weigh.

19Solomon commanded that all of the furnishings of the Temple—the utensils, the altar, and the table for the Bread of the Presence
must be made of gold; 20also the lamps and
lampstands, 21the floral decorations, tongs,
22lamp snuffers, basins, spoons, and firepans—all were made of solid gold. Even the
doorway of the Temple, the main door, and
the inner doors to the Holy of Holies were
overlaid with gold.

CHAPTER 5

The Ark Is Brought to the Temple

So the Temple was finally finished. Then Solomon brought in the gifts dedicated to the
Lord by his father, King David. They were
stored in the Temple treasuries.

2Solomon now summoned to Jerusalem all
of the leaders of Israel—the heads of the tribes
and clans—for the ceremony of transferring
the Ark from the [Tabernacle in the] City of
David, also known as Zion, [to its new home
in the Temple]. 3This celebration took place in
October at the annual Festival of Tabernacles.
4,5As the leaders of Israel watched, the Levites
lifted the Ark and carried it out of the Tabernacle, along with all the other sacred vessels.
6King Solomon and the others sacrificed
sheep and oxen before the Ark in such numbers that no one tried to keep count!

7,8Then the priests carried the Ark into the
inner room of the Temple—the Holy of Holies—and placed it beneath the angels' wings;
their wings spread over the Ark and its carrying poles. 9These carrying poles were so long
that their ends could be seen from the outer
room, but not from the outside doorway.

The Ark is still there at the time of this
writing. 10Nothing was in the Ark except the
two stone tablets that Moses had put there at
Mount Horeb, when the Lord made a covenant with the people of Israel as they were
leaving Egypt.

11,12When the priests had undergone the
purification rites for themselves, they all took
part in the ceremonies without regard to their
normal duties. And how the Levites were
praising the Lord as the priests came out of
the Holy of Holies! The singers were Asaph,
Heman, Jeduthun, and all their sons and
brothers, dressed in finespun linen robes and
standing at the east side of the altar. The choir
was accompanied by 120 priests who were
trumpeters, while others played the cymbals,
lyres, and harps. 13,14The band and chorus
united as one to praise and thank the Lord;
their selections were interspersed with trumpet obbligatos, the clashing of cymbals, and
the loud playing of other musical instruments—all praising and thanking the Lord.

4:20 Light was needed in the Temple's dark interior. Even as the Holy Place would have been dark were it not for the lampstand, so would our life be in total darkness without the presence of the "Light of the World"—Jesus Christ.

Their theme was "He is so good! His loving-
kindness lasts forever!"

And at that moment the glory of the Lord,
coming as a bright cloud, filled the Temple so
that the priests could not continue their work.

CHAPTER 6

Solomon Blesses the People

This is the prayer prayed by Solomon on that
occasion:

"The Lord has said that he would live in
 the thick darkness,
But I have made a Temple for you,
 O Lord, to live in forever!"

[3]Then the king turned around to the people
and they stood to receive his blessing:
[4]"Blessed be the Lord God of Israel," he said
to them, "the God who talked personally to
my father David and has now fulfilled the
promise he made to him. For he told him, [5,6]'I
have never before, since bringing my people
from the land of Egypt, chosen a city anywhere in Israel as the location of my Temple
where my name will be glorified; and never
before have I chosen a king for my people
Israel. But now I have chosen Jerusalem as
that city, and David as that king.'
[7]"My father David wanted to build this
Temple, [8]but the Lord said not to. It was good
to have the desire, the Lord told him, [9]but he
was not the one to build it: his son was chosen
for that task. [10]And now the Lord has done
what he promised, for I have become king in
my father's place, and I have built the Temple
for the Name of the Lord God of Israel [11]and
placed the Ark there. And in the Ark is the
Covenant between the Lord and his people
Israel."

Solomon Dedicates the Temple

[12,13]As he spoke, Solomon was standing before
the people on a platform in the center of the
outer court, in front of the altar of the Lord.
The platform was made of bronze, 7½ feet
square and 4½ feet high. Now, as all the
people watched, he knelt down, reached out
his arms toward heaven, and prayed this
prayer:
[14]"O Lord God of Israel, there is no God like
you in all of heaven and earth. You are the
God who keeps his kind promises to all those
who obey you and who are anxious to do
your will. [15]And you have kept your promise
to my father David, as is evident today. [16]And
now, O God of Israel, carry out your further
promise to him that 'your descendants shall
always reign over Israel if they will obey my
laws as you have.' [17]Yes, Lord God of Israel,
please fulfill this promise too. [18]But will God
really live upon the earth with men? Why,
even the heaven and the heaven of heavens
cannot contain you—how much less this
Temple I have built!
[19]"How I pray that you will heed my prayers, O Lord my God! Listen to my prayer that
I am praying to you now! [20,21]Look down with
favor day and night upon this Temple—upon
this place where you have said that you would
put your name. May you always hear and
answer the prayers I will pray to you as I face
toward this place. Listen to my prayers and to
those of your people Israel when they pray
toward this Temple; yes, hear us from heaven,
and when you hear, forgive.
[22]"Whenever someone commits a crime
and is required to swear to his innocence
before this altar, [23]then hear from heaven and

5:13-14 The trumpets sounded with joy! The singers happily sang out their praises to God. What a beautiful celebration! For the victories in life, we must remember to respond with thanksgiving and praise to God. It is dangerous to emphasize our problems so much that we forget to express joy for the cure!

5:13-14 As the people praised God, his visible presence appeared and entered the Temple. For us to have any hope for recovery, God must be present in our life. No matter what we set out to do, God's help is a necessary ingredient for our success. No wonder God's people responded with such a joyful celebration. They were assured that God was with them! This fact alone gave them confidence in a future filled with joy and success.

6:14 We often become impressed by trendy strategies that claim they can solve all our problems. New techniques or programs promise to accomplish great changes in our life. Usually these programs are filled with human wisdom that requires us to effect change in our own strength. This verse reminds us that there is no substitute for God. He alone is able to empower us for recovery. Notice also that God's promises are realized only when we submit to God's will. Though God gives us the power to recover, he also asks that we give our life into his hands.

6:18 It is a common thing to emphasize our limitations. Our strength is limited; our money is limited; our time is limited; our opportunities are limited. Once again, the Scriptures remind us that God is never limited. God's resources can be counted on in every circumstance we face.

punish him if he is lying, or else declare him innocent.

[24]"If your people Israel are destroyed before their enemies because they have sinned against you, and if they turn to you and call themselves your people, and pray to you here in this Temple, [25]then listen to them from heaven and forgive their sins and give them back this land you gave to their fathers.

[26]"When the skies are shut and there is no rain because of our sins, and then we pray toward this Temple and claim you as our God, and turn from our sins because you have punished us, [27]then listen from heaven and forgive the sins of your people, and teach them what is right; and send rain upon this land that you have given to your people as their own property.

[28]"If there is a famine in the land, or plagues, or crop disease, or attacks of locusts or caterpillars, or if your people's enemies are in the land besieging our cities—whatever the trouble is— [29]listen to every individual's prayer concerning his private sorrow, as well as all the public prayers. [30]Hear from heaven where you live and forgive, and give each one whatever he deserves, for you know the hearts of all mankind. [31]Then they will reverence you forever and will continually walk where you tell them to go.

[32]"And when foreigners hear of your power, and come from distant lands to worship your great name, and to pray toward this Temple, [33]hear them from heaven where you live, and do what they request of you. Then all the peoples of the earth will hear of your fame and will reverence you, just as your people Israel do; and they too will know that this Temple I have built is truly yours.

[34]"If your people go out at your command to fight their enemies, and they pray toward this city of Jerusalem that you have chosen, and this Temple that I have built for your name, [35]then hear their prayers from heaven and give them success.

[36]"If they sin against you (and who has never sinned?) and you become angry with them, and you let their enemies defeat them and take them away as captives to some foreign nation near or far; [37,38]and if in that land of exile they turn to you again, and face toward this land you gave their fathers and this city and your Temple I have built, and plead with you with all their hearts to forgive them, [39]then hear from heaven where you live and help them, and forgive your people who have sinned against you.

[40]"Yes, O my God, be wide awake and attentive to all the prayers made to you in this place. [41]And now, O Lord God, arise and enter this resting place of yours where the Ark of your strength has been placed. Let your priests, O Lord God, be clothed with salvation, and let your people rejoice in your kind deeds. [42]O Lord God, do not ignore me—do not turn your face away from me, your anointed one. Oh, remember your love for David and your kindness to him."

CHAPTER 7

God's Glory Fills the Temple

As Solomon finished praying, fire flashed down from heaven and burned up the sacrifices! And the glory of the Lord filled the Temple, so that the priests couldn't enter! [3]All the people had been watching, and now they fell flat on the pavement and worshiped and thanked the Lord.

"How good he is!" they exclaimed. "He is always so loving and kind."

[4,5]Then the king and all the people dedicated the Temple by sacrificing burnt offerings to the Lord. King Solomon's contribution for this purpose was 22,000 oxen and 120,000 sheep. [6]The priests were standing at their posts of duty, and the Levites were playing their thanksgiving song, "His Loving-kindness Is Forever," using the musical instruments King David himself had made and had used to praise the Lord. Then, when the priests blew the trumpets, all the people stood again. [7]Solomon consecrated the inner court of the Temple for use that day as a place of

---

6:36-40 Prayer is one of our greatest privileges! Solomon pleaded with God, asking him to listen to his people's cries for help and forgiveness. Today, we need not plead with God to listen. Jesus Christ, the Son of God, now mediates our conversations with God. We can approach God at any time through Jesus, whose sacrificial death made possible our reconciliation with God. Solomon had to plead that his prayers would be heard, but we are absolutely assured of a hearing!

7:1-3 A powerful response is called for when we achieve victory over a significant challenge. Solomon and the people had just completed a monumental task—the Temple was now complete! In this verse, the response of the people was genuine and enthusiastic: "How good he is!" They affirmed God's goodness as they thanked him for his help in building the Temple. As we experience great victory, we also need to affirm God's goodness in our life.

sacrifice because there were too many sacrifices for the bronze altar to accommodate.
[8]For the next seven days they celebrated the
Tabernacle Festival, with large crowds coming
in from all over Israel; they arrived from as far
away as Hamath at one end of the country to
the brook of Egypt at the other. [9]A final religious service was held on the eighth day.
[10]Then on October 7 he sent the people home,
joyful and happy because the Lord had been
so good to David and Solomon and to his
people Israel.

God Speaks to Solomon

[11]So Solomon finished building the Temple as
well as his own palace. He completed what he
had planned to do.
[12]One night the Lord appeared to Solomon
and told him, "I have heard your prayer and
have chosen this Temple as the place where I
want you to sacrifice to me. [13]If I shut up the
heavens so that there is no rain, or if I command the locust swarms to eat up all of your
crops, or if I send an epidemic among you,
[14]then if my people will humble themselves
and pray, and search for me, and turn from
their wicked ways, I will hear them from
heaven and forgive their sins and heal their
land. [15]I will listen, wide awake, to every
prayer made in this place. [16]For I have chosen
this Temple and sanctified it to be my home
forever; my eyes and my heart shall always be
here.
[17]"As for yourself, if you follow me as your
father David did, [18]then I will see to it that you
and your descendants will always be the kings
of Israel; [19]but if you don't follow me, if you
refuse the laws I have given you and worship
idols, [20]then I will destroy my people from
this land of mine that I have given them, and
this Temple shall be destroyed even though I
have sanctified it for myself. Instead, I will
make it a public horror and disgrace. [21]Instead
of its being famous, all who pass by will be
incredulous.
"'Why has the Lord done such a terrible
thing to this land and to this Temple?' they
will ask.
[22]"And the answer will be, 'Because his
people abandoned the Lord God of their
fathers, the God who brought them out of the
land of Egypt, and they worshiped other gods
instead. That is why he has done all this to
them.'"

CHAPTER 8

Solomon's Building Projects

It was now twenty years since Solomon had
become king, and the great building projects
of the Lord's Temple and his own royal palace
were completed. [2]He now turned his energies
to rebuilding the cities that King Hiram of
Tyre had given to him, and he relocated some
of the people of Israel into them. [3]It was at this
time, too, that Solomon fought against the
city of Hamath-zobah and conquered it. [4]He
built Tadmor in the desert and built cities in
Hamath as supply centers. [5]He fortified the
cities of upper Beth-horon and lower Beth-
horon, both being supply centers, building
their walls and installing barred gates. [6]He
also built Baalath and other supply centers at
this time and constructed cities where his
chariots and horses were kept. He built to his
heart's desire in Jerusalem and Lebanon and
throughout the entire realm.
[7,8]He began the practice that still continues
of conscripting as slave laborers the Hittites,
Amorites, Perizzites, Hivites, and Jebusites—
the descendants of those nations that the
Israelis had not completely wiped out. [9]How-
ever, he didn't make slaves of any of the Israeli
citizens, but used them as soldiers, officers,
charioteers, and cavalrymen; [10]also, 250 of
them were government officials who administered all public affairs.
[11]Solomon now moved his wife (she was
Pharaoh's daughter) from the City of David
sector of Jerusalem to the new palace he had
built for her. For he said, "She must not live in
King David's palace for the Ark of the Lord
was there, and it is holy ground."
[12]Then Solomon sacrificed burnt offerings

7:14 This verse contains one of God's greatest promises to Israel. Although this promise was given specifically to Old Testament Israel, we know that through Jesus Christ, God does listen to our prayers, and he does forgive our sins as we confess them. It is part of God's nature to be forgiving. This fact should give us great comfort as we seek to deal with past failure in our life.

8:3 Even for Solomon, whose name means "peaceful," some conflict was necessary. As we work toward our recovery, we will discover that conflict is a part of life. Admitting this truth is an important step for all of us in recovery. If we believe that the world should be a bed of roses, we are living in denial. A successful recovery program recognizes that we are in a constant state of warfare against the forces that stand against us. If we fail to recognize this and don't prepare for the onslaught, our recovery is at risk.

to the Lord on the altar he had built in front of the porch of the Temple. [13]The number of sacrifices differed from day to day in accordance with the instructions Moses had given; there were extra sacrifices on the Sabbaths, on new moon festivals, and at the three annual festivals—the Passover celebration, the Festival of Weeks, and the Festival of Tabernacles. [14]In assigning the priests to their posts of duty he followed the organizational chart prepared by his father David; he also assigned the Levites to their work of praise and of helping the priests in each day's duties; and he assigned the gatekeepers to their gates. [15]Solomon did not deviate in any way from David's instructions concerning these matters and concerning the treasury personnel. [16]Thus Solomon successfully completed the construction of the Temple.

[17,18]Then he went to the seaport towns of Ezion-geber and Eloth, in Edom, to launch a fleet presented to him by King Hiram. These ships, with King Hiram's experienced crews working alongside Solomon's men, went to Ophir and brought back to him several milli7on dollars worth of gold on each trip!

CHAPTER 9

The Queen of Sheba

When the queen of Sheba heard of Solomon's fabled wisdom, she came to Jerusalem to test him with hard questions. A very great retinue of aides and servants accompanied her, including camel-loads of spices, gold, and jewels. [2]And Solomon answered all her problems. Nothing was hidden from him; he could explain everything to her. [3]When she discovered how wise he really was, and how breathtaking the beauty of his palace, [4]and how wonderful the food at his tables, and how many servants and aides he had, and when she saw their spectacular uniforms and his stewards in full regalia, and saw the size of the men in his bodyguard, she could scarcely believe it!

[5]Finally she exclaimed to the king, "Everything I heard about you in my own country is true! [6]I didn't believe it until I got here and saw it with my own eyes. Your wisdom is far greater than I could ever have imagined. [7]What a privilege for these men of yours to stand here and listen to you talk! [8]Blessed be the Lord your God! How he must love Israel to give them a just king like you! He wants them to be a great, strong nation forever."

[9]She gave the king a gift of over a million dollars in gold, and great quantities of spices of incomparable quality, and many, many jewels.

[10]King Hiram's and King Solomon's crews brought gold from Ophir, also sandalwood and jewels. [11]The king used the sandalwood to make terraced steps for the Temple and the palace and to construct harps and lyres for the choir. Never before had there been such beautiful instruments in all the land of Judah.

[12]King Solomon gave the queen of Sheba gifts of the same value as she had brought to him, plus everything else she asked for! Then she and her retinue returned to their own land.

Solomon's Wealth

[13,14]Solomon received a quarter of a billion dollars worth of gold each year from the kings of Arabia and many other lands that paid annual tribute to him. In addition, there was a trade balance from the exports of his merchants. [15]He used some of the gold to make 200 large shields, each worth $100,000, [16]and 300 smaller shields, each worth $50,000. The king placed these in the Forest of Lebanon Room in his palace. [17]He also made a huge ivory throne overlaid with pure gold. [18]It had six gold steps and a footstool of gold; also gold armrests, each flanked by a gold lion. [19]Gold lions also stood at each side of each step. No other throne in all the world could be compared with it! [20]All of King Solomon's cups were solid gold, as were all the furnishings in the Forest of Lebanon Room. Silver was too cheap to count for much in those days!

[21]Every three years the king sent his ships to Tarshish, using sailors supplied by King

8:11 In Solomon's day it was common for a head of state to confirm a treaty with a foreign king by marrying one of his daughters. Solomon accepted this worldly practice and married numerous foreign wives to validate his treaties with the surrounding nations. This practice eventually led Solomon into idolatry. We also may be tempted to seek recovery through the latest recovery fad. If any recovery practice or belief system denies God's Word or leads us away from God, we need to avoid it at any cost.

8:16 It is a glorious feeling to complete a worthwhile project. Many Bible students feel that Solomon's greatest accomplishment was the building of the Temple. He did it for God's purposes and in God's way. This is the only kind of building project that honors God.

Hiram, to bring back gold, silver, ivory, apes, and peacocks.

[22]So King Solomon was richer and wiser than any other king in all the earth. [23]Kings from every nation came to visit him and to hear the wisdom God had put into his heart. [24]Each brought him annual tribute of silver and gold bowls, clothing, armor, spices, horses, and mules.

[25]In addition, Solomon had 4,000 stalls of horses and chariots, and 12,000 cavalrymen stationed in the chariot cities as well as in Jerusalem to protect the king. [26]He ruled over all kings and kingdoms from the Euphrates River to the land of the Philistines and as far away as the border of Egypt. [27]He made silver become as plentiful in Jerusalem as stones in the road! And cedar was used as though it were common sycamore. [28]Horses were brought to him from Egypt and other countries.

Solomon's Death

[29]The rest of Solomon's biography is written in the history of Nathan the prophet and in the prophecy of Ahijah the Shilonite, and also in the visions of Iddo the seer concerning Jeroboam the son of Nebat.

[30]So Solomon reigned in Jerusalem over all of Israel for forty years. [31]Then he died and was buried in Jerusalem, and his son Rehoboam became the new king.

CHAPTER 10

Rehoboam Follows Bad Advice

All the leaders of Israel came to Shechem for Rehoboam's coronation. [2,3]Meanwhile, friends of Jeroboam (son of Nebat) sent word to him of Solomon's death. He was in Egypt at the time, where he had gone to escape from King Solomon. He now quickly returned, and was present at the coronation, and led the people's demands on Rehoboam:

[4]"Your father was a hard master," they said. "Be easier on us than he was, and we will let you be our king!"

[5]Rehoboam told them to return in three days for his decision. [6]He discussed their demand with the old men who had counseled his father Solomon.

"What shall I tell them?" he asked.

[7]"If you want to be their king," they replied, "you will have to give them a favorable reply and treat them with kindness."

[8,9]But he rejected their advice and asked the opinion of the young men who had grown up with him. "What do you fellows think I should do?" he asked. "Shall I be easier on them than my father was?"

[10]"No!" they replied. "Tell them, 'If you think my father was hard on you, just wait and see what I'll be like!' Tell them, 'My little finger is thicker than my father's loins! [11]I am going to be tougher on you, not easier! My father used whips on you, but I'll use scorpions!'"

[12]So when Jeroboam and the people returned in three days to hear King Rehoboam's decision, [13]he spoke roughly to them; for he refused the advice of the old men [14]and followed the counsel of the younger ones.

"My father gave you heavy burdens, but I will give you heavier!" he told them. "My father punished you with whips, but I will punish you with scorpions!"

The Northern Tribes Revolt

[15]So the king turned down the people's demands. (God caused him to do it in order to fulfill his prediction spoken to Jeroboam by Ahijah the Shilonite.) [16]When the people realized what the king was saying, they turned their backs and deserted him.

"Forget David and his dynasty!" they shouted angrily. "We'll get someone else to be our king. Let Rehoboam rule his own tribe of Judah! Let's go home!" So they did.

[17]The people of the tribe of Judah, however, remained loyal to Rehoboam. [18]Afterwards, when King Rehoboam sent Hadoram to draft forced labor from the other tribes of Israel, the people stoned him to death. When this news reached King Rehoboam, he jumped into his

---

9:28 When we seek security from any strategy or resource outside of God himself, we are in grave danger. David had refused to trust in horses and the military advantages they offered (1 Chronicles 18:4; see Deuteronomy 17:16). Unfortunately, Solomon did not follow his father's example. We will never succeed in recovery until we learn that God alone is capable of leading us to victory. No other resource is capable of supporting us as we experience the trials of rebuilding.

10:1-14 Rehoboam followed some foolish advice in responding to what seemed a reasonable request. Advice is cheap. We will always have people trying to tell us how to live. Sometimes that advice will be godly; other times it will be foolish. Before heeding the advice of any individual, we should look at the fruits of their own life. Where have their decisions led them? Also check to see whether or not their advice is in line with God's revealed will. If it contradicts God's Word, it must be rejected.

chariot and fled to Jerusalem. [19]And Israel has refused to be ruled by a descendant of David to this day.

CHAPTER 11

Judah Is Forbidden to Reunite

Upon arrival at Jerusalem, Rehoboam mobilized the armies of Judah and Benjamin, 180,000 strong, and declared war against the rest of Israel in an attempt to reunite the kingdom.

[2]But the Lord told Shemaiah the prophet,

[3]"Go and say to King Rehoboam of Judah, Solomon's son, and to the people of Judah and of Benjamin:

[4]"'The Lord says, Do not fight against your brothers. Go home, for I am behind their rebellion.'" So they obeyed the Lord and refused to fight against Jeroboam.

[5-10]Rehoboam stayed in Jerusalem and fortified these cities of Judah with walls and gates to protect himself: Bethlehem, Etam, Tekoa, Beth-zur, Soco, Adullam, Gath, Mareshah, Ziph, Adoraim, Lachish, Azekah, Zorah, Aijalon, and Hebron.

[11]He also rebuilt and strengthened the forts, and manned them with companies of soldiers under their officers, and stored them with food, olive oil, and wine. [12]Shields and spears were placed in armories in every city as a further safety measure. For only Judah and Benjamin remained loyal to him.

Priests and Levites Move to Judah

[13,14]However, the priests and Levites from the other tribes now abandoned their homes and moved to Judah and Jerusalem, for King Jeroboam had fired them, telling them to stop being priests of the Lord. [15]He had appointed other priests instead who encouraged the people to worship idols instead of God and to sacrifice to carved statues of goats and calves, which he placed on the hills. [16]Laymen, too, from all over Israel began moving to Jerusalem where they could freely worship the Lord God of their fathers and sacrifice to him. [17]This strengthened the kingdom of Judah, so King Rehoboam survived for three years without difficulty; for during those years there was an earnest effort to obey the Lord as King David and King Solomon had done.

Rehoboam's Wives and Children

[18]Rehoboam married his cousin Mahalath. She was the daughter of David's son Jerimoth and of Abihail, the daughter of David's brother Eliab. [19]Three sons were born from this marriage—Jeush, Shemariah, and Zaham.

[20]Later he married Maacah, the daughter of

10:15-16 Responding to Rehoboam's foolish decision, the people rebelled and split the kingdom of Israel in two. Two wrongs never make a right. The consequences that followed the rebellion and division were far more harmful to Israel than were the foolish responses of Rehoboam. Their actions eventually led the northern tribes away from God and toward destruction. We are often tempted to take rash measures when we are mistreated by others or when they fail to take our claims seriously. Before doing anything, we must be extremely careful.

10:18-19 When Rehoboam sent Hadoram to draft labor among the rebels, he was headed for trouble. The northern tribes had rebelled in a large part because of the forced labor demanded by Solomon. This automatically caused the rebels to explode. When we seek reconciliation with the people we have wronged, we should do so wisely. We should look for common ground and build on it. We should not foolishly emphasize differences that will impair the recovery process.

11:1-12 Rehoboam was tempted to take matters into his own hands. He was preparing to attack Jeroboam and the northern kingdom when God's messenger came to warn him against the invasion. To Rehoboam's credit, he listened to God and abandoned his plans. Our plans and programs likewise need to be subject to God's leading. We need to be ready to change our course based on the direction God gives us. If we try to do things our own way, the outcome will always be disastrous.

11:15 Most of us try to justify our actions, and it is tempting to use religion to do this. Jeroboam ordained false priests in order to provide religious respectability for his kingdom. We often do the same thing when we face difficulties in life. We attempt to justify our actions by finding something in the Bible to support us or by naming some religious authority figure who agrees with our position. When we do this, however, we usually only compound our problems by defending the sin in our life. In recovery, we must take inventory of our failures and seek, with God's help, to root them out.

11:20-23 The families of most of Israel's kings show us what a family should not be like. Rehoboam was no exception in this regard. His multiple marriages led to favoritism and conflict between the rival brothers. In order to maintain peace in his family, Rehoboam had to give his sons positions of responsibility in separate cities. Apparently the conflict in his family was somewhat explosive. Rehoboam's solution was certainly a wise one, though it was only a Band-Aid solution. The real problem was rooted in his family relationships. Families that are forced to deal with multiple marriages, whether due to polygamy or divorce, always suffer.

Absalom. The children she bore him were
Abijah, Attai, Ziza, and Shelomith. 21He loved
Maacah more than any of his other wives and
concubines (he had eighteen wives and sixty
concubines—with twenty-eight sons and
sixty daughters). 22Maacah's son Abijah was
his favorite, and he intended to make him the
next king. 23He very wisely scattered his other
sons in the fortified cities throughout the
land of Judah and Benjamin, and gave them
large allowances and arranged for them to
have several wives apiece.

CHAPTER 12

Egypt Conquers Jerusalem

But just when Rehoboam was at the height of
his popularity and power he abandoned the
Lord, and the people followed him in this sin.
2As a result, King Shishak of Egypt attacked
Jerusalem in the fifth year of King Rehoboam's reign 3with 1,200 chariots, 60,000 cavalrymen and an unnumbered host of
infantrymen—Egyptians, Libyans, Sukkiim,
and Ethiopians. 4He quickly conquered
Judah's fortified cities and soon arrived at
Jerusalem.

5The prophet Shemaiah now met with Rehoboam and the Judean leaders from every
part of the nation (they had fled to Jerusalem
for safety) and told them, "The Lord says, 'You
have forsaken me, so I have forsaken you and
abandoned you to Shishak.'"

6Then the king and the leaders of Israel
confessed their sins and exclaimed, "The Lord
is right in doing this to us!"

7And when the Lord saw them humble
themselves, he sent Shemaiah to tell them,
"Because you have humbled yourselves, I will
not completely destroy you; some will escape.
I will not use Shishak to pour out my anger
upon Jerusalem. 8But you must pay annual
tribute to him. Then you will realize how
much better it is to serve me than to serve
him!"

9So King Shishak of Egypt conquered Jerusalem and took away all the treasures of the
Temple and of the palace, also all of Solomon's gold shields. 10King Rehoboam replaced them with bronze shields and
committed them to the care of the captain of
his bodyguard. 11Whenever the king went to
the Temple, the guards would carry them and
afterwards return them to the armory. 12When
the king humbled himself, the Lord's anger
was turned aside and he didn't send total
destruction; in fact, even after Shishak's invasion, the economy of Judah remained strong.

Rehoboam's Reign

13King Rehoboam reigned seventeen years in
Jerusalem, the city God had chosen as his
residence after considering all the other cities
of Israel. He had become king at the age of
forty-one, and his mother's name was Naamah the Ammonitess. 14But he was an evil
king, for he never did decide really to please
the Lord. 15The complete biography of Rehoboam is recorded in the histories written by
Shemaiah the prophet and by Iddo the seer
and in *The Genealogical Register.*

There were continual wars between Rehoboam and Jeroboam. 16When Rehoboam died
he was buried in Jerusalem, and his son Abijah became the new king.

12:1-4 When things begin to go well in life, we need to sound the alarm! With success comes the danger of self-sufficiency. When Rehoboam got things established and began to feel secure, he forsook his obligation to lead the people closer to God. As a result, the whole nation fell into sin and was consequently defeated by the Egyptians. In recovery, the same thing tends to happen. When things are going well, we begin to relax. We need to stay alert, realizing that good times often make us more vulnerable to a fall.

12:5 Turning from God has its consequences. Rehoboam had failed to lead his people in godly ways. As a result, they were abandoned by God. The prophet Shemaiah gave God's message in no uncertain terms: "You have forsaken me, so I have forsaken you." God loves us and wants us to live a life that honors him. We cannot sin with impunity. Sin always brings destructive consequences. The most terrible consequence of all might be abandonment by God, without whom our recovery is impossible. If we have failed and sought forgiveness, however, God will return and help us deal with our past failures.

12:13-15 How might our epitaph read? What have we done in our life that is worth remembering? How will people remember our relationship with God when we die? Rehoboam's epitaph reads this way: "He was an evil king, for he never did decide really to please the Lord." Sadly, we spend too little time really seeking God. That is one reason why recovery is so difficult for us. When we die, our wealth and achievements will soon be forgotten. Our relationship with God and the things we do for him are the only things that will last. We would be wise to put our energy into things of eternal value.

CHAPTER 13

Abijah Defeats Jeroboam

Abijah became the new king of Judah in Jerusalem in the eighteenth year of the reign of King Jeroboam of Israel. He lasted three years. His mother's name was Micaiah (daughter of Uriel of Gibeah).

Early in his reign war broke out between Judah and Israel. 3Judah, led by King Abijah, fielded 400,000 seasoned warriors against twice as many Israeli troops—strong, courageous men led by King Jeroboam. 4When the army of Judah arrived at Mount Zemaraim, in the hill country of Ephraim, King Abijah shouted to King Jeroboam and the Israeli army:

5"Listen! Don't you realize that the Lord God of Israel swore that David's descendants would always be the kings of Israel? 6Your King Jeroboam is a mere servant of David's son and was a traitor to his master. 7Then a whole gang of worthless rebels joined him, defying Solomon's son Rehoboam, for he was young and frightened and couldn't stand up to them. 8Do you really think you can defeat the kingdom of the Lord that is led by a descendant of David? Your army is twice as large as mine, but you are cursed with those gold calves you have with you that Jeroboam made for you—he calls them your gods! 9And you have driven away the priests of the Lord and the Levites and have appointed heathen priests instead. Just like the people of other lands, you accept as priests anybody who comes along with a young bullock and seven rams for consecration. Anyone at all can be a priest of these no-gods of yours!

10"But as for us, the Lord is our God and we have not forsaken him. Only the descendants of Aaron are our priests, and the Levites alone may help them in their work. 11They burn sacrifices to the Lord every morning and evening—burnt offerings and sweet incense; and they place the Bread of the Presence upon the holy table. The gold lampstand is lighted every night, for we are careful to follow the instructions of the Lord our God; but you have forsaken him. 12So you see, God is with us; he is our Leader. His priests, trumpeting as they go, will lead us into battle against you. O people of Israel, do not fight against the Lord God of your fathers, for you will not succeed!"

13,14Meanwhile, Jeroboam had secretly sent part of his army around behind the men of Judah to ambush them; so Judah was surrounded, with the enemy before and behind them. Then they cried out to the Lord for mercy, and the priests blew the trumpets. 15,16The men of Judah began to shout. And as they shouted, God used King Abijah and the men of Judah to turn the tide of battle against King Jeroboam and the army of Israel, 17and they slaughtered 500,000 elite troops of Israel that day.

18,19So Judah, depending upon the Lord God of their fathers, defeated Israel, and chased King Jeroboam's troops, and captured some of his cities—Bethel, Jeshanah, Ephron, and their suburbs. 20King Jeroboam of Israel never regained his power during Abijah's lifetime, and eventually the Lord struck him and he died.

21Meanwhile, King Abijah of Judah became very strong. He married fourteen wives and had twenty-two sons and sixteen daughters. 22His complete biography and speeches are recorded in the prophet Iddo's *History of Judah.*

CHAPTER 14

Asa Rules Judah

King Abijah was buried in Jerusalem. Then his son Asa became the new king of Judah, and there was peace in the land for the first ten years of his reign, 2for Asa was careful to obey

13:1-9 Abijah was about to go into a battle in which his army was vastly outnumbered. But instead of giving in to fear, he stood firm because of his faith in God's promises. In the process of recovery we will face many difficult situations. If we try to face them alone, we will fail. We need to stand on the many promises God has given us in Scripture and trust him to deliver us. We need to learn to live by faith when it is impossible to live by sight.

13:10-14 When the going gets tough, it is a good idea to have God on our side. Abijah said, "The Lord is our God and we have not forsaken him." If we draw close to God, he will draw close to us. And as we encounter difficulties or negative patterns in our life, we will certainly need his help to win the battles we face.

13:18-20 There is great danger in rebelling against God. Sometimes it may seem that God is not paying attention—people seem to get away with murder. But what we sow, we will eventually reap. Jeroboam seemed to be successful, but eventually his sins caught up with him. He was soundly defeated by a small army from Judah, which was set firmly in God's hands. Sin has inevitable consequences. We must root it out of our life before it leads to our downfall.

the Lord his God. [3]He demolished the heathen altars on the hills, and broke down the
obelisks, and chopped down the shameful
Asherim-idols, [4]and demanded that the entire
nation obey the commandments of the Lord
God of their ancestors. [5]Also, he removed the
sun-images from the hills and the incense
altars from every one of Judah's cities. That is
why God gave his kingdom peace. [6]This made
it possible for him to build walled cities
throughout Judah.
[7]"Now is the time to do it, while the Lord is
blessing us with peace because of our obedience to him," he told his people. "Let us build
and fortify cities now, with walls, towers,
gates, and bars." So they went ahead with
these projects very successfully.
[8]King Asa's Judean army was 300,000
strong, equipped with light shields and
spears. His army of Benjaminites numbered
280,000, armed with large shields and bows.
Both armies were composed of well-trained,
brave men.
[9,10]But now he was attacked by an army of
1,000,000 troops from Ethiopia with 300
chariots, under the leadership of General Zerah. They advanced to the city of Mareshah,
in the valley of Zephathah, and King Asa sent
his troops to battle with them there.
[11]"O Lord," he cried out to God, "no one
else can help us! Here we are, powerless
against this mighty army. Oh, help us, Lord
our God! For we trust in you alone to rescue
us, and in your name we attack this vast
horde. Don't let mere men defeat you!"
[12]Then the Lord defeated the Ethiopians,
and Asa and the army of Judah triumphed as
the Ethiopians fled. [13]They chased them as far
as Gerar, and the entire Ethiopian army was
wiped out so that not one man remained; for
the Lord and his army destroyed them all.
Then the army of Judah carried off vast quantities of plunder. [14]While they were at Gerar
they attacked all the cities in that area, and
terror from the Lord came upon the residents.
As a result, additional vast quantities of plunder were collected from these cities too.
[15]They not only plundered the cities but destroyed the cattle tents and captured great
herds of sheep and camels before finally returning to Jerusalem.

CHAPTER 15

Asa Rebuilds the Altar

Then the Spirit of God came upon Azariah
(son of Oded), [2]and he went out to meet King
Asa as he was returning from the battle.
"Listen to me, Asa! Listen, armies of Judah
and Benjamin!" he shouted. "The Lord will
stay with you as long as you stay with him!
Whenever you look for him, you will find
him. But if you forsake him, he will forsake
you. [3]For a long time now, over in Israel, the
people haven't worshiped the true God and
have not had a true priest to teach them. They
have lived without God's laws. [4]But whenever
they have turned again to the Lord God of
Israel in their distress and searched for him he
has helped them.[5]In their times of rebellion
against God there was no peace. Problems
troubled the nation on every hand. Crime
was on the increase everywhere. [6]There were
external wars and internal fighting of city
against city, for God was plaguing them with
all sorts of trouble. [7]But you men of Judah,
keep up the good work and don't get discouraged, for you will be rewarded."
[8]When King Asa heard this message from
God, he took courage and destroyed all the
idols in the land of Judah and Benjamin and
in the cities he had captured in the hill country of Ephraim, and he rebuilt the altar of the
Lord in front of the Temple.
[9]Then he summoned all the people of
Judah and Benjamin and the immigrants
from Israel (for many had come from the
territories of Ephraim, Manasseh, and Simeon
in Israel when they saw that the Lord God was

14:1-2 The world's measure of success is not the same as God's measure. Every action, attitude, decision, and feeling needs to be measured by the criterion suggested by Asa's life. "Asa was careful to obey the Lord his God." Obedience to the revealed will of God is an essential step in the rebuilding process. If we are unwilling to obey God's program, there is little hope for our recovery.

14:9-15 Asa was about to be overwhelmed by a mighty enemy army, but he cried out to God, admitting his powerlessness. This was his first step toward victory. Asa was willing to trust that God would deliver him. God comes through when we admit our weakness and look to him for help, but we need to take that all-important first step.

15:4 God is a forgiving God. No matter how deep the stain of sin upon the people of Israel, God would forgive them if they chose to repent. We may have failed so often that we believe we are beyond the point of God's forgiveness and care. It is never too late to turn to God! When we cry out for help, he will respond with restoration and forgiveness. Then he will give us the courage we need to deal with the problems before us.

READ 2 CHRONICLES 15:1-19

GOD grant me the serenity to accept the things I cannot change the courage to change the things I can and the wisdom to know the difference AMEN

There comes a point in recovery when we need to face ourself. We need to acknowledge the wrongs we have committed and the harm we have caused. It takes courage to make the preparations necessary to allow God to change our life and relationships in ways that support our recovery.

King Asa was a man who lived at a time when the people of Israel had given themselves over to the worship of idols. They had turned away from God and the way of life they knew to be right. A messenger of God told the king: "'The Lord will stay with you as long as you stay with him! Whenever you look for him, you will find him. But if you forsake him, he will forsake you.' . . . When King Asa heard this message . . . he took courage and destroyed all the idols in the land . . . and he rebuilt the altar of the Lord" (2 Chronicles 15:2, 8). Asa even removed his mother from her position of power because she had been influential in Israel's idolatry.

Allowing God to remove all our defects of character takes courage because the changes he makes in us will affect every part of our life. The time will come when we need to crush and burn the "idols" we have served, to go against the crowd, to make a commitment to God, and even to separate ourself from those who don't contribute to our recovery. When we do these things, we will find that God will be there for us, encouraging us as we set things straight. ***Turn to page 511, 2 Chronicles 32.***

---

with King Asa). 10They all came to Jerusalem
in June of the fifteenth year of King Asa's
reign 11and sacrificed to the Lord seven hundred oxen and seven thousand sheep—it was
part of the plunder they had captured in the
battle. 12Then they entered into a contract to
worship only the Lord God of their fathers
13and agreed that anyone who refused to do
this must die—whether old or young, man or
woman. 14They shouted out their oath of loyalty to God with trumpets blaring and horns
sounding. 15All were happy for this covenant
with God, for they had entered into it with all
their hearts and wills and wanted him above
everything else, and they found him! And he
gave them peace throughout the nation.

16King Asa even removed his mother
Maacah from being the queen mother because she made an Asherah-idol; he cut down
the idol and crushed and burned it at Kidron
Brook. 17Over in Israel the idol-temples were
not removed. But here in Judah and Benjamin
the heart of King Asa was perfect before God
throughout his lifetime. 18He brought back
into the Temple the silver and gold bowls that
he and his father had dedicated to the Lord.
19So there was no more war until the thirty-
fifth year of King Asa's reign.

CHAPTER 16

Asa Forgets God

In the thirty-sixth year of King Asa's reign,
King Baasha of Israel declared war on him and
built the fortress of Ramah in order to control
the road to Judah. 2Asa's response was to take
the silver and gold from the Temple and from
the palace, and to send it to King Ben-hadad
of Syria at Damascus with this message:

3"Let us renew the mutual security pact that
there was between your father and my father.
See, here is silver and gold to induce you to
break your alliance with King Baasha of Israel,
so that he will leave me alone."

4Ben-hadad agreed to King Asa's request

and mobilized his armies to attack Israel.
They destroyed the cities of Ijon, Dan, Abel-
maim and all of the supply centers in Naphtali. 5As soon as King Baasha of Israel heard
what was happening, he discontinued building Ramah and gave up his plan to attack
Judah. 6Then King Asa and the people of
Judah went out to Ramah and carried away
the building stones and timbers and used
them to build Geba and Mizpah instead.

7About that time the prophet Hanani came
to King Asa and told him, "Because you have
put your trust in the king of Syria instead of
in the Lord your God, the army of the king of
Syria has escaped from you. 8Don't you remember what happened to the Ethiopians
and Libyans and their vast army, with all of
their chariots and cavalrymen? But you relied
then on the Lord, and he delivered them all
into your hand. 9For the eyes of the Lord
search back and forth across the whole earth,
looking for people whose hearts are perfect
toward him, so that he can show his great
power in helping them. What a fool you have
been! From now on you shall have wars."

10Asa was so angry with the prophet for
saying this that he threw him into jail. And
Asa oppressed all the people at that time.

11The rest of the biography of Asa is written
in *The Annals of the Kings of Israel and Judah.*
12In the thirty-ninth year of his reign, Asa
became seriously diseased in his feet, but he
didn't go to the Lord with the problem but to
the doctors. 13,14So he died in the forty-first
year of his reign and was buried in his own
vault that he had hewn out for himself in
Jerusalem. He was laid on a bed perfumed
with sweet spices and ointments, and his
people made a very great burning of incense
for him at his funeral.

CHAPTER 17

Jehoshaphat Rules Judah

Then his son Jehoshaphat became the king
and mobilized for war against Israel. 2He
placed garrisons in all of the fortified cities of
Judah, in various other places throughout the
country, and in the cities of Ephraim that his
father had conquered.

3The Lord was with Jehoshaphat because he
followed in the good footsteps of his father's
early years and did not worship idols. 4He
obeyed the commandments of his father's
God—quite unlike the people across the border in the land of Israel. 5So the Lord strengthened his position as king of Judah. All the
people of Judah cooperated by paying their
taxes, so he became very wealthy as well as
being very popular. 6He boldly followed the
paths of God—even knocking down the heathen altars on the hills and destroying the
Asherim idols.

7-9In the third year of his reign he began a
nationwide religious education program. He
sent out top government officials as teachers
in all the cities of Judah. These men included

16:7-9 Hanani rebuked Asa for depending on Syria instead of trusting in God. No matter what the odds, God could have delivered Judah without the help of Syria's army. We must learn that God is the only one able to deliver us from our dependencies. Though there is an overwhelming array of individuals and programs to help us deal with our problems, none of these programs is sufficient without God's help. We need to put our trust in him.

16:10 When someone honestly points out a problem or failure in our life, we have a decision to make. Either we humbly try to discover the truth behind the charges, or we become angry and take revenge. When Hanani rebuked Asa for hiring the Syrians, the king immediately made the wrong response—he punished Hanani. He would have been wise to listen to God's corrective message. As we take inventory of our life, we need to humbly acknowledge our failures. If we don't, our recovery will ultimately fail.

17:3-4 The role models we follow make a tremendous difference in how we respond to the challenges we face. It is refreshing to discover that Jehoshaphat chose a positive role model to give direction to his life. Based upon the work of his worthy exemplar, Jehoshaphat instituted excellent reforms in Judah. We must be careful not to follow those whose path leads away from the heart of God. We need to look up to people who will lead us to make positive steps in our recovery.

17:5-6 We can learn a lot about people by the way they find fulfillment in life. Jehoshaphat "boldly followed the paths of God." And in following God's paths, he led his kingdom on the path of recovery from idolatry and sin. We can only imagine the fun he had as he broke down the idols and pagan worship areas in his land! Like Jehoshaphat, we need to begin by boldly following the paths of God. We can be sure that by doing this we will also discover the path toward recovery.

17:7-9 Notice that Jehoshaphat used the Word of God as the foundation for his reforms. As we attempt to effect changes in our life, we also need God's Word to direct the changes we make. Scripture furnishes the only adequate foundation for change in our life. We need to take the time to study it so we can discover God's will for us and learn of the power God offers us in recovery.

Ben-hail, Obadiah, Zechariah, Nethanel, and Micaiah. He also used the Levites for this purpose, including Shemaiah, Nethaniah, Zebadiah, Asahel, Shemiramoth, Jehonathan, Adonijah, Tobijah, and Tobadonijah; also the priests, Elishama and Jehoram. They took copies of *The Book of the Law of the Lord* to all the cities of Judah to teach the Scriptures to the people.

10 Then the fear of the Lord fell upon all the surrounding kingdoms so that none of them declared war on King Jehoshaphat.

11 Even some of the Philistines brought him presents and annual tribute, and the Arabs donated 7,700 rams and 7,700 male goats. 12 So Jehoshaphat became very strong and built fortresses and supply cities throughout Judah.

13 His public works program was also extensive, and he had a huge army stationed at Jerusalem, his capital. 14,15 Three hundred thousand Judean troops were there under General Adnah. Next in command was Jehohanan with an army of 280,000 men. 16 Next was Amasiah (son of Zichri), a man of unusual piety, with 200,000 troops. 17 Benjamin supplied 200,000 men equipped with bows and shields under the command of Eliada, a great general. 18 His second in command was Jehozabad, with 180,000 trained men. 19 These were the troops in Jerusalem in addition to those placed by the king in the fortified cities throughout the nation.

CHAPTER 18

Jehoshaphat Joins Forces with Ahab

But rich, popular King Jehoshaphat of Judah made a marriage alliance [for his son] with [the daughter of] King Ahab of Israel. 2 A few years later he went down to Samaria to visit King Ahab, and King Ahab gave a great party for him and his aides, butchering great numbers of sheep and oxen for the feast. Then he asked King Jehoshaphat to join forces with him against Ramoth-gilead.

3-5 "Why, of course!" King Jehoshaphat replied. "I'm with you all the way. My troops are at your command! However, let's check with the Lord first."

So King Ahab summoned 400 of his heathen prophets and asked them, "Shall we go to war with Ramoth-gilead or not?"

And they replied, "Go ahead, for God will give you a great victory!"

6,7 But Jehoshaphat wasn't satisfied. "Isn't there some prophet of the Lord around here too?" he asked. "I'd like to ask him the same question."

"Well," Ahab told him, "there is one, but I hate him, for he never prophesies anything but evil! His name is Micaiah (son of Imlah)."

"Oh, come now, don't talk like that!" Jehoshaphat exclaimed. "Let's hear what he has to say."

8 So the king of Israel called one of his aides. "Quick! Go and get Micaiah (son of Imlah)," he ordered.

9 The two kings were sitting on thrones in full regalia at an open place near the Samaria gate, and all the "prophets" were prophesying before them. 10 One of them, Zedekiah (son of Chenaanah), made some iron horns for the occasion and proclaimed, "The Lord says you will gore the Syrians to death with these!"

11 And all the others agreed. "Yes," they chorused, "go up to Ramoth-gilead and prosper, for the Lord will cause you to conquer."

12 The man who went to get Micaiah told him what was happening and what all the prophets were saying—that the war would end in triumph for the king.

"I hope you will agree with them and give the king a favorable reading," the man ventured.

13 But Micaiah replied, "I vow by God that whatever God says is what I will say."

18:3-5 Generally, when any project is undertaken, companions and allies must be chosen. However, there is grave danger in choosing our allies wrongly. Jehoshaphat's alliance with Ahab almost caused his undoing. In this verse, he not only allied himself with Ahab, but he declared himself to be in complete agreement with this godless king. Companions in recovery are necessary; we cannot accomplish our recovery alone. But choosing the wrong companions can be as destructive as having no companions at all.

18:3-7 Ahab called upon a false prophet; as a result, he got false information. Jehoshaphat wanted to discover what God had to say, so he looked for a true prophet. The false prophets told the people whatever they wanted to hear. True prophets spoke God's word whether the people liked it or not. As we seek God's will in Scripture, we must be careful not to reject messages we don't like. Sometimes the path toward victory is difficult; sometimes we have to do things that we don't really want to do. In the long run, however, God's way is always the fastest and best way to recovery. Looking for quick and easy solutions to our problems will never yield permanent results.

[14]When he arrived before the king, the king
asked him, "Micaiah, shall we go to war
against Ramoth-gilead or not?"
And Micaiah replied, "Sure, go ahead! It
will be a glorious victory!"
[15]"Look here," the king said sharply, "how
many times must I tell you to speak nothing
except what the Lord tells you to?"
[16]Then Micaiah told him, "In my vision I saw
all Israel scattered upon the mountain as sheep
without a shepherd. And the Lord said, 'Their
master has been killed. Send them home.'"
[17]"Didn't I tell you?" the king of Israel exclaimed to Jehoshaphat. "He does it every
time. He *never* prophesies *anything* but evil
against me."
[18]"Listen to what else the Lord has told
me," Micaiah continued. "I saw him upon his
throne surrounded by vast throngs of angels.
[19,20]"And the Lord said, 'Who can get King
Ahab to go to battle against Ramoth-gilead
and be killed there?'
"There were many suggestions, but finally
a spirit stepped forward before the Lord and
said, 'I can do it!'
"'How?' the Lord asked him.
[21]"He replied, 'I will be a lying spirit in the
mouths of all of the king's prophets!'
"'It will work,' the Lord said; 'go and do it.'
[22]"So you see, the Lord has put a lying spirit
in the mouths of these prophets of yours,
when actually he has determined just the
opposite of what they are telling you!"
[23]Then Zedekiah (son of Chenaanah)
walked up to Micaiah and slapped him across
the face. "You liar!" he yelled. "When did the
Spirit of the Lord leave me and enter you?"
[24]"You'll find out soon enough," Micaiah
replied, "when you are hiding in an inner
room!"
[25]"Arrest this man and take him back to
Governor Amon and to my son Joash," the
king of Israel ordered. [26]"Tell them, 'The king
says to put this fellow in prison and feed him
with bread and water until I return safely
from the battle!'"
[27]Micaiah replied, "If you return safely, the
Lord has not spoken through me." Then,
turning to those around them, he remarked,
"Take note of what I have said."

King Ahab Dies in Battle

[28]So the king of Israel and the king of Judah
led their armies to Ramoth-gilead.
[29]The king of Israel said to Jehoshaphat, "I'll
disguise myself so that no one will recognize
me, but you put on your royal robes!" So that
is what they did.
[30]Now the king of Syria had issued these
instructions to his charioteers: "Ignore everyone but the king of Israel!"
[31]So when the Syrian charioteers saw King
Jehoshaphat of Judah in his royal robes,
they went for him, supposing that he was
the man they were after. But Jehoshaphat
cried out to the Lord to save him, and the
Lord made the charioteers see their mistake
and leave him. [32]For as soon as they realized
he was not the king of Israel, they stopped
chasing him. [33]But one of the Syrian soldiers
shot an arrow haphazardly at the Israeli
troops, and it struck the king of Israel at the
opening where the lower armor and the
breastplate meet. "Get me out of here," he
groaned to the driver of his chariot, "for I
am badly wounded." [34]The battle grew hotter and hotter all that day, and King Ahab
went back in, propped up in his chariot, to
fight the Syrians, but just as the sun sank
into the western skies, he died.

CHAPTER 19

A Prophet Rebukes Jehoshaphat

As King Jehoshaphat of Judah returned home,
uninjured, [2]the prophet Jehu (son of Hanani)
went out to meet him.
"Should you be helping the wicked, and
loving those who hate the Lord?" he asked

18:31-34 After hearing God's warning to abandon his plans, Ahab took precautions so he would not be killed in the battle. He dressed as a common soldier so he wouldn't be a target of the enemy. In spite of crafty preparations, however, Ahab was killed by a "chance" arrow. He believed that he could escape God's will, but in trying to do so, he sealed his own doom. When God directs us through his Word or through wise counsel, we would be wise to listen. Following God's will for us, no matter how hard that may be, is the only way toward recovery.

19:1-2 When we make wrong alliances and trust in sources of human strength and ability, there will be consequences to pay. The prophet Jehu met Jehoshaphat to proclaim a message of judgment. Because of Jehoshaphat's cooperation with Ahab, he would have to bear the consequences. We should take this as a warning. Our alliances need to be with people who will encourage us in God's program for recovery. Seeking help from anyone else will lead to negative consequences and suffering.

him. "Because of what you have done, God's wrath is upon you. 3But there are some good things about you in that you got rid of the shame-idols throughout the land, and you have tried to be faithful to God."

Jehoshaphat Appoints Judges

4So Jehoshaphat made no more trips to Israel after that but remained quietly at Jerusalem. Later he went out again among the people, traveling from Beersheba to the hill country of Ephraim to encourage them to worship the God of their ancestors. 5He appointed judges throughout the nation in all the larger cities, 6and instructed them:

"Watch your step—I have not appointed you—God has; and he will stand beside you and help you give justice in each case that comes before you. 7Be very much afraid to give any other decision than what God tells you to. For there must be no injustice among God's judges, no partiality, no taking of bribes."

8Jehoshaphat set up courts in Jerusalem, too, with the Levites and priests and clan leaders and judges. 9These were his instructions to them: "You are to act always in the fear of God, with honest hearts. 10Whenever a case is referred to you by the judges out in the provinces, whether murder cases or other violations of the laws and ordinances of God, you are to clarify the evidence for them and help them to decide justly, lest the wrath of God come down upon you and them; if you do this, you will discharge your responsibility."

11Then he appointed Amariah the High Priest to be the court of final appeal in cases involving violation of sacred affairs; and Zebadiah (son of Ishmael), a ruler in Judah, as the court of final appeal in all civil cases; with the Levites as their assistants. "Be fearless in your stand for truth and honesty. And may God use you to defend the innocent," was his final word to them.

CHAPTER 20

God Gives Jehoshaphat Victory

Later on the armies of the kings of Moab, Ammon, and of the Meunites declared war on Jehoshaphat and the people of Judah. 2Word reached Jehoshaphat that "a vast army is marching against you from beyond the Dead Sea from Syria. It is already at Hazazon-tamar" (also called Engedi). 3Jehoshaphat was badly shaken by this news and determined to beg for help from the Lord; so he announced that all the people of Judah should go without food for a time, in penitence and intercession before God. 4People from all across the nation came to Jerusalem to plead unitedly with him. 5Jehoshaphat stood among them as they gathered at the new court of the Temple and prayed this prayer:

6"O Lord God of our fathers—the only God in all the heavens, the Ruler of all the kingdoms of the earth—you are so powerful, so mighty. Who can stand against you? 7O our God, didn't you drive out the heathen who lived in this land when your people arrived? And didn't you give this land forever to the descendants of your friend Abraham? 8Your people settled here and built this Temple for you, 9truly believing that in a time like this—whenever we are faced with any calamity such as war, disease, or famine—we can stand here before this Temple and before you—for you are here in this Temple—and cry out to you to save us; and that you will hear us and rescue us.

10"And now see what the armies of Ammon, Moab, and Mount Seir are doing. You wouldn't let our ancestors invade those nations when Israel left Egypt, so we went

---

19:5-7 These verses give us excellent instructions for correcting wrong situations in our life. The judicial system in Judah was corrupt, but rather than despairing, Jehoshaphat did something about it. He challenged the judges to pay attention to God's way. He reminded them that the fear of God and his justice was the only proper motivation for action. God's ways should also direct our decisions in recovery. We must take time to seek his wisdom in the Scriptures.

19:11 Jehoshaphat appointed people to make final decisions for justice in the land. He wanted to make sure that the people would be treated justly and that the truth would never be hidden. As we take inventory of our life, we must judge our past performance by God's standards of justice. We must also look honestly at our failures, avoiding our tendency for denial. If we are "fearless in [our] stand for truth and honesty," we will build the foundation for a successful recovery.

20:6-9 God is in charge of our world! He is master over peoples, tongues, and nations! Trust in his sovereignty is the basis for victory in recovery. As we learn to believe in God's control, even when things aren't going our way, our life can be serene in the midst of conflict. We can know that God desires what is best for us. Seeking his will and obeying his direction for our life will always lead to a successful recovery.

around and didn't destroy them. 11 Now see how they reward us! For they have come to throw us out of your land which you have given us. 12 O our God, won't you stop them? We have no way to protect ourselves against this mighty army. We don't know what to do, but we are looking to you."

13 As the people from every part of Judah stood before the Lord with their little ones, wives, and children, 14 the Spirit of the Lord came upon one of the men standing there—Jahaziel (son of Zechariah, son of Benaiah, son of Jeiel, son of Mattaniah the Levite, who was one of the sons of Asaph).

15 "Listen to me, all you people of Judah and Jerusalem, and you, O king Jehoshaphat!" he exclaimed. "The Lord says, 'Don't be afraid! Don't be paralyzed by this mighty army! For the battle is not yours, but God's! 16 Tomorrow, go down and attack them! You will find them coming up the slopes of Ziz at the end of the valley that opens into the wilderness of Jeruel. 17 But you will not need to fight! Take your places; stand quietly and see the incredible rescue operation God will perform for you, O people of Judah and Jerusalem! Don't be afraid or discouraged! Go out there tomorrow, for the Lord is with you!'"

18 Then King Jehoshaphat fell to the ground with his face to the earth, and all the people of Judah and the people of Jerusalem did the same, worshiping the Lord. 19 Then the Levites of the Kohath clan and the Korah clan stood to praise the Lord God of Israel with songs of praise that rang out strong and clear.

20 Early the next morning the army of Judah went out into the wilderness of Tekoa. On the way Jehoshaphat stopped and called them to attention. "Listen to me, O people of Judah and Jerusalem," he said. "Believe in the Lord your God and you shall have success! Believe his prophets and everything will be all right!"

21 After consultation with the leaders of the people, he determined that there should be a choir leading the march, clothed in sanctified garments and singing the song "His Lovingkindness Is Forever" as they walked along praising and thanking the Lord! 22 And at the moment they began to sing and to praise, the Lord caused the armies of Ammon, Moab, and Mount Seir to begin fighting among themselves, and they destroyed each other! 23 For the Ammonites and Moabites turned against their allies from Mount Seir and killed every one of them. And when they had finished that job, they turned against each other! 24 So, when the army of Judah arrived at the watchtower that looks out over the wilderness, as far as they could look there were dead bodies lying on the ground—not a single one of the enemy had escaped. 25 King Jehoshaphat and his people went out to plunder the bodies and came away loaded with money, garments, and jewels stripped from the corpses—so much that it took them three days to cart it all away! 26 On the fourth day they gathered in the Valley of Blessing, as it is called today, and how they praised the Lord!

27 Then they returned to Jerusalem, with Jehoshaphat leading them, full of joy that the Lord had given them this marvelous rescue from their enemies. 28 They marched into Jerusalem accompanied by a band of harps, lyres, and trumpets and proceeded to the Temple. 29 And as had happened before, when the surrounding kingdoms heard that the Lord himself had fought against the enemies of Israel, the fear of God fell upon them. 30 So Jehoshaphat's kingdom was quiet, for his God had given him rest.

Jehoshaphat's Reign

31 A thumbnail sketch of King Jehoshaphat: He became king of Judah when he was thirty-five years old and reigned twenty-five years in Jerusalem. His mother's name was Azubah, the daughter of Shilhi. 32 He was a good king, just as his father Asa was. He continually tried to follow the Lord 33 with the exception that he did not destroy the idol shrines on the hills, nor had the people as yet really decided to follow the God of their ancestors.

20:15 If God is on our side, even the greatest of difficulties will not stand in the way of victory. Just as the prophet spoke to the people of Israel, urging them to hope in God's power to deliver them, God speaks to us in the Bible. He calls upon us to trust in him. The most common command in all of Scripture is "Don't be afraid!" And God always pronounces this command when the surrounding circumstances are terrible. God shows us time and again that no matter how terrible the circumstances, he is able to give the victory. All we need to do is trust in him.

20:17 It is hard for some of us to give up control. We want to do things our way, and we want the credit for success! God told the people of Judah to sit and watch as he gave them a great victory. In recovery we need to learn to give our battles to God. Whether we like it or not, we cannot win them alone. With God's help, however, no enemy is too large or terrible. If we are willing to put our life into God's hands, God will give us the victory.

34The details of Jehoshaphat's reign from
first to last are written in the history of Jehu
the son of Hanani, which is inserted in *The
Annals of the Kings of Israel.*
35But at the close of his life, Jehoshaphat,
king of Judah, went into partnership with
Ahaziah, king of Israel, who was a very wicked
man. 36They made ships in Ezion-geber to sail
to Tarshish. 37Then Eliezer, son of Dodavahu
from Mareshah, prophesied against Jehoshaphat, telling him, "Because you have allied
yourself with King Ahaziah, the Lord has destroyed your work." So the ships met disaster
and never arrived at Tarshish.

CHAPTER 21

Jehoram Rules Judah

When Jehoshaphat died, he was buried in the
cemetery of the kings in Jerusalem, and his
son Jehoram became the new ruler of Judah.
2His brothers—other sons of Jehoshaphat—
were Azariah, Jehiel, Zechariah, Azariah, Michael, and Shephatiah. 3,4Their father had
given each of them valuable gifts of money
and jewels, also the ownership of some of the
fortified cities of Judah. However, he gave the
kingship to Jehoram because he was the oldest. But when Jehoram had become solidly
established as king, he killed all of his brothers and many other leaders of Israel. 5He was
thirty-two years old when he began to reign,
and he reigned eight years in Jerusalem. 6But
he was as wicked as the kings who were over
in Israel. Yes, as wicked as Ahab, for Jehoram
had married one of the daughters of Ahab,
and his whole life was one constant binge of
doing evil. 7However, the Lord was unwilling
to end the dynasty of David, for he had made
a covenant with David always to have one of
his descendants upon the throne.
8At that time the king of Edom revolted,
declaring his independence of Judah. 9Jeho-
ram attacked him with his full army and with
all of his chariots, marching by night, and
almost managed to subdue him. 10But to this
day Edom has been successful in throwing off
the yoke of Judah. Libnah revolted too because Jehoram had turned away from the
Lord God of his fathers. 11What's more, Jehoram constructed idol shrines in the mountains of Judah and led the people of Jerusalem
in worshiping idols; in fact, he compelled his
people to worship them.
12Then Elijah the prophet wrote him this
letter: "The Lord God of your ancestor David
says that because you have not followed in
the good ways of your father Jehoshaphat,
nor the good ways of King Asa, 13but you have
been as evil as the kings over in Israel and
have made the people of Jerusalem and Judah
worship idols just as in the times of King
Ahab, and because you have killed your
brothers who were better than you, 14now the
Lord will destroy your nation with a great
plague. You, your children, your wives, and
all that you have will be struck down. 15You
will be stricken with an intestinal disease and
your bowels will rot away."
16Then the Lord stirred up the Philistines
and the Arabs living next to the Ethiopians to
attack Jehoram. 17They marched against
Judah, broke across the border, and carried
away everything of value in the king's palace,
including his sons and his wives; only his
youngest son, Jehoahaz, escaped.
18It was after this that Jehovah struck him
down with the incurable bowel disease. 19In
the process of time, at the end of two years,
his intestines came out, and he died in terrible
suffering. (The customary pomp and ceremony was omitted at his funeral.) 20He was
thirty-two years old when he began to reign,
and he reigned in Jerusalem eight years and
died unmourned. He was buried in Jerusalem,
but not in the royal cemetery.

CHAPTER 22

Ahaziah Rules Judah

Then the people of Jerusalem chose Ahaziah,
his youngest son, as their new king (for the
marauding bands of Arabs had killed his older
sons). 2Ahaziah was twenty-two years old
when he began to reign, and he reigned one
year in Jerusalem. His mother's name was

21:6-7 What an amazing contrast between father and son! Here we are told about the faithlessness of Jehoram. He patterned his reign after the kings of the northern kingdom, and he even married one of Ahab's wicked daughters. The consequences of turning from God are exhibited in Jehoram's failures. It should encourage us, however, to see that Jehoram's actions could never negate God's promises. No matter how badly we have failed, God will restore us if we turn back to him.

21:18-20 Jehoram's life of rebellion against God and his failure to fulfill his royal responsibilities led to a tragic end. He was disowned and undesired by his own people—they didn't even give him an honorable burial. We can only wonder what would have happened had Jehoram renewed his relationship with God and reconciled himself with his people. Rejecting God's program always leads to failure and shame. God's way is the only way to achieve true recovery.

Athaliah, granddaughter of Omri. 3He, too, walked in the evil ways of Ahab, for his mother encouraged him in doing wrong. 4Yes, he was as evil as Ahab, for Ahab's family became his advisors after his father's death, and they led him on to ruin.

5Following their evil advice, Ahaziah made an alliance with King Joram of Israel (the son of Ahab), who was at war with King Hazael of Syria at Ramoth-gilead. Ahaziah led his army there to join the battle. King Joram of Israel was wounded 6and returned to Jezreel to recover. Ahaziah went to visit him, 7but this turned out to be a fatal mistake; for God had decided to punish Ahaziah for his alliance with Joram. It was during this visit that Ahaziah went out with Joram to challenge Jehu (son of Nimshi), whom the Lord had appointed to end the dynasty of Ahab.

8While Jehu was hunting down and killing the family and friends of Ahab, he met King Ahaziah's nephews, the princes of Judah, and killed them. 9As he and his men were searching for Ahaziah, they found him hiding in the city of Samaria and brought him to Jehu, who killed him. Even so, Ahaziah was given a royal burial because he was the grandson of King Jehoshaphat—a man who enthusiastically served the Lord.

Athaliah Rules Judah

None of his sons, however, except for Joash, lived to succeed him as king, 10for their grandmother Athaliah killed them when she heard the news of her son Ahaziah's death.

11Joash was rescued by his Aunt Jehoshabeath, who was King Ahaziah's sister, and was hidden away in a storage room in the Temple. She was a daughter of King Jehoram and the wife of Jehoiada the priest. 12Joash remained hidden in the Temple for six years while Athaliah reigned as queen. He was cared for by his nurse and by his aunt and uncle.

CHAPTER 23

Young Joash Becomes King

In the seventh year of the reign of Queen Athaliah, Jehoiada the priest got up his courage and took some of the army officers into his confidence: Azariah (son of Jeroham), Ishmael (son of Jehohanan), Azariah (son of Obed), Maaseiah (son of Adaiah), and Elishaphat (son of Zichri). 2,3These men traveled out across the nation secretly to tell the Levites and clan leaders about his plans and to summon them to Jerusalem. On arrival they swore allegiance to the young king, who was still in hiding at the Temple.

"At last the time has come for the king's son to reign!" Jehoiada exclaimed. "The Lord's promise—that a descendant of King David shall be our king—will be true again. 4This is how we'll proceed: A third of you priests and Levites who come off duty on the Sabbath will stay at the entrance as guards. 5,6Another third will go over to the palace, and a third will be at the Lower Gate. Everyone else must stay in the outer courts of the Temple, as required by God's laws. For only the priests and Levites on duty may enter the Temple itself, for they are sanctified. 7You Levites, form a bodyguard for the king, weapons in hand, and kill any unauthorized person entering the Temple. Stay right beside the king."

22:2-4 It is a terrible thing to follow a bad example and listen to foolish advice. Ahaziah had a poisoned heritage and surroundings. His grandparents were Ahab and Jezebel. His mother was godless Athaliah, who served as his chief advisor. Sadly, Ahaziah never turned to God to receive the gift of forgiveness and reconciliation. We may face a heritage similar to Ahaziah's. If so, it is reassuring to know that through Christ, we can overcome the setbacks of even the worst environment or family background.

22:5 Outside of God's direct assistance, it is difficult to overcome family pressures. Just as Jehoshaphat of Judah had joined forces with Ahab of Israel, so Ahaziah of Judah teamed up with his uncle Joram of Israel against the Syrians. This was a ticklish situation. We do owe special allegiance to our family, but not if they try to lead us away from God and his will for our life.

22:10-12 Again and again we are reminded of the truth that God is sovereign. Everything was against Jehoiada and young Joash. They escaped the bloodbath of Jehu and then avoided the slaughter of Ahaziah's family by Athaliah. As we face difficult circumstances, we can find encouragement in the fact that God is ultimately in control. If we entrust our life to him, he will lead us through even the darkest situations.

23:1-11 Some people claim that when we trust in God to deliver us, we need not make any further preparations. This is not what we see in Scripture. Even when we entrust our life to God, he still expects us to take action. In order to accomplish God's will, Jehoiada made painstaking plans. He did everything necessary to restore the royal dynasty of David to Judah's throne. Sometimes doing right requires careful planning and even the use of force. We need to trust that God will lead us to act in a godly way to fulfill his will for our life.

8So all the arrangements were made. Each
of the three leaders led a third of the priests
arriving for duty that Sabbath, and a third of
those whose week's work was done and were
going off duty—for Jehoiada the chief priest
didn't release them to go home. 9Then Jehoiada issued spears and shields to all the army
officers. These had once belonged to King
David and were stored in the Temple. 10These
officers, fully armed, formed a line from one
side to the other in front of the Temple and
around the altar in the outer court. 11Then
they brought out the little prince and placed
the crown upon his head, and handed him a
copy of the law of God, and proclaimed him
king.
A great shout went up, "Long live the
king!" as Jehoiada and his sons anointed him.

Queen Athaliah Is Killed

12When Queen Athaliah heard all the noise
and commotion and the shouts of praise to
the king, she rushed over to the Temple to see
what was going on—and there stood the king
by his pillar at the entrance, with the army
officers and the trumpeters surrounding him,
and people from all over the land rejoicing
and blowing trumpets, and the singers singing, accompanied by an orchestra leading the
people in a great psalm of praise.
Athaliah ripped her clothes and screamed,
"Treason! Treason!"
13,14"Take her out and kill her," Jehoiada the
priest shouted to the army officers. "Don't do
it here at the Temple. And kill anyone who
tries to help her."
15-17So the crowd opened up for them to take
her out, and they killed her at the palace
stables.

Then Jehoiada made a solemn contract
that he and the king and the people would be
the Lord's. And all the people rushed over to
the temple of Baal and knocked it down, and
broke up the altars, and knocked down the
idols, and killed Mattan the priest of Baal
before his altar. 18Jehoiada now appointed the
Levite priests as guards, and to sacrifice the
burnt offering to the Lord as prescribed in the
law of Moses. He made the identical assignments of the Levite clans that King David had.
They sang with joy as they worked. 19The
guards at the Temple gates kept out everything that was not consecrated and all unauthorized personnel.
20Then the army officers, nobles, governors,
and all the people escorted the king from the
Temple, wending their way from the Upper
Gate to the palace, and seated the king upon
his throne. 21So all the people of the land
rejoiced, and the city was quiet and peaceful
because Queen Athaliah was dead.

CHAPTER 24

Joash Repairs the Temple

Joash was seven years old when he became
king, and he reigned forty years in Jerusalem.
His mother's name was Zibiah, from Beer-
sheba. 2Joash tried hard to please the Lord all
during the lifetime of Jehoiada the priest.
3Jehoiada arranged two marriages for him,
and he had sons and daughters.
4Later on Joash decided to repair and recon-
dition the Temple. 5He summoned the priests
and Levites and gave them these instructions:
"Go to all the cities of Judah and collect
offerings for the building fund so that we can
maintain the Temple in good repair. Get at it

23:15-17 After the overthrow of the usurper Athaliah, Jehoiada led the people of Judah to renew their relationship with God. After times of relapse and rebellion, we need to revive our commitment to God. He is always willing to offer us a fresh start—no matter how constant or how deep our failure has been.
23:20-21 The results of conflict are not always negative. After the overthrow of Athaliah, the people rejoiced and there was peace in Jerusalem. We should use conflicts to pinpoint the problems in our life. Then we should take steps to root them out. Hiding from conflict or denying its existence will never lead to personal growth or to victory over our dependencies.
24:1-2 When we are ill-equipped or unprepared for any role in life, it is important that we find a godly mentor to give us direction. The boy-king Joash was greatly blessed to have Jehoiada to guide him in his early decisions. The old priest kept him going in the right direction, leading him in the ways of God. In recovery, all of us need the help of a godly mentor who knows what we are going through. We must avoid the tendency to "go it alone." Let us allow God to use others in our recovery.
24:4-5 Not only must we be committed to doing God's will, we must also be committed to doing things when God wants them done. Procrastinating when God has shown us what he requires is a form of disobedience. Plans to do God's will "tomorrow" should never be mistaken for obedience. If we know what God wants us to do, we need to get on with it!

right away. Don't delay." But the Levites took
their time.

[6]So the king called for Jehoiada the High
Priest and asked him, "Why haven't you demanded that the Levites go out and collect
the Temple taxes from the cities of Judah and
from Jerusalem? The tax law enacted by Moses the servant of the Lord must be enforced
so that the Temple can be repaired."

[7,8](The followers of wicked Athaliah had
ravaged the Temple, and everything dedicated to the worship of God had been removed to the temple of Baalim.) So now the
king instructed that a chest be made and set
outside the Temple gate. [9]Then a proclamation was sent to all the cities of Judah and
throughout Jerusalem telling the people to
bring to the Lord the tax that Moses the
servant of God had assessed upon Israel. [10]And
all the leaders and the people were glad, and
brought the money and placed it in the chest
until it was full.

[11]Then the Levites carried the chest to the
king's accounting office, where the recording
secretary and the representative of the High
Priest counted the money and took the chest
back to the Temple again. This went on day
after day, and money continued to pour in.
[12]The king and Jehoiada gave the money to
the building superintendents, who hired masons and carpenters to restore the Temple,
and to foundrymen, who made articles of
iron and brass. [13]So the work went forward,
and finally the Temple was in much better
condition than before. [14]When all was finished, the remaining money was brought to
the king and Jehoiada, and it was agreed to
use it for making the gold and silver spoons
and bowls used for incense, and for making
the instruments used in the sacrifices and
offerings.

Burnt offerings were sacrificed continually
during the lifetime of Jehoiada the priest. [15]He
lived to a very old age, finally dying at 130.
[16]He was buried in the City of David among
the kings because he had done so much good
for Israel, for God, and for the Temple.

Jehoiada Dies and Joash Sins

[17,18]But after his death, the leaders of Judah
came to King Joash and induced him to abandon the Temple of the God of their ancestors
and to worship shame-idols instead! So the
wrath of God came down upon Judah and
Jerusalem again. [19]God sent prophets to bring
them back to the Lord, but the people
wouldn't listen.

[20]Then the Spirit of God came upon Zechariah, Jehoiada's son. He called a meeting of all
the people. Standing before them upon a platform, he said to them, "God wants to know
why you are disobeying his commandments.
For when you do, everything you try fails. You
have forsaken the Lord, and now he has forsaken you."

[21]Then the leaders plotted to kill Zechariah,
and finally King Joash himself ordered him
executed in the court of the Temple. [22]That
was how King Joash repaid Jehoiada for his
love and loyalty—by killing his son. Zechariah's last words as he died were, "Lord, see
what they are doing and pay them back."

[23]A few months later the Syrian army arrived and conquered Judah and Jerusalem,
killing all the leaders of the nation and sending back great quantities of booty to the king
of Damascus. [24]It was a great triumph for the
tiny Syrian army, but the Lord let the great
army of Judah be conquered by them because
they had forsaken the Lord God of their ancestors. In that way God executed judgment
upon Joash. [25]When the Syrians left—leaving
Joash severely wounded—his own officials
decided to kill him for murdering the son of
Jehoiada the priest. They assassinated him as
he lay in bed, and buried him in the City of
David, but not in the cemetery of the kings.
[26]The conspirators were Zabad, whose mother
was Shimeath, a woman from Ammon; and
Jehozabad, whose mother was Shimrith, a
woman from Moab.

[27]If you want to read about the sons of Joash
and the curses laid upon Joash, and about the
restoration of the Temple, see *The Annals of
the Kings*.

When Joash died, his son Amaziah became
the new king.

CHAPTER 25

Amaziah Rules Judah

Amaziah was twenty-five years old when he
became king, and he reigned twenty-nine

24:17-20 After Jehoiada died, Joash turned away from God. Jehoiada's son Zechariah rebuked Joash for his failure to obey God's laws. Joash was unwilling to face the truth about his behavior and even killed Zechariah to hide from it. When we are confronted with sin in our life, it is tempting to deny its existence. As we take inventory, we need to do so honestly. When confronted with our sin, we need to admit it and then take steps to eliminate it from our life.

years in Jerusalem. His mother's name was Jehoaddan, a native of Jerusalem. 2He did what was right, but sometimes resented it! 3When he was well established as the new king, he executed the men who had assassinated his father. 4However, he didn't kill their children but followed the command of the Lord written in the law of Moses, that the fathers shall not die for the children's sins, nor the children for the father's sins. No, everyone must pay for his own sins.

5,6Another thing Amaziah did was to organize the army, assigning leaders to each clan from Judah and Benjamin. Then he took a census and found that he had an army of 300,000 men twenty years old and older, all trained and highly skilled in the use of spear and sword. He also paid $200,000 to hire 100,000 experienced mercenaries from Israel.

7But a prophet arrived with this message from the Lord: "Sir, do not hire troops from Israel, for the Lord is not with them. 8If you let them go with your troops to battle, you will be defeated no matter how well you fight; for God has power to help or to frustrate."

9"But the money!" Amaziah whined. "What shall I do about that?"

And the prophet replied, "The Lord is able to give you much more than this!"

10So Amaziah sent them home again to Ephraim, which made them very angry and insulted. 11Then Amaziah took courage and led his army to the Valley of Salt and there killed 10,000 men from Seir. 12Another 10,000 were taken alive to the top of a cliff and thrown over so that they were crushed upon the rocks below.

13Meanwhile, the army of Israel that had been sent home raided several of the cities of Judah in the vicinity of Beth-horon toward Samaria, killing 3,000 people and carrying off great quantities of booty.

14When King Amaziah returned from this slaughter of the Edomites, he brought with him idols taken from the people of Seir, set them up as gods, bowed before them, and burned incense to them! 15This made the Lord very angry, and he sent a prophet to demand, "Why have you worshiped gods who couldn't even save their own people from you?"

16"Since when have I asked your advice?" the king retorted. "Be quiet now before I have you killed."

The prophet left with this parting warning: "I know that God has determined to destroy you because you have worshiped these idols and have not accepted my counsel."

17King Amaziah of Judah now took the advice of his counselors and declared war on King Joash of Israel (son of Jehoahaz, grandson of Jehu).

18King Joash replied with this parable: "Out in the Lebanon mountains a thistle demanded of a cedar tree, 'Give your daughter in marriage to my son.' Just then a wild animal came by and stepped on the thistle, crushing it! 19You are very proud about your conquest of Edom, but my advice is to stay home and don't meddle with me, lest you and all Judah get badly hurt."

20But Amaziah wouldn't listen for God was arranging to destroy him for worshiping the gods of Edom. 21The armies met at Beth-shemesh in Judah, 22and Judah was defeated and its army fled home. 23King Joash of Israel captured the defeated King Amaziah of Judah and took him as a prisoner to Jerusalem. Then King Joash ordered 200 yards of the walls of Jerusalem dismantled, from the gate of Ephraim to the Corner Gate. 24He carried off all the treasures and gold bowls from the Temple, as well as the treasures from the palace; and he took hostages, including Obed-edom, and returned to Samaria.

25:1-2 When it came to God's evaluation, Amaziah's grade was good—but not great. He did the right things, but he failed to do them with the right attitude. As we follow God's program for healthy living, we need to do it with a whole heart. We need to seek God sincerely. If we are just going through the motions with hopes of receiving God's blessings, our progress in recovery will be slow and temporary at best.

25:4 Here we are reminded that we all must take responsibility for our own sins. Many of us in recovery have come to realize that much of what we suffer is a consequence of our parents' mistakes. It is easy to use this as an excuse for our failures in life, but this is a big mistake. We need to take responsibility for our own failures. This is part of taking a personal inventory. We must accept the sin in our life and take steps to remove it. We alone are responsible before God for our actions.

25:5-8 As Amaziah faced a powerful enemy, it seemed a good idea to hire a large contingent of mercenaries from the northern kingdom. But God told Amaziah to send all the foreign troops home and to trust him for the outcome. As we face the difficult process of recovery, we may be tempted to try every human resource available to support our recovery. We must be careful to limit the resources we use to the ones that recognize our ultimate need for God's help.

[25]However, King Amaziah of Judah lived on for fifteen years after the death of King Joash of Israel. [26]The complete biography of King Amaziah is written in *The Annals of the Kings of Judah and Israel.* [27]This account includes a report of Amaziah's turning away from God, how his people conspired against him in Jerusalem, and how he fled to Lachish—but they went after him and killed him there. [28]And they brought him back on horses to Jerusalem and buried him in the royal cemetery.

CHAPTER 26

Uzziah Rules Judah

The people of Judah now crowned sixteen-year-old Uzziah as their new king. [2]After his father's death, he rebuilt the city of Eloth and restored it to Judah. [3]In all, he reigned fifty-two years in Jerusalem. His mother's name was Jecoliah, from Jerusalem. [4]He followed in the footsteps of his father Amaziah and was, in general, a good king in the Lord's sight.

[5]While Zechariah was alive Uzziah was always eager to please God. Zechariah was a man who had special revelations from God. And as long as the king followed the paths of God, he prospered, for God blessed him.

[6]He declared war on the Philistines and captured the city of Gath and broke down its walls, also those of Jabneh and Ashdod. Then he built new cities in the Ashdod area and in other parts of the Philistine country. [7]God helped him not only with his wars against the Philistines but also in his battles with the Arabs of Gur-baal and in his wars with the Meunites. [8]The Ammonites paid annual tribute to him, and his fame spread even to Egypt, for he was very powerful.

[9]He built fortified towers in Jerusalem at the Corner Gate, and the Valley Gate, and at the turning of the wall. [10]He also constructed forts in the Negeb and made many water reservoirs, for he had great herds of cattle out in the valleys and on the plains. He was a man who loved the soil and had many farms and vineyards, both on the hillsides and in the fertile valleys.

[11]He organized his army into regiments to which men were drafted under quotas set by Jeiel, the secretary of the army, and his assistant, Maaseiah. The commander-in-chief was General Hananiah. [12]Twenty-six hundred brave clan leaders commanded these regiments. [13]The army consisted of 307,500 men, all elite troops. [14]Uzziah issued to them shields, spears, helmets, coats of mail, bows, and slingstones. [15]And he produced engines of war manufactured in Jerusalem, invented by brilliant men to shoot arrows and huge stones from the towers and battlements. So he became very famous, for the Lord helped him wonderfully until he was very powerful.

[16]But at that point he became proud—and corrupt. He sinned against the Lord his God by entering the forbidden sanctuary of the Temple and personally burning incense upon the altar. [17,18]Azariah the High Priest went in after him with eighty other priests, all brave men, and demanded that he get out.

"It is not for you, Uzziah, to burn incense," they declared. "That is the work of the priests alone, the sons of Aaron who are consecrated to this work. Get out, for you have trespassed, and the Lord is not going to honor you for this!"

[19]Uzziah was furious and refused to set down the incense burner he was holding. But look! Suddenly—leprosy appeared in his forehead! [20]When Azariah and the others saw it, they rushed him out; in fact, he himself was as anxious to get out as they were to get him out because the Lord had struck him.

[21]So King Uzziah was a leper until the day of his death and lived in isolation, cut off from his people and from the Temple. His son Jotham became vice-regent, in charge of the king's affairs and of the judging of the people of the land.

[22]The other details of Uzziah's reign from first to last are recorded by the prophet Isaiah (son of Amoz). [23]When Uzziah died, he was buried in the royal cemetery even though he was a leper, and his son Jotham became the new king.

26:14-16 When everything is going great, we are tempted to feel that we don't need God. Surely this was Uzziah's primary problem. As he became successful, he forgot that he needed God's help. We need to learn from Uzziah's mistake. When our recovery begins to go well, it is easy to think we can go it alone. But as soon as we begin to think this way, we are headed for a fall.

26:16-18 Uzziah had begun his reign so well; he had the potential of being one of the greatest kings in Judah's history. God blessed him in practically everything he did. But then he became proud and entered the Temple sanctuary, something only the priests were allowed to do. Uzziah discovered an important truth—we cannot sin without suffering the consequences.

CHAPTER 27

Jotham Rules Judah

Jotham was twenty-five years old at the time he became king, and he reigned sixteen years in Jerusalem. His mother was Jerushah, daughter of Zadok. 2He followed the generally good example of his father Uzziah—who had, however, sinned by invading the Temple—but even so his people became very corrupt.

3He built the Upper Gate of the Temple and also did extensive rebuilding of the walls on the hill where the Temple was situated. 4And he built cities in the hill country of Judah and erected fortresses and towers on the wooded hills.

5His war against the Ammonites was successful so that for the next three years he received from them an annual tribute of $200,000 in silver, 10,000 sacks of wheat, and 10,000 sacks of barley. 6King Jotham became powerful because he was careful to follow the path of the Lord his God.

7The remainder of his history, including his wars and other activities, is written in *The Annals of the Kings of Israel and Judah.* 8In summary, then, he was twenty-five years old when he began to reign, and he reigned sixteen years in Jerusalem. 9When he died, he was buried in Jerusalem, and his son Ahaz became the new king.

CHAPTER 28

Ahaz Rules Judah

Ahaz was twenty years old when he became king, and he reigned sixteen years in Jerusalem. But he was an evil king, unlike his ancestor King David. 2For he followed the example of the kings over in Israel and worshiped the idols of Baal. 3He even went out to the Valley of Hinnom, and it was not just to burn incense to the idols, for he even sacrificed his own children in the fire, just like the heathen nations that were thrown out of the land by the Lord to make room for Israel. 4Yes, he sacrificed and burned incense at the idol shrines on the hills and under every green tree.

5That is why the Lord God allowed the king of Syria to defeat him and deport large numbers of his people to Damascus. The armies from Israel also slaughtered great numbers of his troops. 6On a single day Pekah, the son of Remaliah, killed 120,000 of his bravest soldiers because they had turned away from the Lord God of their fathers.7Then Zichri, a great warrior from Ephraim, killed the king's son Maaseiah, the king's administrator Azrikam, and the king's second-in-command Elkanah. 8The armies from Israel also captured 200,000 Judean women and children and tremendous amounts of booty, which they took to Samaria.

9But Oded, a prophet of the Lord, was there in Samaria, and he went out to meet the returning army.

"Look!" he exclaimed. "The Lord God of your fathers was angry with Judah and let you capture them, but you have butchered them without mercy, and all heaven is disturbed. 10And now are you going to make slaves of these people from Judah and Jerusalem? What about your own sins against the Lord your God? 11Listen to me and return these relatives of yours to their homes, for now the fierce anger of the Lord is upon *you.*"

12Some of the top leaders of Ephraim also added their opposition. These men were Azariah the son of Johanan, Berechiah the son of Meshillemoth, Jehizkiah the son of Shallum, and Amasa the son of Hadlai.

13"You must not bring the captives here!" they declared. "If you do, the Lord will be angry, and this sin will be added to our many others. We are in enough trouble with God as it is."

14So the army officers turned over the captives and booty to the political leaders to decide what to do. 15Then the four men al-

27:6 What makes a person great? God shows us that Jotham's success was a direct result of his obedience to God. When we are faithful to God's ways, God will lead us to a victorious and productive life. We must remember, however, that God's view of greatness might not correspond with ours.

28:1-2 The northern kingdom of Israel was in the throes of death. It had been vanquished by the Assyrians; most of its people had been taken into captivity and would never return. How foolish for Ahaz to follow the example of the kings of the northern kingdom! He could see where their behavior had led them. We need to be careful about whom we choose to emulate.

28:3-4 Ahaz hadn't learned that the heathen customs of surrounding nations were not appropriate or helpful. In fact, these activities eventually led to his destruction. It is tempting to try recovery programs that prescribe activities or beliefs that contradict God's Word, especially if they seem to be working for people we know. We must measure any program against the truth of God's Word and remember that recovery can only be achieved with God's power.

ready mentioned distributed captured stores of clothing to the women and children who needed it and gave them shoes, food, and wine, and put those who were sick and old on donkeys, and took them back to their families in Jericho, the City of Palm Trees. Then their escorts returned to Samaria.

Ahaz Nails the Temple Shut

16About that time King Ahaz of Judah asked the king of Assyria to be his ally in his war against the armies of Edom. For Edom was invading Judah and capturing many people as
slaves. 17,18Meanwhile, the Philistines had invaded the lowland cities and the Negeb and had already captured Beth-shemesh, Aijalon, Gederoth, Soco, Timnah, and Gimzo with their surrounding villages, and were living
there. 19For the Lord brought Judah very low on account of the evil deeds of King Ahaz of Israel, for he had destroyed the spiritual fiber of Judah and had been faithless to the Lord.
20But when Tilgath-pilneser, king of Assyria, arrived, he caused trouble for King Ahaz in-
stead of helping him. 21So even though Ahaz had given him the Temple gold and the palace treasures, it did no good.

22In this time of deep trial, King Ahaz col-
lapsed spiritually. 23He sacrificed to the gods of the people of Damascus who had defeated him, for he felt that since these gods had helped the kings of Syria, they would help him too if he sacrificed to them. But instead, they were his ruin, and that of all his people.
24The king took the gold bowls from the Temple and slashed them to pieces, and nailed the door of the Temple shut so that no one could worship there, and made altars to the heathen gods in every corner of Jerusa-
lem. 25And he did the same in every city of Judah, thus angering the Lord God of his fathers.

26The other details of his life and activities are recorded in *The Annals of the Kings of Judah and Israel.* 27When King Ahaz died, he was buried in Jerusalem but not in the royal tombs, and his son Hezekiah became the new king.

CHAPTER 29

Hezekiah Reopens the Temple

Hezekiah was twenty-five years old when he became the king of Judah, and he reigned twenty-nine years in Jerusalem. His mother's name was Abijah, the daughter of Zechariah.
2His reign was generally good in the Lord's sight, just as his ancestor David's had been.

3In the very first month of the first year of his reign, he reopened the doors of the Temple and repaired them. 4,5He summoned the priests and Levites to meet him at the open space east of the Temple and addressed them thus:

"Listen to me, you Levites. Sanctify yourselves and sanctify the Temple of the Lord God of your ancestors—clean all the debris
from the holy place. 6For our fathers have committed a deep sin before the Lord our God; they abandoned the Lord and his
Temple and turned their backs on it. 7The doors have been shut tight, the perpetual flame has been put out, and the incense and
burnt offerings have not been offered. 8Therefore, the wrath of the Lord has been upon Judah and Jerusalem. He has caused us to be objects of horror, amazement, and contempt,
as you see us today. 9Our fathers have been killed in war, and our sons and daughters and wives are in captivity because of this.

10"But now I want to make a covenant with the Lord God of Israel so that his fierce anger
will turn away from us. 11My children, don't neglect your duties any longer, for the Lord has chosen you to minister to him and to burn incense."

12-14Then the Levites went into action:

From the Kohath clan, Mahath (son of Amasai) and Joel (son of Azariah);

29:1-2 Hezekiah received a high commendation indeed: he followed the example of his ancestor David. For the kings of Judah, King David was the measure of success. As we seek to rebuild our life, we need to find worthy role models. David is an ideal role model, for though he made many mistakes, he was always willing to humbly admit his failures and seek reconciliation with God and other people.

29:3-5 Hezekiah began his reign in the right way—with steps toward recovery. His father had led Judah into sin and idolatry. The Temple had been closed and its programs of worship discontinued. Hezekiah recognized the failures of his father and set out to make changes. He opened the Temple's doors and enjoined the priests to cleanse themselves and reinstitute the proper worship activities. When our life is filled with problems, denial is not the way to make things better. We need to act like Hezekiah, who assessed the problems and deficiencies of his kingdom and then did what he could to change them.

From the Merari clan, Kish (son of Abdi) and Azariah (son of Jehallelel);
From the Gershon clan, Joah (son of Zimmah) and Eden (son of Joah).
From the Elizaphan clan, Shimri and Jeuel;
From the Asaph clan, Zechariah and Mattaniah;
From the Hemanite clan, Jehuel and Shimei;
From the Jeduthun clan, Shemaiah and Uzziel.

[15]They in turn summoned their fellow Levites and sanctified themselves, and began to clean up and sanctify the Temple, as the king (who was speaking for the Lord) had commanded them. [16]The priests cleaned up the inner room of the Temple and brought out into the court all the filth and decay they found there. The Levites then carted it out to the brook Kidron. [17]This all began on the first day of April, and by the eighth day they had reached the outer court, which took eight days to clean up, so the entire job was completed in sixteen days.

[18]Then they went back to the palace and reported to King Hezekiah, "We have completed the cleansing of the Temple and of the altar of burnt offerings and of its accessories, also the table of the Bread of the Presence and its equipment. [19]What's more, we have recovered and sanctified all the utensils thrown away by King Ahaz when he closed the Temple. They are beside the altar of the Lord."

The Temple Is Consecrated

[20]Early the next morning King Hezekiah went to the Temple with the city officials, [21]taking seven young bulls, seven rams, seven lambs, and seven male goats for a sin offering for the nation and for the Temple.

He instructed the priests, the sons of Aaron, to sacrifice them on the altar of the Lord. [22]So they killed the young bulls, and the priests took the blood and sprinkled it on the altar, and they killed the rams and sprinkled their blood upon the altar, and did the same with the lambs. [23]The male goats for the sin offering were then brought before the king and his officials, who laid their hands upon them. [24]Then the priests killed the animals and made a sin offering with their blood upon the altar to make atonement for all Israel, as the king had commanded—for the king had specified that the burnt offering and sin offering must be sacrificed for the entire nation.

[25,26]He organized Levites at the Temple into an orchestral group, using cymbals, psalteries, and harps. This was in accordance with the directions of David and the prophets Gad and Nathan, who had received their instructions from the Lord. The priests formed a trumpet corps. [27]Then Hezekiah ordered the burnt offering to be placed upon the altar, and as the sacrifice began, the instruments of music began to play the songs of the Lord, accompanied by the trumpets. [28]Throughout the entire ceremony everyone worshiped the Lord as the singers sang and the trumpets blew. [29]Afterwards the king and his aides bowed low before the Lord in worship. [30]Then King Hezekiah ordered the Levites to sing before the Lord some of the psalms of David and of the prophet Asaph, which they gladly did, and bowed their heads and worshiped.

[31]"The consecration ceremony is now ended," Hezekiah said. "Now bring your sacrifices and thank offerings." So the people from every part of the nation brought their sacrifices and thank offerings, and those who wished to brought burnt offerings too. [32,33]In all, there were 70 young bulls for burnt offerings, 100 rams, and 200 lambs. In addition, 600 oxen and 3,000 sheep were brought as holy gifts. [34]But there were too few priests to prepare the burnt offerings, so their brothers the Levites helped them until the work was finished—and until more priests had reported to work—for the Levites were much more ready to sanctify themselves than the priests were. [35]There was an abundance of burnt offerings, and the usual drink offering with each, and many peace offerings. So it was that the Temple was restored to service, and the sacrifices offered again. [36]And Hezekiah and all the people were very happy because of what God had accomplished so quickly.

CHAPTER 30

The Passover Is Celebrated

King Hezekiah now sent letters throughout all of Israel, Judah, Ephraim, and Manasseh, inviting everyone to come to the Temple at Jerusalem for the annual Passover celebration. [2,3]The king, his aides, and all the assembly of Jerusalem had voted to celebrate the Passover in May this time, rather than at the normal time in April, because not enough priests were sanctified at the earlier date, and there wasn't enough time to get notices out. [4]The king and his advisors were in complete agreement in this matter, [5]so they sent a Passover proclamation throughout Israel, from Dan to Beersheba, inviting everyone. They had not kept it in great numbers as prescribed.

6"Come back to the Lord God of Abraham, Isaac, and Israel," the king's letter said, "so that he will return to us who have escaped from the power of the kings of Assyria. 7Do not be like your fathers and brothers who sinned against the Lord God of their fathers and were destroyed. 8Do not be stubborn, as they were, but yield yourselves to the Lord and come to his Temple which he has sanctified forever, and worship the Lord your God so that his fierce anger will turn away from you. 9For if you turn to the Lord again, your brothers and your children will be treated mercifully by their captors, and they will be able to return to this land. For the Lord your God is full of kindness and mercy and will not continue to turn away his face from you if you return to him."

10So the messengers went from city to city throughout Ephraim and Manasseh and as far as Zebulun. But for the most part they were received with laughter and scorn! 11However, some from the tribes of Asher, Manasseh, and Zebulun turned to God and came to Jerusalem. 12But in Judah the entire nation felt a strong, God-given desire to obey the Lord's direction as commanded by the king and his officers. 13And so it was that a very large crowd assembled at Jerusalem in the month of May for the Passover celebration. 14They set to work and destroyed the heathen altars in Jerusalem, and knocked down all the incense altars, and threw them into Kidron Brook.

15On the first day of May the people killed their Passover lambs. Then the priests and Levites became ashamed of themselves for not taking a more active part, so they sanctified themselves and brought burnt offerings into the Temple. 16They stood at their posts as instructed by the law of Moses the man of God; and the priests sprinkled the blood received from the Levites.

17-19Since many of the people arriving from Ephraim, Manasseh, Issachar, and Zebulun were ceremonially impure because they had not undergone the purification rites, the Levites killed their Passover lambs for them, to sanctify them. Then King Hezekiah prayed for them, and they were permitted to eat the Passover anyway, even though this was contrary to God's rules. But Hezekiah said, "May the good Lord pardon everyone who determines to follow the Lord God of his fathers, even though he is not properly sanctified for the ceremony." 20And the Lord listened to Hezekiah's prayer and did not destroy them.

21So the people of Israel celebrated the Passover at Jerusalem for seven days with great joy.

Meanwhile the Levites and priests praised the Lord with music and cymbals day after day. 22(King Hezekiah spoke very appreciatively to the Levites of their excellent music.)

So for seven days the observance continued, and peace offerings were sacrificed, and the people confessed their sins to the Lord God of their fathers. 23The enthusiasm continued, so it was unanimously decided to continue the observance for another seven days. 24King Hezekiah gave the people 1,000 young bulls for offerings and 7,000 sheep; and the princes donated 1,000 young bulls and 10,000 sheep. And at this time another large group of priests stepped forward and sanctified themselves.

25Then the people of Judah, together with the priests, the Levites, the foreign residents, and the visitors from Israel, were filled with deep joy. 26For Jerusalem hadn't seen a celebration like this one since the days of King David's son Solomon. 27Then the priests and Levites stood and blessed the people, and the Lord heard their prayers from his holy temple in heaven.

CHAPTER 31

Hezekiah Restores True Worship

Afterwards a massive campaign against idol worship was begun. Those who were at Jerusalem for the Passover went out to the cities of Judah, Benjamin, Ephraim, and Manasseh and tore down the idol altars, the obelisks,

30:6-8 Hezekiah called his people to break from the dysfunctional patterns set by their parents. Notice that Hezekiah had already broken from the patterns set by his father. He was the ideal person to call his people to do the same. He knew exactly where they were coming from. Some people feel absolutely imprisoned by the failures and wrong patterns set by their parents. However, there is hope for all who trust God. We don't need to be bound by our parents' failures. We have a chance for recovery if we are willing to place our life in God's hands.

30:17-19 God is high and holy; he is sinless and perfect. We can approach him only because he graciously allows us to do so. In the Old Testament, seeking God was prescribed by definite procedures. Hezekiah prayed on behalf of those whose preparations were not as complete as they should have been. Now we can all approach God directly because of what Christ has done on our behalf.

shame-images, and other heathen centers of worship. Then the people who had come to the Passover from the northern tribes returned again to their own homes.

[2]Hezekiah now organized the priests and Levites into service corps to offer the burnt offerings and peace offerings, and to worship and give thanks and praise to the Lord. [3]He also made a personal contribution of animals for the daily morning and evening burnt offerings, as well as for the weekly Sabbath and monthly new moon festivals, and for the other annual feasts as required in the law of God.

[4]In addition, he required the people in Jerusalem to bring their tithes to the priests and Levites so that they wouldn't need other employment but could apply themselves fully to their duties as required in the law of God. [5,6]The people responded immediately and generously with the first of their crops and grain, new wine, olive oil, money, and everything else—a tithe of all they owned, as required by law to be given to the Lord their God. Everything was laid out in great piles. The people who had moved to Judah from the northern tribes and the people of Judah living in the provinces also brought in the tithes of their cattle and sheep, and brought a tithe of the dedicated things to give to the Lord, and piled them up in great heaps. [7,8]The first of these tithes arrived in June, and the piles continued to grow until October. When Hezekiah and his officials came and saw these huge piles, how they blessed the Lord and praised his people!

[9]"Where did all this come from?" Hezekiah asked the priests and Levites.

[10]And Azariah the High Priest from the clan of Zadok replied, "These are tithes! We have been eating from these stores of food for many weeks, but all this is left over, for the Lord has blessed his people."

[11]Hezekiah decided to prepare storerooms in the Temple. [12,13]All the dedicated supplies were brought into the Lord's house. Conaniah the Levite was put in charge, assisted by his brother Shimei and the following aides: Jehiel, Azaziah, Nahath, Asahel, Jerimoth, Jozabad, Eliel, Ismachiah, Mahath, Benaiah.

These appointments were made by King Hezekiah and Azariah the High Priest.

[14,15]Kore (son of Imnah, the Levite), who was the gatekeeper at the East Gate, was put in charge of distributing the offerings to the priests. His faithful assistants were Eden, Miniamin, Jeshua, Shemaiah, Amariah, and Shecaniah. They distributed the gifts to the clans of priests in their cities, dividing them to young and old alike. [16]However, the priests on duty at the Temple and their families were supplied directly from there, so they were not included in this distribution. [17,18]The priests were listed in the genealogical register by clans, and the Levites twenty years old and older were listed under the names of their work corps. A regular food allotment was given to all families of properly registered priests, for they had no other source of income because their time and energies were devoted to the service of the Temple. [19]One of the priests was appointed in each of the cities of the priests to issue food and other supplies to all priests in the area and to all registered Levites.

[20]In this way King Hezekiah handled the distribution throughout all Judah, doing what was just and fair in the sight of the Lord his God. [21]He worked very hard to encourage respect for the Temple, the law, and godly living, and was very successful.

CHAPTER 32

Assyria Invades Judah

Some time later after this good work of King Hezekiah, King Sennacherib of Assyria invaded Judah and laid siege to the fortified cities, planning to place them under tribute. [2]When it was clear that Sennacherib was intending to attack Jerusalem, [3]Hezekiah summoned his princes and officers for a council of war, and it was decided to plug the springs outside the city. [4]They organized a huge work

31:2 Hezekiah here illustrates another important element of recovery. He insured constant praise to God by setting up structures and personnel to lead the people in worship. Here is an element that is often lacking in our programs of recovery. We must never forget to thank God for his help as we seek to overcome the powerful problems in our life. Praising the one who makes our recovery possible is essential to a healthy recovery.

31:4-8 Sometimes doing good is a thankless task. Hezekiah made certain that encouragement was given to the people who took part in Judah's recovery process. When the people gave sacrificially to God, Hezekiah praised them for their generosity. How necessary it is for anyone in recovery to be a part of a comforting and strengthening fellowship. We need to remember to give and to receive the encouragement necessary for a successful recovery.

crew to block them and to cut off the brook running through the fields.

"Why should the king of Assyria come and find water?" they asked.

5Then Hezekiah further strengthened his defenses by repairing the wall wherever it was broken down, and by adding to the fortifications, and constructing a second wall outside it. He also reinforced Fort Millo in the City of David and manufactured large numbers of weapons and shields. 6He recruited an army and appointed officers, and summoned them to the plains before the city, and encouraged them with this address:

7"Be strong, be brave, and do not be afraid of the king of Assyria or his mighty army, for there is someone with us who is far greater than he is! 8He has a great army, but they are all mere men, while we have the Lord our God to fight our battles for us!" This greatly encouraged them.

9Then King Sennacherib of Assyria, while still besieging the city of Lachish, sent ambassadors with this message to King Hezekiah and the citizens of Jerusalem:

10"King Sennacherib of Assyria asks, 'Do you think you can survive my siege of Jerusalem? 11King Hezekiah is trying to persuade you to commit suicide by staying there—to die by famine and thirst—while he promises that "the Lord our God will deliver us from the king of Assyria"! 12Don't you realize that Hezekiah is the very person who destroyed all the idols, and commanded Judah and Jerusalem to use only the one altar at the Temple, and to burn incense upon it alone? 13Don't you realize that I and the other kings of Assyria before me have never yet failed to conquer a nation we attacked? The gods of those nations weren't able to do a thing to save their lands! 14Name just one time when anyone, anywhere, was able to resist us successfully. What makes you think your God can do any better? 15Don't let Hezekiah fool you! Don't believe him. I say it again—no god of any nation has ever yet been able to rescue his people from me or my ancestors; how much less your God!'" 16Thus the ambassador mocked the Lord God and God's servant Hezekiah, heaping up insults.

17King Sennacherib also sent letters scorning the Lord God of Israel.

"The gods of all the other nations failed to save their people from my hand, and the God of Hezekiah will fail too," he wrote.

18The messengers who brought the letters shouted threats in the Jewish language to the people gathered on the walls of the city, trying to frighten and dishearten them. 19These messengers talked about the God of Jerusalem just as though he were one of the heathen gods—a handmade idol!

20Then King Hezekiah and Isaiah the prophet (son of Amoz) cried out in prayer to God in heaven, 21and the Lord sent an angel who destroyed the Assyrian army with all its officers and generals! So Sennacherib returned home in deep shame to his own land. And when he arrived at the temple of his god, some of his own sons killed him there. 22That is how the Lord saved Hezekiah and the people of Jerusalem. And now there was peace at last throughout his realm.

23From then on King Hezekiah became immensely respected among the surrounding nations, and many gifts for the Lord arrived at Jerusalem, with valuable presents for King Hezekiah too.

Hezekiah Gets a Second Chance

24But about that time Hezekiah became deathly sick, and he prayed to the Lord, and the Lord replied with a miracle. 25However, Hezekiah didn't respond with true thanksgiving and praise for he had become proud, and so the anger of God was upon him and upon Judah and Jerusalem. 26But finally Hezekiah and the residents of Jerusalem

32:3-6 Trust in God—and work hard to do his will. Hezekiah gives us an excellent example of how we should act in recovery—with both faith and hard work. He knew that only God could deliver Judah from the Assyrian invasion, but that didn't stop him from doing what he could to protect Jerusalem. One of the engineering marvels of the ancient world is Hezekiah's Tunnel. It brought water from a spring into the city, insuring a steady water supply during a siege. There is no question that Hezekiah trusted God for victory, but he made certain that he did all that he could to prepare for the invasion.

32:20-22 Perhaps the most overlooked resource in the recovery process is prayer. God does hear and answer the call of his people. He does not always send an immediate and miraculous rescue as he did for Hezekiah, but he always answers. God's intervention in this instance is clear. By any human estimation, Sennacherib should have won this battle, but God gave Judah the victory. God is just as able to help us in our "impossible" battles.

READ 2 CHRONICLES 32:1-19

GOD grant me the serenity to accept the things I cannot change the courage to change the things I can and the wisdom to know the difference AMEN

Recovery involves repairing or building healthy boundaries where they have become weak, defective, or torn down through abuse. Boundaries are the limits we set for our protection.

In Bible times each city was fortified by boundary walls that served as protection from outside enemies. If these walls were weak or broken, there was grave danger of invasion and destruction. At one point in Israel's history an enemy was threatening to attack Jerusalem. The king "strengthened his defenses by repairing the wall wherever it was broken down and by adding to the fortifications, and constructing a second wall outside it. He . . . encouraged them with this address: 'Be strong, be brave. . . . We have the Lord our God to fight our battles for us!' This greatly encouraged them" (2 Chronicles 32:5-8).

For some of us, our boundaries have grown weaker as we let people walk all over us or let down our guard against our own destructive behaviors.

Part of the recovery process involves repairing our boundaries. We can also construct a second wall of defense by developing a strong support network around us. We will still need to be brave and remember that no matter what enemies we face in the form of destructive behaviors, there is someone with us who is far greater. This should bring us great encouragement. ***Turn to page 653, Psalm 111.***

---

humbled themselves, so the wrath of the
Lord did not fall upon them during Hezekiah's lifetime.
27So Hezekiah became very wealthy and
was highly honored. He had to construct
special treasury buildings for his silver, gold,
precious stones, and spices, and for his
shields and gold bowls. 28,29He also built
many storehouses for his grain, new wine,
and olive oil, with many stalls for his animals
and folds for the great flocks of sheep and
goats he purchased; and he acquired many
towns, for God had given him great wealth.
30He dammed up the Upper Spring of Gihon
and brought the water down through an aqueduct to the west side of the City of David
sector in Jerusalem. He prospered in everything he did.
31However, when ambassadors arrived
from Babylon to find out about the miracle
of his being healed, God left him to himself
in order to test him and to see what he was
really like.
32The rest of the story of Hezekiah and all of
the good things he did are written in *The Book
of Isaiah* (the prophet, the son of Amoz), and
in *The Annals of the Kings of Judah and Israel.*
33When Hezekiah died, he was buried in the
royal hillside cemetery among the other
kings, and all Judah and Jerusalem honored
him at his death. Then his son Manasseh
became the new king.

CHAPTER 33
Manasseh Rules Judah

Manasseh was only twelve years old when he
became king, and he reigned fifty-five years in
Jerusalem. 2But it was an evil reign, for he
encouraged his people to worship the idols of
the heathen nations destroyed by the Lord
when the people of Israel entered the land.
3He rebuilt the heathen altars his father Heze-

kiah had destroyed—the altars of Baal, and of the shame-images, and of the sun, moon, and stars. 4,5He even constructed heathen altars in both courts of the Temple of the Lord for worshiping the sun, moon and stars—in the very place where the Lord had said that he would be honored forever. 6And Manasseh sacrificed his own children as burnt offerings in the Valley of Hinnom. He consulted spirit-mediums, too, and fortune-tellers and sorcerers, and encouraged every sort of evil, making the Lord very angry.

7Think of it! He placed an idol in the very Temple of God, where God had told David and his son Solomon, "I will be honored here in this Temple and in Jerusalem—the city I have chosen to be honored forever above all the other cities of Israel. 8And if you will only obey my commands—all the laws and instructions given to you by Moses—I won't ever again exile Israel from this land which I gave your ancestors."

9But Manasseh encouraged the people of Judah and Jerusalem to do even more evil than the nations the Lord destroyed when Israel entered the land. 10Warnings from the Lord were ignored by both Manasseh and his people. 11So God sent the Assyrian armies, and they seized him with hooks and bound him with bronze chains and carted him away to Babylon. 12Then at last he came to his senses and cried out humbly to God for help. 13And the Lord listened and answered his plea by returning him to Jerusalem and to his kingdom! At that point Manasseh finally realized that the Lord was really God!

14It was after this that he rebuilt the outer wall of the City of David and the wall from west of the Spring of Gihon in the Kidron Valley, and then to the Fish Gate, and around Citadel Hill, where it was built very high. And he stationed his army generals in all of the fortified cities of Judah. 15He also removed the foreign gods from the hills and took his idol from the Temple, and tore down the altars he had built on the mountain, where the Temple stood, and the altars that were in Jerusalem, and dumped them outside the city. 16Then he rebuilt the altar of the Lord and offered sacrifices upon it—peace offerings and thanksgiving offerings—and demanded that the people of Judah worship the Lord God of Israel. 17However, the people still sacrificed upon the altars on the hills, but only to the Lord their God.

18The rest of Manasseh's deeds, and his prayer to God, and God's reply through the prophets—this is all written in *The Annals of the Kings of Israel.* 19His prayer, and the way God answered, and a frank account of his sins and errors, including a list of the locations where he built idols on the hills and set up shame-idols and graven images (this of course was before the great change in his attitude) are recorded in *The Annals of the Prophets.*

Amon Rules Judah

20,21When Manasseh died, he was buried beneath his own palace, and his son Amon became the new king. Amon was twenty-two years old when he began to reign in Jerusalem, but he lasted for only two years. 22It was an evil reign like the early years of his father Manasseh; for Amon sacrificed to all the idols just as his father had. 23But he didn't change as his father did; instead he sinned more and more. 24At last his own officers assassinated him in his palace. 25But some public-spirited citizens killed all of those who assassinated him and declared his son Josiah to be the new king.

CHAPTER 34

Josiah Rules Judah

Josiah was only eight years old when he became king. He reigned thirty-one years in Jerusalem. 2His was a good reign, as he carefully followed the good example of his ancestor King David. 3For when he was sixteen years old, in the eighth year of his reign, he began to search for the God of his ancestor David; and four years later he began to clean

---

33:1-2 There is biting irony in these verses. Manasseh followed the patterns of the heathen nations—the very ones over whom God had demonstrated his superiority. Manasseh insisted upon a program that had already been proven inadequate. In the recovery process, there are some things that will never work. We need to make sure that the program we follow reflects God's truth as revealed in the Bible.

33:12-13 God placed Manasseh into such dire straits that there was nothing else he could do but seek God. Even though Manasseh had been the worst of all Judah's kings, he was forgiven and restored when he recognized his powerless state and cried out to God for help. God will do no less for each of us today. Sin and failure will ultimately lead us into difficult circumstances. When this happens, we need to let the hard times drive us into God's open and forgiving arms.

Normally the sinful patterns of the parents are duplicated in following generations. Even those who do not want to be like their parents usually turn out to be amazingly similar in their behavior and personality. But it is possible for us to break out of this ongoing spiral of sinful habits through hard personal choices and by facing reality in our life.

Josiah was a young king who chose to stand against a virtual tidal wave of disobedience fostered by his grandfather, Manasseh, and his father, Amon. Breaking from this downward spiral was particularly difficult since Josiah had little knowledge to guide his actions. The Scriptures containing God's laws had been lost for years. But when Hilkiah, the High Priest, discovered the Scriptures in the Temple, young Josiah immediately initiated a recovery program for himself and his people.

It is fair to say that Josiah grew up in a dysfunctional situation. Idolatry and other forms of sinful behavior were an established norm. Josiah had to begin by discovering what God's ideals for living were. Then he was able to establish his own recovery and intervene in the sinful affairs of his nation. In time he was able to break the cycle of sin that had captured Israel in its whirl. He had the faith and commitment to God as well as the courage to pursue both personal and national recovery.

In making his difficult choices, Josiah was seeking to "cut loose" from the sins of the past and to build a new life for himself and the people of Judah. Making a break from long-standing evil practices enabled Judah to proceed with positive reforms and a closer relationship with God. That included one of the most joyful Passover celebrations that Israel had ever known. Josiah was not a perfect man, but he was a true champion of recovery. His stand for God's way made a significant impact on the lives of his people.

STRENGTHS AND ACCOMPLISHMENTS:
- Josiah undertook the long and painful process of personal and national recovery.
- He did away with idolatry and led the people to renew their commitment to God.
- His heart was open to God's will, and he was obedient to God's commands.

WEAKNESSES AND MISTAKES:
- Josiah fought an unnecessary battle against King Neco of Egypt, which resulted in his early death.

LESSONS FROM HIS LIFE:
- We are never too young to pursue recovery and to help others around us.
- One person of faith and courage can have a profound influence in a dysfunctional context.

KEY VERSE:
"There was no other king who so completely turned to the Lord" (2 Kings 23:25).

Josiah's story is told in 2 Kings 21:24–23:30 and 2 Chronicles 33:25–35:26. He is also mentioned in Jeremiah 1:1; 3:6; 22:11-18; Zephaniah 1:1; Zechariah 12:11; and Matthew 1:10-11.

---

up Judah and Jerusalem, destroying the heathen altars and the shame-idols on the hills.
4He went out personally to watch as the altars
of Baal were knocked apart, the obelisks above
the altars chopped down, and the shame-
idols ground into dust and scattered over the
graves of those who had sacrificed to them.
5Then he burned the bones of the heathen
priests upon their own altars, feeling that this
action would clear the people of Judah and
Jerusalem from the guilt of their sin of idol-
worship.

6Then he went to the cities of Manasseh,
Ephraim, and Simeon, even to distant Naphtali, and did the same thing there. 7He broke
down the heathen altars, ground to powder
the shame-idols, and chopped down the obelisks. He did this everywhere throughout the
whole land of Israel before returning to Jerusalem.

8During the eighteenth year of his reign,
after he had purged the land and cleaned up
the situation at the Temple, he appointed
Shaphan (son of Azaliah) and Maaseiah, governor of Jerusalem, and Joah (son of Joahaz),
the city treasurer, to repair the Temple. 9They
set up a collection system for gifts for the
Temple. The money was collected at the
Temple gates by the Levites on guard duty
there. Gifts were brought by the people com-

ing from Manasseh, Ephraim, and other parts of the remnant of Israel, as well as from the people of Jerusalem. The money was taken to Hilkiah the High Priest for accounting, [10,11]and then used by the Levites to pay the carpenters and stonemasons and to purchase building materials—stone building blocks, timber, lumber, and beams. He now rebuilt what earlier kings of Judah had torn down.

[12]The workmen were energetic under the leadership of Jahath and Obadiah, Levites of the subclan of Merari. Zechariah and Meshullam, of the subclan of Kohath, were the building superintendents. The Levites who were skilled musicians played background music while the work progressed. [13]Other Levites superintended the unskilled laborers who carried in the materials to the workmen. Still others assisted as accountants, supervisors, and carriers.

Hilkiah Discovers God's Law

[14]One day when Hilkiah the High Priest was at the Temple recording the money collected at the gates, he found an old scroll that turned out to be the laws of God as given to Moses!

[15,16]"Look!" Hilkiah exclaimed to Shaphan, the king's secretary. "See what I have found in the Temple! These are the laws of God!" Hilkiah gave the scroll to Shaphan, and Shaphan took it to the king, along with his report that there was good progress being made in the reconstruction of the Temple.

[17]"The money chests have been opened and counted, and the money has been put into the hand of the overseers and workmen," he said to the king.

[18]Then he mentioned the scroll and how Hilkiah had discovered it. So he read it to the king. [19]When the king heard what these laws required of God's people, he ripped his clothing in despair [20]and summoned Hilkiah, Ahikam (son of Shaphan), Abdon (son of Micah), Shaphan the treasurer, and Asaiah, the king's personal aide.

[21]"Go to the Temple and plead with the Lord for me!" the king told them. "Pray for all the remnant of Israel and Judah! For this scroll says that the reason the Lord's great anger has been poured out upon us is that our ancestors have not obeyed these laws that are written here."

[22]So the men went to Huldah the prophetess, the wife of Shallum (son of Tokhath, son of Hasrah). (Shallum was the king's tailor, living in the second ward.) When they told her of the king's trouble, [23]she replied, "The Lord God of Israel says, Tell the man who sent you,

[24]"'Yes, the Lord will destroy this city and its people. All the curses written in the scroll will come true. [25]For my people have forsaken me and have worshiped heathen gods, and I am very angry with them for their deeds. Therefore, my unquenchable wrath is poured out upon this place.'

[26]"But the Lord also says this to the king of Judah who sent you to ask me about this: Tell him, the Lord God of Israel says, [27]'Because you are sorry and have humbled yourself before God when you heard my words against this city and its people, and have ripped your clothing in despair and wept before me—I have heard you, says the Lord, [28]and I will not send the promised evil upon this city and its people until after your death.'" So they brought back to the king this word from the Lord. [29]Then the king summoned all the elders of Judah and Jerusalem, [30]and the priests and Levites and all the people great and small, to accompany him to the Temple. There the king read the scroll to them—the covenant of God that was found in the Temple. [31]As the king stood before them, he made a pledge to the Lord to follow his commandments with all his heart and soul and to do what was written in the scroll. [32]And he required every-

---

34:14-19 Even the Scriptures had been lost during the years of spiritual decline. Without them, the people didn't know how God wanted them to live. They had no idea what they were doing wrong or what they needed to do to please God. Without the Bible, it is impossible to effect proper changes in our life. We need some definite standards of right and wrong. Without God's Word, such things become matters of individual opinion. Today, whole systems of faith are based on opinions—what people want to hear rather than what God has to say. Our program must be based on the program that God sets out for us in the Bible.

34:21 As soon as Josiah heard what God expected of his people, he began to take inventory of the situation in Judah. He was open and willing to see how well he and the people measured up against God's standards. The humility and honesty of Josiah here are truly exemplary. He did not try to hide his sin or the sin of his nation. He had no layers of denial to overcome. He openly admitted his failures and sought to change things immediately. As we take inventory in our life, we need to display the same kind of honest humility.

one in Jerusalem and Benjamin to subscribe to this pact with God, and all of them did.

33So Josiah removed all idols from the areas occupied by the Jews and required all of them to worship Jehovah their God. And throughout the remainder of his lifetime they continued serving Jehovah, the God of their ancestors.

CHAPTER 35

Josiah Celebrates Passover

Then Josiah announced that the Passover would be celebrated on the first day of April in Jerusalem. The Passover lambs were slain that evening. 2He also reestablished the priests in their duties and encouraged them to begin their work at the Temple again. 3He issued this order to the sanctified Levites, the religious teachers in Israel:

"Since the Ark is now in Solomon's Temple and you don't need to carry it back and forth upon your shoulders, spend your time ministering to the Lord and to his people. 4,5Form yourselves into the traditional service corps of your ancestors, as first organized by King David of Israel and by his son Solomon. Each corps will assist particular clans of the people who bring in their offerings to the Temple. 6Kill the Passover lambs and sanctify yourselves and prepare to assist the people who come. Follow all of the instructions of the Lord through Moses."

7Then the king contributed 30,000 lambs and young goats for the people's Passover offerings and 3,000 young bulls. 8The king's officials made willing contributions to the priests and Levites. Hilkiah, Zechariah, and Jehiel, the overseers of the Temple, gave the priests 2,600 sheep and goats and 300 oxen as Passover offerings. 9The Levite leaders—Conaniah, Shemaiah, and Nethanel, and his brothers Hashabiah, Jeiel, and Jozabad—gave 5,000 sheep and goats and 500 oxen to the Levites for their Passover offerings.

10When everything was organized and the priests were standing in their places, and the Levites were formed into service corps as the king had instructed, 11then the Levites killed the Passover lambs and presented the blood to the priests, who sprinkled it upon the altar as the Levites removed the skins. 12They piled up the carcasses for each tribe to present its own burnt sacrifices to the Lord, as it is written in the law of Moses. They did the same with the oxen. 13Then, as directed by the laws of Moses, they roasted the Passover lambs and boiled the holy offerings in pots, kettles, and pans, and hurried them out to the people to eat. 14Afterwards the Levites prepared a meal for themselves and for the priests, for they had been busy from morning till night offering the fat of the burnt offerings.

15The singers (the sons of Asaph) were in their places, following directions issued centuries earlier by King David, Asaph, Heman, and Jeduthun the king's prophet. The gatekeepers guarded the gates and didn't need to leave their posts of duty, for their meals were brought to them by their Levite brothers. 16The entire Passover ceremony was completed in that one day. All the burnt offerings were sacrificed upon the altar of the Lord, as Josiah had instructed.

17Everyone present in Jerusalem took part in the Passover observance, and this was followed by the Feast of Unleavened Bread for the next seven days. 18Never since the time of Samuel the prophet had there been such a Passover—not one of the kings of Israel could vie with King Josiah in this respect, involving so many of the priests, Levites, and people from Jerusalem and from all parts of Judah, and from over in Israel. 19This all happened in the eighteenth year of the reign of Josiah.

Josiah Dies in Battle

20Afterwards King Neco of Egypt led his army to Carchemish on the Euphrates River, and Josiah declared war on him.

21But King Neco sent ambassadors to Josiah with this message: "I don't want a fight with you, O king of Judah! I have come only to fight the power with which I am at war. Leave me alone! God has told me to hurry! Don't meddle with God or he will destroy you, for he is with me."

22But Josiah refused to turn back. Instead he led his army into the battle at the Valley of Megiddo. (He laid aside his royal robes so that the enemy wouldn't recognize him.) Josiah

35:1-2 Notice that Josiah took the time to encourage the priests in their Temple activities. Encouragement is extremely important for anyone in a recovery situation. The priests were unaccustomed to leading the people in worship. They needed encouragement to face new and difficult tasks. We are unaccustomed to living without the support of our dependencies. We have to face life directly, without our normal means of escape. We need the encouragement and support of others. Recovery must never be undertaken in a solitary fashion.

refused to believe that Neco's message was from God. 23The enemy archers struck King Josiah with their arrows and fatally wounded him.

"Take me out of the battle," he exclaimed to his aides.

24,25So they lifted him out of his chariot and placed him in his second chariot and brought him back to Jerusalem where he died. He was buried there in the royal cemetery. And all Judah and Jerusalem, including even Jeremiah the prophet, mourned for him, as did the Temple choirs. To this day they still sing sad songs about his death, for these songs of sorrow were recorded among the official lamentations.

26The other activities of Josiah, and his good deeds, and how he followed the laws of the Lord, 27all are written in *The Annals of the Kings of Israel and Judah.*

CHAPTER 36

Jerusalem Is Destroyed

Josiah's son Jehoahaz was selected as the new king. 2He was twenty-three years old when he began to reign, but lasted only three months. 3Then he was deposed by the king of Egypt, who demanded an annual tribute from Judah of $230,000.

4The king of Egypt now appointed Eliakim, the brother of Jehoahaz, as the new king of Judah. (Eliakim's name was changed to Jehoiakim.) Jehoahaz was taken to Egypt as a prisoner.5Jehoiakim was twenty-five years old when he became king, and he reigned eleven years in Jerusalem; but his reign was an evil one. 6Finally Nebuchadnezzar king of Babylon conquered Jerusalem and took away the king in chains to Babylon. 7Nebuchadnezzar also took some of the gold bowls and other items from the Temple, placing them in his own temple in Babylon. 8The rest of the deeds of Jehoiakim and all the evil he did are written in *The Annals of the Kings of Judah*; and his son Jehoiachin became the new king.

9Jehoiachin was eighteen years old when he ascended the throne. But he lasted only three months and ten days, and it was an evil reign as far as the Lord was concerned. 10The following spring he was summoned to Babylon by King Nebuchadnezzar. Many treasures from the Temple were taken away to Babylon at that time, and King Nebuchadnezzar appointed Jehoiachin's brother Zedekiah as the new king of Judah and Jerusalem.

11Zedekiah was twenty-one years old when he became king and he reigned eleven years in Jerusalem. 12His reign, too, was evil so far as the Lord was concerned, for he refused to take the counsel of Jeremiah the prophet, who gave him messages from the Lord. 13He rebelled against King Nebuchadnezzar, even though he had taken an oath of loyalty. Zedekiah was a hard and stubborn man so far as obeying the Lord God of Israel was concerned, for he refused to follow him.

14All the important people of the nation, including the High Priests, worshiped the heathen idols of the surrounding nations, thus polluting the Temple of the Lord in Jerusalem. 15Jehovah the God of their fathers sent his prophets again and again to warn them, for he had compassion on his people and on his Temple. 16But the people mocked these messengers of God and despised their words, scoffing at the prophets until the anger of the Lord could no longer be restrained, and there was no longer any remedy.

17Then the Lord brought the king of Babylon against them and killed their young men, even going after them right into the Temple, and had no pity upon them, killing even young girls and old men. The Lord used the king of Babylon to destroy them completely. 18He also took home with him all the items, great and small, used in the Temple, and treasures from both the Temple and the palace, and took with him all the royal princes. 19Then his army burned the Temple and broke down the walls of Jerusalem and burned all the palaces and destroyed all the valuable Temple utensils. 20Those who survived were taken away to Babylon as slaves to the king and his sons until the kingdom of Persia conquered Babylon.

God Fulfills His Promises

21Thus the word of the Lord spoken through Jeremiah came true, that the land must rest for seventy years to make up for the years when the people refused to observe the Sabbath.

36:14-20 We can never ignore God's will without suffering the consequences. Under Zedekiah the people ignored God's laws and even persecuted the prophets who were sent to remind them of their failure. Is it any wonder that the Temple was destroyed and that the people of Judah were exiled to Babylon? As we discover God's will in the Bible, we need to act on it. His plan will direct us toward a life of recovery and healing. Ignoring his way will lead to sure destruction.

[22,23]But in the first year of King Cyrus of Persia, the Lord stirred up the spirit of Cyrus to make this proclamation throughout his kingdom, putting it into writing:

"All the kingdoms of the earth have been given to me by the Lord God of heaven, and he has instructed me to build him a Temple in Jerusalem, in the land of Judah. All among you who are the Lord's people return to Israel for this task, and the Lord be with you."

This also fulfilled the prediction of Jeremiah the prophet.

36:22-23 These books of woe and doom end with a note of amazing hope. Jerusalem had been destroyed; the Temple had been torn down; the nation had been defeated; the population had been exiled. But the chronicler leaves a burning challenge before God's people. From their exile in Babylon, they were given an opportunity to rebuild, renew, recover, and restore. The books of Chronicles were written for people who had returned to rebuild their Temple and nation. This final passage would show them that despite the failures of their ancestors, God is faithful to his promises. He would help them to recover from centuries of failure. No matter what our past, God holds out the same opportunity for us. With his help, we too can pursue and succeed in our recovery.

REFLECTIONS ON
SECOND
CHRONICLES

insights FROM GOD'S PRIESTS AND PROPHETS

The priests of the northern kingdom found themselves in a difficult position when King Jeroboam ascended to Israel's throne. In **2 Chronicles 11:13-17** we are told that the king ousted the true priests and replaced them with priests who would support his program. The true priests surely wanted to stay in the land of their childhood, but it was obvious that the northern kingdom had turned from God. They moved to the southern kingdom where true worship was still being maintained. We often face similar decisions. We may have to choose between a good job and a healthy or comfortable environment for our family. We would be wise to do as the priests did. They maintained their relationship with God at the cost of personal stability and comfort. Our relationship with God should shape all the decisions we face.

In **2 Chronicles 15:1-8** we are told that God sent a prophet to warn King Asa of Judah that sin would bring suffering to his kingdom, but that trust and obedience would bring blessing. Asa responded to God's warning with appropriate action. He destroyed the idols in his kingdom and rebuilt the altar of God. We also receive warnings from God. He speaks to us through the Bible, through people, and through our conscience. We need to listen for his direction and then act appropriately. Regular times of meditation on God's Word and prayer should help us to be more sensitive to God's leading.

It is often expensive to be absolutely faithful to God, but it is worth the cost. In the account of **2 Chronicles 18:13-22,** the prophet Micaiah knew that he would get into trouble if he told King Ahab he should abandon his plans to attack Ramoth-gilead. At first, he seemingly supported Ahab's plans, but in the end, however, Micaiah took a stand and told the truth. When God speaks to us in his Word or by some other means, we need to do things his way. We must stand for the truth no matter what the people around us are thinking and doing. God's way is always the best way.

insights FROM THE VICTORIES OF JUDAH'S KINGS

Taking God at his word is not always easy, especially when God's promises seem impossible. In the face of Jeroboam's massive armies, King Abijah of Judah had good reason to doubt God's promises. Practically speaking, the army of Judah didn't have a chance. But as we see in **2 Chronicles 13:5-9,** King Abijah still trusted God's promises for the kingly line of David. The positive results of

Abijah's trust should encourage us to do just as he did. When God makes a promise, we should have no doubt that he will keep it.

King Hezekiah of Judah had his armies; he had made elaborate preparations for defense. But in **2 Chronicles 32:7-8** we see that he didn't trust any of these to bring him victory. It is clear that Hezekiah looked only to God for success. We are so prone to depend on our own resources in a crisis. This, however, is never the way to experience success in recovery. We are powerless over our dependencies; only God has the power we need for victory.

When things are in ruin and disarray, it is necessary to rebuild, repair, and clean up. As we see in **2 Chronicles 34:8-11,** such was the situation in Jerusalem at the beginning of King Josiah's reign. During the godless years of King Manasseh, worship of God at the Temple had been discontinued. The Temple itself had fallen into disrepair. Josiah committed the resources of the nation to the restoration of the Temple. We also need to set aside significant resources for the difficult task of recovery. It will demand a great deal of commitment and sacrifice, but no matter what we give up, the gains will be well worth the cost.

Hearing God's Word is important, but we must act on what we hear. If we refuse to act, the hearing is all in vain. In **2 Chronicles 34:31-32** we are told that after hearing the Scriptures, King Josiah pledged himself to obey God's revealed will. Not only did he do so as an individual, but he also called his people to follow. In recovery, we must hear the Word of God and then act on it. Without action, change is impossible; recovery demands that we act—now!

insights FROM THE FAILURES OF JUDAH'S KINGS

In **2 Chronicles 16:12-14,** we find that King Asa's feet became seriously diseased, so he sought a human solution to his problem. Despite the measures he took, however, Asa's condition worsened and he died. Asa failed to look to God for help. In times of trouble, God is often the last resource we turn to. We are willing to try every new human solution to our problem that comes along. Such solutions, however, will never be able to give us true victory. God alone can do that. We would be wise to go to him first.

It is seldom wise for a father to give extravagant gifts to his children. In **2 Chronicles 21:1-6** we see that King Jehoshaphat of Judah gave his children great wealth, but apparently he did little to teach or guide them. Our role as parent includes much more than supplying our children's material needs. They need comfort, direction, and the gift of godly values.

It is a terrible thing for an individual to do evil. It is far more terrible for such a person to lead others into evil. We see in **2 Chronicles 33:9** that King Manasseh of Judah was guilty on both counts. He was even worse than the heathen kings who lived nearby. We must be careful to never lead others into evil. If we have already done so, making restitution demands that we make every effort to lead them out again.

In the final assessment in **2 Chronicles 36:4-8,** King Jehoiakim's reign is condemned as an evil one. By the world's standards, he might have been considered successful. He reigned eleven years through a very difficult time, and he weathered the change of world powers at the Battle of Carchemish. But worldly success is never the final measure. If we fail to live according to God's program, our disobedience will doom us to ultimate failure. In the end, Jehoiakim was exiled to Babylon.

insights FROM THE PERSPECTIVE OF GENESIS

In the book of Genesis, we first learn of the feud between Jacob and Esau. Jacob's descendants became the Israelites, and Esau's descendants became the Edomites. Here in **2 Chronicles 21:8-10** we see that the family feud was still going on hundreds of years later. This should be a lesson to us: the conflicts that we fail to resolve will be passed on to our descendants. For their sake, we would be wise to confront our broken relationships here and now.

EZRA

THE BIG PICTURE

A. REBUILDING THE PLACE (1:1–6:22)
1. The First Exiles Return (1:1–2:70)
2. The Attempt to Rebuild the Temple (3:1-13)
3. The Discouragement of the People (4:1-24)
4. The Joy of the People at the Rebuilt Temple (5:1–6:22)

B. REBUILDING THE PEOPLE (7:1–10:44)
1. The Second Group of Exiles Return with Ezra (7:1–8:36)
2. The Sins of the People (9:1-15)
3. The People Confess Their Sins (10:1-44)

The book of Ezra records two great journeys toward recovery from Babylonian exile. The first journey (1:1–6:22) took place immediately after the decree of Cyrus (539 B.C.) and was led by Zerubbabel, one of King David's descendants. Under his direction the Temple was rebuilt over a twenty-year period (538–515 B.C.). The priest Joshua and the prophets Haggai and Zechariah encouraged the people in this task. The second journey (7:1–10:44) was led by Ezra almost sixty years after to Temple's completion (458 B.C.). Under Ezra's leadership great spiritual and personal rebuilding was accomplished.

Ezra was one of the great men of the Old Testament. Tradition assigns most of Chronicles, Ezra, Nehemiah, and Psalm 119 to his hand. The book of Ezra picks up Israel's history where 2 Chronicles leaves off, approximately forty-eight years after Jerusalem was destroyed by Babylon. After Nebuchadnezzar's glorious rule, Babylon slowly declined until it was conquered by Persia. It was under Cyrus of Persia that Zerubbabel was allowed to lead the first group of Jews home to rebuild the Temple.

Ezra shows us what it means to turn one's life over to God. His desire to know God better motivated him to study God's Word, to believe it, and to obey it. First we need to learn what God's will is; then we need to take action, following the program he lays out for us. But Ezra didn't stop with seeking spiritual growth in his own life. He returned to Jerusalem and led the returned Jews to rebuild their lives as well. Ezra provides us with a model of how we are to carry the message of hope to those still living in bondage.

THE BOTTOM LINE

PURPOSE: To record how the people rebuilt their lives and nation after their exile in Babylon. AUTHOR: Not stated, but probably Ezra. AUDIENCE: The people of Israel after their return from exile in Babylon. DATE WRITTEN: Around the year 446 B.C. SETTING: Ezra picks up where 2 Chronicles left off, covering the period from the decree of Cyrus (538 B.C.) through Ezra's return and reformation (458–446 B.C.). KEY VERSE: "Take courage and tell us how to proceed in setting things straight, and we will fully cooperate" (10:4). KEY PEOPLE: Zerubbabel, Haggai, Zechariah, Ezra.

RECOVERY THEMES

God's Provision for Recovery: God shows his mercy to every one of us. In his love, he seeks our restoration and recovery not only from our sins, but from the consequences of those sins. When we are in captivity to our sins, whether they are addictions or compulsive behaviors, we are never far from God's love and mercy. God is waiting to help us. All we need to do is admit our hopeless situation and come to him for strength and forgiveness. When we know we are helpless, we are closest to his powerful arm. In the book of Ezra we see various examples of how God empowered his people to do what they could never have done without him. All they had to do was give themselves over to his plan.

Resistance to Recovery: There will always be those who do not want to see us recover from our "captivity." People who were associated with our old life-style fight our recovery, just as those within Jerusalem fought against the rebuilding of the Temple. But the most dangerous form of opposition is often found within us. Even though the bigger part of ourself wants to be healed, there is always a part of us that rebels against the good. This does not make us evil, but we need to be aware of this part of our inner self. We don't have to obey this inclination. By turning our will over to God, we can become people "whose hearts' desire is obedience to Christ" (2 Corinthians 10:5).

Starting Over: In the face of opposition, the people of God were not only hindered in their work, they ultimately had to stop the rebuilding process. The same thing often happens to us. Discouragement sets in. We begin to feel like everything we've done was to no avail. In the book of Ezra, the work stopped for ten years. To have our recovery process blocked for ten years could be devastating, giving us a feeling of hopelessness. But be encouraged. Starting over is always a part of God's plan for us. He is patient and long-suffering, and he comes to the aid of those who seek him. As we look at the history of the Jewish people, we see it is a history of new beginnings. God is also the God of our new beginnings!

The Importance of Action: It is one thing to talk about recovery and rebuilding; it is quite another thing to actually do it! God is interested in our *action.* The main characters in this book are all people of action. They didn't sit around and discuss rebuilding the Temple; they organized themselves and started working. The task must have appeared overwhelming at first. But by taking things one day at a time, one task at a time, even overwhelming tasks became possible. The first step is always the most difficult, with the next step almost as hard. Sometimes each step is difficult, but we must focus on today's task and take action, trusting that God will empower us along the way.

CHAPTER 1

King Cyrus Releases Exiled Jews

During the first year of the reign of King Cyrus of Persia, the Lord fulfilled Jeremiah's prophecy by giving King Cyrus the desire to send this proclamation throughout his empire (he also put it into the permanent records of the realm):

2"Cyrus, king of Persia, hereby announces that Jehovah, the God of heaven who gave me my vast empire, has now given me the responsibility of building him a Temple in Jerusalem, in the land of Judah. 3All Jews throughout the kingdom may now return to Jerusalem to rebuild this Temple of Jehovah, who is the God of Israel and of Jerusalem. May his blessings rest upon you. 4Those Jews who do not go should contribute toward the expenses of those who do and also supply them with clothing, transportation, supplies for the journey, and a freewill offering for the Temple."

5Then God gave a great desire to the leaders of the tribes of Judah and Benjamin, and to

1:1 All of us need something that we can count on. The Jews in exile counted on Jeremiah's prophecy—that their captivity would last only seventy years. Today, God has promises for us, too. If we accept Jesus as our Savior, the Holy Spirit will comfort us and help us. We will become a new person—leaving our old ways behind (see 2 Corinthians 5:17). And though our problems may seem overwhelming today, God has provided a way of deliverance.

1:3 When we are in recovery, we need to respond to the opportunities that arise. The Jews had been living in Babylonian exile for many years. King Cyrus gave them an open invitation to return to Jerusalem to rebuild their nation—and their lives. A small group of brave families made the journey home; a majority remained behind in exile. God has given us an open invitation to leave our personal exile through the work of Christ. God is greater than Cyrus, and he is inviting us to rebuild. Will we respond to the opportunity?

the priests and Levites, to return to Jerusalem at once to rebuild the Temple. [6]And all the Jewish exiles who chose to remain in Persia gave them whatever assistance they could, as well as gifts for the Temple.

[7]King Cyrus himself donated the gold bowls and other valuable items, which King Nebuchadnezzar had taken from the Temple at Jerusalem and had placed in the temple of his own gods. [8]He instructed Mithredath, the treasurer of Persia, to present these gifts to Sheshbazzar, the leader of the exiles returning to Judah.

[9,10]The items Cyrus donated included: 1,000 gold trays, 1,000 silver trays, 29 censers, 30 bowls of solid gold, 2,410 silver bowls (of various designs), 1,000 miscellaneous items. [11]In all there were 5,469 gold and silver items turned over to Sheshbazzar to take back to Jerusalem.

CHAPTER 2

Zerubbabel's Group of Returnees

Here is the list of the Jewish exiles who now returned to Jerusalem and to the other cities of Judah, from which their parents had been deported to Babylon by King Nebuchadnezzar.

[2]The leaders were: Zerubbabel, Jeshua, Nehemiah, Seraiah, Reelaiah, Mordecai, Bilshan, Mispar, Bigvai, Rehum, Baanah.

Here is a census of those who returned (listed by subclans):

[3-35]From the subclan of Parosh, 2,172;
From the subclan of Shephatiah, 372;
From the subclan of Arah, 775;
From the subclan of Pahath-moab (the descendants of Jeshua and Joab), 2,812;
From the subclan of Elam, 1,254;
From the subclan of Zattu, 945;
From the subclan of Zaccai, 760;
From the subclan of Bani, 642;
From the subclan of Bebai, 623;
From the subclan of Azgad, 1,222;
From the subclan of Adonikam, 666;
From the subclan of Bigvai, 2,056;
From the subclan of Adin, 454;
From the subclan of Ater (the descendants of Hezekiah), 98;
From the subclan of Bezai, 323;
From the subclan of Jorah, 112;
From the subclan of Hashum, 223;
From the subclan of Gibbar, 95;
From the subclan of Bethlehem, 123;
From the subclan of Netophah, 56;
From the subclan of Anathoth, 128;
From the subclan of Azmaveth, 42;
From the subclans of Kiriath-arim, Chephirah, and Beeroth, 743;
From the subclans of Ramah and Geba, 621;
From the subclan of Michmas, 122;
From the subclans of Bethel and Ai, 223;
From the subclan of Nebo, 52;
From the subclan of Magbish, 156;
From the subclan of Elam, 1,254;
From the subclan of Harim, 320;
From the subclans of Lod, Hadid, and Ono, 725;
From the subclan of Jericho, 345;
From the subclan of Senaah, 3,630.

[36-39]Here are the statistics concerning the returning priests:

From the families of Jedaiah of the subclan of Jeshua, 973;
From the subclan of Immer, 1,052;
From the subclan of Pashhur, 1,247;
From the subclan of Harim, 1,017.

[40-42]Here are the statistics concerning the Levites who returned:

From the families of Jeshua and Kadmiel of the subclan of Hodaviah, 74;
The choir members from the clan of Asaph, 128;
From the descendants of the gatekeepers (the families of Shallum, Ater, Talmon, Akkub, Hatita, and Shobai), 139.

[43-54]The following families of the Temple assistants were represented:

Ziha, Hasupha, Tabbaoth, Keros, Siaha, Padon, Lebanah, Hagabah, Akkub, Hagab, Shamlai, Hanan, Giddel, Gahar, Reaiah, Rezin, Nekoda, Gazzam, Uzza, Paseah, Besai, Asnah, Meunim, Nephisim, Bakbuk, Hakupha, Harhur, Bazluth, Mehida, Harsha, Barkos, Sisera, Temah, Neziah, Hatipha.

[55-57]Those who made the trip also included the descendants of King Solomon's officials:

Sotai, Hassophereth, Peruda, Jaalah, Darkon, Giddel, Shephatiah, Hattil, Pochereth-hazzebaim, Ami.

1:4-6 It is important to have people to encourage us in our recovery. Even though many Jews remained in Persia, they encouraged and supported those who chose to return to Judah. Had those making the return trip not been given assistance, they might not have had the motivation or strength to see the mission through.

58The Temple assistants and the descendants of Solomon's officers numbered 392.

59Another group returned to Jerusalem at this time from the Persian cities of Tel-melah, Tel-harsha, Cherub, Addan, and Immer. However, they had lost their genealogies and could not prove that they were really Israelites. 60This group included the subclans of Delaiah, Tobiah, and Nekoda—a total of 652.

61Three subclans of priests—Habaiah, Hakkoz, and Barzillai (he married one of the daughters of Barzillai the Gileadite and took her family name)—also returned to Jerusalem. 62,63But they too had lost their genealogies, so the leaders refused to allow them to continue as priests; they would not even allow them to eat the priests' share of food from the sacrifices until the Urim and Thummim could be consulted to find out from God whether they actually were descendants of priests or not.

64,65So a total of 42,360 persons returned to Judah; in addition to 7,337 slaves and 200 choir members, both men and women. 66,67They took with them 736 horses, 245 mules, 435 camels, and 6,720 donkeys.

68Some of the leaders were able to give generously toward the rebuilding of the Temple, 69and each gave as much as he could. The total value of their gifts amounted to $300,000 of gold, $170,000 of silver, and 100 robes for the priests.

70So the priests and Levites and some of the common people settled in Jerusalem and its nearby villages; and the singers, the gatekeepers, the Temple workers, and the rest of the people returned to the other cities of Judah from which they had come.

CHAPTER 3

The People Rebuild the Temple

During the month of September everyone who had returned to Judah came to Jerusalem from their homes in the other towns. Then Jeshua (son of Jozadak) with his fellow priests, and Zerubbabel (son of Shealtiel) and his clan, rebuilt the altar of the God of Israel and sacrificed burnt offerings upon it, as instructed in the laws of Moses, the man of God. 3The altar was rebuilt on its old site, and it was used immediately to sacrifice morning and evening burnt offerings to the Lord; for the people were fearful of attack.

4And they celebrated the Feast of Tabernacles as prescribed in the laws of Moses, sacrificing the burnt offerings specified for each day of the feast. 5They also offered the special sacrifices required for the Sabbaths, the new moon celebrations, and the other regular annual feasts of the Lord. Voluntary offerings of the people were also sacrificed. 6It was on the fifteenth day of September that the priests began sacrificing the burnt offerings to the Lord. (This was before they began building the foundation of the Temple.)

7Then they hired masons and carpenters and bought cedar logs from the people of Tyre and Sidon, paying for them with food, wine, and olive oil. The logs were brought down from the Lebanon mountains and floated along the coast of the Mediterranean Sea to Joppa, for King Cyrus had included this provision in his grant.

8The actual construction of the Temple began in June of the second year of their arrival at Jerusalem. The work force was made up of all those who had returned, and they were under the direction of Zerubbabel (son of Shealtiel), Jeshua (son of Jozadak), and their fellow priests and the Levites. The Levites who were twenty years old or older were appointed to supervise the workmen. 9The supervision of the entire project was given to Jeshua, Kadmiel, Henadad, and their sons and relatives, all of whom were Levites.

10When the builders completed the foundation of the Temple, the priests put on their official robes and blew their trumpets; and the descendants of Asaph crashed their cymbals to praise the Lord in the manner or-

---

2:64-65 Surprisingly, when the invitation to rebuild was made, most of the people failed to respond. They chose to remain in a depressing, though comfortable, life-style instead of making the long, hard journey back to Jerusalem to rebuild the Temple and nation. We often choose what is comfortable over what we know is best for us. Recovery is a long, hard journey, but it is far better than the option of continued slavery.

3:1-2 The Temple had been destroyed many years before, so there was no altar for burning sacrifices. The people's means of reconciliation with God had been discontinued; their spiritual life had been cut off. So before the people could proceed with the rebuilding process, they needed to straighten out their relationship with God. These verses show how the Israelites reestablished the sacrifices as a means of reconciliation. Such reconciliation is a necessary step for all of us in recovery. This has been made eternally possible for us through the sacrifice of Jesus Christ.

dained by King David. [11]They sang rounds of praise and thanks to God, singing this song: "He is good, and his love and mercy toward Israel will last forever." Then all the people gave a great shout, praising God because the foundation of the Temple had been laid.

[12]But many of the priests and Levites and other leaders—the old men who remembered Solomon's beautiful Temple—wept aloud, while others were shouting for joy! [13]So the shouting and the weeping mingled together in a loud commotion that could be heard far away!

CHAPTER 4

Enemies Oppose the Rebuilding

When the enemies of Judah and Benjamin heard that the exiles had returned and were rebuilding the Temple, [2]they approached Zerubbabel and the other leaders and suggested, "Let us work with you, for we are just as interested in your God as you are; we have sacrificed to him ever since King Esar-haddon of Assyria brought us here."

[3]But Zerubbabel and Jeshua and the other Jewish leaders replied, "No, you may have no part in this work. The Temple of the God of Israel must be built by the Israelis, just as King Cyrus has commanded."

[4,5]Then the local residents tried to discourage and frighten them by sending agents to tell lies about them to King Cyrus. This went on during his entire reign and lasted until King Darius took the throne.

King Artaxerxes Stops the Work

[6]And afterwards, when King Ahasuerus began to reign, they wrote him a letter of accusation against the people of Judah and Jerusalem [7]and did the same thing during the reign of Artaxerxes. Bishlam, Mithredath, and Tabeel and their associates wrote a letter to him in the Aramaic language, and it was translated to him. [8,9]Others who participated were Governor Rehum, Shimshai (a scribe), several judges and other local leaders, the Persians, the Babylonians, the men of Erech and Susa, [10]and men from several other nations. (They had been taken from their own lands by the great and noble Osnappar and relocated in Jerusalem, Samaria, and throughout the neighboring lands west of the Euphrates River.)

[11]Here is the text of the letter they sent to King Artaxerxes:

"Sir: Greetings from your loyal subjects west of the Euphrates River. [12]Please be informed that the Jews sent to Jerusalem from Babylon are rebuilding this historically rebellious and evil city; they have already rebuilt its walls and have repaired the foundations of the Temple. [13]But we wish you to know that if this city is rebuilt, it will be much to your disadvantage, for the Jews will then refuse to pay their taxes to you.

[14]"Since we are grateful to you as our patron, and we do not want to see you taken advantage of and dishonored in this way, we have decided to send you this information. [15]We suggest that you search the ancient records to discover what a rebellious city this has been in the past; in fact, it was destroyed because of its long history of sedition against the kings and countries who attempted to control it. [16]We wish to declare that if this city is rebuilt and the walls finished, you might as well forget about this part of your empire

3:10-11 Having already built an altar for the sacrifices, the people began the work of rebuilding the Temple itself. Notice that they praised God and celebrated after having laid only the Temple's foundation. Big jobs always seem easier and less intimidating when we break them up into smaller steps. When we face overwhelming or long-term projects, such as recovery, we should take pleasure in completing one step at a time. Realizing that we have completed one phase will encourage us to keep going.

3:12 Some of the old people compared this rebuilding project with their memories of the former Temple. This Temple obviously would never match the glory of Solomon's Temple, built during Israel's golden age. Their expectations were too high. Though Israel would never regain its previous status in the world, God promised that the new Jerusalem would be the center of God's eternal kingdom (see Revelation 21). If our expectations are too high or unrealistic, they may cause us to relapse. We need to focus on how far we have come, not on how things used to be. We may never be able to regain our previous position in life, but that should not make us discouraged and stop our recovery. We will be glorified beyond our wildest dreams at Christ's second coming.

4:1-3 When God's work starts going in a great way, enemies almost invariably rise up against it. There will be adversaries against our work as we establish positive patterns in our life. It is interesting that the enemies of the Temple's rebuilding came in the guise of helpers. We must reject assistance in our recovery that is not God-approved and God-centered.

beyond the Euphrates, for it will be lost to you."

17Then the king made this reply to Governor Rehum and Shimshai the scribe, and to their companions living in Samaria and throughout the area west of the Euphrates River:

18"Gentlemen: Greetings! The letter you sent has been translated and read to me. 19I have ordered a search made of the records and have indeed found that Jerusalem has in times past been a hotbed of insurrection against many kings; in fact, rebellion and sedition are normal there! 20I find, moreover, that there have been some very great kings in Jerusalem who have ruled the entire land beyond the Euphrates River and have received vast tribute, custom, and toll. 21Therefore, I command that these men must stop their work until I have investigated the matter more thoroughly. 22Do not delay, for we must not permit the situation to get out of control!"

23When this letter from King Artaxerxes was read to Rehum and Shimshai, they hurried to Jerusalem and forced the Jews to stop building. 24So the work ended until the second year of the reign of King Darius of Persia.

CHAPTER 5

The Rebuilding Continues

But there were prophets in Jerusalem and Judah at that time—Haggai, and Zechariah (the son of Iddo)—who brought messages from the God of Israel to Zerubbabel (son of Shealtiel) and Jeshua (son of Jozadak), encouraging them to begin building again! So they did and the prophets helped them.

3But Tattenai, the governor of the lands west of the Euphrates, and Shethar-bozenai, and their companions soon arrived in Jerusalem and demanded, "Who gave you permission to rebuild this Temple and finish these walls?"

4They also asked for a list of the names of all the men who were working on the Temple. 5But because the Lord was overseeing the entire situation, our enemies did not force us to stop building, but let us continue while King Darius looked into the matter and returned his decision.

Enemies Inform King Darius

6Following is the letter which Governors Tattenai and Shethar-bozenai and the other officials sent to King Darius:

7"To King Darius:

"Greetings!

8"We wish to inform you that we went to the construction site of the Temple of the great God of Judah. It is being built with huge stones, and timber is being laid in the city walls. The work is going forward with great energy and success. 9We asked the leaders, 'Who has given you permission to do this?' 10And we demanded their names so that we could notify you. 11Their answer was, 'We are the servants of the God of heaven and earth and we are rebuilding the Temple that was constructed here many centuries ago by a great king of Israel. 12But afterwards our ancestors angered the God of heaven, and he abandoned them and let King Nebuchadnezzar destroy this Temple and exile the people to Babylonia.'

13"But they insist that King Cyrus of Babylon, during the first year of his reign, issued a decree that the Temple should be rebuilt,

4:17-23 Often obstacles are placed in the way of rebuilding. In this case it was a work-restraining order from Artaxerxes. Today, we must accept the reality that many will not be supportive of our recovery efforts. We must never allow such people to stand in the way of our recovery program.

4:24 Whether it was a legitimate reason or whether the workers were taking an easy out, the rebuilding work on God's Temple ceased. How often in our own life have outward difficulties stopped our positive progress? We need to guard against interruptions. It is often hard to get back on track once we have stopped or slowed down.

5:1 In this verse, God gave the people fresh encouragement to build. He sent the prophets Haggai and Zechariah to stir up the people to finish their work project. These prophets told the people what God wanted them to do. In this case, it was not the proper time to have a Bible study; it was not the time for a prayer meeting. It was time for them to roll up their sleeves and get to work! There will be times when study and prayer are appropriate, but there will also be times that require immediate action. If God says go, we must go!

5:3-5 Again the work was going smoothly; the people had begun to work with enthusiasm and joy. But again, enemies tried to halt the rebuilding. This time, though, the Jews did not stop their rebuilding task. God was their heavenly foreman, lovingly supervising their work. God cares about us and the outcome of our recovery. If he cared for the rebuilding of the Temple back then, surely he cares for the rebuilding of our life—his temple—today.

14and they say King Cyrus returned the gold
and silver bowls which Nebuchadnezzar had
taken from the Temple in Jerusalem and had
placed in the temple of Babylon. They say
these items were delivered into the safekeeping of a man named Sheshbazzar, whom King
Cyrus appointed as governor of Judah. 15The
king instructed him to return the bowls to
Jerusalem and to let the Temple of God be
built there as before. 16So Sheshbazzar came
and laid the foundations of the Temple at
Jerusalem; and the people have been working
on it ever since, though it is not yet completed. 17We request that you search in the
royal library of Babylon to discover whether
King Cyrus ever made such a decree; and then
let us know your pleasure in this matter."

CHAPTER 6

King Darius Approves the Rebuilding

So King Darius issued orders that a search be
made in the Babylonian archives, where documents were stored.
2Eventually the record was found in the
palace at Ecbatana, in the province of Media.
This is what it said:
3"In this first year of the reign of King
Cyrus, a decree has been sent out concerning
the Temple of God at Jerusalem where the
Jews offer sacrifices. It is to be rebuilt, and the
foundations are to be strongly laid. The
height will be ninety feet and the width will
be ninety feet. 4There will be three layers of
huge stones in the foundation, topped with a
layer of new timber. All expenses will be paid
by the king. 5And the gold and silver bowls,
which were taken from the Temple of God by
Nebuchadnezzar, shall be taken back to Jerusalem and put into the Temple as they were
before."
6So King Darius II sent this message to Governor Shethar-bozenai and the other officials
west of the Euphrates:
"Do not disturb the construction of the
Temple. Let it be rebuilt on its former site,
7and don't molest the governor of Judah and
the other leaders in their work. 8Moreover, I
decree that you are to pay the full construction costs without delay from my taxes collected in your territory. 9Give the priests in
Jerusalem young bulls, rams, and lambs for
burnt offerings to the God of heaven; and
give them wheat, wine, salt, and olive oil each
day without fail. 10Then they will be able to
offer acceptable sacrifices to the God of
heaven and pray for me and my sons. 11Any-
one who attempts to change this message in
any way shall have the beams pulled from his
house and built into a gallows on which he
will be hanged; and his house shall be reduced
to a pile of rubble. 12The God who has chosen
the city of Jerusalem will destroy any king and
any nation that alters this commandment
and destroys this Temple. I, Darius, have issued this decree; let it be obeyed with all
diligence."

The Temple is Completed

13Governors Tattenai and Shethar-bozenai,
and their companions complied at once with
the command of King Darius.
14So the Jewish leaders continued in their
work, and they were greatly encouraged by
the preaching of the prophets Haggai and
Zechariah (son of Iddo).
The Temple was finally finished, as had
been commanded by God and decreed by
Cyrus, Darius, and Artaxerxes, the kings of
Persia. 15The completion date was February 18
in the sixth year of the reign of King Darius II.
16The Temple was then dedicated with great
joy by the priests, the Levites, and all the
people. 17During the dedication celebration
100 young bulls, 200 rams, and 400 lambs
were sacrificed; and twelve male goats were
presented as a sin offering for the twelve tribes
of Israel. 18Then the priests and Levites were
divided into their various service corps to do
the work of God as instructed in the laws of
Moses.

6:14-15 Sometimes (almost always) the recovery process takes more time than we had originally planned. It took more than twenty years, but the Temple was finally finished. The long process had been sometimes tedious, sometimes disillusioning, sometimes actually heartbreaking. But it was done, and it was worth every minute of it! Restoration of our own life is not easy either, but the end result will make the difficult process worth it.

6:16-19 After this long, drawn-out process was finally over, what was the people's response to success? First of all, they acknowledged God in the entire project. Second, they formally recognized the completion in a dedication ceremony. Third, they celebrated this victory with great joy. We need to celebrate our own recovery process. What is worth celebrating more than a life brought back into a right relationship with God and other people?

The People Celebrate Passover

19The Passover was celebrated on the first day of April. 20For by that time many of the priests and Levites had consecrated themselves. 21,22And some of the heathen people who had been relocated in Judah turned from their immoral customs and joined the Israelis in worshiping the Lord God. They, with the entire nation, ate the Passover feast and celebrated the Feast of Unleavened Bread for seven days. There was great joy throughout the land because the Lord had caused the king of Assyria to be generous to Israel and to assist in the construction of the Temple.

CHAPTER 7

Ezra Comes to Teach

Here is the genealogy of Ezra, who traveled from Babylon to Jerusalem during the reign of King Artaxerxes of Persia:

Ezra was the son of Seriah;
Seriah was the son of Azariah;
Azariah was the son of Hilkiah;
Hilkiah was the son of Shallum;
Shallum was the son of Zadok;
Zadok was the son of Ahitub;
Ahitub was the son of Amariah;
Amariah was the son of Meraioth;
Meraioth was the son of Zerahiah;
Zerahiah was the son of Uzzi;
Uzzi was the son of Bukki;
Bukki was the son of Abishua;
Abishua was the son of Phinehas;
Phinehas was the son of Eleazar;
Eleazar was the son of Aaron, the chief priest.

6As a Jewish religious leader, Ezra was well versed in Jehovah's laws, which Moses had given to the people of Israel. He asked to be allowed to return to Jerusalem, and the king granted his request; for the Lord his God was blessing him. 7-9Many ordinary people as well as priests, Levites, singers, gatekeepers, and Temple workers traveled with him. They left Babylon in the middle of March in the seventh year of the reign of Artaxerxes and arrived at Jerusalem in the month of August; for the Lord gave them a good trip. 10This was because Ezra had determined to study and obey the laws of the Lord and to become a Bible teacher, teaching those laws to the people of Israel.

King Artaxerxes Writes to Ezra

11King Artaxerxes presented this letter to Ezra the priest, the student of God's commands:

12"From: Artaxerxes, the king of kings.

"To: Ezra the priest, the teacher of the laws of the God of heaven.

13"I decree that any Jew in my realm, including the priests and Levites, may return to Jerusalem with you. 14I and my Council of Seven hereby instruct you to take a copy of God's laws to Judah and Jerusalem and to send back a report of the religious progress being made there. 15We also commission you to take with you to Jerusalem the silver and gold, which we are presenting as an offering to the God of Israel.

16"Moreover, you are to collect voluntary Temple offerings of silver and gold from the Jews and their priests in all of the provinces of Babylon. 17These funds are to be used primarily for the purchase of oxen, rams, lambs, grain offerings, and drink offerings, all of which will be offered upon the altar of your Temple when you arrive in Jerusalem. 18The money that is left over may be used in whatever way you and your brothers feel is the will of your God. 19And take with you the gold bowls and other items we are giving you for the Temple of your God at Jerusalem. 20If you run short of money for the construction of the Temple or for any similar needs, you may requisition funds from the royal treasury.

21"I, Artaxerxes the king, send this decree to all the treasurers in the provinces west of the Euphrates River: 'You are to give Ezra whatever he requests of you (for he is a priest and teacher of the laws of the God of heaven), 22up to $200,000 in silver; 1,225 bushels of wheat; 990 gallons of wine; any amount of salt; 23and whatever else the God of heaven demands for his Temple; for why should we risk God's wrath against the king and his sons? 24I also

6:20 Before they could lead the people in worshiping God, it was necessary for the priests and Levites to purify themselves. They had to be ritually clean. Now purification is available to all through Jesus Christ. When we trust in Jesus, he purifies us and allows us to commune with him.

7:10 What a noble aspiration is recorded in this verse! This careful student of the Scriptures prepared his heart to seek what God was saying through his Word. Then, he was obedient to its requirements. Ezra also wanted to teach the people the truth he had discovered. It is natural for us to share something that we believe to be worthwhile. Ezra wanted to share God's laws with the people of Israel. We should want to share our testimony of recovery in order to lead others to overcome their dependencies.

decree that no priest, Levite, choir member, gatekeeper, Temple attendant, or other worker in the Temple shall be required to pay taxes of any kind.'

[25]"And you, Ezra, are to use the wisdom God has given you to select and appoint judges and other officials to govern all the people west of the Euphrates River; if they are not familiar with the laws of your God, you
are to teach them. [26]Anyone refusing to obey the law of your God and the law of the king shall be punished immediately by death, banishment, confiscation of goods, or imprisonment."

Ezra Praises God

[27]Well, praise the Lord God of our ancestors, who made the king want to beautify the
Temple of the Lord in Jerusalem! [28]And praise God for demonstrating such loving-kindness to me by honoring me before the king and his Council of Seven and before all of his mighty princes! I was given great status because the Lord my God was with me; and I persuaded some of the leaders of Israel to return with me to Jerusalem.

CHAPTER 8

Ezra's Group of Returnees

These are the names and genealogies of the leaders who accompanied me from Babylon during the reign of King Artaxerxes:

[2-14]From the clan of Phinehas—Gershom;
From the clan of Ithamar—Daniel;
From the subclan of David of the clan of Shecaniah—Hattush;
From the clan of Parosh—Zechariah, and 150 other men;
From the clan of Pahath-moab—Eliehoenai (son of Zerahiah), and 200 other men;
From the clan of Shecaniah—the son of Jahaziel, and 300 other men;
From the clan of Adin—Ebed (son of Jonathan), and 50 other men;
From the clan of Elam—Jeshaiah (son of Athaliah), and 70 other men;
From the clan of Shephatiah—Zebadiah (son of Michael), and 80 other men;
From the clan of Joab—Obadiah (son of Jehiel), and 218 other men;
From the clan of Bani—Shelomith (son of Josiphiah), and 160 other men;
From the clan of Bebai—Zechariah (son of Bebai), and 28 other men;
From the clan of Azgad—Johanan (son of Hakkatan), and 110 other men;
From the clan of Adonikam—Eliphelet, Jeuel, Shemaiah, and 60 other men (they arrived at a later time);
From the clan of Bigvai—Uthai, Zaccur, and 70 other men.

Ezra Goes to Jerusalem

[15]We assembled at the Ahava River and camped there for three days while I went over the lists of the people and the priests who had arrived; and I found that not one Levite had
volunteered! [16]So I sent for Eliezer, Ariel, Shemaiah, Elnathan, Jarib, Elnathan, Nathan, Zechariah, and Meshullam, the Levite leaders; I also sent for Joiarib and Elnathan, who were
very wise men. [17]I sent them to Iddo, the leader of the Jews at Casiphia, to ask him and his brothers and the Temple attendants to send us priests for the Temple of God at Jerusalem. [18]And God was good! He sent us an outstanding man named Sherebiah, along with eighteen of his sons and brothers; he was a very astute man and a descendant of Mahli,
the son of Levi and grandson of Israel. [19]God also sent Hashabiah; and Jeshaiah (the son of Merari), with twenty of his sons and brothers;
[20]and 220 Temple attendants. (The Temple attendants were assistants to the Levites—a job classification of Temple employees first instituted by King David.) These 220 men were all listed by name.

[21]Then I declared a fast while we were at the Ahava River so that we would humble ourselves before our God; and we prayed that he

7:27-28 Many obstacles stood in the way of Ezra's dream of leading the people to learn and obey God's Word. The first obstacle was a governmental one, but God worked in the heart of Artaxerxes to provide permission and resources for Ezra's mission. These two verses record Ezra's prayer of thanks to God. The progress we make is due only to God's love for us. We should praise him for the good work he is accomplishing in our life.

8:15-20 Our recovery generally requires careful preparation and the wise advice of godly people. Ezra knew that his primary task was a spiritual one. These verses detail some of the preparations he made. Here he is arranging for a team of experts (the priests and Levites) to assist him in the task. We will never be able to recover on our own. We need God's help, and we also need others who will encourage us and advise us on how to proceed.

would give us a good journey and protect us, our children, and our goods as we traveled. 22For I was ashamed to ask the king for soldiers and cavalry to accompany us and protect us from the enemies along the way. After all, we had told the king that our God would protect all those who worshiped him, and that disaster could come only to those who had forsaken him! 23So we fasted and begged God to take care of us. And he did.

24I appointed twelve leaders of the priests—Sherebiah, Hashabiah, and ten other priests—25to be in charge of transporting the silver, gold, the gold bowls, and the other items that the king and his council and the leaders and people of Israel had presented to the Temple of God. 26,27I weighed the money as I gave it to them and found it to total $1,300,000 in silver; $200,000 in silver utensils; many millions in gold; and twenty gold bowls worth a total of $100,000. There were also two beautiful pieces of brass that were as precious as gold. 28I consecrated these men to the Lord and then consecrated the treasures—the equipment and money and bowls that had been given as free-will offerings to the Lord God of our fathers.

29"Guard these treasures well!" I told them; "present them without a penny lost to the priests and the Levite leaders and the elders of Israel at Jerusalem, where they are to be placed in the treasury of the Temple."

30So the priests and the Levites accepted the responsibility of taking them to God's Temple in Jerusalem. 31We broke camp at the Ahava River at the end of March and started off to Jerusalem; and God protected us and saved us from enemies and bandits along the way. 32So at last we arrived safely at Jerusalem.

33On the fourth day after our arrival, the silver, gold, and other valuables were weighed in the Temple by Meremoth (the son of Uriah the priest), Eleazar (son of Phinehas), Jozabad (son of Jeshua), and Noadiah (son of Binnui)—all of whom were Levites. 34A receipt was given for each item, and the weight of the gold and silver was noted.

35Then everyone in our party sacrificed burnt offerings to the God of Israel—twelve oxen for the nation of Israel; ninety-six rams; seventy-seven lambs; and twelve goats as a sin offering. 36The king's decrees were delivered to his lieutenants and the governors of all the provinces west of the Euphrates River, and of course they then cooperated in the rebuilding of the Temple of God.

CHAPTER 9

Ezra Prays before the People

But then the Jewish leaders came to tell me that many of the Jewish people and even some of the priests and Levites had taken up the horrible customs of the heathen people who lived in the land—the Canaanites, Hittites, Perizzites, Jebusites, Ammonites, Moabites, Egyptians, and Amorites. 2The men of Israel had married girls from these heathen nations and had taken them as wives for their sons. So the holy people of God were being polluted by these mixed marriages, and the political leaders were some of the worst offenders.

3When I heard this, I tore my clothing and pulled hair from my head and beard and sat

8:24-30 Ezra's group had to transport a great deal of money to Jerusalem, and Ezra made provisions for its safekeeping. He set up lines of accountability; the priests took up the responsibility. In recovery, we also must set up measures of accountability for ourselves. We need to establish goals and then find someone to hold us accountable to them.

8:31-33 Finally Ezra arrived at Jerusalem. He had overcome many obstacles—evidently they faced considerable danger on the road itself. It is interesting that the first thing he did upon arrival was to wait for three days. If we are exhausted or emotionally burned out when we begin a project, our task will seem much tougher than it really is. We need to slow down, develop patience, and gain a godly perspective.

9:1-2 God called the Hebrews to be his special people. He set them apart to be the means of bringing his Son into the world. He intended them to be holy—unique among all the other peoples on earth. Ezra discovered that the Jews were compromising their uniqueness through intermarriage with the neighboring heathen. They were becoming intermingled with the surrounding nations. God has called us to be his people, too. We should not blend in with the unbelievers around us; we must remain clearly identifiable as God's special people.

9:3 Upon realizing the people's sin, Ezra responded with deep mourning. He was heartbroken that the people had forgotten their calling and the special obligations it entailed. As people of God, we must remember that we also have certain responsibilities before God. The temptation is to procrastinate in dealing with tough issues in our life. But God wants us to tackle them head-on, remembering that he is there to give us strength and encouragement.

down utterly baffled. 4Then many who feared
the God of Israel because of this sin of his
people came and sat with me until the time of
the evening burnt offering.

5Finally I stood before the Lord in great
embarrassment; then I fell to my knees and
lifted my hands to the Lord, 6and cried out,
"O my God, I am ashamed; I blush to lift up
my face to you, for our sins are piled higher
than our heads and our guilt is as boundless
as the heavens. 7Our whole history has been
one of sin; that is why we and our kings and
our priests were slain by the heathen kings—
we were captured, robbed, and disgraced, just
as we are today. 8But now we have been given
a moment of peace, for you have permitted a
few of us to return to Jerusalem from our
exile. You have given us a moment of joy and
new life in our slavery. 9For we were slaves, but
in your love and mercy you did not abandon
us to slavery; instead, you caused the kings of
Persia to be favorable to us. They have even
given us their assistance in rebuilding the
Temple of our God and in giving us Jerusalem
as a walled city in Judah.

10"And now, O God, what can we say after
all of this? For once again we have abandoned
you and broken your laws! 11The prophets
warned us that the land we would possess was
totally defiled by the horrible practices of the
people living there. From one end to the other
it is filled with corruption. 12You told us not to
let our daughters marry their sons, and not to
let our sons marry their daughters, and not to
help those nations in any way. You warned us
that only if we followed this rule could we
become a prosperous nation and forever leave
that prosperity to our children as an inheritance. 13And now, even after our punishment
in exile because of our wickedness (and we
have been punished far less than we deserved), and even though you have let some
of us return, 14we have broken your commandments again and intermarried with
people who do these awful things. Surely your
anger will destroy us now until not even this
little remnant escapes. 15O Lord God of Israel,
you are a just God; what hope can we have if
you give us justice as we stand here before you
in our wickedness?"

CHAPTER 10

The People Confess Their Sin

As I lay on the ground in front of the Temple,
weeping and praying and making this confession, a large crowd of men, women, and children gathered around and cried with me.

2Then Shecaniah (the son of Jehiel of the
clan of Elam) said to me, "We acknowledge
our sin against our God, for we have married
these heathen women. But there is hope for
Israel in spite of this. 3For we agree before our
God to divorce our heathen wives and to send
them away with our children; we will follow
your commands and the commands of the
others who fear our God. We will obey the
laws of God. 4Take courage and tell us how to
proceed in setting things straight, and we will
fully cooperate."

5So I stood up and demanded that the leaders of the priests and the Levites and all the
people of Israel swear that they would do as
Shecaniah had said; and they all agreed.
6Then I went into the room of Jehohanan in
the Temple and refused all food and drink, for
I was mourning because of the sin of the
returned exiles.

7,8Then a proclamation was made throughout Judah and Jerusalem that everyone
should appear at Jerusalem within three days
and that the leaders and elders had decided
that anyone who refused to come would be
disinherited and excommunicated from Israel. 9Within three days, on the fifth day of
December, all the men of Judah and Benjamin had arrived and were sitting in the open

9:6-15 Ezra's prayer of confession followed his mourning. He freely admitted the sins of the people and pleaded with God for their restoration. He realized that until they removed this major obstacle to their spiritual success, they would never achieve the victory that God intended for them. Often we hold on to some area of our life that prevents us from experiencing everything that God has for us. What areas do we need to confess and turn over to God's control? We should act immediately so we can get on with our recovery.

10:2 It was all very well and good for Ezra to confess the sins of the people, but until the people confessed their sin, the victory could not take place. If we do nothing about the areas in our life that are out of control, we will never move forward. We must submit these parts of our life to God and then take action against them.

10:3 The people did not stop at mere confession; they also vowed to reform. It is never enough just to acknowledge that we have unacceptable patterns in our life. Even as these people did, we must follow our confession with action. And this is the purpose of recovery—to take active steps to eliminate sinful and destructive behaviors from our life.

space before the Temple; and they were
trembling because of the seriousness of the
matter and because of the heavy rainfall.
10Then I, Ezra the priest, arose and addressed
them:

"You have sinned, for you have married
heathen women; now we are even more
deeply under God's condemnation than we
were before. 11Confess your sin to the Lord
God of your fathers and do what he demands:
separate yourselves from the heathen people
about you and from these women."

12Then all the men spoke up and said, "We
will do what you have said. 13But this isn't
something that can be done in a day or two,
for there are many of us involved in this sinful
affair. And it is raining so hard that we can't
stay out here much longer. 14Let our leaders
arrange trials for us. Everyone who has a heathen wife will come at the scheduled time
with the elders and judges of his city; then
each case will be decided and the situation
will be cleared up, and the fierce wrath of our
God will be turned away from us."

15Only Jonathan (son of Asahel), Jahzeiah
(son of Tikvah), Meshullam, and Shabbethai
the Levite opposed this course of action.

God Forgives the People

16-19So this was the plan that was followed:
Some of the clan leaders and I were designated as judges; we began our work on December 15 and finished by March 15.

Following is the list of priests who had
married heathen wives (they vowed to divorce their wives and acknowledged their
guilt by offering rams as sacrifices): Maaseiah,
Eliezer, Jarib, Gedaliah.

20The sons of Immer: Hanani, Zebadiah.

21The sons of Harim: Maaseiah, Elijah, Shemaiah, Jehiel, Uzziah.

22The sons of Pashhur: Elioenai, Maaseiah,
Ishmael, Nethanel, Jozabad, Elasah.

23The Levites who were guilty: Jozabad,
Shimei, Kelaiah (also called Kelita),
Pethahaiah, Judah, Eliezer.

24Of the singers, there was Eliashib.

Of the gatekeepers, Shallum, Telem, and
Uri.

25Here is the list of ordinary citizens who
were declared guilty:

From the clan of Parosh: Ramiah, Izziah,
Malchijah, Mijamin, Eleazar, Hashabiah, Benaiah.

26From the clan of Elam: Mattaniah, Zechariah, Jehiel, Abdi, Jeremoth, Elijah.

27From the clan of Zattu: Elioenai, Eliashib,
Mattaniah, Jeremoth, Zabad, Aziza.

28From the clan of Bebai: Jehohanan, Hananiah, Zabbai, Athlai.

29From the clan of Bani: Meshullam, Malluch, Adaiah, Jashub, Sheal, Jeremoth.

30From the clan of Pahath-moab: Adna,
Chelal, Benaiah, Maaseiah, Mattaniah,
Bezalel, Binnui, Manasseh.

31,32From the clan of Harim: Eliezer, Isshijah,
Malchijah, Shemaiah, Shimeon, Benjamin,
Malluch, Shemariah.

33From the clan of Hashum: Mattenai, Mat-
tattah, Zabad, Eliphelet, Jeremai, Manasseh,
Shimei.

34-42From the clan of Bani: Maadai, Amram,
Uel, Banaiah, Bedeiah, Cheluhi, Vaniah, Me-
remoth, Eliashib, Mattaniah, Mattenai, Jaasu,
Bani, Binnui, Shimei, Shelemiah, Nathan,
Adaiah, Machnadebai, Shashai, Sharai,
Azarel, Shelemiah, Shemariah, Shallum, Ama-
riah, Joseph.

43From the clan of Nebo: Jeiel, Mattithiah,
Zabad, Zebina, Jaddai, Joel, Benaiah.

44Each of these men had heathen wives,
and many had children by these wives.

10:10-12 Heartily, the people responded, "We will do what you have said." They recognized their special privileges and responsibilities as God's people. When they admitted that they needed to obey God's will, they found victory! Ezra was successful in his recovery mission to the nation! We, too, can know such victory if we follow God's will for our life and trust him to see us through.

NEHEMIAH

THE BIG PICTURE

- A. REBUILDING THE WALL (1:1–7:73)
  - 1. Nehemiah's Call (1:1–2:8)
  - 2. Nehemiah's Preparations (2:9–3:32)
  - 3. The Problems Faced by Nehemiah (4:1–6:14)
    - a. Derision—answered by prayer (4:1-6)
    - b. Discouragement—answered by communication (4:7-23)
    - c. Greed—answered by confrontation (5:1-19)
    - d. Personal attacks—answered by dependence on God (6:1-14)
  - 4. Nehemiah Perseveres (6:15–7:73)
- B. REBUILDING THE WORKERS (8:1–12:47)
  - 1. Ezra Leads in Revival (8:1-18)
  - 2. The Role of Confession (9:1-38)
  - 3. The Response of the People (9:39–10:39)
  - 4. Nehemiah Establishes Policies (11:1–12:47)
- C. REBUILDING THE WORSHIP (13:1-31)

A secure environment is helpful for any rebuilding project. When we lack physical and emotional safety, it is difficult to concentrate on the job at hand. The people of Jerusalem had no physical security—their city wall had been piles of rubble for over a hundred years. The Temple had been rebuilt many years before, but the wall around Jerusalem was still in disrepair. Walls are important boundaries. They protect and shelter inhabitants that live inside; they repel destructive intruders from outside. In the world of the ancient Near East, a city without a wall was vulnerable to raids and all kinds of harassment—it was unthinkable! It was in this unstable situation that Ezra was encouraging the Jews to rebuild their nation and lives.

At this time, Nehemiah worked as the cupbearer for King Artaxerxes of Persia. When he heard about the situation that Ezra faced in Jerusalem, he literally sat down and wept.

Nehemiah decided to approach King Artaxerxes about the problem, and he was given permission to lead a third group of Jews back to Jerusalem. He took responsibility for encouraging the people to rebuild the wall of Jerusalem. Nehemiah's organizational skills and leadership abilities overcame both international and local resistance to the rebuilding project. In the end, by trusting God and pulling together, the people completed the task of rebuilding the wall.

When the work was completed, Nehemiah joined with Ezra to encourage the people to rebuild their lives, their culture, and proper worship of God. Nehemiah's skills were organizational. He handled the logistics of organizing the Levites, the people, and other officials. Ezra complemented Nehemiah as he led the people in the recovery of their spiritual heritage.

THE BOTTOM LINE

PURPOSE: To describe the rebuilding of the wall of Jerusalem and the continued spiritual rebuilding of the people. AUTHOR: Nehemiah; Ezra probably served as an editor. AUDIENCE: The people of Israel after their return from exile in Babylon. DATE WRITTEN: The dates of Nehemiah's first administration were 445–432 B.C., during which time this book was probably written. SETTING: The city of Jerusalem. KEY VERSE: "The laws of God were read aloud to them for two or three hours, and for several more hours they took turns confessing their own sins and those of their ancestors" (9:3). KEY PEOPLE: Ezra, Nehemiah.

RECOVERY THEMES

The Importance of Boundaries: Nehemiah's rebuilding of the wall of Jerusalem illustrates the importance of personal boundaries in our life. When we don't have boundaries, other people feel like they can control us, and they usually can. Our identity often becomes confused with the identities of others to the point of losing touch with who we are. The Jews living in Jerusalem after the return from Babylon also lacked boundaries of protection. They were at the mercy of the people living nearby. The task of rebuilding Jerusalem's boundaries met with opposition, for with a wall, the people of Jerusalem would be able to defend themselves. Rebuilding the wall was a difficult task for Nehemiah, as it is for us, but we must have protective boundaries.

The Importance of Confrontation: Often, directly confronting a person in the wrong is the best way to remedy a bad situation. There are several situations where the enemies of Nehemiah tried to undermine his work through lies and deceit. Each time, Nehemiah was direct in confronting the lies, going right to the source of the problem. He did not allow himself to get discouraged or overwhelmed by the difficulties. Instead, each time something came up as a potential roadblock to God's work, Nehemiah faced the issues squarely and honestly. Then he stayed with the problem until it was resolved.

The Danger of Discouragement: As a wise leader, Nehemiah knew that the discouragement of the people was probably his biggest enemy, just as it is ours. When we get discouraged, we open ourself to defeat, giving the enemy victory for a period of time. Nehemiah shows us that we need to be on guard against discouragement, making certain that we are building into our life protection, healthy relationships, and a heart that seeks after God.

The Power of Confession and Worship: We have a vivid picture in this book of the power of confession and the role of worship in our recovery. Not many days after the end of the Festival of Tabernacles (Nehemiah 8), the people returned for another celebration (Nehemiah 9–10). This one was to celebrate the recovery of not only the Temple, but also the city of Jerusalem. But notice that they started their celebration by listening to the Word of God and confessing not only their own sins, but the sins of their ancestors. This kind of confession brings healing and prepares us for true worship, genuine recovery, and joyous celebration.

CHAPTER 1

Nehemiah Hears about Jerusalem

The autobiography of *Nehemiah, the son of Hecaliah:*

In December of the twentieth year of the reign of King Artaxerxes of Persia, when I was at the palace at Shushan, [2]one of my fellow Jews named Hanani came to visit me with some men who had arrived from Judah. I took the opportunity to inquire about how things were going in Jerusalem.

"How are they getting along—," I asked, "the Jews who returned to Jerusalem from their exile here?"

[3]"Well," they replied, "things are not good; the wall of Jerusalem is still torn down, and the gates are burned."

[4]When I heard this, I sat down and cried. In fact, I refused to eat for several days, for I spent the time in prayer to the God of heaven.

[5]"O Lord God," I cried out; "O great and awesome God who keeps his promises and is so loving and kind to those who love and obey him! Hear my prayer! [6,7]Listen carefully to what I say! Look down and see me praying night and day for your people Israel. I confess that we have sinned against you; yes, I and my people have committed the horrible sin of not obeying the commandments you gave us through your servant Moses. [8]Oh, please remember what you told Moses! You said,

"'If you sin, I will scatter you among the nations; [9]but if you return to me and obey my laws, even though you are exiled to the farthest corners of the universe, I will bring you back to Jerusalem. For Jerusalem is the place in which I have chosen to live.'

[10]"We are your servants, the people you rescued by your great power. [11]O Lord, please

---

1:4-11 For believers, prayer is often an untapped resource or the last resort after every other possibility has been exhausted. It is refreshing to notice that for Nehemiah, prayer was his immediate response. He knew that if the situation was to be corrected, God would be the one to accomplish it! This is a powerful reminder for us—we should fall on our knees so that we don't fall on our face.

1:11 Recovery can never be a solitary procedure. Other people must be involved. Cooperation has to be sought. Sometimes even permission has to be obtained. In this case, Nehemiah recognized the need for the king's favor, and he asked God to secure the necessary response from him. Like Nehemiah, we should determine whose help we need and then ask for their assistance.

NEHEMIAH

Recovery is the process of rebuilding a life, often from the point of near destruction. Nehemiah, the great rebuilder of Jerusalem, leaves us an excellent biblical example of how to pursue and enhance our recovery process.

Nehemiah did not let the long-delayed recovery of Jerusalem discourage him. He realized that it was never too late for God's people to begin the process. Nehemiah's actions were direct and forceful, always based on the realities at hand. His faith, wisdom, and courage kept him focused on his goal, despite considerable opposition. Leaders like Sanballat and Tobiah, who had dominated the land of Judah for some time, used various means to discourage the progress of Nehemiah and the Jews. Painful differences among the Jews themselves also had to be confronted along the way. But all of the obstacles were overcome as the people worked to build a new, more secure life.

The wall of Jerusalem was completed in a miraculous fifty-two days! Soon after this first victory, Nehemiah directed the people toward a second phase of recovery. He called upon the great teacher Ezra to lead the people in a study of the Scriptures. Confronted by God's Word, they were soon in tears, and they repented for their sins and the sins of their ancestors. Ezra, Nehemiah, and the other leaders encouraged the people to be filled with joy because God was with them.

Even at this point, however, all the painful lessons of recovery had not been learned. After Nehemiah went back to Babylon, the people returned once again to their sinful ways. When Nehemiah returned to Jerusalem, he had to put the Jews back on the path toward recovery. This example of short-term recovery and relapse ends the story of Nehemiah on a very realistic note. There will be times when we all fall back into familiar, though destructive, patterns. It should encourage us to realize that no matter how often we fail, there is always another opportunity to get back on track.

STRENGTHS AND ACCOMPLISHMENTS:

- Nehemiah was a man of prayer and unshakable commitment to God.
- He was an effective administrator and an even greater visionary.
- He was secure in himself and had the ability to withstand criticism.
- He had the faith and perseverance to complete the rebuilding process for Jerusalem and the nation.

LESSONS FROM HIS LIFE:

- Prayerful intervention, a realistic vision, and commitment to God are helpful aids to our recovery.
- Confronting and overcoming obstacles to recovery can actually provide momentum for the process.
- The completion of one phase of recovery should motivate us to pursue the next step in the process.
- A relapse should be viewed as a step toward renewed recovery.

KEY VERSE:

"They realized that the work had been done with the help of our God" (Nehemiah 6:16).

Nehemiah's story is told in the book of Nehemiah. He is also mentioned in Ezra 2:2.

---

hear my prayer! Heed the prayers of those of us who delight to honor you. Please help me now as I go in and ask the king for a great favor—put it into his heart to be kind to me." (I was the king's cupbearer.)

CHAPTER 2

Nehemiah Is Allowed to Return

One day in April, four months later, as I was serving the king his wine he asked me, "Why so sad? You aren't sick, are you? You look like a man with deep troubles." (For until then I had always been cheerful when I was with him.) I was badly frightened, 3but I replied, "Sir, why shouldn't I be sad? For the city where my ancestors are buried is in ruins, and the gates have been burned down."

4"Well, what should be done?" the king asked.

With a quick prayer to the God of heaven, I replied, "If it please Your Majesty and if you look upon me with your royal favor, send me to Judah to rebuild the city of my fathers!"

5,6 The king replied, with the queen sitting beside him, "How long will you be gone? When will you return?"

So it was agreed! And I set a time for my departure!

7 Then I added this to my request: "If it please the king, give me letters to the governors west of the Euphrates River instructing them to let me travel through their countries on my way to Judah; 8 also a letter to Asaph, the manager of the king's forest, instructing him to give me timber for the beams and for the gates of the fortress near the Temple, and for the city walls, and for a house for myself."

And the king granted these requests, for God was being gracious to me.

9 When I arrived in the provinces west of the Euphrates River, I delivered the king's letters to the governors there. (The king, I should add, had sent along army officers and troops to protect me!) 10 But when Sanballat (the Horonite) and Tobiah (an Ammonite who was a government official) heard of my arrival, they were very angry that anyone was interested in helping Israel.

Nehemiah Inspects the Wall

11,12 Three days after my arrival at Jerusalem I stole out during the night, taking only a few men with me; for I hadn't told a soul about the plans for Jerusalem that God had put into my heart. I was mounted on my donkey and the others were on foot, 13 and we went out through the Valley Gate toward the Jackal's Well and over to the Dung Gate to see the broken walls and burned gates. 14,15 Then we went to the Fountain Gate and to the King's Pool, but my donkey couldn't get through the rubble. So we circled the city, and I followed the brook, inspecting the wall, and entered again at the Valley Gate.

16 The city officials did not know I had been out there or why, for as yet I had said nothing to anyone about my plans—not to the political or religious leaders, or even to those who would be doing the work.

Nehemiah's Call to Rebuild

17 But now I told them, "You know full well the tragedy of our city; it lies in ruins and its gates are burned. Let us rebuild the wall of Jerusalem and rid ourselves of this disgrace!"

18 Then I told them about the desire God had put into my heart, and of my conversation with the king, and the plan to which he had agreed.

They replied at once, "Good! Let's rebuild the wall!" And so the work began.

19 But when Sanballat, Tobiah, and Geshem the Arab heard of our plan, they scoffed and said, "What are you doing, rebelling against the king like this?"

20 But I replied, "The God of heaven will help us, and we, his servants, will rebuild this wall; but you may have no part in this affair."

CHAPTER 3

The Builders of the Wall

Then Eliashib the High Priest and the other priests rebuilt the wall as far as the Tower of the Hundred and the Tower of Hananel; then they rebuilt the Sheep Gate, hung its doors, and dedicated it. 2 Men from the city of Jericho worked next to them, and beyond them was the work crew led by Zaccur (son of Imri).

3 The Fish Gate was built by the sons of Hassenaah; they did the whole thing—cut the beams, hung the doors, and made the bolts and bars. 4 Meremoth (son of Uriah, son of Hakkoz) repaired the next section of wall, and beyond him were Meshullam (son of Berechiah, son of Meshezabel) and Zadok (son of

---

2:4-8 In answer to Nehemiah's prayer, the king's immediate response was one of encouragement and assistance. One wonders how Artaxerxes would have responded had not Nehemiah first approached God on this matter. Prayer changes things. Prayer changes people. Prayer is a supernatural power at our disposal that enables us to accomplish God's supernatural will. If we try to do things on our own, the odds are against us; we will probably fail. If we try something with God's help, we will definitely succeed.

2:11-16 Taking an inventory is one of the first tasks in any rebuilding project. As soon as Nehemiah came to Jerusalem, he made a nighttime inspection of the city's broken wall. Each of us in recovery needs to take an honest look at all of the circumstances, problems, and resources before us. This is essential for selecting the proper strategy for correcting the problems we face.

3:1-32 Rebuilding the entire wall of Jerusalem was an enormous task. But Nehemiah had a plan to make it easier—he divided the work and assigned it to different groups of people. This way the people felt responsible for their section, and no one got burned out working on the entire task. There is a lesson here for us, too. As we face our recovery, we may become discouraged by the immensity of the task. But if we break up the process into smaller steps—a day or week or month at a time—the task will look less intimidating.

Baana). 5Next were the men from Tekoa, but
their leaders were lazy and didn't help.

6The Old Gate was repaired by Joiada (son
of Paseah) and Meshullam (son of Besodeiah).
They laid the beams, set up the doors, and
installed the bolts and bars. 7Next to them
were Melatiah from Gibeon; Jadon from Meronoth; and men from Gibeon and Mizpah,
who were citizens of the province. 8Uzziel
(son of Harhaiah) was a goldsmith by trade,
but he too worked on the wall. Beyond him
was Hananiah, a manufacturer of perfumes.
Repairs were not needed from there to the
Broad Wall.

9Rephaiah (son of Hur), the mayor of half
of Jerusalem, was next down the wall from
them. 10Jedaiah (son of Harumaph) repaired
the wall beside his own house, and next to
him was Hattush (son of Hashabneiah).
11Then came Malchijah (son of Harim) and
Hasshub (son of Pahath-moab), who repaired
the Furnace Tower in addition to a section of
the wall. 12Shallum (son of Hallohesh) and his
daughters repaired the next section. He was
the mayor of the other half of Jerusalem.

13The people from Zanoah, led by Hanun,
built the Valley Gate, hung the doors, and
installed the bolts and bars; then they repaired the 1,500 feet of wall to the Dung Gate.

14The Dung Gate was repaired by Malchijah
(son of Rechab), the mayor of the Beth-
haccherem area; and after building it, he hung
the doors and installed the bolts and bars.

15Shallum (son of Col-hozeh), the mayor of
the Mizpah district, repaired the Fountain
Gate. He rebuilt it, roofed it, hung its doors,
and installed its locks and bars. Then he repaired the wall from the Pool of Siloam to the
king's garden and the stairs that descend from
the City of David section of Jerusalem. 16Next
to him was Nehemiah (son of Azbuk), the
mayor of half the Beth-zur district; he built as
far as the royal cemetery, the water reservoir,
and the old Officers' Club building. 17Next
was a group of Levites working under the
supervision of Rehum (son of Bani). Then
came Hashabiah, the mayor of half the Keilah
district, who supervised the building of the
wall in his own district. 18Next down the line
were his clan brothers led by Bavvai (son of
Henadad), the mayor of the other half of the
Keilah district.

19Next to them the workers were led by Ezer
(son of Jeshua), the mayor of another part of
Mizpah; they also worked on the section of
wall across from the Armory where the wall
turns. 20Next to him was Baruch (son of Zabbai), who built from the turn in the wall to the
home of Eliashib the High Priest. 21 Meremoth
(son of Uriah, son of Hakkoz) built a section
of the wall extending from a point opposite
the door of Eliashib's house to the side of the
house.

22Then came the priests from the plains
outside the city. 23Benjamin, Hasshub, and
Azariah (son of Maaseiah, son of Ananiah)
repaired the sections next to their own
houses. 24Next was Binnui (son of Henadad),
who built the portion of the wall from Azariah's house to the corner. 25Palal (son of Uzai)
carried on the work from the corner to the
foundations of the upper tower of the king's
castle beside the prison yard. Next was Pedaiah (son of Parosh).

26The Temple attendants living in Ophel
repaired the wall as far as the East Water Gate
and the Projecting Tower. 27Then came the
Tekoites, who repaired the section opposite
the Castle Tower and over to the wall of Ophel. 28The priests repaired the wall beyond the
Horse Gate, each one doing the section immediately opposite his own house.

29Zadok (son of Immer) also rebuilt the wall
next to his own house, and beyond him was
Shemaiah (son of Shecaniah), the gatekeeper
of the East Gate. 30Next was Hananiah (son of
Shelemiah); Hanun (the sixth son of Zalaph);
and Meshullam (son of Berechiah), who built
next to his own house. 31Malchijah, one of the
goldsmiths, repaired as far as the Temple attendants' and merchants' Guild Hall, opposite the Muster Gate; then to the upper room
at the corner. 32The other goldsmiths and merchants completed the wall from that corner to
the Sheep Gate.

CHAPTER 4

Enemies Oppose the Rebuilding

Sanballat was very angry when he learned
that we were rebuilding the wall. He flew into

4:1-4 Whenever we start a recovery process, we will face many kinds of opposition. In this, Nehemiah was no exception. One kind of opposition that he faced was ridicule. The sarcasm expressed by Sanballat and Tobiah must have stung. But Nehemiah did not have his attention focused upon the ridicule; he continued to look to God. We, too, should look to God when we are taunted. The ridicule of others is probably motivated by their desire to continue dominating us or by their jealousy over our recovery.

a rage, and insulted and mocked us and laughed at us, and so did his friends and the Samaritan army officers. "What does this bunch of poor, feeble Jews think they are doing?" he scoffed. "Do they think they can build the wall in a day if they offer enough sacrifices? And look at those charred stones they are pulling out of the rubbish and using again!"

[3]Tobiah, who was standing beside him, remarked, "If even a fox walked along the top of their wall, it would collapse!"

[4]Then I prayed, "Hear us, O Lord God, for we are being mocked. May their scoffing fall back upon their own heads, and may they themselves become captives in a foreign land! [5]Do not ignore their sin. Do not blot it out, for they have despised you in despising us who are building your wall."

[6]At last the wall was completed to half its original height around the entire city—for the workers worked hard.

[7]But when Sanballat and Tobiah and the Arabians, Ammonites, and Ashdodites heard that the work was going right ahead and that the breaks in the wall were being repaired, they became furious. [8]They plotted to lead an army against Jerusalem to bring about riots and confusion. [9]But we prayed to our God and guarded the city day and night to protect ourselves.

[10]Then some of the leaders began complaining that the workmen were becoming tired; and there was so much rubble to be removed that we could never get it done by ourselves. [11]Meanwhile, our enemies were planning to swoop down upon us and kill us, thus ending our work. [12]And whenever the workers who lived in the nearby cities went home for a visit, our enemies tried to talk them out of returning to Jerusalem. [13]So I placed armed guards from each family in the cleared spaces behind the walls.

[14]Then as I looked over the situation, I called together the leaders and the people and said to them, "Don't be afraid! Remember the Lord who is great and glorious; fight for your friends, your families, and your homes!"

[15]Our enemies learned that we knew of their plot, and that God had exposed and frustrated their plan. Now we all returned to our work on the wall; [16]but from then on, only half worked while the other half stood guard behind them. [17]And the masons and laborers worked with weapons within easy reach beside them [18]or with swords belted to their sides. The trumpeter stayed with me to sound the alarm.

[19]"The work is so spread out," I explained to them, "and we are separated so widely from each other, that when you hear the trumpet blow, you must rush to where I am; and God will fight for us."

[20,21]We worked early and late, from sunrise to sunset; and half the men were always on guard. [22]I told everyone living outside the walls to move into Jerusalem so that their servants could go on guard duty as well as work during the day. [23]During this period none of us—I, nor my brothers, nor the servants, nor the guards who were with me—ever took off our clothes except for washing. And we carried our weapons with us at all times.

CHAPTER 5

Nehemiah Defends the Poor

About this time there was a great outcry of protest from parents against some of the rich Jews who were profiteering on them. [2-4]What was happening was that families who ran out of money for food had to sell their children or mortgage their fields, vineyards, and homes to these rich men; and some couldn't even do that, for they already had borrowed to the limit to pay their taxes.

[5]"We are their brothers, and our children are just like theirs," the people protested. "Yet

---

4:10 Rubbish can be very disheartening in itself. With every remodeling project, trash accumulates. This is true not only for physical rebuilding, but for emotional and spiritual recovery as well. The garbage was getting in the way of the workmen, and they were discouraged by it. We experience the same thing as the unresolved emotional garbage from our past discourages us. We must make efforts to recognize the garbage, resolve the problem, and then remove it so we can continue on the path to recovery.

5:1-5 The previous attack had come from the outside; now a new attack came from within. The rebuilding was costing too much! We experience the same emotions as the Jews felt. In overcoming our dependencies, we have to give up some of the things that have brought us security. When times get bad, we may wish we had our addiction back to comfort us, even though we know it was harmful. But in order to rebuild the walls of our life, some pain and sacrifice are necessary. The cost of recovery is worth what we will receive in return—our freedom.

we must sell our children into slavery to get
enough money to live. We have already sold
some of our daughters, and we are helpless to
redeem them, for our fields, too, are mort-
gaged to these men."
[6]I was very angry when I heard this; [7]so after
thinking about it I spoke out against these
rich government officials.
"What is this you are doing?" I demanded.
"How dare you demand a mortgage as a condition for helping another Israelite!"
Then I called a public trial to deal with
them.
[8]At the trial I shouted at them, "The rest of
us are doing all we can to *help* our Jewish
brothers who have returned from exile as
slaves in distant lands, but you are forcing
them right back into slavery again. How often
must we redeem them?"
And they had nothing to say in their own
defense.
[9]Then I pressed further. "What you are doing is very evil," I exclaimed. "Should you not
walk in the fear of our God? Don't we have
enough enemies among the nations around
us who are trying to destroy us? [10]The rest of
us are lending money and grain to our fellow-
Jews without any interest. I beg you, gentlemen, stop this business of usury. [11]Restore
their fields, vineyards, oliveyards, and homes
to them this very day and drop your claims
against them."
[12]So they agreed to do it and said that they
would assist their brothers without requiring
them to mortgage their lands and sell them
their children. Then I summoned the priests
and made these men formally vow to carry
out their promises. [13]And I invoked the curse
of God upon any of them who refused.
"May God destroy your homes and livelihood if you fail to keep this promise," I declared.
And all the people shouted, "Amen," and
praised the Lord. And the rich men did as they
had promised.
[14]I would like to mention that for the entire
twelve years that I was governor of Judah—
from the twentieth until the thirty-second
year of the reign of King Artaxerxes—my
aides and I accepted no salaries or other assistance from the people of Israel. [15]This was
quite a contrast to the former governors who
had demanded food and wine and $100 a day
in cash, and had put the population at the
mercy of their aides who tyrannized them;
but I obeyed God and did not act that way. [16]I
stayed at work on the wall and refused to
speculate in land; I also required my officials
to spend time on the wall. [17]All this despite
the fact that I regularly fed 150 Jewish officials
at my table, besides visitors from other countries! [18]The provisions required for each day
were one ox, six fat sheep, and a large number
of domestic fowls; and we needed a huge
supply of all kinds of wines every ten days. Yet
I refused to make a special levy against the
people, for they were already having a difficult time. [19]O my God, please keep in mind all
that I've done for these people and bless me
for it.

CHAPTER 6

Continued Opposition to Rebuilding

When Sanballat, Tobiah, Geshem the Arab,
and the rest of our enemies found out that we
had almost completed the rebuilding of the
wall—though we had not yet hung all the
doors of the gates— [2]they sent me a message
asking me to meet them in one of the villages
in the Plain of Ono. But I realized they were
plotting to kill me, [3]so I replied by sending
back this message to them:
"I am doing a great work! Why should I
stop to come and visit with you?"
[4]Four times they sent the same message,
and each time I gave the same reply. [5,6]The
fifth time, Sanballat's servant came with an

5:14-19 Leadership by example is the most difficult, yet the most effective, way to lead. Nehemiah gave up many of his rightful privileges in order to be a godly example. Nehemiah did not insist on his own rights. Rather, he was willing to sacrifice them for the good of the people as a part of his response to God.

6:1-2 As the work neared completion, the enemies resorted to trickery—under the guise of negotiation. As we seek to work a godly program, God's enemies may not be excited about us completing it. We should not allow others to distract us from our goal of recovery; they may be diverting us from our program because they do not want us to succeed.

6:3 Nehemiah had set his mind to the task; he had a singleness of purpose. When his enemies tried to lure him away from the work, he answered with the ringing statement, "I am doing a great work!" He allowed nothing to turn him from his purpose. Each of us needs to seek God for such clear direction because we, too, are "doing a great work."

open letter in his hand, and this is what it said:

"Geshem tells me that everywhere he goes he hears that the Jews are planning to rebel, and that is why you are building the wall. He claims you plan to be their king—that is what is being said. [7]He also reports that you have appointed prophets to campaign for you at Jerusalem by saying, 'Look! Nehemiah is just the man we need!'

"You can be very sure that I am going to pass along these interesting comments to King Artaxerxes! I suggest that you come and talk it over with me—for that is the only way you can save yourself !"

[8]My reply was, "You know you are lying. There isn't one bit of truth to the whole story. [9]You're just trying to scare us into stopping our work." (O Lord God, please strengthen me!)

[10]A few days later I went to visit Shemaiah (son of Delaiah, who was the son of Mehetabel), for he said he was receiving a message from God.

"Let us hide in the Temple and bolt the door," he exclaimed, "for they are coming tonight to kill you."

[11]But I replied, "Should I, the governor, run away from danger? And if I go into the Temple, not being a priest, I would forfeit my life. No, I won't do it!"

[12,13]Then I realized that God had not spoken to him, but Tobiah and Sanballat had hired him to scare me and make me sin by fleeing to the Temple; and then they would be able to accuse me.

[14]"O my God," I prayed, "don't forget all the evil of Tobiah, Sanballat, Noadiah the prophetess, and all the other prophets who have tried to discourage me."

The Builders Complete the Wall

[15]The wall was finally finished in early September—just fifty-two days after we had begun!

[16]When our enemies and the surrounding nations heard about it, they were frightened and humiliated, and they realized that the work had been done with the help of our God. [17]During those fifty-two days many letters went back and forth between Tobiah and the wealthy politicians of Judah. [18]For many in Judah had sworn allegiance to him because his father-in-law was Shecaniah (son of Arah) and because his son Jehohanan was married to the daughter of Meshullam (son of Berechiah). [19]They all told me what a wonderful man Tobiah was, and then they told him everything I had said; and Tobiah sent many threatening letters to frighten me.

CHAPTER 7

A Plan for Guarding the Wall

After the wall was finished and we had hung the doors in the gates and had appointed the gatekeepers, singers, and Levites, [2]I gave the responsibility of governing Jerusalem to my brother Hanani and to Hananiah, the commander of the fortress—a very faithful man who revered God more than most people do. [3]I issued instructions to them not to open the Jerusalem gates until well after sunrise, and to close and lock them while the guards were still on duty. I also directed that the guards be residents of Jerusalem, and that they must be on duty at regular times, and that each homeowner who lived near the wall must guard the section of wall next to his own home. [4]For the city was large, but the population was small; and only a few houses were scattered throughout the city.

Nehemiah Registers the People

[5]Then the Lord told me to call together all the leaders of the city, along with the ordinary citizens, for registration. For I had found the record of the genealogies of those who had returned to Judah before, and this is what was written in it:

[6]"The following is a list of the names of the

6:15-16 After overcoming every conceivable kind of evil opposition, the building of the wall was completed in a record fifty-two days. The work was completed so quickly because God had helped the Israelites. A job that had not been done for almost a hundred years was finished within two months. If we have delayed our recovery and now think it is too late, we should look to Nehemiah: he took a long-neglected task and completed it in a short period of time. It is never too late to begin recovery if we go about it with God's help.

7:1-4 It is interesting that after the great project was completed, Nehemiah did not quit. Rather, he set up a careful organization for further building. He made careful provision for the further defense of the city. He wanted God's people to have a safe environment for their individual building projects. Our recovery calls for ongoing attention. Though we may have made the step of breaking with our addiction, we must be on guard for lapses in our resolve or attacks from those who don't want us to succeed.

Jews who returned to Judah after being exiled by King Nebuchadnezzar of Babylon.

7"Their leaders were: Zerubbabel, Jeshua, Nehemiah, Azariah, Raamiah, Nahamani, Mordecai, Bilshan, Mispereth, Bigvai, Nehum, Baanah.

"The others who returned at that time were:

8-38From the subclan of Parosh, 2,172;
From the subclan of Shephatiah, 372;
From the subclan of Arah, 652;
From the families of Jeshua and Joab of the subclan of Pahath-moab, 2,818;
From the subclan of Elam, 1,254;
From the subclan of Zattu, 845;
From the subclan of Zaccai, 760;
From the subclan of Binnui, 648;
From the subclan of Bebai, 628;
From the subclan of Azgad, 2,322;
From the subclan of Adonikam, 667;
From the subclan of Bigvai, 2,067;
From the subclan of Adin, 655;
From the family of Hezekiah of the subclan of Ater, 98;
From the subclan of Hashum, 328;
From the subclan of Bezai, 324;
From the subclan of Hariph, 112;
From the subclan of Gibeon, 95;
From the subclans of Bethlehem and Netophah, 188;
From the subclan of Anathoth, 128;
From the subclan of Beth-azmaveth, 42;
From the subclans of Kiriath-jearim, Chephirah, and Beeroth, 743;
From the subclans of Ramah and Geba, 621;
From the subclan of Michmas, 122;
From the subclans of Bethel and Ai, 123;
From the subclan of Nebo, 52;
From the subclan of Elam, 1,254;
From the subclan of Harim, 320;
From the subclan of Jericho, 345;
From the subclans of Lod, Hadid, and Ono, 721;
From the subclan of Senaah, 3,930.

39-42"Here are the statistics concerning the returning priests:

From the family of Jeshua of the subclan of Jedaiah, 973;
From the subclan of Immer, 1,052;
From the subclan of Pashhur, 1,247;
From the subclan of Harim, 1,017.

43-45"Here are the statistics concerning the Levites:

From the family of Kadmiel of the subclan of Hodevah of the clan of Jeshua, 74;
The choir members from the clan of Asaph, 148;
From the clans of Shallum, (all of whom were gatekeepers), 138.

46-56"Of the Temple assistants, the following subclans were represented: Ziha, Hasupha, Tabbaoth, Keros, Sia, Padon, Lebana, Hagaba, Shalmai, Hanan, Giddel, Gahar, Reaiah, Rezin, Nekoda, Gazzam, Uzza, Paseah, Besai, Asnah, Meunim, Nephushesim, Bakbuk, Hakupha, Harhur, Bazlith, Mehida, Harsha, Barkos, Sisera, Temah, Neziah, Hatipha.

57-59"Following is a list of the descendants of Solomon's officials who returned to Judah: Sotai, Sophereth, Perida, Jaala, Darkon, Giddel, Shephatiah, Hattil, Pochereth-hazzebaim, Amon.

60"In all, the Temple assistants and the descendants of Solomon's officers numbered 392."

61Another group returned to Jerusalem at that time from the Persian cities of Tel-melah, Tel-harsha, Cherub, Addon, and Immer. But they had lost their genealogies and could not prove their Jewish ancestry; 62these were the subclans of Delaiah, Tobiah, and Nekoda—a total of 642.

63There were also several subclans of priests named after Hobaiah. Hakkoz, and Barzillai (he married one of the daughters of Barzillai the Gileadite and took her family name), 64,65whose genealogies had been lost. So they were not allowed to continue as priests or even to receive the priests' share of food from the sacrifices until the Urim and Thummim had been consulted to find out from God whether or not they actually were descendants of priests.

66There was a total of 42,360 citizens who returned to Judah at that time; 67also, 7,337 slaves and 245 choir members, both men and women. 68,69They took with them 736 horses, 245 mules, 435 camels, and 6,720 donkeys.

70Some of their leaders gave gifts for the work. The governor gave $5,000 in gold, 50 gold bowls, and 530 sets of clothing for the priests. 71The other leaders gave a total of $100,000 in gold and $77,000 in silver; 72and the common people gave $100,000 in gold, $70,000 in silver, and sixty-seven sets of clothing for the priests.

73The priests, the Levites, the gatekeepers, the choir members, the Temple attendants, and the rest of the people now returned home to their own towns and villages throughout Judah. But during the month of September, they came back to Jerusalem.

CHAPTER 8

Ezra Reads the Law

Now, in mid-September, all the people assembled at the plaza in front of the Water Gate and requested Ezra, their religious leader, to read to them the law of God, which he had given to Moses.

So Ezra the priest brought out to them the scroll of Moses' laws. He stood on a wooden stand made especially for the occasion so that everyone could see him as he read. He faced the square in front of the Water Gate and read from early morning until noon. Everyone stood up as he opened the scroll. And all who were old enough to understand paid close attention. To his right stood Mattithiah, Shema, Anaiah, Uriah, Hilkiah, and Maaseiah. To his left were Pedaiah, Mishael, Malchijah, Hashum, Hash-baddenah, Zechariah, and Meshullam.

6Then Ezra blessed the Lord, the great God, and all the people said, "Amen," and lifted their hands toward heaven; then they bowed and worshiped the Lord with their faces toward the ground.

7,8As Ezra read from the scroll, Jeshua, Bani, Sherebiah, Jamin, Akkub, Shabbethai, Hodiah, Maaseiah, Kelita, Azariah, Jozabad, Hanan, Pelaiah, and the Levites went among the people and explained the meaning of the passage that was being read. 9All the people began sobbing when they heard the commands of the law.

Then Ezra the priest, and I as governor, and the Levites who were assisting me, said to them, "Don't cry on such a day as this! For today is a sacred day before the Lord your God— 10it is a time to celebrate with a hearty meal and to send presents to those in need, for the joy of the Lord is your strength. You must not be dejected and sad!"

11And the Levites, too, quieted the people, telling them, "That's right! Don't weep! For this is a day of holy joy, not of sadness."

12So the people went away to eat a festive meal and to send presents; it was a time of great and joyful celebration because they could hear and understand God's words.

13The next day the clan leaders and the priests and Levites met with Ezra to go over the law in greater detail. 14As they studied it, they noted that Jehovah had told Moses that the people of Israel should live in tents during the Festival of Tabernacles to be held that month. 15He had said also that a proclamation should be made throughout the cities of the land, especially in Jerusalem, telling the people to go to the hills to get branches from olive, myrtle, palm, and fig trees and to make huts in which to live for the duration of the feast.

16So the people went out and cut branches and used them to build huts on the roofs of their houses, or in their courtyards, or in the court of the Temple, or on the plaza beside the Water Gate, or at the Ephraim Gate Plaza. 17They lived in these huts for the seven days of the feast, and everyone was filled with joy! (This procedure had not been carried out since the days of Joshua.) 18Ezra read from the scroll on each of the seven days of the feast, and on the eighth day there was a solemn closing service as required by the laws of Moses.

CHAPTER 9

The People Confess Their Sins

On October 10 the people returned for another observance; this time they fasted and

---

8:7-8 Not only did Ezra engage in the public reading of Scripture; he also chose a team that was responsible for the public teaching of the Word. This was a group of men that assisted the people in understanding what the Bible meant and how to apply it to their lives. The renewing of the mind always involves the study of Scripture and its application to life. Without Scripture, we would not know what God's purpose is for our life. And without Scripture, we would not hear that we shouldn't "copy the behavior and customs of this world, but be a new and different person with a fresh newness in all [we] do and think" (Romans 12:2).

8:12 The people expressed great joy at understanding God's words. They went out rejoicing. They weren't excited about just hearing God's words; they were excited because they *understood* God's words. They were overwhelmed by God's power and his great love for them. The same message is true for us today: God is all powerful, and he loves us. God sent his Son to die for our sins, so we can live with him forever. Understanding this message should bring us great joy.

9:1-3 Joy was not the people's only response to the Scriptures. Their fresh understanding of the Bible brought about their repentance. They confessed their sins and expressed deep sorrow for disobeying God. They also confessed the sins of their ancestors—a necessary step if we are to break the dysfunctional patterns of our family's past. When we repent, we recognize and admit our disobedience. It is only then that we can turn our life and addictions over to God.

clothed themselves with sackcloth and sprinkled dirt in their hair. And the Israelis separated themselves from all foreigners. 3The
laws of God were read aloud to them for two
or three hours, and for several more hours
they took turns confessing their own sins and
those of their ancestors. And everyone worshiped the Lord their God. 4Some of the Levites were on the platform praising the Lord
God with songs of joy. These men were
Jeshua, Kadmiel, Bani, Shebaniah, Bunni,
Sherebiah, Bani, and Chenani.
5Then the Levite leaders called out to the
people, "Stand up and praise the Lord your
God, for he lives from everlasting to everlasting. Praise his glorious name! It is far greater
than we can think or say."
The leaders in this part of the service were
Jeshua, Kadmiel, Bani, Hashabneiah, Sherebiah, Hodiah, Shebaniah, and Pethahiah.
6Then Ezra prayed, "You alone are God. You
have made the skies and the heavens, the
earth and the seas, and everything in them.
You preserve it all; and all the angels of
heaven worship you.
7"You are the Lord God who chose Abram
and brought him from Ur of the Chaldeans
and renamed him Abraham. 8When he was
faithful to you, you made a contract with him
to forever give him and his descendants the
land of the Canaanites, Hittites, Amorites,
Perizzites, Jebusites, and Girgashites; and now
you have done what you promised, for you
are always true to your word.
9"You saw the troubles and sorrows of our
ancestors in Egypt, and you heard their cries
from beside the Red Sea. 10You displayed great
miracles against Pharaoh and his people, for
you knew how brutally the Egyptians were
treating them; you have a glorious reputation
because of those never-to-be-forgotten deeds.
11You divided the sea for your people so they
could go through on dry land! And then you
destroyed their enemies in the depths of the
sea; they sank like stones beneath the mighty
waters. 12You led our ancestors by a pillar of
cloud during the day and a pillar of fire at
night so that they could find their way.
13"You came down upon Mount Sinai and
spoke with them from heaven and gave them
good laws and true commandments, 14includ-
ing the laws about the holy Sabbath; and you
commanded them, through Moses your servant, to obey them all.
15"You gave them bread from heaven when
they were hungry and water from the rock
when they were thirsty. You commanded

Facing the Sadness

BIBLE READING: Nehemiah 8:7-10

We made a searching and fearless moral inventory of ourselves.

Most of us falter at the prospect of making an honest personal inventory. Rationalizations and excuses abound for avoiding this step. The bottom line is that we know that there is an enormous amount of sadness awaiting us, and we fear the pain that facing the sadness will bring.

The Jewish exiles who returned to Jerusalem after captivity in Babylon had lost touch with God. During the exile, they hadn't been taught his laws; so naturally, they hadn't practiced them either. After rebuilding the city wall and the Temple, the priests gathered the people together to read the book of the law. The people were overwhelmed with grief and began sobbing, because their lives in no way measured up.

The priests said to them, "Don't cry on such a day as this! For today is a sacred day before the Lord your God—it is a time to celebrate with a hearty meal and to send presents to those in need, for the joy of the Lord is your strength" (Nehemiah 8:9-10). That day marked the beginning of the Festival of Tabernacles, a required Jewish feast celebrating their escape from bondage in Egypt and God's care for them while they wandered in the wilderness.

When we set out to face the pain and sadness of making a moral inventory, we will need the "joy of the Lord" to give us strength. This joy comes from recognizing, even celebrating, God's ability to bring us out of bondage and to care for us as we pass through the sadness toward a new way of life. ***Turn to page 543, Nehemiah 9.***

them to go in and conquer the land you had
sworn to give them; 16but our ancestors were
a proud and stubborn lot, and they refused to
listen to your commandments.
17"They refused to obey and didn't pay any
attention to the miracles you did for them;
instead, they rebelled and appointed a leader
to take them back into slavery in Egypt! But
you are a God of forgiveness, always ready to
pardon, gracious and merciful, slow to become angry, and full of love and mercy; you
didn't abandon them, 18even though they
made a calf-idol and proclaimed, 'This is our
God! He brought us out of Egypt!' They
sinned in so many ways, 19but in your great
mercy you didn't abandon them to die in the
wilderness! The pillar of cloud led them forward day by day, and the pillar of fire showed
them the way through the night. 20You sent
your good Spirit to instruct them, and you did
not stop giving them bread from heaven or
water for their thirst. 21For forty years you
sustained them in the wilderness; they lacked
nothing in all that time. Their clothes didn't
wear out, and their feet didn't swell!
22"Then you helped them conquer great
kingdoms and many nations, and you placed
your people in every corner of the land; they
completely took over the land of King Sihon
of Heshbon and King Og of Bashan. 23You
caused a population explosion among the
Israelis and brought them into the land you
had promised to their ancestors. 24You subdued whole nations before them—even the
kings and the people of the Canaanites were
powerless! 25Your people captured fortified cities and fertile land; they took over houses full
of good things, with cisterns and vineyards
and oliveyards and many, many fruit trees; so
they ate and were full and enjoyed themselves
in all your blessings.
26"But despite all this, they were disobedient and rebelled against you. They threw
away your law, killed the prophets who told
them to return to you, and they did many
other terrible things. 27So you gave them to
their enemies. But in their time of trouble
they cried to you, and you heard them from
heaven, and in great mercy you sent them
saviors who delivered them from their ene-
mies.28But when all was going well, your
people turned to sin again, and once more
you let their enemies conquer them. Yet
whenever your people returned to you and
cried to you for help, once more you listened
from heaven, and in your wonderful mercy
delivered them! 29You punished them in order
to turn them toward your laws; but even
though they should have obeyed them, they
were proud and wouldn't listen, and continued to sin. 30You were patient with them for
many years. You sent your prophets to warn
them about their sins, but still they wouldn't
listen. So once again you allowed the heathen
nations to conquer them. 31But in your great
mercy you did not destroy them completely
or abandon them forever. What a gracious
and merciful God you are!
32"And now, O great and awesome God,
you who keep your promises of love and
kindness—do not let all the hardships we
have gone through become as nothing to
you. Great trouble has come upon us and
upon our kings and princes and priests and
prophets and ancestors from the days when
the kings of Assyria first triumphed over us
until now. 33Every time you punished us you
were being perfectly fair; we have sinned so
greatly that you gave us only what we deserved. 34Our kings, princes, priests, and ancestors didn't obey your laws or listen to your
warnings. 35They did not worship you despite
the wonderful things you did for them and
the great goodness you showered upon them.
You gave them a large, fat land, but they
refused to turn from their wickedness.
36"So now we are slaves here in the land of
plenty that you gave to our ancestors! Slaves
among all this abundance! 37The lush yield of
this land passes into the hands of the kings
whom you have allowed to conquer us because of our sins. They have power over our
bodies and our cattle, and we serve them at
their pleasure and are in great misery. 38Be-
cause of all this, we again promise to serve the
Lord! And we and our princes and Levites and
priests put our names to this covenant."

CHAPTER 10

The People Agree to Obey

I, Nehemiah the governor, signed the covenant. The others who signed it were: Zedekiah, Seraiah, Azariah, Jeremiah, Pashhur,
Amariah, Malchijah, Hattush, Shebaniah,

9:38 Every individual believer needs to be a part of some specific structure of accountability. To establish such accountability, the religious leaders in Israel formally wrote out this pact. In this case, the leaders pledged themselves to be accountable to God and each other. We must not try to live a godly life in a solitary fashion. We need others to uplift us, encourage us, and pray for us.

Malluch, Harim, Meremoth, Obadiah, Daniel, Ginnethon, Baruch, Meshullam, Abijah,
Mijamin, Maaziah, Bilgai, Shemaiah. (All
those listed above were priests.)
9-13 These were the Levites who signed:
Jeshua (son of Azaniah), Binnui (son of Henadad), Kadmiel, Shebaniah, Hodiah, Kelita, Pelaiah, Hanan, Mica, Rehob, Hashabiah,
Zaccur, Sherebiah, Shebaniah, Hodiah, Bani,
Beninu.
14-27 The political leaders who signed: Parosh, Pahath-moab, Elam, Zattu, Bani, Bunni,
Azgad, Bebai, Adonijah, Bigvai, Adin, Ater,
Hezekiah, Azzur, Hodiah, Hashum, Bezai, Hariph, Anathoth, Nebai, Magpiash, Meshullam, Hezir, Meshezabel, Zadok, Jaddua,
Pelatiah, Hanan, Anaiah, Hoshea, Hananiah,
Hasshub, Hallohesh, Pilha, Shobek, Rehum,
Hashabnah, Maaseiah, Ahiah, Hanan, Anan,
Malluch, Harim, Baanah.
28 These men signed on behalf of the entire
nation—for the common people, the priests,
the Levites, the gatekeepers, the choir members, the Temple servants, and all the rest
who, with their wives and sons and daughters
who were old enough to understand, had
separated themselves from the heathen
people of the land in order to serve God. 29 For
we all heartily agreed to this oath and vowed
to accept the curse of God unless we obeyed
God's laws as issued by his servant Moses.
30 We also agreed not to let our daughters
marry non-Jewish men and not to let our sons
marry non-Jewish girls.
31 We further agreed that if the heathen
people in the land should bring any grain or
other produce to be sold on the Sabbath or on
any other holy day, we would refuse to buy it.
And we agreed not to do any work every
seventh year and to forgive and cancel the
debts of our brother Jews.
32 We also agreed to charge ourselves annually with a Temple tax so that there would be
enough money to care for the Temple of our
God; 33 for we needed supplies of the special
Bread of the Presence, as well as grain offerings and burnt offerings for the Sabbaths, the
new moon feasts, and the annual feasts. We
also needed to purchase the other items necessary for the work of the Temple and for the
atonement of Israel.
34 Then we tossed a coin to determine
when—at regular times each year—the families of the priests, Levites, and leaders should
supply the wood for the burnt offerings at the
Temple as required in the law.
35 We also agreed always to bring the first

Confession

BIBLE READING: Nehemiah 9:1-3

We made a searching and fearless moral inventory of ourselves.

The heart of our moral inventory will probably deal with our destructive habits, defects of character, the wrongs we have done, the consequences that we now live with, and the hurt we have caused others. It's like sifting through all the garbage. This part is painful, but it is a necessary part of throwing away those rotten habits and behaviors that are spoiling the rest of our life.

The returned Jewish exiles are described as "confessing their own sins" (Nehemiah 9:3). This phrase speaks volumes. The word *confess* means "to bemoan something by wringing of the hands" and also "to throw away." The word *sins* means "offenses against God and their occasions"; it can refer to habitual sinfulness and the consequences of such behavior. This action of the Israelites can serve as a model for us to follow. We can list the occasions of our offenses, our destructive habits, and the consequences we have brought into our life and the lives of others.

In their confession, the Israelites owned, bemoaned, and then discarded their sin. After this they were better able to make a new start. We can "own" the garbage in our own life by taking personal responsibility for our choices and actions. We can "bemoan" it by allowing ourself to grieve. We can "discard" it by leaving it behind and turning toward the future. ***Turn to page 545, Nehemiah 10.***

part of every crop to the Temple—whether it be a ground crop or from our fruit and olive trees.

[36]We agreed to give to God our oldest sons and the firstborn of all our cattle, herds, and flocks, just as the law requires; we presented them to the priests who minister in the Temple of our God. [37]They stored the produce in the Temple of our God—the best of our grain crops, and other contributions, the first of our fruit, and the first of the new wine and olive oil. And we promised to bring to the Levites a tenth of everything our land produced, for the Levites were responsible to collect the tithes in all our rural towns.[38]A priest—a descendant of Aaron—would be with the Levites as they received these tithes, and a tenth of all that was collected as tithes was delivered to the Temple and placed in the storage areas. [39]The people and the Levites were required by law to bring these offerings of grain, new wine, and olive oil to the Temple and place them in the sacred containers for use by the ministering priests, the gatekeepers, and the choir singers.

So we agreed together not to neglect the Temple of our God.

CHAPTER 11

The People Occupy Jerusalem

The Israeli officials were living in Jerusalem, the Holy City, at this time; but now a tenth of the people from the other cities and towns of Judah and Benjamin were selected by lot to live there too. [2]Some who moved to Jerusalem at this time were volunteers, and they were highly honored.

[3]Following is a list of the names of the provincial officials who came to Jerusalem (though most of the leaders, the priests, the Levites, the Temple assistants, and the descendants of Solomon's servants continued to live in their own homes in the various cities of Judah).

[4-6]Leaders from the tribe of Judah:

Athaiah (son of Uzziah, son of Zechariah, son of Amariah, son of Shephatiah, son of Mahalalel, a descendant of Perez);
Maaseiah (son of Baruch, son of Col-hozeh, son of Hazaiah, son of Adaiah, son of Joiarib, son of Zechariah, son of the Shilonite).
These were the 468 stalwart descendants of Perez who lived in Jerusalem.

[7-9]Leaders from the tribe of Benjamin:

Sallu (son of Meshullam, son of Joed, son of Pedaiah, son of Kolaiah, son of Maaseiah, son of Ithiel, son of Jeshaiah).
The 968 descendants of Gabbai and Sallai. Their chief was Joel, son of Zichri, who was assisted by Judah, son of Hassenuah.

[10-14]Leaders from among the priests:

Jedaiah (son of Joiarib);
Jachin;
Seraiah (son of Hilkiah, son of Meshullam, son of Zadok, son of Meraioth, son of Ahitub the chief priest).

In all, there were 822 priests doing the work at the Temple under the leadership of these men. And there were 242 priests under the leadership of Adaiah (son of Jeroham, son of Pelaliah, son of Amzi, son of Zechariah, son of Pashhur, son of Malchijah).

There were also 128 stalwart men under the leadership of Amashsai (son of Azarel, son of Ahzai, son of Meshillemoth, son of Immer); who was assisted by Zabdiel (son of Haggedolim).

[15-17]Levite leaders:

Shemaiah (son of Hasshub, son of Azrikam, son of Hashabiah, son of Bunni);
Shabbethai and Jozabad, who were in charge of the work outside the Temple;
Mattaniah (son of Mica, son of Zabdi, son of Asaph) was the one who began the thanksgiving services with prayer;
Bakbukiah and Abda (son of Shammua, son of Galal, son of Jeduthun) were his assistants.

[18]In all, there were 284 Levites in Jerusalem.

[19]There were also 172 gatekeepers, led by Akkub, Talmon, and others of their clan. [20]The other priests, Levites, and people lived wherever their family inheritance was located. [21]However, the Temple workers (whose leaders were Ziha and Gishpa) all lived in Ophel.

10:39 Here the people agreed not to neglect the Temple, God's dwelling among them. Today, we have a temple to care for, too—our body. "Haven't you yet learned that your body is the home of the Holy Spirit God gave you, and that he lives within you? Your own body does not belong to you" (1 Corinthians 6:19). We should take care of our body and treat it with respect because it is where God dwells. To mistreat our body with an addiction is to mistreat God's own dwelling place.

22,23 The supervisor of the Levites in Jerusalem and of those serving at the Temple was Uzzi (son of Bani, son of Hashabiah, son of Mattaniah, son of Mica), a descendant of Asaph, whose clan became the Tabernacle singers. He was appointed by King David, who also set the pay scale of the singers.

24 Pethahiah (son of Meshezabel, a descendant of Zerah, a son of Judah) assisted in all matters of public administration.

25-30 Some of the towns where the people of Judah lived were: Kiriath-arba, Dibon, Jekabzeel (and their surrounding villages), Jeshua, Moladah, Beth-pelet, Hazar-shual, Beersheba (and its surrounding villages), Ziklag, Meconah and its villages, En-rimmon, Zorah, Jarmuth, Zanoah, Adullam (and their surrounding villages), Lachish and its nearby fields, Azekah and its towns.

So the people spread from Beersheba to the valley of Hinnom.

31-35 The people of the tribe of Benjamin lived at: Geba, Michmash, Aija, Bethel (and its surrounding villages), Anathoth, Nob, Ananiah, Hazor, Ramah, Gittaim, Hadid, Zeboim, Neballat, Lod, Ono (the Valley of the Craftsmen).

36 Some of the Levites who lived in Judah were sent to live with the tribe of Benjamin.

CHAPTER 12

The Priests and Levites

Here is a list of the priests who accompanied Zerubbabel (son of Shealtiel) and Jeshua: Seraiah, Jeremiah, Ezra, Amariah, Malluch, Hattush, Shecaniah, Rehum, Meremoth, Iddo, Ginnethoi, Abijah, Mijamin, Maadiah, Bilgah, Shemaiah, Joiarib, Jedaiah, Sallu, Amok, Hilkiah, Jedaiah.

8 The Levites who went with them were: Jeshua, Binnui, Kadmiel,

Sherebiah, Judah, Mattaniah—who was the one in charge of the thanksgiving service.

9 Bakbukiah and Unni, their fellow clansmen, helped them during the service.

10,11 Jeshua was the father of Joiakim;
Joiakim was the father of Eliashib;
Eliashib was the father of Joiada;
Joiada was the father of Jonathan;
Jonathan was the father of Jaddua.

12-21 The following were the clan leaders of the priests who served under the High Priest Joiakim:

Meraiah, leader of the Seraiah clan;
Hananiah, leader of the Jeremiah clan;
Meshullam, leader of the Ezra clan;

Family Influence

BIBLE READING: Nehemiah 9:34-38

We made a searching and fearless moral inventory of ourselves.

Our family of origin has had an influence on who we are today. Some of us want to pretend that our family was, or is, nearly perfect. Others of us may tend to avoid responsibility for our actions by blaming our family. Whatever the case, when we think about our own life, we also need to deal with our family and the effects it has had on who we are today.

We are told that the returned Jewish exiles "took turns confessing their own sins and those of their ancestors" (Nehemiah 9:3). They blamed their ancestors for their captivity and the difficult situation they were facing. They said, "[Our ancestors] refused to turn from their wickedness. So, now we are slaves here in the land of plenty that you gave to our ancestors! . . . And we serve [conquering kings] at their pleasure and are in great misery" (Nehemiah 9:35-37).

It's all right to admit the truth about what brought us into bondage. This might very well involve the wrongs committed by our parents and family. It's all right to express our anger and regret over what's been done to us. We have a right to hold others accountable and grieve over the negative effects they have had on our life. That is part of the real picture. It's not all right to use this as an excuse for our wrong choices or for staying in bondage. They may be partly responsible for bringing us to this place, but we are responsible for moving on to a better place for ourself and our own children. *Turn to page 1017, Matthew 7.*

Jehohanan, leader of the Amariah clan;
Jonathan, leader of the Malluchi clan;
Joseph, leader of the Shebaniah clan;
Adna, leader of the Harim clan;
Helkai, leader of the Meraioth clan;
Zechariah, leader of the Iddo clan;
Meshullam, leader of the Ginnethon clan;
Zichri, leader of the Abijah clan;
Piltai, leader of the Moadiah and
Miniamin clans;
Shammua, leader of the Bilgah clan;
Jehonathan, leader of the Shemaiah clan;
Mattenai, leader of the Joiarib clan;
Uzzi, leader of the Jedaiah clan;
Kallai, leader of the Sallai clan;
Eber, leader of the Amok clan;
Hashabiah, leader of the Hilkiah clan;
Nethanel, leader of the Jedaiah clan.

22A genealogical record of the heads of the
clans of the priests and Levites was compiled
during the reign of King Darius of Persia, in
the days of Eliashib, Joiada, Johanan, and
Jaddua—all of whom were Levites. 23In *The*
Book of the Chronicles the Levite names were
recorded down to the days of Johanan, the
son of Eliashib.

24These were the chiefs of the Levites at that
time: Hashabiah, Sherebiah, and Jeshua (son
of Kadmiel).

Their fellow-clansmen helped them during
the ceremonies of praise and thanksgiving,
just as commanded by David, the man of
God.

25The gatekeepers who had charge of the
collection centers at the gates were: Mattaniah, Bakbukiah, Obadiah, Meshullam, Talmon, Akkub.

26These were the men who were active in
the time of Joiakim (son of Jeshua, son of
Jozadak), and when I was the governor, and
when Ezra was the priest and teacher of religion.

Dedication of the City Wall

27During the dedication of the new Jerusalem
wall, all the Levites throughout the land came
to Jerusalem to assist in the ceremonies and to
take part in the joyous occasion with their
thanksgiving, cymbals, psaltries, and harps.
28The choir members also came to Jerusalem
from the surrounding villages and from the
villages of the Netophathites; 29they also came
from Beth-gilgal and the area of Geba and
Azmaveth, for the singers had built their own
villages as suburbs of Jerusalem. 30The priests
and Levites first dedicated themselves, then
the people, the gates, and the wall.

31,32I led the Judean leaders to the top of the
wall and divided them into two long lines to
walk in opposite directions along the top of
the wall, giving thanks as they went. The
group which went to the right toward the
Dung Gate consisted of half of the leaders of
Judah, 33including Hoshaiah, Azariah, Ezra,
Meshullam, 34Judah, Benjamin, Shemaiah,
and Jeremiah.

35,36The priests who played the trumpets
were Zechariah (son of Jonathan, son of Shemaiah, son of Mattaniah, son of Micaiah, son
of Zaccur, son of Asaph), Shemaiah, Azarel,
Milalai, Gilalai, Maai, Nethanel, Judah, and
Hanani. (They used the original musical instruments of King David.) Ezra the priest led
this procession. 37When they arrived at the
Fountain Gate they went straight ahead and
climbed the stairs that go up beside the castle
to the old City of David; then they went to the
Water Gate on the east.

38The other group, of which I was a member, went around the other way to meet them.
We walked from the Tower of Furnaces to the
Broad Wall, 39then from the Ephraim Gate to
the Old Gate, passed the Fish Gate and the
Tower of Hananel, and went on to the gate of
the Tower of the Hundred; then we continued
on to the Sheep Gate and stopped at the
Prison Gate.

40,41Both choirs then proceeded to the
Temple. Those with me were joined by the
trumpet-playing priests—Eliakim, Maaseiah,
Miniamin, Micaiah, Elioenai, Zechariah, and
Hananiah, 42and by the singers—Maaseiah,
Shemaiah, Eleazar, Uzzi, Jehohanan, Malchi-
jah, Elam, and Ezer.

They sang loudly and clearly under the
direction of Jezrahiah the choirmaster.

43Many sacrifices were offered on that joyous day, for God had given us cause for great
joy. The women and children rejoiced, too,
and the joy of the people of Jerusalem was
heard far away!

12:27 As God's people, we have the privilege and reason to celebrate. All of the worship leaders were called upon to come to Jerusalem to dedicate the rebuilt wall. This was to be the most joyful occasion in Israel in over half a century! We should take time to joyfully dedicate in our life both the building of healthy boundaries and the tearing down of walls that prevent us from being authentic.

The People Show Appreciation
[44]On that day men were appointed to be in charge of the treasuries, the wave offerings, the tithes, and first-of-the-harvest offerings, and to collect these from the farms as decreed by the laws of Moses. These offerings were assigned to the priests and Levites, for the people of Judah appreciated the priests and Levites and their ministry. [45]They also appreciated the work of the singers and gatekeepers, who assisted them in worshiping God and performing the purification ceremonies as required by the laws of David and his son Solomon. [46](It was in the days of David and Asaph that the custom began of having choir directors to lead the choirs in hymns of praise and thanks to God.) [47]So now, in the days of Zerubbabel and Nehemiah, the people brought a daily supply of food for the members of the choir, the gatekeepers, and the Levites. The Levites, in turn, gave a portion of what they received to the priests.

CHAPTER 13
Foreigners Are Sent Away
On that same day, as the laws of Moses were being read, the people found a statement which said that the Ammonites and Moabites should never be permitted to worship at the Temple. [2]For they had not been friendly to the people of Israel. Instead, they had hired Balaam to curse them—although God turned the curse into a blessing. [3]When this rule was read, all the foreigners were immediately expelled from the assembly.

[4]Before this had happened, Eliashib the priest, who had been appointed as custodian of the Temple storerooms and who was also a good friend of Tobiah, [5]had converted a storage room into a beautiful guest room for Tobiah. The room had previously been used for storing the grain offerings, frankincense, bowls, and tithes of grain, new wine, and olive oil. Moses had decreed that these offerings belonged to the priests, Levites, the members of the choir, and the gatekeepers.

[6]I was not in Jerusalem at the time, for I had returned to Babylon in the thirty-second year of the reign of King Artaxerxes (though I later received his permission to go back again to Jerusalem). [7]When I arrived back in Jerusalem and learned of this evil deed of Eliashib—that he had prepared a guest room in the Temple for Tobiah—[8]I was very upset and threw out all of his belongings from the room. [9]Then I demanded that the room be thoroughly cleaned, and I brought back the Temple bowls, the grain offerings, and frankincense.

The People Support the Levites
[10]I also learned that the Levites had not been given what was due them, so they and the choir singers who were supposed to conduct the worship services had returned to their farms. [11]I immediately confronted the leaders and demanded, "Why has the Temple been forsaken?" Then I called all the Levites back again and restored them to their proper duties. [12]And once more all the people of Judah began bringing their tithes of grain, new wine, and olive oil to the Temple treasury.

[13]I put Shelemiah the priest, Zadok the scribe, and Pedaiah the Levite in charge of the administration of the storehouses; and I appointed Hanan (son of Zaccur, son of Mattaniah) as their assistant. These men had an excellent reputation, and their job was to make an honest distribution to their fellow-Levites.

[14]O my God, remember this good deed and do not forget all that I have done for the Temple.

13:1-3, 23-30 For Israel to accomplish God's purpose of being the nation to bring the Messiah into the world, it was necessary for them to remain pure. They were not to mix themselves with the godless population around them, and certain peoples were not to be allowed at the Temple. However, some of the people had intermarried. Nehemiah had to purge the nation of foreigners so that Israel would not be contaminated by false religions. Our recovery is either strengthened or weakened by our relationships. As we mature, we may need to sacrifice "friends" for the sake of our long-term recovery.

13:4-9 Open union with God's enemies is never an acceptable course of action. In this hideous case, one of the Temple administrators provided a room within the Temple for Tobiah, one of Nehemiah's chief opponents. At this strategic location in the very heart of Jerusalem, Tobiah could have undermined God's authority and his place in the Israelites' lives. Each of us must discern the health of our relationships and act accordingly, either to terminate them or to nurture them. If we allow people into our life who do not recognize God as Lord, we are allowing ourself to be influenced for evil. Much of the work we have done in recovery could be negated by even one such relationship.

Sabbath Work Forbidden

15One day I was on a farm and saw some men
treading winepresses on the Sabbath, hauling
in sheaves, and loading their donkeys with
wine, grapes, figs, and all sorts of produce,
which they took that day into Jerusalem. So I
opposed them publicly. 16There were also
some men from Tyre bringing in fish and all
sorts of wares and selling them on the Sabbath to the people of Jerusalem.

17Then I asked the leaders of Judah, "Why
are you profaning the Sabbath? 18Wasn't it
enough that your fathers did this sort of thing
and brought the present evil days upon us
and upon our city? And now you are bringing
more wrath upon the people of Israel by permitting the Sabbath to be desecrated in this
way."

19So from then on I commanded that the
gates of the city be shut as darkness fell on
Friday evenings and not be opened until the
Sabbath had ended; and I sent some of my
servants to guard the gates so that no
merchandise could be brought in on the Sabbath day. 20The merchants and tradesmen
camped outside Jerusalem once or twice, 21but
I spoke sharply to them and said, "What are
you doing out here, camping around the
wall? If you do this again, I will arrest you."
And that was the last time they came on the
Sabbath.

22Then I commanded the Levites to purify
themselves and to guard the gates in order to
preserve the sanctity of the Sabbath. Remember this good deed, O my God! Have compassion upon me in accordance with your great
goodness.

Marriage to Heathens Forbidden

23About the same time I realized that some of
the Jews had married women from Ashdod,
Ammon, and Moab, 24and that many of their
children spoke in the language of Ashdod and
couldn't speak the language of Judah at all.
25So I confronted these parents and cursed
them and punched a few of them and
knocked them around and pulled out their
hair; and they vowed before God that they
would not let their children intermarry with
non-Jews.

26"Wasn't this exactly King Solomon's problem?" I demanded. "There was no king who
could compare with him, and God loved him
and made him the king over all Israel; but
even so he was led into idolatry by foreign
women. 27Do you think that we will let you
get away with this sinful deed?"

28One of the sons of Jehoiada (the son of
Eliashib the High Priest) was a son-in-law of
Sanballat the Horonite, so I chased him out of
the Temple. 29 Remember them, O my God,
for they have defiled the priesthood and the
promises and vows of the priests and Levites.
30So I purged out the foreigners and assigned
tasks to the priests and Levites, making certain that each knew his work. 31They supplied
wood for the altar at the proper times and
cared for the sacrifices and the first offerings
of every harvest. Remember me, my God,
with your kindness.

13:14, 31 Nehemiah was a great rebuilder. He reconstructed the wall of Jerusalem. He helped the people to rebuild their broken lives. There is no question that God gave credit to this good and faithful servant! And God will honor our attempts to rebuild, too. We also will experience God's kindness in our life.

REFLECTIONS ON
NEHEMIAH

insights FROM THE MINISTRY OF NEHEMIAH

Great affliction and reproach! Ruins and wreckage! In **Nehemiah 1:1-3** we are shown a situation that demanded rebuilding and recovery. When Nehemiah heard of the circumstances in Jerusalem, he was immediately touched. He wanted to do something about it. As we take inventory of our own life, we need to take careful note of what areas need specific work. Rebuilding cannot take place until we know where to begin.

In **Nehemiah 2:17-20** we see that Nehemiah performed a ministry of encouragement. He was completely honest about the people's problems; he didn't deny or underestimate their needs. Then he reminded them of God's powerful hand and challenged them to get on with the work. Every one of us needs a Nehemiah in our life—someone who will honestly tell us what needs fixing and who then will stick close to help us complete the task.

How do we counter ridicule and disdain? In **Nehemiah 4:4-9**, Nehemiah offers us a magnificent example. In such times, it is essential that we seek God and keep our guard up. Nehemiah countered ridicule by prayer. Not only did he pray, but he also set a twenty-four-hour watch, guarding against an attack. While it is important to pray to God for help with our life, we must also be on the lookout for physical attacks from our enemies. Prayer must be balanced with action.

One person can't do everything. In **Nehemiah 4:14-18** we see that Nehemiah recognized this and divided the tasks of defense and construction. This illustrates the truth that exterior attacks don't disappear just because we are busy refurbishing our spiritual interior. Every rebuilder needs to be prepared for attacks from external enemies who will try to take advantage of his busyness. This is especially true in recovery.

✲***insights*** FROM THE MINISTRY OF EZRA

In **Nehemiah 8:1-5** we see that Ezra took on the essential task of spiritual rebuilding in the lives of the citizens. Now that the wall of Jerusalem was rebuilt and its streets were safe, Ezra was able to give attention to the reading of the Law. It is imperative to remember that the Bible contains the directions and resources for rebuilding broken lives. While we may obtain physical recovery, it is also necessary to recover spiritually (through salvation by belief in Jesus Christ) in order to remain free from our addictions. He is the foundation on which we must build our new life.

✲***insights*** FROM THE PEOPLE'S EXPERIENCES OF WORSHIP

In **Nehemiah 2:1-3** we find an example of God's people openly expressing their emotions. Elsewhere in the Bible we see Job expressing his emotions to his friends; King David pouring his heart into his many psalms, pleading with God for his rescue; and Jesus showing emotions, even crying on occasion (see John 11). God expects us to be open and honest in our expression of emotion. Too often, out of a fear of appearing weak, we refuse to express our feelings, only to have them grow in intensity and haunt us for years to come. Venting our emotions is the best way to overcome the grief or despair we experience.

In **Nehemiah 9:4-38** we read pure, unmitigated words of praise to God. As the Levites sang this beautiful hymn, they gloried in the person of God—who he was and what he had done. There is something therapeutic in recognizing God for who he is. We can gain much by reading the words of this hymn of praise and by making the words our own.

ESTHER

The book of Esther tells a story about God's loving care for his people during the Babylonian exile. Although a few Jews had returned to Jerusalem with Zerubbabel to rebuild the Temple, the majority remained in Babylonia. Esther was raised among the Jewish community in exile. King Ahasuerus deposed his queen for disobedience and later held a contest to find a new queen. Esther was chosen.

Soon after Esther became queen, the king appointed Haman, an Agagite, to the position of second in command. All people in the empire were expected to bow down to show him respect. Mordecai, Esther's uncle, refused to bow down, and this so enraged Haman that he had the king enact an irrevocable edict sentencing all Jews to death. Neither the king nor Haman knew that Esther was among the people doomed by the edict. Through Mordecai's prodding, Esther secured the king's favor to deliver her people and brought about Haman's demise.

In the Hebrew Bible, God's name never actually appears in the story. Yet throughout the book we see God's quiet yet effective activity behind the scenes. We see him work through different individuals who are willing to trust him. He brought Esther to a position of influence just at the right time and gave her the courage to act. Esther could have remained selfishly silent. Instead, she risked her life and became an instrument of great deliverance. Even though God's presence is not always obvious in our life, we can be sure that he is behind the scenes, working to protect us and lead us to recovery.

THE BIG PICTURE

A. ESTHER BECOMES QUEEN (1:1–2:23)
   1. Dethronement of Vashti (1:1-22)
   2. Enthronement of Esther (2:1-23)

B. A THREAT AGAINST GOD'S PEOPLE (3:1–7:10)
   1. The Rise of the Enemy of God's People (3:1-15)
   2. The Commitment of a Leader of God's People (4:1–5:14)
   3. The Fall of the Enemy of God's People (6:1–7:10)

C. MORDECAI SECURES THEIR RECOVERY (8:1–10:3)
   1. The Plan of a Rescue Operation (8:1-17)
   2. The Process of a Rescue Operation (9:1-32)
   3. The Product of a Rescue Operation (10:1-3)

THE BOTTOM LINE

PURPOSE: To demonstrate God's loving care for his people and his sovereignty over history and to record the origins of the Jewish holiday of Purim. AUTHOR: Unknown, but it may have been written by Mordecai or Ezra. AUDIENCE: The people of Israel after the Babylonian Exile. DATE WRITTEN: Approximately 470 B.C.; Esther became queen in 479. SETTING: In Susa, the capital of Medo-Persia. KEY VERSE: "If you keep quiet at a time like this, God will deliver the Jews from some other source, but you and your relatives will die; what's more, who can say but that God has brought you into the palace for just such a time as this?" (4:14). KEY PEOPLE AND RELATIONSHIPS: Esther with Mordecai, Haman, King Ahasuerus, Queen Vashti.

RECOVERY THEMES

Hope for the Helpless: When we recognize we are powerless over our problems, we are in a place of great opportunity if we turn things over to God. This was exactly the experience of Esther, Mordecai, and the Jews during their exile under Persian rule. They were the captives. Their life was out of their own control and under the control of Persian rulers. It was in this situation of helplessness that God worked through Esther and Mordecai to bring amazing deliverance to God's people. When we put ourself in God's hands, our success will be defined by God's power, not our weakness.

God's Faithfulness: When we turn our life and our will over to God, we can take courage. We can expect him to display his power in carrying out his will in our life. As we unite our will with his, we benefit from his faithfulness. He does this in spite of our doubts, and even in spite of our desire. One of the great lessons we can learn from Esther is how God acts on our behalf even when we are unaware of what he is doing. He is a God who can be trusted to underwrite our recovery; for even when we are faithless, he always remains faithful!

The Emptiness of Hatred: Haman was driven by racial prejudice and hatred. In the blindness of his own hatred, Haman determined his own punishment and died the death he had planned for the one he hated—Mordecai. Racial hatred is always sinful. It is sinful because it denies the intrinsic value of God's creation. When we hate in this way, we end up with an awful emptiness that works our destruction through bitterness and isolation.

Dealing with Pressures: It takes great wisdom and patience to survive in a world that is not concerned with God or with our recovery. Mordecai shows us how to resist the pressures around us, as he learned all that he could about the Persian system and law but never compromised his own integrity. He continued to respect what was true and good. He was obedient to the God of all truth and was able to show wisdom in the face of everyday pressures.

CHAPTER 1

Queen Vashti Is Deposed

It was the third year of the reign of King
Ahasuerus, emperor of vast Media-Persia,
with its 127 provinces stretching from India
to Ethiopia. This was the year of the great
celebration at Shushan Palace, to which the
emperor invited all his governors, aides, and
army officers, bringing them in from every
part of Media-Persia for the occasion. [4]The
celebration lasted six months, a tremendous
display of the wealth and glory of his empire.
[5]When it was all over, the king gave a special party for the palace servants and officials—janitors and cabinet officials alike—for
seven days of revelry, held in the courtyard of
the palace garden. [6]The decorations were
green, white, and blue, fastened with purple
ribbons tied to silver rings imbedded in marble pillars. Gold and silver benches stood on
pavements of black, red, white, and yellow
marble. [7]Drinks were served in gold goblets of
many designs, and there was an abundance of
royal wine, for the king was feeling very generous. [8]The only restriction on the drinking
was that no one should be compelled to take
more than he wanted, but those who wished
could have as much as they pleased. For the
king had instructed his officers to let everyone decide this matter for himself.
[9]Queen Vashti gave a party for the women
of the palace at the same time.
[10]On the final day when the king was feeling high, half drunk from wine, he told the
seven eunuchs who were his personal aides—
Mehuman, Biztha, Harbona, Bigtha, Abagtha,
Zethar, and Carkas—[11]to bring Queen Vashti
to him with the royal crown upon her head
so that all the men could gaze upon her
beauty—for she was a very beautiful woman.
[12]But when they conveyed the emperor's order to Queen Vashti, she refused to come. The
king was furious [13-15]but first consulted his
lawyers, for he did nothing without their advice. They were men of wisdom who knew
the temper of the times as well as Persian law

1:1-8 Having only recently established his kingdom, King Ahasuerus attempted to curry the favor of his leaders (perhaps to assure their allegiance for an upcoming war) by holding a half-year-long celebration at Susa, the royal winter residence. To further gain the approval of his leaders, King Ahasuerus wisely suspended the custom of each person being forced to drink royal wine. Ahasuerus must have been showing respect for those people whose cultures prohibited the consumption, or abuse, of alcohol. If we are trying to overcome alcohol abuse, we would do well to have friends that show the same respect for us.

ESTHER & MORDECAI

Many of us find ourselves in situations where cruel and unfortunate experiences seem to be the norm. We feel powerless to act, either to defend ourself or to help anyone else. We may wonder how we got there, or why. Esther must have felt this way at times. Esther lived in a community of exiled Jews in Babylonia, far from her homeland of Israel. She was a Jewish foreigner; her people were dominated by pagan Persian rulers. Esther was also an orphan. As a child, she was adopted by her uncle Mordecai, a prominent leader in the Jewish community in exile.

When Esther was probably no more than in her late teens, King Ahasuerus, ruler of the empire, deposed his queen and held an empire-wide beauty contest to find a replacement. Esther competed in the contest and was selected to join the king's harem and to be his queen. But she was instructed by Mordecai not to tell anyone of her Jewish descent.

Even as queen to Ahasuerus, Esther was hardly in a wonderful situation. She was one among many wives and concubines. She would go without seeing her husband for months at a time. And Ahasuerus was hardly an ideal husband. He was known to depose or kill the people close to him at a mere whim. Being close to Ahasuerus was hardly a comfortable position. Esther, as one of God's people, must have often wondered how she had come to be queen and why.

About this time, a man named Haman rose to the position of prime minister, and Esther's uncle Mordecai enraged Haman by not bowing down to him. To get revenge, Haman sought the destruction of all the Jews in the Persian Empire. When Mordecai learned of Haman's plan to kill the Jews, he went to Esther for help. After much prayer and fasting, Esther risked her life by approaching Ahasuerus without an appointment. Within a few days, Esther succeeded in delivering her people from sure destruction.

Esther may not have initially known why she was chosen as queen, but God made his reasons known soon enough: she was there to save her people from sure destruction. God used Esther and Mordecai to work his will in a difficult situation. We may not know why we are placed in our circumstances, but God has a purpose and a plan for us. He may use us, as powerless as we may feel, to work God's will in the lives of many.

STRENGTHS AND ACCOMPLISHMENTS:

- Both of them showed great courage and careful planning.
- Esther was open to wise advice from Mordecai.
- Esther's beauty and character endeared her to King Ahasuerus.
- Esther placed the lives of her people above her own.
- Mordecai refused to worship Haman, disregarding the possible consequences.

LESSONS FROM THEIR LIVES:

- Following God often means that we have to sacrifice our own security.
- We can trust that God will protect his people.
- God may put us in certain circumstances in order to benefit or even rescue others.
- God uses powerless people to work his powerful and perfect will.

KEY VERSE:
"If you keep quiet at a time like this, God will deliver the Jews from some other source, but you and your relatives will die; what's more, who can say but that God has brought you into the palace for just such a time as this?" (Esther 4:14).

Esther and Mordecai's story is told in the book of Esther.

---

and justice, and the king trusted their judgment. These men were Carshena, Shethar, Admatha, Tarshish, Meres, Marsena, and Memucan—seven high officials of Media-Persia. They were his personal friends as well as being the chief officers of the government.

"What shall we do about this situation?" he asked them. "What penalty does the law provide for a queen who refuses to obey the king's orders, properly sent through his aides?"

16Memucan answered for the others, "Queen Vashti has wronged not only the king but every official and citizen of your empire.

17For women everywhere will begin to disobey
their husbands when they learn what Queen
Vashti has done. 18And before this day is out,
the wife of every one of us officials throughout your empire will hear what the queen did
and will start talking to us husbands the same
way, and there will be contempt and anger
throughout your realm. 19We suggest that,
subject to your agreement, you issue a royal
edict, a law of the Medes and Persians that can
never be changed, that Queen Vashti be forever banished from your presence and that
you choose another queen more worthy than
she. 20When this decree is published throughout your great kingdom, husbands everywhere, whatever their rank, will be respected
by their wives!"

21The king and all his aides thought this
made good sense, so he followed Memucan's
counsel 22and sent letters to all of his provinces, in all the local languages, stressing that
every man should rule his home and should
assert his authority.

CHAPTER 2

Esther Becomes Queen

But after King Ahasuerus' anger had cooled, he began brooding over the loss of Vashti, realizing that he would never see her again.

2So his aides suggested, "Let us go and find
the most beautiful girls in the empire and
bring them to the king for his pleasure. 3We
will appoint agents in each province to select
young lovelies for the royal harem. Hegai, the
eunuch in charge, will see that they are given
beauty treatments, 4and after that, the girl
who pleases you most shall be the queen
instead of Vashti."

This suggestion naturally pleased the king very much, and he put the plan into immediate effect.

5Now there was a certain Jew at the palace
named Mordecai (son of Jair, son of Shimei,
son of Kish, a Benjaminite). 6He had been
captured when Jerusalem was destroyed by
King Nebuchadnezzar and had been exiled to
Babylon along with King Jeconiah of Judah
and many others. 7This man had a beautiful
and lovely young cousin, Hadassah (also
called Esther), whose father and mother were
dead, and whom he had adopted into his
family and raised as his own daughter. 8So
now, as a result of the king's decree, Esther
was brought to the king's harem at Shushan
Palace along with many other young girls.
9Hegai, who was responsible for the harem,
was very much impressed with her and did
his best to make her happy; he ordered a
special menu for her, favored her for the
beauty treatments, gave her seven girls from
the palace as her maids, and gave her the most
luxurious apartment in the harem. 10Esther
hadn't told anyone that she was a Jewess, for
Mordecai had said not to. 11He came daily to
the court of the harem to ask about Esther and
to find out what was happening to her.

12-14The instructions concerning these girls
were that before being taken to the king's bed,
each would be given six months of beauty
treatments with oil of myrrh, followed by six
months with special perfumes and ointments. Then, as each girl's turn came for
spending the night with King Ahasuerus, she
was given her choice of clothing or jewelry
she wished, to enhance her beauty. She was
taken to the king's apartment in the evening
and the next morning returned to the second
harem where the king's wives lived. There she
was under the care of Shaashgaz, another of
the king's eunuchs and lived there the rest of
her life, never seeing the king again unless he
had especially enjoyed her and called for her
by name.

15When it was Esther's turn to go to the
king, she accepted the advice of Hegai, the
eunuch in charge of the harem, dressing according to his instructions. And all the other
girls exclaimed with delight when they saw
her. 16So Esther was taken to the palace of the
king in January of the seventh year of his

1:16-22 The wise men evaluated the situation regarding Vashti's disobedience and, realizing the far-reaching effects that such an act could have, suggested quick and final action be taken at once. Anxious to please his allies, the king had made an unwise request of Vashti and now had to live with the consequences. We need to carefully evaluate the requests we make of others, realizing that we may be compromising their rights or desires.

2:15-20 Esther wisely listened to Hegai (a man who knew the king well), taking his advice on how she might please the king. Hence, she succeeded in becoming the king's wife (2:17). She sacrificed her own desires to follow her uncle Mordecai's wishes. Making a major life decision because someone else wants us to is very difficult; we don't want to give up control of our life. But our family and friends may want us to turn from our addictions and return to a normal life. If so, do we have enough commitment to them to motivate us to act?

reign. 17Well, the king loved Esther more than
any of the other girls. He was so delighted
with her that he set the royal crown on her
head and declared her queen instead of
Vashti. 18To celebrate the occasion, he threw
another big party for all his officials and servants, giving generous gifts to everyone and
making grants to the provinces in the form of
remission of taxes.
19Later the king demanded a second bevy of
beautiful girls. By that time Mordecai had
become a government official.
20Esther still hadn't told anyone she was a
Jewess, for she was still following Mordecai's
orders, just as she had in his home.
21One day as Mordecai was on duty at the
palace, two of the king's eunuchs, Bigthan
and Teresh—who were guards at the palace
gate—became angry at the king and plotted
to assassinate him. 22Mordecai heard about it
and passed on the information to Queen Esther, who told the king, crediting Mordecai
with the information. 23An investigation was
made, the two men found guilty, and impaled
alive. This was all duly recorded in the book
of the history of King Ahasuerus' reign.

CHAPTER 3

Haman Plans to Destroy the Jews

Soon afterwards King Ahasuerus appointed
Haman (son of Hammedatha the Agagite) as
prime minister. He was the most powerful
official in the empire next to the king himself.
2Now all the king's officials bowed before him
in deep reverence whenever he passed by, for
so the king had commanded. But Mordecai
refused to bow.
3,4"Why are you disobeying the king's commandment?" the others demanded day after
day, but he still refused. Finally they spoke to
Haman about it to see whether Mordecai
could get away with it because of his being a
Jew, which was the excuse he had given them.
5,6Haman was furious but decided not to lay
hands on Mordecai alone, but to move
against all of Mordecai's people, the Jews, and
destroy all of them throughout the whole
kingdom of Ahasuerus.
7The most propitious time for this action
was determined by throwing dice. This was
done in April of the twelfth year of the reign
of Ahasuerus, and February of the following
year was the date indicated.
8Haman now approached the king about
the matter. "There is a certain race of people
scattered through all the provinces of your
kingdom," he began, "and their laws are different from those of any other nation, and
they refuse to obey the king's laws; therefore,
it is not in the king's interest to let them live.
9If it please the king, issue a decree that they
be destroyed, and I will pay $20,000,000 into
the royal treasury for the expenses involved
in this purge."
10The king agreed, confirming his decision
by removing his ring from his finger and
giving it to Haman, telling him, 11"Keep the
money, but go ahead and do as you like with
these people—whatever you think best."
12Two or three weeks later, Haman called in
the king's secretaries and dictated letters to
the governors and officials throughout the
empire, to each province in its own languages
and dialects; these letters were signed in the
name of King Ahasuerus and sealed with his
ring.
13They were then sent by messengers into
all the provinces of the empire, decreeing that

2:21-23 When Mordecai learned of the guards' plan to kill Ahasuerus, he reported their plot to Queen Esther (2:22). And though he had done something worthy of great honor, Mordecai received no recognition at the time (see 6:1-11). Sometimes the good decisions we make in recovery are only rewarded by our own sense of integrity. Knowing that we made a right decision should be enough for us to continue on the right path.
3:1-6 When Haman heard that Mordecai refused to bow before him, he became furious. Haman wanted revenge for Mordecai's insubordination, so he sought the destruction of all the Jews. His desire to destroy the whole nation may be due to his family's (the Agagites) feud with Mordecai's tribe (the Benjamites; see 1 Samuel 15 for the story of King Saul and King Agag). This illustrates how a legacy of hatred can affect a person's judgment. Haman took drastic measures to settle a conflict that had begun over five hundred years before. Do we have unsettled disagreements with others? If so, we need to forgive them so we can get on with our life and avoid having our children fight our battles long after we are gone.
3:8-15 Without mentioning them by name, Haman convinced the king to allow him to destroy the Jews because they followed different customs and disobeyed the king's laws (3:8). Irresponsibly, without investigating such a serious matter, the king gave Haman complete authority to implement his plan. We should always check into the requests of others, especially when the requests have major implications.

the Jews—young and old, women and children—must all be killed on the 28th day of February of the following year and their property given to those who killed them. 14"A copy of this edict," the letter stated, "must be proclaimed as law in every province and made known to all your people, so that they will be ready to do their duty on the appointed day." 15The edict went out by the king's speediest couriers, after being first proclaimed in the city of Shushan. Then the king and Haman sat down for a drinking spree as the city fell into confusion and panic.

CHAPTER 4

Mordecai Asks Esther for Help

When Mordecai learned what had been done, he tore his clothes, put on sackcloth and ashes, and went out into the city, crying with a loud and bitter wail. 2Then he stood outside the gate of the palace, for no one was permitted to enter in mourning clothes. 3And throughout all the provinces there was great mourning among the Jews, fasting, weeping, and despair at the king's decree; and many lay in sackcloth and ashes.

4When Esther's maids and eunuchs came and told her about Mordecai, she was deeply distressed and sent clothing to him to replace the sackcloth, but he refused it. 5Then Esther sent for Hathach, one of the king's eunuchs who had been appointed as her attendant, and told him to go out to Mordecai and find out what the trouble was and why he was acting like that. 6So Hathach went out to the city square and found Mordecai just outside the palace gates, 7and heard the whole story from him, and about the $20,000,000 Haman had promised to pay into the king's treasury for the destruction of the Jews. 8Mordecai also gave Hathach a copy of the king's decree dooming all Jews, and told him to show it to Esther and to tell her what was happening and that she should go to the king to plead for her people. 9So Hathach returned to Esther with Mordecai's message. 10Esther told Hathach to go back and say to Mordecai,

11"All the world knows that anyone, whether man or woman, who goes into the king's inner court without his summons is doomed to die unless the king holds out his gold scepter; and the king has not called for me to come to him in more than a month."

12So Hathach gave Esther's message to Mordecai.

13This was Mordecai's reply to Esther: "Do you think you will escape there in the palace when all other Jews are killed? 14If you keep quiet at a time like this, God will deliver the Jews from some other source, but you and your relatives will die; what's more, who can say but that God has brought you into the palace for just such a time as this?"

15Then Esther said to tell Mordecai:

16"Go and gather together all the Jews of Shushan and fast for me; do not eat or drink for three days, night or day; and I and my maids will do the same; and then, though it is strictly forbidden, I will go in to see the king; and if I perish, I perish."

17So Mordecai did as Esther told him to.

CHAPTER 5

Esther Intercedes for the Jews

Three days later Esther put on her royal robes and entered the inner court just beyond the royal hall of the palace, where the king was sitting upon his royal throne. 2And when he saw Queen Esther standing there in the inner court, he welcomed her, holding out the golden scepter to her. So Esther approached and touched its tip.

3Then the king asked her, "What do you wish, Queen Esther? What is your request? I

4:1-8 Mordecai and the Jews throughout the empire sensed the hopelessness of their situation and put on mourning clothes (4:1-3). When Esther learned that Mordecai was weeping, she dispatched a servant to determine the reasons for Mordecai's anguish (4:5-6). Then, in a straightforward manner, Mordecai disclosed the gravity of the situation (4:7-8). Realizing our hopelessness is a significant step in our recovery. Had Mordecai denied the truth of Haman's edict, he and the Jews would have faced certain death.

4:9-17 At first Esther wanted to deny the facts about Haman's edict. She focused on her fear that she might be killed for approaching the king uninvited. In doing so, she failed to see the long-term consequences that might result if she refused to act. Esther finally consented to help her people by approching the volatile Ahasuerus, not knowing if he would accept her or have her killed. Her statement "I will go in to see the king; and if I perish, I perish" (4:16) reveals her faith in God and her selflessness. We, too, need to trust in God to deliver us from our dependencies. We also need to look to others for their support and prayers. Like Esther, we need people praying for us if we hope to succeed.

will give it to you, even if it is half the kingdom!"
[4]And Esther replied, "If it please Your Majesty, I want you and Haman to come to a
banquet I have prepared for you today."
[5]The king turned to his aides. "Tell Haman
to hurry!" he said. So the king and Haman
came to Esther's banquet.
[6]During the wine course the king said to
Esther, "Now tell me what you really want,
and I will give it to you, even if it is half of the
kingdom!"
[7,8]Esther replied, "My request, my deepest
wish, is that if Your Majesty loves me and
wants to grant my request, that you come
again with Haman tomorrow to the banquet
I shall prepare for you. And tomorrow I will
explain what this is all about."

Haman Becomes Angry at Mordecai
[9]What a happy man was Haman as he left the
banquet! But when he saw Mordecai there at
the gate, not standing up or trembling before
him, he was furious. [10]However, he restrained
himself, went on home, and gathered together his friends and Zeresh, his wife, [11]and
boasted to them about his wealth, his many
children, and promotions the king had given
him, and how he had become the greatest
man in the kingdom next to the king himself.
[12]Then he delivered his punch line: "Yes,
and Esther the queen invited only me and the
king himself to the banquet she prepared for
us; and tomorrow we are invited again! [13]But
yet," he added, "all this is nothing when I see
Mordecai the Jew just sitting there in front of
the king's gate, refusing to bow to me."
[14]"Well," suggested Zeresh, his wife, and all
his friends, "get ready a 75-foot-high gallows,
and in the morning ask the king to let you
hang Mordecai on it; and when this is done
you can go on your merry way with the king
to the banquet." This pleased Haman immensely, and he ordered the gallows built.

CHAPTER 6
The King Honors Mordecai
That night the king had trouble sleeping and
decided to read awhile. He ordered the historical records of his kingdom from the library,
and in them he came across the item telling
how Mordecai had exposed the plot of Big-
thana and Teresh, two of the king's eunuchs,
watchmen at the palace gates, who had plotted to assassinate him.
[3]"What reward did we ever give Mordecai
for this?" the king asked.
His courtiers replied, "Nothing!"
[4]"Who is on duty in the outer court?" the
king inquired. Now, as it happened, Haman
had just arrived in the outer court of the
palace to ask the king to hang Mordecai from
the gallows he was building.
[5]So the courtiers replied to the king, "Haman is out there."
"Bring him in," the king ordered. [6]So Haman came in, and the king said to him,

5:1-8 Esther courageously faced the danger of approaching the king without first being summoned (5:1). Her fears, however, proved to be unfounded, for the king expressed his willingness to fulfill whatever requests she might make (5:3). Esther asked the king and Haman to two banquets before making her request, knowing that the king would be more receptive to her petition after two great feasts. If we are unsure whether others will help us with our recovery, it can never hurt to "butter them up," as long as we don't compromise our position to gain their favor.
5:9-14 Haman, totally oblivious to Queen Esther's schemes against his life, was overjoyed at being so highly honored by her (5:9, 12). Yet even under such auspicious circumstances, Haman could not fully enjoy himself because he wanted still more. More than anything else, he wanted Mordecai to bow down to him (5:9, 13). In fact, Haman became obsessed with having this one man bow to him. We shouldn't allow what we don't have to overshadow what we do have. Our desire to have everything might cost us the riches we already have.
6:1-6 Even though some time had gone by, the king felt a responsibility to acknowledge his gratitude to Mordecai for saving his life. Expressing gratitude is important for our recovery process. It shows others that we appreciate their help and also that we are not fooling ourself by thinking our progress was accomplished on our own. We should express our thanks to those who have helped us in our recovery: family, friends, employers, God.
6:6-12 Thinking the king was going to honor him, Haman recommended a public display of honor. Haman must have been livid when he was ordered to honor Mordecai according to the plan he himself had outlined. Perhaps Haman's hatred of Mordecai was sparked because Haman had a difficult time honoring others. Showing respect to others would have been a blow to his ego. We should make sure our self-worth does not depend on what others think about us. Once we realize our self-worth is based on our acceptance by God, we can stop competing with others and like them for who they are.

"What should I do to honor a man who truly pleases me?"

Haman thought to himself, "Whom would he want to honor more than me?" 7,8So he replied, "Bring out some of the royal robes the king himself has worn, and the king's own horse, and the royal crown, 9and instruct one of the king's most noble princes to robe the man and to lead him through the streets on the king's own horse, shouting before him, 'This is the way the king honors those who truly please him!'"

10"Excellent!" the king said to Haman. "Hurry and take these robes and my horse, and do just as you have said—to Mordecai the Jew, who works at the Chancellery. Follow every detail you have suggested."

11So Haman took the robes and put them on Mordecai, and mounted him on the king's own steed, and led him through the streets of the city, shouting, "This is the way the king honors those he delights in."

12Afterwards Mordecai returned to his job, but Haman hurried home utterly humiliated. 13When Haman told Zeresh his wife and all his friends what had happened, they said, "If Mordecai is a Jew, you will never succeed in your plans against him; to continue to oppose him will be fatal."

14While they were still discussing it with him, the king's messengers arrived to conduct Haman quickly to the banquet Esther had prepared.

CHAPTER 7

The King Executes Haman

So the king and Haman came to Esther's banquet. 2Again, during the wine course, the king asked her, "What is your petition, Queen Esther? What do you wish? Whatever it is, I will give it to you, even if it is half of my kingdom!"

3And at last Queen Esther replied, "If I have won your favor, O king, and if it please Your Majesty, save my life and the lives of my people. 4For I and my people have been sold to those who will destroy us. We are doomed to destruction and slaughter. If we were only to be sold as slaves, perhaps I could remain quiet, though even then there would be incalculable damage to the king that no amount of money could begin to cover."

5"What are you talking about?" King Ahasuerus demanded. "Who would dare touch you?"

6Esther replied, "This wicked Haman is our enemy."

Then Haman grew pale with fright before the king and queen. 7The king jumped to his feet and went out into the palace garden as Haman stood up to plead for his life to Queen Esther, for he knew that he was doomed. 8In despair he fell upon the couch where Queen Esther was reclining, just as the king returned from the palace garden.

"Will he even rape the queen right here in the palace, before my very eyes?" the king roared. Instantly the death veil was placed over Haman's face.

9Then Harbona, one of the king's aides, said, "Sir, Haman has just ordered a 75-foot gallows constructed, to hang Mordecai, the man who saved the king from assassination! It stands in Haman's courtyard."

"Hang Haman on it," the king ordered.

10So they did, and the king's wrath was pacified.

CHAPTER 8

A Law to Protect the Jews

On that same day King Ahasuerus gave the estate of Haman, the Jews' enemy, to Queen Esther. Then Mordecai was brought before the king, for Esther had told the king that he was her cousin and foster father. 2The king took off his ring—which he had taken back from Haman—and gave it to Mordecai [appointing him Prime Minister]; and Esther appointed Mordecai to be in charge of Haman's estate.

3And now once more Esther came before

7:1-6 Esther presented her petition to the king, seeking his help in saving her and her people from the edict ordering their death. After explaining this life-threatening situation, she wisely waited to see how the king would respond. Noting his rage, she boldly proceeded to denounce Haman as the enemy of her people. Wisely evaluating situations before jumping in further is often necessary. Waiting for the proper timing is much easier than trying to repair damage done by being impetuous.

7:7-10 Haman did not seek forgiveness or make amends for his heinous acts. In the midst of his terror, Haman lost his self-control and committed the impropriety of falling upon Queen Esther's couch (7:8). Had Haman asked for forgiveness and explained the matter to the king, he might have been spared. Ahasuerus condemned him to death after he fell on Esther's couch. There is always a chance for forgiveness and recovery. God will always forgive us, no matter what we have done. But it is our responsibility to ask.

the king, falling down at his feet and begging him with tears to stop Haman's plot against the Jews. [4]And again the king held out the golden scepter to Esther. So she arose and stood before him, [5]and said, "If it please Your Majesty, and if you love me, send out a decree reversing Haman's order to destroy the Jews throughout the king's provinces. [6]For how can I endure it, to see my people butchered and destroyed?"

[7]Then King Ahasuerus said to Queen Esther and Mordecai the Jew, "I have given Esther the palace of Haman, and he has been hanged upon the gallows because he tried to destroy you. [8]Now go ahead and send a message to the Jews, telling them whatever you want to in the king's name, and seal it with the king's ring so that it can never be reversed."

[9,10]Immediately the king's secretaries were called in—it was now the 23rd day of the month of July—and they wrote as Mordecai dictated—a decree to the Jews and to the officials, governors, and princes of all the provinces from India to Ethiopia, 127 in all: the decree was translated into the languages and dialects of all the people of the kingdom. Mordecai wrote in the name of King Ahasuerus and sealed the message with the king's ring and sent the letters by swift carriers—riders on camels, mules, and young dromedaries used in the king's service. [11]This decree gave the Jews everywhere permission to unite in the defense of their lives and their families, to destroy all the forces opposed to them, and to take their property. [12]The day chosen for this throughout all the provinces of King Ahasuerus was the 28th day of February! [13]It further stated that a copy of this decree, which must be recognized everywhere as law, must be broadcast to all the people so that the Jews would be ready and prepared to overcome their enemies. [14]So the mail went out swiftly, carried by the king's couriers and speeded by the king's commandment. The same decree was also issued at Shushan Palace.

[15]Then Mordecai put on the royal robes of blue and white and the great crown of gold, with an outer cloak of fine linen and purple, and went out from the presence of the king through the city streets filled with shouting people. [16]And the Jews had joy and gladness and were honored everywhere. [17]And in every city and province, as the king's decree arrived, the Jews were filled with joy and had a great celebration and declared a holiday. And many of the people of the land pretended to be Jews, for they feared what the Jews might do to them.

CHAPTER 9

The Jews Defeat Their Enemies

So on the 28th day of February, the day the two decrees of the king were to be put into effect—the day the Jews' enemies had hoped to vanquish them, though it turned out quite to the contrary—the Jews gathered in their cities throughout all the king's provinces to defend themselves against any who might try to harm them; but no one tried, for they were greatly feared. [3]And all the rulers of the provinces—the governors, officials, and aides—helped the Jews for fear of Mordecai; [4]for Mordecai was a mighty name in the king's palace and his fame was known throughout all the provinces, for he had become more and more powerful.

[5]But the Jews went ahead on that appointed day and slaughtered their enemies. [6]They even killed 500 men in Shushan. [7-10]They also killed the ten sons of Haman (son of Hammedatha), the Jews' enemy—Parshandatha, Dalphon, Aspatha, Poratha, Adalia, Aridatha, Parmashta, Arisai, Aridai, and Vaizatha.

8:1-6 Esther received Haman's property, and Mordecai became prime minister, but still the Jewish people were in danger. Once again Esther approached Ahasuerus, this time asking for a reversal of Haman's decree. Like Esther, we shouldn't stop with our own recovery. If others still suffer from their addictions, we should help them to escape the disastrous effects of sin.

8:7-14 As before (see 3:10), King Ahasuerus abdicated his management responsibility (8:7-8). This time he put Esther and Mordecai in charge, allowing them to do as they pleased (8:8). We should make sure that those to whom we entrust responsibility are dependable. If we ask someone to hold us accountable or to help us, we need to be able to rely on that person's commitment to our recovery. If he is not trustworthy, we may be doing ourselves more harm than good by asking for his help.

9:5-15 The Jews were finally able to defend themselves from their enemies. Notice that the Jews exhibited self-control by not plundering their enemies' goods even though they had the right to do so (see 8:11). This was a wise move: the Jews could not be accused of rationalizing their slaughter as a cover for becoming rich. We need not always embrace every advantage that the law allows. We would be wise to sacrifice some of our rights to make a statement about our motives.

But they did not try to take Haman's property.

[11]Late that evening, when the king was informed of the number of those slain in Shushan, [12]he called for Queen Esther. "The Jews have killed 500 men in Shushan alone," he exclaimed, "and also Haman's ten sons. If they have done that here, I wonder what has happened in the rest of the provinces! But now, what more do you want? It will be granted to you. Tell me and I will do it."

[13]And Esther said, "If it please Your Majesty, let the Jews who are here at Shushan do again tomorrow as they have done today, and let Haman's ten sons be hanged upon the gallows."

[14]So the king agreed, and the decree was announced at Shushan, and they hung up the bodies of Haman's ten sons. [15]Then the Jews at Shushan gathered together the next day also and killed 300 more men, though again they took no property.

The Feast of Purim

[16]Meanwhile the other Jews throughout the king's provinces had gathered together and stood for their lives and destroyed all their enemies, killing 75,000 of those who hated them; but they did not take their goods. [17]Throughout the provinces this was done on the 28th day of February, and the next day they rested, celebrating their victory with feasting and gladness. [18]But the Jews at Shushan went on killing their enemies the second day also and rested the next day, with feasting and gladness. [19]And so it is that the Jews in the unwalled villages throughout Israel to this day have an annual celebration on the second day when they rejoice and send gifts to each other.

[20]Mordecai wrote a history of all these events and sent letters to the Jews near and far, throughout all the king's provinces, [21]encouraging them to declare an annual holiday on the last two days of the month, [22]to celebrate with feasting, gladness, and the giving of gifts these historic days when the Jews were saved from their enemies, when their sorrow was turned to gladness and their mourning into happiness.

[23]So the Jews adopted Mordecai's suggestion and began this annual custom [24,25]as a reminder of the time when Haman (son of Hammedatha the Agagite), the enemy of all the Jews, had plotted to destroy them at the time determined by a throw of the dice; and to remind them that when the matter came before the king, he issued a decree causing Haman's plot to boomerang, and he and his sons were hanged on the gallows. [26]That is why this celebration is called "Purim" because the word for "throwing dice" in Persian is *pur.* [27]All the Jews throughout the realm agreed to inaugurate this tradition and to pass it on to their descendants and to all who became Jews; they declared they would never fail to celebrate these two days at the appointed time each year. [28]It would be an annual event from generation to generation, celebrated by every family throughout the countryside and cities of the empire, so that the memory of what had happened would never perish from the Jewish race.

[29-31]Meanwhile Queen Esther (daughter of Abihail and later adopted by Mordecai the Jew) had written a letter throwing her full support behind Mordecai's letter inaugurating his annual Feast of Purim. In addition, letters were sent to all the Jews throughout the 127 provinces of the kingdom of Ahasuerus with messages of good will and encouragement to confirm these two days annually as the Feast of Purim, decreed by both Mordecai the Jew and by Queen Esther; indeed, the Jews themselves had decided upon this tradition as a remembrance of the time of their national fasting and prayer. [32]So the commandment of Esther confirmed these dates, and it was recorded as law.

CHAPTER 10

Mordecai Is Rewarded

King Ahasuerus not only laid tribute upon the mainland but even on the islands of the sea.

9:16-19 Upon completing their task, the Jews throughout the empire spontaneously and joyfully celebrated their success. There is nothing wrong with celebrating a great victory, whether it is emotional, spiritual, or physical. If we have been delivered from an addiction or have overcome an emotional problem, we need to rejoice and celebrate! Not only is celebration fun, but it also helps us recharge our batteries for the battles ahead.

9:20-28 Mordecai formalized into an annual event what originally had been a spur-of-the-moment celebration (9:20-21). He named this deliverance of the Jews as an official holiday—Purim. This would remind the Jews annually of their deliverance from near destruction. It is often helpful for us to establish special days to commemorate the important victories in our life. Such days then will serve as reminders of how we were delivered from near self-destruction.

2His great deeds, and also the full account of
the greatness of Mordecai and the honors
given him by the king, are written in *The Book
of the Chronicles of the Kings of Media and
Persia.* 3Mordecai the Jew was the Prime Minister, with authority next to that of King Ahasuerus himself. He was, of course, very great
among the Jews and respected by all his countrymen because he did his best for his people
and was a friend at court for all of them.

10:1-3 Mordecai became known as a great prime minister, no doubt because of his fairness and godliness. Although the book ends with the Jews enjoying much success, it never once mentions the name of God (in the original Hebrew). Yet, despite this seeming oversight, God's handiwork—his timing, his deliverance, and his encouragement—can be seen throughout. God truly works behind the scenes to ensure the full recovery and ultimate success of his people.

JOB

THE BIG PICTURE

A. THE PAIN BEGINS (1:1–2:13)
1. The World of a Faithful Man (1:1-5)
2. The World of a Faithless Angel (1:6-7)
3. God's Choice for Faithfulness (1:8-12)
4. The Trial Begins (1:13–2:10)
5. The Only Friendly Visit (2:11-13)

B. A MAN FORSAKEN (3:1–37:24)
1. Round One: Undependable Friends (3:1–14:22)
2. Round Two: Unnerving Theologies (15:1–21:34)
3. Round Three: Misguided Cures (22:1–26:14)
4. A Painful Remembrance (27:1–31:40)
5. A Self-appointed Spokesman (32:1–37:24)

C. A VOICE OUT OF THE STORM (38:1–41:34)

D. SPIRITUAL RECOVERY: EYES THAT SEE GOD (42:1-6)

E. PHYSICAL RECOVERY: A NEW BEGINNING (42:7-17)

The book of Job addresses head on the problem of the suffering of the innocent. At its opening, Job was a prosperous man, greatly blessed by God. But then God allowed one disaster after another to fall upon Job. We are told that Job's suffering was the consequence of a spiritual conflict, not because of any failure on Job's part. But Job, his wife, and his friends were never made aware of this. They were left to struggle with the pain and to ask the age-old question, *why.*

Job was confused by the devastating losses he had experienced. Even after taking a rigorous inventory of his life, he could find nothing to warrant the punishment he was taking. Amidst his confusion, however, he displayed an amazing faith in God, despite short lapses of anger and despair. Job's wife reacted to Job's suffering as we often do in such situations—she pointed an angry finger at God. The four visiting friends approached Job's suffering with the orthodox theology of their day, which considered all suffering to be the direct result of sin. They could think of no other reason for Job's suffering except his denial of some hidden sin.

The book's prologue makes it clear that Job was innocent. The solution offered by Job's friends was clearly wrong. Why did God allow Job to suffer? Job was never given a clear answer. He did learn, however, to stand humbly and trustingly before his Creator, who alone knew and understood all. Life brings hurts, and there are no guarantees that we will escape. But through suffering we can learn to live by faith rather than our own strength. We can learn that even when suffering leads us to doubt, God is still with us.

THE BOTTOM LINE

PURPOSE: To provide an intimate look into the struggles of a man dealing with the problem of human suffering. AUTHOR: The author is unknown, though either Job or Elihu may have written the initial record. AUDIENCE: The people of Israel. DATE WRITTEN: The date of the book's written completion is unknown. The events probably belong to the patriarchal period (2000–1800 B.C.). SETTING: The land of Uz, probably located in either northeastern Palestine or northwestern Arabia. KEY VERSE: "But as for me, I know that my Redeemer lives, and that he will stand upon the earth at last. And I know that after this body has decayed, this body shall see God!" (19:25-26). KEY PEOPLE AND RELATIONSHIPS: Job, his wife, and his friends Eliphaz, Bildad, Zophar, and Elihu.

RECOVERY THEMES

Dealing with Unfairness: We live in a world filled with injustice and unfairness. The Bible recognizes this hard fact. Joseph suffered unfairly at the hands of his brothers and Potiphar's wife. David suffered unjustly for many years at the hands of King Saul. And here, through no fault of his own, Job lost his possessions, his family, and his health. Job wondered why God allowed him to suffer, but he never got a clear answer. He did discover, however, that through his struggles he came to know God in a new and deeper way. Even though we face unfairness in our world, we can still make it an opportunity to learn more about trusting God.

Honesty with Our Emotions: In the book of Job we discover that it is all right to cry, to doubt, to fear, to question, to need, and to wrestle with the very essence of our existence. As our heart cries out against injustice and pain, Job reassures us of the importance of being honest with God. When we are angry, we should tell him. When we are afraid, we should reach out to him. God will understand our strong feelings. He is never put off or threatened by our anger. In fact, God longs for us to be open and honest with him. He wants to participate in even the darkest parts of our life. Only then will we be able to relate as a whole person to him. Only then will he be able to bring us the healing and hope he longs to give.

God's Goodness: God is all-knowing and all-powerful. His will for each of us is perfect. But he doesn't always act in ways we can understand. Very often he seems to do things that contradict his justice in the world. As Job suffered, his friends believed his pain was the result of something Job had done. Job knew this was not the case. Yet he could not help wondering why he had to suffer so much pain. It would have been easy for Job to wholeheartedly reject God for the apparent injustice he was suffering. But Job still knew that God was good, and, despite lapses of anger and despair, Job trusted that in the end God would deal with him justly.

The Importance of Trust: When our life is going smoothly, trust is easy. The test of trust always comes when life stops making sense. Job gave us a very real example of how trust needs to work in our life. Everything that Job enjoyed had been stripped away for no reason that he could understand or discover. In spite of this, however, Job never gave up on God. He never placed hope in his experience, his wisdom, his friends, or his wealth. His trust was in God, even though he couldn't understand everything he went through. God alone is sufficient to help us deal with the ambiguities in life. We can trust in him.

CHAPTER 1

Job Loses His Family and Wealth

There lived in the land of Uz a man named
Job—a good man who feared God and stayed
away from evil. 2,3He had a large family of
seven sons and three daughters and was immensely wealthy, for he owned 7,000 sheep,
3,000 camels, 500 teams of oxen, 500 female
donkeys, and employed many servants. He
was, in fact, the richest cattleman in that
entire area.
4Every year when Job's sons had birthdays,
they invited their brothers and sisters to their
homes for a celebration. On these occasions
they would eat and drink with great merri-
ment. 5When these birthday parties ended—
and sometimes they lasted several days—Job
would summon his children to him and sanctify them, getting up early in the morning and
offering a burnt offering for each of them. For
Job said, "Perhaps my sons have sinned and
turned away from God in their hearts." This
was Job's regular practice.
6One day as the angels came to present
themselves before the Lord, Satan, the Accuser, came with them.
7"Where have you come from?" the Lord
asked Satan.
And Satan replied, "From Earth, where
I've been watching everything that's going
on."
8Then the Lord asked Satan, "Have you
noticed my servant Job? He is the finest man
in all the earth—a good man who fears God
and will have nothing to do with evil."
9"Why shouldn't he when you pay him so
well?" Satan scoffed. 10"You have always protected him and his home and his property
from all harm. You have prospered everything
he does—look how rich he is! No wonder he
'worships' you! 11But just take away his
wealth, and you'll see him curse you to your
face!"

1:1-5 Job's life-style and heart are revealed to us during this brief introduction. We are told and then shown that Job loved God and desired to lead his children to do the same. This fact will help us to understand the rest of the narrative properly. Job's innocence is established at the beginning of the book so we won't question it as he is judged by his friends.

JOB, HIS FAMILY & FRIENDS

Responding to tragedy is never easy. Maybe it's the terrible sense of loss we feel. Perhaps it's the desire to know *why* that leaves us feeling alienated and alone. Was it something we did? Was it someone else's fault? Why did God allow it to happen? These questions often go unanswered. For many of us, as we make our inventory and dig up the layers of denial, we realize that our suffering is a consequence of our own addictive behavior. But in Job's case this wasn't true. He was a godly man with healthy family relationships. He was willing to honestly examine his life but could find no particular failures or deficiencies. When Job lost everything—wealth and family—in an overnight disaster, the question *why* was especially appropriate.

Yet even after his great losses, Job continued to glorify God. And then, very soon after losing everything he owned, he also lost his good health. Why was all this happening, especially to such a good person? That was the question in the minds of Job, his wife, and the friends who visited Job in his misery. Such *why* questions are ultimately unanswerable from our limited human standpoint, but they are inevitably asked. So we must face them as we seek to navigate our way through the tragedies we face in life.

We will discover that Job's sufferings came as a result of what the New Testament calls spiritual warfare (see Ephesians 6:10-18). But Job and the others had no idea what was happening in the unseen spiritual realm. They could only guess or theorize about what was going on. Job's friends believed that he was living in denial, hiding sins and failures that were the cause of his suffering. Job, knowing his heart to be pure, could not go along with the explanation of his friends. But still, he had no real answer for the nagging question, *why.* As time passed, Job grew increasingly upset and confused, until even he began to question God's sense of justice.

In the end, Job lost his debate with God. While God never explained fully to Job why the disasters had befallen him, he did bring Job to the point of self-examination. This expanded Job's understanding of God and gave him the proper perspective to continue life. Neither Job nor any other person who has suffered a serious loss can ever fully understand why a catastrophe has happened. But if they are willing to trust the God of recovery and put their lives in his powerful hands, balanced restoration can take place, as it did in Job's life.

STRENGTHS AND ACCOMPLISHMENTS:
- Job was rightly known for his godliness.
- Job proved himself to be a good father and husband.
- Job is also justly famous for his patience and perseverance.
- Job's friends had good intentions as they visited him.

WEAKNESSES AND MISTAKES:
- Job's friends made their judgments based on outward appearances, without truly understanding the situation.
- Job's wife let her losses come between her and God.
- Job displayed some pride that needed to be dealt with.

LESSONS FROM THEIR LIVES:
- Disasters touch the lives of even the most moral or godly people.
- As we sustain any major loss, we should not deny our anger; instead, we should work through it.
- In times of loss, we must not let pride stand in the way of a rigorous personal inventory.

KEY VERSE:
"Job is an example of a man who continued to trust the Lord in sorrow; from his experiences we can see how the Lord's plan finally ended in good, for he is full of tenderness and mercy" (James 5:11).

The story of Job, his family, and friends is told in the book of Job. He is also referred to in Ezekiel 14:14, 20 and James 5:11.

[12,13]And the Lord replied to Satan, "You may do anything you like with his wealth, but don't harm him physically."

So Satan went away; and sure enough, not long afterwards when Job's sons and daughters were dining at the oldest brother's house, tragedy struck.

[14,15]A messenger rushed to Job's home with this news: "Your oxen were plowing, with the donkeys feeding beside them,

when the Sabeans raided us, drove away the
animals, and killed all the farmhands except me. I am the only one left."
16While this messenger was still speaking,
another arrived with more bad news: "The
fire of God has fallen from heaven and
burned up your sheep and all the herdsmen,
and I alone have escaped to tell you."
17Before this man finished, still another
messenger rushed in: "Three bands of Chaldeans have driven off your camels and killed
your servants, and I alone have escaped to tell
you."
18As he was still speaking, another arrived
to say, "Your sons and daughters were feasting
in their oldest brother's home, 19when suddenly a mighty wind swept in from the desert
and engulfed the house so that the roof fell in
on them and all are dead; and I alone escaped
to tell you."
20Then Job stood up and tore his robe in
grief and fell down upon the ground before
God. 21"I came naked from my mother's
womb," he said, "and I shall have nothing
when I die. The Lord gave me everything I
had, and they were his to take away. Blessed
be the name of the Lord."
22In all of this Job did not sin or revile God.

CHAPTER 2

Job Loses His Health

Now the angels came again to present themselves before the Lord, and Satan with them.
2"Where have you come from?" the Lord
asked Satan.
"From Earth, where I've been watching
everything that's going on," Satan replied.
3"Well, have you noticed my servant Job?"
the Lord asked. "He is the finest man in all the
earth—a good man who fears God and turns
away from all evil. And he has kept his faith
in me despite the fact that you persuaded me
to let you harm him without any cause."
4,5"Skin for skin," Satan replied. "A man will
give anything to save his life. Touch his body
with sickness, and he will curse you to your
face!"
6"Do with him as you please," the Lord
replied; "only spare his life."
7So Satan went out from the presence of the
Lord and struck Job with a terrible case of
boils from head to foot. 8Then Job took a
broken piece of pottery to scrape himself and
sat among the ashes.
9His wife said to him, "Are you still trying
to be godly when God has done all this to
you? Curse him and die."
10But he replied, "You talk like some heathen woman. What? Shall we receive only
pleasant things from the hand of God and
never anything unpleasant?" So in all this Job
said nothing wrong.

Job's Three Friends

11When three of Job's friends heard of all the
tragedy that had befallen him, they got in
touch with each other and traveled from their
homes to comfort and console him. Their
names were Eliphaz the Temanite, Bildad the
Shuhite, and Zophar the Naamathite. 12Job
was so changed that they could scarcely recognize him. Wailing loudly in despair, they
tore their robes and threw dust into the air
and put earth on their heads to demonstrate
their sorrow. 13Then they sat upon the ground
with him silently for seven days and nights,
no one speaking a word; for they saw that his
suffering was too great for words.

1:13-19 In what seems to be only a few hours' time, everything Job had held significant was stripped away. The pain must have seemed intolerable; the grief, beyond solace. Even though Job mourned his loss, however, his identity was not wrapped up in his possessions. Do we ever get caught in that trap, building our self-worth on what we own—our home, car, job, or wealth? If those were to be taken away, how would we feel? Our self-esteem must be based on the fact that God loves us so much that he sent his Son, Jesus, to die for us while we were still sinners (Romans 5:8). This is something that can never be taken away.

2:1-3 It is important to realize that Satan has no authority apart from God's consent. He is only permitted to test God's beloved; he is not permitted to devour them. When we undergo trials, we should realize that God won't let us be destroyed; if we trust God, he will help us as we face our trials. He wants us to grow in our faith and glorify his name, no matter what difficulties we may be called upon to face.

2:9-10 It is one thing to lose our comforts; it is quite another to lose the support of a spouse. In times of great loss, we desperately need the support of our loved ones. We need our spouse's vote of confidence when no one else is there. The only mention of Job's wife comes at the start of his affliction. She was bitter and unable to share in his pain. As a spouse experiences tough times in recovery, we need to be careful not to taunt or ridicule. He or she needs our support, not our anger or frustration.

CHAPTER 3

Job Wishes for Death

At last Job spoke and cursed the day of his birth.

[2,3]"Let the day of my birth be cursed," he said, "and the night when I was conceived. [4]Let that day be forever forgotten. Let it be lost even to God, shrouded in eternal darkness. [5]Yes, let the darkness claim it for its own, and may a black cloud overshadow it. [6]May it be blotted off the calendar, never again to be counted among the days of the month of that year. [7]Let that night be bleak and joyless. [8]Let those who are experts at cursing curse it. [9]Let the stars of the night disappear. Let it long for light but never see it, never see the morning light. [10]Curse it for its failure to shut my mother's womb, for letting me be born to come to all this trouble.

[11]"Why didn't I die at birth? [12]Why did the midwife let me live? Why did she nurse me at her breasts? [13]For if only I had died at birth, then I would be quiet now, asleep and at rest, [14,15]along with prime ministers and kings with all their pomp, and wealthy princes whose castles are full of rich treasures. [16]Oh, to have been stillborn!—to have never breathed or seen the light. [17]For there in death the wicked cease from troubling, and there the weary are at rest. [18]There even prisoners are at ease, with no brutal jailer to curse them. [19]Both rich and poor alike are there, and the slave is free at last from his master.

[20,21]"Oh, why should light and life be given to those in misery and bitterness, who long for death, and it won't come; who search for death as others search for food or money? [22]What blessed relief when at last they die! [23]Why is a man allowed to be born if God is only going to give him a hopeless life of uselessness and frustration? [24]I cannot eat for sighing; my groans pour out like water. [25]What I always feared has happened to me. [26]I was not fat and lazy, yet trouble struck me down."

CHAPTER 4

A reply to Job from Eliphaz the Temanite:

[2]"Will you let me say a word? For who could keep from speaking out? [3,4]In the past you have told many a troubled soul to trust in God and have encouraged those who are weak or falling, or lie crushed upon the ground or are tempted to despair. [5]But now when trouble strikes, you faint and are broken.

[6]"At such a time as this should not trust in God still be your confidence? Shouldn't you believe that God will care for those who are good? [7,8]Stop and think! Have you ever known a truly good and innocent person who was punished? Experience teaches that it is those who sow sin and trouble who harvest the

---

3:1-19 Even though Job had known amazing success and happiness, he couldn't remember what it had been like. A common element to suffering is a loss of perspective. No matter how hard we try to maintain our point of view, it is difficult to separate yesterday's celebration from today's devastation. But if we can just "hang in there" a little longer, we will experience celebration once again.

3:20-23 Like most sufferers, Job asked *why*. Unfortunately, the answer to that question is often reserved for eternity. We must learn to trust God and stay faithful to him even if we never receive an explanation for our suffering. Sometimes we will never know why things happen the way they do. We can be sure, though, that God is with us in the pain. We can begin the healing process by entrusting our life to God and his will for us.

3:24-26 Even though Job had lived an exemplary life, he faced great suffering. Job thought that he wouldn't have to face this kind of suffering because he had avoided certain behaviors. He had, however, no idea of the supernatural events that precipitated his misery. We, too, may be surprised to find that we are suffering, especially after we have been faithfully following a recovery program. But God has a reason for allowing all the events in our life. We need to persevere in our trust and realize that God's will for us will ultimately bring us great joy.

4:1-6 One thing suffering people don't need is harsh words of judgment, especially from their friends. Most of us are aware of the wrong things we have done and want to make things right. We don't need to be told that our behavior is disappointing to God. Our Father knows better than anyone the pain that we experience. He, too, grows weary and discouraged by our sin. He is not a distant observer of our life, but an intimate companion. When we try to comfort friends or family members, we should let them go through the grief process. Then we can encourage them with the message of God's forgiveness—the only real hope for recovery.

4:7-11 We know that a man reaps what he sows, but we cannot offer this verse as a universal reason for suffering. First, God deals with us by grace, not as we "deserve." Second, suffering is not always a tool of judgment. It can be used to strengthen our faith. Just as gold must be melted to get the impurities out, so we must go through trials to purify our faith.

same. 9They die beneath the hand of God. 10Though they are fierce as young lions, they shall all be broken and destroyed. 11Like aged, helpless lions they shall starve, and all their children shall be scattered.

12"This truth was given me in secret, as though whispered in my ear. 13It came in a nighttime vision as others slept. 14Suddenly, fear gripped me; I trembled and shook with terror, 15as a spirit passed before my face—my hair stood up on end. 16I felt the spirit's presence, but couldn't see it standing there. Then out of the dreadful silence came this voice:

17"'Is mere man more just than God? More pure than his Creator?'

18,19"If God cannot trust his own messengers (for even angels make mistakes), how much less men made of dust, who are crushed to death as easily as moths! 20They are alive in the morning, but by evening they are dead, gone forever with hardly a thought from anyone. 21Their candle of life is snuffed out. They die and no one cares.

CHAPTER 5

"They cry for help but no one listens; they turn to their gods, but none gives them aid. 2They die in helpless frustration, overcome by their own anger. 3Those who turn from God may be successful for the moment, but then comes sudden disaster. 4Their children are cheated, with no one to defend them. 5Their harvests are stolen, and their wealth slakes the thirst of many others, not themselves! 6Misery comes upon them to punish them for sowing seeds of sin. 7Mankind heads for sin and misery as predictably as flames shoot upwards from a fire.

8"My advice to you is this: Go to God and confess your sins to him. 9For he does wonderful miracles, marvels without number. 10He sends the rain upon the earth to water the fields, 11and gives prosperity to the poor and humble, and takes sufferers to safety.

12"He frustrates the plans of crafty men. 13They are caught in their own traps; he thwarts their schemes. 14They grope like blind men in the daylight; they see no better in the daytime than at night.

15"God saves the fatherless and the poor from the grasp of these oppressors. 16And so at last the poor have hope, and the fangs of the wicked are broken.

17"How enviable the man whom God corrects! Oh, do not despise the chastening of the Lord when you sin. 18For though he wounds, he binds and heals again. 19He will deliver you again and again so that no evil can touch you.

20"He will keep you from death in famine and from the power of the sword in time of war.

4:7-21 There are few things more frustrating than a friend who claims to know what is happening, why it is happening, and how we should respond. Job wasn't outside God's favor. He wasn't disobedient and unwilling to follow God. Job was a sufferer, and he needed his friends to trust what they knew about him. Job needed people to share his pain and help him grieve. We don't have to come up with all the answers to be able to comfort our friends. We just have to lovingly support them as they face difficult times.

5:8-16 As we seek to comfort others we must avoid saying, "If I were you, . . ." No matter what we have experienced in the past, we are never really able to understand what other people are going through. We have no idea how we would respond if placed in their situation. We would be wise to respond to another's suffering like this: "Tell me how you're feeling" or "Show me how to stand with you in your grief."

5:17 Eliphaz assumed that Job was rejecting God's discipline. Though Job was not being disciplined by God here, Eliphaz was correct in saying that we should welcome God's correction. God wants only the best for us, and he will discipline us in order to get us back in line with his will. But we shouldn't assume that every experience of suffering in our life is an instance of God's correction.

5:27 The greatest personal resource we possess as believers is the indwelling of the Holy Spirit. He is our intimate connection with God, our heavenly Father. He is our resource, our teacher, our illuminator (see John 14–16). Eliphaz made the mistake of trying to play the role of the Holy Spirit in Job's life. If we feel we need to do the same in order to comfort our friends, we should opt instead to sit quietly with them, as Job's friends did at the start. They came across as more sympathetic when their mouths were shut.

6:14-21 Friends are very important. When we are hurting, we depend on them to listen, to weep, to support, to just be with us. If ever Job needed his friends, it was now. Yet Job found his friends as undependable as a brook. He was deeply disappointed in their failure to support him in his pain. They were long on advice, but short on compassion. When our friends try to comfort us, we should tell them how they can help us better. If we are called upon to comfort others, we need to be sensitive to their needs.

21"You will be safe from slander; no need to
fear the future.
22"You shall laugh at war and famine; wild
animals will leave you alone. 23Dangerous animals will be at peace with you.
24"You need not worry about your home
while you are gone; nothing shall be stolen
from your barns.
25"Your sons shall become important men;
your descendants shall be as numerous as
grass! 26You shall live a long, good life; like
standing grain, you'll not be harvested until
it's time! 27I have found from experience that
all of this is true. For your own good, listen to
my counsel."

CHAPTER 6
Job's reply:
2"Oh, that my sadness and troubles were
weighed. 3For they are heavier than the sand
of a thousand seashores. That is why I spoke
so rashly. 4For the Lord has struck me down
with his arrows; he has sent his poisoned
arrows deep within my heart. All God's terrors
are arrayed against me. 5-7When wild donkeys
bray, it is because their grass is gone; oxen do
not low when they have food; a man com-
plains when there is no salt in his food. And
how tasteless is the uncooked white of an
egg—my appetite is gone when I look at it; I
gag at the thought of eating it!
8,9"Oh, that God would grant the thing I
long for most—to die beneath his hand and
be freed from his painful grip. 10This, at least,
gives me comfort despite all the pain—that I
have not denied the words of the holy God.
11Oh, why does my strength sustain me? How
can I be patient till I die? 12Am I unfeeling, like
stone? Is my flesh made of brass? 13For I am
utterly helpless, without any hope.
14"One should be kind to a fainting friend,
but you have accused me without the slightest fear of God. 15-18My brother, you have
proved as unreliable as a brook; it floods when
there is ice and snow, but in hot weather,
disappears. The caravans turn aside to be refreshed, but there is nothing there to drink,
and so they perish. 19-21When caravans from
Tema and from Sheba stop for water there,
their hopes are dashed. And so my hopes in
you are dashed—you turn away from me in
terror and refuse to help.22But why? Have I
ever asked you for one slightest thing? Have I
begged you for a present? 23Have I ever asked
your help? 24All I want is a reasonable answer—then I will keep quiet. Tell me, what
have I done wrong?

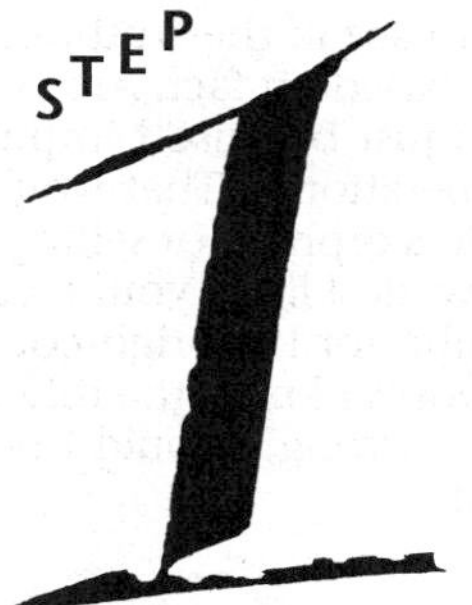

Hope amidst Suffering

BIBLE READING: Job 6:2-13

We admitted that we were powerless over our dependencies—that our life had become unmanageable.

There are times when we are so confused and overwhelmed by the pain in our life that we wish we could die. No matter what we do, we are powerless to change things for the better. The weight of the sadness seems too heavy to bear. We can't see why our heart just doesn't break and allow death to free us.

Job felt that way. He'd lost everything, even though he had always done what was right. His ten children were dead. He had lost his business, his riches, and his health. And all this happened in a matter of days! He was left with a sharp-tongued wife and three friends who blamed him for his own misfortune. Job cried out, "Oh, that my sadness and troubles were weighed. . . . Oh, that God would grant the thing I long for most—to die beneath his hand and be freed from his painful grip. . . . Oh, why does my strength sustain me? How can I be patient till I die? Am I unfeeling, like stone? Is my flesh made of brass? For I am utterly helpless, without any hope" (Job 6:2, 8-9, 11-13).

Job didn't know that the end of his life would be even better than the beginning. God restored everything he had lost, and then some. "Then at last he died, an old, old man, after living a long, good life" (Job 42:17). Even when we're pressed to the point of death, there is still hope that our life will change. Our recovery could be so complete that the final line written about us might read: "At last they died, after living a long, good life." We must remember: life can be good again! ***Turn to page 1071, Mark 10.***

25,26"It is wonderful to speak the truth, but your criticisms are not based on fact. Are you going to condemn me just because I impulsively cried out in desperation? 27That would be like injuring a helpless orphan, or selling a friend. 28Look at me! Would I lie to your face? 29Stop assuming my guilt, for I am righteous. Don't be so unjust. 30Don't I know the difference between right and wrong? Would I not admit it if I had sinned?

CHAPTER 7

"How mankind must struggle. A man's life is long and hard, like that of a slave. 2How he longs for the day to end. How he grinds on to the end of the week and his wages. 3And so to me also have been allotted months of frustration, these long and weary nights. 4When I go to bed I think, 'Oh, that it were morning,' and then I toss till dawn.

5"My skin is filled with worms and blackness. My flesh breaks open, full of pus. 6My life drags by—day after hopeless day. 7My life is but a breath, and nothing good is left. 8You see me now, but not for long. Soon you'll look upon me dead. 9As a cloud disperses and vanishes, so those who die shall go away forever—10gone forever from their family and their home—never to be seen again. 11Ah, let me express my anguish. Let me be free to speak out of the bitterness of my soul.

12"O God, am I some monster that you never let me alone? 13,14Even when I try to forget my misery in sleep, you terrify with nightmares. 15I would rather die of strangulation than go on and on like this. 16I hate my life. Oh, let me alone for these few remaining days. 17What is mere man that you should spend your time persecuting him? 18Must you be his inquisitor every morning and test him every moment of the day? 19Why won't you let me alone—even long enough to spit?

20"Has my sin harmed you, O God, Watcher of mankind? Why have you made me your target, and made my life so heavy a burden to me? 21Why not just pardon my sin and take it all away? For all too soon I'll lie down in the dust and die, and when you look for me, I shall be gone."

CHAPTER 8

Bildad the Shuhite replies to Job:

2"How long will you go on like this, Job, blowing words around like wind? 3Does God twist justice? 4If your children sinned against him, and he punished them, 5and you begged Almighty God for them—6if you were pure and good, he would hear your prayer and answer you and bless you with a happy home. 7And though you started with little, you would end with much.

8"Read the history books and see—9for we were born but yesterday and know so little; our days here on earth are as transient as shadows. 10But the wisdom of the past will teach you. The experience of others will speak to you, reminding you that 11-13those who forget God have no hope. They are like rushes without any mire to grow in; or grass without water to keep it alive. Suddenly it begins to

---

6:30 Job here stated that if he had sinned, he would have admitted it. He wanted to know just what he had done to deserve punishment. Job kept a good moral inventory of his acts and couldn't find anything wrong. We need to keep accurate records of our actions, too. If there is sin in our life, we need to confess it. If we have wronged someone, we need to make restitution. Denying the facts will not help our recovery.

7:1-5 Whether we suffer from physical pain, the loss of a spouse, a disappointing career, divorce, loneliness, depression, an estranged loved one, alcoholism, or any kind of addiction, nights are a difficult time. At least in the daylight hours, our work or other activities can take our mind off our situation. When night falls and we are alone, the reality of our pain stares us in the face with no distractions. It is then we can talk to God about our pain, and he will listen and comfort us. We are never alone—we can always talk to God through prayer.

7:11-21 Job here turned to petition God. Even though he was in anguish, he recognized that God was the only one who could take away the pain (7:21). Whether or not the pain we feel is a result of our own sins, God is there to comfort us. His timing may not be what we would consider ideal, but God's perspective and timing are always best. We can trust in God to rescue us, but in his time, not ours.

8:1-7 "You're getting what you deserve." This is perhaps the most unkind remark we might ever make to a sufferer. In some cases it might be true. Foolish choices do often lead to painful consequences. But if we always got what we deserved, all of us would soon be destroyed. And at times, our suffering is not a consequence of sin at all. Bildad showed his ignorance of God's ways when he tried to connect Job's loss to some hidden sin. We need to be careful not to judge a person who is suffering a setback, for we may not have the whole story. Only God truly knows and understands a person and his circumstances.

wither, even before it is cut. 14A man without
God is trusting in a spider's web. Everything
he counts on will collapse. 15If he counts on
his home for security, it won't last. 16At dawn
he seems so strong and virile, like a green
plant; his branches spread across the garden.
17His roots are in the stream, down among the
stones. 18But when he disappears, he isn't
even missed! 19That is all he can look forward
to! And others spring up from the earth to
replace him!

20"But look! God will not cast away a good
man, nor prosper evildoers. 21He will yet fill
your mouth with laughter and your lips with
shouts of joy. 22Those who hate you shall be
clothed with shame, and the wicked destroyed."

CHAPTER 9

Job's reply:

2"Yes, I know all that. You're not telling me
anything new. But how can a man be truly
good in the eyes of God? 3If God decides to
argue with him, can a man answer even one
question of a thousand he asks? 4For God is so
wise and so mighty. Who has ever opposed
him successfully?

5"Suddenly he moves the mountains, overturning them in his anger. 6He shakes the
earth to its foundations. 7The sun won't rise,
the stars won't shine, if he commands it so!
8Only he has stretched the heavens out and
stalked along the seas. 9He made the Bear,
Orion and the Pleiades, and the constellations
of the southern Zodiac.

10"He does incredible miracles, too many to
count. 11He passes by, invisible; he moves
along, but I don't see him go. 12When he
sends death to snatch a man away, who can
stop him? Who dares to ask him, 'What are
you doing?'

13"And God does not abate his anger. The
pride of man collapses before him. 14And who
am I that I should try to argue with Almighty
God, or even reason with him? 15Even if I were
sinless, I wouldn't say a word. I would only
plead for mercy. 16And even if my prayers were
answered, I could scarce believe that he had
heard my cry. 17For he is the one who destroys, and multiplies my wounds without a
cause. 18He will not let me breathe, but fills me
with bitter sorrows. 19He alone is strong and
just.

20"But I? Am I righteous? My own mouth
says no. Even if I were perfect, God would
prove me wicked. 21And even if I am utterly
innocent, I dare not think of it. I despise what
I am. 22Innocent or evil, it is all the same to
him, for he destroys both kinds. 23He will
laugh when calamity crushes the innocent.
24The whole earth is in the hands of the
wicked. God blinds the eyes of the judges and
lets them be unfair. If not he, then who?

25"My life passes swiftly away, filled with
tragedy. 26My years disappear like swift ships,
like the eagle that swoops upon its prey.

27"If I decided to forget my complaints
against God, to end my sadness and be cheerful, 28then he would pour even greater sorrows
upon me. For I know that you will not hold
me innocent, O God, 29but will condemn me.
So what's the use of trying? 30Even if I were to
wash myself with purest water and cleanse
my hands with lye to make them utterly
clean, 31even so you would plunge me into the
ditch and mud; and even my clothing would
be less filthy than you consider me to be!

32,33"And I cannot defend myself, for you
are no mere man as I am. If you were, then we
could discuss it fairly, but there is no umpire
between us, no middle man, no mediator to
bring us together. 34Oh, let him stop beating
me, so that I need no longer live in terror of
his punishment. 35Then I could speak without
fear to him and tell him boldly that I am not
guilty.

CHAPTER 10

"I am weary of living. Let me complain freely.
I will speak in my sorrow and bitterness. 2I will

8:8-22 Bildad was correct about some of his theology, but he erred in the application of his knowledge. God saw Job as blameless and upright (see 1:8; 2:3), not as unfaithful or disobedient. Job's suffering was not the result of a wayward life. It is not our job to guess the purpose of another person's pain. It is our job to offer comfort and support.

9:1-20 Job knew more than he understood. He knew about God's sovereignty and mercy, and that no man is blameless apart from God's gracious forgiveness. When we feel that God isn't being fair, we should remember that if he were, we would never be able to enter his presence. When God is "unfair," it is always on the side of mercy.

9:32-35 Job lamented the absence of a mediator to stand between himself and God. We cannot make that same plea; God has sent a Mediator—Jesus Christ. We can take our case directly to God because Jesus' death gave us access to God's presence. When we feel as if we cannot stand any more pain, we can go to Jesus with our request for peace. He will listen to us and answer our prayer.

say to God, 'Don't just condemn me—tell me
why you are doing it. [3]Does it really seem right
to you to oppress and despise me, a man you
have made; and to send joy and prosperity to
the wicked? [4-7]Are you unjust like men? Is
your life so short that you must hound me for
sins you know full well I've not committed?
Is it because you know no one can save me
from your hand?
[8]"'You have made me, and yet you destroy
me. [9]Oh, please remember that I'm made of
dust—will you change me back again to dust
so soon? [10]You have already poured me from
bottle to bottle like milk and curdled me like
cheese. [11]You gave me skin and flesh and knit
together bones and sinews. [12]You gave me life
and were so kind and loving to me, and I was
preserved by your care.
[13,14]"'Yet all the time your real motive in
making me was to destroy me if I sinned, and
to refuse to forgive my iniquity.[15]Just the
slightest wickedness, and I am done for. And
if I'm good, that doesn't count. I am filled
with frustration. [16]If I start to get up off the
ground, you leap upon me like a lion and
quickly finish me off. [17]Again and again you
witness against me and pour out an ever-
increasing volume of wrath upon me and
bring fresh armies against me.
[18]"'Why then did you even let me be born?
Why didn't you let me die at birth? [19]Then I
would have been spared this miserable existence. I would have gone directly from the
womb to the grave. [20,21]Can't you see how
little time I have left? Oh, let me alone that I
may have a little moment of comfort before I
leave for the land of darkness and the shadow
of death, never to return—[22]a land as dark as
midnight, a land of the shadow of death
where only confusion reigns and where the
brightest light is dark as midnight.'"

CHAPTER 11

Zophar the Naamathite replies to Job:

[2]"Shouldn't someone stem this torrent of
words? Is a man proved right by all this talk?
[3]Should I remain silent while you boast?
When you mock God, shouldn't someone
make you ashamed? [4]You claim you are pure
in the eyes of God! [5]Oh, that God would
speak and tell you what he thinks! [6]Oh, that
he would make you truly see yourself, for he
knows everything you've done. Listen! God
is doubtless punishing you far less than you
deserve!
[7]"Do you know the mind and purposes of
God? Will long searching make them known
to you? Are you qualified to judge the Almighty? [8]He is as faultless as heaven is high—
but who are you? His mind is
fathomless—what can you know in comparison? [9]His Spirit is broader than the earth and
wider than the sea. [10]If he rushes in and makes
an arrest, and calls the court to order, who is
going to stop him? [11]For he knows perfectly all
the faults and sins of mankind; he sees all sin
without searching.
[12]"Mere man is as likely to be wise as a wild
donkey's colt is likely to be born a man!
[13,14]"Before you turn to God and stretch out
your hands to him, get rid of your sins and
leave all iniquity behind you. [15]Only then,
without the spots of sin to defile you, can you
walk steadily forward to God without fear.
[16]Only then can you forget your misery. It will
all be in the past. [17]And your life will be

10:1-17 Job took a respite from measuring his pain and began to direct his thoughts toward God. This subtle change would become a catalyst for his growth, though he was not yet able to sense any relief. So often we talk about God or about our feelings. A critical step in healing is to address our helpless cries to God. He does not despise our grief; he welcomes its expressions.

10:1-22 There are those who teach that depression is a "negative" emotion. They say that if we have sufficient faith, we need not be depressed. Job's account gives us an honest account of one man's overwhelming grief. When we feel depressed, it is healthy to explore and express the emotions locked up inside us—especially the "negative" ones. By expressing them, we are released from their devastating effects.

10:18-22 Before leaving this world, Jesus assured the disciples that they and we have a place with him in eternity (see John 14:1-4). He gave them a picture of hope that they could hold on to in their impending grief. When we suffer, sometimes hope seems far away. Job couldn't imagine a future of light when he felt so enveloped in darkness. But we can—we have Jesus' promise.

11:7-12 Zophar knew something about God, but his knowledge was limited. God is indeed sovereign, and no one can oppose him and hope to win. But Job wasn't opposing God; he was trying to make sense of his suffering. Just as God allowed Job to meditate on his suffering, he will allow us time to understand why some things are happening to us. We may never find a clear answer, but our faith in God will grow if we learn from our trials and trust God in them, rather than complaining at each new trial.

cloudless; any darkness will be as bright as
morning!
18"You will have courage because you will
have hope. You will take your time and rest in
safety. 19You will lie down unafraid, and many
will look to you for help. 20But the wicked
shall find no way to escape; their only hope is
death."

CHAPTER 12
Job's reply:
2"Yes, I realize you know everything! All
wisdom will die with you! 3Well, I know a few
things myself—you are no better than I am.
And who doesn't know these things you've
been saying? 4I, the man who begged God for
help, and God answered him, have become a
laughingstock to my neighbors. Yes, I, a righteous man, am now the man they scoff at.
5Meanwhile, the rich mock those in trouble
and are quick to despise all those in need. 6For
robbers prosper. Go ahead and provoke
God—it makes no difference! He will supply
your every need anyway!
7-9"Who doesn't know that the Lord does
things like that? Ask the dumbest beast—he
knows that it is so; ask the birds—they will tell
you; or let the earth teach you, or the fish of
the sea. 10For the soul of every living thing is
in the hand of God, and the breath of all
mankind. 11Just as my mouth can taste good
food, so my mind tastes truth when I hear it.
12And as you say, older men like me are wise.
They understand. 13But true wisdom and
power are God's. He alone knows what we
should do; he understands.
14"And how great is his might! What he
destroys can't be rebuilt. When he closes in
on a man, there is no escape. 15He withholds
the rain, and the earth becomes a desert; he
sends the storms and floods the ground. 16Yes,
with him is strength and wisdom. Deceivers
and deceived are both his slaves.
17"He makes fools of counselors and judges.
18He reduces kings to slaves and frees their
servants. 19Priests are led away as slaves. He
overthrows the mighty. 20He takes away the
voice of orators and the insight of the elders.
21He pours contempt upon princes and weak-
ens the strong. 22He floods the darkness with
light, even the dark shadow of death. 23He
raises up a nation and then destroys it. He
makes it great, and then reduces it to nothing.
24,25He takes away the understanding of presidents and kings, and leaves them wandering,
lost and groping, without a guiding light.

CHAPTER 13
"Look, I have seen many instances such as
you describe. I understand what you are saying. 2I know as much as you do. I'm not
stupid. 3Oh, how I long to speak directly to
the Almighty. I want to talk this over with
God himself. 4For you are misinterpreting the

11:13-20 As we devote our heart to God, we will experience a deepening fellowship with him. But this fellowship with God never eliminates all our suffering. Pain is part of life, whether we are close to God or rebellious against him. Zophar's theology could not allow the possibility that Job could suffer and still be righteous. We need to trust in God because of who he is revealed to be. Our faith should never be measured solely by our experience.

12:1-6 We see Job become wiser and wiser because of his pain. He understood well the dilemma faced by Zophar and his companions: "The rich mock those in trouble and are quick to despise all those in need." Theirs was a very comfortable theology. If we are good, God blesses with wealth and comfort. If we are bad, God punishes with poverty and suffering. But as we see here, their assumptions were far from the truth. Job knew that he was innocent of wrongdoing, yet he still suffered greatly. His sufferings gave him the perspective he needed for a better understanding of God and the way he works in our world. Unlike his friends, he knew that suffering was not always a punishment for sin. We should use the difficult times in our life to lead us to a deeper understanding of God.

12:7-25 Job explored the sovereign nature of God. He recognized that God is powerful; man is not. Herein lies one of the most difficult lessons for all of us to learn—God is in ultimate control. Humility does not come easily to us. In our culture, we greatly value power and authority. But we are often powerless over our circumstances and are unable to change our life—only God can do that. Realizing this truth carries us through the first two steps of recovery: recognizing that our life is unmanageable, and acknowledging that God is able to change our life.

13:1-13 Job was clearly angry with his accusers. He saw them as obstacles to his own conversation with God. Like Job's friends, we often find it easy to speak for God when we feel insecure with the circumstances we face. We need to recognize that we never have the whole story on any one situation. God rarely appoints us as intercessors or spokespersons for him. We must be sure that we do not impede someone else's recovery by presuming to speak for God.

whole thing. You are doctors who don't know what they are doing. [5]Oh, please be quiet! That would be your highest wisdom.

[6]"Listen to me now, to my reasons for what I think and to my pleadings.

[7]"Must you go on 'speaking for God' when he never once has said the things that you are putting in his mouth? [8]Does God want your help if you are going to twist the truth for him? [9]Be careful that he doesn't find out what you are doing! Or do you think you can fool God as well as men? [10]No, you will be in serious trouble with him if you use lies to try to help him out. [11]Doesn't his majesty strike terror to your heart? How can you do this thing? [12]These tremendous statements you have made have about as much value as ashes. Your defense of God is as fragile as a clay vase!

[13]"Be silent now and let me alone, that I may speak—and I am willing to face the consequences. [14]Yes, I will take my life in my hand and say what I really think. [15]God may kill me for saying this—in fact, I expect him to. Nevertheless, I am going to argue my case with him. [16]This at least will be in my favor, that I am not godless, to be rejected instantly from his presence. [17]Listen closely to what I am about to say. Hear me out.

[18]"This is my case: *I know that I am righteous.* [19]Who can argue with me over this? If you could prove me wrong, I would stop defending myself and die.

[20]"O God, there are two things I beg you not to do to me; only then will I be able to face you. [21]Don't abandon me. And don't terrify me with your awesome presence. [22]Call to me to come—how quickly I will answer! Or let me speak to you, and you reply. [23]Tell me, what have I done wrong? Help me! Point out my sin to me. [24]Why do you turn away from me? Why hand me over to my enemy? [25]Would you blame a leaf that is blown about by the wind? Will you chase dry, useless straws?

[26]"You write bitter things against me and bring up all the follies of my youth. [27,28]You send me to prison and shut me in on every side. I am like a fallen, rotten tree, like a moth-eaten coat.

CHAPTER 14

"How frail is man, how few his days, how full of trouble! [2]He blossoms for a moment like a flower—and withers; as the shadow of a passing cloud, he quickly disappears. [3]Must you be so harsh with frail men and demand an accounting from them? [4]How can you demand purity in one born impure? [5]You have set mankind so brief a span of life—months is all you give him! Not one bit longer may he live. [6]So give him a little rest, won't you? Turn away your angry gaze and let him have a few moments of relief before he dies.

[7]"For there is hope for a tree—if it's cut down, it sprouts again and grows tender, new branches. [8,9]Though its roots have grown old in the earth, and its stump decays, it may sprout and bud again at the touch of water, like a new seedling. [10]But when a man dies and is buried, where does his spirit go? [11,12]As water evaporates from a lake, as a river disappears in drought, so a man lies down for the last time and does not rise again until the

13:24 Job asked God to show him what he had done wrong. Job had completed a personal moral inventory and had come up with no reasons for his punishment. In our own life, we often have areas of denial. We hesitate to be truly honest about our failures. We need to find the courage to admit any weaknesses we have so we can eliminate all the barriers to our recovery.

14:1-12 We are very fortunate to live after the time of Jesus Christ. We have seen grace demonstrated firsthand, and we have seen the power of resurrection in the risen Christ. Job understood much, but he couldn't quite grasp the idea of eternal life. Our days in the flesh are both numbered and final, and this disturbed Job. Our hope in a future life with Christ should make our troubles here on earth more bearable. We can know with certainty that our sufferings here are not permanent.

14:13-19 All of us face times when we simply want to hide from distress and defeat, and Job was no exception. He pleaded with God for the chance to hide until renewal came. We need to realize that God wasn't punishing Job or taking pleasure in his anguish. He was allowing Job to pass through a fiery trial. God knows the end result of our suffering and despair—a faith that is purer than gold (see 1 Peter 1:6-8). We must look past the difficult times and hope for the positive effects God desires to work in our life. This should encourage us as we face difficult times.

15:1-16 Eliphaz didn't like Job's attitude. He mistook Job's words of grief for words of pride—foolish words. Be careful not to minimize the importance of expressed grief. Grieving is necessary in order to move from despair to hope and to get on with life. We would do well to steer clear of the judgmental attitudes exhibited by Job's friends.

heavens are no more; he shall not awaken, nor be roused from his sleep. 13Oh, that you would hide me with the dead and forget me there until your anger ends; but mark your calendar to think of me again!

14"If a man dies, shall he live again? This thought gives me hope, so that in all my anguish I eagerly await sweet death! 15You would call and I would come, and you would reward all I do. 16But now, instead, you give me so few steps upon the stage of life and notice every mistake I make. 17You bundle them all together as evidence against me.

18,19"Mountains wear away and disappear. Water grinds the stones to sand. Torrents tear away the soil. So every hope of man is worn away. 20,21Always you are against him, and then he passes off the scene. You make him old and wrinkled, then send him away. He never knows it if his sons are honored; or they may fail and face disaster, but he knows it not. 22For him there is only sorrow and pain."

CHAPTER 15

The answer of Eliphaz the Temanite:

2"You are supposed to be a wise man, and yet you give us all this foolish talk. You are nothing but a windbag. 3It isn't right to speak so foolishly. What good do such words do? 4,5Have you no fear of God? No reverence for him? Your sins are telling your mouth what to say! Your words are based on clever deception, 6but why should I condemn you? Your own mouth does!

7,8"Are you the wisest man alive? Were you born before the hills were made? Have you heard the secret counsel of God? Are you called into his counsel room? Do you have a monopoly on wisdom? 9What do you know more than we do? What do you understand that we don't? 10On our side are aged men much older than your father! 11Is God's comfort too little for you? Is his gentleness too rough?

12"What is this you are doing, getting carried away by your anger, with flashing eyes? 13And you turn against God and say all these evil things against him. 14What man in all the earth can be as pure and righteous as you claim to be? 15Why, God doesn't even trust the angels! Even the heavens can't be absolutely pure compared with him! 16How much less someone like you, who is corrupt and sinful, drinking in sin as a sponge soaks up water!

17-19"Listen, and I will answer you from my own experience, confirmed by the experience

Persistent Seeking

BIBLE READING: Job 14:1-6

We came to believe that a Power greater than ourselves could restore us to sanity.

One thing that may make it hard to believe in God is that life often seems unfair to us. We didn't ask to be born into a dysfunctional family! We didn't have any say over the abuses and injustices we suffered! We didn't choose our predisposition toward addiction! And yet we are held accountable for something we can't control on our own! This makes it hard to initially turn to God as the Power to restore our sanity. He seems unreasonable in his demands!

Job understood these feelings. In the midst of his suffering he said, "How frail is man, how few his days, how full of trouble! He blossoms for a moment like a flower—and withers; as the shadow of a passing cloud, he quickly disappears. Must you be so harsh with frail men, and demand an accounting from them? How can you demand purity in one born impure?" (Job 14:1-4). That is a good question—one that most of us have asked in one form or another. Job persisted in his questioning because deep inside he believed God to be good and fair, even though life wasn't. He was honest with his emotions and questions, but he never stopped seeking God.

There is a good answer to the question posed by Job, one that will satisfy both our heart and our mind. It will only be found, however, by those who are willing to work through the pain and unfairness of life and still seek God. Those who seek him will find him; and in God's loving arms, they will also find the answers they seek. ***Turn to page 905, Daniel 4.***

of wise men who have been told this same thing from their fathers—our ancestors to whom alone the land was given—and they have passed this wisdom to us:

20"A wicked man is always in trouble throughout his life. 21He is surrounded by terrors, and if there are good days, they will soon be gone. 22He dares not go out into the darkness lest he be murdered. 23,24He wanders around begging for food. He lives in fear, distress, and anguish. His enemies conquer him as a king defeats his foes. 25,26Armed with his tin shield, he clenches his fist against God, defying the Almighty, stubbornly assaulting him.

27,28"This wicked man is fat and rich, and has lived in conquered cities after killing off their citizens. 29But he will not continue to be rich, or to extend his possessions. 30No, darkness shall overtake him forever; the breath of God shall destroy him; the flames shall burn up all he has.

31"Let him no longer trust in foolish riches; let him no longer deceive himself, for the money he trusts in will be his only reward. 32Before he dies, all this futility will become evident to him. For all he counted on will disappear 33and fall to the ground like a withered grape. How little will come of his hopes! 34For the godless are barren: they can produce nothing truly good. God's fire consumes them with all their possessions. 35The only thing they can 'conceive' is sin, and their hearts give birth only to wickedness."

CHAPTER 16

Job's reply:

2"I have heard all this before. What miserable comforters all of you are. 3Won't you ever stop your flow of foolish words? What have I said that makes you speak so endlessly? 4But perhaps I'd sermonize the same as you—if you were I and I were you. I would spout off my criticisms against you and shake my head at you. 5But no! I would speak in such a way that it would help you. I would try to take away your grief.

6"But now my grief remains no matter how I defend myself; nor does it help if I refuse to speak. 7For God has ground me down and taken away my family. 8O God, you have turned me to skin and bones—as a proof, they say, of my sins. 9God hates me and angrily tears at my flesh; he has gnashed upon me with his teeth and watched to snuff out any sign of life. 10These 'comforters' have gaping jaws to swallow me; they slap my cheek. My enemies gather themselves against me. 11And God has delivered me over to sinners, into the hands of the wicked.

12"I was living quietly until he broke me apart. He has taken me by the neck and dashed me to pieces, then hung me up as his target. 13His archers surround me, letting fly their arrows, so that the ground is wet from my blood. 14Again and again he attacks me, running upon me like a giant. 15Here I sit in sackcloth; and have laid all hope in the dust. 16My eyes are red with weeping, and on my eyelids is the shadow of death.

17"Yet I am innocent, and my prayer is pure. 18O earth, do not conceal my blood. Let it protest on my behalf.

19"Yet even now the Witness to my innocence is there in heaven; my Advocate is there on high. 20My friends scoff at me, but I pour out my tears to God, 21pleading that he will listen as a man would listen to his neighbor. 22For all too soon I must go down that road from which I shall never return.

15:17-35 Eliphaz thought he had *the* explanation for Job's misery: Suffering was reserved for the ungodly. Job was a wicked man, charging at God with a shield of his own making. Why would Eliphaz speak so to Job? What made him think Job was wicked? We may be tempted to adopt Eliphaz's theory as long as things are going well for us. But when things get tough, and there is no clear cause for our suffering, his theory will no longer be a comfort. Hopefully we are not as callous about the pain of others as Eliphaz was. If we are, we will probably bring more harm than help to our friends.

16:1-5 Most of us have known "miserable comforters": those who give advice, those who offer solutions, those who lecture us concerning our failures and mistakes. They generally mean well, but they know little about comfort. Paul tells us that the comfort we offer should grow out of the wealth of comfort we have received from God (2 Corinthians 1:3-7). We should take note of the ways we have been comforted by God; this will help us as we seek to comfort the people we love.

16:18–17:2 How frightening death can be to those who are unaware of God's glorious hope. Job knew God. He even knew that God was his intercessor and friend. But the glory of eternity hadn't yet been revealed to God's people. Though we have God's Word, we, too, fear giving up our mortal body. This world is the home we know; eternity is the home that awaits us.

CHAPTER 17

"I am sick and near to death; the grave is ready to receive me. 2I am surrounded by mockers. I see them everywhere. 3,4Will no one anywhere confirm my innocence? But you, O God, have kept them back from understanding this. Oh, do not let them triumph. 5If they accept bribes to denounce their friends, their children shall go blind.

6"He has made me a mockery among the people; they spit in my face. 7My eyes are dim with weeping and I am but a shadow of my former self. 8Fair-minded men are astonished when they see me.

"Yet, finally, the innocent shall come out on top, above the godless; 9the righteous shall move onward and forward; those with pure hearts shall become stronger and stronger.

10"As for you—all of you please go away; for I do not find a wise man among you. 11My good days are in the past. My hopes have disappeared. My heart's desires are broken. 12They say that night is day and day is night; how they pervert the truth!

13,14"If I die, I go out into darkness, and call the grave my father, and the worm my mother and my sister. 15Where then is my hope? Can anyone find any? 16No, my hope will go down with me to the grave. We shall rest together in the dust!"

CHAPTER 18

The further reply of Bildad the Shuhite:

2"Who are you trying to fool? Speak some sense if you want us to answer! 3Have we become like animals to you, stupid and dumb? 4Just because you tear your clothes in anger, is this going to start an earthquake? Shall we all go and hide?

5"The truth remains that if you do not prosper, it is because you are wicked. And your bright flame shall be put out. 6There will be darkness in every home where there is wickedness.

7"The confident stride of the wicked man will be shortened; he will realize his failing strength. 8,9He walks into traps, and robbers will ambush him. 10There is a booby trap in every path he takes. 11He has good cause for fear—his enemy is close behind him!

12"His vigor is depleted by hunger; calamity stands ready to pounce upon him. 13His skin is eaten by disease. Death shall devour him. 14The wealth he trusted in shall reject him, and he shall be brought down to the King of Terrors. 15His home shall disappear beneath a fiery barrage of brimstone. 16He shall die from the roots up, and all his branches will be lopped off.

17"All memory of his existence will perish from the earth; no one will remember him. 18He will be driven out from the kingdom of light into darkness and chased out of the world. 19He will have neither son nor grandson left, nor any other relatives. 20Old and young alike will be horrified by his fate. 21Yes, that is what happens to sinners, to those rejecting God."

CHAPTER 19

The reply of Job:

2"How long are you going to trouble me, and try to break me with your words? 3Ten times now you have declared I am a sinner. Why aren't you ashamed to deal with me so harshly? 4And if indeed I was wrong, you have yet to prove it. 5You think yourselves so great? Then prove my guilt!

6"The fact of the matter is that God has overthrown me and caught me in his net. 7I scream for help and no one hears me. I shriek, but get no justice. 8God has blocked my path and turned my light to darkness. 9He has stripped me of my glory and removed the crown from my head. 10He has broken me down on every side, and I am done for. He has destroyed all hope. 11His fury burns against me; he counts me as an enemy. 12He sends his troops to surround my tent.

13"He has sent away my brothers and my friends. 14My relatives have failed me; my friends have all forsaken me. 15Those living in

---

17:3-12 Friends are often most supportive at the beginning of our tough times. It is later that they attempt to instruct or judge us. Sometimes they just disappear altogether. Job confronted the meaningless words of his accusers. Unlike his friends, Job offered no reasons for his pain. All he knew was that his heart was heavy, and his friends offered heartless words. If our friends provide us with no comfort, we should either ask them to leave, as Job did, or give them some direction as to how they can help.

18:1-21 We can all see Job's frustration as he longed for just a little comfort from his friends. Bildad wanted to know why Job offered speeches and why he regarded the words of his friends as stupid. The answer is fairly simple: Job's friends didn't know what they were talking about. We should never burden our suffering friends with unnecessary guilt. God is the only one in the position to judge. We should be a support to our friends in need.

my home, even my servants, regard me as a
stranger. I am like a foreigner to them. [16]I call
my servant, but he doesn't come; I even beg
him! [17]My own wife and brothers refuse to
recognize me. [18]Even young children despise
me. When I stand to speak, they mock.

[19]"My best friends abhor me. Those I loved
have turned against me. [20]I am skin and bones
and have escaped death by the skin of my
teeth.

[21]"Oh, my friends, pity me, for the angry
hand of God has touched me. [22]Why must
you persecute me as God does? Why aren't
you satisfied with my anguish? [23,24]Oh, that I
could write my plea with an iron pen in the
rock forever.

[25]"But as for me, I know that my Redeemer
lives, and that he will stand upon the earth at
last. [26]And I know that after this body has
decayed, this body shall see God! [27]Then he
will be on *my* side! Yes, I shall see him, not as
a stranger, but as a friend! What a glorious
hope!

[28]"How dare you go on persecuting me, as
though I were proven guilty? [29]I warn you,
you yourselves are in danger of punishment
for your attitude."

CHAPTER 20

The speech of Zophar the Naamathite:

[2]"I hasten to reply, for I have the answer for
you. [3]You have tried to make me feel ashamed
of myself for calling you a sinner, but my
spirit won't let me stop.

[4]"Don't you realize that ever since man was
first placed upon the earth, [5]the triumph of
the wicked has been short-lived, and the joy
of the godless but for a moment? [6]Though the
godless be proud as the heavens and walk
with his nose in the air, [7]yet he shall perish
forever, cast away like his own dung. Those
who knew him will wonder where he is gone.
[8]He will fade like a dream. [9]Neither his friends
nor his family will ever see him again.

[10]"His children shall beg from the poor,
their hard labor shall repay his debts.
[11]Though still a young man, his bones shall lie
in the dust.

[12]"He enjoyed the taste of his wickedness,
letting it melt in his mouth, [13]sipping it
slowly, lest it disappear.

[14]"But suddenly the food he has eaten turns
sour within him. [15]He will vomit the plunder
he gorged. God won't let him keep it down.
[16]It is like poison and death to him. [17]He shall
not enjoy the goods he stole; they will not be
butter and honey to him after all. [18]His labors
shall not be rewarded; wealth will give him no
joy. [19]For he has oppressed the poor and fore-
closed their homes; he will never recover.
[20]Though he was always greedy, now he has
nothing; of all the things he dreamed of—
none remain. [21]Because he stole at every opportunity, his prosperity shall not continue.

[22]"He shall run into trouble at the peak of
his powers; all the wicked shall destroy him.
[23]Just as he is about to fill his belly, God will
rain down wrath upon him. [24]He will be
chased and struck down. [25]The arrow is pulled
from his body—and the glittering point

19:23-27 Job's growth should encourage us as we struggle with our own pain. As we grieve over losses in this world, we learn to see the reality of eternity. Where once Job saw death as unrelenting darkness (see 10:20-22), here he gave testimony to a living Redeemer. His heart yearned for what he knew to be light and life. The Redeemer Job took comfort in is the one we now know as Jesus Christ. He is waiting to redeem us, just as he did Job. All we have to do is believe in him, and he will rescue us from eternal darkness.

19:28-29 If we live by judgment and condemnation, Job reminds us that we will die by the same. It is critical that we recognize grace. It is by grace that we are saved, and it is by grace that we live in this world. We need to remember that we will be judged by the measure with which we judge others (Matthew 7:1-5; James 2:12-13).

20:4-29 Imagine asking Zophar to paint a portrait of God. What images would we see? Zophar would probably paint an angry God in the act of dealing heavy blows against the ungodly. Where is the God who is patient and kind, compassionate and slow to anger? Where is the God whose love is unfailing? If we have any doubts as to God's compassion, we need only look to Christ. He gave his own life so that we could be forgiven and have fellowship with him. "Since [God] did not spare even his own Son for us but gave him up for us all, won't he also surely give us everything else?" (Romans 8:32).

21:1-21 Job refuted his friends' arguments by saying that the wicked succeed, have large families, great wealth, and long life. He said that "God skips them when he distributes his sorrows and anger." If there are exceptions to the assumptions of Job's friends, there are exceptions to the rule that the godly will not suffer. Of course we know that those who seem to get away with evil acts without judgment on earth will be judged in heaven. We should take comfort in the fact that though we may go through hardships here on earth, in heaven we will be soothed (see Luke 16:19-31).

comes out from his gall. The terrors of death
are upon him.
26"His treasures will be lost in deepest darkness. A raging fire will devour his goods, consuming all he has left. 27The heavens will
reveal his sins, and the earth will give testimony against him. 28His wealth will disappear
beneath the wrath of God. 29This is what
awaits the wicked man, for God prepares it for
him."

CHAPTER 21
Job's reply:
2,3"Listen to me; let me speak, and afterwards, mock on.
4"I am complaining about God, not man;
no wonder my spirit is so troubled. 5Look at
me in horror, and lay your hand upon your
mouth. 6Even I am frightened when I see
myself. Horror takes hold upon me and I
shudder.
7"The truth is that the wicked live on to a
good old age and become great and powerful.
8They live to see their children grow to maturity around them, and their grandchildren
too. 9Their homes are safe from every fear, and
God does not punish them. 10Their cattle are
productive, 11they have many happy children, 12,13they spend their time singing and
dancing. They are wealthy and need deny
themselves nothing; they are prosperous to
the end. 14All this despite the fact that they
ordered God away and wanted no part of him
and his ways.
15"'Who is Almighty God?' they scoff. 'Why
should we obey him? What good will it do
us?'
16"Look, everything the wicked touch has
turned to gold! But I refuse even to deal with
people like that. 17Yet the wicked get away
with it every time. They never have trouble,
and God skips them when he distributes his
sorrows and anger. 18Are they driven before
the wind like straw? Are they carried away by
the storm? Not at all!
19"'Well,' you say, 'at least God will punish
their children!' But I say that God should
punish the man who sins, not his children!
Let him feel the penalty himself. 20Yes, let him
be destroyed for his iniquity. Let him drink
deeply of the anger of the Almighty. 21For
when he is dead, then he will never again be
able to enjoy his family.
22"But who can rebuke God, the supreme
Judge? 23,24He destroys those who are healthy,
wealthy, fat, and prosperous; 25God also destroys those in deep and grinding poverty

Faith

READ JOB 19:8-27

When we experience pain and loss because of something that seems out of our control, we may feel like God is our enemy. The anger and confusion that result don't have to destroy our faith. We may never grasp why God allows such torment, but we can have faith that a time will come when we will understand his will for us.

Job felt this way, too. He said, "God has blocked my path and turned my light to darkness. He has stripped me of my glory and removed the crown from my head. He has broken me down on every side, and I am done for. He has destroyed all hope. His fury burns against me; he counts me as an enemy. He sends his troops to surround my tent. . . . My best friends abhor me. Those I loved have turned against me. I am skin and bones and have escaped death by the skin of my teeth. . . . Oh, that I could write my plea with an iron pen in the rock forever" (Job 19:8-24).

Despite Job's confusion and pain, however, he was able to conclude his complaint with a statement of his faith in God. He said, "But as for me, I know that my Redeemer lives, and that he will stand upon the earth at last. And I know that after this body has decayed, this body shall see God! Then he will be on *my* side! Yes, I shall see him, not as a stranger, but as a friend! What a glorious hope!" (Job 19:25-27). God is on our side, even if we can't see it right now. ***Turn to page 599, Psalm 8.***

who have never known anything good. [26]Both alike are buried in the same dust, both eaten by the same worms.

[27]"I know what you are going to say—[28]you will tell me of rich and wicked men who came to disaster because of their sins. [29]But I reply, Ask anyone who has been around and he can tell you the truth, [30-32]that the evil man is usually spared in the day of calamity and allowed to escape. No one rebukes him openly. No one repays him for what he has done. And an honor guard keeps watch at his grave. [33]A great funeral procession precedes and follows him as the soft earth covers him. [34]How can you comfort me when your whole premise is so wrong?"

CHAPTER 22

Another address from Eliphaz:

[2]"Is mere man of any worth to God? Even the wisest is of value only to himself! [3]Is it any pleasure to the Almighty if you are righteous? Would it be any gain to him if you were perfect? [4]Is it because you are good that he is punishing you? [5]Not at all! It is because of your wickedness! Your sins are endless!

[6]"For instance, you must have refused to loan money to needy friends unless they gave you all their clothing as a pledge—yes, you must have stripped them to the bone. [7]You must have refused water to the thirsty and bread to the starving. [8]But no doubt you gave men of importance anything they wanted and let the wealthy live wherever they chose. [9]You sent widows away without helping them and broke the arms of orphans.[10,11]That is why you are now surrounded by traps and sudden fears, and darkness and waves of horror.

[12]"God is so great—higher than the heavens, higher than the stars. [13]But you reply, 'That is why he can't see what I am doing! How can he judge through the thick darkness? [14]For thick clouds swirl about him so that he cannot see us. He is way up there, walking on the vault of heaven.'

[15,16]"Don't you realize that those treading the ancient paths of sin are snatched away in youth, and the foundations of their lives washed out forever? [17]For they said to God, 'Go away, God! What can you do for us?' [18](God forbid that I should say a thing like that.) Yet they forgot that he had filled their homes with good things. [19]And now the righteous shall see them destroyed; the innocent shall laugh the wicked to scorn. [20]'See,' they will say, 'the last of our enemies have been destroyed in the fire.'

[21]"Quit quarreling with God! Agree with him and you will have peace at last! His favor will surround you if you will only admit that you were wrong. [22]Listen to his instructions and store them in your heart. [23]If you return to God and put right all the wrong in your home, then you will be restored. [24]If you give up your lust for money and throw your gold away, [25]then the Almighty himself shall be your treasure; he will be your precious silver!

[26]"Then you will delight yourself in the Lord and look up to God. [27]You will pray to him, and he will hear you, and you will fulfill all your promises to him. [28]Whatever you wish will happen! And the light of heaven will shine upon the road ahead of you. [29]If you are attacked and knocked down, you will know that there is someone who will lift you up again. Yes, he will save the humble [30]and help even sinners by your pure hands."

CHAPTER 23

The reply of Job:

[2]"My complaint today is still a bitter one, and my punishment far more severe than my

---

21:22-26 Job examined the futility of this world's treasures firsthand. His discovery was simple: those who have known great prosperity meet the same end as those who have known poverty. All will die; all bodies will return to the dust; and the treasures we store up in this world meet the same fate. Earthly conditions don't matter all that much from an eternal perspective. We should store our treasures in heaven, not on earth (see Matthew 6:19-21).

22:1-10 Eliphaz made up a list of sins he was sure Job had committed at one time or another. It is easy for us to project our own sins on other people, claiming others to be guilty of the mistakes we have made. Eliphaz may have been guilty of these sins and perhaps was making himself feel better by condemning Job. We must be careful how we react to the problems or sins of others. Are we being honest with them? Are we using defense mechanisms to soothe our own guilt? If so, we need to stop denying our faults, confess our sins, and start down the road to recovery.

22:21-25 While Eliphaz's advice didn't apply to Job, it is clearly applicable to many of us. The pain we suffer as a consequence of our dependencies should tell us that our way of coping with life is not working. We may have tried living without God, but then we discovered that it led to disaster. All we need to do is give our life over to God, and he will help us in the process of recovery. We can find all we were searching for in God; he is our comfort, our hope, and our "treasure."

fault deserves. [3]Oh, that I knew where to find God—that I could go to his throne and talk with him there. [4,5]I would tell him all about my side of this argument, and listen to his reply, and understand what he wants. [6]Would he merely overpower me with his greatness? No, he would listen with sympathy. [7]Fair and honest men could reason with him and be acquitted by my Judge.

[8]"But I search in vain. I seek him here, I seek him there and cannot find him. [9]I seek him in his workshop in the North but cannot find him there; nor can I find him in the South; there, too, he hides himself. [10]But he knows every detail of what is happening to me; and when he has examined me, he will pronounce me completely innocent—as pure as solid gold!

[11]"I have stayed in God's paths, following his steps. I have not turned aside. [12]I have not refused his commandments but have enjoyed them more than my daily food. [13]Nevertheless, his mind concerning me remains unchanged, and who can turn him from his purposes? Whatever he wants to do, he does. [14]So he will do to me all he has planned, and there is more ahead.

[15]"No wonder I am so terrified in his presence. When I think of it, terror grips me. [16,17]God has given me a fainting heart; he, the Almighty, has terrified me with darkness all around me, thick, impenetrable darkness everywhere.

CHAPTER 24

"Why doesn't God open the court and listen to my case? Why must the godly wait for him in vain? [2]For a crime wave has engulfed us—landmarks are moved, flocks of sheep are stolen, [3]and even the donkeys of the poor and fatherless are taken. Poor widows must surrender the little they have as a pledge to get a loan. [4]The needy are kicked aside; they must get out of the way. [5]Like the wild donkeys in the desert, the poor must spend all their time just getting barely enough to keep soul and body together. They are sent into the desert to search for food for their children. [6]They eat what they find that grows wild and must even glean the vineyards of the wicked. [7]All night they lie naked in the cold, without clothing or covering. [8]They are wet with the showers of the mountains and live in caves for want of a home.

[9]"The wicked snatch fatherless children from their mother's breasts, and take a poor man's baby as a pledge before they will loan him any money or grain. [10]That is why they must go about naked, without clothing, and are forced to carry food while they are starving. [11]They are forced to press out the olive oil without tasting it and to tread out the grape juice as they suffer from thirst. [12]The bones of the dying cry from the city; the wounded cry for help; yet God does not respond to their moaning.

[13]"The wicked rebel against the light and are not acquainted with the right and the good. [14,15]They are murderers who rise in the early dawn to kill the poor and needy; at night they are thieves and adulterers, waiting for the twilight 'when no one will see me,' they say. They mask their faces so no one will know them. [16]They break into houses at night and sleep in the daytime—they are not acquainted with the light. [17]The black night is their morning; they ally themselves with the terrors of the darkness.

[18]"But how quickly they disappear from the face of the earth. Everything they own is cursed. They leave no property for their children. [19]Death consumes sinners as drought

---

23:1-17 Throughout his trials, Job was always honest about what he was thinking and feeling. Strong emotions are a natural part of our response to this life. In and of themselves they should not be labeled either "good" or "bad." We need to give our friends, our family, and our God the gift of honest expression. We should let them know how we feel and what we think. This will make us feel better, too. As we vent our emotions in positive ways, we will be set free from the tensions that build up inside us.

24:1-25 Why aren't the faithful rewarded or even protected? Why don't exploiters meet a speedy punishment? Where is God when we cry for help? As we face a momentous loss, we are often compelled to rediscover the foundations of our faith. Job probed the whole realm of God's justice, judgment, and timing and came to a humble conclusion: God's ways are just. We are often confused by his timing, but his ways are ultimately just.

24:22-25 Our need for security affects our decisions, attitudes, and actions every day. Each of us has a working definition of security, and we fear anything that threatens it. Job's entire foundation in this world had been shaken, and yet he learned an important lesson about security. Real security doesn't lie in what this world has to offer; it lies in the consistency, the justice, the faithfulness, and the overwhelming power and love of God.

and heat consume snow. [20]Even the sinner's own mother shall forget him. Worms shall feed sweetly on him. No one will remember him any more. For wicked men are broken like a tree in the storm.[21]For they have taken advantage of the childless who have no protecting sons. They refuse to help the needy widows.

[22,23]"Yet sometimes it seems as though God preserves the rich by his power and restores them to life when anyone else would die. God gives them confidence and strength, and helps them in many ways. [24]But though they are very great now, yet in a moment they shall be gone like all others, cut off like heads of grain. [25]Can anyone claim otherwise? Who can prove me a liar and claim that I am wrong?"

CHAPTER 25

The further reply of Bildad the Shuhite:

[2]"God is powerful and dreadful. He enforces peace in heaven. [3]Who is able to number his hosts of angels? And his light shines down on all the earth. [4]How can mere man stand before God and claim to be righteous? Who in all the earth can boast that he is clean? [5]God is so glorious that even the moon and stars are less than nothing as compared to him. [6]How much less is man, who is but a worm in his sight?"

CHAPTER 26

Job's reply:

[2]"What wonderful helpers you all are! And how you have encouraged me in my great need! [3]How you have enlightened my stupidity! What wise things you have said! [4]How did you ever think of all these brilliant comments?

[5,6]"The dead stand naked, trembling before God in the place where they go. [7]God stretches out heaven over empty space and hangs the earth upon nothing. [8]He wraps the rain in his thick clouds and the clouds, are not split by the weight. [9]He shrouds his throne with his clouds. [10]He sets a boundary for the ocean, yes, and a boundary for the day and for the night. [11]The pillars of heaven tremble at his rebuke. [12]And by his power the sea grows calm; he is skilled at crushing its pride! [13]The heavens are made beautiful by his Spirit; he pierces the swiftly gliding serpent.

[14]"These are some of the minor things he does, merely a whisper of his power. Who then can withstand his thunder?"

CHAPTER 27

Job's final defense:

[2]"I vow by the living God, who has taken away my rights, even the Almighty God who has embittered my soul, [3]that as long as I live, while I have breath from God, [4]my lips shall speak no evil, my tongue shall speak no lies. [5]I will never, never agree that you are right; until I die I will vow my innocence. [6]I am *not* a sinner—I repeat it again and again. My conscience is clear for as long as I live. [7]Those who declare otherwise are my wicked enemies. They are evil men.

[8]"But what hope has the godless when God cuts him off and takes away his life? [9]Will God listen to his cry when trouble comes upon him? [10]For he does not delight himself in the Almighty or pay any attention to God except in times of crisis.

[11]"I will teach you about God— [12]but really, I don't need to, for you yourselves know as much about him as I do; yet you are saying all these useless things to me.

[13]"This is the fate awaiting the wicked from the hand of the Almighty: [14]If he has a multi-

---

25:1-6 Bildad described a god who thought little of man, but that is not our God. We are made "wonderfully complex" (see Psalm 139:14), crowned with glory and honor (see Psalm 8:5), and fashioned in the image of a God who gives good gifts to his children (see Psalm 8). No matter how difficult life may be, we can count on God's love, commitment, patience, and compassion. We have great worth in God's eyes.

26:1-14 It is difficult for us to admit our powerlessness. We spend years building the illusion that we are in control, only to face events that make it clear that we have no control at all. This is the first step in our recovery from any dependency or compulsion. Job was powerless over his situation. We, too, are powerless over our dependencies and the circumstances that fuel them. But when we call on God for help, we will find he is merciful and willing to help us.

27:1-4 Job vowed here that he would not speak against God—yet he had suffered despite his innocence! Most of us readily denounce God as unjust, even when we are suffering the clear consequences of our actions. This is denial in its greatest form—insisting we have done nothing wrong and blaming our fair and merciful God. To recover successfully, we need to take inventory of our life and see where we have deviated from God's will. Then we need to submit to God's control and ask him to work with us to overcome our dependencies.

tude of children, it is so that they will die in
war or starve to death. 15 Those who survive
shall be brought down to the grave by disease
and plague, with no one to mourn them, not
even their wives.
16"The evil man may accumulate money
like dust, with closets jammed full of clothing—17yes, he may order them made by his
tailor, but the innocent shall wear that clothing and shall divide his silver among them.
18 Every house built by the wicked is as fragile
as a spider web, as full of cracks as a leafy
booth!
19"He goes to bed rich but wakes up to find
that all his wealth is gone. 20 Terror over-
whelms him, and he is blown away in the
storms of the night. 21The east wind carries
him away, and he is gone. It sweeps him into
eternity. 22For God shall hurl at him unspar-
ingly. He longs to flee from God. 23 Everyone
will cheer at his death and boo him into
eternity.

CHAPTER 28

"Men know how to mine silver and refine
gold, 2to dig iron from the earth and melt
copper from stone. 3,4Men know how to put
light into darkness so that a mine shaft can be
sunk into the earth, and the earth searched
and its deep secrets explored. Into the black
rock, shadowed by death, men descend on
ropes, swinging back and forth.
5"Men know how to obtain food from the
surface of the earth, while underneath there
is fire.
6"They know how to find sapphires and
gold dust—7treasures that no bird of prey can
see, no eagle's eye observe—8for they are deep
within the mines. No wild animal has ever
walked upon those treasures; no lion has set
his paw there. 9Men know how to tear apart
flinty rocks and how to overturn the roots of
mountains. 10They drill tunnels in the rocks
and lay bare precious stones. 11They dam up
streams of water and pan the gold.
12"But though men can do all these things,
they don't know where to find wisdom and
understanding. 13They not only don't know
how to get it, but, in fact, it is not to be found
among the living.
14"'It's not here,' the oceans say; and the
seas reply, 'Nor is it here.'
15"It cannot be bought for gold or silver,
16nor for all the gold of Ophir or precious
onyx stones or sapphires. 17Wisdom is far
more valuable than gold and glass. It cannot
be bought for jewels mounted in fine gold.
18Coral or crystal is worthless in trying to get
it; its price is far above rubies. 19Topaz from
Ethiopia cannot purchase it, nor even the
purest gold.
20"Then where can we get it? Where can it
be found? 21For it is hid from the eyes of all
mankind; even the sharp-eyed birds in the sky
cannot discover it.
22"But Destruction and Death speak of
knowing something about it! 23,24And God
surely knows where it is to be found, for he
looks throughout the whole earth, under all
the heavens. 25He makes the winds blow and
sets the boundaries of the oceans. 26He makes
the laws of the rain and a path for the lightning. 27He knows where wisdom is and declares it to all who will listen. He established
it and examined it thoroughly. 28And this is
what he says to all mankind: 'Look, to fear the
Lord is true wisdom; to forsake evil is real
understanding.'"

CHAPTER 29

Job continues:

2"Oh, for the years gone by when God took
care of me, 3when he lighted the way before
me and I walked safely through the darkness;

28:28 "To fear the Lord is true wisdom; to forsake evil is real understanding." This is God's message to man—that wisdom is only found in God and his ways. But how do we know what God expects of us? God has given us his truth in the Bible. We are responsible to study it and discover what he expects of us. We should ask God to show us his truth, and then take the time to listen. As God reveals his truth to us, he will give us the strength and encouragement we need to follow his program for recovery (see James 1:5).

29:1-3 Job found comfort in remembering the days when God took care of him. Those were days when Job felt secure. As hard as it is for us to believe, God continues to take care of us when we suffer. Even when the suffering is brought on by our own actions, he is there, waiting for us to call on him for deliverance.

29:4-17 Here we can almost see Job's countenance change as he recalled the joy of days gone by. A smile, a tear, a glow of remembrance all passed his face as the contentment of a godly life returned to his mind. Where once Job cursed his birth (see 3:1-26), he now remembered the good times. By reflecting on better times in our life, we can begin to feel hope again. We were happy once. If we trust God, we can be sure we will be happy again.

4yes, in my early years, when the friendship of God was felt in my home; 5when the Almighty was still with me and my children were around me; 6when my projects prospered and even the rock poured out streams of olive oil to me!

7"Those were the days when I went out to the city gate and took my place among the honored elders. 8The young saw me and stepped aside, and even the aged rose and stood up in respect at my coming. 9The princes stood in silence and laid their hands upon their mouths. 10The highest officials of the city stood in quietness. 11All rejoiced in what I said. All who saw me spoke well of me.

12"For I, as an honest judge, helped the poor in their need and the fatherless who had no one to help them. 13I helped those who were ready to perish, and they blessed me. And I caused the widows' hearts to sing for joy. 14All I did was just and honest, for righteousness was my clothing! 15I served as eyes for the blind and feet for the lame. 16I was as a father to the poor and saw to it that even strangers received a fair trial. 17I knocked out the fangs of the godless oppressors and made them drop their victims.

18"I thought, 'Surely I shall die quietly in my nest after a long, good life.' 19For everything I did prospered; the dew lay all night upon my fields and watered them. 20Fresh honors were constantly given me, and my abilities were constantly refreshed and renewed. 21Everyone listened to me and valued my advice, and were silent until I spoke. 22And after I spoke, they spoke no more, for my counsel satisfied them. 23They longed for me to speak as those in drought-time long for rain. They waited eagerly with open mouths. 24When they were discouraged, I smiled and that encouraged them and lightened their spirits. 25I told them what they should do and corrected them as their chief, or as a king instructs his army, and as one who comforts those who mourn.

CHAPTER 30

"But now those younger than I deride me—young men whose fathers are less than my dogs. 2Oh, they have strong backs all right, but they are useless, stupid fools. 3They are gaunt with famine and have been cast out into deserts and the wastelands, desolate and gloomy. 4They eat roots and leaves, 5having been driven from civilization. Men shouted after them as after thieves. 6So now they live in frightening ravines, and in caves, and among the rocks. 7They sound like animals among the bushes, huddling together for shelter beneath the nettles. 8These sons of theirs have also turned out to be fools, yes, children of no name, outcasts of civilization.

9"And now I have become the subject of their ribald song! I am a joke among *them!* 10*They* despise me and won't come near me, and don't mind spitting in my face. 11For God has placed my life in jeopardy. These young men, having humbled me, now cast off all restraint before me. 12This rabble trip me and lay traps in my path. 13They block my road and do everything they can to hasten my calamity, knowing full well that I have no one to help me. 14They come at me from all directions. They rush upon me when I am down.

15"I live in terror now. They hold me in contempt, and my prosperity has vanished as a cloud before a strong wind. 16My heart is broken. Depression haunts my days. 17My weary nights are filled with pain as though something were relentlessly gnawing at my bones. 18All night long I toss and turn, and my garments bind about me. 19God has thrown me into the mud. I have become as dust and ashes.

20"I cry to you, O God, but you don't answer me. I stand before you and you don't bother to look. 21You have become cruel toward me and persecute me with great power and effect. 22You throw me into the whirlwind and dissolve me in the storm. 23And I know that your purpose for me is death. 24I expected my fall to be broken, just as one who falls stretches out his hand or cries for help in his calamity.

29:18-19 Our life now may be very different from what we had hoped it would be. We certainly didn't plan on becoming addicted to anything. But even though we have failed to fulfill our youthful dreams, we don't have to give up hope. Once we admit we have the problem, things can still be fixed. But first we have to give our life over to God—only he can overcome the dependencies we face. It is never too late to get our life back on track.

30:20 As his suffering went on, Job began to feel certain that God wasn't listening. Yet Job hadn't given him the chance to answer. We, like Job, talk about God and even talk to God, but we don't stop long enough to let him talk to us. God speaks to us through his Word, the Bible, and through our times of prayer and meditation. We need to sit still and wait for God to speak to our heart.

[25]"And did I not weep for those in trouble? Wasn't I deeply grieved for the needy? [26]I therefore looked for good to come. Evil came instead. I waited for the light. Darkness came. [27]My heart is troubled and restless. Waves of affliction have come upon me. [28,29]I am black but not from sunburn. I stand up and cry to the assembly for help. [But I might as well save my breath,] for I am considered a brother to jackals and a companion to ostriches. [30]My skin is black and peeling. My bones burn with fever. [31]The voice of joy and gladness has turned to mourning.

CHAPTER 31

"I made a covenant with my eyes not to look with lust upon a girl. [2,3]I know full well that Almighty God above sends calamity on those who do. [4]He sees everything I do and every step I take.

[5]"If I have lied and deceived— [6]but God knows that I am innocent— [7,8]or if I have stepped off God's pathway, or if my heart has lusted for what my eyes have seen, or if I am guilty of any other sin, then let someone else reap the crops I have sown and let all that I have planted be rooted out.

[9]"Or if I have longed for another man's wife, [10]then may I die, and may my wife be in another man's home and someone else become her husband. [11]For lust is a shameful sin, a crime that should be punished. [12]It is a devastating fire that destroys to hell and would root out all I have planted.

[13]"If I have been unfair to my servants, [14]how could I face God? What could I say when he questioned me about it? [15]For God made me and made my servant too. He created us both.

[16]"If I have hurt the poor, or caused widows to weep, [17]or refused food to hungry orphans— [18](but we have always cared for orphans in our home, treating them as our own children)— [19,20]or if I have seen anyone freezing and not given him clothing or fleece from my sheep to keep him warm, [21]or if I have taken advantage of an orphan because I thought I could get away with it— [22]if I have done any of these things, then let my arm be torn from its socket! Let my shoulder be wrenched out of place! [23]Rather that than face the judgment sent by God; that I dread more than anything else. For if the majesty of God opposes me, what hope is there?

[24]"If I have put my trust in money, [25]if my happiness depends on wealth, [26]or if I have looked at the sun shining in the skies or the moon walking down her silver pathway [27]and my heart has been secretly enticed, and I have worshiped them by kissing my hand to them, [28]this, too, must be punished by the judges. For if I had done such things, it would mean that I denied the God of heaven.

[29]"If I have rejoiced at harm to an enemy— [30](but actually I have never cursed anyone nor asked for revenge)— [31]or if any of my servants have ever gone hungry— [32](actually I have never turned away even a stranger but have opened my doors to all)— [33]or if, like Adam, I have tried to hide my sins, [34]fearing the crowd and its contempt so that I refused to acknowledge my sin and do not go out of my way to help others— [35](oh, that there were someone who would listen to me and try to see my side of this argument. Look, I will sign my signature to my defense; now let the Almighty show me that I am wrong; let *him* approve the indictments made against me by my enemies. [36]I would treasure it like a crown. [37]Then I would tell him exactly what I have done and why, presenting my defense as one he listens to).

[38,39]"Or if my land accuses me because I stole the fruit it bears, or if I have murdered its owners to get their land for myself, [40]then let thistles grow on that land instead of wheat, and weeds instead of barley."

Job's words are ended.

CHAPTER 32

Elihu Becomes Angry and Speaks

The three men refused to reply further to Job because he kept insisting on his innocence.

[2]Then Elihu (son of Barachel, the Buzite, of the Clan of Ram) became angry because Job refused to admit he had sinned and to acknowledge that God had just cause for punishing him. [3]But he was also angry with Job's three friends because they had been unable to answer Job's arguments and yet had con-

31:35-36 Job wished that God would show him his failure. He was tired and wished desperately for some kind of resolution to his suffering. Job had already taken a critical inventory and had found no clear reason for his suffering. He wanted God to explain what was going on. He was open to any explanation, even the possibility of his own guilt. In recovery we need Job's attitude as we make our personal inventory. Realizing our need for change, we need to honestly examine our life, praying that God will reveal any wrongs we have committed.

demned him. 4Elihu had waited until now to speak because the others were older than he.

5But when he saw that they had no further reply, he spoke out angrily, 6and said, "I am young and you are old, so I held back and did not dare to tell you what I think, 7for those who are older are said to be wiser; 8,9but it is not mere age that makes men wise. Rather, it is the spirit in a man, the breath of the Almighty that makes him intelligent. 10So listen to me awhile and let me express my opinion.

11,12"I have waited all this time, listening very carefully to your arguments, but not one of them has convinced Job that he is a sinner or has proved that he is. 13And don't give me that line about 'only God can convince the sinner of his sin.' 14If Job had been arguing with me, I would not answer with that kind of logic!

15"You sit there baffled, with no further replies. 16Shall I then continue to wait when you are silent? 17No, I will give my answer too. 18For I am pent up and full of words, and the spirit within me urges me on. 19I am like a wine cask without a vent! My words are ready to burst out! 20I must speak to find relief, so let me give my answers. 21,22Don't insist that I be cautious lest I insult someone, and don't make me flatter anyone. Let me be frank lest God should strike me dead.

CHAPTER 33

"Please listen, Job, to what I have to say. 2I have begun to speak; now let me continue. 3I will speak the truth with all sincerity. 4For the Spirit of God has made me, and the breath of the Almighty gives me life. 5Don't hesitate to answer me if you can.

6"Look, I am the one you were wishing for, someone to stand between you and God and to be both his representative and yours. 7You need not be frightened of me. I am not some person of renown to make you nervous and afraid. I, too, am made of common clay.

8"You have said it in my hearing, yes, you've said it again and again— 9'I am pure, I am innocent; I have not sinned.' 10You say God is using a fine-toothed comb to try to find a single fault, and so to count you as his enemy. 11'And he puts my feet in the stocks,' you say, 'and watches every move I make.'

12"All right, here is my reply: In this very thing, you have sinned by speaking of God that way. For God is greater than man. 13Why should you fight against him just because he does not give account to you of what he does?

14"For God speaks again and again, 15in dreams, in visions of the night when deep sleep falls on men as they lie on their beds. 16He opens their ears in times like that and gives them wisdom and instruction, 17,18causing them to change their minds, and keeping them from pride, and warning them of the penalties of sin, and keeping them from falling into some trap.

19"Or God sends sickness and pain, even though no bone is broken, 20so that a man loses all taste and appetite for food and doesn't care for even the daintiest dessert. 21He becomes thin, mere skin and bones, 22and draws near to death.

23,24"But if a messenger from heaven is there to intercede for him as a friend, to show him what is right, then God pities him and says, 'Set him free. Do not make him die, for I have found a substitute.' 25Then his body will become as healthy as a child's, firm and youthful again. 26And when he prays to God, God will hear and answer and receive him with joy, and return him to his duties. 27And he will declare to his friends, 'I sinned, but God let me go. 28He did not let me die. I will go on living in the realm of light.'

29"Yes, God often does these things for man— 30brings back his soul from the pit, so that he may live in the light of the living. 31Mark this well, O Job. Listen to me, and let me say more. 32But if you have anything to say

---

32:6-20 There will always be people who think they have all the answers. They will give us reasons for our actions and condemn our life-style, and they will think that wisdom has been given to them alone. But we need to be careful about listening to these people. We need to consider: (1) Do they have our best interests at heart? (2) Do their words build us up or tear us down? (3) Is what they are saying from God? If any of these questions can be answered no, then they are not the people to help us with our recovery.

33:1-5 Elihu set himself up as someone with an upright heart who spoke sincerely, and yet he accused Job of being prideful for making the same claim (see 33:8-11). The sins we accuse others of are often the very sins we commit. This defense mechanism is called *projection*—we project our areas of weakness or sin onto others. As we begin to identify a particular fault in someone else, we need to ask, "Are we guilty of this, too?" If we hope to progress in recovery, we need to be honest, pinpointing the areas of denial in our own life.

at this point, go ahead. I want to hear it, for I
am anxious to justify you. [33]But if not, then
listen to me. Keep silence and I will teach you
wisdom!"

CHAPTER 34
Elihu continued:
[2]"Listen to me, you wise men. [3]We can
choose the sounds we want to listen to; we
can choose the taste we want in food, [4]and we
should choose to follow what is right. But first
of all we must define among ourselves what is
good. [5]For Job has said, 'I am innocent, but
God says I'm not. [6]I am called a liar, even
though I am innocent. I am horribly punished, even though I have not sinned.'
[7,8]"Who else is as arrogant as Job? He must
have spent much time with evil men, [9]for he
said, 'Why waste time trying to please God?'
[10]"Listen to me, you with understanding.
Surely everyone knows that *God doesn't sin!*
[11]Rather, he punishes the sinners. [12]There is no
truer statement than this: *God is never wicked
or unjust.* [13]He alone has authority over the
earth and dispenses justice for the world. [14]If
God were to withdraw his Spirit, [15]all life
would disappear and mankind would turn
again to dust.
[16]"Listen now and try to understand.
[17]Could God govern if he hated justice? Are
you going to condemn the Almighty Judge?
[18]Are you going to condemn this God who
says to kings and nobles, 'You are wicked and
unjust'? [19]For he doesn't care how great a man
may be, and doesn't pay any more attention
to the rich than to the poor. He made them
all. [20]In a moment they die, and at midnight
great and small shall suddenly pass away, removed by no human hand.
[21]"For God carefully watches the goings on
of all mankind; he sees them all. [22]No darkness is thick enough to hide evil men from his
eyes, [23]so there is no need to wait for some
great crime before a man is called before God
in judgment. [24]Without making a big issue
over it, God simply shatters the greatest of
men and puts others in their places. [25]He
watches what they do and in a single night he
overturns them, destroying them, [26]or openly
strikes them down as wicked men. [27]For they
turned aside from following him, [28]causing
the cry of the poor to come to the attention
of God. Yes, he hears the cries of those being
oppressed. [29,30]Yet when he chooses not to
speak, who can criticize? Again, he may prevent a vile man from ruling, thus saving a
nation from ruin, and he can depose an entire
nation just as easily.
[31]"Why don't people exclaim to their God,
'We have sinned, but we will stop'? [32]Or, 'We
know not what evil we have done; only tell
us, and we will cease at once.'
[33]"Must God tailor his justice to your demands? Must he change the order of the universe to suit your whims? The answer must be
obvious even to you! [34,35]Anyone even half
bright will agree with me that you, Job, are
speaking like a fool. [36]You should be given the
maximum penalty for the wicked way you
have talked about God. [37]For now you have
added rebellion, arrogance, and blasphemy to
your other sins."

CHAPTER 35
Elihu continued:
[2,3]"Do you think it is right for you to claim,
'I haven't sinned, but I'm no better off before
God than if I had'?
[4]"I will answer you and all your friends too.
[5]Look up there into the sky, high above you. [6]If
you sin, does that shake the heavens and knock
God from his throne? Even if you sin again and
again, what effect will it have upon him? [7]Or if
you are good, is this some great gift to him?
[8]Your sins may hurt another man, or your good
deeds may profit him. [9,10]The oppressed may
shriek beneath their wrongs and groan beneath
the power of the rich; yet none of them cry to

34:1-15 Elihu, like Job's other friends, believed that external circumstances are a measuring stick for the quality of a person's faith. If Job was suffering, then he clearly was getting what he deserved. In this case Elihu's assumptions were clearly wrong. Job's grief was not the consequence of a sinful past; it was a testimony to God's faith in his servant Job. As we face the temptation to revert to our dependencies, we might remember that the pain we suffer is a testimony to our faith and our desire to stay free from addiction. We need to remember that "no temptation is irresistible. You can trust God to keep the temptation from becoming so strong that you can't stand up against it" (1 Corinthians 10:13).

34:16-33 In a variety of ways, Elihu displayed his understanding of God. Elihu's God watches our actions, takes note of our deeds, and punishes us without need of further examination. This is not the God of the Bible. God looks at the heart, is endlessly patient, and is slow to anger and quick to forgive. No one can stand before Elihu's god and find mercy. But anyone who honestly submits to God through his Son, Jesus, will find mercy (see Psalm 130).

God, asking, 'Where is God my Maker who gives songs in the night [11]and makes us a little wiser than the animals and birds?'

[12]"But when anyone does cry out this question to him, he never replies by instant punishment of the tyrants. [13]But it is false to say he doesn't hear those cries; [14,15]and it is even more false to say that he doesn't see what is going on. He *does* bring about justice at last if you will only wait. But do you cry out against him because he does not instantly respond in anger? [16]Job, you have spoken like a fool."

CHAPTER 36

Elihu continued:

[2]"Let me go on and I will show you the truth of what I am saying. For I have not finished defending God! [3]I will give you many illustrations of the righteousness of my Maker. [4]I am telling you the honest truth, for I am a man of well-rounded knowledge.

[5]"God is almighty and yet does not despise anyone! And he is perfect in his understanding. [6]He does not reward the wicked with his blessings, but gives them their full share of punishment. [7]He does not ignore the good men but honors them by placing them upon eternal, kingly thrones. [8]If troubles come upon them and they are enslaved and afflicted, [9]then he takes the trouble to point out to them the reason, what they have done that is wrong, or how they have behaved proudly. [10]He helps them hear his instruction to turn away from their sin.

[11]"If they listen and obey him, then they will be blessed with prosperity throughout their lives. [12]If they won't listen to him, they shall perish in battle and die because of their lack of good sense. [13]But the godless reap his anger. They do not even return to him when he punishes them. [14]They die young after lives of dissipation and depravity. [15]He delivers by distress! This makes them listen to him!

[16]"How he wanted to lure you away from danger into a wide and pleasant valley and to prosper you there. [17]But you are too preoccupied with your imagined grievances against others. [18]Watch out! Don't let your anger at others lead you into scoffing at God! Don't let your suffering embitter you at the only one who can deliver you. [19]Do you really think that if you shout loudly enough against God, he will be ashamed and repent? Will this put an end to your chastisement?

[20]"Do not desire the nighttime, with its opportunities for crime. [21]Turn back from evil, for it was to prevent you from getting into a life of evil that God sent this suffering.

[22]"Look, God is all-powerful. Who is a teacher like him? [23]Who can say that what he does is absurd or evil? [24]Instead, glorify him for his mighty works for which he is so famous. [25]Everyone has seen these things from a distance.

[26]"God is so great that we cannot begin to know him. No one can begin to understand eternity. [27]He draws up the water vapor and then distills it into rain, [28]which the skies pour down. [29]Can anyone really understand the spreading of the clouds and the thunders within? [30]See how he spreads the lightning around him, and blankets the tops of the mountains. [31]By his fantastic powers in nature he punishes or blesses the people, giving them food in abundance. [32]He fills his hands with lightning bolts. He hurls each at its target. [33]We feel his presence in the thunder. Even the cattle know when a storm is coming.

CHAPTER 37

"My heart trembles at this. [2]Listen, listen to the thunder of his voice. [3]It rolls across the

---

35:1-16 When we are depressed we tend to speak as Job spoke here. And as we turn to God, displaying our raw emotions, God does hear. We have only to read Jeremiah, Lamentations, Psalms, and the words of Jesus as he approached his death to realize the emotional agony that goes hand in hand with suffering. God hears our complaints and cherishes our openness. It is only as we openly communicate with God that we can truly ask for his forgiveness and maintain an honest relationship with him.

36:5-12 The logic of man is very different from the logic of God. In our mind, justice is simple. When we are good, we should be rewarded. When we sin, we should be punished. When our enemy sins, he should be judged. Elihu spoke well of the majesty and glory of God (see 36:22-26), but he seemed to know little about God's true nature. God is willing to forgive all of us, no matter what we have done or who we are. If we feel we have failed too deeply to be forgiven, we should search the New Testament for people whom God has forgiven—adulterers, homosexuals, alcoholics, thieves (1 Corinthians 6:9-11). No one is ever beyond the reach of God's forgiveness.

37:1-24 God will soon deliver a speech similar to Elihu's, but the words will carry a much different connotation. God is the Creator, the Almighty One, but he is not beyond our reach. He has made himself available to us, even when we fall desperately short of his glorious ideals.

heavens and his lightning flashes out in every direction. [4]Afterwards comes the roaring of the thunder—the tremendous voice of his majesty. [5]His voice is glorious in the thunder. We cannot comprehend the greatness of his power. [6]For he directs the snow, the showers, and storm to fall upon the earth. [7]Man's work stops at such a time so that all men everywhere may recognize his power. [8]The wild animals hide in the rocks or in their dens.

[9]"From the south comes the rain; from the north, the cold. [10]God blows upon the rivers, and even the widest torrents freeze. [11]He loads the clouds with moisture, and they send forth his lightning. [12]The lightning bolts are directed by his hand and do whatever he commands throughout the earth. [13]He sends the storms as punishment or, in his loving-kindness, to encourage.

[14]"Listen, O Job, stop and consider the wonderful miracles of God. [15]Do you know how God controls all nature and causes the lightning to flash forth from the clouds? [16,17]Do you understand the balancing of the clouds with wonderful perfection and skill? Do you know why you become warm when the south wind is blowing and everything is still? [18]Can you spread out the gigantic mirror of the skies as he does?

[19,20]"You who think you know so much, teach the rest of us how we should approach God. For we are too dull to know! With your wisdom, would we then dare to approach him? Well, does a man wish to be swallowed alive? [21]For as we cannot look at the sun for its brightness when the winds have cleared away the clouds, [22]neither can we gaze at the terrible majesty of God breaking forth upon us from heaven, clothed in dazzling splendor. [23]We cannot imagine the power of the Almighty, and yet he is so just and merciful that he does not destroy us. [24]No wonder men everywhere fear him! For he is not impressed by the world's wisest men!"

CHAPTER 38

Then the Lord answered Job from the whirlwind:

[2]"Why are you using your ignorance to deny my providence? [3]Now get ready to fight, for I am going to demand some answers from you, and you must reply.

[4]"Where were you when I laid the foundations of the earth? Tell me, if you know so much. [5]Do you know how its dimensions were determined, and who did the surveying? [6,7]What supports its foundations, and who laid its cornerstone as the morning stars sang together and all the angels shouted for joy?

[8,9]"Who decreed the boundaries of the seas when they gushed from the depths? Who clothed them with clouds and thick darkness [10]and barred them by limiting their shores, [11]and said, 'Thus far and no farther shall you come, and here shall your proud waves stop!'?

[12]"Have you ever once commanded the morning to appear and caused the dawn to rise in the east? [13]Have you ever told the daylight to spread to the ends of the earth, to end the night's wickedness? [14]Have you ever robed the dawn in red, [15]and disturbed the haunts of wicked men, and stopped the arm raised to strike?

[16]"Have you explored the springs from which the seas come, or walked in the sources of their depths? [17,18]Has the location of the gates of Death been revealed to you? Do you realize the extent of the earth? Tell me about it if you know! [19]Where does the light come from, and how do you get there? Or tell me about the darkness. Where does it come from? [20]Can you find its boundaries, or go to its source? [21]But of course you know all this! For you were born before it was all created, and you are so very experienced!

[22,23]"Have you visited the treasuries of the snow, or seen where hail is made and stored? For I have reserved it for the time when I will need it in war. [24]Where is the path to the distribution point of light? Where is the home of the east wind? [25-27]Who dug the valleys for the torrents of rain? Who laid out the path for the lightning, causing the rain to fall upon the barren deserts, so that the parched and barren ground is satisfied with water and tender grass springs up?

[28]"Has the rain a father? Where does dew come from? [29]Who is the mother of the ice and frost? [30]For the water changes and turns to ice as hard as rock.

[31]"Can you hold back the stars? Can you restrain Orion or Pleiades? [32]Can you ensure the proper sequence of the seasons, or guide

38:2–39:30 God used a series of questions to illustrate how little Job knew about Creation and God's ways. If Job knew nothing of these mysteries, how could he know anything about God's character? All Job could do was worship and trust God. We, too, wonder why we suffer. We wonder why bad things happen to us and those we love. But we, like Job, are finite and cannot understand the ways of the infinite God. All we can do is praise him and await his deliverance.

the constellation of the Bear with her satel-
lites across the heavens? 33Do you know the
laws of the universe and how the heavens
influence the earth? 34Can you shout to the
clouds and make it rain? 35Can you make
lightning appear and cause it to strike as you
direct it?

36"Who gives intuition and instinct?
37,38Who is wise enough to number all the
clouds? Who can tilt the water jars of heaven,
when everything is dust and clods? 39,40Can
you stalk prey like a lioness, to satisfy the
young lions' appetites as they lie in their dens
or lie in wait in the jungle? 41Who provides for
the ravens when their young cry out to God
as they try to struggle up from their nest in
hunger?

CHAPTER 39

"Do you know how mountain goats give
birth? Have you ever seen them giving birth
to their young? 2,3Do you know how many
months of pregnancy they have before they
bow themselves to give birth to their young
and carry their burden no longer? 4Their
young grow up in the open field, then leave
their parents and return to them no more.

5"Who makes the wild donkeys wild? 6I
have placed them in the wilderness and given
them salt plains to live in. 7For they hate the
noise of the city and want no drivers shouting
at them! 8The mountain ranges are their pastureland; there they search for every blade of
grass.

9"Will the wild ox be your happy servant?
Will he stay beside your feeding crib? 10Can
you use a wild ox to plow with? Will he pull
the harrow for you? 11Because he is so strong,
will you trust him? Will you let him decide
where to work? 12Can you send him out to
bring in the grain from the threshing-floor?

13"The ostrich flaps her wings grandly but
has no true motherly love. 14She lays her eggs
on top of the earth, to warm them in the dust.
15She forgets that someone may step on them
and crush them, or the wild animals destroy
them. 16She ignores her young as though they
weren't her own and is unconcerned though
they die, 17for God has deprived her of wisdom. 18But whenever she jumps up to run, she
passes the swiftest horse with its rider.

19"Have you given the horse strength or
clothed his neck with a quivering mane?
20Have you made him able to leap forward like
a locust? His majestic snorting is something
to hear! 21-23He paws the earth and rejoices in
his strength, and when he goes to war, he is
unafraid and does not run away though the
arrows rattle against him, or the flashing
spear and javelin. 24Fiercely he paws the
ground and rushes forward into battle when
the trumpet blows. 25At the sound of the bugle
he shouts, 'Aha!' He smells the battle when far
away. He rejoices at the shouts of battle and
the roar of the captain's commands.

26"Do you know how a hawk soars and
spreads her wings to the south? 27Is it at your
command that the eagle rises high upon the
cliffs to make her nest? 28She lives upon the
cliffs, making her home in her mountain fortress. 29From there she spies her prey, from a
very great distance. 30Her nestlings gulp down
blood, for she goes wherever the slain are."

CHAPTER 40

The Lord went on:

2"Do you still want to argue with the Almighty? Or will you yield? Do you—God's
critic—have the answers?"

3*Then Job replied to God:*

4"I am nothing—how could I ever find the
answers? I lay my hand upon my mouth in
silence. 5I have said too much already."

6*Then the Lord spoke to Job again from the
whirlwind:*

7"Stand up like a man and brace yourself for
battle. Let me ask you a question, and give me
the answer. 8Are you going to discredit my
justice and condemn me so that you can say
you are right? 9Are you as strong as God, and
can you shout as loudly as he? 10All right then,
put on your robes of state, your majesty and
splendor. 11Give vent to your anger. Let it
overflow against the proud. 12Humiliate the
haughty with a glance; tread down the wicked
where they stand. 13Knock them into the dust,

40:1–41:34 God used the majesty and power of his creation to remind Job that God is the only one who can save. If Job could not even overpower created beings, such as the crocodile, how could Job save himself from the God who created the crocodile? Everything under heaven belongs to God, and that included Job. God never did give Job an explanation for his suffering; God only let Job know that he was ultimately in control. Likewise, we may be suffering unfairly because of an abusive family member or our codependency with an addict. We may never know why we have to go through the pain, but we need to realize that God is in control of our life. Our faith in him will be rewarded—if not in this life, then in the next.

stone-faced in death. 14If you can do that, then I'll agree with you that your own strength can save you.

15"Take a look at the hippopotamus! I made him, too, just as I made you! He eats grass like an ox. 16See his powerful loins and the muscles of his belly. 17His tail is as straight as a cedar. The sinews of his thighs are tightly knit together. 18His vertebrae lie straight as a tube of brass. His ribs are like iron bars. 19How ferocious he is among all of God's creation, so let whoever hopes to master him bring a sharp sword! 20The mountains offer their best food to him—the other wild animals on which he preys. 21He lies down under the lotus plants, hidden by the reeds, 22covered by their shade among the willows there beside the stream. 23He is not disturbed by raging rivers, not even when the swelling Jordan rushes down upon him. 24No one can catch him off guard or put a ring in his nose and lead him away.

CHAPTER 41

"Can you catch a crocodile with a hook and line? Or put a noose around his tongue? 2Can you tie him with a rope through the nose, or pierce his jaw with a spike? 3Will he beg you to desist or try to flatter you from your intentions? 4Will he agree to let you make him your slave for life? 5Can you make a pet of him like a bird, or give him to your little girls to play with? 6Do fishing partners sell him to the fishmongers? 7Will his hide be hurt by darts, or his head with a harpoon?

8"If you lay your hands upon him, you will long remember the battle that ensues and you will never try it again! 9No, it's useless to try to capture him. It is frightening even to think about it! 10No one dares to stir *him* up, let alone try to conquer him. And if no one can stand before *him,* who can stand before *me?* 11I owe no one anything. Everything under the heaven is mine.

12"I should mention, too, the tremendous strength in his limbs and throughout his enormous frame. 13Who can penetrate his hide, or who dares come within reach of his jaws? 14For his teeth are terrible. 15-17His overlapping scales are his pride, making a tight seal so no air can get between them, and nothing can penetrate.

18"When he sneezes, the sunlight sparkles like lightning across the vapor droplets. His eyes glow like sparks. 19Fire leaps from his mouth. 20Smoke flows from his nostrils, like steam from a boiling pot that is fired by dry rushes. 21Yes, his breath would kindle coals—flames leap from his mouth.

22"The tremendous strength in his neck strikes terror wherever he goes. 23His flesh is hard and firm, not soft and fat. 24His heart is hard as rock, just like a millstone. 25When he stands up, the strongest are afraid. Terror grips them. 26No sword can stop him, nor spear nor dart nor pointed shaft. 27,28Iron is nothing but straw to him, and brass is rotten wood. Arrows cannot make him flee. Slingstones are as ineffective as straw. 29Clubs do no good, and he laughs at the javelins hurled at him. 30His belly is covered with scales as sharp as shards; they tear up the ground as he drags through the mud.

31,32"He makes the water boil with his commotion. He churns the depths. He leaves a shining wake of froth behind him. One would think the sea was made of frost! 33There is nothing else so fearless anywhere on earth. 34Of all the beasts, he is the proudest—monarch of all that he sees."

CHAPTER 42

Then Job replied to God:

2"I know that you can do anything and that no one can stop you. 3You ask who it is who has so foolishly denied your providence. It is I. I was talking about things I knew nothing about and did not understand, things far too wonderful for me.

4"[You said,] 'Listen and I will speak! Let me put the questions to you! See if you can answer them!'

5"[But now I say,] 'I had heard about you before, but now I have seen you, 6and I loathe myself and repent in dust and ashes.'"

7*After the Lord had finished speaking with Job, he said to Eliphaz the Temanite:*

"I am angry with you and with your two friends, for you have not been right in what you have said about me, as my servant Job

42:1-6 Job ventured to answer God, and his reply was filled with gratitude. Where Job had once only heard about God, here he actually saw him—the loving, merciful, all-powerful, majestic Creator. This man, who was known as "blameless and upright" before his suffering, was now even greater because of that suffering. God is good: he gives us good gifts; he works good from all things; and his intentions for us are always good. Pain is a privilege when through it we grow closer to God (Philippians 1:29; 3:10).

was. [8]Now take seven young bulls and seven
rams and go to my servant Job and offer a
burnt offering for yourselves; and my servant Job will pray for you, and I will accept
his prayer on your behalf, and won't destroy you as I should because of your sin,
your failure to speak rightly concerning my
servant Job."

God Blesses Job Once Again

[9]So Eliphaz the Temanite, and Bildad the Shuhite, and Zophar the Naamathite did as the
Lord commanded them, and the Lord accepted Job's prayer on their behalf.[10]Then,
when Job prayed for his friends, the Lord
restored his wealth and happiness! In fact, the
Lord gave him twice as much as before!
[11]Then all of his brothers, sisters, and former
friends arrived and feasted with him in his
home, consoling him for all his sorrow and
comforting him because of all the trials the
Lord had brought upon him. And each of
them brought him a gift of money and a gold
ring.

[12]So the Lord blessed Job at the end of his
life more than at the beginning. For now he
had 14,000 sheep, 6,000 camels, 1,000 teams
of oxen, and 1,000 female donkeys.

[13,14]God also gave him seven more sons and
three more daughters.

These were the names of his daughters: Jemima, Kezia, Keren.

[15]And in all the land there were no other
girls as lovely as the daughters of Job; and
their father put them into his will along with
their brothers.

[16]Job lived 140 years after that, living to see
his grandchildren and great-grandchildren
too. [17]Then at last he died, an old, old man,
after living a long, good life.

42:7-9 How thankful Job's friends must have been that God was not going to deal with them according to their rules, but by grace. They spoke without wisdom and accuracy. They spoke from their fear. They made use of another man's weakness to bolster their own self-esteem. But Job prayed, and God forgave them. When we make mistakes, God is still waiting to forgive us and restore our fellowship with him. We shouldn't let our past actions and attitudes keep us from knowing the true God.

42:10-17 The fact that God restored and even doubled Job's wealth is incidental. Even if Job had continued in his pain, God would still be in control of the universe. And Job probably wouldn't have complained, recognizing that he would be rewarded when he died and went to be with God. We have the same promise. Whether our pain has been caused by our dependencies or by the dysfunctional people around us, God is controlling our life and will reward us in eternity if we submit to his plan. God's future blessings will be greater than anything we could ever imagine!

REFLECTIONS ON JOB

***insights** INTO SATAN'S ACTIVITY

In **Job 1:8-13** we find that God knew the hearts of his servant Job and of Satan, the accuser. The stage was set as God volunteered Job to be the one who would prove Satan wrong. How could God have used Job in this way? It seems somewhat cruel. Perhaps the answer lies in the way we understand suffering. We usually see suffering as an almost crippling tragedy. But for God, suffering is a pathway to maturity (see Romans 5:1-5; Job 42:1-5; James 1:2-4). God would use Job's suffering to bring even greater blessings and strength in the end. We can be sure that God is working his good in our life, even in the midst of our pain.

In **Job 2:4-6** Satan made a keen observation about the character of man. We may grieve when confronted by the loss of possessions, power, friends, or even family; but when confronted by physical illness, we curse God. It is sad to say that Satan has a point. It is difficult to maintain the proper perspective when we are physically afflicted. As we suffer the physical effects of addiction, we may feel that God hates us or that he is punishing us. We should be aware, however, that he may be using our pain to lead us away from our destructive life-style and into recovery.

insights ABOUT JOB'S RELATIONSHIP WITH GOD

We may never know how we'll respond to tragedy until we face it. From Job's response in **Job 1:20-22,** we learn why God labeled him to be "a good man who fears God and will have nothing to do with evil." Job chose to worship God, even in his grief. He chose to make an offering of faith at a time when he needed God the most. When we suffer a loss, praising God for his sovereignty and generosity in allowing us to have the possessions or loved ones for a period of time is often the last thing we feel like doing—but it is the proper response to God.

Job received some comfort from the fact that he hadn't disobeyed God. Even while he was in intense pain, we find in **Job 6:8-13** that he was concerned about his relationship with God. The opposite is often true with us: we suffer and no longer care about God or his laws. Our discouragement touches our spiritual life rather quickly, and the more pain we feel, the quicker we give up on God. But we see from Job that when we suffer, we should focus our thoughts on God, our only hope for salvation.

In **Job 13:14-19** we find Job arguing his case with God. He had confidence in his righteousness and decided to do something about his circumstances. God is never offended by our strong feelings. He welcomes the honest expression of our emotions as we seek to draw closer to him. We, too, must make the decision to do something about our circumstances. We can sit and wallow in our misery, or we can take a chance and try to change things. We would be wise to begin as Job did: with a heart-to-heart talk with God.

Job recognized in **Job 14:4** that no person can make himself pure. This statement reflects the very heart of God's message of grace. Who can make something pure out of something inherently impure? Only our gracious God, and he has done so through the death and resurrection of Jesus. Through him we are holy, just as God himself is holy.

insights ABOUT GIVING AND RECEIVING COMFORT

In **Job 2:11-13,** the three friends saw Job's pain from a distance and were overwhelmed. Then they gave him the best gift they had to offer—they wept and shared in his grief. When others are suffering, we feel that we have to say something comforting, sympathetic, or advisory. But what they may really need is for us just to be with them and experience their pain.

Eliphaz acted like God's prophet sent to straighten out Job's life. He claimed in **Job 5:1-7** to know more about Job than even Job knew! Not all of Eliphaz's words were false, but he spoke about things that he didn't fully understand. It is always easier to analyze than to empathize, because to feel empathy means to put ourself in the sufferer's position. This can be quite frightening—especially if our friend is suffering from something that could happen to us.

Eliphaz's testimony about God in **Job 5:18-26** was not incorrect, but it was insensitive. Job was not doubting God's sovereignty or faithfulness; he was simply mourning his loss. He had, after all, suddenly lost his children, as well as his wealth and health. We, like Job, need to grieve for a period of time. Grief is not an abnormal emotion; it is necessary if we are to move on with our life.

Job's frustration reached a breaking point in **Job 19:1-7.** His friends had repeatedly accused him of sin but had yet to prove any of it. Job knew in his heart that he was not being punished for some hidden, willful sin. He just wanted some comfort and understanding. Sufferers long to be understood. They need comfort, not judgment. We need to keep this in mind as we seek to help our friends who are grieving losses in their lives.

insights ABOUT GRIEF AND SUFFERING

Suffering has a way of stripping us of the protective shields we create to hide behind. As we openly display our pain, we can no longer pretend that things are all right. Job was grieving deeply in the account recorded in **Job 6:1-7.** He felt wounded by God and had no reason to pretend that his pain was not significant. When we can no longer hide our pain, we can talk about it. We can get our emotions out in the open where we can deal with them.

In **Job 11:1-6** Zophar made it clear that he didn't like Job's expressions of grief. To Zophar, Job's words were sacrilegious and unfaithful. God understands our grief. When people are hurting, God does not turn away their words or tears. Intimacy, brokenness, and honesty are part of the purpose for our pain. In those times when we are powerless over our circumstances, we need to give our life over to God's sovereign care. He will lead us out of the painful situations we face.

PSALMS

THE BIG PICTURE

A. PSALMS OF PREPARATION AND PROMISE (1–41)
B. PSALMS OF PETITION AND PRESERVATION (42–72)
C. PSALMS OF PROBLEMS AND POWER (73–89)
D. PSALMS OF PERIL AND PROTECTION (90–106)
E. PSALMS OF PERFECTION AND PRAISE (107–150)

It is impossible to adequately summarize the richness and breadth contained in the book of Psalms. It was Israel's hymnal, containing hymns of praise to God for personal and national salvation. It also contains the laments of God's people in difficult situations. It was Israel's prayer book. The psalmists looked to God in moments of private despair and times of national suffering. Amidst their difficulties they found release by lifting their heartfelt laments and praises to God.

The Psalms are for us, too. They are brimming with honest emotion. Through them we can pour out our anguish and adoration, our suffering and confession, our hopes and fears. Through some we may openly question God's actions or his apparent lack of action. Through others we might express our pain, heartache, and discouragement. Through still others we may praise God as he frees us from oppression and sin. Each psalm is an expression of the heart. None of them are neat little packages of answers tied up with pretty bows. They are living documents, a collection of spiritual diaries from people who honestly sought God's gracious help.

We will find that the Psalms may be read at many different levels depending on the problems we face. They may function as deterrents to keep us out of trouble, as guides to help us through our problems, as reminders of the one who actually delivers us, or as beacons of hope to encourage us in perplexing or painful situations. Through the Psalms we share in the hopes and failures of the entire human race. Yet, as we read them, we are also ushered into the very presence of our loving and merciful God.

THE BOTTOM LINE

PURPOSE: To demonstrate that God is holy and loving and intimately involved in every aspect of our human experience. AUTHORS: David wrote seventy-three psalms; Asaph wrote twelve; the sons of Korah wrote nine; Solomon wrote two; Heman (with the sons of Korah), Ethan, and Moses each wrote one; fifty-one psalms are anonymous. AUDIENCE: The people of Israel. DATE WRITTEN: The psalms were written between the years 1440 and 586 B.C. SETTING: Though the psalms are not generally concerned with recording history, many of them were inspired by historical events. KEY VERSE: "Let everything alive give praises to the Lord! *You* praise him! Hallelujah!" (150:6). KEY PLACE: The Temple in Jerusalem. KEY PEOPLE: David, Asaph, Solomon, Heman, the sons of Korah, Ethan, and Moses.

RECOVERY THEMES

Truth Brings Healing: Above everything else, the psalmists were honest about their experiences and feelings. Again and again they testified to God's faithfulness in hearing and responding to their words of honest confession or praise. It is so easy to try and hedge on the truth, even when we pray to God. This, however, is always a dead end. Only the truth can bring us into the kind of relationship with God that will result in our true healing. When we face the truth about our sins and failures and recognize that we are powerless over them, God will meet us where we are and guide us in the path of recovery and healing.

Legitimate Doubts and Complaints: Most of us act as if doubt is an unforgivable sin. We do everything we can to hide it from God. But God knows all about our doubts. The psalmists were honest about their doubts and brought them straight to God. They were also honest in their complaints. There is a place for complaining before God—it helps us grasp the truth about what is going on in our life. But just as the psalmists did, we will find that our complaining is followed by an affirmation of faith. If we hide our doubts about God, we will be sure to drift away from him. But if we honestly express them, even complaining about his apparent failures in our life, we will discover that our faith is renewed. As happened with the psalmists, our complaints will be followed by words of praise.

God's Power of Deliverance: We can count on the fact that God is all-powerful, and he always chooses to act at the best time possible. God is sovereign over every situation. The psalmists testify again and again that God is able to overcome the despair and pain in life, and that he is always in control. This kind of faith didn't come easily to them. They struggled with this truth, often questioning God's presence in their lives, just as we do. But in the end, their questions were always replaced by praises that affirmed the fact of God's powerful presence.

The Necessity of Forgiveness: Many of the psalms are intense prayers asking God for forgiveness. What the psalmists discovered was that they could be open and honest before God about their failures, emotions, and weaknesses, because God had promised to forgive them. As we experience God's forgiveness, we move away from our dependencies and feelings of alienation and guilt and move into an intimate and loving relationship with God. God's antidote to our past—no matter what our failures and sins—is always forgiveness!

PSALM 1
Oh, the joys of those who do not follow evil
men's advice, who do not hang around with
sinners, scoffing at the things of God. [2]But
they delight in doing everything God wants
them to, and day and night are always meditating on his laws and thinking about ways to
follow him more closely.
[3]They are like trees along a riverbank bearing luscious fruit each season without fail.
Their leaves shall never wither, and all they do
shall prosper.
[4]But for sinners, what a different story!
They blow away like chaff before the wind.
[5]They are not safe on Judgment Day; they
shall not stand among the godly.
[6]For the Lord watches over all the plans and
paths of godly men, but the paths of the
godless lead to doom.

PSALM 2
What fools the nations are to rage against the
Lord! How strange that men should try to
outwit God! [2]For a summit conference of the
nations has been called to plot against the
Lord and his Messiah, Christ the King.
[3]"Come, let us break his chains," they say,

1:1-6 Turning our will over to God means turning away from the kind of people who draw us into temptation. And there is no better source for wisdom and direction than the Word of God. When we fail to study and apply God's Word, we tend to drift through life. We are tossed around by every new fad or philosophy that comes our way. Recognizing our sins and being willing to change our sinful habits is the only way to avoid God's judgment. God wants to help us as we seek to live a godly life. But if we refuse to work on removing the character defects that hinder our recovery, we will certainly suffer the consequences.

2:1-6 If God is in charge of the world, why do we continually try to do things our own way? Here we are told that fighting God's program is a foolish thing to do. Many turn from God because they don't want to be his slave. But if we reject God's rule in our life, we will invariably become a slave to someone or something else. The foolish man, in rejecting God's rule, soon falls into a prison of sin and destructive habits. God shows us here how useless it is to challenge him. The only way we can be in tune with God's plan and receive his help is to accept his loving rule in our life.

"and free ourselves from all this slavery to
God."
4But God in heaven merely laughs! He is
amused by all their puny plans. 5And then in
fierce fury he rebukes them and fills them
with fear.
6For the Lord declares, "This is the King of
my choice, and I have enthroned him in
Jerusalem, my holy city."
7His chosen one replies, "I will reveal the
everlasting purposes of God, for the Lord has
said to me, 'You are my Son. This is your
Coronation Day. Today I am giving you your
glory.'" 8"Only ask and I will give you all the
nations of the world. 9Rule them with an iron
rod; smash them like clay pots!"
10O kings and rulers of the earth, listen
while there is time. 11Serve the Lord with
reverent fear; rejoice with trembling. 12Fall
down before his Son and kiss his feet before
his anger is roused and you perish. I am warning you—his wrath will soon begin. But oh,
the joys of those who put their trust in him!

PSALM 3
A Psalm of David when he fled
from his son Absalom
O Lord, so many are against me. So many seek
to harm me. I have so many enemies. 2So
many say that God will never help me. 3But
Lord, you are my shield, my glory, and my
only hope. You alone can lift my head, now
bowed in shame.
4I cried out to the Lord, and he heard me
from his Temple in Jerusalem. 5Then I lay
down and slept in peace and woke up safely,
for the Lord was watching over me. 6And now,
although ten thousand enemies surround me
on every side, I am not afraid. 7I will cry to
him, "Arise, O Lord! Save me, O my God!"
And he will slap them in the face, insulting
them and breaking off their teeth.
8For salvation comes from God. What joys
he gives to all his people.

PSALM 4
O God, you have declared me perfect in your
eyes; you have always cared for me in my
distress; now hear me as I call again. Have
mercy on me. Hear my prayer.
2The Lord God asks, "Sons of men, will you
forever turn my glory into shame by worshiping these silly idols, when every claim that's
made for them is false?"
3Mark this well: The Lord has set apart the
redeemed for himself. Therefore he will listen
to me and answer when I call to him. 4Stand
before the Lord in awe, and do not sin against
him. Lie quietly upon your bed in silent meditation. 5Put your trust in the Lord, and offer
him pleasing sacrifices.
6Many say that God will never help us.
Prove them wrong, O Lord, by letting the
light of your face shine down upon us. 7Yes,
the gladness you have given me is far greater
than their joys at harvest time as they gaze at
their bountiful crops. 8I will lie down in peace
and sleep, for though I am alone, O Lord, you
will keep me safe.

PSALM 5
O Lord, hear me praying; listen to my plea,
O God my King, for I will never pray to anyone but you. 3Each morning I will look to you
in heaven and lay my requests before you,
praying earnestly.
4I know you get no pleasure from wickedness and cannot tolerate the slightest sin.

3:1-4 Even David, a righteous man, recognized problems in his life that had become unmanageable. When we fail, even our friends sometimes begin to think we are beyond God's help. David, however, knew otherwise. He looked to God for help and encouragement. Calling out to God to increase our knowledge of him is one of the most important steps in the recovery process.
3:5-8 God comforted David so much that he could sleep like a baby in the face of his troubles. What is more, David's worries and anxieties vanished when he focused his thoughts fully on God. Thus David could view life as though all of his problems had been eliminated. By placing his problems in God's hands, David had made the most important step toward solving them. True deliverance and happiness come when we acknowledge God as our helper and the source of our strength.
4:4-5 Turning our will over to God is not a one-time experience; it is a moment-by-moment decision to keep our mind fixed on doing God's will. We don't sacrifice animals on an altar today in order to please God, but we can offer God our life as a living sacrifice. In order to do this, we must seek out and then follow God's plan for holy and healthy living.
4:6-8 Many of the people around us cannot see God at work in our life. They see only our past failures. But as we seek God and with his help make changes, our successful recovery will allow others to see God's power. True joy comes from God—a joy that is greater than all the gladness the world can produce. Nothing will bring us more peaceful nights of sleep than the knowledge that God is with us and helping us to progress in our recovery.

5Therefore, proud sinners will not survive
your searching gaze, for how you hate their
evil deeds. 6You will destroy them for their
lies; how you abhor all murder and deception.
7But as for me, I will come into your Temple
protected by your mercy and your love; I will
worship you with deepest awe.
8Lord, lead me as you promised me you
would; otherwise my enemies will conquer
me. Tell me clearly what to do, which way to
turn. 9For they cannot speak one truthful
word. Their hearts are filled to the brim with
wickedness. Their suggestions are full of the
stench of sin and death. Their tongues are
filled with flatteries to gain their wicked ends.
10O God, hold them responsible. Catch them
in their own traps; let them fall beneath the
weight of their own transgressions, for they
rebel against you.
11But make everyone rejoice who puts his
trust in you. Keep them shouting for joy because you are defending them. Fill all who
love you with your happiness. 12For you bless
the godly man, O Lord; you protect him with
your shield of love.

PSALM 6

No, Lord! Don't punish me in the heat of your
anger. 2Pity me, O Lord, for I am weak. Heal
me, for my body is sick, 3and I am upset and
disturbed. My mind is filled with apprehen-
sion and with gloom. Oh, restore me soon.
4Come, O Lord, and make me well. In your
kindness save me. 5For if I die, I cannot give
you glory by praising you before my friends.
6I am worn out with pain; every night my
pillow is wet with tears. 7My eyes are growing
old and dim with grief because of all my
enemies.
8Go, leave me now, you men of evil deeds,
for the Lord has heard my weeping 9and my
pleading. He will answer all my prayers. 10All
my enemies shall be suddenly dishonored,
terror-stricken, and disgraced. God will turn
them back in shame.

PSALM 7

I am depending on you, O Lord my God, to
save me from my persecutors. 2 Don't let them
pounce upon me as a lion would and maul me
and drag me away with no one to rescue
me.3It would be different, Lord, if I were doing
evil things— 4if I were paying back evil for
good or unjustly attacking those I dislike.
5Then it would be right for you to let my
enemies destroy me, crush me to the ground,
and trample my life in the dust.
6But Lord! Arise in anger against the anger

5:1-7 We have probably tried just about everything to escape our slavery to destructive habits. David understood how foolish it was to look for help from anything or anyone else but God. One by one, he brought his needs daily to God. David understood that God would not accept the prayers of one who was trusting in himself and continuing in his sin. Wherever we go, and whatever we are doing, when we trust God for help in our moment-by-moment walk of obedience, God's wall of protection surrounds us.

5:8-12 David requested God's guidance because he knew that God's plan for him was the only way to avoid the destructive traps he faced. Our old friends, like David's enemies, will tell us the big lie—that one more sin won't hurt us. Their words sound so good, but they prove by their own lives of slavery to sin that they are headed for destruction. In the midst of these snares of the world, however, protection can always be found by trusting in God.

6:1-5 Although we might want instant relief from the anguish of temptation, it doesn't usually come. But when we realize that we are powerless over our dependencies or compulsions, we have taken the first step toward recovery. Once we have acknowledged that God has the power to help us, we have taken the second step. Knowing about these important steps, however, is never enough to help us avoid destruction. We need to act on them, too.

6:6-10 Even though we may be suffering greatly, we can have confidence that God answers our prayers. God will always hear our petitions and rescue us. We should all be as bold as David is here, claiming victory immediately after finishing his prayer. Prayer should not be a last-ditch tactic; it should be the basis for our battle for recovery.

7:11-16 God is patient, but there is a limit to how long he will tolerate those who continue to rebel against him. When we choose to live in ways that stand counter to God's program, we will quickly discover that our problems only grow worse and worse. The plans we make to achieve personal success at the expense of others will destroy us in the end. We will only fall prey to our own schemes (see 9:15).

8:3-9 Many of our problems are rooted in our low self-esteem. Perhaps we were never listened to as children. Or maybe we were abused by people who had authority over us. Whatever the roots of our problems, we are now probably overly sensitive to the attacks of others. We see here that God has made us to be fantastic beings with great powers and privileges. We should never sell ourself short. Our self-esteem should be based on what God thinks of us—not what others say about us.

of my enemies. Awake! Demand justice for
me, Lord! 7,8Gather all peoples before you; sit
high above them, judging their sins. But justify me publicly; establish my honor and
truth before them all. 9End all wickedness,
O Lord, and bless all who truly worship God;
for you, the righteous God, look deep within
the hearts of men and examine all their motives and their thoughts.
10God is my shield; he will defend me. He
saves those whose hearts and lives are true
and right.
11God is a judge who is perfectly fair, and he
is angry with the wicked every day. 12Unless
they repent, he will sharpen his sword and
slay them.
He has bent and strung his bow 13and fitted
it with deadly arrows made from shafts of fire.
14The wicked man conceives an evil plot,
labors with its dark details, and brings to birth
his treachery and lies; 15let him fall into his
own trap. 16May the violence he plans for
others boomerang upon himself; let him die.
17Oh, how grateful and thankful I am to the
Lord because he is so good. I will sing praise
to the name of the Lord who is above all lords.

PSALM 8
O Lord our God, the majesty and glory of
your name fills all the earth and overflows the
heavens. 2You have taught the little children
to praise you perfectly. May their example
shame and silence your enemies!
3When I look up into the night skies and
see the work of your fingers—the moon and
the stars you have made— 4I cannot understand how you can bother with mere puny
man, to pay any attention to him!
5And yet you have made him only a little
lower than the angels and placed a crown of
glory and honor upon his head.
6You have put him in charge of everything
you made; everything is put under his authority: 7all sheep and oxen, and wild animals too,
8the birds and fish, and all the life in the sea.
9O Jehovah, our Lord, the majesty and glory
of your name fills the earth.

PSALM 9
O Lord, I will praise you with all my heart and
tell everyone about the marvelous things you
do. 2I will be glad, yes, filled with joy because
of you. I will sing your praises, O Lord God
above all gods.
3My enemies will fall back and perish in
your presence; 4you have vindicated me; you
have endorsed my work, declaring from your

Self-perception

READ PSALM 8:1-20

We develop our self-perception by noticing how the important people in our life see us. If we grew up in a dysfunctional family, their skewed view of us probably warped our ability to see ourself as we truly are in God's eyes. Understanding how God sees us and the value he has placed on us can help us overcome the negative self-perceptions that many of us have developed.

King David was amazed as he thought about how much God valued him. He said, "I cannot understand how you can bother with mere puny man, to pay any attention to him! And yet you have made him only a little lower than the angels, and placed a crown of glory and honor upon his head. You have put him in charge of everything you made; everything is put under his authority" (Psalm 8:4-6). "How precious it is, Lord, to realize that you are thinking about me constantly! I can't even count how many times a day your thoughts turn toward me. And when I waken in the morning, you are still thinking of me!" (Psalm 139:17-18). The greatest demonstration of how precious we are in God's sight is that Jesus gave his life for us.

God wants us to realize how precious we are to him and to begin to see ourself in the light of his love. Consider this: If God considered us worthy of giving up the most precious thing he had (his only Son), what does that say about our value? ***Turn to page 611, Psalm 32.***

throne that it is good. 5You have rebuked the nations and destroyed the wicked, blotting out their names forever and ever. 6O enemies of mine, you are doomed forever. The Lord will destroy your cities; even the memory of them will disappear.

7,8But the Lord lives on forever; he sits upon his throne to judge justly the nations of the world. 9All who are oppressed may come to him. He is a refuge for them in their times of trouble. 10All those who know your mercy, Lord, will count on you for help. For you have never yet forsaken those who trust in you.

11Oh, sing out your praises to the God who lives in Jerusalem. Tell the world about his unforgettable deeds. 12He who avenges murder has an open ear to those who cry to him for justice. He does not ignore the prayers of men in trouble when they call to him for help.

13And now, O Lord, have mercy on me; see how I suffer at the hands of those who hate me. Lord, snatch me back from the jaws of death. 14Save me, so that I can praise you publicly before all the people at Jerusalem's gates and rejoice that you have rescued me.

15The nations fall into the pitfalls they have dug for others; the trap they set has snapped on them. 16The Lord is famous for the way he punishes the wicked in their own snares!

17The wicked shall be sent away to hell; this is the fate of all the nations forgetting the Lord. 18For the needs of the needy shall not be ignored forever; the hopes of the poor shall not always be crushed.

19O Lord, arise and judge and punish the nations; don't let them defy you! 20Make them tremble in fear; put the nations in their place until at last they know they are but puny men.

PSALM 10

Lord, why are you standing aloof and far away? Why do you hide when I need you the most?

2Come and deal with all these proud and wicked men who viciously persecute the poor. Pour upon these men the evil they planned for others! 3For these men brag of all their evil lusts; they revile God and congratulate those the Lord abhors, whose only goal in life is money.

4These wicked men, so proud and haughty, seem to think that God is dead. They wouldn't think of looking for him! 5Yet there is success in everything they do, and their enemies fall before them. They do not see your punishment awaiting them. 6They boast that neither God nor man can ever keep them down—somehow they'll find a way!

7Their mouths are full of profanity and lies and fraud. They are always boasting of their evil plans. 8They lurk in dark alleys of the city and murder passersby. 9Like lions they crouch silently, waiting to pounce upon the poor. Like hunters they catch their victims in their traps. 10The unfortunate are overwhelmed by their superior strength and fall beneath their blows. 11"God isn't watching," they say to themselves; "he'll never know!"

12O Lord, arise! O God, crush them! Don't forget the poor or anyone else in need. 13Why do you let the wicked get away with this contempt for God? For they think that God will never call them to account. 14Lord, you see what they are doing. You have noted each evil act. You know what trouble and grief they have caused. Now punish them. O Lord, the poor man trusts himself to you; you are known as the helper of the helpless. 15Break

9:1-6 As we experience God's help and begin to change our life for the better, we have the responsibility to carry the message to others so their lives can be changed, too. As we allow God to help us remove the defects in our character, others will see what God has done for us and will receive the gift of hope. Our painful struggle with our addictions and compulsions can be a source of encouragement and guidance to others whose lives are headed toward destruction.

9:15-20 The people who set traps for others will ultimately be trapped themselves. God ensures that such people do not succeed in the long run. Those who realize they need God's help and turn to him will receive it; those who try to control their problems alone will ultimately fail. If we think we are in control of our own destiny and the destinies of others, we have a terrible surprise in store. One day God will step in and demonstrate who truly is in control. And since God is ultimately in control, the only wise plan to follow is God's plan.

10:1-11 God sometimes seems far away when temptation is strong. In truth, he is never far from us. Temptation sometimes becomes strongest when our friends seem to be able to do things without getting trapped the way we do. We tend to follow along and end up in trouble. We need to realize that even though our friends seem to be in control, they also are headed for trouble; they just don't recognize it yet. They may seem to be doing well, but this is only the way things appear. The truth is that they are probably in serious trouble. We need to make sure that the apparent success of others doesn't lead us away from God's program for healthy living.

the arms of these wicked men. Go after them until the last of them is destroyed.

[16]The Lord is King forever and forever. Those who follow other gods shall be swept from his land.

[17]Lord, you know the hopes of humble people. Surely you will hear their cries and comfort their hearts by helping them. [18]You will be with the orphans and all who are oppressed, so that mere earthly man will terrify them no longer.

PSALM 11

How dare you tell me, "Flee to the mountains for safety," when I am trusting in the Lord?

[2]For the wicked have strung their bows, drawn their arrows tight against the bowstrings, and aimed from ambush at the people of God. [3]"Law and order have collapsed," we are told. "What can the righteous do but flee?"

[4]But the Lord is still in his holy temple; he still rules from heaven. He closely watches everything that happens here on earth. [5]He puts the righteous and the wicked to the test; he hates those loving violence. [6]He will rain down fire and brimstone on the wicked and scorch them with his burning wind.

[7]For God is good, and he loves goodness; the godly shall see his face.

PSALM 12

Lord! Help! Godly men are fast disappearing. Where in all the world can dependable men be found? [2]Everyone deceives and flatters and lies. There is no sincerity left.

[3,4]But the Lord will not deal gently with people who act like that; he will destroy those proud liars who say, "We will lie to our hearts' content. Our lips are our own; who can stop us?"

[5]The Lord replies, "I will arise and defend the oppressed, the poor, the needy. I will rescue them as they have longed for me to do." [6]The Lord's promise is sure. He speaks no careless word; all he says is purest truth, like silver seven times refined. [7]O Lord, we know that you will forever preserve your own from the reach of evil men, [8]although they prowl on every side and vileness is praised throughout the land.

PSALM 13

How long will you forget me, Lord? Forever? How long will you look the other way when I am in need? [2]How long must I be hiding daily anguish in my heart? How long shall my enemy have the upper hand?

[3]Answer me, O Lord my God; give me light in my darkness lest I die. [4]Don't let my enemies say, "We have conquered him!" Don't let them gloat that I am down.

[5]But I will always trust in you and in your mercy and shall rejoice in your salvation. [6]I will sing to the Lord because he has blessed me so richly.

PSALM 14

That man is a fool who says to himself, "There is no God!" Anyone who talks like that is warped and evil and cannot really be a good person at all.

10:13-18 Even when it appears that God is blind to the evil deeds of others, we can be sure that one day he will respond with judgment. Those who drag others into sin will be judged harshly by God (see Luke 17:1-3). At times God works quietly behind the scenes, helping those who admit their helplessness to overcome the enemies and problems they face. When we humble ourselves and put our trust in God, we can have hope that one day God will give us a full recovery.

11:1-3 Security from temptation can be found in God; running elsewhere for help will never do any good. If we turn to some other resource for help, the people and problems that threaten to destroy us will lead us astray when we are most vulnerable. They will take advantage of us when the resource we depend on is unavailable. God is always with us. If we put our trust in him, we will have the means to overcome temptation.

12:5-8 We need not worry about the harm that liars may bring us. God has promised to protect us from those who try to destroy us. People make a grave mistake if they don't understand that God is not like us—his words are pure. He never deceives, nor does he ever fail to keep his promises. God has offered to surround us with help if we ask for it. If we really want to avoid tempting situations, God offers us his protection.

13:1-6 The recovery process is often long, with seemingly interminable stretches of spiritual barrenness. At times, we may be convinced that God has forgotten us completely. We may feel completely overwhelmed by our problems and baffled that God has done nothing to help. David began this psalm with feelings like these. But then he demonstrated a helpful way of dealing with the temptation to give in to feelings of discouragement. We can begin by turning our focus away from our problems and allowing God to dominate our vision. When we turn our thoughts to God, we will see that he is already at work in us to complete our recovery and to fill us with joy.

[2]The Lord looks down from heaven on all
mankind to see if there are any who are wise,
who want to please God. [3]But no, all have
strayed away; all are rotten with sin. Not one
is good, not one! [4]They eat my people like
bread and wouldn't think of praying! Don't
they really know any better?
[5]Terror shall grip them, for God is with
those who love him. [6]He is the refuge of the
poor and humble when evildoers are oppressing them. [7]Oh, that the time of their rescue
were already here, that God would come from
Zion now to save his people. What gladness
when the Lord has rescued Israel!

PSALM 15

Lord, who may go and find refuge and shelter
in your tabernacle up on your holy hill?
[2]Anyone who leads a blameless life and is
truly sincere. [3]Anyone who refuses to slander
others, does not listen to gossip, never harms
his neighbor, [4]speaks out against sin, criticizes
those committing it, commends the faithful
followers of the Lord, keeps a promise even if
it ruins him, [5]does not crush his debtors with
high interest rates, and refuses to testify
against the innocent despite the bribes offered him—such a man shall stand firm forever.

PSALM 16

Save me, O God, because I have come to you
for refuge. [2]I said to him, "You are my Lord; I
have no other help but yours." [3]I want the
company of the godly men and women in the
land; they are the true nobility. [4]Those choosing other gods shall all be filled with sorrow;
I will not offer the sacrifices they do or even
speak the names of their gods.
[5]The Lord himself is my inheritance, my
prize. He is my food and drink, my highest
joy! He guards all that is mine. [6]He sees that I
am given pleasant brooks and meadows as my
share! What a wonderful inheritance! [7]I will
bless the Lord who counsels me; he gives me
wisdom in the night. He tells me what to do.
[8]I am always thinking of the Lord; and because he is so near, I never need to stumble or to fall.
[9]Heart, body, and soul are filled with joy.
[10]For you will not leave me among the dead;
you will not allow your beloved one to rot in
the grave. [11]You have let me experience the
joys of life and the exquisite pleasures of your
own eternal presence.

PSALM 17

I am pleading for your help, O Lord; for I have
been honest and have done what is right, and
you must listen to my earnest cry! [2]Publicly
acquit me, Lord, for you are always fair. [3]You
have tested me and seen that I am good. You
have come even in the night and found nothing amiss and know that I have told the truth.
[4]I have followed your commands and have
not gone along with cruel and evil men. [5]My
feet have not slipped from your paths.
[6]Why am I praying like this? Because I

14:1-3 Our refusal to believe in God is the first step toward failure in recovery. Unless we can accept that there is a God who is concerned about us, there is no hope for us. The psalmist gave us a good term to describe the people who refuse to believe in God—fools. The world is filled with evil-minded fools, but we don't have to be like them. We prove we are not such a person by making the decision to turn our will over to God.

15:1-3 If we want to experience recovery, we must be committed to a life of honesty, integrity, and right living. We must quit lying to ourself and to others, and we must stop doing things that hurt other people. These are all essential elements of any effective personal inventory and necessary if we hope to bring reconciliation to our relationships.

16:1-6 Strength and security come from God alone; he is the only one who can restore us to sane living. We can often draw strength from others who are, like us, trying to find and do God's will. And as we recover, we can offer that strength to others. If we look to God as the source of our strength and joy, he will never disappoint us. People and other sources of pleasure will let us down, but God will not.

16:7-11 When we seek through prayer and meditation to improve our relationship with God, we will find in his Word not only peace of mind and heart, but also good counsel that will keep us from falling into sin. Knowing that God is with us and that he will never abandon us should be a constant source of joy and peace. An important principle for our recovery is the realization that God is with us—here and now—and he promises to be with us through all eternity as well.

17:1-5 Taking a careful personal inventory of our life is absolutely necessary for our recovery. If we refuse to examine our life, we will encounter numerous obstacles that will stand in the way of our program for recovery. When we learn to live as we should, we can have confidence that God will respond to our cries for help. We must follow through on our commitment by avoiding involvement with the people who draw us toward the evil things that have overwhelmed us in the past.

know you will answer me, O God! Yes, listen
as I pray. 7Show me your strong love in wonderful ways, O Savior of all those seeking your
help against their foes. 8Protect me as you
would the pupil of your eye; hide me in the
shadow of your wings as you hover over me.

9My enemies encircle me with murder in
their eyes. 10They are pitiless and arrogant.
Listen to their boasting. 11They close in upon
me and are ready to throw me to the ground.
12They are like lions eager to tear me apart, like
young lions hiding and waiting their chance.

13,14Lord, arise and stand against them. Push
them back! Come and save me from these
men of the world whose only concern is
earthly gain—these men whom you have
filled with your treasures so that their children and grandchildren are rich and prosperous.

15But as for me, my contentment is not in
wealth but in seeing you and knowing all is
well between us. And when I awake in
heaven, I will be fully satisfied, for I will see
you face to face.

PSALM 18

This song of David was written at a time
when the Lord had delivered him
from his many enemies, including Saul.

Lord, how I love you! For you have done such
tremendous things for me.

2The Lord is my fort where I can enter and
be safe; no one can follow me in and slay me.
He is a rugged mountain where I hide; he is
my Savior, a rock where none can reach me,
and a tower of safety. He is my shield. He is
like the strong horn of a mighty fighting bull.
3All I need to do is cry to him—oh, praise the
Lord—and I am saved from all my enemies!

4Death bound me with chains, and the
floods of ungodliness mounted a massive attack against me. 5Trapped and helpless, I
struggled against the ropes that drew me on
to death.

6In my distress I screamed to the Lord for
his help. And he heard me from heaven; my
cry reached his ears. 7Then the earth rocked
and reeled, and mountains shook and trembled. How they quaked! For he was angry.
8Fierce flames leaped from his mouth, setting
fire to the earth; smoke blew from his nostrils.
9He bent the heavens down and came to my
defense; thick darkness was beneath his feet.
10Mounted on a mighty angel, he sped swiftly
to my aid with wings of wind. 11He en-
shrouded himself with darkness, veiling his
approach with dense clouds dark as murky
waters. 12Suddenly the brilliance of his presence broke through the clouds with lightning
and a mighty storm of hail.

13The Lord thundered in the heavens; the
God above all gods has spoken—oh, the hailstones; oh, the fire! 14He flashed his fearful
arrows of lightning and routed all my enemies. See how they run! 15Then at your command, O Lord, the sea receded from the
shore. At the blast of your breath the depths
were laid bare.

16He reached down from heaven and took
me and drew me out of my great trials. He
rescued me from deep waters. 17He delivered
me from my strong enemy, from those who
hated me—I who was helpless in their hands.

18On the day when I was weakest, they
attacked. But the Lord held me steady. 19He
led me to a place of safety, for he delights in
me.

20The Lord rewarded me for doing right and
being pure. 21For I have followed his commands and have not sinned by turning back
from following him. 22I kept close watch on all
his laws; I did not refuse a single one. 23I did
my best to keep them all, holding myself back
from doing wrong. 24And so the Lord has paid
me with his blessings, for I have done what is
right, and I am pure of heart. This he knows,
for he watches my every step.

25Lord, how merciful you are to those who
are merciful. And you do not punish those
who run from evil. 26You give blessings to the
pure but pain to those who leave your paths.
27You deliver the humble but condemn the

18:6-15 God used very graphic language in these verses to show us how serious he is about helping those who turn to him for help. The psalmist knew that he would be delivered—not because he was strong or deserving of God's help, but because God loved him and was powerful enough to arouse all the forces of nature to help him. If God is on our side, no enemy is too great. We can always experience victory by depending on God's delivering hand.

18:16-19 When the psalmist realized his helplessness and turned his life over to the Lord, God came to his aid. Many of us know this truth as a theological principle, but now we are in the process of experiencing it in our own life. We also are given a clear warning in these verses. Our enemies or temptations always attack us when we are most vulnerable. A careful moral inventory will help us see just what our weaknesses are and when temptation will be most likely to attack. Then we need to evaluate the situations we encounter and decide which ones should be avoided.

proud and haughty ones. [28]You have turned
on my light! The Lord my God has made my
darkness turn to light. [29]Now in your strength
I can scale any wall, attack any troop.
[30]What a God he is! How perfect in every
way! All his promises prove true. He is a shield
for everyone who hides behind him. [31]For
who is God except our Lord? Who but he is as
a rock?
[32]He fills me with strength and protects me
wherever I go. [33]He gives me the surefooted-
ness of a mountain goat upon the crags. He
leads me safely along the top of the cliffs. [34]He
prepares me for battle and gives me strength
to draw an iron bow!
[35]You have given me your salvation as my
shield. Your right hand, O Lord, supports me;
your gentleness has made me great. [36]You
have made wide steps beneath my feet so that
I need never slip. [37]I chased my enemies; I
caught up with them and did not turn back
until all were conquered. [38]I pinned them to
the ground; all were helpless before me. I
placed my feet upon their necks. [39]For you
have armed me with strong armor for the
battle. My enemies quail before me and fall
defeated at my feet. [40]You made them turn
and run; I destroyed all who hated me. [41]They
shouted for help, but no one dared to rescue
them; they cried to the Lord, but he refused
to answer them. [42]So I crushed them fine as
dust and cast them to the wind. I threw them
away like sweepings from the floor. [43-45]You
gave me victory in every battle. The nations
came and served me. Even those I didn't
know before come now and bow before me.
Foreigners who have never seen me submit
instantly. They come trembling from their
strongholds.
[46]God is alive! Praise him who is the great
rock of protection. [47]He is the God who pays
back those who harm me and subdues the
nations before me.
[48]He rescues me from my enemies; he holds
me safely out of their reach and saves me from
these powerful opponents. [49]For this, O Lord,
I will praise you among the nations. [50]Many
times you have miraculously rescued me, the
king you appointed. You have been loving
and kind to me and will be to my descendants.

PSALM 19
The heavens are telling the glory of God; they
are a marvelous display of his craftsmanship.
[2]Day and night they keep on telling about
God. [3,4]Without a sound or word, silent in the
skies, their message reaches out to all the
world. The sun lives in the heavens where
God placed it [5]and moves out across the skies
as radiant as a bridegroom going to his wedding, or as joyous as an athlete looking forward to a race! [6]The sun crosses the heavens
from end to end, and nothing can hide from
its heat.
[7,8]God's laws are perfect. They protect us,
make us wise, and give us joy and light. [9]God's
laws are pure, eternal, just. [10]They are more
desirable than gold. They are sweeter than
honey dripping from a honeycomb. [11]For
they warn us away from harm and give success to those who obey them.
[12]But how can I ever know what sins are
lurking in my heart? Cleanse me from these
hidden faults. [13]And keep me from deliberate

18:37-42 The battle between us and our dependencies is one that we cannot fight alone. Although at times we may feel that our efforts are overcoming the things that cripple and destroy us, we soon realize that it is God who gives us the strength to fight the battle. Once we bring God into our battles, we begin to experience victory in the places where we were defeated in the past. God alone can guarantee a permanent victory.

18:43-50 The successes that God gives us can become a strong encouragement to others. In recovery we are called upon to share our victories with others. This may be all it takes to give them the courage to go on. They will see God's transforming power in our life and begin to hope that God can do the same for them. Because of who God is and what he does for us, we should constantly give him thanks and praise for the way he helps us. As we do this, we will also be carrying the message of his saving power and love to those who are listening.

19:1-6 No one can rightly say that they have never heard about God. His power can be seen throughout our physical world. Even the sun, though silent in the skies, declares every day what God has done. All humans benefit from the sun, and, whether they like it or not, they cannot hide from the message it declares to all the world. God is not a figment of our imagination. He is with us right now, and he desires to help us in our recovery.

19:7-11 Adhering to God's laws will produce wholeness in our life. Applying God's truth revives our inner being and gives insight—even to the least of us—into how we should live. His Word is not a burden that robs us of the good things of life (see Matthew 11:29-30). Instead, it transforms us, replacing our discouragement with joy.

wrongs; help me to stop doing them. Only then can I be free of guilt and innocent of some great crime.

14May my spoken words and unspoken thoughts be pleasing even to you, O Lord my Rock and my Redeemer.

PSALM 20

In your day of trouble, may the Lord be with you! May the God of Jacob keep you from all harm.2May he send you aid from his sanctuary in Zion. 3May he remember with pleasure the gifts you have given him, your sacrifices and burnt offerings. 4May he grant you your heart's desire and fulfill all your plans. 5May there be shouts of joy when we hear the news of your victory, flags flying with praise to God for all that he has done for you. May he answer all your prayers!

6"God save the king"—I know he does! He hears me from highest heaven and sends great victories. 7Some nations boast of armies and of weaponry, but our boast is in the Lord our God. 8Those nations will collapse and perish; we will arise to stand firm and sure!

9Give victory to our king, O Lord; oh, hear our prayer.

PSALM 21

How the king rejoices in your strength, O Lord! How he exults in your salvation. 2For you have given him his heart's desire, everything he asks you for!

3You welcomed him to the throne with success and prosperity. You set a royal crown of solid gold upon his head. 4He asked for a long, good life, and you have granted his request; the days of his life stretch on and on forever. 5You have given him fame and honor. You have clothed him with splendor and majesty. 6You have endowed him with eternal happiness. You have given him the unquenchable joy of your presence. 7And because the king trusts in the Lord, he will never stumble, never fall; for he depends upon the steadfast love of the God who is above all gods.

8Your hand, O Lord, will find your enemies, all who hate you. 9,10When you appear, they will be destroyed in the fierce fire of your presence. The Lord will destroy them and their children. 11For these men plot against you, Lord, but they cannot possibly succeed. 12They will turn and flee when they see your arrows aimed straight at them.

13Accept our praise, O Lord, for all your glorious power. We will write songs to celebrate your mighty acts!

PSALM 22

My God, my God, why have you forsaken me? Why do you refuse to help me or even to listen to my groans? 2Day and night I keep on weeping, crying for your help, but there is no reply— 3,4for *you are holy.*

The praises of our fathers surrounded your throne; they trusted you and you delivered them. 5You heard their cries for help and saved them; they were never disappointed when they sought your aid.

6But I am a worm, not a man, scorned and despised by my own people and by all mankind. 7Everyone who sees me mocks and sneers and shrugs. 8"Is this the one who rolled his burden on the Lord?" they laugh. "Is this

---

20:1-3 The psalmist counted on God's presence at all times to protect him, especially when his problems were most intense. If God could help Jacob, who was often in trouble, he can also protect all of us. Knowing we need his help, we must remain steadfast in our decision to turn our will and our life over to his care.

20:4-9 God is more than able to give us our greatest desires—even recovery from the consequences of our past mistakes (see Ephesians 3:20-21). Unlike those who trust in their own power to overcome their problems, we can place our trust in God. As a result, we have hope in the future because God is more than able to help us when we call out to him.

21:1-6 As we engage in a thorough evaluation of our life, we come to realize that our strength comes from God as we seek him through prayer and meditation. He wants to give each of us a life that has eternal value and meaning. As we experience such blessings, we will begin to understand that true joy is an outgrowth of being in God's presence. This should motivate us to spend time with God, seeking him through prayer and meditation. We need to draw close to him, not just for what he can do for us, but for who he is.

22:1-5 We all have experienced feelings of abandonment. The words in the first verse were repeated by Jesus Christ as he hung on the cross, indicating that even he experienced isolation from God the Father (see Matthew 27:46; Mark 15:34). When we feel cut off from God, we may be tempted to question God's existence or doubt that he is able to rescue us. At such times, we must rely not on feelings, but on facts. We must remember who God is and what he has done for us in the past.

the one who claims the Lord delights in him?
We'll believe it when we see God rescue him!"
9-11 Lord, how you have helped me before!
You took me safely from my mother's womb
and brought me through the years of infancy.
I have depended upon you since birth; you
have always been my God. Don't leave me
now, for trouble is near and no one else can
possibly help.
12 I am surrounded by fearsome enemies,
strong as the giant bulls from Bashan. 13 They
come at me with open jaws, like roaring lions
attacking their prey. 14 My strength has
drained away like water, and all my bones are
out of joint. My heart melts like wax; 15 my
strength has dried up like sun-baked clay; my
tongue sticks to my mouth, for you have laid
me in the dust of death. 16 The enemy, this
gang of evil men, circles me like a pack of
dogs; they have pierced my hands and feet. 17 I
can count every bone in my body. See these
men of evil gloat and stare; 18 they divide my
clothes among themselves by a toss of the
dice.
19 O Lord, don't stay away. O God my
Strength, hurry to my aid. 20 Rescue me from
death; spare my precious life from all these
evil men. 21 Save me from these lions' jaws and
from the horns of these wild oxen. Yes, God
will answer me and rescue me.
22 I will praise you to all my brothers; I will
stand up before the congregation and testify
of the wonderful things you have done.
23 "Praise the Lord, each one of you who fears
him," I will say. "Each of you must fear and
reverence his name. Let all Israel sing his
praises, 24 for he has not despised my cries of
deep despair; he has not turned and walked
away. When I cried to him, he heard and
came."
25 Yes, I will stand and praise you before all
the people. I will publicly fulfill my vows in
the presence of all who reverence your name.
26 The poor shall eat and be satisfied; all who
seek the Lord shall find him and shall praise
his name. Their hearts shall rejoice with everlasting joy. 27 The whole earth shall see it and
return to the Lord; the people of every nation
shall worship him.
28 For the Lord is King and rules the nations.
29 Both proud and humble together, all who
are mortal—born to die—shall worship him.
30 Our children too shall serve him, for they
shall hear from us about the wonders of the
Lord; 31 generations yet unborn shall hear of
all the miracles he did for us.

PSALM 23

Because the Lord is my Shepherd, I have
everything I need!
2,3 He lets me rest in the meadow grass and
leads me beside the quiet streams. He gives
me new strength. He helps me do what honors him the most.
4 Even when walking through the dark valley of death I will not be afraid, for you are
close beside me, guarding, guiding all the
way.
5 You provide delicious food for me in the
presence of my enemies. You have welcomed
me as your guest; blessings overflow!
6 Your goodness and unfailing kindness
shall be with me all of my life, and afterwards
I will live with you forever in your home.

PSALM 24

The earth belongs to God! Everything in all
the world is his! 2 He is the one who pushed
the oceans back to let dry land appear.
3 Who may climb the mountain of the Lord
and enter where he lives? Who may stand
before the Lord? 4 Only those with pure hands
and hearts, who do not practice dishonesty

22:6-11 When things aren't going well, we may experience low self-esteem, feeling like a "worm." But God cares for us and will help us. Others may mock us, doubting that God can really save us. We should ignore these people because we know God is there to rescue us. He has helped before, ever since birth, and he will surely help us now.

22:12-21 For many of us, these verses describe the results of our addictions. People may torment us, making fun of our problem. The physical pain here reminds us of the effects of drugs or alcohol, or the symptoms of withdrawal. When we seek recovery, we have the help of a God who understands our pain. Jesus Christ experienced these same conditions during his earthly life; he had to face death. He was surrounded, crucified, gawked at, and stripped of his dignity. Jesus knows how we feel, and he is with us through each step in the recovery process.

23:1-6 God is our Shepherd, and he knows what we need better than even we do. God wants us to have what is best for us. As long as we make him our Shepherd, he will be able to lead us to places of safety. He knows how to direct us away from places where we will be tempted to stumble. Even when we fall, he can deliver us from our pain and suffering. God will help us avoid the places where we have stumbled in the past and guide as we make the journey toward recovery.

and lying. 5They will receive God's own goodness as their blessing from him, planted in their lives by God himself, their Savior. 6These are the ones who are allowed to stand before the Lord and worship the God of Jacob.

7Open up, O ancient gates, and let the King of Glory in. 8Who is this King of Glory? The Lord, strong and mighty, invincible in battle. 9Yes, open wide the gates and let the King of Glory in.

10Who is this King of Glory? The Commander of all of heaven's armies!

PSALM 25

To you, O Lord, I pray. 2Don't fail me, Lord, for I am trusting you. Don't let my enemies succeed. Don't give them victory over me. 3None of those who have faith in God will ever be disgraced for trusting him. But all who harm the innocent shall be defeated.

4Show me the path where I should go, O Lord; point out the right road for me to walk. 5Lead me; teach me; for you are the God who gives me salvation. I have no hope except in you. 6,7Overlook my youthful sins, O Lord! Look at me instead through eyes of mercy and forgiveness, through eyes of everlasting love and kindness.

8The Lord is good and glad to teach the proper path to all who go astray; 9he will teach the ways that are right and best to those who humbly turn to him. 10And when we obey him, every path he guides us on is fragrant with his loving-kindness and his truth.

11But Lord, my sins! How many they are. Oh, pardon them for the honor of your name.

12Where is the man who fears the Lord? God will teach him how to choose the best.

13He shall live within God's circle of blessing, and his children shall inherit the earth.

14Friendship with God is reserved for those who reverence him. With them alone he shares the secrets of his promises.

15My eyes are ever looking to the Lord for help, for he alone can rescue me. 16Come, Lord, and show me your mercy, for I am helpless, overwhelmed, in deep distress; 17my problems go from bad to worse. Oh, save me from them all! 18See my sorrows; feel my pain; forgive my sins. 19See how many enemies I have and how viciously they hate me! 20Save me from them! Deliver my life from their power! Oh, let it never be said that I trusted you in vain!

21Assign me Godliness and Integrity as my bodyguards, for I expect you to protect me 22and to ransom Israel from all her troubles.

PSALM 26

Dismiss all the charges against me, Lord, for I have tried to keep your laws and have trusted you without wavering. 2Cross-examine me, O Lord, and see that this is so; test my motives and affections too. 3For I have taken your loving-kindness and your truth as my ideals.4I do not have fellowship with tricky, two-faced men; they are false and hypocritical. 5I hate the sinners' hangouts and refuse to enter them. 6I wash my hands to prove my innocence and come before your altar, 7singing a song of thanksgiving and telling about your miracles.

8Lord, I love your home, this shrine where

24:1-2 Some of us may feel that there is no power great enough to deliver us from the terrible circumstances we have fallen into. In these verses, however, we are shown a God who has enough power to control the entire universe. And we know from his Word that God desires to support us in our recovery from sin and its terrible consequences. God is more than able to overcome our dependencies and lead us to a new life of freedom. All we need to do is bring our failures to him and ask him to help us remove our defects of character.

25:1-7 When we place our faith in God, we can trust him to care for us and to help us overcome the things in our life that would destroy us. We need to ask him to show us how to live according to his will and to forgive our past mistakes. While forgiveness for our sins is important, it is also important for us to forgive others who have harmed us. When we forgive others, we can get rid of our feelings of anger and focus on our own recovery.

25:8-10 We need to let God change us, yet we cannot expect him to work his transformation in our life if we are still proud and unwilling to admit that we are helpless apart from him. The first step in recovery is admitting that we are powerless over our dependencies. Only after we do this can we experience God's healing work in our life.

26:1-7 Even as we stumble, we must keep trying to live an honest and open life, doing all we can to discover and fulfill God's will for us. We don't have to fear God's judgment, since he loves us—even with all our faults. As we seek God's will for us we also need to avoid the activities and people that will lead us back into our destructive life-style. Nothing good can come from trying to associate with the people who formerly dragged us down. We also need to be careful to avoid the situations that will lead to temptation and an eventual fall.

the brilliant, dazzling splendor of your presence lives.

9,10 Don't treat me as a common sinner or murderer who plots against the innocent and demands bribes.

11 No, I am not like that, O Lord; I try to walk a straight and narrow path of doing what is right; therefore in mercy save me.

12 I publicly praise the Lord for keeping me from slipping and falling.

PSALM 27

The Lord is my light and my salvation; he protects me from danger—whom shall I fear? 2 When evil men come to destroy me, they will stumble and fall! 3 Yes, though a mighty army marches against me, my heart shall know no fear! I am confident that God will save me.

4 The one thing I want from God, the thing I seek most of all, is the privilege of meditating in his Temple, living in his presence every day of my life, delighting in his incomparable perfections and glory. 5 There I'll be when troubles come. He will hide me. He will set me on a high rock 6 out of reach of all my enemies. Then I will bring him sacrifices and sing his praises with much joy.

7 Listen to my pleading, Lord! Be merciful and send the help I need.

8 My heart has heard you say, "Come and talk with me, O my people." And my heart responds, "Lord, I am coming."

9 Oh, do not hide yourself when I am trying to find you. Do not angrily reject your servant. You have been my help in all my trials before; don't leave me now. Don't forsake me, O God of my salvation. 10 For if my father and mother should abandon me, you would welcome and comfort me.

11 Tell me what to do, O Lord, and make it plain because I am surrounded by waiting enemies. 12 Don't let them get me, Lord! Don't let me fall into their hands! For they accuse me of things I never did, and all the while are plotting cruelty. 13 I am expecting the Lord to rescue me again, so that once again I will see his goodness to me here in the land of the living.

14 Don't be impatient. Wait for the Lord, and he will come and save you! Be brave, stouthearted, and courageous. Yes, wait and he will help you.

PSALM 28

I plead with you to help me, Lord, for you are my Rock of safety. If you refuse to answer me, I might as well give up and die. 2 Lord, I lift my hands to heaven and implore your help. Oh, listen to my cry.

3 Don't punish me with all the wicked ones who speak so sweetly to their neighbors while planning to murder them. 4 Give them the punishment they so richly deserve! Measure it out to them in proportion to their wickedness; pay them back for all their evil deeds. 5 They care nothing for God or what he has

---

27:11-14 Because temptations are pressing in around us, we need more than ever to learn how God wants us to act in the midst of such troubles. He wants to become the stabilizing factor in our life. Apart from him we have no power against the things that once put us in bondage. We must determine, one day at a time, to follow God, patiently and confidently waiting for him to protect and lead us.

28:1-5 The decision to turn our life over to God for his care is an important step in recovery. We won't find the answers to life's problems anywhere else. The best way to avoid the judgment that will fall on those who lead others astray is to stay away from them. If we don't avoid the people and situations of our past failures, we will almost always get trapped by the same old mistakes and dependencies.

28:6-9 God expects us to do our part in recovery, but we know that only he can empower us to stand against the pressures that seem to drive us back into our old ways. Knowing that God is on our side and will give us victory over our bad habits should be a source of great joy and encouragement. Even when we feel we are powerless and can't go on, God is waiting for us to run into his open and powerful arms.

29:1-9 In this psalm, we are reminded of God's great power over the natural world. Yet even though his power is greater than any words can describe, he knows and loves each one of us. As we realize how powerless we are over the problems we face, the truth about God's power, along with his personal concern for us, should make us more confident and willing to turn our life and will over to him. He is the only one able and willing to help us.

30:1-5 What joy and gratitude we feel when God picks us up and does not allow our problems to defeat or destroy us! One of the hard lessons to learn during recovery is how to delay our gratification. We must go through some long, dark nights struggling with temptation before we experience the joy of victory. But when we do finally overcome, the joy of success will only be that much sweeter.

done or what he has made; therefore God will
dismantle them like old buildings, never to be
rebuilt again.
6Oh, praise the Lord, for he has listened to
my pleadings! 7He is my strength, my shield
from every danger. I trusted in him, and he
helped me. Joy rises in my heart until I burst
out in songs of praise to him. 8The Lord protects his people and gives victory to his
anointed king.
9Defend your people, Lord; defend and
bless your chosen ones. Lead them like a
shepherd and carry them forever in your
arms.

PSALM 29
Praise the Lord, you angels of his; praise his
glory and his strength. 2Praise him for his
majestic glory, the glory of his name. Come
before him clothed in sacred garments.
3The voice of the Lord echoes from the
clouds. The God of glory thunders through
the skies. 4So powerful is his voice; so full of
majesty. 5,6It breaks down the cedars. It splits
the giant trees of Lebanon. It shakes Mount
Lebanon and Mount Sirion. They leap and
skip before him like young calves! 7The voice
of the Lord thunders through the lightning.
8It resounds through the deserts and shakes
the wilderness of Kadesh. 9The voice of the
Lord spins and topples the mighty oaks. It
strips the forests bare. They whirl and sway
beneath the blast. But in his temple all are
praising, "Glory, glory to the Lord."
10At the Flood the Lord showed his control
of all creation. Now he continues to unveil his
power. 11He will give his people strength. He
will bless them with peace.

PSALM 30
I will praise you, Lord, for you have saved me
from my enemies. You refuse to let them
triumph over me. 2O Lord my God, I pleaded
with you, and you gave me my health again.
3You brought me back from the brink of the
grave, from death itself, and here I am alive!
4Oh, sing to him you saints of his; give
thanks to his holy name. 5His anger lasts a
moment; his favor lasts for life! Weeping may
go on all night, but in the morning there is
joy.
6,7In my prosperity I said, "This is forever;
nothing can stop me now! The Lord has
shown me his favor. He has made me steady
as a mountain." Then, Lord, you turned your
face away from me and cut off your river of
blessings. Suddenly my courage was gone; I

Thirst for God

BIBLE READING: Psalm 27:1-6

We sought through prayer and meditation to improve our conscious contact with God, as we understood him, praying only for knowledge of his will for us and the power to carry that out.

Most of us initially turn to God for the help he can give us, namely, his power to free us from the power of our dependencies. We may be surprised to find that, as time passes, we turn to God out of a desire to be near him. As we discover how wonderful he is and how much he loves us, we draw near to him because of the joy we experience in his presence.

King David gave us a glimpse into his relationship with God, saying, "The one thing I want from God, the thing I seek most of all, is the privilege of meditating in his Temple, living in his presence every day of my life, delighting in his incomparable perfections and glory. There I'll be when troubles come. He will hide me. He will set me on a high rock out of reach of all my enemies. Then I will bring him sacrifices and sing his praises with much joy" (Psalm 27:4-6).

David found great joy by improving his conscious contact with God. God is always there, but we are not always aware of his presence. Our relationship with God usually begins with him meeting our desperate needs. But when we begin to focus on getting to know God as an end in itself, we will discover that he will give us what we have always desired—the joy of being close to our loving Creator. Then we will see that he can be trusted with every area of our life.

Turn to page 629, Psalm 65.

was terrified and panic-stricken. [8]I cried to
you, O Lord; oh, how I pled: [9]"What will you
gain, O Lord, from killing me? How can I
praise you then to all my friends? How can
my dust in the grave speak out and tell the
world about your faithfulness? [10]Hear me,
Lord; oh, have pity and help me." [11]Then he
turned my sorrow into joy! He took away my
clothes of mourning and clothed me with joy
[12]so that I might sing glad praises to the Lord
instead of lying in silence in the grave. O Lord
my God, I will keep on thanking you forever!

PSALM 31

Lord, I trust in you alone. Don't let my enemies defeat me. Rescue me because you are
the God who always does what is right. [2]An-
swer quickly when I cry to you; bend low and
hear my whispered plea. Be for me a great
Rock of safety from my foes. [3]Yes, you are my
Rock and my fortress; honor your name by
leading me out of this peril. [4]Pull me from the
trap my enemies have set for me. For you
alone are strong enough. [5,6]Into your hand I
commit my spirit.

You have rescued me, O God who keeps his
promises. I worship only you; how you hate
all those who worship idols, those imitation
gods. [7]I am radiant with joy because of your
mercy, for you have listened to my troubles
and have seen the crisis in my soul. [8]You have
not handed me over to my enemy but have
given me open ground in which to maneuver.

[9,10]O Lord, have mercy on me in my anguish. My eyes are red from weeping; my
health is broken from sorrow. I am pining
away with grief; my years are shortened,
drained away because of sadness. My sins
have sapped my strength; I stoop with sorrow
and with shame. [11]I am scorned by all my
enemies and even more by my neighbors and
friends. They dread meeting me and look the
other way when I go by. [12]I am forgotten like
a dead man, like a broken and discarded pot.
[13]I heard the lies about me, the slanders of my
enemies. Everywhere I looked I was afraid, for
they were plotting against my life.

[14,15]But I am trusting you, O Lord. I said,
"You alone are my God; my times are in your
hands. Rescue me from those who hunt me
down relentlessly. [16]Let your favor shine again
upon your servant; save me just because you
are so kind! [17]Don't disgrace me, Lord, by not
replying when I call to you for aid. But let the
wicked be shamed by what they trust in; let
them lie silently in their graves, [18]their lying
lips quieted at last—the lips of these arrogant
men who are accusing honest men of evil
deeds."

[19]Oh, how great is your goodness to those
who publicly declare that you will rescue

30:6-9 Sometimes we may be in the most danger when everything in our life is going well. We tend to get overconfident and think nothing can happen to us. But pride and overconfidence usually come before a fall. Sometimes God allows us to experience feelings of terror and suffering so we will learn that we can't make it alone. We will only succeed in recovery insofar as we learn to rely on God and follow his program for our recovery.

31:9-13 Sin takes a heavy toll on our life. When we fall into its bondage, everything begins to fall apart. Friends avoid us, afraid we will pull them down. The psalmist understood how we might feel when caught in the trap of sin and continual failure. But he also knew that God is merciful and ready to help us when we call out to him. God is willing to forgive and empower. It is our job to look to him for help.

31:19-22 Actively sharing the joy of our deliverance is an important step in our recovery. Our blessings from God increase when we share with others the good news about his help. Old friends can drag us down, sometimes without meaning to do so. God can protect us from harm if we allow him to take control of our life. In our distress we may wrongly assume that we are alone; yet God is always there, answering our cry for help.

32:1-4 When we get serious about our past sins, admitting each of them and seeking to make amends, we will probably find that most people are more than willing to forgive us. Making amends for our past failures and reconciling our relationships is an important part of our recovery. We see in this psalm that being reconciled to God begins as we admit our sins to him. Then he will forgive us; we can count on it! When we try to hide our sins from God, our life becomes dysfunctional. Our inner being becomes tied up in knots, and we once again begin to lose control. Why fight it? Confessing our sins to God is the first step toward a joyful heart.

32:5-9 Like David, we need to confess our sins before God and admit them to the people we have wronged. By doing so, we set a good example for others who are also having a hard time admitting their sin to God. We also set our heart free of the destructive grip of guilt and reestablish the healthy relationships we all need for a full recovery. God wants to give us a full and productive life, but we must respond willingly to his instruction.

them. For you have stored up great blessings
for those who trust and reverence you.
20Hide your loved ones in the shelter of
your presence, safe beneath your hand, safe
from all conspiring men. 21Blessed is the Lord,
for he has shown me that his never-failing
love protects me like the walls of a fort! 22I
spoke too hastily when I said, "The Lord has
deserted me," for you listened to my plea and
answered me.
23Oh, love the Lord, all of you who are his
people; for the Lord protects those who are
loyal to him, but harshly punishes all who
haughtily reject him. 24So cheer up! Take courage if you are depending on the Lord.

PSALM 32

What happiness for those whose guilt has
been forgiven! What joys when sins are covered over! What relief for those who have
confessed their sins and God has cleared their
record.
3There was a time when I wouldn't admit
what a sinner I was. But my dishonesty made
me miserable and filled my days with frustration. 4All day and all night your hand was
heavy on me. My strength evaporated like
water on a sunny day 5until I finally admitted
all my sins to you and stopped trying to hide
them. I said to myself, "I will confess them to
the Lord." And you forgave me! All my guilt
is gone.
6Now I say that each believer should confess his sins to God when he is aware of them,
while there is time to be forgiven. Judgment
will not touch him if he does.
7You are my hiding place from every storm
of life; you even keep me from getting into
trouble! You surround me with songs of victory. 8I will instruct you (says the Lord) and
guide you along the best pathway for your
life; I will advise you and watch your progress.
9Don't be like a senseless horse or mule that
has to have a bit in its mouth to keep it in line!
10Many sorrows come to the wicked, but
abiding love surrounds those who trust in the
Lord. 11So rejoice in him, all those who are his,
and shout for joy, all those who try to obey
him.

PSALM 33

Let all the joys of the godly well up in praise
to the Lord, for it is right to praise him. 2Play
joyous melodies of praise upon the lyre and
on the harp. 3Compose new songs of praise to
him, accompanied skillfully on the harp; sing
joyfully.

Honesty

READ PSALM 32:1-11

Living a lie is miserable. We may know from personal experience the heavy burden of trying to hide our secret life. If we are avoiding God and withdrawing from people because of our fear of being found out, we are living in needless agony.

Moses understood the price one must pay for trying to live a lie. He prayed, "We die beneath your anger; we are overwhelmed by your wrath. You spread out our sins before you—our secret sins—and see them all. No wonder the years are long and heavy here beneath your wrath. All our days are filled with sighing" (Psalm 90:7-9). David showed us the other side. "What happiness for those whose guilt has been forgiven! . . . What relief for those who have confessed their sins and God has cleared their record. There was a time when I wouldn't admit what a sinner I was. But my dishonesty made me miserable and filled my days with frustration. All day and all night your hand was heavy on me. My strength evaporated like water on a sunny day until I finally admitted all my sins to you and stopped trying to hide them. I said to myself, 'I will confess them to the Lord.' And you forgave me! All my guilt is gone. Now I say that each believer should confess his sins to God when he is aware of them, while there is time to be forgiven. Judgment will not touch him if he does" (Psalm 32:1-6).

Why should we live with the weight of dishonesty when relief is available to us? God already knows our secret sins anyway. Why continue to suffer needless agony when we can be relieved? ***Turn to page 617, Psalm 42.***

4For all God's words are right, and everything he does is worthy of our trust. 5He loves whatever is just and good; the earth is filled with his tender love. 6He merely spoke, and the heavens were formed and all the galaxies of stars. 7He made the oceans, pouring them into his vast reservoirs.

8Let everyone in all the world—men, women and children—fear the Lord and stand in awe of him. 9For when he but spoke, the world began! It appeared at his command! 10And with a breath he can scatter the plans of all the nations who oppose him, 11but his own plan stands forever. His intentions are the same for every generation.

12Blessed is the nation whose God is the Lord, whose people he has chosen as his own. 13-15The Lord gazes down upon mankind from heaven where he lives. He has made their hearts and closely watches everything they do.

16,17The best-equipped army cannot save a king—for great strength is not enough to save anyone. A war horse is a poor risk for winning victories—it is strong, but it cannot save.

18,19But the eyes of the Lord are watching over those who fear him, who rely upon his steady love. He will keep them from death even in times of famine! 20We depend upon the Lord alone to save us. Only he can help us; he protects us like a shield. 21No wonder we are happy in the Lord! For we are trusting him. We trust his holy name. 22Yes, Lord, let your constant love surround us, for our hopes are in you alone.

PSALM 34

I will praise the Lord no matter what happens. I will constantly speak of his glories and grace. 2I will boast of all his kindness to me. Let all who are discouraged take heart. 3Let us praise the Lord together and exalt his name.

4For I cried to him and he answered me! He freed me from all my fears. 5Others too were radiant at what he did for them. Theirs was no downcast look of rejection! 6This poor man cried to the Lord—and the Lord heard him and saved him out of his troubles. 7For the Angel of the Lord guards and rescues all who reverence him.

8Oh, put God to the test and see how kind he is! See for yourself the way his mercies shower down on all who trust in him. 9If you belong to the Lord, reverence him; for everyone who does this has everything he needs. 10Even strong young lions sometimes go hungry, but those of us who reverence the Lord will never lack any good thing.

11Sons and daughters, come and listen and let me teach you the importance of trusting and fearing the Lord. 12Do you want a long, good life? 13Then watch your tongue! Keep your lips from lying. 14Turn from all known sin and spend your time in doing good. Try to live in peace with everyone; work hard at it.

15For the eyes of the Lord are intently watching all who live good lives, and he gives attention when they cry to him. 16But the Lord has made up his mind to wipe out even the memory of evil men from the earth. 17Yes, the Lord hears the good man when he calls to him for help and saves him out of all his troubles.

18The Lord is close to those whose hearts are breaking; he rescues those who are humbly sorry for their sins. 19The good man does not escape all troubles—he has them too. But the Lord helps him in each and every one. 20Not one of his bones is broken.

21Calamity will surely overtake the wicked; heavy penalties are meted out to those who hate the good. 22But as for those who serve the Lord, he will redeem them; everyone who takes refuge in him will be freely pardoned.

33:1-11 Such a powerful God is worthy of our trust. The God who spoke the universe into existence is able to re-create us, and he is filled with tender love for us. He can remove from us the defects that have brought such destruction to us and the people we love. All he asks is that we turn our life over to him so he can work these changes in us.

34:1-7 When we experience deliverance from God, it should be natural for us to praise him and share the good news with others. If we care about other people who suffer as we did, we would be selfish not to tell how we found help. Boasting about our God and the help he has given us is one kind of boasting that is good to do. We will find that this kind of godly boasting will not only encourage others in their recovery, but it will also strengthen our faith in God.

34:8-14 If we have gone through life trusting in our own judgment, we may find it hard to commit our will to God and his plan for us. But if we refuse to seek God's help and direction, we may never know just how good he can be to us. He has the power and the wisdom we need to have victory in our struggles with sin and temptation.

PSALM 35
O Lord, fight those fighting me; declare war
on them for their attacks on me. 2Put on your
armor, take your shield and protect me by
standing in front. 3Lift your spear in my defense, for my pursuers are getting very close.
Let me hear you say that you will save me
from them. 4Dishonor those who are trying to
kill me. Turn them back and confuse them.
5Blow them away like chaff in the wind—
wind sent by the Angel of the Lord. 6Make
their path dark and slippery before them,
with the Angel of the Lord pursuing them.
7For though I did them no wrong, yet they
laid a trap for me and dug a pitfall in my path.
8Let them be overtaken by sudden ruin,
caught in their own net and destroyed.

9But I will rejoice in the Lord. He shall
rescue me! 10From the bottom of my heart
praise rises to him. Where is his equal in all of
heaven and earth? Who else protects the
weak and helpless from the strong, and the
poor and needy from those who would rob
them?

11These evil men swear to a lie. They accuse
me of things I have never even heard about.
12I do them good, but they return me harm. I
am sinking down to death. 13When they were
ill, I mourned before the Lord in sackcloth,
asking him to make them well; I refused to
eat; I prayed for them with utmost earnestness, but God did not listen. 14I went about
sadly as though it were my mother, friend, or
brother who was sick and nearing death. 15But
now that I am in trouble they are glad; they
come together in meetings filled with slander
against me—I didn't even know some of
those who were there. 16For they gather with
the worthless fellows of the town and spend
their time cursing me.

17Lord, how long will you stand there, doing nothing? Act now and rescue me, for I
have but one life and these young lions are
out to get it. 18Save me, and I will thank you
publicly before the entire congregation, before the largest crowd I can find.

19Don't give victory to those who fight me
without any reason! Don't let them rejoice at
my fall—let them die. 20They don't talk of
peace and doing good, but of plots against
innocent men who are minding their own
business. 21They shout that they have seen *me*
doing wrong! "Aha!" they say. "With our own
eyes we saw him do it." 22Lord, you know all
about it. Don't stay silent! Don't desert me
now!

23Rise up, O Lord my God; vindicate me.
24Declare me "not guilty," for you are just.
Don't let my enemies rejoice over me in my
troubles. 25Don't let them say, "Aha! Our dearest wish against him will soon be fulfilled!"
and, "At last we have him!" 26Shame them; let
these who boast against me and who rejoice
at my troubles be themselves overcome by
misfortune that strips them bare of everything they own. Bare them to dishonor. 27But
give great joy to all who wish me well. Let
them shout with delight, "Great is the Lord
who enjoys helping his child!" 28And I will tell
everyone how great and good you are; I will
praise you all day long.

PSALM 36
Sin lurks deep in the hearts of the wicked,
forever urging them on to evil deeds. They
have no fear of God to hold them back. 2In-
stead, in their conceit, they think they can
hide their evil deeds and not get caught.
3Everything they say is crooked and deceitful;
they are no longer wise and good. 4They lie
awake at night to hatch their evil plots instead
of planning how to keep away from wrong.

5Your steadfast love, O Lord, is as great as all
the heavens. Your faithfulness reaches beyond the clouds. 6Your justice is as solid as
God's mountains. Your decisions are as full of
wisdom as the oceans are with water. You are
concerned for men and animals alike. 7How
precious is your constant love, O God! All
humanity takes refuge in the shadow of your
wings. 8You feed them with blessings from

35:17-28 In this psalm, David expressed feelings of desperation; it seemed to him that God had forgotten him. At times we feel the same way, but when relief comes, we should, like David, encourage others who are having the same desperate feelings. The whole world seems to conspire against us when we are fighting to stay free from our dependencies and compulsions. We need to keep crying out to God for his wisdom and power to continue in what we know to be right, knowing that he hears us when we pray.

36:1-4 Sin and repeated failure have taken a toll on our life. Sometimes we aren't fully aware of just how deceitful we have been or how much damage our mistakes have done, to us and to others. That is why it is important to examine our life carefully, to take a careful moral inventory so that God can begin to help us change the things that can be changed.

your own table and let them drink from your
rivers of delight.
[9]For you are the Fountain of life; our light
is from your light. [10]Pour out your unfailing
love on those who know you! Never stop
giving your blessings to those who long to do
your will.
[11]Don't let these proud men trample me.
Don't let their wicked hands push me around.
[12]Look! They have fallen. They are thrown
down and will not rise again.

PSALM 37

Never envy the wicked! [2]Soon they fade away
like grass and disappear. [3]Trust in the Lord
instead. Be kind and good to others; then you
will live safely here in the land and prosper,
feeding in safety.
[4]Be delighted with the Lord. Then he will
give you all your heart's desires. [5]Commit
everything you do to the Lord. Trust him to
help you do it, and he will. [6]Your innocence
will be clear to everyone. He will vindicate
you with the blazing light of justice shining
down as from the noonday sun.
[7]Rest in the Lord; wait patiently for him to
act. Don't be envious of evil men who prosper.
[8]Stop your anger! Turn off your wrath.
Don't fret and worry—it only leads to harm.
[9]For the wicked shall be destroyed, but those
who trust the Lord shall be given every blessing. [10]Only a little while and the wicked shall
disappear. You will look for them in vain.
[11]But all who humble themselves before the
Lord shall be given every blessing and shall
have wonderful peace.
[12,13]The Lord is laughing at those who plot
against the godly, for he knows their judgment day is coming. [14]Evil men take aim to
slay the poor; they are ready to butcher those
who do right. [15]But their swords will be
plunged into their own hearts, and all their
weapons will be broken.
[16]It is better to have little and be godly than
to own an evil man's wealth; [17]for the strength
of evil men shall be broken, but the Lord takes
care of those he has forgiven.
[18]Day by day the Lord observes the good
deeds done by godly men, and gives them
eternal rewards. [19]He cares for them when
times are hard; even in famine, they will have
enough. [20]But evil men shall perish. These
enemies of God will wither like grass and
disappear like smoke. [21]Evil men borrow and
"cannot pay it back"! But the good man returns what he owes with some extra besides.
[22]Those blessed by the Lord shall inherit the
earth, but those cursed by him shall die.
[23]The steps of good men are directed by the
Lord. He delights in each step they take. [24]If
they fall it isn't fatal, for the Lord holds them
with his hand.
[25]I have been young and now I am old. And
in all my years I have never seen the Lord
forsake a man who loves him; nor have I seen
the children of the godly go hungry. [26]Instead,
the godly are able to be generous with their
gifts and loans to others, and their children
are a blessing.
[27]So if you want an eternal home, leave
your evil, low-down ways and live good lives.
[28]For the Lord loves justice and fairness; he
will never abandon his people. They will be
kept safe forever; but all who love wickedness
shall perish.
[29]The godly shall be firmly planted in the
land and live there forever. [30,31]The godly man
is a good counselor because he is just and fair
and knows right from wrong.
[32]Evil men spy on the godly, waiting for an
excuse to accuse them and then demanding
their death. [33]But the Lord will not let these
evil men succeed, nor let the godly be condemned when they are brought before the
judge.
[34]Don't be impatient for the Lord to act!
Keep traveling steadily along his pathway and
in due season he will honor you with every
blessing, and you will see the wicked destroyed. [35,36]I myself have seen it happen: a
proud and evil man, towering like a cedar of

37:1-7 Do not worry about or be jealous of those who seem to be getting away with doing wrong things. Their day in the sun is short; their moment of glory will soon be over. We need to do things that have lasting value—faithfully serving our God and helping the people around us. God's formula for our success is that we develop a relationship with him and determine to serve him in everything we do. Then, in God's perfect timing, we will experience the true joy God promises and freedom from the guilt heaped upon us by others.

37:27-31 God's plan for godly living is the only means to a healthy life. If we really desire to follow God and live a good life, we must saturate our mind with the truth of his Word. God's truth is designed to be the foundation for our life. It will help us to walk securely and make wise and effective decisions. A life lived according to God's program will lead to healthy relationships and freedom from the dependencies that bind us.

Lebanon, but when I looked again, he was gone! I searched but could not find him! 37But the good man—what a different story! For the good man—the blameless, the upright, the man of peace—he has a wonderful future ahead of him. For him there is a happy ending. 38But evil men shall be destroyed, and their posterity shall be cut off.

39The Lord saves the godly! He is their salvation and their refuge when trouble comes. 40Because they trust in him, he helps them and delivers them from the plots of evil men.

PSALM 38

O Lord, don't punish me while you are angry! 2Your arrows have struck deep; your blows are crushing me. 3,4Because of your anger, my body is sick, my health is broken beneath my sins. They are like a flood, higher than my head; they are a burden too heavy to bear. 5,6My wounds are festering and full of pus. Because of my sins, I am bent and racked with pain. My days are filled with anguish. 7My loins burn with inflammation, and my whole body is diseased. 8I am exhausted and crushed; I groan in despair.

9Lord, you know how I long for my health once more. You hear my every sigh. 10My heart beats wildly, my strength fails, and I am going blind. 11My loved ones and friends stay away, fearing my disease. Even my own family stands at a distance.

12Meanwhile my enemies are trying to kill me. They plot my ruin and spend all their waking hours planning treachery. 13,14But I am deaf to all their threats; I am silent before them as a man who cannot speak. I have nothing to say. 15For I am waiting for you, O Lord my God. Come and protect me. 16Put an end to their arrogance, these who gloat when I am cast down!

17How constantly I find myself upon the verge of sin; this source of sorrow always stares me in the face. 18I confess my sins; I am sorry for what I have done. 19But my enemies persecute with vigor and continue to hate me—though I have done nothing against them to deserve it. 20They repay me evil for good and hate me for standing for the right.

21Don't leave me, Lord; don't go away! 22Come quickly! Help me, O my Savior.

PSALM 39

I said to myself, I'm going to quit complaining! I'll keep quiet, especially when the ungodly are around me. 2,3But as I stood there silently the turmoil within me grew to the bursting point. The more I mused, the hotter the fires inside. Then at last I spoke and pled with God: 4Lord, help me to realize how brief my time on earth will be. Help me to know that I am here for but a moment more. 5,6My life is no longer than my hand! My whole lifetime is but a moment to you. Proud man! Frail as breath! A shadow! And all his busy rushing ends in nothing. He heaps up riches for someone else to spend. 7And so, Lord, my only hope is in you.

8Save me from being overpowered by my sins, for even fools will mock me then.

9Lord, I am speechless before you. I will not open my mouth to speak one word of complaint, for my punishment is from you.

10Lord, don't hit me anymore—I am exhausted beneath your hand. 11When you punish a man for his sins, he is destroyed, for he is as fragile as a moth-infested cloth; yes, man is frail as breath.

38:1-8 God's judgment against our sinful habits may seem very harsh, but he intends it for our ultimate good. Our sin does have consequences, and God allows the painful results to remind us that the suffering will only get worse unless we turn from our sin and commit our life to God. Only he can help us overcome our sinful habits and reestablish our relationships. We would be wise to learn from our suffering rather than be destroyed by it.

38:12-22 As we fall deeper into our addictions, our friends may begin to turn away from us. This will make the people who approve of our dependencies and problems even more powerful in our life. We may find that just being with these people draws us deeper and deeper into a destructive trap. If we hope to recover, we need to begin by avoiding the people who want us to remain trapped by our sinful habits. If everyone else has abandoned us, we may find this hard to do. We might begin by looking to God for help and companionship. Staying close to God will demand that we be continually sensitive to our sins and that we confess them and make them right as quickly as possible. This should then lead to the reconciliation of the healthy relationships in our life.

39:1-7 At times, we may become frustrated and explode in anger just as David did in this psalm. We should not be afraid to do this. If we feel afraid, alone, and abandoned, we should voice our feelings of anger and confusion. As we do this, we are admitting our helplessness. This is the first step in turning to God, through whom we can gain a true perspective on life. God is never threatened by our strong emotions. It is our apathy and pride that disturb him the most.

12Hear my prayer, O Lord; listen to my cry! Don't sit back, unmindful of my tears. For I am your guest. I am a traveler passing through the earth, as all my fathers were.

13Spare me, Lord! Let me recover and be filled with happiness again before my death.

PSALM 40

I waited patiently for God to help me; then he listened and heard my cry. 2He lifted me out of the pit of despair, out from the bog and the mire, and set my feet on a hard, firm path, and steadied me as I walked along. 3He has given me a new song to sing, of praises to our God. Now many will hear of the glorious things he did for me, and stand in awe before the Lord, and put their trust in him.4Many blessings are given to those who trust the Lord and have no confidence in those who are proud or who trust in idols.

5O Lord my God, many and many a time you have done great miracles for us, and we are ever in your thoughts. Who else can do such glorious things? No one else can be compared with you. There isn't time to tell of all your wonderful deeds.

6It isn't sacrifices and offerings that you really want from your people. Burnt animals bring no special joy to your heart. But you have accepted the offer of my life-long service. 7Then I said, "See, I have come, just as all the prophets foretold. 8And I delight to do your will, my God, for your law is written upon my heart!"

9I have told everyone the good news that you forgive people's sins. I have not been timid about it, as you well know, O Lord. 10I have not kept this good news hidden in my heart, but have proclaimed your loving-kindness and truth to all the congregation.

11O Lord, don't hold back your tender mercies from me! My only hope is in your love and faithfulness. 12Otherwise I perish, for problems far too big for me to solve are piled higher than my head. Meanwhile my sins, too many to count, have all caught up with me, and I am ashamed to look up. My heart quails within me.

39:8-13 As we suffer God's punishment in our life, there is no point in trying to escape it. The only wise thing to do is beg for mercy. When God reproves us for our sins, we soon learn that everything we hold dear—our possessions, even our life—is ultimately under his divine control. Rather than trying to rationalize our sins, we need to confess them. God is ready and willing to forgive anyone with a humble heart. In confessing our sins and failures to God, we are taking an important step in the process of recovery.

40:1-5 God's timing is always worth waiting for. If we look to him for help, he will rescue us from destruction and despair and from the things that hold us down. He will also bring stability to our life so that we can move forward again with confidence and joy. If we are to experience God's best for our life (which far exceeds all we can imagine), we need to rely on him alone and avoid any entanglements with those who will lead us away from God and his plan for us.

40:11-17 Recovery is rarely a once-and-for-all thing. The psalmist apparently experienced deliverance of a sort (40:1), but then a few verses later he expressed frustration at his continued troubles (40:12). Every time that he felt entrapped, he called out to God for help. This is an important lesson for us to learn as we struggle on the road to full recovery. God will respond as many times as we call out to him. We, however, should never use this as an excuse to stumble time and time again. We need to do what we can to avoid the people and situations that we know will lead to trouble.

41:1-3 As we work through the process of recovery, it is easy to become blind to the needs of others. We focus on our own needs and feelings and often become oblivious to the needs of the people around us. Our recovery, however, demands that we reach out to help others in need. Because of the things we have suffered, we are uniquely gifted to help people seeking freedom from their dependencies. As we reach out to others, we will experience God's help when we are emotionally down or physically sick, or when we face seemingly hopeless situations.

41:4-9 Many people wish us well as we seek to recover. Others, however, seem to gloat over us, continually trying to predict our next failure. We will feel pressure from such people during times when our relationship with God is weak. At such vulnerable moments, our enemies are hard at work trying to ruin our life through lies, deception, and words of discouragement (see Matthew 26:20-25; John 13:18). We need to keep our eyes focused on God; he will never let us down.

42:1-3 We probably developed many destructive appetites during our days of rebellion against God. The solution to our problem is to make God the only object of our desire. The psalmist paints a beautiful picture of the person who aches to be close to God. The language he uses could easily describe the longing we feel for our addictions. We need to realize that only God can satisfy our real needs. We must realize that our addictions will never bring real satisfaction. They may temporarily numb the pain, but in the end they will lead to destruction. If we turn to God, he will help us to change our desires. We can learn to make him the object of our heart's deepest longing.

13Please, Lord, rescue me! Quick! Come and
help me! 14,15Confuse them! Turn them
around and send them sprawling—all these
who are trying to destroy me. Disgrace these
scoffers with their utter failure!
16But may the joy of the Lord be given to
everyone who loves him and his salvation.
May they constantly exclaim, "How great
God is!"
17I am poor and weak, yet the Lord is thinking about me right now! O my God, you are
my helper. You are my Savior; come quickly,
and save me. Please don't delay!

PSALM 41

God blesses those who are kind to the poor.
He helps them out of their troubles. 2He protects them and keeps them alive; he publicly
honors them and destroys the power of their
enemies. 3He nurses them when they are sick
and soothes their pains and worries.
4"O Lord," I prayed, "be kind and heal me,
for I have confessed my sins." 5But my enemies say, "May he soon die and be forgotten!"
6They act so friendly when they come to visit
me while I am sick; but all the time they hate
me and are glad that I am lying there upon my
bed of pain. And when they leave, they laugh
and mock. 7They whisper together about
what they will do when I am dead. 8"It's fatal,
whatever it is," they say. "He'll never get out
of that bed!"
9Even my best friend has turned against
me—a man I completely trusted; how often
we ate together. 10Lord, don't you desert me!
Be gracious, Lord, and make me well again so
I can pay them back! 11I know you are pleased
with me because you haven't let my enemies
triumph over me. 12You have preserved me
because I was honest; you have admitted me
forever to your presence.
13Bless the Lord, the God of Israel, who
exists from everlasting ages past—and on into
everlasting eternity ahead. Amen and amen!

PSALM 42

As the deer pants for water, so I long for you,
O God. 2I thirst for God, the living God.
Where can I find him to come and stand
before him? 3Day and night I weep for his
help, and all the while my enemies taunt me.
"Where is this God of yours?" they scoff.
4,5Take courage, my soul! Do you remember
those times (but how could you ever forget
them!) when you led a great procession to the
Temple on festival days, singing with joy,
praising the Lord? Why then be downcast?

Hope

READ PSALM 42:1-11

During bad times we may get lost in our memories of the "good old days." We may struggle with conflicting emotions, teetering between the extremes of depression and hope.

The psalmist reflected these emotions, saying to himself, "Take courage, my soul! Do you remember those times (but how could you ever forget them!) when you led a great procession to the Temple on festival days, singing with joy, praising the Lord? Why then be downcast? Why be discouraged and sad? Hope in God! I shall yet praise him again. Yes, I shall again praise him for his help. Yet I am standing here depressed and gloomy, but I will meditate upon your kindness. . . . All your waves and billows have gone over me, and floods of sorrow pour upon me like a thundering cataract. Yet day by day the Lord also pours out his steadfast love upon me, and through the night I sing his songs and pray to God who gives me life. . . . O my soul, don't be discouraged. Don't be upset. Expect God to act! For I know that I shall again have plenty of reason to praise him for all that he will do. He is my help! He is my God!" (Psalm 42:4-8, 11).

Look how the psalmist improved his conscious contact with God. He talked to himself, commanding his emotions to "hope in God!" He repeated, "I shall yet praise him again," even though he didn't feel like it at the time. In the dark times he sang songs, thought about God's steadfast love, and prayed. We can do these things, too. ***Turn to page 647, Psalm 103.***

Why be discouraged and sad? Hope in God! I
shall yet praise him again. Yes, I shall again
praise him for his help.
6Yet I am standing here depressed and
gloomy, but I will meditate upon your kindness to this lovely land where the Jordan River
flows and where Mount Hermon and Mount
Mizar stand. 7All your waves and billows have
gone over me, and floods of sorrow pour
upon me like a thundering cataract.
8Yet day by day the Lord also pours out his
steadfast love upon me, and through the
night I sing his songs and pray to God who
gives me life.
9"O God my Rock," I cry, "why have you
forsaken me? Why must I suffer these attacks
from my enemies?" 10Their taunts pierce me
like a fatal wound; again and again they scoff,
"Where is that God of yours?" 11But, O my
soul, don't be discouraged. Don't be upset.
Expect God to act! For I know that I shall
again have plenty of reason to praise him for
all that he will do. He is my help! He is my
God!

PSALM 43
O God, defend me from the charges of these
merciless, deceitful men. 2For you are God,
my only place of refuge. Why have you tossed
me aside? Why must I mourn at the oppression of my enemies?
3Oh, send out your light and your truth—
let them lead me. Let them lead me to your
Temple on your holy mountain, Zion. 4There
I will go to the altar of God, my exceeding joy,
and praise him with my harp. O God—my
God! 5O my soul, why be so gloomy and
discouraged? Trust in God! I shall again praise
him for his wondrous help; he will make me
smile again, *for he is my God!*

PSALM 44
O God, we have heard of the glorious miracles
you did in the days of long ago. Our forefathers have told us how you drove the heathen nations from this land and gave it all to
us, spreading Israel from one end of the country to the other. 3They did not conquer by
their own strength and skill, but by your
mighty power and because you smiled upon
them and favored them.
4You are my King and my God. Decree
victories for your people. 5For it is only by
your power and through your name that we
tread down our enemies; 6I do not trust my
weapons. They could never save me. 7Only
you can give us the victory over those who
hate us.
8My constant boast is God. I can never
thank you enough! 9And yet for a time,
O Lord, you have tossed us aside in dishonor
and have not helped us in our battles. 10You
have actually fought against us and defeated
us before our foes. Our enemies have invaded
our land and pillaged the countryside. 11You
have treated us like sheep in a slaughter pen
and scattered us among the nations. 12You
sold us for a pittance. You valued us at nothing at all. 13The neighboring nations laugh
and mock at us because of all the evil you
have sent. 14You have made the word *Jew* a
byword of contempt and shame among the
nations, disliked by all. 15,16I am constantly
despised, mocked, taunted, and cursed by my
vengeful enemies.
17And all this has happened, Lord, despite
our loyalty to you. We have not violated your
covenant. 18Our hearts have not deserted you!
We have not left your path by a single step.
19If we had, we could understand your punishing us in the barren wilderness and sending us
into darkness and death. 20If we had turned
away from worshiping our God and were worshiping idols, 21would God not know it? Yes,
he knows the secrets of every heart. 22But that
is not our case. For we are facing death threats
constantly because of serving you! We are like
sheep awaiting slaughter.
23Waken! Rouse yourself! Don't sleep,
O Lord! Are we cast off forever? 24Why do you

43:1-5 As we work through the recovery process, those who have lost confidence in us may treat us unfairly. During such times we must look to God, our only dependable source of strength and encouragement. As we turn our life over to him, seeking his wisdom and strength, we will find the help we need. We must learn, as the psalmist did, how to find strength by reading God's Word and allowing him to restore our joy. As our relationship with God grows stronger, we will discover the means for reconciling our other broken relationships.

44:1-7 There are always valuable lessons to be learned from our spiritual predecessors. Those who have progressed farther in the struggle of life and recovery can share how God brought them help and deliverance. The victory God has given others should encourage us, but we must put into practice the principles they share. If we don't act on what we learn, we will never experience the victory they have told us about.

look the other way? Why do you ignore our
sorrows and oppression? 25We lie face downward in the dust. 26Rise up, O Lord, and come
and help us. Save us by your constant love.

PSALM 45
My heart is overflowing with a beautiful
thought! I will write a lovely poem to the
King, for I am as full of words as the speediest
writer pouring out his story.

2You are the fairest of all;
Your words are filled with grace;
God himself is blessing you forever.
3Arm yourself, O Mighty One,
So glorious, so majestic!
4And in your majesty
Go on to victory,
Defending truth, humility, and justice.
Go forth to awe-inspiring deeds!
5Your arrows are sharp
In your enemies' hearts;
They fall before you.
6Your throne, O God, endures forever.
Justice is your royal scepter.
7You love what is good
And hate what is wrong.
Therefore God, your God,
Has given you more gladness
Than anyone else.

8Your robes are perfumed with myrrh, aloes, and cassia. In your palaces of inlaid ivory,
lovely music is being played for your enjoyment. 9Kings' daughters are among your concubines. Standing beside you is the queen,
wearing jewelry of finest gold from Ophir.
10,11"I advise you, O daughter, not to fret
about your parents in your homeland far
away. Your royal husband delights in your
beauty. Reverence him, for he is your lord.
12The people of Tyre, the richest people of our
day, will shower you with gifts and entreat
your favors."
13The bride, a princess, waits within her
chamber, robed in beautiful clothing woven
with gold. 14Lovely she is, led beside her maids
of honor to the king! 15What a joyful, glad
procession as they enter in the palace gates!
16"Your sons will some day be kings like their
father. They shall sit on thrones around the
world!
17"I will cause your name to be honored in
all generations; the nations of the earth will
praise you forever."

PSALM 46
God is our refuge and strength, a tested help
in times of trouble. 2And so we need not fear
even if the world blows up and the mountains
crumble into the sea. 3Let the oceans roar and
foam; let the mountains tremble!
4There is a river of joy flowing through the
city of our God—the sacred home of the God
above all gods. 5God himself is living in that
city; therefore it stands unmoved despite the
turmoil everywhere. He will not delay his
help. 6The nations rant and rave in anger—
but when God speaks, the earth melts in submission and kingdoms totter into ruin.
7The Commander of the armies of heaven
is here among us. He, the God of Jacob, has
come to rescue us.
8Come, see the glorious things that our God
does, how he brings ruin upon the world 9and
causes wars to end throughout the earth,
breaking and burning every weapon. 10"Stand
silent! Know that I am God! I will be honored
by every nation in the world!"
11The Commander of the heavenly armies
is here among *us!* He, the God of Jacob, has
come to rescue *us!*

PSALM 47
Come, everyone, and clap for joy! Shout triumphant praises to the Lord! 2For the Lord,
the God above all gods, is awesome beyond
words; he is the great King of all the earth. 3He
subdues the nations before us 4and will personally select his choicest blessings for his

---

46:1-6 God is more than able to protect us no matter how strong the pull of temptation might be. If we try to resist temptation in our own strength, we have good reason to fear. But if God is with us, we have no reason to be afraid. God's rivers of mercy and strength flow just for us when we are weak and thirsty. No power can draw us out of the circle of his protection once we take refuge in him.

46:7-11 God, the Commander of the heavenly armies, is here among us. If we put our life in his hands, we can rest, confident that he will protect us. He knows our weaknesses and can strengthen us in the needed areas, helping us to overcome the attacks we face each day. It is true that our enemies are strong, but God is far more powerful than anything that might assail us.

47:1-9 Victories, great and small, should be shared with others who are struggling. The psalmist made it a goal to encourage others, reminding them how good and powerful God is and inviting them to join him in praising God.

Jewish people—the very best for those he loves.

[5]God has ascended with a mighty shout, with trumpets blaring. [6,7]Sing out your praises to our God, our King. Yes, sing your highest praises to our King, the King of all the earth. Sing thoughtful praises! [8]He reigns above the nations, sitting on his holy throne. [9]The Gentile rulers of the world have joined with us in praising him—praising the God of Abraham—for the battle shields of all the armies of the world are his trophies. He is highly honored everywhere.

PSALM 48

How great is the Lord! How much we should praise him. He lives upon Mount Zion in Jerusalem. [2]What a glorious sight! See Mount Zion rising north of the city high above the plains for all to see—Mount Zion, joy of all the earth, the residence of the great King.

[3]God himself is the defender of Jerusalem. [4]The kings of the earth have arrived together to inspect the city. [5]They marvel at the sight and hurry home again, [6]afraid of what they have seen; they are filled with panic like a woman in travail! [7]For God destroys the mightiest warships with a breath of wind. [8]We have heard of the city's glory—the city of our God, the Commander of the armies of heaven. And now we see it for ourselves! God has established Jerusalem forever.

[9]Lord, here in your Temple we meditate upon your kindness and your love. [10]Your name is known throughout the earth, O God. You are praised everywhere for the salvation you have scattered throughout the world. [11]O Jerusalem, rejoice! O people of Judah, rejoice! For God will see to it that you are finally treated fairly. [12]Go, inspect the city! Walk around and count her many towers! [13]Note her walls and tour her palaces so that you can tell your children.

[14]For this great God is our God forever and ever. He will be our guide until we die.

PSALM 49

Listen, everyone! High and low, rich and poor, all around the world—listen to my words, [3]for they are wise and filled with insight.

[4]I will tell in song accompanied by harps the answer to one of life's most perplexing problems:

[5]*There is no need to fear when times of trouble come,* even though surrounded by enemies! [6]They trust in their wealth and boast about how rich they are, [7]yet not one of them, though rich as kings, can ransom his own brother from the penalty of sin! For God's forgiveness does not come that way. [8,9]For a soul is far too precious to be ransomed by mere earthly wealth. There is not enough of it in all the earth to buy eternal life for just one soul, to keep it out of hell.

[10]Rich man! Proud man! Wise man! You must die like all the rest! You have no greater lease on life than foolish, stupid men. You must leave your wealth to others. [11]You name your estates after yourselves as though your lands could be forever yours and you could live on them eternally. [12]But man with all his pomp must die like any animal. [13]Such is the folly of these men, though after they die they will be quoted as having great wisdom.

[14]Death is the shepherd of all mankind. And "in the morning" those who are evil will be the slaves of those who are good. For the power of their wealth is gone when they die, they cannot take it with them.

[15]But as for me, God will redeem my soul from the power of death, for he will receive me. [16]So do not be dismayed when evil men grow rich and build their lovely homes. [17]For when they die, they carry nothing with them! Their honors will not follow them. [18]Though a man calls himself happy all through his life—and the world loudly applauds success—[19]yet in the end he dies like everyone else and enters eternal darkness.

[20]For man with all his pomp must die like any animal.

48:9-14 We must take the time to read God's Word and meditate on how God has helped us overcome the problems that once held us in bondage and defeat. Part of our recovery comes as we seek God through prayer and meditation, actions that help us to develop confidence in God. In time we will discover the truth that God loves us and is concerned about us. This will give us added strength as we face the struggles of recovery.

49:5-13 We need to respect our enemy, remembering how we once lost control. But we do not need to fear him, because God won't allow anything to hurt us as long as we trust in him and follow his program for righteous living. The only way we can repay God for his deliverance is to show gratitude and share the good news with others. Though some may seem to prosper and escape the consequences of their wrongdoing in this life, they will face judgment in the next. This truth should be a warning to us not to spend too much time envying others (see 39:5-6; Ecclesiastes 2:15-19).

PSALM 50

The mighty God, the Lord, has summoned all mankind from east to west!

[2]God's glory-light shines from the beautiful Temple on Mount Zion. [3]He comes with the noise of thunder, surrounded by devastating fire; a great storm rages round about him. [4]He has come to judge his people. To heaven and earth he shouts, [5]"Gather together my own people who by their sacrifice upon my altar have promised to obey me." [6]God will judge them with complete fairness, for all heaven declares that he is just.

[7]O my people, listen! For I am your God. Listen! Here are my charges against you: [8]I have no complaint about the sacrifices you bring to my altar, for you bring them regularly. [9]But it isn't sacrificial bullocks and goats that I really want from you. [10,11]For all the animals of field and forest are mine! The cattle on a thousand hills! And all the birds upon the mountains! [12]If I were hungry, I would not mention it to you—for all the world is mine and everything in it. [13]No, I don't need your sacrifices of flesh and blood. [14,15]What I want from you is your true thanks; I want your promises fulfilled. *I want you to trust me in your times of trouble, so I can rescue you and you can give me glory.*

[16]But God says to evil men: Recite my laws no longer and stop claiming my promises, [17]for you have refused my discipline, disregarding my laws. [18]You see a thief and help him, and spend your time with evil and immoral men. [19]You curse and lie, and vile language streams from your mouths. [20]You slander your own brother. [21]I remained silent—you thought I didn't care—but now your time of punishment has come, and I list all the above charges against you. [22]This is the last chance for all of you who have forgotten God, before I tear you apart—and no one can help you then.

[23]But true praise is a worthy sacrifice; this really honors me. Those who walk my paths will receive salvation from the Lord.

PSALM 51

Written after Nathan the prophet had come to inform David of God's judgment against him because of his adultery with Bathsheba, and his murder of Uriah, her husband.

O loving and kind God, have mercy. Have pity upon me and take away the awful stain of my transgressions. [2]Oh, wash me, cleanse me from this guilt. Let me be pure again. [3]For I admit my shameful deed—it haunts me day and night. [4]It is against you and you alone I sinned and did this terrible thing. You saw it all, and your sentence against me is just. [5]But I was born a sinner, yes, from the moment my mother conceived me. [6]You deserve honesty from the heart; yes, utter sincerity and truthfulness. Oh, give me this wisdom.

[7]Sprinkle me with the cleansing blood and I shall be clean again. Wash me and I shall be whiter than snow. [8]And after you have punished me, give me back my joy again. [9]Don't keep looking at my sins—erase them from your sight. [10]Create in me a new, clean heart,

50:1-6 Judgment is coming to those who refuse to recognize God's authority. God is good, but he must deal with those who have harmed others or he would not be a just God after all. Because he is just, we need to take a careful inventory of our life, doing our best to right all the wrongs we have committed.

50:16-23 People who deceive, slander, and encourage others to follow an immoral life-style have no right to claim the promises of God's Word. God sees what goes on and, while it appears his silence means he doesn't care, one day he will present his case against them. The way to avoid such an end is to worship God with thanksgiving and follow him in what he says.

51:5-9 If we fail to admit and confess our sin, it will continue to burden us with destructive guilt. We need to learn to confess and forsake our sin immediately. Then we need to seek God's wisdom as to how we can make amends with the people we have wronged. We won't be able to progress in our recovery or reach out to others until we seek forgiveness for our past failures. Others may not forgive us as quickly as we would like, but we can be sure God will.

51:10-13 David had already seen what happened when God removed his Spirit from King Saul—it was the beginning of his bitter downfall (1 Samuel 15–16). This psalm of repentance was written by David after he committed adultery with Bathsheba and then arranged for her husband's death (2 Samuel 11–12). On the surface, David's sins were far worse than the sins of Saul. Why did God forgive David and offer him forgiveness and restoration? David was humble about his sin. He admitted it and asked for God's help and forgiveness. Saul was never willing to admit his sin; he continued in denial. If we try to hide our sin, we are in grave danger. But if we are sensitive to our failures and humbly seek God's forgiveness, there is hope for us, no matter how great our failures in the past.

O God, filled with clean thoughts and right desires. [11]Don't toss me aside, banished forever from your presence. Don't take your Holy Spirit from me. [12]Restore to me again the joy of your salvation, and make me willing to obey you. [13]Then I will teach your ways to other sinners, and they—guilty like me—will repent and return to you. [14,15]Don't sentence me to death. O my God, you alone can rescue me. Then I will sing of your forgiveness, for my lips will be unsealed—oh, how I will praise you.

[16]You don't want penance; if you did, how gladly I would do it! You aren't interested in offerings burned before you on the altar. [17]It is a broken spirit you want—remorse and penitence. A broken and a contrite heart, O God, you will not ignore.

[18]And Lord, don't punish Israel for my sins—help your people and protect Jerusalem.

[19]And when my heart is right, then you will rejoice in the good that I do and in the bullocks I bring to sacrifice upon your altar.

PSALM 52

Written by David to protest against his enemy Doeg (1 Samuel 22), who later slaughtered eighty-five priests and their families.

You call yourself a *hero,* do you? You *boast* about this evil deed of yours against God's people. [2]You are sharp as a tack in plotting your evil tricks. [3]How you love wickedness—far more than good! And lying more than truth! [4]You love to slander—you love to say anything that will do harm, O man with the lying tongue.

[5]But God will strike you down, pull you from your home, and drag you away from the land of the living. [6]The followers of God will see it happen. They will watch in awe. Then they will laugh and say, [7]"See what happens to those who despise God and trust in their wealth, and become ever more bold in their wickedness."

[8]But I am like a sheltered olive tree protected by the Lord himself. I trust in the mercy of God forever and ever. [9]O Lord, I will praise you forever and ever for your punishment. And I will wait for your mercies—for everyone knows what a merciful God you are.

PSALM 53

Only a fool would say to himself, "There is no God." And why does he say it? Because of his wicked heart, his dark and evil deeds. His life is corroded with sin.

[2]God looks down from heaven, searching among all mankind to see if there is a single one who does right and really seeks for God. [3]But all have turned their backs on him; they are filthy with sin—corrupt and rotten through and through. Not one is good, not one! [4]How can this be? Can't they understand anything? For they devour my people like bread and refuse to come to God. [5]But soon unheard-of terror will fall on them. God will scatter the bones of these, your enemies. They are doomed, for God has rejected them.

[6]Oh, that God would come from Zion now and save Israel! Only when the Lord himself restores them can they ever be really happy again.

52:5-9 In the past we may have valued people for the enjoyment and excitement we experienced while we were with them. We lived for the pleasure and fun of the present moment. With time, however, it became clear that such a life-style always led to painful long-term consequences. We see in this psalm that God is able and willing to snatch us out of the dangerous situations we've walked into. A consistent prayer life can help us keep the right perspective about the world and give us patience and hope as we look to the future.

53:1-6 Coming to believe in God is an essential step in our recovery journey. Ignoring God's plan for healthy living brings only trouble and suffering. We have become prisoners of our own desires, powerless to escape without God's help. Seeing the damage that rebellion has caused us should keep us humble. Our own powerlessness should serve as a continual reminder of our need for God's powerful presence in our life.

54:1-7 We will almost certainly face opposition from people who don't understand our recovery or who feel threatened by it. The words of this psalm should be our prayer for deliverance at such times. God is our protector and sustainer, who will cause our enemies to fall into their own traps. Our response to God's deliverance from those who are against us should be our worship and thanks.

55:16-19 During recovery our relationship with God is extremely important. At times he may be the only friend we have. David was confident that God would rescue and deliver him from his problems. He also depended on God to keep him safe from others who desired his destruction. With God as our friend and helper, there is hope for our recovery no matter what circumstances we have to face.

PSALM 54
Written by David at the time the men of Ziph
tried to betray him to Saul.
Come with great power, O God, and save me!
Defend me with your might! 2Oh, listen to my
prayer. 3For violent men have risen against
me—ruthless men who care nothing for God
are seeking my life.
4But God is my helper. He is a friend of
mine! 5He will cause the evil deeds of my
enemies to boomerang upon them. Do as you
promised and put an end to these wicked
men, O God. 6Gladly I bring my sacrifices to
you; I will praise your name, O Lord, for it is
good.
7God has rescued me from all my trouble,
and triumphed over my enemies.

PSALM 55
Listen to my prayer, O God; don't hide yourself when I cry to you. 2Hear me, Lord! Listen
to me! For I groan and weep beneath my
burden of woe.
3My enemies shout against me and
threaten me with death. They surround me
with terror and plot to kill me. Their fury and
hatred rise to engulf me. 4My heart is in anguish within me. Stark fear overpowers me.
5Trembling and horror overwhelm me. 6Oh,
for wings like a dove, to fly away and rest! 7I
would fly to the far-off deserts and stay there.
8I would flee to some refuge from all this
storm.
9O Lord, make these enemies begin to quarrel among themselves—destroy them with
their own violence and strife. 10Though they
patrol their walls night and day against invaders, their real problem is internal—wickedness and dishonesty are entrenched in the
heart of the city. 11There is murder and robbery there, and cheating in the markets and
wherever you look.
12It was not an enemy who taunted me—
then I could have borne it; I could have hidden and escaped. 13But it was you, a man like
myself, my companion and my friend.
14What fellowship we had, what wonderful
discussions as we walked together to the
Temple of the Lord on holy days.
15Let death seize them and cut them down
in their prime, for there is sin in their homes,
and they are polluted to the depths of their
souls.
16But I will call upon the Lord to save me—
and he will. 17I will pray morning, noon, and
night, pleading aloud with God; and he will
hear and answer. 18Though the tide of battle

Healing the Brokenness

BIBLE READING: Psalm 51:16-19

We were entirely ready to have God remove all these defects of character.

If we have sincerely practiced the previous steps, we have probably found enough pain inside to break our heart. Facing the fact that brokenness is part of the human condition can be crushing. But if we have arrived at this point, it is probably a sign that we are ready for God to change us.

King David, as a young man, wasn't ready for God to change his character because he didn't recognize that it had defects. He prayed, "Don't treat me as a common sinner. . . . No, I am not like that, O Lord; I try to walk a straight and narrow path of doing what is right; therefore in mercy save me" (Psalm 26:9-11). He approached God on the basis of his own merit.

It wasn't until later in his life when he was confronted with his sins of adultery and murder that he was able to say, "I was born a sinner, yes, from the moment my mother conceived me" (Psalm 51:5). He also said, "You don't want penance; if you did, how gladly I would do it! . . . It is a broken spirit you want—remorse and penitence. A broken and a contrite heart, O God, you will not ignore" (Psalm 51:16-17).

Jesus taught, "Those who mourn are fortunate! for they shall be comforted" (Matthew 5:4). God isn't looking for evidence of how good we are or how hard we try. He only wants us to mourn over our brokenness. Then he will not ignore our needs, but will forgive us, comfort us, and cleanse us. ***Turn to page 769, Isaiah 55.***

runs strongly against me, for so many are fighting me, yet he will rescue me. [19]God himself—God from everlasting ages past—will answer them! For they refuse to fear him or even honor his commands.

[20]This friend of mine betrayed me—I who was at peace with him. He broke his promises. [21]His words were oily smooth, but in his heart was war. His words were sweet, but underneath were daggers.

[22]Give your burdens to the Lord. He will carry them. He will not permit the godly to slip or fall. [23]He will send my enemies to the pit of destruction. Murderers and liars will not live out half their days. But I am trusting you to save me.

PSALM 56

Lord, have mercy on me; all day long the enemy troops press in. So many are proud to fight against me; how they long to conquer me.

[3,4]But when I am afraid, I will put my confidence in you. Yes, I will trust the promises of God. And since I am trusting him, what can mere man do to me? [5]They are always twisting what I say. All their thoughts are how to harm me. [6]They meet together to perfect their plans; they hide beside the trail, listening for my steps, waiting to kill me. [7]They expect to get away with it. Don't let them, Lord. In anger cast them to the ground.

[8]You have seen me tossing and turning through the night. You have collected all my tears and preserved them in your bottle! You have recorded every one in your book.

[9]The very day I call for help, the tide of battle turns. My enemies flee! This one thing I *know: God is for me!* [10,11]I am trusting God—oh, praise his promises! I am not afraid of anything mere man can do to me! Yes, praise his promises. [12]I will surely do what I have promised, Lord, and thank you for your help. [13]For you have saved me from death and my feet from slipping, so that I can walk before the Lord in the land of the living.

PSALM 57

O God, have pity, for I am trusting you! I will hide beneath the shadow of your wings until this storm is past. [2]I will cry to the God of heaven who does such wonders for me. [3]He will send down help from heaven to save me because of his love and his faithfulness. He will rescue me from these liars who are so intent upon destroying me. [4]I am surrounded by fierce lions—hotheads whose teeth are sharp as spears and arrows. Their tongues are like swords. [5]Lord, be exalted above the highest heavens! Show your glory high above the earth. [6]My enemies have set a trap for me. Frantic fear grips me. They have dug a pitfall in my path. But look! They themselves have fallen into it!

[7]O God, my heart is quiet and confident. No wonder I can sing your praises! [8]Rouse yourself, my soul! Arise, O harp and lyre! Let us greet the dawn with song! [9]I will thank you publicly throughout the land. I will sing your praises among the nations. [10]Your kindness and love are as vast as the heavens. Your faithfulness is higher than the skies.

[11]Yes, be exalted, O God, above the heavens. May your glory shine throughout the earth.

PSALM 58

Justice? You high and mighty politicians don't even know the meaning of the word! Fairness? Which of you has any left? Not one! All your dealings are crooked: you give "justice" in exchange for bribes. [3]These men are

55:20-23 David's anguish caused him to think about the pain he had suffered at the betrayal of an old friend. Old friends may say all the right words, but deep down they probably want us to continue practicing destructive habits with them. The solution for David, and for us, is to turn burdens over to God. God is able to strengthen us, encourage us, and keep us from falling.

56:8-13 We can learn a helpful lesson from the psalmist here—we should keep our thoughts focused on God and trust him. We will find, as the psalmist did, that God is on our side, even during the times when our struggle is most difficult. God will do his part; we, however, must fulfill our responsibilities of being obedient to God's revealed will. His program is always best for us in the long run.

57:1-3 When we understand the grace of God, we find comfort in turning to him in times of trouble, knowing that he will surround us with his protection until the storm is past. God is there for us; understanding and acting upon this truth are essential to our recovery.

57:7-11 Here the psalmist demonstrates an important principle for recovery: after experiencing God's help, we need to share it with others. In fact, this should be the natural response of our grateful heart. This will not only encourage others in the recovery process, but also help in our own recovery.

born sinners, lying from their earliest words! 4,5 They are poisonous as deadly snakes, cobras that close their ears to the most expert of charmers.

6 O God, break off their fangs. Tear out the teeth of these young lions, Lord. 7 Let them disappear like water into thirsty ground. Make their weapons useless in their hands. 8 Let them be as snails that dissolve into slime and as those who die at birth, who never see the sun. 9 God will sweep away both old and young. He will destroy them more quickly than a cooking pot can feel the blazing fire of thorns beneath it.

10 The godly shall rejoice in the triumph of right; they shall walk the blood-stained fields of slaughtered, wicked men. 11 Then at last everyone will know that good is rewarded, and that there is a God who judges justly here on earth.

PSALM 59

Written by David at the time King Saul set guards at his home to capture and kill him. (1 Samuel 19:11)

O my God, save me from my enemies. Protect me from these who have come to destroy me. 2 Preserve me from these criminals, these murderers. 3 They lurk in ambush for my life. Strong men are out there waiting. And not, O Lord, because I've done them wrong. 4 Yet they prepare to kill me. Lord, waken! See what is happening! Help me! 5 (And O Jehovah, God of heaven's armies, God of Israel, arise and punish the heathen nations surrounding us.) Do not spare these evil, treacherous men. 6 At evening they come to spy, slinking around like dogs that prowl the city. 7 I hear them shouting insults and cursing God, for "No one will hear us," they think. 8 Lord, laugh at them! (And scoff at these surrounding nations too.)

9 O God my Strength! I will sing your praises, for you are my place of safety. 10 My God is changeless in his love for me, and he will come and help me. He will let me see my wish come true upon my enemies. 11 Don't kill them—for my people soon forget such lessons—but stagger them with your power and bring them to their knees. Bring them to the dust, O Lord our shield. 12,13 They are proud, cursing liars. Angrily destroy them. Wipe them out. (And let the nations find out, too, that God rules in Israel and will reign throughout the world.) 14,15 Let these evil men slink back at evening and prowl the city all night before they are satisfied, howling like dogs and searching for food.

16 But as for me, I will sing each morning about your power and mercy. For you have been my high tower of refuge, a place of safety in the day of my distress. 17 O my Strength, to you I sing my praises; for you are my high tower of safety, my God of mercy.

PSALM 60

Written by David at the time he was at war with Syria, with the outcome still uncertain; this was when Joab, captain of his forces, slaughtered twelve thousand men of Edom in the Valley of Salt.

O God, you have rejected us and broken our defenses; you have become angry and deserted us. Lord, restore us again to your favor. 2 You have caused this nation to tremble in fear; you have torn it apart. Lord, heal it now, for it is shaken to its depths. 3 You have been very hard on us and made us reel beneath your blows.

4,5 But you have given us a banner to rally to; all who love truth will rally to it; then you can deliver your beloved people. Use your strong right arm to rescue us. 6,7 God has promised to help us. He has vowed it by his holiness! No wonder I exult! "Shechem, Succoth, Gilead,

58:1-5 The world is unfair. We shouldn't expect everything to go our way; nor should we allow our anger at apparent injustice to cause us to compromise. Regardless of how others act, God still expects us to make amends for the mistakes we have made. He is the only one in the position to judge whether things are ultimately fair or unfair.

59:1-4 Our enemy may not be a person—it could be alcohol or some other addictive substance. Whatever our enemy is, we should see it for what it is—something capable of destroying us. After realizing this, the wisest thing we can do is call out to God for help. He is the only one really capable of helping us; he is our place of refuge.

60:1-5 When God shows his anger because of our sin, we feel both abandoned and overwhelmed. It is at such times that we need to renew our fellowship with him. The consequences of our sins and mistakes often hurt others as well, and we ought to be sensitive to that fact and do our best to make amends. Discipline is never easy to take, but in the midst of it, God provides us with the direction we need to regain his favor and protection. He has revealed his plan for our spiritual recovery in his Word.

Manasseh—still are mine!" he says. "Judah shall continue to produce kings, and Ephraim great warriors. [8]Moab shall become my lowly servant, and Edom my slave. And I will shout in triumph over the Philistines."

[9,10]Who will bring me in triumph into Edom's strong cities? God will! He who cast us off! He who abandoned us to our foes! [11]Yes, Lord, help us against our enemies, for man's help is useless.

[12]With God's help we shall do mighty things, for he will trample down our foes.

PSALM 61

O God, listen to me! Hear my prayer! [2]For wherever I am, though far away at the ends of the earth, I will cry to you for help. When my heart is faint and overwhelmed, lead me to the mighty, towering Rock of safety. [3]For you are my refuge, a high tower where my enemies can never reach me. [4]I shall live forever in your tabernacle; oh, to be safe beneath the shelter of your wings! [5]For you have heard my vows, O God, to praise you every day, and you have given me the blessings you reserve for those who reverence your name.

[6]You will give me added years of life, as rich and full as those of many generations, all packed into one. [7]And I shall live before the Lord forever. Oh, send your loving-kindness and truth to guard and watch over me, [8]and I will praise your name continually, fulfilling my vow of praising you each day.

PSALM 62

I stand silently before the Lord, waiting for him to rescue me. For salvation comes from him alone. [2]Yes, he alone is my Rock, my rescuer, defense and fortress. Why then should I be tense with fear when troubles come?

[3,4]But what is this? They pick on me at a time when my throne is tottering; they plot my death and use lies and deceit to try to force me from the throne. They are so friendly to my face while cursing in their hearts!

[5]But I stand silently before the Lord, waiting for him to rescue me. For salvation comes from him alone. [6]Yes, he alone is my Rock, my rescuer, defense, and fortress—why then should I be tense with fear when troubles come?

[7]My protection and success come from God alone. He is my refuge, a Rock where no enemy can reach me. [8]O my people, trust him all the time. Pour out your longings before him, for he can help! [9]The greatest of men or the lowest—both alike are nothing in his sight. They weigh less than air on scales.

[10]Don't become rich by extortion and robbery; if your riches increase, don't be proud. [11,12]God has said it many times, that power belongs to him (and also, O Lord, steadfast love belongs to you). He rewards each one of us according to what our works deserve.

61:1-8 Wherever we are, whatever the circumstances that we face, we can turn to God for help. He will answer by protecting us with his divine presence. We can ask him for help with confidence because he has proven himself over and over to be a deliverer to those under enemy attack. He is our loving protector who blesses us and gives us a meaningful life, helping us fulfill our vows to live for him day by day.

62:1-8 When we face problems that we cannot overcome alone, the wisest thing to do is wait for God to defend us. We will never totally escape our problems and temptations, but God is with us at all times. He is more than capable of overcoming our most powerful adversaries. And we can rely on him not only for deliverance in times of trouble, but also for strengthening during the times when things are going well and our guard is down. As we realize these truths, we should encourage others to place their full confidence in God. Our recovery is strengthened as we reach out to help others.

63:1-5 The more difficult life is and the more severe the temptations we face, the more important God becomes to us. When we are at our weakest, God's power takes on added significance for us. We begin to understand how precious his compassionate care toward us really is. He is worthy of all our praise, which should flow from the deep emotional contentment he gives.

64:7-10 God knows exactly where our enemies are, and thus he is able to help us thwart their attack. Our part in the recovery process is to turn our life and will over to God for his care. He can't help us without our cooperation. As we allow God to work on our behalf, others will be awed at what he has done for us. And as we share the good news of God's marvelous deeds, our victory will become a cause for the hope and celebration of others, too.

65:5-13 God is more than able to respond effectively to our needs for deliverance, because he is the same God who made the majestic mountains of this world. If he can control the rainfall and the waters of the earth, we can be sure he can take care of us.

PSALM 63
A Psalm of David when he was hiding
in the wilderness of Judea.
O God, my God! How I search for you! How I
thirst for you in this parched and weary land
where there is no water. How I long to find
you! [2]How I wish I could go into your sanctuary to see your strength and glory, [3]for your
love and kindness are better to me than life
itself. How I praise you! [4]I will bless you as
long as I live, lifting up my hands to you in
prayer. [5]At last I shall be fully satisfied; I will
praise you with great joy.
[6]I lie awake at night thinking of you—[7]of
how much you have helped me—and how I
rejoice through the night beneath the protecting shadow of your wings. [8]I follow close
behind you, protected by your strong right
arm. [9]But those plotting to destroy me shall
go down to the depths of hell. [10]They are
doomed to die by the sword, to become the
food of jackals. [11]But I will rejoice in God. All
who trust in him exult, while liars shall be
silenced.

PSALM 64
Lord, listen to my complaint: Oh, preserve
my life from the conspiracy of these wicked
men, these gangs of criminals. [3]They cut me
down with sharpened tongues; they aim their
bitter words like arrows straight at my heart.
[4]They shoot from ambush at the innocent.
Suddenly the deed is done, yet they are not
afraid. [5]They encourage each other to do evil.
They meet in secret to set their traps. "He will
never notice them here," they say. [6]They keep
a sharp lookout for opportunities of crime.
They spend long hours with all their endless
evil thoughts and plans.
[7]But God himself will shoot them down.
Suddenly his arrow will pierce them. [8]They
will stagger backward, destroyed by those
they spoke against. All who see it happening
will scoff at them. [9]Then everyone shall stand
in awe and confess the greatness of the
miracles of God; at last they will realize what
amazing things he does. [10]And the godly shall
rejoice in the Lord, and trust and praise him.

PSALM 65
O God in Zion, we wait before you in silent
praise, and thus fulfill our vow. And because
you answer prayer, all mankind will come to
you with their requests. [3]Though sins fill our
hearts, you forgive them all. [4]How greatly to
be envied are those you have chosen to come
and live with you within the holy tabernacle

Giving Up Control

BIBLE READING: Psalm 61:1-8

We made a decision to turn our will and our life over to the care of God as we understood him.

The thought of turning our will and our life over can be attractive. When we give in to our dependencies and compulsions, aren't we giving control over to another power? Aren't we in some way giving up personal responsibility for our life? When we are overwhelmed and want to escape, our addictions can make us feel strong, safe, attractive, powerful, or happy. So, in a sense, we are very comfortable with the thought of giving up control of our will and our life.

We can simply change our focus and turn our life over to God instead of reverting to the hiding places of the past. The apostle Paul touched on this contrast when he said, "Don't drink too much wine, for many evils lie along that path; be filled instead with the Holy Spirit, and controlled by him" (Ephesians 5:18).

When we are overwhelmed and in need of some kind of escape, we have a new place to turn. King David declared, "All who are oppressed may come to [God]. He is a refuge for them in their times of trouble. All those who know your mercy, Lord, will count on you for help. For you have never yet forsaken those who trust in you" (Psalm 9:9-10).

David also wrote, "For wherever I am, though far away at the ends of the earth, I will cry to you for help. When my heart is faint and overwhelmed, lead me to the mighty, towering Rock of safety. For you are my refuge, a high tower where my enemies can never reach me" (Psalm 61:2-3).

Turn to page 767, Isaiah 54.

courts! What joys await us among all the good things there. 5With dread deeds and awesome power you will defend us from our enemies, O God who saves us. You are the only hope of all mankind throughout the world and far away upon the sea.

6He formed the mountains by his mighty strength. 7He quiets the raging oceans and all the world's clamor. 8In the farthest corners of the earth the glorious acts of God shall startle everyone. The dawn and sunset shout for joy! 9He waters the earth to make it fertile. The rivers of God will not run dry! He prepares the earth for his people and sends them rich harvests of grain. 10He waters the furrows with abundant rain. Showers soften the earth, melting the clods and causing seeds to sprout across the land. 11,12Then he crowns it all with green, lush pastures in the wilderness; hillsides blossom with joy. 13The pastures are filled with flocks of sheep, and the valleys are carpeted with grain. All the world shouts with joy and sings.

PSALM 66

Sing to the Lord, all the earth! 2Sing of his glorious name! Tell the world how wonderful he is.

3How awe-inspiring are your deeds, O God! How great your power! No wonder your enemies surrender! 4All the earth shall worship you and sing of your glories. 5Come, see the glorious things God has done. What marvelous miracles happen to his people! 6He made a dry road through the sea for them. They went across on foot. What excitement and joy there was that day!

7Because of his great power he rules forever. He watches every movement of the nations. O rebel lands, he will deflate your pride.

8Let everyone bless God and sing his praises; 9for he holds our lives in his hands, and he holds our feet to the path. 10You have purified us with fire, O Lord, like silver in a crucible. 11You captured us in your net and laid great burdens on our backs. 12You sent troops to ride across our broken bodies. We went through fire and flood. But in the end, you brought us into wealth and great abundance.

13Now I have come to your Temple with burnt offerings to pay my vows. 14For when I was in trouble, I promised you many offerings. 15That is why I am bringing you these fat male goats, rams, and calves. The smoke of their sacrifice shall rise before you.

16Come and hear, all of you who reverence the Lord, and I will tell you what he did for me: 17For I cried to him for help with praises ready on my tongue. 18He would not have listened if I had not confessed my sins. 19But he listened! He heard my prayer! He paid attention to it!

20Blessed be God, who didn't turn away when I was praying and didn't refuse me his kindness and love.

PSALM 67

O God, in mercy bless us; let your face beam with joy as you look down at us.

2Send us around the world with the news of your saving power and your eternal plan for all mankind. 3How everyone throughout the earth will praise the Lord! 4How glad the nations will be, singing for joy because you are their King and will give true justice to their people! 5Praise God, O world! May all the peoples of the earth give thanks to you. 6,7For the earth has yielded abundant harvests. God, even our own God, will bless us. And peoples from remotest lands will worship him.

66:1-7 When God demonstrates his power and his care for us, we need to carry the message to others. We are not alone in our trouble. Some of our struggling friends face the same problems we do. Our thanks to God for his deliverance can become a source of hope and inspiration for them as they seek victory over their dependencies.

67:1-7 We are called to share with others the good news of God's powerful deliverance and his plan for their life. This should not be a chore that we want to avoid. It should be a natural expression of our joy at being delivered from forces too powerful for us to handle alone. Without God's help we could never resist the tempting call of our addictions. But with his help we can live a life of freedom and joy. Let us celebrate and spread the news of God's powerful deliverance!

68:1-6 There is no security for those who act in opposition to God. But when life has beaten us down, God wants us to know we can find a loving family among his people. He himself is a father to us, a loving deliverer who sets us free from the traps into which we have fallen.

68:24-31 When God helps us gain control over our inner enemies, praise should naturally flow from our lips. The best gifts we can bring to God are our life and our praise. As we thank God for delivering us from our dependencies and problems, others will be encouraged to admit their need for God and call out to him for help.

PSALM 68
Arise, O God, and scatter all your enemies! Chase them away! 2Drive them off like smoke before the wind; melt them like wax in fire! So let the wicked perish at the presence of God.

3But may the godly man exult. May he rejoice and be merry. 4Sing praises to the Lord! Raise your voice in song to him who rides upon the clouds! Jehovah is his name—oh, rejoice in his presence. 5He is a father to the fatherless; he gives justice to the widows, for he is holy. 6He gives families to the lonely, and releases prisoners from jail, singing with joy! But for rebels there is famine and distress.

7O God, when you led your people through the wilderness, 8the earth trembled and the heavens shook. Mount Sinai quailed before you—the God of Israel. 9,10You sent abundant rain upon your land, O God, to refresh it in its weariness! There your people lived, for you gave them this home when they were destitute.

11-13The Lord speaks. The enemy flees. The women at home cry out the happy news: "The armies that came to destroy us have fled!" Now all the women of Israel are dividing the booty. See them sparkle with jewels of silver and gold, covered all over as wings cover doves! 14God scattered their enemies like snowflakes melting in the forests of Zalmon.

15,16O mighty mountains in Bashan! O splendid many-peaked ranges! Well may you look with envy at Mount Zion, the mount where God has chosen to live forever. 17Surrounded by unnumbered chariots, the Lord moves on from Mount Sinai and comes to his holy temple high upon Mount Zion. 18He ascends the heights, leading many captives in his train. He receives gifts for men, even those who once were rebels. God will live among us here.

19What a glorious Lord! He who daily bears our burdens also gives us our salvation.

20He frees us! He rescues us from death. 21But he will crush his enemies, for they refuse to leave their guilty, stubborn ways. 22The Lord says, "Come," to all his people's enemies; they are hiding on Mount Hermon's highest slopes and deep within the sea! 23His people must destroy them. Cover your feet with their blood; dogs will eat them.

24The procession of God my King moves onward to the sanctuary— 25singers in front, musicians behind, girls playing the timbrels in between. 26Let all the people of Israel praise the Lord, who is Israel's fountain. 27The little

Joy in God's Presence

BIBLE READING: Psalm 65:1-4

We sought through prayer and meditation to improve our conscious contact with God, as we understood him, praying only for knowledge of his will for us and the power to carry that out.

Most of us need to desire something before we will wholeheartedly seek after it. Until we realize how much God loves us and cares about the details of our life, we probably won't have the desire to pray to him. Until we sincerely believe that he has completely forgiven us, we will be ashamed to face him. If we hold to our misconceptions about God, this step will be a formidable chore rather than a joy.

The life of King David should give us hope. Long after he had come face to face with his own sinfulness, he was able to sing, "O God in Zion, we wait before you in silent praise, and thus fulfill our vow. And because you answer prayer, all mankind will come to you with their requests. Though sins fill our hearts, you forgive them all. How greatly to be envied are those you have chosen to come and live with you within the holy tabernacle courts! What joys await us among all the good things there" (Psalm 65:1-4). God wants us to be like those who lived and served in his Temple, walking freely into his presence. He wants us to know that we are welcome and valued before him. (See also Matthew 10:29-31.)

The place where God lives can be a place of joy and happiness for us now. We can look forward to spending time with him and living in his presence every day. ***Turn to page 649, Psalm 105.***

tribe of Benjamin leads the way. The princes and elders of Judah, and the princes of Zebulun and Naphtali are right behind. 28Summon your might; display your strength, O God, for you have done such mighty things for us.

29The kings of the earth are bringing their gifts to your temple in Jerusalem. 30Rebuke our enemies, O Lord. Bring them—submissive, tax in hand. Scatter all who delight in war. 31Egypt will send gifts of precious metals. Ethiopia will stretch out her hands to God in adoration. 32Sing to the Lord, O kingdoms of the earth—sing praises to the Lord, 33to him who rides upon the ancient heavens, whose mighty voice thunders from the sky.

34Power belongs to God! His majesty shines down on Israel; his strength is mighty in the heavens. 35What awe we feel, kneeling here before him in the sanctuary. The God of Israel gives strength and mighty power to his people. Blessed be God!

PSALM 69

Save me, O my God. The floods have risen. Deeper and deeper I sink in the mire; the waters rise around me. 3I have wept until I am exhausted; my throat is dry and hoarse; my eyes are swollen with weeping, waiting for my God to act. 4I cannot even count all those who hate me without cause. They are influential men, these who plot to kill me though I am innocent. They demand that I be punished for what I didn't do.

5O God, you know so well how stupid I am, and you know all my sins. 6O Lord God of the armies of heaven, don't let me be a stumbling block to those who trust in you. O God of Israel, don't let me cause them to be confused, 7though I am mocked and cursed and shamed for your sake. 8Even my own brothers pretend they don't know me! 9My zeal for God and his work burns hot within me. And because I advocate your cause, your enemies insult me even as they insult you. 10How they scoff and mock me when I mourn and fast before the Lord! 11How they talk about me when I wear sackcloth to show my humiliation and sorrow for my sins! 12I am the talk of the town and the song of the drunkards. 13But I keep right on praying to you, Lord. For now is the time—you are bending down to hear! You are ready with a plentiful supply of love and kindness. Now answer my prayer and rescue me as you promised. 14Pull me out of this mire. Don't let me sink in. Rescue me from those who hate me, and from these deep waters I am in.

15Don't let the floods overwhelm me or the ocean swallow me; save me from the pit that threatens me. 16O Jehovah, answer my prayers, for your loving-kindness is wonderful; your mercy is so plentiful, so tender and so kind. 17Don't hide from me, for I am in deep trouble. Quick! Come and save me. 18Come, Lord, and rescue me. Ransom me from all my enemies. 19You know how they talk about me, and how they so shamefully dishonor me. You see them all and know what each has said.

20Their contempt has broken my heart; my spirit is heavy within me. If even one would show some pity, if even one would comfort me! 21For food they gave me gall; for my awful thirst they offered vinegar. 22Let their joys turn to ashes and their peace disappear; 23let darkness, blindness, and great feebleness be theirs. 24Pour out your fury upon them; consume them with the fierceness of your anger. 25Let their homes be desolate and abandoned. 26For they persecute the one you have smitten and scoff at the pain of the one you have pierced. 27 Pile their sins high and do not overlook them. 28Let these men be blotted from the list of the living; do not give them the joys of life with the righteous.

29But rescue me, O God, from my poverty and pain. 30Then I will praise God with my singing! My thanks will be his praise—31that

---

69:1-4, 13 As he wrote this psalm, David felt as if his problems were closing in on him. It seemed that no one was around to take his side. We often feel the same desperation as we work through the process of recovery. In times like these, we should do what David did—cry out to God for help, submit to his will, and entrust our life to his care.

69:5-8 David knew how important it was to recognize his faults and to admit them to God. This is an essential step in our own recovery. We must accept responsibility for what we have done in the past. Then, like David, we should turn to God for forgiveness and restoration.

69:9-12 David's visible repentance and desire to change his life brought him intense ridicule. He became a laughingstock among those who were opposed to God. Even the town drunks ridiculed him. As we confess our failures and turn our life over to God, we may experience similar scorn. We may deserve some of the ridicule we receive; it may take people a while to believe that the changes in our life are real. During such trials we should remember that God is more concerned about rebuilding our character than he is about restoring our reputation.

will please him more than sacrificing a bullock or an ox. [32]The humble shall see their God at work for them. No wonder they will be so glad! All who seek for God shall live in joy. [33]For Jehovah hears the cries of his needy ones and does not look the other way.

[34]Praise him, all heaven and earth! Praise him, all the seas and everything in them! [35]For God will save Jerusalem; he rebuilds the cities of Judah. His people shall live in them and not be dispossessed. [36]Their children shall inherit the land; all who love his name shall live there safely.

PSALM 70

Rescue me, O God! Lord, hurry to my aid! [2,3]They are after my life and delight in hurting me. Confuse them! Shame them! Stop them! Don't let them keep on mocking me! [4]But fill the followers of God with joy. Let those who love your salvation exclaim, "What a wonderful God he is!" [5]But I am in deep trouble. Rush to my aid, for only you can help and save me. O Lord, don't delay.

PSALM 71

Lord, you are my refuge! Don't let me down! [2]Save me from my enemies, for you are just! Rescue me! Bend down your ear and listen to my plea and save me. [3]Be to me a great protecting Rock, where I am always welcome, safe from all attacks. For you have issued the order to save me. [4]Rescue me, O God, from these unjust and cruel men. [5]O Lord, you alone are my hope; I've trusted you from childhood. [6]Yes, you have been with me from birth and have helped me constantly—no wonder I am always praising you! [7]My success—at which so many stand amazed—is because you are my mighty protector. [8]All day long I'll praise and honor you, O God, for all that you have done for me.

[9]And now, in my old age, don't set me aside. Don't forsake me now when my strength is failing. [10]My enemies are whispering, [11]"God has forsaken him! Now we can get him. There is no one to help him now!" [12]O God, don't stay away! Come quickly! Help! [13]Destroy them! Cover them with failure and disgrace—these enemies of mine.

[14]I will keep on expecting you to help me. I praise you more and more. [15]I cannot count the times when you have faithfully rescued me from danger. I will tell everyone how good you are, and of your constant, daily care. [16]I walk in the strength of the Lord God. I tell everyone that you alone are just and good. [17]O God, you have helped me from my earliest childhood—and I have constantly testified to others of the wonderful things you do. [18]And now that I am old and gray, don't forsake me. Give me time to tell this new generation (and their children too) about all your mighty miracles. [19]Your power and goodness, Lord, reach to the highest heavens. You have done such wonderful things. Where is there another God like you? [20]You have let me sink down deep in desperate problems. But you will bring me back to life again, up from the depths of the earth. [21]You will give me greater honor than before and turn again and comfort me.

[22]I will praise you with music, telling of your faithfulness to all your promises, O Holy One of Israel. [23]I will shout and sing your praises for redeeming me. [24]I will talk to others all day long about your justice and your goodness. For all who tried to hurt me have been disgraced and dishonored.

PSALM 72

O God, help the king to judge as you would, and help his son to walk in godliness. [2]Help him to give justice to your people, even to the poor. [3]May the mountains and hills flourish in prosperity because of his good reign. [4]Help

---

70:1-5 This prayer by the psalmist is short and to the point. He cried out for help in the face of an immediate emergency. It is possible to pray at any time, and it is especially appropriate when faced with a sudden temptation. For many of us, prayer is the last solution we think of in times of trouble. We try any number of human solutions before looking to God for help. We would be wise to keep prayer always at the tip of our tongue.

71:1-8 The psalmist often described God as his refuge or protecting Rock—a place of safety in times of difficulty and trial. The psalmist gave God heartfelt praise for the shelter he provides. This proves that he had truly experienced God's protection in his life. One way we can show the reality of God's power to others is to praise and thank him for his deliverance. Let us learn from David's praise and pass the same lesson on to the people around us.

71:9-12 We all face difficult times, especially as we undergo the recovery process. As we struggle with our dependencies, our strength often drains to its lowest possible level. When we are powerless, we should seek God's watchful care. He has the power we need to overcome even the most devastating of problems.

him to defend the poor and needy and to
crush their oppressors. 5May the poor and
needy revere you constantly, as long as sun
and moon continue in the skies! Yes, forever!
6May the reign of this son of mine be as
gentle and fruitful as the springtime rains
upon the grass—like showers that water the
earth! 7May all good men flourish in his reign
with abundance of peace to the end of time.
8Let him reign from sea to sea and from the
Euphrates River to the ends of the earth. 9The
desert nomads shall bow before him; his enemies shall fall face downward in the dust.
10Kings along the Mediterranean coast—the
kings of Tarshish and the islands—and those
from Sheba and from Seba—all will bring
their gifts. 11Yes, kings from everywhere! All
will bow before him! All will serve him!
12He will take care of the helpless and poor
when they cry to him; for they have no one
else to defend them. 13He feels pity for the
weak and needy and will rescue them. 14He
will save them from oppression and from
violence, for their lives are precious to him.
15And he shall live; and to him will be given
the gold of Sheba, and there will be constant
praise for him. His people will bless him all
day long. 16Bless us with abundant crops
throughout the land, even on the highland
plains; may there be fruit like that of Lebanon; may the cities be as full of people as the
fields are of grass. 17His name will be honored
forever; it will continue as the sun; and all will
be blessed in him; all nations will praise him.
18Blessed be Jehovah God, the God of Israel,
who only does wonderful things! 19Blessed be
his glorious name forever! Let the whole earth
be filled with his glory. Amen and amen!
20(This ends the psalms of David, son of
Jesse.)

PSALM 73

How good God is to Israel—to those whose
hearts are pure. 2But as for me, I came *so* close
to the edge of the cliff! My feet were slipping
and I was almost gone. 3For I was envious of
the prosperity of the proud and wicked. 4Yes,
all through life their road is smooth! They
grow sleek and fat. 5They aren't always in
trouble and plagued with problems like everyone else, 6so their pride sparkles like a jeweled
necklace, and their clothing is woven of cruelty! 7These fat cats have everything their
hearts could ever wish for! 8They scoff at God
and threaten his people. How proudly they
speak! 9They boast against the very heavens,
and their words strut through the earth.
10And so God's people are dismayed and
confused and drink it all in. 11"Does God
realize what is going on?" they ask. 12"Look at
these men of arrogance; they never have to
lift a finger—theirs is a life of ease; and all the
time their riches multiply."
13Have I been wasting my time? Why take
the trouble to be pure? 14All I get out of it is
trouble and woe—every day and all day long!
15If I had really said that, I would have been a
traitor to your people. 16Yet it is so hard to
explain it—this prosperity of those who hate
the Lord. 17Then one day I went into God's
sanctuary to meditate and thought about the
future of these evil men. 18What a slippery
path they are on—suddenly God will send
them sliding over the edge of the cliff and
down to their destruction: 19an instant end to
all their happiness, an eternity of terror.
20Their present life is only a dream! They will
awaken to the truth as one awakens from a
dream of things that never really were!
21When I saw this, what turmoil filled my
heart! 22I saw myself so stupid and so ignorant; I must seem like an animal to you,
O God.23But even so, you love me! You are
holding my right hand! 24You will keep on
guiding me all my life with your wisdom and
counsel, and afterwards receive me into the
glories of heaven! 25Whom have I in heaven
but you? And I desire no one on earth as
much as you! 26My health fails; my spirits

72:12-14 God acts on behalf of those who have no power to free themselves from their problems. He also helps those who suffer great burdens and have no other source of help. He has great love and compassion for those who are needy. As we face our addictions, we know what it means to be powerless. Alone, we are helpless to overcome the temptation of our dependencies. But with God's help, there is always hope for us. He has the power to overcome any of the problems we face, and he wants to see us through the hard times to a new life of freedom and joy.

73:13-20 The psalmist had begun to wonder whether following God's program was worth it. It seemed to him that evil people were happy and prosperous. It didn't seem to make sense. In these verses, however, the psalmist came to his senses. When all is said and done, God's justice will be served. We all know that our addictions worked for a while, but with time, they became destructive. God's plan is the only recovery program designed to lead to wholeness and eternal life with him. We would be wise to follow his plan no matter how difficult it may seem to us at present.

droop, yet God remains! He is the strength of my heart; he is mine forever!

27But those refusing to worship God will perish, for he destroys those serving other gods.

28But as for me, I get as close to him as I can! I have chosen him, and I will tell everyone about the wonderful ways he rescues me.

PSALM 74

O God, why have you cast us away forever? Why is your anger hot against us—the sheep of your own pasture? 2Remember that we are your people—the ones you chose in ancient times from slavery and made the choicest of your possessions. You chose Jerusalem as your home on earth!

3Walk through the awful ruins of the city and see what the enemy has done to your sanctuary. 4There they shouted their battle cry and erected their idols to flaunt their victory. 5,6Everything lies in shambles like a forest chopped to the ground. They came with their axes and sledgehammers and smashed and chopped the carved paneling; 7they set the sanctuary on fire, and razed it to the ground—your sanctuary, Lord. 8"Let's wipe out every trace of God," they said, and went through the entire country burning down the assembly places where we worshiped you.

9,10There is nothing left to show that we are your people. The prophets are gone, and who can say when it all will end? How long, O God, will you allow our enemies to dishonor your name? Will you let them get away with this forever? 11Why do you delay? Why hold back your power? Unleash your fist and give them a final blow.

12God is my King from ages past; you have been actively helping me everywhere throughout the land. 13,14You divided the Red Sea with your strength; you crushed the sea-god's heads! You gave him to the desert tribes to eat! 15At your command the springs burst forth to give your people water; and then you dried a path for them across the ever-flowing Jordan. 16Day and night alike belong to you; you made the starlight and the sun. 17All nature is within your hands; you make the summer and the winter too. 18Lord, see how these enemies scoff at you. O Jehovah, an arrogant nation has blasphemed your name.

19O Lord, save me! Protect your turtledove from the hawks. Save your beloved people from these beasts. 20Remember your promise! For the land is full of darkness and cruel men. 21O Lord, don't let your downtrodden people be constantly insulted. Give cause for these poor and needy ones to praise your name!22Arise, O God, and state your case against our enemies. Remember the insults these rebels have hurled against you all day long. 23Don't overlook the cursing of these enemies of yours; it grows louder and louder.

PSALM 75

How we thank you, Lord! Your mighty miracles give proof that you care.

2"Yes," the Lord replies, "and when I am ready, I will punish the wicked! 3Though the earth shakes and all its people live in turmoil, yet its pillars are firm, for I have set them in place!"

4I warned the proud to cease their arrogance! I told the wicked to lower their insolent gaze 5and to stop being stubborn and proud. 6,7For promotion and power come

73:21-24 The psalmist had begun to think that God was unjust and had a hard time believing that God was loving and good. In these verses, however, he realized how foolish he had been. God was waiting to restore his relationship with the doubting psalmist. We need God's help if we want to succeed in our recovery. But if we cannot believe that God is good, we will hardly be able to entrust him with our life. Like the psalmist, we need to realize that God does love us and that his plan for us is for the best. If we trust in God and seek to follow his will for us, our recovery is in good hands.

74:12-23 God has proven himself over and over as a God who is able to deliver us. He has shown his power by his control over our enemies, over ferocious animals, and over nature itself. We therefore can call on him and be confident that he is able to overcome all the problems we face. He will be faithful to his Word, watching over us even as we walk through the darkest valleys in this life.

75:1-5 Once we turn our life and will over to God, we begin to see evidence of his care for us. But pride is a powerful enemy. It keeps us from turning to God or other people to get help and perpetuates our tendency for denial. God shows the wrath of his judgment against the proud and boastful, who consider themselves to be self-sufficient. We were never created to stand alone and make our own way in life. We were created by God to fit into his plan for the created universe. God's program for righteous and healthy living has been given for our benefit and joy.

75:6-10 Envy is another great enemy of our soul. The psalmist understood that it was God who lifts up one person and sets down another. We must leave issues of promotion in God's hands. His promise to punish the wicked is given first to warn people away from their evil and then to assure those who suffer at the hands of wicked people that God hasn't forgotten them.

from nowhere on earth, but only from God. He promotes one and deposes another. 8In Jehovah's hand there is a cup of pale and sparkling wine. It is his judgment, poured out upon the wicked of the earth. They must drain that cup to the dregs.

9But as for me, I shall forever declare the praises of the God of Jacob. 10"I will cut off the strength of evil men," says the Lord, "and increase the power of good men in their place."

PSALM 76

God's reputation is very great in Judah and in Israel. 2His home is in Jerusalem. He lives upon Mount Zion. 3There he breaks the weapons of our enemies.

4The everlasting mountains cannot compare with you in glory! 5The mightiest of our enemies are conquered. They lie before us in the sleep of death; not one can lift a hand against us. 6When you rebuked them, God of Jacob, steeds and riders fell. 7No wonder you are greatly feared! Who can stand before an angry God? 8You pronounce sentence on them from heaven; the earth trembles and stands silently before you. 9You stand up to punish the evil-doers and to defend the meek of the earth. 10Man's futile wrath will bring you glory. You will use it as an ornament!

11Fulfill all your vows that you have made to Jehovah your God. Let everyone bring him presents. He should be reverenced and feared, 12for he cuts down princes and does awesome things to the kings of the earth.

PSALM 77

I cry to the Lord; I call and call to him. Oh, that he would listen. 2I am in deep trouble and I need his help so much. All night long I pray, lifting my hands to heaven, pleading. There can be no joy for me until he acts. 3I think of God and moan, overwhelmed with longing for his help. 4I cannot sleep until you act. I am too distressed even to pray!

5I keep thinking of the good old days of the past, long since ended. 6Then my nights were filled with joyous songs. I search my soul and meditate upon the difference now. 7Has the Lord rejected me forever? Will he never again be favorable? 8Is his loving-kindness gone forever? Has his promise failed? 9Has he forgotten to be kind to one so undeserving? Has he slammed the door in anger on his love? 10And I said: This is my fate, that the blessings of God have changed to hate. 11I recall the many miracles he did for me so long ago. 12Those wonderful deeds are constantly in my thoughts. I cannot stop thinking about them.

13O God, your ways are holy. Where is there any other as mighty as you? 14You are the God of miracles and wonders! You still demonstrate your awesome power.

15You have redeemed us who are the sons of Jacob and of Joseph by your might. 16When the Red Sea saw you, how it feared! It trembled to its depths! 17The clouds poured down their rain, the thunder rolled and crackled in the sky. Your lightning flashed. 18There was thunder in the whirlwind; the lightning lighted up the world! The earth trembled and shook.

19Your road led by a pathway through the sea—a pathway no one knew was there! 20You led your people along that road like a flock of sheep, with Moses and Aaron as their shepherds.

PSALM 78

O my people, listen to my teaching. Open your ears to what I am saying. 2,3For I will show you lessons from our history, stories handed down to us from former generations. 4I will reveal these truths to you so that you can describe these glorious deeds of Jehovah to your children and tell them about the mighty miracles he did. 5For he gave his laws to Israel and commanded our fathers to teach them to their children, 6so that they in turn could teach their children too. Thus his laws pass down from generation to generation. 7In this way each generation has been able to

76:11-12 As we make a list of the people we have harmed and make plans for reconciliation, we need to follow through on our plans. We often make promises to act but then fail to do so. If we expect to reconcile our relationships, we need to learn to follow through on our promises. The same principle holds true with God. If we make a promise to him, refusing to follow through will only lead to further pain and separation from God. All relationships are based upon trust. Unless we learn to be trustworthy, our relationships will continue to be shaky, and our recovery is doomed to failure.

77:1-4 As he wrote these verses, the psalmist was feeling anguish so deep he didn't feel like praying. The same thing often happens to us. When we are discouraged, we need to be more persistent in our prayer. God is the only one who can really help us. When our life is out of control, God is able to slow it down and put the pieces back together again.

obey his laws and to set its hope anew on God
and not forget his glorious miracles. [8]Thus
they did not need to be as their fathers were—
stubborn, rebellious, unfaithful, refusing to
give their hearts to God.

[9]The people of Ephraim, though fully
armed, turned their backs and fled when the
day of battle came [10]because they didn't obey
his laws. They refused to follow his ways.
[11,12]And they forgot about the wonderful
miracles God had done for them and for their
fathers in Egypt. [13]For he divided the sea before them and led them through! The water
stood banked up along both sides of them!
[14]In the daytime he led them by a cloud, and
at night by a pillar of fire. [15]He split open the
rocks in the wilderness to give them plenty of
water, as though gushing from a spring.
[16]Streams poured from the rock, flowing like a
river!

[17]Yet they kept on with their rebellion, sinning against the God who is above all gods.
[18]They murmured and complained, demanding other food than God was giving them.
[19,20]They even spoke against God himself.
"Why can't he give us decent food as well as
water?" they grumbled. [21]Jehovah heard them
and was angry; the fire of his wrath burned
against Israel [22]because they didn't believe in
God or trust in him to care for them, [23]even
though he commanded the skies to open—he
opened the windows of heaven—[24]and rained
down manna for their food. He gave them
bread from heaven! [25]They ate angels' food!
He gave them all they could hold.

[26]And he led forth the east wind and guided
the south wind by his mighty power. [27]He
rained down birds as thick as dust, clouds of
them like sands along the shore! [28]He caused
the birds to fall to the ground among the
tents. [29]The people ate their fill. He gave them
what they asked for. [30]But they had hardly
finished eating, and the meat was yet in their
mouths, [31]when the anger of the Lord rose
against them and killed the finest of Israel's
young men. [32]Yet even so the people kept on
sinning and refused to believe in miracles.
[33]So he cut their lives short and gave them
years of terror and disaster.

[34]Then at last, when he had ruined them,
they walked awhile behind him; how earnestly they turned around and followed him!
[35]Then they remembered that God was their
Rock—that their Savior was the God above all
gods. [36]But it was only with their words they
followed him, not with their hearts; [37]their
hearts were far away. They did not keep their
promises. [38]Yet he was merciful and forgave
their sins and didn't destroy them all. Many
and many a time he held back his anger. [39]For
he remembered that they were merely mortal
men, gone in a moment like a breath of wind.

[40]Oh, how often they rebelled against him
in those desert years and grieved his heart.
[41]Again and again they turned away and
tempted God to kill them, and limited the
Holy One of Israel from giving them his blessings. [42]They forgot his power and love and
how he had rescued them from their enemies;
[43]they forgot the plagues he sent upon the
Egyptians in Tanis—[44]how he turned their rivers into blood so that no one could drink,
[45]how he sent vast swarms of flies to fill the
land, and how the frogs had covered all of
Egypt!

[46]He gave their crops to caterpillars. Their
harvest was consumed by locusts. [47]He destroyed their grapevines and their sycamores
with hail. [48]Their cattle died in the fields,
mortally wounded by huge hailstones from
heaven. Their sheep were killed by lightning.
[49]He loosed on them the fierceness of his

78:9-12 God's people, although well equipped to defeat their enemies in the Promised Land, failed to carry out God's command fully. When they should have boldly pressed forward, they ran from the conflict like cowards. This failure was undoubtedly prompted by the fact that they did not consider the full significance of God's past acts of power on behalf of his people. When we fail to count on God's power, either out of unbelief or because of pride, we are bound to fail.

78:17-33 God's anger grew greater against his rebellious people because they continually complained and refused to trust him to deliver them from their wilderness experience. We should pray that this won't happen to us. In spite of our unbelief, God is often merciful to us, giving us benefits we don't deserve (see Exodus 16:4-5; Numbers 11:31). The people had all that they could ever want, but because they still maintained an attitude of rebellion against him, God sent a plague that terrified them greatly, cutting many of them down in the prime of their life (see Numbers 11:32-33). Rebellion can do the same for us.

78:34-39 God knows that we are human, with all the frailties of mortal beings. He is compassionate toward us, forgiving our sins and often turning away his judgment, just as he did to his people in the wilderness. His goodness should encourage us and make us more willing to commit our life to him.

anger, sending sorrow and trouble. He dispatched against them a band of destroying
angels. 50He gave free course to his anger and
did not spare the Egyptians' lives, but handed
them over to plagues and sickness. 51Then he
killed the eldest son in each Egyptian family—he who was the beginning of its strength
and joy.
52But he led forth his own people like a
flock, guiding them safely through the wilderness. 53He kept them safe, so they were not
afraid. But the sea closed in upon their enemies and overwhelmed them. 54He brought
them to the border of his land of blessing, to
this land of hills he made for them. 55He drove
out the nations occupying the land and gave
each tribe of Israel its apportioned place as its
home.
56Yet though he did all this for them, they
still rebelled against the God above all gods
and refused to follow his commands. 57They
turned back from entering the Promised Land
and disobeyed as their fathers had. Like a
crooked arrow, they missed the target of God's
will. 58They made him angry by erecting idols
and altars to other gods.
59When God saw their deeds, his wrath was
strong and he despised his people. 60Then he
abandoned his Tabernacle at Shiloh, where he
had lived among mankind, 61and allowed his
Ark to be captured; he surrendered his glory
into enemy hands. 62He caused his people to
be butchered because his anger was intense.
63Their young men were killed by fire, and
their girls died before they were old enough to
sing their wedding songs. 64The priests were
slaughtered, and their widows died before
they could even begin their lament. 65Then
the Lord rose up as though awakening from
sleep, and like a mighty man aroused by wine,
66he routed his enemies; he drove them back
and sent them to eternal shame. 67But he
rejected Joseph's family, the tribe of Ephraim,
68and chose the tribe of Judah—and Mount
Zion, which he loved. 69There he built his
towering temple, solid and enduring as the
heavens and the earth. 70He chose his servant
David, taking him from feeding sheep 71,72and
from following the ewes with lambs; God
presented David to his people as their shepherd, and he cared for them with a true heart
and skillful hands.

PSALM 79

O God, your land has been conquered by the
heathen nations. Your Temple is defiled, and
Jerusalem is a heap of ruins. 2The bodies of
your people lie exposed—food for birds and
animals. 3The enemy has butchered the entire
population of Jerusalem; blood has flowed
like water. No one is left even to bury them.
4The nations all around us scoff. They heap
contempt on us.
5O Jehovah, how long will you be angry
with us? Forever? Will your jealousy burn
till every hope is gone? 6Pour out your
wrath upon the godless nations—not on
us—on kingdoms that refuse to pray, that
will not call upon your name! 7For they
have destroyed your people Israel, invading
every home. 8Oh, do not hold us guilty for
our former sins! Let your tenderhearted
mercies meet our needs, for we are brought
low to the dust. 9Help us, God of our salvation! Help us for the honor of your name.
Oh, save us and forgive our sins. 10Why
should the heathen nations be allowed to
scoff, "Where is their God?" Publicly
avenge this slaughter of your people!
11Listen to the sighing of the prisoners and
those condemned to die. Demonstrate the
greatness of your power by saving them.
12O Lord, take sevenfold vengeance on these
nations scorning you.
13Then we your people, the sheep of your
pasture, will thank you forever and forever,
praising your greatness from generation to
generation.

PSALM 80

O Shepherd of Israel who leads Israel like a
flock; O God enthroned above the Guardian
Angels, bend down your ear and listen as I
plead. Display your power and radiant glory.
2Let Ephraim, Benjamin, and Manasseh see

78:59-64 Sin has devastating consequences. God loves us, but our continuing in disobedience sometimes causes him to turn away from us and allow our enemies to defeat us. If we are wise, we will understand what has happened, admit our failure, and commit our life again to God's care.

79:5-13 As we face hard times we need to be open to the possibility that God may be allowing our difficulties to call us away from sin. If that is true, we need to plead to God for mercy. God's forgiveness is needed if we are to be restored to wholeness. God delivers us from the controlling influences of our life not merely to give us freedom, but also to bring him honor and to have others recognize his greatness. It is our responsibility to spread the good news of God's deliverance.

you rouse yourself and use your mighty
power to rescue us.
[3]Turn us again to yourself, O God. Look
down on us in joy and love; only then shall
we be saved.
[4]O Jehovah, God of heaven's armies, how
long will you be angry and reject our prayers? [5]You have fed us with sorrow and tears
[6]and have made us the scorn of the neighboring nations. They laugh among themselves.
[7]Turn us again to yourself, O God of Hosts.
Look down on us in joy and love; only then
shall we be saved. [8]You brought us from Egypt
as though we were a tender vine and drove
away the heathen from your land and planted
us. [9]You cleared the ground and tilled the soil,
and we took root and filled the land. [10]The
mountains were covered with our shadow; we
were like the mighty cedar trees, [11]covering
the entire land from the Mediterranean Sea to
the Euphrates River. [12]But now you have broken down our walls, leaving us without protection. [13]The boar from the forest roots
around us, and the wild animals feed on us.
[14]Come back, we beg of you, O God of the
armies of heaven, and bless us. Look down
from heaven and see our plight and care for
this your vine! [15]Protect what you yourself
have planted, this son you have raised for
yourself. [16]For we are chopped and burned by
our enemies. May they perish at your frown.
[17]Strengthen the man you love, the son of
your choice, [18]and we will never forsake you
again. Revive us to trust in you.
[19]Turn us again to yourself, O God of the
armies of heaven. Look down on us, your face
aglow with joy and love—only then shall we
be saved.

PSALM 81

The Lord makes us strong! Sing praises! Sing
to Israel's God!
[2]Sing, accompanied by drums; pluck the
sweet lyre and harp. [3]Sound the trumpet!
Come to the joyous celebrations at full moon,
new moon, and all the other holidays. [4]For
God has given us these times of joy; they are
scheduled in the laws of Israel. [5]He gave them
as reminders of his war against Egypt where
we were slaves on foreign soil.
I heard an unknown voice that said, [6]"Now
I will relieve your shoulder of its burden; I will
free your hands from their heavy tasks." [7]He
said, "You cried to me in trouble, and I saved
you; I answered from Mount Sinai where the
thunder hides. I tested your faith at Meribah,
when you complained there was no water.
[8]Listen to me, O my people, while I give you
stern warnings. O Israel, if you will only
listen! [9]*You must never worship any other god*
nor ever have an idol in your home. [10]For it
was I, Jehovah your God, who brought you
out of the land of Egypt. Only test me! Open
your mouth wide and see if I won't fill it. You
will receive every blessing you can use!
[11]"But no, my people won't listen. Israel
doesn't want me around. [12]So I am letting
them go their blind and stubborn way, living
according to their own desires.
[13]"But oh, that my people would listen to
me! Oh, that Israel would follow me, walking
in my paths! [14]How quickly then I would
subdue her enemies! How soon my hands
would be upon her foes! [15]Those who hate the
Lord would cringe before him; their desolation would last forever. [16]But he would feed
you with the choicest foods. He would satisfy
you with honey for the taking."

80:9-13 God does a marvelous work for us. He frees us from bondage, removes barriers from our life, and firmly establishes us, doing everything we need in order to grow and prosper spiritually. When we begin to act as if we don't need God, he cuts us back down to size and allows our enemies—internal or external—to take advantage of us. Recovery is a lifelong process; our relationship with God also should last a lifetime. We need to realize that without God's help, even when we seem to be doing well, we are in danger of a fall. Our recovery and our relationship with God need constant attention.

80:14-19 When we are beaten down, we need to plead for God's mercy and for his restorative work in our life. Even though we feel overwhelmed by our suffering, we should remember that God can bring an end to all that caused us so much pain. And as he gives us strength and restores us to wholeness, he wants us to share the good news about deliverance with others. As we share the message of God's deliverance, others will begin to hope in God's power, and we will find our own recovery strengthened.

81:6-10 With great power, God takes the burdens away from his people and delivers them when they rely on him. God warns us over and over not to allow any person or thing to take his place in our life. Trusting any resource or power other than God is foolishness. He is far more powerful than any other possible means of deliverance. Only he can satisfy our deepest needs; all we need to do is look to him for help.

PSALM 82

God stands up to open heaven's court. He pronounces judgment on the judges. 2How long will you judges refuse to listen to the evidence? How long will you shower special favors on the wicked? 3Give fair judgment to the poor man, the afflicted, the fatherless, the destitute. 4Rescue the poor and helpless from the grasp of evil men. 5But you are so foolish and so ignorant! Because you are in darkness, all the foundations of society are shaken to the core. 6I have called you all "gods" and "sons of the Most High." 7But in death you are mere men. You will fall as any prince—for all must die.

8Stand up, O God, and judge the earth. For all of it belongs to you. All nations are in your hands.

PSALM 83

O God, don't sit idly by, silent and inactive when we pray. Answer us! Deliver us!

2Don't you hear the tumult and commotion of your enemies? Don't you see what they are doing, these proud men who hate the Lord? 3They are full of craftiness and plot against your people, laying plans to slay your precious ones. 4"Come," they say, "and let us wipe out Israel as a nation—we will destroy the very memory of her existence." 5This was their unanimous decision at their summit conference—they signed a treaty to ally themselves against Almighty God—6these Ishmaelites and Edomites and Moabites and Hagrites; 7people from the lands of Gebal, Ammon, Amalek, Philistia and Tyre; 8Assyria has joined them too, and is allied with the descendants of Lot.

9Do to them as once you did to Midian, or as you did to Sisera and Jabin at the river Kishon, 10and as you did to your enemies at Endor, whose decaying corpses fertilized the soil. 11Make their mighty nobles die as Oreb did, and Zeeb; let all their princes die like Zebah and Zalmunna, 12who said, "Let us seize for our own use these pasturelands of God!"

13O my God, blow them away like dust; like chaff before the wind—14as a forest fire that roars across a mountain. 15Chase them with your fiery storms, tempests, and tornados. 16Utterly disgrace them until they recognize your power and name, O Lord. 17Make them failures in everything they do; let them be ashamed and terrified 18until they learn that you alone, Jehovah, are the God above all gods in supreme charge of all the earth.

PSALM 84

How lovely is your Temple, O Lord of the armies of heaven.

2I long, yes, faint with longing to be able to enter your courtyard and come near to the Living God. 3Even the sparrows and swallows are welcome to come and nest among your altars and there have their young, O Lord of heaven's armies, my King and my God! 4How happy are those who can live in your Temple, singing your praises.

5Happy are those who are strong in the Lord, who want above all else to follow your steps. 6When they walk through the Valley of Weeping, it will become a place of springs where pools of blessing and refreshment collect after rains! 7They will grow constantly in strength, and each of them is invited to meet with the Lord in Zion.

8O Jehovah, God of the heavenly armies,

82:1-4 God executes judgment among his people and particularly holds accountable those who deal unfairly with the innocent and destitute. Many will have to answer for things they have done to cause people to stumble and become addicted to controlling influences. If we have led others astray, part of making amends may be to help them discover their problem and to share the good news of God's deliverance with them.

83:1-8 Encountering problems in our life should motivate us to call out to God for help. All the forces of evil seem to conspire against us as we face temptation. God doesn't want us to fail; he is there to help us. But we need to become aware of the things that weaken and defeat us. By avoiding them, we will find temptation easier to deal with. God's program for healthy living is designed for this very thing—to lead us away from temptation.

83:13-18 Nothing can stand against God. He created everything that exists, and he alone is sovereign over all the world. When we are trying to live for him, our enemies are his enemies, and we can count on him to deal with them as such.

84:1-4 Beauty is found wherever the all-powerful God resides. Although he is a God who rules with great power, he is also a God who cares for the little things of the world—even sparrows and swallows. True blessing and joy come to us when we choose to live in his presence. As we entrust our life to God and do our best to follow his will for us, we will discover the blessings of living in the presence of our righteous and loving God.

hear my prayer! Listen, God of Israel. 9O God,
our Defender and our Shield, have mercy on
the one you have anointed as your king.
10A single day spent in your Temple is better
than a thousand anywhere else! I would
rather be a doorman of the Temple of my God
than live in palaces of wickedness. 11For
Jehovah God is our Light and our Protector.
He gives us grace and glory. No good thing
will he withhold from those who walk along
his paths.
12O Lord of the armies of heaven, blessed
are those who trust in you.

PSALM 85

Lord, you have poured out amazing blessings
on this land! You have restored the fortunes
of Israel, 2and forgiven the sins of your
people—yes, covered over each one, 3so that
all your wrath, your blazing anger, is now
ended.
4Now bring us back to loving you, O Lord,
so that your anger will never need rise against
us again. 5(Or will you be always angry—on
and on to distant generations?) 6Oh, revive us!
Then your people can rejoice in you again.
7Pour out your love and kindness on us, Lord,
and grant us your salvation.
8I am listening carefully to all the Lord is
saying—for he speaks peace to his people, his
saints, if they will only stop their sinning.
9Surely his salvation is near to those who
reverence him; our land will be filled with his
glory.
10Mercy and truth have met together. Grim
justice and peace have kissed! 11Truth rises
from the earth, and righteousness smiles
down from heaven.
12Yes, the Lord pours down his blessings on
the land, and it yields its bountiful crops.
13Justice goes before him to make a pathway
for his steps.

PSALM 86

Bend down and hear my prayer, O Lord, and
answer me, for I am deep in trouble.
2Protect me from death, for I try to follow all
your laws. Save me, for I am serving you and
trusting you. 3Be merciful, O Lord, for I am
looking up to you in constant hope. 4Give me
happiness, O Lord, for I worship only you.
5O Lord, you are so good and kind, so ready to
forgive, so full of mercy for all who ask your aid.
6Listen closely to my prayer, O God. Hear
my urgent cry. 7I will call to you whenever
trouble strikes, and you will help me.
8Where among the heathen gods is there a
god like you? Where are their miracles? 9All
the nations—and you made each one—will
come and bow before you, Lord, and praise
your great and holy name. 10For you are great
and do great miracles. You alone are God.
11Tell me where you want me to go and I
will go there. May every fiber of my being
unite in reverence to your name. 12With all
my heart I will praise you. I will give glory to
your name forever, 13for you love me so much!
You are constantly so kind! You have rescued
me from deepest hell.
14O God, proud and insolent men defy me;
violent, godless men are trying to kill me.
15But you are merciful and gentle, Lord, slow
in getting angry, full of constant loving-kindness and of truth; 16so look down in pity and
grant strength to your servant and save me.
17Send me a sign of your favor. When those
who hate me see it, they will lose face because
you help and comfort me.

84:8-12 Spending just a little while in the presence of God is better than spending a lifetime apart from him. The security, peace, and love that God offers are greater than anything we could receive from other people. When we find the pleasures of our addictions have faded and the promises of our dependencies haven't come true, we can turn to God, and he will fill our soul with true happiness.

85:1-3 It is hard enough to deal with the sins that have us entrapped; how much worse we make it by having to live with a bad conscience. Great relief comes when God helps us to regain control and when we realize that he has forgiven our sins. All we need to do is admit our failures to God and accept the forgiveness he offers.

86:1-5 Even though we may be trying to please God, we often are still faced with grave difficulties from which we need deliverance. Sometimes the answers don't come quickly and, though we pray long and diligently, nothing happens immediately. As we deal with our ongoing anxiety, we may get impatient and begin to wonder if God will ever act. God will ultimately respond with goodness, forgiveness, and compassion to all who call upon him. Sometimes, though, we may have to wait a while before it happens.

86:11-17 We only know God's will as we seek to know him through prayer and the study of his Word. The more we know about God, the more we know of what he expects of us. And as we get to know God better, we will discover that he not only gives us direction, but also gives us the strength and encouragement we need to walk down the pathway he chooses for us.

PSALM 87

High on his holy mountain stands Jerusalem,
the city of God, the city he loves more than
any other!

3O city of God, what wondrous tales are
told of you! 4Nowadays when I mention
among my friends the names of Egypt and
Babylonia, Philistia and Tyre, or even distant
Ethiopia, someone boasts that he was born in
one or another of those countries. 5But someday the highest honor will be to be a native of
Jerusalem! For the God above all gods will
personally bless this city. 6When he registers
her citizens, he will place a checkmark beside
the names of those who were born here. 7And
in the festivals they'll sing, "All my heart is in
Jerusalem."

PSALM 88

O Jehovah, God of my salvation, I have wept
before you day and night. 2Now hear my
prayers; oh, listen to my cry, 3for my life is full
of troubles, and death draws near. 4They say
my life is ebbing out—a hopeless case. 5They
have left me here to die, like those slain on
battlefields from whom your mercies are removed.

6You have thrust me down to the darkest
depths. 7Your wrath lies heavy on me; wave
after wave engulfs me. 8You have made my
friends to loathe me, and they have gone
away. I am in a trap with no way out. 9My eyes
grow dim with weeping. Each day I beg your
help; O Lord, I reach my pleading hands to
you for mercy.

10Soon it will be too late! Of what use are
your miracles when I am in the grave? How
can I praise you then? 11Can those in the grave
declare your loving-kindness? Can they proclaim your faithfulness? 12Can the darkness
speak of your miracles? Can anyone in the
Land of Forgetfulness talk about your help?

13O Lord, I plead for my life and will keep
on pleading day by day. 14O Jehovah, why
have you thrown my life away? Why are you
turning your face from me and looking the
other way?

15From my youth I have been sickly and
ready to die. I stand helpless before your terrors. 16Your fierce wrath has overwhelmed me.
Your terrors have cut me off. 17They flow
around me all day long. 18Lover, friend, acquaintance—all are gone. There is only darkness everywhere.

PSALM 89

Forever and ever I will sing about the tender
kindness of the Lord! Young and old shall
hear about your blessings. 2Your love and
kindness are forever; your truth is as enduring
as the heavens.

3,4The Lord God says, "I have made a solemn agreement with my chosen servant
David. I have taken an oath to establish his
descendants as kings forever on his throne,
from now until eternity!"

5All heaven shall praise your miracles,
O Lord; myriads of angels will praise you for
your faithfulness. 6For who in all of heaven
can be compared with God? What mightiest
angel is anything like him? 7The highest of
angelic powers stand in dread and awe of him.
Who is as revered as he by those surrounding
him? 8O Jehovah, Commander of the heavenly armies, where is there any other Mighty
One like you? Faithfulness is your very character.

9You rule the oceans when their waves arise
in fearful storms; you speak, and they lie still.
10You have cut haughty Egypt to pieces. Your
enemies are scattered by your awesome
power. 11The heavens are yours, the world,
everything—for you created them all. 12You
created north and south! Mount Tabor and

87:1-7 In God's eyes we are like Jerusalem, the city for which he had special love and concern. In the Old Testament, Jerusalem was known as God's dwelling place on earth and the seat of his rule. Since the coming of Jesus Christ, God comes to dwell in our heart; he loves us and longs to direct our decisions and actions. It is a privilege to be called God's beloved and to be considered citizens of his kingdom. It means he cares for us and wants us to enjoy living in his presence.

88:1-5 All of us who have struggled with an addiction know what it means to feel hopeless and overwhelmed by troubles. It is comforting to know that God is listening to our cries. We are privileged to have the Bible, which tells us about God and his power to help us when we call out to him. No situation is hopeless for those who call out to God. When we feel helpless, we need to look to God and hope in his deliverance.

88:6-12 In these verses, the psalmist wrote that God had abandoned him to his problems. It is important to remember that God allows us to stumble and fall, giving us the opportunity to learn personally about the consequences of sin. But it is also important to remember that God does not cause us to fall. Natural consequences should be expected if we sin. If we are suffering for our failures, we should take the opportunity to learn from the past and turn to God.

Mount Hermon rejoice to be signed by your name as their maker! [13]Strong is your arm! Strong is your hand! Your right hand is lifted high in glorious strength.

[14,15]Your throne is founded on two strong pillars—the one is Justice and the other Righteousness. Mercy and Truth walk before you as your attendants. Blessed are those who hear the joyful blast of the trumpet, for they shall walk in the light of your presence. [16]They rejoice all day long in your wonderful reputation and in your perfect righteousness. [17]You are their strength. What glory! Our power is based on your favor! [18]Yes, our protection is from the Lord himself and he, the Holy One of Israel, has given us our king.

[19]In a vision you spoke to your prophet and said, "I have chosen a splendid young man from the common people to be the king—[20]he is my servant David! I have anointed him with my holy oil. [21]I will steady him and make him strong. [22]His enemies shall not outwit him, nor shall the wicked overpower him. [23]I will beat down his adversaries before him and destroy those who hate him. [24]I will protect and bless him constantly and surround him with my love; he will be great because of me. [25]He will hold sway from the Euphrates River to the Mediterranean Sea. [26]And he will cry to me, 'You are my Father, my God, and my Rock of Salvation.'

[27]"I will treat him as my firstborn son and make him the mightiest king in all the earth. [28]I will love him forever and be kind to him always; my covenant with him will never end. [29]He will always have an heir; his throne will be as endless as the days of heaven. [30-32]If his children forsake my laws and don't obey them, then I will punish them, [33]but I will never completely take away my loving-kindness from them, nor let my promise fail. [34]No, I will not break my covenant; I will not take back one word of what I said. [35,36]For I have sworn to David (and a holy God can never lie) that his dynasty will go on forever, and his throne will continue to the end of time. [37]It shall be eternal as the moon, my faithful witness in the sky!"

[38]Then why cast me off, rejected? Why be so angry with the one you chose as king? [39]Have you renounced your covenant with him? For you have thrown his crown in the dust. [40]You have broken down the walls protecting him and laid in ruins every fort defending him. [41]Everyone who comes along has robbed him while his neighbors mock. [42]You have strengthened his enemies against him and made them rejoice. [43]You have struck down his sword and refused to help him in battle. [44]You have ended his splendor and overturned his throne. [45]You have made him old before his time and publicly disgraced him.

[46]O Jehovah, how long will this go on? Will you hide yourself from me forever? How long will your wrath burn like fire? [47]Oh, remember how short you have made man's lifespan. Is it an empty, futile life you give the sons of men? [48]No man can live forever. All will die. Who can rescue his life from the power of the grave?

[49]Lord, where is the love you used to have for me? Where is your kindness that you promised to David with a faithful pledge? [50]Lord, see how all the people are despising me. [51]Your enemies joke about me, the one you anointed as their king.

[52]And yet—blessed be the Lord forever! Amen and amen!

PSALM 90

A prayer of Moses, the man of God.

Lord, through all the generations you have been our home! [2]Before the mountains were created, before the earth was formed, you are God without beginning or end.

[3]You speak, and man turns back to dust. [4]A thousand years are but as yesterday to you! They are like a single hour! [5,6]We glide along the tides of time as swiftly as a racing river and vanish as quickly as a dream. We are like grass that is green in the morning but mowed down and withered before the evening shadows fall. [7]We die beneath your anger; we are overwhelmed by your wrath. [8]You spread out our sins before you—our secret sins—and see

89:11-18 God created and sustains everything that exists. He is extremely powerful, and he displays righteousness, truth, justice, and compassion. When we are powerless, it only makes sense to turn to God. He has the power we need to overcome our dependencies. As we remain close to him and do his will, we will experience deliverance and discover true freedom.

89:38-45 Though God at times may seem to abandon his people and act toward them only in anger, he is just doing what he promised to do. He said he would bless us if we obeyed and punish us if we disobeyed. We sometimes find it hard to understand why God lets some people be seemingly in perfect control of their lives, while we are hopelessly out of control. Deep down, we know the answer: unless God is in control of a person's life, nothing of ultimate good will ever come of it.

them all. 9No wonder the years are long and heavy here beneath your wrath. All our days are filled with sighing.

10Seventy years are given us! And some may even live to eighty. But even the best of these years are often emptiness and pain; soon they disappear, and we are gone. 11Who can realize the terrors of your anger? Which of us can fear you as he should?

12Teach us to number our days and recognize how few they are; help us to spend them as we should.

13O Jehovah, come and bless us! How long will you delay? Turn away your anger from us. 14Satisfy us in our earliest youth with your loving-kindness, giving us constant joy to the end of our lives. 15Give us gladness in proportion to our former misery! Replace the evil years with good. 16Let us see your miracles again; let our children see glorious things, the kind you used to do, 17and let the Lord our God favor us and give us success. May he give permanence to all we do.

PSALM 91

We live within the shadow of the Almighty, sheltered by the God who is above all gods.

2This I declare, that he alone is my refuge, my place of safety; he is my God, and I am trusting him. 3For he rescues you from every trap and protects you from the fatal plague. 4He will shield you with his wings! They will shelter you. His faithful promises are your armor. 5Now you don't need to be afraid of the dark any more, nor fear the dangers of the day; 6nor dread the plagues of darkness, nor disasters in the morning.

7Though a thousand fall at my side, though ten thousand are dying around me, the evil will not touch me. 8I will see how the wicked are punished, but I will not share it. 9For Jehovah is my refuge! I choose the God above all gods to shelter me. 10How then can evil overtake me or any plague come near? 11For he orders his angels to protect you wherever you go. 12They will steady you with their hands to keep you from stumbling against the rocks on the trail. 13You can safely meet a lion or step on poisonous snakes, yes, even trample them beneath your feet!

14For the Lord says, "Because he loves me, I will rescue him; I will make him great because he trusts in my name. 15When he calls on me, I will answer; I will be with him in trouble and rescue him and honor him. 16I will satisfy him with a full life and give him my salvation."

PSALM 92

A song to sing on the Lord's Day.

It is good to say thank you to the Lord, to sing praises to the God who is above all gods.

2Every morning tell him, "Thank you for your kindness," and every evening rejoice in all his faithfulness. 3Sing his praises, accompanied by music from the harp and lute and lyre. 4You have done so much for me, O Lord. No wonder I am glad! I sing for joy.

5O Lord, what miracles you do! And how deep are your thoughts! 6Unthinking people do not understand them! No fool can com-

---

90:10-12 Remembering that life is short and often filled with sorrow, we should ask how God wants us to spend our days and concentrate on making our life count for something. We have wasted enough time creating our own problems. We should focus now on making positive changes in our life so we will be able to accomplish things for God.

90:13-17 Our restoration to sanity and health depends on our cooperation with God. Only he can give us the power to be what we ought to be; yet God won't force changes on us until we want to change. The way we begin is through prayer. We can ask God to make us willing to change and then to give us the strength to follow through with action.

91:1-4 When we discover that we are powerless to fight our addictions alone, we become weak like little children. We feel helpless to protect ourself, caught in a whirlwind of our own making. We turn to God because there is no other answer to our problem. How comforting to know that when we cry out, God protects us as a mother bird protects her young. Our powerful defender will never fail us if we turn to him for shelter and comfort.

91:10-16 We will escape danger because God protects us as his chosen ones. Sometimes his protection will come in the form of angels given the responsibility of caring for us and keeping us safe (see Matthew 4:6). Sometimes God may use other, more natural means, but his help will come. As we cry out to him for help, he will be with us in our troubles and rescue us. Ultimately, he will bring us into his eternal presence forever.

92:1-4 It is a necessary part of recovery to offer praise to God for all that he has done for us. Part of our offering should be a declaration of God's marvelous compassion and his unceasing goodness to us. He truly is the one who brings abiding joy to our life. As we experience his faithfulness in our life, praise and thanks should be our natural response. Our praise will serve as a declaration to others of God's power to deliver us from the bondage of addiction.

prehend this: 7that although the wicked flourish like weeds, there is only eternal destruction ahead of them. 8But the Lord continues forever, exalted in the heavens, 9while his enemies—all evil-doers—shall be scattered.

10But you have made me as strong as a wild bull. How refreshed I am by your blessings! 11I have heard the doom of my enemies announced and seen them destroyed. 12But the godly shall flourish like palm trees and grow tall as the cedars of Lebanon. 13For they are transplanted into the Lord's own garden and are under his personal care. 14Even in old age they will still produce fruit and be vital and green. 15This honors the Lord and exhibits his faithful care. He is my shelter. There is nothing but goodness in him!

PSALM 93

Jehovah is King! He is robed in majesty and strength. The world is his throne.

2O Lord, you have reigned from prehistoric times, from the everlasting past. 3The mighty oceans thunder your praise. 4You are mightier than all the breakers pounding on the seashores of the world! 5Your royal decrees cannot be changed. Holiness is forever the keynote of your reign.

PSALM 94

Lord God, to whom vengeance belongs, let your glory shine out. Arise and judge the earth; sentence the proud to the penalties they deserve. 3Lord, how long shall the wicked be allowed to triumph and exult? 4Hear their insolence! See their arrogance! How these men of evil boast! 5See them oppressing your people, O Lord, afflicting those you love. 6,7They murder widows, immigrants, and orphans, for "The Lord isn't looking," they say, "and besides, he doesn't care."

8Fools! 9Is God deaf and blind—he who makes ears and eyes? 10He punishes the nations—won't he also punish you? He knows everything—doesn't he also know what you are doing?

11The Lord is fully aware of how limited and futile the thoughts of mankind are, 12,13so he helps us by punishing us. This makes us follow his paths and gives us respite from our enemies while God traps them and destroys them. 14The Lord will not forsake his people, for they are his prize. 15Judgment will again be just, and all the upright will rejoice.

16Who will protect me from the wicked? Who will be my shield? 17I would have died unless the Lord had helped me. 18I screamed, "I'm slipping, Lord!" and he was kind and saved me.

19Lord, when doubts fill my mind, when my heart is in turmoil, quiet me and give me renewed hope and cheer. 20Will you permit a corrupt government to rule under your protection—a government permitting wrong to defeat right? 21,22Do you approve of those who condemn the innocent to death? No! The Lord my God is my fortress—the mighty Rock where I can hide. 23God has made the sins of evil men to boomerang upon them! He will destroy them by their own plans. Jehovah our God will cut them off.

PSALM 95

Oh, come, let us sing to the Lord! Give a joyous shout in honor of the Rock of our salvation!

2Come before him with thankful hearts. Let us sing him psalms of praise. 3For the Lord is a great God, the great King of all gods. 4He controls the formation of the depths of the earth and the mightiest mountains; all are his. 5He made the sea and formed the land; they

---

93:1-5 A powerful, holy, unchanging God is able to help us exercise control over our universe—our life. He always keeps his promises. Since he has said he will help us if we turn to him, we can count on it.

94:8-10 The voice of the tempter says, "No one will know or care if we have just one more moment of pleasure." Here we are reminded that God is neither deaf nor blind. Neither are the people who know us well. "Just one more" always translates into a disastrous fall. Remembering that God knows what we are doing and that he cares about us should encourage us to stand against the temptations we face.

94:16-23 In the final analysis, we can count on no one but God to take a stand for us against our enemies. When we stumble into temptation, he is there to keep us from falling. Because he is our defender, he does not allow sin to destroy us beyond hope. Knowing that God is so intimately involved in our life should encourage us to live for him.

95:1-7 We all know how frightening it is to lose control of our life. For this very reason, we may hesitate to entrust it to God. Can he be trusted? God wants us to remember that when we surrender our life to him, he regards us with the same concern that a kind shepherd feels for his sheep. If a watchful shepherd is around, the sheep have little to fear.

too are his. [6]Come, kneel before the Lord our Maker, [7]for he is our God. We are his sheep, and he is our Shepherd. Oh, that you would hear him calling you today and come to him!

[8]Don't harden your hearts as Israel did in the wilderness at Meribah and Massah. [9]For there your fathers doubted me, though they had seen so many of my miracles before. My patience was severely tried by their complaints. [10]"For forty years I watched them in disgust," the Lord God says. "They were a nation whose thoughts and heart were far away from me. They refused to accept my laws. [11]Therefore, in mighty wrath I swore that they would never enter the Promised Land, the place of rest I planned for them."

PSALM 96

Sing a new song to the Lord! Sing it everywhere around the world! [2]Sing out his praises! Bless his name. Each day tell someone that he saves.

[3]Publish his glorious acts throughout the earth. Tell everyone about the amazing things he does. [4]For the Lord is great beyond description and greatly to be praised. Worship only him among the gods! [5]For the gods of other nations are merely idols, but our God made the heavens! [6]Honor and majesty surround him; strength and beauty are in his Temple.

[7]O nations of the world, confess that God alone is glorious and strong. [8]Give him the glory he deserves! Bring your offering and come to worship him. [9]Worship the Lord with the beauty of holy lives. Let the earth tremble before him. [10]Tell the nations that Jehovah reigns! He rules the world. His power can never be overthrown. He will judge all nations fairly.

[11]Let the heavens be glad, the earth rejoice; let the vastness of the roaring seas demonstrate his glory. [12]Praise him for the growing fields, for they display his greatness. Let the trees of the forest rustle with praise. [13]For the Lord is coming to judge the earth; he will judge the nations fairly and with truth!

PSALM 97

Jehovah is King! Let all the earth rejoice! Tell the farthest islands to be glad.

[2]Clouds and darkness surround him. Righteousness and justice are the foundation of his throne. [3]Fire goes forth before him and burns up all his foes. [4]His lightning flashes out across the world. The earth sees and trembles. [5]The mountains melt like wax before the Lord of all the earth. [6]The heavens declare his perfect righteousness; every nation sees his glory.

[7]Let those who worship idols be disgraced—all who brag about their worthless gods—for every god must bow to him! [8,9]Jerusalem and all the cities of Judah have heard of your justice, Lord, and are glad that you reign in majesty over the entire earth and are far greater than these other gods.

[10]The Lord loves those who hate evil; he protects the lives of his people and rescues them from the wicked. [11]Light is sown for the godly and joy for the good. [12]May all who are godly be happy in the Lord and crown him, our holy God.

PSALM 98

Sing a new song to the Lord telling about his mighty deeds! For he has won a mighty victory by his power and holiness. [2,3]He has announced this victory and revealed it to every nation by fulfilling his promise to be kind to Israel. The whole earth has seen God's salvation of his people. [4]That is why the earth

---

96:1-9 The way we live demonstrates what we believe about God. If we stay in our prison of sin, we show that we are either unaware of his power to save us or indifferent about God and the help he wants to offer. If we seek his help to escape the bondage of sin and share the joyful news with others, we show our gratitude to God while also revealing the beauty of a changed life. The world is filled with people who have "remedies" for our problems. Many of them are helpful, but none can offer us the power we need for real change. Only God is mighty enough to offer that kind of help.

97:10-12 When God moves to help us, he cares how we feel about him and about our sins. He is always quick to help those who hate evil and want to please him. God has placed a very close link between our happiness and our holiness. If we want real joy, we need to commit our life to God and his program for joyful and holy living.

98:1-3 God revealed his power to the whole world by the way he rescued the people of Israel. Today he shows his power by delivering us from our powerful addictions and hopeless problems. We are able to win impossible battles, just as the Israelites did, because God is powerful and active in our life. Having found victory, we can share with others our story of God's deliverance. This will give them the hope and wisdom they need to experience God's help in their own lives.

breaks out in praise to God and sings for utter joy!

5Sing your praise accompanied by music from the harp. 6Let the cornets and trumpets shout! Make a joyful symphony before the Lord, the King! 7Let the sea in all its vastness roar with praise! Let the earth and all those living on it shout, "Glory to the Lord."

8,9Let the waves clap their hands in glee and the hills sing out their songs of joy before the Lord, for he is coming to judge the world with perfect justice.

PSALM 99

Jehovah is King! Let the nations tremble! He is enthroned between the Guardian Angels. Let the whole earth shake.

2Jehovah sits in majesty in Zion, supreme above all rulers of the earth. 3Let them reverence your great and holy name.

4This mighty King is determined to give justice. Fairness is the touchstone of everything he does. He gives justice throughout Israel. 5Exalt the Lord our holy God! Bow low before his feet.

6When Moses and Aaron and Samuel, his prophet, cried to him for help, he answered them. 7He spoke to them from the pillar of cloud, and they followed his instructions. 8O Jehovah our God! You answered them and forgave their sins, yet punished them when they went wrong.

9Exalt the Lord our God and worship at his holy mountain in Jerusalem, for he is holy.

PSALM 100

Shout with joy before the Lord, O earth! 2Obey him gladly; come before him, singing with joy.

3Try to realize what this means—the Lord is God! He made us—we are his people, the sheep of his pasture.

4Go through his open gates with great thanksgiving; enter his courts with praise. Give thanks to him and bless his name. 5For the Lord is always good. He is always loving and kind, and his faithfulness goes on and on to each succeeding generation.

PSALM 101

I will sing about your loving-kindness and your justice, Lord. I will sing your praises!

2I will try to walk a blameless path, but how I need your help, especially in my own home, where I long to act as I should.

3Help me to refuse the low and vulgar things; help me to abhor all crooked deals of every kind, to have no part in them. 4I will reject all selfishness and stay away from every evil. 5I will not tolerate anyone who secretly slanders his neighbors; I will not permit conceit and pride. 6I will make the godly of the land my heroes and invite them to my home. Only those who are truly good shall be my servants. 7But I will not allow those who deceive and lie to stay in my house. 8My daily task will be to ferret out criminals and free the city of God from their grip.

PSALM 102

A prayer when overwhelmed with trouble.

Lord, hear my prayer! Listen to my plea!

2Don't turn away from me in this time of my distress. Bend down your ear and give me speedy answers, 3,4for my days disappear like smoke. My health is broken, and my heart is sick; it is trampled like grass and is withered.

99:1-9 Even though God is the God of love, he first made himself known as a holy and righteous God. His love causes him to show mercy toward us, but his holiness means that we can't please him if we continue in sin. We must not presume upon God's loving and forgiving nature, for he also loves justice. Continuing in sin will result in terrible consequences. Our experience of God's delivering power should motivate us to live for him with all our strength.

100:1-5 We always have reasons to rejoice: we live in God's presence, under his continual care, and we experience his love each day. Such a realization should fill us with gratitude and praise each time we come before him in prayer. God never stops showering us with his compassion; he always keeps his promises to help us when we call on him.

101:1-4 Staying free from the sin that used to entrap us depends on our staying close to God and staying away from every evil. It is vital that we not waste our time following a recovery program that tries to undermine our faith in God. We must learn to be discerning about the activities we become involved in. Like the psalmist, we must refuse to tolerate anything in our life that does not recognize the value of our trust in God and obedience to his ways.

102:1-7 When we are beaten down by the events of life, we need with plead to God to respond immediately to our urgent requests. In such times we may feel as though our pain is as searing as a blowtorch; our energy, our very life is withering like grass under the scorching sun. Our agony may become so great that we have no desire even to eat. When there is no other solution to be found, God is still able to deliver us. We need to admit our powerlessness in the situation and trust God to help us through the pain.

My food is tasteless, and I have lost my appetite. 5 I am reduced to skin and bones because of all my groaning and despair. 6 I am like a vulture in a far-off wilderness or like an owl alone in the desert. 7 I lie awake, lonely as a solitary sparrow on the roof.

8 My enemies taunt me day after day and curse at me. 9,10 I eat ashes instead of bread. My tears run down into my drink because of your anger against me, because of your wrath. For you have rejected me and thrown me out. 11 My life is passing swiftly as the evening shadows. I am withering like grass, 12 while you, Lord, are a famous King forever. Your fame will endure to every generation.

13 I know that you will come and have mercy on Jerusalem—and now is the time to pity her—the time you promised help. 14 For your people love every stone in her walls and feel sympathy for every grain of dust in her streets. 15 Now let the nations and their rulers tremble before the Lord, before his glory. 16 For Jehovah will rebuild Jerusalem! He will appear in his glory!

17 He will listen to the prayers of the destitute, for he is never too busy to heed their requests. 18 I am recording this so that future generations will also praise the Lord for all that he has done. And a people that shall be created shall praise the Lord. 19 Tell them that God looked down from his temple in heaven 20 and heard the groans of his people in slavery—they were children of death—and released them, 21,22 so that multitudes would stream to the Temple in Jerusalem to praise him, and his praises were sung throughout the city; and many rulers throughout the earth came to worship him.

23 He has cut me down in middle life, shortening my days. 24 But I cried to him, "O God, you live forever and forever! Don't let me die half through my years! 25 In ages past you laid the foundations of the earth and made the heavens with your hands! 26 They shall perish, but you go on forever. They will grow old like worn-out clothing, and you will change them like a man putting on a new shirt and throwing away the old one! 27 But you yourself never grow old. You are forever, and your years never end.

28 "But our families will continue; generation after generation will be preserved by your protection."

PSALM 103

I bless the holy name of God with all my heart. 2 Yes, I will bless the Lord and not forget the glorious things he does for me.

3 He forgives all my sins. He heals me. 4 He ransoms me from hell. He surrounds me with loving-kindness and tender mercies. 5 He fills my life with good things! My youth is renewed like the eagle's! 6 He gives justice to all who are treated unfairly. 7 He revealed his will and nature to Moses and the people of Israel.

8 He is merciful and tender toward those who don't deserve it; he is slow to get angry and full of kindness and love. 9 He never bears a grudge, nor remains angry forever. 10 He has not punished us as we deserve for all our sins, 11 for his mercy toward those who fear and honor him is as great as the height of the heavens above the earth. 12 He has removed our sins as far away from us as the east is from the west. 13 He is like a father to us, tender and sympathetic to those who reverence him. 14 For he knows we are but dust 15 and that our days are few and brief, like grass, like flowers, 16 blown by the wind and gone forever.

17,18 But the loving-kindness of the Lord is from everlasting to everlasting to those who reverence him; his salvation is to children's

102:17-22 God responds to people who are downtrodden and in distress. Sometimes we may feel that God is too busy or distant, but he is intimately concerned for us. He wants us to have a joyful and meaningful existence—that's what he created us for! When we admit our helplessness and turn to God for help, he will come through for us in one way or another. Then our only natural response to him will be one of joyful praise; we should want to tell others about what God has done for us.

103:13-18 In the same manner that a loving father cares about his children, God has compassion on all who call on him. He is sensitive to our needs and treats us lovingly, since he understands our weaknesses and the transitory nature of our life. God's love never ceases for those who fear him. By serving him obediently now, we can be assured that his love will touch not only our own life, but also the lives of our children and grandchildren.

104:1-24 God created the world to function according to a certain plan—God's plan. God also created us to function best—to live a joyful and healthy life—when we do things God's way. It only makes sense that when we go our own way, we will suffer painful consequences. God created his world and all its creatures. If we seek to live according to God's program revealed in the Bible, we will discover the way to live in peace and harmony with God, other people, and the world we live in.

children of those who are faithful to his covenant and remember to obey him!
19The Lord has made the heavens his
throne; from there he rules over everything
there is. 20Bless the Lord, you mighty angels of
his who carry out his orders, listening for each
of his commands. 21Yes, bless the Lord, you
armies of his angels who serve him constantly.
22Let everything everywhere bless the Lord.
And how I bless him too!

PSALM 104
I bless the Lord: O Lord my God, how great
you are! You are robed with honor and with
majesty and light! You stretched out the starry
curtain of the heavens, 3and hollowed out the
surface of the earth to form the seas. The
clouds are his chariots. He rides upon the
wings of the wind. 4The angels are his messengers—his servants of fire!
5You bound the world together so that it
would never fall apart. 6You clothed the earth
with floods of waters covering up the mountains. 7,8You spoke, and at the sound of your
shout the water collected into its vast ocean
beds, and mountains rose and valleys sank to
the levels you decreed. 9And then you set a
boundary for the seas so that they would
never again cover the earth.
10He placed springs in the valleys and
streams that gush from the mountains. 11They
give water for all the animals to drink. There
the wild donkeys quench their thirst, 12and
the birds nest beside the streams and sing
among the branches of the trees. 13He sends
rain upon the mountains and fills the earth
with fruit. 14The tender grass grows up at his
command to feed the cattle, and there are
fruit trees, vegetables, and grain for man to
cultivate, 15and wine to make him glad, and
olive oil as lotion for his skin, and bread to
give him strength. 16The Lord planted the
cedars of Lebanon. They are tall and flourish-
ing. 17There the birds make their nests, the
storks in the firs. 18High in the mountains are
pastures for the wild goats, and rock-badgers
burrow in among the rocks and find protection there.
19He assigned the moon to mark the
months and the sun to mark the days. 20He
sends the night and darkness, when all the
forest folk come out. 21Then the young lions
roar for their food, but they are dependent on
the Lord. 22At dawn they slink back into their
dens to rest, 23and men go off to work until
the evening shadows fall again. 24O Lord,

Forgiveness

READ PSALM 103:1-22

We may have a hard time believing in God's forgiveness. We may think, *After all I've done, I don't think anyone can completely forgive me.* Maybe we feel that we have done such horrible things, or hurt people so badly, that there's no way our sins could ever be erased entirely. Even if we could be forgiven, who could ever *forget* the things we have done?

When we think of people we know—the people we have hurt—perhaps these fears are well founded. But when it comes to forgiveness from God, we need to remember that his ways are higher than our ways. The psalmist wrote, "[God] has not punished us as we deserve for all our sins, for his mercy toward those who fear and honor him is as great as the height of the heavens above the earth. He has removed our sins as far away from us as the east is from the west" (Psalm 103:10-12). God has said, "Come, let's talk this over! . . . No matter how deep the stain of your sins, I can take it out and make you as clean as freshly fallen snow. Even if you are stained as red as crimson, I can make you white as wool!" (Isaiah 1:18). "I, yes, I alone am he who blots away your sins for my own sake and will never think of them again" (Isaiah 43:25).

Part of our recovery is to accept complete forgiveness from God. When we come to God through the atoning blood of Jesus Christ, his forgiveness is complete. We may keep track of our failures, adding every fall to the long list we have written out against ourselves. But God doesn't keep lists of our past sins; in his eyes we are clean. ***Turn to page 687, Proverbs 15.***

what a variety you have made! And in wisdom you have made them all! The earth is full
of your riches.
25 There before me lies the mighty ocean,
teeming with life of every kind, both great
and small. 26 And look! See the ships! And over
there, the whale you made to play in the sea.
27 Every one of these depends on you to give
them daily food. 28 You supply it, and they
gather it. You open wide your hand to feed
them, and they are satisfied with all your
bountiful provision.
29 But if you turn away from them, then all
is lost. And when you gather up their breath,
they die and turn again to dust.
30 Then you send your Spirit, and new life is
born to replenish all the living of the earth.
31 Praise God forever! How he must rejoice in
all his work! 32 The earth trembles at his
glance; the mountains burst into flame at his
touch.
33 I will sing to the Lord as long as I live. I
will praise God to my last breath! 34 May he be
pleased by all these thoughts about him, for
he is the source of all my joy. 35 Let all sinners
perish—all who refuse to praise him. But I will
praise him. Hallelujah!

PSALM 105

Thank the Lord for all the glorious things he
does; proclaim them to the nations. 2 Sing his
praises and tell everyone about his miracles.
3 Glory in the Lord; O worshipers of God,
rejoice.
4 Search for him and for his strength, and
keep on searching!
5,6 Think of the mighty deeds he did for us,
his chosen ones—descendants of God's servant Abraham, and of Jacob. Remember how
he destroyed our enemies. 7 He is the Lord our
God. His goodness is seen everywhere
throughout the land. 8,9 Though a thousand
generations pass he never forgets his promise,
his covenant with Abraham and Isaac 10,11 and
confirmed with Jacob. This is his never-
ending treaty with the people of Israel: *"I will
give you the land of Canaan as your inheritance."*
12 He said this when they were but few in
number, very few, and were only visitors in
Canaan. 13 Later they were dispersed among
the nations and were driven from one kingdom to another; 14 but through it all he would
not let one thing be done to them apart from
his decision. He destroyed many a king who
tried! 15 "Touch not these chosen ones of
mine," he warned, "and do not hurt my
prophets."
16 He called for a famine on the land of
Canaan, cutting off its food supply. 17 Then he
sent Joseph as a slave to Egypt to save his
people from starvation. 18 There in prison they
hurt his feet with fetters and placed his neck
in an iron collar 19 until God's time finally
came—how God tested his patience! 20 Then
the king sent for him and set him free. 21 He
was put in charge of all the king's possessions.
22 At his pleasure he could imprison the king's
aides and teach the king's advisors.

104:25-35 God controls the destinies of all beings. Every living being depends on him for food and life. We need to realize that if we remove ourself from God's presence, from his control and care, we are without hope, just as the natural world would be without hope if God should withdraw himself from it.

105:5-15 God always keeps his word. When he makes a promise, he fulfills it. God promised Abraham and Jacob that their descendants would inherit the land of Canaan. Generations after Jacob's death, the Israelites entered Canaan with Joshua. Sometimes God's promises take time to come about. In recovery, we often grow impatient with our slow progress. At times we may begin to think our recovery is hopeless, and we may be tempted to give up. We need to realize that our recovery may take time, but this does not mean God is not working on our behalf. We should also remember that the benefits of our recovery will touch not only our life, but also the lives of numerous descendants. Let us embrace God's recovery promises for the long haul.

105:39-45 God is able to care for his people. He responds to our prayers—even our complaints—and meets all the needs we have that no one else could possibly fill. His ultimate purpose is to make us faithful and obedient to his laws. As he helps us to be faithful and obedient to his program, he will fill us with joy. These verses are of special comfort to us in recovery. As we admit our faults to God, we can know that he is listening. As we seek to live according to his will, we can hope for a life of joy and fulfillment. As we entrust our life to God, we can be sure we are in good hands.

106:6-9 The psalmist reflects on the failures of the present generation in Israel and the mistakes of past generations. In recovery, we are called to do the same. Our failures are often closely tied to the mistakes of our parents and grandparents. We need to look back and forgive those who have hurt us. Then we need to honestly assess our own mistakes, taking responsibility for them and seeking forgiveness from those we have hurt. And just as God revealed his goodness by helping the Israelites get back on their feet, he will forgive us and support us in our recovery.

23Then Jacob (Israel) arrived in Egypt and
lived there with his sons. 24In the years that
followed, the people of Israel multiplied ex-
plosively until they were a greater nation than
their rulers. 25At that point God turned the
Egyptians against the Israelis; they hated and
enslaved them.
26But God sent Moses as his representative,
and Aaron with him, 27to call down miracles of
terror upon the land of Egypt. 28They followed
his instructions. He sent thick darkness
through the land 29and turned the nation's
water into blood, poisoning the fish.30Then
frogs invaded in enormous numbers; they
were found even in the king's private rooms.
31When Moses spoke, the flies and other insects swarmed in vast clouds from one end of
Egypt to the other. 32Instead of rain he sent
down murderous hail, and lightning flashes
overwhelmed the nation. 33Their grape vines
and fig trees were ruined; all the trees lay
broken on the ground. 34He spoke, and hordes
of locusts came 35and ate up everything green,
destroying all the crops. 36Then he killed the
oldest child in each Egyptian home, their
pride and joy—37and brought his people safely
out from Egypt, loaded with silver and gold;
there were no sick and feeble folk among them
then. 38Egypt was glad when they were gone,
for the dread of them was great.
39He spread out a cloud above them to
shield them from the burning sun and gave
them a pillar of flame at night to give them
light. 40They asked for meat, and he sent them
quail and gave them manna—bread from
heaven. 41He opened up a rock, and water
gushed out to form a river through the dry
and barren land; 42for he remembered his sacred promises to Abraham his servant.
43So he brought his chosen ones singing
into the Promised Land. 44He gave them the
lands of the Gentiles, complete with their
growing crops; they ate what others planted.
45This was done to make them faithful and
obedient to his laws. Hallelujah!

PSALM 106

Hallelujah! Thank you, Lord! How good you
are! Your love for us continues on forever.
2Who can ever list the glorious miracles of
God? Who can ever praise him half enough?
3Happiness comes to those who are fair to
others and are always just and good.
4Remember me too, O Lord, while you are
blessing and saving your people. 5Let me
share in your chosen ones' prosperity and

Finding God

BIBLE READING: Psalm 105:1-9

We sought through prayer and meditation to improve our conscious contact with God, as we understood him, praying only for knowledge of his will for us and the power to carry that out.

As we work the Twelve Steps, we spend a lot of time looking back. We often think about the wrong things we have done in the past. As we proceed in our recovery, we will need strength to move along the path God wants us to follow. Part of this strength will come as we visualize God's constant presence with us.

The psalmist wrote, "Thank the Lord for all the glorious things he does; proclaim them to the nations. . . . Think of the mighty deeds he did for us. . . . Remember how he destroyed our enemies. He is the Lord our God. His goodness is seen everywhere throughout the land. Though a thousand generations pass he never forgets his promise" (Psalm 105:1, 5-9).

From now on when we look back we will see the "mighty deeds he did for us" and "remember how he destroyed our enemies." We will look around to find his goodness "everywhere throughout the land" and look forward to the fulfillment of his promises. In prayer we thank him for what he's done; we seek him for the strength we need today; and we ask him to fulfill his promises for tomorrow. In meditation we remember our victories, ponder his presence with us today, and consider his faithfulness and the hope that gives us for tomorrow. ***Turn to page 657, Psalm 119.***

rejoice in all their joys, and receive the glory you give to them.

[6]Both we and our fathers have sinned so much. [7]They weren't impressed by the wonder of your miracles in Egypt and soon forgot your many acts of kindness to them. Instead they rebelled against you at the Red Sea. [8]Even so you saved them—to defend the honor of your name and demonstrate your power to all the world. [9]You commanded the Red Sea to divide, forming a dry road across its bottom. Yes, as dry as any desert! [10]Thus you rescued them from their enemies. [11]Then the water returned and covered the road and drowned their foes; not one survived.

[12]Then at last his people believed him. Then they finally sang his praise.

[13]Yet how quickly they forgot again! They wouldn't wait for him to act [14]but demanded better food, testing God's patience to the breaking point. [15]So he gave them their demands but sent them leanness in their souls. [16]They were envious of Moses, yes, and Aaron too, the man anointed by God as his priest. [17]Because of this, the earth opened and swallowed Dathan, Abiram, and his friends; [18]and fire fell from heaven to consume these wicked men. [19,20]For they preferred a statue of an ox that eats grass to the glorious presence of God himself. [21,22]Thus they despised their Savior who had done such mighty miracles in Egypt and at the Sea. [23]So the Lord declared he would destroy them. But Moses, his chosen one, stepped into the breach between the people and their God and begged him to turn from his wrath and not destroy them.

[24]They refused to enter the Promised Land, for they wouldn't believe his solemn oath to care for them. [25]Instead, they pouted in their tents and mourned and despised his command. [26]Therefore he swore that he would kill them in the wilderness [27]and send their children away to distant lands as exiles. [28]Then our fathers joined the worshipers of Baal at Peor and even offered sacrifices to the dead! [29]With all these things they angered him—and so a plague broke out upon them [30]and continued until Phineas executed those whose sins had caused the plague to start. [31](For this good deed Phineas will be remembered forever.)

[32]At Meribah, too, Israel angered God, causing Moses serious trouble, [33]for he became angry and spoke foolishly.

[34]Nor did Israel destroy the nations in the land as God had told them to, [35]but mingled in among the heathen and learned their evil ways, [36]sacrificing to their idols, and were led away from God. [37,38]They even sacrificed their little children to the demons—the idols of Canaan—shedding innocent blood and polluting the land with murder. [39]Their evil deeds defiled them, for their love of idols was adultery in the sight of God. [40]That is why Jehovah's anger burned against his people, and he abhorred them. [41,42]That is why he let the heathen nations crush them. They were ruled by those who hated them and oppressed by their enemies.

[43]Again and again he delivered them from their slavery, but they continued to rebel against him and were finally destroyed by their sin. [44]Yet, even so, he listened to their cries and heeded their distress; [45]he remembered his promises to them and relented because of his great love, [46]and caused even their enemies who captured them to pity them.

[47]O Lord God, save us! Regather us from the nations so we can thank your holy name and rejoice and praise you.

[48]Blessed be the Lord, the God of Israel, from everlasting to everlasting. Let all the people say, "Amen!" Hallelujah!

PSALM 107

Say thank you to the Lord for being so good, for always being so loving and kind. [2]Has the Lord redeemed you? Then speak out! Tell others he has saved you from your enemies.

[3]He brought the exiles back from the farthest corners of the earth. [4]They were wandering homeless in the desert, [5]hungry and thirsty and faint. [6]"Lord, help!" they cried, and he did! [7]He led them straight to safety and a place to live. [8]Oh, that these men would praise the Lord for his loving-kindness, and

---

106:13-15 We all get discouraged when we fail. Like the people of Israel, we sometimes have a very short memory. We learn a lesson one day, only to forget it the next. After failing repeatedly, we need to remember that God has pulled us through in the past, and he is able and willing to do it again. God is always willing to help us if we are sincerely sorry and really desire to change. We must be careful, however, not to test God's patience to the breaking point. If we commit sin willfully, we will suffer the consequences.

106:40-46 God hates sin. When we continue in our old ways, we shouldn't expect him to be pleased with us. God's judgment sometimes follows swiftly and may come from unexpected sources. Yet he never abandons us forever. His goal is still to free us from our bondage.

for all of his wonderful deeds! 9For he satisfies the thirsty soul and fills the hungry soul with good.

10Who are these who sit in darkness, in the shadow of death, crushed by misery and slavery? 11They rebelled against the Lord, scorning him who is the God above all gods. 12That is why he broke them with hard labor; they fell and none could help them rise again. 13Then they cried to the Lord in their troubles, and he rescued them! 14He led them from the darkness and shadow of death and snapped their chains. 15Oh, that these men would praise the Lord for his loving-kindness and for all of his wonderful deeds! 16For he broke down their prison gates of brass and cut apart their iron bars.

17Others, the fools, were ill because of their sinful ways. 18Their appetites were gone, and death was near. 19Then they cried to the Lord in their troubles, and he helped them and delivered them. 20He spoke, and they were healed—snatched from the door of death. 21Oh, that these men would praise the Lord for his loving-kindness and for all of his wonderful deeds! 22Let them tell him thank you as their sacrifice and sing about his glorious deeds.

23And then there are the sailors sailing the seven seas, plying the trade routes of the world. 24They, too, observe the power of God in action. 25He calls to the storm winds; the waves rise high. 26Their ships are tossed to the heavens and sink again to the depths; the sailors cringe in terror. 27They reel and stagger like drunkards and are at their wit's end. 28Then they cry to the Lord in their trouble, and he saves them. 29He calms the storm and stills the waves. 30What a blessing is that stillness as he brings them safely into harbor! 31Oh, that these men would praise the Lord for his loving-kindness and for all of his wonderful deeds! 32Let them praise him publicly before the congregation and before the leaders of the nation.

33He dries up rivers 34and turns the good land of the wicked into deserts of salt. 35Again, he turns deserts into fertile, watered valleys. 36He brings the hungry to settle there and build their cities, 37to sow their fields and plant their vineyards, and reap their bumper crops! 38How he blesses them! They raise big families there and many cattle.

39But others become poor through oppression, trouble, and sorrow. 40For God pours contempt upon the haughty and causes princes to wander among ruins; 41but he rescues the poor who are godly and gives them many children and much prosperity. 42Good men everywhere will see it and be glad, while evil men are stricken silent.

43Listen, if you are wise, to what I am saying. Think about the loving-kindness of the Lord!

PSALM 108

O God, my heart is ready to praise you! I will sing and rejoice before you.

2Wake up, O harp and lyre! We will meet the dawn with song. 3I will praise you everywhere around the world, in every nation. 4For your loving-kindness is great beyond measure, high as the heavens. Your faithfulness reaches the skies. 5His glory is far more vast than the heavens. It towers above the earth. 6Hear the cry of your beloved child—come with mighty power and rescue me.

7God has given sacred promises; no wonder I exult! He has promised to give us all the land of Shechem and also Succoth Valley. 8"Gilead is mine to give to you," he says, "and Manasseh as well; the land of Ephraim is the helmet on my head. Judah is my scepter. 9But Moab and Edom are despised; and I will shout in triumph over the Philistines."

10Who but God can give me strength to

107:10-16 When we reject God and his plan, we live in spiritual darkness; our life hangs by a thread. God punishes evil acts with a heavy penalty, including not only God's divine punishment, but also the natural consequences of disobedience. The psalmist's announcement of punishment, however, should not leave us in despair; his comments end on a hopeful note. If we come to our senses and ask God for his deliverance, he will help us escape from our bondage.

107:23-32 Sometimes we feel we are in a small ship plowing through stormy seas and about to go under. Bad memories and a sense of failure make our world seem dark and hopeless. The longer the storm rages, the more we fear and lose all hope of rescue. God can turn our stormy life into a calm and peaceful sea; he can restore our joy in life. All we have to do is turn to him for help, follow his plan for healthy living, and patiently await his deliverance.

108:1-6 Morning is a wonderful time to praise God. Now that we are in recovery, our nights probably seem long, but another day free of oppression from our addictions should fill our heart with joy. We should let our joy spill out as a message of hope to others in need. Our word of testimony may lead numerous others to the joy we are beginning to experience in the process of recovery.

conquer these fortified cities? Who else can lead me into Edom?

[11]Lord, have you thrown us away? Have you deserted our army? [12]Oh, help us fight against our enemies, for men are useless allies. [13]But with the help of God we shall do mighty acts of valor. For he treads down our foes.

PSALM 109

O God of my praise, don't stand silent and aloof [2]while the wicked slander me and tell their lies. [3]They have no reason to hate and fight me, yet they do! [4]I love them, but even while I am praying for them, they are trying to destroy me. [5]They return evil for good, and hatred for love.

[6]Show him how it feels! Let lies be told about him, and bring him to court before an unfair judge. [7]When his case is called for judgment, let him be pronounced guilty. Count his prayers as sins. [8]Let his years be few and brief; let others step forward to replace him. [9,10]May his children become fatherless and his wife a widow; may they be evicted from the ruins of their home. [11]May creditors seize his entire estate and strangers take all he has earned. [12,13]Let no one be kind to him; let no one pity his fatherless children. May they die. May his family name be blotted out in a single generation. [14]Punish the sins of his father and mother. Don't overlook them. [15]Think constantly about the evil things he has done, and cut off his name from the memory of man.

[16]For he refused all kindness to others, and persecuted those in need, and hounded brokenhearted ones to death. [17]He loved to curse others; now you curse him. He never blessed others; now don't you bless him. [18]Cursing is as much a part of him as his clothing, or as the water he drinks, or the rich food he eats.

[19]Now may those curses return and cling to him like his clothing or his belt. [20]This is the Lord's punishment upon my enemies who tell lies about me and threaten me with death.

[21]But as for me, O Lord, deal with me as your child, as one who bears your name! Because you are so kind, O Lord, deliver me.

[22,23]I am slipping down the hill to death; I am shaken off from life as easily as a man brushes a grasshopper from his arm. [24]My knees are weak from fasting, and I am skin and bones. [25]I am a symbol of failure to all mankind; when they see me they shake their heads.

[26]Help me, O Lord my God! Save me because you are loving and kind. [27]Do it publicly, so all will see that you yourself have done it. [28]Then let them curse me if they like—I won't mind that if you are blessing me! For then all their efforts to destroy me will fail, and I shall go right on rejoicing!

[29]Make them fail in everything they do. Clothe them with disgrace. [30]But I will give repeated thanks to the Lord, praising him to everyone. [31]For he stands beside the poor and hungry to save them from their enemies.

PSALM 110

Jehovah said to my Lord the Messiah, "Rule as my regent—I will subdue your enemies and make them bow low before you."

[2]Jehovah has established your throne in Jerusalem to rule over your enemies. [3]In that day of your power your people shall come to you willingly, dressed in holy altar robes. And your strength shall be renewed day by day like

---

108:7-13 There is no resource for true recovery other than the strength offered by our gracious God. It is futile to trust anyone else for our victory, since God alone can give us the power to overcome our dependencies and compulsions. Ultimately he is the one who does the conquering for us. All we need to do is admit our powerlessness and turn our life over to his care and direction.
109:1-5 We all know what it feels like to be condemned by others—sometimes unjustly. Sometimes we are attacked by painful memories of the abuse we may have suffered. It is then we need to turn to God for relief. He will fill our heart with his love and help us to forgive those who are speaking out against us. We can rest in him and do our best to reconcile with the people who are hurting us. In time, the voices of slander will be silenced.
109:21-31 It takes great humility to entrust our life to God. This is one of the most difficult parts of recovery. As one of God's children, we need to admit how helpless we are to overcome our powerful dependencies alone. By now all of us have discovered what happens when we try to do things our own way: we become enslaved to our own desires and appetites. Dependence on God and his program is the only road to true freedom. We need to remember, however, that though God calls us to be childlike in spirit, he does not want us to be childish in behavior.
111:9-10 We must never forget the ransom price God paid that we might have access to him. God is willing to make sacrifices so we, unworthy as we are, can be restored to a godly and joyful life. This should encourage us as we seek recovery. God wants it to happen even more than we do! That's why we can safely entrust our life into his hands. God has proven his desire for our recovery by giving his own Son to suffer on our behalf.

READ PSALM 111:1-10

GOD grant me the serenity
to accept the things I cannot change
the courage to change the things I can
and the wisdom to know the difference
AMEN

When we lack wisdom, the storms of life can be devastating. When we find our life is in pieces, we may realize that we have acted unwisely and want to change, but where do we start?

"How can men be wise?" the psalmist asks. "The only way to begin is by reverence for God. For growth in wisdom comes from obeying his laws" (Psalm 111:10). God has given clear instructions for life. When we have enough reverence for God that we are willing to accept his instructions as the basis for all of our decisions, we have a good starting point.

Jesus said, "All who listen to my instructions and follow them are wise, like a man who builds his house on solid rock. Though the rain comes in torrents, and the floods rise and the storm winds beat against his house, it won't collapse for it is built on rock" (Matthew 7:24-25). Listening to what the Bible says is the next step toward walking in wisdom. Filling our mind with God's instructions will lead us to follow them. This will also help us turn away from the things forbidden by God. Job tells us, "To fear the Lord is true wisdom; to forsake evil is real understanding" (Job 28:28).

Turning our life over to God is a wise move! Like most aspects of recovery, walking in wisdom is a process that we grow into. These three elements are the groundwork: reverence for God, listening to his instructions, and following them. ***Turn to page 665, Psalm 139.***

---

morning dew. 4Jehovah has taken oath and
will not rescind his vow that you are a priest
forever like Melchizedek. 5God stands beside
you to protect you. He will strike down many
kings in the day of his anger. 6He will punish
the nations and fill them with their dead. He
will crush many heads. 7But he himself shall
be refreshed from springs along the way.

PSALM 111
Hallelujah! I want to express publicly before
his people my heartfelt thanks to God for his
mighty miracles. All who are thankful should
ponder them with me. 3For his miracles
demonstrate his honor, majesty, and eternal
goodness.
4Who can forget the wonders he performs—deeds of mercy and of grace? 5He gives
food to those who trust him; he never forgets
his promises. 6He has shown his great power
to his people by giving them the land of
Israel, though it was the home of many nations living there. 7All he does is just and
good, and all his laws are right, 8for they are
formed from truth and goodness and stand
firm forever. 9He has paid a full ransom for his
people; now they are always free to come to
Jehovah (what a holy, awe-inspiring name
that is).
10How can men be wise? The only way to
begin is by reverence for God. For growth in
wisdom comes from obeying his laws. Praise
his name forever.

PSALM 112
Praise the Lord! For all who fear God and trust
in him are blessed beyond expression. Yes,
happy is the man who delights in doing his
commands.
2His children shall be honored everywhere,
for good men's sons have a special heritage.
3He himself shall be wealthy, and his good
deeds will never be forgotten. 4When darkness overtakes him, light will come bursting

in. He is kind and merciful—5and all goes well
for the generous man who conducts his business fairly.
6Such a man will not be overthrown by evil
circumstances. God's constant care of him
will make a deep impression on all who see it.
7He does not fear bad news, nor live in dread
of what may happen. For he is settled in his
mind that Jehovah will take care of him. 8That
is why he is not afraid but can calmly face his
foes. 9He gives generously to those in need.
His deeds will never be forgotten. He shall
have influence and honor.
10Evil-minded men will be infuriated
when they see all this; they will gnash their
teeth in anger and slink away, their hopes
thwarted.

PSALM 113
Hallelujah! O servants of Jehovah, praise his
name. 2Blessed is his name forever and forever. 3Praise him from sunrise to sunset! 4For
he is high above the nations; his glory is far
greater than the heavens.
5Who can be compared with God enthroned on high? 6Far below him are the
heavens and the earth; he stoops to look, 7and
lifts the poor from the dirt and the hungry
from the garbage dump, 8and sets them
among princes! 9He gives children to the
childless wife, so that she becomes a happy
mother.
Hallelujah! Praise the Lord.

PSALM 114
Long ago when the Israelis escaped from
Egypt, from that land of foreign tongue, 2then
the lands of Judah and of Israel became God's
new home and kingdom.
3The Red Sea saw them coming and quickly
broke apart before them. The Jordan River
opened up a path for them to cross. 4The
mountains skipped like rams, the little hills
like lambs! 5What's wrong, Red Sea, that made
you cut yourself in two? What happened,
Jordan River, to your waters? Why were they
held back? 6Why, mountains, did you skip like
rams? Why, little hills, like lambs?
7Tremble, O earth, at the presence of the
Lord, the God of Jacob. 8For he caused gushing streams to burst from flinty rock.

PSALM 115
Glorify your name, not ours, O Lord! Cause
everyone to praise your loving-kindness and
your truth. 2Why let the nations say, "Their
God is dead!"
3For he is in the heavens and does as he
wishes. 4Their gods are merely man-made
things of silver and of gold. 5They can't talk or
see, despite their eyes and mouths! 6Nor can
they hear, nor smell, 7nor use their hands or
feet, nor speak! 8And those who make and
worship them are just as foolish as their idols
are.
9O Israel, trust the Lord! He is your helper.
He is your shield. 10O priests of Aaron, trust

112:6-10 The best guarantee we have of success in overcoming our habits, our bad thought patterns, and even the hurts in our life is to keep our eyes on God. Making good changes in our life won't make everyone happy. Some of our old enemies—and our old friends who used to lead us astray—will wonder why we no longer relate to them as we did in the past. Some of them may even criticize us or think we are snobbish. As a result, we may find our recovery lonely at first. In times like these, we need to look to God. He is always with us, and with his help we will find new relationships that will strengthen us. We will also learn how to reconcile our old relationships in ways that will support our recovery.

113:5-9 Only God can restore us to sanity; and he alone can lift us up. We may not sit "among princes" again, but we can return to society with dignity when we allow God to help us regain control of our life.

114:1-6 There is no end to the miracles God will perform on behalf of those who seek refuge in him. To bring courage to his readers, the psalmist lists some of God's amazing acts of deliverance in Israel's history. As we face difficulties, we can recall events of God's deliverance—in biblical history or in our own life. This will give us the hope we need to persevere in recovery; it will help us to entrust our life into God's hands without reservation. God is truly an awesome God. He is worthy of our respect, obedience, and praise.

115:1-8 God is the only real resource for recovery. We have probably tried a number of recovery plans, but if God is not a central part of our program, we won't experience a lasting recovery. Some of us look for help in every new fad that comes along. We look for help in places where it will never be found. If we forget to ask God for help, all of these other recovery resources are useless—they are only man-made plans, as powerless as idols. Recovery is never easy. If we hear of a plan that is easy or quick, someone is probably just after our money. God alone knows what we need and has the power to lift us out of our painful circumstances into a life filled with meaning and joy. His program is the only way to a healthy life.

the Lord! He is your helper; he is your shield. 11All of you, his people, trust in him. He is your helper; he is your shield.

12Jehovah is constantly thinking about us, and he will surely bless us. He will bless the people of Israel and the priests of Aaron, 13 and all, both great and small, who reverence him.

14May the Lord richly bless both you and your children. 15Yes, Jehovah who made heaven and earth will personally bless you! 16The heavens belong to the Lord, but he has given the earth to all mankind.

17The dead cannot sing praises to Jehovah here on earth, 18but we can! We praise him forever! Hallelujah! Praise the Lord!

PSALM 116
I love the Lord because he hears my prayers and answers them. 2Because he bends down and listens, I will pray as long as I breathe!

3Death stared me in the face—I was frightened and sad. 4Then I cried, "Lord, save me!" 5How kind he is! How good he is! So merciful, this God of ours! 6The Lord protects the simple and the childlike; I was facing death, and then he saved me. 7Now I can relax. For the Lord has done this wonderful miracle for me. 8He has saved me from death, my eyes from tears, my feet from stumbling. 9I shall live! Yes, in his presence—here on earth!

10,11 In my discouragement I thought, "They are lying when they say I will recover." 12But now what can I offer Jehovah for all he has done for me? 13I will bring him an offering of wine and praise his name for saving me. 14I will publicly bring him the sacrifice I vowed I would. 15His loved ones are very precious to him, and he does not lightly let them die.

16O Lord, you have freed me from my bonds, and I will serve you forever. 17I will worship you and offer you a sacrifice of thanksgiving. 18,19Here in the courts of the Temple in Jerusalem, before all the people, I will pay everything I vowed to the Lord. Praise the Lord.

PSALM 117
Praise the Lord, all nations everywhere. Praise him, all the peoples of the earth. 2For he loves us very dearly, and his truth endures. Praise the Lord.

PSALM 118
Oh, thank the Lord, for he's so good! His loving-kindness is forever.

2Let the congregation of Israel praise him with these same words: "His loving-kindness is forever." 3And let the priests of Aaron chant, "His loving-kindness is forever." 4Let the Gentile converts chant, "His loving-kindness is forever."

5In my distress I prayed to the Lord, and he answered me and rescued me. 6He is for me! How can I be afraid? What can mere man do to me? 7The Lord is on my side; he will help me. Let those who hate me beware.

8It is better to trust the Lord than to put confidence in men. 9It is better to take refuge in him than in the mightiest king!

10Though all the nations of the world attack me, I will march out behind his banner and destroy them. 11Yes, they surround and attack me; but with his flag flying above me I will cut them off. 12They swarm around me like bees; they blaze against me like a roaring flame. Yet beneath his flag I shall destroy them. 13You did your best to kill me, O my enemy, but the Lord helped me. 14He is my strength and song in the heat of battle, and now he has given me the victory. 15,16 Songs of joy at the news of our rescue are sung in the homes of the godly. The strong arm of the Lord has done glorious things! 17I shall not die but live to tell of all his deeds. 18The Lord has punished me but not handed me over to death.

19Open the gates of the Temple—I will go in and give him my thanks. 20 Those gates are the way into the presence of the Lord, and the godly enter there. 21 O Lord, thank you so much for answering my prayer and saving me.

22The stone rejected by the builders has now become the capstone of the arch! 23This

116:1-9 God has a long history of responding to those who turn to him in times of distress. When we were in the grip of our dependencies or addictions, we may have been blind to the fact that we were in danger of losing our reputation, our friends, or even our life. Upon our return to sanity we probably realized just how close to death we actually were. The natural response to this realization should be praise to God—the one who opened our eyes.

116:10-19 We will never be able to repay God for what he has done to help us. But we can at least show our gratitude by fulfilling the promises we made to him when we called out to him for help. God thinks of us as his precious children, so we should show our gratitude by keeping our vows to him. This may include making sure everyone knows it is God who deserves the credit for our deliverance.

is the Lord's doing, and it is marvelous to see!
[24]This is the day the Lord has made. We will
rejoice and be glad in it. [25]O Lord, please help
us. Save us. Give us success. [26]Blessed is the
one who is coming, the one sent by the Lord.
We bless you from the Temple.
[27,28]Jehovah God is our light. I present to
him my sacrifice upon the altar, for you are
my God, and I shall give you this thanks and
this praise. [29]Oh, give thanks to the Lord, for
he is so good! For his loving-kindness is forever.

PSALM 119

Happy are all who perfectly follow the laws of
God. [2]Happy are all who search for God and
always do his will, [3]rejecting compromise
with evil and walking only in his paths. [4]You
have given us your laws to obey—[5]oh, how I
want to follow them consistently. [6]Then I will
not be disgraced, for I will have a clean record.
[7]After you have corrected me, I will thank
you by living as I should! [8]I *will* obey! Oh,
don't forsake me and let me slip back into sin
again.
[9]How can a young man stay pure? By reading your Word and following its rules. [10]I have
tried my best to find you—don't let me wander off from your instructions. [11]I have
thought much about your words and stored
them in my heart so that they would hold me
back from sin.
[12]Blessed Lord, teach me your rules. [13]I have
recited your laws [14]and rejoiced in them more
than in riches. [15]I will meditate upon them
and give them my full respect. [16]I will delight
in them and not forget them.
[17]Bless me with life so that I can continue
to obey you. [18]Open my eyes to see wonderful
things in your Word. [19]I am but a pilgrim here
on earth: how I need a map—and your commands are my chart and guide. [20]I long for
your instructions more than I can tell.
[21]You rebuke those cursed proud ones who
refuse your commands—[22]don't let them
scorn me for obeying you. [23]For even princes
sit and talk against me, but I will continue in
your plans. [24]Your laws are both my light and
my counselors.
[25]I am completely discouraged—I lie in the
dust. Revive me by your Word. [26]I told you my
plans and you replied. Now give me your
instructions. [27] Make me understand what you
want; for then I shall see your miracles.
[28]I weep with grief; my heart is heavy with
sorrow; encourage and cheer me with your
words. [29,30]Keep me far from every wrong; help
me, undeserving as I am, to obey your laws,
for I have chosen to do right. [31]I cling to your
commands and follow them as closely as I
can. Lord, don't let me make a mess of things.
[32]If you will only help me to want your will,
then I will follow your laws even more closely.
[33,34]Just tell me what to do and I will do it,
Lord. As long as I live I'll wholeheartedly

118:22-25 God's ways are not the same as our ways. What people may cast aside as unfit for use, God uses to do awe-inspiring work. This can be true for us, too. We may feel that our life has been ruined beyond repair. We probably think that we will never be used by God for anything significant. God often uses the most unlikely people to work his greatest miracles, proving to the world that God is at work. As willing vessels of God's power, we can be transformed to make an impact on others that goes far beyond our wildest dreams. All we have to do is entrust our life to God.

119:9-16 Obedience to God's Word produces wholeness; it seems only logical that we should do all we can to follow it. This is a significant part of seeking out God's will for us. In the Bible, God has left clear guidelines for how he expects us to live. He has also promised that he will help us to carry out his will if we only ask him. Studying, pondering, and applying God's Word should become a joyful experience that will implant God's truth firmly in our mind and heart.

119:17-24 With God's guidance, we can learn those truths from his Word that will lead us safely through the uncharted territories of life. Because God rebukes those who do not follow his teaching, we need to seek his forgiveness for those times we have strayed. We also must not let the problems of life inhibit our study of God's Word. Without its wisdom and guidance, we will lack the insight we need to experience a successful recovery and a meaningful life.

119:57-64 In recovery we are called to seek out God's will for our life. The Bible should be the first place we look to discover it. Yet once we have been given direction, we must not be merely hearers of his Word. We also need to be doers who take appropriate action once God's will is known (see James 1:22-25). If we learn God's will but fail to act on it, we are no better off than we were before. Our recovery demands that we act—now!

119:71-72 We should be thankful when God disciplines us for our sin. Painful as it may be, it drives us back to his truth, which is far more valuable than all the riches of this world. God only wants what is best for us. We would be wise to learn from God's discipline rather than fight it. It is given for our betterment, not our destruction.

obey. 35 Make me walk along the right paths,
for I know how delightful they really are.
36 Help me to prefer obedience to making
money! 37 Turn me away from wanting any
other plan than yours. Revive my heart toward you. 38 Reassure me that your promises
are for me, for I trust and revere you.
39 How I dread being mocked for obeying,
for your laws are right and good. 40-42 I long to
obey them! Therefore in fairness renew my
life, for this was your promise—yes, Lord, to
save me! Now spare me by your kindness and
your love. Then I will have an answer for
those who taunt me, for I trust your promises.
43 May I never forget your words, for they
are my only hope. 44-46 Therefore I will keep on
obeying you forever and forever, free within
the limits of your laws. I will speak to kings
about their value, and they will listen with
interest and respect.
47 How I love your laws! How I enjoy your
commands! 48 "Come, come to me," I call to
them, for I love them and will let them fill my
life.
49,50 Never forget your promises to me your
servant, for they are my only hope. They give
me strength in all my troubles; how they
refresh and revive me! 51 Proud men hold me
in contempt for obedience to God, but I stand
unmoved. 52 From my earliest youth I have
tried to obey you; your Word has been my
comfort.
53 I am very angry with those who spurn
your commands. 54 For these laws of yours
have been my source of joy and singing
through all these years of my earthly pilgrimage. 55 I obey them even at night and keep my
thoughts, O Lord, on you. 56 What a blessing
this has been to me—to constantly obey.
57 Jehovah is mine! And I promise to obey!
58 With all my heart I want your blessings. Be
merciful just as you promised. 59,60 I thought
about the wrong direction in which I was
headed, and turned around and came running back to you. 61 Evil men have tried to drag
me into sin, but I am firmly anchored to your
laws.
62 At midnight I will rise to give my thanks
to you for your good laws. 63 Anyone is my
brother who fears and trusts the Lord and
obeys him. 64 O Lord, the earth is full of your
loving-kindness! Teach me your good paths.
65 Lord, I am overflowing with your blessings, just as you promised. 66 Now teach me
good judgment as well as knowledge. For your
laws are my guide. 67 I used to wander off until
you punished me; now I closely follow all you

Powerful Secrets

BIBLE READING: Psalm 119:1-11

We sought through prayer and meditation to improve our conscious contact with God, as we understood him, praying only for knowledge of his will for us and the power to carry that out.

The secrets we hide away have enormous power in our life. How many of our addictive/compulsive behaviors have been hidden or covered up? When we took the step to admit the exact nature of our wrongs to another human being, we were probably amazed at the way the addiction lost power as it was exposed. The power of hidden behaviors and secrets can work for us as well as against us.

David said, "I have thought much about [God's] words, and stored them in my heart so that they would hold me back from sin" (Psalm 119:11). The word rendered *stored* can be translated "to hide by covering over" or "to hoard secretly." If we "hide" God's Word in our heart by memorizing and meditating on it, we will find new power to keep our mind and heart clean.

The power of secrets will also work to our advantage in our prayer life. Jesus taught us, "But when you pray, go away by yourself, all alone, and shut the door behind you and pray to your Father secretly, and your Father, who knows your secrets, will reward you" (Matthew 6:6). When we begin to spend time shut away with the Lord in prayer and meditation, we'll find that power working for us. ***Turn to page 755, Isaiah 40.***

say. 68 You are good and do only good; make me follow your lead.

69 Proud men have made up lies about me, but the truth is that I obey your laws with all my heart. 70 Their minds are dull and stupid, but I have sense enough to follow you.

71,72 The punishment you gave me was the best thing that could have happened to me, for it taught me to pay attention to your laws. They are more valuable to me than millions in silver and gold!

73 You made my body, Lord; now give me sense to heed your laws. 74 All those who fear and trust in you will welcome me because I too am trusting in your Word.

75-77 I know, O Lord, that your decisions are right and that your punishment was right and did me good. Now let your loving-kindness comfort me, just as you promised. Surround me with your tender mercies that I may live. For your law is my delight.

78 Let the proud be disgraced, for they have cut me down with all their lies. But I will concentrate my thoughts upon your laws.

79 Let all others join me who trust and fear you, and we will discuss your laws. 80 Help me to love your every wish; then I will never have to be ashamed of myself.

81 I faint for your salvation; but I expect your help, for you have promised it. 82 My eyes are straining to see your promises come true. When will you comfort me with your help? 83 I am shriveled like a wineskin in the smoke, exhausted with waiting. But still I cling to your laws and obey them. 84 How long must I wait before you punish those who persecute me? 85,86 These proud men who hate your truth and laws have dug deep pits for me to fall in. Their lies have brought me into deep trouble. Help me, for you love only truth. 87 They had almost finished me off, yet I refused to yield and disobey your laws. 88 In your kindness, spare my life; then I can continue to obey you.

89 Forever, O Lord, your Word stands firm in heaven. 90,91 Your faithfulness extends to every generation, like the earth you created; it endures by your decree, for everything serves your plans.

92 I would have despaired and perished unless your laws had been my deepest delight. 93 I will never lay aside your laws, for you have used them to restore my joy and health. 94 I am yours! Save me! For I have tried to live according to your desires. 95 Though the wicked hide along the way to kill me, I will quietly keep my mind upon your promises.

96 Nothing is perfect except your words. 97 Oh, how I love them. I think about them all day long. 98 They make me wiser than my enemies because they are my constant guide. 99 Yes, wiser than my teachers, for I am ever thinking of your rules. 100 They make me even wiser than the aged.

101 I have refused to walk the paths of evil, for I will remain obedient to your Word. 102,103 No, I haven't turned away from what you taught me; your words are sweeter than honey. 104 And since only your rules can give me wisdom and understanding, no wonder I hate every false teaching.

105 Your words are a flashlight to light the path ahead of me and keep me from stumbling. 106 I've said it once and I'll say it again and again: I will obey these wonderful laws of yours.

107 I am close to death at the hands of my enemies; oh, give me back my life again, just as you promised me. 108 Accept my grateful thanks and teach me your desires. 109 My life hangs in the balance, but I will not give up obedience to your laws. 110 The wicked have set their traps for me along your path, but I will not turn aside. 111 Your laws are my joyous treasure forever. 112 I am determined to obey you until I die.

113 I hate those who are undecided whether or not to obey you; but my choice is clear—I love your law. 114 You are my refuge and my shield, and your promises are my only source of hope. 115 Begone, you evil-minded men! Don't try to stop me from obeying God's commands. 116 Lord, you promised to let me live! Never let it be said that God failed me. 117 Hold me safe above the heads of all my enemies; then I can continue to obey your laws.

118 But you have rejected all who reject your laws. They are only fooling themselves. 119 The wicked are the scum you skim off and throw away; no wonder I love to obey your laws! 120 I

119:73-77 As we obey God's revealed will, people will begin to see the changes in our life and praise God. All of God's work—even his severe discipline—is done because of his goodness and faithfulness. God wants us to live a joyful life. All we have to do is seek out God's will and do our best, with his help, to follow it. Then, as God transforms us, we will be a living testimony of God's power to transform broken lives.

tremble in fear of you; I fear your punishments.
121Don't leave me to the mercy of my enemies, for I have done what is right; I've been
perfectly fair. 122Commit yourself to bless me!
Don't let the proud oppress me! 123My eyes
grow dim with longing for you to fulfill your
wonderful promise to rescue me. 124Lord, deal
with me in loving-kindness, and teach me,
your servant, to obey; 125for I am your servant;
therefore give me common sense to apply
your rules to everything I do.
126Lord, it is time for you to act. For these
evil men have violated your laws, 127while I
love your commandments more than the finest gold. 128Every law of God is right, whatever
it concerns. I hate every other way.
129Your laws are wonderful; no wonder I
obey them. 130As your plan unfolds, even the
simple can understand it. 131No wonder I wait
expectantly for each of your commands.
132Come and have mercy on me as is your
way with those who love you. 133Guide me
with your laws so that I will not be overcome
by evil. 134Rescue me from the oppression of
evil men; then I can obey you. 135Look down
in love upon me and teach me all your laws.
136I weep because your laws are disobeyed.
137O Lord, you are just and your punishments are fair. 138Your demands are just and
right. 139I am indignant and angry because of
the way my enemies have disregarded your
laws. 140I have thoroughly tested your promises, and that is why I love them so much. 141I
am worthless and despised, but I don't despise
your laws.
142Your justice is eternal for your laws are
perfectly fair. 143In my distress and anguish
your commandments comfort me. 144Your
laws are always fair; help me to understand
them, and I shall live.
145I am praying with great earnestness; answer me, O Lord, and I will obey your laws.
146"Save me," I cry, "for I am obeying." 147Early
in the morning before the sun is up, I am
praying and pointing out how much I trust in
you. 148I stay awake through the night to think
about your promises. 149Because you are so
loving and kind, listen to me and make me
well again.
150Here come these lawless men to attack
me, 151but you are near, O Lord; all your commandments are based on truth. 152I have
known from earliest days that your will never
changes.
153Look down upon my sorrows and rescue
me, for I am obeying your commands. 154Yes,
rescue me and give me back my life again just
as you have promised. 155The wicked are far
from salvation, for they do not care for your
laws. 156Lord, how great is your mercy; oh,
give me back my life again.
157My enemies are so many. They try to
make me disobey, but I have not swerved
from your will. 158I loathed these traitors because they care nothing for your laws. 159Lord,
see how much I really love your demands.
Now give me back my life and health because
you are so kind. 160There is utter truth in all
your laws; your decrees are eternal.
161Great men have persecuted me, though
they have no reason to, but I stand in awe of
only your words. 162I rejoice in your laws like
one who finds a great treasure. 163How I hate
all falsehood, but how I love your laws. 164I
will praise you seven times a day because of
your wonderful laws.
165Those who love your laws have great
peace of heart and mind and do not stumble.
166I long for your salvation, Lord, and so I have
obeyed your laws. 167I have looked for your
commandments, and I love them very much;
168yes, I have searched for them. You know
this because everything I do is known to you.
169O Lord, listen to my prayers; give me the
common sense you promised. 170Hear my
prayers; rescue me as you said you would. 171I
praise you for letting me learn your laws. 172I
will sing about their wonder, for each of them
is just. 173Stand ready to help me because I

119:124-128 Until we turn to God for help, we will never be rescued or have any sure guidance for our life. Following God's plan for our recovery will not be easy, but we can count on his help. Notice how the psalmist asked God to help him follow God's plan. We should do the same. When we are under pressure, we may be tempted to abandon God's way of doing things. Before returning to our old, destructive behaviors, we should turn to God, asking him to help us do what is right. God wants us to recover and is willing to provide not only the plan, but also the encouragement we need to follow it.

119:153-160 As we turn our life over to God, he is willing to restore us to wholeness. By entrusting our life to God, we can be sure that God's compassion for us will never cease. We can count on him to encourage us when our recovery becomes difficult or painful. As we seek out God's will in his Word, we will discover the joyful truth: he is willing and able to restore us to wholeness!

have chosen to follow your will. [174]O Lord, I
have longed for your salvation, and your law
is my delight. [175]If you will let me live, I will
praise you; let your laws assist me.
[176]I have wandered away like a lost sheep;
come and find me, for I have not turned away
from your commandments.

PSALM 120

In my troubles I pled with God to help me and
he did!
[2]Deliver me, O Lord, from liars. [3]O lying
tongue, what shall be your fate? [4]You shall be
pierced with sharp arrows and burned with
glowing coals.
[5,6]My troubles pile high among these haters
of the Lord, these men of Meshech and Kedar.
I am tired of being here among these men
who hate peace. [7]I am for peace, but they are
for war, and my voice goes unheeded in their
councils.

PSALM 121

Shall I look to the mountain gods for help?
[2]No! My help is from Jehovah who made the
mountains! And the heavens too! [3,4]He will
never let me stumble, slip, or fall. For he is
always watching, never sleeping.
[5]Jehovah himself is caring for you! He is
your defender. [6]He protects you day and
night. [7]He keeps you from all evil and preserves your life. [8]He keeps his eye upon you as
you come and go and always guards you.

PSALM 122

I was glad for the suggestion of going to Jerusalem, to the Temple of the Lord. [2,3]Now we
are standing here inside the crowded city. [4]All
Israel—Jehovah's people—have come to worship as the law requires, to thank and praise
the Lord. [5]Look! There are the judges holding
court beside the city gates, deciding all the
people's arguments.
[6]Pray for the peace of Jerusalem. May all
who love this city prosper. [7]O Jerusalem, may
there be peace within your walls and prosperity in your palaces. [8]This I ask for the sake of
all my brothers and my friends who live here;
[9]and may there be peace as a protection to the
Temple of the Lord.

PSALM 123

O God enthroned in heaven, I lift my eyes to
you.
[2]We look to Jehovah our God for his mercy
and kindness just as a servant keeps his eyes
upon his master or a slave girl watches her
mistress for the slightest signal.
[3,4]Have mercy on us, Lord, have mercy. For
we have had our fill of contempt and of the
scoffing of the rich and proud.

PSALM 124

If the Lord had not been on our side (let all
Israel admit it), if the Lord had not been on
our side, [2,3]we would have been swallowed
alive by our enemies, destroyed by their anger. [4,5]We would have drowned beneath the
flood of these men's fury and pride.
[6]Blessed be Jehovah who has not let them
devour us. [7]We have escaped with our lives as
a bird from a hunter's snare. The snare is
broken and we are free!
[8]Our help is from the Lord who made
heaven and earth.

PSALM 125

Those who trust in the Lord are steady as
Mount Zion, unmoved by any circumstance.
[2]Just as the mountains surround and protect Jerusalem, so the Lord surrounds and
protects his people. [3]For the wicked shall not
rule the godly, lest the godly be forced to do
wrong. [4]O Lord, do good to those who are
good, whose hearts are right with the Lord;
[5]but lead evil men to execution. And let Israel
have quietness and peace.

PSALM 126

When Jehovah brought back his exiles to Jerusalem, it was like a dream! [2]How we laughed
and sang for joy. And the other nations said,
"What amazing things the Lord has done for
them."
[3]Yes, glorious things! What wonder! What
joy! [4]May we be refreshed as by streams in the
desert.

121:1-8 God alone is able to give us victory over our dependencies. He watches over us, placing us under his umbrella of protection. He guards us against the dangers that threaten to destroy our life. Simply put, God exercises great care over us day and night.

124:1-8 Without God, there is no hope for deliverance. If he is not fighting our battles with us, we will be overwhelmed by our powerful addictions. We should respond to God's gracious deliverance by praising him for what he has done for us. This is the first step toward sharing the good news of God's love and power with others.

[5]Those who sow tears shall reap joy. [6]Yes, they go out weeping, carrying seed for sowing, and return singing, carrying their sheaves.

PSALM 127
Unless the Lord builds a house, the builders' work is useless. Unless the Lord protects a city, sentries do no good. [2]It is senseless for you to work so hard from early morning until late at night, fearing you will starve to death; for God wants his loved ones to get their proper rest.

[3]Children are a gift from God; they are his reward. [4]Children born to a young man are like sharp arrows to defend him.

[5]Happy is the man who has his quiver full of them. That man shall have the help he needs when arguing with his enemies.

PSALM 128
Blessings on all who reverence and trust the Lord—on all who obey him!

[2]Their reward shall be prosperity and happiness. [3]Your wife shall be contented in your home. And look at all those children! There they sit around the dinner table as vigorous and healthy as young olive trees. [4]That is God's reward to those who reverence and trust him.

[5]May the Lord continually bless you with heaven's blessings as well as with human joys. [6]May you live to enjoy your grandchildren! And may God bless Israel!

PSALM 129
Persecuted from my earliest youth (Israel is speaking), [2]and faced with never-ending discrimination—but not destroyed! My enemies have never been able to finish me off !

[3,4]Though my back is cut to ribbons with their whips, the Lord is good. For he has snapped the chains that evil men had bound me with.

[5]May all who hate the Jews be brought to ignominious defeat. [6,7]May they be as grass in shallow soil, turning sere and yellow when half grown, ignored by the reaper, despised by the binder. [8]And may those passing by refuse to bless them by saying, "Jehovah's blessings be upon you; we bless you in Jehovah's name."

PSALM 130
O Lord, from the depths of despair I cry for your help: [2]"Hear me! Answer! Help me!"

[3,4]Lord, if you keep in mind our sins, then who can ever get an answer to his prayers? But you forgive! What an awesome thing this is! [5]That is why I wait expectantly, trusting God to help, for he has promised. [6]I long for him more than sentinels long for the dawn.

[7]O Israel, hope in the Lord; for he is loving and kind and comes to us with armloads of salvation. [8]He himself shall ransom Israel from her slavery to sin.

PSALM 131
Lord, I am not proud and haughty. I don't think myself better than others. I don't pretend to "know it all." [2]I am quiet now before the Lord, just as a child who is weaned from the breast. Yes, my begging has been stilled.

[3]O Israel, you too should quietly trust in the Lord—now, and always.

PSALM 132
Lord, do you remember that time when my heart was so filled with turmoil? [2-5]I couldn't rest, I couldn't sleep, thinking how I ought to build a permanent home for the Ark of the Lord, a Temple for the mighty one of Israel.

126:1-6 This psalm was written in response to the return of Jewish exiles from captivity. God enabled his people to recover from their many sins by leading them through a period of painful exile. During this time, they admitted their sins and returned to God. Then God allowed them to return to their homeland. This can be our story, too. And as we experience God's restoration, our tears will turn to joy and we can sing our own songs of praise. Change never comes overnight, but God promises to complete our transformation when the time is right.

127:1 As we seek to rebuild our life, we need to make sure that God is involved in the building process. Without him, we have no hope for success. The forces that tear at the building of our life are too strong for us to handle alone. Yet God is able to protect us as the rebuilding goes on, and he will direct us each step of the way. Recovery programs that fail to keep God where he belongs—at the center of our life and recovery—will only lead to disappointment and deeper suffering. "Unless the Lord builds a house, the builders' work is useless."

130:1-8 When we cry out to God, we want quick answers. Yet, we should be thankful that God does not respond on the basis of our worthiness. If he did, we would receive nothing but judgment. God forgives our sins freely so that we might worship him with thankful hearts. He desires our recovery from the sinful forces in our life and will deliver us when we call out to him.

Then I vowed that I would do it; I made a solemn promise to the Lord.

6First the Ark was in Ephrathah, then in the distant countryside of Jaar. 7But now it will be settled in the Temple, in God's permanent home here on earth. That is where we will go to worship him. 8Arise, O Lord, and enter your Temple with the Ark, the symbol of your power.

9We will clothe the priests in white, the symbol of all purity. May our nation shout for joy.

10Do not reject your servant David—the king you chose for your people. 11For you promised me that my son would sit on my throne and succeed me. And surely you will never go back on a promise! 12You also promised that if my descendants will obey the terms of your contract with me, then the dynasty of David shall never end.

13O Lord, you have chosen Jerusalem as your home: 14"This is my permanent home where I shall live," you said, "for I have always wanted it this way. 15I will make this city prosperous and satisfy her poor with food. 16I will clothe her priests with salvation; her saints shall shout for joy. 17David's power shall grow, for I have decreed for him a mighty Son. 18I'll clothe his enemies with shame, but he shall be a glorious King."

PSALM 133

How wonderful it is, how pleasant, when brothers live in harmony! 2For harmony is as precious as the fragrant anointing oil that was poured over Aaron's head and ran down onto his beard and onto the border of his robe. 3Harmony is as refreshing as the dew on Mount Hermon, on the mountains of Israel. And God has pronounced this eternal blessing on Jerusalem, even life forevermore.

PSALM 134

Oh, bless the Lord, you who serve him as watchmen in the Temple every night. 2Lift your hands in holiness and bless the Lord.

3The Lord bless you from Zion—the Lord who made heaven and earth.

PSALM 135

Hallelujah! 2Yes, let his people praise him as they stand in his Temple courts. 3Praise the Lord because he is so good; sing to his wonderful name. 4For the Lord has chosen Israel as his personal possession.

5I know the greatness of the Lord—that he is greater far than any other god. 6He does whatever pleases him throughout all of heaven and earth and in the deepest seas. 7He makes mists rise throughout the earth; he sends the lightning to bring down the rain and sends the winds from his treasuries. 8He destroyed the eldest child in each Egyptian home, along with the firstborn of the flocks. 9He did great miracles in Egypt before Pharaoh and all his people. 10He smote great nations, slaying mighty kings—11Sihon, king of Amorites; and Og, the king of Bashan; and the kings of Canaan—12and gave their land as an eternal gift to his people Israel.

13O Jehovah, your name endures forever; your fame is known to every generation. 14For Jehovah will vindicate his people and have compassion on his servants.

15The heathen worship idols of gold and silver made by men—16idols with speechless mouths, sightless eyes, 17and ears that cannot hear; they cannot even breathe. 18Those who make them become like them! And so do all who trust in them!

19O Israel, bless Jehovah! High priests of Aaron, bless his name. 20O Levite priests, bless the Lord Jehovah! Oh, bless his name, all of you who trust and reverence him. 21All people of Jerusalem, praise the Lord, for he lives here in Jerusalem. Hallelujah!

PSALM 136

Oh, give thanks to the Lord, for he is good; his loving-kindness continues forever.

2Give thanks to the God of gods, for his loving-kindness continues forever. 3Give thanks to the Lord of lords, for his loving-

133:1-3 Reconciling our human relationships is an important part of our recovery. We need people in our life to give us encouragement to overcome our pain and to stand with us against the temptations we face. There is nothing quite like human fellowship and friendship, and God wants to bless us through other people. The kind of friendships most helpful to our recovery will be with people who are trying live according to God's program.

135:1-12 Knowing that God has chosen us as his own should give us the confidence to call on him when we are in trouble. All through the Old Testament we see evidence of God working to save his people. If God is powerful and caring enough to do all these miracles, he can help us when we call on him. No problem is too great for him to solve.

kindness continues forever. 4Praise him who alone does mighty miracles, for his loving-kindness continues forever. 5Praise him who made the heavens, for his loving-kindness continues forever. 6Praise him who planted the water within the earth, for his loving-kindness continues forever. 7Praise him who made the heavenly lights, for his loving-kindness continues forever: 8the sun to rule the day, for his loving-kindness continues forever; 9and the moon and stars at night, for his loving-kindness continues forever. 10Praise the God who smote the firstborn of Egypt, for his loving-kindness to Israel continues forever.

11,12He brought them out with mighty power and upraised fist to strike their enemies, for his loving-kindness to Israel continues forever. 13Praise the Lord who opened the Red Sea to make a path before them, for his loving-kindness continues forever, 14and led them safely through, for his loving-kindness continues forever—15but drowned Pharaoh's army in the sea, for his loving-kindness to Israel continues forever.

16Praise him who led his people through the wilderness, for his loving-kindness continues forever. 17Praise him who saved his people from the power of mighty kings, for his loving-kindness continues forever, 18and killed famous kings who were their enemies, for his loving-kindness to Israel continues forever: 19Sihon, king of Amorites—for God's loving-kindness to Israel continues forever— 20and Og, king of Bashan—for his loving-kindness to Israel continues forever. 21God gave the land of these kings to Israel as a gift forever, for his loving-kindness to Israel continues forever; 22yes, a permanent gift to his servant Israel, for his loving-kindness continues forever.

23He remembered our utter weakness, for his loving-kindness continues forever. 24And saved us from our foes, for his loving-kindness continues forever.

25He gives food to every living thing, for his loving-kindness continues forever. 26Oh, give thanks to the God of heaven, for his loving-kindness continues forever.

PSALM 137

Weeping, we sat beside the rivers of Babylon thinking of Jerusalem. 2We have put away our lyres, hanging them upon the branches of the willow trees, 3,4for how can we sing? Yet our captors, our tormentors, demand that we sing for them the happy songs of Zion! 5,6If I forget you, O Jerusalem, let my right hand forget its skill upon the harp. If I fail to love her more than my highest joy, let me never sing again.

7O Jehovah, do not forget what these Edomites did on that day when the armies of Babylon captured Jerusalem. "Raze her to the ground!" they yelled. 8O Babylon, evil beast, you shall be destroyed. Blessed is the man who destroys you as you have destroyed us. 9Blessed is the man who takes your babies and smashes them against the rocks!

PSALM 138

Lord, with all my heart I thank you. I will sing your praises before the armies of angels. 2I face your Temple as I worship, giving thanks to you for all your loving-kindness and your faithfulness, for your promises are backed by all the honor of your name. 3When I pray, you answer me and encourage me by giving me the strength I need.

4Every king in all the earth shall give you thanks, O Lord, for all of them shall hear your voice. 5Yes, they shall sing about Jehovah's glorious ways, for his glory is very great. 6Yet though he is so great, he respects the humble, but proud men must keep their distance. 7Though I am surrounded by troubles, you will bring me safely through them. You will clench your fist against my angry enemies! Your power will save me. 8The Lord will work out his plans for my life—for your loving-kindness, Lord, continues forever. Don't abandon me—for you made me.

PSALM 139

O Lord, you have examined my heart and know everything about me. 2You know when I sit or stand. When far away you know my every thought. 3You chart the path ahead of me and tell me where to stop and rest. Every moment you know where I am. 4You know

---

136:16-26 Moving through life, struggling with powerful addictions, is like a lonely walk through a wilderness. But God is able to lead us to victory, if we are willing to entrust our life to him. God never abandons us when we are humbled by our enemies—whether internal or external. Instead, he frees us from their clutches because his love for his people "continues forever."

138:6-8 God responds favorably to humility; he sets himself against the proud, who think they have no need of him. When we remain humble and seek his face, he is quick to renew our strength and to help us against our enemies. He will never fail us because he is a good God.

what I am going to say before I even say it.[5]You both precede and follow me and place your hand of blessing on my head.

[6]This is too glorious, too wonderful to believe! [7]I can *never* be lost to your Spirit! I can *never* get away from my God! [8]If I go up to heaven, you are there; if I go down to the place of the dead, you are there. [9]If I ride the morning winds to the farthest oceans, [10]even there your hand will guide me, your strength will support me. [11]If I try to hide in the darkness, the night becomes light around me. [12]For even darkness cannot hide from God; to you the night shines as bright as day. Darkness and light are both alike to you.

[13]You made all the delicate, inner parts of my body and knit them together in my mother's womb. [14]Thank you for making me so wonderfully complex! It is amazing to think about. Your workmanship is marvelous—and how well I know it. [15]You were there while I was being formed in utter seclusion! [16]You saw me before I was born and scheduled each day of my life before I began to breathe. Every day was recorded in your book!

[17,18]How precious it is, Lord, to realize that you are thinking about me constantly! I can't even count how many times a day your thoughts turn toward me. And when I waken in the morning, you are still thinking of me!

[19]Surely you will slay the wicked, Lord! Away, bloodthirsty men! Begone! [20]They blaspheme your name and stand in arrogance against you—how silly can they be? [21]O Lord, shouldn't I hate those who hate you? Shouldn't I be grieved with them? [22]Yes, I hate them, for your enemies are my enemies too.

[23]Search me, O God, and know my heart; test my thoughts. [24]Point out anything you find in me that makes you sad, and lead me along the path of everlasting life.

PSALM 140

O Lord, deliver me from evil men. Preserve me from the violent, [2]who plot and stir up trouble all day long. [3]Their words sting like poisonous snakes. [4]Keep me out of their power. Preserve me from their violence, for they are plotting against me. [5]These proud men have set a trap to catch me, a noose to yank me up and leave me dangling in the air; they wait in ambush with a net to throw over and hold me helpless in its meshes.

[6-8]O Jehovah, my Lord and Savior, my God and my shield—hear me as I pray! Don't let these wicked men succeed; don't let them prosper and be proud. [9]Let their plots boomerang! Let them be destroyed by the very evil they have planned for me. [10]Let burning coals fall down upon their heads, or throw them into the fire or into deep pits from which they can't escape.

139:6-12 God is everywhere. We could never run away from him even if we tried. Such knowledge should keep us from entering into sin and encourage us to follow him, knowing he is there to help us if we need it. Just as he is not limited by space, neither is he limited by time. He works with us day and night to strengthen and encourage us.

139:13-18 The power of our dependencies is often rooted in our low self-esteem. These verses reveal an exciting fact: each of us is an amazing creature—wonderfully made! More than that, God is thinking about us at all times! Our low self-esteem was taught to us. Someone let us know, one way or another, that we were no good. We began to believe this message, and now we have fallen into any number of destructive methods for dealing with the pain. We need to begin to see ourself as God sees us. As we grow to understand this better and better, much of the pain that drives our dependencies should fall away.

140:1-5 We need God's protection against those who might cause our downfall. Some people like to stir up trouble and may dangle enticements before us to the poisonous dependencies that led to our destruction. More than ever, we need God to keep us from being caught in their hidden snares. We may never totally escape the siren call of our addictions. We are never out of the danger zone. For this reason, we must commit ourself to staying close to God, the only one who can keep us safe.

141:1-10 When the flaming desire for our addiction is upon us, we need God's help to put out the fire. God can take away our desire for sin; sometimes we must bear the strain, but we can be sure that if the desire is greater than we can bear, God will help us find a way to escape (see 1 Corinthians 10:13). We should encourage our friends to strengthen us when we feel weak. During times of stress, we need to allow God to be our defender, to keep us safe from the snares that surround us.

142:1-7 Suffering should drive us to God, not to despair. We should feel free to express our feelings to God about the trials we experience. God cares about us. Surrendering our life to him is the thing to do when our dependencies begin to get the better of us. God can help us escape from our bondage and surround us with people who can encourage and strengthen us.

READ PSALM 139:1-16

GOD grant me the serenity
to accept the things I cannot change
the courage to change the things I can
and the wisdom to know the difference
AMEN

Many of us have spent our life trying to be someone we are not. Our addictive/compulsive behaviors may be only a desperate attempt to escape from ourself. Maybe we have difficulty accepting our personality, our appearance, our handicaps, even our talents.

Perhaps we spend our energy and time trying to be what someone else wants us to be because we feel that who we are is not enough. We may do all we can to separate from our inner being because we are so deeply ashamed of who we are. Self-hatred is a defect of character that needs to be removed. It breeds the sin of covetousness, that is, longing to be in someone else's situation or have what they have. The psalmist wrote, "Thank you for making me so wonderfully complex! It is amazing to think about. Your workmanship is marvelous" (Psalm 139:14). Saying we are God's "workmanship" means that we are unique and beautiful masterpieces—works of divine poetry. Beauty and value are designed into our very fiber, by virtue of our Creator.

One important step in our recovery is to allow God to remove self-hatred, helping us to value ourself for who we are. We have been miraculously created, and we are treasured by God. And this has been true since the time in our mother's womb, long before we could *do* anything to earn it! As we begin to see how unique and special we are—embraced and accepted by God himself—our strides toward recovery should grow faster and longer. ***Turn to page 675, Proverbs 2.***

11Don't let liars prosper here in our land;
quickly punish them. 12But the Lord will
surely help those they persecute; he will
maintain the rights of the poor. 13Surely the
godly are thanking you, for they shall live in
your presence.

PSALM 141
Quick, Lord, answer me—for I have prayed.
Listen when I cry to you for help! 2Regard my
prayer as my evening sacrifice and as incense
wafting up to you.
3Help me, Lord, to keep my mouth shut
and my lips sealed. 4Take away my lust for evil
things; don't let me want to be with sinners,
doing what they do, sharing their delicacies.
5Let the godly smite me! It will be a kindness!
If they reprove me, it is medicine! Don't let
me refuse it. But I am in constant prayer
against the wicked and their deeds. 6,7When
their leaders are condemned, and their bones
are strewn across the ground, then these men
will finally listen to me and know that I am
trying to help them.
8I look to you for help, O Lord God. You are
my refuge. Don't let them slay me. 9Keep me
out of their traps. 10Let them fall into their
own snares, while I escape.

PSALM 142
How I plead with God, how I implore his
mercy, pouring out my troubles before him.
3For I am overwhelmed and desperate, and
you alone know which way I ought to turn to
miss the traps my enemies have set for me.
4(There's one—just over there to the right!) No
one gives me a passing thought. No one will
help me; no one cares a bit what happens to
me. 5Then I prayed to Jehovah. "Lord," I pled,
"you are my only place of refuge. Only you
can keep me safe.
6"Hear my cry, for I am very low. Rescue me
from my persecutors, for they are too strong
for me. 7Bring me out of prison so that I can

thank you. The godly will rejoice with me for all your help."

PSALM 143

Hear my prayer, O Lord; answer my plea because you are faithful to your promises. 2Don't bring me to trial! For as compared with you, no one is perfect.

3My enemies chased and caught me. They have knocked me to the ground. They force me to live in the darkness like those in the grave. 4I am losing all hope; I am paralyzed with fear.

5I remember the glorious miracles you did in days of long ago. 6I reach out for you. I thirst for you as parched land thirsts for rain. 7Come quickly, Lord, and answer me, for my depression deepens; don't turn away from me or I shall die. 8Let me see your kindness to me in the morning, for I am trusting you. Show me where to walk, for my prayer is sincere. 9Save me from my enemies. O Lord, I run to you to hide me. 10Help me to do your will, for you are my God. Lead me in good paths, for your Spirit is good.

11Lord, saving me will bring glory to your name. Bring me out of all this trouble because you are true to your promises. 12And because you are loving and kind to me, cut off all my enemies and destroy those who are trying to harm me; for I am your servant.

PSALM 144

Bless the Lord who is my immovable Rock. He gives me strength and skill in battle. 2He is always kind and loving to me; he is my fortress, my tower of strength and safety, my deliverer. He stands before me as a shield. He subdues my people under me.

3O Lord, what is man that you even notice him? Why bother at all with the human race? 4For man is but a breath; his days are like a passing shadow.

5Bend down the heavens, Lord, and come. The mountains smoke beneath your touch.

6Let loose your lightning bolts, your arrows, Lord, upon your enemies, and scatter them.

7Reach down from heaven and rescue me; deliver me from deep waters, from the power of my enemies. 8Their mouths are filled with lies; they swear to the truth of what is false.

9I will sing you a new song, O God, with a ten-stringed harp. 10For you grant victory to kings! You are the one who will rescue your servant David from the fatal sword. 11Save me! Deliver me from these enemies, these liars, these treacherous men.

12-15Here is my description of a truly happy land where Jehovah is God:

Sons vigorous and tall as growing plants.
Daughters of graceful beauty like the
  pillars of a palace wall.
Barns full to the brim with crops of every
  kind.
Sheep by the thousands out in our fields.
Oxen loaded down with produce.
No enemy attacking the walls, but peace
  everywhere.
No crime in our streets.
Yes, happy are those whose God is
  Jehovah.

PSALM 145

I will praise you, my God and King, and bless your name each day and forever.

3Great is Jehovah! Greatly praise him! His greatness is beyond discovery! 4Let each generation tell its children what glorious things he does. 5I will meditate about your glory, splendor, majesty, and miracles. 6Your awe-inspiring deeds shall be on every tongue; I will

---

143:5-12 Our addictions often make it hard to think of anything but the immediate present. It is very important in our recovery, however, that we recall the times in the past when God helped us to overcome our addictions. We also need to take a quick look into the future and remind ourself of the pain we will feel if we fail. Escaping our temptation demands that we give our life to God each and every day.

144:3-8 The mystery we will never understand in this life is why God would ever concern himself with us. The greater mystery is why he would show such great mercy to us when we are overwhelmed by destructive addictions or compulsions. Why is God so good to us? Why does he go out of his way to rescue us? It is in God's nature to do this—he is a loving, gracious, and delivering God. He wants the best for his creation. Ultimately, asking *why* is unimportant. We need to act on God's promises to us and rejoice in his unlimited kindness.

145:1-7 Praise is one of our weapons against the temptation of our dependencies. As we praise God for his deliverance, our mind is fixed on the one who can deliver us. Anything that keeps our mind focused on God is a helpful weapon against our addictions. Our praise of God's work in our life can also be an encouragement to others.

proclaim your greatness. 7Everyone will tell about how good you are and sing about your righteousness.

8Jehovah is kind and merciful, slow to get angry, full of love. 9He is good to everyone, and his compassion is intertwined with everything he does. 10All living things shall thank you, Lord, and your people will bless you. 11They will talk together about the glory of your kingdom and mention examples of your power. 12They will tell about your miracles and about the majesty and glory of your reign. 13For your kingdom never ends. You rule generation after generation.

14The Lord lifts the fallen and those bent beneath their loads. 15The eyes of all mankind look up to you for help; you give them their food as they need it. 16You constantly satisfy the hunger and thirst of every living thing.

17The Lord is fair in everything he does and full of kindness. 18He is close to all who call on him sincerely. 19He fulfills the desires of those who reverence and trust him; he hears their cries for help and rescues them. 20He protects all those who love him, but destroys the wicked.

21I will praise the Lord and call on all men everywhere to bless his holy name forever and forever.

PSALM 146

Praise the Lord! Yes, really praise him! 2I will praise him as long as I live, yes, even with my dying breath.

3Don't look to men for help; their greatest leaders fail; 4for every man must die. His breathing stops, life ends, and in a moment all he planned for himself is ended. 5But happy is the man who has the God of Jacob as his helper, whose hope is in the Lord his God—6the God who made both earth and heaven, the seas and everything in them. He is the God who keeps every promise, 7who gives justice to the poor and oppressed and food to the hungry. He frees the prisoners 8and opens the eyes of the blind; he lifts the burdens from those bent down beneath their loads. For the Lord loves good men. 9He protects the immigrants and cares for the orphans and widows. But he turns topsy-turvy the plans of the wicked.

10The Lord will reign forever. O Jerusalem, your God is King in every generation! Hallelujah! Praise the Lord!

PSALM 147

Hallelujah! Yes, praise the Lord! How good it is to sing his praises! How delightful, and how right!

2He is rebuilding Jerusalem and bringing back the exiles. 3He heals the brokenhearted, binding up their wounds. 4He counts the stars and calls them all by name. 5How great he is! His power is absolute! His understanding is unlimited. 6The Lord supports the humble, but brings the wicked into the dust.

7Sing out your thanks to him; sing praises to our God, accompanied by harps. 8He covers the heavens with clouds, sends down the showers, and makes the green grass grow in mountain pastures. 9He feeds the wild animals, and the young ravens cry to him for food. 10The speed of a horse is nothing to him. How puny in his sight is the strength of a man. 11But his joy is in those who reverence him, those who expect him to be loving and kind.

12Praise him, O Jerusalem! Praise your God, O Zion! 13For he has fortified your gates against all enemies and blessed your children. 14He sends peace across your nation and fills your barns with plenty of the finest wheat.

145:8-13 God showers us with his gifts and often holds back the judgment we deserve. Although he hates our sin, he does not react to it on the basis of his anger. Instead, he shows us great compassion. Someday all creation will recognize what God has done and will praise him. We are part of the host that will demonstrate his great power, especially his work of deliverance in our own life.

146:5-9 God made all things and cares about all his creation, even those on the lowest rungs of the social ladder. He cares for the downtrodden, feeds the hungry, and liberates the captives. He alone can restore us to sanity when sin has caused us to lose control of our life. We may think no one else cares about us, but we can be assured that God does; he even watches over those who have no one else to care for them.

147:2-11 God can restore the good days again. We need to turn to him instead of withering away in our remorse. There is always hope when God is brought into the picture, because there is nothing greater than God's power. He is able to provide for all our needs and is never overwhelmed by the problems or dependencies that we call our enemies.

147:12-20 God is our defender and our peacemaker, the one who meets all of our needs. Since he is the Creator and Sustainer of all nature, we should have no doubt about his ability to care for us once we commit our life to him. He is worthy of our trust.

15He sends his orders to the world. How
swiftly his word flies. 16He sends the snow in
all its lovely whiteness, scatters the frost upon
the ground, 17and hurls the hail upon the
earth. Who can stand before his freezing
cold? 18But then he calls for warmer weather,
and the spring winds blow and all the river ice
is broken. 19He has made known his laws and
ceremonies of worship to Israel—20something
he has not done with any other nation; they
have not known his commands.
Hallelujah! Yes, praise the Lord!

PSALM 148
Praise the Lord, O heavens! Praise him from
the skies! 2Praise him, all his angels, all the
armies of heaven. 3Praise him, sun and moon
and all you twinkling stars. 4Praise him, skies
above. Praise him, vapors high above the
clouds.
5Let everything he has made give praise to
him. For he issued his command, and they
came into being; 6he established them forever
and forever. His orders will never be revoked.
7And praise him down here on earth, you
creatures of the ocean depths. 8Let fire and
hail, snow, rain, wind, and weather, all obey.
9Let the mountains and hills, the fruit trees
and cedars, 10the wild animals and cattle, the
snakes and birds, 11the kings and all the
people with their rulers and their judges,
12young men and maidens, old men and children—13all praise the Lord together. For he
alone is worthy. His glory is far greater than
all of earth and heaven. 14He has made his
people strong, honoring his godly ones—the
people of Israel, the people closest to him.
Hallelujah! Yes, praise the Lord!

PSALM 149
Hallelujah! Yes, praise the Lord! Sing him a
new song. Sing his praises, all his people.
2O Israel, rejoice in your Maker. O people of
Jerusalem, exult in your King. 3Praise his name
with dancing, accompanied by drums and lyre.
4,5For Jehovah enjoys his people; he will
save the humble. Let his people rejoice in this
honor. Let them sing for joy as they lie upon
their beds.
6,7Adore him, O his people! And take a
double-edged sword to execute his punishment upon the nations. 8Bind their kings and
leaders with iron chains, 9and execute their
sentences.
He is the glory of his people. Hallelujah!
Praise him!

PSALM 150
Hallelujah! Yes, praise the Lord!
Praise him in his Temple and in the heavens he made with mighty power. 2Praise him
for his mighty works. Praise his unequaled
greatness. 3Praise him with the trumpet and
with lute and harp. 4Praise him with the
drums and dancing. Praise him with stringed
instruments and horns. 5Praise him with the
cymbals, yes, loud clanging cymbals.
6Let everything alive give praises to the
Lord! *You* praise him!
Hallelujah!

148:1-14 God deserves our praise for all the good that we receive day by day. Not the least of these benefits is the help he gives us in restoring our life to health and sanity. There was a time when we felt out of control; now God is making us strong. That should give us ample reason to join the rest of the universe in a chorus of ceaseless praise.

149:1-9 It should not be hard to commit our life to God. He is known as the one who helps people who are humble and needy—people just like us. Knowing he cares for us as he does, we should find it natural to accept his guidance for our life. God always wants the best for us. All we need to do is turn our life over to him.

150:1-6 Some of the best ways to praise God are by how we live, by how we share the Good News with others, and by submitting to his will for us. All of us are recipients of God's loving forgiveness and restoration. Every living creature—each of us—has ample reason to praise our wonderful and gracious God. "*You* praise him! Hallelujah!"

***insights** INTO GOD'S PROTECTION

In **Psalm 4:1-3** David rejoiced about God's powerful protection. In times of distress our merciful God is the perfect haven of rest. He is listening, and he hears our cries for help. God wants us to put our trust in him. We insult him when we trust in our own resources, or anything else, to deliver us from our problems. When we turn our will and life over to God, we become his own chosen ones, whom he promises to hear when we call out to him.

In **Psalm 7:3-10** David looked to God to defend him against the slanderous judgments of his enemies. Those who attack us or try to undermine our recovery through lies are not just our enemies; they are are God's enemies, too. We can count on him to deal with our common enemies if we are doing what we can to avoid temptation. We ought to hate the things God hates. We don't need to try to defend our choices when we are choosing the right path; God has promised to be our defense.

In **Psalm 18:30-36** David praised God for his ability to protect those who looked to God for help. God will protect us if we are willing to admit our weaknesses and depend on him. He will empower us to do what is right in difficult situations and give us the ability to walk without stumbling, even when the path is slippery. God also teaches his people the ins and outs of spiritual warfare, enabling us to use the most powerful weapons at our disposal. If we will only ask him to help us, God will keep us from the precarious places of temptation that lead to our defeat.

In **Psalm 27:1-6** David praised God for the help and hope he provided. We have nothing to fear in this life if we put our complete trust in God as our guide, deliverer, and protector. With God on our side, there is no need for us to be drawn away by people who formerly led us astray. Today's habits impact tomorrow's ability to achieve success. If we maintain our contact with God, we can be assured that when problems come he will watch over us, make our way secure, and draw us even closer to himself.

In **Psalm 31:1-6** David's words exhibit his dependence on God in a time of stress. God is our strong refuge, our Rock of safety—the one we should turn to when we feel overwhelmed by temptation and danger. Because we know he is such a strong refuge for us, we can with confidence each day turn our will and our life over to his care.

In **Psalm 56:1-7** we find that David trusted God to take care of him during a time of great danger. When we are terrified by tempting or dangerous circumstances, we need to turn our life and our will over to God. We need to trust his promises. He is able to strengthen us so that we won't fall again. Sometimes the enemy we face is obvious. At other times the attacks are very subtle, so we need to be careful.

***insights** INTO GOD'S DELIVERANCE

David probably wrote **Psalm 9:7-14** soon after a great victory over the Philistines. David praised God for delivering him from powerful enemies. God is merciful; he is always ready to help those who are oppressed by their enemies. In God's perfect timing, those who are oppressed will find comfort and encouragement if they put their trust in him. Because God never forsakes those who trust him, we should praise him and tell others that he has rescued us. As we remember his faithfulness to us in our time of distress, we are able to take this message of encouragement to others.

After lamenting the oppressive acts of wicked people, David, in **Psalm 14:4-7,** praised God for delivering him from their clutches. Many of our problems may have been caused by someone else. Someone may have taken advantage of us without considering our feelings. We can find comfort in two facts. First, God will judge the people who have hurt us; we don't have to hold on to our anger and hatred. Second, God is with us; he is there to see us through our recovery. In his perfect timing God will rescue us.

David wrote **Psalm 18:1-5** soon after God delivered him from his enemies. God is more than able to deliver us from our problems. He is our source of strength, our Rock, and the one on whom we must rely as we seek freedom from our bondage. The psalmist learned that his decision to cry out to God for help was a wise choice. We, too, can experience God's deliverance. We should start by admitting our helplessness, the first step in recovery. Then we can look to God to give us the help we need to overcome our dependencies.

In **Psalm 31:14-18** the psalmist shared his confidence that God alone could deliver him from his troubles. He also realized that without God's help he would suffer great humiliation. God is the only one able to solve our problems. He is willing to help us overcome the people and situations that once dragged us down. We need to make sure he is at the center of our own recovery.

In **Psalm 42:4-11** the psalmist honestly shared his feelings of depression over the suffering he was experiencing. Then he declared his faith in God and recognized God's power to deliver. He struggled back and forth between the extremes of despair and faith, and he was always honest about what he was feeling. In the process of recovery, we will all experience times of deep depression; they are to be expected. But God wants us to remember that even as floods of trouble sweep over us, we should keep trusting in him. We should feel free to express our feelings to God. As we pour out our complaints to him, he will pour over us waves of his steadfast love.

In **Psalm 57:4-6** David witnessed to God's faithful help and love in times of trouble. Our dependencies and compulsions are never easy to handle. In fact, without God's help, they are impossible to handle. But God is far more powerful than all our internal and external enemies combined. He rules over heaven and earth and is able and willing to thwart the plans of our enemies.

David wrote **Psalm 60:6-12** during a time of war and affirmed that his help came from God alone. We can turn to God for deliverance because he has promised to help us. God reminds us that we still belong to him, no matter how great our failures in the past. He still offers a good life for any who are willing to do their best to follow his divine program. He can still give us victory if we allow him to help us fight our battles against temptation.

In **Psalm 76:1-12** the psalmist recognized that God was able to overcome even the most powerful opposition we might face. He is even able to use evil deeds to bring about his own plans for good. God's power is far greater than we can even conceive it to be. He is able to overcome even our greatest problems. All we need to do is hand our dependencies over to him, entrusting our life to his care. When he fights for us, none of our enemies—past, present, or future—can stand against us.

In **Psalm 104:19-24** the psalmist praised God for his amazing control over the created world. God uses the sun to regulate the days and the moon to mark the months. Through these heavenly bodies God also defines the seasons of the year and the movement of the tides. Such power and control over the world should encourage us that when we commit our life to God, we have committed ourself to someone who has the power to help us.

In **Psalm 109:16-20** David spoke to God about the undeserved attacks he was forced to endure. All of us have suffered injustice; we all know the feelings that accompany innocent suffering. When we are hurt without just cause we may be tempted to lash out in revenge. This will never resolve our pain or hurt. We need to let go of our anger; it will only lead to more suffering. We can trust God to work his justice according to his timetable. God will return the same kind of evil done to the innocent to those who are guilty. God is the best judge; judgment against the sins of others is best left up to him.

insights INTO GOD'S FORGIVENESS

In **Psalm 103:8-12** David praised God for his great love and kindness. We should be encouraged by the knowledge that God loves us enough not only to forgive our sins but also to put them behind him forever—"as far . . . as the east is from the west." We have all failed, and our mistakes have hurt other people and damaged or destroyed our relationships. Sometimes others have a hard time forgiving us, even when we seek to make amends. God, on the other hand, is waiting to forgive us. All we have to do is admit our sin and turn our life over to him. Knowing that God has forgiven us should give us the courage to continue seeking reconciliation with the people we have wronged.

insights INTO THE VALUE OF CONFESSION

In **Psalm 15:1-5** David reflected on how God's way of doing things leads to a life of stability and peace. If we want to progress in recovery, we must never compromise with sin, whether it's our own or someone else's. No matter how painful it might be, we must confess the sin in our life or, in some cases, confront others with their own. Many times our failures have caused a great deal of pain and loss to the people close to us. We need to become more sensitive to the wrongs we have committed and be specific in our personal inventory. This will help us to escape the cycle of sin we are caught in and protect the people we love from further hurt in the future.

In **Psalm 18:25-29** David recognized God's desire to bestow mercy on those who are merciful toward others and repentant of their sins. When we are ready to admit to God and to others our wrongs, and when we show mercy to others, God is merciful toward us. We do great harm to ourself and to others when we are too proud to admit our failures. But God is quick to help us when we acknowledge who he is and what he can do to help us.

In **Psalm 19:12-14** David asked God to reveal any hidden sins in his life—to break through any denial he might have. He was aware of his need for a moral inventory and asked God to help him do this with absolute honesty. Because our inner being is not always what it should be, we have a tendency to be blind to our sinful tendencies. We need God to clarify our thinking—to reveal the sin that is working its deception within us and to keep us from deliberately doing wrong. When our thought life is right with God, our actions will be right also.

In **Psalm 38:9-16** the psalmist recognized how hideous he had become as a consequence of his sins. Then he turned to the only one who was listening—indeed, the only one able to help—God. The longer we remain in our sin, the more we become disabled. Our heart pounds in fear, our energy ebbs away, and our ability to see ourself as we really are becomes distorted. Even our closest friends and family members steer clear of us for fear that we might drag them down. We would be wise to recognize how helpless we are in the face of our problem and turn to God for help. He is more than able and willing to give us a helping hand.

David wrote **Psalm 51:16-19** after being convicted of his sin with Bathsheba. He realized that no number of sacrifices would cover his sin if he wasn't sorry for what he had done. He knew that God would grant forgiveness to him if he honestly admitted his failures. We don't have to earn forgiveness from God. He is happy to give it to us if we only admit our failures and seek to make changes in our life. God is concerned more with our heartfelt attitudes than mere acts of repentance that do not reflect our true feelings. Actions of repentance can always be faked, but God is never fooled. He is looking for us to take responsibility for our failures and to desire forgiveness and restoration. There is always hope for us if we are willing to confront our failures and seek God's forgiveness. God is looking for people with humble hearts, not perfect records.

insights INTO THE VALUE OF PRAISE

In **Psalm 30:10-12** David concluded his request for deliverance with words of praise to God. Staying close to God through prayer and meditation is an important part of recovery. God wants us to succeed in our recovery, perhaps even more than we do. He wants us to live a meaningful life filled with purpose and joy. When God does help us, we should not hesitate praise him, singing "glad praises to the Lord." Praising God out loud is an excellent way to tell others about God's work in our life. And sharing our experience of deliverance will not only encourage others to persevere in recovery; it will also strengthen our own resolve.

After experiencing God's deliverance, David spoke in **Psalm 40:9-10** about how he shared the good news with others. The news about our deliverance needs to be shared with others who are struggling. God is righteous, faithful, and able to deliver others from their bondage, just as he has delivered us. As we share our victory with others, we will discover that not only will they be encouraged, but our own recovery will be strengthened as well.

Through his words in **Psalm 111:1-8,** the psalmist illustrated what it means to fulfill Step Twelve in recovery. God's work in our life has a twofold purpose—to accomplish our deliverance from bondage and to demonstrate God's power to others who need his help. And our sharing the good news of God's deliverance will not only help others; it will also strengthen our own recovery, giving us the encouragement we need to avoid a relapse.

In **Psalm 112:1-5** the psalmist sings out in exuberant praise to God. When we make the choice to turn our life over to God and commit ourself to do his will, we enter into the joy this passage is talking about. When times get tough for us and we are unsure of what to do, God reveals his path to us. For our part, we need to tell others about what God has given us. This will not only bring hope to other hurting people; it will also strengthen our own program for recovery.

PROVERBS

THE BIG PICTURE

A. PROLOGUE: THE PURPOSE AND WAY OF WISDOM (1:1-7)
B. SOLOMON CHALLENGES YOUNG PEOPLE TO WISE BEHAVIOR (1:8–9:18)
C. SOLOMON CHALLENGES ALL PEOPLE TO WISDOM IN LIVING (10:1–24:34)
D. WISDOM FOR PEOPLE IN LEADERSHIP (25:1–31:9)
E. EPILOGUE: THE WOMAN OF WISDOM (31:10-31)

Common sense—the idea sounds so folksy and simple. Oddly enough, however, we seem to have less and less of it. Perhaps it's because we are too busy or distant to learn from our parents and grandparents. And just as common sense is rare, godly wisdom also is a quality hard to find. The wisdom found in Proverbs can be a helpful resource to fill the lack in our own culture. By reading and heeding its wise words, we will avoid many common destructive mistakes that flow so naturally from our ignorance, denial, and pride.

Although he made numerous costly mistakes, Solomon was the wisest person who ever lived. And because Solomon valued wisdom so highly, he collected many wise proverbs as a guidebook of insight and counsel. Solomon was by no means the only wise man of his day. Agur and Lemuel, also known for their wisdom, are credited with the book's final chapters.

Solomon was particularly aware of the need for young people to develop proper priorities, boundaries, and behavior patterns. However, young people were not Solomon's only concern. His collection of wisdom is invaluable to people of all ages and occupations. King Hezekiah later found it so important that he assigned his men to edit an installment of Solomon's proverbs, speaking to issues like honesty, limits, and healthy relationships.

As dysfunctional thinking and relationships become more prevalent in our society, the wise diagnosis and treatment offered by Proverbs are desperately needed. Its precious nuggets of life-changing counsel are there for us to discover. All of us, no matter how great our failures or hurts, can proceed far down the path of healing by following the God-given wisdom of Proverbs.

THE BOTTOM LINE

PURPOSE: To offer God-given wisdom for protection against dysfunctional behaviors and ungodly practices. AUTHOR: Solomon collected or wrote most of the book; Agur and Lemuel were responsible for the final chapters. AUDIENCE: The people of Israel. DATE WRITTEN: Much of the book was compiled during Solomon's reign (970–930 B.C.); it probably took its final form during Hezekiah's reign (715–686 B.C.). SETTING: This is a book of wise sayings related to the priorities and problems of everyday life. KEY VERSE: "How does a man become wise? The first step is to trust and reverence the Lord! Only fools refuse to be taught" (1:7). KEY PEOPLE AND RELATIONSHIPS: Parents and children, husbands and wives, leaders and citizens, people and God, with warnings against unhealthy relationships.

RECOVERY THEMES

The Importance of Common Sense: Any good recovery program is filled with common sense and wisdom. If our addictive behaviors have roots early in life, we may have missed the opportunity of learning both common sense and wisdom. In recovery, we seek to learn what we have missed, and the book of Proverbs is a primary source. The contrast to a person with common sense is the fool, who is portrayed as a stubborn, willful person who either hates or ignores God. Our own path of recovery should be paved with the common sense of Proverbs.

The Power of Priorities: We all have priorities, whether we're aware of them or not. So it's never a question of having priorities, but rather of straightening them out. A big part of our recovery involves sorting out our priorities, turning them over to God, and getting them to line up with his will. As our priorities become a reflection of God's will, our recovery will progress, and we will avoid the destruction of a relapse. The book of Proverbs contains wisdom and practical advice that reflects God's desires for us. If we follow this advice, we will discover a significant part of God's will for our life.

The Role of Boundaries: A big part of setting personal boundaries in our life is knowing how and when to say no. Solomon recorded for us a large number of situations where saying no is the wisest option—family situations, sexual situations, monetary situations, business situations, and others. As we take these proverbs and make them a part of us, we will develop clearer boundaries and will have a better sense of when we should say no.

Building Healthy Relationships: Our recovery will only be as successful as the health of our relationships. We may have the best of intentions, but if we are surrounded with unhealthy relationships, we are headed for a relapse. The book of Proverbs gives us sound advice for building healthy relationships with friends, family, and coworkers. We are called to be consistent and tactful and to use discipline. If we hope to build the kind of relationships that will help us love and follow after God, high moral standards are essential, both for us and for those close to us.

CHAPTER 1

The Purpose of Proverbs

These are the proverbs of King Solomon of
Israel, David's son:
2He wrote them to teach his people how to
live—how to act in every circumstance, 3for
he wanted them to be understanding, just
and fair in everything they did. 4"I want to
make the simpleminded wise!" he said. "I
want to warn young men about some problems they will face. 5,6I want those already
wise to become the wiser and become leaders
by exploring the depths of meaning in these
nuggets of truth."

The Protection of Wisdom

7-9How does a man become wise? The first step
is to trust and reverence the Lord!
Only fools refuse to be taught. Listen to
your father and mother. What you learn from
them will stand you in good stead; it will gain
you many honors.
10If young toughs tell you, "Come and join
us"—turn your back on them! 11"We'll hide
and rob and kill," they say. 12"Good or bad,
we'll treat them all alike. 13And the loot we'll
get! All kinds of stuff! 14Come on, throw in
your lot with us; we'll split with you in equal
shares."
15Don't do it, son! Stay far from men like
that, 16for crime is their way of life, and murder is their specialty. 17When a bird sees a trap
being set, it stays away, 18but not these men;
they trap themselves! They lay a booby trap
for their own lives. 19Such is the fate of all who
live by violence and murder. They will die a
violent death.

1:2-9 The purpose for writing down these proverbs was to teach people foundational principles about how to live a good life and how to deal with the various problems they would encounter in life. The first step to attaining this kind of wisdom is the hardest: trusting and showing reverence for God. This means admitting that we need help and then allowing God to guide and care for us (see 9:10; 14:26-27; 15:16, 33; 19:23).

1:20-23 Wisdom is personified here, calling out to all who would choose to follow. There is no real secret to obtaining wisdom; all we have to do is ask for it. Indeed, God "is always ready to give a bountiful supply of wisdom to all who ask him" (James 1:5). Unlike experience, which we never get until *after* we need it, God's wisdom is available to us as soon as we are willing to listen to him and obey his plan for our life.

GOD grant me the serenity
to accept the things I cannot change
the courage to change the things I can
and the wisdom to know the difference
AMEN

In recovery we come to realize that we are influenced by the people close to us. We welcome the support of those who are farther along on the road to recovery. We may rely heavily on the encouragement of our sponsor or others who are supportive of our new way of life.

We will also come to see the negative influence of associating with people who are still living the kind of life from which we are trying to escape. Part of our self-inventory may include considering those with whom we choose to spend our time and whether these decisions contribute to our recovery. In Proverbs we are told, "Wisdom and truth will enter the very center of your being, filling your life with joy. You will be given the sense to stay away from evil men who want you to be their partners in crime—men who turn from God's ways to walk down dark and evil paths and exult in doing wrong, for they thoroughly enjoy their sins" (Proverbs 2:10-14). We are encouraged to "follow the steps of the godly instead, and stay on the right path, for only good men enjoy life to the full; evil men lose the good things they might have had, and they themselves shall be destroyed" (Proverbs 2:20-22).

Are we exercising wisdom by following the steps of those who are living the kind of life we truly desire? If we do this, we will find our life to be filled with joy. We will also be spared the loss and destruction that await those who continue down darkened pathways and do not enter into recovery. *Turn to page 677, Proverbs 3.*

Wisdom Demands Our Attention
20 Wisdom shouts in the streets for a hearing.
21 She calls out to the crowds along Main
Street, and to the judges in their courts, and
to everyone in all the land: 22 "You simpletons!" she cries. "How long will you go on
being fools? How long will you scoff at wisdom and fight the facts? 23 Come here and
listen to me! I'll pour out the spirit of wisdom
upon you and make you wise. 24 I have called
you so often, but still you won't come. I have
pleaded, but all in vain. 25 For you have
spurned my counsel and reproof. 26 Some day
you'll be in trouble, and I'll laugh! Mock me,
will you?—I'll mock you! 27 When a storm of
terror surrounds you, and when you are engulfed by anguish and distress, 28 then I will
not answer your cry for help. It will be too late
though you search for me ever so anxiously.
29 "For you closed your eyes to the facts and
did not choose to reverence and trust the
Lord, 30 and you turned your back on me,
spurning my advice. 31 That is why you must
eat the bitter fruit of having your own way
and experience the full terrors of the pathway
you have chosen. 32 For you turned away from
me—to death; your own complacency will
kill you. Fools! 33 But all who listen to me shall
live in peace and safety, unafraid."

CHAPTER 2
Wisdom Is from God
Every young man who listens to me and
obeys my instructions will be given wisdom
and good sense. 3-5 Yes, if you want better insight and discernment, and are searching for
them as you would for lost money or hidden
treasure, then wisdom will be given you and
knowledge of God himself; you will soon
learn the importance of reverence for the
Lord and of trusting him.
6 For the Lord grants wisdom! His every
word is a treasure of knowledge and understanding. 7,8 He grants good sense to the
godly—his saints. He is their shield, protecting them and guarding their pathway. 9 He

shows how to distinguish right from wrong, how to find the right decision every time. [10]For wisdom and truth will enter the very center of your being, filling your life with joy. [11-13]You will be given the sense to stay away from evil men who want you to be their partners in crime—men who turn from God's ways to walk down dark and evil paths [14]and exult in doing wrong, for they thoroughly enjoy their sins. [15]Everything they do is crooked and wrong.

[16,17]Only wisdom from the Lord can save a man from the flattery of prostitutes; these girls have abandoned their husbands and flouted the laws of God. [18]Their houses lie along the road to death and hell. [19]The men who enter them are doomed. None of these men will ever be the same again.

[20]Follow the steps of the godly instead, and stay on the right path, [21]for only good men enjoy life to the full; [22]evil men lose the good things they might have had, and they themselves shall be destroyed.

CHAPTER 3

The Value of Wisdom

My son, never forget the things I've taught you. If you want a long and satisfying life, closely follow my instructions. [3]Never tire of loyalty and kindness. Hold these virtues tightly. Write them deep within your heart. [4,5]If you want favor with both God and man, and a reputation for good judgment and common sense, then trust the Lord completely; don't ever trust yourself. [6]In everything you do, put God first, and he will direct you and crown your efforts with success.

[7,8]Don't be conceited, sure of your own wisdom. Instead, trust and reverence the Lord, and turn your back on evil; when you do that, then you will be given renewed health and vitality.

[9,10]Honor the Lord by giving him the first part of all your income, and he will fill your barns with wheat and barley and overflow your wine vats with the finest wines.

[11,12]Young man, do not resent it when God chastens and corrects you, for his punishment is proof of his love. Just as a father punishes a son he delights in to make him better, so the Lord corrects you.

[13-15]The man who knows right from wrong and has good judgment and common sense is happier than the man who is immensely rich! For such wisdom is far more valuable than precious jewels. Nothing else compares with it. [16,17]Wisdom gives: a long, good life, riches, honor, pleasure, peace. [18]Wisdom is a tree of life to those who eat her fruit; happy is the man who keeps on eating it.

[19]The Lord's wisdom founded the earth; his understanding established all the universe and space. [20]The deep fountains of the earth were broken open by his knowledge, and the skies poured down rain.

[21]Have two goals: wisdom—that is, knowing and doing right—and common sense. Don't let them slip away, [22]for they fill you with living energy and bring you honor and respect. [23]They keep you safe from defeat and disaster and from stumbling off the trail. [24-26]With them on guard you can sleep without fear; you need not be afraid of disaster or the

---

2:1-9 Wisdom is like a hidden treasure that is found only by those who search for it. God will grant us wisdom and good sense. He will also protect us and instruct us on how to make good decisions. We may not have made great decisions in the past, and now we may be suffering the consequences of those decisions. But when we put our trust in God, he will show us the decisions we need to make in order to experience a full recovery.

2:20-22 While we may not be essentially evil, our dependencies certainly are. And we know what our addictions have cost us: our job, friends, family, health, sanity. Now we want to change our life patterns to escape our enslavement. God tells us here that if we get on the right track, we can still enjoy life to the fullest. We may be tempted at times to stray from the path of recovery, but here we are reminded that our addictions will eventually lead to destruction. Recovery is the only real option we have.

3:4-6 What a promise! God will direct us and crown our efforts with success if we put our trust in him rather than trying to do it on our own. Putting God first means turning our life and will over to him. Surrendering to his lordship is humbling, but it is the only way to live a good life.

3:11-12 When God reproves us, he is not doing so because he is angry or likes to see people suffer. He is correcting us because he loves us and doesn't want us to go any farther in our sin. Those of us who have had abusive parents may not be able to easily grasp the concept of a loving, nurturing God, because the only parental figures we have known were anything but loving. To help us see the true nature of God, we need to look to the Gospels and examine the love Jesus had for others. When we understand that Jesus and God are one and the same, we can more readily admit that God loves us and has our best interests in mind when we are punished.

READ PROVERBS 3:13-26

GOD grant me the serenity
to accept the things I cannot change
the courage to change the things I can
and the wisdom to know the difference
AMEN

None of us set out with the goal of becoming addicted. We were seeking something else—escape from pain, perhaps something to make up for our losses and brokenness—or maybe we had an inner desire for self-destruction.

Unfortunately, the things we turned to are not able to satisfy our deepest needs or desires. Our needs are legitimate. What needs to be changed is our tendency to go the wrong way to try to meet them. The Bible says, "Have two goals: wisdom—that is, knowing and doing right—and common sense. Don't let them slip away, for they fill you with living energy and bring you honor and respect. They keep you safe from defeat and disaster and from stumbling off the trail" (Proverbs 3:21-23).

Wisdom leads to the benefits most of us want out of life. When we seek wisdom, as if it were a hidden treasure, we will find the other things we desire. "The man who knows right from wrong and has good judgment and common sense is happier than the man who is immensely rich! For such wisdom is far more valuable than precious jewels. Nothing else compares with it. Wisdom gives: a long, good life, riches, honor, pleasure, and peace" (Proverbs 3:13-17). As we change our focus and begin to seek after wisdom, we will find our life more fulfilled and secure. This may also help us avoid the destructive paths we have previously taken as we tried to fulfill our unmet needs and desires.
Turn to page 679, Proverbs 4.

---

plots of wicked men, for the Lord is with you; he protects you.

27,28 Don't withhold repayment of your debts. Don't say "some other time," if you can pay now. 29 Don't plot against your neighbor; he is trusting you. 30 Don't get into needless fights. 31 Don't envy violent men. Don't copy their ways. 32 For such men are an abomination to the Lord, but he gives his friendship to the godly.

33 The curse of God is on the wicked, but his blessing is on the upright. 34 The Lord mocks at mockers, but helps the humble. 35 The wise are promoted to honor, but fools are promoted to shame!

CHAPTER 4
Wisdom Can Be Learned
Young men, listen to me as you would to your father. Listen, and grow wise, for I speak the truth—don't turn away. 3 For I, too, was once a son, tenderly loved by my mother as an only child, and the companion of my father. 4 He told me never to forget his words. "If you follow them," he said, "you will have a long and happy life. 5 *Learn to be wise,"* he said, *"and develop good judgment and common sense! I cannot overemphasize this point."* 6 Cling to wisdom—she will protect you. Love her—she will guard you.

7 Getting wisdom is the most important thing you can do! And with your wisdom, develop common sense and good judgment. 8,9 If you exalt wisdom, she will exalt you. Hold her fast, and she will lead you to great honor; she will place a beautiful crown upon your head. 10 My son, listen to me and do as I say, and you will have a long, good life.

11 I would have you learn this great fact: that a life of doing right is the wisest life there is. 12 If you live that kind of life, you'll not limp or stumble as you run. 13 Carry out my instruc-

tions; don't forget them, for they will lead you to real living.

14Don't do as the wicked do. 15Avoid their haunts—turn away, go somewhere else, 16for evil men can't sleep until they've done their evil deed for the day. They can't rest unless they cause someone to stumble and fall. 17They eat and drink wickedness and violence!

18But the good man walks along in the ever-brightening light of God's favor; the dawn gives way to morning splendor, 19while the evil man gropes and stumbles in the dark.

20Listen, son of mine, to what I say. Listen carefully. 21Keep these thoughts ever in mind; let them penetrate deep within your heart, 22for they will mean real life for you and radiant health.

23*Above all else, guard your affections.* For they influence everything else in your life. 24Spurn the careless kiss of a prostitute. Stay far from her. 25 Look straight ahead; don't even turn your head to look. 26Watch your step. Stick to the path and be safe. 27Don't sidetrack; pull back your foot from danger.

CHAPTER 5

Warning against Sexual Sin

Listen to me, my son! I know what I am saying; *listen!* 2Watch yourself, lest you be indiscreet and betray some vital information. 3For the lips of a prostitute are as sweet as honey, and smooth flattery is her stock in trade. 4But afterwards only a bitter conscience is left to you, sharp as a double-edged sword. 5She leads you down to death and hell. 6For she does not know the path to life. She staggers down a crooked trail and doesn't even realize where it leads.

7Young men, listen to me, and never forget what I'm about to say: 8*Run from her! Don't go near her house,* 9lest you fall to her temptation and lose your honor, and give the remainder of your life to the cruel and merciless; 10lest strangers obtain your wealth, and you become a slave of foreigners. 11Lest afterwards you groan in anguish and in shame when syphilis consumes your body, 12and you say, "Oh, if only I had listened! If only I had not demanded my own way! 13Oh, why wouldn't I take advice? Why was I so stupid? 14For now I must face public disgrace."

15Drink from your own well, my son—be faithful and true to your wife. 16Why should you beget children with women of the street? 17Why share your children with those outside your home? 18Be happy, yes, rejoice in the wife of your youth. 19Let her breasts and tender embrace satisfy you. Let her love alone fill you with delight. 20Why delight yourself with prostitutes, embracing what isn't yours? 21 *For God is closely watching you,* and he weighs carefully everything you do.

4:11-19 We are all influenced by our environment. That is why we are warned here to stay away from those who do wicked deeds. It is easy to become desensitized to sin. If we spend too much time with people with few moral boundaries, we will begin to think and act as they do. Slipping back into our dependencies will be a very natural thing. However, by spending time with godly people, we will find the encouragement we need to stay on the path of recovery. Then we will be able to enjoy the life God has in mind for us.

4:23-27 The warning to guard our affections is also a warning to not give in to the temptation of sinful pleasures of all kinds. Indulging in sin is pleasurable at first, but in the end its promise is empty and bitter. Sin may satisfy short-term desires, but its consequences are long term. Returning to our addiction may make us feel better for the moment, but it will damage (maybe even undo) our whole recovery process.

5:1-23 Sexual temptation is often very hard to resist, even if we are aware of the dangers and consequences of extramarital affairs. Throughout the book of Proverbs there are warnings against promiscuity (see 2:16-19; 6:25-35; 7:6-27; 9:13-18; 22:14; 23:26-28). Unfaithfulness can destroy our family life and our physical health, and it may result in pregnancy. Also, infidelity is against God's law. If sex is our addiction, we must *run* from any situations where we might be tempted to sin. Also, we should seek help, either from a support group or counselor.

6:16-19 Notice that the seven things God hates are things that stand against recovery. They violate our well-being. To be haughty is to be too proud to begin recovery by admitting we need God's help (Step One). To lie is to fail to take inventory of our life and admit our wrongs (Steps Four and Five). To plot evil is to go in the opposite direction of those who repent of their sin and ask God to cleanse their hearts (Steps Six and Seven). To murder is the opposite of asking forgiveness and making amends (Steps Eight and Nine). To be eager to do wrong is the opposite of being eager to do right by seeking to know God and do his will (Step Eleven). To bear false witness and to sow discord among friends are contrary to carrying the true message of peace to those who are hurting (Step Twelve).

READ PROVERBS 4:1-23

GOD grant me the serenity to accept the things I cannot change the courage to change the things I can and the wisdom to know the difference AMEN

Many of us grew up in families that were crazy. Our parents didn't provide wise guidance for us. This deprivation can leave us wondering how we can fill the void left by what we have missed.

Some people grow up in families where wisdom is modeled and taught by their parents. They have the privilege of receiving wise advice at home. We may feel like the rest of the human race has passed us by. Some of us feel anger, resentment, and a sense of shame because we never learned how to make wise choices. We may ask ourself, *Shouldn't someone have shown me the way?* Ideally, all of us should have had wise and godly instruction. The book of Proverbs records a father instructing his son in the way God intended. "For I, too, was once a son, tenderly loved by my mother . . . and the companion of my father. He told me never to forget his words. . . . *'Learn to be wise,'* he said, *'and develop good judgment and common sense! I cannot overemphasize this point.'* Cling to wisdom—she will protect you. Love her—she will guard you" (Proverbs 4:3-6).

For those of us who were left unprotected and unguarded by our human parents, it's not too late. We have a Father in heaven who is eager to give us the wisdom we need. James once wrote, "If you want to know what God wants you to do, ask him, and he will gladly tell you" (James 1:5). God loves us tenderly, as a parent should. He is always there for us, waiting to give us the wisdom we need whenever we ask.
Turn to page 953, Jonah 4.

22The wicked man is doomed by his own sins; they are ropes that catch and hold him.
23He shall die because he will not listen to the truth; he has let himself be led away into incredible folly.

CHAPTER 6

Warning against Foolish Actions

Son, if you endorse a note for someone you hardly know, guaranteeing his debt, you are in serious trouble.
2You may have trapped yourself by your agreement.
3Quick! Get out of it if you possibly can! Swallow your pride; don't let embarrassment stand in the way. Go and beg to have your name erased.
4Don't put it off. Do it now. Don't rest until you do.
5If you can get out of this trap you have saved yourself like a deer that escapes from a hunter or a bird from the net.

6Take a lesson from the ants, you lazy fellow. Learn from their ways and be wise!
7For though they have no king to make them work,
8yet they labor hard all summer, gathering food for the winter.
9But you—all you do is sleep. When will you wake up?
10"Let me sleep a little longer!" Sure, just a little more!
11And as you sleep, poverty creeps upon you like a robber and destroys you; want attacks you in full armor.

12,13Let me describe for you a worthless and a wicked man; first, he is a constant liar; he signals his true intentions to his friends with eyes and feet and fingers.
14He is always thinking up new schemes to swindle people. He stirs up trouble everywhere.
15But he will be destroyed suddenly, broken beyond hope of healing.

16-19For there are six things the Lord hates—no, seven: haughtiness, lying, murdering, plotting evil, eagerness to do wrong, a false witness, sowing discord among brothers.

Warning against Adultery
[20]Young man, obey your father and your
mother. [21]Take to heart all of their advice;
keep in mind everything they tell you. [22]Every
day and all night long their counsel will lead
you and save you from harm; when you wake
up in the morning, let their instructions guide
you into the new day. [23]For their advice is a
beam of light directed into the dark corners of
your mind to warn you of danger and to give
you a good life. [24]Their counsel will keep you
far away from prostitutes, with all their flatteries, and unfaithful wives of other men.

[25]Don't lust for their beauty. Don't let their
coyness seduce you. [26]For a prostitute will
bring a man to poverty, and an adulteress may
cost him his very life. [27]Can a man hold fire
against his chest and not be burned? [28]Can he
walk on hot coals and not blister his feet? [29]So
it is with the man who commits adultery with
another's wife. He shall not go unpunished
for this sin. [30]Excuses might even be found for
a thief if he steals when he is starving! [31]But
even so, he is fined seven times as much as he
stole, though it may mean selling everything
in his house to pay it back.

[32]But the man who commits adultery is an
utter fool, for he destroys his own soul.
[33]Wounds and constant disgrace are his lot,
[34]for the woman's husband will be furious in
his jealousy, and he will have no mercy on
you in his day of vengeance. [35]You won't be
able to buy him off no matter what you offer.

CHAPTER 7

Wisdom Guards against Immorality
Follow my advice, my son; always keep it in
mind and stick to it. [2]Obey me and live! Guard
my words as your most precious possession.
[3]Write them down, and also keep them deep
within your heart. [4]Love wisdom like a sweet-
heart; make her a beloved member of your
family. [5]Let her hold you back from affairs
with other women—from listening to their
flattery.

[6]I was looking out the window of my house
one day [7]and saw a simple-minded lad, a
young man lacking common sense, [8,9]walking
at twilight down the street to the house of this
wayward girl, a prostitute. [10]She approached
him, saucy and pert, and dressed seductively.
[11,12]She was the brash, coarse type, seen often
in the streets and markets, soliciting at every
corner for men to be her lovers.

[13]She put her arms around him and kissed
him, and with a saucy look she said, "I was
just coming to look for you and here you are!
[14-17]Come home with me, and I'll fix you a
wonderful dinner, and after that—well, my
bed is spread with lovely, colored sheets of
finest linen imported from Egypt, perfumed
with myrrh, aloes, and cinnamon. [18]Come on,
let's take our fill of love until morning, [19]for
my husband is away on a long trip. [20]He has
taken a wallet full of money with him and
won't return for several days."

[21]So she seduced him with her pretty
speech, her coaxing and her wheedling, until
he yielded to her. He couldn't resist her flattery. [22]He followed her as an ox going to the
butcher or as a stag that is trapped, [23]waiting
to be killed with an arrow through its heart.
He was as a bird flying into a snare, not
knowing the fate awaiting it there.

[24]Listen to me, young men, and not only
listen but obey; [25]don't let your desires get out
of hand; don't let yourself think about her.
Don't go near her; stay away from where she
walks, lest she tempt you and seduce you.
[26]For she has been the ruin of multitudes—a
vast host of men have been her victims. [27]If
you want to find the road to hell, look for her
house.

CHAPTER 8

Wisdom Gives Good Advice
Can't you hear the voice of wisdom? She is
standing at the city gates and at every fork in
the road, and at the door of every house.
Listen to what she says: [4,5]"Listen, men!" she
calls. "How foolish and naive you are! Let me
give you understanding. O foolish ones, let
me show you common sense! [6,7]Listen to me!
For I have important information for you.
Everything I say is right and true, for I hate lies
and every kind of deception. [8]My advice is
wholesome and good. There is nothing of evil
in it. [9]My words are plain and clear to anyone
with half a mind—if it is only open! [10]My
instruction is far more valuable than silver or
gold."

[11]For the value of wisdom is far above rubies; nothing can be compared with it. [12]Wis-
dom and good judgment live together, for
wisdom knows where to discover knowledge
and understanding. [13]If anyone respects and
fears God, he will hate evil. For wisdom hates
pride, arrogance, corruption, and deceit of
every kind.

[14-16]"I, Wisdom, give good advice and common sense. Because of my strength, kings
reign in power, and rulers make just laws. [17]I
love all who love me. Those who search for me
shall surely find me. [18]Unending riches, honor,

justice, and righteousness are mine to distribute. 19My gifts are better than the purest gold or sterling silver! 20My paths are those of justice and right. 21Those who love and follow me are indeed wealthy. I fill their treasuries. 22The Lord formed me in the beginning, before he created anything else. 23From ages past, I am. I existed before the earth began. 24I lived before the oceans were created, before the springs bubbled forth their waters onto the earth, 25before the mountains and the hills were made. 26Yes, I was born before God made the earth and fields and the first handfuls of soil.

27-29"I was there when he established the heavens and formed the great springs in the depths of the oceans. I was there when he set the limits of the seas and gave them his instructions not to spread beyond their boundaries. I was there when he made the blueprint for the earth and oceans. 30I was the craftsman at his side. I was his constant delight, rejoicing always in his presence. 31And how happy I was with what he created—his wide world and all his family of mankind! 32And so, young men, listen to me, for how happy are all who follow my instructions.

33"Listen to my counsel—oh, don't refuse it—and be wise. 34Happy is the man who is so anxious to be with me that he watches for me daily at my gates, or waits for me outside my home! 35For whoever finds me finds life and wins approval from the Lord. 36But the one who misses me has injured himself irreparably. Those who refuse me show that they love death."

CHAPTER 9
Wisdom Is Its Own Reward

Wisdom has built a palace supported on seven pillars, 2and has prepared a great banquet, and mixed the wines, 3and sent out her maidens inviting all to come. She calls from the busiest intersections in the city, 4"Come, you simple ones without good judgment; 5come to wisdom's banquet and drink the wines that I have mixed. 6Leave behind your foolishness and begin to live; learn how to be wise."

7,8If you rebuke a mocker, you will only get a smart retort; yes, he will snarl at you. So don't bother with him; he will only hate you for trying to help him. But a wise man, when rebuked, will love you all the more. 9Teach a wise man, and he will be the wiser; teach a good man, and he will learn more. 10*For the reverence and fear of God are basic to all wisdom. Knowing God results in every other kind of understanding.* 11"I, Wisdom, will make the hours of your day more profitable and the years of your life more fruitful." 12Wisdom is its own reward, and if you scorn her, you hurt only yourself.

13A prostitute is loud and brash and never has enough of lust and shame. 14She sits at the door of her house or stands at the street corners of the city, 15whispering to men going by and to those minding their own business. 16"Come home with me," she urges simpletons. 17"Stolen melons are the sweetest; stolen apples taste the best!" 18But they don't realize that her former guests are now citizens of hell.

CHAPTER 10
God's Wisdom Is for Everyone

Happy is the man with a level-headed son; sad the mother of a rebel.

2Ill-gotten gain brings no lasting happiness; right living does.

3The Lord will not let a good man starve to death, nor will he let the wicked man's riches continue forever.

4Lazy men are soon poor; hard workers get rich.

5A wise youth makes hay while the sun shines, but what a shame to see a lad who sleeps away his hour of opportunity.

8:22-36 Solomon portrayed wisdom as a personal being who is eternally existent with God and who was the "craftsman" in Creation. This may be an allusion to Jesus the Messiah, who, in the divine inspiration of Scripture, was the Word that spoke forth God's creation "in the beginning." Those who in faith listen to Christ and follow his wisdom will find life and favor with God. All who follow his instructions will find joy, both in this life and in the next.

9:7-8 When someone tries to help us and correct us, we have two choices. We can either listen and learn, as the wise man does, or we can get angry and rebel, as the mocker does. To mock and hate those who are concerned for us is to deny that we have a problem. The wise man is honest enough to admit there is a problem and that he needs help. This attitude will result in recovery. The mocker will reject good advice and be overtaken by his sins.

10:6 In this and in many of the following proverbs Solomon contrasts good and evil people by the way they live and the consequences they suffer. The basic principle is repeated again and again: moral living is good for us. One key to doing what is right is having an accurate self-perception. As we begin to see ourself as God sees us, we will see that we are lovable and valuable, and we will want to apply the principles of wisdom to our life.

[6]The good man is covered with blessings from head to foot, but an evil man inwardly curses his luck.
[7]We all have happy memories of good men gone to their reward, but the names of wicked men stink after them.
[8]The wise man is glad to be instructed, but a self-sufficient fool falls flat on his face.
[9]A good man has firm footing, but a crook will slip and fall.
[10]Winking at sin leads to sorrow; bold reproof leads to peace.
[11]There is living truth in what a good man says, but the mouth of the evil man is filled with curses.
[12]Hatred stirs old quarrels, but love overlooks insults.
[13]Men with common sense are admired as counselors; those without it are beaten as servants.
[14]A wise man holds his tongue. Only a fool blurts out everything he knows; that only leads to sorrow and trouble.
[15]The rich man's wealth is his only strength. The poor man's poverty is his only curse.
[16]The good man's earnings advance the cause of righteousness. The evil man squanders his on sin.
[17]Anyone willing to be corrected is on the pathway to life. Anyone refusing has lost his chance.
[18]To hide hatred is to be a liar; to slander is to be a fool.
[19]Don't talk so much. You keep putting your foot in your mouth. Be sensible and turn off the flow!
[20]When a good man speaks, he is worth listening to, but the words of fools are a dime a dozen.
[21]A godly man gives good advice, but a rebel is destroyed by lack of common sense.
[22]The Lord's blessing is our greatest wealth. All our work adds nothing to it!
[23]A fool's fun is being bad; a wise man's fun is being wise!
[24]The wicked man's fears will all come true and so will the good man's hopes.
[25]Disaster strikes like a cyclone and the wicked are whirled away. But the good man has a strong anchor.
[26]A lazy fellow is a pain to his employers—like smoke in their eyes or vinegar that sets the teeth on edge.
[27]Reverence for God adds hours to each day; so how can the wicked expect a long, good life?
[28]The hope of good men is eternal happiness; the hopes of evil men are all in vain.
[29]God protects the upright but destroys the wicked.
[30]The good shall never lose God's blessings, but the wicked shall lose everything.
[31]The good man gives wise advice, but the liar's counsel is shunned.
[32]The upright speak what is helpful; the wicked speak rebellion.

CHAPTER 11

The Lord hates cheating and delights in honesty.
[2]Proud men end in shame, but the meek become wise.
[3]A good man is guided by his honesty; the evil man is destroyed by his dishonesty.
[4]Your riches won't help you on Judgment Day; only righteousness counts then.
[5]Good people are directed by their honesty; the wicked shall fall beneath their load of sins.
[6]The good man's goodness delivers him; the evil man's treachery is his undoing.
[7]When an evil man dies, his hopes all perish, for they are based upon this earthly life.
[8]God rescues good men from danger while letting the wicked fall into it.
[9]Evil words destroy; godly skill rebuilds.
[10]The whole city celebrates a good man's success—and also the godless man's death.
[11]The good influence of godly citizens causes a city to prosper, but the moral decay of the wicked drives it downhill.
[12]To quarrel with a neighbor is foolish; a man with good sense holds his tongue.
[13]A gossip goes around spreading rumors, while a trustworthy man tries to quiet them.

10:25 Whether or not our ship continues to sail through the many storms we encounter depends on our readiness to drop the anchor of faith during the storm. The anchor will never make the storm stop, but it will hold us firm so we don't drift to our destruction. When we are encountering difficulties in life, it is a real challenge to be content to weather the storm and to learn what God is teaching us through it. For people of faith, such trials are an opportunity for personal growth (see 24:10).

11:1-3 These proverbs underscore the importance of being honest. In recovery, we need to be honest—with ourself and with others. We need to honestly admit that we can't control our addiction (Step One). We need to be honest as we compile our moral inventory (Steps Four and Ten). And we need to honestly admit to God and others exactly what we have done wrong (Step Five).

[14]Without wise leadership, a nation is in trouble; but with good counselors there is safety.

[15]Be sure you know a person well before you vouch for his credit! Better refuse than suffer later.

[16]Honor goes to kind and gracious women, mere money to cruel men.

[17]Your own soul is nourished when you are kind; it is destroyed when you are cruel.

[18]The evil man gets rich for the moment, but the good man's reward lasts forever.

[19]The good man finds life; the evil man, death.

[20]The Lord hates the stubborn but delights in those who are good.

[21]You can be very sure the evil man will not go unpunished forever. And you can also be very sure God will rescue the children of the godly.

[22]A beautiful woman lacking discretion and modesty is like a fine gold ring in a pig's snout.

[23]The good man can look forward to happiness, while the wicked can expect only wrath.

[24,25]It is possible to give away and become richer! It is also possible to hold on too tightly and lose everything. Yes, the liberal man shall be rich! By watering others, he waters himself.

[26]People curse the man who holds his grain for higher prices, but they bless the man who sells it to them in their time of need.

[27]If you search for good, you will find God's favor; if you search for evil, you will find his curse.

[28]Trust in your money and down you go! Trust in God and flourish as a tree!

[29]The fool who provokes his family to anger and resentment will finally have nothing worthwhile left. He shall be the servant of a wiser man.

[30]Godly men are growing a tree that bears life-giving fruit, and all who win souls are wise.

[31]Even the godly shall be rewarded here on earth; how much more the wicked!

CHAPTER 12

To learn, you must want to be taught. To refuse reproof is stupid.

[2]The Lord blesses good men and condemns the wicked.

[3]Wickedness never brings real success; only the godly have that.

[4]A worthy wife is her husband's joy and crown; the other kind corrodes his strength and tears down everything he does.

[5]A good man's mind is filled with honest thoughts; an evil man's mind is crammed with lies.

[6]The wicked accuse; the godly defend.

[7]The wicked shall perish; the godly shall stand.

[8]Everyone admires a man with good sense, but a man with a warped mind is despised.

[9]It is better to get your hands dirty—and eat, than to be too proud to work—and starve.

[10]A good man is concerned for the welfare of his animals, but even the kindness of godless men is cruel.

[11]Hard work means prosperity; only a fool idles away his time.

[12]Crooks are jealous of each other's loot, while good men long to help each other.

[13]Lies will get any man into trouble, but honesty is its own defense.

[14]Telling the truth gives a man great satisfaction, and hard work returns many blessings to him.

[15]A fool thinks he needs no advice, but a wise man listens to others.

[16]A fool is quick-tempered; a wise man stays cool when insulted.

11:24-25 Some of us may wonder how we can be expected to give anything away. We may have lost everything, or perhaps we just feel too empty and tired to reach out. It might be refreshing to realize that we have a special gift to give others in recovery—encouragement. When we share our victories, even our failures, others will be strengthened for the battles ahead. That is what Step Twelve is all about. As we share our message with others who are in recovery, they will gain the insight and encouragement they need for success. We, in turn, will be encouraged to stay away from our dependencies because of what our recovery has come to mean to others.

12:15 Changing past patterns of behavior and recovering from emotional trauma require the help of people we trust and respect (see 12:26; 15:22; 19:20). We cannot live life successfully alone. Growing toward spiritual and emotional maturity is a process that requires the help of trustworthy people who can guide us with care and hold us accountable as we try to make changes.

12:16 It is foolish for us to lose our temper when we are insulted. We demonstrate maturity by staying self-controlled and expressing our anger calmly and lovingly. By doing so we can offer needed correction to the offender, provide a chance to build intimacy in the relationship, and keep our heart free from resentment (see 19:11).

[17]A good man is known by his truthfulness;
a false man by deceit and lies.
[18]Some people like to make cutting remarks, but the words of the wise soothe and
heal.
[19]Truth stands the test of time; lies are soon
exposed.
[20]Deceit fills hearts that are plotting for evil;
joy fills hearts that are planning for good!
[21]No real harm befalls the good, but there is
constant trouble for the wicked.
[22]God delights in those who keep their
promises and abhors those who don't.
[23]A wise man doesn't display his knowledge, but a fool displays his foolishness.
[24]Work hard and become a leader; be lazy
and never succeed.
[25]Anxious hearts are very heavy, but a word
of encouragement does wonders!
[26]The good man asks advice from friends;
the wicked plunge ahead—and fall.
[27]A lazy man won't even dress the game he
gets while hunting, but the diligent man
makes good use of everything he finds.
[28]The path of the godly leads to life. So why
fear death?

CHAPTER 13

A wise youth accepts his father's rebuke; a
young mocker doesn't.
[2]The good man wins his case by careful
argument; the evil-minded only wants to
fight.
[3]Self-control means controlling the tongue!
A quick retort can ruin everything.
[4]Lazy people want much but get little,
while the diligent are prospering.
[5]A good man hates lies; wicked men lie
constantly and come to shame.
[6]A man's goodness helps him all through
life, while evil men are being destroyed by
their wickedness.
[7]Some rich people are poor, and some poor
people have great wealth!
[8]Being kidnapped and held for ransom
never worries the poor man!
[9]The good man's life is full of light. The
sinner's road is dark and gloomy.
[10]Pride leads to arguments; be humble, take
advice, and become wise.
[11]Wealth from gambling quickly disappears; wealth from hard work grows.
[12]Hope deferred makes the heart sick; but
when dreams come true at last, there is life
and joy.
[13]Despise God's Word and find yourself in
trouble. Obey it and succeed.
[14]The advice of a wise man refreshes like
water from a mountain spring. Those accepting it become aware of the pitfalls on ahead.
[15]A man with good sense is appreciated. A
treacherous man must walk a rocky road.
[16]A wise man thinks ahead; a fool doesn't
and even brags about it!
[17]An unreliable messenger can cause a lot of
trouble. Reliable communication permits
progress.
[18]If you refuse criticism, you will end in
poverty and disgrace; if you accept criticism,
you are on the road to fame.
[19]It is pleasant to see plans develop. That is
why fools refuse to give them up even when
they are wrong.
[20]Be with wise men and become wise. Be
with evil men and become evil.
[21]Curses chase sinners, while blessings
chase the righteous!
[22]When a good man dies, he leaves an inheritance to his grandchildren; but when a
sinner dies, his wealth is stored up for the
godly.
[23]A poor man's farm may have good soil,
but injustice robs him of its riches.
[24]If you refuse to discipline your son, it

13:6 It should not surprise us that evil deeds destroy people. Painful effects are often a direct consequence of a sinful cause. Drug or alcohol abuse will destroy the body; constant lying will ruin a person's reputation; constant gambling will put one in the poorhouse. To avoid the inevitable results of sinful behavior, we need to stay away from our addictions and compulsions and obediently follow God. His ways lead to happiness and will give positive direction to our life.

13:9 Leaving a destructive past to join a recovery program is like walking out of the darkness and into the light. Those who enter the light see their need for help and the reality of a loving God who wants to help them. They can no longer hide their deeds in the darkness of denial and deceit. They must honestly deal with the issues the light has exposed.

13:20 Since we become like the company we keep, it is important to have friends we respect. This is also the reason that involvement in a support group is so important to personal growth. When we are struggling in a certain area, it's helpful to know that we are not alone and that others want to share our pain. It is also helpful to see fellow strugglers modeling the things that will help us to overcome our obstacles—honesty, perseverance, and accountability.

proves you don't love him; for if you love him, you will be prompt to punish him.

25 The good man eats to live, while the evil man lives to eat.

CHAPTER 14

A wise woman builds her house, while a foolish woman tears hers down by her own efforts.

2 To do right honors God; to sin is to despise him.

3 A rebel's foolish talk should prick his own pride! But the wise man's speech is respected.

4 An empty stable stays clean—but there is no income from an empty stable.

5 A truthful witness never lies; a false witness always lies.

6 A mocker never finds the wisdom he claims he is looking for, yet it comes easily to the man with common sense.

7 If you are looking for advice, stay away from fools.

8 The wise man looks ahead. The fool attempts to fool himself and won't face facts.

9 The common bond of rebels is their guilt. The common bond of godly people is good will.

10 Only the person involved can know his own bitterness or joy—no one else can really share it.

11 The work of the wicked will perish; the work of the godly will flourish.

12 Before every man there lies a wide and pleasant road that seems right but ends in death.

13 Laughter cannot mask a heavy heart. When the laughter ends, the grief remains.

14 The backslider gets bored with himself; the godly man's life is exciting.

15 Only a simpleton believes everything he's told! A prudent man understands the need for proof.

16 A wise man is cautious and avoids danger; a fool plunges ahead with great confidence.

17 A short-tempered man is a fool. He hates the man who is patient.

18 The simpleton is crowned with folly; the wise man is crowned with knowledge.

19 Evil men shall bow before the godly.

20,21 Even his own neighbors despise the poor man, while the rich have many "friends." But to despise the poor is to sin. Blessed are those who help them.

22 Those who plot evil shall wander away and be lost, but those who plan good shall be granted mercy and quietness.

23 Work brings profit; talk brings poverty!

24 Wise men are praised for their wisdom; fools are despised for their folly.

25 A witness who tells the truth saves good men from being sentenced to death, but a false witness is a traitor.

26 Reverence for God gives a man deep strength; his children have a place of refuge and security.

27 Reverence for the Lord is a fountain of life; its waters keep a man from death.

28 A growing population is a king's glory; a dwindling nation is his doom.

29 A wise man controls his temper. He knows that anger causes mistakes.

30 A relaxed attitude lengthens a man's life; jealousy rots it away.

31 Anyone who oppresses the poor is insulting God who made them. To help the poor is to honor God.

32 The godly have a refuge when they die, but the wicked are crushed by their sins.

33 Wisdom is enshrined in the hearts of men of common sense, but it must shout loudly before fools will hear it.

34 Godliness exalts a nation, but sin is a reproach to any people.

35 A king rejoices in servants who know what they are doing; he is angry with those who cause trouble.

CHAPTER 15

A gentle answer turns away wrath, but harsh words cause quarrels.

2 A wise teacher makes learning a joy; a rebellious teacher spouts foolishness.

14:15 Trusting God to direct us through the advice of others is an important step in recovery. Solomon, however, gave a wise note of caution in this matter: don't blindly trust others (see 20:6). A healthy trust in others is developed gradually and carefully. This can only happen as we discern when it is safe for us to be vulnerable, and then determine if the guidance we are being given is truly good for us. Also, if any advice is contrary to the truth revealed in the Bible, it should be disregarded, no matter who gives it.

14:26-27 "Reverence for God" is integral in any Twelve Step program. Steps Two, Three, Six, Seven, and Eleven all directly have to do with trusting God and drawing closer to him. God will give us strength and power that we never could have experienced if we had refused to follow his plan for us. He is our security, our strength, and our source of life. If we haven't given our life to Jesus yet, we must do it now. Any hope of recovery depends on our relationship with him.

3 The Lord is watching everywhere and keeps his eye on both the evil and the good.

4 Gentle words cause life and health; griping brings discouragement.

5 Only a fool despises his father's advice; a wise son considers each suggestion.

6 There is treasure in being good, but trouble dogs the wicked.

7 Only the good can give good advice. Rebels can't.

8 The Lord hates the gifts of the wicked but delights in the prayers of his people.

9,10 The Lord despises the deeds of the wicked but loves those who try to be good. If they stop trying, the Lord will punish them; if they rebel against that punishment, they will die.

11 The depths of hell are open to God's knowledge. How much more the hearts of all mankind!

12 A mocker stays away from wise men because he hates to be scolded.

13 A happy face means a glad heart; a sad face means a breaking heart.

14 A wise man is hungry for truth, while the mocker feeds on trash.

15 When a man is gloomy, everything seems to go wrong; when he is cheerful, everything seems right!

16 Better a little with reverence for God than great treasure and trouble with it.

17 It is better to eat soup with someone you love than steak with someone you hate.

18 A quick-tempered man starts fights; a cool-tempered man tries to stop them.

19 A lazy fellow has trouble all through life; the good man's path is easy!

20 A sensible son gladdens his father. A rebellious son saddens his mother.

21 If a man enjoys folly, something is wrong! The sensible stay on the pathways of right.

22 Plans go wrong with too few counselors; many counselors bring success.

23 Everyone enjoys giving good advice, and how wonderful it is to be able to say the right thing at the right time!

24 The road of the godly leads upward, leaving hell behind.

25 The Lord destroys the possessions of the proud but cares for widows.

26 The Lord hates the thoughts of the wicked but delights in kind words.

27 Dishonest money brings grief to all the family, but hating bribes brings happiness.

28 A good man thinks before he speaks; the evil man pours out his evil words without a thought.

29 The Lord is far from the wicked, but he hears the prayers of the righteous.

30 Pleasant sights and good reports give happiness and health.

31,32 If you profit from constructive criticism, you will be elected to the wise men's hall of fame. But to reject criticism is to harm yourself and your own best interests.

33 Humility and reverence for the Lord will make you both wise and honored.

15:14 Truth and sanity go hand in hand. The more honest we are with ourself, others, and God, the healthier we will be. Also, the more we are open to receiving honest feedback from others about how we are coming across, the healthier we will be and the smoother our recovery will be. If people tell us lies about how we are doing, however, we should close our ears to their false compliments. When we are willing to listen to garbage from others—listening to what we *want* to hear instead of what we *need* to hear—our recovery could be put at a significant risk.

15:31-32 If we really want to learn and grow, we must be willing to be held accountable by receiving constructive criticism from others (see 10:8; 13:18; 15:5; 25:12). For many of us it is hard to receive reproof because even when it is shared in love, it hurts. Our tendency may be to ignore correction to avoid the hurt or to collapse emotionally because we are devastated by a word of constructive criticism. We would be wise to ask for feedback from people we respect. That way we will learn from our mistakes and grow in maturity.

16:2 We are incredibly good at rationalizing our actions and motives so that others don't know why we are doing things. But this is dangerous because soon we may believe what we tell others. If we have a drinking problem, it is easy to go into denial about it. We claim that we really don't need to drink or that we only drink to be social. But the truth is quite different. We may even have "proved" to everyone that we don't have a problem—everyone, that is, except God. He knows all our actions, our motives, and our excuses. He is also the one who can make our full recovery possible.

16:9 It is important that we trust our future to God, but it is just as important to plan our recovery, our savings for retirement, our life. Responsible trust in God means taking action to secure what we need in life, letting God's Word and his Spirit guide us in our preparations. Saying "God will provide" and then sitting passively, waiting for God to take care of us, is often an excuse for laziness. We need to get moving and let God direct us in the process.

CHAPTER 16
We can make our plans, but the final outcome
is in God's hands.
2 We can always "prove" that we are right,
but is the Lord convinced?
3 Commit your work to the Lord, then it will
succeed.
4 The Lord has made everything for his own
purposes—even the wicked, for punishment.
5 Pride disgusts the Lord. Take my word for
it—*proud men shall be punished.*
6 Iniquity is atoned for by mercy and truth;
evil is avoided by reverence for God.
7 When a man is trying to please God, God
makes even his worst enemies to be at peace
with him.
8 A little gained honestly is better than great
wealth gotten by dishonest means.
9 We should make plans—counting on God
to direct us.
10 God will help the king to judge the people
fairly; there need be no mistakes.
11 The Lord demands fairness in every business deal. He established this principle.
12 It is a horrible thing for a king to do evil.
His right to rule depends upon his fairness.
13 The king rejoices when his people are
truthful and fair.
14 The anger of the king is a messenger of
death, and a wise man will appease it.
15 Many favors are showered on those who
please the king.
16 How much better is wisdom than gold,
and understanding than silver!
17 The path of the godly leads away from
evil; he who follows that path is safe.
18 Pride goes before destruction and haughtiness before a fall.
19 Better poor and humble than proud and
rich.
20 God blesses those who obey him; happy
the man who puts his trust in the Lord.
21 The wise man is known by his common
sense, and a pleasant teacher is the best.
22 Wisdom is a fountain of life to those possessing it, but a fool's burden is his folly.
23 From a wise mind comes careful and per-
suasive speech.
24 Kind words are like honey—enjoyable
and healthful.
25 Before every man there lies a wide and
pleasant road he thinks is right, but it ends in
death.
26 Hunger is good—if it makes you work to
satisfy it!
27 Idle hands are the devil's workshop; idle
lips are his mouthpiece.

Self-protection

READ PROVERBS 15:16-33

In recovery, we learn new ways of seeing things, new ways of responding, and new guidelines for making decisions. Our old patterns of thinking and living didn't work very well. Now that we are establishing new patterns, we will need counselors. They will supply the support and wisdom we need and will listen as we share our story.

King Solomon gave this advice, "Plans go wrong with too few counselors; many counselors bring success" (Proverbs 15:22). "With good counselors there is safety" (Proverbs 11:14). King David looked to God's Word for counsel saying, "Your laws are both my light and my counselors" (Psalm 119:24). Isaiah prophesied of the Messiah (Jesus), saying, "For unto us a child is born; unto us a son is given; and the government shall be upon his shoulder. These will be his royal titles: 'Wonderful,' 'Counselor,' 'The Mighty God,' 'The Everlasting Father,' 'The Prince of Peace'" (Isaiah 9:6).

When we surround ourselves with dependable counselors, we are developing a safety net. Good counsel can come from the Bible and from godly people. When we admit our wrongs to other people, they can also become a source of counsel for our life. They may be professionals who understand addiction and recovery. They might be people who know us and measure their advice by godly principles. Or perhaps they are people who have experienced what we are now going through. Find someone! ***Turn to page 707, Ecclesiastes 3.***

[28]An evil man sows strife; gossip separates the best of friends.

[29]Wickedness loves company—and leads others into sin.

[30]The wicked man stares into space with pursed lips, deep in thought, planning his evil deeds.

[31]White hair is a crown of glory and is seen most among the godly.

[32]It is better to be slow-tempered than famous; it is better to have self-control than to control an army.

[33]We toss the coin, but it is the Lord who controls its decision.

CHAPTER 17

A dry crust eaten in peace is better than steak every day along with argument and strife.

[2]A wise slave will rule his master's wicked sons and share their estate.

[3]Silver and gold are purified by fire, but God purifies hearts.

[4]The wicked enjoy fellowship with others who are wicked; liars enjoy liars.

[5]Mocking the poor is mocking the God who made them. He will punish those who rejoice at others' misfortunes.

[6]An old man's grandchildren are his crowning glory. A child's glory is his father.

[7]Truth from a rebel or lies from a king are both unexpected.

[8]A bribe works like magic. Whoever uses it will prosper!

[9]Love forgets mistakes; nagging about them parts the best of friends.

[10]A rebuke to a man of common sense is more effective than a hundred lashes on the back of a rebel.

[11]The wicked live for rebellion; they shall be severely punished.

[12]It is safer to meet a bear robbed of her cubs than a fool caught in his folly.

[13]If you repay evil for good, a curse is upon your home.

[14]It is hard to stop a quarrel once it starts, so don't let it begin.

[15]The Lord despises those who say that bad is good and good is bad.

[16]It is senseless to pay tuition to educate a rebel who has no heart for truth.

[17]A true friend is always loyal, and a brother is born to help in time of need.

[18]It is poor judgment to countersign another's note, to become responsible for his debts.

[19]Sinners love to fight; boasting is looking for trouble.

[20]An evil man is suspicious of everyone and tumbles into constant trouble.

[21]It's no fun to be a rebel's father.

[22]A cheerful heart does good like medicine, but a broken spirit makes one sick.

[23]It is wrong to accept a bribe to twist justice.

[24]Wisdom is the main pursuit of sensible men, but a fool's goals are at the ends of the earth!

[25]A rebellious son is a grief to his father and a bitter blow to his mother.

[26]How shortsighted to fine the godly for being good! And to punish nobles for being honest!

[27,28]The man of few words and settled mind is wise; therefore, even a fool is thought to be wise when he is silent. It pays him to keep his mouth shut.

16:33 There is no such thing as luck. All that happens in our life, even the seemingly random toss of a coin, is under the watchful eye and guiding hand of our sovereign God. It is a challenge to our faith to trust that God is truly in control and that he cares about all the details of our life. But we must remember that "all that happens to us is working for our good if we love God and are fitting into his plans" (Romans 8:28).

17:9 The last thing we need to hear in recovery is how much we have messed up our life. We are aware of our mistakes and know that we have done things of which we are ashamed. But by confessing our sins, we receive God's forgiveness and cleansing. He has forgotten our sins and has removed them "as far away from us as the east is from the west" (Psalm 103:12). If God has forgiven and forgotten our past, we have no need to be reminded of it. If friends insist on bringing up the subject, we need to ignore them and not feel guilty for what we have done. The guilt we feel may drag us back into our old life-style.

17:17 A true friend will stick beside us during the hard times. Without a relationship with that kind of friend, recovery and growth can't take place. We all need to be able to express our needs and concerns to someone who will care and encourage us in our efforts to change.

18:1 The selfish person who demands his own way lacks the ability to delay gratification. He ends up satisfying his whims, but he never meets his real needs. Rather than demanding our own way, it is healthier to take the time to reflect on what is truly important to us and to appropriately seek to have those needs met.

CHAPTER 18

The selfish man quarrels against every sound principle of conduct by demanding his own way.

2 A rebel doesn't care about the facts. All he wants to do is yell.

3 Sin brings disgrace.

4 A wise man's words express deep streams of thought.

5 It is wrong for a judge to favor the wicked and condemn the innocent.

6,7 A fool gets into constant fights. His mouth is his undoing! His words endanger him.

8 What dainty morsels rumors are. They are eaten with great relish!

9 A lazy man is brother to the saboteur.

10 The Lord is a strong fortress. The godly run to him and are safe.

11 The rich man thinks of his wealth as an impregnable defense, a high wall of safety. What a dreamer!

12 Pride ends in destruction; humility ends in honor.

13 What a shame—yes, how stupid!—to decide before knowing the facts!

14 A man's courage can sustain his broken body, but when courage dies, what hope is left?

15 The intelligent man is always open to new ideas. In fact, he looks for them.

16 A gift does wonders; it will bring you before men of importance!

17 Any story sounds true until someone tells the other side and sets the record straight.

18 A coin toss ends arguments and settles disputes between powerful opponents.

19 It is harder to win back the friendship of an offended brother than to capture a fortified city. His anger shuts you out like iron bars.

20 Ability to give wise advice satisfies like a good meal!

21 Those who love to talk will suffer the consequences. Men have died for saying the wrong thing!

22 The man who finds a wife finds a good thing; she is a blessing to him from the Lord.

23 The poor man pleads, and the rich man answers with insults.

24 There are "friends" who pretend to be friends, but there is a friend who sticks closer than a brother.

CHAPTER 19

Better be poor and honest than rich and dishonest.

2 It is dangerous and sinful to rush into the unknown.

3 A man may ruin his chances by his own foolishness and then blame it on the Lord!

4 A wealthy man has many "friends"; the poor man has none left.

5 Punish false witnesses. Track down liars.

6 Many beg favors from a man who is generous; everyone is his friend!

7 A poor man's own brothers turn away from him in embarrassment; how much more his friends! He calls after them, but they are gone.

8 He who loves wisdom loves his own best interest and will be a success.

9 A false witness shall be punished, and a liar shall be caught.

10 It doesn't seem right for a fool to succeed or for a slave to rule over princes!

11 A wise man restrains his anger and overlooks insults. This is to his credit.

12 The king's anger is as dangerous as a lion's. But his approval is as refreshing as the dew on grass.

13 A rebellious son is a calamity to his father, and a nagging wife annoys like constant dripping.

14 A father can give his sons homes and riches, but only the Lord can give them understanding wives.

18:12 When we are filled with pride, we cannot see our weaknesses. We build a wall of denial that is almost impregnable. And if we cannot admit our faults, they will never be corrected, and we will suffer the consequences. On the other hand, humility opens the door for correction. When we honestly evaluate our life, we open our eyes to our weaknesses and can then take steps to improve and correct things. This may cause us some pain now, but it will be much more bearable than the pain of a life destroyed by dependencies and compulsions.

19:19 If we rescue impatient friends from their problems once, we will probably rescue them again and again. They will become addicted to being rescued from trouble and will live irresponsibly without having to suffer the consequences. We will become codependent, addicted to the pattern of avoiding our own needs and gaining a sense of importance by helping others with their needs. This pattern is harmful to us and the person who needs our help. Though it is painful to do, we need to let the other person feel the effects of his or her addiction, and then the pain of the experience may bring him or her to admitting the problem and seeking recovery.

15 A lazy man sleeps soundly—and he goes hungry!

16 Keep the commandments and keep your life; despising them means death.

17 When you help the poor you are lending to the Lord—and he pays wonderful interest on your loan!

18 Discipline your son in his early years while there is hope. If you don't you will ruin his life.

19 A short-tempered man must bear his own penalty; you can't do much to help him. If you try once you must try a dozen times!

20 Get all the advice you can and be wise the rest of your life.

21 Man proposes, but God disposes.

22 Kindness makes a man attractive. And it is better to be poor than dishonest.

23 Reverence for God gives life, happiness, and protection from harm.

24 Some men are so lazy they won't even feed themselves!

25 Punish a mocker and others will learn from his example. Reprove a wise man, and he will be the wiser.

26 A son who mistreats his father or mother is a public disgrace.

27 Stop listening to teaching that contradicts what you know is right.

28 A worthless witness cares nothing for truth—he enjoys his sinning too much.

29 Mockers and rebels shall be severely punished.

CHAPTER 20

Wine gives false courage; hard liquor leads to brawls; what fools men are to let it master them, making them reel drunkenly down the street!

2 The king's fury is like that of a roaring lion; to rouse his anger is to risk your life.

3 It is an honor for a man to stay out of a fight. Only fools insist on quarreling.

4 If you won't plow in the cold, you won't eat at the harvest.

5 Though good advice lies deep within a counselor's heart, the wise man will draw it out.

6 Most people will tell you what loyal friends they are, but are they telling the truth?

7 It is a wonderful heritage to have an honest father.

8 A king sitting as judge weighs all the evidence carefully, distinguishing the true from false.

9 Who can ever say, "I have cleansed my heart; I am sinless"?

10 The Lord despises every kind of cheating.

11 The character of even a child can be known by the way he acts—whether what he does is pure and right.

12 If you have good eyesight and good hearing, thank God who gave them to you.

13 If you love sleep, you will end in poverty. Stay awake, work hard, and there will be plenty to eat!

14 "Utterly worthless!" says the buyer as he haggles over the price. But afterwards he brags about his bargain!

15 Good sense is far more valuable than gold or precious jewels.

16 It is risky to make loans to strangers!

17 Some men enjoy cheating, but the cake they buy with such ill-gotten gain will turn to gravel in their mouths.

18 Don't go ahead with your plans without the advice of others; don't go to war until they agree.

19 Don't tell your secrets to a gossip unless you want them broadcast to the world.

20 God puts out the light of the man who curses his father or mother.

21 Quick wealth is not a blessing in the end.

22 Don't repay evil for evil. Wait for the Lord to handle the matter.

23 The Lord loathes all cheating and dishonesty.

20:9 None of us is without sin, but we can receive forgiveness through confession. An important step in recovery involves taking a moral inventory of our life. Through the confession of our sins to God, we can then receive his gracious forgiveness. Taking an inventory is a big job! Many of our sins were committed unconsciously and will require real soul-searching to uncover. And since we have such a strong tendency to sin, we will need to take inventory of our life again and again. We can be sure, however, that each time we confess our sins to God, he will be faithful in forgiving us.

20:22 Seeking revenge against a person who has hurt us will never satisfy our anger; it will only add fuel to the fire. The cycle of retribution often lasts for a long time. Sometimes it continues for years after both parties have forgotten the origin of the conflict. To overcome our anger, we need to start the process of forgiveness right away. We may need to confront our offender in love, seeking to resolve the conflict through mutual understanding. Or we may need to set certain limits on sinful behavior. If reconciliation is not possible, then it is best to give the matter to God and his ultimate justice. Either way, we need to put the sin behind us and move on with life.

[24]Since the Lord is directing our steps, why try to understand everything that happens along the way?

[25]It is foolish and rash to make a promise to the Lord before counting the cost.

[26]A wise king stamps out crime by severe punishment.

[27]A man's conscience is the Lord's searchlight exposing his hidden motives.

[28]If a king is kind, honest, and fair, his kingdom stands secure.

[29]The glory of young men is their strength; of old men, their experience.

[30]Punishment that hurts chases evil from the heart.

CHAPTER 21

Just as water is turned into irrigation ditches, so the Lord directs the king's thoughts. He turns them wherever he wants to.

[2]We can justify our every deed, but God looks at our motives.

[3]God is more pleased when we are just and fair than when we give him gifts.

[4]Pride, lust, and evil actions are all sin.

[5]Steady plodding brings prosperity; hasty speculation brings poverty.

[6]Dishonest gain will never last, so why take the risk?

[7]Because the wicked are unfair, their violence boomerangs and destroys them.

[8]A man is known by his actions. An evil man lives an evil life; a good man lives a godly life.

[9]It is better to live in the corner of an attic than with a crabby woman in a lovely home.

[10]An evil man loves to harm others; being a good neighbor is out of his line.

[11]The wise man learns by listening; the simpleton can learn only by seeing scorners punished.

[12]God, the Righteous One, knows what is going on in the homes of the wicked and will bring the wicked to judgment.

[13]He who shuts his ears to the cries of the poor will be ignored in his own time of need.

[14]An angry man is silenced by giving him a gift!

[15]A good man loves justice, but it is a calamity to evil-doers.

[16]The man who strays away from common sense will end up dead!

[17]A man who loves pleasure becomes poor; wine and luxury are not the way to riches!

[18]The wicked will finally lose; the righteous will finally win.

[19]Better to live in the desert than with a quarrelsome, complaining woman.

[20]The wise man saves for the future, but the foolish man spends whatever he gets.

[21]The man who tries to be good, loving, and kind finds life, righteousness, and honor.

[22]The wise man conquers the strong man and levels his defenses.

[23]Keep your mouth closed and you'll stay out of trouble.

[24]Mockers are proud, haughty, and arrogant.

[25,26]The lazy man longs for many things, but his hands refuse to work. He is greedy to get, while the godly love to give!

[27]God loathes the gifts of evil men, especially if they are trying to bribe him!

[28]No one believes a liar, but everyone respects the words of an honest man.

[29]An evil man is stubborn, but a godly man will reconsider.

[30]No one, regardless of how shrewd or well-advised he is, can stand against the Lord.

[31]Go ahead and prepare for the conflict, but victory comes from God.

CHAPTER 22

If you must choose, take a good name rather than great riches; for to be held in loving esteem is better than silver and gold.

[2]The rich and the poor are alike before the Lord who made them all.

[3]A prudent man foresees the difficulties ahead and prepares for them; the simpleton goes blindly on and suffers the consequences.

20:27 God intends for our conscience to be like a searchlight that illuminates our life, helping us take our moral inventory. When exposing sin, the godly conscience doesn't condemn and blame; it doesn't permissively overlook sin either. Instead, it realizes that sin is not good for us and that it brings pain to others. When we feel that something is not right about our actions, our conscience is probably speaking to us, shining its light on our sin. Once we know that sin is there, then we can confess it and be forgiven.

21:5 Recovery is spelled P-A-T-I-E-N-C-E! We often feel as if we are plodding along, just one short step at a time. Sometimes we even have to go back to repeat steps we have already completed. To experience real change in our life will almost always be a slow process. It takes time to put the principles of recovery into practice. A "quick fix" recovery program will not have lasting results because it will never give us the time we need to make the steps an integral part of our life.

4 True humility and respect for the Lord lead
a man to riches, honor, and long life.
5 The rebel walks a thorny, treacherous road;
the man who values his soul will stay away.
6 Teach a child to choose the right path, and
when he is older, he will remain upon it.
7 Just as the rich rule the poor, so the borrower is servant to the lender.
8 The unjust tyrant will reap disaster, and his
reign of terror shall end.
9 Happy is the generous man, the one who
feeds the poor.
10 Throw out the mocker, and you will be rid
of tension, fighting, and quarrels.
11 He who values grace and truth is the
king's friend.
12 The Lord preserves the upright but ruins
the plans of the wicked.
13 The lazy man is full of excuses. "I can't go
to work!" he says. "If I go outside, I might
meet a lion in the street and be killed!"
14 A prostitute is a dangerous trap; those
cursed of God are caught in it.
15 A youngster's heart is filled with rebellion,
but punishment will drive it out of him.
16 He who gains by oppressing the poor or
by bribing the rich shall end in poverty.
17-19 Listen to this wise advice; follow it
closely, for it will do you good, and you can
pass it on to others: *Trust in the Lord.*
20,21 In the past, haven't I been right? Then
believe what I am telling you now and share
it with others.
22,23 Don't rob the poor and sick! For the
Lord is their defender. If you injure them, he
will punish you.
24,25 Keep away from angry, short-tempered
men, lest you learn to be like them and endanger your soul.
26,27 Unless you have the extra cash on hand,
don't countersign a note. Why risk everything you own? They'll even take your bed!
28 Do not move the ancient boundary
marks. That is stealing.
29 Do you know a hard-working man? He
shall be successful and stand before kings!

CHAPTER 23

When dining with a rich man, be on your
guard and don't stuff yourself, though it all
tastes so good; for he is trying to bribe you,
and no good is going to come of his invitation.
4,5 Don't weary yourself trying to get rich.
Why waste your time? For riches can disappear as though they had the wings of a bird!
6-8 Don't associate with evil men; don't long
for their favors and gifts. Their kindness is a
trick; they want to use you as their pawn. The
delicious food they serve will turn sour in
your stomach, and you will vomit it and have
to take back your words of appreciation for
their "kindness."
9 Don't waste your breath on a rebel. He will
despise the wisest advice.
10,11 Don't steal the land of defenseless orphans by moving their ancient boundary
marks, for their Redeemer is strong; he himself will accuse you.
12 Don't refuse to accept criticism; get all the
help you can.
13,14 Don't fail to correct your children; discipline won't hurt them! They won't die if you
use a stick on them! Punishment will keep
them out of hell.
15,16 My son, how I will rejoice if you become
a man of common sense. Yes, my heart will
thrill to your thoughtful, wise words.
17,18 Don't envy evil men but continue to
reverence the Lord all the time, for surely you
have a wonderful future ahead of you. There
is hope for you yet!
19-21 O my son, be wise and stay in God's
paths; don't carouse with drunkards and glut-

22:6 The most important part of being a parent is teaching our children to follow a godly life-style. If a child learns to respect authority and obey God while he is young, he will stay on that path when he is older. We might have grown up in a dysfunctional family where godly values were shunned or laughed at, and we can see how that led to our codependent life-style. But our children deserve better; they need all the advantages of a moral and loving family environment.

22:17-19 Here Solomon repeated one of his favorite themes in Proverbs: it is wise to put our trust in God. He alone is the source of perfect love and truth. It is only by surrendering to him that we can experience true love and discover how our life should be lived.

23:4-5 Perhaps the most common and unrecognized addiction in our culture today is greed or materialism. Many people weary themselves trying to get more and more money so that they can buy more things and do more things. The pleasure that money buys is temporary; it doesn't satisfy the longings of our heart. The wise learn the secret of delayed gratification and resist the greedy impulses that bring quick and fleeting pleasure. Instead they seek to get their needs met in healthy relationships with God and others.

tons, for they are on their way to poverty. And
remember that too much sleep clothes a man
with rags. 22Listen to your father's advice and
don't despise an old mother's experience.
23Get the facts at any price, and hold on
tightly to all the good sense you can get.
24,25The father of a godly man has cause for
joy—what pleasure a wise son is! So give your
parents joy!
26-28O my son, trust my advice—stay away
from prostitutes. For a prostitute is a deep and
narrow grave. Like a robber, she waits for her
victims as one after another become unfaithful to their wives.
29,30Whose heart is filled with anguish and
sorrow? Who is always fighting and quarreling? Who is the man with bloodshot eyes and
many wounds? It is the one who spends long
hours in the taverns, trying out new mixtures.
31Don't let the sparkle and the smooth taste of
strong wine deceive you. 32For in the end it
bites like a poisonous serpent; it stings like an
adder. 33You will see hallucinations and have
delirium tremens, and you will say foolish,
silly things that would embarrass you no end
when sober. 34You will stagger like a sailor
tossed at sea, clinging to a swaying mast.
35And afterwards you will say, "I didn't even
know it when they beat me up. . . . Let's go
and have another drink!"

CHAPTER 24

Don't envy godless men; don't even enjoy
their company. 2For they spend their days
plotting violence and cheating.
3,4Any enterprise is built by wise planning,
becomes strong through common sense, and
profits wonderfully by keeping abreast of the
facts.
5A wise man is mightier than a strong man.
Wisdom is mightier than strength.
6Don't go to war without wise guidance;
there is safety in many counselors.
7Wisdom is too much for a rebel. He'll not
be chosen as a counselor!
8To plan evil is as wrong as doing it.
9The rebel's schemes are sinful, and the
mocker is the scourge of all mankind.
10You are a poor specimen if you can't stand
the pressure of adversity.
11,12Rescue those who are unjustly sentenced to death; don't stand back and let
them die. Don't try to disclaim responsibility
by saying you didn't know about it. For God,
who knows all hearts, knows yours, and he
knows you knew! And he will reward everyone according to his deeds.
13,14My son, honey whets the appetite and
so does wisdom! When you enjoy becoming
wise, there is hope for you! A bright future lies
ahead!
15,16O evil man, leave the upright man alone
and quit trying to cheat him out of his rights.
Don't you know that this good man, though
you trip him up seven times, will each time
rise again? But one calamity is enough to lay
you low.
17Do not rejoice when your enemy meets
trouble. Let there be no gladness when he
falls— 18for the Lord may be displeased with
you and stop punishing him!
19,20Don't envy the wicked. Don't covet his
riches. For the evil man has no future; his
light will be snuffed out.

23:10-11 Unfortunately, those of us who were not adequately cared for as children often get taken advantage of as adults. Because we have been abandoned, neglected, or violated by people who were supposed to care for us, we have trouble discerning when it's safe to trust others. We often allow others to abuse our rights so we will be liked. We need help learning to set boundaries to protect us from people who might take advantage of our vulnerability. We need to look for godly people who will help us to draw healthy boundaries in our life.

23:26-35 Three thousand years haven't changed the fact that alcohol and sex are two of the most alluring and destructive addictions. They promise pleasure and escape from our troubles, but in the end they release a poison of shame and embarrassment. The only real escape from our troubles, including alcohol abuse and sexual sin, is Jesus Christ. When we turn our life over to him and turn from our sins, addictions, and dependencies, we are freed to pursue a normal life-style. The temptations will still be there, but now we have God working with us to help us resist them. He will help us to persevere in our recovery program.

24:8 This verse is not saying that planning and doing evil are the same thing. But evil actions are born of wrong motives. It is wise to take moral inventory, not just of our actions, but also of our motives. Confessing a sinful action is like pulling a weed but leaving the roots; it will reappear in time. Confessing a sinful motive is like pulling a weed out by its roots; the source of the trouble is gone.

24:15-16 Recovery is a process of being restored again and again. Though we may be tripped up by sin or fall down many times, we will be considered righteous if we rise again and try to learn our lesson. God is forgiving and patient with us in our failings and is quick to help us back to our feet.

[21,22]My son, watch your step before the Lord and the king, and don't associate with radicals. For you will go down with them to sudden disaster, and who knows where it all will end?

[23]It is wrong to sentence the poor and let the rich go free. [24]He who says to the wicked, "You are innocent," shall be cursed by many people of many nations; [25]but blessings shall be showered on those who rebuke sin fearlessly.

[26]It is an honor to receive a frank reply.

[27]Develop your business first before building your house.

[28,29]Don't testify spitefully against an innocent neighbor. Why lie about him? Don't say, "Now I can pay him back for all his meanness to me!"

[30,31]I walked by the field of a certain lazy fellow and saw that it was overgrown with thorns; it was covered with weeds, and its walls were broken down. [32,33]Then, as I looked, I learned this lesson:

"A little extra sleep,
A little more slumber,
A little folding of the hands to rest"

[34]means that poverty will break in upon you suddenly like a robber and violently like a bandit.

CHAPTER 25

Wisdom for Leaders

These proverbs of Solomon were discovered and copied by the aides of King Hezekiah of Judah:

[2,3]It is God's privilege to conceal things, and the king's privilege to discover and invent. You cannot understand the height of heaven, the size of the earth, or all that goes on in the king's mind!

[4,5]When you remove dross from silver, you have sterling ready for the silversmith. When you remove corrupt men from the king's court, his reign will be just and fair.

[6,7]Don't demand an audience with the king as though you were some powerful prince. It is better to wait for an invitation rather than to be sent back to the end of the line, publicly disgraced!

[8-10]Don't be hot-headed and rush to court! You may start something you can't finish and go down before your neighbor in shameful defeat. So discuss the matter with him privately. Don't tell anyone else, lest he accuse you of slander and you can't withdraw what you said.

[11]Timely advice is as lovely as gold apples in a silver basket.

[12]It is a badge of honor to accept valid criticism.

[13]A faithful employee is as refreshing as a cool day in the hot summertime.

[14]One who doesn't give the gift he promised is like a cloud blowing over a desert without dropping any rain.

[15]Be patient and you will finally win, for a soft tongue can break hard bones.

[16]Do you like honey? Don't eat too much of it, or it will make you sick!

[17]Don't visit your neighbor too often, or you will outwear your welcome!

[18]Telling lies about someone is as harmful as hitting him with an axe, or wounding him with a sword, or shooting him with a sharp arrow.

[19]Putting confidence in an unreliable man is like chewing with a sore tooth, or trying to run on a broken foot.

[20]Being happy-go-lucky around a person whose heart is heavy is as bad as stealing his jacket in cold weather or rubbing salt in his wounds.

[21,22]If your enemy is hungry, give him food! If he is thirsty, give him something to drink! This will make him feel ashamed of himself, and God will reward you.

24:30-34 Just as financial poverty comes to those who are lazy, emotional impoverishment comes to those who neglect to work on themselves. As we work on our life, weeding out destructive patterns and sowing the principles of recovery, we will reap a harvest of growth and recovery. Those of us who are lazy, however, will find our soul to be overgrown with weeds.

25:17 We have all known "cling-ons," people who cling to anyone who seems to care for them. Generally, they have been deprived of understanding, love, and respect. The "clingee" ends up feeling suffocated and pulls away, which confirms the cling-on's original insecurity. New and loving relationships in themselves don't make up for our past negative relationships. Recovery from childhood deprivations is a process that must also include working through past issues. Otherwise, our new relationships will follow the same destructive patterns as those in the past.

25:20 People who are troubled need empathy, not just carefree attempts to make their sadness go away. By showing that we understand and care about their feelings, we comfort them and give them the strength to make needed changes in their lives.

[23]As surely as a wind from the north brings cold, just as surely a retort causes anger!

[24]It is better to live in a corner of an attic than in a beautiful home with a cranky, quarrelsome woman.

[25]Good news from far away is like cold water to the thirsty.

[26]If a godly man compromises with the wicked, it is like polluting a fountain or muddying a spring.

[27]Just as it is harmful to eat too much honey, so also it is bad for men to think about all the honors they deserve!

[28]A man without self-control is as defenseless as a city with broken-down walls.

CHAPTER 26

Honor doesn't go with fools any more than snow with summertime or rain with harvesttime!

[2]An undeserved curse has no effect. Its intended victim will be no more harmed by it than by a sparrow or swallow flitting through the sky.

[3]Guide a horse with a whip, a donkey with a bridle, and a rebel with a rod to his back!

[4,5]When arguing with a rebel, don't use foolish arguments as he does, or you will become as foolish as he is! Prick his conceit with silly replies!

[6]To trust a rebel to convey a message is as foolish as cutting off your feet and drinking poison!

[7]In the mouth of a fool a proverb becomes as useless as a paralyzed leg.

[8]Honoring a rebel will backfire like a stone tied to a slingshot!

[9]A rebel will misapply an illustration so that its point will no more be felt than a thorn in the hand of a drunkard.

[10]The master may get better work from an untrained apprentice than from a skilled rebel!

[11]As a dog returns to his vomit, so a fool repeats his folly.

[12]There is one thing worse than a fool, and that is a man who is conceited.

[13]The lazy man won't go out and work. "There might be a lion outside!" he says. [14]He sticks to his bed like a door to its hinges! [15]He is too tired even to lift his food from his dish to his mouth! [16]Yet in his own opinion he is smarter than seven wise men.

[17]Yanking a dog's ears is no more foolish than interfering in an argument that isn't any of your business.

[18,19]A man who is caught lying to his neighbor and says, "I was just fooling," is like a madman throwing around firebrands, arrows, and death!

[20]Fire goes out for lack of fuel, and tensions disappear when gossip stops.

[21]A quarrelsome man starts fights as easily as a match sets fire to paper.

[22]Gossip is a dainty morsel eaten with great relish.

[23]Pretty words may hide a wicked heart, just as a pretty glaze covers a common clay pot.

[24-26]A man with hate in his heart may sound pleasant enough, but don't believe him; for he is cursing you in his heart. Though he pretends to be so kind, his hatred will finally come to light for all to see.

[27]The man who sets a trap for others will get caught in it himself. Roll a boulder down on someone, and it will roll back and crush you.

[28]Flattery is a form of hatred and wounds cruelly.

CHAPTER 27

Don't brag about your plans for tomorrow—wait and see what happens.

[2]Don't praise yourself; let others do it!

[3]A rebel's frustrations are heavier than sand and rocks.

[4]Jealousy is more dangerous and cruel than anger.

[5]Open rebuke is better than hidden love!

[6]Wounds from a friend are better than kisses from an enemy!

[7]Even honey seems tasteless to a man who is full; but if he is hungry, he'll eat anything!

[8]A man who strays from home is like a bird that wanders from its nest.

[9]Friendly suggestions are as pleasant as perfume.

26:11 We almost invariably repeat the patterns of the past; our old problems revisit us again and again. It is easy to slip back into our addictions; that is why we need to be diligent in our recovery. When we relax in our recovery program, we are setting ourself up for a relapse into our old lifestyle. Only through perseverance will we be able to overcome our dependencies.

27:10 Friends are an important resource in recovery. We need people to whom we can be accountable and to whom we can turn in times of need. And we need them to be honest with us and have our best interests at heart. Just as we want our friends to stick by us in times of crisis, we should also support our friends when they need our help. If we are there for others, we will have our own support network in place whenever we need help.

10 Never abandon a friend—either yours or your father's. Then you won't need to go to a distant relative for help in your time of need.

11 My son, how happy I will be if you turn out to be sensible! It will be a public honor to me.

12 A sensible man watches for problems ahead and prepares to meet them. The simpleton never looks and suffers the consequences.

13 The world's poorest credit risk is the man who agrees to pay a stranger's debts.

14 If you shout a pleasant greeting to a friend too early in the morning, he will count it as a curse!

15 A constant dripping on a rainy day and a cranky woman are much alike! 16 You can no more stop her complaints than you can stop the wind or hold onto anything with oil-slick hands.

17 A friendly discussion is as stimulating as the sparks that fly when iron strikes iron.

18 A workman may eat from the orchard he tends; anyone should be rewarded who protects another's interests.

19 A mirror reflects a man's face, but what he is really like is shown by the kind of friends he chooses.

20 Ambition and death are alike in this: neither is ever satisfied.

21 The purity of silver and gold can be tested in a crucible, but a man is tested by his reaction to men's praise.

22 You can't separate a rebel from his foolishness though you crush him to powder.

23,24 Riches can disappear fast. And the king's crown doesn't stay in his family forever—so watch your business interests closely. Know the state of your flocks and your herds; 25-27 then there will be lambs' wool enough for clothing and goats' milk enough for food for all your household after the hay is harvested, and the new crop appears, and the mountain grasses are gathered in.

CHAPTER 28

The wicked flee when no one is chasing them! But the godly are bold as lions!

2 When there is moral rot within a nation, its government topples easily; but with honest, sensible leaders there is stability.

3 When a poor man oppresses those even poorer, he is like an unexpected flood sweeping away their last hope.

4 To complain about the law is to praise wickedness. To obey the law is to fight evil.

5 Evil men don't understand the importance of justice, but those who follow the Lord are much concerned about it.

6 Better to be poor and honest than rich and a cheater.

7 Young men who are wise obey the law; a son who is a member of a lawless gang is a shame to his father.

8 Income from exploiting the poor will end up in the hands of someone who pities them.

9 God doesn't listen to the prayers of those who flout the law.

10 A curse on those who lead astray the godly. But men who encourage the upright to do good shall be given a worthwhile reward.

11 Rich men are conceited, but their real poverty is evident to the poor.

12 When the godly are successful, everyone is glad. When the wicked succeed, everyone is sad.

13 A man who refuses to admit his mistakes can never be successful. But if he confesses and forsakes them, he gets another chance.

14 Blessed is the man who reveres God, but the man who doesn't care is headed for serious trouble.

15 A wicked ruler is as dangerous to the poor as a lion or bear attacking them.

27:20 The ambition referred to here is that of lust or greed. This includes things like sexual gratification, materialism, and greed for power or prestige. Although gratifying these desires can be pleasurable, it is not fulfilling in the long run because these are false substitutes for deeper needs, such as love, intimacy, and security. As time passes we will need more and more of our "drug" of choice to make us feel good, and we will gradually become enslaved to our impulses.

27:21 One way to evaluate our self-perception is to note our response when others praise us. If we discount compliments, this probably means that we suffer from a poor self-image. If we gloat in the praise we receive, we probably have a self-perception that is inflated. We often do this to cover up underlying low self-esteem. The healthy response to praise is to receive it graciously and to balance it with a humble awareness of our weaknesses.

28:13 This verse contains wisdom essential to recovery and change. We must proceed with recovery by honestly assessing our mistakes, confessing our wrongs to one another, resolving to avoid such mistakes in the future, and asking God to change our heart. It is a humbling thing to admit and confess our sin, and it is alarming to commit to change, but that's the only way we can recover from our dependencies and get another chance at life.

[16]Only a stupid prince will oppress his people, but a king will have a long reign if he hates dishonesty and bribes.

[17]A murderer's conscience will drive him into hell. Don't stop him!

[18]Good men will be rescued from harm, but cheaters will be destroyed.

[19]Hard work brings prosperity; playing around brings poverty.

[20]The man who wants to do right will get a rich reward. But the man who wants to get rich quick will quickly fail.

[21]Giving preferred treatment to rich people is a clear case of selling one's soul for a piece of bread.

[22]Trying to get rich quick is evil and leads to poverty.

[23]In the end, people appreciate frankness more than flattery.

[24]A man who robs his parents and says, "What's wrong with that?" is no better than a murderer.

[25]Greed causes fighting; trusting God leads to prosperity.

[26]A man is a fool to trust himself! But those who use God's wisdom are safe.

[27]If you give to the poor, your needs will be supplied! But a curse upon those who close their eyes to poverty.

[28]When the wicked prosper, good men go away; when the wicked meet disaster, good men return.

CHAPTER 29

The man who is often reproved but refuses to accept criticism will suddenly be broken and never have another chance.

[2]With good men in authority, the people rejoice; but with the wicked in power, they groan.

[3]A wise son makes his father happy, but a lad who hangs around with prostitutes disgraces him.

[4]A just king gives stability to his nation, but one who demands bribes destroys it.

[5,6]Flattery is a trap; evil men are caught in it, but good men stay away and sing for joy.

[7]The good man knows the poor man's rights; the godless don't care.

[8]Fools start fights everywhere while wise men try to keep peace.

[9]There's no use arguing with a fool. He only rages and scoffs, and tempers flare.

[10]The godly pray for those who long to kill them.

[11]A rebel shouts in anger; a wise man holds his temper in and cools it.

[12]A wicked ruler will have wicked aides on his staff.

[13]Rich and poor are alike in this: each depends on God for light.

[14]A king who is fair to the poor shall have a long reign.

[15]Scolding and spanking a child helps him to learn. Left to himself, he brings shame to his mother.

[16]When rulers are wicked, their people are too; but good men will live to see the tyrant's downfall.

[17]Discipline your son and he will give you happiness and peace of mind.

[18]Where there is ignorance of God, crime runs wild; but what a wonderful thing it is for a nation to know and keep his laws.

[19]Sometimes mere words are not enough—discipline is needed. For the words may not be heeded.

[20]There is more hope for a fool than for a man of quick temper.

[21]Pamper a servant from childhood, and he will expect you to treat him as a son!

[22]A hot-tempered man starts fights and gets into all kinds of trouble.

[23]Pride ends in a fall, while humility brings honor.

[24]A man who assists a thief must really hate himself! For he knows the consequence but does it anyway.

[25]Fear of man is a dangerous trap, but to trust in God means safety.

29:15, 17 Children cannot grow up to be responsible adults if they are never disciplined, corrected, and held accountable for their actions. Children who are not held accountable fail to learn how to protect themselves from the negative consequences of sin. Children who are punished inconsistently, in anger, or in the absence of a loving relationship will become rebellious toward authority and will resist accountability (see 22:15; 23:13-14). We must be consistent and fair in punishing our children if they are to reap the benefits of discipline.

29:23 Pride always sets us up for a fall. Pride tells us, "I'm strong; I don't need anyone's help." It blinds us to our weaknesses and leads us away from seeking the people and help we need. Humility says, "I do need improvement; could you help me?" Those of us who maintain a humble perspective, realizing that we are weak and vulnerable, will look for the help and support needed for a successful recovery. Humility will protect us from the devastation of a relapse.

26 Do you want justice? Don't fawn on the
judge, but ask the Lord for it!
27 The good hate the badness of the wicked.
The wicked hate the goodness of the
good.

CHAPTER 30

Wise Sayings of Agur

These are the messages of Agur, son of Jakeh, addressed to Ithiel and Ucal:

2 I am tired out, O God, and ready to die. I
am too stupid even to call myself a human
being! 3 I cannot understand man, let alone
God. 4 Who else but God goes back and forth
to heaven? Who else holds the wind in his
fists and wraps up the oceans in his cloak?
Who but God has created the world? If there
is any other, what is his name—and his Son's
name—if you know it?
5 Every word of God proves true. He defends
all who come to him for protection. 6 Do not
add to his words, lest he rebuke you, and you
be found a liar.
7 O God, I beg two favors from you before I
die: 8 First, help me never to tell a lie. Second,
give me neither poverty nor riches! Give me
just enough to satisfy my needs! 9 For if I grow
rich, I may become content without God.
And if I am too poor, I may steal and thus
insult God's holy name.
10 Never falsely accuse a man to his employer, lest he curse you for your sin.
11,12 There are those who curse their father
and mother and feel themselves faultless despite their many sins. 13,14 They are proud beyond description, arrogant, disdainful. They
devour the poor with teeth as sharp as
knives!
15,16 There are two things never satisfied, like
a leech forever craving more: no, three things!
no, four! Hell, the barren womb, a barren
desert, fire.
17 A man who mocks his father and despises
his mother shall have his eye plucked out by
ravens and eaten by vultures.
18,19 There are three things too wonderful for
me to understand—no, four!

How an eagle glides through the sky.
How a serpent crawls upon a rock.
How a ship finds its way across the
heaving ocean.
The growth of love between a man and
a girl.

20 There is another thing too: how a prostitute can sin and then say, "What's wrong with
that?"
21-23 There are three things that make the
earth tremble—no, four it cannot stand:

A slave who becomes a king.
A rebel who prospers.
A bitter woman when she finally marries.
A servant girl who marries her mistress'
husband.

24-28 There are four things that are small but
unusually wise:

Ants: they aren't strong, but store up food
for the winter.
Cliff badgers: delicate little animals who
protect themselves by living among the
rocks.
The locusts: though they have no leader,
they stay together in swarms.
The lizards: they are easy to catch and
kill, yet are found even in king's palaces!

29-31 There are three stately monarchs in the
earth—no, four:

The lion, king of the animals. He won't
turn aside for anyone.
The peacock.
The male goat.
A king as he leads his army.

32 If you have been a fool by being proud or

30:5 The words of God, including these principles in Proverbs, are true and offer protection to those who live by them. Living by God's truth demands that we honestly admit our need for God's wisdom and that we seek to live by it. This will not be easy, and it probably won't be popular. But walking in God's light will place us under God's direction and care, a necessity for any successful recovery.

30:11-12 It is easier to blame others for our problems than it is to admit them. Many of our problems do have roots in the failures of others. Our parents may have failed to love and discipline us as they should have. But these problems have been compounded by bad decisions that we have made. Our sufferings are usually caused by a combination of factors, including the sins of others and sins of our own. We cannot change the failures of others; blame does nothing to speed our recovery. We can, however, change our own attitudes and actions that have perpetuated the suffering. Maturity comes as we take responsibility for our problems by forgiving those who have wronged us and by seeking forgiveness for our own sins.

plotting evil, don't brag about it—cover your
mouth with your hand in shame.
33As the churning of cream yields butter,
and a blow to the nose causes bleeding, so
anger causes quarrels.

CHAPTER 31

Wise Sayings of Lemuel

These are the wise sayings of King Lemuel of Massa, taught to him at his mother's knee:

2O my son, whom I have dedicated to the
Lord, 3do not spend your time with women—
the royal pathway to destruction.
4And it is not for kings, O Lemuel, to drink
wine and whiskey. 5For if they drink they may
forget their duties and be unable to give justice to those who are oppressed. 6,7Hard liquor
is for sick men at the brink of death, and wine
for those in deep depression. Let them drink
to forget their poverty and misery.
8You should defend those who cannot help
themselves. 9Yes, speak up for the poor and
helpless, and see that they get justice.

A Truly Good Wife

10If you can find a truly good wife, she is worth
more than precious gems! 11Her husband can
trust her, and she will richly satisfy his needs.
12She will not hinder him but help him all her
life. 13She finds wool and flax and busily spins
it. 14She buys imported foods brought by ship
from distant ports. 15She gets up before dawn
to prepare breakfast for her household and
plans the day's work for her servant girls. 16She
goes out to inspect a field and buys it; with her
own hands she plants a vineyard. 17She is
energetic, a hard worker, 18and watches for
bargains. She works far into the night!
19,20She sews for the poor and generously
helps those in need. 21She has no fear of winter for her household, for she has made warm
clothes for all of them. 22She also upholsters
with finest tapestry; her own clothing is beautifully made—a purple gown of pure linen.
23Her husband is well known, for he sits in the
council chamber with the other civic leaders.
24She makes belted linen garments to sell to
the merchants.
25She is a woman of strength and dignity
and has no fear of old age. 26When she speaks,
her words are wise, and kindness is the rule
for everything she says. 27She watches carefully all that goes on throughout her household and is never lazy. 28Her children stand
and bless her; so does her husband. He
praises her with these words: 29"There are
many fine women in the world, but you are
the best of them all!"
30Charm can be deceptive and beauty
doesn't last, but a woman who fears and rev-
erences God shall be greatly praised. 31Praise
her for the many fine things she does. These
good deeds of hers shall bring her honor and
recognition from people of importance.

31:10-31 Some women compare themselves to the wife in this chapter and feel inadequate. Actually, the woman of Proverbs 31 represents a description of the ideal wife. No wife ever has or ever will completely measure up to all these standards. A wife should not fall into the perfectionist's trap of striving to measure up to these ideal standards. This will inevitably lead to frustration and despair. Instead, a woman should accept herself for who she is and commit to a process of allowing God to transform her more and more into his likeness. As she grows to be more like him, she will exhibit naturally many of the characteristics of this "ideal wife."

insights INTO OUR RELATIONSHIPS WITH GOD AND OTHERS

As we see in **Proverbs 1:29-33,** many people choose to live life as they please. They give in to their sinful impulses without thinking about God's will for them. It is foolish to fall to temptations just to feel good or escape emotional pain. That path will only lead to addiction and fear. It will also lead us away from God, the only one who can really satisfy our deepest needs. The path to secure freedom and peace is narrow and requires listening to God's wisdom and exercising our self-control. Recovery is a process, not a "quick fix."

According to **Proverbs 10:4-5,** there is little hope for people who are not willing to work hard. Recovery from damaged emotions or addictive patterns is hard work. It requires persevering through each step in the process. But in recovery we will discover that effort alone is not sufficient. We need the faith to reach out and seize the opportunities that God brings our way. God shows his grace and goodness to us by providing chances for us to exercise our faith. He will also provide us with his spiritual support, wisdom, and encouragement as we seek to obey his will for our life.

Proverbs 12:25 reminds us of the value of encouragement. When people are feeling troubled or burdened, few things can help them more than a few words of encouragement. We don't necessarily need to give them a pep talk or an it's-gonna-be-OK speech. Just letting them know we are there for them and that we love them is all the encouraging talk they probably need. Real comfort comes from feeling understood, not from hollow words and clichés.

In **Proverbs 13:17** we are reminded of the importance of reliable communication. It is an essential ingredient of any successful recovery program. We need to be honest with ourself, God, and those who are helping us. If we hold something back, others will not be able to help us completely. Also, if we keep an area of our addiction hidden, it will ruin the progress we have already made. Just as a war can't be won with inaccurate intelligence reports, giving inaccurate information in our recovery will keep us from conquering our dependencies.

We see in **Proverbs 14:2** that sin brings dishonor to God. This is one of the most important motivations we have for seeking recovery from our dependencies. If we are truly seeking after God, we will want to obey and honor him. Like children who want to please their parents, we should want to recover so we can please God, our heavenly Father.

insights FOR EVERYDAY LIFE AND RECOVERY

The words in **Proverbs 10:24** speak of a self-fulfilling prophecy: what we expect to happen will happen. How we look at life often affects what actually happens in life. If we assume that our recovery is hopeless, we have already doomed our recovery program to failure. But if we approach our recovery with a positive outlook, trusting in God to see us through the process, our recovery will progress smoothly.

Proverbs 13:11 emphasizes the importance of hard work. And just as it can produce material riches, it also can produce spiritual riches. Yet few are willing to persevere through pain and difficulty until the job is done. It is easier to roll the dice and go for the "quick fix." There are no short-cuts to recovery or maturity. It is a long path with many small steps that need to be taken over and over again.

As we see in **Proverbs 13:16,** it is wise to process our thoughts and feelings before we act (see also 14:8). Acting on impulses can get us into trouble. Those struggling with addictions to things like drugs, food, sex, work, or shopping know this well. These kinds of things start when we give in to impulses that make us feel good at the moment. The only problem is that the moment doesn't last because the impulsive behaviors don't meet our real needs. It is important to evaluate our real needs and find constructive ways to meet those needs so we can get past our addictive behaviors and find peace.

One thing in life is sure: we will face constant change. As we live in our changing world, it is important that we learn to accept the things that we cannot change. **Proverbs 14:30** reminds us of how important it is for us to find emotional serenity in this life. This is impossible if we fail to accept the things that we cannot control. We cannot change our past, but we must make peace with it by seeking to be forgiven and to forgive. It is easier to remain a victim of our past and seethe with jealousy over those who were given advantages that we weren't given. Yet as we are freed from our past, we can put more energy into making positive changes for the future.

The eyes and ears that Solomon was talking about in **Proverbs 20:12** are known to us as perception and understanding. Accurately sensing what is going on within us and around us is the beginning of recovery from an addictive or unhealthy life-style in which pain and feelings were avoided or repressed. Only by allowing the painful realities of our life to touch us will we be able to admit we need help and begin the healing process of recovery.

We would be wise to listen to the warning in **Proverbs 20:25.** Impulsive promises to change don't work because they are not made wholeheartedly. They come from people who know what they should do, but don't really want to change. Counting the cost involves seriously examining what the promise requires of us and then being willing to fulfill the promise. If we don't want to change, but realize that we probably need to, it is helpful to ask God to make us willing to change. It is only when we totally want to follow through with our promises that we will be able to.

We often look with envy at people who indulge themselves in sinful pleasures. **Proverbs 23:17-18** warns us to avoid the temptation to do this. Such people do whatever they choose without regard for how their actions affect others (see 24:1, 19-20). In the short term they have an easy and pleasurable life. Those who live righteously, however, have it harder initially. But as they move along the pathway of mature living, they have the opportunity to develop a more fulfilling and meaningful life. There is also an eternal perspective to be considered: those who follow God will receive blessings in heaven, and those who live for themselves will face judgment.

ECCLESIASTES

THE BIG PICTURE

A. PROLOGUE: THE FUTILITY OF LIFE (1:1-2)
B. PROOF OF THE FUTILITY OF LIFE IN A FALLEN WORLD (1:3–6:12)
C. COPING WITH LIFE IN A FALLEN WORLD (7:1–12:8)
D. EPILOGUE: LIFE IN A FALLEN WORLD BEGINS AND ENDS WITH GOD (12:9-14)

Sometimes the events of life just don't fit together into a coherent, meaningful pattern. How can we make sense of a past filled with sexual abuse? Why did God allow us to grow up in an alcoholic home? How does being the victim of physical abuse play a part in God's plan? All of these questions are multiplied when we see how our painful past has led us to make bad decisions. We see that we have perpetuated the destruction by attempting to compensate for being sinned against in our developmental years.

The Preacher in Ecclesiastes was searching for the key that would unlock the door to life's meaning. The first part of Ecclesiastes gives us the Preacher's conclusion: "under the sun," that is, on this side of eternity, some things just don't make sense. After recognizing this basic truth, he advised that we should enjoy life the best we can considering the circumstances. We are called to recognize that life is God's good gift to us. The Preacher's final conclusion, which admonishes us to reverence God and obey his commands, puts life into perspective. It creates the necessary boundaries to hold us back from a life of selfish hedonism, while still allowing us to enjoy the good things in life.

Since life is God's good gift to be enjoyed, not a puzzle to be solved, Ecclesiastes helps us cope with our humanity. There will be some things in life that, this side of eternity, we will never be able to understand. Rather than attempting to understand the inscrutable events that make up our life, the Preacher counsels us to enjoy the parts of life that do make sense and to entrust the rest to God's care.

THE BOTTOM LINE

PURPOSE: To show us that life is God's good gift to be responsibly enjoyed, not a puzzle that must be solved. AUTHOR: Attributed to Solomon, although the Hebrew text doesn't clearly name him as the author. AUDIENCE: The people of Israel. DATE WRITTEN: Possibly written toward the end of Solomon's life, around 935 B.C. SETTING: The writer evaluates what he has done in life and ponders the relative value of his activities and accomplishments. KEY VERSE: "Here is my final conclusion: fear God and obey his commandments, for this is the entire duty of man" (12:13). SPECIAL FEATURES: The book uses a variety of literary forms: poems, proverbs, parables, pointed questions, and couplets.

RECOVERY THEMES

The Paralysis of Analysis: The Preacher's search for meaning was almost like a scientific experiment. He seemed desperate to explain life's ambiguities, but he tried every human solution available before finally turning it all over to God. We need to beware of the paralysis that can set in when we get caught up in analyzing our situation in life and seeking human solutions to our problems. It's too easy to get lost on the way and to never reach the right conclusion: our life and will must be turned over to God. Only then will we be able to make true progress in recovery.

Some Things Will Never Make Sense: The Preacher's diligent search for understanding and meaning was ultimately futile. There are some things in life that we will never understand. We all recognize that we suffer for our bad decisions, but it is also true that our failures were influenced by a past that we couldn't control. Our suffering, both past and present, just doesn't seem to be fair in an ultimate sense. We need to stop trying to make sense of it all. We need to take responsible steps toward recovery and seek God's help now. Someday, in eternity, it will make sense. We need to recognize, however, that in this life some things will remain a puzzle. We can only trust that God will love and care for us through the difficult and sometimes meaningless problems we are forced to deal with in this life.

Only God Can Fill Our Emptiness: The Preacher provides us with an accurate picture of the emptiness of our search for answers and meaning apart from God. All around us, people are still pursuing the same empty search, looking at wealth, pleasure, and success as the answer to life's problems. We may have postponed or been sidetracked in our recovery by the same kinds of futile searching. Solomon's experience shows us that until we turn our life over to God, our search will lead only to emptiness. God is the only one who can fill our restless and searching heart.

Life Is to Be Enjoyed Responsibly: The Preacher assessed life very honestly. He was not down on life—only on the futility of seeking happiness and fulfillment apart from God. The Preacher affirmed the value of knowledge, relationships, work, and even pleasure as long as they were put in their proper place. We are to seek balance in our life, knowing that meaning can only be found through a relationship with God. Our recovery is enhanced when we see that life is a gift from God. When he is at the center of all we do—including our recovery—we will find joy during the short time we are given to live under the sun.

CHAPTER 1

Is Life Worth Living?

The author: Solomon of Jerusalem, King David's son, "The Preacher."

[2]In my opinion, nothing is worthwhile; everything is futile. [3-7]For what does a man get for all his hard work?

Generations come and go, but it makes no difference. The sun rises and sets and hurries around to rise again. The wind blows south and north, here and there, twisting back and forth, getting nowhere. The rivers run into the sea, but the sea is never full, and the water returns again to the rivers and flows again to
the sea . . . [8-11]everything is unutterably weary and tiresome. No matter how much we see, we are never satisfied; no matter how much we hear, we are not content.

History merely repeats itself. Nothing is truly new; it has all been done or said before. What can you point to that is new? How do you know it didn't exist long ages ago? We don't remember what happened in those former times, and in the future generations no one will remember what we have done back here.

The Futility of Wisdom

[12-15]I, the Preacher, was king of Israel, living in
Jerusalem. And I applied myself to search for

1:2 Life and its various activities are not meaningless in an absolute sense. They are only meaningless or futile when we make them the ultimate goal and end of our existence. For example, work is not wholly worthless (2:17-24); elsewhere in Ecclesiastes the Preacher encourages us to enjoy our work (3:9-11, 22). But work is meaningless if we try to use it to make sense out of life. Only God can give true meaning to all our activities "under the sun."

1:3-11 The Preacher began his search for meaning in life by looking at the world of nature. In the ancient world, people looked to nature to reveal life's mysteries, since it was the arena in which the gods expressed themselves. He concluded from nature that life is a wearying grind, filled with seemingly endless repetition. Even when we make God the center of our life, we cannot escape the natural grind of life. Yet as we seek to follow God's will for our life, our godly perspective lets us see beyond the bounds of our natural world. This will help us cope with the difficulties of daily life.

understanding about everything in the universe. I discovered that the lot of man, which
God has dealt to him, is not a happy one. It is
all foolishness, chasing the wind. What is
wrong cannot be righted; it is water over the
dam; and there is no use thinking of what
might have been.

16-18 I said to myself, "Look, I am better educated than any of the kings before me in
Jerusalem. I have greater wisdom and knowledge." So I worked hard to be wise instead of
foolish—but now I realize that even this was
like chasing the wind. For the more my wisdom, the more my grief; to increase knowledge only increases distress.

CHAPTER 2

The Futility of Pleasure

I said to myself, "Come now, be merry; enjoy
yourself to the full." But I found that this, too,
was futile. For it is silly to be laughing all the
time; what good does it do?

3 So after a lot of thinking, I decided to try
the road of drink, while still holding steadily
to my course of seeking wisdom.

Next I changed my course again and followed the path of folly, so that I could experience the only happiness most men have
throughout their lives.

4-6 Then I tried to find fulfillment by inaugurating a great public works program: homes,
vineyards, gardens, parks, and orchards for
myself, and reservoirs to hold the water to
irrigate my plantations.

7,8 Next I bought slaves, both men and
women, and others were born within my
household. I also bred great herds and flocks,
more than any of the kings before me. I collected silver and gold as taxes from many
kings and provinces.

In the cultural arts, I organized men's and
women's choirs and orchestras.

And then there were my many beautiful
concubines.

9 So I became greater than any of the kings
in Jerusalem before me, and with it all I remained clear-eyed, so that I could evaluate all
these things. 10 Anything I wanted I took and
did not restrain myself from any joy. I even
found great pleasure in hard work. This pleasure was, indeed, my only reward for all my
labors.

The Futility of Work

11 But as I looked at everything I had tried, it
was all so useless, a chasing of the wind, and
there was nothing really worthwhile anywhere.

12 Now I began a study of the comparative
virtues of wisdom and folly, and anyone else
would come to the same conclusion I did—
13,14 that wisdom is of more value than foolishness, just as light is better than darkness; for
the wise man sees, while the fool is blind. And
yet I noticed that there was one thing that
happened to wise and foolish alike—15 just as
the fool will die, so will I. So of what value is
all my wisdom? Then I realized that even
wisdom is futile. 16 For the wise and fool both
die, and in the days to come both will be long
forgotten. 17 So now I hate life because it is all
so irrational; all is foolishness, chasing the
wind.

18 And I am disgusted about this—that I
must leave the fruits of all my hard work to
others. 19 And who can tell whether my son

1:12-15 The Preacher continued his search for meaning through the way of wisdom. Instead of finding meaning, however, he only discovered the limits of his wisdom and the pain that wisdom brings. Not only is our wisdom limited, it also often brings us pain. Wisdom brings sorrow, and knowledge brings grief (1:18) because we are that much more in touch with the realities of our fallen world. As we face recovery, we are not surprised by this. We have experienced many of the harsh realities of life. True wisdom ultimately leads us back to God. Only by trusting God and obeying his will for us will we find any meaningful direction and joy in this life.

2:1-3 The Preacher tried the pleasure escapes of laughter and alcohol. Had drugs been available in his day as they are now, he may also have included them on his list. But these things ultimately couldn't satisfy his search for meaning. Seeking to escape our painful existence through pleasure leads to substance abuse and addiction. Only God can give us the strength and purpose for a meaningful life. We need to trust him and patiently follow his program for healthy living.

2:4-11 The Preacher next tried to find meaning by building a personal empire. After experiencing incredible success, however, he concluded that it did not give ultimate meaning to his life; all the pieces of life's puzzle didn't fit together. Many of us have made our goals for success the basis for our meaning in life. We are driven to higher and higher goals only to find emptiness at each new success. Many of us even put off our recovery for fear that it might interfere with our career. We need to realize that true success can only be found in seeking God's help in our recovery. He alone is able to give meaning to life in our broken world.

will be a wise man or a fool? And yet all I have
will be given to him—how discouraging!
20-23So I turned in despair from hard work as
the answer to my search for satisfaction. For
though I spend my life searching for wisdom,
knowledge, and skill, I must leave all of it to
someone who hasn't done a day's work in his
life; he inherits all my efforts, free of charge.
This is not only foolish but unfair. So what
does a man get for all his hard work? Days full
of sorrow and grief, and restless, bitter nights.
It is all utterly ridiculous.

Pleasure Comes from God

24-26So I decided that there was nothing better
for a man to do than to enjoy his food and
drink and his job. Then I realized that even
this pleasure is from the hand of God. For
who can eat or enjoy apart from him? For
God gives those who please him wisdom,
knowledge, and joy; but if a sinner becomes
wealthy, God takes the wealth away from him
and gives it to those who please him. So here,
too, we see an example of foolishly chasing
the wind.

CHAPTER 3

A Proper Time for Everything

There is a right time for everything:

2A time to be born;
A time to die;
A time to plant;
A time to harvest;
3A time to kill;
A time to heal;
A time to destroy;
A time to rebuild;
4A time to cry;
A time to laugh;
A time to grieve;
A time to dance;
5A time for scattering stones;
A time for gathering stones;
A time to hug;
A time not to hug;
6A time to find;
A time to lose;
A time for keeping;
A time for throwing away;
7A time to tear;
A time to repair;
A time to be quiet;
A time to speak up;
8A time for loving;
A time for hating;
A time for war;
A time for peace.

God Is in Control

9What does one really get from hard work?
10I have thought about this in connection
with all the various kinds of work God has
given to mankind. 11Everything is appropriate
in its own time. But though God has planted
eternity in the hearts of men, even so, many
cannot see the whole scope of God's work
from beginning to end. 12So I conclude that,
first, there is nothing better for a man than to
be happy and to enjoy himself as long as he

2:24-26 The alternative to the neurotic commitment to work is the enjoyment of life as God's good gift. This includes enjoying our work, while not allowing it to become the key to meaning in our life. This is the first of the Preacher's admonitions to take life less seriously and enjoy it more. Life is too short to waste it on the treadmill of ever-increasing professional accomplishments. In the larger scheme of things, our accomplishments will not last. We need to take the time to enjoy the gifts that God does give.

3:1-8 To analyze each of these "times" individually would most likely miss the Preacher's point. These are figures of speech that present two opposite extremes that cover the entire spectrum between them. For instance, there is a time to be born and a time to die (3:2), but the emphasis is on the lifetime in between. There is a time for everything because God has set the times. That is, all of life is part of a well-orchestrated symphony for which God has written the music. An essential part of our recovery is seeking out God's plan for us and then following it.

3:12-15 Here the Preacher gives us a practical alternative to the desperate search for ultimate meaning in life. He calls us to a responsible enjoyment of life as God's good gift. The Preacher wants us to enjoy life more and to spend less time and energy trying to make sense of it all. Notice that 3:14 sets parameters around our enjoyment of life. Everything we do must be done with the recognition that God is in charge. We must act in ways that demonstrate our respect for him. This will prevent our enjoyment of life from becoming selfish hedonism.

4:9-12 Supportive friendships are absolutely necessary for our recovery. When we fall down, we need help in getting up again. If we stand alone, we are especially vulnerable to inner enemies. Building healthy relationships where there is mutual support is essential to a successful recovery. We must learn to trust others, to reach out to others, and to admit our need for support. This will give us added strength, wisdom, and protection from the attacks of our dependencies and compulsions.

can; [13]and second, that he should eat and drink and enjoy the fruits of his labors, for these are gifts from God.

[14]And I know this, that whatever God does is final—nothing can be added or taken from it; God's purpose in this is that man should fear the all-powerful God.

[15]Whatever is has been long ago; and whatever is going to be has been before; God brings to pass again what was in the distant past and disappeared.

[16]Moreover, I notice that throughout the earth justice is giving way to crime, and even the police courts are corrupt. [17]I said to myself, "In due season God will judge everything man does, both good and bad."

[18]And then I realized that God is letting the world go on its sinful way so that he can test mankind, and so that men themselves will see that they are no better than beasts. [19]For men and animals both breathe the same air, and both die. So mankind has no real advantage over the beasts; what an absurdity! [20]All go to one place—the dust from which they came and to which they must return. [21]For who can prove that the spirit of man goes upward and the spirit of animals goes downward into dust? [22]So I saw that there is nothing better for men than that they should be happy in their work, for that is what they are here for, and no one can bring them back to life to enjoy what will be in the future, so let them enjoy it now.

CHAPTER 4

Sadness in Life

Next I observed all the oppression and sadness throughout the earth—the tears of the oppressed, and no one helping them, while on the side of their oppressors were powerful allies. [2]So I felt that the dead were better off than the living. [3]And most fortunate of all are those who have never been born and have never seen all the evil and crime throughout the earth.

[4]Then I observed that the basic motive for success is the driving force of envy and jealousy! But this, too, is foolishness, chasing the wind. [5,6]The fool won't work and almost starves but feels that it is better to be lazy and barely get by, than to work hard, when in the long run it is all so futile.

[7]I also observed another piece of foolishness around the earth. [8]This is the case of a man who is quite alone, without a son or brother, yet he works hard to keep gaining more riches. And to whom will he leave it all,

D*enial*

READ ECCLESIASTES 3:16–4:1

Some of us avoid or cope with our own pain by trying to fix the world. We try to right every wrong, heal every wound, point out every injustice. We spend our time demanding that the world system reform. We may also dedicate ourself to rescuing and reforming those we love. Our zealousness to set the world aright can be a means of denying that we are powerless to do so.

Solomon said, "Throughout the earth justice is giving way to crime, and even the police courts are corrupt. I said to myself, 'In due season God will judge everything man does.' . . . I observed all the oppression and sadness throughout the earth—the tears of the oppressed, and no one helping them, while on the side of their oppressors were powerful allies" (Ecclesiastes 3:16-17; 4:1). He saw that the world was not as it should be. He also recognized that it was ultimately God's job to judge the injustices in our world.

When we set out to save the world, we err by taking on a role that belongs to God. What we gain by taking on such a massive task is the guarantee that we will always be busy. Then we will never have the time or energy to face our own issues. The Bible makes it clear that the world will never be right until Jesus Christ returns to make it so. We need to accept the fact that we are powerless to do his job. However, when we focus on our own recovery, fixing ourself instead of everyone else, we will be able to be more effective in helping others, too.

Turn to page 793, Jeremiah 9.

and why is he giving up so much now? It is all so pointless and depressing.

The Blessings of Friendship

[9]Two can accomplish more than twice as much as one, for the results can be much better. [10]If one falls, the other pulls him up; but if a man falls when he is alone, he's in trouble.

[11]Also, on a cold night, two under the same blanket gain warmth from each other, but how can one be warm alone? [12]And one standing alone can be attacked and defeated, but two can stand back-to-back and conquer; three is even better, for a triple-braided cord is not easily broken.

Success Does Not Last

[13]It is better to be a poor but wise youth than to be an old and foolish king who refuses all advice. [14]Such a lad could come from prison and succeed. He might even become king though born in poverty. [15]Everyone is eager to help a youth like that, even to help him usurp the throne. [16]He can become the leader of millions of people and be very popular. But, then, the younger generation grows up around him and rejects him! So again, it is all foolishness, chasing the wind.

CHAPTER 5

Have Respect for God

As you enter the Temple, keep your ears open and your mouth shut! Don't be a fool who doesn't even realize it is sinful to make rash promises to God, for he is in heaven and you are only here on earth, so let your words be few. Just as being too busy gives you nightmares, so being a fool makes you a blabbermouth. [4]So when you talk to God and vow to him that you will do something, don't delay in doing it, for God has no pleasure in fools. Keep your promise to him. [5]It is far better not to say you'll do something than to say you will and then not do it. [6,7]In that case, your mouth is making you sin. Don't try to defend yourself by telling the messenger from God that it was all a mistake [to make the vow]. That would make God very angry; and he might destroy your prosperity. Dreaming instead of doing is foolishness, and there is ruin in a flood of empty words; fear God instead.

[8]If you see some poor man being oppressed by the rich, with miscarriage of justice anywhere throughout the land, don't be surprised! For every official is under orders from higher up, and the higher officials look up to their superiors. And so the matter is lost in red tape and bureaucracy. [9]And over them all is the king. Oh, for a king who is devoted to his country! Only he can bring order from this chaos.

[10]He who loves money shall never have enough. The foolishness of thinking that wealth brings happiness! [11]The more you have, the more you spend, right up to the limits of your income. So what is the advantage of wealth—except perhaps to watch it as it runs through your fingers! [12]The man who works hard sleeps well whether he eats little or much, but the rich must worry and suffer insomnia.

[13,14]There is another serious problem I have seen everywhere—savings are put into risky investments that turn sour, and soon there is nothing left to pass on to one's son. [15]The

---

4:13-16 Climbing the ladder of success will never unlock the door to life's meaning. Success is always temporary. Someone will inherit our work, and ultimately it will be forgotten. We must avoid the trap of living for our success in life. Our relationships with God and other people are of far greater importance. Reconciling and building our relationships will lead to true success and a joyful life.

5:10-17 The Preacher here addresses the addiction to accumulating wealth. As is true of all addictions, enough is never enough. This is one reason why wealth is not the key to meaning in life. Here we are given additional reasons to avoid a passionate search for wealth: (1) the more money we have, the more money we spend, saving nothing (5:11); (2) the greater our empire, the more we will worry about it (5:12); (3) we can't take any of it with us when we die (5:13-17). God never intended for us to live for our possessions. We need to make our relationships with God and others the primary concern in our life.

5:18-20 Here we are given an alternative to materialism. We are to celebrate the beauty of God's gift of life and its simple pleasures. If we are content with what we have, we need very little material wealth to really enjoy life. The Preacher shows how important celebration is by stating that the person who fails to do it is worse off than a stillborn child (6:3-6). Though the Preacher probably exaggerated to make his point, his message is clear. The celebration and enjoyment of life is extremely important. The process of recovery is often very painful. We need to take the time to enjoy life's simple pleasures to gain strength for the battles we face.

man who speculates is soon back to where he
began—with nothing. [16]This, as I said, is a
very serious problem, for all his hard work has
been for nothing; he has been working for the
wind. It is all swept away. [17]All the rest of his
life he is under a cloud—gloomy, discouraged,
frustrated, and angry.

Enjoyment Comes from God

[18]Well, one thing, at least, is good: It is for a
man to eat well, drink a good glass of wine,
accept his position in life, and enjoy his work
whatever his job may be, for however long
the Lord may let him live. [19,20]And, of course,
it is very good if a man has received wealth
from the Lord and the good health to enjoy
it. To enjoy your work and to accept your lot
in life—that is indeed a gift from God. The
person who does that will not need to look
back with sorrow on his past, for God gives
him joy.

CHAPTER 6

Is Life Worth Living?

Yes, but there is a very serious evil which I
have seen everywhere—[2]God has given to
some men very great wealth and honor so
that they can have everything they want, but
he doesn't give them the health to enjoy it,
and they die and others get it all! This is
absurd, a hollow mockery, and a serious fault.
[3]Even if a man has a hundred sons and as
many daughters and lives to be very old, but
leaves so little money at his death that his
children can't even give him a decent burial—
I say that he would be better off born dead.
[4]For though his birth would then be futile and
end in darkness, without even a name, [5]never
seeing the sun or even knowing its existence,
yet that is better than to be an old, unhappy
man. [6]Though a man lives a thousand years
twice over but doesn't find contentment—
well, what's the use?
[7,8]Wise men and fools alike spend their lives
scratching for food and never seem to get
enough. Both have the same problem, yet the
poor man who is wise lives a far better life. [9]A
bird in the hand is worth two in the bush;
mere dreaming of nice things is foolish; it's
chasing the wind.
[10]All things are decided by fate; it was
known long ago what each man would be. So
there's no use arguing with God about your
destiny.
[11]The more words you speak, the less they
mean, so why bother to speak at all?
[12]In these few days of our empty lifetimes,

Overcoming Loneliness

BIBLE READING: Ecclesiastes 4:9-12

We made a list of all persons we had harmed and became willing to make amends to them all.

Feelings of loneliness and isolation go along with the guilt and shame we feel about who we are or what we have done. We may feel so cut off from others that we feel lonely even when we are around other people. Our guilt, our fear of being hurt, and our self-hatred can make us unable to believe in the love others have for us. We can feel all alone in the struggle even when there are people beside us who want to help. Being willing to accept their love is part of our preparation for making amends.

Wise King Solomon observed: "Two can accomplish more than twice as much as one, for the results can be much better. If one falls, the other pulls him up; but if a man falls when he is alone, he's in trouble. Also, on a cold night, two under the same blanket gain warmth from each other, but how can one be warm alone? And one standing alone can be attacked and defeated, but two can stand back-to-back and conquer; three is even better, for a triple-braided cord is not easily broken" (Ecclesiastes 4:9-12).

Loneliness can break us and defeat our recovery process. When we prepare to make amends, we also need to prepare our heart to accept whatever love, support, or friendship is offered in return. These supportive relationships, along with the third "strand" of God's supporting hand, will strengthen our life considerably. ***Turn to page 1031, Matthew 18.***

who can say how one's days can best be spent? Who can know what will prove best for the future after he is gone? For who knows the future?

CHAPTER 7

Wise Advice for Living

A good reputation is more valuable than the most expensive perfume.

The day one dies is better than the day he is born! [2]It is better to spend your time at funerals than at festivals. For you are going to die, and it is a good thing to think about it while there is still time. [3]Sorrow is better than laughter, for sadness has a refining influence on us. [4]Yes, a wise man thinks much of death, while the fool thinks only of having a good time now.

[5]It is better to be criticized by a wise man than to be praised by a fool! [6]For a fool's compliment is as quickly gone as paper in fire, and it is silly to be impressed by it.

[7]The wise man is turned into a fool by a bribe; it destroys his understanding.

[8]Finishing is better than starting! Patience is better than pride! [9]Don't be quick-tempered—that is being a fool.

[10]Don't long for "the good old days," for you don't know whether they were any better than these!

[11]To be wise is as good as being rich; in fact, it is better. [12]You can get anything by either wisdom or money, but being wise has many advantages.

[13][See the way God does things and fall into line. Don't fight the facts of nature.] Who can straighten what he has made crooked? [14]Enjoy prosperity whenever you can, and when hard times strike, realize that God gives one as well as the other—so that everyone will realize that nothing is certain in this life.

[15-17]In this silly life I have seen everything, including the fact that some of the good die young and some of the wicked live on and on. So don't be too good or too wise! Why destroy yourself? On the other hand, don't be too wicked either—don't be a fool! Why should you die before your time?

[18]Tackle every task that comes along, and if you fear God you can expect his blessing.

[19]A wise man is stronger than the mayors of ten big cities! [20]And there is not a single man in all the earth who is always good and never sins.

[21,22]Don't eavesdrop! You may hear your servant cursing you! For you know how often you yourself curse others!

[23]I have tried my best to be wise. I declared, "I *will* be wise," but it didn't work. [24]Wisdom is far away and very difficult to find. [25]I searched everywhere, determined to find wisdom and the reason for things, . . . to prove to myself the wickedness of folly and that foolishness is madness.

[26]A prostitute is more bitter than death. May it please God that you escape from her, but sinners don't evade her snares.

[27,28]This is my conclusion, says the Preacher.

6:12 Sometimes our situation in life seems hopeless. No matter where we turn, everything seems painful and ultimately meaningless. "Who knows the future?" We certainly don't, but God does. If we faithfully follow his program for healthy living, we can have hope for the future. We need to begin by recognizing our hopeless state and by placing our life in God's hands. We often allow our lack of understanding or lack of material resources to discourage us. We should realize that if we trust and obey God, our lack of understanding or wealth need not get in the way of a rich and joyful life.

7:1 The style of Ecclesiastes makes a radical shift here, as does the emphasis of the Preacher. The message is presented by using proverbs—short pithy statements of wisdom. He gives us wisdom for coping with everyday life in our fallen world. His search for the meaning of life has essentially ended.

7:13-14 God is in control of our world. He created it and the laws that govern it. It only makes sense that we should follow his plan. Doing things his way will lead us to live in harmony with God, other people, and the world we live in. We will never understand everything about our world or why things happen. There are some things in life that will never make sense. But God is in control. By trusting in him and obeying his plan for healthy living we can live a productive and joyful life. Living at odds with God's plan will only lead to increased suffering and eventual destruction.

7:21-22 We are to listen selectively, being careful about what we take to heart. Many of us grew up in dysfunctional families and had to submit to constant negative criticism. Many of the messages we received just weren't true. We may need to stop listening to people who have been instrumental in destroying our self-esteem. This is not to say that we should filter out constructive criticism. We must learn to tell the difference between legitimate and false criticism. This is a necessary skill for making our personal moral inventory.

Step by step I came to this result after researching in every direction: One tenth of one percent of the men I interviewed could be said to be wise, but not one woman!

29And I found that though God has made men upright, each has turned away to follow his own downward road.

CHAPTER 8

How wonderful to be wise, to understand things, to be able to analyze them and interpret them. Wisdom lights up a man's face, softening its hardness.

2,3Obey the king as you have vowed to do. Don't always be trying to get out of doing your duty, even when it's unpleasant. For the king punishes those who disobey. 4The king's command is backed by great power, and no one can withstand it or question it. 5Those who obey him will not be punished. The wise man will find a time and a way to do what he says. 6,7Yes, there is a time and a way for everything, though man's trouble lies heavy upon him; for how can he avoid what he doesn't know is going to happen?

8No one can hold back his spirit from departing; no one has the power to prevent his day of death, for there is no discharge from that obligation and that dark battle. Certainly a man's wickedness is not going to help him then.

Fearing God Has Great Value

9,10I have thought deeply about all that goes on here in the world, where people have the power of injuring each other. I have seen wicked men buried, and as their friends returned from the cemetery, having forgotten all the dead man's evil deeds, these men were praised in the very city where they had committed their many crimes! How odd! 11Because God does not punish sinners instantly, people feel it is safe to do wrong. 12But though a man sins a hundred times and still lives, I know very well that those who fear God will be better off, 13unlike the wicked, who will not live long, good lives—their days shall pass away as quickly as shadows because they don't fear God.

14There is a strange thing happening here upon the earth: Providence seems to treat some good men as though they were wicked, and some wicked men as though they were good. This is all very vexing and troublesome!

15Then I decided to spend my time having fun because I felt that there was nothing better in all the earth than that a man should eat, drink, and be merry, with the hope that this happiness would stick with him in all the hard work that God gives to mankind everywhere.

Everyone Has a Common Destiny

16,17In my search for wisdom I observed all that was going on everywhere across the earth—ceaseless activity, day and night. (Of course, only God can see everything, and even the wisest man who says he knows everything, doesn't!)

CHAPTER 9

This, too, I carefully explored—that godly and wise men are in God's will; no one knows whether he will favor them or not. All is chance! 2,3The same providence confronts everyone, whether good or bad, religious or irreligious, profane or godly. It seems so unfair that one fate comes to all. That is why men are not more careful to be good but instead choose their own mad course, for they have no hope—there is nothing but death ahead anyway.

4There is hope only for the living. "It is better to be a live dog than a dead lion!" 5For the living at least know that they will die! But the dead know nothing ; they don't even have their memories. 6Whatever they did in their lifetimes—loving, hating, envying—is long

---

8:14 The Preacher noticed something that just didn't make sense. Some good people suffer, and some wicked people prosper. Here we are advised not to trouble our mind with problems we cannot solve. We never have the whole picture. Only God can understand the reasons behind everything. This should give us good reason to trust in God's plan for our life. Knowing that we can trust God to lead us through the ambiguities of life, we should enjoy the simple pleasures that life offers. Some things will never make sense (8:14), but we should enjoy what we can understand (8:15) rather than despairing about the things we cannot (8:16-17).

9:7-10 Because life is short, we should enjoy life while we have it. The Preacher recognized that life under the sun was not the end of the story, but he never minimized the importance of our days here. We need to enjoy good times with the friends and family God gives us. We may sometimes feel that our life is insignificant in the larger scheme of things. We need to realize that in the events of everyday life, we do make a difference. God uses us to touch the lives of others, if we are willing to follow his program. This is one of the greatest lessons of recovery.

gone, and they have no part in anything here on earth any more. [7]So go ahead, eat, drink, and be merry, for it makes no difference to God! [8]Wear fine clothes—with a dash of cologne! [9]Live happily with the woman you love through the fleeting days of life, for the wife God gives you is your best reward down here for all your earthly toil. [10]Whatever you do, do well, for in death, where you are going, there is no working or planning, or knowing, or understanding.

[11]Again I looked throughout the earth and saw that the swiftest person does not always win the race, nor the strongest man the battle, and that wise men are often poor, and skillful men are not necessarily famous; but it is all by chance, by happening to be at the right place at the right time. [12]A man never knows when he is going to run into bad luck. He is like a fish caught in a net, or a bird caught in a snare.

[13]Here is another thing that has made a deep impression on me as I have watched human affairs: [14]There was a small city with only a few people living in it, and a great king came with his army and besieged it. [15]There was in the city a wise man, very poor, and he knew what to do to save the city, and so it was rescued. But afterwards no one thought any more about him. [16]Then I realized that though wisdom is better than strength, nevertheless, if the wise man is poor, he will be despised, and what he says will not be appreciated. [17]But even so, the quiet words of a wise man are better than the shout of a king of fools. [18]Wisdom is better than weapons of war, but one rotten apple can spoil a barrelful.

CHAPTER 10

Living a Balanced Life

Dead flies will cause even a bottle of perfume to stink! Yes, a small mistake can outweigh much wisdom and honor. [2]A wise man's heart leads him to do right, and a fool's heart leads him to do evil. [3]You can identify a fool just by the way he walks down the street!

[4]If the boss is angry with you, don't quit! A quiet spirit will quiet his bad temper.

[5]There is another evil I have seen as I have watched the world go by, a sad situation concerning kings and rulers: [6]For I have seen foolish men given great authority and rich men not given their rightful place of dignity! [7]I have even seen servants riding, while princes walk like servants!

[8,9]Dig a well—and fall into it! Demolish an old wall—and be bitten by a snake! When working in a quarry, stones will fall and crush you! There is risk in each stroke of your axe!

[10]A dull axe requires great strength; be wise and sharpen the blade.

[11]When the horse is stolen, it is too late to lock the barn.

[12,13]It is pleasant to listen to wise words, but a fool's speech brings him to ruin. Since he begins with a foolish premise, his conclusion is sheer madness. [14]A fool knows all about the future and tells everyone in detail! But who can really know what is going to happen? [15]A fool is so upset by a little work that he has no strength for the simplest matter.

[16,17]Woe to the land whose king is a child and whose leaders are already drunk in the morning. Happy the land whose king is a nobleman and whose leaders work hard before they feast and drink, and then only to strengthen themselves for the tasks ahead! [18]Laziness lets the roof leak, and soon the rafters begin to rot. [19]A party gives laughter, and wine gives happiness, and money gives everything! [20]Never curse the king, not even in your thoughts, nor the rich man, either; for a little bird will tell them what you've said.

CHAPTER 11

The Value of Generosity

Give generously, for your gifts will return to you later. [2]Divide your gifts among many, for in the days ahead you yourself may need much help.

[3]When the clouds are heavy, the rains come down; when a tree falls, whether south or north, the die is cast, for there it lies. [4]If you wait for perfect conditions, you will never get anything done. [5]God's ways are as mysterious as the pathway of the wind and as the manner

9:13-18 Even though wisdom in itself cannot give meaning to our life, it is still clearly to be preferred over foolishness. This reinforces the view that wisdom is not meaningless in an absolute sense, but it is limited for the purpose of putting the pieces of the puzzle of life together.

11:5-6 For the last time in the book, the Preacher reminds us of the limits of our understanding. In light of this, he counsels diligence, since we do not know the outcome of our labor. We will never understand all the events of our life. We may never really understand our dependencies or compulsions. But God has given us instructions to follow. We need to be diligent as we obey the will of our faithful and loving God.

in which a human spirit is infused into the little body of a baby while it is yet in its mother's womb. [6]Keep on sowing your seed, for you never know which will grow—perhaps it all will.

The Value of Enjoyment

[7]It is a wonderful thing to be alive! [8]If a person lives to be very old, let him rejoice in every day of life, but let him also remember that eternity is far longer and that everything down here is futile in comparison.

[9]Young man, it's wonderful to be young! Enjoy every minute of it! Do all you want to; take in everything, but realize that you must account to God for everything you do. [10]So banish grief and pain, but remember that youth, with a whole life before it, can make serious mistakes.

CHAPTER 12

Remembering God Right Now

Don't let the excitement of being young cause you to forget about your Creator. Honor him in your youth before the evil years come—when you'll no longer enjoy living. [2]It will be too late then to try to remember him when the sun and light and moon and stars are dim to your old eyes, and there is no silver lining left among your clouds. [3]For there will come a time when your limbs will tremble with age, your strong legs will become weak, and your teeth will be too few to do their work, and there will be blindness too. [4]Then let your lips be tightly closed while eating when your teeth are gone! And you will waken at dawn with the first note of the birds; but you yourself will be deaf and tuneless, with quavering voice. [5]You will be afraid of heights and of falling—a white-haired, withered old man, dragging himself along: without sexual desire, standing at death's door, and nearing his everlasting home as the mourners go along the streets.

[6]Yes, remember your Creator now while you are young—before the silver cord of life snaps and the gold bowl is broken; before the pitcher is broken at the fountain and the wheel is broken at the cistern; [7]then the dust returns to the earth as it was, and the spirit returns to God who gave it. [8]All is futile, says the Preacher; utterly futile.

Fearing and Obeying God

[9]But then, because the Preacher was wise, he went on teaching the people all he knew; and he collected proverbs and classified them. [10]For the Preacher was not only a wise man but a good teacher; he not only taught what he knew to the people, but taught them in an interesting manner. [11]The wise man's words are like goads that spur to action. They nail down important truths. Students are wise who master what their teachers tell them.

[12]But, my son, be warned: there is no end of opinions ready to be expressed. Studying them can go on forever and become very exhausting!

[13]Here is my final conclusion: fear God and obey his commandments, for this is the entire duty of man. [14]For God will judge us for everything we do, including every hidden thing, good or bad.

12:1 Our relationship with God is foundational for coping with life in a fallen world. We need to do more than just acknowledge a higher power. We need to make him the center of our life. Everything we do and say should be inspired by his presence. We are to remember God in our youth, because it gets harder to change as we get older. This is a call to immediate action—the younger, the better! We need to seek out God's will for our life and then do our best to follow it. This may begin with the decision to get into a recovery program.

12:2-7 These verses contain figures of speech that describe the physical effects in the process of aging. Eyesight is lost (12:2); the muscles and bones deteriorate (12:3); hearing fades (12:4); fear sets in, and vitality is lost (12:5); we become unable to hold the water of life (12:6); and our frame returns to dust (12:7). Our addictions often cause these characteristics long before they would naturally happen. God desires that we experience the richest life possible. Yet we can be sure that he will be with us as we face physical deterioration, just as he has walked with us from the days of our youth.

12:13-14 These final verses remind us of the importance of our relationship with God as we live in a fallen world. Life is filled with ambiguity; there are many things that we will never understand. But God has the big picture; he knows what will happen in the future. If we follow his program—obeying his commandments with his help—we will discover joy amidst the ambiguity. As we seek to follow his will, we will discover the only path toward true recovery.

REFLECTIONS ON ECCLESIASTES

✲*insights* ABOUT WORK AND SUCCESS

In **Ecclesiastes 2:1-11** the Preacher shows how living for personal success will ultimately cause us to come up empty. Notice how the first person pronouns—*I, me, my*—dominate this section. The Preacher was committed to the gratification of self-interest as a means of making sense of life. The ultimate failure of this approach to discovering meaning is an important lesson for us to learn. We need to realize that living for the self is ultimately self-destructive. Until we learn this lesson, we will find it unnatural to reach out to help others, an essential step in our own recovery.

In **Ecclesiastes 2:17-23** the Preacher addresses the workaholic. Work is valuable, even necessary, to our well-being (Genesis 2:15; Ecclesiastes 2:24), yet a compulsive commitment to work will lead to sure destruction. The Preacher gives us a number of reasons why looking to work for ultimate meaning is a fruitless endeavor: (1) we don't know who will succeed us in our work (2:17-20); (2) the one who inherits our work will not have the same passion for it as we did (2:21); and (3) workaholism carries a higher emotional and physical cost than its benefits (2:22-23).

Ecclesiastes 4:7-8 makes it clear that if we allow work to control our life, we are headed for trouble. This compulsion will cut us off from the significant relationships necessary to enjoy life. In later years, even if we are successful, we will probably be alone. It is very important that we seek to reconcile and strengthen the relationships God has given us. This is important for our recovery and our ultimate enjoyment of life.

✲*insights* INTO OUR IDENTITY AS HUMAN BEINGS

We are told in **Ecclesiastes 3:11** that eternity has been placed in in our heart. This refers to our innate human desire for ultimate meaning in life. Yet in this life, our perspective and understanding are limited. We can't always understand why we suffer as we do. It is like looking at the underside of an Oriental rug. All we see are knots and loose ends. We can only faintly make out the rug's pattern. This is a key issue in recovery. We must not allow the things we can't understand to drag us down. God tells us enough in the Bible to direct us to a life filled with joy and meaning.

✲*insights* ABOUT GOD

Ecclesiastes 5:1-3 assumes an important truth: God is approachable. He has established ways for us to draw near to him. In the Old Testament, people approached God by worshiping him in the Temple. Now that Jesus Christ has come, however, we can approach God directly. He desires to help us as we struggle with our recovery. Notice that we are warned about how we should come before God. We must never take him for granted. He is to be approached with humble reverence and a grateful heart.

✲*insights* FOR REAL LIFE

We are reminded in **Ecclesiastes 5:4-7** of how important our commitments are. When we make a commitment to God or another person, we need to take it very seriously. This reflects an important principle in our recovery, that of being accountable for the promises we make. If we fail to keep our commitment to recovery, we will cause the people close to us even deeper pain. We also will be headed for sure destruction. It might help us to realize that God takes the commitments we make very seriously.

In **Ecclesiastes 7:15-17** the Preacher does not suggest that we compromise our commitment to righteousness. We all know how destructive sin can be. This was probably the Preacher's way of suggesting that we avoid extremes in all areas of our life. But it also serves as a literal warning against being "so heavenly minded that we are no earthly good." We can become so caught up in following the letter of the law that we fail to fulfill the spirit of the law. There are dangers in being too religious.

SONG OF SOLOMON

THE BIG PICTURE

A. COURTSHIP (1:1–3:5)
B. MARRIAGE CEREMONY AND CONSUMMATION (3:6–5:1)
C. CONFLICT AND SEPARATION (5:2–6:13)
D. RESOLUTION AND STRENGTHENING OF LOVE (7:1–8:14)

No other book in the Bible describes the sexual relationship in such detail and with such affirmation. Ironically, in our society the Bible is often thought to deny the importance of the sexual relationship. God is clearly not embarrassed by the topic. In fact, he is the one who created it in the first place! It thus stands to reason that he is also the best qualified to tell us how to experience sex with the greatest fulfillment.

The Song of Solomon is characterized by the use of rich, figurative language that helps the lovers to express the inexpressible about each other. The words are full of passion and emotion, and the figures of speech are designed to paint visual pictures so we can share in the emotional experience of the lovers.

The song develops a history of the relationship between Solomon and the Shulammite woman. It is not a continuous history, but a series of seemingly isolated snapshots. The couple meets and their love matures through courtship. Then the reader is taken to the wedding ceremony and the wedding night. In an unspecified later time, the couple encounters conflict, and in the course of its resolution, they passionately renew their commitment to each other.

The words of each lover clearly focus on the physical aspects of married love. Even the way Solomon and his bride praise each other is focused almost exclusively on their physical attributes. They have come to see each other as thoroughly beautiful. Marriage in general illustrates the love relationship between Christ and the church (see Ephesians 5:25-33), and Solomon's song has often been used as an illustration of God's love for his people. The primary focus of the Song of Solomon, however, is the celebration of sexual love in the context of marriage.

THE BOTTOM LINE

PURPOSE: To tell of the love between a bridegroom and his bride, affirming the sanctity of marriage and the richness of physical love. AUTHOR: Solomon. AUDIENCE: The people of Israel. DATE WRITTEN: Probably during the early part of Solomon's reign. SETTING: Jerusalem and the surrounding countryside. KEY VERSE: "I am my beloved's and my beloved is mine. He pastures his flock among the lilies" (6:3). KEY PEOPLE AND RELATIONSHIPS: Solomon, his bride, and the young women of Jerusalem.

RECOVERY THEMES

The Beauty of God's Creation: Our past experiences may have limited our ability to see the many beautiful things that God has created for us to enjoy in life. When we have been sexually abused or molested, our legitimate boundaries have been destroyed. The sexual experience becomes an experience of pain and fear. The Song of Solomon helps us to see again what has been taken away from us—a physical love that is shameless and beautiful, even in God's eyes. We can pray that God will restore our vision so that we can see the beauty in what he has created.

The Joy of Committed Love: Our culture's understanding of love is largely distorted and twisted. It is a form of love that is driven by selfish desires, and it usually causes the people involved to be exploited or abused in some way. In the Song of Solomon we see the beauty of a committed love, a love that is protected by God-given boundaries. Sexual intercourse was designed by God as a holy means of celebrating love, producing children, and experiencing pleasure. As we seek to recover God's design in our life, we need to recover God's design for our sexuality. God's plan for our sexuality is always found within the boundaries of marriage.

The Realities of Love: Solomon did not just paint for us an idealized picture of marital bliss. If he had, he would have played into our own fantasies of ideal relationships and left us disappointed with the realities we all face. There will always be problems in any love relationship. As time passes, feelings of loneliness, indifference, and even isolation will be experienced. They are a natural part of any long-term love relationship. In his love song, Solomon did not neglect to reveal the difficult realities we all face in the marriage relationship.

Conflict Should Lead to Recommitment: Just as Solomon revealed the challenging realities of love, he also showed us how to deal with those realities. As conflict entered Solomon's love relationship, the solution was ultimately found: perseverance, honesty, and communication. The same is true for us. Any long-term relationship will face times of conflict. If we learn to face our conflicts and communicate about them, we will find that doing so leads to reconciliation, a new commitment, and a refreshed romance. We must not let walls grow between us and the people we love. We need to face and deal with the problems while they are still small.

CHAPTER 1

The Wedding Day

This song of songs, more wonderful than any other, was composed by King Solomon:

The Girl: 2"Kiss me again and again, for
your love is sweeter than wine. 3How
fragrant your cologne, and how great
your name! No wonder all the young
girls love you! 4Take me with you;
come, let's run!"

The Girl: "The king has brought me into his palace. How happy we will be! Your love is better than wine. No wonder all the young girls love you!"

The Girl: 5"I am dark but beautiful, O girls of Jerusalem, tanned as the dark tents of Kedar."

King Solomon: "But lovely as the silken tents of Solomon!"

The Girl: 6"Don't look down on me, you city girls, just because my complexion is so dark—the sun has tanned me. My brothers were angry with me and sent me out into the sun to tend the vineyards, but see what it has done to me!"

The Girl: 7"Tell me, O one I love, where are you leading your flock today? Where will you be at noon? For I will come and join you there instead of wandering like a vagabond among the flocks of your companions."

King Solomon: 8"If you don't know, O
most beautiful woman in all the world,
follow the trail of my flock to the
shepherds' tents, and there feed your
sheep and their lambs. 9What a lovely
filly you are, my love! 10How lovely
your cheeks are, with your hair falling

1:6 Apparently the bride came from a somewhat dysfunctional family. Her domineering brothers forced her to work in the family's vineyards, something that was apparently not normally done. The tragic result was that she was forced to neglect herself. Many of us have had similar experiences. We may have been abused by family members, and we now try to cover our painful scars by any number of destructive behaviors. As we seek approval, we become slaves of others and neglect our own well-being to fill the emptiness inside. We should know that no matter how ugly we feel, God cares about us and loves us. We need to learn to trust him and obey his loving plan for our life.

down upon them! How stately your
neck with that long string of jewels.
11We shall make you gold earrings and
silver beads."
The Girl: 12"The king lies on his bed,
enchanted by the fragrance of my
perfume. 13My beloved one is a sachet
of myrrh lying between my breasts."
King Solomon: 14"My beloved is a bouquet
of flowers in the gardens of Engedi.
15How beautiful you are, my love, how
beautiful! Your eyes are soft as doves'.
16What a lovely, pleasant thing you are,
lying here upon the grass, 17shaded by
the cedar trees and firs."

CHAPTER 2
The Girl: "I am the rose of Sharon, the lily of
the valley."
King Solomon: 2"Yes, a lily among thorns,
so is my beloved as compared with any
other girls."
The Girl: 3"My lover is an apple tree, the
finest in the orchard as compared with
any of the other youths. I am seated in
his much-desired shade and his fruit is
lovely to eat. 4He brings me to the
banquet hall, and everyone can see how
much he loves me. 5Oh, feed me with
your love—your 'raisins' and your
'apples'—for I am utterly lovesick. 6His
left hand is under my head and with his
right hand he embraces me. 7O girls of
Jerusalem, I adjure you by the gazelles
and deer in the park, that you will not
awaken love until the time is right."

Memories of Courtship

The Girl: 8"Ah, I hear him—my beloved! Here
he comes, leaping upon the mountains
and bounding over the hills. 9My
beloved is like a gazelle or young deer.
Look, there he is behind the wall, now
looking in at the windows.
10"My beloved said to me, 'Rise up,
my love, my fair one, and come away.
11For the winter is past, the rain is over
and gone. 12The flowers are springing
up and the time of the singing of birds
has come. Yes, spring is here. 13The
leaves are coming out, and the
grapevines are in blossom. How
delicious they smell! Arise, my love,
my fair one, and come away.'
14"My dove is hiding behind some
rocks, behind an outcrop of the cliff.
Call to me and let me hear your lovely
voice and see your handsome face.
15"The little foxes are ruining the
vineyards. Catch them, for the grapes
are all in blossom.
16"My beloved is mine and I am his.
He is feeding among the lilies! 17Before
the dawn comes and the shadows flee
away, come to me, my beloved, and be
like a gazelle or a young stag on the
mountains of spices."

CHAPTER 3
The Girl: "One night my lover was missing
from my bed. I got up to look for him
but couldn't find him. 2I went out into
the streets of the city and the roads to
seek him, but I searched in vain. 3The
police stopped me, and I said to them,
'Have you seen him anywhere, this one
I love so much?' 4It was only a little
while afterwards that I found him and
held him and would not let him go
until I had brought him into my
childhood home, into my mother's old
bedroom. 5I adjure you, O women of
Jerusalem, by the gazelles and deer of
the park, not to awaken love until the
time is right."

1:9-17 This is the first of many sections of mutual praise and admiration between the bride and groom. The passionate descriptions that they make of each other undoubtedly remind us of when we met and fell in love with our spouse. There was no hint of criticism or sarcasm, two common elements in any deteriorating relationship. Notice especially the creative ways in which they compliment each other. Our relationships are extremely important to our recovery. We might learn a few lessons here that will help us to reconcile and maintain the relationships that God has given us.

2:7 Though she delighted in simply being with her groom, the bride desired sexual restraint until the proper time—until marriage. It is easy to see how difficult this restraint was for her, which is why she implored her friends for their help in keeping her desire under control until the wedding night. The assumption of the book is that sex should occur only within the parameters of marriage. In recovery, we all need boundaries to give our life direction. God has provided us with numerous healthy boundaries in the Bible. Marriage is a boundary that defines the proper context for sexual activity. We would be wise to develop friendships that will support our marriage relationship and any other boundaries important to our recovery.

Memories of Engagement

The Young Women of Jerusalem: 6"Who is this
sweeping in from the deserts like a
cloud of smoke along the ground,
smelling of myrrh and frankincense
and every other spice that can be
bought? 7Look, it is the chariot of
Solomon with sixty of the mightiest
men of his army surrounding it. 8They
are all skilled swordsmen and
experienced bodyguards. Each one has
his sword upon his thigh to defend his
king against any onslaught in the
night. 9For King Solomon made
himself a chariot from the wood of
Lebanon. 10Its posts are silver, its
canopy gold, the seat is purple; and the
back is inlaid with these words: 'With
love from the girls of Jerusalem!'"

The Girl: 11"Go out and see King Solomon,
O young women of Zion; see the crown
with which his mother crowned him
on his wedding day, his day of
gladness."

CHAPTER 4

King Solomon: "How beautiful you are, my
love, how beautiful! Your eyes are those
of doves. Your hair falls across your
face like flocks of goats that frisk across
the slopes of Gilead. 2Your teeth are
white as sheep's wool, newly shorn and
washed; perfectly matched, without
one missing. 3Your lips are like a thread
of scarlet—and how beautiful your
mouth. Your cheeks are matched
loveliness behind your locks. 4Your
neck is stately as the tower of David,
jeweled with a thousand heroes'
shields. 5Your breasts are like twin
fawns of a gazelle, feeding among the
lilies. 6Until the morning dawns and
the shadows flee away, I will go to the
mountain of myrrh and to the hill of
frankincense. 7You are so beautiful, my
love, in every part of you.

8"Come with me from Lebanon, my
bride. We will look down from the
summit of the mountain, from the top
of Mount Hermon, where the lions
have their dens and panthers prowl.
9You have ravished my heart, my
lovely one, my bride; I am overcome
by one glance of your eyes, by a single
bead of your necklace. 10How sweet is
your love, my darling, my bride. How
much better it is than mere wine. The
perfume of your love is more fragrant
than all the richest spices. 11Your lips,
my dear, are made of honey. Yes,
honey and cream are under your
tongue, and the scent of your garments
is like the scent of the mountains and
cedars of Lebanon.

12"My darling bride is like a private

3:6-11 As was customary in ancient Israel, the groom would come to the home of the bride in an elaborate procession. After the ceremony and wedding feast, the newly married couple would then go to the groom's home to consummate the marriage. They were not to live with his parents, as was typical of other cultures of the ancient Near East. Genesis 2:24 insists that both bride and groom leave their respective families and form a new household, having set proper boundaries with both sets of parents. If our parents have had a negative effect on us, our recovery may demand that we set stronger boundaries between us and them. This may be instrumental in freeing us from some of the destructive patterns in our life.

4:1-7 In perhaps the most sensual part of the book, Solomon described his bride from a lover's perspective. Though she may not have been considered attractive by the general public, or even by herself (see 1:6), he saw her as exquisitely beautiful. Solomon described his bride with figures of speech that are sometimes confusing for us, though in the ancient culture these were glowing compliments. For instance, when he said her hair was "like flocks of goats that frisk across the slopes of Gilead" (4:1), he was saying that her hair was long and flowing; that it glistened like goats frolicking in the evening sun. No matter how broken and sinful our life, God sees past our flaws to see our possibilities. Jesus Christ paid for all our past failures and mistakes by dying for us. Because of this, God can look on us as this lover looks on his bride.

4:12-15 The bride's virginity is compared to a garden, a spring, and a fountain, all of which have been inaccessible to Solomon until now. The sexual enjoyment of the couple is compared to choice fruits that have come out of her garden. Many of us may suffer from the pain of a garden or spring that has been violated by others. We may feel that our sexuality has been spoiled beyond recovery. As the One who created our sexual garden, however, God is capable of restoring it. Notice that each of the symbols used here—the garden, the spring, and the fountain—are symbols of recurring freshness. Even after times of destruction, they soon return to their original condition. With God's help, our sexuality can also be restored to its original beauty.

garden, a spring that no one else can
have, a fountain of my own. 13,14You are
like a lovely orchard bearing precious
fruit, with the rarest of perfumes; nard
and saffron, calamus and cinnamon,
and perfume from every other incense
tree, as well as myrrh and aloes, and
every other lovely spice. 15You are a
garden fountain, a well of living water,
refreshing as the streams from the
Lebanon mountains."

The Girl: 16"Come, north wind, awaken;
come, south wind, blow upon my
garden and waft its lovely perfume to
my beloved. Let him come into his
garden and eat its choicest fruits."

CHAPTER 5

King Solomon: "I am here in my garden, my darling, my bride! I gather my myrrh with my spices and eat my honeycomb with my honey. I drink my wine with my milk."

The Young Women of Jerusalem: "Oh, lover and beloved, eat and drink! Yes, drink deeply!"

A Disturbing Dream

The Girl: 2"One night as I was sleeping, my
heart awakened in a dream. I heard the
voice of my beloved; he was knocking
at my bedroom door. 'Open to me, my
darling, my lover, my lovely dove,' he
said, 'for I have been out in the night
and am covered with dew.'

3"But I said, 'I have disrobed. Shall I
get dressed again? I have washed my
feet, and should I get them soiled?'

4"My beloved tried to unlatch the
door, and my heart was thrilled within
me. 5I jumped up to open it, and my
hands dripped with perfume, my
fingers with lovely myrrh as I pulled
back the bolt. 6I opened to my beloved,
but he was gone. My heart stopped. I
searched for him but couldn't find him
anywhere. I called to him, but there
was no reply. 7The guards found me
and struck and wounded me. The
watchman on the wall tore off my veil.
8I adjure you, O women of Jerusalem,
if you find my beloved one, tell him
that I am sick with love."

The Young Women of Jerusalem: 9"O
woman of rare beauty, what is it about
your loved one that is better than any
other, that you command us this?"

The Girl: 10"My beloved one is tanned and
handsome, better than ten thousand
others! 11His head is purest gold, and he
has wavy, raven hair. 12His eyes are like
doves beside the water brooks, deep
and quiet. 13His cheeks are like sweetly
scented beds of spices. His lips are
perfumed lilies, his breath like myrrh.

5:1 Solomon delighted in his sexual relationship with his bride. He realized that people were created for sexual enjoyment—and celebrated that truth. We often are given the impression that God considers the sexual relationship a necessary evil. This is far from the truth. God gave it as a gift to be enjoyed within marriage. Regaining a healthy view of sex is one of the most difficult problems in recovery, especially when we have suffered from some form of sexual abuse. It is not difficult to see how sex can begin to seem very ugly when practiced outside the proper bounds. If we have suffered in this way, we need to look to God for healing and strength. He will help us to rebuild the boundaries we need for a healthy sex life.

5:2-8 It is not clear how much time had elapsed since the couple's wedding night, but enough time had passed for the realities of married life to set in. Indifference and emotional distance were likely at the root of the conflict described here. The bride had turned in for the night when her husband arrived and wanted to be with her (5:3). She failed to expend the necessary effort to respond to his initiative. As a result, he felt rejected and left, leaving her downcast. We need to be aware of the dangers of indifference in marriage. It happens slowly and is often hard to detect until it is already quite far along. A strong marriage relationship is extremely helpful in the recovery process. We need to strengthen our relationships, especially our marriage, by seeking reconciliation and forgiveness wherever necessary.

5:9-16 The young women of Jerusalem forced the young bride to remind herself of all that she loved about her husband. Her description began with his physical attributes; it concluded with her calling him both her beloved and her friend (5:16). Even though the descriptions in the book emphasize the physical relationship, they had apparently also cultivated a solid friendship. Sexual relationships are often selfishly motivated and probably won't last unless built upon the foundation of a deeper selfless friendship. We need to be careful to judge our relationships carefully, avoiding those that are motivated by our selfish desire for pleasure. We also need to remember that our sexuality has been designed to bring joy within the context of marriage.

14His arms are round bars of gold set
with topaz; his body is bright ivory
encrusted with jewels. 15His legs are as
pillars of marble set in sockets of finest
gold, like cedars of Lebanon; none can
rival him. 16His mouth is altogether
sweet, lovable in every way. Such, O
women of Jerusalem, is my beloved, my
friend."

CHAPTER 6
The Young Women of Jerusalem: "O rarest of
beautiful women, where has your
loved one gone? We will help you find
him."
The Girl: 2"He has gone down to his
garden, to his spice beds, to pasture his
flock and to gather the lilies. 3I am my
beloved's and my beloved is mine. He
pastures his flock among the lilies!"

Praising the Bride's Beauty

King Solomon: 4"O my beloved, you are as
beautiful as the lovely land of Tirzah,
yes, beautiful as Jerusalem, and how
you capture my heart. 5Look the other
way, for your eyes have overcome me!
Your hair, as it falls across your face, is
like a flock of goats frisking down the
slopes of Gilead. 6Your teeth are white
as freshly washed ewes, perfectly
matched and not one missing. 7Your
cheeks are matched loveliness behind
your hair. 8I have sixty other wives, all
queens, and eighty concubines, and
unnumbered virgins available to me;
9but you, my dove, my perfect one, are
the only one among them all, without
an equal! The women of Jerusalem
were delighted when they saw you,
and even the queens and concubines
praise you. 10'Who is this,' they ask,
'arising as the dawn, fair as the moon,
pure as the sun, so utterly
captivating?'"
The Girl: 11"I went down into the orchard
of nuts and out to the valley to see the
springtime there, to see whether the
grapevines were budding or the
pomegranates were blossoming yet.
12Before I realized it, I was stricken with
terrible homesickness and wanted to be
back among my own people."
The Young Women of Jerusalem: 13"Return,
return to us, O maid of Shulam. Come
back, come back, that we may see you
once again."
The Girl: "Why should you seek a mere
Shulammite?"
King Solomon: "Because you dance so
beautifully."

CHAPTER 7
King Solomon: "How beautiful your tripping
feet, O queenly maiden. Your rounded
thighs are like jewels, the work of the
most skilled of craftsmen. 2Your navel
is lovely as a goblet filled with wine.
Your waist is like a heap of wheat set
about with lilies. 3Your two breasts are
like two fawns, yes, lovely twins. 4Your
neck is stately as an ivory tower, your
eyes as limpid pools in Heshbon by the
gate of Bath-rabbim. Your nose is
shapely like the tower of Lebanon
overlooking Damascus.
5"As Mount Carmel crowns the
mountains, so your hair is your crown.
The king is held captive in your
queenly tresses.
6"Oh, how delightful you are; how
pleasant, O love, for utter delight! 7You
are tall and slim like a palm tree, and
your breasts are like its clusters of
dates. 8I said, I will climb up into the
palm tree and take hold of its
branches. Now may your breasts be like
grape clusters, the scent of your breath
like apples, 9and your kisses as exciting
as the best of wine, smooth and sweet,
causing the lips of those who are asleep
to speak."

The Bride's Tender Appeal

The Girl: 10"I am my beloved's and I am the
one he desires. 11Come, my beloved, let
us go out into the fields and stay in the
villages. 12Let us get up early and go out
to the vineyards and see whether the

7:1-9 Solomon's praise of his bride continues. As the couple matured in their love, the passion did not diminish. This is not to say that relationships should go on at a fevered pitch constantly. Clearly there are times of indifference and rejection. But this indicates that passionate love can last as a marriage matures. All relationships go through periods of ebb and flow. It is important for our recovery that we maintain our relationships. We need to do all we can to assess the wrongs we have done against others and to achieve reconciliation and stability.

vines have budded, whether the
blossoms have opened, and whether
the pomegranates are in flower. And
there I will give you my love. 13There
the mandrakes give forth their
fragrance, and the rarest fruits are at
our doors, the new as well as old, for I
have stored them up for my beloved."

CHAPTER 8

The Girl: "Oh, if only you were my brother;
then I could kiss you no matter who
was watching, and no one would laugh
at me. 2I would bring you to my
childhood home, and there you would
teach me. I would give you spiced wine
to drink, sweet pomegranate wine. 3His
left hand would be under my head and
his right hand would embrace me. 4I
adjure you, O women of Jerusalem, not
to awaken love until the time is right."

The Power of Love

The Young Women of Jerusalem: 5"Who is this
coming up from the desert, leaning on
her beloved?"

King Solomon: "Under the apple tree
where your mother gave birth to you in
her travail, there I awakened your love."

The Girl: 6"Seal me in your heart with
permanent betrothal, for love is strong
as death, and jealousy is as cruel as
Sheol. It flashes fire, the very flame of
Jehovah. 7Many waters cannot quench
the flame of love, neither can the
floods drown it. If a man tried to buy it
with everything he owned, he couldn't
do it."

The Girl's Brothers: "We have a little sister
too young for breasts. What will we do
if someone asks to marry her?"

King Solomon: 9If she has no breasts, we
will build upon her a battlement of
silver, and if she is a door, we will
enclose her with cedar boards."

The Girl: 10"I am slim, tall and full-
breasted, and I have found favor in my
lover's eyes. 11Solomon had a vineyard
at Baal-hamon, which he rented out to
some farmers there, the rent being one
thousand pieces of silver from each.
12But as for my own vineyard, you, O
Solomon, shall have my thousand
pieces of silver, and I will give two
hundred pieces to those who care for it.
13O my beloved, living in the gardens,
how wonderful that your companions
may listen to your voice; let me hear it
too. 14Come quickly, my beloved, and
be like a gazelle or young deer upon the
mountains of spices."

7:10-13 The couple returned to the countryside, to the Shulammite woman's home village, to renew their love. They celebrated their renewal in the same place that they met, in the vineyards (7:12). This would have reminded them of the tender moments they shared when they first fell in love, almost as if they knew they were re-creating some of those moments as they were together. The example of Solomon and his bride should inspire us to do what we can to put some sparkle back into our own marriage relationship.

8:6-7 This eloquent statement describing committed love shows the renewed fervor of a love that endures and resolves conflict. The seal, or signet ring, was symbolic of Solomon's commitment to his bride. The jealousy mentioned in 8:6 is a positive emotion; it speaks of the accountability shared between Solomon and his bride. Their commitment was so strong that there would be serious consequences for anyone who threatened it. Given his vast wealth, Solomon could speak from experience about the value of love over riches. True love can never be bought; it must be cultivated. Relationships characterized by commitment, love, and accountability need to be cultivated if we hope to succeed in our recovery.

8:8-12 These verses assume the fact that sexual expression is to be limited to the marriage relationship. The girl's brothers desired to protect their sister from sexual activity prior to her marriage. Sexual activity outside the safety of marriage commitment is always destructive. It may bring pleasure for a while, but it will never lead to a life of stability and fulfillment. We need to build relationships characterized by trust and honesty and keep sexual activity in the proper context—our marriage. This will be of immense help as we seek recovery from the various problems we face in our life.

ISAIAH

THE BIG PICTURE

A. MESSAGE OF CONFRONTATION TO JUDAH (1:1–39:8)
   1. Judah Is Confronted about Her Sin (1:1–12:6)
   2. God Judges Judah's Oppressors (13:1–23:18)
   3. A Promise of God's Final Victory (24:1–27:13)
   4. Judah's Choice of Recovery or Disaster (28:1–31:9)
   5. Salvation Is Coming, but the Path Is Hard (32:1–35:10)
   6. Historical Interlude: Hezekiah's Tests (36:1–39:8)

B. MESSAGE OF HOPE TO BABYLONIAN EXILES (40:1–66:24)
   1. A Promise of God's Deliverance (40:1–48:22)
   2. Deliverance through a Suffering Servant (49:1–55:13)
   3. Israel's Eventual Exaltation (56:1–66:24)

Though it is never easy to face the truth, truth brings healing. God spoke through Isaiah to address the denial of the people of Judah. Over the centuries they had become addicted to the false promises of idolatry. They had developed self-destructive patterns of behavior that included oppressing the poor, accepting bribes, and using lies to get what they wanted. And, though repeatedly confronted by Isaiah, they refused to admit their sin. Instead, they blamed God for their sufferings and wondered why he refused to bless them.

The first part of Isaiah (1:1–39:8) is dominated by a message of judgment. The empire of Assyria had recently destroyed the northern kingdom of Israel and now threatened to destroy Judah. God told the people of Judah that deliverance would come, but only if they repented of their sins and turned to him for help. The people of Judah trusted in God only superficially and sought to save themselves through clever political alliances, first with Assyria and then with Egypt. Their human attempts at escaping the suffering of exile could never bring permanent deliverance. God did allow Judah to survive the attacks of Egypt and Assyria, but just a few generations later, Judah was crushed by the rising power of Babylon.

The second part of Isaiah (40:1–66:24) is dominated by a message of hope. In spite of Judah's unworthiness, God promised that he would lead his people out of Babylonian captivity. He also foretold the miracle of our spiritual salvation through the Suffering Servant and his ultimate cosmic victory culminating in a new heaven and a new earth. Through the words of Isaiah we discover that God's ultimate purpose for his people is always their blessing and recovery.

THE BOTTOM LINE

PURPOSE: To confront the people of Judah with their sin and denial and to inspire them to rebuild their lives based on God's promises. AUTHOR: The prophet Isaiah. AUDIENCE: Isaiah 1–39 was spoken to the people of Judah before their exile; Isaiah 40–66 recorded a message of hope to future generations of exiled Jews. DATE WRITTEN: The book includes oracles given throughout Isaiah's ministry (740–680 B.C.). SETTING: The land of Judah before its destruction by Babylon. KEY VERSE: "But he was wounded and bruised for *our* sins. He was beaten that we might have peace; he was lashed—and we were healed!" (53:5). KEY PLACES: Judah, Egypt, Assyria, Babylonia, and Persia. KEY PEOPLE AND RELATIONSHIPS: Isaiah with kings Ahaz and Hezekiah of Judah and with King Cyrus of Persia.

RECOVERY THEMES

The Truth Brings Healing: Because the truth hurts, we often protect ourself from it. When Isaiah told the people of Judah the truth about their sin, they acted as we often do—they chose to hide in their denial. They refused to admit that they had failed. In doing this, they also refused to experience the healing power of truth. Our recovery program will be effective only if we open ourself to the truth regardless of how painful that might be.

Denial Leads to Blaming: Instead of admitting their sin and responding to that truth, the people of Judah blamed God for the terrible consequences of their sin. If we continue in denial, we will also become expert blamers. If we desire to progress in recovery, however, we need to take responsibility for our actions. The painful circumstances we suffer are often a direct consequence of our own failures.

Recovery through Confrontation: God had a program for Judah's recovery: he confronted them with the truth of their sin. Isaiah's words of confrontation, however, were punctuated by the message of God's love and hope. The model of confrontation found in the book of Isaiah can help us as we intervene in the lives of the people we love who are trapped by their addictions. Our words of confrontation need to be balanced by words and actions that demonstrate our humble love and forgiveness. Angry confrontation causes greater conflict and deeper destruction.

The Importance of Action: God is not an enabler. As we see in Isaiah, he takes our actions very seriously. He does for us what we are unable to do for ourself, but then he leaves the rest to us. Isaiah told the people that despite their impending doom, God would deliver them from Babylonian captivity. God provided the way, but the people had to take the steps to leave. When our prayers for recovery are not answered, it may be time for us to act. Often, it is only after acting in faith that we are able to see the acts God has already accomplished for us.

CHAPTER 1

Messages to a Rebellious People

These are the messages that came to Isaiah, son of Amoz, in the visions he saw during the reigns of King Uzziah, King Jotham, King Ahaz, and King Hezekiah—all kings of Judah. In these messages God showed him what was going to happen to Judah and Jerusalem in the days ahead.

[2]Listen, O heaven and earth, to what the
Lord is saying:

The children I raised and cared for so long
and tenderly have turned against me. [3]Even
the animals—the donkey and the ox—know their owner and appreciate his care for them, but not my people Israel. No matter what I do for them, they still don't care.

[4]Oh, what a sinful nation they are! They walk bent-backed beneath their load of guilt. Their fathers before them were evil too. Born to be bad, they have turned their backs upon the Lord and have despised the Holy One of Israel. They have cut themselves off from his help.

[5,6]Oh, my people, haven't you had enough of punishment? Why will you force me to whip you again and again? Must you forever rebel? From head to foot you are sick and weak and faint, covered with bruises and welts and infected wounds, unanointed and
unbound. [7]Your country lies in ruins; your
cities are burned; while you watch, foreigners are destroying and plundering everything
they see. [8]You stand there helpless and abandoned like a watchman's shanty in the field when the harvesttime is over—or when the crop is stripped and robbed.

[9]If the Lord Almighty had not stepped in to save a few of us, we would have been wiped out

---

1:5-6 Because the people of Judah were in denial and refused to admit the seriousness of their problems, they continued to suffer unnecessarily. When we continue to deny our failures and refuse to admit our need of God's cleansing and forgiveness, we often suffer in ways we don't have to. These are some of the destructive consequences of trying to manage our own life. God wants us to know that we can safely start to deal with truth and come out of denial in his presence. All we have to do is trust him to bring us healing and forgiveness.

1:9-20 Though the people of Judah were very religious, they were accused of being as evil as the people of Sodom and Gomorrah. They gave sacrifices to pay for their sins, but they felt no remorse. They needed to take a moral inventory, acknowledge the depth of their sin, and turn to God for cleansing and renewal. Religious activity is no substitute for a genuine life with God. It is only when we honestly confess our sins and ask God to help us that he will make us "as clean as freshly fallen snow."

ISAIAH

God called Isaiah to be a prophet in "the year King Uzziah died" (Isaiah 6:1), and his ministry extended over more than forty years (740–700 B.C.). He prophesied during the reigns of four kings of Judah: Uzziah, Jotham, Ahaz, and Hezekiah. Isaiah's name means "The Lord is salvation," a meaning especially appropriate since he speaks throughout his book of God's gracious promises of comfort and deliverance.

Isaiah was married and had a family. His sons were given symbolic names: *Shear-jashub* means "a remnant will return"; *Maher-shalal-hash-baz* means "quick to the plunder, swift to the booty." These names carried messages from God to the people of Judah. Isaiah recognized that his sons belonged ultimately to God. Isaiah also called his wife a prophetess. This indicates that his family life was not only consistent with his vocation, but also intimately interwoven with it.

All that we know about the prophet indicates that he was one of the greatest men of his time. His book is an undisputed masterpiece that reveals an author of considerable intelligence and education. Tradition holds that Isaiah belonged to a family of some rank. This would explain his easy access to the king. Because of the greatness of this man, it may be difficult for us to relate to him. Isaiah was a man of God and a statesman. He had the soul of an artist, and he was steadfast in his obedience to God.

Although Isaiah had many gifts, his success was primarily a fruit of his humility and faithfulness to God's will for his life. When God called him, Isaiah had an overwhelming sense of his own sinfulness. He started where we need to start: he admitted his sin and turned to God for cleansing and deliverance. Then, when God revealed his will for Isaiah, the prophet pursued God's plan with determination. He spoke and lived out God's will for him despite the opposition he faced. As a result, God used him to confront his people with their sin, and to comfort his people as they faced a painful future. Through his words and life, Isaiah has blazed a trail for our spiritual growth and recovery.

STRENGTHS AND ACCOMPLISHMENTS:
- Isaiah was a gifted statesman, speaker, and author.
- He followed God's will for his life with determination.
- He recognized his personal need for healing and received God's help.
- He was sensitive, yet strong in his convictions.
- He was faithful to God's call despite great opposition and discouragement.

LESSONS FROM HIS LIFE:
- Our healing begins when we admit our sin and turn to God.
- We can decide to follow God's will and remain faithful to our decision.
- God has gifted each of us, and he will help and lead us as we place our trust in him.

KEY VERSE:
"Then I heard the Lord asking, 'Whom shall I send as a messenger to my people? Who will go?' And I said, 'Lord, I'll go! Send *me*'" (Isaiah 6:8).

The story of Isaiah is told in the book of Isaiah. He is also mentioned in 2 Kings 18–20. His name is also found in the New Testament, where he is recognized for having foretold the coming of the Messiah.

---

as Sodom and Gomorrah were. 10An apt comparison! Listen, you leaders of Israel, you
men of Sodom and Gomorrah, as I call you
now. Listen to the Lord. Hear what he is
telling you! 11I am sick of your sacrifices.
Don't bring me any more of them. I don't
want your fat rams; I don't want to see the
blood from your offerings. 12,13Who wants
your sacrifices when you have no sorrow for
your sins? The incense you bring me is a
stench in my nostrils. Your holy celebrations
of the new moon and the Sabbath, and your
special days for fasting—even your most pious meetings—all are frauds! I want nothing
more to do with them. 14I hate them all; I
can't stand the sight of them. 15From now on,
when you pray with your hands stretched
out to heaven, I won't look or listen. Even
though you make many prayers, I will not
hear, for your hands are those of murderers;
they are covered with the blood of your innocent victims.

16Oh, wash yourselves! Be clean! Let me no
longer see you doing all these wicked things;
quit your evil ways. 17Learn to do good, to be
fair and to help the poor, the fatherless, and
widows.
18Come, let's talk this over! says the Lord;
no matter how deep the stain of your sins, I
can take it out and make you as clean as
freshly fallen snow. Even if you are stained as
red as crimson, I can make you white as wool!
19If you will only let me help you, if you will
only obey, then I will make you rich! 20But if
you keep on turning your backs and refusing
to listen to me, you will be killed by your
enemies; I, the Lord, have spoken.
21Jerusalem, once a faithful wife! And now
a prostitute! Running after other gods! Once
"The City of Fair Play," but now a gang of
murderers. 22Once like sterling silver; now
mixed with worthless alloy! Once so pure, but
now diluted like watered-down wine! 23Your
leaders are rebels, companions of thieves; all
of them take bribes and won't defend the
widows and orphans. 24Therefore the Lord,
the Mighty One of Israel, says: I will pour out
my anger on you, my enemies! 25I myself will
melt you in a smelting pot and skim off your
slag.
26And afterwards I will give you good judges
and wise counselors like those you used to
have. Then your city shall again be called
"The City of Justice" and "The Faithful
Town."
27Those who return to the Lord, who are
just and good, shall be redeemed. 28(But all
sinners shall utterly perish, for they refuse to
come to me.) 29Shame will cover you, and
you will blush to think of all those times you
sacrificed to idols in your groves of "sacred"
oaks. 30You will perish like a withered tree or
a garden without water. 31The strongest
among you will disappear like burning straw;
your evil deeds are the spark that sets the
straw on fire, and no one will be able to put
it out.

CHAPTER 2

Walk in God's Light

This is another message to Isaiah from the
Lord concerning Judah and Jerusalem:
2In the last days Jerusalem and the Temple
of the Lord will become the world's greatest
attraction, and people from many lands will
flow there to worship the Lord.
3"Come," everyone will say, "let us go up
the mountain of the Lord, to the Temple of
the God of Israel; there he will teach us his
laws, and we will obey them." For in those
days the world will be ruled from Jerusalem.
4The Lord will settle international disputes; all
the nations will convert their weapons of war
into implements of peace. Then at the last all
wars will stop and all military training will
end. 5O Israel, come, let us walk in the light of
the Lord and be obedient to his laws!
6The Lord has rejected you because you
welcome foreigners from the East who practice magic and communicate with evil spirits,
as the Philistines do.
7Israel has vast treasures of silver and gold,
and great numbers of horses and chariots
8and idols—the land is full of them! They are
man-made, and yet you *worship* them! 9Small
and great, all bow before them; God will not
forgive you for this sin.
10Crawl into the caves in the rocks and hide
in terror from his glorious majesty, 11for the
day is coming when your proud looks will be
brought low; the Lord alone will be exalted.
12On that day the Lord Almighty will move
against the proud and haughty and bring
them to the dust. 13All the tall cedars of Lebanon and all the mighty oaks of Bashan shall
bend low, 14and all the high mountains and
hills, 15and every high tower and wall, 16and
all the proud ocean ships and trim harbor
craft—*all* shall be crushed before the Lord
that day. 17All the glory of mankind will bow
low; the pride of men will lie in the dust, and
the Lord alone will be exalted. 18And all idols
will be utterly abolished and destroyed.

2:1-5 At the end of history, the entire human race will finally acknowledge that God is supreme. Judah was called to live in light of that future reality. We, too, are called to give up our addictions, compulsions, and other attractions that draw our attention from God. We need to seek out and then live according to God's will for us. As we do this, we will not only be able to restore our present life, we will also be able to share in God's eternal kingdom.

2:6-22 Isaiah declared that when God sets up his kingdom, the people who have put their trust in anything other than God will be humbled and hide in fear. By putting our trust in God, not in any human program or plan, we will have no reason to be ashamed or afraid when he fully reveals his awesome power. Any human program or item that we may choose to trust will one day be destroyed. Therefore, we would be foolish to depend on things like subliminal tapes, crystals, or any other plan that excludes God and his power.

[19]When the Lord stands up from his throne to shake up the earth, his enemies will crawl with fear into the holes in the rocks and into the caves because of the glory of his majesty. [20]Then at last they will abandon their gold and silver idols to the moles and bats [21]and crawl into the caverns to hide among the jagged rocks at the tops of the cliffs, to try to get away from the terror of the Lord and the glory of his majesty when he rises to terrify the earth. [22]Puny man! Frail as his breath! Don't ever put your trust in him!

CHAPTER 3

Well-earned Consequences

The Lord will cut off Jerusalem's and Judah's food and water supplies [2]and kill her leaders; he will destroy her armies, judges, prophets, elders, [3]army officers, businessmen, lawyers, magicians, and politicians. [4]Israel's kings will be like babies, ruling childishly. [5]And the worst sort of anarchy will prevail—everyone stepping on someone else, neighbors fighting neighbors, youths revolting against authority, criminals sneering at honorable men.

[6]In those days a man will say to his brother, "You have some extra clothing, so you be our king and take care of this mess."

[7]"No!" he will reply. "I cannot be of any help! I have no extra food or clothes. Don't get me involved!"

[8]Israel's civil government will be in utter ruin because the Jews have spoken out against their Lord and will not worship him; they offend his glory. [9]The very look on their faces gives them away and shows their guilt. And they boast that their sin is equal to the sin of Sodom; they are not even ashamed. What a catastrophe! They have doomed themselves.

[10]But all is well for the godly man. Tell him, "What a reward you are going to get!" [11]But say to the wicked, "Your doom is sure. You too shall get your just deserts. Your well-earned punishment is on the way."

[12]O my people! Can't you see what fools your rulers are? Weak as women! Foolish as little children playing king. True leaders? No, misleaders! Leading you down the garden path to destruction.

[13]The Lord stands up! He is the great Prosecuting Attorney presenting his case against his people! [14]First to feel his wrath will be the elders and the princes, for they have defrauded the poor. They have filled their barns with grain extorted from the helpless peasants.

[15]"How dare you grind my people in the dust like that?" the Lord Almighty will demand of them.

[16]Next he will judge the haughty Jewish women, who mince along, noses in the air, tinkling bracelets on their ankles, with wanton eyes that rove among the crowds to catch the glances of the men. [17]The Lord will send a plague of scabs to ornament their heads! He will expose their nakedness for all to see. [18]No longer shall they tinkle with self-assurance as they walk. For the Lord will strip away their artful beauty and their ornaments, [19]their necklaces and bracelets and veils of shimmering gauze. [20]Gone shall be their scarves and ankle chains, headbands, earrings, and perfumes; [21]their rings, jewels, [22]party clothes, negligees, capes, ornate combs, and purses; [23]their mirrors, lovely lingerie, beautiful dresses, and veils. [24]Instead of smelling of sweet perfume, they'll stink; for sashes they'll use ropes; their well-set hair will all fall out; they'll wear sacks instead of robes.

All their beauty will be gone; all that will be left to them is shame and disgrace. [25,26]Their husbands shall die in battle; the women, ravaged, shall sit crying on the ground.

CHAPTER 4

Cleansing for God's People

At that time so few men will be left alive that seven women will fight over each of them and

3:1-8 God was going to crush Judah to show them that life is unmanageable without God. The people had refused to listen to God's warnings, so something drastic was needed to shake them out of their denial. Today, we often ignore the warnings God sends us, and we continue with our dependencies and addictions. God may need to send a catastrophe to get us back on the right track. Continuing on our present path will only lead to our destruction. God wants us to have a joyful and meaningful life. We need to pay attention to his warnings before it is too late.

3:9-26 The sins of Sodom and Gomorrah were infamous; God had utterly destroyed those cities for their sin (see Genesis 19). Being compared to wicked Sodom should have made the Israelites realize how evil they had become, but the Israelites weren't even ashamed of the comparison. They weren't denying their sins; they delighted in them. Have we reached the point where we are proud of our addictions, where we flaunt the fact that we behave in a certain way? If so, we may be trying to make ourself believe that our dependent life-style really is fulfilling. But we don't need to fool ourself, because God is willing to help us recover and return to him. All we need to do is ask him.

say, "Let us all marry you! We will furnish our own food and clothing; only let us be called by your name so that we won't be mocked as old maids."

2-4Those whose names are written down to escape the destruction of Jerusalem will be washed and rinsed of all their moral filth by the horrors and the fire. They will be God's holy people. And the land will produce for them its lushest bounty and its richest fruit. 5Then the Lord will provide shade on all Jerusalem—over every home and all its public grounds—a canopy of smoke and cloud throughout the day, and clouds of fire at night, covering the Glorious Land, 6protecting it from daytime heat and from rains and storms.

CHAPTER 5

Sour Grapes in God's Vineyard

Now I will sing a song about his vineyard to the one I love. *My Beloved has a vineyard on a very fertile hill.* 2*He plowed it and took out all the rocks and planted his vineyard with the choicest vines. He built a watchtower and cut a winepress in the rocks. Then he waited for the harvest, but the grapes that grew were wild and sour and not at all the sweet ones he expected.*

3Now, men of Jerusalem and Judah, you have heard the case! You be the judges! 4What more could I have done? Why did my vineyard give me wild grapes instead of sweet? 5I will tear down the fences and let my vineyard go to pasture to be trampled by cattle and sheep. 6I won't prune it or hoe it, but let it be overgrown with briars and thorns. I will command the clouds not to rain on it any more.

7I have given you the story of God's people. They are the vineyard that I spoke about. Israel and Judah are his pleasant acreage! He expected them to yield a crop of justice but found bloodshed instead. He expected righteousness, but the cries of deep oppression met his ears. 8You buy up property so others have no place to live. Your homes are built on great estates so you can be alone in the midst of the earth! 9But the Lord Almighty has sworn your awful fate—with my own ears I heard him say, "Many a beautiful home will lie deserted, their owners killed or gone. 10An acre of vineyard will not produce a gallon of juice! Ten bushels of seed will yield a one-bushel crop!"

11Woe to you who get up early in the morning to go on long drinking bouts that last till late at night—woe to you drunken bums. 12You furnish lovely music at your grand parties; the orchestras are superb! But for the Lord you have no thought or care. 13Therefore I will send you into exile far away because you neither know nor care that I have done so much for you. Your great and honored men will starve, and the common people will die of thirst.

14Hell is licking its chops in anticipation of this delicious morsel, Jerusalem. Her great and small shall be swallowed up, and all her drunken throngs. 15In that day the haughty shall be brought down to the dust; the proud shall be humbled; 16but the Lord Almighty is exalted above all, for he alone is holy, just, and good. 17In those days flocks will feed among the ruins. Lambs and calves and kids will pasture there!

18Woe to those who drag their sins behind them like a bullock on a rope. 19They even mock the Holy One of Israel and dare the Lord to punish them. "Hurry up and punish us, O Lord," they say. "We want to see what you can do!" 20They say that what is right is wrong and what is wrong is right; that black is white and white is black; bitter is sweet and sweet is bitter.

21Woe to those who are wise and shrewd in their own eyes! 22Woe to those who are "heroes" when it comes to drinking and boast about the liquor they can hold. 23They take bribes to pervert justice, letting the wicked go

4:2-4 God wants his people to be characterized by self-respect, honor, and righteousness. Getting there, however, sometimes includes a scorching purification process. Facing up to and dealing with the reality of our inadequacies, dysfunctions, addictions, and compulsive behaviors is not easy or painless, but the end God has prepared for us is worth the price of the process.

5:1-7 God provides us with all we need for a fruitful, functional life, but when we reject him and abandon his way, our life becomes unmanageable, unfruitful, and dysfunctional. If we desire to live a normal, healthy life, we can ask God for his aid, and then turn our life over to him. With God's help, our life will someday bear the "sweet grapes" of God's promises.

5:20-23 When we reject God, our perception of reality becomes distorted. We call our compulsions good, and we become abusive to others. We don't view reality correctly because we have abandoned the one who made reality. To see things in the proper light again, we need to read the Bible—God's Word to us—and talk to God through prayer. As we improve our conscious contact with God, we will discover his will for us and receive a clearer understanding of God's truth.

free and putting innocent men in jail. 24Therefore God will deal with them and burn them. They will disappear like straw on fire. Their roots will rot and their flowers wither, for they have thrown away the laws of God and despised the Word of the Holy One of Israel. 25That is why the anger of the Lord is hot against his people; that is why he has reached out his hand to smash them. The hills will tremble, and the rotting bodies of his people will be thrown as refuse in the streets. But even so, his anger is not ended; his hand is heavy on them still.

26He will send a signal to the nations far away, whistling to those at the ends of the earth, and they will come racing toward Jerusalem. 27They never weary, never stumble, never stop; their belts are tight, their bootstraps strong; they run without stopping for rest or for sleep. 28Their arrows are sharp; their bows are bent; sparks fly from their horses' hoofs, and the wheels of their chariots spin like the wind. 29They roar like lions and pounce upon the prey. They seize my people and carry them off into captivity with none to rescue them. 30They growl over their victims like the roaring of the sea. Over all Israel lies a pall of darkness and sorrow, and the heavens are black.

CHAPTER 6

God Calls Isaiah

The year King Uzziah died I saw the Lord! He was sitting on a lofty throne, and the Temple was filled with his glory. 2Hovering about him were mighty, six-winged angels of fire. With two of their wings they covered their faces with two others they covered their feet, and with two they flew. 3In a great antiphonal chorus they sang, "Holy, holy, holy is the Lord Almighty; the whole earth is filled with his glory." 4Such singing it was! It shook the Temple to its foundations, and suddenly the entire sanctuary was filled with smoke.

5Then I said, "My doom is sealed, for I am a foul-mouthed sinner, a member of a sinful, foul-mouthed race; and I have looked upon the King, the Lord of heaven's armies."

6Then one of the mighty angels flew over to the altar and with a pair of tongs picked out a burning coal. 7He touched my lips with it and said, "Now you are pronounced 'not guilty' because this coal has touched your lips. Your sins are all forgiven."

8Then I heard the Lord asking, "Whom shall I send as a messenger to my people? Who will go?"

And I said, "Lord, I'll go! Send *me."*

9And he said, "Yes, go. But tell my people this: 'Though you hear my words repeatedly, you won't understand them. Though you watch and watch as I perform my miracles, still you won't know what they mean.' 10Dull their understanding, close their ears, and shut their eyes. I don't want them to see or to hear or to understand, or to turn to me to heal them."

11Then I said, "Lord, how long will it be before they are ready to listen?"

And he replied, "Not until their cities are destroyed—without a person left—and the whole country is an utter wasteland, 12and they are all taken away as slaves to other countries far away, and all the land of Israel lies deserted! 13Yet a tenth—a remnant—will survive; and though Israel is invaded again and again and destroyed, yet Israel will be like a tree cut down, whose stump still lives to grow again."

CHAPTER 7

Immanuel—God with Us

During the reign of Ahaz (the son of Jotham and grandson of Uzziah), Jerusalem was attacked by King Rezin of Syria and King Pekah

---

5:24-30 Just as God would use Assyria to invade Israel as judgment for her sins, God also will use the destruction sin brings to our life when we refuse to face the reality of our sins and dysfunctions and try to run our life without God. We, too, may have to face some disaster before we finally admit that our life is unmanageable, but once we do, healing can begin.

6:1-8 Isaiah's recognition of his own uncleanness did not disqualify him from a relationship with God and a life of service to him. In contrast, it set the stage for his cleansing and commission into service. When we hide our sins and failures, we negate the possibility of real recovery. When we admit them, God can cleanse, restore, and use us.

6:8 God is not looking for people who are perfect or who pretend to be perfect. He is looking for people who can say with Isaiah, "Lord, I'll go! Send *me."* If we are willing to turn our past failures over to God, he will not allow them to stand in the way of our future.

6:9-13 Being fruitful does not necessarily mean we have to be a great success in human terms. We need not feel a compulsion to achieve or look good to others; Isaiah certainly did not. Our aim should be to be faithful to God's calling, not to measure up to the world's standards.

of Israel (the son of Remaliah). But it was not
taken; the city stood. 2However, when the
news came to the royal court, "Syria is allied
with Israel against us!" the hearts of the king
and his people trembled with fear as the trees
of a forest shake in a storm.

3Then the Lord said to Isaiah, "Go out to
meet King Ahaz, you and Shear-jashub, your
son. You will find him at the end of the
aqueduct that leads from Gihon Spring to the
upper reservoir, near the road that leads down
to the bleaching field. 4Tell him to quit worrying. Tell him he needn't be frightened by the
fierce anger of those two has-beens, Rezin and
Pekah. 5Yes, the kings of Syria and Israel are
coming against you.

"They say, 6'We will invade Judah and
throw her people into panic. Then we'll fight
our way into Jerusalem and install the son of
Tabeel as their king.'

7"But the Lord God says, This plan will not
succeed, 8for Damascus will remain the capital of Syria alone, and King Rezin's kingdom
will not increase its boundaries. And within
sixty-five years Ephraim, too, will be crushed
and broken. 9Samaria is the capital of Ephraim
alone, and King Pekah's power will not increase. You don't believe me? If you want me
to protect you, you must learn to believe what
I say."

10Not long after this, the Lord sent this
further message to King Ahaz:

11"Ask me for a sign, Ahaz, to prove that I
will indeed crush your enemies as I have said.
Ask anything you like, in heaven or on earth."

12But the king refused. "No," he said, "I'll
not bother the Lord with anything like that."

13Then Isaiah said, O House of David, you
aren't satisfied to exhaust *my* patience; you
exhaust the Lord's as well! 14All right then, the
Lord himself will choose the sign—a child
shall be born to a virgin! And she shall call
him Immanuel (meaning, "God is with us").
15,16By the time this child is weaned and knows
right from wrong, the two kings you fear so
much—the kings of Israel and Syria—will
both be dead.

17But later on, the Lord will bring a terrible curse on you and on your nation and
your family. There will be terror such as has
not been known since the division of Solomon's empire into Israel and Judah—the
mighty king of Assyria will come with his
great army!

18At that time the Lord will whistle for the
army of Upper Egypt, and of Assyria too, to
swarm down upon you like flies and destroy
you, like bees to sting and to kill. 19They will
come in vast hordes, spreading across the
whole land, even into the desolate valleys,
caves, and thorny parts, as well as to all your
fertile acres. 20In that day the Lord will take
this "razor"—these Assyrians you have hired
to save you—and use it on you to shave off
everything you have: your land, your crops,
your people.

21,22When they finally stop plundering, the
whole nation will be a pastureland; whole
flocks and herds will be destroyed, and a
farmer will be fortunate to have a cow and
two sheep left. But the abundant pastureland
will yield plenty of milk, and everyone left
will live on curds and wild honey. 23At that
time the lush vineyards will become patches
of briars. 24All the land will be one vast
thornfield, a hunting ground overrun by
wildlife. 25No one will go to the fertile hillsides
where once the gardens grew, for thorns will
cover them; cattle, sheep, and goats will graze
there.

CHAPTER 8

Assyria's Invasion Predicted

Again the Lord sent me a message: "Make a
large signboard and write on it the birth announcement of the son I am going to give
you. Use capital letters! His name will be
Maher-shalal-hash-baz, which means 'Your
enemies will soon be destroyed.'" 2I asked
Uriah the priest and Zechariah the son of

7:10-12 Ahaz continued in denial and did so with a religious cover-up. Instead of admitting that he didn't believe God or want to obey him, Ahaz claimed that he didn't want to bother God. God is never bothered by our requests; he welcomes them and is waiting to help us. God is a personal God who cares deeply for us. If this were not true, he would never have sent his Son to die so we could be close to him. Fear of bothering God is never a good excuse for not requesting his help.

7:17-25 Confronted with the challenge of invasion from the coalition of Israel and Syria, Ahaz rejected Isaiah's call to trust God and tried to solve the problem his own way: he called on Assyria for protection. Assyria, however, later turned on Judah and did much damage to God's nation and people. We have experienced this with our addictions. The things we originally called on to help us cope with our problems—alcohol, drugs, sex, lies—have now taken over our life and are destroying us. It is not too late to call on the resource we should have turned to in the first place—God.

Jeberechiah, both known as honest men, to watch me as I wrote so they could testify that I had written it [before the child was even on the way]. [3]Then I had sexual intercourse with my wife and she conceived and bore me a son. And the Lord said, "Call him Maher-shalal-hash-baz. [4]This name prophesies that within a couple of years, before this child is even old enough to say 'Daddy' or 'Mommy,' the king of Assyria will invade both Damascus and Samaria and carry away their riches."

[5]Then the Lord spoke to me again and said:

[6]"Since the people of Jerusalem are planning to refuse my gentle care and are enthusiastic about asking King Rezin and King Pekah to come and aid them, [7,8]therefore I will overwhelm my people with Euphrates' mighty flood; the king of Assyria and all his mighty armies will rage against them. This flood will overflow all its channels and sweep into your land of Judah, O Immanuel, submerging it from end to end."

[9,10]Do your worst, O Syria and Israel, our enemies, but you will not succeed—you will be shattered. Listen to me, all you enemies of ours: Prepare for war against us—and perish! Yes! Perish! Call your councils of war, develop your strategies, prepare your plans of attacking us, and perish! For God is with us.

[11]The Lord has said in strongest terms: Do not under any circumstances go along with the plans of Judah to surrender to Syria and Israel. [12]Don't let people call you a traitor for staying true to God. Don't you panic as so many of your neighbors are doing when they think of Syria and Israel attacking you. [13]Don't fear anything except the Lord of the armies of heaven! If you fear him, you need fear nothing else. [14,15]He will be your safety; but Israel and Judah have refused his care and thereby stumbled against the Rock of their salvation and lie fallen and crushed beneath it: God's presence among them has endangered them! [16]Write down all these things I am going to do, says the Lord, and seal them up for the future. Entrust them to some godly man to pass on down to godly men of future generations.

[17]I will wait for the Lord to help us, though he is hiding now. My only hope is in him. [18]I and the children God has given me have symbolic names that reveal the plans of the Lord of heaven's armies for his people: Isaiah means "Jehovah will save (his people)," Shear-jashub means "A remnant shall return," and Maher-shalal-hash-baz means "Your enemies will soon be destroyed." [19]So why are you trying to find out the future by consulting witches and mediums? Don't listen to their whisperings and mutterings. Can the living find out the future from the dead? Why not ask your God?

[20]"Check these witches' words against the Word of God!" he says. "If their messages are different than mine, it is because I have not sent them; for they have no light or truth in them. [21]My people will be led away captive, stumbling, weary and hungry. And because they are hungry, they will rave and shake their fists at heaven and curse their King and their God. [22]Wherever they look there will be trouble and anguish and dark despair. And they will be thrust out into the darkness."

CHAPTER 9

The Coming Messiah

Nevertheless, that time of darkness and despair shall not go on forever. Though soon the land of Zebulun and Naphtali will be under God's contempt and judgment, yet in the future these very lands, Galilee and Northern Transjordan, where lies the road to the sea, will be filled with glory. [2]The people who walk in darkness shall see a great Light—a Light that will shine on all those who live in the land of the shadow of death. [3]For Israel will again be great, filled with joy like that of reapers when the harvest time has come, and like that of men dividing up the plunder they have won. [4]For God will break the chains that

---

8:6-8 Asking Assyria for protection seemed like a good solution to the leaders of Judah, but the long-term consequences would prove to be disastrous. The Assyrian armies would eventually attack Judah and destroy the land. Had the leaders heeded God's warning, they could have avoided the attacks from their former ally. Similarly, if our recovery is grounded in anything other than God and his instructions for our life, we may wind up in greater peril at some later point in life. Unlike Judah, we should seek a recovery plan that includes God.

8:11-15 Isaiah was being pressured to go along with a plan of human origin; God had nothing to do with it. To reject the king's plan, however, amounted to treason, and the king's advisers probably stressed this to Isaiah to get him to go along with the plan. We, too, will face pressure to follow ungodly plans, often leading us back into our addictions. When our "friends" try to coerce us to follow their ways, we shouldn't fear their rejection when we don't go along with them. God says that if we fear him, we need not fear anything else—not friends, coworkers, or family.

bind his people and the whip that scourges them, just as he did when he destroyed the vast host of the Midianites by Gideon's little band. 5In that glorious day of peace there will no longer be the issuing of battle gear; no more the blood-stained uniforms of war; all such will be burned.

6For unto us a child is born; unto us a son is given; and the government shall be upon his shoulder. These will be his royal titles: "Wonderful," "Counselor," "The Mighty God," "The Everlasting Father," "The Prince of Peace." 7His ever-expanding, peaceful government will never end. He will rule with perfect fairness and justice from the throne of his father David. He will bring true justice and peace to all the nations of the world. This is going to happen because the Lord of heaven's armies has dedicated himself to do it!

8-10The Lord has spoken out against that braggart Israel who says that though our land lies in ruins now, we will rebuild it better than before. The sycamore trees are cut down, but we will replace them with cedars! 11,12The Lord's reply to your bragging is to bring your enemies against you—the Syrians on the east and the Philistines on the west. With bared fangs they will devour Israel. And even then the Lord's anger against you will not be satisfied—his fist will still be poised to smash you. 13For after all this punishment you will not repent and turn to him, the Lord of heaven's armies. 14,15Therefore the Lord, in one day, will destroy the leaders of Israel and the lying prophets. 16For the leaders of his people have led them down the paths of ruin.

17That is why the Lord has no joy in their young men and no mercy upon even the widows and orphans, for they are all filthy-mouthed, wicked liars. That is why his anger is not yet satisfied, but his fist is still poised to smash them all. 18He will burn up all this wickedness, these thorns and briars; and the flames will consume the forests too, and send a vast cloud of smoke billowing up from their burning. 19,20The land is blackened by that fire, by the wrath of the Lord of heaven's armies. The people are fuel for the fire. Each fights against his brother to steal his food but will never have enough. Finally they will even eat their own children! 21Manasseh against Ephraim and Ephraim against Manasseh—and both against Judah. Yet even after all of this, God's anger is not yet satisfied. His hand is still heavy upon them to crush them.

CHAPTER 10
Promises of Protection

Woe to unjust judges and to those who issue unfair laws, says the Lord, 2so that there is no justice for the poor, the widows, and orphans. Yes, it is true that they even rob the widows and fatherless children.

3Oh, what will you do when I visit you in that day when I send desolation upon you from a distant land? To whom will you turn then for your help? Where will your treasures be safe? 4I will not help you; you will stumble along as prisoners or lie among the slain. And even then my anger will not be satisfied, but my fist will still be poised to strike you. 5,6Assyria is the whip of my anger; his military strength is my weapon upon this godless nation, doomed and damned; he will enslave them and plunder them and trample them like dirt beneath his feet. 7But the king of Assyria will not know that it is I who sent him. He will merely think he is attacking my people as part of his plan to conquer the world. 8He will declare that every one of his princes will soon be a king, ruling a conquered land.

9"We will destroy Calno just as we did Carchemish," he will say, "and Hamath will go

9:6 God is the one to whom we can turn for deep healing and recovery. He is Wonderful, without equal. He is the Counselor, who can help us sort through our inner mess and guide us into truth and reality. He is the Mighty God, who can supply us with the power to stay on the path of recovery. He is the Everlasting Father, who can love us more deeply than any earthly father can. He is the Prince of Peace, who can fill our mind with peace and our life with wholeness.

9:7 God brings justice and peace to the world and to troubled people. Though injustice seems to prevail and we may suffer from abuses that are not our fault, we can be assured that justice will be served—if not in this lifetime, then in the next. We can have God's peace if we trust in him and give him all our worries, cares, hopes, and ambitions. To have peace in our recovery, we need to ask God to help us through it.

10:1-19 The abused person can find comfort in the theological truth in these verses. Comfort can be found in knowing that (1) God can sovereignly use evil people to work good within his plan (10:5-11, here Assyria is God's instrument in disciplining Judah) and (2) God will punish evildoers (10:12-19, Assyria). It is a comfort to know that our abusers will be held accountable by God (so we can release our hatred) and that even their evil actions can be used by God for our ultimate good.

down before us as Arpad did; and we will
destroy Samaria just as we did Damascus.
10Yes, we have finished off many a kingdom
whose idols were far greater than those in
Jerusalem and Samaria, 11so when we have
defeated Samaria and her idols, we will destroy Jerusalem with hers."

12After the Lord has used the king of Assyria
to accomplish his purpose, then he will turn
upon the Assyrians and punish them too—for
they are proud and haughty men.

13They boast, "We in our own power and
wisdom have won these wars. We are great
and wise. By our own strength we broke down
the walls and destroyed the people and carried off their treasures. 14In our greatness we
have robbed their nests of riches and gathered
up kingdoms as a farmer gathers eggs, and no
one can move a finger or open his mouth to
peep against us!"

15But the Lord says, "Shall the axe boast
greater power than the man who uses it? Is
the saw greater than the man who saws? Can
a rod strike unless a hand is moving it? Can a
cane walk by itself?"

16Because of all your evil boasting, O king of
Assyria, the Lord of Hosts will send a plague
among your proud troops and strike them
down. 17God, the Light and Holy One of Israel, will be the fire and flame that will destroy them. In a single night he will burn
those thorns and briars, the Assyrians who
destroyed the land of Israel. 18Assyria's vast
army is like a glorious forest, yet it will be
destroyed. The Lord will destroy them, soul
and body, as when a sick man wastes away.
19Only a few from all that mighty army will be
left; so few a child could count them!

20Then at last those left in Israel and in
Judah will trust the Lord, the Holy One of
Israel, instead of fearing the Assyrians. 21A
remnant of them will return to the mighty
God. 22But though Israel be now as many as
the sands along the shore, yet only a few of
them will be left to return at that time; God
has rightly decided to destroy his people.
23Yes, it has already been decided by the Lord
God to consume them.

24Therefore the Lord God says, "O my
people in Jerusalem, don't be afraid of the
Assyrians when they oppress you just as the
Egyptians did long ago. 25It will not last very
long; in a little while my anger against you
will end, and then it will rise against them to
destroy them."

26The Lord Almighty will send his angel to
slay them in a mighty slaughter like the time
when Gideon triumphed over Midian at the
rock of Oreb or the time God drowned the
Egyptian armies in the sea. 27On that day God
will end the bondage of his people. He will
break the slave-yoke off their necks and destroy it as decreed.

28,29Look, the mighty armies of Assyria are
coming! Now they are at Aiath, now at Migron; they are storing some of their equipment
at Michmash and crossing over the pass; they
are staying overnight at Geba. Fear strikes the
city of Ramah; all the people of Gibeah—the
city of Saul—are running for their lives. 30Well
may you scream in terror, O people of Gallim.
Shout out a warning to Laish, for the mighty
army comes. O poor Anathoth, what a fate is
yours! 31There go the people of Madmenah, all
fleeing, and the citizens of Gebim are preparing to run. 32But the enemy stops at Nob for
the remainder of that day. He shakes his fist
at Jerusalem on Mount Zion.

33Then, look, look! The Lord, the Lord of
the armies of heaven, is chopping down the
mighty tree! He is destroying all of that vast
army, great and small alike, both officers and
men. 34He, the Mighty One, will cut down the
enemy as a woodsman's axe cuts down the
forest trees in Lebanon.

CHAPTER 11

Promises of a Perfect Ruler

The royal line of David will be cut off,
chopped down like a tree; but from the stump
will grow a Shoot—yes, a new Branch from
the old root. 2And the Spirit of the Lord shall
rest upon him, the Spirit of wisdom, understanding, counsel, and might; the Spirit of
knowledge and of the fear of the Lord. 3His
delight will be obedience to the Lord. He will

10:20 The people of Judah looked to Assyria for help in their military crisis, and Assyria would later oppress Judah. In a similar way, we look to addictive substances and behaviors and to unhealthy relationships to deliver us, and then we are victimized by our inadequate saviors. We must learn, as did the people of Judah, that only God is worthy of our trust.

11:1-10 We may feel deep insecurities and hurt over the abuse, misunderstanding, and injustice we have suffered at the hands of others. Our hope is in God, who will come again and rule the world in justice and truth. He will straighten out all the inequities of the past. When his kingdom is established, we will not have anything to fear: "Nothing will hurt or destroy in all [God's] holy mountain" (11:9).

not judge by appearance, false evidence, or
hearsay, 4but will defend the poor and the
exploited. He will rule against the wicked who
oppress them. 5For he will be clothed with
fairness and with truth.
6In that day the wolf and the lamb will lie
down together, and the leopard and goats will
be at peace. Calves and fat cattle will be safe
among lions, and a little child shall lead them
all. 7The cows will graze among bears; cubs
and calves will lie down together, and lions
will eat grass like the cows. 8Babies will crawl
safely among poisonous snakes, and a little
child who puts his hand in a nest of deadly
adders will pull it out unharmed. 9Nothing
will hurt or destroy in all my holy mountain,
for as the waters fill the sea, so shall the earth
be full of the knowledge of the Lord.
10In that day he who created the royal dynasty of David will be a banner of salvation to
all the world. The nations will rally to him, for
the land where he lives will be a glorious
place. 11At that time the Lord will bring back
a remnant of his people for the second time,
returning them to the land of Israel from
Assyria, Upper and Lower Egypt, Ethiopia,
Elam, Babylonia, Hamath, and all the distant
coastal lands. 12He will raise a flag among the
nations for them to rally to; he will gather the
scattered Israelites from the ends of the earth.
13Then at last the jealousy between Israel and
Judah will end; they will not fight each other
any more. 14Together they will fly against the
nations possessing their land on the east and
on the west, uniting forces to destroy them,
and they will occupy the nations of Edom and
Moab and Ammon.
15The Lord will dry a path through the Red
Sea and wave his hand over the Euphrates,
sending a mighty wind to divide it into seven
streams that can easily be crossed. 16He will
make a highway from Assyria for the remnant
there, just as he did for all of Israel long ago
when they returned from Egypt.

CHAPTER 12

Singing God's Praises

On that day you will say, "Praise the Lord! He
was angry with me, but now he comforts me.
2See, God has come to save me! I will trust and
not be afraid, for the Lord is my strength and
song; he is my salvation. 3Oh, the joy of
drinking deeply from the Fountain of Salvation!"
4In that wonderful day you will say, "Thank
the Lord! Praise his name! Tell the world
about his wondrous love. How mighty he is!"
5Sing to the Lord, for he has done wonderful
things. Make known his praise around the
world. 6Let all the people of Jerusalem shout
his praise with joy. For great and mighty is the
Holy One of Israel, who lives among you.

CHAPTER 13

Babylon's Doom Is Sure

This is the vision God showed Isaiah (son of
Amoz) concerning Babylon's doom.
2See the flags waving as their enemy attacks. Shout to them, O Israel, and wave them
on as they march against Babylon to destroy
the palaces of the rich and mighty. 3I, the

11:11-16 God's power to restore disintegrated families is great. The family of Israel had fallen. Many had been scattered among the nations in the dispersion. The nations of Israel and Judah were locked in destructive patterns of jealousy. Out of this mess, God promised to bring restoration and unity. He can do the same for us, too. If our family is separated because of abuse, addictions, jealousy, etc., God can unify it. Our recovery starts, however, with open communication and complete trust in God.

12:1-6 Once we turn our life over to God, we can rejoice in his salvation. God was angry with us, but now he comforts, heals, and strengthens us. And we will want to share with others the joy and the story of how God has helped us, making "known his praise around the world" (12:5). This is Step Twelve, carrying the message to others who are in need of recovery.

13:1–14:3 Babylon would come under God's judgment. God's anger at the sin of unrepentant people is clearly displayed. God is not, however, like an angry, abusive parent whose anger does not accurately correspond to a child's behavior. Toward the unrepentant unbelievers, God shows judgment. But to those who believe in him, God shows compassion (14:1).

13:1–23:18 These chapters deal with God's judgments on the unbelieving nations. Two lessons stand out for those of us who are on the path of recovery. First, evildoers will come under God's judgment. If we have been seriously hurt by certain people, we can give them up to God. We need not hold on to our pain, seeking revenge, because we know that God will deal with them. Second, those who reject God and think they can manage their lives alone will find they are headed for destruction. We need to make sure we have surrendered our life to God so we can be saved from our dependencies now and be with God in eternity.

Lord, have set apart these armies for this task; I have called those rejoicing in their strength to do this work, to satisfy my anger. [4]Hear the tumult on the mountains! Listen as the armies march! It is the tumult and the shout of many nations. The Lord Almighty has brought them here, [5]from countries far away. They are his weapons against you, O Babylon. They carry his anger with them and will destroy your whole land.

[6]Scream in terror, for the Lord's time has come, the time for the Almighty to crush you. [7]Your arms lie paralyzed with fear; the strongest hearts melt [8]and are afraid. Fear grips you with terrible pangs, like those of a woman in labor. You look at one another, helpless, as the flames of the burning city reflect upon your pallid faces. [9]For see, the day of the Lord is coming, the terrible day of his wrath and fierce anger. The land shall be destroyed and all the sinners with it. [10]The heavens will be black above them. No light will shine from stars or sun or moon.

[11]And I will punish the world for its evil, the wicked for their sin; I will crush the arrogance of the proud man and the haughtiness of the rich. [12]Few will live when I have finished up my work.

Men will be as scarce as gold—of greater value than the gold of Ophir. [13]For I will shake the heavens in my wrath and fierce anger, and the earth will move from its place in the skies.

[14]The armies of Babylon will run until exhausted, fleeing back to their own land like deer chased by dogs, wandering like sheep deserted by their shepherd. [15]Those who don't run will be butchered. [16]Their little children will be dashed to death against the pavement right before their eyes; their homes will be sacked and their wives raped by the attacking hordes. [17]For I will stir up the Medes against Babylon, and no amount of silver or gold will buy them off. [18]The attacking armies will have no mercy on the young people of Babylon or the babies or the children.

[19]And so Babylon, the most glorious of kingdoms, the flower of Chaldean culture, will be as utterly destroyed as Sodom and Gomorrah were when God sent fire from heaven; [20]Babylon will never rise again. Generation after generation will come and go, but the land will never again be lived in. The nomads will not even camp there. The shepherds won't let their sheep stay overnight. [21]The wild animals of the desert will make it their home. The houses will be haunted by howling creatures. Ostriches will live there, and the demons will come there to dance. [22]Hyenas and jackals will den within the palaces. Babylon's days are numbered; her time of doom will soon be here.

CHAPTER 14

Promises of Mercy

But the Lord will have mercy on the Israelis; they are still his special ones. He will bring them back to settle once again in the land of Israel. And many nationalities will come and join them there and be their loyal allies. [2]The nations of the world will help them to return, and those coming to live in their land will serve them. Those enslaving Israel will be enslaved—Israel shall rule her enemies!

[3]In that wonderful day when the Lord gives his people rest from sorrow and fear, from slavery and chains, [4]you will jeer at the king of Babylon and say, "You bully, you! At last you have what was coming to you! [5]For the Lord has crushed your wicked power and broken your evil rule." [6]You persecuted my people with unceasing blows of rage and held the nations in your angry grip. You were unrestrained in tyranny. [7]But at last the whole earth is at rest and is quiet! All the world begins to sing! [8]Even the trees of the woods—the fir trees and cedars of Lebanon—sing out this joyous song: "Your power is broken; no one will bother us now; at last we have peace."

[9]The denizens of hell crowd to meet you as you enter their domain. World leaders and earth's mightiest kings, long dead, are there to see you. [10]With one voice they all cry out, "Now you are as weak as we are!" [11]Your might and power are gone; they are buried with you. All the pleasant music in your palace has ceased; now maggots are your sheet, worms your blanket!

[12]How you are fallen from heaven, O Lucifer, son of the morning! How you are cut down to the ground—mighty though you were against the nations of the world. [13]For you said to yourself, "I will ascend to heaven and rule the angels. I will take the highest throne. I will preside on the Mount of Assem-

14:12-20 Pride was the root of the problem with Babylon and her king. We, too, must beware of this deadly sin. Healthy self-esteem is proper, but the sin of pride makes us think we are better than others, even God. Sometimes our pride is an unhealthy attempt to cover up deep insecurities that can be dealt with only by the love and grace of God.

bly far away in the north. 14I will climb to the highest heavens and be like the Most High." 15But instead, you will be brought down to the pit of hell, down to its lowest depths. 16Everyone there will stare at you and ask, "Can this be the one who shook the earth and the kingdoms of the world? 17Can this be the one who destroyed the world and made it into a shambles, who demolished its greatest cities and had no mercy on his prisoners?"

18The kings of the nations lie in stately glory in their graves, 19but your body is thrown out like a broken branch; it lies in an open grave, covered with the dead bodies of those slain in battle. It lies as a carcass in the road, trampled and mangled by horses' hoofs. 20No monument will be given you, for you have destroyed your nation and slain your people. Your son will not succeed you as the king. 21Slay the children of this sinner. Do not let them rise and conquer the land nor rebuild the cities of the world.

22I, myself, have risen against him, says the Lord of heaven's armies, and will cut off his children and his children's children from ever sitting on his throne.23 I will make Babylon into a desolate land of porcupines, full of swamps and marshes. I will sweep the land with the broom of destruction, says the Lord of the armies of heaven.24He has taken an oath to do it! For this is his purpose and plan. 25I have decided to break the Assyrian army when they are in Israel and to crush them on my mountains; my people shall no longer be their slaves. 26 This is my plan for the whole earth—I will do it by my mighty power that reaches everywhere around the world. 27The Lord, the God of battle, has spoken—who can change his plans? When his hand moves, who can stop him?

Prophecy against Philistia

28This is the message that came to me the year King Ahaz died:

29Don't rejoice, Philistines, that the king who smote you is dead. That rod is broken, yes; but his son will be a greater scourge to you than his father ever was! From the snake will be born an adder, a fiery serpent to destroy you! 30I will shepherd the poor of my people; they shall graze in my pasture! The needy shall lie down in peace. But as for you—I will wipe you out with famine and the sword. 31Weep, Philistine cities—you are doomed. All your nation is doomed. For a perfectly trained army is coming down from the north against you. 32What then shall we tell the reporters? Tell them that the Lord has founded Jerusalem and is determined that the poor of his people will find a refuge within her walls.

CHAPTER 15

Prophecy against Moab

Here is God's message to Moab: In one night your cities of Ar and Kir will be destroyed. 2Your people in Dibon go mourning to their temples to weep for the fate of Nebo and Medeba; they shave their heads in sorrow and cut off their beards. 3They wear sackcloth through the streets, and from every home comes the sound of weeping. 4The cries from the cities of Heshbon and Elealeh are heard far away, even in Jahaz. The bravest warriors of Moab cry in utter terror.

5My heart weeps for Moab! His people flee to Zoar and Eglath. Weeping, they climb the upward road to Luhith, and their crying will be heard all along the road to Horonaim. 6Even Nimrim River is desolate! The grassy banks are dried up and the tender plants are gone. 7The desperate refugees take only the possessions they can carry and flee across the Brook of Willows. 8The whole land of Moab is a land of weeping from one end to the other. 9The stream near Dibon will run red with blood, but I am not through with Dibon yet! Lions will hunt down the survivors, both those who escape and those who remain.

CHAPTER 16

God Rebukes Moab

Moab's refugees at Sela send lambs as a token of alliance with the king of Judah. 2The

14:26-27 We would be foolish to ignore God and his moral laws and still hope that life will go well anyway. The Assyrians thought just that, but they were denying reality. God is sovereign over the whole earth and will uphold his moral laws and purposes whether we believe it or not. Since this is the reality of the matter, we need to follow God and his laws. Even if we have ignored God all our life, it is not too late to turn to him and start living for him now.

15:2-3 The Moabites lamented their suffering, but they never recognized their sins and asked God to forgive them. We face a similar danger in recovery. Unless we admit our problems and dependencies to God and others, we may never get beyond feeling sorry for ourself. Bemoaning the suffering brought on by our dependencies is helpful only if it leads to action that results in changes in our behavior.

women of Moab are left at the fords of the Arnon River like homeless birds. [3][The ambassadors, who accompany the gift to Jerusalem] plead for advice and help. "Give us sanctuary. Protect us. Do not turn us over to our foes. [4,5]Let our outcasts stay among you; hide them from our enemies! God will reward you for your kindness to us. If you let Moab's fugitives settle among you, then when the terror is past, God will establish David's throne forever, and on that throne he will place a just and righteous King."

[6]Is this proud Moab, concerning which we heard so much? His arrogance and insolence are all gone now! [7]Therefore all Moab weeps. Yes, Moab, you will mourn for stricken Kir-hareseth, [8]and for the abandoned farms of Heshbon and the vineyards at Sibmah. The enemy warlords have cut down the best of the grapevines; their armies spread out as far as Jazer in the deserts, and even down to the sea. [9]So I wail and lament for Jazer and the vineyards of Sibmah. My tears shall flow for Heshbon and Elealeh, for destruction has come upon their summer fruits and harvests. [10]Gone now is the gladness, gone the joy of harvest. The happy singing in the vineyards will be heard no more; the treading out of the grapes in the wine presses has ceased forever. I have ended all their harvest joys.

[11]I will weep, weep, weep, for Moab; and my sorrow for Kir-hareseth will be very great. [12]The people of Moab will pray in anguish to their idols at the tops of the hills, but it will do no good; they will cry to their gods in their idol temples, but none will come to save them. [13,14]All this concerning Moab has been said before; but now the Lord says that within three years, without fail, the glory of Moab shall be ended, and few of all its people will be left alive.

CHAPTER 17

Prophecy against Syria

This is God's message to Damascus, capital of Syria:

Look, Damascus is gone! It is no longer a city—it has become a heap of ruins! [2]The cities of Aroer are deserted. Sheep pasture there, lying quiet and unafraid, with no one to chase them away. [3]The strength of Israel and the power of Damascus will end, and the remnant of Syria shall be destroyed. For as Israel's glory departed, so theirs, too, will disappear, declares the Lord Almighty. [4]Yes, the glory of Israel will be very dim when poverty stalks the land. [5]Israel will be as abandoned as the harvested grain fields in the Valley of Rephaim. [6]Oh, a very few of her people will be left, just as a few stray olives are left on the trees when the harvest is ended, two or three in the highest branches, four or five out on the tips of the limbs. That is how it will be in Damascus and Israel—stripped bare of people except for a few of the poor who remain.

[7]Then at last they will think of God their Creator and have respect for the Holy One of Israel. [8]They will no longer ask their idols for help in that day, neither will they worship what their hands have made! They will no longer have respect for the images of Ashtaroth and the sun-idols.

[9]Their largest cities will be as deserted as the distant wooded hills and mountaintops and become like the abandoned cities of the Amorites, deserted when the Israelites approached (so long ago). [10]Why? Because you have turned from the God who can save you—the Rock who can hide you; therefore, even though you plant a wonderful, rare crop of greatest value, [11]and though it grows so well that it will blossom on the very morning that you plant it, yet you will never harvest it—your only harvest will be a pile of grief and incurable pain.

[12]Look, see the armies thundering toward God's land. [13]But though they roar like breakers rolling upon a beach, God will silence them. They will flee, scattered like chaff by the wind, like whirling dust before a storm. [14]In the evening Israel waits in terror, but by

---

16:3-5 This exhortation to Judah could well be applied to our communities and their dealings with hurting people. Have we opened our doors to those with addictions—abused, dysfunctional, and hurting people—so they can find refuge, counsel, and help in an environment of love and grace?

16:12 Judgment would come to humble Moab and to force her to deal with the truth of her sin. Instead of turning to God, she would turn to idols that had no power to help. Moab is like the person who needs recovery but refuses it. Help is there if we will only accept it. Instead of turning to God, we may turn to workaholism, perfectionism, or substance abuse. These "solutions," however, will only add to our problems.

17:3-7 It would take almost complete destruction for Israel to respect God and follow him. Hopefully we won't wait until our life is devastated before turning to God for help. The sooner we admit that our life is unmanageable, the sooner we can ask God to rescue us.

dawn her enemies are dead. This is the just reward of those who plunder and destroy the people of God.

CHAPTER 18
Prophecy against Ethiopia

Ah, land beyond the upper reaches of the Nile, where winged sailboats glide along the river! 2Land that sends ambassadors in fast boats down the Nile! Let swift messengers return to you, O strong and supple nation feared far and wide, a conquering, destroying nation whose land the upper Nile divides. And this is the message sent to you:

3When I raise my battle flag upon the mountain, let all the world take notice! When I blow the trumpet, listen! 4For the Lord has told me this: "Let your mighty army now advance against the land of Israel. God will watch quietly from his Temple in Jerusalem—serene as on a pleasant summer day or a lovely autumn morning during harvesttime." 5But before you have begun the attack, and while your plans are ripening like grapes, he will cut you off as though with pruning shears. He will snip the spreading tendrils. 6Your mighty army will be left dead on the field for the mountain birds and wild animals to eat; the vultures will tear bodies all summer, and the wild animals will gnaw bones all winter. 7But the time will come when that strong and mighty nation, a terror to all both far and near, that conquering, destroying nation whose land the rivers divide, will bring gifts to the Lord Almighty in Jerusalem, where he has placed his name.

CHAPTER 19
Prophecy against Egypt

This is God's message concerning Egypt:

Look, the Lord is coming against Egypt, riding on a swift cloud; the idols of Egypt tremble; the hearts of the Egyptians melt with fear. 2I will set them to fighting against each other—brother against brother, neighbor against neighbor, city against city, province against province. 3Her wise counselors are all at their wits' end to know what to do; they plead with their idols for wisdom and call upon mediums, wizards, and witches to show them what to do. 4I will hand over Egypt to a hard, cruel master, to a vicious king, says the Lord Almighty.

5And the waters of the Nile will fail to rise and flood the fields; the ditches will be parched and dry, 6their channels fouled with rotting reeds. 7All green things along the riverbank will wither and blow away. All crops will perish; everything will die. 8The fishermen will weep for lack of work; those who fish with hooks and those who use the nets will all be unemployed. 9The weavers will have no flax or cotton, for the crops will fail. 10Great men and small—all will be crushed and broken.

11What fools the counselors of Zoan are! Their best counsel to the king of Egypt is utterly stupid and wrong. Will they still boast of their wisdom? Will they dare tell Pharaoh about the long line of wise men they have come from? 12What has happened to your "wise counselors," O Pharaoh? Where has their wisdom gone? If they are wise, let them tell you what the Lord is going to do to Egypt. 13The "wise men" from Zoan are also fools, and those from Memphis are utterly deluded. They are the best you can find, but they have ruined Egypt with their foolish counsel. 14The Lord has sent a spirit of foolishness on them, so that all their suggestions are wrong; they make Egypt stagger like a sick drunkard. 15Egypt cannot be saved by anything or anybody—no one can show her the way.

16In that day the Egyptians will be as weak as women, cowering in fear beneath the upraised fist of God. 17Just to speak the name of Israel will strike deep terror in their hearts, for the Lord Almighty has laid his plans against them.

18At that time five of the cities of Egypt will follow the Lord Almighty and will begin to speak the Hebrew language. One of these will be Heliopolis, "The City of the Sun." 19And there will be an altar to the Lord in the heart of Egypt in those days and a monument to the Lord at its border. 20This will be for a sign of

---

18:7 The enemy nation of Ethiopia would one day come to Jerusalem to worship God. This reminds us that God can do the unexpected and seemingly impossible. What things in our life look impossible? Is it recovering from an addiction, restoring a relationship, putting past abuses behind us? Whatever the situation, God can bring healing. "Is anything too hard for God?" (Genesis 18:14).

19:11-14 The wisdom of the Egyptians turned out to be foolish. The wise men counted on their own logic and were deceived. True wisdom comes from God alone. Our plans will succeed only if we ask God for assistance and rely on him to show us the proper way to go.

loyalty to the Lord Almighty; then when they
cry to the Lord for help against those who
oppress them, he will send them a Savior—
and he shall deliver them.
21In that day the Lord will make himself
known to the Egyptians. Yes, they will know
the Lord and give their sacrifices and offerings
to him; they will make promises to God and
keep them. 22The Lord will smite Egypt and
then restore her! For the Egyptians will turn
to the Lord and he will listen to their plea and
heal them.
23In that day Egypt and Iraq will be connected by a highway, and the Egyptians and
the Iraqi will move freely back and forth between their lands, and they shall worship the
same God. 24And Israel will be their ally; the
three will be together, and Israel will be a
blessing to them. 25For the Lord will bless
Egypt and Iraq because of their friendship
with Israel. He will say, "Blessed be Egypt, my
people; blessed be Iraq, the land I have made;
blessed be Israel, my inheritance!"

CHAPTER 20

The Barefoot Prophet

In the year when Sargon, king of Assyria, sent
the commander-in-chief of his army against
the Philistine city of Ashdod and captured it,
2the Lord told Isaiah, the son of Amoz, to take
off his clothing, including his shoes, and to
walk around naked and barefoot. And Isaiah
did as he was told.
3Then the Lord said, My servant Isaiah,
who has been walking naked and barefoot for
the last three years, is a symbol of the terrible
troubles I will bring upon Egypt and Ethiopia.
4For the king of Assyria will take away the
Egyptians and Ethiopians as prisoners, making them walk naked and barefoot, both
young and old, their buttocks uncovered, to
the shame of Egypt. 5,6Then how dismayed
the Philistines will be, who counted on "Ethiopia's power" and their "glorious ally," Egypt!
And they will say, "If this can happen to
Egypt, what chance have we?"

CHAPTER 21

Prophecy against Babylon

This is God's message concerning Babylon:
Disaster is roaring down upon you from the
terrible desert, like a whirlwind sweeping
from the Negeb. 2I see an awesome vision: oh,
the horror of it all! God is telling me what he
is going to do. I see you plundered and destroyed. Elamites and Medes will take part in
the siege. Babylon will fall, and the groaning
of all the nations she enslaved will end. 3My
stomach constricts and burns with pain;
sharp pangs of horror are upon me, like the
pangs of a woman giving birth to a child. I
faint when I hear what God is planning; I am
terrified, blinded with dismay. 4My mind
reels; my heart races; I am gripped by awful
fear. All rest at night—so pleasant once—is
gone; I lie awake, trembling.
5Look! They are preparing a great banquet!
They load the tables with food; they pull up
their chairs to eat. . . . Quick, quick, grab your
shields and prepare for battle! You are being
attacked!
6,7Meanwhile (in my vision) the Lord had
told me, "Put a watchman on the city wall to
shout out what he sees. When he sees riders
in pairs on donkeys and camels, tell him,
'This is it!'"
8,9So I put the watchman on the wall, and
at last he shouted, "Sir, day after day and
night after night I have been here at my post.
Now at last—look! Here come riders in pairs!"
Then I heard a Voice shout out, "Babylon is
fallen, is fallen; and all the idols of Babylon lie
broken on the ground."
10O my people, threshed and winnowed, I
have told you all that the Lord Almighty, the
God of Israel, has said.

Prophecy against Edom

11This is God's message to Edom:
Someone from among you keeps calling,
calling to me: "Watchman, what of the night?
Watchman, what of the night? How much
time is left?" 12The watchman replies, "Your
judgment day is dawning now. Turn again to
God, so that I can give you better news. Seek
for him, then come and ask again!"

Prophecy against Arabia

13This is God's message concerning Arabia:
O caravans from Dedan, you will hide in

21:5 The Babylonians would choose to continue in denial. Their destruction would be imminent, but they would not face up to reality. They would be feasting when they should have been preparing for battle. As a result, they would fall to the Medes and Persians without a fight (see Daniel 5). Like the Babylonians, we won't know when disaster is ready to strike. We could be reveling in our addiction when *bam,* a major catastrophe hits us. But if we turn our life and addiction over to God, we can avoid any destructive consequences that may otherwise be ahead.

the deserts of Arabia. 14O people of Tema, bring food and water to these weary fugitives! 15They have fled from drawn swords and sharp arrows and the terrors of war! 16"But a long year from now," says the Lord, "the great power of their enemy, the mighty tribe of Kedar, will end. 17Only a few of its stalwart archers will survive." The Lord, the God of Israel, has spoken.

CHAPTER 22

Prophecy about Jerusalem

This is God's message concerning Jerusalem:

What is happening? Where is everyone going? Why are they running to the rooftops? What are they looking at? 2The whole city is in terrible uproar. What's the trouble in this busy, happy city? Bodies! Lying everywhere, slain by plague and not by sword. 3All your leaders flee; they surrender without resistance. The people slip away but they are captured too. 4Let me alone to weep. Don't try to comfort me—let me cry for my people as I watch them being destroyed. 5Oh, what a day of crushing trouble! What a day of confusion and terror from the Lord God of heaven's armies! The walls of Jerusalem are breached, and the cry of death echoes from the mountainsides. 6,7Elamites are the archers; Syrians drive the chariots; the men of Kir hold up the shields. They fill your choicest valleys and crowd against your gates.

8God has removed his protecting care. You run to the armory for your weapons! 9-11You inspect the walls of Jerusalem to see what needs repair! You check over the houses and tear some down for stone for fixing walls. Between the city walls, you build a reservoir for water from the lower pool! But all your feverish plans will not avail, for you never ask for help from God, who lets this come upon you. He is the one who planned it long ago. 12The Lord God called you to repent, to weep and mourn, to shave your heads in sorrow for your sins, and to wear clothes made of sackcloth to show your remorse. 13But instead, you sing and dance and play, and feast and drink. "Let us eat, drink, and be merry," you say: "What's the difference, for tomorrow we die." 14The Lord Almighty has revealed to me that this sin will never be forgiven you until the day you die.

15,16Furthermore, the same Lord God of the armies of heaven has told me this: Go and say to Shebna, the palace administrator: "And who do you think you are, building this beautiful sepulchre in the rock for yourself? 17For the Lord who allowed you to be clothed so gorgeously will hurl you away, sending you into captivity, O strong man! 18He will wad you up in his hands like a ball and toss you away into a distant, barren land; there you will die, O glorious one—you who disgrace your nation!

19"Yes, I will drive you out of office," says the Lord, "and pull you down from your high position. 20And then I will call my servant Eliakim, the son of Hilkiah, to replace you. 21He shall have your uniform and title and authority, and he will be a father to the people of Jerusalem and all Judah. 22I will give him responsibility over all my people; whatever he says will be done; none will be able to stop him. 23,24I will make of him a strong and steady peg to support my people; they will load him with responsibility, and he will be an honor to his family name." 25But the Lord will pull out that other peg that seems to be so firmly fastened to the wall! It will come out and fall to the ground, and everything it supports will fall with it, for the Lord has spoken.

CHAPTER 23

Prophecy against Tyre

This is God's message to Tyre:

Weep, O ships of Tyre, returning home from distant lands! Weep for your harbor, for it is gone! The rumors that you heard in Cyprus are all true. 2,3Deathly silence is everywhere. Stillness reigns where once your hustling port was full of ships from Sidon, bringing merchandise from far across the

22:1-11 Judah was threatened with destruction. They responded by taking an inventory of their situation and weaponry, but they still overlooked one thing—God. They still believed they could stand off the enemy on their own. We do the same thing today. While our dependencies are about to ruin us, we look within ourself to try to handle the situation on our own. We forget to turn to the only resource that can truly help—God. The first steps to recovery include admitting that we are powerless over our problem and recognizing that we can succeed only with God.

22:12-14 Ignoring our problems doesn't make them go away. Rather, the opposite happens—they get worse because we have put off dealing with them. And if we have turned to alcohol, drugs, or food, we have actually added another problem to our list of worries. Instead of giving up hope (as Judah did), we should turn to God and seek his help. If we trust the promises he has given us in the Bible, there is no reason to give up—God is faithful!

ocean, from Egypt and along the Nile. You
were the merchandise mart of the world. 4Be
ashamed, O Sidon, stronghold of the sea. For
you are childless now! 5When Egypt hears the
news, there will be great sorrow. 6Flee to Tarshish, men of Tyre, weeping as you go. 7This
silent ruin is all that's left of your once joyous
land. What a history was yours! Think of all
the colonists you sent to distant lands!

8Who has brought this disaster on Tyre,
empire builder and top trader of the world?
9The Commander of the armies of heaven has
done it to destroy your pride and show his
contempt for all the greatness of mankind.
10Sail on, O ships of Tarshish, for your harbor
is gone. 11The Lord holds out his hand over
the seas; he shakes the kingdoms of the earth;
he has spoken out against this great merchant
city, to destroy its strength.

12He says, "Never again, O dishonored virgin, daughter of Sidon, will you rejoice, will
you be strong. Even if you flee to Cyprus, you
will find no rest."

13It will be the Babylonians, not the Assyrians, who consign Tyre to the wild beasts.
They will lay siege to it, raze its palaces, and
make it a heap of ruins. 14Wail, you ships that
ply the oceans, for your home port is destroyed!

15,16For seventy years Tyre will be forgotten.
Then, in the days of another king, the city will
come back to life again; she will sing sweet
songs as a harlot sings who, long absent from
her lovers, walks the streets to look for them
again and is remembered. 17Yes, after seventy
years, the Lord will revive Tyre, but she will be
no different than she was before; she will
return again to all her evil ways around the
world. 18Yet [the distant time will come when]
her businesses will give their profits to the
Lord! They will not be hoarded but used for
good food and fine clothes for the priests of
the Lord!

CHAPTER 24

Trouble Is Coming!

Look! The Lord is overturning the land of
Judah and making it a vast wasteland of destruction. See how he is emptying out all its
people and scattering them over the face of
the earth. 2Priests and people, servants and
masters, slave girls and mistresses, buyers and
sellers, lenders and borrowers, bankers and
debtors—none will be spared. 3The land will
be completely emptied and looted. The Lord
has spoken. 4,5The land suffers for the sins of
its people. The earth languishes, the crops
wither, the skies refuse their rain. The land is
defiled by crime; the people have twisted the
laws of God and broken his everlasting commands. 6Therefore the curse of God is upon
them; they are left desolate, destroyed by the
drought. Few will be left alive.

7All the joys of life will go: the grape harvest
will fail, the wine will be gone, the merry-
makers will sigh and mourn. 8The melodious
chords of the harp and timbrel are heard no
more; the happy days are ended. 9No more are
the joys of wine and song; strong drink turns
bitter in the mouth.

10The city lies in chaos; every home and
shop is locked up tight to keep out looters.
11Mobs form in the streets, crying for wine;
joy has reached its lowest ebb; gladness has
been banished from the land. 12The city is left
in ruins; its gates are battered down.
13Throughout the land the story is the same—
only a remnant is left.

23:1-12 God pronounced judgment on the prosperous merchant city of Tyre for her pride. Pride is not wrong when it is positive self-esteem ("I was proud of my son's winning home run"), but it is disastrous when it is arrogance like Tyre's, which said, in effect, "I don't need God. I can make my life prosper by my own efforts." We need to constantly take inventory of our pride and make sure we have not replaced our dependence on God with unrealistic confidence in ourself.

23:13-18 At the end of seventy years Tyre would rebuild and return to her old ways of seducing the nations to materialism and idolatry. Without genuine recovery, we, too, go back to the old destructive patterns in our life. Our recovery aim needs to be more than just freedom from drugs or alcohol. We need a whole new life, with God as the foundation. As Jesus said, when we follow him we are like a man who builds a house on rock. Even though the storms of life constantly assail us, we will stand firm (see Matthew 7:24-27).

24:4-7 Our sins do not affect only us; they affect our family, our friends, our nation, and even our planet. It is sobering to realize that what we do has such a great impact on the world. Our whole country is suffering the effects of alcoholism, drug addiction, infidelity, etc., and these problems only seem to be getting worse. Our recovery should be important to us and to those close to us, but there is even more at stake. If each of us were to successfully complete our recovery program, the incidence of dependency and addiction would decline, and our society could gain ground in these areas.

14But all who are left will shout and sing for joy; those in the west will praise the majesty of God, 15,16and those in the east will respond with praise. Hear them singing to the Lord from the ends of the earth, singing glory to the Righteous One!

But my heart is heavy with grief, for evil still prevails and treachery is everywhere. 17Terror and the captivity of hell are still your lot, O men of the world. 18When you flee in terror, you will fall into a pit, and if you escape from the pit, you will step into a trap, for destruction falls from the heavens upon you; the world is shaken beneath you. 19The earth has broken down in utter collapse; everything is lost, abandoned, and confused. 20The world staggers like a drunkard; it shakes like a tent in a storm. It falls and will not rise again, for the sins of the earth are very great.

21On that day the Lord will punish the fallen angels in the heavens and the proud rulers of the nations on earth. 22They will be rounded up like prisoners and imprisoned in a dungeon until they are tried and condemned. 23Then the Lord of heaven's armies will mount his throne in Zion and rule gloriously in Jerusalem, in the sight of all the elders of his people. Such glory there will be that all the brightness of the sun and moon will seem to fade away.

CHAPTER 25
A Day of Rejoicing
O Lord, I will honor and praise your name, for you are my God; you do such wonderful things! You planned them long ago, and now you have accomplished them, just as you said! 2You turn mighty cities into heaps of ruins. The strongest forts are turned to rubble. Beautiful palaces in distant lands disappear and will never be rebuilt. 3Therefore strong nations will shake with fear before you; ruthless nations will obey and glorify your name.

4But to the poor, O Lord, you are a refuge from the storm, a shadow from the heat, a shelter from merciless men who are like a driving rain that melts down an earthen wall. 5As a hot, dry land is cooled by clouds, you will cool the pride of ruthless nations. 6Here on Mount Zion in Jerusalem, the Lord Almighty will spread a wondrous feast for everyone around the world—a delicious feast of good food, with clear, well-aged wine and choice beef. 7At that time he will remove the cloud of gloom, the pall of death that hangs over the earth; 8he will swallow up death forever. The Lord God will wipe away all tears and take away forever all insults and mockery against his land and people. The Lord has spoken—he will surely do it!

9In that day the people will proclaim, "This is our God in whom we trust, for whom we waited. Now at last he is here." What a day of rejoicing! 10For the Lord's good hand will rest upon Jerusalem, and Moab will be crushed as straw beneath his feet and left to rot. 11God will push them down just as a swimmer pushes down the water with his hands. He will end their pride and all their evil works. 12The high walls of Moab will be demolished and brought to dust.

CHAPTER 26
The People Sing to God
Listen to them singing! In that day the whole land of Judah will sing this song:

"Our city is strong! We are surrounded by the walls of his salvation!" 2Open the gates to everyone, for all may enter in who love the Lord. 3He will keep in perfect peace all those who trust in him, whose thoughts turn often to the Lord! 4Trust in the Lord God always, for in the Lord Jehovah is your everlasting strength. 5He humbles the proud and brings the haughty city to the dust; its walls come

24:17-20 The people here were in denial about their circumstances, and Isaiah said that they would get what they deserved. We, too, "get what's coming to us" when we ignore the warning signs and continue in our dependencies and compulsions. To deny the results of our dependencies is to invite disaster into our life. When we are honest with ourself, we can see that what we are doing is wrong and then take steps to recover.

25:1-5 God will comfort those who trust in him and punish those who ignore him. This is a great comfort to those of us who have established a relationship with God. No matter what we have done to mess up our life before, we can rely on God to strengthen us and keep us from our dependencies. If we haven't yet asked God to take control of our unmanageable life, there is still time. No one is too far gone to receive God's mercy.

26:3 When our mind is absorbed with playing back memories of abuse, failure, and shame, we are full of anxiety and turmoil, whether we were the victim of the abuse or the main perpetrator of wrong. But when we learn to work through the past and change our mind-set so that it is fixed on God, we can be flooded with his peace.

crashing down. 6He presents it to the poor and needy for their use.

7But for good men the path is not uphill and rough! God does not give them a rough and treacherous path, but smooths the road before them. 8 O Lord, we love to do your will! Our hearts' desire is to glorify your name. 9All night long I search for you; earnestly I seek for God; for only when you come in judgment on the earth to punish it will people turn away from wickedness and do what is right.

10Your kindness to the wicked doesn't make them good; they keep on doing wrong and take no notice of your majesty. 11They do not listen when you threaten; they will not look to see your upraised fist. Show them how much you love your people. Perhaps then they will be ashamed! Yes, let them be burned up by the fire reserved for your enemies.

12Lord, grant us peace; for all we have and are has come from you. 13 O Lord our God, once we worshiped other gods; but now we worship you alone. 14Those we served before are dead and gone; never again will they return. You came against them and destroyed them, and they are long forgotten. 15O praise the Lord! He has made our nation very great. He has widened the boundaries of our land!

16Lord, in their distress they sought for you. When your punishment was on them, they poured forth a whispered prayer. 17How we missed your presence, Lord! We suffered as a woman giving birth who cries and writhes in pain. 18We too have writhed in agony, but all to no avail. No deliverance has come from all our efforts. 19Yet we have this assurance: Those who belong to God shall live again. Their bodies shall rise again! Those who dwell in the dust shall awake and sing for joy! For God's light of life will fall like dew upon them!

20Go home, my people, and lock the doors! Hide for a little while until the Lord's wrath against your enemies has passed. 21Look! The Lord is coming from the heavens to punish the people of the earth for their sins. The earth will no longer hide the murderers. The guilty will be found.

CHAPTER 27
God Promises Deliverance

In that day the Lord will take his terrible, swift sword and punish leviathan, the swiftly moving serpent, the coiling, writhing serpent, the dragon of the sea.

2In that day [of Israel's freedom] let this anthem be their song:

3Israel is my vineyard; I, the Lord, will tend the fruitful vines; every day I'll water them, and day and night I'll watch to keep all enemies away. 4,5My anger against Israel is gone. If I find thorns and briars bothering her, I will burn them up, unless these enemies of mine surrender and beg for peace and my protection. 6The time will come when Israel will take root and bud and blossom and fill the whole earth with her fruit!

7,8Has God punished Israel as much as he has punished her enemies? No, for he has devastated her enemies, while he has punished Israel but a little, exiling her far from her own land as though blown away in a storm from the east. 9And why did God do it? It was to purge away her sins, to rid her of all her idol altars and her idols. They will never be worshiped again. 10Her walled cities will be silent and empty, houses abandoned, streets grown up with grass, cows grazing through the city munching on twigs and branches.

11My people are like the dead branches of a tree, broken off and used to burn beneath the pots. They are a foolish nation, a witless, stupid people, for they turn away from God. Therefore, he who made them will not have pity on them or show them his mercy. 12Yet the time will come when the Lord will gather them together one by one like handpicked grain, selecting them here and there from his great threshing floor that reaches all the way

26:12-15 These verses summarize the recovery process. The Israelites admitted their sins and turned to God for salvation. They were willing to put aside their false gods, and God came and destroyed the idols. The people then praised God for what he did. Our recovery will follow the same pattern. Our "false gods" are alcohol, drugs, sex, pride—anything that takes us out of God's control. We need to admit our problem and turn to God for help.

27:1 Leviathan was a mythical sea monster that was opposed to God. Its mention here is symbolic; God will destroy his enemies, especially Satan, God's chief rival. This is encouraging to those struggling with drugs, alcohol, sexual sins, eating disorders, or other dependencies that seem like oppressive monsters. God will vanquish these creatures that live in the depths of our life.

27:3 God said he would take care of his people, just as a farmer takes care of his vineyard. He would provide the nourishment and keep enemies away. That truth is the same for us today as it was for the Israelites. God will protect us if we surrender to his power. Once we admit our sins to him, he will help us to stay away from the pull of our dependencies.

from the Euphrates River to the Egyptian boundary. [13]In that day the great trumpet will be blown, and many about to perish among their enemies, Assyria and Egypt, will be rescued and brought back to Jerusalem to worship the Lord in his holy mountain.

CHAPTER 28

Prophecy against Samaria

Woe to the city of Samaria, surrounded by her rich valley—Samaria, the pride and delight of the drunkards of Israel! Woe to her fading beauty, the crowning glory of a nation of men lying drunk in the streets! [2]For the Lord will send a mighty army (the Assyrians) against you; like a mighty hailstorm he will burst upon you and dash you to the ground. [3]The proud city of Samaria—yes, the joy and delight of the drunkards of Israel—will be hurled to the ground and trampled beneath the enemies' feet. [4]Once glorious, her fading beauty surrounded by a fertile valley will suddenly be gone, greedily snatched away as an early fig is hungrily snatched and gobbled up!

[5]Then at last the Lord Almighty himself will be their crowning glory, the diadem of beauty to his people who are left. [6]He will give a longing for justice to your judges and great courage to your soldiers who are battling to the last before your gates. [7]But Jerusalem is now led by drunks! Her priests and prophets reel and stagger, making stupid errors and mistakes. [8]Their tables are covered with vomit; filth is everywhere.

[9]"Who does Isaiah think he is," the people say, "to speak to us like this! Are we little children, barely old enough to talk? [10]He tells us everything over and over again, a line at a time and in such simple words!"

[11]But they won't listen; the only language they can understand is punishment! So God will punish them by sending against them foreigners who speak strange gibberish! Only then will they listen to him! [12]They could have rest in their own land if they would obey him, if they were kind and good. He told them that, but they wouldn't listen to him. [13]So the Lord will spell it out for them again, repeating it over and over in simple words whenever he can; yet over this simple, straightforward message they will stumble and fall and be broken, trapped and captured.

[14]Therefore hear the word of the Lord, you scoffing rulers in Jerusalem:

[15]You have struck a bargain with Death, you say, and sold yourselves to the devil in exchange for his protection against the Assyrians. "They can never touch us," you say, "for we are under the care of one who will deceive and fool them."

[16]But the Lord God says, "See, I am placing a Foundation Stone in Zion—a firm, tested, precious Cornerstone that is safe to build on. He who believes need never run away again. [17]I will take the line and plummet of justice to check the foundation wall you built; it looks so fine, but it is so weak a storm of hail will knock it down! The enemy will come like a flood and sweep it away, and you will be drowned. [18]I will cancel your agreement of compromise with Death and the devil, so when the terrible enemy floods in, you will be trampled into the ground. [19]Again and again that flood will come and carry you off, until at last the unmixed horror of the truth of my warnings will finally dawn on you."

[20]The bed you have made is far too short to lie on; the blankets are too narrow to cover you. [21]The Lord will come suddenly and in anger, as at Mount Perazim and Gibeon, to do

---

28:1-6 The rewards of our addictions are like a crown of flowers whose beauty quickly fades. The high we experience quickly fades and leaves us wanting. In contrast, God is an unfading crown of glory to those who obey his commands. He is able to fill our life completely, and the "high" we feel from him will last throughout eternity.

28:7-13 Judah's leaders belittled Isaiah's message by saying it was infantile (28:9-10) and, by doing so, rejected God's saving rest for them. We, too, can get so caught up in our addictions and dysfunctions that we belittle God's way of recovery, considering it to be elementary and old-fashioned. However, the truth is that God has graciously provided the only means for our recovery. When we reject his methods, we harm only ourself.

28:14-22 The rulers of Jerusalem were in total denial. They thought they were in full control and could stand against the almost certain destruction that Assyria would bring. In reality, though, they were about to fall to the overwhelming scourge of God's judgment through Assyria. Likewise, we commit a fatal error when we are confronted by God's corrections and yet deny that there is any trouble we cannot handle. We cannot overpower God, and it is foolish to try. When King David sinned and faced judgment (see 2 Samuel 24), he said, "It is better to fall into the hand of the Lord (for his mercy is great) than into the hands of men" (2 Samuel 24:14). God will show us mercy if we truly repent and turn from our destructive ways.

a strange, unusual thing—to destroy his own
people! 22So scoff no more, lest your punishment be made even greater, for the Lord God
has plainly told me that he is determined to
crush you.

23,24Listen to me, listen as I plead: Does a
farmer always plow and never sow? Is he
forever harrowing the soil and never planting
it? 25Does he not finally plant his many kinds
of grain, each in its own section of his land?
26 He knows just what to do, for God has made
him see and understand. 27 He doesn't thresh
all grains the same. A sledge is never used on
dill, but it is beaten with a stick. A threshing
wheel is never rolled on cummin, but it is
beaten softly with a flail. 28 Bread grain is easily crushed, so he doesn't keep on pounding
it. 29The Lord Almighty is a wonderful teacher
and gives the farmer wisdom.

CHAPTER 29

No One Can Hide from God

Woe to Jerusalem, the city of David. Year after
year you make your many offerings, 2but I will
send heavy judgment upon you, and there
will be weeping and sorrow. For Jerusalem
shall become as her name "Ariel" means—an
altar covered with blood. 3I will be your enemy. I will surround Jerusalem and lay siege
against it, and build forts around it to destroy
it. 4Your voice will whisper like a ghost from
the earth where you lie buried.

5But suddenly your ruthless enemies will be
driven away like chaff before the wind. 6In an
instant, I, the Lord of Hosts, will come upon
them with thunder, earthquake, whirlwind,
and fire. 7And all the nations fighting Jerusalem will vanish like a dream! 8As a hungry
man dreams of eating but is still hungry, and
as a thirsty man dreams of drinking but is still
faint from thirst when he wakes up, so your
enemies will dream of victorious conquest,
but all to no avail.

9You are amazed, incredulous? You don't
believe it? Then go ahead and be blind if you
must! You are stupid—and not from drinking,
either! Stagger, and not from wine! 10For the
Lord has poured out upon you a spirit of deep
sleep. He has closed the eyes of your prophets
and seers, 11so all of these future events are a
sealed book to them. When you give it to one
who can read, he says, "I can't, for it's sealed."
12When you give it to another, he says, "Sorry,
I can't read."

13And so the Lord says, "Since these people
say they are mine but they do not obey me,
and since their worship amounts to mere
words learned by rote, 14therefore I will take
awesome vengeance on these hypocrites and
make their wisest counselors as fools."

15Woe to those who try to hide their plans
from God, who try to keep him in the dark
concerning what they do! "God can't see us,"
they say to themselves. "He doesn't know
what is going on!" 16How stupid can they be!
Isn't he, the Potter, greater than you, the jars
he makes? Will you say to him, "He didn't
make us"? Does a machine call its inventor
dumb?

17Soon—and it will not be very long—the
wilderness of Lebanon will be a fruitful field
again, a lush and fertile forest. 18In that day
the deaf will hear the words of a book, and out
of their gloom and darkness the blind will see
my plans. 19The meek will be filled with fresh
joy from the Lord, and the poor shall exult in
the Holy One of Israel. 20Bullies will vanish
and scoffers will cease, and all those plotting
evil will be killed—21the violent man who
fights at the drop of a hat, the man who waits
in hiding to beat up the judge who sentenced
him, and the men who use any excuse to be
unfair.

22That is why the Lord who redeemed Abraham says: My people will no longer pale with
fear or be ashamed. 23For when they see the
surging birth rate and the expanding economy, then they will fear and rejoice in my
name; they will praise the Holy One of Israel
and stand in awe of him. 24 Those in error will
believe the truth, and complainers will be
willing to be taught!

29:5-8 God is able to rescue us from certain death. He miraculously saved Jerusalem from her besiegers when all hope had been lost. And he will miraculously save us from our dependencies when we ask him to. If God can save an entire nation from destruction and save the whole world from the consequences of sin, he certainly can rescue us from our addictions.

29:15-16 We can hide nothing from God; he knows all that we have done, are doing, and will do. When we try to hide something from God, often we succeed only in hiding it from ourself. It is necessary to take an inventory of our life and then admit our weaknesses to God, ourself, and others. We tell ourself and others so that we can get help to overcome the problem areas. We tell God not to inform him (he knows already), but to hand our life over to him. Once we do this, we will have the help of the almighty God.

CHAPTER 30

The Tragedy of Misplaced Trust

Woe to my rebellious children, says the Lord; you ask advice from everyone but me and decide to do what I don't want you to do. You yoke yourselves with unbelievers, thus piling up your sins. [2]For without consulting me you have gone down to Egypt to find aid and have put your trust in Pharaoh for his protection. [3]But in trusting Pharaoh, you will be disappointed, humiliated and disgraced, for he can't deliver on his promises to save you. [4]For though his power extends to Zoan and Hanes, [5]yet it will all turn out to your shame—he won't help one little bit!

[6]See them moving slowly across the terrible desert to Egypt—donkeys and camels laden down with treasure to pay for Egypt's aid. On through the badlands they go, where lions and swift venomous snakes live—and Egypt will give you nothing in return! [7]For Egypt's promises are worthless! "The Reluctant Dragon," I call her!

[8]Now go and write down this word of mine concerning Egypt, so that it will stand until the end of time, forever and forever, as an indictment of Israel's unbelief. [9]For if you don't write it, they will claim I never warned them. "Oh no," they'll say, "you never told us that!"

For they are stubborn rebels. [10,11]They tell my prophets, "Shut up—we don't want any more of your reports!" Or they say, "Don't tell us the truth; tell us nice things; tell us lies. Forget all this gloom; we've heard more than enough about your 'Holy One of Israel' and all he says."

[12]This is the reply of the Holy One of Israel:

Because you despise what I tell you and trust instead in frauds and lies and won't repent, [13]therefore calamity will come upon you suddenly, as upon a bulging wall that bursts and falls; in one moment it comes crashing down. [14]God will smash you like a broken dish; he will not act sparingly. Not a piece will be left large enough to use for carrying coals from the hearth, or a little water from the well. [15]For the Lord God, the Holy One of Israel, says: Only in returning to me and waiting for me will you be saved; in quietness and confidence is your strength; but you'll have none of this.

[16]"No," you say. "We will get our help from Egypt; they will give us swift horses for riding to battle." But the only swiftness you are going to see is the swiftness of your enemies chasing you! [17]One of them will chase a thousand of you! Five of them will scatter you until not two of you are left together. You will be like lonely trees on the distant mountaintops. [18]Yet the Lord still waits for you to come to him so he can show you his love; he will conquer you to bless you, just as he said. For the Lord is faithful to his promises. Blessed are all those who wait for him to help them.

[19]O my people in Jerusalem, you shall weep no more, for he will surely be gracious to you at the sound of your cry. He will answer you. [20]Though he give you the bread of adversity and water of affliction, yet he will be with you to teach you—with your own eyes you will see your Teacher. [21]And if you leave God's paths and go astray, you will hear a Voice behind you say, "No, this is the way; walk here." [22]And you will destroy all your silver idols and gold images and cast them out like filthy things you hate to touch. "Ugh!" you'll say to them. "Be gone!"

[23]Then God will bless you with rain at planting time and with wonderful harvests and with ample pastures for your cows. [24]The oxen and young donkeys that till the ground will eat grain, its chaff blown away by the wind. [25]In that day when God steps in to destroy your enemies, he will give you streams of water flowing down each mountain and every hill. [26]The moon will be as bright as the sun, and the sunlight brighter than seven days! So it will be when the Lord

---

30:1-5 In its quest for national recovery, Judah sought help from Egypt and not from God. God here warned Judah's leaders that their plan would only bring defeat because Egypt wasn't able to save them. God alone had the power to deliver them. Our recovery program should include God, too. When we put our trust in people or new fad programs, we will fail. To attempt anything apart from God will only lead to failure and increased suffering.

30:6-11 When we are sinning, we usually try to avoid what God has to say. Deep inside we know what God thinks and how it hurts him to see us behave this way. But if we admit that to ourself, then we become convicted, feeling guilty about our actions and recognizing that we need to change. Instead of wanting to hear God's words, we want to hear people say that we are doing all right, that we have no problems. To continue in this denial will eventually lead to ruin; there will come a point when it is too late for us to admit the truth of God's Word. It is important to accept the truth from God because a little pain now is better than much pain later.

begins to heal his people and to cure the wounds he gave them.

27See, the Lord comes from afar, aflame with wrath, surrounded by thick rising smoke. His lips are filled with fury; his words consume like fire. 28 His wrath pours out like floods upon them all, to sweep them all away. He will sift out the proud nations and bridle them and lead them off to their doom.

29But the people of God will sing a song of solemn joy, like songs in the night when holy feasts are held; his people will have gladness of heart, as when a flutist leads a pilgrim band to Jerusalem to the Mountain of the Lord, the Rock of Israel. 30And the Lord shall cause his majestic voice to be heard and shall crush down his mighty arm upon his enemies with angry indignation and devouring flames, with tornados, terrible storms, and huge hailstones. 31The voice of the Lord shall punish the Assyrians, who had been his rod of punishment. 32And when the Lord smites them, his people will rejoice with music and song. 33The funeral pyre has long been ready, prepared for Molech, the Assyrian god; it is piled high with wood. The breath of the Lord, like fire from a volcano, will set it all on fire.

CHAPTER 31

The Futility of Trusting Egypt

Woe to those who run to Egypt for help, trusting their mighty cavalry and chariots instead of looking to the Holy One of Israel and consulting him. 2In his wisdom, he will send great evil on his people and will not change his mind. He will rise against them for the evil they have done and crush their allies too. 3For these Egyptians are mere men, not God! Their horses are puny flesh, not mighty spirits! When the Lord clenches his fist against them, they will stumble and fall among those they are trying to help. All will fail together.

4,5But the Lord has told me this: When a lion, even a young one, kills a sheep, he pays no attention to the shepherd's shouts and noise. He goes right on and eats. In such manner the Lord will come and fight upon Mount Zion. He will not be frightened away! He, the Lord Almighty, will hover over Jerusalem as birds hover round their nests, and he will defend the city and deliver it.

6Therefore, O my people, though you are such wicked rebels, come, return to God. 7I know the glorious day will come when every one of you will throw away his gold idols and silver images—which in your sinfulness you have made.

8The Assyrians will be destroyed, but not by swords of men. The "sword of God" will smite them. They will panic and flee, and the strong young Assyrians will be taken away as slaves. 9Even their generals will quake with terror and flee when they see the battle flags of Israel, says the Lord. For the flame of God burns brightly in Jerusalem.

CHAPTER 32

A Promise of Peace

Look, a righteous King is coming, with honest princes! 2He will shelter Israel from the storm and wind. He will refresh her as a river in the desert and as the cooling shadow of a mighty rock within a hot and weary land. 3Then at last the eyes of Israel will open wide to God; his people will listen to his voice. 4Even the hotheads among them will be full of sense and understanding, and those who stammer in uncertainty will speak out plainly.

5In those days the ungodly, the atheists, will not be heroes! Wealthy cheaters will not be spoken of as generous, outstanding men! 6Everyone will recognize an evil man when he sees him, and hypocrites will fool no one at all. Their lies about God and their cheating of

31:1-5 Judah turned to Egypt instead of God for help, and destruction followed. Egypt can be a symbol for us of all those things we turn to for relief from our inner pain: work, sex, alcohol, drugs, food, unhealthy relationships. They look good, like the mighty chariots and horses of Egypt, but their help is just as illusory. Only God can bring us true deliverance.

31:6-9 We might think that with such rebellion and stubbornness in Judah, God would have become fed up with them and written them off. Incredibly, God continued to invite them to return to him and find his blessings. What an encouragement this is for us, especially if we have begun to wonder if God still cares about us after repeated failure. God wants all of us to turn to him and find salvation.

32:1-2 This King who was to come is Jesus—we don't have to wait for him. The future blessings described in these verses are ours now. The Jews were asked to trust in help that was yet to come. We can trust in help that has already come; it is ours for the asking. To claim God's aid, we need to confess Jesus as our Savior, realizing that he died and rose again; ask for forgiveness for our sins and addictions; and give God control of our life so he can purify us from our dependencies and compulsions.

the hungry will be plain for all to see. 7The smooth tricks of evil men will be exposed, as will all the lies they use to oppress the poor in the courts. 8But good men will be generous to others and will be blessed of God for all they do.

9Listen, you women who loll around in lazy ease; listen to me and I will tell you your reward: 10In a short time—in just a little more than a year—suddenly you'll care, O careless ones. For the crops of fruit will fail; the harvest will not take place. 11Tremble, O women of ease; throw off your unconcern. Strip off your pretty clothes—wear sackcloth for your grief. 12Beat your breasts in sorrow for those bountiful farms of yours that will soon be gone, and for those fruitful vines of other years. 13For your lands will thrive with thorns and briars; your joyous homes and happy cities will be gone. 14Palaces and mansions will all be deserted, the crowded cities empty. Wild herds of donkeys and goats will graze upon the mountains where the watchtowers are, 15until at last the Spirit is poured down on us from heaven. Then once again enormous crops will come. 16Then justice will rule through all the land, 17and out of justice, peace. Quietness and confidence will reign forever more.

18My people will live in safety, quietly at home, 19but the Assyrians will be destroyed and their cities laid low. 20And God will greatly bless his people. Wherever they plant, bountiful crops will spring up, and their flocks and herds will graze in green pastures.

CHAPTER 33

God's Great Forgiveness

Woe to you, Assyrians, who have destroyed everything around you but have never felt destruction for yourselves. You expect others to respect their promises to you, while you betray them! Now you, too, will be betrayed and destroyed.

2But to us, O Lord, be merciful, for we have waited for you. Be our strength each day and our salvation in the time of trouble. 3The enemy runs at the sound of your voice. When you stand up, the nations flee. 4Just as locusts strip the fields and vines, so Jerusalem will strip the fallen army of Assyria!

5The Lord is very great and lives in heaven. He will make Jerusalem the home of justice and goodness and righteousness. 6An abundance of salvation is stored up for Judah in a safe place, along with wisdom and knowledge and reverence for God.

7But now your ambassadors weep in bitter disappointment, for Assyria has refused their cry for peace. 8Your roads lie in ruins; travelers detour on back roads. The Assyrians have broken their peace pact and care nothing for the promises they made in the presence of witnesses—they have no respect for anyone. 9All the land of Israel is in trouble; Lebanon has been destroyed; Sharon has become a wilderness; Bashan and Carmel are plundered.

10But the Lord says, I will stand up and show my power and might. 11You Assyrians will gain nothing by all your efforts. Your own breath will turn to fire and kill you. 12Your armies will be burned to lime, like thorns cut down and tossed in the fire. 13Listen to what I have done, O nations far away! And you that are near, acknowledge my might!

14The sinners among my people shake with fear. "Which one of us," they cry, "can live here in the presence of this all-consuming, Everlasting Fire?" 15I will tell you who can live here: All who are honest and fair, who reject making profit by fraud, who hold back their hands from taking bribes, who refuse to listen to those who plot murder, who shut their eyes to all enticement to do wrong. 16Such as these shall dwell on high. The rocks of the mountains will be their fortress of safety; food will be supplied to them, and they will have all the water they need.

17Your eyes will see the King in his beauty and the highlands of heaven far away. 18Your mind will think back to this time of terror when the Assyrian officers outside your walls are counting your towers and estimating how much they will get from your fallen city. 19But soon they will all be gone. These fierce, violent people with a strange, jabbering language you can't understand will disappear.

20Instead you will see Jerusalem at peace, a place where God is worshiped, a city quiet and unmoved. 21The glorious Lord will be to us as a wide river of protection, and no enemy

33:1 Assyria's foreign policy was based on a double standard—lies told *to* Assyria were punished while lies told *by* Assyria were overlooked. This hypocrisy would be judged by God. God hates lies just as much today as he did then. We will be held responsible by God for our lies, and our relationships will be destroyed by them. If we want a good reputation, we must be honest with everyone and fulfill our promises.

can cross. 22For the Lord is our Judge, our Lawgiver and our King; he will care for us and save us. 23The enemies' sails hang loose on broken masts with useless tackle. Their treasure will be divided by the people of God; even the lame will win their share. 24The people of Israel will no longer say, "We are sick and helpless," for the Lord will forgive them their sins and bless them.

CHAPTER 34

Destruction for God's Enemies

Come here and listen, O nations of the earth; let the world and everything in it hear my words. 2For the Lord is enraged against the nations; his fury is against their armies. He will utterly destroy them and deliver them to slaughter. 3Their dead will be left unburied, and the stench of rotting bodies will fill the land; the mountains will flow with their blood. 4At that time the heavens above will melt away and disappear just like a rolled-up scroll, and the stars will fall as leaves, as ripe fruit from the trees.

5And when my sword has finished its work in the heavens, then watch, for it will fall upon Edom, the people I have doomed. 6The sword of the Lord is sated with blood; it is gorged with flesh as though used for slaying lambs and goats for sacrifice. For the Lord will slay a great sacrifice in Edom and make a mighty slaughter there. 7The strongest will perish, young boys and veterans too. The land will be soaked with blood, and the soil made rich with fat. 8For it is the day of vengeance, the year of recompense for what Edom has done to Israel. 9The streams of Edom will be filled with burning pitch, and the ground will be covered with fire.

10This judgment on Edom will never end. Its smoke will rise up forever. The land will lie deserted from generation to generation; no one will live there anymore. 11There the hawks and porcupines will live, and owls and ravens. For God will observe that land and find it worthy of destruction. He will test its nobles and find them worthy of death. 12It will be called "The Land of Nothing," and its princes soon will all be gone. 13Thorns will overrun the palaces, nettles will grow in its forts, and it will become the haunt of jackals and a home for ostriches. 14The wild animals of the desert will mingle there with wolves and hyenas. Their howls will fill the night. There the night-monsters will scream at each other, and the demons will come there to rest. 15There the owl will make her nest and lay her eggs; she will hatch her young and nestle them beneath her wings, and the kites will come, each one with its mate.

16Search the book of the Lord and see all that he will do; not one detail will he miss; not one kite will be there without a mate, for the Lord has said it, and his Spirit will make it all come true. 17He has surveyed and subdivided the land and deeded it to those doleful creatures; they shall possess it forever, from generation to generation.

CHAPTER 35

Streams in the Desert

Even the wilderness and desert will rejoice in those days; the desert will blossom with flowers. 2Yes, there will be an abundance of flowers and singing and joy! The deserts will become as green as the Lebanon mountains, as lovely as Mount Carmel's pastures and Sharon's meadows; for the Lord will display his glory there, the excellency of our God.

3With this news bring cheer to all discouraged ones. 4Encourage those who are afraid. Tell them, "Be strong, fear not, for your God

33:24 God will heal the sick and helpless people who turn to him. That is wonderful news for us. We have all committed sins, some of which have led to our addictions as an escape from the guilt. We don't need the drugs, alcohol, work, or anything else to feel better about ourself. God will heal us, forgiving our sins and blessing us. And once God has forgiven us, we no longer need to feel the guilt, because the sins are gone—God will never remember them again.

34:1-17 God's judgment of Edom reminds us that rejecting God and his program brings disaster. It may mean physical destruction, such as the deterioration of our health, emotional destruction, and/or eternal destruction at the second coming of Christ. Accepting God and his plan for our life will ensure that we finish life on the right path, and we will enjoy God's presence throughout eternity.

35:3-7 God proclaims a message of hope to all who are discouraged, frightened, and injured. God will save us and heal our weaknesses; that is his promise. Part of this has already been fulfilled (see Jesus' healing ministry throughout the Gospels), and we can ask God for his healing and salvation. The other part of this will be fulfilled at the end of history when Christ returns. Following God means that we are able to ask him to help us recover in this lifetime and that we are able to share eternal glory with him in the next.

is coming to destroy your enemies. He is coming to save you." 5And when he comes, he will open the eyes of the blind and unstop the ears of the deaf. 6The lame man will leap up like a deer, and those who could not speak will shout and sing! Springs will burst forth in the wilderness, and streams in the desert. 7The parched ground will become a pool, with springs of water in the thirsty land. Where desert jackals lived, there will be reeds and rushes!

8And a main road will go through that once-deserted land; it will be named "The Holy Highway." No evil-hearted men may walk upon it. God will walk there with you; even the most stupid cannot miss the way. 9No lion will lurk along its course, nor will there be any other dangers; only the redeemed will travel there. 10These, the ransomed of the Lord, will go home along that road to Zion, singing the songs of everlasting joy. For them all sorrow and all sighing will be gone forever; only joy and gladness will be there.

CHAPTER 36

Assyria Threatens Judah

So in the fourteenth year of King Hezekiah's reign, Sennacherib, king of Assyria, came to fight against the walled cities of Judah and conquered them. 2Then he sent his personal representative with a great army from Lachish to confer with King Hezekiah in Jerusalem. He camped near the outlet of the upper pool, along the road going past the field where cloth is bleached.

3Then Eliakim, Hilkiah's son, who was the prime minister of Israel, and Shebna, the king's scribe, and Joah, Asaph's son, the royal secretary, formed a truce team and went out of the city to meet with him. 4The Assyrian ambassador told them to go and say to Hezekiah, "The mighty king of Assyria says you are a fool to think that the king of Egypt will help you. 5What are the Pharaoh's promises worth? Mere words won't substitute for strength, yet you rely on him for help and have rebelled against me!6Egypt is a dangerous ally. She is a sharpened stick that will pierce your hand if you lean on it. That is the experience of everyone who has ever looked to her for help. 7But perhaps you say, 'We are trusting in the Lord our God!' Oh? Isn't he the one your king insulted, tearing down his temples and altars in the hills and making everyone in Judah worship only at the altars here in Jerusalem? 8,9My master, the king of Assyria, wants to make a little bet with you!—that you don't have 2,000 men left in your entire army! If you do, he will give you 2,000 horses for them to ride on! With that tiny army, how can you think of proceeding against even the smallest and worst contingent of my master's troops? For you'll get no help from Egypt. 10What's more, do you think I have come here without the Lord's telling me to take this land? The Lord said to me, 'Go and destroy it!'"

11Then Eliakim, Shebna, and Joah said to him, "Please talk to us in Aramaic, for we understand it quite well. Don't speak in Hebrew, for the people on the wall will hear."

12But he replied, "My master wants everyone in Jerusalem to hear this, not just you. He wants them to know that if you don't surrender, this city will be put under siege until everyone is so hungry and thirsty that he will eat his own dung and drink his own urine."

13Then he shouted in Hebrew to the Jews listening on the wall, "Hear the words of the great king, the king of Assyria:

14"Don't let Hezekiah fool you—nothing he can do will save you. 15Don't let him talk you into trusting in the Lord by telling you the

35:8-10 This "Holy Highway" was God's recovery program for his people. He would provide a way for them to return from exile. God also provides us with a passage through the desert of our pain and suffering into his presence. And the road is without danger because God is traveling with us. We are not alone as we fight against our addictions and compulsions—God is with us, giving us strength to resist the temptations.

36:1-12 The Assyrians besieged Jerusalem and mocked Judah for thinking they could find deliverance through trusting in God. In a similar way, people may mock us for thinking our hope for recovery can come from God. "That's a religious cop-out," they say. "Face reality." The reality is that God loves us, cares about us, and wants the best for us. The reality is that God is the only one who can effect our recovery. To trust in anything else is to deny reality.

36:13-22 The king of Assyria appealed to Judah to trust him, instead of God, to care for them. That's tantamount to asking the three little pigs to trust the big, bad wolf and open the door to let him in. In the same way, we are enticed to trust the things to which we are addicted, instead of turning to God for help, in spite of the fact that they are our enemies bent on our destruction. It is imperative that we stop believing the lies our addictions tell us and begin trusting God.

Lord won't let you be conquered by the king
of Assyria. 16Don't listen to Hezekiah, for here
is the king of Assyria's offer to you: Give me a
present as a token of surrender; open the gates
and come out, and I will let you each have
your own farm and garden and water, 17until
I can arrange to take you to a country very
similar to this one—a country where there are
bountiful harvests of grain and grapes, a land
of plenty. 18Don't let Hezekiah deprive you of
all this by saying the Lord will deliver you
from my armies. Have any other nation's gods
ever gained victory over the armies of the
king of Assyria? 19Don't you remember what I
did to Hamath and Arpad? Did their gods save
them? And what about Sepharvaim and Samaria? Where are their gods now? 20Of all the
gods of these lands, which one has ever delivered their people from my power? Name just
one! And do you think this God of yours can
deliver Jerusalem from me? Don't be ridiculous!"

21But the people were silent and answered
not a word, for Hezekiah had told them to say
nothing in reply. 22Then Eliakim (son of Hilkiah), the prime minister, and Shebna, the
royal scribe, and Joah (son of Asaph), the
royal secretary, went back to Hezekiah with
clothes ripped to shreds as a sign of their
despair and told him all that had happened.

CHAPTER 37

God Will Deliver Jerusalem

When King Hezekiah heard the results of the
meeting, he tore his robes and wound himself
in coarse cloth used for making sacks, as a sign
of humility and mourning, and went over to
the Temple to pray. 2Meanwhile he sent Eliakim his prime minister, and Shebna his royal
scribe, and the older priests—all dressed in
sackcloth—to Isaiah the prophet, son of
Amoz. 3They brought him this message from
Hezekiah:

"This is a day of trouble and frustration and
blasphemy; it is a serious time, as when a
woman is in heavy labor trying to give birth
and the child does not come. 4But perhaps the
Lord your God heard the blasphemy of the
king of Assyria's representative as he scoffed
at the living God. Surely God won't let him
get away with this. Surely God will rebuke
him for those words. Oh, Isaiah, pray for us
who are left!"

5So they took the king's message to Isaiah.

6Then Isaiah replied, "Tell King Hezekiah
that the Lord says, Don't be disturbed by this
speech from the servant of the king of Assyria
and his blasphemy. 7For a report from Assyria
will reach the king that he is needed at home
at once, and he will return to his own land,
where I will have him killed."

8,9Now the Assyrian envoy left Jerusalem
and went to consult his king, who had left
Lachish and was besieging Libnah. But at this
point the Assyrian king received word that
Tirhakah, crown prince of Ethiopia, was leading an army against him [from the south].
Upon hearing this, he sent messengers back
to Jerusalem to Hezekiah with this message:

10"Don't let this God you trust in fool you
by promising that Jerusalem will not be captured by the king of Assyria! 11Just remember
what has happened wherever the kings of
Assyria have gone, for they have crushed
everyone who has opposed them. Do you
think you will be any different? 12Did their
gods save the cities of Gozan, Haran, or Rezeph, or the people of Eden in Telassar? No,
the Assyrian kings completely destroyed
them! 13And don't forget what happened to
the king of Hamath, to the king of Arpad, and
to the kings of the cities of Sepharvaim, Hena,
and Ivvah."

14As soon as King Hezekiah had read this
letter, he went over to the Temple and spread
it out before the Lord 15and prayed, saying,

37:1-4 Hezekiah shows us the right thing to do when we face overwhelming trouble. He humbled himself before God, prayed about the problem, and sought help from a godly person. Too often we deny the seriousness of our problems and refuse to turn to God or others for help. But recovery is not possible without asking God for help and without the encouragement and instruction of godly friends.

37:8-20 The king of Assyria tried to dissuade Hezekiah from trusting God by lumping the God of Israel with the false gods of the people he had already conquered. Hezekiah recognized that those gods were man-made and easy to destroy, but that Israel's God was real and able to rescue his people. Our addictions seem powerful and may have already survived our human attempts to overcome them. Recovery programs that ignore God's power function as false gods in our life and can easily be overcome by our dependencies. But God is different than any of our humanistic recovery programs—he created the world and can do anything he desires. No addiction can ever stand against God's transforming work in our life.

[16,17]"O Lord, Almighty God of Israel enthroned between the Guardian Angels, *you alone* are God of all the kingdoms of the earth. You alone made heaven and earth. Listen as I plead; see me as I pray. Look at this letter from King Sennacherib, for he has mocked the living God. [18]It is true, O Lord, that the kings of Assyria have destroyed all those nations, just as the letter says, [19]and thrown their gods into the fire; for they weren't gods at all but merely idols, carved by men from wood and stone. Of course the Assyrians could destroy them. [20]O Lord our God, save us so that all the kingdoms of the earth will know that you are God, and you alone."

God Will Destroy Sennacherib

[21]Then Isaiah, the son of Amoz, sent this message to King Hezekiah: The Lord God of Israel says, This is my answer to your prayer against Sennacherib, Assyria's king.

[22]"The Lord says to him: My people—the helpless virgin daughter of Zion—laughs at you and scoffs and shakes her head at you in scorn. [23]Who is it you scoffed against and mocked? Whom did you revile? At whom did you direct your violence and pride? It was against the Holy One of Israel! [24] You have sent your messengers to mock the Lord. You boast, 'I came with my mighty army against the nations of the west. I cut down the tallest cedars and choicest cypress trees. I conquered their highest mountains and destroyed their thickest forests.'

[25]"You boast of wells you've dug in many a conquered land, and Egypt with all its armies is no obstacle to you! [26]But do you not yet know that it was I who decided all this long ago? That it was I who gave you all this power from ancient times? I have caused all this to happen as I planned—that you should crush walled cities into ruined heaps. [27]That's why their people had so little power and were such easy prey for you. They were as helpless as the grass, as tender plants you trample down beneath your feet, as grass upon the housetops, burnt yellow by the sun. [28]But I know you well—your comings and goings and all you do—and the way you have raged against me. [29]Because of your anger against the Lord—and I heard it all!—I have put a hook in your nose and a bit in your mouth and led you back to your own land by the same road you came."

[30]Then God said to Hezekiah, "Here is the proof that I am the one who is delivering this city from the king of Assyria: This year he will abandon his siege. Although it is too late now to plant your crops, and you will have only volunteer grain this fall, still it will give you enough seed for a small harvest next year, and two years from now you will be living in luxury again. [31]And you who are left in Judah will take root again in your own soil and flourish and multiply. [32]For a remnant shall go out from Jerusalem to repopulate the land; the power of the Lord Almighty will cause all this to come to pass.

[33]"As for the king of Assyria, his armies shall not enter Jerusalem, nor shoot their arrows there, nor march outside its gates, nor build up an earthen bank against its walls. [34]He will return to his own country by the road he came on and will not enter this city, says the Lord. [35]For my own honor I will defend it and in memory of my servant David."

[36]That night the Angel of the Lord went out to the camp of the Assyrians and killed 185,000 soldiers; when the living wakened the next morning, all these lay dead before them. [37]Then Sennacherib, king of Assyria, returned to his own country, to Nineveh. [38]And one day while he was worshiping in the temple of Nisroch his god, his sons Adrammelech and Sharezer killed him with their swords; then they escaped into the land of Ararat, and Esar-haddon his son became king.

CHAPTER 38

Hezekiah Asks for a Miracle

It was just before all this that Hezekiah became deathly sick, and Isaiah the prophet (Amoz' son) went to visit him and gave him this message from the Lord:

"Set your affairs in order, for you are going to die; you will not recover from this illness."

37:33-38 What an impossible situation! Jerusalem was surrounded and besieged by the army of the largest empire on earth. All the Assyrians had to do was starve out Jerusalem and success was theirs. God is not bound by what seems possible to man. He can bring deliverance to those who trust in him in the most hopeless of situations.

38:1-8 Hezekiah's situation seemed totally hopeless. He even received a word from God that his life was over. We are reminded that no situation is so hopeless that it is beyond God's ability to help. Hezekiah turned to God in prayer, and God spared his life. We are never without hope because our God is a God of mercy. When we admit our weakness and ask him to save us, he will.

2When Hezekiah heard this, he turned his face to the wall and prayed:

3"O Lord, don't you remember how true I've been to you and how I've always tried to obey you in everything you said?" Then he broke down with great sobs.

4So the Lord sent another message to Isaiah: 5"Go and tell Hezekiah that the Lord God of your forefather David hears you praying and sees your tears and will let you live fifteen more years. 6He will deliver you and this city from the king of Assyria. I will defend you, says the Lord, 7and here is my guarantee: 8I will send the sun backwards ten degrees as measured on Ahaz' sundial!"

So the sun retraced ten degrees that it had gone down!

9When King Hezekiah was well again, he wrote this poem about his experience:

10"My life is but half done and I must leave it all. I am robbed of my normal years, and now I must enter the gates of Sheol. 11Never again will I see the Lord in the land of the living. Never again will I see my friends in this world. 12My life is blown away like a shepherd's tent; it is cut short as when a weaver stops his working at the loom. In one short day my life hangs by a thread.

13"All night I moaned; it was like being torn apart by lions. 14Delirious, I chattered like a swallow and mourned like a dove; my eyes grew weary of looking up for help. 'O God,' I cried, 'I am in trouble—help me.' 15But what can I say? For he himself has sent this sickness. All my sleep has fled because of my soul's bitterness. 16O Lord, your discipline is good and leads to life and health. Oh, heal me and make me live!

17"Yes, now I see it all—it was good for me to undergo this bitterness, for you have lovingly delivered me from death; you have forgiven all my sins. 18For dead men cannot praise you. They cannot be filled with hope and joy. 19The living, only the living, can praise you as I do today. One generation makes known your faithfulness to the next. 20Think of it! The Lord healed me! Every day of my life from now on I will sing my songs of praise in the Temple, accompanied by the orchestra."

21(For Isaiah had told Hezekiah's servants, "Make an ointment of figs and spread it over the boil, and he will get well again."

22And then Hezekiah had asked, "What sign will the Lord give me to prove that he will heal me?")

CHAPTER 39

Messengers from Babylon

Soon afterwards, the king of Babylon (Merodach-baladan, the son of Baladan) sent Hezekiah a present and his best wishes, for he had heard that Hezekiah had been very sick and now was well again. 2Hezekiah appreciated this and took the envoys from Babylon on a tour of the palace, showing them his treasure house full of silver, gold, spices, and perfumes. He took them into his jewel rooms, too, and opened to them all his treasures—everything.

3Then Isaiah the prophet came to the king and said, "What did they say? Where are they from?"

"From far away in Babylon," Hezekiah replied.

4"How much have they seen?" asked Isaiah.

And Hezekiah replied, "I showed them everything I own, all my priceless treasures."

5Then Isaiah said to him, "Listen to this message from the Lord Almighty:

6"The time is coming when everything you have—all the treasures stored up by your fathers—will be carried off to Babylon. Nothing will be left. 7And some of your own sons will become slaves, yes, eunuchs, in the palace of the king of Babylon."

8"All right," Hezekiah replied. "Whatever the Lord says is good. At least there will be peace during my lifetime!"

CHAPTER 40

God Will Feed His Flock

"Comfort, yes, comfort my people," says your God. 2"Speak tenderly to Jerusalem and tell her that her sad days are gone. Her sins are

38:10-22 Hezekiah saw that his illness was actually good for him because it enabled him to find God's deliverance. Often our suffering works some good because it breaks our selfish life-style and brings us to the point where we realize we need God. We should take a moral inventory and see if we are living for God or ourself. If God is not first in our life, now is a great time to put him there.

39:1-7 Hezekiah foolishly received the Babylonians and showed them the extent of his treasury; he failed to perceive that they would be the next conquerors of Judah. We often fail to discern the things that are our true enemies and "make friends" with unhealthy relationships and activities that end up destroying us. To avoid this pitfall, we need to ask one question of our "alliances": Would God approve of this relationship, activity, habit, or environment?

pardoned, and I have punished her in full for
all her sins."

3Listen! I hear the voice of someone shouting, "Make a road for the Lord through the
wilderness; make him a straight, smooth road
through the desert. 4Fill the valleys; level the
hills; straighten out the crooked paths, and
smooth off the rough spots in the road. 5The
glory of the Lord will be seen by all mankind
together." The Lord has spoken—it shall be.

6The voice says, "Shout!"

"What shall I shout?" I asked.

"Shout that man is like the grass that dies
away, and all his beauty fades like dying flowers. 7The grass withers, the flower fades beneath the breath of God. And so it is with
fragile man. 8The grass withers, the flowers
fade, but the Word of our God shall stand
forever."

9O Crier of good news, shout to Jerusalem
from the mountaintops! Shout louder—don't
be afraid—tell the cities of Judah, "Your God
is coming!" 10Yes, the Lord God is coming
with mighty power; he will rule with awesome strength. See, his reward is with him, to
each as he has done. 11He will feed his flock
like a shepherd; he will carry the lambs in his
arms and gently lead the ewes with young.

12Who else has held the oceans in his hands
and measured off the heavens with his ruler?
Who else knows the weight of all the earth
and weighs the mountains and the hills?
13Who can advise the Spirit of the Lord or be
his teacher or give him counsel? 14Has he ever
needed anyone's advice? Did he need instruction as to what is right and best? 15No, for all
the peoples of the world are nothing in comparison with him—they are but a drop in the
bucket, dust on the scales. He picks up the
islands as though they had no weight at all.
16All of Lebanon's forests do not contain sufficient fuel to consume a sacrifice large enough
to honor him, nor are all its animals enough
to offer to our God. 17All the nations are as
nothing to him; in his eyes they are less than
nothing—mere emptiness and froth.

18How can we describe God? With what can
we compare him? 19With an idol? An idol
made from a mold, overlaid with gold, and
with silver chains around its neck? 20The man
too poor to buy expensive gods like that will
find a tree free from rot and hire a man to
carve a face on it, and that's his god—a god
that cannot even move!

21Are you so ignorant? Are you so deaf to
the words of God—the words he gave before
the world began? Have you never heard nor
understood? 22It is God who sits above the
circle of the earth. (The people below must
seem to him like grasshoppers!) He is the one
who stretches out the heavens like a curtain
and makes his tent from them. 23He dooms
the great men of the world and brings them
all to naught. 24They hardly get started, barely
take root, when he blows on them and their
work withers, and the wind carries them off
like straw.

25"With whom will you compare me? Who
is my equal?" asks the Holy One.

26Look up into the heavens! Who created all
these stars? As a shepherd leads his sheep,
calling each by its pet name, and counts them
to see that none are lost or strayed, so God
does with stars and planets!

27O Jacob, O Israel, how can you say that
the Lord doesn't see your troubles and isn't
being fair? 28Don't you yet understand? Don't
you know by now that the everlasting God,
the Creator of the farthest parts of the earth,
never grows faint or weary? No one can
fathom the depths of his understanding. 29He
gives power to the tired and worn out, and

40:1-5 After the judgments of chapters 1–39, God's message to his people is one of comfort and blessing. God never gives up on us, no matter how bad the things we have done. The punishment will end, and God will restore us to a loving relationship with himself. To make a straight path for him means to clear out the obstacles in our life: sin, pride, addictions, hypocrisy, greed. When those obstacles are gone, we are free to become the people God wants us to be.

40:10-17 When we doubt God's power, we need to reread these verses. He is the Creator and will rule with "awesome strength." He has perfect wisdom and is greater than any person or nation. When we doubt that God can really help us overcome our dependencies, we need to remember that he is bigger and more powerful than anything on earth. And this God is also compassionate and loving. He will carry his sheep (that's us!) in his arms and "gently lead" us. God will lead us down the road to recovery because he loves us.

41:11-14 God promises that he will crush our enemies, and what greater enemies are there in our life right now than our addictions and compulsions? We won't be able to destroy them on our own, but only with God's help. He will be there for us, holding our hand and helping us all the way. Though we may be despised by others now for our life-style, God will redeem us and make us whole again.

strength to the weak. 30Even the youths shall
be exhausted, and the young men will all give
up. 31But they that wait upon the Lord shall
renew their strength. They shall mount up
with wings like eagles; they shall run and not
be weary; they shall walk and not faint.

CHAPTER 41

God Will Help Israel

Listen in silence before me, O lands beyond
the sea. Bring your strongest arguments.
Come now and speak. The court is ready for
your case.
2Who has stirred up this one from the east,
whom victory meets at every step? Who, indeed, but the Lord? God has given him victory over many nations and permitted him to
trample kings underfoot and to put entire
armies to the sword. 3He chases them away
and goes on safely, though the paths he treads
are new. 4Who has done such mighty deeds,
directing the affairs of generations of mankind as they march by? It is I, the Lord, the
First and Last; I alone am he.
5The lands beyond the sea watch in fear and
wait for word of Cyrus' new campaigns. Remote lands tremble and mobilize for war.
6,7The craftsmen encourage each other as they
rush to make new idols to protect them. The
carver hurries the goldsmith, and the molder
helps at the anvil. "Good," they say. "It's
coming along fine. Now we can solder on the
arms." Carefully they join the parts together
and then fasten the thing in place so it won't
fall over!
8But as for you, O Israel, you are mine, my
chosen ones; for you are Abraham's family,
and he was my friend. 9I have called you back
from the ends of the earth and said that you
must serve but me alone, for I have chosen
you and will not throw you away. 10Fear not,
for I am with you. Do not be dismayed. I am
your God. I will strengthen you; I will help
you; I will uphold you with my victorious
right hand.
11See, all your angry enemies lie confused
and shattered. Anyone opposing you will die.
12You will look for them in vain—they will all
be gone. 13I am holding you by your right
hand—I, the Lord your God—and I say to
you, Don't be afraid; I am here to help you.
14Despised though you are, fear not, O Israel;
for I will help you. I am the Lord, your Redeemer; I am the Holy One of Israel. 15You
shall be a new and sharp-toothed threshing
instrument to tear all enemies apart, making
chaff of mountains. 16You shall toss them in

Patient Waiting

BIBLE READING: Isaiah 40:28-31

We sought through prayer and meditation to improve our conscious contact with God, as we understood him, praying only for knowledge of his will for us and the power to carry that out.

We all want to recover as quickly as possible. It's hard to be patient as we wait for the process to work. Sure, we realize that we didn't get to the difficult spot we are in overnight. We understand that we cannot undo a lifetime of damage in a moment. But still, it is a challenge to wait patiently. Every part of our recovery requires time and patience. This step also requires that we learn to wait for God.

The prophet Isaiah gave us this promise: "They that wait upon the Lord shall renew their strength. They shall mount up with wings like eagles; they shall run and not be weary; they shall walk and not faint" (Isaiah 40:31). Jeremiah said, "The Lord is wonderfully good to those who wait for him, to those who seek for him. It is good both to hope and wait quietly for the salvation of the Lord" (Lamentations 3:25-26).

Waiting for the Lord has its rewards. We can remain calm when it appears that nothing is happening in our recovery. As we learn to respond to life in new ways, the winds of adversity will lift us up, like wind beneath the wings of an eagle, instead of knocking us down. As we develop a patient faith in God we will be able to endure to the end of the race—and win. ***Turn to page 1145, John 3.***

the air; the wind shall blow them all away; whirlwinds shall scatter them. And the joy of the Lord shall fill you full; you shall glory in the God of Israel.

17When the poor and needy seek water and there is none, and their tongues are parched from thirst, then I will answer when they cry to me. I, Israel's God, will not ever forsake them. 18I will open up rivers for them on high plateaus! I will give them fountains of water in the valleys! In the deserts will be pools of water, and rivers fed by springs shall flow across the dry, parched ground. 19I will plant trees—cedars, myrtle, olive trees, the cypress, fir and pine—on barren land. 20Everyone will see this miracle and understand that it is God who did it, Israel's Holy One.

21Can your idols make such claims as these? Let them come and show what they can do! says God, the King of Israel. 22Let them try to tell us what occurred in years gone by or what the future holds. 23Yes, that's it! If you are gods, tell what will happen in the days ahead! Or do some mighty miracle that makes us stare, amazed. 24But no! You are less than nothing and can do nothing at all. Anyone who chooses you needs to have his head examined!

25But I have stirred up (Cyrus) from the north and east; he will come against the nations and call on my name, and I will give him victory over kings and princes. He will tread them as a potter tramples clay.

26Who but I have told you this would happen? Who else predicted this, making you admit that he was right? No one else! None other said one word! 27I was the first to tell Jerusalem, "Look! Look! Help is on the way!" 28Not one of your idols told you this. Not one gave any answer when I asked. 29 See, they are all foolish, worthless things; your idols are all as empty as the wind.

CHAPTER 42

God's Chosen One

See my servant, whom I uphold; my Chosen One in whom I delight. I have put my Spirit upon him; he will reveal justice to the nations of the world. 2He will be gentle—he will not shout nor quarrel in the streets. 3He will not break the bruised reed, nor quench the dimly burning flame. He will encourage the fainthearted, those tempted to despair. He will see full justice given to all who have been wronged. 4He won't be satisfied until truth and righteousness prevail throughout the earth, nor until even distant lands beyond the seas have put their trust in him.

5The Lord God who created the heavens and stretched them out, who created the earth and everything in it, who gives life and breath and spirit to everyone in all the world, he is the one who says [to his Servant, the Messiah],

6"I the Lord have called you to demonstrate my righteousness. I will guard and support you, for I have given you to my people as the personal confirmation of my covenant with them. You shall also be a light to guide the nations unto me. 7You will open the eyes of the blind and release those who sit in prison darkness and despair. 8I am the Lord! That is my name, and I will not give my glory to anyone else; I will not share my praise with carved idols. 9Everything I prophesied came true, and now I will prophesy again. I will tell you the future before it happens."

10Sing a new song to the Lord; sing his praises, all you who live in earth's remotest corners! Sing, O sea! Sing, all you who live in distant lands beyond the sea! 11Join in the chorus, you desert cities—Kedar and Sela! And you, too, dwellers in the mountaintops. 12Let the western coastlands glorify the Lord and sing his mighty power.

13The Lord will be a mighty warrior, full of fury toward his foes. He will give a great shout and prevail. 14Long has he been silent; he has restrained himself. But now he will give full vent to his wrath; he will groan and cry like a woman delivering her child. 15He will level the mountains and hills and blight their greenery. He will dry up the rivers and pools. 16He will bring blind Israel along a path they

41:17-20 God calls us to himself to receive wholeness in life, pictured here by the images of water in a dry place and trees growing from barren land. To receive his fullness, however, requires that we admit we are inadequate and needy, unable to control our life without him.

42:1-4 This Servant song describes Jesus the Messiah and his ministry. No description could be more encouraging to us as we seek deliverance from injuries and fragile emotions. He is gentle; he will not shame us. He will encourage us and bring justice for the wrongs we have suffered. Even as children, many of us have endured abuse or wrongdoing that we did nothing to instigate. But we are able to let go of the hatred and bitterness we feel because Christ will judge the people who have pained us. We need to ask God to help us put these events behind us so we can move on with our recovery.

have not seen before. He will make the darkness bright before them and smooth and
straighten out the road ahead. He will not
forsake them. 17But those who trust in idols
and call them gods will be greatly disappointed; they will be turned away.

Blind and Deaf toward God

18Oh, how blind and deaf you are toward God!
Why won't you listen? Why won't you see?
19Who in all the world is as blind as my own
people, who are designed to be my messengers of truth? Who is so blind as my "dedicated one," the "servant of the Lord"? 20You
see and understand what is right but won't
heed nor do it; you hear, but you won't listen.

21The Lord has magnified his law and made
it truly glorious. Through it he had planned
to show the world that he is righteous. 22But
what a sight his people are—these who were
to demonstrate to all the world the glory of
his law; for they are robbed, enslaved, imprisoned, trapped, fair game for all, with no one
to protect them. 23Won't even one of you
apply these lessons from the past and see the
ruin that awaits you up ahead? 24Who let
Israel be robbed and hurt? Did not the Lord?
It is the Lord they sinned against, for they
would not go where he sent them nor listen
to his laws. 25That is why God poured out
such fury and wrath on his people and destroyed them in battle. Yet, though set on fire
and burned, they will not understand the
reason why—that it is God, wanting them to
repent.

CHAPTER 43

No Other Savior

But now the Lord who created you, O Israel,
says, Don't be afraid, for I have ransomed you;
I have called you by name; you are mine.
2When you go through deep waters and great
trouble, I will be with you. When you go
through rivers of difficulty, you will not
drown! When you walk through the fire of
oppression, you will not be burned up—the
flames will not consume you. 3For I am the
Lord your God, your Savior, the Holy One of
Israel. I gave Egypt and Ethiopia and Seba [to
Cyrus] in exchange for your freedom, as your
ransom. 4Others died that you might live; I
traded their lives for yours because you are
precious to me and honored, and I love you.

5Don't be afraid, for I am with you. I will
gather you from east and west, 6from north
and south. I will bring my sons and daughters
back to Israel from the farthest corners of the
earth. 7All who claim me as their God will
come, for I have made them for my glory; I
created them. 8Bring them back to me—blind
as they are and deaf when I call (although
they see and hear!).

9Gather the nations together! Which of all
their idols ever has foretold such things?
Which can predict a single day ahead? Where
are the witnesses of anything they said? If
there are no witnesses, then they must confess that only God can prophesy.

10But I have witnesses, O Israel, says the
Lord! You are my witnesses and my servants,
chosen to know and to believe me and to
understand that I alone am God. There is no
other God; there never was and never will be.
11I am the Lord, and there is no other Savior.
12Whenever you have thrown away your
idols, I have shown you my power. With one
word I have saved you. You have seen me do
it; you are my witnesses that it is true. 13From
eternity to eternity I am God. No one can
oppose what I do.

God Promises Victory

14The Lord, your Redeemer, the Holy One of
Israel, says:

For your sakes I will send an invading army
against Babylon that will walk in, almost unscathed. The boasts of the Babylonians will
turn to cries of fear. 15I am the Lord, your Holy

42:20-23 God here encourages us to do two things: first, we are to do what we know is right; second, we are to learn lessons from our past. Israel's flouting of God's righteous laws led to her ruin. Haven't we been "robbed, enslaved, imprisoned, trapped" by our addictions? We can become free only when we stop denying reality and confess our addictions to God.

43:1-3 God loves us and will be there for us in times of trouble and turmoil. As we "go through rivers of difficulty," we have a choice. We can either trust in our own ability and drown, or put our trust in God and be rescued. If we are honest, we will realize that our life-style has made our life unmanageable and that God is the only one who can redeem us.

43:9-13 There are people around us who can witness to God's power of deliverance: those who have overcome addictions or past abuses. When we have doubts about our recovery or feel like giving in to temptation, we need to look for encouragement to people who have been successful in the recovery process. Their lives can give us helpful hints as to how we can overcome our dependencies. They will also show us God's ability to transform a broken life.

One, Israel's Creator and King. 16 I am the
Lord, who opened a way through the waters,
making a path right through the sea. 17 I called
forth the mighty army of Egypt with all its
chariots and horses, to lie beneath the waves,
dead, their lives snuffed out like candlewicks.
18 But forget all that—it is nothing compared to what I'm going to do! 19 For I'm going
to do a brand new thing. See, I have already
begun! Don't you see it? I will make a road
through the wilderness of the world for my
people to go home, and create rivers for them
in the desert! 20 The wild animals in the fields
will thank me, the jackals and ostriches too,
for giving them water in the wilderness, yes,
springs in the desert, so that my people, my
chosen ones, can be refreshed. 21 I have made
Israel for myself, and these my people will
some day honor me before the world.
22 But O my people, you won't ask my help;
you have grown tired of me! 23 You have not
brought me the lambs for burnt offerings; you
have not honored me with sacrifices. Yet my
requests for offerings and incense have been
very few! I have not treated you as slaves.
24 You have brought me no sweet-smelling incense nor pleased me with the sacrificial fat.
No, you have presented me only with sins
and wearied me with all your faults.
25 I, yes, I alone am he who blots away your
sins for my own sake and will never think of
them again. 26 Oh, remind me of this promise
of forgiveness, for we must talk about your
sins. Plead your case for my forgiving you.
27 From the very first your ancestors sinned
against me—all your forebears transgressed
my law. 28 That is why I have deposed your
priests and destroyed Israel, leaving her to
shame.

CHAPTER 44

Idols Are False Gods

Listen to me, O my servant Israel, O my chosen ones:
2 The Lord who made you, who will help
you, says, O servant of mine, don't be afraid.
O Jerusalem, my chosen ones, don't be afraid.
3 For I will give you abundant water for your
thirst and for your parched fields. And I will
pour out my Spirit and my blessings on your
children. 4 They shall thrive like watered grass,
like willows on a riverbank. 5 "I am the Lord's,"
they'll proudly say, or, "I am a Jew," and
tattoo upon their hands the name of God or
the honored name of Israel.
6 The Lord, the King of Israel, says—yes, it is
Israel's Redeemer, the Lord Almighty, who
says it—I am the First and Last; there is no
other God. 7 Who else can tell you what is
going to happen in the days ahead? Let them
tell you if they can and prove their power. Let
them do as I have done since ancient times.
8 Don't, don't be afraid. Haven't I proclaimed
from ages past [that I would save you]? You
are my witnesses—is there any other God?
No! None that I know about! There is no other
Rock!
9 What fools they are who manufacture
idols for their gods. Their hopes remain unanswered. They themselves are witnesses that
this is so, for their idols neither see nor know.
No wonder those who worship them are so
ashamed. 10 Who but a fool would make his
own god—an idol that can help him not one
whit! 11 All that worship these will stand before
the Lord in shame, along with all these carpenters—mere men—who claim that they
have made a god. Together they will stand in
terror. 12 The metalsmith stands at his forge to
make an axe, pounding on it with all his
might. He grows hungry and thirsty, weak
and faint. 13 Then the woodcarver takes the
axe and uses it to make an idol. He measures
and marks out a block of wood and carves the
figure of a man. Now he has a wonderful idol
that can't so much as move from where it is
placed. 14 He cuts down cedars, he selects the
cypress and the oak, he plants the ash in the
forest to be nourished by the rain. 15 And after
his care, he uses part of the wood to make a
fire to warm himself and bake his bread, and
then—he really does—he takes the rest of it
and makes himself a god—a god for men to
worship! An idol to fall down before and

44:6-8 God is our Redeemer and the Rock on whom we should build our life. He has promised to save us from our addictions and from the sure penalty of sin—death. When we have the promise of the all-powerful God, why look to other sources for our recovery?

44:21-28 Through Isaiah, God named Cyrus as the king who would free his people to return from captivity. But Cyrus would not rise to power until 150 years after Isaiah's ministry! Once we have committed our life to God, we can have confidence in his provision for us. He will take care of our needs and lead us to a fulfilling life of trust in him. If God could name the king who would allow Israel to rebuild Jerusalem, 150 years before he came to power, God can do anything in our life to bring about our recovery.

praise! [16]Part of the tree he burns to roast his
meat and to keep him warm and fed and well
content, [17]and with what's left he makes his
god: a carved idol! He falls down before it and
worships it and prays to it. "Deliver me," he
says. "You are my god!"
[18]Such stupidity and ignorance! God has
shut their eyes so that they cannot see and
closed their minds from understanding. [19]The
man never stops to think or figure out, "Why,
it's just a block of wood! I've burned it for heat
and used it to bake my bread and roast my
meat. How can the rest of it be a god? Should
I fall down before a chunk of wood?" [20]The
poor, deluded fool feeds on ashes; he is trusting what can never give him any help at all.
Yet he cannot bring himself to ask, "Is this
thing, this idol that I'm holding in my hand,
a lie?"
[21]Pay attention, Israel, for you are my servant; I made you, and I will not forget to help
you. [22]I've blotted out your sins; they are gone
like morning mist at noon! Oh, return to me,
for I have paid the price to set you free.
[23]Sing, O heavens, for the Lord has done
this wondrous thing. Shout, O earth; break
forth into song, O mountains and forests, yes,
and every tree; for the Lord redeemed Jacob
and is glorified in Israel! [24]The Lord, your Redeemer who made you, says, "All things were
made by me; I alone stretched out the heavens. By myself I made the earth and everything in it.
[25]I am the one who shows what liars all false
prophets are, by causing something else to
happen than the things they say. I make wise
men give opposite advice to what they should
and make them into fools. [26]But what my
prophets say, I do; when they say Jerusalem
will be delivered and the cities of Judah lived
in once again—it shall be done! [27]When I
speak to the rivers and say, "Be dry!" they
shall be dry. [28]When I say of Cyrus, "He is my
shepherd," he will certainly do as I say; and
Jerusalem will be rebuilt and the Temple restored, for I have spoken it.

CHAPTER 45

The One True God

This is Jehovah's message to Cyrus, God's
anointed, whom he has chosen to conquer
many lands. God shall empower his right
hand, and he shall crush the strength of
mighty kings. God shall open the gates of
Babylon to him; the gates shall not be shut
against him any more. [2]I will go before you,
Cyrus, and level the mountains and smash
down the city gates of brass and iron bars.
[3]And I will give you treasures hidden in the
darkness, secret riches; and you will know
that I am doing this—I, the Lord, the God of
Israel, the one who calls you by your name.
[4]And why have I named you for this work?
For the sake of Jacob, my servant—Israel, my
chosen. I called you by name when you didn't
know me. [5]I am Jehovah; there is no other
God. I will strengthen you and send you out
to victory even though you don't know me,
[6]and all the world from east to west will know
there is no other God. I am Jehovah and there
is no one else. I alone am God. [7]I form the
light and make the dark. I send good times
and bad. I, Jehovah, am he who does these
things. [8]Open up, O heavens. Let the skies
pour out their righteousness. Let salvation
and righteousness sprout up together from
the earth. I, Jehovah, created them.
[9]Woe to the man who fights with his Creator. Does the pot argue with its maker? Does
the clay dispute with him who forms it, saying, "Stop, you're doing it wrong!" or the pot
exclaim, "How clumsy can you be!"? [10]Woe to
the baby just being born who squalls to his
father and mother, "Why have you produced
me? Can't you do anything right at all?"
[11]Jehovah, the Holy One of Israel, Israel's
Creator, says: What right have you to question what I do? Who are you to command me
concerning the work of my hands? [12]I have

45:1-6 God was able to take a pagan king like Cyrus and use him for his purposes without Cyrus's realizing it. If he can use someone who doesn't even know him, imagine how much more he can do with us who trust in him. There are great possibilities with God. We need to have the faith to follow him.

45:9-13 The example of the book of Psalms makes clear that it is acceptable to pour out our complaints and arguments to God as we try to wrestle through the problems of life to achieve faith. What is rebuked here is the stubborn and chronic unbelief of Israel, who charged God with fumbling his control of history in raising Cyrus to power. Their immediate perception was that God was just helping another enemy. However, their limited view of life did not allow the Israelites to see God's true purpose. Likewise, we may not understand why God is allowing certain things to happen, but we can trust that God is working according to his perfect plan.

made the earth and created man upon it. With my hands I have stretched out the heavens and commanded all the vast myriads of stars. 13I have raised up Cyrus to fulfill my righteous purpose, and I will direct all his paths. He shall restore my city and free my captive people—and not for a reward!

14Jehovah says: The Egyptians, Ethiopians, and Sabeans shall be subject to you. They shall come to you with all their merchandise, and it shall all be yours. They shall follow you as prisoners in chains and fall down on their knees before you and say, "The only God there is, is your God!"

15Truly, O God of Israel, Savior, you work in strange, mysterious ways. 16All who worship idols shall be disappointed and ashamed. 17But Israel shall be saved by Jehovah with eternal salvation; they shall never be disappointed in their God through all eternity. 18For Jehovah created the heavens and earth and put everything in place, and he made the world to be lived in, not to be an empty chaos. I am Jehovah, he says, and there is no other! 19I publicly proclaim bold promises; I do not whisper obscurities in some dark corner so that no one can know what I mean. And I didn't tell Israel to ask me for what I didn't plan to give! No, for I, Jehovah, speak only truth and righteousness.

20Gather together and come, you nations that escape from Cyrus' hand. What fools they are who carry around the wooden idols and pray to gods that cannot save! 21Consult together, argue your case and state your proofs that idol-worship pays! Who but God has said that these things concerning Cyrus would come true? What idol ever told you they would happen? For there is no other God but me—a just God and a Savior—no, not one! 22Let all the world look to me for salvation! For I am God; there is no other. 23I have sworn by myself, and I will never go back on my word, for it is true—that every knee in all the world shall bow to me, and every tongue shall swear allegiance to my name.

24"In Jehovah is all my righteousness and strength," the people shall declare. And all who were angry with him shall come to him and be ashamed. 25In Jehovah all the generations of Israel shall be justified, triumphant.

CHAPTER 46

The False God's of Babylon

The idols of Babylon, Bel and Nebo, are being hauled away on ox carts! But look! The beasts are stumbling! The cart is turning over! The gods are falling out onto the ground! Is that the best that they can do? If they cannot even save themselves from such a fall, how can they save their worshipers from Cyrus?

3"Listen to me, all Israel who are left; I have created you and cared for you since you were born. 4I will be your God through all your lifetime, yes, even when your hair is white with age. I made you and I will care for you. I will carry you along and be your Savior.

5"With what in all of heaven and earth do I compare? Whom can you find who equals me? 6Will you compare me with an idol made lavishly with silver and with gold? They hire a goldsmith to take your wealth and make a god from it! Then they fall down and worship it! 7They carry it around on their shoulders, and when they set it down, it stays there, for it cannot move! And when someone prays to it, there is no answer, for it cannot get him out of his trouble.

8"Don't forget this, O guilty ones. 9And don't forget the many times I clearly told you what was going to happen in the future. For I am God—I only—and there is no other like me 10who can tell you what is going to happen. All I say will come to pass, for I do whatever I wish. 11I will call that swift bird of prey from the east—that man Cyrus from far away. And he will come and do my bidding. I have said I would do it and I will. 12Listen to me, you stubborn, evil men! 13For I am offering you my deliverance; not in the distant future, but right now! I am ready to save you, and I will restore Jerusalem and Israel, who is my glory."

CHAPTER 47

God's Revenge against Babylon

"O Babylon, the unconquered, come sit in the dust; for your days of glory, pomp, and honor are ended. O daughter of Chaldea, never again will you be the lovely princess, tender and delicate. 2Take heavy millstones and grind the corn; remove your veil; strip off your robe; expose yourself to public view.

46:1-13 God calls us to reality and truth. People turn to many things to fill their inner needs. All that is less than God, whether idols of old or addictions and unhealthy relationships today, will fail like an idol that cannot even hold itself on a cart. In contrast, God is the everlasting, sovereign Lord of history who can (and will!) do what he says. Putting the hope of our recovery in God's hands is the only way to achieve our goal.

[3]You shall be in nakedness and shame. I will
take vengeance upon you and will not repent."
[4]So speaks our Redeemer, who will save
Israel from Babylon's mighty power; the Lord
Almighty is his name, the Holy One of Israel.
[5]Sit in darkness and silence, O Babylon;
never again will you be called "The Queen of
Kingdoms." [6]For I was angry with my people
Israel and began to punish them a little by
letting them fall into your hands, O Babylon.
But you showed them no mercy. You have
made even the old folks carry heavy burdens.
[7]You thought your reign would never end,
Queen Kingdom of the world. You didn't care
a whit about my people or think about the
fate of those who do them harm.
[8]O pleasure-mad kingdom, living at ease,
bragging as the greatest in the world—listen
to the sentence of my court upon your sins.
You say, "I alone am God! I'll never be a
widow; I'll never lose my children." [9]Well,
those two things shall come upon you in one
moment, in full measure in one day: widowhood and the loss of your children, despite all
your witchcraft and magic.
[10]You felt secure in all your wickedness.
"No one sees me," you said. Your "wisdom"
and "knowledge" have caused you to turn
away from me and claim that you yourself
are Jehovah. [11]That is why disaster shall overtake you suddenly—so suddenly that you
won't know where it comes from. And there
will be no atonement then to cleanse away
your sins.
[12]Call out the demon hordes you've worshiped all these years. Call on them to help
you strike deep terror into many hearts again.
[13]You have advisors by the ton—your astrologers and stargazers, who try to tell you what
the future holds. [14]But they are as useless as
dried grass burning in the fire. They cannot
even deliver themselves! You'll get no help
from them at all. Theirs is no fire to sit beside
to make you warm! [15]And all your friends of
childhood days shall slip away and disappear,
unable to help.

CHAPTER 48

No Peace for the Wicked

Hear me, my people: you swear allegiance to
the Lord without meaning a word of it when
you boast of living in the Holy City and brag
about depending on the God of Israel. [3]Time
and again I told you what was going to happen in the future. My words were scarcely
spoken when suddenly I did just what I said.
[4]I knew how hard and obstinate you are. Your
necks are as unbending as iron; you are as
hardheaded as brass. [5]That is why I told you
ahead of time what I was going to do, so that
you could never say, "My idol did it; my
carved image commanded it to happen!" [6]You
have heard my predictions and seen them
fulfilled, but you refuse to agree it is so. Now
I will tell you new things I haven't mentioned
before, secrets you haven't heard.
[7]Then you can't say, "We knew that all the
time!"
[8]Yes, I'll tell you things entirely new, for I
know so well what traitors you are, rebels
from earliest childhood, rotten through and
through. [9]Yet for my own sake and for the
honor of my name I will hold back my anger
and not wipe you out. [10]I refined you in the
furnace of affliction, but found no silver
there. You are worthless, with nothing good
in you at all. [11]Yet for my own sake—yes, *for
my own sake*—I will save you from my anger
and not destroy you lest the heathen say their
gods have conquered me. I will not let them
have my glory.
[12]Listen to me, my people, my chosen ones!
I alone am God. I am the First; I am the Last.
[13]It was my hand that laid the foundations of
the earth; the palm of my right hand spread
out the heavens above; I spoke and they came
into being.
[14]Come, all of you, and listen. Among all
your idols, which one has ever told you this:
'The Lord loves Cyrus. He will use him to put

47:1-15 Babylon can be compared to those who ruthlessly oppress or mistreat us. Though they think they are getting away with their evil deeds, God has kept track of their sins and is going to punish them. We need not waste our time plotting revenge or secretly hating these people. God will exact justice; we need to focus on the rest of our life, dealing with the damage that has been done.

48:12-15 Amidst the uncertainties and turmoils of life, we can derive comfort from knowing who God is. He is the God of the past, who knows all of the troubles that have brought the pain we experience today. He is the God of the future, who knows what lies ahead and can be trusted with guiding us in the right path. He is the Creator, who has power over all his creation and sovereignty over all history. We can surely trust a God this powerful to see our recovery to completion.

an end to the empire of Babylonia. He will utterly rout the armies of the Chaldeans'? 15But I am saying it. I have called Cyrus; I have sent him on this errand, and I will prosper him.

16Come closer and listen. I have always told you plainly what would happen, so that you could clearly understand. And now the Lord God and his Spirit have sent me (with this message):

17The Lord, your Redeemer, the Holy One of Israel, says, I am the Lord your God, who punishes you for your own good and leads you along the paths that you should follow.

18Oh, that you had listened to my laws! Then you would have had peace flowing like a gentle river, and great waves of righteousness. 19Then you would have become as numerous as the sands along the seashores of the world, too many to count, and there would have been no need for your destruction.

20Yet even now, be free from your captivity! Leave Babylon, singing as you go; shout to the ends of the earth that the Lord has redeemed his servants, the Jews. 21They were not thirsty when he led them through the deserts; he divided the rock, and water gushed out for them to drink. 22But there is no peace, says the Lord, for the wicked.

CHAPTER 49

A Light for the World

Listen to me, all of you in far-off lands: The Lord called me before my birth. From within the womb he called me by my name. 2God will make my words of judgment sharp as swords. He has hidden me in the shadow of his hand; I am like a sharp arrow in his quiver.

3He said to me: "You are my Servant, a Prince of Power with God, and you shall bring me glory."

4I replied, "But my work for them seems all in vain; I have spent my strength for them without response. Yet I leave it all with God for my reward."

5"And now," said the Lord—the Lord who formed me from my mother's womb to serve him who commissioned me to restore to him his people Israel, who has given me the strength to perform this task and honored me for doing it!— 6"you shall do more than restore Israel to me. I will make you a Light to the nations of the world to bring my salvation to them too."

7The Lord, the Redeemer and Holy One of Israel, says to the One who is despised, rejected by mankind, and kept beneath the heel of the world's rulers: "Kings shall stand at attention when you pass by; princes shall bow low because the Lord has chosen you; he, the faithful Lord, the Holy One of Israel, chooses you."

Comfort for God's People

8,9The Lord says, "Your request has come at a favorable time. I will keep you from harm and give you as a token and pledge to Israel, proof that I will reestablish the land of Israel and reassign it to its own people again. Through you I am saying to the prisoners of darkness, 'Come out! I am giving you your freedom!' They will be my sheep, grazing in green pastures and on the grassy hills. 10They shall neither hunger nor thirst; the searing sun and scorching desert winds will not reach them any more. For the Lord in his mercy will lead them beside the cool waters. 11And I will make my mountains into level paths for them; the highways shall be raised above the valleys.

48:16-22 God would bring deliverance from Babylon in spite of Judah's unworthiness, but they would forfeit peace of mind because of their resistance to God. We, too, can have a relationship with God and be assured of eternal peace, but we may be sacrificing the peace God wants for us on earth if we are continuing in our addictions. Our life can be stable if we are willing to give up our dependencies and the turmoil they bring.

49:1-7 There will be many times when it seems like our godly acts are all for nothing. Since starting recovery, we have lost some old friends and strained some relationships, and we struggle with our own temptations. There doesn't seem to be any good coming out of this process. But we are honoring God, and he will reward us for our faith.

49:8-12 We see here what God wants for and offers to the downtrodden through his Messiah. To those who are in spiritual and emotional bondage and depression, he offers freedom. To those who feel inner emptiness and aimlessness, he offers guidance, care, and fulfillment. To those who feel battered by life, he offers comfort. To those who are ensnared by addictions, he offers liberation.

49:13-26 The people of Judah felt abandoned by God because of the troubles they were experiencing at that time. We can be assured that even though we might feel abandoned by God because of the troubles we are going through, God will never abandon us. In spite of present appearances, God is working out his plan for us and will bring deliverance from our enemies.

12See, my people shall return from far away, from north and west and south."

13Sing for joy, O heavens; shout, O earth. Break forth with song, O mountains, for the Lord has comforted his people and will have compassion upon them in their sorrow.

14Yet they say, "My Lord deserted us; he has forgotten us."

15"Never! Can a mother forget her little child and not have love for her own son? Yet even if that should be, I will not forget you. 16See, I have tattooed your name upon my palm, and ever before me is a picture of Jerusalem's walls in ruins. 17Soon your rebuilders shall come and chase away all those destroying you. 18Look and see, for the Lord has vowed that all your enemies shall come and be your slaves. They will be as jewels to display, as bridal ornaments.

19"Even the most desolate parts of your abandoned land shall soon be crowded with your people, and your enemies who enslaved you shall be far away. 20The generations born in exile shall return and say, 'We need more room! It's crowded here!' 21Then you will think to yourself, 'Who has given me all these? For most of my children were killed, and the rest were carried away into exile, leaving me here alone. Who bore these? Who raised them for me?'"

22The Lord God says, "See, I will give a signal to the Gentiles, and they shall carry your little sons back to you in their arms, and your daughters on their shoulders. 23Kings and queens shall serve you; they shall care for all your needs. They shall bow to the earth before you and lick the dust from off your feet; then you shall know I am the Lord. Those who wait for me shall never be ashamed."

24Who can snatch the prey from the hands of a mighty man? Who can demand that a tyrant let his captives go? 25But the Lord says, "Even the captives of the most mighty and most terrible shall all be freed; for I will fight those who fight you, and I will save your children. 26I will feed your enemies with their own flesh, and they shall be drunk with rivers of their own blood. All the world shall know that I, the Lord, am your Savior and Redeemer, the Mighty One of Israel."

CHAPTER 50

God's Servant Obeys

The Lord asks, Did I sell you to my creditors? Is that why you aren't here? Is your mother gone because I divorced her and sent her away? No, you went away as captives because of your sins. And your mother, too, was taken in payment for your sins. 2Was I too weak to save you? Is that why the house is silent and empty when I come home? Have I no longer power to deliver? No, that is not the reason! For I can rebuke the sea and make it dry! I can turn the rivers into deserts, covered with dying fish. 3I am the one who sends the darkness out across the skies.

4The Lord God has given me his words of wisdom so that I may know what I should say to all these weary ones. Morning by morning he wakens me and opens my understanding to his will. 5The Lord God has spoken to me, and I have listened; I do not rebel nor turn away. 6I give my back to the whip, and my cheeks to those who pull out the beard. I do not hide from shame—they spit in my face.

7Because the Lord God helps me, I will not be dismayed; therefore, I have set my face like flint to do his will, and I know that I will triumph. 8He who gives me justice is near. Who will dare to fight against me now? Where are my enemies? Let them appear! 9See, the Lord God is for me! Who shall declare me guilty? All my enemies shall be destroyed like old clothes eaten up by moths!

10Who among you fears the Lord and obeys his Servant? If such men walk in darkness, without one ray of light, let them trust the Lord, let them rely upon their God. 11But see here, you who live in your own light and

---

50:4-6 The Messiah is speaking here of his own determination to follow God's call to him in spite of the hardships involved. He serves as a model to us in times when we need courage to follow through with God's will. Sometimes God's program for us is difficult. It may involve receiving rebuke, suffering shame, or being misunderstood by those who do not like the path we are on. We will face opposition to our recovery because many people don't want to lose their influence over us, or they feel threatened by our change in life-style. We must stand up to them and follow through with God's plan for us.

50:7-9 We are encouraged to persevere because God is close to us, defending us from our enemies. Any time we enter recovery, we rock the boat of the relationships in which we are entangled. Others become uncomfortable at the prospect of change and will resist us, even trying to get us to fall back into old patterns of behavior. If we stand firm in our resolve to follow God, he will see to it that we triumph.

warm yourselves from your own fires and not from God's; you will live among sorrows.

CHAPTER 51

The People Must Fear God

Listen to me, all who hope for deliverance, who seek the Lord! Consider the quarry from which you were mined, the rock from which you were cut! Yes, think about your ancestors Abraham and Sarah, from whom you came. You worry at being so small and few, but Abraham was only *one* when I called him. But when I blessed him, he became a great nation. 3And the Lord will bless Israel again, and make her deserts blossom; her barren wilderness will become as beautiful as the Garden of Eden. Joy and gladness will be found there, thanksgiving and lovely songs.

4Listen to me, my people; listen, O Israel, for I will see that right prevails. 5My mercy and justice are coming soon; your salvation is on the way. I will rule the nations; they shall wait for me and long for me to come. 6Look high in the skies and watch the earth beneath, for the skies shall disappear like smoke, the earth shall wear out like a garment, and the people of the earth shall die like flies. But my salvation lasts forever; my righteous rule will never die nor end.

7Listen to me, you who know the right from wrong and cherish my laws in your hearts: don't be afraid of people's scorn or their slanderous talk. 8For the moth shall destroy them like garments; the worm shall eat them like wool; but my justice and mercy shall last forever, and my salvation from generation to generation.

9Awake, O Lord! Rise up and robe yourself with strength. Rouse yourself as in the days of old when you slew Egypt, the dragon of the Nile. 10Are you not the same today, the mighty God who dried up the sea, making a path right through it for your ransomed ones? 11The time will come when God's redeemed will all come home again. They shall come with singing to Jerusalem, filled with joy and everlasting gladness; sorrow and mourning will all disappear.

12I, even I, am he who comforts you and gives you all this joy. So what right have you to fear mere mortal men, who wither like the grass and disappear? 13And yet you have no fear of God, your Maker—you have forgotten him, the one who spread the stars throughout the skies and made the earth. Will you be in constant dread of men's oppression, and fear their anger all day long? 14Soon, soon you slaves shall be released; dungeon, starvation and death are not your fate. 15For I am the Lord your God, the Lord Almighty, who dried a path for you right through the sea, between the roaring waves. 16And I have put my words in your mouth and hidden you safe within my hand. I planted the stars in place and molded all the earth. I am the one who says to Israel, "You are mine."

17Wake up, wake up, Jerusalem! You have drunk enough from the cup of the fury of the Lord. You have drunk to the dregs the cup of terror and squeezed out the last drops. 18Not one of her sons is left alive to help or tell her what to do. 19These two things have been your lot: desolation and destruction. Yes, famine and the sword. And who is left to sympathize? Who is left to comfort you? 20For your sons have fainted and lie in the streets, helpless as wild goats caught in a net. The Lord has poured out his fury and rebuke upon them. 21But listen now to this, afflicted ones—full of troubles and in a stupor (but not from being drunk)— 22this is what the Lord says, the Lord your God who cares for his people: "See, I take from your hands the terrible cup; you shall drink no more of my fury; it is gone at last. 23But I will put that terrible cup into the hands of those who tormented you and trampled your souls to the dust and walked upon your backs."

CHAPTER 52

God's People Will Come Home

Wake up, wake up, Jerusalem, and clothe yourselves with strength [from God]. Put on

---

51:7-8 When we set proper boundaries, stop enabling the dysfunctions of others, and deal with abusive relationships, we will experience scorn and slander. Though their rejection will hurt, we need to see the bigger picture. These people, and eventually the entire earth, will pass away, but God's justice, mercy, and salvation will last. So we should concentrate on pleasing God, not people, because God is permanent, while people and their criticism are not.

51:12-23 God is the one who is in control of our life, yet we don't fear him as we should. Instead, we fear people—people who don't really have any authority over us. We are tempted to retreat from God's ways and lapse back into dysfunctional ways, just to please others. We should strive to please God because he has the power to bless us for seeking his will or to discipline us for disobeying.

your beautiful clothes, O Zion, Holy City; for sinners—those who turn from God—will no longer enter your gates. 2Rise from the dust, Jerusalem; take off the slave bands from your neck, O captive daughter of Zion. 3For the Lord says, When I sold you into exile, I asked no fee from your oppressors; now I can take you back again and owe them not a cent! 4My people were tyrannized without cause by Egypt and Assyria, and I delivered them.

5And now, what is this? asks the Lord. Why are my people enslaved again and oppressed without excuse? Those who rule them shout in exultation, and my name is constantly blasphemed day by day. 6Therefore I will reveal my name to my people, and they shall know the power in that name. Then at last they will recognize that it is I, yes, I, who speaks to them.

7How beautiful upon the mountains are the feet of those who bring the happy news of peace and salvation, the news that the God of Israel reigns. 8The watchmen shout and sing with joy, for right before their eyes they see the Lord God bring his people home again. 9Let the ruins of Jerusalem break into joyous song, for the Lord has comforted his people; he has redeemed Jerusalem. 10The Lord has bared his holy arm before the eyes of all the nations; the ends of the earth shall see the salvation of our God.

11Go now, leave your bonds and slavery. Put Babylon and all it represents far behind you—it is unclean to you. You are the holy people of the Lord; purify yourselves, all you who carry home the vessels of the Lord. 12You shall not leave in haste, running for your lives; for the Lord will go ahead of you, and he, the God of Israel, will protect you from behind.

God's Suffering Servant

13See, my Servant shall prosper; he shall be highly exalted. 14,15Yet many shall be amazed when they see him—yes, even far-off foreign nations and their kings; they shall stand dumbfounded, speechless in his presence. For they shall see and understand what they had not been told before. They shall see my Servant beaten and bloodied, so disfigured one would scarcely know it was a person standing there. So shall he cleanse many nations.

CHAPTER 53

But, oh, how few believe it! Who will listen? To whom will God reveal his saving power? 2In God's eyes he was like a tender green shoot, sprouting from a root in dry and sterile ground. But in our eyes there was no attractiveness at all, nothing to make us want him. 3We despised him and rejected him—a man of sorrows, acquainted with bitterest grief. We turned our backs on him and looked the other way when he went by. He was despised, and we didn't care.

4Yet it was *our* grief he bore, *our* sorrows that weighed him down. And we thought his troubles were a punishment from God, for his *own* sins! 5But he was wounded and bruised for *our* sins. He was beaten that we might have peace; he was lashed—and we were healed! 6*We*—every one of us—have strayed away like sheep! *We,* who left God's paths to follow our own. Yet God laid on *him* the guilt and sins of every one of us!

7He was oppressed and he was afflicted, yet he never said a word. He was brought as a lamb to the slaughter; and as a sheep before her shearers is dumb, so he stood silent before the ones condemning him. 8From prison and

---

52:1-6 We know what it feels like to be a slave—a slave to alcohol, drugs, sex, or power. God promises to free us from our enslavement; he wants to remove our "slave bands." God is greater than any addiction we may have, and when we believe that he can free us from our bondage, he will save us.

52:7-10 God's message of deliverance is so wonderful that it deserves to be shared near and far. "Beautiful" are the feet of those who make the effort to share such news with others. Just as the message of Judah's deliverance from captivity deserved to be shared abroad, our message of salvation and recovery through Christ deserves to be shared. This is the essence of Step Twelve, which calls us to share what we have learned with others as part of our continuing recovery.

52:13–53:12 This marvelous passage describes in detail the atoning death of Jesus the Messiah, God's Suffering Servant. His death for us is the basis of true and full recovery. Because he died for our sins, we don't have to pay for all the garbage for which we are responsible. We have to endure the consequences of whatever we have done, and we will have to make restitution, but we do not have to pay the penalty for our sins, which is eternal death (see Romans 6:23).

53:7-12 It was not easy for Jesus the Messiah to bear such abuse and shame—and it was wholly undeserved! The outcome, however, was a ministry that would change the world. This is the same pattern we can expect. When we suffer in God's will for doing what is right, we can be assured that God will use it to minister to others and will vindicate us in due time, either in this life or the next.

trial they led him away to his death. But who among the people of that day realized it was their sins that he was dying for—that he was suffering their punishment? 9He was buried like a criminal, but in a rich man's grave; but he had done no wrong and had never spoken an evil word.

10But it was the Lord's good plan to bruise him and fill him with grief. However, when his soul has been made an offering for sin, then he shall have a multitude of children, many heirs. He shall live again, and God's program shall prosper in his hands. 11And when he sees all that is accomplished by the anguish of his soul, he shall be satisfied; and because of what he has experienced, my righteous Servant shall make many to be counted righteous before God, for he shall bear all their sins. 12Therefore, I will give him the honors of one who is mighty and great because he has poured out his soul unto death. He was counted as a sinner, and he bore the sins of many, and he pled with God for sinners.

CHAPTER 54

Israel Will Be Rebuilt

Sing, O childless woman! Break out into loud and joyful song, Jerusalem, for she who was abandoned has more blessings now than she whose husband stayed! 2Enlarge your house; build on additions; spread out your home! 3For you will soon be bursting at the seams! And your descendants will possess the cities left behind during the exile and rule the nations that took their lands.

4Fear not; you will no longer live in shame. The shame of your youth and the sorrows of widowhood will be remembered no more, 5for your Creator will be your "husband." The Lord Almighty is his name; he is your Redeemer, the Holy One of Israel, the God of all the earth. 6For the Lord has called you back from your grief—a young wife abandoned by her husband. 7For a brief moment I abandoned you. But with great compassion I will take you back. 8In a moment of anger I turned my face a little while; but with everlasting love I will have pity on you, says the Lord, your Redeemer.

9Just as in the time of Noah I swore that I would never again permit the waters of a flood to cover the earth and destroy its life, so now I swear that I will never again pour out my anger on you. 10For the mountains may depart and the hills disappear, but my kindness shall not leave you. My promise of peace for you will never be broken, says the Lord who has mercy upon you.

11O my afflicted people, tempest-tossed and troubled, I will rebuild you on a foundation of sapphires and make the walls of your houses from precious jewels. 12I will make your towers of sparkling agate and your gates and walls of shining gems. 13And all your citizens shall be taught by me, and their prosperity shall be great. 14You will live under a government that is just and fair. Your enemies will stay far away; you will live in peace. Terror shall not come near. 15If any nation comes to fight you, it will not be sent by me to punish you. Therefore, it will be routed, for I am on your side. 16I have created the smith who blows the coals beneath the forge and makes the weapons of destruction. And I have created the armies that destroy. 17But in that coming day, no weapon turned against you shall succeed, and you will have justice against every courtroom lie. This is the heritage of the servants of the Lord. This is the blessing I have given you, says the Lord.

CHAPTER 55

A Promise of Joy and Peace

Say there! Is anyone thirsty? Come and drink—even if you have no money! Come, take your choice of wine and milk—it's all free! 2Why spend your money on food that

---

54:10 Here is a promise we can hang on to during those times when everything seems to be falling apart and nobody, not even God, seems to care. Things that are apparently permanent, such as mountains and hills, will not last as long as God's mercy for his people. God's promise to us for kindness and peace in the midst of our troubles will stand forever.

55:6 We need to seek God while we have the opportunity. He does not make himself unavailable to us, but if we procrastinate and make excuses long enough, we will find that without knowing it we have been hardening our heart. Someday our heart may be so hard that God's call to us can no longer be heard. The time to turn to God is now!

56:1-2 God rescues us free of charge; it is a gift. It is not something we can earn by being "good enough." While our salvation is not based on the good things we do, our deeds are an important demonstration of our faith in God. By following God's instructions for living, we are demonstrating our obedience to and respect for God. And God's laws lead to a rich, full, addiction-free life. Since he created the world and us, he knows what works best for us.

doesn't give you strength? Why pay for groceries that do you no good? Listen and I'll tell you where to get good food that fattens up the soul!

[3]Come to me with your ears wide open. Listen, for the life of your soul is at stake. I am ready to make an everlasting covenant with you, to give you all the unfailing mercies and love that I had for King David. [4]He proved my power by conquering foreign nations. [5]You also will command the nations, and they will come running to obey, not because of your own power or virtue, but because I, the Lord your God, have glorified you.

[6]Seek the Lord while you can find him. Call upon him now while he is near. [7]Let men cast off their wicked deeds; let them banish from their minds the very thought of doing wrong! Let them turn to the Lord that he may have mercy upon them, and to our God, for he will abundantly pardon! [8]This plan of mine is not what you would work out, neither are my thoughts the same as yours! [9]For just as the heavens are higher than the earth, so are my ways higher than yours, and my thoughts than yours.

[10]As the rain and snow come down from heaven and stay upon the ground to water the earth, and cause the grain to grow and to produce seed for the farmer and bread for the hungry, [11]so also is my Word. I send it out, and it always produces fruit. It shall accomplish all I want it to and prosper everywhere I send it. [12]You will live in joy and peace. The mountains and hills, the trees of the field—all the world around you—will rejoice. [13]Where once were thorns, fir trees will grow; where briars grew, the myrtle trees will sprout up. This miracle will make the Lord's name very great and be an everlasting sign [of God's power and love].

CHAPTER 56

Blessings for All People

Be just and fair to all, the Lord God says. Do what's right and good, for I am coming soon to rescue you. [2]Blessed is the man who refuses to work during my Sabbath days of rest, but honors them; and blessed is the man who checks himself from doing wrong.

[3]And my blessings are for Gentiles, too, when they accept the Lord; don't let them think that I will make them second-class citizens. And this is for the eunuchs too. They can be as much mine as anyone. [4]For I say this to the eunuchs who keep my Sabbaths holy, who choose the things that please me and

Redeeming the Past

BIBLE READING: Isaiah 54:4-8

We made a decision to turn our will and our life over to the care of God as we understood him.

We all come to God with a past. In turning our life over to him, we give him our past with all its losses and shame. We hand over every moment of disgrace, every tear we have ever cried, every word we wish we could take back, all the broken promises, the loneliness, all the dreams that died, the dashed hopes, the broken relationships, our successes and failures, all of our yesterdays and the scars they have left in our life.

Under Old Testament law, if someone lost freedom, property, or spouse because of a disaster or a debt, the next of kin was looked to as a "redeemer." If property had been lost because of an inability to pay, the redeemer would pay for it and return it to the original owner. If a woman lost her husband, the redeemer would marry her, providing her with protection and love. God tells us, "Fear not; you will no longer live in shame. The shame of your youth and the sorrows of widowhood will be remembered no more, for your Creator will be your 'husband.' The Lord Almighty is his name; he is your Redeemer. . . . For the Lord has called you back from your grief" (Isaiah 54:4-6).

God is our Redeemer, the restorer of our losses. He is Lord of all, even of the days and dreams in our past. When we give God our past, he can make up for all that we have lost. He can rid us of the shame. He can fill the empty places in our heart. ***Turn to page 1021, Matthew 11.***

obey my laws: 5I will give them—in my house,
within my walls—a name far greater than the
honor they would receive from having sons
and daughters. For the name that I will give
them is an everlasting one; it will never disappear.

6As for the Gentiles, the outsiders who join
the people of the Lord and serve him and love
his name, who are his servants and don't
desecrate the Sabbath, and have accepted his
covenant and promises, 7I will bring them
also to my holy mountain of Jerusalem and
make them full of joy within my House of
Prayer.

I will accept their sacrifices and offerings,
for my Temple shall be called "A House of
Prayer for All People"! 8For the Lord God who
brings back the outcasts of Israel says, I will
bring others too besides my people Israel.

9Come, wild animals of the field; come, tear
apart the sheep; come, wild animals of the
forest, devour my people. 10For the leaders of
my people—the Lord's watchmen, his shepherds—are all blind to every danger. They are
featherbrained and give no warning when
danger comes. They love to lie there, love to
sleep, to dream. 11And they are as greedy as
dogs, never satisfied; they are stupid shepherds who only look after their own interest,
each trying to get as much as he can for
himself from every possible source.

12"Come," they say. "We'll get some wine
and have a party; let's all get drunk. This is
really living; let it go on and on, and tomorrow will be even better!"

CHAPTER 57

The Godly Will Rest in Peace

The good men perish; the godly die before
their time, and no one seems to care or wonder why. No one seems to realize that God is
taking them away from evil days ahead. 2For
the godly who die shall rest in peace.

3But you—come here, you witches' sons,
you offspring of adulterers and harlots! 4Who
is it you mock, making faces and sticking out
your tongues? You children of sinners and
liars! 5You worship your idols with great zeal
beneath the shade of every tree and slay your
children as human sacrifices down in the valleys, under overhanging rocks. 6Your gods are
the smooth stones in the valleys. You worship
them, and they, not I, are your inheritance.
Does all this make me happy? 7,8You have
committed adultery on the tops of the mountains, for you worship idols there, deserting
me. Behind closed doors you set your idols up
and worship someone other than me. This is
adultery, for you are giving these idols your
love instead of loving me. 9You have taken
pleasant incense and perfume to Molech as
your gift. You have traveled far, even to hell
itself, to find new gods to love. 10You grew
weary in your search, but you never gave up.
You strengthened yourself and went on.
11Why were you more afraid of them than of
me? How is it that you gave not even a second
thought to me? Is it because I've been too
gentle that you have no fear of me?

12And then there is your "righteousness"
and your "good works"—none of which will
save you. 13Let's see if the whole collection of
your idols can help you when you cry to them
to save you! They are so weak that the wind
can carry them off ! A breath can puff them
away. But he who trusts in me shall possess
the land and inherit my Holy Mountain. 14I
will say, Rebuild the road! Clear away the
rocks and stones. Prepare a glorious highway
for my people's return from captivity.

56:9-12 The evil leaders of God's people will be chastised. We must be aware of those whom we follow. There will be those who want to give us advice and guidance but cannot be trusted because they are not following God's principles. Anything that goes against what God wants should be avoided.

57:1-14 Recovery is God's desire for us, but it does not happen automatically. Here God judges those who turn their backs on him and plunge headlong into sin. These people deliberately reject God and don't care about following his ways. God is not judging those who struggle with doing what is right and fail. Making mistakes is common to all of us and should be expected from time to time because we are not perfect. But by asking for forgiveness and for help from God, we can continue toward our goal—even after a fall.

58:1-5 The lives of the people of Judah were full of religious activities, but their religion was just a front. They led dysfunctional lives, devoid of obedience to God and concern for his laws. Not realizing that their own empty religious acts were at fault, they blamed God for not doing anything for them. While we may go through the motions of being religious, are we really trying to serve and honor God? Have we tried to recover from our addictions, or are we covering over our dysfunctions with religious acts? If we don't truly seek to live as God wants us to, he will ignore our false religious acts.

15The high and lofty One who inhabits eternity, the Holy One, says this: I live in that
high and holy place where those with contrite, humble spirits dwell; and I refresh the
humble and give new courage to those with
repentant hearts. 16For I will not fight against
you forever, nor always show my wrath; if I
did, all mankind would perish—the very souls
that I have made. 17I was angry and smote
these greedy men. But they went right on
sinning, doing everything their evil hearts
desired. 18I have seen what they do, but I will
heal them anyway! I will lead them and comfort them, helping them to mourn and to
confess their sins. 19Peace, peace to them,
both near and far, for I will heal them all. 20But
those who still reject me are like the restless
sea, which is never still, but always churns up
mire and dirt. 21There is no peace, says my
God, for them!

CHAPTER 58
A Call to Just Living
Shout with the voice of a trumpet blast; tell
my people of their sins! 2Yet they act so pious!
They come to the Temple every day and are so
delighted to hear the reading of my laws—just
as though they would obey them—just as
though they don't despise the commandments of their God! How anxious they are to
worship correctly; oh, how they love the
Temple services!
3"We have fasted before you," they say.
"Why aren't you impressed? Why don't you
see our sacrifices? Why don't you hear our
prayers? We have done much penance, and
you don't even notice it!" I'll tell you why!
Because you are living in evil pleasure even
while you are fasting, and you keep right on
oppressing your workers. 4Look, what good is
fasting when you keep on fighting and quarreling? This kind of fasting will never get you
anywhere with me. 5Is this what I want—this
doing of penance and bowing like reeds in the
wind, putting on sackcloth and covering
yourselves with ashes? Is this what you call
fasting?
6No, the kind of fast I want is that you stop
oppressing those who work for you and treat
them fairly and give them what they earn. 7I
want you to share your food with the hungry
and bring right into your own homes those
who are helpless, poor, and destitute. Clothe
those who are cold, and don't hide from relatives who need your help.
8If you do these things, God will shed his
own glorious light upon you. He will heal

God's Abundant Pardon

BIBLE READING: Isaiah 55:1-9

We were entirely ready to have God remove all these defects of character.

People tell us to repent and stop thinking the way we do. Most of us would give anything to do this. If it were only that simple to put a stop to our obsessive thoughts! When we are starving emotionally, it is almost impossible to stop thinking about what has fed that hunger, even when we realize it doesn't satisfy.

People don't seem to understand. They may quote a verse like, "Let men cast off their wicked deeds; let them banish from their minds the very thought of doing wrong!" (Isaiah 55:7). But we think, *How? My thoughts seem to be out of my control.*

God does understand. He put that verse into the larger context of dealing with the hunger within our soul. He said, "Why spend your money on food that doesn't give you strength? Why pay for groceries that do you no good? Listen and I'll tell you where to get good food that fattens up the soul! Come to me with your ears wide open. Listen, for the life of your soul is at stake. . . . Let them turn to the Lord that he may have mercy upon them, and to our God, for he will abundantly pardon!" (Isaiah 55:2-3, 7). The word translated *abundantly* can be understood to mean "in progressively increasing measure each time we come."

We fight our addictions on two fronts: dealing with the hunger deep inside us, and changing our thoughts of doing wrong. Neither battle is easily won; each requires our daily readiness for God to satisfy our hunger and remove our defects of character. ***Turn to page 955, Jonah 4.***

you; your godliness will lead you forward,
goodness will be a shield before you, and the
glory of the Lord will protect you from behind. 9Then, when you call, the Lord will
answer. "Yes, I am here," he will quickly reply.
All you need to do is to stop oppressing the
weak and stop making false accusations and
spreading vicious rumors!

10Feed the hungry! Help those in trouble!
Then your light will shine out from the darkness, and the darkness around you shall be as
bright as day. 11And the Lord will guide you
continually, and satisfy you with all good
things, and keep you healthy too; and you
will be like a well-watered garden, like an
ever-flowing spring. 12Your sons will rebuild
the long-deserted ruins of your cities, and you
will be known as "The People Who Rebuild
Their Walls and Cities."

13If you keep the Sabbath holy, not having
your own fun and business on that day, but
enjoying the Sabbath, speaking of it with delight as the Lord's holy day, and honoring the
Lord in what you do, not following your own
desires and pleasure nor talking idly—14then
the Lord will be your delight, and I will see to
it that you ride high and get your full share of
the blessings I promised to Jacob, your father.
The Lord has spoken.

CHAPTER 59

A Call to Obedience

Listen now! The Lord isn't too weak to save
you. And he isn't getting deaf! He can hear
you when you call! 2But the trouble is that
your sins have cut you off from God. Because
of sin he has turned his face away from you
and will not listen anymore. 3For your hands
are those of murderers and your fingers are
filthy with sin. You lie and grumble and oppose the good. 4No one cares about being fair
and true. Your lawsuits are based on lies; you
spend your time plotting evil deeds and doing
them. 5You spend your time and energy in
spinning evil plans that end up in deadly
actions. 6You cheat and shortchange everyone. Everything you do is filled with sin;
violence is your trademark. 7Your feet run to
do evil and rush to murder; your thoughts are
only of sinning, and wherever you go you
leave behind a trail of misery and death. 8You
don't know what true peace is, nor what it
means to be just and good; you continually
do wrong and those who follow you won't
experience any peace either.

9It is because of all this evil that you aren't
finding God's blessings; that's why he doesn't
punish those who injure you. No wonder you
are in darkness when you expected light. No
wonder you are walking in the gloom. 10No
wonder you grope like blind men and stumble along in broad daylight, yes, even at
brightest noontime, as though it were the
darkest night! No wonder you are like corpses
when compared with vigorous young men!
11You roar like hungry bears; you moan with
mournful cries like doves. You look for God to
keep you, but he doesn't. He has turned away.
12For your sins keep piling up before the righteous God and testify against you.

Yes, we know what sinners we are. 13We
know our disobedience; we have denied the

58:6-12 The path of recovery includes performing compassionate acts toward others. If we focus our attention on our own life and make excuses to ignore others, we will not progress very far in recovery. As we learn to deal with others righteously and learn to love and serve them in healthy ways, we will find that God will bring healing and protection to us.

58:13-14 The Old Testament Sabbath regulation provided a structure within which people would regularly take a rest from the pressures of life, worship God, and relax with their families. We still need to set boundaries on our workaholic tendencies so we can take care of ourself, our family, and our relationship with God. Not only will we strengthen these relationships, but we will also be refreshed physically and ready to face the work ahead of us.

59:13 We often fear dealing honestly with life's problems. We are afraid that if we start opening up to the truth, we will be devastated. So we start lying to cover up and hide from the truth. Before long we are fooled by our own lies. Honesty with God, with ourself, and with others is essential for our growth. We can never recover in the areas where we deny that there is a problem.

59:15 It is true that people are attacked as they try to improve themselves. Friends don't want us to deal truthfully with our hang-ups because our doing so might expose their own. People may exert a great deal of influence over us, and they may not want to lose their power. The forces against us and our recovery are great because the world stands contrary to God's program. We must resist what the world says and follow God.

60:1-3 God's people are called to let their light shine to the nations. God's desire is to transform all of us and then to use us to bring his truth to others. We are reminded of Step Twelve, which tells us that an important part of our recovery is sharing our life as living proof that recovery is possible with God's help.

Lord our God. We know what rebels we are
and how unfair we are, for we carefully plan
our lies. 14Our courts oppose the righteous
man; fairness is unknown. Truth falls dead in
the streets, and justice is outlawed.
15Yes, truth is gone, and anyone who tries a
better life is soon attacked. The Lord saw all
the evil and was displeased to find no steps
taken against sin. 16He saw no one was helping
you and wondered that no one intervened.
Therefore he himself stepped in to save you
through his mighty power and justice. 17He
put on righteousness as armor and the helmet
of salvation on his head. He clothed himself
with robes of vengeance and of godly fury.
18He will repay his enemies for their evil
deeds—fury for his foes in distant lands.
19Then at last they will reverence and glorify
the name of God from west to east. For he will
come like a flood tide driven by Jehovah's
breath. 20He will come as a Redeemer to those
in Zion who have turned away from sin.
21"As for me, this is my promise to them,"
says the Lord: "My Holy Spirit shall not leave
them, and they shall want the good and hate
the wrong—they and their children and their
children's children forever."

CHAPTER 60

Glory for God's People

Arise, my people! Let your light shine for all
the nations to see! For the glory of the Lord is
streaming from you. 2Darkness as black as
night shall cover all the peoples of the earth,
but the glory of the Lord will shine from you.
3All nations will come to your light; mighty
kings will come to see the glory of the Lord
upon you.
4Lift up your eyes and see! For your sons
and daughters are coming home to you from
distant lands. 5Your eyes will shine with joy,
your hearts will thrill, for merchants from
around the world will flow to you, bringing
you the wealth of many lands. 6Vast droves of
camels will converge upon you, dromedaries
from Midian and Sheba and Ephah too, bringing gold and incense to add to the praise of
God. 7The flocks of Kedar shall be given you,
and the rams of Nabaioth for my altars, and I
will glorify my glorious Temple in that day.
8And who are these who fly like a cloud to
Israel, like doves to their nests? 9I have reserved the ships of many lands, the very best,
to bring the sons of Israel home again from far
away, bringing their wealth with them. For
the Holy One of Israel, known around the
world, has glorified you in the eyes of all.

Clearing the Mess

BIBLE READING: Isaiah 57:12-19

We humbly asked him to remove our shortcomings.

In many ways Step Seven represents a turning point in our recovery. It forms a bridge between the inner work of the first six steps and the final steps, which emphasize outer work—changes in behavior. Our shortcomings may seem to clutter the road out of our past. Just because we are working the steps doesn't mean that our life is as it should be. Will God really come into the mess and lead us out?

"I will say, Rebuild the road! Clear away the rocks and stones. Prepare a glorious highway for my people's return from captivity. The high and lofty one who inhabits eternity, the Holy One, says this: I live in that high and holy place where those with contrite, humble spirits dwell; and I refresh the humble and give new courage to those with repentant hearts. . . . I have seen what they do, but I will heal them anyway! I will lead them and comfort them, helping them to mourn and to confess their sins" (Isaiah 57:14-15, 18).

God is a great help when it comes to clearing the way to a better future. He looks forward to removing our shortcomings so we can better avoid being tripped up. When we come to him with humility, admitting that we still struggle with many of our short-comings, he refreshes us and gives us the courage we need to go on. He isn't put off by the things we do. He sees what we do, but chooses to heal us anyway! He'll keep leading us toward recovery, one step at a time.

Turn to page 803, Jeremiah 18.

10 Foreigners will come and build your cities.
Presidents and kings will send you aid. For
though I destroyed you in my anger, I will
have mercy on you through my grace. 11 Your
gates will stay wide open around the clock to
receive the wealth of many lands. The kings
of the world will cater to you. 12 For the nations refusing to be your allies will perish;
they shall be destroyed. 13 The glory of Lebanon will be yours—the forests of firs, pines,
and box trees—to beautify my sanctuary. My
Temple will be glorious.

14 The sons of anti-Semites will come and
bow before you! They will kiss your feet! They
will call Jerusalem "The City of the Lord" and
"The Glorious Mountain of the Holy One of
Israel."

15 Though once despised and hated and re-
buffed by all, you will be beautiful forever, a
joy for all the generations of the world, for I
will make you so. 16 Powerful kings and
mighty nations shall provide you with the
choicest of their goods to satisfy your every
need, and you will know at last and really
understand that I, the Lord, am your Savior
and Redeemer, the Mighty One of Israel. 17 I
will exchange your brass for gold, your iron
for silver, your wood for brass, your stones for
iron. Peace and righteousness shall be your
taskmasters! 18 Violence will disappear out of
your land—all war will end. Your walls will be
"Salvation" and your gates "Praise."

19 No longer will you need the sun or moon
to give you light, for the Lord your God will
be your everlasting light, and he will be your
glory. 20 Your sun shall never set; the moon
shall not go down—for the Lord will be your
everlasting light; your days of mourning all
will end. 21 All your people will be good. They
will possess their land forever, for I will plant
them there with my own hands; this will
bring me glory. 22 The smallest family shall
multiply into a clan; the tiny group shall be a
mighty nation. I, the Lord, will bring it all to
pass when it is time.

CHAPTER 61

Hope for Suffering People

The Spirit of the Lord God is upon me, because the Lord has anointed me to bring good
news to the suffering and afflicted. He has
sent me to comfort the brokenhearted, to
announce liberty to captives, and to open the
eyes of the blind. 2 He has sent me to tell those
who mourn that the time of God's favor to
them has come, and the day of his wrath to
their enemies. 3 To all who mourn in Israel he
will give: beauty for ashes; joy instead of
mourning; praise instead of heaviness.

For God has planted them like strong and
graceful oaks for his own glory.

4 And they shall rebuild the ancient ruins,
repairing cities long ago destroyed, reviving
them though they have lain there many generations. 5 Foreigners shall be your servants;
they shall feed your flocks and plow your
fields and tend your vineyards. 6 You shall be
called priests of the Lord, ministers of our
God. You shall be fed with the treasures of the
nations and shall glory in their riches. 7 Instead of shame and dishonor, you shall have
a double portion of prosperity and everlasting
joy.

8 For I, the Lord, love justice; I hate robbery
and wrong. I will faithfully reward my people
for their suffering and make an everlasting
covenant with them. 9 Their descendants shall
be known and honored among the nations;

60:4-22 The restoration and exaltation of Israel at the end of history are described in these verses. How unbelievable this description must have seemed to the Jews of Isaiah's day, who were under the threat of Assyrian domination, and to the subsequent generations, who would be held captive in Babylonia. But God can do the seemingly impossible. He could restore them, and he can restore us, too. (See Ephesians 3:20-21.)

61:4-7 God promises rebuilding, prosperity, ministry, and honor to the people of Israel in their final restoration at the end of history. Right now God promises these same things, though in different forms, to all of his children, whether Jew or Gentile. He wants to rebuild our broken life, make us spiritually prosperous, give our life significance through ministry to others, and fill us with honor through his love and grace.

62:1-5 God promised a glorious restoration for Jerusalem and her people in the future. She who had been degraded and abused by conquerors would be lifted up and honored. This is God's desire for us, too. Whether we have been abused by parents, spouse, friends, or strangers, or whether our pain has been self-inflicted through our addictions, God desires to cleanse us and restore us to health and honor. He can do this if we believe in him and ask him to save us.

62:6-7 The intercessors here were asked to cry out to God, reminding him of his promises to Jerusalem. They were to keep praying until he had fulfilled his word. We should not neglect prayer in our recovery. It is not just a way to bring us peace of mind, but a way to bring change in the world.

all shall realize that they are a people God has
blessed.
10 Let me tell you how happy God has made
me! For he has clothed me with garments of
salvation and draped about me the robe of
righteousness. I am like a bridegroom in his
wedding suit or a bride with her jewels. 11 The
Lord will show the nations of the world his
justice; all will praise him. His righteousness
shall be like a budding tree, or like a garden in
early spring, full of young plants springing up
everywhere.

CHAPTER 62
Isaiah's Prayer
Because I love Zion, because my heart yearns
for Jerusalem, I will not cease to pray for her
or to cry out to God on her behalf until she
shines forth in his righteousness and is glorious in his salvation. 2 The nations shall see
your righteousness. Kings shall be blinded by
your glory; and God will confer on you a new
name. 3 He will hold you aloft in his hands for
all to see—a splendid crown for the King of
kings. 4 Never again shall you be called "The
God-forsaken Land" or the "Land That God
Forgot." Your new name will be "The Land of
God's Delight" and "The Bride," for the Lord
delights in you and will claim you as his own.
5 Your children will care for you, O Jerusalem,
with joy like that of a young man who marries
a virgin; and God will rejoice over you as a
bridegroom with his bride.
6,7 O Jerusalem, I have set intercessors on
your walls who shall cry to God all day and all
night for the fulfillment of his promises. Take
no rest, all you who pray, and give God no rest
until he establishes Jerusalem and makes her
respected and admired throughout the earth.
8 The Lord has sworn to Jerusalem with all his
integrity: "I will never again give you to your
enemies; never again shall foreign soldiers
come and take away your grain and wine.
9 You raised it; you shall keep it, praising God.
Within the Temple courts you yourselves
shall drink the wine you pressed."
10 Go out! Go out! Prepare the roadway for
my people to return! Build the roads, pull out
the boulders, raise the flag of Israel.
11 See, the Lord has sent his messengers to
every land and said, "Tell my people, I, the
Lord your God, am coming to save you and
will bring you many gifts." 12 And they shall be
called "The Holy People" and "The Lord's
Redeemed," and Jerusalem shall be called
"The Land of Desire" and "The City God Has
Blessed."

Our Mission

BIBLE READING: Isaiah 61:1-3

Having had a spiritual awakening as the result of these steps, we tried to carry this message to others and to practice these principles in all our affairs.

A life that has been set free from addiction is a beautiful sight to behold. When we practice these principles, people will gain hope and see the glory of God in our life. We know from experience the depths of suffering, affliction, and brokenness. We know the pain of being enslaved to our passions and blinded by our denial. We have endured our season of grieving. We can relate to those who struggle to be free. We also know that there is more to life than bondage. There is healing and freedom; there is clarity and mercy; there is beauty and joy; there is heaven as well as hell.

When Jesus came to earth he had a mission, which was expressed in these words, "The Spirit of the Lord God is upon me, because the Lord has anointed me to bring good news to the suffering and afflicted. He has sent me to comfort the broken-hearted, to announce liberty to captives, and to open the eyes of the blind. He has sent me to tell those who mourn that the time of God's favor to them has come. . . . To all who mourn . . . he will give: beauty for ashes; joy instead of mourning; praise instead of heaviness" (Isaiah 61:1-3).

This mission has been passed on to us. Some people talk about "preaching the gospel" but may alienate those who need the Good News the most. We are in a unique position to share our experience, strength, and hope in a way that broken people can receive it. ***Turn to page 1083, Mark 16.***

CHAPTER 63
God Is Loving and Kind

Who is this who comes from Edom, from the
city of Bozrah, with his magnificent garments
of crimson? Who is this in royal robes, marching in the greatness of his strength?
“It is I, the Lord, announcing your salvation; I, the Lord, the one who is mighty to
save!”
2“Why are your clothes so red, as from
treading out the grapes?”
3“I have trodden the winepress alone. No
one was there to help me. In my wrath I have
trodden my enemies like grapes. In my fury I
trampled my foes. It is their blood you see
upon my clothes. 4For the time has come for
me to avenge my people, to redeem them
from the hands of their oppressors. 5I looked
but no one came to help them; I was amazed
and appalled. So I executed vengeance alone;
unaided, I meted out judgment. 6I crushed the
heathen nations in my anger and made them
stagger and fall to the ground.”
7I will tell of the loving-kindnesses of God.
I will praise him for all he has done; I will
rejoice in his great goodness to Israel, which
he has granted in accordance with his mercy
and love. 8He said, “They are my very own;
surely they will not be false again.” And he
became their Savior. 9In all their affliction he
was afflicted, and he personally saved them.
In his love and pity he redeemed them and
lifted them up and carried them through all
the years.
10But they rebelled against him and grieved
his Holy Spirit. That is why he became their
enemy and personally fought against them.
11Then they remembered those days of old
when Moses, God’s servant, led his people out
of Egypt, and they cried out, “Where is the
One who brought Israel through the sea, with
Moses as their shepherd? Where is the God
who sent his Holy Spirit to be among his
people? 12Where is he whose mighty power
divided the sea before them when Moses
lifted up his hand, and established his reputation forever? 13Who led them through the
bottom of the sea? Like fine stallions racing
through the desert, they never stumbled.
14Like cattle grazing in the valleys, so the Spirit
of the Lord gave them rest. Thus he gave
himself a magnificent reputation.”
15O Lord, look down from heaven and see
us from your holy, glorious home; where is
the love for us you used to show—your power,
your mercy, and your compassion? Where are
they now? 16Surely you are still our Father!
Even if Abraham and Jacob would disown us,
still you would be our Father, our Redeemer
from ages past. 17O Lord, why have you hardened our hearts and made us sin and turn
against you? Return and help us, for we who
belong to you need you so. 18How briefly we
possessed Jerusalem! And now our enemies
have destroyed her. 19O God, why do you treat
us as though we weren’t your people, as
though we were a heathen nation that never
called you “Lord”?

CHAPTER 64
God Is like a Potter

Oh, that you would burst forth from the skies
and come down! How the mountains would
quake in your presence! 2The consuming fire
of your glory would burn down the forests
and boil the oceans dry. The nations would
tremble before you; then your enemies would
learn the reason for your fame! 3So it was
before when you came down, for you did

63:10-14 Isaiah recounted the history of Israel. In spite of God’s deliverance from Egypt, they rebelled against God, worshiped idols, and then wondered why their lives were such a mess. We may be in danger of doing the same if we think that trusting God is only a stage in our recovery. After we have achieved a certain level of healing and maturity, we may stop depending on God and try to take care of things ourself. If we do, we will only experience disaster. Trusting God is critical in every stage of recovery.

63:17-19 We see that turning back to God and renewing that relationship is not a push-button experience that happens instantly. We have allowed our heart to become hardened (though Israel here blames God for this), and it takes time to soften it again. We can begin this process in a moment, but God will not necessarily seem immediately near. We need to keep moving in his direction, and our relationship with him will blossom in time. God is there; we just have trouble seeing him.

64:1-4 We see two key elements in this passage that are essential to recovery: faith and patience. The people of Israel looked at the awesome nature of their glorious, powerful, incomparable God. This increased their faith. Then they patiently waited for him to bring about their deliverance. Such matters do not happen instantly or according to our timetable. If we persevere in doing our part, God will bring about the results in due time. If we are faithful and trust God, our recovery will be achieved.

awesome things beyond our highest expectations, and how the mountains quaked! [4]For since the world began no one has seen or heard of such a God as ours, who works for those who wait for him! [5]You welcome those who cheerfully do good, who follow godly ways.

But we are not godly; we are constant sinners and have been all our lives. Therefore your wrath is heavy on us. How can such as we be saved? [6]We are all infected and impure with sin. When we put on our prized robes of righteousness, we find they are but filthy rags. Like autumn leaves we fade, wither and fall. And our sins, like the wind, sweep us away. [7]Yet no one calls upon your name or pleads with you for mercy. Therefore, you have turned away from us and turned us over to our sins.

[8]And yet, O Lord, you are our Father. We are the clay and you are the Potter. We are all formed by your hand. [9]Oh, be not so angry with us, Lord, nor forever remember our sins. Oh, look and see that we are all your people.

[10]Your holy cities are destroyed; Jerusalem is a desolate wilderness. [11]Our holy, beautiful Temple where our fathers praised you is burned down, and all the things of beauty are destroyed. [12]After all of this, must you still refuse to help us, Lord? Will you stand silent and still punish us?

CHAPTER 65

New Heavens and New Earth

The Lord says, People who never before inquired about me are now seeking me out. Nations who never before searched for me are finding me.

[2]But my own people—though I have been spreading out my arms to welcome them all day long—have rebelled; they follow their own evil paths and thoughts. [3]All day long they insult me to my face by worshiping idols in many gardens and burning incense on the rooftops of their homes. [4]At night they go out among the graves and caves to worship evil spirits, and they eat pork and other forbidden foods. [5]Yet they say to one another, "Don't come too close, you'll defile me! For I am holier than you!" They stifle me. Day in and day out they infuriate me.

[6]See, here is my decree all written out before me: *I will not stand silent; I will repay. Yes, I will repay them*— [7]not only for their own sins but for those of their fathers too, says the Lord, for they also burned incense on the mountains and insulted me upon the hills. I will pay them back in full.

[8]But I will not destroy them all, says the Lord; for just as good grapes are found among a cluster of bad ones (and someone will say, "Don't throw them all away—there are some good grapes there!") so I will not destroy all Israel, for I have true servants there. [9]I will preserve a remnant of my people to possess the land of Israel; those I select will inherit it and serve me there. [10]As for my people who have sought me, the plains of Sharon shall again be filled with flocks, and the valley of Achor shall be a place to pasture herds.

[11]But because the rest of you have forsaken the Lord and his Temple and worship gods of "Fate" and "Destiny," [12]therefore I will "destine" you to the sword, and your "fate" shall be a dark one; for when I called, you didn't answer; when I spoke, you wouldn't listen.

64:5 Isaiah admitted that he and his people were all sinners, and he asked how they could be saved. The answer includes the first two steps of recovery: admitting they were powerless and that life was unmanageable, and that God could restore them. Of course we must go further than this if we are to recover; we need to give our life to God and let him work in us. If we do this, we can be delivered from our dependencies.

65:3-5 Not all religious behavior is good. The Israelites had turned from the true God by trying to mix idol worship and occult practices with their worship of God. In our desperation for help, we may feel tempted to turn to Ouija boards, New Age spirituality, or other occult practices. Such practices promise help, but they really only turn us away from God. To draw closer to God, we should get involved with a Bible study, attend a community of Bible-believing people, pray, and receive encouragement from godly friends. Following any teachings or practices contrary to what we learn from these sources is a modern form of idol worship.

65:8-10 In the midst of national judgment, God will deal righteously with each individual, preserving the remnant who seek him. We need not fear that God will deal with us abusively and unfairly, basing his judgment on our family or friends. God deals with us as individuals, examining our relationship with him. This gives us hope, especially if we come from or are presently in a dysfunctional environment.

You deliberately sinned before my very eyes, choosing to do what you know I despise.

[13]Therefore, the Lord God says, You shall starve, but my servants shall eat; you shall be thirsty while they drink; you shall be sad and ashamed, but they shall rejoice. [14]You shall cry in sorrow and vexation and despair, while they sing for joy. [15]Your name shall be a curse word among my people, for the Lord God will slay you and call his true servants by another name.

[16]And yet, the days will come when all who invoke a blessing or take an oath shall swear by the God of Truth; for I will put aside my anger and forget the evil that you did. [17]For see, I am creating new heavens and a new earth—so wonderful that no one will even think about the old ones anymore. [18]Be glad; rejoice forever in my creation. Look! I will recreate Jerusalem as a place of happiness, and her people shall be a joy! [19]And I will rejoice in Jerusalem and in my people; and the voice of weeping and crying shall not be heard there any more.

[20]No longer will babies die when only a few days old; no longer will men be considered old at 100! Only sinners will die that young! [21,22]In those days, when a man builds a house, he will keep on living in it—it will not be destroyed by invading armies as in the past. My people will plant vineyards and eat the fruit themselves—their enemies will not confiscate it. For my people will live as long as trees and will long enjoy their hard-won gains. [23]Their harvests will not be eaten by their enemies; their children will not be born to be cannon fodder. For they are the children of those the Lord has blessed; and their children, too, shall be blessed. [24]I will answer them before they even call to me. While they are still talking to me about their needs, I will go ahead and answer their prayers! [25]The wolf and lamb shall feed together, the lion shall eat straw as the ox does, and poisonous snakes shall strike no more! In those days nothing and no one shall be hurt or destroyed in all my Holy Mountain, says the Lord.

CHAPTER 66

A Vision of God's Goodness

Heaven is my throne and the earth is my footstool: What Temple can you build for me as good as that? [2]My hand has made both earth and skies, and they are mine. Yet I will look with pity on the man who has a humble and a contrite heart, who trembles at my word.

[3]But those who choose their own ways, delighting in their sins, are cursed. God will not accept their offerings. When such men sacrifice an ox on the altar of God, it is no more acceptable to him than human sacrifice. If they sacrifice a lamb or bring an offering of grain, it is as loathsome to God as putting a dog or the blood of a swine on his altar! When they burn incense to him, he counts it the same as though they blessed an idol. [4]I will send great troubles upon them—all the things they feared, for when I called them, they refused to answer, and when I spoke to them, they would not hear. Instead, they did wrong before my eyes and chose what they knew I despised.

[5]Hear the words of God, all you who fear him, and tremble at his words: Your brethren hate you and cast you out for being loyal to my name. "Glory to God," they scoff. "Be happy in the Lord!" But they shall be put to shame.

[6]What is all the commotion in the city? What is that terrible noise from the Temple? It is the voice of the Lord taking vengeance upon his enemies.

[7,8]Who has heard or seen anything as strange as this? For in one day, suddenly, a nation, Israel, shall be born, even before the

---

65:16-25 The new heaven and new earth will be wonderful; there will be no pain, suffering, sorrow, or want. God will answer our prayers while we are still speaking them. There will be peace everywhere, even among the animals. While this level of blessing will not be achieved in this earthly lifetime, we can look forward to this in the next life if we are children of God. Our recovery will take away many of our pains; the coming in glory of God's Kingdom will take away the rest.

66:2 God will respond to us when we follow these key recovery principles: the humility to acknowledge our faults, the willingness to turn from and deal with our wrongs (contrite heart), and a desire to do what is right, no matter how difficult (tremble at God's Word). There is a double blessing when we follow these principles: we are able to overcome our addictions, and we are able to share in God's Kingdom.

66:3-4 God is not fooled by our religious games. If we "play church" and have no desire to follow God, we will be judged. God's deliverance comes from seeking his will and honoring and trusting him. The process of recovery will succeed when we learn to really depend on God, not just go through the motions of following him.

birth pains come. In a moment, just as Israel's
anguish starts, the baby is born; the nation
begins. 9Shall I bring to the point of birth and
then not deliver? asks the Lord your God. No!
Never!
10Rejoice with Jerusalem; be glad with her,
all you who love her, you who mourned for
her. 11Delight in Jerusalem; drink deep of her
glory even as an infant at a mother's generous
breasts. 12Prosperity shall overflow Jerusalem
like a river, says the Lord, for I will send it; the
riches of the Gentiles will flow to her. Her
children shall be nursed at her breasts, carried
on her hips and dandled on her knees. 13I will
comfort you there as a little one is comforted
by its mother.
14When you see Jerusalem, your heart will
rejoice; vigorous health will be yours. All the
world will see the good hand of God upon his
people and his wrath upon his enemies. 15For
see, the Lord will come with fire and with
swift chariots of doom to pour out the fury of
his anger and his hot rebuke with flames of
fire. 16For the Lord will punish the world by
fire and by his sword, and the slain of the Lord
shall be many!
17Those who worship idols that are hidden
behind a tree in the garden, feasting there on
pork and mouse and all forbidden meat—
they will come to an evil end, says Jehovah.
18I see full well what they are doing; I know
what they are thinking, so I will gather together all nations and people against Jerusalem, where they shall see my glory. 19I will
perform a mighty miracle against them, and
I will send those who escape, as missionaries
to the nations—to Tarshish, Put, Lud, Meshech, Rosh, Tubal, Javan, and to the lands
beyond the sea that have not heard my fame
nor seen my glory. There they shall declare
my glory to the Gentiles. 20And they shall
bring back all your brethren from every nation as a gift to the Lord, transporting them
gently on horses and in chariots, and in lit-
ters, and on mules and camels, to my holy
mountain, to Jerusalem, says the Lord. It will
be like offerings flowing into the Temple of
the Lord at harvesttime, carried in vessels
consecrated to the Lord. 21And I will appoint
some of those returning to be my priests and
Levites, says the Lord.
22As surely as my new heavens and earth
shall remain, so surely shall you always be my
people, with a name that shall never disappear. 23All mankind shall come to worship me
from week to week and month to month.
24And they shall go out and look at the dead
bodies of those who have rebelled against me,
for their worm shall never die; their fire shall
not be quenched; and they shall be a disgusting sight to all mankind.

66:22-24 Isaiah ends his book with a twofold promise. First, those who follow God will live with God forever; their names "shall never disappear." Second, those who oppose God (and his people) will suffer eternal punishment; "they shall be a disgusting sight to all mankind." The choice is clear: we either follow God and experience healing and blessing in this life and the next, or we rebel against God and experience turmoil and pain in this life and the next.

REFLECTIONS ON

insights ABOUT OUR RESPONSIBILITY

We find in **Isaiah 1:2-4** that even though the people of Judah had God—the perfect parent—to lead them, they still went wrong. They were responsible for their sins and the consequences that would surely follow. This should remind us that we are often the originating cause of our hang-ups and dependencies. And even though some of our problems are inherited from our parents, we are ultimately held accountable for our actions. Taking responsibility for our problems is an essential part of the recovery process.

The key to renewal and recovery is summed up in **Isaiah 30:12-17.** We can be like Judah, frantically turning to every source of help besides God to find instant relief from our problems. Or we can admit our need for God and return to him, trusting him for deliverance. Scripture makes clear which choice will lead to recovery and which will lead to ruin. Which will we choose?

When troubles fill our life, we may be tempted to think that God has turned on us or is powerless to help. But Isaiah made it clear in **Isaiah 50:1-2** that Judah's problems had been brought on by her own sins, not God's injustice. Most of our problems, too, are brought on by our own sins, and those that aren't are not sent by God to abuse us. We suffer at times because we live in a world corrupted by sin. But we are reminded that the God who controls all nature can certainly care for us if we turn to him.

In **Isaiah 54:1-8** we are told that Israel strayed from God, and that God punished them so they would see the error of their ways and return to him. But after a period of punishment, God promised to restore them to himself and bless them. Today we may suffer pains from our addictions—pains which serve to warn us of the dangers we are courting and serve to get us back on God's program for life. When we make a decision to seek recovery, we are also making a decision to follow God and turn from our old life-style. By doing so, we are allowing God to work in us and give us his blessings.

In **Isaiah 59:1-14** we find that the people of Israel blamed God for failing to deliver them from their troubles. Sometimes we do the same thing. We get mad at God because he seems too weak to follow through with his promises to us. God isn't too weak, and it isn't that he can't hear us; our sin cuts us off from God. If it seems that God isn't with us anymore, we should take a moral inventory to see where our problem is. Once we isolate the area where we are out of God's will, we can repent and work to correct it. Until we admit those sins, we will remain cut off from God.

God doesn't tolerate inaction—not helping those who are suffering is as bad as adding to their misery. In **Isaiah 59:16** God made it clear that his plan for us includes our helping one another. We need to pray for others when they are in trouble. We need to hold others accountable for their actions. We may also need to humbly intervene to help others deal with the problems they refuse to face.

insights ABOUT THE PERSON OF GOD

In **Isaiah 4:5-6** the prophet used the imagery of the cloud of smoke and fire to remind the people of Judah of God's protection in the desert wanderings (see Exodus 13:21–14:31). God is still there to protect us and rescue us, even though we can't see the pillar of smoke and fire. The Holy Spirit will care for us and guide us through our recovery if we let him.

God will bless us, but God's ways take time. An essential factor in the recovery process is highlighted in **Isaiah 30:18:** we may need to wait! Trying to hurry the process only leads to disaster. "Blessed are all those who wait for [God] to help them."

In **Isaiah 40:27-31** we find that God knows everything and understands all our pain. There is nothing he doesn't know. But evil things still happen in the world, and our recovery process will take time and suffer some setbacks. We may get tired of trying to do right and want to give up and go back to old habits. If we endure and keep faith in God, he will renew our strength so we can continue with our recovery.

We may be afraid to come to God because we think he will hold our sins against us. But God promises in **Isaiah 43:25-28** to blot out our sins when we come to him, forgetting them and cleansing us. Approaching God in humility is the only way to have the shame of our sin removed.

As we are on the path to recovery, it is comforting to know that God is with us, bringing us out of our slavery. In **Isaiah 52:12** we are told that he goes ahead of us, showing us the way to a productive, normal life. And he protects us from behind, guarding us from being attacked by our dependencies.

In **Isaiah 59:20-21** the prophet makes it clear that God desires our recovery. He provides us with his Holy Spirit to empower us and the Bible, his written Word, to guide us. His desire is to change us and to begin a pattern of health that will be passed on to our children and grandchildren. If we want to know how to "want the good and hate the wrong," we need to ask God to show us, and he will!

In **Isaiah 61:8-9** God shows us that he hates injustice, so he himself is not going to treat us unjustly. When we have been abused and mistreated by others, we become afraid that everyone, even

God, will treat us in the same manner. But we are assured that God will treat his people justly and reward them for their undue suffering.

When we find that we have fallen away from God, we can be encouraged to seek him again, just as Isaiah was doing on behalf of his people in **Isaiah 63:15-16.** Even if our own parents should disown us because of how far we have fallen, God will never disown us. He will welcome us back to himself and love us (see Luke 15:11-32).

In **Isaiah 63:1-6** God is pictured as a warrior returning victoriously from a battle he has had to fight alone against the enemies of his people. Because of the troubles we encounter and the pain we bear, we sometimes wonder if God is for us or against us. As we see in these verses, God is definitely for us. He is seen dripping with the blood of our, and his, enemies. He loves us so much that he is willing to fight single-handedly to deliver us.

When we consider our sins and failures, we often think that God must be disgusted with us and want nothing to do with us. We see in **Isaiah 65:1-2,** however, that God stands with open arms, ready to receive us in spite of our moral blemishes. He welcomes those who have never sought him before, and he longs for those who have rebelled to come back to him.

Isaiah 66:7-9 shows us that God will fulfill his promises, just as a baby will be born and cannot be stopped. When we started recovery, we asked God to remove our character defects and lead us to a normal life. But the initial zeal soon wore off, and we struggled and were tempted to give up. Knowing that God will carry through his promise for our recovery can give us the courage to continue with the process.

insights ABOUT THE DANGERS OF IDOLATRY

Isaiah 44:9-20 shows us the utter folly of idolatry. All man-made gods will fail us, whether they are alcohol, drugs, greed, career success (workaholism), perfectionism, or false religions with their trinkets, such as crystals and charms. Belief that such things will deliver us is a clue that we are denying reality. We need to take a moral inventory to truly see where our trust lies. If it is in anything other than God, we should reevaluate our beliefs and seek God.

Isaiah 55:1-5 reminds us that God alone can satisfy our soul's hunger and thirst. He calls us to stop seeking our ultimate fulfillment in things that cannot satisfy—work, sex, or various other obsessions. These things are like junk food; they satisfy cravings but have no nutritional value. We spend our time chasing after these "groceries that do [us] no good" while we should be seeking God and his will, the only real nourishment for us.

In **Isaiah 65:11-15** we are told that the people of Israel abandoned the true God by dabbling in occult practices. They worshiped pagan gods called "Fate" and "Destiny," hoping to influence their own future. It is ironic that what they were trying to avoid (suffering and judgment) came down upon them because they sought help from these gods. God is our only reliable source of help in recovery. Any source or program that is contrary to God will leave us in worse shape than before—we will still have our dependencies, and we will be further from God than we ever were.

insights ABOUT GOD'S GRACE

What encouragement we find in **Isaiah 48:1-11!** Once we have committed our life to God, we belong to him. He is then committed to bringing spiritual blessings to us. Even our stubborn rebelliousness and spiritual incompetence do not keep God's grace away from us. Even when we mess things up completely and deserve nothing, he will still act on behalf of his own name.

In **Isaiah 51:1-6** the prophet reminds us that when Judah looked to herself, there was no hope for deliverance from her troubles. But when she looked to God, she could see that he was able to bring a whole nation out of one man, Abraham. He could certainly bring joy, comfort, and deliverance to her. When we look to our own abilities, our hope for recovery from the complex and confusing issues that entangle us vanishes. When we look to God, that hope can return. To trust in anything other than God for our recovery is to plan on failure. Success will come from relying on God alone.

As long as we can hear the call of God to us, it is not too late to follow him. In **Isaiah 55:7-9** we are told that no matter how great our sins, no matter how unlikely it seems that God could forgive us, God offers forgiveness. While people may have given up on us, God hasn't, because God's ways are not our ways. Asking God for forgiveness and guidance is the only requirement for receiving his help. (For examples of "hopeless sinners" who received God's salvation, see Luke 19:1-10; 23:32-43; Acts 9:1-19.)

Both Gentiles and eunuchs were excluded from full participation in the worship ceremonies in Israel, and the Jews generally despised them. But in **Isaiah 56:3-8** we are all welcomed into God's family: men, women, victims of abuse, people with AIDS, alcoholics, drug abusers, murderers, etc. God loves everyone and wants the whole world to believe in him (see 1 Timothy 2:4). All who believe are welcome in his love.

Isaiah 57:15 tells us that God does not promise blessings only to those who can clean up their life and be perfect. His blessings are given to all who are humble enough to admit their sins and weaknesses and who repent of their wrongs. If there is a willingness on our part, we will find that God's arms are open wide to accept us.

The prophet reminds us in **Isaiah 57:17-21** that God is gracious and blesses us beyond what we deserve. Even though we may have led a dysfunctional life-style for years, God's healing is still available. He still promises to help us in the recovery process "to mourn and confess sins." Those who persist in their sins and dysfunctions, however, will eventually lose their opportunity for peace, in this life and the next.

Isaiah 60:17 is a wonderful verse for a recovery meditation. God's desire is to exchange all that is worthless in our life with things of value and to exchange our abusive taskmasters with a situation dominated by peace and righteousness. In order to exchange our worthless addictions for peace and righteousness, we need to turn the management of our life over to God.

In **Isaiah 64:8-12** the Israelites were asking God to act graciously toward them. They had admitted that they sinned and that their punishment was deserved. Now they asked God to turn away his wrath and forget their sins. In Isaiah's day there was no final provision for their request; today there is. If we put our trust in Jesus the Messiah, his blood will cleanse us from all the sin in our life, so we can spend eternity in God's presence.

⁂*insights* ABOUT THE MESSIAH AND HIS KINGDOM

In **Isaiah 53:4-6** the prophet described the Messiah who would come and suffer on our behalf. Jesus Christ fulfilled Isaiah's prophecy. He came not because *some* of us needed to be saved from sin, but because *all* of us have strayed from God's path and need salvation. Jesus suffered the punishment for the sins we committed, and he can completely understand what it feels like to suffer the pain of abuse. We can confess our anguish and feelings of hatred, shame, and sorrow to Jesus, and he will sympathize with us and send us comfort.

In **Isaiah 54:11-17** we are given a vision of what lies ahead for those who look to God for forgiveness and deliverance. There will be blessings, fairness, and justice in God's messianic kingdom. This should encourage us as we struggle with our dependencies, the oppression of cruel people, and the injustice that pervades our society. No matter how rough life gets, we have the hope of eternal security and peace with God.

The prophecy in **Isaiah 61:1-3** of the Messiah's healing ministry was quoted by Jesus as a description of himself (Luke 4:18-19). He is the Anointed One (the Christ), who calls all who are suffering and afflicted to come to him and find comfort, healing, joy, and beauty. There is nothing we can do to earn these gifts from Christ; they are free to all who ask.

How much does God want to help us? The Messiah speaks in **Isaiah 61:10** and is overwhelmed with joy at the fact that God has promised future blessings for his people. God does not give to us begrudgingly, as some people we know may do. He wants to bless us! He is happy when people find salvation in him. He wants everyone to trust him and none to suffer eternal judgment (see 1 Timothy 2:4).

JEREMIAH

THE BIG PICTURE

A. JEREMIAH'S SPECIAL APPOINTMENT (1:1-19)

B. THE PROPHET DELIVERS GOD'S MESSAGES (2:1–45:5)

1. God's Warnings to Judah (2:1–29:32)
2. The Coming Exile and Restoration (30:1–33:26)
3. The Fall of Jerusalem (34:1–45:5)

C. GOD'S JUDGMENT ON THE NATIONS (46:1–51:64)

D. A PAINFUL REMINDER OF PAINFUL DAYS (52:1-34)

Most of us, when thinking of the future, create dreams in which we are needed, loved, successful, and sought after. Rarely do we hope for deep sorrow, thankless service, and unwarranted persecution, particularly at the hands of the people we care about. When God called him, Jeremiah probably had visions of people listening and responding to his words. He probably hoped that his ministry would inspire the recovery of the people of Judah. Jeremiah's hopes for success never came to be.

Jeremiah faithfully warned the Israelites of the sure punishment that would come because of their sin, but the people ignored his passionate pleas. Instead of admitting their sins and failures, they rejected, imprisoned, and abused God's prophet. No one wanted to hear what Jeremiah had to say. King Zedekiah put him into an empty cistern where the prophet sank not only into the mud, but also into a mire of disdain. Virtually no one respected him or the messages he spoke. The consequences of rejecting Jeremiah and his message were great; Judah fell deeper into sin and eventually suffered almost complete destruction.

Like Jeremiah, we end up in circumstances that are far from ideal. Many of us are suffering for our own mistakes. Jeremiah suffered innocently at the hands of selfish people. We may know how that feels, too. From a human standpoint, Jeremiah was not very successful. But in the eyes of God, he was one of the most successful people in all history. He remained faithful despite the opposition he faced. We may also experience opposition and suffering. Much of it may even be self-inflicted. Even so, just as he did for Jeremiah, God will fulfill his purposes for us if we are faithful to him and his program.

THE BOTTOM LINE

PURPOSE: To warn the people of Judah to turn from their sin and denial, and to obey God's good plan for them. AUTHOR: The prophet Jeremiah. AUDIENCE: The people of Judah, before and during the Babylonian exile. DATE WRITTEN: The book includes oracles given throughout Jeremiah's ministry (627–586 B.C.). SETTING: The land of Judah, from the initial threats by Assyria and Egypt (627 B.C.) until after her eventual destruction by Babylon (586 B.C.). KEY VERSE: "Your words are what sustain me; they are food to my hungry soul. They bring joy to my sorrowing heart and delight me. How proud I am to bear your name, O Lord" (15:16). KEY PEOPLE AND RELATIONSHIPS: Jeremiah with God and with the people of Judah.

RECOVERY THEMES

Faithfulness Overcomes Failure: From our human perspective, Jeremiah was a failure. But from God's point of view, Jeremiah was one of the great success stories in the Bible. He remained faithful to God and his commands despite the powerful opposition he faced. In our recovery, we may begin to feel that our suffering has no purpose whatsoever. The obstacles may seem too big to overcome; our weaknesses, too much of a liability. When we feel discouraged, we need to remember that God simply calls us to be faithful—to keep on going. We don't have to be a raving success. We just need to be faithful in the long haul. God will honor our faithfulness by providing us with the strength we need for the next step.

God's Way May Be Painful: In order to avoid pain, the people of Judah refused to listen to Jeremiah's call for repentance and change in their lives. At times we may be tempted to avoid painful memories or necessary changes, but such avoidance and denial will only retard our recovery. If we refuse to hear God's message of truth, we will create suffering even deeper than the pain we are trying to avoid. We would be wise to face the pain now and allow it to lead us to inner healing and righteous living.

God Understands Our Emotions: Jeremiah has often been called the weeping prophet. But he did more than weep—he was bitter, angry, discouraged, depressed, and lonely. We have all experienced those ugly feelings. Jeremiah even complained to God, "You have failed me in my time of need! . . . Your help is as uncertain as a seasonal mountain brook—sometimes a flood, sometimes as dry as a bone" (15:17-18). God's acceptance of Jeremiah's emotions frees us to bring all of our failures and strong feelings straight to God. He accepts and understands us just as we are, and he is ready to heal our broken and hurting parts. All we need to do is be honest with him.

Hope despite Disaster: Jeremiah's warnings of approaching judgment are punctuated by promises of ultimate deliverance. Jeremiah told the people about the "new contract" that God had for them (see 31:1-40). Despite their impending doom, he told them that God loved them and had a wonderful future planned for them: "For I know the plans I have for you, says the Lord. They are plans for good and not for evil, to give you a future and a hope" (29:11). When God confronts us with the truth about our sin, he always concludes with a message of hope. He is the God of hope and recovery.

CHAPTER 1

God Calls Jeremiah

These are God's messages to Jeremiah the
priest (the son of Hilkiah) who lived in the
town of Anathoth in the land of Benjamin.
The first of these messages came to him in the
thirteenth year of the reign of Amon's son
Josiah, king of Judah. 3Others came during
the reign of Josiah's son Jehoiakim, king of
Judah, and at various other times until July of
the eleventh year of the reign of Josiah's son
Zedekiah, king of Judah, when Jerusalem was
captured and the people were taken away as
slaves.
4The Lord said to me, 5"I knew you before
you were formed within your mother's womb;
before you were born I sanctified you and appointed you as my spokesman to the world."
6"O Lord God," I said, "I can't do that! I'm
far too young! I'm only a youth!"
7"Don't say that," he replied, "for you will
go wherever I send you and speak whatever I
tell you to. 8And don't be afraid of the people,
for I, the Lord, will be with you and see you
through."
9Then he touched my mouth and said,
"See, I have put my words in your mouth!
10Today your work begins, to warn the nations

1:1-3 Some of Jeremiah's messages were given to warn the Jews of the impending Babylonian captivity; others were given after Judah had already fallen to Babylon. God often tries to warn us of the consequences of our present actions; we would be wise to listen when he does. But we should be grateful that God still reaches out to help us, even after we have failed.

1:4-5 God probably doesn't want us to be a prophet like Jeremiah, but he does have a plan for us. It is our responsibility to cooperate with God now so that we can return to the path he intended for us before we failed. Recovery of our life also means the recovery of God's plan for us. We need to seek out God's will and then follow it. God will help and encourage us as we do.

1:11-16 God used signs to show Jeremiah that Judah would be judged for her continued idolatry. We also worship idols. Power, wealth, comfort, prestige, possessions, and position are only a few of the idols we tend to build and protect. When our idols cease to satisfy, God is showing us that something is wrong with the gods we worship. Those who worship the true God will find complete satisfaction. No false god can promise that.

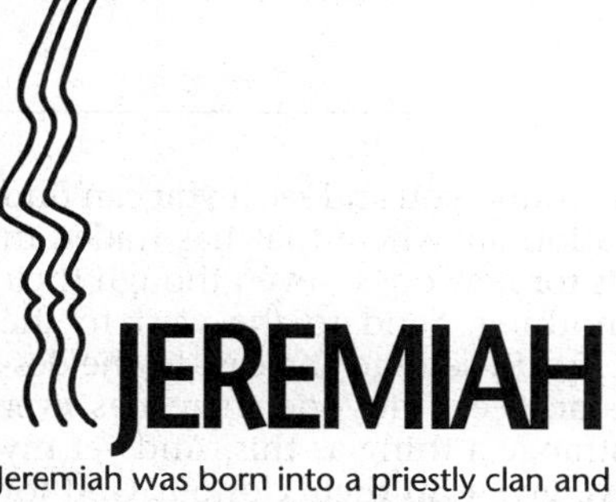

JEREMIAH

Jeremiah was born into a priestly clan and was called to the prophetic ministry when he was just a youth. Even though he was young, Jeremiah was humble and eager to serve God. Jeremiah's ministry stretched from the thirteenth year of Josiah's reign (626 B.C.) until after the destruction of Jerusalem (586 B.C.).

Josiah's reign was the last high point in Judah's spiritual history, and Jeremiah was an ally in the king's reforms. After Josiah's death, Judah quickly declined spiritually, which caused great sorrow to Jeremiah. During those years, Jeremiah preached against the hypocrisy and corruption of prophets, priests, and government officials alike. He also prophesied that the nation faced sure destruction as a consequence of her sins—a message that few believed. The people preferred to believe the false prophets, who predicted a rosy future for Judah.

During his years of ministry, Jeremiah suffered intense persecution. He was thrown into a dungeon, beaten, put in stocks, threatened, and almost killed. Extrabiblical tradition says that he was stoned to death. Jeremiah was a man of prayer and deep spirituality, and he faced his trials with courage. Despite the opposition he faced, he remained true to the messages God gave him. He confronted the Jews with their denial and called them to admit their failures and ask God for forgiveness. As God directed him, he also spoke words of comfort to a people facing disaster.

Jeremiah was always honest about how he felt. He is known as the weeping prophet. He never wept for his own suffering, but he shed many tears for the sin of his people and the destructive consequences he knew they would face. After Jerusalem was destroyed and the people exiled, Jeremiah wept for the pain and loss of his people. There were times when Jeremiah openly and honestly complained to God about the work God had given him to do. Yet even in the midst of his "down times," Jeremiah never lost faith in God's power to judge righteously, to reward liberally, and to restore his broken and sinful people.

STRENGTHS AND ACCOMPLISHMENTS:
- Jeremiah was faithful to God's call despite the persecution he suffered.
- He showed great compassion for his people, even though they mistreated him.
- He did not hesitate to tell God exactly what he was feeling.
- He fearlessly confronted the Jews with their sins.

LESSONS FROM HIS LIFE:
- Sin is always accompanied by painful consequences.
- No matter how great our sin, God still loves us and desires our recovery.
- God is not shocked when we openly share of our feelings with him.
- True success is defined by our faithfulness to God's will for our life.

KEY VERSES:
"'For see, today I have made you impervious to their attacks. They cannot harm you. . . . They will try, but they will fail. For I am with you,' says the Lord. 'I will deliver you'" (Jeremiah 1:18-19).

Jeremiah's story is told primarily in the book of Jeremiah. He is also mentioned in 2 Chronicles 35–36; Ezra 1; Daniel 9; and Matthew 2; 16; 27.

---

and the kingdoms of the world. In accord with my words spoken through your mouth I will tear down some and destroy them, and plant others, nurture them, and make them strong and great."

11Then the Lord said to me, "Look, Jeremiah! What do you see?"

And I replied, "I see a whip made from the branch of an almond tree."

12And the Lord replied, "That's right, and it means that I will surely carry out my threats of punishment."

13Then the Lord asked me, "What do you see now?"

And I replied, "I see a pot of boiling water, tipping southward, spilling over Judah."

14"Yes," he said, "for terror from the north
will boil out upon all the people of this land.
15I am calling the armies of the kingdoms of
the north to come to Jerusalem and set their
thrones at the gates of the city and all along
its walls, and in all the other cities of Judah.
16This is the way I will punish my people for
deserting me and for worshiping other gods—

yes, idols they themselves have made! 17Get up and dress and go out and tell them whatever I tell you to say. Don't be afraid of them, or else I will make a fool of you in front of them. 18For see, today I have made you impervious to their attacks. They cannot harm you. You are strong like a fortified city that cannot be captured, like an iron pillar and heavy gates of brass. All the kings of Judah, its officers, priests, and people will not be able to prevail against you. 19They will try, but they will fail. For I am with you," says the Lord. "I will deliver you."

CHAPTER 2

Israel Turns from God

Again the Lord spoke to me and said:

2Go and shout this in Jerusalem's streets: The Lord says, I remember how eager you were to please me as a young bride long ago, how you loved me and followed me even through the barren deserts. 3In those days Israel was a holy people, the first of my children. All who harmed them were counted deeply guilty, and great evil fell on anyone who touched them.

4,5O Israel, says the Lord, why did your fathers desert me? What sin did they find in me that turned them away and changed them into fools who worship idols? 6They ignore the fact that it was I, the Lord, who brought them safely out of Egypt and led them through the barren wilderness, a land of deserts and rocks, of drought and death, where no one lives or even travels. 7And I brought them into a fruitful land, to eat of its bounty and goodness, but they made it into a land of sin and corruption and turned my inheritance into an evil thing. 8Even their priests cared nothing for the Lord, and their judges ignored me; their rulers turned against me, and their prophets worshiped Baal and wasted their time on nonsense.

9But I will not give you up—I will plead for you to return to me and will keep on pleading; yes, even with your children's children in the years to come!

10,11Look around you and see if you can find another nation anywhere that has traded in its old gods for new ones—even though their gods are nothing. Send to the west to the island of Cyprus; send to the east to the deserts of Kedar. See if anyone there has ever heard so strange a thing as this. And yet my people have given up their glorious God for silly idols! 12The heavens are shocked at such a thing and shrink back in horror and dismay. 13For my people have done two evil things: They have forsaken me, the Fountain of Life-giving Water; and they have built for themselves broken cisterns that can't hold water!

14Why has Israel become a nation of slaves? Why is she captured and led far away?

15I see great armies marching on Jerusalem with mighty shouts to destroy her and leave her cities in ruins, burned and desolate. 16I see the armies of Egypt rising against her, marching from their cities of Memphis and Tahpanhes to utterly destroy Israel's glory and power. 17And you have brought this on yourselves by rebelling against the Lord your God when he wanted to lead you and show you the way!

18What have you gained by your alliances with Egypt and with Assyria? 19Your own wickedness will punish you. You will see what an evil, bitter thing it is to rebel against the Lord your God, fearlessly forsaking him, says the Lord Almighty. 20Long ago you shook off my yoke and broke away from my ties. Defiant, you would not obey me. On every hill and under every tree you've bowed low before idols.

21How could this happen? How could this be? For when I planted you, I chose my seed so carefully—the very best. Why have you become this degenerate race of evil men? 22No amount of soap or lye can make you clean. You are stained with guilt that cannot ever be washed away. I see it always before me, the Lord God says. 23You say it isn't so, that you haven't worshiped idols? How can you say a thing like that? Go and look in any valley in the land! Face the awful sins that you have done, O restless female camel, seeking for a

2:9 God was persistent in his efforts to deliver Israel from the bondage of Egypt and of sin. He never gives up on those he loves; neither will he give up on us. He will continue to seek us out. As we wander from him and try to take back control of our life, he lovingly pleads for us to return to him. We would be wise to listen to him and respond with loving obedience.

2:26-27 So often we feel guilty only if we get caught. That is why hitting bottom can be so instructive, since failure helps us understand and admit our true condition. Feeling the shame, seeing our life being wasted—these show us our need for God. What can follow, if we turn to him, is the wonderful joy of knowing there is still hope for us. We can begin this process by admitting our failures to God and looking to him for the help we need.

male! 24You are a wild donkey, sniffing the wind at mating time. (Who can restrain your lust?) Any jack wanting you need not search, for you come running to him! 25Why don't you turn from all this weary running after other gods? But you say, "Don't waste your breath. I've fallen in love with these strangers and I can't stop loving them now!"

26,27Like a thief, the only shame that Israel knows is getting caught. Kings, princes, priests, and prophets—all are alike in this. They call a carved-up wooden post their father, and for their mother they have an idol chiseled out from stone. Yet in time of trouble they cry to me to save them! 28Why don't you call on these gods you have made? When danger comes, let *them* go out and save you if they can! For you have as many gods as there are cities in Judah. 29Don't come to me—you are all rebels, says the Lord. 30I have punished your children, but it did them no good; they still will not obey. And you yourselves have killed my prophets as a lion kills its prey.

31O my people, listen to the words of God: Have I been unjust to Israel? Have I been to them a land of darkness and of evil? Why then do my people say, "At last we are free from God; we won't have anything to do with him again!" 32How can you disown your God like that? Can a girl forget her jewels? What bride will seek to hide her wedding dress? Yet for years on end my people have forgotten me—the most precious of their treasures.

33How you plot and scheme to win your lovers. The most experienced harlot could learn a lot from you! 34Your clothing is stained with the blood of the innocent and the poor. Brazenly you murder without a cause. 35And yet you say, "I haven't done a thing to anger God. I'm sure he isn't angry!" I will punish you severely because you say, "I haven't sinned!"

36First here, then there, you flit about, going from one ally to another for their help; but it's all no good—your new friends in Egypt will forsake you as Assyria did before. 37You will be left in despair and cover your face with your hands, for the Lord has rejected the ones that you trust. You will not succeed despite their aid.

CHAPTER 3

There is a law that if a man divorces a woman who then remarries, he is not to take her back again, for she has become corrupted. But though you have left me and married many lovers, yet I have invited you to come to me again, the Lord says. 2Is there a single spot in all the land where you haven't been defiled by your adulteries—your worshiping these other gods? You sit like a prostitute beside the road waiting for a client! You sit alone like a Bedouin in the desert. You have polluted the land with your vile prostitution. 3That is why even the springtime rains have failed. For you are a prostitute and completely unashamed. 4,5And yet you say to me, "O Father, you have always been my Friend; surely you won't be angry about such a little thing! Surely you will just forget it?" So you talk and keep right on doing all the evil that you can.

God's People Worship Idols

6This message from the Lord came to me during the reign of King Josiah:

Have you seen what Israel does? Like a wanton wife who gives herself to other men at every chance, so Israel has worshiped other gods on every hill, beneath every shady tree. 7I thought that someday she would return to me and once again be mine; but she didn't come back. And her faithless sister Judah saw the continued rebellion of Israel. 8Yet she paid no attention, even though she saw that I divorced faithless Israel. But now Judah too has left me and given herself to prostitution, for she has gone to other gods to worship them. 9She treated it all so lightly—to her it was nothing at all that she should worship idols made of wood and stone. And so the land was greatly polluted and defiled. 10Then, afterwards, this faithless one "returned" to me, but her "sorrow" was only faked, the Lord

2:34-35 The worst result of our loss of control is the hurt we bring to the innocent. Recovery means we can be free of the shame we feel over the pain we have caused people who deserve better from us. Saying no to sin is difficult but liberating. We must accept God's forgiveness and make restitution for our mistakes. In the Kingdom of God, no one is expected to wallow in remorse over sins that have already been forgiven. God forgives us as soon as we repent. We can expect God's judgment, however, if we continue living in denial.

3:8 God likens our worship of other gods to prostitution. When we worship our dependencies, money, success, power, or prestige, we are acting like a well-loved wife who runs elsewhere for others to satisfy her desire for pleasure instead of remaining faithful to her loving husband. We all know that these false gods can never really satisfy. We would be wise to turn our life over to the only true God. He will care for us and love us as a faithful and loving husband.

God says. [11]In fact, faithless Israel is less guilty than treacherous Judah!

[12]Therefore, go and say to Israel, O Israel, my sinful people, come home to me again, for I am merciful; I will not be forever angry with you. [13]Only acknowledge your guilt; admit that you rebelled against the Lord your God and committed adultery against him by worshiping idols under every tree; confess that you refused to follow me. [14]O sinful children, come home, for I am your Master, and I will bring you again to the land of Israel—one from here and two from there, wherever you are scattered. [15]And I will give you leaders after my own heart, who will guide you with wisdom and understanding.

[16]Then, when your land is once more filled with people, says the Lord, you will no longer wish for "the good old days of long ago" when you possessed the Ark of God's covenant. Those days will not be missed or even thought about, and the Ark will not be reconstructed, for the Lord himself will be among you. [17]The whole city of Jerusalem will be known as the throne of the Lord; all nations will come to him there and no longer stubbornly follow their evil desires. [18]At that time the people of Judah and of Israel will return together from their exile in the north, to the land I gave their fathers as an inheritance forever. [19]And I thought how wonderful it would be for you to be here among my children. I planned to give you part of this beautiful land, the finest in the world. I looked forward to your calling me "Father" and thought that you would never turn away from me again. [20]But you have betrayed me; you have gone off and given yourself to a host of foreign gods; you have been like a faithless wife who leaves her husband.

[21]I hear a voice high upon the windswept mountains, crying, crying. It is the sons of Israel who have turned their backs on God and wandered far away. [22]O my rebellious children, come back to me again and I will heal you from your sins.

And they reply, Yes, we will come, for you are the Lord our God. [23]We are weary of worshiping idols on the hills and of having orgies on the mountains. It is all a farce. Only in the Lord our God can Israel ever find her help and her salvation. [24]From our childhood we have seen everything our fathers had—flocks and herds and sons and daughters—squandered on priests and idols. [25]We lie in shame and in dishonor, for we and our fathers have sinned from childhood against the Lord our God; we have not obeyed him.

CHAPTER 4

The Land Is Destroyed

O Israel, if you will truly return to me and absolutely discard your idols, [2]and if you will swear by me alone, the living God, and begin to live good, honest, clean lives, then you will be a testimony to the nations of the world, and they will come to me and glorify my name.

[3]The Lord is saying to the men of Judah and Jerusalem, Plow up the hardness of your hearts; otherwise the good seed will be wasted among the thorns. [4]Cleanse your minds and hearts, not just your bodies, or else my anger will burn you to a crisp because of all your sins. And no one will be able to put the fire out.

[5]Shout to Jerusalem and to all Judea, telling them to sound the alarm throughout the land. "Run for your lives! Flee to the fortified cities!" [6]Send a signal from Jerusalem: "Flee

---

3:16-17 Sometimes we stubbornly refuse to change because we are afraid we will miss the good old days, old acquaintances, even old hangouts. But when we turn our life over to God, the experience of his love will so radically change our heart that we will not miss these things at all. We will be so fulfilled that the former days of superficial living will mean nothing to us. No one has ever been disappointed by a life turned totally over to God. We may lose some of the old things, but we will gain so much more than we lost!

3:21-22 We look for healing in many different places. Many people offer solutions to help us escape our guilt feelings, but many of these lead only to a deeper denial. The only sure way to remove the guilt feelings is to get rid of the guilt by asking God to forgive our sins. If we don't turn to God for help, we will be left to cry alone in the wilderness.

4:1-2 God had always planned that his people would be living proof of his power and goodness. He wanted others to believe in him because of the blessings that Israel received through a healthy relationship with God. God also wants to use us as a testimony to his loving power. When we turn our life over to God, our increasing goodness, purity, and honesty will stand out as a testimony of the kind of life that is possible through him. What an honor it is for us to be used by our Creator to touch the lives of others! Our success in recovery will bring hope and encouragement to others as they struggle with their dependencies.

now, don't delay!" For I the Lord am bringing vast destruction on you from the north. 7A lion—a destroyer of nations—stalks from his lair; and he is headed for your land. Your cities will lie in ruin without inhabitant. 8Put on clothes of mourning and weep with broken hearts, for the fierce anger of the Lord has not stopped yet. 9In that day, says the Lord, "the king and the princes will tremble in fear; and the priests and the prophets will be stricken with horror.

10(Then I said, "But Lord, the people have been deceived by what you said, for you promised great blessings on Jerusalem. Yet the sword is even now poised to strike them dead!")

11,12At that time he will send a burning wind from the desert upon them—not in little gusts but in a roaring blast—and he will pronounce their doom. 13The enemy shall roll down upon us like a storm wind; his chariots are like a whirlwind; his steeds are swifter than eagles. Woe, woe upon us, for we are doomed.

14O Jerusalem, cleanse your hearts while there is time. You can yet be saved by casting out your evil thoughts. 15From Dan and from Mount Ephraim your doom has been announced. 16Warn the other nations that the enemy is coming from a distant land, and they shout against Jerusalem and the cities of Judah. 17They surround Jerusalem like shepherds moving in on some wild animal! For my people have rebelled against me, says the Lord. 18Your ways have brought this down upon you; it is a bitter dose of your own medicine, striking deep within your hearts.

19My heart, my heart—I writhe in pain; my heart pounds within me. I cannot be still because I have heard, O my soul, the blast of the enemies' trumpets and the enemies' battle cries. 20Wave upon wave of destruction rolls over the land, until it lies in utter ruin; suddenly, in a moment, every house is crushed. 21How long must this go on? How long must I see war and death surrounding me?

22"Until my people leave their foolishness, for they refuse to listen to me; they are dull, retarded children who have no understanding. They are smart enough at doing wrong, but for doing right they have no talent, none at all."

23I looked down upon their land, and as far as I could see in all directions everything was ruins. And all the heavens were dark. 24I looked at the mountains and saw that they trembled and shook. 25I looked, and mankind was gone, and the birds of the heavens had fled.

26The fertile valleys were wilderness, and all the cities were broken down before the presence of the Lord, crushed by his fierce anger. 27The Lord's decree of desolation covers all the land.

"Yet," he says, "there will be a little remnant of my people left. 28The earth shall mourn, the heavens shall be draped with black, because of my decree against my people; I have made up my mind and will not change it."

29All the cities flee in terror at the noise of marching armies coming near. The people hide in the bushes and flee to the mountains. All the cities are abandoned—all have fled in terror. 30Why do you put on your most beautiful clothing and jewelry and brighten your eyes with mascara? It will do you no good! Your allies despise you and will kill you.

31I have heard great crying like that of a woman giving birth to her first child; it is the cry of my people gasping for breath, pleading for help, prostrate before their murderers.

CHAPTER 5
No Respect for God

Run up and down through every street in all Jerusalem; search high and low and see if you

4:14 It isn't easy to rid our mind of evil or destructive thoughts, especially if we have spent much of our life developing our mental habits. When we turn our life over to God, spend time with him, and ask him to lead us, he will reveal his will for us and begin to reshape our thought patterns. As we continue to meditate on God's Word, improving our conscious contact with our loving God, his thoughts will become our own. He will replace our evil thoughts with good and healthy ones. Developing healthy thought patterns is an essential part of our recovery.

4:30 As they faced imminent destruction, the people of Israel sought to make external changes that they hoped would bring deliverance. We sometimes do the same thing, making whatever changes we can on the outside to somehow survive the next onslaught from our dependencies. We try to look good to cover the terrible pain we feel. Covering up our failures and pain in this way only deepens our denial. Recovery begins when we display our broken heart to God and admit our failures. God will help us make changes on the inside. When we are concerned about what we look like to others, we can't deal with the real problems hidden beneath the surface.

can find even one person who is fair and
honest! Search every square, and if you find
just one, I'll not destroy the city! 2Even under
oath, they all lie.
3O Lord, you are looking for faithfulness.
You have tried to get them to be honest, for
you have punished them, but they won't
change! You have destroyed them, but they
refuse to turn from their sins. They are determined, with faces hard as rock, not to repent.
4Then I said, "But what can we expect from
the poor and ignorant? They don't know the
ways of God. How can they obey him?"
5I will go now to their leaders, the men of
importance, and speak to them, for they
know the ways of the Lord and the judgment
that follows sin. But they too had utterly
rejected their God.
6So I will send upon them the wild fury of
the "lion from the forest"; the "desert wolves"
shall pounce upon them, and a "leopard"
shall lurk around their cities so that all who
go out shall be torn apart. For their sins are
very many; their rebellion against me is great.
7How can I pardon you? For even your
children have turned away and worship gods
that are not gods at all. I fed my people until
they were fully satisfied, and their thanks was
to commit adultery wholesale and to gang up
at the city's brothels. 8They are well-fed, lusty
stallions, each neighing for his neighbor's
mate. 9Shall I not punish them for this? Shall
I not send my vengeance on such a nation as
this? 10Go down the rows of the vineyards and
destroy them! But leave a scattered few to live.
Strip the branches from each vine, for they are
not the Lord's.
11For the people of Israel and Judah are full
of treachery against me, says the Lord. 12They
have lied and said, "He won't bother us! No
evil will come upon us! There will be neither
famine nor war! 13God's prophets," they say,
"are windbags full of words with no divine
authority. Their claims of doom will fall upon
themselves, not us!"
14Therefore, this is what the Lord God of
Hosts says to his prophets: Because of talk like
this, I'll take your words and prophecies and
turn them into raging fire and burn up these
people like kindling wood. 15See, I will bring a
distant nation against you, O Israel, says the
Lord. It is a mighty nation, an ancient nation
whose language you don't understand.
16Their weapons are deadly; the men are all
mighty. 17And they shall eat your harvest and
your children's bread, your flocks of sheep
and herds of cattle, yes, and your grapes and
figs; and they shall sack your walled cities that
you think are safe.
18But I will not completely blot you out. So
says the Lord.
19And when your people ask, "Why is it
that the Lord is doing this to us?" then you
shall say, "You rejected him and gave yourselves to other gods while in your land; now
you must be slaves to foreigners in their
lands."
20"Make this announcement to Judah and
to Israel:
21Listen, O foolish, senseless people—you
with the eyes that do not see and the ears that
do not listen— 22have you no respect at all for
me? the Lord God asks. How can it be that you
don't even tremble in my presence? I set the
shorelines of the world by perpetual decrees,
so that the oceans, though they toss and roar,
can never pass those bounds. Isn't such a God
to be feared and worshiped?
23,24But my people have rebellious hearts;
they have turned against me and gone off
into idolatry. Though I am the one who gives
them rain each year in spring and fall and

5:1 It is a great honor to be called fair and honest. If one person had been working at being consistently honest, the course of Israel's history could have been changed. We can change history today. Our honesty can have a profound impact on the people around us and on the many generations to come. Our failure to deal honestly with our problems will hurt the people close to us and will also cause suffering to many in the future. It is up to us to take responsibility for our failures, admitting them to God and receiving the help we need for recovery.

5:19 Everyone who rejects God will become a slave to something else. Rebelling against God's power and control, we become controlled by destructive dependencies such as drugs, alcohol, immoral sex, or other manifestations of appetites out of control. The only way to escape from this type of slavery is to allow God to take control of our life. He is the only truly kind and loving master. Trust and obedience to his will for us is always our best program for recovery.

5:21-22 A proper reverence for God inspires us to trust God and obey his will for our life. Such an attitude protects us from the dependencies and problems that devour us. Disregard for God sets us up for failure as we grapple with life's difficulties with our own limited resources and understanding. Fearing God leads to faith, obedience, honesty, and love, all important aspects of a solid recovery program.

sends the harvesttimes, yet they have no respect or fear for me. 25And so I have taken away these wondrous blessings from them. This sin has robbed them of all of these good things.

26Among my people are wicked men who lurk for victims like a hunter hiding in a blind. They set their traps for men. 27Like a coop full of chickens their homes are full of evil plots. And the result? Now they are great and rich, 28they are well fed and well groomed, and there is no limit to their wicked deeds. They refuse justice to orphans and the rights of the poor. 29Should I sit back and act as though nothing is going on? the Lord God asks. Shouldn't I punish a nation such as this?

30A horrible thing has happened in this land— 31the priests are ruled by false prophets, and my people like it so! But your doom is certain.

CHAPTER 6

One Last Warning

Run, people of Benjamin, run for your lives! Flee from Jerusalem! Sound the alarm in Tekoa; send up a smoke signal at Beth-haccherem; warn everyone that a powerful army is on the way from the north, coming to destroy this nation! 2Helpless as a girl, you are beautiful and delicate—and doomed. 3Evil shepherds shall surround you. They shall set up camp around the city and divide your pastures for their flocks. 4See them prepare for battle. At noon it has begun. All afternoon it rages until the evening shadows fall. 5"Come," they say. "Let us attack by night and destroy her palaces!"

6For the Lord Almighty has said to them, Cut down her trees for battering rams; smash down the walls of Jerusalem. This is the city to be punished, for she is vile through and through. 7She spouts evil like a fountain! Her streets echo with the sounds of violence; her sickness and wounds are ever before me.

8This is your last warning, O Jerusalem. If you don't listen, I will empty the land. 9Disaster on disaster shall befall you. Even the few who remain in Israel shall be gleaned again, the Lord Almighty has said; for as a grape-gatherer checks each vine to pick what he has missed, so the remnant of my people shall be destroyed again.

10But who will listen when I warn them? Their ears are closed, and they refuse to hear. The word of God has angered them; they don't want it at all.

11For all this I am full of the wrath of God against them. I am weary of holding it in. I will pour it out over Jerusalem, even upon the children playing in the streets, upon the gatherings of young men, and on husbands and wives and grandparents. 12Their enemies shall live in their homes and take their fields and wives. For I will punish the people of this land, the Lord has said. 13They are swindlers and liars, from the least of them right to the top! Yes, even my prophets and priests! 14You can't heal a wound by saying it's not there! Yet the priests and prophets give assurances of peace when all is war. 15Were my people ashamed when they worshiped idols? No, not at all—they didn't even blush. Therefore they shall lie among the slain. They shall die beneath my anger.

16Yet the Lord pleads with you still: Ask where the good road is, the godly paths you used to walk in, in the days of long ago. Travel there, and you will find rest for your souls. But you reply, "No, that is not the road we want!" 17I set watchmen over you who warned you: "Listen for the sound of the trumpet! It will let you know when trouble comes." But you said, "No! We won't pay any attention!"

18,19This, then, is my decree against my people: (Listen to it, distant lands; listen to it, O my people in Jerusalem; listen to it, all the earth!) I will bring evil upon this people; it will be the fruit of their own sin because they will not listen to me. They reject my law. 20There is no use now in burning sweet incense from Sheba before me! Keep your expensive perfumes! I cannot accept your offerings; they have no sweet fragrance for me. 21I will make an obstacle course of the

6:1 Sometimes our recovery is protected by the one act all of us can do—run from sin! God warns us to flee temptation, to run before we have to experience the dreadful consequences of being out of control. The next time we find our recovery on shaky ground, perhaps we should run first, then analyze our situation later.

6:8-10 God always warns us many times before finally allowing us to experience the full consequences of our destructive behavior. He does all he can to get our attention before we have to face significant suffering. If we don't listen, however, we eventually hit bottom. Hopefully, through such experiences we discover how helpless we are without God, turn our life over to him, and submit to his will for us. Even God's punishment is meant to lead us back to himself, but we would be wise to act before we have to deal with the terrible consequences of chronic sins and dependencies.

pathway of my people; fathers and sons shall be frustrated; neighbors and friends shall collapse together. 22The Lord God says, See the armies marching from the north—a great nation is rising against you. 23They are a cruel, merciless people, fully armed, mounted for war. The noise of their army is like a roaring sea.

24We have heard the fame of their armies, and we are weak with fright. Fright and pain have gripped us like that of women in travail. 25Don't go out to the fields! Don't travel the roads! For the enemy is everywhere, ready to kill; we are terrorized at every turn.

26O Jerusalem, pride of my people, put on mourning clothes and sit in ashes; weep bitterly as for an only son. For suddenly the destroying armies will be upon you.

27Jeremiah, I have made you an assayer of metals that you may test this my people and determine their value. Listen to what they are saying and watch what they are doing. 28Are they not the worst of rebels, full of evil talk against the Lord? They are insolent as brass, hard and cruel as iron. 29The bellows blow fiercely; the refining fire grows hotter, but it can never cleanse them, for there is no pureness in them to bring out. Why continue the process longer? All is dross. No matter how hot the fire, they continue in their wicked ways. 30I must label them "Impure, Rejected Silver," and I have discarded them.

CHAPTER 7

False Worship

Then the Lord said to Jeremiah:

2Go over to the entrance of the Temple of the Lord and give this message to the people: O Judah, listen to this message from God. Listen to it, all of you who worship here. 3The Lord, the God of Israel says: Even yet, if you quit your evil ways, I will let you stay in your own land. 4But don't be fooled by those who lie to you and say that since the Temple of the Lord is here, God will never let Jerusalem be destroyed. 5You may remain under these conditions only: If you stop your wicked thoughts and deeds and are fair to others; 6if you stop exploiting orphans, widows, and foreigners, and stop your murdering; if you stop worshiping idols as you do now to your hurt, 7then, and only then, will I let you stay in this land that I gave to your fathers to keep forever.

8You think that because the Temple is here, you will never suffer? Don't fool yourselves! 9Do you really think that you can steal, murder, commit adultery, lie, and worship Baal and all of those new gods of yours, 10and then come here and stand before me in my Temple and chant, "We are saved!"—only to go right back to all these evil things again? 11Is my Temple but a den of robbers in your eyes? For I see all the evil going on in there.

12Go to Shiloh, the city I first honored with my name, and see what I did to her because of all the wickedness of my people Israel. 13,14And now, says the Lord, I will do the same thing here because of all this evil you have done. Again and again I spoke to you about it, rising up early and calling, but you refused to hear or answer. Yes, I will destroy this Temple, as I did in Shiloh—this Temple called by my name, which you trust for help, and this place I gave to you and to your fathers. 15And I will send you into exile, just as I did your brothers, the people of Ephraim.

6:26 The mourning and grief from the loss of an only son are too painful to imagine. Yet our grief and sorrow over our misguided life should be as much a cause for mourning. These are words of warning; we have an opportunity today to make good choices that will lead us away from the losses we are now headed for. If we follow God's program, life can become worth living again.

7:8-11 Many of God's chosen people had come to believe that God's presence in the Temple would protect them from enemy attack, regardless of whether or not they obeyed God's laws. But the people of Judah were not excused from obedience; neither are we. We may claim to be an exception to the rule for any number of reasons: "I have special needs," "I have a special plan," "I understand this; others don't." This, however, will only support our denial, allowing us to falsely believe that we are not accountable to God's plans, rules, and judgment. Such an attitude will only lead to destruction. God controls our world, and his plan for healthy living is the only program worth following.

7:12 By examining the lives of those who have gone before us, we will see the blessings experienced by those who obeyed God and the terrible consequences suffered by those who rebelled against him. Greed, denial, and pursuit of pleasure have destroyed the lives of thousands of our ancestors. If we are willing to act upon this bit of wisdom, we can make the changes we need to avoid their terrible fate.

[16]Pray no more for these people, Jeremiah. Neither weep for them nor pray nor beg that I should help them, for I will not listen. [17]Don't you see what they are doing throughout the cities of Judah and in the streets of Jerusalem? [18]No wonder my anger is great! Watch how the children gather wood and the fathers build fires, and the women knead dough and make cakes to offer to The Queen of Heaven and to their other idol-gods! [19] Am I the one that they are hurting? asks the Lord. Most of all they hurt themselves, to their own shame. [20]So the Lord God says, I will pour out my anger, yes, my fury on this place—people, animals, trees, and plants will be consumed by the unquenchable fire of my anger.

[21]The Lord, the God of Israel says, Away with your offerings and sacrifices! [22]It wasn't offerings and sacrifices I wanted from your fathers when I led them out of Egypt. That was not the point of my command. [23]But what I told them was: *Obey* me, and I will be your God and you shall be my people; only do as I say, and all shall be well!

[24]But they wouldn't listen; they kept on doing whatever they wanted to, following their own stubborn, evil thoughts. They went backward instead of forward. [25]Ever since the day your fathers left Egypt until now, I have kept on sending them my prophets, day after day. [26]But they wouldn't listen to them or even try to hear. They are hard and stubborn and rebellious—worse even than their fathers were.

[27]Tell them everything that I will do to them, but don't expect them to listen. Cry out your warnings, but don't expect them to respond. [28]Say to them: This is the nation that refuses to obey the Lord its God and refuses to be taught. She continues to live a lie.

[29]O Jerusalem, shave your head in shame and weep alone upon the mountains; for the Lord has rejected and forsaken this people of his wrath. [30]For the people of Judah have sinned before my very eyes, says the Lord. They have set up their idols right in my own Temple, polluting it. [31]They have built the altar called Topheth in the Valley of Ben-hinnom, and there they burn to death their little sons and daughters as sacrifices to their gods—a deed so horrible I've never even thought of it, let alone commanded it to be done. [32] The time is coming, says the Lord, when that valley's name will be changed from Topheth, or the Valley of Ben-hinnom, to the Valley of Slaughter; for there will be so many slain to bury that there won't be room enough for all the graves, and they will dump the bodies in that valley.

[33]The bodies of my people shall be food for the birds and animals, and no one shall be left to scare them away. [34]I will end the happy singing and laughter and the joyous voices of the bridegrooms and brides in the streets of Jerusalem and in the cities of Judah. For the land shall lie in desolation.

CHAPTER 8

Then, says the Lord, the enemy shall break open the graves of the kings of Judah and of the princes, and the graves of the priests, prophets, and people, [2]and dig out their bones and spread them out on the ground before the sun and moon and stars—the gods of my people!—whom they have loved and worshiped. Their bones shall not be gathered up again nor buried but shall be scattered like dung upon the ground. [3]And those of this evil nation who are still left alive shall long to die rather than live where I will scatter them, says the Lord Almighty.

The People Believe Lies

[4,5]Once again give them this message from the Lord: When a person falls, he jumps up again; when he is on the wrong road and discovers his mistake, he goes back to the fork where he made the wrong turn. But these people keep on along their evil path, even though I warn them. [6]I listen to their conversation and what do I hear? Is anyone sorry for sin? Does anyone say, "What a terrible thing I have done"? No, all are rushing pell-mell down the path of sin as swiftly as a horse rushing to the battle! [7]The stork knows the time of her migration,

---

7:30-34 The depth of Judah's sin was revealed in their practice of child sacrifice, a heinous act that God had clearly forbidden. This is a sin that might turn the stomach of even a hardened sinner. How could God's people have grown so distant from God's plan for them? How are we lured so far from God's plan for us? We need to take a regular moral inventory in order to detect the sin and denial in our life. When we don't, one sin leads to another. As we continue to fail, we become blind to our sin, and our failures grow ever greater. When we take an honest moral inventory on a regular basis, we can make the changes needed to root out our problems before they lead us to destruction.

as does the turtledove, the crane, and the swallow. They all return at God's appointed time each year; but not my people! They don't accept the laws of God.

[8]How can you say, "We understand his laws," when your teachers have twisted them up to mean a thing I never said? [9]These wise teachers of yours will be shamed by exile for this sin, for they have rejected the word of the Lord. Are they then so wise? [10]I will give their wives and their farms to others; for all of them, great and small, prophet and priest, have one purpose in mind—to get what isn't theirs. [11]They give useless medicine for my people's grievous wounds, for they assure them all is well when that isn't so at all! [12]Are they ashamed because they worship idols? No, not in the least; they don't even know how to blush! That is why I will see to it that they lie among the fallen. I will visit them with death. [13]Their figs and grapes will disappear, their fruit trees will die, and all the good things I prepared for them will soon be gone.

[14]Then the people will say, "Why should we wait here to die? Come, let us go to the walled cities and perish there. For the Lord our God has decreed our doom and given us a cup of poison to drink because of all our sins. [15]We expected peace, but no peace came; we looked for health, but there was only terror."

[16]The noise of war resounds from the northern border. The whole land trembles at the approach of the terrible army, for the enemy is coming and is devouring the land and everything in it—the cities and people alike. [17]For I will send these enemy troops among you like poisonous snakes that you cannot charm. No matter what you do, they will bite you and you shall die.

[18]My grief is beyond healing; my heart is broken. [19]Listen to the weeping of my people all across the land.

"Where is the Lord?" they ask. "Has God deserted us?"

"Oh, why have they angered me with their carved idols and strange evil rites?" the Lord replies.

[20]"The harvest is finished; the summer is over, and we are not saved."

[21]I weep for the hurt of my people; I stand amazed, silent, dumb with grief. [22]Is there no medicine in Gilead? Is there no physician there? Why doesn't God do something? Why doesn't he help?

CHAPTER 9

Jeremiah Weeps

Oh, that my eyes were a fountain of tears; I would weep forever; I would sob day and night for the slain of my people! [2]Oh, that I could go away and forget them and live in some wayside shack in the desert, for they are all adulterous, treacherous men.

[3]"They bend their tongues like bows to

8:7 One of the reasons so many of us fall prey to addictive behaviors is that we don't accept God's principles for healthy living. Another reason is that we foolishly seek to find truth and meaning apart from God. Not finding it, we fill the void with whatever is most convenient. Even the animals show more wisdom than we do. They know that God's way is the only way for survival. We would be wise to follow their lead.

8:8-9 People who lead others astray will face severe judgment from God. People in recovery are often told that there are quick, easy methods for overcoming addictions. We are also told by many that recovery requires no commitment to God. Those who claim these things are trying to sell us something. Recovery from deep-rooted dependencies or other personal problems is never fast and easy. And God isn't interested in quick fixes. He is interested in a full recovery based on a strong relationship with him. We may hear claims that there is another way, but any program that excludes God and his Word should be avoided.

8:18-19 The people of Judah had strayed from God in disobedience and then complained that God had deserted them. We often do the same thing. But God never moves away from us. If we are far from God, we are the ones who have moved. Recovery comes as we seek to rebuild our relationship with God through trust in his person and obedience to his plan. God is eager to help all those who humbly turn to him for help.

9:7-8 God had come to a critical point in his relationship with the people of Judah. They had ignored his warnings and continued to disobey his will for them. God now had to bring a destructive punishment upon them. Notice, however, that even their punishment was designed to lead to their betterment. God would melt them down through the Babylonian exile and reshape his people into a nation that could be used by him. God also uses the trials in our life to refine and test us. He may even allow us to hit bottom in order to promote our spiritual growth. We often try to escape such testing, but God uses it to remind us of how much we need him. Unless we continue to place our life in God's hands on a daily basis, our recovery is at risk.

shoot their arrows of untruth. They care nothing for right and go from bad to worse; they care nothing for me," says the Lord.

4Beware of your neighbor! Beware of your brother! All take advantage of one another and spread their slanderous lies. 5With practiced tongues they fool and defraud each other; they wear themselves out with all their sinning.

6"They pile evil upon evil, lie upon lie, and utterly refuse to come to me," says the Lord.

7Therefore, the Lord Almighty says this: "See, I will melt them in a crucible of affliction. I will refine them and test them like metal. What else can I do with them? 8For their tongues aim lies like poisoned spears. They speak cleverly to their neighbors while planning to kill them. 9Should not I punish them for such things as this?" asks the Lord. "Shall not my soul be avenged on such a nation as this?"

10Sobbing and weeping, I point to their mountains and pastures, for now they are desolate, without a living soul. Gone is the lowing of cattle, gone the birds and wild animals. All have fled.

11"And I will turn Jerusalem into heaps of ruined houses where only jackals have their dens. The cities of Judah shall be ghost towns, with no one living in them."

12Who is wise enough to understand all this? Where is the Lord's messenger to explain it? Why is the land a wilderness so that no one dares even to travel through?

13"Because," the Lord replies, "my people have forsaken my commandments and not obeyed my laws. 14Instead, they have done whatever they pleased and worshiped the idols of Baal, as their fathers told them to."
15Therefore, this is what the Lord, the God of Israel, says: "Look! I will feed them with bitterness and give them poison to drink. 16I will scatter them around the world, to be strangers in distant lands; and even there the sword of destruction shall chase them until I have utterly destroyed them."

17,18The Lord Almighty says: "Send for the mourners! Quick! Begin your crying! Let the tears flow from your eyes. 19Hear Jerusalem weeping in despair. 'We are ruined! Disaster has befallen us! We must leave our land and homes!'" 20Listen to the words of God, O women who wail. Teach your daughters to wail and your neighbors too. 21For death has crept in through your windows into your homes. He has killed off the flower of your

Honesty

READ JEREMIAH 9:1-9

Most of us know the pain caused by deceit, both for the deceiver and for the one who has been betrayed. We may be trying to learn to trust again after living in situations in which we haven't been given any reason to trust.

David cried, "Lord! Help! Godly men are fast disappearing. Where in all the world can dependable men be found? Everyone deceives and flatters and lies. There is no sincerity left. But the Lord will not deal gently with . . . those proud liars who say, 'We will lie to our hearts' content. Our lips are our own; who can stop us?'" (Psalm 12:1-4).

Jeremiah prophesied, "Beware of your neighbor! Beware of your brother! All take advantage of one another and spread their slanderous lies. With practiced tongues they fool and defraud each other; they wear themselves out with all their sinning. 'They pile evil upon evil, lie upon lie, and utterly refuse to come to me,' says the Lord. Therefore the Lord Almighty says this: 'See, I will melt them in a crucible of affliction. I will refine them and test them like metal'" (Jeremiah 9:4-7).

When we turn our life over to God, learning to trust him is a process. He understands that this will be hard. God is absolutely trustworthy. We should be cautious as we put our trust in people, trusting only those who have proven themselves trustworthy. ***Turn to page 801, Jeremiah 17.***

youth. Children no longer play in the streets;
the young men gather no more in the squares.
22Tell them this, says the Lord: Bodies shall
be scattered across the fields like manure, like
sheaves after the mower, and no one will bury
them.
23The Lord says: Let not the wise man bask
in his wisdom, nor the mighty man in his
might, nor the rich man in his riches. 24Let
them boast in this alone: That they truly
know me, and understand that I am the Lord
of justice and of righteousness whose love is
steadfast; and that I love to be this way.
25,26A time is coming, says the Lord, when I
will punish all those who are circumcised in
body but not in spirit—the Egyptians, Edomites, Ammonites, Moabites, Arabs, and yes,
even you people of Judah. For all these pagan
nations also circumcise themselves. Unless
you circumcise your hearts by loving me,
your circumcision is only a heathen rite like
theirs, and nothing more.

CHAPTER 10

The God of Creation

Hear the word of the Lord, O Israel:
2,3Don't act like the people who make horo-
scopes and try to read their fate and future in
the stars! Don't be frightened by predictions
such as theirs, for it is all a pack of lies. Their
ways are futile and foolish. They cut down a
tree and carve an idol; 4they decorate it with
gold and silver and fasten it securely in place
with hammer and nails so that it won't fall
over. 5And there stands their god like a helpless scarecrow in a garden! It cannot speak,
and it must be carried, for it cannot walk.
Don't be afraid of such a god, for it can neither harm nor help nor do you any good.
6O Lord, there is no other god like you. For
you are great, and your name is full of power.
7Who would not fear you, O King of nations?
(And that title belongs to you alone!) Among
all the wise men of the earth and in all the
kingdoms of the world there isn't anyone like
you.
8The wisest of men who worship idols are
altogether stupid and foolish. 9They bring
beaten sheets of silver from Tarshish and gold
from Uphaz and give them to skillful goldsmiths who make their idols; then they clothe
these gods in royal purple robes that expert
tailors make.
10But the Lord is the only true God, the
living God, the everlasting King. The whole
earth shall tremble at his anger; the world
shall hide before his displeasure.
11Say this to those who worship other gods:
Your so-called gods, who have not made the
heavens and earth, shall vanish from the
earth. 12But our God formed the earth by his
power and wisdom, and by his intelligence he
hung the stars in space and stretched out the
heavens. 13It is his voice that echoes in the
thunder of the storm clouds. He causes mist
to rise upon the earth; he sends the lightning
and brings the rain, and from his treasuries he
brings the wind.
14But foolish men without knowledge of
God bow before their idols. It is a shameful
business that these men are in, for what they
make are frauds, gods without life or power in
them. 15All are worthless, silly; they will be
crushed when their makers perish. 16But the
God of Jacob is not like these foolish idols. He
is the Creator of all, and Israel is his chosen
nation. The Lord Almighty is his name.
17Pack your bags, he says. Get ready now to
leave; the siege will soon begin. 18For suddenly I'll fling you from this land and pour
great troubles down; at last you shall feel my
wrath.
19*Desperate is my wound. My grief is great. My*
sickness is incurable, but I must bear it. 20*My*
home is gone; my children have been taken away,
and I will never see them again. There is no one
left to help me rebuild my home. 21The shepherds
of my people have lost their senses; they no
longer follow God nor ask his will. Therefore
they perish, and their flocks are scattered.
22Listen! Hear the terrible sound of great armies coming from the north. The cities of
Judah shall become dens of jackals.
23O Lord, I know it is not within the power

10:2-3 A horoscope is just a bad substitute for a relationship with God; it is a way of seeking for truth apart from him. Instead of looking at the stars to find God's will, we should look to the Creator of the stars and to the Bible—his Word to us. As we seek to strengthen our relationship with God, we will discover that we have also strengthened our recovery.

10:4-5 Trusting in anything that is a substitute for God is as foolish as propping up an idol. This may refer to our dependencies, which we use to face problems that are too big for us to face alone. It may refer to unhealthy relationships on which we have placed too much importance. It may even refer to a recovery program that excludes or ignores our need for God. Only God can help us overcome our dependencies and the underlying suffering that drives them.

of man to map his life and plan his course—
24so you correct me, Lord; but please be gentle.
Don't do it in your anger, for I would die.
25Pour out your fury on the nations who don't
obey the Lord, for they have destroyed Israel
and made a wasteland of this entire country.

CHAPTER 11

Remember God's Promise

Then the Lord spoke to Jeremiah once again
and said:

Remind the men of Judah and all the
people of Jerusalem that I made a contract
with their fathers—and cursed is the man
who does not heed it! 4For I told them at the
time I brought them out of slavery in Egypt
that if they would obey me and do whatever
I commanded them, then they and all their
children would be mine and I would be their
God. 5And now, Israel, obey me, says the Lord,
so that I can do for you the wonderful things
I swore I would if you obeyed. I want to give
you a land that "flows with milk and honey,"
as it is today.

Then I replied, "So be it, Lord!"

6Then the Lord said: Broadcast this message
in Jerusalem's streets—go from city to city
throughout the land and say, Remember this
agreement that your fathers made with God,
and do all the things they promised him they
would. 7For I solemnly said to your fathers
when I brought them out of Egypt—and have
kept on saying it over and over again until
this day: "Obey my every command!" 8But
your fathers didn't do it. They wouldn't even
listen. Each followed his own stubborn will
and his proud heart. Because they refused to
obey, I did to them all the evils stated in the
contract.

9Again the Lord spoke to me and said: I
have discovered a conspiracy against me
among the men of Judah and Jerusalem.
10They have returned to the sins of their
fathers, refusing to listen to me and worshiping idols. The agreement I made with their
fathers is broken and canceled. 11Therefore,
the Lord says, I am going to bring calamity
down upon them, and they shall not escape.
Though they cry for mercy, I will not listen to
their pleas. 12Then they will pray to their idols
and burn incense before them, but that cannot save them from their time of anguish and
despair. 13O my people, you have as many
gods as there are cities, and your altars of
shame (your altars to burn incense to Baal) are
along every street in Jerusalem.

14Therefore, Jeremiah, pray no longer for
this people, neither weep nor plead for them;
for I will not listen to them when they are
finally desperate enough to beg me for help.
15What right do my beloved people have to
come any more to my Temple? For you have
been unfaithful and worshiped other gods.
Can promises and sacrifices now avert your
doom and give you life and joy again?

16The Lord used to call you his green olive
tree, beautiful to see and full of good fruit; but
now he has sent the fury of your enemies to
burn you up and leave you broken and
charred. 17It is because of the wickedness of
Israel and Judah in offering incense to Baal
that the Lord Almighty who planted the tree
has ordered it destroyed.

18Then the Lord told me all about their
plans and showed me their evil plots. 19I had
been as unsuspecting as a lamb or ox on the
way to slaughter. I didn't know that they were
planning to kill me! "Let's destroy this man
and all his messages," they said. "Let's kill him
so that his name will be forever forgotten."

20O Lord Almighty, you are just. See the
hearts and motives of these men. Repay them
for all that they have planned! I look to you
for justice.

10:23-25 The prophet acknowledged his inability to map out his life and recognized his powerlessness. This is the first step in God's program for recovery. Sadly, the people of Judah didn't share Jeremiah's sentiments. The prophet begged God to let his people off lightly, but punishment was the only solution for their denial. It was painful for Jeremiah to watch as they lived out the consequences of their own sin.

11:1-17 God gave his people the terms for their restoration: he asked for their obedience. We can see from this passage that God already knew that they would refuse to repent. They had enjoyed their father's sins and preferred idols to the true God. We may consider God's price too high and the reward too delayed for giving up the pleasures of our sin. When this is our attitude, we will reap a harvest of suffering when the time is ripe. Keeping the long view in mind helps us to choose God's way.

11:5 God is waiting to do wonderful things for those who simply trust and obey him. When we decide to reject God's program, we automatically choose the world's rules for life and the consequences that accompany them. The world will always hand us disappointment in the long run. God promises that wonderful things will be ours when we decide to obey him.

[21,22]And the Lord replied, The men of the city of Anathoth shall be punished for planning to kill you. They will tell you not to prophesy in God's name on pain of death. And so their young men shall die in battle; their boys and girls shall starve. [23]Not one of these plotters of Anathoth shall survive, for I will bring a great disaster upon them. Their time has come.

CHAPTER 12

Jeremiah Complains to God

O Lord, you always give me justice when I bring a case before you to decide. Now let me bring you this complaint: Why are the wicked so prosperous? Why are evil men so happy? [2]You plant them. They take root and their business grows. Their profits multiply, and they are rich. They say, "Thank God!" But in their hearts they give no credit to you. [3]But as for me—Lord, you know my heart—you know how much it longs for you. (And I am poor, O Lord!) Lord, drag them off like helpless sheep to the slaughter. Judge them, O God!

[4]How long must this land of yours put up with all their goings on? Even the grass of the field groans and weeps over their wicked deeds! The wild animals and birds have moved away, leaving the land deserted. Yet the people say, "God won't bring judgment on us. We're perfectly safe!"

[5]The Lord replied to me: If racing with mere men—these men of Anathoth—has wearied you, how will you race against horses, against the king, his court and all his evil priests? If you stumble and fall on open ground, what will you do in Jordan's jungles? [6]Even your own brothers, your own family, have turned against you. They have plotted to call for a mob to lynch you. Don't trust them, no matter how pleasantly they speak. Don't believe them.

God Abandons His People

[7]Then the Lord said: I have abandoned my people, my inheritance; I have surrendered my dearest ones to their enemies. [8]My people have roared at me like a lion of the forest, so I have treated them as though I hated them. [9]My people have fallen. I will bring upon them swarms of vultures and wild animals to pick the flesh from their corpses.

[10]Many foreign rulers have ravaged my vineyard, trampling down the vines, and turning all its beauty into barren wilderness. [11]They have made it desolate; I hear its mournful cry. The whole land is desolate and no one cares. [12]Destroying armies plunder the land; the sword of the Lord devours from one end of the nation to the other; nothing shall escape. [13]My people have sown wheat but reaped thorns; they have worked hard, but it does them no good. They shall harvest a crop of shame, for the fierce anger of the Lord is upon them.

[14]And now the Lord says this to the evil nations, the nations surrounding the land God gave his people Israel: See, I will force you from your land just as Judah will be forced from hers; [15]but afterwards I will return and have compassion on all of you and will bring you home to your own land again, each man to his inheritance. [16]And if these heathen nations quickly learn my people's ways and claim me as their God instead of Baal (whom they taught my people to worship), then they shall be strong among my people. [17]But any nation refusing to obey me will be expelled again and finished, says the Lord.

CHAPTER 13

Good for Nothing

The Lord said to me, Go and buy a linen loincloth and wear it, but don't wash it—don't put it in water at all. [2]So I bought the loincloth and put it on. [3]Then the Lord's message came to me again. This time he said, [4]Take the loincloth out to the Euphrates River and hide it in a hole in the rocks.

[5]So I did; I hid it as the Lord had told me to. [6]Then, a long time afterwards, the Lord said: Go out to the river again and get the loincloth. [7]And I did; I dug it out of the hole where

12:1-17 It is no wonder that Jeremiah struggled deeply with his calling. He was living in the midst of Judah's sin; he could see the godless life-style of Judah's people, and he knew God's concern about their sin. So he asked the question we often ask: Why do the wicked prosper? God responded by revealing that the wicked never prosper for long. We should not allow ourself to be bothered by their apparent success. If we do, we are the ones who will stumble (see Psalm 73). As difficult as it is to be patient, God's truth and righteousness do prevail—always.

12:13 Often our actions produce a crop of shame, but God can turn our shameful experiences into meaningful lessons if we will submit to him. Our challenge is to take our failure and shame to God and allow him to forgive us and heal our heart. Then, with renewed humility and faith, we can make significant forward progress in our recovery.

I had hidden it. But now it was mildewed and falling apart. It was utterly useless!

[8,9]Then the Lord said: This illustrates the way that I will rot the pride of Judah and Jerusalem. [10]This evil nation refuses to listen to me and follows its own evil desires, and worships idols; therefore, it shall become as this loincloth—good for nothing. [11]Even as a loincloth clings to a man's loins, so I made Judah and Israel to cling to me, says the Lord. They were my people, an honor to my name. But then they turned away.

[12]Tell them this: The Lord God of Israel says, All your wine jugs will be full of wine. And they will reply, Of course, you don't need to tell us how prosperous we will be! [13]Then tell them: That's not what I mean. I mean that I will fill everyone living in this land with helpless bewilderment—from the king sitting on David's throne, and the priests and the prophets right on down to all the people. [14]And I will smash fathers and sons against each other, says the Lord. I will not let pity nor mercy spare them from utter destruction.

[15]Oh, that you were not so proud and stubborn! Then you would listen to the Lord, for he has spoken. [16]Give glory to the Lord your God before it is too late, before he causes deep, impenetrable darkness to fall upon you so that you stumble and fall upon the dark mountains; then, when you look for light, you will find only terrible darkness. [17]Do you still refuse to listen? Then in loneliness my breaking heart shall mourn because of your pride. My eyes will overflow with tears because the Lord's flock shall be carried away as slaves.

[18]Say to the king and queen-mother, Come down from your thrones and sit in the dust, for your glorious crowns are removed from your heads. They are no longer yours. [19]The cities of the Negeb to the south of Jerusalem have closed their gates against the enemy. They must defend themselves, for Jerusalem cannot help; and all Judah shall be taken away as slaves.

[20]See the armies marching from the north! Where is your flock, Jerusalem, your beautiful flock he gave you to take care of ? [21]How will you feel when he sets your allies over you as your rulers? You will writhe in pain like a woman having a child. [22]And if you ask yourself, Why is all this happening to me? it is because of the grossness of your sins; that is why you have been raped and destroyed by the invading army. [23]Can the Ethiopian change the color of his skin? or a leopard take away his spots? Nor can you who are so used to doing evil now start being good.

[24,25]Because you have put me out of your mind and put your trust in false gods, I will scatter you as chaff is scattered by the fierce winds off the desert. This then is your allotment, that which is due you, which I have measured out especially for you. [26]I myself will expose you to utter shame. [27]I am keenly aware of your apostasy, your faithlessness to me, and your abominable idol worship in the fields and on the hills. Woe upon you, O Jerusalem! How long before you will be pure?

CHAPTER 14

Doom for Jerusalem

This message came to Jeremiah from the Lord, explaining why he was holding back the rain:

[2]Judah mourns; business has ground to a halt; all the people prostrate themselves to

13:1-11 God used an object lesson to prepare Jeremiah for the devastation he would soon see. In this illustration God compared himself to Jeremiah. He also compared his people to Jeremiah's new loincloth. Jeremiah was told to bury it and, after a period of time, dig it up again. When Jeremiah retrieved the loincloth, it was rotten. This illustrated how the people of Judah had become spiritually rotten by going their own way in life. Following our selfish inclinations always leads to destruction. Following God's will leads to health and spiritual renewal.

13:15 Stubbornness and pride are two of the greatest barriers to our recovery. When we hit bottom, we reach a point of emptiness in which these two personal characteristics lose their power over us. At this point, we become willing to comply with God's will for us. When we find ourself becoming stubborn and proud, it will sober us to be reminded that these problems have led people to destruction for thousands of years. Stubbornness and pride are nothing new, but we can provide a new response to them as we continue to give control of our life to God.

13:23 We often try to change by making resolutions to do what we know to be right. But change doesn't happen overnight, and we don't have the power to do it alone. Taking action is a good thing to do, but if we set out to change in our own power, we will be sure to fail. Our actions will produce no lasting changes in our life. We must begin by admitting that we are powerless to change. This is the first step toward allowing God to transform our heart and life from the inside out. If we are willing to cooperate, God can and will make permanent changes in our life.

the earth, and a great cry rises from Jerusalem. 3The nobles send servants for water from the wells, but the wells are dry. The servants return, baffled and desperate, and cover their heads in grief. 4The ground is parched and cracked for lack of rain; the farmers are afraid. 5The deer deserts her fawn because there is no grass. 6The wild donkeys stand upon the bare hills panting like thirsty jackals. They strain their eyes looking for grass to eat, but there is none to be found.

7O Lord, we have sinned against you grievously, yet help us for the sake of your own reputation! 8O Hope of Israel, our Savior in times of trouble, why are you as a stranger to us, as one passing through the land who is merely stopping for the night? 9Are you also baffled? Are you helpless to save us? O Lord, you are right here among us, and we carry your name; we are known as your people. O Lord, don't desert us now!

10But the Lord replies: You have loved to wander far from me and have not tried to follow in my paths. Now I will no longer accept you as my people; now I will remember all the evil you have done and punish your sins.

11The Lord told me again: Don't ask me any more to bless this people. Don't pray for them any more. 12When they fast, I will not pay any attention; when they present their offerings and sacrifices to me, I will not accept them. What I will give them in return is war and famine and disease.

13Then I said, O Lord God, their prophets are telling them that all is well—that no war or famine will come. They tell the people you will surely send them peace, that you will bless them.

14Then the Lord said: The prophets are telling lies in my name. I didn't send them or tell them to speak or give them any message. They prophesy of visions and revelations they have never seen nor heard; they speak foolishness concocted out of their own lying hearts. 15Therefore, the Lord says, I will punish these lying prophets who have spoken in my name though I did not send them, who say no war shall come nor famine. By war and famine they themselves shall die! 16And the people to whom they prophesy—their bodies shall be thrown out into the streets of Jerusalem, victims of famine and war; there shall be no one to bury them. Husbands, wives, sons, and daughters—all will be gone. For I will pour out terrible punishment upon them for their sins.

17Therefore, tell them this: Night and day my eyes shall overflow with tears; I cannot stop my crying, for my people have been run through with a sword and lie mortally wounded on the ground. 18If I go out in the fields, there lie the bodies of those the sword has killed; and if I walk in the streets, there lie those dead from starvation and disease. And yet the prophets and priests alike have made it their business to travel through the whole country, reassuring everyone that all is well, speaking of things they know nothing about.

19"O Lord," the people will cry, "have you completely rejected Judah? Do you abhor Jerusalem? Even after punishment, will there be no peace? We thought, Now at last he will heal us and bind our wounds. But no peace has come, and there is only trouble and terror everywhere. 20O Lord, we confess our wickedness, and that of our fathers too. 21Do not hate us, Lord, for the sake of your own name. Do not disgrace yourself and the throne of your glory by forsaking your promise to bless us! 22What heathen god can give us rain? Who but you alone, O Lord our God, can do such things as this? Therefore we will wait for you to help us."

CHAPTER 15

Jerusalem Is Persecuted

Then the Lord said to me, Even if Moses and Samuel stood before me pleading for these

---

14:1-10 As the people of Judah faced a period of drought, they turned to God in desperation. How quickly we turn to God when something goes wrong in our life! Where yesterday's happiness found us only vaguely aware of God's power and grace, today's pain finds us begging for his mercy. If we wait until disaster strikes to beg for mercy, God will answer our cries, but we should realize that our healing will come only through great suffering. We would be wiser to remain close to God even when things are going well for us. Then we will know God will deliver us when we face the difficult times in life.

14:13 Many of us would go merrily on our self-destructive way if God didn't somehow intervene to stop us. We often choose to live in denial, somehow hoping that God will protect us if difficult times strike. The sooner we accept that our actions will lead to painful consequences, the sooner we will turn to God and begin to recover his plan for our life. God allows us to experience the consequences of our actions to wake us up and lead us back to himself and the healing he offers.

people, even then I wouldn't help them—away with them! Get them out of my sight! 2And if they say to you, But where can we go? tell them the Lord says: Those who are destined for death, to death; those who must die by the sword, to the sword; those doomed to starvation, to famine; and those for captivity, to captivity. 3I will appoint over them four kinds of destroyers, says the Lord: the sword to kill, the dogs to tear, and the vultures and wild animals to finish up what's left. 4Because of the wicked things Manasseh, son of Hezekiah, king of Judah, did in Jerusalem, I will punish you so severely that your fate will horrify the peoples of the world.

5Who will feel sorry for you, Jerusalem? Who will weep for you? Who will even bother to ask how you are? 6You have forsaken me and turned your backs upon me. Therefore, I will clench my fists against you to destroy you. I am tired of always giving you another chance. 7I will sift you at the gates of your cities and take from you all that you hold dear, and I will destroy my own people because they refuse to turn back to me from all their evil ways. 8There shall be countless widows; at noontime I will bring death to the young men and sorrow to their mothers. I will cause anguish and terror to fall upon them suddenly. 9The mother of seven sickens and faints, for all her sons are dead. Her sun is gone down while it is yet day. She sits childless now, disgraced, for all her children have been killed.

10Then Jeremiah said, "What sadness is mine, my mother; oh, that I had died at birth. For I am hated everywhere I go. I am neither a creditor soon to foreclose nor a debtor refusing to pay—yet they all curse me. 11Well, let them curse! Lord, you know how I have pled with you on their behalf—how I have begged you to spare these enemies of mine."

12,13Can a man break bars of northern iron or bronze? This people's stubborn will can't be broken either. So, because of all your sins against me, I will deliver your wealth and treasures as loot to the enemy. 14I will have your enemies take you as slaves to a land where you have never been before, for my anger burns like fire, and it shall consume you.

15Then Jeremiah replied, "Lord, you know it is for your sake that I am suffering. They are persecuting me because I have proclaimed your word to them. Don't let them kill me! Rescue me from their clutches, and give them what they deserve! 16Your words are what sustain me; they are food to my hungry soul. They bring joy to my sorrowing heart and delight me. How proud I am to bear your name, O Lord. 17,18I have not joined the people in their merry feasts. I sit alone beneath the hand of God. I burst with indignation at their sins. Yet you have failed me in my time of need! You have let them keep right on with all their persecutions. Will they never stop hurting me? Your help is as uncertain as a seasonal mountain brook—sometimes a flood, sometimes as dry as a bone."

19The Lord replied: "Stop this foolishness and talk some sense! Only if you return to trusting me will I let you continue as my spokesman. You are to influence *them,* not let them influence *you!* 20They will fight against you like a besieging army against a high city wall. But they will not conquer you, for I am with you to protect and deliver you," says the Lord. 21"Yes, I will certainly deliver you from these wicked men and rescue you from their ruthless hands."

CHAPTER 16

A Prophecy of Disaster

On yet another occasion God spoke to me, and said:

2You must not marry and have children

15:3-9 God named Manasseh as the king primarily responsible for Judah's great suffering. Manasseh had died several generations before the ministry of Jeremiah began, yet his sinful life-style had infected the entire nation of Judah with sin. The consequences of his behavior were suffered by generations of God's people. Our behavior is important not only for us and our immediate family, but also for our descendants and all the people who will come in contact with them. Knowing this truth should motivate us to follow God's program for our life. If we do things God's way, we will pass peace and joy to future generations.

16:1-13 God had worked with his people for centuries, warning them, forgiving them, and healing them; but the people had continued to ignore God and follow their own selfish ways. As a result, God withdrew his blessings from his people. God did not do this out of spite; rather, he hoped that his children's experience in exile would lead them back to his ways. Painful discipline often gets our attention when everything else fails. We should learn from our painful experiences and turn to God; we should never allow punishment to drive us away from him. His discipline is a clear sign that he loves us and wants to have a close relationship with us.

here. [3]For the children born in this city and their mothers and fathers [4]shall die from terrible diseases. No one shall mourn for them or bury them, but their bodies shall lie on the ground to rot and fertilize the soil. They shall die from war and famine, and their bodies shall be picked apart by vultures and wild animals. [5]Do not mourn or weep for them, for I have removed my protection and my peace from them—taken away my loving-kindness and my mercies. [6]Both great and small shall die in this land, unburied and unmourned, and their friends shall not cut themselves nor shave their heads as signs of sorrow (as is their heathen custom). [7]No one shall comfort the mourners with a meal nor send them a cup of wine expressing grief for their parents' death.

[8]As a sign to them of these sad days ahead, don't you join them any more in their feasts and parties—don't even eat a meal with them. [9]For the Lord Almighty, the God of Israel, says: In your own lifetime, before your very eyes, I will end all laughter in this land—the happy songs, the marriage feasts, the songs of bridegrooms and of brides.

[10]And when you tell the people all these things and they ask, "Why has the Lord decreed such terrible things against us? What have we done to merit such treatment? What is our sin against the Lord our God?" [11]tell them the Lord's reply is this: Because your fathers forsook me. They worshiped other gods and served them; they did not keep my laws, [12]*and you have been worse than your fathers were!* You follow evil to your hearts' content and refuse to listen to me. [13]Therefore, I will throw you out of this land and chase you into a foreign land where neither you nor your fathers have been before, and there you can go ahead and worship your idols all you like—and I will grant you no favors!

[14,15]But there will come a glorious day, says the Lord, when the whole topic of conversation will be that God is bringing his people home from a nation in the north, and from many other lands where he had scattered them. You will look back no longer to the time when I rescued you from your slavery in Egypt. That mighty miracle will scarcely be mentioned any more. Yes, I will bring you back again, says the Lord, to this same land I gave your fathers.

[16]Now I am sending for many fishermen to fish you from the deeps where you are hiding from my wrath. I am sending for hunters to chase you down like deer in the forests or mountain goats on inaccessible crags. Wherever you run to escape my judgment, I will find you and punish you. [17]For I am closely watching you, and I see every sin. You cannot hope to hide from me.

[18]And I will punish you doubly for all your sins because you have defiled my land with your detestable idols and filled it up with all your evil deeds.

[19]O Lord, my Strength and Fortress, my Refuge in the day of trouble, nations from around the world will come to you saying, Our fathers have been foolish, for they have worshiped worthless idols! [20]Can men make God? The gods they made are not real gods at all.

[21]And when they come in that spirit, I will show them my power and might and make them understand at last that I alone am God.

CHAPTER 17

Jeremiah Warns the People

My people sin as though commanded to, as though their evil were laws chiseled with an iron pen or diamond point upon their stony hearts or on the corners of their altars. [2,3]Their youths do not forget to sin, worshiping idols beneath each tree, high in the mountains or in the open country down below. And so I will give all your treasures to your enemies as the price that you must pay for all your sins. [4]And the wonderful heritage I reserved for you will

---

16:8 In this verse, God was telling Jeremiah not to be an enabler. The prophet was to break through the people's denial by refusing to celebrate with them. It takes a great deal of courage to confront loved ones' denial. They will certainly question our choices and may even actively pressure us to continue our enabling behavior. Sometimes we can help the people we love by gently showing them that they are in need of recovery. Often, though, a more direct approach may become necessary. Jesus was hardly gentle when he threw the moneychangers out of the Temple! If the situation calls for it, direct confrontation may be the best approach to take.

17:5-6 In recovery, it is often tempting to trust someone who claims to speak for God, but here we are reminded that God alone is worthy of our trust. Many contemporary recovery programs do not assume our need to trust and obey God and his Word. Such a program can be dangerous, causing us to place our trust in people or activities that have no real power to deliver. We need to be sure we adhere to godly wisdom, not one individual's distortion of it. The analogy of the stunted shrub accurately describes what it feels like for us to live without nourishment from God.

slip out of your hand, and I will send you
away as slaves to your enemies in distant
lands. For you have kindled a fire of my anger
that shall burn forever.
5The Lord says: Cursed is the man who
puts his trust in mortal man and turns his
heart away from God. 6He is like a stunted
shrub in the desert, with no hope for the
future; he lives on the salt-encrusted plains in
the barren wilderness; good times pass him
by forever.
7But blessed is the man who trusts in the
Lord and has made the Lord his hope and
confidence. 8He is like a tree planted along a
riverbank, with its roots reaching deep into
the water—a tree not bothered by the heat
nor worried by long months of drought. Its
leaves stay green, and it goes right on producing all its luscious fruit.
9The heart is the most deceitful thing there
is and desperately wicked. No one can really
know how bad it is! 10Only the Lord knows!
He searches all hearts and examines deepest
motives so he can give to each person his
right reward, according to his deeds—how he
has lived.
11Like a bird that fills her nest with young
she has not hatched and which will soon
desert her and fly away, so is the man who
gets his wealth by unjust means. Sooner or
later he will lose his riches and at the end of
his life become a poor old fool.
12But our refuge is your throne, eternal,
high and glorious. 13O Lord, the Hope of Israel, all who turn away from you shall be
disgraced and shamed; they are registered for
earth and not for glory, for they have forsaken
the Lord, the Fountain of living waters.
14Lord, you alone can heal me, you alone can
save, and my praises are for you alone.
15Men scoff at me and say, "What is this
word of the Lord you keep talking about? If
these threats of yours are really from God,
why don't they come true?"
16Lord, I don't want the people crushed by
terrible calamity. The plan is yours, not mine.
It is *your* message I've given them, not my
own. *I* don't want them doomed! 17Lord,
don't desert me now! You alone are my hope.
18Bring confusion and trouble on all who persecute me, but give me peace. Yes, bring double destruction upon them!

Jerusalem's Gates Will Burn

19Then the Lord said to me, Go and stand in
the gates of Jerusalem, first at the gate where
the king goes out, and then at each of the

Hope

READ JEREMIAH 17:1-14

We may have learned a long time ago that hoping only brings disappointment. Our hopes were dashed. The promises we believed were broken. We were left feeling like fools for ever hoping in the first place. But perhaps we were devastated because we put our hope in the wrong place.

"The Lord says: Cursed is the man who puts his trust in mortal man and turns his heart away from God. He is like a stunted shrub in the desert, with no hope for the future; he lives on the salt-encrusted plains in the barren wilderness; good times pass him by forever. But blessed is the man who trusts in the Lord and has made the Lord his hope and confidence. He is like a tree planted along a riverbank, with its roots reaching deep into the water—a tree not bothered by the heat nor worried by long months of drought. Its leaves stay green, and it goes right on producing all its luscious fruit" (Jeremiah 17:5-8).

Turning our life over to God includes placing our hope in him, even if people have disappointed us. When we place *all* of our hope in other people, it's like expecting a tree to flourish in a barren desert. Our thirst continues, and they are unable to satisfy our deepest needs. Placing our hope in God changes everything. Jesus said, "The water I give . . . becomes a perpetual spring within them, watering them forever with eternal life" (John 4:14). When our hope is in God, and our life is in his care, we are sustained when we otherwise would be devastated. ***Turn to page 843, Lamentations 3.***

other gates, 20and say to all the people: Hear the word of the Lord, kings of Judah and all the people of this nation, and all you citizens of Jerusalem. 21,22The Lord says: Take warning and live; do no unnecessary work on the Sabbath day, but make it a holy day. I gave this commandment to your fathers, 23but they didn't listen or obey. They stubbornly refused to pay attention and be taught.

24But if you obey me, says the Lord, and refuse to work on the Sabbath day and keep it separate, special and holy, 25then this nation shall continue forever. There shall always be descendants of David sitting on the throne here in Jerusalem; there shall always be kings and princes riding in pomp and splendor among the people, and this city shall remain forever. 26And from all around Jerusalem and from the cities of Judah and Benjamin, from the Negeb and from the lowlands west of Judah, the people shall come with their burnt offerings and grain offerings and incense, bringing their sacrifices to praise the Lord in his Temple.

27But if you will not listen to me, if you refuse to keep the Sabbath holy, if on the Sabbath you bring in loads of merchandise through these gates of Jerusalem, just as on other days, then I will set fire to these gates. The fire shall spread to the palaces and utterly destroy them, and no one shall be able to put out the raging flames.

CHAPTER 18

The People Refuse to Listen

Here is another message to Jeremiah from the Lord:

2Go down to the shop where clay pots and jars are made, and I will talk to you there. 3I did as he told me and found the potter working at his wheel. 4But the jar that he was forming didn't turn out as he wished, so he kneaded it into a lump and started again.

5Then the Lord said: 6O Israel, can't I do to you as this potter has done to his clay? As the clay is in the potter's hand, so are you in my hand.7Whenever I announce that a certain nation or kingdom is to be taken up and destroyed, 8then if that nation renounces its evil ways, I will not destroy it as I had planned. 9And if I announce that I will make a certain nation strong and great, 10but then that nation changes its mind, turns to evil, and refuses to obey me, then I, too, will change my mind and not bless that nation as I had said I would.

11Therefore, go and warn all Judah and Jerusalem, saying: Hear the word of the Lord. I am planning evil against you now instead of good; turn back from your evil paths and do what is right.

12But they replied, "Don't waste your breath. We have no intention whatever of doing what God says. We will continue to live as we want to, free from any restraint, full of stubbornness and wickedness!"

13Then the Lord said: Even among the heathen, no one has ever heard of such a thing! My people have done something too horrible to understand. 14The snow never melts high up in the Lebanon mountains. The cold, flowing streams from the crags of Mount Hermon never run dry. 15These can be counted on. But not my people! For they have deserted me and turned to foolish idols. They have turned away from the ancient highways of good and walk the muddy paths of sin. 16Therefore, their land shall become desolate, so that all who pass by will gasp and shake their heads in amazement at its utter desolation. 17I will scatter my people before their enemies as the east wind scatters dust;

17:19-27 We often lose sight of what God intended by the laws he gave us. The people of Judah had forsaken the Sabbath day, not realizing that the day had been set aside for their benefit. God's laws were not given to inconvenience us, but to minister to us and help us be all that God intends us to be. He loves us, and his laws were given because of his love. That is why following God's program is the only way to experience fulfillment and freedom in this life.

18:11-17 God gave the people of Judah the warning they needed to avoid judgment, but they would not respond. They preferred their own sinful ways to God's ways. God's ways are simple; his paths are straight; his burden is light. But we, at times, become stubborn, proud, and arrogant, choosing to do things our own way—a way that leads ultimately to despair and pain.

18:12-15 The people of Judah were aware of their sin and even admitted it openly, yet they proudly refused to change. The only recourse left to God was the destruction of his holy nation and the exile of his people. His love led him to punish his people in hope that they would finally respond with repentance. We are most hopeless when we know we have a problem and admit it to others, yet still continue on the path toward destruction. Admission without change is meaningless. The more we know about ourself, the greater our responsibility to change what we know needs changing.

and in all their trouble I will turn my back on
them and refuse to notice their distress.
18Then the people said, "Come, let's get rid
of Jeremiah. We have our own priests and
wise men and prophets—we don't need his
advice. Let's silence him that he may speak no
more against us, nor bother us again."
19*O Lord, help me! See what they are planning
to do to me!* 20Should they repay evil for good?
They have set a trap to kill me, yet I spoke well
of them to you and tried to defend them from
your anger. 21Now, Lord, let their children
starve to death and let the sword pour out
their blood! Let their wives be widows and be
bereft of all their children! Let their men die
in epidemics and their youths die in battle!
22Let screaming be heard from their homes as
troops of soldiers come suddenly upon them,
for they have dug a pit for me to fall in, and
they have hidden traps along my path. 23Lord,
you know all their murderous plots against
me. Don't forgive them, don't blot out their
sin, but let them perish before you; deal with
them in your anger.

CHAPTER 19

God Will Shatter Jerusalem

The Lord said, Buy a clay jar and take it out
into the valley of Ben-hinnom by the east
gate of the city. Take some of the elders of the
people and some of the older priests with
you, and speak to them whatever words I
give you.
3Then the Lord spoke to them and said:
Listen to the word of the Lord, kings of Judah
and citizens of Jerusalem! The Lord Almighty,
the God of Israel, says, I will bring terrible evil
upon this place, so terrible that the ears of
those who hear it will prickle. 4For Israel has
forsaken me and turned this valley into a
place of shame and wickedness. The people
burn incense to idols—idols that neither this
generation nor their forefathers nor the kings
of Judah have worshiped before—and they
have filled this place with the blood of innocent children. 5They have built high altars to
Baal, and there they burn their sons in sacrifice—a thing I never commanded them nor
even thought of !
6The day is coming, says the Lord, when
this valley shall no longer be called Topheth
or Ben-hinnom Valley, but The Valley of
Slaughter. 7For I will upset the battle plans of
Judah and Jerusalem, and I will let invading
armies kill you here and leave your dead bodies for vultures and wild animals to feed upon.
8And I will wipe Jerusalem off the earth, so

Giving Up Control

BIBLE READING: Jeremiah 18:1-6

We humbly asked him to remove our shortcomings.

Giving up control may be difficult for us. When we get ready for God to remove our shortcomings, we still may want to control how he does it. We are so used to calling the shots that we'll ask for God's help as long as he does it on our terms. We may demand that the changes happen on our timetable, or in the order we feel ready to give them up, or at a speed convenient to us.

God doesn't work that way. That is why humility is such an important part of this step. God told Jeremiah to go to the house of the potter to learn a lesson. Jeremiah said, "I did as he told me and found the potter working at his wheel. But the jar that he was forming didn't turn out as he wished, so he kneaded it into a lump and started again. Then the Lord said: . . . Can't I do to you as this potter has done to his clay? As the clay is in the potter's hand, so are you in my hand" (Jeremiah 18:3-6). God told Isaiah, "Woe to the man who fights with his Creator. Does the pot argue with its maker? Does the clay dispute with him who forms it, saying, 'Stop, you're doing it wrong!' or the pot exclaim, 'How clumsy can you be!'?" (Isaiah 45:9).

When we put our life in God's hands he will reshape it as he sees fit. It is our humility that allows us to accept the fact that he is the Creator. Our new life may be similar to the one we left behind, or entirely different. God is the master craftsman. Whatever he does, we can trust that he will recreate our life beautifully, once we get out of his way! ***Turn to page 1111, Luke 11.***

that everyone going by will gasp with astonishment at all that I have done to her. [9]I will see to it that your enemies lay siege to the city until all food is gone and those trapped inside begin to eat their own children and friends.

[10]And now, Jeremiah, as these men watch, smash the jar you brought with you, [11]and say to them, This is the message to you from the Lord Almighty: As this jar lies shattered, so I will shatter the people of Jerusalem; and as this jar cannot be mended, neither can they. The slaughter shall be so great that there won't be room enough for decent burial anywhere, and their bodies shall be heaped in this valley. [12]And as it will be in this valley, so it will be in Jerusalem. For I will fill Jerusalem with dead bodies too. [13]And I will defile all the homes in Jerusalem, including the palace of the kings of Judah—wherever incense has been burned upon the roofs to your stargods, and libations poured out to them.

[14]As Jeremiah returned from Topheth where he had delivered this message, he stopped in front of the Temple of the Lord and said to all the people, [15]The Lord Almighty, the God of Israel, says: I will bring upon this city and her surrounding towns all the evil I have promised because you have stubbornly refused to listen to the Lord.

CHAPTER 20

Jeremiah Is Arrested

Now when Pashhur (son of Immer), the priest in charge of the Temple of the Lord, heard what Jeremiah was saying, [2]he arrested Jeremiah and had him whipped and put in the stocks at Benjamin Gate near the Temple. [3]He left him there all night.

The next day when Pashhur finally released him, Jeremiah said, "Pashhur, the Lord has changed your name. He says from now on to call you 'The Man Who Lives in Terror.' [4]For the Lord will send terror on you and all your friends, and you will see them die by the swords of their enemies. I will hand over Judah to the king of Babylon, says the Lord, and he shall take away these people as slaves to Babylon and kill them. [5]And I will let your enemies loot Jerusalem. All the famed treasures of the city, with the precious jewels and gold and silver of your kings, shall be carried off to Babylon. [6]And as for you, Pashhur, you and all your family and household shall become slaves in Babylon and die there—you and those to whom you lied when you prophesied that everything would be all right."

[7]O Lord, you deceived me when you promised me your help. I have to give them your messages because you are stronger than I am, but now I am the laughingstock of the city, mocked by all. [8]You have never once let me speak a word of kindness to them; always it is disaster and horror and destruction. No wonder they scoff and mock and make my name a household joke. [9]And I can't quit! For if I say I'll never again mention the Lord—never more speak in his name—then his word in my heart is like fire that burns in my bones, and I can't hold it in any longer. [10]Yet on every side I hear their whispered threats and am afraid. "We will report," they say. Even those who were my friends are watching me, waiting for a fatal slip. "He will trap himself," they say, "and then we will get our revenge on him."

[11]But the Lord stands beside me like a great warrior, and before him, the Mighty, Terrible One, they shall stumble. They cannot defeat me; they shall be shamed and thoroughly humiliated, and they shall have a stigma upon them forever. [12]O Lord Almighty, who knows those who are righteous and examines the deepest thoughts of hearts and minds, let me see your vengeance on them. For I have committed my cause to you. [13]Therefore, I will sing out in thanks to the Lord! Praise him! For he has delivered me, poor and needy, from my oppressors.

[14]Yet, cursed be the day that I was born! [15]Cursed be the man who brought my father the news that a son was born. [16]Let that messenger be destroyed like the cities of old which God overthrew without mercy. Terrify him all day long with battle shouts [17]because

---

19:1-15 It is hard to imagine God's people sacrificing their own children on an altar. For those who had turned away from the true God, turning to Baal and other false gods was the expected step. Then making hideous sacrifices was the next step. One mistake almost always leads to another. When we turn to any resource other than the true God, all kinds of problems and sins creep into our life. False sources of help, such as alcohol or drugs, make us a prisoner to one failure after another. When we bring our pain to God, he will set us free.

20:7-18 The beauty of the prophet's relationship with God lies in the freedom of the exchange. Jeremiah was free to question and to lament, and he was free to praise God for his faithfulness even when hope seemed far away. God longs for such a freedom of exchange with each of us. He longs for open and honest communication.

he did not kill me at my birth! Oh, that I had
died within my mother's womb, that it had
been my grave! 18Why was I ever born? For my
life has been but trouble and sorrow and
shame.

CHAPTER 21

God Refuses the King's Request

Then King Zedekiah sent Pashhur (son of Malchiah) and Zephaniah the priest (son of Maaseiah) to Jeremiah and begged, "Ask the Lord
to help us, for Nebuchadnezzar, king of Babylon, has declared war on us! 2Perhaps the Lord
will be gracious to us and do a mighty miracle
as in olden times and force Nebuchadnezzar
to withdraw his forces."

3,4Jeremiah replied, "Go back to King Zedekiah and tell him the Lord God of Israel says,
I will make all your weapons useless against
the king of Babylon and the Chaldeans besieging you. In fact, I will bring your enemies
right into the heart of this city, 5and I myself
will fight against you, for I am very angry.
6And I will send a terrible plague on this city,
and both men and animals shall die. 7And
finally I will deliver King Zedekiah himself
and all the remnant left in the city into the
hands of King Nebuchadnezzar of Babylon, to
slaughter them without pity or mercy.

8Tell these people, The Lord says: Take your
choice of life or death! 9Stay here in Jerusalem
and die—slaughtered by your enemies, killed
by starvation and disease—or go out and surrender to the Chaldean army and live. 10For I
have set my face against this city; I will be its
enemy and not its friend, says the Lord. It
shall be captured by the king of Babylon and
he shall reduce it to ashes.

11"And to the king of Judah, the Lord says:
12I am ready to judge you because of all the
evil you are doing. Quick! Give justice to these
you judge! Begin doing what is right before
my burning fury flashes out upon you like a
fire no man can quench. 13I will fight against
this city of Jerusalem, that boasts, 'We are
safe; no one can touch us here!' 14And I myself
will destroy you for your sinfulness, says the
Lord. I will light a fire in the forests that will
burn up everything in its path."

CHAPTER 22

Evil Kings to Be Judged

Then the Lord said to me: Go over and speak
directly to the king of Judah and say, 2Listen
to this message from God, O king of Judah,
sitting on David's throne; and let your servants and your people listen too.

3The Lord says: Be fair-minded. Do what is
right! Help those in need of justice! Quit your
evil deeds! Protect the rights of aliens and
immigrants, orphans and widows; stop murdering the innocent! 4If you put an end to all
these terrible deeds you are doing, then I will
deliver this nation and once more give kings
to sit on David's throne, and there shall be
prosperity for all. 5But if you refuse to pay
attention to this warning, I swear by my own
name, says the Lord, that this palace shall
become a shambles.

6For this is the Lord's message concerning
the palace: You are as beloved to me as fruitful
Gilead and the green forests of Lebanon; but
I will destroy you and leave you deserted and
uninhabited. 7I will call for a wrecking crew to
bring out its tools to dismantle you. They will
tear out all of your fine cedar beams and
throw them on the fire. 8Men from many
nations will pass by the ruins of this city and

20:14-18 In our moments of greatest despair, we wish we were dead and regret we were ever born. Knowing that God's power can restore us may help us cling to our life at this point. We can take solace in knowing that others, including Jeremiah, have felt the way we do. Despite our feelings of loss and despair, the reality is that God does love us. He is with us, even when we cannot feel his presence.

21:1-14 There comes a time when it is too late to avoid the painful consequences of our actions. As Nebuchadnezzar bore down on Jerusalem, King Zedekiah wanted the persecuted prophet to petition God for help. God responded by telling his people that it was too late. Since they had failed to respond to God's numerous warnings through his prophets, they would have to endure incredible devastation. We would be wise to listen to the warnings we receive, before it's too late.

22:1-30 All of us are responsible for our own actions, but leaders and teachers are held to even greater degrees of responsibility. In this chapter, Jeremiah confronted the leaders of Judah for their sins. He called the kings to rule as David had ruled, but they refused. Instead, they encouraged their people to turn to idols. As a result, the entire nation suffered destruction. We are all leaders in some context. What do we teach our children, employees, or students by our words and actions? What we do and say does affect others, whether we like it or not. We need to take responsibility for the sin and suffering we have passed on to others, whether intentionally or by mistake, and make amends the best we can.

say to one another, "Why did the Lord do it?
Why did he destroy such a great city?" [9]And
the answer will be, "Because the people living
here forgot the Lord their God and violated
his agreement with them, for they worshiped
idols."

[10]Don't weep for the dead! Instead weep for
the captives led away! For they will never
return to see their native land again. [11]For the
Lord says this about Jehoahaz who succeeded
his father King Josiah and was taken away as
a captive: [12]He shall die in a distant land and
never again see his own country.

[13]And woe to you, King Jehoiakim, for you
are building your great palace with forced
labor. By not paying wages you are building
injustice into its walls and oppression into its
doorframes and ceilings. [14]You say, "I will
build a magnificent palace with huge rooms
and many windows, paneled throughout
with fragrant cedar and painted a lovely red."
[15]But a beautiful palace does not make a great
king! Why did your father Josiah reign so
long? Because he was just and fair in all his
dealings. That is why God blessed him. [16]He
saw to it that justice and help were given the
poor and the needy and all went well for him.
This is how a man lives close to God. [17]But
you! You are full of selfish greed and all dishonesty! You murder the innocent, oppress
the poor, and reign with ruthlessness.

[18]Therefore this is God's decree of punishment against King Jehoiakim, who succeeded
his father Josiah on the throne: His family will
not weep for him when he dies. His subjects
will not even care that he is dead. [19]He shall
be buried like a dead donkey—dragged out of
Jerusalem and thrown on the garbage dump
beyond the gate! [20]Weep, for your allies are
gone. Search for them in Lebanon; shout for
them at Bashan; seek them at the fording
points of Jordan. See, they are all destroyed.
Not one is left to help you! [21]When you were
prosperous I warned you, but you replied,
"Don't bother me." Since childhood you have
been that way—you just won't listen! [22]And
now all your allies have disappeared with a
puff of wind; all your friends are taken off as
slaves. Surely at last you will see your wickedness and be ashamed. [23]It's very nice to live
graciously in a beautiful palace among the
cedars of Lebanon, but soon you will cry and
groan in anguish—anguish as of a woman in
labor.

[24,25]And as for you, Coniah, son of Jehoiakim king of Judah—even if you were the signet ring on my right hand, I would pull you
off and give you to those who seek to kill you,
of whom you are so desperately afraid—to
Nebuchadnezzar, king of Babylon, and his
mighty army. [26]I will throw you and your
mother out of this country, and you shall die
in a foreign land. [27]You will never again return
to the land of your desire. [28]This man Coniah
is like a discarded, broken dish. He and his
children will be exiled to distant lands.

[29]O earth, earth, earth! Hear the word of the
Lord! [30]The Lord says: Record this man Coniah as childless, for none of his children
shall ever sit upon the throne of David or rule
in Judah. His life will amount to nothing.

CHAPTER 23

A Righteous King Will Come

The Lord declares:

I will send disaster upon the leaders of my
people—the shepherds of my sheep—for they
have destroyed and scattered the very ones
they were to care for. [2]Instead of leading my
flock to safety, you have deserted them and
driven them to destruction. And now I will
pour out judgment upon you for the evil you
have done to them. [3]And I will gather together the remnant of my flock from wherever I have sent them and bring them back
into their own fold, and they shall be fruitful

22:8-9 Sometimes we look at the destruction in our life or someone else's life and ask, Why did God do it? Such destruction is never God's fault. Sometimes our suffering is brought on by someone else's sin. Quite often, however, our suffering comes as a result of our own failures. Our destruction is masterminded by our own decisions and actions. God creates; we destroy through our rebellion, then we blame him for the results. It is important to our recovery that we accept responsibility for what we have done to ourself and avoid blaming God or someone else for problems resulting from our own choices.

22:21 When the people of Judah were prospering, they didn't think they needed God and refused to listen to his warnings. When our recovery is progressing rapidly, we may be in great danger of a relapse. As we experience success, we begin to grow confident in our own ability to stand up to our dependencies. We forget the first all-important step: "We admitted we were powerless over our dependencies. . . ." We need to be continually reminded that our addictions are too strong for us to handle alone. We need God to help us—even when things are going well! Those who deal with reality best plan for hard times when times are good.

and increase. [4]And I will appoint responsible shepherds to care for them, and they shall not need to be afraid again; all of them shall be accounted for continually.

[5,6]For the time is coming, says the Lord, when I will place a righteous Branch upon King David's throne. He shall be a King who shall rule with wisdom and justice and cause righteousness to prevail everywhere throughout the earth. And this is his name: *The Lord Our Righteousness.* At that time Judah will be saved and Israel will live in peace.

[7]In that day people will no longer say when taking an oath, "As the Lord lives who rescued the people of Israel from the land of Egypt," [8]but they will say, "As the Lord lives who brought the Jews back to their own land of Israel from the countries to which he had exiled them."

Warnings about False Prophets

[9]My heart is broken for the false prophets, full of deceit. I awake with fear and stagger as a drunkard does from wine because of the awful fate awaiting them, for God has decreed holy words of judgment against them. [10]For the land is full of adultery, and the curse of God is on it. The land itself is mourning—the pastures are dried up—for the prophets do evil, and their power is used wrongly.

[11]The priests are like the prophets, all ungodly, wicked men. I have seen their despicable acts right here in my own Temple, says the Lord. [12]Therefore, their paths will be dark and slippery; they will be chased down dark and treacherous trails and fall. For I will bring evil upon them and see to it, when their time has come, that they pay their penalty in full for all their sins.

[13]I knew the prophets of Samaria were unbelievably evil, for they prophesied by Baal and led my people Israel into sin; [14]but the prophets of Jerusalem are even worse! The things they do are horrible; they commit adultery and love dishonesty. They encourage and compliment those who are doing evil instead of turning them back from their sins. These prophets are as thoroughly depraved as the men of Sodom and Gomorrah were.

[15]Therefore the Lord Almighty says: I will feed them with bitterness and give them poison to drink. For it is because of them that wickedness fills this land. [16]This is my warning to my people, says the Lord Almighty. Don't listen to these false prophets when they prophesy to you, filling you with futile hopes. They are making up everything they say. They do not speak for me! [17]They keep saying to these rebels who despise me, "Don't worry! All is well"; and to those who live the way they want to, "The Lord has said you shall have peace!"

[18]But can you name even one of these prophets who lives close enough to God to hear what he is saying? Has even one of them cared enough to listen? [19]See, the Lord is sending a furious whirlwind to sweep away these wicked men. [20]The terrible anger of the Lord will not abate until it has carried out the full penalty he decrees against them. Later, when Jerusalem has fallen, you will see what I mean.

[21]I have not sent these prophets, yet they claim to speak for me; I gave them no mes-

---

23:1-4 Shepherds who were supposed to care for God's people had scattered and forsaken them. Since Judah's leaders had only led God's people astray, God himself promised to guide his people back to pasture. He vowed to place them in the care of shepherds who would love and tend them. Jesus is our Good Shepherd, loving us and tending us as his flock (see John 10:1-18). If we are willing to seek out and follow his will for our life, there is hope for us, no matter how far we may have strayed.

23:5-8 The people of Judah faced a future filled with suffering, but Jeremiah gave them hope that after the destruction there would be a time of rebuilding. Even in the darkest times, when judgment seems most severe, God reminds us that a better day is coming. How sweet these promises must have sounded to the weary prophet! As we face suffering in our own life, we can know that God desires to restore us and give us a hopeful future. Perhaps our suffering will even help us admit our powerlessness and lead us to turn to God for help—the first steps in our recovery.

23:21-22 The people of Judah still hoped they would escape destruction, and the false prophets supported their hope with false predictions of deliverance. This allowed the people to continue in their sin with no thought to the consequences. Jeremiah, however, called the people to deal with reality. He demanded that they face the truth of their sin and warned them of the inevitable consequences. This, of course, upset the people, who rejected his message. Jeremiah spoke for God and was rejected by the people. The false prophets spoke for the people and were accepted by them. The answer to a simple question will often help us determine whether or not a prophet speaks for God: "What is the prophet or leader getting out of his ministry?" If someone is getting rich, powerful, or famous, we have good grounds for at least questioning his or her legitimacy.

sage, yet they say their words are mine. [22]If they were mine, they would try to turn my people from their evil ways. [23]Am I a God who is only in one place and cannot see what they are doing? [24]Can anyone hide from me? Am I not everywhere in all of heaven and earth?

[25]"Listen to the dream I had from God last night," they say. And then they proceed to lie in my name. [26]How long will this continue? If they are "prophets," they are prophets of deceit, inventing everything they say. [27]By telling these false dreams they are trying to get my people to forget me in the same way as their fathers did, who turned away to the idols of Baal. [28]Let these false prophets tell their dreams and let my true messengers faithfully proclaim my every word. There is a difference between chaff and wheat! [29]Does not my word burn like fire? asks the Lord. Is it not like a mighty hammer that smashed the rock to pieces? [30,31]So I stand against these "prophets" who get their messages from each other—these smooth-tongued prophets who say, "This message is from God!" [32]Their made-up dreams are flagrant lies that lead my people into sin. I did not send them, and they have no message at all for my people, says the Lord.

[33]When one of the people or one of their "prophets" or priests asks you, "Well, Jeremiah, what is the sad news from the Lord today?" you shall reply, "What sad news? You are the sad news, for the Lord has cast you away!" [34]And as for the false prophets and priests and people who joke about "today's sad news from God," I will punish them and their families for saying this. [35]You can ask each other, "What is God's message? What is he saying?" [36]But stop using this term, "God's sad news." For what is sad is you and your lying. You are twisting my words and inventing "messages from God" that I didn't speak. [37]You may respectfully ask Jeremiah, "What is the Lord's message? What has he said to you?" [38,39]But if you ask him about "today's sad news from God," when I have warned you not to mock like that, then I, the Lord God, will unburden myself of the burden you are to me. I will cast you out of my presence, you and this city I gave to you and your fathers. [40] And I will bring reproach upon you and your name shall be infamous through the ages.

CHAPTER 24

Vision of the Figs

After Nebuchadnezzar, king of Babylon, had captured and enslaved Jeconiah (son of Jehoiakim), king of Judah, and exiled him to Babylon along with the princes of Judah and the skilled tradesmen—the carpenters and blacksmiths—the Lord gave me this vision. [2]I saw two baskets of figs placed in front of the Temple in Jerusalem. In one basket there were fresh, just-ripened figs, but in the other the figs were spoiled and moldy—too rotten to eat. [3]Then the Lord said to me, "What do you see, Jeremiah?"

I replied, "Figs, some very good and some very bad."

[4,5]Then the Lord said: "The good figs represent the exiles sent to Babylon. I have done it for their good. [6]I will see that they are well treated, and I will bring them back here again. I will help them and not hurt them; I will plant them and not pull them up. [7]I will give them hearts that respond to me. They shall be my people and I will be their God, for they shall return to me with great joy.

[8]"But the rotten figs represent Zedekiah, king of Judah, his officials, and all the others of Jerusalem left here in this land; those too who live in Egypt. I will treat them like spoiled figs, too bad to use. [9]I will make them repulsive to every nation of the earth, and they shall be mocked and taunted and cursed wherever I compel them to go. [10]And I will send massacre and famine and disease among them until they are destroyed from the land of Israel, which I gave to them and to their fathers."

CHAPTER 25

Jeremiah Predicts Captivity

This message for all the people of Judah came from the Lord to Jeremiah during the fourth year of the reign of King Jehoiakim of Judah

---

24:1-10 Jeremiah was given another illustration to help us understand the fate of the Jews taken into captivity. The exiles who followed God would be like good figs, full of nourishment. They would be well treated in exile and would be allowed to return to their homeland. King Zedekiah and those who had led the people falsely would be like bad figs, tasteless and fit only for destruction. God made it clear that the Exile was intended to bring healing to his shattered and sin-scarred people. Our suffering works the same way. If it leads us to admit our failures and follow God's will for our life, we will be blessed by God and experience both physical and spiritual recovery.

(son of Josiah). This was the year Nebuchadnezzar, king of Babylon, began his reign.

[2,3]For the past twenty-three years, Jeremiah said, from the thirteenth year of the reign of Josiah (son of Amon) king of Judah, until now, God has been sending me his messages. I have faithfully passed them on to you, but you haven't listened. [4]Again and again down through the years, God has sent you his prophets, but you have refused to hear. [5]Each time the message was this: Turn from the evil road you are traveling and from the evil things you are doing. Only then can you continue to live here in this land which the Lord gave to you and to your ancestors forever. [6]*Don't anger me by worshiping idols; but if you are true to me, then I'll not harm you.* [7]But you won't listen; you have gone ahead and made me furious with your idols. So you have brought upon yourselves all the evil that has come your way.

[8,9]And now the Lord God says, Because you have not listened to me, I will gather together all the armies of the north under Nebuchadnezzar, king of Babylon (I have appointed him as my deputy), and I will bring them all against this land and its people and against the other nations near you, and I will utterly destroy you and make you a byword of contempt forever. [10]I will take away your joy, your gladness, and your wedding feasts; your businesses shall fail, and all your homes shall lie in silent darkness. [11]This entire land shall become a desolate wasteland; all the world will be shocked at the disaster that befalls you. Israel and her neighboring lands shall serve the king of Babylon for seventy years.

[12]Then, after these years of slavery are ended, I will punish the king of Babylon and his people for their sins; I will make the land of Chaldea an everlasting waste. [13]I will bring upon them all the terrors I have promised in this book—all the penalties announced by Jeremiah against the nations. [14]For many nations and great kings shall enslave the Chaldeans, just as they enslaved my people; I will punish them in proportion to their treatment of my people.

A Whirlwind of Anger

[15]For the Lord God said to me: "Take from my hand this wine cup filled to the brim with my fury, and make all the nations to whom I send you drink from it. [16]They shall drink from it and reel, crazed by the death blows I rain upon them."

[17]So I took the cup of fury from the Lord and made all the nations drink from it—every nation God had sent me to; [18]I went to Jerusalem and to the cities of Judah, and their kings and princes drank of the cup so that from that day until this they have been desolate, hated and cursed, just as they are today. [19,20]I went to Egypt, and Pharaoh, his servants, the princes, and the people—they too drank from that terrible cup, along with all the foreign population living in his land. So did all the kings of the land of Uz and the kings of the Philistine cities: Ashkelon, Gaza, Ekron, and what remains of Ashdod, [21]and I visited the nations of Edom, Moab, and Ammon; [22]and all the kings of Tyre and Sidon, and the kings of the regions across the sea; [23]Dedan, Tema, and Buz, and the other heathen there; [24]and all the kings of Arabia and of the nomadic tribes of the desert; [25]and all the kings of Zimri, Elam, and Media; [26]and all the kings of the northern countries, far and near, one after the other; and all the kingdoms of the world. And finally, the king of Babylon himself drank from this cup of God's wrath.

[27]Tell them, "The Lord of heaven's armies, the God of Israel, says, Drink from this cup of my wrath until you are drunk and vomit and fall to rise no more, for I am sending terrible wars upon you." [28]And if they refuse to accept the cup, tell them, "The Lord of heaven's armies says you *must* drink it! You cannot escape! [29]I have begun to punish my own

---

25:1-14 How impatient we become when the consequences of our failures last for days or weeks, much less years. The Israelites served Nebuchadnezzar for seventy years! Many of them finally learned to honor God in the midst of captivity. Since their return from Babylonian captivity, the Jews have never been known to fall into the sin of physical idolatry. It is important to face the consequences of our behavior. One way we can honor God is to accept his discipline and build upon the lessons learned from the sorrow.

25:15-38 Sometimes when we are doing our best to serve God, we notice that God allows people to prosper who care nothing about him or his ways. In these verses, we are reminded that God will make all things right in his time. Sometimes God uses the ungodly for his own purposes; at other times he seems to allow the ungodly to thrive for a time; but the end result is clear. All people and all nations are subject to God, and he rewards those who earnestly seek him (see Hebrews 11:6).

people, so should you go free? No, you shall not evade punishment. I will call for war against all the peoples of the earth."

30 Therefore prophesy against them. Tell them the Lord will shout against his own from his holy temple in heaven and against all those living on the earth. He will shout as the harvesters do who tread the juice from the grapes. 31 That cry of judgment will reach the farthest ends of the earth, for the Lord has a case against all the nations—all mankind. He will slaughter all the wicked. 32 See, declares the Lord Almighty, the punishment shall go from nation to nation—a great whirlwind of wrath shall rise against the farthest corners of the earth. 33 On that day those the Lord has slain shall fill the earth from one end to the other. No one shall mourn for them nor gather up the bodies to bury them; they shall fertilize the earth.

34 Weep and moan, O evil shepherds; let the leaders of mankind beat their heads upon the stones, for their time has come to be slaughtered and scattered; they shall fall like fragile women. 35 And you will find no place to hide, no way to escape.

36 Listen to the frantic cries of the shepherds and to the leaders shouting in despair, for the Lord has spoiled their pastures. 37 People now living undisturbed will be cut down by the fierceness of the anger of the Lord. 38 He has left his lair like a lion seeking prey; their land has been laid waste by warring armies—because of the fierce anger of the Lord.

CHAPTER 26

Jeremiah Escapes Death

This message came to Jeremiah from the Lord during the first year of the reign of Jehoiakim (son of Josiah), king of Judah:

2 Stand out in front of the Temple of the Lord and make an announcement to all the people who have come there to worship from many parts of Judah. Give them the entire message; don't leave out one word of all I have for them to hear. 3 For perhaps they will listen and turn from their evil ways, and then I can withhold all the punishment I am ready to pour out upon them because of their evil deeds. 4 Tell them the Lord says: If you will not listen to me and obey the laws I have given you, 5 and if you will not listen to my servants, the prophets—for I sent them again and again to warn you, but you would not listen to them— 6 then I will destroy this Temple as I destroyed the Tabernacle at Shiloh, and I will make Jerusalem a curse word in every nation of the earth.

7,8 When Jeremiah had finished his message, saying everything the Lord had told him to, the priests and false prophets and all the people in the Temple mobbed him, shouting, "Kill him! Kill him! 9 What right do you have to say the Lord will destroy this Temple like the one at Shiloh?" they yelled. "What do you mean—Jerusalem destroyed and not one survivor?"

10 When the high officials of Judah heard what was going on, they rushed over from the palace and sat down at the door of the Temple to hold court. 11 Then the priests and the false prophets presented their accusations to the officials and the people. "This man should die!" they said. "You have heard with your own ears what a traitor he is, for he has prophesied against this city."

12 Then Jeremiah spoke in his defense. "The Lord sent me," he said, "to prophesy against this Temple and this city. He gave me every word of all that I have spoken. 13 But if you stop your sinning and begin obeying the Lord your God, he will cancel all the punishment he has announced against you. 14 As for me, I am helpless and in your power—do with me as you think best. 15 But there is one thing sure, if you kill me, you will be killing an innocent

---

26:1-24 Without question, it is most difficult to serve God when others mock, question, or entice us to doubt. The rulers of Judah tried nearly everything to silence Jeremiah, and finally they threatened him with physical death. Though threats can discourage, sometimes they only fuel the fire of our commitment (see Philippians 1:12-14). As we experience God's power in our recovery, we need to share the good news. Some people might laugh at us; others may oppose us. But we should not allow this to stop us. God's deliverance is available to all who entrust their lives to his loving direction.

26:12-15 Because of Jeremiah's faith, he was able to speak boldly for God, even when his life was threatened. Sometimes we, like Peter, deny that we know God when we face opposition. Anyone can claim to have faith when everything is going well. The depth of our faith is measured when we are under pressure. We should never allow the opinions of others to keep us from sharing what we know about God and his power to deliver us from the bondage of our dependencies. Someone else's life and our own recovery may rest on it!

man, and the responsibility will lie upon you and upon this city and upon every person living in it; for it is absolutely true that the Lord sent me to speak every word that you have heard from me."

[16]Then the officials and people said to the priests and false prophets, "This man does not deserve the death sentence, for he has spoken to us in the name of the Lord our God."

[17]Then some of the wise old men stood and spoke to all the people standing around and said:

[18]"The decision is right; for back in the days when Micah the Morasthite prophesied in the days of King Hezekiah of Judah, he told the people that God said: 'This hill shall be plowed like an open field and this city of Jerusalem razed into heaps of stone, and a forest shall grow at the top where the great Temple now stands!' [19]But did King Hezekiah and the people kill him for saying this? No, they turned from their wickedness and worshiped the Lord and begged the Lord to have mercy upon them; and the Lord held back the terrible punishment he had pronounced against them. If we kill Jeremiah for giving us the messages of God, who knows what God will do to us!"

[20]Another true prophet of the Lord, Uriah (son of Shemaiah) from Kiriath-jearim, was also denouncing the city and the nation at the same time as Jeremiah was. [21]But when King Jehoiakim and the army officers and officials heard what he was saying, the king sent to kill him. Uriah heard about it and fled to Egypt. [22]Then King Jehoiakim sent Elnathan (son of Achbor) to Egypt along with several other men to capture Uriah. [23]They took him prisoner and brought him back to King Jehoiakim, who butchered him with a sword and had him buried in an unmarked grave.

[24]But Ahikam (son of Shaphan), the royal secretary, stood with Jeremiah and persuaded the court not to turn him over to the mob to kill him.

CHAPTER 27

The People Will Be Enslaved

This message came to Jeremiah from the Lord at the beginning of the reign of Jehoiakim (son of Josiah), king of Judah:

[2]Make a yoke and fasten it on your neck with leather thongs as you would strap a yoke on a plow-ox. [3]Then send messages to the kings of Edom, Moab, Ammon, Tyre, and Sidon, through their ambassadors in Jerusalem, [4]saying, Tell your masters that the Lord, the God of Israel, sends you this message:

[5]"By my great power I have made the earth and all mankind and every animal; and I give these things of mine to anyone I want to. [6]So now I have given all your countries to King Nebuchadnezzar of Babylon, who is my deputy. And I have handed over to him all your cattle for his use. [7]All the nations shall serve him and his son and his grandson until his time is up, and then many nations and great kings shall conquer Babylon and make him their slave. [8]Submit to him and serve him—put your neck under Babylon's yoke! I will punish any nation refusing to be his slave; I will send war, famine, and disease upon that nation until he has conquered it.

[9]"Do not listen to your false prophets, fortune-tellers, dreamers, mediums, and magicians who say the king of Babylon will not enslave you. [10]For they are all liars, and if you follow their advice and refuse to submit to the king of Babylon, I will drive you out of your land and send you far away to perish. [11]But the people of any nation submitting to the king of Babylon will be permitted to stay in their own country and farm the land as usual."

[12]Jeremiah repeated all these prophecies to

27:1-15 Sometimes God uses the unrighteous to achieve his righteous ends. Nebuchadnezzar is not the kind of king God would normally honor, yet God would use him to discipline his wayward people and lead them to repentance. God had the good of his people in mind, and he saw that his will for them was carried out. When we suffer at the hands of people who care nothing for God, we should know that God is with us through our trials. And if we are listening, we may learn some important things about ourself and our loving God during the process.

27:16-22 The people of Judah chose to listen to the pleasant messages of the false prophets, but this only blinded them to their sin and its inevitable consequences. All of us are impressionable, and even more so when we are young or going through difficult times. It is important that we build our life on a foundation of truth rather than on convenient or pleasant messages. God calls us to do some unpleasant things. He requires that we take an honest look at our life, admit our sin, and humbly seek to make amends with those we have hurt. Recovery is never easy; it is always painful. We would be wise to face the truth. The road of pleasant experiences will only lead to denial and destruction.

Zedekiah, king of Judah. “If you want to live, submit to the king of Babylon,” he said. 13“Why do you insist on dying—you and your people? Why should you choose war and famine and disease, which the Lord has promised to every nation that will not submit to Babylon’s king? 14Don’t listen to the false prophets who keep telling you the king of Babylon will not conquer you, for they are liars. 15I have not sent them, says the Lord, and they are telling you lies in my name. If you insist on heeding them, I must drive you from this land to die—you and all these ‘prophets’ too.”

16I spoke again and again to the priests and all the people and told them: “The Lord says, Don’t listen to your prophets who are telling you that soon the gold dishes taken from the Temple will be returned from Babylon. It is all a lie. 17Don’t listen to them. Surrender to the king of Babylon and live, for otherwise this whole city will be destroyed. 18If they are really God’s prophets, then let them pray to the Lord Almighty that the gold dishes still here in the Temple, left from before; and that those in the palace of the king of Judah and in the palaces in Jerusalem will not be carried away with you to Babylon!

19-21“For the Lord Almighty says, The pillars of bronze standing before the Temple, the great bronze basin in the Temple court, the metal stands, and all the other ceremonial articles left here by Nebuchadnezzar, king of Babylon, when he exiled all the important people of Judah and Jerusalem to Babylon, along with Jeconiah (son of Jehoiakim), king of Judah, 22will all yet be carried away to Babylon and will stay there until I send for them. Then I will bring them all back to Jerusalem again.”

CHAPTER 28

A False Prophet

On a December day in that same year—the fourth year of the reign of Zedekiah, king of Judah—Hananiah (son of Azzur), a false prophet from Gibeon, addressed me publicly in the Temple while all the priests and people listened. He said:

2“The Lord of Hosts, the God of Israel, declares: I have removed the yoke of the king of Babylon from your necks. 3Within two years I will bring back all the Temple treasures that Nebuchadnezzar carried off to Babylon, 4and I will bring back King Jeconiah, son of Jehoiakim, king of Judah, and all the other captives exiled to Babylon, says the Lord. I will surely remove the yoke put on your necks by the king of Babylon.”

5Then Jeremiah said to Hananiah, in front of all the priests and people, 6“Amen! May your prophecies come true! I hope the Lord will do everything you say and bring back from Babylon the treasures of this Temple, with all our loved ones. 7But listen now to the solemn words I speak to you in the presence of all these people. 8The ancient prophets who preceded you and me spoke against many nations, always warning of *war, famine,* and *plague.* 9So a prophet who foretells *peace* has the burden of proof on him to prove that God has really sent him. Only when his message comes true can it be known that he really is from God.”

10Then Hananiah, the false prophet, took the yoke off Jeremiah’s neck and broke it. 11And Hananiah said again to the crowd that had gathered, “The Lord has promised that within two years he will release all the nations now in slavery to King Nebuchadnezzar of Babylon.” At that point Jeremiah walked out.

12Soon afterwards the Lord gave this message to Jeremiah: 13Go and tell Hananiah that the Lord says, You have broken a wooden yoke, but these people have yokes of iron on their necks. 14The Lord, the God of Israel, says: I have put a yoke of iron on the necks of all these nations, forcing them into slavery to Nebuchadnezzar, king of Babylon. And nothing will change this decree, for I have even given him all your flocks and herds.

15Then Jeremiah said to Hananiah, the false prophet, “Listen, Hananiah, the Lord has not sent you, and the people are believing your lies. 16Therefore the Lord says you must die. This very year your life will end because you have rebelled against the Lord.”

17And sure enough, two months later Hananiah died.

CHAPTER 29

Warnings about False Prophets

After Jeconiah the king, the queen-mother, the court officials, the tribal officers, and craftsmen had been deported to Babylon by Nebuchadnezzar, Jeremiah wrote them a letter from Jerusalem, addressing it to the Jewish elders, priests, prophets, and to all the people. 3He sent the letter with Elasah (son of Shaphan) and Gemariah (son of Hilkiah) when they went to Babylon as King Zedekiah’s ambassadors to Nebuchadnezzar. And this is what the letter said:

4The Lord Almighty, the God of Israel,

sends this message to all the captives he has exiled to Babylon from Jerusalem:

5Build homes and plan to stay; plant vineyards, for you will be there many years. 6Marry and have children, and then find mates for them and have many grandchildren. Multiply! Don't dwindle away! 7And work for the peace and prosperity of Babylon. Pray for her, for if Babylon has peace, so will you.

8The Lord Almighty, the God of Israel, says: Don't let the false prophets and mediums who are there among you fool you. Don't listen to the dreams that they invent, 9for they prophesy lies in my name. I have not sent them, says the Lord. 10The truth is this: You will be in Babylon for seventy years. But then I will come and do for you all the good things I have promised and bring you home again. 11For I know the plans I have for you, says the Lord. They are plans for good and not for evil, to give you a future and a hope. 12In those days when you pray, I will listen. 13You will find me when you seek me, if you look for me in earnest.

14Yes, says the Lord, I will be found by you, and I will end your slavery and restore your fortunes; I will gather you out of the nations where I sent you and bring you back home again to your own land.

15But now, because you accept the false prophets among you and say the Lord has sent them, 16,17I will send war, famine, and plague upon the people left here in Jerusalem—on your relatives who were not exiled to Babylon, and on the king who sits on David's throne—and make them like rotting figs, too bad to eat. 18And I will scatter them around the world. And in every nation where I place them they will be cursed and hissed and mocked, 19for they refuse to listen to me though I spoke to them again and again through my prophets.

20Therefore listen to the word of God, all you Jewish captives over there in Babylon. 21The Lord Almighty, the God of Israel, says this about your false prophets, Ahab (son of Kolaiah) and Zedekiah (son of Maaseiah), who are declaring lies to you in my name: Look, I am turning them over to Nebuchadnezzar to execute publicly. 22Their fate shall become proverbial of all evil, so that whenever anyone wants to curse someone he will say, "The Lord make you like Zedekiah and Ahab whom the king of Babylon burned alive!" 23For these men have done a terrible thing among my people. They have committed adultery with their neighbors' wives and have lied in my name. I know, for I have seen everything they do, says the Lord.

24And say this to Shemaiah the dreamer: 25The Lord, the God of Israel, says: You have written a letter to Zephaniah (son of Maaseiah) the priest, and sent copies to all the other priests and to everyone in Jerusalem. 26And in this letter you have said to Zephaniah, "The Lord has appointed you to replace Jehoiada as priest in Jerusalem. And it is your responsibility to arrest any madman who claims to be a prophet and to put him in the stocks and collar. 27Why haven't you done something about this false prophet Jeremiah of Anathoth? 28For he has written to us here in Babylon saying that our captivity will be long; that we should build permanent homes and plan to stay many years; that we should plant fruit trees, for we will be here to eat the fruit from them for a long time to come."

29Zephaniah took the letter over to Jeremiah and read it to him! 30Then the Lord gave this message to Jeremiah:

31Send an open letter to all the exiles in Babylon and tell them this: The Lord says that because Shemaiah the Nehelamite has "prophesied" to you when I didn't send him and has fooled you into believing his lies, 32I will punish him and his family. None of his descendants shall see the good I have waiting for my people, for he has taught you to rebel against the Lord.

CHAPTER 30

Restoration Will Follow Exile

This is another of the Lord's messages to Jeremiah:

2The Lord God of Israel says, Write down for the record all that I have said to you. 3For the time is coming when I will restore the

29:11 What comfort this verse offers! In our moments of despair, we must remember that God has a plan for us, and we can be sure that it is designed for our blessing. Our challenge is to act on that knowledge. In recovery, we are to pray for knowledge of God's will and the power to carry it out. We can be sure that our recovery is an important part of God's will for us. We can begin the process by recognizing how helpless we are against our dependencies and entrusting our life into God's powerful yet loving hands. God has a special place for us in his overall plan. Realizing this gives us hope for the future.

fortunes of my people, Israel and Judah, and I will bring them home to this land that I gave to their fathers; they shall possess it and live here again.

[4]And write this also concerning Israel and Judah:

[5]"Where shall we find peace?" they cry. "There is only fear and trembling. [6]Do men give birth? Then why do they stand there, ashen-faced, hands pressed against their sides like women in labor?"

[7]Alas, in all history when has there ever been a time of terror such as in that coming day? It is a time of trouble for my people—for Jacob—such as they have never known before. Yet God will rescue them! [8]For on that day, says the Lord Almighty, I will break the yoke from their necks and snap their chains, and foreigners shall no longer be their masters! [9]For they shall serve the Lord their God, and David their King, whom I will raise up for them, says the Lord.

[10]So don't be afraid, O Jacob my servant; don't be dismayed, O Israel; for I will bring you home again from distant lands, and your children from their exile. They shall have rest and quiet in their own land, and no one shall make them afraid. [11]For I am with you and I will save you, says the Lord. Even if I utterly destroy the nations where I scatter you, I will not exterminate you; I will punish you, yes—you will not go unpunished.

[12]For your sin is an incurable bruise, a terrible wound. [13]There is no one to help you or to bind up your wound, and no medicine does any good. [14]All your lovers have left you and don't care anything about you any more; for I have wounded you cruelly, as though I were your enemy; mercilessly, as though I were an implacable foe; for your sins are so many, your guilt is so great.

[15]Why do you protest your punishment? Your sin is so scandalous that your sorrow should never end! It is because your guilt is great that I have had to punish you so much.

[16]But in that coming day, all who are destroying you shall be destroyed, and all your enemies shall be slaves. Those who rob you shall be robbed; and those attacking you shall be attacked. [17]I will give you back your health again and heal your wounds. Now you are called "The Outcast" and "Jerusalem, the Place Nobody Wants."

[18]But, says the Lord, when I bring you home again from your captivity and restore your fortunes, Jerusalem will be rebuilt upon her ruins; the palace will be reconstructed as it was before. [19]The cities will be filled with joy and great thanksgiving, and I will multiply my people and make of them a great and honored nation. [20]Their children shall prosper as in David's reign; their nations shall be established before me, and I will punish anyone who hurts them. [21]They will have their own ruler again. He will not be a foreigner. And I will invite him to be a priest at my altars, and he shall approach me, for who would dare to come unless invited. [22]And you shall be my people, and I will be your God.

[23]Suddenly the devastating whirlwind of the Lord roars with fury; it shall burst upon the heads of the wicked. [24]The Lord will not call off the fierceness of his wrath until it has finished all the terrible destruction he has planned. Later on you will understand what I am telling you.

CHAPTER 31

God Will Rebuild His Land

At that time, says the Lord, all the families of Israel shall recognize me as the Lord; they shall act like my people. [2]I will care for them as I did those who escaped from Egypt, to whom I showed my mercies in the wilderness, when Israel sought for rest. [3]For long ago the Lord had said to Israel: I have loved you, O my people, with an everlasting love; with loving-

30:1-24 The people of Judah hungered for God's judgment to end, just as every child eagerly awaits the end of discipline. Before his wrath was fully upon them, God told his people that they would be renewed and restored. Such a promise unveils the unfailing love God has for us. His punishment is real, but it is motivated by a desire for healing and true restoration. Just like the people of Judah, we often resist God's will for us until we discover that doing things our own way leads to destruction. We can be sure that if we repent and follow God's will for our life, he will use our punishment as a significant step in our recovery.

31:1-40 Here God paints a joyful picture of recovery, with all the details of repentance, sorrow, forgiveness, laughter, restoration, and hope. Once again God's people would follow his plan for them, and he would receive their worship and praise. We can experience this kind of restoration, too. We start the process by admitting our need for God's healing power in our life. God desires to rebuild his relationship with us, no matter how far we may have strayed from him. He delights in finding new ways to exhibit his love to those who belong to him.

kindness I have drawn you to me. [4]I will rebuild your nation, O virgin of Israel. You will again be happy and dance merrily with the timbrels. [5]Again you will plant your vineyards upon the mountains of Samaria and eat from your own gardens there.

[6]The day shall come when watchmen on the hills of Ephraim will call out and say, Arise, and let us go up to Zion to the Lord our God." [7]For the Lord says, Sing with joy for all that I will do for Israel, the greatest of the nations! Shout out with praise and joy: "The Lord has saved his people, the remnant of Israel." [8]For I will bring them from the north and from earth's farthest ends, not forgetting their blind and lame, young mothers with their little ones, those ready to give birth. It will be a great company who comes. [9]Tears of joy shall stream down their faces, and I will lead them home with great care. They shall walk beside the quiet streams and not stumble. For I am a Father to Israel, and Ephraim is my oldest child.

[10]Listen to this message from the Lord, you nations of the world, and publish it abroad: The Lord who scattered his people will gather them back together again and watch over them as a shepherd does his flock. [11]He will save Israel from those who are too strong for them! [12]They shall come home and sing songs of joy upon the hills of Zion and shall be radiant over the goodness of the Lord—the good crops, the wheat, the wine, and the oil, and the healthy flocks and herds. Their life shall be like a watered garden, and all their sorrows shall be gone. [13]The young girls will dance for joy, and menfolk—old and young—will take their part in all the fun; for I will turn their mourning into joy, and I will comfort them and make them rejoice, for their captivity with all its sorrows will be behind them. [14]I will feast the priests with the abundance of offerings brought to them at the Temple; I will satisfy my people with my bounty, says the Lord.

[15]The Lord spoke to me again, saying: In Ramah there is bitter weeping—Rachel weeping for her children and cannot be comforted, for they are gone. [16]But the Lord says: Don't cry any longer, for I have heard your prayers and you will see them again; they will come back to you from the distant land of the enemy. [17]There is hope for your future, says the Lord, and your children will come again to their own land.

[18]I have heard Ephraim's groans: "You have punished me greatly; but I needed it all, as a calf must be trained for the yoke. Turn me again to you and restore me, for you alone are the Lord, my God. [19]I turned away from God, but I was sorry afterwards. I kicked myself for my stupidity. I was thoroughly ashamed of all I did in younger days."

[20]And the Lord replies: Ephraim is still my son, my darling child. I had to punish him, but I still love him. I long for him and surely will have mercy on him.

[21]As you travel into exile, set up road signs pointing back to Israel. Mark your pathway well. For you shall return again, O virgin Israel, to your cities here. [22]How long will you vacillate, O wayward daughter? For the Lord will cause something new and different to happen—Israel will search for God.

[23]The Lord, the God of Israel, says: When I bring them back again, they shall say in Judah and her cities, "The Lord bless you, O center of righteousness, O holy hill!" [24]And city dwellers and farmers and shepherds alike shall live together in peace and happiness. [25]For I have given rest to the weary and joy to all the sorrowing.

[26](Then Jeremiah wakened. "Such sleep is very sweet!" he said.)

[27]The Lord says: The time will come when I will greatly increase the population and multiply the number of cattle here in Israel. [28]In the past I painstakingly destroyed the nation, but now I will carefully build it up. [29]The people shall no longer quote this proverb—"Children pay for their fathers' sins." [30]For everyone shall die for his own sins—the person eating sour grapes is the one whose teeth are set on edge.

[31]The day will come, says the Lord, when I will make a new contract with the people of Israel and Judah. [32]It won't be like the one I made with their fathers when I took them by the hand to bring them out of the land of Egypt—a contract they broke, forcing me to reject them, says the Lord. [33]But this is the new contract I will make with them: I will inscribe my laws upon their hearts, so that they shall want to honor me; then they shall truly be my people and I will be their God. [34]At that time it will no longer be necessary to admonish one another to know the Lord. For everyone, both great and small, shall really know me then, says the Lord, and I will forgive and forget their sins.

[35]The Lord who gives us sunlight in the daytime and the moon and stars to light the night, and who stirs the sea to make the

roaring waves—his name is Lord Almighty—says this:

[36]I am as likely to reject my people Israel as I am to do away with these laws of nature! [37]Not until the heavens can be measured and the foundations of the earth explored, will I consider casting them away forever for their sins!

[38,39]For the time is coming, says the Lord, when all Jerusalem shall be rebuilt for the Lord, from the Tower of Hananel at the northeast corner, to the Corner Gate at the northwest; and from the Hill of Gareb at the southwest, across to Goah on the southeast. [40]And the entire city, including the graveyard and ash dump in the valley, and all the fields out to the brook of Kidron, and from there to the Horse Gate on the east side of the city, all shall be holy to the Lord; it shall never again be captured or destroyed.

CHAPTER 32

Jeremiah Buys Land

The following message came to Jeremiah from the Lord in the tenth year of the reign of Zedekiah, king of Judah (which was the eighteenth year of Nebuchadnezzar's reign). [2]At this time Jeremiah was imprisoned in the dungeon beneath the palace, while the Babylonian army was besieging Jerusalem. [3]King Zedekiah had put him there for continuing to prophesy that the city would be conquered by the king of Babylon, [4]and that King Zedekiah would be caught and taken as a prisoner before the king of Babylon for trial and sentencing.

[5]"He shall take you to Babylon and imprison you there for many years until you die. Why fight the facts? You can't win! Surrender now!" Jeremiah had told him again and again.

[6,7]Then this message from the Lord came to Jeremiah: Your cousin Hanamel (son of Shallum) will soon arrive to ask you to buy the farm he owns in Anathoth, for by law you have a chance to buy before it is offered to anyone else.

[8]So Hanamel came, as the Lord had said he would, and visited me in the prison. "Buy my field in Anathoth, in the land of Benjamin," he said, "for the law gives you the first right to purchase it." Then I knew for sure that the message I had heard was really from the Lord.

[9]So I bought the field, paying Hanamel seventeen pieces of silver. [10]I signed and sealed the deed of purchase before witnesses, weighed out the silver, and paid him. [11]Then I took the sealed deed containing the terms and conditions and also the unsealed copy, [12]and publicly, in the presence of my cousin Hanamel and the witnesses who had signed the deed, and as the prison guards watched, I handed the papers to Baruch (son of Neriah, who was the son of Mahseiah). [13]And I said to him as they all listened:

[14]"The Lord, God of Israel, says: Take both this sealed deed and the copy and put them into a pottery jar to preserve them for a long time. [15]For the Lord, God of Israel, says, In the future these papers will be valuable. Someday people will again own property here in this country and will be buying and selling houses and vineyards and fields."

[16]Then after I had given the papers to Baruch I prayed:

[17]"O Lord God! You have made the heavens and earth by your great power; nothing is too hard for you! [18]You are loving and kind to thousands, yet children suffer for their fathers' sins; you are the great and mighty God, the Lord Almighty. [19]You have all wisdom and do great and mighty miracles; for your eyes are open to all the ways of men, and you reward everyone according to his life and

32:1-5 Even though Jeremiah's prophecies were coming to pass, King Zedekiah still ignored his message. He and his people suffered from a severe case of denial. We also are very good at hiding from the truth. We unconsciously work out schemes to hide our dependencies and other problems from others. We even hide the truth from ourself. Jeremiah asked the king, "Why fight the facts?" We need to ask the same question of ourself. We cannot recover from problems that we refuse to admit. We need to face the fact that our life is out of control and we are headed for destruction. Once we have done that, we can give the problem to God and allow him to deliver and restore us.

32:6-15 Jeremiah was instructed to buy land, even though the Babylonians would soon conquer Judah and their laws of ownership would no longer apply. God used Jeremiah's actions to show that there was still hope. Despite the losses they would soon experience, God would once again restore the Promised Land to his people. Jeremiah's investment in real estate would someday be of value. We may be facing the devastating consequences of our dependencies and see little hope for the future. But just as Jeremiah invested in Israel's future, God has invested in our future through the atoning death of Jesus Christ. Through him we can receive the comfort and power needed to recover from total devastation.

deeds. [20]You have done incredible things in the land of Egypt—things still remembered to this day. And you have continued to do great miracles in Israel and all around the world. You have made your name very great, as it is today.

[21]"You brought Israel out of Egypt with mighty miracles and great power and terror. [22]You gave Israel this land that you promised their fathers long ago—a wonderful land that 'flows with milk and honey.' [23]Our fathers came and conquered it and lived in it, but they refused to obey you or to follow your laws; they have hardly done one thing you told them to. That is why you have sent all this terrible evil upon them. [24]See how the siege mounds have been built against the city walls, and the Babylonians shall conquer the city by sword, famine, and disease. Everything has happened just as you said—as you determined it should! [25]And yet you say to buy the field—paying good money for it before these witnesses—even though the city will belong to our enemies."

[26]Then this message came to Jeremiah: [27]I am the Lord, the God of all mankind; is there anything too hard for me? [28]Yes, I will give this city to the Babylonians and to Nebuchadnezzar, king of Babylon; he shall conquer it. [29]And the Babylonians outside the walls shall come in and set fire to the city and burn down all these houses, where the roofs have been used to offer incense to Baal and to pour out libations to other gods, causing my fury to rise! [30]For Israel and Judah have done nothing but wrong since their earliest days; they have infuriated me with all their evil deeds. [31]From the time this city was built until now it has done nothing but anger me; so I am determined to be rid of it.

[32]The sins of Israel and Judah—the sins of the people, of their kings, officers, priests and prophets—stir me up. [33]They have turned their backs upon me and refused to return; day after day, year after year, I taught them right from wrong, but they would not listen or obey. [34]They have even defiled my own Temple by worshiping their abominable idols there. [35]And they have built high altars to Baal in the Valley of Hinnom. There they have burnt their children as sacrifices to Molech—something I never commanded and cannot imagine suggesting. What an incredible evil, causing Judah to sin so greatly!

[36]Now therefore the Lord God of Israel says concerning this city that it will fall to the king of Babylon through warfare, famine, and disease, [37]but I will bring my people back again from all the countries where in my fury I will scatter them. I will bring them back to this very city and make them live in peace and safety. [38]And they shall be my people, and I will be their God. [39]And I will give them one heart and mind to worship me forever, for their own good and for the good of all their descendants.

[40]And I will make an everlasting covenant with them, promising never again to desert them but only to do them good. I will put a desire into their hearts to worship me, and they shall never leave me. [41]I will rejoice to do them good and will replant them in this land with great joy. [42]Just as I have sent all these terrors and evils upon them, so will I do all the good I have promised them.

[43]Fields will again be bought and sold in this land now ravaged by the Babylonians, where men and animals alike have disappeared. [44]Yes, fields shall once again be bought and sold—deeds signed and sealed and witnessed—in the country of Benjamin and here in Jerusalem, in the cities of Judah and in the hill country, in the Philistine plain and in the Negeb too, for some day I will restore prosperity to them.

CHAPTER 33

A Wonderful Promise

While Jeremiah was still in jail, the Lord sent him this second message:

[2]The Lord, the Maker of heaven and earth—Jehovah is his name—says this: [3]Ask me and I will tell you some remarkable secrets about what is going to happen here. [4]For though you have torn down the houses of this city, and the king's palace too, for

32:27-39 God wanted his people to accept responsibility for their sins, bad choices, and failures; their suffering in exile would force them to do this. But their story would not end with destruction and exile. God promised that he would deliver his people from captivity, restore them to their homeland, and reconcile his relationship with them. These promises must have sounded impossible to a people facing the devastation of warfare, famine, and disease. God introduced these verses with a question to answer his people's doubt: "Is there anything too hard for me?" As we face problems and dependencies that are beyond our power to control, there is still hope. Nothing is too hard for God!

materials to strengthen the walls against the siege weapons of the enemy, [5]yet the Babylonians will enter, and the men of this city are already as good as dead, for I have determined to destroy them in my furious anger. I have abandoned them because of all their wickedness, and I will not pity them when they cry for help.

[6]Nevertheless the time will come when I will heal Jerusalem's damage and give her prosperity and peace. [7]I will rebuild the cities of both Judah and Israel and restore their fortunes. [8]And I will cleanse away all their sins against me and pardon them. [9]Then this city will be an honor to me, and it will give me joy and be a source of praise and glory to me before all the nations of the earth! The people of the world will see the good I do for my people and will tremble with awe!

[10,11]The Lord declares that the happy voices of bridegrooms and of brides and the joyous song of those bringing thanksgiving offerings to the Lord will be heard again in this doomed land. The people will sing: "Praise the Lord! For he is good and his mercy endures forever!" For I will make this land happier and more prosperous than it has ever been before. [12]This land—though every man and animal and city is doomed—will once more see shepherds leading sheep and lambs. [13]Once again their flocks will prosper in the mountain villages and in the cities east of the Philistine plain, in all the cities of the Negeb, in the land of Benjamin, in the vicinity of Jerusalem, and in all the cities of Judah. [14]Yes, the day will come, says the Lord, when I will do for Israel and Judah all the good I promised them.

[15]At that time I will bring to the throne the true Son of David, and he shall rule justly. [16]In that day the people of Judah and Jerusalem shall live in safety and their motto will be, "The Lord is our righteousness!" [17]For the Lord declares that from then on, David shall forever have an heir sitting on the throne of Israel. [18]And there shall always be Levites to offer burnt offerings and meal offerings and sacrifices to the Lord.

[19]Then this message came to Jeremiah from the Lord: [20,21]If you can break my covenant with the day and with the night so that day and night don't come on their usual schedule, only then will my covenant with David, my servant, be broken so that he shall not have a son to reign upon his throne; and my covenant with the Levite priests, my ministers, is noncancelable. [22]And as the stars cannot be counted nor the sand upon the seashores measured, so the descendants of David my servant and the line of the Levites who minister to me will be multiplied.

[23]The Lord spoke to Jeremiah again and said: [24]Have you heard what people are saying?—that the Lord chose Judah and Israel and then abandoned them! They are sneering and saying that Israel isn't worthy to be counted as a nation. [25,26]But this is the Lord's reply: I would no more reject my people than I would change my laws of night and day, of earth and sky. I will never abandon the Jews, or David my servant, or change the plan that his child will someday rule these descendants of Abraham, Isaac, and Jacob. Instead I will restore their prosperity and have mercy on them.

CHAPTER 34

Zedekiah Will Be Captured

This is the message that came to Jeremiah from the Lord when Nebuchadnezzar, king of Babylon, and all his armies from all the kingdoms he ruled, came and fought against Jerusalem and the cities of Judah:

[2]Go tell Zedekiah, king of Judah, that the Lord says this: I will give this city to the king of Babylon and he shall burn it. [3]You shall not escape; you shall be captured and taken before the king of Babylon; he shall pronounce sentence against you and you shall be exiled to Babylon. [4]But listen to this, O Zedekiah, king of Judah: God says you won't be killed in war and carnage [5]but that you will die quietly

33:1-26 When everything in life seems an unstable disaster, there is one thing we can count on: God is committed to us and to our recovery. No matter how gray our life may be, no matter how dark our future, our loving and faithful God can restore our hope and lead us toward recovery. As we trust him with our disappointments, failures, and confusion, we will find him faithful to comfort, forgive, and guide us.

34:1-7 The errant Zedekiah would not die by the sword, even though his deeds had caused suffering to many. Instead of death, God promised grace to Zedekiah. We always deserve far more punishment that we actually receive. If we always received what we deserved, even the best of us would suffer terrible punishment. God deals with us by grace (see Ephesians 2:8-9), not by a strict code of justice. Such is the heart of the gospel. No matter what we have done in the past, there is still hope. If we honestly admit our sins and turn to God, he will be gracious to us.

among your people, and they will burn incense in your memory, just as they did for your fathers. They will weep for you and say, "Alas, our king is dead!" This I have decreed, says the Lord.

6So Jeremiah delivered the message to King Zedekiah. 7At this time the Babylonian army was besieging Jerusalem, Lachish, and Azekah—the only walled cities of Judah still standing.

Slaves Will Be Set Free

8This is the message that came to Jeremiah from the Lord after King Zedekiah of Judah had freed all the slaves in Jerusalem—9(for King Zedekiah had ordered everyone to free his Hebrew slaves, both men and women. He had said that no Jew should be the master of another Jew for all were brothers. 10The princes and all the people had obeyed the king's command and freed their slaves, but the action was only temporary. 11They changed their minds and made their servants slaves again. 12That is why the Lord gave the following message to Jerusalem.)

13The Lord, the God of Israel, says: I made a covenant with your fathers long ago when I brought them from their slavery in Egypt. 14I told them that every Hebrew slave must be freed after serving six years. But this was not done. 15Recently you began doing what was right, as I commanded you, and freed your slaves. You had solemnly promised me in my Temple that you would do it. 16But now you refuse and have defiled my name by shrugging off your oath and have made them slaves again.

17Therefore, says the Lord, because you will not listen to me and release them, I will release you to the power of death by war and famine and disease. And I will scatter you over all the world as exiles. 18,19Because you have refused the terms of our contract, I will cut you apart just as you cut apart the calf when you walked between its halves to solemnize your vows. Yes, I will butcher you, whether you are princes, court officials, priests, or people—for you have broken your oath. 20I will give you to your enemies, and they shall kill you. I will feed your dead bodies to the vultures and wild animals. 21And I will surrender Zedekiah, king of Judah, and his officials to the army of the king of Babylon, though he has departed from the city for a little while. 22I will summon the Babylonian armies back again, and they will fight against it and capture this city and burn it. And I will see to it that the cities of Judah are completely destroyed and left desolate without a living soul.

CHAPTER 35

The Obedient Rechabites

This is the message the Lord gave Jeremiah when Jehoiakim (son of Josiah) was the king of Judah:

2Go to the settlement where the families of the Rechabites live and invite them to the Temple. Take them into one of the inner rooms and offer them a drink of wine.

3So I went over to see Jaazaniah (son of Jeremiah, who was the son of Habazziniah) and brought him and all his brothers and sons—representing all the Rechab families—4to the Temple, into the room assigned for the use of the sons of Hanan the prophet (the son of Igdaliah). This room was located next to the one used by the palace official, directly above the room of Maaseiah (son of Shallum), who was the temple doorman. 5I set cups and jugs of wine before them and invited them to have a drink, 6but they refused.

"No," they said. "We don't drink, for Jonadab our father (son of Rechab) commanded that none of us should ever drink, neither we nor our children forever. 7He also told us not to build houses or plant crops or vineyards and not to own farms, but always to live in tents; and that if we obeyed, we would live long, good lives in our own land. 8And we

---

34:8-22 Zedekiah accepted God's grace to him and, in turn, extended grace to others. He called his people to free all their Hebrew slaves, one of God's requirements in the law. While the people initially responded well to Zedekiah's request, they soon went back to their old ways of disobedience. As a result, all the gains they had made toward healing were soon lost. Recovery is never a one-time act; it is a long-term process. If we fail to persevere in our recovery, we may end up worse off than we were before. When God calls us to change, he calls us to change permanently.

35:1-19 This chapter contains a fascinating story about a family that faithfully obeyed the direction of its ancestors, choosing to submit to a program that fostered its physical, social, and spiritual well-being. God held up this family as an example for the people of Judah. He longed for his people to obey his will just as the Rechabites adhered to the direction of their leaders. Trusting God and obeying his will for our life is the only true path to recovery.

have obeyed him in all these things. We have never had a drink of wine since then, nor have our wives or our sons or daughters either. [9]We haven't built houses or owned farms or planted crops. [10]We have lived in tents and have fully obeyed everything that Jonadab our father commanded us. [11]But when Nebuchadnezzar, king of Babylon, arrived in this country, we were afraid and decided to move to Jerusalem. That's why we are here."

[12]Then the Lord gave this message to Jeremiah:

[13]The Lord, the God of Israel, says: Go and say to Judah and Jerusalem, Won't you learn a lesson from the families of Rechab? [14]They don't drink because their father told them not to. But I have spoken to you again and again, and you won't listen or obey. [15]I have sent you prophet after prophet to tell you to turn back from your wicked ways and to stop worshiping other gods, and that if you obeyed, then I would let you live in peace here in the land I gave to you and your fathers. But you wouldn't listen or obey. [16]The families of Rechab have obeyed their father completely, but you have refused to listen to me. [17]Therefore, the Lord Almighty, the God of Israel, says: Because you refuse to listen or answer when I call, I will send upon Judah and Jerusalem all the evil I have ever threatened.

[18,19]Then Jeremiah turned to the Rechabites and said: "The Lord, the God of Israel, says that because you have obeyed your father in every respect, he shall always have descendants who will worship me."

CHAPTER 36

The King Burns the Scroll

In the fourth year of the reign of King Jehoiakim of Judah (son of Josiah) the Lord gave this message to Jeremiah:

[2]"Get a scroll and write down all my messages against Israel, Judah, and the other nations. Begin with the first message back in the days of Josiah, and write down every one of them. [3]Perhaps when the people of Judah see in writing all the terrible things I will do to them, they will repent. And then I can forgive them."

[4]So Jeremiah sent for Baruch (son of Neriah), and as Jeremiah dictated, Baruch wrote down all the prophecies.

[5]When all was finished, Jeremiah said to Baruch, "Since I am a prisoner here, [6]you read the scroll in the Temple on the next day of fasting, for on that day people will be there from all over Judah. [7]Perhaps even yet they will turn from their evil ways and ask the Lord to forgive them before it is too late, even though these curses of God have been pronounced upon them."

[8]Baruch did as Jeremiah told him to and read all these messages to the people at the Temple. [9]This occurred on the day of fasting held in December of the fifth year of the reign of King Jehoiakim (son of Josiah). People came from all over Judah to attend the services at the Temple that day. [10]Baruch went to the office of Gemariah the Scribe (son of Shaphan) to read the scroll. (This room was just off the upper assembly hall of the Temple, near the door of the New Gate.)

[11]When Micaiah (son of Gemariah, son of Shaphan) heard the messages from God, [12]he went down to the palace to the conference room where the administrative officials were meeting. Elishama (the scribe) was there, as well as Delaiah (son of Shamaiah), Elnathan (son of Achbor), Gemariah (son of Shaphan), Zedekiah (son of Hananiah), and all the others with similar responsibilities. [13]When Micaiah told them about the messages Baruch was reading to the people, [14,15]the officials sent Jehudi (son of Nethaniah, son of Shelemiah, son of Cushi) to ask Baruch to come and read the messages to them too, and Baruch did.

[16]By the time he finished they were badly frightened. "We must tell the king," they said. [17]"But first, tell us how you got these messages. Did Jeremiah himself dictate them to you?" [18]So Baruch explained that Jeremiah had dictated them to him word by word, and he had written them down in ink upon the scroll. [19]"You and Jeremiah both hide," the officials said to Baruch. "Don't tell a soul

36:1-32 King Zedekiah refused to listen to Jeremiah's predictions of coming destruction. He preferred the comforting lies of the false prophets to the terrifying truth of God's prophet. He tried to deny his sin and its consequences by ignoring them. We must face the truth about our actions and circumstances if we hope to overcome them. Living in denial can never solve our problems; it only compounds them. Are there false prophets in our life calling us away from the truth? Are we living in denial about our dependencies and the consequences sure to follow? Only in admitting our dependencies can we hope to avoid the consequences.

where you are!" [20]Then the officials hid the
scroll in the room of Elishama the scribe and
went to tell the king.

[21]The king sent Jehudi to get the scroll.
Jehudi brought it from Elishama the scribe
and read it to the king as all his officials stood
by. [22]The king was in a winterized part of the
palace at the time, sitting in front of a fire-
place, for it was December and cold. [23]And
whenever Jehudi finished reading three or
four columns, the king would take his knife,
slit off the section, and throw it into the fire,
until the whole scroll was destroyed. [24,25]And
no one protested except Elnathan, Delaiah,
and Gemariah. They pled with the king not to
burn the scroll, but he wouldn't listen to
them. Not another of the king's officials
showed any signs of fear or anger at what he
had done.

[26]Then the king commanded Jerahmeel (a
member of the royal family) and Seraiah (son
of Azriel) and Shelemiah (son of Abdeel) to
arrest Baruch and Jeremiah. But the Lord hid
them!

[27]After the king had burned the scroll, the
Lord said to Jeremiah: [28]Get another scroll
and write everything again just as you did
before, [29]and say this to the king: "The Lord
says, You burned the scroll because it said the
king of Babylon would destroy this country
and everything in it. [30]And now the Lord
adds this concerning you, Jehoiakim, king of
Judah: He shall have no one to sit upon the
throne of David. His dead body shall be
thrown out to the hot sun and frosty nights,
[31]and I will punish him and his family and his
officials because of their sins. I will pour out
upon them all the evil I promised—upon
them and upon all the people of Judah and
Jerusalem, for they wouldn't listen to my
warnings."

[32]Then Jeremiah took another scroll and
dictated again to Baruch all he had written
before, only this time the Lord added a lot
more!

CHAPTER 37

Jeremiah Is Put in Prison

Nebuchadnezzar, King of Babylon, did not
appoint Coniah (King Jehoiakim's son) to be
the new king of Judah. Instead he chose Zedekiah (son of Josiah). [2]But neither King Zedekiah nor his officials nor the people who were
left in the land listened to what the Lord said
through Jeremiah. [3]Nevertheless, King Zedekiah sent Jehucal (son of Shelemiah) and Zephaniah the priest (son of Maaseiah) to ask
Jeremiah to pray for them. [4](Jeremiah had not
been imprisoned yet, so he could come and
go as he pleased.)

[5]When the army of Pharaoh Hophra of
Egypt appeared at the southern border of
Judah to relieve the besieged city of Jerusalem, the Babylonian army withdrew from Jerusalem to fight the Egyptians.

[6]Then the Lord sent this message to Jeremiah: [7]The Lord, the God of Israel, says: Tell
the king of Judah, who sent you to ask me
what is going to happen, that Pharaoh's army,
though it came here to help you, is about to
return in flight to Egypt! The Babylonians
shall defeat them and send them scurrying
home. [8]These Babylonians shall capture this
city and burn it to the ground. [9]Don't fool
yourselves that the Babylonians are gone for
good. They aren't! [10]Even if you destroyed the
entire Babylonian army until there was only
a handful of survivors and they lay wounded
in their tents, yet they would stagger out and
defeat you and put this city to the torch!"

[11]When the Babylonian army set out from
Jerusalem to engage Pharaoh's army in battle,
[12]Jeremiah started to leave the city to go to the
land of Benjamin, to see the property he had
bought. [13]But as he was walking through the
Benjamin Gate, a sentry arrested him as a
traitor, claiming he was defecting to the Babylonians. The guard making the arrest was
Irijah (son of Shelemiah, grandson of Hananiah).

[14]"That's not true," Jeremiah said. "I have
no intention whatever of doing any such
thing!"

But Irijah wouldn't listen; he took Jeremiah
before the city officials. [15,16]They were incensed with Jeremiah and had him flogged
and put into the dungeon under the house of
Jonathan the scribe, which had been converted into a prison. Jeremiah was kept there
for several days, [17]but eventually King Zedekiah sent for him to come to the palace secretly. The king asked him if there was any
recent message from the Lord. "Yes," said
Jeremiah, "there is! You shall be defeated by
the king of Babylon!"

[18]Then Jeremiah broached the subject of his
imprisonment. "What have I ever done to
deserve this?" he asked the king. "What crime
have I committed? Tell me what I have done
against you or your officials or the people?
[19]Where are those prophets now who told you
that the king of Babylon would not come?
[20]Listen, O my lord the king: I beg you, don't

send me back to that dungeon, for I'll die there."

21 Then King Zedekiah commanded that Jeremiah not be returned to the dungeon but be placed in the palace prison instead, and that he be given a small loaf of fresh bread every day as long as there was any left in the city. So Jeremiah was kept in the palace prison.

CHAPTER 38

Jeremiah Is Rescued

But when Shephatiah (son of Mattan) and Gedaliah (son of Pashhur) and Jucal (son of Shelemiah) and Pashhur (son of Malchiah) heard what Jeremiah had been telling the people— 2 that everyone remaining in Jerusalem would die by sword, starvation, or disease, but anyone surrendering to the Babylonians would live, 3 and that the city of Jerusalem would surely be captured by the king of Babylon— 4 they went to the king and said: "Sir, this fellow must die. That kind of talk will undermine the morale of the few soldiers we have left, and of all the people too. This man is a traitor."

5 So King Zedekiah agreed. "All right," he said. "Do as you like—I can't stop you."

6 They took Jeremiah from his cell and lowered him by ropes into an empty cistern in the prison yard. (It belonged to Malchiah, a member of the royal family.) There was no water in it, but there was a thick layer of mire at the bottom, and Jeremiah sank down into it.

7 When Ebed-melech the Ethiopian, an important palace official, heard that Jeremiah was in the cistern, 8 he rushed out to the Gate of Benjamin where the king was holding court.

9 "My lord the king," he said, "these men have done a very evil thing in putting Jeremiah into the cistern. He will die of hunger, for almost all the bread in the city is gone."

10 Then the king commanded Ebed-melech to take thirty men with him and pull Jeremiah out before he died. 11 So Ebed-melech took thirty men and went to a palace depot for discarded supplies where used clothing was kept. There he found some old rags and discarded garments which he took to the cistern and lowered to Jeremiah on a rope. 12 Ebed-melech called down to Jeremiah, "Use these rags under your armpits to protect you from the ropes." Then, when Jeremiah was ready, 13 they pulled him out and returned him to the palace prison, where he remained.

Zedekiah Questions Jeremiah

14 One day King Zedekiah sent for Jeremiah to meet him at the side entrance of the Temple.

"I want to ask you something," the king said, "and don't try to hide the truth."

15 Jeremiah said, "If I tell you the truth, you will kill me. And you won't listen to me anyway."

16 So King Zedekiah swore before Almighty God his Creator that he would not kill Jeremiah or give him to the men who were after his life.

17 Then Jeremiah said to Zedekiah, "The Almighty Lord, the God of Israel, says: If you will surrender to Babylon, you and your family shall live and the city will not be burned. 18 If you refuse to surrender, this city shall be set afire by the Babylonian army and you will not escape."

19 "But I am afraid to surrender," the king said, "for the Babylonians will hand me over to the Jews who have defected to them, and who knows what they will do to me?"

20 Jeremiah replied, "You won't get into their hands if only you will obey the Lord; your life will be spared, and all will go well for you. 21,22 But if you refuse to surrender, the Lord has said that all the women left in your palace will be brought out and given to the officers of the Babylonian army; and these women will taunt you with bitterness. 'Fine friends you have,' they'll say, 'those Egyptians. They have betrayed you and left you to your fate!' 23 All your wives and children will be led out to the Babylonians, and you will not escape. You will be seized by the king of Babylon, and this city will be burned."

24 Then Zedekiah said to Jeremiah, "On pain of death, don't tell anyone you told me this! 25 And if my officials hear that I talked with you and they threaten you with death unless you tell them what we discussed, 26 just say that you begged me not to send you back to

---

38:11-28 Jeremiah gave Zedekiah clear direction from God, but the king was too insecure to follow the prophet's advice. We often fall into the same trap. God gives us clear direction in his Word, but we fail to act on what we know. Sometimes we are afraid of what others will think, or we are afraid of what God is asking; other times we simply don't want to comply, or we just feel too tired to act. Seeking out God's will for us is only part of the task. We must act on our knowledge before it will become effective in our life.

the dungeon in Jonathan's house, for you would die there."

[27]And sure enough, it wasn't long before all the city officials came to Jeremiah and asked him why the king had called for him. So he said what the king had told him to, and they left without finding out the truth, for the conversation had not been overheard by anyone. [28]And Jeremiah remained confined to the prison yard until the day Jerusalem was captured.

CHAPTER 39

Jerusalem Is Captured

It was in January of the ninth year of the reign of King Zedekiah of Judah that King Nebuchadnezzar and all his army came against Jerusalem again and besieged it. [2]Two years later, in the month of July, they breached the wall, and the city fell, [3]and all the officers of the Babylonian army came in and sat in triumph at the middle gate. Nergal-sharezer was there, Samgar-nebo, Sarsechim, Nergal-sharezer the king's chief assistant, and many others.

[4]When King Zedekiah and his soldiers realized that the city was lost, they fled during the night, going out through the gate between the two walls back of the palace garden and across the fields toward the Jordan valley. [5]But the Babylonians chased the king and caught him on the plains of Jericho and brought him to Nebuchadnezzar, king of Babylon who was at Riblah, in the land of Hamath, where he pronounced judgment upon him. [6]The king of Babylon made Zedekiah watch as they killed his children and all the nobles of Judah. [7]Then he gouged out Zedekiah's eyes and bound him in chains to send him away to Babylon as a slave.

[8]Meanwhile the army burned Jerusalem, including the palace, and tore down the walls of the city. [9]Then Nebuzaradan, the captain of the guard, and his men sent the remnant of the population and all those who had defected to him to Babylon. [10]But throughout the land of Judah he left a few people, the very poor, and gave them fields and vineyards.

[11,12]Meanwhile King Nebuchadnezzar had told Nebuzaradan to find Jeremiah. "See that he isn't hurt," he said. "Look after him well and give him anything he wants." [13]So Nebuzaradan, the captain of the guard, and Nebushazban, the chief of the eunuchs, and Nergal-sharezer, the king's advisor, and all the officials took steps to do as the king had commanded. [14]They sent soldiers to bring Jeremiah out of the prison, and put him into the care of Gedaliah (son of Ahikam, son of Shaphan), to take him back to his home. And Jeremiah lived there among his people who were left in the land.

[15]The Lord gave the following message to Jeremiah before the Babylonians arrived, while he was still in prison: [16]"Send this word to Ebed-melech the Ethiopian: The Lord, the God of Israel, says: I will do to this city everything I threatened; I will destroy it before your eyes, [17]but I will deliver you. You shall not be killed by those you fear so much. [18]As a reward for trusting me, I will preserve your life and keep you safe."

CHAPTER 40

Jeremiah Is Released

Nebuzaradan, captain of the guard, took Jeremiah to Ramah along with all the exiled people of Jerusalem and Judah who were being sent to Babylon, but then released him.

[2,3]The captain called for Jeremiah and said, "The Lord your God has brought this disaster on this land, just as he said he would. For these people have sinned against the Lord. That is why it happened. [4]Now I am going to take off your chains and let you go. If you want to come with me to Babylon, fine; I will see that you are well cared for. But if you don't want to come, don't. The world is before you—go where you like. [5]If you decide to stay, then return to Gedaliah, who has been appointed as governor of Judah by the king of Babylon, and stay with the remnant he rules. But it's up to you; go where you like."

Then Nebuzaradan gave Jeremiah some food and money and let him go. [6]So Jeremiah returned to Gedaliah and lived in Judah with the people left in the land.

[7]Now when the leaders of the Jewish guerrilla bands in the countryside heard that the

---

39:1-18 Tragic scenes of murder and destruction filled Jerusalem as Jeremiah's prophecy became a reality. Even when we are expecting the consequences of our sin, the resulting pain is no less difficult to bear. God doesn't enjoy our pain; he longs for us to learn from the devastation.

40:1-12 For the first time since Jeremiah's prophetic work began, we see peace and harmony in the lives of God's people. The reason was simple. They were following God's directive to serve Nebuchadnezzar. They were obeying God. There is peace both within and among us when we seek to follow God's will for us.

king of Babylon had appointed Gedaliah as
governor over the poor of the land who were
left behind, and had not exiled everyone to
Babylon, 8they came to see Gedaliah at Mizpah, where his headquarters were. These are
the names of the leaders who came: Ishmael
(son of Nethaniah), Johanan and Jonathan
(sons of Kareah), Seraiah (son of Tanhumeth),
the sons of Ephai (the Netophathite), Jeza-
niah (son of a Maacathite), and their men.
9 And Gedaliah assured them that it would be
safe to surrender to the Babylonians.

"Stay here and serve the king of Babylon,"
he said, "and all will go well for you. 10As for
me, I will stay at Mizpah and intercede for you
with the Babylonians who will come here to
oversee my administration. Settle in any city
you wish and live off the land. Harvest the
grapes and summer fruits and olives and store
them away."

11When the Jews in Moab and among the
Ammonites and in Edom and the other
nearby countries heard that a few people were
still left in Judah, and that the king of Babylon
had not taken them all away, and that Gedaliah was the governor, 12they all began to
return to Judah from the many places to
which they had fled. They stopped at Mizpah
to discuss their plans with Gedaliah and then
went out to the deserted farms and gathered
a great harvest of wine grapes and other crops.

13,14But soon afterwards Johanan (son of
Kareah) and the other guerrilla leaders came
to Mizpah to warn Gedaliah that Baalis, king
of the Ammonites, had sent Ishmael (son of
Nethaniah) to assassinate him. But Gedaliah
wouldn't believe them. 15Then Johanan had a
private conference with Gedaliah. Johanan
volunteered to kill Ishmael secretly.

"Why should we let him come and murder
you?" Johanan asked. "What will happen
then to the Jews who have returned? Why
should this remnant be scattered and lost?"

16But Gedaliah said, "I forbid you to do any
such thing, for you are lying about Ishmael."

CHAPTER 41

Gedaliah Is Assassinated

But in October, Ishmael (son of Nethaniah,
son of Elishama), who was a member of the
royal family and one of the king's top officials, arrived in Mizpah, accompanied by ten
men. Gedaliah invited them to dinner. 2While
they were eating, Ishmael and the ten men in
league with him suddenly jumped up, pulled
out their swords, and killed Gedaliah. 3Then
they went out and slaughtered all the Jewish
officials and Babylonian soldiers who were in
Mizpah with Gedaliah.

4The next day, before the outside world
knew what had happened, 5eighty men approached Mizpah from Shechem, Shiloh, and
Samaria, to worship at the Temple of the Lord.
They had shaved off their beards, torn their
clothes, and cut themselves, and were bringing offerings and incense. 6Ishmael went out
from the city to meet them, crying as he went.
When he faced them he said, "Oh, come and
see what has happened to Gedaliah!"

7Then, when they were all inside the city,
Ishmael and his men killed all but ten of them
and threw their bodies into a cistern. 8The ten
had talked Ishmael into letting them go by
promising to bring him their treasures of
wheat, barley, oil, and honey they had hidden
away. 9The cistern where Ishmael dumped the
bodies of the men he murdered was the large
one constructed by King Asa when he fortified Mizpah to protect himself against Baasha,
king of Israel.

10Ishmael made captives of the king's
daughters and of the people who had been
left under Gedaliah's care in Mizpah by
Nebuzaradan, captain of the guard. Soon after, he took them with him when he headed
toward the country of the Ammonites.

11But when Johanan (son of Kareah) and
the rest of the guerrilla leaders heard what
Ishmael had done, 12they took all their men
and set out to stop him. They caught up with
him at the pool near Gibeon. 13,14The people
with Ishmael shouted for joy when they saw
Johanan and his men and ran to meet them.

15Meanwhile Ishmael escaped with eight of
his men into the land of the Ammonites.

16,17Then Johanan and his men went to the
village of Geruth Chimham, near Bethlehem,
taking with them all those they had rescued—
soldiers, women, children, and eunuchs, to
prepare to leave for Egypt. 18For they were

40:13–43:13 When turmoil again threatened the security of the people, they chose to take matters back into their own hands. Sometimes the lessons we think we have learned must be learned all over again. When things begin to go well in our recovery, we may forget our need for God and go back to doing things our way. This tendency toward pride, however, will only lead us toward a relapse. If we forget that our dependencies are too strong for us and try to go it alone, there is little hope for our ultimate success.

afraid of what the Babylonians would do when the news reached them that Ishmael had killed Gedaliah the governor, for he had been chosen and appointed by the Babylonian emperor.

CHAPTER 42

God Warns against Going to Egypt

Then Johanan and the army captains and all the people, great and small, came to Jeremiah 2and said, "Please pray for us to the Lord your God, for as you know so well, we are only a tiny remnant of what we were before. 3Beg the Lord your God to show us what to do and where to go."

4"All right," Jeremiah replied. "I will ask him and I will tell you what he says. I will hide nothing from you."

5Then they said to Jeremiah, "May the curse of God be on us if we refuse to obey whatever he says we should do! 6Whether we like it or not, we will obey the Lord our God, to whom we send you with our plea. For if we obey him, everything will turn out well for us."

7Ten days later the Lord gave his reply to Jeremiah. 8So he called for Johanan and the captains of his forces, and for all the people, great and small, 9and said to them: "You sent me to the Lord, the God of Israel, with your request, and this is his reply:

10"Stay here in this land. If you do, I will bless you, and no one will harm you. For I am sorry for all the punishment I have had to give to you. 11Don't fear the king of Babylon any more, for I am with you to save you and to deliver you from his hand. 12And I will be merciful to you by making him kind so that he will not kill you or make slaves of you but will let you stay here in your land.

13,14"But if you refuse to obey the Lord and say, 'We will not stay here,'—and insist on going to Egypt where you think you will be free from war and hunger and alarms, 15then this is what the Lord replies, O remnant of Judah: The Lord Almighty, the God of Israel, says: If you insist on going to Egypt, 16the war and famine you fear will follow close behind you, and you will perish there. 17That is the fate awaiting every one of you who insists on going to live in Egypt. Yes, you will die from sword, famine, and disease. None of you will escape from the evil I will bring upon you there.

18"For the Lord, the God of Israel, says: Just as my anger and fury were poured out upon the people of Jerusalem, so it will be poured out on you when you enter Egypt. You will be received with disgust and with hatred—you will be cursed and reviled. And you will never again see your own land. 19For the Lord has said: O remnant of Judah, do not go to Egypt!"

Jeremiah concluded: "Never forget the warning I have given you today. 20If you go, it will be at the cost of your lives. For you were deceitful when you sent me to pray for you and said, 'Just tell us what God says and we will do it!' 21And today I have told you exactly what he said, but you will not obey any more now than you did the other times. 22Therefore know for a certainty that you will die by sword, famine, and disease in Egypt, where you insist on going."

CHAPTER 43

The People Refuse to Listen

When Jeremiah had finished giving this message from God to all the people, 2,3Azariah (son of Hoshaiah) and Johanan (son of Kareah) and all the other proud men, said to Jeremiah, "You lie! The Lord our God hasn't told you to tell us not to go to Egypt! Baruch (son of Neriah) has plotted against us and told you to say this so that we will stay here and be killed by the Babylonians or carried off to Babylon as slaves."

4So Johanan and all the guerrilla leaders and all the people refused to obey the Lord and stay in Judah. 5All of them, including all those who had returned from the nearby countries where they had fled, now started off for Egypt with Johanan and the other captains in command. 6In the crowd were men, women and children, the king's daughters, and all those whom Nebuzaradan, the captain of the guard, had left with Gedaliah. They even forced Jeremiah and Baruch to go with them too. 7And so they arrived in Egypt at the city of Tahpanhes, for they would not obey the Lord.

8Then at Tahpanhes, the Lord spoke to Jeremiah again and said: 9"Call together the men of Judah and, as they watch you, bury large rocks between the pavement stones at the entrance of Pharaoh's palace here in Tahpanhes, 10and tell the men of Judah this: The Lord Almighty, the God of Israel, says: I will surely bring Nebuchadnezzar, king of Babylon, here to Egypt, for he is my servant. I will set his throne upon these stones that I have hidden. He shall spread his royal canopy over them. 11And when he comes, he shall destroy the land of Egypt, killing all those I want killed and capturing those I want captured, and many shall die of plague. [12]He will set fire to the temples of the gods of Egypt and burn the idols and carry off the people as his captives. And he shall plunder the land of Egypt as a shepherd picks fleas from his cloak! And he himself shall leave unharmed. [13]And he shall break down the obelisks standing in the city of Heliopolis and burn down the temples of the gods of Egypt."

CHAPTER 44

Judgment because of Idolatry

This is the message God gave to Jeremiah concerning all the Jews who were living in the north of Egypt in the cities of Migdol, Tahpanhes, and Memphis, and throughout southern Egypt as well:

[2,3]The Lord Almighty, the God of Israel, says: You saw what I did to Jerusalem and to all the cities of Judah. Because of all their wickedness they lie in heaps and ashes, without a living soul. For my anger rose high against them for worshiping other gods—"gods" that neither they nor you nor any of your fathers have ever known.

[4]I sent my servants, the prophets, to protest over and over again and to plead with them not to do this horrible thing I hate, [5]but they wouldn't listen and wouldn't turn back from their wicked ways; they have kept right on with their sacrifices to these "gods." [6]And so my fury and anger boiled over and fell as fire upon the cities of Judah and into the streets of Jerusalem, and there is desolation until this day.

[7]And now the Lord, the Lord Almighty, the God of Israel, asks you: Why are you destroying yourselves? For not one of you shall live—not a man, woman or child among you who has come here from Judah, not even the babies in arms. [8]For you are rousing my anger with the idols you have made and worshiped here in Egypt, burning incense to them, and causing me to destroy you completely and to make you a curse and a stench in the nostrils of all the nations of the earth. [9]Have you forgotten the sins of your fathers, the sins of the kings and queens of Judah, your own sins, and the sins of your wives in Judah and Jerusalem? [10]And even until this very hour there has been no apology; no one has wanted to return to me or follow the laws I gave you and your fathers before you.

[11]Therefore the Lord, the God of Israel, says: There is fury in my face and I will destroy every one of you! [12]I will take this remnant of Judah that insisted on coming here to Egypt, and I will consume them. They shall fall here in Egypt, killed by famine and sword; all shall die, from the least important to the greatest. They shall be despised and loathed, cursed and hated. [13]I will punish them in Egypt just as I punished them in Jerusalem, by sword, famine, and disease. [14]Not one of them shall escape from my wrath except those who repent of their coming and escape from the others by returning again to their own land.

[15]Then all the women present and all the men who knew that their wives had burned incense to idols (it was a great crowd of all the Jews in southern Egypt) answered Jeremiah:

[16]"We will not listen to your false 'Messages from God'! [17]We will do whatever we want to. We will burn incense to the Queen of Heaven and sacrifice to her just as much as we like—just as we and our fathers before us, and our kings and princes have always done in the cities of Judah and in the streets of Jerusalem; for in those days we had plenty to eat, and we were well off and happy! [18]But ever since we quit burning incense to the Queen of Heaven and stopped worshiping her, we have been in great trouble and have been destroyed by sword and famine."

[19]"And," the women added, "do you suppose that we were worshiping the Queen of Heaven and pouring out our libations to her and making cakes for her with her image on them, without our husbands knowing it and helping us? Of course not!"

[20]Then Jeremiah said to all of them, men and women alike, who had given him that answer:

[21]"Do you think the Lord didn't know that you and your fathers, your kings and princes, and all the people were burning incense to idols in the cities of Judah and in the streets of Jerusalem? [22]It was because he could no longer bear all the evil things you were doing

44:1-30 Jeremiah encouraged the remnant in Egypt to heed lessons learned from Judah's recent fall and to turn away from their idolatry. Their response betrayed them: "Ever since we quit burning incense to the 'Queen of Heaven' and stopped worshiping her we have been in great trouble." Sadly, their love for God was conditional. Unless God rewarded them in the ways they expected, they would not obey him. God is worthy of our love and obedience, whether or not he gives us what we want. God can be trusted at the deepest level, and his program for us is always best.

that he made your land desolate, an incredible ruin, cursed, without an inhabitant, as it
is today. 23The very reason all these terrible
things have befallen you is because you have
burned incense and sinned against the Lord
and refused to obey him."
24Then Jeremiah said to them all, including
the women: "Listen to the word of the Lord,
all you citizens of Judah who are here in
Egypt! 25The Lord, the God of Israel, says: Both
you and your wives have said that you will
never give up your devotion and sacrifices to
the Queen of Heaven, and you have proved it
by your actions. Then go ahead and carry out
your promises and vows to her! 26But listen to
the word of the Lord, all you Jews who are
living in the land of Egypt: I have sworn by
my great name, says the Lord, that it will do
you no good to seek my help and blessing any
more, saying, 'O Lord our God, help us!' 27For
I will watch over you, but *not* for good! I will
see to it that evil befalls you, and you shall be
destroyed by war and famine until all of you
are dead.
28"Only those who return to Judah (it will
be but a tiny remnant) shall escape my wrath,
but all who refuse to go back—who insist on
living in Egypt—shall find out who tells the
truth, I or they! 29And this is the proof I give
you that all I have threatened will happen to
you and that I will punish you here: 30I will
turn Pharaoh Hophra, king of Egypt, over to
those who seek his life, just as I turned Zedekiah, king of Judah, over to Nebuchadnezzar,
king of Babylon."

CHAPTER 45
A Warning for Baruch
This is the message Jeremiah gave to Baruch in the fourth year of the reign of King Jehoiakim (son of Josiah), after Baruch had written down all God's messages as Jeremiah was dictating them to him:
2O Baruch, the Lord God of Israel says this
to you: 3You have said, Woe is me! Don't I
have troubles enough already? And now the
Lord has added more! I am weary of my own
sighing and I find no rest. 4But tell Baruch
this, The Lord says: I will destroy this nation
that I built; I will wipe out what I established.
5Are you seeking great things for yourself?
Don't do it! For though I will bring great evil
upon all these people, I will protect you wherever you go, as your reward.

CHAPTER 46
Here are the messages given to Jeremiah concerning foreign nations:

A Message to Egypt
2This message was given against Egypt at the occasion of the battle of Carchemish when Pharaoh Necho, king of Egypt, and his army were defeated beside the Euphrates River by Nebuchadnezzar, king of Babylon, in the fourth year of the reign of Jehoiakim (son of Josiah), king of Judah:
3Buckle on your armor, you Egyptians and
advance to battle! 4Harness the horses and
prepare to mount them—don your helmets,
sharpen your spears, put on your armor. 5But
look! The Egyptian army flees in terror; the
mightiest of its soldiers run without a backward glance. Yes, terror shall surround them
on every side, says the Lord. 6The swift will
not escape, nor the mightiest of warriors. In
the north, by the river Euphrates, they have
stumbled and fallen.
7What is this mighty army, rising like the
Nile at flood time, overflowing all the land?
8It is the Egyptian army, boasting that it will
cover the earth like a flood, destroying every
foe. 9Then come, O horses and chariots and
mighty soldiers of Egypt! Come, all of you
from Cush and Put and Lud who handle the
shield and bend the bow! 10For this is the day
of the Lord, the Lord Almighty, a day of
vengeance upon his enemies. The sword shall
devour until it is sated, yes, drunk with your
blood, for the Lord, the Lord Almighty will
receive a sacrifice today in the north country
beside the river Euphrates! 11 Go up to Gilead
for medicine, O virgin daughter of Egypt! Yet
there is no cure for your wounds. Though you
have used many medicines, there is no healing for you. 12The nations have heard of your

45:1-5 As is often the case in our own life, Baruch's eyes turned toward his own comfort and security. It is rarely easy to serve others when we feel our own contentment is threatened, but God longs for us to trust him even then—especially then.

46:1–51:64 Words of judgment were pronounced on the nations who had mistreated God's chosen people. Without exception, Egypt, Philistia, Moab, Ammon, Edom, Damascus, Kedar, Hazor, Elam, and Babylon would all receive God's judgment for their wicked and ungodly practices. The wicked never prosper for long, though it may appear that they do for a time. We can rely on God's righteousness to prevail. He disciplines us as a parent does a child, and that discipline is always just and designed for our improvement.

shame. The earth is filled with your cry of despair and defeat; your mightiest soldiers will stumble across each other and fall together.

13Then God gave Jeremiah this message concerning the coming of Nebuchadnezzar, king of Babylon, to attack Egypt:

14Shout it out in Egypt; publish it in the cities of Migdol, Memphis, and Tahpanhes! Mobilize for battle, for the sword of destruction shall devour all around you. 15Why has Apis, your bull god, fled in terror? Because the Lord knocked him down before your enemies. 16Vast multitudes fall in heaps. (Then the remnant of the Jews will say, "Come, let us return again to Judah where we were born and get away from all this slaughter here!")

17Rename Pharaoh Hophra and call him "The Man with No Power But with Plenty of Noise!"

18As I live, says the King, the Lord of Hosts, one is coming against Egypt who is as tall as Mount Tabor or Mount Carmel by the sea! 19Pack up; get ready to leave for exile, you citizens of Egypt, for the city of Memphis shall be utterly destroyed and left without a soul alive. 20,21Egypt is sleek as a heifer, but a gadfly sends her running—a gadfly from the north! Even her famed mercenaries have become like frightened calves. They turn and run, for it is the day of great calamity for Egypt, a time of great punishment. 22,23Silent as a serpent gliding away, Egypt flees; the invading army marches in. The numberless soldiers cut down your people like woodsmen who clear a forest of its trees. 24Egypt is as helpless as a girl before these men from the north.

25The Lord, the God of Israel, says: I will punish Amon, god of Thebes, and all the other gods of Egypt. I will punish Pharaoh too, and all who trust in him. 26I will deliver them into the hands of those who want them killed—into the hands of Nebuchadnezzar, king of Babylon, and his army. But afterwards the land shall recover from the ravages of war.

27But don't you be afraid, O my people who return to your own land, don't be dismayed; for I will save you from far away and bring your children from a distant land. Yes, Israel shall return and be at rest, and nothing shall make her afraid. 28Fear not, O Jacob, my servant, says the Lord, for I am with you. I will destroy all the nations to which I have exiled you, but I will not destroy you. I will punish you, but only enough to correct you.

CHAPTER 47

A Message to Philistia

This is God's message to Jeremiah concerning the Philistines of Gaza, before the city was captured by the Egyptian army:

2The Lord says: A flood is coming from the north to overflow the land of the Philistines; it will destroy their cities and everything in them. Strong men will scream in terror, and all the land will weep. 3Hear the clattering hoofs and rumbling wheels as the chariots go rushing by; fathers flee without a backward glance at their helpless children, 4for the time has come when all the Philistines and their allies from Tyre and Sidon will be destroyed. For the Lord is destroying the Philistines, those colonists from Caphtor. 5The cities of Gaza and Ashkelon will be razed to the ground and lie in ruins. O descendants of the Anakim, how you will lament and mourn!

6O sword of the Lord, when will you be at rest again? Go back into your scabbard; rest and be still! 7But how can it be still when the Lord has sent it on an errand? For the city of Ashkelon and those living along the sea must be destroyed.

CHAPTER 48

A Message to Moab

This is the message of the Lord of Hosts, the God of Israel, against Moab:

Woe to the city of Nebo, for it shall lie in ruins. The city of Kiriathaim and its forts are overwhelmed and captured. 2-4No one will ever brag about Moab any more, for there is a plot against her life. In Heshbon plans have been completed to destroy her. "Come," they say, "we will cut her off from being a nation." In Madmen all is silent. And then the roar of battle will surge against Horonaim, for all Moab is being destroyed. Her crying will be heard as far away as Zoar. 5Her refugees will climb the hills of Luhith, weeping bitterly, while cries of terror rise from the city below. 6Flee for your lives; hide in the wilderness! 7For you trusted in your wealth and skill; therefore, you shall perish. Your god Chemosh, with his priests and princes, shall be taken away to distant lands!

8All the villages and cities, whether they be on the plateaus or in the valleys, shall be destroyed, for the Lord has said it. 9Oh, for wings for Moab that she could fly away, for her cities shall be left without a living soul. 10Cursed be those withholding their swords from your blood, refusing to do the work that God has given them!

11From her earliest history Moab has lived there undisturbed from all invasions. She is like wine that has not been poured from flask to flask and is fragrant and smooth. But now she shall have the pouring out of exile! 12The time is coming soon, the Lord has said, when he will send troublemakers to spill her out from jar to jar and then shatter the jars! 13Then at last Moab shall be ashamed of her idol Chemosh, as Israel was of her calf-idol at Bethel.

14Do you remember that boast of yours: "We are heroes, mighty men of war"? 15But now Moab is to be destroyed; her destroyer is on the way; her choicest youth are doomed to slaughter, says the King, the Lord Almighty. 16Calamity is coming fast to Moab.

17O friends of Moab, weep for her and cry! See how the strong, the beautiful is shattered! 18Come down from your glory and sit in the dust, O people of Dibon, for those destroying Moab shall shatter Dibon too, and tear down all her towers. 19Those in Aroer stand anxiously beside the road to watch, and shout to those who flee from Moab, "What has happened there?"

20And they reply, "Moab lies in ruins; weep and wail. Tell it by the banks of the Arnon, that Moab is destroyed."

21All the cities of the tableland lie in ruins too, for God's judgment has been poured out upon them all—on Holon and Jahzah and Mephaath, 22and Dibon and Nebo and Beth-diblathaim, 23and Kiriathaim and Beth-gamul and Beth-meon, 24and Kerioth and Bozrah—and all the cities of the land of Moab, far and near.

25The strength of Moab is ended—her horns are cut off; her arms are broken. 26Let her stagger and fall like a drunkard, for she has rebelled against the Lord. Moab shall wallow in her vomit, scorned by all. 27For you scorned Israel and robbed her and were happy at her fall.

28O people of Moab, flee from your cities and live in the caves like doves that nest in the clefts of the rocks. 29We have all heard of the pride of Moab, for it is very great. We know your loftiness, your arrogance, and your haughty heart. 30I know her insolence, the Lord has said, but her boasts are false—her helplessness is great. 31Yes, I wail for Moab, my heart is broken for the men of Kir-heres.

32O men of Sibmah, rich in vineyards, I weep for you even more than for Jazer. For the destroyer has cut off your spreading tendrils and harvested your grapes and summer fruits. He has plucked you bare! 33Joy and gladness are gone from fruitful Moab. The presses yield no wine; no one treads the grapes with shouts of joy. There is shouting, yes, but not the shouting of joy. 34Instead the awful cries of terror and pain rise from all over the land—from Heshbon clear across to Elealeh and to Jahaz; from Zoar to Horonaim and to Eglath-shelishiyah. The pastures of Nimrim are deserted now.

35For the Lord says: I have put a stop to Moab's worshiping false gods and burning incense to idols. 36Sad sings my heart for Moab and Kir-heres, for all their wealth has disappeared. 37They shave their heads and beards in anguish; they slash their hands and put on clothes of sackcloth. 38Crying and sorrow will be in every Moabite home and on the streets; for I have smashed and shattered Moab like an old, unwanted bottle. 39How it is broken! Hear the wails! See the shame of Moab! For she is a sign of horror and of scoffing to her neighbors now.

40A vulture circles ominously above the land of Moab, says the Lord. 41Her cities are fallen; her strongholds are seized. The hearts of her mightiest warriors fail with fear like women in the pains of giving birth. 42Moab shall no longer be a nation, for she has boasted against the Lord. 43Fear and traps and treachery shall be your lot, O Moab, says the Lord. 44He who flees shall fall in a trap, and he who escapes from the trap shall run into a snare. I will see to it that you do not get away, for the time of your judgment has come. 45They flee to Heshbon, unable to go farther. But a fire comes from Heshbon—Sihon's ancestral home—and devours the land from end to end with all its rebellious people.

46Woe to you, O Moab; the people of the god Chemosh are destroyed, and your sons and daughters are taken away as slaves. 47But in the latter days, says the Lord, I will reestablish Moab.

(Here the prophecy concerning Moab ends.)

CHAPTER 49

A Message to Ammon

What is this you are doing? Why are you living in the cities of the Jews? Aren't there Jews enough to fill them up? Didn't they inherit them from me? Why then have you, who worship Milcom, taken over Gad and all its cities? 2I will punish you for this, the Lord

declares, by destroying your city of Rabbah. It
shall become a desolate heap, and the neighboring towns shall be burned. Then Israel
shall come and take back her land from you
again. She shall dispossess those who dispossessed her, says the Lord.
3Cry out, O Heshbon, for Ai is destroyed!
Weep, daughter of Rabbah! Put on garments
of mourning; weep and wail, hiding in the
hedges, for your god Milcom shall be exiled
along with his princes and priests. 4You are
proud of your fertile valleys, but they will
soon be ruined. O wicked daughter, you
trusted in your wealth and thought no one
could ever harm you. 5But see, I will bring
terror upon you, says the Lord, the Lord Almighty. For all your neighbors shall drive you
from your land and none shall help your
exiles as they flee. 6But afterward I will restore
the fortunes of the Ammonites, says the Lord.

A Message to Edom

7The Lord says: Where are all your wise men
of days gone by? Is there not one left in all of
Teman? 8Flee to the remotest parts of the
desert, O people of Dedan; for when I punish
Edom, I will punish you! 9,10Those who gather
grapes leave a few for the poor, and even
thieves don't take everything, but I will strip
bare the land of Esau, and there will be no
place to hide. Her children, her brothers, her
neighbors—all will be destroyed—and she
herself will perish too. 11(But I will preserve
your fatherless children who remain, and let
your widows depend upon me.)
12The Lord says to Edom: If the innocent
must suffer, how much more must you! You
shall not go unpunished! You must drink this
cup of judgment! 13For I have sworn by my
own name, says the Lord, that Bozrah shall
become heaps of ruins, cursed and mocked;
and her cities shall be eternal wastes.
14I have heard this message from the Lord:
He has sent a messenger to call the nations to
form a coalition against Edom and destroy
her.
15I will make her weak among the nations
and despised by all, says the Lord. 16You have
been fooled by your fame and your pride,
living there in the mountains of Petra, in the
clefts of the rocks. But though you live among
the peaks with the eagles, I will bring you
down, says the Lord.
17The fate of Edom will be horrible; all who
go by will be appalled and gasp at the sight.
18Your cities will become as silent as Sodom
and Gomorrah and their neighboring towns,
says the Lord. No one will live there anymore.
19I will send against them one who will come
like a lion from the wilds of Jordan stalking
the sheep in the fold. Suddenly Edom shall be
destroyed, and I will appoint over the Edomites the person of my choice. For who is like
me, and who can call me to account? What
shepherd can defy me?
20Take note: The Lord will certainly do this
to Edom and also the people of Teman—even
little children will be dragged away as slaves!
It will be a shocking thing to see. 21The earth
shakes with the noise of Edom's fall; the cry
of the people is heard as far away as the Red
Sea. 22The one who will come will fly as swift
as a vulture and will spread his wings against
Bozrah. Then the courage of the mightiest
warriors will disappear like that of women in
labor.

A Message to Damascus

23The cities of Hamath and Arpad are stricken
with fear, for they have heard the news of
their doom. Their hearts are troubled like a
wild sea in a raging storm. 24Damascus has
become feeble, and all her people turn to flee.
Fear, anguish, and sorrow have gripped her as
they do women in labor. 25O famous city, city
of joy, how you are forsaken now! 26Your
young men lie dead in the streets; your entire
army shall be destroyed in one day, says the
Lord Almighty. 27And I will start a fire at the
edge of Damascus that shall burn up the palaces of Benhadad.

A Message to Kedar and Hazor

28This prophecy is about Kedar and the kingdoms of Hazor that are going to be destroyed
by Nebuchadnezzar, king of Babylon, for the
Lord will send him to destroy them:
29Their flocks and their tents will be captured, says the Lord, with all their household
goods. Their camels will be taken away, and
all around will be the shouts of panic, "We are
surrounded and doomed!" 30Flee for your
lives, says the Lord. Go deep into the deserts,
O people of Hazor, for Nebuchadnezzar, king
of Babylon, has plotted against you and is
preparing to destroy you.
31"Go," said the Lord to King Nebuchadnezzar. "Attack those wealthy Bedouin tribes living alone in the desert without a care in the
world, boasting that they are self-sufficient—
that they need neither walls nor gates. 32Their
camels and cattle shall all be yours, and I will
scatter these heathen to the winds. From all
directions I will bring calamity upon them.

33"Hazor shall be a home for wild animals
of the desert. No one shall ever live there
again. It shall be desolate forever."

A Message to Elam

34God's message against Elam came to Jeremiah in the beginning of the reign of Zedekiah, king of Judah:
35The Lord says: I will destroy the army of
Elam, 36and I will scatter the people of Elam to
the four winds; they shall be exiled to countries throughout the world. 37My fierce anger
will bring great evil upon Elam, says the Lord,
and I will cause her enemies to wipe her out.
38And I will set my throne in Elam, says the
Lord. I will destroy her king and princes. 39But
in the latter days I will bring the people back,
says the Lord.

CHAPTER 50

A Message to Babylon

This is the message from the Lord against
Babylon and the Chaldeans, spoken by Jeremiah the prophet:
2Tell all the world that Babylon will be
destroyed; her god Marduk will be utterly
disgraced! 3For a nation shall come down
upon her from the north with such destruction that no one shall live in her again; all
shall be gone—both men and animals shall
flee.
4Then the people of Israel and Judah shall
join together, weeping and seeking the Lord
their God. 5They shall ask the way to Zion and
start back home again. "Come," they will say,
"let us be united to the Lord with an eternal
pledge that will never be broken again."
6My people have been lost sheep. Their
shepherds led them astray and then turned
them loose in the mountains. They lost their
way and didn't remember how to get back to
the fold. 7All who found them devoured them
and said, "We are permitted to attack them
freely, for they have sinned against the Lord,
the God of justice, the hope of their fathers."
8But now, flee from Babylon, the land of the
Chaldeans; lead my people home again. 9For
see, I am raising up an army of great nations
from the north, and I will bring them against
Babylon to attack her, and she shall be destroyed. The enemies' arrows go straight to
the mark; they do not miss! 10And Babylon
shall be sacked until everyone is sated with
loot, says the Lord.
11Though you were glad, O Chaldeans,
plunderers of my people, and are fat as cows
that feed in lush pastures, and neigh like
stallions, 12yet your mother shall be overwhelmed with shame, for you shall become
the least of the nations—a wilderness, a dry
and desert land. 13Because of the anger of the
Lord, Babylon shall become deserted wasteland, and all who pass by shall be appalled
and shall mock at her for all her wounds.
14Yes, prepare to fight with Babylon, all you
nations round about; let the archers shoot at
her; spare no arrows, for she has sinned
against the Lord. 15Shout against her from
every side. Look! She surrenders! Her walls
have fallen. The Lord has taken vengeance.
Do to her as she has done! 16Let the farmhands
all depart. Let them rush back to their own
lands as the enemies advance.
17The Israelites are like sheep the lions
chase. First the king of Assyria ate them up;
then Nebuchadnezzar, the king of Babylon,
crunched their bones. 18Therefore the Lord,
the God of Israel, says: Now I will punish the
king of Babylon and his land as I punished the
king of Assyria. 19And I will bring Israel home
again to her own land, to feed in the fields of
Carmel and Bashan and to be happy once
more on Mount Ephraim and Mount Gilead.
20In those days, says the Lord, no sin shall be
found in Israel or in Judah, for I will pardon
the remnant I preserve.
21Go up, O my warriors, against the land of
Merathaim and against the people of Pekod.
Yes, march against Babylon, the land of rebels, a land that I will judge! Annihilate them,
as I have commanded you. 22Let there be the
shout of battle in the land, a shout of great
destruction. 23Babylon, the mightiest hammer in all the earth, lies broken and shattered. Babylon is desolate among the
nations! 24O Babylon, I have set a trap for you
and you are caught, for you have fought
against the Lord.
25The Lord has opened his armory and
brought out weapons to explode his wrath
upon his enemies. The terror that befalls Babylon will be the work of the Lord God. 26Yes,
come against her from distant lands; break
open her granaries; knock down her walls and
houses into heaps of ruins and utterly destroy
her; let nothing be left. 27Not even her cattle—
woe to them too! Kill them all! For the time
has come for Babylon to be devastated.
28But my people will flee; they will escape
back to their own country to tell how the Lord
their God has broken forth in fury upon those
who destroyed his Temple.
29Send out a call for archers to come to
Babylon; surround the city so that none can

escape. Do to her as she has done to others,
for she has haughtily defied the Lord, the
Holy One of Israel. 30 Her young men will fall
in the streets and die; her warriors will all be
killed. 31 For see, I am against you, O people so
proud; and now your day of reckoning has
come. 32 Land of pride, you will stumble and
fall, and no one will raise you up; for the Lord
will light a fire in the cities of Babylon that
will burn everything around them.

33 The Lord says: The people of Israel and
Judah have been wronged. Their captors hold
them and refuse to let them go. 34 But their
Redeemer is strong. His name is the Lord
Almighty. He will plead for them and see that
they are freed to live again in quietness in
Israel.

As for the people of Babylon—there is no
rest for them! 35 The sword of destruction shall
smite the Chaldeans, says the Lord. It shall
smite the people of Babylon—her princes and
wise men too. 36 All her wise counselors shall
become fools! Panic shall seize her mightiest
warriors! 37 War shall devour her horses and
chariots, and her allies from other lands shall
become as weak as women. Her treasures shall
all be robbed; 38 even her water supply will fail.
And why? Because the whole land is full of
images, and the people are madly in love with
their idols.

39 Therefore this city of Babylon shall become inhabited by ostriches and jackals; it
shall be a home for the wild animals of the
desert. Never again shall it be lived in by
human beings; it shall lie desolate forever.
40 The Lord declares that he will destroy Babylon just as he destroyed Sodom and Gomorrah and their neighboring towns. No one has
lived in them since, and no one will live again
in Babylon.

41 See them coming! A great army from the
north! It is accompanied by many kings called
by God from many lands. 42 They are fully
armed for slaughter; they are cruel and show
no mercy; their battle cry roars like the surf
against the shoreline. O Babylon, they ride
against you fully ready for the battle.

43 When the king of Babylon received the
dispatch, his hands fell helpless at his sides;
pangs of terror gripped him like the pangs of
a woman in labor.

44 *I will send against them an invader who will
come upon them suddenly, like a lion from the
jungles of Jordan that leaps upon the grazing
sheep. I will put her defenders to flight and appoint over them whomsoever I please. For who is
like me? What ruler can oppose my will? Who
can call me to account?*

45 Listen to the plan of the Lord against
Babylon, the land of the Chaldeans. For even
little children shall be dragged away as slaves;
oh, the horror; oh, the terror. 46 The whole
earth shall shake at Babylon's fall, and her cry
of despair shall be heard around the world.

CHAPTER 51

The Fall of Babylon

The Lord says: I will stir up a destroyer against
Babylon, against that whole land of the Chaldeans, and destroy it. 2 Winnowers shall come
and winnow her and blow her away; they
shall come from every side to rise against her
in her day of trouble. 3 The arrows of the
enemy shall strike down the bowmen of Babylon and pierce her warriors in their coats of
mail. No one shall be spared; both young and
old alike shall be destroyed. 4 They shall fall
down slain in the land of the Chaldeans,
slashed to death in her streets. 5 For the Lord
Almighty has not forsaken Israel and Judah.
He is still their God, but the land of the
Chaldeans is filled with sin against the Holy
One of Israel.

6 Flee from Babylon! Save yourselves! Don't
get trapped! If you stay, you will be destroyed
when God takes his vengeance on all of Babylon's sins. 7 Babylon has been as a gold cup in
the Lord's hands, a cup from which he made
the whole earth drink and go mad. 8 But now,
suddenly Babylon too has fallen. Weep for
her; give her medicine; perhaps she can yet be
healed. 9 We would help her if we could, but
nothing can save her now. Let her go. Abandon her and return to your own land, for God
is judging her from heaven. 10 The Lord has
vindicated us. Come, let us declare in Jerusalem all the Lord our God has done.

11 Sharpen the arrows! Lift up the shields!
For the Lord has stirred up the spirit of the
kings of the Medes to march on Babylon and
destroy her. This is his vengeance on those
who wronged his people and desecrated his
Temple. 12 Prepare your defenses, Babylon! Set
many watchmen on your walls; send out an
ambush, for the Lord will do all he has said he
would concerning Babylon. 13 O wealthy port,
great center of commerce, your end has come;
the thread of your life is cut. 14 The Lord Almighty has taken this vow and sworn to it in
his own name: Your cities shall be filled with
enemies, like fields filled with locusts in a
plague, and they shall lift to the skies their
mighty shouts of victory.

15God made the earth by his power and wisdom. He stretched out the heavens by his understanding. 16When he speaks there is thunder in the heavens, and he causes the vapors to rise around the world; he brings the lightning with the rain and the winds from his treasuries. 17Compared to him, all men are stupid beasts. They have no wisdom—none at all! The silversmith is dulled by the images he makes, for in making them he lies; for he calls them gods when there is not a breath of life in them at all! 18Idols are nothing! They are lies! And the time is coming when God will come and see, and shall destroy them all. 19But the God of Israel is no idol! For he made everything there is, and Israel is his nation; the Lord Almighty is his name.

20Cyrus is God's battleaxe and sword. I will use you, says the Lord, to break nations in pieces and to destroy many kingdoms. 21With you I will crush armies, destroying the horse and his rider, the chariot and the charioteer—22yes, and the civilians too, both old and young, young men and maidens, 23shepherds and flocks, farmers and oxen, captains and rulers; 24 before your eyes I will repay Babylon and all the Chaldeans for all the evil they have done to my people, says the Lord.

25For see, I am against you, O mighty mountain, Babylon, destroyer of the earth! I will lift my hand against you, roll you down from your heights, and leave you, a burnt-out mountain. 26You shall be desolate forever; even your stones shall never be used for building again. You shall be completely wiped out.

27Signal many nations to mobilize for war on Babylon. Sound the battle cry; bring out the armies of Ararat, Minni, and Ashkenaz. Appoint a leader; bring a multitude of horses! 28Bring against her the armies of the kings of the Medes and their generals, and the armies of all the countries they rule.

29Babylon trembles and writhes in pain, for all that the Lord has planned against her stands unchanged. Babylon will be left desolate without a living soul. 30Her mightiest soldiers no longer fight; they stay in their barracks. Their courage is gone; they have become as women. The invaders have burned the houses and broken down the city gates. 31Messengers from every side come running to the king to tell him all is lost! 32All the escape routes are blocked; the fortifications are burning, and the army is in panic.

33For the Lord, the God of Israel, says: Babylon is like the wheat upon a threshing floor; in just a little while the flailing will begin.

34,35The Jews in Babylon say, "Nebuchadnezzar, king of Babylon, has eaten and crushed us and emptied out our strength; he has swallowed us like a great monster and filled his belly with our riches; he has cast us out of our own country. May Babylon be repaid for all she did to us! May she be paid in full for all our blood she spilled!"

36And the Lord replies: I will be your lawyer; I will plead your case; I will avenge you. I will dry up her river, her water supply, 37and Babylon shall become a heap of ruins, haunted by jackals, a land horrible to see, incredible, without a living soul. 38In their drunken feasts, the men of Babylon roar like lions. 39And while they lie inflamed with all their wine, I will prepare a different kind of feast for them and make them drink until they fall unconscious to the floor, to sleep forever, never to waken again, says the Lord. 40I will bring them like lambs to the slaughter, like rams and goats.

41How Babylon is fallen—great Babylon, lauded by all the earth! The world can scarcely believe its eyes at Babylon's fall! 42The sea has risen upon Babylon; she is covered by its waves. 43Her cities lie in ruins—she is a dry wilderness where no one lives nor even travelers pass by. 44And I will punish Bel, the god of Babylon, and pull from his mouth what he has taken. The nations shall no longer come and worship him; the wall of Babylon has fallen.

45O my people, flee from Babylon; save yourselves from the fierce anger of the Lord. 46But don't panic when you hear the first rumor of approaching forces. For rumors will keep coming year by year. Then there will be a time of civil war as the governors of Babylon fight against each other. 47For the time is surely coming when I will punish this great city and all her idols; her dead shall lie in the streets. 48Heaven and earth shall rejoice, for out of the north shall come destroying armies against Babylon, says the Lord. 49Just as Babylon killed the people of Israel, so must she be killed. 50Go, you who escaped the sword! Don't stand and watch—flee while you can! Remember the Lord and return to Jerusalem far away!

51*"We are ashamed because the Temple of the Lord has been defiled by foreigners from Babylon."*

52Yes, says the Lord. But the time is coming for the destruction of the idols of Babylon. All through the land will be heard the groans of the wounded. 53Though Babylon be as powerful as heaven, though she increase her strength immeasurably, she shall die, says the Lord.

54Listen! Hear the cry of great destruction out of Babylon, the land the Chaldeans rule! 55For the Lord is destroying Babylon; her mighty voice is stilled as the waves roar in upon her. 56Destroying armies come and slay her mighty men; all her weapons break in her hands, for the Lord God gives just punishment and is giving Babylon all her due. 57I will make drunk her princes, wise men, rulers, captains, warriors. They shall sleep and not wake up again! So says the King, the Lord Almighty. 58For the wide walls of Babylon shall be leveled to the ground, and her high gates shall be burned; the builders from many lands have worked in vain—their work shall be destroyed by fire!

59During the fourth year of Zedekiah's reign, this message came to Jeremiah to give to Seraiah (son of Neriah, son of Mahseiah), concerning Seraiah's capture and exile to Babylon along with Zedekiah, king of Judah. (Seraiah was quartermaster of Zedekiah's army.) 60Jeremiah wrote on a scroll all the terrible things God had scheduled against Babylon—all the words written above— 61,62and gave the scroll to Seraiah and said to him, "When you get to Babylon, read what I have written and say, 'Lord, you have said that you will destroy Babylon so that not a living creature will remain, and it will be abandoned forever.' 63Then, when you have finished reading the scroll, tie a rock to it, and throw it into the Euphrates River, 64and say, 'So shall Babylon sink, never more to rise, because of the evil I am bringing upon her.'"

(This ends Jeremiah's messages.)

CHAPTER 52

Details of Jerusalem's Fall

(Events told about in chapter 39.)

Zedekiah was twenty-one years old when he became king, and he reigned eleven years in Jerusalem. His mother's name was Hamutal (daughter of Jeremiah of Libnah). 2But he was a wicked king, just as Jehoiakim had been. 3Things became so bad at last that the Lord, in his anger, saw to it that Zedekiah rebelled against the king of Babylon until he and the people of Israel were ejected from the Lord's presence in Jerusalem and Judah, and were taken away as captives to Babylon.

4In the ninth year of Zedekiah's reign, on the tenth day of the tenth month, Nebuchadnezzar, king of Babylon, came with all his army against Jerusalem and built forts around it, 5and laid siege to the city for two years. 6Then finally, on the ninth day of the fourth month, when the famine in the city was very serious, with the last of the food entirely gone, 7the people in the city tore a hole in the city wall and all the soldiers fled from the city during the night, going out by the gate between the two walls near the king's gardens (for the city was surrounded by the Chaldeans), and made a dash for it across the fields, toward Arabah.

8But the Chaldean soldiers chased them and caught King Zedekiah in some fields near Jericho—for all his army was scattered from him. 9They brought him to the king of Babylon who was staying in the city of Riblah in the kingdom of Hamath, and there judgment was passed upon him. 10He made Zedekiah watch while his sons and all the princes of Judah were killed before his eyes. 11Then his eyes were gouged out, and he was taken in chains to Babylon and put in prison for the rest of his life.

12On the tenth day of the fifth month during the nineteenth year of the reign of Nebuchadnezzar, king of Babylon, Nebuzaradan, captain of the guard, arrived in Jerusalem, 13and burned the Temple and the palace and all the larger homes, 14and set the Chaldean army to work tearing down the walls of the city. 15Then he took to Babylon, as captives, some of the poorest of the people—along with those who survived the city's destruction, and those who had deserted Zedekiah and had come over to the Babylonian army, and the tradesmen who were left. 16But he left

52:1-34 There is, perhaps, no greater suffering than the reminder of our sin and the memory of the suffering we have caused others. As Jerusalem fell, the people could avoid the destructive consequences of their sin no longer. And memories of Jerusalem's broken walls would bring their past failures back to haunt them again and again. What a burden to carry into exile! As we face recovery and are surrounded by the devastation of our poor choices and selfish actions, we can turn to God and still have hope for restoration. God loves us as no one else can. He desires a relationship with us more than we can know. The pain of our sin is grievous to us and to God, but God always desires our restoration and wants to give us a chance to begin again.

some of the poorest people to care for the crops as vinedressers and plowmen.

[17]The Babylonians dismantled the two large bronze pillars that stood at the entrance of the Temple, and the bronze laver and bronze bulls on which it stood, and carted them off to
Babylon. [18]And he took along all the bronze pots and kettles, the ash shovels used at the altar, the snuffers, spoons, bowls, and all the
other items used in the Temple. [19]He also took the firepans, the solid gold and silver candlesticks, and the cups and bowls.

[20]The weight of the two enormous pillars, the laver, and twelve bulls was tremendous. They had no way of estimating it. (They had been made in the days of King Solomon.)
[21]For the pillars were each 27 feet high and 18 feet in circumference, hollow, with 3-inch
walls. [22]The top 7 1/2 feet of each column had bronze carvings, a network of bronze pomegranates. [23]There were 96 pomegranates on the sides, and on the network round about there were a hundred more.

[24,25]The captain of the guard took along with him as his prisoners: Seraiah the chief priest, Zephaniah his assistant, the three chief Temple guards, one of the commanding officers of the army, seven of the king's special counselors discovered in the city, the secretary of the general-in-chief of the Jewish army (who was in charge of recruitment), and sixty
other men of importance found hiding. [26]He took them to the king of Babylon at Riblah,
[27]where the king killed them all.

So it was that Judah's exile was accomplished.

[28]The number of captives taken to Babylon in the seventh year of Nebuchadnezzar's reign
was 3,023. [29]Then, eleven years later, he took
832 more; [30]five years after that he sent Nebuzaradan, his captain of the guard, and took 745—a total of 4,600 captives in all.

[31]On February 25 of the thirty-seventh year of the imprisonment in Babylon of Jehoiachin, king of Judah, Evil-merodach, who became king of Babylon that year, was kind to King Jehoiachin and brought him out of
prison. [32]He spoke pleasantly to him and gave him preference over all the other kings in
Babylon; [33]he gave him new clothes and fed him from the king's kitchen as long as he
lived. [34]And he was given a regular allowance to cover his daily needs until the day of his death.

REFLECTIONS ON JEREMIAH

✲*insights* ABOUT THE DANGER OF IDOLATRY

Our idols differ from the idols of the people of Judah. As we see in **Jeremiah 1:16,** their gods were handmade, often statues of clay or precious metals. Ours may come in the form of alcohol, drugs, sex, or work. Whatever consumes our time and energy and permeates our thought life has become our god. Our idolatry will destroy our relationship with God and ruin our life if we allow it to go on unchecked.

In **Jeremiah 2:13** we see that idolatry involves two grave mistakes: first, we turn away from our powerful God, the only one who can really help us; second, we turn to idols that have no power to help us. When we choose to turn from God, we often turn to alcohol, drugs, sex, or work to deal with pain that only God can heal. We know from experience, however, that these temporary solutions only deepen our pain in the long run. God invites us to put these things away. He wants us to return to his loving care. He wants a relationship with us, free of the distractions of our destructive addictions.

In **Jeremiah 2:24-25** the prophet compared Israel with a female donkey at mating time, running to one male donkey after another to satisfy her lusts. Israel was willing to try out any god without even thinking about it—she was out of control! When we reject God's control in our life, we will find ourself out of control. We will mindlessly chase after the old addictions that brought us so much destruction in the past. We need to recognize how helpless we are against the pull of our dependencies and put our life into God's hands. Only then will we begin to experience his power in our recovery.

✲*insights* ABOUT DENIAL AND HYPOCRISY

In **Jeremiah 3:9-10** we find that the people of Israel were in denial and took their sins lightly. We often do the same thing, perhaps because the consequences don't come immediately. Nothing bad happens for a while, and we are lulled into thinking we can get away with our destructive behavior. If the consequences struck us instantly, we would probably take our actions more seriously. We must realize that God does not take our sin lightly. The consequences for sinful behavior will inevitably come sooner or later.

Jeremiah's audience was in denial. In **Jeremiah 5:11-13** the prophet warned them that their behavior would lead to terrible consequences, but they refused to listen. We often do the same thing. When confronted with the consequences of our behavior, we foolishly defend our actions. We even begin to project our own destruction onto others. Next time someone goes to the trouble of confronting us, we need to listen; they may be right. When this happens, we would be wise to take an inventory of our life to see whether or not our recovery needs renovation.

In **Jeremiah 16:16–17:13** it becomes clear that we can fool others with our actions, but we can never fool God. Judgment came to Judah not simply because the actions of the people were grievous, but also because their hearts were unrepentant. God searches our innermost parts and knows our heart. He cares about who we are, not just about what we do. For this reason, our recovery does not begin with a heroic act on our part. It begins as we admit that we are powerless and unable to do anything. All we need is a humble and repentant heart.

Jeremiah 23:23-24 leaves us with a clear reminder that although we may hide our behavior from others, we can never hide from God. He knows about our failures; he is aware of our deepest pain. We are never alone! This should comfort us as we admit our failures to God. Despite the fact that he knows all about us, he still loves us and wants us to experience his healing and grace. Knowing that God is aware of all our thoughts and actions should also help us stand against temptation. We all know that it is easier to fall when we think no one is watching.

✲*insights* ABOUT THE PERSON OF GOD

In **Jeremiah 1:6-8** God asked his prophet to do some difficult things. He does the same for us: he asks us to put the past behind us; he wants us to fight lust, greed, fear, and despair. But in his love, he never sends us into battle alone. He will always be by our side, encouraging us along and showing us the way.

In **Jeremiah 3:1** we discover that God goes beyond what anyone would reasonably expect from another human to show his grace. No matter how far we wander, no matter how many other false gods (our dependencies, godless recovery programs, unhealthy relationships) we have worshiped, he will take us back. When we stop living life in our own power, God invites us to recover through his power. No sin is so awful that God's love won't forgive it.

In **Jeremiah 3:6–4:4** God is portrayed as feeling intense emotion. He is hurt deeply by the sin of Israel and Judah, just as he is hurt by our sin. God longs for his people to return and receive forgiveness. Sin is painful to all who are touched by its perversion, yet no one grieves over sin's devastating consequences more than God. He wants us to turn to him for deliverance from the grip of sin in our life; he wants to set us free from the painful consequences we are creating for ourself with each passing day.

In **Jeremiah 3:19-20** God reminded his people that he had wanted to be like a loving Father to them. Few of us understand the depth of God's fatherly love. What a wonderful God who waits patiently for the day when we turn to him and utter the word *Father!* For us to say it, we have to daily allow him to be our Father by turning our focus to him. Since he always desires the best for us, we can seek out his will for us and do our best to follow it. As we do, he will be with us each step of the way, giving us the strength and encouragement we need to succeed in our recovery.

✲*insights* INTO THE PROCESS OF RECOVERY

God tells us, every day, exactly what he told his prophet in **Jeremiah 1:10:** "Today your work begins." It is never too late to make a new start, and today can be that time for us. We are to be about our Father's business of confronting and dealing with our sin and encouraging others to do the same. Today is the day to begin!

In marriage there is a honeymoon period when we are eager to please our new spouse. In **Jeremiah 2:2-3** God remembered the time when Israel was his eager bride, happy to be faithful to him. We also have a honeymoon period in our recovery when we are eager to please God and focus on him. However, a period of disillusionment sets in when the honeymoon turns into a relapse. By taking time daily to be renewed by God's love and power, we can avoid such a relapse. Temptations will lose their power to divert us as we daily surrender our life to God's control.

Though the world has gone its own way, in **Jeremiah 4:27-28** God calls us to be a steadfast remnant, living to honor him. Even in recovery groups there often is only a small remnant who truly seek after God. Making God the center of our recovery and seeking direction from his Word will keep us from straying from the truth. With God's help we can be part of the remnant that prevails, standing for God even when a majority of the people around us forsake him.

In **Jeremiah 9:4-6** the prophet warned his people about the power of others to lead us away from God. When our heart is focused on God, it won't matter what others do to us or think of us. Some people may be threatened by our recovery; others may stand to lose something. Such people may do everything they can to drag us down with slanderous lies. Even when this happens, we need to remain obedient to the truth and steadfast in our relationship with God. He will protect us if we trust in him.

The cry to God for help in **Jeremiah 17:14** is the cry of recovery. When we acknowledge that only God can save us and heal our hurts, we can begin a new life. Hope doesn't come from within; we don't have the power to produce it. Only God can give us hope and then provide the help we need.

✲*insights* FROM ISRAEL'S HISTORY

The prophet's message in **Jeremiah 2:1–3:5** was intended for the people of Judah. God spoke about Judah's early days as a parent might reflect on the sweeter days in the life of a troubled child. Judah had forsaken God to create her own idols (see 2:13), and God's heart had been broken. The idols in our life never bring satisfaction. A careful inventory will reveal the things in our life that we put before God. These need to be removed before we can move forward in our relationship with God and with our recovery.

In **Jeremiah 2:6-8** the prophet recalls how the people of Israel soon forgot who had saved them from their bondage in Egypt. As a result, they wandered for years in the wilderness. Without God, we, too, will find ourself wandering in a terrible wilderness. Relapsing into our destructive, selfish ways is a certainty without God's help. If we refuse to acknowledge and take advantage of God's power in our life, we will find ourself in humbling situations, forced once again to acknowledge our need for God's power in our life. Why would we ever want to turn away from him?

In **Jeremiah 3:12-13** we find God's plan for change, and his plan has not changed any since that time. He expects us to admit our guilt and confess that we have been following someone or something other than God. We cannot change until we are willing to confess our mistakes to God and someone else. Recovery begins today as it did thousands of years ago. We need to openly confess that we have wandered from God and ask for his forgiveness and restoring power. As we give our life into his hands, trusting him to help us, he will work the process of recovery in our life.

✲*insights* INTO THE VALUE OF GOD'S DISCIPLINE

Perhaps the most difficult part of discipline is allowing those we love to live with the consequences of their mistakes. No parent enjoys the process of discipline, but without it, love is incomplete. In **Jeremiah 4:5–6:30** we find that God allows the people to suffer the consequences of their sins (see 4:18; 5:3, 19, 31; 6:18-19), yet his heart is heavy. He suffers when we suffer, and the suffering he brings upon us is designed to lead us to healing and recovery.

Jeremiah 8:4–10:22 is filled with predictions of God's judgment. There is nothing good left to salvage from among the people of Judah. There is no truth in the mouths of God's people. The wound is incurable. The people will soon suffer terrible punishment. We also may reach a point in life where God allows the consequences of our sins to catch up to us; we may lose everything. Even if we have reached that point, we can take courage. God brings punishment into our life to get our attention. He disciplines us because he loves us. It is never too late for recovery. All we have to do is admit that we are powerless against our dependencies and hand things over to God. He is able to rebuild our life from the ashes of destruction.

Tucked away in a long passage of judgment, the words of **Jeremiah 16:14-15** reveal God's forgiving heart. The sins of Judah would lead to punishment in exile, but God's plans for his people didn't stop there. Through their suffering, God's people were forced to recognize their sin and look to God for deliverance. God then redeemed his people from exile and led them back to the Promised Land. No matter how badly we have sinned and how terrible the consequences we have suffered, God desires to work good in our life. If we admit our failures and turn to him for help, he will be faithful to restore us to wholeness.

insights INTO THE VALUE OF GOD'S LAWS

In **Jeremiah 6:16** God promises rest for our soul if we are willing to do things his way. A life spent rejecting God's laws, however, only drains our resources. We end up exhausted and distant from God. The road back to God is always the right road. It allows our soul to experience the rest and serenity possible only for those who put their lives in God's hands.

We find in **Jeremiah 8:14-15** that no matter how hard we struggle in our pursuit of health and peace, it can only be found where God says it will be found. Recovery can only begin as we commit our life to God's intended plan for us. It only progresses as we develop our relationship with God by seeking conscious contact with God through prayer and meditation on his Word.

In **Jeremiah 17:11** we discover that ill-gotten gain will never bring satisfaction. We often try to obtain things in ways God would never allow: money through greed and extortion, a spouse through adultery, or prestige through oppression of the poor. If we gain our possessions and relationships through actions God forbids, we should expect to lose them. In recovery, we are called to make amends with those we have wronged. We must give up the possessions we have gained wrongly and seek to reconcile the relationships broken by our wrong actions.

An important recovery principle can be found in **Jeremiah 17:27.** When we don't obey God's command to take a day of rest and reflection, we bring about our own destruction. We lose perspective on our priorities. We need a Sabbath to do nothing but reaffirm that God is in control—not us. One of the most important steps in recovery involves our realization of this truth. We need to reaffirm this on a regular basis. We are safe from relapse only when we allow God to take control. The more control we try to take back, the greater our danger of relapse. As we set aside time for God, we are reaffirming his importance and lordship in our life.

insights CONCERNING FALSE TEACHERS

Throughout the Bible there are warnings to watch out for false prophets and false teachers. In **Jeremiah 23:9-40** we find the false prophets of Judah claiming that the people had nothing to fear. They said that God's presence with them in the Temple was a guarantee of their protection. This sounded pious, but these prophets failed to recognize the seriousness of the people's sin. Their words only supported the people's denial. There are recovery programs that offer easy methods to overcome addiction. This kind of teaching will only lead to denial. It is never easy to deal with the failure and pain that drive our dependencies and compulsions. God calls us to face our sins honestly and to receive the forgiveness and restoration that only he can give. Anyone who teaches otherwise, or who offers a program that excludes God, should be shunned as a false prophet.

LAMENTATIONS

THE BIG PICTURE

A. JEREMIAH'S GRIEF IS EXPRESSED (1:1-22)
B. THE AGONY OF THE CONSEQUENCES (2:1-22)
C. THE PROPHET'S DEEP PAIN AND CONSOLATION (3:1-66)
D. THE PAST AND THE PRESENT IN FULL VIEW (4:1-22)
E. AN IMPASSIONED PRAYER FOR FORGIVENESS (5:1-22)

With head bowed in humility and pain, Jeremiah penned the words of Lamentations. His heart was broken. He wept to see the great city of Jerusalem destroyed and God's people in exile. Gone were the days of obedience and prosperity. The prophet had only his memories to hold on to, and a faint hope of future recovery.

Jeremiah's pain was like that of a father with an errant child. He had lived with God's people and pleaded with them to return to God. But his pleas fell on deaf ears. The prophet's tears were God's tears, for God weeps for our sin and mourns with us in our loss. Jeremiah didn't mince his words or hide his pain. He wept openly and fully. His example can help us as we grieve our own losses.

Lamentations does not provide pat answers for the suffering we experience in life. As we read, we discover that it is all right to be real, to be angry with God, to be disappointed with life, and to despair about what tomorrow holds for us. Jeremiah gained comfort as he honestly told God how he hurt. God accepted Jeremiah as he was—angry, tired, and discouraged.

Jeremiah has given us a model for expressing our pain to God. In response to his honest cries, God listened to him and comforted him. In the midst of his agony, Jeremiah found one ray of hope despite the destruction around him—"[God's] compassion never ends!" As we face great losses in our life, we also can find hope as we tell God what we are feeling. He really does hear us.

THE BOTTOM LINE

PURPOSE: To lament the destruction of Jerusalem and the sins of Judah and to pray for recovery and restoration. AUTHOR: The prophet Jeremiah. AUDIENCE: The people of Judah, shortly after they were exiled to Babylon. DATE WRITTEN: Soon after the fall of Jerusalem (around 586 B.C.). SETTING: Jeremiah lamented for the exiled Jews from the ruins of Jerusalem. KEY VERSES: *"Yet there is one ray of hope: his compassion never ends.* It is only the Lord's mercies that have kept us from complete destruction" (3:21-22). SPECIAL FEATURES: Lamentations is written in the rhythm and style of ancient Jewish funeral songs or chants. Each chapter contains an acrostic poem: each new verse opens with a successive letter of the Hebrew alphabet.

RECOVERY THEMES

The Importance of Grief: Grief is the process that helps us to recover from our losses. In it we come to terms with our past and find freedom to live in the reality of the present. It also lays the groundwork for our hope for the future. When we harden ourself to the pain involved in the grieving process, recovery cannot take place. We see that God honored the tears and grief of Jeremiah. He will also honor our honesty as we share our pain with him. Then he will use our grief to bring healing for the present and hope for the future.

The Pain of Consequences: God does not always protect us from the consequences of our attitudes and behaviors. Those of us in recovery know, however, that the painful consequences we suffer are really a special gift from God. Through them we learn to take responsibility for the mistakes we have made. We learn to allow our pain to inspire our personal and spiritual growth. As we discover that even our suffering is part of God's recovery program, we will more readily trust and obey him and do all we can to get to know him better.

The Gift of Our Emotions: Nothing is closer to the core of our being than our emotions. If we have developed a pattern of denying or hiding our feelings, we will lose the sense of who we are before God. Jeremiah shows us that we have nothing to fear in bringing even our most raw or embarrassing emotions to God. The more honest we are about how we feel, the more completely we will become involved in our relationships with God and with others.

Forgiveness—A Way of Life: Jeremiah finished his grieving and turned to God to seek forgiveness. The book ends with a question of remorse, *"Are you angry with us still?"* Behind this question is Jeremiah's humility, coupled with his hope that God will start the process toward reconciliation and forgiveness. Jeremiah knew God's heart, so he knew that God would forgive. We can be sure that God will forgive us, too, no matter how great our sin and failure. We need to come humbly before him and place our life in his strong, gentle hands.

CHAPTER 1

Jeremiah Weeps for Jerusalem

Jerusalem's streets, once thronged with people, are silent now. Like a widow broken with grief, she sits alone in her mourning. She, once queen of nations, is now a slave.

2She sobs through the night; tears run down her cheeks. Among all her lovers, there is none to help her. All her friends are now her enemies.

3Why is Judah led away, a slave? Because of all the wrong she did to others, making them her slaves. Now she sits in exile far away. There is no rest, for those she persecuted have turned and conquered her.

4The roads to Zion mourn, no longer filled with joyous throngs who come to celebrate the Temple feasts; the city gates are silent, her priests groan, her virgins have been dragged away. Bitterly she weeps.

5Her enemies prosper, for the Lord has punished Jerusalem for all her many sins; her young children are captured and taken far away as slaves.

6All her beauty and her majesty are gone; her princes are like starving deer that search for pasture—helpless game too weak to keep on running from their foes.

7And now in the midst of all Jerusalem's sadness she remembers happy bygone days. She thinks of all the precious joys she had before her mocking enemy struck her down—and there was no one to give her aid.

8For Jerusalem sinned so horribly; therefore, she is tossed away like dirty rags. All who honored her despise her now, for they have seen her stripped naked and humiliated. She groans and hides her face.

9She indulged herself in immorality and refused to face the fact that punishment was sure to come. Now she lies in the gutter with no one left to lift her out. "O Lord," she cries, "see my plight. The enemy has triumphed."

10Her enemies have plundered her completely, taking everything precious she owns. She has seen foreign nations violate her sacred Temple—foreigners you had forbidden even to enter.

1:1-11 The sins of Judah's people led to their destruction and exile. The once-prosperous nation was now only a memory. Its capital city, Jerusalem, lay in ruins. The magnificent Temple built by Solomon had been leveled. The people felt abandoned by their God. The prophet Jeremiah mourned the terrible losses, recognizing that the people's sins had brought them about. Our sin also yields devastating consequences if we allow it to continue unchecked. If we are suffering terrible losses in our life, we should assess whether or not our sin is at the heart of them. Recovery begins as we mourn our losses and admit our failures to God. If we do this, God can rebuild our life from the ruins.

11 Her people groan and cry for bread; they have sold all they have for food to give a little strength. "Look, O Lord," she prays, "and see how I'm despised."

12 Is it nothing to you, all you who pass by? Look and see if there is any sorrow like my sorrow because of all the Lord has done to me in the day of his fierce wrath.

13 He has sent fire from heaven that burns within my bones; he has placed a pitfall in my path and turned me back. He has left me sick and desolate the whole day through.

14 He wove my sins into ropes to hitch me to a yoke of slavery. He sapped my strength and gave me to my enemies; I am helpless in their hands.

15 The Lord has trampled all my mighty men. A great army has come at his command to crush the noblest youth. The Lord has trampled his beloved city as grapes in a winepress.

16 For all these things I weep; tears flow down my cheeks. My Comforter is far away—he who alone could help me. My children have no future; we are a conquered land.

17 Jerusalem pleads for help, but no one comforts her. For the Lord has spoken: "Let her neighbors be her foes! Let her be thrown out like filthy rags!"

18 And the Lord is right, for we rebelled. And yet, O people everywhere, behold and see my anguish and despair, for my sons and daughters are taken far away as slaves to distant lands.

19 I begged my allies for their help. False hope—they could not help at all. Nor could my priests and elders—they were starving in the streets while searching through the garbage dumps for bread.

20 *See, O Lord, my anguish;* my heart is broken and my soul despairs, for I have terribly rebelled. In the streets the sword awaits me; at home, disease and death.

21 *Hear my groans!* And there is no one anywhere to help. All my enemies have heard my troubles, and they are glad to see what you have done. And yet, O Lord, the time will surely come—for you have promised it—when you will do to them as you have done to me.

22 Look also on their sins, O Lord, and punish them as you have punished me, for my sighs are many and my heart is faint.

CHAPTER 2

God's Anger at Sin

A cloud of anger from the Lord has overcast Jerusalem; the fairest city of Israel lies in the dust of the earth, cast from the heights of heaven at his command. In his day of awesome fury he has shown no mercy even to his Temple.

2 The Lord without mercy has destroyed every home in Israel. In his wrath he has broken every fortress, every wall. He has brought the kingdom to dust, with all its rulers.

3 All the strength of Israel vanishes beneath his wrath. He has withdrawn his protection as the enemy attacks. God burns across the land of Israel like a raging fire.

4 He bends his bow against his people as though he were an enemy. His strength is used against them to kill their finest youth. His fury is poured out like fire upon them.

5 Yes, the Lord has vanquished Israel like an enemy. He has destroyed her forts and palaces. Sorrows and tears are his portion for Jerusalem.

6 He has violently broken down his Temple as though it were a booth of leaves and branches in a garden! No longer can the people celebrate their holy feasts and Sabbaths. Kings and priests together fall before his wrath.

7 The Lord has rejected his own altar, for he despises the false "worship" of his people; he has given their palaces to their enemies, who carouse in the Temple as Israel used to do on days of holy feasts!

8 The Lord determined to destroy Jerusalem.

1:18-22 After suffering through Jerusalem's devastation and exile, many of the Jews were forced to recognize that they had sinned. Before Jerusalem's destruction, many believed that God would protect Jerusalem and the Temple regardless of how they lived. This belief only supported the people's denial. The destruction of Jerusalem forced them to face reality. They had sinned, and their sins had terrible consequences. Accepting responsibility for our failures is an essential part of the recovery process.

2:1-18 God's anger is described in detail in these verses, as are the devastating consequences of that anger. It should be noted that God is always slow to anger and quick to forgive. The Israelites had been warned by God's prophets for centuries before their enemies finally destroyed the Holy City of Jerusalem. We need to remember that God's anger is motivated by his love; it is his last resort as he seeks to get our attention. His purpose is not to destroy, but to bring repentance and restoration to our life.

He laid out an unalterable line of destruction. Therefore the ramparts and walls fell down before him.

9 Jerusalem's gates are useless. All their locks and bars are broken, for he has crushed them. Her kings and princes are enslaved in far-off lands, without a temple, without a divine law to govern them or prophetic vision to guide them.

10 The elders of Jerusalem sit upon the ground in silence, clothed in sackcloth; they throw dust upon their heads in sorrow and despair. The virgins of Jerusalem hang their heads in shame.

11 I have cried until the tears no longer come; my heart is broken, my spirit poured out, as I see what has happened to my people; little children and tiny babies are fainting and dying in the streets.

12 "Mama, Mama, we want food," they cry, and then collapse upon their mothers' shrunken breasts. Their lives ebb away like those wounded in battle.

13 In all the world has there ever been such sorrow? O Jerusalem, what can I compare your anguish to? How can I comfort you? For your wound is deep as the sea. Who can heal you?

14 Your "prophets" have said so many foolish things, false to the core. They have not tried to hold you back from slavery by pointing out your sins. They lied and said that all was well.

15 All who pass by scoff and shake their heads and say, "Is this the city called 'Most Beautiful in All the World,' and 'Joy of All the Earth'?"

16 All your enemies deride you. They hiss and grind their teeth and say, "We have destroyed her at last! Long have we waited for this hour, and it is finally here! With our own eyes we've seen her fall."

17 But it is the Lord who did it, just as he had warned. He has fulfilled the promises of doom he made so long ago. He has destroyed Jerusalem without mercy and caused her enemies to rejoice over her and boast of their power.

18 Then the people wept before the Lord. O walls of Jerusalem, let tears fall down upon you like a river; give yourselves no rest from weeping day or night.

19 Rise in the night and cry to your God. Pour out your hearts like water to the Lord; lift up your hands to him; plead for your children as they faint with hunger in the streets.

20 *O Lord, think! These are your own people to whom you are doing this.* Shall mothers eat their little children, those they bounced upon their knees? Shall priests and prophets die within the Temple of the Lord?

21 See them lying in the streets—old and young, boys and girls, killed by the enemies' swords. You have killed them, Lord, in your anger; you have killed them without mercy.

22 You have deliberately called for this destruction; in the day of your anger none escaped or remained. All my little children lie dead upon the streets before the enemy.

2:19-22 Jeremiah called the people to admit their helplessness and turn to God for deliverance. This is how all of us begin our recovery. Many of us can relate to the terrible losses the Jews had experienced. And many of us can point to failures in our life that brought the suffering upon us. All of us, no matter what our problem, can recognize how helpless we are and then turn to God for help. As we do this, we set the process of recovery in motion.

3:1-20 The prophet's words took a personal turn in this chapter. He was heartbroken and weary, discouraged and completely undone. He felt alone and helpless and very much afflicted by God. Jeremiah was probably sharing something of his experience as God's prophet among a people who refused to listen. Notice that he spoke frankly with God; he didn't hide his despair or anger. Expressing his feelings was an important step toward his recovery of hope (3:21). Sometimes we hide our feelings from God, fearing that he will condemn us for them. God is never offended by our honest anger. Unless we speak it, we cannot deal with it and escape its destructive grip.

3:21-26 After Jeremiah shared his pain with God, he reflected upon God's faithfulness. What could possibly save him from his terrible anguish? Nothing, except the compassion of a gracious and loving God. God's love is unfailing; his purposes, clear; his righteousness, unquestionable. When we come to God with our pain, we are sure to get a fair hearing. And God, in his mercy and grace, is able to give us the help we need to overcome our setbacks and gain a new perspective on life.

3:27-39 God disciplines us because he loves us. When we are following a dangerous path, we need to be stopped. Sometimes the only way God can get our attention is by knocking us down. Though we may get angry at God for his discipline, it is an opportunity for change. We should take a moral inventory to discover the root of the problem. Then we can turn our problems over to God and seek to live according to his program. As we face the pain of discipline, we would be wise to ask Jeremiah's question: "Why then should we, mere humans as we are, murmur and complain when punished for our sins?"

CHAPTER 3

Hope amidst Affliction

I am the man who has seen the afflictions that
come from the rod of God's wrath. 2He has
brought me into deepest darkness, shutting
out all light. 3He has turned against me. Day
and night his hand is heavy on me. 4He has
made me old and has broken my bones.

5He has built forts against me and surrounded me with anguish and distress. 6He
buried me in dark places, like those long dead.
7He has walled me in; I cannot escape; he has
fastened me with heavy chains. 8And though
I cry and shout, he will not hear my prayers!
9He has shut me into a place of high, smooth
walls; he has filled my path with detours.

10He lurks like a bear, like a lion, waiting
to attack me. 11He has dragged me into the
underbrush and torn me with his claws,
leaving me bleeding and desolate.

12He has bent his bow and aimed it squarely
at me, 13and sent his arrows deep within my
heart.

14My own people laugh at me; all day long
they sing their ribald songs.

15He has filled me with bitterness and given
me a cup of deepest sorrows to drink. 16He has
made me eat gravel and broken my teeth; he
has rolled me in ashes and dirt. 17O Lord, all
peace and all prosperity have long since gone,
for you have taken them away. I have forgotten what enjoyment is. 18 All hope is gone; my
strength has turned to water, for the Lord has
left me. 19 Oh, remember the bitterness and
suffering you have dealt to me! 20For I can
never forget these awful years; always my soul
will live in utter shame.

21*Yet there is one ray of hope:* 22*his compassion
never ends.* It is only the Lord's mercies that
have kept us from complete destruction.
23Great is his faithfulness; his loving-kindness
begins afresh each day. 24My soul claims the
Lord as my inheritance; therefore I will hope
in him. 25The Lord is wonderfully good to
those who wait for him, to those who seek for
him. 26It is good both to hope and wait quietly
for the salvation of the Lord.

27It is good for a young man to be under
discipline, 28for it causes him to sit apart in
silence beneath the Lord's demands, 29to lie
face downward in the dust; then at last
there is hope for him. 30Let him turn the
other cheek to those who strike him and
accept their awful insults, 31for the Lord will
not abandon him forever. 32Although God
gives him grief, yet he will show compassion too, according to the greatness of his

H*ope*

READ LAMENTATIONS 3:1-26

Perhaps we are brokenhearted because of the bitter suffering in our family. Maybe our once-good reputations have been ruined and now we are ashamed. Our life has been taken captive and destroyed before the watchful eyes of friend and foe alike.

Jeremiah watched this happen to his beloved nation, Israel. It's no wonder he is known as the weeping prophet. The people of God refused to listen to Jeremiah's warnings and were taken captive by a heathen nation as a result. Lamentations is a record of Jeremiah's lament over the shameful fate of God's people. He wept, "O Lord, all peace and all prosperity have long since gone, for you have taken them away. I have forgotten what enjoyment is. All hope is gone; my strength has turned to water, for the Lord has left me. Oh, remember the bitterness and suffering you have dealt to me! For I can never forget these awful years; always my soul will live in utter shame. *Yet there is one ray of hope: his compassion never ends.* It is only the Lord's mercies that have kept us from complete destruction. Great is his faithfulness; his loving-kindness begins afresh each day. My soul claims the Lord as my inheritance; therefore I will hope in him. . . . It is good both to hope and to wait quietly for the salvation of the Lord" (Lamentations 3:17-26).

Turning our life over to God includes giving him our pain and suffering. In our times of grief and shame, we can hope for the time when God will overcome the problems we face. God is strong enough to lift our burdens and loving enough to mend our broken heart. ***Turn to page 921, Hosea 3.***

loving-kindness. 33For he does not enjoy afflicting men and causing sorrow.

34-36But you have trampled and crushed beneath your feet the lowly of the world, and deprived men of their God-given rights, and refused them justice. No wonder the Lord has had to deal with you! 37For who can act against you without the Lord's permission? 38It is the Lord who helps one and harms another.

39Why then should we, mere humans as we are, murmur and complain when punished for our sins? 40Let us examine ourselves instead, and let us repent and turn again to the Lord. 41Let us lift our hearts and hands to him in heaven, 42for we have sinned; we have rebelled against the Lord, and he has not forgotten it.

43You have engulfed us by your anger, Lord, and slain us without mercy. 44You have veiled yourself as with a cloud so that our prayers do not reach through. 45You have made us as refuse and garbage among the nations. 46All our enemies have spoken out against us. 47We are filled with fear, for we are trapped and desolate, destroyed.

48,49My eyes flow day and night with never-ending streams of tears because of the destruction of my people. 50Oh, that the Lord might look down from heaven and respond to my cry! 51My heart is breaking over what is happening to the young girls of Jerusalem.

52My enemies, whom I have never harmed, chased me as though I were a bird. 53They threw me in a well and capped it with a rock. 54The water flowed above my head. I thought, This is the end! 55But I called upon your name, O Lord, from deep within the well, 56and you heard me! You listened to my pleading; you heard my weeping! 57Yes, you came at my despairing cry and told me not to fear.

58O Lord, you are my lawyer! Plead my case! For you have redeemed my life. 59You have seen the wrong they did to me; be my Judge, to prove me right. 60You have seen the plots my foes have laid against me. 61You have heard the vile names they have called me, 62and all they say about me and their whispered plans. 63See how they laugh and sing with glee, preparing my doom.

64O Lord, repay them well for all the evil they have done. 65Harden their hearts and curse them, Lord. 66Go after them in fierce pursuit and wipe them off the earth, beneath the heavens of the Lord.

CHAPTER 4

God's Anger Satisfied

How the finest gold has lost its luster! For the inlaid Temple walls are scattered in the streets! 2The cream of our youth—the finest of the gold—are treated as earthenware pots. 3,4Even the jackals feed their young, but not my people, Israel. They are like cruel desert ostriches, heedless of their babies' cries. The children's tongues stick to the roofs of their mouths for thirst, for there is not a drop of water left. Babies cry for bread, but no one can give them any. 5Those who used to eat fastidiously are begging in the streets for anything at all. Those brought up in palaces now scratch in garbage pits for food. 6For the sin of my people is greater than that of Sodom, where utter disaster struck in a moment without the hand of man.

7Our princes were lean and tanned, the finest specimens of men; 8but now their faces are as black as soot. No one can recognize them. Their skin sticks to their bones; it is dry and hard and withered. 9Those killed by the sword are far better off than those who die of slow starvation. 10Tenderhearted women have cooked and eaten their own children; thus they survived the siege.

11But now at last the anger of the Lord is satisfied; his fiercest anger has been poured out. He started a fire in Jerusalem that burned it down to its foundations. 12Not a king in all the earth—no one in all the world—would have believed an enemy could enter through Jerusalem's gates! 13Yet God permitted it because of the sins of her prophets and priests, who defiled the city by shedding innocent blood. 14Now these same men are blindly staggering through the streets, covered with blood, defiling everything they touch.

15"Get away!" the people shout at them. "You are defiled!" They flee to distant lands and wander there among the foreigners; but none will let them stay. 16The Lord himself has

---

4:1-22 In this chapter, Jeremiah took a moment to reflect on the ravaged city of Jerusalem. His memory turned to a time when Jerusalem knew splendor and majesty. Now even the children were begging for bread. There was a time when no one would have believed that Jerusalem would be destroyed, but the Holy City was now in ruins. We may think that our life is safe from this kind of destruction. But if we are controlled by our sins and addictions, we are headed there fast. We need to take steps toward recovery while there is still time.

dealt with them; he no longer helps them, for
they persecuted the priests and elders who
stayed true to God.
17We look for our allies to come and save us,
but we look in vain. The nation we expected
most to help us makes no move at all.
18We can't go into the streets without danger to our lives. Our end is near—our days are
numbered. We are doomed. 19Our enemies are
swifter than the eagles; if we flee to the mountains they find us. If we hide in the wilderness,
they are waiting for us there. 20Our king—the
life of our life, the Lord's anointed—was captured in their snares. Yes, even our mighty
king, about whom we had boasted that under
his protection we could hold our own against
any nation on earth!
21Do you rejoice, O people of Edom, in the
land of Uz? But you, too, will feel the awful
anger of the Lord. 22Israel's exile for her sins
will end at last, but Edom's never.

CHAPTER 5

Jeremiah Prays for Restoration

O Lord, remember all that has befallen us; see
what sorrows we must bear! 2Our homes, our
nation, now are filled with foreigners. 3We are
orphans—our fathers dead, our mothers widowed. 4We must even pay for water to drink;
our fuel is sold to us at the highest of prices.
5We bow our necks beneath the victors' feet;
unending work is now our lot. 6We beg for
bread from Egypt, and Assyria too.
7Our fathers sinned but died before the
hand of judgment fell. We have borne the
blow that they deserved!
8Our former servants have become our masters; there is no one left to save us. 9We went
into the wilderness to hunt for food, risking
death from enemies. 10Our skin was black from
famine. 11They rape the women of Jerusalem
and the girls in Judah's cities. 12Our princes are
hanged by their thumbs. Even aged men are
treated with contempt. 13They take away the
young men to grind their grain, and the little
children stagger beneath their heavy loads.
14The old men sit no longer in the city
gates; the young no longer dance and sing.
15The joy of our hearts has ended; our dance
has turned to death. 16Our glory is gone. The
crown is fallen from our head. Woe upon us
for our sins. 17Our hearts are faint and weary;
our eyes grow dim. 18Jerusalem and the
Temple of the Lord are desolate, deserted by
all but wild animals lurking in the ruins.
19O Lord, forever you remain the same!
Your throne continues from generation to
generation. 20Why do you forget us forever?
Why do you forsake us for so long? 21Turn us
around and bring us back to you again! That
is our only hope! Give us back the joys we
used to have! 22*Or have you utterly rejected us?
Are you angry with us still?*

5:1-18 The prophet asked God to remember the suffering of his people. He took great care to list the abuses that they had endured. Notice how bold Jeremiah was in his relationship with God. When we feel upset about the situations we face, we often remain silent or complain under our breath. In doing so, we allow our relationship with God to grow distant. Jeremiah went directly to God with his complaints, allowing his relationship with God to be strengthened in the process. God does hear, and he does care. We need to share our significant feelings and struggles with him.

5:19-22 Jeremiah made a final and impassioned plea to God to remember and restore his broken people. And God did restore Israel after the years of Babylonian captivity. Under the leadership of men like Zerubbabel, Ezra, and Nehemiah, God led his people home to rebuild the Holy City and Temple. And God still restores his people. Regardless of the intensity of our pain, he is able to bring deep and abiding comfort.

EZEKIEL

THE BIG PICTURE

A. CONDEMNATION FOR JUDAH (1:1–24:27)
  1. God's Glory in Ezekiel's Vision and Commission (1:1–3:27)
  2. Messages of Gloom for Israel (4:1–24:27)

B. CONSOLATION FOR JUDAH (25:1–48:35).
  1. Judgment against Foreign Nations (25:1–32:32)
  2. Messages of Hope for Judah (33:1–39:29)
  3. The New Temple in Jerusalem (40:1–48:35)

Discouragement. Despair. Disillusionment. These are just a few of the feelings experienced by the audience to whom Ezekiel ministered. The prophet Ezekiel was deported with other Jews to Babylonia about ten years before the destruction of Jerusalem. He prophesied to the Babylonian exiles at the Chebar Canal during the last years of Jerusalem's survival and in the years closely following its fall. He was called by God to confront and then to comfort his people.

As the book of Ezekiel begins, one hope for the exiles still remained. Jerusalem was still standing; there was hope that the holy city and Temple would yet be spared. The Jews, however, were in denial. The popular theology of the day assumed that God's presence in the Temple would protect Jerusalem. The people failed to realize that there was no escaping the painful consequences of their sins. During this time of false hope, God called Ezekiel to proclaim that Jerusalem's destruction was a sure thing. The people needed to realize that their sins had consequences and their humble repentance was required.

The final chapters (25:1–48:35) were given after Jerusalem's destruction and are filled with words of hope for God's broken people. With the fall of Jerusalem (24:1-27), the predicted consequences of Israel's sins had come to pass. The people of Judah now could no longer deny their sin, and they turned to God for help. God's response was a promise of future restoration and peace. Through a vision of dry bones coming to life, the exiled Jews received hope for a new life. God would do the impossible! He would lead his people home and rebuild his nation from a state of total ruin.

THE BOTTOM LINE

PURPOSE: To help the people in exile understand how God's glory and righteousness made their present judgment necessary and their future restoration certain. AUTHOR: The prophet Ezekiel. AUDIENCE: The Jews of the Babylonian exile, before and after the fall of Jerusalem. DATE WRITTEN: The book was probably written shortly after the time period it covers (from 592 to 570 B.C.). SETTING: Ezekiel lived near the Chebar Canal in Babylon and ministered to the Jews in exile. KEY VERSE: "I will give you a new heart—I will give you new and right desires—and put a new spirit within you. I will take out your stony hearts of sin and give you new hearts of love" (36:26). KEY PLACES: Jerusalem, Babylon, and Egypt. KEY PEOPLE: Ezekiel, his wife, Israel's leaders, and Nebuchadnezzar.

RECOVERY THEMES

Recovery through Confrontation: During the first part of Ezekiel, the Jews were in denial. They believed that God would preserve Jerusalem regardless of how they behaved. So during the first half of Ezekiel, God's program for Judah's recovery came in the form of direct confrontation. Ezekiel told the Jews the truth about their sin; their nation would soon suffer the consequence of complete destruction. When we are in denial, direct confrontation may be the last resort to get our attention. If we fail to listen to the truth, God will let us suffer the consequences. We would be wise to humbly listen to any legitimate confrontation sent our way.

Hope in Failure: Whenever we have slipped or relapsed, our dominant feeling is one of helplessness. We feel that all is lost, that nothing good can happen. After the destruction of Jerusalem, God's people felt like this. Ezekiel's message of judgment had been proven true. The people came to the humbling realization that they were sinful and that their suffering was a consequence of their sin. As the people realized how bleak their situation was, God sent them a message of hope and recovery. When we feel defeated because of our failures, God brings us a message of hope. We never want to fail, but when we do fail, God is our strength and hope for recovery.

God Is Always Available: The exiles in Babylon lived in a place that reminded them daily of their failure and shame. They felt abandoned by God. Yet God, who isn't limited by geographical boundaries, was right there in Babylon with them. He met Ezekiel on foreign soil, and through him spoke to his broken people. God wants to meet us no matter where are, even when we are at our worst. And when he comes, he comes in glory, bringing light to the darkness and hope for recovery. God is always available—even in the midst of our shame.

No Situation Is Hopeless: Many of us suffer the consequences of having been raised in a dysfunctional family. Sometimes the bad decisions we make affect our life for a long period of time. We probably feel a lot like the exiles in Babylon felt. Many of them were suffering in exile because of the sins of their fathers. They felt overwhelmed and helpless. But God entered into that hopeless situation and transformed it into something that brought honor and glory to his name. God hasn't changed. He still wants to come into our hopeless situations and transform them. He wants to free us from our bondage to past sins and failures.

CHAPTER 1

A Vision of Heavenly Beings

Ezekiel was a priest (the son of Buzi) who lived
with the Jewish exiles beside the Chebar Canal in Babylon.
One day late in June, when I was thirty
years old, the heavens were suddenly opened
to me and I saw visions from God. 4 I saw, in
this vision, a great storm coming toward me
from the north, driving before it a huge cloud
glowing with fire, with a mass of fire inside
that flashed continually; and in the fire there
was something that shone like polished brass.
5 Then from the center of the cloud, four
strange forms appeared that looked like men,
6 except that each had four faces and two pairs
of wings! 7 Their legs were like those of men,
but their feet were cloven like calves' feet,
and shone like burnished brass. 8 And beneath each of their wings I could see human
hands.
9 The four living beings were joined wing to
wing, and they flew straight forward without
turning. 10 Each had the face of a man [in
front], with a lion's face on the right side [of
his head], and the face of an ox on the left

1:1-3 Ezekiel was among the people of Judah exiled to Babylon about ten years prior to Jerusalem's destruction. The people had lost their homeland and their property. Yet in the early chapters of the book (1:1–24:27), the people still clung to a slim measure of hope. Jerusalem and its Temple still stood; complete destruction had not yet fallen. Because of this, many of the people continued in their denial, believing that God would not allow their homeland to be destroyed. They refused to admit their sins and the sins of their ancestors. So in the early chapters, the prophet confronted the exiles with their sins and predicted Jerusalem's destruction. Ezekiel's early ministry was one of confrontation.

1:1-3 Having been trained as a priest, Ezekiel would have naturally associated God's presence with the Temple in Jerusalem. But he and his companions had been uprooted from their land—and specifically from their Temple. Many wondered whether or not they would be able to experience God's presence in Babylonia. Through Ezekiel's visions, it became clear that God is not limited by geography. He even revealed himself in godless Babylon! God can reach out to us no matter where we are or what we have done. If we are willing to turn our life over to him, there is always hope for recovery.

EZEKIEL

Little is known of Ezekiel, the man. We do know, however, that he was a priest who faithfully obeyed God's laws and was called by God to be a prophet. He began to prophesy at age thirty, five years after he had been taken into Babylonian captivity. He settled near the Chebar Canal, where he prophesied to the exiles during the final years of Jerusalem's survival and in the years closely following her destruction.

The fact that Ezekiel said little about himself may indicate his humility. The prophetic work that God called him to do was certainly humbling. He was called to act out publicly God's message for his people. On one occasion, he was told to lie on his left side for 390 days to symbolize the years of Israel's sin, and then on his right side for 40 days to depict the years of Judah's sin. Another time, he was forbidden to mourn his wife's death, to show that no one would mourn over Jerusalem after her impending demise.

Ezekiel's name means "God strengthens," a name appropriate to the man and his message. Ezekiel needed God's strength as he carried a message of judgment to a people that did not want to hear it. Ezekiel also carried a message of strengthening hope after Jerusalem's destruction and the loss of Israel's hope. God wanted his people to know that they could not escape the consequences of their sins. Ezekiel's message was intended to break through their denial. But God also wanted the Jews to realize that his mercy was available to those who would admit their sins and turn to him. The suffering was designed to bring his people's recovery, not their destruction.

Ezekiel's messages of confrontation and comfort are for us, too. If we tend to ignore the sin in our life, we would be wise to listen to his words of warning. Denial only leads to suffering and destruction. If we have been broken by our failures and have turned to God for help, Ezekiel's words of comfort are meant for us as well. God can rebuild our life, no matter how broken it is. Ezekiel saw a vision in which God reassembled the scattered, dry bones of his people and brought them back to life. He can do the same thing in our life.

STRENGTHS AND ACCOMPLISHMENTS:

- Ezekiel was completely dedicated to God.
- He communicated God's message clearly despite opposition.
- He did not complain about the difficult task that God gave him.
- He was willing to be humiliated for God's cause.

LESSONS FROM HIS LIFE:

- Sin and denial lead to suffering and destruction.
- Through repentance we can receive forgiveness and restoration.
- God may call us to do difficult things to accomplish his will.
- When God calls us to speak, we must not be swayed by the opposition.

KEY VERSES:

"Then [God] added: 'Son of dust, let all my words sink deep into your own heart first; listen to them carefully for yourself. Then, afterward, go to your people in exile, and whether or not they will listen, tell them: "This is what the Lord God says!"'" (Ezekiel 3:10-11).

Ezekiel's story is told in the book of Ezekiel.

---

side, and the face of an eagle at the back!
11Each had two pairs of wings spreading out
from the middle of his back. One pair
stretched out to attach to the wings of the
living beings on each side, and the other pair
covered his body. 12Wherever their spirit went
they went, going straight forward without
turning.
13Going up and down among them were
other forms that glowed like bright coals of
fire or brilliant torches, and it was from these
the lightning flashed. 14The living beings
darted to and fro, swift as lightning.
15As I stared at all of this, I saw four wheels
on the ground beneath them, one wheel belonging
to each. 16The wheels looked as if they
were made of polished amber, and each wheel
was constructed with a second wheel crosswise
inside. 17They could go in any of the four
directions without having to face around.
18The four wheels had rims and spokes, and the
rims were filled with eyes around their edges.

19-21When the four living beings flew forward, the wheels moved forward with them.
When they flew upwards, the wheels went up
too. When the living beings stopped, the
wheels stopped. For the spirit of the four
living beings was in the wheels; so wherever
their spirit went, the wheels and the living
beings went there too.
22The sky spreading out above them looked
as though it were made of crystal; it was
inexpressibly beautiful.
23The wings of each stretched straight out
to touch the others' wings, and each had two
wings covering his body. 24And as they flew,
their wings roared like waves against the
shore, or like the voice of God, or like the
shouting of a mighty army. When they
stopped, they let down their wings. 25And
every time they stopped, there came a voice
from the crystal sky above them.
26For high in the sky above them was what
looked like a throne made of beautiful blue
sapphire stones, and upon it sat someone
who appeared to be a Man.
27,28From his waist up, he seemed to be all
glowing bronze, dazzling like fire; and from
his waist down he seemed to be entirely
flame, and there was a glowing halo like a
rainbow all around him. That was the way the
glory of the Lord appeared to me. And when
I saw it, I fell face downward on the ground
and heard the voice of someone speaking to
me:

CHAPTER 2

God Calls Ezekiel

And he said to me: "Stand up, son of dust, and
I will talk to you."
2And the Spirit entered into me as he spoke,
and set me on my feet.
3"Son of dust," he said, "I am sending you
to the nation of Israel, to a nation rebelling
against me. They and their fathers have kept
on sinning against me until this very hour.
4For they are a hardhearted, stiff-necked
people. But I am sending you to give them my
messages—the messages of the Lord God.
5And whether they listen or not (for remember, they are rebels), they will at least know
they have had a prophet among them.
6"Son of dust, don't be afraid of them; don't
be frightened even though their threats are
sharp and barbed and sting like scorpions.
Don't be dismayed by their dark scowls. For
remember, they are rebels! 7You must give
them my messages whether they listen or not
(but they won't, for they are utter rebels).
8Listen, son of dust, to what I say to you.
Don't you be a rebel too! Open your mouth
and eat what I give you."
9,10Then I looked and saw a hand holding
out to me a scroll, with writing on both sides.
He unrolled it, and I saw that it was full of
warnings and sorrows and pronouncements
of doom.

CHAPTER 3

Ezekiel Will Be a Watchman

And he said to me: "Son of dust, eat what I am
giving you—eat this scroll! Then go and give
its message to the people of Israel."
2So I took the scroll.
3"Eat it all," he said. And when I ate it, it
tasted sweet as honey.
4Then he said: "Son of dust, I am sending
you to the people of Israel with my messages.
5I am not sending you to some far-off foreign
land where you can't understand the language— 6no, not to tribes with strange, difficult tongues. (If I did, they would listen!) 7I am
sending you to the people of Israel, and they
won't listen to you any more than they listen
to me! For the whole lot of them are hard,
impudent, and stubborn. 8But see, I have
made you hard and stubborn too—as tough
as they are. 9I have made your forehead as

2:3-5 Why did God send a message of judgment to a group of people already in exile? At the time of this message, Jerusalem still stood, and a majority of the people still lived in Israel. Ezekiel was among a small group that had been exiled in 597 B.C., and many of these early exiles believed their captivity would be short. Ezekiel was called to make it clear that the consequences of their sins had not yet fully fallen upon them. Jerusalem was yet to be destroyed. The people would need to admit their sins and turn to God in repentance in order to fulfill God's purpose for their exile. Like the exiles, we often hold on to our denial long after we have begun to feel the destructive consequences of our actions. We would be wise to wake up and act before the full consequences of our addictions fall upon us.

3:1-3 Ezekiel was commanded to eat the scroll that contained God's Word, an act that enabled him to perform his difficult ministry. He was sustained and directed by the words he received from God. As we face the trials of recovery, God's sustaining words in the Bible can provide us with the direction and strength we need. As we daily read and meditate on God's truths, we will discover God's power helping us to progress successfully in the recovery process.

hard as rock. So don't be afraid of them, or
fear their sullen, angry looks, even though
they are such rebels."
10Then he added: "Son of dust, let all my
words sink deep into your own heart first;
listen to them carefully for yourself. 11Then,
afterward, go to your people in exile, and
whether or not they will listen, tell them:
'This is what the Lord God says!'"
12Then the Spirit lifted me up, and the glory
of the Lord began to move away, accompanied by the sound of a great earthquake. 13It
was the noise of the wings of the living beings
as they touched against each other, and the
sound of their wheels beside them.
14,15The Spirit lifted me up, and took me
away to Tel Abib, another colony of Jewish
exiles beside the Chebar River. I went in bitterness and anger, but the hand of the Lord
was strong upon me. And I sat among them,
overwhelmed, for seven days.
16At the end of the seven days, the Lord said
to me:
17"Son of dust, I have appointed you as a
watchman for Israel; whenever I send my
people a warning, pass it on to them at once.
18If you refuse to warn the wicked when I want
you to tell them, 'You are under the penalty
of death; therefore repent and save your life,'
they will die in their sins, but I will punish
you. I will demand your blood for theirs. 19But
if you warn them, and they keep on sinning
and refuse to repent, they will die in their sins,
but you are blameless—you have done all you
could. 20And if a good man becomes bad, and
you refuse to warn him of the consequences,
and the Lord destroys him, his previous good
deeds won't help him—he shall die in his sin.
But I will hold you responsible for his death
and punish you. 21But if you warn him and he
repents, he shall live, and you have saved
your own life too."
22I was helpless in the hand of God, and
when he said to me, "Go out into the valley
and I will talk to you there"— 23I arose and
went, and oh, I saw the glory of the Lord
there, just as in my first vision! And I fell to
the ground on my face.
24Then the Spirit entered into me and set
me on my feet. He talked to me and said: "Go,
imprison yourself in your house, 25and I will
paralyze you so you can't leave; 26and I will
make your tongue stick to the roof of your
mouth so that you can't reprove them; for
they are rebels. 27But whenever I give you a
message, then I will loosen your tongue and
let you speak, and you shall say to them: 'The
Lord God says.' Let anyone listen who wants
to, and let anyone refuse who wants to, for
they are rebels."

CHAPTER 4
Ezekiel Draws a Map

"And now, son of dust, take a large brick and
lay it before you and draw a map of the city
of Jerusalem on it. Draw a picture of siege
mounds being built against the city, put enemy camps around it and battering rams surrounding the walls. 3And put an iron plate
between you and the city, like a wall of iron.
Demonstrate how an enemy army will capture Jerusalem!
"There is special meaning in each detail of
what I have told you to do. For it is a warning
to the people of Israel.
4,5"Now lie on your left side for 390 days, to
show that Israel will be punished for 390 years
by captivity and doom. Each day you lie there
represents a year of punishment ahead for
Israel. 6Afterwards, turn over and lie on your
right side for forty days, to signify the years of
Judah's punishment. Each day will represent
one year.
7"Meanwhile continue your demonstration
of the siege of Jerusalem; lie there with your
arm bared [to signify great strength and
power in the attack against her]. This will
prophesy her doom. 8And I will paralyze you

3:24 Ezekiel had just been commissioned with a gigantic ministry. He was overwhelmed by the scope of it. At this point, the Spirit entered him to empower him for the work he had to do. In recovery we are faced with major challenges, and spiritual enablement is essential for our success in performing the required tasks. As we examine our life, we should rejoice about the small miracles God has worked for us. Such things would never have happened without the Holy Spirit's intervention.
4:9-11 Bad news is never welcome, but it often comes anyway. In this little drama, Ezekiel illustrated what it would be like for his people during the coming famine. They needed to realize that though things were already bad, the situation was only going to get worse. As long as the people had any reason for hope, they would never admit their sin and trust God for recovery. Our own life probably had to deteriorate to an intolerable state before we were willing to admit our failures and start the rebuilding process. It is essential that we recognize our need for God and daily turn our life over to him and his power.

so that you can't turn over from one side to
the other until you have completed all the
days of your siege.
9"During the first 390 days eat bread made
of flour mixed from wheat, barley, beans,
lentils, and spelt. Mix the various kinds of
flour together in a jar. 10You are to ration this
out to yourself at the rate of eight ounces at a
time, one meal a day. 11And use one quart of
water a day; don't use more than that. 12Each
day take flour from the barrel and prepare it
as you would barley cakes. While all the
people are watching, bake it over a fire, using
dried human dung as fuel, and eat it. 13For the
Lord declares, Israel shall eat defiled bread in
the Gentile lands to which I exile them!"
14Then I said, "O Lord God, must I be defiled by using dung? For I have never been
defiled before in all my life. From the time I
was a child until now I have never eaten any
animal that died of sickness or that I found
injured or dead; and I have never eaten any of
the kinds of animals our law forbids."
15Then the Lord said, "All right, you may
use cow dung instead of human dung."
16Then he told me, "Son of dust, bread will
be tightly rationed in Jerusalem. It will be
weighed out with great care and eaten fear-
fully. And the water will be portioned out in
driblets, and the people will drink it with
dismay. 17I will cause the people to lack both
bread and water; they will look at one another
in frantic terror and waste away beneath their
punishment."

CHAPTER 5

Ezekiel Shaves His Head

"Son of dust, take a sharp sword and use it as
a barber's razor to shave your head and beard;
use balances to weigh the hair into three
equal parts. 2Place a third of it at the center of
your map of Jerusalem. After your siege, burn
it there. Scatter another third across your map
and slash at it with a knife. Scatter the last
third to the wind, for I will chase my people
with the sword. 3Keep just a bit of the hair and
tie it up in your robe; 4then take a few hairs
out and throw them into the fire, for a fire
shall come from this remnant and destroy all
Israel."
5-7The Lord God says, "This illustrates what
will happen to Jerusalem, for she has turned
away from my laws and has been even more
wicked than the nations surrounding her."
8Therefore the Lord God says, I, even I, am
against you and will punish you publicly
while all the nations watch. 9Because of the
terrible sins you have committed, I will punish you more terribly than I have ever done
before or ever will again. 10Fathers will eat
their own sons, and sons will eat their fathers;
and those who survive will be scattered into
all the world.
11"For I promise you: Because you have
defiled my Temple with idols and evil sacrifices, therefore I will not spare you nor pity
you at all. 12One-third of you will die from
famine and disease; one-third will be slaughtered by the enemy; and one-third I will scatter to the winds, sending the sword of the
enemy chasing after you. 13Then at last my
anger will be appeased. And all Israel will
know that what I threaten I do.
14"So I will make a public example of you
before all the surrounding nations and before
everyone traveling past the ruins of your land.
15You will become a laughingstock to the
world and an awesome example to everyone,
for all to see what happens when the Lord
turns against an entire nation in furious rebuke. I, the Lord, have spoken it!
16"I will shower you with deadly arrows of
famine to destroy you. The famine will become more and more serious until every bit
of bread is gone. 17And not only famine will
come, but wild animals will attack and kill

5:8-10 God's judgment is righteous and cannot be avoided. Its inevitability was announced by Ezekiel in no uncertain terms. If we refuse to repent, we also must face God's judgment for our sin. It is a question not of *if,* but of *when.* Sin has terrible and unavoidable consequences. We cannot live a life that is out of control and hope to slip past the consequences of our rebellion. God certainly does love us and is willing to restore us if we confess our failures to him and ask his forgiveness. But this does not mean we can do whatever we want to. God is just and must discipline his people when they continue to sin.

5:14-15 God judged Israel for her rebellion to show the world what happens to those who disobey him. Rebellion against God always has painful consequences. We all have seen how destructive addiction and its accompanying sins can be; many of us have firsthand experience. We would be wise to learn from the pain of others and seek God's help and forgiveness. If we don't, we will become one more of God's object lessons to show others what happens to those who rebel against God and his ways.

you and your families; disease and war will
stalk your land, and the sword of the enemy
will slay you; I, the Lord, have spoken it!"

CHAPTER 6
Ezekiel Speaks to the Mountains
Again a message came from the Lord:
2"Son of dust, look over toward the mountains of Israel and prophesy against them.
3Say to them, 'O mountains of Israel, hear the
message of the Lord God against you and
against the rivers and valleys. I, even I the
Lord, will bring war upon you to destroy your
idols. 4-7All your cities will be smashed and
burned, and the idol altars abandoned. Your
gods will be shattered; the bones of their
worshipers will lie scattered among the altars.
Then at last you will know I am the Lord.
8"'But I will let a few of my people escape—
to be scattered among the nations of the
world. 9Then when they are exiled among the
nations, they will remember me, for I will take
away their adulterous hearts—their love of
idols—and I will blind their lecherous eyes
that long for other gods. Then at last they will
loathe themselves for all this wickedness.
10They will realize that I alone am God and
that I wasn't fooling when I told them that all
this would happen to them.'"
11The Lord God says: "Raise your hands in
horror and shake your head with deep remorse and say, 'Alas for all the evil we have
done!' For you are going to perish from war
and famine and disease. 12Disease will strike
down those in exile; war will destroy those in
the land of Israel; and any who remain will
die by famine and siege. So at last I will expend my fury on you. 13When your slain lie
scattered among your idols and altars on
every hill and mountain and under every
green tree and great oak where they offered
incense to their gods—you will realize that I
alone am God. 14I will crush you and make
your cities desolate from the wilderness in the
south to Riblah in the north. Then you will
know I am the Lord.'"

CHAPTER 7
Jerusalem Will Be Punished
This further message came to me from God:
2"Tell Israel, 'Wherever you look—east,
west, north or south—your land is finished.
3No hope remains, for I will loose my anger
on you for your worshiping of idols. 4I will
turn my eyes away and show no pity; I will
repay you in full, and you shall know I am the
Lord.'"
5,6The Lord God says: "With one blow after
another I will finish you. The end has come;
your final doom is waiting. 7O Israel, the day
of your damnation dawns; the time has come;
the day of trouble nears. It is a day of shouts
of anguish, not shouts of joy! 8,9Soon I will
pour out my fury and let it finish its work of
punishing you for all your evil deeds. I will
not spare nor pity you, and you will know
that I, the Lord, am doing it. 10,11The day of
judgment has come; the morning dawns, for
your wickedness and pride have run their
course and reached their climax—none of
these rich and wicked men of pride shall live.
All your boasting will die away, and no one
will be left to bewail your fate.
12"Yes, the time has come; the day draws
near. There will be nothing to buy or sell, for
the wrath of God is on the land. 13And even if

6:8-10 God rebuked his people for their sins and assured them of coming judgment, but he did not leave them in despair. He gave them hope for recovery. God would spare a remnant who would escape captivity to rebuild the nation. In order to rebuild, it was necessary for God to first tear down. This pattern has been repeated many times in the lives of nations and individuals who have hit bottom but then found new hope as they turned to God. No matter how great our present suffering, there is always hope for the future. We can begin by viewing our pain as an important step in recovery. Then we must turn to God for the forgiveness and healing he promises.
6:14 "Then you will know I am the Lord." The people of Israel needed to learn this lesson if they hoped to recover from their punishment in exile. This is an important lesson for all of us to learn. Each of us must discover who God is and what he requires, if we hope to succeed in our recovery. When we give God control of our life, doing our best to obey his will, we are on the way to recovery. As we do things his way, we will discover how to rebuild our life on a solid foundation.
7:5-11 Even though the evaluation is disheartening, honest recognition of our circumstances and failures is essential before any positive steps can be taken for our recovery. Until we recognize where we are, we can never take measures to get to where we should be. The people of Israel were in denial about their sinful past and were therefore unable to receive God's forgiveness, healing, and direction. God forced them to stop their denial with his acts of judgment. We would be wise to admit our problems and humbly turn to God for help before we are forced to by sin's painful consequences.

a merchant lives, his business will be gone, for God has spoken against all the people of Israel; all will be destroyed. Not one of those whose lives are filled with sin will recover.

14"The trumpets shout to Israel's army, 'Mobilize!' but no one listens, for my wrath is on them all. 15If you go outside the walls, there stands the enemy to kill you. If you stay inside, famine and disease will devour you. 16Any who escape will be lonely as mourning doves hiding on the mountains, each weeping for his sins. 17All hands shall be feeble, and all knees as weak as water. 18You shall clothe yourselves with sackcloth, and horror and shame shall cover you; you shall shave your heads in sorrow and remorse.

19"Throw away your money! Toss it out like worthless rubbish, for it will have no value in that day of wrath. It will neither satisfy nor feed you, for your love of money is the reason for your sin. 20I gave you gold to use in decorating the Temple, and you used it instead to make idols! Therefore, I will take it all away from you. 21I will give it to foreigners and to wicked men as booty. They shall defile my Temple. 22I will not look when they defile it, nor will I stop them. Like robbers, they will loot the treasures and leave the Temple in ruins.

23"Prepare chains for my people, for the land is full of bloody crimes. Jerusalem is filled with violence, so I will enslave her people. 24I will crush your pride by bringing to Jerusalem the worst of the nations to occupy your homes, break down your fortifications you are so proud of, and defile your Temple. 25For the time has come for the cutting off of Israel. You will sue for peace, but you won't get it. 26,27Calamity upon calamity will befall you; woe upon woe, disaster upon disaster! You will long for a prophet to guide you, but the priests and elders and the kings and princes will stand helpless, weeping in despair. The people will tremble with fear, for I will do to them the evil they have done and give them all their just deserts. They shall learn that I am the Lord."

CHAPTER 8

The Sins of the People

Then, late in August of the sixth year of King Jehoiachin's captivity, as I was talking with the elders of Judah in my home, the power of the Lord God fell upon me. 2I saw what appeared to be a Man; from his waist down, he was made of fire; from his waist up, he was all amber-colored brightness. 3He put out what seemed to be a hand and took me by the hair. And the Spirit lifted me up into the sky and seemed to transport me to Jerusalem, to the entrance of the north gate, where the large idol was that had made the Lord so angry. 4Suddenly the glory of the God of Israel was there, just as I had seen it before in the valley.

5He said to me, "Son of dust, look toward the north." So I looked and, sure enough, north of the altar gate in the entrance stood the idol.

6And he said: "Son of dust, do you see what they are doing? Do you see what great sins the people of Israel are doing here, to push me from my Temple? But come, and I will show you greater sins than these!"

7Then he brought me to the door of the Temple court, where I could see an opening in the wall.

8"Now dig into the wall," he said. I did and uncovered a door to a hidden room.

9"Go in," he said, "and see the wickedness going on in there!"

10So I went in. The walls were covered with pictures of all kinds of snakes, lizards, and hideous creatures, besides all the various idols worshiped by the people of Israel. 11Seventy

7:19 The people of Israel couldn't use their wealth to escape the coming judgment. In fact, all of their human resources proved inadequate for the task. Only God was able to deliver them, but since they were in denial about their sin, there was no hope of escape from the judgment to come. When it comes to dealing with our dependencies and destructive habits, human resources alone are of no avail. If we refuse to allow God to take part in our recovery, we have little hope for success. We must avoid programs that exclude God; he is our only hope for recovery. If we depend wholly on any other resource, we are on the slippery slide toward destruction.

8:1-17 The religious activities of Israel's leaders were revealed to Ezekiel in a vision. They were involved in idolatrous pagan practices and had the gall to believe that God didn't see what they were doing or perhaps had gone away. This misconception about God is still prevalent today. Either we believe we can actually hide our sins from God, or we believe that he is somehow looking the other way. Such a belief is clearly false and extremely dangerous. It feeds our denial and leads to painful consequences and, ultimately, destruction. God is deeply concerned about our destructive habits and sins. The terrible fate of Israel's leaders should serve as a warning to us.

elders of Israel were standing there along with Ja-azaniah (son of Shaphan) worshiping the pictures. Each of them held a censer of burning incense, so there was a thick cloud of smoke above their heads.

[12]Then the Lord said to me: "Son of dust, have you seen what the elders of Israel are doing in their minds? For they say, 'The Lord doesn't see us; he has gone away!'" [13]Then he added, "Come, and I will show you greater sins than these!"

[14]He brought me to the north gate of the Temple, and there sat women weeping for Tammuz, their god.

[15]"Have you seen this?" he asked. "But I will show you greater evils than these!"

[16]Then he brought me into the inner court of the Temple, and there at the door, between the porch and the bronze altar, were about twenty-five men standing with their backs to the Temple of the Lord, facing east, worshiping the sun!

[17]"Have you seen this?" he asked. "Is it nothing to the people of Judah that they commit these terrible sins, leading the whole nation into idolatry, thumbing their noses at me and arousing my fury against them? [18]Therefore, I will deal with them in fury. I will neither pity nor spare. And though they scream for mercy, I will not listen."

CHAPTER 9

The Death of Idolaters

Then he thundered, "Call those to whom I have given the city! Tell them to bring their weapons with them!"

[2]Six men appeared at his call, coming from the upper north gate, each one with his sword. One of them wore linen clothing and carried a writer's case strapped to his side. They all went into the Temple and stood beside the bronze altar. [3]And the glory of the God of Israel rose from between the Guardian Angels where it had rested and stood above the entrance to the Temple.

And the Lord called to the man with the writer's case [4]and said to him, "Walk through the streets of Jerusalem and put a mark on the foreheads of the men who weep and sigh because of all the sins they see around them."

[5]Then I heard the Lord tell the other men: "Follow him through the city and kill everyone whose forehead isn't marked. Spare not nor pity them— [6]kill them all—old and young, girls, women and little children; but don't touch anyone with the mark. And begin right here at the Temple." And so they began by killing the seventy elders.

[7]And he said, "Defile the Temple! Fill its courts with the bodies of those you kill! Go!" And they went out through the city and did as they were told.

[8]While they were fulfilling their orders, I was alone. I fell to the ground on my face and cried out: "O Lord God! Will your fury against Jerusalem wipe out everyone left in Israel?"

[9]But he said to me, "The sins of the people of Israel and Judah are very great and all the land is full of murder and injustice, for they say, 'The Lord doesn't see it! He has gone away!' [10]And so I will not spare them nor have any pity on them, and I will fully repay them for all that they have done."

[11]Just then the man in linen clothing, carrying the writer's case, reported back and said, "I have finished the work you gave me to do."

CHAPTER 10

Burning Coals Rain Down

Suddenly a throne of beautiful blue sapphire appeared in the sky above the heads of the Guardian Angels.

[2]Then the Lord spoke to the man in linen clothing and said: "Go in between the whirling wheels beneath the Guardian Angels, and take a handful of glowing coals and scatter them over the city."

9:1-6 In Ezekiel's day many in Israel believed they had nothing to fear because they had favored status as God's people. They thought that God's presence in the Jerusalem Temple guaranteed their safety. From these verses, however, it is clear that God was not blind to their sin. He was concerned about the people's blatant disregard for God's laws and would make sure the offenders were punished. Sin always has consequences. God will not stand idly by and allow people to rebel against his program forever. We would be wise to listen and take appropriate action before it is too late.

10:1-22 In these chapters (Ezekiel 8–11) we see God's glory departing from the Temple. It moved to the door (9:3), then to the south side of the Temple (10:3), to the eastern gate (10:18-19; 11:1), and finally to the mountain east of the Temple (11:23). God was leaving Jerusalem. Many of the Jews believed they were immune to enemy attack because of God's presence among them. This attitude made them deaf to Ezekiel's condemnation of their sin and the predicted consequence of Jerusalem's destruction. When God left the Temple, however, the people could no longer claim his divine presence to support their denial. Their sin was real, and God's judgment was near.

He did so while I watched. 3The Guardian Angels were standing at the south end of the Temple when the man went in. And the cloud of glory filled the inner court. 4Then the glory of the Lord rose from above the Guardian Angels and went over to the door of the Temple. The Temple was filled with the cloud of glory, and the court of the Temple was filled with the brightness of the glory of the Lord. 5And the sound of the wings of the Guardian Angels was as the voice of Almighty God when he speaks and could be heard clear out in the outer court.

6When the Lord told the man in linen clothing to go between the Guardian Angels and take some burning coals from between the wheels, the man went in and stood beside one of the wheels, 7,8and one of the Guardian Angels reached out his hand (for each of the mighty angels had, beneath his wings, what looked like human hands) and took some live coals from the flames between the Angels and put them into the hands of the man in linen clothes, who took them and went out.

9-13Each of the four Guardian Angels had a wheel beside him—"The Whirl-Wheels," as I heard them called, for each one had a second wheel crosswise within—sparkling like chrysolite, giving off a greenish-yellow glow. Because of the construction of these wheels, the Angels could go straight forward in each of four directions; they did not turn when they changed direction but could go in any of the four ways their faces looked. Each of the four wheels was covered with eyes, including the rims and spokes. 14Each of the four Guardian Angels had four faces—the first was that of an ox; the second, a man's; the third, a lion's; and the fourth, an eagle's.

15,16These were the same beings I had seen beside the Chebar Canal, and when they rose into the air, the wheels rose with them and stayed beside them as they flew. 17When the Guardian Angels stood still, so did the wheels, for the spirit of the Guardian Angels was in the wheels.

18Then the glory of the Lord moved from the door of the Temple and stood above the Guardian Angels. 19And as I watched, the Guardian Angels flew with their wheels beside them to the east gate of the Temple. And the glory of the God of Israel was above them.

20These were the living beings I had seen beneath the God of Israel beside the Chebar Canal. I knew they were the same, 21for each had four faces and four wings, with what looked like human hands under their wings. 22Their faces too were identical to the faces of those I had seen at the Canal, and they traveled straight ahead, just as the others did.

CHAPTER 11

God Will Regather Israel

Then the Spirit lifted me and brought me over to the east gate of the Temple, where I saw twenty-five of the most prominent men of the city, including two officers, Jaazaniah (son of Azzur) and Pelatiah (son of Benaiah).

Then the Spirit said to me, "Son of dust, these are the men who are responsible for all of the wicked counsel being given out in this city. 3For they say to the people, 'It is time to rebuild Jerusalem, for our city is an iron shield and will protect us from all harm.' 4Therefore, son of dust, prophesy against them loudly and clearly."

5Then the Spirit of the Lord came upon me and told me to say: "The Lord says to the people of Israel: Is that what you are saying? Yes, I know it is, for I know everything you think—every thought that comes into your minds. 6You have murdered endlessly and filled your streets with the dead."

7Therefore the Lord God says: "You think this city is an iron shield? No, it isn't! It will not protect you. Your slain will lie within it, but you will be dragged out and slaughtered. 8I will expose you to the war you have so greatly feared, says the Lord God, 9and I will take you from Jerusalem and hand you over to foreigners who will carry out my judgments against you. 10You will be slaughtered all the way to the borders of Israel, and you will know I am the Lord. 11No, this city will not be an iron shield for you, and you safe within. I will chase you even to the borders of Israel, 12and you will know I am the Lord—you who have not obeyed me but rather have copied the nations all around you."

13While I was still speaking and telling them this, Pelatiah (son of Benaiah) suddenly died. Then I fell to the ground on my face and cried out: "O Lord God, are you going to kill everyone in all Israel?"

14Again a message came from the Lord:

15"Son of dust, the remnant left in Jerusalem are saying about your brother exiles: 'It is because they were so wicked that the Lord has deported them. Now the Lord has given us their land!'

16"But tell the exiles that the Lord God says: Although I have scattered you in the countries of the world, yet I will be a sanctuary to you for the time that you are there, 17and I will

gather you back from the nations where you
are scattered and give you the land of Israel
again. [18]And when you return, you will remove every trace of all this idol worship. [19]I
will give you one heart and a new spirit; I will
take from you your hearts of stone and give
you tender hearts of love for God, [20]so that
you can obey my laws and be my people, and
I will be your God. [21]But as for those now in
Jerusalem who long for idols, I will repay
them fully for their sins," the Lord God says.

[22]Then the Guardian Angels lifted their
wings and rose into the air with their wheels
beside them, and the glory of the God of Israel
stood above them. [23]Then the glory of the
Lord rose from over the city and stood above
the mountain on the east side.

[24]Afterwards the Spirit of God carried me
back again to Babylon, to the Jews in exile
there. And so ended the vision of my visit to
Jerusalem. [25]And I told the exiles everything
the Lord had shown me.

CHAPTER 12

Ezekiel Digs a Tunnel

Again a message came to me from the Lord:

[2]"Son of dust," he said, "you live among
rebels who could know the truth if they
wanted to, but they don't want to; they could
hear me if they would listen, but they won't,
[3]for they are rebels. So now put on a demonstration to show them what being exiled will
be like. Pack whatever you can carry on your
back and leave your home—go somewhere
else. Go in the daylight so they can see, for
perhaps even yet they will consider what this
means, even though they are such rebels.
[4]Bring your baggage outside your house during the daylight so they can watch. Then
leave the house at night, just as captives do
when they begin their long march to distant
lands. [5]Dig a tunnel through the city wall
while they are observing and carry your possessions out through the hole. [6]As they watch,
lift your pack to your shoulders and walk
away into the night; muffle your face and
don't gaze around. All this is a sign to the
people of Israel of the evil that will come
upon Jerusalem."

[7]So I did as I was told. I brought my pack
outside in the daylight—all I could take into
exile—and in the evening I dug through the
wall with my hands. I went out into the
darkness with my pack on my shoulder while
the people looked on. [8]The next morning this
message came to me from the Lord:

[9]"Son of dust, these rebels, the people of
Israel, have asked what all this means. [10]Tell
them the Lord God says it is a message to King
Zedekiah in Jerusalem and to all the people of
Israel. [11]Explain that what you did was a demonstration of what is going to happen to
them, for they shall be driven out of their
homes and sent away into exile.

[12]"Even King Zedekiah shall go out at night
through a hole in the wall, taking only what
he can carry with him, with muffled face, for
he won't be able to see. [13]I will capture him in
my net and bring him to Babylon, the land of
the Chaldeans; but he shall not see it, and he
shall die there. [14]I will scatter his servants and
guards to the four winds and send the sword
after them. [15]And when I scatter them among
the nations, then they shall know I am the

11:16-21 God had a purpose behind the devastation he brought upon his people. His intervention was the only thing that would penetrate their denial and motivate them to change. We are often as stubborn as the people of Israel. God may have to visit us with a devastating setback to get our attention. As we face suffering in our life, we should be encouraged by the future God has planned for his people. God would use the Exile to transform them into people who loved God. Ezekiel's prophecy can come true for us, too. As we admit our failures and character flaws to God, he will bring us forgiveness and healing through Jesus Christ. We too can become God's special people.

11:23 God's glory departed from the Temple and then from the Holy City itself. God's presence in Jerusalem had been the basis for the people's hope for deliverance; its departure was a portent of the destruction to come. If we continue with our destructive habits, we will have to face devastating consequences. We would be wise to shed our denial through a rigorous personal inventory before it is too late. If we admit our sin to God, he will be more than willing to help us deal with the difficult situations we have created. Then, in time, we will be able to build for a better future.

12:1-3 When we see the rebellion of God's people here, we tend to judge them for being spiritually blind and deaf. As we make such judgments, however, we may be like the person Jesus spoke about, who tried to remove the speck from another person's eye while having a log in his own. The people referred to in this verse are totally unaware of their spiritual disorder. This reminds us how easy it is to live in denial. We need to work out our own program, not someone else's. We have enough problems in our own life.

Lord. 16But I will spare a few of them from
death by war and famine and disease. I will
save them to confess to the nations how
wicked they have been, and they shall know
I am the Lord."
17Then this message came to me from the
Lord:
18"Son of dust, tremble as you eat your
meals; ration out your water as though it were
your last, 19and say to the people, the Lord
God says that the people of Israel and Jerusalem shall ration their food with utmost care
and sip their tiny portions of water in utter
despair because of all their sins. 20Your cities
shall be destroyed and your farmlands deserted, and you shall know I am the Lord."
21Again a message came to me from the
Lord:
22"Son of dust, what is that proverb they
quote in Israel—'The days as they pass make
liars out of every prophet.' 23The Lord God
says, I will put an end to this proverb and they
will soon stop saying it. Give them this one
instead: 'The time has come for all these
prophecies to be fulfilled.'
24"Then you will see what becomes of all
the false predictions of safety and security for
Jerusalem. 25For I am the Lord! What I
threaten always happens. There will be no
more delays, O rebels of Israel! I will do it in
your own lifetime!" says the Lord God.
26Then this message came:
27"Son of dust, the people of Israel say, 'His
visions won't come true for a long, long time.'
28Therefore say to them: 'The Lord God says,
All delay has ended! I will do it now!'"

CHAPTER 13

False Prophets Are Judged

Then this message came to me:
2,3"Son of dust, prophesy against the false
prophets of Israel who are inventing their
own visions and claiming to have messages
from me when I have never told them anything at all. Woe upon them!
4"O Israel, these 'prophets' of yours are as
useless as foxes for rebuilding your walls! 5O
evil prophets, what have you ever done to
strengthen the walls of Israel against her enemies—by strengthening Israel in the Lord?
6Instead you have lied when you said, 'My
message is from God!' God did not send you.
And yet you expect him to fulfill your prophecies. 7Can you deny that you have claimed to
see 'visions' you never saw, and that you have
said, 'This message is from God,' when I never
spoke to you at all?"
8Therefore the Lord God says: "I will destroy you for these 'visions' and lies. 9My
hand shall be against you, and you shall be
cut off from among the leaders of Israel; I will
blot out your names, and you will never see
your own country again. And you shall know
I am the Lord. 10For these evil men deceive my
people by saying, 'God will send peace,' when
that is not my plan at all! My people build a

12:18-20 In these verses Ezekiel prophesied, through symbolic actions, the coming destruction of Jerusalem. Since negative people warn us continually that "the worst is yet to come," we usually discount their dire predictions. Ezekiel's harsh predictions, however, were driven by God's truth, not Ezekiel's gloomy disposition. Again and again, he attempted to turn the people's focus from hope in Jerusalem's survival to hope in God—the only means to their ultimate deliverance. In order to escape the troubles ahead, the people would have to face the truth about their sin and act quickly to make some changes.

12:26-28 No matter how unlikely something might seem, if God predicts it will happen, it will happen. It was now time for God to follow through on his warnings of judgment. But God's promises are not all filled with gloom. There are many promises given to encourage us in the difficult circumstances we face. Ezekiel's messages throughout the first half of the book are concerned with judgment. Jerusalem still stood, and the people believed God would protect the Holy City, whether they sinned or not. They would soon learn that they were accountable for their actions and that their sin would have consequences. The final half of Ezekiel, given after Jerusalem's fall, is filled with promises of restoration and forgiveness.

13:2-3 We all face the danger of following ungodly men's leadership. The people of Israel faced terrible destruction, and God's truth was the only real pathway to their deliverance. They were surrounded by false prophets who claimed the people had nothing to worry about—a message the people were only too glad to believe. These prophets gave the people an easy way out when an easy way out didn't exist. We need to be careful that we don't fall into the same trap. If someone claims to have an easy path to recovery, or if a friend assures us that we don't have a problem, we need to steer clear. God's way demands that we face our sin and its consequences and take responsibility for the suffering we have caused, as painful as that might be. Recovery is never easy, but we can be sure that if we do things God's way, he will stand by us as we take each step.

flimsy wall, and these prophets praise them
for it—and cover it with whitewash!
11“Tell these evil builders that their wall will
fall. A heavy rainstorm will undermine it;
great hailstones and mighty winds will knock
it down. 12And when the wall falls, the people
will cry out, ‘Why didn’t you tell us that it
wasn’t good enough? Why did you whitewash it and cover up its faults?’ 13Yes, it will
surely fall.” The Lord God says: “I will sweep
it away with a storm of indignation, with a
great flood of anger, and with hailstones of
wrath. 14I will break down your whitewashed
wall; it will fall on you and crush you, and you
shall know I am the Lord. 15Then at last my
wrath against the wall will be completed; and
concerning those who praised it, I will say:
The wall and its builders both are gone. 16For
they were lying prophets, claiming Jerusalem
will have peace when there is no peace,” says
the Lord God.
17“Son of dust, speak out against the
women prophets too who pretend the Lord
has given them his messages. 18Tell them,
“The Lord God says: Woe to these women
who are damning the souls of my people, of
both young and old alike, by tying magic
charms on their wrists, furnishing them with
magic veils, and selling them indulgences.
They refuse to even offer help unless they get
a profit from it. 19For the sake of a few paltry
handfuls of barley or a piece of bread will you
turn away my people from me? You have led
those to death who should not die! And you
have promised life to those who should not
live by lying to my people—and how they
love it!’”
20And so the Lord says: “I will crush you
because you hunt my people’s souls with all
your magic charms. I will tear off the charms
and set my people free like birds from cages.
21I will tear off the magic veils and save my
people from you; they will no longer be your
victims, and you shall know I am the Lord.
22Your lies have discouraged the righteous
when I didn’t want it so. And you have encouraged the wicked by promising life,
though they continue in their sins. 23But you
will lie no more; no longer will you talk of
seeing ‘visions’ that you never saw nor practice your magic, for I will deliver my people
out of your hands by destroying you, and you
shall know I am the Lord.”

CHAPTER 14

Idolatry Is Condemned

Then some of the elders of Israel visited me to
ask me for a message from the Lord, 2and this
is the message that came to me to give to
them:
3“Son of dust, these men worship idols in
their hearts—should I let them ask me anything? 4Tell them, ‘The Lord God says: I the
Lord will personally deal with anyone in Israel who worships idols and then comes to
ask my help. 5For I will punish the minds and
hearts of those who turn from me to idols.’
6,7“Therefore, warn them that the Lord God
says: ‘Repent and destroy your idols, and stop
worshiping them in your hearts. I the Lord
will personally punish everyone, whether
people of Israel or the foreigners living among
you, who rejects me for idols and then comes
to a prophet to ask for my help and advice. 8I
will turn upon him and make a terrible example of him, destroying him; and you shall
know I am the Lord. 9And if one of the false
prophets gives him a message anyway, it is a
lie. His prophecy will not come true, and I will
stand against that ‘prophet’ and destroy him
from among my people Israel. 10False prophets and hypocrites—evil people who say they
want my words—all will be punished for their
sins, 11so that the people of Israel will learn
not to desert me and not to be polluted any
longer with sin. They will be my people and I
their God.’ So says the Lord.”
12Then this message of the Lord came to me:

13:10 There may be significant problems in our life, but claiming everything is all right will never solve them. In fact, such denial will only make things worse. It is unwise to proclaim peace when there is no peace. If problems exist, we need to admit them and respond with the appropriate action. Many of us tend to look the other way, pretending everything is all right. This will only lead us into deeper slavery and eventual destruction.

14:1-5 Very often a third party is involved in the breakdown of important relationships. For example, a third party may come between a husband and wife. Our relationship with God tends to suffer in a similar way, and the third party is identified here as an idol. If we hope to succeed in our recovery, we should allow nothing to come between us and God. Our dependencies already have done this. As we seek to overcome them, we need to be careful not to replace God with a recovery program or a relationship with another person. Only God has the power to give us true and permanent deliverance. Everything else in our life must be shaped and directed by our relationship with him.

13"Son of dust, if the people of a land sin against me, then I will crush them with my fist, break off their food supply, and send famine to destroy both man and beast. 14Even if Noah, Daniel, and Job were in it, they alone would be saved by their righteousness, and I would destroy the remainder of Israel," says the Lord God.

15"If I send an invasion of dangerous wild animals into the land to devastate the land, 16even if these three men were there, the Lord God swears that it would do no good—it would not save the people from their doom. Those three only would be saved, but the land would be devastated.

17"Or if I bring war against that land and tell the armies of the enemy to come and destroy everything, 18even if these three men were in the land, the Lord God declares that they alone would be saved.

19"And if I pour out my fury by sending an epidemic of disease into the land, and the plague kills man and beast alike, 20though Noah, Daniel, and Job were living there, the Lord God says that only they would be saved because of their righteousness."

21And the Lord says: "Four great punishments await Jerusalem to destroy all life: war, famine, ferocious beasts, plague. 22If there are survivors and they come here to join you as exiles in Babylon, you will see with your own eyes how wicked they are, and you will know it was right for me to destroy Jerusalem. 23You will agree, when you meet them, that it is not without cause that all these things are being done to Israel."

CHAPTER 15
A Useless Vine

Then this message came to me from the Lord:

2"Son of dust, what good are vines from the forest? Are they as useful as trees? Are they even as valuable as a single branch? 3No, for vines can't be used even for making pegs to hang up pots and pans! 4All they are good for is fuel—and even so, they burn but poorly! 5,6So they are useless both before and after being put in the fire!

"This is what I mean," the Lord God says: "The people of Jerusalem are like the vines of the forest—useless before being burned and certainly useless afterwards! 7And I will set myself against them to see to it that if they escape from one fire, they will fall into another; and then you shall know I am the Lord. 8And I will make the land desolate because they worship idols," says the Lord God.

CHAPTER 16
Israel's Terrible Sins

Then again a message came to me from the Lord.

2"Son of dust," he said, "speak to Jerusalem about her loathsome sins. 3Tell her, 'The Lord God says: You are no better than the people of Canaan—your father must have been an Amorite and your mother a Hittite! 4When you were born, no one cared for you. When I first saw you, your umbilical cord was uncut, and you had been neither washed nor rubbed with salt nor clothed. 5No one had the slightest interest in you; no one pitied you or cared for you. On that day when you were born, you were dumped out into a field and left to die, unwanted.

6,7"'But I came by and saw you there, covered with your own blood, and I said, "Live! Thrive like a plant in the field!" And you did! You grew up and became tall, slender and supple, a jewel among jewels. And when you reached the age of maidenhood, your breasts were full-formed and your pubic hair had grown; yet you were naked.

8"'Later, when I passed by and saw you

14:21-23 Even Ezekiel seems to have struggled with the impending destruction of Jerusalem. He couldn't understand how God could destroy his Holy City. In these verses, Ezekiel was told that God's judgments would come true, just as he had predicted. He was also assured that the judgments on Jerusalem were completely just. We can trust God; his actions are always right. Even when we don't fully understand the circumstances we face, we can trust God to do the right thing.

16:6-15 In this passage, Ezekiel compared God's people to a young, helpless girl who was nurtured by God to become queenlike in power and beauty. God took unruly Israel from Egyptian slavery and strengthened her until she became one of the great nations of the ancient world. He made a covenant with her, similar in many respects to a marriage covenant. But rather than being devoted to her husband and provider, the wife (Israel) became far more interested in prostituting herself to others. We face a similar trap in our recovery. After we struggle through the early phases of recovery, leaning heavily on God's loving power, we tend to forget how much we owe him. It is easy to become self-satisfied and take credit for our growth. Such attitudes will lead only one way—downward. God is the only one able to deliver us from our dependencies; he is also the only one able to maintain our freedom.

again, you were old enough for marriage; and I wrapped my cloak around you to legally declare my marriage vow. I signed a covenant with you, and you became mine. [9,10]Then, when the marriage had taken place, I gave you beautiful clothes of linens and silk, embroidered, and sandals made of dolphin hide. [11]I gave you lovely ornaments, bracelets, and beautiful necklaces, [12]a ring for your nose and two more for your ears, and a lovely tiara for your head. [13]And so you were made beautiful with gold and silver, and your clothes were silk and linen and beautifully embroidered. You ate the finest foods and became more beautiful than ever. You looked like a queen, and so you were! [14]Your reputation was great among the nations for your beauty; it was perfect because of all the gifts I gave you,'" says the Lord God.

[15]"'But you thought you could get along without me—you trusted in your beauty instead; and you gave yourself as a prostitute to every man who came along. Your beauty was his for the asking. [16]You used the lovely things I gave you for making idol shrines and to decorate your bed of prostitution. Unbelievable! There has never been anything like it before! [17]You took the very jewels and gold and silver ornaments I gave to you and made statues of men and worshiped them, which is adultery against me. [18]You used the beautifully embroidered clothes I gave you—to cover your idols! And used my oil and incense to worship *them!* [19]You set before *them* as a lovely sacrifice—imagine it—the fine flour and oil and honey I gave you! [20]And you took my sons and daughters you had borne to me and sacrificed them to your gods; and they are gone. Wasn't it enough that you should be a prostitute? [21]Must you also slay my children by sacrificing them to idols?

[22]"'And in all these years of adultery and sin you have not thought of those days long ago when you were naked and covered with blood.

[23]"'And then, in addition to all your other wickedness—woe, woe upon you, says the Lord God— [24]you built a spacious brothel for your lovers and idol altars on every street, [25]and there you offered your beauty to every man who came by, in an endless stream of prostitution. [26]And you added lustful Egypt to your prostitutions by your alliance with her. My anger is great.

[27]"'Therefore I have crushed you with my fist; I have reduced your boundaries and delivered you into the hands of those who hate you—the Philistines—and even they are ashamed of you.

[28]"'You have committed adultery with the Assyrians too [by making them your allies and worshiping their gods]; it seems that you can never find enough new gods. After your adultery there, you still weren't satisfied, [29]so you worshiped the gods of that great merchant land of Babylon—and you still weren't satisfied. [30]What a filthy heart you have, says the Lord God, to do such things as these; you are a brazen prostitute, [31]building your idol altars, your brothels, on every street. You have been worse than a prostitute, so eager for sin that you have not even charged for your love! [32]Yes, you are an adulterous wife who lives with other men instead of her own husband. [33,34]Prostitutes charge for their services—men pay with many gifts. But not you, you give *them* gifts, bribing them to come to you! So you are different from other prostitutes. But you had to pay them, for no one wanted you.

[35]"'O prostitute, hear the word of the Lord: [36]The Lord God says: Because I see your filthy sins, your adultery with your lovers—your worshiping of idols—and the slaying of your children as sacrifices to your gods, [37]this is what I am going to do: I will gather together all your allies—these lovers of yours you have sinned with, both those you loved and those you hated—and I will make you naked before them that they may see you. [38]I will punish you as a murderess is punished and as a woman breaking wedlock living with other men. [39]I will give you to your lovers—these many nations—to destroy, and they will knock down your brothels and idol altars. They will strip you, take your beautiful jewels, and leave you naked and ashamed. [40,41]They will burn your homes, punishing you before the eyes of many women. And I will see to it that you stop your adulteries with other gods and end your payments to your allies for their love.

[42]"'Then at last my fury against you will die away; my jealousy against you will end, and I will be quiet and not be angry with you anymore. [43]But first, because you have not remembered your youth but have angered me by all these evil things you do, I will fully repay you for all of your sins,'" says the Lord. "'For you are thankless in addition to all your other faults.

[44]"'"Like mother, like daughter"—that is what everyone will say of you. [45]For your mother loathed her husband and her children, and you do too. And you are exactly like

your sisters, for they despised their husbands
and their children. Truly, your mother must
have been a Hittite and your father an Amorite.
[46]"'Your older sister is Samaria, living with
her daughters north of you; your younger
sister is Sodom and her daughters, in the
south. [47]You have not merely sinned as they
do—no, that was nothing to you; in a very
short time you far surpassed them.
[48]"'As I live, the Lord God says, Sodom and
her daughters have never been as wicked as
you and your daughters. [49]Your sister Sodom's
sins were pride, laziness, and too much food,
while the poor and needy suffered outside her
door. [50]She insolently worshiped many idols
as I watched. Therefore I crushed her.
[51]"'Even Samaria has not committed half
your sins. You have worshiped idols far more
than your sisters have; they seem almost righteous in comparison with you! [52]Don't be
surprised then by the lighter punishment
they get. For your sins are so awful that in
comparison with you, your sisters seem innocent! [53](But someday I will restore the fortunes
of Sodom and Samaria again, and those of
Judah too.) [54]Your terrible punishment will be
a consolation to them, for it will be greater
than theirs.
[55]"'Yes, your sisters, Sodom and Samaria,
and all their people will be restored again, and
Judah, too, will prosper in that day. [56]In your
proud days you held Sodom in unspeakable
contempt. [57]But now your greater wickedness
has been exposed to all the world, and you are
the one who is scorned—by Edom and all her
neighbors and by all the Philistines. [58]This is
part of your punishment for all your sins,'"
says the Lord.
[59,60]For the Lord God says: "I will repay you
for your broken promises. You lightly broke
your solemn vows to me, yet I will keep the
pledge I made to you when you were young.
I will establish an everlasting covenant with
you forever, [61]and you will remember with
shame all the evil you have done; and you will
be overcome by my favor when I take your
sisters, Samaria and Sodom, and make them
your daughters, for you to rule over. You will
know you don't deserve this gracious act, for
you did not keep my covenant. [62]I will reaffirm my covenant with you, and you will
know I am the Lord. [63]Despite all you have
done, I will be kind to you again; you will
cover your mouth in silence and in shame
when I forgive you all that you have done,"
says the Lord God.

CHAPTER 17

The Great Eagle

Then this message came to me from the Lord:
[2]"Son of dust, give this riddle to the people
of Israel:
[3,4]"A great eagle with broad wings full of
many-colored feathers came to Lebanon and
plucked off the shoot at the top of the tallest
cedar tree and carried it into a city filled with
merchants. [5]There he planted it in fertile
ground beside a broad river, where it would
grow as quickly as a willow tree. [6]It took root
and grew and became a low but spreading
vine that turned toward the eagle and produced strong branches and luxuriant leaves.
[7]But when another great, broad-winged, full-
feathered eagle came along, this tree sent its
roots and branches out toward him instead,
[8]even though it was already in good soil with
plenty of water to become a splendid vine,
producing leaves and fruit.
[9]The Lord God asks: "Shall I let this tree
grow and prosper? No! I will pull it out, roots
and all! I will cut off its branches and let its
leaves wither and die. It will pull out easily
enough—it won't take a big crew or a lot of

16:59-63 Even though Israel had failed God, and even though her punishment was certain, God's promises of blessing would still be fulfilled in the end. The judgment Israel would suffer was designed as part of her recovery. The same is true for us. As we face the consequences of our failures, we should not blame God. We must face the truth that we have failed God and others. But no matter how great our failures, we can hope for future restoration. If we are willing to listen and respond humbly to our sufferings, God will use them to play a significant part in our recovery. Even if we have failed God, he will never fail us if we admit our sin and seek to follow his will for our life.

17:1-24 This chapter contains a review of Judah's final years. It mentions the times when Jews were exiled to Babylon prior to Jerusalem's destruction and predicts the ultimate destruction of Jerusalem. The exiles who heard Ezekiel's words had been among those exiled during the events he described, but they still hoped that his final prediction—Jerusalem's destruction—would not take place. They were still in denial about their sin and its consequences. We often resist the truth about ourself just as the people of Judah did. This is never a solution to our problems and dependencies. Since God and his Word warns us about our sins, we would be wise to listen and then act accordingly. When God speaks, we can be sure his plan will be carried out.

equipment to do that. [10]Though the vine began so well, will it thrive? No, it will wither
away completely when the east wind touches
it, dying in the same choice soil where it had
grown so well."
[11]Then this message came to me from the
Lord:
[12,13]"Ask these rebels of Israel: Don't you
understand what this riddle of the eagles
means? I will tell you. Nebuchadnezzar, king
of Babylon [the first of the two eagles], came
to Jerusalem, took away her king and princes
[her topmost buds and shoots], and brought
them to Babylon. Nebuchadnezzar made a
covenant with a member of the royal family
[Zedekiah], and made him take an oath of
loyalty. He took a seedling and planted it in
fertile ground beside a broad river. He also
exiled the top men of Israel's government, [14]so
that Israel would not be strong again and
revolt. But by keeping her promises, Israel
could be respected and maintain her identity.
[15]"Nevertheless, Zedekiah rebelled against
Babylon, sending ambassadors to Egypt to
seek for a great army and many horses to fight
against Nebuchadnezzar. But will Israel prosper after breaking all her promises like that?
Will she succeed? [16]No! For as I live," says the
Lord, "the king of Israel shall die. (Nebuchadnezzar will pull out the tree, roots and all!)
Zedekiah shall die in Babylon, where the king
lives who gave him his power, and whose
covenant he despised and broke. [17]Pharaoh
and all his mighty army shall fail to help Israel
when the king of Babylon lays siege to Jerusalem again and slaughters many lives. [18]For the
king of Israel broke his promise after swearing
to obey; therefore he shall not escape."
[19]The Lord God says: "As I live, surely I will
punish him for despising the solemn oath he
made in my name. [20]I will throw my net over
him, and he shall be captured in my snare; I
will bring him to Babylon and deal with him
there for this treason against me. [21]And all the
best soldiers of Israel will be killed by the
sword, and those remaining in the city will be
scattered to the four winds. Then you will
know that I, the Lord, have spoken these
words."
[22,23]The Lord God says: "I will take a tender
sprout from the top of a tall cedar, and I will
plant it on the top of Israel's highest mountain. It shall become a noble cedar, bringing
forth branches and bearing seed. Animals of
every sort will gather under it; its branches
will shelter every kind of bird. [24]And everyone
shall know that it is I, the Lord, who cuts
down the high trees and exalts the low, that I
make the green tree wither and the dead tree
grow. I, the Lord, have said that I would do it,
and I will."

CHAPTER 18

Personal Responsibility for Sin

Then the Lord's message came to me again.
[2]"Why do people use this proverb about the
land of Israel: The children are punished for
their fathers' sins? [3]As I live," says the Lord
God, "you will not use this proverb any more
in Israel, [4]for all souls are mine to judge—
fathers and sons alike—and my rule is this: It
is for a man's own sins that he will die.
[5]"But if a man is just and does what is lawful
and right, [6]and has not gone out to the mountains to feast before the idols of Israel and
worship them, and does not commit adultery
nor lie with any woman during the time of
her menstruation; [7]if he is a merciful creditor,
not holding onto the items given to him in
pledge by poor debtors, and is no robber but
gives food to the hungry and clothes to those
in need; [8]and if he grants loans without interest, stays away from sin, is honest and fair
when judging others, [9]and obeys my laws—
that man is just," says the Lord, "and he shall
surely live.
[10]"But if that man has a son who is a robber
or murderer and who fulfills none of his responsibilities, [11]who refuses to obey the laws
of God but worships idols on the mountains
and commits adultery, [12]oppresses the poor
and helpless, robs his debtors by refusing to
let them redeem what they have given him in
pledge, loves idols and worships them, [13]and
loans out his money at interest—shall that

18:2-4 Here we are reminded that we are held accountable by God for our actions. Many of us have suffered innocently at the hands of others. As we become aware of this, it is tempting to blame others for our problems and dependencies. As much as others may have hurt us, it is never valid to blame others for the mistakes we have made. We cannot change the behavior of others, and we must forgive them and put the pain of these experiences behind us. Recovery requires that we accept responsibility for our own failures and do what we can to make amends with those we have harmed. This will break the chain of suffering in our family line. We cannot change how we are treated, but we can change how we treat others.

man live? No! He shall surely die, and it is his own fault.

14“But if this sinful man has, in turn, a son who sees all his father’s wickedness, so that he fears God and decides against that kind of life; 15he doesn’t go up on the mountains to feast before the idols and worship them and does not commit adultery; 16he is fair to those who borrow from him and doesn’t rob them, but feeds the hungry, clothes the needy, 17helps the poor, does not loan money at interest, and obeys my laws—he shall not die because of his father’s sins; he shall surely live. 18But his father shall die for his own sins because he is cruel and robs and does wrong.

19“‘What?’ you ask. ‘Doesn’t the son pay for his father’s sins?’ No! For if the son does what is right and keeps my laws, he shall surely live. 20The one who sins is the one who dies. The son shall not be punished for his father’s sins, nor the father for his son’s. The righteous person will be rewarded for his own goodness and the wicked person for his wickedness. 21But if a wicked person turns away from all his sins and begins to obey my laws and do what is just and right, he shall surely live and not die. 22All his past sins will be forgotten, and he shall live because of his goodness.

23“Do you think I like to see the wicked die?” asks the Lord. “Of course not! I only want him to turn from his wicked ways and live. 24However, if a righteous person turns to sinning and acts like any other sinner, should he be allowed to live? No, of course not. All his previous goodness will be forgotten and he shall die for his sins.

25“Yet you say: ‘The Lord isn’t being fair!’ Listen to me, O people of Israel. Am I the one who is unfair, or is it you? 26When a good man turns away from being good, begins sinning, and dies in his sins, he dies for the evil he has done. 27And if a wicked person turns away from his wickedness and obeys the law and does right, he shall save his soul, 28for he has thought it over and decided to turn from his sins and live a good life. He shall surely live—he shall not die.

29“And yet the people of Israel keep saying: ‘The Lord is unfair!’ O people of Israel, it is you who are unfair, not I. 30I will judge each of you, O Israel, and punish or reward each according to his own actions. Oh, turn from your sins while there is yet time. 31Put them behind you and receive a new heart and a new spirit. For why will you die, O Israel? 32I do not enjoy seeing you die,” the Lord God says. “Turn, turn and live!”

CHAPTER 19

A Death Dirge

“Sing this death dirge for the leaders of Israel: 2What a woman your mother was—like a lioness! Her children were like lion’s cubs! 3One of her cubs [King Jehoahaz] grew into a strong young lion and learned to catch prey and became a man-eater. 4Then the nations called out their hunters; they trapped him in a pit and brought him in chains to Egypt.

5“When Israel, the mother lion, saw that all her hopes for him were gone, she took another of her cubs [King Jehoiachin] and taught him to be ‘king of the beasts.’ 6He became a leader among the lions and learned to catch prey, and he too became a man-eater. 7He demolished the palaces of the surrounding nations and ruined their cities; their farms were desolated, their crops destroyed; everyone in the land shook with terror when they heard him roar. 8Then the armies of the nations surrounded him, coming from every side, and trapped him in a pit and captured him. 9They prodded him into a cage and brought him before the king of Babylon. He was held in captivity so that his voice could never again be heard upon the mountains of Israel.

10“Your mother was like a vine beside an irrigation ditch, with lush, green foliage because of all the water. 11Its strongest branch became a ruler’s scepter, and it was very great, towering above the others and noticed from far away. 12But the vine was uprooted in fury and thrown down to the ground. Its branches were broken and withered by a strong wind from the east; the fruit was destroyed by fire. 13Now the vine is planted in the wilderness where the ground is hard and dry. 14It is decaying from within; no strong branch remains. The fulfillment of this sad prophecy has already begun, and there is more ahead.”

18:30-32 Some say that God is too good to damn anybody. Certainly, it is true that God takes no pleasure in the death of the wicked. But he created us to be responsible individuals. God desires that each person choose him. If a person should choose not to turn from his sin, the only alternative is eternal separation from God himself. God wants us all to live. If we admit our sin to God, he will always help us to rebuild our life, no matter how extensive the devastation.

CHAPTER 20

Remembering Past Rebellion

Late in July, six years after King Jeconiah was
captured, some of the elders of Israel came to
ask instructions from the Lord and sat before
me awaiting his reply.
[2]Then the Lord gave me this message:

[3]"Son of dust, say to the elders of Israel,
'The Lord God says: How dare you come to
ask my help? I swear that I will tell you nothing.' [4]Judge them, son of dust; condemn
them; tell them of all the sins of this nation
from the times of their fathers until now.
[5,6]Tell them, 'The Lord God says: When I chose
Israel and revealed myself to her in Egypt, I
swore to her and her descendants that I would
bring them out of Egypt to a land I had
discovered and explored for them—a good
land, flowing as it were with milk and honey,
the best of all lands anywhere.'
[7]"Then I said to them: 'Get rid of every idol;
do not defile yourselves with the Egyptian
gods, for I am the Lord your God.' [8]But they
rebelled against me and would not listen.
They didn't get rid of their idols nor forsake
the gods of Egypt. Then I thought, I will pour
out my fury upon them and fulfill my anger
against them while they are still in Egypt.
[9,10]"But I didn't do it, for I acted to protect
the honor of my name, lest the Egyptians
laugh at Israel's God who couldn't keep them
back from harm. So I brought my people out
of Egypt right before the Egyptians' eyes and
led them into the wilderness. [11]There I gave
them my laws so they could live by keeping
them. If anyone keeps them, he will live.
[12]And I gave them the Sabbath—a day of rest
every seventh day—as a symbol between
them and me, to remind them that it is I, the
Lord, who sanctifies them—that they are
truly my people.
[13]"But Israel rebelled against me. There in
the wilderness they refused my laws. They
would not obey my rules even though obeying them means life. And they misused my
Sabbaths. Then I thought, I will pour out my
fury upon them and utterly consume them in
the desert.
[14]"But again I refrained in order to protect
the honor of my name, lest the nations who
saw me bring them out of Egypt would say
that it was because I couldn't care for them
that I destroyed them. [15]But I swore to them
in the wilderness that I would not bring them
into the land I had given them, a land full of
milk and honey, the choicest spot on earth,
[16]because they laughed at my laws, ignored
my wishes, and violated my Sabbaths—their
hearts were with their idols! [17]Nevertheless, I
spared them. I didn't finish them off in the
wilderness.
[18]"Then I spoke to their children and said:
'Don't follow your fathers' footsteps. Don't
defile yourselves with their idols, [19]for I am
the Lord your God. Follow my laws; keep my
ordinances; [20]hallow my Sabbaths; for they
are a symbol of the contract between us to
help you remember that I am the Lord your
God.'
[21]"But their children, too, rebelled against
me. They refused my laws—the laws that if a
person keeps them, he will live. And they
defiled my Sabbaths. So then I said: 'Now at
last I will pour out my fury upon you in the
wilderness.'
[22]"Nevertheless, again I withdrew my judgment against them to protect my name
among the nations who had seen my power
in bringing them out of Egypt. [23,24]But I took a
solemn oath against them while they were in
the wilderness that I would scatter them, dis-
persing them to the ends of the earth because
they did not obey my laws but scorned them
and violated my Sabbaths and longed for
their fathers' idols. [25]I let them adopt customs
and laws which were worthless. Through the
keeping of them they could not attain life.
[26]In the hope that they would draw back in
horror and know that I alone am God, I let
them pollute themselves with the very gifts I
gave them. They burnt their firstborn children as offerings to their gods!
[27,28]"Son of dust, tell them that the Lord
God says: 'Your fathers continued to blaspheme and betray me when I brought them
into the land I promised them, for they offered sacrifices and incense on every high hill
and under every tree! They roused my fury as
they offered up their sacrifices to
those "gods." They brought their perfumes

20:1-8 God's program for healthy living is defined by him alone; he sets up the terms, not us. God is not a recovery gimmick. He is not a Power we try to accommodate into our own recovery program. If we want to succeed in recovery, we will have to fit into God's plan. As the one who created us and loves us, God is uniquely qualified to lead us into the best possible future. If we try to do things our own way, however, we are only asking for trouble. The experience of the people of Judah in these verses should make these truths clear.

and incense and poured out their drink offerings to them! 29I said to them: "What is this
place of sacrifice where you go?" And so it is
still called 'The Place of Sacrifice'—that is how
it got its name.
30"The Lord God wants to know whether
you are going to pollute yourselves just as
your fathers did and keep on worshiping
idols. 31For when you offer gifts to them and
give your little sons to be burned to ashes as
you do even today, shall I listen to you or help
you, Israel? As I live," the Lord God says, "I
will not give you any message, though you
have come to me to ask.
32"What you have in mind will not be
done—to be like the nations all around you,
serving gods of wood and stone. 33I will rule
you with an iron fist and in great anger and
with power. 34With might and fury I will bring
you out from the lands where you are scattered, 35,36and will bring you into my desert
judgment hall. I will judge you there and get
rid of the rebels, just as I did in the wilderness
after I brought you out of Egypt. 37I will count
you carefully and let only a small quota return. 38And the others—the rebels and all
those who sin against me—I will purge from
among you. They shall not enter Israel, but I
will bring them out of the countries where
they are in exile. And when that happens, you
will know I am the Lord.
39"O Israel," the Lord God says: "If you
insist on worshiping your idols, go right
ahead, but then don't bring your gifts to me
as well! Such desecration of my holy name
must stop!
40"For at Jerusalem in my holy mountain,"
says the Lord, "all Israel shall worship me.
There I will accept you and require you to
bring me your offerings and the finest of your
gifts. 41You will be to me as an offering of
perfumed incense when I bring you back
from exile, and the nations will see the great
change in your hearts. 42Then, when I have
brought you home to the land I promised
your fathers, you will know I am the Lord.
43Then you will look back at all your sins and
loathe yourselves because of the evil you have
done. 44And when I have honored my name
by blessing you despite your wickedness,
then, O Israel, you will know I am the Lord."
45Then this message came to me from the
Lord:
46"Son of dust, look toward Jerusalem and
speak out against it and the forest lands of the
Negeb. 47Prophesy to it and say: 'Hear the
word of the Lord. I will set you on fire, O
forest, and every tree will die, green and dry
alike. The terrible flames will not be
quenched, and they will scorch the world.
48And all the world will see that I, the Lord,
have set the fire. It shall not be put out.'"
49Then I said, "O Lord God, they say of me,
'He only talks in riddles!'"

CHAPTER 21
Babylon Will Attack Judah

Then this message came to me from the Lord:
2"Son of dust, face toward Jerusalem and
prophesy against Israel and against my
Temple! 3For the Lord says: 'I am against you,
Israel. I will unsheath my sword and destroy
your people, good and bad alike—4I will not
spare even the righteous. I will make a clean
sweep throughout the land from the Negeb to
your northern borders. 5All the world shall
know that it is I, the Lord. His sword is in his
hand, and it will not return to its sheath again
until its work is finished.'
6"Sigh and groan before the people, son of

20:40-42 Here Ezekiel gave God's exiled people a precious promise for the future. After a period of suffering, the people would repent and experience God's cleansing; then they would be restored to the Promised Land. But, of even greater significance, they would be restored to God's fellowship. Doing things God's way—admitting our sin and seeking his plan for us—is the beginning of our recovery and the foundation of our hope for the future.

21:3 These ominous words are addressed to the nation of Israel. Notice that God would punish the entire nation, including the few good people. Our sin always has consequences, and very often those consequences are experienced by the innocent people around us. Our mistakes and dependencies cause undeserved pain for spouses, children, coworkers, and employees. This should motivate us to seek changes in our life and make amends to those we have hurt.

21:6-7 God called Ezekiel to express his grief at the coming destruction of Jerusalem. He was to hold nothing back. This would be a further warning to the people that Jerusalem's destruction was a sure thing. In contrast to the norms of our culture, uninhibited emotional expressions of this kind were normal in ancient Israel. Not only is this kind of emotional honesty good therapy for a wounded heart, it also allows others to enter into our suffering and learn from it. God's call to honesty should extend even into the realm of our emotions.

dust, in your bitter anguish; sigh with grief
and broken heart. [7]When they ask you why,
tell them: 'Because of the fearsome news that
God has given me. When it comes true, the
boldest heart will melt with fear; all strength
will disappear. Every spirit will faint; strong
knees will tremble and become as weak as
water.' And the Lord God says: 'Your doom is
on the way; my judgments will be fulfilled!'"

[8]Then again this message came to me from
God:

[9-11]"Son of dust, tell them this: 'A sword is
being sharpened and polished for terrible
slaughter. Now will you laugh? For those far
stronger than you have perished beneath its
power. It is ready now to hand to the executioner.' [12]Son of dust, with sobbing, beat upon
your thigh, for that sword shall slay my
people and all their leaders. All alike shall die.
[13]It will put them all to the test—and what
chance do they have?" the Lord God asks.

[14]"Prophesy to them in this way: Clap your
hands vigorously, then take a sword and brandish it twice, thrice, to symbolize the great
massacre they face! [15]Let their hearts melt
with terror, for a sword glitters at every gate;
it flashes like lightning; it is razor-edged for
slaughter. [16]O sword, slash to the right and
slash to the left, wherever you will, wherever
you want. [17]And you have prophesied with
clapping hands that I, the Lord, will smite
Jerusalem and satisfy my fury."

[18]Then this message came to me. The Lord
said:

[19,20]"Son of dust, make a map and on it trace
two routes for the king of Babylon to follow—
one to Jerusalem and the other to Rabbah in
Trans-Jordan. And put a signpost at the fork
in the road from Babylon. [21]For the king of
Babylon stands at a fork, uncertain whether
to attack Jerusalem or Rabbah. He will call his
magicians to use divination; they will cast lots
by shaking arrows from the quiver; they will
sacrifice to idols and inspect the liver of their
sacrifice. [22]They will decide to turn toward
Jerusalem! With battering rams they will go
against the gates, shouting for the kill; they
will build siege towers and make a hill against
the walls to reach the top. [23]Jerusalem won't
understand this treachery; how could the diviners make this terrible mistake? For Babylon
is Judah's ally and has sworn to defend Jerusalem! But (the king of Babylon) will think
only of the times the people rebelled. He will
attack and defeat them.

[24]The Lord God says: "Again and again your
guilt cries out against you, for your sins are
open and unashamed. Wherever you go,
whatever you do, all is filled with sin. And
now the time of punishment has come.

[25]"O King Zedekiah, evil prince of Israel,
your final day of reckoning is here. [26]Take off
your jeweled crown," the Lord God says. "The
old order changes. Now the poor are exalted
and the rich brought very low. [27]I will overturn, overturn, overturn the kingdom, so that
even the new order that emerges will not
succeed until the Man appears who has a right
to it. And I will give it all to him.

[28]"Son of dust, prophesy to the Ammonites
too, for they mocked my people in their woe.
Tell them this:

"'Against you also my glittering sword is
drawn from its sheath; it is sharpened and
polished and flashed like lightning. [29]Your
magicians and false prophets have told you
lies of safety and success—that your gods will
save you from the king of Babylon. Thus they
have caused your death along with all the
other wicked, for when the day of final reckoning has come, you will be wounded unto
death. [30]Shall I return my sword to its sheath
before I deal with you? No, I will destroy you
in your own country where you were born. [31]I
will pour out my fury upon you and blow
upon the fire of my wrath until it becomes a
roaring conflagration, and I will deliver you
into the hands of cruel men skilled in destruction. [32]You are the fuel for the fire; your blood
will be spilled in your own country, and you
will be utterly wiped out, your memory lost in
history. For I, the Lord, have spoken it.'"

CHAPTER 22

A List of Jerusalem's Sins

Now another message came from the Lord.
He said:

[2]"Son of dust, indict Jerusalem as the City of

22:2-4 In contemporary culture the reality of personal guilt is often rejected as an illusion. There are programs that seek to ignore the guilt we feel rather than dealing with the sin that lies at its root. This is not to say that false guilt does not exist. Yet any therapy that denies the existence of sin and tries to find excuses rather than remedies is not in agreement with God's program. God has provided salvation from the guilt of sin. There is no reason for us to hide or ignore it. We must choose God's remedy, which starts with our recognition of our helplessness and the admission of our sins.

Murder. Publicly denounce her terrible deeds.
3City of Murder, doomed and damned—City
of Idols, filthy and foul—4you are guilty both
of murder and idolatry. Now comes your day
of doom. You have reached the limit of your
years. I will make you a laughingstock and a
reproach to all the nations of the world. 5Near
and far they will mock you, a city of infamous
rebels.

6"Every leader in Israel who lives within
your walls is bent on murder. 7Fathers and
mothers are contemptuously ignored; immigrants and visitors are forced to pay you for
your 'protection'; orphans and widows are
wronged and oppressed. 8The things of God
are all despised; my Sabbaths are ignored.
9Prisoners are falsely accused and sent to their
death. Every mountaintop is filled with idols;
lewdness is everywhere. 10There are men who
commit adultery with their fathers' wives and
lie with menstruous women. 11Adultery with
a neighbor's wife, a daughter-in-law, a half
sister—this is common. 12Hired murderers,
loan racketeers, and extortioners are everywhere. You never even think of me and my
commands," the Lord God says.

13"But now I snap my fingers and call a halt
to your dishonest gain and bloodshed. 14How
strong and courageous will you be then, in
my day of reckoning? For I, the Lord, have
spoken, and I will do all that I have said. 15I
will scatter you throughout the world and
burn out the wickedness within you. 16You
will be dishonored among the nations, and
you shall know I am the Lord."

17Then the Lord said this:

18-20"Son of dust, the people of Israel are the
worthless slag left when silver is smelted.
They are the dross, compounded from the
brass, the tin, the iron and the lead. Therefore
the Lord God says: 'Because you are worthless
dross, I will bring you to my crucible in Jerusalem, to smelt you with the heat of my
wrath. 21I will blow the fire of my wrath upon
you, 22and you will melt like silver in fierce
heat, and you will know that I, the Lord, have
poured my wrath upon you.'"

23Again the message of the Lord came to
me, saying:

24"Son of dust, say to the people of Israel:
'In the day of my indignation you shall be like
an uncleared wilderness or a desert without
rain.' 25Your 'prophets' have plotted against
you like lions stalking prey. They devour
many lives; they seize treasures and extort
wealth; they multiply the widows in the land.
26Your priests have violated my laws and defiled my Temple and my holiness. To them
the things of God are no more important than
any daily task. They have not taught my
people the difference between right and
wrong, and they disregard my Sabbaths, so
my holy name is greatly defiled among them.
27Your leaders are like wolves, who tear apart
their victims, and they destroy lives for profit.
28Your 'prophets' describe false visions and
speak false messages they claim are from God,
when he hasn't spoken one word to them at
all. Thus they repair the walls with whitewash! 29Even the common people oppress and
rob the poor and needy and cruelly extort
from aliens.

30"I looked in vain for anyone who would
build again the wall of righteousness that
guards the land, who could stand in the gap
and defend you from my just attacks, but I
found not one." 31And so the Lord God says:
"I will pour out my anger upon you; I will
consume you with the fire of my wrath. I have
heaped upon you the full penalty for all your
sins."

CHAPTER 23

Parable of Two Sisters

The Lord's message came to me again, saying:

2,3"Son of dust, there were two sisters who
as young girls became prostitutes in Egypt.

4,5"The older girl was named Oholah; her
sister was Oholibah. (I am speaking of Samaria and Jerusalem!) I married them, and
they bore me sons and daughters. But then
Oholah turned to other gods instead of me
and gave her love to the Assyrians, her neighbors, 6for they were all attractive young men,
captains and commanders, in handsome

23:1-49 Throughout this chapter Ezekiel compared the kingdoms of Judah and Israel to two adulterous sisters. Despite all the blessings God had given them, they sold themselves to idols and were thus unfaithful to God. God's people were guilty of spiritual harlotry. We are guilty of this same sin when we allow anything to take God's proper place in our life. This may involve using an unhealthy dependency—drugs, alcohol, overwork, illicit sexual activity—to hide from inner pain that only God can heal. It may involve using a recovery program that ignores God and leads us away from his way of life. Whatever idols we have, they must be removed if we hope to deal with our failures and rebuild for a meaningful future.

blue, dashing about on their horses. 7And so
she sinned with them—the choicest men of
Assyria—worshiping their idols, defiling herself. 8For when she left Egypt, she did not
leave her spirit of prostitution behind, but
was still as lewd as in her youth when the
Egyptians poured out their lusts upon her and
robbed her of her virginity.

9"And so I delivered her into the evil
clutches of the Assyrians whose gods she
loved so much. 10They stripped her and killed
her and took away her children as their slaves.
Her name was known to every woman in the
land as a sinner who had received what she
deserved.

11"But when Oholibah [Jerusalem] saw
what had happened to her sister she went
right ahead in the same way and sinned even
more than her sister. 12She fawned over her
Assyrian neighbors, those handsome young
men on fine steeds, those army officers in
handsome uniforms—all of them desirable.
13I saw the way she was going, following right
along behind her older sister.

14,15"She was in fact more debased than Samaria, for she fell in love with pictures she
saw painted on a wall! They were pictures of
Babylonian military officers, outfitted in
striking red uniforms, with handsome belts,
and flowing turbans on their heads. 16When
she saw these paintings, she longed to give
herself to the men pictured, so she sent messengers to Chaldea to invite them to come to
her. 17And they came and committed adultery
with her, defiling her in the bed of love, but
afterward she hated them and broke off all
relations with them.

18"And I despised her, just as I despised her
sister, because she flaunted herself before
them and gave herself to their lust. 19,20But
that didn't bother her. She turned to even
greater prostitution, sinning with the lustful
men she remembered from her youth when
she was a prostitute in Egypt. 21And thus you
celebrated those former days when as a young
girl you gave your virginity to those from
Egypt.

22"And now the Lord God says that he will
raise against you, O Oholibah [Jerusalem],
those very nations from which you turned
away, disgusted. 23For the Babylonians will
come, and all the Chaldeans from Pekod and
Shoa and Koa; and all the Assyrians with
them—handsome young men of high rank,
riding their steeds. 24They will come against
you from the north with chariots, wagons,
and a great army fully prepared for attack.
They will surround you on every side with
armored men, and I will let them at you, to do
with you as they wish. 25And I will send my
jealousy against you and deal furiously with
you. They will cut off your nose and ears; your
survivors will be killed; your children will be
taken away as slaves, and everything left will
be burned. 26They will strip you of your beautiful clothes and jewels.

27"And so I will put a stop to your lewdness
and prostitution brought from the land of
Egypt; you will no more long for Egypt and
her gods." 28For the Lord God says: "I will
surely deliver you over to your enemies, to
those you loathe. 29They will deal with you in
hatred and rob you of all you own, leaving
you naked and bare. And the shame of your
prostitution shall be exposed to all the world.

30"You brought all this upon yourself by
worshiping the gods of other nations, defiling
yourself with all their idols. 31You have followed in your sister's footsteps, so I will punish
you with the same terrors that destroyed her.
32Yes, the terrors that fell upon her will fall
upon you—and the cup from which she drank
was full and large. And all the world will mock
you for your woe. 33You will reel like a drunkard beneath the awful blows of sorrow and
distress, just as your sister Samaria did. 34In
deep anguish you will drain that cup of terror
to the very bottom and will lick the inside to
get every drop. For I have spoken," says the
Lord. 35"Because you have forgotten me and
turned your backs on me, therefore you must
bear the consequence of all your sin.

36"Son of dust, you must accuse Jerusalem
and Samaria of all their awful deeds. 37For they
have committed both adultery and murder;
they have worshiped idols and murdered my
children whom they bore to me, burning
them as sacrifices on their altars. 38On the
same day they defiled my Temple and ignored
my Sabbaths, 39for when they had murdered
their children in front of their idols, then
even that same day they actually came into
my Temple to worship! That is how much
regard they have for me!

40"You even sent away to distant lands for
priests to come with other gods for you to
serve, and they have come and been welcomed! You bathed yourself, painted your
eyelids, and put on your finest jewels for
them. 41You sat together on a beautifully embroidered bed and put my incense and my oil
upon a table spread before you. 42From your
apartment came the sound of many men carousing—lewd men and drunkards from the

wilderness, who put bracelets on your wrists and beautiful crowns upon your head. 43Will they commit adultery with these who have become old harlot hags? 44Yet that is what they did. They went in to them—to Samaria and Jerusalem, these shameless harlots—with all the zest of lustful men who visit prostitutes. 45But just persons everywhere will judge them for what they really are—adulteresses and murderers. They will mete out to them the sentences the law demands.

46The Lord God says: "Bring an army against them and hand them out to be crushed and despised. 47For their enemies will stone them and kill them with swords; they will butcher their sons and daughters and burn their homes. 48Thus will I make lewdness and idolatry to cease from the land. My judgment will be a lesson against idolatry for all to see. 49For you will be fully repaid for all your harlotry, your worshiping of idols. You will suffer the full penalty, and you will know that I alone am God."

CHAPTER 24

Parable of a Cooking Pot

One day late in December of the ninth year (of King Jehoiachin's captivity), another message came to me from the Lord.

2"Son of dust," he said, "write down this date, for today the king of Babylon has attacked Jerusalem. 3And now give this parable to these rebels, Israel; tell them, 'The Lord God says: Put a pot of water on the fire to boil. 4Fill it with choicest mutton, the rump and shoulder and all the most tender cuts. 5Use only the best sheep from the flock, and heap fuel on the fire beneath the pot. Boil the meat well, until the flesh falls off the bones.'

6For the Lord God says: "Woe to Jerusalem, City of Murderers; you are a pot that is pitted with rust and with wickedness. So take out the meat chunk by chunk in whatever order it comes—for none is better than any other. 7For her wickedness is evident to all—she boldly murders, leaving blood upon the rocks in open view for all to see; she does not even try to cover it. 8And I have left it there, uncovered, to shout to me against her and arouse my wrath and vengeance.

9"Woe to Jerusalem, City of Murderers. I will pile on the fuel beneath her. 10Heap on the wood; let the fire roar and the pot boil. Cook the meat well, and then empty the pot and burn the bones. 11Now set it empty on the coals to scorch away the rust and corruption. 12But all for naught—it all remains despite the hottest fire. 13It is the rust and corruption of your filthy lewdness, of worshiping your idols. And now, because I wanted to cleanse you and you refused, remain filthy until my fury has accomplished all its terrors upon you! 14I, the Lord, have spoken it; it shall come to pass and I will do it."

15Again a message came to me from the Lord, saying:

16"Son of dust, I am going to take away your lovely wife. Suddenly, she will die. Yet you must show no sorrow. Do not weep; let there be no tears. 17You may sigh, but only quietly. Let there be no wailing at her grave; don't bare your head nor feet, and don't accept the food brought to you by consoling friends."

18I proclaimed this to the people in the morning, and in the evening my wife died. The next morning I did all the Lord had told me to.

19Then the people said: "What does all this mean? What are you trying to tell us?"

20,21And I answered, "The Lord told me to say to the people of Israel: 'I will destroy my lovely, beautiful Temple, the strength of your nation. And your sons and daughters in Judea will be slaughtered by the sword. 22And you will do as I have done; you may not mourn in public or console yourself by eating the food brought to you by sympathetic friends. 23Your head and feet shall not be bared; you shall not mourn or weep. But you will sorrow to one another for your sins and mourn privately for all the evil you have done. 24Ezekiel is an example to you,' the Lord God says. 'You will do as he has done. And when that time comes, then you will know I am the Lord.'"

25"Son of dust, on the day I finish taking from them in Jerusalem the joy of their hearts and their glory and joys—their wives and their sons and their daughters— 26on that day a refugee from Jerusalem will start on a journey to come to you in Babylon to tell you what has happened. 27And on the day of his arrival, your voice will suddenly return to you

---

24:1-14 In these verses God predicted the destruction of Jerusalem. God had delayed his punishment for many years, giving his people ample opportunity to repent and seek forgiveness. His people had failed, however, and the time of their final destruction had arrived. God gives us numerous opportunities to admit our failures and ask his forgiveness before he allows our destruction. We would be wise to listen before it is too late.

so that you can talk with him; and you will be a symbol for these people, and they shall know I am the Lord."

CHAPTER 25

A Prophecy against Ammon

Then the Lord's message came to me again. He said:

[2]"Son of dust, look toward the land of Ammon and prophesy against its people. [3]Tell them: 'Listen to what the Lord God says. Because you scoffed when my Temple was destroyed, and mocked Israel in her anguish, and laughed at Judah when she was marched away captive, [4]therefore I will let the Bedouins from the desert to the east of you overrun your land. They will set up their encampments among you. They will harvest all your fruit and steal your dairy cattle. [5]And I will turn the city of Rabbah into a pasture for camels and all the country of the Ammonites into a wasteland where flocks of sheep can graze. Then you will know I am the Lord.'"

[6]For the Lord God says: "Because you clapped and stamped and cheered with glee at the destruction of my people, [7]therefore I will lay my hand heavily upon you, delivering you to many nations for devastation. I will cut you off from being a nation any more. I will destroy you; then you shall know I am the Lord."

A Prophecy against Moab

[8]And the Lord God says: "Because the Moabites have said that Judah is no better off than any other nation, [9,10]therefore I will open up the eastern flank of Moab, wiping out her frontier cities, the glory of the nation—Beth-jeshimoth, Baal-meon and Kiriathaim. And Bedouin tribes from the desert to the east will pour in upon her, just as they will upon Ammon. And Moab will no longer be counted among the nations. [11]Thus I will bring down my judgment upon the Moabites, and they shall know I am the Lord."

A Prophecy against Edom

[12]And the Lord God says: "Because the people of Edom have sinned so greatly by avenging themselves upon the people of Judah, [13]I will smash Edom with my fist and wipe out her people, her cattle, and her flocks. The sword will destroy everything from Teman to Dedan. [14]By the hand of my people, Israel, this shall be done. They will carry out my furious vengeance."

A Prophecy against Philistia

[15]And the Lord God says: "Because the Philistines have acted against Judah out of revenge and long-standing hatred, [16]I will shake my fist over the land of the Philistines, and I will wipe out the Cherithites and utterly destroy those along the seacoast. [17]I will execute terrible vengeance upon them to rebuke them for what they have done. And when all this happens, then they shall know I am the Lord."

CHAPTER 26

A Prophecy against Tyre

Another message came to me from the Lord on the first day of the month, in the eleventh year (after King Jehoiachin was taken away to captivity).

[2]"Son of dust, Tyre has rejoiced over the fall of Jerusalem, saying, 'Ha! She who controlled the lucrative north-south trade routes along the coast and along the course of the Jordan

24:25-27 These verses conclude the long section of judgment (1:1–24:27). The people already in Babylon would soon hear news of Jerusalem's destruction. They would discover that Ezekiel's predictions had been true. This would confirm the truth of all his words, including his condemnation of the people for their sin. Their only response could be one of mourning and repentance. They would have to humble themselves before God, their Judge and their Redeemer. From this point on, Ezekiel is called upon to bring a message of hope to the exiled Jews. God's judgment was not the end. He began by showing his people that the foreign nations would also be judged for their sin (25:1–32:32). Then he also promised the restoration of his scattered people to the land of Israel (33:1–39:29).

25:1-17 After God finished punishing his people, he turned to punish Israel's foreign neighbors. God's people are precious to him, so he turned his wrath against those who had treated them badly. God is just, and his justice will stand in the end, no matter how bad things may look at present. Israel had been destroyed and her people left in hopeless exile. God began his ministry among them by punishing the nations that had acted to harm Israel in earlier days. Even though these nations had seemed to get away with injustice, they were held accountable for their sin in the end. This should give us hope if we have been wronged, but it should also warn us to act now to make amends for our past failures. The consequences of past sins will always come back to haunt us and our descendants.

River has been broken, and I have fallen heir! Because she has been laid waste, I shall become wealthy!'

3Therefore the Lord God says: "I stand against you, Tyre, and I will bring nations against you like ocean waves. 4They will destroy the walls of Tyre and tear down her towers. I will scrape away her soil and make her a bare rock! 5Her island shall become uninhabited, a place for fishermen to spread their nets, for I have spoken it," says the Lord God. "Tyre shall become the prey of many nations, 6and her mainland city shall perish by the sword. Then they shall know I am the Lord."

7For the Lord God says: "I will bring Nebuchadnezzar, king of Babylon—the king of kings from the north—against Tyre with a great army and cavalry and chariots. 8First he will destroy your suburbs; then he will attack your mainland city by building a siege wall and raising a roof of shields against it. 9He will set up battering rams against your walls and with sledgehammers demolish your forts. 10The hoofs of his cavalry will choke the city with dust, and your walls will shake as the horses gallop through your broken gates, pulling chariots behind them. 11Horsemen will occupy every street in the city; they will butcher your people, and your famous, huge pillars will topple.

12"They will plunder all your riches and merchandise and break down your walls. They will destroy your lovely homes and dump your stones and timber and even your dust into the sea. 13I will stop the music of your songs. No more will there be the sound of harps among you. 14I will make your island a bare rock, a place for fishermen to spread their nets. You will never be rebuilt, for I, the Lord, have spoken it." So says the Lord. 15"The whole country will shake with your fall; the wounded will scream as the slaughter goes on.

16"Then all the seaport rulers shall come down from their thrones and lay aside their robes and beautiful garments and sit on the ground shaking with fear at what they have seen. 17And they shall wail for you, singing this dirge: 'O mighty island city, with your naval power that terrorized the mainland, how you have vanished from the seas! 18How the islands tremble at your fall! They watch dismayed.'"

19For the Lord God says: "I will destroy Tyre to the ground. You will sink beneath the terrible waves of enemy attack. Great seas shall swallow you. 20I will send you to the pit of hell to lie there with those of long ago. Your city will lie in ruins, dead, like the bodies of those in the underworld who entered long ago the nether world of the dead. Never again will you be inhabited or be given beauty here in the land of those who live. 21I will bring you to a dreadful end; no search will be enough to find you," says the Lord.

CHAPTER 27

The Greatness of Tyre

Then this message came to me from the Lord. He said:

2"Son of dust, sing this sad dirge for Tyre:

3"'O mighty seaport city, merchant center of the world, the Lord God speaks. You say, "I am the most beautiful city in all the world." 4You have extended your boundaries out into the sea; your architects have made you glorious. 5You are like a ship built of finest fir from Senir. They took a cedar from Lebanon to make a mast for you. 6They made your oars from oaks of Bashan. The walls of your cabin are of cypress from the southern coast of Cyprus. 7Your sails are made of Egypt's finest linens; you stand beneath awnings bright with purple and scarlet dyes from eastern Cyprus.

26:1-21 This entire chapter focuses on God's judgment of Tyre. In the ancient world, Tyre was considered to be impregnable. The city was surrounded by water and therefore was safe from a siege. Tyre's ships could keep her continually supplied with food and water. Her people believed that no one could conquer her and that her future was secure. Her people were blind to the pain they had caused others. But in this chapter we see that her destruction was assured. We may think we are strong enough to stand against the power of our besetting dependencies. Such an attitude, however, will only lead to destruction. Our recovery is only possible if we give up our control to God. We can only escape destruction by seeking and obeying God's will for our life.

27:3-25 Tyre congratulated herself on her beauty (27:3-7), her military might (27:8-11), and her wealth (27:12-25), but none of these would be able to avert the disaster she would soon face. When we are gifted with intelligence, beauty, strength, or wealth, it is easy to deceive ourself into thinking we can overcome our dependencies on our own. If we have this attitude, however, our strengths are only a liability. Recovery can only begin when we are ready to throw in the towel, when we realize that we can't win the fight alone. We must never let our strengths blind us to our weaknesses and lead us down the garden path toward destruction.

[8]"'Your sailors come from Sidon and Arvad;
your helmsmen are skilled men from Zemer.
[9]Wise old craftsmen from Gebal do the calk-
ing. Ships come from every land with all their
goods to barter for your trade.
[10]"'Your army includes men from far-off
Paras, Lud, and Put. They serve you—it is a
feather in your cap to have their shields hang
upon your walls; it is the ultimate of honor.
[11]Men from Arvad and from Helech are the
sentinels upon your walls; your towers are
manned by men from Gamad. Their shields
hang row on row upon the walls, perfecting
your glory.
[12]"'From Tarshish come all kinds of riches
to your markets—silver, iron, tin, and lead.
[13]Merchants from Javan, Tubal, and Meshech
bring slaves and bronze dishes, [14]while from
Togarmah come chariot horses, steeds, and
mules.
[15]"'Merchants come to you from Rhodes,
and many coastlands are your captive markets, giving payment in ebony and ivory.
[16]Edom sends her traders to buy your many
wares. They bring emeralds, purple dyes, embroidery, fine linen, and jewelry of coral and
agate. [17]Judah and the cities in what was once
the kingdom of Israel send merchants with
wheat from Minnith and Pannag, and with
honey, oil, and balm. [18]Damascus comes. She
brings wines from Helbon and white Syrian
wool to trade for all the rich variety of goods
you make. [19]Vedan and Javan bring Arabian
yarn, wrought iron, cassia, and calamus,
[20]while Dedan brings expensive saddlecloths
for riding.
[21]"'The Arabians and Kedar's wealthy merchant princes bring you lambs and rams and
goats. [22]The merchants of Sheba and Raamah
come with all kinds of spices, jewels, and
gold. [23]Haran, Canneh, Eden, Asshur, and
Chilmad all send their wares. [24]They bring
choice fabrics to trade—blue cloth, embroidery, and many-colored carpets bound with
cords and made secure. [25]The ships of Tarshish
are your ocean caravans; your island ware-
house is filled to the brim!
[26]"'But now your statesmen bring your ship
of state into a hurricane! Your mighty vessel
flounders in the heavy eastern gale, and you
are wrecked in the heart of the seas! [27]Every-
thing is lost. Your riches and wares, your sailors and pilots, your shipwrights, merchants,
and soldiers; and all the people sink into the
sea on the day of your vast ruin.
[28]"'The surrounding cities quake at the
sound as your pilots scream with fright. [29]All
your sailors out at sea come to land and watch
upon the mainland shore, [30]weeping bitterly
and casting dust upon their heads and
wallowing in ashes. [31]They shave their heads
in grief, put on sackcloth, and weep for you
with bitterness of heart and deep mourning.
[32]"'And this is the song of their sorrow:
"Where in all the world was there ever such a
wondrous city as Tyre, destroyed in the midst
of the sea? [33]Your merchandise satisfied the
desires of many nations. Kings at the ends of
the earth rejoiced in the riches you sent them.
[34]Now you lie broken beneath the sea; all your
merchandise and all your crew have perished
with you. [35]All who live along the coastlands
watch, incredulous. Their kings are horribly
afraid and look on with twisted faces. [36]The
merchants of the nations shake their heads,
for your fate is dreadful; you have forever
perished."'"

CHAPTER 28
The King of Tyre Condemned
Here is another message given to me from the
Lord:
[2,3]"Son of dust, say to the prince of Tyre,
'The Lord God says: You are so proud you
think you are God, sitting on the throne of a
god on your island home in the midst of the

27:26-36 Tyre had achieved success of all kinds—except the kind that really mattered. She believed that she was sufficiently able to handle any crisis. This city was able to stand against invaders for over two hundred years, but in the end she was destroyed. Alexander the Great, as God's instrument, proved once again that we cannot stand against the destruction set in motion by our sin. No matter how great our material success, we are headed for destruction if our life is not in line with God's will for us.

28:2-10 The first lie ever told was Satan's promise to Eve, "You will become like [God]" (Genesis 3:5). It seems that the prince of Tyre believed that old recycled falsehood. And he was not the last person to believe that lie. If we choose to live according to our personal program for success and pleasure, we are doing the same thing. Doing things our way is evidence that we believe we are our own god. Those of us in recovery have discovered how destructive this way of life can be. God is the only one able to see things objectively, and his plan for us is always the best one. We would be wise to abdicate the throne of our life to the only one who can give us a life filled with meaning and freedom—God himself.

seas. But you are only a man and not a god, though you boast yourself to be like God. You are wiser than Daniel, for no secret is hidden from you. 4You have used your wisdom and understanding to get great wealth—gold and silver and many treasures. 5Yes, your wisdom has made you very rich and very proud."

6Therefore the Lord God says: "Because you claim that you are as wise as God, 7an enemy army, the terror of the nations, shall suddenly draw their swords against your marvelous wisdom and defile your splendor! 8They will bring you to the pit of hell, and you shall die as those pierced with many wounds, there on your island in the heart of the seas. 9Then will you boast as a god? At least to these invaders you will be no god, but merely man! 10You will die like an outcast at the hands of foreigners. For I have spoken it," the Lord God says.

11Then this further message came to me from the Lord:

12"Son of dust, weep for the king of Tyre. Tell him, 'The Lord God says: You were the perfection of wisdom and beauty. 13You were in Eden, the garden of God; your clothing was bejeweled with every precious stone—ruby, topaz, diamond, chrysolite, onyx, jasper, sapphire, carbuncle, and emerald—all in beautiful settings of finest gold. They were given to you on the day you were created. 14I appointed you to be the anointed Guardian Angel. You had access to the holy mountain of God. You walked among the stones of fire.

15"'You were perfect in all you did from the day you were created until that time when wrong was found in you. 16Your great wealth filled you with internal turmoil, and you sinned. Therefore, I cast you out of the mountain of God like a common sinner. I destroyed you, O Guardian Angel, from the midst of the stones of fire. 17Your heart was filled with pride because of all your beauty; you corrupted your wisdom for the sake of your splendor. Therefore, I have cast you down to the ground and exposed you helpless before the curious gaze of kings. 18You defiled your holiness with lust for gain; therefore, I brought forth fire from your own actions and let it burn you to ashes upon the earth in the sight of all those watching you. 19All who know you are appalled at your fate; you are an example of horror; you are destroyed forever.'"

20Then another message came to me from the Lord:

21"Son of dust, look toward the city of Sidon and prophesy against it. Say to it, 22'The Lord God says: I am your enemy, O Sidon, and I will reveal my power over you. When I destroy you and show forth my holiness upon you, then all who see shall know I am the Lord. 23I will send an epidemic of disease and an army to destroy; the wounded shall be slain in your streets by troops on every side. Then you will know I am the Lord. 24No longer shall you and Israel's other neighbor nations prick and tear at Israel like thorns and briars, though they formerly despised her and treated her with great contempt.

25"'The people of Israel will once more live in their own land, the land I gave their father Jacob. For I will gather them back again from distant lands where I have scattered them, and I will show the nations of the world my holiness among my people. 26They will live safely in Israel and build their homes and plant their vineyards. When I punish all the bordering nations that treated them with such contempt, then they shall know I am the Lord their God.'"

CHAPTER 29

A Prophecy against Egypt

Late in December of the tenth year (of the imprisonment of King Jehoiachin), this message came to me from the Lord:

2"Son of dust, face toward Egypt and prophesy against Pharaoh her king and all her

---

28:25-26 By every human measure, the day of Israel's success was in the past. The elite of Israel's population had been in forced captivity for years. Jerusalem itself was on the verge of destruction. But God always controls the final outcome; no matter how far a nation or a person falls, God can pick up such a nation or individual and bring victory when defeat seemed a certainty.

29:2-16 When Israel was in deep trouble, her leaders often turned to Egypt for help. Their hope in Egypt, however, was always in vain. Egypt lacked the power necessary to bring true and permanent deliverance. We often make the same mistake. When we face terrible problems or inner pain, we may turn to strategies that provide only temporary respite or fail altogether. We may look to alcohol, drugs, sex, or work to help us forget our pain. We all know how destructive that can be. As we face the problem of our dependencies, we may be tempted to try a humanistic recovery program that excludes God. We must be careful to deal with our problems with the only Power able to bring true deliverance—God. In dealing with the problems of our life, we must be careful not to turn to resources that offer only false security.

people. 3Tell them that the Lord God says: 'I
am your enemy, Pharaoh, king of Egypt—
mighty dragon lying in the middle of your
rivers. For you have said, "The Nile is mine; I
have made it for myself!" 4I will put hooks
into your jaws and drag you out onto the land
with fish sticking to your scales. 5And I will
leave you and all the fish stranded in the
desert to die, and you won't be buried, for I
have given you as food to the wild animals
and birds.

6"'Because of the way your might collapsed
when Israel called on you for aid [instead of
trusting me], all of you shall know I am the
Lord. 7Israel leaned on you but, like a cracked
staff, you snapped beneath her hand and
wrenched her shoulder out of joint and made
her stagger with the pain. 8Therefore the Lord
God says: I will bring an army against you, O
Egypt, and destroy both men and herds. 9The
land of Egypt shall become a desolate wasteland, and the Egyptians will know that I, the
Lord, have done it.

10"'Because you said: "The Nile is mine! I
made it!" therefore I am against you and your
river, and I will utterly destroy the land of
Egypt, from Migdol to Syene, as far south as
the border of Ethiopia. 11For forty years not a
soul will pass that way, neither men nor animals. It will be completely uninhabited. 12I
will make Egypt desolate, surrounded by desolate nations, and her cities will lie as wastelands for forty years. I will exile the Egyptians
to other lands.

13"'But the Lord God says that at the end of
the forty years he will bring the Egyptians
home again from the nations to which they
will be banished. 14And I will restore the fortunes of Egypt and bring her people back to
the land of Pathros in southern Egypt where
they were born, but she will be an unimportant, minor kingdom. 15She will be the lowliest of all the nations; never again will she raise
herself above the other nations; never again
will Egypt be great enough for that.

16"'Israel will no longer expect any help
from Egypt. Whenever she thinks of asking
for it, then she will remember her sin in
seeking it before. Then Israel will know that I
alone am God.'"

17In the twenty-seventh year of King Jehoi-
achin's captivity, around the middle of
March, this message came to me from the
Lord:

18"Son of dust, the army of King Nebuchadnezzar of Babylon fought hard against Tyre.
The soldiers' heads were bald (from carrying
heavy basketfuls of earth); their shoulders
were raw and blistered (from burdens of
stones for the siege). And Nebuchadnezzar
received no compensation and could not pay
the army for all this work." 19Therefore, the
Lord God says, "I will give the land of Egypt
to Nebuchadnezzar, king of Babylon, and he
will carry off her wealth, plundering everything she has, for his army. 20Yes, I have given
him the land of Egypt for his salary because
he was working for me during those thirteen
years at Tyre," says the Lord. 21"And the day
will come when I will cause the ancient glory
of Israel to revive, and then at last her words
will be respected, and Egypt shall know I am
the Lord."

CHAPTER 30

Egypt Faces Doom

Another message from the Lord!

2,3"Son of dust, prophesy and say: The Lord
God says, 'Weep, for the terrible day is almost
here; the day of the Lord; a day of clouds and
gloom; a day of despair for the nations! 4A
sword shall fall on Egypt; the slain shall cover
the ground. Her wealth is taken away, her
foundations destroyed. The land of Cush has
been ravished. 5For Cush, Put, Lud, Arabia,

29:18-21 God used King Nebuchadnezzar of Babylon as an agent to achieve his sovereign will. It may be hard for us to accept the fact that God could use an evil dictator as a part of his plan. Nebuchadnezzar was just such a man: he disposed of people and treaties without a thought about the consequences. He even considered himself a god. Sometimes God may use hostile forces to accomplish his purposes in our life. We may wonder how God could allow such a thing. But we can be sure that if we trust in God, we will receive his best in the end. We can also be sure that the evil people used by God will ultimately be held accountable for their terrible deeds. God destroyed Nebuchadnezzar and his empire, just as he destroyed the other nations cataloged in these chapters.

30:2-3 In the Old Testament the Day of the Lord is a term used to refer to a specific time of God's intervention in the affairs of this world. When God breaks into history, judgment follows—a time of purification of his people and destruction of his enemies. Following this purging, wonderful blessings come. Although this passage refers to a specific historical event—Egypt's destruction—let us consider what it would mean for us if we faced the Day of the Lord today. Would we be judged or blessed?

and Libya, and all the countries leagued with them shall perish in that war."

6For the Lord says: "All Egypt's allies shall fall, and the pride of her power shall end. From Migdol to Syene they shall perish by the sword. 7She shall be desolate, surrounded by desolate nations, and her cities shall be in ruins, surrounded by other ruined cities. 8And they will know I am the Lord when I have set Egypt on fire and destroyed her allies. 9At that time I will send swift messengers to bring panic to the Ethiopians; great terror shall befall them at that time of Egypt's doom. This will all come true."

10For the Lord God says: "Nebuchadnezzar, king of Babylon, will destroy the multitudes of Egypt. 11He and his armies—the terror of the nations—are sent to demolish the land. They shall war against Egypt and cover the ground with the slain. 12I will dry up the Nile and sell the whole land to wicked men. I will destroy Egypt and everything in it, using foreigners to do it. I, the Lord, have spoken it.

13"And I will smash the idols of Egypt and the images at Memphis, and there will be no king in Egypt; anarchy shall reign!

14"The cities of Pathros [along the upper Nile], Zoan, and Thebes shall lie in ruins by my hand. 15And I will pour out my fury upon Pelusium, the strongest fortress of Egypt, and I will stamp out the people of Thebes. 16Yes, I will set fire to Egypt; Pelusium will be racked with pain. Thebes will be torn apart; Memphis will be in daily terror. 17The young men of Heliopolis and Bubastis shall die by the sword, and the women will be taken away as slaves. 18When I come to break the power of Egypt, it will be a dark day for Tahpanhes too; a dark cloud will cover her, and her daughters will be taken away as captives. 19And so I will greatly punish Egypt and they shall know I am the Lord."

20A year later, around the middle of March of the eleventh year of King Jehoiachin's captivity, this message came to me:

21"Son of dust, I have broken the arm of Pharaoh, king of Egypt, and it has not been set nor put into a cast to make it strong enough to hold a sword again. 22For the Lord God says, I am against Pharaoh, king of Egypt, and I will break both his arms—the strong one and the one that was broken before, and I will make his sword clatter to the ground. 23And I will banish the Egyptians to many lands. 24And I will strengthen the arms of the king of Babylon and place my sword in his hand. But I will break the arms of Pharaoh, king of Egypt, and he shall groan before the king of Babylon as one who has been wounded unto death. 25I will strengthen the hands of the king of Babylon, while the arms of Pharaoh fall useless to his sides. Yes, when I place my sword into the hand of the king of Babylon, and he swings it over the land of Egypt, Egypt shall know I am the Lord. 26I will scatter the Egyptians among the nations; then they shall know I am the Lord."

CHAPTER 31

Egypt's Destructive Pride

In mid-May of the eleventh year of King Jehoiachin's captivity, this message came to me from the Lord:

2,3"Son of dust, tell Pharaoh, king of Egypt, and all his people: 'You are as Assyria was—a great and mighty nation—like a cedar of Lebanon, full of thick branches and forest shade, with its head high up among the clouds. 4Its roots went deep into the moist earth. It grew luxuriantly and gave streamlets of water to all the trees around. 5It towered above all the other trees. It prospered and grew long thick branches because of all the water at its roots. 6The birds nested in its branches, and in its shade the flocks and herds gave birth to young. All the great nations of the world lived

---

30:21-26 God is absolutely sovereign in international affairs. And if God can work his will among hostile superpowers, how simple it must be for him to work his will in willing individuals! God wants us to succeed in our recovery, and, if we are willing to submit to his will for us, he will accomplish just that. God is both willing and able to work miraculous changes in this world. If we turn to him for the help he offers, we can become a part of God's plan for the recovery of his people and his created world.

31:2-9 In Ezekiel's day Egypt's pharaoh was second only to Nebuchadnezzar of Babylon in power and greatness. The pharaoh was reminded here that the great empire of Assyria, once the greatest power on earth, had already been destroyed by Babylon. Pharaoh needed to learn that no one, even a nation as powerful as Egypt, could stand against God's ultimate plan for the world. God has created all people and things to live in a close relationship with himself. Our only hope for survival and blessing can be found in seeking and obeying his plan for healthy living. If we refuse to take part in his program, we will face the painful consequences.

beneath its shadow. 7It was strong and beautiful, for its roots went deep to water. 8This tree
was taller than any other in the garden of
God; no cypress had branches equal to it;
none had boughs to compare; none equaled
it in beauty. 9Because of the magnificence that
I gave it, it was the envy of all the other trees
of Eden.'
10"But Egypt has become proud and arrogant," the Lord God says. "Therefore because
she has set herself so high above the others,
reaching to the clouds, 11I will deliver her into
the hands of a mighty nation, to destroy her
as her wickedness deserves. I, myself, will cut
her down. 12A foreign army (from Babylon)—
the terror of the nations—will invade her land
and cut her down and leave her fallen on the
ground. Her branches will be scattered across
the mountains and valleys and rivers of the
land. All those who live beneath her shade
will go away and leave her lying there. 13The
birds will pluck off her twigs, and the wild
animals will lie among her branches; 14let no
other nation exult with pride for its own
prosperity, though it be higher than the
clouds, for all are doomed, and they will land
in hell along with all the proud men of the
world."
15The Lord God says: "When she fell, I
made the oceans mourn for her and restrained their tides. I clothed Lebanon in
black and caused the trees of Lebanon to
weep. 16I made the nations shake with fear at
the sound of her fall, for I threw her down to
hell with all the others like her. And all the
other proud trees of Eden, the choicest and
the best of Lebanon, the ones whose roots
went deep into the water, are comforted to
find her there with them in hell. 17Her allies,
too, are all destroyed and perish with her.
They went down with her to the nether
world—those nations that had lived beneath
her shade.
18"O Egypt, you are great and glorious
among the trees of Eden—the nations of the
world. And you will be brought down to the
pit of hell with all these other nations. You
will be among the nations you despise, killed
by the sword. This is the fate of Pharaoh and
all his teeming masses," says the Lord.

CHAPTER 32

Israel's Enemies Will Perish

In mid-February of the twelfth year of King
Jehoiachin's captivity, this message came to
me from the Lord:
2"Son of dust, mourn for Pharaoh, king of
Egypt and say to him: 'You think of yourself
as a strong young lion among the nations, but
you are merely a crocodile along the banks of
the Nile, making bubbles and muddying the
stream.'"
3The Lord God says: "I will send a great
army to catch you with my net. I will haul you
out 4and leave you stranded on the land to
die. And all the birds of the heavens will light
upon you, and the wild animals of the whole
earth will devour you until they are glutted
and full. 5And I will cover the hills with your
flesh and fill the valleys with your bones.
6And I will drench the earth with your gushing blood, filling the ravines to the tops of the
mountains. 7I will blot you out, and I will veil
the heavens and darken the stars. I will cover
the sun with a cloud, and the moon shall not
give you her light. 8Yes, darkness will be everywhere across your land—even the bright stars
will be dark above you.
9"And when I destroy you, grief will be in
many hearts among the distant nations you
have never seen. 10Yes, terror shall strike in
many lands, and their kings shall be terribly
afraid because of all I do to you. They shall
shudder with terror when I brandish my
sword before them. They shall greatly tremble
for their lives on the day of your fall."
11For the Lord God says: "The sword of the
king of Babylon shall come upon you. 12I will

31:18 God's assessment of greatness was certainly different from Pharaoh's. Pharaoh thought of himself as a beautiful and sturdy tree—to be compared even with the splendor of the trees of the Garden of Eden. But as magnificent and stalwart as Pharaoh and his nation were, they would be cut down and destroyed. No one can reject God and hope to succeed for long. Pride always comes before a fall. We must learn this lesson in recovery. As soon as we begin to think we can do things our way and in our own power, we are headed for disaster.

32:2-8 It is always dangerous when we begin to think of ourself more highly than we ought to. Pharaoh thought of himself as a lion spreading fear among all who saw him. But the following verses reveal just how vulnerable to capture and death he actually was. If we begin to think we can go it alone in recovery, we are headed for trouble. None of us is strong enough to endure the pull of our addictions without help. If we think we can stand alone, we will reject the help and support offered by God and others. We need to be reminded continually that we are powerless over our dependencies.

destroy you with Babylon's mighty army—the terror of the nations. It will smash the pride of Egypt and all her people; all will perish. 13I will destroy all your flocks and herds that graze beside the streams, and neither man nor animal will disturb those waters any more. 14Therefore, the waters of Egypt will be as clear and flow as smoothly as olive oil," the Lord God says. 15"And when I destroy Egypt and wipe out everything she has, then she shall know that I, the Lord, have done it. 16Yes, cry for the sorrows of Egypt. Let all the nations weep for her and for her people," says the Lord.

17Two weeks later, another message came to me from the Lord. He said:

18"Son of dust, weep for the people of Egypt and for the other mighty nations. Send them down to the nether world among the denizens of death. 19 What nation is as beautiful as you, O Egypt? Yet your doom is the pit; you will be laid beside the people you despise. 20The Egyptians will die with the multitudes slain by the sword, for the sword is drawn against the land of Egypt. She will be drawn down to judgment. 21The mighty warriors in the nether world will welcome her as she arrives with all her friends, to lie there beside the nations she despised, all victims of the sword.

22"The princes of Assyria lie there surrounded by the graves of all her people, those the sword has slain. 23Their graves are in the depths of hell, surrounded by their allies. All these mighty men who once struck terror into the hearts of everyone are now dead at the hands of their foes.

24"Great kings of Elam lie there with their people. They scourged the nations while they lived, and now they lie undone in hell; their fate is the same as that of ordinary men. 25They have a resting place among the slain, surrounded by the graves of all their people. Yes, they terrorized the nations while they lived, but now they lie in shame in the pit, slain by the sword.

26"The princes of Meshech and Tubal are there, surrounded by the graves of all their armies—all of them idolaters—who once struck terror to the hearts of all; now they lie dead. 27They are buried in a common grave and not as the fallen lords who are buried in great honor with their weapons beside them, with their shields covering them and their swords beneath their heads. They were a terror to all while they lived. 28Now you will lie crushed and broken among the idolaters, among those who are slain by the sword.

29"Edom is there with her kings and her princes; mighty as they were, they too lie among the others whom the sword has slain, with the idolaters who have gone down to the pit. 30All the princes of the north are there and the Sidonians, all slain. Once a terror, now they lie in shame; they lie in ignominy with all the other slain who go down to the pit.

31"When Pharaoh arrives, he will be comforted to find that he is not alone in having all his army slain," says the Lord God. 32"For I have caused my terror to fall upon all the living. And Pharaoh and his army shall lie among the idolaters who are slain by the sword."

CHAPTER 33

God Will Be the Judge

Once again a message came to me from the Lord. He said:

2"Son of dust, tell your people: 'When I bring an army against a country, and the people of that land choose a watchman, 3and when he sees the army coming and blows the alarm to warn them, 4then anyone who hears the alarm but refuses to heed it—well, if he dies, the fault is his own. 5For he heard the warning and wouldn't listen; the fault is his. If he had heeded the warning, he would have saved his life. 6But if the watchman sees the enemy coming and doesn't sound the alarm and warn the people, he is responsible for their deaths. They will die in their sins, but I will charge the watchman with their deaths.'

7"So with you, son of dust. I have appointed you as a watchman for the people of Israel;

32:9-10 There is something terrifying about the fall of a person or nation of great power. Pharaoh had been a figure of great domination; his authority had been almost absolute. When he was judged, the world was horrified and filled with fear. We would be wise to learn from the failures of others. People with far greater strength than ours have been destroyed by their addictions. What hope do we have of standing against ours? We must accept our powerlessness and turn for help to the only one with the power to deliver us—God himself.

33:2-6 The solemn responsibility of a watchman in an Old Testament town was to warn the citizens of impending danger. If the watchman was unfaithful, the result would be the tragic loss of life and property. We are watchmen for others as well. We should, as recovering people, be careful not to lead others astray or fail to warn them of the dangers of our former life-style.

therefore, listen to what I say and warn them
for me. 8When I say to the wicked, 'O wicked
man, you will die!' and you don't tell him
what I say, so that he does not repent—that
wicked person will die in his sins, but I will
hold you responsible for his death. 9But if you
warn him to repent and he doesn't, he will die
in his sin, and you will not be responsible.

10"O people of Israel, you are saying: 'Our
sins are heavy upon us; we pine away with
guilt. How can we live?' 11Tell them: 'As I live,
says the Lord God, I have no pleasure in the
death of the wicked; *I desire that the wicked
turn from his evil ways and live.* Turn, turn from
your wickedness, for why will you die, O
Israel? 12For the good works of a righteous
man will not save him if he turns to sin; and
the sins of an evil man will not destroy him if
he repents and turns from his sins.'

13"I have said the good man will live. But if
he sins, expecting his past goodness to save
him, then none of his good deeds will be
remembered. I will destroy him for his sins.
14And when I tell the wicked he will die, and
then he turns from his sins and does what is
fair and right— 15if he gives back the borrower's pledge, returns what he has stolen, and
walks along the paths of right, not doing
evil—he shall surely live. He shall not die.
16None of his past sins shall be brought up
against him, for he has turned to the good
and shall surely live.

17"And yet your people are saying the Lord
isn't fair. The trouble is *they* aren't fair. 18For
again I say, when the good man turns to evil,
he shall die. 19But if the wicked turns from his
wickedness and does what's fair and just, he
shall live. 20Yet you are saying the Lord isn't
fair. But I will judge each of you in accordance
with his deeds."

The People Refuse to Listen

21In the eleventh year of our exile, late in
December, one of those who escaped from
Jerusalem arrived to tell me, "The city has
fallen!" 22Now the hand of the Lord had been
upon me the previous evening, and he had
healed me so that I could speak again by the
time the man arrived.

23Then this message came to me:

24"Son of dust, the scattered remnants of
Judah living among the ruined cities keep
saying, 'Abraham was only one man and yet
he got possession of the whole country! We
are many, so we should certainly be able to get
it back!' 25But the Lord God says: 'You are
powerless, for you do evil! You eat meat with

Covering the Past

BIBLE READING: Ezekiel 33:10-16

We made direct amends to such people wherever possible, except when to do so would injure them or others.

When we walk down the wrong paths in life, we end up in bad places and experience devastating losses. If we go far enough down those paths, we endanger our very life. We may wonder if we have already gone too far. Is a new way of life really possible, even if we turn from our old ways and make amends?

Even under the Old Testament laws, there was hope for those who chose to turn around and make amends. God spoke through Ezekiel, saying, "O people of Israel, you are saying: 'Our sins are heavy upon us; we pine away with guilt. How can we live?' Tell them: 'As I live, says the Lord God, I have no pleasure in the death of the wicked; *I desire that the wicked turn from his evil ways and live.* Turn, turn from your wickedness, for why will you die, O Israel? For the good works of a righteous man will not save him if he turns to sin; and the sins of an evil man will not destroy him if he repents and turns from his sins.' . . . When I tell the wicked he will die, and then he turns from his sins and does what is fair and right—if he gives back the borrower's pledge, returns what he has stolen, and walks along the paths of right, not doing evil—he shall surely live. He shall not die. None of his past sins shall be brought up against him, for he has turned to the good and shall surely live" (Ezekiel 33:10-12, 14-16).

There is hope for everyone who turns around and makes amends. Our past sins can be overshadowed by the new life ahead of us. ***Turn to page 1011, Matthew 5.***

the blood, you worship idols, and murder. Do you suppose I'll let you have the land? 26Murderers! Idolators! Adulterers! Should you possess the land?'

27"Tell them, 'The Lord God says: As I live, surely those living in the ruins shall die by the sword. Those living in the open fields shall be eaten by wild animals, and those in the forts and caves shall die of disease. 28I will desolate the land and her pride, and her power shall come to an end. And the mountain villages of Israel shall be so ruined that no one will even travel through them. 29When I have ruined the land because of their sins, then they shall know I am the Lord.'

30"Son of dust, your people are whispering behind your back. They talk about you in their houses and whisper about you at the doors, saying, 'Come on, let's have some fun! Let's go hear him tell us what the Lord is saying!' 31So they come as though they are sincere and sit before you listening. But they have no intention of doing what I tell them to; they talk very sweetly about loving the Lord, but with their hearts they are loving their money. 32You are very entertaining to them, like someone who sings lovely songs with a beautiful voice or plays well on an instrument. They hear what you say but don't pay any attention to it! 33But when all these terrible things happen to them—as they will—then they will know a prophet has been among them."

CHAPTER 34

Israel Is God's Flock

Then this message came to me from the Lord: 2"Son of dust, prophesy against the shepherds, the leaders of Israel. Say to them, 'The Lord God says to you: Woe to the shepherds who feed themselves instead of their flocks. Shouldn't shepherds feed the sheep? 3You eat the best food and wear the finest clothes, but you let your flocks starve. 4You haven't taken care of the weak, nor tended the sick, nor bound up the broken bones, nor gone looking for those who have wandered away and are lost. Instead, you have ruled them with force and cruelty. 5So they were scattered, without a shepherd. They have become a prey to every animal that comes along. 6My sheep wandered through the mountains and hills and over the face of the earth, and there was no one to search for them or care about them.

7"'Therefore, O shepherds, hear the word of the Lord: 8As I live, says the Lord God, you abandoned my flock, leaving them to be attacked and destroyed, and you were no real shepherds at all, for you didn't search for them. You fed yourselves and let them starve; 9,10therefore, I am against the shepherds, and I will hold them responsible for what has happened to my flock. I will take away their right to feed the flock—and take away their right to eat. I will save my flock from being taken for their food.'"

11For the Lord God says: "I will search and find my sheep. 12I will be like a shepherd looking for his flock. I will find my sheep and rescue them from all the places they were scattered in that dark and cloudy day. 13And I will bring them back from among the people and nations where they were, back home to their own land of Israel, and I will feed them upon the mountains of Israel and by the rivers where the land is fertile and good. 14Yes, I will give them good pasture on the high hills of Israel. There they will lie down in peace and feed in luscious mountain pastures. 15,16I myself will be the Shepherd of my sheep and cause them to lie down in peace," the Lord God says. "I will seek my lost ones, those who strayed away, and bring them safely home again. I will put splints and bandages upon their broken limbs and heal the sick. And I

33:33 There is an inescapable certainty to God's pronouncements. When God's Word is faithfully proclaimed, as it was by Ezekiel, then the message is vindicated when the declarations come to pass. When God says something—anything—we can be assured that his word will come to pass. God declares much of his will for us in the Scriptures. We would be wise to listen to what God has to say and act on it. Doing anything else will lead to painful consequences.

34:2-10 Leaders are accountable to God for their actions. The more people they lead, the greater their accountability. The spiritual leaders of Israel were like evil shepherds who could not be trusted and would therefore be judged. They were opportunists who took advantage of the people under their care. In any phase of recovery, we must be aware of our leadership responsibilities. All of us touch the lives of others in some way. Some of us may only be responsible for our children. Others of us may only be responsible for our friends. We must be careful to lead according to God's program. If we don't, we will suffer great consequences and cause suffering to many who are innocent. If we have already failed in this area, we need to take immediate steps toward making amends, seeking to undo some of the damage we have already done.

will destroy the powerful, fat shepherds; I will feed them, yes—feed them punishment!

17"And as for you, O my flock—my people," the Lord God says, "I will judge you and separate good from bad, sheep from goats.

18"Is it a small thing to you, O evil shepherds, that you not only keep the best of the pastures for yourselves, but trample down the rest? That you take the best water for yourselves and muddy the rest with your feet? 19All that's left for my flock is what you've trampled down; all they have to drink is water that you've fouled."

20Therefore the Lord God says: "I will surely judge between these fat shepherds and their scrawny sheep. 21For these shepherds push and butt and crowd my sick and hungry flock until they're scattered far away. 22So I myself will save my flock; no more will they be picked on and destroyed. And I will notice which is plump and which is thin, and why!

23"And I will set one Shepherd over all my people, even my Servant David. He shall feed them and be a Shepherd to them.

24"And I, the Lord, will be their God, and my Servant David shall be a Prince among my people. I, the Lord, have spoken it.

25"I will make a peace pact with them and drive away the dangerous animals from the land, so that my people can safely camp in the wildest places and sleep safely in the woods. 26I will make my people and their homes around my hill a blessing. And there shall be showers, showers of blessing, for I will not shut off the rains but send them in their seasons. 27Their fruit trees and fields will yield bumper crops, and everyone will live in safety. When I have broken off their chains of slavery and delivered them from those who profiteered at their expense, they shall know I am the Lord. 28No more will other nations conquer them nor wild animals attack. They shall live in safety and no one shall make them afraid.

29"And I will raise up a notable Vine [the Messiah], in Israel so that my people will never again go hungry nor be shamed by heathen conquest. 30In this way they will know that I, the Lord their God, am with them, and that they, the people of Israel, are my people," says the Lord God. 31"You are my flock, the sheep of my pasture. You are my men and I am your God, so says the Lord."

CHAPTER 35

Edom Will Be Destroyed

Again a message came from the Lord. He said:

2"Son of dust, face toward Mount Seir and prophesy against the people saying, 3'The Lord God says: I am against you, and I will smash you with my fist and utterly destroy you. 4,5Because you hate my people Israel, I will demolish your cities and make you desolate, and then you shall know I am the Lord. You butchered my people when they were helpless, when I had punished them for all their sins. 6As I live, the Lord God says, since you enjoy blood so much, I will give you a blood bath—your turn has come! 7I will utterly wipe out the people of Mount Seir, killing off all those who try to escape and all those who return. 8I will fill your mountains with the dead—your hills, your valleys, and your rivers will be filled with those the sword has killed. 9Never again will you revive. You will be abandoned forever; your cities will never be rebuilt. Then you shall know I am the Lord.

10"'For you said, "Both Israel and Judah shall be mine. We will take possession of them. What do we care that God is there!" 11Therefore as I live, the Lord God says, I will pay back your angry deeds with mine—I will punish you for all your acts of envy and of hate. And I will honor my name in Israel by what I do to you. 12And you shall know that I have heard each evil word you spoke against the Lord, saying, "His people are helpless; they are food for us to eat!" 13Saying that, you boasted great words against the Lord. And I have heard them all!

14"'The whole world will rejoice when I make you desolate. 15You rejoiced at Israel's fearful fate. Now I will rejoice at yours! You

34:11-16 Even though Israel was now a conquered nation and Jerusalem had fallen; even though the deportation of the population had been accomplished and the people had no real hope for the future—God had given his people a promise that could be counted on. No matter what our circumstances, we can be assured of God's constant care and concern for us.

34:23-24 God had promised David that he would provide someone from his family line who would rule his people in peace; this descendant would be the promised Messiah. This promise was fulfilled in the person of Jesus the Messiah. He is the true Shepherd—the Good Shepherd. We can trust him for guidance and sustenance through every situation in our life. He promises to give us help and power to overcome the areas in our life that are drawing us downward toward destruction.

will be wiped out, O people of Mount Seir and all who live in Edom! And then you will know I am the Lord!'

CHAPTER 36

Good Times Will Return

"Son of dust, prophesy to Israel's mountains. Tell them: 'Listen to this message from the Lord.

2"'Your enemies have sneered at you and claimed your ancient heights as theirs; 3they have destroyed you on every side and sent you away as slaves to many lands. You are mocked and slandered. 4Therefore, O mountains of Israel, hear the word of the Lord God. He says to the hills and mountains, dales and valleys, and to the ruined farms and the long-deserted cities, destroyed and mocked by heathen nations all around: 5My anger is afire against these nations, especially Edom, for grabbing my land with relish, in utter contempt for me, to take it for themselves.'

6"Therefore prophesy and say to the hills and mountains, dales and valleys of Israel: 'The Lord God says, I am full of fury because you suffered shame before the surrounding nations. 7Therefore, I have sworn with hand held high that those nations are going to have their turn of being covered with shame, 8but for Israel good times will return. There will be heavy crops of fruit to prepare for my people's return—and they will be coming home again soon! 9See, I am for you, and I will come and help you as you prepare the ground and sow your crops. 10I will greatly increase your population throughout all Israel, and the ruined cities will be rebuilt and filled with people. 11Not only the people, but your flocks and herds will also greatly multiply. O mountains of Israel, again you will be filled with homes. I will do even more for you than I did before. Then you shall know I am the Lord. 12My people will walk upon you once again, and you will belong to them again; and you will no longer be a place for burning their children on idol altars.'"

13The Lord God says: "Now the other nations taunt you, saying, 'Israel is a land that devours her people!' 14But they will not say this any more. Your birth rate will rise, and your infant mortality rate will drop off sharply," says the Lord. 15"No longer will those heathen nations sneer, for you will no longer be a nation of sinners," the Lord God says.

16Then this further word came to me from the Lord:

17"Son of dust, when the people of Israel were living in their own country, they defiled it by their evil deeds; to me their worship was as foul as filthy rags. 18They polluted the land with murder and with the worshiping of idols, so I poured out my fury upon them. 19And I exiled them to many lands; that is how I punished them for the evil way they lived. 20But when they were scattered out among the nations, then they were a blight upon my holy name because the nations said, 'These are the people of God and he couldn't protect them from harm!' 21I am concerned about my reputation that was ruined by my people throughout the world.

22"Therefore say to the people of Israel, 'The Lord God says: I am bringing you back again, but not because you deserve it; I am doing it to protect my holy name, which you tarnished among the nations. 23I will honor my great name, that you defiled, and the people of the world shall know I am the Lord. I will be honored before their eyes by delivering you from exile among them. 24For I will bring you back home again to the land of Israel.

25"'Then it will be as though I had sprinkled clean water on you, for you will be clean—your filthiness will be washed away, your idol worship gone. 26And I will give you a new heart—I will give you new and right desires—and put a new spirit within you. I will take out your stony hearts of sin and give you new hearts of love. 27And I will put my Spirit within you so that you will obey my laws and do whatever I command.

28"'And you shall live in Israel, the land which I gave your fathers long ago. And you shall be my people, and I will be your God. 29I will cleanse away your sins. I will abolish crop failures and famine. 30I will give you huge harvests from your fruit trees and fields, and

36:17-24 God promised the people of Israel that their nation would be restored, but not because the people deserved it. They really deserved destruction. God had promised to reveal himself to the world through the nation of Israel, and God's will would not be thwarted. He would deliver his people from exile and rebuild his nation so that the whole world would benefit. Through this tiny nation, the Messiah would be born to change the face of history and to transform all who give their lives to him. God went to painful lengths to bring his Deliverer into the world. We would be wise to take advantage of God's gift of forgiveness and restoration through Jesus the Messiah.

never again will the surrounding nations be
able to scoff at your land for its famines.
[31]Then you will remember your past sins and
loathe yourselves for all the evils you did.
[32]But always remember this: It is not for your
own sakes that I will do this, but for mine. O
my people Israel, be utterly ashamed of all
that you have done!'"

[33]The Lord God says: "When I cleanse you
from your sins, I will bring you home again to
Israel, and rebuild the ruins. [34]Acreage will be
cultivated again that through the years of
exile lay empty as a barren wilderness; all who
passed by were shocked to see the extent of
ruin in your land. [35]But when I bring you
back, they will say, 'This God-forsaken land
has become like Eden's garden! The ruined
cities are rebuilt and walled and filled with
people!' [36]Then the nations all around—all
those still left—will know that I, the Lord,
rebuilt the ruins and planted lush crops in the
wilderness. For I, the Lord, have promised it,
and I will do it."

[37,38]The Lord God says: "I am ready to hear
Israel's prayers for these blessings and to grant
them their requests. Let them but ask, and I
will multiply them like the flocks that fill
Jerusalem's streets at time of sacrifice. The
ruined cities will be crowded once more, and
everyone will know I am the Lord."

CHAPTER 37

A Valley of Dry Bones

The power of the Lord was upon me and I was
carried away by the Spirit of the Lord to a
valley full of old, dry bones that were scattered everywhere across the ground. He led
me around among them, [3]and then he said to
me:

"Son of dust, can these bones become
people again?"

I replied, "Lord, you alone know the answer to that."

[4]Then he told me to speak to the bones and
say: "O dry bones, listen to the words of God,
[5]for the Lord God says, 'See! I am going to
make you live and breathe again! [6]I will replace the flesh and muscles on you and cover
you with skin. I will put breath into you, and
you shall live and know I am the Lord.'"

[7]So I spoke these words from God, just as he
told me to; and suddenly there was a rattling
noise from all across the valley, and the bones
of each body came together and attached to
each other as they used to be. [8]Then, as I
watched, the muscles and flesh formed over
the bones, and skin covered them, but the
bodies had no breath. [9]Then he told me to call
to the wind and say: "The Lord God says:
Come from the four winds, O Spirit, and
breathe upon these slain bodies, that they
may live again." [10]So I spoke to the winds as
he commanded me, and the bodies began
breathing; they lived and stood up—a very
great army.

[11]Then he told me what the vision meant:
"These bones," he said, "represent all the
people of Israel. They say: 'We have become a
heap of dried-out bones—all hope is gone.'
[12]But tell them, 'The Lord God says: My
people, I will open your graves of exile and
cause you to rise again and return to the land
of Israel. [13]And, then at last, O my people, you
will know I am the Lord. [14]I will put my Spirit
into you, and you shall live and return home
again to your own land. Then you will know
that I, the Lord, have done just what I promised you.'"

36:25-27 How can any individual please God? We have experienced how helpless we are against the destructive evils in our life, but these verses should fill us with hope. As we respond to God's gracious provision of forgiveness and restoration, God promises to give us a new heart and fill us with his Spirit so that we can make decisions that follow God's program. This new heart is his gift to those who believe in the work of Jesus on their behalf.

36:33 Before the nation of Israel could be rebuilt, it had to be cleansed of sin. Sin separates us from God and leads to destructive consequences. Until the sin question is dealt with, we will not experience the power God offers to help us overcome our dependencies. It is impossible to rebuild a country or a life without first dealing with the sin that is destroying it. Before we can achieve success, we must first admit our sin and accept the forgiveness and cleansing that God offers.

37:1-10 Ezekiel was shown an old battlefield filled with dry bones. There was no life in them whatsoever—no possibility of life for the people to whom the bones had once belonged. It would be difficult to find a better illustration of powerlessness! The bones were helpless to act for themselves. But as the dry bones were a picture of complete need, so God's Spirit provided a picture of complete supply. When God entered the picture, defeat became uncompromising victory. This principle applies to us as we deal with the devastation of our addictions. Alone, our failures and their terrible consequences are already accomplished, but with God's help we are assured of victory and new life.

Ezekiel's Carved Stick

15Again a message from the Lord came to me, saying:

16"Take a stick and carve on it these words: 'This stick represents Judah and her allied tribes.' Then take another stick and carve these words on it: 'This stick represents all the other tribes of Israel.' 17Now hold them together in your hand as one stick. 18-20Tell these people (holding the sticks so they can see what you are doing), the Lord God says: 'I will take the tribes of Israel and join them to Judah and make them one stick in my hand.'"

21For the Lord God says: "I am gathering the people of Israel from among the nations and bringing them home from around the world to their own land, 22to unify them into one nation. One king shall be king of them all; no longer shall they be divided into two nations. 23They shall stop polluting themselves with idols and their other sins, for I will save them from all this foulness. Then they shall truly be my people and I their God.

24"And David, my Servant—the Messiah—shall be their King, their only Shepherd; and they shall obey my laws and all my wishes. 25They shall live in the land of Israel where their fathers lived, the land I gave my servant Jacob. They and their children after them shall live there, and their grandchildren, for all generations. And my Servant David, their Messiah, shall be their Prince forever. 26And I will make a covenant of peace with them, an everlasting pact. I will bless them and multiply them and put my Temple among them forever. 27And I will make my home among them. Yes, I will be their God, and they shall be my people. 28And when my Temple remains among them forever, then the nations will know that I, the Lord, have chosen Israel as my very own."

CHAPTER 38

Ezekiel's Message to Gog

Here is another message to me from the Lord:

2,3"Son of dust, face northward toward the land of Magog and prophesy against Gog king of Meshech and Tubal. Tell him that the Lord God says: 'I am against you, Gog. 4I will put hooks into your jaws and pull you to your doom. I will mobilize your troops and armored cavalry and make you a mighty host, all fully armed. 5Peras, Cush, Put shall join you too with all their weaponry, 6and so shall Gomer and all his hordes and the armies of Togarmah from the distant north, as well as many others. 7Be prepared! Stay mobilized. You are their leader, Gog!

8"'A long time from now you will be called to action. In distant years you will swoop down onto the land of Israel that will be lying in peace after the return of its people from many lands. 9You and all your allies—a vast and awesome army—will roll down upon them like a storm and cover the land like a cloud. 10For at that time an evil thought will have come to your mind. 11You will have said, "Israel is an unprotected land of unwalled villages! I will march against her and destroy these people living in such confidence! 12I will go to those once-desolate cities that are now filled with people again—those who have returned from all the nations—and I will capture vast amounts of loot and many slaves. For the people are rich with cattle now, and the whole earth revolves around them!"

13"But Sheba and Dedan and the merchant princes of Tarshish with whom she trades will ask, 'Who are you to rob them of silver and gold and drive away their cattle and seize their goods and make them poor?'"

14The Lord God says to Gog: "When my people are living in peace in their land, then you will rouse yourself. 15,16You will come from all over the north with your vast host of cavalry and cover the land like a cloud. This will happen in the distant future—in the latter years of history. I will bring you against my land, and my holiness will be vindicated in your terrible destruction before their eyes, so that all the nations will know that I am God."

17The Lord God says: "You are the one I spoke of long ago through the prophets of Israel, saying that after many years had passed, I would bring you against my people. 18But when you come to destroy the land of Israel, my fury will rise! 19For in my jealousy and blazing wrath, I promise a mighty shak-

37:24-28 God promised that one day he would make his home among his people. This took place as God became a man in the person of Jesus Christ. As we study the life of Jesus on earth, we can discover what God is really like—who he really is. And God still lives among us in the person of his Spirit. Though our world is far from perfect because of sin, we can all look forward to the day when Jesus Christ, the true Shepherd, will return to guide his people in righteousness and truth. We can begin this period of God's reign in our own life today by obeying God's program for joyful and healthy living.

ing in the land of Israel on that day. 20All
living things shall quake in terror at my presence; mountains shall be thrown down; cliffs
shall tumble; walls shall crumble to the earth.
21I will summon every kind of terror against
you," says the Lord God, "and you will fight
against yourselves in mortal combat! 22I will
fight you with sword, disease, torrential
floods, great hailstones, fire, and brimstone!
23Thus will I show my greatness and bring
honor upon my name, and all the nations of
the world will hear what I have done and
know that I am God!"

CHAPTER 39

God's Holiness Vindicated

"Son of dust, prophesy this also against Gog.
Tell him:

"'I stand against you, Gog, leader of Meshech and Tubal. 2I will turn you and drive
you toward the mountains of Israel, bringing
you from the distant north. And I will destroy
85 percent of your army in the mountains. 3I
will knock your weapons from your hands
and leave you helpless. 4You and all your vast
armies will die upon the mountains. I will
give you to the vultures and wild animals to
devour you. 5You will never reach the cities—
you will fall upon the open fields; for I have
spoken, the Lord God says. 6And I will rain
down fire on Magog and on all your allies
who live safely on the coasts, and they shall
know I am the Lord.

7"'Thus I will make known my holy name
among my people Israel; I will not let it be
mocked at anymore. And the nations, too,
shall know I am the Lord, the Holy One of
Israel. 8That day of judgment will come;
everything will happen just as I have declared
it.

9"'The people of the cities of Israel will go
out and pick up your shields and bucklers,
bows and arrows, javelins and spears, to use
for fuel—enough to last them seven years.
10For seven years they will need nothing else
for their fires. They won't cut wood from the
fields or forests, for these weapons will give
them all they need. They will use the possessions of those who abused them.

11"'And I will make a vast graveyard for Gog
and his armies in the Valley of the Travelers,
east of the Dead Sea. It will block the path of
the travelers. There Gog and all his armies will
be buried. And they will change the name of
the place to "The Valley of Gog's Army." 12It
will take seven months for the people of Israel
to bury the bodies. 13Everyone in Israel will
help, for it will be a glorious victory for Israel
on that day when I demonstrate my glory,
says the Lord. 14At the end of the seven
months, they will appoint men to search the
land systematically for any skeletons left and
bury them, so that the land will be cleansed.
15,16Whenever anyone sees some bones, he
will put up a marker beside them so that the
buriers will see them and take them to the
Valley of Gog's Army to bury them. A city
named "Multitude" is there! And so the land
will finally be cleansed.'

17"And now, son of dust, call all the birds
and animals and say to them: 'Gather together for a mighty sacrificial feast. Come
from far and near to the mountains of Israel.
Come, eat the flesh and drink the blood! 18Eat
the flesh of mighty men and drink the blood
of princes—they are the rams, the lambs, the
goats, and the fat young bulls of Bashan for
my feast! 19Gorge yourselves with flesh until
you are glutted, drink blood until you are
drunk; this is the sacrificial feast I have prepared for you. 20Feast at my banquet table—
feast on horses, riders, and valiant warriors,
says the Lord God.'

21"Thus I will demonstrate my glory among
the nations; all shall see the punishment of
Gog and know that I have done it. 22And from
that time onward the people of Israel will
know I am the Lord their God. 23And the

38:17-23 In these verses God declared his power in no uncertain terms. The greatest powers of military and political strength that the world could offer would array themselves against God and his people. But when God intervened, the unthinkable would happen—even the greatest enemies would be destroyed by his powerful hand. We all face powerful enemies, both internal and external; these may be enemies whom we are powerless to stop or control. If we turn our situation over to God, however, even the most powerful enemies can be defeated. With God on our side, no enemy is too powerful, no life is beyond recovery.

39:1-6 God was against Gog, but it must be remembered that first Gog was against God. Every creature with the power of choice either chooses to obey God or stands against him. Gog had ranged his mighty array of forces against God's people; he had left God and his divine will out of his thinking altogether. The destruction of Gog promised by Ezekiel reveals the consequences of choosing to stand against God and his will. As we see these terrible consequences, we should be encouraged to admit our own failures and take steps to follow God's will for our life.

nations will know why Israel was sent away to exile—it was punishment for sin, for they acted in treachery against their God. Therefore, I turned my face away from them and let their enemies destroy them. 24I turned my face away and punished them in proportion to the vileness of their sins.

25"But now," the Lord God says, "I will end the captivity of my people and have mercy upon them and restore their fortunes, for I am concerned about my reputation! 26Their time of treachery and shame will all be in the past; they will be home again, in peace and safety in their own land, with no one bothering them or making them afraid. 27I will bring them home from the lands of their enemies—and my glory shall be evident to all the nations when I do it. Through them I will vindicate my holiness before the nations. 28Then my people will know I am the Lord their God—responsible for sending them away to exile, and responsible for bringing them home. I will leave none of them remaining among the nations. 29And I will never hide my face from them again, for I will pour out my Spirit upon them," says the Lord God.

CHAPTER 40

The New Temple

Early in April of the twenty-fifth year of our exile—the fourteenth year after Jerusalem was captured—the hand of the Lord was upon me, 2and in a vision he took me to the land of Israel and set me down on a high mountain where I saw what appeared to be a city opposite me. 3Going nearer, I saw a man whose face shone like bronze, standing beside the Temple gate, holding in his hand a measuring tape and a measuring stick.

4He said to me: "Son of dust, watch and listen and take to heart everything I show you, for you have been brought here so I can show you many things; and then you are to return to the people of Israel to tell them all you have seen." 5The man began to measure the wall around the outside of the Temple area with his measuring stick, which was 10½ feet long. He told me, "This wall is 10½ feet high and 10½ feet wide." 6Then he took me over to the passageway that goes through the eastern wall. We climbed the seven steps into the entrance, and he measured the entry hall of the passage; it was 10½ feet wide.

7-12Walking on through the passageway I saw that there were three guardrooms on each side; each of these rooms was 10½ feet square, with a distance of 8¾ feet along the wall between them. In front of these rooms was a low barrier 18 inches high and 18 inches wide. Beyond the guardrooms was a 10½-foot doorway opening into a 14-foot hall with 3½-foot columns. Beyond this hall, at the inner end of the passageway, was a vestibule 22¾ feet wide and 17½ feet long.

13Then he measured the entire outside width of the passageway, measuring across the roof from the outside doors of the guardrooms; this distance was 43¾ feet. 14Then he estimated the pillars on each side of the porch to be about 100 feet high. 15The full length of the entrance passage was 87½ feet from one end to the other. 16There were windows that narrowed inward through the walls along both sides of the passageway and along the guardroom walls. The windows were also in

39:25-29 Without God, the future of Israel was dark and hopeless. But no matter what their present suffering, they could hope in the future, knowing that God still had great things in store for them. God is a God of recovery and restoration. It is part of his plan for creation that the power of sin be broken and the destruction of sin be reversed. God restored his people so his promise of a Savior—Jesus the Messiah—could be fulfilled. And through this Savior, the restoration of our life is possible, no matter how great our past sin or how terrible our present circumstances.

40:1–48:35 The final chapters of Ezekiel contain a description of a new Temple in a new Jerusalem. Through the restoration of the Temple, we see that proper worship is also being restored. In every age, God considers worship one of the most important factors of life. Life itself ought to be an expression of worship. Our hope for future restoration must involve a restoration of our relationship with God and our proper worship of him. Without a healthy relationship with God, a permanent and healthy recovery is not possible.

40:1 Notice that God spoke to his people through Ezekiel while they were still in exile. God is never limited by where we are or what we have done. Ezekiel discovered that even under the adverse circumstances of exile, God was still reaching out to communicate with his people. We may feel that the terrible circumstances we face because of our foolish choices make us ineligible for God's help. We may feel that we have sinned too deeply to be forgiven by God. But, even in times of "exile," God is still reaching out to us. He desires to help us; all we need to do is admit that we need him.

the exit and in the entrance halls. The pillars were decorated with palm tree decorations.

[17]And so we passed through the passageway to the court inside. A stone pavement ran around the inside of the walls, and thirty rooms were built against the walls, opening onto this pavement. [18]This was called "the lower pavement." It extended out from the walls into the court the same distance as the passageway did.

[19]Then he measured across to the wall on the other side of this court (which was called "the outer court" of the Temple) and found that the distance was 175 feet. [20]As I followed, he left the eastern passageway and went over to the passage through the northern wall and measured it. [21]Here, too, there were three guardrooms on each side, and all the measurements were the same as for the east passageway—$87\frac{1}{2}$ feet long and $43\frac{3}{4}$ feet from side to side across the top of the guardrooms. [22]There were windows, an entry hall, and the palm tree decorations just the same as on the east side. And there were seven steps leading up to the doorway to the entry hall inside.

[23]Here at the north entry, just as at the east, if one walked through the passageway into the court and straight across it, he came to an inner wall and a passageway through it to an inner court. The distance between the two passageways was 175 feet. [24]Then he took me around to the south gate and measured the various sections of its passageway and found they were just the same as in the others. [25]It had windows along the walls as the others did, and an entry hall. And like the others, it was $87\frac{1}{2}$ feet long and $43\frac{3}{4}$ feet wide. [26]It, too, had a stairway of seven steps leading up to it, and there were palm tree decorations along the walls. [27]And here again, if one walked through the passageway into the court and straight across it, he came to the inner wall and a passageway through it to the inner court. And the distance between the passageways was 175 feet.

[28]Then he took me over to the inner wall and its south passageway. He measured this passageway and found that it had the same measurements as the passageways of the outer wall. [29,30] Its guardrooms, pillars, and entrance and exit hall were identical to all the others, and so were the windows along its walls and entry. And, like the others, it was $87\frac{1}{2}$ feet long by $43\frac{3}{4}$ feet wide. [31]The only difference was that it had eight steps leading up to it instead of seven. It had palm tree decorations on the pillars, just as the others.

[32]Then he took me along the court to the eastern entrance of the inner wall, and measured it. It, too, had the same measurements as the others. [33]Its guardrooms, pillars, and entrance hall were the same size as those of the other passageways, and there were windows along the walls and in the entry hall; and it was $87\frac{1}{2}$ feet long by $43\frac{3}{4}$ feet wide. [34]Its entry hall faced the outer court, and there were palm tree decorations on its columns, but there were eight steps instead of seven going up to the entrance.

[35]Then he took me around to the north gate of the inner wall, and the measurements there were just like the others: [36]The guardrooms, pillars, and entry hall of this passageway were the same as the others, with a length of $87\frac{1}{2}$ feet and a width of $43\frac{3}{4}$ feet. [37]Its entry hall faced toward the outer court; it had palm tree decorations on the walls of each side of the passageway, and there were eight steps leading up to the entrance.

[38]But a door led from its entry hall into a side room where the flesh of the sacrifices was washed before being taken to the altar; [39]on each side of the entry hall of the passageway there were two tables where the animals for sacrifice were slaughtered for the burnt offerings, sin offerings, and guilt offerings to be presented in the Temple. [40]Outside the entry hall, on each side of the stairs going up to the north entrance, there were two more tables. [41]So, in all there were eight tables, four inside and four outside, where the sacrifices were cut up and prepared. [42]There were also four stone tables where the butchering knives and other implements were laid. These tables were about $2\frac{5}{8}$ feet square and $1\frac{3}{4}$ feet high. [43]There were hooks, 3 or 4 inches long, fastened along the walls of the entry hall, and on the tables the flesh of the offering was to be laid.

[44]In the inner court there were two one-room buildings, one beside the northern entrance, facing south, and one beside the southern entrance, facing north.

[45]And he said to me: "The building beside the inner northern gate is for the priests who supervise the maintenance. [46]The building beside the inner southern entrance is for the priests in charge of the altar—the descendants of Zadok—for they alone of all the Levites may come near to the Lord to minister to him."

[47]Then he measured the inner court [in front of the Temple] and found it to be 175 feet square, and there was an altar in the

court, standing in front of the Temple. 48,49Then he brought me to the entrance hall of the Temple. Ten steps led up to it from the inner court. Its walls extended up on either side to form two pillars, each of them 8 3/4 feet thick. The entrance was 24 1/2 feet wide with 5 1/4-foot walls. Thus the entry hall was 35 feet wide and 19 1/4 feet long.

CHAPTER 41

The Holy of Holies

Afterward he brought me into the nave, the large main room of the Temple, and measured the pillars that formed its doorway. They were 10 1/2 feet square. 2The entrance hall was 17 1/2 feet wide and 8 3/4 feet deep. The nave itself was 70 feet long by 35 feet.

3Then he went into the inner room at the end of the nave and measured the columns at the entrance and found them to be 3 1/2 feet thick; its doorway was 10 1/2 feet wide, with a hallway 12 1/4 feet deep behind it. 4The inner room was 35 feet square. "This," he told me, "is the Most Holy Place."

5Then he measured the wall of the Temple and found that it was 10 1/2 feet thick, with a row of rooms along the outside. Each room was 7 feet wide. 6These rooms were in three tiers, one above the other, with thirty rooms in each tier. The whole structure was supported by girders and not attached to the Temple wall for support. 7Each tier was wider than the one below it, corresponding to the narrowing of the Temple wall as it rose higher. A stairway at the side of the Temple led up from floor to floor.

8I noticed that the Temple was built on a terrace and that the bottom row of rooms extended out 10 1/2 feet onto the terrace. 9The outer wall of these rooms was 8 3/4 feet thick, leaving a free space of 8 3/4 feet out to the edge of the terrace, the same on both sides.

10Thirty-five feet away from the terrace, on both sides of the Temple, was another row of rooms down in the inner court. 11Two doors opened from the tiers of rooms to the terrace yard, which was 8 3/4 feet wide; one door faced north and the other south.

12A large building stood on the west, facing the Temple yard, measuring 122 1/2 feet wide by 157 1/2 feet long. Its walls were 8 3/4 feet thick. 13Then he measured the Temple and its immediately surrounding yards. The area was 175 feet square. 14The inner court at the east of the Temple was also 175 feet wide, 15,16and so was the building west of the Temple, including its two walls.

The nave of the Temple and the Holy of Holies and the entry hall were paneled, and all three had recessed windows. The inner walls of the Temple were paneled with wood above and below the windows. 17,18The space above the door leading into the Holy of Holies was also paneled. The walls were decorated with carvings of Guardian Angels, each with two faces, and of palm trees alternating with the Guardian Angels. 19,20One face—that of a man—looked toward the palm tree on one side, and the other face—that of a young lion—looked toward the palm tree on the other side. And so it was, all around the inner wall of the Temple.

21There were square doorposts at the doors of the nave, and in front of the Holy of Holies was what appeared to be an altar, but it was made of wood. 22This altar was 3 1/2 feet square and 5 1/4 feet high; its corners, base, and sides were all of wood. "This," he told me, "is the Table of the Lord."

23Both the nave and the Holy of Holies had double doors, 24each with two swinging sections. 25The doors leading into the nave were decorated with cherubim and palm trees, just as on the walls. And there was a wooden canopy over the entry hall. 26There were recessed windows and carved palm trees on both sides of the entry hall, the hallways beside the Temple, and on the canopy over the entrance.

CHAPTER 42

Rooms for the Priests

Then he led me out of the Temple, back into the inner court to the rooms north of the Temple yard, and to another building. 2This group of structures was 175 feet long by 87 1/2 feet wide. 3The rows of rooms behind this building were the inner wall of the court. The rooms were in three tiers, overlooking the outer court on one side, and having a 35-foot strip of inner court on the other. 4A 17 1/2-foot walk ran between the building and the tiers of rooms, extending the entire length, with the doors of the building facing north. 5The upper two tiers of rooms were not as wide as the lower one, because the upper tiers had wider walkways beside them. 6And since the building was not built with girders as those in the outer court were, the upper stories were set back from the ground floor.

7,8The north tiers, next to the outer court, were 87 1/2 feet long—only half as long as the inner wing that faced the Temple court, which was 175 feet long. But a wall extended from the end of the shorter wing, parallel to the longer wing. 9,10And there was an entrance from the outer court to these rooms from the east. On the opposite side of the Temple a similar building composed of two units of tiers was on the south side of the inner court, between the Temple and the outer court, arranged the same as the other. 11There was a walk between the two wings of the building, the same as in the other building across the court—the same length and width and the same exits and doors—they were identical units. 12And there was a door from the outer court at the east.

13Then he told me: "These north and south tiers of rooms facing the Temple yard are holy; there the priests who offer up the sacrifices to the Lord shall eat of the most holy offerings and store them—the cereal offerings, sin offerings, and guilt offerings, for these rooms are holy. 14When the priests leave the Holy Place—the nave of the Temple—they must change their clothes before going out to the outer court. The special robes in which they have been ministering must first be removed, for these robes are holy. They must put on other clothes before entering the parts of the building open to the public."

15When he had finished making these measurements, he led me out through the east passageway to measure the entire Temple area. 16-20He found that it was in the form of a square, 875 feet long on each side, with a wall all around it to separate the restricted area from the public places.

CHAPTER 43

Sacrifices in the Temple

Afterward he brought me out again to the passageway through the outer wall leading to the east. 2And suddenly the glory of the God of Israel appeared from the east. The sound of his coming was like the roar of rushing waters, and the whole landscape lighted up with his glory. 3It was just as I had seen it in the other visions, first by the Chebar Canal, and then later at Jerusalem when he came to destroy the city. And I fell down before him with my face in the dust. 4And the glory of the Lord came into the Temple through the eastern passageway.

5Then the Spirit took me up and brought me into the inner court; and the glory of the Lord filled the Temple. 6And I heard the Lord speaking to me from within the Temple (the man who had been measuring was still standing beside me).

7And the Lord said to me:

"Son of dust, this is the place of my throne and my footstool, where I shall remain, living among the people of Israel forever. They and their kings will not defile my holy name any longer through the adulterous worship of other gods or by worshiping the totem poles erected by their kings. 8They built their idol temples beside mine, with only a wall between, and worshiped their idols. Because they sullied my holy name by such wickedness, I consumed them in my anger. 9Now let them put away their idols and the totem poles erected by their kings, and I will live among them forever.

10"Son of dust, describe the Temple I have shown you to the people of Israel. Tell them its appearance and its plan so they will be ashamed of all their sins. 11And if they are truly ashamed of what they have done, then explain to them the details of its construction—its doors and entrances—and everything about it. Write out all the directions and the rules for them to keep. 12And this is the basic law of the Temple: *Holiness!* The entire top of the hill where the Temple is built is *holy.* Yes, this is the primary law concerning it.

13"And these are the measurements of the altar: The base is 21 inches high, with a 9 inch rim around its edge, and it extends 21 inches beyond the altar on all sides. 14The first stage of the altar is a stone platform 3½ feet high. This platform is 21 inches narrower than the base block on all sides. Rising from this is a narrower platform, 21 inches narrower on all sides, and 7 feet high. 15From it a still narrower platform rises 7 feet, and this is the top of the altar, with four horns projecting 21 inches up from the corners. 16This top platform of the

43:1-5 Ezekiel had seen the glory of God leave the Jerusalem Temple early in his prophetic career (10:1–11:23). Here he had the joy of seeing it return. As a descendant of priests, Ezekiel must have been greatly encouraged by this vision. It signaled God's renewed presence among his people and hope for their restoration. God did restore his people and then came to live among us in the person of his Son, Jesus the Messiah. And through a relationship with him, we are assured of God's presence with us as we undergo the process of recovery. God promises us his transforming presence through his Spirit, giving us hope as we face the painful process of confession and change necessary for a full recovery.

altar is 21 feet square. 17 The platform beneath it is $24\frac{1}{2}$ feet square with a $10\frac{1}{2}$-inch curb around the edges. The entire platform extends out from the top 21 inches on all sides. On the east side are steps to climb the altar."

18 And he said to me:

"Son of dust, the Lord God says: These are the measurements of the altar to be made in the future, when it is erected for the burning of offerings and the sprinkling of blood upon it. 19 At that time the Zadok family of the Levite tribe, who are my ministers, are to be given a bullock for a sin offering. 20 You shall take some of its blood and smear it on the four horns of the altar and on the four corners of the top platform and in the curb around it. This will cleanse and make atonement for the altar. 21 Then take the bullock for the sin offering and burn it at the appointed place outside the Temple area.

22 "The second day, sacrifice a young male goat without any defects—without sickness, deformities, cuts or scars—for a sin offering. Thus the altar shall be cleansed, as it was by the bullock. 23 When you have finished this cleansing ceremony, offer another perfect bullock and a perfect ram from the flock. 24 Present them before the Lord, and the priests shall sprinkle salt upon them as a burnt offering.

25 "Every day for seven days a male goat, a bullock and a ram from the flock shall be sacrificed as a sin offering. None are to have any defects or unhealthiness of any kind. 26 Do this each day for seven days to cleanse and make atonement for the altar, thus consecrating it. 27 On the eighth day, and on each day afterward, the priests will sacrifice on the altar the burnt offerings and thank offerings of the people, and I will accept you, says the Lord God."

CHAPTER 44

Requirements for the Priests

Then the Lord brought me back to the outer wall's eastern passageway, but it was closed. 2 And he said to me:

"This gate shall remain closed; it shall never be opened. No man shall pass through it; for the Lord, the God of Israel, entered here, and so it shall remain shut. 3 Only the prince—because he is the prince—may sit inside the passageway to feast there before the Lord. But he shall go and come only through the entry hall of the passage."

4 Then he brought me through the north passageway to the front of the Temple. I looked and saw that the glory of the Lord filled the Temple of the Lord, and I fell to the ground with my face in the dust.

5 And the Lord said to me:

"Son of dust, notice carefully; use your eyes and ears. Listen to all I tell you about the laws and rules of the Temple of the Lord. Note carefully who may be admitted to the Temple and who is to be excluded from it. 6 And say to these rebels, the people of Israel, 'The Lord God says: O Israel, you have sinned greatly 7 by letting the uncircumcised into my sanctuary—those who have no heart for God—when you offer me my food, the fat and the blood. Thus you have broken my covenant in addition to all your other sins. 8 You have not kept the laws I gave you concerning these holy affairs, for you have hired foreigners to take charge of my sanctuary.'"

9 The Lord God says: "No foreigner of all the many among you shall enter my sanctuary if he has not been circumcised and does not love the Lord. 10 And the men of the tribe of Levi who abandoned me when Israel strayed away from God to idols must be punished for their unfaithfulness. 11 They may be Temple guards and gatemen; they may slay the animals brought for burnt offerings and be present to help the people. 12 But because they encouraged the people to worship other gods, causing Israel to fall into deep sin, I have raised my hand and taken oath," says the Lord God, "that they must be punished. 13 They shall not come near me to minister as priests; they may not touch any of my holy things, for they must bear their shame for all the sins they have committed. 14 They are the Temple caretakers, to do maintenance work and to assist the people in a general way.

15 "However, the sons of Zadok, of the tribe of Levi, continued as my priests in the Temple when Israel abandoned me for idols. These men shall be my ministers; they shall stand

---

44:6-7 Refusing to obey God's will always has painful consequences. God had clearly revealed his will for his people, but they had ignored the guidelines God had graciously provided. They had rebelled against the plan God had laid out for them. God has clearly revealed much of his will for us in the Bible. It is our responsibility to follow it. Since there are consequences for failing to obey God's will, we would be wise to diligently seek God's will for our life and then do what we can to carry it out. If we take these steps, God will be glad to help us.

before me to offer the fat and blood of the sacrifices," says the Lord God. 16"They shall enter my sanctuary and come to my Table to minister to me; they shall fulfill my requirements.

17"They must wear only linen clothing when they enter the passageway to the inner court, for they must wear no wool while on duty in the inner court or in the Temple. 18They must wear linen turbans and linen trousers; they must not wear anything that would cause them to perspire. 19When they return to the outer court, they must take off the clothes they wear while ministering to me, leaving them in the sacred chambers, and put on other clothes lest they harm the people by touching them with this clothing.

20"They must not let their hair grow too long nor shave it off. Regular, moderate haircuts are all they are allowed. 21No priest may drink wine before coming to the inner court. 22He may marry only a Jewish maiden, or the widow of a priest; he may not marry a divorced woman.

23"He shall teach my people the difference between what is holy and what is secular, what is right and what is wrong.

24"They will serve as judges to resolve any disagreements among my people. Their decisions must be based upon my laws. And the priests themselves shall obey my rules and regulations at all the sacred festivals, and they shall see to it that the Sabbath is kept a sacred day.

25"A priest must not defile himself by being in the presence of a dead person, unless it is his father, mother, child, brother, or unmarried sister. In such cases it is all right. 26But afterward he must wait seven days before he is cleansed and able to perform his Temple duties again. 27The first day he returns to work and enters the inner court and the sanctuary, he must offer a sin offering for himself," the Lord God says.

28"As to property, they shall not own any, for I am their heritage! That is enough!

29"Their food shall be the gifts and sacrifices brought to the Temple by the people—the cereal offerings, the sin offerings, and the guilt offerings. Whatever anyone gives to the Lord shall be the priests'. 30The first of the first-ripe fruits and all the gifts for the Lord shall go to the priests. The first samples of each harvest of grain shall be donated to the priests too, so that the Lord will bless your homes. 31Priests may never eat meat from any bird or animal that dies a natural death or that dies after being attacked by other animals."

CHAPTER 45

God's Portion of the Land

"When you divide the land among the tribes of Israel, you shall first give a section of it to the Lord as his holy portion. This piece shall be 8 1/3 miles long and 6 2/3 miles wide. It shall all be holy ground.

2"A section of this land, 875 feet square, shall be designated for the Temple. An additional 87 1/2-foot strip all around is to be left empty. 3The Temple shall be built within the area which is 8 1/3 miles long and 3 1/3 miles wide. 4All this section shall be holy land; it will be used by the priests, who minister in the sanctuary, for their homes and for my Temple.

5"The strip next to it, 8 1/3 miles long and 3 1/3 miles wide, shall be the residence area for the Levites who work at the Temple. 6Adjacent to the holy lands will be a section 8 1/3 miles by 1 2/3 miles for a city open to everyone in Israel.

7"Two special sections of land shall be set apart for the prince—one on each side of the holy lands and city; it is contiguous with them in length, and its eastern and western boundaries are the same as those of the tribal sections. 8This shall be his allotment. My princes shall no longer oppress and rob my people but shall assign all the remainder of the land to the people, giving a portion to each tribe."

9For the Sovereign Lord says to the rulers: "Quit robbing and cheating my people out of their land and expelling them from their homes. Always be fair and honest. 10You must use honest scales, honest bushels, honest gallons. 11A homer [about five bushels] shall be your standard unit of measurement for both liquid and dry measure. Smaller units shall be the ephah [about one half bushel] for dry measure, and the bath [about seventeen quarts] for liquid. 12The unit of weight shall be the silver shekel [about half an ounce]; it must always be exchanged for twenty gerahs, no less; five shekels shall be valued at five shekels, no less; and ten shekels at ten shekels! Fifty shekels shall always equal one mina.

13"This is the tax you must give to the prince: a bushel of wheat or barley for every sixty you reap; 14and one percent of your olive oil; 15from each 200 sheep in all your flocks in Israel, give him one sheep. These are the meal offerings, burnt offerings and thank offerings to make atonement for those who bring them," says the Lord God. 16"All the people of Israel shall bring their offerings to the prince.

17"The prince shall be required to furnish the people with sacrifices for public worship—sin offerings, burnt offerings, meal offerings, drink offerings, and thank offerings—to make reconciliation for the people of Israel. This shall be done at the time of the religious feasts, the new moon ceremonies, the Sabbaths, and all other similar occasions.

18The Lord God says: "On each New Year's Day sacrifice a young bull with no blemishes, to purify the Temple. 19The priest shall take some of the blood of this sin offering and put it on the door posts of the Temple, upon the four corners of the base of the altar, and upon the walls at the entry of the inner court. 20Do this also on the seventh day of that month for anyone who has sinned through error or ignorance, and so the Temple will be cleansed.

21"On the fourteenth day of the same month, you shall celebrate the Passover. It will be a seven-day feast. Only bread without yeast shall be eaten during those days. 22On the day of Passover the prince shall provide a young bull for a sin offering for himself and all the people of Israel. 23On each of the seven days of the feast he shall prepare a burnt offering to the Lord. This daily offering will consist of seven young bulls and seven rams without blemish. A male goat shall also be given each day for a sin offering. 24And the prince shall provide one half bushel of grain with each bullock and ram for a meal offering, and three quarts of olive oil.

25"Early in October during each of the seven days of the annual festival of shelters, he shall provide these same sacrifices for the sin offering, burnt offering, meal offering, and oil offering."

CHAPTER 46

Special Offerings

The Lord God says, "The inner wall's eastern entrance shall be closed during the six work days but open on the Sabbath and on the days of the new moon celebrations. 2The prince shall enter the outside entry hall of the passageway and proceed to the inner wall at the other end while the priest offers his burnt offering and peace offering. He shall worship inside the passageway and then return back to the entrance, which shall not be closed until evening. 3The people shall worship the Lord in front of this passageway on the Sabbaths and on the days of the new moon celebrations.

4"The burnt offering that the prince sacrifices to the Lord on the Sabbath days shall be six lambs and a ram, all unblemished. 5He shall present a meal offering of one half bushel of flour to go with the ram and whatever amount he is willing for to go with each lamb. And he shall bring three quarts of olive oil for each half bushel of flour. 6At the new moon celebration, he shall bring one young bull in perfect condition, six lambs, and one ram, all without any blemish. 7With the young bull, he must bring one half bushel of flour for a meal offering. With the ram he must bring one half bushel of flour. With the lamb he is to bring whatever he is willing to give. With each half bushel of grain he is to bring three quarts of olive oil.

8"The prince shall go in at the entry hall of the passageway and out the same way; 9but when the people come in through the north passageway to sacrifice during the religious feasts, they must go out through the south passageway. Those coming in from the south must go out by the north. They must never go out the same way they come in, but must always use the opposite passageway. 10The prince shall enter and leave with the common people on these occasions.

11"To summarize: At the special feasts and sacred festivals the meal offering shall be one half bushel with the young bull; one half bushel with the ram; as much as the prince is willing to give with each lamb; and three quarts of oil with each half bushel of grain. 12Whenever the prince offers an extra burnt

46:1-24 This chapter contains a long list of regulations relating to the giving of sacrifices. Sacrifices were a means for paying for the sins of the people and reestablishing the people's relationship with God. Slaughtering animals for our sins may seem terribly barbaric, and we may wonder why God chose to do things this way. If we react negatively to this practice, however, it is easy for us to miss the point. God provided a way to pay for his people's sins without bringing their complete destruction. God didn't expect them to be perfect. He only expected them to admit their sins and follow his program for their forgiveness. God expects the same of us today. Since Ezekiel's day, God has provided the ultimate sacrifice, Jesus Christ, to pay for our sins. He has provided a means for our recovery. All we have to do is accept the gift he has provided.

offering or peace offering to be sacrificed to the Lord, the inner eastern gate shall be opened up for him to enter, and he shall offer his sacrifices just as on the Sabbaths. Then he shall turn around and go out, and the passage shall be shut behind him.

13 "Each morning a yearling lamb must be sacrificed as a burnt offering to the Lord. 14,15 And there must be a meal offering each morning—five pounds of flour with one quart of oil with which to mix it. This is a permanent ordinance—the lamb, the grain offering, and the olive oil shall be provided every morning for the daily sacrifice.

16 The Sovereign Lord says: "If the prince gives a gift of land to one of his sons, it will belong to him forever. 17 But if he gives a gift of land to one of his servants, the servant may keep it only until the Year of Release (every seventh year) when he is set free; then the land returns to the prince. Only gifts to his sons are permanent. 18 And the prince may never take anyone's property by force. If he gives property to his sons, it must be from his own land, for I don't want my people losing their property and having to move away."

19,20 After that, using the door through the wall at the side of the main passageway, he led me through the entrance to the block of sacred chambers that faced north. There, at the extreme west end of these rooms, I saw a place where, my guide told me, the priests boil the meat of the trespass offering and sin offering and bake the flour of the flour offerings into bread. They do it here to avoid the necessity of carrying the sacrifices through the outer court, in case they harm the people.

21,22 Then he brought me out to the outer court again and led me to each of the four corners of the court. I saw that in each corner there was a room 70 feet long by $52\frac{1}{2}$ feet wide, enclosed by walls. 23 Around the inside of these walls there ran a line of brick boiling vats with ovens underneath. 24 He said these rooms were where the Temple assistants—the Levites—boil the sacrifices the people offer.

CHAPTER 47

The River of Healing

Then he brought me back to the door of the Temple. I saw a stream flowing eastward from beneath the Temple and passing to the right of the altar, that is, on its south side. 2 Then he brought me outside the wall through the north passageway and around to the eastern entrance, where I saw the stream flowing along on the south side [of the eastern passageway]. 3 Measuring as he went, he took me 1,500 feet east along the stream and told me to go across. At that point the water was up to my ankles. 4 He measured off another 1,500 feet and told me to cross again. This time the water was up to my knees. 5 Fifteen hundred feet after that it was up to my waist. Another 1,500 feet and it had become a river so deep I wouldn't be able to get across unless I were to swim. It was too deep to cross on foot.

6 He told me to keep in mind what I had seen, then led me back along the bank. 7 And now, to my surprise, many trees were growing on both sides of the river!

8 He told me: "This river flows east through the desert and the Jordan Valley to the Dead Sea, where it will heal the salty waters and make them fresh and pure. 9 Everything touching the water of this river shall live. Fish will abound in the Dead Sea, for its waters will be healed. Wherever this water flows, everything will live. 10 Fishermen will stand along the shores of the Dead Sea, fishing all the way from Engedi to Eneglaim. The shores will be filled with nets drying in the sun. Fish of every kind will fill the Dead Sea just as they do the Mediterranean! 11 But the marshes and swamps will not be healed; they will still be salty. 12 All kinds of fruit trees will grow along the riverbanks. The leaves will never turn brown and fall, and there will always be fruit. There will be a new crop every month—without fail! For they are watered by the river flowing from the Temple. The fruit will be for food and the leaves for medicine."

47:1-12 A river of healing is described in these verses. It will flow throughout the land, restoring its arid landscape with vitality and life. The land had been destroyed by the foolish choices of God's people, but God will restore what man has destroyed. This is our hope in the coming of Jesus the Messiah. During his first coming, Jesus made our personal restoration possible through the power of his miraculous resurrection. We now look forward to his second coming, when God will bring about a cosmic restoration. The sin of humanity has devastated God's perfect plan for the world. In the end, however, God's plan of peace and prosperity on earth will come to pass. God will restore us and the universe we live in from the devastating consequences of sin. We can take part in God's program for recovery today by seeking his will for us and then doing everything possible to follow it.

The Nation's Boundaries

13 The Lord God says: "Here are the instructions for dividing the land to the twelve tribes
of Israel: The tribe of Joseph (Ephraim and
Manasseh) shall be given two sections. 14 Otherwise, each tribe will have an equal share. I
promised with hand raised in oath of truth to
give the land to your fathers, and you shall
inherit it now.

15 "The northern boundary will run from the
Mediterranean toward Hethlon, then on
through Labweh to Zedad; 16 then to Berothah
and Sibraim, which are on the border between
Damascus and Hamath, and finally to Hazer-
hatticon, on the border of Hauran. 17 So the
northern border will be from the Mediterranean to Hazar-enan, on the border with Hamath to the north and Damascus to the south.

18 "The eastern border will run south from
Hazar-enan to Mount Hauran, where it will
bend westward to the Jordan at the southern
tip of the Sea of Galilee, and down along the
Jordan River separating Israel from Gilead,
past the Dead Sea to Tamar.

19 "The southern border will go west from
Tamar to the springs at Meribath-kadesh and
then follow the course of the Brook of Egypt
(Wadi el-Arish) to the Mediterranean.

20 "On the west side, the Mediterranean itself will be your boundary, from the southern
boundary to the point where the northern
boundary begins.

21 "Divide the land within these boundaries
among the tribes of Israel. 22 Distribute the
land as an inheritance for yourselves and for
the foreigners who live among you with their
families. All children born in the land—
whether or not their parents are foreigners—
are to be considered citizens and have the
same rights your own children have. 23 All
these immigrants are to be given land according to the tribe where they now live."

CHAPTER 48

The Land Is Divided

"Here is the list of the tribes and the territory
each is to get. For Dan: From the northwest
boundary at the Mediterranean, across to
Hethlon, then to Labweh, and then on to
Hazar-enan on the border between Damascus
to the south and Hamath to the north. Those
are the eastern and western limits of the land.
2 Asher's territory lies south of Dan's and has
the same east and west boundaries. 3 Naphtali's land lies south of Asher's, with the same
boundary lines on the east and the west.
4 Then comes Manasseh, south of Naphtali,
with the same eastern and western boundary
lines. 5-7 Next, to the south, is Ephraim, and
then Reuben and then Judah, all with the
same boundaries on the east and the west.

8 "South of Judah is the land set aside for the
Temple. It has the same eastern and western
boundaries as the tribal units, with the
Temple in the center. 9 This Temple area will be
8 1/3 miles long and 6 2/3 miles wide.

10 "A strip of land measuring 8 1/3 miles long
by 3 1/3 miles wide, north to south, surrounds
the Temple. 11 It is for the priests, that is, the
sons of Zadok who obeyed me and didn't go
into sin when the people of Israel and the rest
of their tribe of Levi did. 12 It is their special
portion when the land is distributed, the most
sacred land of all. Next to it lies the area where
the other Levites will live. 13 It will be of the
same size and shape as the first. Together they
measure 8 1/3 miles by 6 2/3 miles. 14 None of this
special land shall ever be sold or traded or
used by others, for it belongs to the Lord; it is
holy.

15 "The strip of land 8 1/3 miles long by 1 2/3
miles wide, south of the Temple section, is for
public use—homes, pasture, and parks, with a
city in the center. 16 The city itself is to be 1 1/2
miles square. 17 Open land for pastures shall
surround the city for approximately a tenth of
a mile. 18 Outside the city, stretching east and
west for three miles alongside the holy
grounds, is garden area belonging to the city,
for public use. 19 It is open to anyone working
in the city, no matter where he comes from in
Israel.

20 "The entire area—including sacred lands
and city lands—is 8 1/3 miles square.

21,22 "The land on both sides of this area,
extending clear out to the eastern and western boundaries of Israel, shall belong to the
prince. This land, lying between the sections
alloted to Judah and Benjamin, is 8 1/3 miles
square on each side of the sacred and city
lands.

23 "The sections given to the remaining
tribes are as follows: Benjamin's section extends across the entire country of Israel, from
its eastern border clear across to the western
border. 24 South of Benjamin's area lies that of
Simeon, also extending out to these same
eastern and western borders. 25 Next is Issachar, with the same boundaries. 26 Then comes
Zebulun, also extending all the way across.
27,28 Then Gad, with the same borders on east
and west, while its south border runs from
Tamar to the Spring at Meribath-kadesh, and
then follows the Brook of Egypt (Wadi el-

Arish) to the Mediterranean. 29These are the
allotments to be made to each tribe," says the
Lord God.

The City Gates

30,31"Each city gate will be named in honor
of one of the tribes of Israel. On the north
side, with its 1½-mile wall, there will be
three gates, one named for Reuben, one for
Judah, and one for Levi. 32On the east side,
with its 1½-mile wall, the gates will be
named for Joseph, Benjamin, and Dan.
33The south wall, also the same length, will
have the gates of Simeon, Issachar, and Zebulun; 34on the 1½ miles of the west side,
they will be named for Gad, Asher, and
Naphtali.

35"The entire circumference of the city is six
miles. And the name of the city will be 'The
City of God.'"

REFLECTIONS ON
EZEKIEL

insights ABOUT THE PERSON OF GOD

Ezekiel 1:4-28 contains a magnificent vision! The glory of God was revealed to God's people in captivity. Many of them doubted whether God was even able to be there in a foreign land. Some believed that when they were defeated by Babylon, their God had been defeated by the gods of Babylon. To counteract their confusion, God revealed his glory to his people in Babylon. As is true with us, the people of Judah needed to believe that God could act on their behalf before they were able to entrust their recovery to him. God helped them to trust him by revealing himself in this way.

In **Ezekiel 2:1-2** the prophet was awestruck by God's glory and found himself facedown on the ground, unable to stand in God's presence. When we realize the depth of our helplessness and begin to understand God's limitless power, we may also find ourself falling down before him. But notice that it was God's Spirit who lifted Ezekiel back to his feet. God acted for the stricken prophet and prepared him to receive his message. As we begin our recovery, we need to throw ourself on the mercy of God, recognizing our helplessness. As we give our life to God, he will lift us up and set us on the road to recovery. When we are unable to help ourself, God will give us the strength needed to take the next step.

insights INTO THE RESPONSIBILITIES OF RECOVERY

In **Ezekiel 2:6** the prophet was warned of the great difficulties he would face as he obeyed God's will for his life. But God also made it clear that he would be with Ezekiel as the prophet trusted and obeyed him. When we seek to follow God's will in our recovery, we can count on God's protection and help. That doesn't mean things will be easy for us. In fact, sometimes things get much worse before they get better. Close friends may reject us or make fun of us. People who stand to lose something through our recovery may even try to stop us. In spite of great opposition, we don't have to be afraid. Fear incapacitates and debilitates. God's promise to Ezekiel should give us courage as we follow God's will in our recovery.

For most of us, interpersonal confrontation is never comfortable, yet in **Ezekiel 3:7-8** the prophet was warned that his ministry would be filled with it. If God's work was to be accomplished, Ezekiel would have to speak directly to God's people and condemn them for their sins. In recovery, our times of confrontation are seldom pleasant, but sometimes they are necessary. We need to remember that what we fail to deal with today often becomes a much bigger problem tomorrow.

What is our responsibility to other individuals? Do we have any obligation to others in need of recovery? Are we responsible to warn them of impending danger? People in need of recovery are often blind to the dangers they face. Some of us are in physical peril from our dependencies long before we become aware of it. We also may be in danger of damaging our relationships and the lives of the people close to us. In **Ezekiel 3:17-21** the prophet was commissioned as a guard to warn his people of approaching danger. We should love our fellow strugglers enough to warn them before it is too late to avoid destruction.

Ezekiel 33:10-16 contains a wonderful promise for our recovery. Even as we suffer terrible consequences for our failures and sins, we can be sure that if we repent, God will forgive us. God does not punish us out of anger or vengeance; he punishes us because he loves us. He doesn't desire our destruction; he desires our restoration and recovery. Yet our responsibility is clear: we must repent and turn from our sins. As we do this each day, we will discover that God will help and strengthen us in the battles we face. And though we may still suffer the consequences for our past actions, our ultimate recovery is assured.

insights ABOUT DENIAL

In **Ezekiel 4:1-3** the prophet made it clear to the Jewish exiles that their troubles were not over. Many were in denial about their sin and hoped they would soon return to Jerusalem and the Temple. Ezekiel told them that their beloved homeland would soon be destroyed. He had to help the people recognize their sin before he could help them resolve it. A clear understanding of our problems is essential to our recovery. If we know what we are fighting, we won't spend our efforts working on the wrong issues. Sometimes facing our problems is unpleasant; it certainly was painful for the exiles from Judah. But as hard as it is to face our sins and dependencies, we must admit them if we want to overcome them.

DANIEL

THE BIG PICTURE

A. THE CAPTURE OF INNOCENT BYSTANDERS (1:1-21)
B. GOD HUMBLES THE PROUD (2:1–7:28)
C. HOPE FOR ULTIMATE RECOVERY (8:1–12:4)
D. LIMITED ANSWERS TO LIFE'S PAINFUL QUESTIONS (12:5-13)

Innocent bystanders often get hurt by the mistakes and crimes of other people. Disasters happen that haunt us for life, even though we have no responsibility for the events that take place. Such events are not fair, but they happen anyway. When we suffer innocently, only in facing the realities of our situation can we recover from the problems we have inherited.

Daniel and his friends were innocent bystanders. They suffered a lifelong exile to Babylon because of Judah's prolonged disobedience to God. But they did not remain victims forever. With courage and faith in God, they faced the realities of exile and lived successful lives—even by Babylonian standards. Their recovery gives us insight into how to deal with the unfair circumstances in our life.

After being taken from Jerusalem to Babylon, Daniel and his three friends were trained for service in the Babylonian government. Their captors often demanded that they do things that stood in opposition to God's revealed will for their lives. To protect their relationship with God, Daniel and his friends set clear boundaries for their behavior. They followed God's program for their lives, despite its conflict with the commands of their strong-willed captors. God protected his faithful men from the foreign laws and unstable tyrants they lived under.

Daniel and his friends were exiled to Babylon for the sins of their ancestors, but they did not use that as an excuse for continued failure. Instead, they trusted God and determined to live according to his will. Because of their faith and courage, God not only repeatedly delivered them from difficult circumstances; he also used them to prove his existence and power to others.

THE BOTTOM LINE

PURPOSE: To show how God humbles proud oppressors and vindicates those who trust God through their days of suffering. AUTHOR: The prophet Daniel. AUDIENCE: God's people during and after the Babylonian exile. DATE WRITTEN: The book was probably written around 535 B.C., recording events that happened between 605 and 535 B.C. SETTING: The land of Babylon after Daniel and his friends were exiled there in 605 B.C. KEY VERSE: "And those who are wise—the people of God—shall shine as brightly as the sun's brilliance, and those who turn many to righteousness will glitter like stars forever" (12:3). KEY PLACES: Jerusalem, Babylon, and Susa. KEY PEOPLE AND RELATIONSHIPS: Daniel, Shadrach, Meshach, and Abednego; and foreign rulers Nebuchadnezzar, Belshazzar, and Darius.

RECOVERY THEMES

Life Is Unfair: When we experience unfairness in life, the examples of Daniel and his three friends give us some encouragement and direction. Despite his life of obedience, Daniel was not protected from God's judgment on Judah. We do not have automatic protection from the unfairness of life. We will all face it at one time or another. But we do have the assurance that God is concerned about what we are doing and will honor our faithfulness and obedience.

Not Victims Forever: Daniel was a victim. He was controlled by a powerful group of people and had no say in his future. The dynamics are similar in cases of sexual abuse or in other forms of victimization. Daniel did not remain a victim, however. He discovered that when he turned his life over to God and sought to do God's will, he was no longer at the mercy of selfish and unstable foreign rulers. He was in God's powerful and protecting hands. As Daniel was faithful to God and his program, God delivered Daniel from terrible situations, giving him freedom in the midst of his slavery.

God Can Do Anything: Shadrach, Meshach, and Abednego could have decided that God was unable to protect them from the fiery furnace. Daniel could have decided that God could not handle the den of hungry lions. They might have decided that fudging a little on God's will for them was better than risking their lives. If they had done this, however, they would not have experienced the glorious victories God gave them. God can do anything in our life if we are willing to hand it all over to him and follow his will for us. This may mean that we have to face new conflicts with people who don't approve, but staying faithful to God's program is the only way to a lasting recovery.

Pain in Recovery: Daniel and his friends sought to live according to God's program, but found that others opposed their efforts. This led initially to great danger, but ultimately to glorious victory. Shadrach, Meshach, and Abednego had to walk through a fiery furnace because they obeyed God's will for them. But notice that only the ropes that bound them were burned by the fire. Daniel had to sleep in a den of lions because he was faithful to God. Notice that when he left the lions' den, he was far better off than when he was before. God used these trials to bring blessings to his servants and glory to himself. As we seek to do God's will, he may lead us into some difficult situations. God often uses such trials to bless us. We need to stick to his program, no matter what the difficulties we face.

CHAPTER 1

Daniel Refuses to Compromise

Three years after King Jehoiakim began to rule
in Judah, Babylon's King Nebuchadnezzar attacked Jerusalem with his armies, and the
Lord gave him victory over Jehoiakim. When
he returned to Babylon, he took along some
of the sacred cups from the Temple of God
and placed them in the treasury of his god in
the land of Shinar.
3,4Then he ordered Ashpenaz, who was in
charge of his palace personnel, to select some
of the Jewish youths brought back as captives—young men of the royal family and
nobility of Judah—and to teach them the
Chaldean language and literature. "Pick
strong, healthy, good-looking lads," he said;
"those who have read widely in many fields,
are well informed, alert and sensible, and have
enough poise to look good around the palace."
5The king assigned them the best of food
and wine from his own kitchen during their
three-year training period, planning to make
them his counselors when they graduated.
6Daniel, Hananiah, Mishael, and Azariah
were four of the young men chosen, all from
the tribe of Judah. 7However, their superintendent gave them Babylonian names, as follows:

Daniel was called Belteshazzar;
Hananiah was called Shadrach;

1:1-6 Daniel, Hananiah, Mishael, and Azariah faced troubled times: their city was conquered, and they were captured by the enemy and marched across the desert to Babylon. Life must have seemed over for the four young men. But then their fortune changed. After a three-year training period they were chosen to be Nebuchadnezzar's counselors. No one knows what the future holds. Our current bad times may be temporary; recovery may be just around the corner. We shouldn't give up hope, because God has a good plan for our life, and he will see it through.

1:7-16 When authority figures and personalities try to squeeze us into their mold and get us to compromise our values, the natural thing to do is give in to their wishes. The healthy response, and the one that indicates progress toward recovery, is to courageously set boundaries as Daniel did by not eating food contrary to God's laws. With proper boundaries set up, we will be less tempted to give in to compromise.

DANIEL

Daniel experienced all the forces that normally lead to discouragement and defeat, yet he stood firm in his faith and convictions. He was exiled from Judah as a youth, separated from the healthy boundaries supported by his family and Jewish faith. The Babylonian government chose him for government service and hoped he would discard his faith and religious practices to become a Babylonian. He was even named after one of the gods of Babylon to discourage his allegiance to his own God and homeland.

Daniel experienced the turmoil of transition from one culture to another, yet he was able to recognize that God had everything under control. He knew that no matter what happened around him, God and his will would remain the same. Daniel knew what God expected of him and remained faithful to God's program, despite the opposition and temptations he faced. So God blessed him, and Daniel became a great success in the courts of Babylon and Persia.

Daniel's rise to power in Nebuchadnezzar's court, though a great blessing, posed many difficulties and dangers. Leaders in Babylon's government were often destroyed by the plots of power-hungry nobles; the king himself was known to dispose of his counselors on a whim. Daniel narrowly escaped destruction from both of these quarters. He trusted in God to keep him safe in the dangerous world of Babylonian politics. He refused to compromise his faith in God, despite opposition and the increased danger it caused him during the reign of Darius.

As God delivered Daniel from one difficulty after another, even the kings of Babylon and Persia came to believe in God's power. At times, Daniel's faith led him into difficult situations—he was forced to spend a whole night with hungry lions! But God always delivered him, strengthening Daniel's faith and proving that God was in control. Daniel proved time and time again that doing things God's way is always best. And in that world of shifting power and changing governments, Daniel held important positions for over sixty years.

STRENGTHS AND ACCOMPLISHMENTS:
- Daniel refused to let the abuse he suffered affect his future.
- He had an accurate understanding of who he was as one of God's people.
- He remained faithful to God despite much opposition and many temptations.
- He handled the power given to him with humility, and he was a just leader.
- He always followed God's will for him, even when it was dangerous to do so.

LESSONS FROM HIS LIFE:
- God's help in the past can strengthen our faith for the future.
- Doing things God's way is always best.
- God's unchanging character can give stability in our changing world.
- As we follow God's will for us, others will come to believe in God's power.
- A disciplined relationship with God will help us to obey God's will for us.

KEY VERSE:
"Call for this man, Daniel—or Belteshazzar, as the king called him—for his mind is filled with divine knowledge and understanding. He can interpret dreams, explain riddles, and solve knotty problems. He will tell you what the writing means" (Daniel 5:12).

Daniel's story is told in the book of Daniel. He is also mentioned in Matthew 24:15.

Mishael was called Meshach;
Azariah was called Abednego.

[8]But Daniel made up his mind not to eat the food and wine given to them by the king. He asked the superintendent for permission to eat other things instead. [9]Now as it happened, God had given the superintendent a special appreciation for Daniel and sympathy for his predicament. [10]But he was alarmed by Daniel's suggestion.

"I'm afraid you will become pale and thin compared with the other youths your age," he said, "and then the king will behead me for neglecting my responsibilities."

[11]Daniel talked it over with the steward who was appointed by the superintendent to look after Daniel, Hananiah, Mishael, and Azariah, [12]and suggested a ten-day diet of only vegetables and water; [13]then, at the end of this trial period the steward could see how they looked in comparison with the other fellows who ate

the king's rich food and decide whether or not to let them continue their diet.

[14]The steward finally agreed to the test. [15]Well, at the end of the ten days, Daniel and his three friends looked healthier and better nourished than the youths who had been eating the food supplied by the king! [16]So after that the steward fed them only vegetables and water, without the rich foods and wines!

[17]God gave these four youths great ability to learn, and they soon mastered all the literature and science of the time; and God gave to Daniel special ability in understanding the meanings of dreams and visions.

[18,19]When the three-year training period was completed, the superintendent brought all the young men to the king for oral exams, as he had been ordered to do. King Nebuchadnezzar had long talks with each of them, and none of them impressed him as much as Daniel, Hananiah, Mishael, and Azariah. So they were put on his regular staff of advisors. [20]And in all matters requiring information and balanced judgment, the king found these young men's advice ten times better than that of all the skilled magicians and wise astrologers in his realm.

[21]Daniel held this appointment as the king's counselor until the first year of the reign of King Cyrus.

CHAPTER 2
Daniel Interprets a Dream

One night in the second year of his reign, Nebuchadnezzar had a terrifying nightmare and awoke trembling with fear. And to make matters worse, he couldn't remember his dream! He immediately called in all his magicians, incantationists, sorcerers, and astrologers, and demanded that they tell him what his dream had been.

"I've had a terrible nightmare," he said as they stood before him, "and I can't remember what it was. Tell me, for I fear some tragedy awaits me."

[4]Then the astrologers (speaking in Aramaic) said to the king, "Sir, tell us the dream and then we can tell you what it means."

[5]But the king replied, "I tell you the dream is gone—I can't remember it. And if you won't tell me what it was and what it means, I'll have you torn limb from limb and your houses made into heaps of rubble! [6]But I will give you many wonderful gifts and honors if you tell me what the dream was and what it means. So, begin!"

[7]They said again, "How can we tell you what the dream means unless you tell us what it was?"

[8,9]The king retorted, "I can see your trick! You're trying to stall for time until the calamity befalls me that the dream foretells. But if you don't tell me the dream, you certainly can't expect me to believe your interpretation!"

[10]The astrologers replied to the king, "There isn't a man alive who can tell others what they have dreamed! And there isn't a king in all the world who would ask such a thing! [11]This is an impossible thing the king requires. No one except the gods can tell you your dream, and they are not here to help."

[12]Upon hearing this, the king was furious and sent out orders to execute all the wise men of Babylon. [13]And Daniel and his companions were rounded up with the others to be killed.

[14]But when Arioch, the chief executioner, came to kill them, Daniel handled the situation with great wisdom by asking, [15]"Why is the king so angry? What is the matter?"

Then Arioch told him all that had happened.

[16]So Daniel went in to see the king. "Give me a little time," he said, "and I will tell you the dream and what it means."

[17]Then he went home and told Hananiah, Mishael, and Azariah, his companions. [18]They asked the God of heaven to show them his mercy by telling them the secret, so they would not die with the others. [19]And that night in a vision God told Daniel what the king had dreamed.

Then Daniel praised the God of heaven, [20]saying, "Blessed be the name of God forever and ever, for he alone has all wisdom and all power. [21]World events are under his control. He removes kings and sets others on their thrones. He gives wise men their wisdom and scholars their intelligence. [22]He reveals pro-

2:26-28 Daniel wisely gave God the credit for the discovery of the dream. He could easily have told Nebuchadnezzar that *he* knew the dream, and thus elevated himself above all the counselors. But he acknowledged God and God's power. God works in our life, too, bringing recovery where once there was pain and despair. Have we given God the credit for our recovery, or have we told others we did it on our own? We need to follow Daniel's example and give credit where credit is due.

found mysteries beyond man's understanding. He knows all hidden things, for he
is light, and darkness is no obstacle to him. 23I
thank and praise you, O God of my fathers,
for you have given me wisdom and glowing
health, and now even this vision of the king's
dream and the understanding of what it
means."
24Then Daniel went in to see Arioch, who
had been ordered to execute the wise men of
Babylon, and said, "Don't kill them. Take me
to the king, and I will tell him what he wants
to know."
25Then Arioch hurried Daniel in to the king
and said, "I've found one of the Jewish captives who will tell you your dream!"
26The king said to Daniel, "Is this true? Can
you tell me what my dream was and what it
means?"
27Daniel replied, "No wise man, astrologer,
magician, or wizard can tell the king such
things, 28but there is a God in heaven who
reveals secrets, and he has told you in your
dream what will happen in the future. This
was your dream:
29"You dreamed of coming events. He who
reveals secrets was speaking to you. 30(But
remember, it's not because I am wiser than
any living person that I know this secret of
your dream, for God showed it to me for your
benefit.)
31"O king, you saw a huge and powerful
statue of a man, shining brilliantly, frightening and terrible. 32The head of the statue was
made of purest gold, its chest and arms were
of silver, its belly and thighs of brass, 33its legs
of iron, its feet part iron and part clay. 34But as
you watched, a Rock was cut from the mountainside by supernatural means. It came hurtling toward the statue and crushed the feet of
iron and clay, smashing them to bits. 35Then
the whole statue collapsed into a heap of iron,
clay, brass, silver, and gold; its pieces were
crushed as small as chaff, and the wind blew
them all away. But the Rock that knocked the
statue down became a great mountain that
covered the whole earth.
36"That was the dream; now for its meaning:
37"Your Majesty, you are a king over many
kings, for the God of heaven has given you
your kingdom, power, strength, and glory.
38You rule the farthest provinces, and even
animals and birds are under your control, as
God decreed. You are that head of gold.
39"But after your kingdom has come to an
end, another world power will arise to take
your place. This empire will be inferior to
yours. And after that kingdom has fallen, yet
a third great power —represented by the
bronze belly of the statue—will rise to rule the
world. 40Following it, the fourth kingdom will
be strong as iron—smashing, bruising, and
conquering. 41,42The feet and toes you saw—
part iron and part clay—show that later on,
this kingdom will be divided. Some parts of it
will be as strong as iron, and some as weak as
clay. 43This mixture of iron with clay also
shows that these kingdoms will try to
strengthen themselves by forming alliances
with each other through intermarriage of
their rulers; but this will not succeed, for iron
and clay don't mix.
44"During the reigns of those kings, the God
of heaven will set up a kingdom that will
never be destroyed; no one will ever conquer
it. It will shatter all these kingdoms into nothingness, but it shall stand forever, indestructible.
45That is the meaning of the Rock cut from the
mountain without human hands—the Rock
that crushed to powder all the iron and brass,
the clay, the silver, and the gold.
"Thus the great God has shown what will
happen in the future, and this interpretation
of your dream is as sure and certain as my
description of it."
46Then Nebuchadnezzar fell to the ground
before Daniel and worshiped him and commanded his people to offer sacrifices and burn
sweet incense before him.
47"Truly, O Daniel," the king said, "your
God is the God of gods, Ruler of kings, the
Revealer of mysteries, because he has told you
this secret."
48Then the king made Daniel very great; he
gave him many valuable gifts and appointed
him to be ruler over the whole province of
Babylon, as well as chief over all his wise men.
49Then, at Daniel's request, the king appointed Shadrach, Meshach, and Abednego
as Daniel's assistants, to be in charge of all
the affairs of the province of Babylon; Daniel served as chief magistrate in the king's
court.

2:29-45 In this vision, a prominent theme of the book of Daniel is introduced: how God is ultimately in control, even over seemingly unshakable human power. This passage provides the framework for interpreting all the prophetic visions of Daniel, but it also tells us that God will defeat those who are against his people. He will establish his kingdom for those who follow his ways.

CHAPTER 3
Four Men in the Furnace
King Nebuchadnezzar made a gold statue
ninety feet high and nine feet wide and set it
up on the Plain of Dura, in the province of
Babylon; 2then he sent messages to all the
princes, governors, captains, judges, treasurers, counselors, sheriffs, and rulers of all the
provinces of his empire, to come to the dedication of his statue. 3When they had all arrived and were standing before the
monument, 4a herald shouted out, "O people
of all nations and languages, this is the king's
command:
5"When the band strikes up, you are to fall
flat on the ground to worship King Nebuchadnezzar's gold statue; 6anyone who refuses
to obey will immediately be thrown into a
flaming furnace."
7So when the band began to play, everyone—whatever his nation, language, or religion—fell to the ground and worshiped the
statue.
8But some officials went to the king and
accused some of the Jews of refusing to worship!
9"Your Majesty," they said to him, 10"you
made a law that everyone must fall down and
worship the gold statue when the band begins
to play, 11and that anyone who refuses will be
thrown into a flaming furnace. 12But there are
some Jews out there—Shadrach, Meshach,
and Abednego, whom you have put in charge
of Babylonian affairs—who have defied you,
refusing to serve your gods or to worship the
gold statue you set up."
13Then Nebuchadnezzar, in a terrible rage,
ordered Shadrach, Meshach, and Abednego
to be brought in before him.
14"Is it true, O Shadrach, Meshach, and Abednego," he demanded, "that you are refusing to serve my gods or to worship the gold
statue I set up? 15I'll give you one more
chance. When the music plays, if you fall
down and worship the statue, all will be well.
But if you refuse, you will be thrown into a
flaming furnace within the hour. And what
god can deliver you out of my hands then?"
16Shadrach, Meshach, and Abednego replied, "O Nebuchadnezzar, we are not worried
about what will happen to us. 17If we are
thrown into the flaming furnace, our God is
able to deliver us; and he will deliver us out of
your hand, Your Majesty. 18But if he doesn't,
please understand, sir, that even then we will
never under any circumstance serve your gods
or worship the gold statue you have erected."
19Then Nebuchadnezzar was filled with
fury and his face became dark with anger at
Shadrach, Meshach, and Abednego. He commanded that the furnace be heated up seven
times hotter than usual, 20and called for some
of the strongest men of his army to bind
Shadrach, Meshach, and Abednego, and
throw them into the fire. 21So they bound
them tight with ropes and threw them into
the furnace, fully clothed. 22And because the
king, in his anger, had demanded such a hot
fire in the furnace, the flames leaped out and
killed the soldiers as they threw them in! 23So
Shadrach, Meshach, and Abednego fell down
bound into the roaring flames.
24But suddenly, as he was watching, Nebuchadnezzar jumped up in amazement and
exclaimed to his advisors, "Didn't we throw
three men into the furnace?"
"Yes," they said, "we did indeed, Your Majesty."
25"Well, look!" Nebuchadnezzar shouted. "I
see *four* men, unbound, walking around in
the fire, and they aren't even hurt by the
flames! And the fourth looks like a god!"
26Then Nebuchadnezzar came as close as he
could to the open door of the flaming furnace
and yelled: "Shadrach, Meshach, and Abednego, servants of the Most High God! Come
out! Come here!" So they stepped out of the
fire.
27Then the princes, governors, captains, and
counselors crowded around them and saw that
the fire hadn't touched them—not a hair of

3:7-15 Shadrach, Meshach, and Abednego displayed great faith and courage as they refused to bow to the statue. When Nebuchadnezzar confronted them, he issued an ultimatum: either bow down or die! He reminds us of the people who bully their way through life, abusing people who won't give in to their pressure. But those people are no match for God—he will stand by us, protecting us from the various abusive personalities we encounter.

3:24-30 Nebuchadnezzar was amazed at what he saw and immediately worshiped the God of Shadrach, Meshach, and Abednego. If the Hebrews had not stood up to Nebuchadnezzar, he never would have seen the great power of God. The best way we can tell someone about God is to demonstrate his power in our life. This will encourage those who seek him and help in their recovery. It may even win over those who were against us at the beginning.

NEBUCHADNEZZAR

Nebuchadnezzar was one of the greatest conquerors in the history of our world. He came to dominate the people of many nations, including Judah. He possessed power, fame, wealth, and influence. At one point, he even considered himself to be a god. But, like so many others, he lacked the one thing he needed the most: peace. His insecurities would not allow him to be at peace with himself. So how could he be at peace with others? He was a man who was unhappy with himself and hostile toward the people around him.

Nebuchadnezzar never truly discovered the peace that could have been found had he recognized his powerlessness and surrendered his life to God. He did everything he could to maintain his power over others. Daniel and his friends were perfect examples of how success and peace could be found through complete dependence on God and surrender to his will. After Shadrach, Meshach, and Abednego walked out of the fiery furnace unscathed, Nebuchadnezzar realized that he had been thwarted by a higher Power. He also saw that the three friends, by turning their lives over to God, had far greater power at their disposal than even he had. Despite his recognition of God's power, however, the king's pride continued to get the best of him.

Nebuchadnezzar continued to brag about his greatness and claimed that he alone was responsible for the great city of Babylon. He refused to recognize that all power—even his power—was granted by God. So God judged Nebuchadnezzar's pride by afflicting him with madness, and the king was forced from his throne. After a time, Nebuchadnezzar turned to God and admitted his sin of pride, and God restored his sanity and rule. Nebuchadnezzar had been reminded once again that he was not ultimately in control of his world.

Sadly, it seems that Nebuchadnezzar never understood the true nature of submission to God. He saw God act in the lives of others, and even in his own life. He clearly believed in God's presence and power. Yet he could not seem to put his life into God's hands on a permanent basis. Although he may have experienced religious conviction, it seems that he never experienced spiritual conversion and transformation.

STRENGTHS AND ACCOMPLISHMENTS:

- Nebuchadnezzar achieved great success and accumulated astounding wealth.
- He was used by God, in spite of himself, to accomplish God's purposes.
- He was a great leader of men.

WEAKNESSES AND MISTAKES:

- He demanded rather than earned loyalty from his subordinates.
- He wanted his people to worship him as if he were a god.
- He failed to act on his knowledge that God was ultimately in control.
- His pride kept him from submitting to God's will for his life.

LESSONS FROM HIS LIFE:

- Submitting to God's will is the first step toward receiving his power.
- If we refuse to trust God with our life, we will be plagued by fear.
- A life of peace can only be found by entrusting our life to God.
- Playing God by controlling others only leads to insecurity and hostility.
- Healing comes when we admit our sin to God and look to him for help.

KEY VERSES:

"[Nebuchadnezzar] was strolling on the roof of the royal palace in Babylon, and saying, 'I, by my own mighty power, have built this beautiful city as my royal residence. . . .' While he was still speaking these words, a voice called down from heaven, 'O King Nebuchadnezzar, this message is for you: You are no longer ruler of this kingdom'" (Daniel 4:29-31).

Nebuchadnezzar's story is told in Daniel 1–5. He is also mentioned in 2 Kings 24–25 and 2 Chronicles 36.

---

their heads was singed; their coats were unscorched, and they didn't even smell of smoke!
28Then Nebuchadnezzar said, "Blessed be the
God of Shadrach, Meshach, and Abednego, for he sent his angel to deliver his trusting servants when they defied the king's commandment and were willing to die rather than serve or worship any god except their own. 29Therefore,
I make this decree, that any person of any nation, language, or religion who speaks a word against the God of Shadrach, Meshach, and Abednego shall be torn limb from limb and his house knocked into a heap of rubble. For no other God can do what this one does."
30Then the king gave promotions to Shadrach, Meshach, and Abednego, so that they prospered greatly there in the province of Babylon.

CHAPTER 4

A Dream about a Tree

This is the proclamation of Nebuchadnezzar the king, which he sent to people of every language in every nation of the world:

Greetings:

[2]I want you all to know about the strange thing that the Most High God did to me. [3]It was incredible—a mighty miracle! And now I know for sure that his kingdom is everlasting; he reigns forever and ever.

[4]I, Nebuchadnezzar, was living in peace and prosperity, [5]when one night I had a dream that greatly frightened me. [6]I called in all the wise men of Babylon to tell me the meaning of my dream, [7]but when they came—the magicians, astrologers, fortune-tellers, and wizards—and I told them the dream, they couldn't interpret it. [8]At last Daniel came in—the man I named Belteshazzar after my god—the man in whom is the spirit of the holy gods, and I told him the dream.

[9]"O Belteshazzar, master magician," I said, "I know that the spirit of the holy gods is in you and no mystery is too great for you to solve. Tell me what my dream means:

[10,11]"I saw a very tall tree out in a field, growing higher and higher into the sky until it could be seen by everyone in all the world. [12]Its leaves were fresh and green, and its branches were weighted down with fruit, enough for everyone to eat. Wild animals rested beneath its shade and birds sheltered in its branches, and all the world was fed from it. [13]Then as I lay there dreaming, I saw one of God's angels coming down from heaven.

[14]"He shouted, 'Cut down the tree; lop off its branches; shake off its leaves, and scatter its fruit. Get the animals out from under it and the birds from its branches, [15]but leave its stump and roots in the ground, banded with a chain of iron and brass, surrounded by the tender grass. Let the dew of heaven drench him and let him eat grass with the wild animals! [16]For seven years let him have the mind of an animal instead of a man. [17]For this has been decreed by the Watchers, demanded by the Holy Ones. The purpose of this decree is that all the world may understand that the Most High dominates the kingdoms of the world and gives them to anyone he wants to, even the lowliest of men!'

[18]"O Belteshazzar, that was my dream; now tell me what it means. For no one else can help me; all the wisest men of my kingdom have failed me. But you can tell me, for the spirit of the holy gods is in you."

[19]Then Daniel sat there stunned and silent for an hour, aghast at the meaning of the dream. Finally the king said to him: "Belteshazzar, don't be afraid to tell me what it means."

Daniel replied: "Oh, that the events foreshadowed in this dream would happen to your enemies, my lord, and not to you! [20]For the tree you saw growing so tall, reaching high into the heavens for all the world to see, [21]with its fresh green leaves, loaded with fruit for all to eat, the wild animals living in its shade, with its branches full of birds— [22]that tree, Your Majesty, is you. For you have grown strong and great; your greatness reaches up to heaven, and your rule to the ends of the earth.

[23]"Then you saw God's angel coming down from heaven and saying, 'Cut down the tree and destroy it, but leave the stump and the roots in the earth surrounded by tender grass, banded with a chain of iron and brass. Let him be wet with the dew of heaven. For seven years let him eat grass with the animals of the field.'

[24]"Your Majesty, the Most High God has decreed—and it will surely happen—[25]that your people will chase you from your palace, and you will live in the fields like an animal, eating grass like a cow, your back wet with dew from heaven. For seven years this will be your life, until you learn that the Most High God dominates the kingdoms of men and gives power to anyone he chooses. [26]But the stump and the roots were left in the ground! This means that you will get your kingdom

---

4:18-27 Nebuchadnezzar's dream was interpreted by Daniel (Belteshazzar) through the wisdom given by God's Spirit (4:18). The king's tragic breakdown would soon take place unless he made some drastic changes in his life. Similarly, we may be heading for a humbling experience if we continue to think we are in control of our life. Our recovery is dependent on our trust in God and obedience to his will for our life.

4:28-37 Even after a warning, Nebuchadnezzar did not change his life-style and give God the credit for his power. The result was seven years of humiliating insanity. But God restored Nebuchadnezzar to the throne when he turned toward heaven for deliverance. We should notice that the king praised and honored God; he didn't curse him for his many years of madness. If we experience a painful setback, God is giving us a chance to change our ways. God will remove our suffering when we have learned the lesson he wanted to teach us.

back again when you have learned that
heaven rules.
27"O King Nebuchadnezzar, listen to me—
stop sinning; do what you know is right; be
merciful to the poor. Perhaps even yet God
will spare you."
28But all these things happened to Nebuchadnezzar. 29Twelve months after this
dream, he was strolling on the roof of the
royal palace in Babylon, 30and saying, "I, by
my own mighty power, have built this beautiful city as my royal residence and as the
capital of my empire."
31While he was still speaking these words, a
voice called down from heaven, "O King Nebuchadnezzar, this message is for you: You are
no longer ruler of this kingdom. 32You will be
forced out of the palace to live with the animals in the fields and to eat grass like the cows
for seven years, until you finally realize that
God parcels out the kingdoms of men and
gives them to anyone he chooses."
33That very same hour this prophecy was
fulfilled. Nebuchadnezzar was chased from
his palace and ate grass like the cows, and his
body was wet with dew; his hair grew as long
as eagles' feathers, and his nails were like
birds' claws.
34"At the end of seven years I, Nebuchadnezzar, looked up to heaven, and my sanity
returned, and I praised and worshiped the
Most High God and honored him who lives
forever, whose rule is everlasting, his kingdom evermore. 35All the people of the earth
are nothing when compared to him; he does
whatever he thinks best among the angels of
heaven, as well as here on earth. No one can
stop him or challenge him, saying, 'What do
you mean by doing these things?' 36When my
mind returned to me, so did my honor and
glory and kingdom. My counselors and officers came back to me, and I was reestablished
as head of my kingdom, with even greater
honor than before.
37"Now, I, Nebuchadnezzar, praise and glorify and honor the King of Heaven, the Judge
of all, whose every act is right and good; for
he is able to take those who walk proudly and
push them into the dust!"

CHAPTER 5
The Writing on the Wall
Belshazzar the king invited a thousand of his
officers to a great feast where the wine flowed
freely. 2-4While Belshazzar was drinking, he
was reminded of the gold and silver cups
taken long before from the Temple in Jerusa-

Grandiose Thinking

BIBLE READING: Daniel 4:19-33

We came to believe that a Power greater than ourselves could restore us to sanity.

When we are caught up in our addiction, it's common for us to deny the truth about our situation with grandiose thinking. We may believe that we're above it all, a god unto ourself, accountable to no one.

In his day, Nebuchadnezzar, king of ancient Babylon, was the most powerful ruler on earth. He believed himself to be a god and demanded worship as such. God said to him, "The Most High God has decreed . . . that your people will chase you from your palace, and you will live in the fields like an animal. . . . This will be your life, until you learn that the Most High God dominates the kingdoms of men, and gives power to anyone he chooses" (Daniel 4:24-25).

All this happened just as it had been predicted. At the end of the king's time in exile, he said, "I . . . looked up to heaven, and my sanity returned, and I praised and worshiped the Most High God and honored him who lives forever. . . . When my mind returned to me, so did my honor and glory and kingdom . . . with even greater honor than before. Now I, Nebuchadnezzar, praise and glorify and honor the King of Heaven, the Judge of all, whose every act is right and good; for he is able to take those who walk proudly and push them into the dust!" (Daniel 4:34, 36-37).

We are not God; we are accountable to a higher Power. But this higher Power can remedy our "madness" and restore our life to be even better than it was before our season of insanity. He will do so if we entrust our life to him. ***Turn to page 1061, Mark 5.***

lem during Nebuchadnezzar's reign and brought to Babylon. Belshazzar ordered that these sacred cups be brought in to the feast, and when they arrived, he and his princes, wives, and concubines drank toasts from them to their idols made of gold and silver, brass and iron, wood and stone.

[5]Suddenly, as they were drinking from these cups, they saw the fingers of a man's hand writing on the plaster of the wall opposite the lampstand. The king himself saw the fingers as they wrote. [6]His face blanched with fear, and such terror gripped him that his knees knocked together and his legs gave way beneath him.

[7]"Bring the magicians and astrologers!" he screamed. "Bring the Chaldeans! Whoever reads that writing on the wall and tells me what it means will be dressed in purple robes of royal honor, with a gold chain around his neck, and he will become the third ruler in the kingdom!"

[8]But when they came, none of them could understand the writing or tell him what it meant.

[9]The king grew more and more hysterical; his face reflected the terror he felt, and his officers too were shaken.[10]But when the queen-mother heard what was happening, she rushed to the banquet hall and said to Belshazzar, "Calm yourself, Your Majesty, don't be so pale and frightened over this. [11]For there is a man in your kingdom who has within him the spirit of the holy gods. In the days of your father this man was found to be as full of wisdom and understanding as though he were himself a god. And in the reign of King Nebuchadnezzar, he was made chief of all the magicians, astrologers, Chaldeans, and soothsayers of Babylon. [12]Call for this man, Daniel—or Belteshazzar, as the king called him—for his mind is filled with divine knowledge and understanding. He can interpret dreams, explain riddles, and solve knotty problems. He will tell you what the writing means."

[13]So Daniel was rushed in to see the king. The king asked him, "Are you the Daniel brought from Israel as a captive by King Nebuchadnezzar? [14]I have heard that you have the spirit of the gods within you and that you are filled with enlightenment and wisdom. [15]My wise men and astrologers have tried to read that writing on the wall and tell me what it means, but they can't. [16]I am told you can solve all kinds of mysteries. If you can tell me the meaning of those words, I will clothe you in purple robes, with a gold chain around your neck, and make you the third ruler in the kingdom."

[17]Daniel answered, "Keep your gifts or give them to someone else, but I will tell you what the writing means. [18]Your Majesty, the Most High God gave Nebuchadnezzar, who long ago preceded you, a kingdom and majesty and glory and honor. [19]He gave him such majesty that all the nations of the world trembled before him in fear. He killed any who offended him and spared any he liked. At his whim they rose or fell. [20]But when his heart and mind were hardened in pride, God removed him from his royal throne and took away his glory. [21]He was chased out of his palace into the fields. His thoughts and feelings became those of an animal, and he lived among the wild donkeys; he ate grass like the cows, and his body was wet with the dew of heaven, until at last he knew that the Most High overrules the kingdoms of men and appoints anyone he desires to reign over them.

[22]"And you, his successor, O Belshazzar—you knew all this, yet you have not been humble. [23]For you have defied the Lord of Heaven and brought here these cups from his Temple; and you and your officers and wives and concubines have been drinking wine

---

5:1-6 One of the worst types of denial is that of drowning our fears and problems in a compulsive action. Alcohol, drugs, and sex are all compulsive behaviors that people turn to in order to avoid or forget. While such things may mask the fear and pain momentarily, the circumstances that led to our addiction are still there. In fact, they are probably only getting worse. In Belshazzar's case, the "writing was on the wall"—the Medo-Persian army had surrounded Babylon during Belshazzar's feast and would soon capture the city. We need to pay attention to problems when they arise and not hide behind our dependencies. If we don't act right away, it may be too late to escape disaster when we come down from our high.

5:18-31 Tragically, it is possible to wait too long to enter recovery. Belshazzar had not learned from the experiences of his ancestor Nebuchadnezzar, and now his time had run out. His pride and arrogance had led him to the point where there could be no recovery; he would die before the night was over. It doesn't have to be too late—we can find recovery when we turn to God for help. The time to trust God is now, while our heart is soft enough for us to hear God calling. Without God, we may as well apply the writing on the wall to our own life.

from them while praising gods of silver, gold, brass, iron, wood, and stone—gods that neither see nor hear nor know anything at all. But you have not praised the God who gives you the breath of life and controls your destiny! 24,25And so God sent those fingers to write this message: *'Mene,' 'Mene,' 'Tekel,' 'Parsin.'*

26"This is what it means:

"Mene means 'numbered'—God has numbered the days of your reign, and they are ended.

27*"Tekel* means 'weighed'—you have been weighed in God's balances and have failed the test.

28*"Parsin* means 'divided'—your kingdom will be divided and given to the Medes and Persians."

29Then at Belshazzar's command, Daniel was robed in purple, a gold chain was hung around his neck, and he was proclaimed third ruler in the kingdom.

30That very night Belshazzar, the Chaldean king, was killed, 31and Darius the Mede entered the city and began reigning at the age of sixty-two.

CHAPTER 6

Daniel in the Lion's Den

Darius divided the kingdom into 120 provinces, each under a governor. 2The governors were accountable to three presidents (Daniel was one of them) so the king could administer the kingdom efficiently.

3Daniel soon proved himself more capable than all the other presidents and governors, for he had great ability, and the king began to think of placing him over the entire empire as his administrative officer.

4This made the other presidents and governors very jealous, and they began searching for some fault in the way Daniel was handling his affairs so that they could complain to the king about him. But they couldn't find anything to criticize! He was faithful and honest and made no mistakes. 5So they concluded, "Our only chance is his religion!"

6They decided to go to the king and say, "King Darius, live forever! 7We presidents, governors, counselors, and deputies have unanimously decided that you should make a law, irrevocable under any circumstance, that for the next thirty days anyone who asks a favor of God or man—except from you, Your Majesty—shall be thrown to the lions. 8Your Majesty, we request your signature on this law; sign it so that it cannot be canceled or changed; it will be a 'law of the Medes and Persians' that cannot be revoked."

9So King Darius signed the law.

10But though Daniel knew about it, he went home and knelt down as usual in his upstairs bedroom, with its windows open toward Jerusalem, and prayed three times a day, just as he always had, giving thanks to his God.

11Then the men thronged to Daniel's house and found him praying there, asking favors of his God. 12They rushed back to the king and reminded him about his law. "Haven't you signed a decree," they demanded, "that permits no petitions to any God or man—except you—for thirty days? And anyone disobeying will be thrown to the lions?"

"Yes," the king replied, "it is 'a law of the Medes and Persians,' that cannot be altered or revoked."

13Then they told the king, "That fellow Daniel, one of the Jewish captives, is paying no attention to you or your law. He is asking favors of his God three times a day."

14Hearing this, the king was very angry with himself for signing the law and determined to save Daniel. He spent the rest of the day trying to think of some way to get Daniel out of this predicament.

15In the evening the men came again to the king and said, "Your Majesty, there is nothing you can do. You signed the law, and it cannot be changed."

16So at last the king gave the order for Daniel's arrest, and he was taken to the den

6:1-4 Just because a person is healthy and balanced from an emotional and spiritual standpoint, it doesn't guarantee his popularity or acceptance. Such wholeness, especially if it is matched with ability, can be quite intimidating to those who do not understand recovery. There will always be those who are threatened by our progress in recovery. They may do anything to keep us from achieving our goals just so they can feel important or powerful. When we are prepared for this, we won't be swayed by their intimidation.

6:11-17 We need to always consider how our actions will affect others. The king satisfied his ego but failed to realize the impact of this new law. As a result, Daniel, who was obviously close to the king, was sentenced to die. Before doing anything, it is important to evaluate the significance of our decisions. Will anyone be hurt? Is it morally wrong? Will we regret the outcome? If any of these questions can be answered yes, we need to consider another plan of action.

of lions. The king said to him, "May your God, whom you worship continually, deliver you." And then they threw him in. 17A stone was brought and placed over the mouth of the den; and the king sealed it with his own signet ring and with that of his government, so that no one could rescue Daniel from the lions.

18Then the king returned to his palace and went to bed without dinner. He refused his usual entertainment and didn't sleep all night. 19Very early the next morning he hurried out to the lions' den 20and called out in anguish, "O Daniel, servant of the Living God, was your God, whom you worship continually, able to deliver you from the lions?"

21Then he heard a voice! "Your Majesty, live forever!" It was Daniel! 22"My God has sent his angel," he said, "to shut the lions' mouths so that they can't touch me, for I am innocent before God; nor, sir, have I wronged you."

23The king was beside himself with joy and ordered Daniel lifted from the den. And not a scratch was found on him because he believed in his God.

24Then the king issued a command to bring the men who had accused Daniel and throw them into the den along with their children and wives, and the lions leaped upon them and tore them apart before they even hit the bottom of the den.

25,26Afterward King Darius wrote this message addressed to everyone in his empire:

"Greetings! I decree that everyone shall tremble and fear before the God of Daniel in every part of my kingdom. For his God is the living, unchanging God whose kingdom shall never be destroyed and whose power shall never end. 27He delivers his people, preserving them from harm; he does great miracles in heaven and earth; it is he who delivered Daniel from the power of the lions."

28So Daniel prospered in the reign of Darius and in the reign of Cyrus the Persian.

CHAPTER 7

Daniel Dreams of Four Beasts

One night during the first year of Belshazzar's reign over the Babylonian Empire, Daniel had a dream and he wrote it down. This is his description of what he saw:

2In my dream I saw a great storm on a mighty ocean, with strong winds blowing from every direction. 3Then four huge animals came up out of the water, each different from the other. 4The first was like a lion, but it had eagle's wings! And as I watched, its wings were pulled off so that it could no longer fly, and it was left standing on the ground, on two feet, like a man; and a man's mind was given to it. 5The second animal looked like a bear with its paw raised, ready to strike. It held three ribs between its teeth, and I heard a voice saying to it, "Get up! Devour many people!" 6The third of these strange animals looked like a leopard, but on its back it had wings like those of birds, and it had four heads! And great power was given to it over all mankind.

7Then, as I watched in my dream, a fourth animal rose up out of the ocean, too dreadful to describe and incredibly strong. It devoured some of its victims by tearing them apart with its huge iron teeth, and others it crushed beneath its feet. It was far more brutal and vicious than any of the other animals, and it had ten horns.

8As I was looking at the horns, suddenly another small horn appeared among them, and three of the first ones were yanked out, roots and all, to give it room; this little horn had a man's eyes and a bragging mouth.

9I watched as thrones were put in place and the Ancient of Days—the Almighty God—sat down to judge. His clothing was as white as snow, his hair like whitest wool. He sat upon a fiery throne brought in on flaming wheels, and 10a river of fire flowed from before him. Millions of angels ministered to him, and

6:25-27 Not only will we benefit from God's work in our life, but others will also reap a profit. Darius was able to see the awesome power of Daniel's God, and he was also relieved of the guilt he felt for sentencing Daniel to death. As we are patient in our sufferings, we may find that God is using us to reach others. Those who abuse or persecute us, whether intentionally or unintentionally, need God as much as we do. When God reveals himself to them through us, their lives will change, and they will want to tell others of the power of God.

7:1-14 This vision parallels Nebuchadnezzar's vision of the grand statue in chapter 2. Here, however, the presentation of the successive world empires is made from a godly perspective: they are "beastly" in their thirst for power and control. Their violence and pride stand in direct opposition to what biblical recovery is all about. We can choose to be proud and abusive, but we will suffer the same terrible fate as the fourth beast. We can also choose to enter recovery, obeying God's will for our life. If we do, we will enjoy the glory of God's kingdom forever.

hundreds of millions of people stood before him, waiting to be judged. Then the court began its session, and the books were opened.

11As I watched, the brutal fourth animal was killed and its body handed over to be burned because of its arrogance against Almighty God and the boasting of its little horn. 12As for the other three animals, their kingdoms were taken from them, but they were allowed to live a short time longer.

13Next I saw the arrival of a Man—or so he seemed to be—brought there on clouds from heaven; he approached the Ancient of Days and was presented to him. 14He was given the ruling power and glory over all the nations of the world, so that all people of every language must obey him. His power is eternal—it will never end; his government shall never fall.

15I was confused and disturbed by all I had seen [Daniel wrote in his report], 16so I approached one of those standing beside the throne and asked him the meaning of all these things, and he explained them to me.

17"These four huge animals," he said, "represent four kings who will someday rule the earth. 18But in the end the people of the Most High God shall rule the governments of the world forever and forever."

19Then I asked about the fourth animal, the one so brutal and shocking, with its iron teeth and brass claws that tore men apart and stamped others to death with its feet. 20I asked, too, about the ten horns and the little horn that came up afterward and destroyed three of the others—the horn with the eyes and the loud, bragging mouth, the one that was stronger than the others. 21For I had seen this horn warring against God's people and winning, 22until the Ancient of Days came and opened his court and vindicated his people, giving them worldwide powers of government.

23"This fourth animal," he told me, "is the fourth world power that will rule the earth. It will be more brutal than any of the others; it will devour the whole world, destroying everything before it. 24His ten horns are ten kings that will rise out of his empire; then another king will arise, more brutal than the other ten, and will destroy three of them. 25He will defy the Most High God and wear down the saints with persecution, and he will try to change all laws, morals, and customs. God's people will be helpless in his hands for three and a half years.

26"But then the Ancient of Days will come and open his court of justice and take all power from this vicious king, to consume and destroy it until the end. 27Then all nations under heaven and their power shall be given to the people of God; they shall rule all things forever, and all rulers shall serve and obey them."

28That was the end of the dream. When I awoke, I was greatly disturbed, and my face was pale with fright, but I told no one what I had seen.

CHAPTER 8

Daniel Dreams of a Ram and Goat

In the third year of the reign of King Belshazzar, I had another dream similar to the first.

2This time I was at Susa, the capital in the province of Elam, standing beside the Ulai River. 3As I was looking around, I saw a ram with two long horns standing on the riverbank; and as I watched, one of these horns began to grow, so that it was longer than the other. 4The ram butted everything out of its way, and no one could stand against it or help its victims. It did as it pleased and became very great.

5While I was wondering what this could mean, suddenly a buck goat appeared from the west so swiftly that it didn't even touch the ground. This goat, which had one very large horn between its eyes, 6rushed furiously at the two-horned ram. 7And the closer he came, the angrier he was. He charged into the ram and broke off both his horns. Now the ram was helpless, and the buck goat knocked him down and trampled him, for there was no one to rescue him.

8The victor became both proud and powerful, but suddenly, at the height of his power, his horn was broken, and in its place grew four good-sized horns pointing in four directions. 9One of these, growing slowly at first, soon became very strong and attacked the south and east, and warred against the land of Israel. 10He fought against the people of God and defeated some of their leaders. 11He even

8:5-8, 21 Although not the most prominent figure in this vision of the future, Alexander the Great, the "first great king" of Greece (8:21), presents an important lesson for those in recovery. While oppressors may seem to have great power and be invincible, God is in control of their fate. There is no one in authority who has not been put there by God (see John 19:10-11). When God deems the time right, we will be delivered and our persecutors will be judged.

challenged the Commander of the army of heaven by canceling the daily sacrifices offered to him and by defiling his Temple. 12But the army of heaven was restrained from destroying him for this transgression. As a result, truth and righteousness perished, and evil triumphed and prospered.

13Then I heard two of the holy angels talking to each other. One of them said, "How long will it be until the daily sacrifice is restored again? How long until the destruction of the Temple is avenged and God's people triumph?"

14The other replied, "Twenty-three hundred days must first go by."

15As I was trying to understand the meaning of this vision, suddenly a man was standing in front of me—or at least he looked like a man— 16and I heard a man's voice calling from across the river, "Gabriel, tell Daniel the meaning of his dream."

17So Gabriel started toward me. But as he approached, I was too frightened to stand and fell down with my face to the ground. "Son of man," he said, "you must understand that the events you have seen in your vision will not take place until the end times come."

18Then I fainted, lying face downward on the ground. But he roused me with a touch and helped me to my feet. 19"I am here," he said, "to tell you what is going to happen in the last days of the coming time of terror—for what you have seen pertains to that final event in history.

20"The two horns of the ram you saw are the kings of Media and Persia; 21the shaggy-haired goat is the nation of Greece, and its long horn represents the first great king of that country. 22When you saw the horn break off and four smaller horns replace it, this meant that the Grecian Empire will break into four sections with four kings, none of them as great as the first.

23"Toward the end of their kingdoms, when they have become morally rotten, an angry king shall rise to power with great shrewdness and intelligence. 24His power shall be mighty, but it will be satanic strength and not his own. Prospering wherever he turns, he will destroy all who oppose him, though their armies be mighty, and he will devastate God's people.

25"He will be a master of deception, defeating many by catching them off guard as they bask in false security. Without warning he will destroy them. So great will he fancy himself to be that he will even take on the Prince of Princes in battle; but in so doing he will seal his own doom, for he shall be broken by the hand of God, though no human means could overpower him.

26"And then in your vision you heard about the twenty-three hundred days to pass before the rights of worship are restored. This number is literal, and means just that. But none of these things will happen for a long time, so don't tell anyone about them yet."

27Then I grew faint and was sick for several days. Afterward I was up and around again and performed my duties for the king, but I was greatly distressed by the dream and did not understand it.

CHAPTER 9

Daniel Prays for His People

It was now the first year of the reign of King Darius, the son of Ahasuerus. (Darius was a Mede but became king of the Chaldeans.) 2In that first year of his reign, I, Daniel, learned from the book of Jeremiah the prophet, that Jerusalem must lie desolate for seventy years. 3So I earnestly pleaded with the Lord God [to end our captivity and send us back to our own land].

As I prayed, I fasted and wore rough sackcloth, and I sprinkled myself with ashes 4and confessed my sins and those of my people.

"O Lord," I prayed, "you are a great and awesome God; you always fulfill your promises of mercy to those who love you and keep

---

8:9-14, 25 This prophetic description of the domination of the Jewish people and of the Jerusalem Temple by the Greek king, Antiochus IV, carries with it an important point for recovery. Antiochus was allowed to get away with his atrocities for a period of time, but not indefinitely. The days of his abuse were numbered (8:25), and the Temple worship would begin again (8:14). The abuse we suffer is being watched by God, and he has set a limit on the amount of pain we will have to endure. In recovery we can pray to God for comfort and guidance, asking for help to get through our anguish until we are set free.

9:1-3 Daniel makes it clear that victims of dysfunctional systems need recovery, too. Because of his nation's sins, Daniel and other "innocent bystanders" were forced into captivity. But Daniel's innocence did not stop him from mourning and praying to God for release. We all suffer from the injustices of others. We don't enjoy being victimized. Our pain is real, and we need real healing. Asking God for comfort and recovery is the best thing we can do to experience healing.

your laws. [5]But we have sinned so much; we have rebelled against you and scorned your commands. [6]We have refused to listen to your servants the prophets, whom you sent again and again down through the years, with your messages to our kings and princes and to all the people.

[7]"O Lord, you are righteous; but as for us, we are always shamefaced with sin, just as you see us now; yes, all of us—the men of Judah, the people of Jerusalem, and all Israel, scattered near and far wherever you have driven us because of our disloyalty to you. [8]O Lord, we and our kings and princes and fathers are weighted down with shame because of all our sins.

[9]"But the Lord our God is merciful and pardons even those who have rebelled against him.

[10]"O Lord our God, we have disobeyed you; we have flouted all the laws you gave us through your servants, the prophets. [11]All Israel has disobeyed; we have turned away from you and haven't listened to your voice. And so the awesome curse of God has crushed us—the curse written in the law of Moses your servant. [12]And you have done exactly as you warned us you would do, for never in all history has there been a disaster like what happened at Jerusalem to us and our rulers. [13]Every curse against us written in the law of Moses has come true; all the evils he predicted—all have come. But even so we still refuse to satisfy the Lord our God by turning from our sins and doing right.

[14]"And so the Lord deliberately crushed us with the calamity he prepared; he is fair in everything he does, but we would not obey. [15]O Lord our God, you brought lasting honor to your name by removing your people from Egypt in a great display of power. Lord, do it again! Though we have sinned so much and are full of wickedness, [16]yet because of all your faithful mercies, Lord, please turn away your furious anger from Jerusalem, your own city, your holy mountain. For the heathen mock at you because your city lies in ruins for our sins.

[17]"O our God, hear your servant's prayer! Listen as I plead! Let your face shine again with peace and joy upon your desolate sanctuary—for your own glory, Lord.

[18]"O my God, bend down your ear and listen to my plea. Open your eyes and see our wretchedness, how your city lies in ruins—for everyone knows that it is yours. We don't ask because we merit help, but because you are so merciful despite our grievous sins.

[19]"O Lord, hear; O Lord, forgive. O Lord, listen to me and act! Don't delay—for your own sake, O my God, because your people and your city bear your name."

[20]Even while I was praying and confessing my sin and the sins of my people, desperately pleading with the Lord my God for Jerusalem, his holy mountain, [21]Gabriel, whom I had seen in the earlier vision, flew swiftly to me at the time of the evening sacrifice [22]and said to me, "Daniel, I am here to help you understand God's plans. [23]The moment you began praying a command was given. I am here to tell you what it was, for God loves you very much. Listen and try to understand the meaning of the vision that you saw!

[24]"The Lord has commanded 490 years of further punishment upon Jerusalem and your people. Then at last they will learn to stay away from sin, and their guilt will be cleansed; then the kingdom of everlasting righteousness will begin, and the Most Holy Place (in the Temple) will be rededicated, as the prophets have declared. [25]Now listen! It will be 49 years plus 434 years from the time the command is given to rebuild Jerusalem until the Anointed One comes! Jerusalem's streets and walls will be rebuilt despite the perilous times.

[26]"After this period of 434 years, the Anointed One will be killed, his kingdom still unrealized . . . and a king will arise whose armies will destroy the city and the Temple.

9:10-14 Denial is incredibly powerful. Daniel said that the people of Israel had suffered all the curses that God had promised to send for their disobedience. Yet even after all their suffering, the people still wouldn't do right and follow God. Had the Israelites been spiritually honest, they could have been aware of their first mistakes and corrected the situation immediately. They could have avoided much of their severe punishment. When we first feel the harmful effects of our addiction, we need to be honest with ourself and God and ask him to help us overcome the problem. It is not necessary for us to wait for destruction before turning to God for help and healing.

9:20-27 Though Daniel was worried about his people and country, God had a plan for their recovery. The road would not be easy, and Israel would have many years of pain ahead, but God's time to judge his enemies would come (after a symbolic 490 years). God hasn't abandoned us in our hour of need. He is there, waiting to work his plan for our life. We are to follow God and trust in his timing for our complete recovery.

They will be overwhelmed as with a flood, and war and its miseries are decreed from that time to the very end. 27This king will make a seven-year treaty with the people, but after half that time, he will break his pledge and stop the Jews from all their sacrifices and their offerings; then, as a climax to all his terrible deeds, the Enemy shall utterly defile the sanctuary of God. But in God's time and plan, his judgment will be poured out upon this Evil One."

CHAPTER 10

A Heavenly Messenger

In the third year of the reign of Cyrus, king of Persia, Daniel (also called Belteshazzar) had another vision. It concerned events certain to happen in the future: times of great tribulation—wars and sorrows, and this time he understood what the vision meant.

2When this vision came to me [Daniel said later], I had been in mourning for three full weeks. 3All that time I tasted neither wine nor meat, and, of course, I went without desserts. I neither washed nor shaved nor combed my hair.

4Then one day early in April, as I was standing beside the great Tigris River, 5,6I looked up, and suddenly there before me stood a person robed in linen garments, with a belt of purest gold around his waist and glowing, lustrous skin! From his face came blinding flashes like lightning, and his eyes were pools of fire; his arms and feet shone like polished brass, and his voice was like the roaring of a vast multitude of people.

7I, Daniel, alone saw this great vision; the men with me saw nothing, but they were suddenly filled with unreasoning terror and ran to hide, 8so I was left alone. When I saw this frightening vision, my strength left me, and I grew pale and weak with fright.

9Then he spoke to me, and I fell to the ground face downward in a deep faint. 10But a hand touched me and lifted me, still trembling, to my hands and knees. 11And I heard his voice—"O Daniel, greatly beloved of God," he said, "stand up and listen carefully to what I have to say to you, for God has sent me to you." So I stood up, still trembling with fear.

12Then he said, "Don't be frightened, Daniel, for your request has been heard in heaven and was answered the very first day you began to fast before the Lord and pray for understanding; that very day I was sent here to meet you. 13But for twenty-one days the mighty Evil Spirit who overrules the kingdom of Persia blocked my way. Then Michael, one of the top officers of the heavenly army, came to help me, so that I was able to break through these spirit rulers of Persia. 14Now I am here to tell you what will happen to your people, the Jews, at the end times—for the fulfillment of this prophecy is many years away."

15All this time I was looking down, unable to speak a word. 16Then someone—he looked like a man—touched my lips and I could talk again, and I said to the messenger from heaven, "Sir, I am terrified by your appearance and have no strength. 17How can such a person as I even talk to you? For my strength is gone, and I can hardly breathe."

18Then the one who seemed to be a man touched me again, and I felt my strength returning. 19"God loves you very much," he said; "don't be afraid! Calm yourself; be strong—yes, strong!"

Suddenly, as he spoke these words, I felt stronger and said to him, "Now you can go ahead and speak, sir, for you have strengthened me."

20,21He replied, "Do you know why I have come? I am here to tell you what is written in the 'Book of the Future.' Then, when I leave, I will go again to fight my way back, past the prince of Persia; and after him, the prince of Greece. Only Michael, the angel who guards your people Israel, will be there to help me."

10:11, 18 God twice assured Daniel of his great and personal love. And God also loves each one of us. When we realize that the Creator of the universe finds value in us, we will then understand that our identity isn't wrapped up in our job, possessions, or power. When we truly believe this, we can stop our workaholism and begin to feel good about ourself because God loves us.

10:12-13 An important but largely overlooked aspect of recovery has to do with our prayer life and the spiritual warfare we face in the unseen realm. Those of us seeking recovery often have a difficult time praying and tend to give up easily if our prayers are not quickly answered. Satan is aware of this and uses unseen warriors to intercept God's messengers and to discourage God's people (see also Ephesians 6:11-12). It may well be that God actually answers the recovering believer's prayer quickly, but the answer is delayed because of unseen spiritual conflict. If we want answers to our prayers, we should keep on praying until we get our responses.

CHAPTER 11

Predictions for the Future

"I was the one sent to strengthen and help Darius the Mede in the first year of his reign. 2But now I will show you what the future holds. Three more Persian kings will reign, to be succeeded by a fourth, far richer than the others. Using his wealth for political advantage, he will plan total war against Greece.

3"Then a mighty king will rise in Greece, a king who will rule a vast kingdom and accomplish everything he sets out to do. 4But at the zenith of his power, his kingdom will break apart and be divided into four weaker nations, not even ruled by his sons. For his empire will be torn apart and given to others.5One of them, the king of Egypt, will increase in power, but this king's own officials will rebel against him and take away his kingdom and make it still more powerful.

6"Several years later an alliance will be formed between the king of Syria and the king of Egypt. The daughter of the king of Egypt will be given in marriage to the king of Syria as a gesture of peace, but she will lose her influence over him, and not only will her hopes be blighted, but those of her father, the king of Egypt, and of her ambassador and child. 7But when her brother takes over as king of Egypt, he will raise an army against the king of Syria and march against him and defeat him. 8When he returns again to Egypt, he will carry back their idols with him, along with priceless gold and silver dishes; and for many years afterward he will leave the Syrian king alone.

9"Meanwhile, the king of Syria will invade Egypt briefly but will soon return again to his own land. 10,11However, the sons of this Syrian king will assemble a mighty army that will overflow across Israel into Egypt, to a fortress there. Then the king of Egypt, in great anger, will rally against the vast forces of Syria and defeat them. 12Filled with pride after this great victory, he will have many thousands of his enemies killed, but his success will be short-lived.

13"A few years later the Syrian king will return with a fully-equipped army far greater than the one he lost, 14and other nations will join him in a crusade against Egypt. Insurgents among your own people, the Jews, will join them, thus fulfilling prophecy, but they will not succeed. 15Then the Syrian king and his allies will come and lay siege to a fortified city of Egypt and capture it, and the proud armies of Egypt will go down to defeat.

16"The Syrian king will march onward unopposed; none will be able to stop him. And he will also enter 'The Glorious Land' of Israel and pillage it. 17This will be his plot for conquering all Egypt: he, too, will form an alliance with the Egyptian king, giving him a daughter in marriage, so that she can work for him from within. But the plan will fail.

18"After this he will turn his attention to the coastal cities and conquer many. But a general will stop him and cause him to retreat in shame. 19He will turn homeward again but will have trouble on the way and disappear.

20"His successor will be remembered as the king who sent a tax collector into Israel, but after a very brief reign, he will die mysteriously, though neither in battle nor in riot.

21"Next to come to power will be an evil man not directly in line for royal succession. But during a crisis he will take over the kingdom by flattery and intrigue. 22Then all opposition will be swept away before him, including a leader of the priests. 23His promises will be worthless. From the first his method will be deceit; with a mere handful of followers, he will become strong. 24He will enter the richest areas of the land without warning and do something never done before: he will take the property and wealth of the rich and scatter it out among the people. With great success he will besiege and capture powerful strongholds throughout his dominions, but this will last for only a short while. 25Then he will stir up his courage and raise a great army against Egypt; and Egypt, too, will raise a mighty army, but to no avail, for plots against him will succeed.

26"Those of his own household will bring his downfall; his army will desert, and many be killed.

27"Both these kings will be plotting against each other at the conference table, attempting to deceive each other. But it will make no

11:12 The king of Egypt's success would be short-lived, probably as God's judgment against his pride. If there is anyone God cannot help, it is the proud person who thinks he should be credited with all his successes. God is the one effecting changes within us. When we begin to believe that *we* have made progress because of our own work, we only distance ourself from God and lose ground in our recovery. Remembering to thank God for the work he is doing in us and giving him the credit he deserves will help us to keep depending on him.

difference, for neither can succeed until God's
appointed time has come.
28"The Syrian king will then return home
with great riches, first marching through Israel and destroying it. 29Then at the predes-
tined time he will once again turn his armies
southward, as he had threatened, but now it
will be a very different story from those first
two occasions. 30,31For Roman warships will
scare him off, and he will withdraw and return home. Angered by having to retreat, the
Syrian king will again pillage Jerusalem and
pollute the sanctuary, putting a stop to the
daily sacrifices, and worshiping idols inside
the Temple. He will leave godless Jews in
power when he leaves—men who have abandoned their fathers' faith. 32He will flatter
those who hate the things of God and win
them over to his side. But the people who
know their God shall be strong and do great
things.
33"Those with spiritual understanding will
have a wide ministry of teaching in those
days. But they will be in constant danger,
many of them dying by fire and sword, or
being jailed and robbed. 34Eventually these
pressures will subside, and some ungodly
men will come, pretending to offer a helping
hand, only to take advantage of them.
35"And some who are most gifted in the
things of God will stumble in those days and
fall, but this will only refine and cleanse them
and make them pure until the final end of all
their trials, at God's appointed time.
36"The king will do exactly as he pleases,
claiming to be greater than every god there is,
even blaspheming the God of gods, and prospering—until his time is up. For God's plans
are unshakable. 37He will have no regard for
the gods of his fathers, nor for the god beloved of women, nor any other god, for he
will boast that he is greater than them all.
38Instead of these, he will worship the Fortress
god—a god his fathers never knew—and lavish on him costly gifts! 39Claiming this god's
help, he will have great success against the
strongest fortresses. He will honor those who
submit to him, appointing them to positions
of authority and dividing the land to them as
their reward.
40"Then at the time of the end, the king of
the south will attack him again, and the
northern king will react with the strength and
fury of a whirlwind; his vast army and navy
will rush out to bury him with their might.
41He will invade various lands on the way,
including Israel, the Pleasant Land, and overthrow the governments of many nations.
Moab, Edom, and most of Ammon will escape, 42but Egypt and many other lands will
be occupied. 43 He will capture all the treasures
of Egypt, and the Libyans and Ethiopians
shall be his servants.
44"But then news from the east and north
will alarm him, and he will return in great
anger to destroy as he goes. 45He will halt
between Jerusalem and the sea and there
pitch his royal tents, but while he is there his
time will suddenly run out, and there will be
no one to help him."

CHAPTER 12

A Prophecy of the Last Days

"At that time Michael, the mighty angelic
prince who stands guard over your nation,
will stand up [and fight for you in heaven
against satanic forces], and there will be a
time of anguish for the Jews greater than any
previous suffering in Jewish history. And yet
every one of your people whose names are
written in the Book will endure it.
2"And many of those whose bodies lie dead
and buried will rise up, some to everlasting
life and some to shame and everlasting contempt.
3"And those who are wise—the people of
God—shall shine as brightly as the sun's bril-

11:35 Stumbling in our recovery can serve to cleanse and strengthen us. We can look at these times when we stumble as a weight lifter looks at weights. If they weren't hard to lift, he wouldn't gain any muscle. At first we may stumble a lot, but as we struggle, we grow stronger in our recovery. Eventually we will be able to resist greater and greater temptations where we once would have fallen. Through these spiritual workouts we gradually are transformed from a ninety-five-pound weakling to a strongman.

12:1-4, 13 As we face recovery, we would probably like to believe that life will never again be as painful as it was before recovery. That, however, cannot be guaranteed. Prior to the Resurrection at the end of the age, there will be a time of unparalleled suffering for God's people, and, between now and then, there will be consistent tribulation for God's people (see Acts 14:22). While we may distinguish ourself by our faith, courage, and wisdom during that time, we will never have answers to all our questions in this life. However, we have the assurance that we will be with God and will understand everything in the end.

liance, and those who turn many to righteousness will glitter like stars forever.

[4]"But Daniel, keep this prophecy a secret; seal it up so that it will not be understood until the end times, when travel and education shall be vastly increased!"

[5]Then I, Daniel, looked and saw two men on each bank of a river. [6]And one of them asked the man in linen robes who was standing now above the river, "How long will it be until all these terrors end?"

[7]He replied, with both hands lifted to heaven, taking oath by him who lives forever and ever, that they will not end until three and a half years after the power of God's people has been crushed.

[8]I heard what he said, but I didn't understand what he meant. So I said, "Sir, how will all this finally end?"

[9]But he said, "Go now, Daniel, for what I have said is not to be understood until the time of the end. [10]Many shall be purified by great trials and persecutions. But the wicked shall continue in their wickedness, and none of them will understand. Only those who are willing to learn will know what it means.

[11]"From the time the daily sacrifice is taken away and the Horrible Thing is set up to be worshiped, there will be 1,290 days. [12]And blessed are those who wait and remain until the 1335th day!

[13]"But go on now to the end of your life and your rest; for you will rise again and have your full share of those last days."

12:10 The suffering that may have to be endured by those in recovery will, thankfully, have a very positive effect. These difficult trials will teach us lessons to help us in the future. But for those who deny the truth, there will be no learning and no purification. Through openness, honesty, and self-examination we will gain our recovery and become the people God wants us to be.

insights FROM DANIEL'S LIFE

When we use the talents and abilities given to us by God, others will notice. In **Daniel 1:17-21** King Nebuchadnezzar saw that Daniel and his friends had more insight than any of his other magicians or astrologers. The wisdom of these young men is what set them apart from the other advisers and allowed them to overcome their disastrous past. God supplies us with all that we need to triumph over our past.

In **Daniel 2:16-22** we are given a model for action when we are in trouble. Daniel needed help, so he gathered his godly friends and prayed. Then, after the prayer was granted, Daniel praised God for his blessings. Praying with others to overcome our dependencies, and thanking God for the power to do what we asked, is essential to our recovery. It is easy to forget that God is in control of our recovery and instead think that we have defeated our addiction on our own. Thanking God for the progress he allows us to accomplish will help us maintain a proper focus on God.

In **Daniel 6:6-10** the prophet chose to ignore the manipulation of his rivals and continued to worship God, who had cared for Daniel throughout his life. Fortunately prayer doesn't earn the death penalty for most of us, but there are other drawbacks to following God. We can be made fun of, discriminated against, or beaten up by people who are threatened by our faith. No matter what opposition we face, however, God is still worthy of our trust. Our recovery depends on our worshiping him despite the consequences.

In **Daniel 6:19-23** God rescued Daniel from what seemed a sure death. The lions didn't harm Daniel, just as the fire hadn't touched Shadrach, Meshach, and Abednego (see 3:1-30). It is clear that God protects those who obey his will. He is able to save us when no one else can. Even when we are in abusive situations with no hope of escape, God is still able to deliver us. We need to continue to trust in him.

Everyone is guilty of sinning against God, and we all need recovery from the eternal consequences of sin—death (see Romans 6:23). In **Daniel 9:7-9** even the godly prophet, Daniel, admitted his sins, asked for God's mercy, and turned his life over to God. These are the same steps needed in our recovery from powerful dependencies and their consequences. Twenty-five centuries have not changed the way God works in people's lives.

***insights** FROM THE LIVES OF THE THREE FRIENDS

We all face situations in which we are tempted to do things that are wrong. Sometimes there are consequences for not going along with the crowd. This fact is clearly illustrated in **Daniel 3:1-30,** the story of the fiery furnace. The penalty for not going with the flow was death by burning. When we stand for what is right and refuse to go along with the crowd, we may suffer any number of consequences: ostracism, ridicule, or physical abuse, to name a few. But we must have the courage to do what is right and resist those who want us to step outside our established boundaries of godly behavior.

In **Daniel 3:16-23** Shadrach, Meshach, and Abednego put their faith on the line by not giving in to Nebuchadnezzar's threats. They risked their lives in order to obey what they knew to be God's will for them. To die was better than to live with the guilt and shame of disobeying God. Do we have the faith we need to stand up against our oppressors in order to follow God? If we do, we will be rewarded. If not, our recovery will fail.

HOSEA

THE BIG PICTURE

A. HOSEA'S MARRIAGE: A PICTURE OF GOD'S UNFAILING LOVE (1:1–3:5)
   1. Hosea's Dysfunctional Family (1:1–2:1)
   2. The Unfaithful Wife and Mother (2:2-13)
   3. The Reconciliation of Husband and Wife (2:14-23)
   4. The Recovery of the Unfaithful Wife (3:1-5)

B. HOSEA'S MESSAGES: TEACHING ABOUT GOD'S UNFAILING LOVE (4:1–14:9)
   1. God's Complaints against Israel (4:1-19)
   2. Israel's Refusal to Return to God (5:1–8:14)
   3. God Uses "Tough Love" (9:1-9)
   4. Israel's History of Rejecting God's Love (9:10–13:16)
   5. The Reconciliation of God and Israel (14:1-9)

God called Hosea to reveal through word and deed that God loved his people and desired to restore his relationship with them. God initiated his message by commanding Hosea to marry a woman whom both God and Hosea knew from the start would never be a faithful wife. As soon as Hosea and his wife's children were born, she prostituted herself and, in time, became enslaved. In response to God's command, Hosea then redeemed his wife from slavery and restored her to the family. God intended this demonstration of unconditional love to be a symbol of his own love for the people of Israel.

The book of Hosea tells the story of God's stormy relationship with his people. God treated them with mercy and compassion even though they rejected him and his will for them time and again. But though God was angered by the unfaithfulness of his people, he never rejected them completely. Neither did he enable their sin by extending unqualified mercy, but allowed Israel to suffer the consequences of their disobedience. He made their restoration possible through repentance and perseverance during a period of painful exile.

The story of Hosea's gracious love for Gomer is the story of God's love for the wayward Israelites. It is also the story of God's love for us. We, too, sometimes choose the way of disobedience that leads inevitably toward suffering and exile. But as God did with Israel, he often uses the pain of exile to bring us to our senses and lead us back to him. It is then that we experience God's unfailing love and the healing that is possible through an intimate relationship with him.

THE BOTTOM LINE

PURPOSE: To reveal God's unending love for his sinful people and God's desire to restore their relationship with him. AUTHOR: The prophet Hosea. AUDIENCE: The people of the northern kingdom of Israel. DATE WRITTEN: Approximately 715 B.C., shortly after the years of Hosea's ministry (755–722 B.C.). SETTING: The northern kingdom of Israel just prior to its conquest by Assyria in 722 B.C.. KEY VERSE: "Plant the good seeds of righteousness, and you will reap a crop of my love; plow the hard ground of your hearts, for now is the time to seek the Lord, that he may come and shower salvation upon you" (10:12). KEY PEOPLE AND RELATIONSHIPS: Hosea, his wife Gomer, and their children.

RECOVERY THEMES

The Power of Committed Love: It is always hard to love people who don't deserve it, but these are the people who need to be loved the most. The kind of love that God pours out on us is unconditional. It has a powerful healing effect, especially when we are helplessly trapped by our dependencies and feel unworthy of love. Throughout the book of Hosea we hear this message again and again: God loves us and reaches out to us no matter how unworthy we are. Understanding this fact is foundational for our healing and recovery.

Tough Love Leads to Recovery: God will never enable us to live a destructive life-style. His love is tough; it is confrontational. He cares enough to stop us before we are destroyed by our decisions and activities. Sometimes God uses suffering to help us realize that our life-style has destructive consequences. God revealed his love for his people by allowing them to suffer the pain of captivity in a foreign land. All too often our love becomes enabling instead of healing. Not so with God. He knows that it takes tough love to help us accept how powerless we are and how much we need his help in the process of recovery.

God Is Merciful: When Hosea found Gomer, his intent was not punishment but mercy. He was concerned about her restoration and recovery. When God allowed Israel to be conquered by Assyria, this was an expression of his mercy toward her. It was a significant part of God's program for Israel's restoration and recovery. We can be confident that as we put our life in God's hands, he will use even the painful periods in our life to bring healing. God is ready and willing to show mercy to all who turn to him for help.

Never "Too Far Gone" for God: Gomer was a failure; she ended up selling herself into slavery in order to survive. But Hosea did not give up on her. Israel likewise was a failure; she turned to other gods in her rebellion. But God did not give up on her. If we have become slaves of our dependencies and feel powerless to change, we can be sure that God will never give up on us.

CHAPTER 1

Hosea's Wife and Children

These are the messages from the Lord to Hosea, son of Beeri, during the reigns of these
four kings of Judah:
Uzziah, Jotham, Ahaz, and Hezekiah; and
one of the kings of Israel, Jeroboam, son of
Joash.
2Here is the first message:
The Lord said to Hosea, "Go and marry a
girl who is a prostitute, so that some of her
children will be born to you from other men.
This will illustrate the way my people have
been untrue to me, committing open adultery
against me by worshiping other gods."
3So Hosea married Gomer, daughter of Dib-
laim, and she conceived and bore him a son.
4,5And the Lord said, "Name the child Jezreel, for in the Valley of Jezreel I am about to
punish King Jehu's dynasty to avenge the
murders he committed; in fact, I will put an
end to Israel as an independent kingdom,
breaking the power of the nation in the Valley
of Jezreel."
6Soon Gomer had another child—this one
a daughter. And God said to Hosea, "Name
her Lo-ruhamah (meaning 'No more mercy')
for I will have no more mercy upon Israel, to
forgive her again. 7But I *will* have mercy on
the tribe of Judah. I will personally free her
from her enemies without any help from her
armies or her weapons."
8After Gomer had weaned Lo-ruhamah, she
again conceived and this time gave birth to a

1:2-3 God told Hosea to marry a woman who would become a prostitute. Their relationship would symbolize God's relationship with Israel, who prostituted herself to the false gods of her pagan neighbors. Using this analogy, it becomes easy to see how it must hurt God when we seek other sources for our recovery, whether psychics and crystals, or any recovery program that ignores our need for God. When we are in trouble, we should turn to God, our "husband" (see 2 Corinthians 11:2). He loves us and wants to take care of us, no matter how great our past failures.

1:6 At first glance, God seemed to be saying that his relationship with Israel had ended. But naming the daughter Lo-ruhamah ("No more mercy") indicated a situation of tough love. God had shown mercy in the past despite Israel's unrepentant condition. Now genuine love demanded that he withdraw that mercy to allow her to suffer the consequences of her actions, bringing her to abandon all of her false hopes. Allowing others to experience the consequences of their wrong actions is often hard for us to do because (1) we don't want our loved ones to suffer, and (2) we feel a sense of importance when we help our loved ones. But codependent relationships don't teach addicted people the lessons of responsibility and accountability. Often the best thing we can do for people who keep falling is to refuse to catch them. We may need to let them fall so they can learn from the painful consequences of their actions and seek recovery.

son. 9And God said, "Call him Lo-ammi
(meaning 'Not mine'), for Israel is not mine
and I am not her God.
10"Yet the time will come when Israel shall
prosper and become a great nation; in that
day her people will be too numerous to
count—like sand along a seashore! Then, instead of saying to them, 'You are not my
people,' I will tell them, 'You are my sons,
children of the Living God.' 11Then the people
of Judah and Israel will unite and have one
leader; they will return from exile together;
what a day that will be—the day when God
will sow his people in the fertile soil of their
own land again."

CHAPTER 2

Punishment and Restoration

"O Jezreel, rename your brother and sister.
Call your brother Ammi (which means "Now
you are mine"); name your sister Ruhamah
("Pitied"), for now God will have mercy upon
her!
2"Plead with your mother, for she has become another man's wife—I am no longer her
husband. Beg her to stop her harlotry, to quit
giving herself to others. 3If she doesn't, I will
strip her as naked as the day she was born and
cause her to waste away and die of thirst as in
a land riddled with famine and drought. 4And
I will not give special favors to her children as
I would to my own, for they are not my
children; they belong to other men.
5"For their mother has committed adultery.
She did a shameful thing when she said, 'I'll
run after other men and sell myself to them
for food and drinks and clothes.'
6"But I will fence her in with briars and
thornbushes; I'll block the road before her to
make her lose her way, so that 7when she runs
after her lovers she will not catch up with
them. She will search for them but not find
them. Then she will think, 'I might as well
return to my husband, for I was better off with
him than I am now.'
8"She doesn't realize that all she has, has
come from me. It was I who gave her all the
gold and silver she used in worshiping Baal,
her god!
9"But now I will take back the wine and
ripened corn I constantly supplied, and the
clothes I gave her to cover her nakedness—I
will no longer give her rich harvests of grain
in its season or wine at the time of the grape
harvest. 10Now I will expose her nakedness in
public for all her lovers to see, and no one will
be able to rescue her from my hand.
11"I will put an end to all her joys, her
parties, holidays, and feasts. 12I will destroy
her vineyards and her orchards—gifts she
claims her lovers gave her—and let them
grow into a jungle; wild animals will eat their
fruit.
13"For all the incense she burned to Baal her
idol and for the times when she put on her
earrings and jewels and went out looking for
her lovers and deserted me—for all these
things I will punish her," says the Lord.
14"But I will court her again and bring her
into the wilderness, and I will speak to her
tenderly there. 15There I will give back her
vineyards to her and transform her Valley of
Troubles into a Door of Hope. She will respond to me there, singing with joy as in days
long ago in her youth after I had freed her
from captivity in Egypt.
16"In that coming day," says the Lord, "she
will call me 'My Husband' instead of 'My
Master.' 17O Israel, I will cause you to forget
your idols, and their names will not be spoken
anymore.
18"At that time I will make a treaty between
you and the wild animals, birds, and snakes,
not to fear each other any more; and I will
destroy all weapons, and all wars will end.
"Then you will lie down in peace and
safety, unafraid; 19and I will bind you to me
forever with chains of righteousness and justice and love and mercy. 20I will betroth you
to me in faithfulness and love, and you will

2:5-13 Our addictions and compulsions are like Israel's worship of foreign gods, because in them we search for the joy and fulfillment that only God can give. And while God is patient with us, if we put off our recovery there will come the day when he will turn us over to the consequences of our addictions. We will feel shame and suffer physical pain as well. God will refuse to rescue us because we need to see just what our "gods" have given us. But even though we have failed, we can have hope because God loves us; we don't have to die in our sins. If we turn to God for help, we will be redeemed.

2:21-22 God is in control of nature, and nature praises him. If God can control the rain and the growth of plants, he certainly can control the events of our life. We, too, like nature, must proclaim that God "has given all," because without his help, we would still be in the parched desert of our addictions. As we sing out our story of deliverance, we will not only encourage others to persevere, but we will also find renewed strength for our own recovery.

really know me then as you never have before.

[21,22]"In that day," says the Lord, "I will answer the pleading of the sky for clouds, to pour down water on the earth in answer to its cry for rain. Then the earth can answer the parched cry of the grain, the grapes, and the olive trees for moisture and for dew—and the whole grand chorus shall sing together that "God sows!" He has given all!

[23]"At that time I will sow a crop of Israelites and raise them for myself! I will pity those who are 'not pitied,' and I will say to those who are 'not my people,' 'Now you are my people'; and they will reply, 'You are our God!'"

CHAPTER 3
Hosea Is Reconciled to His Wife

Then the Lord said to me, "Go, and get your wife again and bring her back to you and love her, even though she loves adultery. For the Lord still loves Israel though she has turned to other gods and offered them choice gifts."

[2]So I bought her [back from her slavery] for a couple of dollars and eight bushels of barley, [3]and I said to her, "You must live alone for many days; do not go out with other men nor be a prostitute, and I will wait for you."

[4]This illustrates the fact that Israel will be a long time without a king or prince, and without an altar, temple, priests, or even idols!

[5]Afterward they will return to the Lord their God and to the Messiah, their King, and they shall come trembling, submissive to the Lord and to his blessings in the end times.

CHAPTER 4
God's Case against Israel

Hear the word of the Lord, O people of Israel. The Lord has filed a lawsuit against you listing the following charges: "There is no faithfulness, no kindness, no knowledge of God in your land. [2]You swear and lie and kill and steal and commit adultery. There is violence everywhere, with one murder after another.

[3]"That is why your land is not producing; it is filled with sadness, and all living things grow sick and die; the animals, the birds, and even the fish begin to disappear.

[4]"Don't point your finger at someone else and try to pass the blame to him! Look, priest, I am pointing my finger at *you*. [5]As a sentence for your crimes, you priests will stumble in broad daylight as well as in the night, and so will your false 'prophets' too; and I will destroy your mother, Israel. [6]My people are destroyed because they don't know me, and it is all your fault, you priests, for you yourselves refuse to know me; therefore, I refuse to rec-

3:1-2 Hosea was able to heal his broken family by redeeming, or buying back, his wife Gomer. His extraordinary love is highlighted by this unexpected action. She did not come back to him, so he went to her and paid money to get her back. This symbolizes God's love, which is even more extraordinary. While we were still sinners, God sent his son, Jesus, who gave his life for us (Romans 5:8). We can experience the ultimate recovery by accepting a relationship with Christ, becoming his "bride." In this relationship God offers us his constant help and companionship.

4:1-2 God wanted his people to examine their lives honestly. They had ignored the healthy boundaries set up by the Ten Commandments (see Exodus 20:1-17; Deuteronomy 5:6-21). Their lack of commitment to God was at the root of their destructive behaviors (cursing, lying, murdering, stealing, and committing adultery). This should encourage us to take a moral inventory so we can become aware of any shortcomings and correct them before we stray too far from God's laws. If we are honest in our self-examination and confession, God will give us the healing forgiveness we need for recovery.

4:7-9 Leaders carry great responsibility. They are responsible not only for their own spiritual well-being, but also for the well-being of those who follow them. If we are at the point in recovery in which we are sharing the good news of God's deliverance in our life, we must be sure to stay on the right path and not lapse back into destructive patterns. Those who look to us for guidance will do as we do, not as we say. If we hope to help others stay on the road to recovery, we need to stay on the road, too.

4:15-17 Judah was warned to stay away from Israel, lest she be tempted to follow in the footsteps of her unfaithful sister nation. We can heed this warning, too. Since we tend to conform to the people around us, it makes sense to stay away from those who are engaging in immoral or addictive behaviors. To stay firmly on the path of recovery, we would do well to surround ourself with people who are following God and the principles of recovery.

5:3-4 The guilt and love of adultery kept the people away from God. In their arrogance they refused to admit their wrongdoing and turn their life back over to God. Though our addictions may bring us a temporary thrill, we can never escape their destructive consequences. Like Israel, we will stumble and fall unless we turn to God for forgiveness and healing.

ognize you as my priests. Since you have
forgotten my laws, I will 'forget' to bless your
children. 7The more my people multiplied,
the more they sinned against me. They exchanged the glory of God for the disgrace of
idols.
8"The priests rejoice in the sins of the
people; they lap it up and lick their lips for
more! 9And thus it is: 'Like priests, like
people'—because the priests are wicked, the
people are too. Therefore, I will punish both
priests and people for all their wicked deeds.
10They will eat and still be hungry. Though
they do a big business as prostitutes, they
shall have no children, for they have deserted
me and turned to other gods.
11"Wine, women, and song have robbed my
people of their brains. 12For they are asking a
piece of wood to tell them what to do. 'Divine
Truth' comes to them through tea leaves!
Longing after idols has made them foolish.
For they have played the harlot, serving other
gods, deserting me. 13They sacrifice to idols on
the tops of mountains; they go up into the
hills to burn incense in the pleasant shade of
oaks and poplars and sumac trees.
"There your daughters turn to prostitution
and your brides commit adultery. 14But why
should I punish them? For you men are doing
the same thing, sinning with harlots and
temple prostitutes. Fools! Your doom is
sealed, for you refuse to understand.
15"But though Israel is a prostitute, may
Judah stay far from such a life. O Judah, do
not join with those who insincerely worship
me at Gilgal and at Bethel. Their worship is
mere pretense. 16Don't be like Israel, stubborn
as a heifer, resisting the Lord's attempts to
lead her in green pastures. 17Stay away from
her, for she is wedded to idolatry.
18"The men of Israel finish up their drinking bouts, and off they go to find some
whores. Their love for shame is greater than
for honor.
19"Therefore, a mighty wind shall sweep
them away; they shall die in shame because
they sacrifice to idols."

CHAPTER 5

Israel Is Declared Guilty

"Listen to this, you priests and all of Israel's
leaders; listen, all you men of the royal family:
You are doomed! For you have deluded the
people with idols at Mizpah and Tabor 2and
dug a deep pit to trap them at Acacia. But
never forget—I will settle up with all of you
for what you've done.

Love

READ HOSEA 3:1-5

If we have broken trust with a spouse, especially if we have violated our marriage vows, making amends will take time. Perhaps we have made so many false promises in the past that our spouse will need time before fully trusting our love.

The prophet Hosea was told by God to marry a prostitute. His marriage was to be a living example to the nation of Israel of her infidelity toward God. It had to hurt Hosea deeply when she returned to her life of prostitution. Hosea said, "Then the Lord said to me, 'Go, and get your wife again and bring her back to you and love her, even though she loves adultery. For the Lord still loves Israel though she has turned to other gods and offered them choice gifts.' So I bought her [back from her slavery] for a couple of dollars and eight bushels of barley, and I said to her, 'You must live alone for many days; do not go out with other men nor be a prostitute, and I will wait for you'" (Hosea 3:1-3).

Hosea needed some time before he could be close to his wife again. Sometimes the best way we can make amends with our mate is to allow time to go by. During that time, we can demonstrate to our spouse that there is no reason to fear that our wrong behavior has continued. Love and trust must come together. If our spouse feels the need for a time of separation to see that our commitment is real, we need to give him or her that time and focus on our own recovery. ***Turn to page 925, Hosea 10.***

3I have seen your evil deeds: Israel, you have left me as a prostitute leaves her husband; you are utterly defiled. 4Your deeds won't let you come to God again, for the spirit of adultery is deep within you, and you cannot know the Lord.

5"The very arrogance of Israel testifies against her in my court. She will stumble under her load of guilt, and Judah, too, shall fall. 6Then at last, they will come with their flocks and herds to sacrifice to God, but it will be too late—they will not find him. He has withdrawn from them and they are left alone.

7"For they have betrayed the honor of the Lord, bearing children that aren't his. Suddenly they and all their wealth will disappear. 8Sound the alarm! Warn with trumpet blasts in Gibeah and Ramah, and on over to Beth-aven; tremble, land of Benjamin! 9Hear this announcement, Israel: When your day of punishment comes, you will become a heap of rubble.

10"The leaders of Judah have become the lowest sort of thieves. Therefore, I will pour my anger down upon them like a waterfall, 11and Ephraim will be crushed and broken by my sentence because she is determined to follow idols. 12I will destroy her as a moth does wool; I will sap away the strength of Judah like dry rot.

13"When Ephraim and Judah see how sick they are, Ephraim will turn to Assyria, to the great king there, but he can neither help nor cure.

14"I will tear Ephraim and Judah as a lion rips apart its prey; I will carry them off and chase all rescuers away.

15"I will abandon them and return to my home until they admit their guilt and look to me for help again, for as soon as trouble comes, they will search for me and say:

CHAPTER 6

"'Come, let us return to the Lord; it is he who has torn us—he will heal us. He has wounded—he will bind us up. 2In just a couple of days, or three at the most, he will set us on our feet again to live in his kindness! 3Oh, that we might know the Lord! Let us press on to know him, and he will respond to us as surely as the coming of dawn or the rain of early spring.'"

God Wants Israel's Love

4"O Ephraim and Judah, what shall I do with you? For your love vanishes like morning clouds, and disappears like dew. 5I sent my prophets to warn you of your doom; I have slain you with the words of my mouth, threatening you with death. Suddenly, without warning, my judgment will strike you as surely as day follows night.

6"I don't want your sacrifices—I want your love; I don't want your offerings—I want you to know me.

7"But like Adam, you broke my covenant; you refused my love. 8Gilead is a city of sinners, tracked with footprints of blood. 9Her citizens are gangs of robbers, lying in ambush for their victims; packs of priests murder along the road to Shechem and practice every kind of sin. 10Yes, I have seen a horrible thing in Israel—Ephraim chasing other gods, Israel utterly defiled.

11"O Judah, for you also there is a plentiful harvest of punishment waiting—and I wanted so much to bless you!"

5:13 The people of Israel and Judah would recognize their need for help, but they would turn to the wrong source for recovery, and they would pay for it with their lives. If we are honest enough in our self-examination, and penetrate deeply enough, we will see that no one is able to heal our disease except God. Turning to any other source for healing would be like refusing to have surgery performed by a doctor and choosing a butcher instead!

6:1-3 These verses contain several of the steps to recovery. The people admitted their helplessness, viewing themselves as "torn" and "wounded" (Step One). They committed their lives to God, deciding to "return to the Lord" (Step Three). They decided to let God change them, affirming that he would "heal" and "bind" them (Step Seven). They sought to improve their relationship with God, saying, "Oh, that we might know the Lord!" (Step Eleven). Finally, they wanted to help others by encouraging each other in the process of returning to God, "Let us press on to know him" (Step Twelve).

6:6 The way we treat other people gives us a good idea of how committed we are to God. Our religious worship activities can be acted out without any true feeling. They may prove nothing more than that we know the rituals. Acting kindly toward others and forgiving those who have hurt us not only proves that we are growing spiritually; it also helps us to grow even more. God is not saying here that he does not value our sincere acts of worship; he values them greatly. But if our worship is sincere, it will always be coupled with an active obedience to his will.

CHAPTER 7

Israel Is like a Crooked Bow

"I wanted to forgive Israel, but her sins were far too great—no one can even live in Samaria without being a liar, thief, and bandit!

2"Her people never seem to recognize that I am watching them. Their sinful deeds give them away on every side; I see them all. 3The king is glad about their wickedness; the princes laugh about their lies. 4They are all adulterers; as a baker's oven is constantly aflame—except after he kneads the dough and waits for it to rise again—so are these people constantly aflame with lust.

5"On the king's birthday, the princes get him drunk; he makes a fool of himself and drinks with those who mock him. 6Their hearts blaze like a furnace with intrigue. Their plot smolders through the night, and in the morning it flames forth like raging fire.

7"They kill their kings one after another, and none cries out to me for help.

8"My people mingle with the heathen, picking up their evil ways; thus they become as good-for-nothing as a half-baked cake!

9"Worshiping foreign gods has sapped their strength, but they don't know it. Ephraim's hair is turning gray, and he doesn't even realize how weak and old he is. 10His pride in other gods has openly condemned him; yet he doesn't return to his God, nor even try to find him.

11"Ephraim is a silly, witless dove, calling to Egypt, flying to Assyria. 12But as she flies, I throw my net over her and bring her down like a bird from the sky; I will punish her for all her evil ways.

13"Woe to my people for deserting me; let them perish, for they have sinned against me. I wanted to redeem them but their hard hearts would not accept the truth. 14They lie there sleepless with anxiety but won't ask my help. Instead, they worship heathen gods, asking them for crops and for prosperity.

15"I have helped them and made them strong, yet now they turn against me.

16"They look everywhere except to heaven, to the Most High God. They are like a crooked bow that always misses targets; their leaders will perish by the sword of the enemy for their insolence to me. And all Egypt will laugh at them."

CHAPTER 8

Israel Will Reap the Whirlwind

"Sound the alarm! They are coming! Like a vulture, the enemy descends upon the people of God because they have broken my treaty and revolted against my laws.

2"Now Israel pleads with me and says, 'Help us, for you are our God!' 3But it is too late! Israel has thrown away her chance with contempt, and now her enemies will chase her. 4She has appointed kings and princes, but not with my consent. They have cut themselves off from my help by worshiping the idols that they made from their silver and gold.

5"O Samaria, I reject this calf—this idol you have made. My fury burns against you. How long will it be before one honest man is found among you? 6When will you admit this calf

7:5-7 Alcohol affects our ability to perceive reality accurately and leads us to act unwisely. Notice that the king's drunkenness leads him to drink with the very people who are seeking his destruction. We, also, tend to associate with our enemies—dangerous people, bad habits, or harmful substances—while under the influence. An important step toward overcoming our involvement with destructive people and activities is to keep our mind clear and sober. We can then turn to God and pray for his help as we seek to overcome the powerful temptations in our life.

7:10 Pride is a very destructive sin. It lets us assume the place of God in our own life. It tells us to take the credit for our successes and blame others for our failures. The sin of pride robs us of recovery because it won't let us admit we have a problem. If we really want to overcome our addictions, it is necessary to come to God with a humble heart, admitting our weaknesses and seeking change.

7:13 God longs to redeem us, to bring us to complete recovery. But what hinders him from doing that? Hearts hardened by rebellion and denial. If we are to be open to God's powerful help, it is important that we commit ourself to following God's will. It is necessary that we learn to accept reality, admitting our faults and addictions. Only when we open our life up to God will he be able to help us.

8:5-6 Jeroboam set up two golden calves in Israel in an attempt to consolidate his power. He feared losing control of the northern kingdom should everyone go to Jerusalem (in the southern kingdom) to worship God. So he made the idols and told his people that these were the gods who led the people out of Egypt (1 Kings 12:28-30). God had promised to give Jeroboam the kingdom of Israel, but Jeroboam had gone to another source to secure God's promise. This led to the destruction of Jeroboam's dynasty (1 Kings 13:33-34). When God promises us something, we can trust him to complete it in his way and in his time. Taking matters into our own hands is always harmful and will impede our recovery.

you worship was made by human hands! It is not God! Therefore, it must be smashed to bits.

7“They have sown the wind, and they will reap the whirlwind. Their cornstalks stand there barren, withered, sickly, with no grain; if it has any, foreigners will eat it.

8“Israel is destroyed; she lies among the nations as a broken pot. 9She is a lonely, wandering wild ass. The only friends she has are those she hires; Assyria is one of them.

10“But though she hires ‘friends’ from many lands, I will send her off to exile. Then for a while at least she will be free of the burden of her wonderful king! 11Ephraim has built many altars, but they are not to worship me! They are altars of sin! 12Even if I gave her ten thousand laws, she'd say they weren't for her—that they applied to someone far away. 13Her people love the ritual of their sacrifice, but to me it is meaningless! I will call for an accounting of their sins and punish them; they shall return to Egypt.

14“Israel has built great palaces; Judah has constructed great defenses for her cities, but they have forgotten their Maker. Therefore, I will send down fire upon those palaces and burn those fortresses.”

CHAPTER 9

Wandering without God

O Israel, rejoice no more as others do, for you have deserted your God and sacrificed to other gods on every threshing floor.

2Therefore your harvests will be small; your grapes will blight upon the vine.

3You may no longer stay here in this land of God; you will be carried off to Egypt and Assyria and live there on scraps of food. 4There, far from home, you are not allowed to pour out wine for sacrifice to God. For no sacrifice that is offered there can please him; it is polluted, just as food of mourners is; all who eat such sacrifices are defiled. They may eat this food to feed themselves, but may not offer it to God. 5What then will you do on holy days, on days of feasting to the Lord, 6when you are carried off to Assyria as slaves? Who will inherit your possessions left behind? Egypt will! She will gather your dead; Memphis will bury them. And thorns and thistles will grow up among the ruins.

7The time of Israel's punishment has come; the day of recompense is almost here, and soon Israel will know it all too well. “The prophets are crazy”; “The inspired men are mad.” Yes, so they mock, for the nation is weighted with sin and shows only hatred for those who love God.

8“I appointed the prophets to guard my people, but the people have blocked them at every turn and publicly declared their hatred, even in the Temple of the Lord. 9The things my people do are as depraved as what they did in Gibeah long ago. The Lord does not forget. He will surely punish them.

10“O Israel, how well I remember those first

8:12 God's laws apply to everyone, not just the people who obey them. Those who believe that God's principles for life apply only to others are only harming themselves. If we drive at 90 m.p.h. in a 55 m.p.h. zone and get pulled over, the officer will never let us off if we claim, “Well, officer, I saw the speed limit sign, but it doesn't apply to me.” And neither will God let us off when we refuse to obey his revealed will in the Bible. Knowing that God holds us accountable to know and obey his will should motivate us to read and understand his Word. The Bible is God's book of traffic laws for our life in this world. If we refuse to listen to what he has to say, we deny reality and risk being crushed by the consequences.

9:7 It is difficult to have the courage to change when society's values are turned on end. Those who speak for the truth are thought of as fools; those who represent God are classed with the insane. But when we know that God values what the world counts as foolish (1 Corinthians 1:27), it becomes easier to bear men's abuse when we are following God. To some, our recovery program and relationship with God may seem foolish, but in reality they are valuable and necessary.

10:1 The more prosperous the people of Israel became, the further they moved from God. Unfortunately, most people think that success is measured in direct proportion to wealth. Even when our addictions are killing us, we tend to think everything is all right if we are financially successful. However, money is never the key to a successful life; in fact, it is often a major part of the problem. Our relationship with God is what measures true success. Living an addiction-free, godly life is infinitely better than being rich and out of control.

10:8 When the addictions we have trusted fail us, and we begin to experience the painful consequences, it usually seems like a quick death would be better than trying to turn our life around. A quick end to our pain may be the easiest way out, but it is never the best or right way. There is always hope for a good life in the future, no matter how terrible things may seem in the present. We can begin by giving our life over to our merciful God. He wants all of us to come to him, no matter how great our past failures.

delightful days when I led you through the
wilderness! How refreshing was your love!
How satisfying, like the early figs of summer
in their first season! But then you deserted me
for Baal-peor, to give yourselves to other gods,
and soon you were as foul as they. 11The glory
of Israel flies away like a bird, for your children will die at birth, or perish in the womb,
or never even be conceived. 12And if your
children grow, I will take them from you; all
are doomed. Yes, it will be a sad day when I
turn away and leave you alone."
13In my vision I have seen the sons of Israel
doomed. The fathers are forced to lead their
sons to slaughter. 14O Lord, what shall I ask for
your people? I will ask for wombs that don't
give birth, for breasts that cannot nourish.
15"All their wickedness began at Gilgal;
there I began to hate them. I will drive them
from my land because of their idolatry. I will
love them no more, for all their leaders are
rebels. 16Ephraim is doomed. The roots of Israel are dried up; she shall bear no more fruit.
And if she gives birth, I will slay even her
beloved child."
17My God will destroy the people of Israel
because they will not listen or obey. They will
be wandering Jews, homeless among the nations.

CHAPTER 10
Hosea Predicts Punishment
"How prosperous Israel is—a luxuriant vine
all filled with fruit! But the more wealth I give
her, the more she pours it on the altars of her
heathen gods; the richer the harvests I give
her, the more beautiful the statues and idols
she erects. 2The hearts of her people are false
toward God. They are guilty and must be
punished. God will break down their heathen
altars and smash their idols."
3Then they will say, "We deserted the Lord
and he took away our king. But what's the
difference? We don't need one anyway!"
4They make promises they don't intend to
keep. Therefore punishment will spring up
among them like poisonous weeds in the furrows of the field. 5The people of Samaria tremble lest their calf-god idols at Beth-aven
should be hurt; the priests and people, too,
mourn over the departed honor of their shattered gods. 6This idol—this calf-god thing—
will be carted with them when they go as
slaves to Assyria, a present to the great king
there. Ephraim will be laughed at for trusting
in this idol; Israel will be put to shame. 7As for
Samaria, her king shall disappear like a chip

Accountability

READ HOSEA 10:1-12

While in recovery, we learn to accept responsibility for our actions, even when we are powerless over our addictions. We come to realize that all our actions yield consequences. Some of us may have deceived ourself into thinking we could escape the consequences of the things we have done. But with time, it becomes clear that God has made accountability a necessary element of healthy human living.

"A man will always reap just the kind of crop he sows! If he sows to please his own wrong desires, he will be planting seeds of evil and he will surely reap a harvest of spiritual decay and death; but if he plants the good things of the Spirit, he will reap the everlasting life that the Holy Spirit gives him" (Galatians 6:7-8).

The law of sowing and reaping can also work to our benefit. God spoke through the prophet Hosea: "Plant the good seeds of righteousness, and you will reap a crop of my love; plow the hard ground of your hearts, for now is the time to seek the Lord, that he may come and shower salvation upon you" (Hosea 10:12).

God says we *always* reap what we have sown. Even after we have been forgiven, we must deal with the consequences of our actions. It may take a season of time to finish harvesting the negative consequences from our past, but this need not discourage us. Making our list of those we have harmed is a step toward planting good seeds. In time we will see a good crop beginning to grow. ***Turn to page 989, Zechariah 9.***

of wood upon an ocean wave. [8]And the idol
altars of Aven at Bethel where Israel sinned
will crumble. Thorns and thistles will grow up
to surround them. And the people will cry to
the mountains and hills to fall upon them
and crush them.
[9]"O Israel, ever since that awful night in
Gibeah, there has been only sin, sin, sin! You
have made no progress whatever. Was it not
right that the men of Gibeah were wiped out?
[10]I will come against you for your disobedience; I will gather the armies of the nations
against you to punish you for your heaped-up
sins.
[11]"Ephraim is accustomed to treading out
the grain—an easy job she loves. I have never
put her under a heavy yoke before; I have
spared her tender neck. But now I will harness
her to the plow and harrow. Her days of ease
are gone.
[12]"Plant the good seeds of righteousness,
and you will reap a crop of my love; plow the
hard ground of your hearts, for now is the
time to seek the Lord, that he may come and
shower salvation upon you.
[13]"But you have cultivated wickedness and
raised a thriving crop of sins. You have earned
the full reward of trusting in a lie—believing
that military might and great armies can
make a nation safe!
[14]"Therefore, the terrors of war shall rise
among your people, and all your forts will fall,
just as at Beth-arbel, which Shalman destroyed; even mothers and children were
dashed to death there. [15]That will be your fate,
too, you people of Israel, because of your great
wickedness. In one morning the king of Israel
shall be destroyed.

CHAPTER 11

God's Love for Israel

"When Israel was a child I loved him as a son
and brought him out of Egypt. [2]But the more
I called to him, the more he rebelled, sacrificing to Baal and burning incense to idols. [3]I
trained him from infancy, I taught him to
walk, I held him in my arms. But he doesn't
know or even care that it was I who raised him.
[4]"As a man would lead his favorite ox, so I
led Israel with my ropes of love. I loosened his
muzzle so he could eat. I myself have stooped
and fed him. [5]But my people shall return to
Egypt and Assyria because they won't return
to me.
[6]"War will swirl through their cities; their
enemies will crash through their gates and
trap them in their own fortresses. [7]For my
people are determined to desert me. And so I
have sentenced them to slavery, and no one
shall set them free.
[8]"Oh, how can I give you up, my Ephraim?
How can I let you go? How can I forsake you
like Admah and Zeboiim? My heart cries out
within me; how I long to help you! [9]No, I will
not punish you as much as my fierce anger
tells me to. This is the last time I will destroy
Ephraim. For I am God and not man; I am the
Holy One living among you, and I did not
come to destroy.
[10]"For the people shall walk after the Lord.
I shall roar as a lion [at their enemies] and my
people shall return trembling from the west.
[11]Like a flock of birds, they will come from
Egypt—like doves flying from Assyria. And I
will bring them home again; it is a promise
from the Lord."
[12]Israel surrounds me with lies and deceit,
but Judah still trusts in God and is faithful to
the Holy One.

11:1-3 Hosea here compared God's love for Israel to a father's love for his son. He paints a poignant picture of our complete dependence on God. God did everything right in raising his child, but Israel rebelled against God and sought the favor of false gods who could not protect her from the destruction to come. We can learn from Israel's catastrophe and accept the guidance of our heavenly Father before our life is destroyed by our addictions.

12:2-5 The patriarch Jacob changed from being a deceiver to one who sought God's blessing. In his struggles with God he finally faced his own inadequacies and earnestly sought God's favor. Healing and growth will be found only through honest communion with God.

12:6 God asks his people to love him by loving others. This means that we are to seek the best interests of others in a manner consistent with God's revealed will. When we are tempted to take advantage of others for personal gain, we need to ask God to help us to be just and loving. It is only through God that we will treat others as God would have them treated.

13:1-3 Israel's downfall came after it had forsaken God for false gods, not before. Likewise, we will find, if we closely examine our life, that our problems began when we replaced God with our addictions. We cannot blame God for our situation, because he lovingly cares for us. It is we who abandoned him. We can begin our recovery by admitting our failures and dependencies to God and asking him to take control of our life. He will lovingly come to our rescue.

CHAPTER 12
God Invites His People Back
Israel is chasing the wind, yes, shepherding a
whirlwind—a dangerous game! For she has
given gifts to Egypt and Assyria to get their
help, and in return she gets their worthless
promises.
2But the Lord is bringing a lawsuit against
Judah. Jacob will be justly punished for his
ways. 3When he was born, he struggled with
his brother; when he became a man, he even
fought with God. 4Yes, he wrestled with the
Angel and prevailed. He wept and pleaded for
a blessing from him. He met God there at
Bethel face to face. God spoke to him— 5the
Lord, the God of heaven's armies—Jehovah is
his name.
6Oh, come back to God. Live by the principles of love and justice, and always be expecting much from him, your God.
7But no, my people are like crafty merchants selling from dishonest scales—they
love to cheat. 8Ephraim boasts, "I am so rich!
I have gotten it all by myself!" But riches can't
make up for sin.
9I am the same Lord, the same God, who
delivered you from slavery in Egypt, and I am
the one who will consign you to living in
tents again, as you do each year at the Tabernacle Feast. 10I sent my prophets to warn you
with many a vision and many a parable and
dream."
11But the sins of Gilgal flourish just the
same. Row on row of altars—like furrows in a
field—are used for sacrifices to your idols. And
Gilead, too, is full of fools who worship idols.
12Jacob fled to Syria and earned a wife by
tending sheep. 13Then the Lord led his people
out of Egypt by a prophet, who guided and
protected them. 14But Ephraim has bitterly
provoked the Lord. The Lord will sentence
him to death as payment for his sins.

CHAPTER 13
God Is Angry at Israel
It used to be when Israel spoke, the nations
shook with fear, for he was a mighty prince;
but he worshiped Baal and sealed his doom.
2And now the people disobey more and
more. They melt their silver to mold into
idols, formed with skill by the hands of men.
"Sacrifice to these!" they say—men kissing
calves! 3They shall disappear like morning
mist, like dew that quickly dries away, like
chaff blown by the wind, like a cloud of
smoke.
4"I alone am God, your Lord, and have

Unending Love

BIBLE READING: Hosea 11:8-11

We admitted to God, to ourselves, and to another human being the exact nature of our wrongs.

We may be sorely aware of the deep shame, trouble, and pain inflicted on our family because someone (ourself or someone we love) is acting out his addictions. We may be afraid of admitting the exact nature of our wrongs because we don't understand how God could love someone who is so bad.

Hosea was a prophet to the rebellious nation of Israel. God used Hosea's life to demonstrate his unconditional love for us. The Lord told Hosea to marry a prostitute. He married her, loved her, and devoted himself to her. She relapsed into her old ways, broke Hosea's heart, and brought shame on their family. She ended up falling into slavery. God then baffled Hosea by telling him, "Go, and get your wife again and bring her back to you and love her, even though she loves adultery. For the Lord still loves Israel though she has turned to other gods" (Hosea 3:1).

We may be asking, *How could God (or anyone) still love me?* But God asks, "Oh, how can I give you up. . . ? How can I let you go? How can I forsake you. . . ? My heart cries out within me; how I long to help you! . . . For I am God and not man; I am the Holy One living among you, and I did not come to destroy" (Hosea 11:8-9). There is absolutely nothing we can do or admit that would cause God to stop loving us! (See Romans 8:38-39.) ***Turn to page 943, Amos 7.***

been ever since I brought you out from Egypt. You have no God but me, for there is no other Savior. 5I took care of you in the wilderness, in that dry and thirsty land. 6But when you had eaten and were satisfied, then you became proud and forgot me. 7So I will come upon you like a lion, or a leopard lurking along the road. 8I will rip you to pieces like a bear whose cubs have been taken away, and like a lion I will devour you.

9"O Israel, if I destroy you, who can save you? 10Where is your king? Why don't you call on him for help? Where are all the leaders of the land? You asked for them, now let them save you! 11I gave you kings in my anger, and I took them away in my wrath. 12Ephraim's sins are harvested and stored away for punishment.

13"New birth is offered him, but he is like a child resisting in the womb—how stubborn! how foolish! 14Shall I ransom him from hell? Shall I redeem him from Death? O Death, bring forth your terrors for his tasting! O Grave, demonstrate your plagues! For I will not relent!

15"He was called the most fruitful of all his brothers, but the east wind—a wind of the Lord from the desert—will blow hard upon him and dry up his land. All his flowing springs and green oases will dry away, and he will die of thirst. 16Samaria must bear her guilt, for she rebelled against her God. Her people will be killed by the invading army, her babies dashed to death against the ground, her pregnant women ripped open with a sword."

CHAPTER 14

Repentance Will Bring Restoration

O Israel, return to the Lord, your God, for you have been crushed by your sins. 2Bring your petition. Come to the Lord and say, "O Lord, take away our sins; be gracious to us and receive us, and we will offer you the sacrifice of praise. 3Assyria cannot save us, nor can our strength in battle; never again will we call the idols we have made 'our gods'; for in you alone, O Lord, the fatherless find mercy."

4"Then I will cure you of idolatry and faithlessness, and my love will know no bounds, for my anger will be forever gone! 5I will refresh Israel like the dew from heaven; she will blossom as the lily and root deeply in the soil like cedars in Lebanon. 6Her branches will spread out as beautiful as olive trees, fragrant as the forests of Lebanon. 7Her people will return from exile far away and rest beneath my shadow. They will be a watered garden and blossom like grapes; they will be as fragrant as the wines of Lebanon.

8"O Ephraim! Stay away from idols! I am living and strong! I look after you and care for you. I am like an evergreen tree, yielding my fruit to you throughout the year. My mercies never fail."

9Whoever is wise, let him understand these things. Whoever is intelligent, let him listen. For the paths of the Lord are true and right, and good men walk along them. But sinners trying them will fail.

13:4, 13 There is no salvation except that offered by the God of the Bible. He offers salvation to all who will accept it (John 3:3, 16). Anyone who refuses this offer and looks to another source for salvation is like a stubborn "child resisting in the womb," not wanting the life being offered. Are we resisting God's offer, or have we gladly accepted the new life God has in store for us?

14:1-4 These verses contain a paradigm for recovery. The people admitted their helplessness apart from God, examined themselves, and found that they were responsible for their condition. They showed their willingness to let God change them, renounced any further dealings with gods of their own making, and committed their lives to God alone. We can follow the same steps to our own recovery, renouncing our own false gods—our addictive thoughts and behaviors—and committing our life to God and his will.

14:4-8 God's people would experience unprecedented spiritual growth as they committed their lives more and more to him. As they allowed God to heal them, they would find that he also was the source of the water they needed for nourishment and growth. They would become blossoming plants that would send out their roots to start new shoots. We can have the same hope today. The problems caused by our dependencies can be resolved as we repent and accept God's acts of mercy on our behalf.

14:9 We need God's wisdom to discern the areas of our life that need to be changed. The prophet Hosea spoke often of sin and judgment, but his message never ended there. He always pointed the way to salvation through humble repentance. Wise people will listen and learn from the prophet's words, seeing the inherent rightness in all that God asks of them. God cares about our welfare and wants to see us healed because he loves us.

insights ABOUT GOD'S COMPASSION

In **Hosea 1:7–2:1** the prophet was told to name his second child Lo-ammi, which means "Not mine." This illustrated the fact that the people of Israel were no longer God's people. In essence, God was granting her a divorce because of her unfaithfulness. God's declaration of rejection, however, was only to be a temporary condition. Lo-ammi was to be renamed Ammi, which means "Now you are mine." The troubles of punishment and exile that were soon to arrive would someday be replaced with complete restoration and healing. That is the hope for all who are following God's path to recovery. Today's pain and suffering are here only for a season; "in the morning there [will be] joy" (Psalm 30:5).

In **Hosea 10:12** God tried to break through the people's blindness by announcing his desire to restore their broken relationship. Earlier we saw that the people planted the wind and then reaped the whirlwind (8:7). In other words, they sinned and then harvested the chaotic and painful consequences. Here they were asked to plant righteousness and reap the unfailing love of God. That same offer is open to us. If we seek God and let him come into our life, he will save us, both from our addictions and from eternal punishment.

In **Hosea 11:8-11** we see just how painful it is for God when people stray from him and seek out false sources of security. Even though our dependencies may have almost totally destroyed our life, we have not suffered what we deserved; God has compassion on us, his wayward people. What a wonderful God he is! He shows us mercy and provides a way to end our pain and restore our relationship with him. Our recovery is possible only if we seek God and let him fill the empty places that our addictions could never fill.

insights INTO THE IMPORTANCE OF A RELATIONSHIP WITH GOD

A healthy relationship with God requires an intimate knowledge of his revelation in the Bible. The knowledge God desires us to have goes beyond a mere acquaintance with the facts of his Word, however—he wants us to get to know him personally. In **Hosea 4:6** we find that God wants his people to know him personally. The priests of Israel were well acquainted with the laws of God, but they lived an immoral life-style because they didn't really know God. Without a growing and intimate relationship with God, we will have great difficulty as we work through the process of our recovery.

The people of Israel started down the path of recovery, but they soon turned back. In **Hosea 6:4-5** God wonders what he should do with his wayward people. Why did they fail? Perhaps the Israelites were never really committed to following God and his will for them. Perhaps they responded only with their emotions and were soon lured away by something that seemed more attractive. The depth of our commitment to God will determine whether we recover or relapse. As with anything else, the more we want recovery, the better our chances are of achieving it. And, if we look to God for help in the process, we will achieve it. But if we are just going through the motions, relapse is just around the corner.

JOEL

THE BIG PICTURE

A. A LOCUST PLAGUE: FROM CATASTROPHE TO RECOVERY (1:1–2:27)
1. Locusts Terrify the Land (1:1-14)
2. God Judges the Land (1:15–2:11)
3. God Has Mercy on the Land (2:12-27)

B. THE DAY OF THE LORD: CHOOSING DENIAL OR RECOVERY (2:28–3:21)
1. Power to Live Rightly: The Gift of the Spirit (2:28-29)
2. Terror on the Earth: The Day of the Lord (2:30-31)
3. Deliverance from Judgment: An Invitation to All (2:32)
4. Judgment on the Earth: The Wars of God (3:1-15)
5. Restoration of the Land: God's Kingdom (3:16-21)

Earthquakes, hurricanes, floods, tornadoes—natural catastrophes of various kinds—have a way of making us feel helpless. We can do nothing to stop them. We can only do our best to avoid them and then pick up the pieces after they have passed. The first part of Joel's prophecy is concerned with natural disasters that would lead to great suffering for God's people—a drought of major proportions and a plague of locusts. God used these natural events to warn his people of even worse suffering in the future, should they refuse to recognize their need for him.

Disasters are even more painful when they are a consequence of our own behavior. Joel realized that the natural disasters suffered by the people of Judah were God's way of getting their attention. Centuries earlier, Moses had warned that disobedience to God's plan would lead to such catastrophes (Deuteronomy 28:38-39). God sought to restore his people to a healthy relationship with himself by showing them how helpless they really were and how much they needed him. Through these natural disasters, God broke through their illusions of security and self-sufficiency, showing them how important their relationship with him was.

Many of us have suffered from "locust plagues" in our own life. Through actions of our own, we have suffered painful consequences and find ourself helpless to combat the powers that assail us. As we experience this helplessness, we should realize that it is not the end of our life. It is a wonderful opportunity for a new start! In discovering our powerlessness and recognizing our need for God, we have already started the process of recovery.

THE BOTTOM LINE

PURPOSE: To warn God's people of impending judgment, and to urge them to admit their sins and turn back to God. AUTHOR: The prophet Joel. AUDIENCE: The people of the southern kingdom of Judah. DATE WRITTEN: The book was probably written about 800 B.C., when the High Priest Jehoiada governed Judah for young King Joash (2 Kings 11; 2 Chronicles 23–24). SETTING: Jerusalem during a period of prosperity; the people had become complacent about their relationship with God. KEY VERSE: "Return to the Lord your God, for he is gracious and merciful. He is not easily angered; he is full of kindness and anxious not to punish you" (2:13). KEY PEOPLE AND RELATIONSHIPS: Political and religious leaders, parents and children, bride and groom, Joel and God's people.

RECOVERY THEMES

The Power of Confrontation: God's people had lost sight of their need for God and had become complacent about following the plan God had laid out for them. So to break through their denial, God allowed them to suffer a series of disasters. Through their sufferings and the words of the prophet Joel, God let his people know that they were headed for disaster and needed to make some changes in their lives. God often intervenes in our life in similar ways. He allows us to suffer the consequences of our behavior to awaken us from our denial and complacency. He confronts us with the painful reality of our choices and actions. But we should find comfort in this, because he confronts us not to destroy us, but to initiate the process of our restoration.

The Importance of Forgiveness: Joel stated that the day of accountability was coming. But with his message of warning and judgment, he also gave his listeners the grounds for hope through repentance. Repentance would allow God's people to experience the healing available through God's forgiveness. Like the nation of Judah, each of us would love to change some of our actions and choices in the past. Rather than changing the past, God provides a means of resolving our past failures through forgiveness. Our recovery is built on the foundation of both receiving and granting forgiveness.

God's Power Is Limitless: We can easily be overwhelmed by the power of nature when it unleashes its fury in an earthquake, volcano, or hurricane. When we look at the coastline of the Pacific Northwest and see how the ocean has carved out cliffs and caves, we marvel at the power of the ocean. But none of these powerful acts of nature can compare to the overwhelming power of God. When we feel powerless, God invites us to come to him for help. In him we have all the power we need to overcome our problems and dependencies.

God's Power within Us: Joel predicted a time when the limitless power of God would be poured out upon us through his Holy Spirit. This promise implied that God would be directly available to his people, and it was fulfilled in the coming of God's Son, Jesus the Messiah, and in the pouring out of God's Spirit after Jesus ascended to heaven. This truth is of utmost importance to us in the process of recovery. God is with us, and his power is available to us as we persevere in the struggle. God provides us with the power we need to overcome the powerful dependencies and compulsions with which we struggle.

CHAPTER 1

A Plague of Locusts

This message came from the Lord to Joel, son
of Pethuel:
2Listen, you aged men of Israel! Everyone,
listen! In all your lifetime, yes, in all your
history, have you ever heard of such a thing
as I am going to tell you? 3In years to come,
tell your children about it; pass the awful
story down from generation to generation.
4After the cutter-locusts finish eating your
crops, the swarmer-locusts will take what's
left! After them will come the hopper-locusts!
And then the stripper-locusts too!
5Wake up and weep, you drunkards, for all
the grapes are ruined, and all your wine is
gone! 6A vast army of locusts covers the land.
It is a terrible army too numerous to count,
with teeth as sharp as those of lions! 7They
have ruined my vines and stripped the bark
from the fig trees, leaving trunks and
branches white and bare.
8Weep with sorrow, as a virgin weeps
whose fiancé is dead. 9Gone are the offerings of grain and wine to bring to the
Temple of the Lord; the priests are starving.
Hear the crying of these ministers of God.
10The fields are bare of crops. Sorrow and

1:2-3 The people of Joel's generation barely escaped with their lives, and Joel urged them to share with their children what they had learned. When we share our recovery with others, we need to tell the whole story so that others can see just how bad things once were. We may be able to keep others away from the addictions we endured by showing them the horrors and pain associated with our addictions. And we may be able to show those who have already experienced the torture of addiction that it is never too late to enter recovery and regain a normal life.

1:4–2:11 The people needed to admit their helplessness before God could intervene on their behalf. Joel led them to do this in three areas. First, their physical resources were depleted by the locust plague and drought (1:4-12). Second, they were spiritually destitute and could not find God through the standard method of presenting sacrifices (1:13-20). Third, they could not rely on courage and self-defense, because the locusts were too great a foe to overcome (2:1-11). Once we admit we cannot do anything to save ourself, then we can turn to God and ask him to mercifully rescue us from our pain.

sadness are everywhere. The grain, the grapes, the olive oil are gone.

11Well may you farmers stand so shocked and stricken; well may you vinedressers weep. Weep for the wheat and the barley, too, for they are gone. 12The grapevines are dead; the fig trees are dying; the pomegranates wither; the apples shrivel on the trees; all joy has withered with them.

A Call to Repentance

13O priests, robe yourselves in sackcloth. O ministers of my God, lie all night before the altar, weeping. For there are no more offerings of grain and wine for you. 14Announce a fast; call a solemn meeting. Gather the elders and all the people into the Temple of the Lord your God, and weep before him there.

15Alas, this terrible day of punishment is on the way. Destruction from the Almighty is almost here! 16Our food will disappear before our eyes; all joy and gladness will be ended in the Temple of our God. 17The seed rots in the ground; the barns and granaries are empty; the grain has dried up in the fields. 18The cattle groan with hunger; the herds stand perplexed, for there is no pasture for them; the sheep bleat in misery.

19Lord, help us! For the heat has withered the pastures and burned up all the trees. 20Even the wild animals cry to you for help, for there is no water for them. The creeks are dry, and the pastures are scorched.

CHAPTER 2

A Warning of Judgment

Sound the alarm in Jerusalem! Let the blast of the warning trumpet be heard upon my holy mountain! Let everyone tremble in fear, for the day of the Lord's judgment approaches.

2It is a day of darkness and gloom, of black clouds and thick darkness. What a mighty army! It covers the mountains like night! How great, how powerful these "people" are! The likes of them have not been seen before, and never will again throughout the generations of the world! 3Fire goes before them and follows them on every side! Ahead of them the land lies fair as Eden's Garden in all its beauty, but they destroy it to the ground; not one thing escapes. 4They look like tiny horses, and they run as fast. 5Look at them leaping along the tops of the mountain! Listen to the noise they make, like the rumbling of chariots, or the roar of fire sweeping across a field, and like a mighty army moving into battle.

6Fear grips the waiting people; their faces grow pale with fright. 7These "soldiers" charge like infantry; they scale the walls like picked and trained commandos. Straight forward they march, never breaking ranks. 8They never crowd each other. Each is right in place. No weapon can stop them. 9They swarm upon the city; they run upon the walls; they climb up into the houses, coming like thieves through the windows. 10The earth quakes before them and the heavens tremble. The sun and moon are obscured and the stars are hid.

11The Lord leads them with a shout. This is his mighty army, and they follow his orders. The day of the judgment of the Lord is an awesome, terrible thing. Who can endure it?

A Call to Return to God

12That is why the Lord says, "Turn to me now, while there is time. Give me all your hearts. Come with fasting, weeping, mourning. 13Let your remorse tear at your hearts and not your garments." Return to the Lord your God, for he is gracious and merciful. He is not easily angered; he is full of kindness and anxious not to punish you.

14Who knows? Perhaps even yet he will decide to let you alone and give you a blessing instead of his terrible curse. Perhaps he will give you so much that you can offer your grain and wine to the Lord as before!

15Sound the trumpet in Zion! Call a fast and gather all the people together for a solemn meeting. 16Bring everyone—the elders, the children, and even the babies. Call the bridegroom from his quarters and the bride from her privacy.

17The priests, the ministers of God, will stand between the people and the altar, weeping; and they will pray, "Spare your people, O our God; don't let the heathen rule them, for they belong to you. Don't let them be disgraced by the taunts of the heathen who say, 'Where is this God of theirs? How weak and helpless he must be!'"

18Then the Lord will pity his people and be

2:12-17 Instead of responding to God's judgment with the prescribed ritual (tearing garments), God wanted the people of Judah to come to him with broken hearts, admitting their guilt and helplessness. The people needed to commit themselves to God, examine themselves, and let God change them. Since God is known for his graciousness and compassion (2:13), it makes sense to commit our life to him. He may yet change our pain into joy.

indignant for the honor of his land! 19He will reply, "See, I am sending you much corn and wine and oil, to fully satisfy your need. No longer will I make you a laughingstock among the nations. 20I will remove these armies from the north and send them far away; I will turn them back into the parched wastelands where they will die; half shall be driven into the Dead Sea and the rest into the Mediterranean, and then their rotting stench will rise upon the land. The Lord has done a mighty miracle for you."

21Fear not, my people; be glad now and rejoice, for he has done amazing things for you. 22Let the flocks and herds forget their hunger; the pastures will turn green again. The trees will bear their fruit; the fig trees and grape vines will flourish once more. 23Rejoice, O people of Jerusalem, rejoice in the Lord your God! For the rains he sends are tokens of forgiveness. Once more the autumn rains will come, as well as those of spring. 24The threshing floors will pile high again with wheat, and the presses overflow with olive oil and wine.

25"And I will give you back the crops the locusts ate!—my great destroying army that I sent against you. 26Once again you will have all the food you want.

"Praise the Lord, who does these miracles for you. Never again will my people experience disaster such as this. 27And you will know that I am here among my people Israel, and that I alone am the Lord your God. And my people shall never again be dealt a blow like this.

God Will Pour out His Spirit

28"After I have poured out my rains again, I will pour out my Spirit upon all of you! Your sons and daughters will prophesy; your old men will dream dreams, and your young men see visions. 29And I will pour out my Spirit even on your slaves, men and women alike, 30and put strange symbols in the earth and sky—blood and fire and pillars of smoke.

31"The sun will be turned into darkness and the moon to blood before the great and terrible Day of the Lord shall come.

32"Everyone who calls upon the name of the Lord will be saved; even in Jerusalem some will escape, just as the Lord has promised, for he has chosen some to survive."

CHAPTER 3

The Day of the Lord

"At that time, when I restore the prosperity of Judah and Jerusalem," says the Lord, 2"I will gather the armies of the world into the 'Valley Where Jehovah Judges' and punish them there for harming my people, for scattering my inheritance among the nations and dividing up my land.

3"They divided up my people as their slaves; they traded a young lad for a prostitute, and a little girl for wine enough to get drunk. 4Tyre and Sidon, don't you try to interfere! Are you trying to take revenge on me, you cities of Philistia? Beware, for I will strike back swiftly and return the harm to your own heads.

5"You have taken my silver and gold and all my precious treasures and carried them off to your heathen temples. 6You have sold the people of Judah and Jerusalem to the Greeks, who took them far from their own land. 7But I will bring them back again from all these places you have sold them to, and I will pay

---

2:18-27 When the people of Judah admitted their sin, God would take away their pain and replace it with his blessing. Likewise, when we admit our addictions and dependencies and turn our life over to God, he will take away the things that torment us and replace them with his wonderful provisions. The parched, barren areas of our life will flourish. He promises that we will never have to go through the pain of our addictions again as long as we are following him.

2:28-29 Since this prophecy was fulfilled at Pentecost (see Acts 2), we can receive the gift of the Holy Spirit. The Holy Spirit has been changing dysfunctional lives since he was poured out: Peter and the apostles (Acts 2), Paul (Acts 9), a demon-possessed slave girl and a prison guard (Acts 16), and others. The Spirit Joel prophesied about, and who changed first-century lives, is available to change our life, too. We can trust the God of the Old and New Testaments to heal our broken life and work our recovery.

2:32 To call "upon the name of the Lord" is to commit our life to God. When we do this, we will find deliverance. No failure in our past is too great to prevent this. No disadvantage of any kind can keep us from God's grace. When God comes to judge the world, his grace is able to keep us from all harm.

3:1-14 Those who have harmed us will not get away with their abuses. God will judge his enemies; and God's enemies are those who oppress his people and ignore his power. Since they will face God in the Valley of Judgment, we can let go of our hatred and desire for revenge and focus on our own recovery.

you back for all that you have done. 8I will sell your sons and daughters to the people of Judah, and they will sell them to the Sabeans far away. This is a promise from the Lord."

9Announce this far and wide: Get ready for war! Conscript your best soldiers; collect all your armies. 10Melt your plowshares into swords, and beat your pruning hooks into spears. Let the weak be strong. 11Gather together and come, all nations everywhere. And now, O Lord, bring down your warriors!

12"Collect the nations; bring them to the Valley of Jehoshaphat, for there I will sit to pronounce judgment on them all. 13Now let the sickle do its work; the harvest is ripe and waiting. Tread the winepress, for it is full to overflowing with the wickedness of these men."

14Multitudes, multitudes waiting in the valley for the verdict of their doom! For the Day of the Lord is near, in the Valley of Judgment. 15The sun and moon will be darkened and the stars withdraw their light. 16The Lord shouts from his Temple in Jerusalem, and the earth and sky begin to shake. But to his people Israel, the Lord will be very gentle. He is their Refuge and Strength.

17"Then you shall know at last that I am the Lord your God in Zion, my holy mountain. Jerusalem shall be mine forever; the time will come when no foreign armies will pass through her any more.

18"Sweet wine will drip from the mountains, and the hills shall flow with milk. Water will fill the dry stream beds of Judah, and a fountain will burst forth from the Temple of the Lord to water Acacia Valley. 19Egypt will be destroyed, and Edom, too, because of their violence against the Jews, for they killed innocent people in those nations.

20"But Israel will prosper forever, and Jerusalem will thrive as generations pass. 21For I will avenge the blood of my people; I will not clear their oppressors of guilt. For my home is in Jerusalem with my people."

3:16-21 God has a good future planned for all who trust in him. Restoration and recovery will be complete; salvation will be forever. With this hope for the future, we can find the courage we need to persevere through our problems today (Romans 8:18-21). Since the final goal of our recovery process is assured, we need not fear the dark days still ahead.

AMOS

THE BIG PICTURE

A. THINGS THAT OFFEND GOD (1:1–2:16)
1. Inhumane Conduct between Nations (1:1–2:3)
2. Rejecting God and His Laws (2:4-5)
3. Oppressing the Poor and Helpless (2:6-8)
4. Rejecting God's Pleas to Change Behavior (2:9-16)

B. WARNINGS FROM GOD (3:1–6:14)
1. The People Break the Covenant (3:1-15)
2. The People Refuse to Change Their Behavior (4:1-13)
3. The People Must Choose Life or Death (5:1-27)
4. Danger in Putting Confidence in the Wrong Things (6:1-14)

C. GOD'S LOVING PUNISHMENT (7:1–9:15)
1. The Context for Punishment: Merciful Love (7:1-6)
2. The Time for Punishment: The Near Future (7:7–8:14)
3. The Extent of Punishment: The Entire Nation (9:1-6)
4. The Result of Punishment: Recovery and Restoration (9:7-15)

God is just and righteous, yet he always expresses his justice in the context of his love and compassion. He expects us to act in the same way. God's Word asks that we show mercy and understanding toward others, promoting fairness in our relationships. In Amos's day, Israel was a prosperous nation, but with their prosperity came corruption, injustice toward the poor and helpless, and religious apostasy. God had given his chosen people laws for governing human relationships, but they had refused to obey them.

In response, God called Amos, a shepherd from Tekoa, to awaken his people from their denial and to warn them of the painful consequences that would follow. Amos confronted the people of Israel with their ill-treatment of the poor and oppressed, demanding that they act mercifully and with justice. God gave this warning of punishment in hope that his people would change. They were reminded of their responsibilities as God's chosen people and were called to evaluate their behavior honestly. Sadly, their behavior had fallen to a level lower than that of their pagan neighbors!

God desired to show mercy toward his people, but they refused to repent. So Amos's predictions for Israel's future were dark and dismal. God would allow his people to suffer through a period of destruction and exile. Despite his predictions of doom, however, Amos also spoke of the future with hope. If only the people would admit their sin and ask for forgiveness, God would purify and restore them completely. It is never too late to begin the recovery process. God is waiting for us to recognize how helpless we are and to call out to him for his loving help.

THE BOTTOM LINE

PURPOSE: To confront the people of Israel with their sin, calling them to confession and repentance. AUTHOR: The prophet Amos. AUDIENCE: The people of the northern kingdom of Israel. DATE WRITTEN: Between 760 and 750 B.C., when Jeroboam II was king of Israel and Uzziah was king of Judah. SETTING: The northern kingdom of Israel during a time of material prosperity and spiritual complacency. KEY VERSE: "I will restore the fortunes of my people Israel, and they will rebuild their ruined cities and live in them again; they will plant vineyards and gardens; they will eat their crops and drink their wine" (9:14). KEY PLACES: Samaria, the northern kingdom's capital, and the temple at Bethel. KEY PEOPLE AND RELATIONSHIPS: Amos and Amaziah, the priest at Bethel, the people of Israel, and the Edomites.

RECOVERY THEMES

Complacency Leads to Relapse: When life is going smoothly, we need to be careful. We are ripe for complacency and relapse. In Amos's day, the people of Israel were prosperous and began to think they could make it without God. This led them down a steep pathway toward destruction. Even when life is going well, we still need God. If we keep this in mind, we will recognize our need for God and his help when life becomes difficult. God is the source of power for our recovery; all success must be attributed to him. A complacent, self-sufficient attitude will only lead to a relapse.

Created for Relationship: The people in the time of Amos acted like they were isolated individuals. They exploited the weak and poor. They were indifferent to the pain of those around them. They enslaved the helpless through extortion and heavy taxation. God has created us to live in relationship with others, not in isolation. Our recovery calls us to recognize our need for others and to do what we can to make amends with those we have wronged. God is in the business of restoring our broken relationships.

God Honors Upright Hearts: Many of the people of Israel carried on the outward appearances of religion even though they had abandoned their faith in God. Sometimes we work our recovery program in the same way. We perform to get the approval of others, and genuine internal change never takes place. We begin to hide our failures from others, pretending we are faithfully following our program. This only leads to denial. God wants us to have genuine hearts that seek to know him better and trust him more. He doesn't care how we appear on the surface; he sees through our false appearances even if other people don't. God cares about the attitudes of our heart.

Recovery Begins with Helplessness: When the people of Israel went into captivity, with their society crumbling about them, their denial was broken. They knew that they needed God. The dark times of life often lead us to recovery. Our helplessness shatters our denial; it awakens us from our false illusions about reality. When our life is totally out of control and crumbling around us, our attempts to deny that we need God are futile. We can acknowledge our need and be open to God and his healing power. As we recognize our helplessness, our recovery can begin.

CHAPTER 1

God Will Punish Israel's Neighbors

Amos was a herdsman living in the village of Tekoa. [All day long he sat on the hillsides watching the sheep, keeping them from straying.]

2One day, in a vision, God told him some of the things that were going to happen to his nation, Israel. This vision came to him at the time Uzziah was king of Judah and while Jeroboam (son of Joash) was king of Israel—two years before the earthquake.

This is his report of what he saw and heard: The Lord roared—like a ferocious lion from his lair—from his Temple on Mount Zion. And suddenly the lush pastures of Mount Carmel withered and dried, and all the shepherds mourned.

3The Lord says, "The people of Damascus have sinned again and again, and I will not forget it. I will not leave her unpunished any more. For they have threshed my people in
Gilead as grain is threshed with iron rods. 4So
I will set fire to King Hazael's palace, destroying the strong fortress of Ben-hadad. 5I will
snap the bars that locked the gates of Damascus and kill her people as far away as the plain of Aven, and the people of Syria shall return to Kir as slaves." The Lord has spoken.

6The Lord says, "Gaza has sinned again and again, and I will not forget it. I will not leave her unpunished any more. For she sent my people into exile, selling them as slaves in
Edom. 7So I will set fire to the walls of Gaza,
and all her forts shall be destroyed. 8I will kill
the people of Ashdod and destroy Ekron and the king of Ashkelon; all Philistines left will perish." The Lord has spoken.

9The Lord says, "The people of Tyre have sinned again and again, and I will not forget it. I will not leave them unpunished any more. For they broke their treaty with their brother, Israel; they attacked and conquered
him, and led him into slavery to Edom. 10So I

1:3–2:3 All the people of the earth are accountable to God for their actions. There are certain boundaries of human behavior that God will not allow people to cross without punishment. Yet, as Jesus said, God has mercy even on the unrighteous (Matthew 5:45). God will send judgment, but only after giving all people time to repent and change their ways. God does the same thing with us today. We may seem to prosper in our addictions, but this will only last a short while. If we do not admit our problem and turn our life over to God, he will leave us to the consequences of our sin.

will set fire to the walls of Tyre, and it will
burn down all his forts and palaces."
11The Lord says, "Edom has sinned again
and again, and I will not forget it. I will not
leave him unpunished any more. For he
chased his brother, Israel, with the sword; he
was pitiless in unrelenting anger. 12So I will set
fire to Teman, and it will burn down all the
forts of Bozrah."

13The Lord says, "The people of Ammon
have sinned again and again, and I will not
forget it. I will not leave them unpunished
any more. For in their wars in Gilead to enlarge their borders they committed cruel
crimes, ripping open pregnant women with
their swords.

14"So I will set fire to the walls of Rabbah,
and it will burn down their forts and palaces;
there will be wild shouts of battle like a whirlwind in a mighty storm. 15And their king and
his princes will go into exile together." The
Lord has spoken.

CHAPTER 2

The Lord says, "The people of Moab have
sinned again and again, and I will not forget
it. I will not leave them unpunished any
more. For they desecrated the tombs of the
kings of Edom, with no respect for the dead.
2Now in return I will send fire upon Moab,
and it will destroy all the palaces in Kerioth.
Moab shall go down in tumult as the warriors
shout and trumpets blare. 3 And I will destroy
their king and slay all the leaders under him."
The Lord has spoken.

4The Lord says, "The people of Judah have
sinned again and again, and I will not forget
it. I will not leave them unpunished any
more. For they have rejected the laws of God,
refusing to obey him. They have hardened
their hearts and sinned as their fathers did.
5So I will destroy Judah with fire and burn
down all Jerusalem's palaces and forts."

God Will Punish Israel

6The Lord says, "The people of Israel have
sinned again and again, and I will not forget
it. I will not leave them unpunished any
more. For they have perverted justice by accepting bribes and sold into slavery the poor
who can't repay their debts; they trade them
for a pair of shoes. 7They trample the poor in
the dust and kick aside the meek.

"And a man and his father defile the same
temple-girl, corrupting my holy name. 8At
their religious feasts they lounge in clothing
stolen from their debtors, and in my own
Temple they offer sacrifices of wine they purchased with stolen money.

9"Yet think of all I did for them! I cleared
the land of the Amorites before them—the
Amorites, as tall as cedar trees, and strong as
oaks! But I lopped off their fruit and cut their
roots. 10And I brought you out from Egypt and
led you through the desert forty years, to
possess the land of the Amorites. 11And I
chose your sons to be Nazirites and prophets—can you deny this, Israel?" asks the Lord.
12"But you caused the Nazirites to sin by urging them to drink your wine, and you silenced my prophets, telling them, 'Shut up!'

13"Therefore, I will make you groan as a
wagon groans that is loaded with sheaves.
14Your swiftest warriors will stumble in flight.
The strong will all be weak, and the great ones
can no longer save themselves. 15The archer's
aim will fail, the swiftest runners won't be fast
enough to flee, and even the best of horsemen
can't outrun the danger then. 16The most
courageous of your mighty men will drop
their weapons and run for their lives that
day." The Lord God has spoken.

CHAPTER 3

Sin Separates the People from God

Listen! This is your doom! It is spoken by the
Lord against both Israel and Judah—against
the entire family I brought from Egypt:

2:4-8 The sins of Judah and Israel stemmed from their rejection of God's laws. They oppressed and took advantage of the poor; they took bribes, engaged in sexual sins, and overstepped God's boundaries for healthy living in many other ways. Obeying God's regulations would have brought them blessing, but their evil deeds ensured their punishment. While our world may have changed since Bible times, God and his laws have not. These same behaviors will still bring punishment from God. And if we have been the victim of any such sins, we can rest assured that God will judge our oppressors.

3:2 The people of Israel knew how God wanted them to act, yet they chose to sin anyway. They knew the laws and the consequences for disobedience, yet still flouted them. So God would send the appropriate curses outlined in his laws. We know the dangers and consequences of our compulsions and addictions. If we engage in them and don't expect the consequences, we are in denial about our destructive attitudes and actions. The only way to avoid the consequences of our addictions is to avoid the addictive behaviors that cause them.

2"Of all the peoples of the earth, I have chosen you alone. That is why I must punish you the more for all your sins. 3For how can we walk together with your sins between us?

4"Would I be roaring as a lion unless I had a reason? The fact is, I am getting ready to destroy you. Even a young lion, when it growls, shows it is ready for its food. 5A trap doesn't snap shut unless it is stepped on; your punishment is well deserved. 6The alarm has sounded—listen and fear! For I, the Lord, am sending disaster into your land.

7"But always, first of all, I warn you through my prophets. This I now have done."

8The Lion has roared—tremble in fear. The Lord God has sounded your doom—I dare not refuse to proclaim it.

9"Call together the Assyrian and Egyptian leaders, saying, 'Take your seats now on the mountains of Samaria to witness the scandalous spectacle of all Israel's crimes.' 10My people have forgotten what it means to do right," says the Lord. "Their beautiful homes are full of the loot from their thefts and banditry. 11Therefore," the Lord God says, "an enemy is coming! He is surrounding them and will shatter their forts and plunder those beautiful homes."

12The Lord says, "A shepherd tried to rescue his sheep from a lion, but it was too late; he snatched from the lion's mouth two legs and a piece of ear. So it will be when the Israelites in Samaria are finally rescued—all they will have left is half a chair and a tattered pillow.

13"Listen to this announcement and publish it throughout all Israel," says the Lord, the Lord Almighty: 14"On the same day that I punish Israel for her sins I will also destroy the idol altars at Bethel. The horns of the altar will be cut off and fall to the ground.

15"And I will destroy the beautiful homes of the wealthy—their winter mansions and their summer houses too—and demolish their ivory palaces."

CHAPTER 4

The People Refuse to Repent

Listen to me, you "fat cows" of Bashan living in Samaria—you women who encourage your husbands to rob the poor and crush the needy—you who never have enough to drink! 2The Lord God has sworn by his holiness that the time will come when he will put hooks in your noses and lead you away like the cattle you are; they will drag the last of you away with fishhooks! 3You will be hauled from your beautiful homes and tossed out through the nearest breach in the wall. The Lord has said it.

4Go ahead and sacrifice to idols at Bethel and Gilgal. Keep disobeying—your sins are mounting up. Sacrifice each morning and bring your tithes twice a week! 5Go through all your proper forms and give extra offerings. How you pride yourselves and crow about it everywhere!

6"I sent you hunger," says the Lord, "but it did no good; you still would not return to me. 7I ruined your crops by holding back the rain three months before the harvest. I sent rain on one city but not another. While rain fell on one field, another was dry and withered. 8People from two or three cities would make their weary journey for a drink of water to a city that had rain, but there wasn't ever enough. Yet you wouldn't return to me," says the Lord.

3:3-8 We all receive warnings before our addictions and dysfunctional behaviors overtake us. God's prophets had warned the people of Israel on a regular basis, and they had all seen the pain suffered by their ancestors for disobedience. We receive regular warnings, too, from medical reports, friends and family members, and the Bible. Continuing in our addictions and ignoring the warnings is as bad as hearing a smoke alarm go off and then waiting to be burned in the fire. We should listen to the warnings we receive before it is too late.

4:4-5 It is easy to find substitutes for a genuine relationship with God. One tempting substitute is religious activity. If we go to church regularly, perhaps even sing in the choir, won't that be enough? God required the Israelites to give sacrifices and tithes, but he demanded even more. An offering given because the giver is already committed to God pleases God. But if an offering is given in place of true commitment, then God regards even the offering as a sin. Our heartfelt devotion is what God really wants.

4:6-11 Modern-day parallels to these verses could be: "I took away your job and your family left you, yet you still wouldn't give up your alcohol and drugs." "You are empty despite all you possess, yet you still won't turn to me." "I've sent you AIDS and venereal disease, yet you continue to practice sexual sins." All the negative effects of our compulsions and addictions are signs for us to give up these detrimental pursuits and turn back to God, the giver of all that is good and perfect (James 1:17).

9"I sent blight and mildew on your farms
and your vineyards; the locusts ate your figs
and olive trees. And still you wouldn't return
to me," says the Lord. 10"I sent you plagues like
those of Egypt long ago. I killed your lads in
war and drove away your horses. The stench
of death was terrible to smell. And yet you
refused to come. 11I destroyed some of your
cities, as I did Sodom and Gomorrah; those
left are like half-burned firebrands snatched
away from fire. And still you won't return to
me," says the Lord.
12"Therefore, I will bring upon you all these
further evils I have spoken of. Prepare to meet
your God in judgment, Israel. 13For you are
dealing with the One who formed the mountains, made the winds, and knows your every
thought; he turns the morning to darkness
and crushes down the mountains underneath
his feet: Jehovah, the Lord, the Lord Almighty, is his name."

CHAPTER 5

Amos Mourns for Israel

Sadly I sing this song of grief for you, O Israel:
2Beautiful Israel lies broken and crushed
upon the ground and cannot rise. No one will
help her. She is left alone to die." 3For the Lord
God says, "The city that sends a thousand
men to battle, a hundred will return. The city
that sends a hundred, only ten will come back
alive."
4The Lord says to the people of Israel, "Seek
me—and live. 5Don't seek the idols of Bethel,
Gilgal, or Beersheba; for the people of Gilgal
will be carried off to exile, and those of Bethel
shall surely come to grief."
6Seek the Lord and live, or else he will
sweep like fire through Israel and consume
her, and none of the idols in Bethel can put it
out.
7O evil men, you make "justice" a bitter pill
for the poor and oppressed. "Righteousness"
and "fair play" are meaningless fictions to
you!
8Seek him who created the Seven Stars and
the constellation Orion, who turns darkness
into morning and day into night, who calls
forth the water from the ocean and pours it
out as rain upon the land. The Lord, Jehovah,
is his name. 9With blinding speed and violence he brings destruction on the strong,
breaking all defenses.
10How you hate honest judges! How you
despise people who tell the truth! 11You trample the poor and steal their smallest crumb by
all your taxes, fines, and usury; therefore, you
will never live in the beautiful stone houses
you are building, nor drink the wine from the
lush vineyards you are planting.
12For many and great are your sins. I know
them all so well. You are the enemies of everything good; you take bribes; you refuse justice
to the poor. 13Therefore, those who are wise
will not try to interfere with the Lord in the
dread day of your punishment.
14Be good, flee evil—and live! Then the
Lord, the Lord Almighty, will truly be your
Helper, as you have claimed he is. 15Hate evil
and love the good; remodel your courts into
true halls of justice. Perhaps even yet the Lord
God of Hosts will have mercy on his people
who remain.
16Therefore the Lord God says this: "There
will be crying in all the streets and every road.
Call for the farmers to weep with you too; call
for professional mourners to wail and lament.
17There will be sorrow and crying in every
vineyard, for I will pass through and destroy.
18You say, 'If only the Day of the Lord were
here, for then God would deliver us from all
our foes.' But you have no idea what you ask.
For that day will *not* be light and prosperity,
but darkness and doom! How terrible the
darkness will be for you; not a ray of joy or
hope will shine. 19In that day you will be as a
man who is chased by a lion and is met by a
bear, or a man in a dark room who leans
against a wall and puts his hand on a snake.
20Yes, that will be a dark and hopeless day for
you.
21"I hate your show and pretense—your
hypocrisy of 'honoring' me with your religious feasts and solemn assemblies. 22I will

5:4-5 Israel was warned not to worship false idols, since those who do will soon face trouble. Anything we look to for comfort other than God is a false god. We may not worship carved images, but we do turn to alcohol, drugs, work, materialism, sex, and other compulsions to hide from our painful problems. God is there waiting to help us. He doesn't want us chasing after things that will only lead to disappointment and death. Instead, he calls out to us: "Seek me—and live."

5:18-20 It is possible to fool ourself into thinking we are spiritually right with God. Amos calls here for honest self-examination. When Jesus Christ returns, it will be a time of joy and of the completion of recovery for those whose faith is genuine. Those of us who have not been honest with ourself will be lost forever (Matthew 7:21-23). Let us take a moral inventory right now. Where do we stand with God? How can we change to be more like he wants us to be?

not accept your burnt offerings and thank offerings. I will not look at your offerings of peace. 23 Away with your hymns of praise—they are mere noise to my ears. I will not listen to your music, no matter how lovely it is.

24"I want to see a mighty flood of justice—a torrent of doing good.

25-27"You sacrificed to me for forty years while you were in the desert, Israel—but always your real interest has been in your heathen gods—in Sakkuth your king, and in Kaiwan, your god of the stars, and in all the images of them you made. So I will send them into captivity with you far to the east of Damascus," says the Lord, the Lord Almighty.

CHAPTER 6

God Hates Israel's Pride

Woe to those lounging in luxury at Jerusalem and Samaria, so famous and popular among the people of Israel. 2Go over to Calneh and see what happened there; then go to great Hamath and down to Gath in the Philistines' land. Once they were better and greater than you, but look at them now. 3You push away all thought of punishment awaiting you, but by your deeds you bring the Day of Judgment near.

4You lie on ivory beds surrounded with luxury, eating the meat of the tenderest lambs and the choicest calves. 5You sing idle songs to the sound of the harp and fancy yourselves to be as great musicians as King David was.

6You drink wine by the bucketful and perfume yourselves with sweet ointments, caring nothing at all that your brothers need your help. 7Therefore you will be the first to be taken as slaves; suddenly your revelry will end.

8Jehovah the Almighty Lord has sworn by his own name, "I despise the pride and false glory of Israel and hate their beautiful homes. I will turn over this city and everything in it to her enemies."

9If there are as few as ten of them left and only one house, they too will perish. 10A man's uncle will be the only one left to bury him, and when he goes in to carry his body from the house, he will ask the only one still alive inside, "Are any others left?" And the answer will be, "No," and he will add, "Shhh . . . don't mention the name of the Lord—he might hear you."

11For the Lord commanded this: That homes both great and small should be smashed to pieces. 12Can horses run on rocks? Can oxen plow the sea? Stupid even to ask—but no more stupid than what you do when you make a mockery of justice and corrupt and sour all that should be good and right. 13 And just as stupid is your rejoicing in how great you are when you are less than nothing—and priding yourselves on your own tiny power!

5:21-24 No amount of religious activity is going to make up for our dysfunctional life-style. We may fool others, leading them to believe that we are all right because we go to church three times a week or give 20 percent of our income to the church. But God will not look favorably upon our religious behavior if we are not doing good to others and following his guidelines for a healthy life.

6:4-7 Addiction to "the good life" can be one of the deadliest of all addictions. God has no quarrel with his people enjoying the good things he provides for them. The problem with the Israelites was that they craved their enjoyments so much that they no longer cared who they hurt in the process of getting them. Many of us are in the same situation; we get wrapped up in our pleasures and don't care who we step on to get them. Maybe we have ruined our family life or friendships in the pursuit of more "things" or because of an addiction. If we turn these areas over to God, he can help us recover our life and our relationships.

7:7-9 God would not hold back his judgment any longer. He took a plumbline to see just how Israel measured up to his righteous standards. God looks at our life with a plumbline, too—the Bible, his Word to us. On our own, when we look at our life it may seem straight and strong. But if we compared it to God's plumbline, we would see that our life is really weak and leaning to the side of sin. Praying to God for help is the way to start the process toward a life in line with God's plan for us.

7:10-17 Notice how Amos faced opposition. He was sure of his commitment to God and persevered in what he knew to be God's will. God had called him to enter new territory, and he had done it courageously. We will face opposition to our recovery, especially when we bring others the message of a better life. People may feel threatened by our progress, and they would love to see us fail so they won't feel guilty about their own life-style. When we are being attacked, we may feel like giving up and giving in to others. But we must persevere, trusting God for protection and strength.

14"O Israel, I will bring against you a nation
that will bitterly oppress you from your
northern boundary to your southern tip, all
the way from Hamath to the brook of Arabah," says the Lord, the Lord Almighty.

CHAPTER 7

Amos's Visions of Judgment

This is what the Lord God showed me in a
vision: He was preparing a vast swarm of
locusts to destroy all the main crop that
sprang up after the first mowing, which went
as taxes to the king. 2They ate everything in
sight. Then I said, "O Lord God, please forgive
your people! Don't send them this plague! If
you turn against Israel, what hope is there?
For Israel is so small!"
3So the Lord relented and did not fulfill the
vision. "I won't do it," he told me.
4Then the Lord God showed me a great fire
he had prepared to punish them; it had
burned up the waters and was devouring the
entire land.
5Then I said, "O Lord God, please don't do
it. If you turn against them, what hope is
there? For Israel is so small!"
6Then the Lord turned from this plan too,
and said, "I won't do that either."
7Then he showed me this: The Lord was
standing beside a wall built with a plumbline,
checking it with a plumbline to see if it was
straight. 8And the Lord said to me, "Amos,
what do you see?"
I answered, "A plumbline."
And he replied, "I will test my people with
a plumbline. I will no longer turn away from
punishing. 9The idol altars and temples of
Israel will be destroyed, and I will destroy the
dynasty of King Jeroboam by the sword."
10But when Amaziah, the priest of Bethel,
heard what Amos was saying, he rushed a
message to Jeroboam, the king: "Amos is a
traitor to our nation and is plotting your
death. This is intolerable. It will lead to rebellion all across the land. 11He says you will be
killed and Israel will be sent far away into
exile and slavery."
12Then Amaziah sent orders to Amos, "Get
out of here, you prophet, you! Flee to the land
of Judah and do your prophesying there!
13Don't bother us here with your visions, not
here in the capital where the king's chapel is!"
14But Amos replied, "I am not really one of
the prophets. I do not come from a family of
prophets. I am just a herdsman and fruit
picker. 15But the Lord took me from caring for

The Plumbline

BIBLE READING: Amos 7:7-8

We admitted to God, to ourselves, and to another human being the exact nature of our wrongs.

The kind of instrument we use to measure our life will often determine the kinds of problems we uncover. If we use a faulty guideline, we won't be able to make an accurate assessment. We may wonder why we aren't progressing in our recovery program. It may be that we need to look closely at the measuring stick we are using to uncover our problem areas.

The prophet Amos recorded this vision: "The Lord was standing beside a wall built with a plumbline, checking it with a plumbline to see if it was straight. And the Lord said, . . . 'I will test my people with a plumbline'" (Amos 7:7-8).

A plumbline is a length of string that has a weight tied to one end. When the string is held up with the weighted end hanging down, gravity ensures that the string is perfectly vertical. When held next to a building structure, the plumbline provides something sure by which to check whether or not the building is "in line" with the physical universe. If a building is built in line with the plumbline, the structure will be sturdy and function well.

The same holds true in the spiritual realm. God's Word is our spiritual plumbline. Just as we can't argue with the law of gravity, we can't change the spiritual laws revealed in the Bible. It is to our advantage to measure our life by the plumbline of God's Word. When things don't measure up, it is important that we admit there is a problem and start rebuilding accordingly. ***Turn to page 1151, John 8.***

the flocks and told me, 'Go and prophesy to
my people Israel.'
16"Now, therefore, listen to this message to
you from the Lord. You say, 'Don't prophesy
against Israel.' 17The Lord's reply is this: 'Because of your interference, your wife will become a prostitute in this city, your sons and
daughters will be killed, and your land divided up. You yourself will die in a heathen
land, and the people of Israel will certainly
become slaves in exile, far from their land.'"

CHAPTER 8

Amos Sees a Basket of Fruit

Then the Lord God showed me, in a vision, a
basket full of ripe fruit.
2"What do you see, Amos?" he asked.
I replied, "A basket full of ripe fruit."
Then the Lord said, "This fruit represents
my people Israel—ripe for punishment. I will
not defer their punishment again. 3The riot-
ous sound of singing in the Temple will turn
to weeping then. Dead bodies will be scattered everywhere. They will be carried out of
the city in silence." The Lord has spoken.
4Listen, you merchants who rob the poor,
trampling on the needy; 5you who long for
the Sabbath to end and the religious holidays
to be over so you can get out and start cheating again—using your weighted scales and
undersized measures; 6you who make slaves
of the poor, buying them for their debt of a
piece of silver or a pair of shoes, or selling
them your moldy wheat:
7The Lord, the Pride of Israel, has sworn: "I
won't forget your deeds! 8The land will tremble as it awaits its doom, and everyone will
mourn. It will rise up like the river Nile at
floodtime, toss about, and sink again. 9At that
time I will make the sun go down at noon and
darken the earth in the daytime. 10And I will
turn your parties into times of mourning, and
your songs of joy will be turned to cries of
despair. You will wear funeral clothes and
shave your heads as signs of sorrow, as if your
only son had died; bitter, bitter will be that
day.
11"The time is surely coming," says the Lord
God, "when I will send a famine on the
land—not a famine of bread or water, but of
hearing the words of the Lord. 12Men will
wander everywhere from sea to sea, seeking
the word of the Lord, searching, running here
and going there, but will not find it. 13Beauti-
ful girls and fine young men alike will grow
faint and weary, thirsting for the word of God.
14And those who worship the idols of Samaria,
Dan, and Beersheba shall fall and never rise
again."

CHAPTER 9

Israel Will Be Destroyed

I saw the Lord standing beside the altar, saying, "Smash the tops of the pillars and shake
the Temple until the pillars crumble and the
roof crashes down upon the people below.
Though they run, they will not escape; they
all will be killed.
2"Though they dig down to Sheol, I will
reach down and pull them up; though they
climb into the heavens, I will bring them
down. 3Though they hide among the rocks at
the top of Carmel, I will search them out and
capture them. Though they hide at the bot-

8:4-6 Instead of serving God, the Israelites served material wealth. They were not honest about this, however, even with themselves. They sat through worship services, but spent the time thinking up new ways to cheat their customers. And Israel experienced the negative consequences of their addiction to material goods: dishonesty, morbid dependence on others, irresponsibility, and spiritual deadness. Serving wealth has become quite common in our society, maybe even a way of life for some of us. But if we are devoted to money, we cannot be serving God (see Matthew 6:24). We must decide who our master will be—God, who offers eternal life and peace, or money, which can never satisfy us.

8:11-14 Why would the people not be able to find "the word of the Lord"? It wasn't because God was silent. Other prophets followed: Hosea, Isaiah, Micah, and many others. The people couldn't find God's words because they looked in the wrong places. They looked for revelations from the prevalent false gods. God's people would not be able to hear God speaking to them until they admitted their sin and helplessness. They would need to seek God alone and nothing else. We, too, need to stop trusting the "idols" we count on to get us through the day in order to be able to hear the truth of God's Word. Only the hope God's Word offers us can truly satisfy.

9:1-4 It is our responsibility to commit our life to God; we cannot begin recovery unless we do. Psalm 139 speaks reassuringly of God's presence with those who seek him; Amos speaks of the terrible consequences for those who refuse to commit their lives to him (see Revelation 6:15-17). Earthly and eternal recovery are available to all who are willing to ask God to rescue them from their past sins and mistakes.

tom of the ocean, I will send the sea-serpent
after them to bite and destroy them. [4]Though
they volunteer for exile, I will command the
sword to kill them there. I will see to it that
they receive evil and not good."
[5]The Lord Almighty touches the land and it
melts, and all its people mourn. It rises like
the river Nile in Egypt and then sinks again.
[6]The upper stories of his home are in the
heavens, the first floor on the earth. He calls
for the vapor to rise from the ocean and pours
it down as rain upon the ground. Jehovah, the
Lord, is his name.
[7]"O people of Israel, are you any more to
me than the Ethiopians are? Have not I, who
brought you out of Egypt, done as much for
other people too? I brought the Philistines
from Caphtor and the Syrians out of Kir.
[8]"The eyes of the Lord God are watching
Israel, that sinful nation, and I will root her up
and scatter her across the world. *Yet I have
promised that this rooting out will not be permanent.* [9]For I have commanded that Israel be
sifted by the other nations as grain is sifted in
a sieve, yet not one true kernel will be lost.
[10]But all these sinners who say, 'God will not
touch us,' will die by the sword.

Israel Will Be Restored

[11]"Then, at that time I will rebuild the City of
David, which is now lying in ruins, and return
it to its former glory, [12]and Israel will possess
what is left of Edom and of all the nations that
belong to me." For so the Lord, who plans it
all, has said.
[13]"The time will come when there will be
such abundance of crops that the harvesttime
will scarcely end before the farmer starts again
to sow another crop, and the terraces of
grapes upon the hills of Israel will drip sweet
wine! [14]I will restore the fortunes of my people
Israel, and they will rebuild their ruined cities
and live in them again; they will plant vineyards and gardens; they will eat their crops
and drink their wine. [15]I will firmly plant
them there upon the land that I have given
them; they shall not be pulled up again," says
the Lord your God.

9:10 Refusal to admit the truth can be dangerous. Outward appearances seemed to deny the truth of what Amos was saying. The nation was prosperous; enemies were weak; the military was strong; alliances were made with Egypt and other nations. Inwardly, however, the people were diseased (see Amos 6:6). Israel's spiritual sickness would lead ultimately to her physical destruction. The people denied the truth, their country was destroyed, and they were taken captive to Assyria. Let's not let denial cost us our life and happiness. Let's admit the truth to ourself and to God so we can begin recovery and enjoy the fulfillment he offers.

9:11-15 God has committed himself to helping his people recover. He plans to restore what is broken and in ruin, changing barren land to a place of unprecedented fruitfulness. This can only happen when we see how helpless we are without God's help and commit our life into his hands. The process will be painful as we grow spiritually, but the end result will be worth it.

REFLECTIONS ON AMOS

insights INTO GOD'S PERSON AND WILL

In **Amos 5:6, 14** the prophet describes the life of recovery. It comes from God alone, not from anywhere else. To seek God means to admit our helplessness and to commit our life to him, letting him change us. But how do we avoid the various failures mentioned in these verses? God reveals himself uniquely in the Bible; it is our infallible guide to the truth. We need to seek out God's will in his Word and then seek, with his help, to live by it.

In **Amos 5:8-9** the Creator and Sustainer of the universe is described (see also 4:13; 9:6). When we seek God, we seek the Creator of all things. He is all-powerful, controlling both day and night. He pours out the sea like water from a pitcher. He cannot be stopped by the best efforts of the human race. When we commit our life to him, we can be sure that he is capable of changing us.

OBADIAH

THE BIG PICTURE

A. FREEDOM THROUGH SEEING GOD'S PRINCIPLE OF JUSTICE (1:1-9)
   1. Betrayal Begets Betrayal (1:1)
   2. No One Can Stand against the Lord (1:2-4)
   3. Betrayers Must Lose Everything (1:5-9)

B. FREEDOM THROUGH SEEING GOD'S VIEW OF INJUSTICE (1:10-14)
   1. Gloating while Others Are Hurting (1:10-12)
   2. Inflicting Pain (1:13-14)

C. FREEDOM THROUGH SEEING GOD'S PLAN FOR THE FUTURE (1:15-21)

Betrayal always produces feelings of agony, and the closer our relationship with someone, the greater the pain we feel when that person betrays us. In this short book, Obadiah condemned the people of Edom for betraying their kinsmen in Judah, who were under attack by the Babylonian armies. The people of Judah were descendants of Jacob, while the Edomites were descended from Jacob's twin brother, Esau. The two nations were closely related, yet Edom's acts of aggression toward Israel over the years had been great.

When Judah needed help to stand against the armies of Babylon, the Edomites stood by and encouraged the attackers. They cheered the enemy on! They gloated while the Babylonians sacked Jerusalem. And when the Babylonians left, the Edomites entered the Holy City and helped themselves to the remaining plunder. They even captured Judeans who were trying to escape and turned them over to the Babylonians.

Obadiah reassured the hurting Judeans that justice would be done. In God's timing, Edom would experience the same kind of destruction that Judah did. God promised that Judah and Israel would someday come out on top, and he has been true to his word. The nation of Israel still exists, but the nation of Edom has been gone for thousands of years. When we have been betrayed and are struggling with hatred and the desire to "get even," we can leave justice in God's hands. We can rest in the knowledge that someday he will right all wrongs. Then, as we release the burden of anger and hatred to God, we can get on with our recovery.

THE BOTTOM LINE

PURPOSE: To demonstrate how God would accomplish recovery for his people after they had been betrayed by their allies. AUTHOR: The prophet Obadiah. AUDIENCE: The people of Judah and the Edomites. DATE WRITTEN: Either shortly after Judah and Jerusalem fell to the Babylonians in 586 B.C., or perhaps much earlier when Jehoram was king of Judah in 845 B.C. SETTING: The prophet speaks alternately to the nation of Edom and to the people of Judah in Jerusalem. KEY VERSE: "For deliverers will come to Jerusalem and rule all Edom. And the Lord shall be King!" (1:21). KEY PEOPLE AND RELATIONSHIPS: The book focuses on the relationship between the descendants of Isaac's twin sons: Jacob (the ancestor of the Judeans) and Esau (the ancestor of the Edomites).

RECOVERY THEMES

Justice Belongs to God: When we have been betrayed by someone we trusted, and realize the enormity of their offense, we may become obsessed with the desire for revenge. Our soul might resound with the words, "Justice must prevail!" Although these feelings are natural, God makes it very clear that we are not to act on them. Revenge will only bring even more pain and devastation into our life. We are to confidently place justice in God's hands. He can be trusted to bring about true and total justice. Then we can be free from the destructive hatred that will only impede our recovery.

The Danger of Self-sufficiency: The Edomites were proud of their self-sufficiency and felt secure in their mountain fortress. However, there is no lasting security apart from God. We need to guard our heart as we progress in our recovery. Success can subtly lead us to think we can go it alone, an attitude that invariably leads to relapse and despair. As we begin to feel good about our recovery, we must remember that God is the one who empowers us. We cannot stand on our own; we need God's constant sustenance and strength.

CHAPTER 1

Edom's Destruction Is Sure

In a vision the Lord God showed Obadiah the future of the land of Edom.

"A report has come from the Lord," he said,
"that God has sent an ambassador to the
nations with this message: 'Attention! You are
to send your armies against Edom and destroy
her!'"
2"I will cut you down to size among the
nations, Edom, making you small and despised.
3"You are proud because you live in those
high, inaccessible cliffs. 'Who can ever
reach us way up here!' you boast. Don't fool
yourselves! 4Though you soar as high as
eagles, and build your nest among the stars,
I will bring you plummeting down," says
the Lord.
5"Far better it would be for you if thieves
had come at night to plunder you—for they
would not take everything! Or if your vineyards were robbed of all their fruit—for at
least the gleanings would be left! 6Every nook
and cranny will be searched and robbed, and
every treasure found and taken.
7"All your allies will turn against you and
help to push you out of your land. They will
promise peace while plotting your destruction. Your trusted friends will set traps for
you, and all your counterstrategy will fail. 8In
that day not one wise man will be left in all of
Edom!" says the Lord. "For I will fill the wise
men of Edom with stupidity. 9The mightiest
soldiers of Teman will be confused, and helpless to prevent the slaughter.
10"And why? Because of what you did to
your brother Israel. Now your sins will be
exposed for all to see; ashamed and defenseless, you will be cut off forever. 11For you

---

1:3-4 Pride had distorted the thinking of the Edomites. They thought they were too great and powerful for God, but God let them know that no one is beyond the reach of his power. We may think that we don't need God because of our status in society or because of our wealth and prestige. Harboring this kind of pride is always destructive; whether we like it or not, we are helpless without God. If we are not able to admit the fact that we need God, there is little hope for our recovery. No matter how capable we are, our dependencies will overwhelm us if we don't have God on our side in the battle.

1:10 The nation of Edom was called Israel's "brother" for good reason. The Edomites and Israelites were descended from Esau and Jacob, the twin sons of the patriarch Isaac. Throughout their lives these brothers had lived in conflict, and, though they made a sort of reconciliation later in life, they were never able to live together for long. Down through the centuries, the anger felt between the two families continued. Unresolved conflict always brings long-term consequences. We have suffered for the conflicts of our ancestors; we carry many of their traits and dysfunctions within ourself. We need to resolve such conflicts and painful issues in our own life to avoid passing them on to future generations. Now is the time to deal with our deep-seated problems!

1:10-15 God held the Edomites accountable for taking advantage of their helpless neighbors in Israel. People who are undergoing tribulations are precious to God, and he will not tolerate those who gain from their misfortunes. God will see to it that justice is served; he says that their "acts will boomerang upon [their] heads." We may have suffered unjustly in the past. If so, we can let go of our feelings of hatred, because God will see that our enemies get what they deserve. If we have taken unfair advantage of others, we need to admit our failures to God and seek to make amends. If we don't, God will not allow us to go unpunished.

deserted Israel in his time of need. You stood aloof, refusing to lift a finger to help him when invaders carried off his wealth and divided Jerusalem among them by lot; you were as one of his enemies.

12"You should not have done it. You should not have gloated when they took him far away to foreign lands; you should not have rejoiced in the day of his misfortune; you should not have mocked in his time of need. 13You yourselves went into the land of Israel in the day of his calamity and looted him. You made yourselves rich at his expense. 14You stood at the crossroads and killed those trying to escape; you captured the survivors and returned them to their enemies in that terrible time of his distress.

15The Lord's vengeance will soon fall upon all Gentile nations. As you have done to Israel, so will it be done to you. Your acts will boomerang upon your heads. 16 You drank my cup of punishment upon my holy mountain, and the nations round about will drink it too; yes, they will drink and stagger back and disappear from history, no longer nations any more.

Israel Will Be Restored

17"But Jerusalem will become a refuge, a way of escape. Israel will reoccupy the land. 18Israel will be a fire that sets the dry fields of Edom aflame. There will be no survivors," for the Lord has spoken.

19Then my people who live in the Negeb shall occupy the hill country of Edom; those living in Judean lowlands shall possess the Philistine plains and repossess the fields of Ephraim and Samaria. And the people of Benjamin shall possess Gilead.

20The Israeli exiles shall return and occupy the Phoenician coastal strip as far north as Zarephath. Those exiled in Asia Minor shall return to their homeland and conquer the Negeb's outlying villages. 21For deliverers will come to Jerusalem and rule all Edom. And the Lord shall be King!

1:17-21 Obadiah's words were for God's people in Israel, but they apply to all people who suffer. While we may have troubles now, God will preserve his people and bless them in the future. We will live with God as our King, while our oppressors will be destroyed. And though life may be rough now, God's promises offer us hope for our future restoration.

JONAH

THE BIG PICTURE

A. JONAH REJECTS GOD'S PROGRAM (1:1-17)
B. JONAH IS DELIVERED FROM THE CONSEQUENCES (2:1-10)
C. GOD SPARES THE PEOPLE OF NINEVEH (3:1-10)
D. THE DEBATE BETWEEN GOD AND JONAH (4:1-10)

God called Jonah to warn the people of Nineveh that they faced sure destruction if they refused to repent of their sins. But Jonah would rather have died than obey God's command to confront the Ninevites with their sin. Jonah wanted God to destroy the wicked Assyrian capital; he didn't want her people to repent and receive God's forgiveness. So Jonah boarded a ship and headed in the opposite direction.

When Jonah chose to disobey God's call, he was not the only person to suffer. The life of everyone on Jonah's ship was threatened by the great storm that God sent. Terrified, the sailors sought out the guilty party, and Jonah quickly volunteered to be thrown overboard. It seems he preferred death to the prospect of preaching to the godless Ninevites.

It is difficult to begin the process of forgiveness once bitterness has set in. God had to put Jonah in the belly of a great fish for three days to get his attention. In the end, Jonah finally admitted he was helpless and asked God for deliverance. Then he grudgingly went to Nineveh to warn the people of their impending punishment. Jonah was not happy when the people responded to his message and repented, for God responded to their humility with mercy.

Even though Jonah quit on God, God never gave up on Jonah. The process of forgiving someone is never easy. God used numerous object lessons—a storm, a great fish, a large bush, a small worm, and a scorching wind—to teach Jonah about compassion and forgiveness. And in spite of Jonah's resistance to God's call, God used him to spread the good news that God desires to bring his salvation to the entire human race.

THE BOTTOM LINE

PURPOSE: To show that God has compassion not only for the Jews, but for all peoples and nations. AUTHOR: The prophet Jonah. AUDIENCE: The people of God in Israel's northern and southern kingdoms. DATE WRITTEN: Probably around 760 B.C. SETTING: Jonah was a prophet in Israel during the time of Jeroboam II, one of the northern kingdom's most powerful kings. He was sent to preach to the people of Nineveh, the capital of Assyria, the nation that would conquer the northern kingdom in 722 B.C. KEY VERSE: "In my great trouble I cried to the Lord and he answered me; from the depths of death I called, and Lord, you heard me!" (2:2). KEY PEOPLE AND RELATIONSHIPS: Jonah, the ship's captain and crew, and the people of Nineveh.

RECOVERY THEMES

God Delivers the Powerless: None of us likes to be powerless, whether we like being in control or whether we are accustomed to playing the victim. However, it is only when we acknowledge our powerlessness that our recovery can begin. In the darkness inside the great fish, Jonah came to realize how helpless he was. It was there that he finally turned to God and received his help. As we recognize our helplessness, we too can receive the help God offers. Only he can redeem and deliver us from our dependencies and compulsions. If we try to go it alone, we are headed for sure disaster.

Keeping God's Priorities: Since Jonah was a prophet of God, we might have expected him to share God's priorities. But when God told him to go to Nineveh, Jonah's response reflected his cultural heritage rather than God's values. Jonah hated the people of Nineveh just as all the people of Israel did—they were the enemy. But God had compassion on this wicked and bloodthirsty people. Jonah needed to get his priorities in line with God's. God desires the salvation of all people, regardless of their race, religion, or nationality. As we share the story of our deliverance, we need to keep this truth in mind.

God's Patience: There are many painful aspects of the recovery process. We, like Jonah, are often tempted to drag our feet. We even pout when life does not go as we would like it to. But God is patient with us, just as he was with Jonah. Rather than running *from* God and trying to avoid the pain of recovery, we need to run *to* God, who is in control and who is trustworthy. He will walk with us all the way, step after painful step.

Forgiveness for Everyone: Jonah was so bitter toward the people of Nineveh that he would have chosen to die rather than proclaim God's good news to them. We, too, can become possessed with the desire for revenge to the point of destroying our own life. Bitterness destroys our peace, takes away our joy, and impedes our recovery. It is not a natural thing to want God to forgive those who have hurt us. But God is merciful to our enemies, even as he has been merciful to us. When we experience God's forgiveness, we can respond with joy when someone else receives the same. We may even become an instrument of healing to the people who have hurt us in the past.

CHAPTER 1

Jonah Runs Away from God

The Lord sent this message to Jonah, the son
of Amittai:
2"Go to the great city of Nineveh, and give
them this announcement from the Lord: 'I
am going to destroy you, for your wickedness
rises before me; it smells to highest heaven.'"
3But Jonah was afraid to go and ran away
from the Lord. He went down to the seacoast,
to the port of Joppa, where he found a ship
leaving for Tarshish. He bought a ticket, went
on board, and climbed down into the dark
hold of the ship to hide there from the Lord.
4But as the ship was sailing along, suddenly
the Lord flung a terrific wind over the sea,
causing a great storm that threatened to send
them to the bottom. 5Fearing for their lives,
the desperate sailors shouted to their gods for
help and threw the cargo overboard to lighten
the ship. And all this time Jonah was sound
asleep down in the hold.
6So the captain went down after him.
"What do you mean," he roared, "sleeping at
a time like this? Get up and cry to your god,
and see if he will have mercy on us and save
us!"
7Then the crew decided to draw straws to

1:1-3 God's ways are not always our ways. God gave Jonah a message that he didn't want to hear, much less obey. It appears here that Jonah was afraid to confront this godless people with the truth about their sin. Later on, however, we are given another reason for Jonah's reticence (4:1-2). Jonah was afraid that the Ninevites would repent and that God would spare them. The prophet was bitter against this bloodthirsty nation and wanted them to be destroyed. He refused to acknowledge that even they could receive God's forgiveness. Part of our recovery includes sharing the story of deliverance with others. Is there someone in our life with whom we refuse to share the Good News for fear he will repent? Harboring such bitterness will lead to our own destruction. God excludes no one from his forgiveness and restoration.

1:4-17 God created a great storm, putting the sailors in a dangerous position over which they had no control. Jonah, who was responsible for their plight, was asleep in the bottom of the boat. Often our irresponsible actions put the lives of others in jeopardy. Our dependencies bring pain, and sometimes long-term consequences, into the lives of family members and friends. We, like Jonah, need to wake up from the sleep of denial and take responsibility for our failures. Then we must do what we can to make amends with the innocent people around us.

READ JONAH 4:1-4

GOD grant me the serenity to accept the things I cannot change the courage to change the things I can and the wisdom to know the difference AMEN

When people have hurt us deeply, it is easy to hate and wish for vengeance. But holding tightly to these feelings can easily become a defect of character.

The bitterness we experience threatens our recovery because it causes us to blame others for our problems. It may scare us to think of forgiving those who have hurt us. We may be afraid that releasing our hatred will require us to condone the bad things people have done to us.

Jonah felt this way, too. He hated the people of Nineveh for their cruelty toward Israel. God told Jonah to go and warn them of the destruction planned for them. Instead, he tried to run away by boarding a ship going the opposite direction. God caused a life-threatening storm, and Jonah ended up in the belly of a great fish. Suddenly, God had Jonah's attention, and Jonah reluctantly obeyed. Jonah preached to the people of Nineveh, they changed their ways, and God put off his planned destruction. Jonah complained, "This is exactly what I thought you'd do. . . . That's why I ran away. . . . I knew how easily you could cancel your plans for destroying these people" (Jonah 4:2).

We will never be able to remove our bitterness on our own. And it will never be easy to accept that God wants to rescue even the people we hate. We will need to allow God to change our heart as we work toward forgiving those who have hurt us. This will take time. God asks only that we be willing to let him begin the work. ***Turn to page 1013, Matthew 6.***

---

see which of them had offended the gods and
caused this terrible storm; and Jonah drew the
short one.
8"What have you done," they asked, "to
bring this awful storm upon us? Who are you?
What is your work? What country are you
from? What is your nationality?"
9,10And he said, "I am a Jew; I worship
Jehovah, the God of heaven, who made the
earth and sea." Then he told them he was
running away from the Lord.
The men were terribly frightened when
they heard this. "Oh, why did you do it?" they
shouted. 11"What should we do to you to stop
the storm?" For it was getting worse and
worse.
12"Throw me out into the sea," he said,
"and it will become calm again. For I know
this terrible storm has come because of me."
13They tried harder to row the boat ashore,
but couldn't make it. The storm was too fierce
to fight against. 14Then they shouted out a
prayer to Jehovah, Jonah's God. "O Jehovah,"
they pleaded, "don't make us die for this
man's sin, and don't hold us responsible for
his death, for it is not our fault—you have
sent this storm upon him for your own good
reasons."
15Then they picked up Jonah and threw
him overboard into the raging sea—and the
storm stopped!
16The men stood there in awe before
Jehovah, and they sacrificed to him and
vowed to serve him.
17Now the Lord had arranged for a great fish
to swallow Jonah. And Jonah was inside the
fish three days and three nights.

CHAPTER 2

Jonah Prays inside the Fish

Then Jonah prayed to the Lord his God from
inside the fish:
2"In my great trouble I cried to the Lord and
he answered me; from the depths of death I

called, and Lord, you heard me! [3]You threw
me into the ocean depths; I sank down into
the floods of waters and was covered by your
wild and stormy waves. [4]Then I said, 'O Lord,
you have rejected me and cast me away. How
shall I ever again see your holy Temple?'
[5]"I sank beneath the waves, and death was
very near. The waters closed above me; the
seaweed wrapped itself around my head. [6]I
went down to the bottoms of the mountains
that rise from off the ocean floor. I was locked
out of life and imprisoned in the land of
death. But, O Lord my God, you have
snatched me from the yawning jaws of death!
[7]"When I had lost all hope, I turned my
thoughts once more to the Lord. And my
earnest prayer went to you in your holy
Temple. [8](Those who worship false gods have
turned their backs on all the mercies waiting
for them from the Lord!)
[9]"I will never worship anyone but you! For
how can I thank you enough for all you have
done? I will surely fulfill my promises. For my
deliverance comes from the Lord alone."
[10]And the Lord ordered the fish to spit up
Jonah on the beach, and it did.

CHAPTER 3

Jonah Preaches at Nineveh

Then the Lord spoke to Jonah again: "Go to
that great city, Nineveh," he said, "and warn
them of their doom, as I told you to before!"
[3]So Jonah obeyed and went to Nineveh.
Now Nineveh was a very large city with many
villages around it—so large that it would take
three days to walk through it.
[4,5]But the very first day when Jonah entered
the city and began to preach, the people repented. Jonah shouted to the crowds that
gathered around him, "Forty days from now
Nineveh will be destroyed!" And they believed him and declared a fast; from the king
on down, everyone put on sackcloth—the
rough, coarse garments worn at times of
mourning.
[6]For when the king of Nineveh heard what
Jonah was saying, he stepped down from his
throne, laid aside his royal robes, put on sackcloth, and sat in ashes. [7]And the king and his

2:1-10 It took Jonah three days in the stomach of the fish to realize that he would have to follow God's plan for his life. God had called Jonah to do something he didn't want to do. Jonah tried to do things his own way and had to suffer the consequences. We all have the same choice Jonah did. We can do things God's way and receive his help and blessing, or we can do things our way and suffer the painful consequences. God will go a long way to rescue his wayward children and lead them back to himself. Sometimes that path will lead down to the depths, if that's what it takes to show us that God's way is the only way.

3:4-9 God's message penetrated to all levels of Ninevite society. The people immediately admitted their faults before God and dressed in clothes of mourning and repentance. The king then took responsibility for his people, making sure that they understood how serious their situation was. He called both great and small to humble themselves before God. When we obey God and share God's transforming message with others, it brings not only deliverance for us but recovery for others as well.

3:10 God does not always use the same methods to deliver people. He saved the sailors by having Jonah willingly thrown from the boat. Here he delivered the Ninevites when Jonah unwillingly brought God's message to them. And God is able to forgive and deliver even the worst of sinners. When people truly repent of their wickedness, God delivers them from judgment. God is merciful toward those who confess their sins and allow God to change them.

4:4-6 God was very patient with Jonah. Rather than condemning him for his anger or punishing him for his actions, God taught Jonah another lesson. He used a fast-growing plant to deliver Jonah from the misery of the scorching heat of the Mesopotamian day. This kind act, however, did not mean God approved of Jonah's behavior. Sometimes physical blessings from God don't necessarily equal spiritual blessings, nor do they imply the spiritual well-being of the person receiving the blessings.

4:7-9 When the vine died and the hot desert wind and sun beat fiercely against Jonah, he was miserable. In fact, Jonah became so upset by his personal discomfort and the mercy God had shown the Ninevites that he wanted to die. He made the mistake of thinking that the world revolved around him rather than around God and his program. As long as we have the same self-centered attitude that Jonah had, there will be little hope for our recovery. We need to humble ourself before God and submit to his plan for us. God's plan may not be the easiest way, and it may not lead us in the direction we want to go, but we can be sure that God's way is always the best way in the long run.

nobles sent this message throughout the city:
"Let no one, not even the animals, eat anything at all, nor even drink any water. 8Every-
one must wear sackcloth and cry mightily to
God, and let everyone turn from his evil ways,
from his violence and robbing. 9Who can tell?
Perhaps even yet God will decide to let us live
and will hold back his fierce anger from destroying us."
10And when God saw that they had put a
stop to their evil ways, he abandoned his plan
to destroy them and didn't carry it through.

CHAPTER 4

God's Mercy Makes Jonah Angry

This change of plans made Jonah very angry.
2He complained to the Lord about it: "This is
exactly what I thought you'd do, Lord, when
I was there in my own country and you first
told me to come here. That's why I ran away
to Tarshish. For I knew you were a gracious
God, merciful, slow to get angry, and full of
kindness; I knew how easily you could cancel
your plans for destroying these people.
3"Please kill me, Lord; I'd rather be dead
than alive [when nothing that I told them
happens]."
4Then the Lord said, "Is it right to be *angry*
about *this?"*
5So Jonah went out and sat sulking on the
east side of the city, and he made a leafy
shelter to shade him as he waited there to see
if anything would happen to the city. 6And
when the leaves of the shelter withered in the
heat, the Lord arranged for a vine to grow up
quickly and spread its broad leaves over Jonah's head to shade him. This made him
comfortable and very grateful.
7But God also prepared a worm! The next
morning the worm ate through the stem of
the plant, so that it withered away and died.
8Then when the sun was hot, God ordered
a scorching east wind to blow on Jonah, and
the sun beat down upon his head until he
grew faint and wished to die. For he said,
"Death is better than this!"
9And God said to Jonah, "Is it right for you
to be angry because the plant died?"
"Yes," Jonah said, "it is; it is right for me to
be angry enough to die!"
10Then the Lord said, "You feel sorry for
yourself when your shelter is destroyed,
though you did no work to put it there, and
it is, at best, short-lived. 11And why shouldn't
I feel sorry for a great city like Nineveh with
its 120,000 people in utter spiritual darkness
and all its cattle?"

Removing Deeper Hurts

BIBLE READING: Jonah 4:4-8

We were entirely ready to have God remove all these defects of character.

When we are upset, we often depend on our addictions to make us feel better. As we get rid of our addictions, we then face the deeper character defects that God wants to heal. Our addictions function as places of "shelter" from our pain. But when those "shelters" are removed, deep anger may surface, exposing yet deeper character flaws that need healing.

Jonah had a glaring defect of character: he couldn't seem to forgive and have compassion on the people he hated. When God decided not to destroy them, Jonah threw a temper tantrum. "Then the Lord said, 'Is it right to be *angry* about *this?'* So Jonah went out and sat sulking on the east side of the city. . . . The Lord arranged for a vine to grow up quickly and spread its broad leaves over Jonah's head to shade him. . . . The next morning . . . [the vine] withered away and died. Then when the sun was hot, God ordered a scorching east wind to blow on Jonah, and the sun beat down upon his head until he grew faint and wished to die" (Jonah 4:4-8).

God did this to show Jonah that the real problem wasn't the loss of his shelter. Hatred was the real problem. The removal of our sheltering addictions may expose deeper problems. This may spark defensive anger as God touches our deepest hurts. It is all right to let the anger out. But it is important to let God take care of the real problem, too. ***Turn to page 1147, John 5.***

REFLECTIONS ON JONAH

insights FROM JONAH'S LIFE

In **Jonah 3:1-3** God once again commanded Jonah to go to Nineveh to proclaim his message. This time, deciding that it was better to obey God than to face his wrath, Jonah obeyed God and preached to the people of Nineveh whom he despised. Sometimes God calls us to do things that we would rather not do. The easy road is usually the wrong road; the right road costs us something. In the end, however, the right way always leads to recovery, blessing, and deliverance.

That which ordinarily would have been considered a great success became a source of great agitation to Jonah. In **Jonah 4:1-3** we find that the prophet became incensed because God decided to forgive the wicked Ninevites. God often chooses to answer our prayers in ways we would never ask for, but that bring a much greater good. If we hope to please God and strengthen our relationship with him, we need to commit ourself to obeying his will. If we do things our own way, we will face a life of frustration and pain. Jonah needed to learn that God's way is the only good way.

In **Jonah 4:10-11** we find the prophet putting his own desires before the needs of others. God was concerned for the spiritual well-being of the more than 600,000 Ninevites, 120,000 of whom were innocent children. As we give in to our dependencies, we often put our own needs before the needs of others around us. We seek to salve our inner pain at the expense of causing great suffering in the lives of those who love us. When God begins to work recovery in our life, we begin to see, as Jonah finally did, just how foolish our selfish attitudes are and how we can begin to act responsibly toward God and others.

MICAH

THE BIG PICTURE

A. THE DOWNFALL OF THE HAUGHTY (1:1–2:13)
   1. Judgment Comes to Those Who Live Disruptive Lives (1:1–2:11)
   2. Hope Comes to Those Who Live Dedicated Lives (2:12-13)

B. THE DELIVERANCE OF THE HELPLESS (3:1–5:15)
   1. Judgment Comes to Those Who Serve Themselves (3:1-12)
   2. Hope Comes from the One Who Serves Others (4:1–5:15)

C. THE DEFEAT OF THE OPPRESSORS (6:1–7:20)
   1. Judgment Comes to Those Who Give Misery to Others (6:1–7:13)
   2. Hope Comes for the One Who Gives Meaning to Others (7:14-20)

The people of Micah's day were not much different than people today. Many of them lived self-centered lives driven by greed and false pride. They spent their nights plotting against the helpless and their days taking advantage of the weak. Their spiritual lives were hypocritical, and they used religion for their personal gain. They lied to make themselves look good and deceived others to cover their corruption. The kingdoms of Israel and Judah had wandered far from God's plan for them, and they would soon suffer the painful consequences.

Centuries before, God had agreed to bless the people of Israel in a unique way in return for their faithfulness. The people had agreed to follow God's will for them, but they had never lived up to their promise. So through his prophet Micah, God took his wayward people to court. God was the prosecutor and plaintiff, Micah was the plaintiff's spokesman, Israel was the defendant, and the witnesses were heaven and earth. God could do nothing but judge them guilty as charged. The consequence would be judgment through exile. The northern kingdom of Israel fell to Assyria soon after this prophecy; the southern kingdom of Judah fell to Babylon a few centuries later.

Micah made it clear that no satisfaction can be found in this life apart from God. Only when we accept our own weaknesses and submit to his program for healthy living can we hope to escape the destructive consequences of a self-centered life. Through our repentance, God always offers us his forgiveness, compassion, and unfailing love. By admitting that we are trapped by our dependencies, and turning to God for help, we can have hope for the future.

THE BOTTOM LINE

PURPOSE: To warn God's people of the destructive consequences of disobedience and to offer a life of peace to those willing to obey God's revealed will. AUTHOR: The prophet Micah. AUDIENCE: The people of God in Israel's northern and southern kingdoms. DATE WRITTEN: Sometime between 742 and 687 B.C. SETTING: Micah spoke to God's people in the northern and southern kingdoms during the period described in 2 Kings 15–20 and 2 Chronicles 26–30. KEY VERSE: "No, [God] has told you what he wants, and this is all it is: *to be fair, just, merciful, and to walk humbly with your God"* (6:8). KEY PLACES: Samaria, Jerusalem, and Bethlehem. KEY PEOPLE AND RELATIONSHIPS: Micah and the people of Samaria and Jerusalem.

RECOVERY THEMES

The Dangers of Pretense: The people in Micah's day were extremely hypocritical. All their religious activities were designed only to make them look good to others. Making an honest assessment of our actions and doing away with pretense are necessary if we want to progress in recovery. To mix selfish motives with an empty display of religious or recovery activities is to pervert the meaning of faith. But to turn to God in our need and to honestly repent of our destructive behaviors and attitudes is a genuine response that leads to healing. Anything less will only set us up for failure and relapse.

God Delivers the Powerless: Even though God's judgment against his rebellious people was sure, he promised that a remnant would trust him and survive the trials ahead. Out of hopelessness, God can bring hope. God's ways are different than the ways of the world. To prove this to us, he often ignores what we consider significant and brings deliverance in ways that we least expect. Micah makes it clear that when we acknowledge our weaknesses, God will step into the gap to deliver us.

God Cares for the Hurting: God cares for those who are hurting and helpless. He shows tenderness to those who suffer and have been rejected. He reaches out in love and mercy to bring healing and hope. And he calls on us to do the same. As we progress in our recovery, we can become instruments of God to bring healing to others. An important part of our recovery is to carry the story of our healing to those who are still in bondage. As we do this, we will give hope to others and experience renewed encouragement to persevere in our own recovery.

CHAPTER 1

The Trial of Israel and Judah

These are messages from the Lord to Micah, who lived in the town of Moresheth during the reigns of King Jotham, King Ahaz, and King Hezekiah, all kings of Judah. The messages were addressed to both Samaria and Judah and came to Micah in the form of visions.

2 Attention! Let all the peoples of the world
listen. For the Lord in his holy Temple has
made accusations against you!
3 Look! He is coming! He leaves his throne
in heaven and comes to earth, walking on the
mountaintops. 4 They melt beneath his feet
and flow into the valleys like wax in fire, like
water pouring down a hill.
5 And why is this happening? Because of the
sins of Israel and Judah. What sins? The idolatry and oppression centering in the capital
cities, Samaria and Jerusalem!
6 Therefore, the entire city of Samaria will
crumble into a heap of rubble and become an
open field, her streets plowed up for planting
grapes! The Lord will tear down her wall and
her forts, exposing their foundations, and
pour their stones into the valleys below. 7 All
her carved images will be smashed to pieces;
her ornate idol temples, built with the gifts of
worshipers, will all be burned.
8 I will wail and lament, howling as a jackal,
mournful as an ostrich crying across the desert sands at night. I will walk naked and barefoot in sorrow and shame; 9 for my people's
wound is far too deep to heal. The Lord stands
ready at Jerusalem's gates to punish her. 10 Woe
to the city of Gath. Weep, men of Bakah. In
Beth-le-aphrah roll in the dust in your anguish and shame. 11 There go the people of
Shaphir, led away as slaves—stripped, naked
and ashamed. The people of Zaanan dare not
show themselves outside their walls. The
foundations of Beth-ezel are swept away—the

1:2-7 God announced the coming of a sudden and intense judgment on his people, who had refused to trust and obey him. They had rebelled and sought help from powerless idols. God showed them how useless their idol worship was by allowing them to suffer the consequences of seeking help from a source that could not deliver. Our addictions may be idols that we call upon to escape our inner pain—a pain that only God is able to truly heal. We may make a recovery fad an idol and call upon it to lead us down an easy road to recovery. If we pursue help from idols, however, we will only be disappointed. Only God has the power to help us persevere in the process of recovery.

1:12-16 If we don't repent of our dependencies and failures, we cannot expect God's blessing. And we should never expect to experience good times when God is dealing with the sin in our life. When there is no repentance, sin is contagious, and its effects are far-reaching. Notice that even the innocent children will be sold into slavery because of their parents' sins. We often fail to realize that our dependencies may cause great suffering for generations into the future. We need to act now, admitting our failures and giving our life into God's gracious hands. With God's help we will yet be able to overcome our addictions and set our children and grandchildren free from a painful future.

very ground on which it stood. 12The people
of Maroth vainly hope for better days, but
only bitterness awaits them as the Lord stands
poised against Jerusalem.
13Quick! Use your swiftest chariots and flee,
O people of Lachish, for you were the first of
the cities of Judah to follow Israel in her sin of
idol worship. Then all the cities of the south
began to follow your example.
14Write off Moresheth of Gath; there is no
hope of saving her. The town of Achzib has
deceived the kings of Israel, for she promised
help she cannot give. 15You people of Mareshah will be a prize to your enemies. They will
penetrate to Adullum, the "Pride of Israel."
16Weep, weep for your little ones. For they
are snatched away, and you will never see
them again. They have gone as slaves to distant lands. Shave your heads in sorrow.

CHAPTER 2

God Punishes Injustice

Woe to you who lie awake at night, plotting
wickedness; you rise at dawn to carry out your
schemes; because you can, you do. 2You want
a certain piece of land or someone else's house
(though it is all he has); you take it by fraud
and threats and violence.
3But the Lord God says, "I will reward your
evil with evil; nothing can stop me; never
again will you be proud and haughty after I
am through with you. 4Then your enemies
will taunt you and mock your dirge of despair:
'We are finished, ruined. God has confiscated
our land and sent us far away; he has given
what is ours to others.'" 5Others will set your
boundaries then. "The People of the Lord"
will live where they are sent.
6"Don't say such things," the people say.
"Don't harp on things like that. It's disgraceful, that sort of talk. Such evils surely will not
come our way."
7Is that the right reply for you to make, O
House of Jacob? Do you think the Spirit of the
Lord likes to talk to you so roughly? No! His
threats are for your good, to get you on the
path again.
8Yet to this very hour my people rise against
me. For you steal the shirts right off the backs
of those who trusted you, who walk in peace.
9You have driven out the widows from their
homes and stripped their children of every
God-given right. 10Up! Begone! This is no
more your land and home, for you have filled
it with sin, and it will vomit you out.
11"I'll preach to you the joys of wine and
drink"—that is the kind of drunken, lying
prophet that you like!
12"The time will come, O Israel, when I will
gather you—all that are left—and bring you
together again like sheep in a fold, like a flock
in a pasture—a noisy, happy crowd. 13The
Messiah will lead you out of exile and bring
you through the gates of your cities of captivity, back to your own land. Your King will go
before you—the Lord leads on.

CHAPTER 3

Punishment for the Leaders

Listen, you leaders of Israel—you are supposed to know right from wrong, 2yet you are
the very ones who hate good and love evil;

2:1-5 Many of Israel's influential people spent their time planning ways to ruin the lives of others. They sought personal wealth and influence, and the more they took for themselves, the more they hurt those around them. They were blind to much of the pain they were causing and unaware of the judgment they were piling up for themselves. Our addictions often drive us to make the same mistake. As we make an inventory of our life, we should think clearly about those we have hurt and seek ways to make amends. If we don't, God will defend the helpless from our selfish actions and bring judgment against us.

2:12-13 Even though God warned his people of sure destruction to come, he also gave them a reason to hope for the future: someday he would restore the nation he was about to punish. As we face the inescapable consequences of our past actions, we can still have hope for the future. Even though there may be hard times ahead, if we trust God and obey his will for our life, there is always hope for recovery. No matter how great our sin and suffering, God is able to bring about our forgiveness and restoration.

3:1-4 The leaders of Israel failed to fulfill their responsibilities before God—to defend the poor and helpless in society. In fact, they took advantage of the very people they were supposed to protect. They could expect only punishment from God for such actions. We may have suffered innocently at the hands of our parents or some other person in authority. Perhaps their sin against us is at the root of our own destructive behaviors. We can be sure that God will punish those who have wronged us. We can leave the situation in God's hands and spend our energy dealing with our own problems and dependencies. If we have harmed the innocent people in our charge, it is time to repent and make amends.

you skin my people and strip them to the bone.

3You devour them, flog them, break their bones, and chop them up like meat for the cooking pot—4and then you plead with the Lord for his help in times of trouble! Do you really expect him to listen? He will look the other way! 5You false prophets! You who lead his people astray! You who cry "Peace" to those who give you food and threaten those who will not pay!

This is God's message to you: 6"The night will close about you and cut off all your visions; darkness will cover you with never a word from God. The sun will go down upon you, and your day will end. 7Then at last you will cover your faces in shame and admit that your messages were not from God."

8But as for me, I am filled with power, with the Spirit of the Lord, fearlessly announcing God's punishment on Israel for her sins.

9Listen to me, you leaders of Israel who hate justice and love unfairness 10and fill Jerusalem with murder and sin of every kind— 11you leaders who take bribes; you priests and prophets who won't preach and prophesy until you're paid. (And yet you fawn upon the Lord and say, "All is well—the Lord is here among us. No harm can come to us.") 12It is because of you that Jerusalem will be plowed like a field and become a heap of rubble; the mountaintop where the Temple stands will be overgrown with brush.

CHAPTER 4

God Will Be King

But in the last days Mount Zion will be the most renowned of all the mountains of the world, praised by all nations; people from all over the world will make pilgrimages there.

2"Come," they will say to one another, "let us visit the mountain of the Lord, and see the Temple of the God of Israel; he will tell us what to do, and we will do it." For in those days the whole world will be ruled by the Lord from Jerusalem! He will issue his laws and announce his decrees from there.

3He will arbitrate among the nations and dictate to strong nations far away. They will beat their swords into plowshares and their spears into pruning-hooks; nations shall no longer fight each other, for all war will end. There will be universal peace, and all the military academies and training camps will be closed down.

4Everyone will live quietly in his own home in peace and prosperity, for there will be nothing to fear. The Lord himself has promised this. 5(Therefore we will follow the Lord our God forever and ever, even though all the nations around us worship idols!)

6In that coming day, the Lord says that he will bring back his punished people—sick and lame and dispossessed— 7and make them strong again in their own land, a mighty nation, and the Lord himself shall be their King from Mount Zion forever. 8O Jerusalem—the Watchtower of God's people—your royal might and power will come back to you again, just as before.

9But for now, now you scream in terror. Where is your king to lead you? He is dead! Where are your wise men? All are gone! Pain has gripped you like a woman in labor. 10Writhe and groan in your terrible pain, O people of Zion, for you must leave this city and live in the fields; you will be sent far away into exile in Babylon. But there I will rescue you and free you from the grip of your enemies.

11True, many nations have gathered together against you, calling for your blood, eager to destroy you. 12But they do not know the thoughts of the Lord nor understand his plan, for the time will come when the Lord will gather together the enemies of his people

---

3:5-12 Some of us serve God only for what we can get out of it. When all is going well, we act piously; when things don't go our way, however, we use pressure tactics to secure personal gain. Manipulation of others must stop if our recovery is to be complete. God does not always pick up the pieces of our mistakes and bad decisions. He may allow us to experience the full negative impact of our actions. Sometimes it takes such suffering to awaken us from our denial and to help us realize how much we need God.

4:1-5 If God's will was obeyed by everyone, our world would be filled with peace and prosperity. Life would be filled with meaning and joy. For some reason, however, we continually reject God's program and continue to do things our own way. We live for personal gratification and blind ourselves to the needs of others. As we recognize the destruction and pain we have caused by doing things our own way, it might help to reflect on how things could be if we did things God's way. God desires that we live in a world of joy and harmony. If we admit our failures and seek to live according to his will for us, there is still hope that our corner of the world can reflect God's good intentions for wellness and peace.

like sheaves upon the threshing floor, helpless before Israel.

13Rise, thresh, O daughter of Zion; I will give you horns of iron and hoofs of brass; you will trample to pieces many people, and you will give their wealth as offerings to the Lord, the Lord of all the earth.

CHAPTER 5

A Ruler from Bethlehem

Mobilize! The enemy lays siege to Jerusalem! With a rod they shall strike the Judge of Israel on the face.

2"O Bethlehem Ephrathah, you are but a small Judean village, yet you will be the birthplace of my King who is alive from everlasting ages past!" 3God will abandon his people to their enemies until she who is to give birth has her son; then at last his fellow countrymen—the exile remnants of Israel—will rejoin their brethren in their own land.

4And he shall stand and feed his flock in the strength of the Lord, in the majesty of the name of the Lord his God, and his people shall remain there undisturbed, for he will be greatly honored all around the world. 5He will be our Peace. And when the Assyrian invades our land and marches across our hills, he will appoint seven shepherds to watch over us, eight princes to lead us. 6They will rule Assyria with drawn swords and enter the gates of the land of Nimrod. He will deliver us from the Assyrians when they invade our land.

7Then the nation of Israel will refresh the world like a gentle dew or the welcome showers of rain, 8and Israel will be as strong as a lion. The nations will be like helpless sheep before her! 9She will stand up to her foes; all her enemies will be wiped out.

10"At that same time," says the Lord, "I will destroy all the weapons you depend on, 11tear down your walls, and demolish the defenses of your cities. 12I will put an end to all witchcraft—there will be no more fortune-tellers to consult— 13and destroy all your idols. Never again will you worship what you have made, 14for I will abolish the heathen shrines from among you, and destroy the cities where your idol temples stand.

15"I will pour out my vengeance upon the nations who refuse to obey me."

CHAPTER 6

God's Case against His People

Listen to what the Lord is saying to his people:

"Stand up and state your case against me. Let the mountains and hills be called to witness your complaint.

2"And now, O mountains, listen to the Lord's complaint! For he has a case against his people Israel! He will prosecute them to the full. 3O my people, what have I done that makes you turn away from me? Tell me why your patience is exhausted! Answer me! 4For I brought you out of Egypt and cut your chains of slavery. I gave you Moses, Aaron, and Miriam to help you.

5"Don't you remember, O my people, how

4:9-13 God's people needed to accept the consequences of their actions. God had to remove their world of false security and send them into exile in order to help them realize that they needed him. But God did this only to make them a stronger and more righteous people. His punishments were only a small part of his much bigger plan to restore and heal them. God works the same way in our life. The pain we face now for our past failures is real, but it is only a small part of God's plan for our recovery. In the end, God's judgments will become a source of great blessing for us if we trust God and obey his will for our life.

5:1-5 Out of a place that the world considered insignificant, God would bring greatness. God made the tiny town of Bethlehem an internationally famous place when he chose it as the birthplace of his Messiah. God is famous for using "insignificant" people and places to achieve great things. He can take our broken and useless life and turn it into a blessing to others if we turn it over to him. This can begin as we share our story of how God delivered us. As others hear how God has blessed us, they will experience hope that God can do the same for them. Out of a hopeless situation, God can bring hope. Out of the confusion and chaos we have created, God can rebuild a world of peace.

5:10-15 Here God promised to destroy all the useless things his people had depended on for security. They relied on their weapons and walled cities for protection from their enemies. They sought spiritual guidance in the occult, astrology, and idol worship. God's people would discover that their so-called strengths were only illusions; they were depending on things that could never help them. We do the same thing when we turn to our dependencies—drugs, alcohol, sex, work—to help us deal with our inner pain. Sometimes we turn to other "spiritual" remedies for our addictions, which only leads us away from the one true source of help—God. If we depend on useless resources, we will find that they go up in smoke as soon as we really need them. Only God can offer the deliverance and healing that we really need.

Balak, king of Moab, tried to destroy you
through the curse of Balaam, son of Beor, but
I made him bless you instead? That is the
kindness I showed you again and again. Have
you no memory at all of what happened at
Acacia and Gilgal and how I blessed you
there?"
6"How can we make up to you for what
we've done?" you ask. "Shall we bow before
the Lord with offerings of yearling calves?"
Oh no! 7For if you offered him thousands
of rams and ten thousands of rivers of olive
oil—would that please him? Would he be
satisfied? If you sacrificed your oldest child,
would that make him glad? Then would he
forgive your sins? Of course not!
8No, he has told you what he wants, and
this is all it is: *to be fair, just, merciful, and to
walk humbly with your God.*
9The Lord's voice calls out to all Jerusalem—listen to the Lord if you are wise! "The
armies of destruction are coming; the Lord is
sending them. 10For your sins are very great—
is there to be no end of getting rich by cheating? The homes of the wicked are full of
ungodly treasures and lying scales. 11Shall I
say 'Good!' to all your merchants with their
bags of false, deceitful weights? How could
God be just while saying that? 12Your rich men
are wealthy through extortion and violence;
your citizens are so used to lying that their
tongues can't tell the truth!
13"Therefore I will wound you! I will make
your hearts miserable for all your sins. 14You
will eat but never have enough; hunger pangs
and emptiness will still remain. And though
you try and try to save your money, it will
come to nothing at the end, and what little
you succeed in storing up I'll give to those
who conquer you! 15You will plant crops but
not harvest them; you will press out the oil
from the olives and not get enough to anoint
yourself! You will trample the grapes but get
no juice to make your wine.
16"The only commands you keep are those
of Omri; the only example you follow is that
of Ahab! Therefore, I will make an awesome
example of you—I will destroy you. I will
make you the laughingstock of the world; all
who see you will snicker and sneer!"

CHAPTER 7

Hard Times for Everyone

Woe is me! It is as hard to find an honest man
as grapes and figs when harvest days are over.
Not a cluster to eat, not a single early fig,
however much I long for it! The good men
have disappeared from the earth; not one
fair-minded man is left. They are all murderers, turning against even their own brothers.
3They go at their evil deeds with both
hands, and how skilled they are in using
them! The governor and judge alike demand
bribes. The rich man pays them off and tells
them whom to ruin. Justice is twisted between them. 4Even the best of them are
prickly as briars; the straightest is more
crooked than a hedge of thorns. But your
judgment day is coming swiftly now; your
time of punishment is almost here; confusion, destruction, and terror will be yours.
5Don't trust anyone, not your best friend—
not even your wife! 6For the son despises his
father; the daughter defies her mother; the
bride curses her mother-in-law. Yes, a man's
enemies will be found in his own home.

6:4-5 The people of Israel had become smug and self-sufficient, forgetting that they were helpless without God's power. When we begin to experience success in our recovery, it can be easy to forget that God was the one who delivered us. We tend to take some of the credit and place less importance on our relationship to God. When we fail to recognize God's help in our earlier successes, we can almost count on a painful relapse. God was the only one able to deliver us from bondage, and he is the only one able to sustain us in recovery.

6:6-8 When we consider who God is and who we are, we realize that there is nothing we can truly give to him—neither our possessions nor our most prized treasures—that will impress him or win his favor for us. God, in the final sense, does not desire our religious acts of worship, unless those acts are accompanied by a life that is pleasing to him. His desire is that we treat others responsibly, that we demonstrate compassion toward others, and that we exhibit a full reliance on him. These are important features of any godly recovery program.

7:1-6 When people live for personal gain and turn away from God, the results are always disastrous. Following God's program should lead to a society of peace and prosperity. Following the program of personal gratification leads to a world where business becomes unproductive and competition becomes cruel. The leaders of the government become corrupt and no one can be trusted—even members of one's own family! Instead of following our selfish inclinations, we can choose to obey God's will for our life; it will lead to a life of peace.

God Promises Eventual Restoration
7As for me, I look to the Lord for his help; I
wait for God to save me; he will hear me. 8Do
not rejoice against me, O my enemy, for
though I fall, I will rise again! When I sit in
darkness, the Lord himself will be my Light. 9I
will be patient while the Lord punishes me,
for I have sinned against him; then he will
defend me from my enemies and punish
them for all the evil they have done to me.
God will bring me out of my darkness into the
light, and I will see his goodness. 10Then my
enemy will see that God is for me and be
ashamed for taunting, "Where is that God of
yours?" Now with my own eyes I see them
trampled down like mud in the street.
11Your cities, people of God, will be rebuilt,
much larger and more prosperous than before. 12Citizens of many lands will come and
honor you—from Assyria to Egypt, and from
Egypt to the Euphrates, from sea to sea and
from distant hills and mountains.
13But first comes terrible destruction to Israel for the great wickedness of her people.
14O Lord, come and rule your people; lead
your flock; make them live in peace and prosperity; let them enjoy the fertile pastures of
Bashan and Gilead as they did long ago.
15"Yes," replies the Lord, "I will do mighty
miracles for you, like those when I brought
you out of slavery in Egypt. 16All the world
will stand amazed at what I will do for you
and be embarrassed at their puny might. They
will stand in silent awe, deaf to all around
them." 17They will see what snakes they are,
lowly as worms crawling from their holes.
They will come trembling out from their
fortresses to meet the Lord our God. They will
fear him; they will stand in awe.
18Where is another God like you, who pardons the sins of the survivors among his
people? You cannot stay angry with your
people, for you love to be merciful. 19Once
again you will have compassion on us. You
will tread our sins beneath your feet; you will
throw them into the depths of the ocean!
20You will bless us as you promised Jacob long
ago. You will set your love upon us, as you
promised our father Abraham!

7:15-20 What beautiful words of comfort! No matter how terrible our past, there is always hope for the future when we turn our life over to God. As we follow God's will for us, we will begin to experience God's full pardon and will be the beneficiaries of God's perfect compassion. He will free us from the clutches of our dependencies and make us a blessing to others. We can be assured of God's promises by looking back at how he has kept his promises in the past. As we hear the stories of others in recovery, we can take God's work in their life as a promise for our own healing. We can depend on God to come through for us.

REFLECTIONS ON MICAH

✲*insights* ABOUT GOD'S DISCIPLINE

The people of Israel did not want to face up to their sins and tried to ignore Micah's messages predicting punishment from God. But since they refused to listen to God's warnings, they would have to face the consequences of their actions. Perhaps their suffering would lead them to repentance. Notice that in **Micah 2:6-7,** God told his wayward people that he planned to punish them because he loved them, not because he wanted vengeance. God wanted to lead his people back into a healthy relationship with himself. The painful consequences we suffer for our addictive behaviors are one way God uses to call us back into a relationship with himself. Sometimes our denial is so strong that nothing short of disaster can get our attention. We can be sure that no matter how much pain we feel now, God still loves us and desires to get us into the process of recovery.

In **Micah 4:6-7** we are shown how much God cares about hurting people. He consistently shows deep tenderness to those rejected by society. God also demonstrates a fatherly concern toward those he has disciplined. In fact, his very discipline is a clear sign of his love (see Hebrews 12:6-7). Although God's discipline may hurt, it helps us recognize the destructive forces in our life and is often the impetus to our recovery. As we recover from the consequences of past failures, we need to remember that God hasn't forgotten us, no matter how others have turned against us and are reluctant to forgive us.

In **Micah 7:9-14** the prophet spoke for God's people, recognizing that they had sinned and that their suffering was a part of God's plan for their restoration. The prophet was willing to face the consequences of his people's behavior, knowing that God would use their suffering to bring healing and recovery in the end. Instead of seeking to escape the pain of well-deserved consequences in a relapse, we can turn our life over to God. He will use our pain to help us grow. God is in the business of recovery. Just as he recovered his people from the exile caused by their sin, he desires to deliver us from our bondage and give us a life filled with meaning and joy.

insights ABOUT GOD'S JUSTICE

The prophet made it clear in **Micah 6:10-16** that God despises those who treat others unfairly or who cheat others for personal gain (see Deuteronomy 25:13-16; Proverbs 11:1; 20:10, 23). God will bring sickness to the souls of such people, and they will experience an emptiness that cannot be satisfied by the things of this world. Ultimately they will not enjoy the rewards of their labor; instead, they will suffer destruction, derision, and reproach. As we humbly accept the defects in our character, we will become less prone to victimize fellow strugglers. Learning such humility is an important part of the recovery process.

NAHUM

THE BIG PICTURE

A. JUDAH'S COMFORT IN GOD'S CHARACTER (1:1-15)
   1. God's Justice (1:1-3)
   2. God's Sovereignty (1:3-6)
   3. God's Mercy toward His People (1:7)
   4. God's Judgment toward His Enemies (1:8)
   5. God's Good News of Restoration and Recovery (1:9-15)

B. ASSYRIA'S FEAR AT GOD'S JUDGMENT (2:1–3:19)
   1. Judgment Predicted (2:1-2)
   2. Judgment Described (2:3-10)
   3. Judgment Justified (2:11–3:19)

The prophet Nahum ministered in Judah during a time of great fear. Judah had barely survived attacks from the brutal Assyrians, and her sister nation, the kingdom of Israel, had long since been destroyed by Assyria's bloodthirsty armies. The people of Judah lived in constant fear of being overrun. Their enemy was indifferent to their suffering and well known for its cruelty and oppression.

Nahum, whose name means *comfort,* was God's prophet of consolation during these troubled times. His words were meant to lift the hearts of Judah's oppressed people and to address their unspoken doubts. Nahum began by reminding the people that God is a powerful refuge for people in trouble. He told them that God would judge Judah's cruel oppressors and that Judah would someday regain her status of significance and wholeness.

Nahum's words were also for the people of Nineveh, Assyria's capital. He predicted its imminent doom, and God's judgment arrived soon after the prophet spoke. The city was plundered by the Medes and Babylonians, and the Assyrian empire soon crumbled. Nineveh's demise was a consequence of her harsh treatment of others, especially the people of God.

A century earlier, the prophet Jonah had gone to Nineveh, and the city had been spared destruction because her people had repented. But their failure to stay on the right track led to severe consequences in Nahum's day. Repentance is never a onetime thing. It is something we need to do on a regular basis. True repentance means that we act on our promises to change. Apparently the Assyrians repented only because they feared destruction, not because they had a sincere desire for change. We are in a position to learn from Assyria's mistakes.

THE BOTTOM LINE

PURPOSE: To prophesy the overthrow of Assyria, showing that God is all-powerful and fully able to help those who are oppressed and in trouble. AUTHOR: The prophet Nahum. AUDIENCE: The people of Judah and Nineveh. DATE WRITTEN: Sometime between 663 and 612 B.C., during the period preceding Nineveh's fall in 612 B.C. SETTING: In Nahum's day, Assyria controlled most of the ancient Near East and had already destroyed the northern kingdom of Israel (722 B.C.). KEY VERSE: "The Lord is good. When trouble comes, he is the place to go! And he knows everyone who trusts in him!" (1:7). KEY PLACE: Nineveh, the capital of Assyria. KEY PEOPLE AND RELATIONSHIPS: Nahum, the people of Judah, and the people of Nineveh.

RECOVERY THEMES

Rescued from Fear: Our fears can destroy us if we allow them to control our life. The people of Judah lived under the threat of Assryian attack for many years. Nahum comforted them by helping them turn their eyes away from their cruel enemy and toward their powerful and loving God. He called them to make God their source of strength. As we contend daily with the powerful enemies of our dependencies, we can easily be overcome by fear. We may begin to feel so helpless that we give in to the constant temptation. If we can turn our eyes away from our enemy and toward God, who loves and desires our recovery, our fear and helplessness will melt away. God is there to help us when we come to the end of our rope.

Recovery Occurs within Boundaries: God created us to function best when we do things his way. The people of Nineveh broke all of God's principles for healthy living, and they were allowed to continue in their destructive behavior for quite some time before the consequences caught up with them. But God's inevitable judgment did come down on them. We need to live life within the boundaries of God's revealed will so our recovery can take place without delay. Rejecting God's program always leads to pain and devastation.

The Importance of Perseverance: Nahum was not the first of God's prophets to warn Nineveh of destruction. Over one hundred years earlier, Jonah had gone to call the Ninevites to repentance. Amazingly, the Assyrians had responded to Jonah's message and were spared destruction. But they failed to follow through on their initial promises. They did little to change their behavior and, before long, were worse off than when they started. Recovery doesn't happen all at once. It is something we need to keep up on a regular basis. And it demands action—we need to follow through on our promises to change. Without perseverance, we will end up as Nineveh did—wrecked beyond recognition.

CHAPTER 1

God's Patience and Power

This is the vision God gave to Nahum, who
lived in Elkosh, concerning the impending
doom of Nineveh:
2God is jealous over those he loves; that is
why he takes vengeance on those who hurt
them. He furiously destroys their enemies.
3He is slow in getting angry, but when
aroused, his power is incredible, and he does
not easily forgive. He shows his power in the
terrors of the cyclone and the raging storms;
clouds are billowing dust beneath his feet! 4At
his command the oceans and rivers become
dry sand; the lush pastures of Bashan and
Carmel fade away; the green forests of Lebanon wilt. 5In his presence mountains quake
and hills melt; the earth crumbles, and its
people are destroyed.
6Who can stand before an angry God? His
fury is like fire; the mountains tumble down
before his anger.
7The Lord is good. When trouble comes, he
is the place to go! And he knows everyone
who trusts in him! 8But he sweeps away his
enemies with an overwhelming flood; he pur-
sues them all night long.

God Will Rescue Judah

9What are you thinking of, Nineveh, to defy
the Lord? He will stop you with one blow; he
won't need to strike again. 10He tosses his
enemies into the fire like a tangled mass of
thorns. They burst into flames like straw.
11Who is this king of yours who dares to plot
against the Lord? 12But the Lord is not afraid
of him! "Though he build his army millions
strong," the Lord declares, "it will vanish.
"O my people, I have punished you
enough! 13Now I will break your chains and
release you from the yoke of slavery to this
Assyrian king." 14And to the king he says, "I
have ordered an end to your dynasty; your

1:2-8 The people of Judah were helpless against the great power of Assyria. There was no way they could have withstood an extended attack without God's help. In recovery we begin by recognizing that we can't stand against our dependencies without God's help. We need a power greater than ourself to help us make the changes needed for a restored life. Here we see that God is all-knowing, righteous, compassionate, all-powerful, good, and holy. He is slow to anger but has the power to take radical steps to arrest the progression of injustice and further the recovery of his people.

1:15 This same language was used in Isaiah 52:7 of heralds poised on the hills of Judah shouting the good news of Judah's liberation. The kingdom of Israel had already been destroyed by Assyria, and Judah had lived under a continual threat of attack for many years. The conquest of Nineveh by the Babylonians and Medes would be good news for the desperate, helpless people of Judah. This event took place in 612 B.C., and Nahum 2:3-10 records an account of Nineveh's defeat.

sons will never sit upon your throne. And I
will destroy your gods and temples, and I will
bury you! For how you stink with sin!"
15 See, the messengers come running down
the mountains with glad news: "The invaders
have been wiped out and we are safe!" O
Judah, proclaim a day of thanksgiving and
worship only the Lord, as you have vowed.
For this enemy from Nineveh will never come
again. He is cut off forever; he will never be
seen again.

CHAPTER 2
Nineveh Will Fall

Nineveh, you are finished! You are already
surrounded by enemy armies! Sound the
alarm! Man the ramparts! Muster your defenses, full force, and keep a sharp watch for
the enemy attack to begin! 2 For the land of the
people of God lies empty and broken after
your attacks, but the Lord will restore their
honor and power again!
3 Shields flash red in the sunlight! The attack
begins! See their scarlet uniforms! See their
glittering chariots moving forward side by
side, pulled by prancing steeds! 4 Your own
chariots race recklessly along the streets and
through the squares, darting like lightning,
gleaming like torches. 5 The king shouts for his
officers; they stumble in their haste, rushing
to the walls to set up their defenses. 6 But too
late! The river gates are open! The enemy has
entered! The palace is in panic!
7 The queen of Nineveh is brought out naked to the streets and led away, a slave, with
all her maidens weeping after her; listen to
them mourn like doves and beat their breasts!
8 Nineveh is like a leaking water tank! Her
soldiers slip away, deserting her; she cannot
hold them back. "Stop, stop," she shouts, but
they keep on running.
9 Loot the silver! Loot the gold! There seems
to be no end of treasures. Her vast, uncounted
wealth is stripped away. 10 Soon the city is an
empty shambles; hearts melt in horror; knees
quake; her people stand aghast, pale-faced
and trembling.
11 Where now is that great Nineveh, lion of
the nations, full of fight and boldness, where
even the old and feeble, as well as the young
and tender, lived unafraid?
12 O Nineveh, once mighty lion! You
crushed your enemies to feed your children
and your wives and filled your city and your
homes with captured goods and slaves.
13 But now the Lord Almighty has turned
against you. He destroys your weapons. Your
chariots stand there, silent and unused. Your
finest youth lie dead. Never again will you
bring back slaves from conquered nations;
never again will you rule the earth.

CHAPTER 3
Assyria Will Be Destroyed

Woe to Nineveh, City of Blood, full of lies,
crammed with plunder. 2 Listen! Hear the
crack of the whips as the chariots rush forward against her, wheels rumbling, horses'
hoofs pounding, and chariots clattering as
they bump wildly through the streets! 3 See the
flashing swords and glittering spears in the
upraised arms of the cavalry! The dead are
lying in the streets—bodies, heaps of bodies,
everywhere. Men stumble over them, scram-
ble to their feet, and fall again.
4 All this because Nineveh sold herself to the
enemies of God. The beautiful and faithless
city, mistress of deadly charms, enticed the
nations with her beauty, then taught them all
to worship her false gods, bewitching people
everywhere.
5 "No wonder I stand against you," says the
Lord Almighty; "and now all the earth will see
your nakedness and shame. 6 I will cover you
with filth and show the world how really vile
you are." 7 All who see you will shrink back in
horror: "Nineveh lies in utter ruin." Yet no
one anywhere regrets your fate!
8 Are you any better than Thebes, straddling
the Nile, protected on all sides by the river?

2:2 Assyria had rendered God's people powerless. However, because of God's righteous character and his faithfulness to his people, Nahum gave God's promise that the past glories of Judah and Israel would be restored with the defeat of God's enemies. There is always hope for recovery for those who trust in God.

2:13–3:1 Assyria's defeat was certain. God's people would be delivered, and those who supported Assyria would be silenced forever. God's justice is always administered according to his timetable. It is easy to become discouraged as we see injustices happening all around us. We may wonder why God seems to be doing so little about them. Here we see that God will hold unjust people accountable when the time is right. Our recovery can be slowed if we worry constantly about the injustices we have suffered. God wants us to remember that he is just and will deal with those who have hurt us. It is our job to focus on our own failures and do what we can to follow God's perfect will for our life.

9Ethiopia and the whole land of Egypt were her mighty allies, and she could call on them for infinite assistance, as well as Put and Libya. 10Yet Thebes fell and her people were led off as slaves; her babies were dashed to death against the stones of the streets. Soldiers drew straws to see who would get her officers as servants. All her leaders were bound in chains.

11Nineveh, too, will stagger like a drunkard and hide herself in fear. 12All your forts will fall. They will be devoured like first-ripe figs that fall into the mouths of those who shake the trees. 13Your troops will be weak and helpless as women. The gates of your land will be opened wide to the enemy and set on fire and burned. 14Get ready for the siege! Store up water! Strengthen the forts! Prepare many bricks for repairing your walls! Go into the pits to trample the clay, and pack it in the molds!

15But in the middle of your preparations, the fire will devour you; the sword will cut you down; the enemy will consume you like young locusts that eat up everything before them. There is no escape, though you multiply like grasshoppers. 16Merchants, numerous as stars, filled your city with vast wealth, but your enemies swarm like locusts and carry it away. 17Your princes and officials crowd together like grasshoppers in the hedges in the cold, but all of them will flee away and disappear, like locusts when the sun comes up and warms the earth.

18O Assyrian king, your princes lie dead in the dust; your people are scattered across the mountains; there is no shepherd now to gather them. 19There is no healing for your wound—it is far too deep to cure. All who hear your fate will clap their hands for joy, for where can one be found who has not suffered from your cruelty?

HABAKKUK

THE BIG PICTURE

A. HABAKKUK'S PERPLEXITY AND DOUBT (1:1-17)
B. HABAKKUK PERCEIVES GOD'S PURPOSES (2:1-20)
C. HABAKKUK PRAISES GOD (3:1-19)

Habakkuk was troubled by the evil he saw running rampant in Judah. He brought his honest concern to God, but was not prepared for God's answer. God planned to use the cruel and violent Chaldeans to punish Judah! Judah, even with all her sin, was far more righteous than Babylon. How could God support Babylon's success while bringing destruction on Judah?

Life is filled with such questions. Injustice is a familiar thing in our society; often the bad guys seem to win. Why does God allow it? The words of Habakkuk's prophecy assure us that no matter what we face in life, God never changes his personality or his promises. His holy and loving character remains the same, even when everything seems to be falling apart. He will fulfill all the good promises of his Word, even when our future seems to hold nothing but pain. God is powerful enough to use even the bad things in life to bring about his good will for us and his world.

This prophecy is unique because the prophet never took the role of God's spokesman. Instead, he recorded how God responded to his honest questions about life. God wants us to come to him with our questions and doubts. If we listen to God's reply, we, like Habakkuk, can have our heart stirred to a renewed trust and hope in God. Habakkuk came to realize that remembering past displays of God's power would give him faith in God for future struggles. This is part of the value of sharing our story of deliverance with others. As we remember how God has worked in our recovery, we and others will be strengthened for the conflicts yet to come.

THE BOTTOM LINE

PURPOSE: To deal with doubt by affirming that in spite of the evil in the world, God has not changed in his person or purpose. AUTHOR: The prophet Habakkuk. AUDIENCE: The people of the southern kingdom of Judah. DATE WRITTEN: Between 612 and 589 B.C. SETTING: The kingdom of Judah, just prior to the beginning of the Babylonian invasions and the destruction of Jerusalem. KEY VERSE: "Note this: Wicked men trust themselves alone [as these Chaldeans do], and fail; but the righteous man trusts in me and lives!" (2:4). KEY PEOPLE AND RELATIONSHIPS: Habakkuk and the Chaldeans (Babylonians), Habakkuk and God.

RECOVERY THEMES

The Value of Doubt: We all have our questions; they are a part of life. We may not always find the answers, but we always have the right to ask them. Habakkuk felt the freedom to ask such questions, even of God. We have the same freedom. When circumstances around us or within us seem unbearable, we can remember: God is in control. He does care, and he wants us to come to him with our doubts. It is often during times of doubt that our recovery takes a surge forward. In these times of honest confusion, we are able to recognize our helplessness and entrust our life to God. This is the only way to move forward in recovery.

God Never Changes: For most of us, life is hard and filled with struggle. As we seek to overcome our problems and dependencies, pondering God's faithfulness to us in the past can be a source of continual strength. The prophet Habakkuk was greatly encouraged as he remembered all that God had done for his people. Because God never changes, we can be confident that what he has done in the past, he will continue to do in the future. This is one of the reasons why sharing our story is so important. By telling others about what God has done for us, we give them a reason to believe that he will work the same miracle for them.

God Is Our Source of Hope: Our hope must be built upon the foundation of our powerful and loving God. Because Habakkuk's hope was in God, he could patiently wait for God to bring the day of judgment against Babylon. We live—really live—by trusting God. We will make progress in recovery as we improve our relationship with him and seek his face each day. He is our strength and our place of safety. He is the basis of our hope for recovery.

CHAPTER 1

Habakkuk Questions God

This is the message that came to the prophet Habakkuk in a vision from God:

[2]O Lord, how long must I call for help before you will listen? I shout to you in vain; there is no answer. "Help! Murder!" I cry, but no one comes to save. [3]Must I forever see this sin and sadness all around me?

Wherever I look I see oppression and bribery and men who love to argue and to fight. [4]The law is not enforced, and there is no justice given in the courts, for the wicked far outnumber the righteous, and bribes and trickery prevail.

[5]The Lord replied: "Look, and be amazed! You will be astounded at what I am about to do! For I am going to do something in your own lifetime that you will have to see to believe. [6]I am raising a new force on the world scene, the Chaldeans, a cruel and violent nation who will march across the world and conquer it. [7]They are notorious for their cruelty. They do as they like, and no one can interfere. [8]Their horses are swifter than leopards. They are a fierce people, more fierce than wolves at dusk. Their cavalry move proudly forward from a distant land; like eagles they come swooping down to pounce upon their prey. [9]All opposition melts away before the terror of their presence. They collect captives like sand.

[10]"They scoff at kings and princes and scorn their forts. They simply heap up dirt against their walls and capture them! [11] They sweep past like wind and are gone, but their guilt is deep, for they claim their power is from their gods."

[12]O Lord my God, my Holy One, you who are eternal—is your plan in all of this to wipe us out? Surely not! O God our Rock, you have decreed the rise of these Chaldeans to chasten and correct us for our awful sins. [13]We are wicked, but they far more! Will you, who cannot allow sin in any form, stand idly by while they swallow us up? Should you be silent while the wicked destroy those who are better than they?

1:1-4 Habakkuk, a contemporary of the prophets Jeremiah, Daniel, and Ezekiel, was appalled at the wickedness that swirled about him like a windstorm. Lawlessness and injustice were rampant in the nation of Judah. The prophet, sensitive to the sin around him, called out to God. Today's society is not much different. We often find ourself wondering, *Will this ever end?* The rest of Habakkuk's book provides an answer to this question.

1:5-11 God's solution for Judah's sin was exile in Babylonia. He would allow the Babylonians to destroy Judah and Jerusalem to teach them that ignoring his plan for them was not a healthy way to live. It was God's way of helping his people reach bottom so they could begin the process of recovery. God often does the same thing with us. He allows us to live out our dependencies for just so long before he allows the consequences to catch up with us. As we hit bottom, we realize that we can't make it alone. We can then turn to God and discover that his plan for us is the way to recovery.

14Are we but fish, to be caught and killed? Are we but creeping things that have no leader to defend them from their foes? 15Must we be strung up on their hooks and dragged out in their nets, while they rejoice? 16Then they will worship their nets and burn incense before them! "These are the gods who make us rich," they'll say.

17Will you let them get away with this forever? Will they succeed forever in their heartless wars?

CHAPTER 2

God Explains His Ways

I will climb my watchtower now and wait to see what answer God will give to my complaint.

2And the Lord said to me, "Write my answer on a billboard, large and clear, so that anyone can read it at a glance and rush to tell the others. 3But these things I plan won't happen right away. Slowly, steadily, surely, the time approaches when the vision will be fulfilled. If it seems slow, do not despair, for these things will surely come to pass. Just be patient! They will not be overdue a single day!

4"Note this: Wicked men trust themselves alone [as these Chaldeans do], and fail; but the righteous man trusts in me and lives! 5What's more, these arrogant Chaldeans are betrayed by all their wine, for it is treacherous. In their greed they have collected many nations, but like death and hell, they are never satisfied. 6The time is coming when all their captives will taunt them, saying: 'You robbers! At last justice has caught up with you! Now you will get your just deserts for your oppression and extortion!'

7"Suddenly your debtors will rise up in anger and turn on you and take all you have, while you stand trembling and helpless. 8You have ruined many nations; now they will ruin you. You murderers! You have filled the countryside with lawlessness and all the cities too.

9"Woe to you for getting rich by evil means, attempting to live beyond the reach of danger. 10By the murders you commit, you have shamed your name and forfeited your lives. 11The very stones in the walls of your homes cry out against you, and the beams in the ceilings echo what they say.

12"Woe to you who build cities with money gained from murdering and robbery! 13Has not the Lord decreed that godless nations' gains will turn to ashes in their hands? They work so hard, but all in vain!

14("The time will come when all the earth is filled, as the waters fill the sea, with an awareness of the glory of the Lord.)

15"Woe to you for making your neighboring lands reel and stagger like drunkards beneath your blows, and then gloating over their nakedness and shame. 16Soon your own glory will be replaced by shame. Drink down God's judgment on yourselves. Stagger and fall! 17You cut down the forests of Lebanon—now you will be cut down! You terrified the wild animals you caught in your traps—now terror will strike you because of all your murdering and violence in cities everywhere.

18"What profit was there in worshiping all your man-made idols? What a foolish lie that they could help! What fools you were to trust what you yourselves had made. 19Woe to those who command their lifeless wooden idols to arise and save them, who call out to the speechless stone to tell them what to do. Can images speak for God? They are overlaid with gold and silver, but there is no breath at all inside!

20"But the Lord is in his holy Temple; let all the earth be silent before him."

1:12–2:3 When faced with the coming of the Chaldeans, it seemed to Habakkuk that the cure was worse than the disease. How could God bless the godless Babylonians so they would be able to destroy his own people? It didn't seem right. Like Habakkuk, we sometimes wonder how people even more wicked than we are can be allowed to prosper. But rather than turn away in confusion and resentment, we would be wise to turn and face our own problems and dependencies. God will deal with the other people when the time is right. He is ultimately in control.

2:4 Wicked people are characterized by the fact that they trust in themselves. They proudly believe they can make their own way in the world under their own power. Most of us have experienced the consequences of such an attitude. We have discovered that without God, we cannot live a healthy and meaningful life. We soon become enslaved to something—alcohol, drugs, sexual pleasure, work, religious activities—in an effort to fill the empty space inside that only God can fill. God knows what is best for us; we can trust him to lead us into the most meaningful life possible. Notice that being righteous does not depend on our doing the right things. It has to do with trusting God. We can be righteous, no matter how terrible our past, by believing and following God's plan for us.

CHAPTER 3

Habakkuk's Prayer

This is the prayer of triumph that Habakkuk sang before the Lord:

2 O Lord, now I have heard your report, and I worship you in awe for the fearful things you are going to do. In this time of our deep need, begin again to help us, as you did in years gone by. Show us your power to save us. In your wrath, remember mercy.

3 I see God moving across the deserts from Mount Sinai. His brilliant splendor fills the earth and sky; his glory fills the heavens, and the earth is full of his praise! What a wonderful God he is! 4 From his hands flash rays of brilliant light. He rejoices in his awesome power. 5 Pestilence marches before him; plague follows close behind. 6 He stops; he stands still for a moment, gazing at the earth. Then he shakes the nations, scattering the everlasting mountains and leveling the hills. His power is just the same as always! 7 I see the people of Cushan and of Midian in mortal fear.

8,9 Was it in anger, Lord, you smote the rivers and parted the sea? Were you displeased with them? No, you were sending your chariots of salvation! All saw your power! Then springs burst forth upon the earth at your command! 10 The mountains watched and trembled. Onward swept the raging water. The mighty deep cried out, announcing its surrender to the Lord. 11 The lofty sun and moon began to fade, obscured by brilliance from your arrows and the flashing of your glittering spear.

12 You marched across the land in awesome anger and trampled down the nations in your wrath. 13 You went out to save your chosen people. You crushed the head of the wicked and laid bare his bones from head to toe. 14 You destroyed with their own weapons those who came out like a whirlwind, thinking Israel would be an easy prey.

15 Your horsemen marched across the sea; the mighty waters piled high. 16 I tremble when I hear all this; my lips quiver with fear. My legs give way beneath me, and I shake in terror. I will quietly wait for the day of trouble to come upon the people who invade us.

17 Even though the fig trees are all destroyed, and there is neither blossom left nor fruit; though the olive crops all fail, and the fields lie barren; even if the flocks die in the fields and the cattle barns are empty, 18 yet I will rejoice in the Lord; I will be happy in the God of my salvation. 19 The Lord God is my strength; he will give me the speed of a deer and bring me safely over the mountains.

(A note to the choir director: When singing this ode, the choir is to be accompanied by stringed instruments.)

3:1-2 Habakkuk praised God, not only for answering his questions, but also for the knowledge he had gained about the person of God. Habakkuk had come to realize how much his people needed God's discipline (Hebrews 12:5-6), so he acknowledged God's righteousness in their coming judgment. Then he looked past the coming punishment to a time of restoration. God's punishment is always meted for the purpose of growth and blessing in the end. If we are willing to recognize our need for God and follow his good plans for us, we can experience the blessings God intended for us to gain through our painful experiences.

3:3-16 Remembering the powerful acts of God in the past can give us confidence in what God can do now and in the future. During recovery, it is of immeasurable help to read what God has done in the lives of his people and receive the encouragement that their examples and words can provide (see Romans 15:4; 1 Corinthians 10:11). God's work in our own life can also be of great help to others. As we share how God has delivered us in the past, not only will others receive new hope for their recovery, but we also will find encouragement by remembering what God has already done for us.

3:17-19 Habakkuk's prayer came to a climax in a beautiful affirmation of faith. Though there would be hard times ahead, Habakkuk knew that he could trust in God to provide him with the strength he needed to persevere. The words of 3:19 provide a stunning picture of the surefooted confidence we can have in our God of strength and safety, a great assurance for all of us in recovery.

ZEPHANIAH

THE BIG PICTURE

A. PROPHECIES OF JUDGMENT AGAINST JUDAH (1:1–2:3)
   1. Judah's Moral and Spiritual Irresponsibility (1:1-13)
   2. Judah's Accountability before God (1:14-18)
   3. Judah's Opportunity for Recovery (2:1-3)

B. PROPHECIES OF JUDGMENT AGAINST THE NATIONS (2:4-15)

C. PROPHECIES OF JUDGMENT AGAINST JERUSALEM (3:1-8)

D. PROMISES OF BLESSING TO THOSE WHO TRUST IN GOD (3:9-20)

"If only . . ." is a haunting phrase. It implies that we have failed and that we wish we could go back and do things differently. As we work the process of recovery, we often become sad and ashamed when we reflect on our past. We regret our irresponsible and destructive behaviors and wish we could erase past mistakes. This must have been how the people of Judah felt when they heard the prophetic words of Zephaniah. *If only* they had obeyed and trusted God!

God called Zephaniah during the days of King Josiah, the last of Judah's good kings. The prophet's condemnation of Judah's idol worship and self-centered living fit well with the early part of Josiah's reign, when his purges against idolatry were just beginning. Zephaniah's prophetic support of these purges would certainly have bolstered Josiah's efforts. However, the apostasy of Judah's previous kings, Manasseh and Amon, had left deep spiritual wounds in Judah. And despite Zephaniah's ministry and Josiah's noble reforms, scars remained visible in Judah even at the end of his reign.

The people of Judah were in need of some major changes. They had seen the northern kingdom of Israel exiled to Assyria, but assumed that the presence of God in the Jerusalem Temple would protect them from foreign invaders. They needed to be shocked out of their denial and spiritual indifference. Zephaniah warned the people that Judah would be destroyed if they didn't act right away. He also let them know that recovery was still possible. Spiritual awakening could still occur if they would admit their sins and trust in God. Josiah and the people listened to Zephaniah, responded, and experienced revival and recovery.

THE BOTTOM LINE

PURPOSE: To shake the people of Judah out of their complacency and to get them back on the path of recovery. AUTHOR: The prophet Zephaniah. AUDIENCE: The people of the southern kingdom of Judah. DATE WRITTEN: Sometime between 640 and 621 B.C., just prior to King Josiah's great reformation. SETTING: The kingdom of Judah during the years of King Josiah; Zephaniah's ministry may have helped to motivate the young king's reforms. KEY VERSE: "You will no longer need to be ashamed of yourselves, for you will no longer be rebels against me. I will remove all your proud and arrogant people from among you; there will be no pride or haughtiness on my holy mountain" (3:11). KEY PLACE: Jerusalem. KEY PEOPLE AND RELATIONSHIPS: Zephaniah and the people of Judah.

RECOVERY THEMES

The Consequences of Irresponsibility: Many of our troubles are direct consequences of our irresponsibility. Judah was irresponsible in her covenant relationship with God. She worshiped false gods and ignored God's laws that were intended for her own good. But Zephaniah made it clear that their irresponsibility would carry heavy consequences. Encouraged by Zephaniah and led by Josiah, the people of Judah took responsibility for their sins and turned their lives over to God. As a result, they received substantial healing. When we are irresponsible in our relationship with God and others, our situation in life will grow progressively worse. But as we learn to live a responsible life, we begin to experience the blessings of God.

Complacency Leads to Relapse: Prosperity and success often lead to complacency. Josiah's great-grandfather, Hezekiah, had been one of Judah's greatest kings. He had led his people back to God, and God had greatly blessed them. However, Judah's next two kings, Manasseh and Amon, led their people into a period of complacency. And with time, the complacency led to sin and its consequences. Josiah followed in the footsteps of Hezekiah and helped lead the people back to God. Often our greatest failures follow our greatest victories. In order to prevent a relapse, we need to take inventory of our life on a regular basis. We want to have a heart that is vulnerable and dependent on God, regardless of our successes in recovery. For this to happen, we must remain dependent on God.

Recovery Leads to Joy: The process of recovery almost always starts out painfully. When we tell the truth about ourself, it hurts. But as we admit our failures to God, to ourself, and to another person, we discover the great relief and hope that God offers. Then we can look forward to the joy and celebration we will experience as God restores us to himself and to the people we love.

CHAPTER 1

A Grim Prediction for Judah

Subject: a message from the Lord.

To: Zephaniah (son of Cushi, grandson of Gedaliah, great-grandson of Amariah, and great-great-grandson of Hezekiah). *When:* During the reign of Josiah (son of Amon) king of Judah.

2"I will sweep away everything in all your land," says the Lord. "I will destroy it to the ground. 3I will sweep away both men and animals alike. Mankind and all the idols that he worships—all will vanish. Even the birds of the air and the fish in the sea will perish. 4I will crush Judah and Jerusalem with my fist and destroy every remnant of those who worship Baal; I will put an end to their idolatrous priests, so that even the memory of them will disappear. 5They go up on their roofs and bow to the sun, moon, and stars. They 'follow the Lord,' but worship Molech too! I will destroy them. 6And I will destroy those who formerly worshiped the Lord, but now no longer do, and those who never loved him and never wanted to."

7Stand in silence in the presence of the Lord. For the awesome Day of his Judgment has come; he has prepared a great slaughter of his people and has chosen their executioners. 8"On that Day of Judgment I will punish the leaders and princes of Judah and all others wearing heathen clothing. 9Yes, I will punish those who follow heathen customs and who rob and kill to fill their masters' homes with evil gain of violence and fraud. 10A cry of alarm will begin at the farthest gate of Jerusalem, coming closer and closer until the noise of the advancing army reaches the very top of the hill where the city is built.

11"Wail in sorrow, you people of Jerusalem. All your greedy businessmen, all your loan sharks—all will die.

12"I will search with lanterns in Jerusalem's darkest corners to find and punish those who sit contented in their sins, indifferent to God, thinking he will let them alone. 13They are the very ones whose property will be plundered by the enemy, whose homes will be ransacked; they will never have a chance to live in the new homes they have built. They will

1:4-13 Through Zephaniah, God condemned the irresponsible behavior of Judah's leaders. He was probably referring to the recent reigns of Manasseh and Amon, two of Judah's most wicked kings. During their reigns, the people of Judah had become increasingly dependent upon false gods, had ceased to worship the true God, and had built a society in which deceitful and immoral people could prosper. The progression is clear: when we turn from the true God, our society and its members begin to deteriorate. We all need God. Unless we recognize this fact, our life will continue on a downhill trend. As we recognize our powerlessness and turn to God for help, he gives us the power we need to live a healthy and meaningful life.

never drink wine from the vineyards they
have planted.
14“That terrible day is near. Swiftly it
comes—a day when strong men will weep
bitterly. 15It is a day of the wrath of God
poured out; it is a day of terrible distress and
anguish, a day of ruin and desolation, a day
of darkness and gloom, of clouds, blackness,
16trumpet calls, and battle cries; down go the
walled cities and strongest battlements!
17“I will make you as helpless as a blind man
searching for a path because you have sinned
against the Lord; therefore, your blood will be
poured out into the dust and your bodies will
lie there rotting on the ground.”
18Your silver and gold will be of no use to
you in that day of the Lord's wrath. You cannot ransom yourselves with it. For the whole
land will be devoured by the fire of his jealousy. He will make a speedy riddance of all the
people of Judah.

CHAPTER 2
Gather together and pray, you shameless nation, 2while there still is time—before judgment begins and your opportunity is blown
away like chaff; before the fierce anger of the
Lord falls and the terrible day of his wrath
begins. 3Beg him to save you, all who are
humble—all who have tried to obey.
Walk humbly and do what is right; perhaps
even yet the Lord will protect you from his
wrath in that day of doom.

Punishment for Judah's Neighbors

4Gaza, Ashkelon, Ashdod, Ekron—these Philistine cities, too, will be rooted out and left in
desolation. 5And woe to you Philistines living
on the coast and in the land of Canaan, for
the judgment is against you too. The Lord will
destroy you until not one of you is left. 6The
coastland will become a pasture, a place of
shepherd camps and folds for sheep.
7There the little remnant of the tribe of
Judah will be pastured. They will lie down to
rest in the abandoned houses in Ashkelon.
For the Lord God will visit his people in kindness and restore their prosperity again.
8“I have heard the taunts of the people of
Moab and Ammon, mocking my people and
invading their land. 9Therefore as I live,” says
the Lord Almighty, God of Israel, “Moab and
Ammon will be destroyed like Sodom and
Gomorrah and become a place of stinging
nettles, salt pits, and eternal desolation; those
of my people who are left will plunder and
possess them.”
10They will receive the wages of their pride,
for they have scoffed at the people of the Lord
Almighty. 11The Lord will do terrible things to
them. He will starve out all those gods of foreign powers, and everyone shall worship him,
each in his own land throughout the world.
12You Ethiopians, too, will be slain by his
sword, 13and so will the lands of the north; he
will destroy Assyria and make its great capital
Nineveh a desolate wasteland like a wilderness. 14That once proud city will become a
pastureland for sheep. All sorts of wild animals will have their homes in her. Hedgehogs
will burrow there; the vultures and the owls
will live among the ruins of her palaces, hoot-
ing from the gaping windows; the ravens will
croak from her doors. All her cedar paneling
will lie open to the wind and weather.
15This is the fate of that vast, prosperous

1:14-18 The prophet warned of the coming "Day of Judgment"—a day of reckoning with God. At that time, Judah would be conquered and her people led away as slaves to Babylon. God mercifully offered his people numerous chances to repent, but there would come a time when judgment would fall. We should be thankful that God will not allow us to reject his way forever. When we do things our way, we only hurt ourself and the people we love. If we listen to the early warnings we receive and act appropriately, we need not fear a future day of reckoning.

2:1-3 The purpose of God's judgment was to encourage the people of Judah to depend on him. The prophet called the people to repent, hoping that they would be spared the coming devastation. The people responded favorably to Zephaniah's message, and King Josiah led them in a great reformation. This led to the last high point in Judah's history. Though the day of reckoning did come, it was delayed for several generations. If we respond to the warnings we receive, admitting our failures and asking God to help us, we may escape the painful consequences we deserve.

2:4-15 Zephaniah listed the nations that had influenced Judah in their idolatrous practices. These nations would come under God's judgment and lose their corrupting influence. God gives us great potential to influence others for good. However, we often end up leading others in the wrong direction. Taking responsibility for those we have led astray in some way is part of our moral inventory. It may be one of our children or, perhaps, a friend or coworker. Part of making amends with such people is doing what we can to get them back on the right track.

city that lived in such security, that said to herself, "In all the world there is no city as great as I." But now—see how she has become a place of utter ruins, a place for animals to live! Everyone passing that way will mock or shake his head in disbelief.

CHAPTER 3

Judgment for Jerusalem

Woe to filthy, sinful Jerusalem, city of violence and crime. 2In her pride she won't listen even to the voice of God. No one can tell her anything; she refuses all correction. She does not trust the Lord nor seek for God.

3Her leaders are like roaring lions hunting for their victims—out for everything that they can get. Her judges are like ravenous wolves at evening time, who by dawn have left no trace of their prey.

4Her "prophets" are liars seeking their own gain; her priests defile the Temple by their disobedience to God's laws.

5But the Lord is there within the city, and he does no wrong. Day by day his justice is more evident, but no one heeds—the wicked know no shame.

6"I have cut off many nations, laying them waste to their farthest borders; I have left their streets in silent ruin and their cities deserted without a single survivor to remember what happened. 7I thought, 'Surely they will listen to me now—surely they will heed my warnings, so that I'll not need to strike again.' But no; however much I punish them, they continue all their evil ways from dawn to dusk and dusk to dawn."8But the Lord says, "Be patient; the time is coming soon when I will stand up and accuse these evil nations. For it is my decision to gather together the kingdoms of the earth and pour out my fiercest anger and wrath upon them. All the earth shall be devoured with the fire of my jealousy.

A Promise of Hope

9"At that time I will change the speech of my returning people to pure Hebrew so that all can worship the Lord together. 10My scattered people who live in the Sudan, beyond the rivers of Ethiopia, will come with their offerings, asking me to be their God again. 11And then you will no longer need to be ashamed of yourselves, for you will no longer be rebels against me. I will remove all your proud and arrogant people from among you; there will be no pride or haughtiness on my holy mountain. 12Those who are left will be the poor and the humble, and they will trust in the name of the Lord. 13They will not be sinners, full of lies and deceit. They will live quietly, in peace, and lie down in safety, and no one will make them afraid."

14Sing, O daughter of Zion; shout, O Israel; be glad and rejoice with all your heart, O daughter of Jerusalem. 15For the Lord will remove his hand of judgment and disperse the armies of your enemy. And the Lord himself, the King of Israel, will live among you! At last your troubles will be over—you need fear no more.

16On that day the announcement to Jerusalem will be, "Cheer up, don't be afraid. 17,18For the Lord your God has arrived to live among you. He is a mighty Savior. He will give you victory. He will rejoice over you with great gladness; he will love you and not accuse you." Is that a joyous choir I hear? No, it is the Lord himself exulting over you in happy song.

"I have gathered your wounded and taken away your reproach. 19And I will deal severely with all who have oppressed you. I will save the weak and helpless ones, and bring together those who were chased away. I will give glory to my former exiles, mocked and shamed.

20"At that time, I will gather you together and bring you home again, and give you a good name, a name of distinction among all the peoples of the earth, and they will praise you when I restore your fortunes before your very eyes," says the Lord.

3:1-5 The destructive behavior of Judah's people, though influenced by other nations, was ultimately her responsibility. The people refused to admit their sins to God. Instead, they rejected all his attempts at warning and correction. We have all been influenced negatively by others, but pointing the finger at them will slow our recovery. They are responsible to deal with their problems; we are responsible for our own. As we take responsibility for our actions, recognizing how much we need God, we will take the needed steps toward recovery. If we continue to blame others for our problems, we are headed for destruction.

3:9-20 Zephaniah described a future age that would follow the ultimate "Day of Judgment." This will be an age of blessing marked by an honest and pure worship of God. God will remove all dysfunctions from our personalities and relationships; sorrows and burdens will no longer exist; and the nation of Israel will finally be restored to its land of hope and security. As we journey toward full recovery, even in a physical sense, we can rejoice in this promise.

HAGGAI

THE BIG PICTURE

A. INTRODUCTION (1:1)
B. THE FIRST SERMON: REBUKE (1:2-15)
  1. The Prophet's Challenge to Rebuild the Temple (1:2-11)
  2. The People Respond with Action (1:12-15)
C. THE SECOND SERMON: RENEWAL (2:1-9)
D. THE THIRD SERMON: RESTORATION (2:10-19)
E. THE FOURTH SERMON: REASSURANCE (2:20-23)

Haggai was called to encourage the people of Jerusalem to return to the task of rebuilding God's house. About eighteen years had passed since Cyrus released Zerubbabel with a group of Jewish exiles to return to Jerusalem to rebuild the Temple. They had arrived filled with hope, but pressure from the local authorities and selfish decisions led them to quit the task. They turned instead to the task of building their own homes. Their priorities were out of order.

Haggai's task was to arouse the people to complete the task of rebuilding God's Temple. Over a six-month period, he gave four messages designed to get the people back on track. He began by telling the people to stop making excuses and get back to work. He showed them how their present sufferings were a result of their failure to put God first in their lives. They needed to get their spiritual lives in shape and let their actions prove that they had done so before they could expect God's blessings. Haggai's next messages continued the encouragement by promising God's help as they continued the task.

The task of rebuiding the Temple was difficult; so is the task of rebuilding our life. There will always be obstacles, but we don't have to let them stop us. When we feel like quitting, we can remember the message of Haggai. God is there to help and protect us each step of the way. As God's people had to reassess their spiritual lives in the rebuilding process, we need to examine our life and act to prove our inner changes. We, like the people of Jerusalem, can respond to Haggai's message and move forward in the rebuilding process.

THE BOTTOM LINE

PURPOSE: To challenge the people to complete the rebuilding of God's Temple, their community, and their lives. AUTHOR: The prophet Haggai. AUDIENCE: The people living in Jerusalem, including those who had returned from Babylonian exile. DATE WRITTEN: Between August and December, 520 B.C. SETTING: Jerusalem had been in ruins since her destruction by the Babylonians in 586 B.C. The people had started to rebuild the Temple but had failed to complete the task. KEY VERSE: "'Think it over,' says the Lord Almighty. 'Consider how you have acted and what has happened as a result!'" (1:7). KEY PLACES: Jerusalem and the Temple. KEY PEOPLE AND RELATIONSHIPS: Zerubbabel (the political leader), Joshua (the priestly leader), and the prophets Haggai and Zechariah.

RECOVERY THEMES

God's Plan Must Come First: When we face obstacles to God's plan for us, it is easy to get sidetracked; it is tempting to follow the way of least resistance. The people of Jerusalem started rebuilding God's Temple but then met with stiff opposition. Instead of trusting God and standing up to the opposition, the people turned away from the rebuilding project God had for them and built their own homes instead. We tend to make the same mistake. When we face an obstacle to God's program for recovery, we turn away and take the way of least resistance. We hang on to destructive habits, activities, and relationships. We may even start on a recovery program that looks easier but excludes God. But when we reject God's program for our recovery, we also reject his power and blessings in our life.

We Will Face Obstacles: The rebuilding process is never easy. Old friends may be threatened by the changes in our life and set out to stop us. Codependent spouses may become insecure as we begin to grow and may make things difficult for us. We might fear the pain we begin to feel and try to escape it. Temptation will rear its ugly head time and again as we work our program. The Judeans faced numerous obstacles as they sought to rebuild the Temple. Local leaders tried to stop the work again and again. The people became afraid and gave up on the task God had given them to do. With God's help and the encouragement of Haggai, however, the task went on, and the rebuilding of God's Temple was completed. God wants us to recover, and he will help us to overcome the obstacles if we look to him for help.

Recovery Requires Action: It is much easier to recognize a problem than it is to do something about it. God's people in Jerusalem knew the Temple needed to be rebuilt if their nation was to get back on the right track spiritually. They had set out to complete the task, but had then become discouraged and failed to follow through. Their failure to act over a period of years brought continued suffering upon them. Haggai called the people to act; he calls us to do the same. Our recovery project must go beyond our recognition of the problem. We need to take active steps toward reconciliation with God, ourself, and others. As we take these steps, as painful as they may be, we will be moving toward the recovery of our life and relationships.

CHAPTER 1

A Call to Rebuild the Temple

Subject: a message from the Lord.
To: Haggai the prophet, who delivered it to
Zerubbabel (son of Shealtiel), governor of
Judah; and to Joshua (son of Josedech), the
High Priest—for it was addressed to them.
When: In late August of the second year of
the reign of King Darius I.
2"Why is everyone saying it is not the right
time for rebuilding my Temple?" asks the
Lord.
3,4His reply to them is this: "Is it then the
right time for you to live in luxurious homes,
when the Temple lies in ruins? 5Look at the
result: 6You plant much but harvest little. You
have scarcely enough to eat or drink and not
enough clothes to keep you warm. Your income disappears, as though you were putting
it into pockets filled with holes!
7"Think it over," says the Lord Almighty.
"Consider how you have acted and what has
happened as a result! 8Then go up into the
mountains, bring down timber, and rebuild
my Temple, and I will be pleased with it and
appear there in my glory," says the Lord.
9"You hope for much but get so little. And
when you bring it home, I blow it away—it
doesn't last at all. Why? Because my Temple
lies in ruins, and you don't care. Your only
concern is your own fine homes. 10That is why
I am holding back the rains from heaven and
giving you such scant crops. 11In fact, I have
called for a drought upon the land, yes, and
in the highlands too—a drought to wither the
grain and grapes and olives and all your other
crops, a drought to starve both you and all
your cattle and ruin everything you have
worked so hard to get."
12Then Zerubbabel (son of Shealtiel), the
governor of Judah, and Joshua (son of Josedech), the High Priest, and the few people

1:2-8 God called the people in Jerusalem to take an inventory of their priorities. The people had returned from exile and started to rebuild the Temple, but they had stopped when they faced opposition. They chose to build beautiful homes for themselves instead of finishing God's house. They had proven by their actions that they considered their personal comfort to be more important than God. As a result, they suffered the consequences of hard times. When we put God in the backseat of our life, we become enslaved to something else—alcohol, sex, work, a relationship, money, pleasure, even religious activity. We need to begin our recovery by putting God back in the driver's seat. If we put God first in our life and seek to follow his will, no addiction will be too great to overcome.

remaining in the land obeyed Haggai's message from the Lord their God; they began to worship him in earnest.

[13]Then the Lord told them (again sending the message through Haggai, his messenger), "I am with you; I will bless you." [14,15]And the Lord gave them a desire to rebuild his Temple; so they all gathered in early September of the second year of King Darius' reign and volunteered their help.

CHAPTER 2

God Promises to Bless His People

In early October of the same year, the Lord sent them this message through Haggai:

[2]"Ask this question of the governor and High Priest and everyone left in the land:

[3]"'Who among you can remember the Temple as it was before? How glorious it was! In comparison, it is nothing now, is it? [4]But take courage, O Zerubbabel and Joshua and all the people; take courage and work, for I am with you, says the Lord Almighty. [5]For I promised when you left Egypt that my Spirit would remain among you; so don't be afraid.'"

[6]"For the Lord Almighty says, 'In just a little while I will begin to shake the heavens and earth—and the oceans, too, and the dry land. [7]I will shake all nations, and the Desire of All Nations shall come to this Temple, and I will fill this place with my glory,' says the Lord Almighty. [8,9]'The future splendor of this Temple will be greater than the splendor of the first one! For I have plenty of silver and gold to do it! And here I will give peace," says the Lord.

[10]In early December, in the second year of the reign of King Darius, this message came from the Lord through Haggai the prophet:

[11]"Ask the priests this question about the law: [12]'If one of you is carrying a holy sacrifice in his robes and happens to brush against some bread or wine or meat, will it too become holy?'"

"No," the priests replied. "Holiness does not pass to other things that way."

[13]Then Haggai asked, "But if someone touches a dead person, and so becomes ceremonially impure, and then brushes against something, does it become contaminated?"

And the priests answered, "Yes."

[14]Haggai then made his meaning clear. "'You people,'" he said (speaking for the Lord), "'were contaminating your sacrifices by living with selfish attitudes and evil hearts—and not only your sacrifices, but everything else that you did as a "service" to me. [15]And so everything you did went wrong. But all is different now because you have begun to build the Temple. [16,17]Before, when you expected a twenty-bushel crop, there were only ten. When you came to draw fifty gallons from the olive press, there were only twenty. I rewarded all your labor with rust and mildew and hail. Yet, even so, you refused to return to me,'" says the Lord.

[18,19]"'But now note this: From today, this 24th day of the month, as the foundation of the Lord's Temple is finished, and from this day onward, I will bless you. Notice, I am giving you this promise now before you have even begun to rebuild the Temple structure, and before you have harvested your grain, and before the grapes, the figs, the pomegranates, and olives have produced their next crops: *From this day I will bless you.*'"

[20]Another message came to Haggai from the Lord that same day:

1:13-15 There is a point in recovery when we need to get beyond mere self-examination, a time when we need to stop talking about our problems and take concrete steps to change. We are like the people in Haggai's day who already knew God's will for them—they were to rebuild God's Temple. They just needed to act on their knowledge. Here we see that they finally took concrete steps to complete the task God had given them. As we take our inventory on a regular basis, we soon become aware of the things we need to change. We know whom we have hurt and have a good idea of what we should do. When we reach this point, it is time to act! If we don't take concrete, active steps, we cannot progress in our recovery.

2:3-9 The former Temple had been destroyed at least sixty-seven years earlier, so there were few alive who could remember it. The few elderly people who had seen Solomon's Temple were sad because the new Temple would never match the old one in splendor. God made it clear, however, that their rebuilding project would result in a Temple even more glorious than the first. As we work toward recovery, the pain over what we have lost through our addictions need not distract us from building for a worthwhile future. There is always hope when we rebuild with God's help.

2:12-13 Purity and cleanness do not rub off; impurity and dirtiness do rub off. This is true not only in a physical sense, but in a spiritual sense as well. That is one reason why we are told to avoid people associated with our addictions, especially in the early years of our recovery. They are far more likely to lead us astray than we are to influence them for good. In recovery, our associations—circumstantial and personal—must pass the test of God's approval.

[21]"Tell Zerubbabel, the governor of Judah, 'I
am about to shake the heavens and the earth,
[22]to overthrow thrones, destroy the strength
of the kingdoms of the nations. I will overthrow their armed might, and brothers and
companions will kill each other. [23]But when
that happens, I will take you, O Zerubbabel
my servant, and honor you like a signet ring
upon my finger; for I have specially chosen
you,'" says the Lord Almighty.

ZECHARIAH

THE BIG PICTURE

A. THE PROPHET'S INTRODUCTION (1:1-6)
B. A PROGRAM FOR THE PEOPLE'S RECOVERY (1:7–6:15)
   1. A Vision of Preparation (1:7-17)
   2. A Vision of Reflection (1:18-21)
   3. A Vision of Reconstruction (2:1-13)
   4. A Vision of Justification (3:1-10)
   5. A Vision of Evangelization (4:1-14)
   6. A Vision of Liberation (5:1-11)
   7. A Vision of Retribution (6:1-8)
   8. The Crowning of Joshua (6:9-15)
C. A SPIRITUAL PROBLEM IN THE PEOPLE'S RECOVERY (7:1–8:23)
   1. The Problem of Religious Formality (7:1-14)
   2. The Solution of Genuine Spirituality (8:1-23)
D. A SPECIFIC PROCESS IN THE PEOPLE'S RECOVERY (9:1–14:21)
   1. The Way of Failure: Rejection of the Savior (9:1–11:17)
   2. The Way of Deliverance: Receiving the Savior (12:1–14:21)

At times life seems intolerable, especially for those of us who have been victims most of our life. Though we may finally escape abusive or dysfunctional homes, we are not automatically freed from the emotional grasp of the past. As a result, we feel that people are hostile or that they do not care about us. Eventually, immobilizing despair sets in. Motivation and enthusiasm for life are gone. We become emotionally crippled.

That was probably what it was like for God's people in Judah. As a result of the repeated sins of their fathers, their families had been displaced from Palestine to Assyria and Babylonia. Seventy years later, at the decree of Cyrus, a remnant of Jews returned to Jerusalem under the leadership of Zerubbabel. Their first goal was to rebuild the house of God, but their initial enthusiasm was dampened by opposition from local residents. The work of rebuilding the Temple was soon stopped.

To counter this hopelessness, God appointed the elderly Haggai and the young Zechariah to prophesy, encouraging the returned exiles to rebuild God's Temple in Jerusalem. Zechariah, whose name means "God remembers," reminded the Jews that God had not forgotten them. Rather, he had a certain and dynamic plan for their restoration.

Hope for the future can provide great encouragement for the present. The promise of deliverance makes it possible to be renewed and to continue in the process of recovery. This book is a fascinating study of how God, through his prophets, led his hurting people from hopelessness to commitment, through self-examination and transformation to a deepening spiritual perception. It is an account of rebuilding and recovery.

THE BOTTOM LINE

PURPOSE: To encourage God's people to complete the task of rebuilding God's Temple, their society, and their lives. AUTHOR: The prophet Zechariah. AUDIENCE: The people living in Jerusalem, including those who had returned from Babylonian exile. DATE WRITTEN: Chapters 1–8 were written between 528 and 520 B.C., and chapters 9–14 were written around 480 B.C. SETTING: The people had started to rebuild God's Temple in Jerusalem but had failed to complete the task. KEY VERSE: "Come to the place of safety, all you prisoners, for there is yet hope! I promise right now, I will repay you two mercies for each of your woes!" (9:12). KEY PLACES: Jerusalem and the Temple. KEY PEOPLE AND RELATIONSHIPS: Zerubbabel, Joshua the priest, and the prophets Haggai and Zechariah.

RECOVERY THEMES

Disappointment Leads to Despair: When faced with disappointment we have a choice: we can nurture our negative feelings, or we can confront them and find a solution. The people of God chose to hold on to their disappointment. This led to despair. To avoid despair we need to give our disappointments to God and confront those aspects of them that we can change. As we take small steps toward our recovery, we will find that our feelings of despair will pass. But we cannot just wait for our healing. We need to become actively involved in God's program for our recovery.

Hope Encourages Us Today: Zechariah's visions of the future gave hope to the people, helping them face the tasks of their present. The hope that we have of God's final healing can encourage us to endure the pain that is involved in our recovery today. We won't always feel so hurt and confused. If we follow God's will for us in faith, we will experience God's healing in our life and discover the joy that only God can give.

Recovery Involves the Heart: Zechariah told the people that God did not care about their fasts and religious observances. He did care about the attitudes of their hearts. Our spiritual recovery involves the attitudes of our heart; it is not a matter of just doing and saying the right things. It is only as our mind and heart are changed by God that our true deliverance can occur. As our heart is transformed, our attitudes and actions will also be transformed. If we go through the motions of recovery without ever being changed on the inside, our recovery will never last. We need to be changed from the inside out. Just as this was true for the people in Jerusalem in Zechariah's day, it is true for us today.

CHAPTER 1

A Call to Repentance

Subject: messages from the Lord. These messages from the Lord were given to Zechariah
(son of Berechiah and grandson of Iddo the
prophet) in early November of the second
year of the reign of King Darius.
2The Lord Almighty was very angry with
your fathers. 3But he will turn again and favor
you if only you return to him. 4Don't be like
your fathers were! The earlier prophets pled in
vain with them to turn from all their evil
ways.
"Come, return to me," the Lord God said.
But no, they wouldn't listen; they paid no
attention at all.
5,6Your fathers and their prophets are now
long dead, but remember the lesson they
learned, that *God's Word endures!* It caught up
with them and punished them. Then at last
they repented.
"We have gotten what we deserved from
God," they said. "He has done just what he
warned us he would."

A Man among the Myrtle Trees

7The following February, still in the second
year of the reign of King Darius, another message from the Lord came to Zechariah (son of
Berechiah and grandson of Iddo the prophet),
in a vision in the night: 8I saw a Man sitting
on a red horse that was standing among the
myrtle trees beside a river. Behind him were
other horses, red and bay and white, each
with its rider.
9An angel stood beside me, and I asked him,
"Sir, what are all those horses for?"
"I'll tell you," he replied.
10Then the rider on the red horse—he was
the Angel of the Lord—answered me, "The
Lord has sent them to patrol the earth for
him."
11Then the other riders reported to the Angel of the Lord, "We have patrolled the whole
earth, and everywhere there is prosperity and
peace."
12Upon hearing this, the Angel of the Lord
prayed this prayer: "O Lord Almighty, for seventy years your anger has raged against Jerusalem and the cities of Judah. How long will
it be until you again show mercy to them?"
13And the Lord answered the angel who
stood beside me, speaking words of comfort
and assurance.
14Then the angel said, "Shout out this message from the Lord Almighty: 'Don't you
think I care about what has happened to
Judah and Jerusalem? I am as jealous as a
husband for his captive wife. 15I am very angry
with the heathen nations sitting around at

1:7-17 This vision of a red horse among the myrtle trees was a vision of preparation. It was the first of eight apocalyptic visions that Zechariah saw. It pointed to a time of peace that would come before God intervened on Israel's behalf. Outward peace can be deceiving. It may hide deep trauma within the heart of a victimized person. For those who are troubled, however, God has "words of comfort and assurance" (1:13).

ease, for I was only a little displeased with my
people, but the nations afflicted them far beyond my intentions.' [16]Therefore the Lord declares: 'I have returned to Jerusalem filled
with mercy; my Temple will be rebuilt,' says
the Lord Almighty, 'and so will all Jerusalem.'
[17]Say it again: 'The Lord Almighty declares
that the cities of Israel will again overflow
with prosperity, and the Lord will again comfort Jerusalem and bless her and live in her.' "

Four Horns and Four Blacksmiths

[18]Then I looked and saw four animal horns!
[19]"What are these?" I asked the angel.
He replied, "They represent the four world
powers that have scattered Judah, Israel, and
Jerusalem."
[20]Then the Lord showed me four blacksmiths.
[21]"What have these men come to do?" I
asked.
The angel replied, "They have come to take
hold of the four horns that scattered Judah so
terribly, and to pound them on the anvil and
throw them away."

CHAPTER 2

A Man with a Yardstick

When I looked around me again, I saw a man
carrying a yardstick in his hand.
[2]"Where are you going?" I asked.
"To measure Jerusalem," he said. "I want to
see whether it is big enough for all the
people!"
[3]Then the angel who was talking to me
went over to meet another angel coming toward him.
[4]"Go tell this young man," said the other
angel, "that Jerusalem will some day be so full
of people that she won't have room enough
for all! Many will live outside the city walls,
with all their many cattle—and yet they will
be safe. [5]For the Lord himself will be a wall of
fire protecting them and all Jerusalem; he will
be the glory of the city.
[6,7]"Come, flee from the land of the north,
from Babylon," says the Lord to all his exiles
there; "I scattered you to the winds, but I will
bring you back again. Escape, escape to Zion
now!" says the Lord.
[8]"The Lord of Glory has sent me against the
nations that oppressed you, for he who harms
you sticks his finger in Jehovah's eye!
[9]"I will smash them with my fist and their
slaves will be their rulers! *Then you will know
it was the Lord Almighty who sent me.* [10]Sing,
Jerusalem, and rejoice! For I have come to live
among you," says the Lord. [11,12]"At that time
many nations will be converted to the Lord,
and they too shall be my people; I will live
among them all. *Then you will know it was the
Lord Almighty who sent me to you.* And Judah
shall be the Lord's inheritance in the Holy
Land, for God shall once more choose to bless
Jerusalem.
[13]"Be silent, all mankind, before the Lord,
for he has come to earth from heaven, from
his holy home."

CHAPTER 3

The High Priest, Joshua

Then the Angel showed me (in my vision)
Joshua the High Priest standing before the
Angel of the Lord; and Satan was there too, at

1:18-21 The vision of the four horns (the horn being a symbol of power) and the four blacksmiths was a vision of reflection. The first three horns were smashed in turn by the hammers of the blacksmiths, but the fourth was unscathed. Similar to one of Daniel's visions, it pointed to the four world empires that would oppress the Jews: Babylon, Medo-Persia, Greece, and Rome. God's dejected people can find courage and hope in the fact that he will eventually overthrow the oppressive powers that dominate them.

2:1-13 The vision of the man with a yardstick concerned the reconstruction and repatriation of Israel. Many of the Jews had become comfortable in exile and were reluctant to return to Palestine. They were probably afraid they would return to a land of confusion and strife. There was no need to fear, however, for God had promised a future of prosperity and peace. For any of us who wrestle with fear in the wake of traumatic experiences, we also are given the assurance of God's special protection. If we want to escape our bondage, we need to trust God and follow his plan for our deliverance.

3:1-4 This vision of Joshua the High Priest teaches us much about God's merciful forgiveness. The historical figure, Joshua ben-Jehozadak, the High Priest at that time, appeared here in soiled garments. Satan stood at his right, accusing him of Israel's failures. The filthy High Priest symbolized what Israel looked like to God in their sinful state (Romans 10:3). We still wrestle with sin today, and Satan is always there to accuse us before God for things in our life that have demoralized and immobilized us. Yet, God is always there to defend us if we have come to him for forgiveness and cleansing.

the Angel's right hand, accusing Joshua of many things.

2And the Lord said to Satan, "I reject your accusations, Satan; yes, I, the Lord, for I have decided to be merciful to Jerusalem—I rebuke you. I have decreed mercy to Joshua and his nation; they are like a burning stick pulled out of the fire."

3Joshua's clothing was filthy as he stood before the Angel of the Lord.

4Then the Angel said to the others standing there, "Remove his filthy clothing." And turning to Joshua he said, "See, I have taken away your sins, and now I am giving you these fine new clothes."

5,6Then I said, "Please, could he also have a clean turban on his head?" So they gave him one.

Then the Angel of the Lord spoke very solemnly to Joshua and said, 7"The Lord Almighty declares: 'If you will follow the paths I set for you and do all I tell you to, then I will put you in charge of my Temple, to keep it holy; and I will let you walk in and out of my presence with these angels. 8Listen to me, O Joshua the High Priest, and all you other priests, you are illustrations of the good things to come. Don't you see?—Joshua represents my servant the Branch whom I will send. 9He will be the Foundation Stone of the Temple that Joshua is standing beside, and I will engrave this inscription on it seven times: *I will remove the sins of this land in a single day.* 10And after that,' the Lord Almighty declares, 'you will all live in peace and prosperity, and each of you will own a home of your own where you can invite your neighbors.'"

CHAPTER 4

The Golden Lampstand

Then the angel who had been talking with me woke me, as though I had been asleep.

2"What do you see now?" he asked.

I answered, "I see a gold lampstand holding seven lamps, and at the top there is a reservoir for the olive oil that feeds the lamps, flowing into them through seven tubes. 3And I see two olive trees carved upon the lampstand, one on each side of the reservoir. 4What is it, sir?" I asked. "What does this mean?"

5"Don't you really know?" the angel asked.

"No, sir," I said, "I don't."

6Then he said, "This is God's message to Zerubbabel: 'Not by might, nor by power, but by my Spirit, says the Lord Almighty—you will succeed because of my Spirit, though you are few and weak.' 7Therefore no mountain, however high, can stand before Zerubbabel! For it will flatten out before him! And Zerubbabel will finish building this Temple with mighty shouts of thanksgiving for God's mercy, declaring that all was done by grace alone."

8Another message that I received from the Lord said:

9"Zerubbabel laid the foundation of this Temple, and he will complete it. (Then you will know these messages are from God, the Lord Almighty.) 10Do not despise this small beginning, for the eyes of the Lord rejoice to

---

3:5-10 God would purify Joshua, the High Priest, and he would be a living illustration of the good leadership that would be experienced under the Messiah's rule. There is a real word of hope here. When God's restoration is complete, suffering people will experience his healing. Their sorrow and isolation will be replaced by joy and true fellowship with friends and neighbors. As we experience God's powerful deliverance in our life, we, like Joshua, can illustrate what happens to a life that is ruled and directed by our loving God. As we share God's deliverance with others through both word and deed, they too will experience the healing power he offers.

4:1-5 The vision of the lampstand and the olive trees teaches us about God's sustaining provision (4:1-14). This strange vision of the gold lampstand into whose reservoir two olive trees pour their oil points to the power by which Messiah's kingdom shall be inaugurated, namely that of the Holy Spirit (see 4:6). Zechariah should have known from Scripture what the symbols meant. Likewise, we become confused when we don't know what God's Word has promised us. In studying the Bible, we discover the truth we need in order to understand God's will for us, and the promise of God's power to help us as we seek to follow it.

4:6-14 Zerubbabel had led a contingent of Jews to Jerusalem to rebuild the Temple, but their efforts had been stopped by political opposition. The people became discouraged, and they began to wonder if God was with them. Here God gave Zechariah a message of encouragement for his disheartened people. They needed to remember that success was not the result of human strength or ingenuity, but a fruit of the Holy Spirit's power. With his power, the difficult task of rebuilding could yet be accomplished. We often become discouraged as we face the massive task of our own recovery, especially when we experience regular opposition from people, emotions, and temptations. But when we recognize our own powerlessness, we are able to allow God to step in. His power is more than sufficient for the task of our recovery.

see the work begin, to see the plumbline in
the hand of Zerubbabel. For these seven
lamps represent the eyes of the Lord that see
everywhere around the world."
11Then I asked him about the two olive trees
on each side of the lampstand, 12and about
the two olive branches that emptied oil into
gold bowls through two gold tubes.
13"Don't you know?" he asked.
"No, sir," I said.
14Then he told me, "They represent the two
anointed ones who assist the Lord of all the
earth."

CHAPTER 5

A Flying Scroll

I looked up again and saw a scroll flying
through the air.
2"What do you see?" he asked.
"A flying scroll!" I replied. "It appears to be
about thirty feet long and fifteen feet wide!"
3"This scroll," he told me, "represents the
words of God's curse going out over the entire
land. It says that all who steal and lie have
been judged and sentenced to death."
4"I am sending this curse into the home of
every thief and everyone who swears falsely
by my name," says the Lord Almighty. "And
my curse shall remain upon his home and
completely destroy it."

A Flying Basket

5Then the angel left me for awhile, but he
returned and said, "Look up! Something is
traveling through the sky!"
6"What is it?" I asked.
He replied, "It is a bushel basket filled with
the sin prevailing everywhere throughout the
land."
7Suddenly the heavy lead cover on the basket was lifted off, and I could see a woman
sitting inside the basket!
8He said, "She represents wickedness," and
he pushed her back into the basket and
clamped down the heavy lid again.
9Then I saw two women flying toward us,
with wings like those of a stork. And they took
the bushel basket and flew off with it, high in
the sky.
10"Where are they taking her?" I asked the
angel.
11He replied, "To Babylon where they will
build a temple for the basket, to worship it!"

CHAPTER 6

Four Chariots

Then I looked up again and saw four chariots
coming from between what looked like two
mountains made of brass. 2The first chariot
was pulled by red horses, the second by black
ones, 3the third by white horses and the
fourth by dappled-grays.
4"And what are these, sir?" I asked the angel.
5He replied, "These are the four heavenly
spirits who stand before the Lord of all the
earth; they are going out to do his work. 6The
chariot pulled by the black horses will go
north, and the one pulled by white horses will
follow it there, while the dappled-grays will
go south."
7The red horses were impatient to be off, to
patrol back and forth across the earth, so the
Lord said, "Go. Begin your patrol." So they
left at once.
8Then the Lord summoned me and said,
"Those who went north have executed my
judgment and quieted my anger there."

5:5-11 The vision of the bushel basket was about liberation. The strange imagery graphically portrays the liberation of God's people from a long-standing curse of materialism and commercialism. This affliction was, in fact, the result of their abuse of one of God's blessings (Deuteronomy 15:6). We who are controlled by enslaving attitudes or habits need to realize, as did the Jews, that deliverance comes when we allow God to change us.

6:1-8 The vision of the four chariots was God's way of promising his righteous judgment against the Gentile nations. Famine, war, and pestilence would be his divine weapons. We who are wrestling with recovery from victimization must remember that God knows all about our suffering and will deal in his own time with those who have hurt us. We can release our hatred and desire for revenge, because vengeance belongs to God (Leviticus 19:18; Deuteronomy 32:35; Romans 12:17-19). Only when we stop blaming others for our problems can we take responsible steps toward recovery.

6:9-15 In this climax to the visions, Zechariah was instructed to receive gifts from a delegation of Jews from Babylon designated for the work of rebuilding the Temple. From the silver and gold, he was to make a crown that he would set upon Joshua's head. This would foreshadow the royal priesthood that would come with the Messiah (Psalm 110:1-4; Hebrews 7:1-3). Once again, however, the obligation upon God's people was clear. There would be no blessing from God unless they were willing to follow his will for them. The same is true for us. There is little hope for our recovery unless we recognize our need for God and seek to do things his way.

The Crowning of Joshua

[9]In another message the Lord said:

[10,11]"Heldai, Tobijah, and Jedaiah will bring gifts of silver and gold from the Jews exiled in Babylon. The same day they arrive, meet them at the home of Josiah (son of Zephaniah), where they will stay. Accept their gifts and make from them a crown from the silver and gold. Then put the crown on the head of Joshua (son of Josedech) the High Priest. [12]Tell him that the Lord Almighty says, 'You represent the Man who will come, whose name is "The Branch"—he will grow up from himself—and will build the Temple of the Lord. [13]To him belongs the royal title. He will rule both as King and as Priest, with perfect harmony between the two!'

[14]"Then put the crown in the Temple of the Lord, to honor those who gave it—Heldai, Tobijah, Jedaiah, and also Josiah. [15]These three who have come from so far away represent many others who will some day come from distant lands to rebuild the Temple of the Lord. And when this happens, you will know my messages have been from God, the Lord Almighty. But none of this will happen unless you carefully obey the commandments of the Lord your God."

CHAPTER 7

A Call to Justice and Mercy

Another message came to me from the Lord in late November of the fourth year of the reign of King Darius.

[2]The Jews of the city of Bethel had sent a group of men headed by Sharezer, the chief administrative officer of the king, and Regemmelech, to the Lord's Temple at Jerusalem, to seek his blessing [3]and to speak with the priests and prophets about whether they must continue their traditional custom of fasting and mourning during the month of August each year, as they had been doing so long.

[4]This was the Lord's reply:

[5]"When you return to Bethel, say to all your people and your priests, 'During those seventy years of exile when you fasted and mourned in August and October, were you really in earnest about leaving your sins behind and coming back to me? No, not at all! [6]And even now in your holy feasts to God, you don't think of me, but only of the food and fellowship and fun. [7]Long years ago, when Jerusalem was prosperous and her southern suburbs out along the plain were filled with people, the prophets warned them that this attitude would surely lead to ruin, as it has.'"

[8,9]Then this message from the Lord came to Zechariah. "Tell them to be honest and fair—and not to take bribes—and to be merciful and kind to everyone. [10]Tell them to stop oppressing widows and orphans, foreigners and poor people, and to stop plotting evil against each other. [11]Your fathers would not listen to this message. They turned stubbornly away and put their fingers in their ears to keep from hearing me. [12]They hardened their hearts like flint, afraid to hear the words that God, the Lord Almighty, commanded them—the laws he had revealed to them by his Spirit through the early prophets. That is why such great wrath came down on them from God. [13]I called, but they refused to listen, so when they cried to me, I turned away. [14]I scattered them as with a whirlwind among the far-off nations. Their land became desolate; no one even traveled through it; the Pleasant Land lay bare and blighted."

CHAPTER 8

Blessings for Judah

Again the Lord's message came to me:

[2]The Lord Almighty says, "I am greatly concerned—yes, furiously angry—because of all that Jerusalem's enemies have done to her.

7:1-7 Two years had elapsed since Zechariah received the visions of the first six chapters. Since then, the work on the Temple had progressed, and the minds of the people had been turned back toward God. The citizens of Bethel sent a delegation to Jerusalem asking whether or not their ceremonies of fasting for the destruction of Jerusalem were legitimate, especially since the Temple was being rebuilt. God made it clear through Zechariah's answer that he was more concerned about the attitudes of their hearts than whether or not they fasted. Many of us have come to realize that true recovery, whether from addictive or abusive behaviors, codependency, or victimization, must involve deep internal change. Only as our heart is changed by God can real deliverance occur.

7:8-10 For the recovering exiles, the test of their faith was simple: love for others (Leviticus 19:18), especially the helpless—widows, orphans, foreigners, and the poor. The final step, and ultimate proof, of our recovery is our desire to help others who are suffering under the burden of their dependencies. As we reach out to them to offer them the second chance that we have already received, we will discover the joy of loving others, and our own recovery will be strengthened as a result.

3Now I am going to return to my land, and I,
myself, will live within Jerusalem. Then Jerusalem shall be called 'The Faithful City,' and
'The Holy Mountain,' and 'The Mountain of
the Lord Almighty.'"
4The Lord Almighty declares that Jerusalem
will have peace and prosperity so long that
there will once again be aged men and
women hobbling through her streets on
canes, 5and the streets will be filled with boys
and girls at play.
6The Lord says, "This seems unbelievable to
you—a remnant, small, discouraged as you
are—but it is no great thing for me. 7You can
be sure that I will rescue my people from east
and west, wherever they are scattered. 8I will
bring them home again to live safely in Jerusalem, and they will be my people, and I will
be their God, just and true and yet forgiving
them their sins!"
9The Lord Almighty says, "Get on with the
job and finish it! You have been listening long
enough! For since you began laying the foundation of the Temple, the prophets have been
telling you about the blessings that await you
when it's finished. 10Before the work began
there were no jobs, no wages, no security; if
you left the city, there was no assurance you
would ever return, for crime was rampant.
11"But it is all so different now!" says the
Lord Almighty. 12"For I am sowing peace and
prosperity among you. Your crops will prosper; the grapevines will be weighted down
with fruit; the ground will be fertile, with
plenty of rain; all these blessings will be given
to the people left in the land. 13'May you be as
poor as Judah,' the heathen used to say to
those they cursed! But no longer! For now
Judah is a word of blessing, not a curse. 'May
you be as prosperous and happy as Judah is,'
they'll say. So don't be afraid or discouraged!
Get on with rebuilding the Temple! 14,15If you
do, I will certainly bless you. And don't think
that I might change my mind. I did what I
said I would when your fathers angered me
and I promised to punish them, and I won't
change this decision of mine to bless you.
16Here is your part: Tell the truth. Be fair. Live
at peace with everyone. 17Don't plot harm to
others; don't swear that something is true
when it isn't! How I hate all that sort of
thing!" says the Lord.
18Here is another message that came to me
from the Lord Almighty:
19"The traditional fasts and times of mourning you have kept in July, August, October,
and January are ended. They will be changed
to joyous festivals if you love truth and peace!
20,21People from around the world will come
on pilgrimages and pour into Jerusalem from
many foreign cities to attend these celebrations. People will write their friends in other
cities and say, 'Let's go to Jerusalem to ask the
Lord to bless us and be merciful to us. I'm
going! Please come with me. Let's go *now!'*
22Yes, many people, even strong nations, will
come to the Lord Almighty in Jerusalem to
ask for his blessing and help. 23In those days
ten men from ten different nations will clutch
at the coat sleeves of one Jew and say, 'Please
be my friend, for I know that God is with
you.'"

CHAPTER 9

Punishment for Israel's Enemies

This is the message concerning God's curse on
the lands of Hadrach and Damascus, for the
Lord is closely watching all mankind, as well
as Israel.
2"Doomed is Hamath, near Damascus, and
Tyre and Zidon too, shrewd though they be.
3Though Tyre has armed herself to the hilt
and become so rich that silver is like dirt to
her, and fine gold like dust in the streets, 4yet

8:1-17 The most important way to identify true religion is to see how it affects our daily life. God promised wonderful blessings, should the Jews complete the task of rebuilding his Temple. Their action in rebuilding God's house would prove their commitment to his revealed will. Our recovery cannot stop with self-examination; taking a moral inventory must lead to appropriate action. Our attempts to obey God's will for us prove that we trust his program to the point of shaping our life around it. This is the kind of faith we need for genuine spirituality and a successful recovery.

9:1-8 These verses introduce a long declaration by God against the Gentile nations. Although all of Israel's neighbors would be overrun, God would protect his land from the invading armies. This prophecy probably referred to the conquests of Alexander the Great that would take place during the intertestamental period. These verses trace Alexander's campaign through Syria, Phoenicia, and Philistia (334–332 B.C.). But in Jerusalem, God would stop Alexander from destroying the Temple. This word would have given hope to the Jews, who had lived for centuries with the threat of invading armies. Fear is often the source of paralysis in life. God's assurance, however, leads to courage. As we face the difficulties of recovery, God's promise to stay with us should give us the courage to persevere.

the Lord will dispossess her and hurl her fortifications into the sea; and she shall be set on fire and burned to the ground.

5"Ashkelon will see it happen and be filled with fear; Gaza will huddle in desperation, and Ekron will shake with terror, for their hopes that Tyre would stop the enemies' advance will all be dashed. Gaza will be conquered, her king killed, and Ashkelon will be completely destroyed.

6"Foreigners will take over the city of Ashdod, the rich city of the Philistines. 7I will yank her idolatry out of her mouth and pull from her teeth her sacrifices that she eats with blood. Everyone left will worship God and be adopted into Israel as a new clan: the Philistines of Ekron will intermarry with the Jews, just as the Jebusites did so long ago. 8And I will surround my Temple like a guard to keep invading armies from entering Israel. I am closely watching their movements, and I will keep them away; no foreign oppressors will again overrun my people's land.

The King Is Coming

9"Rejoice greatly, O my people! Shout with joy! For look—your King is coming! He is the Righteous One, the Victor! Yet he is lowly, riding on a donkey's colt! 10I will disarm all peoples of the earth, including my people in Israel, and he shall bring peace among the nations. His realm shall stretch from sea to sea, from the river to the ends of the earth.

11"I have delivered you from death in a waterless pit because of the covenant I made with you, sealed with blood. 12Come to the place of safety, all you prisoners, for there is yet hope! I promise right now, I will repay you two mercies for each of your woes! 13Judah, you are my bow! Ephraim, you are my arrow! Both of you will be my sword, like the sword of a mighty soldier brandished against the sons of Greece."

14The Lord shall lead his people as they fight! His arrows shall fly like lightning; the Lord God shall sound the trumpet call and go out against his enemies like a whirlwind off the desert from the south. 15He will defend his people, and they will subdue their enemies, treading them beneath their feet. They will taste victory and shout with triumph. They will slaughter their foes, leaving horrible carnage everywhere. 16,17The Lord their God will save his people in that day, as a Shepherd caring for his sheep. They shall shine in his land as glittering jewels in a crown. How wonderful and beautiful all shall be! The abundance of grain and grapes will make the young men and girls flourish; they will be radiant with health and happiness.

CHAPTER 10

The Lost Sheep of Israel

Ask the Lord for rain in the springtime, and he will answer with lightning and showers. Every field will become a lush pasture. 2How foolish to ask the idols for anything like that! Fortune-tellers' predictions are all a bunch of silly lies; what comfort is there in promises that don't come true? Judah and Israel have been led astray and wander like lost sheep; everyone attacks them, for they have no shepherd to protect them.

3"My anger burns against your 'shepherds'—your leaders—and I will punish them—these goats. For the Lord Almighty has arrived to help his flock of Judah. I will make them strong and glorious like a proud steed in battle. 4From them will come the Cornerstone, the Peg on which all hope hangs, the Bow that wins the battle, the Ruler over all the earth. 5They will be mighty warriors for God, grinding their enemies' faces into the dust beneath their feet. The Lord is with them as they fight; their enemy is doomed.

6"I will strengthen Judah, yes, and Israel too; I will reestablish them because I love them. It will be as though I had never cast

9:13–10:1 Recovery is a matter of committing our life to God and patiently waiting for his timely intervention. The Jews' victory over the Greek tyrants is described here in a series of rapidly changing metaphors. God's people are seen as instruments of conquest: the bow and arrow, a hero's sword. God would give his people victory over the oppressive powers that assailed them. We may feel trapped by powerful dependencies or an oppressive relationship, but God is fully capable of bringing deliverance. Through his bountiful power, he can restore beauty and freedom to any damaged life.

10:8-12 Like a shepherd who whistles to his flocks, God will call his people back from exile. Political restoration would not be enough, however; the Jews needed to return in faith to their God. Similarly, God has a perfect plan for each of us, and he will not rest until each one has been perfected according to his sovereign will (Romans 8:30-32). In recovery, we are called to seek out God's will for us and do all we can to follow it. If we seek to follow God's plan, he will help us along the way.

them all away, for I, the Lord their God, will
hear their cries. 7They shall be like mighty
warriors. They shall be happy as with wine.
Their children, too, shall see the mercies of
the Lord and be glad. Their hearts shall rejoice
in the Lord. 8When I whistle to them, they'll
come running, for I have bought them back
again. From the few that are left, their population will grow again to former size. 9Though
I have scattered them like seeds among the
nations, still they will remember me and return again to God; with all their children,
they will come home again to Israel. 10I will
bring them back from Egypt and Assyria and
resettle them in Israel—in Gilead and Lebanon; there will scarcely be room for all of
them! 11They shall pass safely through the sea
of distress, for the waves will be held back.
The Nile will become dry—the rule of Assyria
and Egypt over my people will end."
12The Lord says, "I will make my people
strong with power from me! They will go
wherever they wish, and wherever they go
they will be under my personal care."

CHAPTER 11
Open your doors, O Lebanon, to judgment.
You will be destroyed as though by fire raging
through your forests. 2Weep, O cypress trees,
for all the ruined cedars; the tallest and most
beautiful of them are fallen. Cry in fear, you
oaks of Bashan, as you watch the thickest
forests felled. 3Listen to the wailing of Israel's
leaders—all these evil shepherds—for their
wealth is gone. Hear the young lions roaring—the princes are weeping, for their glorious Jordan valley lies in ruins.

The Two Shepherds

4Then said the Lord my God to me, "Go and
take a job as shepherd of a flock being fat-
tened for the butcher. 5This will illustrate the
way my people have been bought and slain by
wicked leaders, who go unpunished. 'Thank
God, now I am rich!' say those who have
betrayed them—their own shepherds have
sold them without mercy. 6And I won't spare
them either," says the Lord, "for I will let
them fall into the clutches of their own
wicked leaders, and they will slay them. They
shall turn the land into a wilderness, and I will
not protect it from them."
7So I took two shepherd's staffs, naming
one Grace and the other Union, and I fed the
flock as I had been told to do. 8And I got rid
of their three evil shepherds in a single

Hope

READ ZECHARIAH 9:9-17

We may feel like our life is a battlefield. We may be a prisoner in the ongoing war between good and evil. When we turn our life over to God, will he rescue us and keep us safe?

Five hundred years before the birth of Jesus, the prophet Zechariah wrote these words: "Rejoice greatly, O my people! Shout with joy! For look—your King is coming! He is the Righteous One, the Victor! Yet he is lowly, riding on a donkey's colt! [This prophecy was fulfilled by the coming of Jesus (see Matthew 21:4-11).] I will disarm all peoples of the earth, including my people in Israel, and he shall bring peace among the nations. His realm shall stretch from sea to sea, from the river to the ends of the earth. I have delivered you from death in a waterless pit because of the covenant I made with you, sealed with blood. Come to the place of safety, all you prisoners, for there is yet hope! I promise right now, I will repay you two mercies for each of your woes!" (Zechariah 9:9-12).

Jesus fulfilled part of these prophecies when he came the first time. He did deliver us from death by shedding his own blood to seal our pardon. When he comes again, as he promised, he will bring peace on earth. For now, we can take refuge in Jesus. When the war is over and Jesus is crowned King of kings, he will repay all those who are his, two mercies for every woe suffered in the war! No matter how terrible the battles we face, we can turn our life over to God and have a sure hope for the future.
Turn to page 1009, Matthew 4.

month. But I became impatient with these
sheep—this nation—and they hated me too.
9So I told them, "I won't be your shepherd
any longer. If you die, you die; if you are
killed, I don't care. Go ahead and destroy
yourselves!"
10And I took my staff called Grace and
snapped it in two, showing that I had broken
my contract to lead and protect them. 11That
was the end of the agreement. Then those
who bought and sold sheep, who were watching, realized that God was telling them something through what I did.
12And I said to their leaders, "If you like,
give me my pay, whatever I am worth; but
only if you want to."
So they counted out thirty little silver coins
as my wages.
13And the Lord told me, "Use it to buy a
field from the pottery makers—this magnificent sum they value you at!"
So I took the thirty coins and threw them
into the Temple for the pottery makers.
14Then I broke my other staff, "Union," to
show that the bond of unity between Judah
and Israel was broken.
15Then the Lord told me to go again and get
a job as a shepherd; this time I was to act the
part of a worthless, wicked shepherd.
16And he said to me, "This illustrates how I
will give this nation a shepherd who will not
care for the dying ones, nor look after the
young, nor heal the broken bones, nor feed
the healthy ones, nor carry the lame that
cannot walk; instead, he will eat the fat ones,
even tearing off their feet. 17Woe to this
worthless shepherd who doesn't care for the
flock. God's sword will cut his arm and pierce
through his right eye; his arm will become
useless and his right eye blinded."

CHAPTER 12

God Defends His People

This is the fate of Israel, as pronounced by the
Lord, who stretched out the heavens, laid the
foundation of the earth, and formed the spirit
of man within him:
2"I will make Jerusalem and Judah like a cup
of poison to all the nearby nations that send
their armies to surround Jerusalem. 3Jerusalem
will be a heavy stone burdening the world. And
though all the nations of the earth unite in an
attempt to move her, they will all be crushed.
4"In that day," says the Lord, "I will bewil-
der the armies drawn up against her, and
make fools of them, for I will watch over the
people of Judah, but blind all her enemies.
5"And the clans of Judah shall say to themselves, 'The people of Jerusalem have found
strength in the Lord Almighty, their God.'
6"In that day I will make the clans of Judah
like a little fire that sets the forest aflame—like
a burning match among the sheaves; they will
burn up all the neighboring nations right and
left, while Jerusalem stands unmoved. 7The
Lord will give victory to the rest of Judah first,
before Jerusalem, so that the people of Jerusalem and the royal line of David won't be filled
with pride at their success.
8"The Lord will defend the people of Jerusalem; the weakest among them will be as
mighty as King David! And the royal line will
be as God, like the Angel of the Lord who goes
before them! 9For my plan is to destroy all the
nations that come against Jerusalem.
10"Then I will pour out the spirit of grace
and prayer on all the people of Jerusalem.
They will look on him they pierced, and
mourn for him as for an only son, and grieve
bitterly for him as for an oldest child who
died. 11The sorrow and mourning in Jerusalem
at that time will be even greater than the
grievous mourning for the godly King Josiah,
who was killed in the valley of Megiddo.
12-14"All of Israel will weep in profound sorrow. The whole nation will be bowed down
with universal grief—king, prophet, priest,
and people. Each family will go into private
mourning, husbands and wives apart, to face
their sorrow alone.

12:1-9 Zechariah again spoke of a time when the nations would try to oppress Israel, but this time they would not succeed. Though they would suffer confusion and panic, Israel would be encouraged by God's delivering intervention. When we who have been victimized turn to God, he will deliver us. Our oppressors cannot ultimately prevail against his limitless power.

12:10–13:1 These verses describe a national conversion in Israel, but they are also an outline of our own spiritual conversion. Here is the secret for anyone who is trapped in an abusive or codependent situation with no apparent hope. First, we must recognize that we are helpless without God and depend on him to show us the areas of sin and failure in our life (12:10). Second, we need to admit our failures and seek to follow God's will for our life (12:11-14). Next, we must accept the free cleansing that God offers us (13:1). Because of what Jesus Christ has done on our behalf, we can be confident of God's total forgiveness of all our past failures.

CHAPTER 13

A Fountain of Cleansing

"At that time a Fountain will be opened to the people of Israel and Jerusalem, a Fountain to cleanse them from all their sins and defilement."

[2]And the Lord Almighty declares, "In that day I will get rid of every vestige of idol worship throughout the land, so that even the names of the idols will be forgotten. All false prophets and fortune-tellers will be wiped out, [3]and if anyone begins false prophecy again, his own father and mother will slay him! 'You must die,' they will tell him, 'for you are prophesying lies in the name of the Lord.'

[4]"No one will be boasting then of his prophetic gift! No one will wear prophet's clothes to try to fool the people then.

[5]"'No,' he will say. 'I am not a prophet; I am a farmer. The soil has been my livelihood from my earliest youth.'

[6]"And if someone asks, 'Then what are these scars on your chest and your back?' he will say, 'I got into a brawl at the home of a friend!'

[7]"Awake, O sword, against my Shepherd, the man who is my associate and equal," says the Lord Almighty. "Strike down the Shepherd and the sheep will scatter, but I will come back and comfort and care for the lambs. [8]Two-thirds of all the nation of Israel will be cut off and die, but a third will be left in the land. [9]I will bring the third that remain through the fire and make them pure, as gold and silver are refined and purified by fire. They will call upon my name and I will hear them; I will say, 'These are my people,' and they will say, 'The Lord is our God.'"

CHAPTER 14

God Will Rule the Earth

Watch, for the day of the Lord is coming soon! On that day the Lord will gather together the nations to fight Jerusalem; the city will be taken, the houses rifled, the loot divided, the women raped; half the population will be taken away as slaves, and half will be left in what remains of the city.

[3]Then the Lord will go out fully armed for war, to fight against those nations. [4]That day his feet will stand upon the Mount of Olives, to the east of Jerusalem, and the Mount of Olives will split apart, making a very wide valley running from east to west, for half the mountain will move toward the north and half toward the south. [5]You will escape through that valley, for it will reach across to the city gate. Yes, you will escape as your people did long centuries ago from the earthquake in the days of Uzziah, king of Judah, and the Lord my God shall come, and all his saints and angels with him.

[6]The sun and moon and stars will no longer shine, [7]yet there will be continuous day! Only the Lord knows how! There will be no normal day and night—at evening time it will still be light. [8]Life-giving waters will flow out from Jerusalem, half toward the Dead Sea and half toward the Mediterranean, flowing continuously both in winter and in summer.

[9]And the Lord shall be King over all the earth. In that day there shall be one Lord—his name alone will be worshiped. [10]All the land from Geba (the northern border of Judah) to Rimmon (the southern border) will become one vast plain, but Jerusalem will be on an elevated site, covering the area all the way from the Gate of Benjamin over to the site of the old gate, then to the Corner Gate, and from the Tower of Hananel to the king's wine presses. [11]And Jerusalem shall be inhabited, safe at last, never again to be cursed and destroyed.

[12]And the Lord will send a plague on all the people who fought Jerusalem. They will be-

---

13:2-4 Part of God's program for Israel's recovery included getting rid of her idols and false prophets. The people had learned to depend upon teachings and objects that had no power to deliver. God would remove those sources of false hope so the people could learn to depend on him alone. We, too, are often guilty of bowing to idols or following false prophets. Our dependencies themselves are idols, since we use them to deal with pain in our life that only God is able to heal. The false prophets of recovery fads and New Age spirituality can also lead us away from true dependence on God. Our recovery depends upon our removing idols and false prophets from our life. God is the only one able to fulfill his promises of deliverance.

14:8-15 At last Zechariah reached the goal of his prophecy—and of all history—the messianic kingdom. The Messiah will be king over all the earth, and all of earth's inhabitants will know, worship, and serve him. When the whole world runs according to God's program, life for everyone will be characterized by peace and joy. Part of our recovery requires that we live according to God's will—today. We don't have to wait until the end of the world to put him in charge of our life. When God occupies the place of absolute authority, radical changes will take place. Our life will take on a new beauty and peace as we become a part of God's program of cosmic restoration.

come like walking corpses, their flesh rotting
away; their eyes will shrivel in their sockets,
and their tongues will decay in their mouths.
13They will be seized with terror, panic-
stricken from the Lord, and will fight against
each other in hand-to-hand combat. 14All
Judah will be fighting at Jerusalem. The
wealth of all the neighboring nations will be
confiscated—great quantities of gold and silver and fine clothing. 15(This same plague
will strike the horses, mules, camels, donkeys, and all the other animals in the enemy
camp.)
16In the end, those who survive the plague
will go up to Jerusalem each year to worship
the King, the Lord Almighty, to celebrate a
time of thanksgiving. 17And any nation anywhere in all the world that refuses to come to
Jerusalem to worship the King, the Lord Almighty, will have no rain. 18But if Egypt refuses to come, God will punish her with some
other plague. 19And so Egypt and the other
nations will all be punished if they refuse to
come.
20In that day the bells on the horses will
have written on them, "These Are Holy Property"; and the trash cans in the Temple of the
Lord will be as sacred as the bowls beside the
altar. 21In fact, every container in Jerusalem
and Judah shall be sacred to the Lord Almighty; all who come to worship may use any
of them free of charge to boil their sacrifices
in; there will be no more grasping traders in
the Temple of the Lord Almighty!

14:16-21 When the Messiah rules, Israel will be sanctified as God's priestly nation, and it will be characterized by holiness. Nothing unclean will be allowed to defile the Temple precincts. We are reminded here that God desires his people to be holy, just as he is holy. We are made holy by accepting God's work on our behalf through Jesus Christ. Because God dwells in us through his Holy Spirit, our body becomes his temple, where nothing unclean should be allowed to enter (1 Corinthians 6:19-20). This provides a strong motivation for us to stay free of enslavement to our addictions.

REFLECTIONS ON

insights ABOUT GOD'S DISCIPLINE

In **Zechariah 1:1-6** the prophet confronted the Jews with their sin. These people had recently returned from Babylonian exile, so the prophet reminded them that God would deal with their sins just as he had punished their ancestors with the captivity they had recently escaped. It is never safe to ignore such a call to turn back to God. Hearing demands heeding! God's promises of future comfort, victory, and deliverance must not lead us to a false sense of security. Neglected spiritual opportunities are lost opportunities.

In **Zechariah 7:11-14** we are reminded of how the ancestors of Zechariah's Jewish audience had ignored all of God's appeals to show compassion to the poor and helpless. Because they would not listen to God, he refused to listen to their prayers. Merely attending church or saying formal prayers to some "God as we understand him," will be of no profit for our recovery. True emotional and spiritual healing always involves obedience to God's revealed will. We cannot do things our own way and expect God's help in our deliverance. It is only as we give our life over to God and submit to his perfect plan for us that real progress can be made in our recovery.

insights INTO THE HOPE GOD OFFERS

At the very center of Israel's hope was the Messiah, whose promised coming was a source of great hope and joy. As we see in **Zechariah 9:9-10,** his credentials were his righteousness, his offer of salvation, and his lowliness, distinguishing him from all other earthly rulers. The one who demonstrated these credentials was, of course, Jesus of Nazareth. Clearly, God's people must place their hope for recovery not primarily in human sources, but in their personal relationship with God through Jesus Christ. If we put our hope in God, no problem is too great for us to overcome.

In **Zechariah 14:1-7** the prophet foresaw a time of terrible desolation, but in the midst of the horrible suffering, God would step in to deliver his people. Throughout the Scriptures we find God transforming terrible situations into amazing victories. This prophecy looks forward to a time in the future when God will do this in an ultimate sense. We all have experienced deep pain, and many of us are experiencing it even today. Sometimes we must reach a point of extreme desperation before we can understand our helplessness and realize how useless it is to go on alone. God is able to heal our deepest hurts and restore our life, no matter how terrible our past.

THE BIG PICTURE

A. DESCRIPTION OF THE BOOK (1:1)
B. DIALOGUES ABOUT FAILURE (1:2-14)
  1. A Dialogue about Love (1:2-5)
  2. A Dialogue about Faithlessness (1:6-10)
  3. A Dialogue about Holiness (1:11-14)
C. SERMONS ABOUT FAILURE (2:1-17)
  1. The Failure of the Priests (2:1-9)
  2. The Failure of the People (2:10-17)
D. A MESSAGE OF HOPE: GOD'S PROMISED INTERVENTION (3:1-6)
E. ANOTHER MESSAGE TO THOSE IN RECOVERY (3:7-18)
  1. Failure in Fiscal Responsibility (3:7-15)
  2. Success of the Remnant (3:16-18)
F. A MESSAGE OF JUDGMENT: GOD'S PROMISED INTERVENTION (4:1-6)

When recovery comes only in terms of external behavioral changes without internal change, there is the constant threat of relapse. This seemed to be the case with the people in Jerusalem. Under Nehemiah's leadership, the people had rebuilt the walls of the city and their lives. But when Nehemiah returned to Persia, all the excellent activities and attitudes that he had fostered in them disappeared.

Malachi preached to a nation of backsliders—a people who had relapsed. Even the spiritual leaders had fallen into old, sinful patterns. As a result, they were suffering the consequences of economic depression, poor crops, and the attacks of foreign marauders. Family life had gone to pieces, and divorce was rampant. Their religious life could be characterized as cold and empty formalism.

Malachi gave a message of hope to a nation that knew repeated failure. After being restored to their homeland, the Jews had forgotten the one who had delivered them. We tend to make the same mistake. As soon as we overcome our pressing problems, we forget the one who helped us escape—God. Without a continued relationship with God, our hope of sustaining our recovery is slim at best. We need to keep our eyes on God, the source and means for our success in recovery.

Although Malachi presented a long list of the people's failures, woven throughout his words of judgment is a clear message of hope and forgiveness. As the final book of the Old Testament, Malachi forms a bridge with the New as it concludes with a promise of the coming of another "prophet like Elijah" (4:5-6). This promise was fulfilled in the coming of John the Baptist, who prepared the way for the Messiah—Jesus Christ. With God, there is always hope!

THE BOTTOM LINE

PURPOSE: To confront the people about getting back on track after they had relapsed into old patterns of sin. AUTHOR: The prophet Malachi. AUDIENCE: The people in Judah shortly after Nehemiah rebuilt Jerusalem's walls. DATE WRITTEN: Sometime between 432 and 420 B.C. SETTING: After the Temple and Jerusalem's walls were rebuilt, the people began to fall back into destructive behavior patterns. Malachi confronted God's people with their sins and called them to restore their relationship with God. KEY VERSE: "For I am the Lord—I do not change. That is why you are not already utterly destroyed [for my mercy endures forever]" (3:6). KEY PLACES: Jerusalem and the Temple. KEY PEOPLE: Malachi and the priests.

RECOVERY THEMES

God Always Loves Us: God's love to the people of Jerusalem and to us cannot be explained. God knows the depth of our sin; he knows how weak we are; yet he still loves us. There is nothing that we can do to lose this love that we never deserved in the first place. God's love has the power to heal the broken places in our life, and our failures, relapses, and defenses cannot stop God from wanting to heal us. This fact should give us hope for recovery, no matter how terrible our failures in the past.

Forgiveness Is Foundational for Recovery: The way of forgiveness always leads us on the path back to a relationship with God. God wants us not only to receive his forgiveness, but also to be a forgiving people, passing on to others what he has so freely given to us. If we can receive God's forgiveness and grant forgiveness to others, we will have laid a solid foundation for our recovery.

God Is Always with Us: God wants us to turn to him for healing and forgiveness. He was patient for hundreds of years with the people of Israel in spite of their sin. He is just as patient with us now. When he spoke through the prophets, he had a message of hope woven into his warnings of judgment. In Malachi, he continued the theme of hope by promising the "prophet like Elijah" who would come and bring forgiveness and freedom to all people. God is with us even now to help us manage our unmanageable life. We can receive his help by trusting him and seeking to obey his will for our life.

CHAPTER 1

God Loves His People

Here is the Lord's message to Israel, given
through the prophet Malachi:
[2,3]"I have loved you very deeply," says the
Lord.
But you retort, "Really? When was this?"
And the Lord replies, "I showed my love
for you by loving your father, Jacob. I didn't
need to. I even rejected his very own
brother, Esau, and destroyed Esau's mountains and inheritance, to give it to the jackals of the desert. [4]And if his descendants
should say, 'We will rebuild the ruins,' then
the Lord Almighty will say, 'Try to if you
like, but I will destroy it again,' for their
country is named 'The Land of Wickedness,'
and their people are called 'Those Whom
God Does Not Forgive.'"
[5]O Israel, lift your eyes to see what God is
doing all around the world; then you will say,
"Truly, the Lord's great power goes far beyond
our borders!"

Imperfect Sacrifices for God

[6]"A son honors his father, a servant honors his
master. I am your Father and Master, yet you
don't honor me, O priests, but you despise my
name."
"Who? Us?" you say. "When did we ever
despise your name?"
[7]"When you offer polluted sacrifices on my
altar."
"Polluted sacrifices? When have we ever
done a thing like that?"
"Every time you say, 'Don't bother bringing
anything very valuable to offer to God!' [8]You
tell the people, 'Lame animals are all right to
offer on the altar of the Lord—yes, even the
sick and the blind ones.' And you claim this
isn't evil? Try it on your governor sometime—
give him gifts like that—and see how pleased
he is!
[9]"'God have mercy on us,' you recite; 'God
be gracious to us!' But when you bring that
kind of gift, why should he show you any
favor at all?

1:5 The Judeans had experienced many recent triumphs through God's power. God had allowed them to return to the Promised Land after years in exile. Then, with God's help, they overcame great obstacles to rebuild the Temple and the city of Jerusalem. The people had many reasons to be thankful to God and to recognize his power of restoration. Despite the great triumphs they had experienced, however, the people had quickly returned to doing things their own way. It is easy for us to do the same thing. After experiencing great victories with God's help, we fall back into old destructive patterns. We need to be reminded on a regular basis of what God has done and can do. We can get such reminders as we swap stories of deliverance with friends in recovery.

1:7-14 God did not want mere words of repentance; he wanted the people to back up their words with appropriate action. If they were really sorry for their sins and honored God in their hearts, they would have brought their best offerings to God. They exposed their insincerity by bringing blemished sacrifices. They kept the best for themselves. If we don't back up our mental resolutions with action, all our thoughts and resolutions pertaining to recovery will achieve nothing.

[10]"Oh, to find one priest among you who
would shut the doors and refuse this kind of
sacrifice! I have no pleasure in you," says the
Lord Almighty, "and I will not accept your
offerings.
[11]"But my name will be honored by the
Gentiles from morning till night. All around
the world they will offer sweet incense and
pure offerings in honor of my name. For my
name shall be great among the nations," says
the Lord Almighty. [12]"But you dishonor it,
saying that my altar is not important and
encouraging people to bring cheap, sick animals to offer to me on it.
[13]"You say, 'Oh, it's too difficult to serve the
Lord and do what he asks.' And you turn up
your noses at the rules he has given you to
obey. Think of it! Stolen animals, lame and
sick—as offerings to God! Should I accept
such offerings as these?" asks the Lord.
[14]"Cursed is that man who promises a fine
ram from his flock and substitutes a sick one
to sacrifice to God. For I am a Great King,"
says the Lord Almighty, "and my name is to
be mightily revered among the Gentiles."

CHAPTER 2

God Warns His Priests

Listen, you priests, to this warning from the
Lord Almighty:
"If you don't change your ways and give
glory to my name, then I will send terrible
punishment upon you, and instead of giving
you blessings as I would like to, I will turn on
you with curses. Indeed, I have cursed you
already because you haven't taken seriously
the things that are most important to me.
[3]"Take note that I will rebuke your children;
I will spread on your faces the manure of these
animals you offer me and throw you out like
dung. [4]Then at last you will know it was I who
sent you this warning to return to the laws I
gave your father Levi," says the Lord Almighty.
[5]"The purpose of these laws was to give him
life and peace, to be a means of showing his
respect and awe for me by keeping them. [6]He
passed on to the people all the truth he got
from me. He did not lie or cheat; he walked
with me, living a good and righteous life, and
turned many from their lives of sin.
[7]"Priests' lips should flow with the knowledge of God so the people will learn God's
laws. The priests are the messengers of the
Lord Almighty, and men should come to
them for guidance. [8]But not to you! For you
have left God's paths. Your 'guidance' has
caused many to stumble in sin. You have
distorted the covenant of Levi and made it
into a grotesque parody," says the Lord Almighty. [9]"Therefore, I have made you con-
temptible in the eyes of all the people; for you
have not obeyed me, but you let your favorites break the law without rebuke."

A Call to Faithfulness

[10]We are children of the same father, Abraham, all created by the same God. And yet we
are faithless to each other, violating the covenant of our fathers! [11]In Judah, in Israel, and
in Jerusalem, there is treachery, for the men
of Judah have defiled God's holy and beloved
Temple by marrying heathen women who
worship idols. [12]May the Lord cut off from his
covenant every last man, whether priest or
layman, who has done this thing!
[13]Yet you cover the altar with your tears
because the Lord doesn't pay attention to
your offerings anymore, and you receive no
blessing from him. [14]"Why has God abandoned us?" you cry. I'll tell you why; it is
because the Lord has seen your treachery in
divorcing your wives who have been faith-

2:1-9 Even Israel's religious leaders failed to show God proper respect. God singled these people out for special punishment because they used their influence to hurt rather than help the people under them. We are all in positions of influence at one level or another. Some of us are responsible for many; others of us influence only our family, spouse, or a few friends. No matter what our position, however, we can influence people for either good or evil. If we have led someone astray, our responsibility is to acknowledge our failure and do what we can to make amends. This may mean doing what we can to help this person overcome a dependency that we got him or her started in.

2:14-16 Some of the Judeans had divorced their wives for no reason other than personal gratification. They pushed their wives into a world where they had no means of supporting themselves. This practice was not only unethical; it was also terribly cruel. God hates divorce. The family was his idea, and family commitments were intended to be binding. Many of us have experienced firsthand the pain of a broken marriage. For some of us, that is the pain driving our addictions. For others of us, our addictions were a primary cause of our family's dissolution. A broken family is a serious hindrance to recovery. We need strong relationships to hold us accountable and keep us on the right track. Part of our recovery includes making amends to family members and rebuilding our damaged relationships.

ful to you through the years, the companions you promised to care for and keep. 15You were united to your wife by the Lord. In God's wise plan, when you married, the two of you became one person in his sight. And what does he want? Godly children from your union. Therefore, guard your passions! Keep faith with the wife of your youth.

16For the Lord, the God of Israel, says he hates divorce and cruel men. Therefore, control your passions—let there be no divorcing of your wives.

17You have wearied the Lord with your words.

"Wearied him?" you ask in fake surprise. "How have we wearied him?"

By saying that evil is good, that it pleases the Lord! Or by saying that God won't punish us—he doesn't care.

CHAPTER 3

The Messiah's Coming

"Listen: I will send my messenger before me to prepare the way. And then the One you are looking for will come suddenly to his Temple—the Messenger of God's promises, to bring you great joy. Yes, he is surely coming," says the Lord Almighty. 2"But who can live when he appears? Who can endure his coming? For he is like a blazing fire refining precious metal, and he can bleach the dirtiest garments! 3Like a refiner of silver he will sit and closely watch as the dross is burned away. He will purify the Levites, the ministers of God, refining them like gold or silver, so that they will do their work for God with pure hearts. 4Then once more the Lord will enjoy the offerings brought to him by the people of Judah and Jerusalem, as he did before. 5At that time my punishments will be quick and certain; I will move swiftly against wicked men who trick the innocent, against adulterers and liars, against all those who cheat their hired hands, who oppress widows and orphans, or defraud strangers, and do not fear me," says the Lord Almighty.

6"For I am the Lord—I do not change. That is why you are not already utterly destroyed [for my mercy endures forever].

The People Rob God

7"Though you have scorned my laws from earliest time, yet you may still return to me," says the Lord Almighty. "Come and I will forgive you.

"But you say, 'We have never even gone away!'

8"Will a man rob God? Surely not! And yet you have robbed me.

"'What do you mean? When did we ever rob you?'

"You have robbed me of the tithes and offerings due to me. 9And so the awesome curse of God is cursing you, for your whole nation has been robbing me. 10Bring all the tithes into the storehouse so that there will be food enough in my Temple; if you do, I will open up the windows of heaven for you and pour out a blessing so great you won't have room enough to take it in!

"Try it! Let me prove it to you! 11Your crops will be large, for I will guard them from insects and plagues. Your grapes won't shrivel away before they ripen," says the Lord Almighty. 12"And all nations will call you blessed, for you will be a land sparkling with happiness. These are the promises of the Lord Almighty.

13"Your attitude toward me has been proud and arrogant," says the Lord.

"But you say, 'What do you mean? What have we said that we shouldn't?'

2:17 God's standards cannot be ignored with impunity. The people had built walls of denial so thick that they considered their evil deeds to be good. If we refuse to recognize and respect God's standards, we will suffer severe consequences. Our recovery is possible only if we recognize our need for God and the value of his program. As long as we fight it, we will face a steady decline leading to disaster. If we trust God and follow his will, we can be sure he will strengthen us as we work our program.

3:3-4 Precious metals are refined by the searing heat of the furnace. Cleansing of filthy fabric requires the use of caustic soap. God often uses the fire of difficult times to ready us for his restoring work. He uses suffering to lead us to the first step in recovery—a recognition that we are powerless. If we recognize this fact and turn to God for help, he will deliver us from destruction and encourage us as we walk the upward path of recovery.

3:7 The denial of God's people was great. God confronted them directly with their sin, but they still refused to acknowledge it. Our addictions can lead us into denial that is equally powerful. While we may refuse to admit our failures, however, there is no hope for our recovery. We can receive help only after we have recognized that we have a problem. As long as we think we are all right, God's hands are tied.

14,15"Listen; you have said, 'It is foolish to worship God and obey him. What good does it do to obey his laws, and to sorrow and mourn for our sins? From now on, as far as we're concerned, "Blessed are the arrogant." For those who do evil shall prosper, and those who dare God to punish them shall get off scot-free.'"

The Faithful Remnant

16Then those who feared and loved the Lord spoke often of him to each other. And he had a Book of Remembrance drawn up in which he recorded the names of those who feared him and loved to think about him.

17"They shall be mine," says the Lord Almighty, "in that day when I make up my jewels. And I will spare them as a man spares an obedient and dutiful son. 18Then you will see the difference between God's treatment of good men and bad, between those who serve him and those who don't.

CHAPTER 4

A Great Day of Judgment

"Watch now," the Lord Almighty declares, "the day of judgment is coming, burning like a furnace. The proud and wicked will be burned up like straw; like a tree, they will be consumed—roots and all.

2"But for you who fear my name, the Sun of Righteousness will rise with healing in his wings. And you will go free, leaping with joy like calves let out to pasture. 3Then you will tread upon the wicked as ashes underfoot," says the Lord Almighty. 4"Remember to obey the laws I gave all Israel through Moses my servant on Mount Horeb.

5"See, I will send you another prophet like Elijah before the coming of the great and dreadful judgment day of God. 6His preaching will bring fathers and children together again, to be of one mind and heart, for they will know that if they do not repent, I will come and utterly destroy their land."

4:1 It is not a popular theme, but the Bible is filled with warnings against proud and sinful people. People who think they don't need God are doomed to destruction. We may react negatively to God's warnings because we don't really understand his heart. God warns us of destruction in hope that we will change and experience deliverance and recovery. If we were left to our selfish ways, we would destroy not only our own life, but also the lives of most of the people with whom we come into contact. When we hit bottom, we come to this hard realization. If we never realize this, however, we will never experience the rich and meaningful life that God wants for all of us.

4:2-6 Fear is never a pleasant subject, but healthy fear is the beginning of a proper view of God. And as we recognize God's goodness and power, we learn to trust him and become willing to follow his program for healthy living. A proper view of God will lead to healing in our life. Someday the entire world will recognize God for who he is and will worship and obey him. Life in God's kingdom will be characterized by wholeness and peace. Until that time, however, we can put God in charge of our life, and we can experience his healing in our own corner of the world. As we grow to respect God as he deserves, we will joyfully follow his perfect plan for us.

THE NEW TESTAMENT

MATTHEW

THE BIG PICTURE

A. JESUS' INTRODUCTION AS THE PROMISED KING (1:1–4:11)
   1. His Family History (1:1-17)
   2. His Birth and Development (1:18–2:23)
   3. His Baptism and Temptation (3:1–4:11)

B. JESUS' KINGLY MINISTRY AND MESSAGE (4:12–20:34)
   1. Jesus' Early Ministry (4:12-25)
   2. Jesus' Sermon on the Mount (5:1–7:29)
   3. Jesus Performs Many Miracles (8:1–10:42)
   4. Jesus Teaches about His Kingdom (11:1–20:34)

C. JESUS, THE REJECTED REDEEMER (21:1–27:66)
   1. Jesus the King Enters Jerusalem (21:1-17)
   2. Jesus Teaches His Disciples (21:18–25:46)
   3. Jesus Is Rejected and Crucified (26:1–27:66)

D. JESUS, THE RESURRECTED SAVIOR (28:1-20)

Many Jews of Jesus' day harbored some form of "messianic hope." They were suffering miserably at the hands of their Roman oppressors and clung to the belief that a Savior would emerge to deliver them. Based on the Old Testament promises of a delivering king, they eagerly awaited the Messiah's coming.

God wanted the world to accept Jesus as the Messiah and Savior. Through Jesus' ancestry, Virgin Birth, fulfillment of Old Testament prophecies, teachings, and miracles, God demonstrated who Jesus was. But during Jesus' earthly ministry, most people were unwilling to face the reality of his identity. Instead of looking to him as their long-awaited Messiah, they crucified him. And instead of finding deliverance, they remained in a state of oppression.

To deal with our problems, we have probably focused our hope on various "deliverers." Some of us are still looking to our addictions for deliverance from inner pain, a solution that only leads to greater suffering. Some of us hope for "freedom" through a recovery program that emphasizes "self-actualization," but this only leads us away from our true Deliverer. The Gospel of Matthew makes it clear that our only hope for recovery lies in Jesus the Messiah.

Jesus deserves our trust and commitment as we seek recovery from our dependencies and sin. When we rely on the power of forgiveness gained through his death and the hope for new life found in his resurrection, we have true hope for a genuine recovery. But it is up to us to place our hope in God. We must each let go of our selfish denial and make Jesus the King of our life. He alone is worthy of that honor and responsibility.

THE BOTTOM LINE

PURPOSE: To prove that Jesus was the promised Messiah and to show that God offers recovery to anyone through him. AUTHOR: Matthew, the apostle and former tax collector. AUDIENCE: Matthew wrote primarily for Jewish readers. DATE WRITTEN: Probably between A.D. 60 and 65. SETTING: Matthew emphasized the fulfillment of Old Testament prophecy in the person of Jesus Christ, making this Gospel the connecting link between Old and New Testaments. KEY VERSE: "Don't misunderstand why I have come—it isn't to cancel the laws of Moses and the warnings of the prophets. No, I came to fulfill them" (5:17). KEY PEOPLE AND RELATIONSHIPS: Jesus in relationship with his ancestors, Mary and Joseph, John the Baptist, Jesus' disciples, and the Jewish and Roman leaders.

RECOVERY THEMES

The Power of the Resurrection: Sometimes we want to find the power for our recovery within ourself. We don't want to depend on a power that is outside of us. But the power within us can only be as strong as we are, and we have already recognized that we are powerless. God demonstrated his power in the Gospels in many ways, but the ultimate example was in the resurrection of Jesus Christ. In his victory over sin and death, Jesus established his credentials as King and his power and authority over all evil. That's the kind of power we need in our recovery, and it is available when we turn our life over to him.

The Importance of Hope: Without hope, we are miserable; hope is the driving force behind our recovery. If we had no hope, there would be no possibility of our recovery. Understanding who Jesus is gives each of us a hope that can transcend even the deepest despair. In the Gospel of Matthew, we see and hear the message of hope that is available to everyone, not just to a select group of people. His resurrection forms the basis of our hope because in it God demonstrated his control over the power of death.

The Dangers of Denial: Often people say that if they could just see a miracle, they would believe. But as we see in Matthew, many people denied the truth about Jesus despite the miracles he did for them. Our denial systems are well-entrenched. God can handle our doubts and our fears, but cynicism and unbelief shut us off from his transforming power. Let us be like the disciples, who stood in awe on the Mount of Transfiguration, and wondered what kind of man Jesus was. That kind of openness facilitates our recovery.

God's Kingdom—A Model for Recovery: Jesus came to earth to inaugurate his Kingdom. His complete rule, however, will only be realized when he returns. His Kingdom will be made up of all those who, in faith, have turned their lives over to God and sought to follow him. We begin our recovery by believing in him. But then, living as a child of the King is a moment-by-moment act of faith and trust. Our recovery works the same way. And just as in this life we never fully enter into God's Kingdom, we never really are finished with our recovery. We look forward to that day when we will see Jesus, face-to-face, and know that our recovery is complete—in him.

CHAPTER 1

Jesus' Family Tree

These are the ancestors of Jesus Christ, a descendant of King David and of Abraham:
2 Abraham was the father of Isaac; Isaac was
the father of Jacob; Jacob was the father of
Judah and his brothers.
3 Judah was the father of Perez and Zerah
(Tamar was their mother); Perez was the
father of Hezron; Hezron was the father of
Aram;
4 Aram was the father of Amminadab; Amminadab was the father of Nahshon; Nahshon was the father of Salmon;
5 Salmon was the father of Boaz (Rahab was
his mother); Boaz was the father of Obed
(Ruth was his mother); Obed was the father of
Jesse;
6 Jesse was the father of King David. David
was the father of Solomon (his mother was
the widow of Uriah);
7 Solomon was the father of Rehoboam; Rehoboam was the father of Abijah; Abijah was
the father of Asa;
8 Asa was the father of Jehoshaphat; Jehoshaphat was the father of Joram; Joram was
the father of Uzziah;
9 Uzziah was the father of Jotham; Jotham
was the father of Ahaz; Ahaz was the father of
Hezekiah;

1:1-16 Notice that the family tree of Jesus, the sinless God-man, was far from perfect. Judah fathered Perez with his daughter-in-law Tamar, thinking she was a prostitute (1:3; see Genesis 38); Salmon married Rahab, the former prostitute of Jericho (1:5; see Joshua 6); and David had an adulterous affair with Uriah's wife, Bathsheba (1:6; see 2 Samuel 11). Throughout history God has used imperfect people to work his will. He was more concerned about the attitude of their heart than about the mistakes they had made. God is never fooled or discouraged by people's past mistakes. This should give us hope that God can give us a productive future no matter how destructive our past. For a new start, all we need to do is admit our failures and hand our life over to God.

1:18-19 Joseph reacted to the implications of Mary's pregnancy by deciding to break their engagement. Although he was a man of principle and was well intentioned, the choice was still shortsighted (see 1:20-23). Attitudes and decisions based on a half-baked understanding are a significant problem related to recovery. Patience, honesty, and perseverance in communication are crucial to preventing far-reaching mistakes, such as broken relationships.

JOSEPH & MARY

Trust can be rebuilt when it has been broken, but this does not happen automatically. Such a process takes work and commitment, especially when a relationship has been threatened by unfaithfulness. This was the challenge that Joseph and Mary faced.

Months before their planned wedding, Mary became pregnant. Because Joseph knew that this was not his child, he assumed that she had been unfaithful to him. Though he was troubled by doubts and anger, he chose to break off the engagement as inconspicuously as possible. He was a man of integrity and mercy, so he did not want to hurt or embarrass Mary.

God had other plans, however. He sent an angel to speak to Joseph and assured him that Mary's baby had been supernaturally conceived by the Holy Spirit. The child's name would be Jesus, and he would be the Savior of the world, the one who would offer spiritual recovery to all. Because Joseph believed God, his perspective changed. Mary and Joseph's mutual commitment to and trust in God served as a foundation upon which their trust in each other could again be established.

Mary and Joseph humbly and joyfully entered a new life together. Joseph did all that was possible to protect Mary and the baby Jesus when he was born. He became a loving father who carefully taught his son the carpentry trade. Mary was an attentive and caring mother. This relationship demonstrates that it is possible to rebuild trust and repair love in a relationship that was once very fragile.

The story of Joseph and Mary is told in the Gospels, notably in Matthew 1–2 and Luke 1–2. Mary is also mentioned in Acts 1:14.

STRENGTHS AND ACCOMPLISHMENTS:
- Joseph and Mary's relationship was founded on their commitment to God.
- They were open to God's will and were willing to change their opinions.
- They obeyed God despite the embarrassment they would suffer.

WEAKNESSES AND MISTAKES:
- Joseph did not give Mary the benefit of the doubt early in her pregnancy.
- They failed to understand Jesus' need to spend time in his Father's house.

LESSONS FROM THEIR LIVES:
- Relationships should not be destroyed by unsubstantiated doubts.
- Trust can always be rebuilt if God is at the center of a relationship.
- Things are not always what they seem to be.
- Trust in God is foundational for trust between people.

KEY VERSES:
"Then Joseph . . . decided to break the engagement but to do it quietly, as he didn't want to publicly disgrace her. As he lay awake . . . [he] saw an angel standing beside him. 'Joseph, son of David,' the angel said, 'don't hesitate to take Mary as your wife! For the child within her has been conceived by the Holy Spirit'" (Matthew 1:19-20).

10Hezekiah was the father of Manasseh; Manasseh was the father of Amos; Amos was the father of Josiah;

11Josiah was the father of Jechoniah and his brothers (born at the time of the exile to Babylon).

12After the exile: Jechoniah was the father of Shealtiel; Shealtiel was the father of Zerubbabel;

13Zerubbabel was the father of Abiud; Abiud was the father of Eliakim; Eliakim was the father of Azor;

14Azor was the father of Zadok; Zadok was the father of Achim; Achim was the father of Eliud;

15Eliud was the father of Eleazar; Eleazar was the father of Matthan; Matthan was the father of Jacob;

16Jacob was the father of Joseph (who was the husband of Mary, the mother of Jesus Christ the Messiah).

17These are fourteen of the generations from Abraham to King David; and fourteen from King David's time to the exile; and fourteen from the exile to Christ.

An Angel Visits Joseph

18These are the facts concerning the birth of Jesus Christ: His mother, Mary, was engaged to be married to Joseph. But while she was still a virgin she became pregnant by the Holy Spirit.
19Then Joseph, her fiancé, being a man of stern principle, decided to break the engagement but to do it quietly, as he didn't want to publicly disgrace her.

20As he lay awake considering this, he fell into a dream, and saw an angel standing beside him. "Joseph, son of David," the angel said, "don't hesitate to take Mary as your wife!

For the child within her has been conceived
by the Holy Spirit. 21And she will have a Son,
and you shall name him Jesus (meaning 'Savior'), for he will save his people from their
sins. 22This will fulfill God's message through
his prophets—

> 23'*Listen! The virgin shall conceive a child!*
> She shall give birth to a Son, and he
> shall be called "Emmanuel" (meaning
> "God is with us").'"

24When Joseph awoke, he did as the angel
commanded and brought Mary home to be
his wife, 25but she remained a virgin until her
Son was born; and Joseph named him "Jesus."

CHAPTER 2

Visitors Arrive from the East

Jesus was born in the town of Bethlehem, in
Judea, during the reign of King Herod.
At about that time some astrologers from
eastern lands arrived in Jerusalem, asking,
2"Where is the newborn King of the Jews? for
we have seen his star in far-off eastern lands
and have come to worship him."
3King Herod was deeply disturbed by their
question, and all Jerusalem was filled with
rumors. 4He called a meeting of the Jewish
religious leaders.
"Did the prophets tell us where the Messiah
would be born?" he asked.
5"Yes, in Bethlehem," they said, "for this is
what the prophet Micah wrote:

> 6'O little town of Bethlehem, you are not
> just an unimportant Judean village, for
> a Governor shall rise from you to rule
> my people Israel.'"

7Then Herod sent a private message to the
astrologers, asking them to come to see him;
at this meeting he found out from them the
exact time when they first saw the star. Then
he told them, 8"Go to Bethlehem and search
for the child. And when you find him, come
back and tell me so that I can go and worship
him too!"
9After this interview the astrologers started
out again. And look! The star appeared to
them again, standing over Bethlehem. 10Their
joy knew no bounds!

11Entering the house where the baby and
Mary, his mother, were, they threw themselves down before him, worshiping. Then
they opened their presents and gave him
gold, frankincense, and myrrh. 12But when
they returned to their own land, they didn't
go through Jerusalem to report to Herod, for
God had warned them in a dream to go home
another way.

The Escape to Egypt

13After they were gone, an angel of the Lord
appeared to Joseph in a dream. "Get up and
flee to Egypt with the baby and his mother,"
the angel said, "and stay there until I tell you
to return, for King Herod is going to try to kill
the child." 14That same night he left for Egypt
with Mary and the baby, 15and stayed there
until King Herod's death. This fulfilled the
prophet's prediction,

> "I have called my Son from Egypt."

16Herod was furious when he learned that
the astrologers had disobeyed him. Sending
soldiers to Bethlehem, he ordered them to kill
every baby boy two years old and under, both
in the town and on the nearby farms, for the
astrologers had told him the star first appeared
to them two years before. 17This brutal action
of Herod's fulfilled the prophecy of Jeremiah,

> 18"Screams of anguish come from Ramah,
> Weeping unrestrained;
> Rachel weeping for her children,
> Uncomforted—
> For they are dead."

19When Herod died, an angel of the Lord
appeared in a dream to Joseph in Egypt and
told him, 20"Get up and take the baby and his
mother back to Israel, for those who were
trying to kill the child are dead."
21So he returned immediately to Israel with
Jesus and his mother. 22But on the way he was
frightened to learn that the new king was
Herod's son, Archelaus. Then, in another
dream, he was warned not to go to Judea, so
they went to Galilee instead 23and lived in
Nazareth. This fulfilled the prediction of the
prophets concerning the Messiah,

> "He shall be called a Nazarene."

2:3-8, 12-18 King Herod was a tyrannical personality who turned on the charm and manipulated others to achieve his ends. Herod thought he could get information about the identity and whereabouts of the Messiah from the wise men by feigning interest and a desire to worship. Frequently, abusive or oppressive persons will "play along" in the earliest stages of recovery, hoping to crush any resistance to their domination later. We need to be careful to avoid such people, as did the wise men and Joseph.

CHAPTER 3

John Preaches about the Kingdom

While they were living in Nazareth, John the Baptist began preaching out in the Judean wilderness. His constant theme was, 2"Turn from your sins . . . turn to God . . . for the Kingdom of Heaven is coming soon." 3Isaiah the prophet had told about John's ministry centuries before! He had written,

"I hear a shout from the wilderness,
'Prepare a road for the Lord—straighten out the path where he will walk.'"

4John's clothing was woven from camel's hair and he wore a leather belt; his food was locusts and wild honey. 5People from Jerusalem and from all over the Jordan Valley, and, in fact, from every section of Judea went out to the wilderness to hear him preach, 6and when they confessed their sins, he baptized them in the Jordan River.

7But when he saw many Pharisees and Sadducees coming to be baptized, he denounced them.

"You sons of snakes!" he warned. "Who said that you could escape the coming wrath of God? 8Before being baptized, prove that you have turned from sin by doing worthy deeds. 9Don't try to get by as you are, thinking, 'We are safe for we are Jews—descendants of Abraham.' That proves nothing. God can change these stones here into Jews!

10"And even now the axe of God's judgment is poised to chop down every unproductive tree. They will be chopped and burned.

11"With water I baptize those who repent of their sins; but someone else is coming, far greater than I am, so great that I am not worthy to carry his shoes! He shall baptize you with the Holy Spirit and with fire. 12He will separate the chaff from the grain, burning the chaff with never-ending fire and storing away the grain."

John Baptizes Jesus

13Then Jesus went from Galilee to the Jordan River to be baptized there by John. 14John didn't want to do it.

"This isn't proper," he said. "I am the one who needs to be baptized by you."

15But Jesus said, "Please do it, for I must do all that is right." So then John baptized him.

16After his baptism, as soon as Jesus came up out of the water, the heavens were opened to him and he saw the Spirit of God coming down in the form of a dove. 17And a voice from heaven said, "This is my beloved Son, and I am wonderfully pleased with him."

CHAPTER 4

Satan Tempts Jesus

Then Jesus was led out into the wilderness by the Holy Spirit, to be tempted there by Satan. 2For forty days and forty nights he ate nothing and became very hungry. 3Then Satan tempted him to get food by changing stones into loaves of bread.

"It will prove you are the Son of God," he said.

4But Jesus told him, "No! For the Scriptures tell us that bread won't feed men's souls: obedience to every word of God is what we need."

5Then Satan took him to Jerusalem to the roof of the Temple. 6"Jump off," he said, "and prove you are the Son of God; for the

3:1-2 John the Baptist preached a centuries-old message: repentance. People could have easily dismissed his message by saying, "I've heard this before," or "I'll quit sinning tomorrow." But John presented with fresh urgency the need for an immediate moral U-turn: "The Kingdom of Heaven is coming soon." Repentance requires honest self-examination. The sense of urgency in John's message is similar to the urgency of recovery. There is no time like the present to face reality and turn from our self-destructive behaviors.

3:16-17 After Jesus' baptism, the Holy Spirit was seen in visible form, and the voice of the Father was heard commending the Son. Jesus is thus shown to be in perfect harmony with his Father and the Holy Spirit. While those of us seeking recovery will never have perfect unity in our relationships, we can draw support from those who affirm us. As we study the Bible, God's love letter to the human race, we will find numerous evidences of God's unlimited love for us. Repeated "I love you" messages from our heavenly Father can help to offset the lack of explicit affirmation from our earthly relationships.

4:3-7 Notice that Satan did not doubt that Jesus was the Son of God. Rather, he appealed to real needs and possible doubts that were common to his humanity. Jesus, like us, had need for food, security, protection, significance, and achievement. Had Jesus faltered at the point of his humanity, Satan could have called into question Jesus' right to rule and his perfection as the unique God-man. Similarly, Satan and his forces will attack those of us pursuing recovery at our most vulnerable points. It is important that we be on guard against these attacks.

Scriptures declare, 'God will send his angels to
keep you from harm,' . . . they will prevent
you from smashing on the rocks below."
[7]Jesus retorted, "It also says not to put the
Lord your God to a foolish test!"
[8]Next Satan took him to the peak of a very
high mountain and showed him the nations
of the world and all their glory. [9]"I'll give it all
to you," he said, "if you will only kneel and
worship me."
[10]"Get out of here, Satan," Jesus told him.
"The Scriptures say, 'Worship only the Lord
God. Obey only him.'"
[11]Then Satan went away, and angels came
and cared for Jesus.

Jesus Teaches in Galilee

[12,13]When Jesus heard that John had been ar-
rested, he left Judea and returned home to
Nazareth in Galilee; but soon he moved to
Capernaum, beside the Lake of Galilee, close
to Zebulun and Naphtali. [14]This fulfilled
Isaiah's prophecy:

[15,16]"The land of Zebulun and the land of
Naphtali, beside the Lake, and the
countryside beyond the Jordan River,
and Upper Galilee where so many
foreigners live—there the people who
sat in darkness have seen a great Light;
they sat in the land of death, and the
Light broke through upon them."

[17]From then on, Jesus began to preach,
"Turn from sin and turn to God, for the Kingdom of Heaven is near."

Four Fishermen Follow Jesus

[18]One day as he was walking along the beach
beside the Lake of Galilee, he saw two brothers—Simon, also called Peter, and Andrew—
out in a boat fishing with a net, for they were
commercial fishermen.
[19]Jesus called out, "Come along with me
and I will show you how to fish for the souls
of men!" [20]And they left their nets at once and
went with him.
[21]A little farther up the beach he saw two
other brothers, James and John, sitting in a
boat with their father, Zebedee, mending
their nets; and he called to them to come too.
[22]At once they stopped their work and, leaving their father behind, went with him.

Jesus Teaches about the Kingdom

[23]Jesus traveled all through Galilee teaching in
the Jewish synagogues, everywhere preaching
the Good News about the Kingdom of
Heaven. And he healed every kind of sickness
and disease. [24]The report of his miracles
spread far beyond the borders of Galilee so
that sick folk were soon coming to be healed
from as far away as Syria. And whatever their
illness and pain, or if they were possessed by
demons, or were insane, or paralyzed—he
healed them all. [25]Enormous crowds followed
him wherever he went—people from Galilee,
and the Ten Cities, and Jerusalem, and from
all over Judea, and even from across the Jordan River.

CHAPTER 5

The Sermon on the Mount

One day as the crowds were gathering, he
went up the hillside with his disciples and sat
down and taught them there.
[3]"Humble men are very fortunate!" he told
them, "for the Kingdom of Heaven is given to
them. [4]Those who mourn are fortunate! for
they shall be comforted. [5]The meek and lowly

4:12-16 The way of recovery through Jesus Christ is open to everyone, not just the "religious." Jesus can heal anyone, regardless of past history, religious affiliation, or national background. Jesus himself proved this by spending his early years in the cosmopolitan region of Galilee. The Jews in this area were not considered "good Jews" by those in Judea because of their contact with the many Gentiles who lived there. But Jesus showed God's love for them. And he continues to show his love to all who trust him, no matter who we are or how great our mistakes in the past.

5:3-5 We cannot experience God-blessed recovery without true humility. Pride stands in the way of our dealing with painful problems and destructive dependencies. If we cannot admit our problems and failures, there can be no real cure for us. When we humble ourself before God, we mourn and grieve over our mistakes and losses. As we do this, we will experience the wonderful comfort that only God can offer (see 2 Corinthians 1:3-5).

5:21-22, 27-29 Anger and lust are two dangerous pitfalls that threaten all of us in one way or another. Intense emotions and desires must be dealt with from the inside out. Those of us burning with rage, lust, or some other addictive behavior generally think we can control it from the outside in. But we eventually and invariably lose control. Jesus shows how the patterns of anger and lust are serious and far too powerful for us to control alone. However, we can begin the path toward victory by admitting that we are powerless and looking to our powerful God for help.

are fortunate! for the whole wide world belongs to them.
[6]"Happy are those who long to be just and
good, for they shall be completely satisfied.
[7]Happy are the kind and merciful, for they
shall be shown mercy. [8]Happy are those
whose hearts are pure, for they shall see God.
[9]Happy are those who strive for peace—they
shall be called the sons of God. [10]Happy are
those who are persecuted because they are
good, for the Kingdom of Heaven is theirs.
[11]"When you are reviled and persecuted
and lied about because you are my followers—wonderful! [12]Be *happy* about it! Be *very*
glad! for a *tremendous reward* awaits you up in
heaven. And remember, the ancient prophets
were persecuted too.

Being like Salt and Light

[13]"You are the world's seasoning, to make it
tolerable. If you lose your flavor, what will
happen to the world? And you yourselves will
be thrown out and trampled underfoot as
worthless. [14]You are the world's light—a city
on a hill, glowing in the night for all to see.
[15,16]Don't hide your light! Let it shine for all;
let your good deeds glow for all to see, so that
they will praise your heavenly Father.

Teachings about God's Laws

[17]"Don't misunderstand why I have come—it
isn't to cancel the laws of Moses and the
warnings of the prophets. No, I came to fulfill
them and to make them all come true. [18]With
all the earnestness I have I say: Every law in
the Book will continue until its purpose is
achieved. [19]And so if anyone breaks the least
commandment and teaches others to, he
shall be the least in the Kingdom of Heaven.
But those who teach God's laws *and obey them*
shall be great in the Kingdom of Heaven.
[20]"But I warn you—unless your goodness is
greater than that of the Pharisees and other
Jewish leaders, you can't get into the Kingdom of Heaven at all!

Teachings about Anger

[21]"Under the laws of Moses the rule was, 'If
you murder, you must die.' [22]But I have added
to that rule and tell you that if you are only
angry, even in your own home, you are in
danger of judgment! If you call your friend an
idiot, you are in danger of being brought
before the court. And if you curse him, you
are in danger of the fires of hell.
[23]"So if you are standing before the altar in
the Temple, offering a sacrifice to God, and

Delayed gratification

READ MATTHEW 4:1-11

We may be searching for a shortcut to happiness. The road of life often takes us through painful places we would rather avoid. Some of us have gotten off the right track, lured away by hopes of a faster and easier way to "the good life."

Jesus faced this same temptation. He was destined to become the King of all the earth. The plan was that he would come to earth as a man, live a sinless life, die to pay for our sins, rise from the dead, and return to heaven to wait for those who would be his. Then he would return to earth to claim his people and his rightful place as King of kings. Satan offered him a shortcut. "Satan . . . showed [Jesus] the nations of the world and all their glory. 'I'll give it all to you,' he said, 'if you will only kneel and worship me.' 'Get out of here, Satan,' Jesus told him. 'The Scriptures say, "Worship only the Lord God. Obey only him"'" (Matthew 4:8-10). If Jesus had fallen for this trick, he would have sinned and lost everything.

We need to beware of "shortcuts" that take us even one step outside of God's will. We are warned, "Resist the devil and he will flee from you" (James 4:7). This resistance is sometimes shown by ignoring offers that are "too good to be true." There are really no quick fixes in life. The path of recovery can be long and hard, but many have gone before us and made it. As we stay on the path, taking one step at a time, we'll find the good things in life. ***Turn to page 1015, Matthew 6.***

suddenly remember that a friend has something against you, [24]leave your sacrifice there beside the altar and go and apologize and be reconciled to him, and then come and offer your sacrifice to God. [25]Come to terms quickly with your enemy before it is too late and he drags you into court and you are thrown into a debtor's cell, [26]for you will stay there until you have paid the last penny.

Teachings about Adultery

[27]"The laws of Moses said, 'You shall not commit adultery.' [28]But I say: Anyone who even looks at a woman with lust in his eye has already committed adultery with her in his heart. [29]So if your eye—even if it is your best eye! —causes you to lust, gouge it out and throw it away. Better for part of you to be destroyed than for all of you to be cast into hell. [30]And if your hand—even your right hand—causes you to sin, cut it off and throw it away. Better that than find yourself in hell.

[31]"The law of Moses says, 'If anyone wants to be rid of his wife, he can divorce her merely by giving her a letter of dismissal.' [32]But I say that a man who divorces his wife, except for fornication, causes her to commit adultery if she marries again. And he who marries her commits adultery.

Teachings about Making Vows

[33]"Again, the law of Moses says, 'You shall not break your vows to God but must fulfill them all.' [34]But I say: Don't make any vows! And even to say 'By heavens!' is a sacred vow to God, for the heavens are God's throne. [35]And if you say 'By the earth!' it is a sacred vow, for the earth is his footstool. And don't swear 'By Jerusalem!' for Jerusalem is the capital of the great King. [36]Don't even swear 'By my head!' for you can't turn one hair white or black. [37]Say just a simple 'Yes, I will' or 'No, I won't.' Your word is enough. To strengthen your promise with a vow shows that something is wrong.

Teachings about Getting Even

[38]"The law of Moses says, 'If a man gouges out another's eye, he must pay with his own eye. If a tooth gets knocked out, knock out the tooth of the one who did it.' [39]But I say: Don't resist violence! If you are slapped on one cheek, turn the other too. [40]If you are ordered to court, and your shirt is taken from you, give your coat too. [41]If the military demand that you carry their gear for a mile, carry it two. [42]Give to those who ask, and don't turn away from those who want to borrow.

Loving Our Enemies

[43]"There is a saying, 'Love your *friends* and hate your enemies.' [44]But I say: Love your *enemies!* Pray for those who *persecute* you! [45]In that way you will be acting as true sons of your Father in heaven. For he gives his sunlight to both the evil and the good, and sends rain on the just and on the unjust too. [46]If you love only those who love you, what good is that? Even scoundrels do that much. [47]If you are friendly only to your friends, how are you different from anyone else? Even the heathen do that. [48]But you are to be perfect, even as your Father in heaven is perfect.

CHAPTER 6

Giving to the Needy

"Take care! Don't do your good deeds publicly, to be admired, for then you will lose the

---

5:43-48 When we find ourself able to love our enemies, we can be sure that we are making progress in recovery. Loving our enemies doesn't mean we have to like them, but it does mean we must forgive them and desire what is best for them. If we harbor anger and bitterness toward others, we only hurt ourself; such emotions keep us from making progress in our own recovery. God loved us while we were still his enemies (see Romans 5:8); he loves us even though we are far from perfect. Recovery is not perfectionism; it is the development of the ability to follow God and shape our actions according to his good plans for us.

6:5-8 Public prayer is open to many distortions and abuses. Some individuals use majestic-sounding, churchy jargon that impresses people, but not God. Others think that the key to answered prayer is repetition, thus reducing it almost to the level of a chant or mantra. Both attitudes miss the mark because they assume prayer has more to do with technique than internal attitudes and realities. True heart-to-heart communication with God, whether private or public, is rewarded and will have a profound effect on our recovery.

6:12, 14-15 True forgiveness is an essential part of any recovery program. We often experience difficulty in getting past our anger and bitterness toward those who have mistreated or abused us. However, asking God's forgiveness for our personal shortcomings and sins is hypocritical unless we are willing to forgive others. To the detriment of our recovery program, we forfeit forgiveness from God by denying forgiveness to others. Not only is this selfish; it is also self-destructive.

reward from your Father in heaven. 2When
you give a gift to a beggar, don't shout about
it as the hypocrites do—blowing trumpets in
the synagogues and streets to call attention to
their acts of charity! I tell you in all earnestness, they have received all the reward they
will ever get. 3But when you do a kindness to
someone, do it secretly—don't tell your left
hand what your right hand is doing. 4And
your Father, who knows all secrets, will reward you.

Teachings about Prayer

5"And now about prayer. When you pray,
don't be like the hypocrites who pretend piety
by praying publicly on street corners and in
the synagogues where everyone can see them.
Truly, that is all the reward they will ever get.
6But when you pray, go away by yourself, all
alone, and shut the door behind you and pray
to your Father secretly, and your Father, who
knows your secrets, will reward you.
7,8"Don't recite the same prayer over and
over as the heathen do, who think prayers are
answered only by repeating them again and
again. Remember, your Father knows exactly
what you need even before you ask him!
9"Pray along these lines: 'Our Father in
heaven, we honor your holy name. 10We ask
that your kingdom will come now. May your
will be done here on earth, just as it is in
heaven. 11Give us our food again today, as
usual, 12and forgive us our sins, just as we have
forgiven those who have sinned against us.
13Don't bring us into temptation, but deliver
us from the Evil One. Amen.' 14,15Your heavenly Father will forgive you if you forgive
those who sin against you; but if *you* refuse to
forgive *them, he* will not forgive *you.*

Teachings about Fasting

16"And now about fasting. When you fast,
declining your food for a spiritual purpose,
don't do it publicly, as the hypocrites do, who
try to look wan and disheveled so people will
feel sorry for them. Truly, that is the only
reward they will ever get. 17But when you fast,
put on festive clothing, 18so that no one will
suspect you are hungry, except your Father
who knows every secret. And he will reward
you.

Teachings about Money

19"Don't store up treasures here on earth
where they can erode away or may be stolen.
20Store them in heaven where they will never
lose their value and are safe from thieves. 21If

Making Peace

BIBLE READING: Matthew 5:23-25

We made direct amends to such people wherever possible, except when to do so would injure them or others.

We all suffer brokenness in our life, in our relationship with God, and in our relationships with others. Brokenness tends to weigh us down and can easily lead us back into our addictions. Recovery isn't complete until all areas of brokenness are mended.

Jesus taught, "So if you are standing before the altar in the Temple, offering a sacrifice to God, and suddenly remember that a friend has something against you, leave your sacrifice there beside the altar and go and apologize and be reconciled to him, and then come and offer your sacrifice to God" (Matthew 5:23-24). The apostle John wrote, "If anyone says 'I love God,' but keeps on hating his brother, he is a liar; for if he doesn't love his brother who is right there in front of him, how can he love God whom he has never seen?" (1 John 4:20).

Much of recovery involves repairing the brokenness in our life. This requires that we make peace with God, with ourself, and with others whom we have alienated. Unresolved issues in relationships can keep us from being at peace with God and ourself. Once we go through the process of making amends, we must keep our mind and heart open to anyone we may have overlooked. God will often remind us of relationships that need attention. When these come to mind, we should not delay going to those we have offended, seeking to repair the damage. *Turn to page 1125, Luke 19.*

your profits are in heaven, your heart will be
there too.
22"If your eye is pure, there will be sunshine
in your soul. 23But if your eye is clouded with
evil thoughts and desires, you are in deep
spiritual darkness. And oh, how deep that
darkness can be!
24"You cannot serve two masters: God and
money. For you will hate one and love the
other, or else the other way around.
25"So my counsel is: Don't worry about
things—food, drink, and clothes. For you already have life and a body—and they are far
more important than what to eat and wear.
26Look at the birds! They don't worry about
what to eat—they don't need to sow or reap
or store up food—for your heavenly Father
feeds them. And you are far more valuable to
him than they are. 27Will all your worries add
a single moment to your life?
28"And why worry about your clothes?
Look at the field lilies! They don't worry
about theirs. 29Yet King Solomon in all his
glory was not clothed as beautifully as they.
30And if God cares so wonderfully for flowers
that are here today and gone tomorrow,
won't he more surely care for you, O men of
little faith?
31,32"So don't worry at all about having
enough food and clothing. Why be like the
heathen? For they take pride in all these
things and are deeply concerned about them.
But your heavenly Father already knows perfectly well that you need them, 33and he will
give them to you if you give him first place in
your life and live as he wants you to.
34"So don't be anxious about tomorrow.
God will take care of your tomorrow too. Live
one day at a time.

CHAPTER 7

Teachings about Criticizing Others

"Don't criticize, and then you won't be criticized. 2For others will treat you as you treat
them. 3And why worry about a speck in the
eye of a brother when you have a board in
your own? 4Should you say, 'Friend, let me
help you get that speck out of your eye,'
when you can't even see because of the
board in your own? 5Hypocrite! First get rid
of the board. Then you can see to help your
brother.
6"Don't give holy things to depraved men.
Don't give pearls to swine! They will trample
the pearls and turn and attack you.

God Gives Good Gifts

7"Ask, and you will be given what you ask for.
Seek, and you will find. Knock, and the door
will be opened. 8For everyone who asks, receives. Anyone who seeks, finds. If only you
will knock, the door will open. 9If a child asks
his father for a loaf of bread, will he be given
a stone instead? 10If he asks for fish, will he be
given a poisonous snake? Of course not!
11And if you hardhearted, sinful men know
how to give good gifts to your children,
won't your Father in heaven even more certainly give good gifts to those who ask him
for them?
12"Do for others what you want them to do
for you. This is the teaching of the laws of
Moses in a nutshell.

Heaven's Narrow Gate

13"Heaven can be entered only through the
narrow gate! The highway to hell is broad,
and its gate is wide enough for all the multitudes who choose its easy way. 14But the Gateway to Life is small, and the road is narrow,
and only a few ever find it.

The Danger of False Teachers

15"Beware of false teachers who come disguised as harmless sheep, but are wolves and
will tear you apart. 16You can detect them by
the way they act, just as you can identify a tree
by its fruit. You need never confuse grape-

7:7-11 Prayer is an opportunity for perseverance. Each of the three commands ("ask," "seek," and "knock") are positive habits meant to be developed. We will persist in prayer with realistic hope once we fully appreciate the kind of Father who hears our prayers. Many of us in recovery have suffered at the hands of dysfunctional, even abusive, parents who often gave us "stones" and "snakes." Thus, we often must completely rethink our concept of God as a Father who gives good gifts to his children. As we discover his loving character, we will be encouraged to ask him for the good gift of recovery.

7:15-20 The good fruit that our life should be evidencing is "love, joy, peace, patience, kindness, goodness, faithfulness, gentleness and self-control" (Galatians 5:22-23). To be in the throes of an addiction, however, means that we are without peace and totally out of control. If we are honest as we take our moral inventory, we will admit that the fruits of our life are not those that God intends for us. Once we admit the reality of our failure, we can enter recovery and work to produce the life that God wants for us.

READ MATTHEW 6:25-34

GOD grant me the serenity
to accept the things I cannot change
the courage to change the things I can
and the wisdom to know the difference
AMEN

Living one day at a time is a discipline we all have to focus on when we are in recovery.

It is easy to slip back into worrying about tomorrow, dwelling on the "what ifs" and the "if onlys." Each day brings with it a host of things we cannot change. We face the continual reality of circumstances beyond our control. There is also the reality of who we are—human beings confined within the slice of life we call today. It is tempting to deny the present, but escaping reality is part of the insanity of our addictive way of life.

Jesus once said, "Will all your worries add a single moment to your life? . . . God will take care of your tomorrow too. Live one day at a time" (Matthew 6:27, 34). The prophet Jeremiah said, "It is only the Lord's mercies that have kept us from complete destruction. Great is his faithfulness; his loving-kindness begins afresh each day" (Lamentations 3:22-23). Since God's grace comes in daily doses, that's the best way to face life.

We need to ask at every turn in life, "Am I accepting this present moment, or am I pretending—trying to escape into the past or the future?" For each day, there is something to find joy in, and there is strength promised for the troubles of that day. The psalmist wrote, "This is the day that the Lord has made. We will rejoice and be glad in it" (Psalm 118:24). We, too, can choose to find joy, strength, and sanity when we accept today's realities. ***Turn to page 1025, Matthew 14.***

---

vines with thorn bushes or figs with thistles.
17Different kinds of fruit trees can quickly be
identified by examining their fruit. 18A variety
that produces delicious fruit never produces
an inedible kind. And a tree producing an
inedible kind can't produce what is good. 19So
the trees having the inedible fruit are
chopped down and thrown on the fire. 20Yes,
the way to identify a tree or a person is by the
kind of fruit produced.

21"Not all who sound religious are really
godly people. They may refer to me as 'Lord,'
but still won't get to heaven. For the decisive
question is whether they obey my Father in
heaven. 22At the Judgment many will tell me,
'Lord, Lord, we told others about you and
used your name to cast out demons and to do
many other great miracles.' 23But I will reply,
'You have never been mine. Go away, for your
deeds are evil.'

Building on Rock or Sand

24"All who listen to my instructions and follow them are wise, like a man who builds his
house on solid rock. 25Though the rain comes
in torrents, and the floods rise and the storm
winds beat against his house, it won't collapse, for it is built on rock.

26"But those who hear my instructions and
ignore them are foolish, like a man who
builds his house on sand. 27For when the rains
and floods come, and storm winds beat
against his house, it will fall with a mighty
crash." 28The crowds were amazed at Jesus'
sermons, 29for he taught as one who had great
authority, and not as their Jewish leaders.

CHAPTER 8

Jesus Heals a Leper

Large crowds followed Jesus as he came down
the hillside.

2Look! A leper is approaching. He kneels before
him, worshiping. "Sir," the leper pleads, "if you
want to, you can heal me."
3Jesus touches the man. "I want to," he says.
"Be healed." And instantly the leprosy disap-
pears.
4Then Jesus says to him, "Don't stop to talk to
anyone; go right over to the priest to be examined;
and take with you the offering required by Moses'
law for lepers who are healed—a public testimony
of your cure."

A Roman Soldier's Faith

5,6When Jesus arrived in Capernaum, a Roman
army captain came and pled with him to
come to his home and heal his servant boy
who was in bed paralyzed and racked with
pain.
7"Yes," Jesus said, "I will come and heal
him."
8,9Then the officer said, "Sir, I am not worthy to have you in my home; [and it isn't
necessary for you to come]. If you will only
stand here and say, 'Be healed,' my servant
will get well! I know, because I am under the
authority of my superior officers and I have
authority over my soldiers, and I say to one,
'Go,' and he goes, and to another, 'Come,'
and he comes, and to my slave boy, 'Do this
or that,' and he does it. And I know you have
authority to tell his sickness to go—and it will
go!"
10Jesus stood there amazed! Turning to the
crowd he said, "I haven't seen faith like this
in all the land of Israel! 11And I tell you this,
that many Gentiles [like this Roman officer],
shall come from all over the world and sit
down in the Kingdom of Heaven with Abraham, Isaac, and Jacob. 12And many an Israelite—those for whom the Kingdom was
prepared—shall be cast into outer darkness,
into the place of weeping and torment."
13Then Jesus said to the Roman officer, "Go
on home. What you have believed has happened!" And the boy was healed that same
hour!

Jesus Heals Many

14When Jesus arrived at Peter's house, Peter's
mother-in-law was in bed with a high fever.
15But when Jesus touched her hand, the fever
left her; and she got up and prepared a meal
for them!
16That evening several demon-possessed
people were brought to Jesus; and when he
spoke a single word, all the demons fled; and
all the sick were healed. 17This fulfilled the
prophecy of Isaiah, "He took our sicknesses
and bore our diseases."

The Cost of Following Jesus

18When Jesus noticed how large the crowd
was growing, he instructed his disciples to get
ready to cross to the other side of the lake.
19Just then one of the Jewish religious
teachers said to him, "Teacher, I will follow
you no matter where you go!"
20But Jesus said, "Foxes have dens and birds
have nests, but I, the Messiah, have no home
of my own—no place to lay my head."

8:2-4 Jesus' healing of the leper demonstrated his ability to bring about instant physical recovery in response to faith. Jesus then directed the grateful leper to an immediate examination, calling him to display his deliverance and faith in a public way. Emotional and spiritual recovery is generally more of a prolonged process for us than was the physical healing of this leper. Yet both timetables for recovery have the same starting and ending points. The same Jesus who can effect instant healing is also the Author and Finisher of our recovery program.

8:5-13 The healing of the servant of the Roman army captain has much to teach all of us who are in recovery. The officer understood and humbly admitted his need, believing that Jesus could heal his young servant even at a distance. Jesus marveled because such faith was rare, even among God's chosen people, the Jews. We see here that Jesus came to bring deliverance to all people, whether Jew or Gentile, man or woman, rich or poor, religious or nonreligious. With God's help we can all have hope for recovery, no matter who we are or what we have done.

8:23-32 In this passage Jesus exhibited power over both the weather and the demonic realm. In both cases his disciples learned lessons about faith in the incredible power of God. Since Jesus has the ability to calm a mighty storm and rid people of demonic influence, he can certainly empower our recovery process. We can experience God's power in our life by first recognizing how powerless we are and then giving our life to him.

9:1-7 The Jewish religious leaders thought it blasphemous for Jesus to claim to forgive sins, but they considered it just as impossible for him to heal the paralyzed man. So by doing the impossible—healing the paralytic—Jesus made it clear to his critics that he also had the power to forgive sins. Implicit in his actions was a claim to deity, because only God is able to forgive sins. Knowing this truth should give us the courage to turn to Jesus for help. As God's own Son, he has the power to offer forgiveness and recovery to all who trust in him.

[21]Another of his disciples said, "Sir, when
my father is dead, then I will follow you."
[22]But Jesus told him, "Follow me *now!* Let
those who are spiritually dead care for their
own dead."

Jesus Calms a Storm

[23]Then he got into a boat and started across
the lake with his disciples. [24]Suddenly a terrible
storm came up, with waves higher than
the boat. But Jesus was asleep.
[25]The disciples went to him and wakened
him, shouting, "Lord, save us! We're sinking!"
[26]But Jesus answered, "O you men of little
faith! Why are you so frightened?" Then he
stood up and rebuked the wind and waves,
and the storm subsided and all was calm.
[27]The disciples just sat there, awed! "Who is
this," they asked themselves, "that even the
winds and the sea obey him?"

Jesus Heals a Demon-possessed Man

[28]When they arrived on the other side of the
lake, in the country of the Gadarenes, two
men with demons in them met him. They
lived in a cemetery and were so dangerous
that no one could go through that area.
[29]They began screaming at him, "What do
you want with us, O Son of God? You have no
right to torment us yet."
[30]A herd of pigs was feeding in the distance,
[31]so the demons begged, "If you cast us out,
send us into that herd of pigs."
[32]"All right," Jesus told them. "Begone."
And they came out of the men and entered
the pigs, and the whole herd rushed over a
cliff and drowned in the water below. [33]The
herdsmen fled to the nearest city with the
story of what had happened, [34]and the entire
population came rushing out to see Jesus and
begged him to go away and leave them alone.

CHAPTER 9

Jesus Heals a Paralyzed Man

So Jesus climbed into a boat and went across
the lake to Capernaum, his hometown.
[2]Soon some men brought him a paralyzed
boy on a mat. When Jesus saw their faith, he
said to the sick boy, "Cheer up, son! For I have
forgiven your sins!"
[3]"Blasphemy! This man is saying he is
God!" exclaimed some of the religious leaders
to themselves.
[4]Jesus knew what they were thinking and
asked them, "Why are you thinking such evil
thoughts? [5,6]I, the Messiah, have the authority
on earth to forgive sins. But talk is cheap—

Forgiveness

READ MATTHEW 6:9-15

Some of us become so focused on our personal failures in recovery that we don't deal with the pain we have suffered at the hands of others. Some of us, on the other hand, focus too much on the way we have been mistreated and use this as an excuse for our behavior. Either approach to past abuse leaves us with emotional baggage that will hinder our progress in recovery. Forgiving others is an important part of turning our will over to God.

Jesus taught his disciples, "Pray along these lines: 'Our Father in heaven, we honor your holy name. We ask that your kingdom will come now. May your will be done here on earth, just as it is in heaven. Give us our food again today, as usual, and forgive us our sins, just as we have forgiven those who have sinned against us. Don't bring us into temptation, but deliver us from the Evil One. Amen.' Your heavenly Father will forgive you if you forgive those who sin against you; but if *you* refuse to forgive *them, he* will not forgive *you*" (Matthew 6:9-15).

Being forgiven for the wrongs we have done against others does not excuse us from our actions or make our actions right. And when we forgive others of the wrongs they have committed against us, we do not excuse what they have done. We simply recognize that we have been hurt unjustly and then turn the matter over to God. This helps us face the truth about our own pain. It also frees us from any excuse to continue our compulsive behavior because of what has been done to us. ***Turn to page 1027, Matthew 15.***

anybody could say that. So I'll prove it to you
by healing this man." Then, turning to the
paralyzed man, he commanded, "Pick up
your stretcher and go on home, for you are
healed."
7And the boy jumped up and left!
8A chill of fear swept through the crowd as
they saw this happen right before their eyes.
How they praised God for giving such authority to a man!

Jesus Eats at Matthew's House

9As Jesus was going on down the road, he saw
a tax collector, Matthew, sitting at a tax collection booth. "Come and be my disciple,"
Jesus said to him, and Matthew jumped up
and went along with him.
10Later, as Jesus and his disciples were eating dinner [at Matthew's house], there were
many notorious swindlers there as guests!
11The Pharisees were indignant. "Why does
your teacher associate with men like that?"
12"Because people who are well don't need
a doctor! It's the sick people who do!" was
Jesus' reply. 13Then he added, "Now go away
and learn the meaning of this verse of Scripture,

'It isn't your sacrifices and your gifts I
want—I want you to be merciful.'

For I have come to urge sinners, not the
self-righteous, back to God."

Questions about Fasting

14One day the disciples of John the Baptist
came to Jesus and asked him, "Why don't
your disciples fast as we do and as the Pharisees do?"
15"Should the bridegroom's friends mourn
and go without food while he is with them?"
Jesus asked. "But the time is coming when I
will be taken from them. Time enough then
for them to refuse to eat.
16"And who would patch an old garment
with unshrunk cloth? For the patch would
tear away and make the hole worse. 17And
who would use old wineskins to store new
wine? For the old skins would burst with the
pressure, and the wine would be spilled and
skins ruined. Only new wineskins are used to
store new wine. That way both are preserved."

Two Wonderful Miracles

18As he was saying this, the rabbi of the local
synagogue came and worshiped him. "My
little daughter has just died," he said, "but
you can bring her back to life again if you will
only come and touch her."
19As Jesus and the disciples were going to
the rabbi's home, 20a woman who had been
sick for twelve years with internal bleeding
came up behind him and touched a tassel of
his robe, 21for she thought, "If I only touch
him, I will be healed."
22Jesus turned around and spoke to her.
"Daughter," he said, "all is well! Your faith has
healed you." And the woman was well from
that moment.
23When Jesus arrived at the rabbi's home
and saw the noisy crowds and heard the funeral music, 24he said, "Get them out, for the
little girl isn't dead; she is only sleeping!"
Then how they all scoffed and sneered at him!
25When the crowd was finally outside, Jesus
went in where the little girl was lying and
took her by the hand, and she jumped up and
was all right again! 26The report of this wonderful miracle swept the entire countryside.

Jesus Heals the Blind and the Mute

27As Jesus was leaving her home, two blind
men followed along behind, shouting, "O
Son of King David, have mercy on us."
28They went right into the house where he
was staying, and Jesus asked them, "Do you
believe I can make you see?"
"Yes, Lord," they told him, "we do."

9:14-17 Jesus contrasted religious ritualism that cannot save with true spiritual power that can lead to a transformed life. He used two analogies here. The unshrunk cloth and new wine represent the power for recovery that Jesus offers. The old garment and wineskins refer to the ritualistic life-styles and outward appearances characteristic of many Jews in Jesus' day. He could just as well have been speaking directly to us who need recovery today. Small, external adjustments will not bring us relief from our addictions. We need the newness of full recovery in Jesus Christ.

9:18-33 More and more proof stacks up that Jesus is the Messiah and the source of recovery for all kinds of people. Jesus restored life to a dead girl and stopped a woman's chronic hemorrhage. Then he healed two blind men, and a demon-possessed man who was unable to speak. Jesus thus showed his ability to help people living, and even dying, under the power of personal demons. No matter what the recovery issue, recognizing our need and turning to God in faith are the first steps to recovery.

29Then he touched their eyes and said, "Because of your faith it will happen."
30And suddenly they could see! Jesus sternly
warned them not to tell anyone about it, 31but
instead they spread his fame all over the
town.
32Leaving that place, Jesus met a man who
couldn't speak because a demon was inside
him. 33So Jesus cast out the demon, and instantly the man could talk. How the crowds
marveled! "Never in all our lives have we seen
anything like this," they exclaimed.
34But the Pharisees said, "The reason he can
cast out demons is that he is demon-possessed
himself—possessed by Satan, the demon
king!"

Jesus' Need for Workers

35Jesus traveled around through all the cities
and villages of that area, teaching in the Jewish synagogues and announcing the Good
News about the Kingdom. And wherever he
went he healed people of every sort of illness.
36And what pity he felt for the crowds that
came, because their problems were so great
and they didn't know what to do or where to
go for help. They were like sheep without a
shepherd.
37"The harvest is so great, and the workers
are so few," he told his disciples. 38"So pray to
the one in charge of the harvesting, and ask
him to recruit more workers for his harvest
fields."

CHAPTER 10

Jesus Sends Out His Disciples

Jesus called his twelve disciples to him and
gave them authority to cast out evil spirits
and to heal every kind of sickness and disease.
2-4Here are the names of his twelve disciples:
Simon (also called Peter), Andrew (Peter's
brother), James (Zebedee's son), John (James'
brother), Philip, Bartholomew, Thomas, Matthew (the tax collector), James (Alphaeus'
son), Thaddaeus, Simon (a member of "The
Zealots," a subversive political party), Judas
Iscariot (the one who betrayed him).
5Jesus sent them out with these instructions: "Don't go to the Gentiles or the Samaritans, 6but only to the people of Israel—God's
lost sheep. 7Go and announce to them that
the Kingdom of Heaven is near. 8Heal the sick,
raise the dead, cure the lepers, and cast out
demons. Give as freely as you have received!
9"Don't take any money with you; 10don't
even carry a duffle bag with extra clothes and
shoes, or even a walking stick; for those you

Finger Pointing

BIBLE READING: Matthew 7:1-5

We made a searching and fearless moral inventory of ourselves.

There have probably been times when we have avoided our own wrongs and problems by pointing the finger at someone else. We may be out of touch with our internal affairs because we are still blaming others for our moral choices. Or perhaps we avoid self-examination by making moral inventories of the people around us.

When God asked Adam and Eve about their sin, they each pointed a finger at someone else. "'Have you eaten fruit from the tree I warned you about?' 'Yes,' Adam admitted, 'but it was the woman you gave me who brought me some, and I ate it.' Then the Lord God asked the woman, 'How could you do such a thing?' 'The serpent tricked me,' she replied" (Genesis 3:11-13). It seems to be human nature to blame others as our first line of defense.

We also may avoid our own problems by evaluating and criticizing others. Jesus tells us, "And why worry about a speck in the eye of a brother when you have a board in your own? . . . Hypocrite! First get rid of the board. Then you can see to help your brother" (Matthew 7:3, 5).

While doing this step, we must constantly remind ourself that this is a season of *self*-examination. We must guard against drifting off into blaming and examining the lives of others. There will be time in the future for helping others after we have taken responsibility for our own life. ***Turn to page 1291, 2 Corinthians 7.***

help should feed and care for you. 11When-
ever you enter a city or village, search for a
godly man and stay in his home until you
leave for the next town. 12When you ask permission to stay, be friendly, 13and if it turns
out to be a godly home, give it your blessing;
if not, keep the blessing. 14Any city or home
that doesn't welcome you—shake off the dust
of that place from your feet as you leave.
15Truly, the wicked cities of Sodom and Gomorrah will be better off at Judgment Day
than they.

Preparation for Persecution

16"I am sending you out as sheep among
wolves. Be as wary as serpents and harmless as
doves. 17But beware! For you will be arrested
and tried, and whipped in the synagogues.
18Yes, and you must stand trial before governors and kings for my sake. This will give you
the opportunity to tell them about me, yes, to
witness to the world.
19"When you are arrested, don't worry
about what to say at your trial, for you will be
given the right words at the right time. 20For
it won't be you doing the talking—it will be
the Spirit of your heavenly Father speaking
through you!
21"Brother shall betray brother to death,
and fathers shall betray their own children.
And children shall rise against their parents
and cause their deaths. 22Everyone shall hate
you because you belong to me. But all of you
who endure to the end shall be saved.
23"When you are persecuted in one city, flee
to the next! I will return before you have
reached them all!
24"A student is not greater than his teacher.
A servant is not above his master. 25The student shares his teacher's fate. The servant
shares his master's! And since I, the master of
the household, have been called 'Satan,' how
much more will you! 26But don't be afraid of
those who threaten you. For the time is coming when the truth will be revealed: their
secret plots will become public information.
27"What I tell you now in the gloom, shout
abroad when daybreak comes. What I whisper
in your ears, proclaim from the housetops!
28"Don't be afraid of those who can kill
only your bodies—but can't touch your souls!
Fear only God who can destroy both soul and
body in hell. 29Not one sparrow (What do they
cost? Two for a penny?) can fall to the ground
without your Father knowing it. 30And the
very hairs of your head are all numbered. 31So
don't worry! You are more valuable to him
than many sparrows.
32"If anyone publicly acknowledges me as
his friend, I will openly acknowledge him as
my friend before my Father in heaven. 33But if
anyone publicly denies me, I will openly deny
him before my Father in heaven.
34"Don't imagine that I came to bring peace
to the earth! No, rather, a sword. 35I have come
to set a man against his father, and a daughter
against her mother, and a daughter-in-law
against her mother-in-law— 36a man's worst
enemies will be right in his own home! 37If
you love your father and mother more than
you love me, you are not worthy of being
mine; or if you love your son or daughter
more than me, you are not worthy of being
mine. 38If you refuse to take up your cross and
follow me, you are not worthy of being mine.
39"If you cling to your life, you will lose it;
but if you give it up for me, you will save it.
40"Those who welcome you are welcoming
me. And when they welcome me they are
welcoming God who sent me. 41If you wel-

10:16-26 Those of us living for God and pursuing recovery may feel like sheep in the presence of wolves. But, when wisdom and honesty define our behavior and relationships, we can face the inevitable misunderstandings and persecutions. Jesus suffered much at the hands of godless men, and those who are committed to him often receive similar treatment. But if we can persevere in following God's will for us, we will receive a tremendous reward (see 5:11-12).

10:39 The only way to gain our life (and get control of our life!) is to submit ourself to God through Jesus Christ. By living for ourself, we have become slaves to material success, work, alcohol, illicit sex, or any number of other destructive behaviors. We have lost control of our life and are in trouble. By giving our life to Jesus, we allow him to cleanse us of our addictions and show us the way to real life—a life free of destructive dependencies. And as we follow God's will for us, we will begin to experience a meaningful life in the present, while also finding eternal peace with God.

11:2-6 Doubt is a troubling reality for those of us in recovery. We doubt ourself, and we doubt others. Here even John the Baptist doubted that Jesus was the promised Messiah, the one who would come to offer physical and spiritual recovery to his people. Jesus challenged John's doubts by pointing to his impressive track record of miraculous healings and restorations. Such a résumé should also convince us that Jesus is willing and able to meet even our greatest needs for recovery and restoration.

MATTHEW & SIMON THE ZEALOT

It has been said that opposites attract; just as often, however, opposites repel. The differences between some people result in a complementary relationship in which the strengths of one make up for the weaknesses of the other. In some cases, however, the differences only lead to continual strife. Marriage relationships are often comprised of two opposites, resulting in either great teamwork or terrible conflict.

Two of Jesus' twelve disciples, Matthew and Simon the Zealot, were opposites. Matthew was a Jew who worked for the Roman government as a tax collector. People of this occupation were known for their corruption. They grew rich by extorting excess taxes from their own, oppressed people. These tax collectors were nonreligious and, needless to say, were hated and despised as traitors by their countrymen.

From his title, "the Zealot," Simon, at the very least, was a religious fanatic. This term was sometimes used to label people with intense zeal for the law of Moses and Jewish religious tradition. This term was also used to identify someone who belonged to the religious-political party known as the Zealots, which wanted to overthrow the Roman government. If Simon was a member, he would have been strongly opposed to the Roman occupation of Judea, while Matthew signed on as an integral part of its government. These men were clearly opposites.

Both Matthew and Simon met Jesus and realized the emptiness and futility of their former callings. Both gave up what they had been in order to follow Christ in faith and experienced the new life that developed from the inside out. Both were transformed by the God of recovery into people who could love and accept those who were very different from themselves.

The story of the apostles Matthew and Simon the Zealot is found in the Gospels. Both men are also mentioned in Acts 1:14.

STRENGTHS AND ACCOMPLISHMENTS:
- Matthew and Simon both apparently were capable men.
- Both men were willing to recognize that they needed to change.
- Both men made Jesus the center of their lives, enabling them to work with people quite different from themselves.

WEAKNESSES AND MISTAKES:
- Both had been driven by shortsighted motivations before following Jesus.
- As a tax collector, Matthew had probably used his position to extort money from the poor.
- As a Zealot, Simon probably condoned the use of violence for achieving his political ends.

LESSONS FROM THEIR LIVES:
- Financial success cannot replace our need for a relationship with God.
- If Christ is at the center of a relationship, no differences are too great to overcome.
- Differences can be used to strengthen a relationship and should not be used as an excuse to destroy it.

KEY VERSES:
"[The disciples] held a prayer meeting in an upstairs room of the house where they were staying. Here is the list of those who were present at the meeting: . . . Matthew, . . . Simon (also called 'The Zealot')" (Acts 1:13-14).

come a prophet because he is a man of God, you will be given the same reward a prophet gets. And if you welcome good and godly men because of their godliness, you will be given a reward like theirs.

42"And if, as my representatives, you give even a cup of cold water to a little child, you will surely be rewarded."

CHAPTER 11

Jesus Eases John's Doubt

When Jesus had finished giving these instructions to his twelve disciples, he went off preaching in the cities where they were scheduled to go.

2John the Baptist, who was now in prison,
heard about all the miracles the Messiah was
doing, so he sent his disciples to ask Jesus,
3"Are you really the one we are waiting for, or
shall we keep on looking?"
4Jesus told them, "Go back to John and tell
him about the miracles you've seen me do—
5the blind people I've healed, and the lame
people now walking without help, and the
cured lepers, and the deaf who hear, and the
dead raised to life; and tell him about my
preaching the Good News to the poor. 6Then
give him this message, 'Blessed are those who
don't doubt me.'"
7When John's disciples had gone, Jesus be-

gan talking about him to the crowds. "When you went out into the barren wilderness to see John, what did you expect him to be like? Grass blowing in the wind? 8Or were you expecting to see a man dressed as a prince in a palace? 9Or a prophet of God? Yes, and he is more than just a prophet. 10For John is the man mentioned in the Scriptures—a messenger to precede me, to announce my coming, and prepare people to receive me.

11"Truly, of all men ever born, none shines more brightly than John the Baptist. And yet, even the lesser lights in the Kingdom of Heaven will be greater than he is! 12And from the time John the Baptist began preaching and baptizing until now, ardent multitudes have been crowding toward the Kingdom of Heaven, 13for all the laws and prophets looked forward [to the Messiah]. Then John appeared, 14and if you are willing to understand what I mean, he is Elijah, the one the prophets said would come [at the time the Kingdom begins]. 15If ever you were willing to listen, listen now!

16"What shall I say about this nation? These people are like children playing, who say to their little friends, 17'We played wedding and you weren't happy, so we played funeral but you weren't sad.' 18For John the Baptist doesn't even drink wine and often goes without food, and you say, 'He's crazy.' 19And I, the Messiah, feast and drink, and you complain that I am 'a glutton and a drinking man, and hang around with the worst sort of sinners!' But brilliant men like you can justify your every inconsistency!"

Jesus Promises Rest for the Soul

20Then he began to pour out his denunciations against the cities where he had done most of his miracles, because they hadn't turned to God.

21"Woe to you, Chorazin, and woe to you, Bethsaida! For if the miracles I did in your streets had been done in wicked Tyre and Sidon their people would have repented long ago in shame and humility. 22Truly, Tyre and Sidon will be better off on the Judgment Day than you! 23And Capernaum, though highly honored, shall go down to hell! For if the marvelous miracles I did in you had been done in Sodom, it would still be here today. 24Truly, Sodom will be better off at the Judgment Day than you."

25And Jesus prayed this prayer: "O Father, Lord of heaven and earth, thank you for hiding the truth from those who think themselves so wise, and for revealing it to little children. 26Yes, Father, for it pleased you to do it this way! . . .

27"Everything has been entrusted to me by my Father. Only the Father knows the Son, and the Father is known only by the Son and by those to whom the Son reveals him. 28Come to me and I will give you rest—all of you who work so hard beneath a heavy yoke. 29,30Wear my yoke—for it fits perfectly—and let me teach you; for I am gentle and humble, and you shall find rest for your souls; for I give you only light burdens."

CHAPTER 12

Teachings about the Sabbath

About that time, Jesus was walking one day through some grainfields with his disciples. It was on the Sabbath, the Jewish day of worship, and his disciples were hungry; so they began breaking off heads of wheat and eating the grain.

2But some Pharisees saw them do it and

11:16-19 When we are in denial, we tend to resist those who challenge our comfort zones. We find excuses not to accept the good advice of others no matter what they do or say. We become cynical and try to justify our inconsistencies. The message of recovery is too joyful and hopeful for some, or it is too realistic and direct for others. Recovery is too structured for those of us who are used to doing our own thing; it is too liberating for those of us from a legalistic background. But such perspectives are only blind excuses that we use to keep from facing our need for recovery.

12:1-8 God's standards were intended for our good; he gave them to mercifully meet the needs of his people. But his laws can also be abused through legalism. By seeking to follow God's laws to the letter it is easy to violate the very reasons that God gave his laws in the first place. God gave the Sabbath laws to protect his people from overwork, but the Pharisees had applied this law so rigidly that the Sabbath became a day of rigorous self-denial. This is the opposite of what God had originally intended. The Pharisees were determined to employ God's Word for restrictive and enslaving purposes, rather than for spiritual freedom and balance. People do the same thing today. But God wants to be merciful to us, offering recovery and hope instead of condemnation. If God had wanted to crush us with legalism, he would never have sent Jesus to die for us. He would have let us die in our sins.

Things To Do Today

ELIZABETH G REARDON

protested, "Your disciples are breaking the
law. They are harvesting on the Sabbath."
[3]But Jesus said to them, "Haven't you ever
read what King David did when he and his
friends were hungry? [4]He went into the
Temple and they ate the special bread permitted to the priests alone. That was breaking the
law too. [5]And haven't you ever read in the law
of Moses how the priests on duty in the
Temple may work on the Sabbath? [6]And truly,
one is here who is greater than the Temple!
[7]But if you had known the meaning of this
Scripture verse, 'I want you to be merciful
more than I want your offerings,' you would
not have condemned those who aren't guilty!
[8]For I, the Messiah, am master even of the
Sabbath."

Jesus Heals on the Sabbath

[9]Then he went over to the synagogue [10]and
noticed there a man with a deformed hand.
The Pharisees asked Jesus, "Is it legal to work
by healing on the Sabbath day?" (They were,
of course, hoping he would say yes, so they
could arrest him!) [11]This was his answer: "If
you had just one sheep, and it fell into a well
on the Sabbath, would you work to rescue it
that day? Of course you would. [12]And how
much more valuable is a person than a sheep!
Yes, it is right to do good on the Sabbath."
[13]Then he said to the man, "Stretch out your
arm." And as he did, his hand became normal, just like the other one!
[14]Then the Pharisees called a meeting to
plot Jesus' arrest and death.
[15]But he knew what they were planning and
left the synagogue, with many following him.
He healed all the sick among them, [16]but he
cautioned them against spreading the news
about his miracles. [17]This fulfilled the prophecy of Isaiah concerning him:

[18]"Look at my Servant.
See my Chosen One.
He is my Beloved, in whom my soul
delights.
I will put my Spirit upon him,
And he will judge the nations.
[19]He does not fight nor shout;
He does not raise his voice!
[20]He does not crush the weak,
Or quench the smallest hope;
He will end all conflict with his final
victory,
[21]And his name shall be the hope
Of all the world."

Submission and Rest

BIBLE READING: Matthew 11:27-30

We made a decision to turn our will and our life over to the care of God as we understood him.

When our burdens become heavy and we find that our way of life is leading us toward death, we may finally become willing to let someone else do the driving. We have probably worked hard at trying to get our life on the right track, but still feel like we always end up on a dead-end street.

Proverbs tells us, "Before every man there lies a wide and pleasant road that seems right but ends in death" (Proverbs 14:12). When we began our addictive behaviors, we were probably seeking pleasure or looking for a way to overcome the pain of living. The way seemed right at first, but it wasn't long before it became clear that we were on the wrong track. But then we were unable to turn around on our own. Jesus said, "Come to me and I will give you rest—all of you who work so hard beneath a heavy yoke. Wear my yoke—for it fits perfectly—and let me teach you; for I am gentle and humble, and you shall find rest for your souls" (Matthew 11:28-30).

Taking on a yoke implies being united to another in order to work together. Those who are yoked together must go in the same direction, but when they do so, their work is made considerably easier. Jesus is saying that when we finally decide to submit our life and our will to his direction, our burdens will become manageable. When we let him do the driving, we will be able to "find rest" for our soul. He knows the way and has the strength to turn us around and get us on the road toward life. ***Turn to page 1207, Acts 17.***

Jesus Accused of Being of Satan

22Then a demon-possessed man—he was both
blind and unable to talk—was brought to
Jesus, and Jesus healed him so that he could
both speak and see. 23The crowd was amazed.
"Maybe Jesus is the Messiah!" they exclaimed.
24But when the Pharisees heard about the
miracle they said, "He can cast out demons
because he is Satan, king of devils."
25Jesus knew their thoughts and replied, "A
divided kingdom ends in ruin. A city or home
divided against itself cannot stand. 26And if
Satan is casting out Satan, he is fighting himself and destroying his own kingdom. 27And
if, as you claim, I am casting out demons by
invoking the powers of Satan, then what
power do your own people use when they cast
them out? Let them answer your accusation!
28But if I am casting out demons by the Spirit
of God, then the Kingdom of God has arrived
among you. 29One cannot rob Satan's kingdom without first binding Satan. Only then
can his demons be cast out! 30Anyone who
isn't helping me is harming me.
31,32"Even blasphemy against me or any
other sin can be forgiven—all except one:
speaking against the Holy Spirit shall never be
forgiven, either in this world or in the world
to come.
33"A tree is identified by its fruit. A tree from
a select variety produces good fruit; poor varieties don't. 34You brood of snakes! How
could evil men like you speak what is good
and right? For a man's heart determines his
speech. 35A good man's speech reveals the rich
treasures within him. An evil-hearted man is
filled with venom, and his speech reveals it.
36And I tell you this, that you must give account on Judgment Day for every idle word
you speak. 37Your words now reflect your fate
then: either you will be justified by them or
you will be condemned."

A Request for a Miracle

38One day some of the Jewish leaders, including some Pharisees, came to Jesus asking him
to show them a miracle.
39,40But Jesus replied, "Only an evil, faithless
nation would ask for further proof; and none
will be given except what happened to Jonah
the prophet! For as Jonah was in the great fish
for three days and three nights, so I, the
Messiah, shall be in the heart of the earth
three days and three nights. 41The men of
Nineveh shall arise against this nation at the
judgment and condemn you. For when Jonah
preached to them, they repented and turned
to God from all their evil ways. And now a
greater than Jonah is here—and you refuse to
believe him. 42The Queen of Sheba shall rise
against this nation in the judgment and condemn it; for she came from a distant land to
hear the wisdom of Solomon; and now a
greater than Solomon is here—and you refuse
to believe him.
43-45"This evil nation is like a man possessed
by a demon. For if the demon leaves, it goes
into the deserts for a while, seeking rest but
finding none. Then it says, 'I will return to the
man I came from.' So it returns and finds the
man's heart clean but empty! Then the demon finds seven other spirits more evil than
itself, and all enter the man and live in him.
And so he is worse off than before."

Jesus Describes His True Family

46,47As Jesus was speaking in a crowded house
his mother and brothers were outside, wanting to talk with him. When someone told him
they were there, 48he remarked, "Who is my

12:17-21 Centuries earlier the prophet Isaiah had described the Messiah (Isaiah 42:1-4), and Matthew recognized how Jesus fulfilled that prophecy. This passage offers a powerful message of hope for those of us in recovery. Jesus the Messiah is both our servant and our leader. He is strong enough to lead and judge the nations, yet tender enough to care for the weak and helpless. He is the world's hope for salvation and our hope for recovery.

12:22-32 Only God through Jesus Christ is able to offer us the power we need for recovery. If we look to any other source of power, our recovery will be limited at best. Secular, New Age, even occult approaches to recovery are available. It is tragic enough that Christ-centered recovery is often doubted by many who need it the most, but it is even more tragic when people who find deliverance through a relationship with Jesus are later told that it is all a lie. God's way of recovery is the way of Jesus Christ. It is through him that we can receive the power we need for recovery and restoration.

12:43-45 Incomplete recovery can leave a person "worse off than before." To be rid of what afflicts us is only half the battle. Once we kick an addiction or dependency, there is a void in our life that was once filled with the old behavior. We must be sure to fill that emptiness with God's Spirit and godly attitudes and actions. Otherwise, new addictions and dependencies will move in and lead to further problems in our life.

mother? Who are my brothers?" 49He pointed
to his disciples. "Look!" he said, "these are my
mother and brothers." 50Then he added,
"Anyone who obeys my Father in heaven is
my brother, sister, and mother!"

CHAPTER 13

A Story about Four Soils

Later that same day, Jesus left the house and
went down to the shore, 2,3where an immense
crowd soon gathered. He got into a boat and
taught from it while the people listened on
the beach. He used many illustrations such as
this one in his sermon:

"A farmer was sowing grain in his fields. 4As
he scattered the seed across the ground, some
fell beside a path, and the birds came and ate
it. 5And some fell on rocky soil where there
was little depth of earth; the plants sprang up
quickly enough in the shallow soil, 6but the
hot sun soon scorched them and they withered and died, for they had so little root.
7Other seeds fell among thorns, and the
thorns choked out the tender blades. 8But
some fell on good soil and produced a crop
that was thirty, sixty, and even a hundred
times as much as he had planted. 9If you have
ears, listen!"

10His disciples came and asked him, "Why
do you always use these hard-to-understand
illustrations?"

11Then he explained to them that only they
were permitted to understand about the Kingdom of Heaven, and others were not.

12,13"For to him who has will more be
given," he told them, "and he will have great
plenty; but from him who has not, even the
little he has will be taken away. That is why I
use these illustrations, so people will hear and
see but not understand.

14"This fulfills the prophecy of Isaiah:

'They hear, but don't understand; they
look, but don't see! 15For their hearts are
fat and heavy, and their ears are dull,
and they have closed their eyes in sleep,
16so they won't see and hear and
understand and turn to God again, and
let me heal them.'

But blessed are your eyes, for they see; and
your ears, for they hear. 17Many a prophet and
godly man has longed to see what you have
seen and hear what you have heard, but
couldn't.

18"Now here is the explanation of the story
I told about the farmer planting grain: 19The
hard path where some of the seeds fell represents the heart of a person who hears the
Good News about the Kingdom and doesn't
understand it; then Satan comes and snatches
away the seeds from his heart. 20The shallow,
rocky soil represents the heart of a man who
hears the message and receives it with real joy,
21but he doesn't have much depth in his life,
and the seeds don't root very deeply, and after
a while when trouble comes, or persecution
begins because of his beliefs, his enthusiasm
fades, and he drops out. 22The ground covered
with thistles represents a man who hears the
message, but the cares of this life and his
longing for money choke out God's Word,
and he does less and less for God. 23The good
ground represents the heart of a man who
listens to the message and understands it and
goes out and brings thirty, sixty, or even a
hundred others into the Kingdom."

13:2-8, 18-23 The story about the sower and the four soils applies quite directly to recovery. The varied responses to the "seed" of the gospel are like the many responses to recovery. Some embrace recovery wholeheartedly, some only halfheartedly or temporarily, and some pass up the opportunity, denying they need it. Generally, various trials will make clear which recovery category we fit into. If we hope to succeed in recovery and experience new life, we must allow God to plow up the soil of our heart and make it ready to receive his healing message.

13:10-17 Jesus' explanation for teaching with stories and illustrations fits well with the dynamics of recovery and denial. Those of us who respond in faith to what we already know will be given more insight as we make progress in recovery. We who do not respond properly, however, will become more and more spiritually blind and hardened in our denial. Amazingly, God continues to offer recovery even to those who have turned their back on him in unbelieving denial. When we are ready to ask God what to do, he will be there with the answer (see James 1:5).

13:24-30, 36-43 The story about the wheat and the thistles applies to those of us considering recovery. Ultimately, there are two kinds of people in the world: some submit to God's will and experience the restoration he offers in Jesus Christ; the others, whether they realize it or not, have submitted themselves to the control of Satan. This stark but realistic contrast shows us that if we do not choose God, we choose Satan by default. If we have already undertaken a form of recovery but have not yet committed our life to Jesus Christ, we still have one more step to go before experiencing the victory available in God's recovery program.

A Story of Wheat and Thistles

[24]Here is another illustration Jesus used: "The Kingdom of Heaven is like a farmer sowing good seed in his field; [25]but one night as he slept, his enemy came and sowed thistles among the wheat. [26]When the crop began to grow, the thistles grew too.

[27]"The farmer's men came and told him, 'Sir, the field where you planted that choice seed is full of thistles!'

[28]"'An enemy has done it,' he exclaimed.

"'Shall we pull out the thistles?' they asked.

[29]"'No,' he replied. 'You'll hurt the wheat if you do. [30]Let both grow together until the harvest, and I will tell the reapers to sort out the thistles and burn them, and put the wheat in the barn.'"

A Story about a Mustard Seed

[31,32]Here is another of his illustrations: "The Kingdom of Heaven is like a tiny mustard seed planted in a field. It is the smallest of all seeds but becomes the largest of plants, and grows into a tree where birds can come and find shelter."

A Story about Yeast in Bread

[33]He also used this example:

"The Kingdom of Heaven can be compared to a woman making bread. She takes a measure of flour and mixes in the yeast until it permeates every part of the dough."

[34,35]Jesus constantly used these illustrations when speaking to the crowds. In fact, because the prophets said that he would use so many, he never spoke to them without at least one illustration. For it had been prophesied, "I will talk in parables; I will explain mysteries hidden since the beginning of time."

Jesus Explains His Stories

[36]Then, leaving the crowds outside, he went into the house. His disciples asked him to explain to them the illustration of the thistles and the wheat.

[37]"All right," he said, "I am the farmer who sows the choice seed. [38]The field is the world, and the seed represents the people of the Kingdom; the thistles are the people belonging to Satan. [39]The enemy who sowed the thistles among the wheat is the devil; the harvest is the end of the world, and the reapers are the angels.

[40]"Just as in this story the thistles are separated and burned, so shall it be at the end of the world: [41]I will send my angels, and they will separate out of the Kingdom every temptation and all who are evil, [42]and throw them into the furnace and burn them. There shall be weeping and gnashing of teeth. [43]Then the godly shall shine as the sun in their Father's Kingdom. Let those with ears, listen!

A Story of Hidden Treasure

[44]"The Kingdom of Heaven is like a treasure a man discovered in a field. In his excitement, he sold everything he owned to get enough money to buy the field—and get the treasure, too!

A Story about a Pearl

[45]"Again, the Kingdom of Heaven is like a pearl merchant on the lookout for choice pearls. [46]He discovered a real bargain—a pearl of great value—and sold everything he owned to purchase it!

A Story about Some Fish

[47,48]"Again, the Kingdom of Heaven can be illustrated by a fisherman—he casts a net into the water and gathers in fish of every kind, valuable and worthless. When the net is full, he drags it up onto the beach and sits down and sorts out the edible ones into crates and throws the others away. [49]That is the way it will be at the end of the world—the angels will come and separate the wicked people from the godly, [50]casting the wicked into the fire; there shall be weeping and gnashing of teeth. [51]Do you understand?"

"Yes," they said, "we do."

[52]Then he added, "Those experts in Jewish law who are now my disciples have double treasures—from the Old Testament as well as from the New!"

Jesus Is Rejected in Nazareth

[53,54]When Jesus had finished giving these illustrations, he returned to his hometown, Naza-

13:53-58 We must always fight the preconceived notions that others have of us. We might leave the presence of our dysfunctional family or friends and enter a successful recovery program. When we return, we shouldn't be surprised to find that others will ignore our message of recovery, saying that we are *just* so-and-so or *just* the kid they went to school with. They won't listen to us because they are too close to who we were and are not able to see who we have become through God's grace. As we share our story of recovery with those who are familiar with our past, it may take some time to convince them of our sincerity.

READ MATTHEW 14:23-33

GOD grant me the serenity to accept the things I cannot change the courage to change the things I can and the wisdom to know the difference AMEN

Having God remove our defects can be frightening. We may stay trapped in destructive life patterns because we fear change.

If we wait for all our fear to go away before we take courageous steps, we will never make significant progress in recovery. Courage isn't the absence of fear. Courage means that we take advantage of the little strength we find within us, that we find little ways to encourage ourself, and that we are stubborn in sticking to God's program for us. It doesn't mean being free of fear. It means finding enough strength to take the next step.

In the account where Jesus walked on the water, the disciples were terrified when they saw him. "Then Peter called to him, 'Sir, if it is really you, tell me to come over to you, walking on the water.' 'All right,' the Lord said, 'come along!' So Peter went over the side of the boat and walked on the water toward Jesus. But when he looked around at the high waves, he was terrified and began to sink. 'Save me, Lord!' he shouted. Instantly Jesus reached out his hand and rescued him" (Matthew 14:28-31).

Peter gathered up enough courage to take one step. He ventured out into a new experience. When he got in over his head, he called out and found the help he needed. We, too, only need to summon the courage to take the next step. This doesn't mean that we won't feel fear or need help. It does mean that with God's help, we will make it. All we need is the courage to take just one more step. ***Turn to page 1045, Matthew 26.***

---

reth in Galilee, and taught there in the synagogue and astonished everyone with his wisdom and his miracles.
55"How is this possible?" the people exclaimed. "He's just a carpenter's son, and we
know Mary his mother and his brothers—
James, Joseph, Simon, and Judas. 56And his
sisters—they all live here. How can he be so
great?" 57And they became angry with him!
Then Jesus told them, "A prophet is honored everywhere except in his own country,
and among his own people!" 58And so he did
only a few great miracles there, because of
their unbelief.

CHAPTER 14

Herod Kills John the Baptist

When King Herod heard about Jesus, 2he said
to his men, "This must be John the Baptist,
come back to life again. That is why he can do
these miracles." 3For Herod had arrested John
and chained him in prison at the demand of
his wife Herodias, his brother Philip's ex-wife,
4because John had told him it was wrong for
him to marry her. 5He would have killed John
but was afraid of a riot, for all the people
believed John was a prophet.
6But at a birthday party for Herod, Herodias' daughter performed a dance that greatly
pleased him, 7so he vowed to give her anything she wanted. 8Consequently, at her
mother's urging, the girl asked for John the
Baptist's head on a tray.
9The king was grieved, but because of his
oath, and because he didn't want to back
down in front of his guests, he issued the
necessary orders.
10So John was beheaded in the prison, 11and
his head was brought on a tray and given to
the girl, who took it to her mother.

12 Then John's disciples came for his body and buried it, and came to tell Jesus what had happened.

Jesus Feeds Five Thousand

13 As soon as Jesus heard the news, he went off by himself in a boat to a remote area to be alone. But the crowds saw where he was headed and followed by land from many villages.

14 So when Jesus came out of the wilderness, a vast crowd was waiting for him, and he pitied them and healed their sick.

15 That evening the disciples came to him and said, "It is already past time for supper, and there is nothing to eat here in the desert; send the crowds away so they can go to the villages and buy some food."

16 But Jesus replied, "That isn't necessary—you feed them!"

17 "What!" they exclaimed. "We have exactly five small loaves of bread and two fish!"

18 "Bring them here," he said.

19 Then he told the people to sit down on the grass; and he took the five loaves and two fish, looked up into the sky, and asked God's blessing on the meal, then broke the loaves apart and gave them to the disciples to place before the people. 20 And everyone ate until full! And when the scraps were picked up afterwards, there were twelve basketfuls left over! 21 (About five thousand men were in the crowd that day, besides all the women and children.)

Jesus Walks on Water

22 Immediately after this, Jesus told his disciples to get into their boat and cross to the other side of the lake while he stayed to get the people started home.

23,24 Then afterwards he went up into the hills to pray. Night fell, and out on the lake the disciples were in trouble. For the wind had risen and they were fighting heavy seas.

25 About four o'clock in the morning Jesus came to them, walking on the water! 26 They screamed in terror, for they thought he was a ghost.

27 But Jesus immediately spoke to them, reassuring them. "Don't be afraid!" he said.

28 Then Peter called to him: "Sir, if it is really you, tell me to come over to you, walking on the water."

29 "All right," the Lord said, "come along!"

So Peter went over the side of the boat and walked on the water toward Jesus. 30 But when he looked around at the high waves, he was terrified and began to sink. "Save me, Lord!" he shouted.

31 Instantly Jesus reached out his hand and rescued him. "O man of little faith," Jesus said. "Why did you doubt me?" 32 And when they had climbed back into the boat, the wind stopped.

33 The others sat there, awestruck. "You really are the Son of God!" they exclaimed.

Jesus Heals Many

34 They landed at Gennesaret. 35 The news of their arrival spread quickly throughout the city, and soon people were rushing around, telling everyone to bring in their sick to be healed. 36 The sick begged him to let them touch even the tassel of his robe, and all who did were healed.

14:15-21 Jesus fed multitudes of hungry people on more than one occasion (see also 15:32-39). This illustrates not only that Jesus is able to do the impossible, but also that he is concerned with our pressing human needs. Since Jesus is committed to meeting even our most basic physical needs, how much more is he committed to meeting our emotional needs related to recovery! And notice that Jesus did not do everything himself; he used his disciples to help meet the people's needs. Jesus often meets the needs in our life through human instruments. God may well be working our recovery through concerned friends or others who are hurting like us. We should never refuse the help offered by godly brothers and sisters. And as we are given opportunities to encourage others in their recovery, we can be thankful that God has chosen to use us.

14:22-24 Time alone to focus on our tasks and to pray is necessary if we are engaged in any form of prolonged recovery program. Though we may feel we are wasting time, it is important to recharge our batteries, physically, emotionally, and spiritually. If we don't, we will experience burnout. Since Jesus took time out to pray and recharge, we should never feel guilty for doing the same.

15:1-20 There will be those people who will look down on us and criticize us for our dependencies and our need for recovery. They will assume a self-righteous posture because they fulfill all their proper "religious" obligations, while we are far from being a model church member. However, Jesus says that our outward activities don't necessarily correspond to our inner righteousness. If we do all the right things and have a proud and selfish heart, we will be judged by God. If we have accepted Jesus in our heart and are humbly trying to recover, God is pleased with us, no matter what others may say.

CHAPTER 15

Teachings about Inner Purity

Some Pharisees and other Jewish leaders now
arrived from Jerusalem to interview Jesus.
2“Why do your disciples disobey the ancient Jewish traditions?” they demanded.
“For they ignore our ritual of ceremonial
handwashing before they eat.” 3He replied,
“And why do your traditions violate the direct
commandments of God? 4For instance, God’s
law is ‘Honor your father and mother; anyone
who reviles his parents must die.’ 5,6But you
say, ‘Even if your parents are in need, you may
give their support money to the church instead.’ And so, by your man-made rule, you
nullify the direct command of God to honor
and care for your parents. 7You hypocrites!
Well did Isaiah prophesy of you, 8‘These
people say they honor me, but their hearts are
far away. 9Their worship is worthless, for they
teach their man-made laws instead of those
from God.’”
10Then Jesus called to the crowds and said,
“Listen to what I say and try to understand:
11You aren’t made unholy by eating nonkosher food! It is what you *say* and *think* that
makes you unclean.”
12Then the disciples came and told him,
“You offended the Pharisees by that remark.”
13,14Jesus replied, “Every plant not planted
by my Father shall be rooted up, so ignore
them. They are blind guides leading the blind,
and both will fall into a ditch.”
15Then Peter asked Jesus to explain what he
meant when he said that people are not defiled by nonkosher food.
16“Don’t you understand?” Jesus asked him.
17“Don’t you see that anything you eat passes
through the digestive tract and out again?
18But evil words come from an evil heart and
defile the man who says them. 19For from the
heart come evil thoughts, murder, adultery,
fornication, theft, lying, and slander. 20These
are what defile; but there is no spiritual defilement from eating without first going through
the ritual of ceremonial handwashing!”

Jesus Frees a Girl from a Demon

21Jesus then left that part of the country and
walked the fifty miles to Tyre and Sidon.
22A woman from Canaan who was living
there came to him, pleading, “Have mercy on
me, O Lord, King David’s Son! For my daughter has a demon within her, and it torments
her constantly.”
23But Jesus gave her no reply—not even a
word. Then his disciples urged him to send

Faith

READ MATTHEW 15:22-28

Sometimes the insanity of living with our own addictions or with someone who is acting in bizarre ways can cause us to become desperate for help. Jesus once dealt with a woman who was driven to him out of desperation.

“A woman from Canaan who was living there came to him [Jesus], pleading, ‘Have mercy on me, O Lord, King David’s Son! For my daughter has a demon within her, and it torments her constantly.’ But Jesus gave her no reply—not even a word. Then his disciples urged him to send her away. . . . Then he said to the woman, ‘I was sent to help the Jews—the lost sheep of Israel—not the Gentiles.’ But she came and worshiped him and pled again, ‘Sir, help me!’ ‘It doesn’t seem right to take bread from the children and throw it to the dogs,’ he said. ‘Yes, it is!’ she replied, ‘for even the puppies beneath the table are permitted to eat the crumbs that fall.’ ‘Woman,’ Jesus told her, ‘your faith is large, and your request is granted.’ And her daughter was healed right then” (Matthew 15:22-28).

It took a lot of courage for this woman to even speak to Jesus because of the racism of their time. She was despised and ridiculed for seeking an end to her family’s torment, but she didn’t give up. She believed God was the only one who could help her, and she would not be deterred. Our own desperation can lead to a sincere faith that can be of tremendous help in our recovery.

Turn to page 1029, Matthew 16.

her away. "Tell her to get going," they said, "for she is bothering us with all her begging."

[24]Then he said to the woman, "I was sent to help the Jews—the lost sheep of Israel—not the Gentiles."

[25]But she came and worshiped him and pled again, "Sir, help me!"

[26]"It doesn't seem right to take bread from the children and throw it to the dogs," he said.

[27]"Yes, it is!" she replied, "for even the puppies beneath the table are permitted to eat the crumbs that fall."

[28]"Woman," Jesus told her, "your faith is large, and your request is granted." And her daughter was healed right then.

Jesus Amazes the Crowds

[29]Jesus now returned to the Sea of Galilee and climbed a hill and sat there. [30]And a vast crowd brought him their lame, blind, maimed, and those who couldn't speak, and many others, and laid them before Jesus, and he healed them all. [31]What a spectacle it was! Those who hadn't been able to say a word before were talking excitedly, and those with missing arms and legs had new ones; the crippled were walking and jumping around, and those who had been blind were gazing about them! The crowds just marveled, and praised the God of Israel.

Jesus Feeds Four Thousand

[32]Then Jesus called his disciples to him and said, "I pity these people—they've been here with me for three days now and have nothing left to eat; I don't want to send them away hungry or they will faint along the road."

[33]The disciples replied, "And where would we get enough here in the desert for all this mob to eat?"

[34]Jesus asked them, "How much food do you have?" And they replied, "Seven loaves of bread and a few small fish!"

[35]Then Jesus told all of the people to sit down on the ground, [36]and he took the seven loaves and the fish, and gave thanks to God for them, and divided them into pieces, and gave them to the disciples who presented them to the crowd. [37,38]And everyone ate until full—four thousand men besides the women and children! And afterwards, when the scraps were picked up, there were seven basketfuls left over!

[39]Then Jesus sent the people home and got into the boat and crossed to Magadan.

CHAPTER 16

Another Request for a Miracle

One day the Pharisees and Sadducees came to test Jesus' claim of being the Messiah by asking him to show them some great demonstrations in the skies.

[2,3]He replied, "You are good at reading the weather signs of the skies—red sky tonight means fair weather tomorrow; red sky in the morning means foul weather all day—but you can't read the obvious signs of the times! [4]This evil, unbelieving nation is asking for some strange sign in the heavens, but no further proof will be given except the miracle that happened to Jonah." Then Jesus walked out on them.

15:32-38 The feeding of the four thousand is both similar to and different from the previous feeding of the five thousand (see 14:15-21). In both cases Jesus pitied those in need; he took a small amount of food and fed a large number of people; he used the disciples to distribute the resources; and much more was left over at the end than they had in the beginning. Since the reason for pity was somewhat different, as was the location of the event and the number of people fed, we see that Jesus, the only true source of recovery, tailored his resources to meet pressing needs. We can count on God to show similar concern for us and to lend his unlimited power to support our recovery.

16:1-4 The Pharisees had the kind of attitude that is often a hindrance to recovery. They wanted an amazing miracle to prove that Jesus was the Messiah. We make the same mistake when we expect an instant cure or supernatural intervention for our recovery. Looking for a quick fix to a lifelong problem is tantamount to seeking "a sign in the sky." God rarely gives us an instant cure for our dependencies; it often takes a lifetime of hard work to maintain our sobriety. When we recognize this truth, we will be less likely to be disappointed by the difficulties of the recovery process. We will also be more aware of the small victories that God gives us with each passing day.

16:13-17 There are many answers to the question, Who is Jesus? but only one of them is correct. The insight that Jesus is the promised Messiah and the Son of God comes from God himself. It doesn't come from any human source. Likewise, the realization that the God of the Bible is the higher Power that we need for recovery is a revelation from God's Word. To put our trust in any other power for recovery will only lead to disappointment and continued failure.

A Warning about False Teachings

5Arriving across the lake, the disciples discovered they had forgotten to bring any food.
6"Watch out!" Jesus warned them; "beware
of the yeast of the Pharisees and Sadducees."
7They thought he was saying this because
they had forgotten to bring bread.
8Jesus knew what they were thinking and
told them, "O men of little faith! Why are you
so worried about having no food? 9Won't you
ever understand? Don't you remember at all
the five thousand I fed with five loaves, and
the basketfuls left over? 10Don't you remember the four thousand I fed, and all that was
left? 11How could you even think I was talking
about food? But again I say, 'Beware of the
yeast of the Pharisees and Sadducees.'"
12Then at last they understood that by *yeast*
he meant the *wrong teaching* of the Pharisees
and Sadducees.

Peter Says Jesus Is the Messiah

13When Jesus came to Caesarea Philippi, he
asked his disciples, "Who are the people saying I am?"
14"Well," they replied, "some say John the
Baptist; some, Elijah; some, Jeremiah or one
of the other prophets."
15Then he asked them, "Who do *you* think
I am?"
16Simon Peter answered, "The Christ, the
Messiah, the Son of the living God."
17"God has blessed you, Simon, son of Jonah," Jesus said, "for my Father in heaven has
personally revealed this to you—this is not
from any human source. 18You are Peter, a
stone; and upon this rock I will build my
church; and all the powers of hell shall not
prevail against it. 19And I will give you the
keys of the Kingdom of Heaven; whatever
doors you lock on earth shall be locked in
heaven; and whatever doors you open on
earth shall be open in heaven!"
20Then he warned the disciples against telling others that he was the Messiah.

Jesus Talks of His Death

21From then on Jesus began to speak plainly to
his disciples about going to Jerusalem, and
what would happen to him there—that he
would suffer at the hands of the Jewish leaders, that he would be killed, and that three
days later he would be raised to life again.
22But Peter took him aside to remonstrate
with him. "Heaven forbid, sir," he said. "This
is not going to happen to you!"
23Jesus turned on Peter and said, "Get away

Delayed gratification

READ MATTHEW 16:24-26

Some of us are addicted to chaos. We may be so used to crisis that we don't know how to enjoy the calm. Life in recovery may seem boring in comparison to our old ways. We may miss the excitement and danger. The rewards may seem too slow in coming.

The apostle Paul said, "And let us not get tired of doing what is right, for after a while we will reap a harvest of blessing if we don't get discouraged and give up" (Galatians 6:9). Weeds spring up immediately. The good crops must be tended steadily, even before we can see anything growing. It's only in time that we will enjoy the fruit.

Jesus suggested that we expand our perspective even further, with a view toward eternity. "Jesus said to the disciples, 'If anyone wants to be a follower of mine, let him deny himself and take up his cross and follow me. For anyone who keeps his life for himself shall lose it; and anyone who loses his life for me shall find it again. What profit is there if you gain the whole world—and lose eternal life?'" (Matthew 16:24-26).

It is God's will for us to have a rewarding and fulfilled life. It may be easier to adjust to our new way of life if we remember that denying ourself immediate pleasures will bring a harvest of rich rewards, in this life and the life to come. ***Turn to page 1041, Matthew 25.***

from me, you Satan! You are a dangerous trap to me. You are thinking merely from a human point of view, and not from God's."

[24]Then Jesus said to the disciples, "If anyone wants to be a follower of mine, let him deny himself and take up his cross and follow me. [25]For anyone who keeps his life for himself shall lose it; and anyone who loses his life for me shall find it again. [26]What profit is there if you gain the whole world—and lose eternal life? What can be compared with the value of eternal life? [27]For I, the Son of Mankind, shall come with my angels in the glory of my Father and judge each person according to his deeds. [28]And some of you standing right here now will certainly live to see me coming in my Kingdom."

CHAPTER 17

Jesus Is Transfigured

Six days later Jesus took Peter, James, and his brother John to the top of a high and lonely hill, [2]and as they watched, his appearance changed so that his face shone like the sun and his clothing became dazzling white.

[3]Suddenly Moses and Elijah appeared and were talking with him. [4]Peter blurted out, "Sir, it's wonderful that we can be here! If you want me to, I'll make three shelters, one for you and one for Moses and one for Elijah."

[5]But even as he said it, a bright cloud came over them, and a voice from the cloud said, "*This* is my beloved Son, and I am wonderfully pleased with him. Obey him."

[6]At this the disciples fell face downward to the ground, terribly frightened. [7]Jesus came over and touched them. "Get up," he said, "don't be afraid."

[8]And when they looked, only Jesus was with them.

[9]As they were going down the mountain, Jesus commanded them not to tell anyone what they had seen until after he had risen from the dead.

[10]His disciples asked, "Why do the Jewish leaders insist Elijah must return before the Messiah comes?"

[11]Jesus replied, "They are right. Elijah must come and set everything in order. [12]And, in fact, he has already come, but he wasn't recognized, and was badly mistreated by many. And I, the Messiah, shall also suffer at their hands."

[13]Then the disciples realized he was speaking of John the Baptist.

Jesus Frees a Boy of a Demon

[14]When they arrived at the bottom of the hill, a huge crowd was waiting for them. A man came and knelt before Jesus and said, [15]"Sir, have mercy on my son, for he is mentally deranged and in great trouble, for he often falls into the fire or into the water; [16]so I brought him to your disciples, but they couldn't cure him."

[17]Jesus replied, "Oh, you stubborn, faithless people! How long shall I bear with you? Bring him here to me." [18]Then Jesus rebuked the demon in the boy and it left him, and from that moment the boy was well.

[19]Afterwards the disciples asked Jesus privately, "Why couldn't we cast that demon out?"

[20]"Because of your little faith," Jesus told them. "For if you had faith even as small as a tiny mustard seed you could say to this mountain, 'Move!' and it would go far away. Nothing would be impossible. [21]But this kind

17:1-8 Even before the event of Jesus' transfiguration, Jesus was the glorious Son of God. It was just that Peter, James, and John had never seen Jesus in that way. After their experience on the Mount of Transfiguration, however, these disciples would never again be able to consider Jesus as anything less than God's Son without being in full-scale denial. Through the words of Matthew and the testimony of other believers, we too are witnesses of God's glory in Jesus Christ. To deny his authority over our life is to assure the failure of any recovery program. Jesus is the only one who can transfigure our broken life.

17:14-21 This account of the disciples' failure to cast out a demon teaches us a crucial lesson about the role of faith in recovery. Jesus criticized the disciples for their lack of faith in God's powerful ability to heal the boy. We don't need large amounts of faith to begin the healing process in our life; we need only a small amount, "as small as a tiny mustard seed," to effect change. Prayer and faith in God are the tools we need for recovery; with these we can move mountains!

18:2-6 By calling the little children to come to him, Jesus revealed how much he loves each of us. He warned that terrible judgment would come upon those who harm his followers or cause them to lose faith. This is encouraging for those of us who have suffered injustices or abuse from others, especially when we were children. We don't have to carry our hate with us or waste our energy dreaming of revenge. God will judge those who have harmed us. Our focus should be on our recovery, not on the punishment of the people who have hurt us.

of demon won't leave unless you have prayed
and gone without food."

Jesus again Speaks of His Death
22,23 One day while they were still in Galilee,
Jesus told them, "I am going to be betrayed
into the power of those who will kill me, and
on the third day afterwards I will be brought
back to life again." And the disciples' hearts
were filled with sorrow and dread.

Money in a Fish's Mouth
24 On their arrival in Capernaum, the Temple
tax collectors came to Peter and asked him,
"Doesn't your master pay taxes?"
25 "Of course he does," Peter replied.
Then he went into the house to talk to Jesus
about it, but before he had a chance to speak,
Jesus asked him, "What do you think, Peter?
Do kings levy assessments against their own
people or against conquered foreigners?"
26,27 "Against the foreigners," Peter replied.
"Well, then," Jesus said, "the citizens are
free! However, we don't want to offend them,
so go down to the shore and throw in a line,
and open the mouth of the first fish you
catch. You will find a coin to cover the taxes
for both of us; take it and pay them."

CHAPTER 18
Who Is the Greatest?
About that time the disciples came to Jesus to
ask which of them would be greatest in the
Kingdom of Heaven!
2 Jesus called a small child over to him and
set the little fellow down among them, 3 and
said, "Unless you turn to God from your sins
and become as little children, you will never
get into the Kingdom of Heaven. 4 Therefore
anyone who humbles himself as this little
child is the greatest in the Kingdom of
Heaven. 5 And any of you who welcomes a
little child like this because you are mine is
welcoming me and caring for me. 6 But if any
of you causes one of these little ones who
trusts in me to lose his faith, it would be better
for you to have a rock tied to your neck and
be thrown into the sea.
7 "Woe upon the world for all its evils. Temptation to do wrong is inevitable, but woe to the
man who does the tempting. 8 So if your hand
or foot causes you to sin, cut it off and throw
it away. Better to enter heaven crippled than
to be in hell with both of your hands and feet.
9 And if your eye causes you to sin, gouge it out
and throw it away. Better to enter heaven with
one eye than to be in hell with two.

Forgiven to Forgive

BIBLE READING: Matthew 18:23-35

We made a list of all persons we had harmed and became willing to make amends to them all.

Listing all the people we have harmed will probably trigger a natural defensiveness. With each name we put on our list, another mental list may begin to form—a list of the wrongs that have been done against us. How can we deal with the resentment we hold toward others, so we can move toward making amends?

Jesus told a story: "A king . . . decided to bring his accounts up to date. In the process, one of his debtors was brought in who owed him $10 million!" (Matthew 18:23-24). The man begged for forgiveness. "Then the king was filled with pity for him and released him and forgave his debt. But when the man left the king, he went to a man who owed him $2,000 and grabbed him by the throat and demanded instant payment" (18:27-28). This was reported to the king. "And the king called before him the man he had forgiven and said, 'You evil-hearted wretch! Here I forgave you all that tremendous debt, just because you asked me to—shouldn't you have mercy on others. . . ?' Then the angry king sent the man to the torture chamber until he had paid every last penny due. So shall my heavenly Father do to you if you refuse to truly forgive your brothers" (18:32-35).

When we look at all that God has forgiven us, it makes sense to choose to forgive others. This also frees us from the torture of festering resentment. We can't change what others have done to us, but we can write off their debt and become willing to make amends. ***Turn to page 1283, 2 Corinthians 2.***

A Story about a Lamb

10"Beware that you don't look down upon a single one of these little children. For I tell you that in heaven their angels have constant access to my Father. 11And I, the Messiah, came to save the lost.

12"If a man has a hundred sheep, and one wanders away and is lost, what will he do? Won't he leave the ninety-nine others and go out into the hills to search for the lost one? 13And if he finds it, he will rejoice over it more than over the ninety-nine others safe at home! 14Just so, it is not my Father's will that even one of these little ones should perish.

Dealing with People Who Harm Us

15"If a brother sins against you, go to him privately and confront him with his fault. If he listens and confesses it, you have won back a brother. 16But if not, then take one or two others with you and go back to him again, proving everything you say by these witnesses. 17If he still refuses to listen, then take your case to the church, and if the church's verdict favors you, but he won't accept it, then the church should excommunicate him. 18And I tell you this—whatever you bind on earth is bound in heaven, and whatever you free on earth will be freed in heaven.

19"I also tell you this—if two of you agree down here on earth concerning anything you ask for, my Father in heaven will do it for you. 20For where two or three gather together because they are mine, I will be right there among them."

A Story about Forgiveness

21Then Peter came to him and asked, "Sir, how often should I forgive a brother who sins against me? Seven times?"

22"No!" Jesus replied, "seventy times seven!

23"The Kingdom of Heaven can be compared to a king who decided to bring his accounts up to date. 24In the process, one of his debtors was brought in who owed him $10 million! 25He couldn't pay, so the king ordered him sold for the debt, also his wife and children and everything he had.

26"But the man fell down before the king, his face in the dust, and said, 'Oh, sir, be patient with me and I will pay it all.'

27"Then the king was filled with pity for him and released him and forgave his debt.

28"But when the man left the king, he went to a man who owed him $2,000 and grabbed him by the throat and demanded instant payment.

29"The man fell down before him and begged him to give him a little time. 'Be patient and I will pay it,' he pled.

30"But his creditor wouldn't wait. He had the man arrested and jailed until the debt would be paid in full.

31"Then the man's friends went to the king and told him what had happened. 32And the king called before him the man he had forgiven and said, 'You evil-hearted wretch! Here I forgave you all that tremendous debt, just because you asked me to— 33shouldn't you have mercy on others, just as I had mercy on you?'

34"Then the angry king sent the man to the torture chamber until he had paid every last penny due. 35So shall my heavenly Father do to you if you refuse to truly forgive your brothers."

CHAPTER 19

Teachings about Marriage

After Jesus had finished this address, he left Galilee and circled back to Judea from across the Jordan River. 2Vast crowds followed him, and he healed their sick. 3Some Pharisees came to interview him and tried to trap him into saying something that would ruin him.

"Do you permit divorce?" they asked.

4"Don't you read the Scriptures?" he replied. "In them it is written that at the beginning God created man and woman, 5,6and that a man should leave his father and mother, and be forever united to his wife. The two shall become one—no longer two, but one! And no man may divorce what God has joined together."

7"Then, why," they asked, "did Moses say a man may divorce his wife by merely writing her a letter of dismissal?"

8Jesus replied, "Moses did that in recognition of your hard and evil hearts, but it was

18:10-14 Many children and adults have bought the lie that they are worthless to other people and insignificant to God. Jesus indicated that his mission was to save the lost, no matter how few or how "insignificant" they were considered to be. God the Father does not want anyone to miss the opportunity for salvation or recovery in Jesus Christ. God values each one of us, no matter how painful our past or how far we have strayed. If we admit our need for him and seek to follow his will for us, we will discover how very important we are to God and the people close to us.

not what God had originally intended. 9And I tell you this, that anyone who divorces his wife, except for fornication, and marries another, commits adultery."

10Jesus' disciples then said to him, "If that is how it is, it is better not to marry!"

11"Not everyone can accept this statement," Jesus said. "Only those whom God helps. 12Some are born without the ability to marry, and some are disabled by men, and some refuse to marry for the sake of the Kingdom of Heaven. Let anyone who can, accept my statement."

Jesus Blesses the Children

13Little children were brought for Jesus to lay his hands on them and pray. But the disciples scolded those who brought them. "Don't bother him," they said.

14But Jesus said, "Let the little children come to me, and don't prevent them. For of such is the Kingdom of Heaven." 15And he put his hands on their heads and blessed them before he left.

Jesus and the Rich Young Man

16Someone came to Jesus with this question: "Good master, what must I do to have eternal life?"

17"When you call me good you are calling me God," Jesus replied, "for God alone is truly good. But to answer your question, you can get to heaven if you keep the commandments."

18"Which ones?" the man asked.

And Jesus replied, "Don't kill, don't commit adultery, don't steal, don't lie, 19honor your father and mother, and love your neighbor as yourself!"

20"I've always obeyed every one of them," the youth replied. "What else must I do?"

21Jesus told him, "If you want to be perfect, go and sell everything you have and give the money to the poor, and you will have treasure in heaven; and come, follow me." 22But when the young man heard this, he went away sadly, for he was very rich.

23Then Jesus said to his disciples, "It is almost impossible for a rich man to get into the Kingdom of Heaven. 24I say it again—it is easier for a camel to go through the eye of a needle than for a rich man to enter the Kingdom of God!"

25This remark confounded the disciples. "Then who in the world can be saved?" they asked.

26Jesus looked at them intently and said, "Humanly speaking, no one. But with God, everything is possible."

27Then Peter said to him, "We left everything to follow you. What will we get out of it?"

28And Jesus replied, "When I, the Messiah, shall sit upon my glorious throne in the Kingdom, you my disciples shall certainly sit on twelve thrones judging the twelve tribes of Israel. 29And anyone who gives up his home, brothers, sisters, father, mother, wife, children, or property, to follow me, shall receive a hundred times as much in return, and shall have eternal life. 30But many who are first now will be last then; and some who are last now will be first then."

CHAPTER 20

A Story about a Vineyard

Here is another illustration of the Kingdom of Heaven. "The owner of an estate went out

---

19:3-12 Jesus affirmed the importance of the marriage relationship. We may find it confining to be without an "escape hatch" in marriage, but God has always intended that marriage be a lifelong relationship. Realizing that marriage is permanent, and that a husband and wife become one through marriage, should make us consider how much our sin and dependencies affect our spouse. Our addictions always harm our mate in one way or another. And even though divorce may end the conflict a couple is having, it will not correct the attitudes or behaviors that brought about the conflict. Unless we correct the root problems, we will have the same conflicts in any future relationship.

19:16-24 The rich young man was trying to work (and buy) his way to heaven. Jesus played along with this man's shortsighted attempt to claim he was perfect. But it soon became clear that he was addicted to his material wealth and the security it bought him. His possessions had a higher priority in his life than God had. Materialism is a form of addiction or compulsion that makes it nearly impossible to humble ourselves and trust Jesus Christ alone for salvation and recovery. As long as we believe we can buy our way out of our problems, we will never be able to achieve a lasting recovery.

19:25-26 These verses are true not only for salvation, but also for recovery. Left on our own, we would only fall deeper into the pit of our addictions, never gaining control over them. But with God's help, the inconceivable is made possible. He can take our life and turn it around, bringing hope and health where once despair and pain had reigned. Giving God control of our life is the only way to regain independence from our addictions and other compulsive behaviors.

early one morning to hire workers for his
harvest field. 2He agreed to pay them $20 a
day and sent them out to work.

3"A couple of hours later he was passing a
hiring hall and saw some men standing
around waiting for jobs, 4so he sent them
also into his fields, telling them he would
pay them whatever was right at the end of
the day. 5At noon and again around three
o'clock in the afternoon he did the same
thing.

6"At five o'clock that evening he was in
town again and saw some more men standing
around and asked them, 'Why haven't you
been working today?'

7"'Because no one hired us,' they replied.

"'Then go on out and join the others in my
fields,' he told them.

8"That evening he told the paymaster to
call the men in and pay them, beginning with
the last men first. 9When the men hired at five
o'clock were paid, each received $20. 10So
when the men hired earlier came to get theirs,
they assumed they would receive much more.
But they, too, were paid $20.

11,12"They protested, 'Those fellows worked
only one hour, and yet you've paid them just
as much as those of us who worked all day in
the scorching heat.'

13"'Friend,' he answered one of them, 'I did
you no wrong! Didn't you agree to work all
day for $20? 14Take it and go. It is my desire to
pay all the same; 15is it against the law to give
away my money if I want to? Should you be
angry because I am kind?' 16And so it is that
the last shall be first, and the first, last."

Jesus Talks about His Death

17As Jesus was on the way to Jerusalem, he
took the twelve disciples aside 18and talked to
them about what would happen to him when
they arrived.

"I will be betrayed to the chief priests and
other Jewish leaders, and they will condemn
me to die. 19And they will hand me over to the
Roman government, and I will be mocked
and crucified, and the third day I will rise to
life again."

The Importance of Serving Others

20Then the mother of James and John, the
sons of Zebedee, brought them to Jesus and
respectfully asked a favor.

21"What is your request?" he asked. She
replied, "In your Kingdom, will you let my
two sons sit on two thrones next to yours?"

22But Jesus told her, "You don't know what
you are asking!" Then he turned to James and
John and asked them, "Are you able to drink
from the terrible cup I am about to drink
from?"

"Yes," they replied, "we are able!"

23"You shall indeed drink from it," he told
them. "But I have no right to say who will sit
on the thrones next to mine. Those places are
reserved for the persons my Father selects."

24The other ten disciples were indignant
when they heard what James and John had
asked for.

25But Jesus called them together and said,
"Among the heathen, kings are tyrants and
each minor official lords it over those beneath
him. 26But among you it is quite different.
Anyone wanting to be a leader among you
must be your servant. 27And if you want to be
right at the top, you must serve like a slave.
28Your attitude must be like my own, for I, the
Messiah, did not come to be served, but to
serve, and to give my life as a ransom for
many."

Jesus Heals Two Blind Men

29As Jesus and the disciples left the city of
Jericho, a vast crowd surged along behind.

30Two blind men were sitting beside the
road, and when they heard that Jesus was
coming that way, they began shouting, "Sir,
King David's Son, have mercy on us!"

31The crowd told them to be quiet, but they
only yelled the louder.

20:1-16 The story about the workers and their pay speaks strongly about the grace of God. No matter when we begin to follow Jesus, we receive the same amount of grace from God. That may seem unfair to some; however, God in his mercy accepts all people who turn to him for salvation and recovery, no matter how early (or late) in life. It is never too late to begin the process of recovery!

20:20-28 The disciples were indignant at James and John's request for special recognition because they, too, wanted to achieve a high position of honor in God's Kingdom. This prideful attitude was contrary to what Jesus was teaching, and such an attitude is always detrimental to our recovery. The path to becoming great in God's sight is through humbly serving others. This is also one of our goals in recovery. As we receive God's grace and experience his restoration, we are then called to carry God's message to others and do what we can to help them in their recovery.

[32,33]When Jesus came to the place where they were, he stopped in the road and called, "What do you want me to do for you?"

"Sir," they said, "we want to see!"

[34]Jesus was moved with pity for them and touched their eyes. And instantly they could see, and followed him.

CHAPTER 21

Jesus Rides into Jerusalem

As Jesus and the disciples approached Jerusalem, and were near the town of Bethphage on the Mount of Olives, Jesus sent two of them into the village ahead.

[2]"Just as you enter," he said, "you will see a donkey tied there, with its colt beside it.
Untie them and bring them here. [3]If anyone asks you what you are doing, just say, 'The Master needs them,' and there will be no trouble."

[4]This was done to fulfill the ancient prophecy,
[5]"Tell Jerusalem her King is coming to her, riding humbly on a donkey's colt!"

[6]The two disciples did as Jesus said, [7]and brought the animals to him and threw their garments over the colt for him to ride on.
[8]And some in the crowd threw down their coats along the road ahead of him, and others cut branches from the trees and spread them out before him.

[9]Then the crowds surged on ahead and pressed along behind, shouting, "God bless King David's Son!" . . . "God's Man is here!". . . Bless him, Lord!" . . . "Praise God in highest heaven!"

[10]The entire city of Jerusalem was stirred as he entered. "Who is this?" they asked.

[11]And the crowds replied, "It's Jesus, the prophet from Nazareth up in Galilee."

Jesus Clears the Temple

[12]Jesus went into the Temple, drove out the merchants, and knocked over the moneychangers' tables and the stalls of those selling doves.

[13]"The Scriptures say my Temple is a place of prayer," he declared, "but you have turned it into a den of thieves."

[14]And now the blind and crippled came to him, and he healed them there in the Temple.
[15]But when the chief priests and other Jewish leaders saw these wonderful miracles and heard even the little children in the Temple shouting, "God bless the Son of David," they were disturbed and indignant and asked him, "Do you hear what these children are saying?"

[16]"Yes," Jesus replied. "Didn't you ever read the Scriptures? For they say, 'Even little babies shall praise him!'"

[17]Then he returned to Bethany, where he stayed overnight.

Power through Faith in God

[18]In the morning, as he was returning to Jerusalem, he was hungry [19]and noticed a fig tree beside the road. He went over to see if there were any figs, but there were only leaves. Then he said to it, "Never bear fruit again!" And soon the fig tree withered up.

[20]The disciples were utterly amazed and asked, "How did the fig tree wither so quickly?"

[21]Then Jesus told them, "Truly, if you have faith and don't doubt, you can do things like this and much more. You can even say to this Mount of Olives, 'Move over into the ocean,'
and it will. [22]You can get anything—*anything* you ask for in prayer—if you believe."

Religious Leaders Challenge Jesus

[23]When he had returned to the Temple and was teaching, the chief priests and other Jewish leaders came up to him and demanded to know by whose authority he had thrown out the merchants the day before.

[24]"I'll tell you if you answer one question

20:29-34 Jesus' sensitivity to the needs of two blind men in the midst of a huge crowd shows that God cares very much for individuals who hurt. Jesus healed the blind men because they believed in him and they asked him to. Notice that they did not listen to the discouraging remarks of the other bystanders. They persevered despite opposition and continued with their humble pleas for help. As we continue in recovery, we may encounter similar opposition. If this happens, we may need to swallow our pride and just keep going. We can be sure that even if others are laughing at us, God is listening and will respond by helping us in our recovery.

21:18-22 Jesus again commented on the power of faith. Seemingly impossible answers to prayer, including the life-transforming recovery process, can occur as we live by faith and grow in our commitment to God. This passage does not suggest that we pray for the withering of a fig tree or the actual relocation of a mountain. It does tell us, however, that incredible answers are given when we pray to God in faith.

first," Jesus replied. 25"Was John the Baptist
sent from God or not?"

They talked it over among themselves. "If
we say, 'From God,'" they said, "then he will
ask why we didn't believe what John said.
26And if we deny that God sent him, we'll be
mobbed, for the crowd all think he was a
prophet." 27So they finally replied, "We don't
know!"

And Jesus said, "Then I won't answer your
question either.

A Story about Two Sons

28"But what do you think about this? A man
with two sons told the older boy, 'Son, go out
and work on the farm today.' 29'I won't,' he
answered, but later he changed his mind and
went. 30Then the father told the youngest,
'You go!' and he said, 'Yes, sir, I will.' But he
didn't. 31Which of the two was obeying his
father?"

They replied, "The first, of course."

Then Jesus explained his meaning: "Surely
evil men and prostitutes will get into the
Kingdom before you do. 32For John the Baptist
told you to repent and turn to God, and you
wouldn't, while very evil men and prostitutes
did. And even when you saw this happening,
you refused to repent, and so you couldn't
believe.

A Story about Wicked Farmers

33"Now listen to this story: A certain land-
owner planted a vineyard with a hedge
around it, and built a platform for the watchman, then leased the vineyard to some farmers on a sharecrop basis, and went away to live
in another country.

34"At the time of the grape harvest he sent
his agents to the farmers to collect his share.
35But the farmers attacked his men, beat one,
killed one, and stoned another.

36"Then he sent a larger group of his men to
collect for him, but the results were the same.
37Finally the owner sent his son, thinking they
would surely respect him.

38"But when these farmers saw the son
coming they said among themselves, 'Here
comes the heir to this estate; come on, let's
kill him and get it for ourselves!' 39So they
dragged him out of the vineyard and killed
him.

40"When the owner returns, what do you
think he will do to those farmers?"

41The Jewish leaders replied, "He will put
the wicked men to a horrible death and lease
the vineyard to others who will pay him
promptly."

42Then Jesus asked them, "Didn't you ever
read in the Scriptures: 'The stone rejected by
the builders has been made the honored cornerstone; how remarkable! what an amazing
thing the Lord has done'?

43"What I mean is that the Kingdom of God
shall be taken away from you, and given to a
nation that will give God his share of the
crop. 44All who stumble on this rock of truth
shall be broken, but those it falls on will be
scattered as dust."

45When the chief priests and other Jewish
leaders realized that Jesus was talking about
them—that they were the farmers in his
story—46they wanted to get rid of him but
were afraid to try because of the crowds, for
they accepted Jesus as a prophet.

CHAPTER 22

A Story about a Wedding

Jesus told several other stories to show what
the Kingdom of Heaven is like.

"For instance," he said, "it can be illustrated by the story of a king who prepared a
great wedding dinner for his son. 3Many
guests were invited, and when the banquet
was ready he sent messengers to notify everyone that it was time to come. But all refused!

21:28-32 Before our recovery, we were like the first son, saying no to his father's wishes. We turned our back to God and indulged in our desires. But later we changed our mind, seeing where we were headed, and followed our Father. Although we have messed up our life, we are now obeying God. This is in sharp contrast to the son who said he would obey and then didn't. People like this may be part of the established "church" who think they are following God, but are far from his ways. Our change of life-style will gain us eternal favor; their denial will earn them eternal punishment.

22:1-10 When the king's servants brought everyone they could find, there were good people and bad people alike. The offer was open to anyone who wanted to come. So it is with heaven: everyone is invited, and anyone can turn down the offer. The same principles apply to recovery—God wants everyone to lead a healthy, productive, godly life, and anyone can turn down the opportunity to start the recovery process. Will we be like the first group of guests and suffer for our decision, or will we be like the second and enjoy what God has to offer us?

4So he sent other servants to tell them, 'Everything is ready and the roast is in the oven.
Hurry!'
5"But the guests he had invited merely
laughed and went on about their business,
one to his farm, another to his store; 6others
beat up his messengers and treated them
shamefully, even killing some of them.
7"Then the angry king sent out his army
and destroyed the murderers and burned
their city. 8And he said to his servants, 'The
wedding feast is ready, and the guests I invited
aren't worthy of the honor. 9Now go out to
the street corners and invite everyone you
see.'
10"So the servants did, and brought in all
they could find, good and bad alike; and the
banquet hall was filled with guests. 11But
when the king came in to meet the guests, he
noticed a man who wasn't wearing the wedding robe [provided for him].
12"'Friend,' he asked, 'how does it happen
that you are here without a wedding robe?'
And the man had no reply.
13"Then the king said to his aides, 'Bind him
hand and foot and throw him out into the
outer darkness where there is weeping and
gnashing of teeth.' 14For many are called, but
few are chosen."

A Question about Taxes

15Then the Pharisees met together to try to
think of some way to trap Jesus into saying
something for which they could arrest him.
16They decided to send some of their men
along with the Herodians to ask him this
question: "Sir, we know you are very honest
and teach the truth regardless of the consequences, without fear or favor. 17Now tell us,
is it right to pay taxes to the Roman government or not?"
18But Jesus saw what they were after. "You
hypocrites!" he exclaimed. "Who are you trying to fool with your trick questions? 19Here,
show me a coin." And they handed him a
penny.
20"Whose picture is stamped on it?" he
asked them. "And whose name is this beneath
the picture?"
21"Caesar's," they replied.
"Well, then," he said, "give it to Caesar if it
is his, and give God everything that belongs
to God."
22His reply surprised and baffled them, and
they went away.

Questions about the Resurrection

23But that same day some of the Sadducees,
who say there is no resurrection after death,
came to him and asked, 24"Sir, Moses said that
if a man died without children, his brother
should marry the widow and their children
would get all the dead man's property. 25Well,
we had among us a family of seven brothers.
The first of these men married and then died,
without children, so his widow became the
second brother's wife. 26This brother also died
without children, and the wife was passed to
the next brother, and so on until she had been
the wife of each of them. 27And then she also
died. 28So whose wife will she be in the resurrection? For she was the wife of all seven of
them!"
29But Jesus said, "Your error is caused by
your ignorance of the Scriptures and of God's
power! 30For in the resurrection there is no
marriage; everyone is as the angels in heaven.
31But now, as to whether there is a resurrection of the dead—don't you ever read the
Scriptures? Don't you realize that God was
speaking directly to you when he said, 32'I *am*
the God of Abraham, Isaac, and Jacob'? So
God is not the God of the dead, but of the
living."

The Greatest Commandment

33The crowds were profoundly impressed by
his answers—34,35but not the Pharisees! When
they heard that he had routed the Sadducees
with his reply, they thought up a fresh question of their own to ask him. One of them, a
lawyer, spoke up: 36"Sir, which is the most
important command in the laws of Moses?"
37Jesus replied, "'Love the Lord your God
with all your heart, soul, and mind.' 38,39This
is the first and greatest commandment. The
second most important is similar: 'Love your
neighbor as much as you love yourself.' 40All

22:33-40 To simplify our priorities, Jesus boiled down the six hundred–plus regulations of the law of Moses into two foundational responsibilities. We are to love God with everything we are and have; we are to love our neighbor as ourself. To do these is to obey every other law. A better two-point summary of the Twelve Steps could not be found. When we love God with our very life, we will not want to do anything to disgrace him or make him angry. Loving others should make us aware of the pain others feel when we engage in our addictions, and our concern and love for them should make us think twice before causing them to suffer.

the other commandments and all the demands of the prophets stem from these two laws and are fulfilled if you obey them. Keep only these and you will find that you are obeying all the others."

A Question about the Messiah

41Then, surrounded by the Pharisees, he asked them a question: 42"What about the Messiah? Whose son is he?"

"The son of David," they replied.

43"Then why does David, speaking under the inspiration of the Holy Spirit, call him 'Lord'?" Jesus asked. "For David said,

> 44'God said to my Lord, Sit at my right
> hand until I put your enemies beneath
> your feet.'

45Since David called him 'Lord,' how can he be merely his son?"

46They had no answer. And after that no one dared ask him any more questions.

CHAPTER 23

A Warning about the Religious Leaders

Then Jesus said to the crowds, and to his disciples, 2"You would think these Jewish leaders and these Pharisees were Moses, the way they keep making up so many laws! 3And of course you should obey their every whim! It may be all right to do what they say, but above anything else, *don't follow their example.* For they don't do what they tell you to do. 4They load you with impossible demands that they themselves don't even try to keep.

5"Everything they do is done for show. They act holy by wearing on their arms little prayer boxes with Scripture verses inside, and by lengthening the memorial fringes of their robes. 6And how they love to sit at the head table at banquets and in the reserved pews in the synagogue! 7How they enjoy the deference paid them on the streets and to be called 'Rabbi' and 'Master'! 8Don't ever let anyone call you that. For only God is your Rabbi and all of you are on the same level, as brothers. 9And don't address anyone here on earth as 'Father,' for only God in heaven should be addressed like that. 10And don't be called 'Master,' for only one is your master, even the Messiah.

11"The more lowly your service to others, the greater you are. To be the greatest, be a servant. 12But those who think themselves great shall be disappointed and humbled; and those who humble themselves shall be exalted.

Woes against the Religious Leaders

13,14"Woe to you, Pharisees, and you other religious leaders. Hypocrites! For you won't let others enter the Kingdom of Heaven and won't go in yourselves. And you pretend to be holy, with all your long, public prayers in the streets, while you are evicting widows from their homes. Hypocrites! 15Yes, woe upon you hypocrites. For you go to all lengths to make one convert, and then turn him into twice the son of hell you are yourselves. 16Blind guides! Woe upon you! For your rule is that to swear 'By God's Temple' means nothing—you can break that oath, but to swear 'By the gold in the Temple' is binding! 17Blind fools! Which is greater, the gold, or the Temple that sanctifies the gold? 18And you say that to take an oath 'By the altar' can be broken, but to swear 'By the gifts on the altar' is binding! 19Blind! For which is greater, the gift on the altar, or the altar itself that sanctifies the gift? 20When you swear 'By the altar' you are swearing by it and everything on it, 21and when you swear 'By the Temple' you are swearing by it and by God who lives in it. 22And when you swear 'By heavens' you are swearing by the Throne of God and by God himself.

23"Yes, woe upon you, Pharisees, and you other religious leaders—hypocrites! For you tithe down to the last mint leaf in your garden, but ignore the important things—justice and mercy and faith. Yes, you should tithe, but you shouldn't leave the more important

---

23:1-12 The Pharisees and Jewish leaders are classic examples of people who live by a double standard. They made the standards of behavior for others impossibly difficult, but they failed to keep these stipulations themselves. In spite of their shortcomings, they demanded to be called by titles fit only for God. They did not realize that true greatness begins with humility and is proven by a willingness to help others. The Pharisees' pride kept them from seeing their true need for God.

23:13-36 As a result of their hypocritical behavior, Jesus pronounced "woes" of judgment on all the spiritually blind religious leaders. Their external rhetoric and ritualism were a mere sham, all show with no inner reality. Such people cause great pain to others and are far from recovery themselves. However, there is hope for everyone—even hypocrites! Both Joseph of Arimathea and Nicodemus, once numbered with the hypocrites, eventually found recovery through belief in Jesus (see John 19:38-42). If we search for Jesus, we will find him, and he will work our recovery.

things undone. 24Blind guides! You strain out a gnat and swallow a camel.

25"Woe to you, Pharisees, and you religious leaders—hypocrites! You are so careful to polish the outside of the cup, but the inside is foul with extortion and greed. 26Blind Pharisees! First cleanse the inside of the cup, and then the whole cup will be clean.

27"Woe to you, Pharisees, and you religious leaders! You are like beautiful mausoleums—full of dead men's bones, and of foulness and corruption. 28You try to look like saintly men, but underneath those pious robes of yours are hearts besmirched with every sort of hypocrisy and sin.

29,30"Yes, woe to you, Pharisees, and you religious leaders—hypocrites! For you build monuments to the prophets killed by your fathers and lay flowers on the graves of the godly men they destroyed, and say, 'We certainly would never have acted as our fathers did.'

31"In saying that, you are accusing yourselves of being the sons of wicked men. 32And you are following in their steps, filling up the full measure of their evil. 33Snakes! Sons of vipers! How shall you escape the judgment of hell?

34"I will send you prophets, and wise men, and inspired writers, and you will kill some by crucifixion, and rip open the backs of others with whips in your synagogues, and hound them from city to city, 35so that you will become guilty of all the blood of murdered godly men from righteous Abel to Zechariah (son of Barachiah), slain by you in the Temple between the altar and the sanctuary. 36Yes, all the accumulated judgment of the centuries shall break upon the heads of this very generation.

37"O Jerusalem, Jerusalem, the city that kills the prophets and stones all those God sends to her! How often I have wanted to gather your children together as a hen gathers her chicks beneath her wings, but you wouldn't let me. 38And now your house is left to you, desolate. 39For I tell you this, you will never see me again until you are ready to welcome the one sent to you from God."

CHAPTER 24

Jesus Tells about the Future

As Jesus was leaving the Temple grounds, his disciples came along and wanted to take him on a tour of the various Temple buildings.

2But he told them, "All these buildings will be knocked down, with not one stone left on top of another!"

3"When will this happen?" the disciples asked him later, as he sat on the slopes of the Mount of Olives. "What events will signal your return and the end of the world?"

4Jesus told them, "Don't let anyone fool you. 5For many will come claiming to be the Messiah and will lead many astray. 6When you hear of wars beginning, this does not signal my return; these must come, but the end is not yet. 7The nations and kingdoms of the earth will rise against each other, and there will be famines and earthquakes in many places. 8But all this will be only the beginning of the horrors to come.

9"Then you will be tortured and killed and hated all over the world because you are mine, 10and many of you shall fall back into sin and betray and hate each other. 11And many false prophets will appear and lead many astray. 12Sin will be rampant everywhere and will cool the love of many. 13But those enduring to the end shall be saved.

14"And the Good News about the Kingdom will be preached throughout the whole world, so that all nations will hear it, and then, finally, the end will come.

15"So, when you see the horrible thing (told about by Daniel the prophet) standing in a holy place (Note to the reader: You know what is meant!), 16then those in Judea must flee into the Judean hills. 17Those on their porches must not even go inside to pack before they flee. 18Those in the fields should not return to their homes for their clothes.

24:2-8 Many people in need of or seeking recovery are greatly discouraged by the fear that things will go on indefinitely in the same miserable, dysfunctional way they are now. As Jesus began his Olivet discourse (Matthew 24–25), he looked ahead to events surrounding his return to earth, and he promised that someday true recovery would take place (24:13). But things will get worse before they get better, which parallels the normal course for recovery. We need to hang in there until our program is complete and we experience the restoration we seek.

24:14 Because God loves everyone, he is delaying the world's judgment until all parts of the earth have heard the message of salvation. This does not mean that everyone will accept the gospel; it just means that every group will have had a chance to respond. As we get closer to world evangelization, we get closer to Christ's second coming. Have we accepted Jesus and his plan for our recovery? If not, time is running out.

19"And woe to pregnant women and to
those with babies in those days. 20And pray
that your flight will not be in winter, or on the
Sabbath. 21For there will be persecution such
as the world has never before seen in all its
history and will never see again.

22"In fact, unless those days are shortened,
all mankind will perish. But they will be
shortened for the sake of God's chosen
people.

Jesus Tells about His Return

23"Then if anyone tells you, 'The Messiah has
arrived at such and such a place, or has appeared here or there,' don't believe it. 24For
false Christs shall arise, and false prophets,
and will do wonderful miracles so that if it
were possible, even God's chosen ones would
be deceived. 25See, I have warned you.

26"So if someone tells you the Messiah has
returned and is out in the desert, don't bother
to go and look. Or, that he is hiding at a
certain place, don't believe it! 27For as the
lightning flashes across the sky from east to
west, so shall my coming be, when I, the
Messiah, return. 28And wherever the carcass is,
there the vultures will gather.

29"Immediately after the persecution of
those days the sun will be darkened, and the
moon will not give light, and the stars will
seem to fall from the heavens, and the powers
overshadowing the earth will be convulsed.

30"And then at last the signal of my coming
will appear in the heavens, and there will be
deep mourning all around the earth. And the
nations of the world will see me arrive in the
clouds of heaven, with power and great glory.
31And I shall send forth my angels with the
sound of a mighty trumpet blast, and they
shall gather my chosen ones from the farthest
ends of the earth and heaven.

32"Now learn a lesson from the fig tree.
When her branch is tender and the leaves
begin to sprout, you know that summer is
almost here. 33Just so, when you see all these
things beginning to happen, you can know
that my return is near, even at the doors.
34Then at last this age will come to its close.

35"Heaven and earth will disappear, but my
words remain forever.

A Warning to Stay Alert

36But no one knows the date and hour when
the end will be—not even the angels. No, nor
even God's Son. Only the Father knows.

37,38"The world will be at ease—banquets
and parties and weddings—just as it was in
Noah's time before the sudden coming of the
flood; 39people wouldn't believe what was going to happen until the flood actually arrived
and took them all away. So shall my coming
be.

40"Two men will be working together in the
fields, and one will be taken, the other left.
41Two women will be going about their household tasks; one will be taken, the other left.

42"So be prepared, for you don't know what
day your Lord is coming.

43"Just as a man can prevent trouble from
thieves by keeping watch for them, 44so you
can avoid trouble by always being ready for
my unannounced return.

45"Are you a wise and faithful servant of the
Lord? Have I given you the task of managing
my household, to feed my children day by
day? 46Blessings on you if I return and find
you faithfully doing your work. 47I will put
such faithful ones in charge of everything I
own!

48"But if you are evil and say to yourself,
'My Lord won't be coming for a while,' 49and
begin oppressing your fellow servants, party-
ing and getting drunk, 50your Lord will arrive
unannounced and unexpected, 51and severely
whip you and send you off to the judgment
of the hypocrites; there will be weeping and
gnashing of teeth.

CHAPTER 25

A Story about Ten Bridesmaids

"The Kingdom of Heaven can be illustrated by
the story of ten bridesmaids who took their
lamps and went to meet the bridegroom.

24:36-51 Jesus did not let us know when the final redemption of this evil world would come. In the same way, we may not know when our personal recovery is to be complete. All of us are still recovering, one day at a time. None of us has arrived. Not until the Second Coming will we be relieved of daily working, watching, and recovering.

25:1-13 The story of the ten bridesmaids reinforces the need for wise preparation and readiness for Christ's coming. Those who have not readied themselves for the return of Jesus, the heavenly Bridegroom—by faith, commitment, and responsible living—will be ashamed. For those of us who have suffered from a dysfunctional background, the process of recovery is a very important part of that preparation.

[2-4]But only five of them were wise enough to
fill their lamps with oil, while the other five
were foolish and forgot.
[5,6]"So, when the bridegroom was delayed,
they lay down to rest until midnight, when
they were roused by the shout, 'The bridegroom is coming! Come out and welcome
him!'
[7,8]"All the girls jumped up and trimmed
their lamps. Then the five who hadn't any oil
begged the others to share with them, for
their lamps were going out.
[9]"But the others replied, 'We haven't
enough. Go instead to the shops and buy
some for yourselves.'
[10]"But while they were gone, the bridegroom came, and those who were ready went
in with him to the marriage feast, and the
door was locked.
[11]"Later, when the other five returned, they
stood outside, calling, 'Sir, open the door for
us!'
[12]"But he called back, 'Go away! It is too
late!'
[13]"So stay awake and be prepared, for you
do not know the date or moment of my
return.

A Story about Using Gifts Wisely

[14]"Again, the Kingdom of Heaven can be illustrated by the story of a man going into another country, who called together his
servants and loaned them money to invest for
him while he was gone.
[15]"He gave $5,000 to one, $2,000 to another, and $1,000 to the last—dividing it in
proportion to their abilities—and then left on
his trip. [16]The man who received the $5,000
began immediately to buy and sell with it and
soon earned another $5,000. [17]The man with
$2,000 went right to work, too, and earned
another $2,000.
[18]"But the man who received the $1,000
dug a hole in the ground and hid the money
for safekeeping.
[19]"After a long time their master returned
from his trip and called them to him to account for his money. [20]The man to whom he
had entrusted the $5,000 brought him
$10,000.
[21]"His master praised him for good work.
'You have been faithful in handling this small
amount,' he told him, 'so now I will give you
many more responsibilities. Begin the joyous
tasks I have assigned to you.'
[22]"Next came the man who had received

Perfectionism

READ MATTHEW 25:14-30

Perfectionism can paralyze us. Perhaps we have been shamed for not being exactly what others wanted us to be. Now the shadow of their unrealistic expectations is cast over how we see ourself, creating unrealistic expectations for our progress.

Jesus told a story of a man who loaned three servants money to invest for him while he was away. The first two men invested and doubled the money; the third hid his money in a hole. The third servant saw the master through the eyes of fear. He "came and said, 'Sir, I knew you were a hard man, and I was afraid you would rob me of what I earned, so I hid your money in the earth and here it is!' But his master replied, ' . . . Since you knew I would demand your profit, you should at least have put my money into the bank so I could have some interest'" (Matthew 25:24-27).

When we measure ourself by the expectations of others or by our own need to be perfect, we may not even try to succeed. All God asks is that we try to do something with our abilities and resources. When we allow ourself the option of just making modest progress, we will find the courage to progress in our recovery. Even the least improvement is better than being doomed to complete failure by our perfectionism.
Turn to page 1099, Luke 6.

the $2,000, with the report, 'Sir, you gave me
$2,000 to use, and I have doubled it.'
23"'Good work,' his master said. 'You are a
good and faithful servant. You have been
faithful over this small amount, so now I will
give you much more.'
24,25"Then the man with the $1,000 came
and said, 'Sir, I knew you were a hard man,
and I was afraid you would rob me of what I
earned, so I hid your money in the earth and
here it is!'
26"But his master replied, 'Wicked man!
Lazy slave! Since you knew I would demand
your profit, 27you should at least have put my
money into the bank so I could have some
interest. 28Take the money from this man and
give it to the man with the $10,000. 29For the
man who uses well what he is given shall be
given more, and he shall have abundance. But
from the man who is unfaithful, even what
little responsibility he has shall be taken from
him. 30And throw the useless servant out into
outer darkness: there shall be weeping and
gnashing of teeth.'

The Sheep and the Goats
31"But when I, the Messiah, shall come in my
glory, and all the angels with me, then I shall
sit upon my throne of glory. 32And all the
nations shall be gathered before me. And I
will separate the people as a shepherd separates the sheep from the goats, 33and place the
sheep at my right hand, and the goats at my
left.
34"Then I, the King, shall say to those at my
right, 'Come, blessed of my Father, into the
Kingdom prepared for you from the founding
of the world. 35For I was hungry and you fed
me; I was thirsty and you gave me water; I was
a stranger and you invited me into your
homes; 36naked and you clothed me; sick and
in prison, and you visited me.'
37"Then these righteous ones will reply, 'Sir,
when did we ever see you hungry and feed
you? Or thirsty and give you anything to
drink? 38Or a stranger, and help you? Or naked, and clothe you? 39When did we ever see
you sick or in prison, and visit you?'
40"And I, the King, will tell them, 'When
you did it to these my brothers you were
doing it to me!' 41Then I will turn to those on
my left and say, 'Away with you, you cursed
ones, into the eternal fire prepared for the
devil and his demons. 42For I was hungry and
you wouldn't feed me; thirsty, and you
wouldn't give me anything to drink; 43a
stranger, and you refused me hospitality; naked, and you wouldn't clothe me; sick, and in
prison, and you didn't visit me.'
44"Then they will reply, 'Lord, when did we
ever see you hungry or thirsty or a stranger or
naked or sick or in prison, and not help you?'
45"And I will answer, 'When you refused to
help the least of these my brothers, you were
refusing help to me.'
46"And they shall go away into eternal punishment; but the righteous into everlasting
life."

CHAPTER 26
A Plot to Kill Jesus
When Jesus had finished this talk with his
disciples, he told them,
2"As you know, the Passover celebration
begins in two days, and I shall be betrayed
and crucified."
3At that very moment the chief priests and
other Jewish officials were meeting at the
residence of Caiaphas the High Priest, 4to discuss ways of capturing Jesus quietly and killing him. 5"But not during the Passover
celebration," they agreed, "for there would be
a riot."

A Woman Anoints Jesus' Feet
6Jesus now proceeded to Bethany, to the
home of Simon the leper. 7While he was eating, a woman came in with a bottle of very
expensive perfume and poured it over his
head.
8,9The disciples were indignant. "What a
waste of good money," they said. "Why, she

25:31-46 We will all ultimately be accountable to God on Judgment Day. Not only will we be responsible for our own recovery, we will also be responsible for how we have helped others. The last step in recovery is to tell others about our recovery and to encourage them in the recovery process. Since Jesus identifies himself with those who suffer, we should follow his example and be especially alert to the needs of others.

26:6-13 This woman expressed her love for Jesus the best way she knew how. The disciples criticized her wastefulness, but Jesus commended her action. There will always be someone who thinks we are foolish for expressing our gratitude to God. But we should continue to praise him because this act reminds us that God is the one who is working our recovery, it gives us a chance to tell others what God has done for us, and God appreciates the gesture.

could have sold it for a fortune and given it to the poor."

[10]Jesus knew what they were thinking and said, "Why are you criticizing her? For she has done a good thing to me. [11]You will always have the poor among you, but you won't always have me. [12]She has poured this perfume on me to prepare my body for burial. [13]And she will always be remembered for this deed. The story of what she has done will be told throughout the whole world, wherever the Good News is preached."

Judas Agrees to Betray Jesus

[14]Then Judas Iscariot, one of the twelve apostles, went to the chief priests [15]and asked, "How much will you pay me to get Jesus into your hands?" And they gave him thirty silver coins. [16]From that time on, Judas watched for an opportunity to betray Jesus to them.

Jesus Prepares for Passover

[17]On the first day of the Passover ceremonies, when bread made with yeast was purged from every Jewish home, the disciples came to Jesus and asked, "Where shall we plan to eat the Passover?"

[18]He replied, "Go into the city and see Mr. So-and-So, and tell him, 'Our Master says, my time has come, and I will eat the Passover meal with my disciples at your house.'" [19]So the disciples did as he told them and prepared the supper there.

The Last Supper

[20,21]That evening as he sat eating with the Twelve, he said, "One of you will betray me."

[22]Sorrow chilled their hearts, and each one asked, "Am I the one?"

[23]He replied, "It is the one I served first. [24]For I must die just as was prophesied, but woe to the man by whom I am betrayed. Far better for that one if he had never been born."

[25]Judas, too, had asked him, "Rabbi, am I the one?" And Jesus had told him, "Yes."

[26]As they were eating, Jesus took a small loaf of bread and blessed it and broke it apart and gave it to the disciples and said, "Take it and eat it, for this is my body."

[27]And he took a cup of wine and gave thanks for it and gave it to them and said, "Each one drink from it, [28]for this is my blood, sealing the New Covenant. It is poured out to forgive the sins of multitudes. [29]Mark my words—I will not drink this wine again until the day I drink it new with you in my Father's Kingdom."

Jesus Predicts Peter's Denial

[30]And when they had sung a hymn, they went out to the Mount of Olives.

[31]Then Jesus said to them, "Tonight you will all desert me. For it is written in the Scriptures that God will smite the Shepherd, and the sheep of the flock will be scattered. [32]But after I have been brought back to life again, I will go to Galilee and meet you there."

[33]Peter declared, "If everyone else deserts you, I won't."

[34]Jesus told him, "The truth is that this very night, before the cock crows at dawn, you will deny me three times!"

[35]"I would die first!" Peter insisted. And all the other disciples said the same thing.

Jesus Agonizes in the Garden

[36]Then Jesus brought them to a garden grove, Gethsemane, and told them to sit down and wait while he went on ahead to pray. [37]He took Peter with him and Zebedee's two sons James and John, and began to be filled with anguish and despair.

26:14-16, 20-25 Judas thought he could hide his dealings with the chief priests, but Jesus saw right through his false front. Jesus discreetly yet openly made Judas aware that he knew exactly what was going on. Judas, however, passed up an opportunity to confess his actions and restore his relationship with Jesus. When we are confronted with our sin, will we do as Judas did and deny our involvement, or will we use the chance to turn to God?

26:26-28 Through the activities of the Last Supper, Jesus communicated the reason why he came to earth to die on the cross. His body would be broken, like the bread, so we could receive continued spiritual sustenance. His blood, represented by the wine, was the eternal payment for our sins. When we acknowledge Jesus as the Lord of our life, we become a member of his body, forgiven by his blood. There are no restrictions based on race, sex, occupation, or past failures. All who look to Jesus are forgiven through the blood he shed on the cross.

26:31-75 Like Peter, we often go through several stages as we fall prey to our weaknesses. First we claim that we will never fail in a certain way (26:31-35). Then we find ourself doing what we promised we wouldn't do (26:56, 69-74). Next we realize that we have failed miserably (26:75). From there we have two options: we can work to overcome our weakness and learn from the experience, as Peter did; or we can wallow in our sin and never grow spiritually, as Judas did (27:5).

[38]Then he told them, "My soul is crushed with horror and sadness to the point of death . . . stay here . . . stay awake with me."

[39]He went forward a little, and fell face downward on the ground, and prayed, "My Father! If it is possible, let this cup be taken away from me. But I want your will, not mine."

[40]Then he returned to the three disciples and found them asleep. "Peter," he called, "couldn't you even stay awake with me one hour? [41]Keep alert and pray. Otherwise temptation will overpower you. For the spirit indeed is willing, but how weak the body is!"

[42]Again he left them and prayed, "My Father! If this cup cannot go away until I drink it all, your will be done."

[43]He returned to them again and found them sleeping, for their eyes were heavy, [44]so he went back to prayer the third time, saying the same things again.

[45]Then he came to the disciples and said, "Sleep on now and take your rest . . . but no! The time has come! I am betrayed into the hands of evil men! [46]Up! Let's be going! Look! Here comes the man who is betraying me!"

Judas Betrays Jesus

[47]At that very moment while he was still speaking, Judas, one of the Twelve, arrived with a great crowd armed with swords and clubs, sent by the Jewish leaders. [48]Judas had told them to arrest the man he greeted, for that would be the one they were after. [49]So now Judas came straight to Jesus and said, "Hello, Master!" and embraced him in friendly fashion.

[50]Jesus said, "My friend, go ahead and do what you have come for." Then the others grabbed him.

[51]One of the men with Jesus pulled out a sword and slashed off the ear of the High Priest's servant.

[52]"Put away your sword," Jesus told him. "Those using swords will get killed. [53]Don't you realize that I could ask my Father for thousands of angels to protect us, and he would send them instantly? [54]But if I did, how would the Scriptures be fulfilled that describe what is happening now?" [55]Then Jesus spoke to the crowd. "Am I some dangerous criminal," he asked, "that you had to arm yourselves with swords and clubs before you could arrest me? I was with you teaching daily in the Temple and you didn't stop me then. [56]But this is all happening to fulfill the words of the prophets as recorded in the Scriptures."

At that point, all the disciples deserted him and fled.

Caiaphas Questions Jesus

[57]Then the mob led him to the home of Caiaphas, the High Priest, where all the Jewish leaders were gathering. [58]Meanwhile, Peter was following far to the rear, and came to the courtyard of the High Priest's house and went in and sat with the soldiers, and waited to see what was going to be done to Jesus.

[59]The chief priests and, in fact, the entire Jewish Supreme Court assembled there and looked for witnesses who would lie about Jesus, in order to build a case against him that would result in a death sentence. [60,61]But even though they found many who agreed to be false witnesses, these always contradicted each other.

Finally two men were found who declared, "This man said, 'I am able to destroy the Temple of God and rebuild it in three days.'"

[62]Then the High Priest stood up and said to Jesus, "Well, what about it? Did you say that, or didn't you?" [63]But Jesus remained silent.

Then the High Priest said to him, "I demand in the name of the living God that you tell us whether you claim to be the Messiah, the Son of God."

[64]"Yes," Jesus said, "I am. And in the future you will see me, the Messiah, sitting at the right hand of God and returning on the clouds of heaven."

[65,66]Then the High Priest tore at his own clothing, shouting, "Blasphemy! What need have we for other witnesses? You have all heard him say it! What is your verdict?"

They shouted, "Death!—Death!—Death!"

[67]Then they spat in his face and struck him and some slapped him, [68]saying, "Prophesy to us, you Messiah! Who struck you that time?"

27:3-8 The religious leaders refused to accept the blood money that Judas tried to return. It was probably their way of denying that they were responsible for the death of Jesus. If we are not careful, we can fall into this kind of hypocrisy and denial. Sometimes we hide behind righteous activities to conceal terrible sins. We should take a moral inventory of our whole life and see which actions are not lined up with God's desires. Denying even one area of our life can jeopardize our entire recovery.

READ MATTHEW 26:36-39

GOD grant me the serenity
to accept the things I cannot change
the courage to change the things I can
and the wisdom to know the difference
AMEN

As we work through the steps of recovery, we look up a long, difficult road toward a better life.

Although we know our goal of recovery is worthy of our commitment, we often find the challenge of the process overwhelming. As God goes about removing our defects, we may wish there were some other way. We may feel fear, a lack of confidence, deep anguish, and a host of other emotions that threaten to stop us in our tracks.

Jesus understands how we feel. He had similar emotions the night he was arrested. His friends were nearby, but when he needed them they were asleep. He told his friends, "My soul is crushed with horror and sadness to the point of death" (Matthew 26:38). As he realized the enormity of the pain he would face, he looked for some other way. He was not immediately able to accept the path set before him. Instead, he struggled and prayed the same thing three times, "My Father! If it is possible, let this cup be taken away from me. But I want your will, not mine" (26:39). Finally he found the grace to accept God's plan.

We may be overwhelmed as we face our own cross on the way to a new life. But during such times of stress, we can go to Jesus for encouragement and express our deepest emotions about our struggle. As we cry out for help, we can be confident that we will be given the strength we need for the next step. *Turn to page 1079, Mark 14.*

Peter Denies Knowing Jesus
69Meanwhile, as Peter was sitting in the courtyard, a girl came over and said to him, "You
were with Jesus, for both of you are from
Galilee."
70But Peter denied it loudly. "I don't even
know what you are talking about," he angrily
declared.
71Later, out by the gate, another girl noticed
him and said to those standing around, "This
man was with Jesus—from Nazareth."
72Again Peter denied it, this time with an
oath. "I don't even know the man," he said.
73But after a while the men who had been
standing there came over to him and said,
"We know you are one of his disciples, for we
can tell by your Galilean accent."
74Peter began to curse and swear. "I don't
even know the man," he said.
And immediately the cock crowed. 75Then
Peter remembered what Jesus had said, "Before the cock crows, you will deny me three
times." And he went away, crying bitterly.

CHAPTER 27
The Council Condemns Jesus
When it was morning, the chief priests and Jewish leaders met again to discuss how to induce the Roman government to sentence
Jesus to death. 2Then they sent him in chains
to Pilate, the Roman governor.

Judas Hangs Himself
3About that time Judas, who betrayed him, when he saw that Jesus had been condemned to die, changed his mind and deeply regretted what he had done, and brought back the money to the chief priests and other Jewish leaders.
4"I have sinned," he declared, "for I have betrayed an innocent man."
"That's your problem," they retorted.

5Then he threw the money onto the floor of the Temple and went out and hanged himself. 6The chief priests picked the money up. "We can't put it in the collection," they said, "since it's against our laws to accept money paid for murder."

7They talked it over and finally decided to buy a certain field where the clay was used by potters, and to make it into a cemetery for foreigners who died in Jerusalem. 8That is why the cemetery is still called "The Field of Blood."

9This fulfilled the prophecy of Jeremiah which says,

> "They took the thirty pieces of silver—the price at which he was valued by the people of Israel—10and purchased a field from the potters as the Lord directed me."

Jesus Is Tried by Pilate

11Now Jesus was standing before Pilate, the Roman governor. "Are you the Jews' Messiah?" the governor asked him.

"Yes," Jesus replied.

12But when the chief priests and other Jewish leaders made their many accusations against him, Jesus remained silent.

13"Don't you hear what they are saying?" Pilate demanded.

14But Jesus said nothing, much to the governor's surprise.

15Now the governor's custom was to release one Jewish prisoner each year during the Passover celebration—anyone they wanted. 16This year there was a particularly notorious criminal in jail named Barabbas, 17and as the crowds gathered before Pilate's house that morning he asked them, "Which shall I release to you—Barabbas, or Jesus your Messiah?" 18For he knew very well that the Jewish leaders had arrested Jesus out of envy because of his popularity with the people.

19Just then, as he was presiding over the court, Pilate's wife sent him this message: "Leave that good man alone; for I had a terrible nightmare concerning him last night."

20Meanwhile the chief priests and Jewish officials persuaded the crowds to ask for Barabbas' release, and for Jesus' death. 21So when the governor asked again, "Which of these two shall I release to you?" the crowd shouted back their reply: "Barabbas!"

22"Then what shall I do with Jesus, your Messiah?" Pilate asked.

And they shouted, "Crucify him!"

23"Why?" Pilate demanded. "What has he done wrong?" But they kept shouting, "Crucify! Crucify!"

24When Pilate saw that he wasn't getting anywhere and that a riot was developing, he sent for a bowl of water and washed his hands before the crowd, saying, "I am innocent of the blood of this good man. The responsibility is yours!"

25And the mob yelled back, "His blood be on us and on our children!"

26Then Pilate released Barabbas to them. And after he had whipped Jesus, he gave him to the Roman soldiers to take away and crucify.

Roman Soldiers Mock Jesus

27But first they took him into the armory and called out the entire contingent. 28They stripped him and put a scarlet robe on him, 29and made a crown from long thorns and put it on his head, and placed a stick in his right hand as a scepter and knelt before him in mockery. "Hail, King of the Jews," they yelled. 30And they spat on him and grabbed the stick and beat him on the head with it.

31After the mockery, they took off the robe and put his own garment on him again, and took him out to crucify him.

Jesus Is Hung on the Cross

32As they were on the way to the execution grounds they came across a man from Cyrene, in Africa—Simon was his name—and

---

27:11-26 Pontius Pilate's handling of Jesus' trial indicates that he was a man consumed with pleasing others. Although he was convinced that Jesus was innocent and righteous (27:24), he bowed to public opinion and the special interest groups outside his residence. Pilate was a classic example of someone in need of recovery who knew the right thing to do, but did not have the courage to follow through and risk angering others. Since it is impossible to please everyone all the time, we must make sure that what we are doing is honest and pleasing to God. We should be more concerned about sinning against God than about angering someone who is trying to manipulate us.

27:26-54 The narrative of Jesus' crucifixion and death records one act of brutal abuse after another. Jesus was beaten, ridiculed, tortured, and killed. Thus, he can directly understand the feelings of others who have been abused or oppressed. Jesus can also redeem oppressors or abusers who come to faith, as did the soldiers and their sergeant at the cross. Jesus' death and resurrection were intended to bring deliverance for everyone.

forced him to carry Jesus' cross. 33Then they went out to an area known as Golgotha, that is, "Skull Hill," 34where the soldiers gave him drugged wine to drink; but when he had tasted it, he refused.

35After the crucifixion, the soldiers threw dice to divide up his clothes among themselves. 36Then they sat around and watched him as he hung there. 37And they put a sign above his head, "This is Jesus, the King of the Jews."

38Two robbers were also crucified there that morning, one on either side of him. 39And the people passing by hurled abuse, shaking their heads at him and saying, 40"So! You can destroy the Temple and build it again in three days, can you? Well, then, come on down from the cross if you are the Son of God!"

41-43And the chief priests and Jewish leaders also mocked him. "He saved others," they scoffed, "but he can't save himself! So you are the King of Israel, are you? Come down from the cross and we'll believe you! He trusted God—let God show his approval by delivering him! Didn't he say, 'I am God's Son'?"

44And the robbers also threw the same in his teeth.

Jesus Dies on the Cross

45That afternoon, the whole earth was covered with darkness for three hours, from noon until three o'clock.

46About three o'clock, Jesus shouted, "Eli, Eli, lama sabachthani?" which means, "My God, my God, why have you forsaken me?"

47Some of the bystanders misunderstood and thought he was calling for Elijah. 48One of them ran and filled a sponge with sour wine and put it on a stick and held it up to him to drink. 49But the rest said, "Leave him alone. Let's see whether Elijah will come and save him."

50Then Jesus shouted out again, dismissed his spirit, and died.

51And look! The curtain secluding the Holiest Place in the Temple was split apart from top to bottom; and the earth shook, and rocks broke, 52and tombs opened, and many godly men and women who had died came back to life again. 53After Jesus' resurrection, they left the cemetery and went into Jerusalem, and appeared to many people there.

54The soldiers at the crucifixion and their sergeant were terribly frightened by the earthquake and all that happened. They exclaimed, "Surely this was God's Son."

55And many women who had come down from Galilee with Jesus to care for him were watching from a distance. 56Among them were Mary Magdalene and Mary the mother of James and Joseph, and the mother of James and John (the sons of Zebedee).

Jesus Is Placed in the Tomb

57When evening came, a rich man from Arimathea named Joseph, one of Jesus' followers, 58went to Pilate and asked for Jesus' body. And Pilate issued an order to release it to him. 59Joseph took the body and wrapped it in a clean linen cloth, 60and placed it in his own new rock-hewn tomb, and rolled a great stone across the entrance as he left. 61Both Mary Magdalene and the other Mary were sitting nearby watching.

62The next day—at the close of the first day of the Passover ceremonies—the chief priests and Pharisees went to Pilate, 63and told him, "Sir, that liar once said, 'After three days I will come back to life again.' 64So we request an order from you sealing the tomb until the third day, to prevent his disciples from coming and stealing his body and then telling everyone he came back to life! If that happens, we'll be worse off than we were at first."

27:57-60 Joseph of Arimathea was a secret disciple who came out of the closet at a crisis point (see John 19:38). He was like the people who toy with recovery in a limited and private sense, but then come to the point of decision where they either have to reject their program or make a deeper commitment to it. Joseph's willingness to approach Pilate, as well as his generous burial of Jesus, indicates that he took the step toward faith and a stronger commitment. What kind of crisis will it take to inspire us to devote our life wholeheartedly to God and his program of recovery?

27:62–28:15 The religious leaders went to a lot of trouble to be free of Jesus' message. They spent time and energy trying to discredit him in front of the crowds. Then they plotted his murder. When they caught him, they tried to come up with witnesses and then had to convince Rome that Jesus was worthy of the death penalty. Once Jesus was dead, the leaders feared he would come back to life, either in fact or through rumor, so they got permission to seal and guard the tomb. Finally, they had to come up with a story to explain the disappearance of Jesus' body. Obviously the easier path would have been to accept Jesus' message and make the appropriate changes in their lives and beliefs. We must make sure we don't become so hardened by denial that we, like the Jewish leaders, go to great lengths to avoid accepting the lifesaving message of the gospel.

65"Use your own Temple police," Pilate told
them. "They can guard it safely enough."
66So they sealed the stone and posted
guards to protect it from intrusion.

CHAPTER 28

Jesus Rises from the Dead

Early on Sunday morning, as the new day was
dawning, Mary Magdalene and the other
Mary went out to the tomb.
2Suddenly there was a great earthquake; for
an angel of the Lord came down from heaven
and rolled aside the stone and sat on it. 3His
face shone like lightning and his clothing was
a brilliant white. 4The guards shook with fear
when they saw him, and fell into a dead faint.
5Then the angel spoke to the women.
"Don't be frightened!" he said. "I know you
are looking for Jesus, who was crucified, 6but
he isn't here! For he has come back to life
again, just as he said he would. Come in and
see where his body was lying. . . . 7And now,
go quickly and tell his disciples that he has
risen from the dead, and that he is going to
Galilee to meet them there. That is my message to them."
8The women ran from the tomb, badly
frightened, but also filled with joy, and rushed
to find the disciples to give them the angel's
message. 9And as they were running, suddenly Jesus was there in front of them!

"Good morning!" he said. And they fell to the ground before him, holding his feet and worshiping him.
10Then Jesus said to them, "Don't be frightened! Go tell my brothers to leave at once for Galilee, to meet me there."

The Guards Are Bribed

11As the women were on the way into the city,
some of the Temple police who had been
guarding the tomb went to the chief priests
and told them what had happened. 12,13A
meeting of all the Jewish leaders was called,
and it was decided to bribe the police to say
they had all been asleep when Jesus' disciples
came during the night and stole his body.
14"If the governor hears about it," the
Council promised, "we'll stand up for you
and everything will be all right."
15So the police accepted the bribe and said
what they were told to. Their story spread
widely among the Jews and is still believed by
them to this very day.

Jesus Commissions His Disciples

16Then the eleven disciples left for Galilee,
going to the mountain where Jesus had said
they would find him. 17There they met him
and worshiped him—but some of them
weren't sure it really was Jesus!
18He told his disciples, "I have been given
all authority in heaven and earth. 19Therefore
go and make disciples in all the nations, baptizing them into the name of the Father and
of the Son and of the Holy Spirit, 20and then
teach these new disciples to obey all the commands I have given you; and be sure of this—
that I am with you always, even to the end of
the world."

28:16-20 Some disciples adjusted to the new reality of Jesus' resurrection quite readily, while others were more reticent. But Jesus' resurrection life was not an end in itself, nor was it given for just his closest disciples. The message of new life through faith in the crucified and resurrected Christ was to be offered to all the nations of the world. Those who by faith enter true spiritual recovery are baptized to display their commitment. Continual instruction in the faith helps those in recovery grow spiritually. God's recovery process is available until Jesus returns at the end of the age.

REFLECTIONS ON MATTHEW

insights ABOUT THE PERSON OF JESUS

The mention of Tamar, Rahab, Ruth, and Bathsheba in Jesus' lineage in **Matthew 1:1-16** is significant. Each of these women was almost certainly non-Jewish in ethnic background. Yet God used them along the way to prepare for the coming of the Jewish Messiah. Similarly, God often employs people from diverse and unusual backgrounds to accomplish his purposes. His grace is stronger than the presumed limitations of our past. He can use us regardless of our background.

In **Matthew 3:13-15** Jesus was baptized by John the Baptist. Jesus had no real reason to follow John's call to baptism because he had never sinned and had no reason to repent. However, Jesus proceeded to be baptized anyway because it was the right thing to do, and his actions modeled the importance of baptism to others. We who seek recovery need examples of those who do the right things for the right reasons, thus modeling a balanced life. As we proceed in our own recovery, we can become models for others in need of recovery. Being an example for others through word and deed will not only help others, but it will also encourage us to persevere in our own recovery.

In **Matthew 4:23-25** we discover that Jesus offers healing and restoration, not just physically, but also spiritually and interpersonally. He provides recovery from the pain of abuse and dysfunctional relationships, areas that trouble an ever-increasing mass of people. Such recovery is extended as part and parcel of the gospel of faith in Jesus Christ. True recovery is open to all. No part of our life is beyond his healing touch.

insights CONCERNING OBSTACLES TO RECOVERY

In **Matthew 1:18-25** we find Joseph in a difficult predicament. His fiancée, Mary, had become pregnant, and Joseph was thinking about how he could break their engagement quietly. But, when Joseph was shown that God was responsible for the pregnancy, he immediately changed his decision about breaking off the engagement with Mary. He married her just as God had requested, despite the rumors that would be sure to surround their marriage. Pride can easily become an obstacle to the restoration of our damaged relationships. We should resist the urgings of pride and do what God wants us to do, just as Joseph did.

When we enter recovery, we should not mistakenly think that our faith and spiritual growth will insulate us from temptation. On the contrary, in **Matthew 4:1-2** Jesus was actually led into the wilderness by the Holy Spirit for a prolonged siege of temptation. This should serve as a fair warning that temptation may follow quickly on the heels of a spiritual high. God often uses such trials in our life to remind us of how helpless we are without him.

In **Matthew 5:10-12** we are reminded that persecution can be a real problem for us as we try to live by God's principles. Old friends may try to intimidate us into giving up on recovery. Family members may be threatened by the changes we are making and do what they can to discourage us. We need to realize that it is more important to please God than other people. Then, as we do things God's way, we will be set free from our destructive and codependent relationships. Then we can begin to build healthy relationships with others and continue to strengthen our all-important relationship with God.

In **Matthew 6:19-34** Jesus made it clear that living for personal gain will only lead to great anxiety. Materialism and anxiety are two enemies of recovery. They often work together to lead us away from a balanced life. We need to realize that the essence of life is not found in the possession of things, and that worry about the future availability of material things is never helpful. We are powerless to change the future and must trust God to take care of us and empower our recovery. As we entrust our life to him, we will no longer need to worry about what is around the corner.

People who refuse to admit their own need for recovery are usually the first to stand in the way of someone else's recovery. Instead of praising God for the miracle that Jesus performed, in **Matthew 12:9-12** the Pharisees judged Jesus for breaking the Sabbath laws. To the Pharisees, it was more important to preserve their legalistic observances than to see a man healed of his deformity. They wanted to be ruled by their interpretations of the law and rejected the rule of the compassionate Messiah-King. There will be people who oppose our attempts at recovery, doing anything they can to keep us enslaved to our addictions. We should make every effort to overcome our dependencies, regardless of the pressures of the people that surround us. And with God's help, no obstacles are too great to overcome.

In **Matthew 14:1-11** we are told that John the Baptist was arrested because he had condemned Herod Antipas for marrying his brother's wife, Herodias. Rather than admitting his sin, Herod put John in prison, hoping to silence him. Herodias wanted John silenced too, only she was more vicious than her husband and wanted him executed. In the end, Herod was too weak to refuse his wife's request, and the prophet was beheaded. Our shame from one sin often leads us to commit greater sins. To avoid the downward spiral, we must have the courage to admit our smaller sins and problems before they grow larger. As we turn our sins and failures over to God, we can be confident that we will receive his healing help.

insights ABOUT HONESTY AND DENIAL

It is clear from **Matthew 3:5-9** that not everyone who went to listen to John the Baptist wanted to repent and find a new life. John saw that the Pharisees, and others like them, were merely going through the motions, trusting external appearances for their salvation. Similarly, some of us who claim to be entering recovery are simply going through the motions, appearing to fix the addiction while not changing the problems that drive our dependencies. If this is the case in our life, we are headed for a painful relapse. We need to begin with an honest assessment of our weaknesses and failures before we can receive God's help and forgiveness.

In **Matthew 3:7-11** John the Baptist confronted the Pharisees with the denial in their lives. These religious leaders had blinded themselves to the sins of their hearts and believed themselves to be beyond the reach of God's judgment. Perhaps we once acted as if the consequences of our actions would never catch up with us. Our denial may have been so deep that we weren't even aware of the serious consequences we would have to face. It is only a matter of time before God sees fit to take an axe to "unproductive trees"—those who are not following him. However, for those of us willing to truly repent, God fuels our recovery by the power of his Holy Spirit. The choice is up to us: either we continue as we are and await God's judgment, or we turn from our present life-style and enter recovery, counting on God's Spirit to help us change.

In **Matthew 7:1-5** Jesus warned against our tendency of being critical of others. It is easy to hide from the sins and dependencies ("boards") in our own life by pointing out the small failures ("specks") in the lives of others. This kind of denial destroys the relationships we need for recovery and blinds us to our own sin and its destructive consequences. To be truly helpful to others, we must first recognize that we have sin in our own life, and then we need to deal with that sin. After humbling ourself in this way, we will be ready to confront others about their need for recovery.

The tax collectors in Judea during the time of Jesus were Jews who had sold out to the oppressive Roman government. They used their position to extort money from their own people. So, for good reason, they were hated by the Jewish population, who considered them traitors to God and homeland. In **Matthew 9:9-13** we see that the Jews were surprised that Jesus would even speak to such people. Matthew, the author of this Gospel, and his friends were surprisingly open to the gospel of grace and forgiveness. As dysfunctional as they were, they admitted their need and responded with humility to Jesus. On the other hand, the Pharisees clung to their self-righteous denial, not recognizing their own desperate need for recovery. It is not how we appear to others that matters; it is whether or not we are willing to let God heal us from the power of sin in our life.

In **Matthew 10:14-15** we discover that the danger of denial is eternal in its ramifications. Those who refuse the offer of recovery in Christ are making a huge mistake. This message may seem threatening at the moment, but it is meant to bring peace and serenity. In the end, we who have tried to establish a comfort zone in our ever-increasing denial will have to answer to God at the time of our final judgment.

insights ABOUT GOD'S PRIORITIES

The Beatitudes in **Matthew 5:1-12** contain much of what God desires of us as we seek to follow his will for our life. This life-style affirms God's perspective, priorities, and boundaries. As we look over God's program in this passage, we may wonder how anyone could live up to it. The truth is, no one can do it without God's help. Following God's program requires wisdom and grace from above. But the life-style found in these verses can replace our warped human outlook with God's enduring perspective.

In **Matthew 6:1-4** we find that God's priorities are very different from ours. God is clearly more interested in our quiet service of others than our outward success in worldly terms. All of us have both public and private lives, but the reward systems for each are very different. While we may succeed to some degree by becoming famous or wealthy, we will never receive further reward from God for our public success. However, if we humbly seek to help others, we will be openly rewarded by our heavenly Father. What seems private and unnoticed by other people is public, even center stage, before God.

✲insights INTO SHARING THE GOOD NEWS

In **Matthew 5:13-16** Jesus described what we should be like. If we have been delivered by God's power, we are witnesses to his power to save. We can carry the light of his good news to people imprisoned in the darkness of addiction and sin. Dysfunctional behaviors and warped relationships abound, in part due to our lack of healthy, seasoned, radiant role models. People are desperate for seasoning and light. We can make a significant impact on individuals, relationships, and even societal structures if we are willing to shine our spiritual light for others to see. As we experience God's deliverance, our recovery calls us to share the story with others. This will not only extend hope to hurting people, but it will also encourage us as we face new trials ahead.

Jesus had great compassion for those who had no protection or guidance. So in **Matthew 9:36–10:8** we find Jesus training his closest disciples to help fill the need. They were to go out and use God's power to offer healing and encouragement for those in need of physical or spiritual recovery. They were not expected to reach everyone, but they were to make a difference in at least one needy target group. As we seek to share our story of recovery with others, we cannot expect to reach everyone with the good news of recovery. We can, however, share the message with a few, who will also share their story with others. As we use our own recovery to encourage the recovery of others, we will start a chain reaction that will touch the lives of many.

The story recorded in **Matthew 25:14-30** is about using our gifts wisely, and it provides both needed encouragement and sobering reality to those of us in recovery. Even though this parable is about money, it can, by extension, also refer to God-given abilities. Everyone has been given abilities of various kinds by God; no one is untalented or worthless. That should encourage us. On the other hand, we are each responsible to use our abilities for God. After suffering for years as a slave to a destructive addiction, some of us may wonder if we have anything to offer. Yet even if we have nothing else, we do have our story to tell. As we share our experience of deliverance, we will give others hope for recovery. Our years of suffering may become the gift of life to someone in need.

✲insights ABOUT PRAYER

In **Matthew 6:9-13** Jesus gave his disciples a model prayer to follow. This prayer, however, is more than just a model for our prayers: it is a model for our life in recovery. We are to acknowledge and praise God's supremacy and desire his Kingdom to enter into this world. We are to ask for God's will to be achieved, both in our life and in the world in general. God's daily provision for us is another petition important for recovery. Also, we must ask for forgiveness for our sins while forgiving those who have wronged us in the past. Finally, God wants us to ask for protection from the evil temptations we face each day. If we find we are praying these things and living them in our walk with God, we are truly on the path of recovery.

✲insights CONCERNING TRUE FAITH

In **Matthew 7:24-27** we are told that two kinds of life-building foundations are available. One foundation is as solid as rock—the foundation of faith in Jesus Christ. The other foundation is like shifting sand—the foundation of human pride and selfish endeavor. Our life might be outwardly impressive, but if it is built on the wrong foundation, difficult circumstances will soon level what we have built. Like a fragile house of cards, our life will come crashing down. How much better to build our life on the solid foundation of faith in Jesus Christ. Then when the inevitable storms of life come, we will not be moved.

In **Matthew 11:25-30** we are told of the importance of childlike faith. Only when we come to Jesus as a little child can we find recovery and relief for our emotional pain. Many of us think we can work things out our own way. In doing this, however, we miss the simple truth that God alone has the power to enable our recovery. We cannot even begin the recovery process until we are willing to admit how powerless we are; this is the importance of childlike faith. Children are powerless and are very aware of that fact. As a result, they entrust themselves to their parents each and every day. As we recognize how powerless we are over our dependencies, we can entrust ourself to God's loving care. He has all the power we need for a full recovery.

In **Matthew 14:25-33** we find that Jesus walked on water and then enabled Peter, through faith, to do the same. Before we began the process of recovery, our life was as turbulent as a stormy sea. When we trusted God to effect our recovery, we, like Peter, stepped out in faith into the storm. As long as we hold on to our faith and keep our eyes on Jesus, we will succeed, skimming over the waves of life. It is when we focus on the troubled waters around us and forget God's assistance that we start to sink and are overwhelmed by our dependencies and flaws of character. If we want to make continued progress, we need to keep our eyes on God.

In **Matthew 15:21-28** a Gentile woman showed great perseverance and faith, and Jesus rewarded her for it. When we seek recovery, we must truly believe that God is able to effect our recovery. We also must be prepared to persist in our program, not giving up even when there seems to be little hope for success. God will reward us in our efforts if we are fully committed to following his will for our life and prove it by our actions.

MARK

THE BIG PICTURE

A. JESUS PREPARES FOR SERVICE (1:1-13)
B. JESUS SERVES THROUGH WORD AND DEED (1:14–13:37)
   1. Jesus Serves in Galilee (1:14–9:50)
   2. Jesus Serves beyond Jerusalem (10:1-45)
   3. Jesus Serves in Jerusalem (10:46–13:37)
C. JESUS SERVES THROUGH SELF-SACRIFICE (14:1–16:20)

When our life was out of control, we responded to our trials in various ways: with anger, bitterness, or rebellion. Our addictions determined our behavior and attitudes. We eventually realized that our life had become unmanageable and that we were destroying not only ourself, but our loved ones, too. We needed to break the cycle, but we were powerless to do so.

The Gospel of Mark is written for people like us; it shows that Jesus is powerful and wants to help us. In this Gospel we see Jesus' power displayed again and again: he raised the dead, gave sight to the blind, restored deformed limbs, made lame people walk, cast out demons, healed incurable skin diseases, and quieted stormy waters. Though Mark is the shortest Gospel, it records more miracles than any of the others. It proves that Jesus is a powerful Savior and is more than able to help suffering people.

This Gospel also emphasizes the fact that Jesus wants to help us. Jesus spent his energy to the point of exhaustion in order to heal those who came to him for help. By recording a rapid succession of vivid pictures of Jesus in action, the Gospel writer has shown that Jesus came to help us. And this truth is driven home by Jesus' willingness to suffer a painful death to free us from our bondage to sin.

Jesus has power over the problems that bind us. He is more powerful than our dependencies, problems, and weaknesses. He has the power to help us all with recovery, no matter how terrible our past. All we have to do is look to him and admit that we need his help.

THE BOTTOM LINE

PURPOSE: To encourage us to continue trusting and serving God, especially through life's difficulties. AUTHOR: John Mark. AUDIENCE: The Christians in Rome. DATE WRITTEN: Probably between A.D. 55 and 65. SETTING: The Roman Empire had unified the known world, and its use of a common language made conditions ideal for the spread of the gospel in written form. KEY VERSE: "For even I, the Messiah, am not here to be served, but to help others, and to give my life as a ransom for many" (10:45). SPECIAL FEATURES: The Gospel of Mark is characterized by its fast-paced narrative. KEY PEOPLE AND RELATIONSHIPS: Jesus with his disciples, especially Peter.

RECOVERY THEMES

Jesus as the Servant: The Twelfth Step tells us that our recovery should lead us to be servants and to share our story of deliverance with others. Real greatness in God's eyes is proven by a willingness to serve and to sacrifice for others. Jesus didn't come as a conquering king; he came as a servant. He chose to obey his Father and to die for us. When personal ambition and a hunger for power control our life, we live in contradiction to our recovery and to God's will for our life.

The Power of God: The Gospel of Mark is filled with amazing events that display the awesome power of God in Jesus. Mark recorded more miracles than sermons. He wanted us to see God's power in action. The more we are convinced that Jesus is God, the more we will see his power and his love in action in our own life. His greatest miracles are still those that involve forgiveness, healing of relationships, and the restoration of a lost or wasted past. The same power we see in Mark's Gospel is available to us today.

Recovery Is Not the Goal: Some people are afraid of recovery because it seems all-consuming. They have a distorted image of what recovery is all about. Our goal is not recovery; our goal is spiritual and emotional growth, accompanied by sacrificial service. That is one reason we can never claim to have recovered. Jesus set the pace for us with his example of service. His whole purpose in coming was to serve, not to be served. That principle—that we seek to give away what we have gained—is an essential part of our recovery.

Sharing the Message: There is no such thing as a secret disciple or a private recovery. Discipleship and recovery take place within relationships. And God's Good News is meant to be shared. As we share the joys and struggles of our own recovery, we encourage others in their recovery. And the message transcends national, racial, and economic barriers, reaching out to those who are willing to admit their powerlessness. The message of our recovery is worth sharing with others.

CHAPTER 1

John Prepares the Way

Here begins the wonderful story of Jesus the Messiah, the Son of God.

2In the book written by the prophet Isaiah,
God announced that he would send his Son to
earth, and that a special messenger would arrive first to prepare the world for his coming.
3"This messenger will live out in the barren
wilderness," Isaiah said, "and will proclaim
that everyone must straighten out his life to
be ready for the Lord's arrival."
4This messenger was John the Baptist. He
lived in the wilderness and taught that all
should be baptized as a public announcement
of their decision to turn their backs on sin, so
that God could forgive them. 5People from
Jerusalem and from all over Judea traveled out
into the Judean wastelands to see and hear
John, and when they confessed their sins he
baptized them in the Jordan River. 6His
clothes were woven from camel's hair and he
wore a leather belt; locusts and wild honey
were his food. 7Here is a sample of his preaching:
"Someone is coming soon who is far
greater than I am, so much greater that I am
not even worthy to be his slave. 8I baptize you
with water but he will baptize you with God's
Holy Spirit!"

John Baptizes Jesus

9Then one day Jesus came from Nazareth in
Galilee, and was baptized by John there in the
Jordan River. 10The moment Jesus came up out
of the water, he saw the heavens open and the
Holy Spirit in the form of a dove descending
on him, 11and a voice from heaven said, "You
are my beloved Son; you are my Delight."

Satan Tempts Jesus

12,13Immediately the Holy Spirit urged Jesus
into the desert. There, for forty days, alone
except for desert animals, he was subjected to
Satan's temptations to sin. And afterwards the
angels came and cared for him.

Jesus Preaches in Galilee

14Later on, after John was arrested by King
Herod, Jesus went to Galilee to preach God's
Good News.

1:1-13 Only belief in a Power greater than ourself can restore us to sanity. That's how John the Baptist saw Jesus—as one far greater than he was. Jesus demonstrated his great power through victory over Satan and his temptations. Jesus' victory over temptation should encourage us as we face temptation in our own life. With his help, we can stand up to anything. Under our own power, we are helpless against the power of our dependencies. We can tap into God's power by making a conscious decision to turn our back on sin (1:4) and by entrusting our life to the care of God.

SIMON PETER

Simon the fisherman was reckless, vacillating, and often thoughtless. We would never nickname such a person *Peter,* which means "Rock." Jesus did. What greater evidence could there be that Jesus accepted Simon as he was but also had a vision for the man he would become? By the end of Simon's life his nickname, Peter, appropriately described his steadfast maturity. What an amazing transformation took place in that burly fisherman!

Most of us readily identify with Simon Peter. His intentions were usually good, but he was impetuous in speech and impulsive in action. Instead of standing in awe at the Transfiguration, he blurted out the first idea that came into his head. When Jesus revealed that his divine mission would involve a painful death, Peter rashly told Jesus to stop talking that way. At the Last Supper he brazenly objected to letting Jesus wash his feet. When Jesus was arrested, Peter bravely but brashly cut off the ear of the high priest's servant. Finally, at a critical point in his life, Peter denied Jesus three times. Even as Jesus was restoring Peter from this failure, Peter's attention was on John rather than on what God was doing for him.

Later in Simon's life we see what Jesus saw when he called him "Rock." He presided over the meeting to select a successor to Judas. At Pentecost he preached publicly about Jesus despite the opposition he knew he would face. Peter worked several miracles and was himself miraculously rescued from prison. Peter was the apostle who had the spiritual insight to proclaim the great confession at Caesarea Philippi, stating clearly that Jesus Christ was the only means to salvation.

In Simon Peter's life we see hope for our transformation and recovery. He was amazingly transformed by God, but we should remember that he was never made perfect. The apostle Paul described in Galatians 2:11-14 how Peter acted hypocritically. Despite his imperfections, however, his transformation had a profound effect on the world around him, and his words, actions, and letters became a significant part of the early church's spiritual foundation.

STRENGTHS AND ACCOMPLISHMENTS:
- Simon's natural boldness was used to spread the Good News of Jesus Christ.
- He was the recognized leader and spokesman for the twelve disciples.
- He was inspired to write letters to encourage believers (1 and 2 Peter).
- His natural enthusiasm was later channeled into disciplined courage.

WEAKNESSES AND MISTAKES:
- Simon often spoke and acted before he thought about the consequences.
- His temperament was mercurial; he quickly moved from professed loyalty to betrayal.
- Even after his transformation, he at least once allowed a situation to govern his actions (Galatians 2:11-14).

LESSONS FROM HIS LIFE:
- Jesus Christ has enough power to transform even the most unlikely people.
- God can transform our faults into powerful tools for use in his Kingdom.
- When people make themselves available, they can always be used by God.

KEY VERSE:
"You are Peter, a stone; and upon this rock I will build my church; and all the powers of hell shall not prevail against it" (Matthew 16:18).

There is extensive biblical material on Simon Peter in the Gospels and Acts 1–15. In Paul's letters, Peter is mentioned in 1 Corinthians 1:12; 3:22; 9:5; 15:5; and Galatians 1:18; 2:7-14. Some material about him may also be gleaned from his two letters, 1 and 2 Peter.

15"At last the time has come!" he announced. "God's Kingdom is near! Turn from your sins and act on this glorious news!"

Four Fishermen Follow Jesus

16One day as Jesus was walking along the shores of the Sea of Galilee, he saw Simon and his brother Andrew fishing with nets, for they were commercial fishermen.

17Jesus called out to them, "Come, follow me! And I will make you fishermen for the souls of men!" 18At once they left their nets and went along with him.

19A little farther up the beach, he saw Zebedee's sons, James and John, in a boat mending their nets. 20He called them too, and immediately they left their father Zebedee in the boat with the hired men and went with him.

Jesus Teaches with Authority

21 Jesus and his companions now arrived at the town of Capernaum and on Saturday morning went into the Jewish place of worship—the synagogue—where he preached. 22 The congregation was surprised at his sermon because he spoke as an authority and didn't try to prove his points by quoting others—quite unlike what they were used to hearing!

23 A man possessed by a demon was present and began shouting, 24 "Why are you bothering us, Jesus of Nazareth—have you come to destroy us demons? I know who you are—the holy Son of God!"

25 Jesus curtly commanded the demon to say no more and to come out of the man. 26 At that the evil spirit screamed and convulsed the man violently and left him. 27 Amazement gripped the audience and they began discussing what had happened.

"What sort of new religion is this?" they asked excitedly. "Why, even evil spirits obey his orders!"

28 The news of what he had done spread quickly through that entire area of Galilee.

Jesus Heals Many

29,30 Then, leaving the synagogue, he and his disciples went over to Simon and Andrew's home, where they found Simon's mother-in-law sick in bed with a high fever. They told Jesus about her right away. 31 He went to her bedside, and as he took her by the hand and helped her to sit up, the fever suddenly left, and she got up and prepared dinner for them!

32,33 By sunset the courtyard was filled with the sick and demon-possessed, brought to him for healing; and a huge crowd of people from all over the city of Capernaum gathered outside the door to watch. 34 So Jesus healed great numbers of sick folk that evening and ordered many demons to come out of their victims. (But he refused to allow the demons to speak, because they knew who he was.)

Jesus Ministers throughout Galilee

35 The next morning he was up long before daybreak and went out alone into the wilderness to pray.

36,37 Later, Simon and the others went out to find him, and told him, "Everyone is asking for you."

38 But he replied, "We must go on to other towns as well, and give my message to them too, for that is why I came."

39 So he traveled throughout the province of Galilee, preaching in the synagogues and releasing many from the power of demons.

Jesus Heals a Leper

40 Once a leper came and knelt in front of him and begged to be healed. "If you want to, you can make me well again," he pled.

41 And Jesus, moved with pity, touched him and said, "I want to! Be healed!" 42 Immediately the leprosy was gone—the man was healed!

43,44 Jesus then told him sternly, "Go and be examined immediately by the Jewish priest. Don't stop to speak to anyone along the way. Take along the offering prescribed by Moses for a leper who is healed, so that everyone will have proof that you are well again."

45 But as the man went on his way he began to shout the good news that he was healed; as a result, such throngs soon surrounded Jesus that he couldn't publicly enter a city anywhere, but had to stay out in the barren wastelands. And people from everywhere came to him there.

CHAPTER 2

Jesus Heals a Paralyzed Man

Several days later he returned to Capernaum, and the news of his arrival spread quickly through the city. 2 Soon the house where he was staying was so packed with visitors that there wasn't room for a single person more, not even outside the door. And he preached the Word to them. 3 Four men arrived carrying a paralyzed man on a stretcher. 4 They couldn't get to Jesus through the crowd, so they dug through the clay roof above his head and lowered the sick man on his stretcher, right down in front of Jesus.

5 When Jesus saw how strongly they believed that he would help, Jesus said to the sick man, "Son, your sins are forgiven!"

6 But some of the Jewish religious leaders said to themselves as they sat there, 7 "What?

1:35-39 If Jesus, the Son of God, took time from his busy schedule to pray to his Father, how much more do we need to do so. By placing a priority on prayer, Jesus was able to persevere in his ministry and keep from burning out. We who seek our own recovery, and recovery for others, can hardly get by without prayer. The busier the day ahead, the more we need to meditate on God's Word and pray for his strength and wisdom.

This is blasphemy! Does he think he is God? For only God can forgive sins."

[8]Jesus could read their minds and said to them at once, "Why does this bother you? [9-11]I, the Messiah, have the authority on earth to forgive sins. But talk is cheap—anybody could say that. So I'll prove it to you by healing this man." Then, turning to the paralyzed man, he commanded, "Pick up your stretcher and go on home, for you are healed!"

[12]The man jumped up, took the stretcher, and pushed his way through the stunned onlookers! Then how they praised God. "We've never seen anything like this before!" they all exclaimed.

Jesus Eats at Matthew's House

[13]Then Jesus went out to the seashore again and preached to the crowds that gathered around him. [14]As he was walking up the beach he saw Levi, the son of Alphaeus, sitting at his tax collection booth. "Come with me," Jesus told him. "Come be my disciple."

And Levi jumped to his feet and went along.

[15]That night Levi invited his fellow tax collectors and many other notorious sinners to be his dinner guests so that they could meet Jesus and his disciples. (There were many men of this type among the crowds that followed him.) [16]But when some of the Jewish religious leaders saw him eating with these men of ill repute, they said to his disciples, "How can he stand it, to eat with such scum?"

[17]When Jesus heard what they were saying, he told them, "Sick people need the doctor, not healthy ones! I haven't come to tell good people to repent, but the bad ones."

A Question about Fasting

[18]John's disciples and the Jewish leaders sometimes fasted, that is, went without food as part of their religion. One day some people came to Jesus and asked why his disciples didn't do this too.

[19]Jesus replied, "Do friends of the bridegroom refuse to eat at the wedding feast? Should they be sad while he is with them? [20]But some day he will be taken away from them, and then they will mourn. [21][Besides, going without food is part of the old way of doing things.] It is like patching an old garment with unshrunk cloth! What happens? The patch pulls away and leaves the hole worse than before. [22]You know better than to put new wine into old wineskins. They would burst. The wine would be spilled out and the wineskins ruined. New wine needs fresh wineskins."

Teachings about the Sabbath

[23]Another time, on a Sabbath day as Jesus and his disciples were walking through the fields, the disciples were breaking off heads of wheat and eating the grain.

[24]Some of the Jewish religious leaders said to Jesus, "They shouldn't be doing that! It's against our laws to work by harvesting grain on the Sabbath."

[25,26]But Jesus replied, "Didn't you ever hear about the time King David and his companions were hungry, and he went into the house of God—Abiathar was High Priest then—and

---

2:1-12 Jesus came not only to heal physical problems, but also to solve the sin problem. If we have not yet come to know Jesus, we are paralyzed in spirit, as powerless to help ourself as was this paralytic. If our faith is still too weak to carry us to the point of healing, the faith of "four friends" may be enough to get us there. Notice that it was not enough for Jesus to mouth the words of forgiveness; he had to prove his authority and intent with action. In the same way, it is not enough for us to mouth words of faith. We must take responsible action if we expect spiritual cleansing and physical healing.

2:13-17 Because of their reputed cheating and support of pagan Rome, tax collectors were considered notorious sinners by the Jews, especially by the self-righteous religious leaders. But it was for people like this that Jesus came to bring his salvation. Levi (Matthew) proved he meant business with Jesus by immediately witnessing to his friends, colleagues, and collaborators in sin. Some may question whether a person so new and immature in his faith should be telling his story to others. But the account here illustrates the truth that our recovery is strengthened when we share our story with others, no matter the extent of our knowledge, skill, or experience.

2:18-22 The old wineskins of Jewish religious practice were too rigid to carry the expansive, life-changing message of God's love in Jesus Christ. Religious activities are never enough, unless they are coupled with genuine repentance. We must start by recognizing the failures in our life and then look to the only one who is able to make things right again—God in Jesus Christ. If we look to him for help, he is more than able to forgive us and get us back on the right track. God will make our hard heart open and pliable, like a fresh wineskin, so we can receive his gifts of grace.

they ate the special bread only priests were allowed to eat? That was against the law too. 27But the Sabbath was made to benefit man, and not man to benefit the Sabbath. 28And I, the Messiah, have authority even to decide what men can do on Sabbath days!"

CHAPTER 3

Jesus Heals on the Sabbath

While in Capernaum Jesus went over to the synagogue again, and noticed a man there with a deformed hand.

2Since it was the Sabbath, Jesus' enemies watched him closely. Would he heal the man's hand? If he did, they planned to arrest him!

3Jesus asked the man to come and stand in front of the congregation. 4Then turning to his enemies he asked, "Is it all right to do kind deeds on Sabbath days? Or is this a day for doing harm? Is it a day to save lives or to destroy them?" But they wouldn't answer him. 5Looking around at them angrily, for he was deeply disturbed by their indifference to human need, he said to the man, "Reach out your hand." He did, and instantly his hand was healed!

6At once the Pharisees went away and met with the Herodians to discuss plans for killing Jesus.

Large Crowds Follow Jesus

7,8Meanwhile, Jesus and his disciples withdrew to the beach, followed by a huge crowd from all over Galilee, Judea, Jerusalem, Idumea, from beyond the Jordan River, and even from as far away as Tyre and Sidon. For the news about his miracles had spread far and wide and vast numbers came to see him for themselves.

9He instructed his disciples to bring around a boat and to have it standing ready to rescue him in case he was crowded off the beach. 10For there had been many healings that day and as a result great numbers of sick people were crowding around him, trying to touch him.

11And whenever those possessed by demons caught sight of him they would fall down before him shrieking, "You are the Son of God!" 12But he strictly warned them not to make him known.

Jesus Selects Twelve Disciples

13Afterwards he went up into the hills and summoned certain ones he chose, inviting them to come and join him there; and they did. 14,15Then he selected twelve of them to be his regular companions and to go out to preach and to cast out demons. 16-19These are the names of the twelve he chose: Simon (he renamed him "Peter"), James and John (the sons of Zebedee, but Jesus called them "Sons of Thunder"), Andrew, Philip, Bartholomew, Matthew, Thomas, James (the son of Alphaeus), Thaddaeus, Simon (a member of a political party advocating violent overthrow of the Roman government), Judas Iscariot (who later betrayed him).

Jesus Accused of Being of Satan

20When he returned to the house where he was staying, the crowds began to gather again, and soon it was so full of visitors that he couldn't even find time to eat. 21When his friends heard what was happening they came to try to take him home with them.

"He's out of his mind," they said.

22But the Jewish teachers of religion who had arrived from Jerusalem said, "His trouble is that he's possessed by Satan, king of demons. That's why demons obey him."

23Jesus summoned these men and asked them (using proverbs they all understood), "How can Satan cast out Satan? 24A kingdom divided against itself will collapse. 25A home filled with strife and division destroys itself. 26And if Satan is fighting against himself, how

---

3:7-19 Despite being rejected by the religious establishment, Jesus enjoyed an ever-growing following, even from places he had not yet ministered in. Nearly halfway through three years of public ministry, Jesus' popularity was at a high point. The great demands on Jesus for service may have prompted him to summon and appoint the twelve members of his close support group. Not even Jesus attempted to minister alone. We need to surround ourself with those who will support us and help us maintain what we have gained through recovery.

3:20-30 Although Satan causes a great deal of trouble in our world, God has power over him. And since Jesus is God, he has the power to work his will with Satan. Binding Satan's stronghold of demons and loosening his grip on our lives is the solemn work of recovery. There is no sin in our past so heinous that it cannot be forgiven, no hurt so deep that it cannot be healed. The one exception to this is "blasphemy against the Holy Spirit," which is the denial of God's power through his Son, Jesus Christ.

JAMES & JOHN

Sons of Thunder! Why would Jesus use such a powerful description for two Galilean fishermen, James and John? We are given a glimpse of their fiery personalities when, after they were rejected by the people of a Samaritan village, James and John asked Jesus if they should call down fire from heaven to consume the village. Jesus rebuked them for their impulse to retaliate.

Jesus worked in these brothers' lives so that they became people known not for anger and revenge, but for love and forgiveness. John, "the disciple Jesus loved," wrote powerful words on the importance of love. He had discovered that he didn't have to earn God's love, but that he could freely receive it and pass it on to others.

James was the first of the twelve disciples to give his life for his faith. He was killed in Jerusalem by order of Herod Agrippa. John became an important leader in the church of Asia Minor and was later exiled to the island of Patmos, where he wrote the book of Revelation. He apparently outlived the rest of the twelve disciples.

Though the two brothers had once been ambitious for personal advancement, they became ambitious to advance the lives of others by sharing God's love with them. The brothers had discovered that when we understand and experience God's love, we are free to live and grow. And as we grow and share our discovery with others, we can be used by God to touch the lives of many in need of God's healing help.

STRENGTHS AND ACCOMPLISHMENTS:
- With Peter, James and John formed the inner circle of Jesus' disciples.
- Both men were important leaders in the early church.
- John was inspired to write five New Testament books (The Gospel of John; 1, 2, 3 John; and Revelation).

WEAKNESSES AND MISTAKES:
- They apparently had a tendency to react angrily to anyone who opposed them.
- They selfishly tried to promote themselves ahead of the other disciples.

LESSONS FROM THEIR LIVES:
- It is important to experience God's love and act with love toward others.
- God can take our weaknesses and mold them into strengths.

KEY VERSES:
"Then [Jesus] selected twelve of them to be his regular companions. . . . These are the names of the twelve he chose: . . . James and John (the sons of Zebedee, but Jesus called them 'Sons of Thunder')" (Mark 3:14-19).

The stories of James and John are told in Matthew 4:21-22; 20:20-28; Mark 1:19; 3:13-19; 9:1-9; 10:35-40; Luke 9:49-56; John 13:23-25; 19:26-27; 21:20-24; Acts 4:1-23; 8:14-25; 12:2; and Revelation 1:1-2, 9; 22:8.

---

can he accomplish anything? He would never
survive. 27[Satan must be bound before his
demons are cast out], just as a strong man must be tied up before his house can be ransacked and his property robbed.
28"I solemnly declare that any sin of man can be forgiven, even blasphemy against me;
29but blasphemy against the Holy Spirit can never be forgiven. It is an eternal sin."
30He told them this because they were saying he did his miracles by Satan's power [instead of acknowledging it was by the Holy Spirit's power].

Jesus Describes His True Family

31,32Now his mother and brothers arrived at the crowded house where he was teaching, and they sent word for him to come out and talk with them. "Your mother and brothers are outside and want to see you," he was told.
33He replied, "Who is my mother? Who are
my brothers?" 34Looking at those around him he said, "These are my mother and brothers!
35Anyone who does God's will is my brother, and my sister, and my mother."

CHAPTER 4

A Story about Four Soils

Once again an immense crowd gathered around him on the beach as he was teaching, so he got into a boat and sat down and talked
from there. 2His usual method of teaching was to tell the people stories. One of them went like this:
3"Listen! A farmer decided to sow some
grain. As he scattered it across his field, 4some
of it fell on a path, and the birds came and picked it off the hard ground and ate it.
5,6Some fell on thin soil with underlying rock. It grew up quickly enough, but soon wilted beneath the hot sun and died because the roots had no nourishment in the shallow soil.
7Other seeds fell among thorns that shot up and crowded the young plants so that they
produced no grain. 8But some of the seeds fell
into good soil and yielded thirty times as

much as he had planted—some of it even sixty or a hundred times as much! [9]If you have ears, listen!"

Jesus Explains His Story

[10]Afterwards, when he was alone with the twelve and with his other disciples, they asked him, "What does your story mean?"

[11,12]He replied, "You are permitted to know some truths about the Kingdom of God that are hidden to those outside the Kingdom:

> 'Though they see and hear, they will not
> understand or turn to God, or be
> forgiven for their sins.'

[13]But if you can't understand *this* simple illustration, what will you do about all the others I am going to tell?

[14]"The farmer I talked about is anyone who brings God's message to others, trying to plant good seed within their lives. [15]The hard pathway, where some of the seed fell, represents the hard hearts of some of those who hear God's message; Satan comes at once to try to make them forget it. [16]The rocky soil represents the hearts of those who hear the message with joy, [17]but, like young plants in such soil, their roots don't go very deep, and though at first they get along fine, as soon as persecution begins, they wilt.

[18]"The thorny ground represents the hearts of people who listen to the Good News and receive it, [19]but all too quickly the attractions of this world and the delights of wealth, and the search for success and lure of nice things come in and crowd out God's message from their hearts, so that no crop is produced.

[20]"But the good soil represents the hearts of those who truly accept God's message and produce a plentiful harvest for God—thirty, sixty, or even a hundred times as much as was planted in their hearts." [21]Then he asked them, "When someone lights a lamp, does he put a box over it to shut out the light? Of course not! The light couldn't be seen or used. A lamp is placed on a stand to shine and be useful.

[22]"All that is now hidden will someday come to light. [23]If you have ears, listen! [24]And be sure to put into practice what you hear. The more you do this, the more you will understand what I tell you. [25]To him who has shall be given; from him who has not shall be taken away even what he has.

A Story about Planting Seed

[26]"Here is another story illustrating what the Kingdom of God is like:

"A farmer sowed his field [27]and went away, and as the days went by, the seeds grew and grew without his help. [28]For the soil made the seeds grow. First a leaf-blade pushed through, and later the wheat-heads formed and finally the grain ripened, [29]and then the farmer came at once with his sickle and harvested it."

A Story about a Mustard Seed

[30]Jesus asked, "How can I describe the Kingdom of God? What story shall I use to illustrate it? [31,32]It is like a tiny mustard seed!

4:1-20 Some welcome recovery, while others reject it. The mystery of this is revealed in the stories Jesus tells about the Kingdom, four of which are given in 4:1-34. God's Kingdom refers to God's hidden reign in the world, a reign that will be made visible at the return of Christ. This first story dramatizes varying responses to God's reign in the hearts of his people. As we proceed with recovery and learn to seek out God's will for us, we are placing ourself under the just and loving rule of God. And we can be sure that as we plow the soil of our heart through self-examination, we will experience a fruitful and meaningful life.

4:21-25 The lamp in this illustration represents the truth about Jesus. We hide that light every time we put a box over it. As we progress in recovery, it is important that we remove the boxes of guilt, bitterness, anger, shame, or denial that we hide behind. It is extremely important that we humbly share our story of pain and deliverance with others. We may need to start by taking a moral inventory of our life to uncover the attitudes that keep us from sharing who we are and what God has done for us. As we discover the things that cause us to hide the light, we can give them to God and ask for his help in removing them. We can shine, but we may need to remove the boxes first.

4:35-41 Jesus demonstrated his power over nature: even the wind and the seas obeyed him! The disciples were awed by the power Jesus displayed. Seeing this incredible display of power should strengthen our faith in God. Just as he was able to calm the stormy sea, he has the power to calm our out-of-control life. With Jesus in our boat, we need not fear the storms of life that threaten to drown us. There is no storm so violent or powerful that Jesus is unable to calm it. We should never hesitate to cry out in desperation: "Teacher, don't you even care that we are all about to drown?" (4:38).

Though this is one of the smallest of seeds, yet
it grows to become one of the largest of
plants, with long branches where birds can
build their nests and be sheltered."
33He used many such illustrations to teach
the people as much as they were ready to
understand. 34In fact, he taught only by illustrations in his public teaching, but afterwards,
when he was alone with his disciples, he
would explain his meaning to them.

Jesus Calms a Storm
35As evening fell, Jesus said to his disciples,
"Let's cross to the other side of the lake." 36So
they took him just as he was and started out,
leaving the crowds behind (though other
boats followed). 37But soon a terrible storm
arose. High waves began to break into the
boat until it was nearly full of water and about
to sink. 38Jesus was asleep at the back of the
boat with his head on a cushion. Frantically
they wakened him, shouting, "Teacher, don't
you even care that we are all about to drown?"
39Then he rebuked the wind and said to the
sea, "Quiet down!" And the wind fell, and
there was a great calm!
40And he asked them, "Why were you so
fearful? Don't you even yet have confidence
in me?"
41And they were filled with awe and said
among themselves, "Who is this man, that
even the winds and seas obey him?"

CHAPTER 5
Jesus Heals a Man with Demons
When they arrived at the other side of the
lake, a demon-possessed man ran out from a
graveyard, just as Jesus was climbing from the
boat.
3,4This man lived among the gravestones
and had such strength that whenever he was
put into handcuffs and shackles—as he often
was—he snapped the handcuffs from his
wrists and smashed the shackles and walked
away. No one was strong enough to control
him. 5All day long and through the night he
would wander among the tombs and in the
wild hills, screaming and cutting himself with
sharp pieces of stone.
6When Jesus was still far out on the water,
the man had seen him and had run to meet
him, and fell down before him.
7,8Then Jesus spoke to the demon within
the man and said, "Come out, you evil spirit."
It gave a terrible scream, shrieking, "What
are you going to do to me, Jesus, Son of the

Internal Bondage

BIBLE READING: Mark 5:1-13

We came to believe that a Power greater than ourselves could restore us to sanity.

When we are under the influence of our addiction, its hold may seem to have supernatural force. We may give up on living, throwing ourself into self-destructive behaviors with reckless abandon. People also may give up on us. They may distance themselves from us, as though we were already dead. Whether our "insanity" is self-induced, or even if it has a more sinister origin, there is power available to restore us to sanity and wholeness.

Jesus helped a man who was known to be acting insanely. "This man lived among the gravestones and had such strength that whenever he was put into handcuffs and shackles—as he often was—he snapped the handcuffs from his wrists and smashed the shackles and walked away. No one was strong enough to control him. All day long and through the night he would wander among the tombs and in the wild hills, screaming and cutting himself with sharp pieces of stone" (Mark 5:3-5). Jesus went into the graveyard and assessed the situation. He dealt with the forces of darkness that were afflicting the man and restored him to sanity. He then sent him home to his friends and family.

We may be so far gone that we have broken all restraints. We struggle to be free from the control of society and loved ones, only to discover that our bondage doesn't come from outside sources. All hope seems lost, but where there is still life, there is still hope. God can come into our "graveyard" and restore us to sanity. ***Turn to page 1103, Luke 8.***

Most High God? For God's sake, don't torture me!"

9"What is your name?" Jesus asked, and the demon replied, "Legion, for there are many of us here within this man."

10Then the demons begged him again and again not to send them to some distant land.

11Now as it happened there was a huge herd of hogs rooting around on the hill above the lake. 12"Send us into those hogs," the demons begged.

13And Jesus gave them permission. Then the evil spirits came out of the man and entered the hogs, and the entire herd plunged down the steep hillside into the lake and drowned.

14The herdsmen fled to the nearby towns and countryside, spreading the news as they ran. Everyone rushed out to see for themselves. 15And a large crowd soon gathered where Jesus was; but as they saw the man sitting there, fully clothed and perfectly sane, they were frightened. 16Those who saw what happened were telling everyone about it, 17and the crowd began pleading with Jesus to go away and leave them alone! 18So he got back into the boat. The man who had been possessed by the demons begged Jesus to let him go along. 19But Jesus said no.

"Go home to your friends," he told him, "and tell them what wonderful things God has done for you; and how merciful he has been."

20So the man started off to visit the Ten Towns of that region and began to tell everyone about the great things Jesus had done for him; and they were awestruck by his story.

A Woman Touches Jesus' Clothes

21When Jesus had gone across by boat to the other side of the lake, a vast crowd gathered around him on the shore.

22The leader of the local synagogue, whose name was Jairus, came and fell down before him, 23pleading with him to heal his little daughter.

"She is at the point of death," he said in desperation. "Please come and place your hands on her and make her live."

24Jesus went with him, and the crowd thronged behind. 25In the crowd was a woman who had been sick for twelve years with a hemorrhage. 26She had suffered much from many doctors through the years and had become poor from paying them, and was no better but, in fact, was worse. 27She had heard all about the wonderful miracles Jesus did, and that is why she came up behind him through the crowd and touched his clothes.

28For she thought to herself, "If I can just touch his clothing, I will be healed." 29And sure enough, as soon as she had touched him, the bleeding stopped and she knew she was well!

30Jesus realized at once that healing power had gone out from him, so he turned around in the crowd and asked, "Who touched my clothes?"

31His disciples said to him, "All this crowd pressing around you, and you ask who touched you?"

32But he kept on looking around to see who it was who had done it. 33Then the frightened woman, trembling at the realization of what had happened to her, came and fell at his feet and told him what she had done. 34And he said to her, "Daughter, your faith has made you well; go in peace, healed of your disease."

5:21-43 Jairus was among a minority of Jewish leaders who responded positively to Jesus. Driven by love for his daughter and by faith that Jesus could help her, Jairus risked the scorn of his peers by publicly seeking Jesus' help. In the end, we see that his humble faith paid off. Some of us avoid recovery because we are too ashamed to admit we have a problem. We are afraid to go public. If we cannot humbly admit our problem, there is little hope for our healing. We must, like Jairus, risk the scorn of friends and enemies and admit our failures and mistakes. If we do this, we can be sure that Jesus will be there to help us. With his help, no problem is too great to solve; no wound is too deep to heal.

5:25-34 Sometimes we feel so ashamed of our problems that we think God's opinion of us must mirror the social ostracism or self-loathing we have experienced. Such was the case with the woman who had been bleeding for twelve years. This hemorrhage was likely a menstrual or uterine disorder, which would have made her ritually "unclean" (see Leviticus 15:25-27). So, according to Jewish law, anyone who touched her would also be rendered unclean. This woman had likely lived as an outcast for some time. It is little wonder that she shrank back from touching Jesus. But instead of making Jesus unclean, she reached out in faith and was miraculously healed. We must never allow fear or shame to keep us from approaching God for forgiveness and healing. He is waiting for us to reach out and touch him.

A Girl Is Raised from the Dead

35 While he was still talking to her, messengers
arrived from Jairus' home with the news that
it was too late—his daughter was dead and
there was no point in Jesus' coming now.
36 But Jesus ignored their comments and said
to Jairus, "Don't be afraid. Just trust me."
37 Then Jesus halted the crowd and wouldn't
let anyone go on with him to Jairus' home
except Peter and James and John. 38 When
they arrived, Jesus saw that all was in great
confusion, with unrestrained weeping and
wailing. 39 He went inside and spoke to the
people.
"Why all this weeping and commotion?"
he asked. "The child isn't dead; she is only
asleep!"
40 They laughed at him in bitter derision,
but he told them all to leave, and taking the
little girl's father and mother and his three
disciples, he went into the room where she
was lying.
41,42 Taking her by the hand he said to her,
"Get up, little girl!" (She was twelve years old.)
And she jumped up and walked around! Her
parents just couldn't get over it. 43 Jesus instructed them very earnestly not to tell what
had happened and told them to give her
something to eat.

CHAPTER 6

Jesus Is Rejected at Nazareth

Soon afterwards he left that section of the
country and returned with his disciples to
Nazareth, his hometown. 2,3 The next Sabbath
he went to the synagogue to teach, and the
people were astonished at his wisdom and his
miracles because he was just a local man like
themselves.
"He's no better than we are," they said.
"He's just a carpenter, Mary's boy, and a
brother of James and Joseph, Judas and Simon. And his sisters live right here among
us." And they were offended!
4 Then Jesus told them, "A prophet is honored everywhere except in his hometown and
among his relatives and by his own family."
5 And because of their unbelief he couldn't do
any mighty miracles among them except to
place his hands on a few sick people and heal
them. 6 And he could hardly accept the fact
that they wouldn't believe in him.
Then he went out among the villages,
teaching.

Jesus Sends Out His Disciples

7 And he called his twelve disciples together
and sent them out two by two, with power to
cast out demons. 8,9 He told them to take nothing with them except their walking sticks—no
food, no knapsack, no money, not even an
extra pair of shoes or a change of clothes.
10 "Stay at one home in each village—don't
shift around from house to house while you
are there," he said. 11 "And whenever a village
won't accept you or listen to you, shake off
the dust from your feet as you leave; it is a sign
that you have abandoned it to its fate."
12 So the disciples went out, telling everyone
they met to turn from sin. 13 And they cast out
many demons and healed many sick people,
anointing them with olive oil.

Herod Kills John the Baptist

14 King Herod soon heard about Jesus, for his
miracles were talked about everywhere. The
king thought Jesus was John the Baptist come
back to life again. So the people were saying,
"No wonder he can do such miracles."
15 Others thought Jesus was Elijah the ancient
prophet, now returned to life again; still
others claimed he was a new prophet like the
great ones of the past.
16 "No," Herod said, "it is John, the man I
beheaded. He has come back from the dead."
17,18 For Herod had sent soldiers to arrest and
imprison John because he kept saying it was
wrong for the king to marry Herodias, his
brother Philip's wife. 19 Herodias wanted John
killed in revenge, but without Herod's approval she was powerless. 20 And Herod respected John, knowing that he was a good
and holy man, and so he kept him under his
protection. Herod was disturbed whenever he
talked with John, but even so he liked to listen
to him.

6:7-13 When we experience the joy of recovery, we naturally want to share the good news with others. Yet we are not always well received. So it was with the disciples, who were paired off and sent out to share the good news of the Messiah's coming. They were told what to take and what not to take, where to stay and for how long, and what to do when rejected. In the face of rejection, they kept up the good work of preaching repentance, deliverance, and healing. As we share the healing we have experienced in our recovery, not everyone will be responsive. When ridiculed or rejected, we can still press on to share our hope with the next fellow struggler we meet. Sharing our message may be the difference between life and death for someone in need.

[21]Herodias' chance finally came. It was Herod's birthday and he gave a stag party for his palace aides, army officers, and the leading citizens of Galilee. [22,23]Then Herodias' daughter came in and danced before them and greatly pleased them all.

"Ask me for anything you like," the king vowed, "even half of my kingdom, and I will give it to you!"

[24]She went out and consulted her mother, who told her, "Ask for John the Baptist's head!"

[25]So she hurried back to the king and told him, "I want the head of John the Baptist—right now—on a tray!"

[26]Then the king was sorry, but he was embarrassed to break his oath in front of his guests. [27]So he sent one of his bodyguards to the prison to cut off John's head and bring it to him. The soldier killed John in the prison, [28]and brought back his head on a tray, and gave it to the girl and she took it to her mother.

[29]When John's disciples heard what had happened, they came for his body and buried it in a tomb.

Jesus Feeds Five Thousand

[30]The apostles now returned to Jesus from their tour and told him all they had done and what they had said to the people they visited.

[31]Then Jesus suggested, "Let's get away from the crowds for a while and rest." For so many people were coming and going that they scarcely had time to eat. [32]So they left by boat for a quieter spot. [33]But many people saw them leaving and ran on ahead along the shore and met them as they landed. [34]So the usual vast crowd was there as he stepped from the boat; and he had pity on them because they were like sheep without a shepherd, and he taught them many things they needed to know.

[35,36]Late in the afternoon his disciples came to him and said, "Tell the people to go away to the nearby villages and farms and buy themselves some food, for there is nothing to eat here in this desolate spot, and it is getting late."

[37]But Jesus said, "*You* feed them."

"With what?" they asked. "It would take a fortune to buy food for all this crowd!"

[38]"How much food do we have?" he asked. "Go and find out."

They came back to report that there were five loaves of bread and two fish. [39,40]Then Jesus told the crowd to sit down, and soon colorful groups of fifty or a hundred each were sitting on the green grass.

[41]He took the five loaves and two fish and looking up to heaven, gave thanks for the food. Breaking the loaves into pieces, he gave some of the bread and fish to each disciple to place before the people. [42]And the crowd ate until they could hold no more!

[43,44]There were about 5,000 men there for that meal, and afterwards twelve basketfuls of scraps were picked up off the grass!

Jesus Walks on Water

[45]Immediately after this Jesus instructed his disciples to get back into the boat and strike out across the lake to Bethsaida, where he would join them later. He himself would stay and tell the crowds good-bye and get them started home.

[46]Afterwards he went up into the hills to pray. [47]During the night, as the disciples in their boat were out in the middle of the lake, and he was alone on land, [48]he saw that they were in serious trouble, rowing hard and struggling against the wind and waves.

About three o'clock in the morning he walked out to them on the water. He started past them, [49]but when they saw something walking along beside them they screamed in

---

6:30-34 The disciples demonstrated accountability to Jesus by reporting their activities to him. At the same time, Jesus encouraged his disciples to take care of themselves by drawing them away for rest and solitude. For the disciples to continue helping others, they would need time apart for personal reflection and refreshment. Unfortunately, their time apart was delayed by the many who followed after them. We need to make sure that our life is balanced, too. We need time apart to recharge our spiritual and emotional batteries. As we take time to reflect, we will learn the lessons of humility and dependence on God that are necessary for our progress in recovery.

6:45-52 We may lose sight of Jesus, but Jesus never loses sight of us. That's the lesson for people in "deep water" who appreciate his threefold miracle: (1) Jesus walked on water; (2) he calmed the storm; and (3) he saw the disciples' boat safely to shore (see John 6:21). Despite many such miracles, the disciples still had not realized just how powerful Jesus was. All of us can recall some time when Jesus intervened in our life to show us how much he cares. When we begin to waver in our faith, we should recall the times when he has helped us in the past. This should give us the courage to submit our life once again to his loving care.

HEROD & FAMILY

There are certain names in history that immediately bring to mind images of horror, violence, greed, and cruelty. Several Herods are mentioned in the New Testament. The first, Herod the Great, was called "great" because of his ambitious and lavish building projects, including the rebuilding of the Temple in Jerusalem. His character, however, was anything but great. He was known for his cruelty, jealousy, and insatiable lust for power and wealth.

Herod was appointed king by the Romans, but many of his Jewish subjects never really accepted him as a legitimate ruler. Herod was not really of Jewish descent; he was actually an Idumean from the land south of Judea. Because of this, Herod was uneasy about any threat to his position and responded with swift cruelty to the slightest rumor of disloyalty. The Herods didn't hesitate to have even their own family members murdered if it would be to their own advantage.

Herod Antipas, Herod the Great's son, is well known for his role in killing John the Baptist. Another descendent, Herod Agrippa I, was responsible for the death of the apostle James. A grandson, Agrippa II, heard the truth of the gospel directly from the apostle Paul. In fact, each of the Herods had an encounter with a messenger from God but refused to respond to the truth.

Herod's inability to hear God's truth grew out of his greed and insecurity. As a result, Herod left his children a heritage of greed and cruelty. It is important that we ask ourself what heritage we are leaving for our children. We can either remain in our denial and pass on our dysfunctions, or we can choose the path of recovery and build a happy and meaningful future for our children and grandchildren. There is a great deal at stake in our recovery. We are fighting for more than just our own life; we are fighting for the lives of countless descendants as well.

STRENGTHS AND ACCOMPLISHMENTS:
- Herod and his family were industrious builders.
- They were extremely clever at political maneuvering.

WEAKNESSES AND MISTAKES:
- Herod and his family lusted for power and possessions.
- They didn't hesitate to destroy innocent people who stood in their way.
- They were extremely insecure and were suspicious of the people around them.

LESSONS FROM THEIR LIVES:
- Having power and wealth doesn't guarantee success and happiness.
- We must carefully consider the heritage we will leave our children.
- Those who live for themselves at the expense of others will pay the price in the end.

KEY VERSE:
"Herod was furious when he learned that the astrologers had disobeyed him. Sending soldiers to Bethlehem, he ordered them to kill every baby boy two years old and under" (Matthew 2:16).

Herod and members of his family are mentioned in Matthew 2:1-11; Mark 6:14-29; Luke 1:5; and Acts 4:27; 12:1-23; 13:1; and 25:13–26:32.

---

terror, thinking it was a ghost, [50]for they all saw him.

But he spoke to them at once. "It's all right," he said. "It is I! Don't be afraid." [51]Then he climbed into the boat and the wind stopped!

They just sat there, unable to take it in! [52]For they still didn't realize who he was, even after the miracle the evening before! For they didn't want to believe!

Jesus Heals Many

[53]When they arrived at Gennesaret on the other side of the lake, they moored the boat
[54]and climbed out.

The people standing around there recognized him at once, [55]and ran throughout the whole area to spread the news of his arrival, and began carrying sick folks to him on mats and stretchers. [56]Wherever he went—in villages and cities, and out on the farms—they laid the sick in the market plazas and streets, and begged him to let them at least touch the fringes of his clothes; and as many as touched him were healed.

CHAPTER 7

Teachings about Inner Purity

One day some Jewish religious leaders arrived from Jerusalem to investigate him, [2]and noticed that some of his disciples failed to follow the usual Jewish rituals before eating. 3(For the Jews, especially the Pharisees, will never eat until they have sprinkled their arms to the elbows, as required by their ancient traditions. 4So when they come home from the market they must always sprinkle themselves in this way before touching any food. This is but one of many examples of laws and regulations they have clung to for centuries, and still follow, such as their ceremony of cleansing for pots, pans and dishes.)

5So the religious leaders asked him, "Why don't your disciples follow our age-old customs? For they eat without first performing the washing ceremony."

6,7Jesus replied, "You bunch of hypocrites! Isaiah the prophet described you very well when he said, 'These people speak very prettily about the Lord but they have no love for him at all. Their worship is a farce, for they claim that God commands the people to obey their petty rules.' How right Isaiah was! 8For you ignore God's specific orders and substitute your own traditions. 9You are simply rejecting God's laws and trampling them under your feet for the sake of tradition.

10For instance, Moses gave you this law from God: 'Honor your father and mother.' And he said that anyone who speaks against his father or mother must die. 11But you say it is perfectly all right for a man to disregard his needy parents, telling them, 'Sorry, I can't help you! For I have given to God what I could have given to you.' 12,13And so you break the law of God in order to protect your man-made tradition. And this is only one example. There are many, many others."

14Then Jesus called to the crowd to come and hear. "All of you listen," he said, "and try to understand. 15,16Your souls aren't harmed by what you eat, but by what you think and say!"

17Then he went into a house to get away from the crowds, and his disciples asked him what he meant by the statement he had just made.

18"Don't you understand either?" he asked. "Can't you see that what you eat won't harm your soul? 19For food doesn't come in contact with your heart, but only passes through the digestive system." (By saying this he showed that every kind of food is kosher.)

20And then he added, "It is the thought-life that pollutes. 21For from within, out of men's hearts, come evil thoughts of lust, theft, murder, adultery, 22wanting what belongs to others, wickedness, deceit, lewdness, envy, slander, pride, and all other folly. 23All these vile things come from within; they are what pollute you and make you unfit for God."

Jesus Frees a Girl from a Demon

24Then he left Galilee and went to the region of Tyre and Sidon, and tried to keep it a secret that he was there, but couldn't. For as usual the news of his arrival spread fast.

25Right away a woman came to him whose little girl was possessed by a demon. She had heard about Jesus and now she came and fell at his feet, 26and pled with him to release her child from the demon's control. (But she was Syrophoenician—a "despised Gentile!")

27Jesus told her, "First I should help my own family—the Jews. It isn't right to take the children's food and throw it to the dogs."

28She replied, "That's true, sir, but even the

7:1-13 For many of the Jewish leaders, human tradition had begun to supersede God's revealed Word. Ritual had begun to replace a relationship with God; reputation had become more important than godliness. Jesus called this hypocrisy, and it is a dangerous form of denial. If we hide the pain we feel and the mistakes we make, we will never be able to deal with them and experience healing. Our recovery can succeed only if we are willing to make a fearless moral inventory, using God's Word as the measuring stick. As we seek to follow God's will for our life, we will experience his powerful help and direction.

7:14-23 Jesus explained that defilement does not start with our external behavior, but that it comes from within our heart. Most of us have tried to control our dependencies by changing various aspects of our external behavior. The fact that this never works for long is clear evidence that our real problem lies within. We should find it encouraging that God goes right to the root of the problem; he works his healing from the inside out. By recognizing our need for internal healing, we open our life to God's healing power.

7:24-30 By helping this Gentile woman, Jesus made it clear that his message of hope was for everyone, not just a privileged few. Jesus responded not only to the woman's humility and accurate self-perception, but also to her great faith and perseverance. The more we trust in God, the more he can do for us and through us. Conversely, a lack of faith and perseverance will prevent God from working his healing in our life and in the lives of our loved ones.

puppies under the table are given some scraps
from the children's plates."
29"Good!" he said. "You have answered
well—so well that I have healed your little
girl. Go on home, for the demon has left her!"
30And when she arrived home, her little girl
was lying quietly in bed, and the demon was
gone.

The Crowd Is Amazed by Jesus

31From Tyre he went to Sidon, then back to
the Sea of Galilee by way of the Ten Towns. 32A
deaf man with a speech impediment was
brought to him, and everyone begged Jesus to
lay his hands on the man and heal him.
33Jesus led him away from the crowd and
put his fingers into the man's ears, then spat
and touched the man's tongue with the spittle. 34Then, looking up to heaven, he sighed
and commanded, "Open!" 35Instantly the
man could hear perfectly and speak plainly!
36Jesus told the crowd not to spread the
news, but the more he forbade them, the
more they made it known, 37for they were
overcome with utter amazement. Again and
again they said, "Everything he does is wonderful; he even corrects deafness and stam-
mering!"

CHAPTER 8

Jesus Feeds Four Thousand

One day about this time as another great
crowd gathered, the people ran out of food
again. Jesus called his disciples to discuss the
situation.
"I pity these people," he said, "for they
have been here three days and have nothing
left to eat. 3And if I send them home without
feeding them, they will faint along the road!
For some of them have come a long distance."
4"Are we supposed to find food for them
here in the desert?" his disciples scoffed.
5"How many loaves of bread do you have?"
he asked.
"Seven," they replied. 6So he told the crowd
to sit down on the ground. Then he took the
seven loaves, thanked God for them, broke
them into pieces and passed them to his disciples; and the disciples placed them before
the people. 7A few small fish were found, too,
so Jesus also blessed these and told the disciples to serve them.
8,9And the whole crowd ate until they were
full, and afterwards he sent them home.
There were about 4,000 people in the crowd
that day and when the scraps were picked up
after the meal, there were seven very large
basketfuls left over!

The Leaders Demand a Miracle

10Immediately after this he got into a boat
with his disciples and came to the region of
Dalmanutha.
11When the local Jewish leaders learned of
his arrival, they came to argue with him.
"Do a miracle for us," they said. "Make
something happen in the sky. Then we will
believe in you."
12He sighed deeply when he heard this and
he said, "Certainly not. How many more
miracles do you people need?"

A Warning about False Teachings

13So he got back into the boat and left them,
and crossed to the other side of the lake. 14But
the disciples had forgotten to stock up on

7:31-37 A key to our recovery may have been another person who led us to get the help we needed. In this account, a group of people apparently cared enough for this deaf man to do something about his problem. They brought their friend to Jesus and then begged Jesus to heal him. We may be the one God will use to give another hurting person hope and direction for recovery. As we share the story of our own deliverance and God's power for bringing recovery, we can give others the gift of life and health. And when we share our story, we will not only give hope to others, but we will also experience a renewed commitment to our own recovery.

8:1-9 We sometimes feel like our prayers never get beyond the ceiling. We wonder if the hot line to God is busy and if we have been left indefinitely on hold. The truth is, God is never too busy to concern himself with the daily needs of his people. Jesus was moved by pity to feed four thousand hungry people, even though he was busy with a preaching and healing campaign. There is no need too small or request too large that God will not hear and respond to.

8:10-21 Jesus was troubled by his disciples' lack of faith and their seeming inability to learn the basic lessons he was trying to teach them. As slow to catch on as they were, Jesus still nurtured them in faith. We may tend to progress in recovery in a series of lurches and falls. When we fail, we can recover by quickly admitting our limitations, accepting God's forgiveness, and continuing to depend on his power, day by day. God will be patient with us if we are willing to stick with his program for our recovery.

food before they left and had only one loaf of bread in the boat.

15 As they were crossing, Jesus said to them very solemnly, "Beware of the yeast of King Herod and of the Pharisees."

16 "What does he mean?" the disciples asked each other. They finally decided that he must be talking about their forgetting to bring bread.

17 Jesus realized what they were discussing and said, "No, that isn't it at all! Can't you understand? Are your hearts too hard to take it in? 18 'Your eyes are to see with—why don't you look? Why don't you open your ears and listen?' Don't you remember anything at all?

19 "What about the 5,000 men I fed with five loaves of bread? How many basketfuls of scraps did you pick up afterwards?"

"Twelve," they said.

20 "And when I fed the 4,000 with seven loaves, how much was left?"

"Seven basketfuls," they said.

21 "And yet you think I'm worried that we have no bread?"

Jesus Heals a Blind Man

22 When they arrived at Bethsaida, some people brought a blind man to him and begged him to touch and heal him. 23 Jesus took the blind man by the hand and led him out of the village, and spat upon his eyes, and laid his hands over them.

"Can you see anything now?" Jesus asked him.

24 The man looked around. "Yes!" he said, "I see men! But I can't see them very clearly; they look like tree trunks walking around!"

25 Then Jesus placed his hands over the man's eyes again and as the man stared intently, his sight was completely restored, and he saw everything clearly, drinking in the sights around him.

26 Jesus sent him home to his family. "Don't even go back to the village first," he said.

Peter Says Jesus Is the Messiah

27 Jesus and his disciples now left Galilee and went out to the villages of Caesarea Philippi. As they were walking along he asked them, "Who do the people think I am? What are they saying about me?"

28 "Some of them think you are John the Baptist," the disciples replied, "and others say you are Elijah or some other ancient prophet come back to life again."

29 Then he asked, "Who do you think I am?" Peter replied, "You are the Messiah." 30 But Jesus warned them not to tell anyone!

Jesus Speaks of His Death

31 Then he began to tell them about the terrible things he would suffer, and that he would be rejected by the elders and the Chief Priests and the other Jewish leaders—and be killed, and that he would rise again three days afterwards. 32 He talked about it quite frankly with them, so Peter took him aside and chided him. "You shouldn't say things like that," he told Jesus.

33 Jesus turned and looked at his disciples and then said to Peter very sternly, "Satan, get behind me! You are looking at this only from a human point of view and not from God's."

The Cost of Following Jesus

34 Then he called his disciples and the crowds to come over and listen. "If any of you wants to be my follower," he told them, "you must put aside your own pleasures and shoulder your cross, and follow me closely. 35 If you insist on saving your life, you will lose it. Only those who throw away their lives for my sake and for the sake of the Good News will ever know what it means to really live.

36 "And how does a man benefit if he gains the whole world and loses his soul in the process? 37 For is anything worth more than his soul? 38 And anyone who is ashamed of me and my message in these days of unbelief and sin, I, the Messiah, will be ashamed of him when I return in the glory of my Father, with the holy angels."

CHAPTER 9

Jesus went on to say to his disciples, "Some of you who are standing here right now will live to see the Kingdom of God arrive in great power!"

8:31–9:1 When Jesus told his disciples that his ministry would lead to suffering and death, he was sharing a basic truth about life. When dealing with the destructive effects of sin, victory is usually experienced only after traveling a journey of pain and tears. No cross, no resurrection. No pain, no gain. Jesus had to suffer in order to overcome the destructive power of sin in our world. Our recovery from destructive habits will also involve pain, but we should not let this discourage us. Jesus has already paid the price for our sins. If we admit our failures and accept God's forgiveness, we can be sure of our victory over our addiction with God's daily help.

Jesus Is Transfigured

[2]Six days later Jesus took Peter, James and
John to the top of a mountain. No one else
was there.
Suddenly his face began to shine with
glory, [3]and his clothing became dazzling
white, far more glorious than any earthly
process could ever make it! [4]Then Elijah and
Moses appeared and began talking with Jesus!
[5]"Teacher, this is wonderful!" Peter exclaimed. "We will make three shelters here,
one for each of you. . . ."
[6]He said this just to be talking, for he didn't
know what else to say and they were all terribly frightened.
[7]But while he was still speaking these
words, a cloud covered them, blotting out the
sun, and a voice from the cloud said, *"This* is
my beloved Son. Listen to *him."*
[8]Then suddenly they looked around and
Moses and Elijah were gone, and only Jesus
was with them.
[9]As they descended the mountainside he
told them never to mention what they had
seen until after he had risen from the dead.
[10]So they kept it to themselves, but often
talked about it, and wondered what he meant
by "rising from the dead."
[11]Now they began asking him about something the Jewish religious leaders often spoke
of, that Elijah must return [before the Messiah
could come]. [12,13]Jesus agreed that Elijah must
come first and prepare the way—and that he
had, in fact, already come! And that he had
been terribly mistreated, just as the prophets
had predicted. Then Jesus asked them what
the prophets could have been talking about
when they predicted that the Messiah would
suffer and be treated with utter contempt.

Jesus Heals a Demon-possessed Boy

[14]At the bottom of the mountain they found
a great crowd surrounding the other nine
disciples, as some Jewish leaders argued with
them. [15]The crowd watched Jesus in awe as he
came toward them, and then ran to greet him.
[16]"What's all the argument about?" he asked.
[17]One of the men in the crowd spoke up
and said, "Teacher, I brought my son for you
to heal—he can't talk because he is possessed
by a demon. [18]And whenever the demon is in
control of him it dashes him to the ground
and makes him foam at the mouth and grind
his teeth and become rigid. So I begged your
disciples to cast out the demon, but they
couldn't do it."
[19]Jesus said [to his disciples], "Oh, what tiny
faith you have; how much longer must I be
with you until you believe? How much longer
must I be patient with you? Bring the boy to
me."
[20]So they brought the boy, but when he saw
Jesus the demon convulsed the child horribly,
and he fell to the ground writhing and foam-
ing at the mouth.
[21]"How long has he been this way?" Jesus
asked the father.
And he replied, "Since he was very small,
[22]and the demon often makes him fall into
the fire or into water to kill him. Oh, have
mercy on us and do something if you can."
[23]"If I can?" Jesus asked. *"Anything* is possible if you have faith."
[24]The father instantly replied, "I *do* have
faith; oh, help me to have *more!"*
[25]When Jesus saw the crowd was growing
he rebuked the demon.
"O demon of deafness and dumbness," he
said, "I command you to come out of this
child and enter him no more!"
[26]Then the demon screamed terribly and
convulsed the boy again and left him; and the
boy lay there limp and motionless, to all
appearance dead. A murmur ran through the

9:14-29 In a moment of honest self-examination, the father of the demon-possessed boy acknowledged both belief and unbelief. He believed that Jesus could restore his son to health, but he questioned whether Jesus would do so. Sometimes we feel the same way. We see how God has delivered others and believe that God is able to help, but we are afraid that God will refuse to help us. Perhaps we are afraid that God will think us unworthy of his deliverance. God never works that way. Not only is he able to help us, but he also wants to help us. All we have to do is turn to him in faith, ask for his help and forgiveness, and do what we can to follow his revealed will for us. God will do the rest.

9:30-37 The argument over who would be the greatest in God's Kingdom ran counter to everything Jesus stood for. True greatness is measured by how we serve others. That service, for the disciples, included showing loving care for all people, even a little child. We may not be tempted to turn away from little children in need, but what about the many adults who need our help? Do we turn away people who are poor, homeless, hungry, and addicted? God heals our hurts so we can help others get the healing they need, not so we can rise to a higher position in society. If we fail to help the people who are in need, we are pushing Jesus right out of our life.

crowd—"He is dead." 27But Jesus took him by
the hand and helped him to his feet and he
stood up and was all right! 28Afterwards, when
Jesus was alone in the house with his disciples, they asked him, "Why couldn't we cast
that demon out?"
29Jesus replied, "Cases like this require
prayer."

Jesus Again Predicts His Death

30,31Leaving that region they traveled through
Galilee where he tried to avoid all publicity in
order to spend more time with his disciples,
teaching them. He would say to them, "I, the
Messiah, am going to be betrayed and killed
and three days later I will return to life again."

Who Is the Greatest?

32But they didn't understand and were afraid
to ask him what he meant.
33And so they arrived at Capernaum. When
they were settled in the house where they
were to stay he asked them, "What were you
discussing out on the road?"
34But they were ashamed to answer, for they
had been arguing about which of them was
the greatest!
35He sat down and called them around him
and said, "Anyone wanting to be the greatest
must be the least—the servant of all!"
36Then he placed a little child among them;
and taking the child in his arms he said to
them, 37"Anyone who welcomes a little child
like this in my name is welcoming me, and
anyone who welcomes me is welcoming my
Father who sent me!"
38One of his disciples, John, told him one
day, "Teacher, we saw a man using your name
to cast out demons; but we told him not to,
for he isn't one of our group."
39"Don't forbid him!" Jesus said. "For no
one doing miracles in my name will quickly
turn against me. 40Anyone who isn't against
us is for us. 41If anyone so much as gives you
a cup of water because you are Christ's—I say
this solemnly—he won't lose his reward. 42But
if someone causes one of these little ones who
believe in me to lose faith—it would be better
for that man if a huge millstone were tied
around his neck and he were thrown into the
sea.

Jesus Warns about Temptation

43,44 "If your hand does wrong, cut it off. Better
live forever with one hand than be thrown
into the unquenchable fires of hell with two!
45,46 If your foot carries you toward evil, cut it
off! Better be lame and live forever than have
two feet that carry you to hell.
47"And if your eye is sinful, gouge it out.
Better enter the Kingdom of God half blind
than have two eyes and see the fires of hell,
48where the worm never dies, and the fire
never goes out—49where all are salted with
fire.
50"Good salt is worthless if it loses its saltiness; it can't season anything. So don't lose
your flavor! Live in peace with each other."

CHAPTER 10

Teachings about Marriage

Then he left Capernaum and went southward
to the Judean borders and into the area east of
the Jordan River. And as always there were the
crowds; and as usual he taught them.
2Some Pharisees came and asked him, "Do

9:38-42 Cooperation and peace, not cutthroat competition, must characterize our interpersonal relationships. Notice that Jesus instructed his disciples to fully and peacefully accept others who ministered in his name. He accepted those not under his own direct authority but who were building up the Kingdom of God. So must we. If we fail to do so and cause others to lose faith, then we will suffer the painful consequences.

9:43-50 Through a series of startling statements, Jesus admonished his disciples to get rid of anything in their lives that might draw them away from God. For us, this can be taken to refer to our besetting addiction and the emotional baggage that supports it. We can identify our weaknesses by making a searching and fearless moral inventory of our life. Then we need to take action to "cut off" the offensive parts of ourself so we can begin the process of healing. It is usually wise to have the help of a support group as we follow through on such drastic measures.

10:1-12 The Pharisees were not looking for guidance when they asked Jesus about divorce; they were only looking for a means to discredit him. Jesus offered no grounds for divorce, with the possible exception of infidelity (see Matthew 19:9). In our society, many believe divorce to be a good way to deal with conflict. Most of us have discovered, however, that interpersonal conflict follows us wherever we go because it is only an evidence of much deeper problems. These same problems may also drive our dependencies. Marriage is not always easy; neither is recovery. But both can be of great help to each other. Marriage gives us a context of accountability and loving support necessary to help us through the process of recovery. Recovery gives us the program for personal growth and for reestablishing our family and marriage relationships.

you permit divorce?" Of course they were
trying to trap him.
3"What did Moses say about divorce?" Jesus
asked them.
4"He said it was all right," they replied. "He
said that all a man has to do is write his wife
a letter of dismissal."
5"And why did he say that?" Jesus asked.
"I'll tell you why—it was a concession to your
hardhearted wickedness. 6,7But it certainly
isn't God's way. For from the very first he
made man and woman to be joined together
permanently in marriage; therefore a man is
to leave his father and mother, 8and he and
his wife are united so that they are no longer
two, but one. 9And no man may separate what
God has joined together."
10Later, when he was alone with his disciples in the house, they brought up the subject
again.
11He told them, "When a man divorces his
wife to marry someone else, he commits adultery against her. 12And if a wife divorces her
husband and remarries, she, too, commits
adultery."

Jesus Blesses the Children
13Once when some mothers were bringing
their children to Jesus to bless them, the disciples shooed them away, telling them not to
bother him.
14But when Jesus saw what was happening
he was very much displeased with his disciples and said to them, "Let the children come
to me, for the Kingdom of God belongs to
such as they. Don't send them away! 15I tell
you as seriously as I know how that anyone
who refuses to come to God as a little child
will never be allowed into his Kingdom."
16Then he took the children into his arms
and placed his hands on their heads and he
blessed them.

Jesus and the Rich Young Man
17As he was starting out on a trip, a man came
running to him and knelt down and asked,
"Good Teacher, what must I do to get to
heaven?"
18"Why do you call me good?" Jesus asked.
"Only God is truly good! 19But as for your
question—you know the commandments:
don't kill, don't commit adultery, don't steal,
don't lie, don't cheat, respect your father and
mother."
20"Teacher," the man replied, "I've never
once broken a single one of those laws."
21Jesus felt genuine love for this man as he

Like Little Children

BIBLE READING: Mark 10:13-16

We admitted that we were powerless over our dependencies—that our life had become unmanageable.

For many of us in recovery, memories of childhood are memories of the terrors associated with being powerless. If we were raised in families that were out of control, where we were neglected, abused, or exposed to domestic violence and family dysfunction, the thought of being powerless might be very frightening. We may have silently vowed never again to be as vulnerable as we were when we were children.

Jesus tells us that in order to enter the Kingdom of God we must become like a little child, and this involves being powerless. He said, "I tell you as seriously as I know how that anyone who refuses to come to God as a little child will never be allowed into his Kingdom" (Mark 10:15).

In any society, children are the most dependent members. They have no inherent power for self-protection—no means to insure that their lives will be safe, comfortable, or fulfilling. Little children are singularly reliant on the love, care, and nurture of others for their most basic needs. They *must* cry out even though they may not know exactly what they need. They *must* trust their lives to someone who is more powerful than they, and, hopefully, they will be heard and lovingly cared for.

We, too, must admit that we are truly powerless if our life is to become healthy. This doesn't mean we have to become victims again. Admitting our powerlessness is an honest appraisal of our situation in life and a positive step toward recovery. ***Turn to page 1193, Acts 9.***

looked at him. "You lack only one thing," he
told him; "go and sell all you have and give
the money to the poor—and you shall have
treasure in heaven—and come, follow me."
22 Then the man's face fell, and he went
sadly away, for he was very rich.
23 Jesus watched him go, then turned
around and said to his disciples, "It's almost
impossible for the rich to get into the Kingdom of God!"
24 This amazed them. So Jesus said it again:
"Dear children, how hard it is for those who
trust in riches to enter the Kingdom of God.
25 It is easier for a camel to go through the eye
of a needle than for a rich man to enter the
Kingdom of God."
26 The disciples were incredulous! "Then
who in the world can be saved, if not a rich
man?" they asked.
27 Jesus looked at them intently, then said,
"Without God, it is utterly impossible. But
with God everything is possible."
28 Then Peter began to mention all that he
and the other disciples had left behind.
"We've given up everything to follow you,"
he said.
29 And Jesus replied, "Let me assure you that
no one has ever given up anything—home,
brothers, sisters, mother, father, children, or
property—for love of me and to tell others the
Good News, 30 who won't be given back, a
hundred times over, homes, brothers, sisters,
mothers, children, and land—with persecutions!
"All these will be his here on earth, and in
the world to come he shall have eternal life.
31 But many people who seem to be important
now will be the least important then; and
many who are considered least here shall be
greatest there."

Jesus again Speaks of His Death

32 Now they were on the way to Jerusalem, and
Jesus was walking along ahead; and as the
disciples were following they were filled with
terror and dread.
Taking them aside, Jesus once more began
describing all that was going to happen to
him when they arrived at Jerusalem.
33 "When we get there," he told them, "I,
the Messiah, will be arrested and taken before
the chief priests and the Jewish leaders, who
will sentence me to die and hand me over to
the Romans to be killed. 34 They will mock me
and spit on me and flog me with their whips
and kill me; but after three days I will come
back to life again."

The Importance of Serving Others

35 Then James and John, the sons of Zebedee,
came over and spoke to him in a low voice.
"Master," they said, "we want you to do us a
favor."
36 "What is it?" he asked.
37 "We want to sit on the thrones next to
yours in your Kingdom," they said, "one at
your right and the other at your left!"
38 But Jesus answered, "You don't know
what you are asking! Are you able to drink
from the bitter cup of sorrow I must drink
from? Or to be baptized with the baptism of
suffering I must be baptized with?"
39 "Oh, yes," they said, "we are!"
And Jesus said, "You shall indeed drink
from my cup and be baptized with my baptism, 40 but I do not have the right to place you
on thrones next to mine. Those appointments have already been made."
41 When the other disciples discovered what
James and John had asked, they were very
indignant. 42 So Jesus called them to him and

10:23-31 Most people in Jesus' day believed that wealth was a reward from God for being good. Thus, the wealthy usually enjoyed a measure of prestige. Jesus amazed his audience by showing how very difficult it was for the rich to enter God's Kingdom. Wealthy people have a hard time recognizing their need for anything, and the only way to receive God's help is by recognizing how much we need him. The rich young man would have to see his helplessness before he could be helped. Notice, however, that even this problem is not too big for God. He has ways of getting the attention of even the proud and self-sufficient. Many of us have learned through painful experience that we are helpless and in need of God's intervention in our life. God often lets us hit bottom so we can begin to experience his healing and forgiveness.

10:46-52 Faith brought recovery of sight to blind Bartimaeus. He had to persevere in faith despite the initial opposition he experienced from Jesus' followers. In that day, blindness was thought to be a divine curse for sin (see John 9:2), but Jesus refuted this notion by both word and deed. We sometimes face opposition to our recovery. Sometimes those who claim to be God's people reject us and make us feel unwelcome because we are trapped by our dependencies. Even when rejected by others, we can be sure that Jesus will never turn us away. We should persevere like Bartimaeus did, knowing that Jesus has both the power and the desire to help us overcome our besetting weaknesses.

said, "As you know, the kings and great men of the earth lord it over the people; [43]but among you it is different. Whoever wants to be great among you must be your servant. [44]And whoever wants to be greatest of all must be the slave of all. [45]For even I, the Messiah, am not here to be served, but to help others, and to give my life as a ransom for many."

Jesus Heals a Blind Beggar

[46]And so they reached Jericho. Later, as they left town, a great crowd was following. Now it happened that a blind beggar named Bartimaeus (the son of Timaeus) was sitting beside the road as Jesus was going by.

[47]When Bartimaeus heard that Jesus from Nazareth was near, he began to shout out, "Jesus, Son of David, have mercy on me!"

[48]"Shut up!" some of the people yelled at him.

But he only shouted the louder, again and again, "O Son of David, have mercy on me!"

[49]When Jesus heard him, he stopped there in the road and said, "Tell him to come here."

So they called the blind man. "You lucky fellow," they said, "come on, he's calling you!" [50]Bartimaeus yanked off his old coat and flung it aside, jumped up and came to Jesus.

[51]"What do you want me to do for you?" Jesus asked.

"O Teacher," the blind man said, "I want to see!"

[52]And Jesus said to him, "All right, it's done. Your faith has healed you."

And instantly the blind man could see and followed Jesus down the road!

CHAPTER 11

Jesus Rides into Jerusalem

As they neared Bethphage and Bethany on the outskirts of Jerusalem and came to the Mount of Olives, Jesus sent two of his disciples on ahead.

[2]"Go into that village over there," he told them, "and just as you enter you will see a colt tied up that has never been ridden. Untie him and bring him here. [3]And if anyone asks you what you are doing, just say, 'Our Master needs him and will return him soon.'"

[4,5]Off went the two men and found the colt standing in the street, tied outside a house. As they were untying it, some who were standing there demanded, "What are you doing, untying that colt?"

[6]So they said what Jesus had told them to, and then the men agreed.

[7]So the colt was brought to Jesus, and the disciples threw their cloaks across its back for him to ride on. [8]Then many in the crowd spread out their coats along the road before him, while others threw down leafy branches from the fields.

[9]He was in the center of the procession with crowds ahead and behind, and all of them shouting, "Hail to the King!" "Praise God for him who comes in the name of the Lord!" . . . [10]"Praise God for the return of our father David's kingdom . . ." "Hail to the King of the universe!"

[11]And so he entered Jerusalem and went into the Temple. He looked around carefully at everything and then left—for now it was late in the afternoon—and went out to Bethany with the twelve disciples.

Jesus Clears the Temple

[12]The next morning as they left Bethany, he felt hungry. [13]A little way off he noticed a fig tree in full leaf, so he went over to see if he could find any figs on it. But no, there were only leaves, for it was too early in the season for fruit.

[14]Then Jesus said to the tree, "You shall

11:1-10 As we suffer the pain of our addictions, we often look for instant deliverance. We wish some white knight would sweep us off our feet and take care of all our problems at once. The Judeans were expecting the same kind of deliverance from their Messiah. They wanted some glorious political king on a war-horse to ride into Jerusalem and sweep the Romans out of power. Instead, Jesus came riding on a lowly donkey, in peace. Few of us, if any, ever experience an instant cure for our dependencies. God works our recovery through a process of personal growth, from the inside out. He helps us to recognize our failures and our need for help, and he gives us the strength to take the necessary steps toward recovery. Looking for an instant cure will only put us on the road to a relapse.

11:11-19 The barren fig tree is analogous to a spiritually bankrupt people. If the fig tree did not produce fruit, as it was designed to do, then it had no real reason to exist. If the Temple did not produce true worship and prayer, but only ill-gotten gain for the money-changers, then the Temple had to be judged and cleansed as well. So also in our recovery program: if our life in recovery is not bearing the fruit of new behavior patterns, then it must be overhauled. If we only go through the motions of recovery, then our faith has no substance, and our attempt to recover is only a pretense.

never bear fruit again!" And the disciples heard him say it.

15 When they arrived back to Jerusalem he went to the Temple and began to drive out the merchants and their customers, and knocked over the tables of the moneychangers and the stalls of those selling doves, 16 and stopped everyone from bringing in loads of merchandise.

17 He told them, "It is written in the Scriptures, 'My Temple is to be a place of prayer for all nations,' but you have turned it into a den of robbers."

18 When the chief priests and other Jewish leaders heard what he had done, they began planning how best to get rid of him. Their problem was their fear of riots because the people were so enthusiastic about Jesus' teaching.

19 That evening as usual they left the city.

Teachings about Prayer

20 Next morning, as the disciples passed the fig tree he had cursed, they saw that it was withered from the roots! 21 Then Peter remembered what Jesus had said to the tree on the previous day and exclaimed, "Look, Teacher! The fig tree you cursed has withered!"

22,23 In reply Jesus said to the disciples, "If you only have faith in God—this is the absolute truth—you can say to this Mount of Olives, 'Rise up and fall into the Mediterranean,' and your command will be obeyed. All that's required is that you really believe and have no doubt! 24 Listen to me! You can pray for *anything,* and *if you believe, you have it;* it's yours! 25 But when you are praying, first forgive anyone you are holding a grudge against, so that your Father in heaven will forgive you your sins too."

Leaders Challenge Jesus' Authority

26-28 By this time they had arrived in Jerusalem again, and as he was walking through the Temple area, the chief priests and other Jewish leaders came up to him demanding, "What's going on here? Who gave you the authority to drive out the merchants?"

29 Jesus replied, "I'll tell you if you answer one question! 30 What about John the Baptist? Was he sent by God, or not? Answer me!"

31 They talked it over among themselves. "If we reply that God sent him, then he will say, 'All right, why didn't you accept him?' 32 But if we say God didn't send him, then the people will start a riot." (For the people all believed strongly that John was a prophet.)

33 So they said, "We can't answer. We don't know."

To which Jesus replied, "Then I won't answer your question either!"

CHAPTER 12

A Story about Wicked Farmers

Here are some of the story-illustrations Jesus gave to the people at that time:

"A man planted a vineyard and built a wall around it and dug a pit for pressing out the grape juice, and built a watchman's tower. Then he leased the farm to tenant farmers and moved to another country. 2 At grape-picking time he sent one of his men to collect his share of the crop. 3 But the farmers beat up the man and sent him back empty-handed.

4 "The owner then sent another of his men, who received the same treatment, only worse, for his head was seriously injured. 5 The next man he sent was killed; and later, others were either beaten or killed, until 6 there was only one left—his only son. He finally sent him, thinking they would surely give him their full respect.

7 "But when the farmers saw him coming

11:19-25 God wants us to pray for his will to be done in our recovery, much as he wants us to pray for fruitfulness in his Kingdom work. Moving mountains into the sea is probably not God's will for us. It is God's will, however, to remove mountains of resistance or denial from our life. God has the power to do miracles—but not as a result of a positive mental attitude. The God of the Kingdom and of our recovery is the God of the impossible. If we want God to work a miracle of healing in our life, we cannot just pretend to believe. We need to admit our helplessness and put our life into God's hands. He will then walk with us as we face each new step in recovery.

12:1-12 By telling this story, Jesus confronted the religious leaders with their hypocrisy and denial. The leaders were the wicked farmers who had rejected God, the owner of his people (who were represented by the vineyard). These leaders pretended to be in touch with God, but their actions and attitudes proved otherwise. Jesus confronted them, hoping they would listen and change. We also need to be awakened from our denial if we hope to recover. God often brings people into our life to wake us up. We would be wise to listen, unlike the proud Pharisees. If we refuse to admit our sins and mistakes, we will never be able to receive the help God offers for our recovery.

they said, 'He will own the farm when his
father dies. Come on, let's kill him—and then
the farm will be ours!' 8So they caught him
and murdered him and threw his body out of
the vineyard.
9"What do you suppose the owner will do
when he hears what happened? He will come
and kill them all, and lease the vineyard to
others. 10Don't you remember reading this
verse in the Scriptures? 'The Rock the builders
threw away became the cornerstone, the most
honored stone in the building! 11This is the
Lord's doing and it is an amazing thing to
see.'"
12The Jewish leaders wanted to arrest him
then and there for using this illustration, for
they knew he was pointing at them—they
were the wicked farmers in his story. But they
were afraid to touch him for fear of a mob. So
they left him and went away.

A Question about Taxes

13But they sent other religious and political
leaders to talk with him and try to trap him
into saying something he could be arrested
for.
14"Teacher," these spies said, "we know you
tell the truth no matter what! You aren't influenced by the opinions and desires of men, but
sincerely teach the ways of God. Now tell us,
is it right to pay taxes to Rome, or not?"
15Jesus saw their trick and said, "Show me a
coin and I'll tell you."
16When they handed it to him he asked,
"Whose picture and title is this on the coin?"
They replied, "The emperor's."
17"All right," he said, "if it is his, give it to
him. But everything that belongs to God must
be given to God!" And they scratched their
heads in bafflement at his reply.

Questions about the Resurrection

18Then the Sadducees stepped forward—a
group of men who say there is no resurrection. Here was their question:
19"Teacher, Moses gave us a law that when
a man dies without children, the man's
brother should marry his widow and have
children in his brother's name. 20-22Well, there
were seven brothers and the oldest married
and died, and left no children. So the second
brother married the widow, but soon he died
too and left no children. Then the next
brother married her and died without children, and so on until all were dead, and still
there were no children; and last of all, the
woman died too.
23"What we want to know is this: In the
resurrection, whose wife will she be, for she
had been the wife of each of them?"
24Jesus replied, "Your trouble is that you
don't know the Scriptures and don't know the
power of God. 25For when these seven brothers and the woman rise from the dead, they
won't be married—they will be like the angels.
26"But now as to whether there will be a
resurrection—have you never read in the
book of Exodus about Moses and the burning
bush? God said to Moses, 'I *am* the God of
Abraham, and I *am* the God of Isaac, and I *am*
the God of Jacob.'
27"God was telling Moses that these men,
though dead for hundreds of years, were still
very much alive, for he would not have said,
'I *am* the God' of those who don't exist! You
have made a serious error."

The Greatest Commandment

28One of the teachers of religion who was
standing there listening to the discussion realized that Jesus had answered well. So he
asked, "Of all the commandments, which is
the most important?"
29Jesus replied, "The one that says, 'Hear, O
Israel! The Lord our God is the one and only
God. 30And you must love him with all your
heart and soul and mind and strength.'
31"The second is: 'You must love others as
much as yourself.' No other commandments
are greater than these."
32The teacher of religion replied, "Sir, you
have spoken a true word in saying that there
is only one God and no other. 33And I know it
is far more important to love him with all my
heart and understanding and strength, and to
love others as myself, than to offer all kinds of
sacrifices on the altar of the Temple."

12:18-27 Jesus avoided another trick question, this one by the Sadducees, who did not believe in the possibility of the resurrection after death. Again Jesus cleverly exposed the moral shortcomings of those who had the form of religion but denied its power. Book learning, even Scripture memory, is not enough to keep us from sin or help us recover from our dependencies. We must know the living God personally and accept the help he offers as our higher Power. The God of the patriarchs is not the God of philosophical speculation. He is our God, active today in our recovery. He is the God of hope and resurrection; all we have to do is accept the many gifts he offers.

34Realizing this man's understanding, Jesus
said to him, "You are not far from the Kingdom of God." And after that, no one dared ask
him any more questions.

A Question about the Messiah

35Later, as Jesus was teaching the people in the
Temple area, he asked them this question:
"Why do your religious teachers claim that
the Messiah must be a descendant of King
David? 36For David himself said—and the
Holy Spirit was speaking through him when
he said it—'God said to my Lord, sit at my
right hand until I make your enemies your
footstool.' 37Since David called him his Lord,
how can he be his *son?"*
(This sort of reasoning delighted the crowd
and they listened to him with great interest.)

Jesus Warns about the Religious Leaders

38Here are some of the other things he taught
them at this time:
"Beware of the teachers of religion! For they
love to wear the robes of the rich and schol-
arly, and to have everyone bow to them as
they walk through the markets. 39They love to
sit in the best seats in the synagogues and at
the places of honor at banquets—40but they
shamelessly cheat widows out of their homes
and then, to cover up the kind of men they
really are, they pretend to be pious by praying
long prayers in public. Because of this, their
punishment will be the greater."

A Poor Widow's Great Gift

41Then he went over to the collection boxes in
the Temple and sat and watched as the crowds
dropped in their money. Some who were rich
put in large amounts. 42Then a poor widow
came and dropped in two pennies.
43,44He called his disciples to him and remarked, "That poor widow has given more
than all those rich men put together! For they
gave a little of their extra fat, while she gave
up her last penny."

CHAPTER 13

Jesus Tells about the Future

As he was leaving the Temple that day, one of
his disciples said, "Teacher, what beautiful
buildings these are! Look at the decorated
stonework on the walls."
2Jesus replied, "Yes, look! For not one stone
will be left upon another, except as ruins."
3,4And as he sat on the slopes of the Mount
of Olives across the valley from Jerusalem,
Peter, James, John, and Andrew got alone
with him and asked him, "Just when is all this
going to happen to the Temple? Will there be
some warning ahead of time?"
5So Jesus launched into an extended reply.
"Don't let anyone mislead you," he said, 6"for
many will come declaring themselves to be
your Messiah and will lead many astray. 7And
wars will break out near and far, but this is not
the signal of the end-time.
8"For nations and kingdoms will proclaim
war against each other, and there will be
earthquakes in many lands, and famines.
These herald only the early stages of the anguish ahead. 9But when these things begin to
happen, watch out! For you will be in great
danger. You will be dragged before the courts,
and beaten in the synagogues, and accused
before governors and kings of being my followers. This is your opportunity to tell them
the Good News. 10And the Good News must
first be made known in every nation before
the end-time finally comes. 11But when you
are arrested and stand trial, don't worry about
what to say in your defense. Just say what God
tells you to. Then you will not be speaking,
but the Holy Spirit will.
12"Brothers will betray each other to death,
fathers will betray their own children, and
children will betray their parents to be killed.

12:28-34 Many think of religion, with all its commandments, as a burdensome straitjacket, antithetical to true recovery. This may have been true, in some sense, of the Judaism in Jesus' day, and it is sometimes true among people today, who claim to belong to God. Jesus wanted to correct this wrong understanding of true faith. He summed up the numerous Jewish laws in two simple but profound commandments: We are to love God totally, and we are to love others as much as ourself. If we allow these two thoughts to rule our heart and mind, we will be well along the path toward recovery.

13:1-20 The Olivet discourse (13:1-37) speaks to the all-too-human preoccupation with an uncertain future. The disciples worried about the future of their nation after Jesus predicted the destruction of the Temple that was then being reconstructed. We, like the disciples, may tend to worry about whether or not we will survive future conflicts and temptations. As we face an uncertain future, we are encouraged to live one day at a time. God makes it clear that despite the trials we may face, we should not worry. If we entrust our life to God, his Spirit will be with us during our difficult times. Recovery is never easy, but it is always possible with God's help.

13And everyone will hate you because you are mine. But all who endure to the end without renouncing me shall be saved.

14"When you see the horrible thing standing in the Temple —reader, pay attention!—flee, if you can, to the Judean hills. 15,16Hurry! If you are on your rooftop porch, don't even go back into the house. If you are out in the fields, don't even return for your money or clothes.

17"Woe to pregnant women in those days, and to mothers nursing their children. 18And pray that your flight will not be in winter. 19For those will be days of such horror as have never been since the beginning of God's creation, nor will ever be again. 20And unless the Lord shortens that time of calamity, not a soul in all the earth will survive. But for the sake of his chosen ones he will limit those days.

Jesus Tells about His Return

21"And then if anyone tells you, 'This is the Messiah,' or, 'That one is,' don't pay any attention. 22For there will be many false Messiahs and false prophets who will do wonderful miracles that would deceive, if possible, even God's own children. 23Take care! I have warned you!

24"After the tribulation ends, then the sun will grow dim and the moon will not shine, 25and the stars will fall—the heavens will convulse.

26"Then all mankind will see me, the Messiah, coming in the clouds with great power and glory. 27And I will send out the angels to gather together my chosen ones from all over the world—from the farthest bounds of earth and heaven.

28"Now, here is a lesson from a fig tree. When its buds become tender and its leaves begin to sprout, you know that spring has come. 29And when you see these things happening that I've described, you can be sure that my return is very near, that I am right at the door.

30"Yes, these are the events that will signal the end of the age. 31Heaven and earth shall disappear, but my words stand sure forever.

A Call to Stay Alert

32"However, no one, not even the angels in heaven, nor I myself, knows the day or hour when these things will happen; only the Father knows. 33And since you don't know when it will happen, stay alert. Be on the watch [for my return].

34"My coming can be compared with that of a man who went on a trip to another country. He laid out his employees' work for them to do while he was gone and told the gatekeeper to watch for his return.

35-37"Keep a sharp lookout! For you do not know when I will come, at evening, at midnight, early dawn or late daybreak. Don't let me find you sleeping. *Watch for my return!* This is my message to you and to everyone else."

CHAPTER 14

A Plot to Kill Jesus

The Passover observance began two days later—an annual Jewish holiday when no bread made with yeast was eaten. The chief priests and other Jewish leaders were still looking for an opportunity to arrest Jesus secretly and put him to death.

2"But we can't do it during the Passover," they said, "or there will be a riot."

A Gift of Love for Jesus

3Meanwhile Jesus was in Bethany, at the home of Simon the leper; during supper a woman came in with a beautiful flask of expensive perfume. Then, breaking the seal, she poured it over his head.

4,5Some of those at the table were indignant among themselves about this "waste," as they called it.

"Why, she could have sold that perfume for a fortune and given the money to the poor!" they snarled.

6But Jesus said, "Let her alone; why berate her for doing a good thing? 7You always have the poor among you, and they badly need your help, and you can aid them whenever you want to; but I won't be here much longer.

8"She has done what she could and has anointed my body ahead of time for burial.

13:21-37 Jesus did not reveal when the end would come, but this should motivate us to remain alert and watchful from now until the end. And as we are unsure of the future of our world, we also are uncertain concerning the timing and difficulties we will face in recovery. In reality, we are never completely recovered; we are always in recovery. We will experience total victory only after Jesus has returned to make us into new people. Preparation for his return must be made one day at a time. We cannot calculate the day of his return and plan to change just before the final event. Our daily preparation and action are an important key to our spiritual health and our recovery.

9And I tell you this in solemn truth, that wherever the Good News is preached throughout the world, this woman's deed will be remembered and praised."

Judas Agrees to Betray Jesus

10Then Judas Iscariot, one of his disciples, went to the chief priests to arrange to betray Jesus to them.

11When the chief priests heard why he had come, they were excited and happy and promised him a reward. So he began looking for the right time and place to betray Jesus.

The Last Supper

12On the first day of the Passover, the day the lambs were sacrificed, his disciples asked him where he wanted to go to eat the traditional Passover supper. 13He sent two of them into Jerusalem to make the arrangements.

"As you are walking along," he told them, "you will see a man coming toward you carrying a pot of water. Follow him. 14At the house he enters, tell the man in charge, 'Our Master sent us to see the room you have ready for us, where we will eat the Passover supper this evening!' 15He will take you upstairs to a large room all set up. Prepare our supper there."

16So the two disciples went on ahead into the city and found everything as Jesus had said, and prepared the Passover.

17In the evening Jesus arrived with the other disciples, 18and as they were sitting around the table eating, Jesus said, "I solemnly declare that one of you will betray me, one of you who is here eating with me."

19A great sadness swept over them, and one by one they asked him, "Am I the one?"

20He replied, "It is one of you twelve eating with me now. 21I must die, as the prophets declared long ago; but, oh, the misery ahead for the man by whom I am betrayed. Oh, that he had never been born!"

22As they were eating, Jesus took bread and asked God's blessing on it and broke it in pieces and gave it to them and said, "Eat it—this is my body."

23Then he took a cup of wine and gave thanks to God for it and gave it to them; and they all drank from it. 24And he said to them, "This is my blood, poured out for many, sealing the new agreement between God and man. 25I solemnly declare that I shall never again taste wine until the day I drink a different kind in the Kingdom of God."

Jesus Predicts Peter's Denial

26Then they sang a hymn and went out to the Mount of Olives.

27"All of you will desert me," Jesus told them, "for God has declared through the prophets, 'I will kill the Shepherd, and the sheep will scatter.' 28But after I am raised to life again, I will go to Galilee and meet you there."

29Peter said to him, "I will never desert you no matter what the others do!"

14:10-25 We are often shocked by the story of Judas's betrayal of Jesus. Since Judas had spent about three years in close friendship with Jesus, we wonder what could have prompted him to act as he did. Yet if we are as honest as we should be, we can probably see the same potential in our own heart. Whenever we refuse to give Jesus authority over a certain area of our life, we act like Judas. Whenever we promise to do one thing and then do another, we act like Judas. We all have betrayed God in some way or another. We should use Judas's failure as an opportunity to take a hard look at our own life. In what ways are we betraying God?

14:26-31 Peter wasn't honest with himself when he promised that he would stay with Jesus no matter what the cost. He still did not realize that following Jesus would lead him to the foot of the cross. So when things got tough, Peter backed out of his commitment. We often do the same thing in recovery. We determine to escape the pain of our addictions, so we commit ourself to recovery. But we still may be unaware of the hard times we will have to face along the way. As our recovery becomes difficult and we experience opposition, we become tempted to give up and fall back into our destructive habits. We would be wise to consider the difficulties we may face before we start the journey. That way, we won't be devastated when we have to face them.

14:32-42 Jesus opened his heart to Peter, James, and John: "My soul is crushed by sorrow" (14:34) and "though the spirit is willing enough, the body is weak" (14:38). Jesus demonstrated some qualities that are important for us in recovery: honesty, transparency, and trust. Jesus evidently needed others for support in this hour of agony shortly before his death. If Jesus needed human support to face his trials, we must need it even more. It is important that we develop a support group that will hold us accountable to our commitments in recovery. Unless we can develop and maintain meaningful human relationships, it will be nearly impossible to sustain our recovery.

READ MARK 14:3-9

GOD grant me the serenity to accept the things I cannot change the courage to change the things I can and the wisdom to know the difference AMEN

As we pray the serenity prayer, we learn to think in new ways. We learn to ask questions that will lead us away from our destructive past and into a productive future.

We begin to ask, What can we change in our situation? What things are beyond our control? What are our responsibilities in the situations we face? As we develop these new thought processes, we may lack confidence in our own wisdom and common sense. We may hesitate to carry out God's will if we are afraid of the criticism of the people around us.

Common sense could be defined as our ability to figure out in advance what the likely consequences of our choices and actions will be. We are told, "Getting wisdom is the most important thing you can do! And with your wisdom, develop common sense and good judgment" (Proverbs 4:7). We can exercise our common sense by thinking about what we can do and then doing the things that we can.

A woman wanted to do something to display her love for Jesus, so she poured some expensive perfume on him. When she did this, she was criticized by the disciples. Jesus came to her defense with these words, "Let her alone; why berate her for doing a good thing? . . . She has done what she could" (Mark 14:6-8). These are words we also can cling to.

God wants to renew our mind and help us develop wisdom and common sense. As we try to sort out our choices and develop common sense, people may criticize us. But we can trust that God will come to our defense, as long as we do what we can. ***Turn to page 1113, Luke 11.***

30"Peter," Jesus said, "before the cock crows
a second time tomorrow morning you will
deny me three times."
31"No!" Peter exploded. "Not even if I have
to die with you! I'll *never* deny you!" And all
the others vowed the same.

Jesus Agonizes in the Garden

32And now they came to an olive grove called
the Garden of Gethsemane, and he instructed
his disciples, "Sit here, while I go and pray."
33He took Peter, James, and John with him
and began to be filled with horror and deepest
distress. 34And he said to them, "My soul is
crushed by sorrow to the point of death; stay
here and watch with me."
35He went on a little further and fell to the
ground and prayed that if it were possible the
awful hour awaiting him might never come.
36"Father, Father," he said, "everything is
possible for you. Take away this cup from me.
Yet I want your will, not mine."
37Then he returned to the three disciples
and found them asleep.
"Simon!" he said. "Asleep? Couldn't you
watch with me even one hour? 38Watch with
me and pray lest the Tempter overpower you.
For though the spirit is willing enough, the
body is weak."
39And he went away again and prayed, repeating his pleadings. 40Again he returned to
them and found them sleeping, for they were
very tired. And they didn't know what to say.
41The third time when he returned to them
he said, "Sleep on; get your rest! But no! The
time for sleep has ended! Look! I am betrayed
into the hands of wicked men. 42Come! Get
up! We must go! Look! My betrayer is here!"

Judas Betrays Jesus

43 And immediately, while he was still speaking, Judas (one of his disciples) arrived with a
mob equipped with swords and clubs, sent
out by the chief priests and other Jewish leaders.

44 Judas had told them, "You will know
which one to arrest when I go over and greet
him. Then you can take him easily." 45 So as
soon as they arrived he walked up to Jesus.
"Master!" he exclaimed, and embraced him
with a great show of friendliness. 46 Then the
mob arrested Jesus and held him fast. 47 But
someone pulled a sword and slashed at the
High Priest's servant, cutting off his ear.

48 Jesus asked them, "Am I some dangerous
robber, that you come like this, armed to the
teeth to capture me? 49 Why didn't you arrest
me in the Temple? I was there teaching every
day. But these things are happening to fulfill
the prophecies about me."

50 Meanwhile, all his disciples had fled.
51,52 There was, however, a young man following along behind, clothed only in a linen
nightshirt. When the mob tried to grab him,
he escaped, though his clothes were torn off
in the process, so that he ran away completely
naked.

Jesus before the Council

53 Jesus was led to the High Priest's home
where all of the chief priests and other Jewish
leaders soon gathered. 54 Peter followed far behind and then slipped inside the gates of the
High Priest's residence and crouched beside a
fire among the servants.

55 Inside, the chief priests and the whole
Jewish Supreme Court were trying to find
something against Jesus that would be sufficient to condemn him to death. But their
efforts were in vain. 56 Many false witnesses
volunteered, but they contradicted each
other.

57 Finally some men stood up to lie about
him and said, 58 "We heard him say, 'I will
destroy this Temple made with human hands
and in three days I will build another, made
without human hands!'" 59 But even then they
didn't get their stories straight!

60 Then the High Priest stood up before the
Court and asked Jesus, "Do you refuse to
answer this charge? What do you have to say
for yourself?"

61 To this Jesus made no reply.

Then the High Priest asked him. "Are you
the Messiah, the Son of God?"

62 Jesus said, "I am, and you will see me
sitting at the right hand of God, and returning
to earth in the clouds of heaven."

63,64 Then the High Priest tore at his clothes
and said, "What more do we need? Why wait
for witnesses? You have heard his blasphemy.
What is your verdict?" And the vote for the
death sentence was unanimous.

65 Then some of them began to spit at him,
and they blindfolded him and began to hammer his face with their fists.

"Who hit you that time, you prophet?"
they jeered. And even the bailiffs were using
their fists on him as they led him away.

Peter Denies Knowing Jesus

66,67 Meanwhile Peter was below in the courtyard. One of the maids who worked for the
High Priest noticed Peter warming himself at
the fire.

She looked at him closely and then announced, "*You* were with Jesus, the Nazarene."

68 Peter denied it. "I don't know what you're
talking about!" he said, and walked over to
the edge of the courtyard.

Just then, a rooster crowed.

69 The maid saw him standing there and
began telling the others, "There he is! There's
that disciple of Jesus!"

70 Peter denied it again.

A little later others standing around the fire
began saying to Peter, "You are, too, one of
them, for you are from Galilee!"

14:53-65 Jesus was a victim of abuse and injustice: he was lied about, falsely accused and convicted, and physically assaulted. But, instead of returning words or blows in kind, he entrusted himself to his Father's care (1 Peter 2:23). Jesus thus modeled the kind of trust that a person with a history of abuse might emulate. As we experience the pain of past abuse in our life, we, too, can turn all the hurtful events and vengeful feelings over to God's care. We can focus our attention on our own problems and dependencies, knowing that God will deal justly with the people in our past.

14:66-72 Peter apparently didn't know himself as well as he thought. Earlier he had claimed that he would never deny Jesus; here he denied his Master three times. Peter could have profited from Jesus' earlier prediction of his denial. Instead of shrugging it off, he should have responded to Jesus' words with honest self-examination. Denying the sad truth about ourself usually leads to the loss of important opportunities to correct our character flaws. This, in turn, stops our progress in recovery and slows our spiritual growth.

71 He began to curse and swear. "I don't even know this fellow you are talking about," he said.

72 And immediately the rooster crowed the second time. Suddenly Jesus' words flashed through Peter's mind: "Before the cock crows twice, you will deny me three times." And he began to cry.

CHAPTER 15

Pilate Questions Jesus

Early in the morning the chief priests, elders and teachers of religion—the entire Supreme Court—met to discuss their next steps. Their decision was to send Jesus under armed guard to Pilate, the Roman governor.

2 Pilate asked him, "Are you the King of the Jews?"

"Yes," Jesus replied, "it is as you say."

3,4 Then the chief priests accused him of many crimes, and Pilate asked him, "Why don't you say something? What about all these charges against you?"

5 But Jesus said no more, much to Pilate's amazement.

Pilate Allows Jesus' Crucifixion

6 Now, it was Pilate's custom to release one Jewish prisoner each year at Passover time—any prisoner the people requested. 7 One of the prisoners at that time was Barabbas, convicted along with others for murder during an insurrection.

8 Now a mob began to crowd in toward Pilate, asking him to release a prisoner as usual.

9 "How about giving you the 'King of Jews'?" Pilate asked. "Is he the one you want released?" 10 (For he realized by now that this was a frameup, backed by the chief priests because they envied Jesus' popularity.)

11 But at this point the chief priests whipped up the mob to demand the release of Barabbas instead of Jesus.

12 "But if I release Barabbas," Pilate asked them, "what shall I do with this man you call your king?"

13 They shouted back, "Crucify him!"

14 "But why?" Pilate demanded. "What has he done wrong?" They only roared the louder, "Crucify him!"

15 Then Pilate, afraid of a riot and anxious to please the people, released Barabbas to them. And he ordered Jesus flogged with a leaded whip, and handed him over to be crucified.

Roman Soldiers Mock Jesus

16,17 Then the Roman soldiers took him into the barracks of the palace, called out the entire palace guard, dressed him in a purple robe, and made a crown of long, sharp thorns and put it on his head. 18 Then they saluted, yelling, "Yea! King of the Jews!" 19 And they beat him on the head with a cane, and spat on him, and went down on their knees to "worship" him.

20 When they finally tired of their sport, they took off the purple robe and put his own clothes on him again, and led him away to be crucified.

21 Simon of Cyrene, who was coming in from the country just then, was pressed into service to carry Jesus' cross. (Simon is the father of Alexander and Rufus.)

22 And they brought Jesus to a place called Golgotha. (Golgotha means skull.) 23 Wine drugged with bitter herbs was offered to him there, but he refused it. 24 And then they crucified him—and threw dice for his clothes.

Jesus Is Hung on the Cross

25 It was about nine o'clock in the morning when the crucifixion took place.

26 A signboard was fastened to the cross above his head, announcing his crime. It read, "The King of the Jews."

27 Two robbers were also crucified that morning, their crosses on either side of his. 28 And so the Scripture was fulfilled that said, "He was counted among evil men."

15:1-15 Pilate stated at least three times that he found no guilt in Jesus, yet he handed him over for execution. Strong emotions on the part of the Jews and Pilate's desire to pacify them at all cost led to the punishment of an innocent man. We have a lot in common with Pilate. When we sacrifice the truth in order to please the crowd, we, too, crucify Jesus. Our challenge in recovery is to stand firm in our faith and not succumb to cynicism, compromises, or moral laxity. When we take the first step toward relapse, we must recover our footing with courage and wisdom.

15:16-32 Jesus suffered the ultimate in verbal and physical abuse when he was spat upon, beaten up, mocked, and nailed to a cross. Knowing that Jesus did all this to provide a powerful means for our recovery should give us hope. No matter how terrible our past, no matter how great our mistakes, Jesus has paid the penalty for our sins. Because of his suffering, we can have a true relationship with our powerful God. As we grow in our relationship with him, we will discover that there is more than enough power available for our recovery.

[29,30]The people jeered at him as they walked
by, and wagged their heads in mockery.
"Ha! Look at you now!" they yelled at him.
"Sure, you can destroy the Temple and rebuild
it in three days! If you're so wonderful, save
yourself and come down from the cross."
[31]The chief priests and religious leaders
were also standing around joking about Jesus.
"He's quite clever at 'saving' others," they
said, "but he can't save himself!"
[32]"Hey there, Messiah!" they yelled at him.
"You 'King of Israel'! Come on down from the
cross and we'll believe you!"
And even the two robbers dying with him,
cursed him.

Jesus Dies on the Cross

[33]About noon, darkness fell across the entire
land, lasting until three o'clock that afternoon.
[34]Then Jesus called out with a loud voice,
"Eli, Eli, lama sabachthani?" ("My God, my
God, why have you deserted me?")
[35]Some of the people standing there
thought he was calling for the prophet Elijah.
[36]So one man ran and got a sponge and filled
it with sour wine and held it up to him on a
stick.
"Let's see if Elijah will come and take him
down!" he said.
[37]Then Jesus uttered another loud cry and
dismissed his spirit.
[38]And the curtain in the Temple was split
apart from top to bottom.
[39]When the Roman officer standing beside
his cross saw how he dismissed his spirit, he
exclaimed, "Truly, this was the Son of God!"
[40]Some women were there watching from
a distance—Mary Magdalene, Mary (the
mother of James the Younger and of Joses),
Salome, and others. [41]They and many other
Galilean women who were his followers
had ministered to him when he was up in
Galilee, and had come with him to Jerusalem.

Jesus Is Placed in a Tomb

[42,43]This all happened the day before the Sabbath. Late that afternoon Joseph from Arimathea, an honored member of the Jewish
Supreme Court (who personally was eagerly
expecting the arrival of God's Kingdom),
gathered his courage and went to Pilate and
asked for Jesus' body.
[44]Pilate couldn't believe that Jesus was already dead so he called for the Roman officer
in charge and asked him. [45]The officer confirmed the fact, and Pilate told Joseph he
could have the body.
[46]Joseph bought a long sheet of linen cloth
and, taking Jesus' body down from the cross,
wound it in the cloth and laid it in a rock-
hewn tomb, and rolled a stone in front of the
entrance.
[47](Mary Magdalene and Mary the mother of
Joses were watching as Jesus was laid away.)

CHAPTER 16

Jesus Rises from the Dead

The next evening, when the Sabbath ended,
Mary Magdalene and Salome and Mary the
mother of James went out and purchased
embalming spices.
Early the following morning, just at sun-

15:33-41 The purpose for which Jesus came to earth, and the key thought of Mark's Gospel (10:45), can be found in Jesus' sacrificial death as a payment for our sins. At this excruciating moment, the Savior bore the pain and punishment for all the sins ever committed (1 Peter 2:24). This is truly good news! Although we are never good enough to gain God's favor, Jesus' sacrifice provides the eternal security necessary for our recovery. No matter how hard we try, we can never attain recovery from sin and its effects under our own power or effort. But by looking to God for help, however, we can overcome even the most terrible sins, dependencies, and compulsions.

16:3-7 The women were wondering how they would ever roll the great stone from the tomb entrance, when, to their amazement, they found it already gone. The tomb was empty! Notice that the women had only wanted to roll back the stone. But God had accomplished so much more: he had raised Jesus from the dead! If God can give life to a dead body, he surely can restore our life from addiction. All we need to do is put our trust in him. There is always hope. With God, all things are possible! He specializes in rolling away burdens too great for our feeble human strength to handle. And, if we set out to do all we can, we will likely discover that God has already accomplished our goals—and even more!

16:9-20 Many of the disciples had a hard time believing that Jesus had risen from the dead. When they finally met the resurrected Jesus, he rebuked them for their unbelief. Then Jesus rewarded his followers as they came to believe. Faith is foundational for our salvation and recovery; unbelief leads to condemnation and relapse. As we grow in our faith in Jesus, we will discover that the power of his resurrection will touch and transform our life. Then we will become a source of encouragement to others as we share the story of God's deliverance.

rise, they carried them out to the tomb. [3]On
the way they were discussing how they could
ever roll aside the huge stone from the entrance.
[4]But when they arrived they looked up and
saw that the stone—a *very* heavy one—was
already moved away and the entrance was
open! [5]So they entered the tomb—and there
on the right sat a young man clothed in
white. The women were startled, [6]but the angel said, "Don't be so surprised. Aren't you
looking for Jesus, the Nazarene who was crucified? He isn't here! He has come back to life!
Look, that's where his body was lying. [7]Now
go and give this message to his disciples including Peter:
"'Jesus is going ahead of you to Galilee. You
will see him there, just as he told you before
he died!'"
[8]The women fled from the tomb, trembling
and bewildered, too frightened to talk.

Jesus Talks to Mary Magdalene

[9] It was early on Sunday morning when Jesus
came back to life, and the first person who
saw him was Mary Magdalene—the woman
from whom he had cast out seven demons.
[10,11]She found the disciples wet-eyed with grief
and exclaimed that she had seen Jesus, and he
was alive! But they didn't believe her!

Jesus Appears to Two Believers

[12]Later that day he appeared to two who were
walking from Jerusalem into the country, but
they didn't recognize him at first because he
had changed his appearance. [13]When they
finally realized who he was, they rushed back
to Jerusalem to tell the others, but no one
believed them.

Jesus Appears to the Disciples

[14]Still later he appeared to the eleven disciples
as they were eating together. He rebuked
them for their unbelief—their stubborn refusal to believe those who had seen him alive
from the dead.

The Great Commission

[15]And then he told them, "You are to go into
all the world and preach the Good News to
everyone, everywhere. [16]Those who believe
and are baptized will be saved. But those who
refuse to believe will be condemned.
[17]"And those who believe shall use my authority to cast out demons, and they shall
speak new languages. [18]They will be able even
to handle snakes with safety, and if they drink

Our Story

BIBLE READING: Mark 16:14-18

Having had a spiritual awakening as the result of these steps, we tried to carry this message to others and to practice these principles in all our affairs.

Each one of us has a valuable story to tell. We may be shy and feel awkward about speaking. We may think that what we have to share is too trivial. Is it actually going to help anyone else? We may struggle to get beyond the shame of our past. But our recovery story can help others who are trapped back where we were. Are we willing to allow God to use us to help free others?

Jesus left us with this vital task: "You are to go into all the world and preach the Good News [of salvation from the bondage and penalty of sin] to everyone, everywhere" (Mark 16:15). The apostle Paul traveled the world over telling everyone the story of his conversion. He ended up in chains, but his spirit was free. He presented his defense (and his own story of redemption) before kings. King Agrippa interrupted him to say, "'With trivial proofs like these, you expect me to become a Christian?' And Paul replied, 'Would to God that whether my arguments are trivial or strong, both you and everyone here in this audience might become the same as I am, except for these chains'" (Acts 26:28-29).

Within each personal story of the journey from bondage to freedom is a microcosm of the gospel. When people hear our story, even if it seems trivial, we are offering them the chance to loosen their chains and begin a recovery story of their own. ***Turn to page 1167, John 15.***

anything poisonous, it won't hurt them; and they will be able to place their hands on the sick and heal them."

Jesus Ascends into Heaven
[19]When the Lord Jesus had finished talking
with them, he was taken up into heaven and sat down at God's right hand.
[20]And the disciples went everywhere
preaching, and the Lord was with them and confirmed what they said by the miracles that followed their messages.

✲insights CONCERNING TRUE FAITH

In **Mark 1:16-20** Jesus called four burly fishermen to be his disciples. We are not sure how many times Jesus had to call Simon Peter, Andrew, James, and John to follow him. On two other occasions, a similar call went out to these four fishermen (see Luke 5:1-11; John 1:35-42). Their response to Jesus' call on any one occasion, as here, seems to have been "immediate." But it seems that they soon went back to their old occupation and way of life. So also it is in recovery. Our faith in God will grow over time, at uneven rates, with uncertain steps. Each step of faith we take requires that we drop whatever else we are doing and follow Jesus wholeheartedly.

In **Mark 10:13-22,** two kinds of people are contrasted: the little children, who came to Jesus with innocent trust; and a wealthy young man, who trusted in his wealth and was unwilling to follow Jesus. The only way we can enter the Kingdom of God is through childlike trust. This is also the only way we can enter recovery. As long as we think we can make it on our own, we are hopelessly entrapped by our dependencies. Anyone who has tried to recover alone has discovered that it is a losing battle. We must begin by assuming that we are helpless, just like little children. Then we must put our life into the hands of God and do what we can to follow his program for us. If we trust in our abilities or wealth for deliverance, we are doomed to self-inflicted destruction.

The women who followed Jesus to the cross in **Mark 15:47–16:11** were not in a position to stop the Crucifixion. But instead of running away, they did what they could. They stayed at the foot of the cross, watched to see where Jesus would be buried, and prepared spices to embalm his body. They were willing to do this even though the twelve disciples had run for their lives. Their resourcefulness and faithful devotion to the very end was honored by an opportunity to see the risen Jesus. As we continue in the process of recovery, we should never waste time waiting for opportunities that will never arrive. We need to take full advantage of the opportunities God gives for recovery and experience his power in our life.

✲insights ABOUT GOD'S POWER TO SAVE

In **Mark 1:21-28** God's power to change lives was demonstrated as Jesus cast out an unclean spirit. If Jesus has the power to cast out evil spirits, he certainly has enough power to free us from our defects of character, even our dependencies and compulsions. All we need to do is recognize that we have a problem and call out to him for help.

In **Mark 1:40-45** Jesus displayed his power by healing a man with leprosy. Leprosy is a progressive, contagious, and crippling skin disease. In ancient times, it was often considered a form of divine retribution (see Numbers 12:9-10; 2 Chronicles 26:16-23). Since there was no hope for a cure, except by a miracle from God, leprosy was treated by social ostracism (see Leviticus 13). Modern medicine has all but eliminated the disease of leprosy, but we can still relate to what it must have been like. In fact, we all are "lepers," infected by the incurable disease of sin. This has made us ugly and caused our separation from the people we love. Yet there is hope for us. We can be restored to healthy living and fellowship by the healing touch of Jesus. First, like the leper, we must realize our inability to cure ourself. Then we can trust Jesus' power and love for cleansing and recovery.

In **Mark 4:26-29** Jesus used an illustration to show us how God works in our recovery. Just as seeds silently grow in the soil, God gradually and relentlessly changes us from the inside out. We have come to recognize how helpless we are against our dependencies. We already know that we are powerless to change alone. We have already failed many times by trying to participate in the right activities and behaviors. We know we can't change from the outside in. Here we are given a wonderful message of hope! God changes us from the inside out! He has the power to make us into a new person and will sustain us in our recovery.

In **Mark 4:30-34** Jesus used the illustration of the mustard seed to make another point about how God works in our recovery. God's healing work in our life may have a small beginning. We may even wonder if anything has happened at all. But as God's power and grace begin to work their way in our life, we will experience significant changes for the better. In time, our recovery will be made complete (see Philippians 1:6) and, just as the mustard tree grew up to shelter birds in its branches, we will make a profound impact for good on the lives of the people around us.

The miracle of **Mark 6:35-44** displays an important recovery principle: our needs are never greater than God's supply. That's the lesson for people in recovery who appreciate Jesus' miraculous supply of food for more than five thousand people. The twelve disciples should have learned this lesson through Jesus' ample provision, but failed to do so (6:52). They should have learned that when confronted with an impossible situation, Jesus could be trusted to meet the momentary need. We also need to remember that no obstacle to recovery is too great for God. He is more than able to meet all of our needs.

In **Mark 9:2-13** we see Jesus transfigured on the mountain. In this amazing event, we are given a picture of what we can hope for in our own life. Someday, we will be changed; we will be made perfect. We may be struggling with destructive dependencies, in despair about our devastated life. In such times, it might help to reflect on who we will become if we only entrust our life to God in Jesus Christ. God wants to begin the process of leading us toward a healthy and productive life right now. And when he returns in glory, he will restore us and his entire creation to perfection. With this hope in mind, let us do what we can now to start the process of recovery.

insights ABOUT GOD'S PRIORITIES

God gave the Sabbath laws (Exodus 34:21) to protect God's people from overwork and to keep their lives in proper balance. Like all of God's laws, these laws were intended for the good of his people. When the disciples picked grain at the edge of a farmer's field in **Mark 2:23-28,** they were actually following one of the provisions God had prescribed in his Law (Leviticus 19:9-10). Yet the Pharisees, with their made-up rules and false assumptions, accused Jesus of breaking the Law by working on the Sabbath. Sadly, as they pretended to uphold the Law, the Pharisees actually stood counter to God's intentions. So today, our preconceptions about disease, sin, or God's plan can motivate us to block the path of recovery for others. We must never set up roadblocks to the healing of hurting people, especially by using God's Word. It is part of God's plan that people should live healthy lives; we should do all we can to support his plan.

We find in **Mark 10:32-45** that immediately after Jesus warned his disciples of his impending suffering and death, James and John turned around and requested positions of honor and authority. They were blind to the fact that the call to follow Jesus would involve suffering and persecution. Following Jesus on the road to recovery is never easy. It demands that we swallow our pride and admit our mistakes. It calls us to give up the dependencies that have helped us escape our inner pain. It means that we have to come out of hiding and show the world how ugly we are inside. We must humble ourselves before the people we have wronged. Following Jesus is never the easiest path, but it is the only path that leads to a life of restoration, joy, and fulfillment.

Jesus expressed his true feelings in **Mark 14:35-36,** as he begged his Father to remove the cup of suffering that he faced, but he never rebelled against God's will. He was willing to suffer and die so that all of us could experience forgiveness from sin and recovery from its painful effects. And, as much as we might want to escape certain unpleasant tasks in our recovery, we must submit all such desires to God's will. God may lead us into some tough experiences, but, as painful as they may be, we can be assured that he has our best in mind. We can also be sure that he will stand with us throughout the process.

✲*insights* CONCERNING OBSTACLES TO RECOVERY

The Sabbath controversy recorded in **Mark 3:1-6** reveals two ways of dealing with anger. Anger itself is a normal human emotion; it is morally neutral. What we do with our anger is what counts. Jesus was angry at the Pharisees for making up rules about the Sabbath that stood counter to God's real intentions in the Law. Jesus used his anger constructively—not to tear people down, but to heal a man's deformed hand. The Pharisees and Herodians, in their anger, plotted to kill Jesus. Anger expressed in selfish or harmful ways will always stand in the way of our recovery.

In **Mark 5:1-20,** after healing the demon-possessed man, Jesus faced opposition from the people of the nearby town. The demons had left the man and entered a herd of pigs, causing them to run wildly into the lake to be drowned. The people of the town did not like losing their source of livelihood. They felt threatened when the status quo of their world was disturbed. We may experience similar opposition when God begins to make changes in our life. Friends and family members may feel threatened by the changes and try to stop us. If we experience opposition from codependents, we should be neither surprised nor discouraged. We should simply continue trusting God to change us so we will be able to help our friends and family in ways they may never have imagined possible.

In **Mark 14:1-9,** a woman (Mary) showed her devotion to Jesus by anointing him with expensive perfume (equal in value to a year's wages), as if preparing a king for burial. Her devotion was mocked by some of the disciples, but it was praised by Jesus as an example for all believers to follow. Our faith in God and commitment to recovery often receive the criticism of others. Sometimes family members have a hard time believing we are sincere. Our friends may even feel threatened by the changes they see in our life. We can be sure, however, that no matter what others might say, Jesus is in favor of the steps we are taking. And, if we persevere, we will discover that others will someday praise our efforts, too.

✲*insights* ABOUT THE PERSON OF JESUS

In **Mark 6:1-6** Jesus visited his hometown of Nazareth. During his visit, Jesus was looked upon as a mere man, a carpenter, Mary's boy. In short, Jesus was just a regular guy to this hometown crowd. This attitude of unbelief effectively kept Jesus from doing a more extensive ministry in Nazareth. Unfortunately for the people of Nazareth, their familiarity with Jesus bred contempt. Fortunately for us, Jesus left and went elsewhere to do his ministry, to those who would believe in his miracles and message. Our world has tried to pass Jesus off as just another man, a good teacher, or a wise prophet. Anyone who focuses on Jesus' humanity to the exclusion of his divinity makes a grave mistake. If Jesus is not the Son of God, there is little hope for our recovery.

✲*insights* ABOUT HONESTY AND DENIAL

Herod Antipas did not like being corrected. So in **Mark 6:14-29,** when John the Baptist confronted him concerning his immoral marriage to his brother's wife, the prophet paid for it with his life. Herod was in denial about his sin and did not like to be reminded of what he had done. But his denial only led to an even greater sin—murder. We are guilty of the same thing when we refuse to listen to warnings about our destructive behaviors. We need to learn that our denial will never help things; it will only lead to even greater suffering and devastation. We would be wise to act immediately upon the warnings we receive. If we don't, we are headed for even greater trouble.

LUKE

THE BIG PICTURE

A. THE SAVIOR'S BIRTH AND PREPARATION (1:1–4:13)
B. THE SAVIOR'S MINISTRY IN WORD AND DEED (4:14–21:38)
   1. Jesus' Ministry in Galilee (4:14–9:50)
   2. Jesus' Ministry on the Way to Jerusalem (9:51–19:27)
   3. Jesus' Ministry in Jerusalem (19:28–21:38)
C. THE SAVIOR'S DEATH AND RESURRECTION (22:1–24:53)

Luke was a physician and historian. He wrote about Jesus as a man who cared greatly for suffering and downtrodden people, a man who brought healing to the hurting. In the genealogy of Jesus, Luke traced Jesus' human ancestors back to Adam, the father of the human race. And Luke's stories about Jesus focused on his relationships with individual people. Jesus paid special attention to people who were often ignored in society—women, children, the poor, prostitutes, despised tax collectors, and sinners of every sort.

Jesus offered salvation, strength, and spiritual recovery to everyone he met, but his greatest concern was for the outcasts of society. Luke stressed the humanity and compassion of Jesus more than any of the other Gospel writers did. His narrative made it clear that God, through his Son Jesus, reaches out in love to the unlovable of our world. Ever since Adam and Eve's first sin in the Garden of Eden, God has passionately desired and pursued the recovery of broken people. His love and concern for us are unstoppable!

As we work our recovery, many of us discover just how terrible and destructive our mistakes have been. As the levels of denial peel away, we begin to see how sick and broken we really are. We may wonder whether there is any hope for us. How could God care for us after all we have done? In reading the Gospel of Luke, we can gain hope from the compassion God showed toward people who were a lot like us. God wants to show us how much he loves us, regardless of our mistakes in the past. He wants to have an active role in our recovery.

THE BOTTOM LINE

PURPOSE: To confirm the historical record of the life of Jesus Christ, whose universal message offers hope and salvation to all who turn to him. AUTHOR: Luke, the physician. AUDIENCE: Theophilus, whose name means "lover of God." DATE WRITTEN: Probably about A.D. 60. KEY VERSES: "Jesus told him, 'This shows that salvation has come to this home today. This man was one of the lost sons of Abraham, and I, the Messiah, have come to search for and to save such souls as his'" (19:9-10). SPECIAL FEATURES: Luke focused on Jesus' relationships with people, particularly those who were in need, and he placed special emphasis on the role of women. KEY PEOPLE AND RELATIONSHIPS: Jesus and his disciples, Zacharias and Elizabeth, Mary, Mary Magdalene, and John the Baptist.

RECOVERY THEMES

Jesus Loves the Outcast: Jesus paid special attention to the poor, the despised, the hurt, and the sinful. He rejected no one; he ignored no one. And no one today is beyond the scope of his love or beyond his ability to help—including us. He cares for us no matter what we have done or what we have suffered. Only this kind of deep love can satisfy our deepest needs and mobilize us to recovery. When our life is most unmanageable and we are faced with our powerlessness, we often feel that no one can understand or care. Luke shows us that God both understands and cares. We can safely turn our life over to him!

The Power of the Resurrection: Paul wrote to the Philippians and told them that he longed to "experience the mighty power that brought [Jesus] back to life again" (Philippians 3:10). Like the other Gospel writers, Luke showed in detail the events surrounding the death and resurrection of Jesus. There is no greater example of God's power at work than that which can bring the dead back to life again. God specializes in demonstrating that kind of power. In our recovery, we experience his power at work within us, bringing back to life our soul and body. With God, nothing is too difficult.

God's Passion for Our Recovery: God cares about our recovery even more than we do—that's how much he loves and cares for us. Jesus showed this by revealing his intense interest in people and relationships. He cared for his followers and friends. He was interested in all types of people—men, women, and children. His concern transcended all barriers and extended to any and all that he met. He longed to see people whole, well, and growing. As we come to know him and share his heart, we experience his passion for our wholeness and recovery. He died that we might live.

The Power of the Holy Spirit: Jesus lived his life in complete dependence on the Holy Spirit. The Holy Spirit was present at the birth of Jesus, at his baptism, in his ministry, and in his resurrection. The Holy Spirit was sent by the Father to confirm Jesus' authority. Today the Holy Spirit is given to empower us to live as God wants us to live. By faith, we can have the Holy Spirit's presence and power within us, enabling us in our recovery and spiritual growth.

CHAPTER 1

Luke's Purpose in Writing

Dear friend who loves God:

1,2Several biographies of Christ have already been written using as their source material the reports circulating among us from the early disciples and other eyewitnesses. 3However, it occurred to me that it would be well to recheck all these accounts from first to last and after thorough investigation to pass this summary on to you, 4to reassure you of the truth of all you were taught.

An Angel Visits Zacharias

5My story begins with a Jewish priest, Zacharias, who lived when Herod was king of Judea. Zacharias was a member of the Abijah division of the Temple service corps. (His wife, Elizabeth, was, like himself, a member of the priest tribe of the Jews, a descendant of Aaron.) 6Zacharias and Elizabeth were godly folk, careful to obey all of God's laws in spirit as well as in letter. 7But they had no children, for Elizabeth was barren; and now they were both very old.

1:1-4 In this preface, Luke testified that the gospel of Jesus is based upon historical facts and not theories or myths. Speculative religions, secular philosophies, or political leaders do not meet the deepest needs of the human heart. History is filled with people who aspired to be gods, but only one was truly God. All the other would-be "messiahs" or gods—Alexander the Great, King Tut, Julius Caesar, Napoleon, Adolf Hitler—fall short. Jesus alone can meet the deepest needs of our recovery.

1:5-7 Zacharias and Elizabeth were godly people, but they were also childless, and Elizabeth was well past the childbearing years. Their situation was discouraging, even depressing, as many couples in our society can testify. Yet in their society, childlessness was typically taken as a sign of God's curse or displeasure. Zacharias and Elizabeth were faithful in trusting God, even though God seemed to be against them. This was a key to the blessings they received later on. Their example of patient perseverance is a good example for those of us in recovery.

1:16-17 John the Baptist's ministry was one that would turn the hearts of fathers to their children (Malachi 4:5-6). This is a need felt by many in recovery. His message called for personal repentance and the restoration of broken family relationships. Even though the complete fulfillment of these words is still in the future, the principle has always been true. Spiritual cleansing by God is the first and foundational step to the rebuilding of hurting and broken family relationships. When God is at work, even the most resistant hearts can be softened and the most dysfunctional families restored.

LUKE

Luke wrote more of the New Testament than did any other author. He gave a detailed account of the life of Jesus in his Gospel and a description of the early church in Acts. He was a physician by profession, and his writing reveals his compassion for people. Even his efforts to write his two books were motivated by a concern to help a friend grow in the faith. Consistent with this, Luke pointed his readers to the healing work and person of Jesus, the Great Physician.

Luke's concern for the spiritual health of others was matched by his concern for their physical well-being. Throughout his books he made a point to notice the physical suffering of people and the care that those people received. He recounted how Jesus and his apostles again and again brought physical and spiritual healing into hurting and broken lives. Luke also noticed how Jesus paid special attention to the helpless in society. Jesus didn't help only the wealthy or religious, but he made a special point of helping diseased outcasts, prostitutes, and hated tax collectors. As he wrote his account, Luke's compassionate heart led him to emphasize the compassion of Jesus for the rejects of society.

Luke was also noted for his commitment and loyalty to the apostle Paul as they traveled together spreading the gospel in Asia Minor and Greece. In prison, near the end of his life, Paul wrote of his appreciation for Luke. He called Luke a beloved friend, for he had stayed with Paul even when most of Paul's friends had deserted him. Luke was willing to follow God, even when it led him to share in Paul's sufferings.

Luke did not aspire to greatness or try to grab the spotlight. His goal in life was to serve and care for others. We need people like Luke in our life and should do what we can to establish relationships with compassionate, godly people. Perhaps even more, however, we need to learn how we can become an instrument of healing in the lives of the people around us. Sharing our story and our life in order to help others is one of the important goals of our recovery.

STRENGTHS AND ACCOMPLISHMENTS:
- Luke proclaimed the merits of Jesus without promoting himself.
- He used his talents in medicine and writing to help others.
- He had great compassion for the physical and spiritual needs of others.
- He was a loyal and faithful friend to the apostle Paul.
- He persevered in following God, even when he encountered tough times.

LESSONS FROM HIS LIFE:
- Our care for others should meet spiritual, emotional, and physical needs.
- Being loyal to our friends during hard times is very important.
- God's good will for us sometimes leads us through difficult times.
- If we offer our abilities to God, he will use them to do something of eternal significance.

KEY VERSES:
"Demas has left me. He loved the good things of this life and went to Thessalonica. Crescens has gone to Galatia, Titus to Dalmatia. Only Luke is with me" (2 Timothy 4:10-11).

Luke included himself in the "we" sections of Acts 16–28. He is also mentioned in Luke 1:3; Acts 1:1-2; Colossians 4:14; 2 Timothy 4:11; and Philemon 1:24.

8,9One day as Zacharias was going about his
work in the Temple—for his division was on
duty that week—the honor fell to him by lot
to enter the inner sanctuary and burn incense
before the Lord. 10Meanwhile, a great crowd
stood outside in the Temple court, praying as
they always did during that part of the service
when the incense was being burned.
11,12Zacharias was in the sanctuary when
suddenly an angel appeared, standing to the
right of the altar of incense! Zacharias was
startled and terrified.
13But the angel said, "Don't be afraid, Zacharias! For I have come to tell you that God has
heard your prayer, and your wife, Elizabeth,
will bear you a son! And you are to name him
John. 14You will both have great joy and gladness at his birth, and many will rejoice with
you. 15For he will be one of the Lord's great
men. He must never touch wine or hard liquor—and he will be filled with the Holy
Spirit, even from before his birth! 16And he
will persuade many a Jew to turn to the Lord
his God. 17He will be a man of rugged spirit
and power like Elijah, the prophet of old; and
he will precede the coming of the Messiah,

preparing the people for his arrival. He will soften adult hearts to become like little children's, and will change disobedient minds to the wisdom of faith."

18Zacharias said to the angel, "But this is impossible! I'm an old man now, and my wife is also well along in years."

19Then the angel said, "I am Gabriel! I stand in the very presence of God. It was he who sent me to you with this good news! 20And now, because you haven't believed me, you are to be stricken silent, unable to speak until the child is born. For my words will certainly come true at the proper time."

21Meanwhile the crowds outside were waiting for Zacharias to appear and wondered why he was taking so long. 22When he finally came out, he couldn't speak to them, and they realized from his gestures that he must have seen a vision in the Temple. 23He stayed on at the Temple for the remaining days of his Temple duties and then returned home. 24Soon afterwards Elizabeth his wife became pregnant and went into seclusion for five months.

25"How kind the Lord is," she exclaimed, "to take away my disgrace of having no children!"

An Angel Visits Mary

26The following month God sent the angel Gabriel to Nazareth, a village in Galilee, 27to a virgin, Mary, engaged to be married to a man named Joseph, a descendant of King David.

28Gabriel appeared to her and said, "Congratulations, favored lady! The Lord is with you!"

29Confused and disturbed, Mary tried to think what the angel could mean.

30"Don't be frightened, Mary," the angel told her, "for God has decided to wonderfully bless you! 31Very soon now, you will become pregnant and have a baby boy, and you are to name him 'Jesus.' 32He shall be very great and shall be called the Son of God. And the Lord God shall give him the throne of his ancestor David. 33And he shall reign over Israel forever; his Kingdom shall never end!"

34Mary asked the angel, "But how can I have a baby? I am a virgin."

35The angel replied, "The Holy Spirit shall come upon you, and the power of God shall overshadow you; so the baby born to you will be utterly holy—the Son of God. 36Furthermore, six months ago your Aunt Elizabeth—'the barren one,' they called her—became pregnant in her old age! 37For every promise from God shall surely come true."

38Mary said, "I am the Lord's servant, and I am willing to do whatever he wants. May everything you said come true." And then the angel disappeared.

Mary Visits Elizabeth

39,40A few days later Mary hurried to the highlands of Judea to the town where Zacharias lived, to visit Elizabeth.

41At the sound of Mary's greeting, Elizabeth's child leaped within her and she was filled with the Holy Spirit.

42She gave a glad cry and exclaimed to Mary, "You are favored by God above all other women, and your child is destined for God's mightiest praise. 43What an honor this is, that the mother of my Lord should visit me! 44When you came in and greeted me, the instant I heard your voice, my baby moved in me for joy! 45You believed that God would do what he said; that is why he has given you this wonderful blessing."

46Mary responded, "Oh, how I praise the Lord. 47How I rejoice in God my Savior! 48For he took notice of his lowly servant girl, and now generation after generation forever shall call me blest of God. 49For he, the mighty Holy One, has done great things to me. 50His mercy

1:18-20 As godly as Zacharias was, he still could not believe the angel Gabriel's promise. From a natural frame of reference, it seemed totally impossible that he and Elizabeth could conceive a child in their old age. The consequence of even this short-term unbelief was substantial and tragic—Zacharias could not speak throughout the term of Elizabeth's miraculous pregnancy. Unbelief can have a numbing effect on our recovery, as well. Confession of faith, before God and others, by lips and life, as Zacharias was eventually able to do (1:63-64), will help us along the path of recovery. Honestly admitting our doubts is a good place to start.

1:51-55 These words from Mary's song reflect God's priorities standing in stark contrast to the way our world thinks. How important it is, when life seems unfair and does not turn out the way we might have chosen, to realize that God's ways are often not man's ways. Personal fulfillment and genuine recovery do not necessarily come through human greatness and success, but through sincere humility. The most important relationships in life are not always with the rich and famous, but often with the lowly, the needy, and those in recovery.

ELIZABETH & ZACHARIAS

Many loving couples who long for children are unable to have them. Often, their attempts to conceive a child go on for a very long time. As each month passes, they go through a painful progression from hope, to fear, to terrible disappointment. And as the years roll by, all their lingering hopes disappear; they are left with a sort of empty resignation.

This was what it was like for Elizabeth and Zacharias. Their desire for children had not been fulfilled, and they concluded that they would remain childless for the rest of their lives. But suddenly life changed for them. While serving in the Jerusalem Temple, Zacharias was visited by an angel, who announced that he and Elizabeth would have a son. He was to be called John and would become the forerunner of the Messiah.

Understandably shocked, Zacharias doubted the words of the angel. Because of his unbelief, he was rendered speechless until the child's birth. When Elizabeth heard the news, she believed the angel's message and was excited about her forthcoming pregnancy. She indeed became pregnant and, in her sixth month, was visited by her cousin, Mary, who was pregnant with the child Jesus. Filled with the Holy Spirit, Elizabeth praised Mary's faith.

When Elizabeth's baby was born, Zacharias, who still could not speak, wrote down the name the angel had given him—John. At that point, God restored his voice. With his first joyful words, Zacharias praised God for the great gift of a son and his intimate concern with their pain. Whether God blesses the childless with a child, or the helpless with his powerful presence, we see from the lives of Elizabeth and Zacharias that God is intimately involved in our pain and that he desires to fill the empty places in our life.

STRENGTHS AND ACCOMPLISHMENTS:
- Zacharias and Elizabeth were known as godly people.
- Zacharias overcame his doubt and praised God for his power.
- Zacharias obeyed the angel and named his son John.
- Elizabeth commended Mary for her role as the Messiah's mother.

WEAKNESSES AND MISTAKES:
- Zacharias doubted God's ability to give them a child in their older years.

LESSONS FROM THEIR LIVES:
- God is fully aware of the painful disappointment of childless people.
- God is intimately aware of the pain of hurting people.
- All things are possible with God.
- God can use older people to make significant contributions to his plan.

KEY VERSE:
"Zacharias and Elizabeth were godly folk, careful to obey all of God's laws in spirit as well as in letter" (Luke 1:6).

The story of Elizabeth and Zacharias is told in Luke 1:5-80.

---

goes on from generation to generation, to all
who reverence him.
51"How powerful is his mighty arm! How he
scatters the proud and haughty ones! 52He has
torn princes from their thrones and exalted
the lowly. 53He has satisfied the hungry hearts
and sent the rich away with empty hands.
54And how he has helped his servant Israel! He
has not forgotten his promise to be merciful.
55For he promised our fathers—Abraham and
his children—to be merciful to them forever."
56Mary stayed with Elizabeth about three
months and then went back to her own
home.

John the Baptist Is Born

57By now Elizabeth's waiting was over, for the
time had come for the baby to be born—and
it was a boy. 58The word spread quickly to her
neighbors and relatives of how kind the Lord
had been to her, and everyone rejoiced.
59When the baby was eight days old, all the
relatives and friends came for the circumcision ceremony. They all assumed the baby's
name would be Zacharias, after his father.
60But Elizabeth said, "No! He must be
named John!"
61"What?" they exclaimed. "There is no one
in all your family by that name." 62So they
asked the baby's father, talking to him by
gestures.
63He motioned for a piece of paper and to
everyone's surprise wrote, "His name is *John!*"
64Instantly Zacharias could speak again, and
he began praising God.
65Wonder fell upon the whole neighbor-

hood, and the news of what had happened
spread through the Judean hills. 66And everyone who heard about it thought long
thoughts and asked, "I wonder what this
child will turn out to be? For the hand of the
Lord is surely upon him in some special way."
67Then his father, Zacharias, was filled with
the Holy Spirit and gave this prophecy:
68"Praise the Lord, the God of Israel, for he
has come to visit his people and has redeemed
them. 69He is sending us a Mighty Savior from
the royal line of his servant David, 70just as he
promised through his holy prophets long
ago—71someone to save us from our enemies,
from all who hate us.
72,73"He has been merciful to our ancestors,
yes, to Abraham himself, by remembering his
sacred promise to him, 74and by granting us
the privilege of serving God fearlessly, freed
from our enemies, 75and by making us holy
and acceptable, ready to stand in his presence
forever.
76"And you, my little son, shall be called the
prophet of the glorious God, for you will
prepare the way for the Messiah. 77You will tell
his people how to find salvation through forgiveness of their sins. 78All this will be because
the mercy of our God is very tender, and
heaven's dawn is about to break upon us, 79to
give light to those who sit in darkness and
death's shadow, and to guide us to the path of
peace."
80The little boy greatly loved God and when
he grew up he lived out in the lonely wilderness until he began his public ministry to
Israel.

CHAPTER 2

Jesus Is Born

About this time Caesar Augustus, the Roman
emperor, decreed that a census should be
taken throughout the nation. 2(This census
was taken when Quirinius was governor of
Syria.)
3Everyone was required to return to his
ancestral home for this registration. 4And because Joseph was a member of the royal line,
he had to go to Bethlehem in Judea, King
David's ancient home—journeying there
from the Galilean village of Nazareth. 5He
took with him Mary, his fiancée, who was
obviously pregnant by this time.
6And while they were there, the time came
for her baby to be born; 7and she gave birth to
her first child, a son. She wrapped him in a
blanket and laid him in a manger, because
there was no room for them in the village inn.

Angels Appear to Shepherds

8That night some shepherds were in the fields
outside the village, guarding their flocks of
sheep. 9Suddenly an angel appeared among
them, and the landscape shone bright with
the glory of the Lord. They were badly frightened, 10but the angel reassured them.
"Don't be afraid!" he said. "I bring you the
most joyful news ever announced, and it is for
everyone! 11The Savior—yes, the Messiah, the
Lord—has been born tonight in Bethlehem!
12How will you recognize him? You will find a
baby wrapped in a blanket, lying in a manger!"
13Suddenly, the angel was joined by a vast
host of others—the armies of heaven—praising God:
14"Glory to God in the highest heaven,"
they sang, "and peace on earth for all those
pleasing him."
15When this great army of angels had returned again to heaven, the shepherds said to
each other, "Come on! Let's go to Bethlehem!
Let's see this wonderful thing that has happened, which the Lord has told us about."
16They ran to the village and found their

2:6-7 The welcome that Jesus received in Bethlehem is a good illustration of how most people respond to him today. The original manger scene was hardly an idyllic place like the ones pictured on our beautiful Christmas cards. It was probably a cold, damp, dark, dirty cave with a hollowed-out feeding trough or manger. In the original manger scene, Jesus entered a world unfit for his royal presence. God's willingness to enter our world, darkened and dirtied by sin, is a reason to be thankful. We don't have to clean up our act first in order to make room for him. When Jesus comes into our life, he accepts us as we are—that's when the real housecleaning and moral inventory begins. Thankfully, he is there to help us with the process.

2:8-12 Encounters with the living God inevitably elicit fear. So the angels had to reassure the shepherds: "Don't be afraid!" Once the shepherds realized the fact that God accepted them and wanted to communicate with them, they were free to worship the Christ child. The fact that Jesus came in the flesh reassures us that our holy and almighty God is also a personal God. God is with us and for us. We need not fear the unknown future or the all-too-familiar past. When we put our faith in the living God of yesterday, today, and tomorrow, his perfect love casts out all fear (see 1 John 4:18).

way to Mary and Joseph. And there was the baby, lying in the manger. [17]The shepherds told everyone what had happened and what the angel had said to them about this child. [18]All who heard the shepherds' story expressed astonishment, [19]but Mary quietly treasured these things in her heart and often thought about them.

[20]Then the shepherds went back again to their fields and flocks, praising God for the visit of the angels, and because they had seen the child, just as the angel had told them.

Jesus Is Brought to the Temple

[21]Eight days later, at the baby's circumcision ceremony, he was named Jesus, the name given him by the angel before he was even conceived.

[22]When the time came for Mary's purification offering at the Temple, as required by the laws of Moses after the birth of a child, his parents took him to Jerusalem to present him to the Lord; [23]for in these laws God had said, "If a woman's first child is a boy, he shall be dedicated to the Lord."

[24]At that time Jesus' parents also offered their sacrifice for purification—"either a pair of turtledoves or two young pigeons" was the legal requirement. [25]That day a man named Simeon, a Jerusalem resident, was in the Temple. He was a good man, very devout, filled with the Holy Spirit and constantly expecting the Messiah to come soon. [26]For the Holy Spirit had revealed to him that he would not die until he had seen him—God's anointed King. [27]The Holy Spirit had impelled him to go to the Temple that day; and so, when Mary and Joseph arrived to present the baby Jesus to the Lord in obedience to the law, [28]Simeon was there and took the child in his arms, praising God.

[29-31]"Lord," he said, "now I can die content! For I have seen him as you promised me I would. I have seen the Savior you have given to the world. [32]He is the Light that will shine upon the nations, and he will be the glory of your people Israel!"

[33]Joseph and Mary just stood there, marveling at what was being said about Jesus.

[34,35]Simeon blessed them but then said to Mary, "A sword shall pierce your soul, for this child shall be rejected by many in Israel, and this to their undoing. But he will be the greatest joy of many others. And the deepest thoughts of many hearts shall be revealed."

[36,37]Anna, a prophetess, was also there in the Temple that day. She was the daughter of Phanuel, of the Jewish tribe of Asher, and was very old, for she had been a widow for eighty-four years following seven years of marriage. She never left the Temple but stayed there night and day, worshiping God by praying and often fasting.

[38]She came along just as Simeon was talking with Mary and Joseph, and she also began thanking God and telling everyone in Jerusalem who had been awaiting the coming of the Savior that the Messiah had finally arrived.

[39]When Jesus' parents had fulfilled all the requirements of the Law of God they returned home to Nazareth in Galilee. [40]There the child became a strong, robust lad, and was known for wisdom beyond his years; and God poured out his blessings on him.

2:19 In our recovery, painful thoughts of a guilt-ridden past or an uncertain future often intrude and disrupt the present. Some days these disrupting thoughts cause us to feel depressed. Certainly these darker issues must be faced for us to break free from the patterns of the past. But Mary shows us how thoughts about positive things can lift our spirits and give us the courage to take the next step. She meditated on the things God was doing and wanted to do in her life. When we do the same, we take a step toward recovery and wholeness. Pondering the joy with the sorrow, the awesome with the awful, the gain with the pain will lead to emotional and spiritual healing.

2:29-32 Simeon's words reflect the universality of God's plan of salvation. It was a rare thing for a Jew to declare that the Messiah would bring deliverance to the whole world, not just the Jews. God reaches out to not just one ethnic group, but to all people. He still brings light, life, and contentment to all who put their faith in him through Jesus Christ. God will accept any of us who are willing to turn to him for help, regardless of our background or situation in life. He is the universal Savior. With faith in Jesus we can go through life and death "content," as did Simeon.

2:36-38 Anna modeled how the power of faith can bring a life of meaning for people in recovery. After a relatively short marriage and the lifelong loss of a husband, most of us would have allowed bitterness to set in. Decades of unwanted singleness can drive many of us to find love in all the wrong places. Not so with Anna. Instead, she found her singleness gave her more opportunities to serve God in the Temple. She overcame adversity by drawing closer to God through prayer and fasting, and she was given the gift of prophecy. Anna accepted God's plan for her, which included a glimpse of the Messiah she had been longing for.

Jesus Teaches the Teachers

[41,42]When Jesus was twelve years old he accompanied his parents to Jerusalem for the annual Passover Festival, which they attended each year. [43]After the celebration was over they started home to Nazareth, but Jesus stayed behind in Jerusalem. His parents didn't miss him the first day, [44]for they assumed he was with friends among the other travelers. But when he didn't show up that evening, they started to look for him among their relatives and friends; [45]and when they couldn't find him, they went back to Jerusalem to search for him there.

[46,47]Three days later they finally discovered him. He was in the Temple, sitting among the teachers of Law, discussing deep questions with them and amazing everyone with his understanding and answers.

[48]His parents didn't know what to think. "Son!" his mother said to him. "Why have you done this to us? Your father and I have been frantic, searching for you everywhere."

[49]"But why did you need to search?" he asked. "Didn't you realize that I would be here at the Temple, in my Father's House?" [50]But they didn't understand what he meant.

[51]Then he returned to Nazareth with them and was obedient to them; and his mother stored away all these things in her heart. [52]So Jesus grew both tall and wise, and was loved by God and man.

CHAPTER 3

John Prepares the Way

In the fifteenth year of the reign of Emperor Tiberius Caesar, a message came from God to John (the son of Zacharias), as he was living out in the deserts. (Pilate was governor over Judea at that time; Herod, over Galilee; his brother Philip, over Iturea and Trachonitis; Lysanias, over Abilene; and Annas and Caiaphas were High Priests.) [3]Then John went from place to place on both sides of the Jordan River, preaching that people should be baptized to show that they had turned to God and away from their sins, in order to be forgiven.

[4]In the words of Isaiah the prophet, John was "a voice shouting from the barren wilderness, 'Prepare a road for the Lord to travel on! Widen the pathway before him! [5]Level the mountains! Fill up the valleys! Straighten the curves! Smooth out the ruts! [6]And then all mankind shall see the Savior sent from God.'"

[7]Here is a sample of John's preaching to the crowds that came for baptism: "You brood of snakes! You are trying to escape hell without truly turning to God! That is why you want to be baptized! [8]First go and prove by the way you live that you really have repented. And don't think you are safe because you are descendants of Abraham. That isn't enough. God can produce children of Abraham from these desert stones! [9]The axe of his judgment is poised over you, ready to sever your roots and cut you down. Yes, every tree that does not produce good fruit will be chopped down and thrown into the fire."

[10]The crowd replied, "What do you want us to do?"

[11]"If you have two coats," he replied, "give one to the poor. If you have extra food, give it away to those who are hungry."

[12]Even tax collectors—notorious for their corruption—came to be baptized and asked, "How shall we prove to you that we have abandoned our sins?"

[13]"By your honesty," he replied. "Make sure you collect no more taxes than the Roman government requires you to."

[14]"And us," asked some soldiers, "what about us?"

John replied, "Don't extort money by threats and violence; don't accuse anyone of what you know he didn't do; and be content with your pay!"

[15]Everyone was expecting the Messiah to come soon, and eager to know whether or not John was he. This was the question of the hour and was being discussed everywhere.

[16]John answered the question by saying, "I baptize only with water; but someone is coming soon who has far higher authority than mine; in fact, I am not even worthy of being his slave. He will baptize you with fire—with the Holy Spirit. [17]He will separate chaff from grain, and burn up the chaff with eternal fire and store away the grain." [18]He used many such warnings as he announced the Good News to the people.

3:1-6 The road to recovery can be as treacherous, as fatiguing, as dry, and as deserted as a trek through the Judean wilderness. John knew that, and so he preached a discomforting message about God's bulldozer preparing the way for the world's Savior. Those who were honest with themselves in their heart of hearts knew that John was right. All that remained was a public confession of faith. Those of us in recovery need to take responsibility for our sinful actions, turn our life over to God, and experience God's power to "smooth out" our life.

[19,20](But after John had publicly criticized Herod, governor of Galilee, for marrying Herodias, his brother's wife, and for many other wrongs he had done, Herod put John in prison, thus adding this sin to all his many others.)

John Baptizes Jesus

[21]Then one day, after the crowds had been baptized, Jesus himself was baptized; and as he was praying, the heavens opened, [22]and the Holy Spirit in the form of a dove settled upon him, and a voice from heaven said, "You are my much loved Son, yes, my delight."

Joseph's Family Tree

[23-38]Jesus was about thirty years old when he began his public ministry.

Jesus was known as the son of Joseph. Joseph's father was Heli; Heli's father was Matthat; Matthat's father was Levi; Levi's father was Melchi; Melchi's father was Jannai; Jannai's father was Joseph; Joseph's father was Mattathias; Mattathias' father was Amos; Amos' father was Nahum; Nahum's father was Esli; Esli's father was Naggai; Naggai's father was Maath; Maath's father was Mattathias; Mattathias' father was Semein; Semein's father was Josech; Josech's father was Joda; Joda's father was Joanan; Joanan's father was Rhesa; Rhesa's father was Zerubbabel; Zerubbabel's father was Shealtiel; Shealtiel's father was Neri; Neri's father was Melchi; Melchi's father was Addi; Addi's father was Cosam; Cosam's father was Elmadam; Elmadam's father was Er; Er's father was Joshua; Joshua's father was Eliezer; Eliezer's father was Jorim; Jorim's father was Matthat; Matthat's father was Levi; Levi's father was Simeon; Simeon's father was Judah; Judah's father was Joseph; Joseph's father was Jonam; Jonam's father was Eliakim; Eliakim's father was Melea; Melea's father was Menna; Menna's father was Mattatha; Mattatha's father was Nathan; Nathan's father was David; David's father was Jesse; Jesse's father was Obed; Obed's father was Boaz; Boaz' father was Salmon; Salmon's father was Nahshon; Nahshon's father was Amminadab; Amminadab's father was Admin; Admin's father was Arni; Arni's father was Hezron; Hezron's father was Perez; Perez' father was Judah; Judah's father was Jacob; Jacob's father was Isaac; Isaac's father was Abraham; Abraham's father was Terah; Terah's father was Nahor; Nahor's father was Serug; Serug's father was Reu; Reu's father was Peleg; Peleg's father was Eber; Eber's father was Shelah; Shelah's father was Cainan; Cainan's father was Arphaxad; Arphaxad's father was Shem; Shem's father was Noah; Noah's father was Lamech; Lamech's father was Methuselah; Methuselah's father was Enoch; Enoch's father was Jared; Jared's father was Mahalaleel; Mahalaleel's father was Cainan; Cainan's father was Enos; Enos' father was Seth; Seth's father was Adam; Adam's father was God.

CHAPTER 4

Jesus Resists Temptation

Then Jesus, full of the Holy Spirit, left the Jordan River, being urged by the Spirit out into the barren wastelands of Judea, where

---

3:21-22 By settling upon him in the form of a dove, God the Holy Spirit visibly showed not only that he identified with Jesus, but that God's power was with him. God the Father showed how much he was pleased with his Son by speaking directly from heaven. Through recovery in Jesus, we can experience God's heavenly power upon us, his fatherly love for us, and his supreme identification with us. Thus, we, too, are God's "delight," though not in the unique way that Jesus was.

3:23-28 Even though Jesus apparently knew from his youth what his mission on earth would be, this "son of Joseph" patiently persevered as an obscure carpenter in Nazareth until the age of thirty. He was never in a rush to accomplish his ambitious God-given task. He modeled for us the need for patience and trust in God's timing as we progress through recovery. As we are faithful, God will work his healing power within us over time.

3:23-38 Luke's genealogy of Jesus traces his roots to the very beginning of the human race. This shows Jesus' close identification with all humanity. Jesus' genealogy is sprinkled with people known for their mistakes. Judah fathered Perez through an illicit relationship with his daughter Tamar. Salmon fathered Boaz through his marriage with Rahab, a former prostitute from Jericho. Boaz fathered Obed through his marriage with the Moabitess, Ruth. David fathered Solomon through Bathsheba, the rightful wife of another man (see Matthew 1:1-17). From Jesus' genealogy we discover that Jesus is clearly "one of us." No problem in our life is "foreign" to him. By taking on our flesh, God in Jesus Christ was subject to the weaknesses of humanity and even suffered death for us. Jesus truly understands the difficulties we face in our recovery.

Satan tempted him for forty days. He ate
nothing all that time and was very hungry.
3 Satan said, "If you are God's Son, tell this
stone to become a loaf of bread."
4 But Jesus replied, "It is written in the
Scriptures, 'Other things in life are much
more important than bread!'"
5 Then Satan took him up and revealed to
him all the kingdoms of the world in a moment of time; 6,7 and the devil told him, "I will
give you all these splendid kingdoms and
their glory—for they are mine to give to anyone I wish—if you will only get down on your
knees and worship me."
8 Jesus replied, "We must worship God, and
him alone. So it is written in the Scriptures."
9-11 Then Satan took him to Jerusalem to a
high roof of the Temple and said, "If you are
the Son of God, jump off! For the Scriptures
say that God will send his angels to guard you
and to keep you from crashing to the pavement below!"
12 Jesus replied, "The Scriptures also say, 'Do
not put the Lord your God to a foolish test.'"
13 When the devil had ended all the temptations, he left Jesus for a while and went away.
14 Then Jesus returned to Galilee, full of the
Holy Spirit's power. Soon he became well
known throughout all that region 15 for his
sermons in the synagogues; everyone praised
him.

Jesus Is Rejected at Nazareth

16 When he came to the village of Nazareth, his
boyhood home, he went as usual to the synagogue on Saturday, and stood up to read the
Scriptures. 17 The book of Isaiah the prophet
was handed to him, and he opened it to the
place where it says:
18,19 "The Spirit of the Lord is upon me; he
has appointed me to preach Good News to
the poor; he has sent me to heal the brokenhearted and to announce that captives shall
be released and the blind shall see, that the
downtrodden shall be freed from their oppressors, and that God is ready to give blessings to all who come to him."
20 He closed the book and handed it back to
the attendant and sat down, while everyone
in the synagogue gazed at him intently.
21 Then he added, "These Scriptures came true
today!"
22 All who were there spoke well of him and
were amazed by the beautiful words that fell
from his lips. "How can this be?" they asked.
"Isn't this Joseph's son?"
23 Then he said, "Probably you will quote
me that proverb, 'Physician, heal yourself'—
meaning, 'Why don't you do miracles here in
your hometown like those you did in Capernaum?' 24 But I solemnly declare to you that
no prophet is accepted in his own hometown!
25,26 For example, remember how Elijah the
prophet used a miracle to help the widow of
Zarephath—a foreigner from the land of Sidon. There were many Jewish widows needing help in those days of famine, for there had
been no rain for three and a half years, and
hunger stalked the land; yet Elijah was not
sent to them. 27 Or think of the prophet Elisha,
who healed Naaman, a Syrian, rather than the
many Jewish lepers needing help."
28 These remarks stung them to fury; 29 and
jumping up, they mobbed him and took him

4:1-2 Jesus was sorely tempted for forty days, alone in the Judean wastelands. Here, as in every aspect of his life, he overcame adversity by depending on the power of the Holy Spirit working through him. This same higher Power is available for us today. By virtue of God's Holy Spirit dwelling within, believers are given immediate access to this Power. This Power within our heart is great enough to help us resist the most tempting of sins the world, the flesh, or the devil has to throw at us (1 John 2:16; 4:4). Even the most powerful of addictions is no match for the higher Power of the Holy Spirit.

4:13 Temptation by the devil is an ongoing reality. After tempting Jesus in the wilderness, Satan gave up, but only temporarily. He would save his best punch for later (at the cross). This time around he had to admit defeat, having exhausted his most compelling temptations to no avail. But the devil continued to try to undermine Jesus' ministry, especially through the people around him (see Luke 11:14-22). Similarly, if we, in our recovery, withstand a certain temptation at one point, Satan will eventually try again, either in the same area, or in another.

4:18-21 When Jesus claimed to fulfill the words of Isaiah 61, he was making a direct claim to being Israel's long-awaited Messiah. Isaiah's words beautifully characterized a major focus of the Messiah's ministry. The Messiah would heal people who were brokenhearted and in distress. He would deliver those who were captives to the power of sin and spiritual discouragement. He would give sight to the physically and spiritually blind. He would bring triumph to the downcast and inwardly bruised. A relationship with God through Jesus Christ provides these limitless resources to all of us who are in recovery.

to the edge of the hill on which the city was built, to push him over the cliff. 30But he walked away through the crowd and left them.

Jesus Teaches with Authority

31Then he returned to Capernaum, a city in Galilee, and preached there in the synagogue every Saturday. 32Here, too, the people were amazed at the things he said. For he spoke as one who knew the truth, instead of merely quoting the opinions of others as his authority.

33Once as he was teaching in the synagogue, a man possessed by a demon began shouting at Jesus, 34"Go away! We want nothing to do with you, Jesus from Nazareth. You have come to destroy us. I know who you are—the Holy Son of God."

35Jesus cut him short. "Be silent!" he told the demon. "Come out!" The demon threw the man to the floor as the crowd watched, and then left him without hurting him further.

36Amazed, the people asked, "What is in this man's words that even demons obey him?" 37The story of what he had done spread like wildfire throughout the whole region.

Jesus Heals Many

38After leaving the synagogue that day, he went to Simon's home where he found Simon's mother-in-law very sick with a high fever. "Please heal her," everyone begged.

39Standing at her bedside he spoke to the fever, rebuking it, and immediately her temperature returned to normal, and she got up and prepared a meal for them!

40As the sun went down that evening, all the villagers who had any sick people in their homes, no matter what their diseases were, brought them to Jesus; and the touch of his hands healed every one! 41Some were possessed by demons; and the demons came out at his command, shouting, "You are the Son of God." But because they knew he was the Christ, he stopped them and told them to be silent.

Jesus Preaches Throughout Galilee

42Early the next morning he went out into the desert. The crowds searched everywhere for him, and when they finally found him, they begged him not to leave them but to stay at Capernaum. 43But he replied, "I must preach the Good News of the Kingdom of God in other places too, for that is why I was sent." 44So he continued to travel around preaching in synagogues throughout Judea.

CHAPTER 5

An Amazing Catch of Fish

One day as he was preaching on the shore of Lake Gennesaret, great crowds pressed in on him to listen to the Word of God. 2He noticed two empty boats standing at the water's edge while the fishermen washed their nets. 3Stepping into one of the boats, Jesus asked Simon, its owner, to push out a little into the water, so that he could sit in the boat and speak to the crowds from there.

4When he had finished speaking, he said to Simon, "Now go out where it is deeper and let down your nets and you will catch a lot of fish!"

5"Sir," Simon replied, "we worked hard all last night and didn't catch a thing. But if you say so, we'll try again."

6And this time their nets were so full that they began to tear! 7A shout for help brought their partners in the other boat, and soon both boats were filled with fish and on the verge of sinking.

8When Simon Peter realized what had happened, he fell to his knees before Jesus and said, "Oh, sir, please leave us—I'm too much

4:28-30 The response of this hardhearted, hometown crowd in Nazareth to Jesus' remarks is a classic example of what happens when denial is mixed with anger. When Jesus challenged their unbelief, their surface appreciation of his ministry gave way to outrage. They wondered how this hometown boy could claim to be a prophet. Their attempt at mob violence showed how hysterical and resistant to the truth even religious people can be. We need to overcome the areas of denial in our life if we want God to step in and transform us into new and healthy people. God cannot heal us until we are willing to recognize our problems and our unbelief.

5:4-10 The disciples were certainly persistent in their fishing, but doing things their way just wasn't enough. As soon as they followed Jesus' advice, as crazy as it sounded, they experienced abundant success. We may be struggling along to attain recovery on our own. We may be diligent, hard working, and disciplined. However, if we don't do things God's way, no amount of hard work will bring the desired results. Following God's will for our life is the only program that will lead to success. We may think the truth found in God's Word seems crazy. But as we follow God's program obediently and with his gracious help, we will experience his powerful help for our recovery.

of a sinner for you to have around." 9For he was awestruck by the size of their catch, as were the others with him, 10and his partners too—James and John, the sons of Zebedee. Jesus replied, "Don't be afraid! From now on you'll be fishing for the souls of men!"

11And as soon as they landed, they left everything and went with him.

Jesus Heals a Leper

12One day in a certain village he was visiting, there was a man with an advanced case of leprosy. When he saw Jesus he fell to the ground before him, face downward in the dust, begging to be healed.

"Sir," he said, "if you only will, you can clear me of every trace of my disease."

13Jesus reached out and touched the man and said, "Of course I will. Be healed." And the leprosy left him instantly! 14Then Jesus instructed him to go at once without telling anyone what had happened and be examined by the Jewish priest. "Offer the sacrifice Moses' law requires for lepers who are healed," he said. "This will prove to everyone that you are well." 15Now the report of his power spread even faster and vast crowds came to hear him preach and to be healed of their diseases. 16But he often withdrew to the wilderness for prayer.

Jesus Heals a Paralyzed Man

17One day while he was teaching, some Jewish religious leaders and teachers of the Law were sitting nearby. (It seemed that these men showed up from every village in all Galilee and Judea, as well as from Jerusalem.) And the Lord's healing power was upon him.

18,19Then—look! Some men came carrying a paralyzed man on a sleeping mat. They tried to push through the crowd to Jesus but couldn't reach him. So they went up on the roof above him, took off some tiles and lowered the sick man down into the crowd, still on his sleeping mat, right in front of Jesus.

20Seeing their faith, Jesus said to the man, "My friend, your sins are forgiven!"

21"Who does this fellow think he is?" the Pharisees and teachers of the Law exclaimed among themselves. "This is blasphemy! Who but God can forgive sins?"

22Jesus knew what they were thinking, and he replied, "Why is it blasphemy? 23,24I, the Messiah, have the authority on earth to forgive sins. But talk is cheap—anybody could say that. So I'll prove it to you by healing this man." Then, turning to the paralyzed man, he commanded, "Pick up your stretcher and go on home, for you are healed!"

25And immediately, as everyone watched, the man jumped to his feet, picked up his mat and went home praising God! 26Everyone present was gripped with awe and fear. And they praised God, remarking over and over again, "We have seen strange things today."

Jesus Eats at Matthew's House

27Later on as Jesus left the town he saw a tax collector—with the usual reputation for cheating—sitting at a tax collection booth. The man's name was Levi. Jesus said to him, "Come and be one of my disciples!" 28So Levi left everything, sprang up and went with him.

29Soon Levi held a reception in his home with Jesus as the guest of honor. Many of Levi's fellow tax collectors and other guests were there.

30But the Pharisees and teachers of the Law complained bitterly to Jesus' disciples about his eating with such notorious sinners.

31Jesus answered them, "It is the sick who need a doctor, not those in good health. 32My purpose is to invite sinners to turn from their

---

5:30-32 In order to receive Jesus' help and begin recovery, we must first recognize and admit how helpless we are. Jesus' greatest priority was ministry to the so-called notorious sinners (social outcasts) because they admitted their lowly, helpless position. The Pharisees were also sinners, but they were in denial about their sin. Because of their self-righteousness and self-sufficiency, Jesus could do nothing for them. When we are willing to recognize our need for help and admit our failures to God and others, Jesus will reach out and help us.

6:6-11 Jesus routinely healed people on the Sabbath, and this angered his opponents. Getting well didn't always play well with the Pharisees. So also, not everyone will be pleased with our recovery. Sometimes our recovery enrages the people who are closest to us. Friends who are also caught in the trap of addiction may be threatened by the changes in our life. People who have used our addiction to gain power over us may also be upset as they lose their ability to manipulate us. Such legalistic friends may resemble the scribes and Pharisees. Sometimes our recovery frustrates and angers such people, and they go to great lengths to keep us trapped by our addictions. No matter how great the opposition to our recovery, Jesus wants us to be healed. As we trust in him and obey his program for healthy living, we will experience the healing he intends for us.

sins, not to spend my time with those who
think themselves already good enough."

A Question about Fasting
33Their next complaint was that Jesus' disciples were feasting instead of fasting. "John the
Baptist's disciples are constantly going without food and praying," they declared, "and so
do the disciples of the Pharisees. Why are
yours wining and dining?"
34Jesus asked, "Do happy men fast? Do wedding guests go hungry while celebrating with
the groom? 35But the time will come when the
bridegroom will be killed; then they won't
want to eat."
36Then Jesus used this illustration: "No one
tears off a piece of a new garment to make a
patch for an old one. Not only will the new
garment be ruined, but the old garment will
look worse with a new patch on it! 37And no
one puts new wine into old wineskins, for the
new wine bursts the old skins, ruining the
skins and spilling the wine. 38New wine must
be put into new wineskins. 39But no one after
drinking the old wine seems to want the fresh
and the new. 'The old ways are best,' they
say."

CHAPTER 6
Teachings about the Sabbath
One Sabbath as Jesus and his disciples were
walking through some grainfields, they were
breaking off the heads of wheat, rubbing off
the husks in their hands and eating the grains.
2But some Pharisees said, "That's illegal!
Your disciples are harvesting grain, and it's
against the Jewish law to work on the Sabbath."
3Jesus replied, "Don't you read the Scriptures? Haven't you ever read what King David
did when he and his men were hungry? 4He
went into the Temple and took the shew-
bread, the special bread that was placed before the Lord, and ate it—illegal as this
was—and shared it with others." 5And Jesus
added, "I am master even of the Sabbath."

Jesus Heals on the Sabbath
6On another Sabbath he was in the synagogue
teaching, and a man was present whose right
hand was deformed. 7The teachers of the Law
and the Pharisees watched closely to see
whether he would heal the man that day,
since it was the Sabbath. For they were eager
to find some charge to bring against him.
8How well he knew their thoughts! But he
said to the man with the deformed hand,

Forgiveness

READ LUKE 6:27-36

As we set out to mend relationships, there may be some things that are beyond our control. Some people may refuse to be reconciled, even when we do our best to make amends. This may leave us feeling like a victim. Once again we are stuck with the pain of unresolved issues. We may be left with negative feelings that continue to surface. What can we do to gain control in these situations?

Jesus said, "Listen, all of you. Love your *enemies.* Do *good* to those who *hate* you. Pray for the happiness of those who *curse* you; implore God's blessing on those who *hurt* you. . . . Love your *enemies!* Do good to *them!* Lend to *them!* And don't be concerned about the fact that they won't repay. Then your reward from heaven will be very great, and you will truly be acting as sons of God: for he is kind to the *unthankful* and to those who are *very wicked"* (Luke 6:27-28, 35).

We no longer need to be controlled by other people's dispositions and actions. Even when we have done our best to make amends for the wrongs we have done, the situations may not change. And even when we have come to terms with the wrongs that have been done against us, our feelings may not change. But we don't have to be held captive by our feelings or the feelings of others. We can choose to forgive and act in a loving way. This will free us from being controlled by anyone other than God. As we choose to forgive others and do good, our feelings will follow with time. ***Turn to page 1121, Luke 17.***

"Come and stand here where everyone can
see." So he did.
9 Then Jesus said to the Pharisees and teachers of the Law, "I have a question for you. Is it
right to do good on the Sabbath day, or to do
harm? To save life, or to destroy it?"
10 He looked around at them one by one and
then said to the man, "Reach out your hand."
And as he did, it became completely normal
again. 11 At this, the enemies of Jesus were wild
with rage and began to plot his murder.

Jesus Chooses His Disciples

12 One day soon afterwards he went out into
the mountains to pray, and prayed all night.
13 At daybreak he called together his followers
and chose twelve of them to be the inner
circle of his disciples. (They were appointed as
his "apostles," or "missionaries.") 14-16 Here are
their names:

Simon (he also called him Peter), Andrew
(Simon's brother), James, John, Philip,
Bartholomew, Matthew, Thomas, James
(the son of Alphaeus), Simon (a
member of the Zealots, a subversive
political party), Judas (son of James),
Judas Iscariot (who later betrayed him).

Jesus Teaches on a Mountainside

17,18 When they came down the slopes of the
mountain, they stood with Jesus on a large,
level area, surrounded by many of his followers who, in turn, were surrounded by the
crowds. For people from all over Judea and
from Jerusalem and from as far north as the
seacoasts of Tyre and Sidon had come to hear
him or to be healed. And he cast out many
demons. 19 Everyone was trying to touch him,
for when they did, healing power went out
from him and they were cured.
20 Then he turned to his disciples and said,
"What happiness there is for you who are
poor, for the Kingdom of God is yours! 21 What
happiness there is for you who are now hungry, for you are going to be satisfied! What
happiness there is for you who weep, for the
time will come when you shall laugh with
joy! 22 What happiness it is when others hate
you and exclude you and insult you and
smear your name because you are mine!
23 When that happens, rejoice! Yes, leap for
joy! For you will have a great reward awaiting
you in heaven. And you will be in good company—the ancient prophets were treated that
way too!
24 "But, oh, the sorrows that await the rich.
For they have their only happiness down
here. 25 They are fat and prosperous now, but a
time of awful hunger is before them. Their
careless laughter now means sorrow then.
26 And what sadness is ahead for those praised
by the crowds—for *false* prophets have *always*
been praised.

A Call to Love Our Enemies

27 "Listen, all of you. Love your *enemies*. Do
good to those who *hate* you. 28 Pray for the
happiness of those who *curse* you; implore
God's blessing on those who *hurt* you.
29 "If someone slaps you on one cheek, let
him slap the other too! If someone demands
your coat, give him your shirt besides. 30 Give
what you have to anyone who asks you for it;
and when things are taken away from you,
don't worry about getting them back. 31 Treat
others as you want them to treat you.
32 "Do you think you deserve credit for
merely loving those who love you? Even the
godless do that! 33 And if you do good only to
those who do you good—is that so wonderful? Even sinners do that much! 34 And if you
lend money only to those who can repay you,
what good is that? Even the most wicked will
lend to their own kind for full return!
35 "Love your *enemies!* Do good to *them!*
Lend to *them!* And don't be concerned about
the fact that they won't repay. Then your
reward from heaven will be very great, and
you will truly be acting as sons of God: for he
is kind to the *unthankful* and to those who are
very wicked.
36 "Try to show as much compassion as your
Father does.

Jesus Teaches about Judging Others

37 "Never criticize or condemn—or it will all
come back on you. Go easy on others; then
they will do the same for you. 38 For if you give,

6:20-26 When Jesus spoke about Kingdom values, he left no question about the importance of priorities in life. He pronounced woes to shake people out of their selfishness and denial. He pronounced blessings to awaken joy and gratitude in those who depend on God and live one day at a time. By his strong words, Jesus was creating a crisis intervention of sorts. Those who, for example, put their greatest trust in money and material goods on this earth—and who do not realize their need for God—they will meet the great Equalizer. Pride goes before a fall, especially on the path to recovery.

you will get! Your gift will return to you in full and overflowing measure, pressed down, shaken together to make room for more, and running over. Whatever measure you use to give—large or small—will be used to measure what is given back to you."

39Here are some of the story-illustrations Jesus used in his sermons: "What good is it for one blind man to lead another? He will fall into a ditch and pull the other down with him. 40How can a student know more than his teacher? But if he works hard, he may learn as much.

41"And why quibble about the speck in someone else's eye—his little fault—when a board is in your own? 42How can you think of saying to him, 'Brother, let me help you get rid of that speck in your eye,' when you can't see past the board in yours? Hypocrite! First get rid of the board, and then perhaps you can see well enough to deal with his speck!

A Tree and Its Fruit

43"A tree from good stock doesn't produce scrub fruit nor do trees from poor stock produce choice fruit. 44A tree is identified by the kind of fruit it produces. Figs never grow on thorns, or grapes on bramble bushes. 45A good man produces good deeds from a good heart. And an evil man produces evil deeds from his hidden wickedness. Whatever is in the heart overflows into speech.

Building on Rock or Sand

46"So why do you call me 'Lord' when you won't obey me? 47,48But all those who come and listen and obey me are like a man who builds a house on a strong foundation laid upon the underlying rock. When the floodwaters rise and break against the house, it stands firm, for it is strongly built.

49"But those who listen and don't obey are like a man who builds a house without a foundation. When the floods sweep down against that house, it crumbles into a heap of ruins."

CHAPTER 7

The Faith of a Roman Soldier

When Jesus had finished his sermon he went back into the city of Capernaum.

2Just at that time the highly prized slave of a Roman army captain was sick and near death. 3When the captain heard about Jesus, he sent some respected Jewish elders to ask him to come and heal his slave. 4So they began pleading earnestly with Jesus to come with them and help the man. They told him what a wonderful person the captain was.

"If anyone deserves your help, it is he," they said, 5"for he loves the Jews and even paid personally to build us a synagogue!"

6-8Jesus went with them; but just before arriving at the house, the captain sent some friends to say, "Sir, don't inconvenience yourself by coming to my home, for I am not worthy of any such honor or even to come and meet you. Just speak a word from where you are, and my servant boy will be healed! I know, because I am under the authority of my superior officers, and I have authority over my men. I only need to say 'Go!' and they go; or 'Come!' and they come; and to my slave, 'Do this or that,' and he does it. So just say, 'Be healed!' and my servant will be well again!"

9Jesus was amazed. Turning to the crowd he said, "Never among all the Jews in Israel have I met a man with faith like this."

10And when the captain's friends returned to his house, they found the slave completely healed.

A Widow's Son Raised from the Dead

11Not long afterwards Jesus went with his disciples to the village of Nain, with the usual great crowd at his heels. 12A funeral proces-

---

7:1-10 The qualities possessed by the centurion are key elements for anyone wishing to receive God's greatest blessings in life. The centurion was unusually compassionate to people of a lower social class and people of another race and religion. He was humble and recognized his own unworthiness despite being a man of authority. Nonetheless, he wholeheartedly placed his faith in Jesus. Jesus himself marveled at such faith and answered his request. Those who have been raised in religious circles are expected to have faith, but very often do not. Sometimes true faith is best found in places we least expect to find it: among the unchurched and the outcasts, who recognize their need for help and cry out to God in their helplessness. It is this kind of faith that is necessary to our recovery.

7:11-15 By raising the young boy from the dead, Jesus showed his compassion for people experiencing great loss. This woman had previously lost her husband, and now her only son was dead. This miracle shows us that no situation in our life is beyond the restoring power of God. Even in the midst of what seems like a dead end, God is not limited. Power that can raise the dead can certainly bring health for the sick and freedom for the addicted.

sion was coming out as he approached the
village gate. The boy who had died was the
only son of his widowed mother, and many
mourners from the village were with her.
13When the Lord saw her, his heart overflowed with sympathy. "Don't cry!" he said.
14Then he walked over to the coffin and
touched it, and the bearers stopped. "Laddie,"
he said, "come back to life again."
15Then the boy sat up and began to talk to
those around him! And Jesus gave him back
to his mother.
16A great fear swept the crowd, and they
exclaimed with praises to God, "A mighty
prophet has risen among us," and, "We have
seen the hand of God at work today."
17The report of what he did that day raced
from end to end of Judea and even out across
the borders.

Jesus Eases John's Doubts

18The disciples of John the Baptist soon heard
of all that Jesus was doing. When they told
John about it, 19he sent two of his disciples to
Jesus to ask him, "Are you really the Messiah?
Or shall we keep on looking for him?"
20-22The two disciples found Jesus while he
was curing many sick people of their various
diseases—healing the lame and the blind and
casting out evil spirits. When they asked him
John's question, this was his reply: "Go back
to John and tell him all you have seen and
heard here today: how those who were blind
can see. The lame are walking without a limp.
The lepers are completely healed. The deaf
can hear again. The dead come back to life.
And the poor are hearing the Good News.
23And tell him, 'Blessed is the one who does
not lose his faith in me.'"
24After they left, Jesus talked to the crowd
about John. "Who is this man you went out
into the Judean wilderness to see?" he asked.
"Did you find him weak as grass, moved by
every breath of wind? 25Did you find him
dressed in expensive clothes? No! Men who
live in luxury are found in palaces, not out in
the wilderness. 26But did you find a prophet?
Yes! And more than a prophet. 27He is the one
to whom the Scriptures refer when they say,
'Look! I am sending my messenger ahead of
you, to prepare the way before you.' 28In all
humanity there is no one greater than John.
And yet the least citizen of the Kingdom of
God is greater than he."
29And all who heard John preach—even the
most wicked of them—agreed that God's requirements were right, and they were baptized by him. 30All, that is, except the
Pharisees and teachers of Moses' Law. They
rejected God's plan for them and refused
John's baptism.
31"What can I say about such men?" Jesus
asked. "With what shall I compare them?
32They are like a group of children who complain to their friends, 'You don't like it if we
play "wedding" and you don't like it if we
play "funeral"'! 33For John the Baptist used to
go without food and never took a drop of
liquor all his life, and you said, 'He must be
crazy!' 34But I eat my food and drink my wine,
and you say, 'What a glutton Jesus is! And he
drinks! And has the lowest sort of friends!'
35But I am sure you can always justify your
inconsistencies."

A Woman Kisses Jesus' Feet

36One of the Pharisees asked Jesus to come to
his home for lunch and Jesus accepted the
invitation. As they sat down to eat, 37a woman
of the streets—a prostitute—heard he was
there and brought an exquisite flask filled
with expensive perfume. 38Going in, she knelt
behind him at his feet, weeping, with her
tears falling down upon his feet; and she

7:18-19 This account of John the Baptist shows that even the strongest believers will go through times of discouragement and doubt. John had been imprisoned and was facing death (Matthew 11:2). The seeming inability or unwillingness of Jesus to set up his Kingdom led John to send these inquirers. Jesus had deep respect for John (Luke 7:28), even with his doubts. John's questions were honestly asked in a time of acute suffering, so Jesus affirmed him and answered him accordingly. God invites us to do likewise and bring our doubts to Jesus, who will gently move us along the path of discovery and recovery.

7:24-28 Because of his strength of character, John the Baptist did not allow himself to be squeezed into anyone else's mold. Rather, he committed himself to fulfill his role as a prophet and forerunner of the Messiah. He knew the boundaries of his role and fulfilled his God-given purpose on earth. John is a good example for us in this regard. God has a purpose for each one of us. As we discover what our role in his plan is, following the vision he gives us will bring us contentment. As we follow his will, he will always be with us, guiding and strengthening us along the way. Trying to be someone we were never intended to be only slows our spiritual growth and our progress in recovery.

wiped them off with her hair and kissed them
and poured the perfume on them.
[39]When Jesus' host, a Pharisee, saw what
was happening and who the woman was, he
said to himself, "This proves that Jesus is no
prophet, for if God had really sent him, he
would know what kind of woman this one
is!"
[40]Then Jesus spoke up and answered his
thoughts. "Simon," he said to the Pharisee, "I
have something to say to you."
"All right, Teacher," Simon replied, "go
ahead."
[41]Then Jesus told him this story: "A man
loaned money to two people—$5,000 to one
and $500 to the other. [42]But neither of them
could pay him back, so he kindly forgave
them both, letting them keep the money!
Which do you suppose loved him most after
that?"
[43]"I suppose the one who had owed him the
most," Simon answered.
"Correct," Jesus agreed.
[44]Then he turned to the woman and said to
Simon, "Look! See this woman kneeling here!
When I entered your home, you didn't bother
to offer me water to wash the dust from my
feet, but she has washed them with her tears
and wiped them with her hair. [45]You refused
me the customary kiss of greeting, but she has
kissed my feet again and again from the time
I first came in. [46]You neglected the usual courtesy of olive oil to anoint my head, but she
has covered my feet with rare perfume.
[47]Therefore her sins—and they are many—are
forgiven, for she loved me much; but one
who is forgiven little, shows little love."
[48]And he said to her, "Your sins are forgiven."
[49]Then the men at the table said to themselves, "Who does this man think he is, going
around forgiving sins?"
[50]And Jesus said to the woman, "Your faith
has saved you; go in peace."

CHAPTER 8

Women Follow Jesus

Not long afterwards he began a tour of the
cities and villages of Galilee to announce the
coming of the Kingdom of God, and took his
twelve disciples with him. [2]Some women
went along, from whom he had cast out demons or whom he had healed; among them
were Mary Magdalene (Jesus had cast out
seven demons from her), [3]Joanna, Chuza's
wife (Chuza was King Herod's business manager and was in charge of his palace and

Healing Faith

BIBLE READING: Luke 8:43-48

We came to believe that a Power greater than ourselves could restore us to sanity.

Faith is a key to successfully working the second step. For some of us faith comes easily. For others, especially if we have experienced betrayal, it may be more difficult. Sometimes we must exhaust all of our own resources in trying to overcome our addictive "disease" before we will risk believing in a higher Power.

When Jesus was on earth, he was so renowned for his healing power that crowds of sick people constantly pressed in on him. One day "a woman who wanted to be healed came up behind and touched him, for she had been slowly bleeding for twelve years, and could find no cure. . . . But the instant she touched the edge of his robe, the bleeding stopped." Jesus realized that someone had deliberately touched him, because he felt the healing power go out from him. When the woman confessed that she was the one who had been healed, Jesus said, "Your faith has healed you. Go in peace" (Luke 8:43-48).

In order to recover we need to follow the example of this woman. We cannot afford to stand back, hoping for a "cure," and avoid deliberate action because of our lack of faith. We may have lived with our condition for many years, spending our resources on promising "cures" without success. When we can come to believe in a Power greater than ourselves and have the faith to take hold of our own recovery, we will find the healing power we have been looking for. ***Turn to page 1119, Luke 15.***

domestic affairs), Susanna, and many others who were contributing from their private means to the support of Jesus and his disciples.

A Story about Four Soils

4One day he gave this illustration to a large crowd that was gathering to hear him—while many others were still on the way, coming from other towns.

5"A farmer went out to his field to sow grain. As he scattered the seed on the ground, some of it fell on a footpath and was trampled on; and the birds came and ate it as it lay exposed. 6Other seed fell on shallow soil with rock beneath. This seed began to grow, but soon withered and died for lack of moisture. 7Other seed landed in thistle patches, and the young grain stalks were soon choked out. 8Still other fell on fertile soil; this seed grew and produced a crop one hundred times as large as he had planted." (As he was giving this illustration he said, "If anyone has listening ears, use them now!")

Jesus Explains His Story

9His apostles asked him what the story meant.

10He replied, "God has granted you to know the meaning of these parables, for they tell a great deal about the Kingdom of God. But these crowds hear the words and do not understand, just as the ancient prophets predicted.

11"This is its meaning: The seed is God's message to men. 12The hard path where some seed fell represents the hard hearts of those who hear the words of God, but then the devil comes and steals the words away and prevents people from believing and being saved. 13The stony ground represents those who enjoy listening to sermons, but somehow the message never really gets through to them and doesn't take root and grow. They know the message is true, and sort of believe for awhile; but when the hot winds of persecution blow, they lose interest. 14The seed among the thorns represents those who listen and believe God's words but whose faith afterwards is choked out by worry and riches and the responsibilities and pleasures of life. And so they are never able to help anyone else to believe the Good News.

15"But the good soil represents honest, good-hearted people. They listen to God's words and cling to them and steadily spread them to others who also soon believe."

A Story about a Lamp

16[Another time he asked,] "Who ever heard of someone lighting a lamp and then covering it up to keep it from shining? No, lamps are mounted in the open where they can be seen. 17This illustrates the fact that someday everything [in men's hearts] shall be brought to light and made plain to all. 18So be careful how you listen; for whoever has, to him shall be given more; and whoever does not have, even what he thinks he has shall be taken away from him."

Jesus Describes His True Family

19Once when his mother and brothers came to see him, they couldn't get into the house where he was teaching because of the crowds. 20When Jesus heard they were standing outside and wanted to see him, 21he remarked, "My mother and my brothers are all those who hear the message of God and obey it."

Jesus Calms the Storm

22One day about that time, as he and his disciples were out in a boat, he suggested that they cross to the other side of the lake. 23On the way across he lay down for a nap, and while he was sleeping the wind began to rise. A fierce storm developed that threatened to swamp them, and they were in real danger.

24They rushed over and woke him up. "Master, Master, we are sinking!" they screamed.

So he spoke to the storm: "Quiet down," he said, and the wind and waves subsided and all

---

8:4-15 This story about the farmer and the soils emphasizes accountability and discipleship in our relationship with God. The attitudes and condition of our heart matter more than our outward profession of faith. The pressures that draw us back into a life of addiction are well known to those of us in recovery. We face continual temptation to give in to destructive habits, and it is essential to be consistent and watchful in the recovery process. By taking a regular moral inventory, we can avoid the problems that tend to creep into our life through the back door. As we keep our heart open to the new life that God wants to build for us, he gives us a new lease on life.

8:16-17 Just as lamps expose everything else to the light, so God will someday bring our thoughts out into the open. Our thoughts and habits are already known to God (see Psalm 139:1-4); someday others will know them, too. As we are open, honest, and transparent in confessing our shortcomings, God can work his plan of recovery and healing in us.

was calm! 25Then he asked them, "Where is
your faith?"
And they were filled with awe and fear of
him and said to one another, "Who is this
man, that even the winds and waves obey
him?"

Jesus Frees a Demon-possessed Man

26So they arrived at the other side, in the
Gerasene country across the lake from Galilee. 27As he was climbing out of the boat a
man from the city of Gadara came to meet
him, a man who had been demon-possessed
for a long time. Homeless and naked, he lived
in a cemetery among the tombs. 28As soon as
he saw Jesus he shrieked and fell to the
ground before him, screaming, "What do you
want with me, Jesus, Son of God Most High?
Please, I beg you, oh, don't torment me!"
29For Jesus was already commanding the
demon to leave him. This demon had often
taken control of the man so that even when
shackled with chains he simply broke them
and rushed out into the desert, completely
under the demon's power. 30"What is your
name?" Jesus asked the demon. "Legion,"
they replied—for the man was filled with
thousands of them! 31They kept begging Jesus
not to order them into the Bottomless Pit.
32A herd of pigs was feeding on the mountainside nearby, and the demons pled with
him to let them enter into the pigs. And Jesus
said they could. 33So they left the man and
went into the pigs, and immediately the
whole herd rushed down the mountainside
and fell over a cliff into the lake below, where
they drowned. 34The herdsmen rushed away
to the nearby city, spreading the news as they
ran.
35Soon a crowd came out to see for themselves what had happened and saw the man
who had been demon-possessed sitting quietly at Jesus' feet, clothed and sane! And the
whole crowd was badly frightened. 36Then
those who had seen it happen told how the
demon-possessed man had been healed.
37And everyone begged Jesus to go away and
leave them alone (for a deep wave of fear had
swept over them). So he returned to the boat
and left, crossing back to the other side of the
lake.
38The man who had been demon-possessed
begged to go too, but Jesus said no.
39"Go back to your family," he told him,
"and tell them what a wonderful thing God
has done for you."
So he went all through the city telling
everyone about Jesus' mighty miracle.

A Woman Is Healed

40On the other side of the lake the crowds
received him with open arms, for they had
been waiting for him.
41And now a man named Jairus, a leader of
a Jewish synagogue, came and fell down at
Jesus' feet and begged him to come home
with him, 42for his only child was dying, a
little girl twelve years old. Jesus went with
him, pushing through the crowds.
43,44As they went a woman who wanted to
be healed came up behind and touched him,
for she had been slowly bleeding for twelve
years, and could find no cure (though she had
spent everything she had on doctors). But the
instant she touched the edge of his robe, the
bleeding stopped.
45"Who touched me?" Jesus asked.
Everyone denied it, and Peter said, "Master,
so many are crowding against you. . . ."
46But Jesus told him, "No, it was someone
who deliberately touched me, for I felt healing power go out from me."
47When the woman realized that Jesus
knew, she began to tremble and fell to her
knees before him and told why she had
touched him and that now she was well.
48"Daughter," he said to her, "your faith has
healed you. Go in peace."

8:26-37 The life of this demon-possessed man was a complete disaster. Desperately in need of healing from demonic influence, he was a physical and emotional wreck, an embarrassing social outcast. As hopeless as his case was, Jesus had, and still has, the power to break satanic bondage and bring recovery. Yet the people of the community were more concerned about their loss of a herd of pigs than they were with the healing of this helpless and broken man. Regrettably, we sometimes experience similar opposition to our own recovery. No matter what obstacles we face, however, Jesus desires our recovery and will help us make progress toward that goal.

8:43-44 Luke, with his background in medicine, noted that medical doctors had been able to do nothing for this woman's chronic illness. By faith, God's power did the impossible. As with many of Jesus' miracles, this incident shows that one who trusts in God can experience hope where previously there had been only despair. Recovery may seem beyond the scope of most doctors, but it is still well within the normal range of miracles that God does for people who look to him in faith.

A Girl Is Raised from the Dead

49While he was still speaking to her, a messenger arrived from the Jairus' home with the
news that the little girl was dead. "She's
gone," he told her father; "there's no use
troubling the Teacher now."

50But when Jesus heard what had happened, he said to the father, "Don't be afraid!
Just trust me, and she'll be all right."

51When they arrived at the house, Jesus
wouldn't let anyone into the room except
Peter, James, John, and the little girl's father
and mother. 52The home was filled with
mourning people, but he said, "Stop the
weeping! She isn't dead; she is only asleep!"
53This brought scoffing and laughter, for they
all knew she was dead.

54Then he took her by the hand and called,
"Get up, little girl!" 55And at that moment her
life returned and she jumped up! "Give her
something to eat!" he said. 56Her parents were
overcome with happiness, but Jesus insisted
that they not tell anyone the details of what
had happened.

CHAPTER 9

Jesus Sends Out His Disciples

One day Jesus called together his twelve apostles and gave them authority over all demons—power to cast them out—and to heal
all diseases. 2Then he sent them away to tell
everyone about the coming of the Kingdom
of God and to heal the sick.

3"Don't even take along a walking stick," he
instructed them, "nor a beggar's bag, nor
food, nor money. Not even an extra coat. 4Be
a guest in only one home at each village.

5"If the people of a town won't listen to you
when you enter it, turn around and leave,
demonstrating God's anger against it by shaking its dust from your feet as you go."

6So they began their circuit of the villages,
preaching the Good News and healing the
sick.

Herod Kills John the Baptist

7When reports of Jesus' miracles reached
Herod, the governor, he was worried and puzzled, for some were saying, "This is John the
Baptist come back to life again"; 8and others,
"It is Elijah or some other ancient prophet
risen from the dead." These rumors were circulating all over the land.

9"I beheaded John," Herod said, "so who is
this man about whom I hear such strange
stories?" And he tried to see him.

Jesus Feeds Five Thousand

10After the apostles returned to Jesus and reported what they had done, he slipped quietly
away with them toward the city of Bethsaida.
11But the crowds found out where he was
going and followed. And he welcomed them,
teaching them again about the Kingdom of
God and curing those who were ill.

12Late in the afternoon all twelve of the
disciples came and urged him to send the
people away to the nearby villages and farms,
to find food and lodging for the night. "For
there is nothing to eat here in this deserted
spot," they said.

13But Jesus replied, *"You* feed them!"

"Why, we have only five loaves of bread
and two fish among the lot of us," they protested; "or are you expecting us to go and buy
enough for this whole mob?" 14For there were
about 5,000 men there!

"Just tell them to sit down on the ground
in groups of about fifty each," Jesus replied.
15So they did.

16Jesus took the five loaves and two fish and
looked up into the sky and gave thanks; then
he broke off pieces for his disciples to set
before the crowd. 17And everyone ate and ate;
still, twelve basketfuls of scraps were picked
up afterwards!

Peter Says Jesus Is the Messiah

18One day as he was alone, praying, with his
disciples nearby, he came over and asked
them, "Who are the people saying I am?"

19"John the Baptist," they told him, "or
perhaps Elijah or one of the other ancient
prophets risen from the dead."

20Then he asked them, "Who do you think
I am?"

9:10-20 This episode demonstrates, once again, Jesus' desire to meet needs at various levels. In feeding the five thousand he supplied even their most basic need—food. Before this incident, Jesus had been dealing primarily with various problems that called for physical healing. Notice also that, during this incident, Jesus met the intellectual and emotional needs of his disciples. As God helps us down the path toward recovery, he ultimately meets our spiritual need for a right relationship with God. The recovery that Jesus the Messiah offers touches every area of our life and world. As we look to him for help, we can take steps to live in harmony with God, the people around us, and the world in which we live.

Peter replied, "The Messiah—the Christ of
God!"

Jesus Speaks of His Death

21He gave them strict orders not to speak of
this to anyone. 22"For I, the Messiah, must
suffer much," he said, "and be rejected by the
Jewish leaders—the elders, chief priests, and
teachers of the Law—and be killed; and three
days later I will come back to life again!"

23Then he said to all, "Anyone who wants
to follow me must put aside his own desires
and conveniences and carry his cross with
him every day and *keep close to me!* 24Whoever
loses his life for my sake will save it, but
whoever insists on keeping his life will lose it;
25and what profit is there in gaining the whole
world when it means forfeiting one's self?

26"When I, the Messiah, come in my glory
and in the glory of the Father and the holy
angels, I will be ashamed then of all who are
ashamed of me and of my words now. 27But
this is the simple truth—some of you who are
standing here right now will not die until you
have seen the Kingdom of God."

Jesus Is Transfigured

28Eight days later he took Peter, James, and
John with him into the hills to pray. 29And as
he was praying, his face began to shine, and
his clothes became dazzling white and blazed
with light. 30Then two men appeared and began talking with him—Moses and Elijah!
31They were splendid in appearance, glorious
to see; and they were speaking of his death at
Jerusalem, to be carried out in accordance
with God's plan.

32Peter and the others had been very
drowsy and had fallen asleep. Now they woke
up and saw Jesus covered with brightness and
glory, and the two men standing with him.
33As Moses and Elijah were starting to leave,
Peter, all confused and not even knowing
what he was saying, blurted out, "Master, this
is wonderful! We'll put up three shelters—one
for you and one for Moses and one for Elijah!"

34But even as he was saying this, a bright
cloud formed above them; and terror gripped
them as it covered them. 35And a voice from
the cloud said, *"This* is my Son, my Chosen
One; listen to *him."*

36Then, as the voice died away, Jesus was
there alone with his disciples. They didn't tell
anyone what they had seen until long afterwards.

Jesus Heals a Demon-possessed Boy

37The next day as they descended from the
hill, a huge crowd met him, 38and a man in
the crowd called out to him, "Teacher, this
boy here is my only son, 39 and a demon keeps
seizing him, making him scream; and it
throws him into convulsions so that he foams
at the mouth; it is always hitting him and
hardly ever leaves him alone. 40I begged your
disciples to cast the demon out, but they
couldn't."

41"O you stubborn faithless people," Jesus
said [to his disciples], "how long should I put
up with you? Bring him here."

42As the boy was coming the demon
knocked him to the ground and threw him
into a violent convulsion. But Jesus ordered
the demon to come out, and healed the boy
and handed him over to his father.

43Awe gripped the people as they saw this
display of the power of God.

Meanwhile, as they were exclaiming over
all the wonderful things he was doing, Jesus
said to his disciples, 44"Listen to me and remember what I say. I, the Messiah, am going
to be betrayed." 45But the disciples didn't
know what he meant, for their minds had
been sealed and they were afraid to ask him.

9:23-27 In this classic confrontation of wills, Jesus shows the critical importance of submitting our will to God's will. Jesus has a prior claim on the life of his followers, a claim that supersedes all personal conveniences or desires. Clinging to the conveniences of our world and the desires of the flesh may destroy our very life. Paradoxically, "losing one's life" in a relationship with God through Jesus is the only sure way of finding ultimate meaning and purpose. This teaching stands opposed to our natural inclinations and can only be accepted by faith. But if we are willing to submit our will to God's will, we will begin to experience the meaningful life that God wants us to have.

9:28-36 While initial impressions do mean a lot, and while many judge others based on appearances, things often are not as they initially appear to be. This principle is important in recovery and comes into play on the Mount of Transfiguration. Peter relied too much on first impressions and outward appearances, so he jumped to some foolish conclusions. Here two great Old Testament prophets appeared to be on a par with Jesus. Yet God's voice and later events confirmed that Jesus was in reality God himself. If our recovery is to progress, we need to explore inner realities, suspending judgment and listening to God.

Who Is the Greatest?

46Now came an argument among them as to
which of them would be greatest [in the coming Kingdom]! 47But Jesus knew their
thoughts, so he stood a little child beside him
48and said to them, "Anyone who takes care of
a little child like this is caring for me! And
whoever cares for me is caring for God who
sent me. Your care for others is the measure of
your greatness." 49His disciple John came to
him and said, "Master, we saw someone using
your name to cast out demons. And we told
him not to. After all, he isn't in our group."
50But Jesus said, "You shouldn't have done
that! For anyone who is not against you is for
you."

The Cost of Following Jesus

51As the time drew near for his return to
heaven, he moved steadily onward toward
Jerusalem with an iron will.
52One day he sent messengers ahead to reserve rooms for them in a Samaritan village.
53But they were turned away! The people of
the village refused to have anything to do
with them because they were headed for Jerusalem.
54When word came back of what had happened, James and John said to Jesus, "Master,
shall we order fire down from heaven to burn
them up?" 55But Jesus turned and rebuked
them, 56and they went on to another village.
57As they were walking along someone said
to Jesus, "I will always follow you no matter
where you go."
58But Jesus replied, "Remember, I don't
even own a place to lay my head. Foxes have
dens to live in, and birds have nests, but I, the
Messiah, have no earthly home at all."
59Another time, when he invited a man to
come with him and to be his disciple, the man
agreed—but wanted to wait until his father's
death.
60Jesus replied, "Let those without eternal
life concern themselves with things like that.
Your duty is to come and preach the coming
of the Kingdom of God to all the world."
61Another said, "Yes, Lord, I will come, but
first let me ask permission of those at home."
62But Jesus told him, "Anyone who lets
himself be distracted from the work I plan for
him is not fit for the Kingdom of God."

CHAPTER 10

Jesus Sends Out Seventy Messengers

The Lord now chose seventy other disciples
and sent them on ahead in pairs to all the
towns and villages he planned to visit later.
2These were his instructions to them:
"Plead with the Lord of the harvest to send
out more laborers to help you, for the harvest
is so plentiful and the workers so few. 3Go
now, and remember that I am sending you
out as lambs among wolves. 4Don't take any
money with you, or a beggar's bag, or even an
extra pair of shoes. And don't waste time
along the way.
5"Whenever you enter a home, give it your
blessing. 6If it is worthy of the blessing, the
blessing will stand; if not, the blessing will
return to you.
7"When you enter a village, don't shift
around from home to home, but stay in one
place, eating and drinking without question
whatever is set before you. And don't hesitate
to accept hospitality, for the workman is worthy of his wages!
8,9"If a town welcomes you, follow these
two rules:

(1) Eat whatever is set before you.
(2) Heal the sick; and as you heal them, say, 'The Kingdom of God is very near you now.'

10"But if a town refuses you, go out into its
streets and say, 11'We wipe the dust of your
town from our feet as a public announcement
of your doom. Never forget how close you
were to the Kingdom of God!' 12Even wicked
Sodom will be better off than such a city on
the Judgment Day. 13What horrors await you,
you cities of Chorazin and Bethsaida! For if
the miracles I did for you had been done in
the cities of Tyre and Sidon, their people
would have sat in deep repentance long ago,
clothed in sackcloth and throwing ashes on
their heads to show their remorse. 14Yes, Tyre
and Sidon will receive less punishment on the
Judgment Day than you. 15And you people of
Capernaum, what shall I say about you? Will

10:10-16 The disciples were given the ambitious task and privilege of sharing the message of the Messiah throughout the land. Their ministry would not always be well received. One who follows Jesus on the path to recovery will encounter similar setbacks. Rejection and ridicule often accompany recovery. As we begin to share our story of deliverance with others, we may find we are not always welcome in our old stomping grounds. When we experience rejection, we can be prepared to make a timely exit, to go in peace, and to find a more receptive audience.

MARY & MARTHA

As with all siblings, Mary and Martha each had her own unique gifts and personality. Martha was industrious and concerned about detail, while Mary, the contemplative one, treasured the role of being a student of Jesus.

We are given a glimpse into the heart of Mary when we see her anoint Jesus with costly perfume shortly before his death. Mary's extravagant act of love and devotion was hypocritically criticized by Judas. In the process of recovery it may be necessary to take steps that others will criticize, but we must remember that the bottom line is whether or not God is pleased with our actions.

When their brother Lazarus died, the events that followed allowed each of the sisters to grow in her understanding of Jesus. Jesus knew that if he delayed coming to them, he wouldn't arrive until after Lazarus's death. If he had come before Lazarus died, he certainly could have healed him; but by coming later, Jesus was able to do something even more glorious—raise him from the dead!

For Mary and Martha, the delay was painful. The ultimate outcome, however, was a deeper faith and a fuller experience of the joy that comes from trusting God with the details of life. As we go through difficult times, we may not always understand what God is doing, but we will grow in strength and faith as we patiently endure. There is always hope when the God who can raise the dead is on our side.

The story of Mary and Martha is found in Matthew 26:6-13; Luke 10:38-42; and John 11:1-45; 12:1-8.

STRENGTHS AND ACCOMPLISHMENTS:
- Both were devoted followers of Jesus.
- Martha was hardworking, efficient, and conscientious.
- Mary had a heart that was devoted to God.

WEAKNESSES AND MISTAKES:
- Martha was so worried about details that she missed spending time with Jesus.

LESSONS FROM THEIR LIVES:
- We may get so busy doing things in our recovery—even good things—that we forget to spend time with Jesus.
- Jesus valued the contribution of these women among his followers.
- It is important to see each of our children as a unique individual.

KEY VERSES:
"[Martha] came to Jesus and said, 'Sir, doesn't it seem unfair to you that my sister just sits here while I do all the work? Tell her to come and help me.' But the Lord said to her, 'Martha, dear friend, you are so upset over all these details! There is really only one thing worth being concerned about. Mary has discovered it—and I won't take it away from her!'" (Luke 10:40-42).

---

you be exalted to heaven? No, you shall be brought down to hell."
16Then he said to the disciples, "Those who welcome you are welcoming me. And those who reject you are rejecting me. And those who reject me are rejecting God who sent me."

The Messengers Return

17When the seventy disciples returned, they joyfully reported to him, "Even the demons obey us when we use your name."
18"Yes," he told them, "I saw Satan falling from heaven as a flash of lightning! 19And I
have given you authority over all the power of the Enemy, and to walk among serpents and scorpions and to crush them. Nothing shall injure you! 20However, the important
thing is not that demons obey you, but that your names are registered as citizens of heaven."
21Then he was filled with the joy of the Holy Spirit and said, "I praise you, O Father, Lord of heaven and earth, for hiding these things from the intellectuals and worldly wise and for revealing them to those who are as trusting as little children. Yes, thank you, Father, for that is the way you wanted it. 22I
am the Agent of my Father in everything; and no one really knows the Son except the Father, and no one really knows the Father except the Son and those to whom the Son chooses to reveal him."
23Then, turning to the twelve disciples, he said quietly, "How privileged you are to see what you have seen. 24Many a prophet and
king of old has longed for these days, to see and hear what you have seen and heard!"

A Story about a Good Samaritan

25One day an expert on Moses' laws came to test Jesus' orthodoxy by asking him this ques-

tion: "Teacher, what does a man need to do to
live forever in heaven?"
[26]Jesus replied, "What does Moses' law say
about it?"
[27]"It says," he replied, "that you must love
the Lord your God with all your heart, and
with all your soul, and with all your strength,
and with all your mind. And you must love
your neighbor just as much as you love yourself."
[28]"Right!" Jesus told him. *"Do* this and *you*
shall live!"
[29]The man wanted to justify (his lack of love
for some kinds of people), so he asked,
"Which neighbors?"
[30]Jesus replied with an illustration: "A Jew
going on a trip from Jerusalem to Jericho was
attacked by bandits. They stripped him of his
clothes and money, and beat him up and left
him lying half dead beside the road.
[31]"By chance a Jewish priest came along;
and when he saw the man lying there, he
crossed to the other side of the road and
passed him by. [32]A Jewish Temple-assistant
walked over and looked at him lying there,
but then went on.
[33]"But a despised Samaritan came along,
and when he saw him, he felt deep pity.
[34]Kneeling beside him the Samaritan soothed
his wounds with medicine and bandaged
them. Then he put the man on his donkey
and walked along beside him till they came to
an inn, where he nursed him through the
night. [35]The next day he handed the inn-
keeper two twenty-dollar bills and told him to
take care of the man. 'If his bill runs higher
than that,' he said, 'I'll pay the difference the
next time I am here.'
[36]"Now which of these three would you say
was a neighbor to the bandits' victim?"
[37]The man replied, "The one who showed
him some pity."
Then Jesus said, "Yes, now go and do the
same."

Jesus Visits Mary and Martha

[38]As Jesus and the disciples continued on their
way to Jerusalem they came to a village where
a woman named Martha welcomed them into
her home. [39]Her sister Mary sat on the floor,
listening to Jesus as he talked.
[40]But Martha was the jittery type and was
worrying over the big dinner she was preparing.
She came to Jesus and said, "Sir, doesn't it
seem unfair to you that my sister just sits here

10:25-37 The story of the Good Samaritan teaches that true love for God will express itself in caring for the needs of others. According to the Jewish religious leaders in Jesus' day, the person least likely to help the wounded man was the Samaritan. When the despised Samaritan proved to be the good neighbor, Jesus was turning the tables to show that concern for others has no such boundaries. When God has done a work of healing and recovery in our life, we become the most effective instrument in reaching others with similar needs. Sharing the good news of our deliverance is a responsibility we receive when we experience God's powerful help in our life. As we share the Good News, we will experience great joy as others gain hope for recovery. We will also find our own faith and recovery strengthened as we remember what God has done on our behalf.

10:38-42 There is a difference between being spiritually committed to our recovery and being preoccupied with our recovery. This story about Mary and Martha illustrates the difference. Martha was so busy "doing for others" that she had no time or energy left for simply being with Jesus. Mary, on the other hand, took time out to listen to Jesus. In all her doing, Martha even became irritated at Mary for not being equally busy. Our recovery needs to be a recovery from the heart, not just a recovery where we act compulsively to look the part.

11:2 The opening address of this prayer, "Father," describes the attitude and relationship with which we are to approach God. Luke used an intimate word that a child might use in speaking to his earthly father. The equivalent in our everyday speech would be addressing God as "Daddy." Only through this kind of intimate prayer relationship with our heavenly Father can we find strength to tackle the big challenges involved in lifelong recovery.

11:4 God's forgiveness of us and our forgiveness of others are inextricably linked together. This tight connection refers to the experiential aspect of forgiveness. To fully experience God's forgiveness, we must be able and willing to forgive others. Conversely, an unforgiving spirit hinders our ability to enjoy the freedom found in God's forgiveness. To harbor anger and an unforgiving spirit when God has forgiven us so much is not only hypocritical, it is a roadblock to our recovery.

11:4 The honesty of this prayer recognizes our own weakness and vulnerability to temptation. The prayer of faith asks for life's circumstances to lead away from rather than through temptation. As a model prayer, this principle is especially important when we are seeking victory over an area of our life where sin has gained a stronghold. The recovery process involves not only recognizing our own shortcomings and character defects, but also avoiding situations that might lead to temptation and a fall.

while I do all the work? Tell her to come and help me."

[41]But the Lord said to her, "Martha, dear friend, you are so upset over all these details![42]There is really only one thing worth being concerned about. Mary has discovered it—and I won't take it away from her!"

CHAPTER 11
Jesus Teaches about Prayer
Once when Jesus had been out praying, one of his disciples came to him as he finished and said, "Lord, teach us a prayer to recite just as John taught one to his disciples."

[2]And this is the prayer he taught them: "Father, may your name be honored for its holiness; send your Kingdom soon. [3]Give us our food day by day. [4]And forgive our sins—for we have forgiven those who sinned against us. And don't allow us to be tempted."

[5,6]Then, teaching them more about prayer, he used this illustration: "Suppose you went to a friend's house at midnight, wanting to borrow three loaves of bread. You would shout up to him, 'A friend of mine has just arrived for a visit and I've nothing to give him to eat.' [7]He would call down from his bedroom, 'Please don't ask me to get up. The door is locked for the night and we are all in bed. I just can't help you this time.'

[8]"But I'll tell you this—though he won't do it as a friend, if you keep knocking long enough, he will get up and give you everything you want—just because of your persistence. [9]And so it is with prayer—keep on asking and you will keep on getting; keep on looking and you will keep on finding; knock and the door will be opened. [10]Everyone who asks, receives; all who seek, find; and the door is opened to everyone who knocks.

[11]"You men who are fathers—if your boy asks for bread, do you give him a stone? If he asks for fish, do you give him a snake? [12]If he asks for an egg, do you give him a scorpion? [Of course not!]

[13]"And if even sinful persons like yourselves give children what they need, don't you realize that your heavenly Father will do at least as much, and give the Holy Spirit to those who ask for him?"

Jesus Answers Accusations
[14]Once, when Jesus cast out a demon from a man who couldn't speak, his voice returned to him. The crowd was excited and enthusiastic, [15]but some said, "No wonder he can cast them out. He gets his power from Satan, the

Pride Born of Hurt
BIBLE READING: Luke 11:5-13
We humbly asked him to remove our shortcomings.
Our pride can keep us from asking for what we need. We may have grown up in a family where we were consistently ignored or disappointed. No one listened when we asked that certain needs be met. Some of us may have reacted by becoming self-sufficient. We determined never to ask anyone for help. In fact, we were going to strive to never need anyone's help ever again!

It is this type of pride, born of hurt, that will hold us back from asking God to remove our shortcomings. Jesus said, "Keep on asking and you will keep on getting; keep on looking and you will keep on finding; knock and the door will be opened. Everyone who asks, receives; all who seek, find; and the door is opened to everyone who knocks" (Luke 11:9-10). "If a child asks his father for a loaf of bread, will he be given a stone instead? If he asks for fish, will he be given a poisonous snake? Of course not! And if you hardhearted, sinful men know how to give good gifts to your children, won't your Father in heaven even more certainly give good gifts to those who ask him for them?" (Matthew 7:9-11).

We must come to the place of giving up our prideful self-sufficiency; we must be willing to ask for help. And we can't ask for help just once and be done with it. We must be persistent and ask repeatedly as the needs arise. When we practice Step Seven in this way, we can be assured that our loving heavenly Father will respond by giving us good gifts and by removing our shortcomings. ***Turn to page 1123, Luke 18.***

king of demons!" 16Others asked for something to happen in the sky to prove his claim of being the Messiah.

17He knew the thoughts of each of them, so he said, "Any kingdom filled with civil war is doomed; so is a home filled with argument and strife. 18Therefore, if what you say is true, that Satan is fighting against himself by empowering me to cast out his demons, how can his kingdom survive? 19And if I am empowered by Satan, what about your own followers? For they cast out demons! Do you think this proves they are possessed by Satan? Ask *them* if you are right! 20But if I am casting out demons because of power from God, it proves that the Kingdom of God has arrived.

21"For when Satan, strong and fully armed, guards his palace, it is safe—22until someone stronger and better-armed attacks and overcomes him and strips him of his weapons and carries off his belongings.

23"Anyone who is not for me is against me; if he isn't helping me, he is hurting my cause.

24"When a demon is cast out of a man, it goes to the deserts, searching there for rest; but finding none, it returns to the person it left, 25and finds that its former home is all swept and clean. 26Then it goes and gets seven other demons more evil than itself, and they all enter the man. And so the poor fellow is seven times worse off than he was before."

27As he was speaking, a woman in the crowd called out, "God bless your mother—the womb from which you came, and the breasts that gave you suck!"

28He replied, "Yes, but even more blessed are all who hear the Word of God and put it into practice."

Jesus Warns against Unbelief

29,30As the crowd pressed in upon him, he preached them this sermon: "These are evil times, with evil people. They keep asking for some strange happening in the skies [to prove I am the Messiah], but the only proof I will give them is a miracle like that of Jonah, whose experiences proved to the people of Nineveh that God had sent him. My similar experience will prove that God has sent me to these people.

31"And at the Judgment Day the Queen of Sheba shall arise and point her finger at this generation, condemning it, for she went on a long, hard journey to listen to the wisdom of Solomon; but one far greater than Solomon is here [and few pay any attention].

32"The men of Nineveh, too, shall arise and condemn this nation, for they repented at the preaching of Jonah; and someone far greater than Jonah is here [but this nation won't listen].

A Call to Shine Brightly

33"No one lights a lamp and hides it! Instead, he puts it on a lampstand to give light to all who enter the room. 34Your eyes light up your inward being. A pure eye lets sunshine into your soul. A lustful eye shuts out the light and plunges you into darkness. 35So watch out that the sunshine isn't blotted out. 36If you are filled with light within, with no dark corners, then your face will be radiant too, as though a floodlight is beamed upon you."

Jesus Criticizes the Religious Leaders

37,38As he was speaking, one of the Pharisees asked him home for a meal. When Jesus arrived, he sat down to eat without first performing the ceremonial washing required by Jewish custom. This greatly surprised his host.

39Then Jesus said to him, "You Pharisees wash the outside, but inside you are still dirty—full of greed and wickedness! 40Fools! Didn't God make the inside as well as the outside? 41Purity is best demonstrated by generosity.

42"But woe to you Pharisees! For though you are careful to tithe even the smallest part of your income, you completely forget about justice and the love of God. You should tithe, yes, but you should not leave these other things undone.

43"Woe to you Pharisees! For how you love the seats of honor in the synagogues and the respectful greetings from everyone as you walk through the markets! 44Yes, awesome judgment is awaiting you. For you are like hidden graves in a field. Men go by you with no knowledge of the corruption they are passing."

45"Sir," said an expert in religious law who was standing there, "you have insulted my profession, too, in what you just said."

46"Yes," said Jesus, "the same horrors await you! For you crush men beneath impossible religious demands—demands that you yourselves would never think of trying to keep. 47Woe to you! For you are exactly like your ancestors who killed the prophets long ago. 48Murderers! You agree with your fathers that

READ LUKE 11:37-44

GOD grant me the serenity to accept the things I cannot change the courage to change the things I can and the wisdom to know the difference AMEN

We often protect ourself by focusing our attention on other people and their behaviors. That way we don't have to examine our own.

We often stay in relationships in which we seem powerless, for in doing so, we maintain built-in excuses for failure. We may also spend time looking down on others who are "worse" than we are, thus avoiding an examination of our own corruption. But in doing these things, we fail to take responsibility for our own recovery by honest self-examination.

Jesus confronted the Pharisees, saying, "You Pharisees wash the outside, but inside you are still dirty—full of greed and wickedness!" (Luke 11:39). Can you imagine washing only the outside of a cup that is moldy on the inside, and then drinking from it? Of course not! But we do this in a spiritual sense because it is hard to deal with the "dirt" inside our heart.

Changing those things in our life that we can change involves taking steps to clean out the inside of our cup. We must begin by turning our eyes away from everyone around us, including those we blame for our condition in life or those we condemn to make our wrongs seem less in comparison. Then we can get back to looking within ourself. We all have some residue of wrongdoing in our life. When we admit this to God, to ourself, and to another human being, we will experience the cleansing of humility and forgiveness. Then we will have a life that can bring refreshment to others. ***Turn to page 1269, 1 Corinthians 10.***

---

what they did was right—you would have done the same yourselves.

[49]"This is what God says about you: 'I will send prophets and apostles to you, and you will kill some of them and chase away the others.'

[50]"And you of this generation will be held responsible for the murder of God's servants from the founding of the world— [51]from the murder of Abel to the murder of Zechariah who perished between the altar and the sanctuary. Yes, it will surely be charged against you.

[52]"Woe to you experts in religion! For you hide the truth from the people. You won't accept it for yourselves, and you prevent others from having a chance to believe it."

[53,54]The Pharisees and legal experts were furious; and from that time on they plied him fiercely with a host of questions, trying to trap him into saying something for which they could have him arrested.

CHAPTER 12

Warnings against Hypocrisy

Meanwhile the crowds grew until thousands upon thousands were milling about and crushing each other. He turned now to his disciples and warned them, "More than anything else, beware of these Pharisees and the way they pretend to be good when they aren't. But such hypocrisy cannot be hidden forever. [2]It will become as evident as yeast in dough. [3]Whatever they have said in the dark shall be heard in the light, and what you have whispered in the inner rooms shall be broadcast from the housetops for all to hear!

[4]"Dear friends, don't be afraid of these who want to murder you. They can only kill the body; they have no power over your souls.

5But I'll tell you whom to fear—fear God who
has the power to kill and then cast into hell.
6"What is the price of five sparrows? A
couple of pennies? Not much more than that.
Yet God does not forget a single one of them.
7And he knows the number of hairs on your
head! Never fear, you are far more valuable to
him than a whole flock of sparrows.
8"And I assure you of this: I, the Messiah,
will publicly honor you in the presence of
God's angels if you publicly acknowledge me
here on earth as your Friend. 9But I will deny
before the angels those who deny me here
among men. 10(Yet those who speak against
me may be forgiven—while those who speak
against the Holy Spirit shall never be forgiven.)
11"And when you are brought to trial before
these Jewish rulers and authorities in the synagogues, don't be concerned about what to
say in your defense, 12for the Holy Spirit will
give you the right words even as you are
standing there."

A Story about a Rich Fool

13Then someone called from the crowd, "Sir,
please tell my brother to divide my father's
estate with me."
14But Jesus replied, "Man, who made me a
judge over you to decide such things as that?
15Beware! Don't always be wishing for what
you don't have. For real life and real living are
not related to how rich we are."
16Then he gave an illustration: "A rich man
had a fertile farm that produced fine crops.
17In fact, his barns were full to overflowing—
he couldn't get everything in. He thought
about his problem, 18and finally exclaimed, 'I
know—I'll tear down my barns and build
bigger ones! Then I'll have room enough.
19And I'll sit back and say to myself, "Friend,
you have enough stored away for years to
come. Now take it easy! Wine, women, and
song for you!"'
20"But God said to him, 'Fool! Tonight you
die. Then who will get it all?'
21"Yes, every man is a fool who gets rich on
earth but not in heaven."

Jesus Warns about Worry

22Then turning to his disciples he said, "Don't
worry about whether you have enough food
to eat or clothes to wear. 23For life consists of
far more than food and clothes. 24Look at the
ravens—they don't plant or harvest or have
barns to store away their food, and yet they
get along all right—for God feeds them. And
you are far more valuable to him than any
birds!
25"And besides, what's the use of worrying?
What good does it do? Will it add a single day
to your life? Of course not! 26And if worry
can't even do such little things as that, what's
the use of worrying over bigger things?
27"Look at the lilies! They don't toil and
spin, and yet Solomon in all his glory was not
robed as well as they are. 28And if God provides clothing for the flowers that are here
today and gone tomorrow, don't you suppose
that he will provide clothing for you, you
doubters? 29And don't worry about food—
what to eat and drink; don't worry at all that
God will provide it for you. 30All mankind
scratches for its daily bread, but your heavenly Father knows your needs. 31He will always give you all you need from day to day if
you will make the Kingdom of God your
primary concern.
32"So don't be afraid, little flock. For it gives
your Father great happiness to give you the
Kingdom. 33Sell what you have and give to
those in need. This will fatten your purses in

12:6-7 If God cares for even the smallest sparrow, then he cares even more for us. If he cares enough to count the hairs on our head, then he cares even more about the thoughts and feelings inside. Dwelling on this reality can help us when we feel depressed or lonely. The most powerful and important Person in the universe cares deeply and personally for us.

12:13-21 Jesus continually emphasized the dangers of materialism. Materialism is not just a problem for the rich people Jesus encountered or for the characters in his stories. The tendency to desire more of everything is endemic to human nature. Notice that Jesus was concerned not so much with how much we possess, but with how much our wealth possesses us. True freedom and contentment cannot be found in the things we own; our recovery can never be bought. These gifts are freely given to us as we humbly turn to God for his gracious help.

12:22-31 True freedom and contentment are found by depending exclusively on God. The argument here confronts the worthlessness of spending time worrying about things God has already taken care of. Since neither animals nor plants worry about food and clothing, neither should we. As God takes care of them while they live their life from day to day, so also God will take care of us while we seek his Kingdom. Knowing God's supreme providential care enables people in recovery to live one day at a time.

heaven! And the purses of heaven have no rips or holes in them. Your treasures there will never disappear; no thief can steal them; no moth can destroy them. 34Wherever your treasure is, there your heart and thoughts will also be.

A Warning to Be Prepared

35"Be prepared—all dressed and ready— 36for your Lord's return from the wedding feast. Then you will be ready to open the door and let him in the moment he arrives and knocks. 37There will be great joy for those who are ready and waiting for his return. He himself will seat them and put on a waiter's uniform and serve them as they sit and eat! 38He may come at nine o'clock at night—or even at midnight. But whenever he comes, there will be joy for his servants who are ready!

39"Everyone would be ready for him if they knew the exact hour of his return—just as they would be ready for a thief if they knew when he was coming. 40So be ready all the time. For I, the Messiah, will come when least expected."

41Peter asked, "Lord, are you talking just to us or to everyone?"

42-44And the Lord replied, "I'm talking to any faithful, sensible man whose master gives him the responsibility of feeding the other servants. If his master returns and finds that he has done a good job, there will be a reward—his master will put him in charge of all he owns.

45"But if the man begins to think, 'My Lord won't be back for a long time,' and begins to whip the men and women he is supposed to protect, and to spend his time at drinking parties and in drunkenness— 46well, his master will return without notice and remove him from his position of trust and assign him to the place of the unfaithful. 47He will be severely punished, for though he knew his duty he refused to do it.

48"But anyone who is not aware that he is doing wrong will be punished only lightly. Much is required from those to whom much is given, for their responsibility is greater.

Jesus Warns of Coming Division

49"I have come to bring fire to the earth, and, oh, that my task were completed! 50There is a terrible baptism ahead of me, and how I am pent up until it is accomplished!

51"Do you think I have come to give peace to the earth? *No!* Rather, strife and division! 52From now on families will be split apart, three in favor of me, and two against—or perhaps the other way around. 53A father will decide one way about me; his son, the other; mother and daughter will disagree; and the decision of an honored mother-in-law will be spurned by her daughter-in-law."

Jesus Warns of a Future Crisis

54Then he turned to the crowd and said, "When you see clouds beginning to form in the west, you say, 'Here comes a shower.' And you are right.

55"When the south wind blows you say, 'Today will be a scorcher.' And it is. 56Hypocrites! You interpret the sky well enough, but you refuse to notice the warnings all around you about the crisis ahead. 57Why do you refuse to see for yourselves what is right?

58"If you meet your accuser on the way to court, try to settle the matter before it reaches the judge, lest he sentence you to jail; 59for if that happens, you won't be free again until the last penny is paid in full."

CHAPTER 13

A Call to Repentance

About this time he was informed that Pilate had butchered some Jews from Galilee as they were sacrificing at the Temple in Jerusalem.

2"Do you think they were worse sinners than other men from Galilee?" he asked. "Is that why they suffered? 3Not at all! And don't you realize that you also will perish unless you leave your evil ways and turn to God?

4"And what about the eighteen men who died when the Tower of Siloam fell on them? Were they the worst sinners in Jerusalem? 5Not at all! And you, too, will perish unless you repent."

6Then he used this illustration: "A man planted a fig tree in his garden and came again and again to see if he could find any

---

12:32-34 The heart represents all that motivates us—our thoughts, ideals, inclinations, priorities, convictions, worries, and fears. If we want genuine recovery in some problem area of our life, we must first release our heartfelt attachment to the dependency or compulsion we are struggling with. The things we value most and spend time and money pursuing—that's where our heartfelt attachments and personal identity can be found. Our checkbook and date book are barometers of our heart condition and our progress in recovery.

fruit on it, but he was always disappointed.
7Finally he told his gardener to cut it down.
'I've waited three years and there hasn't been
a single fig!' he said. 'Why bother with it any
longer? It's taking up space we can use for
something else.'
8"'Give it one more chance,' the gardener
answered. 'Leave it another year, and I'll give
it special attention and plenty of fertilizer. 9If
we get figs next year, fine; if not, I'll cut it
down.'"

Jesus Heals on the Sabbath

10One Sabbath as he was teaching in a synagogue, 11he saw a seriously handicapped
woman who had been bent double for eighteen years and was unable to straighten herself.
12Calling her over to him Jesus said,
"Woman, you are healed of your sickness!"
13He touched her, and instantly she could
stand straight. How she praised and thanked
God!
14But the local Jewish leader in charge of the
synagogue was very angry about it because
Jesus had healed her on the Sabbath day.
"There are six days of the week to work," he
shouted to the crowd. "Those are the days to
come for healing, not on the Sabbath!"
15But the Lord replied, "You hypocrite! You
work on the Sabbath! Don't you untie your
cattle from their stalls on the Sabbath and
lead them out for water? 16And is it wrong for
me, just because it is the Sabbath day, to free
this Jewish woman from the bondage in
which Satan has held her for eighteen years?"
17This shamed his enemies. And all the
people rejoiced at the wonderful things he
did.

Teachings about God's Kingdom

18Now he began teaching them again about
the Kingdom of God: "What is the Kingdom
like?" he asked. "How can I illustrate it? 19It is
like a tiny mustard seed planted in a garden;
soon it grows into a tall bush and the birds
live among its branches.
20,21"It is like yeast kneaded into dough,
which works unseen until it has risen high
and light."
22He went from city to city and village to
village, teaching as he went, always pressing
onward toward Jerusalem.
23Someone asked him, "Will only a few be
saved?"
And he replied, 24,25"The door to heaven is
narrow. Work hard to get in, for the truth is
that many will try to enter but when the head
of the house has locked the door, it will be too
late. Then if you stand outside knocking, and
pleading, 'Lord, open the door for us,' he will
reply, 'I do not know you.'
26"'But we ate with you, and you taught in
our streets,' you will say.
27"And he will reply, 'I tell you, I don't know
you. You can't come in here, guilty as you are.
Go away.'
28"And there will be great weeping and
gnashing of teeth as you stand outside and see
Abraham, Isaac, Jacob, and all the prophets
within the Kingdom of God— 29for people
will come from all over the world to take their
places there. 30And note this: some who are
despised now will be greatly honored then;
and some who are highly thought of now will
be least important then."

Jesus Grieves over Jerusalem

31A few minutes later some Pharisees said to
him, "Get out of here if you want to live, for
King Herod is after you!"
32Jesus replied, "Go tell that fox that I will
keep on casting out demons and doing
miracles of healing today and tomorrow; and
the third day I will reach my destination.
33Yes, today, tomorrow, and the next day! For
it wouldn't do for a prophet of God to be
killed except in Jerusalem!
34"O Jerusalem, Jerusalem! The city that
murders the prophets. The city that stones

13:10-13 Jesus cared for social outcasts, emotional and physical cripples, and those in spiritual bondage. This handicapped woman was hurting in all three respects. The longevity of her ailment indicates she had probably tried everything but now was resigned to her painful limitations. The religious powers in her society, as well as the powers of the underworld, wanted to keep her that way. However, the power of Jesus Christ knows no such limitations. Jesus healed this woman who had given up all hope for a new life. He can do the same for us by empowering our recovery process.

13:22-30 Appearances can be deceiving. But God is not fooled—he knows the real intent of our heart. We can go to church, teach Sunday school, or sing in the choir and, like the religious hypocrites of Jesus' day, still lack a real relationship with God. Being real, not merely religious, is crucial to our recovery. God will judge religious hypocrisy, and he will honor honest attempts to obey him and know him better—no matter how many times we may fail.

those sent to help her. How often I have
wanted to gather your children together even
as a hen protects her brood under her wings,
but you wouldn't let me. 35And now—now
your house is left desolate. And you will never
again see me until you say, 'Welcome to him
who comes in the name of the Lord.'"

CHAPTER 14

Jesus Heals a Man with Dropsy

One Sabbath as he was in the home of a
member of the Jewish Council, the Pharisees
were watching him like hawks to see if he
would heal a man who was present who was
suffering from dropsy.
3Jesus said to the Pharisees and legal experts
standing around, "Well, is it within the Law
to heal a man on the Sabbath day, or not?"
4And when they refused to answer, Jesus
took the sick man by the hand and healed
him and sent him away.
5Then he turned to them: "Which of you
doesn't work on the Sabbath?" he asked. "If
your cow falls into a pit, don't you proceed at
once to get it out?"
6Again they had no answer.

Jesus Teaches about Seeking Honor

7When he noticed that all who came to the
dinner were trying to sit near the head of the
table, he gave them this advice: 8"If you are
invited to a wedding feast, don't always head
for the best seat. For if someone more respected than you shows up, 9the host will
bring him over to where you are sitting and
say, 'Let this man sit here instead.' And you,
embarrassed, will have to take whatever seat
is left at the foot of the table!
10"Do this instead—start at the foot; and
when your host sees you he will come and say,
'Friend, we have a better place than this for
you!' Thus you will be honored in front of all
the other guests. 11For everyone who tries to
honor himself shall be humbled; and he who
humbles himself shall be honored." 12Then he
turned to his host. "When you put on a dinner," he said, "don't invite friends, brothers,
relatives, and rich neighbors! For they will
return the invitation. 13Instead, invite the
poor, the crippled, the lame, and the blind.
14Then at the resurrection of the godly, God
will reward you for inviting those who can't
repay you."

A Story about a Great Feast

15Hearing this, a man sitting at the table with
Jesus exclaimed, "What a privilege it would be
to get into the Kingdom of God!"
16Jesus replied with this illustration: "A man
prepared a great feast and sent out many
invitations. 17When all was ready, he sent his
servant around to notify the guests that it was
time for them to arrive. 18But they all began
making excuses. One said he had just bought
a field and wanted to inspect it, and asked to
be excused. 19Another said he had just bought
five pair of oxen and wanted to try them out.
20Another had just been married and for that
reason couldn't come.
21"The servant returned and reported to his
master what they had said. His master was
angry and told him to go quickly into the
streets and alleys of the city and to invite the
beggars, crippled, lame, and blind. 22But even
then, there was still room.
23"'Well, then,' said his master, 'go out into
the country lanes and out behind the hedges
and urge anyone you find to come, so that the
house will be full. 24For none of those I invited
first will get even the smallest taste of what I
had prepared for them.'"

The Cost of Following Jesus

25Great crowds were following him. He turned
around and addressed them as follows:
26"Anyone who wants to be my follower must
love me far more than he does his own father,
mother, wife, children, brothers, or sisters—
yes, more than his own life—otherwise he
cannot be my disciple. 27And no one can be

14:12-24 This story about the great feast illustrates one of the major themes in Luke's Gospel. God extends his grace and blessing to the poor and the handicapped of society, who in almost every case are ignored, even abused. Extending mercy to such people will be rewarded by God. An important step in following Jesus, and in our own recovery program, is our willingness to help others less fortunate than we.

14:26-33 "Counting the cost" applies not only to our decision to follow Jesus, but it also speaks of our need to weigh the cost of our recovery. A searching and fearless moral inventory of our life is required in both cases. If commitment to Jesus and recovery is more valuable to us than our compulsions, addictions, or dysfunctions, then recovery in the fullest sense will be realized. If we cannot give up the pleasures of our dependencies, our recovery will be short-lived. We will end up compromising our commitments and remain enslaved to our dependencies and the painful consequences that inevitably result.

my disciple who does not carry his own cross and follow me.

28"But don't begin until you count the cost. For who would begin construction of a building without first getting estimates and then checking to see if he has enough money to pay the bills? 29Otherwise he might complete only the foundation before running out of funds. And then how everyone would laugh!

30"'See that fellow there?' they would mock. 'He started that building and ran out of money before it was finished!'

31"Or what king would ever dream of going to war without first sitting down with his counselors and discussing whether his army of 10,000 is strong enough to defeat the 20,000 men who are marching against him? 32"If the decision is negative, then while the enemy troops are still far away, he will send a truce team to discuss terms of peace. 33So no one can become my disciple unless he first sits down and counts his blessings—and then renounces them all for me.

34"What good is salt that has lost its saltiness? 35Flavorless salt is fit for nothing—not even for fertilizer. It is worthless and must be thrown out. Listen well if you would understand my meaning."

CHAPTER 15

A Story about a Lost Sheep

Dishonest tax collectors and other notorious sinners often came to listen to Jesus' sermons; 2but this caused complaints from the Jewish religious leaders and the experts on Jewish law because he was associating with such despicable people—even eating with them!

3,4So Jesus used this illustration: "If you had a hundred sheep and one of them strayed away and was lost in the wilderness, wouldn't you leave the ninety-nine others to go and search for the lost one until you found it? 5And then you would joyfully carry it home on your shoulders. 6When you arrived you would call together your friends and neighbors to rejoice with you because your lost sheep was found.

7"Well, in the same way heaven will be happier over one lost sinner who returns to God than over ninety-nine others who haven't strayed away!

A Story about a Lost Coin

8"Or take another illustration: A woman has ten valuable silver coins and loses one. Won't she light a lamp and look in every corner of the house and sweep every nook and cranny until she finds it? 9And then won't she call in her friends and neighbors to rejoice with her? 10In the same way there is joy in the presence of the angels of God when one sinner repents."

A Story about a Lost Son

11To further illustrate the point, he told them this story: "A man had two sons. 12When the younger told his father, 'I want my share of your estate now, instead of waiting until you die!' his father agreed to divide his wealth between his sons.

13"A few days later this younger son packed all his belongings and took a trip to a distant land, and there wasted all his money on parties and prostitutes. 14About the time his money was gone a great famine swept over the land, and he began to starve. 15He persuaded a local farmer to hire him to feed his pigs. 16The boy became so hungry that even

---

15:3-10 The stories of the lost coin and the lost sheep show God's grace toward those who have strayed and his great joy in finding them. Though our past may be tarnished, we are extremely valuable in the eyes of God. This value is reflected in the symbolism of the coin and sheep (valuable commodities in that day). That the owner would stop everything else to search for the one lost shows even more how valuable we are to the One who owns us.

15:20-24 The father's great compassion for his younger son portrays God's response to anyone who repents. Like the father in this story, God waits for the addict or sinner to come to his senses and return of his own volition. The waiting father, however, does not wait for total amends or a cleanup act. (Those steps in the recovery process can wait.) The father runs to his penitent son, hugs and kisses him, and throws a party—thus wiping away all shame and guilt. Thus God actively seeks those who do not have a personal relationship with him, as well as those of us who have strayed in our walk of faith.

15:25-30 God asks us to share his great concern for those who are helpless and lost, and to be willing to carry the message of hope to them. The older brother in this story is a significant character because his selfish attitude is shown to be sinful and self-centered. He represents the religious leadership of that time, as well as those of us who still cling to our own self-sufficiency. The father in this story demonstrates God's attitude toward people who are lost. God desires our restoration more than anything, whether the people around us like it or not. He also wants to use us to support fellow strugglers in the recovery process.

the pods he was feeding the swine looked
good to him. And no one gave him anything.
17"When he finally came to his senses, he
said to himself, 'At home even the hired men
have food enough and to spare, and here I
am, dying of hunger! 18I will go home to my
father and say, "Father, I have sinned against
both heaven and you, 19and am no longer
worthy of being called your son. Please take
me on as a hired man."'
20"So he returned home to his father. And
while he was still a long distance away, his
father saw him coming, and was filled with
loving pity and ran and embraced him and
kissed him.
21"His son said to him, 'Father, I have
sinned against heaven and you, and am not
worthy of being called your son—'
22"But his father said to the slaves, 'Quick!
Bring the finest robe in the house and put it
on him. And a jeweled ring for his finger; and
shoes! 23And kill the calf we have in the fattening pen. We must celebrate with a feast, 24for
this son of mine was dead and has returned to
life. He was lost and is found.' So the party
began.
25"Meanwhile, the older son was in the
fields working; when he returned home, he
heard dance music coming from the house,
26and he asked one of the servants what was
going on.
27"'Your brother is back,' he was told, 'and
your father has killed the calf we were fattening and has prepared a great feast to celebrate
his coming home again unharmed.'
28"The older brother was angry and
wouldn't go in. His father came out and
begged him, 29but he replied, 'All these years
I've worked hard for you and never once
refused to do a single thing you told me to;
and in all that time you never gave me even
one young goat for a feast with my friends.
30Yet when this son of yours comes back after
spending your money on prostitutes, you celebrate by killing the finest calf we have on the
place.'
31"'Look, dear son,' his father said to him,
'you and I are very close, and everything I
have is yours. 32But it is right to celebrate. For
he is your brother; and he was dead and has
come back to life! He was lost and is found!'"

CHAPTER 16
A Story about a Shrewd Accountant
Jesus now told this story to his disciples: "A
rich man hired an accountant to handle his

Restoration

BIBLE READING: Luke 15:11-24

We came to believe that a Power greater than ourselves could restore us to sanity.

In the natural progression of addiction, life necessarily degenerates. In one way or another, many of us wake up one day to realize that we are living like animals. How true this is depends on the nature of our addiction. Some of us may be living like animals in terms of our physical surroundings. Others of us may be slaves to our animal passions—powerful emotions that dehumanize us.

A young man took an early inheritance and wandered away from home. When the money was spent, the women just a memory, and the "high" long gone, he resorted to slopping pigs to earn a meager living. When he became so hungry that he was eyeing the pig's slop with envy, he realized he had a problem. "When he finally came to his senses, he said to himself, 'At home even the hired men have food enough and to spare, and here I am, dying of hunger! I will go home to my father. . . .' So he returned home to his father. And while he was still a long distance away, his father saw him coming, and was filled with loving pity and ran and embraced him and kissed him" (Luke 15:17-18, 20).

The fact that we are able to recognize our life as degenerate or insane proves that there is hope for a better way of life. We are reminded of a time when life was good, and we long to have it restored. When we turn in the direction of God who is more powerful, who represents the memory of something better, we will find the Power who can restore us to sanity. ***Turn to page 1229, Romans 1.***

affairs, but soon a rumor went around that the accountant was thoroughly dishonest.

[2]“So his employer called him in and said, ‘What’s this I hear about your stealing from me? Get your report in order, for you are to be dismissed.’

[3]“The accountant thought to himself, ‘Now what? I’m through here, and I haven’t the strength to go out and dig ditches, and I’m too proud to beg. [4]I know just the thing! And then I’ll have plenty of friends to take care of me when I leave!’

[5,6]“So he invited each one who owed money to his employer to come and discuss the situation. He asked the first one, ‘How much do you owe him?’ ‘My debt is 850 gallons of olive oil,’ the man replied. ‘Yes, here is the contract you signed,’ the accountant told him. ‘Tear it up and write another one for half that much!’

[7]“‘And how much do you owe him?’ he asked the next man. ‘A thousand bushels of wheat,’ was the reply. ‘Here,’ the accountant said, ‘take your note and replace it with one for only 800 bushels!’

[8]“The rich man had to admire the rascal for being so shrewd. And it is true that the citizens of this world are more clever [in dishonesty!] than the godly are. [9]But shall I tell *you* to act that way, to buy friendship through cheating? Will this ensure your entry into an everlasting home in heaven? [10]*No!* For unless you are honest in small matters, you won’t be in large ones. If you cheat even a little, you won’t be honest with greater responsibilities. [11]And if you are untrustworthy about worldly wealth, who will trust you with the true riches of heaven? [12]And if you are not faithful with other people’s money, why should you be entrusted with money of your own?

[13]“For neither you nor anyone else can serve two masters. You will hate one and show loyalty to the other, or else the other way around—you will be enthusiastic about one and despise the other. You cannot serve both God and money.”

[14]The Pharisees, who dearly loved their money, naturally scoffed at all this.

[15]Then he said to them, “You wear a noble, pious expression in public, but God knows your evil hearts. Your pretense brings you honor from the people, but it is an abomination in the sight of God. [16]Until John the Baptist began to preach, the laws of Moses and the messages of the prophets were your guides. But John introduced the Good News that the Kingdom of God would come soon. And now eager multitudes are pressing in. [17]But that doesn’t mean that the Law has lost its force in even the smallest point. It is as strong and unshakable as heaven and earth.

[18]“So anyone who divorces his wife and marries someone else commits adultery, and anyone who marries a divorced woman commits adultery.”

The Rich Man and Lazarus

[19]“There was a certain rich man,” Jesus said, “who was splendidly clothed and lived each day in mirth and luxury. [20]One day Lazarus, a diseased beggar, was laid at his door. [21]As he lay there longing for scraps from the rich man’s table, the dogs would come and lick his open sores. [22]Finally the beggar died and was carried by the angels to be with Abraham in the place of the righteous dead. The rich man

---

16:1-13 This story teaches the importance of using our material possessions to help bring eternal life and spiritual blessing to others. If the shrewd accountant is commended for cleverly using his talent for winning friends and influencing people, how much more the honest steward who dedicates all to God. Using material possessions and God-given talent merely for personal enjoyment, with no concern for others, is wrong. That may mean that our possessions have possessed us, or that our goods have become our god. Serving God alone will lead us down the path of recovery.

16:19-31 In this story we are shown the consequences of selfishness. Insulated by all the material comforts of life, the rich man never took inventory of his deepest needs and shortcomings. Because he was hardhearted and selfish, refusing to feed Lazarus, he was consigned to hell. The beggar Lazarus, however, lacked basic material needs and suffered physical pain in his lifetime, but he was prepared for eternity. Death proved to be the great equalizer, effecting a reversal of fortune for these two. God wants us to have the proper attitude toward money and possessions and to use them unselfishly to help others.

17:1-4 Knowing when to forgive and when to confront is critical to the recovery process. Jesus taught that forgiveness is to be freely and frequently extended to others, with no strings attached. On the other hand, the recovery process sometimes calls for tough love. If our friends are acting in ways clearly counter to God’s will, we need to confront them for their own good. Woe to the person, however, who puts temptation in the way of a person in recovery. Strong drink or drugs, for example, should never be offered to people in recovery. Those who offer such temptation will pay dearly when they stand before God.

also died and was buried, [23]and his soul went
into hell. There, in torment, he saw Lazarus in
the far distance with Abraham.
[24]"'Father Abraham,' he shouted, 'have
some pity! Send Lazarus over here if only to
dip the tip of his finger in water and cool my
tongue, for I am in anguish in these flames.'
[25]"But Abraham said to him, 'Son, remember that during your lifetime you had everything you wanted, and Lazarus had nothing.
So now he is here being comforted and you
are in anguish. [26]And besides, there is a great
chasm separating us, and anyone wanting to
come to you from here is stopped at its edge;
and no one over there can cross to us.'
[27]"Then the rich man said, 'O Father Abraham, then please send him to my father's
home— [28]for I have five brothers—to warn
them about this place of torment lest they
come here when they die.'
[29]"But Abraham said, 'The Scriptures have
warned them again and again. Your brothers
can read them any time they want to.'
[30]"The rich man replied, 'No, Father Abraham, they won't bother to read them. But if
someone is sent to them from the dead, then
they will turn from their sins.'
[31]"But Abraham said, 'If they won't listen to
Moses and the prophets, they won't listen
even though someone rises from the dead.'"

CHAPTER 17

Teachings about Forgiveness and Faith

"There will always be temptations to sin,"
Jesus said one day to his disciples, "but woe to
the man who does the tempting. [2,3]If he were
thrown into the sea with a huge rock tied to
his neck, he would be far better off than
facing the punishment in store for those who
harm these little children's souls. I am warning you!
"Rebuke your brother if he sins, and forgive
him if he is sorry.[4]Even if he wrongs you seven
times a day and each time turns again and
asks forgiveness, forgive him."
[5]One day the apostles said to the Lord, "We
need more faith; tell us how to get it."
[6]"If your faith were only the size of a mustard seed," Jesus answered, "it would be large
enough to uproot that mulberry tree over
there and send it hurtling into the sea! Your
command would bring immediate results!
[7-9]When a servant comes in from plowing or
taking care of sheep, he doesn't just sit down
and eat, but first prepares his master's meal
and serves him his supper before he eats his
own. And he is not even thanked, for he is

Faith

READ LUKE 17:1-10

How many times have we wished that we could overcome the addictions and compulsions that keep us in bondage? We know what it is to struggle with the effects of addiction and the craziness this brings to our life. We may feel despair and wonder if there really is any way out of the insanity of our current circumstances. Maybe our plight is impossible, at least without God's help, but faith can make even the impossible happen.

"One day the apostles said to the Lord, 'We need more faith; tell us how to get it.' 'If your faith were only the size of a mustard seed,' Jesus answered, 'it would be large enough to uproot that mulberry tree over there and send it hurtling into the sea! Your command would bring immediate results!'" (Luke 17:5-6). Matthew also recorded Jesus' words, "For if you had faith even as small as a tiny mustard seed you could say to this mountain, 'Move!' and it would go far away. Nothing would be impossible" (Matthew 17:20).

Faith is a mysterious commodity. Jesus says that if we have faith, real faith, it only takes a small amount to make a big difference. We may be exercising faith without even realizing it. It takes faith to believe that a Power greater than ourself could restore us to sanity. It takes faith to work through the steps of a recovery program. It is comforting to know that God only needs a tiny bit of faith in order to work in powerful ways to restore our sanity. ***Turn to page 1131, Luke 22.***

merely doing what he is supposed to do. [10]Just so, if you merely obey me, you should not consider yourselves worthy of praise. For you have simply done your duty!"

Jesus Heals Ten Lepers

[11]As they continued onward toward Jerusalem, they reached the border between Galilee and Samaria, [12]and as they entered a village there, ten lepers stood at a distance, [13]crying out, "Jesus, sir, have mercy on us!"

[14]He looked at them and said, "Go to the Jewish priest and show him that you are healed!" And as they were going, their leprosy disappeared.

[15]One of them came back to Jesus, shouting, "Glory to God, I'm healed!" [16]He fell flat on the ground in front of Jesus, face downward in the dust, thanking him for what he had done. This man was a despised Samaritan.

[17]Jesus asked, "Didn't I heal ten men? Where are the nine? [18]Does only this foreigner return to give glory to God?"

[19]And Jesus said to the man, "Stand up and go; your faith has made you well."

Teachings about the Kingdom

[20]One day the Pharisees asked Jesus, "When will the Kingdom of God begin?" Jesus replied, "The Kingdom of God isn't ushered in with visible signs. [21]You won't be able to say, 'It has begun here in this place or there in that part of the country.' For the Kingdom of God is within you."

[22]Later he talked again about this with his disciples. "The time is coming when you will long for me to be with you even for a single day, but I won't be here," he said. [23]"Reports will reach you that I have returned and that I am in this place or that; don't believe it or go out to look for me. [24]For when I return, you will know it beyond all doubt. It will be as evident as the lightning that flashes across the skies. [25]But first I must suffer terribly and be rejected by this whole nation.

[26]"[When I return] the world will be [as indifferent to the things of God] as the people were in Noah's day. [27]They ate and drank and married—everything just as usual right up to the day when Noah went into the ark and the flood came and destroyed them all.

[28]"And the world will be as it was in the days of Lot: people went about their daily business—eating and drinking, buying and selling, farming and building— [29]until the morning Lot left Sodom. Then fire and brimstone rained down from heaven and destroyed them all. [30]Yes, it will be 'business as usual' right up to the hour of my return.

[31]"Those away from home that day must not return to pack; those in the fields must not return to town— [32]remember what happened to Lot's wife! [33]Whoever clings to his life shall lose it, and whoever loses his life shall save it. [34]That night two men will be asleep in the same room, and one will be taken away, the other left. [35,36]Two women will be working together at household tasks; one will be taken, the other left; and so it will be with men working side by side in the fields."

[37]"Lord, where will they be taken?" the disciples asked.

Jesus replied, "Where the body is, the vultures gather!"

17:11-19 The story of the ten lepers illustrates Jesus' great compassion for the hurting and his desire to make them whole. Only one of the ten lepers returned to say thanks, and that one was a Samaritan. So also in the recovery movement, most people will not appreciate our efforts at intervention on their behalf. Those few who are grateful are the faithful ones who get well.

18:1-8 Many of us have experienced injustice at the hands of some authority figure. Perhaps a family court judge, a mean boss, or a parole officer acted unfairly toward us. This story contrasts God to the unfair judge and makes the point that even if life is unfair, at least God is fair. If even an unjust judge will answer the pleas of a persistent widow, how much more will a just God respond to those in need who pray to him in faith. When trials and challenges make it seem like life is unfair, we can still trust God to deliver us. Seeking God in prayer requires patience and persistence, but it always pays off in the end.

18:15-17 Children are naturally given to trusting, and God wants our relationship with him to be driven by that kind of simple trust. Any other kind of "faith" is inappropriate, unnatural, and ineffective. If we find ourself unable to trust, it may be helpful for us to understand the hurts in our past that make it so difficult to do this. Childlike faith is itself a gift from God that may take time for him to restore in us, especially if we have been abused (spiritually, emotionally, sexually, or physically). In recovery we are told to keep it simple; a simple faith in an almighty God is what we need for a successful recovery.

CHAPTER 18

A Story of a Persistent Widow

One day Jesus told his disciples a story to
illustrate their need for constant prayer and to
show them that they must keep praying until
the answer comes.
2 "There was a city judge," he said, "a very
godless man who had great contempt for
everyone. 3 A widow of that city came to him
frequently to appeal for justice against a man
who had harmed her. 4,5 The judge ignored her
for a while, but eventually she got on his
nerves.
"'I fear neither God nor man,' he said to
himself, 'but this woman bothers me. I'm
going to see that she gets justice, for she is
wearing me out with her constant coming!'"
6 Then the Lord said, "If even an evil judge
can be worn down like that, 7 don't you think
that God will surely give justice to his people
who plead with him day and night? 8 Yes! He
will answer them quickly! But the question is:
When I, the Messiah, return, how many will
I find who have faith [and are praying]?"

The Prayers of Two Men

9 Then he told this story to some who boasted
of their virtue and scorned everyone else:
10 "Two men went to the Temple to pray.
One was a proud, self-righteous Pharisee, and
the other a cheating tax collector. 11 The proud
Pharisee 'prayed' this prayer: 'Thank God, I
am not a sinner like everyone else, especially
like that tax collector over there! For I never
cheat, I don't commit adultery, 12 I go without
food twice a week, and I give to God a tenth
of everything I earn.'
13 "But the corrupt tax collector stood at a
distance and dared not even lift his eyes to
heaven as he prayed, but beat upon his chest
in sorrow, exclaiming, 'God, be merciful to
me, a sinner.' 14 I tell you, this sinner, not the
Pharisee, returned home forgiven! For the
proud shall be humbled, but the humble shall
be honored."

Jesus Blesses the Children

15 One day some mothers brought their babies
to him to touch and bless. But the disciples
told them to go away.
16,17 Then Jesus called the children over to
him and said to the disciples, "Let the little
children come to me! Never send them away!
For the Kingdom of God belongs to men who
have hearts as trusting as these little children's. And anyone who doesn't have their

A Humble Heart

BIBLE READING: Luke 18:10-14

We humbly asked him to remove our shortcomings.

After examining our life closely (as we did in Steps Four, Five, and Six), we may feel cut off from God. Considering the scope of what we have done, we may feel unworthy to ask God for anything. Maybe our problem behaviors are despised as the lowest kind of evil by those whom we consider respectable. We may struggle with self-hatred. Our genuine remorse may cause us to wonder if we even dare approach God to ask for his help.

We are welcome to come to God, even when we feel this way. Jesus told this story: "Two men went to the Temple to pray. One was a proud, self-righteous Pharisee, and the other a cheating tax collector. The proud Pharisee 'prayed' this prayer: 'Thank God, I am not a sinner like everyone else, especially like that tax collector over there! For I never cheat, I don't commit adultery, I go without food twice a week, and I give to God a tenth of everything I earn.' But the corrupt tax collector stood at a distance and dared not even lift his eyes to heaven as he prayed, but beat upon his chest in sorrow, exclaiming, 'God, be merciful to me, a sinner.' I tell you, this sinner, not the Pharisee, returned home forgiven!" (Luke 18:10-14).

Tax collectors were among the most despised members of Jewish society. Pharisees, on the other hand, commanded the highest respect. Jesus purposely chose this illustration to show that it doesn't matter where we fit in society's hierarchy. It is the humble heart that opens the door to God's forgiveness. ***Turn to page 1235, Romans 3.***

kind of faith will never get within the Kingdom's gates."

Jesus and the Rich Young Man

[18]Once a Jewish religious leader asked him this
question: "Good sir, what shall I do to get to
heaven?"
[19]"Do you realize what you are saying when
you call me 'good'?" Jesus asked him. "Only
God is truly good, and no one else.
[20]"But as to your question, you know what
the Ten Commandments say—don't commit
adultery, don't murder, don't steal, don't lie,
honor your parents, and so on." [21]The man
replied, "I've obeyed every one of these laws
since I was a small child."
[22]"There is still one thing you lack," Jesus
said. "Sell all you have and give the money to
the poor—it will become treasure for you in
heaven—and come, follow me."
[23]But when the man heard this he went
sadly away, for he was very rich.
[24]Jesus watched him go and then said to his
disciples, "How hard it is for the rich to enter
the Kingdom of God! [25]It is easier for a camel
to go through the eye of a needle than for a
rich man to enter the Kingdom of God."
[26]Those who heard him say this exclaimed,
"If it is that hard, how can *anyone* be saved?"
[27]He replied, "God can do what men can't!"
[28]And Peter said, "We have left our homes
and followed you."
[29]"Yes," Jesus replied, "and everyone who
has done as you have, leaving home, wife,
brothers, parents, or children for the sake of
the Kingdom of God, [30]will be repaid many
times over now, as well as receiving eternal
life in the world to come."

Jesus Again Predicts His Death

[31]Gathering the Twelve around him he told
them, "As you know, we are going to Jerusalem. And when we get there, all the predictions of the ancient prophets concerning me
will come true. [32]I will be handed over to the
Gentiles to be mocked and treated shamefully
and spat upon, [33]and lashed and killed. And
the third day I will rise again."
[34]But they didn't understand a thing he
said. He seemed to be talking in riddles.

Jesus Heals a Blind Beggar

[35]As they approached Jericho, a blind man
was sitting beside the road, begging from travelers. [36]When he heard the noise of a crowd
going past, he asked what was happening.
[37]He was told that Jesus from Nazareth was
going by, [38]so he began shouting, "Jesus, Son
of David, have mercy on me!"
[39]The crowds ahead of Jesus tried to hush
the man, but he only yelled the louder, "Son
of David, have mercy on me!"
[40]When Jesus arrived at the spot, he
stopped. "Bring the blind man over here," he
said. [41]Then Jesus asked the man, "What do
you want?"
"Lord," he pleaded, "I want to see!"
[42]And Jesus said, "All right, begin seeing!
Your faith has healed you."
[43]And instantly the man could see and followed Jesus, praising God. And all who saw it
happen praised God too.

CHAPTER 19

Zacchaeus Gets a Second Chance

As Jesus was passing through Jericho, a man
named Zacchaeus, one of the most influential
Jews in the Roman tax-collecting business
(and, of course, a very rich man), [3]tried to get
a look at Jesus, but he was too short to see over
the crowds. [4]So he ran ahead and climbed into
a sycamore tree beside the road, to watch
from there.
[5]When Jesus came by, he looked up at Zacchaeus and called him by name! "Zacchaeus!"
he said. "Quick! Come down! For I am going
to be a guest in your home today!"
[6]Zacchaeus hurriedly climbed down and

18:31-34 Jesus here predicted the suffering he would go through on the way to the cross. While the pain and disgrace he would experience was extreme, he was willing to accept it as a necessary part of the process toward the goal. In recovery, the process of spiritual growth often involves pain and sacrifice. Sometimes reversing patterns of former sinful or addictive behavior can be extremely difficult. This can be discouraging, so it is essential that we keep our focus on the goal—our recovery—which is worth the sacrifice we make.

19:11-27 This story teaches the principle of stewardship—our accountability before God to use wisely the gifts, abilities, and possessions he has entrusted to us. To wisely use what God has given will result in generous reward; to refuse to do so will bring a stern reprimand from God. Whatever opportunities and resources God gives us—whether time, money, talents, or relationships—we are to multiply in the lives of others. After years of pain and devastation, we may wonder what we have to offer. Our story of deliverance may be all someone needs to take a step toward God and recovery. By sharing ourself with others, we may be saving the life of a needy person.

took Jesus to his house in great excitement
and joy.
[7]But the crowds were displeased. "He has
gone to be the guest of a notorious sinner,"
they grumbled.
[8]Meanwhile, Zacchaeus stood before the
Lord and said, "Sir, from now on I will give
half my wealth to the poor, and if I find I have
overcharged anyone on his taxes, I will penalize myself by giving him back four times as
much!"
[9,10]Jesus told him, "This shows that salvation has come to this home today. This man
was one of the lost sons of Abraham, and I,
the Messiah, have come to search for and to
save such souls as his."

Wise and Foolish Investors

[11]And because Jesus was nearing Jerusalem, he
told a story to correct the impression that the
Kingdom of God would begin right away.
[12]"A nobleman living in a certain province
was called away to the distant capital of the
empire to be crowned king of his province.
[13]Before he left he called together ten assistants and gave them each $2,000 to invest
while he was gone. [14]But some of his people
hated him and sent him their declaration of
independence, stating that they had rebelled
and would not acknowledge him as their
king.
[15]"Upon his return he called in the men to
whom he had given the money, to find out
what they had done with it, and what their
profits were.
[16]"The first man reported a tremendous
gain—ten times as much as the original
amount!
[17]"'Fine!' the king exclaimed. 'You are a
good man. You have been faithful with the
little I entrusted to you, and as your reward,
you shall be governor of ten cities.'
[18]"The next man also reported a splendid
gain—five times the original amount.
[19]"'All right!' his master said. 'You can be
governor over five cities.'
[20]"But the third man brought back only the
money he had started with. 'I've kept it safe,'
he said, [21]'because I was afraid [you would
demand my profits], for you are a hard man
to deal with, taking what isn't yours and even
confiscating the crops that others plant.'
[22]'You vile and wicked slave,' the king roared.
'Hard, am I? That's exactly how I'll be toward
you! If you knew so much about me and how
tough I am, [23]then why didn't you deposit the

From Taker to Giver

BIBLE READING: Luke 19:1-10

We made direct amends to such people wherever possible, except when to do so would injure them or others.

When we are feeding our addictions, it is easy to become consumed by our own needs. Nothing matters except getting what we crave so desperately. We may have to lie, cheat, kill, or steal; but that doesn't stop us. Within our family and community we become known as "takers," trampling over the unseen needs of others.

Zacchaeus had the same problem. His hunger for riches drove him to betray his own people by collecting taxes for the oppressive Roman government. He was hated by his own people as a thief, an extortioner, and a traitor. But when Jesus reached out to him, he changed dramatically. "Zacchaeus stood before the Lord and said, 'Sir, from now on I will give half my wealth to the poor, and if I find I have overcharged anyone on his taxes, I will penalize myself by giving him back four times as much!' Jesus told him, 'This shows that salvation has come to this home today'" (Luke 19:8-9).

Zacchaeus went beyond just paying back what he had taken. For the first time in a long time, he saw the needs of others and wanted to be a "giver." Making amends includes paying back what we have taken, whenever possible. Some of us may even seize the opportunity to go further, giving even more. As we begin to see the needs of others and respond by choice, our self-esteem will rise. We will begin to realize that we can give to others, instead of just being a burden. ***Turn to page 1377, Philemon 1.***

money in the bank so that I could at least get
some interest on it?'
24"Then turning to the others standing by
he ordered, 'Take the money away from him
and give it to the man who earned the most.'
25"'But, sir,' they said, 'he has enough already!'
26"'Yes,' the king replied, 'but it is always
true that those who have, get more, and those
who have little, soon lose even that. 27And
now about these enemies of mine who revolted—bring them in and execute them before me.'"

Jesus Rides into Jerusalem

28After telling this story, Jesus went on toward
Jerusalem, walking along ahead of his disciples. 29As they came to the towns of Bethphage and Bethany, on the Mount of Olives,
he sent two disciples ahead, 30with instructions to go to the next village, and as they
entered they were to look for a donkey tied
beside the road. It would be a colt, not yet
broken for riding.
"Untie him," Jesus said, "and bring him
here. 31And if anyone asks you what you are
doing, just say, 'The Lord needs him.'"
32They found the colt as Jesus said, 33and
sure enough, as they were untying it, the
owners demanded an explanation.
"What are you doing?" they asked. "Why
are you untying our colt?"
34And the disciples simply replied, "The
Lord needs him!" 35So they brought the colt to
Jesus and threw some of their clothing across
its back for Jesus to sit on.
36,37Then the crowds spread out their robes
along the road ahead of him, and as they
reached the place where the road started
down from the Mount of Olives, the whole
procession began to shout and sing as they
walked along, praising God for all the wonderful miracles Jesus had done.
38"God has given us a King!" they exulted.
"Long live the King! Let all heaven rejoice!
Glory to God in the highest heavens!"
39But some of the Pharisees among the
crowd said, "Sir, rebuke your followers for
saying things like that!"
40He replied, "If they keep quiet, the stones
along the road will burst into cheers!"
41But as they came closer to Jerusalem and
he saw the city ahead, he began to cry. 42"Eternal peace was within your reach and you
turned it down," he wept, "and now it is too
late. 43Your enemies will pile up earth against
your walls and encircle you and close in on
you, 44and crush you to the ground, and your
children within you; your enemies will not
leave one stone upon another—for you have
rejected the opportunity God offered you."

Jesus Clears the Temple

45Then he entered the Temple and began to
drive out the merchants from their stalls,
46saying to them, "The Scriptures declare, 'My
Temple is a place of prayer; but you have
turned it into a den of thieves.'"
47After that he taught daily in the Temple,
but the chief priests and other religious leaders and the business community were trying
to find some way to get rid of him. 48But they
could think of nothing, for he was a hero to
the people—they hung on every word he said.

CHAPTER 20

Religious Leaders Challenge Jesus

On one of those days when he was teaching
and preaching the Good News in the Temple,
he was confronted by the chief priests and
other religious leaders and councilmen. 2They
demanded to know by what authority he had
driven out the merchants from the Temple.
3"I'll ask you a question before I answer," he
replied. 4"Was John sent by God, or was he
merely acting under his own authority?"
5They talked it over among themselves. "If
we say his message was from heaven, then we
are trapped because he will ask, 'Then why
didn't you believe him?' 6But if we say John
was not sent from God, the people will mob
us, for they are convinced that he was a
prophet." 7Finally they replied, "We don't
know!"
8And Jesus responded, "Then I won't answer your question either."

A Story about Wicked Farmers

9Now he turned to the people again and told
them this story: "A man planted a vineyard
and rented it out to some farmers, and went
away to a distant land to live for several years.

19:45-48 Just how dysfunctional the people's worship had become is evident by the fact that Jesus had to drive the merchants out of God's Temple. Correcting this gross injustice was not appreciated and did not produce the desired effect of change in the worshipers. Instead, Jesus' act of cleaning house was met with anger and a desire for vengeance. Change, even much-needed change for the better, is resisted by those in denial.

[10]When harvest time came, he sent one of his men to the farm to collect his share of the crops. But the tenants beat him up and sent him back empty-handed. [11]Then he sent another, but the same thing happened; he was beaten up and insulted and sent away without collecting. [12]A third man was sent and the same thing happened. He, too, was wounded and chased away.

[13]"'What shall I do?' the owner asked himself. 'I know! I'll send my cherished son. Surely they will show respect for him.'

[14]"But when the tenants saw his son, they said, 'This is our chance! This fellow will inherit all the land when his father dies. Come on. Let's kill him, and then it will be ours.' [15]So they dragged him out of the vineyard and killed him.

"What do you think the owner will do? [16]I'll tell you—he will come and kill them and rent the vineyard to others."

"But they would never do a thing like that," his listeners protested.

[17]Jesus looked at them and said, "Then what does the Scripture mean where it says, 'The Stone rejected by the builders was made the cornerstone'?" [18]And he added, "Whoever stumbles over that Stone shall be broken; and those on whom it falls will be crushed to dust."

[19]When the chief priests and religious leaders heard about this story he had told, they wanted him arrested immediately, for they realized that he was talking about them. They were the wicked tenants in his illustration. But they were afraid that if they themselves arrested him, there would be a riot. So they tried to get him to say something that could be reported to the Roman governor as reason for arrest by him.

A Question about Taxes

[20]Watching their opportunity, they sent secret agents pretending to be honest men. [21]They said to Jesus, "Sir, we know what an honest teacher you are. You always tell the truth and don't budge an inch in the face of what others think, but teach the ways of God. [22]Now tell us—is it right to pay taxes to the Roman government or not?"

[23]He saw through their trickery and said, [24]"Show me a coin. Whose portrait is this on it? And whose name?"

They replied, "Caesar's—the Roman emperor's."

[25]He said, "Then give the emperor all that is his—and give to God all that is his!"

[26]Thus their attempt to outwit him before the people failed; and marveling at his answer, they were silent.

Questions about the Resurrection

[27]Then some Sadducees—men who believed that death is the end of existence, that there is no resurrection—[28]came to Jesus with this:

"The laws of Moses state that if a man dies without children, the man's brother shall marry the widow, and their children will legally belong to the dead man, to carry on his name. [29]We know of a family of seven brothers. The oldest married and then died without any children. [30]His brother married the widow and he, too, died. Still no children. [31]And so it went, one after the other, until each of the seven had married her and died, leaving no children. [32]Finally the woman died also. [33]Now here is our question: Whose wife will she be in the resurrection? For all of them were married to her!"

[34,35]Jesus replied, "Marriage is for people here on earth, but when those who are counted worthy of being raised from the dead get to heaven, they do not marry. [36]And they never die again; in these respects they are like angels, and are sons of God, for they are raised up in new life from the dead.

[37,38]"But as to your real question—whether or not there is a resurrection—why, even the writings of Moses himself prove this. For when he describes how God appeared to him in the burning bush, he speaks of God as 'the God of Abraham, the God of Isaac, and the God of Jacob.' To say that the Lord *is* some person's God means that person is *alive,* not dead! So from God's point of view, all men are living."

[39]"Well said, sir!" remarked some of the

20:9-18 This story is unmistakably blunt. No one likes being confronted with their denial and blindness. The Pharisees were no exception. They didn't like the message, so they killed the messenger. That was true of the farmers in the story, the Pharisees in Jesus' day, and us while we remain in denial. When we choose to deny the truth, there is not much God or others can do. Sometimes the truth can penetrate our denial when someone speaks plainly but indirectly. Nathan did this effectively with David by telling him a story, which motivated David to repent of his sin (2 Samuel 12). Yet some people in denial, like these Pharisees, will resist to their dying day.

experts in the Jewish law who were standing
there. 40And that ended their questions, for
they dared ask no more!

A Question about the Messiah

41Then he presented *them* with a question.
"Why is it," he asked, "that Christ, the Messiah, is said to be a descendant of King David?
42,43For David himself wrote in the book of
Psalms: 'God said to my Lord, the Messiah,
"Sit at my right hand until I place your enemies beneath your feet."' 44How can the Messiah be both David's son and David's God at
the same time?"

Warnings about Religious Leaders

45Then, with the crowds listening, he turned
to his disciples and said, 46"Beware of these
experts in religion, for they love to parade in
dignified robes and to be bowed to by the
people as they walk along the street. And how
they love the seats of honor in the synagogues and at religious festivals! 47But even
while they are praying long prayers with great
outward piety, they are planning schemes to
cheat widows out of their property. Therefore
God's heaviest sentence awaits these men."

CHAPTER 21

A Poor Widow's Great Gift

As he stood in the Temple, he was watching
the rich tossing their gifts into the collection
box. 2Then a poor widow came by and
dropped in two small copper coins.

3"Really," he remarked, "this poor widow
has given more than all the rest of them
combined. 4For they have given a little of
what they didn't need, but she, poor as she is,
has given everything she has."

Jesus Tells about the Future

5Some of his disciples began talking about the
beautiful stonework of the Temple and the
memorial decorations on the walls.

6But Jesus said, "The time is coming when
all these things you are admiring will be
knocked down, and not one stone will be left
on top of another; all will become one vast
heap of rubble."

7"Master!" they exclaimed. "When? And
will there be any warning ahead of time?"

8He replied, "Don't let anyone mislead you.
For many will come announcing themselves
as the Messiah, and saying, 'The time has
come.' But don't believe them! 9And when
you hear of wars and insurrections beginning,
don't panic. True, wars must come, but the
end won't follow immediately—10for nation
shall rise against nation and kingdom against
kingdom, 11and there will be great earthquakes, and famines in many lands, and epidemics, and terrifying things happening in
the heavens.

12"But before all this occurs, there will be a
time of special persecution, and you will be
dragged into synagogues and prisons and before kings and governors for my name's sake.
13But as a result, the Messiah will be widely
known and honored. 14Therefore, don't be
concerned about how to answer the charges
against you, 15for I will give you the right
words and such logic that none of your opponents will be able to reply! 16Even those closest
to you—your parents, brothers, relatives, and
friends will betray you and have you arrested;
and some of you will be killed. 17And everyone
will hate you because you are mine and are
called by my name. 18But not a hair of your
head will perish! 19For if you stand firm, you
will win your souls.

20"But when you see Jerusalem surrounded
by armies, then you will know that the time
of its destruction has arrived. 21Then let the
people of Judea flee to the hills. Let those in
Jerusalem try to escape, and those outside the
city must not attempt to return. 22For those
will be days of God's judgment, and the words
of the ancient Scriptures written by the

21:1-4 God has an altogether different standard by which to measure giving and givers. With God, attitude counts more than amount, so this widow was praised by Jesus. A generous person is not one who gives conveniently and comfortably out of abundance. A generous person in God's eyes is one who risks all, sacrifices cheerfully, and gives without demanding attention or expecting a reward. Whether it's our time, talents, or money, God wants us to risk them all and turn our life over to his care. One small step in giving may become one giant leap toward recovery.

21:16-17 What happened to Jesus leading up to the cross, and what would happen to his disciples afterwards, illustrates an important principle in recovery. Family and friends are not always overjoyed at the prospect of our changed life. Our faith in Jesus, as well as our freedom from sin and addiction, often threatens the status quo. Often those closest to us become the greatest source of hurt and misunderstanding, as they resist what we know is best for us. As we become aware of this, we will not allow them to slow us down. In time they will discover that our recovery is not only good for us, but for them, too.

prophets will be abundantly fulfilled. [23]Woe to expectant mothers in those days, and those with tiny babies. For there will be great distress upon this nation and wrath upon this people. [24]They will be brutally killed by enemy weapons, or sent away as exiles and captives to all the nations of the world; and Jerusalem shall be conquered and trampled down by the Gentiles until the period of Gentile triumph ends in God's good time.

Jesus Tells about His Return

[25]"Then there will be strange events in the skies—warnings, evil omens and portents in the sun, moon and stars; and down here on earth the nations will be in turmoil, perplexed by the roaring seas and strange tides. [26]The courage of many people will falter because of the fearful fate they see coming upon the earth, for the stability of the very heavens will be broken up. [27]Then the peoples of the earth shall see me, the Messiah, coming in a cloud with power and great glory. [28]So when all these things begin to happen, stand straight and look up! For your salvation is near."

[29]Then he gave them this illustration: "Notice the fig tree, or any other tree. [30]When the leaves come out, you know without being told that summer is near. [31]In the same way, when you see the events taking place that I've described you can be just as sure that the Kingdom of God is near.

[32]"I solemnly declare to you that when these things happen, the end of this age has come. [33]And though all heaven and earth shall pass away, yet my words remain forever true.

A Call to Stay Alert

[34,35]"Watch out! Don't let my sudden coming catch you unawares; don't let me find you living in careless ease, carousing and drinking, and occupied with the problems of this life, like all the rest of the world. [36]Keep a constant watch. And pray that if possible you may arrive in my presence without having to experience these horrors."

[37,38]Every day Jesus went to the Temple to teach, and the crowds began gathering early in the morning to hear him. And each evening he returned to spend the night on the Mount of Olives.

CHAPTER 22

A Plot to Kill Jesus

And now the Passover celebration was drawing near—the Jewish festival when only bread made without yeast was used. [2]The chief priests and other religious leaders were actively plotting Jesus' murder, trying to find a way to kill him without starting a riot—a possibility they greatly feared.

Judas Agrees to Betray Jesus

[3]Then Satan entered into Judas Iscariot, who was one of the twelve disciples, [4]and he went over to the chief priests and captains of the Temple guards to discuss the best way to betray Jesus to them. [5]They were, of course, delighted to know that he was ready to help them and promised him a reward. [6]So he began to look for an opportunity for them to arrest Jesus quietly when the crowds weren't around.

Jesus Prepares for Passover

[7]Now the day of the Passover celebration arrived, when the Passover lamb was killed and eaten with the unleavened bread. [8]Jesus sent Peter and John ahead to find a place to prepare their Passover meal.

[9]"Where do you want us to go?" they asked.

21:34-36 This charge follows a lengthy prophecy about the coming days of destruction (21:5-31), and it illustrates the biblical purpose of prophecy. Prophecy is never given simply to satisfy the curiosity of those who wonder about God's plan for the future. Prophecy is primarily a call for believers to repent, stay alert, and prepare spiritually for the coming of God's Kingdom. As we await the triumphant return of Christ, or even the recovery of normal sanity, God warns about the danger of a life controlled by sin. We only fool ourself if we think we have all the time in the world to get ready. If we continue to put off recovery until tomorrow, one day tomorrow will not come!

22:3-6 At the deepest level, the brokenness, the bondage, and the out-of-control nature of our life is due to Satan's influence. Spiritual warfare (see Ephesians 6:10-17) plays itself out in personal relationships—in Judas' betrayal of Jesus, and in the breakup of our own relationships. Spiritual warfare undermines and destroys relational boundaries and renders our life unmanageable. (Judas would later commit suicide.) But Satan's involvement does not excuse human sin, addiction, and betrayal. Whatever role Satan may have in undoing our best-laid plans or human commitments, God is never thwarted. Jesus' death (at the hands of Satan) was part of God's plan all along. No matter what Satan does to harm us, God is able to use Satan's plans for evil to work his good plan of deliverance for us and his world. He does this when we trust and obey him.

10And he replied, "As soon as you enter Jerusalem, you will see a man walking along carrying a pitcher of water. Follow him into the house he enters, 11and say to the man who lives there, 'Our Teacher says for you to show us the guest room where he can eat the Passover meal with his disciples.' 12He will take you upstairs to a large room all ready for us. That is the place. Go ahead and prepare the meal there."

13They went off to the city and found everything just as Jesus had said, and prepared the Passover supper.

The Last Supper

14Then Jesus and the others arrived, and at the proper time all sat down together at the table; 15and he said, "I have looked forward to this hour with deep longing, anxious to eat this Passover meal with you before my suffering begins. 16For I tell you now that I won't eat it again until what it represents has occurred in the Kingdom of God."

17Then he took a glass of wine, and when he had given thanks for it, he said, "Take this and share it among yourselves. 18For I will not drink wine again until the Kingdom of God has come."

19Then he took a loaf of bread; and when he had thanked God for it, he broke it apart and gave it to them, saying, "This is my body, given for you. Eat it in remembrance of me."

20After supper he gave them another glass of wine, saying, "This wine is the token of God's new agreement to save you—an agreement sealed with the blood I shall pour out to purchase back your souls. 21But here at this table, sitting among us as a friend, is the man who will betray me. 22I must die. It is part of God's plan. But, oh, the horror awaiting that man who betrays me."

23Then the disciples wondered among themselves which of them would ever do such a thing.

24And they began to argue among themselves as to who would have the highest rank [in the coming Kingdom].

25Jesus told them, "In this world the kings and great men order their slaves around, and the slaves have no choice but to like it! 26But among you, the one who serves you best will be your leader. 27Out in the world the master sits at the table and is served by his servants. But not here! For I am your servant. 28Nevertheless, because you have stood true to me in these terrible days, 29and because my Father has granted me a Kingdom, I, here and now, grant you the right 30to eat and drink at my table in that Kingdom; and you will sit on thrones judging the twelve tribes of Israel.

Jesus Predicts Peter's Denial

31"Simon, Simon, Satan has asked to have you, to sift you like wheat, 32but I have pleaded in prayer for you that your faith should not completely fail. So when you have repented and turned to me again, strengthen and build up the faith of your brothers."

33Simon said, "Lord, I am ready to go to jail with you, and even to die with you."

34But Jesus said, "Peter, let me tell you something. Between now and tomorrow morning when the rooster crows, you will deny me three times, declaring that you don't even know me."

35Then Jesus asked them, "When I sent you out to preach the Good News and you were without money, duffle bag, or extra clothing, how did you get along?"

"Fine," they replied.

36"But now," he said, "take a duffle bag if you have one and your money. And if you don't have a sword, better sell your clothes and buy one! 37For the time has come for this prophecy about me to come true: 'He will be condemned as a criminal!' Yes, everything written about me by the prophets will come true."

22:24-30 This upper room discourse contrasts Jesus' humility and servant's heart with the selfish intentions of his twelve closest followers. In going to the cross, Jesus showed his disciples what it meant to be a servant-leader. The disciples' desire for a special place at God's table was not what Jesus had intended to teach them. Jesus calls us to put the needs of others before our own and asks that we serve others rather than expecting to be served. We can never go wrong when our life is defined and motivated by humility.

22:39-46 Jesus' prayer in the Garden of Gethsemane reflected the awesome task before him: he was about to shoulder the sins of the world. He persevered through fear and faith to submit to God's sovereign will. His absolute commitment to God is an example for us of prayer and perseverance. Jesus could have selfishly seized the privileges of deity and avoided the cross (see Philippians 2:6-8). Instead, he was willing to delay the gratification of heaven's glory and accomplish the task set before him. Although our challenges in life are not of this magnitude, God enables us to persevere through the tough stages of recovery to reap the rewards that follow.

[38]"Master," they replied, "we have two swords among us."
"Enough!" he said.

Jesus Agonizes in the Garden
[39]Then, accompanied by the disciples, he left
the upstairs room and went as usual to the
Mount of Olives. [40]There he told them, "Pray
God that you will not be overcome by temptation."
[41,42]He walked away, perhaps a stone's
throw, and knelt down and prayed this
prayer: "Father, if you are willing, please take
away this cup of horror from me. But I want
your will, not mine." [43]Then an angel from
heaven appeared and strengthened him, [44]for
he was in such agony of spirit that he broke
into a sweat of blood, with great drops falling
to the ground as he prayed more and more
earnestly. [45]At last he stood up again and returned to the disciples—only to find them
asleep, exhausted from grief.
[46]"Asleep!" he said. "Get up! Pray God that
you will not fall when you are tempted."

Jesus Is Betrayed
[47]But even as he said this, a mob approached,
led by Judas, one of his twelve disciples. Judas
walked over to Jesus and kissed him on the
cheek in friendly greeting.
[48]But Jesus said, "Judas, how can you do
this—betray the Messiah with a kiss?"
[49]When the other disciples saw what was
about to happen, they exclaimed, "Master,
shall we fight? We brought along the swords!"
[50]And one of them slashed at the High Priest's
servant and cut off his right ear.
[51]But Jesus said, "Don't resist any more."
And he touched the place where the man's ear
had been and restored it. [52]Then Jesus addressed the chief priests and captains of the
Temple guards and the religious leaders who
headed the mob. "Am I a robber," he asked,
"that you have come armed with swords and
clubs to get me? [53]Why didn't you arrest me
in the Temple? I was there every day. But this
is your moment—the time when Satan's
power reigns supreme."

Peter Denies Knowing Jesus
[54]So they seized him and led him to the High
Priest's residence, and Peter followed at a distance. [55]The soldiers lit a fire in the courtyard
and sat around it for warmth, and Peter
joined them there.
[56]A servant girl noticed him in the firelight

Faith

READ LUKE 22:31-34

It is easy to lose faith when we are troubled. As we are buffeted about by life, we may feel like the faith we once had has slipped away. We may begin to feel anger toward God.

Simon Peter had his ups and downs with God. On the night Simon Peter would deny him, Jesus said to him, "Simon, Simon, Satan has asked to have you, to sift you like wheat, but I have pleaded in prayer for you that your faith should not completely fail. So when you have repented and turned to me again, strengthen and build up the faith of your brothers" (Luke 22:31-32).

Jesus pointed out that Simon had an assailant in the spiritual realm. Jesus knew Peter would be attacked and "sifted," but he also was confident that afterwards Peter would return to God. Wheat is sifted by throwing it repeatedly into the air and catching it. The kernels are separated from the chaff as the lighter chaff is carried away by the wind. All that remain are the solid wheat kernels, which are good.

We should not be surprised that we face times when our faith seems to disappear. We may feel like we are being ripped open and our faith is being blown away. But we needn't worry. We will find the core of our faith again. And when we do, we will be all the better for it—and better able to encourage others, too. ***Turn to page 1155, John 8.***

and began staring at him. Finally she spoke:
"This man was with Jesus!"
57Peter denied it. "Woman," he said, "I
don't even know the man!"
58After a while someone else looked at him
and said, "You must be one of them!"
"No sir, I am not!" Peter replied.
59About an hour later someone else flatly
stated, "I know this fellow is one of Jesus'
disciples, for both are from Galilee."
60But Peter said, "Man, I don't know what
you are talking about." And as he said the
words, a rooster crowed.
61At that moment Jesus turned and looked
at Peter. Then Peter remembered what he had
said—"Before the rooster crows tomorrow
morning, you will deny me three times."
62And Peter walked out of the courtyard, crying bitterly.
63,64Now the guards in charge of Jesus began
mocking him. They blindfolded him and hit
him with their fists and asked, "Who hit you
that time, prophet?" 65And they threw all
sorts of other insults at him.

The Council Condemns Jesus

66Early the next morning at daybreak the Jewish Supreme Court assembled, including the
chief priests and all the top religious authorities of the nation. Jesus was led before this
Council 67,68and instructed to state whether or
not he claimed to be the Messiah.
But he replied, "If I tell you, you won't
believe me or let me present my case. 69But the
time is soon coming when I, the Messiah,
shall be enthroned beside Almighty God."
70They all shouted, "Then you claim you
are the Son of God?"
And he replied, "Yes, I am."
71"What need do we have for other
witnesses?" they shouted. "For we ourselves
have heard him say it."

CHAPTER 23

Jesus Is Tried by Pilate

Then the entire Council took Jesus over to
Pilate, the governor. 2They began at once accusing him: "This fellow has been leading our
people to ruin by telling them not to pay their
taxes to the Roman government and by
claiming he is our Messiah—a King."
3So Pilate asked him, "Are you their Messiah—their King?"
"Yes," Jesus replied, "it is as you say."
4Then Pilate turned to the chief priests and
to the mob and said, "So? That isn't a crime!"
5Then they became desperate. "But he is
causing riots against the government everywhere he goes, all over Judea, from Galilee to
Jerusalem!"

Jesus Is Tried by Herod

6"Is he then a Galilean?" Pilate asked.
7When they told him yes, Pilate said to take
him to King Herod, for Galilee was under
Herod's jurisdiction; and Herod happened to
be in Jerusalem at the time. 8Herod was delighted at the opportunity to see Jesus, for he
had heard a lot about him and had been
hoping to see him perform a miracle.
9He asked Jesus question after question, but
there was no reply. 10Meanwhile, the chief
priests and the other religious leaders stood
there shouting their accusations.
11Now Herod and his soldiers began mocking and ridiculing Jesus; and putting a kingly
robe on him, they sent him back to Pilate.

22:54-62 Peter's denial of Jesus is a classic story of recovery. Though Peter believed he could never stoop so low (22:31-34), he denied Jesus completely when the heat was on. Peter not only disappointed Jesus, he disappointed himself, but even then, all was not lost. His experience led to genuine sorrow and healthy repentance. Peter's threefold denial was followed by a threefold affirmation and his restoration to full-fledged service (John 21:15-19). Later, Peter became the leading spokesman of the early church, powerfully proclaiming the message of the risen Christ. Only through complete forgiveness by God could Peter have so effectively recovered from the depths of despair.

23:1-5 The Sanhedrin attempted to manipulate Pontius Pilate's verdict about Jesus by telling multiple half-truths, even outright lies. In denial, the subtle (and not-so-subtle) lies we tell ourself and others keep us from making progress in recovery. Lying is often used by others to knock us off track and to maintain the status quo. Often others are not even aware of their need to keep everything, including us, in place. Recovery is based on the principle of truth and honesty.

23:13-25 Pilate initially saw through all the lies of the Sanhedrin. That is an indictment of his accusers, not Jesus. Yet Pilate could not follow through on these convictions. He acquiesced to political expediency and moral compromise to save his job. In seeing Jesus as a political threat, Pilate denied him his human dignity and rights. Often the truth does come out, vindicating the innocent person, but not before a price has been paid. In the recovery process, telling the truth and doing the right thing are always crucial.

12That day Herod and Pilate—enemies before—became fast friends.

Jesus Is to Be Crucified

13Then Pilate called together the chief priests
and other Jewish leaders, along with the
people, 14and announced his verdict:

"You brought this man to me, accusing
him of leading a revolt against the Roman
government. I have examined him thoroughly on this point and find him innocent.
15Herod came to the same conclusion and sent
him back to us—nothing this man has done
calls for the death penalty. 16I will therefore
have him scourged with leaded thongs and
release him."

17,18 But now a mighty roar rose from the
crowd as with one voice they shouted. "Kill
him, and release Barabbas to us!" 19(Barabbas
was in prison for starting an insurrection in
Jerusalem against the government, and for
murder.) 20Pilate argued with them, for he
wanted to release Jesus. 21But they shouted,
"Crucify him! Crucify him!"

22Once more, for the third time, he demanded, "Why? What crime has he committed? I have found no reason to sentence him
to death. I will therefore scourge him and let
him go." 23But they shouted louder and
louder for Jesus' death, and their voices prevailed.

24So Pilate sentenced Jesus to die as they
demanded. 25And he released Barabbas, the
man in prison for insurrection and murder, at
their request. But he delivered Jesus over to
them to do with as they would.

Jesus Is Led Away

26As the crowd led Jesus away to his death,
Simon of Cyrene, who was just coming into
Jerusalem from the country, was forced to
follow, carrying Jesus' cross. 27Great crowds
trailed along behind, and many grief-stricken
women.

28But Jesus turned and said to them,
"Daughters of Jerusalem, don't weep for me,
but for yourselves and for your children. 29For
the days are coming when the women who
have no children will be counted fortunate
indeed. 30Mankind will beg the mountains to
fall on them and crush them, and the hills to
bury them. 31For if such things as this are done
to me, the Living Tree, what will they do to
you?"

Jesus Is Hung on the Cross

32,33Two others, criminals, were led out to be
executed with him at a place called "The
Skull." There all three were crucified—Jesus
on the center cross, and the two criminals on
either side.

34"Father, forgive these people," Jesus said,
"for they don't know what they are doing."

And the soldiers gambled for his clothing,
throwing dice for each piece. 35The crowd
watched. And the Jewish leaders laughed and
scoffed. "He was so good at helping others,"
they said, "let's see him save himself if he is
really God's Chosen One, the Messiah."

36The soldiers mocked him, too, by offering
him a drink—of sour wine. 37And they called
to him, "If you are the King of the Jews, save
yourself!"

38A signboard was nailed to the cross above
him with these words: "This is the King of the
Jews."

39One of the criminals hanging beside him
scoffed, "So you're the Messiah, are you?
Prove it by saving yourself—and us, too, while
you're at it!"

40,41But the other criminal protested. "Don't
you even fear God when you are dying? We
deserve to die for our evil deeds, but this man
hasn't done one thing wrong." 42Then he said,
"Jesus, remember me when you come into
your Kingdom."

43And Jesus replied, "Today you will be with
me in Paradise. This is a solemn promise."

Jesus Dies on the Cross

44By now it was noon, and darkness fell across
the whole land for three hours, until three

23:32-34 Jesus forgave those who nailed him to the cross. Here in the most unjust situation in history, forgiveness was extended without limit. If Christ forgave in this way from the cross, no sin we've committed is too great for his forgiveness. As we experience his forgiveness, we are freed to forgive those who have sinned against us. Christ helps us to release our bitterness and resentment, which only imprison us. His forgiveness empowers us to be forgiving people—forgiving ourself as well as those who have hurt us.

23:40-43 The piercing self-examination of the criminal crucified next to Jesus was the prelude to his salvation. His attitude stands in stark contrast to the self-sufficient bitterness and cynicism of the other criminal, who died in bondage to sin and despair. God always preserves the element of choice in our recovery, right up to the end of life. It is never too late to begin the process!

o'clock. [45]The light from the sun was gone—and suddenly the thick veil hanging in the Temple split apart.

[46]Then Jesus shouted, "Father, I commit my spirit to you," and with those words he died.

[47]When the captain of the Roman military unit handling the executions saw what had happened, he was stricken with awe before God and said, "Surely this man was innocent."

[48]And when the crowd that came to see the crucifixion saw that Jesus was dead they went home in deep sorrow. [49]Meanwhile, Jesus' friends, including the women who had followed him down from Galilee, stood in the distance watching.

Jesus Is Placed in a Tomb

[50-52]Then a man named Joseph, a member of the Jewish Supreme Court, from the city of Arimathea in Judea, went to Pilate and asked for the body of Jesus. He was a godly man who had been expecting the Messiah's coming and had not agreed with the decision and actions of the other Jewish leaders. [53]So he took down Jesus' body and wrapped it in a long linen cloth and laid it in a new, unused tomb hewn into the rock [at the side of a hill]. [54]This was done late on Friday afternoon, the day of preparation for the Sabbath.

[55]As the body was taken away, the women from Galilee followed and saw it carried into the tomb. [56]Then they went home and prepared spices and ointments to embalm him; but by the time they were finished it was the Sabbath, so they rested all that day as required by the Jewish law.

CHAPTER 24

Jesus Rises from the Dead

But very early on Sunday morning they took the ointments to the tomb—[2]and found that the huge stone covering the entrance had been rolled aside. [3]So they went in—but the Lord Jesus' body was gone.

[4]They stood there puzzled, trying to think what could have happened to it. Suddenly two men appeared before them, clothed in shining robes so bright their eyes were dazzled. [5]The women were terrified and bowed low before them.

Then the men asked, "Why are you looking in a tomb for someone who is alive? [6,7]He isn't here! He has come back to life again! Don't you remember what he told you back in Galilee—that the Messiah must be betrayed into the power of evil men and be crucified and that he would rise again the third day?"

[8]Then they remembered [9]and rushed back to Jerusalem to tell his eleven disciples—and everyone else—what had happened. [10](The women who went to the tomb were Mary Magdalene and Joanna and Mary the mother of James, and several others.) [11]But the story sounded like a fairy tale to the men—they didn't believe it.

[12]However, Peter ran to the tomb to look. Stooping, he peered in and saw the empty linen wrappings; and then he went back home again, wondering what had happened.

Jesus on the Road to Emmaus

[13]That same day, Sunday, two of Jesus' followers were walking to the village of Emmaus, seven miles out of Jerusalem. [14]As they walked along they were talking of Jesus' death, [15]when suddenly Jesus himself came along and joined them and began walking beside them. [16]But they didn't recognize him, for God kept them from it.

[17]"You seem to be in a deep discussion about something," he said. "What are you so concerned about?" They stopped short, sadness written across their faces. [18]And one of them, Cleopas, replied, "You must be the only person in Jerusalem who hasn't heard about

---

24:1-12 During the arrest and trial of Jesus, the disciples showed complete helplessness in dealing with the circumstances at hand. But after the Resurrection, in the book of Acts, a new Power enabled them to recover their courage and go into the world with the message of God's Good News. The Resurrection is both a historical fact and an experiential power. This Power is greater than death itself and is more than able to help us overcome our dependencies and compulsions. The Resurrection is the very source of our recovery. As we experience Christ's resurrection in our life, we will enjoy victory over temptation and power to live free of bondage and addiction.

24:13-24 The two disciples on the road to Emmaus were obviously deeply discouraged and grieved by the events of the past few days. They did not fully comprehend who Jesus was, nor the kind of faith needed to recover from their pain. By a short step of faith, however, they were lifted from their grief to become people who would help change the world. By meeting and speaking with their higher Power, the road from the cross to Emmaus became their path of recovery and wholeness.

the terrible things that happened there last week."

19"What things?" Jesus asked.

"The things that happened to Jesus, the Man from Nazareth," they said. "He was a Prophet who did incredible miracles and was a mighty Teacher, highly regarded by both God and man. 20But the chief priests and our religious leaders arrested him and handed him over to the Roman government to be condemned to death, and they crucified him. 21We had thought he was the glorious Messiah and that he had come to rescue Israel.

"And now, besides all this—which happened three days ago— 22,23some women from our group of his followers were at his tomb early this morning and came back with an amazing report that his body was missing, and that they had seen some angels there who told them Jesus is alive! 24Some of our men ran out to see, and sure enough, Jesus' body was gone, just as the women had said."

25Then Jesus said to them, "You are such foolish, foolish people! You find it so hard to believe all that the prophets wrote in the Scriptures! 26Wasn't it clearly predicted by the prophets that the Messiah would have to suffer all these things before entering his time of glory?"

27Then Jesus quoted them passage after passage from the writings of the prophets, beginning with the book of Genesis and going right on through the Scriptures, explaining what the passages meant and what they said about himself.

28By this time they were nearing Emmaus and the end of their journey. Jesus would have gone on, 29but they begged him to stay the night with them, as it was getting late. So he went home with them. 30As they sat down to eat, he asked God's blessing on the food and then took a small loaf of bread and broke it and was passing it over to them, 31when suddenly—it was as though their eyes were opened—they recognized him! And at that moment he disappeared!

32They began telling each other how their hearts had felt strangely warm as he talked with them and explained the Scriptures during the walk down the road. 33,34Within the hour they were on their way back to Jerusalem, where the eleven disciples and the other followers of Jesus greeted them with these words, "The Lord has really risen! He appeared to Peter!"

35Then the two from Emmaus told their story of how Jesus had appeared to them as they were walking along the road and how they had recognized him as he was breaking the bread.

Jesus Appears to His Disciples

36And just as they were telling about it, Jesus himself was suddenly standing there among them, and greeted them. 37But the whole group was terribly frightened, thinking they were seeing a ghost!

38"Why are you frightened?" he asked. "Why do you doubt that it is really I? 39Look at my hands! Look at my feet! You can see that it is I, myself ! Touch me and make sure that I am not a ghost! For ghosts don't have bodies, as you see that I do!" 40As he spoke, he held out his hands for them to see [the marks of the nails], and showed them [the wounds in] his feet.

41Still they stood there undecided, filled with joy and doubt.

Then he asked them, "Do you have anything here to eat?"

42They gave him a piece of broiled fish, 43and he ate it as they watched!

44Then he said, "When I was with you before, don't you remember my telling you that everything written about me by Moses and the prophets and in the Psalms must all come true?" 45Then he opened their minds to understand at last these many Scriptures! 46And he said, "Yes, it was written long ago that the Messiah must suffer and die and rise again from the dead on the third day; 47and that this message of salvation should be taken from Jerusalem to all the nations: *There is forgiveness of sins for all who turn to me.* 48You have seen these prophecies come true.

49"And now I will send the Holy Spirit upon you, just as my Father promised. Don't begin

---

24:36-49 Jesus is alive and well, yet this was not immediately evident to his first followers in the upper room. They were banded together as fellow strugglers in their grief and pain. That's when the living Christ appeared. So also the living Christ is present in our support groups when we realize that only he can calm our fears and doubts. The task of spreading the good news of resurrection and recovery was an overwhelming job. Through the promised Holy Spirit (see Acts 2), Jesus gave them the peace and power to do all things through Christ. He can do the same for anyone in recovery who trusts in him.

telling others yet—stay here in the city until the Holy Spirit comes and fills you with power from heaven."

Jesus Ascends into Heaven

50Then Jesus led them out along the road to
Bethany, and lifting his hands to heaven, he
blessed them, 51and then began rising into the
sky, and went on to heaven. 52And they worshiped him, and returned to Jerusalem filled
with mighty joy, 53and were continually in the
Temple, praising God.

REFLECTIONS ON LUKE

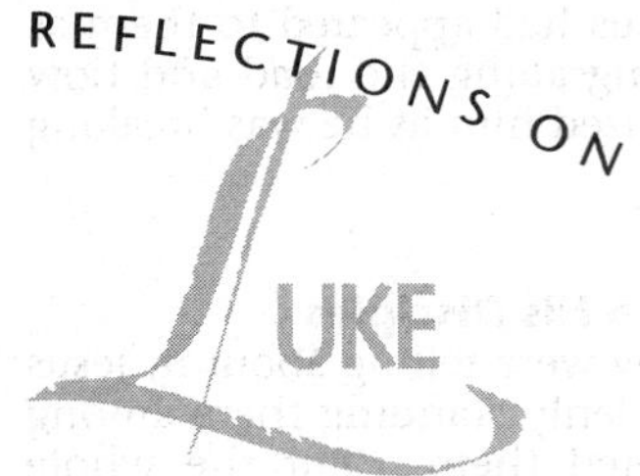

insights ABOUT THE PERSON OF JESUS

Jesus Christ is portrayed in **Luke 1:76-79** as light shining on those living in darkness. Hearing this metaphor, the original readers would probably have thought of a group of travelers overtaken by darkness, who were left in danger by the roadside all night. Such people, helpless to defend themselves against the attacks of robbers, would have welcomed the light of the rising sun. This is a picture of what Jesus can do for any of us who are in "in darkness," helpless to defend ourself against the draw of our powerful dependencies. We move from darkness into light as we receive God's gift of forgiveness and make a personal commitment to him. As we experience new hope in Jesus, we can tell fellow strugglers about the sunrise that is just around the corner.

Jesus, of course, did not need recovery because he was the sinless God-man. Yet from **Luke 2:52** it is clear that he lived out the perfect model of balanced growth from childhood to adulthood. He developed physically, intellectually, spiritually, and socially. He displayed both personal and interpersonal growth. No dimension was overemphasized, underdeveloped, or rejected. Our own recovery needs to be balanced in a similar way.

Jesus did not succumb to temptation, yet he fully experienced, in one form or another, every temptation known to humanity. The Bible clearly affirms that Jesus was vulnerable to sin. Jesus did not sin, true enough, but in his humanity he was certainly able to do so. If Jesus would have been unable to sin because of his deity, then the temptations given by Satan in **Luke 4:3-13** would not have been in any way tempting. And, if Jesus was beyond temptation, he would be unable to sympathize with our weaknesses (see Hebrews 4:15). When we experience temptation, especially from the injuries or addictions of our past, we can remember that Jesus understands.

insights ABOUT GOD'S POWER TO SAVE

In **Luke 4:33-37** Jesus displayed his ability to deliver people from demon possession. Luke and the other Gospel writers repeatedly affirmed Jesus' power in this arena. In that day, being possessed by a demon was believed to be the greatest infirmity one could suffer. By his absolute control over demons, Jesus was overruling all the adversity that this world and the world below could heap against humanity. To this day, no evil or adversity in life is too great for God's power to overcome.

The story of Zacchaeus in **Luke 19:1-10** beautifully illustrates God's acceptance and restoration of a repentant sinner. After admitting his failures to God, to himself, and to others, Zacchaeus was willing to repay the people he had wronged. Making restitution to those we have harmed or cheated is crucial to repentance and recovery, unless the process of making amends will only cause further injury to people we have wronged. In such a case, it is enough to admit our wrongdoing to God, to ourself, and to another person.

Luke 19:9-10 captures the central theme of Luke's Gospel: Jesus' passion to find and restore those who are lost and alienated from God. This priority has been on the heart of God since the first sin in the Garden of Eden. Immediately after Adam and Eve sinned, it was God who sought them out as they hid in fear. He restored fellowship with them and offered them a way of recovery from their sin (Genesis 3). The work of Jesus on the cross represents the culmination of God's plan for forgiveness, hope, and restored fellowship with God.

The glass of wine shared by Jesus and his disciples in **Luke 22:20** symbolized the blood of Jesus, which would institute the New Covenant (see Jeremiah 31:31-34). Jesus Christ was the ultimate sacrificial Lamb of God, who has taken away the sins of the world (see John 1:29). Without this provision for sin once and for all, we have no peace or serenity. Without taking the cup of the Lord's Supper, we are still in our sins and insecurity. Without the cup of God's salvation, many will keep looking for salvation in a bottle. We have an open invitation to receive God's gracious forgiveness. We can now rest secure in God's grace, which allows us to escape the guilt of our past.

insights ABOUT PRAYER

In **Luke 6:12-16** we find that Jesus spent an entire night in prayer before choosing his twelve disciples. Despite the care he took, however, among them was Judas Iscariot, who would betray him. Jesus did not make a mistake; Judas was chosen purposely and prayerfully. Unlike Jesus, we make foolish choices no matter how careful we are. Yet, we are like Jesus in that the prayerful choices we make in our recovery may still result in our betrayal. Even though, through no fault of our own, we may still be betrayed, we can take comfort from the fact that God can and will use this for good in our life.

The story in **Luke 11:8-13** emphasizes that God wants us to approach him with shameless persistence. The commands to ask, seek, and knock are all given in the present tense, emphasizing continuous, persistent action on our part. That which produces the greatest results is the persistence of the seeker, not necessarily the kindness of the giver. To practice this quality in our prayer life and recovery program, we must first have a personal relationship with the Giver of all good gifts. Through faith, we can have great expectations from our relationship with God. He is good—gentler and kinder than any human father—and he wants our recovery more than anyone else.

insights CONCERNING TRUE FAITH

Luke 10:21 tells us where to look for true wisdom. Many of us have spent years looking for wisdom that will help us in our recovery. We may have begun to think it is hard, if not impossible, to come by. Often the reason we find true wisdom so elusive is that it is divinely and simply revealed to "those who are as trusting as little children." The greatest of wisdom does not come from the worldly wise or from ivory-tower intellectuals. God's wisdom for recovery can be gleaned by simply trusting him, one day at a time, as children are prone to do. People in recovery can gain a great deal by following God's leading in childlike simplicity and humility.

In **Luke 15:1-2** we see that Jesus attracted many of the outcasts of Jewish religious and social life. Perhaps this was because he was the only one who did not despise and reject them. Jesus preferred these downcast people because they were aware of their sinfulness and because they approached God with a humble attitude. In contrast, the religious leaders, who were outwardly moral but inwardly proud, were not at all attracted to Jesus. To this day, religion can still hinder recovery. But an admission of powerlessness and a relationship with Jesus will help the recovery process.

The story of the lost son in **Luke 15:11-32** wonderfully illustrates the theme of Luke's Gospel (Luke 19:9-10) and the steps of recovery. Like the younger son, we have been guilty of choosing a life of pleasure. With time, however, we discovered that we became a slave to our selfish life-style. Some of us never even saw how lost we were until we hit bottom. The bottom for the younger son in this story was his realization that the pigs were eating better than he was. When we realize that our life is hopelessly out of control, we have made the first step toward recovery. When we are humbled by our helplessness, we are in the best situation to establish a healthy relationship with our gracious God.

In **Luke 18:40-43** Jesus miraculously healed a blind man. Jesus would not have healed this man, however, had he not trusted in his power to do so. On the other hand, it was not simply the blind man's faith that healed him. Faith heals to the extent that it is clearly focused on the proper and powerful object of faith—God in Jesus Christ. Our recovery is based not on our own power or our faith, but on our loving God, who has the power and desire to heal us. Our part is to look to him for help.

insights CONCERNING OBSTACLES TO RECOVERY

In **Luke 11:14-23** Jesus was accused of being an ally of Satan. Through Jesus' words and actions, however, it became clear that these accusations were false. Unseen powers of darkness are agents of Satan's kingdom and are behind a great deal of human bondage. When we understand this, then "riding the fence" between living for God and living for ourself is no longer an option. Our success in recovery leaves no room for neutrality or living a life of moral compromise. Not to decide for God in Jesus Christ is to decide for Satan and his world of bondage. Only through uncompromising faith in Jesus Christ can we achieve victory and lifelong recovery.

We see in **Luke 22:31-34** that Simon Peter, along with Judas (see 22:3-6), was influenced by Satan to break his commitment to Jesus and found his life careening out of control. While it must have pained Peter to hear that he would betray Jesus, Jesus held out to him the hope of repentance and restoration. Jesus knows when we will betray or deny him, and he makes gracious provision for that. Though we may have been "sifted by Satan," it is never too late to turn back to Jesus. By continuing to take a personal moral inventory, our relapses from recovery will become shorter in duration and fewer in number.

insights ABOUT HONESTY AND DENIAL

The Pharisee in **Luke 18:10-14** did not have an accurate self-perception. He looked upon himself as better than others; his pride hindered his ability to see himself or others as God did. He is a good example of what we are like when we are in denial. Most of us are guilty of ignoring our own dependencies by pointing a hypocritical finger at someone worse off than ourself. Some of us have hidden behind the respect we command in our community. God sees the heart and will reward us (forgive us, heal us, aid us in recovery) according to our humble faith. The tax collector in this story, with humble and honest self-awareness, was well on his way to recovery. The Pharisee was headed for spiritual disaster.

Our true spiritual condition is not so much evidenced by our religious activities as it is by what we depend on for security. In **Luke 18:18-23** Jesus exposed a wealthy young man's dependence on his possessions. In doing this, Jesus was bringing him face to face with a common human problem—denial. We don't know whether or not this young man ever repented of his attachment to his belongings, but each of us is faced with the same choice. Only by renouncing our unhealthy dependencies will we be able to receive lasting spiritual treasure—a healthy, fulfilling relationship with ourself, God, and others.

JOHN

THE BIG PICTURE

A. THE GLORIOUS SOURCE OF RECOVERY IS REVEALED (1:1-18)
B. JESUS GIVES NEW LIFE (1:19–3:36)
C. SATISFYING THE LONGINGS OF YOUR SOUL (4:1–7:53)
D. COMING INTO THE LIGHT TO BE FREED FROM A PAINFUL PAST (8:1–9:41)
E. EMBRACING AND CELEBRATING AN ABUNDANT LIFE (10:1–12:50)
F. LOVING OTHERS AS JESUS HAS LOVED US (13:1–17:26)
G. THE CRUCIFIXION: EVERYTHING SEEMS TO FALL APART (18:1–19:42)
H. THE RESURRECTION: MIRACULOUS RECOVERY (20:1–21:25)

From the vast stretches of eternity to the confines of time—so the Son of God entered into this world. Jesus was the Creator of this world, but then he immersed himself in his creation. God became a man and willingly sacrificed himself so that all who would receive him could have forgiveness and redemption.

John used a number of images to illustrate who Jesus is and how he gives us eternal life: Jesus is the unblemished Lamb who is sacrificed for us; the Bread who satisfies our spiritual hunger; the Living Water who satisfies our spiritual thirst; the Light who guides us; the Shepherd who leads us; the Vine who gives us life; and the Counselor who comforts and teaches us. Through these images, John demonstrated that Jesus can give us all we need for a new, abundant life.

John also used the miracles Jesus performed to show us Jesus' power to transform lives. This Gospel is filled with examples of the power of God in lives needing recovery. With God's help, we can drink the new wine of a changed life; take responsibility to walk away from the sin that paralyzes us; recover from our sicknesses; be healed of our blindness to the truth; escape from our sinful addictions and the people who condemn us; and be raised to new life from a dead and empty existence.

John collected this series of images and miracles to help us recognize Jesus for who he is—the Son of God. When we recognize Jesus for who he is, we can begin to experience the new life that he offers to all who believe.

THE BOTTOM LINE

PURPOSE: To reveal Jesus as the Son of God and show that by faith in him we can experience true love, forgiveness, and recovery. AUTHOR: John the apostle, brother of James, called a "Son of Thunder." AUDIENCE: All people everywhere. DATE WRITTEN: Probably between A.D. 80 and 90. SETTING: After many years of reflecting on his experience as a disciple of Jesus, the apostle John recorded his unique perspective on the gospel. KEY VERSES: "These [things] are recorded so that you will believe that [Jesus] is the Messiah, the Son of God, and that believing in him you will have life" (20:30-31). KEY PEOPLE AND RELATIONSHIPS: Jesus with John the Baptist, the disciples, Mary, Martha, Lazarus, the religious leaders, Pilate, and Mary Magdalene.

RECOVERY THEMES

The Power of God: Each of the miracles recorded by John, six of which are not recorded in the other Gospels, clearly demonstrates God's power. Jesus healed a man born blind; he walked on water and then calmed a storm; he healed the nobleman's son without even being there; and he raised Lazarus from the dead after the man had been dead for more than three days. John did not simply tell us about the life of Christ—he made the important point that Jesus is the embodiment of all of God's power. That power is promised to us when we come to him in our powerlessness and turn our life over to him.

God's Power Can Be within Us: Our recovery is based on God's power at work within us. Jesus gave us several pictures of how we can have God's power. He described how the branch abides in the trunk of the vine and draws life and power from the vine. He told us that he is the Bread of Life, and that we are to eat that bread. He said that he has water for us to drink that will quench our thirst forever. Each of these images illustrated the promise he made in the upper room that the Holy Spirit would be available to teach us, comfort us, and empower us daily. When we turn our life over to God, the Holy Spirit comes to live within us and take us step-by-step to wholeness and healing.

The Dangers of Denial: In Jesus' early ministry, large crowds followed him. But as Jesus confronted the people with the truth of their sin, the crowds gradually grew smaller and smaller. Eventually, as people were unwilling to face the realities he exposed in their lives, they rejected the only one who could help them. Times have changed, but the pattern of denial remains the same: We begin with some question about the truth and over time develop rigid resistance to it. Gradually our heart becomes hardened, and we no longer see the obvious truth. As he confronted the crowds, Jesus also confronts us with the changes we need to make. It takes courage to be open and willing to face the truth, but admitting the truth is the first step in recovery.

The Invitation to Relationship: Although each of the Gospels shows us the love of Jesus, John presented it as a central theme. In the upper room, Jesus said that the mark of following him is having love for others. He prayed that we would be united in love as he and the Father are. John referred to himself in this Gospel as "the disciple Jesus loved" (21:20). In one of his later letters, he wrote that the greatest evidence of God's presence in our life is our love for others (see 1 John 4:11-12, 20-21). Central to our recovery and to our walk with God is our recognition of God's love for us and our willingness to value and respect others.

CHAPTER 1

God Becomes a Human Being

Before anything else existed, there was Christ,
with God. He has always been alive and is
himself God. [3]He created everything there
is—nothing exists that he didn't make. [4]Eter-
nal life is in him, and this life gives light to all
mankind. [5]His life is the light that shines
through the darkness—and the darkness can
never extinguish it.

[6,7]God sent John the Baptist as a witness to
the fact that Jesus Christ is the true Light.
[8]John himself was not the Light; he was only
a witness to identify it.

[9]Later on, the one who is the true Light
arrived to shine on everyone coming into the
world.

[10]But although he made the world, the
world didn't recognize him when he came.
[11,12]Even in his own land and among his own
people, the Jews, he was not accepted. Only a
few would welcome and receive him. But to
all who received him, he gave the right to
become children of God. All they needed to
do was to trust him to save them. [13]All those
who believe this are reborn!—not a physical
rebirth resulting from human passion or
plan—but from the will of God.

1:1-13 The same Power that created the universe (1:3) is available to create a new life from our shattered hopes. The Light of life that exposes and drives away the darkness of the human race (1:4-5) is the same Light that brightens the dark corners of our world. This source of all life and true Light of the world is the source of our recovery. Eternal life and true recovery are ours when we believe what God says, renounce our tendency to do things our way, and receive the one whom God sent to help us (1:11-13).

1:14-18 The true Light of the world (1:1-9) became a human being, known to us as Jesus Christ. Through Jesus, who was both fully God and fully human, we can know what God is like and enjoy a relationship with him. Jesus Christ came to bring us God's forgiveness from sin and to reveal God's truth to us. God's forgiving grace says, "I forgive you for your wrongs; I love and accept you freely for the person you are." His truth says, "I will show you what is true about me, about life, about yourself and others."

JOHN THE BAPTIST

A thunderstorm swept in from the wilderness of Judea, stirring many from their slumber, demolishing old structures, and soaking the moisture-starved fields. Many were afraid of the fierce deluge, but others were thankful for the future bounty its rain would provide. In the same way, John the Baptist broke onto the scene in Judea. He challenged the power structure of the Jewish leadership and paved the way for what was to come.

From the day an angel appeared to John's father to announce his birth, it was clear that John was special, set aside for a unique purpose. John boldly preached a clear and powerful message: the kingdom of God was coming, and people were called to turn from their sins and be baptized as a symbol of their repentance.

Some were deeply moved by the words of John and humbly sought to change their lives; others were hardened in their pride and arrogance. When King Herod married Herodias, his brother's wife, John did not remain silent, but pointed out the king's neglect of God's Law. Herodias was angered by John's words of condemnation and had him killed. She was able to stomp out the messenger but not the message. The way had been prepared; the Messiah had broken onto the scene. John had done his job.

John felt he was not worthy to be Jesus' slave. Jesus, however, said that there was no one greater than John in the history of the human race. John did not have a self-esteem problem; he had appropriate humility. When we truly understand the greatness of Jesus, our own self-importance, pride, and self-sufficiency will be transformed into gratitude and a desire to please him.

STRENGTHS AND ACCOMPLISHMENTS:
- John spoke the truth, no matter what the cost.
- He cared about God's opinion, not what others thought.
- He fulfilled God's will for him by preparing the way for the Messiah.
- He put God first in everything he did and said.
- He honestly expressed his feelings of confusion and doubt.

LESSONS FROM HIS LIFE:
- Standing for the truth may be costly, but it is worthwhile in the end.
- There is joy in telling others about God's Kingdom and the King, Jesus.
- An accurate self-perception is a key to faithful service.

KEY VERSE:
"[John] replied, 'I am a voice from the barren wilderness, shouting as Isaiah prophesied, "Get ready for the coming of the Lord!"'" (John 1:23).

John's story is found in Matthew 3:1-17; 11:18-19; 14:1-12; Mark 1:1-11; 6:14-29; Luke 1:5-25, 39-45, 57-80; 3:1-22; 7:18-35; 9:7-9; John 1:6-9, 19-37. He is also mentioned in Acts 1:5, 21-22; 10:36-37; 11:16; 13:24-25; 18:25-26; 19:3-4.

14And Christ became a human being and
lived here on earth among us and was full of
loving forgiveness and truth. And some of us
have seen his glory—the glory of the only Son
of the heavenly Father!
15John pointed him out to the people, telling the crowds, "This is the one I was talking
about when I said, 'Someone is coming who
is greater by far than I am—for he existed long
before I did!'" 16We have all benefited from
the rich blessings he brought to us—blessing
upon blessing heaped upon us! 17For Moses
gave us only the Law with its rigid demands
and merciless justice, while Jesus Christ
brought us loving forgiveness as well. 18No
one has ever actually seen God, but, of course,
his only Son has, for he is the companion of
the Father and has told us all about him.

John the Baptist's Mission

19The Jewish leaders sent priests and assistant
priests from Jerusalem to ask John whether he
claimed to be the Messiah.
20He denied it flatly. "I am not the Christ,"
he said.
21"Well then, who are you?" they asked.
"Are you Elijah?"
"No," he replied.
"Are you the Prophet?"
"No."
22"Then who are you? Tell us, so we can give
an answer to those who sent us. What do you
have to say for yourself?"
23He replied, "I am a voice from the barren
wilderness, shouting as Isaiah prophesied,
'Get ready for the coming of the Lord!'"
24,25Then those who were sent by the Phari-

sees asked him, "If you aren't the Messiah or
Elijah or the Prophet, what right do you have
to baptize?"
26John told them, "I merely baptize with
water, but right here in the crowd is someone
you have never met, 27who will soon begin his
ministry among you, and I am not even fit to
be his slave."
28This incident took place at Bethany, a
village on the other side of the Jordan River
where John was baptizing.

Jesus, the Promised Messiah

29The next day John saw Jesus coming toward
him and said, "Look! There is the Lamb of
God who takes away the world's sin! 30He is
the one I was talking about when I said, 'Soon
a man far greater than I am is coming, who
existed long before me!' 31I didn't know he
was the one, but I am here baptizing with
water in order to point him out to the nation
of Israel."
32Then John told about seeing the Holy
Spirit in the form of a dove descending from
heaven and resting upon Jesus.
33"I didn't know he was the one," John said
again, "but at the time God sent me to baptize
he told me, 'When you see the Holy Spirit
descending and resting upon someone—he is
the one you are looking for. He is the one who
baptizes with the Holy Spirit.' 34I saw it happen to this man, and I therefore testify that he
is the Son of God."

Jesus' First Followers

35The following day as John was standing with
two of his disciples, 36Jesus walked by. John
looked at him intently and then declared,
"See! There is the Lamb of God!"
37Then John's two disciples turned and followed Jesus.
38Jesus looked around and saw them following. "What do you want?" he asked them.
"Sir," they replied, "where do you live?"
39"Come and see," he said. So they went
with him to the place where he was staying
and were with him from about four o'clock
that afternoon until the evening. 40(One of
these men was Andrew, Simon Peter's
brother.)
41Andrew then went to find his brother
Peter and told him, "We have found the Messiah!" 42And he brought Peter to meet Jesus.
Jesus looked intently at Peter for a moment
and then said, "You are Simon, John's son—
but you shall be called Peter, the rock!"
43The next day Jesus decided to go to Galilee. He found Philip and told him, "Come
with me." 44(Philip was from Bethsaida, Andrew and Peter's hometown.)
45Philip now went off to look for Nathanael
and told him, "We have found the Messiah!—
the very person Moses and the prophets told
about! His name is Jesus, the son of Joseph
from Nazareth!"
46"Nazareth!" exclaimed Nathanael. "Can
anything good come from there?"
"Just come and see for yourself," Philip
declared.
47As they approached, Jesus said, "Here
comes an honest man—a true son of Israel."
48"How do you know what I am like?" Nathanael demanded.
And Jesus replied, "I could see you under
the fig tree before Philip found you."
49Nathanael replied, "Sir, you are the Son of
God—the King of Israel!"
50Jesus asked him, "Do you believe all this
just because I told you I had seen you under
the fig tree? You will see greater proofs than
this. 51You will even see heaven open and the
angels of God coming back and forth to me,
the Messiah."

CHAPTER 2

Jesus Turns Water into Wine

Two days later Jesus' mother was a guest at a
wedding in the village of Cana in Galilee, 2and

1:19-28 John the Baptist was an original messenger of repentance and recovery. He himself was not the true Light or source of recovery; he merely pointed to the one who was (1:6-8, 26-27, 30-31, 34). Likewise, those of us in recovery reflect God's light and merely point the way to recovery. We should not draw followers to ourself any more than John did. We are mere beggars telling other beggars where to find food. When we lay aside pride in our achievements and abilities as John the Baptist did, we are better able to serve Christ by showing fellow strugglers the way to recovery.

2:1-12 Jesus was at a wedding celebration with family and friends when the wine ran out. So Jesus turned the water from six stone waterpots into enough wine for the rest of the celebration. If we are in recovery, this abundance of wine might seem dangerous. But one truth should be encouraging for us all: Jesus wanted the people at this wedding to have a good time. Even though his life's mission was a very sobering one, he valued the joy of people at a wedding feast. God wants us to live a joyful life as well. He may call us to do some painful things in the process of recovery, but his ultimate goal for us is a life filled with joy.

Jesus and his disciples were invited too. 3The wine supply ran out during the festivities, and Jesus' mother came to him with the problem.

4"I can't help you now," he said. "It isn't yet my time for miracles."

5But his mother told the servants, "Do whatever he tells you to."

6Six stone waterpots were standing there; they were used for Jewish ceremonial purposes and held perhaps twenty to thirty gallons each. 7,8Then Jesus told the servants to fill them to the brim with water. When this was done he said, "Dip some out and take it to the master of ceremonies."

9When the master of ceremonies tasted the water that was now wine, not knowing where it had come from (though, of course, the servants did), he called the bridegroom over.

10"This is wonderful stuff !" he said. "You're different from most. Usually a host uses the best wine first, and afterwards, when everyone is full and doesn't care, then he brings out the less expensive brands. But you have kept the best for the last!"

11This miracle at Cana in Galilee was Jesus' first public demonstration of his heaven-sent power. And his disciples believed that he really was the Messiah.

12After the wedding he left for Capernaum for a few days with his mother, brothers, and disciples.

Jesus Clears the Temple

13Then it was time for the annual Jewish Passover celebration, and Jesus went to Jerusalem.

14In the Temple area he saw merchants selling cattle, sheep, and doves for sacrifices, and moneychangers behind their counters. 15Jesus made a whip from some ropes and chased them all out, and drove out the sheep and oxen, scattering the moneychangers' coins over the floor and turning over their tables! 16Then, going over to the men selling doves, he told them, "Get these things out of here. Don't turn my Father's House into a market!"

17Then his disciples remembered this prophecy from the Scriptures: "Concern for God's House will be my undoing."

18"What right have you to order them out?" the Jewish leaders demanded. "If you have this authority from God, show us a miracle to prove it."

19"All right," Jesus replied, "this is the miracle I will do for you: Destroy this sanctuary and in three days I will raise it up!"

20"What!" they exclaimed. "It took forty-six years to build this Temple, and you can do it in three days?" 21But by "this sanctuary" he meant his body. 22After he came back to life again, the disciples remembered his saying this and realized that what he had quoted from the Scriptures really did refer to him, and had all come true!

23Because of the miracles he did in Jerusalem at the Passover celebration, many people were convinced that he was indeed the Messiah. 24,25But Jesus didn't trust them, for he knew mankind to the core. No one needed to tell him how changeable human nature is!

CHAPTER 3

Jesus Talks with Nicodemus

After dark one night a Jewish religious leader named Nicodemus, a member of the sect of the Pharisees, came for an interview with Jesus. "Sir," he said, "we all know that God has sent you to teach us. Your miracles are proof enough of this."

3Jesus replied, "With all the earnestness I possess I tell you this: Unless you are born again, you can never get into the Kingdom of God."

4"Born again!" exclaimed Nicodemus. "What do you mean? How can an old man go back into his mother's womb and be born again?"

5Jesus replied, "What I am telling you so

2:13-16 Jesus was angry at those who turned the Temple courts into a marketplace of unjust profit. People were forced to buy "approved" sacrificial animals at exorbitant prices. They also were required to exchange their currency for Temple currency at inflated rates. Jesus cleared the Temple with a whip to demonstrate God's anger at those who abused the public trust and mocked holy worship. Anger that is measured and authorized by God's purposes is justified. Sometimes this kind of anger can play an important role in our spiritual, emotional, and physical recovery. We may need to stand up to the abusive forces in our life and make changes that will set us free from their grip. As we do this, God will stand by us.

3:1-12 Spiritual rebirth is as necessary to the recovery process as it is to entering God's Kingdom. Being born again is the easy, passive part—a baby step in the process. The hard part comes each subsequent day as we submit our stubborn heart and will to the control of God's Spirit. True recovery is not attained by trying harder to live a better life. It is a gift of cleansing and forgiveness that is bestowed as we entrust our life to God and seek to follow his will for our life.

earnestly is this: Unless one is born of water
and the Spirit, he cannot enter the Kingdom
of God. 6Men can only reproduce human life,
but the Holy Spirit gives new life from
heaven; 7so don't be surprised at my statement that you must be born again! 8Just as
you can hear the wind but can't tell where it
comes from or where it will go next, so it is
with the Spirit. We do not know on whom he
will next bestow this life from heaven."

9"What do you mean?" Nicodemus asked.

10,11Jesus replied, "You, a respected Jewish
teacher, and yet you don't understand these
things? I am telling you what I know and have
seen—and yet you won't believe me. 12But if
you don't even believe me when I tell you
about such things as these that happen here
among men, how can you possibly believe if
I tell you what is going on in heaven? 13For
only I, the Messiah, have come to earth and
will return to heaven again. 14And as Moses in
the wilderness lifted up the bronze image of a
serpent on a pole, even so I must be lifted up
upon a pole, 15so that anyone who believes in
me will have eternal life. 16For God loved the
world so much that he gave his only Son so
that anyone who believes in him shall not
perish but have eternal life. 17God did not
send his Son into the world to condemn it,
but to save it.

18"There is no eternal doom awaiting those
who trust him to save them. But those who
don't trust him have already been tried and
condemned for not believing in the only Son
of God. 19Their sentence is based on this fact:
that the Light from heaven came into the
world, but they loved the darkness more than
the Light, for their deeds were evil. 20They
hated the heavenly Light because they
wanted to sin in the darkness. They stayed
away from that Light for fear their sins would
be exposed and they would be punished. 21But
those doing right come gladly to the Light to
let everyone see that they are doing what God
wants them to."

John the Baptist Speaks of Jesus

22Afterwards Jesus and his disciples left Jerusalem and stayed for a while in Judea and baptized there.

23,24At this time John the Baptist was not yet
in prison. He was baptizing at Aenon, near
Salim, because there was plenty of water
there. 25One day someone began an argument
with John's disciples, telling them that Jesus'
baptism was best. 26So they came to John and
said, "Master, the man you met on the other
side of the Jordan River—the one you said was
the Messiah—he is baptizing too, and everybody is going over there instead of coming
here to us."

27John replied, "God in heaven appoints
each man's work. 28My work is to prepare the
way for that man so that everyone will go to
him. You yourselves know how plainly I told
you that I am not the Messiah. I am here to
prepare the way for him—that is all. 29The
crowds will naturally go to the main attraction—the bride will go where the bridegroom
is! A bridegroom's friends rejoice with him. I
am the Bridegroom's friend, and I am filled
with joy at his success. 30He must become
greater and greater, and I must become less
and less.

31"He has come from heaven and is greater
than anyone else. I am of the earth, and my
understanding is limited to the things of
earth. 32He tells what he has seen and heard,
but how few believe what he tells them!
33,34Those who believe him discover that God
is a fountain of truth. For this one—sent by
God—speaks God's words, for God's Spirit is
upon him without measure or limit. 35The
Father loves this man because he is his Son,

3:16-18 Faith says yes to God's loving overtures to us. God cared enough to send his own Son to pay for our failures—Jesus Christ. True faith has nothing to do with our human efforts, social achievements, or material wealth. Instead, saving faith says to God: "I'm a helpless sinner, unable to effect my own recovery. I trust your forgiveness, which you freely offer me in Jesus Christ." That kind of faith in God delivers us from the ultimate consequences of our sins—eternal separation from God. It also gives us the power to make changes in the present that will plant the seeds for a new life.

4:4-27 The disciples were surprised to find Jesus speaking with the woman at the well for a number of reasons: She was a Samaritan (half Jew and half Gentile); she was a woman; and she had a questionable history. Any one of these factors would have disqualified her from speaking with a "righteous" Jewish man. But Jesus broke down all the traditional barriers to accept her as she was and gave her a chance to experience a fresh start in life. In doing this, Jesus demonstrated God's love for all who have been rejected, condemned, or shunned. This can be a source of great encouragement to us. No matter what we have done in the past, God still offers us his unconditional acceptance in Jesus. With his powerful help, nothing can stand in the way of our recovery.

and God has given him everything there is.
36And all who trust him—God's Son—to save
them have eternal life; those who don't believe and obey him shall never see heaven,
but the wrath of God remains upon them."

CHAPTER 4

Jesus Talks to a Samaritan Woman

When the Lord knew that the Pharisees had
heard about the greater crowds coming to
him than to John to be baptized and to become his disciples—(though Jesus himself
didn't baptize them, but his disciples did)—
3he left Judea and returned to the province of
Galilee.
4He had to go through Samaria on the way,
5,6and around noon as he approached the village of Sychar, he came to Jacob's Well, located on the parcel of ground Jacob gave to
his son Joseph. Jesus was tired from the long
walk in the hot sun and sat wearily beside the
well.
7Soon a Samaritan woman came to draw
water, and Jesus asked her for a drink. 8He was
alone at the time as his disciples had gone
into the village to buy some food. 9The
woman was surprised that a Jew would ask a
"despised Samaritan" for anything—usually
they wouldn't even speak to them!—and she
remarked about this to Jesus.
10He replied, "If you only knew what a
wonderful gift God has for you, and who I
am, you would ask me for some *living* water!"
11"But you don't have a rope or a bucket,"
she said, "and this is a very deep well! Where
would you get this living water? 12And besides, are you greater than our ancestor Jacob?
How can you offer better water than this
which he and his sons and cattle enjoyed?"
13Jesus replied that people soon became
thirsty again after drinking this water. 14"But
the water I give them," he said, "becomes a
perpetual spring within them, watering them
forever with eternal life."
15"Please, sir," the woman said, "give me
some of that water! Then I'll never be thirsty
again and won't have to make this long trip
out here every day."
16"Go and get your husband," Jesus told
her.
17,18"But I'm not married," the woman replied.
"All too true!" Jesus said. "For you have had
five husbands, and you aren't even married to
the man you're living with now."
19"Sir," the woman said, "you must be a
prophet. 20But say, tell me, why is it that you

Friends of the Light

BIBLE READING: John 3:18-21

We sought through prayer and meditation to improve our conscious contact with God, as we understood him, praying only for knowledge of his will for us and the power to carry that out.

Sometimes we don't want to know God's will because there are areas in our life that we aren't ready to deal with yet. Recovery is a process for us. We may be ready to pray for God's will in some areas but feel uncomfortable with having God's light shine into the areas that are still hidden in shame.

When talking about those who refuse to trust him with their life, Jesus said, "The Light from heaven came into the world, but they loved the darkness more than the Light, for their deeds were evil. . . . They stayed away from that Light for fear their sins would be exposed and they would be punished" (John 3:19-20). "Later, in one of his talks, Jesus said to the people, 'I am the Light of the world. So if you follow me, you won't be stumbling through the darkness, for living light will flood your path'" (John 8:12).

Darkness is great when we are trying to hide something; but light is needed when we are trying to walk without stumbling. When we were hiding our shameful behaviors and holding on to our addictions, the darkness seemed like our friend. Now that we are trying to walk in the steps of recovery, we need the light to keep us from stumbling. We don't have to be afraid of God's light anymore since we have his forgiveness through Christ. He wants to safely guide us on the right path. ***Turn to Step Twelve, page 773, Isaiah 61.***

Jews insist that Jerusalem is the only place of
worship, while we Samaritans claim it is here
[at Mount Gerizim], where our ancestors worshiped?"
21-24 Jesus replied, "The time is coming,
ma'am, when we will no longer be concerned
about whether to worship the Father here or
in Jerusalem. For it's not *where* we worship
that counts, but *how* we worship—is our worship spiritual and real? Do we have the Holy
Spirit's help? For God is Spirit, and we must
have his help to worship as we should. The
Father wants this kind of worship from us. But
you Samaritans know so little about him,
worshiping blindly, while we Jews know all
about him, for salvation comes to the world
through the Jews."
25 The woman said, "Well, at least I know
that the Messiah will come—the one they call
Christ—and when he does, he will explain
everything to us."
26 Then Jesus told her, "I am the Messiah!"
27 Just then his disciples arrived. They were
surprised to find him talking to a woman, but
none of them asked him why, or what they
had been discussing.
28,29 Then the woman left her waterpot beside the well and went back to the village and
told everyone, "Come and meet a man who
told me everything I ever did! Can this be the
Messiah?" 30 So the people came streaming
from the village to see him.
31 Meanwhile, the disciples were urging
Jesus to eat. 32 "No," he said, "I have some food
you don't know about."
33 "Who brought it to him?" the disciples
asked each other.
34 Then Jesus explained: "My nourishment
comes from doing the will of God who sent
me, and from finishing his work. 35 Do you
think the work of harvesting will not begin
until the summer ends four months from
now? Look around you! Vast fields of human
souls are ripening all around us, and are ready
now for reaping. 36 The reapers will be paid
good wages and will be gathering eternal
souls into the granaries of heaven! What joys
await the sower and the reaper, both together!
37 For it is true that one sows and someone else
reaps. 38 I sent you to reap where you didn't
sow; others did the work, and you received
the harvest."

Many Samaritans Believe in Jesus

39 Many from the Samaritan village believed
he was the Messiah because of the woman's
report: "He told me everything I ever did!"
40,41 When they came out to see him at the
well, they begged him to stay at their village;
and he did, for two days, long enough for
many of them to believe in him after hearing
him. 42 Then they said to the woman, "Now
we believe because we have heard him ourselves, not just because of what you told us.
He is indeed the Savior of the world."

Jesus Heals an Official's Son

43,44 At the end of the two days' stay he went on
into Galilee. Jesus used to say, "A prophet is
honored everywhere except in his own country!" 45 But the Galileans welcomed him with
open arms, for they had been in Jerusalem at
the Passover celebration and had seen some
of his miracles.
46,47 In the course of his journey through
Galilee he arrived at the town of Cana, where
he had turned the water into wine. While he
was there, a man in the city of Capernaum, a
government official, whose son was very sick,
heard that Jesus had come from Judea and
was traveling in Galilee. This man went over
to Cana, found Jesus, and begged him to
come to Capernaum with him and heal his
son, who was now at death's door.
48 Jesus asked, "Won't any of you believe in
me unless I do more and more miracles?"
49 The official pled, "Sir, please come now
before my child dies."

4:39-42 The Samaritan woman put her faith in Jesus, who knew all about her faults yet still loved and respected her. She responded to God's gracious forgiveness by immediately sharing her story with others. She told her neighbors about the Messiah who had offered her a new life. As a result, many were blessed with the benefits of faith in Jesus Christ. As we experience God's powerful deliverance in our life, it is important that we share the good news with others. The message we share may be the difference between life and death for someone we know. And when we share our story, we will experience anew the great joy of our victory in Christ.

4:46-53 The government official demonstrated his faith in Jesus by humbly asking him to heal his son, and then by taking him at his word. He believed Jesus' word to be true even though he hadn't yet seen the results. Our faith is expressed in similar ways. We can begin by humbly and honestly seeking God's help. He will help us even though we don't see immediate results. The recovery process usually takes a while. We can believe that God is working and persevere, even when the results of his work in our life are not immediately evident.

[50]Then Jesus told him, "Go back home.
Your son is healed!" And the man believed
Jesus and started home. [51]While he was on his
way, some of his servants met him with the
news that all was well—his son had recovered.
[52]He asked them when the lad had begun to
feel better, and they replied, "Yesterday afternoon at about one o'clock his fever suddenly
disappeared!" [53]Then the father realized it was
the same moment that Jesus had told him,
"Your son is healed." And the officer and his
entire household believed that Jesus was the
Messiah.
[54]This was Jesus' second miracle in Galilee
after coming from Judea.

CHAPTER 5
Jesus Heals a Lame Man
Afterwards Jesus returned to Jerusalem for
one of the Jewish religious holidays. [2]Inside
the city, near the Sheep Gate, was Bethesda
Pool, with five covered platforms or porches
surrounding it. [3]Crowds of sick folks—lame,
blind, or with paralyzed limbs—lay on the
platforms (waiting for a certain movement of
the water, [4]for an angel of the Lord came from
time to time and disturbed the water, and the
first person to step down into it afterwards
was healed).
[5]One of the men lying there had been sick
for thirty-eight years. [6]When Jesus saw him
and knew how long he had been ill, he asked
him, "Would you like to get well?"
[7]"I can't," the sick man said, "for I have no
one to help me into the pool at the movement of the water. While I am trying to get
there, someone else always gets in ahead of
me."
[8]Jesus told him, "Stand up, roll up your
sleeping mat and go on home!"
[9]Instantly, the man was healed! He rolled
up the mat and began walking!
But it was on the Sabbath when this miracle
was done. [10]So the Jewish leaders objected.
They said to the man who was cured, "You
can't work on the Sabbath! It's illegal to carry
that sleeping mat!"
[11]"The man who healed me told me to,"
was his reply.
[12]"Who said such a thing as that?" they
demanded.
[13]The man didn't know, and Jesus had disappeared into the crowd. [14]But afterwards
Jesus found him in the Temple and told him,
"Now you are well; don't sin as you did before, or something even worse may happen to
you."

Discovering Hope

BIBLE READING: John 5:1-15

We were entirely ready to have God remove all these defects of character.

How can we honestly say that we are *entirely* ready for God to remove our defects of character? If we think in terms of all or nothing, we may get stuck here because we will never feel entirely ready. It is important to keep in mind that the Twelve Steps are guiding ideals. No one can work them perfectly. Our part is to keep moving, to get as close as we can to being ready.

In Jesus' day there was a pool where people came in hope of experiencing a miraculous healing. "One of the men lying there had been sick for thirty-eight years. When Jesus saw him and knew how long he had been ill, he asked him, 'Would you like to get well?' 'I can't,' the sick man said, 'for I have no one to help me into the pool at the movement of the water. While I am trying to get there, someone else always gets in ahead of me.' Jesus told him, 'Stand up, roll up your sleeping mat and go on home!' Instantly, the man was healed! He rolled up the mat and began walking!" (John 5:5-9).

This man was so crippled that he couldn't go any farther on his own. He camped as near as he could to a place where there was hope for recovery. God met him there and brought him the rest of the way. For us, "entirely ready" may mean getting as close to the hope of healing as we can in our crippled condition. When we do, God will meet us there and take us the rest of the way. ***Turn to page 1241, Romans 6.***

15 Then the man went to find the Jewish
leaders and told them it was Jesus who had
healed him.

Jesus Claims to Be God's Son

16 So they began harassing Jesus as a Sabbath
breaker.
17 But Jesus replied, "My Father constantly
does good, and I'm following his example."
18 Then the Jewish leaders were all the more
eager to kill him because in addition to disobeying their Sabbath laws, he had spoken of
God as his Father, thereby making himself
equal with God.
19 Jesus replied, "The Son can do nothing by
himself. He does only what he sees the Father
doing, and in the same way. 20 For the Father
loves the Son, and tells him everything he is
doing; and the Son will do far more awesome
miracles than this man's healing. 21 He will
even raise from the dead anyone he wants to,
just as the Father does. 22 And the Father leaves
all judgment of sin to his Son, 23 so that everyone will honor the Son, just as they honor the
Father. But if you refuse to honor God's Son,
whom he sent to you, then you are certainly
not honoring the Father.
24 "I say emphatically that anyone who
listens to my message and believes in God
who sent me has eternal life, and will never be
damned for his sins, but has already passed
out of death into life.
25 "And I solemnly declare that the time is
coming, in fact, it is here, when the dead shall
hear my voice—the voice of the Son of God—
and those who listen shall live. 26 The Father
has life in himself, and has granted his Son to
have life in himself, 27 and to judge the sins of
all mankind because he is the Son of Man.
28 Don't be so surprised! Indeed the time is
coming when all the dead in their graves shall
hear the voice of God's Son, 29 and shall rise
again—those who have done good, to eternal
life; and those who have continued in evil, to
judgment.
30 "But I pass no judgment without consulting the Father. I judge as I am told. And my
judgment is absolutely fair and just, for it is
according to the will of God who sent me and
is not merely my own.

Jesus Supports His Claim

31 "When I make claims about myself they
aren't believed, 32,33 but someone else, yes,
John the Baptist, is making these claims for
me too. You have gone out to listen to his
preaching, and I can assure you that all he
says about me is true! 34 But the truest witness I have is not from a man, though I have
reminded you about John's witness so that
you will believe in me and be saved. 35 John
shone brightly for a while, and you benefited and rejoiced, 36 but I have a greater
witness than John. I refer to the miracles I
do; these have been assigned me by the
Father, and they prove that the Father has
sent me. 37 And the Father himself has also
testified about me, though not appearing to
you personally, or speaking to you directly.
38 But you are not listening to him, for you
refuse to believe me—the one sent to you
with God's message.
39 "You search the Scriptures, for you believe
they give you eternal life. And the Scriptures
point to me! 40 Yet you won't come to me so
that I can give you this life eternal!
41,42 "Your approval or disapproval means
nothing to me, for as I know so well, you
don't have God's love within you. 43 I know,
because I have come to you representing my
Father and you refuse to welcome me, though
you readily enough receive those who aren't
sent from him, but represent only themselves! 44 No wonder you can't believe! For you
gladly honor each other, but you don't care
about the honor that comes from the only
God!
45 "Yet it is not I who will accuse you of this
to the Father—Moses will! Moses, on whose
laws you set your hopes of heaven. 46 For you
have refused to believe Moses. He wrote about
me, but you refuse to believe him, so you refuse

5:39-40 The Jewish leaders knew the Scriptures backwards and forwards, yet they were spiritually dead. That's because they missed the whole purpose of the Scriptures: to bring people into a vital relationship with the God of grace. Intellectual knowledge about the Bible does not bring us into a transforming relationship with God unless we act on that knowledge. Knowing about God's truth concerning recovery, without applying it personally, will result in a failed recovery program. Real growth and recovery come through knowing the person of God in Jesus Christ.

5:41-44 Jesus called the Pharisees to task for being more concerned about what others thought of them than about what God thought. At times during recovery it may be necessary to do things that are neither understood nor approved by those around us. The bottom line for us is whether or not God approves of what we are doing, not what others think. As we take our moral inventory, God and his Word, not the opinions of our peers, are the measuring stick for our behavior.

to believe in me. [47]And since you don't believe
what he wrote, no wonder you don't believe
me either."

CHAPTER 6

Jesus Feeds Five Thousand

After this, Jesus crossed over the Sea of Galilee, also known as the Sea of Tiberias. [2-5]And a
huge crowd, many of them pilgrims on their
way to Jerusalem for the annual Passover celebration, were following him wherever he
went, to watch him heal the sick. So when
Jesus went up into the hills and sat down with
his disciples around him, he soon saw a great
multitude of people climbing the hill, looking
for him.

Turning to Philip he asked, "Philip, where
can we buy bread to feed all these people?"
[6](He was testing Philip, for he already knew
what he was going to do.)

[7]Philip replied, "It would take a fortune to
begin to do it!"

[8,9]Then Andrew, Simon Peter's brother,
spoke up. "There's a youngster here with five
barley loaves and a couple of fish! But what
good is that with all this mob?"

[10]"Tell everyone to sit down," Jesus ordered.
And all of them—the approximate count of
the men only was five thousand—sat down on
the grassy slopes. [11]Then Jesus took the loaves
and gave thanks to God and passed them out
to the people. Afterwards he did the same with
the fish. And everyone ate until full!

[12]"Now gather the scraps," Jesus told his
disciples, "so that nothing is wasted." [13]And
twelve baskets were filled with the leftovers!

[14]When the people realized what a great
miracle had happened, they exclaimed,
"Surely, he is the Prophet we have been expecting!"

[15]Jesus saw that they were ready to take him
by force and make him their king, so he went
higher into the mountains alone.

Jesus Walks on Water

[16]That evening his disciples went down to the
shore to wait for him. [17]But as darkness fell
and Jesus still hadn't come back, they got into
the boat and headed out across the lake toward Capernaum. [18,19]But soon a gale swept
down upon them as they rowed, and the sea
grew very rough. They were three or four
miles out when suddenly they saw Jesus walking toward the boat! They were terrified, [20]but
he called out to them and told them not to be
afraid. [21]Then they were willing to let him in,
and immediately the boat was where they
were going!

Jesus, the Bread of Life

[22,23]The next morning, back across the lake,
crowds began gathering on the shore [waiting
to see Jesus]. For they knew that he and his
disciples had come over together and that the
disciples had gone off in their boat, leaving
him behind. Several small boats from Tiberias
were nearby, [24]so when the people saw that
Jesus wasn't there, nor his disciples, they got
into the boats and went across to Capernaum
to look for him.

[25]When they arrived and found him, they
said, "Sir, how did you get here?" [26]Jesus replied, "The truth of the matter is that you
want to be with me because I fed you, not
because you believe in me. [27]But you
shouldn't be so concerned about perishable
things like food. No, spend your energy seeking the eternal life that I, the Messiah, can
give you. For God the Father has sent me for
this very purpose."

[28]They replied, "What should we do to satisfy God?"

[29]Jesus told them, "This is the will of God,
that you believe in the one he has sent."

[30,31]They replied, "You must show us more
miracles if you want us to believe you are the
Messiah. Give us free bread every day, like our

6:1-15 It is interesting that Jesus often used people as channels of his grace. In feeding 5,000 hungry men (plus women and children), Jesus used what was provided by a young boy. So also in effecting our recovery, or another's recovery God allows us to have a part in what he does. When we willingly dedicate our own small resources—time, talents, or possessions—to God, he can work miracles of recovery for us and others. God can take our limited resources and multiply them beyond our wildest expectations.

6:16-21 It was a dark and stormy night on Lake Galilee. The disciples were cold, wet, and exhausted from rowing almost four miles in storm-tossed waters. They might have cried out, "Where's Jesus when we really need him?" But, in fact, they had been impatient and had left safe shores without him. Jesus came to their rescue anyway—walking on the stormy sea toward their boat! And when Jesus got in with them, he brought them safely to shore. There are important lessons for us in this story. We would be wise to stay with Jesus and his plan for us. Going off on our own will inevitably lead us into some stormy situations. When we do leave Jesus behind, however, he will still come through for us if we look to him for help.

fathers had while they journeyed through the
wilderness! As the Scriptures say, 'Moses gave
them bread from heaven.'"
32Jesus said, "Moses didn't give it to them.
My Father did. And now he offers you true
Bread from heaven. 33The true Bread is a Person—the one sent by God from heaven, and
he gives life to the world."
34"Sir," they said, "give us that bread every
day of our lives!"
35Jesus replied, "I am the Bread of Life. No
one coming to me will ever be hungry
again. Those believing in me will never
thirst. 36But the trouble is, as I have told you
before, you haven't believed even though
you have seen me. 37But some will come to
me—those the Father has given me—and I
will never, never reject them. 38For I have
come here from heaven to do the will of
God who sent me, not to have my own way.
39And this is the will of God, that I should
not lose even one of all those he has given
me, but that I should raise them to eternal
life at the Last Day. 40For it is my Father's
will that everyone who sees his Son and
believes on him should have eternal life—
that I should raise him at the Last Day."

The Jews Disagree about Jesus

41Then the Jews began to murmur against him
because he claimed to be the Bread from
heaven.
42"What?" they exclaimed. "Why, he is
merely Jesus the son of Joseph, whose father
and mother we know. What is this he is saying, that he came down from heaven?"
43But Jesus replied, "Don't murmur among
yourselves about my saying that. 44For no one
can come to me unless the Father who sent
me draws him to me, and at the Last Day I will
cause all such to rise again from the dead. 45As
it is written in the Scriptures, 'They shall all be
taught of God.' Those the Father speaks to,
who learn the truth from him, will be attracted to me. 46(Not that anyone actually sees
the Father, for only I have seen him.)
47"How earnestly I tell you this—anyone
who believes in me already has eternal life!
48-51Yes, I am the Bread of Life! When your
fathers in the wilderness ate bread from the
skies, they all died. But the Bread from heaven
gives eternal life to everyone who eats it. I am
that Living Bread that came down out of
heaven. Anyone eating this Bread shall live
forever; this Bread is my flesh given to redeem
humanity."
52Then the Jews began arguing with each
other about what he meant. "How can this
man give us his flesh to eat?" they asked.
53So Jesus said it again, "With all the earnestness I possess I tell you this: Unless you
eat the flesh of the Messiah and drink his
blood, you cannot have eternal life within
you. 54But anyone who does eat my flesh and
drink my blood has eternal life, and I will raise
him at the Last Day. 55For my flesh is the true
food, and my blood is the true drink. 56Every-
one who eats my flesh and drinks my blood is
in me, and I in him. 57I live by the power of
the living Father who sent me, and in the
same way those who partake of me shall live
because of me! 58I am the true Bread from
heaven; and anyone who eats this Bread shall
live forever, and not die as your fathers did—

6:32-40 After feeding more than 5,000 hungry people with five loaves of bread and two fish, Jesus explained that he himself was the Bread of Life. Jesus feeds the hungry with himself. His is a perfect love that never rejects us, no matter what our failures have been in the past. He satisfies the deepest longings of our soul and wants to fulfill our need for recovery. Until the end of time, Jesus will work toward the recovery of all the broken people in his world. Our part is to turn to him and believe in his power to help us.

6:53-58 The sight of human flesh and blood is offensive to most of us, and Jesus' words here are jarring. In saying we need to eat his flesh and drink his blood to have eternal life, Jesus offended many people, but he made some important points. Jesus' flesh reminds us that he was fully human. As one of us, Jesus understands our temptations and struggles in this life. Jesus' mention of his blood anticipated his death on the cross—in our place, for our sins. The call to partake of his flesh and blood was a call to make him and his teachings more than just an intellectual activity. We are called to make Jesus the very center of our being—emotional, spiritual, and physical. As we feed our body with food, we are to feed our soul with the spiritual reality represented by the body and blood of Christ.

6:68-69 Many sales pitches for enticing products assault us daily. Publisher's sweepstakes, lottery games, television specials, political causes, religious gurus—they all call for our time, money, and devotion. They promise to give us what we all need and desire. When all is said and done, however, we are left with Peter's question, "Master, to whom shall we go?" Jesus is the answer to our need for recovery. He alone can deliver us from powerful addictions and compulsions; he alone deserves our total commitment.

though they ate bread from heaven." [59](He
preached this sermon in the synagogue in
Capernaum.)

Many Followers Desert Jesus
[60]Even his disciples said, "This is very hard to
understand. Who can tell what he means?"
[61]Jesus knew within himself that his disciples were complaining and said to them,
"Does *this* offend you? [62]Then what will you
think if you see me, the Messiah, return to
heaven again? [63]Only the Holy Spirit gives
eternal life. Those born only once, with physical birth, will never receive this gift. But now
I have told you how to get this true spiritual
life. [64]But some of you don't believe me." (For
Jesus knew from the beginning who didn't
believe and knew the one who would betray
him.)
[65]And he remarked, "That is what I meant
when I said that no one can come to me
unless the Father attracts him to me."
[66]At this point many of his disciples turned
away and deserted him.
[67]Then Jesus turned to the Twelve and
asked, "Are you going too?"
[68]Simon Peter replied, "Master, to whom
shall we go? You alone have the words that
give eternal life, [69]and we believe them and
know you are the holy Son of God."
[70]Then Jesus said, "I chose the twelve of
you, and one is a devil." [71]He was speaking of
Judas, son of Simon Iscariot, one of the
Twelve, who would betray him.

CHAPTER 7
Jesus' Brothers Ridicule Him
After this, Jesus went to Galilee, going from
village to village, for he wanted to stay out of
Judea where the Jewish leaders were plotting
his death. [2]But soon it was time for the Tabernacle Ceremonies, one of the annual Jewish
holidays, [3]and Jesus' brothers urged him to go
to Judea for the celebration.
"Go where more people can see your
miracles!" they scoffed. [4]"You can't be famous
when you hide like this! If you're so great,
prove it to the world!" [5]For even his brothers
didn't believe in him.
[6]Jesus replied, "It is not the right time for
me to go now. But you can go anytime and it
will make no difference, [7]for the world can't
hate you; but it does hate me, because I accuse
it of sin and evil. [8]You go on, and I'll come
later when it is the right time." [9]So he remained in Galilee.

Feelings of Shame

BIBLE READING: John 8:3-11

We admitted to God, to ourselves, and to another human being the exact nature of our wrongs.

Shame has kept many of us in hiding. The thought of revealing ourself to another human being stirs up feelings of shame and the fear of being publicly exposed.

"The Jewish leaders . . . brought a woman caught in adultery and placed her out in front of the staring crowd. 'Teacher,' they said to Jesus, '. . . Moses' law says to kill her. What about it?' . . . Jesus stooped down and wrote in the dust with his finger. They kept demanding an answer, so he stood up again and said, 'All right, hurl the stones at her until she dies. But only he who never sinned may throw the first!' Then he stooped down again and wrote some more in the dust. And the Jewish leaders slipped away one by one . . until only Jesus was left in front of the crowd with the woman" (John 8:3-9).

Many believe that it was Jesus' writing in the dust that caused the accusers to leave. Perhaps he was listing the secret sins of the Jewish leaders. If this is true, it gives us a beautiful picture of the kind of person Jesus is—a person to whom we can safely expose our secrets. Our confessor needs to be someone who is not surprised by sin and will not be waiting to condemn us. Such a person needs to take private note of our wrongs, writing them in the soft dust, not etching them in stone and posting them in public. Since shame can be a trigger for addictive behavior, we need to be careful about whom we choose to confide in. ***Turn to page 1221, Acts 26.***

Jesus Teaches at the Temple

10But after his brothers had left for the celebration, then he went too, though secretly, staying out of the public eye. 11The Jewish leaders
tried to find him at the celebration and kept
asking if anyone had seen him. 12There was a
lot of discussion about him among the
crowds. Some said, "He's a wonderful man,"
while others said, "No, he's duping the public." 13But no one had the courage to speak out
for him in public for fear of reprisals from the
Jewish leaders.

14Then, midway through the festival, Jesus
went up to the Temple and preached openly.
15The Jewish leaders were surprised when they
heard him. "How can he know so much when
he's never been to our schools?" they asked.

16So Jesus told them, "I'm not teaching you
my own thoughts, but those of God who sent
me. 17If any of you really determines to do
God's will, then you will certainly know
whether my teaching is from God or is merely
my own. 18Anyone presenting his own ideas is
looking for praise for himself, but anyone
seeking to honor the one who sent him is a
good and true person. 19None of *you* obeys the
laws of Moses! So why pick on *me* for breaking
them? Why kill *me* for this?"

20The crowd replied, "You're out of your
mind! Who's trying to kill you?"

21-23Jesus replied, "I worked on the Sabbath
by healing a man, and you were surprised. But
you work on the Sabbath, too, whenever you
obey Moses' law of circumcision (actually,
however, this tradition of circumcision is
older than the Mosaic law); for if the correct
time for circumcising your children falls on
the Sabbath, you go ahead and do it, as you
should. So why should I be condemned for
making a man completely well on the Sabbath? 24Think this through and you will see
that I am right."

25Some of the people who lived there in
Jerusalem said among themselves, "Isn't this
the man they are trying to kill? 26But here he
is preaching in public, and they say nothing
to him. Can it be that our leaders have
learned, after all, that he really is the Messiah?
27But how could he be? For we know where
this man was born; when Christ comes, he
will just appear and no one will know where
he comes from."

28So Jesus, in a sermon in the Temple, called
out, "Yes, you know me and where I was born
and raised, but I am the representative of one
you don't know, and he is Truth. 29I know him
because I was with him, and he sent me to
you."

30Then the Jewish leaders sought to arrest
him; but no hand was laid on him, for God's
time had not yet come.

31Many among the crowds at the Temple
believed on him. "After all," they said, "what
miracles do you expect the Messiah to do that
this man hasn't done?"

Leaders Try to Arrest Jesus

32When the Pharisees heard that the crowds
were in this mood, they and the chief priests
sent officers to arrest Jesus. 33But Jesus told
them, "[Not yet!] I am to be here a little
longer. Then I shall return to the one who
sent me. 34You will search for me but not find
me. And you won't be able to come where I
am!"

35The Jewish leaders were puzzled by this
statement. "Where is he planning to go?"
they asked. "Maybe he is thinking of leaving
the country and going as a missionary among
the Jews in other lands, or maybe even to the
Gentiles! 36What does he mean about our
looking for him and not being able to find
him, and, 'You won't be able to come where I
am'?"

7:3-10 Jesus experienced firsthand the ridicule and rejection from family that many of us in recovery have also experienced. Jesus knew what was right and when to do it. He resisted the timetables, agendas, and expectations that others—even his own brothers—foisted upon him. Jesus' example reminds us that timetables for recovery, going public, or staging a comeback will vary from person to person. Premature publicity of our conversion to Christ or commitment to recovery may lead to unnecessary attacks from others or an inflated sense of personal pride about our success. Either of these will stand in the way of what God is trying to accomplish in and through our life. Often it is best to remain anonymous until "the time is right."

7:10-15, 25-27, 40-49 In this chapter the author polled the audience for different opinions about who Jesus actually was. Some believed he was a wonderful teacher (7:12, 46). Others thought he was a fraud (7:12) or a madman (7:20). Still others conceded he might be the Messiah (7:26, 48-49), or at least a prophet (7:40). The minority who were in power saw him as a political threat and wanted him arrested, even killed (7:1, 20, 44). We, too, must decide who Jesus is and what he means to us. Our decision about Jesus is very important. It will not only affect our recovery from addiction; it will have eternal consequences as well (see 8:24).

37On the last day, the climax of the holidays, Jesus shouted to the crowds, "If anyone
is thirsty, let him come to me and drink. 38For
the Scriptures declare that rivers of living water shall flow from the inmost being of anyone who believes in me." 39(He was speaking
of the Holy Spirit, who would be given to
everyone believing in him; but the Spirit had
not yet been given, because Jesus had not yet
returned to his glory in heaven.)
40When the crowds heard him say this,
some of them declared, "This man surely is
the prophet who will come just before the
Messiah." 41,42Others said, "He *is* the Messiah."
Still others, "But he *can't* be! Will the Messiah
come from *Galilee?* For the Scriptures clearly
state that the Messiah will be born of the royal
line of David, in *Bethlehem,* the village where
David was born." 43So the crowd was divided
about him. 44And some wanted him arrested,
but no one touched him.
45The Temple police who had been sent to
arrest him returned to the chief priests and
Pharisees. "Why didn't you bring him in?"
they demanded.
46"He says such wonderful things!" they
mumbled. "We've never heard anything like
it."
47"So you also have been led astray?" the
Pharisees mocked. 48"Is there a single one of
us Jewish rulers or Pharisees who believes he
is the Messiah? 49These stupid crowds do, yes;
but what do they know about it? A curse upon
them anyway!"
50Then Nicodemus spoke up. (Remember
him? He was the Jewish leader who came
secretly to interview Jesus.) 51"Is it legal to
convict a man before he is even tried?" he
asked.
52They replied, "Are you a wretched Galilean too? Search the Scriptures and see for
yourself—no prophets will come from Galilee!"
53 Then the meeting broke up and everybody went home.

CHAPTER 8

Jesus Forgives an Adulterous Woman

Jesus returned to the Mount of Olives, 2but
early the next morning he was back again at
the Temple. A crowd soon gathered, and he
sat down and talked to them. 3As he was
speaking, the Jewish leaders and Pharisees
brought a woman caught in adultery and
placed her out in front of the staring crowd.
4"Teacher," they said to Jesus, "this woman
was caught in the very act of adultery. 5Moses'
law says to kill her. What about it?"
6They were trying to trap him into saying
something they could use against him, but
Jesus stooped down and wrote in the dust
with his finger. 7They kept demanding an
answer, so he stood up again and said, "All
right, hurl the stones at her until she dies. But
only he who never sinned may throw the
first!"
8Then he stooped down again and wrote
some more in the dust. 9And the Jewish leaders slipped away one by one, beginning with
the eldest, until only Jesus was left in front of
the crowd with the woman.
10Then Jesus stood up again and said to her,
"Where are your accusers? Didn't even one of
them condemn you?"
11"No, sir," she said.
And Jesus said, "Neither do I. Go and sin no
more."

Jesus, the Light of the World

12Later, in one of his talks, Jesus said to the
people, "I am the Light of the world. So if you
follow me, you won't be stumbling through
the darkness, for living light will flood your
path."
13The Pharisees replied, "You are boasting—
and lying!"
14Jesus told them, "These claims are true
even though I make them concerning myself.
For I know where I came from and where I am
going, but you don't know this about me.
15You pass judgment on me without knowing

7:37-39 Jesus is the Living Water who satisfies our thirst (see 4:10). When we put our faith in him and ask for a drink, he gives us his Spirit. The Holy Spirit becomes an inexhaustible river of living water, welling up in us and flowing through us. The indwelling and eternal Holy Spirit goes with us wherever we go and can quench even our strongest spiritual thirst. Having this water "on tap" is the key to resisting the temptation to escape through alcohol, food, sex, work, codependent relationships, and other compulsions.

8:12 As the Light of the world, Jesus exposes what has been hidden and guides us down the path of life and recovery. To walk in the light is to be honest and vulnerable with others and in fellowship with God (see 1 John 1:5-7). As we express our needs and feelings, our sins and struggles, with the people we trust, light will fall on our failures and strengths. This will give us the direction we need to make significant progress in recovery. (See also 1:4-9; 3:19-21; 12:35, 46.)

the facts. I am not judging you now; 16but if I
were, it would be an absolutely correct judgment in every respect, for I have with me the
Father who sent me. 17Your laws say that if
two men agree on something that has happened, their witness is accepted as fact. 18Well,
I am one witness, and my Father who sent me
is the other."

19"Where is your father?" they asked.

Jesus answered, "You don't know who I am,
so you don't know who my Father is. If you
knew me, then you would know him too."

20Jesus made these statements while in the
section of the Temple known as the Treasury.
But he was not arrested, for his time had not
yet run out.

Jesus Warns of Coming Judgment

21Later he said to them again, "I am going
away; and you will search for me, and die in
your sins. And you cannot come where I am
going."

22The Jews asked, "Is he planning suicide?
What does he mean, 'You cannot come where
I am going'?"

23Then he said to them, "You are from below; I am from above. You are of this world; I
am not. 24That is why I said that you will die
in your sins; for unless you believe that I am
the Messiah, the Son of God, you will die in
your sins."

25"Tell us who you are," they demanded.

He replied, "I am the one I have always
claimed to be. 26I could condemn you for
much and teach you much, but I won't, for I
say only what I am told to by the one who
sent me; and he is Truth." 27But they still
didn't understand that he was talking to them
about God.

28So Jesus said, "When you have killed the
Messiah, then you will realize that I am he
and that I have not been telling you my own
ideas, but have spoken what the Father taught
me. 29And he who sent me is with me—he has
not deserted me—for I always do those things
that are pleasing to him."

True Children of God

30,31Then many of the Jewish leaders who
heard him say these things began believing
him to be the Messiah.

Jesus said to them, "You are truly my disciples if you live as I tell you to, 32and you will
know the truth, and the truth will set you
free."

33"But we are descendants of Abraham,"
they said, "and have never been slaves to any
man on earth! What do you mean, 'set free'?"

34Jesus replied, "You are slaves of sin, every
one of you. 35And slaves don't have rights, but
the Son has every right there is! 36So if the Son
sets you free, you will indeed be free—37(Yes, I
realize that you are descendants of Abraham!)
And yet some of you are trying to kill me
because my message does not find a home
within your hearts. 38I am telling you what I
saw when I was with my Father. But you are
following the advice of *your* father."

39"Our father is Abraham," they declared.

"No!" Jesus replied, "for if he were, you
would follow his good example. 40But instead
you are trying to kill me—and all because I
told you the truth I heard from God. Abraham
wouldn't do a thing like that! 41No, you are
obeying your *real* father when you act that
way."

They replied, "We were not born out of
wedlock—our true Father is God himself."

42Jesus told them, "If that were so, then you
would love me, for I have come to you from
God. I am not here on my own, but he sent
me. 43Why can't you understand what I am
saying? It is because you are prevented from
doing so! 44For you are the children of your
father the devil and you love to do the evil
things he does. He was a murderer from the
beginning and a hater of truth—there is not
an iota of truth in him. When he lies, it is
perfectly normal; for he is the father of liars.
45And so when I tell the truth, you just naturally don't believe it!

46"Which of you can truthfully accuse me
of one single sin? [No one!] And since I am
telling you the truth, why don't you believe
me? 47Anyone whose Father is God listens

8:30-36 To be "set free" is to know the truth—the truth about ourself and the truth about Jesus our Liberator. The truth is this: we are slaves to sin and powerless to manage our life effectively. With God's truth as a measuring stick for our moral inventory, we can recognize and confess our needs and struggles, our sins and addictions. As we confess these to God, to ourself, and to at least one other person, we share the truth about our life. And when we turn our broken life over to God, who alone can make us whole, we are again acknowledging the truth. These many different applications of the truth can all combine to set us free from sinful habits, chemical dependencies, and emotional bondage.

gladly to the words of God. Since you don't, it proves you aren't his children."

Jesus Angers Religious Leaders

48"You Samaritan! Foreigner! Devil!" the Jewish leaders snarled. "Didn't we say all along
you were possessed by a demon?"
49"No," Jesus said, "I have no demon in me.
For I honor my Father—and you dishonor
me. 50And though I have no wish to make
myself great, God wants this for me and
judges [those who reject me]. 51With all the
earnestness I have I tell you this—no one who
obeys me shall ever die!"
52The leaders of the Jews said, "Now we
know you are possessed by a demon. Even
Abraham and the mightiest prophets died,
and yet you say that obeying you will keep a
man from dying! 53So you are greater than our
father Abraham, who died? And greater than
the prophets, who died? Who do you think
you are?" 54Then Jesus told them this: "If I am
merely boasting about myself, it doesn't
count. But it is my Father—and you claim
him as your God—who is saying these glorious things about me. 55But you do not even
know him. I do. If I said otherwise, I would be
as great a liar as you! But it is true—I know
him and fully obey him. 56Your father Abraham rejoiced to see my day. He knew I was
coming and was glad."
57*The Jewish leaders:* "You aren't even fifty
years old—sure, you've seen Abraham!"
58*Jesus:* "The absolute truth is that I was in
existence before Abraham was ever born!"
59At that point the Jewish leaders picked up
stones to kill him. But Jesus was hidden from
them, and walked past them and left the
Temple.

CHAPTER 9

Jesus Heals a Blind Man

As he was walking along, he saw a man blind
from birth.
2"Master," his disciples asked him, "why
was this man born blind? Was it a result of his
own sins or those of his parents?"
3"Neither," Jesus answered. "But to demonstrate the power of God. 4All of us must
quickly carry out the tasks assigned us by the
one who sent me, for there is little time left
before the night falls and all work comes to an
end. 5But while I am still here in the world, I
give it my light."
6Then he spat on the ground and made
mud from the spittle and smoothed the mud
over the blind man's eyes, 7and told him, "Go

Honesty

READ JOHN 8:30-36

Living in denial is living dishonestly. How many times have we lied to ourself and others, saying, "I can stop any time I want to!" Or "I have the right to choose how I live my own life!" Or "My behavior doesn't affect anyone but me!" Ironically, as we asserted our freedom to live as we chose, we soon lost the freedom to choose anything other than our dependencies; we became enslaved to them.

Jesus said to some would-be disciples, "'You are truly my disciples if you live as I tell you to, and you will know the truth, and the truth will set you free. . . . You are slaves of sin, every one of you. And slaves don't have rights, but the Son has every right there is! So if the Son sets you free, you will indeed be free. . . . Why can't you understand what I am saying? It is because you are prevented [by the devil] from doing so! . . . He was a murderer from the beginning and a hater of truth—there is not an iota of truth in him. When he lies, it is perfectly normal; for he is the father of liars'" (John 8:31-36, 43-44).

The spiritual forces that sway our life have roots in either truth or deceit. Truth leads to freedom; deceit leads to bondage and death. Denial is a lie that keeps us in slavery. When we are slaves to our addictions, we lose the right to choose any other way of life. It is only when we break the cycle of denial, when we become brutally honest about our bondage, that there is any chance for real freedom. ***Turn to page 1165, John 14.***

and wash in the Pool of Siloam" (the word *Siloam* means "Sent"). So the man went where he was sent and washed and came back seeing!

[8]His neighbors and others who knew him as a blind beggar asked each other, "Is this the same fellow—that beggar?"

[9]Some said yes, and some said no. "It can't be the same man," they thought, "but he surely looks like him!"

And the beggar said, "I *am* the same man!"

[10]Then they asked him how in the world he could see. What had happened?

[11]And he told them, "A man they call Jesus made mud and smoothed it over my eyes and told me to go to the Pool of Siloam and wash off the mud. I did, and I can see!"

[12]"Where is he now?" they asked.

"I don't know," he replied.

Leaders Question the Blind Man

[13]Then they took the man to the Pharisees. [14]Now as it happened, this all occurred on a Sabbath. [15]Then the Pharisees asked him all about it. So he told them how Jesus had smoothed the mud over his eyes, and when it was washed away, he could see!

[16]Some of them said, "Then this fellow Jesus is not from God because he is working on the Sabbath."

Others said, "But how could an ordinary sinner do such miracles?" So there was a deep division of opinion among them.

[17]Then the Pharisees turned on the man who had been blind and demanded, "This man who opened your eyes—who do you say he is?"

"I think he must be a prophet sent from God," the man replied.

[18]The Jewish leaders wouldn't believe he had been blind, until they called in his parents [19]and asked them, "Is this your son? Was he born blind? If so, how can he see?"

[20]His parents replied, "We know this is our son and that he was born blind, [21]but we don't know what happened to make him see, or who did it. He is old enough to speak for himself. Ask him."

[22,23]They said this in fear of the Jewish leaders who had announced that anyone saying Jesus was the Messiah would be excommunicated.

[24]So for the second time they called in the man who had been blind and told him, "Give the glory to God, not to Jesus, for we know Jesus is an evil person."

[25]"I don't know whether he is good or bad," the man replied, "but I know this: *I was blind, and now I see!*"

[26]"But what did he do?" they asked. "How did he heal you?"

[27]"Look!" the man exclaimed. "I told you once; didn't you listen? Why do you want to hear it again? Do you want to become his disciples too?"

[28]Then they cursed him and said, "You are his disciple, but we are disciples of Moses. [29]We know God has spoken to Moses, but as for this fellow, we don't know anything about him."

[30]"Why, that's very strange!" the man replied. "He can heal blind men, and yet you don't know anything about him! [31]Well, God doesn't listen to evil men, but he has open ears to those who worship him and do his will. [32]Since the world began there has never been anyone who could open the eyes of someone born blind. [33]If this man were not from God, he couldn't do it."

[34]"You illegitimate bastard, you!" they shouted. "Are you trying to teach *us?*" And they threw him out.

9:1-12, 35-41 Imagine being blind from birth, not being able to see the people we love and the world around us. Then to add insult to injury, people insinuate that we are blind because of our personal sin or the sins of our parents! Jesus healed this man's blindness, but the real miracle occurred later when the man's spiritual blindness was healed. He learned to see through eyes of faith that Jesus truly was the Messiah, the Savior of the world. This kind of spiritual vision is what we need to recognize that God has the power and the desire to free us from habitual sin, chemical dependencies, and other character flaws. When we recognize Jesus as our deliverer, we have begun to gain our spiritual sight.

9:13-34 Some people are so blinded by their legalistic attitudes that they cannot see a wonderful miracle of healing taking place right in front of them. This was true of the Pharisees. They were more concerned about the letter of the law and the threat Jesus posed to their authority than the amazing healing that had taken place. Even though they were exposed to the power of God, they chose to remain blind to the truth. Those who are teachable and humble will discover that God can heal even the most terrible afflictions. It is often the people we think least likely to make progress in recovery who experience healing and deliverance; they are the ones humble enough to ask God for help.

35When Jesus heard what had happened, he
found the man and said, "Do you believe in
the Messiah?"
36The man answered, "Who is he, sir, for I
want to."
37"You have seen him," Jesus said, "and he
is speaking to you!"
38"Yes, Lord," the man said, "I believe!" And
he worshiped Jesus.
39Then Jesus told him, "I have come into
the world to give sight to those who are spiritually blind and to show those who think
they see that they are blind."
40The Pharisees who were standing there
asked, "Are you saying we are blind?"
41"If you were blind, you wouldn't be
guilty," Jesus replied. "But your guilt remains
because you claim to know what you are
doing.

CHAPTER 10

Jesus, the Good Shepherd

"Anyone refusing to walk through the gate
into a sheepfold, who sneaks over the wall,
must surely be a thief! 2For a shepherd comes
through the gate. 3The gatekeeper opens the
gate for him, and the sheep hear his voice and
come to him; and he calls his own sheep by
name and leads them out. 4He walks ahead of
them; and they follow him, for they recognize
his voice. 5They won't follow a stranger but
will run from him, for they don't recognize
his voice."
6Those who heard Jesus use this illustration
didn't understand what he meant, 7so he explained it to them.
"I am the Gate for the sheep," he said. 8"All
others who came before me were thieves and
robbers. But the true sheep did not listen to
them. 9Yes, I am the Gate. Those who come in
by way of the Gate will be saved and will go
in and out and find green pastures. 10The
thief's purpose is to steal, kill and destroy. My
purpose is to give life in all its fullness.
11"I am the Good Shepherd. The Good
Shepherd lays down his life for the sheep. 12A
hired man will run when he sees a wolf coming and will leave the sheep, for they aren't
his and he isn't their shepherd. And so the
wolf leaps on them and scatters the flock.
13The hired man runs because he is hired and
has no real concern for the sheep.
14"I am the Good Shepherd and know my
own sheep, and they know me, 15just as my
Father knows me and I know the Father; and
I lay down my life for the sheep. 16I have other
sheep, too, in another fold. I must bring them
also, and they will heed my voice; and there
will be one flock with one Shepherd.
17"The Father loves me because I lay down
my life that I may have it back again. 18No one
can kill me without my consent—I lay down
my life voluntarily. For I have the right and
power to lay it down when I want to and also
the right and power to take it again. For the
Father has given me this right."
19When he said these things, the Jewish
leaders were again divided in their opinions
about him. 20Some of them said, "He has a
demon or else is crazy. Why listen to a man
like that?"
21Others said, "This doesn't sound to us like
a man possessed by a demon! Can a demon
open the eyes of blind men?"

Leaders Try to Stone Jesus

22,23It was winter, and Jesus was in Jerusalem at
the time of the Dedication Celebration. He
was at the Temple, walking through the section known as Solomon's Hall. 24The Jewish
leaders surrounded him and asked, "How
long are you going to keep us in suspense? If
you are the Messiah, tell us plainly."
25"I have already told you, and you don't
believe me," Jesus replied. "The proof is in the
miracles I do in the name of my Father. 26But
you don't believe me because you are not part
of my flock. 27My sheep recognize my voice,
and I know them, and they follow me. 28I give
them eternal life and they shall never perish.

10:1-5 The shepherd knows each of his sheep by name, and they know and respond only to his voice. In like manner, Jesus knows our personality, needs, feelings, and desires. He even knows our faults and our sins, yet he still loves us! He calls out to us and leads us in the way that is best for us. To be set free from the pain of our past, we need to respond to the guiding voice of our Shepherd, who knows us fully and loves us completely.

10:7-18 At night, shepherds in Bible times led their flocks to lie down in a natural sheep pen (an area boxed in by brush or rock). The shepherd slept in the opening and literally became the gate to the sheepfold. With his own body he would protect the sheep from wild animals and robbers. This is what Jesus, the Gate and the Good Shepherd, does for us. By sacrificing his life he has provided the means for our protection from temptation and addiction. Not that we won't ever fail again, but that in Christ we can find security and serenity. God is able to use our sins and failures to bring about our ultimate good if we are willing to trust him and obey his plan for our life.

No one shall snatch them away from me 29for my Father has given them to me, and he is more powerful than anyone else, so no one can kidnap them from me. 30I and the Father are one."

31Then again the Jewish leaders picked up stones to kill him.

32Jesus said, "At God's direction I have done many a miracle to help the people. For which one are you killing me?"

33They replied, "Not for any good work, but for blasphemy; you, a mere man, have declared yourself to be God."

34-36"In your own Law it says that men are gods!" he replied. "So if the Scripture, which cannot be untrue, speaks of those as gods to whom the message of God came, do you call it blasphemy when the one sanctified and sent into the world by the Father says, 'I am the Son of God'? 37Don't believe me unless I do miracles of God. 38But if I do, believe them even if you don't believe me. Then you will become convinced that the Father is in me, and I in the Father."

39Once again they started to arrest him. But he walked away and left them, 40and went beyond the Jordan River to stay near the place where John was first baptizing. 41And many followed him.

"John didn't do miracles," they remarked to one another, "but all his predictions concerning this man have come true." 42And many came to the decision that he was the Messiah.

CHAPTER 11

Lazarus Becomes Sick and Dies

Do you remember Mary, who poured the costly perfume on Jesus' feet and wiped them with her hair? Well, her brother Lazarus, who lived in Bethany with Mary and her sister Martha, was sick. 3So the two sisters sent a message to Jesus telling him, "Sir, your good friend is very, very sick."

4But when Jesus heard about it he said, "The purpose of his illness is not death, but for the glory of God. I, the Son of God, will receive glory from this situation."

5Although Jesus was very fond of Martha, Mary, and Lazarus, 6he stayed where he was for the next two days and made no move to go to them. 7Finally, after the two days, he said to his disciples, "Let's go to Judea."

8But his disciples objected. "Master," they said, "only a few days ago the Jewish leaders in Judea were trying to kill you. Are you going there again?"

9Jesus replied, "There are twelve hours of daylight every day, and during every hour of it a man can walk safely and not stumble. 10Only at night is there danger of a wrong step, because of the dark." 11Then he said, "Our friend Lazarus has gone to sleep, but now I will go and waken him!"

12,13The disciples, thinking Jesus meant Lazarus was having a good night's rest, said, "That means he is getting better!" But Jesus meant Lazarus had died.

14Then he told them plainly, "Lazarus is dead. 15And for your sake, I am glad I wasn't there, for this will give you another opportunity to believe in me. Come, let's go to him."

16Thomas, nicknamed "The Twin," said to his fellow disciples, "Let's go too—and die with him."

10:27-29 When we entrust our life to Jesus, we can feel safe and secure. No one can take us away from him and his care, not even the devil! Such security is sometimes hard for us to grasp emotionally, especially if we have been a victim of abuse. If we have suffered abuse in the past, we may have been so emotionally damaged that life can seem very unsafe. Unsure of whom we can trust and not wanting to be hurt again, we keep everyone at a distance—even God. Recovery from abuse can occur only in a safe relationship in which divine love and protection are expressed. This is the kind of relationship that God offers to us.

10:30-38 For Jesus to say that he and the Father were one was a clear claim to divinity (see 1:1-2; 8:58). Jesus was God in human flesh (1:14). He was one with his Father in essence, in purpose, in words, and in thoughts. All of Jesus' miracles attest to his divine authority (10:37-38); so do the Scriptures (5:39). Only such a God-man could perfectly understand our all-too-human weaknesses, yet still command our complete trust. Only the divine Miracle Worker, Jesus, can effect the everyday and everlasting recovery that we need.

11:3-4 When faced with a critical illness or a hopeless situation, we have options. We can whine and look around for some pity; we can complain and blame God; or we can see the crisis as an opportunity to make a request of God. Mary and Martha asked Jesus to help them with their great loss. Then they gave him the glory for the amazing miracle he did—raising their brother, Lazarus, from the dead. If we can learn to humbly ask God for help, we will make progress in our recovery. If he is able to raise someone from the dead, he is more than able to help us overcome our dependencies and character flaws.

Jesus Comforts Mary and Martha

17 When they arrived at Bethany, they were told that Lazarus had already been in his tomb for four days. 18 Bethany was only a couple of miles down the road from Jerusalem, 19 and many of the Jewish leaders had come to pay their respects and to console Martha and Mary on their loss. 20 When Martha got word that Jesus was coming, she went to meet him. But Mary stayed at home.

21 Martha said to Jesus, "Sir, if you had been here, my brother wouldn't have died. 22 And even now it's not too late, for I know that God will bring my brother back to life again, if you will only ask him to."

23 Jesus told her, "Your brother will come back to life again."

24 "Yes," Martha said, "when everyone else does, on Resurrection Day."

25 Jesus told her, "I am the one who raises the dead and gives them life again. Anyone who believes in me, even though he dies like anyone else, shall live again. 26 He is given eternal life for believing in me and shall never perish. Do you believe this, Martha?"

27 "Yes, Master," she told him. "I believe you are the Messiah, the Son of God, the one we have so long awaited."

28 Then she left him and returned to Mary and, calling her aside from the mourners, told her, "He is here and wants to see you." 29 So Mary went to him at once.

30 Now Jesus had stayed outside the village, at the place where Martha met him. 31 When the Jewish leaders who were at the house trying to console Mary saw her leave so hastily, they assumed she was going to Lazarus' tomb to weep; so they followed her.

32 When Mary arrived where Jesus was, she fell down at his feet, saying, "Sir, if you had been here, my brother would still be alive."

33 When Jesus saw her weeping and the Jewish leaders wailing with her, he was moved with indignation and deeply troubled. 34 "Where is he buried?" he asked them.

They told him, "Come and see." 35 Tears came to Jesus' eyes.

36 "They were close friends," the Jewish leaders said. "See how much he loved him."

Jesus Resurrects Lazarus

37,38 But some said, "This fellow healed a blind man—why couldn't he keep Lazarus from dying?"

And again Jesus was moved with deep anger. Then they came to the tomb. It was a cave with a heavy stone rolled across its door.

39 "Roll the stone aside," Jesus told them.

But Martha, the dead man's sister, said, "By now the smell will be terrible, for he has been dead four days."

40 "But didn't I tell you that you will see a wonderful miracle from God if you believe?" Jesus asked her.

41 So they rolled the stone aside. Then Jesus looked up to heaven and said, "Father, thank you for hearing me. 42 (You always hear me, of course, but I said it because of all these people standing here, so that they will believe you sent me.)" 43 Then he shouted, "Lazarus, come out!"

44 And Lazarus came—bound up in the gravecloth, his face muffled in a head swath. Jesus told them, "Unwrap him and let him go!"

Leaders Plot to Kill Jesus

45 And so at last many of the Jewish leaders who were with Mary and saw it happen, finally believed on him. 46 But some went away to the Pharisees and reported it to them.

47 Then the chief priests and Pharisees convened a council to discuss the situation.

"What are we going to do?" they asked each other. "For this man certainly does miracles. 48 If we let him alone the whole nation will follow him—and then the Roman army will come and kill us and take over the Jewish government."

49 And one of them, Caiaphas, who was High Priest that year, said, "You stupid idiots— 50 let this one man die for the people—why should the whole nation perish?"

51 This prophecy that Jesus should die for the entire nation came from Caiaphas in his position as High Priest—he didn't think of it by himself, but was inspired to say it. 52 It was a prediction that Jesus' death would not be for Israel only, but for all the children of God scattered around the world. 53 So from that

11:37-44 Imagine being there when Jesus raised Lazarus from the dead. The man had been dead for four days, and his body had begun to stink. Then, suddenly, he responded to Jesus' voice and came walking out of the grave wrapped up like a mummy! Lazarus was free to leave the tomb and get on with the rest of his life, but his gravecloth had to go. The one who has power over the grave has power to bring new life to us, too (11:25-27). Jesus Christ has set us free from the bondage of sin and death, but our bandages—destructive habits and dependencies—have got to go!

time on the Jewish leaders began plotting Jesus' death.
[54]Jesus now stopped his public ministry and left Jerusalem; he went to the edge of the desert, to the village of Ephraim, and stayed there with his disciples.
[55]The Passover, a Jewish holy day, was near, and many country people arrived in Jerusalem several days early so that they could go through the cleansing ceremony before the
Passover began. [56]They wanted to see Jesus, and as they gossiped in the Temple, they asked each other, "What do you think? Will
he come for the Passover?" [57]Meanwhile the chief priests and Pharisees had publicly announced that anyone seeing Jesus must report him immediately so that they could arrest him.

CHAPTER 12

Mary Anoints Jesus' Feet

Six days before the Passover ceremonies began, Jesus arrived in Bethany where Lazarus
was—the man he had brought back to life. [2]A
banquet was prepared in Jesus' honor. Martha served, and Lazarus sat at the table with him.
[3]Then Mary took a jar of costly perfume made from essence of nard, and anointed Jesus' feet with it and wiped them with her hair. And the house was filled with fragrance.
[4]But Judas Iscariot, one of his disciples—the
one who would betray him—said, [5]"That perfume was worth a fortune. It should have been sold and the money given to the poor."
[6]Not that he cared for the poor, but he was in charge of the disciples' funds and often dipped into them for his own use!
[7]Jesus replied, "Let her alone. She did it in
preparation for my burial. [8]You can always help the poor, but I won't be with you very long."
[9]When the ordinary people of Jerusalem heard of his arrival, they flocked to see him and also to see Lazarus—the man who had
come back to life again. [10]Then the chief
priests decided to kill Lazarus too, [11]for it was
because of him that many of the Jewish leaders had deserted and believed in Jesus as their Messiah.

Jesus Rides into Jerusalem

[12]The next day, the news that Jesus was on the way to Jerusalem swept through the city, and
a huge crowd of Passover visitors [13]took palm
branches and went down the road to meet him, shouting, "The Savior! God bless the King of Israel! Hail to God's Ambassador!"
[14]Jesus rode along on a young donkey, ful-
filling the prophecy that said: [15]"Don't be
afraid of your King, people of Israel, for he will come to you meekly, sitting on a donkey's colt!"
[16](His disciples didn't realize at the time that this was a fulfillment of prophecy; but after Jesus returned to his glory in heaven, then they noticed how many prophecies of Scripture had come true before their eyes.)
[17]And those in the crowd who had seen Jesus call Lazarus back to life were telling all
about it. [18]That was the main reason why so

12:1-8 Mary's faith in Jesus is a testimony to us all. Scripture records three times in which she knelt in humble faith at Jesus' feet: she sat at Jesus' feet listening to his every word (Luke 10:39); she threw herself at his feet crying and seeking comfort (John 11:32); and here she knelt to clean and anoint his feet with expensive perfume. Jesus was first in her heart, and she surrendered herself to him. The decision to surrender all we are and have to God, as we understand him, is a crucial step in the recovery process. When we do this, God is able and willing to help us with the problems we face.

12:12-19 Jesus was hailed by the crowds as the promised Messiah, but his days of popularity would be few. He had just raised Lazarus from the dead in front of many witnesses, and the people were hailing Jesus as their Messiah. In a few days, however, they would stand back and do nothing as the Jewish leaders and Roman governors crowned Jesus with thorns and executed him as a pretentious "King of the Jews" (18:39–19:21). Our recovery process can be like that—full of heated curiosity one week and hollow commitment the next. If we hope to benefit from our program, our commitment to recovery must be wholehearted. A halfhearted recovery is likely to leave us even worse off than we were before we started.

12:23-25 Instead of giving a king's acceptance speech, Jesus explained why he would have to die. He said, in effect: "I must die so that I can bring new life to you. If you want this new life, then turn away from your current way of living!" This message can be hard for us to accept, too. But in order to move through recovery—from addiction to freedom, brokenness to healing, guilt to forgiveness, or isolation to intimacy—we must accept it. No longer can we embrace a life of escapism and denial. From now on, we must honestly embrace the painful realities in our life and patiently allow God's love to make us whole.

JUDAS ISCARIOT

In the life of Judas we find a terrible tragedy—the tragedy of having been so close to Jesus yet never really knowing him. For Judas the bottom line was profit. He was always looking for a way to gain something for himself. In following Jesus, Judas thought he was on a sure road to political and financial success. Indeed, Judas was excited about the role that he would have in the kingdom that Jesus would set up.

When faced with Jesus' talk of death and sacrifice, Judas, as well as the other disciples, couldn't see how that could be part of God's plan. In his disappointment, Judas failed to perceive that Jesus would do much more than simply challenge the political system in one corner of the world, disposing of the hated Roman oppressors. Instead, by his sacrificial death, he would be striking a blow for true freedom—freedom from spiritual oppression; freedom from the darkness of sin.

Judas betrayed Jesus with a kiss, turning a sign of affection and respect into a token of betrayal. Judas did feel great remorse for his actions, but his feelings of guilt never led to true repentance. In contrast to Peter, who also betrayed Jesus, Judas destroyed himself instead of turning to the mercy and forgiveness of God. For those of us in recovery, it is vital to remember that Jesus waits for us with open arms, wanting to give us the gifts of mercy and forgiveness. We can run to him in times of need because he does not condemn us—he longs to change us and heal the pain and guilt in our life.

The story of Judas Iscariot is found in the Gospels; see especially Luke 22:3-6 and John 12:4-6. He is also mentioned in Acts 1:16-19.

STRENGTHS AND ACCOMPLISHMENTS:
- He was the only non-Galilean disciple.
- He was trusted enough to be made treasurer of the group.
- He recognized how wrong his betrayal of Jesus was.

WEAKNESSES AND MISTAKES:
- Judas valued material wealth over spiritual wealth.
- He was more interested in what he could get from Jesus than in who Jesus was.

LESSONS FROM HIS LIFE:
- Spiritual wealth is more valuable than material wealth.
- God always offers us what is best for us, not always what we want.
- It is easy to underestimate the value of spiritual growth when we are preoccupied with material gain.
- We cannot stop at admitting our sin; we must also turn to God for healing and forgiveness.

KEY VERSES:
"Then Satan entered into Judas Iscariot, who was one of the twelve disciples, and he went over to the chief priests . . . to discuss the best way to betray Jesus to them" (Luke 22:3-4).

---

many went out to meet him—because they
had heard about this mighty miracle.
19Then the Pharisees said to each other,
"We've lost. Look—the whole world has gone
after him!"

Jesus Speaks of His Death

20Some Greeks who had come to Jerusalem to
attend the Passover 21paid a visit to Philip,
who was from Bethsaida, and said, "Sir, we
want to meet Jesus." 22Philip told Andrew
about it, and they went together to ask Jesus.
23,24Jesus replied that the time had come for
him to return to his glory in heaven, and that
"I must fall and die like a kernel of wheat that
falls into the furrows of the earth. Unless I die
I will be alone—a single seed. But my death
will produce many new wheat kernels—a
plentiful harvest of new lives. 25If you love
your life down here—you will lose it. If you
despise your life down here—you will exchange it for eternal glory.
26"If these Greeks want to be my disciples,
tell them to come and follow me, for my
servants must be where I am. And if they
follow me, the Father will honor them. 27Now
my soul is deeply troubled. Shall I pray,
'Father, save me from what lies ahead'? But
that is the very reason why I came! 28Father,
bring glory and honor to your name."

Then a voice spoke from heaven saying, "I
have already done this, and I will do it again."
29When the crowd heard the voice, some of
them thought it was thunder, while others
declared an angel had spoken to him.
30Then Jesus told them, "The voice was for
your benefit, not mine. 31The time of judgment for the world has come—and the time
when Satan, the prince of this world, shall be
cast out. 32And when I am lifted up [on the

cross], I will draw everyone to me." 33He said this to indicate how he was going to die.

34"Die?" asked the crowd. "We understood that the Messiah would live forever and never die. Why are you saying he will die? What Messiah are you talking about?"

35Jesus replied, "My light will shine out for you just a little while longer. Walk in it while you can, and go where you want to go before the darkness falls, for then it will be too late for you to find your way. 36Make use of the Light while there is still time; then you will become light bearers."

After saying these things, Jesus went away and was hidden from them.

Many Refuse to Believe Jesus

37But despite all the miracles he had done, most of the people would not believe he was the Messiah. 38This is exactly what Isaiah the prophet had predicted: "Lord, who will believe us? Who will accept God's mighty miracles as proof?" 39But they couldn't believe, for as Isaiah also said: 40"God has blinded their eyes and hardened their hearts so that they can neither see nor understand nor turn to me to heal them." 41Isaiah was referring to Jesus when he made this prediction, for he had seen a vision of the Messiah's glory.

42However, even many of the Jewish leaders believed him to be the Messiah but wouldn't admit it to anyone because of their fear that the Pharisees would excommunicate them from the synagogue; 43for they loved the praise of men more than the praise of God.

Jesus Summarizes His Message

44Jesus shouted to the crowds, "If you trust me, you are really trusting God. 45For when you see me, you are seeing the one who sent me. 46I have come as a Light to shine in this dark world, so that all who put their trust in me will no longer wander in the darkness. 47If anyone hears me and doesn't obey me, I am not his judge—for I have come to save the world and not to judge it. 48But all who reject me and my message will be judged at the Day of Judgment by the truths I have spoken. 49For these are not my own ideas, but I have told you what the Father said to tell you. 50And I know his instructions lead to eternal life; so whatever he tells me to say, I say!"

CHAPTER 13

Jesus Washes the Disciples' Feet

Jesus knew on the evening of Passover Day that it would be his last night on earth before returning to his Father. During supper the devil had already suggested to Judas Iscariot, Simon's son, that this was the night to carry out his plan to betray Jesus. Jesus knew that the Father had given him everything and that he had come from God and would return to God. And how he loved his disciples! 4So he got up from the supper table, took off his robe, wrapped a towel around his loins, 5poured water into a basin, and began to wash the disciples' feet and to wipe them with the towel he had around him.

6When he came to Simon Peter, Peter said to him, "Master, you shouldn't be washing our feet like this!"

7Jesus replied, "You don't understand now why I am doing it; some day you will."

8"No," Peter protested, "you shall never wash my feet!"

"But if I don't, you can't be my partner," Jesus replied.

9Simon Peter exclaimed, "Then wash my hands and head as well—not just my feet!"

10Jesus replied, "One who has bathed all

12:42-43 Many of the Jewish leaders believed in Jesus, but their faith was rendered ineffective by their fear and isolation. They were more concerned with what their peers thought of them than they were with what God thought. This kind of faith will never take us very far in recovery. If we hope to make real progress in recovery, we need to share our belief in God with at least one other person. When we tell others what we believe and what direction our life is heading, we are inviting them to hold us accountable. Accountability for our intentions, attitudes, and actions is a necessary part of recovery. Making others a significant part of our life is crucial to our recovery and growth. Remaining isolated from others will only lead to defeat.

13:1-7 The Son of God came not as a proud master who demanded service from others, but as a humble servant who delighted in helping others. In stooping down to do the most menial of jobs (washing his disciples' feet), Jesus showed them that true leaders serve their followers. To follow Jesus' example and serve others, we start by allowing him to serve us. As we experience his cleansing power in our life, we can help others by serving them—sharing our story, listening to their confessions, feeling their pain, and standing by them in the tough times. We will find that as we support others in their recovery, our own recovery also will be strengthened.

over needs only to have his feet washed to be entirely clean. Now you are clean—but that isn't true of everyone here." 11For Jesus knew who would betray him. That is what he meant when he said, "Not all of you are clean."

12After washing their feet he put on his robe again and sat down and asked, "Do you understand what I was doing? 13You call me 'Master' and 'Lord,' and you do well to say it, for it is true. 14And since I, the Lord and Teacher, have washed your feet, you ought to wash each other's feet. 15I have given you an example to follow: do as I have done to you. 16How true it is that a servant is not greater than his master. Nor is the messenger more important than the one who sends him. 17You know these things—now do them! That is the path of blessing.

18"I am not saying these things to all of you; I know so well each one of you I chose. The Scripture declares, 'One who eats supper with me will betray me,' and this will soon come true. 19I tell you this now so that when it happens, you will believe on me.

20"Truly, anyone welcoming my messenger is welcoming me. And to welcome me is to welcome the Father who sent me."

The Last Supper

21Now Jesus was in great anguish of spirit and exclaimed, "Yes, it is true—one of you will betray me." 22The disciples looked at each other, wondering whom he could mean. 23Since I was sitting next to Jesus at the table, being his closest friend, 24Simon Peter motioned to me to ask him who it was who would do this terrible deed.

25So I turned and asked him, "Lord, who is it?"

26He told me, "It is the one I honor by giving the bread dipped in the sauce."

And when he had dipped it, he gave it to Judas, son of Simon Iscariot.

27As soon as Judas had eaten it, Satan entered into him. Then Jesus told him, "Hurry—do it now."

28None of the others at the table knew what Jesus meant. 29Some thought that since Judas was their treasurer, Jesus was telling him to go and pay for the food or to give some money to the poor. 30Judas left at once, going out into the night.

Jesus Predicts Peter's Denial

31As soon as Judas left the room, Jesus said, "My time has come; the glory of God will soon surround me—and God shall receive great praise because of all that happens to me. 32And God shall give me his own glory, and this so very soon. 33Dear, dear children, how brief are these moments before I must go away and leave you! Then, though you search for me, you cannot come to me—just as I told the Jewish leaders.

34"And so I am giving a new commandment to you now—love each other just as much as I love you. 35Your strong love for each other will prove to the world that you are my disciples."

36Simon Peter said, "Master, where are you going?"

And Jesus replied, "You can't go with me now; but you will follow me later."

37"But why can't I come now?" he asked, "for I am ready to die for you."

38Jesus answered, "Die for me? No—three times before the cock crows tomorrow morning, you will deny that you even know me!

CHAPTER 14

Jesus, the Way, Truth, and Life

"Let not your heart be troubled. You are trusting God, now trust in me. 2,3There are many homes up there where my Father lives, and I am going to prepare them for your coming. When everything is ready, then I will come

---

13:20 God expresses himself to us primarily through chosen messengers. In doing so, he makes all of our relationships with others sacred. We experience God's healing love for our wounds through the godly people we let into our life. This may be very difficult for us if we have been a victim of abuse. We may never want to be close to other people. But as we allow godly people into our life, we will discover that they bring the healing touch of Jesus with them. And, as we reach out to others in the name of Jesus, we in turn become his messengers. God will use us to bring his powerful deliverance into their lives.

13:34-35 Our ability to love others (and ourself) is based upon the degree to which we have received God's love (most often through other people). In this sense it is appropriate to consider our need to be loved before we think of giving love to others. Otherwise, we will be trying to give something that we don't have. If we try to do this, we will end up giving to others in hope of receiving something in return. This kind of selfish gift never feels good to us or to the person we are trying to help. When we love one another out of the overflow of God's love, then our witness and service can be effective toward recovery.

and get you, so that you can always be with
me where I am. If this weren't so, I would tell
you plainly. 4And you know where I am going
and how to get there."
5"No, we don't," Thomas said. "We haven't
any idea where you are going, so how can we
know the way?"
6Jesus told him, "I am the Way—yes, and
the Truth and the Life. No one can get to the
Father except by means of me. 7If you had
known who I am, then you would have
known who my Father is. From now on you
know him—and have seen him!"
8Philip said, "Sir, show us the Father and we
will be satisfied."
9Jesus replied, "Don't you even yet know
who I am, Philip, even after all this time I
have been with you? Anyone who has seen
me has seen the Father! So why are you asking
to see him? 10Don't you believe that I am in
the Father and the Father is in me? The words
I say are not my own but are from my Father
who lives in me. And he does his work
through me. 11Just believe it—that I am in the
Father and the Father is in me. Or else believe
it because of the mighty miracles you have
seen me do.
12,13"In solemn truth I tell you, anyone believing in me shall do the same miracles I
have done, and even greater ones, because I
am going to be with the Father. You can ask
him for *anything,* using my name, and I will
do it, for this will bring praise to the Father
because of what I, the Son, will do for you.
14Yes, ask *anything,* using my name, and I will
do it!

Jesus Promises the Holy Spirit

15,16"If you love me, obey me; and I will ask the
Father and he will give you another Comforter, and he will never leave you. 17He is the
Holy Spirit, the Spirit who leads into all truth.
The world at large cannot receive him, for it
isn't looking for him and doesn't recognize
him. But you do, for he lives with you now
and some day shall be in you. 18No, I will not
abandon you or leave you as orphans in the
storm—I will come to you. 19In just a little
while I will be gone from the world, but I will
still be present with you. For I will live again—
and you will too. 20When I come back to life
again, you will know that I am in my Father,
and you in me, and I in you. 21The one who
obeys me is the one who loves me; and because he loves me, my Father will love him;
and I will too, and I will reveal myself to him."
22Judas (not Judas Iscariot, but his other
disciple with that name) said to him, "Sir,

14:1-4 We receive lasting comfort by putting our trust in God. Sometimes God gives us immediate deliverance from a painful situation. More often than not, however, he walks with us as we struggle with problems that just won't seem to let go. Our pain may be a direct consequence of the mistakes we have made in the past; it may be the result of someone else's failure. God allows us to experience such trying circumstances to build our character and strengthen our faith. When we place our trust in Jesus, we receive his peace in this life and the promise of an eternal home with him in the next.

14:5-11 Faith in Jesus is the only way to truly know God and to receive the meaningful life that God wants for each of us. Despite living with Jesus for many months, Thomas and Philip had not yet come to know God through his Son, Jesus. Many people know all about God and Jesus Christ, but they don't know God personally. Genuine faith is personal and relational. It is based upon the truth that can be known about God through the Scriptures. God in Jesus Christ is the Way, the Truth, and the Life for anyone going step-by-step through recovery. He has the power to overcome our failures and addictions, and to give us a new life.

14:27 Many of us are dealing with stress and anxiety, grief and loss; we long for peace of mind and heart. So did the early disciples—they were about to lose their best friend and their Messiah, with whom they had planned to rule the world. Their souls were indeed troubled, like many of us recovering from the loss of a job, spouse, or child, or from chemical addictions. They were looking for something to fill the void. Yet Jesus said he was leaving them with wholesome, fulfilling peace—*shalom*—unlike worldly peace, which is merely an absence of conflict. God can bring us peace even in the midst of our troubles (see 16:33).

15:1-8 God desires that our life be like the fruitful branches of a grapevine. The only way to be fruitful is to remain connected to Jesus, the Vine, and to allow God, the Gardener, to prune our life in ways that will stimulate growth and fruitfulness. It is God's cultivating, weeding, and pruning in our life that brings forth spiritual fruit, character development, and progress in recovery. Just as sustenance for the desired fruit comes through the vine, so fullness of life comes through faith in Jesus Christ. We need to stay close to God in Jesus Christ, the source of power and practical help for our recovery.

why are you going to reveal yourself only to
us disciples and not to the world at large?"
23Jesus replied, "Because I will only reveal
myself to those who love me and obey me.
The Father will love them too, and we will
come to them and live with them. 24Anyone
who doesn't obey me doesn't love me. And
remember, I am not making up this answer to
your question! It is the answer given by the
Father who sent me.
25"I am telling you these things now while
I am still with you. 26But when the Father
sends the Comforter instead of me—and by
the Comforter I mean the Holy Spirit—he will
teach you much, as well as remind you of
everything I myself have told you.
27"I am leaving you with a gift—peace of
mind and heart! And the peace I give isn't
fragile like the peace the world gives. So don't
be troubled or afraid. 28Remember what I told
you—I am going away, but I will come back
to you again. If you really love me, you will be
very happy for me, for now I can go to the
Father, who is greater than I am. 29I have told
you these things before they happen so that
when they do, you will believe [in me].
30"I don't have much more time to talk to
you, for the evil prince of this world approaches. He has no power over me, 31but I
will freely do what the Father requires of me
so that the world will know that I love the
Father. Come, let's be going.

CHAPTER 15

Jesus, the Vine

"I am the true Vine, and my Father is the
Gardener. 2He lops off every branch that
doesn't produce. And he prunes those
branches that bear fruit for even larger crops.
3He has already tended you by pruning you
back for greater strength and usefulness by
means of the commands I gave you. 4Take
care to live in me, and let me live in you. For
a branch can't produce fruit when severed
from the vine. Nor can you be fruitful apart
from me.
5"Yes, I am the Vine; you are the branches.
Whoever lives in me and I in him shall produce a large crop of fruit. For apart from me
you can't do a thing. 6If anyone separates
from me, he is thrown away like a useless
branch, withers, and is gathered into a pile
with all the others and burned. 7But if you
stay in me and obey my commands, you may
ask any request you like, and it will be
granted! 8My true disciples produce bountiful
harvests. This brings great glory to my Father.

Love

READ JOHN 14:15-26

Real love brings security into our life. For many of us, feelings of insecurity contribute to the power of our dependencies. Believing that love can bring lasting security may be hard for those of us who have been abandoned. Maybe someone we loved betrayed our trust. Perhaps someone turned away from us when we betrayed theirs. It could be that someone we needed died, leaving us permanently.

Jesus promised, "I will not abandon you or leave you as orphans in the storm—I will come to you" (John 14:18). We may ask, "How can I trust in God's love when it feels like all I've ever known is love that disappoints?" Here's the difference: Jesus is the only one who entered our life through the "one way" door of death. "God showed how much he loved us by sending his only Son into this wicked world to bring to us eternal life through his death. In this act we see what real love is: it is not our love for God but his love for us when he sent his Son to satisfy God's anger against our sins" (1 John 4:9-10). The psalmist wrote, "For [God] knows we are but dust and that our days are few and brief. . . . But the loving-kindness of the Lord is from everlasting to everlasting to those who reverence him" (Psalm 103:14-18).

God's love is unconditional and always waiting for us. Turning our life over to God involves opening the door of our heart to his love. Filling up on God's love helps us to avoid relapse. It meets us at our deepest need and eases our most powerful insecurities. ***Turn to page 1175, John 21.***

9"I have loved you even as the Father has
loved me. Live within my love. 10When you
obey me you are living in my love, just as I
obey my Father and live in his love. 11I have
told you this so that you will be filled with my
joy. Yes, your cup of joy will overflow! 12I
demand that you love each other as much as
I love you. 13And here is how to measure
it—the greatest love is shown when a person
lays down his life for his friends; 14and you are
my friends if you obey me. 15I no longer call
you slaves, for a master doesn't confide in his
slaves; now you are my friends, proved by the
fact that I have told you everything the Father
told me.

Jesus Warns about Persecution

16"You didn't choose me! I chose you! I appointed you to go and produce lovely fruit
always, so that no matter what you ask for
from the Father, using my name, he will give
it to you. 17I demand that you love each
other,18for you get enough hate from the
world! But then, it hated me before it hated
you. 19The world would love you if you belonged to it; but you don't—for I chose you to
come out of the world, and so it hates you.
20Do you remember what I told you? 'A slave
isn't greater than his master!' So since they
persecuted me, naturally they will persecute
you. And if they had listened to me, they
would listen to you! 21The people of the world
will persecute you because you belong to me,
for they don't know God who sent me.

22"They would not be guilty if I had not
come and spoken to them. But now they have
no excuse for their sin. 23Anyone hating me is
also hating my Father. 24If I hadn't done such
mighty miracles among them they would not
be counted guilty. But as it is, they saw these
miracles and yet they hated both of us—me
and my Father. 25This has fulfilled what the
prophets said concerning the Messiah, 'They
hated me without reason.'

26"But I will send you the Comforter—the
Holy Spirit, the source of all truth. He will
come to you from the Father and will tell you
all about me. 27And you also must tell everyone about me because you have been with me
from the beginning.

CHAPTER 16

"I have told you these things so that you
won't be staggered [by all that lies ahead.] 2For
you will be excommunicated from the synagogues, and indeed the time is coming when
those who kill you will think they are doing
God a service. 3This is because they have
never known the Father or me. 4Yes, I'm telling you these things now so that when they
happen you will remember I warned you. I
didn't tell you earlier because I was going to
be with you for a while longer.

Teachings about the Holy Spirit

5"But now I am going away to the one who
sent me; and none of you seems interested in
the purpose of my going; none wonders why.
6Instead you are only filled with sorrow. 7But
the fact of the matter is that it is best for you
that I go away, for if I don't, the Comforter
won't come. If I do, he will—for I will send
him to you.

8"And when he has come he will convince
the world of its sin, and of the availability of
God's goodness, and of deliverance from

15:15 Jesus demonstrated God's desire to be our friend, not our taskmaster. Many of us in recovery have never experienced God on such friendly, intimate terms. Rare in our experience is the authority figure who, rather than lording his power over us, actually seeks to confide in us and befriend us. And so we find it hard to imagine God to be any different. Jesus urges us to think again and trust in him. By becoming our friend through Jesus, God empowers us and enables us to become accountable, responsible, and trustworthy.

16:20-22 Jesus' followers certainly grieved the imminent loss of their friend and Master. Losing someone we love is a painful and universal experience. We grieve the loss of our childhood, our innocence, our spouse, or our only means of livelihood. We even have to grieve the loss of an addiction that we have used to numb our inner pain. Abuse, abandonment, or neglect by someone we trust is painful—indeed, it can cause enough pain for a lifetime. But we can never suffer so much pain that Jesus cannot heal it. When we find the courage to honestly face and grieve over our losses and injuries, we can discover what lies on the other side of grief—freedom and joy!

16:33 In this world, especially in recovery, we encounter "many trials and sorrows." Some of these difficulties are inevitable and beyond our control. These can be endured with God's help. On the other hand, some of our suffering is self-inflicted and can be avoided. In such situations, God still offers us peace as we muster the courage to make needed changes in our life. God's forgiveness and loving acceptance can give us peace as we face our trials and sorrows, even when the pain we face is ultimately our own fault. He has the power to lead us down the path of recovery; he has already overcome all the obstacles that stand in our way!

judgment. 9The world's sin is unbelief in me;
10there is righteousness available because I go
to the Father and you shall see me no more;
11there is deliverance from judgment because
the prince of this world has already been
judged.
12"Oh, there is so much more I want to tell
you, but you can't understand it now. 13When
the Holy Spirit, who is truth, comes, he shall
guide you into all truth, for he will not be
presenting his own ideas, but will be passing
on to you what he has heard. He will tell you
about the future. 14He shall praise me and
bring me great honor by showing you my
glory. 15All the Father's glory is mine; this is
what I mean when I say that he will show you
my glory.
16"In just a little while I will be gone, and
you will see me no more; but just a little while
after that, and you will see me again!"

Teachings on Prayer

17,18"Whatever is he saying?" some of his disciples asked. "What is this about 'going to the
Father'? We don't know what he means."
19Jesus realized they wanted to ask him so
he said, "Are you asking yourselves what I
mean? 20The world will greatly rejoice over
what is going to happen to me, and you will
weep. But your weeping shall suddenly be
turned to wonderful joy [when you see me
again]. 21It will be the same joy as that of a
woman in labor when her child is born—her
anguish gives place to rapturous joy and the
pain is forgotten. 22You have sorrow now, but
I will see you again and then you will rejoice;
and no one can rob you of that joy. 23At that
time you won't need to ask me for anything,
for you can go directly to the Father and ask
him, and he will give you what you ask for
because you use my name. 24You haven't tried
this before, [but begin now]. Ask, using my
name, and you will receive, and your cup of
joy will overflow.
25"I have spoken of these matters very
guardedly, but the time will come when this
will not be necessary and I will tell you plainly
all about the Father. 26Then you will present
your petitions over my signature! And I won't
need to ask the Father to grant you these
requests, 27for the Father himself loves you
dearly because you love me and believe that I
came from the Father. 28Yes, I came from the
Father into the world and will leave the world
and return to the Father."
29"At last you are speaking plainly," his disciples said, "and not in riddles. 30Now we

Sharing Together

BIBLE READING: John 15:5-15

Having had a spiritual awakening as the result of these steps, we tried to carry this message to others and to practice these principles in all our affairs.

Since we have worked through the Twelve Steps, we are in a special position to carry the message to others. We can recognize the warning signs of addictive/compulsive tendencies in those around us, as well as in ourself. When touching on such deep and sensitive issues, it is important to speak in the language of love, not condemnation.

The Bible tells us that if someone "is overcome by some sin, you who are godly should gently and humbly help him back onto the right path, remembering that next time it might be one of you who is in the wrong. Share each other's troubles and problems, and so obey our Lord's command" (Galatians 6:1-2). The command was the one Jesus taught his disciples, "And so I am giving a new commandment to you now—love each other just as much as I love you" (John 13:34). "I demand that you love each other as much as I love you. And here is how to measure it—the greatest love is shown when a person lays down his life for his friends" (15:12-13).

We are not the Savior, but we can love others as he has loved us. Love goes beyond mere words. Sometimes it is spoken in silence, when we don't condemn someone who comes to us looking for help. Love doesn't just tell them what the problem is. It helps carry the weight of their burdens. We can be part of a support network to help carry our friends until they are able to take steps toward recovery on their own initiative. *Turn to page 1191, Acts 8.*

understand that you know everything and don't need anyone to tell you anything. From this we believe that you came from God."

31"Do you finally believe this?" Jesus asked. 32"But the time is coming—in fact, it is here—when you will be scattered, each one returning to his own home, leaving me alone. Yet I will not be alone, for the Father is with me. 33I have told you all this so that you will have peace of heart and mind. Here on earth you will have many trials and sorrows; but cheer up, for I have overcome the world."

CHAPTER 17

Jesus Prays for Himself

When Jesus had finished saying all these things he looked up to heaven and said, "Father, the time has come. Reveal the glory of your Son so that he can give the glory back to you. 2For you have given him authority over every man and woman in all the earth. He gives eternal life to each one you have given him. 3And this is the way to have eternal life—by knowing you, the only true God, and Jesus Christ, the one you sent to earth! 4I brought glory to you here on earth by doing everything you told me to. 5And now, Father, reveal my glory as I stand in your presence, the glory we shared before the world began.

Jesus Prays for His Disciples

6"I have told these men all about you. They were in the world, but then you gave them to me. Actually, they were always yours, and you gave them to me; and they have obeyed you. 7Now they know that everything I have is a gift from you, 8for I have passed on to them the commands you gave me; and they accepted them and know of a certainty that I came down to earth from you, and they believe you sent me.

9"My plea is not for the world but for those you have given me because they belong to you. 10And all of them, since they are mine, belong to you; and you have given them back to me with everything else of yours, and so *they are my glory!* 11Now I am leaving the world, and leaving them behind, and coming to you. Holy Father, keep them in your own care—all those you have given me—so that they will be united just as we are, with none missing. 12During my time here I have kept safe within your family all of these you gave me. I guarded them so that not one perished, except the son of hell, as the Scriptures foretold.

13"And now I am coming to you. I have told them many things while I was with them so that they would be filled with my joy. 14I have given them your commands. And the world hates them because they don't fit in with it, just as I don't. 15I'm not asking you to take them out of the world, but to keep them safe from Satan's power. 16They are not part of this world any more than I am. 17Make them pure and holy through teaching them your words of truth. 18As you sent me into the world, I am sending them into the world, 19and I consecrate myself to meet their need for growth in truth and holiness.

Jesus Prays for Future Believers

20"I am not praying for these alone but also for the future believers who will come to me because of the testimony of these. 21My prayer for all of them is that they will be of one heart and mind, just as you and I are, Father—that just as you are in me and I am in you, so they will be in us, and the world will believe you sent me.

22"I have given them the glory you gave me—the glorious unity of being one, as we are—23I in them and you in me, all being perfected into one—so that the world will know you sent me and will understand that you love them as much as you love me. 24Father, I want them with me—these you've given me—so that they can see my glory. You gave me the glory because you loved me before the world began!

25"O righteous Father, the world doesn't know you, but I do; and these disciples know you sent me. 26And I have revealed you to them and will keep on revealing you so that the mighty love you have for me may be in them, and I in them."

17:1-26 Jesus is our High Priest and intercessor: he makes God's will known to us and our heartfelt needs known to God. Through his words and deeds he reveals to us God's mercy, justice, glory, and truth, and his desire to establish a personal relationship with us. Jesus also intercedes with God the Father on our behalf, bringing our needs and requests continually before God's throne. He prays that we would know his perfect joy, be protected from all evil, grow in truth and holiness, and show love toward all people. Jesus prayed this prayer for his twelve disciples as they faced his imminent death. Yet this prayer is for all of us as we follow Jesus through the process of recovery.

CHAPTER 18

Jesus Is Arrested

After saying these things Jesus crossed the
Kidron ravine with his disciples and entered a
grove of olive trees. 2Judas, the betrayer, knew
this place, for Jesus had gone there many
times with his disciples.
3The chief priests and Pharisees had given
Judas a squad of soldiers and police to accompany him. Now with blazing torches, lanterns, and weapons they arrived at the olive
grove.
4,5Jesus fully realized all that was going to
happen to him. Stepping forward to meet
them he asked, "Whom are you looking for?"
"Jesus of Nazareth," they replied.
"I am he," Jesus said. 6And as he said it, they
all fell backwards to the ground!
7Once more he asked them, "Whom are
you searching for?"
And again they replied, "Jesus of Nazareth."
8"I told you I am he," Jesus said; "and since
I am the one you are after, let these others go."
9He did this to carry out the prophecy he had
just made, "I have not lost a single one of
those you gave me. . . . "
10Then Simon Peter drew a sword and
slashed off the right ear of Malchus, the High
Priest's servant.
11But Jesus said to Peter, "Put your sword
away. Shall I not drink from the cup the
Father has given me?"

Annas Questions Jesus

12So the Jewish police, with the soldiers and
their lieutenant, arrested Jesus and tied him.
13First they took him to Annas, the father-in-
law of Caiaphas, the High Priest that year.
14Caiaphas was the one who told the other
Jewish leaders, "Better that one should die for
all."
15Simon Peter followed along behind, as did
another of the disciples who was acquainted
with the High Priest. So that other disciple
was permitted into the courtyard along with
Jesus, 16while Peter stood outside the gate.
Then the other disciple spoke to the girl
watching at the gate, and she let Peter in.
17The girl asked Peter, "Aren't you one of Jesus'
disciples?"
"No," he said, "I am not!"
18The police and the household servants
were standing around a fire they had made,
for it was cold. And Peter stood there with
them, warming himself.
19Inside, the High Priest began asking Jesus
about his followers and what he had been
teaching them.
20Jesus replied, "What I teach is widely
known, for I have preached regularly in the
synagogue and Temple; I have been heard by
all the Jewish leaders and teach nothing in
private that I have not said in public. 21Why
are you asking me this question? Ask those
who heard me. You have some of them here.
They know what I said."
22One of the soldiers standing there struck
Jesus with his fist. "Is that the way to answer
the High Priest?" he demanded.
23"If I lied, prove it," Jesus replied. "Should
you hit a man for telling the truth?"
24Then Annas sent Jesus, bound, to Caiaphas the High Priest.

Peter Denies Knowing Jesus

25Meanwhile, as Simon Peter was standing by
the fire, he was asked again, "Aren't you one
of his disciples?"
"Of course not," he replied.
26But one of the household slaves of the
High Priest—a relative of the man whose ear
Peter had cut off—asked, "Didn't I see you out
there in the olive grove with Jesus?"
27Again Peter denied it. And immediately a
rooster crowed.

Jesus Stands before Pilate

28Jesus' trial before Caiaphas ended in the
early hours of the morning. Next he was
taken to the palace of the Roman governor.
His accusers wouldn't go in themselves for
that would "defile" them, they said, and they
wouldn't be allowed to eat the Passover lamb.
29So Pilate, the governor, went out to them
and asked, "What is your charge against this
man? What are you accusing him of doing?"

18:15-18, 25-27 The arrest, trial, and crucifixion of Jesus unfolds over several chapters. The injustice of it all makes us angry. We may find ourself pointing a blaming finger at the religious leaders who instigated Jesus' downfall. We also see Peter deny Jesus not only once, but three times—all this despite his earlier assurances of loyalty. We have often done the same thing. We have made steps of faith, only to turn around and deny Christ's lordship over a crucial area of our life. Peter meant well when he assured Jesus of his loyalty, but he still failed. Yet his relapse was not the end of the story (see 21:15-19), just as the relapses we experience don't have to be the end of our recovery. With Jesus Christ, there is always the opportunity for restoration.

30“We wouldn’t have arrested him if he weren’t a criminal!” they retorted.

31“Then take him away and judge him yourselves by your own laws,” Pilate told them.

“But we want him crucified,” they demanded, “and your approval is required.” 32This fulfilled Jesus’ prediction concerning the method of his execution.

33Then Pilate went back into the palace and called for Jesus to be brought to him. “Are you the King of the Jews?” he asked him.

34“‘King’ as *you* use the word or as the *Jews* use it?” Jesus asked.

35“Am I a Jew?” Pilate retorted. “Your own people and their chief priests brought you here. Why? What have you done?”

36Then Jesus answered, “I am not an earthly king. If I were, my followers would have fought when I was arrested by the Jewish leaders. But my Kingdom is not of the world.”

37Pilate replied, “But you are a king then?”

“Yes,” Jesus said. “I was born for that purpose. And I came to bring truth to the world. All who love the truth are my followers.”

38“What is truth?” Pilate exclaimed. Then he went out again to the people and told them, “He is not guilty of any crime. 39But you have a custom of asking me to release someone from prison each year at Passover. So if you want me to, I’ll release the ‘King of the Jews.’”

40But they screamed back. “No! Not this man, but Barabbas!” Barabbas was a robber.

CHAPTER 19

Jesus Is Mocked

Then Pilate laid open Jesus’ back with a leaded whip, 2and the soldiers made a crown of thorns and placed it on his head and robed him in royal purple. 3“Hail, ‘King of the Jews!’” they mocked, and struck him with their fists.

4Pilate went outside again and said to the Jews, “I am going to bring him out to you now, but understand clearly that I find him *not guilty.”*

5Then Jesus came out wearing the crown of thorns and the purple robe. And Pilate said, “Behold the man!”

6At sight of him the chief priests and Jewish officials began yelling, “Crucify! Crucify!”

“You crucify him,” Pilate said. “I find him *not guilty.”*

7They replied, “By our laws he ought to die because he called himself the Son of God.”

8When Pilate heard this, he was more frightened than ever. 9He took Jesus back into the palace again and asked him, “Where are you from?” but Jesus gave no answer.

10“You won’t talk to me?” Pilate demanded. “Don’t you realize that I have the power to release you or to crucify you?”

11Then Jesus said, “You would have no power at all over me unless it were given to you from above. So those who brought me to you have the greater sin.”

12Then Pilate tried to release him, but the Jewish leaders told him, “If you release this man, you are no friend of Caesar’s. Anyone who declares himself a king is a rebel against Caesar.”

13At these words Pilate brought Jesus out to them again and sat down at the judgment bench on the stone-paved platform. 14It was now about noon of the day before Passover.

And Pilate said to the Jews, “Here is your king!”

15“Away with him,” they yelled. “Away with him—crucify him!”

“What? Crucify your king?” Pilate asked.

“We have no king but Caesar,” the chief priests shouted back.

18:28-38 Many people believe that truth is relative, as did Pilate. Modern moral relativists live without absolute guidelines for right and wrong, not realizing how destructive even the most private sins can be. Since we are all tempted at times to disregard God’s guidelines for healthy living, we need to be held accountable to God’s truth. We need the help of godly people who can help us measure our attitudes and actions against the truth of God’s Word. If we try to write our own rules for life, we are headed for a painful relapse.

19:4-16 The people who were shouting “Crucify! Crucify!” (19:6, 15) had just days before hailed Jesus as their King (12:12-13). Sometimes we are tempted to do the same thing. We may have entrusted our life to God only to discover that his program for recovery wasn’t quite what we had in mind. We may have wanted a quick fix for our problems—a way out of the pain. When we realized that recovery was painful, even with God’s help, we turned against him and the help he offered. The people in Jerusalem, even Jesus’ twelve disciples, gave up hope as Jesus hung on the cross. But three days later, they discovered that even death gave way to God’s power! The path of pain and death led to the greatest of victories—the Resurrection! The same is true in the process of our recovery.

MARY MAGDALENE

The people who have been healed of the worst afflictions are often the most grateful for their new lease on life. Once enslaved by seven demons, but freed by Jesus, Mary Magdalene became a shining example of a life filled with gratitude and loyalty to Jesus.

We know few details of Mary's life. She was apparently from Magdala in Galilee and was an early follower of Jesus. Her life was dramatically changed by Jesus when he released her from demons. She traveled with Jesus and the disciples and helped meet the practical needs of the group. During Jesus' crucifixion, when many of the disciples were not to be found, she was one of the few courageous ones to stay at the foot of the cross. She was also one of the women who wanted to make sure Jesus had a proper burial.

Some have suggested that since the twelve disciples were all men, Jesus must not have considered women very important to his ministry. But the role of Mary Magdalene and the other women who followed Jesus shows that this was definitely not the case. Jesus treated women in a manner far beyond the cultural expectation of the day, respecting them fully as persons, and he considered them to be a necessary part of his ministry.

We may identify with Mary Magdalene, either as a woman or as one who has been delivered from a life of total bondage. She was an outcast in society, a woman of ill repute. But by her desire for healing and her trusting obedience of Jesus, she became a significant person in the history of our world. Her life gives us the courage to come boldly before God, knowing that his love extends to all of us, regardless of our situation. He specializes in tough cases.

STRENGTHS AND ACCOMPLISHMENTS:

- Mary supported the work of Jesus and his disciples.
- She was present at Jesus' death.
- She was the first to see the risen Jesus.
- She was given the responsibility of telling the disciples about the Resurrection.

WEAKNESSES AND MISTAKES:

- Mary had somehow become enslaved by demonic forces.

LESSONS FROM HER LIFE:

- Those who receive the most from God are often the most grateful.
- God intends women to play an essential role in his ministry.
- The forgiveness we experience can motivate us to live our life for God.

KEY VERSE:

"It was early on Sunday morning when Jesus came back to life, and the first person who saw him was Mary Magdalene—the woman from whom he had cast out seven demons" (Mark 16:9).

Mary Magdalene's story is found in Matthew 27:55–28:10; Mark 15:40–16:11; Luke 8:1-3; and John 20:1-18.

---

16 Then Pilate gave Jesus to them to be crucified.

Jesus Is Nailed to the Cross

17 So they had him at last, and he was taken out
of the city, carrying his cross to the place
known as "The Skull," in Hebrew, "Golgotha." 18 There they crucified him and two
others with him, one on either side, with
Jesus between them. 19 And Pilate posted a sign
over him reading, "Jesus of Nazareth, the King
of the Jews." 20 The place where Jesus was crucified was near the city; and the signboard
was written in Hebrew, Latin, and Greek, so
that many people read it.
21 Then the chief priests said to Pilate,
"Change it from 'The King of the Jews' to *'He
said,* I am King of the Jews.'"
22 Pilate replied, "What I have written, I
have written. It stays exactly as it is."
23,24 When the soldiers had crucified Jesus,
they put his garments into four piles, one for
each of them. But they said, "Let's not tear up
his robe," for it was seamless. "Let's throw
dice to see who gets it." This fulfilled the
Scripture that says,

"They divided my clothes among them
and cast lots for my robe."

25 So that is what they did.
Standing near the cross were Jesus' mother,
Mary, his aunt, the wife of Cleopas, and Mary
Magdalene. 26 When Jesus saw his mother
standing there beside me, his close friend, he
said to her, "He is your son."

27And to me he said, "She is your mother!"
And from then on I took her into my home.

Jesus Dies and Is Buried

28Jesus knew that everything was now finished, and to fulfill the Scriptures said, "I'm
thirsty." 29A jar of sour wine was sitting there,
so a sponge was soaked in it and put on a
hyssop branch and held up to his lips.
30When Jesus had tasted it, he said, "It is
finished," and bowed his head and dismissed
his spirit.
31The Jewish leaders didn't want the victims
hanging there the next day, which was the
Sabbath (and a very special Sabbath at that,
for it was the Passover), so they asked Pilate to
order the legs of the men broken to hasten
death; then their bodies could be taken down.
32So the soldiers came and broke the legs of
the two men crucified with Jesus; 33but when
they came to him, they saw that he was dead
already, so they didn't break his. 34However,
one of the soldiers pierced his side with a
spear, and blood and water flowed out. 35I saw
all this myself and have given an accurate
report so that you also can believe. 36,37The
soldiers did this in fulfillment of the Scripture
that says, "Not one of his bones shall be
broken," and, "They shall look on him whom
they pierced."
38Afterwards Joseph of Arimathea, who had
been a secret disciple of Jesus for fear of the
Jewish leaders, boldly asked Pilate for permission to take Jesus' body down; and Pilate told
him to go ahead. So he came and took it away.
39Nicodemus, the man who had come to Jesus
at night, came too, bringing a hundred
pounds of embalming ointment made from
myrrh and aloes. 40Together they wrapped
Jesus' body in a long linen cloth saturated
with the spices, as is the Jewish custom of
burial. 41The place of crucifixion was near a
grove of trees, where there was a new tomb,
never used before. 42And so, because of the
need for haste before the Sabbath, and because the tomb was close at hand, they laid
him there.

CHAPTER 20

Jesus Rises from the Dead

Early Sunday morning, while it was still dark,
Mary Magdalene came to the tomb and found
that the stone was rolled aside from the entrance.
2She ran and found Simon Peter and me
and said, "They have taken the Lord's body
out of the tomb, and I don't know where they
have put him!"
3,4We ran to the tomb to see; I outran Peter
and got there first, 5and stooped and looked
in and saw the linen cloth lying there, but I
didn't go in. 6Then Simon Peter arrived and
went on inside. He also noticed the cloth
lying there, 7while the swath that had covered
Jesus' head was rolled up in a bundle and was
lying at the side. 8Then I went in too, and saw,
and believed [that he had risen]—9for until
then we hadn't realized that the Scriptures
said he would come to life again!

Jesus Appears to Mary Magdalene

10We went on home, 11and by that time Mary
had returned to the tomb and was standing
outside crying. And as she wept, she stooped
and looked in 12and saw two white-robed angels sitting at the head and foot of the place
where the body of Jesus had been lying.
13"Why are you crying?" the angels asked
her.
"Because they have taken away my Lord,"
she replied, "and I don't know where they
have put him."
14She glanced over her shoulder and saw
someone standing behind her. It was Jesus,
but she didn't recognize him!
15"Why are you crying?" he asked her.
"Whom are you looking for?"
She thought he was the gardener. "Sir," she

19:28-30 What did Jesus finish? The underlying word means "paid in full." Jesus on the cross finished the work he was sent to do (4:21-24; 17:4) and fully paid for our sin (1 Peter 3:18). In the greatest act of love in history, and in fulfillment of a complicated, centuries-old system of sacrifices, he became the perfect sacrificial Lamb of God (see 1:29; Hebrews 8:1–10:18). The miracle of the Resurrection (20:1-9) confirmed that Jesus is the Savior who can bring forgiveness, new life, and recovery to all of us.

20:10-18 Mary Magdalene modeled an essential part of the recovery process—telling others the Good News. Once healed of seven demons (Mark 16:9), Mary had supported the ministry of Jesus financially (Luke 8:3) and was a faithful follower from early in his ministry (John 19:25; 20:11). Her faithfulness was honored when the risen Christ appeared and spoke to her before he spoke to anyone else! After seeing the resurrected Jesus, she went immediately and told the disciples the good news. When we finally begin to realize the power that the risen Christ can bring to our recovery, we can pay our debt of gratitude by doing as Mary did, by carrying the message to others.

THOMAS

Though distrust or wavering faith is a reality for most of us, it is painful to be labeled a "doubting Thomas." We might wonder what it was like for Thomas, the disciple of Jesus who became known for his doubting. He simply did not believe that Jesus had risen from the dead. But that is not the end of his story.

Didymus was the other name given for Thomas in the Gospels; it means "Twin." Thomas was likely raised the way most twins are. Probably he was compared to, often in conflict with, and forced to share with his twin sibling. This background could easily have instilled a habit of doubt into his outlook on life. In spite of this, however, Thomas became one of the inner circle of Jesus' followers and at times exhibited great courage. When Jesus went with his disciples to Bethany to raise Lazarus from the dead, they were walking into a dangerous situation. The religious leaders were actively plotting to kill Jesus. Thomas and the other disciples bravely chose to go along.

Thomas did not doubt Jesus' resurrection out of fear. He continued to meet with the followers of Jesus in the upper room. He just happened to be absent when the risen Jesus first appeared to them. He wanted some kind of proof that his companions had not just been seeing things. Thomas was given the undeniable evidence that he asked for when Jesus appeared a second time. This permanently dispelled his doubts.

We also have undeniable evidence for the Resurrection; we can experience God's transforming power in our own life. As we look to Jesus for our recovery, we will experience his power to transform our life, giving us firsthand knowledge of his power. We can overcome our troubling doubts as we continue to trust God to show his power in our life. And when Thomas overcame his doubts, he set out on a ministry that exhibited extraordinary faith. As we experience God's power for deliverance, we, too, can use this to motivate our ministry to others.

STRENGTHS AND ACCOMPLISHMENTS:
- Thomas was willing to give up everything to follow Jesus.
- He was a man of conviction and courage.
- He was a keen thinker and analyst of events.
- He was willing to admit his mistake.

WEAKNESSES AND MISTAKES:
- Thomas discounted the supernatural explanation of the Resurrection.
- He wanted unquestionable evidence before he was willing to believe.

LESSONS FROM HIS LIFE:
- People from difficult family backgrounds can recover by following Jesus.
- Doubt can lead to deeper faith if faced honestly.
- Undeniable evidence is not necessary to begin a life of faith.
- God's work in our life can lead to deeper faith.

KEY VERSE:
"Then Jesus told [Thomas], 'You believe because you have seen me. But blessed are those who haven't seen me and believe anyway'" (John 20:29).

Thomas's story is told in several passages in the Gospels. His final mention is in Acts 1:14.

---

said, "if you have taken him away, tell me
where you have put him, and I will go and get
him."
16"Mary!" Jesus said. She turned toward him.
"Master!" she exclaimed.
17"Don't touch me," he cautioned, "for I
haven't yet ascended to the Father. But go
find my brothers and tell them that I ascend
to my Father and your Father, my God and
your God."
18Mary Magdalene found the disciples and
told them, "I have seen the Lord!" Then she
gave them his message.

Jesus Appears to His Disciples
19That evening the disciples were meeting behind locked doors, in fear of the Jewish leaders, when suddenly Jesus was standing there
among them! After greeting them, 20he
showed them his hands and side. And how
wonderful was their joy as they saw their Lord!
21He spoke to them again and said, "As the
Father has sent me, even so I am sending
you." 22Then he breathed on them and told
them, "Receive the Holy Spirit. 23If you forgive
anyone's sins, they are forgiven. If you refuse
to forgive them, they are unforgiven."

Jesus Talks with Thomas

24 One of the disciples, Thomas, "The Twin," was not there at the time with the others. 25 When they kept telling him, "We have seen the Lord," he replied, "I won't believe it unless I see the nail wounds in his hands—and put my fingers into them—and place my hand into his side."

26 Eight days later the disciples were together again, and this time Thomas was with them. The doors were locked; but suddenly, as before, Jesus was standing among them and greeting them.

27 Then he said to Thomas, "Put your finger into my hands. Put your hand into my side. Don't be faithless any longer. Believe!"

28 "My Lord and my God!" Thomas said.

29 Then Jesus told him, "You believe because you have seen me. But blessed are those who haven't seen me and believe anyway."

30,31 Jesus' disciples saw him do many other miracles besides the ones told about in this book, but these are recorded so that you will believe that he is the Messiah, the Son of God, and that believing in him you will have life.

CHAPTER 21

A Great Catch of Fish

Later Jesus appeared again to the disciples beside the Lake of Galilee. This is how it happened:

2 A group of us were there—Simon Peter, Thomas, "The Twin," Nathanael from Cana in Galilee, my brother James and I and two other disciples.

3 Simon Peter said, "I'm going fishing."

"We'll come too," we all said. We did, but caught nothing all night. 4 At dawn we saw a man standing on the beach but couldn't see who he was.

5 He called, "Any fish, boys?"

"No," we replied.

6 Then he said, "Throw out your net on the right-hand side of the boat, and you'll get plenty of them!" So we did, and couldn't draw in the net because of the weight of the fish, there were so many!

7 Then I said to Peter, "It is the Lord!" At that, Simon Peter put on his tunic (for he was stripped to the waist) and jumped into the water [and swam ashore]. 8 The rest of us stayed in the boat and pulled the loaded net to the beach, about 300 feet away. 9 When we got there, we saw that a fire was kindled and fish were frying over it, and there was bread.

10 "Bring some of the fish you've just caught," Jesus said. 11 So Simon Peter went out and dragged the net ashore. By his count

20:22-23 The risen Christ did as he had promised (see 14:15-20; 15:26; 16:7) and breathed his Spirit into his disciples. This life-giving, truth-revealing, sin-convicting, comfort-giving Spirit is also a Spirit of forgiveness. Just as we receive God's forgiveness for our sins, so we are exhorted and enabled to forgive those who sin against us. If we refuse to forgive others, we will miss the blessed freedom that God offers. He wants us to experience the emotional healing that comes only from working through our anger and hurt to the point of releasing it to God. By God's Spirit, our recovery from a painful past can be completed.

20:24-29 This is where doubting Thomas earned his reputation. He refused to believe in Jesus' resurrection until he saw and felt the risen Christ with his own eyes and hands. In recovery we often experience doubt of a similar nature. We have a hard time believing God is at work in our life when we don't see immediate changes or miraculous results. Recovery can be a painstaking process without much to show for it at first. Even when evidence of God's power is not immediate, when we persevere in faith we will experience the peace that comes from trusting God with our present problems and our unknown future.

21:1-14 Just imagine what the disciples must have felt. They were professional fisherman who had spent an entire night fishing. They had tried every trick they knew, but still hadn't caught anything. Then Jesus called out to them and told them to throw the net on the other side of the boat! The disciples' first response must have been to laugh. But when they did as Jesus said, they caught so many fish that the net began to break. As strange as it may sound, that is how our recovery works. When we have tried everything and come to realize our helplessness, we need to follow God's instructions for healthy living. It may seem foolish at first, but as we trust God and obey his will, we will discover that God has the power we need to rebuild our life.

21:15-17 Whereas Peter had denied Jesus three times, here Jesus allows Peter to declare his love for him three times. Each time Jesus affirms his confidence in Peter by commissioning him to feed his flock. Peter was later able to fulfill this commission when he was filled with the mighty power of the Holy Spirit at Pentecost. He became a key leader in the early church. Though we may experience failure and relapse, when we open our heart to God, he is willing and able to restore us—even to the point where our life becomes a model of recovery to others.

there were 153 large fish; and yet the net hadn't torn.

12"Now come and have some breakfast!" Jesus said; and none of us dared ask him if he really was the Lord, for we were quite sure of it. 13Then Jesus went around serving us the bread and fish.

14This was the third time Jesus had appeared to us since his return from the dead.

Jesus Talks with Peter

15After breakfast Jesus said to Simon Peter, "Simon, son of John, do you love me more than these others?"

"Yes," Peter replied, "you know I am your friend."

"Then feed my lambs," Jesus told him.

16Jesus repeated the question: "Simon, son of John, do you *really* love me?"

"Yes, Lord," Peter said, "you know I am your friend."

"Then take care of my sheep," Jesus said.

17Once more he asked him, "Simon, son of John, are you even my friend?"

Peter was grieved at the way Jesus asked the question this third time. "Lord, you know my heart; you know I am," he said.

Jesus said, "Then feed my little sheep.
18When you were young, you were able to do as you liked and go wherever you wanted to; but when you are old, you will stretch out your hands and others will direct you and take you where you don't want to go."
19Jesus said this to let him know what kind of death he would die to glorify God. Then Jesus told him, "Follow me."

20Peter turned around and saw the disciple Jesus loved following, the one who had leaned around at supper that time to ask Jesus, "Master, which of us will betray you?"
21Peter asked Jesus, "What about him, Lord? What sort of death will he die?"

22Jesus replied, "If I want him to live until I return, what is that to you? *You* follow me."

23So the rumor spread among the brotherhood that that disciple wouldn't die! But that isn't what Jesus said at all! He only said, "If I want him to live until I come, what is that to you?"

24*I am that disciple!* I saw these events and have recorded them here. And we all know that my account of these things is accurate.

25And I suppose that if all the other events in Jesus' life were written, the whole world could hardly contain the books!

Love

READ JOHN 21:14-25

We may wonder how we can love others but still hurt them. This paradox causes shame, sometimes erecting a barrier between us and the ones we love. We may be afraid to say that we love them, thinking, *If I really loved them, I wouldn't let them down the way I have.*

Peter had once sworn his love for Jesus. But then, after Jesus was arrested, Peter protected himself by denying that he even knew him. Jesus wasn't surprised. But Peter had a hard time forgiving himself. After Jesus rose from the dead, he had this conversation with Peter. "Jesus said to Simon Peter, 'Simon, son of John, do you love me more than these others?' 'Yes,' Peter replied, 'you know I am your friend.' . . . [A third time] he asked him, 'Simon, son of John, are you even my friend?' Peter was grieved at the way Jesus asked the question this third time. 'Lord, you know my heart; you know I am,' he said" (John 21:15-17).

Jesus allowed Peter to affirm his love the best he could and accepted him as he was. In this way, Jesus reduced the shame and restored the relationship. Shame and isolation can lead us back to our addictions. For the sake of our recovery, we must not let our shame cause us to avoid the people we love. It is all right if we love others imperfectly—no one is perfect. But we must keep our love relationships together until they have had time to heal. ***Turn to page 1233, Romans 3.***

REFLECTIONS ON JOHN

✲*insights* FROM JESUS' WORDS AND DEEDS

Jesus was a perfect picture of God and a perfect teacher of God's truth. In **John 1:29-31** we find that he was also the perfect sacrifice—the Lamb of God. The Old Testament sacrificial system required that an unblemished lamb be slain on the altar in place of the people. Through its death the people could be forgiven of their sins and given a fresh start. By dying on the cross, Jesus fulfilled the requirements of that sacrificial system completely and forever. He is the Lamb of God who deals with our sin, our powerlessness, and our shortcomings. He gives us a chance for a new start, no matter how terrible our past.

Those who witnessed Jesus' actions and words had to choose between belief and unbelief. Our choice, like that of the Pharisees in **John 2:17-25,** is to accept or reject what Jesus' actions indicate about his mission and authority. Was he just a fascinating man who did amazing deeds? Was he just a good teacher with an interesting message? Was he a madman with delusions of grandeur? Or was Jesus actually God, who came to live among us? According to the Bible, Jesus is God, and he has the power to offer us a new life. The disciples discovered this truth and were transformed from rough fishermen into some of the greatest leaders of their day. God has the power to do the same for us.

The paralyzed man mentioned in **John 5:1-15** had waited at the Bethesda pool for thirty-eight years, hoping to be healed. He was as hopelessly trapped by his physical handicap as we are by our dependencies. Notice that he was full of excuses for why things weren't working out for him. He couldn't stand up and walk until he took responsibility for his life and put his faith in Jesus' power to heal him. When healed by Jesus, he also stood up to Jesus' critics and witnessed to others about God's power to save. Recovery does not come to those who wallow in the blame game, but only to those who are willing to take small steps of faith.

In **John 8:1-11** the Pharisees brought to Jesus a woman who had been caught in the act of adultery. Jewish law required that she be stoned to death (Leviticus 20:10; Deuteronomy 22:22). In asking Jesus to judge the situation, the Pharisees hoped to trap him. If Jesus had told them to stone her, they could have brought Jesus before the Roman authorities. The Romans did not allow the Jews to implement their own death sentences. Yet, if Jesus had granted this woman a pardon, the Pharisees could have claimed he was a false prophet for ignoring God's Law. Jesus wisely escaped the trap by showing the Pharisees that they had no grounds for judging since they, too, were sinful. Then, Jesus told the woman to go and sin no more. Jesus did not ignore this woman's sin, but he forgave her and gave her a new start in life. When others shake their fingers at us, Jesus can give us a new start in life, no matter how terrible our past behaviors.

When we are ridiculed, rejected, or abused, that is the time to look up—to Jesus' experiences leading to the cross. In **John 19:1-3** we see that Jesus suffered the shame and humiliation of being mocked, crowned with thorns, and struck in the face. He was shamefully exposed on the cross, yet held his head high enough to shout, "It is finished!" (19:30). Because of the shame Jesus suffered, we can hold our head high as we look to God. We have been forgiven of our sins and failures. Through Jesus, our sin and shame are removed, and we have been offered another chance at life.

✲*insights* FROM THE DISCIPLES' LIVES

Once Andrew had met Jesus and realized who he was, he was quick to carry the saving message to others. In **John 1:40-42** we see him rushing off to find his brother, Simon, whom he immediately brought to Jesus. When we experience God's power in our life, we will be just as eager to share our newfound hope with others. As we know, this is an essential part of our recovery. As we share the

Good News of God and his power to deliver, we will give great hope to fellow strugglers. We will also be encouraged to persevere when we remember all the great things God has done for us.

Throughout his Gospel (see **John 13:23; 19:26; 21:20**), the apostle John referred to himself as "the disciple Jesus loved" or Jesus' "close friend." John was probably Jesus' closest friend during the years of his ministry, but John was not boasting about this. Rather, the apostle was basing his self-perception solely upon God's unconditional love for him. To the extent that we see ourself as God does—as deeply loved—then we will have an accurate self-image and make healthy progress toward recovery.

It is easy to fall into the trap of comparing ourself to others, as Peter did with John in **John 21:20-25**. We sometimes take solace in comparing ourself to someone who is still in bondage to an addiction. Or we may look at others in recovery and become jealous of how quickly they seem to have progressed. Focusing on the failures and successes of others in recovery is an easy distraction from our own life and recovery. Our challenge is to make a searching inventory of our own life, not the lives of others. When we keep our eyes on our own issues, we will soon begin to make progress in our recovery.

insights ABOUT OUR RELATIONSHIP WITH GOD

In **John 6:28-29** the people asked Jesus, "What should we do to satisfy God?" That question has plagued the human race ever since the first sin by Adam and Eve. Many of us live by a list of "shoulds" and "shouldn'ts" in our effort to earn God's acceptance. Some of us learned to do this as children, when our parents persistently pressured us to "measure up" to their ideals. In turn, we may do this to our own children. The good news is that we don't have to do anything to receive God's help and forgiveness! God in Jesus Christ has taken all the initiative; we simply receive him by faith. Each step of our growth begins as we respond to God's love for us.

As we see in **John 15:9-12,** genuine, unconditional love overflows from the abundant love God has shown us. Conversely, unhealthy, codependent love starts with our emptiness and need for love. We try to love others in an attempt to earn their love in return. This kind of love is selfish and driven by our inner emptiness. Only when we experience and remain in God's love (shared by people we trust and respect) can we genuinely love ourself and others. God's joy is made complete in us when we experience his love in our life. Only then can we offer his unselfish love to others out of an overflowing heart (see 13:34-35).

insights CONCERNING THE HOLY SPIRIT

God desires to have a special kind of relationship with us. When Jesus ascended to the Father in heaven, he sent his Spirit to live within his followers. In **John 14:15-18** the Holy Spirit is called the Comforter. Other translations call him the Counselor, or Advocate. By whatever name, he ministers God's compassion to us, brings to mind Jesus' teachings, guides us into doing justice and knowing all truth, and he brings our needs before God the Father (see 14:26; 15:26; 16:5-16). Many of us in recovery feel like emotional orphans or cripples who have been abandoned or neglected. God, the Holy Spirit, will never leave or forsake us. He is with us at all times, and he has the power to help us overcome the problems in our life.

In recovery it is crucial that we learn to depend on the Holy Spirit. In **John 15:26-27** we find that the Holy Spirit provides comfort in times of doubt, despair, and affliction. As the "source of all truth" he gives wisdom to help us examine our life; he helps us see past our denial and self-deception. The Holy Spirit reveals the truth of God's Word, holds us accountable to other believers, and conforms us to the image of his Son. He can guide us to an accurate perception of ourself, just like an unflattering mirror. The result will be convicting, but fulfilling—so much so, that we cannot help but share the good news with others.

ACTS

THE BIG PICTURE

A. TO JERUSALEM: TELLING THEIR STORY AT HOME (1:1–8:40)
B. TO JUDEA AND SAMARIA: TRANSITION TO OUTSIDERS (9:1–12:25)
C. TO THE WHOLE WORLD: HOW OUTSIDERS BECOME INSIDERS (13:1–21:40)
D. JERUSALEM TO ROME: THE COST OF FOLLOWING JESUS (22:1–28:31)

What occurred during the brief years of Jesus' earthly life was limited to a small corner of the world. Most of civilization never noticed Jesus bringing hope to a hurting and seemingly forsaken group of people. But just as he predicted, the small band of disciples that met in Jerusalem following his death and resurrection "turned the world upside down." Life on planet earth has never been the same since.

Written by Luke as a sequel to his Gospel, Acts records a history of the early believers and the church. Through the examples of these early believers, we see that the Holy Spirit has the power to change lives. We learn that God can transform our life and help us live at peace with himself and others.

The first half of this book focuses on the ministry of Peter—how he was transformed from an impulsive and unreliable, though well-intentioned, follower of Jesus to a bold and dedicated leader. The second half of the book presents us with the life and ministry of Paul. Paul and his companions faced all kinds of difficulties and opposition, but through the power of God they spread the Good News about Jesus throughout the Mediterranean world.

These men should be an encouragement to us. Both made serious mistakes as younger men, but as they turned their lives over to God, they gradually were changed. Paul, who as an angry young man helped to kill the first Christian martyr, Stephen, later became a selfless and dedicated missionary. Peter, whose cockiness often prevented him from overcoming his weaknesses, became a humble and effective leader. The changes in both men demonstrate what God can do in our lives, too.

THE BOTTOM LINE

PURPOSE: To trace the story of how the Jewish Jesus movement became a worldwide movement through the impetus of the Holy Spirit. AUTHOR: Luke, the physician. AUDIENCE: Theophilus, whose name means "lover of God." DATE WRITTEN: Sometime between A.D. 63 and 70. SETTING: Acts provides a history of the events that follow the resurrection of Jesus. KEY VERSE: "But when the Holy Spirit has come upon you, you will receive power to testify about me with great effect, to the people in Jerusalem, throughout Judea, in Samaria, and to the ends of the earth" (1:8). SPECIAL FEATURES: The book of Acts is a sequel to the Gospel of Luke. KEY PEOPLE: Peter, John, Stephen, Philip, Paul, Barnabas, Silas, Timothy, and Luke.

RECOVERY THEMES

The Power of the Holy Spirit: Jesus promised the disciples that after he left, the Holy Spirit would bring them power. Little did they know just what kind of power would be made available to them! As they learned firsthand, the Holy Spirit and his power are real. When we compare Peter in the Gospels with Peter in the book of Acts, we can tell that his life had been changed. When we look at Saul doing his utmost to destroy the early church and then see his dedicated missionary service, we can tell that he was radically transformed by God. The power of God changed their hearts, giving them confidence to tell the truth about him. In our powerlessness, God makes his power available to us through the Holy Spirit. With his help, no problem is too great to overcome; no life is so far gone that it cannot be made new.

Commitment That Overcomes Opposition: Luke did not idealize the people of the early church. They did not have an easy task that swiftly and smoothly moved to its objective. Instead, they struggled with controversy, opposition, and discouragement. They were misunderstood by religious and irreligious people alike. But their common thread was a commitment to God at any cost. As we commit our life to God and to our recovery, we can expect to face obstacles, but we can also expect to overcome any problems or opposing forces with God's powerful help.

Living beyond Circumstances: When we read about the early Christians and how they shared what they had and took care of each other, it is easy to think that somehow they were above the kinds of problems we experience. It was, rather, that they learned how to live beyond their circumstances. They weren't in denial, but were more conscious of God than they were of their problems. When we focus on the problems in our life, we lose sight of our source of power. We try to generate the power from within, only to fail and become discouraged. It does us no good to deny or ignore our circumstances, but it does us a world of good to trust God as we turn our life and our circumstances over to him.

Sharing the Message: As Peter, John, Philip, Paul, Barnabas, and others came to faith in Jesus, they shared the Good News with others. God's healing power is good news! As we carry the message of our own spiritual awakening to others in need, we find that we share the good news of God's healing power, as did those early disciples. In so doing, we become stronger in our own recovery and stronger in our faith in God.

CHAPTER 1

Jesus Ascends to Heaven

Dear friend who loves God:

In my first letter I told you about Jesus' life
and teachings and how he returned to heaven
after giving his chosen apostles further instructions from the Holy Spirit. 3During the
forty days after his crucifixion he appeared to
the apostles from time to time, actually alive,
and proved to them in many ways that it was
really he himself they were seeing. And on
these occasions he talked to them about the
Kingdom of God.

4In one of these meetings he told them not
to leave Jerusalem until the Holy Spirit came
upon them in fulfillment of the Father's
promise, a matter he had previously discussed
with them.

5"John baptized you with water," he reminded them, "but you shall be baptized with
the Holy Spirit in just a few days."

6And another time when he appeared to
them, they asked him, "Lord, are you going to
free Israel [from Rome] now and restore us as
an independent nation?"

7"The Father sets those dates," he replied,

1:1-5 This is the sequel to Luke's Gospel, and it picks up where the Gospel left off. It records the activities of the apostles, beginning soon after Jesus' resurrection. Before ascending to heaven, Jesus assured his followers that the Holy Spirit he had promised to send would come upon them as they waited in Jerusalem. At the appointed time, the early Christians received the power they needed to reach the world with the Good News of Jesus Christ. God offers us the same powerful help in overcoming the barriers in our recovery.

1:6-11 When the disciples asked Jesus about the coming of his earthly Kingdom, they displayed a deep yearning for the Messiah's reign of freedom and peace. Jesus responded by telling them not to worry about the future. Instead, he turned their eyes to the present. With the power of the Holy Spirit, they were to share the Good News of salvation in Jesus Christ with others. Sometimes we make the mistake the disciples did, looking forward to a time of complete freedom and peace while we could be taking productive steps of action here and now. The Holy Spirit makes available to us the power necessary for a successful recovery. An important part of that recovery process is to share the Good News with others.

"and they are not for you to know. 8But when
the Holy Spirit has come upon you, you will
receive power to testify about me with great
effect, to the people in Jerusalem, throughout
Judea, in Samaria, and to the ends of the
earth, about my death and resurrection."
9It was not long afterwards that he rose into
the sky and disappeared into a cloud, leaving
them staring after him. 10As they were straining their eyes for another glimpse, suddenly
two white-robed men were standing there
among them, 11and said, "Men of Galilee, why
are you standing here staring at the sky? Jesus
has gone away to heaven, and some day, just
as he went, he will return!"

Matthias Replaces Judas

12They were at the Mount of Olives when this
happened, so now they walked the half mile
back to Jerusalem 13and held a prayer meeting
in an upstairs room of the house where they
were staying.
14Here is the list of those who were present
at the meeting: Peter, John, James, Andrew,
Philip, Thomas, Bartholomew, Matthew,
James (son of Alphaeus), Simon (also called
"The Zealot"), Judas (son of James), and the
brothers of Jesus. Several women, including
Jesus' mother, were also there.
15This prayer meeting went on for several
days. During this time, on a day when about
120 people were present, Peter stood up and
addressed them as follows:
16"Brothers, it was necessary for the
Scriptures to come true concerning Judas,
who betrayed Jesus by guiding the mob to
him, for this was predicted long ago by the
Holy Spirit, speaking through King David.
17Judas was one of us, chosen to be an apostle
just as we were. 18He bought a field with the
money he received for his treachery and falling headlong there, he burst open, spilling
out his bowels. 19The news of his death spread
rapidly among all the people of Jerusalem,
and they named the place 'The Field of
Blood.' 20King David's prediction of this appears in the Book of Psalms, where he says,
'Let his home become desolate with no one
living in it.' And again, 'Let his work be given
to someone else to do.'
21,22"So now we must choose someone else
to take Judas' place and to join us as witnesses
of Jesus' resurrection. Let us select someone
who has been with us constantly from our
first association with the Lord—from the time
he was baptized by John until the day he was
taken from us into heaven."
23The assembly nominated two men: Joseph Justus (also called Barsabbas) and Matthias. 24,25Then they all prayed for the right
man to be chosen. "O Lord," they said, "you
know every heart; show us which of these
men you have chosen as an apostle to replace
Judas the traitor, who has gone on to his
proper place."
26Then they drew straws, and in this manner Matthias was chosen and became an apostle with the other eleven.

CHAPTER 2

The Holy Spirit Comes

Seven weeks had gone by since Jesus' death
and resurrection, and the Day of Pentecost
had now arrived. As the believers met together that day, 2suddenly there was a sound
like the roaring of a mighty windstorm in the
skies above them and it filled the house where
they were meeting. 3Then, what looked like
flames or tongues of fire appeared and settled
on their heads. 4And everyone present was
filled with the Holy Spirit and began speaking
in languages they didn't know, for the Holy
Spirit gave them this ability.
5Many godly Jews were in Jerusalem that
day for the religious celebrations, having arrived from many nations. 6And when they
heard the roaring in the sky above the house,
crowds came running to see what it was all
about, and were stunned to hear their own
languages being spoken by the disciples.
7"How can this be?" they exclaimed. "For
these men are all from Galilee, 8and yet we
hear them speaking all the native languages
of the lands where we were born! 9Here we
are—Parthians, Medes, Elamites, men from
Mesopotamia, Judea, Cappadocia, Pontus,
Asia Minor, 10Phrygia, Pamphylia, Egypt, the

2:1-4 On the day of Pentecost, the disciples waited in Jerusalem just as Jesus had told them to. Suddenly the Holy Spirit manifested his presence by sound (wind), sight (fire), and speech (new languages). The believers were filled with the Holy Spirit, and God's renewing power began its work of transforming them from the inside out. This marked a new era in history as God's powerful presence entered the lives of all believers. We still live in the era introduced at Pentecost, and God's powerful presence can still indwell our life, transforming our defects and healing our wounds. As we entrust our life to God, his Spirit enters our life to empower our recovery.

Cyrene language areas of Libya, visitors from
Rome—both Jews and Jewish converts—
11Cretans, and Arabians. And we all hear these
men telling in our own languages about the
mighty miracles of God!"
12They stood there amazed and perplexed.
"What can this mean?" they asked each other.
13But others in the crowd were mocking.
"They're drunk, that's all!" they said.

Peter Preaches to a Crowd

14Then Peter stepped forward with the eleven
apostles and shouted to the crowd, "Listen, all
of you, visitors and residents of Jerusalem
alike! 15Some of you are saying these men are
drunk! It isn't true! It's much too early for
that! People don't get drunk by 9:00 A.M.!
16No! What you see this morning was predicted centuries ago by the prophet Joel—17'In
the last days,' God said, 'I will pour out my
Holy Spirit upon all mankind, and your sons
and daughters shall prophesy, and your
young men shall see visions, and your old
men dream dreams. 18Yes, the Holy Spirit shall
come upon all my servants, men and women
alike, and they shall prophesy. 19And I will
cause strange demonstrations in the heavens
and on the earth—blood and fire and clouds
of smoke; 20the sun shall turn black and the
moon blood-red before that awesome Day of
the Lord arrives. 21But anyone who asks for
mercy from the Lord shall have it and shall be
saved.'
22"O men of Israel, listen! God publicly endorsed Jesus of Nazareth by doing tremendous miracles through him, as you well know.
23But God, following his prearranged plan, let
you use the Roman government to nail him
to the cross and murder him. 24Then God
released him from the horrors of death and
brought him back to life again, for death
could not keep this man within its grip.
25"King David quoted Jesus as saying:

'I know the Lord is always with me. He is
helping me. God's mighty power
supports me.
26'No wonder my heart is filled with joy
and my tongue shouts his praises! For I
know all will be well with me in death—
27'You will not leave my soul in hell or let
the body of your Holy Son decay.
28'You will give me back my life and give
me wonderful joy in your presence.'

29"Dear brothers, think! David wasn't referring to himself when he spoke these words I
have quoted, for he died and was buried, and
his tomb is still here among us. 30But he was a
prophet, and knew God had promised with
an unbreakable oath that one of David's own
descendants would [be the Messiah and] sit
on David's throne. 31David was looking far
into the future and predicting the Messiah's
resurrection, and saying that the Messiah's
soul would not be left in hell and his body
would not decay. 32He was speaking of Jesus,
and we all are witnesses that Jesus rose from
the dead.
33"And now he sits on the throne of highest
honor in heaven, next to God. And just as
promised, the Father gave him the authority
to send the Holy Spirit—with the results you
are seeing and hearing today.
34"[No, David was not speaking of himself
in these words of his I have quoted], for he
never ascended into the skies. Moreover, he
further stated, 'God spoke to my Lord, the
Messiah, and said to him, Sit here in honor
beside me 35until I bring your enemies into
complete subjection.'
36"Therefore I clearly state to everyone in
Israel that God has made this Jesus you crucified to be the Lord, the Messiah!"
37These words of Peter's moved them
deeply, and they said to him and to the other
apostles, "Brothers, what should we do?"

2:14-21 After asserting his sobriety, Peter told the crowd about the power behind his transformation. The amazing power of the Holy Spirit had been promised by the prophet Joel centuries earlier. By quoting Joel 2:28-32, Peter stressed the universal impact of the Holy Spirit. The Holy Spirit would be given to all God's people—young and old, men and women, masters and servants. God's power for living is for everyone—regardless of race, gender, or social class—who recognizes his or her helpless state and asks for God's mercy (2:21). No one with a humble heart is beyond the reach of God's powerful help.

2:37-39 Peter's preaching led the people to examine their lives and ask the apostle what to do. They readily recognized their need for salvation in Christ and went on to receive God's powerful help. Peter assured them that by turning from their sins and entrusting their life to God, they would be forgiven and receive the powerful presence of the Holy Spirit into their lives. We can expect the same blessings if we bring our failures before God. His forgiveness of our sins will set us free from bondage to our past. The presence of his Holy Spirit will give us the power to persevere through hard times. If God is in our life, we are never too far gone for a successful recovery.

[38]And Peter replied, "Each one of you must
turn from sin, return to God, and be baptized
in the name of Jesus Christ for the forgiveness
of your sins; then you also shall receive this
gift, the Holy Spirit. [39]For Christ promised
him to each one of you who has been called
by the Lord our God, and to your children
and even to those in distant lands!"

[40]Then Peter preached a long sermon, telling about Jesus and strongly urging all his
listeners to save themselves from the evils of
their nation.

The Believers Meet Together

[41]And those who believed Peter were baptized—about three thousand in all! [42]They
joined with the other believers in regular at-
tendance at the apostles' teaching sessions
and at the Communion services and prayer
meetings.

[43]A deep sense of awe was on them all, and
the apostles did many miracles.

[44]And all the believers met together constantly and shared everything with each
other, [45]selling their possessions and dividing
with those in need. [46]They worshiped together regularly at the Temple each day, met
in small groups in homes for Communion,
and shared their meals with great joy and
thankfulness, [47]praising God. The whole city
was favorable to them, and each day God
added to them all who were being saved.

CHAPTER 3

Peter Heals a Crippled Beggar

Peter and John went to the Temple one afternoon to take part in the three o'clock daily
prayer meeting. [2]As they approached the
Temple, they saw a man lame from birth
carried along the street and laid beside the
Temple gate—the one called The Beautiful
Gate—as was his custom every day. [3]As Peter
and John were passing by, he asked them for
some money.

[4]They looked at him intently, and then
Peter said, "Look here!"

[5]The lame man looked at them eagerly,
expecting a gift.

[6]But Peter said, "We don't have any money
for you! But I'll give you something else! I
command you in the name of Jesus Christ of
Nazareth, *walk!* "

[7,8]Then Peter took the lame man by the
hand and pulled him to his feet. And as he
did, the man's feet and ankle-bones were
healed and strengthened so that he came up
with a leap, stood there a moment and began
walking! Then, walking, leaping, and praising
God, he went into the Temple with them.

[9]When the people inside saw him walking
and heard him praising God, [10]and realized he
was the lame beggar they had seen so often at
The Beautiful Gate, they were inexpressibly
surprised! [11]They all rushed out to Solomon's
Hall, where he was holding tightly to Peter
and John! Everyone stood there awed by the
wonderful thing that had happened.

Peter Preaches in the Temple

[12]Peter saw his opportunity and addressed the
crowd. "Men of Israel," he said, "what is so
surprising about this? And why look at us as
though we by our own power and godliness
had made this man walk? [13]For it is the God
of Abraham, Isaac, Jacob and of all our ancestors who has brought glory to his servant
Jesus by doing this. I refer to the Jesus whom
you rejected before Pilate, despite Pilate's determination to release him. [14]You didn't want
him freed—this holy, righteous one. Instead
you demanded the release of a murderer.
[15]And you killed the Author of Life; but God
brought him back to life again. And John and

2:42-47 In these verses, Luke mentioned a number of activities that characterized the early Christian community. They committed themselves to spiritual growth by studying the Scriptures together, sharing together, and praying together. They helped those in need by sharing their food, their clothing, and even their homes. Their faith, joy, and loving support were so contagious that large numbers soon joined them. Our recovery follows the same pattern as we grow in faith—it is never done in isolation. We need people to walk along with us, encouraging us when we become discouraged and holding us accountable when we stray.

3:1-11 This crippled man was truly helpless, making him a prime candidate for God's powerful help. Notice the steps in this healing. Peter established personal contact by asking the man to look at him. Next, Peter awakened hope in the man by telling him that Jesus Christ could deliver him from his helpless condition. Then, at Peter's command and touch, the man was suddenly on his feet, leaping and praising God. Our healing comes as God touches our life through the ministry of others. As we experience healing in our own life and share our story, we can bestow the same blessings on others by leading them to Jesus Christ.

I are witnesses of this fact, for after you killed
him we saw him alive!
16"Jesus' name has healed this man—and
you know how lame he was before. Faith in
Jesus' name—faith given us from God—has
caused this perfect healing.
17"Dear brothers, I realize that what you did
to Jesus was done in ignorance; and the same
can be said of your leaders. 18But God was
fulfilling the prophecies that the Messiah
must suffer all these things. 19Now change
your mind and attitude to God and turn to
him so he can cleanse away your sins and
send you wonderful times of refreshment
from the presence of the Lord 20and send Jesus
your Messiah back to you again. 21,22For he
must remain in heaven until the final recovery of all things from sin, as prophesied from
ancient times. Moses, for instance, said long
ago, 'The Lord God will raise up a Prophet
among you, who will resemble me! Listen
carefully to everything he tells you. 23Anyone
who will not listen to him shall be utterly
destroyed.'
24"Samuel and every prophet since have all
spoken about what is going on today. 25You
are the children of those prophets; and you
are included in God's promise to your ancestors to bless the entire world through the
Jewish race—that is the promise God gave to
Abraham. 26And as soon as God had brought
his servant to life again, he sent him first of all
to you men of Israel, to bless you by turning
you back from your sins."

CHAPTER 4

Peter and John before the Council

While they were talking to the people, the
chief priests, the captain of the Temple police,
and some of the Sadducees came over to
them, 2very disturbed that Peter and John
were claiming that Jesus had risen from the
dead. 3They arrested them and since it was
already evening, jailed them overnight. 4But
many of the people who heard their message
believed it, so that the number of believers
now reached a new high of about five thousand men!
5The next day it happened that the Council
of all the Jewish leaders was in session in
Jerusalem— 6Annas the High Priest was there,
and Caiaphas, John, Alexander, and others of
the High Priest's relatives. 7So the two disciples were brought in before them.
"By what power, or by whose authority
have you done this?" the Council demanded.
8Then Peter, filled with the Holy Spirit, said
to them, "Honorable leaders and elders of our
nation, 9if you mean the good deed done to
the cripple, and how he was healed, 10let me
clearly state to you and to all the people of
Israel that it was done in the name and power
of Jesus from Nazareth, the Messiah, the man
you crucified—but God raised back to life
again. It is by his authority that this man
stands here healed! 11For Jesus the Messiah is
(the one referred to in the Scriptures when
they speak of) a 'stone discarded by the builders which became the capstone of the arch.'
12There is salvation in no one else! Under all
heaven there is no other name for men to call
upon to save them."
13When the Council saw the boldness of
Peter and John and could see that they were
obviously uneducated non-professionals,
they were amazed and realized what being
with Jesus had done for them! 14And the
Council could hardly discredit the healing
when the man they had healed was standing
right there beside them! 15So they sent them
out of the Council chamber and conferred
among themselves.
16"What shall we do with these men?" they
asked each other. "We can't deny that they
have done a tremendous miracle, and everybody in Jerusalem knows about it. 17But perhaps we can stop them from spreading their
propaganda. We'll tell them that if they do it

4:1-12 Peter consistently held his listeners accountable for their actions (4:10; see 2:36; 3:12-23), but he never concluded his messages on a negative note. He always went on to declare that God can do what we are powerless to do—deliver us from the destructive grip of sin. We all need the forgiveness and recovery offered only by Jesus Christ. Jesus desires our complete recovery—spiritual, emotional, and physical—and he has the power to bring it about.

4:13-22 Peter's courage and power took the religious leaders by surprise, and they were uncertain about how they should proceed. They decided to command Peter to stop his preaching and healing ministry, but Peter refused to obey, affirming his commitment to an even higher Power. The leaders were unable to stop the spread of Jesus' message in Jerusalem and beyond. God wants people the world over to find forgiveness and freedom, despite what the government authorities might say. Once we have experienced the reality of God's power and direction in our life, no one can take that away from us.

again we'll really throw the book at them."
[18]So they called them back in, and told them
never again to speak about Jesus.
[19]But Peter and John replied, "You decide
whether God wants us to obey you instead of
him! [20]We cannot stop telling about the wonderful things we saw Jesus do and heard him
say."
[21]The Council then threatened them further and finally let them go because they
didn't know how to punish them without
starting a riot. For everyone was praising God
for this wonderful miracle— [22]the healing of a
man who had been lame for forty years.

Believers Pray for Courage

[23]As soon as they were freed, Peter and John
found the other disciples and told them what
the Council had said.
[24]Then all the believers united in this
prayer:
"O Lord, Creator of heaven and earth and
of the sea and everything in them— [25,26]you
spoke long ago by the Holy Spirit through our
ancestor King David, your servant, saying,
'Why do the heathen rage against the Lord,
and the foolish nations plan their little plots
against Almighty God? The kings of the earth
unite to fight against him and against the
anointed Son of God!'
[27]"That is what is happening here in this
city today! For Herod the king, and Pontius
Pilate the governor, and all the Romans—as
well as the people of Israel—are united against
Jesus, your anointed Son, your holy servant.
[28]They won't stop at anything that you in
your wise power will let them do. [29]And now,
O Lord, hear their threats, and grant to your
servants great boldness in their preaching,
[30]and send your healing power, and may
miracles and wonders be done by the name of
your holy servant Jesus."
[31]After this prayer, the building where they
were meeting shook, and they were all filled
with the Holy Spirit and boldly preached
God's message.

Believers Share Their Possessions

[32]All the believers were of one heart and mind,
and no one felt that what he owned was his
own; everyone was sharing. [33]And the apostles preached powerful sermons about the resurrection of the Lord Jesus, and there was
warm fellowship among all the believers,
[34,35]and no poverty—for all who owned land
or houses sold them and brought the money
to the apostles to give to others in need.
[36]For instance, there was Joseph (the one
the apostles nicknamed "Barnabas, the encourager"! He was of the tribe of Levi, from
the island of Cyprus). [37]He was one of those
who sold a field he owned and brought the
money to the apostles for distribution to
those in need.

CHAPTER 5

Ananias and Sapphira Are Judged

But there was a man named Ananias (with his
wife Sapphira) who sold some property [2]and
brought only part of the money, claiming it
was the full price. (His wife had agreed to this
deception.)

4:23-31 When Peter and John were released by the religious leaders, they returned to their support group. There they dealt with their difficulties by discussing the issues, worshiping God, and spending time in prayer. This resulted in a new manifestation of God's presence among them and a new boldness empowered by the Holy Spirit. We can learn from the way these early believers dealt with the obstacles before them. We, too, can find help in a support group, a context in which our problems can safely be discussed and prayed over. As we express our dependence on God, he gives us the power to persevere despite the difficulties we face. When we bring our problems to God, he can turn seemingly devastating circumstances into occasions for joy.

4:32-37 The early Christians were growing spiritually by caring for each other, by meeting each other's basic needs, and by carrying the Good News to people who hadn't yet heard. Barnabas was a model believer, even in this exemplary community. His original name was Joseph, but the apostles renamed him Barnabas, which means "son of encouragement." As a part of our recovery, we may need to give ourself a new name that reflects what we are becoming in Christ. Who knows? We might also become a son or daughter of encouragement.

5:1-11 God's judgment of Ananias and Sapphira is a unique event in the history of the church but universal in its application. The fact that God does not normally punish denial and misrepresentation with immediate death makes it unique. It is universal in application because we all are guilty of denial and of trying to impress others with lies and half-truths. Although the consequences for imitating Ananias and Sapphira may not be as serious today, such attitudes and actions are always destructive to our recovery. Our regular moral inventory needs to focus on our tendency to harbor this kind of destructive denial. Then we can take the necessary steps to root it out.

3But Peter said, "Ananias, Satan has filled your heart. When you claimed this was the full price, you were lying to the Holy Spirit. 4The property was yours to sell or not, as you wished. And after selling it, it was yours to decide how much to give. How could you do a thing like this? You weren't lying to us, but to God."

5As soon as Ananias heard these words, he fell to the floor, dead! Everyone was terrified, 6and the younger men covered him with a sheet and took him out and buried him.

7About three hours later his wife came in, not knowing what had happened. 8Peter asked her, "Did you people sell your land for such and such a price?"

"Yes," she replied, "we did."

9And Peter said, "How could you and your husband even think of doing a thing like this—conspiring together to test the Spirit of God's ability to know what is going on? Just outside that door are the young men who buried your husband, and they will carry you out too."

10Instantly she fell to the floor, dead, and the young men came in and, seeing that she was dead, carried her out and buried her beside her husband. 11Terror gripped the entire church and all others who heard what had happened.

The Apostles Heal Many

12Meanwhile, the apostles were meeting regularly at the Temple in the area known as Solomon's Hall, and they did many remarkable miracles among the people. 13The other believers didn't dare join them, though, but all had the highest regard for them. 14And more and more believers were added to the Lord, crowds both of men and women. 15Sick people were brought out into the streets on beds and mats so that at least Peter's shadow would fall across some of them as he went by! 16And crowds came in from the Jerusalem suburbs, bringing their sick folk and those possessed by demons; and every one of them was healed.

The Apostles Meet Opposition

17The High Priest and his relatives and friends among the Sadducees reacted with violent jealousy 18and arrested the apostles, and put them in the public jail.

19But an angel of the Lord came at night, opened the gates of the jail and brought them out. Then he told them, 20"Go over to the Temple and preach about this Life!"

21They arrived at the Temple about daybreak and immediately began preaching! Later that morning the High Priest and his courtiers arrived at the Temple, and, convening the Jewish Council and the entire Senate, they sent for the apostles to be brought for trial. 22But when the police arrived at the jail, the men weren't there, so they returned to the Council and reported, 23"The jail doors were locked, and the guards were standing outside, but when we opened the gates, no one was there!"

24When the police captain and the chief priests heard this, they were frantic, wondering what would happen next and where all this would end! 25Then someone arrived with

---

5:9-11 Peter confronted Ananias and Sapphira about their dishonesty, holding them accountable for their sins. This kind of honest confrontation is as necessary for our recovery as it was for maintaining the spiritual health of this early Christian community. Confrontation and discipline are vital components in any community, whether a Christian church, a recovery group, or a family. As we are confronted with the truth about ourself, we need to humbly and honestly admit our mistakes and defects of character. As we do this, God will give us the help we need to overcome them.

5:12-16 We may wonder how God could possibly do anything for us. We probably have never seen, heard, or felt him. In the activities of the early church, we are shown the primary means that God uses to work in people's lives. He touches hurting people with the help of other hurting people. God channels his power through people like us so others can experience his powerful help for healing and recovery. God has probably touched our life through the help of an individual or group. As we carry the Good News to others in both word and deed, we can be used to bring hope and healing to others.

5:24-42 This power struggle between the religious establishment and the apostles is instructive for our recovery. We probably have already faced opposition similar to that experienced by the apostles. People may have tried to stand in our way as we grew in our relationship with God or participated in recovery activities. They may have sought to impose their will on us without first trying to discover what God's will for us might be. If such people do not speak for God, their advice will not lead to a successful recovery. But if our recovery is centered around God and his will for us, nothing will be able to stop our progress. The key is to obey God rather than other people.

the news that the men they had jailed were
out in the Temple, preaching to the people!
26,27The police captain went with his officers
and arrested them (without violence, for they
were afraid the people would kill them if they
roughed up the disciples) and brought them
in before the Council.
28"Didn't we tell you never again to preach
about this Jesus?" the High Priest demanded.
"And instead you have filled all Jerusalem
with your teaching and intend to bring the
blame for this man's death on us!"
29But Peter and the apostles replied, "We
must obey God rather than men. 30The God of
our ancestors brought Jesus back to life again
after you had killed him by hanging him on a
cross. 31Then, with mighty power, God exalted him to be a Prince and Savior, so that the
people of Israel would have an opportunity
for repentance, and for their sins to be forgiven. 32And we are witnesses of these things
and so is the Holy Spirit, who is given by God
to all who obey him."
33At this, the Council was furious and decided to kill them. 34But one of their members,
a Pharisee named Gamaliel (an expert on religious law and very popular with the people),
stood up and requested that the apostles be
sent outside the Council chamber while he
talked.
35Then he addressed his colleagues as follows:
"Men of Israel, take care what you are planning to do to these men! 36Some time ago
there was that fellow Theudas, who pretended
to be someone great. About four hundred
others joined him, but he was killed, and his
followers were harmlessly dispersed.
37"After him, at the time of the taxation,
there was Judas of Galilee. He drew away
some people as disciples, but he also died, and
his followers scattered.
38"And so my advice is, leave these men
alone. If what they teach and do is merely on
their own, it will soon be overthrown. 39But if
it is of God, you will not be able to stop them,
lest you find yourselves fighting even against
God."
40The Council accepted his advice, called in
the apostles, had them beaten, and then told
them never again to speak in the name of
Jesus, and finally let them go. 41They left the
Council chamber rejoicing that God had
counted them worthy to suffer dishonor for
his name. 42And every day, in the Temple and
in their home Bible classes, they continued to
teach and preach that Jesus is the Messiah.

CHAPTER 6
Seven Deacons Are Chosen

But with the believers multiplying rapidly,
there were rumblings of discontent. Those
who spoke only Greek complained that their
widows were being discriminated against,
that they were not being given as much food
in the daily distribution as the widows who
spoke Hebrew. 2So the Twelve called a meeting
of all the believers.
"We should spend our time preaching, not
administering a feeding program," they said.
3"Now look around among yourselves, dear
brothers, and select seven men, wise and full
of the Holy Spirit, who are well thought of by
everyone; and we will put them in charge of
this business. 4Then we can spend our time in
prayer, preaching, and teaching."
5This sounded reasonable to the whole assembly, and they elected the following: Stephen (a man unusually full of faith and the
Holy Spirit), Philip, Prochorus, Nicanor, Ti-
mon, Parmenas, Nicolaus of Antioch (a Gentile convert to the Jewish faith, who had
become a Christian).
6These seven were presented to the apos-

6:2-6 Conflict resolution is vital to our recovery, just as it was to the early church. To accomplish this difficult task, the early believers acknowledged their limitations, set their priorities, and laid out specific tasks that would fulfill their needs. They sought God's wisdom and had the congregation select seven new leaders to better represent the cultural mix in their community. By delegating leadership to Spirit-filled, Greek-speaking Jews, they overcame their food distribution problem. No problem in recovery is insurmountable. With God's wisdom and a godly network of support, we can work through old dysfunctional patterns and find healthy, balanced ways to rebuild our life and meet the needs of the people around us.

6:8-15 Stephen was noted for his courage, boldness, and faith. He was dedicated to carrying the message of deliverance in Jesus Christ to the people around him. The Jewish establishment accused Stephen of attacking their institutions, especially the laws of Moses and the Jerusalem Temple. Stephen confronted them with their false religion and denial and called them to face the truth. We may need to do the same for our fellow strugglers. If so, this will require God's wisdom and power from above, attributes that Stephen exhibited abundantly. We can receive God's wisdom and power by entrusting our life to God and faithfully obeying his will for our life.

tles, who prayed for them and laid their hands
on them in blessing.
[7]God's message was preached in ever-
widening circles, and the number of disciples
increased vastly in Jerusalem; and many of
the Jewish priests were converted too.

Stephen Is Arrested

[8]Stephen, the man so full of faith and the
Holy Spirit's power, did spectacular miracles
among the people.
[9]But one day some of the men from the
Jewish cult of "The Freedmen" started an argument with him, and they were soon joined
by Jews from Cyrene, Alexandria in Egypt,
and the Turkish provinces of Cilicia, and Asia
Minor. [10]But none of them was able to stand
against Stephen's wisdom and spirit.
[11]So they brought in some men to lie about
him, claiming they had heard Stephen curse
Moses, and even God.
[12]This accusation roused the crowds to fury
against Stephen, and the Jewish leaders arrested him and brought him before the Council. [13]The lying witnesses testified again that
Stephen was constantly speaking against the
Temple and against the laws of Moses.
[14]They declared, "We have heard him say
that this fellow Jesus of Nazareth will destroy
the Temple and throw out all of Moses' laws."
[15]At this point everyone in the Council chamber saw Stephen's face become as radiant as an
angel's!

CHAPTER 7

Stephen Addresses the Council

Then the High Priest asked him, "Are these
accusations true?"
[2]This was Stephen's lengthy reply: "The glorious God appeared to our ancestor Abraham
in Iraq before he moved to Syria, [3]and told
him to leave his native land, to say good-bye
to his relatives and to start out for a country
that God would direct him to. [4]So he left the
land of the Chaldeans and lived in Haran, in
Syria, until his father died. Then God brought
him here to the land of Israel, [5]but gave him
no property of his own, not one little tract of
land.
"However, God promised that eventually
the whole country would belong to him and
his descendants—though as yet he had no
children! [6]But God also told him that these
descendants of his would leave the land and
live in a foreign country and there become
slaves for 400 years. [7]'But I will punish the
nation that enslaves them,' God told him,
'and afterwards my people will return to this
land of Israel and worship me here.'
[8]"God also gave Abraham the ceremony of
circumcision at that time, as evidence of the
covenant between God and the people of
Abraham. And so Isaac, Abraham's son, was
circumcised when he was eight days old. Isaac
became the father of Jacob, and Jacob was the
father of the twelve patriarchs of the Jewish
nation. [9]These men were very jealous of Joseph and sold him to be a slave in Egypt. But
God was with him, [10]and delivered him out of
all of his anguish, and gave him favor before
Pharaoh, king of Egypt. God also gave Joseph
unusual wisdom so that Pharaoh appointed
him governor over all Egypt, as well as putting
him in charge of all the affairs of the palace.
[11]"But a famine developed in Egypt and
Canaan, and there was great misery for our
ancestors. When their food was gone, [12]Jacob
heard that there was still grain in Egypt, so he
sent his sons to buy some. [13]The second time
they went, Joseph revealed his identity to his
brothers, and they were introduced to Pharaoh. [14]Then Joseph sent for his father Jacob
and all his brothers' families to come to
Egypt, seventy-five persons in all. [15]So Jacob
came to Egypt, where he died, and all his
sons. [16]All of them were taken to Shechem
and buried in the tomb Abraham bought
from the sons of Hamor, Shechem's father.
[17,18]"As the time drew near when God
would fulfill his promise to Abraham to free
his descendants from slavery, the Jewish
people greatly multiplied in Egypt; but then a
king was crowned who had no respect for
Joseph's memory. [19]This king plotted against
our race, forcing parents to abandon their
children in the fields.
[20]"About that time Moses was born—a child
of divine beauty. His parents hid him at home
for three months, [21]and when at last they
could no longer keep him hidden and had to

7:1-53 Stephen did not get defensive about, or take personally, the accusations of his fellow Jews. Instead, he took control of the situation and shared his faith with them. Like Stephen, we do not need to be defensive about our faith or recovery. When we are experiencing God's healing power in our life, we can boldly carry that message to others without apology, fear, or shame. Others may yet try to harm us, as they did Stephen, but that does not negate the reality of God's power in our life.

STEPHEN

Stephen was a man filled with the Holy Spirit, exhibiting God's power and love in everything he did. He was known for doing spectacular miracles and helping people in need. He was called to be one of the first deacons, and it was his job to make sure that no one (even the helpless widow) was overlooked in the distribution of food. Stephen also proclaimed the Good News of Jesus with boldness and power. Even as he was stoned to death by religious fanatics, God's hand was clearly upon him.

Stephen demonstrated God's message publicly through the miracles he did in Jesus' name. Those who tried to disprove the truth about Jesus Christ were not able to stand against his wisdom and spirit. So they lied about him in order to have him arrested and brought before the council of Jewish leaders.

Stephen responded to the inquisition by telling the history of the Jewish people, beginning with Abraham, progressing through Moses, and ending with the coming of Jesus, the Messiah. He concluded with a scathing attack on the religious leaders who, like many of their ancestors, resisted the essential message of God's revealed Word and the leading of the Holy Spirit.

Stephen's words angered the Jewish leaders so much that they rushed him out of the city and stoned him to death. As he stumbled under the rain of stones, Stephen called upon God to receive his spirit and to forgive the people who were killing him. Unlike Stephen, many of us hold on to grudges and past hurts and allow them to control our life. This makes complete healing and recovery impossible. If we entrust our life to God's hands, we can both live and die with joy, knowing that God will take care of the details we cannot control or change.

STRENGTHS AND ACCOMPLISHMENTS:
- Stephen really knew God, both personally and through the Scriptures.
- Because he trusted God, he was able to rise above his circumstances.
- He had a passion for God and a compassion for others.
- He used his many gifts to serve the poor and helpless.

LESSONS FROM HIS LIFE:
- Serving others is a natural activity when we have given our life to God.
- If we can trust God in daily life, we will be able to face death with joy.
- We can face even the most terrible circumstances if God is with us.

KEY VERSE:
"Stephen, the man so full of faith and the Holy Spirit's power, did spectacular miracles among the people" (Acts 6:8).

Stephen's story is told in Acts 6–8, 11, and 22.

---

abandon him, Pharaoh's daughter found him
and adopted him as her own son, 22and taught
him all the wisdom of the Egyptians, and he
became a mighty prince and orator.
23"One day as he was nearing his fortieth
birthday, it came into his mind to visit his
brothers, the people of Israel. 24During this
visit he saw an Egyptian mistreating a man of
Israel. So Moses killed the Egyptian. 25Moses
supposed his brothers would realize that God
had sent him to help them, but they didn't.
26"The next day he visited them again and
saw two men of Israel fighting. He tried to be
a peacemaker. 'Gentlemen,' he said, 'you are
brothers and shouldn't be fighting like this! It
is wrong!'
27"But the man in the wrong told Moses to
mind his own business. 'Who made *you* a
ruler and judge over us?' he asked. 28'Are you
going to kill me as you killed that Egyptian
yesterday?'
29"At this, Moses fled the country and lived
in the land of Midian, where his two sons
were born.
30"Forty years later, in the desert near
Mount Sinai, an Angel appeared to him in a
flame of fire in a bush. 31Moses saw it and
wondered what it was, and as he ran to see,
the voice of the Lord called out to him, 32'I am
the God of your ancestors—of Abraham, Isaac
and Jacob.' Moses shook with terror and
dared not look.

33"And the Lord said to him, 'Take off your
shoes, for you are standing on holy ground.
34I have seen the anguish of my people in
Egypt and have heard their cries. I have come
down to deliver them. Come, I will send you
to Egypt.' 35And so God sent back the same
man his people had previously rejected by
demanding, 'Who made *you* a ruler and judge
over us?' Moses was sent to be their ruler and
savior. 36And by means of many remarkable
miracles he led them out of Egypt and
through the Red Sea, and back and forth
through the wilderness for forty years.

37"Moses himself told the people of Israel,
'God will raise up a Prophet much like me
from among your brothers.' 38How true this
proved to be, for in the wilderness, Moses was
the go-between—the mediator between the
people of Israel and the Angel who gave them
the Law of God—the Living Word—on
Mount Sinai.

39"But our fathers rejected Moses and
wanted to return to Egypt. 40They told Aaron,
'Make idols for us, so that we will have gods
to lead us back; for we don't know what has
become of this Moses, who brought us out of
Egypt.' 41So they made a calf-idol and sacrificed to it, and rejoiced in this thing they had
made.

42"Then God turned away from them and
gave them up, and let them serve the sun,
moon, and stars as their gods! In the book of
Amos' prophecies the Lord God asks, 'Was it
to me you were sacrificing during those forty
years in the desert, Israel? 43No, your real
interest was in your heathen gods—Sakkuth,
and the star god Kaiway, and in all the images
you made. So I will send you into captivity far
away beyond Babylon.'

44"Our ancestors carried along with them a
portable Temple, or Tabernacle, through the
wilderness. In it they kept the stone tablets
with the Ten Commandments written on
them. This building was constructed in exact
accordance with the plan shown to Moses by
the Angel. 45Years later, when Joshua led the
battles against the Gentile nations, this Tabernacle was taken with them into their new
territory, and used until the time of King
David.

46"God blessed David greatly, and David
asked for the privilege of building a permanent Temple for the God of Jacob. 47But it was
Solomon who actually built it. 48,49However,
God doesn't live in temples made by human
hands. 'The heaven is my throne,' says the
Lord through his prophets, 'and earth is my
footstool. What kind of home could you

7:44-50 Stephen referred to the Temple to make a point that is important to us in recovery. Israel had gradually limited God to the Temple and the institutions that surrounded the worship there. They had taken the eternal God—the Master of the universe—and had figuratively bound him inside the Temple walls. Sometimes we make the same mistake, defining God in ways we can understand and control. We shape and limit him with our theological systems, our church dogmas, our political presuppositions, and our personal experience. God is much bigger than any conception we could ever have of him. His omnipresence and abundant grace fill the entire universe! As we get a more accurate vision of God and his power, we will discover that he is far bigger than the problems that trouble us.

7:51-60 Stephen confronted the religious leaders about their denial. They were resisting the Holy Spirit and didn't like being rebuked. We would think that as mature adults, these leaders would have pondered Stephen's words and made some kind of honest self-assessment. However, they reacted in anger and set out to kill Stephen. Despite their rage, Stephen did not desire revenge or harbor a grudge. Instead, he kept his focus on Christ, forgiving the people who were killing him. Stephen's peace and self-control are gifts of the Holy Spirit that are available to us all through faith.

8:1-3 The people who seem the most unlikely candidates for recovery are often at the top of God's list. Paul of Tarsus was one such unlikely candidate. At Stephen's death, Paul was one of the dreaded enemies of the fledgling Christian movement. He went from house to house, devastating believers with his mission to search and destroy. Yet, Paul's story is really a story of God's amazing grace. Paul the persecutor became Paul the apostle, one of the greatest leaders in Christian history. Many of us began our recovery as unlikely candidates, but there is no limit to what we can become with God's powerful and gracious help.

8:4-8 God used the terrible circumstances of persecution for his glory. The believers were driven from their homes in Jerusalem, but they used the opportunity to share the Good News wherever they went. God often uses painful circumstances for his glory. Many of us would not be in recovery were it not for the suffering caused by our addictions. Our pain has awakened us to the opportunity to build a new life of faith. We can rebuild our broken relationships and make amends with the people we have hurt. God has used our painful circumstances to give us a second chance.

build?' asks the Lord. 'Would I stay in it?
50Didn't I make both heaven and earth?'
51"You stiff-necked heathen! Must you forever resist the Holy Spirit? But your fathers
did, and so do you! 52Name one prophet your
ancestors didn't persecute! They even killed
the ones who predicted the coming of the
Righteous One—the Messiah whom you
betrayed and murdered. 53Yes, and you deliberately destroyed God's laws, though you received them from the hands of angels."

Stephen Is Killed by Stoning

54The Jewish leaders were stung to fury by
Stephen's accusation and ground their teeth
in rage. 55But Stephen, full of the Holy Spirit,
gazed steadily upward into heaven and saw
the glory of God and Jesus standing at God's
right hand. 56And he told them, "Look, I see
the heavens opened and Jesus the Messiah
standing beside God, at his right hand!"
57Then they mobbed him, putting their
hands over their ears, and drowning out his
voice with their shouts, 58and dragged him
out of the city to stone him. The official
witnesses—the executioners—took off their
coats and laid them at the feet of a young man
named Paul.
59And as the murderous stones came hurtling at him, Stephen prayed, "Lord Jesus,
receive my spirit." 60And he fell to his knees,
shouting, "Lord, don't charge them with this
sin!" and with that, he died.

CHAPTER 8

Persecution Scatters the Believers

Paul was in complete agreement with the
killing of Stephen.
And a great wave of persecution of the
believers began that day, sweeping over the
church in Jerusalem, and everyone except the
apostles fled into Judea and Samaria. 2(But
some godly Jews came and with great sorrow
buried Stephen.) 3Paul was like a wild man,
going everywhere to devastate the believers,
even entering private homes and dragging
out men and women alike and jailing them.
4But the believers who had fled Jerusalem
went everywhere preaching the Good News
about Jesus! 5Philip, for instance, went to the
city of Samaria and told the people there
about Christ. 6Crowds listened intently to
what he had to say because of the miracles he
did. 7Many evil spirits were cast out, screaming as they left their victims, and many who
were paralyzed or lame were healed, 8so there
was much joy in that city!

Listening First

BIBLE READING: Acts 8:26-40

Having had a spiritual awakening as the result of these steps, we tried to carry this message to others and to practice these principles in all our affairs.

We may be so excited about what God has done for us that we want to rush right out and tell everyone our story. Or we may be very shy and hesitate to tell anyone, especially if we think they are better than we are. We all have a valuable story to tell; we just need to discover the best way to communicate it.

The evangelist Philip was led to meet an influential traveler who "had gone to Jerusalem to worship and was now returning . . . reading aloud from the book of the prophet Isaiah. The Holy Spirit said to Philip, 'Go over and walk along beside the chariot.' Philip ran over and heard what he was reading and asked, 'Do you understand it?' 'Of course not!' the man replied. 'How can I when there is no one to instruct me?' . . . So Philip began with this same Scripture and then used many others to tell him about Jesus" (Acts 8:27-31, 35).

The way Philip communicated is a model for us. He was sensitive to allow God to lead him to someone who was ready. He wasn't so intimidated by the man's status that he hesitated to share his story. Philip began by listening carefully. He tuned into the man's need and interests and then explained their relationship to the message he was prepared to share. Whether we are zealous or shy, following this model can help us communicate our message in a way that people can understand and receive it.

Turn to page 1357, 1 Timothy 4.

Philip and Simon the Sorcerer

9-11 A man named Simon had formerly been a
sorcerer there for many years; he was a very
influential, proud man because of the amazing things he could do—in fact, the Samaritan
people often spoke of him as the Messiah.
12 But now they believed Philip's message that
Jesus was the Messiah, and his words concerning the Kingdom of God; and many men and
women were baptized. 13 Then Simon himself
believed and was baptized and began following Philip wherever he went, and was amazed
by the miracles he did.
14 When the apostles back in Jerusalem
heard that the people of Samaria had accepted God's message, they sent down Peter
and John. 15 As soon as they arrived, they began praying for these new Christians to receive the Holy Spirit, 16 for as yet he had not
come upon any of them. For they had only
been baptized in the name of the Lord Jesus.
17 Then Peter and John laid their hands upon
these believers, and they received the Holy
Spirit.
18 When Simon saw this—that the Holy
Spirit was given when the apostles placed
their hands upon people's heads—he offered
money to buy this power.
19 "Let me have this power too," he exclaimed, "so that when I lay my hands on
people, they will receive the Holy Spirit!"
20 But Peter replied, "Your money perish
with you for thinking God's gift can be
bought! 21 You can have no part in this, for
your heart is not right before God. 22 Turn
from this great wickedness and pray. Perhaps
God will yet forgive your evil thoughts— 23 for
I can see that there is jealousy and sin in your
heart."
24 "Pray for me," Simon exclaimed, "that
these terrible things won't happen to me."
25 After testifying and preaching in Samaria,
Peter and John returned to Jerusalem, stopping at several Samaritan villages along the
way to preach the Good News to them too.

Philip and the Ethiopian

26 But as for Philip, an angel of the Lord said to
him, "Go over to the road that runs from
Jerusalem through the Gaza Desert, arriving
around noon." 27 So he did, and who should
be coming down the road but the Treasurer of
Ethiopia, a eunuch of great authority under
Candace the queen. He had gone to Jerusalem
to worship 28 and was now returning in his
chariot, reading aloud from the book of the
prophet Isaiah.
29 The Holy Spirit said to Philip, "Go over
and walk along beside the chariot."
30 Philip ran over and heard what he was
reading and asked, "Do you understand it?"
31 "Of course not!" the man replied. "How
can I when there is no one to instruct me?"
And he begged Philip to come up into the
chariot and sit with him.
32 The passage of Scripture he had been reading from was this:

"He was led as a sheep to the slaughter,
and as a lamb is silent before the
shearers, so he opened not his mouth;
33 in his humiliation, justice was denied
him; and who can express the
wickedness of the people of his

8:9-17 Philip had preached boldly to the Samaritans, who were considered by the Jews to be no better than Gentiles because of their mixed ancestry. The Samaritans responded to the gospel message in great numbers. Hearing about the successful ministry there, Peter and John came to join Philip, and the Samaritan believers received the Holy Spirit. This proved that the Good News of salvation in Christ was not just for the Jews. It was for all people, including the Samaritans. The Good News of Jesus Christ is for us, too, no matter who we are or what we have done.

8:18-25 When Simon the sorcerer saw the ministry of Peter and John, he offered to buy the secret of their power. This was proof to Peter that Simon did not understand his relationship with God. He only sought God for what he might get out of the relationship. Perhaps he wanted to gain back the prestige he had lost when Philip came to town (see 8:9-13). Peter warned Simon that he was heading for disaster and that he needed to examine himself and repent. This problem of impure motives also applies to recovery. If we are in recovery just to look good, we are in it for the wrong reason. When we look to God for help, we are also committing ourself to make his will our own. We succeed in recovery only as we become willing to submit completely to God's will for our life.

9:10-16 During Paul's intense self-examination, God sent Ananias to befriend him, pray for him, and restore his sight. Ananias was afraid at first because he wasn't sure that Paul had really changed. When he met with Paul, however, Ananias discovered that no one is too far gone for God. By coming to help Paul, Ananias discovered a truth that we learn in recovery. When we reach out to others and share the Good News, God not only uses us to help others, he also strengthens our own faith.

generation? For his life is taken from
the earth."

34The eunuch asked Philip, "Was Isaiah
talking about himself or someone else?"
35So Philip began with this same Scripture
and then used many others to tell him about
Jesus.
36As they rode along, they came to a small
body of water, and the eunuch said, "Look!
Water! Why can't I be baptized?"
37 "You can," Philip answered, "if you believe with all your heart."
And the eunuch replied, "I believe that
Jesus Christ is the Son of God."
38He stopped the chariot, and they went
down into the water and Philip baptized him.
39And when they came up out of the water,
the Spirit of the Lord caught away Philip, and
the eunuch never saw him again, but went on
his way rejoicing. 40Meanwhile, Philip found
himself at Azotus! He preached the Good
News there and in every city along the way, as
he traveled to Caesarea.

CHAPTER 9

Paul Meets Jesus

But Paul, threatening with every breath and
eager to destroy every Christian, went to the
High Priest in Jerusalem. 2He requested a letter
addressed to synagogues in Damascus, requiring their cooperation in the persecution of
any believers he found there, both men and
women, so that he could bring them in chains
to Jerusalem.
3As he was nearing Damascus on this mission, suddenly a brilliant light from heaven
spotted down upon him! 4He fell to the
ground and heard a voice saying to him,
"Paul! Paul! Why are you persecuting me?"
5"Who is speaking, sir?" Paul asked.
And the voice replied, "I am Jesus, the one
you are persecuting! 6Now get up and go into
the city and await my further instructions."
7The men with Paul stood speechless with
surprise, for they heard the sound of someone's voice but saw no one! 8,9As Paul picked
himself up off the ground, he found that he
was blind. He had to be led into Damascus
and was there three days, blind, going without food and water all that time.
10Now there was in Damascus a believer
named Ananias. The Lord spoke to him in a
vision, calling, "Ananias!"
"Yes, Lord!" he replied.
11And the Lord said, "Go over to Straight
Street and find the house of a man named
Judas and ask there for Paul of Tarsus. He is

A Time to Choose

BIBLE READING: Acts 9:1-9

We admitted we were powerless over our dependencies—that our life had become unmanageable.

There are important moments in life that can bring about changes in our very destiny. These are often times when we are confronted with how powerless we are over the events of our life. These moments can either destroy us or forever set the course of our life in a much better direction.

Paul of Tarsus had such a moment. After Jesus' ascension, Paul took it upon himself to rid the world of Christians. As he took off on his quest, "suddenly a brilliant light from heaven spotted down upon him! He fell to the ground and heard a voice saying to him, 'Paul! Paul! Why are you persecuting me? . . . I am Jesus, the one you are persecuting! Now, get up and go into the city and await my further instructions.' . . . [Paul] found that he was blind. He had to be led into Damascus and was there three days, blind, going without food and water all that time" (Acts 9:3-6, 8-9).

Paul was suddenly confronted with the fact that his life wasn't as perfect as he had thought. Self-righteousness had been his trademark. By letting go of his illusions of power, however, he became one of the most powerful men ever: the apostle Paul. When we are confronted with the fact that our life isn't in our control, we have a choice. We can continue in denial and self-righteousness, or we can face the fact that we have been blind to some important issues. If we become willing to be led into recovery and a whole new way of life, we will find true power. ***Turn to page 1287, 2 Corinthians 4.***

praying to me right now, for 12I have shown
him a vision of a man named Ananias coming
in and laying his hands on him so that he can
see again!"
13"But Lord," exclaimed Ananias, "I have
heard about the terrible things this man has
done to the believers in Jerusalem! 14And we
hear that he has arrest warrants with him
from the chief priests, authorizing him to
arrest every believer in Damascus!"
15But the Lord said, "Go and do what I say.
For Paul is my chosen instrument to take my
message to the nations and before kings, as
well as to the people of Israel. 16And I will
show him how much he must suffer for me."
17So Ananias went over and found Paul and
laid his hands on him and said, "Brother Paul,
the Lord Jesus, who appeared to you on the
road, has sent me so that you may be filled
with the Holy Spirit and get your sight back."
18Instantly (it was as though scales fell from
his eyes) Paul could see and was immediately
baptized. 19Then he ate and was strengthened.
He stayed with the believers in Damascus
for a few days 20and went at once to the
synagogue to tell everyone there the Good
News about Jesus—that he is indeed the Son
of God!
21All who heard him were amazed. "Isn't
this the same man who persecuted Jesus' followers so bitterly in Jerusalem?" they asked.
"And we understand that he came here to
arrest them all and take them in chains to the
chief priests."
22Paul became more and more fervent in his
preaching, and the Damascus Jews couldn't
withstand his proofs that Jesus was indeed the
Christ.
23After a while the Jewish leaders determined to kill him. 24But Paul was told about
their plans, that they were watching the gates
of the city day and night prepared to murder
him. 25So during the night some of his converts let him down in a basket through an
opening in the city wall!
26Upon arrival in Jerusalem he tried to meet
with the believers, but they were all afraid of
him. They thought he was faking! 27Then Barnabas brought him to the apostles and told
them how Paul had seen the Lord on the way
to Damascus, what the Lord had said to him,
and all about his powerful preaching in the
name of Jesus. 28Then they accepted him, and
after that he was constantly with the believers
29and preached boldly in the name of the
Lord. But then some Greek-speaking Jews
with whom he had argued plotted to murder
him. 30However, when the other believers
heard about his danger, they took him to
Caesarea and then sent him to his home in
Tarsus.
31Meanwhile, the church had peace
throughout Judea, Galilee and Samaria, and
grew in strength and numbers. The believers
learned how to walk in the fear of the Lord
and in the comfort of the Holy Spirit.

Peter Heals Aeneas and Dorcas

32Peter traveled from place to place to visit
them, and in his travels came to the believers
in the town of Lydda. 33There he met a man
named Aeneas, paralyzed and bedridden for
eight years.
34Peter said to him, "Aeneas! Jesus Christ
has healed you! Get up and make your bed."
And he was healed instantly. 35Then the
whole population of Lydda and Sharon
turned to the Lord when they saw Aeneas
walking around.
36In the city of Joppa there was a woman
named Dorcas ("Gazelle"), a believer who was
always doing kind things for others, especially for the poor. 37About this time she became ill and died. Her friends prepared her for

---

9:20-25 Paul quickly joined the Christians in Damascus and began to share the Good News of salvation in Jesus Christ. In this way, he demonstrated that his transformation was real. Both Jews and Christians were astounded at the changes in Paul. The Jews quickly turned against him and sought to kill him, but his new Christian friends helped him escape. We may also experience opposition from our old friends when we enter the recovery process. They may begin to feel guilty about their own dependencies; or they may be afraid they are about to lose a friend. Whatever the reason, our old friends may try to thwart our recovery. This is where our new support group takes on an essential role, protecting and guiding us through these difficult times.

9:26-30 Paul returned to Jerusalem and tried to join the Christian movement. He was immediately met with skepticism. They couldn't believe that such a cruel enemy could have changed so quickly. In time, though, Paul proved his sincerity and was accepted. When we enter recovery, we may meet similar skepticism for a while. As we seek to restore our relationships and make amends, friends and family members may turn away. In time, however, if we continue to follow God's will for our life, relationships we have broken will begin to heal. Our broken relationships, like our addictions, took time to develop. Our recovery also will take time.

burial and laid her in an upstairs room. [38]But when they learned that Peter was nearby at Lydda, they sent two men to beg him to return with them to Joppa. [39]This he did; as soon as he arrived, they took him upstairs where Dorcas lay. The room was filled with weeping widows who were showing one another the coats and other garments Dorcas had made for them. [40]But Peter asked them all to leave the room; then he knelt and prayed. Turning to the body he said, "Get up, Dorcas," and she opened her eyes! And when she saw Peter, she sat up! [41]He gave her his hand and helped her up and called in the believers and widows, presenting her to them.

[42]The news raced through the town, and many believed in the Lord. [43]And Peter stayed a long time in Joppa, living with Simon, the tanner.

CHAPTER 10

Cornelius Calls for Peter

In Caesarea there lived a Roman army officer, Cornelius, a captain of an Italian regiment. [2]He was a godly man, deeply reverent, as was his entire household. He gave generously to charity and was a man of prayer. [3]While wide awake one afternoon he had a vision—it was about three o'clock—and in this vision he saw an angel of God coming toward him.

"Cornelius!" the angel said.

[4]Cornelius stared at him in terror. "What do you want, sir?" he asked the angel.

And the angel replied, "Your prayers and charities have not gone unnoticed by God! [5,6]Now send some men to Joppa to find a man named Simon Peter, who is staying with Simon, the tanner, down by the shore, and ask him to come and visit you."

[7]As soon as the angel was gone, Cornelius called two of his household servants and a godly soldier, one of his personal bodyguard, [8]and told them what had happened and sent them off to Joppa.

Peter Visits Cornelius

[9,10]The next day as they were nearing the city, Peter went up on the flat roof of his house to pray. It was noon and he was hungry, but while lunch was being prepared, he fell into a trance. [11]He saw the sky open and a great canvas sheet, suspended by its four corners, settle to the ground. [12]In the sheet were all sorts of animals, snakes, and birds [forbidden to the Jews for food].

[13]Then a voice said to him, "Go kill and eat any of them you wish."

[14]"Never, Lord," Peter declared, "I have never in all my life eaten such creatures, for they are forbidden by our Jewish laws."

[15]The voice spoke again, "Don't contradict God! If he says something is kosher, then it is."

[16]The same vision was repeated three times. Then the sheet was pulled up again to heaven.

[17]Peter was very perplexed. What could the vision mean? What was he supposed to do?

Just then the men sent by Cornelius had found the house and were standing outside at the gate, [18]inquiring whether this was the place where Simon Peter lived!

[19]Meanwhile, as Peter was puzzling over the vision, the Holy Spirit said to him, "Three men have come to see you. [20]Go down and meet them and go with them. All is well, I have sent them."

[21]So Peter went down. "I'm the man you're looking for," he said. "Now what is it you want?"

[22]Then they told him about Cornelius the Roman officer, a good and godly man, well thought of by the Jews, and how an angel had instructed him to send for Peter to come and tell him what God wanted him to do.

9:36-43 Peter received a call for help from grieving friends in nearby Joppa. Dorcas, a disciple who constantly served other widows and the poor, had just died, and those who loved her had sent for Peter. Imitating Jesus and implementing God's power over death (see Luke 8:41-42, 49-56), Peter brought this woman back to life. When God's power is at work within us, nothing is impossible. God's power can pull us out of our addictions, as if from death, and give us a new life in Jesus Christ.

10:9-20 God sent a special vision to Peter to confront the apostle about some of his hidden prejudices. In this vision, Peter saw a sheet covered with all sorts of animals that according to Jewish Law were unclean. At first, Peter refused to have anything to do with them. But God sent the vision three times, challenging Peter's view of what was clean or unclean. God was preparing Peter to carry the Good News to the Gentiles in the "unclean" home of Cornelius. Peter needed to realize that in Christ people of all backgrounds are acceptable to God. This truth is important for us as well. As we share the Good News with others, we must not allow our prejudices to stand in the way of God's will for us. If God opens a door for us to share his hope with someone, we need to step through it in faith. God will go with us as we spread his message of hope.

23So Peter invited them in and lodged them
overnight.
The next day he went with them, accompanied by some other believers from Joppa.
24They arrived in Caesarea the following
day, and Cornelius was waiting for him and
had called together his relatives and close
friends to meet Peter. 25As Peter entered his
home, Cornelius fell to the floor before him
in worship.
26But Peter said, "Stand up! I'm not a god!"
27So he got up, and they talked together for
a while and then went in where the others
were assembled.
28Peter told them, "You know it is against
the Jewish laws for me to come into a Gentile
home like this. But God has shown me in a
vision that I should never think of anyone as
inferior. 29So I came as soon as I was sent for.
Now tell me what you want."
30Cornelius replied, "Four days ago I was
praying as usual at this time of the afternoon,
when suddenly a man was standing before me
clothed in a radiant robe! 31He told me, 'Cornelius, your prayers are heard and your charities have been noticed by God! 32Now send
some men to Joppa and summon Simon Peter, who is staying in the home of Simon, a
tanner, down by the shore.' 33So I sent for you
at once, and you have done well to come so
soon. Now here we are, waiting before the
Lord, anxious to hear what he has told you to
tell us!"

Peter Shares the Good News

34Then Peter replied, "I see very clearly that
the Jews are not God's only favorites! 35In
every nation he has those who worship him
and do good deeds and are acceptable to him.
36,37I'm sure you have heard about the Good
News for the people of Israel—that there is
peace with God through Jesus, the Messiah,
who is Lord of all creation. This message has
spread all through Judea, beginning with
John the Baptist in Galilee. 38And you no
doubt know that Jesus of Nazareth was
anointed by God with the Holy Spirit and
with power, and he went around doing good
and healing all who were possessed by demons, for God was with him.
39"And we apostles are witnesses of all he
did throughout Israel and in Jerusalem, where
he was murdered on a cross. 40,41But God
brought him back to life again three days later
and showed him to certain witnesses God had
selected beforehand—not to the general public, but to us who ate and drank with him after
he rose from the dead. 42And he sent us to
preach the Good News everywhere and to
testify that Jesus is ordained of God to be the
Judge of all—living and dead. 43And all the
prophets have written about him, saying that
everyone who believes in him will have their
sins forgiven through his name."
44Even as Peter was saying these things, the
Holy Spirit fell upon all those listening! 45The
Jews who came with Peter were amazed that

10:21-33 Peter didn't want to visit the home of this "unclean" Gentile. But when Peter and Cornelius got together, they excitedly shared with one another the unusual things they had just seen and heard. God had worked undercover to cut away the prejudices that would have kept them from speaking to each other. As a result, the Holy Spirit filled all the Gentiles who were in the home of Cornelius. God was able to draw people close who had once been separated by immense barriers. We may have relationships in our life that seem broken beyond repair. The harsh emotions and prejudices formed during our years in bondage have made communication almost impossible. As hopeless as such relationships might seem, God can work to soften our defenses and enhance our communication. He will do this as we entrust our life to him and seek to follow his will for our life.

11:1-3 Even before Peter arrived home, the Jewish believers heard that Gentiles had believed in Christ. In their prejudice they did not accept what they had heard, so they immediately confronted Peter. Earlier, when faced with opposition before Christ's death (Luke 22:54-62), Peter had relapsed in his faith. But Peter did not fold this time; God had made some amazing changes in him since that time of painful failure. Peter defended the truth that had been revealed to him without concern for the cost to him. Sometimes we may be surprised by the changes that God has worked in our life. Recognizing how far we have already come can help to increase our resolve to persevere in the process.

11:4-18 The Jewish believers were slow to accept Gentile believers into the fellowship of Christians. They resisted an event that actually was reason for rejoicing. They had succeeded in obeying Jesus' mandate to testify about him "in Jerusalem, throughout Judea, in Samaria, and to the ends of the earth" (1:8). Numerous Samaritans had already believed in Christ (8:1-25), and now Gentiles from the ends of the earth had joined the Christian community (see also 8:26-40). We may have friends who cannot recognize our moments of triumph in recovery. They may try to discourage us as we take significant steps to follow God's will for us. Like Peter, we need not allow them to dampen our faith or discourage our progress while God is helping us to follow his will.

CORNELIUS & FAMILY

Recovery usually doesn't happen overnight; it is a process. When Cornelius and his family came into the spotlight in Acts 10, the process of their recovery had already begun. Out of a Roman religious and military background, this centurion and his family had become "God-fearers." They worshiped the God of Israel and lived godly lives. They were deeply reverent and generous, and they were people of prayer.

The family of Cornelius had undoubtedly changed many of the habit patterns and perspectives that had emerged out of their background. At this point, God intervened to make it possible for them to proceed to a deeper and eternally decisive level of recovery. God met them by sending the apostle Peter who came to them with the needed spiritual insight.

That scene in Cornelius's home was a model of family recovery. As Cornelius and his family came to believe in the redemption of Jesus, they also entered a phase of spiritual recovery augmented by the power of the Holy Spirit. This wasn't the end of their recovery process by any means. But they were well on their way because they had established healthy relationships with each other and with God.

When the family of Cornelius received the gift of the Holy Spirit, a new era of history was born. For the first time, God showed that all people were acceptable to God through Jesus Christ—even "unclean" Gentiles. Because of his cultural prejudices, Peter had a hard time accepting this truth, but when Cornelius and his family received the Holy Spirit, he could no longer deny it. God desires to make the Holy Spirit's power a part of all our lives. If we accept God's forgiveness on the basis of the work of Jesus Christ, we can experience God's power in our life. With God's help, no problem or dependency is too great to overcome.

STRENGTHS AND ACCOMPLISHMENTS:
- Cornelius believed God to the degree that he understood him.
- He led his family to know God the best way he knew how.
- He was not satisfied with his level of maturity and sought to grow further.
- He and his family were open to change and embraced new life in Jesus Christ.

WEAKNESSES AND MISTAKES:
- Cornelius's understanding was limited, and he initially worshiped Peter.

LESSONS FROM THEIR LIVES:
- God reaches out to those who want to know him better.
- The power of Jesus is for everyone, regardless of race or background.
- Recovery often requires guidance from others who have already been there.

KEY VERSE:
"Everyone who believes in [Jesus Christ] will have their sins forgiven through his name" (Acts 10:43).

The story of Cornelius and his family is told in Acts 10–11.

---

the gift of the Holy Spirit would be given to
Gentiles too! 46,47But there could be no doubt
about it, for they heard them speaking in
tongues and praising God.
Peter asked, "Can anyone object to my
baptizing them, now that they have received
the Holy Spirit just as we did?" 48So he did,
baptizing them in the name of Jesus, the
Messiah. Afterwards Cornelius begged him to
stay with them for several days.

CHAPTER 11

The Inclusion of the Gentiles

Soon the news reached the apostles and other
brothers in Judea that Gentiles also were being converted! 2But when Peter arrived back in
Jerusalem, the Jewish believers argued with
him.
3"You fellowshiped with Gentiles and even
ate with them," they accused.
4Then Peter told them the whole story.
5"One day in Joppa," he said, "while I was
praying, I saw a vision—a huge sheet, let down
by its four corners from the sky. 6Inside the
sheet were all sorts of animals, reptiles, and
birds [which we are not to eat]. 7And I heard a
voice say, 'Kill and eat whatever you wish.'
8"'Never, Lord,' I replied. 'For I have never
yet eaten anything forbidden by our Jewish
laws!'
9"But the voice came again, 'Don't say it
isn't right when God declares it is!'

10“This happened *three times* before the sheet and all it contained disappeared into heaven. 11Just then three men who had come to take me with them to Caesarea arrived at the house where I was staying! 12The Holy Spirit told me to go with them and not to worry about their being Gentiles! These six brothers here accompanied me, and we soon arrived at the home of the man who had sent the messengers. 13He told us how an angel had appeared to him and told him to send messengers to Joppa to find Simon Peter! 14‘He will tell you how you and all your household can be saved!’ the angel had told him.

15“Well, I began telling them the Good News, but just as I was getting started with my sermon, the Holy Spirit fell on them, just as he fell on us at the beginning! 16Then I thought of the Lord’s words when he said, ‘Yes, John baptized with water, but you shall be baptized with the Holy Spirit.’ 17And since it was *God* who gave these Gentiles the same gift he gave us when we believed on the Lord Jesus Christ, who was I to argue?”

18When the others heard this, all their objections were answered and they began praising God! “Yes,” they said, “God has given to the Gentiles, too, the privilege of turning to him and receiving eternal life!”

A New Church in Antioch

19Meanwhile, the believers who fled from Jerusalem during the persecution after Stephen’s death traveled as far as Phoenicia, Cyprus, and Antioch, scattering the Good News, but only to Jews. 20However, some of the believers who went to Antioch from Cyprus and Cyrene also gave their message about the Lord Jesus to some Greeks. 21And the Lord honored this effort so that large numbers of these Gentiles became believers.

22When the church at Jerusalem heard what had happened, they sent Barnabas to Antioch to help the new converts. 23When he arrived and saw the wonderful things God was doing, he was filled with excitement and joy, and encouraged the believers to stay close to the Lord, whatever the cost. 24Barnabas was a kindly person, full of the Holy Spirit and strong in faith. As a result, large numbers of people were added to the Lord.

25Then Barnabas went on to Tarsus to hunt for Paul. 26When he found him, he brought him back to Antioch; and both of them stayed there for a full year teaching the many new converts. (It was there at Antioch that the believers were first called “Christians.”)

27During this time some prophets came down from Jerusalem to Antioch, 28and one of them, named Agabus, stood up in one of the meetings to predict by the Spirit that a great famine was coming upon the land of Israel. (This was fulfilled during the reign of Claudius.) 29So the believers decided to send relief to the Christians in Judea, each giving as much as he could. 30This they did, consigning their gifts to Barnabas and Paul to take to the elders of the church in Jerusalem.

CHAPTER 12

An Angel Rescues Peter

About that time King Herod moved against some of the believers 2and killed the apostle James (John’s brother). 3When Herod saw how much this pleased the Jewish leaders, he arrested Peter during the Passover celebration 4and imprisoned him, placing him under the guard of sixteen soldiers. Herod’s intention was to deliver Peter to the Jews for execution after the Passover. 5But earnest prayer was going up to God from the church for his safety all the time he was in prison.

6The night before he was to be executed, he was asleep, double-chained between two soldiers with others standing guard before the prison gate, 7when suddenly there was a light in the cell and an angel of the Lord stood beside Peter! The angel slapped him on the side to awaken him and said, “Quick! Get up!” And the chains fell off his wrists! 8Then the angel told him, “Get dressed and put on your shoes.” And he did. “Now put on your coat and follow me!” the angel ordered.

9So Peter left the cell, following the angel. But all the time he thought it was a dream or vision and didn’t believe it was really happening. 10They passed the first and second cell blocks and came to the iron gate to the street,

12:1-11 Peter’s escape from prison shows that nothing can thwart God’s plan for our life. God can always overcome the obstacles that stand in our way. He may even use supernatural means to deliver us—against all human odds and in response to prayer. This does not mean we will never face difficulties in our walk with God. Even as the early church enjoyed phenomenal success, it still suffered severe trials. We will always face some obstacles as we seek to live out God’s plan for our life. But since God wants us to succeed in recovery, nothing can stand in the way of our success if we entrust our life to his care.

and this opened to them of its own accord! So
they passed through and walked along together for a block, and then the angel left
him.
11Peter finally realized what had happened!
"It's really true!" he said to himself. "The Lord
has sent his angel and saved me from Herod
and from what the Jews were hoping to do to
me!"
12After a little thought he went to the home
of Mary, mother of John Mark, where many
were gathered for a prayer meeting.
13He knocked at the door in the gate, and a
girl named Rhoda came to open it. 14When
she recognized Peter's voice, she was so overjoyed that she ran back inside to tell everyone
that Peter was standing outside in the street.
15They didn't believe her. "You're out of your
mind," they said. When she insisted they
decided, "It must be his angel. [They must
have killed him.]"
16Meanwhile Peter continued knocking.
When they finally went out and opened the
door, their surprise knew no bounds. 17He
motioned for them to quiet down and told
them what had happened and how the Lord
had brought him out of jail. "Tell James and
the others what happened," he said—and left
for safer quarters.
18At dawn, the jail was in great commotion.
What had happened to Peter? 19When Herod
sent for him and found that he wasn't there,
he had the sixteen guards arrested, court-
martialed and sentenced to death. Afterwards
he left to live in Caesarea for a while.

King Herod Dies

20While he was in Caesarea, a delegation from
Tyre and Sidon arrived to see him. He was
highly displeased with the people of those
two cities, but the delegates made friends with
Blastus, the royal secretary, and asked for
peace, for their cities were economically dependent upon trade with Herod's country.
21An appointment with Herod was granted,
and when the day arrived he put on his royal
robes, sat on his throne, and made a speech
to them. 22At its conclusion the people gave
him a great ovation, shouting, "It is the voice
of a god and not of a man!"
23Instantly, an angel of the Lord struck
Herod with a sickness so that he was filled
with maggots and died—because he accepted
the people's worship instead of giving the
glory to God.
24God's Good News was spreading rapidly
and there were many new believers.
25Barnabas and Paul now visited Jerusalem
and as soon as they had finished their business, returned to Antioch, taking John Mark
with them.

CHAPTER 13

Barnabas and Paul Are Sent Out

Among the prophets and teachers of the
church at Antioch were Barnabas and Symeon
(also called "The Black Man"), Lucius (from
Cyrene), Manaen (the foster-brother of King
Herod), and Paul. 2One day as these men were
worshiping and fasting the Holy Spirit said,
"Dedicate Barnabas and Paul for a special job
I have for them." 3So after more fasting and
prayer, the men laid their hands on them—
and sent them on their way.

A Sorcerer Is Blinded

4Directed by the Holy Spirit they went to
Seleucia and then sailed for Cyprus. 5There, in
the town of Salamis, they went to the Jewish
synagogue and preached. (John Mark went
with them as their assistant.)
6,7Afterwards they preached from town to
town across the entire island until finally they
reached Paphos where they met a Jewish sor-

12:20-24 Herod Agrippa pompously considered himself to be entirely self-sufficient, with no need of others, much less any higher Power. He enjoyed the worship he received from his people, playing the role of a god in their lives. What a contrast to the helpless way he died. Death is the great leveler of all members of the human race. God will not be mocked; he will judge those who try to displace him on the throne of their lives. When we give up our self-sufficiency and turn our life over to God our true King, we come to know that his mercy and justice are sufficient for each day and for eternity.

13:1-3 However reluctant the church in Antioch may have been to lose Paul and Barnabas, they immediately submitted to the voice of the Holy Spirit. Although it meant a major change, they participated with the Holy Spirit by releasing and commissioning these key leaders to missionary service. To send them on their way, they fasted, prayed, and laid their hands on them. In like manner, we can show support for one another in the process of recovery. If God is number one in our life, we will be willing to give up our possessions, life-style, and codependent relationships to follow God's will for our life. Although this may include a great deal of personal sacrifice, it will lead to a life of joy and serenity.

cerer, a fake prophet named Bar-Jesus. He had attached himself to the governor, Sergius Paulus, a man of considerable insight and understanding. The governor invited Barnabas and Paul to visit him, for he wanted to hear their message from God. 8But the sorcerer, Elymas (his name in Greek), interfered and urged the governor to pay no attention to what Paul and Barnabas said, trying to keep him from trusting the Lord.

9Then Paul, filled with the Holy Spirit, glared angrily at the sorcerer and said, 10"You son of the devil, full of every sort of trickery and villainy, enemy of all that is good, will you never end your opposition to the Lord? 11And now God has laid his hand of punishment upon you, and you will be stricken awhile with blindness."

Instantly mist and darkness fell upon him, and he began wandering around begging for someone to take his hand and lead him. 12When the governor saw what happened, he believed and was astonished at the power of God's message.

Paul Preaches to Jews in Antioch

13Now Paul and those with him left Paphos by ship for Turkey, landing at the port town of Perga. There John deserted them and returned to Jerusalem. 14But Barnabas and Paul went on to Antioch, a city in the province of Pisidia.

On the Sabbath they went into the synagogue for the services. 15After the usual readings from the Books of Moses and from the Prophets, those in charge of the service sent them this message: "Brothers, if you have any word of instruction for us come and give it!"

16So Paul stood, waved a greeting to them and began. "Men of Israel," he said, "and all others here who reverence God, [let me begin my remarks with a bit of history].

17"The God of this nation Israel chose our ancestors and honored them in Egypt by gloriously leading them out of their slavery. 18And he nursed them through forty years of wandering around in the wilderness. 19,20Then he destroyed seven nations in Canaan and gave Israel their land as an inheritance. Judges ruled for about four hundred and fifty years and were followed by Samuel the prophet.

21"Then the people begged for a king, and God gave them Saul (son of Kish), a man of the tribe of Benjamin, who reigned for forty years. 22But God removed him and replaced him with David as king, a man about whom God said, 'David (son of Jesse) is a man after my own heart, for he will obey me.' 23And it is one of King David's descendants, Jesus, who is God's promised Savior of Israel!

24"But before he came, John the Baptist preached the need for everyone in Israel to turn from sin to God. 25As John was finishing his work he asked, 'Do you think I am the Messiah? No! But he is coming soon—and in comparison with him, I am utterly worthless.'

26"Brothers—you sons of Abraham, and also all of you Gentiles here who reverence God—this salvation is for all of us! 27The Jews in Jerusalem and their leaders fulfilled prophecy by killing Jesus; for they didn't recognize him or realize that he is the one the prophets had written about, though they heard the prophets' words read every Sabbath. 28They found no just cause to execute him, but asked Pilate to have him killed anyway. 29When they had fulfilled all the prophecies concerning his death, he was taken from the cross and placed in a tomb.

30"But God brought him back to life again! 31And he was seen many times during the next few days by the men who had accompanied him to Jerusalem from Galilee—these men have constantly testified to this in public witness.

32,33"And now Barnabas and I are here to bring you this Good News—that God's promise to our ancestors has come true in our own time, in that God brought Jesus back to life again. This is what the second Psalm is talking about when it says concerning Jesus, 'Today I have honored you as my Son.'

34"For God had promised to bring him back to life again, no more to die. This is stated in the Scripture that says, 'I will do for you the wonderful thing I promised David.' 35In another Psalm he explained more fully, saying,

---

13:13-14 John Mark left the missionary team and returned home to Jerusalem. We aren't sure why he deserted the team, but perhaps it was due to his lack of faith, his disappointment in Paul's leadership, culture shock, homesickness, or fear. His failure here may remind us of our experiences of relapse. It is encouraging to see that later John Mark was restored to fellowship with Barnabas and Paul. Barnabas took John Mark under his wing, even when Paul rejected him (15:37-39). From Paul's letters a decade later (Colossians 4:10; 2 Timothy 4:11), we know that John Mark became a faithful minister in the early church. Our failures can become opportunities to start over and then take steps to keep learning and growing.

PAUL

Paul the Pharisee was exemplary in his religious fervor, and he backed up his convictions with immediate and decisive action; no one could doubt his sincerity. His number one priority was to wipe out the church of Jesus Christ—and he thought this was what God wanted him to do. He pursued the first Christians with a vengeance.

One day Jesus Christ confronted this proud religious leader on the road to Damascus. He intervened in Paul's life at a point when he was driven by an angry religious addiction. Though God blinded Paul physically, he gave him clear spiritual insight. In one moment, Paul was broken, humbled, and set on the road to recovery. He was freed from the legalistic mind-set that had controlled his life. Paul had experienced the transforming power of God.

With the kind of commitment and intensity that he displayed as a Pharisee, Paul set out to tell the world about Jesus Christ. He endured sickness, rejection, and repeated attacks on his life to bring the message of God's forgiveness to needy people. He spoke before Jews, Greeks, and Romans. He defended his faith before kings and emperors. By the end of his life, much of the Mediterranean world had been reached with the gospel. This former Pharisee was destined to become the greatest missionary of the early church.

As we rejoice in the transformation of Paul's life, it is important to remember that this change took place because of the marvelous grace of God. Originally he was highly dysfunctional. As a result of his conversion, however, he was set free from his unhealthy behaviors and activities. We, like Paul, can experience this freeing and transforming grace of God. Through it we can be healed and transformed, no matter how dark our past or how great our mistakes.

STRENGTHS AND ACCOMPLISHMENTS:
- Paul displayed great commitment to the causes he pursued.
- He was a brilliant spokesperson for Jesus Christ.
- He was no longer driven to self-serving achievement after his conversion.
- Paul was largely responsible for the dramatic spread of the gospel.

WEAKNESSES AND MISTAKES:
- Before his conversion, Paul sought to destroy the church of Jesus Christ.
- Before he came to believe, Paul denied the truth about Jesus vehemently.

LESSONS FROM HIS LIFE:
- Zeal and energy alone do not impress God or make a person successful.
- A person can be healed from the past and find hope for the future.
- No matter when we begin recovery, we can still make an impact on others.

KEY VERSES:
"No, dear brothers, I am still not all I should be, but I am bringing all my energies to bear on this one thing: Forgetting the past and looking forward to what lies ahead, I strain to reach the end of the race and receive the prize for which God is calling us up to heaven because of what Christ Jesus did for us" (Philippians 3:13-14).

Paul's story is told in Acts 7–28; additional information can be found in the various letters he wrote. He is also mentioned in 2 Peter 3:15-16.

'God will not let his Holy One decay.' 36This
was not a reference to David, for after David
had served his generation according to the
will of God, he died and was buried, and his
body decayed. 37[No, it was a reference to
another]—someone God brought back to life,
whose body was not touched at all by the
ravages of death.
38"Brothers! Listen! In this man Jesus there
is forgiveness for your sins! 39Everyone who
trusts in him is freed from all guilt and declared righteous—something the Jewish law
could never do. 40Oh, be careful! Don't let the
prophets' words apply to you. For they said,
41'Look and perish, you despisers [of the
truth], for I am doing something in your day—something that you won't believe when you hear it announced.'"
42As the people left the synagogue that day,
they asked Paul to return and speak to them
again the next week. 43And many Jews and
godly Gentiles who worshiped at the synagogue followed Paul and Barnabas down the street as the two men urged them to accept
the mercies God was offering. 44The following
week almost the entire city turned out to hear them preach the Word of God.

Paul Turns to the Gentiles

45But when the Jewish leaders saw the crowds,

they were jealous, and cursed and argued against whatever Paul said.

46 Then Paul and Barnabas spoke out boldly and declared, “It was necessary that this Good News from God should be given first to you Jews. But since you have rejected it and shown yourselves unworthy of eternal life—well, we will offer it to Gentiles. 47 For this is as the Lord commanded when he said, ‘I have made you a light to the Gentiles, to lead them from the farthest corners of the earth to my salvation.’ ”

48 When the Gentiles heard this, they were very glad and rejoiced in Paul’s message; and as many as wanted eternal life, believed. 49 So God’s message spread all through that region.

50 Then the Jewish leaders stirred up both the godly women and the civic leaders of the city and incited a mob against Paul and Barnabas, and ran them out of town. 51 But they shook off the dust of their feet against the town and went on to the city of Iconium. 52 And their converts were filled with joy and with the Holy Spirit.

CHAPTER 14

Paul and Barnabas Preach at Iconium

At Iconium, Paul and Barnabas went together to the synagogue and preached with such power that many—both Jews and Gentiles—believed.

2 But the Jews who spurned God’s message stirred up distrust among the Gentiles against Paul and Barnabas, saying all sorts of evil things about them. 3 Nevertheless, they stayed there a long time, preaching boldly, and the Lord proved their message was from him by giving them power to do great miracles. 4 But the people of the city were divided in their opinion about them. Some agreed with the Jewish leaders, and some backed the apostles.

5,6 When Paul and Barnabas learned of a plot to incite a mob of Gentiles, Jews, and Jewish leaders to attack and stone them, they fled for their lives, going to the cities of Lycaonia, Lystra, Derbe, and the surrounding area, 7 and preaching the Good News there.

Paul Heals a Cripple at Lystra

8 While they were at Lystra, they came upon a man with crippled feet who had been that way from birth, so he had never walked. 9 He was listening as Paul preached, and Paul noticed him and realized he had faith to be healed. 10 So Paul called to him, “Stand up!” and the man leaped to his feet and started walking!

11 When the listening crowd saw what Paul had done, they shouted (in their local dialect, of course), “These men are gods in human bodies!” 12 They decided that Barnabas was the Greek god Jupiter, and that Paul, because he was the chief speaker, was Mercury! 13 The local priest of the Temple of Jupiter, located on the outskirts of the city, brought them cartloads of flowers and prepared to sacrifice oxen to them at the city gates before the crowds.

14 But when Barnabas and Paul saw what was happening, they ripped at their clothing in dismay and ran out among the people, shouting, 15 “Men! What are you doing? We are merely human beings like yourselves! We have come to bring you the Good News that you are invited to turn from the worship of these foolish things and to pray instead to the living God, who made heaven and earth and sea and everything in them. 16 In bygone days he permitted the nations to go their own ways, 17 but he never left himself without a witness; there were always his reminders—the kind things he did such as sending you rain and good crops and giving you food and gladness.”

18 But even so, Paul and Barnabas could scarcely restrain the people from sacrificing to them!

19 Yet only a few days later, some Jews ar-

13:45–14:6 Jealousy, rejection, ridicule, revenge, physical abuse, murder plots—Paul and Barnabas experienced all that and more as they preached the Good News to others. Sometimes Paul and Barnabas stayed in a town for weeks; other times they had to run for their lives after only a short stay. When we reach out to others in recovery, we may need courage to hang in there with unreceptive people who present challenges to our message. In other cases we may need to cut our losses and run. It takes wisdom from above to know how to react in any given situation.

14:14-20 The crowds at Lystra erroneously thought Paul and Barnabas were Greek gods. The missionaries were horrified by such badly mistaken identification and sadly misplaced worship. They quickly sought to clear up the misunderstanding. Soon after this, Jews from the neighboring town of Iconium persuaded the locals that Paul was a charlatan. As a result, Paul was nearly killed, but God intervened to spare his life. The people at Lystra changed their attitudes and opinions about God very quickly and on very little evidence. The result was destructive. If we will determine to persevere in our faith, proving God’s faithfulness, we will enjoy long-term recovery.

BARNABAS & JOHN MARK

Discouragement often drains our energy, especially when we face the trials of recovery. At such times, it is very helpful to spend time with people who know how to encourage. Some people know just what to do or say to remind us that life is worthwhile, even in the midst of pain and failure. They know how to inspire hope when there seems to be nothing to hope for. Barnabas, whose name means "son of encouragement," was just that kind of person.

Barnabas's gift of encouragement was demonstrated through his financial generosity, his leadership, his teaching of new believers at Antioch, and his acceptance of Paul when others were afraid of him and doubted his conversion. It is probably accurate to say that Barnabas changed the course of church history and even the shape of the New Testament itself by persevering in his encouragement of John Mark.

Unfortunately, John Mark bailed out of his responsibilities on the first missionary journey with Paul and Barnabas. Barnabas was willing to give the younger man an opportunity for recovery by including him in a second journey, but Paul wouldn't hear of it. The disagreement was so great that Barnabas and Paul parted company. Paul went back to Asia Minor with his new partner, Silas; Barnabas went on his own missionary journey with John Mark at his side.

With Barnabas's encouragement, Mark was faithful in his missionary ministry and soon regained Paul's respect. Later, Mark would also work with the apostle Peter. He was the author of the Gospel of Mark, written to encourage others to consider faith in Jesus Christ. Just as was true for John Mark, failure need not be the end for us. The recovery offered by Jesus Christ gives each of us the chance for a new start. As we recover, we also have the privilege of encouraging others along the way.

STRENGTHS AND ACCOMPLISHMENTS:
- Barnabas was a gifted encourager.
- Barnabas was willing to invest in John Mark even after his failure.
- John Mark became a great minister and writer.

WEAKNESSES AND MISTAKES:
- John Mark gave up and went home during Paul's first missionary journey.

LESSONS FROM THEIR LIVES:
- As we work our recovery, we need encouragers to give us perspective.
- At times, we may need to make personal sacrifices to encourage others.
- Though it can lead to disappointment, encouragement can pay huge dividends.

KEY VERSES:
"Barnabas . . . wanted to take along John Mark. But Paul didn't like that idea at all, since John had deserted them in Pamphylia. Their disagreement over this was so sharp that they separated. Barnabas took Mark with him and sailed for Cyprus" (Acts 15:37-39).

The story of Barnabas and John Mark is told in Acts 12:25–15:39. Both also are mentioned in Colossians 4:10. Barnabas is referred to in Acts 4, 9, and 11; 1 Corinthians 9; and Galatians 2. John Mark is referred to in 2 Timothy 4; Philemon 1:24; and 1 Peter 5.

---

rived from Antioch and Iconium and turned
the crowds into a murderous mob that stoned
Paul and dragged him out of the city, apparently dead. 20But as the believers stood around
him, he got up and went back into the city!

Paul and Barnabas Appoint Elders

The next day he left with Barnabas for Derbe.
21After preaching the Good News there and
making many disciples, they returned again
to Lystra, Iconium and Antioch, 22where they
helped the believers to grow in love for God
and each other. They encouraged them to
continue in the faith in spite of all the persecution, reminding them that they must enter
into the Kingdom of God through many tribulations. 23Paul and Barnabas also appointed
elders in every church and prayed for them
with fasting, turning them over to the care of
the Lord in whom they trusted.
24Then they traveled back through Pisidia
to Pamphylia, 25preached again in Perga, and
went on to Attalia.

Paul and Barnabas Return to Antioch

26Finally they returned by ship to Antioch,
where their journey had begun and where
they had been committed to God for the work
now completed.
27Upon arrival they called together the be-

lievers and reported on their trip, telling how God had opened the door of faith to the Gentiles too. [28]And they stayed there with the believers at Antioch for a long while.

CHAPTER 15

The Leaders Meet in Jerusalem

While Paul and Barnabas were at Antioch, some men from Judea arrived and began to teach the believers that unless they adhered to the ancient Jewish custom of circumcision, they could not be saved. [2]Paul and Barnabas argued and discussed this with them at length, and finally the believers sent them to Jerusalem, accompanied by some local men, to talk to the apostles and elders there about this question. [3]After the entire congregation had escorted them out of the city, the delegates went on to Jerusalem, stopping along the way in the cities of Phoenicia and Samaria to visit the believers, telling them—much to everyone's joy—that the Gentiles, too, were being converted.

[4]Arriving in Jerusalem, they met with the church leaders—all the apostles and elders were present—and Paul and Barnabas reported on what God had been doing through their ministry. [5]But then some of the men who had been Pharisees before their conversion stood to their feet and declared that all Gentile converts must be circumcised and required to follow all the Jewish customs and ceremonies.

[6]So the apostles and church elders set a further meeting to decide this question.

[7]At the meeting, after long discussion, Peter stood and addressed them as follows: "Brothers, you all know that God chose me from among you long ago to preach the Good News to the Gentiles so that they also could believe. [8]God, who knows men's hearts, confirmed the fact that he accepts Gentiles by giving them the Holy Spirit, just as he gave him to us. [9]He made no distinction between them and us, for he cleansed their lives through faith, just as he did ours. [10]And now are you going to correct God by burdening the Gentiles with a yoke that neither we nor our fathers were able to bear? [11]Don't you believe that all are saved the same way, by the free gift of the Lord Jesus?"

[12]There was no further discussion, and everyone now listened as Barnabas and Paul told about the miracles God had done through them among the Gentiles.

[13]When they had finished, James took the floor. "Brothers," he said, "listen to me. [14]Peter has told you about the time God first visited the Gentiles to take from them a people to bring honor to his name. [15]And this fact of Gentile conversion agrees with what the prophets predicted. For instance, listen to this passage from the prophet Amos:

> [16]'Afterwards' [says the Lord], 'I will return
> and renew the broken contract with
> David, [17]so that Gentiles, too, will find
> the Lord—all those marked with my
> name.'

[18]That is what the Lord says, who reveals his plans made from the beginning.

[19]"And so my judgment is that we should not insist that the Gentiles who turn to God must obey our Jewish laws, [20]except that we should write to them to refrain from eating meat sacrificed to idols, from all fornication, and also from eating unbled meat of strangled animals. [21]For these things have been preached against in Jewish synagogues in every city on every Sabbath for many generations."

15:1-5 The Jerusalem Council marked a crisis point in the history of Christianity. At the center of this crisis was the issue of the Jewish Law. Should Gentiles be required to keep the Law of Moses, including the rite of circumcision? Jewish Christians thought Gentile Christians should have to comply. The answer of the council would affect the basis for faith, fellowship, outreach, and leadership in the church. The very gospel of grace was at stake in this crisis. Is Christ's work alone sufficient for our salvation? Or do we also have to follow the Mosaic Law? In the end, the sufficiency of Christ was defended. Self-examination and crisis intervention were essential to the health of the early church, just as they are to our recovery. Reaffirming our basis of faith, regularly and at crucial moments, is important to the recovery and renewal process.

15:12-21 At this council meeting in Jerusalem, James concluded the discussion and confirmed Peter's view that Gentiles were acceptable to God in Christ without adhering to Jewish Law. James defended his view by appealing to the Scriptures as his final authority for faith and practice. Henceforth, Gentile believers did not have to keep the Jewish Law in order to be accepted in the Christian community. Just as the Jews wisely did not add unnecessary requirements for salvation in Christ, we must be careful to keep the requirements for involvement in recovery simple. God is the ultimate director of our recovery. As we continue to submit to his will, he will show us what is essential.

A Letter for Gentile Believers

22Then the apostles and elders and the whole
congregation voted to send delegates to Antioch with Paul and Barnabas, to report on this
decision. The men chosen were two of the
church leaders—Judas (also called Barsabbas)
and Silas.
23This is the letter they took along with
them:
"From: The apostles, elders and brothers at
Jerusalem.
"To: The Gentile brothers in Antioch, Syria
and Cilicia. Greetings!
24"We understand that some believers from
here have upset you and questioned your
salvation, but they had no such instructions
from us. 25So it seemed wise to us, having
unanimously agreed on our decision, to send
to you these two official representatives,
along with our beloved Barnabas and Paul.
26These men—Judas and Silas, who have
risked their lives for the sake of our Lord Jesus
Christ—will confirm orally what we have decided concerning your question.
27-29"For it seemed good to the Holy Spirit
and to us to lay no greater burden of Jewish
laws on you than to abstain from eating food
offered to idols and from unbled meat of
strangled animals, and, of course, from fornication. If you do this, it is enough. Farewell."
30The four messengers went at once to Antioch, where they called a general meeting of
the Christians and gave them the letter. 31And
there was great joy throughout the church
that day as they read it.
32Then Judas and Silas, both being gifted
speakers, preached long sermons to the believers, strengthening their faith. 33They
stayed several days, and then Judas and Silas
returned to Jerusalem taking greetings and
appreciation to those who had sent them.
34,35Paul and Barnabas stayed on at Antioch to
assist several others who were preaching and
teaching there.

Paul and Barnabas Separate

36Several days later Paul suggested to Barnabas
that they return again to Turkey and visit each
city where they had preached before, to see
how the new converts were getting along.
37Barnabas agreed and wanted to take along
John Mark. 38But Paul didn't like that idea at
all, since John had deserted them in Pamphylia. 39Their disagreement over this was so
sharp that they separated. Barnabas took
Mark with him and sailed for Cyprus,
40,41while Paul chose Silas and, with the blessing of the believers, left for Syria and Cilicia
to encourage the churches there.

CHAPTER 16

Timothy Joins Paul and Silas

Paul and Silas went first to Derbe and then on
to Lystra where they met Timothy, a believer
whose mother was a Christian Jewess, but his
father a Greek. 2Timothy was well thought of
by the brothers in Lystra and Iconium, 3so
Paul asked him to join them on their journey.
In deference to the Jews of the area, he circumcised Timothy before they left, for everyone knew that his father was a Greek [and
hadn't permitted this before]. 4Then they
went from city to city, making known the
decision concerning the Gentiles, as decided
by the apostles and elders in Jerusalem. 5So
the church grew daily in faith and numbers.

A Call from Macedonia

6Next they traveled through Phrygia and Galatia because the Holy Spirit had told them
not to go into the Turkish province of Asia
Minor at that time. 7Then going along the
borders of Mysia they headed north for the
province of Bithynia, but again the Spirit of

15:36-41 Recovery and spiritual growth are processes we never outgrow. This fact is demonstrated in the conflict between Paul and Barnabas over John Mark. Paul could not forgive John Mark for abandoning them on the first missionary journey (see 13:13-14). This resulted in a sharp disagreement and split between Paul and Barnabas. Even as mature men of faith, Paul and Barnabas had to deal with conflict and anger. They still needed to examine their motives and make amends. We know from Paul's letters that all three later reconciled, due in part to Barnabas's willingness to take John Mark with him. Like these godly men, we are never beyond the need for recovery and restoration.

16:1-3 Paul advised Timothy to submit to the Jewish practice of circumcision, even though it wasn't necessary for his salvation—the Jerusalem Council had established that fact (see 15:12-21). Timothy voluntarily followed Paul's advice in order to remove any possible stumbling block to his communicating with a Jewish audience. As we seek to share with others the Good News of God's powerful deliverance, we need to be willing to remove any cultural or social barriers to effective communication. In this way we will be able to get the message out to as many people in need of recovery as possible.

Jesus said no. 8So instead they went on through Mysia province to the city of Troas.

9That night Paul had a vision. In his dream he saw a man over in Macedonia, Greece, pleading with him, "Come over here and help us." 10Well, that settled it. We would go to Macedonia, for we could only conclude that God was sending us to preach the Good News there.

Lydia Believes in Jesus

11We went aboard a boat at Troas, and sailed straight across to Samothrace, and the next day on to Neapolis, 12and finally reached Philippi, a Roman colony just inside the Macedonian border, and stayed there several days.

13On the Sabbath we went a little way outside the city to a riverbank where we understood some people met for prayer; and we taught the Scriptures to some women who came. 14One of them was Lydia, a saleswoman from Thyatira, a merchant of purple cloth. She was already a worshiper of God and as she listened to us, the Lord opened her heart and she accepted all that Paul was saying. 15She was baptized along with all her household and asked us to be her guests. "If you agree that I am faithful to the Lord," she said, "come and stay at my home." And she urged us until we did.

A Philippian Jailer Believes

16One day as we were going down to the place of prayer beside the river, we met a demon-possessed slave girl, who was a fortune-teller and earned much money for her masters. 17She followed along behind us shouting, "These men are servants of God, and they have come to tell you how to have your sins forgiven."

18This went on day after day until Paul, in great distress, turned and spoke to the demon within her. "I command you in the name of Jesus Christ to come out of her," he said. And instantly it left her.

19Her masters' hopes of wealth were now shattered; they grabbed Paul and Silas and dragged them before the judges at the marketplace.

20,21"These Jews are corrupting our city," they shouted. "They are teaching the people to do things that are against the Roman laws."

22A mob was quickly formed against Paul and Silas, and the judges ordered them stripped and beaten with wooden whips. 23Again and again the rods slashed down across their bared backs; and afterwards they were thrown into prison. The jailer was threatened with death if they escaped, 24so he took no chances, but put them into the inner dungeon and clamped their feet into the stocks.

25Around midnight, as Paul and Silas were praying and singing hymns to the Lord—and the other prisoners were listening— 26suddenly there was a great earthquake; the prison was shaken to its foundations, all the doors flew open—and the chains of every prisoner fell off! 27The jailer wakened to see the prison doors wide open, and assuming the prisoners

---

16:11-18 In Macedonia Paul's first converts were women. One was a businesswoman named Lydia who sold expensive purple cloth to be worn by the wealthy. Another female convert was a slave girl who had been demon-possessed. These two women from entirely different economic and social levels in society both played a key role in the growth of the Philippian church. We are all welcome into the throne room of God through our relationship with Christ. We may be tempted to discriminate on the basis of gender, age, social class, employment status, marital status, handicaps, or the like. But God has made a relationship with himself and his power for recovery available to everyone.

16:25-34 Paul and Silas were beaten and jailed in violation of their rights as Roman citizens. Yet they sang praises to God despite the painful circumstances they faced. God was not finished with Paul and Silas, and he delivered them from this abusive situation. In so doing he taught a clear lesson to the Philippian rulers. God is able to deliver and sustain us in even the most abusive of circumstances. When our focus is on him and all that he has done for us, our identity and inner strength will be sustained. Our inner joy and ability to praise God in the midst of persecution and hardship is a sign of God's power and may even result in our enemies admitting their need for him.

17:1-9 At Thessalonica, Paul presented the Good News in a way that took into account the questions and needs of his largely Jewish audience. As a result, many Jews and many Gentiles turned their lives over to God. Nevertheless, many more Jews objected to Paul's message. They stirred up the crowds and city officials to run Paul out of town—not just out of Thessalonica, but out of Berea, too. This kind of mixed response is similar to the response generated by the recovery movement. Just because some people do not agree with our God-centered approach to recovery doesn't mean it is wrong. We can keep God central to our program and persevere in the face of opposition, just as Paul and Silas did.

had escaped, he drew his sword to kill himself.
28But Paul yelled to him, "Don't do it! We
are all here!"
29Trembling with fear, the jailer called for
lights and ran to the dungeon and fell down
before Paul and Silas. 30He brought them out
and begged them, "Sirs, what must I do to be
saved?"
31They replied, "Believe on the Lord Jesus
and you will be saved, and your entire household."
32Then they told him and all his household
the Good News from the Lord. 33That same
hour he washed their stripes, and he and all
his family were baptized. 34Then he brought
them up into his house and set a meal before
them. How he and his household rejoiced
because all were now believers! 35The next
morning the judges sent police officers over
to tell the jailer, "Let those men go!" 36So the
jailer told Paul they were free to leave.
37But Paul replied, "Oh no they don't! They
have publicly beaten us without trial and
jailed us—and we are Roman citizens! So now
they want us to leave secretly? Never! Let
them come themselves and release us!"
38The police officers reported to the judges,
who feared for their lives when they heard
Paul and Silas were Roman citizens. 39So they
came to the jail and begged them to go, and
brought them out and pled with them to
leave the city. 40Paul and Silas then returned
to the home of Lydia, where they met with
the believers and preached to them once
more before leaving town.

CHAPTER 17

Paul Preaches in Thessalonica

Now they traveled through the cities of Am-
phipolis and Apollonia and came to Thessalonica, where there was a Jewish synagogue. 2As
was Paul's custom, he went there to preach,
and for three Sabbaths in a row he opened the
Scriptures to the people, 3explaining the
prophecies about the sufferings of the Messiah and his coming back to life, and proving
that Jesus is the Messiah. 4Some who listened
were persuaded and became converts—including a large number of godly Greek men
and also many important women of the city.
5But the Jewish leaders were jealous and
incited some worthless fellows from the
streets to form a mob and start a riot. They
attacked the home of Jason, planning to take
Paul and Silas to the City Council for punishment.

STEP 3

Discovering God

BIBLE READING: Acts 17:23-28

We made a decision to turn our will and our life over to the care of God as we understood him.

Before we can turn our life over to God, we need to have an accurate understanding of who he is. It is crucial that we entrust ourself to the God who loves us, and not to the "god" of this world who seeks only to deceive and destroy. The apostle Paul described the deceiver this way: "Satan, who is the god of this evil world, has made him [the deceived person] blind, unable to see the glorious light of the Gospel that is shining upon him or to understand the amazing message we preach about the glory of Christ, who is God" (2 Corinthians 4:4). Has Satan deceived us? How can we be sure that we have a true understanding of God?

When Paul addressed the men of Athens, he said, "I saw your many altars, and one of them had this inscription on it—'To the Unknown God.' You have been worshiping him without knowing who he is, and now I wish to tell you about him. . . . His purpose in all of this is that they [all people] should seek after God, and perhaps feel their way toward him and find him—though he is not far from any one of us. For in him we live and move and are!" (Acts 17:23, 27-28).

Even though God may be unknown to us, he is near and willing to reveal himself. God has promised, "You will find me when you seek me, if you look for me in earnest" (Jeremiah 29:13). Turning over our will involves becoming willing to accept God as he is, instead of insisting on creating him in our own image. When we seek God with an open heart and mind, we will find him.

Turn to page 1409, James 4.

6Not finding them there, they dragged out
Jason and some of the other believers, and
took them before the Council instead. "Paul
and Silas have turned the rest of the world
upside down, and now they are here disturb-
ing our city," they shouted, 7"and Jason has
let them into his home. They are all guilty of
treason, for they claim another king, Jesus,
instead of Caesar."
8,9The people of the city, as well as the
judges, were concerned at these reports and
let them go only after they had posted bail.

Paul and Silas in Beroea

10That night the Christians hurried Paul and
Silas to Beroea, and, as usual, they went to the
synagogue to preach. 11But the people of
Beroea were more open-minded than those in
Thessalonica, and gladly listened to the message. They searched the Scriptures day by day
to check up on Paul and Silas' statements to
see if they were really so. 12As a result, many
of them believed, including several prominent Greek women and many men also.
13But when the Jews in Thessalonica
learned that Paul was preaching in Beroea,
they went over and stirred up trouble. 14The
believers acted at once, sending Paul on to the
coast, while Silas and Timothy remained behind. 15Those accompanying Paul went on
with him to Athens and then returned to
Beroea with a message for Silas and Timothy
to hurry and join him.

Paul Preaches in Athens

16While Paul was waiting for them in Athens,
he was deeply troubled by all the idols he saw
everywhere throughout the city. 17He went to
the synagogue for discussions with the Jews
and the devout Gentiles, and spoke daily in
the public square to all who happened to be
there.
18He also had an encounter with some of
the Epicurean and Stoic philosophers. Their
reaction, when he told them about Jesus and
his resurrection, was, "He's a dreamer," or,
"He's pushing some foreign religion."
19But they invited him to the forum at Mars
Hill. "Come and tell us more about this new
religion," they said, 20"for you are saying some
rather startling things and we want to hear
more." 21(I should explain that all the Atheni-
ans as well as the foreigners in Athens seemed
to spend all their time discussing the latest
new ideas!)
22So Paul, standing before them at the Mars
Hill forum, addressed them as follows:
"Men of Athens, I notice that you are very
religious, 23for as I was out walking I saw your
many altars, and one of them had this inscription on it—'To the Unknown God.' You have
been worshiping him without knowing who
he is, and now I wish to tell you about him.
24"He made the world and everything in it,
and since he is Lord of heaven and earth, he
doesn't live in man-made temples; 25and human hands can't minister to his needs—for he
has no needs! He himself gives life and breath
to everything, and satisfies every need there
is. 26He created all the people of the world
from one man, Adam, and scattered the nations across the face of the earth. He decided
beforehand which should rise and fall, and
when. He determined their boundaries.
27"His purpose in all of this is that they
should seek after God, and perhaps feel their
way toward him and find him—though he is
not far from any one of us. 28For in him we

17:10-12 At Berea, Paul enjoyed a most eager response from the Jewish community. The Bereans searched the Scriptures to confirm Paul's testimonial experience and anecdotal evidence against God's final authority. How exciting when someone is ready to hear the Good News of God's plan of recovery for his life. But no one should have to simply take our word alone as the gospel truth. Fortunately, we have the Scriptures to back up every claim we make about God's grace and his power to deliver.

17:22-31 In Athens, Paul did not preach in the synagogue as he normally did upon entering a new town. Instead, he took a tour through Athens and then shared the Good News with intellectuals and philosophers in their marketplace. He began by acknowledging their belief in an unnamed higher Power—"the Unknown God." Paul described that higher Power as the heavenly Father, as the Creator, as the risen Lord and future Judge. Thanks to Jesus and his messengers, we can know God personally (John 1:18; 1 John 1:1-3). We don't have to look to some unnamed or unknowable higher Power for help in our recovery. We can trust in a powerful, loving, and personal God.

18:1-9 Perhaps Paul was discouraged because his Athens ministry had resulted in very few converts. That might explain the discouragement he felt in Corinth and account for the direct encouragement he received from God while there. We all go through hard times, especially as we pursue recovery. If we follow God's will, however, he will be there to encourage us when times get tough. God doesn't help us along to a certain point just to leave us to be destroyed.

PRISCILLA & AQUILA

Priscilla and Aquila were united not only in marriage, but also in ministry. In writing of this godly couple, Paul and Luke never mentioned them apart from each other. Their abilities and talents were complementary: together, they were able to enrich the lives of the people around them.

Priscilla and Aquila moved to Corinth, Greece, to build a new life after the Jews were commanded to leave the city of Rome. While adjusting to this change, they opened their home to the apostle Paul. He had recently experienced intense trials in his ministry and needed a place to rest and recuperate. In the home of Priscilla and Aquila, Paul found not only acceptance and love, but a livelihood as well. Paul joined them in their tentmaking business.

Paul rested and was greatly encouraged from his time with Priscilla and Aquila. Refreshed from his time in this godly home, Paul responded to God's challenge and entered new territories of ministry. Aquila and Priscilla moved to Ephesus with Paul and helped him in the ministry. Their faithful friendship provided Paul with a relationship of both accountability and encouragement.

When Paul left Ephesus, Aquila and Priscilla oversaw the ministry there. They became aware that a young Jew, Apollos, was speaking with great zeal but with incomplete knowledge of the truth. They solved this problem by patiently explaining the things of God to him. Apollos soon became one of the most gifted preachers in the early church.

As a result of their perseverance in God's work, Priscilla and Aquila eventually had a church meeting in their home. Their strong relationship and godly example made them ideal leaders in the early church. Though they were never famous preachers or leaders themselves, they were used by God to minister to some of the greatest leaders of the early church.

STRENGTHS AND ACCOMPLISHMENTS:
- Priscilla and Aquila shared responsibilities in their marriage.
- They enjoyed a marriage built on respect and love.
- They were willing to take risks and accept new challenges.
- They were able to open their home for the help and encouragement of others.

LESSONS FROM THEIR LIVES:
- A healthy marriage allows both husband and wife the opportunity to exercise their gifts.
- A godly and healthy home is always open to minister to others in need.
- Rest is often needed before and after a time of stress and change.

KEY VERSES:
"Tell Priscilla and Aquila hello. They have been my fellow workers in the affairs of Christ Jesus. In fact, they risked their lives for me, and I am not the only one who is thankful to them; so are all the Gentile churches" (Romans 16:3-4).

Priscilla and Aquila's story is told in Acts 18. Both are also mentioned in Romans 16:3; 1 Corinthians 16:19; and 2 Timothy 4:19.

---

live and move and are! As one of your own
poets says it, 'We are the sons of God.' [29]If this
is true, we shouldn't think of God as an idol
made by men from gold or silver or chipped
from stone. [30]God tolerated man's past ignorance about these things, but now he commands everyone to put away idols and
worship only him. [31]For he has set a day for
justly judging the world by the man he has
appointed, and has pointed him out by bringing him back to life again."

[32]When they heard Paul speak of the resurrection of a person who had been dead, some
laughed, but others said, "We want to hear
more about this later." [33]That ended Paul's
discussion with them, [34]but a few joined him
and became believers. Among them was Dio-
nysius, a member of the City Council, and a
woman named Damaris, and others.

CHAPTER 18

Paul Meets Priscilla and Aquila

Then Paul left Athens and went to Corinth.
[2,3]There he became acquainted with a Jew
named Aquila, born in Pontus, who had recently arrived from Italy with his wife, Priscilla. They had been expelled from Italy as a
result of Claudius Caesar's order to deport all

Jews from Rome. Paul lived and worked with them, for they were tentmakers just as he was.

[4]Each Sabbath found Paul at the synagogue, trying to convince the Jews and Greeks alike. [5]And after the arrival of Silas and Timothy from Macedonia, Paul spent his full time preaching and testifying to the Jews that Jesus is the Messiah. [6]But when the Jews opposed him and blasphemed, hurling abuse at Jesus, Paul shook off the dust from his robe and said, "Your blood be upon your own heads—I am innocent—from now on I will preach to the Gentiles."

[7]After that he stayed with Titus Justus, a Gentile who worshiped God and lived next door to the synagogue. [8]However, Crispus, the leader of the synagogue, and all his household believed in the Lord and were baptized—as were many others in Corinth.

[9]One night the Lord spoke to Paul in a vision and told him, "Don't be afraid! Speak out! Don't quit! [10]For I am with you and no one can harm you. Many people here in this city belong to me." [11]So Paul stayed there the next year and a half, teaching the truths of God.

Paul Is Taken to Court

[12]But when Gallio became governor of Achaia, the Jews rose in concerted action against Paul and brought him before the governor for judgment. [13]They accused Paul of "persuading men to worship God in ways that are contrary to Roman law." [14]But just as Paul started to make his defense, Gallio turned to his accusers and said, "Listen, you Jews, if this were a case involving some crime, I would be obliged to listen to you, [15]but since it is merely a bunch of questions of semantics and personalities and your silly Jewish laws, you take care of it. I'm not interested and I'm not touching it." [16]And he drove them out of the courtroom.

[17]Then the mob grabbed Sosthenes, the new leader of the synagogue, and beat him outside the courtroom. But Gallio couldn't have cared less.

Paul Returns to Antioch

[18]Paul stayed in the city several days after that and then said good-bye to the Christians and sailed for the coast of Syria, taking Priscilla and Aquila with him. At Cenchreae Paul had his head shaved according to Jewish custom, for he had taken a vow. [19]Arriving at the port of Ephesus, he left us aboard ship while he went over to the synagogue for a discussion with the Jews. [20]They asked him to stay for a few days, but he felt that he had no time to lose.

[21]"I must by all means be at Jerusalem for the holiday," he said. But he promised to return to Ephesus later if God permitted; and so he set sail again.

[22]The next stop was at the port of Caesarea from where he visited the church [at Jerusalem] and then sailed on to Antioch. [23]After spending some time there, he left for Turkey again, going through Galatia and Phrygia visiting all the believers, encouraging them and helping them grow in the Lord.

Apollos Is Instructed at Ephesus

[24]As it happened, a Jew named Apollos, a wonderful Bible teacher and preacher, had just arrived in Ephesus from Alexandria in Egypt. [25,26]While he was in Egypt, someone had told him about John the Baptist and what John had said about Jesus, but that is all he knew. He had never heard the rest of the story! So he was preaching boldly and enthusiastically in the synagogue, "The Messiah is coming! Get ready to receive him!" Priscilla and Aquila were there and heard him—and it was a powerful sermon. Afterwards they met with him and explained what had happened to Jesus since the time of John, and all that it meant!

[27]Apollos had been thinking about going to Greece, and the believers encouraged him in this. They wrote to their fellow-believers there, telling them to welcome him. And upon his arrival in Greece, he was greatly used of God to strengthen the church, [28]for he powerfully refuted all the Jewish arguments

18:24-28 Apollos was very well-educated, both in philosophy and in the Scriptures, and was a skilled orator. Yet after hearing him speak in the synagogue, Priscilla and Aquila realized that, as gifted as he was, he still needed to know more about Jesus Christ. They invited him home and explained the gospel to him, filling him in on the things he didn't yet know or understand. We may know people who seem to have it all together, yet they are missing an essential element to a healthy life—a true understanding of and relationship with God. Their giftedness need not intimidate us from sharing the truth with them. We may find that they sense a need for recovery in their life and are ready to respond to our message.

APOLLOS

Apollos was a Jewish Bible teacher and skilled orator from Alexandria. He had heard about John the Baptist's message concerning the coming Messiah. Because he had studied the Scriptures seriously, he knew John's message was true. Apollos traveled north to Ephesus, preaching the message of God's Kingdom and zealously debating the skeptics.

Priscilla and Aquila heard Apollos preach in Ephesus. They were two devoted followers of Christ who had been greatly impacted by Paul's ministry. Though they appreciated his zeal, they discerned that he had incomplete knowledge of the Scriptures. They invited him to their home and more fully explained the truth about Jesus Christ, the salvation he brought, and the Holy Spirit that indwelt and empowered believers. For the first time, Apollos was able to put it all together!

With this new understanding, Apollos went to minister in the city of Corinth. His ministry was so effective that Paul had to warn the believers there to keep their eyes on Christ, rather than on Apollos or himself. Apollos continued to travel and speak throughout Greece. Paul appreciated him so much that he encouraged Titus to support Apollos as much as possible.

The story of Apollos demonstrates the tremendous value of wise counsel in our life. Unfortunately, the counsel many seek lacks true spiritual understanding. Some of us stumble through life with a very limited view of the love and power available in Jesus Christ. The more we are exposed to truth through wise counsel, the more we will fully comprehend Christ's work on our behalf. As this occurs, we can internalize the healing nature of the gospel and become better equipped to minister to others in need.

STRENGTHS AND ACCOMPLISHMENTS:
- Apollos believed God and was committed to him.
- He used his strengths and abilities for the Kingdom of God.
- He was teachable when confronted with the truth.

WEAKNESSES AND MISTAKES:
- Initially, Apollos was operating on an incomplete understanding of the truth.

LESSONS FROM HIS LIFE:
- God's wisdom and truth are available for our personal healing.
- As we discover God's truth and experience his power we are better able to help our fellow strugglers.
- If we are willing to act upon the little we know, God will make it possible for us to learn the full truth.

KEY VERSES:
"Priscilla and Aquila were there and heard [Apollos]—and it was a powerful sermon. Afterwards they met with him and explained what had happened to Jesus since the time of John, and all that it meant!" (Acts 18:25-26).

The story of Apollos is told in Acts 18:24-28. He is also mentioned in 1 Corinthians 1:12; 3:4-6, 22; 4:1, 6; 16:12; and Titus 3:13.

---

in public debate, showing by the Scriptures that Jesus is indeed the Messiah.

CHAPTER 19

The Holy Spirit in Ephesus

While Apollos was in Corinth, Paul traveled through Turkey and arrived in Ephesus, where he found several disciples. 2"Did you receive the Holy Spirit when you believed?" he asked them.

"No," they replied, "we don't know what you mean. What is the Holy Spirit?"

3"Then what beliefs did you acknowledge at your baptism?" he asked.

And they replied, "What John the Baptist taught."

4Then Paul pointed out to them that John's baptism was to demonstrate a desire to turn from sin to God and that those receiving his baptism must then go on to believe in Jesus, the one John said would come later.

5As soon as they heard this, they were baptized in the name of the Lord Jesus. 6Then, when Paul laid his hands upon their heads, the Holy Spirit came on them, and they spoke in other languages and prophesied. 7The men involved were about twelve in number.

Paul Ministers in Ephesus

8Then Paul went to the synagogue and preached boldly each Sabbath day for three months, telling what he believed and why,

and persuading many to believe in Jesus. 9But
some rejected his message and publicly spoke
against Christ, so he left, refusing to preach to
them again. Pulling out the believers, he began a separate meeting at the lecture hall of
Tyrannus and preached there daily. 10This
went on for the next two years, so that everyone in the Turkish province of Asia Minor—
both Jews and Greeks—heard the Lord's
message.

11And God gave Paul the power to do unusual miracles, 12so that even when his hand-
kerchiefs or parts of his clothing were placed
upon sick people, they were healed, and any
demons within them came out.

13A team of itinerant Jews who were traveling from town to town casting out demons
planned to experiment by using the name of
the Lord Jesus. The incantation they decided
on was this: "I adjure you by Jesus, whom
Paul preaches, to come out!" 14Seven sons of
Sceva, a Jewish priest, were doing this. 15But
when they tried it on a man possessed by a
demon, the demon replied, "I know Jesus and
I know Paul, but who are you?" 16And he
leaped on two of them and beat them up, so
that they fled out of his house naked and
badly injured.

17The story of what happened spread
quickly all through Ephesus, to Jews and
Greeks alike; and a solemn fear descended on
the city, and the name of the Lord Jesus was
greatly honored. 18,19Many of the believers
who had been practicing black magic confessed their deeds and brought their incantation books and charms and burned them at a
public bonfire. (Someone estimated the value
of the books at $10,000.) 20This indicates how
deeply the whole area was stirred by God's
message.

The Silversmiths Cause a Riot

21Afterwards Paul felt impelled by the Holy
Spirit to go across to Greece before returning
to Jerusalem. "And after that," he said, "I
must go on to Rome!" 22He sent his two assistants, Timothy and Erastus, on ahead to
Greece while he stayed awhile longer in Asia
Minor.

23But about that time, a big blowup developed in Ephesus concerning the Christians.
24It began with Demetrius, a silversmith who
employed many craftsmen to manufacture
silver shrines of the Greek goddess Diana. 25He
called a meeting of his men, together with
others employed in related trades, and addressed them as follows:

"Gentlemen, this business is our income.
26As you know so well from what you've seen
and heard, this man Paul has persuaded
many, many people that handmade gods
aren't gods at all. As a result, our sales volume
is going down! And this trend is evident not
only here in Ephesus, but throughout the
entire province! 27Of course, I am not only
talking about the business aspects of this situation and our loss of income, but also of the
possibility that the temple of the great goddess Diana will lose its influence, and that
Diana—this magnificent goddess worshiped
not only throughout this part of Turkey but
all around the world—will be forgotten!"

28At this their anger boiled and they began
shouting, "Great is Diana of the Ephesians!"

29A crowd began to gather, and soon the
city was filled with confusion. Everyone
rushed to the amphitheater, dragging along
Gaius and Aristarchus, Paul's traveling companions, for trial. 30Paul wanted to go in, but
the disciples wouldn't let him. 31Some of the
Roman officers of the province, friends of
Paul, also sent a message to him, begging him
not to risk his life by entering.

32Inside the people were all shouting, some
one thing and some another—everything was
in confusion. In fact, most of them didn't
even know why they were there.

33Alexander was spotted among the crowd
by some of the Jews and dragged forward. He
motioned for silence and tried to speak. 34But
when the crowd realized he was a Jew, they
started shouting again and kept it up for two
hours: "Great is Diana of the Ephesians! Great
is Diana of the Ephesians!"

35At last the mayor was able to quiet them

19:11-20 The people of Ephesus were in bondage to their fear of the spiritual realm, and the seven sons of Sceva made their living by allaying their fears. When they were confronted by a real demon, however, these men were powerless. But the demon recognized the authority of Jesus Christ and Paul because they were representatives of God himself. When the people heard the story that proved God's sovereignty over the demonic realm, they were filled with a healthy awe of Jesus Christ and his true representatives. Like the evil spirits, our compulsions and addictions are more powerful than we are. That is why we need God's power to be at work in our life. No other power can overcome our destructive habits and sustain us in a life of recovery.

down enough to speak. "Men of Ephesus," he
said, "everyone knows that Ephesus is the
center of the religion of the great Diana,
whose image fell down to us from heaven.
[36]Since this is an indisputable fact, you
shouldn't be disturbed no matter what is said,
and should do nothing rash. [37]Yet you have
brought these men here who have stolen
nothing from her temple and have not de-
famed her. [38]If Demetrius and the craftsmen
have a case against them, the courts are cur-
rently in session and the judges can take the
case at once. Let them go through legal channels. [39]And if there are complaints about other
matters, they can be settled at the regular City
Council meetings; [40]for we are in danger of
being called to account by the Roman government for today's riot, since there is no cause
for it. And if Rome demands an explanation,
I won't know what to say."

[41]Then he dismissed them, and they dispersed.

CHAPTER 20

On to Greece and Macedonia

When it was all over, Paul sent for the disciples, preached a farewell message to them,
said good-bye and left for Greece, [2]preaching
to the believers along the way in all the cities
he passed through. [3]He was in Greece three
months and was preparing to sail for Syria
when he discovered a plot by the Jews against
his life, so he decided to go north to Macedonia first.

[4]Several men were traveling with him, going as far as Turkey; they were Sopater of
Beroea, the son of Pyrrhus; Aristarchus and
Secundus, from Thessalonica; Gaius, from
Derbe; and Timothy; and Tychicus and Trophimus, who were returning to their homes
in Turkey, [5]and had gone on ahead and were
waiting for us at Troas. [6]As soon as the Passover ceremonies ended, we boarded ship at
Philippi in northern Greece and five days later
arrived in Troas, Turkey, where we stayed a
week.

Paul Resurrects Eutychus

[7]On Sunday we gathered for a Communion
service, with Paul preaching. And since he
was leaving the next day, he talked until midnight! [8]The upstairs room where we met was
lighted with many flickering lamps; [9]and as
Paul spoke on and on, a young man named
Eutychus, sitting on the windowsill, went fast
asleep and fell three stories to his death below.
[10-12]Paul went down and took him into his
arms. "Don't worry," he said, "he's all right!"
And he was! What a wave of awesome joy
swept through the crowd! They all went back
upstairs and ate the Lord's Supper together;
then Paul preached another long sermon—so
it was dawn when he finally left them!

Paul Meets the Ephesian Elders

[13]Paul was going by land to Assos, and we
went on ahead by ship. [14]He joined us there
and we sailed together to Mitylene; [15]the next
day we passed Chios; the next, we touched at
Samos; and a day later we arrived at Miletus.

[16]Paul had decided against stopping at Eph-
esus this time, as he was hurrying to get to
Jerusalem, if possible, for the celebration of
Pentecost.

[17]But when we landed at Miletus, he sent a
message to the elders of the church at Ephesus
asking them to come down to the boat to
meet him.

[18]When they arrived he told them, "You
men know that from the day I set foot in
Turkey until now [19]I have done the Lord's
work humbly—yes, and with tears—and have
faced grave danger from the plots of the Jews
against my life. [20]Yet I never shrank from

20:1-6 Paul was not a hit-and-run artist, nor did he operate as a lone ranger. He was accountable and responsible to and for others. He didn't just make converts, he followed them up. He cared for them and helped them to grow spiritually. When we carry our message of hope and recovery to others, it is important to do more than just share the Good News. We need to walk through each new step in recovery with those who desire to change. Paul's entourage pulled together as a team for the sake of the common welfare of growing believers. So we also can join hands with other believers to help hurting people make progress and to receive encouragement for our own daily struggle.

20:7-12 Eutychus fell asleep while Paul was preaching and fell to his death. However, Paul brought him back to life. When we know the happy outcome, this story can seem somewhat humorous—especially since we sense a kindred spirit with Eutychus. (Who among us has not fallen asleep during a sermon?) Luke recounts this event to remind us that God has the power to restore the dead to new life. God works beyond our own natural capabilities, doing what we would consider impossible. He can do the same for those of us who are dead in sin and gripped by addiction. We can find hope for restoration in this amazing story of resurrection.

telling you the truth, either publicly or in your homes. 21I have had one message for Jews and Gentiles alike—the necessity of turning from sin to God through faith in our Lord Jesus Christ.

22"And now I am going to Jerusalem, drawn there irresistibly by the Holy Spirit, not knowing what awaits me, 23except that the Holy Spirit has told me in city after city that jail and suffering lie ahead. 24But life is worth nothing unless I use it for doing the work assigned me by the Lord Jesus—the work of telling others the Good News about God's mighty kindness and love.

25"And now I know that none of you among whom I went about teaching the Kingdom will ever see me again. 26Let me say plainly that no man's blood can be laid at my door, 27for I didn't shrink from declaring all God's message to you.

28"And now beware! Be sure that you feed and shepherd God's flock—his church, purchased with his blood—for the Holy Spirit is holding you responsible as overseers. 29I know full well that after I leave you, false teachers, like vicious wolves, will appear among you, not sparing the flock. 30Some of you yourselves will distort the truth in order to draw a following. 31Watch out! Remember the three years I was with you—my constant watchcare over you night and day and my many tears for you.

32"And now I entrust you to God and his care and to his wonderful words that are able to build your faith and give you all the inheritance of those who are set apart for himself.

33"I have never been hungry for money or fine clothing— 34you know that these hands of mine worked to pay my own way and even to supply the needs of those who were with me. 35And I was a constant example to you in helping the poor; for I remembered the words of the Lord Jesus, 'It is more blessed to give than to receive.'"

36When he had finished speaking, he knelt and prayed with them, 37and they wept aloud as they embraced him in farewell, 38sorrowing most of all because he said that he would never see them again. Then they accompanied him down to the ship.

CHAPTER 21

Paul Returns to Jerusalem

After parting from the Ephesian elders, we sailed straight to Cos. The next day we reached Rhodes and then went to Patara. 2There we boarded a ship sailing for the Syrian province of Phoenicia. 3We sighted the island of Cyprus, passed it on our left, and landed at the harbor of Tyre, in Syria, where the ship unloaded. 4We went ashore, found the local believers, and stayed with them a week. These disciples warned Paul—the Holy Spirit prophesying through them—not to go on to Jerusalem. 5At the end of the week when we returned to the ship, the entire congregation including wives and children walked down to the beach with us where we prayed and said our farewells. 6Then we went aboard, and they returned home.

7The next stop after leaving Tyre was Ptolemais, where we greeted the believers but stayed only one day. 8Then we went on to Caesarea and stayed at the home of Philip the Evangelist, one of the first seven deacons. 9He had four unmarried daughters who had the gift of prophecy.

10During our stay of several days, a man named Agabus, who also had the gift of prophecy, arrived from Judea 11and visited us. He took Paul's belt, bound his own feet and hands with it, and said, "The Holy Spirit declares, 'So shall the owner of this belt be bound by the Jews in Jerusalem and turned over to the Romans.'" 12Hearing this, all of

---

20:22-38 As Paul met with the Ephesian elders, he told them of his plans to return to Jerusalem. Paul sensed a clear leading by the Holy Spirit and was determined to follow it. Apparently, Paul was aware that God's plan might lead him through difficult, even fatal, circumstances. Yet this knowledge didn't slow him down at all. Following God's will in recovery is not necessarily an easy path either. Sometimes it leads to a time of loneliness and loss. Sometimes it causes conflict with our friends and family members. Even though following God's will can be hard at times, it is always the best way to go. Paul's example encourages us to pray for clear knowledge of God's will and the power to obey it.

21:7-9 The last recorded event involving Philip had taken place some twenty-five years earlier while he traveled to Caesarea (8:40). After that time, Philip not only had a continuing ministry, but he also had a godly family with four gifted daughters. Philip had instilled in them his faith in Christ and God's power for life and ministry. This indicates that Christianity, though new, had the power to transform lives on a permanent basis. Philip demonstrated the kind of perseverance and fruitfulness we can have as we work our program today.

us—the local believers and his traveling companions—begged Paul not to go on to Jerusalem.
13But he said, "Why all this weeping? You
are breaking my heart! For I am ready not
only to be jailed at Jerusalem but also to die
for the sake of the Lord Jesus." 14When it was
clear that he wouldn't be dissuaded, we gave
up and said, "The will of the Lord be done."
15So shortly afterwards we packed our
things and left for Jerusalem. 16Some disciples
from Caesarea accompanied us, and on arrival we were guests at the home of Mnason,
originally from Cyprus, one of the early believers; 17and all the believers at Jerusalem
welcomed us cordially.

Paul Arrives at Jerusalem

18The second day Paul took us with him to
meet with James and the elders of the Jerusalem church. 19After greetings were exchanged,
Paul recounted the many things God had
accomplished among the Gentiles through
his work.
20They praised God but then said, "You
know, dear brother, how many thousands of
Jews have also believed, and they are all very
insistent that Jewish believers must continue
to follow the Jewish traditions and customs.
21Our Jewish Christians here at Jerusalem
have been told that you are against the laws
of Moses, against our Jewish customs, and
that you forbid the circumcision of their children. 22Now what can be done? For they will
certainly hear that you have come.
23"We suggest this: We have four men here
who are preparing to shave their heads and
take some vows. 24Go with them to the
Temple and have your head shaved too—and
pay for theirs to be shaved.

"Then everyone will know that you approve of this custom for the Hebrew Christians and that you yourself obey the Jewish laws and are in line with our thinking in these matters.
25"As for the Gentile Christians, we aren't
asking them to follow these Jewish customs at
all—except for the ones we wrote to them
about: not to eat food offered to idols, not to
eat unbled meat from strangled animals, and
not to commit fornication."

Paul Is Arrested

26,27So Paul agreed to their request and the
next day went with the men to the Temple for
the ceremony, thus publicizing his vow to
offer a sacrifice seven days later with the
others.

The seven days were almost ended when
some Jews from Turkey saw him in the
Temple and roused a mob against him. They
grabbed him, 28yelling, "Men of Israel! Help!
Help! This is the man who preaches against
our people and tells everybody to disobey the
Jewish laws. He even talks against the Temple
and defiles it by bringing Gentiles in!" 29(For
down in the city earlier that day, they had
seen him with Trophimus, a Gentile from
Ephesus in Turkey, and assumed that Paul had
taken him into the Temple.)
30The whole population of the city was electrified by these accusations and a great riot
followed. Paul was dragged out of the Temple,
and immediately the gates were closed behind him. 31As they were killing him, word
reached the commander of the Roman garrison that all Jerusalem was in an uproar. 32He
quickly ordered out his soldiers and officers
and ran down among the crowd. When the
mob saw the troops coming, they quit beating
Paul. 33The commander arrested him and ordered him bound with double chains. Then
he asked the crowd who he was and what he
had done. 34Some shouted one thing and
some another. When he couldn't find out
anything in all the uproar and confusion, he
ordered Paul to be taken to the armory. 35As
they reached the stairs, the mob grew so violent that the soldiers lifted Paul to their shoulders to protect him, 36and the crowd surged
behind shouting, "Away with him, away with
him!"

Paul Speaks to the Crowd

37,38As Paul was about to be taken inside, he
said to the commander, "May I have a word
with you?"

"Do you know Greek?" the commander

21:18-27 Paul had been accused of encouraging Jews to live a Gentile life-style. So James suggested that Paul participate in a special vow to show the Jews that he was still one of them. Paul's love for his brothers and sisters led him to do what he could to remove anything that might destroy the faith of a Jewish believer. Thus, Paul followed James's advice and participated in the prescribed Temple worship. Like Paul, we may need to make some personal sacrifices in order to encourage someone else in the recovery process. As we learn to give up our own rights for the sake of others, we will discover the joy that can be found only by serving God and his people.

asked, surprised. "Aren't you that Egyptian who led a rebellion a few years ago and took 4,000 members of the Assassins with him into the desert?"

39"No," Paul replied, "I am a Jew from Tarsus in Cilicia which is no small town. I request permission to talk to these people."

40The commander agreed, so Paul stood on the stairs and motioned to the people to be quiet; soon a deep silence enveloped the crowd, and he addressed them in Hebrew as follows:

CHAPTER 22

"Brothers and fathers, listen to me as I offer my defense." 2(When they heard him speaking in Hebrew, the silence was even greater.) 3"I am a Jew," he said, "born in Tarsus, a city in Cilicia, but educated here in Jerusalem under Gamaliel, at whose feet I learned to follow our Jewish laws and customs very carefully. I became very anxious to honor God in everything I did, just as you have tried to do today. 4And I persecuted the Christians, hounding them to death, binding and delivering both men and women to prison. 5The High Priest or any member of the Council can testify that this is so. For I asked them for letters to the Jewish leaders in Damascus, with instructions to let me bring any Christians I found to Jerusalem in chains to be punished.

6"As I was on the road, nearing Damascus, suddenly about noon a very bright light from heaven shone around me. 7And I fell to the ground and heard a voice saying to me, 'Paul, Paul, why are you persecuting me?'

8"'Who is it speaking to me, sir?' I asked. And he replied, 'I am Jesus of Nazareth, the one you are persecuting.' 9The men with me saw the light but didn't understand what was said.

10"And I said, 'What shall I do, Lord?'

"And the Lord told me, 'Get up and go into Damascus, and there you will be told what awaits you in the years ahead.'

11"I was blinded by the intense light and had to be led into Damascus by my companions. 12There a man named Ananias, as godly a man as you could find for obeying the law and well thought of by all the Jews of Damascus, 13came to me, and standing beside me said, 'Brother Paul, receive your sight!' And that very hour I could see him!

14"Then he told me, 'The God of our fathers has chosen you to know his will and to see the Messiah and hear him speak. 15You are to take his message everywhere, telling what you have seen and heard. 16And now, why delay? Go and be baptized and be cleansed from your sins, calling on the name of the Lord.'

17,18"One day after my return to Jerusalem, while I was praying in the Temple, I fell into a trance and saw a vision of God saying to me, 'Hurry! Leave Jerusalem, for the people here won't believe you when you give them my message.'

19"'But Lord,' I argued, 'they certainly know that I imprisoned and beat those in every synagogue who believed on you. 20And when your witness Stephen was killed, I was standing there agreeing—keeping the coats they laid aside as they stoned him.'

21"But God said to me, 'Leave Jerusalem, for I will send you far away to the *Gentiles!*'"

22The crowd listened until Paul came to that word, then with one voice they shouted, "Away with such a fellow! Kill him! He isn't fit to live!" 23They yelled and threw their coats in the air and tossed up handfuls of dust.

Paul Reveals His Citizenship

24So the commander brought him inside and ordered him lashed with whips to make him confess his crime. He wanted to find out why the crowd had become so furious!

25As they tied Paul down to lash him, Paul said to an officer standing there, "Is it legal for you to whip a Roman citizen who hasn't even been tried?"

26The officer went to the commander and asked, "What are you doing? This man is a Roman citizen!"

27So the commander went over and asked Paul, "Tell me, are you a Roman citizen?"

"Yes, I certainly am."

22:1-21 In this second account of Paul's conversion (see 9:1-18), we learn one additional detail: Paul studied under the great rabbinic scholar, Gamaliel. We are impressed once again with Paul's rage against the believers prior to his conversion. But despite Paul's former self-sufficiency, he quickly admitted his helplessness when Christ appeared to him in a blinding light. His powerless state was so complete that others had to lead him by the hand due to his temporary blindness. Fortunately, we don't all need such a dramatic event to force us to face our powerlessness. However, we must all realize that without God we cannot overcome our compulsions and addictions. When we come to understand this truth, we have started down the road of recovery.

28"I am too," the commander muttered, "and it cost me plenty!"

"But I am a citizen by birth!"

29The soldiers standing ready to lash him, quickly disappeared when they heard Paul was a Roman citizen, and the commander was frightened because he had ordered him bound and whipped.

Paul Before the Jewish Council

30The next day the commander freed him from his chains and ordered the chief priests into session with the Jewish Council. He had Paul brought in before them to try to find out what the trouble was all about.

CHAPTER 23

Gazing intently at the Council, Paul began: "Brothers, I have always lived before God in all good conscience!"

2Instantly Ananias the High Priest commanded those close to Paul to slap him on the mouth.

3Paul said to him, "God shall slap you, you whitewashed pigpen. What kind of judge are you to break the law yourself by ordering me struck like that?"

4Those standing near Paul said to him, "Is that the way to talk to God's High Priest?"

5"I didn't realize he was the High Priest, brothers," Paul replied, "for the Scriptures say, 'Never speak evil of any of your rulers.'"

6Then Paul thought of something! Part of the Council were Sadducees, and part were Pharisees! So he shouted, "Brothers, I am a Pharisee, as were all my ancestors! And I am being tried here today because I believe in the resurrection of the dead!"

7This divided the Council right down the middle—the Pharisees against the Sadducees— 8for the Sadducees say there is no resurrection or angels or even eternal spirit within us, but the Pharisees believe in all of these.

9So a great clamor arose. Some of the Jewish leaders jumped up to argue that Paul was all right. "We see nothing wrong with him," they shouted. "Perhaps a spirit or angel spoke to him [there on the Damascus road]."

10The shouting grew louder and louder, and the men were tugging at Paul from both sides, pulling him this way and that. Finally the commander, fearing they would tear him apart, ordered his soldiers to take him away from them by force and bring him back to the armory.

11That night the Lord stood beside Paul and said, "Don't worry, Paul; just as you have told the people about me here in Jerusalem, so you must also in Rome."

The Plan to Kill Paul

12,13The next morning some forty or more of the Jews got together and bound themselves by a curse neither to eat nor drink until they had killed Paul! 14Then they went to the chief priests and elders and told them what they had done. 15"Ask the commander to bring Paul back to the Council again," they requested. "Pretend you want to ask a few more questions. We will kill him on the way."

16But Paul's nephew got wind of their plan and came to the armory and told Paul.

17Paul called one of the officers and said, "Take this boy to the commander. He has something important to tell him."

18So the officer did, explaining, "Paul, the prisoner, called me over and asked me to bring this young man to you to tell you something."

19The commander took the boy by the hand, and leading him aside asked, "What is it you want to tell me, lad?"

20"Tomorrow," he told him, "the Jews are going to ask you to bring Paul before the Council again, pretending they want to get some more information. 21But don't do it! There are more than forty men hiding along the road ready to jump him and kill him. They have bound themselves under a curse to neither eat nor drink till he is dead. They are out there now, expecting you to agree to their request."

22"Don't let a soul know you told me this," the commander warned the boy as he left.

Paul Is Sent to Caesarea

23,24Then the commander called two of his

23:12-35 This chapter in Paul's life features the courage of a young boy. Paul's young nephew risked his life to warn his uncle of a plot against his life. With this intelligence information, the Roman commander was able to make adjustments in his plan and move Paul safely to Caesarea. A military escort accompanied Paul on his journey that very night, and a cover letter to the governor, Felix, won Paul another chance to speak for himself and God. Thus God providentially worked through a variety of people to move Paul one step closer to Rome. God uses people—little children and governors alike—to accomplish his divine will.

officers and ordered, "Get 200 soldiers ready
to leave for Caesarea at nine o'clock tonight!
Take 200 spearmen and 70 mounted cavalry.
Give Paul a horse to ride and get him safely to
Governor Felix."
25Then he wrote this letter to the governor:
26"*From:* Claudius Lysias
"*To:* His Excellency, Governor Felix.
"Greetings!
27"This man was seized by the Jews, and
they were killing him when I sent the soldiers
to rescue him, for I learned that he was a
Roman citizen. 28Then I took him to their
Council to try to find out what he had done.
29I soon discovered it was something about
their Jewish beliefs, certainly nothing worthy
of imprisonment or death. 30But when I was
informed of a plot to kill him, I decided to
send him on to you and will tell his accusers
to bring their charges before you."
31So that night, as ordered, the soldiers took
Paul to Antipatris. 32They returned to the armory the next morning, leaving him with the
cavalry to take him on to Caesarea.
33When they arrived in Caesarea, they presented Paul and the letter to the governor.
34He read it and then asked Paul where he was
from.
"Cilicia," Paul answered.
35"I will hear your case fully when your
accusers arrive," the governor told him, and
ordered him kept in the prison at King Herod's palace.

CHAPTER 24

Paul Appears before Felix

Five days later Ananias the High Priest arrived
with some of the Jewish leaders and the lawyer Tertullus, to make their accusations
against Paul. 2When Tertullus was called forward, he laid charges against Paul in the following address to the governor:
"Your Excellency, you have given quietness
and peace to us Jews and have greatly reduced
the discrimination against us. 3And for this we
are very, very grateful to you. 4But lest I bore
you, kindly give me your attention for only a
moment as I briefly outline our case against
this man. 5For we have found him to be a
troublemaker, a man who is constantly incit-
ing the Jews throughout the entire world to
riots and rebellions against the Roman government. He is a ringleader of the sect known
as the Nazarenes. 6Moreover, he was trying to
defile the Temple when we arrested him.
"We would have given him what he justly
deserves, 7but Lysias, the commander of the
garrison, came and took him violently away
from us, 8demanding that he be tried by Roman law. You can find out the truth of our
accusations by examining him yourself."
9Then all the other Jews chimed in, declaring that everything Tertullus said was true.
10Now it was Paul's turn. The governor motioned for him to rise and speak.
Paul began: "I know, sir, that you have been
a judge of Jewish affairs for many years, and
this gives me confidence as I make my defense. 11You can quickly discover that it was
no more than twelve days ago that I arrived
in Jerusalem to worship at the Temple, 12and
you will discover that I have never incited a
riot in any synagogue or on the streets of any
city; 13and these men certainly cannot prove
the things they accuse me of doing.
14"But one thing I do confess, that I believe
in the way of salvation, which they refer to as
a sect; I follow that system of serving the God
of our ancestors; I firmly believe in the Jewish
law and everything written in the books of
prophecy; 15and I believe, just as these men
do, that there will be a resurrection of both
the righteous and ungodly. 16Because of this, I
try with all my strength to always maintain a
clear conscience before God and man.
17"After several years away, I returned to
Jerusalem with money to aid the Jews and to
offer a sacrifice to God. 18My accusers saw me
in the Temple as I was presenting my thank
offering. I had shaved my head as their laws
required, and there was no crowd around me,
and no rioting! But some Jews from Turkey
were there 19(who ought to be here if they
have anything against me)— 20but look! Ask
these men right here what wrongdoing their
Council found in me, 21except that I said one
thing I shouldn't when I shouted out, 'I am
here before the Council to defend myself for
believing that the dead will rise again!'"
22Felix, who knew Christians didn't go
around starting riots, told the Jews to wait for
the arrival of Lysias, the garrison commander,
and then he would decide the case. 23He ordered Paul to prison but instructed the guards
to treat him gently and not to forbid any of
his friends from visiting him or bringing him
gifts to make his stay more comfortable.
24A few days later Felix came with Drusilla,
his legal wife, a Jewess. Sending for Paul, they
listened as he told them about faith in Christ
Jesus. 25And as he reasoned with them about
righteousness and self-control and the judgment to come, Felix was terrified.
"Go away for now," he replied, "and when

I have a more convenient time, I'll call for you
again."
[26]He also hoped that Paul would bribe him,
so he sent for him from time to time and
talked with him. [27]Two years went by in this
way; then Felix was succeeded by Porcius Festus. And because Felix wanted to gain favor
with the Jews, he left Paul in chains.

CHAPTER 25

Paul Appears before Festus

Three days after Festus arrived in Caesarea to
take over his new responsibilities, he left for
Jerusalem, [2]where the chief priests and other
Jewish leaders got hold of him and gave him
their story about Paul. [3]They begged him to
bring Paul to Jerusalem at once. (Their plan
was to waylay and kill him.) [4]But Festus replied that since Paul was at Caesarea and he
himself was returning there soon, [5]those with
authority in this affair should return with him
for the trial.

[6]Eight or ten days later he returned to Caesarea and the following day opened Paul's
trial.

[7]On Paul's arrival in court the Jews from
Jerusalem gathered around, hurling many serious accusations which they couldn't prove.
[8]Paul denied the charges: "I am not guilty," he
said. "I have not opposed the Jewish laws or
desecrated the Temple or rebelled against the
Roman government."

[9]Then Festus, anxious to please the Jews,
asked him, "Are you willing to go to Jerusalem
and stand trial before me?"

[10,11]But Paul replied, "No! I demand my
privilege of a hearing before the emperor himself. You know very well I am not guilty. If I
have done something worthy of death, I don't
refuse to die! But if I am innocent, neither you
nor anyone else has a right to turn me over to
these men to kill me. *I appeal to Caesar."*

[12]Festus conferred with his advisors and
then replied, "Very well! You have appealed to
Caesar, and to Caesar you shall go!"

[13]A few days later King Agrippa arrived with
Bernice for a visit with Festus. [14]During their
stay of several days Festus discussed Paul's case
with the king. "There is a prisoner here," he
told him, "whose case was left for me by Felix.
[15]When I was in Jerusalem, the chief priests
and other Jewish leaders gave me their side of
the story and asked me to have him killed. [16]Of
course I quickly pointed out to them that
Roman law does not convict a man before he
is tried. He is given an opportunity to defend
himself face to face with his accusers.

[17]"When they came here for the trial, I
called the case the very next day and ordered
Paul brought in. [18]But the accusations made
against him weren't at all what I supposed
they would be. [19]It was something about their
religion and about someone called Jesus who
died, but Paul insists is alive! [20]I was perplexed
as to how to decide a case of this kind and
asked him whether he would be willing to
stand trial on these charges in Jerusalem. [21]But
Paul appealed to Caesar! So I ordered him
back to jail until I could arrange to get him to
the emperor."

[22]"I'd like to hear the man myself," Agrippa
said.

And Festus replied, "You shall—tomorrow!"

Paul Speaks before Agrippa

[23]So the next day, after the king and Bernice
had arrived at the courtroom with great
pomp, accompanied by military officers and
prominent men of the city, Festus ordered
Paul brought in.

[24]Then Festus addressed the audience:
"King Agrippa and all present," he said, "this
is the man whose death is demanded both by
the local Jews and by those in Jerusalem! [25]But
in my opinion he has done nothing worthy
of death. However, he appealed his case to
Caesar, and I have no alternative but to send
him. [26]But what shall I write the emperor? For
there is no real charge against him! So I have
brought him before you all, and especially
you, King Agrippa, to examine him and then
tell me what to write. [27]For it doesn't seem
reasonable to send a prisoner to the emperor
without any charges against him!"

CHAPTER 26

Then Agrippa said to Paul, "Go ahead. Tell us
your story."

24:26-27 Felix made no decision on Paul's case. He probably was afraid that if he set Paul free, the Jews would respond with rebellion. In the end, Felix just left Paul in prison. Perhaps he hoped Paul would be able to muster a bribe to buy his release. Whatever his reason for keeping Paul, Felix allowed the apostle to languish in jail for at least two years. No doubt the miserable prison conditions challenged Paul to the depth of his being. By the grace of God he endured his long stay with incredible patience. If Paul could survive his years in bondage, depending on God to help him one day at a time, we can do the same.

So Paul, with many gestures, presented his
defense:
2"I am fortunate, King Agrippa," he began,
"to be able to present my answer before you,
3for I know you are an expert on Jewish laws
and customs. Now please listen patiently!
4"As the Jews are well aware, I was given a
thorough Jewish training from my earliest
childhood in Tarsus and later at Jerusalem,
and I lived accordingly. 5If they would admit
it, they know that I have always been the
strictest of Pharisees when it comes to obedience to Jewish laws and customs. 6But the real
reason behind their accusations is something
else—it is because I am looking forward to the
fulfillment of God's promise made to our ancestors. 7The twelve tribes of Israel strive night
and day to attain this same hope I have! Yet,
O King, for me it is a crime, they say! 8But is it
a crime to believe in the resurrection of the
dead? Does it seem incredible to you that God
can bring men back to life again?
9"I used to believe that I ought to do many
horrible things to the followers of Jesus of
Nazareth. 10I imprisoned many of the saints in
Jerusalem, as authorized by the High Priests;
and when they were condemned to death, I
cast my vote against them. 11I used torture to
try to make Christians everywhere curse
Christ. I was so violently opposed to them
that I even hounded them in distant cities in
foreign lands.
12"I was on such a mission to Damascus,
armed with the authority and commission of
the chief priests, 13when one day about noon,
sir, a light from heaven brighter than the sun
shone down on me and my companions.
14We all fell down, and I heard a voice speaking to me in Hebrew, 'Paul, Paul, why are you
persecuting me? You are only hurting yourself.'
15"'Who are you, sir?' I asked.
"And the Lord replied, 'I am Jesus, the one
you are persecuting. 16Now stand up! For I
have appeared to you to appoint you as my
servant and my witness. You are to tell the
world about this experience and about the
many other occasions when I shall appear to
you. 17And I will protect you from both your
own people and the Gentiles. Yes, I am going
to send you to the Gentiles 18to open their
eyes to their true condition so that they may
repent and live in the light of God instead of
in Satan's darkness, so that they may receive
forgiveness for their sins and God's inheritance along with all people everywhere whose

26:1-23 This is the third account of Paul's conversion in the book of Acts (see 9:1-20; 22:1-21). It seems that Paul has become quite skilled at sharing his story with anyone who is willing to listen. Paul's story has its before, during, and after stages. Before meeting Christ, Paul was a powerful enemy of the Christian faith and did "horrible things" to try and stop its growth (26:9-11). Paul then met Jesus in a dramatic way, which led to his painful spiritual awakening (26:12-16). After catching his breath, Paul went on to carry his story to others who needed to hear the message (26:18). If we aren't sure how to share our story with others, it might help to follow Paul's lead by telling others what happened in our life before, during, and after we experienced God's deliverance.

26:19-23 Paul assured King Agrippa that he was suffering persecution, not because he had done anything wrong, but because he was now preaching the faith he had once tried to destroy. Paul showed that what he was preaching as a Christian was really in agreement with the Old Testament Scriptures. The basic teaching of both Old and New Testaments is that God desires to deliver people from the power of sin and has done so perfectly through the work of God's anointed one—the Messiah. That scriptural message of God's desire to save us is essential to the recovery process.

26:24-29 Paul was so concerned about the salvation of other people that he had little time to worry about his own problems. Here he risked his life to share his testimony with a man who had the power to have him killed. This conversation with Herod Agrippa II shows Paul's burning desire to soften and reclaim even the most hardened of hearts. For everyone in recovery, as for Paul, it can be helpful to get our eyes off our own afflictions to focus on the needs of others. As we help others discover the way to recovery, we will be freed from our tendency to have an inward focus. This will help to strengthen our own recovery.

27:1-15 It was part of God's plan that Paul go to Rome, but his journey there was hardly straightforward. After years in prison, he was finally put on a ship bound for Rome, but he arrived there only after surviving a life-threatening storm and shipwreck. Paul had no control over the means or timing of getting to his destination. But since Paul knew God wanted him in Rome, he was confident he would eventually get there. Similarly, we can be sure that God wants us to make progress in recovery. Yet, like Paul, we have no control over the route we will take to get there. Our faithfulness does not ensure a life without storms or shipwrecks. Yet God does guarantee that his presence and power will be right there with us and that we will arrive at our destination in the end.

sins are cleansed away, who are set apart by
faith in me.'
19"And so, O King Agrippa, I was not disobedient to that vision from heaven! 20I
preached first to those in Damascus, then in
Jerusalem and through Judea, and also to the
Gentiles that all must forsake their sins and
turn to God—and prove their repentance by
doing good deeds. 21The Jews arrested me in
the Temple for preaching this and tried to kill
me, 22but God protected me so that I am still
alive today to tell these facts to everyone,
both great and small. I teach nothing except
what the Prophets and Moses said— 23that the
Messiah would suffer and be the First to rise
from the dead, to bring light to Jews and
Gentiles alike."
24Suddenly Festus shouted, "Paul, you are
insane. Your long studying has broken your
mind!"
25But Paul replied, "I am not insane, Most
Excellent Festus. I speak words of sober truth.
26And King Agrippa knows about these things.
I speak frankly for I am sure these events are
all familiar to him, for they were not done in
a corner! 27King Agrippa, do you believe the
Prophets? But I know you do—"
28Agrippa interrupted him. "With trivial
proofs like these, you expect me to become a
Christian?"
29And Paul replied, "Would to God that
whether my arguments are trivial or strong,
both you and everyone here in this audience
might become the same as I am, except for
these chains."
30Then the king, the governor, Bernice, and
all the others stood and left. 31As they talked
it over afterwards they agreed, "This man
hasn't done anything worthy of death or imprisonment."
32And Agrippa said to Festus, "He could be
set free if he hadn't appealed to Caesar!"

CHAPTER 27

Paul Sails for Rome

Arrangements were finally made to start us on
our way to Rome by ship; so Paul and several
other prisoners were placed in the custody of
an officer named Julius, a member of the
imperial guard. 2We left on a boat that was
scheduled to make several stops along the
Turkish coast. I should add that Aristarchus, a
Greek from Thessalonica, was with us.
3The next day when we docked at Sidon,
Julius was very kind to Paul and let him go
ashore to visit with friends and receive their
hospitality. 4Putting to sea from there, we

Receiving Forgiveness

BIBLE READING: Acts 26:12-18

We admitted to God, to ourselves, and to another human being the exact nature of our wrongs.

As we work our recovery program, we go through a process of accepting the truth about our life and the consequences of our choices. We may feel like we have to earn forgiveness instead of just receiving it. We may find it easier to forgive others who have hurt us than to forgive ourself for the hurt we have caused.

When Jesus confronted the apostle Paul, he gave him this mission: "Now stand up! For I have appeared to you to appoint you as my servant and my witness. . . . Yes, I am going to send you to the Gentiles to open their eyes to their true condition so that they may repent and live in the light of God instead of in Satan's darkness, so that they may receive forgiveness for their sins and God's inheritance along with all people everywhere whose sins are cleansed away, who are set apart by faith in me" (Acts 26:16-18).

God's goal in sending his Word to us is that we may receive forgiveness and a full inheritance. The process involves first opening our eyes to our true condition, which happens in Steps One, Two, and Four. This allows us the opportunity to repent, changing our minds so that we are in agreement with God and ready to admit our wrongs. God wants us to receive immediate forgiveness, based on the finished work of Jesus Christ. We are not second-class citizens in the Kingdom of God. We don't have to work the rest of the Twelve Steps as a form of penance. Forgiveness awaits us right now, if we will only receive it. ***Turn to page 1231, Romans 2.***

encountered headwinds that made it difficult
to keep the ship on course, so we sailed north
of Cyprus between the island and the mainland 5and passed along the coast of the provinces of Cilicia and Pamphylia, landing at
Myra, in the province of Lycia. 6There our
officer found an Egyptian ship from Alexandria, bound for Italy, and put us aboard.
7,8We had several days of rough sailing, and
finally neared Cnidus; but the winds had become too strong, so we ran across to Crete,
passing the port of Salome. Beating into the
wind with great difficulty and moving slowly
along the southern coast, we arrived at Fair
Havens, near the city of Lasea. 9There we
stayed for several days. The weather was becoming dangerous for long voyages by then
because it was late in the year, and Paul spoke
to the ship's officers about it.
10"Sirs," he said, "I believe there is trouble
ahead if we go on—perhaps shipwreck, loss of
cargo, injuries, and death." 11But the officers
in charge of the prisoners listened more to the
ship's captain and the owner than to Paul.
12And since Fair Havens was an exposed harbor—a poor place to spend the winter—most
of the crew advised trying to go further up the
coast to Phoenix in order to winter there;
Phoenix was a good harbor with only a northwest and southwest exposure.

The Storm at Sea

13Just then a light wind began blowing from
the south, and it looked like a perfect day for
the trip; so they pulled up anchor and sailed
along close to shore.
14,15But shortly afterwards the weather
changed abruptly, and a heavy wind of ty-
phoon strength (a "northeaster," they called
it) caught the ship and blew it out to sea. They
tried at first to face back to shore but couldn't,
so they gave up and let the ship run before the
gale.
16We finally sailed behind a small island
named Claude, where with great difficulty we
hoisted aboard the lifeboat that was being
towed behind us, 17and then banded the ship
with ropes to strengthen the hull. The sailors
were afraid of being driven across to the
quicksands of the African coast, so they lowered the topsails and were thus driven before
the wind.
18The next day as the seas grew higher, the
crew began throwing the cargo overboard.
19The following day they threw out the tackle
and anything else they could lay their hands
on. 20The terrible storm raged unabated many
days, until at last all hope was gone.
21No one had eaten for a long time, but
finally Paul called the crew together and said,
"Men, you should have listened to me in the
first place and not left Fair Havens—you
would have avoided all this injury and loss!
22But cheer up! Not one of us will lose our
lives, even though the ship will go down.
23"For last night an angel of the God to
whom I belong and whom I serve stood beside me 24and said, 'Don't be afraid, Paul—for
you will surely stand trial before Caesar!
What's more, God has granted your request
and will save the lives of all those sailing with
you.' 25So take courage! For I believe God! It
will be just as he said! 26But we will be shipwrecked on an island."

The Shipwreck

27About midnight on the fourteenth night of
the storm, as we were being driven to and fro
on the Adriatic Sea, the sailors suspected land
was near. 28They sounded and found 120 feet
of water below them. A little later they
sounded again and found only 90 feet. 29At
this rate they knew they would soon be driven
ashore; and fearing rocks along the coast,
they threw out four anchors from the stern
and prayed for daylight.
30Some of the sailors planned to abandon
the ship and lowered the emergency boat as

27:13-26 After two storm-tossed weeks, the ship had begun to fall apart, the sailors had given up hope, and everyone was hungry and terrified. Yet Paul urged all to believe his promise from God that they would survive. The fate of 276 people—passengers and crew—hung in the balance. Paul's courageous faith was met with assurances that he would reach Rome, yet not without still more hardships. Life in recovery is often like that. We are assured by faith of a positive outcome, but it is usually attained by persevering through difficult times.

27:27-42 Earlier the sailors had ignored Paul (27:9-12), but this time they listened carefully (27:30-32). Paul assured them that even though the ship would be destroyed, all the passengers would reach land safely. This happened just as Paul said it would. The next day the ship was grounded on a sandbar and destroyed by the winds and waves, but not before all the passengers safely reached shore. Few of us have an awareness of the future like Paul did. But we can have the same confidence in the power of God to protect us when we follow his will. We can have success in recovery by walking obediently by faith, one step at a time.

though they were going to put out anchors
from the prow. [31]But Paul said to the soldiers
and commanding officer, "You will all die
unless everyone stays aboard." [32]So the soldiers cut the ropes and let the boat fall off.

[33]As the darkness gave way to the early
morning light, Paul begged everyone to eat.
"You haven't touched food for two weeks," he
said. [34]"Please eat something now for your
own good! For not a hair of your heads shall
perish!"

[35]Then he took some hardtack and gave
thanks to God before them all, and broke off
a piece and ate it. [36]Suddenly everyone felt
better and began eating, [37]all 276 of us—for
that is the number we had aboard. [38]After
eating, the crew lightened the ship further by
throwing all the wheat overboard.

[39]When it was day, they didn't recognize
the coastline, but noticed a bay with a beach
and wondered whether they could get between the rocks and be driven up onto the
beach. [40]They finally decided to try. Cutting
off the anchors and leaving them in the sea,
they lowered the rudders, raised the foresail,
and headed ashore. [41]But the ship hit a sandbar and ran aground. The bow of the ship
stuck fast, while the stern was exposed to the
violence of the waves and began to break
apart.

[42]The soldiers advised their commanding
officer to let them kill the prisoners lest any of
them swim ashore and escape. [43]But Julius
wanted to spare Paul, so he told them no.
Then he ordered all who could swim to jump
overboard and make for land, [44]and the rest to
try for it on planks and debris from the broken ship. So everyone escaped safely ashore!

CHAPTER 28

Paul Survives a Snake Bite

We soon learned that we were on the island
of Malta. The people of the island were very
kind to us, building a bonfire on the beach to
welcome and warm us in the rain and cold.

[3]As Paul gathered an armful of sticks to lay
on the fire, a poisonous snake, driven out by
the heat, fastened itself onto his hand! [4]The
people of the island saw it hanging there and
said to each other, "A murderer, no doubt!
Though he escaped the sea, justice will not
permit him to live!"

[5]But Paul shook off the snake into the fire
and was unharmed. [6]The people waited for
him to begin swelling or suddenly fall dead;
but when they had waited a long time and no
harm came to him, they changed their minds
and decided he was a god.

[7]Near the shore where we landed was an
estate belonging to Publius, the governor of
the island. He welcomed us courteously and
fed us for three days. [8]As it happened, Publius'
father was ill with fever and dysentery. Paul
went in and prayed for him, and laying his
hands on him, healed him! [9]Then all the
other sick people in the island came and were
cured. [10]As a result we were showered with
gifts, and when the time came to sail, people
put on board all sorts of things we would need
for the trip.

[11]It was three months after the shipwreck
before we set sail again, and this time it was in
The Twin Brothers of Alexandria, a ship that had
wintered at the island. [12]Our first stop was
Syracuse, where we stayed three days. [13]From
there we circled around to Rhegium; a day later
a south wind began blowing, so the following
day we arrived at Puteoli, [14]where we found
some believers! They begged us to stay with
them seven days. Then we went on to Rome.

Paul Under Guard in Rome

[15]The brothers in Rome had heard we were
coming and came to meet us at the Forum on
the Appian Way. Others joined us at The
Three Taverns. When Paul saw them, he
thanked God and took courage.

[16]When we arrived in Rome, Paul was permitted to live wherever he wanted to, though
guarded by a soldier.

[17]Three days after his arrival, he called together the local Jewish leaders and spoke to
them as follows:

"Brothers, I was arrested by the Jews in
Jerusalem and handed over to the Roman
government for prosecution, even though I
had harmed no one nor violated the customs
of our ancestors. [18]The Romans gave me a trial

28:1-10 Safe on the island of Malta, the ship's crew and passengers spent the winter there. If stormy seas and a shipwreck couldn't thwart God's plan for Paul, neither would the bite of a poisonous snake. Paul was bitten by a deadly snake, yet he suffered no ill effects. The credit for this miracle was given to God, the power behind all real miracles. While Paul was deterred from reaching Rome, he spent his time and talents helping the people around him. To Paul, even obstacles were opportunities to serve others and share his faith. As we work through the process of recovery, we, too, can turn our obstacles into wonderful opportunities for growth and service.

and wanted to release me, for they found no
cause for the death sentence demanded by
the Jewish leaders. 19But when the Jews protested the decision, I felt it necessary, with no
malice against them, to appeal to Caesar. 20I
asked you to come here today so we could get
acquainted and I could tell you that it is
because I believe the Messiah has come that I
am bound with this chain."
21They replied, "We have heard nothing
against you! We have had no letters from Judea or reports from those arriving from Jerusalem. 22But we want to hear what you believe,
for the only thing we know about these Christians is that they are denounced everywhere!"
23So a time was set, and on that day large
numbers came to his house. He told them
about the Kingdom of God and taught them
about Jesus from the Scriptures—from the
five books of Moses and the books of prophecy. He began lecturing in the morning and
went on into the evening!
24Some believed and some didn't. 25But after
they had argued back and forth among themselves, they left with this final word from Paul
ringing in their ears: "The Holy Spirit was
right when he said through Isaiah the
prophet,

> 26"'Say to the Jews, "You will hear and see
> but not understand, 27for your hearts
> are too fat and your ears don't listen
> and you have closed your eyes against
> understanding, for you don't want to
> see and hear and understand and turn
> to me to heal you."'

28,29 So I want you to realize that this salvation
from God is available to the Gentiles too, and
they will accept it."
30Paul lived for the next two years in his
rented house and welcomed all who visited
him, 31telling them with all boldness about
the Kingdom of God and about the Lord Jesus
Christ; and no one tried to stop him.

28:30-31 Even under house arrest, Paul experienced the peace and contentment that come only by following God's will. Paul used his time in prison to carry the message of salvation to people in need. The apostle's life is an example to each of us, showing the importance and benefits of persisting in our relationship with God and sharing our faith. As we get to know God better, learn to trust in his love and power, and share this power for recovery with others, we can live each new day with serenity and courage.

insights CONCERNING THE HOLY SPIRIT

In **Acts 2:5-15,** when the Holy Spirit came in power, the results were immediately apparent in the apostles, especially Peter. This man, who had previously failed to live up to his commitment to Christ (Luke 22:54-62), was now confidently preaching and helping others discover this new power for living. When we experience God's power in our life, we will never be the same, nor will we be able to keep the Good News to ourself.

insights FROM THE EARLY CHRISTIAN COMMUNITY

As the Christian community grew, various problems arose. One such problem is mentioned in **Acts 6:1** concerning the distribution of food to needy widows. The conflict was apparently rooted in the cultural differences between the various church members. Most of the church members were Aramaic-speaking Palestinian Jews, but there were also Greek-speaking Jews among them who had been raised outside of Palestine. Apparently, the Greek-speaking Jews were being neglected by the Jews native to Palestine. Relationships within the church, as well as in the recovery movement, can be stretched, even broken, if members refuse to accept one another. As we humbly recognize our own need for God's gracious forgiveness, we will have less trouble accepting others who are different from us.

✲*insights* FROM PHILIP'S LIFE

In **Acts 8:26-40** Philip was called to share the Good News with an Ethiopian eunuch and serves as an excellent model of how we can effectively engage in this important recovery activity. He didn't rush in and start preaching. He took time to understand where the Ethiopian was concerning his faith. Then, he proceeded humbly and confidently to share what he knew to be true—that Jesus was the Messiah and that through him we can experience deliverance from sin and its power. When we follow Philip's example here, we will find people receptive to what we have to say. Sharing our faith this way takes time; it requires patience and sensitivity. But as we follow Philip's example, we will learn to share our faith with not only words, but also with deeds.

✲*insights* FROM PAUL'S LIFE

In **Acts 9:3-9** we find Paul traveling to Damascus to persecute the Christians there. As he neared his destination, he was suddenly struck down and blinded by the risen Christ. Blind and helpless, Paul was led to Damascus to await further instructions from God. For three days he ate and drank nothing. He was forced into a period of rigorous self-examination. This kind of experience is often helpful in recovery. Some of us were probably confronted suddenly and dramatically with the painful truth about our life. But whether it happened with a bang or a whisper, we all have come face-to-face with our sins and character flaws. Recovery begins as we discover our helplessness; it continues with serious self-examination and continued dependence on God's power.

ROMANS

THE BIG PICTURE

The church in Rome was a testimony to God's power. It had flourished despite the obstacles posed by the surrounding pagan culture. Yet these believers were not perfect; in fact, they had some serious problems. Though they were well established in their faith, their convictions and unity as a group were threatened by racial and cultural division.

The main topic in this letter is the gospel—the good news that salvation from sin is available through Jesus Christ. At the core of the gospel is the truth that God is bigger than our past. No matter who we are or what we have done, we can be saved by grace (undeserved favor from God) through faith (complete trust) in Christ. We can stand before God justified—declared "not guilty." That's good news!

In Romans, Paul explained four major points. First, God makes no distinction between us as individuals—we are all guilty, and we are all offered his free gift of salvation (1:17–4:25). Second, we can all be freed from sin's power through God's grace and the Holy Spirit inside us (5:1–8:39). Third, we are all "in recovery," and therefore have no grounds for arrogance (9:1–11:36). And fourth, because of God's mercy we all must respect one another, despite the differences between us (12:1–15:13).

Many people have called this letter the greatest theological treatise ever written, but it's really a letter about how to live. It teaches us how to deal with our sinful attitudes and behaviors and how to get back on the right track. Paul's letter has direct application to us, showing us how to recover from the effects of sin and dysfunction in our life.

THE BOTTOM LINE

PURPOSE: To introduce Paul to the church at Rome and summarize his message before he arrived there. AUTHOR: The apostle Paul. AUDIENCE: The church at Rome. DATE WRITTEN: A.D. 57, from Corinth, just before Paul's return to Jerusalem. SETTING: Paul wrote this letter in anticipation of a future visit to the believers in Rome. KEY VERSES: "For I am convinced that nothing can ever separate us from his love. Death can't, and life can't. The angels won't, and all the powers of hell itself cannot keep God's love away. . . . nothing will ever be able to separate us from the love of God" (8:38-39). KEY PEOPLE AND RELATIONSHIPS: Paul with the believers in Rome and with Phoebe, who helped Paul in his ministry.

RECOVERY THEMES

Our Universal Need: All of us have sinned; we have each fallen short of God's standards. Regardless of whether we have fallen deeply into controlling addictions, been abused by dysfunctional family members, or escaped severe trauma—we are all in need of recovery from sin of one kind or another. Ever since Adam and Eve rebelled against God, our nature has been to disobey him; we have been addicted to ignoring God's will. We are all powerless in our sin and need God to save us.

God's Power to Deliver: Our need for recovery involves our need to be forgiven and to forgive, as well as to be cleansed from the effects of the past. Although we are powerless to help ourself and don't really deserve to be helped, God, in his love, reaches out to us, offering to forgive us, cleanse us, and empower us to become what he wants us to be. This is truly good news! Our part is to admit our powerlessness and turn our life and will over to this loving God.

Recovery Leads to Freedom: Because God has attacked our problems at the roots—that is, he has made it possible for us to be freed from our sin—we can be free from controlling addictions. Through God's power, our life can become manageable. Though the process is never easy, over time we can become more and more like Christ as we walk one day at a time with God. The better we get to know him, the more empowered we can be. By continuing to take inventory, putting our sins and defects into God's hands, and seeking to make amends to those whom we have wronged, we can discover what it is to experience true freedom.

The Role of Faith: Much of this letter is a description of the importance of faith or trust in God. "The man who finds life will find it through trusting God" (1:17). There is no other way to recovery; the role of faith is central. Our recovery began with faith when we turned our will and our life over to the care of God, and each step of the way built on that first step of faith. There is no magic formula for this—it is a daily act of trust, putting our hand in the hand of the all-powerful God, who promises never to forsake us, and to always love us no matter how unlovable we are.

CHAPTER 1

Greetings from Paul

Dear friends in Rome: 1This letter is from Paul,
Jesus Christ's slave, chosen to be a missionary,
and sent out to preach God's Good News.
2This Good News was promised long ago by
God's prophets in the Old Testament. 3It is the
Good News about his Son, Jesus Christ our
Lord, who came as a human baby, born into
King David's royal family line; 4and by being
raised from the dead he was proved to be the
mighty Son of God, with the holy nature of
God himself.
5And now, through Christ, all the kindness
of God has been poured out upon us undeserving sinners; and now he is sending us out
around the world to tell all people everywhere
the great things God has done for them, so
that they, too, will believe and obey him.
6,7And you, dear friends in Rome, are
among those he dearly loves; you, too, are
invited by Jesus Christ to be God's very own—
yes, his holy people. May all God's mercies
and peace be yours from God our Father and
from Jesus Christ our Lord.

God's Powerful Good News

8Let me say first of all that wherever I go I hear
you being talked about! For your faith in God
is becoming known around the world. How I
thank God through Jesus Christ for this good
report, and for each one of you. 9God knows
how often I pray for you. Day and night I
bring you and your needs in prayer to the one

1:1 In this letter, Paul introduced himself as a slave of Jesus Christ. Paul was a Roman citizen, and for him to choose a life of slavery was unthinkable. But Paul purposely used this word to demonstrate his humility and dependence upon God. Paul demonstrated the type of humility we need in our recovery. We will begin to make progress in recovery when we recognize how helpless we are and how much we need God. Only when we joyfully submit to God's will for our life can we begin the recovery process.

1:16-17 All of us have failed in one way or another, and we all know what shame feels like. We are ashamed of our past failures, our bad habits, or even the abuses we have suffered. Paul tells us that the Good News of Jesus Christ is God's power to deliver us from all the shameful things in our life. And it's for everyone! God has the power to deliver and transform us when we turn our life over to him. The Good News is certainly nothing to be ashamed of!

I serve with all my might, telling others the
Good News about his Son.
10And one of the things I keep on praying
for is the opportunity, God willing, to come
at last to see you and, if possible, that I will
have a safe trip. 11,12For I long to visit you so
that I can impart to you the faith that will
help your church grow strong in the Lord.
Then, too, I need your help, for I want not
only to share my faith with you but to be
encouraged by yours: Each of us will be a
blessing to the other.
13I want you to know, dear brothers, that I
planned to come many times before (but was
prevented) so that I could work among you
and see good results, just as I have among the
other Gentile churches. 14For I owe a great
debt to you and to everyone else, both to
civilized people and uncivilized alike; yes, to
the educated and uneducated alike. 15So, to
the fullest extent of my ability, I am ready to
come also to you in Rome to preach God's
Good News.
16For I am not ashamed of this Good News
about Christ. It is God's powerful method of
bringing all who believe it to heaven. This
message was preached first to the Jews alone,
but now everyone is invited to come to God
in this same way. 17This Good News tells us
that God makes us ready for heaven—makes
us right in God's sight—when we put our faith
and trust in Christ to save us. This is accomplished from start to finish by faith. As the
Scripture says it, "The man who finds life will
find it through trusting God."

The Sinful Human Race

18But God shows his anger from heaven
against all sinful, evil men who push away the
truth from them. 19For the truth about God is
known to them instinctively; God has put
this knowledge in their hearts. 20Since earliest
times men have seen the earth and sky and all
God made, and have known of his existence
and great eternal power. So they will have no
excuse [when they stand before God at Judgment Day].
21Yes, they knew about him all right, but
they wouldn't admit it or worship him or
even thank him for all his daily care. And after
awhile they began to think up silly ideas of
what God was like and what he wanted them
to do. The result was that their foolish minds
became dark and confused. 22Claiming themselves to be wise without God, they became
utter fools instead. 23And then, instead of worshiping the glorious, ever-living God, they

Coming to Believe

BIBLE READING: Romans 1:18-20

We came to believe that a Power greater than ourselves could restore us to sanity.
Saying that we "came to believe" in anything describes a process. Belief is the result of consideration, doubt, reasoning, and concluding. The ability to form beliefs is the mark of God's image in our life. It involves emotion and logic. It leads to action. What, then, is the process that leads to solid belief, which leads us to change our life?

We start with our own experience. We see what doesn't work. Looking at the condition of our life, we realize that we don't have enough power to overcome our dependencies. We try with all our might, but to no avail. When we are quiet enough to listen, we hear that still, small voice inside us saying, "There is a God, and he is extremely powerful." The apostle Paul said it this way, "For the truth about God is known to [all people] instinctively; God has put this knowledge in their hearts" (Romans 1:19).

Recognizing our internal weaknesses is the first step. When we look beyond ourself, we will see that there are others who have struggled with addictions and recovered. We can see that they, too, were unable to heal themselves, yet they are able to live free of addictive behaviors. We conclude that there must be a greater Power that helped them. Since we can see the similarities between their struggle and our own, we come to believe that there must be a Power that can restore us to sanity. This is where many people are when they get to Step Two, and it's a good place to be on the way to recovery. ***Turn to page 1391, Hebrews 11.***

took wood and stone and made idols for
themselves, carving them to look like mere
birds and animals and snakes and puny men.
24So God let them go ahead into every sort
of sex sin, and do whatever they wanted to—
yes, vile and sinful things with each other's
bodies. 25Instead of believing what they knew
was the truth about God, they deliberately
chose to believe lies. So they prayed to the
things God made, but wouldn't obey the
blessed God who made these things.
26That is why God let go of them and let
them do all these evil things, so that even
their women turned against God's natural
plan for them and indulged in sex sin with
each other. 27And the men, instead of having
normal sex relationships with women,
burned with lust for each other, men doing
shameful things with other men and, as a
result, getting paid within their own souls
with the penalty they so richly deserved.
28So it was that when they gave God up and
would not even acknowledge him, God gave
them up to doing everything their evil minds
could think of. 29Their lives became full of
every kind of wickedness and sin, of greed
and hate, envy, murder, fighting, lying, bitterness, and gossip.
30They were backbiters, haters of God, insolent, proud, braggarts, always thinking of new
ways of sinning and continually being disobedient to their parents. 31They tried to misunderstand, broke their promises, and were
heartless—without pity. 32They were fully
aware of God's death penalty for these crimes,
yet they went right ahead and did them anyway and encouraged others to do them, too.

CHAPTER 2

God's Judgment of Sin

"Well," you may be saying, "what terrible
people you have been talking about!" But wait
a minute! You are just as bad. When you say
they are wicked and should be punished, you
are talking about yourselves, for you do these
very same things. 2And we know that God, in
justice, will punish anyone who does such
things as these. 3Do you think that God will
judge and condemn others for doing them
and overlook you when you do them, too?
4Don't you realize how patient he is being
with you? Or don't you care? Can't you see
that he has been waiting all this time without
punishing you, to give you time to turn from
your sin? His kindness is meant to lead you to
repentance.
5But no, you won't listen; and so you are
saving up terrible punishment for yourselves
because of your stubbornness in refusing to
turn from your sin; for there is going to come
a day of wrath when God will be the just
Judge of all the world. 6He will give each one
whatever his deeds deserve. 7He will give eternal life to those who patiently do the will of
God, seeking for the unseen glory and honor
and eternal life that he offers. 8But he will
terribly punish those who fight against the
truth of God and walk in evil ways—God's
anger will be poured out upon them. 9There
will be sorrow and suffering for Jews and
Gentiles alike who keep on sinning. 10But

1:21-32 When we refuse to admit our powerlessness, and hold on to our self-sufficiency, we follow the downward path that Paul describes here. First, we exchange our worship of God for the worship of things—our addictions and compulsions. Second, we exchange our worship of the living God for a willful form of sin. Third, we move beyond these forms of sin to a state of deep denial—we believe lies and reject truth. This passage describes a life that has become totally unmanageable, the natural consequence of pride and self-sufficiency. The only way to escape such destruction is to recognize our powerlessness and turn our life over to God.

2:1-4 In the previous chapter Paul described a life that was completely out of control. As we read that description, it is easy to point our finger at someone else. Paul quickly corrects our tendency to do this by showing that everyone is in the same boat. We all do things that are wrong; we hide all kinds of problems, habits, and failures in the dark recesses of our life. If we find ourself applying this passage to someone else, we probably really need to apply it to ourself. Our recovery begins with an honest personal inventory.

2:6-16 God is impartial. He doesn't forgive us because we are members of a special group of people. He doesn't judge us by the way we talk, walk, or dress. He judges us by whether or not we obey his will for our life. There is no in-group in God's eyes. The Jewish people of Paul's day believed that they had special privileges from God, but here we find that God treats all people the same. If we admit our failures and seek to follow God's will for us, we are his special people. We are also on the way to recovery. Some of us have felt like outsiders all our life. We may have been rejected by various groups because of our problems or failures. If we feel this way, Paul's message is for us: God will never reject us if we confess our sins, accept his forgiveness, and seek to follow his will for our life.

there will be glory and honor and peace from
God for all who obey him, whether they are
Jews or Gentiles. 11For God treats everyone the
same.
12-15He will punish sin wherever it is found.
He will punish the heathen when they sin,
even though they never had God's written
laws, for down in their hearts they know right
from wrong. God's laws are written within
them; their own conscience accuses them, or
sometimes excuses them. And God will punish the Jews for sinning because they have his
written laws but don't obey them. They know
what is right but don't do it. After all, salvation is not given to those who know what to
do, unless they do it. 16The day will surely
come when at God's command Jesus Christ
will judge the secret lives of everyone, their
inmost thoughts and motives; this is all part
of God's great plan, which I proclaim.

The Inadequacy of God's Laws

17You Jews think all is well between yourselves
and God because he gave his laws to you; you
brag that you are his special friends. 18Yes, you
know what he wants; you know right from
wrong and favor the right because you have
been taught his laws from earliest youth.
19You are so sure of the way to God that you
could point it out to a blind man. You think
of yourselves as beacon lights, directing men
who are lost in darkness to God. 20You think
that you can guide the simple and teach even
children the affairs of God, for you really
know his laws, which are full of all knowledge
and truth.
21Yes, you teach others—then why don't
you teach yourselves? You tell others not to
steal—do *you* steal? 22You say it is wrong to
commit adultery—do *you* do it? You say
"Don't pray to idols" and then make money
your god instead.
23You are so proud of knowing God's laws,
but you dishonor him by breaking them. 24No
wonder the Scriptures say that the world
speaks evil of God because of you.
25Being a Jew is worth something if you
obey God's laws; but if you don't, then you
are no better off than the heathen. 26And if the
heathen obey God's laws, won't God give
them all the rights and honors he planned to
give the Jews? 27In fact, those heathen will be
much better off than you Jews who know so
much about God and have his promises but
don't obey his laws.
28For you are not real Jews just because you
were born of Jewish parents or because you

Freedom through Confession

BIBLE READING: Romans 2:12-15

We admitted to God, to ourselves, and to another human being the exact nature of our wrongs.

All of us struggle with our conscience, trying to make peace within our own heart. We may deny what we have done, find excuses, or try to squirm out from beneath the full weight of our conduct. We may work hard to be "good," trying to counteract our wrongs. We do everything we can to even out the score. In order to put the past to rest, however, we must stop rationalizing our failures and admit the truth.

We are all born with a built-in alarm that alerts us to what is wrong. God holds everyone accountable, "for down in their hearts they know right from wrong. God's laws are written within them; their own conscience accuses them, or sometimes excuses them" (Romans 2:12-15).

In Step Five we set out to stop this internal struggle and admit that wrong is wrong. It is a time to agree with God and our own conscience about our cover-up and the exact nature of our wrongs. We are people who have been accused of crimes that we have actually committed. We may have spent years constructing alibis, coming up with excuses, and trying to plea-bargain. It is time to come clean. It is time to admit what we know deep down inside to be true: "Yes, I'm guilty as charged."

There is no real freedom without confession. What a relief it is to finally give up the weight of our lies and excuses. When we do confess, we will find the internal peace we lost so long ago. We will also be one step closer to full recovery. ***Turn to page 1305, Galatians 6.***

have gone through the Jewish initiation ceremony of circumcision. 29No, a real Jew is anyone whose heart is right with God. For God is
not looking for those who cut their bodies in
actual body circumcision, but he is looking
for those with changed hearts and minds.
Whoever has that kind of change in his life
will get his praise from God, even if not from
you.

CHAPTER 3

God Remains Faithful

Then what's the use of being a Jew? Are there
any special benefits for them from God? Is
there any value in the Jewish circumcision
ceremony? 2Yes, being a Jew has many advantages.

First of all, God trusted them with his laws
[so that they could know and do his will].
3True, some of them were unfaithful, but just
because they broke their promises to God,
does that mean God will break his promises?
4Of course not! Though everyone else in the
world is a liar, God is not. Do you remember
what the book of Psalms says about this? That
God's words will always prove true and right,
no matter who questions them.

5"But," some say, "our breaking faith with
God is good, our sins serve a good purpose,
for people will notice how good God is when
they see how bad we are. Is it fair, then, for
him to punish us when our sins are helping
him?" (That is the way some people talk.)
6God forbid! Then what kind of God would he
be, to overlook sin? How could he ever condemn anyone? 7For he could not judge and
condemn me as a sinner if my dishonesty
brought him glory by pointing up his honesty
in contrast to my lies. 8If you follow through
with that idea you come to this: the worse we
are, the better God likes it! But the damnation
of those who say such things is just. Yet some
claim that this is what I preach!

All People Are Sinners

9Well, then, are we Jews *better* than others?
No, not at all, for we have already shown that
all men alike are sinners, whether Jews or
Gentiles. 10As the Scriptures say,

"No one is good—no one in all the world is
innocent."

11No one has ever really followed God's
paths or even truly wanted to.

12Every one has turned away; all have gone
wrong. No one anywhere has kept on doing
what is right; not one.

13Their talk is foul and filthy like the stench
from an open grave. Their tongues are loaded
with lies. Everything they say has in it the
sting and poison of deadly snakes.

14Their mouths are full of cursing and bitterness.

15They are quick to kill, hating anyone who
disagrees with them.

16Wherever they go they leave misery and
trouble behind them, 17and they have never

2:28-29 Paul made an important point very clear in these verses: God is concerned that our heart be open and obedient to him. Our outward religious or recovery activities are important only if they are a reflection of our love for God and others. We can always fake our recovery, just as we can fake our relationship with God. If we just go through the motions and make no real commitment to God, we cannot make progress for long. But if we are motivated by our love for God and other people, no obstacles to recovery are too great to overcome.

3:20 The more we know about God's laws, God's heart, and God's claim on our life, the clearer it becomes that we don't measure up. God's laws in the Old Testament represent God's will for us, as following them would lead to a healthy life. But none of us can follow these ideals under our own power. As we realize this, we recognize our need for God's gracious forgiveness and his power on a daily basis to help us follow his program for healthy living. When we fail in our walk with the God of recovery, we can use such times to remind us that we are powerless. This is the first step back into the process of recovery.

3:21-26 This is one of the richest sections in the Bible for understanding why Jesus died on the cross. We are all made right with God through faith in Jesus Christ. None of us are so good that we don't need God's help; none of us are so bad that we are beyond the reach of God's loving help. Paul says that Jesus has set us free from God's wrath against sin. Our salvation is freely given, but it was expensively purchased by God!

3:27 Again, Paul emphasized God's impartiality. God deals with all people on the same basis, regardless of race or social class. In a contemporary setting, Paul might have said that God gives the same attention to the homeless alcoholic that he gives to the richest person in the world. All must come to recovery through faith and trust in God. This leaves us nothing to boast about; none of us can be saved by anything we could do or say. But there is no reason for us to hide from God either; there can be nothing so bad in our life that it cannot be forgiven completely by our gracious God.

known what it is to feel secure or enjoy God's
blessing.
18 They care nothing about God nor what he
thinks of them.
19 So the judgment of God lies very heavily
upon the Jews, for they are responsible to
keep God's laws instead of doing all these evil
things; not one of them has any excuse; in
fact, all the world stands hushed and guilty
before Almighty God.
20 Now do you see it? No one can ever be
made right in God's sight by doing what the
law commands. For the more we know of
God's laws, the clearer it becomes that we
aren't obeying them; his laws serve only to
make us see that we are sinners.

Christ Took Our Punishment

21,22 But now God has shown us a different way
to heaven—not by "being good enough" and
trying to keep his laws, but by a new way
(though not new, really, for the Scriptures told
about it long ago). Now God says he will
accept and acquit us—declare us "not
guilty"—if we trust Jesus Christ to take away
our sins. And we all can be saved in this same
way, by coming to Christ, no matter who we
are or what we have been like. 23 Yes, all have
sinned; all fall short of God's glorious ideal;
24 yet now God declares us "not guilty" of
offending him if we trust in Jesus Christ, who
in his kindness freely takes away our sins.
25 For God sent Christ Jesus to take the punishment for our sins and to end all God's
anger against us. He used Christ's blood and
our faith as the means of saving us from his
wrath. In this way he was being entirely fair,
even though he did not punish those who
sinned in former times. For he was looking
forward to the time when Christ would come
and take away those sins. 26 And now in these
days also he can receive sinners in this same
way because Jesus took away their sins.
But isn't this unfair for God to let criminals
go free, and say that they are innocent? No,
for he does it on the basis of their trust in Jesus
who took away their sins.
27 Then what can we boast about doing to
earn our salvation? Nothing at all. Why? Because our acquittal is not based on our good
deeds; it is based on what Christ has done and
our faith in him. 28 So it is that we are saved by
faith in Christ and not by the good things we
do.
29 And does God save only the Jews in this
way? No, the Gentiles, too, may come to him
in this same manner. 30 God treats us all the

Self-perception

READ ROMANS 3:10-12

We may feel that we are different from other people—either much worse or much better. We may look down on ourself and continually compare ourself with "good" people. Or perhaps our addiction is more socially acceptable. We may tend to console ourself by looking down on others whose sins seem worse than ours.

"As the Scriptures say, 'No one is good—no one in all the world is innocent.' No one has ever really followed God's paths or even truly wanted to. Every one has turned away; all have gone wrong" (Romans 3:10-12).

The first chapter of Romans is often used to condemn sexual sins or sexual addictions. People often skip over the last few verses, which condemn the more "acceptable" sins, such as backbiting, disobeying parents, or being a braggart. Right after this chapter, the apostle Paul speaks to people who see themselves as better than others: "'Well,' you may be saying, 'what terrible people you have been talking about!' But wait a minute! You are just as bad. When you say they are wicked and should be punished, you are talking about yourselves, for you do these very same things" (Romans 2:1).

Every one of us is made of the same stuff, both good and bad. We may act out in different ways; but in God's eyes, we are all the same. When we focus on admitting our wrongs, it helps us remember that we are not so different from others after all. As we admit our helplessness, we can begin the steps toward healing and recovery. ***Turn to page 1237, Romans 4.***

same; all, whether Jews or Gentiles, are acquitted if they have faith. [31]Well then, if we are saved by faith, does this mean that we no longer need obey God's laws? Just the opposite! In fact, only when we trust Jesus can we truly obey him.

CHAPTER 4

The Faith of Abraham

Abraham was, humanly speaking, the founder of our Jewish nation. What were his experiences concerning this question of being saved by faith? Was it because of his good deeds that God accepted him? If so, then he would have something to boast about. But from God's point of view Abraham had no basis at all for pride. [3]For the Scriptures tell us Abraham *believed God,* and that is why God canceled his sins and declared him "not guilty."

[4,5]But didn't he earn his right to heaven by all the good things he did? No, for being saved is a gift; if a person could earn it by being good, then it wouldn't be free—but it is! It is *given* to those who do *not* work for it. For God declares sinners to be good in his sight if they have faith in Christ to save them from God's wrath.

[6]King David spoke of this, describing the happiness of an undeserving sinner who is declared "not guilty" by God. [7]"Blessed and to be envied," he said, "are those whose sins are forgiven and put out of sight. [8]Yes, what joy there is for anyone whose sins are no longer counted against him by the Lord."

[9]Now then, the question: Is this blessing given only to those who have faith in Christ but also keep the Jewish laws, or is the blessing also given to those who do not keep the Jewish rules but only trust in Christ? Well, what about Abraham? We say that he received these blessings through his faith. Was it by faith alone, or because he also kept the Jewish rules?

[10]For the answer to that question, answer this one: *When* did God give this blessing to Abraham? It was *before he became a Jew*—before he went through the Jewish initiation ceremony of circumcision.

[11]It wasn't until later on, *after* God had promised to bless him *because of his faith,* that he was circumcised. The circumcision ceremony was a sign that Abraham already had faith and that God had already accepted him and declared him just and good in his sight—before the ceremony took place. So Abraham is the spiritual father of those who believe and are saved without obeying Jewish laws. We see, then, that those who do not keep these rules are justified by God through faith. [12]And Abraham is also the spiritual father of those Jews who have been circumcised. They can see from his example that it is not this ceremony that saves them, for Abraham found favor with God by faith alone *before he was circumcised.*

[13]It is clear, then, that God's promise to give the whole earth to Abraham and his descendants was not because Abraham obeyed God's laws but because he trusted God to keep his promise. [14]So if you still claim that God's blessings go to those who are "good enough," then you are saying that God's promises to those who have faith are meaningless, and faith is foolish. [15]But the fact of the matter is this: when we try to gain God's blessing and salvation by keeping his laws we always end up under his anger, for we always fail to keep them. The only way we can keep from breaking laws is not to have any to break!

[16]So God's blessings are given to us by faith, as a free gift; we are certain to get them whether or not we follow Jewish customs if we have faith like Abraham's, for Abraham is the father of us all when it comes to these matters of faith. [17]That is what the Scriptures mean when they say that God made Abraham the father of many nations. God will accept all people in every nation who trust God as Abraham did. And this promise is from God

---

4:6-8 Many of us have failed desperately; we have hurt others in ways that cannot easily be repaired. What can we do with our guilt? King David was guilty of serious sins—adultery, deceit, and murder—yet when he acknowledged his guilt, turned it over to God, and experienced God's forgiveness, he found joy. Each of these steps was an act of faith, but the result was joy. Each of the steps we take in our recovery is also an act of faith, but as we faithfully work each step, we also will experience God's forgiveness and joy.

4:23-25 When we believe in God and the restoration he offers in Jesus Christ, an exchange takes place. We turn our unmanageable life over to God, including all our sin and guilt, and he gives us his goodness and forgiveness in return. When Jesus died on the cross, he took our sins and guilt away. When Jesus rose from the grave, God demonstrated his power to transform us and fill us with his goodness. As we follow God's program for restoration, we die to our sins and failures and then rise to a new and better life.

himself, who makes the dead live again and
speaks of future events with as much certainty
as though they were already past.
18So, when God told Abraham that he
would give him a son who would have many
descendants and become a great nation, Abraham believed God even though such a promise just couldn't come to pass! 19And because
his faith was strong, he didn't worry about the
fact that he was too old to be a father at the
age of one hundred, and that Sarah his wife,
at ninety, was also much too old to have a
baby.
20But Abraham never doubted. He believed
God, for his faith and trust grew ever stronger,
and he praised God for this blessing even
before it happened. 21He was completely sure
that God was well able to do anything he
promised. 22And because of Abraham's faith
God forgave his sins and declared him "not
guilty."
23Now this wonderful statement—that he
was accepted and approved through his
faith—wasn't just for Abraham's benefit. 24It
was for us, too, assuring us that God will
accept us in the same way he accepted Abraham—when we believe the promises of God
who brought back Jesus our Lord from the
dead. 25He died for our sins and rose again to
make us right with God, filling us with God's
goodness.

CHAPTER 5
Faith Brings Joy
So now, since we have been made right in
God's sight by faith in his promises, we can
have real peace with him because of what
Jesus Christ our Lord has done for us. 2For
because of our faith, he has brought us into
this place of highest privilege where we now
stand, and we confidently and joyfully look
forward to actually becoming all that God has
had in mind for us to be.
3We can rejoice, too, when we run into
problems and trials, for we know that they are
good for us—they help us learn to be patient.
4And patience develops strength of character
in us and helps us trust God more each time
we use it until finally our hope and faith are
strong and steady. 5Then, when that happens,
we are able to hold our heads high no matter
what happens and know that all is well, for we
know how dearly God loves us, and we feel
this warm love everywhere within us because
God has given us the Holy Spirit to fill our
hearts with his love.
6When we were utterly helpless, with no

Declared "Not Guilty"

BIBLE READING: Romans 3:23-28

We humbly asked him to remove our shortcomings.

What are our shortcomings? We all realize that we have them. Is this just another way of saying that we have fallen short of our personal ideals? At some time, all of us have held high ideals. We have used them to define what we think life should be like. But most of us learned early on that we couldn't measure up to them. Worse yet, we have often fallen short of the expectations of others and the desires of God. Oh, the weight of guilt we carry! Oh, the pain to think of how we have disappointed those we love! Oh, the longing for some way to make up the difference between what we are and what we should be!

The apostle Paul once wrote, "Yes, all have sinned; all fall short of God's glorious ideal; yet now God declares us 'not guilty' of offending him if we trust in Jesus Christ, who in his kindness freely takes away our sins" (Romans 3:23-24). Paul goes on to ask, "Then what can we boast about doing to earn our salvation? Nothing at all. Why? Because our acquittal is not based on our good deeds; it is based on what Christ has done and our faith in him. So it is that we are saved by faith in Christ and not by the good things we do" (3:27-28).

When God removes our shortcomings, he does a great job! "He has removed our sins as far away from us as the east is from the west" (Psalm 103:12). We can trust God to remove our shortcomings, moment by moment, if we humble ourself to accept his way. That means having faith in Jesus Christ to make up for our weaknesses in both character and action. ***Turn to page 1325, Philippians 2.***

way of escape, Christ came at just the right
time and died for us sinners who had no use
for him. 7Even if we were good, we really
wouldn't expect anyone to die for us, though,
of course, that might be barely possible. 8But
God showed his great love for us by sending
Christ to die for us while we were still sinners.
9And since by his blood he did all this for us
as sinners, how much more will he do for us
now that he has declared us not guilty? Now
he will save us from all of God's wrath to
come. 10And since, when we were his enemies,
we were brought back to God by the death of
his Son, what blessings he must have for us
now that we are his friends and he is living
within us!

11Now we rejoice in our wonderful new
relationship with God—all because of what
our Lord Jesus Christ has done in dying for
our sins—making us friends of God.

Adam's Sin; Christ's Forgiveness

12When Adam sinned, sin entered the entire
human race. His sin spread death throughout
all the world, so everything began to grow old
and die, for all sinned. 13[We know that it was
Adam's sin that caused this] because although, of course, people were sinning from
the time of Adam until Moses, God did not in
those days judge them guilty of death for
breaking his laws—because he had not yet
given his laws to them nor told them what he
wanted them to do. 14So when their bodies
died it was not for their own sins since they
themselves had never disobeyed God's special
law against eating the forbidden fruit, as
Adam had.

What a contrast between Adam and Christ
who was yet to come! 15And what a difference
between man's sin and God's forgiveness!

For this one man, Adam, brought death to
many through his *sin*. But this one man, Jesus
Christ, brought forgiveness to many through
God's *mercy*. 16Adam's *one* sin brought the penalty of death to many, while Christ freely
takes away *many* sins and gives glorious life
instead. 17The sin of this one man, Adam,
caused *death to be king over all*, but all who will
take God's gift of forgiveness and acquittal are
kings of life because of this one man, Jesus
Christ. 18Yes, Adam's *sin* brought *punishment*
to all, but Christ's *righteousness* makes men
right with God, so that they can live. 19Adam
caused many to be sinners because he *disobeyed* God, and Christ caused many to be
made acceptable to God because he *obeyed*.

20The Ten Commandments were given so
that all could see the extent of their failure to

5:12-13 How can we be judged for something Adam did thousands of years ago? It doesn't seem fair. Many of us find it easy to point our finger at others, blaming them for our problems. We might want to blame Adam for our failures; most of us probably blame our parents in some way or another. Here, Paul made it clear that Adam's failure and the failures of our ancestors should not be our primary concern. Our problems may have started with the mistakes of others, but we have all solidly aligned ourselves with Adam by repeatedly making the same mistakes. We are made of the same stuff, prone to rebel against God and his ways. We will suffer the consequences for the sins we have committed if God doesn't intervene. We don't need fairness from God; we need his mercy. And that is what God provides for all who look to him for deliverance.

5:15-21 Paul had already asserted that we stand forgiven and joyful in God's grace (5:2), and here he added more punch to that reality. The essential nature of God's grace is that it rules over the presence of sin and death in our world. While Adam's failure brought on the reign of sin and death, Jesus Christ has brought the reign of life through his grace for all who are willing to receive it. Our old unmanageable life represented the rule of death through Adam. Our life in recovery through Jesus Christ represents the rule of God's grace, kindness, and love. As we turn our life over to God, we can begin to receive the wonderful life that he offers.

6:1-3 If God loves to forgive, why not sin to give him added opportunities to forgive us? We may not admit it, but we act on this principle all too often. Paul's response to our use of this excuse for sin is an emphatic *no.* Such an attitude presumes upon God's grace and is clear evidence that we are in denial. When we think or act that way, we are making light of the tremendous cost of our salvation. It is unthinkable that we would continue to allow sin to be our master when we have turned our life over to God.

6:12-14 When we are recovering from an addiction or compulsive behavior, we may become very impatient because the old desires still bother us. Paul recognized that temptation would be an ongoing reality, so he gave us this warning: "Do not give in." The temptations we experience are an extension of the defects of character that exist in each of our lives. Though we cannot overcome our sinful nature alone, we can ask God to help us. As God helps us to clear the destructive patterns from our life, we can then replace them with healthy patterns and desires. As we are transformed with God's help, we will overcome the powerful temptations in our life.

obey God's laws. But the more we see our
sinfulness, the more we see God's abounding
grace forgiving us. 21Before, sin ruled over all
men and brought them to death, but now
God's kindness rules instead, giving us right
standing with God and resulting in eternal
life through Jesus Christ our Lord.

CHAPTER 6

Sin's Power Is Broken

Well then, shall we keep on sinning so that
God can keep on showing us more and more
kindness and forgiveness?
2,3Of course not! Should we keep on sinning
when we don't have to? For sin's power over
us was broken when we became Christians
and were baptized to become a part of Jesus
Christ; through his death the power of your
sinful nature was shattered. 4Your old sin-loving nature was buried with him by baptism
when he died; and when God the Father, with
glorious power, brought him back to life
again, you were given his wonderful new life
to enjoy.
5For you have become a part of him, and so
you died with him, so to speak, when he died;
and now you share his new life and shall rise
as he did. 6Your old evil desires were nailed to
the cross with him; that part of you that loves
to sin was crushed and fatally wounded, so
that your sin-loving body is no longer under
sin's control, no longer needs to be a slave to
sin; 7for when you are deadened to sin you are
freed from all its allure and its power over
you. 8And since your old sin-loving nature
"died" with Christ, we know that you will
share his new life. 9Christ rose from the dead
and will never die again. Death no longer has
any power over him. 10He died once for all to
end sin's power, but now he lives forever in
unbroken fellowship with God. 11So look
upon your old sin nature as dead and unre-
sponsive to sin, and instead be alive to God,
alert to him, through Jesus Christ our Lord.
12Do not let sin control your puny body any
longer; do not give in to its sinful desires. 13Do
not let any part of your bodies become tools
of wickedness, to be used for sinning; but give
yourselves completely to God—every part of
you—for you are back from death and you
want to be tools in the hands of God, to be
used for his good purposes. 14Sin need never
again be your master, for now you are no
longer tied to the law where sin enslaves you,
but you are free under God's favor and mercy.

Faith

READ ROMANS 4:1-5

When our addictive patterns represent "sinful" behavior, it is common to feel awkward about getting close to God. We may feel ineligible to receive God's love and, instead, expect his angry judgment. We might feel guilty and be afraid that God will reject us. Secretly, we wish that we could have a loving relationship with God, but we are afraid we could never be good enough.

The apostle Paul has shown us that we can have the love and acceptance we desire. He wrote, "For the Scriptures tell us Abraham *believed God,* and that is why God canceled his sins and declared him 'not guilty.' . . . Being saved is a gift; if a person could earn it by being good, then it wouldn't be free—but it is! It is *given* to those who do *not* work for it. For God declares sinners to be good in his sight if they have faith in Christ to save them from God's wrath. . . . God will accept us in the same way he accepted Abraham—when we believe the promises of God who brought back Jesus our Lord from the dead. He died for our sins and rose again to make us right with God" (Romans 4:3-5, 24-25).

There are free gifts waiting for us that are essential to our recovery: God's forgiveness, acceptance, and powerful support. God makes it clear that we have been declared "not guilty" in his court of justice if we have trusted Christ. He promises to give us a special home in heaven with our name on it. There is no need for us to do anything but accept his free gifts. When we turn our life over to God, we gain far more than we could ever lose! ***Turn to page 1243, Romans 7.***

Freedom to Obey God

15Does this mean that now we can go ahead
and sin and not worry about it? (For our
salvation does not depend on keeping the law
but on receiving God's grace!) Of course not!
16Don't you realize that you can choose
your own master? You can choose sin (with
death) or else obedience (with acquittal). The
one to whom you offer yourself—he will take
you and be your master, and you will be his
slave. 17Thank God that though you once
chose to be slaves of sin, now you have
obeyed with all your heart the teaching to
which God has committed you. 18And now
you are free from your old master, sin; and
you have become slaves to your new master,
righteousness.
19I speak this way, using the illustration of
slaves and masters, because it is easy to understand: just as you used to be slaves to all kinds
of sin, so now you must let yourselves be
slaves to all that is right and holy.
20In those days when you were slaves of sin
you didn't bother much with goodness. 21And
what was the result? Evidently not good, since
you are ashamed now even to think about
those things you used to do, for all of them
end in eternal doom. 22But now you are free
from the power of sin and are slaves of God,
and his benefits to you include holiness and
everlasting life. 23For the wages of sin is death,
but the free gift of God is eternal life through
Jesus Christ our Lord.

CHAPTER 7

No Longer Bound to the Law

Don't you understand yet, dear Jewish brothers in Christ, that when a person dies the law
no longer holds him in its power?
2Let me illustrate: when a woman marries,
the law binds her to her husband as long as he
is alive. But if he dies, she is no longer bound
to him; the laws of marriage no longer apply
to her. 3Then she can marry someone else if
she wants to. That would be wrong while he
was alive, but it is perfectly all right after he
dies.
4Your "husband," your master, used to be
the Jewish law; but you "died," as it were,
with Christ on the cross; and since you are
"dead," you are no longer "married to the
law," and it has no more control over you.
Then you came back to life again when Christ
did and are a new person. And now you are
"married," so to speak, to the one who rose
from the dead, so that you can produce good
fruit, that is, good deeds for God. 5When your
old nature was still active, sinful desires were
at work within you, making you want to do
whatever God said not to and producing sinful deeds, the rotting fruit of death. 6But now
you need no longer worry about the Jewish

6:19-22 It is impossible to be neutral. We all have a master—either sin or God. Making sin our master may seem fun for a while, but it will lead only to a life that is painfully out of control. When we turn our life over to God and work on our recovery, we are affirming that God is our master. This is the only way we can hope to experience restoration for our life. At first God's way may look harder than the way of sin, but in time we will discover that God's way is the only way to a joyful and meaningful life.

7:1-6 Paul used a marriage analogy to clarify his reasoning. If the person we have been married to dies, that person no longer has any power in our life. If we remarry, we give someone else that position of authority in our life. In the same way, when we turn our life over to God, our old way of life has died. We now are "married" to God, giving him a position of power and authority in our life. If we are willing to live under God's authority, we will experience the meaningful life that he wants for all his people.

7:13 Paul didn't want to leave us with the impression that God's laws are bad. God's laws were meant to lead us to a meaningful life in close fellowship with our gracious God. The real problem is our inability to live up to the standards God has set. By nature we are flawed and sinful creatures. Few of us set out to become enslaved to a destructive substance or relationship, but we are overcome by our inherent tendency to sin. We can be thankful that God has made a provision for our weaknesses, solving the sin problem through the work of Jesus Christ. Now, if we turn our life over to God, we can experience his transforming power in our life. He will provide us with the help we need to overcome our destructive behaviors.

7:14-17 In these verses, Paul described a struggle all of us can identify with. We long to do what is good, healthy, and right, but we end up doing the same old destructive things. As we take our personal inventory, we admit our failures and seek to change, but then we fall right back into our destructive habits once again. We are not alone in this process—it is part of being human. For this reason, we need not allow this struggle to discourage us. Instead, we can use our failures to inspire a new moral inventory and then get on with recovery once again. In time, we will discover that our failures become less frequent as God begins to transform our life.

laws and customs because you "died" while in
their captivity, and now you can really serve
God; not in the old way, mechanically obeying a set of rules, but in the new way, [with all
of your hearts and minds].

God's Law Reveals Our Sin

[7]Well then, am I suggesting that these laws of
God are evil? Of course not! No, the law is not
sinful, but it was the law that showed me my
sin. I would never have known the sin in my
heart—the evil desires that are hidden there—
if the law had not said, "You must not have
evil desires in your heart." [8]But sin used this
law against evil desires by reminding me that
such desires are wrong, and arousing all kinds
of forbidden desires within me! Only if there
were no laws to break would there be no
sinning.

[9]That is why I felt fine so long as I did not
understand what the law really demanded.
But when I learned the truth, I realized that I
had broken the law and was a sinner, doomed
to die. [10]So as far as I was concerned, the good
law which was supposed to show me the way
of life resulted instead in my being given the
death penalty. [11]Sin fooled me by taking the
good laws of God and using them to make me
guilty of death. [12]But still, you see, the law
itself was wholly right and good.

[13]But how can that be? Didn't the law cause
my doom? How then can it be good? No, it
was sin, devilish stuff that it is, that used what
was good to bring about my condemnation.
So you can see how cunning and deadly and
damnable it is. For it uses God's good laws for
its own evil purposes.

The Struggle Within

[14]The law is good, then, and the trouble is not
there but with *me* because I am sold into
slavery with Sin as my owner.

[15]I don't understand myself at all, for I
really want to do what is right, but I can't. I
do what I don't want to—what I hate. [16]I
know perfectly well that what I am doing is
wrong, and my bad conscience proves that I
agree with these laws I am breaking. [17]But I
can't help myself because I'm no longer doing
it. It is sin inside me that is stronger than I am
that makes me do these evil things.

[18]I know I am rotten through and through
so far as my old sinful nature is concerned. No
matter which way I turn I can't make myself
do right. I want to but I can't. [19]When I want
to do good, I don't; and when I try not to do
wrong, I do it anyway. [20]Now if I am doing

Repeated Forgiveness

BIBLE READING: Romans 5:3-5

We continued to take personal inventory and when we were wrong promptly admitted it.

We may grow impatient with ourself when we continue to run into the same sins over and over again. This may cause us to get discouraged, or we may be afraid that we are doomed to relapse.

Peter asked Jesus, "'Sir, how often should I forgive a brother who sins against me? Seven times?' 'No!' Jesus replied, 'seventy times seven!'" (Matthew 18:21-22). If this is to be our attitude toward others, doesn't it make sense that we should extend the same grace to ourself? We need to be as patient with ourself as God expects us to be with others.

Paul wrote, "We can rejoice, too, when we run into problems and trials, for we know that they are good for us—they help us learn to be patient. And patience develops strength of character in us and helps us trust God more each time we use it until finally our hope and faith are strong and steady. Then, when that happens . . . we know how dearly God loves us, and we feel this warm love everywhere within us because God has given us the Holy Spirit to fill our hearts with his love" (Romans 5:3-5).

Learning to wait patiently is an important characteristic for us to develop. Each time we admit wrong and accept God's forgiveness, our hope and faith have a chance to be exercised and to grow stronger. We no longer have to hide in shame every time we slip. We can admit our wrongs and move on. God's love is reaffirmed every time we rely on it. In this way, God helps us to hold our heads high no matter what happens. ***Turn to page 1317, Ephesians 4.***

what I don't want to, it is plain where the
trouble is: sin still has me in its evil grasp.
21It seems to be a fact of life that when I
want to do what is right, I inevitably do what
is wrong. 22I love to do God's will so far as my
new nature is concerned; 23-25but there is
something else deep within me, in my lower
nature, that is at war with my mind and wins
the fight and makes me a slave to the sin that
is still within me. In my mind I want to be
God's willing servant, but instead I find myself still enslaved to sin.

So you see how it is: my new life tells me to
do right, but the old nature that is still inside
me loves to sin. Oh, what a terrible predicament I'm in! Who will free me from my slavery to this deadly lower nature? Thank God!
It has been done by Jesus Christ our Lord. He
has set me free.

CHAPTER 8

The Holy Spirit Offers Freedom

So there is now no condemnation awaiting
those who belong to Christ Jesus. 2For the
power of the life-giving Spirit—and this
power is mine through Christ Jesus—has
freed me from the vicious circle of sin and
death. 3We aren't saved from sin's grasp by
knowing the commandments of God because
we can't and don't keep them, but God put
into effect a different plan to save us. He sent
his own Son in a human body like ours—except that ours are sinful—and destroyed sin's
control over us by giving himself as a sacrifice
for our sins. 4So now we can obey God's laws
if we follow after the Holy Spirit and no
longer obey the old evil nature within us.
5Those who let themselves be controlled by
their lower natures live only to please themselves, but those who follow after the Holy
Spirit find themselves doing those things that
please God. 6Following after the Holy Spirit
leads to life and peace, but following after the
old nature leads to death 7because the old
sinful nature within us is against God. It never
did obey God's laws and it never will. 8That's
why those who are still under the control of
their old sinful selves, bent on following their
old evil desires, can never please God.
9But you are not like that. You are controlled
by your new nature if you have the Spirit of
God living in you. (And remember that if
anyone doesn't have the Spirit of Christ living
in him, he is not a Christian at all.) 10Yet, even
though Christ lives within you, your body will
die because of sin; but your spirit will live, for
Christ has pardoned it. 11And if the Spirit of
God, who raised up Jesus from the dead, lives
in you, he will make your dying bodies live
again after you die, by means of this same
Holy Spirit living within you.

We Are God's Children

12So, dear brothers, you have no obligations
whatever to your old sinful nature to do what
it begs you to do. 13For if you keep on following it you are lost and will perish, but if
through the power of the Holy Spirit you
crush it and its evil deeds, you shall live. 14For
all who are led by the Spirit of God are sons of
God.

8:1 This is one of the great affirmations of Scripture. We will never be condemned by God for our sins, because Jesus Christ has paid the price once and for all. When we decide to turn our life over to God's care, we can be confident that we will not be condemned by him. If we have accepted God's offer of forgiveness in Christ, there is "no condemnation."

8:2-4 Once we recognize how helpless we are to fight our dependencies, the next step is to look outside ourself to God for the power we need. The life-giving Spirit that Paul mentioned here is the Holy Spirit. He was present at the creation of the world (Genesis 1–2) and is available to help us as we seek to rebuild our life. We cannot overcome our addictions and compulsions alone, but God is more than able to help us. He sent his Son and destroyed the power of sin through his death and resurrection. Now we can follow God's program for healthy living through the power of the Holy Spirit who is always with us.

8:5-6 Paul puts people in two categories—those who let themselves be controlled by their self-serving "lower natures" and those who follow after the Holy Spirit. Once we have made the decision to turn our life over to God, it is a daily decision to consciously choose to follow his way for our continued recovery. We need to continually reassess our progress, taking a regular moral inventory of our life.

8:9-11 Either we have the Spirit of God living in us, or we don't. How does the Spirit of God come to live within us? By our act of faith in turning our life over to God and by our acceptance of the work of Christ on our behalf. Can we feel the Spirit of God within us? Sometimes, but we can know he is there whether we feel his presence or not. God has promised to give us the Holy Spirit when we ask. We receive the same Holy Spirit who raised Jesus from the dead. God will put his power to work within us to bring about our recovery.

15 And so we should not be like cringing,
fearful slaves, but we should behave like God's
very own children, adopted into the bosom of
his family, and calling to him, "Father,
Father." 16 For his Holy Spirit speaks to us deep
in our hearts and tells us that we really are
God's children. 17 And since we are his children, we will share his treasures—for all God
gives to his Son Jesus is now ours too. But if
we are to share his glory, we must also share
his suffering.

Our Future Reward

18 Yet what we suffer now is nothing compared
to the glory he will give us later. 19 For all
creation is waiting patiently and hopefully for
that future day when God will resurrect his
children. 20,21 For on that day thorns and thistles, sin, death, and decay—the things that
overcame the world against its will at God's
command—will all disappear, and the world
around us will share in the glorious freedom
from sin which God's children enjoy.
22 For we know that even the things of nature, like animals and plants, suffer in sickness and death as they await this great event.
23 And even we Christians, although we have
the Holy Spirit within us as a foretaste of
future glory, also groan to be released from
pain and suffering. We, too, wait anxiously
for that day when God will give us our full
rights as his children, including the new bodies he has promised us—bodies that will never
be sick again and will never die.
24 We are saved by trusting. And trusting
means looking forward to getting something
we don't yet have—for a man who already has
something doesn't need to hope and trust that
he will get it. 25 But if we must keep trusting
God for something that hasn't happened yet,
it teaches us to wait patiently and confidently.
26 And in the same way—by our faith—the
Holy Spirit helps us with our daily problems
and in our praying. For we don't even know
what we should pray for nor how to pray as
we should, but the Holy Spirit prays for us
with such feeling that it cannot be expressed
in words. 27 And the Father who knows all
hearts knows, of course, what the Spirit is
saying as he pleads for us in harmony with
God's own will. 28 And we know that all that
happens to us is working for our good if we
love God and are fitting into his plans.

Nothing Separates Us from God's Love

29 For from the very beginning God decided
that those who came to him—and all along

Removed, Not Improved

BIBLE READING: Romans 6:5-11

We were entirely ready to have God remove all these defects of character.

Most of us have made numerous attempts at self-improvement. Perhaps we have consciously tried to improve our attitudes, our education, our appearance, or our habits. We probably have had success in self-improvement on some level. However, when it comes to our struggles with defects of character, chances are we have only experienced deep frustration.

There is a reason for our frustration. These character defects can only be removed, never improved! The illustration given us in the Bible is that these defects of character must be put to death, as Jesus was, with the hope of new life to follow. The apostle Paul wrote, "Your old evil desires were nailed to the cross with [Jesus]; that part of you that loves to sin was crushed and fatally wounded, so that your sin-loving body is no longer under sin's control, no longer needs to be a slave to sin" (Romans 6:6). "Those who belong to Christ have nailed their natural evil desires to his cross and crucified them there" (Galatians 5:24).

There is no Band-Aid cure for these defects of character. They have been fatally wounded and must die on the cross. This process is never easy. Who goes to a crucifixion without some measure of anxiety? But when we accept this and allow God to remove our defects, we will be pleasantly surprised by the new life that greets us on the other side. ***Turn to page 1327, Philippians 3.***

he knew who would—should become like his Son, so that his Son would be the First, with many brothers. [30]And having chosen us, he called us to come to him; and when we came, he declared us "not guilty," filled us with Christ's goodness, gave us right standing with himself, and promised us his glory.

[31]What can we ever say to such wonderful things as these? If God is on our side, who can ever be against us? [32]Since he did not spare even his own Son for us but gave him up for us all, won't he also surely give us everything else?

[33]Who dares accuse us whom God has chosen for his own? Will God? No! He is the one who has forgiven us and given us right standing with himself.

[34]Who then will condemn us? Will Christ? *No!* For he is the one who died for us and came back to life again for us and is sitting at the place of highest honor next to God, pleading for us there in heaven.

[35]Who then can ever keep Christ's love from us? When we have trouble or calamity, when we are hunted down or destroyed, is it because he doesn't love us anymore? And if we are hungry or penniless or in danger or threatened with death, has God deserted us?

[36]No, for the Scriptures tell us that for his sake we must be ready to face death at every moment of the day—we are like sheep awaiting slaughter; [37]but despite all this, overwhelming victory is ours through Christ who loved us enough to die for us. [38]For I am convinced that nothing can ever separate us from his love. Death can't, and life can't. The angels won't, and all the powers of hell itself cannot keep God's love away. Our fears for today, our worries about tomorrow, [39]or where we are—high above the sky, or in the deepest ocean—nothing will ever be able to separate us from the love of God demonstrated by our Lord Jesus Christ when he died for us.

CHAPTER 9

God's Sovereignty

O Israel, my people! O my Jewish brothers! How I long for you to come to Christ. My heart is heavy within me, and I grieve bitterly day and night because of you. Christ knows and the Holy Spirit knows that it is no mere pretense when I say that I would be willing to be forever damned if that would save you. [4]God has given you so much, but still you will not listen to him. He took you as his own special, chosen people and led you along with a bright cloud of glory and told you how very much he wanted to bless you. He gave you his rules for daily life so you would know what he wanted you to do. He let you worship him and gave you mighty promises. [5]Great men of God were your fathers, and Christ himself was one of you, a Jew so far as his human nature is concerned, he who now rules over all things. Praise God forever!

[6]Well then, has God failed to fulfill his promises to the Jews? No! [For these promises are only to those who are truly Jews.] And not everyone born into a Jewish family is truly a Jew! [7]Just the fact that they come from Abraham doesn't make them truly Abraham's children. For the Scriptures say that the promises apply only to Abraham's son Isaac and Isaac's descendants, though Abraham had other children too. [8]This means that not all of Abraham's children are children of God, but only those who believe the promise of salvation which he made to Abraham.

[9]For God had promised, "Next year I will give you and Sarah a son." [10-13]And years later, when this son Isaac was grown up and married and Rebecca his wife was about to bear him twin children, God told her that Esau, the child born first, would be a servant to Jacob, his twin brother. In the words of the Scripture, "I chose to bless Jacob but not Esau." And God said this before the children were even born, before they had done any-

8:31-39 Our security in recovery is based on God's unshakable love for us. The love God has for us is not just an emotion, but a matter of historical record. God proved his love for us by willingly sending his Son to suffer and die. So why would he hold back any lesser gift? In fact, there is nothing in the whole universe that can separate us from God's love! What more could God say to us to make us more secure in his love?

9:25-26 God specializes in loving those who are unlovely and undeserving. The fact is, none of us deserve God's love, and those of us who think we deserve it are in denial. God's love is bestowed on all who admit their need and respond to his love for them. It is sometimes the most undeserving who are the first to admit their need for God. That is why God so often reaches out to the broken and unlovely. No one is entirely innocent of wrongdoing; yet no sin is too great for God to forgive. Thus, desperate addicts who have admitted their failures are better off than "respectable" people who are in denial about their need for God. Admitting that we have failed and that we need God is an essential part of the recovery process.

thing either good or bad. This proves that God was doing what he had decided from the beginning; it was not because of what the children did but because of what God wanted and chose.

14 Was God being unfair? Of course not. 15 For God had said to Moses, "If I want to be kind to someone, I will. And I will take pity on anyone I want to." 16 And so God's blessings are not given just because someone decides to have them or works hard to get them. They are given because God takes pity on those he wants to.

17 Pharaoh, king of Egypt, was an example of this fact. For God told him he had given him the kingdom of Egypt for the very purpose of displaying the awesome power of God against him, so that all the world would hear about God's glorious name. 18 So you see, God is kind to some just because he wants to be, and he makes some refuse to listen.

19 Well then, why does God blame them for not listening? Haven't they done what he made them do?

20 No, don't say that. Who are you to criticize God? Should the thing made say to the one who made it, "Why have you made me like this?" 21 When a man makes a jar out of clay, doesn't he have a right to use the same lump of clay to make one jar beautiful, to be used for holding flowers, and another to throw garbage into? 22 Does not God have a perfect right to show his fury and power against those who are fit only for destruction, those he has been patient with for all this time? 23,24 And he has a right to take others such as ourselves, who have been made for pouring the riches of his glory into, whether we are Jews or Gentiles, and to be kind to us so that everyone can see how very great his glory is.

25 Remember what the prophecy of Hosea says? There God says that he will find other children for himself (who are not from his Jewish family) and will love them, though no one had ever loved them before. 26 And the heathen, of whom it once was said, "You are not my people," shall be called "sons of the Living God."

27 Isaiah the prophet cried out concerning the Jews that though there would be millions of them, only a small number would ever be saved. 28 "For the Lord will execute his sentence upon the earth, quickly ending his dealings, justly cutting them short."

29 And Isaiah says in another place that except for God's mercy all the Jews would be

Self-perception

READ ROMANS 7:18-25

We may have begun to realize that we have character flaws that are beyond our control. Deep down inside there is a sense of brokenness that is a constant reminder of our humanity. Hopefully, we will get to a place where our behavior is under control, and we will be able to maintain sobriety. But as long as we are in this human body, we will have to contend with our lower nature.

Paul said of himself, "I know I am rotten through and through so far as my old sinful nature is concerned. No matter which way I turn I can't make myself do right. I want to but I can't. . . . There is something else deep within me, in my lower nature, that is at war with my mind and wins the fight and makes me a slave to the sin that is still within me" (Romans 7:18, 23-25). King David described God's tenderness toward us because of our human condition: "He is like a father to us, tender and sympathetic to those who reverence him. For he knows we are but dust and that our days are few and brief" (Psalm 103:13-15).

No matter how far we progress, our lower nature will always be inclined toward and susceptible to the lure of our addictions. We can't afford to forget this or let down our guard. Maintaining sobriety is something we will need to nurture for the rest of our life, one day at a time. But we also have a reason for great hope. By recognizing our helplessness against the power of sin, we open our life to the transforming power of God. ***Turn to page 1247, Romans 12.***

destroyed—all of them—just as everyone in the cities of Sodom and Gomorrah perished.

Israel's Rejection of the Good News

30Well then, what shall we say about these things? Just this, that God has given the Gentiles the opportunity to be acquitted by faith, even though they had not been really seeking God. 31But the Jews, who tried so hard to get right with God by keeping his laws, never succeeded. 32Why not? Because they were trying to be saved by keeping the law and being good instead of by depending on faith. They have stumbled over the great stumbling stone. 33God warned them of this in the Scriptures when he said, "I have put a Rock in the path of the Jews, and many will stumble over him (Jesus). Those who believe in him will never be disappointed."

CHAPTER 10

Dear brothers, the longing of my heart and my prayer is that the Jewish people might be saved. 2I know what enthusiasm they have for the honor of God, but it is misdirected zeal. 3For they don't understand that Christ has died to make them right with God. Instead they are trying to make themselves good enough to gain God's favor by keeping the Jewish laws and customs, but that is not God's way of salvation. 4They don't understand that Christ gives to those who trust in him everything they are trying to get by keeping his laws. He ends all of that.

5For Moses wrote that if a person could be perfectly good and hold out against temptation all his life and never sin once, only then could he be pardoned and saved. 6But the salvation that comes through faith says, "You don't need to search the heavens to find Christ and bring him down to help you," and, 7"You don't need to go among the dead to bring Christ back to life again."

8For salvation that comes from trusting Christ—which is what we preach—is already within easy reach of each of us; in fact, it is as near as our own hearts and mouths. 9For if you tell others with your own mouth that Jesus Christ is your Lord and believe in your own heart that God has raised him from the dead, you will be saved. 10For it is by believing in his heart that a man becomes right with God; and with his mouth he tells others of his faith, confirming his salvation.

11For the Scriptures tell us that no one who believes in Christ will ever be disappointed. 12Jew and Gentile are the same in this respect: they all have the same Lord who generously gives his riches to all those who ask him for them. 13Anyone who calls upon the name of the Lord will be saved.

14But how shall they ask him to save them unless they believe in him? And how can they believe in him if they have never heard about him? And how can they hear about him unless someone tells them? 15And how will anyone go and tell them unless someone sends him? That is what the Scriptures are talking about when they say, "How beautiful are the feet of those who preach the Gospel of peace with God and bring glad tidings of good things." In other words, how welcome are those who come preaching God's Good News!

16But not everyone who hears the Good News has welcomed it, for Isaiah the prophet said, "Lord, who has believed me when I told them?" 17Yet faith comes from listening to this Good News—the Good News about Christ.

18But what about the Jews? Have they heard God's Word? Yes, for it has gone wherever they are; the Good News has been told to the ends of the earth. 19And did they understand [that God would give his salvation to others if they refused to take it]? Yes, for even back in the time of Moses, God had said that he would make his people jealous and try to wake them up by giving his salvation to the foolish heathen nations. 20And later on Isaiah said boldly that God would be found by people who weren't even looking for him. 21In the meantime, he keeps on reaching out his hands to the Jews, but they keep arguing and refusing to come.

CHAPTER 11

God's Mercy on Israel

I ask then, has God rejected and deserted his people the Jews? Oh no, not at all. Remember

---

10:8-15 Our salvation comes by trusting Jesus Christ; there is nothing we can do to earn it. Many of us have spent our entire life trying to earn the approval of others. Perhaps the pain we feel at our failure to achieve perfection is at the heart of our compulsive behavior. We can be thankful that God does not accept us on the basis of our performance. He accepts us because of what Christ has done on our behalf, no matter how great our failures have been. We have no reason to hide our mistakes from God; he wants only to relieve us of the burdens we carry. He invites us to entrust our life to him and seek to follow his will for our life.

that I myself am a Jew, a descendant of Abraham and a member of Benjamin's family.

[2,3]No, God has not discarded his own people whom he chose from the very beginning. Do you remember what the Scriptures say about this? Elijah the prophet was complaining to God about the Jews, telling God how they had killed the prophets and torn down God's altars; Elijah claimed that he was the only one left in all the land who still loved God, and now they were trying to kill him too.

[4]And do you remember how God replied? God said, "No, you are not the only one left. I have seven thousand others besides you who still love me and have not bowed down to idols!"

[5]It is the same today. Not all the Jews have turned away from God; there are a few being saved as a result of God's kindness in choosing them. [6]And if it is by God's kindness, then it is not by their being good enough. For in that case the free gift would no longer be free—it isn't free when it is earned.

[7]So this is the situation: Most of the Jews have not found the favor of God they are looking for. A few have—the ones God has picked out—but the eyes of the others have been blinded. [8]This is what our Scriptures refer to when they say that God has put them to sleep, shutting their eyes and ears so that they do not understand what we are talking about when we tell them of Christ. And so it is to this very day.

[9]King David spoke of this same thing when he said, "Let their good food and other blessings trap them into thinking all is well between themselves and God. Let these good things boomerang on them and fall back upon their heads to justly crush them. [10]Let their eyes be dim," he said, "so that they cannot see, and let them walk bent-backed forever with a heavy load."

[11]Does this mean that God has rejected his Jewish people forever? Of course not! His purpose was to make his salvation available to the Gentiles, and then the Jews would be jealous and begin to want God's salvation for themselves. [12]Now if the whole world became rich as a result of God's offer of salvation, when the Jews stumbled over it and turned it down, think how much greater a blessing the world will share in later on when the Jews, too, come to Christ.

[13]As you know, God has appointed me as a special messenger to you Gentiles. I lay great stress on this and remind the Jews about it as often as I can, [14]so that if possible I can make them want what you Gentiles have and in that way save some of them. [15]And how wonderful it will be when they become Christians! When God turned away from them it meant that he turned to the rest of the world to offer his salvation; and now it is even more wonderful when the Jews come to Christ. It will be like dead people coming back to life. [16]And since Abraham and the prophets are God's people, their children will be too. For if the roots of the tree are holy, the branches will be too.

[17]But some of these branches from Abraham's tree, some of the Jews, have been broken off. And you Gentiles who were branches from, we might say, a wild olive tree, were grafted in. So now you, too, receive the blessing God has promised Abraham and his children, sharing in God's rich nourishment of his own special olive tree.

[18]But you must be careful not to brag about being put in to replace the branches that were broken off. Remember that you are important only because you are now a part of God's tree; you are just a branch, not a root.

[19]"Well," you may be saying, "those branches were broken off to make room for me, so I must be pretty good."

[20]Watch out! Remember that those branches, the Jews, were broken off because they didn't believe God, and you are there only because you do. Do not be proud; be humble and grateful—and careful. [21]For if God did not spare the branches he put there in the first place, he won't spare you either.

[22]Notice how God is both kind and severe. He is very hard on those who disobey, but very good to you if you continue to love and trust him. But if you don't, you too will be cut off. [23]On the other hand, if the Jews leave their

---

11:1-10 Paul asked, "Has God rejected and deserted his people the Jews?" The apostle answered his own question with a resounding *no.* Even though a majority of Jews had rejected Jesus' messianic claims, there was still hope for them. It is never too late to turn our life over to God to experience his healing power and grace. As long as we have breath, we can still ask for God's help and forgiveness. Even though this is true, however, an extended period of denial is always costly. During our years of denial we may cause great pain to others, and the longer we wait, the more difficult it will be to change. The time to seek change is now!

unbelief behind them and come back to God,
God will graft them back into the tree again.
He has the power to do it.
24For if God was willing to take you who
were so far away from him—being part of a
wild olive tree—and graft you into his own
good tree—a very unusual thing to do—don't
you see that he will be far more ready to put
the Jews back again, who were there in the
first place?

God's Mercy Is for Everyone

25I want you to know about this truth from
God, dear brothers, so that you will not feel
proud and start bragging. Yes, it is true that
some of the Jews have set themselves against
the Gospel now, but this will last only until all
of you Gentiles have come to Christ—those of
you who will. 26And then all Israel will be
saved.

Do you remember what the prophets said
about this? "There shall come out of Zion a
Deliverer, and he shall turn the Jews from all
ungodliness. 27At that time I will take away
their sins, just as I promised."
28Now many of the Jews are enemies of the
Gospel. They hate it. But this has been a
benefit to you, for it has resulted in God's
giving his gifts to you Gentiles. Yet the Jews
are still beloved of God because of his promises to Abraham, Isaac, and Jacob. 29For God's
gifts and his call can never be withdrawn; he
will never go back on his promises. 30Once
you were rebels against God, but when the
Jews refused his gifts God was merciful to you
instead. 31And now the Jews are the rebels, but
some day they, too, will share in God's mercy
upon you. 32For God has given them all up to
sin so that he could have mercy upon all alike.
33Oh, what a wonderful God we have! How
great are his wisdom and knowledge and
riches! How impossible it is for us to understand his decisions and his methods! 34For
who among us can know the mind of the
Lord? Who knows enough to be his counselor
and guide? 35And who could ever offer to the
Lord enough to induce him to act? 36For
everything comes from God alone. Everything lives by his power, and everything is for
his glory. To him be glory evermore.

CHAPTER 12

A Living Sacrifice to God

And so, dear brothers, I plead with you to give
your bodies to God. Let them be a living
sacrifice, holy—the kind he can accept. When
you think of what he has done for you, is this
too much to ask? 2Don't copy the behavior
and customs of this world, but be a new and
different person with a fresh newness in all
you do and think. Then you will learn from

11:33-36 After sketching out the broad contours of God's plan for us, Paul could only fall on his knees in worship of God's majesty. God's plan, wisdom, knowledge, and ways are all so far beyond ours that we have only one option: to humbly give him the praise he deserves! For those of us who recognize how limited and helpless we are, the fact that God's power and wisdom are great can be an encouragement, especially since he loves us and wants to help us.

12:3 This verse is a call to honesty and true humility. We are to take a personal inventory of our life, making an honest assessment of both our strengths and weaknesses. An honest inventory will teach us humility as we uncover our faults. It will also help us develop a grateful attitude toward God as we discover the many gifts he has given us.

12:4-8 God has an important role for each of us to play. We are all given special gifts that are needed by the people around us. Some of us may look at our life and wonder how we could ever be used to accomplish anything significant. Our addictions may have decimated our resources and destroyed our relationships. We may feel useless, isolated, and alone. Notice that Paul mentioned the gift of giving comfort to others. This is something that we in recovery are especially suited to do. Who could better help a person devastated by addiction than someone who has already been there? Part of our recovery involves sharing our story with others. We may think our life isn't worth much, but our story of deliverance may mean the difference between life and death for a person in need. As we reach out to comfort others, we will discover that our isolation has given way to fellowship.

12:9-21 We are called to let love govern all our attitudes and actions as we continue in the process of recovery. We are called to love even those we consider to be our enemies. We have all been wronged by others. God's love allows us to forgive them and seek reconciliation. All of us have hurt others. Love enables us to ask for their forgiveness and do what we can to make amends for the trouble and pain we have caused. Often we need to make a special effort to reach out to immediate family members—parents, siblings, children, a spouse. Love is not easy; it demands that we swallow our pride and admit our wrongs to others. As painful as love may be, however, it is the only way we can experience the joy of rebuilding our relationships and progressing in recovery.

your own experience how his ways will really
satisfy you.
[3]As God's messenger I give each of you
God's warning: Be honest in your estimate of
yourselves, measuring your value by how
much faith God has given you. [4,5]Just as there
are many parts to our bodies, so it is with
Christ's body. We are all parts of it, and it takes
every one of us to make it complete, for we
each have different work to do. So we belong
to each other, and each needs all the others.
[6]God has given each of us the ability to do
certain things well. So if God has given you
the ability to prophesy, then prophesy whenever you can—as often as your faith is strong
enough to receive a message from God. [7]If
your gift is that of serving others, serve them
well. If you are a teacher, do a good job of
teaching. [8]If you are a preacher, see to it that
your sermons are strong and helpful. If God
has given you money, be generous in helping
others with it. If God has given you administrative ability and put you in charge of
the work of others, take the responsibility
seriously. Those who offer comfort to the sorrowing should do so with Christian cheer.
[9]Don't just pretend that you love others:
really love them. Hate what is wrong. Stand
on the side of the good. [10]Love each other
with brotherly affection and take delight in
honoring each other. [11]Never be lazy in your
work, but serve the Lord enthusiastically.
[12]Be glad for all God is planning for you. Be
patient in trouble, and prayerful always.
[13]When God's children are in need, you be the
one to help them out. And get into the habit
of inviting guests home for dinner or, if they
need lodging, for the night.
[14]If someone mistreats you because you are
a Christian, don't curse him; pray that God
will bless him. [15]When others are happy, be
happy with them. If they are sad, share their
sorrow. [16]Work happily together. Don't try to
act big. Don't try to get into the good graces
of important people, but enjoy the company
of ordinary folks. And don't think you know
it all!
[17]Never pay back evil for evil. Do things in
such a way that everyone can see you are
honest clear through. [18]Don't quarrel with
anyone. Be at peace with everyone, just as
much as possible.
[19]Dear friends, never avenge yourselves.
Leave that to God, for he has said that he will
repay those who deserve it. [Don't take the
law into your own hands.] [20]Instead, feed your
enemy if he is hungry. If he is thirsty give him

Self-perception

READ ROMANS 12:1-2

How many times have we wished that we could be someone else? Perhaps one reason we act out our addictions is that we hate ourself. Self-hatred is often associated with addictive/compulsive personalities. If we don't like who we are and feel helpless to change, it is reassuring to know that God has the power to change us dramatically.

The apostle Paul wrote, "I plead with you to give your bodies to God. Let them be a living sacrifice, holy—the kind he can accept. When you think of what he has done for you, is this too much to ask? Don't copy the behavior and customs of this world, but be a new and different person with a fresh newness in all you do and think. Then you will learn from your own experience how his ways will really satisfy you" (Romans 12:1-2).

We are told here to avoid being like the world around us. If we copy the behavior and customs of this world, we will head straight toward selfish ways and destructive dependencies. Our part is to turn our will and our life over to the care of God. As we give our life to him, he will work changes in our life, making us into a new person. God wants to change us from the inside out. As we are changed on the inside, we will begin to evidence those changes in our external attitudes and actions.

We all have great potential for change, but we cannot do it under our own power. As we yield our life and will to God, we can depend on him to renew our mind and heart. He will begin to remove our defects of character, transforming us from the inside out. ***Turn to page 1263, 1 Corinthians 6.***

something to drink and you will be "heaping coals of fire on his head." In other words, he will feel ashamed of himself for what he has done to you. [21]Don't let evil get the upper hand, but conquer evil by doing good.

CHAPTER 13

Respect for Authority

Obey the government, for God is the one who has put it there. There is no government anywhere that God has not placed in power. [2]So those who refuse to obey the laws of the land are refusing to obey God, and punishment will follow. [3]For the policeman does not frighten people who are doing right; but those doing evil will always fear him. So if you don't want to be afraid, keep the laws and you will get along well. [4]The policeman is sent by God to help you. But if you are doing something wrong, of course you should be afraid, for he will have you punished. He is sent by God for that very purpose. [5]Obey the laws, then, for two reasons: first, to keep from being punished, and second, just because you know you should.

[6]Pay your taxes too, for these same two reasons. For government workers need to be paid so that they can keep on doing God's work, serving you. [7]Pay everyone whatever he ought to have: pay your taxes and import duties gladly, obey those over you, and give honor and respect to all those to whom it is due.

Love Fulfills God's Requirements

[8]Pay all your debts except the debt of love for others—never finish paying that! For if you love them, you will be obeying all of God's laws, fulfilling all his requirements. [9]If you love your neighbor as much as you love yourself you will not want to harm or cheat him, or kill him or steal from him. And you won't sin with his wife or want what is his, or do anything else the Ten Commandments say is wrong. All ten are wrapped up in this one, to love your neighbor as you love yourself. [10]Love does no wrong to anyone. That's why it fully satisfies all of God's requirements. It is the only law you need.

[11]Another reason for right living is this: you know how late it is; time is running out. Wake up, for the coming of the Lord is nearer now than when we first believed. [12,13]The night is far gone, the day of his return will soon be here. So quit the evil deeds of darkness and put on the armor of right living, as we who live in the daylight should! Be decent and true in everything you do so that all can approve your behavior. Don't spend your time in wild parties and getting drunk or in adultery and lust or fighting or jealousy. [14]But ask the Lord Jesus Christ to help you live as you should, and don't make plans to enjoy evil.

CHAPTER 14

The Danger of Criticism

Give a warm welcome to any brother who wants to join you, even though his faith is weak. Don't criticize him for having different

---

13:1-7 Our life-style in recovery includes the way we relate to the authorities of civil government. Paul pointed out that government exists because God allows it to exist. Therefore, we are asked to submit to the government as we would submit to God himself. Some of us may have suffered great abuse by someone in a position of authority. How could God want us to submit to authorities who do not act justly toward their people? Elsewhere in Scripture we find that there is a place for civil disobedience (see Acts 4:13-22). Sometimes we need to resist the injustices that are being done against us. We can do this by communicating with trustworthy people about the abuses we have suffered. We are called to support and obey authorities that seek to uphold justice. But when they stand in direct contradiction to God's will, we need to seek the support of others and try to change the situation.

13:8-10 Progress in recovery can take place only as we learn to love others. Love is not an emotion we feel; it is an attitude of unselfish concern for others. If we love God and the people around us, we will treat others with the respect we normally give ourself. We would never harm them, steal from them, or deprive them to satisfy our own selfish desires. Love is the opposite of being selfish. As we continue to take a regular personal inventory, we can use love as the standard by which we judge our behavior. Do we act with the best interests of others in mind? If we measure all our actions against the measuring stick of love, we will experience great progress in our recovery.

13:12-14 When we turn our life over to God, we are given a new identity; we become children of the light. People who live in the light are awake—their eyes are open. They are not in the darkness of denial. In other words, they have the ability to see and admit the truth about themselves. One way we can make sure we are walking in the light is to take a regular moral inventory. This will keep our eyes open to the truth about our life.

ideas from yours about what is right and
wrong. 2For instance, don't argue with him
about whether or not to eat meat that has
been offered to idols. You may believe there is
no harm in this, but the faith of others is
weaker; they think it is wrong and will go
without any meat at all and eat vegetables
rather than eat that kind of meat. 3Those who
think it is all right to eat such meat must not
look down on those who won't. And if you
are one of those who won't, don't find fault
with those who do. For God has accepted
them to be his children. 4They are God's servants, not yours. They are responsible to him,
not to you. Let him tell them whether they
are right or wrong. And God is able to make
them do as they should.

5Some think that Christians should observe
the Jewish holidays as special days to worship
God, but others say it is wrong and foolish to
go to all that trouble, for every day alike
belongs to God. On questions of this kind
everyone must decide for himself. 6If you
have special days for worshiping the Lord,
you are trying to honor him; you are doing a
good thing. So is the person who eats meat
that has been offered to idols; he is thankful
to the Lord for it; he is doing right. And the
person who won't touch such meat, he, too,
is anxious to please the Lord, and is thankful.
7We are not our own bosses to live or die as we
ourselves might choose. 8Living or dying we
follow the Lord. Either way we are his. 9Christ
died and rose again for this very purpose, so
that he can be our Lord both while we live
and when we die.

10You have no right to criticize your brother
or look down on him. Remember, each of us
will stand personally before the Judgment
Seat of God. 11For it is written, "As I live," says
the Lord, "every knee shall bow to me and
every tongue confess to God." 12Yes, each of
us will give an account of himself to God.

13So don't criticize each other anymore. Try
instead to live in such a way that you will
never make your brother stumble by letting
him see you doing something he thinks is
wrong.

14As for myself, I am perfectly sure on the
authority of the Lord Jesus that there is nothing really wrong with eating meat that has
been offered to idols. But if someone believes
it is wrong, then he shouldn't do it because
for him it is wrong. 15And if your brother is
bothered by what you eat, you are not acting
in love if you go ahead and eat it. Don't let
your eating ruin someone for whom Christ
died. 16Don't do anything that will cause criticism against yourself even though you know
that what you do is right.

17For, after all, the important thing for us as
Christians is not what we eat or drink but
stirring up goodness and peace and joy from
the Holy Spirit. 18If you let Christ be Lord in
these affairs, God will be glad; and so will
others. 19In this way aim for harmony in the
church, and try to build each other up.

20Don't undo the work of God for a chunk
of meat. Remember, there is nothing wrong
with the meat, but it is wrong to eat it if it
makes another stumble. 21The right thing to
do is to quit eating meat or drinking wine or
doing anything else that offends your brother
or makes him sin. 22You may know that there
is nothing wrong with what you do, even
from God's point of view, but keep it to yourself; don't flaunt your faith in front of others
who might be hurt by it. In this situation,
happy is the man who does not sin by doing
what he knows is right. 23But anyone who

14:1-4 We may find it easy to judge others who are still struggling in recovery, with one foot still in the old patterns of the past. We might even be tempted to show them how "strong" we are by participating in activities that would still lead them into a destructive fall. Even if we have progressed in recovery to the point that certain circumstances no longer trouble us, we still need to be sensitive to the fact that our friends may be led astray by our activities. Our love for others will lead us to avoid activities that might lead to their downfall. The more mature we are, the more responsible we will be to respond to others in a loving way.

14:10-12 Paul reminds us that we are not to take inventory for others. Many of us find it easier to point out the failures of others than to look critically at our own life. But it isn't our primary responsibility to straighten out other people's lives. Besides, the job of straightening out our own life is more than enough to keep us busy, at least in the initial stages. If we spend our time pointing the finger at others, we will never make progress in our own recovery.

14:22-23 In the process of recovery, we sometimes become tempted to do things that are not necessarily wrong, but that will lead us toward a fall. We know such activities are dangerous, but it is hard to turn away, especially if our friends are involved. We need to learn that when we *feel* something is wrong for us, it *is* wrong for us. It may not be wrong for someone else, but that is not our concern. We are to pray for the knowledge of God's will for our life, and for the power to do it.

believes that something he wants to do is wrong shouldn't do it. He sins if he does, for he thinks it is wrong, and so for him it *is* wrong. Anything that is done apart from what he feels is right is sin.

CHAPTER 15
Living to Please Others

Even if we believe that it makes no difference to the Lord whether we do these things, still we cannot just go ahead and do them to please ourselves; for we must bear the "burden" of being considerate of the doubts and fears of others—of those who feel these things are wrong. Let's please the other fellow, not ourselves, and do what is for his good and thus build him up in the Lord. 3Christ didn't please himself. As the Psalmist said, "He came for the very purpose of suffering under the insults of those who were against the Lord." 4These things that were written in the Scriptures so long ago are to teach us patience and to encourage us so that we will look forward expectantly to the time when God will conquer sin and death.

5May God who gives patience, steadiness, and encouragement help you to live in complete harmony with each other—each with the attitude of Christ toward the other. 6And then all of us can praise the Lord together with one voice, giving glory to God, the Father of our Lord Jesus Christ.

7So warmly welcome each other into the church, just as Christ has warmly welcomed you; then God will be glorified. 8Remember that Jesus Christ came to show that God is true to his promises and to help the Jews. 9And remember that he came also that the Gentiles might be saved and give glory to God for his mercies to them. That is what the psalmist meant when he wrote: "I will praise you among the Gentiles and sing to your name."

10And in another place, "Be glad, O you Gentiles, along with his people the Jews."

11And yet again, "Praise the Lord, O you Gentiles; let everyone praise him."

12And the prophet Isaiah said, "There shall be an Heir in the house of Jesse, and he will be King over the Gentiles; they will pin their hopes on him alone."

13So I pray for you Gentiles that God who gives you hope will keep you happy and full of peace as you believe in him. I pray that God will help you overflow with hope in him through the Holy Spirit's power within you.

Paul Explains Why He Is Writing

14I know that you are wise and good, my brothers, and that you know these things so well that you are able to teach others all about them. 15,16But even so I have been bold enough to emphasize some of these points, knowing that all you need is this reminder from me; for I am, by God's grace, a special messenger from Jesus Christ to you Gentiles, bringing you the Gospel and offering you up as a fragrant sacrifice to God; for you have been made pure and pleasing to him by the Holy Spirit. 17So it is right for me to be a little proud of all Christ Jesus has done through me. 18I dare not judge how effectively he has used others, but I know this: he has used me to win the Gentiles to God. 19I have won them by my message and by the good way I have lived before them and by the miracles done through me as signs from God—all by the Holy Spirit's power. In this way I have preached the full Gospel of Christ all the way from Jerusalem clear over into Illyricum.

20But all the while my ambition has been to go still farther, preaching where the name of Christ has never yet been heard, rather than where a church has already been started by someone else. 21I have been following the plan spoken of in the Scriptures where Isaiah says that those who have never heard the name of Christ before will see and understand. 22In fact, that is the very reason I have been so long in coming to visit you.

Paul Explains His Travel Plans

23But now at last I am through with my work here, and I am ready to come after all these long years of waiting. 24For I am planning to take a trip to Spain, and when I do, I will stop off there in Rome; and after we have had a

---

15:1-6 Showing consideration to others is crucial for a successful recovery. Our human relationships are second in importance only to our relationship with God. If we are not at peace with others, we will be at war within ourself. And that is a perfect recipe for a relapse. We need to learn to delay our personal gratification for the sake of others. This will help us form healthy relationships with the significant people in our life, a necessity for progress in any recovery program. Such relationships will help us find a balance between meeting the needs of others and finding healthy ways to meet our own needs.

good time together for a little while, you can
send me on my way again.
25But before I come, I must go down to
Jerusalem to take a gift to the Jewish Christians there. 26For you see, the Christians in
Macedonia and Achaia have taken up an offering for those in Jerusalem who are going
through such hard times. 27They were very
glad to do this, for they feel that they owe a
real debt to the Jerusalem Christians. Why?
Because the news about Christ came to these
Gentiles from the church in Jerusalem. And
since they received this wonderful spiritual
gift of the Gospel from there, they feel that
the least they can do in return is to give some
material aid. 28As soon as I have delivered this
money and completed this good deed of
theirs, I will come to see you on my way to
Spain. 29And I am sure that when I come the
Lord will give me a great blessing for you.
30Will you be my prayer partners? For the
Lord Jesus Christ's sake and because of your
love for me—given to you by the Holy
Spirit—pray much with me for my work.
31Pray that I will be protected in Jerusalem
from those who are not Christians. Pray also
that the Christians there will be willing to
accept the money I am bringing them. 32Then
I will be able to come to you with a happy
heart by the will of God, and we can refresh
each other.
33And now may our God, who gives peace,
be with you all. Amen.

CHAPTER 16

Paul Greets His Friends

Phoebe, a dear Christian woman from the
town of Cenchreae, will be coming to see you
soon. She has worked hard in the church
there. Receive her as your sister in the Lord,
giving her a warm Christian welcome. Help
her in every way you can, for she has helped
many in their needs, including me. 3Tell Priscilla and Aquila hello. They have been my
fellow workers in the affairs of Christ Jesus.
4In fact, they risked their lives for me, and I
am not the only one who is thankful to them;
so are all the Gentile churches.
5Please give my greetings to all those who
meet to worship in their home. Greet my
good friend Epaenetus. He was the very first
person to become a Christian in Asia. 6Re-
member me to Mary, too, who has worked so
hard to help us. 7Then there are Andronicus
and Junias, my relatives who were in prison
with me. They are respected by the apostles
and became Christians before I did. Please
give them my greetings. 8Say hello to Ampli-
atus, whom I love as one of God's own children, 9and Urbanus, our fellow worker, and
beloved Stachys.
10Then there is Apelles, a good man whom
the Lord approves; greet him for me. And
give my best regards to those working at the
house of Aristobulus. 11Remember me to He-
rodion my relative. Remember me to the
Christian slaves over at Narcissus House.
12Say hello to Tryphaena and Tryphosa, the
Lord's workers, and to dear Persis, who has
worked so hard for the Lord. 13Greet Rufus for
me, whom the Lord picked out to be his very
own; and also his dear mother who has been
such a mother to me. 14And please give my
greetings to Asyncritus, Phlegon, Hermes,
Patrobas, Hermas, and the other brothers
who are with them. 15Give my love to Philol-
ogus, Julia, Nereus and his sister, and to
Olympas, and all the Christians who are with
them. 16Shake hands warmly with each other.
All the churches here send you their greetings.

Paul Gives Final Instructions

17And now there is one more thing to say
before I end this letter. Stay away from those
who cause divisions and are upsetting
people's faith, teaching things about Christ
that are contrary to what you have been
taught. 18Such teachers are not working for
our Lord Jesus but only want gain for themselves. They are good speakers, and simple-
minded people are often fooled by them.
19But everyone knows that you stand loyal
and true. This makes me very happy. I want
you always to remain very clear about what is
right and to stay innocent of any wrong. 20The
God of peace will soon crush Satan under
your feet. The blessings from our Lord Jesus
Christ be upon you.
21Timothy my fellow worker, and Lucius
and Jason and Sosipater, my relatives, send
you their good wishes. 22I, Tertius, the one
who is writing this letter for Paul, send my
greetings too, as a Christian brother. 23Gaius
says to say hello to you for him. I am his guest,
and the church meets here in his home. Erastus, the city treasurer, sends you his greetings
and so does Quartus, a Christian brother.
24Good-bye. May the grace of our Lord Jesus
Christ be with you all.
25-27I commit you to God, who is able to
make you strong and steady in the Lord, just
as the Gospel says, and just as I have told you.
This is God's plan of salvation for you Gen-

tiles, kept secret from the beginning of time. But now as the prophets foretold and as God commands, this message is being preached everywhere, so that people all around the world will have faith in Christ and obey him. To God, who alone is wise, be the glory forever through Jesus Christ our Lord. Amen.

Sincerely, Paul

insights ABOUT THE POWER OF CHRIST'S RESURRECTION

For the apostle Paul, the Good News was more than just the events of Christ's death, burial, and resurrection. It certainly included these facts, but the Good News moves beyond the amazing events of Jesus' life into our own sinful and broken lives. In **Romans 1:1-5** we are told that we can die to the power of sin because of what Jesus has done. Then we can be resurrected into a new life! The Good News is a promise that there is power available to help us change. It is the story of God's kindness to us through Jesus Christ, no matter what we have done in the past. This Good News is for us. As we put our life in God's hands, he will give us the power we need to change. Then, as we grow, we will experience God's joy in our life and the desire to share our story of deliverance with others.

In **Romans 6:2-11** Paul examined how we can receive new life through the death and resurrection of Jesus Christ. He traced the history of Jesus' life: (1) his earthly body under death's mastery; (2) his death, burial, and resurrection; (3) his resurrection body that was no longer under the power of death. Next, Paul showed how our own life can be parallel to that of Jesus: (1) we begin under the mastery of sin and death; (2) we identify with Jesus' death, burial, and resurrection; (3) we receive a new life, free from the power of sin and death. God has the power to take a life headed for destruction and set it on the road to new life.

insights ABOUT OUR HELPLESSNESS

In **Romans 3:9-10** Paul summarized his earlier discussion by concluding that "all men alike are sinners." No one is exempt—we are all fallen and dysfunctional; we are all in need of salvation and recovery. If we pretend to be healthy and without defect, we only prove that we are in denial. Recovery can begin only after we have admitted this truth. When we recognize that we are broken and helpless, God steps in and provides the power we need for recovery.

In **Romans 5:1-11** Paul used several phrases to describe our painful condition: "we were utterly helpless, with no way of escape" (5:6); we were "sinners" (5:6, 8-9); and we were God's "enemies" (5:10). It was precisely when we were in this condition that God decided to solve our sin problem for us. He loved us so much that he sent his Son to die on the cross to set us free from the power of sin. We cannot be any worse than the way Paul described us here, so God's love and acceptance of us can never be negated by our behavior! With a Savior like that, we can confidently turn our life over to him.

In **Romans 7:18-20** Paul recognized the power of sin in his life and admitted how helpless he was against its persistent power. As he admitted his powerlessness, he was starting down the lifelong road toward recovery. When we can admit how powerless we are over our dependencies, we will have made a significant step toward recovery. Only then will we be ready to accept the help that God offers; and only with God's power will we be able to overcome the temptations we face.

insights ABOUT FAITH

In **Romans 4:1-3** Paul referred to Abraham as an example of what it means to come to God in faith. As we look at Abraham in the book of Genesis, we find a man who was set apart for God. Despite his mistakes, he could be considered a person who had it all together. But Abraham had to come to God the same way we do—through faith. He did nothing to deserve the special promises that God gave him. In the same way, we can do nothing to deserve the promises of forgiveness and recovery that God offers us. No social status or good deed can make us deserving of God's gracious forgiveness; yet no failure is too great an obstacle for God's restoring power. When we entrust our life to God and believe that he can help us, God then gives us the power and courage to move forward one step at a time.

insights ABOUT PRAYER

Prayer is listed in **Romans 8:26-28** as one of the ways we improve our conscious contact with God, and Paul assures us that the indwelling power of the Holy Spirit is at work within us as we pray. We are not left alone to work out our problems. As we entrust our life to God, he directs the events of our life, even the painful ones, for our good. He can turn even our mistakes into the means for our growth and blessing.

insights ABOUT THE BENEFITS OF SUBMISSION TO GOD

In **Romans 12:1-2** we are called to offer our life to God as a living sacrifice. We are exhorted to make the decision to turn our life and will over to God, so he can care for us and transform us into the holy people he wants us to be. We are called to follow God's program for our life, utilizing the power he offers. As we do this, we will become a showcase to others of what God's power can do. And as we grow, we will discover the joy and meaning that can be experienced when we offer our life to God. When we sacrifice all we are and have to God, he will return what we gave up, multiplied many times over.

THE BIG PICTURE

A. THE CHURCH IN DENIAL (1:1–6:20)
  1. Divisions: Infighting among the Believers (1:1–4:21)
  2. Disorders: Serving Self before God (5:1–6:20)

B. THE CHURCH IN RECOVERY (7:1–16:24)
  1. Contentment: Being Happy Where We Are (7:1-40)
  2. Instruction: Personal Worship (8:1–10:33)
  3. Instruction: Public Worship (11:1–14:40)
  4. Encouragement: Christ Is with Us (15:1–16:24)

The Greek city of Corinth was known for its corruption, immorality, and pagan religion. Following Christ in that setting meant leaving behind many of the practices accepted by the larger culture. This presented the new believers with all kinds of temptations and problems.

Though the Corinthian believers had received new life in Christ, they had much to learn; Paul called them "baby Christians" (3:3). It would take time for them to mature. In short, their intentions were fine, but they needed further instructions about following Christ. They needed to get a handle on God's perspectives concerning right and wrong. Paul wrote this letter to help them make progress—to give them advice about how to change.

Our recovery often requires a similar struggle against the surrounding environment. Though we determine to change, the world in which we live stays much the same. We live and work with the same people, go to many of the same places, and do many of the same things—all while trying to make radical changes in our life. The feelings of loneliness that result can make us as vulnerable as the Corinthian believers once were.

Despite the difficulties we face, God understands our struggle. That is why he has given us his Word, his power, and his people; they are all available to help us take one step at a time. This letter alone contains numerous insights for recovery (too many to list here). Through it we can learn how to separate ourself from our old way of life and open ourself to God's new standards. The transformation may be slow or even painful, but by God's grace and our commitment, it will happen.

THE BOTTOM LINE

PURPOSE: To encourage the believers living in Corinth to resolve their problems and honor God. AUTHOR: The apostle Paul. AUDIENCE: The church at Corinth, a city in Greece. DATE WRITTEN: Around A.D. 55, near the end of Paul's three-year stay in Ephesus. SETTING: Corinth was a large cosmopolitan city that teemed with idolatry and immorality. The church in Corinth was fairly new and made up primarily of non-Jewish (Gentile) believers. KEY VERSE: "But whatever I am now it is all because God poured out such kindness and grace upon me—and not without results: for I have worked harder than all the other apostles, yet actually I wasn't doing it, but God working in me" (15:10). KEY PEOPLE AND RELATIONSHIPS: Paul with Timothy, Chloe's household, and the Corinthian believers.

RECOVERY THEMES

Jesus Is the Center of Our Recovery: The believers in Corinth show us what happens when we take our eyes off Jesus Christ. Though they were followers of Christ, they identified themselves primarily with their various teachers. This caused unnecessary divisions among them and kept them from making progress in spiritual growth. While the support and advice of others are important, our Savior is Jesus Christ. He is the center of all our efforts; we must focus on him. People and recovery techniques are his tools, not ours.

Freedom with Loving Restraint: The new believers in Corinth had to make a clean break with their past. Some of these believers were quite mature and were no longer bothered by the temptations that had plagued them before. But others were not so secure. Paul therefore instructed the more mature ones not to flaunt their freedom around those who still struggled. Our successful recovery doesn't give us license to be inconsiderate or insensitive to others. We can show support for one another by being careful how we use our freedom. We will always have this responsibility to look out for one another.

Life Is to Be Enjoyed Responsibly: The believers at Corinth lived in a very immoral, pleasure-seeking society. The standards of conduct that God had for them were quite different from what they were used to. But if they thought those standards seemed too restrictive, they were mistaken. Longing for "freedom" from God's laws is like longing for the "fun" of being an alcoholic. It is like wanting to be trapped in a life of addictions, compulsions, or other destructive behaviors, reasoning that turning our life over to God would keep us from having fun. On the contrary, God challenges us to live an uncompromising life, because that is the way to enjoy life at its deepest level. The same is true for us in our recovery—we are discovering what life was meant to be!

The Invitation to Love: One of the most beautiful passages on love ever written is found in this letter to the Corinthians, in chapter 13. It goes beyond the idea of love as merely an emotion and describes it strictly in terms of selfless action. If we love, then we will act in selfless ways. When we don't feel loving or don't feel loved, 1 Corinthians 13 is a wonderful reminder of how God loves us and how we can show love to others.

CHAPTER 1

Greetings from Paul

From: Paul, chosen by God to be Jesus Christ's
missionary, and from brother Sosthenes.
2*To:* The Christians in Corinth, invited by
God to be his people and made acceptable to
him by Christ Jesus. *And to:* All Christians
everywhere—whoever calls upon the name of
Jesus Christ, our Lord and theirs.
3May God our Father and the Lord Jesus
Christ give you all of his blessings, and great
peace of heart and mind.

Paul Thanks God

4I can never stop thanking God for all the
wonderful gifts he has given you, now that
you are Christ's: 5he has enriched your
whole life. He has helped you speak out for
him and has given you a full understanding
of the truth; 6what I told you Christ could
do for you has happened! 7Now you have
every grace and blessing; every spiritual gift
and power for doing his will are yours during this time of waiting for the return of our
Lord Jesus Christ. 8And he guarantees right
up to the end that you will be counted free
from all sin and guilt on that day when he
returns. 9God will surely do this for you, for
he always does just what he says, and he is
the one who invited you into this wonderful friendship with his Son, even Christ our
Lord.

1:2 Corinth was a giant cultural melting pot with a great diversity of ethnic groups, religions, intellectual perspectives, and moral standards. It had a reputation for being fiercely independent and was as decadent as any city in the world. Idolatry flourished, and there were more than a dozen pagan temples that at one time had employed at least a thousand religious prostitutes. The new believers in this city had to deal with many deep-rooted habits and attitudes as they sought to nurture their new life in Christ. For a person in recovery from any kind of destructive habit, the temptation to fall would have been constant. The world of Corinth was not unlike the world we live in today. The apostle Paul's advice to these early believers will touch on many of the issues we face today.

1:4-9 Although there were problems among the Corinthian believers, Paul began his letter to them on a positive note. He understood that confronting others about their failures is more effective when we approach them diplomatically. We need to gain a hearing by recognizing the good things in the lives of those we need to confront. In this way, we show that we are concerned about them and value them as people. Our interventions will only be effective when we first show that we love the people we are trying to help.

An Appeal for Harmony

10But, dear brothers, I beg you in the name of
the Lord Jesus Christ to stop arguing among
yourselves. Let there be real harmony so that
there won't be splits in the church. I plead
with you to be of one mind, united in
thought and purpose. 11For some of those
who live at Chloe's house have told me of
your arguments and quarrels, dear brothers.
12Some of you are saying, "I am a follower of
Paul"; and others say that they are for Apollos
or for Peter; and some that they alone are the
true followers of Christ. 13And so, in effect,
you have broken Christ into many pieces.

But did I, Paul, die for your sins? Were any
of you baptized in my name? 14I am so thankful now that I didn't baptize any of you except
Crispus and Gaius. 15For now no one can
think that I have been trying to start something new, beginning a "Church of Paul."
16Oh, yes, and I baptized the family of Stephanas. I don't remember ever baptizing anyone
else. 17For Christ didn't send me to baptize,
but to preach the Gospel; and even my
preaching sounds poor, for I do not fill
my sermons with profound words and high
sounding ideas, for fear of diluting the
mighty power there is in the simple message
of the cross of Christ.

Christ Gives New Life from God

18I know very well how foolish it sounds to
those who are lost, when they hear that Jesus
died to save them. But we who are saved
recognize this message as the very power of
God. 19For God says, "I will destroy all human
plans of salvation no matter how wise they
seem to be, and ignore the best ideas of men,
even the most brilliant of them."

20So what about these wise men, these scholars, these brilliant debaters of this world's great
affairs? God has made them all look foolish
and shown their wisdom to be useless nonsense. 21For God in his wisdom saw to it that
the world would never find God through human brilliance, and then he stepped in and
saved all those who believed his message,
which the world calls foolish and silly. 22It
seems foolish to the Jews because they want a
sign from heaven as proof that what is
preached is true; and it is foolish to the Gentiles because they believe only what agrees
with their philosophy and seems wise to them.
23So when we preach about Christ dying to
save them, the Jews are offended and the Gentiles say it's all nonsense. 24But God has opened
the eyes of those called to salvation, both Jews
and Gentiles, to see that Christ is the mighty
power of God to save them; Christ himself is
the center of God's wise plan for their salvation. 25This so-called "foolish" plan of God is
far wiser than the wisest plan of the wisest
man, and God in his weakness—Christ dying
on the cross—is far stronger than any man.

26Notice among yourselves, dear brothers,
that few of you who follow Christ have big
names or power or wealth. 27Instead, God has
deliberately chosen to use ideas the world
considers foolish and of little worth in order
to shame those people considered by the
world as wise and great. 28He has chosen a
plan despised by the world, counted as nothing at all, and used it to bring down to nothing those the world considers great, 29so that
no one anywhere can ever brag in the presence of God.

30For it is from God alone that you have
your life through Christ Jesus. He showed us
God's plan of salvation; he was the one who
made us acceptable to God; he made us pure
and holy and gave himself to purchase our
salvation. 31As it says in the Scriptures, "If
anyone is going to boast, let him boast only
of what the Lord has done."

1:12 The Corinthian believers had begun to elevate various leaders to unhealthy positions in their lives. They were attributing power and wisdom to these people that no one but God could legitimately claim. This is a form of idolatry, one of the sins God forbids (see Exodus 20:3). All too often we give a person, perhaps a religious leader or the leader of a recovery movement, the position of a god in our life. We believe everything they say and are willing to do anything they ask us to do. This is a dangerous practice. Each of us must remember that all people are powerless—the only one worthy of worship is Christ himself. We must remember to measure everything we hear against the eternal truth of God's Word.

1:18-19 Some of the Corinthian believers followed the human wisdom of the day, which called the idea of salvation in Christ into question. It seemed too simple! How could God forgive us freely through of what Christ did on the cross? Surely we need to do something special or know something special to be saved! Paul made it clear that we need nothing but a willing heart to receive God's power and forgiveness. We have no power or ability that can overcome the power of sin in our life. In fact, a life of self-sufficiency is ultimately self-destructive. When we turn our life over to God, we accept his way—the way of the cross. Only then can we experience the power of God in our life.

CHAPTER 2

The Holy Spirit Gives Wisdom

Dear brothers, even when I first came to you I didn't use lofty words and brilliant ideas to tell you God's message. [2]For I decided that I would speak only of Jesus Christ and his death on the cross. [3]I came to you in weakness—timid and trembling. [4]And my preaching was very plain, not with a lot of oratory and human wisdom, but the Holy Spirit's power was in my words, proving to those who heard them that the message was from God. [5]I did this because I wanted your faith to stand firmly upon God, not on man's great ideas.

[6]Yet when I am among mature Christians I do speak with words of great wisdom, but not the kind that comes from here on earth, and not the kind that appeals to the great men of this world, who are doomed to fall. [7]Our words are wise because they are from God, telling of God's wise plan to bring us into the glories of heaven. This plan was hidden in former times, though it was made for our benefit before the world began. [8]But the great men of the world have not understood it; if they had, they never would have crucified the Lord of Glory.

[9]That is what is meant by the Scriptures which say that no mere man has ever seen, heard, or even imagined what wonderful things God has ready for those who love the Lord. [10]But we know about these things because God has sent his Spirit to tell us, and his Spirit searches out and shows us all of God's deepest secrets. [11]No one can really know what anyone else is thinking or what he is really like except that person himself. And no one can know God's thoughts except God's own Spirit. [12]And God has actually given us his Spirit (not the world's spirit) to tell us about the wonderful free gifts of grace and blessing that God has given us. [13]In telling you about these gifts we have even used the very words given to us by the Holy Spirit, not words that we as men might choose. So we use the Holy Spirit's words to explain the Holy Spirit's facts. [14]But the man who isn't a Christian can't understand and can't accept these thoughts from God, which the Holy Spirit teaches us. They sound foolish to him because only those who have the Holy Spirit within them can understand what the Holy Spirit means. Others just can't take it in. [15]But the spiritual man has insight into everything, and that bothers and baffles the man of the world, who can't understand him at all. [16]How could he? For certainly he has never been one to know the Lord's thoughts, or to discuss them with him, or to move the hands of God by prayer. But, strange as it seems, we Christians actually do have within us a portion of the very thoughts and mind of Christ.

CHAPTER 3

An Appeal for Unity

Dear brothers, I have been talking to you as though you were still just babies in the Christian life who are not following the Lord but your own desires; I cannot talk to you as I would to healthy Christians who are filled with the Spirit. [2]I have had to feed you with milk and not with solid food because you

---

2:1-5 Many times, when we seek to help others, we overwhelm them with a series of complicated theories and instructions. Paul realized that doing this would only confuse the Corinthians, making them think that salvation was dependent on some kind of special wisdom or knowledge. So he brought them the plain message of the gospel—there is nothing we can do to save ourself, but God has done everything necessary for our deliverance. Paul kept the message simple. As we share the story of our deliverance with others, we need to keep things simple and trust the power of the Holy Spirit to work in the life of the people we are trying to help.

2:7 God has had a good plan for us from the beginning of time. If we allow him to work in our life, that plan will come about. No matter how many mistakes we have made, God can still turn things around so they work out according to his program. Our part is to entrust our life to him and seek to follow his will as he reveals it to us. No matter what we have done in the past, God still chooses to love us and to work his restoration within us.

2:9-10 When our life is unmanageable and we feel as if we have lost our direction, we often blame God or feel that somehow he is making things worse. Paul reminded the Corinthians that God had wonderful things planned for them, things even more wonderful than they could imagine. This message is for us, too. If we turn our life and will over to God, he can build a new life for us that is beyond our wildest dreams.

2:14-15 The person who refuses to turn his or her life over to the care of God cannot understand God's plan. That's why recovery begins not with understanding, but with a decision to follow God. Prior to that decision, God's way would probably seem like madness. Only when we face the fact that our life is insane can we open ourself to God and his good plan for us.

couldn't digest anything stronger. And even now you still have to be fed on milk. 3For you are still only baby Christians, controlled by your own desires, not God's. When you are jealous of one another and divide up into quarreling groups, doesn't that prove you are still babies, wanting your own way? In fact, you are acting like people who don't belong to the Lord at all. 4There you are, quarreling about whether I am greater than Apollos, and dividing the church. Doesn't this show how little you have grown in the Lord?

5Who am I, and who is Apollos, that we should be the cause of a quarrel? Why, we're just God's servants, each of us with certain special abilities, and with our help you believed. 6My work was to plant the seed in your hearts, and Apollos' work was to water it, but it was God, not we, who made the garden grow in your hearts. 7The person who does the planting or watering isn't very important, but God is important because he is the one who makes things grow. 8Apollos and I are working as a team, with the same aim, though each of us will be rewarded for his own hard work. 9We are only God's coworkers. You are *God's* garden, not ours; you are *God's* building, not ours.

10God, in his kindness, has taught me how to be an expert builder. I have laid the foundation and Apollos has built on it. But he who builds on the foundation must be very careful. 11And no one can ever lay any other real foundation than that one we already have—Jesus Christ. 12But there are various kinds of materials that can be used to build on that foundation. Some use gold and silver and jewels; and some build with sticks and hay or even straw! 13There is going to come a time of testing at Christ's Judgment Day to see what kind of material each builder has used. Everyone's work will be put through the fire so that all can see whether or not it keeps its value, and what was really accomplished. 14Then every workman who has built on the foundation with the right materials, and whose work still stands, will get his pay. 15But if the house he has built burns up, he will have a great loss. He himself will be saved, but like a man escaping through a wall of flames.

16Don't you realize that all of you together are the house of God, and that the Spirit of God lives among you in his house? 17If anyone defiles and spoils God's home, God will destroy him. For God's home is holy and clean, and you are that home.

18Stop fooling yourselves. If you count yourself above average in intelligence, as judged by this world's standards, you had better put this all aside and be a fool rather

3:1-4 Part of becoming mature is realizing that following our own desires only leads down a dead-end street. We remain "babies" as long as we try to do things our own way. Maturing happens only as we begin to follow God's will for our life. As we do this, we will consider what God wants and what others need before we act. This will mean that we have to give the control of our life and will over to God. It may also mean that we have to delay self-gratification at times for the sake of others. This is not easy, but when we do, we will experience the meaningful life that God wants for each of us.

3:5-6 As we progress in recovery, we are called upon to reach out to others. As we tell them our story of deliverance, hoping it will help them turn their lives around, these verses are an encouragement to us. Even when the message doesn't seem to be getting through, we can leave the results in God's hands. Sometimes people respond to our story immediately and get involved in recovery. At other times our words only plant seeds that over time will lead someone to be changed by God's power. Perhaps we are just one in a long line of people God will use to change someone's life. One thing is for certain: if we speak out, God will use our efforts to change lives.

3:13-15 Many of us struggle with denial because the truth is so painful. We avoid the truth about our failures so we won't have to make difficult changes in our life. It might help to be reminded that no matter how much we hide from our mistakes, in time they will come back to haunt us. Allowing our dependencies to continue unchecked will lead to painful consequences. In these verses, we are reminded that those consequences may even continue into eternity. There will come a day of reckoning! Have we put our life in God's hands? As we turn our life over to him, he will help us build it on a solid foundation. When the day of reckoning arrives, we will still be standing.

3:18-20 It is possible for our intelligence to get in the way of our progress in recovery. As we analyze the steps we are asked to take, we may find them somewhat foolish or demeaning. The truth is, sometimes following God's plan will not make perfect sense to us. We may wonder how entrusting our life to God can change anything. We might even find that following God's revealed will is embarrassing at times. We need to realize that true understanding often happens only as we take steps to obey God's program for our healing. We may be better off throwing aside our need to analyze and understand so that we can experience God's healing power in our life through faith and obedience.

than let it hold you back from the true wisdom from above. 19For the wisdom of this world is foolishness to God. As it says in the book of Job, God uses man's own brilliance to trap him; he stumbles over his own "wisdom" and falls. 20And again, in the book of Psalms, we are told that the Lord knows full well how the human mind reasons and how foolish and futile it is.

21So don't be proud of following the wise men of this world. For God has already given you everything you need. 22He has given you Paul and Apollos and Peter as your helpers. He has given you the whole world to use, and life and even death are your servants. He has given you all of the present and all of the future. All are yours, 23and you belong to Christ, and Christ is God's.

CHAPTER 4

Paul's Counsel to the Corinthians

So Apollos and I should be looked upon as Christ's servants who distribute God's blessings by explaining God's secrets. 2Now the most important thing about a servant is that he does just what his master tells him to. 3What about me? Have I been a good servant? Well, I don't worry over what you think about this or what anyone else thinks. I don't even trust my own judgment on this point. 4My conscience is clear, but even that isn't final proof. It is the Lord himself who must examine me and decide.

5So be careful not to jump to conclusions before the Lord returns as to whether someone is a good servant or not. When the Lord comes, he will turn on the light so that everyone can see exactly what each one of us is really like, deep down in our hearts. Then everyone will know why we have been doing the Lord's work. At that time God will give to each one whatever praise is coming to him.

6I have used Apollos and myself as examples to illustrate what I have been saying: that you must not have favorites. You must not be proud of one of God's teachers more than another. 7What are you so puffed up about? What do you have that God hasn't given you? And if all you have is from God, why act as though you are so great, and as though you have accomplished something on your own?

8You seem to think you already have all the spiritual food you need. You are full and spiritually contented, rich kings on your thrones, leaving us far behind! I wish you really were already on your thrones, for when that time comes you can be sure that we will be there, too, reigning with you. 9Sometimes I think God has put us apostles at the very end of the line, like prisoners soon to be killed, put on display at the end of a victor's parade, to be stared at by men and angels alike.

10Religion has made us foolish, you say, but of course you are all such wise and sensible Christians! We are weak, but not you! You are well thought of, while we are laughed at. 11To this very hour we have gone hungry and thirsty, without even enough clothes to keep us warm. We have been kicked around without homes of our own. 12We have worked wearily with our hands to earn our living. We have blessed those who cursed us. We have been patient with those who injured us. 13We have replied quietly when evil things have been said about us. Yet right up to the present moment we are like dirt underfoot, like garbage.

14I am not writing about these things to make you ashamed, but to warn and counsel you as beloved children. 15For although you may have ten thousand others to teach you about Christ, remember that you have only me as your father. For I was the one who brought you to Christ when I preached the Gospel to you. 16So I beg you to follow my example and do as I do.

4:6-13 How easy it is to become puffed up about our success and forget that pride leads to a fall. The Corinthians were very self-sufficient, looking down on Paul and his ministry with them. Their prideful attitudes led them away from Paul's teachings about Christ, a dangerous thing for anyone living in a diverse religious environment like theirs. It is just as dangerous for us to become proud about our success in recovery. We forget that it was God's power that delivered us and that we continue to need his help. If we allow pride to get a foothold in our life, we will discover that self-sufficiency leads directly to a relapse.

4:17 Paul sent Timothy to remind the Corinthian believers of what Paul had taught them. The apostle realized that they needed someone to hold them accountable to the truth they had been taught and to encourage them to persevere in their faith. One of the best ways to protect ourself from a spirit of self-sufficiency is to be accountable to someone else. Mentors and sponsors are there to help us remember what works in recovery. They are also there to help us learn how to develop faithfulness in our life, an essential part of our spiritual growth.

[17]That is the very reason why I am sending Timothy—to help you do this. For he is one of those I won to Christ, a beloved and trustworthy child in the Lord. He will remind you of what I teach in all the churches wherever I go.

[18]I know that some of you will have become proud, thinking that I am afraid to come to deal with you. [19]But I will come, and soon, if the Lord will let me, and then I'll find out whether these proud men are just big talkers or whether they really have God's power. [20]The Kingdom of God is not just talking; it is living by God's power. [21]Which do you choose? Shall I come with punishment and scolding, or shall I come with quiet love and gentleness?

CHAPTER 5

Paul Condemns Immorality

Everyone is talking about the terrible thing that has happened there among you, something so evil that even the heathen don't do it: you have a man in your church who is living in sin with his father's wife. [2]And are you still so conceited, so "spiritual"? Why aren't you mourning in sorrow and shame and seeing to it that this man is removed from your membership?

[3,4]Although I am not there with you, I have been thinking a lot about this, and in the name of the Lord Jesus Christ I have already decided what to do, just as though I were there. You are to call a meeting of the church—and the power of the Lord Jesus will be with you as you meet, and I will be there in spirit—[5]and cast out this man from the fellowship of the church and into Satan's hands, to punish him, in the hope that his soul will be saved when our Lord Jesus Christ returns.

[6]What a terrible thing it is that you are boasting about your purity and yet you let this sort of thing go on. Don't you realize that if even one person is allowed to go on sinning, soon all will be affected? [7]Remove this evil cancer—this wicked person—from among you, so that you can stay pure. Christ, God's Lamb, has been slain for us. [8]So let us feast upon him and grow strong in the Christian life, leaving entirely behind us the cancerous old life with all its hatreds and wickedness. Let us feast instead upon the pure bread of honor and sincerity and truth.

[9]When I wrote to you before I said not to mix with evil people. [10]But when I said that I wasn't talking about unbelievers who live in sexual sin or are greedy cheats and thieves and idol worshipers. For you can't live in this world without being with people like that. [11]What I meant was that you are not to keep company with anyone who claims to be a brother Christian but indulges in sexual sins, or is greedy, or is a swindler, or worships idols, or is a drunkard, or abusive. Don't even eat lunch with such a person.

[12]It isn't our job to judge outsiders. But it certainly is our job to judge and deal strongly with those who are members of the church and who are sinning in these ways. [13]God

5:1-5 We face many of the same forms of sexual immorality that the Corinthians faced. Like the people of Corinth, we tend to put on a blindfold and tell ourself that everything is all right. Our denial of the problems of illicit sexual activity and sexual abuse, however, only builds barriers between ourself and others. In time, we even grow distant from God. Such denial allows the problems in our churches and communities to fester until individuals and families are torn apart. We need to open our eyes to the problems around us and confront them together as a community, just as Paul advised the Corinthians to do.

5:6-8 Paul called the Corinthian believers to remove the unrepentant sinner from among their fellowship. If they didn't do this, his destructive activities would eat away at their church fellowship like a cancer. This principle is important in our recovery. As we begin our program, we need to give up the relationships and activities that are likely to lead to our downfall. This will keep us out of situations in which we are almost sure to fail. Notice that when Paul called the Corinthians to excommunicate this unrepentant sinner, he also reminded them to involve themselves in wholesome activities. In the same way, when we pull away from our destructive activities and relationships, we need to replace them with wholesome activities and people who will encourage us in our recovery.

5:9-13 Paul did warn his people to avoid close relationships with people who were in denial about their sin. But that didn't mean they were to totally isolate themselves from unbelievers. They were still to share the Good News with people who needed to hear the message. The same principle holds true for our recovery. We need to avoid close relationships with people who will drag us down and try to get us to quit our program. Yet as we experience God's power in our life, we need to share the Good News with others. Our story of deliverance MAY save the life of someone in bondage. As we share the message, not only will we be a source of hope to others, but we will also find renewed strength to continue in our own recovery.

alone is the Judge of those on the outside. But
you yourselves must deal with this man and
put him out of your church.

CHAPTER 6

Avoiding Lawsuits with Believers

How is it that when you have something
against another Christian, you "go to law"
and ask a heathen court to decide the matter
instead of taking it to other Christians to
decide which of you is right? [2]Don't you know
that someday we Christians are going to judge
and govern the world? So why can't you decide even these little things among yourselves? [3]Don't you realize that we Christians
will judge and reward the very angels in
heaven? So you should be able to decide your
problems down here on earth easily enough.
[4]Why then go to outside judges who are not
even Christians? [5]I am trying to make you
ashamed. Isn't there anyone in all the church
who is wise enough to decide these arguments? [6]But, instead, one Christian sues another and accuses his Christian brother in
front of unbelievers.

[7]To have such lawsuits at all is a real defeat
for you as Christians. Why not just accept
mistreatment and leave it at that? It would be
far more honoring to the Lord to let yourselves be cheated. [8]But, instead, you yourselves are the ones who do wrong, cheating
others, even your own brothers.

Behavior that Gives Glory to God

[9,10]Don't you know that those doing such
things have no share in the Kingdom of God?
Don't fool yourselves. Those who live immoral lives, who are idol worshipers, adulterers or homosexuals—will have no share in his
Kingdom. Neither will thieves or greedy
people, drunkards, slanderers, or robbers.
[11]There was a time when some of you were
just like that but now your sins are washed
away, and you are set apart for God; and he
has accepted you because of what the Lord
Jesus Christ and the Spirit of our God have
done for you.

[12]I can do anything I want to if Christ has
not said no, but some of these things aren't
good for me. Even if I am allowed to do them,
I'll refuse to if I think they might get such a
grip on me that I can't easily stop when I want
to. [13]For instance, take the matter of eating.
God has given us an appetite for food and
stomachs to digest it. But that doesn't mean
we should eat more than we need. Don't
think of eating as important because someday
God will do away with both stomachs and
food.

But sexual sin is never right: our bodies
were not made for that but for the Lord, and
the Lord wants to fill our bodies with himself.
[14]And God is going to raise our bodies from
the dead by his power just as he raised up the
Lord Jesus Christ. [15]Don't you realize that

6:1-6 Taking someone to court, as painful as it may be, is often the easy way out of a conflict. Instead of working our problems out, we take them to an impartial judge. Though this can be helpful at times, we usually end up handing our conflicts over to someone else. Dealing with conflict in such an indirect way usually leads to separation rather than reconciliation. Paul warned the Corinthian believers not to go to unbelieving judges to settle their disputes. If God's power is at work within us, we can depend on the wisdom and guidance of the Holy Spirit to settle our conflicts. We need to keep this in mind as we seek to make amends with those we have harmed.

6:18-20 Sexual sin affects us like no other sin. It isn't that it is the heaviest on some imaginary sin scale, but rather, that its effects are broad and devastating. In sexual sin, we sin not only against ourself, but also against other people and against God. Our body is the dwelling place of God's Holy Spirit, and it belongs to God. This is one more reason for taking care of our body and seeking a new life in recovery.

7:2-5 Marriage is the place for sexual expression and fulfillment. Our body doesn't belong to us; it belongs to God. But here Paul is saying that it also belongs to our spouse. If we seek sexual fulfillment outside of marriage, we will find ourself in the trap of selfish pleasure seeking. Only in marriage can our sexuality be acted out with concern for the other person involved. If we belong to God and to our spouse, we have the potential to act in ways to bring them great joy. Our challenge is to not seek only our personal gratification. As we keep our sexuality within the bounds of marriage, we can discover the joy that comes from living faithfully with another person and before God.

7:8-9 If we are single, we may feel that our recovery would be easier if we had the help of a spouse. If we are married, we may think we could focus more on our recovery if we were unmarried. Whether we are single or married, there are difficulties that we will have to deal with. When we find ourself wishing we were in a different state, we are usually wanting to avoid the responsibilities of our present situation. We would be wise to seek ways to improve the situation we are in rather than abandoning it for something else. Abandoning a relationship or desperately grasping at a new one will never solve our problems in life.

your bodies are actually parts and members of
Christ? So should I take part of Christ and join
him to a prostitute? Never! 16And don't you
know that if a man joins himself to a prostitute she becomes a part of him and he becomes a part of her? For God tells us in the
Scripture that in his sight the two become one
person. 17But if you give yourself to the Lord,
you and Christ are joined together as one
person.
18That is why I say to run from sex sin. No
other sin affects the body as this one does.
When you sin this sin it is against your own
body. 19Haven't you yet learned that your
body is the home of the Holy Spirit God gave
you, and that he lives within you? Your own
body does not belong to you. 20For God has
bought you with a great price. So use every
part of your body to give glory back to God
because he owns it.

CHAPTER 7

Questions about Marriage

Now about those questions you asked in your
last letter: my answer is that if you do not
marry, it is good. 2But usually it is best to be
married, each man having his own wife, and
each woman having her own husband, because otherwise you might fall back into sin.
3The man should give his wife all that is her
right as a married woman, and the wife
should do the same for her husband: 4for a girl
who marries no longer has full right to her
own body, for her husband then has his rights
to it, too; and in the same way the husband
no longer has full right to his own body, for it
belongs also to his wife. 5So do not refuse
these rights to each other. The only exception
to this rule would be the agreement of both
husband and wife to refrain from the rights of
marriage for a limited time, so that they can
give themselves more completely to prayer.
Afterwards, they should come together again
so that Satan won't be able to tempt them
because of their lack of self-control.
6I'm not saying you *must* marry, but you
certainly *may* if you wish. 7I wish everyone
could get along without marrying, just as I do.
But we are not all the same. God gives some
the gift of a husband or wife, and others he
gives the gift of being able to stay happily
unmarried. 8So I say to those who aren't married and to widows—better to stay unmarried
if you can, just as I am. 9But if you can't
control yourselves, go ahead and marry. It is
better to marry than to burn with lust.
10Now, for those who are married I have a

Delayed gratification

READ 1 CORINTHIANS 6:1-13

Our appetites can overtake and enslave us. Perfectly good activities can get us into trouble when we fail to practice them in moderation. Or there may be times when we don't feed our appetites in a balanced way. Then we find ourself so starved that we fall to our addictions at the first opportunity.

This happened to Esau. One day he came home so hungry that he promised his birthright to his younger brother in exchange for a bowl of porridge. We are warned, "Watch out that no one becomes involved in sexual sin or becomes careless about God as Esau did: he traded his rights as the oldest son for a single meal. And afterwards, when he wanted those rights back again, it was too late, even though he wept bitter tears of repentance. So remember, and be careful" (Hebrews 12:16-17). The apostle Paul wrote, "I can do anything I want to if Christ has not said no, but some of these things aren't good for me. Even if I am allowed to do them, I'll refuse to if I think they might get such a grip on me that I can't easily stop when I want to" (1 Corinthians 6:12).

We need to satisfy our appetites in appropriate ways so we don't become starved and thus more susceptible to temptation. There may be some good things that have such control over us that it's best to avoid them altogether. If we allow the demands of our appetites to become overpowering, we risk losing things (or people) that we might never get back. ***Turn to page 1273, 1 Corinthians 13.***

command, not just a suggestion. And it is not a command from me, for this is what the Lord himself has said: A wife must not leave her husband. 11But if she is separated from him, let her remain single or else go back to him. And the husband must not divorce his wife.

12Here I want to add some suggestions of my own. These are not direct commands from the Lord, but they seem right to me: If a Christian has a wife who is not a Christian, but she wants to stay with him anyway, he must not leave her or divorce her. 13And if a Christian woman has a husband who isn't a Christian, and he wants her to stay with him, she must not leave him. 14For perhaps the husband who isn't a Christian may become a Christian with the help of his Christian wife. And the wife who isn't a Christian may become a Christian with the help of her Christian husband. Otherwise, if the family separates, the children might never come to know the Lord; whereas a united family may, in God's plan, result in the children's salvation.

15But if the husband or wife who isn't a Christian is eager to leave, it is permitted. In such cases the Christian husband or wife should not insist that the other stay, for God wants his children to live in peace and harmony. 16For, after all, there is no assurance to you wives that your husbands will be converted if they stay; and the same may be said to you husbands concerning your wives.

Learning to Be Content

17But be sure in deciding these matters that you are living as God intended, marrying or not marrying in accordance with God's direction and help, and accepting whatever situation God has put you into. This is my rule for all the churches.

18For instance, a man who already has gone through the Jewish ceremony of circumcision before he became a Christian shouldn't worry about it; and if he hasn't been circumcised, he shouldn't do it now. 19For it doesn't make any difference at all whether a Christian has gone through this ceremony or not. But it makes a lot of difference whether he is pleasing God and keeping God's commandments. That is the important thing.

20Usually a person should keep on with the work he was doing when God called him. 21Are you a slave? Don't let that worry you—but of course, if you get a chance to be free, take it. 22If the Lord calls you, and you are a slave, remember that Christ has set you free from the awful power of sin; and if he has called you and you are free, remember that you are now a slave of Christ. 23You have been bought and paid for by Christ, so you belong to him—be free now from all these earthly prides and fears. 24So, dear brothers, whatever situation a person is in when he becomes a Christian, let him stay there, for now the Lord is there to help him.

Questions about Being Single

25Now I will try to answer your other question. What about girls who are not yet married? Should they be permitted to do so? In answer to this question, I have no special command for them from the Lord. But the Lord in his kindness has given me wisdom that can be trusted, and I will be glad to tell you what I think.

26Here is the problem: We Christians are facing great dangers to our lives at present. In times like these I think it is best for a person

---

7:10-15 Many of us have been hurt by divorce, either as a participant or as a child of divorced parents. Paul began his words on the subject with a firm reminder of God's command to avoid divorce at all cost. Yet he then recognizes that there are situations in which divorce is a legitimate option. The principle that comes from the command and supports Paul's suggestions is found here: God wants us to live in harmony with one another. When we are not experiencing harmony, we need to examine our life to see if there is anything we can do to change. If, after making appropriate changes in our life, we still face significant problems, we may need to help our spouse go through a similar process. Often a marriage counselor is needed to facilitate this process. Divorce is an option only when one of the partners refuses to remain faithful to his or her marriage commitment.

7:20-24 The Roman world was filled with oppressed people, many of whom had been taken as children to a foreign land to serve as slaves. Some of these slaves came to believe in Christ, and naturally, they yearned for their freedom. They would have been tempted to think they could be better Christians if only they were free. It is easy for us to fall into the same trap. We look at others and think that different circumstances would make our recovery easier. Instead of wishing for a miracle, we can start our recovery no matter what our situation in life. Once we have made a decision to turn our will and our life over to God, we have a new power at work within us—regardless of our outward circumstances.

to remain unmarried. 27Of course, if you already are married, don't separate because of
this. But if you aren't, don't rush into it at this
time. 28But if you men decide to go ahead
anyway and get married now, it is all right;
and if a girl gets married in times like these, it
is no sin. However, marriage will bring extra
problems that I wish you didn't have to face
right now.

29The important thing to remember is that
our remaining time is very short, [and so are
our opportunities for doing the Lord's work].
For that reason those who have wives should
stay as free as possible for the Lord; 30happiness
or sadness or wealth should not keep anyone
from doing God's work. 31Those in frequent
contact with the exciting things the world
offers should make good use of their opportunities without stopping to enjoy them; for the
world in its present form will soon be gone.

32In all you do, I want you to be free from
worry. An unmarried man can spend his time
doing the Lord's work and thinking how to
please him. 33But a married man can't do that
so well; he has to think about his earthly
responsibilities and how to please his wife.
34His interests are divided. It is the same with
a girl who marries. She faces the same problem. A girl who is not married is anxious to
please the Lord in all she is and does. But a
married woman must consider other things
such as housekeeping and the likes and dislikes of her husband.

35I am saying this to help you, not to try to
keep you from marrying. I want you to do
whatever will help you serve the Lord best,
with as few other things as possible to distract
your attention from him.

36But if anyone feels he ought to marry
because he has trouble controlling his passions, it is all right; it is not a sin; let him
marry. 37But if a man has the willpower not to
marry and decides that he doesn't need to and
won't, he has made a wise decision. 38So the
person who marries does well, and the person
who doesn't marry does even better.

39The wife is part of her husband as long as
he lives; if her husband dies, then she may
marry again, but only if she marries a Christian. 40But in my opinion she will be happier
if she doesn't marry again; and I think I am
giving you counsel from God's Spirit when I
say this.

CHAPTER 8

Food Offered to Idols

Next is your question about eating food that
has been sacrificed to idols. On this question
everyone feels that only his answer is the
right one! But although being a "know-it-all"
makes us feel important, what is really needed
to build the church is love. 2If anyone thinks
he knows all the answers, he is just showing
his ignorance. 3But the person who truly loves
God is the one who is open to God's knowledge.

4So now, what about it? Should we eat meat
that has been sacrificed to idols? Well, we all
know that an idol is not really a god, and that
there is only one God, and no other. 5Accord-
ing to some people, there are a great many
gods, both in heaven and on earth. 6But we
know that there is only one God, the Father,
who created all things and made us to be his
own; and one Lord Jesus Christ, who made
everything and gives us life.

7However, some Christians don't realize
this. All their lives they have been used to
thinking of idols as alive, and have believed
that food offered to the idols is really being
offered to actual gods. So when they eat such
food it bothers them and hurts their tender
consciences. 8Just remember that God doesn't
care whether we eat it or not. We are no worse
off if we don't eat it, and no better off if we
do. 9But be careful not to use your freedom to
eat it, lest you cause some Christian brother
to sin whose conscience is weaker than yours.

8:1-3 Love is a way of life in which we allow all our thoughts and actions to be guided by our concern for others. Most of us are in need of recovery because we lived for our own personal gratification. As we sought to escape from our inner pain through the fleeting pleasures of addictive activities and substances, we became blind to the needs of the people around us. This life-style has left our past littered with hurt people and broken relationships. A life governed by selfless love is the only path to rebuilding our broken past. The fact that God loves us, no matter what our past, is the place where we start.

8:10-13 Our personal freedom is a precious right until it deprives someone else of his or her personal freedom. We can try to justify our actions by intellectualizing them, but love is the only principle that will guide us to make a legitimate moral inventory. When we love, our freedom to do certain things will not be as important as our relationships with others. We will learn to put the needs of others before our own desires. Love is to be the measuring stick for our moral inventory and the motivation for making amends with the people we have wronged.

10You see, this is what may happen: Someone who thinks it is wrong to eat this food will see you eating at a temple restaurant, for you know there is no harm in it. Then he will become bold enough to do it too, although all the time he still feels it is wrong. 11So because you "know it is all right to do it," you will be responsible for causing great spiritual damage to a brother with a tender conscience for whom Christ died. 12And it is a sin against Christ to sin against your brother by encouraging him to do something he thinks is wrong. 13So if eating meat offered to idols is going to make my brother sin, I'll not eat any of it as long as I live because I don't want to do this to him.

CHAPTER 9

The Rights of Apostles

I am an apostle, God's messenger, responsible to no mere man. I am one who has actually seen Jesus our Lord with my own eyes. And your changed lives are the result of my hard work for him. 2If in the opinion of others, I am not an apostle, I certainly am to you, for you have been won to Christ through me. 3This is my answer to those who question my rights.

4Or don't I have any rights at all? Can't I claim the same privilege the other apostles have of being a guest in your homes? 5If I had a wife, and if she were a believer, couldn't I bring her along on these trips just as the other disciples do, and as the Lord's brothers do, and as Peter does? 6And must Barnabas and I alone keep working for our living while you supply these others? 7What soldier in the army has to pay his own expenses? And have you ever heard of a farmer who harvests his crop and doesn't have the right to eat some of it? What shepherd takes care of a flock of sheep and goats and isn't allowed to drink some of the milk? 8And I'm not merely quoting the opinions of men as to what is right. I'm telling you what God's law says. 9For in the law God gave to Moses he said that you must not put a muzzle on an ox to keep it from eating when it is treading out the wheat. Do you suppose God was thinking only about oxen when he said this? 10Wasn't he also thinking about us? Of course he was. He said this to show us that Christian workers should be paid by those they help. Those who do the plowing and threshing should expect some share of the harvest.

11We have planted good spiritual seed in your souls. Is it too much to ask, in return, for mere food and clothing? 12You give them to others who preach to you, and you should. But shouldn't we have an even greater right to them? Yet we have *never* used this right but supply our own needs without your help. We have never demanded payment of any kind for fear that, if we did, you might be less interested in our message to you from Christ.

13Don't you realize that God told those working in his temple to take for their own needs some of the food brought there as gifts to him? And those who work at the altar of God get a share of the food that is brought by those offering it to the Lord. 14In the same way the Lord has given orders that those who preach the Gospel should be supported by those who accept it.

15Yet I have never asked you for one penny. And I am not writing this to hint that I would like to start now. In fact, I would rather die of hunger than lose the satisfaction I get from preaching to you without charge. 16For just preaching the Gospel isn't any special credit to me—I couldn't keep from preaching it if I wanted to. I would be utterly miserable. Woe unto me if I don't.

17If I were volunteering my services of my

9:4-12 Paul set himself up as a model for what he had just said about giving up personal freedom in order to show love toward others. Paul had all the rights we have, but he willingly gave them up because of his relationship with Jesus Christ and his desire to help others. We may feel that we have certain freedoms and rights, but if we desire to make progress in recovery, we may have to give up some of those rights. We may have the right to take part in certain activities or frequent certain places, but we probably know that some of these things will only lead to a fall. In order to recover, we need to give up any activities and relationships that will lead to a relapse. We may also need to relinquish some of our rights in order to support our friends in recovery.

9:15-18 Paul gave up his right to be paid for his work in the ministry, choosing instead to work to support himself. The point wasn't whether or not he should have been paid. He was illustrating the principle that when something is important in our life, we may have to give up some of our rights and freedoms to accomplish it. If we hope to make progress in recovery, our relationship with Jesus Christ and his program for our recovery need to take a central place in our life. We may need to give up some of our possessions, activities, and codependent relationships in order to achieve the freedom that we long for.

own free will, then the Lord would give me a special reward; but that is not the situation, for God has picked me out and given me this sacred trust, and I have no choice. [18]Under this circumstance, what is my pay? It is the special joy I get from preaching the Good News without expense to anyone, never demanding my rights.

[19]And this has a real advantage: I am not bound to obey anyone just because he pays my salary; yet I have freely and happily become a servant of any and all so that I can win them to Christ. [20]When I am with the Jews I seem as one of them so that they will listen to the Gospel and I can win them to Christ. When I am with Gentiles who follow Jewish customs and ceremonies I don't argue, even though I don't agree, because I want to help them. [21]When with the heathen I agree with them as much as I can, except of course that I must always do what is right as a Christian. And so, by agreeing, I can win their confidence and help them too.

[22]When I am with those whose consciences bother them easily, I don't act as though I know it all and don't say they are foolish; the result is that they are willing to let me help them. Yes, whatever a person is like, I try to find common ground with him so that he will let me tell him about Christ and let Christ save him. [23]I do this to get the Gospel to them and also for the blessing I myself receive when I see them come to Christ.

[24]In a race everyone runs, but only one person gets first prize. So run your race to win. [25]To win the contest you must deny yourselves many things that would keep you from doing your best. An athlete goes to all this trouble just to win a blue ribbon or a silver cup, but we do it for a heavenly reward that never disappears. [26]So I run straight to the goal with purpose in every step. I fight to win. I'm not just shadow-boxing or playing around. [27]Like an athlete I punish my body, treating it roughly, training it to do what it should, not what it wants to. Otherwise I fear that after enlisting others for the race, I myself might be declared unfit and ordered to stand aside.

CHAPTER 10

Lessons about Idol Worship

For we must never forget, dear brothers, what happened to our people in the wilderness long ago. God guided them by sending a cloud that moved along ahead of them; and he brought them all safely through the waters of the Red Sea. [2]This might be called their "baptism"—baptized both in sea and cloud!—as followers of Moses—their commitment to him as their leader. [3,4]And by a miracle God sent them food to eat and water to drink there in the desert; they drank the water that Christ gave them. He was there with them as a mighty Rock of spiritual refreshment. [5]Yet after all this most of them did not obey God, and he destroyed them in the wilderness.

[6]From this lesson we are warned that we must not desire evil things as they did, [7]nor worship idols as they did. (The Scriptures tell us, "The people sat down to eat and drink and then got up to dance" in worship of the golden calf.)

9:19-23 An essential part of recovery is sharing the Good News of God's forgiveness and help. Paul left us with some helpful hints about how to do this effectively. He shows us that if we want to communicate, we must first take the time to understand where another person is coming from. Paul listened to his audience and found common ground with them before he took steps to help them change. As we seek to help others, we begin by gaining their confidence. We don't need to be good at winning arguments; we need to be good at listening and showing that we care. Paul listened to the needs of people and then presented his message in a way that met their specific needs. We can do the same as we carry the message of hope to hurting people.

9:24-27 The process of recovery is a lot like training for a title bout in the boxing ring or getting ready for a marathon. These activities require a great deal of endurance and strict discipline for those who want to win. No one ever said recovery would be easy, and Paul makes it clear that growing in our relationship with God is a tough task. If we want to succeed in recovery and grow spiritually, we need to live a life focused on those goals. We need to give up the destructive activities that will slow us down and take part in a rigorous training program. If we recognize that things won't be easy at the outset of our program and do what we can to persevere, we will experience God's powerful help in our life and experience the freedom of recovery.

10:1-13 Paul had just used himself as an example of the disciplined, vigilant athlete; here he used the history of Israel to show us what not to be like. Israel's lack of self-discipline and vigilance against temptation led them into sin. They were over-confident, and that attitude led to a self-destructive pride that we must avoid. Notice that Paul held up Israel's failure as a warning to us. If we follow their example, we will suffer the same painful consequences that they did.

8Another lesson for us is what happened when some of them sinned with other men's wives, and 23,000 fell dead in one day. 9And don't try the Lord's patience—they did and died from snake bites. 10And don't murmur against God and his dealings with you as some of them did, for that is why God sent his Angel to destroy them.

11All these things happened to them as examples—as object lessons to us—to warn us against doing the same things; they were written down so that we could read about them and learn from them in these last days as the world nears its end.

12So be careful. If you are thinking, "Oh, I would never behave like that"—let this be a warning to you. For you too may fall into sin. 13But remember this—the wrong desires that come into your life aren't anything new and different. Many others have faced exactly the same problems before you. And no temptation is irresistible. You can trust God to keep the temptation from becoming so strong that you can't stand up against it, for he has promised this and will do what he says. He will show you how to escape temptation's power so that you can bear up patiently against it.

14So, dear friends, carefully avoid idol worship of every kind.

15You are intelligent people. Look now and see for yourselves whether what I am about to say is true. 16When we ask the Lord's blessing upon our drinking from the cup of wine at the Lord's Table, this means, doesn't it, that all who drink it are sharing together the blessing of Christ's blood? And when we break off pieces of the bread from the loaf to eat there together, this shows that we are sharing together in the benefits of his body. 17No matter how many of us there are, we all eat from the same loaf, showing that we are all parts of the one body of Christ. 18And the Jewish people, all who eat the sacrifices, are united by that act.

19What am I trying to say? Am I saying that the idols to whom the heathen bring sacrifices are really alive and are real gods, and that these sacrifices are of some value? No, not at all. 20What I am saying is that those who offer food to these idols are united together in sacrificing to demons, certainly not to God. And I don't want any of you to be partners with demons when you eat the same food, along with the heathen, that has been offered to these idols. 21You cannot drink from the cup at the Lord's Table and at Satan's table, too. You cannot eat bread both at the Lord's Table and at Satan's table.

22What? Are you tempting the Lord to be angry with you? Are you stronger than he is?

23You are certainly free to eat food offered to idols if you want to; it's not against God's laws to eat such meat, but that doesn't mean that you should go ahead and do it. It may be perfectly legal, but it may not be best and helpful. 24Don't think only of yourself. Try to think of the other fellow, too, and what is best for him.

25Here's what you should do. Take any meat you want that is sold at the market. Don't ask whether or not it was offered to idols, lest the answer hurt your conscience. 26For the earth and every good thing in it belongs to the Lord and is yours to enjoy.

27If someone who isn't a Christian asks you out to dinner, go ahead; accept the invitation if you want to. Eat whatever is on the table and don't ask any questions about it. Then you won't know whether or not it has been used as a sacrifice to idols, and you won't risk having a bad conscience over eating it. 28But if someone warns you that this meat has been offered to idols, then don't eat it for the sake of the man who told you, and of his conscience. 29In this case *his* feeling about it is the important thing, not yours.

But why, you may ask, must I be guided and limited by what someone else thinks? 30If I

10:19-22 We cannot serve both Christ and the devil. We cannot be in recovery and dabble in our old life-style. Compromising our personal standards to please those who represent our dysfunctional past is walking on a dangerous middle ground. If we continue in this pattern, our relationship with God will soon falter, and our recovery will be in jeopardy. Recovery requires a choice, and that choice means we have to leave some things behind.

10:23-33 Paul sought to balance his argument here, for it is easy to become too legalistic as we work our recovery program. The balance can be found by being willing to give up any of our rights that might cause another to fall, while also not forcing our standards on anyone else. This middle road does not lead to codependency, where we seek to please others for unhealthy reasons. Paul sought to please others for the specific purpose of leading them to salvation and recovery. If our actions are governed by our love for others, we will be well on the way to developing strong relationships and overcoming the problems that drive our addictions and compulsions. We will also be powerful instruments of help in the lives of other hurting people.

READ 1 CORINTHIANS 10:12-14

GOD grant me the serenity to accept the things I cannot change the courage to change the things I can and the wisdom to know the difference AMEN

Belief in an instant cure for addiction will put our recovery at risk; belief that we will someday be beyond the reach of temptation is also dangerous.

Unfortunately, temptation is a permanent part of our world and of human experience. The Bible says, "The wrong desires that come into your life aren't anything new and different. Many others have faced exactly the same problems before you" (1 Corinthians 10:13). Not only is temptation all around us; it is within us as well. "Temptation is the pull of man's own evil thoughts and wishes" (James 1:14). Even if we could rid ourself of all external temptations, we would still have to live with the destructive desires within our secret self.

Even Jesus Christ faced temptation; and yet he never sinned. Before he was tempted, he spent an extended period of time alone in the wilderness, and during that time he went without food. We are usually tempted the most during the times when we are lonely and hungry.

Facing temptation is a part of accepting reality. We need to accept that we will always be susceptible to temptation in our areas of weakness and predisposition. When we receive Christ as our Savior, God gives us a new nature, but it is unrealistic to believe that our old sinful nature will ever get better. When we put away the belief that temptation will magically disappear, we will be more aware and better able to avoid falling under temptation's power. We need to prayerfully seek God's help in dealing with this reality of life. ***Turn to page 1329, Philippians 4.***

---

can thank God for the food and enjoy it, why
let someone spoil everything just because he
thinks I am wrong? 31Well, I'll tell you why. It
is because you must do everything for the
glory of God, even your eating and drinking.
32So don't be a stumbling block to anyone,
whether they are Jews or Gentiles or Christians. 33That is the plan I follow, too. I try to
please everyone in everything I do, not doing
what I like or what is best for me but what is
best for them, so that they may be saved.

CHAPTER 11

Instructions for Public Worship

And you should follow my example, just as I follow Christ's.

2I am so glad, dear brothers, that you have
been remembering and doing everything I
taught you. 3But there is one matter I want to
remind you about: that a wife is responsible
to her husband, her husband is responsible to
Christ, and Christ is responsible to God. 4That
is why, if a man refuses to remove his hat
while praying or preaching, he dishonors
Christ. 5And that is why a woman who publicly prays or prophesies without a covering
on her head dishonors her husband [for her
covering is a sign of her subjection to him].
6Yes, if she refuses to wear a head covering,
then she should cut off all her hair. And if it
is shameful for a woman to have her head
shaved, then she should wear a covering. 7But
a man should not wear anything on his head
[when worshiping, for his hat is a sign of
subjection to men].

God's glory is man made in his image, and
man's glory is the woman. 8The first man
didn't come from woman, but the first
woman came out of man. 9And Adam, the
first man, was not made for Eve's benefit, but

Eve was made for Adam. [10]So a woman should wear a covering on her head as a sign that she is under man's authority, a fact for all the angels to notice and rejoice in.

[11]But remember that in God's plan men and women need each other. [12]For although the first woman came out of man, all men have been born from women ever since, and both men and women come from God their Creator.

[13]What do you yourselves really think about this? Is it right for a woman to pray in public without covering her head? [14,15]Doesn't even instinct itself teach us that women's heads should be covered? For women are proud of their long hair, while a man with long hair tends to be ashamed. [16]But if anyone wants to argue about this, all I can say is that we never teach anything else than this—that a woman should wear a covering when prophesying or praying publicly in the church, and all the churches feel the same way about it.

Order at the Lord's Supper

[17]Next on my list of items to write you about is something else I cannot agree with. For it sounds as if more harm than good is done when you meet together for your communion services. [18]Everyone keeps telling me about the arguing that goes on in these meetings, and the divisions developing among you, and I can just about believe it. [19]But I suppose you feel this is necessary so that you who are always right will become known and recognized!

[20]When you come together to eat, it isn't the Lord's Supper you are eating, [21]but your own. For I am told that everyone hastily gobbles all the food he can without waiting to share with the others, so that one doesn't get enough and goes hungry while another has too much to drink and gets drunk. [22]What? Is this really true? Can't you do your eating and drinking at home to avoid disgracing the church and shaming those who are poor and can bring no food? What am I supposed to say about these things? Do you want me to praise you? Well, I certainly do not!

[23]For this is what the Lord himself has said about his Table, and I have passed it on to you before: That on the night when Judas betrayed him, the Lord Jesus took bread, [24]and when he had given thanks to God for it, he broke it and gave it to his disciples and said, "Take this and eat it. This is my body, which is given for you. Do this to remember me." [25]In the same way, he took the cup of wine after supper, saying, "This cup is the new agreement between God and you that has been established and set in motion by my blood. Do this in remembrance of me whenever you drink it." [26]For every time you eat this bread and drink this cup you are retelling the message of the Lord's death, that he has died for you. Do this until he comes again.

[27]So if anyone eats this bread and drinks from this cup of the Lord in an unworthy manner, he is guilty of sin against the body and the blood of the Lord. [28]That is why a man should examine himself carefully before eating the bread and drinking from the cup. [29]For if he eats the bread and drinks from the cup unworthily, not thinking about the body of Christ and what it means, he is eating and drinking God's judgment upon himself; for he is trifling with the death of Christ. [30]That is why many of you are weak and sick, and some have even died.

[31]But if you carefully examine yourselves before eating you will not need to be judged and punished. [32]Yet, when we are judged and punished by the Lord, it is so that we will not be condemned with the rest of the world. [33]So,

---

11:17-22 Paul spent some time here trying to solve a problem in the Corinthian church. Apparently some of the wealthier believers looked down on the poorer members and refused to share from their abundance at the communion meal. Paul made it clear that attitudes of superiority are extremely destructive. As we undergo recovery, we must share the process with others. There may be people in our group whom we feel are below us, but this kind of attitude is destructive. In God's eyes, no one is better than another. We are all broken by sin and need God's transforming power. Our material well-being or educational level does not make us better people. When we recognize this and humbly share our failures with others, we will be able to make progress in recovery.

11:17-30 In these verses, Paul called the Corinthians to make a searching and fearless moral inventory of their lives. Some of them needed to recognize the pride they were harboring and take steps to remove it. This is something we all need to do on a regular basis. We cannot do it just once and expect to be finished with it; it must be a way of life for us. Spiritual growth, emotional growth, and our recovery depend on our faithfulness in taking our personal inventory. Paul noted here that even physical illness can be the result of an unexamined life. When we take the time to make a regular moral inventory we will gain victory over the destructive forces in our life.

dear brothers, when you gather for the Lord's Supper—the communion service—wait for each other; 34if anyone is really hungry he should eat at home so that he won't bring punishment upon himself when you meet together.

I'll talk to you about the other matters after I arrive.

CHAPTER 12

Teachings about Spiritual Gifts

And now, brothers, I want to write about the special abilities the Holy Spirit gives to each of you, for I don't want any misunderstanding about them. 2You will remember that before you became Christians you went around from one idol to another, not one of which could speak a single word. 3But now you are meeting people who claim to speak messages from the Spirit of God. How can you know whether they are really inspired by God or whether they are fakes? Here is the test: no one speaking by the power of the Spirit of God can curse Jesus, and no one can say, "Jesus is Lord," and really mean it, unless the Holy Spirit is helping him.

4Now God gives us many kinds of special abilities, but it is the same Holy Spirit who is the source of them all. 5There are different kinds of service to God, but it is the same Lord we are serving. 6There are many ways in which God works in our lives, but it is the same God who does the work in and through all of us who are his. 7The Holy Spirit displays God's power through each of us as a means of helping the entire church.

8To one person the Spirit gives the ability to give wise advice; someone else may be especially good at studying and teaching, and this is his gift from the same Spirit. 9He gives special faith to another, and to someone else the power to heal the sick. 10He gives power for doing miracles to some, and to others power to prophesy and preach. He gives someone else the power to know whether evil spirits are speaking through those who claim to be giving God's messages—or whether it is really the Spirit of God who is speaking. Still another person is able to speak in languages he never learned; and others, who do not know the language either, are given power to understand what he is saying. 11It is the same and only Holy Spirit who gives all these gifts and powers, deciding which each one of us should have.

Many Parts but One Body

12Our bodies have many parts, but the many parts make up only one body when they are all put together. So it is with the "body" of Christ. 13Each of us is a part of the one body of Christ. Some of us are Jews, some are Gentiles, some are slaves, and some are free. But the Holy Spirit has fitted us all together into one body. We have been baptized into Christ's body by the one Spirit, and have all been given that same Holy Spirit.

14Yes, the body has many parts, not just one part. 15If the foot says, "I am not a part of the body because I am not a hand," that does not make it any less a part of the body. 16And what would you think if you heard an ear say, "I am not part of the body because I am only an ear and not an eye"? Would that make it any less a part of the body? 17Suppose the whole body were an eye—then how would you hear? Or if your whole body were just one big ear, how could you smell anything?

18But that isn't the way God has made us. He has made many parts for our bodies and has put each part just where he wants it. 19What a strange thing a body would be if it had only one part! 20So he has made many parts, but still there is only one body.

21The eye can never say to the hand, "I

12:4-11 Each of us is gifted in some way. No one is without talent and special abilities, and these talents and abilities are gifts from God. When we "put ourself down," we are rejecting these gifts from God rather than delighting in them. We don't need to build up our self-esteem; we just need a more accurate sense of who we are and how God has gifted us. Whether we have recognized it or not, being in recovery is a unique gift in itself. Having suffered through the process of failure and deliverance, we are uniquely gifted to help others struggling in similar ways. By sharing our story of deliverance with others, we may be giving the gift of life to a person in need.

12:12-26 When we become proud of our gifts and accomplishments, we invariably end up hurting ourself and others. All of us are gifted in some way or another, and our gifts ultimately come from God. If we do not recognize this truth, we will tend to take credit for our progress in recovery and flaunt our success before others. This kind of pride causes pain to others and leads us toward a fall. When we have an accurate view of ourself, we will give God the credit for the gifts he has given us and be thankful for the help he has given us in our recovery. If we cannot do this, we need to go back to Step One and once again admit how powerless we really are.

don't need you." The head can't say to the feet, "I don't need you."

22And some of the parts that seem weakest and least important are really the most necessary. 23Yes, we are especially glad to have some parts that seem rather odd! And we carefully protect from the eyes of others those parts that should not be seen, 24while of course the parts that may be seen do not require this special care. So God has put the body together in such a way that extra honor and care are given to those parts that might otherwise seem less important. 25This makes for happiness among the parts, so that the parts have the same care for each other that they do for themselves. 26If one part suffers, all parts suffer with it, and if one part is honored, all the parts are glad.

27Now here is what I am trying to say: All of you together are the one body of Christ, and each one of you is a separate and necessary part of it. 28Here is a list of some of the parts he has placed in his Church, which is his body:

Apostles,
Prophets—those who preach God's Word,
Teachers,
Those who do miracles,
Those who have the gift of healing;
Those who can help others,
Those who can get others to work together,
Those who speak in languages they have never learned.

29Is everyone an apostle? Of course not. Is everyone a preacher? No. Are all teachers? Does everyone have the power to do miracles? 30Can everyone heal the sick? Of course not. Does God give all of us the ability to speak in languages we've never learned? Can just anyone understand and translate what those are saying who have that gift of foreign speech? 31No, but try your best to have the more important of these gifts.

First, however, let me tell you about something else that is better than any of them!

CHAPTER 13

What Is Real Love?

If I had the gift of being able to speak in other languages without learning them and could speak in every language there is in all of heaven and earth, but didn't love others, I would only be making noise. 2If I had the gift of prophecy and knew all about what is going to happen in the future, knew everything about *everything,* but didn't love others, what good would it do? Even if I had the gift of faith so that I could speak to a mountain and make it move, I would still be worth nothing at all without love. 3If I gave everything I have to poor people, and if I were burned alive for preaching the Gospel but didn't love others, it would be of no value whatever.

4Love is very patient and kind, never jealous or envious, never boastful or proud, 5never haughty or selfish or rude. Love does not demand its own way. It is not irritable or touchy. It does not hold grudges and will hardly even notice when others do it wrong. 6It is never glad about injustice, but rejoices whenever truth wins out. 7If you love someone, you will be loyal to him no matter what the cost. You will always believe in him, always expect the best of him, and always stand your ground in defending him.

8All the special gifts and powers from God

13:1-3 Paul was writing to a group of believers who had started to forget what real love is all about. He began his reminder by showing them that all their abilities, talents, and spiritual gifts amounted to nothing if they didn't love each other. Without selfless love, we have nothing. Loving relationships are also essential to our recovery.

13:11-13 Recovery and growth are never complete in this life; we are always in recovery—always growing. We are still like children, needing to grow and mature. Only when we see God face-to-face will we be complete and whole. Paul shares this truth not to discourage us, but to give us hope that someday we will be made perfect. We will persevere in the process of recovery if we have *faith* in God and those around us. We need *hope* to endure and be healed from the painful problems and addictions in our life. Most of all we need genuine *love* to conquer the barriers and bondage of our past. Faith, hope, and love are all necessary ingredients to a successful recovery. Genuine love, however, is the greatest healer of all.

14:1-12 In these verses, Paul returned to the subject of spiritual gifts. He warned us not to use our gifts to build ourself up or to reinforce our sense of self-sufficiency. All spiritual gifts are just that—gifts. They are given to us by God to be used to build others up and encourage them in their spiritual growth. Using our God-given gifts for our own purposes shows that we have forgotten the one who gave the gifts in the first place—God. This kind of attitude invariably leads to failure. We will succeed as we remind ourself that we are powerless and in need of God's powerful help.

will someday come to an end, but love goes
on forever. Someday prophecy and speaking
in unknown languages and special knowledge—these gifts will disappear. 9Now we
know so little, even with our special gifts, and
the preaching of those most gifted is still so
poor. 10But when we have been made perfect
and complete, then the need for these inadequate special gifts will come to an end, and
they will disappear.
11It's like this: when I was a child I spoke
and thought and reasoned as a child does. But
when I became a man my thoughts grew far
beyond those of my childhood, and now I
have put away the childish things. 12In the
same way, we can see and understand only a
little about God now, as if we were peering at
his reflection in a poor mirror; but someday
we are going to see him in his completeness,
face to face. Now all that I know is hazy and
blurred, but then I will see everything clearly,
just as clearly as God sees into my heart right
now.
13There are three things that remain—faith,
hope, and love—and the greatest of these is
love.

CHAPTER 14

The Gifts of Prophecy and Tongues

Let love be your greatest aim; nevertheless,
ask also for the special abilities the Holy Spirit
gives, and especially the gift of prophecy, being able to preach the messages of God.
2But if your gift is that of being able to
"speak in tongues," that is, to speak in languages you haven't learned, you will be talking to God but not to others, since they won't
be able to understand you. You will be speaking by the power of the Spirit, but it will all be
a secret. 3But one who prophesies, preaching
the messages of God, is helping others grow
in the Lord, encouraging and comforting
them. 4So a person "speaking in tongues"
helps himself grow spiritually, but one who
prophesies, preaching messages from God,
helps the entire church grow in holiness and
happiness.
5I wish you all had the gift of "speaking in
tongues," but even more I wish you were all
able to prophesy, preaching God's messages,
for that is a greater and more useful power
than to speak in unknown languages—unless,
of course, you can tell everyone afterwards
what you were saying, so that they can get
some good out of it too.
6Dear friends, even if I myself should come
to you talking in some language you don't

Love

READ 1 CORINTHIANS 13:1-7

We may have given up on love. Perhaps we have waited for love to find us, only to be disappointed. Maybe our loved ones have hurt us so badly that we needed to numb ourself from the pain. In the past our addictions helped to keep us numb, but now that we are in recovery, we have to find a way to deal with the issue of love once again.

It is God's will that we love; without love nothing else matters (see 1 Corinthians 13:1-3). Love is more than a feeling. It is a choice of behaviors that grows in our life; it is a fruit of the Holy Spirit, produced in our life as we yield to God. The Bible defines it this way: "Love is very patient and kind, never jealous or envious, never boastful or proud, never haughty or selfish or rude. . . . If you love someone, you will be loyal to him no matter what the cost. You will always believe in him, always expect the best of him, and always stand your ground in defending him" (1 Corinthians 13:4-7).

This passage is a description of how God loves us. As we begin to absorb his love, we will find ourself reaching out to love again. No one loves perfectly, but we must not give up on loving. We can accept the responsibility to love others and stop waiting for them to love us, playing the role of the victim. We cannot expect to be good at loving right away; we can be patient as God's love grows within us. When we choose to act in loving ways, the emotions will follow, and we will find that love comes back to us.
Turn to page 1289, 2 Corinthians 5.

understand, how would that help you? But if
I speak plainly what God has revealed to me,
and tell you the things I know, and what is
going to happen, and the great truths of God's
Word—that is what you need; that is what
will help you. 7Even musical instruments—
the flute, for instance, or the harp—are examples of the need for speaking in plain, simple
English rather than in unknown languages.
For no one will recognize the tune the flute is
playing unless each note is sounded clearly.
8And if the army bugler doesn't play the right
notes, how will the soldiers know that they
are being called to battle? 9In the same way, if
you talk to a person in some language he
doesn't understand, how will he know what
you mean? You might as well be talking to an
empty room.

10I suppose that there are hundreds of different languages in the world, and all are
excellent for those who understand them,
11but to me they mean nothing. A person
talking to me in one of these languages will be
a stranger to me and I will be a stranger to
him. 12Since you are so anxious to have special
gifts from the Holy Spirit, ask him for the very
best, for those that will be of real help to the
whole church.

13If someone is given the gift of speaking in
unknown tongues, he should pray also for the
gift of knowing what he has said, so that he
can tell people afterwards plainly. 14For if I
pray in a language I don't understand, my
spirit is praying, but I don't know what I am
saying.

15Well, then, what shall I do? I will do both.
I will pray in unknown tongues and also in
ordinary language that everyone understands. I will sing in unknown tongues and
also in ordinary language so that I can understand the praise I am giving; 16for if you praise
and thank God with the spirit alone, speaking
in another language, how can those who
don't understand you be praising God along
with you? How can they join you in giving
thanks when they don't know what you are
saying? 17You will be giving thanks very
nicely, no doubt, but the other people present
won't be helped.

18I thank God that I "speak in tongues"
privately more than any of the rest of you.
19But in public worship I would much rather
speak five words that people can understand
and be helped by than ten thousand words
while "speaking in tongues" in an unknown
language.

20Dear brothers, don't be childish in your
understanding of these things. Be innocent
babies when it comes to planning evil, but be
men of intelligence in understanding matters
of this kind. 21We are told in the ancient
Scriptures that God would send men from
other lands to speak in foreign languages to
his people, but even then they would not
listen. 22So you see that being able to "speak
in tongues" is not a sign to God's children
concerning his power, but is a sign to the
unsaved. However, prophecy (preaching the
deep truths of God) is what the Christians
need, and unbelievers aren't yet ready for it.
23Even so, if an unsaved person, or someone
who doesn't have these gifts, comes to church
and hears you all talking in other languages,
he is likely to think you are crazy. 24But if you
prophesy, preaching God's Word, [even
though such preaching is mostly for believ-
ers] and an unsaved person or a new Christian
comes in who does not understand about
these things, all these sermons will convince
him of the fact that he is a sinner, and his
conscience will be pricked by everything he
hears. 25As he listens, his secret thoughts will
be laid bare, and he will fall down on his
knees and worship God, declaring that God is
really there among you.

A Call to Orderly Worship

26Well, my brothers, let's add up what I am
saying. When you meet together some will
sing, another will teach, or tell some special
information God has given him, or speak in
an unknown language, or tell what someone
else is saying who is speaking in the unknown
language, but everything that is done must be

14:26-39 In these verses, Paul returned to the subject of relationships characterized by a healthy interdependence. We are called to live in community with others, seeking to build them up and meet their needs. It is important to make the distinction between this kind of relationship and a codependent relationship, in which we relate to others for some ulterior motive, perhaps seeking to meet our own lack or need. Interdependence describes a healthy relationship in which we attempt to meet one another's needs without seeking some hidden reward. When we learn to love selflessly as Paul proposed, the physical and emotional needs of everyone in our community will be met. One of the goals of our recovery is restoring our broken, dysfunctional relationships, turning them into healthy and interdependent ones.

useful to all, and build them up in the Lord.
27No more than two or three should
speak in an unknown language, and they
must speak one at a time, and someone must
be ready to interpret what they are saying.
28But if no one is present who can interpret,
they must not speak out loud. They must talk
silently to themselves and to God in the unknown language but not publicly.

29,30Two or three may prophesy, one at a
time, if they have the gift, while all the others
listen. But if, while someone is prophesying,
someone else receives a message or idea from
the Lord, the one who is speaking should stop.
31In this way all who have the gift of prophecy
can speak, one after the other, and everyone
will learn and be encouraged and helped. 32Re-
member that a person who has a message from
God has the power to stop himself or wait his
turn. 33God is not one who likes things to be
disorderly and upset. He likes harmony, and
he finds it in all the other churches.

34Women should be silent during the
church meetings. They are not to take part in
the discussion, for they are subordinate to
men as the Scriptures also declare. 35If they
have any questions to ask, let them ask their
husbands at home, for it is improper for
women to express their opinions in church
meetings.

36You disagree? And do you think that the
knowledge of God's will begins and ends with
you Corinthians? Well, you are mistaken!
37You who claim to have the gift of prophecy
or any other special ability from the Holy
Spirit should be the first to realize that what I
am saying is a commandment from the Lord
himself. 38But if anyone still disagrees—well,
we will leave him in his ignorance.

39So, my fellow believers, long to be prophets so that you can preach God's message
plainly; and never say it is wrong to "speak in
tongues"; 40however, be sure that everything
is done properly in a good and orderly way.

CHAPTER 15

The Resurrection of Christ

Now let me remind you, brothers, of what the
Gospel really is, for it has not changed—it is
the same Good News I preached to you before. You welcomed it then and still do now,
for your faith is squarely built upon this wonderful message; 2and it is this Good News that
saves you if you still firmly believe it, unless of
course you never really believed it in the first
place.

3I passed on to you right from the first what
had been told to me, that Christ died for our
sins just as the Scriptures said he would, 4and
that he was buried, and that three days afterwards he arose from the grave just as the
prophets foretold. 5He was seen by Peter and
later by the rest of "the Twelve." 6After that he
was seen by more than five hundred Christian
brothers at one time, most of whom are still
alive, though some have died by now. 7Then
James saw him, and later all the apostles. 8Last
of all I saw him too, long after the others, as
though I had been born almost too late for
this. 9For I am the least worthy of all the
apostles, and I shouldn't even be called an
apostle at all after the way I treated the church
of God.

10But whatever I am now it is all because
God poured out such kindness and grace
upon me—and not without results: for I have
worked harder than all the other apostles, yet
actually I wasn't doing it, but God working in
me, to bless me. 11It makes no difference who
worked the hardest, I or they; the important
thing is that we preached the Gospel to you
and you believed it.

15:10 In recovery, we often say something beginning with "But for the grace of God, I. . . ." Such statements started with Paul's own recognition that without God's grace, he never would have achieved any of the success for which he is famous. Our success in recovery also must be accompanied by our recognition of God's help in the process. When we fail to give the credit to God for what has happened in our life, we negate our progress by forgetting the lessons of its earliest steps. Notice, however, that Paul also recognized his own hard work in the process. Our own recovery is based on the grace of God and his desire to help us, but we still have a part in the equation: we have to work hard! Our recovery takes a combination of God's gracious power and our faithful willingness to follow his plan for our life.

15:12-20 Some of the Corinthians had begun to question the hope we have of being resurrected to new life at Christ's second coming. So Paul reemphasized the importance of the Resurrection and the hope it offers to all of us, even those who are already dead. The greatest expression of God's power was raising Jesus from the grave. If God could do that, then he has the power to do anything! If God did not raise Jesus from the grave, however, then our God is powerless, and we are lost. Paul affirmed the truth that Jesus did rise from the dead and, in so doing, also affirmed the fact that we have access to the greatest power in the universe—God himself.

The Resurrection of the Dead

12But tell me this! Since you believe what we preach, that *Christ* rose from the dead, why are some of you saying that dead people will never come back to life again? 13For if there is no resurrection of the dead, then Christ must still be dead. 14And if he is still dead, then all our preaching is useless and your trust in God is empty, worthless, hopeless; 15and we apostles are all liars because we have said that God raised Christ from the grave, and of course that isn't true if the dead do not come back to life again. 16If they don't, then Christ is still dead, 17and you are very foolish to keep on trusting God to save you, and you are still under condemnation for your sins; 18in that case, all Christians who have died are lost! 19And if being a Christian is of value to us only now in this life, we are the most miserable of creatures.

20But the fact is that Christ did actually rise from the dead and has become the first of millions who will come back to life again someday.

21Death came into the world because of what one man (Adam) did, and it is because of what this other man (Christ) has done that now there is the resurrection from the dead. 22Everyone dies because all of us are related to Adam, being members of his sinful race, and wherever there is sin, death results. But all who are related to Christ will rise again. 23Each, however, in his own turn: Christ rose first; then when Christ comes back, all his people will become alive again.

24After that the end will come when he will turn the Kingdom over to God the Father, having put down all enemies of every kind. 25For Christ will be King until he has defeated all his enemies, 26including the last enemy—death. This too must be defeated and ended. 27For the rule and authority over all things has been given to Christ by his Father; except, of course, Christ does not rule over the Father himself, who gave him this power to rule. 28When Christ has finally won the battle against all his enemies, then he, the Son of God, will put himself also under his Father's orders, so that God who has given him the victory over everything else will be utterly supreme.

29If the dead will not come back to life again, then what point is there in people being baptized for those who are gone? Why do it unless you believe that the dead will someday rise again?

30And why should we ourselves be continually risking our lives, facing death hour by hour? 31For it is a fact that I face death daily; that is as true as my pride in your growth in the Lord. 32And what value was there in fighting wild beasts—those men of Ephesus—if it was only for what I gain in this life down here? If we will never live again after we die, then we might as well go and have ourselves a good time: let us eat, drink, and be merry. What's the difference? For tomorrow we die, and that ends everything!

33Don't be fooled by those who say such things. If you listen to them you will start acting like them. 34Get some sense and quit your sinning. For to your shame I say it; some of you are not even Christians at all and have never really known God.

The Resurrection Body

35But someone may ask, "How will the dead be brought back to life again? What kind of bodies will they have?" 36What a foolish question! You will find the answer in your own garden! When you put a seed into the ground it doesn't grow into a plant unless it "dies" first. 37And when the green shoot comes up out of the seed, it is very different from the seed you first planted. For all you put into the ground is a dry little seed of wheat or whatever it is you are planting, 38then God gives it a beautiful new body—just the kind he wants

---

15:29-34 If death is the end of everything, then a selfish, pleasure-seeking life-style may be a justifiable alternative. But Paul reminds us that our hope and our recovery lead to an existence beyond the grave. It is this truth about the Resurrection that motivates us to make right choices and leave behind our old way of life. If we do things God's way, we have an eternity of joy and peace to look forward to. If we decide to do things our own way, we face an eternity of suffering.

15:35-58 No matter how terrifying our dependencies may have become, death is probably still our greatest fear. Sometimes our fear of death can motivate us to seek God for help with our destructive problems. Yet, our fear of death can also lead us to despair and may actually feed our dependencies. It can bring out the best and the worst in us. Paul reminds us of a fact that can remove our fear of death: Jesus Christ has conquered death. His resurrection conquered death and the "sting of death," which is sin. When we have the resurrection power of Jesus Christ at work within us, nothing we do is ever wasted. God will use even our failures and relapses to teach us something for his glory.

it to have; a different kind of plant grows from
each kind of seed. 39 And just as there are
different kinds of seeds and plants, so also
there are different kinds of flesh. Humans,
animals, fish, and birds are all different.
40 The angels in heaven have bodies far different from ours, and the beauty and the glory
of their bodies is different from the beauty
and the glory of ours. 41 The sun has one kind
of glory while the moon and stars have another kind. And the stars differ from each
other in their beauty and brightness.
42 In the same way, our earthly bodies which
die and decay are different from the bodies we
shall have when we come back to life again,
for they will never die. 43 The bodies we have
now embarrass us, for they become sick and
die; but they will be full of glory when we
come back to life again. Yes, they are weak,
dying bodies now, but when we live again
they will be full of strength. 44 They are just
human bodies at death, but when they come
back to life they will be superhuman bodies.
For just as there are natural, human bodies,
there are also supernatural, spiritual bodies.
45 The Scriptures tell us that the first man,
Adam, was given a natural, human body but
Christ is more than that, for he was life-giving
Spirit.
46 First, then, we have these human bodies,
and later on God gives us spiritual, heavenly
bodies. 47 Adam was made from the dust of the
earth, but Christ came from heaven above.
48 Every human being has a body just like
Adam's, made of dust, but all who become
Christ's will have the same kind of body as
his—a body from heaven. 49 Just as each of us
now has a body like Adam's, so we shall some
day have a body like Christ's.
50 I tell you this, my brothers: an earthly
body made of flesh and blood cannot get into
God's Kingdom. These perishable bodies of
ours are not the right kind to live forever.
51 But I am telling you this strange and wonderful secret: we shall not all die, but we shall
all be given new bodies! 52 It will all happen in
a moment, in the twinkling of an eye, when
the last trumpet is blown. For there will be a
trumpet blast from the sky, and all the Christians who have died will suddenly become
alive, with new bodies that will never, never
die; and then we who are still alive shall
suddenly have new bodies too. 53 For our
earthly bodies, the ones we have now that can
die, must be transformed into heavenly bodies that cannot perish but will live forever.
54 When this happens, then at last this Scripture will come true—"Death is swallowed up
in victory." 55,56 O death, where then your victory? Where then your sting? For sin—the
sting that causes death—will all be gone; and
the law, which reveals our sins, will no longer
be our judge. 57 How we thank God for all of
this! It is he who makes us victorious through
Jesus Christ our Lord!
58 So, my dear brothers, since future victory
is sure, be strong and steady, always abounding in the Lord's work, for you know that
nothing you do for the Lord is ever wasted as
it would be if there were no resurrection.

CHAPTER 16

Directions for the Offering

Now here are the directions about the money
you are collecting to send to the Christians in
Jerusalem; (and, by the way, these are the
same directions I gave to the churches in
Galatia). 2 On every Lord's Day each of you
should put aside something from what you
have earned during the week, and use it for
this offering. The amount depends on how
much the Lord has helped you earn. Don't
wait until I get there and then try to collect it
all at once. 3 When I come I will send your
loving gift with a letter to Jerusalem, to be
taken there by trustworthy messengers you
yourselves will choose. 4 And if it seems wise
for me to go along too, then we can travel
together.

Paul's Final Instructions

5 I am coming to visit you after I have been to
Macedonia first, but I will be staying there
only for a little while. 6 It could be that I will
stay longer with you, perhaps all winter, and
then you can send me on to my next destination. 7 This time I don't want to make just a
passing visit and then go right on; I want to
come and stay awhile, if the Lord will let me.
8 I will be staying here at Ephesus until the
holiday of Pentecost, 9 for there is a wide open
door for me to preach and teach here. So
much is happening, but there are many enemies.

16:5-18 Throughout this letter, Paul encouraged the Corinthians in their recovery and spiritual growth. In closing, Paul revealed his love and trust in them by making personal requests. There is always a balance between caring for the hurts and needs of others and being able to ask for what we need as well. Healthy relationships are characterized by this kind of balanced give-and-take.

10 If Timothy comes make him feel at home,
for he is doing the Lord's work just as I am.
11 Don't let anyone despise or ignore him [be-
cause he is young], but send him back to me
happy with his time among you; I am looking
forward to seeing him soon, along with the
others who are returning.
12 I begged Apollos to visit you along with
the others, but he thought that it was not at
all God's will for him to go now; he will be
seeing you later on when he has the opportunity.
13 Keep your eyes open for spiritual danger;
stand true to the Lord; act like men; be strong;
14 and whatever you do, do it with kindness
and love.
15 Do you remember Stephanas and his
family? They were the first to become Christians in Greece, and they are spending their
lives helping and serving Christians everywhere. 16 Please follow their instructions and
do everything you can to help them as well
as all others like them who work hard at your
side with such real devotion. 17 I am so glad
that Stephanas, Fortunatus, and Achaicus
have arrived here for a visit. They have been
making up for the help you aren't here to
give me. 18 They have cheered me greatly and
have been a wonderful encouragement to
me, as I am sure they were to you, too. I hope
you properly appreciate the work of such
men as these.
19 The churches here in Asia send you their
loving greetings. Aquila and Priscilla send you
their love, and so do all the others who meet
in their home for their church service. 20 All
the friends here have asked me to say hello to
you for them. And give each other a loving
handshake when you meet.
21 I will write these final words of this letter
with my own hand: 22 if anyone does not love
the Lord, that person is cursed. Lord Jesus,
come! 23 May the love and favor of the Lord
Jesus Christ rest upon you. 24 My love to all of
you, for we all belong to Christ Jesus.

Sincerely, Paul

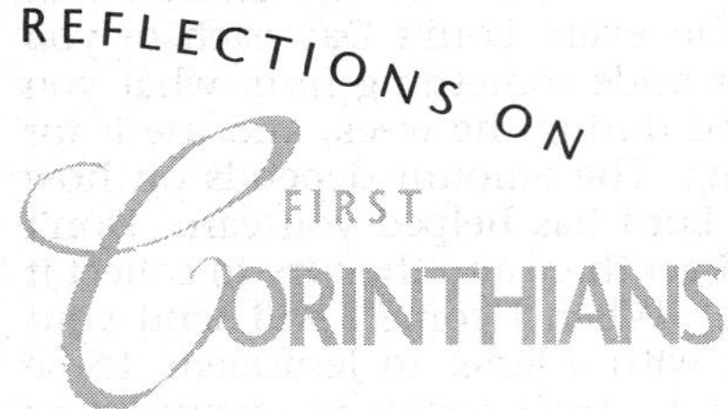
REFLECTIONS ON
FIRST
CORINTHIANS

✲insights ABOUT OUR POWERLESSNESS AND GOD'S POWER

Through a series of illustrations in **1 Corinthians 1:26-31,** Paul pointed out that God's plan for our recovery doesn't utilize our human wisdom, strength, or skill. And we don't have to be famous or rich to receive God's forgiveness and power. For people who are self-sufficient, this may be hard to accept. We want to feel worthy of our salvation or our recovery. But until we can admit that we are powerless to change without God's help, we are doomed to cycles of painful failure. God's free gift of forgiveness and the power to live a new life may appear foolish to us. But once we turn our will and our life over to God's care, we will discover genuine power and release from the bondage of our past.

✲insights INTO FINDING GOD'S WILL

Some of us may wonder how we could ever know God's will for our life. In **1 Corinthians 2:11-12** we find that we can know God's mind and heart because he has placed his Holy Spirit within us to communicate these things to us. Often the Holy Spirit uses God's Word in the Scriptures to communicate with us. What a privilege! God's presence in our life will help us know how to deal with our painful past, facilitating our ability to make an accurate personal inventory. This will lead to a healthy view of ourself and the restoration of our broken relationships. If we are willing to consistently follow God's direction in our life through the Holy Spirit, our recovery is assured.

✲insights INTO HEALTHY RELATIONSHIPS

In **1 Corinthians 6:12** Paul told the Corinthian believers to avoid involvement in activities that would be likely to seduce them back into their old way of life. This warning is important for us in recovery, too. Many of our old activities and relationships are not wrong in themselves, but staying involved in these things will naturally lead us toward a relapse. If this is the case, these activities are not good for us or our recovery. We need to avoid anything that might stop or slow our spiritual growth.

✲***insights*** ABOUT LOVE

Most of us define love as an emotion and stop there. But Paul in **1 Corinthians 13:4-7** defined love as a commitment to act in a certain way toward others. We may not be able to conjure up the emotions and feelings of love, but we can certainly practice the behaviors he listed in these verses. The apostle knew that when we behave in loving ways, feelings of love soon follow. As we seek to restore our relationships and make amends, we will find that Paul's description of loving action is a sure prescription for restoration and healing.

SECOND CORINTHIANS

THE BIG PICTURE

A. PAUL DISCUSSES HIS MOTIVES AND ACTIONS (1:1–2:13)
B. PAUL RELATES HIS MINISTRY TO THE NEW COVENANT (2:14–7:16)
C. PAUL APPEALS TO HIS READERS FOR SUPPORT (8:1–9:15)
D. PAUL DEFENDS HIS APOSTOLIC AUTHORITY (10:1–13:14)

Paul wrote this letter mainly to defend the authority of his teachings about Christ. The church at Corinth was struggling, and one of its problems was the presence of members who openly challenged Paul's authority. These challengers slandered Paul's character and questioned the message he preached. They also introduced a number of dangerous false teachings. Since the believers in Corinth had come to faith through Paul's ministry, this put the entire church at risk.

The false teachers claimed that following the Jewish laws was a requirement for salvation. To counteract this false teaching, Paul emphasized the truth that God changes us from the inside out. We cannot change ourself by changing our external behaviors. As we are reconciled to God, he transforms us into an entirely new person; our old self is changed in a fundamental sense.

Of course, change is never easy when it involves our lifestyle. Old habits die hard, and positive habits have a way of falling prey to neglect. Typically the habits that die hardest are our negative or unhealthy thoughts and behavioral patterns. "Out with the old, in with the new!" sounds simple, but even as we long for an end to our bad habits, we cling to them.

Fortunately, God has done something about our helpless situation. That is why we can admit our powerlessness and come to him for help. It is essential for recovery that we turn our life over to God. Through Christ's death and resurrection, God made it possible for us to experience the changes we long for. By being reconciled to him, we can have a new life in Christ, transformed from the inside out.

THE BOTTOM LINE

PURPOSE: To explain new life in Christ while also defending Paul's authority to preach. AUTHOR: The apostle Paul. AUDIENCE: The church at Corinth, a city in Greece. DATE WRITTEN: About A.D. 55 from Macedonia. SETTING: After hearing several accusations against him circulating at Corinth, Paul wrote to the Corinthian believers to correct their misunderstandings and help them with other problems. KEY VERSE: "When someone becomes a Christian, he becomes a brand new person inside. He is not the same anymore. A new life has begun!" (5:17). KEY PLACES: Corinth, Macedonia, Troas, Jerusalem. KEY PEOPLE AND RELATIONSHIPS: Paul with Timothy, Titus, the Corinthian believers, and some false apostles.

RECOVERY THEMES

God's Power for Our Recovery: All of us have made resolutions about how we are going to change. The results are usually the same—we end up falling back into the same old bad habits we promised to change. The Corinthians were apparently doing the same kind of thing, with the same results. What they failed to grasp as they listened to the false teachers was that only God's power can enable us to make changes in our life. Our own efforts always fall short. Instead of merely making resolutions, we need to admit our powerlessness and turn our life over to God. Then we can allow his power to change us from within.

Learning to Accept Criticism: One of Paul's purposes in writing this letter was to discipline those who needed to be corrected. Criticism usually hurts. Yet it also helps us see what we need to change and forces us to face our problems. If we are going to be effective in our recovery, we must confront and solve problems, not ignore them; that means being open to criticism.

Conflict Can Inspire Growth: Interpersonal conflicts are an inevitable part of being human. They can also be so discouraging that they cause us to give in to failure. But what conflicts do to us depends on how we handle them. If we view them as opportunities for growth, as Paul urged the Corinthians to do, we can turn them into something productive. If we face them and try to solve them in loving ways, they can motivate us to make progress in our recovery and recommitment to each other. If we ignore them, they can eat away at us like a cancer, destroying the work of recovery not only within us, but also in others around us. Conflicts are opportunities for growth if we use them as such.

God's Strength in Our Weakness: In this letter of Paul's, he told about a particular "thorn" in his flesh (12:7). We don't know what this problem was because he didn't tell us. Some have suggested that it was a physical ailment, or even a disease affecting his eyes. Whatever it was, it was debilitating and chronic, and at times, it interfered with his work. It also kept Paul humble because it forced him to depend on God. Through this hardship, Paul learned to thank God for his weakness. In each of us there will always be weaknesses holding us back and bogging us down. But our weaknesses have a purpose—to bring us to God. For those of us in recovery, to what better place can our weaknesses take us?

CHAPTER 1

Greetings from Paul

Dear friends: This letter is from me, Paul,
appointed by God to be Jesus Christ's messenger; and from our dear brother Timothy. We
are writing to all of you Christians there in
Corinth and throughout Greece. [2]May God
our Father and the Lord Jesus Christ mightily
bless each one of you and give you peace.

God Offers Comfort to All

[3,4]What a wonderful God we have—he is the
Father of our Lord Jesus Christ, the source of
every mercy, and the one who so wonderfully
comforts and strengthens us in our hardships
and trials. And why does he do this? So that
when others are troubled, needing our sympathy and encouragement, we can pass on to
them this same help and comfort God has
given us. [5]You can be sure that the more we
undergo sufferings for Christ, the more he
will shower us with his comfort and encouragement. [6,7]We are in deep trouble for bringing you God's comfort and salvation. But in
our trouble God has comforted us—and this,
too, to help you: to show you from our personal experience how God will tenderly comfort you when you undergo these same
sufferings. He will give you the strength to
endure.

[8]I think you ought to know, dear brothers,
about the hard time we went through in Asia.
We were really crushed and overwhelmed, and
feared we would never live through it. [9]We felt
we were doomed to die and saw how powerless we were to help ourselves; but that was

---

1:1-7 Not only is God the God of peace, but he is also the God of mercy and comfort. That's good news, both when we are going through a particular trial and when we are trying to recover from a dysfunctional or abusive situation. Jesus Christ suffered greatly and unjustly when he went to the cross. He fully understands and identifies with our suffering, and he knows the kind of comfort we need. He is worthy of our trust and able to deliver us from our painful circumstances.

1:8-10 Paul wrote of his own recent need for comfort from God (see 1:3-7). Apparently, Paul and his missionary group had been almost killed as they ministered in the Roman province of Asia, now southwestern Turkey. Yet, even though Paul and his companions thought the end had come, God delivered them. Many of us have experienced God's delivering power in our own life. Even when everything seems to be coming apart, God can rescue us from what appears to be sure destruction.

good, for then we put everything into the
hands of God, who alone could save us, for he
can even raise the dead. 10And he did help us
and saved us from a terrible death; yes, and we
expect him to do it again and again. 11But you
must help us too by praying for us. For much
thanks and praise will go to God from you
who see his wonderful answers to your prayers
for our safety!

Paul's Change of Plans

12We are so glad that we can say with utter
honesty that in all our dealings we have been
pure and sincere, quietly depending upon the
Lord for his help and not on our own skills.
And that is even more true, if possible, about
the way we have acted toward you. 13,14My
letters have been straightforward and sincere;
nothing is written between the lines! And
even though you don't know me very well (I
hope someday you will), I want you to try to
accept me and be proud of me as you already
are to some extent; just as I shall be of you on
that day when our Lord Jesus comes back
again.

15,16It was because I was so sure of your
understanding and trust that I planned to
stop and see you on my way to Macedonia, as
well as afterwards when I returned, so that I
could be a double blessing to you and so that
you could send me on my way to Judea.

17Then why, you may be asking, did I
change my plan? Hadn't I really made up my
mind yet? Or am I like a man of the world
who says yes when he really means no?
18Never! As surely as God is true, I am not that
sort of person. My yes means yes.

19Timothy and Silvanus and I have been
telling you about Jesus Christ the Son of God.
He isn't one to say yes when he means no. He
always does exactly what he says. 20He carries
out and fulfills all of God's promises, no matter how many of them there are; and we have
told everyone how faithful he is, giving glory
to his name. 21It is this God who has made you
and me into faithful Christians and commissioned us apostles to preach the Good News.
22He has put his brand upon us—his mark of
ownership—and given us his Holy Spirit in
our hearts as guarantee that we belong to him
and as the first installment of all that he is
going to give us.

23I call upon this God to witness against me
if I am not telling the absolute truth: the
reason I haven't come to visit you yet is that
I don't want to sadden you with a severe
rebuke. 24When I come, although I can't do

The Fruit of Forgiveness

BIBLE READING: 2 Corinthians 2:5-8

We made a list of all persons we had harmed and became willing to make amends to them all.

Some of the things we have done have earned us disapproval and possibly a loss of love. We have found that some people in our life love us only if they can approve of our behavior. We may have struggled with bitterness toward them because we feel as if they have been trying to punish us. If our "sins" have been made public, we may assume that we have lost the love of everyone who disapproves of our actions. This fear of rejection might deter us from reaching out to make amends.

In the young Corinthian church, a man was cut off from church fellowship when his sins were made public. After he turned around and tried to make amends, some people refused to welcome him back into the church. The apostle Paul told them: "Remember that . . . man I wrote about, who caused all the trouble. . . . I don't want to be harder on him than I should. He has been punished enough by your united disapproval. Now it is time to forgive him and comfort him. Otherwise he may become so bitter and discouraged that he won't be able to recover. Please show him now that you still do love him very much" (2 Corinthians 2:5-8). Some people will follow this advice and reaffirm their love for you when you go to them.

There will be some people who will respond with forgiveness, comfort, acceptance, and love. This will help us overcome the grief, the bitterness, and the discouragement we may feel. Their forgiveness will help us to move on with our recovery. ***Turn to page 1307, Galatians 6.***

much to help your faith, for it is strong already, I want to be able to do something about your joy: I want to make you happy, not sad.

CHAPTER 2

"No," I said to myself, "I won't do it. I'll not make them unhappy with another painful visit." [2]For if I make you sad, who is going to make me happy? You are the ones to do it, and how can you if I cause you pain? [3]That is why I wrote as I did in my last letter, so that you will get things straightened out before I come. Then, when I do come, I will not be made sad by the very ones who ought to give me greatest joy. I felt sure that your happiness was so bound up in mine that you would not be happy either unless I came with joy.

[4]Oh, how I hated to write that letter! It almost broke my heart, and I tell you honestly that I cried over it. I didn't want to hurt you, but I had to show you how very much I loved you and cared about what was happening to you.

Reinstating the Repentant Sinner

[5,6]Remember that the man I wrote about, who caused all the trouble, has not caused sorrow to me as much as to all the rest of you—though I certainly have my share in it too. I don't want to be harder on him than I should. He has been punished enough by your united disapproval. [7]Now it is time to forgive him and comfort him. Otherwise he may become so bitter and discouraged that he won't be able to recover. [8]Please show him now that you still do love him very much.

[9]I wrote to you as I did so that I could find out how far you would go in obeying me. [10]When you forgive anyone, I do too. And whatever I have forgiven (to the extent that this affected me too) has been by Christ's authority, and for your good. [11]A further reason for forgiveness is to keep from being outsmarted by Satan, for we know what he is trying to do.

[12]Well, when I got as far as the city of Troas, the Lord gave me tremendous opportunities to preach the Gospel. [13]But Titus, my dear brother, wasn't there to meet me and I couldn't rest, wondering where he was and what had happened to him. So I said goodbye and went right on to Macedonia to try to find him.

The Fragrance of Christ

[14]But thanks be to God! For through what Christ has done, he has triumphed over us so that now wherever we go he uses us to tell others about the Lord and to spread the Gospel like a sweet perfume. [15]As far as God is concerned there is a sweet, wholesome fragrance in our lives. It is the fragrance of Christ within us, an aroma to both the saved and the unsaved all around us. [16]To those who are not being saved, we seem a fearful smell of death and doom, while to those who know Christ we are a life-giving perfume. But who is adequate for such a task as this? [17]Only those who, like ourselves, are men of integrity, sent by God, speaking with Christ's power, with God's eye upon us. We are not like those hucksters—and there are many of them—whose idea in getting out the Gospel is to make a good living out of it.

CHAPTER 3

Our Success Comes from God

Are we beginning to be like those false teachers of yours who must tell you all about themselves and bring long letters of recommendation with them? I think you hardly need someone's letter to tell you about

---

1:23–2:4 For all of his strength of personality, Paul was not insensitive to the pain of his readers. In this case, the apostle knew that the strong rebuke he needed to give them would be devastating. He truly wanted to be positive, but he concluded that there was no way to avoid confronting them about their responsibilities before God and others. Sometimes we need to be comforted; sometimes we need to be confronted. The apostle Paul recognized that this was a time for honest confrontation. When we confront others about their failures, we must make sure that we are seeking their best, just as Paul did. It is sometimes tempting to judge others in order to cover up our own shortcomings.

2:14-17 We all know that our continued recovery is based on our sharing the Good News of God's deliverance. For some of us, this may seem an impossible and terrifying task. Paul shows us here that it is a natural outworking of God's grace in our life. As God transforms us, giving us victory over our dependencies, we begin to reflect his grace in our life. The fragrance of God's transforming work will be readily evident to others if we are open and transparent with them. We don't have to be a wonderful speaker to share the Good News. We can reach out to others in the ways we are able to and be willing to share our story. Our humble message passed along by word and deed may be all the encouragement someone needs to get his life back on track.

us, do you? And we don't need a recommendation from you, either! 2The only letter I
need is you yourselves! By looking at the good
change in your hearts, everyone can see that
we have done a good work among you. 3They
can see that you are a letter from Christ,
written by us. It is not a letter written with
pen and ink, but by the Spirit of the living
God; not one carved on stone, but in human
hearts.

4We dare to say these good things about
ourselves only because of our great trust in
God through Christ, that he will help us to be
true to what we say, 5and not because we
think we can do anything of lasting value by
ourselves. Our only power and success comes
from God. 6He is the one who has helped us
tell others about his new agreement to save
them. We do not tell them that they must
obey every law of God or die; but we tell them
there is life for them from the Holy Spirit. The
old way, trying to be saved by keeping the Ten
Commandments, ends in death; in the new
way, the Holy Spirit gives them life.

A New Plan for Salvation

7Yet that old system of law that led to death
began with such glory that people could not
bear to look at Moses' face. For as he gave
them God's law to obey, his face shone out
with the very glory of God—though the
brightness was already fading away. 8Shall we
not expect far greater glory in these days
when the Holy Spirit is giving life? 9If the plan
that leads to doom was glorious, much more
glorious is the plan that makes men right with
God. 10In fact, that first glory as it shone from
Moses' face is worth nothing at all in comparison with the overwhelming glory of the new
agreement. 11So if the old system that faded
into nothing was full of heavenly glory, the
glory of God's new plan for our salvation is
certainly far greater, for it is eternal.

12Since we know that this new glory will
never go away, we can preach with great boldness, 13and not as Moses did, who put a veil
over his face so that the Israelis could not see
the glory fade away.

14Not only Moses' face was veiled, but his
people's minds and understanding were
veiled and blinded too. Even now when the
Scripture is read it seems as though Jewish
hearts and minds are covered by a thick veil,
because they cannot see and understand the
real meaning of the Scriptures. For this veil of
misunderstanding can be removed only by
believing in Christ. 15Yes, even today when
they read Moses' writings their hearts are
blind and they think that obeying the Ten
Commandments is the way to be saved.

16But whenever anyone turns to the Lord
from his sins, then the veil is taken away.
17The Lord is the Spirit who gives them life,
and where he is there is freedom [from trying
to be saved by keeping the laws of God]. 18But
we Christians have no veil over our faces; we
can be mirrors that brightly reflect the glory
of the Lord. And as the Spirit of the Lord
works within us, we become more and more
like him.

CHAPTER 4

Satan Blinds, but God Gives Light

It is God himself, in his mercy, who has given
us this wonderful work [of telling his Good
News to others], and so we never give up. 2We

3:4-5 In his letters, Paul frequently comes across as a very confident person. He explained here, however, that his confidence was not so much self-confidence, as a "God-inspired" confidence. If we trust our competent God to work in and through us, we can know with confidence that the resources are available to overcome any problem we might face. The most healthy foundation for self-esteem is the knowledge that we are made in God's image (see Genesis 1:26-27) and that we are competent because of Christ's work on our behalf.

3:6-16 Paul's contrast between the Old Covenant (the law of Moses) and the New Covenant (salvation through Jesus Christ) is instructive for the recovery process. The glory of the law, as well as the glow on Moses' face from when he met God on Mount Sinai, was substantial. But it faded, implying that the law was not a long-term solution to the sin problem. Likewise, the many humanistic recovery programs and other means for dealing with our pain and dependencies may seem "gloriously" effective in the short run, but the success we experience through them will rapidly fade. The new life that God offers through an ongoing relationship with God through Jesus Christ is the only means to a permanent recovery.

3:17-18 The glory of God is seen in the new covenant as well as the old. But rather than being reflected on the outside, as with Moses' face, the glory of the New Covenant is a transformation from the inside out. This glory shines through the lives of all who trust Jesus Christ and pursue true recovery in the power of the Holy Spirit. The further we progress in our relationship with God, the more visible God's glory becomes in our life.

do not try to trick people into believing—we
are not interested in fooling anyone. We
never try to get anyone to believe that the
Bible teaches what it doesn't. All such shameful methods we forego. We stand in the presence of God as we speak and so we tell the
truth, as all who know us will agree.

3If the Good News we preach is hidden to
anyone, it is hidden from the one who is on
the road to eternal death. 4Satan, who is the
god of this evil world, has made him blind,
unable to see the glorious light of the Gospel
that is shining upon him or to understand the
amazing message we preach about the glory
of Christ, who is God. 5We don't go around
preaching about ourselves but about Christ
Jesus as Lord. All we say of ourselves is that we
are your slaves because of what Jesus has done
for us. 6For God, who said, "Let there be light
in the darkness," has made us understand
that it is the brightness of his glory that is seen
in the face of Jesus Christ.

7But this precious treasure—this light and
power that now shine within us—is held in a
perishable container, that is, in our weak bodies. Everyone can see that the glorious power
within must be from God and is not our own.

8We are pressed on every side by troubles,
but not crushed and broken. We are perplexed because we don't know why things
happen as they do, but we don't give up and
quit. 9We are hunted down, but God never
abandons us. We get knocked down, but we
get up again and keep going. 10These bodies of
ours are constantly facing death just as Jesus
did; so it is clear to all that it is only the living
Christ within [who keeps us safe].

11Yes, we live under constant danger to our
lives because we serve the Lord, but this gives
us constant opportunities to show forth the
power of Jesus Christ within our dying bodies.
12Because of our preaching we face death, but
it has resulted in eternal life for you.

13We boldly say what we believe [trusting
God to care for us], just as the psalm writer did
when he said, "I believe and therefore I
speak." 14We know that the same God who
brought the Lord Jesus back from death will
also bring us back to life again with Jesus and
present us to him along with you. 15These
sufferings of ours are for your benefit. And the
more of you who are won to Christ, the more
there are to thank him for his great kindness,
and the more the Lord is glorified.

16That is why we never give up. Though our
bodies are dying, our inner strength in the
Lord is growing every day. 17These troubles
and sufferings of ours are, after all, quite small
and won't last very long. Yet this short time
of distress will result in God's richest blessing
upon us forever and ever! 18So we do not look
at what we can see right now, the troubles all
around us, but we look forward to the joys in
heaven which we have not yet seen. The

4:3-4 If we are not willing to recognize the sin in our life, we are in denial and are headed for destruction. If we cannot recognize that we have a problem with sin and addiction, we cannot accept the gift of forgiveness that God offers us through a relationship with Jesus Christ. The only way to overcome the powerful effects of sin in our life is to recognize our helplessness and entrust our life to God's care. He will help us take an honest inventory of our life and empower us to make the needed changes. But we begin the process by shedding our denial and accepting the Good News of salvation through Jesus Christ.

4:16-18 When we entrust our life to God, two opposite and somewhat confusing processes are simultaneously at work. On the one hand, physical deterioration and eventual death are inevitable, as are the distressing trials that accompany them. On the other hand, the glorious inner growth is preparing us day-by-day for the overwhelming glory and blessing we will experience in the presence of God throughout eternity. We may have to wait a while for God's eternal blessings. But if we trust God to help us in this life of decay and death, we can be sure of his blessings in the future.

5:6-9 The fact that God is preparing a better body and better place of residence for us at the end of the recovery process cannot be proven scientifically. There is strong unseen spiritual evidence, but it must be accepted by faith (see Hebrews 11:1). Such faith always pleases God, and it also helps us overcome our great fear of death, which is just the doorway to our eternal life with God (see John 14:2-3). It is important in recovery that we entrust our life to God and seek to do his will. Knowing that God wants to give us something special after this life motivates us to put our life in his hands right now.

5:10-11 Consequences and motives are both major issues in the recovery process. Consequences for selfish and destructive behavior reach even beyond the boundaries of this life. All of us will have to stand before God's judgment seat and receive his piercing evaluation. For those of us who have believed in Jesus Christ for salvation, this judgment will also include the giving of rewards. Understanding that our actions and commitments do have eternal consequences can help us to think twice before we act and can motivate us to do things according to God's program.

troubles will soon be over, but the joys to
come will last forever.

CHAPTER 5
Earthly Bodies Are Weak
For we know that when this tent we live in
now is taken down—when we die and leave
these bodies—we will have wonderful new
bodies in heaven, homes that will be ours
forevermore, made for us by God himself and
not by human hands. 2How weary we grow of
our present bodies. That is why we look forward eagerly to the day when we shall have
heavenly bodies that we shall put on like new
clothes. 3For we shall not be merely spirits
without bodies. 4These earthly bodies make us
groan and sigh, but we wouldn't like to think
of dying and having no bodies at all. We want
to slip into our new bodies so that these dying
bodies will, as it were, be swallowed up by
everlasting life. 5This is what God has prepared for us, and as a guarantee he has given
us his Holy Spirit.

6Now we look forward with confidence to
our heavenly bodies, realizing that every moment we spend in these earthly bodies is time
spent away from our eternal home in heaven
with Jesus. 7We know these things are true by
believing, not by seeing. 8And we are not
afraid but are quite content to die, for then we
will be at home with the Lord. 9So our aim is
to please him always in everything we do,
whether we are here in this body or away
from this body and with him in heaven. 10For
we must all stand before Christ to be judged
and have our lives laid bare—before him.
Each of us will receive whatever he deserves
for the good or bad things he has done in his
earthly body.

We Are God's Ambassadors
11It is because of this solemn fear of the Lord,
which is ever present in our minds, that we
work so hard to win others. God knows our
hearts, that they are pure in this matter, and I
hope that, deep within, you really know it
too.

12Are we trying to pat ourselves on the back
again? No, I am giving you some good ammu-
nition! You can use this on those preachers of
yours who brag about how well they look and
preach but don't have true and honest hearts.
You can boast about us that we, at least, are
well intentioned and honest.

13,14Are we insane [to say such things about
ourselves]? If so, it is to bring glory to God.
And if we are in our right minds, it is for your

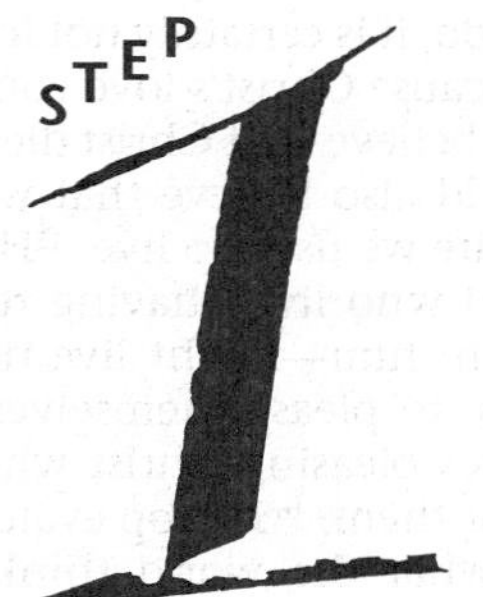

The Paradox of Powerlessness

BIBLE READING: 2 Corinthians 4:7-10

We admitted that we were powerless over our dependencies—that our life had become unmanageable.

We may be afraid to admit that we are powerless and that our life is unmanageable. If we admit that we are powerless, won't we be tempted to give up completely in the struggle against our addiction? It doesn't seem to make sense that we can admit powerlessness and still find the power to go on. This paradox will be dealt with as we go on to Steps Two and Three.

Life is full of paradoxes. The apostle Paul tells us, "This precious treasure—this light and power that now shine within us—is held in a perishable container, that is, in our weak bodies. Everyone can see that the glorious power within must be from God and is not our own. We are pressed on every side by troubles, but not crushed and broken" (2 Corinthians 4:7-8).

The picture here presents a contrast between a precious treasure and the simple clay pot in which the treasure is stored. The living power poured into our life from above is the treasure. Our human life, with all the everyday pressures and problems, is represented by the clay pot, the perishable container. As human beings, we have inherent weaknesses.

Once we recognize the paradox of powerlessness it can be quite a relief. We don't have to always be strong or pretend to be perfect. We can live a real life, with daily struggles, in a human body beset with weakness and still find the power from above to keep going without being crushed and broken. ***Turn to Step Two, page 575, Job 14.***

benefit. Whatever we do, it is certainly not for
our own profit but because Christ's love controls us now. Since we believe that Christ died
for all of us, we should also believe that we
have died to the old life we used to live. 15He
died for all so that all who live—having received eternal life from him—might live no
longer for themselves, to please themselves,
but to spend their lives pleasing Christ who
died and rose again for them. 16So stop evaluating Christians by what the world thinks
about them or by what they seem to be like
on the outside. Once I mistakenly thought of
Christ that way, merely as a human being like
myself. How differently I feel now! 17When
someone becomes a Christian, he becomes a
brand new person inside. He is not the same
anymore. A new life has begun!

18All these new things are from God who
brought us back to himself through what
Christ Jesus did. And God has given us the
privilege of urging everyone to come into his
favor and be reconciled to him. 19For God was
in Christ, restoring the world to himself, no
longer counting men's sins against them but
blotting them out. This is the wonderful message he has given us to tell others. 20We are
Christ's ambassadors. God is using us to speak
to you: we beg you, as though Christ himself
were here pleading with you, receive the love
he offers you—be reconciled to God. 21For
God took the sinless Christ and poured into
him our sins. Then, in exchange, he poured
God's goodness into us!

CHAPTER 6

As God's partners, we beg you not to toss aside
this marvelous message of God's great kindness. 2For God says, "Your cry came to me at
a favorable time, when the doors of welcome

5:17 The new life we experience in Jesus Christ is so far-reaching and complete that it can be said we become a brand-new person through him. That does not mean that our thoughts and habits, including our compulsions or addictions, will automatically vanish. But it does mean that from God's point of view, we have been forgiven—we are new creatures in his sight. And through the power of God's Holy Spirit, we have all the power necessary for a complete transformation in every area of our life.

5:18-21 One of the great needs in most recovery contexts is the reconciliation of dysfunctional or fractured relationships. At the human level, this is very difficult to do. But in the case of our broken relationship with God, he has already met us more than halfway by offering us reconciliation through Jesus Christ. God's work of reconciliation is even more profound since God committed none of the wrongs in our relationship with him. By accepting the forgiveness he offers, we can have our relationship with God restored. We are also called to follow God and to offer the gift of forgiveness to others. And if the gift of forgiveness is offered by someone else, we can humbly accept it. In this way we can begin the process of rebuilding our relationships and making amends to the people we have wronged.

6:8-10 When we live for God and follow his program for healthy living, we will find that others react to us in one of two ways. Some honor us as genuine and support what we are trying to do; others will malign and dishonor us. If we are trying to impress others to bolster our self-esteem, we will be devastated when people react negatively. This may lead us to give up on what we have started. Paul received his self-esteem from his relationship with God and did not need to be honored by others. He knew that he could never please everyone anyway. As we live to please God, however, we will find that we are building healthy relationships with others along the way.

6:11-13 Paul went the extra mile to reconcile his relationship with the Corinthians. Having defended his sincerity toward them earlier (see 1:12-23), he once again pledged his honest affection to his readers, challenging them to do the same for him. In recovering relationships, it is often the case that one party withholds affection to childishly punish the other. This only leads to deeper alienation and loss. We may not be able to control how another person acts in a broken relationship, but we can control how we act. We need never be the one to withhold forgiveness. We can be like Paul, extending the invitation of restoration to others, humbly and without reservation.

6:14-18 Since we started the process of recovery, we probably have struggled with our past friendships. Some of our old friends may be uncomfortable with us because they feel guilty about their own dependencies. Others may be threatened by the changes we are making because they no longer have a means to control us. These kinds of people are likely to try to stop us from making any progress. Very often we need to put our codependent relationships on hold for a time, sometimes even permanently, because of their potential to ruin our recovery. This does not mean we do not reach out to unbelievers; it only means that we do not become too close to people who will lead us away from God and the recovery he desires for us. Our primary relationships need to be with unselfish, godly people who will support our life in recovery.

were wide open. I helped you on a day when salvation was being offered." Right now God is ready to welcome you. Today he is ready to save you.

Paul Patiently Endures Hardship

3We try to live in such a way that no one will ever be offended or kept back from finding the Lord by the way we act, so that no one can find fault with us and blame it on the Lord. 4In fact, in everything we do we try to show that we are true ministers of God.

We patiently endure suffering and hardship and trouble of every kind. 5We have been beaten, put in jail, faced angry mobs, worked to exhaustion, stayed awake through sleepless nights of watching, and gone without food. 6We have proved ourselves to be what we claim by our wholesome lives and by our understanding of the Gospel and by our patience. We have been kind and truly loving and filled with the Holy Spirit. 7We have been truthful, with God's power helping us in all we do. All of the godly man's arsenal—weapons of defense, and weapons of attack—have been ours.

8We stand true to the Lord whether others honor us or despise us, whether they criticize us or commend us. We are honest, but they call us liars.

9The world ignores us, but we are known to God; we live close to death, but here we are, still very much alive. We have been injured but kept from death. 10Our hearts ache, but at the same time we have the joy of the Lord. We are poor, but we give rich spiritual gifts to others. We own nothing, and yet we enjoy everything.

11Oh, my dear Corinthian friends! I have told you all my feelings; I love you with all my heart. 12Any coldness still between us is not because of any lack of love on my part but because your love is too small and does not reach out to me and draw me in. 13I am talking to you now as if you truly were my very own children. Open your hearts to us! Return our love!

The Danger of Unhealthy Relationships

14Don't be teamed with those who do not love the Lord, for what do the people of God have in common with the people of sin? How can light live with darkness? 15And what harmony can there be between Christ and the devil? How can a Christian be a partner with one who doesn't believe? 16And what union can there be between God's temple and idols? For

Self-perception

READ 2 CORINTHIANS 5:12-21

Our addictions may be so ingrained in us that we define our identity by them. We may even begin to feel that we are predisposed to behave as we do. We may grow discouraged as we are condemned for behavior that seems beyond our control. How can we escape our self-perception that views us in terms of the addictions that dominate our life?

One passage in Scripture seems to identify people by their behavior. It says, "Those who live immoral lives, who are idol worshipers, adulterers or homosexuals—will have no share in his Kingdom. Neither will thieves or greedy people, drunkards, slanderers, or robbers." This doesn't seem fair. We feel like we will never be able to escape our addictive nature. But the passage goes on, "There was a time when some of you were just like that but now your sins are washed away, and you are set apart for God; and he has accepted you because of what the Lord Jesus Christ and the Spirit of our God have done for you" (1 Corinthians 6:9-11). "When someone becomes a Christian, he becomes a brand new person inside. He is not the same anymore. A new life has begun!" (2 Corinthians 5:17).

God doesn't just erase our behaviors. When we identify ourself with Christ, he gives us a new identity. We will always remember what we were and realize that our sinful nature and our body may always be predisposed to a particular addiction. We may even still slip up at times, but we need no longer see our addiction as the definition of who we are. In Christ, we are the forgiven, cleansed, and holy child of God.
Turn to page 1303, Galatians 5.

you are God's temple, the home of the living God, and God has said of you, "I will live in them and walk among them, and I will be their God and they shall be my people." [17]That is why the Lord has said, "Leave them; separate yourselves from them; don't touch their filthy things, and I will welcome you [18]and be a Father to you, and you will be my sons and daughters."

CHAPTER 7

Paul's Joy at the Church's Repentance

Having such great promises as these, dear friends, let us turn away from everything wrong, whether of body or spirit, and purify ourselves, living in the wholesome fear of God, giving ourselves to him alone. [2]Please open your hearts to us again, for not one of you has suffered any wrong from us. Not one of you was led astray. We have cheated no one nor taken advantage of anyone. [3]I'm not saying this to scold or blame you, for, as I have said before, you are in my heart forever, and I live and die with you. [4]I have the highest confidence in you, and my pride in you is great. You have greatly encouraged me; you have made me so happy in spite of all my suffering.

[5]When we arrived in Macedonia there was no rest for us; outside, trouble was on every hand and all around us; within us, our hearts were full of dread and fear. [6]Then God who cheers those who are discouraged refreshed us by the arrival of Titus. [7]Not only was his presence a joy, but also the news that he brought of the wonderful time he had with you. When he told me how much you were looking forward to my visit, and how sorry you were about what had happened, and about your loyalty and warm love for me, well, I overflowed with joy!

[8]I am no longer sorry that I sent that letter to you, though I was very sorry for a time, realizing how painful it would be to you. But it hurt you only for a little while. [9]Now I am glad I sent it, not because it hurt you but because the pain turned you to God. It was a good kind of sorrow you felt, the kind of sorrow God wants his people to have, so that I need not come to you with harshness. [10]For God sometimes uses sorrow in our lives to help us turn away from sin and seek eternal life. We should never regret his sending it. But the sorrow of the man who is not a Christian is not the sorrow of true repentance and does not prevent eternal death.

[11]Just see how much good this grief from the Lord did for you! You no longer shrugged your shoulders but became earnest and sincere and very anxious to get rid of the sin that I wrote you about. You became frightened about what had happened and longed for me to come and help. You went right to work on the problem and cleared it up [punishing the man who sinned]. You have done everything you could to make it right.

7:5-7 For all his determined and aggressive style of ministry, Paul was definitely not a man without emotions. Here he freely admitted the fears he felt during a very difficult time. But he was greatly comforted by God (see 1:3-7) through the arrival of Titus from Corinth (see 2:12-13). Titus brought news that the Corinthian believers had changed their negative attitudes toward Paul. In our recovery, it is important that we keep a similar balance between our personal tasks and our relationships. If we get so focused on the tasks of recovery that we undervalue our relationships with others, our recovery is at risk. The most important part of recovery is our reconciliation with other people, without which long-term success is impossible.

7:11-13 When we admit our failures to God and others and do what we can to follow God's will, wonderful changes take place in our life. In these verses, we see that such repentance produces fruit on three fronts. First, it purifies and revitalizes our life and emotions in a remarkable way (7:11). Next, it renews our relationship with God (7:12). Finally, it has an amazing effect for good on our relationships with other people, both those we have wronged (7:12) and onlookers who are wonderfully encouraged by the refreshing changes that have taken place (7:13).

7:15 For all the mistakes the Corinthians made in their relationship with Paul, they did do one thing right. They were willing to listen when Titus presented Paul's version of some earlier events that they had misinterpreted. This teachability and lack of defensiveness drew great admiration and love from both Titus and Paul. A willingness to listen and be teachable is necessary for a successful recovery. It will help us to take an honest moral inventory and follow God's good plan for our life.

8:9 The perfect model for graciously helping others is Jesus Christ. He became a lowly human being and died the death of a criminal on the cross to conquer our enemies of sin and death. He gave up his heavenly glory and willingly suffered on our behalf (see Philippians 2:6-8). Thus, besides "enriching" our life spiritually, Christ can also strongly identify with the pain and temptation we have suffered (see Hebrews 4:15). He is available and able to help us in our recovery. As we receive his help, we can then reach out a helping hand to others in need.

[12]I wrote as I did so the Lord could show
how much you really do care for us. That was
my purpose even more than to help the man
who sinned or his father to whom he did the
wrong.
[13]In addition to the encouragement you
gave us by your love, we were made happier
still by Titus' joy when you gave him such a
fine welcome and set his mind at ease. [14]I told
him how it would be—told him before he left
me of my pride in you—and you didn't disappoint me. I have always told you the truth
and now my boasting to Titus has also proved
true! [15]He loves you more than ever when he
remembers the way you listened to him so
willingly and received him so anxiously and
with such deep concern. [16]How happy this
makes me, now that I am sure all is well
between us again. Once again I can have perfect confidence in you.

CHAPTER 8

A Call to Generous Giving

Now I want to tell you what God in his grace
has done for the churches in Macedonia.
[2]Though they have been going through
much trouble and hard times, they have
mixed their wonderful joy with their deep
poverty, and the result has been an overflow
of giving to others. [3]They gave not only what
they could afford but far more; and I can
testify that they did it because they wanted to
and not because of nagging on my part. [4]They
begged us to take the money so they could
share in the joy of helping the Christians in
Jerusalem. [5]Best of all, they went beyond our
highest hopes, for their first action was to
dedicate themselves to the Lord and to us, for
whatever directions God might give to them
through us. [6]They were so enthusiastic about
it that we have urged Titus, who encouraged
your giving in the first place, to visit you and
encourage you to complete your share in this
ministry of giving. [7]You people there are leaders in so many ways—you have so much faith,
so many good preachers, so much learning, so
much enthusiasm, so much love for us. Now
I want you to be leaders also in the spirit of
cheerful giving.
[8]I am not giving you an order; I am not
saying you must do it, but others are eager for
it. This is one way to prove that your love is
real, that it goes beyond mere words.
[9]You know how full of love and kindness
our Lord Jesus was: though he was so very
rich, yet to help you he became so very poor,
so that by being poor he could make you rich.

Constructive Sorrow

BIBLE READING: 2 Corinthians 7:8-11

We made a searching and fearless moral inventory of ourselves.

We all have to deal with sorrow. We may try to stuff it down and ignore it. We may try to drown it or avoid feeling it by intellectualizing. But sorrow doesn't go away. We need to accept the sorrow that will be a part of the inventory process.

Not all sorrow is bad for us. The apostle Paul had written a letter to the church in Corinth that made them very sad because Paul was confronting them about something that they were doing wrong. At first he was sorry that he had hurt them, but later he said, "Now I am glad I sent it, not because it hurt you but because the pain turned you to God. It was a good kind of sorrow you felt, the kind of sorrow God wants his people to have. . . . For God sometimes uses sorrow in our lives to help us turn away from sin and seek eternal life. We should never regret his sending it. . . . Just see how much good this grief from the Lord did for you! You no longer shrugged your shoulders but became earnest and sincere and very anxious to get rid of the sin" (2 Corinthians 7:9-11).

Jeremiah said, "Although God gives . . . grief, yet he will show compassion too, according to the greatness of his loving-kindness. For he does not enjoy afflicting men and causing sorrow" (Lamentations 3:32-33).

This grief was good—it came from honest self-evaluation, not morbid self-condemnation. We can learn to accept our sorrow as a positive part of our recovery, not as punishment. ***Turn to page 1467, Revelation 20.***

10I want to suggest that you finish what you
started to do a year ago, for you were not only
the first to propose this idea, but the first to
begin doing something about it. 11Having
started the ball rolling so enthusiastically, you
should carry this project through to completion just as gladly, giving whatever you can
out of whatever you have. Let your enthusiastic idea at the start be equalled by your realistic action now. 12If you are really eager to give,
then it isn't important how much you have to
give. God wants you to give what you have,
not what you haven't.
13Of course, I don't mean that those who
receive your gifts should have an easy time of
it at your expense, 14but you should divide
with them. Right now you have plenty and
can help them; then at some other time they
can share with you when you need it. In this
way, each will have as much as he needs. 15Do
you remember what the Scriptures say about
this? "He that gathered much had nothing
left over, and he that gathered little had
enough." So you also should share with those
in need.
16I am thankful to God that he has given
Titus the same real concern for you that I
have. 17He is glad to follow my suggestion that
he visit you again—but I think he would have
come anyway, for he is very eager to see you!
18I am sending another well-known brother
with him, who is highly praised as a preacher
of the Good News in all the churches. 19In
fact, this man was elected by the churches to
travel with me to take the gift to Jerusalem.
This will glorify the Lord and show our eagerness to help each other. 20By traveling together we will guard against any suspicion, for
we are anxious that no one should find fault
with the way we are handling this large gift.
21God knows we are honest, but I want everyone else to know it too. That is why we have
made this arrangement.
22And I am sending you still another
brother, whom we know from experience to
be an earnest Christian. He is especially interested as he looks forward to this trip because
I have told him all about your eagerness to
help.
23If anyone asks who Titus is, say that he is
my partner, my helper in helping you, and
you can also say that the other two brothers
represent the assemblies here and are splendid examples of those who belong to the
Lord.
24Please show your love for me to these men
and do for them all that I have publicly
boasted you would.

CHAPTER 9

God Prizes Cheerful Givers

I realize that I really don't even need to mention this to you, about helping God's people.
2For I know how eager you are to do it, and I
have boasted to the friends in Macedonia that
you were ready to send an offering a year ago.
In fact, it was this enthusiasm of yours that
stirred up many of them to begin helping.
3But I am sending these men just to be sure
that you really are ready, as I told them you
would be, with your money all collected; I
don't want it to turn out that this time I was
wrong in my boasting about you. 4I would be
very much ashamed—and so would you—if
some of these Macedonian people come with
me, only to find that you still aren't ready
after all I have told them!
5So I have asked these other brothers to
arrive ahead of me to see that the gift you
promised is on hand and waiting. I want it to
be a real gift and not look as if it were being
given under pressure.
6But remember this—if you give little, you

8:10-12 It is much easier to start something than to finish it. This is especially true as we work on our recovery. Thus, the principle of perseverance is a crucial one for those of us with the tendency to "run out of gas." In this case, the Corinthians had enthusiastically started a relief fund for the Jerusalem church, but then failed to follow through on their commitment. So Paul confronted them and encouraged them to persevere in this worthy task. Our recovery is no less worthy of our perseverance. We need to do more than make promises and verbal commitments to recovery; we need to follow through on them as well.

9:6-9 The more spiritual seeds we plant by generously helping others, the greater will be our harvest of spiritual fruit. God never forces us to give; he wants us to give with a willing heart. This shows that God is not only interested in what we do; he is also interested in the attitudes and motives behind our actions. Some of us may feel that we don't have much to offer people in need. Our life may be destroyed; we may have gone into debt to support a destructive habit. But even if we have nothing else to give, we can share our life with them. We can share the story of how God gave us a second chance. As little as this may seem to us, it may be the gift of life to someone in the throes of an addiction.

will get little. A farmer who plants just a few seeds will get only a small crop, but if he plants much, he will reap much. 7Everyone must make up his own mind as to how much he should give. Don't force anyone to give more than he really wants to, for cheerful givers are the ones God prizes. 8God is able to make it up to you by giving you everything you need and more so that there will not only be enough for your own needs but plenty left over to give joyfully to others. 9It is as the Scriptures say: "The godly man gives generously to the poor. His good deeds will be an honor to him forever."

10For God, who gives seed to the farmer to plant, and later on good crops to harvest and eat, will give you more and more seed to plant and will make it grow so that you can give away more and more fruit from your harvest.

11Yes, God will give you much so that you can give away much, and when we take your gifts to those who need them they will break out into thanksgiving and praise to God for your help. 12So two good things happen as a result of your gifts—those in need are helped, and they overflow with thanks to God. 13Those you help will be glad not only because of your generous gifts to themselves and to others, but they will praise God for this proof that your deeds are as good as your doctrine. 14And they will pray for you with deep fervor and feeling because of the wonderful grace of God shown through you.

15Thank God for his Son—his Gift too wonderful for words.

CHAPTER 10

Paul Defends His Authority

I plead with you—yes, I, Paul—and I plead gently, as Christ himself would do. Yet some of you are saying, "Paul's letters are bold enough when he is far away, but when he gets here he will be afraid to raise his voice!"

2I hope I won't need to show you when I come how harsh and rough I can be. I don't want to carry out my present plans against some of you who seem to think my deeds and words are merely those of an ordinary man. 3It is true that I am an ordinary, weak human being, but I don't use human plans and methods to win my battles. 4I use God's mighty weapons, not those made by men, to knock down the devil's strongholds. 5These weapons can break down every proud argument against God and every wall that can be built to keep men from finding him. With these weapons I can capture rebels and bring them back to God and change them into men whose hearts' desire is obedience to Christ. 6I will use these weapons against every rebel who remains after I have first used them on you yourselves and you surrender to Christ.

7The trouble with you is that you look at me and I seem weak and powerless, but you don't look beneath the surface. Yet if anyone can claim the power and authority of Christ, I certainly can. 8I may seem to be boasting more than I should about my authority over you—authority to help you, not to hurt you—but I shall make good every claim. 9I say this so that you will not think I am just blustering when I scold you in my letters.

10"Don't bother about his letters," some say. "He sounds big, but it's all noise. When he gets here you will see that there is nothing great about him, and you have never heard a worse preacher!" 11This time my personal presence is going to be just as rough on you as my letters are!

12Oh, don't worry, I wouldn't dare say that I am as wonderful as these other men who tell you how good they are! Their trouble is that they are only comparing themselves with each other and measuring themselves against their own little ideas. What stupidity!

13But we will not boast of authority we do not have. Our goal is to measure up to God's plan for us, and this plan includes our working there with you. 14We are not going too far when we claim authority over you, for we were the first to come to you with the Good News concerning Christ. 15It is not as though we were trying to claim credit for the work someone else has done among you. Instead, we hope that your faith will grow and that,

10:13-15 From a recovery perspective, it is illuminating to note that Paul had set limits on his ministry based on his understanding of God's will for him. Our recovery activities also need to be in line with God's plan. We must concentrate our limited energy on focused priorities that reflect God's will. Paul was sensitive to God's will for his life, and he was confident that his leadership over the Corinthian church was a part of that plan. We can be sure that recovery is part of God's plan for us. We still need to discover, however, what activities he might want us to be involved in on a daily basis. Insight concerning God's will for us is likely to come through our study of the Scriptures, the help of godly friends, or the counsel we receive from the Holy Spirit.

still within the limits set for us, our work among you will be greatly enlarged.

[16]After that, we will be able to preach the Good News to other cities that are far beyond you, where no one else is working; then there will be no question about being in someone else's field. [17]As the Scriptures say, "If anyone is going to boast, let him boast about what the Lord has done and not about himself." [18]When someone boasts about himself and how well he has done, it doesn't count for much. But when the Lord commends him, that's different!

CHAPTER 11

Paul and the False Teachers

I hope you will be patient with me as I keep on talking like a fool. Do bear with me and let me say what is on my heart. [2]I am anxious for you with the deep concern of God himself—anxious that your love should be for Christ alone, just as a pure maiden saves her love for one man only, for the one who will be her husband. [3]But I am frightened, fearing that in some way you will be led away from your pure and simple devotion to our Lord, just as Eve was deceived by Satan in the Garden of Eden. [4]You seem so gullible: you believe whatever anyone tells you even if he is preaching about another Jesus than the one we preach, or a different spirit than the Holy Spirit you received, or shows you a different way to be saved. You swallow it all.

[5]Yet I don't feel that these marvelous "messengers from God," as they call themselves, are any better than I am. [6]If I am a poor speaker, at least I know what I am talking about, as I think you realize by now, for we have proved it again and again.

[7]Did I do wrong and cheapen myself and make you look down on me because I preached God's Good News to you without charging you anything? [8,9]Instead I "robbed" other churches by taking what they sent me and using it up while I was with you so that I could serve you without cost. And when that was gone and I was getting hungry, I still didn't ask you for anything, for the Christians from Macedonia brought me another gift. I have never yet asked you for one cent, and I never will. [10]I promise this with every ounce of truth I possess—that I will tell everyone in Greece about it! [11]Why? Because I don't love you? God knows I do. [12]But I will do it to cut out the ground from under the feet of those who boast that they are doing God's work in just the same way we are.

[13]God never sent those men at all; they are "phonies" who have fooled you into thinking they are Christ's apostles. [14]Yet I am not surprised! Satan can change himself into an angel of light, [15]so it is no wonder his servants can do it too, and seem like godly ministers. In the end they will get every bit of punishment their wicked deeds deserve.

Paul's Many Trials

[16]Again I plead, don't think that I have lost my wits to talk like this; but even if you do, listen to me anyway—a witless man, a fool—while I also boast a little as they do. [17]Such bragging isn't something the Lord commanded me to do, for I am acting like a brainless fool. [18]Yet those other men keep telling you how wonderful they are, so here I go: [19,20](You think you are so wise—yet you listen gladly to those fools; you don't mind at all when they make you their slaves and take everything you

11:2-3 Paul was worried that the Corinthian believers would replace their faith in Jesus with a false faith, and he was concerned for good reason. Corinth was a cosmopolitan city, and numerous religions and cults were practiced there. Paul also was concerned because rejecting Christ would lead to painful consequences. It would be as if the believers had rejected the abundant life offered by Jesus Christ for a life of ultimate disaster. We also live in a world of multiple religions, and programs for recovery can be found that represent most of them. But our recovery is only possible through the work of Jesus Christ and the power offered by the Holy Spirit. Leaving the hope offered in Christ is a rejection of the only real power available for recovery. Looking to any other power will lead to disappointment and failure.

11:13-15 The Corinthian believers had apparently rejected Paul's teachings to follow a number of false teachers who had twisted the Christian message. These false leaders were probably Judaizers who taught that salvation came through a combination of faith in Christ and adherence to the Jewish law (see 11:22). Paul made it clear in all of his letters that salvation is a free gift, paid for by the sacrificial work of Jesus Christ. Sometimes we are tempted to follow the same heresy. We want to earn our recovery by working hard. Most of us who have tried this approach, however, have had to admit that we are powerless over our dependencies. We discovered that we couldn't do it by just trying harder. We needed God's help. This is what Paul preached. Without God, we are helpless against the power of sin in our life. But with his help, no problem is too great to overcome.

have, and take advantage of you, and put on
airs, and slap you in the face. 21I'm ashamed
to say that I'm not strong and daring like that!
But whatever they can boast about—I'm
talking like a fool again—I can boast about it,
too.)

22They brag that they are Hebrews, do they?
Well, so am I. And they say that they are
Israelites, God's chosen people? So am I. And
they are descendants of Abraham? Well, I am
too.

23They say they serve Christ? But I have
served him far more! (Have I gone mad to
boast like this?) I have worked harder, been
put in jail more often, been whipped times
without number, and faced death again and
again and again. 24Five different times the
Jews gave me their terrible thirty-nine lashes.
25Three times I was beaten with rods. Once I
was stoned. Three times I was shipwrecked.
Once I was in the open sea all night and the
whole next day. 26I have traveled many weary
miles and have been often in great danger
from flooded rivers and from robbers and
from my own people, the Jews, as well as from
the hands of the Gentiles. I have faced grave
dangers from mobs in the cities and from
death in the deserts and in the stormy seas
and from men who claim to be brothers in
Christ but are not. 27I have lived with weariness and pain and sleepless nights. Often I
have been hungry and thirsty and have gone
without food; often I have shivered with cold,
without enough clothing to keep me warm.

28Then, besides all this, I have the constant
worry of how the churches are getting along:
29Who makes a mistake and I do not feel his
sadness? Who falls without my longing to
help him? Who is spiritually hurt without my
fury rising against the one who hurt him?

30But if I must brag, I would rather brag
about the things that show how weak I am.
31God, the Father of our Lord Jesus Christ,
who is to be praised forever and ever, knows I
tell the truth. 32For instance, in Damascus the
governor under King Aretas kept guards at the
city gates to catch me; 33but I was let down by
rope and basket from a hole in the city wall,
and so I got away! [What popularity!]

CHAPTER 12

Paul's Vision and His Weakness

This boasting is all so foolish, but let me go
on. Let me tell about the visions I've had, and
revelations from the Lord.

2,3Fourteen years ago I was taken up to
heaven for a visit. Don't ask me whether my
body was there or just my spirit, for I don't
know; only God can answer that. But anyway,
there I was in paradise, 4and heard things so
astounding that they are beyond a man's
power to describe or put in words (and anyway I am not allowed to tell them to others).
5That experience is something worth bragging about, but I am not going to do it. I am
going to boast only about how weak I am and
how great God is to use such weakness for his
glory. 6I have plenty to boast about and would
be no fool in doing it, but I don't want anyone
to think more highly of me than he should
from what he can actually see in my life and
my message.

7I will say this: because these experiences I
had were so tremendous, God was afraid I
might be puffed up by them; so I was given a
physical condition which has been a thorn in
my flesh, a messenger from Satan to hurt and
bother me and prick my pride. 8Three different times I begged God to make me well
again.

9Each time he said, "No. But I am with you;
that is all you need. My power shows up best
in weak people." Now I am glad to boast
about how weak I am; I am glad to be a living
demonstration of Christ's power, instead of
showing off my own power and abilities.

11:23-29 Paul demonstrated his commitment to Jesus Christ by listing a number of the tremendous hardships he had suffered. If nothing else, such ongoing mistreatment, deprivation, and ministry responsibility revealed his perseverance. Paul was definitely no fair-weather minister or friend. If we display the kind of commitment to our recovery that Paul had for his ministry, we will receive the same kind of powerful help in our recovery that Paul experienced in his service of Christ.

11:30; 12:1-10 Paul's "bragging" was not intended to make him look better than he really was. He spoke this way to establish the truth about his person and apostolic authority. Even though the apostle told of his incredible visit to heaven (12:1-4), he quickly balanced the scales by admitting his own weaknesses (11:30; 12:5). He also recounted how he sensed God's grace at work even through his chronic physical suffering and spiritual warfare (12:9-10). Paul made an honest assessment of his life, recognizing both his strengths and weaknesses. Then he accepted and received the powerful help that God offers to all who look to him. Paul is a good model for us to follow. As we make an honest assessment of our life and learn to depend upon God's infinite resources, we will make significant progress in our recovery.

10Since I know it is all for Christ's good, I am
quite happy about "the thorn," and about
insults and hardships, persecutions and difficulties; for when I am weak, then I am
strong—the less I have, the more I depend on
him.

Paul's Concern for the Corinthians

11You have made me act like a fool—boasting
like this—for you people ought to be writing
about me and not making me write about
myself. There isn't a single thing these other
marvelous fellows have that I don't have too,
even though I am really worth nothing at all.
12When I was there I certainly gave you every
proof that I was truly an apostle, sent to you
by God himself, for I patiently did many
wonders and signs and mighty works among
you. 13The only thing I didn't do for you,
which I do everywhere else in all other
churches, was to become a burden to you—I
didn't ask you to give me food to eat and a
place to stay. Please forgive me for this wrong!
14Now I am coming to you again, the third
time; and it is still not going to cost you
anything, for I don't want your money. I want
you! And anyway, you are my children, and
little children don't pay for their father's and
mother's food—it's the other way around;
parents supply food for their children. 15I am
glad to give you myself and all I have for your
spiritual good, even though it seems that the
more I love you, the less you love me.
16Some of you are saying, "It's true that his
visits didn't seem to cost us anything, but he
is a sneaky fellow, that Paul, and he fooled us.
As sure as anything he must have made
money from us some way."
17But how? Did any of the men I sent to you
take advantage of you? 18When I urged Titus
to visit you and sent our other brother with
him, did they make any profit? No, of course
not. For we have the same Holy Spirit and
walk in each other's steps, doing things the
same way.
19I suppose you think I am saying all this to
get back into your good graces. That isn't it at
all. I tell you, with God listening as I say it,
that I have said this to help *you,* dear friends—
to build you up spiritually—and not to help
myself. 20For I am afraid that when I come to
visit you I won't like what I find, and then you
won't like the way I will have to act. I am
afraid that I will find you quarreling, and
envying each other, and being angry with
each other, and acting big, and saying wicked
things about each other and whispering behind each other's backs, filled with conceit
and disunity. 21Yes, I am afraid that when I
come God will humble me before you and I
will be sad and mourn because many of you
who have sinned before and don't even care
about the wicked, impure things you have

12:19-21 Everything that Paul said to the Corinthians, both negative and positive, was intended for their good. Paul was concerned that they mature in their faith, and he did what he could to encourage their spiritual growth. The demands he made on the Corinthians were motivated by his love and concern for them. Many of us have come to realize that we often communicate with others for selfish reasons. When we compliment people, we are looking for something in return rather than trying to build them up. When we criticize others, we are seeking to destroy rather than correct. As we take our moral inventory, we need to be aware of our tendency to use others for our own ends. As we seek to restore our damaged relationships, the apostle Paul is an excellent model to follow.

13:2-3 Paul had warned the Corinthians at an earlier time that discipline would be forthcoming if they did not face their personal and interpersonal sins. Here he gave them an additional warning because he had been away from Corinth for longer than he had intended. He wanted to make sure that the people knew his warning was not hollow. Paul would indeed follow through forcefully and hold the Corinthian believers accountable to their commitments to God. We all need someone like Paul in our life: a godly person who can hold us accountable to our recovery commitments and our intention to follow God's will.

13:5-6 Paul urged the Corinthian believers to engage in serious self-examination. He wanted them to assess the nature of their commitment to God by looking closely at their own lives. This is an essential part of the recovery process. We need to engage in honest self-examination if we hope to uncover the problems that tear down our relationships and drive our dependencies. And as we admit our failures to God, he will forgive us and help us make progress in recovery.

13:11 As Paul closed this letter to the Corinthians, he left them with some worthy applications and goals to pursue. In essence, he admonished the people to open their minds and hearts to personal change and the healing of their relationships. Such spiritual growth and interpersonal harmony can be fueled by faith in God, the ultimate source of healing love and peace. As modern readers of this letter, we, too, can benefit by acting on Paul's wise advice.

done: your lust and immorality, and the taking of other men's wives.

CHAPTER 13

Paul's Final Advice

This is the third time I am coming to visit you. The Scriptures tell us that if two or three have seen a wrong, it must be punished. [Well, this is my third warning as I come now for this visit.] [2]I have already warned those who had been sinning when I was there last; now I warn them again and all others, just as I did then, that this time I come ready to punish severely and I will not spare them.

[3]I will give you all the proof you want that Christ speaks through me. Christ is not weak in his dealings with you but is a mighty power within you. [4]His weak, human body died on the cross, but now he lives by the mighty power of God. We, too, are weak in our bodies, as he was, but now we live and are strong, as he is, and have all of God's power to use in dealing with you.

[5]Check up on yourselves. Are you really Christians? Do you pass the test? Do you feel Christ's presence and power more and more within you? Or are you just pretending to be Christians when actually you aren't at all? [6]I hope you can agree that I have stood that test and truly belong to the Lord.

[7]I pray that you will live good lives, not because that will be a feather in our caps, proving that what we teach is right; no, for we want you to do right even if we ourselves are despised. [8]Our responsibility is to encourage the right at all times, not to hope for evil. [9]We are glad to be weak and despised if you are really strong. Our greatest wish and prayer is that you will become mature Christians.

[10]I am writing this to you now in the hope that I won't need to scold and punish when I come; for I want to use the Lord's authority that he has given me, not to punish you but to make you strong.

[11]I close my letter with these last words: Be happy. Grow in Christ. Pay attention to what I have said. Live in harmony and peace. And may the God of love and peace be with you.

[12]Greet each other warmly in the Lord. [13]All the Christians here send you their best regards. [14]May the grace of our Lord Jesus Christ be with you all. May God's love and the Holy Spirit's friendship be yours.

Paul

REFLECTIONS ON

insights ABOUT PRAYER

It is essential that we learn to encourage others in recovery without giving up the balance in our own life. That is exactly what Paul was asking the Corinthians to do in **2 Corinthians 1:11** when he requested their prayers. By interceding in prayer for the needs of the apostle and his companions, the Corinthian believers would be helping and strengthening them from a distance. Because of our own weaknesses, we sometimes are unable to help some of the people we care about. To maintain our own recovery, we have to keep our distance. But this does not mean that we need to forget about them. We can help them by praying that they will discover how helpless they are without God and that they will turn to him for help. God has the power to do for them what we may not be able to do through direct contact.

insights ABOUT RESTORING RELATIONSHIPS

A problem in the Corinthian church (probably the one described in 1 Corinthians 5:1-11) was the basis for Paul's rebuke in **2 Corinthians 2:5-11.** When the troublemaker in question repented of his sin and honestly faced the consequences of his behavior, the Corinthian believers refused to forgive him. Paul pointed out how cruel it was to withhold forgiveness. The apostle explained that through their lack of forgiveness they were actually playing right into Satan's hands by discouraging the repentant party. We need to make sure that when others repent of their failures, we do our part to encourage the process of restoration and healing. Most of us have experienced the pain of being rejected, even after admitting our mistakes and trying to change. We should be the last to cause the same kind of pain to someone else.

insights FOR SURVIVAL DURING TOUGH TIMES

In **2 Corinthians 4:8-11** Paul reflects on the value of suffering. The hard times in life tend to either crush and disillusion or challenge and stimulate us. It is hard for us to keep going when the going gets tough. But it can be a real encouragement to know that God is with us in the midst of the trials we face, and that he can use even our weaknesses for his glory. In fact, our need for recovery from an addiction may be the gift of life to other people in bondage to a powerful dependency. As they see God's work in our life, they may gain the courage to face and conquer their own addictions with God's powerful help.

In **2 Corinthians 5:1-5** Paul reminded his readers that their weak bodies will someday be replaced by glorious new ones. To many of us, the aging process is a depressing reality, one we'd like to avoid. The fact that we pay great sums of money for cosmetic surgery, hair coloring, and the like is evidence of that. But there is a comforting side to aging if we trust Jesus Christ for our salvation and recovery. Before long, we will "check in" our present physical body and receive a glorified eternal body. The Holy Spirit's presence in our life is the guarantee that we are drawing ever closer to that point.

insights ABOUT SHARING THE GOOD NEWS

We find in **2 Corinthians 6:3-4** that Paul sought to live in such a way that no one would be offended or kept away from God on his account. He was a model for other believers to look up to and follow. Some of us who have been in recovery for a while may have grown tired of playing this role. We have found it exhausting to be a model for the recovery of others. We feel the burden of numerous expectations. As a result, some of us may have quit trying to help others in recovery. As we grow spiritually, the responsibility to help others will always be there. The apostle Paul took this responsibility very seriously and acted out of concern for the well-being of others. Though this may be a difficult burden for some of us, it may help us to realize that being a model for others in recovery is one of the ways that God keeps us on the road toward wholeness.

insights ABOUT CONFRONTATION

Paul had apparently written a short letter between 1 and 2 Corinthians that was not included among the New Testament books. From his mention of the letter in **2 Corinthians 7:8-10**, it must have been quite sharp in tone. He admits that he had mixed feelings about sending that letter. But because of the Corinthians' positive response to his tough love, all his regrets had vanished. In recovery situations, we must realize that when we confront others, we are taking a calculated risk that might lead to either healing or alienation. When we do confront people about their problems, we must do so with humility and love, and entrust the situation to God. If we do this, God will work things out according to his perfect will.

GALATIANS

THE BIG PICTURE

A. GREETINGS (1:1-5)
B. THE PEOPLE'S REJECTION OF GOD'S GRACE (1:6-10)
C. PAUL'S DEFENSE OF THE GOSPEL OF GRACE (1:11–6:10)
1. Confirmed by the Apostles (1:11–2:21)
2. Confirmed by the People's Membership in God's Family (3:1–4:31)
3. Confirmed by the People's Deliverance from Sin's Power (5:1–6:10)
D. CONCLUSION (6:11-18)

Paul planted the churches in Galatia during his first missionary journey in Asia Minor. But within months of Paul's ministry there, certain people began to contradict the Good News Paul had preached. These teachers claimed that non-Jewish converts to Christ had to keep the Jewish law in order to be saved. This meant that all Gentiles who sought membership in the church would have to be circumcised.

This alternative gospel was very enticing to the Galatian believers. For one thing, its proponents claimed to have the direct blessing of the apostles back in Jerusalem. Their arguments from the Old Testament seemed to be flawless and irrefutable. But because Paul knew how destructive this teaching could be, he wrote this letter to correct them.

Paul made it clear to the Galatians that in Christ, they were truly free. They were free from the demands of the Jewish law, free from the power of sin, and free to live under God's grace. We may wonder why the Galatians would ever want to give up the freedom they had in Christ. But bondage is subtle. No one ever starts drinking with a determination to become an alcoholic. We slowly become dependent on certain behaviors, substances, and attitudes. And, in a pathetic sort of way, our bondage gives us security.

This letter to the Galatian believers challenges us to hold on to our freedom. Being controlled by alcohol or drugs means living a life of slavery. So does being involved in any recovery program that is based on our ability and strength. We cannot escape the grip of addiction and sin alone, but as we turn our life over to God, he will graciously give us the power we need to overcome our dependencies.

THE BOTTOM LINE

PURPOSE: To encourage readers to depend on Christ alone for salvation and daily strength. AUTHOR: The apostle Paul. AUDIENCE: Several churches in southern Galatia. DATE WRITTEN: Probably around A.D. 49. SETTING: The most pressing controversy in the early church was whether new non-Jewish converts needed to accept Jewish laws to be a part of the church. Paul wrote this letter to answer that question. KEY VERSE: "So Christ has made us free. Now make sure that you stay free, and don't get all tied up again in the chains of slavery" (5:1). KEY PEOPLE AND RELATIONSHIPS: Paul with the Galatian believers and with the Jerusalem apostles, as well as the false teachers.

RECOVERY THEMES

The Seduction of the Law: For some of us, following a set of rules may seem easier than working on a personal inventory, praying, meditating on Scripture, or engaging in some other activity that leads to a deeper relationship with God. We would rather have someone tell us what to do. Perhaps the Galatians felt the same way. They may have said, "Just give us some rules to follow, like the Mosaic law." Following a set of rules for recovery is never the way to success. Not only is it impossible for us to do, but it also leads us away from our dependence on God, the only real means we have for success.

Recovery Leads to True Freedom: This letter was written to show us how to find true spiritual freedom. Paul's advice to the Galatians is also for us as we search for freedom from our addictions, dysfunctional families, compulsive behaviors, or codependent relationships. True freedom is found as we turn our life over to God, depending not on our own self-sufficiency, but on his powerful and firm intervention. Having faith in Christ is the only way we can have true freedom from sin and its consequences, and from bondage to our defects of character.

The Power of the Holy Spirit: We become believers through the work of the Holy Spirit, the personal expression of the power of God. We also are empowered in our recovery by the Holy Spirit. He brings new life to us; even the faith to believe and the courage to admit our own powerlessness are gifts from him. The Holy Spirit instructs, guides, leads, and gives us power. It is he who ends our bondage to evil desires and addictive patterns, and who creates in us love, joy, peace, and serenity.

The Necessity of Faith: Many of us have been frustrated, even discouraged to the point of giving up, by our failed efforts to change. Recovery from sin and its destructive effects, including our dependencies, is only possible through trust in Jesus Christ. Turning our will and our life over to God does not miraculously and instantly transform us (though some changes may happen right away). But by placing our trust and confidence in Jesus Christ, we do experience forgiveness and unconditional acceptance from God. Then his power begins to work within us to inspire our continued growth and recovery.

CHAPTER 1

Greetings from Paul

From: Paul the missionary and all the other
Christians here.
To: The churches of Galatia.
I was not called to be a missionary by any
group or agency. My call is from Jesus Christ
himself and from God the Father who raised
him from the dead. 3May peace and blessing
be yours from God the Father and from the
Lord Jesus Christ. 4He died for our sins just
as God our Father planned, and rescued us
from this evil world in which we live. 5All
glory to God through all the ages of eternity. Amen.

There Is Only One Gospel

6I am amazed that you are turning away so
soon from God who, in his love and mercy,
invited you to share the eternal life he gives
through Christ; you are already following a
different "way to heaven," which really
doesn't go to heaven at all. 7For there is no
other way than the one we showed you; you
are being fooled by those who twist and
change the truth concerning Christ.
8Let God's curses fall on anyone, including
myself, who preaches any other way to be
saved than the one we told you about; yes, if
an angel comes from heaven and preaches
any other message, let him be forever cursed.

1:1-5 In this letter, Paul gave much more than the normal brief, customary greeting. He introduced the main themes of his letter: his God-given apostolic authority, and clear teachings about the fatherhood of God and the delivering power of Jesus Christ. The good news to us is that God, the supreme higher Power, is to be regarded as a loving Father. When we turn our life over to him, he is able through his Son, Jesus, to help us overcome our problems and shortcomings.

1:7-10 The Galatians obviously faced a choice between what they thought were two gospels. However, Paul quickly pointed out that their choice was really between the true gospel he preached and the false gospel preached by his opponents. The choice we face as we look for a way to deal with our past sins and failures is just as clear. We can listen to those who offer us amazing and easy recovery fads. Or we can fall prey to a legalistic system where we are manipulated through our guilt to try to effect our own recovery by adhering to a set of standards or rules. Or we can accept what God says about the power of sin and God's ability to set us free if we keep our eyes on him. Only God in Jesus Christ can offer us the power we need for recovery. No other solution to our problems and dependencies will ever lead to real or permanent change.

[9]I will say it again: if anyone preaches any other gospel than the one you welcomed, let God's curse fall upon him.

[10]You can see that I am not trying to please you by sweet talk and flattery; no, I am trying to please God. If I were still trying to please men I could not be Christ's servant.

Paul's Message Comes from God

[11]Dear friends, I solemnly swear that the way to heaven that I preach is not based on some mere human whim or dream. [12]For my message comes from no less a person than Jesus Christ himself, who told me what to say. No one else has taught me.

[13]You know what I was like when I followed the Jewish religion—how I went after the Christians mercilessly, hunting them down and doing my best to get rid of them all. [14]I was one of the most religious Jews of my own age in the whole country and tried as hard as I possibly could to follow all the old, traditional rules of my religion.

[15]But then something happened! For even before I was born, God had chosen me to be his and called me—what kindness and grace—[16]to reveal his Son within me so that I could go to the Gentiles and show them the Good News about Jesus.

When all this happened to me I didn't go at once and talk it over with anyone else; [17]I didn't go up to Jerusalem to consult with those who were apostles before I was. No, I went away into the deserts of Arabia and then came back to the city of Damascus.[18]It was not until three years later that I finally went to Jerusalem for a visit with Peter and stayed there with him for fifteen days. [19]And the only other apostle I met at that time was James, our Lord's brother. [20](Listen to what I am saying, for I am telling you this in the very presence of God. This is exactly what happened—I am not lying to you.) [21]Then after this visit I went to Syria and Cilicia. [22]And still the Christians in Judea didn't even know what I looked like. [23]All they knew was what people were saying, that "our former enemy is now preaching the very faith he tried to wreck." [24]And they gave glory to God because of me.

CHAPTER 2

The Apostles Accepted Paul

Then fourteen years later I went back to Jerusalem again, this time with Barnabas; and Titus came along too. [2]I went there with definite orders from God to confer with the brothers there about the message I was preaching to the Gentiles. I talked privately to the leaders of the church so that they would all understand just what I had been teaching and, I hoped, agree that it was right. [3]And they did agree; they did not even demand that Titus, my companion, should be circumcised, though he was a Gentile.

[4]Even that question wouldn't have come up except for some so-called "Christians" there—false ones, really—who came to spy on us and see what freedom we enjoyed in Christ Jesus, as to whether we obeyed the Jewish laws or not. They tried to get us all tied up in their rules, like slaves in chains. [5]But we did not listen to them for a single moment, for we did not want to confuse you into thinking that salvation can be earned by being circumcised and by obeying Jewish laws.

[6]And the great leaders of the church who were there had nothing to add to what I was preaching. (By the way, their being great lead-

1:11-24 As Paul looked back on his conversion experience, he recalled how he had once been an extremely religious Jew. He had actively worked to defend his faith against the threat of Christianity. But then, by grace, God in Jesus Christ reached out and radically transformed him. Paul came to recognize that all his religious activities were ultimately fruitless; through them, he could never be delivered from the power of sin in his life. Only God could forgive his past failings and give him the power to start over again. If we have tried to overcome our dependencies through behavior modification or religious activity, we already know what it means to fail. But if we have entrusted our life to God's hands and learned to live by his power, we know the secret of victory. God's power through Jesus Christ is the only means to a lasting recovery.

2:1-10 In this letter, Paul wanted to present a clear argument against the teachings of the Judaizers. These people recognized that God's work through Jesus Christ was important, but they also believed that people were required to follow the Jewish laws to obtain salvation. For them, salvation was based on actions, not solely on God's gracious gift. Paul wanted the Galatians to realize that none of us are able to follow God's laws adequately on our own. He taught that Christ alone has the power to release us from sin and its destructive consequences. Most of us have already discovered how powerless we are against sin. We know that we need a higher Power to help us overcome our addictions and compulsions. Paul's message of grace is a source of hope for us as we look to God to help us overcome our dependencies.

ers made no difference to me, for all are the
same to God.) 7-9In fact, when Peter, James,
and John, who were known as the pillars of
the church, saw how greatly God had used me
in winning the Gentiles, just as Peter had
been blessed so greatly in his preaching to the
Jews—for the same God gave us each our
special gifts—they shook hands with Barnabas and me and encouraged us to keep right
on with our preaching to the Gentiles while
they continued their work with the Jews.
10The only thing they did suggest was that we
must always remember to help the poor, and
I, too, was eager for that.

Paul Confronts Peter

11But when Peter came to Antioch I had to
oppose him publicly, speaking strongly
against what he was doing, for it was very
wrong. 12For when he first arrived, he ate with
the Gentile Christians [who don't bother with
circumcision and the many other Jewish
laws]. But afterwards, when some Jewish
friends of James came, he wouldn't eat with
the Gentiles anymore because he was afraid of
what these Jewish legalists, who insisted that
circumcision was necessary for salvation,
would say; 13and then all the other Jewish
Christians and even Barnabas became hypocrites too, following Peter's example, though
they certainly knew better. 14When I saw what
was happening and that they weren't being
honest about what they really believed and
weren't following the truth of the Gospel, I
said to Peter in front of all the others,
"Though you are a Jew by birth, you have
long since discarded the Jewish laws; so why,
all of a sudden, are you trying to make these
Gentiles obey them? 15You and I are Jews by
birth, not mere Gentile sinners, 16and yet we
Jewish Christians know very well that we cannot become right with God by obeying our
Jewish laws but only by faith in Jesus Christ
to take away our sins. And so we, too, have
trusted Jesus Christ, that we might be accepted by God because of faith—and not because we have obeyed the Jewish laws. For no
one will ever be saved by obeying them."

17But what if we trust Christ to save us and
then find that we are wrong and that we
cannot be saved without being circumcised
and obeying all the other Jewish laws?
Wouldn't we need to say that faith in Christ
had ruined us? God forbid that anyone
should dare to think such things about our
Lord. 18Rather, we are sinners if we start rebuilding the old systems I have been destroying of trying to be saved by keeping Jewish
laws, 19for it was through reading the Scripture that I came to realize that I could never
find God's favor by trying—and failing—to
obey the laws. I came to realize that acceptance with God comes by believing in Christ.

20I have been crucified with Christ: and I

2:11-14 The apostle Peter, a Jewish Christian, recognized that salvation is a free gift of grace. So, while in Antioch, he freely associated with the Gentile Christians there, despite the fact that they had not fulfilled the Jewish law of circumcision. When other Jewish Christian leaders arrived there, however, Peter pulled back in his relationships with the Gentile believers. He was influenced by his Jewish peers and began to act as if obeying the Jewish laws was necessary for salvation. Paul confronted Peter about his prejudice, and the problem was resolved. Some of us know how Peter felt when his Jewish friends arrived. As we became involved in recovery, we were probably embarrassed when our old friends came around. We may have succumbed to the pressure to turn from our commitment to the truth about our need for recovery. Like Peter, we can humbly assess our failure and get back on the right track.

2:20-21 In this verse, Paul was showing that our old life-style has died on the cross with Jesus Christ. For the Jewish Christians, this meant that they had to give up their old life of trying to earn salvation by following the Jewish law. Many of us have struggled with this very problem. Some of us have worked very hard to overcome our addictions but have achieved no real freedom. Paul wanted the Jewish believers to realize that they could gain nothing by trying harder. They had to give up control and allow God to heal them and empower their recovery from sin. We also need to give up our old way of looking for deliverance and accept God's program for recovery—the free gift of forgiveness and healing offered by Jesus Christ.

3:1-14 Paul appealed to the physical evidence the Galatians had experienced when they, upon believing in Christ, received the Holy Spirit. We become true sons of Abraham, as spoken of here in the Bible, when we receive the redemption available to us through the sacrifice of Jesus Christ. The evidence of becoming Abraham's sons and daughters is not circumcision, but the presence of the Holy Spirit in our life (3:14). We can be sure of the Holy spirit's presence when we begin to see changes in our life. Knowing God and being in a right relationship with him enables us to know his will and to follow it. But trying to follow God's laws in our human strength will never bring us into a right relationship with God.

myself no longer live, but Christ lives in me. And the real life I now have within this body is a result of my trusting in the Son of God, who loved me and gave himself for me.
21 I am not one of those who treats Christ's death as meaningless. For if we could be saved by keeping Jewish laws, then there was no need for Christ to die.

CHAPTER 3

The Jewish Law and Faith in Christ

Oh, foolish Galatians! What magician has hypnotized you and cast an evil spell upon you? For you used to see the meaning of Jesus Christ's death as clearly as though I had waved a placard before you with a picture on it of Christ dying on the cross.
2 Let me ask you this one question: Did you receive the Holy Spirit by trying to keep the Jewish laws? Of course not, for the Holy Spirit came upon you only after you heard about Christ and trusted him to save you.
3 Then have you gone completely crazy? For if trying to obey the Jewish laws never gave you spiritual life in the first place, why do you think that trying to obey them now will make you stronger Christians?
4 You have suffered so much for the Gospel. Now are you going to just throw it all overboard? I can hardly believe it!

5 I ask you again, does God give you the power of the Holy Spirit and work miracles among you as a result of your trying to obey the Jewish laws? No, of course not. It is when you believe in Christ and fully trust him.

6 Abraham had the same experience—God declared him fit for heaven only because he believed God's promises.
7 You can see from this that the real children of Abraham are all the men of faith who truly trust in God.

8,9 What's more, the Scriptures looked forward to this time when God would save the Gentiles also, through their faith. God told Abraham about this long ago when he said, "I will bless those in every nation who trust in me as you do." And so it is: all who trust in Christ share the same blessing Abraham received.

10 Yes, and those who depend on the Jewish laws to save them are under God's curse, for the Scriptures point out very clearly, "Cursed is everyone who at any time breaks a single one of these laws that are written in God's Book of the Law."
11 Consequently, it is clear that no one can ever win God's favor by trying to keep the Jewish laws because God has said that the only way we can be right in his sight is by faith. As the prophet Habakkuk

Self-control

READ GALATIANS 5:16-23

There's a struggle going on inside of us—a fight for control. Our willpower fails us repeatedly. Where can we turn when we realize that we can't get control of our life?

The apostle Paul says, "I advise you to obey only the Holy Spirit's instructions. He will tell you where to go and what to do, and then you won't always be doing the wrong things your evil nature wants you to. For we naturally love to do evil things that are just the opposite from the things that the Holy Spirit tells us to do; and the good things we want to do when the Spirit has his way with us are just the opposite of our natural desires. These two forces within us are constantly fighting each other to win control over us, and our wishes are never free from their pressures. . . . But when the Holy Spirit controls our lives he will produce this kind of fruit in us: love, joy, peace, patience, kindness, goodness, faithfulness, gentleness and self-control" (Galatians 5:16-17, 22-23).

Self-control is not willpower. It is not something we get by gritting our teeth and forcing ourself to "just say no." Self-control is called a fruit. Fruit doesn't instantly pop out on the tree. As the tree grows and seasons pass, the fruit naturally develops. As we continue to follow God's guidance, taking one step at a time, our self-control will naturally grow. Our job is to stay connected to God. It is the Holy Spirit's job to produce the fruit of self-control in our life.
Turn to page 1313, Ephesians 2.

says it, "The man who finds life will find it through trusting God." [12]How different from this way of faith is the way of law, which says that a man is saved by obeying every law of God, without one slip. [13]But Christ has bought us out from under the doom of that impossible system by taking the curse for our wrongdoing upon himself. For it is written in the Scripture, "Anyone who is hanged on a tree is cursed" [as Jesus was hung upon a wooden cross].

[14]Now God can bless the Gentiles, too, with this same blessing he promised to Abraham; and all of us as Christians can have the promised Holy Spirit through this faith.

The Jewish Law and God's Promises

[15]Dear brothers, even in everyday life a promise made by one man to another, if it is written down and signed, cannot be changed. He cannot decide afterward to do something else instead.

[16]Now, God gave some promises to Abraham and his Child. And notice that it doesn't say the promises were to his *children,* as it would if all his sons—all the Jews—were being spoken of, but to his *Child*—and that, of course, means Christ. [17]Here's what I am trying to say: God's promise to save through faith—and God wrote this promise down and signed it—could not be canceled or changed four hundred and thirty years later when God gave the Ten Commandments. [18]If *obeying those laws* could save us, then it is obvious that this would be a different way of gaining God's favor than Abraham's way, for he simply accepted God's promise.

[19]Well then, why were the laws given? They were added after the promise was given, to show men how guilty they are of breaking God's laws. But this system of law was to last only until the coming of Christ, the Child to whom God's promise was made. (And there is this further difference. God gave his laws to angels to give to Moses, who then gave them to the people; [20]but when God gave his promise to Abraham, he did it by himself alone, without angels or Moses as go-betweens.)

[21,22]Well then, are God's laws and God's promises against each other? Of course not! If we could be saved by his laws, then God would not have had to give us a different way to get out of the grip of sin—for the Scriptures insist we are all its prisoners. The only way out is through faith in Jesus Christ; the way of escape is open to all who believe him.

[23]Until Christ came we were guarded by the law, kept in protective custody, so to speak, until we could believe in the coming Savior.

God's Children through Faith

[24]Let me put it another way. The Jewish laws were our teacher and guide until Christ came to give us right standing with God through our faith. [25]But now that Christ has come, we don't need those laws any longer to guard us and lead us to him. [26]For now we are all children of God through faith in Jesus Christ, [27]and we who have been baptized into union with Christ are enveloped by him. [28]We are no

---

3:15-29 God's relationship with us is not based on our keeping the law, but on the promises made to Abraham to bless all humanity through his offspring, Jesus Christ. The law shows us that we are sinners deserving punishment and in need of a Savior. Following the law is not the solution to the sin problem; the law is a measuring stick that reveals the sin problem. None of us are capable of true and complete obedience. Despite our helplessness, though, God desires to bless us, not curse us. His blessings come when we trust in his promises, not when we perform according to his perfect standards. Knowing that God loves us enough to pay for our failures can help us to be more fearless as we take our moral inventory. Jesus Christ has paid for our failures. When we admit them to God, he will set us free from their destructive power.

3:26-29 When we entrust our life to God in Jesus Christ, we become God's children. What an amazing truth! We are given a place in God's family, no matter what our past mistakes; no matter how dysfunctional our family; no matter how deeply we have been hurt. As children of God, we can entrust our life to him. He has a plan for each of us, and like any parent, he wants to help us succeed. Faith in Christ is all we need to enter into this privileged status. Each of us is important to God, and he is concerned enough to help us overcome our weaknesses and character flaws.

4:8-11 If we are not willing to trust and obey God in Jesus Christ, we soon become enslaved to something else. We turn to other activities or substances to help us deal with our problems in life. Most of us realize that this often leads to various forms of addiction. We have discovered that looking to drugs, alcohol, sexual activity, work, or even religious activity can never solve our problems. In fact, depending on anything other than God himself leads to even deeper problems. Only God can offer us the power to be delivered from bondage to build a new life. Turning to him for help is really the only valid option we have.

longer Jews or Greeks or slaves or free men or
even merely men or women, but we are all the
same—we are Christians; we are one in Christ
Jesus. [29]And now that we are Christ's we are
the true descendants of Abraham, and all of
God's promises to him belong to us.

CHAPTER 4
But remember this, that if a father dies and
leaves great wealth for his little son, that child
is not much better off than a slave until he
grows up, even though he actually owns
everything his father had. [2]He has to do what
his guardians and managers tell him to until
he reaches whatever age his father set.
[3]And that is the way it was with us before
Christ came. We were slaves to Jewish laws
and rituals, for we thought they could save us.
[4]But when the right time came, the time God
decided on, he sent his Son, born of a woman,
born as a Jew, [5]to buy freedom for us who were
slaves to the law so that he could adopt us as
his very own sons. [6]And because we are his
sons, God has sent the Spirit of his Son into
our hearts, so now we can rightly speak of
God as our dear Father. [7] Now we are no longer
slaves but God's own sons. And since we are
his sons, everything he has belongs to us, for
that is the way God planned.

Paul's Concern for the Galatians
[8]Before you Gentiles knew God you were
slaves to so-called gods that did not even
exist. [9]And now that you have found God (or
I should say, now that God has found you),
how can it be that you want to go back again
and become slaves once more to another
poor, weak, useless religion of trying to get to
heaven by obeying God's laws? [10]You are trying to find favor with God by what you do or
don't do on certain days or months or seasons
or years. [11]I fear for you. I am afraid that all my
hard work for you was worth nothing.
[12]Dear brothers, please feel as I do about
these things, for I am as free from these chains
as you used to be. You did not despise me then
when I first preached to you, [13]even though I
was sick when I first brought you the Good
News of Christ. [14]But even though my sickness was revolting to you, you didn't reject
me and turn me away. No, you took me in and
cared for me as though I were an angel from
God or even Jesus Christ himself.
[15]Where is that happy spirit that we felt
together then? For in those days I know you
would gladly have taken out your own eyes

Escaping Self-deception

BIBLE READING: Galatians 6:7-10

We admitted to God, to ourselves, and to another human being the exact nature of our wrongs.

We may fool ourself into believing that we can simply bury our wrongs and go on, without ever having to admit them. In time, we all discover that those deeds we thought were buried once and for all were actually seeds. They grow and bear fruit. Eventually we have to deal with a crop of consequences and face the fact that self-deception doesn't work to our advantage.

"A man will always reap just the kind of crop he sows! If he sows to please his own wrong desires, he will be planting seeds of evil and he will surely reap a harvest of spiritual decay and death; but if he plants the good things of the Spirit, he will reap the everlasting life that the Holy Spirit gives him" (Galatians 6:7-8). "If we say that we have no sin, we are only fooling ourselves and refusing to accept the truth. But if we confess our sins to [God], he can be depended on to forgive us and to cleanse us from every wrong" (1 John 1:8-9).

Step Five says good-bye to self-deception and hello to forgiveness and cleansing. We should note that there is cleansing from every wrong, not from "wrongdoing" in a general sense. Admitting the exact nature of our wrongs includes giving an account in exact and specific terms. It is only when we get specific that we will no longer be able to fool ourself about the nature of our wrongs. Since we cannot ignore God and get away with it anyway, we might as well come clean and be forgiven. ***Turn to Step Six, page 27, Genesis 23.***

and given them to replace mine if that would have helped me.

[16]And now have I become your enemy because I tell you the truth?

[17]Those false teachers who are so anxious to win your favor are not doing it for your good. What they are trying to do is to shut you off from me so that you will pay more attention to them. [18]It is a fine thing when people are nice to you with good motives and sincere hearts, especially if they aren't doing it just when I am with you! [19]Oh, my children, how you are hurting me! I am once again suffering for you the pains of a mother waiting for her child to be born—longing for the time when you will finally be filled with Christ. [20]How I wish I could be there with you right now and not have to reason with you like this, for at this distance I frankly don't know what to do.

Abraham's Two Children

[21]Listen to me, you friends who think you have to obey the Jewish laws to be saved: Why don't you find out what those laws really mean? [22]For it is written that Abraham had two sons, one from his slave-wife and one from his freeborn wife. [23]There was nothing unusual about the birth of the slave-wife's baby. But the baby of the freeborn wife was born only after God had especially promised he would come.

[24,25]Now this true story is an illustration of God's two ways of helping people. One way was by giving them his laws to obey. He did this on Mount Sinai, when he gave the Ten Commandments to Moses. Mount Sinai, by the way, is called "Mount Hagar" by the Arabs—and in my illustration, Abraham's slave-wife Hagar represents Jerusalem, the mother-city of the Jews, the center of that system of trying to please God by trying to obey the Commandments; and the Jews, who try to follow that system, are her slave children. [26]But our mother-city is the heavenly Jerusalem, and she is not a slave to Jewish laws.

[27]That is what Isaiah meant when he prophesied, "Now you can rejoice, O childless woman; you can shout with joy though you never before had a child. For I am going to give you many children—more children than the slave-wife has."

[28]You and I, dear brothers, are the children that God promised, just as Isaac was. [29]And so we who are born of the Holy Spirit are persecuted now by those who want us to keep the Jewish laws, just as Isaac, the child of promise, was persecuted by Ishmael, the slave-wife's son.

[30]But the Scriptures say that God told Abraham to send away the slave-wife and her son, for the slave-wife's son could not inherit Abraham's home and lands along with the free woman's son. [31]Dear brothers, we are not slave children, obligated to the Jewish laws, but children of the free woman, acceptable to God because of our faith.

CHAPTER 5

Living in Christ's Freedom

So Christ has made us free. Now make sure that you stay free, and don't get all tied up again in the chains of slavery to Jewish laws and ceremonies. [2]Listen to me, for this is serious: *if you are counting on circumcision and keeping the Jewish laws to make you right with God, then Christ cannot save you.* [3]I'll say it again. Anyone trying to find favor with God by being circumcised must always obey every other Jewish law or perish. [4]Christ is useless to you if you are counting on clearing your debt to God by keeping those laws; you are lost from God's grace.

[5]But we by the help of the Holy Spirit are counting on Christ's death to clear away our sins and make us right with God. [6]And we to whom Christ has given eternal life don't need to worry about whether we have been circum-

---

4:17-20 Paul was trying to help the Galatians experience the new life that God offers in Jesus Christ. The false teachers were trying to lead the people back into bondage under the Jewish law. Paul wanted to help the Galatians without asking anything in return. The false teachers offered only lies and demanded a position of authority in return. There is a distinct contrast between Paul's attitudes and actions and those of the false teachers. We have all come across recovery fads that promise amazing results. Usually, however, these programs cost a lot of money and yield, at best, only temporary results. The only real means to recovery is God's power—and it's free of charge! All we have to do is accept it.

5:1-12 The Galatians faced the same basic choice that all of us face. Should we choose a life of power and freedom in Christ or a life of slavery through useless and destructive solutions? If we make a bad choice, we risk being cut off from the deliverance available to God's people. There is no deliverance from the power of sin except through Christ and his powerful presence in our life. Only his power can restore us to sanity.

cised or not, or whether we are obeying the
Jewish ceremonies or not; for all we need is
faith working through love.
7You were getting along so well. Who has
interfered with you to hold you back from
following the truth? 8It certainly isn't God
who has done it, for he is the one who has
called you to freedom in Christ. 9But it takes
only one wrong person among you to infect
all the others.
10I am trusting the Lord to bring you back
to believing as I do about these things. God
will deal with that person, whoever he is, who
has been troubling and confusing you.
11Some people even say that I myself am
preaching that circumcision and Jewish laws
are necessary to the plan of salvation. Well, if
I preached that, I would be persecuted no
more—for that message doesn't offend anyone. The fact that I am still being persecuted
proves that I am still preaching salvation
through faith in the cross of Christ alone.
12I only wish these teachers who want you
to cut yourselves by being circumcised would
cut themselves off from you and leave you
alone!
13For, dear brothers, you have been given
freedom: not freedom to do wrong, but freedom to love and serve each other. 14For the
whole Law can be summed up in this one
command: "Love others as you love yourself."
15But if instead of showing love among yourselves you are always critical and catty, watch
out! Beware of ruining each other.

Living by the Spirit's Power

16I advise you to obey only the Holy Spirit's
instructions. He will tell you where to go and
what to do, and then you won't always be
doing the wrong things your evil nature
wants you to. 17For we naturally love to do evil
things that are just the opposite from the
things that the Holy Spirit tells us to do; and
the good things we want to do when the Spirit
has his way with us are just the opposite of
our natural desires. These two forces within us
are constantly fighting each other to win control over us, and our wishes are never free
from their pressures. 18When you are guided
by the Holy Spirit, you need no longer force
yourself to obey Jewish laws.
19But when you follow your own wrong
inclinations, your lives will produce these evil
results: impure thoughts, eagerness for lustful
pleasure, 20idolatry, spiritism (that is, encouraging the activity of demons), hatred and
fighting, jealousy and anger, constant effort

Reaping Goodness

BIBLE READING: Galatians 6:7-10

We made a list of all persons we had harmed and became willing to make amends to them all.

While in recovery, we learn to accept responsibility for our actions, even when we are powerless over our addictions. We come to realize that all our actions yield consequences. Some of us may have fooled ourselves into thinking we could escape the consequences of the things we did. But with time, it has become clear that God has made accountability a necessary element of healthy human living.

"A man will always reap just the kind of crop he sows! If he sows to please his own wrong desires, he will be planting seeds of evil and he will surely reap a harvest of spiritual decay and death; but if he plants the good things of the Spirit, he will reap the everlasting life that the Holy Spirit gives him" (Galatians 6:7-8).

The law of sowing and reaping can also work for us. God spoke through the prophet Hosea: "Plant the good seeds of righteousness, and you will reap a crop of my love; plow the hard ground of your hearts, for now is the time to seek the Lord, that he may come and shower salvation upon you" (Hosea 10:12).

God says we *always* reap what we have sown. Even after we have been forgiven, we must deal with the consequences of our actions. It may take a season of time to finish harvesting the negative consequences from our past, but we don't have to let this discourage us. Making our list of those we have harmed is a step toward planting good seeds. In time we will see a good crop begin to grow. ***Turn to Step Nine, page 41, Genesis 33.***

to get the best for yourself, complaints and criticisms, the feeling that everyone else is wrong except those in your own little group—and there will be wrong doctrine, 21envy, murder, drunkenness, wild parties, and all that sort of thing. Let me tell you again, as I have before, that anyone living that sort of life will not inherit the Kingdom of God.

22But when the Holy Spirit controls our lives he will produce this kind of fruit in us: love, joy, peace, patience, kindness, goodness, faithfulness, 23 gentleness and self-control; and here there is no conflict with Jewish laws.

24Those who belong to Christ have nailed their natural evil desires to his cross and crucified them there.

25If we are living now by the Holy Spirit's power, let us follow the Holy Spirit's leading in every part of our lives. 26Then we won't need to look for honors and popularity, which lead to jealousy and hard feelings.

CHAPTER 6

We Reap What We Sow

Dear brothers, if a Christian is overcome by some sin, you who are godly should gently and humbly help him back onto the right path, remembering that next time it might be one of you who is in the wrong. 2Share each other's troubles and problems, and so obey our Lord's command. 3If anyone thinks he is too great to stoop to this, he is fooling himself. He is really a nobody.

4Let everyone be sure that he is doing his very best, for then he will have the personal satisfaction of work well done and won't need to compare himself with someone else. 5Each of us must bear some faults and burdens of his own. For none of us is perfect!

6Those who are taught the Word of God should help their teachers by paying them.

7Don't be misled; remember that you can't ignore God and get away with it: a man will always reap just the kind of crop he sows! 8If he sows to please his own wrong desires, he will be planting seeds of evil and he will surely reap a harvest of spiritual decay and death; but if he plants the good things of the Spirit, he will reap the everlasting life that the Holy Spirit gives him. 9And let us not get tired of doing what is right, for after a while we will reap a harvest of blessing if we don't get discouraged and give up. 10That's why whenever we can we should always be kind to everyone, and especially to our Christian brothers.

Paul's Final Advice

11I will write these closing words in my own handwriting. See how large I have to make the letters! 12Those teachers of yours who are trying to convince you to be circumcised are doing it for just one reason: so that they can be popular and avoid the persecution they would get if they admitted that the cross of Christ alone can save. 13And even those teachers who submit to circumcision don't try to keep the other Jewish laws; but they want you to be circumcised in order that they can boast that you are their disciples.

14As for me, God forbid that I should boast about anything except the cross of our Lord Jesus Christ. Because of that cross, my inter-

5:22-24 These characteristics are a product of the Holy Spirit's work in a life submitted to God and his plan. Just as a tree bears fruit by means of God's silent work behind the scenes, we experience these fruits of the Spirit by means of God's power alone. Our part is to entrust our life to him. When the Holy Spirit begins to bear these fruits in our life, our dependencies lose their power. With *joy* and *peace* we overcome the pain of our broken past. With *love, kindness, goodness, faithfulness,* and *gentleness* we restore our relationships and make amends. With *patience* we persevere through the difficult times. With *self-control* we stand against our tendency toward a relapse. God's Spirit can supply everything necessary for a successful recovery.

6:1-3 Paul told the Galatians to share their troubles with one another. He knew that this would bring healing to hurting people and provide opportunities for the believers to help one another. Since Paul knew some would be too proud to admit their problems, he jotted a special note to encourage everyone's participation. An essential part of recovery is admitting to others the exact nature of our wrongs. As we do this, we will discover that much of the burden of our sins will be lifted. The burden of our painful past and addictive tendencies will be shared by others. With their encouragement and call to accountability, we will be able to shed our painful past and move on toward a productive future.

6:11-18 In these concluding verses, Paul recapped his major arguments with a closing emotional appeal to stand firm against false teachers who try to attract people away from the liberating message of the gospel. Admitting that we are helpless to overcome our sins and accepting God's help are responsible decisions. Rather than humiliating us, God bestows dignity and healing upon us when we enter the process of recovery through faith in Christ. As God works his healing in our life, we can take the Good News to others as Paul did with the Galatian believers.

est in all the attractive things of the world
was killed long ago, and the world's interest
in me is also long dead. 15It doesn't make any
difference now whether we have been circumcised or not; what counts is whether we
really have been changed into new and different people.
16May God's mercy and peace be upon all of
you who live by this principle and upon those
everywhere who are really God's own.
17From now on please don't argue with me
about these things, for I carry on my body the
scars of the whippings and wounds from
Jesus' enemies that mark me as his slave.
18Dear brothers, may the grace of our Lord
Jesus Christ be with you all.

Sincerely, Paul

REFLECTIONS ON
GALATIANS

✲*insights* INTO GOD'S WILL

Very often, God's will for us stands in direct opposition to our natural desires. Our recovery depends on our acceptance of the fact that following our own selfish desires is destructive. In **Galatians 5:16-21,** we find a whole list of destructive behaviors that flow out of a self-centered life. When we turn our life over to God, however, we allow his Spirit to help us control the desires that lead us to sin. More and more God's desires become our own desires. Considering the facts, submitting our life to God's will is the best choice we can make.

✲*insights* ABOUT CONSEQUENCES

In **Galatians 6:7-10,** Paul left an important reminder for us all. We will always reap what we have sown. In other words, sins and addictions have painful consequences. We might be able to fool ourself for a while into thinking that certain activities and relationships are all right. But when the consequences catch up with us, there will be no denying the facts. We need to take this warning seriously and take steps to change now. We don't have to wait to hit bottom before we act. Using God's Word as a measuring stick, we can take a fearless moral inventory and make the necessary adjustments before it's too late.

EPHESIANS

THE BIG PICTURE

A. GREETINGS (1:1-2)
B. ASSURANCE OF GOD'S PROGRAM FOR SPIRITUAL WHOLENESS (1:3–3:21)
C. ACCEPTANCE OF OUR RESPONSIBILITY FOR SPIRITUAL WHOLENESS (4:1–6:9)
D. AWARENESS OF OUR ROLE IN SPIRITUAL WARFARE (6:10-20)
E. CLOSING REMARKS (6:21-24)

The Ephesian church had been planted through Paul's influence (Acts 18:19-21), and for a few years he had served as its pastor (Acts 19:8-10; 20:31). This church thrived in a city renowned as a center for the worship of the goddess Artemis (also known as Diana). While Paul was there, the Ephesian believers maintained a strong attachment to him, and when he left they openly expressed their sorrow.

How could the Ephesian church survive for the long haul in its hostile environment? They could not depend on Paul's presence forever; they would have to learn to stand on their own, with God's help. Paul wrote this letter to remind the Ephesian believers to place their faith in the only solid foundation for healthy living—God in Jesus Christ.

How can we maintain our recovery in a hostile environment? None of us have the resources or strength to initiate and sustain our recovery alone. Paul assumed one important fact: we can change! But our transformation is possible only on God's terms. We can recover if we break with our former way of life and depend on God's power to help us change. While programs and supportive people are helpful, lasting recovery happens only when we recognize our need for a higher Power—the God who created us and sustains our life.

Belief in God and obedience to his will are keys to a genuine and stable recovery. If our attitudes and actions reflect God's truth, and we adopt a new attitude of submission to God's authority and care, we will indeed make progress. Recovery that ignores God is doomed to fail; recovery that depends on God will succeed.

THE BOTTOM LINE

PURPOSE: To strengthen the believers in Ephesus in their relationship with God and with each other. AUTHOR: The apostle Paul. AUDIENCE: The believers in Ephesus, a city in western Asia Minor, and all believers everywhere. DATE WRITTEN: Around A.D. 60, during Paul's imprisonment in Rome. SETTING: This letter was not sent to solve any particular problem. Rather, it was a somewhat personal message from Paul to some close and dear friends in the mother church of Asia. Paul probably intended this to be a circular letter passed from church to church for encouragement. KEY VERSE: "Last of all I want to remind you that your strength must come from the Lord's mighty power within you" (6:10). KEY PEOPLE AND RELATIONSHIPS: Paul with Tychicus, and with his close friends in the Ephesian church.

RECOVERY THEMES

God's Desire for Our Recovery: God has had a plan for us since the beginning of time. His plan for us doesn't include our bondage to sin or the past. He wants us to have a relationship with him so we can enjoy his love and presence. He wants us to recover even more than we do! Many of us have distorted images of God based on painful images of authority figures in our past. This letter shows us that God is a Father who has loved us from the beginning of time. He will continue to love us, no matter what we do.

The Importance of Jesus Christ: In the New Testament, and especially in Ephesians, Jesus Christ is exalted as the focus of all history and as the only means for experiencing a meaningful life. Only through God in Jesus Christ can the power of sin be overcome. This letter urges us to keep Jesus Christ at the center of all we do, maintaining conscious contact with him on a daily basis.

True Recovery Leads to Wise Conduct: It is easy to think of recovery only in terms of stopping destructive behavior patterns. But it is important to see that the best way to stop destructive habits is to build constructive ones with which to replace them. We are able to lay aside old patterns when we consciously turn our life over to God, seeking his will for us each day. As we begin to live out God's will for our life, we will find we are no longer following the path toward destruction.

Adoption into God's Family: Many of us have painful memories from the past, particularly from the experiences we had in our family. Some of us have no positive memories of our family life at all. The letter to the Ephesians reminds us that when we turn our life over to God, he adopts us into a new family. In this family, God is our perfect and loving Father. Even God's family, the church, has its limitations and imperfections. But our Father is perfect, and becoming a part of his family is an important step in our recovery.

CHAPTER 1

Greetings from Paul

Dear Christian friends at Ephesus, ever loyal to
the Lord: This is Paul writing to you, chosen
by God to be Jesus Christ's messenger. 2May his
blessings and peace be yours, sent to you from
God our Father and Jesus Christ our Lord.

God's Overflowing Kindness

3How we praise God, the Father of our Lord
Jesus Christ, who has blessed us with every
blessing in heaven because we belong to
Christ.
4Long ago, even before he made the world,
God chose us to be his very own through
what Christ would do for us; he decided then
to make us holy in his eyes, without a single
fault—we who stand before him covered with
his love. 5His unchanging plan has always
been to adopt us into his own family by
sending Jesus Christ to die for us. And he did
this because he wanted to!
6Now all praise to God for his wonderful
kindness to us and his favor that he has
poured out upon us because we belong to his
dearly loved Son. 7So overflowing is his kind-

1:3-6 Recovery cannot begin until we admit that our life is unmanageable and that we are powerless over the circumstances we face. The apostle Paul reminds us that God is sovereign over all the details of our life. God has a special plan for each of us, and that plan includes adopting us into his family. We have already realized that doing things our way leads to painful consequences that are beyond our control. With this in mind, we can be motivated to submit to God's perfect will for our life. God wants only what is best for us. It is always God's will for us to find new life in him.

1:11-12 Some of us may wonder how we can know God's will for our life. While there are details we may never know in advance, God's Word points us in the right direction. There are many things that God desires for all of us, and these are revealed in Scripture. Here we find that God wants us to experience an intimate relationship with him in Christ. In this relationship, God will delight in us and we will praise him in return. For many of us, this is an amazing truth. God wants to have a close relationship with us, no matter who we are or what we have done. Because of what God has done for us in Jesus Christ, we can live a life of praise, sharing the Good News with others in need.

1:13-14 God's program for our salvation is completed by the sealing work of the Holy Spirit. Just as an official marks a document as being genuine, so the Holy Spirit's work within us guarantees our identity as one of God's adopted children. This is all made possible by Jesus Christ and his saving work on our behalf. It becomes a reality in our life when we place our faith in him. Our knowledge of God's concern for us and the help he offers gives us a reason for hope as we seek to overcome our problems and dependencies. When we trust God, we become a part of the powerful solution he has provided to deal with the sin problem in our world.

ness toward us that he took away all our sins
through the blood of his Son, by whom we are
saved; [8]and he has showered down upon us
the richness of his grace—for how well he
understands us and knows what is best for us
at all times.
[9]God has told us his secret reason for sending Christ, a plan he decided on in mercy long
ago; [10]and this was his purpose: that when the
time is ripe he will gather us all together from
wherever we are—in heaven or on earth—to
be with him in Christ forever. [11]Moreover,
because of what Christ has done, we have
become gifts to God that he delights in, for as
part of God's sovereign plan we were chosen
from the beginning to be his, and all things
happen just as he decided long ago. [12]God's
purpose in this was that we should praise God
and give glory to him for doing these mighty
things for us, who were the first to trust in
Christ.
[13]And because of what Christ did, all you
others too, who heard the Good News about
how to be saved, and trusted Christ, were
marked as belonging to Christ by the Holy
Spirit, who long ago had been promised to all
of us Christians. [14]His presence within us is
God's guarantee that he really will give us all
that he promised; and the Spirit's seal upon us
means that God has already purchased us and
that he guarantees to bring us to himself. This
is just one more reason for us to praise our
glorious God.

Paul Prays for the Ephesians

[15]That is why, ever since I heard of your strong
faith in the Lord Jesus and of the love you
have for Christians everywhere, [16,17]I have
never stopped thanking God for you. I pray
for you constantly, asking God, the glorious
Father of our Lord Jesus Christ, to give you
wisdom to see clearly and really understand
who Christ is and all that he has done for you.
[18]I pray that your hearts will be flooded with
light so that you can see something of the
future he has called you to share. I want you
to realize that God has been made rich because we who are Christ's have been given to
him! [19]I pray that you will begin to understand how incredibly great his power is to
help those who believe him. It is that same
mighty power [20]that raised Christ from the
dead and seated him in the place of honor at
God's right hand in heaven, [21]far, far above
any other king or ruler or dictator or leader.
Yes, his honor is far more glorious than that
of anyone else either in this world or in the

Self-perception

READ EPHESIANS 2:1-13

We may feel like we are not good enough to be an example for others. We may realize that we need other people, but find it hard to believe that our story could help anyone else.

The apostle Paul said, "Just as there are many parts to our bodies, so it is with Christ's body. We are all parts of it, and it takes every one of us to make it complete, for we each have different work to do. So we belong to each other, and each needs all the others" (Romans 12:4-5). "It is God himself who has made us what we are and given us new lives from Christ Jesus; and long ages ago he planned that we should spend these lives in helping others" (Ephesians 2:10).

To have a true view of where we fit in the scheme of things, we need to see that God has a purpose for our life. God created each of us with abilities and talents. He likens us to a part of a body where every part is needed for the proper working of the whole. If you isolate any one part of a body and examine it, apart from its proper place among the other members, it may seem odd and useless. It is only when it is connected to the body and doing its appointed job that it realizes its usefulness. And so it is with us.

We need to find a place where our talents and abilities can be used to help others. Doing this will show that we have gained an honest understanding of whom God created us to be. He loves us and wants to help us realize our place in the body of Christ and our purpose in life. ***Turn to page 1315, Ephesians 4.***

world to come. [22]And God has put all things under his feet and made him the supreme Head of the Church—[23]which is his body, filled with himself, the Author and Giver of everything everywhere.

CHAPTER 2

From Death to New Life

Once you were under God's curse, doomed forever for your sins. [2]You went along with the crowd and were just like all the others, full of sin, obeying Satan, the mighty prince of the power of the air, who is at work right now in the hearts of those who are against the Lord. [3]All of us used to be just as they are, our lives expressing the evil within us, doing every wicked thing that our passions or our evil thoughts might lead us into. We started out bad, being born with evil natures, and were under God's anger just like everyone else.

[4]But God is so rich in mercy; he loved us so much [5]that even though we were spiritually dead and doomed by our sins, he gave us back our lives again when he raised Christ from the dead—only by his undeserved favor have we ever been saved—[6]and lifted us up from the grave into glory along with Christ, where we sit with him in the heavenly realms—all because of what Christ Jesus did. [7]And now God can always point to us as examples of how very, very rich his kindness is, as shown in all he has done for us through Jesus Christ.

[8]Because of his kindness, you have been saved through trusting Christ. And even trusting is not of yourselves; it too is a gift from God. [9]Salvation is not a reward for the good we have done, so none of us can take any credit for it. [10]It is God himself who has made us what we are and given us new lives from Christ Jesus; and long ages ago he planned that we should spend these lives in helping others.

[11]Never forget that once you were heathen and that you were called godless and "unclean" by the Jews. (But their hearts, too, were still unclean, even though they were going through the ceremonies and rituals of the godly, for they circumcised themselves as a sign of godliness.) [12]Remember that in those days you were living utterly apart from Christ; you were enemies of God's children, and he had promised you no help. You were lost, without God, without hope.

[13]But now you belong to Christ Jesus, and though you once were far away from God, now you have been brought very near to him because of what Jesus Christ has done for you with his blood.

Christ Is the Way to Peace

[14]For Christ himself is our way of peace. He has made peace between us Jews and you Gentiles by making us all one family, breaking down the wall of contempt that used to separate us. [15]By his death he ended the angry resentment between us, caused by the Jewish laws that favored the Jews and excluded the Gentiles, for he died to annul that whole system of Jewish laws. Then he took the two groups that had been opposed to each other and made them parts of himself; thus he fused us together to become one new person, and at last there was peace. [16]As parts of the same body, our anger against each other has disappeared, for both of us have been reconciled to God. And so the feud ended at last at the cross. [17]And he has brought this Good News of peace to you Gentiles who were very far away from him, and to us Jews who were near. [18]Now all of us, whether Jews or Gentiles, may come to God the Father with the

---

2:1-10 In these verses, Paul affirms two essential truths related to our recovery. He begins by recognizing that we are broken creatures, powerless to stand against our tendency toward sin and failure. Paul then recognizes God's wealth of mercy and love, and he reminds us that even though we are far from God and entrapped by sin, God graciously reaches out to us. God wants to forgive us and give us the power to rebuild our life. Through the work of Jesus Christ, God has already conquered the power of sin and death. When we admit that we need God's help and ask him to act on our behalf, God's power is made available to us to overcome our problems and dependencies.

2:14-19 Through Jesus Christ, the barrier between God and his sinful creatures has been removed. But Christ's work of reconciliation does not stop there. He can also remove the obstacles that alienate us from other people. In Christ, we can have peace both with God and with others. This restoration of our broken relationships is a necessary part of the recovery process. Some of us may feel that our relationships could never be salvaged. But realizing that Christ can give us the power to live at peace with others gives us new hope. It is his power that will enable us to make amends with the people we have wronged. All who believe in Christ are made brothers and sisters in him.

Holy Spirit's help because of what Christ has
done for us.
19Now you are no longer strangers to God
and foreigners to heaven, but you are members of God's very own family, citizens of
God's country, and you belong in God's
household with every other Christian.
20What a foundation you stand on now: the
apostles and the prophets; and the cornerstone of the building is Jesus Christ himself!
21We who believe are carefully joined together
with Christ as parts of a beautiful, constantly
growing temple for God. 22And you also are
joined with him and with each other by the
Spirit and are part of this dwelling place of
God.

CHAPTER 3

Salvation Is for Everyone

I, Paul, the servant of Christ, am here in jail
because of you—for preaching that you Gentiles are a part of God's house. 2,3No doubt you
already know that God has given me this
special work of showing God's favor to you
Gentiles, as I briefly mentioned before in one
of my letters. God himself showed me this
secret plan of his, that the Gentiles, too, are
included in his kindness. 4I say this to explain
to you how I know about these things. 5In
olden times God did not share this plan with
his people, but now he has revealed it by the
Holy Spirit to his apostles and prophets.
6And this is the secret: that the Gentiles will
have their full share with the Jews in all the
riches inherited by God's sons; both are invited to belong to his Church, and all of God's
promises of mighty blessings through Christ
apply to them both when they accept the
Good News about Christ and what he has
done for them. 7God has given me the wonderful privilege of telling everyone about this
plan of his; and he has given me his power
and special ability to do it well.
8Just think! Though I did nothing to deserve it, and though I am the most useless
Christian there is, yet I was the one chosen for
this special joy of telling the Gentiles the
Glad News of the endless treasures available
to them in Christ; 9and to explain to everyone
that God is the Savior of the Gentiles too, just
as he who made all things had secretly
planned from the very beginning.
10And his reason? To show to all the rulers
in heaven how perfectly wise he is when all of
his family—Jews and Gentiles alike—are seen
to be joined together in his Church 11in just

Honesty

READ EPHESIANS 4:12-27

We probably grew up believing lies about life, about ourself, about our family. We may still experience confusion and uncertainty because we don't have a strong sense of what is really true. The lies we believe can contribute to our addictive ways, so we need to reexamine our life in the light of what is true.

The apostle Paul talked about how the people who believed in Christ were to function like a single body. Each member is to be "filled full with Christ" (Ephesians 4:13), offering the gifts he has to help the whole body grow up into maturity. Since Jesus described himself as "the Truth" (John 14:6), and we are to be filled with him, our recovery process involves becoming "truth-full." Paul continued, "Then we will no longer be like children, forever changing our minds about what we believe because someone has told us something different or has cleverly lied to us and made the lie sound like the truth. Instead, we will lovingly follow the truth at all times" (Ephesians 4:14-16).

Recovery can be like growing up all over again. As we grow, we are to continue to aim for what is true. In the past we measured truth against whatever sounded right to us at the time. Now we can have the sure measurement of God's Word and Jesus Christ himself. From this perspective we can reevaluate our beliefs. What is true about God? What is true about me? What is right? What is wrong? ***Turn to page 1323, Philippians 1.***

the way he had always planned it through Jesus Christ our Lord.

[12]Now we can come fearlessly right into God's presence, assured of his glad welcome when we come with Christ and trust in him.

[13]So please don't lose heart at what they are doing to me here. It is for you I am suffering, and you should feel honored and encouraged.

The Greatness of God's Love

[14,15]When I think of the wisdom and scope of his plan, I fall down on my knees and pray to the Father of all the great family of God—some of them already in heaven and some down here on earth—[16]that out of his glorious, unlimited resources he will give you the mighty inner strengthening of his Holy Spirit.
[17]And I pray that Christ will be more and more at home in your hearts, living within you as you trust in him. May your roots go down deep into the soil of God's marvelous love;
[18,19]and may you be able to feel and understand, as all God's children should, how long, how wide, how deep, and how high his love really is; and to experience this love for yourselves, though it is so great that you will never see the end of it or fully know or understand it. And so at last you will be filled up with God himself.

[20]Now glory be to God, who by his mighty power at work within us is able to do far more than we would ever dare to ask or even dream of—infinitely beyond our highest prayers, desires, thoughts, or hopes. [21]May he be given glory forever and ever through endless ages because of his master plan of salvation for the Church through Jesus Christ.

CHAPTER 4

We Are One Body in Christ

I beg you—I, a prisoner here in jail for serving the Lord—to live and act in a way worthy of those who have been chosen for such wonderful blessings as these. [2]Be humble and gentle. Be patient with each other, making allowance for each other's faults because of your love. [3]Try always to be led along together by the Holy Spirit and so be at peace with one another.

[4]We are all parts of one body, we have the same Spirit, and we have all been called to the same glorious future. [5]For us there is only one

3:1-13 In these verses one truth stands out: God accepts all of us through faith. Our race, reputation, and position have no bearing on God's forgiveness. Paul wrote these words to convince the believers of their oneness in Christ. Apparently some of the Jewish believers claimed superiority because of their relationship to God in the Old Testament Scriptures. Paul refuted their view by reminding them that our relationship with God is based on our trust in Jesus Christ. It has nothing to do with our personal history or position in society. This important truth is encouraging for us in recovery. Even though many of us were respected in the past, our addictions probably have destroyed the reputation we once commanded. None of this matters to God. If we seek his forgiveness, he will accept us and help us make a new start.

3:14-21 For the church or a small group to function effectively as a vehicle for recovery, it must be driven by God's dynamic and unlimited love. Paul prayed that his friends might be deeply anchored in and strengthened by God's love. As we begin to discover how much God loves us, we will become confident that anything is possible with God. In fact, God is able to do far more in and through us than we could ever imagine! This is a truth to bank our recovery on! We may feel that our life is in a hopeless state, well beyond the point of recovery. If we trust God to help us, however, we will discover that restoration and healing are never impossible. When we are grounded in God's love, our recovery is assured.

4:1-6 Even though God's program for recovery is centered on his sovereign purposes and power, we have important responsibilities as well. What we believe about God is crucial, but so is the manner in which we live. For many of us, the recovery process is hindered by a stubborn pride that prevents us from taking a searching and fearless inventory of our life. Our recovery is impossible until we humbly admit that we are powerless and need God's help. Then, as we trust God to help us, his Holy Spirit will replace our character flaws with humility, love, and patience. When God asks us to live a certain way, he provides the power we need to succeed.

4:7-16 We have been gifted in ways that make us necessary to others. Others have been gifted in ways that make them necessary to us. Some of us have special gifts for teaching others about God. Others of us may have the gift of caring for hurting people. Whatever gifts we might have, they are important for the emotional and spiritual growth of others. Since God has a purpose for each of us, it is important that we strive to know him better through prayer and meditation on his Word. As we seek him, he will show us what our gifts are and how we can use them to help others. As we share our gifts and receive the benefits of other people's gifts, we will find the body of Christ growing stronger and healthier.

Lord, one faith, one baptism, [6]and we all have
the same God and Father who is over us all
and in us all, and living through every part of
us. [7]However, Christ has given each of us
special abilities—whatever he wants us to
have out of his rich storehouse of gifts.
[8]The psalmist tells about this, for he says
that when Christ returned triumphantly to
heaven after his resurrection and victory over
Satan, he gave generous gifts to men. [9]Notice
that it says he returned to heaven. This means
that he had first come down from the heights
of heaven, far down to the lowest parts of the
earth. [10]The same one who came down is the
one who went back up, that he might fill all
things everywhere with himself, from the
very lowest to the very highest.
[11]Some of us have been given special ability
as apostles; to others he has given the gift of
being able to preach well; some have special
ability in winning people to Christ, helping
them to trust him as their Savior; still others
have a gift for caring for God's people as a
shepherd does his sheep, leading and teaching them in the ways of God.
[12]Why is it that he gives us these special
abilities to do certain things best? It is that
God's people will be equipped to do better
work for him, building up the Church, the
body of Christ, to a position of strength and
maturity; [13]until finally we all believe alike
about our salvation and about our Savior,
God's Son, and all become full-grown in the
Lord—yes, to the point of being filled full
with Christ.
[14]Then we will no longer be like children,
forever changing our minds about what we
believe because someone has told us something different or has cleverly lied to us and
made the lie sound like the truth. [15,16]Instead,
we will lovingly follow the truth at all times—
speaking truly, dealing truly, living truly—
and so become more and more in every way
like Christ who is the Head of his body, the
Church. Under his direction, the whole body
is fitted together perfectly, and each part in its
own special way helps the other parts, so that
the whole body is healthy and growing and
full of love.

Living as a New Person

[17,18]Let me say this, then, speaking for the
Lord: Live no longer as the unsaved do, for
they are blinded and confused. Their closed
hearts are full of darkness; they are far away
from the life of God because they have shut
their minds against him, and they cannot

Dealing with Anger

BIBLE READING: Ephesians 4:26-27

We continued to take personal inventory and when we were wrong promptly admitted it.

Many of us have a hard time dealing with anger. Some of us have a history of rage, so we try to stifle our feelings. Others of us stuff down the feelings of anger, pretending they don't exist because we were never allowed to express them in the past. If some of our problems stem from not knowing how to express anger properly, we may try to avoid dealing with it altogether. We may try to just "put it off" and hope it goes away. Evaluating how to deal with anger appropriately is an important part of our daily inventory.

The apostle Paul once said, "If you are angry, don't sin by nursing your grudge. Don't let the sun go down with you still angry—get over it quickly; for when you are angry, you give a mighty foothold to the devil" (Ephesians 4:26-27). One key is to have a daily time limit for handling our feelings of anger—a time to find a way to express the feelings and then let them go.

Dealing with anger promptly is important because when it is left to fester, it becomes bitterness. Bitterness is anger that has been buried and given time to grow. The Bible warns us, "Watch out that no bitterness takes root among you, for as it springs up it causes deep trouble, hurting many in their spiritual lives" (Hebrews 12:15).

Alcoholics Anonymous teaches that we should never allow ourself to become too hungry, angry, lonely, or tired. We can accomplish this by promptly dealing with our anger as it occurs. ***Turn to page 1355, 1 Timothy 4.***

understand his ways. 19They don't care anymore about right and wrong and have given
themselves over to impure ways. They stop at
nothing, being driven by their evil minds and
reckless lusts.
20But that isn't the way Christ taught you!
21If you have really heard his voice and
learned from him the truths concerning himself, 22then throw off your old evil nature—the
old you that was a partner in your evil ways—
rotten through and through, full of lust and
sham.
23Now your attitudes and thoughts must all
be constantly changing for the better. 24Yes,
you must be a new and different person, holy
and good. Clothe yourself with this new nature.
25Stop lying to each other; tell the truth, for
we are parts of each other and when we lie to
each other we are hurting ourselves. 26If you
are angry, don't sin by nursing your grudge.
Don't let the sun go down with you still
angry—get over it quickly; 27for when you are
angry, you give a mighty foothold to the
devil.
28If anyone is stealing he must stop it and
begin using those hands of his for honest
work so he can give to others in need. 29Don't
use bad language. Say only what is good and
helpful to those you are talking to, and what
will give them a blessing.
30Don't cause the Holy Spirit sorrow by the
way you live. Remember, he is the one who
marks you to be present on that day when
salvation from sin will be complete.
31Stop being mean, bad-tempered, and
angry. Quarreling, harsh words, and dislike of
others should have no place in your lives.
32Instead, be kind to each other, tenderhearted, forgiving one another, just as God
has forgiven you because you belong to
Christ.

CHAPTER 5

Living as a Child of the Light

Follow God's example in everything you do
just as a much-loved child imitates his father.
2Be full of love for others, following the example of Christ who loved you and gave himself
to God as a sacrifice to take away your sins.
And God was pleased, for Christ's love for you
was like sweet perfume to him.
3Let there be no sex sin, impurity or greed
among you. Let no one be able to accuse you
of any such things. 4Dirty stories, foul talk,
and coarse jokes—these are not for you. Instead, remind each other of God's goodness,
and be thankful.
5You can be sure of this: The Kingdom of
Christ and of God will never belong to anyone who is impure or greedy, for a greedy
person is really an idol worshiper—he loves
and worships the good things of this life more
than God. 6Don't be fooled by those who try
to excuse these sins, for the terrible wrath of
God is upon all those who do them. 7Don't
even associate with such people. 8For though
once your heart was full of darkness, now it is
full of light from the Lord, and your behavior
should show it! 9Because of this light within
you, you should do only what is good and
right and true.
10Learn as you go along what pleases the
Lord. 11Take no part in the worthless pleasures
of evil and darkness, but instead, rebuke and
expose them. 12It would be shameful even to
mention here those pleasures of darkness
that the ungodly do. 13But when you expose
them, the light shines in upon their sin and
shows it up, and when they see how wrong
they really are, some of them may even become children of light! 14That is why God says
in the Scriptures, "Awake, O sleeper, and rise
up from the dead; and Christ shall give you
light."
15,16So be careful how you act; these are

4:31-32 A life of recovery is a life committed to knowing God better through prayer and meditation on his Word. In examining our life, we realize just how demanding God's standards for righteous living are, but since it is God's grace that helps us conform to his will, we need not despair. As we obey him, he will teach us humility and help us forgive the people who have hurt us. God is in the business of healing our relationships. When we do things his way, we are well on the way to reconciling with our alienated friends and building a solid foundation for recovery.

5:1-7 In recovery, we are told to follow God's will for our life. Some of us may wonder how we can know what God wants us to do. Here we see that God wants us to be like Jesus Christ. As we look at his life, we can see how God would like us to think and act. We are to love our enemies, just as Jesus did. We are to avoid sexual impurity, greed, and obscene speech, since they stand counter to the character of God. These requirements are right in line with what is needed in recovery. We are to seek to rebuild our broken relationships, even when someone else is in the wrong. We are to avoid destructive behaviors, admit our wrongs, and seek to make amends for the pain we have caused. As difficult as imitating Christ might sound, anything is possible with God's powerful help.

difficult days. Don't be fools; be wise: make
the most of every opportunity you have for
doing good. 17Don't act thoughtlessly, but try
to find out and do whatever the Lord wants
you to. 18Don't drink too much wine, for
many evils lie along that path; be filled instead with the Holy Spirit and controlled by
him.

19Talk with each other much about the
Lord, quoting psalms and hymns and singing
sacred songs, making music in your hearts to
the Lord. 20Always give thanks for everything
to our God and Father in the name of our
Lord Jesus Christ.

Advice for Wives and Husbands

21Honor Christ by submitting to each other.
22You wives must submit to your husbands'
leadership in the same way you submit to the
Lord. 23 For a husband is in charge of his wife
in the same way Christ is in charge of his body
the Church. (He gave his very life to take care
of it and be its Savior!) 24 So you wives must
willingly obey your husbands in everything,
just as the Church obeys Christ.

25And you husbands, show the same kind of
love to your wives as Christ showed to the
Church when he died for her, 26to make her
holy and clean, washed by baptism and God's
Word; 27so that he could give her to himself as
a glorious Church without a single spot or
wrinkle or any other blemish, being holy and
without a single fault. 28That is how husbands
should treat their wives, loving them as parts
of themselves. For since a man and his wife
are now one, a man is really doing himself a
favor and loving himself when he loves his
wife! 29,30No one hates his own body but lovingly cares for it, just as Christ cares for his
body the Church, of which we are parts.

31(That the husband and wife are one body
is proved by the Scripture, which says, "A
man must leave his father and mother when
he marries so that he can be perfectly joined
to his wife, and the two shall be one.") 32I
know this is hard to understand, but it is an
illustration of the way we are parts of the body
of Christ.

33So again I say, a man must love his wife as
a part of himself; and the wife must see to it
that she deeply respects her husband—obeying, praising, and honoring him.

CHAPTER 6

Advice for Children and Parents

Children, obey your parents; this is the right
thing to do because God has placed them in
authority over you. 2Honor your father and
mother. This is the first of God's Ten Commandments that ends with a promise. 3And
this is the promise: that if you honor your
father and mother, yours will be a long life,
full of blessing.

4And now a word to you parents. Don't
keep on scolding and nagging your children,
making them angry and resentful. Rather,
bring them up with the loving discipline the
Lord himself approves, with suggestions and
godly advice.

Advice for Slaves and Masters

5Slaves, obey your masters; be eager to give
them your very best. Serve them as you would
Christ. 6,7Don't work hard only when your
master is watching and then shirk when he
isn't looking; work hard and with gladness all
the time, as though working for Christ, doing
the will of God with all your hearts. 8Remem-
ber, the Lord will pay you for each good thing
you do, whether you are slave or free.

9And you slave owners must treat your
slaves right, just as I have told them to treat

5:21-33 When our life is out of control, family tensions and violence are a part of everyday life. Paul tells us that the home should be a place where love and mutual submission are exhibited. Husbands and wives need to show love to each other and be sensitive to each other's needs. As they do this, they reflect the loving relationship that God has established between Christ and the Christian community. The painful consequences of our addictions are most deeply felt by our close family members. By selfishly seeking to meet our own needs through addictive behaviors, we have neglected and hurt the people it was our responsibility to love and support. So rebuilding our family relationships is one of the most important tasks we face in recovery. As we admit the nature of our wrongs and seek to make amends with our loved ones, we can begin to reestablish a family atmosphere characterized by love and mutual submission.

6:1-4 In these verses, Paul directed both parents and children to show love toward one another. Children are to show due respect to their parents. The widespread disrespect shown toward parents today leads to deep emotional scars both in parents and children. Paul also warned parents to treat their children with love and respect. Through ridicule and neglect parents can create resentment that may stay with their children for life. Whether we are a parent or a child who has failed, we need to admit our failures and seek to make amends wherever possible.

you. Don't keep threatening them; remember, you yourselves are slaves to Christ; you have the same Master they do, and he has no favorites.

Wearing the Armor of God

[10]Last of all I want to remind you that your
strength must come from the Lord's mighty
power within you. [11]Put on all of God's armor
so that you will be able to stand safe against
all strategies and tricks of Satan. [12]For we are
not fighting against people made of flesh and
blood, but against persons without bodies—
the evil rulers of the unseen world, those
mighty satanic beings and great evil princes
of darkness who rule this world; and against
huge numbers of wicked spirits in the spirit
world.

[13]So use every piece of God's armor to resist
the enemy whenever he attacks, and when it
is all over, you will still be standing up.

[14]But to do this, you will need the strong
belt of truth and the breastplate of God's
approval. [15]Wear shoes that are able to speed
you on as you preach the Good News of peace
with God. [16]In every battle you will need faith
as your shield to stop the fiery arrows aimed
at you by Satan. [17]And you will need the helmet of salvation and the sword of the Spirit—
which is the Word of God.

[18]Pray all the time. Ask God for anything in
line with the Holy Spirit's wishes. Plead with
him, reminding him of your needs, and keep
praying earnestly for all Christians everywhere. [19]Pray for me, too, and ask God to give
me the right words as I boldly tell others
about the Lord and as I explain to them that
his salvation is for the Gentiles too. [20]I am in
chains now for preaching this message from
God. But pray that I will keep on speaking out
boldly for him even here in prison, as I
should.

Paul's Final Greetings

[21]Tychicus, who is a much-loved brother and
faithful helper in the Lord's work, will tell you
all about how I am getting along. [22]I am sending him to you for just this purpose: to let you
know how we are and be encouraged by his
report.

[23]May God give peace to you, my Christian
brothers, and love, with faith from God the
Father and the Lord Jesus Christ. [24]May God's
grace and blessing be upon all who sincerely
love our Lord Jesus Christ.

Sincerely, Paul

6:10-13 While we may be firmly grounded in sound doctrine and accept our responsibility to live a godly life, we need to be aware of the fierce, invisible warfare being waged against us. Much of our struggle with addiction could be the result of a direct attack by a spiritual enemy. Since we continue to struggle with dependencies that once rendered us powerless, we need to admit our inability to manage our life. Then as we turn our life and will over to God, he will stand with us in the battle.

6:13-20 Notice that each piece of our spiritual armor (except the sword) is defensive in nature. As a recovering addict, we need to seek to improve our conscious contact with God, to know him better, and to surround ourself with truth, righteousness, faith, and prayer. These will protect us against the assault of hostile spiritual forces. The forces arrayed against us are powerful, but the weapons God gives us are adequate for our defense. Notice that a part of our armor—the shoes—enables us to share the Good News of God's delivering power with others. By sharing our story, we give hope to others while also strengthening our own recovery.

HILIPPIANS

THE BIG PICTURE

A. JOY IN THE MIDST OF DIFFICULT CIRCUMSTANCES (1:1-30)
B. THE SECRET OF VICTORIOUS LIVING (2:1-30)
C. HAVING A VICTORIOUS FOCUS (3:1-21)
D. FINDING A JOYFUL FELLOWSHIP (4:1-23)

As a missionary and a traveling pastor, Paul depended on others for financial support. The Philippian church, which Paul planted during his second missionary journey, had supported him for ten years. They were compassionate people whose commitment to Christ and support of Christ's work were well known.

Paul wrote this letter to thank the Philippians and to challenge them to remain true to Christ and joyful in their circumstances. Wholeness of life, he reminded them, does not come from material things or pleasant circumstances. Genuine joy, meaning, and satisfaction come as we follow Christ and help others to grow spiritually.

Paul knew what he was talking about. He wrote this encouraging letter while facing a trial in Rome that, for all he knew, might lead to his execution. Paul had been both rich and poor; comfortable and in pain; healthy and sick; popular and the target of mobs. He had learned to be content, even joyful, no matter what the surrounding circumstances.

The letter to the Philippians has much to say to us. Our life had become unmanageable; we had hurt people we loved; and we had come to the end of our rope. Though the worst is behind us, we still must contend with day-to-day frustration, anger, and conflict. Yet, despite our painful circumstances, Christ can be our joy. Recovery will probably never be pleasant, but at the same time we need to remember that we have God with us. Because of that, we can have joy. The secret of getting and maintaining our joy can be found by increasing our knowledge of Christ and making him the center of our life each day.

THE BOTTOM LINE

PURPOSE: To thank the Philippian believers for their support of Paul's ministry, and to encourage them. AUTHOR: The apostle Paul. AUDIENCE: The believers in Philippi, a city in Macedonia. DATE WRITTEN: Around A.D. 61–62. SETTING: Paul, a prisoner in Rome, wrote this warm letter to the believers at Philippi after they sent him a generous gift. KEY VERSE: "Keep putting into practice all you learned from me and saw me doing, and the God of peace will be with you" (4:9). KEY PEOPLE AND RELATIONSHIPS: Paul with Timothy, Epaphroditus, and the Philippian believers.

RECOVERY THEMES

The Importance of Humility: When we turn our life over to God, we experience his power at work within us. He changes our life and gives us the control we once lacked. But a long time in successful recovery can make us prone to pride. We may begin to forget the source of power in our life and start to see ourself as self-sufficient. The letter to the Philippians reminds us to be humble, to adopt the attitude of Christ, who, "though he was God, did not demand and cling to his rights as God" (2:6). Our recovery must always involve a spirit of humility.

Recovery Leads to True Joy: Our life has been crazy, unmanageable, and out of control. When we admit our powerlessness and turn our life over to God, we not only start our recovery but also take the first steps toward finding true joy. We can have joy even during the tough times—because joy does not come from outward circumstances, but from inward strength. Joy comes from knowing Christ personally and from depending on his strength and power on a daily basis.

Recovery Requires Sacrifice: A sure sign of progress in our own recovery is when we begin to care about those around us who are still in bondage to their addictions. As Christ suffered and died so we might have life, we must make it our goal to sacrifice for others as well. It takes maturity to lay aside our own interests and carry the message of hope and recovery to others. But such a sacrifice is a part of our own recovery. Staying self-absorbed can set us up for pride and relapse; carrying the message of recovery to others will always strengthen us.

Fighting the Real Enemies: As we struggle with the recovery process, it is easy to have conflicts with other people. We are in pain and it can be very easy to turn against the people who are causing that pain. The believers at Philippi also "picked at each other." But as this letter reminds us, our battle should not be waged against one another. We need to concentrate our energy against much greater enemies: our powerful dependencies and destructive pride.

CHAPTER 1

Greetings from Paul

From: Paul and Timothy, slaves of Jesus Christ.
To: The pastors and deacons and all the Christians in the city of Philippi.
2May God bless you all. Yes, I pray that God
our Father and the Lord Jesus Christ will give each of you his fullest blessings and his peace in your hearts and your lives.

Paul Prays for the Philippians

3All my prayers for you are full of praise to
God! 4When I pray for you, my heart is full of
joy 5because of all your wonderful help in
making known the Good News about Christ
from the time you first heard it until now.
6And I am sure that God who began the good
work within you will keep right on helping
you grow in his grace until his task within you

1:3-11 Paul told the Philippians about how he had been praying for them. This would have been a great encouragement to those early believers. Our spiritual awakening will lead us to feel a growing concern for people in need. As we share the message of hope with others, we may also make prayer for their progress a part of our service to them. Our commitment to pray for other people struggling with addictions will have a significant impact on their spiritual growth. As we let them know we are behind them, not only will they grow in their faith, but we also will experience the encouragement we need to persevere in recovery.

1:12-14 In retrospect, Paul could see that the events of his life, both good and bad, had been allowed by God to help him spread the Good News. If we take an honest look at our life, we will probably find the same thing to be true. Through our painful addictions we gained the perspective needed to share the message of hope with others. Our personal story of deliverance is an essential tool for reaching others in need of recovery. As with Paul, our painful past and God's powerful deliverance open the door to our serving God and helping others in need.

1:19-24 We cannot lose if we belong to God. Whether we live or die, we know we will win in the end. During times of relapse and failure we may be tempted to give up on life completely. Paul's primary motivation for persevering was his deep concern for others who still needed to hear the good news of God's loving power. No matter how bad things are, if we entrust our life to God, he will come through for us. We will then have one more victory story to share with others. No matter how deeply we have failed or how many times we have fallen, God can still use us to help others. There is always a reason to live. God still wants to use us to save the lives of others just like us.

is finally finished on that day when Jesus
Christ returns.
[7]How natural it is that I should feel as I do about you, for you have a very special place in my heart. We have shared together the blessings of God, both when I was in prison and when I was out, defending the truth and telling others about Christ. [8]Only God knows how deep is my love and longing for you—with the tenderness of Jesus Christ. [9]My prayer for you is that you will overflow more and more with love for others, and at the same time keep on growing in spiritual knowledge and insight, [10]for I want you always to see clearly the difference between right and wrong, and to be inwardly clean, no one being able to criticize you from now until our Lord returns. [11]May you always be doing those good, kind things that show you are a child of God, for this will bring much praise and glory to the Lord.

A Call to Preach the Good News

[12]And I want you to know this, dear brothers: Everything that has happened to me here has been a great boost in getting out the Good News concerning Christ. [13]For everyone around here, including all the soldiers over at the barracks, knows that I am in chains simply because I am a Christian. [14]And because of my imprisonment, many of the Christians here seem to have lost their fear of chains! Somehow my patience has encouraged them, and they have become more and more bold in telling others about Christ.

[15]Some, of course, are preaching the Good News because they are jealous of the way God has used me. They want reputations as fearless preachers! But others have purer motives, [16,17]preaching because they love me, for they know that the Lord has brought me here to use me to defend the Truth. And some preach to make me jealous, thinking that their success will add to my sorrows here in jail! [18]But whatever their motive for doing it, the fact remains that the Good News about Christ is being preached, and I am glad.

[19]I am going to keep on being glad, for I know that as you pray for me, and as the Holy Spirit helps me, this is all going to turn out for my good. [20]For I live in eager expectation and hope that I will never do anything that will cause me to be ashamed of myself but that I will always be ready to speak out boldly for Christ while I am going through all these trials here, just as I have in the past; and that I will always be an honor to Christ, whether I

Perseverance

READ PHILIPPIANS 1:2-6

Sometimes we may feel like giving up the struggle. We try, to persevere, only to fall once again. We take two steps forward, but then stumble backwards. We feel condemned, and we fear that even God may give up on us. At times there are so many difficulties, so many issues to work through, so many patterns in our life that have to be changed, that we begin to feel like we are going crazy.

God acknowledges the difficulties we face, but he also promises us victory in the end. The apostle Paul once wrote, "Overwhelming victory is ours through Christ who loved us enough to die for us. For I am convinced that nothing can ever separate us from [Christ's] love. Death can't, and life can't. The angels won't, and all the powers of hell itself cannot keep God's love away. . . . Nothing will ever be able to separate us from the love of God demonstrated by our Lord Jesus Christ when he died for us" (Romans 8:37-39). Paul also said, "I am sure that God who began the good work within you will keep right on helping you grow in his grace until his task within you is finally finished on that day when Jesus Christ returns" (Philippians 1:6).

When we feel like we are going crazy and don't think that we can handle life, God is there. He is determined not to give up on us. We can rely on his persistent love. God has promised to keep working on us until we are whole. There will still be crazy times, but with his help we can handle life, one day at a time. ***Turn to page 1335, Colossians 3.***

live or whether I must die. [21]For to me, living
means opportunities for Christ, and dying—
well, that's better yet! [22]But if living will give
me more opportunities to win people to
Christ, then I really don't know which is
better, to live or die! [23]Sometimes I want to
live, and at other times I don't, for I long to
go and be with Christ. How much happier for
me than being here! [24]But the fact is that I can
be of more help to *you* by staying!

[25]Yes, I am still needed down here, and so I
feel certain I will be staying on earth a little
longer, to help you grow and become happy
in your faith; [26]my staying will make you glad
and give you reason to glorify Christ Jesus for
keeping me safe when I return to visit you
again.

[27]But whatever happens to me, remember
always to live as Christians should, so that
whether I ever see you again or not, I will keep
on hearing good reports that you are standing
side by side with one strong purpose—to tell
the Good News [28]fearlessly, no matter what
your enemies may do. They will see this as a
sign of their downfall, but for you it will be a
clear sign from God that he is with you, and
that he has given you eternal life with him.
[29]For to you has been given the privilege not
only of trusting him but also of suffering for
him. [30]We are in this fight together. You have
seen me suffer for him in the past; and I am
still in the midst of a great and terrible struggle now, as you know so well.

CHAPTER 2

Following Christ in Humility

Is there any such thing as Christians cheering
each other up? Do you love me enough to
want to help me? Does it mean anything to
you that we are brothers in the Lord, sharing
the same Spirit? Are your hearts tender and
sympathetic at all? [2]Then make me truly
happy by loving each other and agreeing
wholeheartedly with each other, working together with one heart and mind and purpose.

[3]Don't be selfish; don't live to make a good
impression on others. Be humble, thinking of
others as better than yourself. [4]Don't just
think about your own affairs, but be interested in others, too, and in what they are
doing.

[5]Your attitude should be the kind that was
shown us by Jesus Christ, [6]who, though he
was God, did not demand and cling to his
rights as God, [7]but laid aside his mighty power
and glory, taking the disguise of a slave and
becoming like men. [8]And he humbled himself

2:1-4 We are never an island unto ourself; we are a part of a whole, a member of Christ's body. If we are part of a loving community, when others hurt, we hurt; when we hurt, others hurt. Early in the recovery process we probably need to concentrate on our own welfare. But as we grow, we have to move beyond a self-centered focus and learn to be available to others. A necessary part of making amends with the people we have harmed is to prove to them that we have changed. As we learn to love others, we will find that others will learn to love us. As our relationships grow stronger, our addictions will lose their grip on our life.

2:5-11 Paul set Jesus Christ up as an ideal model for our humility in service. Our thoughts, attitudes, and actions are to become more and more like those exhibited by Christ during his earthly life. His willingness to humble himself is a great example for us. As we take an honest moral inventory of our life, we can be humble enough to admit our faults. Then we can begin to change the destructive patterns in our life. If we can follow Jesus Christ in humility, learning to admit our failures without hesitation, nothing will be able to stop our recovery.

2:12-18 Here we are reminded that obedience to God's program is one of the requirements for spiritual growth. Some of us may wonder how we are supposed to succeed at doing what God wants us to do. How can we be perfect? We have already admitted that we are powerless over the pull of our addictions. But God not only asks us to live a godly life, he also provides us with the power to do it (2:13). He is working in our life, helping us to obey him. As we get to know God by reading the Bible and spending time with him in prayer, he can begin to transform us from the inside out.

2:25-28 Being a believer in Christ is not always easy. As Epaphroditus clearly demonstrated, we need stamina to do the work and a servant's attitude to succeed in the spiritual battles we face. We must be willing to give ourself to the cause of Christ, choosing to put the needs of others before our personal comforts. The same is true in recovery. As we grow spiritually, we learn to put the needs of others before our own. We carry the message to fellow strugglers, despite difficulties and ridicule. As we do this, we begin to realize that when we give up our desires to meet the needs of others, we also leave behind the burden of our addictions. As we serve others, we build meaningful relationships and a strong foundation for a permanent recovery. By helping others, we have helped ourself.

even further, going so far as actually to die a
criminal's death on a cross.
[9]Yet it was because of this that God raised
him up to the heights of heaven and gave
him a name which is above every other name,
[10]that at the name of Jesus every knee shall
bow in heaven and on earth and under the
earth, [11]and every tongue shall confess that
Jesus Christ is Lord, to the glory of God the
Father.

Shining Lights in a Dark World

[12]Dearest friends, when I was there with you,
you were always so careful to follow my instructions. And now that I am away you must
be even more careful to do the good things
that result from being saved, obeying God
with deep reverence, shrinking back from all
that might displease him. [13]For God is at work
within you, helping you want to obey him,
and then helping you do what he wants.
[14]In everything you do, stay away from
complaining and arguing [15]so that no one can
speak a word of blame against you. You are to
live clean, innocent lives as children of God
in a dark world full of people who are crooked
and stubborn. Shine out among them like
beacon lights, [16]holding out to them
the Word of Life.

Then when Christ returns, how glad I will
be that my work among you was so worthwhile. [17]And if my lifeblood is, so to speak, to
be poured out over your faith, which I am
offering up to God as a sacrifice—that is, if I
am to die for you—even then I will be glad
and will share my joy with each of you. [18]For
you should be happy about this, too, and
rejoice with me for having this privilege of
dying for you.

Timothy and Epaphroditus Are Coming

[19]If the Lord is willing, I will send Timothy to
see you soon. Then when he comes back, he
can cheer me up by telling me all about you
and how you are getting along. [20]There is no
one like Timothy for having a real interest in
you; [21]everyone else seems to be worrying
about his own plans and not those of Jesus
Christ. [22]But you know Timothy. He has been
just like a son to me in helping me preach the
Good News. [23]I hope to send him to you just
as soon as I find out what is going to happen
to me here. [24]And I am trusting the Lord that
soon I myself may come to see you.
[25]Meanwhile, I thought I ought to send
Epaphroditus back to you. You sent him to
help me in my need; well, he and I have been

Into the Open

BIBLE READING: Philippians 2:5-9

We humbly asked him to remove our shortcomings.

Because of our pride, we may hide behind defenses during the recovery process. We may hide behind our good reputation, our position, or delusions of superiority. We may feel such inner shame that we go overboard to cover up with a self-righteous public identity. Those of us who have tried to protect ourself in this way will need a dramatic change of attitude.

The apostle Paul wrote, "Your attitude should be the kind that was shown us by Jesus Christ, who, though he was God, did not demand and cling to his rights as God, but laid aside his mighty power and glory, taking the disguise of a slave and becoming like men. And he humbled himself even further, going so far as actually to die a criminal's death on a cross. Yet it was because of this that God raised him up to the heights of heaven and gave him a name which is above every other name" (Philippians 2:5-9). The author of Hebrews wrote, "Keep your eyes on Jesus, our leader and instructor. He was willing to die a shameful death on the cross because of the joy he knew would be his afterwards; and now he sits in the place of honor by the throne of God" (Hebrews 12:2).

We can ask God to change our attitudes. When he deals with our pride, we will be able to stop hiding behind our reputation. We will allow ourself to become "anonymous," known as just another person struggling with addiction. When we humbly yield to God in recovery, he promises us future honor and the restoration of a good name. ***Turn to page 1435, 1 John 5.***

real brothers, working and battling side by side. [26]Now I am sending him home again, for he has been homesick for all of you and upset because you heard that he was ill. [27]And he surely was; in fact, he almost died. But God had mercy on him and on me, too, not allowing me to have this sorrow on top of everything else.

[28]So I am all the more anxious to get him back to you again, for I know how thankful you will be to see him, and that will make me happy and lighten all my cares. [29]Welcome him in the Lord with great joy, and show your appreciation, [30]for he risked his life for the work of Christ and was at the point of death while trying to do for me the things you couldn't do because you were far away.

CHAPTER 3

The Value of Knowing Christ

Whatever happens, dear friends, be glad in the Lord. I never get tired of telling you this, and it is good for you to hear it again and again.

[2]Watch out for those wicked men—dangerous dogs, I call them—who say you must be circumcised to be saved. [3]For it isn't the *cutting of our bodies* that makes us children of God; it is *worshiping him with our spirits*. That is the only true "circumcision." We Christians glory in what Christ Jesus has done for us and realize that we are helpless to save ourselves.

[4]Yet if anyone ever had reason to hope that he could save himself, it would be I. If others could be saved by what they are, certainly I could! [5]For I went through the Jewish initiation ceremony when I was eight days old, having been born into a pure-blooded Jewish home that was a branch of the old original Benjamin family. So I was a real Jew if there ever was one! What's more, I was a member of the Pharisees who demand the strictest obedience to every Jewish law and custom. [6]And sincere? Yes, so much so that I greatly persecuted the Church; and I tried to obey every Jewish rule and regulation right down to the very last point.

[7]But all these things that I once thought very worthwhile—now I've thrown them all away so that I can put my trust and hope in Christ alone. [8]Yes, everything else is worthless when compared with the priceless gain of knowing Christ Jesus my Lord. I have put aside all else, counting it worth less than nothing, in order that I can have Christ, [9]and become one with him, no longer counting on being saved by being good enough or by obeying God's laws, but by trusting Christ to

3:2-3 The world is filled with deceivers. We must be especially alert for those who offer recovery plans that exclude our need for God. The false teachers mentioned by Paul demanded that Gentile Christians obey the Jewish law of circumcision in order to be saved. The apostle stood against this claim, reminding the Philippians that only God through Jesus Christ could bring them the deliverance they sought. This message is for us, too. If someone claims we don't need God for a successful recovery, we should walk the other way. A program that depends on our actions will never succeed for long. In fact, until we admit that we are powerless to help ourself, our recovery won't even get off the ground.

3:4-11 In these verses, Paul made a detailed inventory of his past. And of all his past behaviors—including his religious activities—he found nothing worth hanging on to. He threw out his past life and replaced it with his new life in Christ. By means of Paul's personal illustration, we are urged to engage in an honest inventory of our heritage and accomplishments. As we compare the value of our past accomplishments to the power offered by Christ, we will find the new life God offers is the obvious choice. Our personal inventory helps us discover that the things of this world can't satisfy our eternal needs; only God can.

3:17-21 On the human level, we need to pattern our life after those who, despite difficulties, have been successful in managing their lives for Christ. Those who fail to examine themselves end up spending all their efforts living only for themselves, enslaved by destructive habits and dependencies. Full recovery, however, can be experienced by trusting Jesus Christ and following in his steps. Some of us may wonder if we will ever get beyond the pain we experience on a daily basis. But even if the pain remains throughout our life, we will be changed completely when Jesus Christ returns. If we trust in Jesus, our pain will not last forever.

4:1-3 Since we know with certainty what our ultimate destiny will be, we can have confidence to face the hardships of life. Paul set a good example for how we grow spiritually and encourage others in their growth. To encourage these two Christian women to reestablish their formerly harmonious relationship, he complimented them on their previous service to God. He was assuming that they were humble enough to take criticism and change for the better. When we keep a close watch on our own life, as Paul did, we will be better able to hold others accountable to their recovery commitments.

save me; for God's way of making us right
with himself depends on faith—counting on
Christ alone. 10Now I have given up everything else—I have found it to be the only way
to really know Christ and to experience the
mighty power that brought him back to life
again, and to find out what it means to suffer
and to die with him. 11So whatever it takes, I
will be one who lives in the fresh newness of
life of those who are alive from the dead.

Forgetting the Past; Reaching for the Goal

12I don't mean to say I am perfect. I haven't
learned all I should even yet, but I keep working toward that day when I will finally be all
that Christ saved me for and wants me to be.
13No, dear brothers, I am still not all I
should be, but I am bringing all my energies
to bear on this one thing: Forgetting the past
and looking forward to what lies ahead, 14I
strain to reach the end of the race and receive
the prize for which God is calling us up to
heaven because of what Christ Jesus did
for us.
15I hope all of you who are mature Christians will see eye-to-eye with me on these
things, and if you disagree on some point, I
believe that God will make it plain to you—
16if you fully obey the truth you have.
17Dear brothers, pattern your lives after
mine, and notice who else lives up to my
example. 18For I have told you often before,
and I say it again now with tears in my eyes,
there are many who walk along the Christian
road who are really enemies of the cross of
Christ. 19Their future is eternal loss, for their
god is their appetite: they are proud of what
they should be ashamed of; and all they think
about is this life here on earth. 20But our
homeland is in heaven, where our Savior, the
Lord Jesus Christ, is; and we are looking forward to his return from there. 21When he
comes back, he will take these dying bodies of
ours and change them into glorious bodies
like his own, using the same mighty power
that he will use to conquer all else everywhere.

CHAPTER 4

Thinking on Pure and Lovely Things

Dear brother Christians, I love you and long
to see you, for you are my joy and my reward
for my work. My beloved friends, stay true to
the Lord.
2And now I want to plead with those two
dear women, Euodias and Syntyche. Please,

Attitudes and Actions

BIBLE READING: Philippians 3:12-14

We were entirely ready to have God remove all these defects of character.

Getting "entirely ready" to have God remove "all" our defects of character sounds impossible. In reality we know that such perfection is out of reach. This is another way of saying that we are going to do our best to approach a lifelong goal that no one ever reaches this side of eternity.

The apostle Paul expressed a similar thought. He said, "I don't mean to say I am perfect. I haven't learned all I should even yet, but I keep working toward that day when I will finally be all that Christ saved me for and wants me to be. . . . Forgetting the past and looking forward to what lies ahead, I strain to reach the end of the race and receive the prize for which God is calling us up to heaven" (Philippians 3:12-14).

This combination of a positive attitude and energetic effort is a part of the mystery of our cooperation with God. Paul said, "Be even more careful to do the good things that result from being saved, obeying God with deep reverence, shrinking back from all that might displease him. For God is at work within you, helping you want to obey him, and then helping you do what he wants" (Philippians 2:12-13).

We will need to practice these steps the rest of our life. We don't have to demand perfection; it is enough to keep moving ahead as best we can. We can look forward to our rewards with the hope of becoming all that God intends us to be. God will strengthen and encourage us as we do so.

Turn to Step Seven, page 771, Isaiah 57.

please, with the Lord's help, quarrel no more—be friends again. [3]And I ask you, my true teammate, to help these women, for they worked side by side with me in telling the Good News to others; and they worked with Clement, too, and the rest of my fellow workers whose names are written in the Book of Life.

[4]Always be full of joy in the Lord; I say it again, rejoice! [5]Let everyone see that you are unselfish and considerate in all you do. Remember that the Lord is coming soon. [6]Don't worry about anything; instead, pray about everything; tell God your needs, and don't forget to thank him for his answers. [7]If you do this, you will experience God's peace, which is far more wonderful than the human mind can understand. His peace will keep your thoughts and your hearts quiet and at rest as you trust in Christ Jesus.

[8]And now, brothers, as I close this letter, let me say this one more thing: Fix your thoughts on what is true and good and right. Think about things that are pure and lovely, and dwell on the fine, good things in others. Think about all you can praise God for and be glad about. [9]Keep putting into practice all you learned from me and saw me doing, and the God of peace will be with you.

God Supplies Our Needs

[10]How grateful I am and how I praise the Lord that you are helping me again. I know you have always been anxious to send what you could, but for a while you didn't have the chance. [11]Not that I was ever in need, for I have learned how to get along happily whether I have much or little. [12]I know how to live on almost nothing or with everything. I have learned the secret of contentment in every situation, whether it be a full stomach or hunger, plenty or want; [13]for I can do everything God asks me to with the help of Christ who gives me the strength and power. [14]But even so, you have done right in helping me in my present difficulty.

[15]As you well know, when I first brought the Gospel to you and then went on my way, leaving Macedonia, only you Philippians became my partners in giving and receiving. No other church did this. [16]Even when I was over in Thessalonica you sent help twice. [17]But though I appreciate your gifts, what makes me happiest is the well-earned reward you will have because of your kindness.

[18]At the moment I have all I need—more than I need! I am generously supplied with the gifts you sent me when Epaphroditus came. They are a sweet-smelling sacrifice that pleases God well. [19]And it is he who will supply all your needs from his riches in glory because of what Christ Jesus has done for us. [20]Now unto God our Father be glory forever and ever. Amen.

Sincerely, Paul

Paul's Final Greetings

P.S. [21]Say hello for me to all the Christians there; the brothers with me send their greetings, too. [22]And all the other Christians here want to be remembered to you, especially those who work in Caesar's palace. [23]The blessings of our Lord Jesus Christ be upon your spirits.

4:4-9 True happiness can be found in any situation of life when we recognize that God is at work. Because Christ is with us and his return is certain, we can act calmly in the face of painful and difficult situations. Peace comes when we focus on those things that provide lasting value to our life. The more we commit ourself to knowing God's will through prayer and the study of his Word, the better prepared we are to help ourself and others in the process of recovery.

4:12-13 Some of us may wonder if we will ever have a peaceful life again. Our battle against addiction seems endless and hard. We find ourself in a continually helpless situation. When we get discouraged and recognize that recovery is too hard for us to achieve alone, we can return to these verses for renewed hope. God wants us to make progress in recovery, and he has the power to help us do it. As we entrust our life to God, we will be able to make progress in recovery with the help of Christ who gives us the strength we need. With God, nothing is impossible!

4:15-20 Paul's relationship with the Philippian believers was characterized by mutual respect and sharing. These are important qualities in any strong relationship and should characterize our relationships in recovery. Paul was a great Christian leader, respected by thousands of believers in the early church. Many in his position would have had a hard time accepting the help the Philippians offered and might have tried to go it alone. It is sometimes difficult to accept the help offered by others. Perhaps we feel they really don't understand where we are coming from or are just trying to manipulate us, doing things that make them feel good about themselves. If we hope to succeed in recovery, however, we need to follow Paul's example. He joyfully received the help offered by the Philippian believers and, as a result, was able to stand firm through some tough, lonely times.

READ PHILIPPIANS 4:10-14

GOD grant me the serenity to accept the things I cannot change the courage to change the things I can and the wisdom to know the difference AMEN

Serenity hints at tranquility, having an inner calm in the midst of the ups and downs of life. It involves learning to be content with the things that cannot be changed in our life.

Some of us have never accepted the hurtful circumstances of our life. We may be living in denial to avoid the pain. We continue to struggle against the painful realities, to rebel against who we are or what has happened to us. There are others of us who have accepted the bad, even to the point that it feels normal and comfortable. Therefore, we repeat destructive cycles of behavior.

The apostle Paul wrote, "I have learned how to get along happily whether I have much or little. I know how to live on almost nothing or with everything. I have learned the secret of contentment in every situation, whether it be a full stomach or hunger, plenty or want" (Philippians 4:11-12). When Paul wrote these words, he was in a Roman prison waiting to hear if he would be executed. And yet we hear no whining or complaining. Instead, he learned to accept the circumstances he could not change.

The process of recovery is a time of learning to find serenity while also accepting life as it is. Life isn't fair. It isn't predictable or controllable. It can be wonderfully rich in some ways and terribly difficult in others. When we become willing to face the hurt in our life and consider how we have reacted to it, then our discomfort can lead us to break the destructive cycles. Then we can learn to be content with the things we cannot change. ***Turn to page 1333, Colossians 1.***

COLOSSIANS

THE BIG PICTURE

A. THE POWER OF JESUS CHRIST (1:1–2:23)
B. CHRIST'S POWER WITHIN US (3:1–4:18)

Colossians is a letter about the greatness of Christ. Since their conversion, the believers in Colosse had heard many theories about salvation, all of which diminished Christ in some way. Some people had faith in angels, some in rituals, and others in various religious philosophies or practices. Paul wrote to correct them all: Christ is God in the flesh and the only one sufficient to save us from sin and its destructive power.

In this letter, Paul included some practical advice about the kind of life the believers were to live. He called them to adhere to the truth, to live sexually pure lives, to live in peace with their friends and neighbors, and to live in dependence on God. Paul did not expect the Colossians to accomplish these things on their own. He emphasized the fact that when we seek to do God's will, we can depend on God's help. Our actions can be energized by the greatest power in the universe—the power of God in Jesus Christ.

Recovery is easier when we lean on others, but ultimately God is the only one who can rescue us completely. We need God's power to begin the process of healing in our recovery. The same power that made salvation possible is the power that makes it possible for us to recover. We can trust Christ to save us, and we can "trust him, too, for each day's problems" (2:6). In Christ we have the power to live each day as it comes.

THE BOTTOM LINE

PURPOSE: To show us that Christ is the only real source of power in our life. AUTHOR: The apostle Paul. AUDIENCE: The believers at Colosse, a city in Asia Minor. DATE WRITTEN: Around A.D. 60, while Paul was in prison in Rome. SETTING: Paul was writing to a church that he had never visited. It had been started by some of his converts, including a man named Epaphras. KEY VERSES: "For in Christ there is all of God in a human body; *so you have everything when you have Christ,* and you are filled with God through your union with Christ. He is the highest Ruler, with authority over every other power" (2:9-10). KEY PEOPLE AND RELATIONSHIPS: Paul with Timothy, Tychicus, Onesimus, John Mark, and Epaphras.

RECOVERY THEMES

Recovery Is a Lifelong Process: It is easy to long for a day when we will be totally free from the bondage of our past—a day when our recovery will be complete and we can go on with life. But our recovery is a lifelong process, with daily challenges to maintain contact with our powerful and loving God. From this letter to the Colossian believers, we learn that our life with Christ is not just a one-time rescue operation, but a lifelong commitment.

True Recovery Involves Faith in God: One danger we face after a period of successful recovery is our tendency to forget how much we need God. It is easy to start thinking we can go it alone, depending on rules or formulas for "success." Paul warned the Colossians about this danger, urging them to live in daily contact and communication with God. It is true that with maturity comes strength of character, but it is not true that we can end our need for faith in God. Self-sufficiency got us into trouble in the first place, and it can lead to relapse as well. If we are to experience true recovery, we need to acknowledge our ongoing need for faith in God.

Jesus Is Lord of the Universe: The entire universe is being held together by the power of Jesus Christ. He is the supreme ruler and Lord of all creation. He is the reflection of the invisible God. He is eternal, preexistent, omnipotent, and equal with the Father. He is also the Lord of every successful recovery. What a privilege to depend not merely on some anonymous "higher Power," but on the highest Power of all. How incredible that he invites us to have a personal relationship with him!

Healthy Relationships: An important part of the recovery process involves making amends with the people we have wronged. This letter to the Colossians gives us practical guidance in this area. Paul calls us to live according to the principles of selfless love and to share mutual respect with all the people in our life. If we can treat others in ways that build them up, we will discover that our relationships grow stronger and support us in the recovery process.

CHAPTER 1

Greetings from Paul

From: Paul, chosen by God to be Jesus Christ's
messenger, and from Brother Timothy.
2*To:* The faithful Christian brothers—God's
people—in the city of Colosse.

May God our Father shower you with blessings and fill you with his great peace.

Paul's Prayer for the Colossians

3Whenever we pray for you, we always begin
by giving thanks to God the Father of our
Lord Jesus Christ, 4for we have heard how
much you trust the Lord, and how much you
love his people. 5And you are looking forward
to the joys of heaven, and have been ever
since the Gospel first was preached to you.
6The same Good News that came to you is
going out all over the world and changing
lives everywhere, just as it changed yours that
very first day you heard it and understood
about God's great kindness to sinners.
7Epaphras, our much-loved fellow worker,
was the one who brought you this Good
News. He is Jesus Christ's faithful slave, here
to help us in your place. 8And he is the one
who has told us about the great love for others
that the Holy Spirit has given you.
9So ever since we first heard about you we
have kept on praying and asking God to help
you understand what he wants you to do;
asking him to make you wise about spiritual

1:11-14 As always, Paul was careful to point out that our strength and power come not from ourself, but from God. Only God's power at work within our life can give us the ability to make progress in recovery. We have already admitted that we are powerless over our dependencies. By recognizing that God has the power to restore us to sanity, we can begin to think more positively about our recovery.

1:15-17 These verses describe God in Jesus Christ, our higher Power. As the Creator of our world, he has the means to rebuild our life no matter how broken it is. In fact, the entire universe would dissolve if he stopped holding it together. Even people who seem to have things under control could not exist a moment longer if it wasn't for the power of God expended on their behalf. We all need God and his power, whether we admit it or not. God is our infinite power source, and he can provide all the power we need to pursue recovery.

1:20-23 Here Paul describes how we feel when our life is unmanageable and spinning out of control. In that state we are God's enemies, and our thoughts and actions separate us from him. It is, however, precisely at that point that God in Christ reaches out to make us his friends. That is why turning our life and our will over to him is a reasonable thing to do.

READ COLOSSIANS 1:2-14

GOD grant me the serenity
to accept the things I cannot change
the courage to change the things I can
and the wisdom to know the difference
AMEN

Many of us in recovery are learning to think and act in new ways. We may find it hard to recognize true wisdom, even when it's staring us in the face.

We may need some guidelines to help us identify wisdom in our thoughts and choices of action. According to the Bible, there are two aspects of wisdom: the spiritual and the practical. Spiritual wisdom gives insight into the true nature of things. It includes things like "asking God to help you understand what he wants you to do; asking him to make you wise about spiritual things; . . . learning to know God better and better" (Colossians 1:9-10). Special wisdom is also sometimes given "that your hearts will be flooded with light so that you can see something of the future he has called you to share" (Ephesians 1:18).

Wisdom can be evaluated by its qualities. The Bible tells us that God's wisdom is "first of all pure and full of quiet gentleness. Then it is peace-loving and courteous. It allows discussion and is willing to yield to others; it is full of mercy and good deeds. It is wholehearted and straightforward and sincere" (James 3:17).

On the practical level, our wisdom can be judged by whether or not our actions conform to God's instructions. God's instructions were given to us because they naturally lead to healthy living. Using them, we can find the wisdom we need to walk toward wholeness. This can be one of the standards we use in our continuing daily inventory. ***Turn to page 1365, 2 Timothy 4.***

---

things; 10and asking that the way you live will
always please the Lord and honor him, so that
you will always be doing good, kind things for
others, while all the time you are learning to
know God better and better.

11We are praying, too, that you will be filled
with his mighty, glorious strength so that you
can keep going no matter what happens—always full of the joy of the Lord, 12and always
thankful to the Father who has made us fit to
share all the wonderful things that belong to
those who live in the Kingdom of light. 13For
he has rescued us out of the darkness and
gloom of Satan's kingdom and brought us
into the Kingdom of his dear Son, 14who
bought our freedom with his blood and forgave us all our sins.

Who Is Jesus Christ?

15Christ is the exact likeness of the unseen
God. He existed before God made anything at
all, and, in fact, 16Christ himself is the Creator
who made everything in heaven and earth,
the things we can see and the things we can't;
the spirit world with its kings and kingdoms,
its rulers and authorities; all were made by
Christ for his own use and glory. 17He was
before all else began and it is his power that
holds everything together. 18He is the Head of
the body made up of his people—that is, his
Church—which he began; and he is the
Leader of all those who arise from the dead,
so that he is first in everything; 19for God
wanted all of himself to be in his Son.

20It was through what his Son did that God
cleared a path for everything to come to
him—all things in heaven and on earth—for
Christ's death on the cross has made peace
with God for all by his blood. 21This includes
you who were once so far away from God. You
were his enemies and hated him and were
separated from him by your evil thoughts and

actions, yet now he has brought you back as his friends. 22He has done this through the death on the cross of his own human body, and now as a result Christ has brought you into the very presence of God, and you are standing there before him with nothing left against you—nothing left that he could even chide you for; 23the only condition is that you fully believe the Truth, standing in it steadfast and firm, strong in the Lord, convinced of the Good News that Jesus died for you, and never shifting from trusting him to save you. This is the wonderful news that came to each of you and is now spreading all over the world. And I, Paul, have the joy of telling it to others.

Paul's Mission and Concern

24But part of my work is to suffer for you; and I am glad, for I am helping to finish up the remainder of Christ's sufferings for his body, the Church.

25God has sent me to help his Church and to tell his secret plan to you Gentiles. 26,27He has kept this secret for centuries and generations past, but now at last it has pleased him to tell it to those who love him and live for him, and the riches and glory of his plan are for you Gentiles, too. And this is the secret: *Christ in your hearts is your only hope of glory.*

28So everywhere we go we talk about Christ to all who will listen, warning them and teaching them as well as we know how. We want to be able to present each one to God, perfect because of what Christ has done for each of them. 29This is my work, and I can do it only because Christ's mighty energy is at work within me.

CHAPTER 2

I wish you could know how much I have struggled in prayer for you and for the church at Laodicea, and for my many other friends who have never known me personally. 2This is what I have asked of God for you: that you will be encouraged and knit together by strong ties of love, and that you will have the rich experience of knowing Christ with real certainty and clear understanding. *For God's secret plan, now at last made known, is Christ himself.* 3In him lie hidden all the mighty, untapped treasures of wisdom and knowledge.

New Life in Christ

4I am saying this because I am afraid that someone may fool you with smooth talk. 5For though I am far away from you my heart is with you, happy because you are getting along so well, happy because of your strong faith in Christ. 6And now just as you trusted Christ to save you, trust him, too, for each day's problems; live in vital union with him. 7Let your roots grow down into him and draw up nourishment from him. See that you go on growing in the Lord, and become strong and vigorous in the truth you were taught. Let your lives overflow with joy and thanksgiving for all he has done.

1:28-29 An essential part of rebuilding our life is to carry the message of our recovery in Jesus Christ to others. We were far away from God, yet he provided not only the solution to our problem, but also the power to change. That is news worth sharing! We may be afraid to do this at first, but the power available for our recovery is also available to help us share our story.

2:6-7 The same faith that we exercised when we turned our life over to God is to be used daily as we walk with God. Paul urges us to improve our conscious contact with God, so that his power will be at work within us, filling us with joy and thanksgiving. Without God's power feeding into our life, we are at the mercy of our destructive habits and dependencies.

2:9-10 When we tried to change through our own efforts, we realized just how powerless we were. It was then that we realized the truth found in Paul's statement—that everything we need is found not in ourself, nor even in others, but in Jesus Christ. A recovery that does not build itself on the person and power of Jesus Christ will always be incomplete.

2:11-15 The power of Christ is able to restore us to sanity and to help us overcome the destructive patterns from our past. Since he has authority over every other power, including the power of evil in our life, Jesus can set us free. Our freedom is not just from the bondage of the past, but also from the spiritual bondage of our old evil nature. In Christ, we can experience the life of peace and joy that God intends for us.

2:20-23 There are many programs for recovery with strict rules that need to be followed. Perhaps the program with the most rules is the one we have tried to create for ourself in order to break free from our bondage. "We just need to try harder," we tell ourselves. But Paul tells us that this kind of program will never work in the long run because it looks to our own strength as a means to success. It leads us away from the only adequate power source—God in Jesus Christ. He is the only one with the power to transform us and help us rebuild our life.

8Don't let others spoil your faith and joy
with their philosophies, their wrong and shallow answers built on men's thoughts and
ideas, instead of on what Christ has said. 9For
in Christ there is all of God in a human body;
10*so you have everything when you have Christ,*
and you are filled with God through your
union with Christ. He is the highest Ruler,
with authority over every other power.
11When you came to Christ, he set you free
from your evil desires, not by a bodily operation of circumcision but by a spiritual operation, the baptism of your souls. 12For in
baptism you see how your old, evil nature
died with him and was buried with him; and
then you came up out of death with him into
a new life because you trusted the Word of the
mighty God who raised Christ from the dead.
13You were dead in sins, and your sinful
desires were not yet cut away. Then he gave
you a share in the very life of Christ, for he
forgave all your sins, 14and blotted out the
charges proved against you, the list of his
commandments which you had not obeyed.
He took this list of sins and destroyed it by
nailing it to Christ's cross. 15In this way God
took away Satan's power to accuse you of sin,
and God openly displayed to the whole world
Christ's triumph at the cross where your sins
were all taken away.

Freedom from Jewish Law

16So don't let anyone criticize you for what
you eat or drink, or for not celebrating Jewish
holidays and feasts or new moon ceremonies
or Sabbaths. 17For these were only temporary
rules that ended when Christ came. They
were only shadows of the real thing—of
Christ himself. 18Don't let anyone declare you
lost when you refuse to worship angels, as
they say you must. They have seen a vision,
they say, and know you should. These proud
men (though they claim to be so humble)
have a very clever imagination. 19But they are
not connected to Christ, the Head to which
all of us who are his body are joined; for we
are joined together by his strong sinews, and
we grow only as we get our nourishment and
strength from God.
20Since you died, as it were, with Christ and
this has set you free from following the
world's ideas of how to be saved—by doing
good and obeying various rules—why do you
keep right on following them anyway, still
bound by such rules as 21not eating, tasting, or
even touching certain foods? 22Such rules are
mere human teachings, for food was made to

Self-protection

READ COLOSSIANS 3:1-4

The world doesn't get any better just because we are in recovery! We still have to pay our bills, deal with people, and face the stressful changes that recovery can bring. There are pressures beyond our control that will tend to wear us down if we aren't careful to protect ourself from the world's onslaught of anxiety.

The apostle Paul gave us a strategy to help guard against the troubles of daily life. He wrote, "Let heaven fill your thoughts; don't spend your time worrying about things down here" (Colossians 3:2). The apostle also wrote, "Don't worry about anything; instead, pray about everything; tell God your needs, and don't forget to thank him for his answers. If you do this, you will experience God's peace, which is far more wonderful than the human mind can understand. His peace will keep your thoughts and your hearts quiet and at rest as you trust in Christ Jesus" (Philippians 4:6-7).

The word translated "keep" is a military term that means to keep under guard, like one protected by a sentry. The image is one of a guard marching around the border of our heart and mind to keep out the pressing anxieties of life. This is only promised if we routinely turn every worry and need over to God and develop an attitude of gratitude. When we turn our worries over to the care of God, we will discover his protection and experience the inner peace that passes all understanding. ***Turn to page 1347, 2 Thessalonians 3.***

be eaten and used up. 23These rules may seem good, for rules of this kind require strong devotion and are humiliating and hard on the body, but they have no effect when it comes to conquering a person's evil thoughts and desires. They only make him proud.

CHAPTER 3

Principles to Live By

Since you became alive again, so to speak, when Christ arose from the dead, now set your sights on the rich treasures and joys of heaven where he sits beside God in the place of honor and power. 2Let heaven fill your thoughts; don't spend your time worrying about things down here. 3You should have as little desire for this world as a dead person does. Your real life is in heaven with Christ and God. 4And when Christ who is our real life comes back again, you will shine with him and share in all his glories.

5Away then with sinful, earthly things; deaden the evil desires lurking within you; have nothing to do with sexual sin, impurity, lust, and shameful desires; don't worship the good things of life, for that is idolatry. 6God's terrible anger is upon those who do such things. 7You used to do them when your life was still part of this world; 8but now is the time to cast off and throw away all these rotten garments of anger, hatred, cursing, and dirty language.

9Don't tell lies to each other; it was your old life with all its wickedness that did that sort of thing; now it is dead and gone. 10You are living a brand new kind of life that is continually learning more and more of what is right, and trying constantly to be more and more like Christ who created this new life within you. 11In this new life one's nationality or race or education or social position is unimportant; such things mean nothing. Whether a person has Christ is what matters, and he is equally available to all.

12Since you have been chosen by God who has given you this new kind of life, and because of his deep love and concern for you, you should practice tenderhearted mercy and kindness to others. Don't worry about making a good impression on them, but be ready to suffer quietly and patiently. 13Be gentle and ready to forgive; never hold grudges. Remember, the Lord forgave you, so you must forgive others.

14Most of all, let love guide your life, for then the whole church will stay together in perfect harmony. 15Let the peace of heart that comes from Christ be always present in your hearts and lives, for this is your responsibility and privilege as members of his body. And always be thankful.

16Remember what Christ taught, and let his words enrich your lives and make you wise; teach them to each other and sing them out in psalms and hymns and spiritual songs, singing to the Lord with thankful hearts. 17And whatever you do or say, let it be as a representative of the Lord Jesus, and come with him into the presence of God the Father to give him your thanks.

3:1-3 Paul isn't urging us to deny the harsh realities of life; he is simply reminding us of where our focus should be. When our eyes are on Christ, we see the matters of this life from a different perspective. We realize that there is hope, even when everything seems dark and hopeless. When we learn to see with an eternal perspective, the struggles of our recovery don't disappear; rather, they are seen in the proper light. They no longer have the terrifying power that they once did. When we keep our eyes on Christ and his promises for our recovery, no obstacle is too great for us to overcome.

3:9-11 To make progress in recovery it is essential that we take a personal inventory and then make amends to the people we have hurt. This involves shedding our denial and learning to be truly honest about our failures. As we recognize our character flaws and seek to change with God's help, we begin to live a new kind of life. This new life with God at the center involves taking an honest personal inventory on a regular basis. Although we will never reach a state of perfection in this life, by allowing God to show us our progress, we affirm the new life that God is creating within us through Jesus Christ.

3:12-13 Paul urges us to maintain our relationships with other people. This advice is especially important for those of us in recovery. Our addictions have probably destroyed or severely strained all our important relationships, and we have a lot of work to do on this front. We need to make amends where necessary, to seek forgiveness from those we have hurt, and to forgive those who have hurt us. Obviously, there are some situations where we cannot, or should not, directly involve the people we have harmed. In such cases Paul urges caution, telling us to be gentle and not to hold grudges. As we seek to make amends, our actions are to be governed by the principle of selfless love.

Principles for Healthy Relationships
18You wives, submit yourselves to your husbands, for that is what the Lord has planned
for you. 19And you husbands must be loving
and kind to your wives and not bitter against
them nor harsh.
20You children must always obey your
fathers and mothers, for that pleases the Lord.
21Fathers, don't scold your children so much
that they become discouraged and quit trying.
22You slaves must always obey your earthly
masters, not only trying to please them when
they are watching you but all the time; obey
them willingly because of your love for the
Lord and because you want to please him.
23Work hard and cheerfully at all you do, just
as though you were working for the Lord and
not merely for your masters, 24remembering
that it is the Lord Christ who is going to pay
you, giving you your full portion of all he
owns. He is the one you are really working for.
25And if you don't do your best for him, he
will pay you in a way that you won't like—for
he has no special favorites who can get away
with shirking.

CHAPTER 4
You slave owners must be just and fair to all
your slaves. Always remember that you, too,
have a Master in heaven who is closely watching you.
2Don't be weary in prayer; keep at it; watch
for God's answers, and remember to be thankful when they come. 3Don't forget to pray for
us too, that God will give us many chances to
preach the Good News of Christ for which I
am here in jail. 4Pray that I will be bold
enough to tell it freely and fully and make it
plain, as, of course, I should.
5Make the most of your chances to tell
others the Good News. Be wise in all your
contacts with them. 6Let your conversation be
gracious as well as sensible, for then you will
have the right answer for everyone.

Paul's Final Greetings
7Tychicus, our much-loved brother, will tell
you how I am getting along. He is a hard
worker and serves the Lord with me. 8I have
sent him on this special trip just to see how
you are and to comfort and encourage you. 9I
am also sending Onesimus, a faithful and
much-loved brother, one of your own people.
He and Tychicus will give you all the latest
news.
10Aristarchus, who is with me here as a
prisoner, sends you his love, and so does
Mark, a relative of Barnabas. And as I said
before, give Mark a hearty welcome if he
comes your way. 11Jesus Justus also sends his
love. These are the only Jewish Christians
working with me here, and what a comfort
they have been!
12Epaphras, from your city, a servant of
Christ Jesus, sends you his love. He is always
earnestly praying for you, asking God to make
you strong and perfect and to help you know
his will in everything you do. 13I can assure
you that he has worked hard for you with his
prayers, and also for the Christians in Laodicea and Hierapolis.
14Dear Doctor Luke sends his love, and so
does Demas.
15Please give my greeting to the Christian
friends at Laodicea, and to Nymphas, and to
those who meet in his home. 16By the way,
after you have read this letter, will you pass it
on to the church at Laodicea? And read the
letter I wrote to them. 17And say to Archippus,
"Be sure that you do all the Lord has told you
to."
18Here is my own greeting in my own handwriting: Remember me here in jail. May God's
blessings surround you.

Sincerely, Paul

4:2-3 Paul encouraged the Colossian believers to persevere in prayer. This is good advice for us, too. As we pray, we acknowledge our need for a higher Power and are reminded to keep our eyes on God. As we make prayer a daily priority, we are reminded to thank God for his help, and we become increasingly aware of his activity in our life. And when we are feeling weak, we can still come to God in prayer. He will then empower us to "keep at it." As we turn to God in prayer, we embrace the power sufficient to meet our needs in recovery.

FIRST THESSALONIANS

THE BIG PICTURE

A. GREETINGS (1:1)
B. CONGRATULATIONS (1:2–3:13)
   1. Paul's Commendation for Their Progress (1:2-10)
   2. Paul's Conduct while with Them (2:1-12)
   3. Paul's Concern for Their Continued Recovery (2:13–3:13)
C. CONSULTATIONS (4:1–5:22)
   1. Concerning Morality (4:1-8)
   2. Concerning Mutual Love (4:9-12)
   3. Concerning Deceased Christians (4:13-18)
   4. Concerning Accountability before God (5:1-11)
   5. Concerning Our Conduct in Relationships (5:12-22)
D. BENEDICTION AND CLOSING THOUGHTS (5:23-28)

Paul and his companions Silas and Timothy first traveled to Thessalonica on their second missionary journey (see Acts 17:1-4). Many people there who had worshiped idols turned their lives over to God, and for this Paul commended them. The believers in Thessalonica had gone from a life of dependency upon material things and empty ritual to a life of serving the living and true God.

Their new life of faith was not easy, though. Many of their friends and relatives opposed it. Despite the positive changes God had made in their lives, some people harassed and teased them. This persecution forced Paul and his companions to leave Thessalonica. After he left, Paul became concerned about the new believers he had left there. Had they been grounded in their new faith in God? Would they relapse into old patterns of belief and practice? Paul sent Timothy to check on them, and, encouraged by Timothy's report, Paul sent them this letter of encouragement.

When we meet with opposition in our recovery, we can identify with Paul and the believers at Thessalonica. Friends and family members may not understand our faith; old habits may be a source of pressure, pushing us from within to return to our old ways. But we can be encouraged by the progress we have already made. God's power is at work within us. We don't have to quit just because we face opposition.

THE BOTTOM LINE

PURPOSE: To commend the believers in Thessalonica for their trust in God, to encourage them to continue trusting him, and to reassure them that Christ would return. AUTHOR: The apostle Paul. AUDIENCE: The believers in Thessalonica, a city in Macedonia. DATE WRITTEN: About A.D. 50–51, during Paul's second missionary journey. SETTING: The church in Thessalonica was only two or three years old when Paul wrote this letter. The believers there needed to mature spiritually, and they needed some help in understanding what to expect at the return of Christ. KEY VERSE: "For you are all children of the light and of the day, and do not belong to darkness and night" (5:5). KEY PEOPLE AND RELATIONSHIPS: Paul with the believers at Thessalonica and with Timothy.

RECOVERY THEMES

God Is Our Source of Hope: If we have placed our trust in Christ to save us from sin, we will live with him forever—we have eternal life. But we can have hope in more than just life beyond the grave; we can also have hope in what God brings to our life in the present. The power that raised Jesus Christ from the dead is nothing less than the power of God—the God to whom we have entrusted our life. With this kind of power available to us, there is always hope!

Recovery Is a Way of Life: Paul challenged the Thessalonians to live at all times in humble anticipation of Christ's coming—to live each day as if it were important. In a similar way, we need to live one day at a time, realizing that our recovery will never be complete in this life. We need to live responsibly, working and living in dependence on God at all times. We are always in recovery; when we become complacent and forget that fact, we set ourself up for a relapse.

Commitment That Overcomes Obstacles: We are all flawed human beings, with numerous limitations and problems. Because of this, we will always face obstacles to our continued recovery. Living in this world means we need to stand firm in our commitment to recovery, knowing that the Holy Spirit empowers us with God's strength. Though God's power is available to all of us, God will not do the work of recovery for us. To make progress, we must commit ourself to the task.

CHAPTER 1

Opening Greetings

From: Paul, Silas, and Timothy.

To: The church at Thessalonica—to you who belong to God the Father and the Lord Jesus Christ: May blessing and peace of heart be your rich gifts from God our Father and from Jesus Christ our Lord.

Paul Commends the Thessalonians

2We always thank God for you and pray for
you constantly. 3We never forget your loving
deeds as we talk to our God and Father about
you, and your strong faith and steady looking
forward to the return of our Lord Jesus Christ.
4We know that God has chosen you, dear
brothers, much beloved of God. 5For when we
brought you the Good News, it was not just
meaningless chatter to you; no, you listened
with great interest. What we told you produced a powerful effect upon you, for the
Holy Spirit gave you great and full assurance
that what we said was true. And you know
how our very lives were further proof to you
of the truth of our message. 6So you became
our followers and the Lord's; for you received
our message with joy from the Holy Spirit in
spite of the trials and sorrows it brought you.
7Then you yourselves became an example
to all the other Christians in Greece. 8And
now the Word of the Lord has spread out from
you to others everywhere, far beyond your
boundaries, for wherever we go we find
people telling us about your remarkable faith
in God. We don't need to tell *them* about it,
9for *they* keep telling *us* about the wonderful
welcome you gave us, and how you turned
away from your idols to God so that now the
living and true God only is your Master. 10And
they speak of how you are looking forward to

1:2-3 Paul is thankful for the Thessalonian believers and their love for each other, their faith in God, and their hope in Christ's return. The triad of faith, love, and hope is a summary of the Christian life (see 1 Corinthians 13:13). Faith in an all-powerful God is demonstrated by living one day at a time. Love is shown as principles of truth are demonstrated through sacrificial service to others. Hope carries us through the hard times as we depend upon God.

1:4-6 The Thessalonians had been restored to productive roles in God's Kingdom and had gained freedom from bondage to idols because they believed in Jesus Christ and experienced his transforming power in their lives. This same power—our higher Power—makes all the difference between a doomed do-it-yourself recovery and true, God-centered recovery. When we recognize our powerlessness and entrust our life to God, we allow God's infinite resources to work on our behalf.

1:7-9 The Thessalonian believers had experienced a spiritual awakening through belief in Jesus Christ. As they imitated his ways, despite the persecution it brought them, they became an example that led many in the surrounding area to experience the healing offered by God in Jesus Christ. An essential part of our recovery is sharing the Good News of God's powerful deliverance with others. We can allow this to be the natural outflow of our experience of salvation. As God delivers us from our dependencies, we can give hope to others by sharing our story. And as we do so, we will not only inspire hope in others; we will also experience personal encouragement as we recall all the great things God has done in our life.

the return of God's Son from heaven—Jesus, whom God brought back to life—and he is our only Savior from God's terrible anger against sin.

CHAPTER 2

Paul Remembers His Friends

You yourselves know, dear brothers, how worthwhile that visit was. 2You know how badly we had been treated at Philippi just before we came to you and how much we suffered there. Yet God gave us the courage to boldly repeat the same message to you, even though we were surrounded by enemies. 3So you can see that we were not preaching with any false motives or evil purposes in mind; we were perfectly straightforward and sincere.

4For we speak as messengers from God, trusted by him to tell the truth; we change his message not one bit to suit the taste of those who hear it; for we serve God alone, who examines our hearts' deepest thoughts. 5Never once did we try to win you with flattery, as you very well know, and God knows we were not just pretending to be your friends so that you would give us money! 6As for praise, we have never asked for it from you or anyone else, although as apostles of Christ we certainly had a right to some honor from you. 7But we were as gentle among you as a mother feeding and caring for her own children. 8We loved you dearly—so dearly that we gave you not only God's message, but our own lives too.

9Don't you remember, dear brothers, how hard we worked among you? Night and day we toiled and sweated to earn enough to live on so that our expenses would not be a burden to anyone there, as we preached God's Good News among you. 10You yourselves are our witnesses—as is God—that we have been pure and honest and faultless toward every one of you. 11We talked to you as a father to his own children—don't you remember?—pleading with you, encouraging you and even demanding 12that your daily lives should not embarrass God but bring joy to him who invited you into his Kingdom to share his glory.

13And we will never stop thanking God for this: that when we preached to you, you didn't think of the words we spoke as being just our own, but you accepted what we said as the very Word of God—which, of course, it was—and it changed your lives when you believed it.

14And then, dear brothers, you suffered what the churches in Judea did, persecution from your own countrymen, just as they suffered from their own people, the Jews. 15After they had killed their own prophets, they even executed the Lord Jesus; and now they have brutally persecuted us and driven us out. They are against both God and man, 16trying to keep us from preaching to the Gentiles for fear some might be saved; and so their sins continue to grow. But the anger of God has caught up with them at last.

17Dear brothers, after we left you and had been away from you but a very little while (though our hearts never left you), we tried hard to come back to see you once more. 18We wanted very much to come, and I, Paul, tried again and again, but Satan stopped us. 19For what is it we live for, that gives us hope and joy and is our proud reward and crown? It is you! Yes, you will bring us much joy as we stand together before our Lord Jesus Christ when he comes back again. 20For you are our trophy and joy.

CHAPTER 3

Timothy's Good Report

Finally, when I could stand it no longer, I decided to stay alone in Athens 2,3and send

---

2:3-12 Paul did not minister in Thessalonica to secure personal gain. Yet to discredit Paul, his enemies charged him of that very thing. The apostle recalled his ministry among them, showing that he had gained nothing from it. His work among the Thessalonians had been motivated by the apostle's sincere love and empathy. In recovery, we are called to carry the message of hope to others. But before getting involved in the life of someone else, we need to examine our motives. Are we helping them for reasons of personal gain or because we are sincerely concerned about them? It will be helpful to make this question an integral part of our personal moral inventory.

2:19-20 Paul had discovered the message of hope in the gospel of Jesus Christ. As he grew in the faith, he joyfully began to share it with others. Notice that Paul's ministry not only helped the Thessalonians, but it also helped Paul. As Paul saw the Thessalonians grow spiritually, he experienced incredible joy in his own life. Just as their sorrow had been his sorrow, their victory became his victory. The Thessalonians became Paul's "reward and crown" and "trophy and joy." The common bond that we share with others in Christ can be a source of great encouragement as we continue in recovery.

Timothy, our brother and fellow worker,
God's minister, to visit you to strengthen your
faith and encourage you and to keep you
from becoming fainthearted in all the
troubles you were going through. (But of
course you know that such troubles are a part
of God's plan for us Christians. 4Even while
we were still with you we warned you ahead
of time that suffering would soon come—and
it did.)
5As I was saying, when I could bear the
suspense no longer, I sent Timothy to find out
whether your faith was still strong. I was
afraid that perhaps Satan had gotten the best
of you and that all our work had been useless.
6And now Timothy has just returned and
brings the welcome news that your faith and
love are as strong as ever and that you remember our visit with joy and want to see us just
as much as we want to see you. 7So we are
greatly comforted, dear brothers, in all of our
own crushing troubles and suffering here,
now that we know you are standing true to
the Lord. 8We can bear anything as long as we
know that you remain strong in him.
9How can we thank God enough for you
and for the joy and delight you have given us
in our praying for you? 10For night and day we
pray on and on for you, asking God to let us
see you again, to fill up any little cracks there
may yet be in your faith.
11May God our Father himself and our Lord
Jesus send us back to you again. 12And may the
Lord make your love to grow and overflow to
each other and to everyone else, just as our
love does toward you. 13This will result in your
hearts being made strong, sinless, and holy by
God our Father so that you may stand before
him guiltless on that day when our Lord Jesus
Christ returns with all those who belong to
him.

CHAPTER 4

Living to Please God

Let me add this, dear brothers: You already
know how to please God in your daily living,
for you know the commands we gave you
from the Lord Jesus himself. Now we beg
you—yes, we demand of you in the name of
the Lord Jesus—that you live more and more
closely to that ideal. 3,4For God wants you to
be holy and pure and to keep clear of all
sexual sin so that each of you will marry in
holiness and honor— 5not in lustful passion
as the heathen do, in their ignorance of God
and his ways.
6And this also is God's will: that you never
cheat in this matter by taking another man's
wife because the Lord will punish you terribly
for this, as we have solemnly told you before.
7For God has not called us to be dirty-minded
and full of lust but to be holy and clean. 8If
anyone refuses to live by these rules, he is not
disobeying the rules of men but of God who
gives his *Holy* Spirit to you.
9But concerning the pure brotherly love

3:2-4 Paul made it clear that troubles are to be expected in life, even a life of recovery in Christ. When we entrust our life to God, we cannot expect everything to go smoothly. God never promised to miraculously remove our dependencies, though he may do so on rare occasions. In most cases, God stands with us as we face our problems, giving us strength to confront each new challenge as it arises. Realizing that we will always face troubles in this life can help us to survive the hard times in the recovery process. As we face the struggles inherent to human existence, we can count on God's presence with us.

3:6-8 Timothy returned with good news from Thessalonica. The spiritual well-being of the Thessalonians was a great encouragement to Paul, and it helped him make it through his own tough times. Our relationships with others in recovery can be an essential source of shared mutual help. When we are down, the successes of others can lift us up. When we are up, our joy can lift others out of their despair. As we share our lives with one another, we will build each other up and provide the needed encouragement for a successful recovery.

3:11-13 Paul concluded this portion of his letter with a short prayer for the Thessalonian believers. Paul prayed that these spiritually transformed people would continue to mature before God. He requested that their new life and love for God would flow out to others. Paul's prayer for these believers can be a model for us as we seek to encourage others in their recovery. We can continually lift others to God in prayer and then rejoice as we see God working his transformation in their lives.

4:3-8 The Bible paints a clear picture of what God wants us to be like. Here we are given a list of characteristics we will exemplify if we are following God's will. This positive list is then followed by a list of things we should not be involved in. Passages like this can serve as a measuring stick for us as we take our personal inventory. If we don't measure up to God's ideals, we can admit our failures to him and allow him to help us change. As we entrust our life to him, we will begin to see the positive characteristics growing in our life.

that there should be among God's people, I
don't need to say very much, I'm sure! For
God himself is teaching you to love one another. 10Indeed, your love is already strong
toward all the Christian brothers throughout
your whole nation. Even so, dear friends, we
beg you to love them more and more. 11This
should be your ambition: to live a quiet life,
minding your own business and doing your
own work, just as we told you before. 12As a
result, people who are not Christians will
trust and respect you, and you will not need
to depend on others for enough money to pay
your bills.

Hope in the Resurrection

13And now, dear brothers, I want you to know
what happens to a Christian when he dies so
that when it happens, you will not be full of
sorrow, as those are who have no hope. 14For
since we believe that Jesus died and then
came back to life again, we can also believe
that when Jesus returns, God will bring back
with him all the Christians who have died.

15I can tell you this directly from the Lord:
that we who are still living when the Lord
returns will not rise to meet him ahead of
those who are in their graves. 16For the Lord
himself will come down from heaven with a
mighty shout and with the soul-stirring cry of
the archangel and the great trumpet-call of
God. And the believers who are dead will be
the first to rise to meet the Lord. 17Then we
who are still alive and remain on the earth
will be caught up with them in the clouds to
meet the Lord in the air and remain with him
forever. 18So comfort and encourage each
other with this news.

CHAPTER 5

A Call to Stay Alert

When is all this going to happen? I really
don't need to say anything about that, dear
brothers, 2for you know perfectly well that no
one knows. That day of the Lord will come
unexpectedly, like a thief in the night. 3When
people are saying, "All is well; everything is
quiet and peaceful"—then, all of a sudden,
disaster will fall upon them as suddenly as a
woman's birth pains begin when her child is
born. And these people will not be able to get
away anywhere—there will be no place to
hide.

4But, dear brothers, you are not in the dark
about these things, and you won't be surprised as by a thief when that day of the Lord
comes. 5For you are all children of the light
and of the day, and do not belong to darkness
and night. 6So be on your guard, not asleep
like the others. Watch for his return and stay
sober. 7Night is the time for sleep and the time
when people get drunk. 8But let us who live in
the light keep sober, protected by the armor
of faith and love, and wearing as our helmet
the happy hope of salvation.

9For God has not chosen to pour out his
anger upon us but to save us through our Lord
Jesus Christ; 10he died for us so that we can
live with him forever, whether we are dead or
alive at the time of his return. 11So encourage
each other to build each other up, just as you
are already doing.

Paul's Final Instructions

12Dear brothers, honor the officers of your
church who work hard among you and warn
you against all that is wrong. 13Think highly
of them and give them your wholehearted
love because they are straining to help you.
And remember, no quarreling among yourselves.

14Dear brothers, warn those who are lazy,
comfort those who are frightened, take tender
care of those who are weak, and be patient
with everyone. 15See that no one pays back
evil for evil, but always try to do good to each

4:13-18 Apparently the Thessalonian believers wondered what would happen to the Christians who had already died. They were afraid that believers who died before Jesus returned would lose the opportunity of sharing in Christ's glorious reign. Paul explained that dead Christians would be raised and would share in the fellowship and reign of Jesus in God's Kingdom. We all have this hope in our future as well. All believers can be sure that they will have a special part to play when Christ returns. It doesn't matter whether we are dead or alive; God has a plan that includes us.

5:1-11 Paul warns us of a day when God will hold all people accountable for their attitudes and actions. Since this time will come unexpectedly, we need to stay alert and ready at all times. This is especially important for those of us who are procrastinating, thinking we can start our recovery any time. God wants us to act immediately to receive his forgiveness and his power to help us change. Those of us who belong to God will give evidence of our faith by acting in ways that testify to God's work in our life. If we entrust our life to God and seek to follow his will, we have nothing to fear. If we continue to do things our own way, rejecting God's plan of salvation, this day of accountability will be our day of doom.

other and to everyone else. [16]Always be joyful.
[17]Always keep on praying. [18]No matter what
happens, always be thankful, for this is God's
will for you who belong to Christ Jesus.
[19]Do not smother the Holy Spirit. [20]Do not
scoff at those who prophesy, [21]but test everything that is said to be sure it is true, and if it
is, then accept it. [22]Keep away from every kind
of evil. [23]May the God of peace himself make
you entirely pure and devoted to God; and
may your spirit and soul and body be kept
strong and blameless until that day when our
Lord Jesus Christ comes back again. [24]God,
who called you to become his child, will do
all this for you, just as he promised. [25]Dear
brothers, pray for us. [26]Shake hands for me
with all the brothers there. [27]I command you
in the name of the Lord to read this letter to
all the Christians. [28]And may rich blessings
from our Lord Jesus Christ be with you, every
one.

Sincerely, Paul

5:14-28 In these verses, Paul leaves us with a collection of good advice. If we follow these many instructions, as we can with God's help, we will be well on our way in the recovery process. We are called to minister to others, a part of recovery that gives hope to others and reinforces our own success. Paul calls us to rebuild our relationships by repaying the wrongs of others with kindness. We are called to live a joyful life, always prayerful, continually seeking God's will for our life. We are reminded of the gift of the Holy Spirit, God's continual helping presence in our life. God gives us what we need to succeed in recovery. Our part is to participate in the good plan he has set out for us.

SECOND THESSALONIANS

THE BIG PICTURE

A. GREETINGS (1:1-2)
B. COMMENDATIONS IN THE MIDST OF PERSECUTION (1:3-12)
C. CORRECTION CONCERNING THE DAY OF THE LORD (2:1-17)
D. ENCOURAGEMENT FOR PRAYER AND A DISCIPLINED LIFE (3:1-15)
E. CONCLUDING REMARKS (3:16-18)

The message we receive is not always the message that was sent. Paul's first letter to the Thessalonians had made an impact on its readers, but it wasn't the impact intended by the apostle. Paul had affirmed that Jesus would return soon. In response, some of the people assumed that they should stop everything and wait for Christ to return. Some even stopped working, expecting that they would no longer need food and other supplies.

Not every believer in Thessalonica thought that way; many continued to act responsibly even as they anticipated Christ's return. But this only added to the tension between church members. The diligent ones felt pressure to pick up the slack left by the others. The lazy ones claimed they were living a life of true faith. After hearing about this problem, Paul sent the Thessalonians this second letter.

Though Paul wrote to correct his audience's misunderstanding, he commended them for their faithfulness to God. He was confident, because of their commitment to doing God's will, that God would help them resolve this issue. Paul's message was simple. He urged them to be content with their situation and disciplined about fulfilling their responsibilities.

Second Thessalonians is a good reminder for us in recovery. While we have turned our life over to God, and we look forward to the day when all our problems will be behind us, we have to live here and now. Being in recovery does not mean we can neglect our family, work, or friends. Continuing with the responsibilities God has given us helps us get our life back to normal. Recovery involves taking on our responsibilities, not laying them aside.

THE BOTTOM LINE

PURPOSE: To encourage the Thessalonian believers to fulfill their day-to-day responsibilities while anticipating Christ's return. AUTHOR: The apostle Paul. AUDIENCE: The church at Thessalonica, a city in Macedonia. DATE WRITTEN: About A.D. 51–52, during Paul's second missionary journey; shortly after he had written 1 Thessalonians. SETTING: Some of these young believers had misunderstood Paul's first letter; they thought that Christ was to return at any moment, and they used that assumption as an excuse for being lazy and disruptive while waiting for Christ to return. KEY VERSE: "May the Lord bring you into an ever deeper understanding of the love of God and of the patience that comes from Christ" (3:5). KEY PEOPLE AND RELATIONSHIPS: Paul with Silas, Timothy, and the believers at Thessalonica.

RECOVERY THEMES

God Is the Source of Our Hope: Sometimes we get our eyes off God and too much on our recovery. We tell ourself that if we only keep up our resolve, all will be well. But when we place our hope in anything other than God, we set ourself up for a relapse. Part of the reason we are in recovery is that we recognized that our life had become unmanageable and that we needed God's help. If we depend on our resolve alone, we will eventually get so tired of the burden that we will want to quit. But if we depend on God, he will provide us with the strength and joy we need to persevere.

The Importance of Perseverance: Some of the believers in Thessalonica were sitting back and waiting for the return of Christ. Their lazy, indifferent attitude toward the concerns of everyday life kept them from living responsible lives. They soon became a burden to others. Entrusting our life to God does not give us license to just sit around. We must continue to put forth effort, trusting God to sustain us and bring about the desired result of recovery. Our dependence on God is a partnership with him; he doesn't become our slave. Expecting him to do all the work leads to relapse and will alienate the people who have to pick up after us.

God's Reassuring Power and Presence: We live in a time when evil seems to be on the increase, as it was in Thessalonica. From the New Testament we know that until Christ returns, evil will continue to increase. But we don't need to be surprised or afraid; God is sovereign over the earth, no matter how evil our world becomes. As we consciously work on our relationship with God and continue to turn our life and will over to him, he promises to guard us from evil. We can have victory over the evil in our life by remaining faithful to God.

CHAPTER 1

Opening Greetings

From: Paul, Silas, and Timothy.
To: The church of Thessalonica—kept safe
in God our Father and in the Lord Jesus Christ.
2May God the Father and the Lord Jesus
Christ give you rich blessings and peace-filled
hearts and minds.

Paul Encourages Persecuted Believers

3Dear brothers, giving thanks to God for you
is not only the right thing to do, but it is our
duty to God because of the really wonderful
way your faith has grown and because of your
growing love for each other. 4We are happy to
tell other churches about your patience and
complete faith in God, in spite of all the
crushing troubles and hardships you are going through.
5This is only one example of the fair, just
way God does things, for he is using your
sufferings to make you ready for his Kingdom,
6while at the same time he is preparing judgment and punishment for those who are
hurting you.
7And so I would say to you who are suffering, God will give you rest along with us when
the Lord Jesus appears suddenly from heaven

1:3-5 Paul rejoiced that the Thessalonians were maturing in their faith. Notice that their hardships were an important impetus to their spiritual growth. Paul reminds us that hardships are something to learn from. Most of us would not be in recovery except for the painful experiences caused by our dependencies. Just as God used hardships to inspire growth among the Thessalonians, he does the same with us. Painful situations force us to admit that we cannot make it without God. When we realize that we are powerless, we can begin to rebuild our life on the only sure foundation—Jesus Christ.

1:5-8 We often look upon difficulties as something to avoid at all cost. We run from painful situations, however, only to be trapped by other serious problems. Sometimes our desire to escape pain is the foundation for our destructive addictions and compulsions. As we learn to face painful circumstances with God's help, we will be freed from the addictive habits that we once used as an escape. Our hardships can become an impetus for our spiritual growth, not a cause for failure and relapse.

1:9-10 Everlasting hell refers not to complete annihilation, but to a shipwrecked existence, eternally separated from God's healing presence. The Thessalonians escaped such a terrible fate by committing their lives to God. We have an opportunity to do the same, beginning the process of faith that leads to emotional, physical, and spiritual recovery.

2:3-10 Paul warned the Thessalonians of an evil power at work in our world. These new believers had experienced the work of this oppressor during their years as idol worshipers. We experience that same evil power at work in our addictions, compulsions, and other dysfunctional behaviors. We can rejoice that when Jesus Christ returns, he will completely overcome the evil powers in this world. And if we entrust our life to him now, he will begin his delivering work in our life right away.

in flaming fire with his mighty angels, 8bring-
ing judgment on those who do not wish to
know God and who refuse to accept his plan
to save them through our Lord Jesus Christ.
9They will be punished in everlasting hell,
forever separated from the Lord, never to see
the glory of his power 10when he comes to
receive praise and admiration because of all
he has done for his people, his saints. And you
will be among those praising him because you
have believed what we told you about him.
11And so we keep on praying for you, that
our God will make you the kind of children
he wants to have—will make you as good as
you wish you could be!—rewarding your faith
with his power. 12Then everyone will be praising the name of the Lord Jesus Christ because
of the results they see in you; and your greatest glory will be that you belong to him. The
tender mercy of our God and of the Lord Jesus
Christ has made all this possible for you.

CHAPTER 2

Paul Writes about the Antichrist

And now, what about the coming again of our
Lord Jesus Christ and our being gathered together to meet him? Please don't be upset and
excited, dear brothers, by the rumor that this
day of the Lord has already begun. If you hear
of people having visions and special messages
from God about this, or letters that are supposed to have come from me, don't believe
them. 3Don't be carried away and deceived
regardless of what they say.
For that day will not come until two things
happen: first, there will be a time of great
rebellion against God, and then the man of
rebellion will come—the son of hell. 4He will
defy every god there is and tear down every
other object of adoration and worship. He
will go in and sit as God in the temple of God,
claiming that he himself is God. 5Don't you
remember that I told you this when I was with
you? 6And you know what is keeping him
from being here already; for he can come only
when his time is ready.
7As for the work this man of rebellion and
hell will do when he comes, it is already going
on, but he himself will not come until the one
who is holding him back steps out of the way.
8Then this wicked one will appear, whom the
Lord Jesus will burn up with the breath of his
mouth and destroy by his presence when he
returns. 9This man of sin will come as Satan's
tool, full of satanic power, and will trick
everyone with strange demonstrations, and
will do great miracles. 10He will completely

Self-protection

READ 2 THESSALONIANS 3:1-8

Many of us know what it is like to be a burden to others. It is a common side effect of being controlled by an addictive/compulsive behavior. Sometimes our behaviors have caused us to lose our jobs or have made us unable to hold one. As a result, we have found ourself in financial need. This humiliation can affect our family in many ways. We may have caused loved ones great stress and shame because we haven't provided for their needs.

The apostle Paul taught us to follow this standard: "For you well know that you ought to follow our example: you never saw us loafing; we never accepted food from anyone without buying it; we worked hard day and night" (2 Thessalonians 3:7-8). "This should be your ambition: to live a quiet life, minding your own business and doing your own work. . . . [People] will trust and respect you, and you will not need to depend on others for enough money to pay your bills" (1 Thessalonians 4:11-12).

It is important for us to think about how our irresponsibility has affected others. Much pain may have been caused by our failure to provide for our family's needs. We need to reflect on how this failure has caused us to lose their respect and trust. The shame of not facing this aspect of our life can be terribly discouraging. Once we face this and become willing to make amends, our self-respect will get quite a boost. This step will help us get rid of some of our daily stress, freeing us up to proceed with recovery. ***Turn to page 1389, Hebrews 10.***

fool those who are on their way to hell because they have said no to the Truth; they have refused to believe it and love it and let it save them, 11so God will allow them to believe lies with all their hearts, 12and all of them will be justly judged for believing falsehood, refusing the Truth, and enjoying their sins.

A Call to Stand Firm

13But we must forever give thanks to God for you, our brothers loved by the Lord, because God chose from the very first to give you salvation, cleansing you by the work of the Holy Spirit and by your trusting in the Truth. 14Through us he told you the Good News. Through us he called you to share in the glory of our Lord Jesus Christ.

15With all these things in mind, dear brothers, stand firm and keep a strong grip on the truth that we taught you in our letters and during the time we were with you.

16May our Lord Jesus Christ himself and God our Father, who has loved us and given us everlasting comfort and hope, which we don't deserve, 17comfort your hearts with all comfort, and help you in every good thing you say and do.

CHAPTER 3

Paul Requests Prayer

Finally, dear brothers, as I come to the end of this letter, I ask you to pray for us. Pray first that the Lord's message will spread rapidly and triumph wherever it goes, winning converts everywhere as it did when it came to you. 2Pray, too, that we will be saved out of the clutches of evil men, for not everyone loves the Lord. 3But the Lord is faithful; he will make you strong and guard you from satanic attacks of every kind. 4And we trust the Lord that you are putting into practice the things we taught you, and that you always will. 5May the Lord bring you into an ever deeper understanding of the love of God and of the patience that comes from Christ.

A Call to Responsible Living

6Now here is a command, dear brothers, given in the name of our Lord Jesus Christ by his authority: Stay away from any Christian who spends his days in laziness and does not follow the ideal of hard work we set up for you. 7For you well know that you ought to follow our example: you never saw us loafing; 8we never accepted food from anyone without buying it; we worked hard day and night for the money we needed to live on, in order that we would not be a burden to any of you. 9It wasn't that we didn't have the right to ask you to feed us, but we wanted to show you firsthand how you should work for your living. 10Even while we were still there with you, we gave you this rule: "He who does not work shall not eat."

11Yet we hear that some of you are living in laziness, refusing to work, and wasting your time in gossiping. 12In the name of the Lord Jesus Christ we appeal to such people—we command them—to quiet down, get to work, and earn their own living. 13And to the rest of you I say, dear brothers, never be tired of doing right.

14If anyone refuses to obey what we say in this letter, notice who he is and stay away from him, that he may be ashamed of himself. 15Don't think of him as an enemy, but

---

2:15-16 Paul praised the Thessalonians for their exemplary faith and then went on to encourage them to continue to seek God, his will, and his power. Paul also reminded them to hold on to the truth they had been taught. We must do the same if we hope to make progress in recovery. If we cannot face the truth about our own life, we cannot even begin the process. We need to recognize that we are powerless and that we need God's help to survive and grow spiritually. Recognizing this truth is a foundational step toward our recovery.

3:1-2 Paul drew his readers into his life and ministry by asking them to pray for him. He didn't set himself above them but rather shared how he needed their prayers, just as he needed the power of God for continued safety. Paul shows us how his own survival was tied to the spiritual growth of others. As the Thessalonians prayed for Paul, they shared in his life. And as Paul experienced deliverance, they rejoiced and were strengthened by God's clear answers to their prayers. By involving the Thessalonians in his struggles, Paul also involved them in his victories. Our relationships in recovery yield mutual encouragement in similar ways.

3:6-10 Apparently many of the Thessalonian believers, in anticipation of Christ's return, had stopped working. Their false understanding had led them to live irresponsibly. So Paul set things straight by telling these believers to get back to work. If they refused to work, they would have to face the consequences—they wouldn't be allowed to eat. Since God has promised to help us in recovery, we might be tempted to think we can sit idly by and watch it happen. This is not the case. We need to participate in the plan God has for us. If we don't take the necessary steps of faith, we will have to face the consequences—a failed recovery.

speak to him as you would to a brother who needs to be warned.

Paul's Final Greetings

[16]May the Lord of peace himself give you his peace no matter what happens. The Lord be with you all.

[17]Now here is my greeting, which I am writing with my own hand, as I do at the end of all my letters, for proof that it really is from me. This is in my own handwriting. [18]May the blessing of our Lord Jesus Christ be upon you all.

Sincerely, Paul

3:11-13 Some of the Thessalonians who had stopped working had also begun to gossip about other people. This practice is extremely destructive to the process of recovery. Not only does it breed discouragement among the people being talked about, but it also keeps us from examining our own life as we should. Instead of taking inventory of our own life, we focus on the lives of others. Paul exhorted the Thessalonians to set things straight and to live in the power of God. If they didn't, their gossiping life-style would cause them to shrink away from their own recovery, while also discouraging others.

FIRST TIMOTHY

THE BIG PICTURE

A. A CALL TO SOUND DOCTRINE (1:1-20)
B. A CALL TO ORDER AMONG THE BELIEVERS (2:1–4:16)
C. A CALL TO PROPER RELATIONSHIPS (5:1–6:2)
D. A CALL TO SPIRITUAL DISCERNMENT (6:3-21)

Paul and Timothy had a special relationship. Timothy came to faith in Christ as a result of Paul's ministry, and he quickly joined the apostle's traveling team. As they traveled and ministered together, the two became as close as a father and son. As Timothy matured in his faith, Paul sent him to lead the church in Ephesus. As a young minister, Timothy faced many challenges and problems. Paul wrote this letter to counsel and encourage his young protégé.

Although this letter is personal in nature, Paul included in it a wealth of advice about how to deal with problems in the church context. Along the way, he also painted a clear picture of what the Christian church should be like. Every church, for example, should have sound spiritual teaching, faithful worship, strong leadership, dedication to God's Word, and caring ministries. These characteristics are what make church communities places of redemption and healing.

Recovery is a long-term process. In our search for wholeness we need a safe, nurturing environment in which we can set things straight and build a new life. A professional counselor or our recovery group is limited in this respect. We need to find a more permanent context for long-term care and support.

The ideal context for this kind of help is a healthy church community. Not all churches, however, qualify for this distinction. A healing church provides a context of loving accountability, like the ideal church described in this letter. A good church is a hospital for the hurting, a place where our old wounds can heal and our life can be rebuilt. We all need a healthy church family to help us in the long-term process of recovery.

THE BOTTOM LINE

PURPOSE: To encourage Timothy, a young pastor, at a time when he was facing difficult circumstances. AUTHOR: The apostle Paul. AUDIENCE: Timothy, a young pastor. DATE WRITTEN: Around A.D. 64, just before Paul was imprisoned in Rome. SETTING: Timothy was one of Paul's closest friends. Paul had sent him to help the church at Ephesus and was now writing to offer him practical advice on issues Timothy was facing. KEY VERSE: "Cling tightly to your faith in Christ and always keep your conscience clear, doing what you know is right" (1:19). KEY PEOPLE AND RELATIONSHIPS: Paul with Timothy.

RECOVERY THEMES

The Truth Brings Healing: Paul urged Timothy to preserve the Christian faith and to speak only the truth. Timothy was opposing false teachers who were trying to undermine his work. The only weapons he had were the truth about Christ and a godly life-style that would back up everything he taught. Paul knew that only the truth about God in Jesus Christ could bring healing and recovery to broken people, and he wanted Timothy to be convinced of that as well. It is still true—only Jesus Christ can offer us the freedom we seek. Our job is to defend and share the message of God's healing power through belief in Christ. We can do this by speaking the truth about God's power and by backing up our words with a transformed life.

The Importance of Discipline: Paul urged Timothy to discipline himself. Self-discipline does not negate our need for God's power, just as God's gracious help does not negate our need for self-discipline. Both are necessary parts of a successful recovery program. We need to stay in good spiritual and emotional condition in order to receive the powerful help that God offers us. We must continue to take our personal inventory and right the wrongs we uncover. We also must involve ourself in activities that increase our conscious contact with God. These disciplines will encourage our spiritual growth and keep our recovery on track.

God Works through People: An important part of recovery involves our relationships with other people. Paul gave Timothy specific instructions on how to relate to the people in his church. His advice relates to our relationships as well, especially as we carry the message of hope to others. Caring for each other demonstrates God's power at work within us. It is also a reminder of how we were cared for when we entered recovery.

Taking Inventory Leads to Wise Conduct: Recovery always takes place in the context of relationships. So taking inventory in the recovery process must lead us to make improvements in the way we relate to others. We may not be in a position of leadership, but we are always an example to someone else. When we are taking inventory on a regular basis, everyone wins: we do because we grow; others do because they are encouraged. A successful recovery will lead to the healing of our broken relationships.

CHAPTER 1

Greetings from Paul

From: Paul, a missionary of Jesus Christ, sent out by the direct command of God our Savior and by Jesus Christ our Lord—our only hope.

[2]*To:* Timothy.

Timothy, you are like a son to me in the things of the Lord. May God our Father and Jesus Christ our Lord show you his kindness and mercy and give you great peace of heart and mind.

Paul Warns about False Teachers

[3,4]As I said when I left for Macedonia, please stay there in Ephesus and try to stop the men who are teaching such wrong doctrine. Put an end to their myths and fables, and their idea of being saved by finding favor with an endless chain of angels leading up to God—wild ideas that stir up questions and arguments instead of helping people accept God's plan of faith. [5]What I am eager for is that all the Christians there will be filled with love that comes from pure hearts, and that their minds will be clean and their faith strong.

[6]But these teachers have missed this whole idea and spend their time arguing and talking foolishness. [7]They want to become famous as teachers of the laws of Moses when they haven't the slightest idea what those laws really show us. [8]Those laws are good when used as God intended. [9]But they were not made for us, whom God has saved; they are for sinners who hate God, have rebellious hearts, curse and swear, attack their fathers and mothers, and murder. [10,11]Yes, these laws are made to identify as sinners all who are immoral and impure: homosexuals, kidnappers, liars, and all others who do things that contradict the glorious Good News of our blessed God, whose messenger I am.

God's Amazing Kindness

[12]How thankful I am to Christ Jesus our Lord

1:3-7 Apparently, the false teachers in Ephesus were claiming that certain knowledge and activities were necessary for salvation. Their teachings were causing division and pride among the believers, since some of them claimed to have special knowledge. This also led the believers away from the essentials of the faith and the only real power for salvation—faith in Jesus Christ. There are many today who claim to have solutions to our recovery, and many of their programs assume we can accomplish our recovery without God's help. We would be wise to heed Paul's exhortation and steer clear of people who teach such things. Only God in Jesus Christ has the power to deliver us.

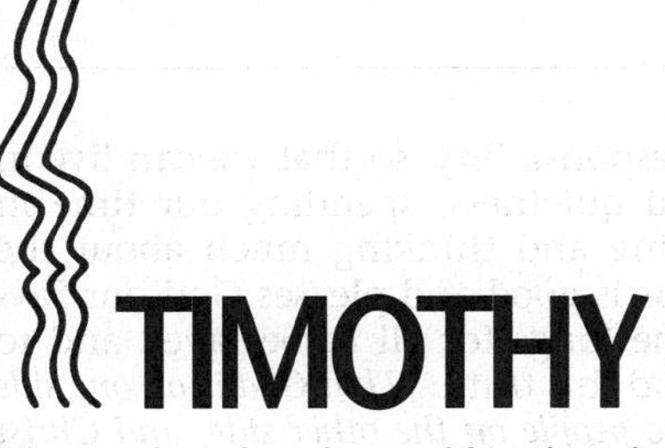

TIMOTHY

When we have found a good friend, we have found a treasure. This is especially true as we struggle through the stages of recovery. We need people who are faithful and willing to persevere with us through the hard times. We need the love and acceptance that only a true friend can offer. The friendship between young Timothy and the apostle Paul brought significant support and encouragement to both men.

Paul described Timothy as a faithful brother with a solid reputation. Timothy was devoted to Paul and shared many of his triumphant victories in the ministry. But Timothy didn't stay around only when things were going well. He persevered with Paul during the difficult times of imprisonment, torture, and mockery as well. Their years of shared ministry grew into a lifelong friendship.

Paul referred to Timothy with admiration in many of his letters. He called him "a beloved and trustworthy child in the Lord" (1 Corinthians 4:17) and "my fellow worker" (Romans 16:21). In his letter to the Philippians, Paul referred to Timothy with the highest praise, and then added that he had been "just like a son" to him (Philippians 2:22). In his letters to Timothy, Paul expressed great affection for him. Paul's personal involvement in Timothy's ministry was shown when Paul reminded him "to stir into flame the strength and boldness that is in you, that entered into you when I laid my hands upon your head and blessed you" (2 Timothy 1:6).

Timothy was never known as a charismatic or strong leader. He was apparently somewhat timid and afraid to confront his people, especially the older men. But he was faithful and persevered in his ministry despite his fears and trials. Paul supported Timothy in his ministry, realizing that God had called this young man into special service for him. Despite his weaknesses, Timothy was used by God to build the church and to encourage his more charismatic coworker, Paul.

Our recovery requires that we allow people into our life for both support and accountability. We need to ask God for a "Timothy"—someone who has integrity, who can be trusted, and who will stand by our side through anything. When we find our "Timothy," we will be equipped to face the trials of recovery.

STRENGTHS AND ACCOMPLISHMENTS:

- Timothy had an excellent reputation for his faithfulness.
- He was a special friend to the apostle Paul.
- He stood by Paul even in the most difficult circumstances.
- He was a faithful minister of the gospel.

WEAKNESSES AND MISTAKES:

- Timothy struggled with his youth and timidity.
- He had stomach problems, possibly related to anxiety.

LESSONS FROM HIS LIFE:

- Our fears and inadequacies need not stop us from serving God.
- Good friendships are extremely valuable, especially in recovery.

KEY VERSES:

"Finally, when I could stand it no longer, I decided to stay alone in Athens and send Timothy, our brother and fellow worker, God's minister, to visit you to strengthen your faith and encourage you and to keep you from becoming fainthearted in all the troubles you were going through" (1 Thessalonians 3:1-3).

Timothy is first named in Acts 16:1-5 and is mentioned at various other points in the book. He is the recipient of Paul's letters 1 and 2 Timothy. He is also mentioned in Romans 16:21; 1 Corinthians 4:17; 16:10-11; 2 Corinthians 1:1, 19; Philippians 1:1; 2:19-23; Colossians 1:1; 1 Thessalonians 1:1-10; 3:2-6; Philemon 1:1; and Hebrews 13:23.

---

for choosing me as one of his messengers, and
giving me the strength to be faithful to him,
13even though I used to scoff at the name of
Christ. I hunted down his people, harming
them in every way I could. But God had
mercy on me because I didn't know what I
was doing, for I didn't know Christ at that
time. 14Oh, how kind our Lord was, for he
showed me how to trust him and become full
of the love of Christ Jesus.
15How true it is, and how I long that everyone should know it, that Christ Jesus came
into the world to save sinners—and I was the
greatest of them all. 16But God had mercy on
me so that Christ Jesus could use me as an
example to show everyone how patient he is

with even the worst sinners, so that others
will realize that they, too, can have everlasting
life. 17Glory and honor to God forever and
ever. He is the King of the ages, the unseen
one who never dies; he alone is God, and full
of wisdom. Amen.

A Call to Stand Firm

18Now, Timothy, my son, here is my command to you: Fight well in the Lord's battles,
just as the Lord told us through his prophets
that you would. 19Cling tightly to your faith
in Christ and always keep your conscience
clear, doing what you know is right. For some
people have disobeyed their consciences and
have deliberately done what they knew was
wrong. It isn't surprising that soon they lost
their faith in Christ after defying God like
that. 20Hymenaeus and Alexander are two examples of this. I had to give them over to
Satan to punish them until they could learn
not to bring shame to the name of Christ.

CHAPTER 2

Instructions about Worship

Here are my directions: Pray much for others;
plead for God's mercy upon them; give
thanks for all he is going to do for them.

2Pray in this way for kings and all others
who are in authority over us, or are in places
of high responsibility, so that we can live in
peace and quietness, spending our time in
godly living and thinking much about the
Lord. 3This is good and pleases God our Savior, 4for he longs for all to be saved and to
understand this truth: 5*That God is on one side
and all the people on the other side, and Christ
Jesus, himself man, is between them to bring
them together,* 6*by giving his life for all mankind.*

This is the message that at the proper time
God gave to the world. 7And I have been
chosen—this is the absolute truth—as God's
minister and missionary to teach this truth to
the Gentiles and to show them God's plan of
salvation through faith.

8So I want men everywhere to pray with
holy hands lifted up to God, free from sin and
anger and resentment. 9,10And the women
should be the same way, quiet and sensible in
manner and clothing. Christian women
should be noticed for being kind and good,
not for the way they fix their hair or because
of their jewels or fancy clothes. 11Women
should listen and learn quietly and humbly.

12I never let women teach men or lord it
over them. Let them be silent in your church
meetings. 13Why? Because God made Adam
first, and afterwards he made Eve. 14And it was
not Adam who was fooled by Satan, but Eve,
and sin was the result. 15So God sent pain and

1:18-20 Paul commanded Timothy to fight God's battles well. In one sense this continued his earlier thoughts about upholding God's truth against the false teachers. Yet the real battle was not in the realm of ideas; it involved acting in ways that reflected a healthy relationship with God. Paul told Timothy to cling to his faith and to keep his conscience clear. He was to live in ways that showed God's power. The same thing is true in the process of recovery. Our beliefs are important, but we must go beyond just thinking the right things to doing the right things. That is where God's real battles are won. Our voiced commitment to recovery is evidenced when we take the necessary steps, some of them painful, and live out our relationship with God in ways that show others the comfort and deliverance that can be found in him.

2:1-2 Here Paul shows why prayer is essential for establishing a peaceful context for spiritual growth. Through prayer, both public and private, order and peace are promoted and strengthened. Prayer involves thanksgiving for God's blessings and intercession for others. It is one of the assets we often overlook as we work our program. We can easily become so focused on our own activities that we forget to turn to God for help. Prayer is a primary means for improving our conscious contact with God. Regular prayer is also a helpful reminder that we are helpless without God's continual and powerful help.

2:3-5 That God wants everyone to be saved is encouraging news. No matter how hopeless our life may seem, how bad we have been, or how badly others have treated us, God wants us to come to him. The truth is that all of us are separated from God by sin until we give our life to Christ, the one who bridges the gulf between man and God. God gives us power for recovery, in this life and the next, when we confess our powerlessness and ask Jesus for forgiveness, salvation, and assistance.

3:1-7 Paul described the prospective pastor as someone who has self-control and spiritual maturity. Notice Paul's emphasis upon a pastor's strong record of leadership within his own family. The home is the most reliable proving ground for potential leaders. It is also the place where we can give evidence of our progress in recovery. Since our family members have probably been hurt by our dependencies, it is essential that we make amends to them. Sometimes it is hardest to restore our closest relationships. But a successful recovery always involves the people in our family and leads to the restoration of broken family relationships.

suffering to women when their children are
born, but he will save their souls if they trust
in him, living quiet, good, and loving lives.

CHAPTER 3

Standards for Church Leaders

It is a true saying that if a man wants to be a
pastor he has a good ambition. 2For a pastor
must be a good man whose life cannot be
spoken against. He must have only one wife,
and he must be hard working and thoughtful,
orderly, and full of good deeds. He must enjoy
having guests in his home and must be a
good Bible teacher. 3He must not be a drinker
or quarrelsome, but he must be gentle and
kind and not be one who loves money. 4He
must have a well-behaved family, with children who obey quickly and quietly. 5For if a
man can't make his own little family behave,
how can he help the whole church?

6The pastor must not be a new Christian
because he might be proud of being chosen so
soon, and pride comes before a fall. (Satan's
downfall is an example.) 7Also, he must be
well spoken of by people outside the church—
those who aren't Christians—so that Satan
can't trap him with many accusations and
leave him without freedom to lead his flock.

8The deacons must be the same sort of
good, steady men as the pastors. They must
not be heavy drinkers and must not be greedy
for money. 9They must be earnest, wholehearted followers of Christ, who is the hidden
Source of their faith. 10Before they are asked to
be deacons, they should be given other jobs
in the church as a test of their character and
ability, and if they do well, then they may be
chosen as deacons.

11Their wives must be thoughtful, not
heavy drinkers, not gossipers, but faithful in
everything they do. 12Deacons should have
only one wife, and they should have happy,
obedient families. 13Those who do well as deacons will be well rewarded both by respect
from others and also by developing their own
confidence and bold trust in the Lord.

14I am writing these things to you now,
even though I hope to be with you soon, 15so
that if I don't come for awhile, you will know
what kind of men you should choose as officers for the church of the living God, which
contains and holds high the truth of God.

16It is quite true that the way to live a godly
life is not an easy matter. But the answer lies
in Christ, who came to earth as a man, was
proved spotless and pure in his Spirit, was
served by angels, was preached among the

Spiritual Exercises

BIBLE READING: 1 Timothy 4:7-8

We continued to take personal inventory and when we were wrong promptly admitted it.

It is amazing to behold what a human being can achieve through a consistent disciplined effort. How many times have we watched seasoned gymnasts or other athletes and marveled at the ease with which they performed their sport? We realize that they developed that ability through rigorous training, which is what sets the true athlete apart from the spectator. Continuing our regular personal inventory requires similar self-discipline.

Paul wrote to Timothy, "Spend your time and energy in the exercise of keeping spiritually fit. Bodily exercise is all right, but spiritual exercise is much more important" (1 Timothy 4:7-8). The word translated *exercise* referred specifically to the disciplined training done by gymnasts in Paul's day.

Spiritual strength and agility only come through practice. We need to develop our spiritual muscles through consistent effort and daily discipline. Continuing to take our personal inventory is one of the disciplines we can develop. Like the athlete, we can motivate ourself to continue in a disciplined routine by looking to our reward. This kind of discipline "will help [us] not only now in this life, but in the next life too" (1 Timothy 4:8). Results won't happen overnight. But as we continue practicing these disciplines each day, we will eventually grow to enjoy the benefits. ***Turn to page 1363, 2 Timothy 2.***

nations, was accepted by men everywhere,
and was received up again to his glory in
heaven.

CHAPTER 4

The Danger of False Teachers

But the Holy Spirit tells us clearly that in the
last times some in the church will turn away
from Christ and become eager followers of
teachers with devil-inspired ideas. [2]These
teachers will tell lies with straight faces and do
it so often that their consciences won't even
bother them.

[3]They will say it is wrong to be married and
wrong to eat meat, even though God gave
these things to well-taught Christians to enjoy and be thankful for. [4]For everything God
made is good, and we may eat it gladly if we
are thankful for it, [5]and if we ask God to bless
it, for it is made good by the Word of God and
prayer.

[6]If you explain this to the others you will be
doing your duty as a worthy pastor who is fed
by faith and by the true teaching you have
followed.

[7]Don't waste time arguing over foolish
ideas and silly myths and legends. Spend your
time and energy in the exercise of keeping
spiritually fit. [8]Bodily exercise is all right, but
spiritual exercise is much more important
and is a tonic for all you do. So exercise
yourself spiritually, and practice being a better
Christian because that will help you not only
now in this life, but in the next life too. [9,10]This

3:16 Paul reminds us that the way to a godly and healthy life is never easy. We all know this. We have already recognized that we cannot do it alone. Even with God's powerful help, each step of confession and healing can be painful. Yet Jesus Christ has paid the debt for our sins and failures. He has paved the way for our recovery and will stand beside us each step of the way. As difficult as our recovery may be, Jesus Christ can give us the power to start over. He already has been resurrected to a new life; he now offers us the same.

4:1-5 Notice that one of the errors Paul warned Timothy about was a religiously motivated self-denial. What is wrong with this? Wasn't it self-indulgence that got most of us in trouble in the first place? Paul points out that the good pleasures offered by God should be enjoyed with thanksgiving and not rejected in the name of spirituality. We have probably heard of recovery leaders who call their followers to give up all forms of pleasure to purge their lives of the tendency toward addiction. If we have tried this, however, we know that deprivation leads us to a deeper hunger and an eventual relapse. God has given us many legitimate pleasures in this life. When we learn how to replace our enslaving dependencies with legitimate forms of enjoyment, we will find that the temptation to escape life through our addictive habits will melt away.

4:7-10 Here Paul warns young Timothy not to argue about insignificant issues and tells him to focus on taking the necessary steps to grow spiritually. In recovery, it is easy to get sidetracked by new ideas and solutions to our problems. We may enjoy debating the strengths and weaknesses of one program over another. Recovery and spiritual growth cannot be achieved by arguing about the finer points of one program or another. We can keep spiritually fit only by taking a regular moral inventory, admitting our failures, and seeking to make amends with those we have wronged. We can make progress in our journey only if we are willing to take the first steps.

4:11-16 Timothy is admonished to share the Good News of new life in Christ through both word and deed. We sometimes forget that the most effective way we share our story of deliverance is to live it out. Nothing we could ever say can witness as powerfully to God's power as the changes people can see in our life. Some people will always question the legitimacy of what we say, but no one can question the fact of a transformed life. The best way to share the Good News of God's transforming power is to live it. When we entrust our life to God, we can experience the new life promised in Jesus Christ. Allowing God to change us is the best way to help others enter the path of recovery.

5:1-2 Paul reminded Timothy to treat all people with respect. In doing so, he reminds us of the importance of healthy relationships in the Christian community. Sound doctrine, proper worship, and godly leadership are all important, but unless we treat people with love and respect, the church will never be a place where people in recovery can grow. The godly courtesy and affection requested by Paul will make the Christian community a place where healing can take place and lives can be rebuilt.

5:3-10 Paul made it clear that the Christian community was to show special attention to the widows in their midst. Paul's directions here reflect God's Scripture-wide concern for the helpless and rejected in society. This is encouraging to us because we all know what it feels like to be helpless and to be rejected. But God wants us to be included among his people; there is a place for everyone in his church. No matter who we are or what we have done, we are acceptable on the basis of our faith in Jesus Christ. God reaches out to us, as helpless and rejected as we may be, and calls us to be a part of his family.

is the truth and everyone should accept it. We
work hard and suffer much in order that
people will believe it, for our hope is in the
living God who died for all, and particularly
for those who have accepted his salvation.
11Teach these things and make sure everyone learns them well. 12Don't let anyone
think little of you because you are young. Be
their ideal; let them follow the way you teach
and live; be a pattern for them in your love,
your faith, and your clean thoughts. 13Until I
get there, read and explain the Scriptures to
the church; preach God's Word.
14Be sure to use the abilities God has given
you through his prophets when the elders of
the church laid their hands upon your head.
15Put these abilities to work; throw yourself
into your tasks so that everyone may notice
your improvement and progress. 16Keep a
close watch on all you do and think. Stay true
to what is right and God will bless you and use
you to help others.

CHAPTER 5

Helping Others in God's Family

Never speak sharply to an older man, but
plead with him respectfully just as though he
were your own father. Talk to the younger
men as you would to much-loved brothers.
2Treat the older women as mothers, and the
girls as your sisters, thinking only pure
thoughts about them.
3The church should take loving care of
women whose husbands have died if they
don't have anyone else to help them. 4But if
they have children or grandchildren, these
are the ones who should take the responsibility, for kindness should begin at home, supporting needy parents. This is something that
pleases God very much.
5The church should care for widows who
are poor and alone in the world if they are
looking to God for his help and spending
much time in prayer; 6but not if they are
spending their time running around gossiping, seeking only pleasure and thus ruining
their souls. 7This should be your church rule
so that the Christians will know and do what
is right.
8But anyone who won't care for his own
relatives when they need help, especially
those living in his own family, has no right to
say he is a Christian. Such a person is worse
than the heathen.
9A widow who wants to become one of the
special church workers should be at least sixty
years old and have been married only once.

Talking the Walk

BIBLE READING: 1 Timothy 4:14-16

Having had a spiritual awakening as the result of these steps, we tried to carry this message to others and to practice these principles in all our affairs.

When we wake up to realize everything we have gained by following the Twelve Steps, it will be natural to want to share this life-giving message with others. If we think back to the time before we entered recovery, we will probably recall that we didn't respond very well to "preaching." Yet we also realize that there are people in our life who could be helped by our message. That is why we need to communicate our story, but do it in a sensitive way.

The apostle Paul taught Timothy that to get the message across, he needed to combine putting his beliefs into practice with telling others about them. He said, "Throw yourself into your tasks so that everyone may notice your improvement and progress. Keep a close watch on all you do and think. Stay true to what is right and God will . . . use you to help others" (1 Timothy 4:15-16). When we practice the principles of the Twelve Steps, others will be watching and will notice the changes. This will open the door for us to be able to tell them our story.

Every addict is a precious lost soul whom God loves and wants to rescue. "If anyone has slipped away . . . that person who brings him back to God will have saved a wandering soul from death, bringing about the forgiveness of his many sins" (James 5:19-20). ***Turn to page 1373, Titus 3.***

[10]She must be well thought of by everyone because of the good she has done. Has she brought up her children well? Has she been kind to strangers as well as to other Christians? Has she helped those who are sick and hurt? Is she always ready to show kindness?

[11]The younger widows should not become members of this special group because after awhile they are likely to disregard their vow to Christ and marry again. [12]And so they will stand condemned because they broke their first promise. [13]Besides, they are likely to be lazy and spend their time gossiping around from house to house, getting into other people's business. [14]So I think it is better for these younger widows to marry again and have children and take care of their own homes; then no one will be able to say anything against them. [15]For I am afraid that some of them have already turned away from the church and been led astray by Satan.

[16]Let me remind you again that a widow's relatives must take care of her and not leave this to the church to do. Then the church can spend its money for the care of widows who are all alone and have nowhere else to turn.

[17]Pastors who do their work well should be paid well and should be highly appreciated, especially those who work hard at both preaching and teaching. [18]For the Scriptures say, "Never tie up the mouth of an ox when it is treading out the grain—let him eat as he goes along!" And in another place, "Those who work deserve their pay!"

[19]Don't listen to complaints against the pastor unless there are two or three witnesses to accuse him. [20]If he has really sinned, then he should be rebuked in front of the whole church so that no one else will follow his example.

[21]I solemnly command you in the presence of God and the Lord Jesus Christ and of the holy angels to do this whether the pastor is a special friend of yours or not. All must be treated exactly the same. [22]Never be in a hurry about choosing a pastor; you may overlook his sins, and it will look as if you approve of them. Be sure that you yourself stay away from all sin. [23](By the way, this doesn't mean you should completely give up drinking wine. You ought to take a little sometimes as medicine for your stomach because you are sick so often.)

[24]Remember that some men, even pastors, lead sinful lives, and everyone knows it. In such situations you can do something about it. But in other cases only the judgment day will reveal the terrible truth. [25]In the same way, everyone knows how much good some pastors do, but sometimes their good deeds aren't known until long afterward.

CHAPTER 6

Money Isn't Everything

Christian slaves should work hard for their owners and respect them; never let it be said that Christ's people are poor workers. Don't let the name of God or his teaching be laughed at because of this.

[2]If their owner is a Christian, that is no excuse for slowing down; rather they should work all the harder because a brother in the faith is being helped by their efforts.

Teach these truths, Timothy, and encourage all to obey them.

[3]Some may deny these things, but they are the sound, wholesome teachings of the Lord Jesus Christ and are the foundation for a godly life. [4]Anyone who says anything different is both proud and stupid. He is quibbling over the meaning of Christ's words and stirring up arguments ending in jealousy and anger, which only lead to name-calling, accusations, and evil suspicions. [5]These arguers—their minds warped by sin—don't know how to tell the truth; to them the Good News is

---

5:24-25 Paul called Timothy to confront his fellow church leaders who were living sinful lives. By confronting them about their failures, Timothy would save them from the consequences that continued disobedience would bring them on Judgment Day. This advice to confront wrongdoers is a call to tough love. Sometimes we must do the same for the people we love. As we notice the growing power of someone's addictive behavior, we can say something before he hits bottom. In so doing, we will give him the opportunity to admit his helplessness and receive God's transforming help.

6:3-10 Paul warned Timothy about those who spread false teachings among the believers. The apostle wanted to protect the free salvation offered by Jesus Christ from the distorting lies of money-hungry charlatans. Paul's advice for Timothy is valuable also for us in recovery. Anyone promising recovery through any power other than God in Jesus Christ is trying to sell something. Only God can deliver us from our besetting weaknesses. If someone claims to have another solution to our problems, it is likely that he has something to gain from the program he is offering. We would be wise to hold on to our money when this kind of person comes around. God's solution in Jesus Christ can heal our deepest wounds, and the power he offers is free of charge.

just a means of making money. Keep away from them.

[6]Do you want to be truly rich? You already are if you are happy and good. [7]After all, we didn't bring any money with us when we came into the world, and we can't carry away a single penny when we die. [8]So we should be well satisfied without money if we have enough food and clothing. [9]But people who long to be rich soon begin to do all kinds of wrong things to get money, things that hurt them and make them evil-minded and finally send them to hell itself. [10]For the love of money is the first step toward all kinds of sin. Some people have even turned away from God because of their love for it, and as a result have pierced themselves with many sorrows.

Paul's Final Instructions

[11]O Timothy, you are God's man. Run from all these evil things, and work instead at what is right and good, learning to trust him and love others and to be patient and gentle. [12]Fight on for God. Hold tightly to the eternal life that God has given you and that you have confessed with such a ringing confession before many witnesses.

[13]I command you before God, who gives life to all, and before Christ Jesus, who gave a fearless testimony before Pontius Pilate, [14]that you fulfill all he has told you to do so that no one can find fault with you from now until our Lord Jesus Christ returns. [15]For in due season Christ will be revealed from heaven by the blessed and only Almighty God, the King of kings and Lord of lords, [16]who alone can never die, who lives in light so terrible that no human being can approach him. No mere man has ever seen him nor ever will. Unto him be honor and everlasting power and dominion forever and ever. Amen.

[17]Tell those who are rich not to be proud and not to trust in their money, which will soon be gone, but their pride and trust should be in the living God who always richly gives us all we need for our enjoyment. [18]Tell them to use their money to do good. They should be rich in good works and should give happily to those in need, always being ready to share with others whatever God has given them. [19]By doing this they will be storing up real treasure for themselves in heaven—it is the only safe investment for eternity! And they will be living a fruitful Christian life down here as well.

[20]Oh, Timothy, don't fail to do these things that God entrusted to you. Keep out of foolish arguments with those who boast of their "knowledge" and thus prove their lack of it. [21]Some of these people have missed the most important thing in life—they don't know God. May God's mercy be upon you.

Sincerely, Paul

6:11-16 Paul warned Timothy about the pitfall of trusting in money. Some of us may have already experienced the emptiness of such misplaced trust. We may have thought that wealth could buy a solution to all of our problems. We now know, however, that no amount of money can deliver us from the power of our dependencies. Whether we are rich or poor, the pull of our addictions can only be overcome when we admit our helplessness and turn to God for help. The only way to a successful life in God's eyes is to pursue the virtues of godliness. Paul compares this pursuit to an agonizing athletic competition (6:12; see 1 Corinthians 9:24-26; Philippians 3:14). By taking steps of faith in God we can experience his help in our recovery and the renewed life he offers.

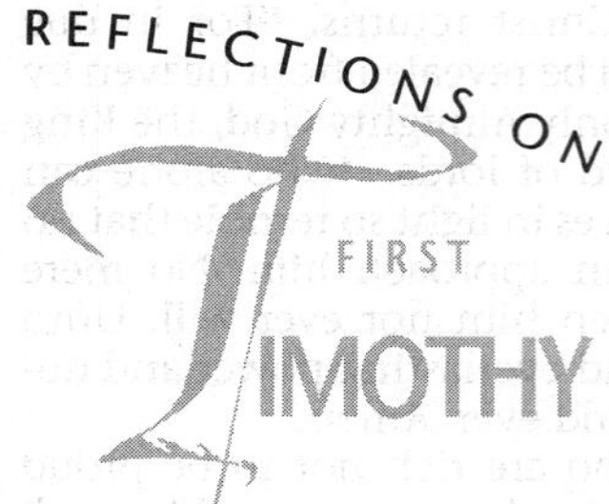
REFLECTIONS ON
FIRST
TIMOTHY

✲*insights* ABOUT GOD'S LAW

In **1 Timothy 1:8-11** Paul pointed out that God's law is intended to convict us of our sins, leading us to admit our helplessness and receive his forgiveness. It is not primarily a set of rules for us to live by. It is true that recovery involves acknowledging that there are healthy boundaries for our actions. But our recovery will never be helped by an attempt to observe the Old Testament law, which is beyond our ability to keep (see Acts 15:10). Attempting to do so will lead to frustration and guilt, which will stymie rather than encourage our recovery. We need to use the law as a means for discovering how helpless we are. Then we can entrust our life to God and trust him to help us take each new step in recovery.

✲*insights* ABOUT GOD'S TRANSFORMING POWER

In **1 Timothy 1:12-17** Paul recounted how he had once done everything he could to stop the growth of the Christian community. But God mercifully intervened in Paul's life, transforming him into one of the most dynamic leaders of the Christian church. As he shared his story, his previous status as an enemy made his message all the more powerful. The amazing changes in his life were a testimony to God's transforming power. Some of us may feel that we will never be able to make an impact on the lives of others. We may feel that we are so terrible that we are beyond the point of recovery. God can change us no matter who we are or what we have done. As we share our story of deliverance, others will receive hope as they see what God has done in our life.

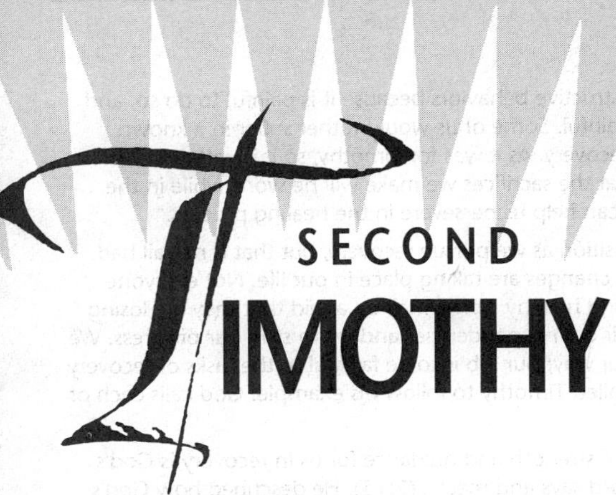

SECOND TIMOTHY

THE BIG PICTURE

A. GREETINGS (1:1-2)
B. ENCOURAGEMENT TO PERSEVERE (1:3–2:26)
   1. The Need to Be Faithful (1:3-18)
   2. The Reality of Hardships (2:1-13)
   3. The Need to Behave Responsibly (2:14-26)
C. EXHORTATIONS CONCERNING THE LAST DAYS (3:1–4:8)
D. PAUL SHARES HIS OWN PERSONAL NEEDS (4:9-22)

When a loved one is about to die, we strain to hear any whispered words of blessing or advice, knowing they will be the last. When an important person is lying on his deathbed, people crowd around for words of enduring wisdom. In this letter, Paul wrote his final words of blessing, advice, and comfort. It is Paul's deathbed communication to Timothy, his son in the faith.

As he wrote this letter, Paul was awaiting his execution in a Roman prison. He expected the end to come soon, so he penned these words of advice and encouragement to his young protégé in Ephesus. He wanted to make sure that Timothy had all the tools he needed to be an effective minister of the gospel.

Paul told Timothy to develop his relationship with God and to serve God faithfully. Paul knew that Timothy would face many problems as a church leader, so he encouraged Timothy to persevere. He challenged the young pastor to be faithful to his duties, to use the gifts God had given him, to hold on to the truth of God's Word, to teach others, and to be willing to suffer for the sake of Christ.

Paul had made mistakes in the past, but that didn't disqualify him from helping Timothy. Neither do our mistakes disqualify us from reaching out to others. Rather, God gives each of us something to share from our experiences in life. Paul had much to pass on to Timothy. Through our recovery, God has given us important insights from which others can benefit. Carrying those insights to others is a small but important part of our own journey toward wholeness.

THE BOTTOM LINE

PURPOSE: To encourage a faithful but discouraged Timothy in continuing to do God's work. AUTHOR: The apostle Paul. AUDIENCE: Timothy, a young pastor. DATE WRITTEN: Sometime between A.D. 66 and 67, shortly before Paul's death during the reign of Emperor Nero. SETTING: When Paul wrote this letter, he was virtually alone in prison; only his friend Luke was with him. This is a very personal letter, showing Paul's vulnerability and loneliness. It also reveals his inner strength as he continued, even in his desperate situation, to encourage young Timothy. KEY VERSE: "Run from anything that gives you the evil thoughts that young men often have, but stay close to anything that makes you want to do right" (2:22). KEY PEOPLE AND RELATIONSHIPS: Paul, with Timothy, Luke, and Mark.

RECOVERY THEMES

God's Way Can Be Difficult: We don't like giving up destructive behaviors because it is painful to do so, and the changes required for recovery are often especially painful. Some of us would rather suffer in a known situation than risk moving into the unknown world of recovery. As it was for Timothy, so it is with us: our growth involves some pain, but we can be confident that the sacrifices we make will be worthwhile in the end. Knowing that there will be hard times in recovery can help us persevere in the healing process.

The Importance of Faithfulness: We can count on opposition as we pursue recovery, but that is not all bad. The opposition can clue us in to the fact that important changes are taking place in our life. Not everyone likes to see us change, even if those changes are good and healthy. Some may be afraid that they are losing an old friend. Others may begin to feel guilty about their own dependencies and try to stop our progress. We don't have to figure out why people want to stand in our way; our job is to be faithful to the tasks of recovery and spiritual growth. Paul was faithful to God, and he called Timothy to follow his example. God calls each of us to do the same.

The Power of God's Word: One of the primary sources of strength and guidance for us in recovery is God's Word. Paul challenged Timothy to know what God's Word says and means (2:15). He described how God's Word helps us as it teaches us what is true, makes us realize what is wrong in our life, points us in the right direction, and helps us do what is right (3:16). Our praying and thinking are to be focused on God's Word, for it equips us to live as God wants us to live.

CHAPTER 1

Greetings from Paul

From: Paul, Jesus Christ's missionary, sent out
by God to tell men and women everywhere
about the eternal life he has promised them
through faith in Jesus Christ.
2 *To:* Timothy, my dear son. May God the
Father and Christ Jesus our Lord shower you
with his kindness, mercy, and peace.

Paul Encourages Timothy

3 How I thank God for you, Timothy. I pray for
you every day, and many times during the
long nights I beg my God to bless you richly.
He is my fathers' God and mine, and my only
purpose in life is to please him.
4 How I long to see you again. How happy I
would be, for I remember your tears as we left
each other.
5 I know how much you trust the Lord, just
as your mother Eunice and your grandmother
Lois do; and I feel sure you are still trusting
him as much as ever.
6 This being so, I want to remind you to stir
into flame the strength and boldness that is in
you, that entered into you when I laid my

1:5 Whether we like it or not, we all learn from our parents and pass on the lessons we learn to our children. Sometimes the lessons we learn and teach are good; at times, however, they are destructive. We complain because our parents have passed defects of character on to us. We weep because we have passed those same defects on to our children. Notice that Timothy's faith in Christ had been modeled by his mother and grandmother. We can stop the cycle of passing destructive traits from one generation to the next by turning our life over to God. As we seek to live according to God's plan, we will model a transformed life to our children. As they see the power of our vibrant faith in God, they will be likely to follow in our steps. Like Timothy's mother and grandmother, we will be able to rejoice in the godly children who come after us.

1:7-14 Timothy did not have the character traits normally expected of a leader. Paul implied that Timothy lacked courage, strength, love, and self-discipline. But Paul told Timothy not to let his weaknesses stop him from ministering to others. His success was not based on his ability, skill, or courage; it was based on the Holy Spirit's power working in him. This is true also in recovery. We don't have the inherent strength, courage, and self-discipline needed to overcome our dependencies. With God's powerful help, however, no problem is too great to overcome. We can succeed in recovery by depending on him.

1:15-18 Paul was in prison when he wrote this letter. Soon after being locked up, he was deserted by most of his friends and followers. His friend Onesiphorus, however, stood with Paul even though it was a risky thing to do. Onesiphorus's example teaches us what it means to show loyalty and love to someone in need. Like Paul, we may have been abandoned by many of our friends as we entered recovery. We may also know what Paul must have felt toward his loyal friend. We may have an Onesiphorus in our life, too. Realizing how essential this kind of person is to our recovery encourages us to take every opportunity to be a loyal friend to others. This is part of sharing the message of hope with others and helping them take steps toward recovery.

hands upon your head and blessed you. 7For
the Holy Spirit, God's gift, does not want you
to be afraid of people, but to be wise and
strong, and to love them and enjoy being
with them.
8If you will stir up this inner power, you will
never be afraid to tell others about our Lord
or to let them know that I am your friend
even though I am here in jail for Christ's sake.
You will be ready to suffer with me for the
Lord, for he will give you strength in suffering.
9It is he who saved us and chose us for his
holy work not because we deserved it but
because that was his plan long before the
world began—to show his love and kindness
to us through Christ. 10And now he has made
all of this plain to us by the coming of our
Savior Jesus Christ, who broke the power of
death and showed us the way of everlasting
life through trusting him. 11And God has chosen me to be his missionary, to preach to the
Gentiles and teach them.
12That is why I am suffering here in jail, and
I am certainly not ashamed of it, for I know
the one in whom I trust, and I am sure that he
is able to safely guard all that I have given him
until the day of his return.
13Hold tightly to the pattern of truth I
taught you, especially concerning the faith
and love Christ Jesus offers you. 14Guard well
the splendid, God-given ability you received
as a gift from the Holy Spirit who lives within
you.
15As you know, all the Christians who came
here from Asia have deserted me; even Phy-
gellus and Hermogenes are gone. 16May the
Lord bless Onesiphorus and all his family
because he visited me and encouraged me
often. His visits revived me like a breath of
fresh air, and he was never ashamed of my
being in jail. 17In fact, when he came to Rome,
he searched everywhere trying to find me,
and finally did. 18May the Lord give him a
special blessing at the day of Christ's return.
And you know better than I can tell you how
much he helped me at Ephesus.

CHAPTER 2

Being a Good Soldier

O Timothy, my son, be strong with the
strength Christ Jesus gives you. 2For you must
teach others those things you and many
others have heard me speak about. Teach
these great truths to trustworthy men who
will, in turn, pass them on to others.
3Take your share of suffering as a good

Perseverance

BIBLE READING: 2 Timothy 2:1-8

We continued to take personal inventory and when we were wrong promptly admitted it.

Recovery is a lifelong process. There will be times when we grow weary, times when we want to throw in the towel. We will experience pain, fear, and a host of other emotions. We will win some battles but lose others in our war to gain wholeness. We may get discouraged at times when we can't see any progress, even though we have been working hard. But if we persevere through it all, we will hold on to the ground we have gained.

The apostle Paul used three illustrations to teach about perseverance. He wrote to Timothy, "Take your share of suffering as a good soldier of Jesus Christ, just as I do; and as Christ's soldier, do not let yourself become tied up in worldly affairs, for then you cannot satisfy the one who has enlisted you in his army. Follow the Lord's rules for doing his work, just as an athlete either follows the rules or is disqualified and wins no prize. Work hard like a farmer who gets paid well if he raises a large crop. Think over these three illustrations, and may the Lord help you to understand how they apply to you" (2 Timothy 2:3-7).

Like the soldier, we are in a war that we can win only if we fight to the end. Like the athlete, we must train for a new way of life and follow the steps of recovery to the finish line. Like the farmer, we must do our work in every season and then wait patiently until we see the growth. If we stop working our program before reaching our goal, we may lose everything we have fought, trained, and worked hard for. *Turn to page 1403, James 1.*

soldier of Jesus Christ, just as I do; 4and as
Christ's soldier, do not let yourself become
tied up in worldly affairs, for then you cannot
satisfy the one who has enlisted you in his
army. 5Follow the Lord's rules for doing his
work, just as an athlete either follows the rules
or is disqualified and wins no prize. 6Work
hard like a farmer who gets paid well if he
raises a large crop. 7Think over these three
illustrations, and may the Lord help you to
understand how they apply to you.

8Don't ever forget the wonderful fact that
Jesus Christ was a man, born into King
David's family; and that he was God, as
shown by the fact that he rose again from the
dead. 9It is because I have preached these great
truths that I am in trouble here and have been
put in jail like a criminal. But the Word of God
is not chained, even though I am. 10I am more
than willing to suffer if that will bring salvation and eternal glory in Christ Jesus to those
God has chosen.

11I am comforted by this truth, that when
we suffer and die for Christ it only means that
we will begin living with him in heaven.
12And if we think that our present service for
him is hard, just remember that some day we
are going to sit with him and rule with him.
But if we give up when we suffer, and turn
against Christ, then he must turn against us.
13Even when we are too weak to have any faith
left, he remains faithful to us and will help us,
for he cannot disown us who are part of
himself, and he will always carry out his
promises to us.

Being a Good Worker

14Remind your people of these great facts, and
command them in the name of the Lord not
to argue over unimportant things. Such arguments are confusing and useless and even
harmful. 15Work hard so God can say to you,
"Well done." Be a good workman, one who
does not need to be ashamed when God examines your work. Know what his Word says
and means. 16Steer clear of foolish discussions
that lead people into the sin of anger with
each other. 17Things will be said that will burn
and hurt for a long time to come. Hymenaeus
and Philetus, in their love of argument, are
men like that. 18They have left the path of
truth, preaching the lie that the resurrection
of the dead has already occurred; and they
have weakened the faith of some who believe
them.

19But God's truth stands firm like a great
rock, and nothing can shake it. It is a foundation stone with these words written on it:
"The Lord knows those who are really his,"

2:1-2 Notice that Paul didn't tell Timothy just to be strong; he told him to be strong in Jesus Christ. The apostle knew that Timothy could never succeed in his ministry by depending on his own strength. He needed the only Power sufficient for successful living—God in Jesus Christ. The truth that God gives us the power to live transformed lives is good news! It is something we need to pass on to others. Paul reminded Timothy that the Good News of God's transforming power should be passed from one person to the next. That is what recovery is all about. As each of us hears about and experiences God's power, we pass the word on to someone else. In this way others receive God's gracious help, and we discover the joy of helping others and growing in our faith.
2:3-7 The process of recovery and spiritual growth is never easy. Progress requires that we follow principles of disciplined faith on a daily basis. Like the soldier, we need to put aside the obstacles to our spiritual growth—our dependencies, our pursuit of pleasure, our denial. Like the athlete, we need to follow the rules for healthy living—God's will for our life. Like the farmer, we need to work hard, even when nature seems to stand in the way—persevering through the tough times. If we follow these examples, we will find God at work in our life. He will help us win life's hard battles; he will reward us with a prize at the end of the race; and we will harvest a rich crop of blessings.
2:15 Timothy was told to work hard to receive God's commendation and blessing. Notice that Paul applied Timothy's hard work to the task of understanding the Scriptures. Timothy was told to study God's Word to discover God's will for him in both attitude and action. We cannot know God's will unless we know what the Bible says. And since our recovery is dependent upon our following God's will, we need to take time to discover how God wants us to live. By seeking God's will through the hard work of study, we can take steps to follow his instructions for rebuilding our broken life.
2:22 Paul's advice to Timothy is appropriate for us, too. We need to run from the places and situations that are likely to lead to temptation. We are to avoid spending time with people who will lead us to a fall. Instead, we are to spend time with people who will support our progress in recovery and spiritual growth. This simple advice, though at times difficult to follow, can go a long way in supporting our progress in recovery. If we don't have friends or activities that support our recovery, we need to get involved in a community of godly and supportive people.

READ 2 TIMOTHY 4:5-15

GOD grant me the serenity to accept the things I cannot change the courage to change the things I can and the wisdom to know the difference AMEN

We cannot change our past, yet it is hard to accept the truth about it. It is hard to face the things that others have done to us and all the mistakes we have made.

In recovery we all struggle to move out of a difficult past and into a healthier future. Our energy can easily be spent trying to rewrite the past, a hopeless task. In the recovery process we need to honestly evaluate our life, including everything in our past.

Jesus said, "You will know the truth, and the truth will set you free" (John 8:32). The path to freedom always leads through the truth, even the truth about our past. The apostle Paul once wrote to young Timothy: "Alexander the coppersmith has done me much harm. The Lord will punish him" (2 Timothy 4:14). Paul states the truth about someone who had hurt him but leaves the matter in God's hands. We, too, need to honestly accept what has been done to us and then let it go, leaving it in God's hands.

Elsewhere, Paul examined his past, making an honest review of his earthly accomplishments, his wrongs, his mistakes, his family, his gains, and his losses. It was from this broad perspective that he could write these words: "I haven't learned all I should even yet, but I keep working toward that day when I will finally be all that Christ saved me for and wants me to be" (Philippians 3:12). When we face the truth about our past, we can finally let go of it. Then we can journey on into a healthier future. *Turn to page 1371, Titus 2.*

---

and "A person who calls himself a Christian
should not be doing things that are wrong."
20In a wealthy home there are dishes made
of gold and silver as well as some made from
wood and clay. The expensive dishes are used
for guests, and the cheap ones are used in the
kitchen or to put garbage in. 21If you stay away
from sin you will be like one of these dishes
made of purest gold—the very best in the
house—so that Christ himself can use you for
his highest purposes.
22Run from anything that gives you the evil
thoughts that young men often have, but stay
close to anything that makes you want to do
right. Have faith and love, and enjoy the
companionship of those who love the Lord
and have pure hearts.
23Again I say, don't get involved in foolish
arguments, which only upset people and
make them angry. 24God's people must not be
quarrelsome; they must be gentle, patient
teachers of those who are wrong. 25Be humble
when you are trying to teach those who are
mixed up concerning the truth. For if you talk
meekly and courteously to them, they are
more likely, with God's help, to turn away
from their wrong ideas and believe what is
true. 26Then they will come to their senses and
escape from Satan's trap of slavery to sin,
which he uses to catch them whenever he
likes, and then they can begin doing the will
of God.

CHAPTER 3

Faith Can Lead to Suffering

You may as well know this too, Timothy, that
in the last days it is going to be very difficult
to be a Christian. 2For people will love only
themselves and their money; they will be
proud and boastful, sneering at God, disobedient to their parents, ungrateful to them,
and thoroughly bad. 3They will be hard-

headed and never give in to others; they will be constant liars and troublemakers and will think nothing of immorality. They will be rough and cruel, and sneer at those who try to be good. [4]They will betray their friends; they will be hotheaded, puffed up with pride, and prefer good times to worshiping God. [5]They will go to church, yes, but they won't really believe anything they hear. Don't be taken in by people like that.

[6]They are the kind who craftily sneak into other people's homes and make friendships with silly, sin-burdened women and teach them their new doctrines. [7]Women of that kind are forever following new teachers, but they never understand the truth. [8]And these teachers fight truth just as Jannes and Jambres fought against Moses. They have dirty minds, warped and twisted, and have turned against the Christian faith.

[9]But they won't get away with all this forever. Someday their deceit will be well known to everyone, as was the sin of Jannes and Jambres.

Paul's Charge to Timothy

[10]But you know from watching me that I am not that kind of person. You know what I believe and the way I live and what I want. You know my faith in Christ and how I have suffered. You know my love for you, and my patience. [11]You know how many troubles I have had as a result of my preaching the Good News. You know about all that was done to me while I was visiting in Antioch, Iconium, and Lystra, but the Lord delivered me. [12]Yes, and those who decide to please Christ Jesus by living godly lives will suffer at the hands of those who hate him. [13]In fact, evil men and false teachers will become worse and worse, deceiving many, they themselves having been deceived by Satan.

[14]But you must keep on believing the things you have been taught. You know they are true, for you know that you can trust those of us who have taught you. [15]You know how, when you were a small child, you were taught the holy Scriptures; and it is these that make you wise to accept God's salvation by trusting in Christ Jesus. [16]The whole Bible was given to us by inspiration from God and is useful to teach us what is true and to make us realize what is wrong in our lives; it straightens us out and helps us do what is right. [17]It is God's way of making us well prepared at every point, fully equipped to do good to everyone.

CHAPTER 4

A Call to Share God's Truth

And so I solemnly urge you before God and before Christ Jesus—who will someday judge the living and the dead when he appears to set up his Kingdom— [2]to preach the Word of God urgently at all times, whenever you get the chance, in season and out, when it is convenient and when it is not. Correct and rebuke your people when they need it, encourage them to do right, and all the time be feeding them patiently with God's Word.

[3]For there is going to come a time when

3:1-9 These verses describe people we should not imitate. Sadly, under the influence of our addictions, however, many of us fit this description very well. We lived selfishly, with little thought for the other people in our life. Many of us may be suffering the consequences for our actions right now. We feel alone, lost, and abandoned. Paul made it clear that these attitudes and actions have severe consequences. Most of us have already discovered this the hard way. By continuing to take an inventory of our attitudes and actions, we can uncover our destructive character traits and ask God for his transforming help. We don't have to fit this description forever. With the help God offers in Jesus Christ, we can become a new person.

3:14-17 Paul reminded Timothy of the wonderful resource that God has left for us—the Bible. It is the ultimate guide to help us realize what is wrong in our life. It is the only accurate measuring stick available to help us make an honest moral inventory. It reveals God's program for healthy living and shows us how to relate properly and unselfishly to God and other people. God's Word offers more than just good advice. It promises God's powerful help to all who turn to him with a humble heart. God has given us a wonderful resource in his Word. Our recovery will benefit when we take the time to understand what it says.

4:1-5 Paul strongly encouraged Timothy to share the Good News of Jesus Christ with others. This is an integral part of Christian living. The good news of our recovery in Christ is also something to be shared. In fact, a strong and permanent recovery is impossible unless we make sharing our story an integral part of our life. By sharing our story of deliverance, we will offer new life to many needy people. In the process, we will be reminded of God's wonderful work in our life and be encouraged to persevere. We will build strong relationships with others as we walk through recovery with them. This will lead to the healthy community life necessary to support our recovery on a permanent basis.

people won't listen to the truth but will go
around looking for teachers who will tell
them just what they want to hear. [4]They
won't listen to what the Bible says but will
blithely follow their own misguided ideas.
[5]Stand steady, and don't be afraid of suffering for the Lord. Bring others to Christ. Leave
nothing undone that you ought to do.
[6]I say this because I won't be around to help
you very much longer. My time has almost
run out. Very soon now I will be on my way
to heaven. [7]I have fought long and hard for
my Lord, and through it all I have kept true to
him. And now the time has come for me to
stop fighting and rest. [8]In heaven a crown is
waiting for me, which the Lord, the righteous
Judge, will give me on that great day of his
return. And not just to me but to all those
whose lives show that they are eagerly looking forward to his coming back again.

Paul's Final Words

[9]Please come as soon as you can, [10]for Demas
has left me. He loved the good things of this
life and went to Thessalonica. Crescens has
gone to Galatia, Titus to Dalmatia. [11]Only
Luke is with me. Bring Mark with you when
you come, for I need him. [12](Tychicus is gone
too, as I sent him to Ephesus.) [13]When you
come, be sure to bring the coat I left at Troas
with Brother Carpus, and also the books, but
especially the parchments.
[14]Alexander the coppersmith has done me
much harm. The Lord will punish him, [15]but
be careful of him, for he fought against everything we said.
[16]The first time I was brought before the
judge, no one was here to help me. Everyone
had run away. I hope that they will not be
blamed for it. [17]But the Lord stood with me
and gave me the opportunity to boldly preach
a whole sermon for all the world to hear. And
he saved me from being thrown to the lions.
[18]Yes, and the Lord will always deliver me
from all evil and will bring me into his heavenly Kingdom. To God be the glory forever
and ever. Amen.
[19]Please say hello for me to Priscilla and
Aquila and those living at the home of Onesiphorus. [20]Erastus stayed at Corinth, and I left
Trophimus sick at Miletus.
[21]Do try to be here before winter. Eubulus
sends you greetings, and so do Pudens, Linus,
Claudia, and all the others. [22]May the Lord
Jesus Christ be with your spirit.

Farewell, Paul

4:6-8 Paul left his young protégé with these reflections to encourage him as he faced the long struggle to live a godly life. Paul had fought hard to live for God and had suffered greatly for the sake of others. Now he could look forward to the wonderful blessings he would receive in God's presence. Giving Timothy an eternal perspective would help him approach the tough times with the hope of future blessings. We are given this same hope. It is not easy to walk the path of recovery and spiritual growth. We will experience painful times as we recognize our desperate need for God's help. We will experience rejection as we seek to share the hope we have experienced with others. But God will reward our perseverance with eternal peace and joy. It all will be worth it in the end.

4:11 Mark had forsaken Paul and Barnabas during their first missionary journey (see Acts 13:13). Because of Mark's failure, Paul refused to allow his participation in the second journey, resulting in the separation of Paul and Barnabas (Acts 15:36-41). Though Mark had failed miserably at an earlier time, it is clear in this passage that his relationship with Paul had been fully restored. Mark's recovery from an earlier mistake can give hope to all who have failed and wondered whether recovery was even possible. Mark went on to write the Gospel of Mark, which has touched the lives of millions of people over the past twenty centuries. No matter how great our failures in the past, God can use us in amazing ways if we are willing to entrust our life—failures and all—to him.

4:16-18 Paul recalled the loneliness he felt during his first Roman imprisonment. He remembered how God had stayed with him even after all his human companions had forsaken him. Only God was able to bring him deliverance and restoration when he was a helpless prisoner. Some of us know what it is like to be forsaken by our friends. Under the influence of our addictions we may have destroyed our healthy family relationships. And when we entered recovery, the friends who supported our addictions soon left us. We don't have to face the dark days of recovery alone; God is always with us. As we grow in our faith, God will provide the healthy relationships we need to support our progress.

TITUS

THE BIG PICTURE

A. THREATS TO THE TRUTH ABOUT GOD'S GRACE (1:1-16)
B. SOUND TEACHINGS WITH RESPECT TO GOD'S GRACE (2:1–3:11)
   1. Applying God's Truth to Various Age-Groups (2:1-10)
   2. God's Grace As a Motivation for Godly Living (2:11–3:8)
   3. Applying God's Truth to the Problem of Legalism (3:9-11)
C. FINAL PERSONAL REMARKS (3:12-15)

Paul wrote this letter to Titus, a young pastor on the island of Crete. Titus faced two primary problems in his church. On the one hand, some claimed that immoral living was all right because God's grace was sufficient for forgiveness. On the other hand, there were those who claimed that acceptance by God came through obeying God's laws. Paul encouraged Titus to confront both groups for undermining God's gracious gift of forgiveness in Christ.

Paul solved Titus's dual problem by reminding him of the importance of God's grace. When we discover the amazing grace that God has bestowed on us, we will feel an incredible sense of gratitude. This will motivate us to delight in obeying God's will for our life, not to live a life of immorality because our forgiveness is guaranteed. God is not a harsh taskmaster whose favor depends on our slavish obedience to his rules. He is a gracious Father who offers us a relationship with him, both now and throughout eternity. We can live godly lives out of gratitude to God because he loves and forgives us.

The fact that God is gracious and forgiving is essential to our recovery. We already know that we are powerless against sin and our dependencies. We have all failed many times over. But because God is gracious, we don't need to be afraid to admit our failures to God. He will forgive us and give us a chance to start over again. Because God is gracious, we can continue our honest self-examination without fear. God will never write us off for our failures and mistakes. God accepts us just as we are.

THE BOTTOM LINE

PURPOSE: To encourage Titus to be faithful in applying the grace of God to various circumstances. AUTHOR: The apostle Paul. AUDIENCE: Titus, a pastor on the island of Crete. DATE WRITTEN: Between Paul's first and second Roman imprisonments (A.D. 63–66). SETTING: Titus pastored the believers on the island of Crete, a place well known for its immorality. Also, a group of Jewish legalists had made inroads into the church. Titus thus had to deal with both immorality and legalism. KEY VERSES: "For the free gift of eternal salvation is now being offered to everyone; and along with this gift comes the realization that God wants us to turn from godless living and sinful pleasures and to live good, God-fearing lives day after day" (2:11-12). KEY PEOPLE AND RELATIONSHIPS: Paul with Titus.

RECOVERY THEMES

The Blessings of God's Grace: Salvation in Jesus Christ is good news! This is especially true because God offers it to us freely, even though we do not deserve it. This Good News goes beyond God's offer to pay for our sins; God also seeks to transform our life so that we can live day by day with the reality of his power inside us. We don't need to be afraid as we come before God, regardless of our past or our failures. Our relationship with God is not based on our success at following his laws. It is based on his gracious provision for the forgiveness of our sin—Jesus Christ. As we entrust our life to God, he forgives us and empowers us to live according to his perfect plan.

The Importance of Accountability: We can never make much progress in recovery when we are isolated from others. Developing healthy relationships goes right along with turning our life over to God. On our own, all of us are helpless against the power of our dependencies. God often uses other people to give us the help and encouragement we need to persevere. Paul urged Titus to be accountable to others. By depending on others, he was able to stand firm and reflect God's love and power in his life. Relationships that hold us accountable can give us the courage to do as Titus did.

Recovery Requires Sacrifice: When we enter into recovery, we also enter into new relationships. As we see in this letter, there is an order to all our relationships. Everyone's role is important, and if we are going to be faithful to our role, we must make sacrifices for others. Recovery, like salvation, can begin as a very selfish process. We tend to focus on our own problems and needs. But a healthy recovery moves beyond this self-focus to reach out to others. Each of us has something to share. We can make the sacrifices necessary to be helpful to others in need of recovery.

CHAPTER 1

Greetings from Paul

From: Paul, the slave of God and the messenger of Jesus Christ.
I have been sent to bring faith to those God
has chosen and to teach them to know God's
truth—the kind of truth that changes lives—
so that they can have eternal life, which God
promised them before the world began—and
he cannot lie. [3]And now in his own good time
he has revealed this Good News and permits
me to tell it to everyone. By command of God
our Savior, I have been trusted to do this work
for him.
[4]*To:* Titus, who is truly my son in the affairs
of the Lord.
May God the Father and Christ Jesus our
Savior give you his blessings and his peace.

1:4-5 Paul had planted churches on the island of Crete, and Titus was called upon to finish Paul's work. He was to strengthen the believers and appoint leaders to serve them. Paul recognized that Titus could not do everything alone. He probably also recognized that having a single leader is never ideal. Organizations that revolve around one person are likely to reproduce the flaws of their leaders. Having a leadership group provides balance for the weaknesses of the individuals. If church or recovery leaders try to control everything, refusing to share their responsibilities and power with others, we should wonder whether they are there to help other people or to help themselves. We need to steer clear of this kind of group or organization.

1:6-9 This list of qualifications for church leadership makes no mention of social standing, financial resources, or professional accomplishments. It is a simple list of character traits. Church leaders must be good spouses and parents; they need to have a good reputation; they need to be humble, patient, self-controlled, hospitable, sensible, and fair. These character traits have nothing to do with whether or not we are wealthy or poor, famous or unknown, powerful or lowly. No one can buy these character traits; no one can demand them. We can get them only by entrusting our life to God and making his will our own. God can help these character traits grow in our life, regardless of the circumstances we face. Whether we are respected millionaires or homeless addicts, God can transform us into people worthy of being leaders in his church.

1:10-14 Paul encouraged Titus to confront both the Cretans, who abused God's grace by living in sin (1:12-13), and the Jewish legalists, who denied God's grace by requiring believers to do good works to earn salvation (1:10, 14). Paul's primary concern was with the legalists, since they undermined a life of grace with their rules and traditions (see Mark 7:1-8). Legalism makes our obedience to rules and traditions more important than a personal and transforming relationship with God. It assumes that we can be good under our own power, an assumption we know to be false. In recovery we have come to recognize our powerlessness. We cannot change without the help of a higher Power. We have put our life into God's hands, trusting him to help us. So in these verses Paul was defending some of the basic tenets of recovery: our powerlessness and God's sufficiency.

READ TITUS 2:11-14

GOD grant me the serenity to accept the things I cannot change the courage to change the things I can and the wisdom to know the difference AMEN

No matter how terrible our past, we can make changes for the better in mind, body, and spirit.

Some of us may have come to the conclusion that we just can't change. But if we are willing to place our life in God's hands, there is always hope for positive change and a bright future. The apostle Paul wrote, "May the God of peace himself make you entirely pure and devoted to God; and may your spirit and soul and body be kept strong and blameless until that day when our Lord Jesus Christ comes back again. God, who called you to become his child, will do all this for you, just as he promised" (1 Thessalonians 5:23-24).

"For the free gift of eternal salvation is now being offered to everyone; and along with this gift comes the realization that God wants us to turn from godless living and sinful pleasures and to live good, God-fearing lives day after day, looking forward to that wonderful time we've been expecting, when his glory shall be seen. . . . He died under God's judgment against our sins so that he could rescue us from constant falling into sin and make us his very own people, with cleansed hearts and real enthusiasm for doing kind things for others" (Titus 2:11-14).

God has promised us a wonderful future! In the present, he is in the process of rescuing us from constantly falling into sin. Our willingness to let go of the things we cannot change in our past will free us to make positive changes for a healthy future. ***Turn to page 1469, Revelation 21.***

Guidelines for Church Leaders

5I left you there on the island of Crete so that
you could do whatever was needed to help
strengthen each of its churches, and I asked
you to appoint pastors in every city who
would follow the instructions I gave you. 6The
men you choose must be well thought of for
their good lives; they must have only one wife
and their children must love the Lord and not
have a reputation for being wild or disobedient to their parents.

7These pastors must be men of blameless
lives because they are God's ministers. They
must not be proud or impatient; they must
not be drunkards or fighters or greedy for
money. 8They must enjoy having guests in
their homes and must love all that is good.
They must be sensible men, and fair. They
must be clean minded and level headed.
9Their belief in the truth that they have been
taught must be strong and steadfast so that
they will be able to teach it to others and
show those who disagree with them where
they are wrong.

Warning against False Teachers

10For there are many who refuse to obey; this
is especially true among those who say that all
Christians must obey the Jewish laws. But this
is foolish talk; it blinds people to the truth,
11and it must be stopped. Already whole families have been turned away from the grace of
God. Such teachers are only after your money.
12One of their own men, a prophet from
Crete, has said about them, "These men of
Crete are all liars; they are like lazy animals,
living only to satisfy their stomachs." 13And
this is true. So speak to the Christians there as
sternly as necessary to make them strong in
the faith 14and to stop them from listening to

Jewish folk tales and the demands of men who have turned their backs on the truth.

15 A person who is pure of heart sees goodness and purity in everything; but a person whose own heart is evil and untrusting finds evil in everything, for his dirty mind and rebellious heart color all he sees and hears.
16 Such persons claim they know God, but from seeing the way they act, one knows they don't. They are rotten and disobedient, worthless so far as doing anything good is concerned.

CHAPTER 2

Guidelines for Healthy Living

But as for you, speak up for the right living that goes along with true Christianity.
2 Teach the older men to be serious and unruffled; they must be sensible, knowing and believing the truth and doing everything with love and patience.

3 Teach the older women to be quiet and respectful in everything they do. They must not go around speaking evil of others and must not be heavy drinkers, but they should be teachers of goodness.
4 These older women must train the younger women to live quietly, to love their husbands and their children,
5 and to be sensible and clean minded, spending their time in their own homes, being kind and obedient to their husbands so that the Christian faith can't be spoken against by those who know them.

6 In the same way, urge the young men to behave carefully, taking life seriously.
7 And here you yourself must be an example to them of good deeds of every kind. Let everything you do reflect your love of the truth and the fact that you are in dead earnest

2:1-5 Paul called older men and women to take a special role in the Christian community. They were to be role models for others, teaching by the way they lived. Many of us have experienced the importance of having a godly mentor to encourage us. The most helpful recovery groups have a healthy mix of people, with sponsors who provide encouragement not only with their words, but also with their actions. As we grow spiritually and make progress in recovery, we can become healthy role models to others in need of recovery. As they see our transformed life and hear our story of deliverance, they will be encouraged to take the steps necessary for building a new life.

2:6 Paul told Titus to warn the young people in his church to think before acting. Young people often are blind to the consequences of certain activities. They often act first and think about it later. Many of us were very short-sighted when we became involved in our addictive behaviors. We probably started out innocently enough, using alcohol or other addictive substances socially. We didn't think through the possible consequences before we took the first dangerous steps toward addiction. Now we are reaping the painful consequences of our impetuous actions. Paul here calls young Christians to "behave carefully." If we think before we act, conforming our activities to God's revealed will, we will build for a meaningful future.

2:11-15 When we realize that God loves us and provides the power for us to live a godly life, we are motivated to entrust our life to him and seek out his will. The proper response to God's grace is right living. In the Bible, guilt and fear are never considered appropriate motivations for righteousness. We obey God because he loves us and desires to help us succeed. Seeing God as accepting, gracious, and compassionate instead of harsh, condemning, and punitive is critical for our spiritual growth. We don't need to fear God because of the mistakes we have made. He still loves us and will help us rebuild our life when we admit our failures to him. God wants us to make progress in recovery even more than we do! This can give us hope as we work through the process.

3:3 This verse describes what we are like when enslaved by an addiction. We become slaves to our dependencies, filled with resentment, envy, and hate. But this verse is only the dark backdrop that will magnify the beauty of the deliverance God offers in the person of Jesus Christ. Our broken life can be like black velvet, against which the bright diamond of God's gracious salvation can be displayed. The darker our life before meeting Christ, the better it will magnify God's mercy toward us. None of us deserves God's gracious help. He loves us simply because he chooses to, more in spite of us than because we deserve it. This truth makes it easier to admit our powerlessness and commit our life to God. No matter how terrible our past, God is willing to forgive and transform us.

3:4-8 Notice the terms used to describe God's grace: "kindness and love" (3:4), "kindness and pity" (3:5), and "great kindness" (3:7). We are justified by God's grace; that is, we are declared "good in God's eyes" by virtue of belonging to Christ. This takes us off the performance treadmill, relieving us of the need to measure up to God's standards. Some of us have spent our life trying to measure up. We bear a load of guilt for failing to fulfill the unrealistic ideals of our parents, teachers, or bosses. The anger and pain caused by this heavy burden have helped to drive our addictions. But God accepts us just as we are. He doesn't expect us to be perfect; he knows we cannot go it alone. When he calls us to holy living, he also provides the power and direction we need to succeed at building a new life.

about it. 8Your conversation should be so
sensible and logical that anyone who wants
to argue will be ashamed of himself because
there won't be anything to criticize in anything you say!
9Urge slaves to obey their masters and to try
their best to satisfy them. They must not talk
back, 10nor steal, but must show themselves to
be entirely trustworthy. In this way they will
make people want to believe in our Savior and
God.
11For the free gift of eternal salvation is
now being offered to everyone; 12and along
with this gift comes the realization that God
wants us to turn from godless living and
sinful pleasures and to live good, God-fearing
lives day after day, 13looking forward to that
wonderful time we've been expecting, when
his glory shall be seen—the glory of our great
God and Savior Jesus Christ. 14He died under
God's judgment against our sins so that he
could rescue us from constant falling into sin
and make us his very own people, with
cleansed hearts and real enthusiasm for doing kind things for others. 15You must teach
these things and encourage your people to
do them, correcting them when necessary as
one who has every right to do so. Don't let
anyone think that what you say is not important.

CHAPTER 3

Showing Respect for Authority

Remind your people to obey the government
and its officers, and always to be obedient and
ready for any honest work. 2They must not
speak evil of anyone, nor quarrel, but be gentle and truly courteous to all.
3Once we, too, were foolish and disobedient; we were misled by others and became
slaves to many evil pleasures and wicked desires. Our lives were full of resentment and
envy. We hated others and they hated us.
4But when the time came for the kindness
and love of God our Savior to appear, 5then he
saved us—not because we were good enough
to be saved but because of his kindness and
pity—by washing away our sins and giving us
the new joy of the indwelling Holy Spirit,
6whom he poured out upon us with wonderful fullness—and all because of what Jesus
Christ our Savior did 7so that he could declare
us good in God's eyes—all because of his great
kindness; and now we can share in the wealth
of the eternal life he gives us, and we are
eagerly looking forward to receiving it. 8These
things I have told you are all true. Insist on

Never Forget

BIBLE READING: Titus 3:1-5

Having had a spiritual awakening as the result of these steps, we tried to carry this message to others and to practice these principles in all our affairs.

As we get further along in our recovery, the memory of how bad our life really was may begin to fade. Do we vividly remember what we once were? Can we recall the dark emotions that filled our soul? Do we have true compassion and humble sympathy for those to whom we try to carry the message?

When we take the message of recovery to others, it is vital that we never forget where we came from and how we got where we are. Paul told Titus: "Once we, too, were foolish and disobedient; we were misled by others and became slaves to many evil pleasures and wicked desires. . . . But when the time came for the kindness and love of God our Savior to appear, then he saved us—not because we were good enough to be saved but because of his kindness and pity—by washing away our sins and giving us the new joy of the indwelling Holy Spirit" (Titus 3:3-5).

As we share our message, let us never forget the following truths. We, too, were slaves, just as others are today. Our heart was filled with the confusion and painful emotions that others still feel. We were saved because of the love and kindness of God, not because we were good enough. We must also remember that we are able to stay free because God is with us, upholding us every step of the way. ***Turn to page 1419, 1 Peter 4.***

them so that Christians will be careful to do good deeds all the time, for this is not only right, but it brings results.

Avoiding Useless Arguments

9Don't get involved in arguing over unanswerable questions and controversial theological ideas; keep out of arguments and quarrels about obedience to Jewish laws, for this kind of thing isn't worthwhile; it only does harm.
10If anyone is causing divisions among you, he should be given a first and second warning. After that have nothing more to do with him,
11for such a person has a wrong sense of values. He is sinning, and he knows it.

Paul's Final Instructions

12I am planning to send either Artemas or Tychicus to you. As soon as one of them arrives, please try to meet me at Nicopolis as quickly as you can, for I have decided to stay there for the winter. 13Do everything you can to help Zenas the lawyer and Apollos with their trip; see that they are given everything they need. 14For our people must learn to help all who need their assistance, that their lives will be fruitful.

15Everybody here sends greetings. Please say hello to all of the Christian friends there. May God's blessings be with you all.

Sincerely, Paul

PHILEMON

THE BIG PICTURE

A. GREETINGS (1:1-3)
B. PAUL COMMENDS PHILEMON (1:4-7)
C. PAUL REQUESTS CONSIDERATION FOR ONESIMUS (1:8-21)
D. CONCLUDING REMARKS (1:22-25)

There were millions of slaves in the Roman Empire; Onesimus was one of them. He was owned by a kind Christian leader named Philemon, but he was still a slave. Out of desperation, Onesimus stole from his master and ran away. But as so often happens, his attempt at a solution only added to his problem. According to the law, a runaway slave could be branded on the forehead or even executed.

Onesimus went to hide in Rome, and while there he met Paul. Through the apostle's influence, he came to believe in Jesus Christ. Paul, himself a prisoner at the time, wrote to his friend Philemon to tell him of Onesimus's conversion. The apostle begged Philemon to forgive Onesimus and welcome him home as a "beloved brother." We do not know how Philemon responded, but it seems reasonable to assume that he forgave Onesimus.

We all know what it's like to be a slave. We have been slaves to addictive substances, to other people, to compulsive behaviors, and even to the injuries of the past. Slavery of any kind takes away our humanity, turning us into mere tools in the hands of our owners. We know the utter powerlessness we felt when in that condition.

Paul's letter to Philemon reminds us that God still loves us. God cares for us, just as he cared for Onesimus, no matter what we have done in the past. God can step into the middle of our unmanageable life and offer us real hope for the future. As long as we do our part—facing our powerlessness, turning our life over to God, confessing our wrongs, and seeking to make amends—we can count on a life of freedom.

THE BOTTOM LINE

PURPOSE: To convince Philemon, a slave owner, to forgive a slave for running away. AUTHOR: The apostle Paul. AUDIENCE: Philemon, a believer in the early church. DATE WRITTEN: About A.D. 60, during Paul's imprisonment in Rome. SETTING: Slavery was common in the Roman Empire, even among the new believers. Paul did not speak directly against slavery, but he did take a radical step by calling the slave Onesimus "a beloved brother" (1:16). KEY VERSE: "Onesimus (whose name means 'Useful') hasn't been of much use to you in the past, but now he is going to be of real use to both of us" (1:11). KEY PEOPLE AND RELATIONSHIPS: Paul with Onesimus and Philemon.

RECOVERY THEMES

God Cares for the Dispossessed: Onesimus was one of the rejects of his society. As a slave, he had no worth apart from what he was able to do for his master. When he intensified his problems by stealing and running away, his value was diminished even further—he was worthless. But to God he was highly valuable; no one is ever worthless in the eyes of God. God's values are different from ours: he cares deeply about all people who have been broken and dispossessed. No matter what we have done in the past, he calls us to himself and offers us a life of recovery and hope.

The Necessity of Forgiveness: Anyone in the Roman Empire would have expected Onesimus to be condemned to death for what he had done. But from God's perspective, Onesimus was deemed worthy of forgiveness because of his relationship with Jesus Christ. The foundation of the change in Onesimus's life was the forgiveness he received from God. And the foundation of his continued relationship with Philemon was the forgiveness he received from his master. The forgiveness granted by God and by others makes our recovery possible. We can rejoice that when we entrust our life to God, he forgives us and transforms our life. Then he helps us to make amends with the people we have harmed, paving the way for our forgiveness and restoration.

CHAPTER 1

Greetings from Paul

From: Paul, in jail for preaching the Good News about Jesus Christ, and from Brother Timothy.

To: Philemon, our much-loved fellow worker, and to the church that meets in your home, and to Apphia our sister, and to Archippus who, like myself, is a soldier of the cross.

[3]May God our Father and the Lord Jesus Christ give you his blessings and his peace.

[4]I always thank God when I am praying for you, dear Philemon, [5]because I keep hearing of your love and trust in the Lord Jesus and in his people. [6]And I pray that as you share your faith with others it will grip their lives too, as they see the wealth of good things in you that come from Christ Jesus. [7]I myself have gained much joy and comfort from your love, my

---

1:3-9 Before bringing up the problem of the runaway Onesimus, Paul took some time to establish his lines of communication with Philemon. The apostle showed an appreciation for Philemon and a real concern for his family. Paul's example here may be helpful for us in recovery. There are times when we are called upon to confront others about their dependencies or deal with some other touchy problem. As we face situations that require confrontation, we need to make sure we value the people involved and take the time to establish strong lines of communication. If we jump in too soon, they may feel we are just trying to hurt them. If we prove our love beforehand, however, they will be more likely to listen to what we have to say.

1:10-13 Onesimus had been reconciled to God; he had experienced God's forgiveness in his life. But the fact that God had forgiven him did not exempt him from the consequences of his earlier actions. He still had to return to Philemon to make amends for his wrongs. Restitution is one of the hardest parts of recovery. Our actions have painful consequences; they hurt other people. Even after we have been reconciled to God, we still need to make amends with the people we have wronged. As hard as this may be, we can be sure that God will stand with us in the process. Onesimus returned to his master bearing this letter from Paul. And though there is no record of the outcome of Onesimus's return, it is unlikely that this letter would have survived had Philemon not taken Paul's advice to forgive Onesimus.

1:14-17 Both Onesimus and Philemon had a responsibility. Onesimus was responsible to do what he could to make amends to Philemon; Philemon was responsible to accept the overtures of repentant Onesimus. Old resentments had to be set aside, and Philemon was called upon to forgive and accept his repentant brother. If we have wronged someone else, we need to take clear steps toward making amends. It is equally important, however, that we respond with forgiveness when someone humbly seeks to make amends with us. Bearing a grudge against someone else is destructive not only to the person we turn away; it also will fill us with unresolved bitterness, making progress in our own recovery impossible.

1:18-21 With the phrase "charge me for it," Paul was asking Philemon to reckon Onesimus's debt against Paul's account. Philemon was to welcome Onesimus back into his household as if Paul was the one returning. Paul intervened to arrest the progression of resentment and brokenness in this relationship. This is a beautiful illustration of what God does for us through Jesus Christ. God reckons all our sins and failures to the account of Jesus Christ, who has paid the price through his death on the cross. Then God joyfully receives us into his family, just as if he was welcoming his own Son (see 2 Corinthians 5:21).

brother, because your kindness has so often
refreshed the hearts of God's people.

Paul's Appeal for Onesimus

8,9Now I want to ask a favor of you. I could
demand it of you in the name of Christ because it is the right thing for you to do, but I
love you and prefer just to ask you—I, Paul,
an old man now, here in jail for the sake of
Jesus Christ. 10My plea is that you show kindness to my child Onesimus, whom I won to
the Lord while here in my chains. 11Onesimus
(whose name means "Useful") hasn't been of
much use to you in the past, but now he is
going to be of real use to both of us. 12I am
sending him back to you, and with him
comes my own heart.

13I really wanted to keep him here with me
while I am in these chains for preaching the
Good News, and you would have been helping me through him, 14but I didn't want to do
it without your consent. I didn't want you to
be kind because you had to but because you
wanted to. 15Perhaps you could think of it this
way: that he ran away from you for a little
while so that now he can be yours forever,
16no longer only a slave, but something much
better—a beloved brother, especially to me.
Now he will mean much more to you too,
because he is not only a servant but also your
brother in Christ.

17If I am really your friend, give him the
same welcome you would give to me if I were
the one who was coming. 18If he has harmed
you in any way or stolen anything from you,
charge me for it. 19I will pay it back (I, Paul,
personally guarantee this by writing it here
with my own hand) but I won't mention how
much you owe me! The fact is, you even owe
me your very soul! 20Yes, dear brother, give me
joy with this loving act and my weary heart
will praise the Lord.

21I've written you this letter because I am
positive that you will do what I ask and even
more!

Final Greetings

22Please keep a guest room ready for me, for I
am hoping that God will answer your prayers
and let me come to you soon.

23Epaphras my fellow prisoner, who is also
here for preaching Christ Jesus, sends you his
greetings. 24So do Mark, Aristarchus, Demas,
and Luke, my fellow workers.

25The blessings of our Lord Jesus Christ be
upon your spirit.

Paul

Unfinished Business

BIBLE READING: Philemon 1:13-16

We made direct amends to such people wherever possible, except when to do so would injure them or others.

Sometimes we need to complete unfinished business before we can move forward toward new opportunities in life. Some of us may have left a trail of broken laws and relationships—things we need to address before moving on.

A new life doesn't excuse us from past obligations. While the apostle Paul was in prison, he led a runaway slave named Onesimus into a new life. Then Paul sent him back to his master, even though Onesimus faced a possible death penalty for his offense. Since his previous master was a friend of Paul's and a Christian brother, they hoped that Onesimus would be forgiven.

Onesimus carried a letter to his master from Paul, which read "I really wanted to keep [Onesimus] here with me . . . but I didn't want to do it without your consent. . . . He ran away from you for a little while so that now he can be yours forever, no longer only a slave, but something much better—a beloved brother. . . . If he has harmed you in any way or stolen anything from you, charge me for it" (Philemon 1:13-16, 18).

Before we can move ahead, we must face the unfinished business of the past. This includes offering to pay back what we owe, coming clean with the law, and going back to the people from whom we ran away. We can't assume forgiveness from people, although we can hope for it. In some cases we may be surprised to find pardon and release from the bondage of our past. *Turn to page 1415, 1 Peter 2.*

THE BIG PICTURE

A. THE SUPERIORITY OF JESUS AS OUR POWER FOR RECOVERY (1:1–10:18)
   1. He Is More Powerful than the Angels (1:1–2:18)
   2. He Is Greater than Moses and Joshua (3:1–4:13)
   3. He Surpasses Everything in the Old Covenant Priesthood (4:14–7:28)
   4. His New Covenant Is Superior (8:1–10:18)

B. THE FREEING POWER OF FAITH AND HUMILITY (10:19–13:25)
   1. Faith Needed in Hard Times (10:19-39)
   2. Faith Seen in Old Testament Times (11:1-40)
   3. Faithfulness and the Loving Discipline of God (12:1-29)
   4. Faithfulness and the Trustworthy Foundation of Christ (13:1-25)

All of us have felt the tug of an old habit or a former way of life. We have known the frustration it creates as we long for the familiar, even if it is destructive. Perhaps at times the challenge of recovery seems too hard for us. Our old life beckons, tempting us with familiar sources of comfort.

Many of the Jewish Christians of the first century thought about returning to the Jewish faith. Some of Jesus' teachings didn't seem to line up with the teachings of the Jewish rabbis. Was Jesus really the Messiah? Did following him mean they had to give up their old, familiar forms of worship? Would it be wrong to go back to their old beliefs and traditions? Did it make sense to follow this "new way" when it led to harsh persecution?

The writer of Hebrews dealt with the doubts of Jewish believers by showing how salvation in Jesus Christ is clearly superior to the way of the Jewish law. The Jewish readers are told to hold on to their new faith, to encourage each other, and to look forward to Jesus the Messiah's return. They are warned of the consequences of rejecting the salvation offered by God in Christ and reminded of the blessings promised to those who entrust their lives to him.

Entering recovery requires that we entrust our life to God in Jesus Christ and follow his ways. From time to time we will almost certainly feel a temptation to return to our former life. But God is the only one who can empower our recovery. When we give our life over to him, we take the leap of faith necessary to begin the process of recovery.

THE BOTTOM LINE

PURPOSE: To demonstrate the wisdom of following Christ and the foolishness of looking elsewhere for salvation. AUTHOR: The author is unknown, but Paul, Luke, Barnabas, Apollos, Silas, Philip, Priscilla, and others have been suggested as possibilities. AUDIENCE: Jewish believers. DATE WRITTEN: Probably shortly before the destruction of the Jerusalem Temple in A.D. 70. SETTING: Hebrews was written to encourage Jewish believers who were being severely persecuted. They needed to be reassured that Jesus was who he claimed to be—the Son of God and the promised Messiah. KEY VERSE: "God's Son shines out with God's glory, and all that God's Son is and does marks him as God" (1:3). KEY PEOPLE AND RELATIONSHIPS: Jesus Christ, along with many men and women of faith.

RECOVERY THEMES

The Primacy of Jesus Christ: The book of Hebrews describes Jesus as God. It explains that Jesus is the ultimate power and authority in the universe, superior to any and every other leader in history. He is the full and complete revelation of God to us. And Jesus is the one who can forgive us of our sins. Christ is the center of our hope and trust, and for that reason he is our only real hope for recovery.

God Delivers the Powerless: Because Jesus was the perfect sacrifice, he fulfilled all that the Old Testament sacrifices represented—he was the means of God's complete forgiveness of our sins. That means every sin can be forgiven completely—past, present, and future. Through Christ, God did for us what we could not do. Jesus removed the barrier of sin between us and God so we could have access to God's very presence. Christ's complete sacrifice removed the guilt that accompanied our sin. Through his sacrificial death and powerful resurrection, he has delivered the powerless!

The Necessity of Faith: Faith is "the confident assurance that something we want is going to happen. It is the certainty that what we hope for is waiting for us, even though we cannot see it up ahead" (11:1). Our recovery is based on faith—our confident trust in God that he will help us do what we are powerless to do. As we place our trust in God, he will transform us with his power. He has promised this to all who believe.

The Importance of Perseverance: It is one thing to know that our recovery is a lifelong process; it is another to persevere when obstacles and problems block our way. The first readers of the book of Hebrews experienced incredible persecution for their faith. But the writer assured them that they would be able to endure it if they did not give up or turn back. We need to pray for the strength to endure, because perseverance is essential to any successful recovery.

CHAPTER 1

Jesus Christ Is God's Son

Long ago God spoke in many different ways
to our fathers through the prophets [in visions, dreams, and even face to face], telling
them little by little about his plans.
2But now in these days he has spoken to us
through his Son to whom he has given everything and through whom he made the world
and everything there is.
3God's Son shines out with God's glory, and
all that God's Son is and does marks him as
God. He regulates the universe by the mighty
power of his command. He is the one who
died to cleanse us and clear our record of all
sin, and then sat down in highest honor beside the great God of heaven.

Christ Is Greater than the Angels

4Thus he became far greater than the angels,
as proved by the fact that his name "Son of
God," which was passed on to him from his
Father, is far greater than the names and titles
of the angels. 5,6For God never said to any
angel, "You are my Son, and today I have
given you the honor that goes with that
name." But God said it about Jesus. Another
time he said, "I am his Father and he is my
Son." And still another time—when his firstborn Son came to earth—God said, "Let all
the angels of God worship him."
7God speaks of his angels as messengers
swift as the wind and as servants made of
flaming fire; 8but of his Son he says, "Your
Kingdom, O God, will last forever and ever;

1:1-2 Jesus Christ, the Son of God, is God's final and most perfect revelation. Yet God the Son shaped the original creation as well. As "A and Z, the Beginning and the Ending" (Revelation 1:8), he is the only Power capable of the re-creation and transformation we seek in recovery. As the heir of all the treasures of heaven and earth, Jesus Christ stands ready and able to help those who come to him with empty hands, acknowledging their needs and problems.

1:3 There is a vast difference between the divine infinite Being (God) and a limited human being (ourself). The only way a person can come to understand something of God's glory and power is to get to know Jesus Christ by faith. Christ is simultaneously both an incredibly powerful expression of God's person and the one who lovingly entered sinful human existence to redeem and renew needy souls. When we acknowledge how powerless we are to save ourself, we need to come to the only Power who can accomplish what we cannot—God in Jesus Christ.

1:4-6 Largely because of their role in the Old Testament, angels were greatly esteemed by the Jews as servants of God. However, as glorious as they are, there is still no comparison between the angels and Jesus Christ. Not only is he clearly superior in his person and in the purposes he accomplished; he also has a declared Son-to-Father relationship with the heavenly Father that is unique (see Psalm 2:7; 2 Samuel 7:14). It is into this wonderful Father-child relationship that he draws us (2:11). Through Jesus, we have access to a Father who loves us and cares for our every need tenderly and with infinite wisdom (see Galatians 4:6; Ephesians 2:18). This is good news indeed!

its commands are always just and right. 9You
love right and hate wrong; so God, even your
God, has poured out more gladness upon you
than on anyone else."

10God also called him "Lord" when he said,
"Lord, in the beginning you made the earth,
and the heavens are the work of your hands.
11They will disappear into nothingness, but
you will remain forever. They will become
worn out like old clothes, 12and some day you
will fold them up and replace them. But you
yourself will never change, and your years
will never end."

13And did God ever say to an angel, as he
does to his Son, "Sit here beside me in honor
until I crush all your enemies beneath your
feet"?

14No, for the angels are only spirit-messen-
gers sent out to help and care for those who
are to receive his salvation.

CHAPTER 2

A Warning against Drifting Away

So we must listen very carefully to the truths
we have heard, or we may drift away from
them. 2For since the messages from angels
have always proved true and people have
always been punished for disobeying them,
3what makes us think that we can escape if we
are indifferent to this great salvation announced by the Lord Jesus himself and passed
on to us by those who heard him speak?

4God always has shown us that these messages are true by signs and wonders and various miracles and by giving certain special
abilities from the Holy Spirit to those who
believe; yes, God has assigned such gifts to
each of us.

God Became a Human Being

5And the future world we are talking about
will not be controlled by angels. 6No, for in
the book of Psalms David says to God, "What
is mere man that you are so concerned about
him? And who is this Son of Man you
honor so highly? 7For though you made him
lower than the angels for a little while, now
you have crowned him with glory and honor.
8And you have put him in complete charge of
everything there is. Nothing is left out."

We have not yet seen all of this take place,
9but we do see Jesus—who for awhile was a
little lower than the angels—crowned now by
God with glory and honor because he suffered death for us. Yes, because of God's great
kindness, Jesus tasted death for everyone in
all the world.

10And it was right and proper that God,
who made everything for his own glory,
should allow Jesus to suffer, for in doing this
he was bringing vast multitudes of God's
people to heaven; for his suffering made Jesus
a perfect Leader, one fit to bring them into
their salvation.

11We who have been made holy by Jesus,
now have the same Father he has. That is why
Jesus is not ashamed to call us his brothers.
12For he says in the book of Psalms, "I will talk
to my brothers about God my Father, and
together we will sing his praises." 13At another
time he said, "I will put my trust in God along
with my brothers." And at still another time,

2:1-3 This is the first of many "warning" passages in Hebrews. By it, the author sought to alert the Jewish readers to the subtle danger of drifting back into their former life-style in Judaism. In recovery, too, there is always the danger of falling back into old ways. This passage makes clear the consequences of our decisions: there will be either just punishment for ignoring the opportunity for recovery in Christ or wonderful salvation by trusting God and the strongly confirmed gospel of renewal.

2:5-8 The writer of Hebrews applied a well-known psalm to Christ (Psalm 8:4-6), most likely because of a reference to the "Son of Man." In Psalm 8 itself it is not obvious that these verses are messianic (i.e., referring to Christ). Rather, they seem to refer to humanity's status: lower than the angels, yet ruler of the earth. In applying these verses to Christ, the writer of Hebrews put a new twist on this. As the Son of Man, Christ was made lower than the angels for a time, but now is exalted to a position of authority over all things. He went before us, and now gives us hope as we look ahead to our ultimate future. No matter how difficult things are for us on this earth, our eventual destiny is to rule in heaven with Christ.

2:8-14 Believers who are in recovery are on the way to an eternity with God, moving through difficult territory where Christ has already been. It was God's kindness that led Jesus to his death—because by his death, salvation was made available to all. It is also God's kindness that leads us through suffering in recovery. Often it is only through the refining fire of suffering that we achieve balance and true holiness. When we suffer, we can be sure that Jesus is with us, that he went before us, and that God will use our pain for his purposes.

"See, here am I and the children God gave me."

14Since we, God's children, are human beings—made of flesh and blood—he became flesh and blood too by being born in human form; for only as a human being could he die and in dying break the power of the devil who had the power of death. 15Only in that way could he deliver those who through fear of death have been living all their lives as slaves to constant dread.

16We all know he did not come as an angel but as a human being—yes, a Jew. 17And it was necessary for Jesus to be like us, his brothers, so that he could be our merciful and faithful High Priest before God, a Priest who would be both merciful to us and faithful to God in dealing with the sins of the people. 18For since he himself has now been through suffering and temptation, he knows what it is like when we suffer and are tempted, and he is wonderfully able to help us.

CHAPTER 3

Christ Is Greater than Moses

Therefore, dear brothers whom God has set apart for himself—you who are chosen for heaven—I want you to think now about this Jesus who is God's Messenger and the High Priest of our faith.

2For Jesus was faithful to God who appointed him High Priest, just as Moses also faithfully served in God's house. 3But Jesus has far more glory than Moses, just as a man who builds a fine house gets more praise than his house does. 4And many people can build houses, but only God made everything.

5Well, Moses did a fine job working in God's house, but he was only a servant; and his work was mostly to illustrate and suggest those things that would happen later on. 6But Christ, God's faithful Son, is in complete charge of God's house. And we Christians are God's house—he lives in us!—if we keep up our courage firm to the end, and our joy and our trust in the Lord.

A Call to Listen to God

7,8And since Christ is so much superior, the Holy Spirit warns us to listen to him, to be careful to hear his voice today and not let our hearts become set against him, as the people of Israel did. They steeled themselves against his love and complained against him in the desert while he was testing them. 9But God was patient with them forty years, though they tried his patience sorely; he kept right on doing his mighty miracles for them to see. 10"But," God says, "I was very angry with them, for their hearts were always looking somewhere else instead of up to me, and they never found the paths I wanted them to follow."

11Then God, full of this anger against them, bound himself with an oath that he would never let them come to his place of rest.

12Beware then of your own hearts, dear brothers, lest you find that they, too, are evil

---

2:17-18 When we are depressed or struggling in recovery, we may feel that nobody cares about us or understands what we are going through. No person has ever gone to greater lengths to identify with us than Jesus Christ; though he was limitless God, he subjected himself to all our limitations. He lived in our world as a human being, and he suffered as we do—therefore he understands our pain and suffering from personal experience. He has been where we are, and he is both eager and able to help us.

3:1 The writer of Hebrews reminded his readers that they were God's special people, set apart, chosen for heaven. Periodically in our recovery work we need to be reminded of who we are and where we are headed. Formerly, before we began recovery, our past controlled our present. Now, in recovery, because of the faith we exercise, our future sets the direction and tone of our life. As often as we need to, we can affirm who we are in Christ and the glorious destiny he holds for us.

3:2-6 Christ's superiority to Moses was underlined by comparing the positions held by each. Christ was like a builder (as Creator), while Moses was like a house the builder constructed, or even a servant—though an esteemed one—in that house. God may use many means to help us in our recovery: a therapist, a recovery group, a pastor, a sponsor, books, meetings, taped messages, journaling, prayer. But let us remember that it is God who is in loving control of the reconstruction of our life. In that knowledge we can find comfort, confidence, and joy.

3:7–4:13 In this second and more extended "warning section" (see 2:1-4), the readers are cautioned to avoid the mistake made by the Israelites who received the Law at Mount Sinai. In spite of all their spiritual privileges and visual awareness of God's awesome power, they still refused to exercise faith and enter the Promised Land that God graciously offered. Many of us have made similar mistakes with respect to entering recovery. Either we don't persevere, or we don't anchor our recovery in Christ, the only true source of healing. The book of Hebrews, and all of Scripture, is geared toward helping us put our full trust in God as he is revealed in Jesus Christ.

and unbelieving and are leading you away from the living God. 13Speak to each other about these things every day while there is still time so that none of you will become hardened against God, being blinded by the glamor of sin. 14For if we are faithful to the end, trusting God just as we did when we first became Christians, we will share in all that belongs to Christ.

15But *now* is the time. Never forget the warning, "*Today* if you hear God's voice speaking to you, do not harden your hearts against him, as the people of Israel did when they rebelled against him in the desert."

16And who were those people I speak of, who heard God's voice speaking to them but then rebelled against him? They were the ones who came out of Egypt with Moses their leader. 17And who was it who made God angry for all those forty years? These same people who sinned and as a result died in the wilderness. 18And to whom was God speaking when he swore with an oath that they could never go into the land he had promised his people? He was speaking to all those who disobeyed him. 19And why couldn't they go in? Because they didn't trust him.

CHAPTER 4

Promised Rest for God's People

Although God's promise still stands—his promise that all may enter his place of rest—we ought to tremble with fear because some of you may be on the verge of failing to get there after all. 2For this wonderful news—the message that God wants to save us—has been given to us just as it was to those who lived in the time of Moses. But it didn't do them any good because they didn't believe it. They didn't mix it with faith. 3For only we who believe God can enter into his place of rest. He has said, "I have sworn in my anger that those who don't believe me will never get in," even though he has been ready and waiting for them since the world began.

4We know he is ready and waiting because it is written that God rested on the seventh day of creation, having finished all that he had planned to make.

5Even so they didn't get in, for God finally said, "They shall never enter my rest." 6Yet the promise remains and some get in—but not those who had the first chance, for they disobeyed God and failed to enter.

7But he has set another time for coming in, and that time is now. He announced this through King David long years after man's first failure to enter, saying in the words already quoted, "Today when you hear him calling, do not harden your hearts against him."

8This new place of rest he is talking about does not mean the land of Israel that Joshua led them into. If that were what God meant, he would not have spoken long afterwards about "today" being the time to get in. 9So there is a full complete rest *still waiting* for the people of God. 10Christ has already entered there. He is resting from his work, just as God did after the creation. 11Let us do our best to go into that place of rest, too, being careful not to disobey God as the children of Israel did, thus failing to get in.

12For whatever God says to us is full of living power: it is sharper than the sharpest dagger, cutting swift and deep into our inner-

---

4:1-3 God is always ready and willing to fulfill his promises of freedom and rest. There is only one thing that stops him: our unbelief or lack of faith. God wants us to receive wonderful blessings and freedom from our dependencies, but these can only be received by faith. Just as the Jews of Moses' day turned back from entering the Promised Land, sometimes we allow the difficulties of the present to cause us to doubt God's ability to keep his promises. Recovery is hard, painful work at times. When the going seems the hardest, that is when we must consciously fix our minds on God's promises. Faith in Christ, not in our own efforts, is the only way to true recovery.

4:4-11 Though he is by no means presently inactive, God, in a very real sense, entered his "rest" at the end of the creation (see Genesis 2:1-3). The writer understood David's renewed offer of rest in Psalm 95 to mean that the final rest was not secured when Joshua and Israel entered the Promised Land. Therefore, God's offer of rest, which certainly includes the goals of recovery (peace with God, self, and others; healthy relationships; the ability to cope with life) remains available to those who pursue it with faith and perseverance.

4:12-13 During hard times our faith tends to dwindle; it is easy to grow angry and harden our heart to the truth about ourself. There is an antidote to this problem: the Word of God, which has spiritual power to penetrate even the deepest denial. This is good news for those of us struggling to overcome a dysfunctional life-style characterized by a tendency to distort reality. God knows everything about us, even the things we try to hide from ourself. We can count on him, through his Word, to uncover the problems and needs we will face in recovery.

most thoughts and desires with all their parts, exposing us for what we really are. 13He knows about everyone, everywhere. Everything about us is bare and wide open to the all-seeing eyes of our living God; nothing can be hidden from him to whom we must explain all that we have done.

Christ Is Our High Priest

14But Jesus the Son of God is our great High Priest who has gone to heaven itself to help us; therefore let us never stop trusting him. 15This High Priest of ours understands our weaknesses since he had the same temptations we do, though he never once gave way to them and sinned. 16So let us come boldly to the very throne of God and stay there to receive his mercy and to find grace to help us in our times of need.

CHAPTER 5

The Jewish high priest is merely a man like anyone else, but he is chosen to speak for all other men in their dealings with God. He presents their gifts to God and offers to him the blood of animals that are sacrificed to cover the sins of the people and his own sins too. And because he is a man, he can deal gently with other men, though they are foolish and ignorant, for he, too, is surrounded with the same temptations and understands their problems very well.

4Another thing to remember is that no one can be a high priest just because he wants to be. He has to be called by God for this work in the same way God chose Aaron.

5That is why Christ did not elect himself to the honor of being High Priest; no, he was chosen by God. God said to him, "My Son, today I have honored you." 6And another time God said to him, "You have been chosen to be a priest forever, with the same rank as Melchizedek."

7Yet while Christ was here on earth he pleaded with God, praying with tears and agony of soul to the only one who would save him from [premature] death. And God heard his prayers because of his strong desire to obey God at all times.

8And even though Jesus was God's Son, he had to learn from experience what it was like to obey when obeying meant suffering. 9It was after he had proved himself perfect in this experience that Jesus became the Giver of eternal salvation to all those who obey him. 10For remember that God has chosen him to be a High Priest with the same rank as Melchizedek.

A Call to Spiritual Growth

11There is much more I would like to say along these lines, but you don't seem to listen, so it's hard to make you understand.

12,13You have been Christians a long time now, and you ought to be teaching others, but instead you have dropped back to the place where you need someone to teach you all over again the very first principles in God's Word. You are like babies who can drink only milk, not old enough for solid food. And when a person is still living on milk it shows he isn't very far along in the Christian life, and doesn't know much about the difference between right and wrong. He is still a baby Christian! 14You will never be able to eat solid spiritual food and understand the deeper

---

5:4-10 Like any high priest, Jesus Christ had to be chosen for his role. But Christ's was a different priesthood than the Jewish priesthood descended from Aaron. Jesus is the final (and eternal) High Priest in the order of Melchizedek (see 7:1-21; Psalm 110:4). To prepare for that unique calling, Jesus, who was and is perfect as God (see Hebrews 13:8), had to go through a painful growing and learning process (see Luke 2:52) that culminated in his death on the cross. His success in that process lends us great hope as we pursue recovery. He is the one who goes before us and has prepared the way, and he is with us in every step we take.

5:11-13 The writer interrupted his discussion of Melchizedek (see 5:6-10; 7:1-21) in order to give a lengthy warning (5:11–6:12) about the spiritual dynamics underlying the readers' stalled growth in Christ. Having adequate time to grow and change was not a problem. But the readers (like many of us today) continued to manifest childlike behavior instead of growing to spiritual adulthood. Sometimes in recovery it takes a long time to see any progress. But this passage suggests that growth is the norm, even though it is often slow. If we don't see any progress in our recovery, it may be time to reconsider our approach.

5:14 Spiritual growth, eventual maturity, and balance can happen only through application: acting on what we know to be true (see 4:12). The idea implied by the word *practice* is that we need to continue to do the right things, and the more we do them, the more they become second nature to us. Like the athlete training for physical prowess, our recovery involves moral conditioning through making right choices, which will lead to spiritual and emotional maturity.

things of God's Word until you become better
Christians and learn right from wrong by
practicing doing right.

CHAPTER 6
Let us stop going over the same old ground
again and again, always teaching those first
lessons about Christ. Let us go on instead to
other things and become mature in our understanding, as strong Christians ought to be.
Surely we don't need to speak further about
the foolishness of trying to be saved by being
good, or about the necessity of faith in God;
2you don't need further instruction about
baptism and spiritual gifts and the resurrection of the dead and eternal judgment.
3The Lord willing, we will go on now to
other things.
4There is no use trying to bring you back to
the Lord again if you have once understood
the Good News and tasted for yourself the
good things of heaven and shared in the Holy
Spirit, 5and know how good the Word of God
is, and felt the mighty powers of the world to
come, 6and then have turned against God.
You cannot bring yourself to repent again if
you have nailed the Son of God to the cross
again by rejecting him, holding him up to
mocking and to public shame.
7When a farmer's land has had many showers upon it and good crops come up, that land
has experienced God's blessing upon it. 8But
if it keeps on having crops of thistles and
thorns, the land is considered no good and is
ready for condemnation and burning off.
9Dear friends, even though I am talking like
this I really don't believe that what I am
saying applies to you. I am confident you are
producing the good fruit that comes along
with your salvation. 10For God is not unfair.
How can he forget your hard work for him, or
forget the way you used to show your love for
him—and still do—by helping his children?
11And we are anxious that you keep right on
loving others as long as life lasts, so that you
will get your full reward.
12Then, knowing what lies ahead for you,
you won't become bored with being a Christian nor become spiritually dull and indifferent, but you will be anxious to follow the
example of those who receive all that God has
promised them because of their strong faith
and patience.

God's Promises Bring Hope

13For instance, there was God's promise to
Abraham: God took an oath in his own name,
since there was no one greater to swear by,
14that he would bless Abraham again and
again, and give him a son and make him the
father of a great nation of people. 15Then
Abraham waited patiently until finally God
gave him a son, Isaac, just as he had promised.
16When a man takes an oath, he is calling
upon someone greater than himself to force
him to do what he has promised or to punish
him if he later refuses to do it; the oath ends
all argument about it. 17God also bound himself with an oath, so that those he promised
to help would be perfectly sure and never
need to wonder whether he might change his
plans.
18He has given us both his promise and his
oath, two things we can completely count on,
for it is impossible for God to tell a lie. Now
all those who flee to him to save them can

6:4-8 This section refers either to believers who turned from their salvation or to unbelievers who came close to salvation but then turned away. Either way, the agricultural analogy brings out the truth that if there is real spiritual life, there will be some evidence of it. In our recovery, let us look for and cherish any and all signs of growth, even if they are only tiny, green shoots where before there was dry, barren ground. If we are seeking wholeness through faith in Christ, we can be assured that there will, in good time, be fruit.

6:9-12 In confronting his readers regarding their spiritual lethargy (see 5:11-14), the writer's words were strong and direct, though he still chose to be positive and think the best about them. On the one hand, he knew from the past what positive things they were capable of doing. However, he also faced the reality of their immaturity and challenged them to persevere in spiritual growth and recovery with a patient faith. In our recovery, we sometimes need to hear hard words of correction and challenge. This passage is both an example of how to confront when necessary and a challenge to be open to correction from the people who love us.

6:13-20 Abraham, the father of the Jewish nation, was a classic example of patient faith. After waiting for many years, he received his promised son, Isaac, the first of many descendants (see Genesis 12:1-3; 22:16-18). Abraham's persevering faith (see 11:8-19) was anchored in God's promises, which were based on God's unchanging nature. Like Abraham, we can trust God's promises and find absolute security in the resurrected Christ, who is our High Priest and who connects us with the living God.

take new courage when they hear such assurances from God; now they can know without
doubt that he will give them the salvation he
has promised them.
[19]This certain hope of being saved is a
strong and trustworthy anchor for our souls,
connecting us with God himself behind the
sacred curtains of heaven, [20]where Christ has
gone ahead to plead for us from his position
as our High Priest, with the honor and rank of
Melchizedek.

CHAPTER 7

Melchizedek Is Compared to Abraham

This Melchizedek was king of the city of Salem and also a priest of the Most High God.
When Abraham was returning home after
winning a great battle against many kings,
Melchizedek met him and blessed him; [2]then
Abraham took a tenth of all he had won in the
battle and gave it to Melchizedek.
Melchizedek's name means "Justice," so he
is the King of Justice; and he is also the King
of Peace because of the name of his city,
Salem, which means "Peace." [3]Melchizedek
had no father or mother and there is no
record of any of his ancestors. He was never
born and he never died but his life is like that
of the Son of God—a priest forever.
[4]See then how great this Melchizedek is:
*(a)*Even Abraham, the first and most honored of all God's chosen people, gave Melchizedek a tenth of the spoils he took from the
kings he had been fighting. [5]One could understand why Abraham would do this if Melchizedek had been a Jewish priest, for later on
God's people were required by law to give gifts
to help their priests because the priests were
their relatives. [6]But Melchizedek was not a
relative, and yet Abraham paid him.
*(b)*Melchizedek placed a blessing upon
mighty Abraham, [7]and as everyone knows, a
person who has the power to bless is always
greater than the person he blesses.
[8]*(c)*The Jewish priests, though mortal, received tithes; but we are told that Melchizedek lives on.
[9]*(d)*One might even say that Levi himself
(the ancestor of all Jewish priests, of all who
receive tithes), paid tithes to Melchizedek
through Abraham. [10]For although Levi wasn't
born yet, the seed from which he came was in
Abraham when Abraham paid the tithes to
Melchizedek.
[11]*(e)*If the Jewish priests and their laws had
been able to save us, why then did God need
to send Christ as a priest with the rank of
Melchizedek, instead of sending someone
with the rank of Aaron—the same rank all
other priests had?
[12-14]And when God sends a new kind of
priest, his law must be changed to permit it.
As we all know, Christ did not belong to the
priest-tribe of Levi, but came from the tribe of
Judah, which had not been chosen for priesthood; Moses had never given them that work.

Christ Is like Melchizedek

[15]So we can plainly see that God's method
changed, for Christ, the new High Priest who
came with the rank of Melchizedek, [16]did not
become a priest by meeting the old requirement of belonging to the tribe of Levi, but on
the basis of power flowing from a life
that cannot end. [17]And the psalmist points
this out when he says of Christ, "You are a
priest forever with the rank of Melchizedek."

7:1-3 The discussion here returned to the consideration of Melchizedek (see 5:6-10). These ideas may have been too deep for the original readers to fully understand in their state of spiritual lethargy, but the writer thought it was crucial that they try to understand. Aspects of Melchizedek's life (see Genesis 14:18-20) were amazingly parallel to events in the life of Christ. This was to make it clear that Christ truly did qualify as a priest in Melchizedek's order (see 6:20), and thus as our perpetual anchor for recovery and reconciliation.

7:4-10 This entire section argued that Abraham recognized Melchizedek as greater than himself, and thus obviously greater than any of Abraham's descendants, including Levi and the priesthood descended from him. It also established that the priesthood Christ holds, according to the order of Melchizedek, is actually older (implying more stability) than that of Aaron. Such stability can be a great comfort to a person in the turmoil of recovery. Our life may seem to fall apart, and circumstances may constantly change, but Christ will never change.

7:11-19 The new priesthood of Christ was desperately needed because the Levitical priesthood and the Mosaic law were incapable of producing true spiritual maturity. A better priesthood, a better law, and a better hope for living in a growing relationship with God were necessary. Christ's qualification for his High Priesthood came not through tribal descent, but because of his resurrection to new life. The Mosaic law could not make people right with God. Only Christ could do that. In our recovery, Jesus will work his lasting changes in our life.

[18]Yes, the old system of priesthood based on
family lines was canceled because it didn't
work. It was weak and useless for saving
people. [19]It never made anyone really right
with God. But now we have a far better hope,
for Christ makes us acceptable to God, and
now we may draw near to him.
[20]God took an oath that Christ would always be a Priest, [21]although he never said that
of other priests. Only to Christ he said, "The
Lord has sworn and will never change his
mind: You are a Priest forever, with the rank
of Melchizedek." [22]Because of God's oath,
Christ can guarantee forever the success of
this new and better arrangement.
[23]Under the old arrangement there had to
be many priests so that when the older ones
died off, the system could still be carried on
by others who took their places.
[24]But Jesus lives forever and continues to be
a Priest so that no one else is needed. [25]He is
able to save completely all who come to God
through him. Since he will live forever, he will
always be there to remind God that he has
paid for their sins with his blood.
[26]He is, therefore, exactly the kind of High
Priest we need; for he is holy and blameless,
unstained by sin, undefiled by sinners, and to
him has been given the place of honor in
heaven. [27]He never needs the daily blood of
animal sacrifices, as other priests did, to cover
over first their own sins and then the sins of
the people; for he finished all sacrifices, once
and for all, when he sacrificed himself on the
cross. [28]Under the old system, even the high
priests were weak and sinful men who could
not keep from doing wrong, but later God
appointed by his oath his Son who is perfect
forever.

CHAPTER 8

Christ Is Our High Priest

What we are saying is this: Christ, whose
priesthood we have just described, is our
High Priest and is in heaven at the place of
greatest honor next to God himself. [2]He ministers in the temple in heaven, the true place
of worship built by the Lord and not by human hands.
[3]And since every high priest is appointed to
offer gifts and sacrifices, Christ must make an
offering too. [4]The sacrifice he offers is far
better than those offered by the earthly
priests. (But even so, if he were here on earth
he wouldn't even be permitted to be a priest
because down here the priests still follow
the old Jewish system of sacrifices.) [5]Their
work is connected with a mere earthly model
of the real tabernacle in heaven; for when
Moses was getting ready to build the tabernacle, God warned him to follow exactly the
pattern of the heavenly tabernacle as shown
to him on Mount Sinai. [6]But Christ, as a
Minister in heaven, has been rewarded with a
far more important work than those who
serve under the old laws because the new
agreement that he passes on to us from God
contains far more wonderful promises.
[7]The old agreement didn't even work. If it
had, there would have been no need for another to replace it. [8]But God himself found
fault with the old one, for he said, "The day
will come when I will make a new agreement
with the people of Israel and the people of
Judah. [9]This new agreement will not be like
the old one I gave to their fathers on the day
when I took them by the hand to lead them
out of the land of Egypt; they did not keep
their part in that agreement, so I had to cancel

7:20-26 The unchangeable oath of God regarding Christ's priesthood, stated prophetically in Psalm 110:4, meant that Christ's ministry was related to a better and final covenant. This sense of permanence means, among other things, that Christ will see our recovery through to the end, that he is always available to help, and that he is always our perfect model of right living.

8:1-6 Christ is not only a superior heavenly High Priest, but he also serves in a superior heavenly sanctuary. In fact, the earthly tabernacle was never intended as anything but a limited copy of the ultimate heavenly sanctuary. So it doesn't matter that Christ was never recognized as an earthly priest. Through the death and resurrection of Christ, the limited, earthly priesthood gave way to the perfect, heavenly priesthood. It is the heavenly priesthood that provides the needed resources for recovery; any other means is inadequate.

8:7-13 Six centuries before Christ died on the cross to provide a new way for us to relate to God (see Luke 22:20), the prophet Jeremiah predicted that a "new contract," totally unlike the Old Testament law, was needed to breach the separation between God and the human race (see Jeremiah 31:31-34). Thus, rather than turning back to the old legalistic ways of Judaism, the readers should have been aware that God's old program had been on its way out for a long time. They were looking for recovery in the wrong place. There is only one way to experiencing recovery and reconciliation—through faith in Jesus Christ.

it. 10But this is the new agreement I will make with the people of Israel, says the Lord: I will write my laws in their minds so that they will know what I want them to do without my even telling them, and these laws will be in their hearts so that they will want to obey them, and I will be their God and they shall be my people. 11And no one then will need to speak to his friend or neighbor or brother, saying, 'You, too, should know the Lord,' because everyone, great and small, will know me already. 12And I will be merciful to them in their wrongdoings, and I will remember their sins no more."

13God speaks of these new promises, of this new agreement, as taking the place of the old one; for the old one is out of date now and has been put aside forever.

CHAPTER 9

Old Rules about Worship

Now in that first agreement between God and his people there were rules for worship and there was a sacred tent down here on earth. Inside this place of worship there were two rooms. The first one contained the golden candlestick and a table with special loaves of holy bread upon it; this part was called the Holy Place. 3Then there was a curtain, and behind the curtain was a room called the Holy of Holies. 4In that room there were a golden incense-altar and the golden chest, called the ark of the covenant, completely covered on all sides with pure gold. Inside the ark were the tablets of stone with the Ten Commandments written on them, and a golden jar with some manna in it, and Aaron's wooden cane that budded. 5Above the golden chest were statues of angels called the cherubim—the guardians of God's glory—with their wings stretched out over the ark's golden cover, called the mercy seat. But enough of such details.

6Well, when all was ready, the priests went in and out of the first room whenever they wanted to, doing their work. 7But only the high priest went into the inner room, and then only once a year, all alone, and always with blood that he sprinkled on the mercy seat as an offering to God to cover his own mistakes and sins and the mistakes and sins of all the people.

8And the Holy Spirit uses all this to point out to us that under the old system the common people could not go into the Holy of Holies as long as the outer room and the entire system it represents were still in use.

9This has an important lesson for us today. For under the old system, gifts and sacrifices were offered, but these failed to cleanse the hearts of the people who brought them. 10For the old system dealt only with certain rituals—what foods to eat and drink, rules for washing themselves, and rules about this and that. The people had to keep these rules to tide them over until Christ came with God's new and better way.

Christ Is the Perfect Sacrifice

11He came as High Priest of this better system that we now have. He went into that greater, perfect tabernacle in heaven, not made by men nor part of this world, 12and once for all took blood into that inner room, the Holy of Holies, and sprinkled it on the mercy seat; but it was not the blood of goats and calves. No,

---

8:10-13 The new plan to establish our relationship with God through Jesus Christ is exciting indeed. In Christ we can receive the spiritual and emotional healing we seek: moral codes written in the heart, rather than imposed from without; a new desire and ability to obey God; a special, close relationship with God; a new fellowship with other believers; ready mercy from God, with full forgiveness of past sins and character defects. In Christ, we have all the help necessary to make progress in our recovery.

9:1-10 The regulations and order of the Old Testament priesthood were striking in their beauty and powerfully symbolized the painful consequences of sin. But even though these sacrifices were effective on a short term basis, they were not a permanent solution to the sin problem. They could not produce immediate personal access to God or a clear conscience. Their role was to tide the people over until God's final and complete revelation could arrive in the person of Jesus Christ. Again we see that for those of us in need of recovery and spiritual transformation, Christ is the only viable option. Only in him can God effect permanent changes in our life.

9:11-15 There was absolutely no comparison between the ongoing sacrifices of the earthly Temple in Jerusalem and the sacrifice provided by Christ, our great High Priest and mediator. Christ accomplished what the Old Testament sacrificial system never could: a once-for-all, completed redemption. Trusting the work that he did is the only way to secure a clear conscience, complete forgiveness, and eternal life. Now when we put our faith in Christ, we are free to joyfully know and serve God.

he took his own blood, and with it he, by
himself, made sure of our eternal salvation.
13And if under the old system the blood of
bulls and goats and the ashes of young cows
could cleanse men's bodies from sin, 14just
think how much more surely the blood of
Christ will transform our lives and hearts. His
sacrifice frees us from the worry of having to
obey the old rules and makes us want to serve
the living God. For by the help of the eternal
Holy Spirit, Christ willingly gave himself to
God to die for our sins—he being perfect,
without a single sin or fault. 15Christ came
with this new agreement so that all who are
invited may come and have forever all the
wonders God has promised them. For Christ
died to rescue them from the penalty of the
sins they had committed while still under
that old system.
16Now, if someone dies and leaves a will—a
list of things to be given away to certain
people when he dies—no one gets anything
until it is proved that the person who wrote
the will is dead. 17The will goes into effect only
after the death of the person who wrote it.
While he is still alive no one can use it to get
any of those things he has promised them.
18That is why blood was sprinkled [as proof
of Christ's death] before even the first agreement could go into effect. 19For after Moses
had given the people all of God's laws, he took
the blood of calves and goats, along with
water, and sprinkled the blood over the book
of God's laws and over all the people, using
branches of hyssop bushes and scarlet wool to
sprinkle with. 20Then he said, "This is the
blood that marks the beginning of the agreement between you and God, the agreement
God commanded me to make with you."
21And in the same way he sprinkled blood on
the sacred tent and on whatever instruments
were used for worship. 22In fact we can say
that under the old agreement almost everything was cleansed by sprinkling it with
blood, and without the shedding of blood
there is no forgiveness of sins.
23That is why the sacred tent down here on
earth and everything in it—all copied from
things in heaven—all had to be made pure by
Moses in this way, by being sprinkled with the
blood of animals. But the real things in
heaven, of which these down here are copies,
were made pure with far more precious offerings.
24For Christ has entered into heaven itself
to appear now before God as our Friend. It
was not in the earthly place of worship that

Self-protection

READ HEBREWS 10:23-34

Recovery is not a battle anyone wins alone. We help each other to think and live in new ways. Alone, we are vulnerable to temptation; together, we form a shield of protection for one another.

The apostle Paul wrote, "In every battle you will need faith as your shield to stop the fiery arrows aimed at you by Satan" (Ephesians 6:16). Faith here refers to trusting in Christ for salvation. In general terms it also means having constancy in our convictions. This can apply to our convictions about God's wisdom in the Bible or our confidence in the Twelve Steps. The shield of faith was likened to the shields carried by Roman soldiers, which were able to cover the entire body. To advance in battle, a group of soldiers would assemble together, making a wall of shields for protection as they moved forward.

In like manner, we are told to stick together. The writer of Hebrews wrote, "Let us not neglect our church meetings, as some people do, but encourage and warn each other" (Hebrews 10:25). We are to take our place in a fellowship of people that provides us with the mutual protection we need to stand firm in our recovery.

We need to assemble with others who share the common beliefs helpful in our recovery. Our encouragement of one another, our shared faith in God and his Word, and the principles of the Twelve Steps will be a form of protection as we continue to advance in the recovery process. ***Turn to page 1393, Hebrews 12.***

he did this, for that was merely a copy of the
real temple in heaven. 25Nor has he offered
himself again and again, as the high priest
down here on earth offers animal blood in the
Holy of Holies each year. 26If that had been
necessary, then he would have had to die
again and again, ever since the world began.
But no! He came once for all, at the end of the
age, to put away the power of sin forever by
dying for us.

27And just as it is destined that men die only
once, and after that comes judgment, 28so also
Christ died only once as an offering for the
sins of many people; and he will come again,
but not to deal again with our sins.

This time he will come bringing salvation
to all those who are eagerly and patiently
waiting for him.

CHAPTER 10

A Sacrifice Once for All

The old system of Jewish laws gave only a dim
foretaste of the good things Christ would do
for us. The sacrifices under the old system
were repeated again and again, year after year,
but even so they could never save those who
lived under their rules. 2If they could have,
one offering would have been enough; the
worshipers would have been cleansed once
for all and their feeling of guilt would
be gone.

3But just the opposite happened: those
yearly sacrifices reminded them of their disobedience and guilt instead of relieving their
minds. 4For it is not possible for the blood of
bulls and goats really to take away sins.

5That is why Christ said as he came into the
world, "O God, the blood of bulls and goats
cannot satisfy you, so you have made ready
this body of mine for me to lay as a sacrifice
upon your altar. 6You were not satisfied with
the animal sacrifices, slain and burnt before
you as offerings for sin. 7Then I said, 'See, I
have come to do your will, to lay down my
life, just as the Scriptures said that I would.'"

8After Christ said this about not being satisfied with the various sacrifices and offerings
required under the old system, 9he then added,
"Here I am. I have come to give my life."

He cancels the first system in favor of a far
better one. 10Under this new plan we have
been forgiven and made clean by Christ's
dying for us once and for all.

11Under the old agreement the priests stood
before the altar day after day offering sacrifices that could never take away our sins. 12But
Christ gave himself to God for our sins as one
sacrifice for all time and then sat down in the
place of highest honor at God's right hand,
13waiting for his enemies to be laid under his
feet. 14For by that one offering he made forever perfect in the sight of God all those
whom he is making holy.

15And the Holy Spirit testifies that this is so,
for he has said, 16"This is the agreement I will
make with the people of Israel, though they
broke their first agreement: I will write my
laws into their minds so that they will always

9:27-28 Hope for the future must be based on the reality of the past and present. Death (and the following judgment) is the ultimate reality of this life; even Jesus Christ died! But, because his redemption and resurrection were successful, he is able to offer salvation and spare believers from the fear of judgment for their sins. This blend of reality and hope through faith can calm our fearful heart as we struggle with recovery issues. We can face any sin, any character defect, any hurt, knowing that Christ's sacrifice is completely sufficient to offer cleansing and new life.

10:3-10 As this section on the superiority of the New Covenant (8:1–10:18) draws to a close, the writer crowns his argument by asserting that the frustrating repetition of Old Covenant sacrifices has now been replaced by Christ coming and offering himself in accord with the will of God (10:7, 9-10). To not pursue recovery by faith in Christ is to openly reject the superior nature of God's will for history and for individual human lives. If we reject God's offer of salvation and transformation in Jesus Christ, we are rejecting the only means available to sustain our recovery on a permanent basis.

10:19-25 This climactic instructional section of Hebrews (10:19–13:25) begins with a summary of the argument for Christ's superiority, then shifts to the transformed attitudes that are necessary as a result. Since Christ is the final redemptive sacrifice and great High Priest, we can enjoy the full privileges he has secured: personal access to God through Christ without an elaborate system, full assurance of our faith and salvation, hope for what the future holds, and encouragement from other people of faith. Through Christ and a community of believers we receive everything necessary for a successful recovery.

10:24-25 Sometimes in recovery we may find ourself pulling away from healthy relationships or falling into codependent or negative situations that undermine our momentum toward recovery. These verses remind us that accountable and encouraging relationships with other believers are crucial to our spiritual growth. No one can stand alone for long in the recovery process. If we run from healthy relationships, we are running straight toward a painful relapse.

know my will, and I will put my laws in their
hearts so that they will want to obey them."
17And then he adds, "I will never again remember their sins and lawless deeds."
18Now, when sins have once been forever
forgiven and forgotten, there is no need to
offer more sacrifices to get rid of them.

Living by Faith

19And so, dear brothers, now we may walk
right into the very Holy of Holies, where God
is, because of the blood of Jesus. 20This is the
fresh, new, life-giving way that Christ has
opened up for us by tearing the curtain—his
human body—to let us into the holy presence
of God.
21And since this great High Priest of ours
rules over God's household, 22let us go right in
to God himself, with true hearts fully trusting
him to receive us because we have been sprinkled with Christ's blood to make us clean and
because our bodies have been washed with
pure water.
23Now we can look forward to the salvation
God has promised us. There is no longer any
room for doubt, and we can tell others that
salvation is ours, for there is no question that
he will do what he says.
24In response to all he has done for us, let us
outdo each other in being helpful and kind to
each other and in doing good.
25Let us not neglect our church meetings, as
some people do, but encourage and warn
each other, especially now that the day of his
coming back again is drawing near.
26If anyone sins deliberately by rejecting
the Savior after knowing the truth of forgiveness, this sin is not covered by Christ's death;
there is no way to get rid of it. 27There will be
nothing to look forward to but the terrible
punishment of God's awful anger, which will
consume all his enemies. 28A man who refused to obey the laws given by Moses was
killed without mercy if there were two or
three witnesses to his sin. 29Think how much
more terrible the punishment will be for
those who have trampled underfoot the Son
of God and treated his cleansing blood as
though it were common and unhallowed,
and insulted and outraged the Holy Spirit
who brings God's mercy to his people.
30For we know him who said, "Justice belongs to me; I will repay them"; who also said,
"The Lord himself will handle these cases."
31It is a fearful thing to fall into the hands of
the living God.
32Don't ever forget those wonderful days

Hope in Faith

BIBLE READING: Hebrews 11:1-10

We came to believe that a Power greater than ourselves could restore us to sanity.

Step Two is often referred to as "the hope step." In coming to believe that a Power greater than ourself can restore us to sanity, we will remember what it was like to live sanely and have the faith to hope that sanity can return.

"What is faith?" the Bible asks. "It is the confident assurance that something we want is going to happen. It is the certainty that what we hope for is waiting for us, even though we cannot see it up ahead" (Hebrews 11:1). How can we be confident that something we want is going to happen, especially if all of our hopes have been dashed? How can we risk believing that the life we hope for is waiting for us around the bend?

The Bible tells us that the key is in the nature of the higher Power we look to. We are told, "Anyone who wants to come to God must believe that there is a God and that he rewards those who sincerely look for him" (Hebrews 11:6). If we see God as one waiting to reward us, we will be more eager to look for him. If our faith has not matured to that point yet, we can ask for help. There was one man who came to Jesus and asked him to help his young son who was afflicted by a demon. He said to Jesus, "'Oh, have mercy on us and do something if you can.' 'If I can?' Jesus asked. '*Anything* is possible if you have faith.' The father instantly replied, 'I *do* have faith; oh, help me to have *more!*'" (Mark 9:22-24). We can start by asking God to help us have more faith. Then we can ask him for the courage to hope for a better future. ***Turn to Step Three, page 173, Numbers 23.***

when you first learned about Christ. Remember how you kept right on with the Lord even though it meant terrible suffering. 33Sometimes you were laughed at and beaten, and sometimes you watched and sympathized with others suffering the same things. 34You suffered with those thrown into jail, and you were actually joyful when all you owned was taken from you, knowing that better things were awaiting you in heaven, things that would be yours forever.

35Do not let this happy trust in the Lord die away, no matter what happens. Remember your reward! 36You need to keep on patiently doing God's will if you want him to do for you all that he has promised. 37His coming will not be delayed much longer. 38And those whose faith has made them good in God's sight must live by faith, trusting him in everything. Otherwise, if they shrink back, God will have no pleasure in them.

39But we have never turned our backs on God and sealed our fate. No, our faith in him assures our souls' salvation.

CHAPTER 11

Great Heroes of Faith

What is faith? It is the confident assurance that something we want is going to happen. It is the certainty that what we hope for is waiting for us, even though we cannot see it up ahead. 2Men of God in days of old were famous for their faith.

3By faith—by believing God—we know that the world and the stars—in fact, all things—were made at God's command; and that they were all made from things that can't be seen.

4It was by faith that Abel obeyed God and brought an offering that pleased God more than Cain's offering did. God accepted Abel and proved it by accepting his gift; and though Abel is long dead, we can still learn lessons from him about trusting God.

5Enoch trusted God too, and that is why God took him away to heaven without dying; suddenly he was gone because God took him. Before this happened God had said how pleased he was with Enoch. 6You can never please God without faith, without depending on him. Anyone who wants to come to God must believe that there is a God and that he rewards those who sincerely look for him.

7Noah was another who trusted God. When he heard God's warning about the future, Noah believed him even though there was then no sign of a flood, and wasting no time, he built the ark and saved his family. Noah's belief in God was in direct contrast to the sin and disbelief of the rest of the world—which refused to obey—and because of his faith he became one of those whom God has accepted.

8Abraham trusted God, and when God told him to leave home and go far away to another land that he promised to give him, Abraham obeyed. Away he went, not even knowing where he was going. 9And even when he reached God's promised land, he lived in tents like a mere visitor as did Isaac and Jacob,

---

10:26-39 This was the first "warning section" in the application portion of the book (see 12:14-29). It summarizes the only way to a wholehearted pursuit of emotional and spiritual healing. First, we can find release by repenting of sinful patterns and receiving forgiveness. Then we can take positive steps by strengthening our healthy behavioral patterns and attitudes, particularly our faith in God.

11:5-7 Enoch was unique (along with Elijah; see 2 Kings 2) in that he did not die (11:5; see Genesis 5:21-24). Noah also played a unique role with the ark, the Flood, and a new beginning (see Genesis 6–9). These two biblical characters illustrate the utter necessity of the faith and earnest perseverance described in 11:6. As we trust and depend on God for each aspect of our recovery, we can be confident that such trust pleases God and will be rewarded with his powerful help.

11:8-19 This portion about Abraham and Sarah is the longest in the Hebrews 11 "Hall of Faith," probably because Abraham fathered the Jewish nation. His life repeatedly demonstrated faith as, again and again, he encountered circumstances that seemed to undermine the fulfillment of God's promises. Sometimes in recovery it seems like forever before we see any changes. At such times we can remind ourself that even the biblical characters who are most famous for their faith had to persevere without seeing visible results. We can trust that God will come through for us, even when the struggle seems to drag on forever. Abraham had to wait most of a lifetime to see God's promises even partially fulfilled.

11:20-31 The writer demonstrated that every crucial person and event between the life of Abraham and Israel's entrance into the Promised Land exhibited exemplary faith (11:1, 6). God accomplishes his purposes, great and small, through the faith of his people. As we trust him with every aspect of our life and our recovery, he will accomplish the healing that is surely his will for us. If we trust in God, nothing is impossible!

to whom God gave the same promise. 10Abra-
ham did this because he was confidently waiting for God to bring him to that strong
heavenly city whose designer and builder is
God.
11Sarah, too, had faith, and because of this
she was able to become a mother in spite of
her old age, for she realized that God, who
gave her his promise, would certainly do what
he said. 12And so a whole nation came from
Abraham, who was too old to have even one
child—a nation with so many millions of
people that, like the stars of the sky and the
sand on the ocean shores, there is no way to
count them.
13These men of faith I have mentioned died
without ever receiving all that God had promised them; but they saw it all awaiting them
on ahead and were glad, for they agreed that
this earth was not their real home but that
they were just strangers visiting down here.
14And quite obviously when they talked like
that, they were looking forward to their real
home in heaven.
15If they had wanted to, they could have
gone back to the good things of this world.
16But they didn't want to. They were living for
heaven. And now God is not ashamed to be
called their God, for he has made a heavenly
city for them.
17While God was testing him, Abraham still
trusted in God and his promises, and so he
offered up his son Isaac and was ready to slay
him on the altar of sacrifice; 18yes, to slay even
Isaac, through whom God had promised to
give Abraham a whole nation of descendants!
19He believed that if Isaac died God would
bring him back to life again; and that is just
about what happened, for as far as Abraham
was concerned, Isaac was doomed to death,
but he came back again alive! 20It was by faith
that Isaac knew God would give future blessings to his two sons, Jacob and Esau.
21By faith Jacob, when he was old and dying, blessed each of Joseph's two sons as he
stood and prayed, leaning on the top of his
cane.
22And it was by faith that Joseph, as he
neared the end of his life, confidently spoke
of God bringing the people of Israel out of
Egypt; and he was so sure of it that he made
them promise to carry his bones with them
when they left!
23Moses' parents had faith too. When they
saw that God had given them an unusual
child, they trusted that God would save him
from the death the king commanded, and

Faith

READ HEBREWS 12:1-4

Our addictions interfere with our ability to win in the race of life. Many of us feel like losers who have just dropped out. Faith in God can give us the motivation to run the race, with a real chance at winning life's rewards.

Hebrews 11 has been called the "Hall of Faith." It mentions a long list of people whose lives were used by God because of their faith. The following chapter begins this way: "Since we have such a huge crowd of men of faith watching us from the grandstands, let us strip off anything that slows us down or holds us back, and especially those sins that wrap themselves so tightly around our feet and trip us up; and let us run with patience the particular race that God has set before us" (Hebrews 12:1).

This illustration referred to the Olympic games. In Bible times men wore flowing robes. At the time of an event, the athletes would strip off their robes and lay them aside to run without encumbrance. If someone tried to compete in his robes, he would get tangled up, losing both the race and the prize.

It is God's will for us to win the race of life. The robes of our recurrent sins need to be laid aside. There will be pain from the exertion, but we are told to pace ourself and to bear the pain with patience. And remember, others who have run the same race and finished well are cheering us on!
Turn to page 1395, Hebrews 12.

they hid him for three months and were not afraid.

[24,25]It was by faith that Moses, when he grew up, refused to be treated as the grandson of the king, but chose to share ill-treatment with God's people instead of enjoying the fleeting pleasures of sin. [26]He thought that it was better to suffer for the promised Christ than to own all the treasures of Egypt, for he was looking forward to the great reward that God would give him. [27]And it was because he trusted God that he left the land of Egypt and wasn't afraid of the king's anger. Moses kept right on going; it seemed as though he could see God right there with him. [28]And it was because he believed God would save his people that he commanded them to kill a lamb as God had told them to and sprinkle the blood on the doorposts of their homes so that God's terrible Angel of Death could not touch the oldest child in those homes as he did among the Egyptians.

[29]The people of Israel trusted God and went right through the Red Sea as though they were on dry ground. But when the Egyptians chasing them tried it, they all were drowned.

[30]It was faith that brought the walls of Jericho tumbling down after the people of Israel had walked around them seven days as God had commanded them. [31]By faith—because she believed in God and his power—Rahab the harlot did not die with all the others in her city when they refused to obey God, for she gave a friendly welcome to the spies.

[32]Well, how much more do I need to say? It would take too long to recount the stories of the faith of Gideon and Barak and Samson and Jephthah and David and Samuel and all the other prophets. [33]These people all trusted God and as a result won battles, overthrew kingdoms, ruled their people well, and received what God had promised them; they were kept from harm in a den of lions [34]and in a fiery furnace. Some, through their faith, escaped death by the sword. Some were made strong again after they had been weak or sick. Others were given great power in battle; they made whole armies turn and run away. [35]And some women, through faith, received their loved ones back again from death. But others trusted God and were beaten to death, preferring to die rather than turn from God and be free—trusting that they would rise to a better life afterwards.

[36]Some were laughed at and their backs cut open with whips, and others were chained in dungeons. [37,38]Some died by stoning and some by being sawed in two; others were promised freedom if they would renounce their faith, then were killed with the sword. Some went about in skins of sheep and goats, wandering over deserts and mountains, hiding in dens and caves. They were hungry and sick and ill-treated—too good for this world. [39]And these men of faith, though they trusted God and won his approval, none of them received all that God had promised them; [40]for God wanted them to wait and share the even better rewards that were prepared for us.

CHAPTER 12

God's Discipline Proves His Love

Since we have such a huge crowd of men of faith watching us from the grandstands, let us

---

11:32-38 Here the writer rapidly lists more people from Old Testament history who demonstrated powerful faith. Despite the brevity of this overview, it is clear that even in Old Testament times, faith was not just a strict obedience to Mosaic law. It was a heartfelt trust in our personal God. This would have shown the readers that many before them had faced difficult times and hung in there, persevering by faith (11:33-38; see 10:32-36). When we feel our faith faltering, it is good to be reminded of others who have gone before us. We may turn both to the Bible and to other Christians in recovery for real-life testimonies of how God works through faith.

12:14-29 This was the last of the "warning passages" spaced purposefully throughout Hebrews (see 2:1-4; 3:7–4:13; 5:11–6:12; 10:26-39). In effect, it served as the climactic confrontation between writer and readers over their apparent in-process defection from Christ back to Judaism and the Mosaic law. After exhorting the readers not to squander God's grace, the writer shifted to considering the huge consequences of rejecting faith in Christ and the recovery he offers. Our choices have eternal consequences! If we reject Christ, we also reject the only means for eternal salvation and recovery from our destructive dependencies.

12:15 When we are dealing with difficult circumstances or facing painful recovery issues, it is easy to grow angry or bitter. Sometimes we can't even perceive our own bitterness taking root; we need others to point it out to us. The feelings are understandable, especially if we have been victimized. And allowing ourself to feel them can be a first step in recovery. But we then need to be willing to forgive and to release the injustices and hurts in order to experience God's overwhelming forgiveness (see Matthew 18:21-35). When we hang on to our bitterness, we not only stall our own healing, but also hurt others along the way.

strip off anything that slows us down or holds
us back, and especially those sins that wrap
themselves so tightly around our feet and trip
us up; and let us run with patience the particular race that God has set before us.
2Keep your eyes on Jesus, our leader and
instructor. He was willing to die a shameful
death on the cross because of the joy he knew
would be his afterwards; and now he sits in
the place of honor by the throne of God.
3If you want to keep from becoming fainthearted and weary, think about his patience
as sinful men did such terrible things to him.
4After all, you have never yet struggled against
sin and temptation until you sweat great
drops of blood.
5And have you quite forgotten the encouraging words God spoke to you, his child? He
said, "My son, don't be angry when the Lord
punishes you. Don't be discouraged when he
has to show you where you are wrong. 6For
when he punishes you, it proves that he loves
you. When he whips you, it proves you are
really his child."
7Let God train you, for he is doing what any
loving father does for his children. Whoever
heard of a son who was never corrected? 8If
God doesn't punish you when you need it, as
other fathers punish their sons, then it means
that you aren't really God's son at all—that
you don't really belong in his family. 9Since
we respect our fathers here on earth, though
they punish us, should we not all the more
cheerfully submit to God's training so that we
can begin really to live?
10Our earthly fathers trained us for a few
brief years, doing the best for us that they
knew how, but God's correction is always
right and for our best good, that we may share
his holiness. 11Being punished isn't enjoyable
while it is happening—it hurts! But afterwards
we can see the result, a quiet growth in grace
and character.
12So take a new grip with your tired hands,
stand firm on your shaky legs, 13and mark out
a straight, smooth path for your feet so that
those who follow you, though weak and
lame, will not fall and hurt themselves but
become strong.

A Call to Listen to God

14Try to stay out of all quarrels, and seek to live
a clean and holy life, for one who is not holy
will not see the Lord. 15Look after each other
so that not one of you will fail to find God's
best blessings. Watch out that no bitterness
takes root among you, for as it springs up it

Faith

READ HEBREWS 12:5-11

Some phases of our recovery may be very painful; we may feel that we are being punished for our failures. We may assume that bad things are happening to us because we are bad. And we may begin to believe that God doesn't love us.

It may hurt when God removes our defects, but this in itself is a display of love. The Bible says, "'My son, don't be angry when the Lord punishes you. . . . For when he punishes you, it proves that he loves you. When he whips you, it proves you are really his child.' Let God train you, for he is doing what any loving father does for his children. Whoever heard of a son who was never corrected? . . . God's correction is always right and for our best good, that we may share his holiness. Being punished isn't enjoyable while it is happening—it hurts! But afterwards we can see the result, a quiet growth in grace and character" (Hebrews 12:5-7, 10-11).

Our recovery is a time of correction; it is a time of facing problems and character flaws and changing incorrect beliefs. There may be seasons when we do have to pay for our past. God will use this time to redirect our life toward something better. His correction isn't arbitrary or abusive, but it is still painful. Knowing that God's discipline demonstrates his love for us can be comforting in the midst of the pain. It helps to remember that his love will allow only that which is for our ultimate good. ***Turn to page 1407, James 3.***

causes deep trouble, hurting many in their spiritual lives. 16Watch out that no one becomes involved in sexual sin or becomes careless about God as Esau did: he traded his rights as the oldest son for a single meal. 17And afterwards, when he wanted those rights back again, it was too late, even though he wept bitter tears of repentance. So remember, and be careful.

18You have not had to stand face to face with terror, flaming fire, gloom, darkness, and a terrible storm as the Israelites did at Mount Sinai when God gave them his laws. 19For there was an awesome trumpet blast and a voice with a message so terrible that the people begged God to stop speaking. 20They staggered back under God's command that if even an animal touched the mountain it must die. 21Moses himself was so frightened at the sight that he shook with terrible fear.

22But you have come right up into Mount Zion, to the city of the living God, the heavenly Jerusalem, and to the gathering of countless happy angels; 23and to the church, composed of all those registered in heaven; and to God who is Judge of all; and to the spirits of the redeemed in heaven, already made perfect; 24and to Jesus himself, who has brought us his wonderful new agreement; and to the sprinkled blood, which graciously forgives instead of crying out for vengeance as the blood of Abel did.

25So see to it that you obey him who is speaking to you. For if the people of Israel did not escape when they refused to listen to Moses, the earthly messenger, how terrible our danger if we refuse to listen to God who speaks to us from heaven! 26When he spoke from Mount Sinai his voice shook the earth, but, "Next time," he says, "I will not only shake the earth but the heavens too." 27By this he means that he will sift out everything without solid foundations so that only unshakable things will be left.

28Since we have a Kingdom nothing can destroy, let us please God by serving him with thankful hearts and with holy fear and awe. 29For our God is a consuming fire.

CHAPTER 13

Following God's Program

Continue to love each other with true brotherly love. 2Don't forget to be kind to strangers, for some who have done this have entertained angels without realizing it! 3Don't forget about those in jail. Suffer with them as though you were there yourself. Share the sorrow of those being mistreated, for you know what they are going through.

4Honor your marriage and its vows, and be pure; for God will surely punish all those who are immoral or commit adultery.

5Stay away from the love of money; be satisfied with what you have. For God has said, "I will never, *never* fail you nor forsake you." 6That is why we can say without any doubt or fear, "The Lord is my Helper, and I am not afraid of anything that mere man can do to me."

7Remember your leaders who have taught you the Word of God. Think of all the good that has come from their lives, and try to trust the Lord as they do.

8Jesus Christ is the same yesterday, today, and forever. 9So do not be attracted by strange, new ideas. Your spiritual strength comes as a gift from God, not from ceremonial rules about eating certain foods—a method which, by the way, hasn't helped those who have tried it!

12:22-24 There is a wonderful reward waiting for those who, by faith, have endured in the recovery process (see 11:1, 6). The clustered references to Mount Zion, Jerusalem, angels, the firstborn, God, mediation, and blood were intended to show that the New Covenant and Christ offer the very things that the readers mistakenly sought by returning to Judaism. Again we see that full spiritual recovery is available only through faith in Jesus Christ.

13:1-6 This section lists a series of practical commands for faithfulness in service to others, in the marriage relationship, and in attitudes toward possessions. This faithfulness is based on God's empowerment and protection. Perhaps the readers were seriously wavering in these areas, even as many professing believers waver today. Since many of us with dysfunctional backgrounds struggle to determine which behaviors and attitudes are acceptable, God's clear standards can be a great help. As we practice right living, God's presence and power are available to help us.

13:7, 17 Many of us in recovery have difficulty dealing with authority figures. Apparently the readers of Hebrews, in turning back to their former Judaic life-style, were ignoring the proper authorities in their Jewish-Christian setting. So the writer admonished his readers to imitate the faith and life-style of their former leaders and cooperate with their present leaders for the good of all involved. In our recovery work, let us remember the importance of other people, especially those who model recovery and spiritual growth for us.

[10]We have an altar—the cross where Christ was sacrificed—where those who continue to seek salvation by obeying Jewish laws can never be helped. [11]Under the system of Jewish laws, the high priest brought the blood of the slain animals into the sanctuary as a sacrifice for sin, and then the bodies of the animals were burned outside the city. [12]That is why Jesus suffered and died outside the city, where his blood washed our sins away.

[13]So let us go out to him beyond the city walls [that is, outside the interests of this world, being willing to be despised] to suffer with him there, bearing his shame. [14]For this world is not our home; we are looking forward to our everlasting home in heaven.

[15]With Jesus' help we will continually offer our sacrifice of praise to God by telling others of the glory of his name. [16]Don't forget to do good and to share what you have with those in need, for such sacrifices are very pleasing to him. [17]Obey your spiritual leaders and be willing to do what they say. For their work is to watch over your souls, and God will judge them on how well they do this. Give them reason to report joyfully about you to the Lord and not with sorrow, for then you will suffer for it too.

Final Words

[18]Pray for us, for our conscience is clear and we want to keep it that way. [19]I especially need your prayers right now so that I can come back to you sooner.

[20,21]And now may the God of peace, who brought again from the dead our Lord Jesus, equip you with all you need for doing his will. May he who became the great Shepherd of the sheep by an everlasting agreement between God and you, signed with his blood, produce in you through the power of Christ all that is pleasing to him. To him be glory forever and ever. Amen.

[22]Brethren, please listen patiently to what I have said in this letter, for it is a short one. [23]I want you to know that Brother Timothy is now out of jail; if he comes here soon, I will come with him to see you. [24,25]Give my greetings to all your leaders and to the other believers there. The Christians from Italy who are here with me send you their love. God's grace be with you all. Good-bye.

13:8, 15-16 Even if our human leaders were to fail or be abusive, Jesus Christ is totally consistent and trustworthy. He will always be there for us, no matter what. As that kind of God and Friend, Christ also deserves to receive the new covenant equivalent of old covenant sacrifices: (1) praise for who he is and what he has done; (2) good works of service; and (3) sharing with others in need (see 13:2-3). These activities all support an essential step in our ongoing recovery: telling others what God has done in our life and reaching out to people in need.

13:20-25 The letter to the Hebrews concluded with a double benediction. The first was a summary prayer, asking for the power of Christ's resurrection to enable the readers to do God's will and please him. Unlike some human fathers, God the Father readily helps his children to succeed. That idea led beautifully to the final concept of the letter: grace. These last lines speak volumes to those of us who are seeking recovery: God will provide us with what we need to overcome our dependencies, and he will relate to us according to the principles of grace and mercy.

REFLECTIONS ON

insights ABOUT THE PERSON OF CHRIST

The cascade of quotations in **Hebrews 1:7-13** from several messianic psalms gives angels their just due as powerful spirits, but then contrasts the greater glory of Christ: his clear right to rule as messianic King; his power over the original creation and the final re-creation when it occurs; and his current status of honor beside the Father. Christ can provide all the resources necessary for our recovery when we entrust our life to his loving plan.

It would be terrifying to admit our failures to a perfect God if Jesus wasn't our High Priest. But we see in **Hebrews 4:14–5:3** that Jesus became a man and is able to deal gently with our weaknesses because he understands our problems. And unlike the human priests, Jesus Christ, the ultimate High Priest, has already been glorified in heaven. He suffered the same temptations we do, but did not sin; he offered a sacrifice, but for the sins of the world, not his own. That combination of glory and understanding beckons us to pray confidently for God's grace and mercy on an ongoing basis. The first steps in recovery are concerned with admitting powerlessness over our problems, acknowledging that only God can restore us, and turning our will and life over to God. Hebrews 4:14-16 gives us the scriptural confidence that as we work those steps, God is willing and able to shower us with the mercy and grace we need.

insights ABOUT ANGELS

Although Jesus is far superior to the angels, in **Hebrews 1:14** we are also told that angels are involved in helping God's people in the recovery process. In fact, angels constantly serve and protect those who have already entered the process of recovery through faith in Christ. We may also interpret this verse to mean that God's "guardian angels" are somehow watching over all those who will yet receive salvation by faith in this life.

insights ABOUT GOD'S TRANSFORMING POWER

As is mentioned in **Hebrews 2:4,** the power of God to confirm the message of salvation through faith in Christ is tremendously impressive. In the generation of the apostles (see 2 Corinthians 12:12), which was drawing to a close by this point, "signs and wonders" were more the rule in the newborn church than the exception. Though miraculous healings and immediate transformations may still happen today, it seems more the rule that recovery is a process—often an excruciatingly long process, even for committed believers with great faith. Nevertheless, the signs and wonders God demonstrated in the past remind us that he still works just as powerfully, though perhaps in different ways. The "special abilities" God assigns to us may have more to do with perseverance or a new ability to resist temptation, but they are no less miraculous than an immediate healing by God.

insights ABOUT ACCOUNTABILITY AND RESPONSIBILITY

Most of **Hebrews 3:7-13** is a paraphrase of Psalm 95:7-11. The writer was reminding his Jewish audience of the mistakes their ancestors had made, recalling how they had been unfaithful to God and had suffered the painful consequences. The writer used past events to show his readers that they would be held accountable to live out their faith in whatever context God placed them. Most recovery programs incorporate this kind of accountability through such things as attending meetings and working with a sponsor. These verses underline the importance of such measures.

In **Hebrews 3:14-19** the writer confirmed the need to act immediately, as well as the necessity for his readers to accept full responsibility for their wrong actions. The urgency to act immediately is underlined here by the emphasis on "today" in Psalm 95:7. The importance of taking responsibility becomes clear as we see that Israel truly had no one to blame but themselves for the fiasco in the wilderness. Acting immediately and taking responsibility for our life are both crucial aspects of the recovery process.

insights ABOUT TRUE FAITH

In **Hebrews 11:1-3, 39-40** we find that faith is an active mixture of our trust in the dependability of God working in the unseen spiritual realm and our reliance upon the reality of God's past actions in the world. Those who want a vibrant spiritual life have always had to live by such faith (11:2). Amazingly, by trusting in God we can still make a place for ourself in the "Hall of Faith." The day of induction is still in the future! Seeking approval from other people is a constant battle for some of us in recovery. We need to remember that we cannot please everyone. We will make progress only when we stop trying to please others and put our trust in God, doing what we can to follow his will for our life.

Hebrews 12:1-3 shows us that many, including some very unlikely candidates, have "won" the race of faith along the rocky road of recovery. The author of Hebrews advises readers to forcefully cut loose from sinful patterns—chemical dependencies, illicit sex, unbalanced work habits, even false religious activities—and focus on Christ every step of the way, knowing that Jesus has been where we are and emerged victorious (see 4:14-15). Such perseverance in faith can help us face the reality of delayed gratification, preventing burnout on the recovery trail.

insights ABOUT GOD'S DISCIPLINE

We are reminded in **Hebrews 12:5-10** that true discipline is a form of loving correction, not hateful destruction. Many of us have suffered painful consequences for our dependencies. We may have become angry and wondered why God allowed us to suffer so deeply. Often, the consequences we suffer for our sins are used by God for discipline. But God does not allow us to suffer because he wants revenge or because he wants to destroy us. He allows us to suffer because he loves us. Sometimes harsh discipline is the only way to break through our denial and get us on the road to recovery. As we look back, we can realize that our most painful days led to our first steps in recovery. Through them we realized how powerless we were and turned to God for help. By allowing us to suffer, God was leading us into a vital relationship with himself.

JAMES

THE BIG PICTURE

A. WISDOM: THE FOUNDATION OF RECOVERY (1:1-27)
B. FAITH: THE SUBSTANCE OF RECOVERY (2:1-26)
C. SELF-CONTROL: SETTING BOUNDARIES IN RECOVERY (3:1-18)
D. HUMILITY: THE ATTITUDE OF RECOVERY (4:1-17)
E. GIVING OF OURSELF: THE EVIDENCE OF RECOVERY (5:1-20)

When we think of hypocrisy, we tend to think of those who live an overtly inconsistent life, people who live in constant denial. Yet in one way or another we are all hypocrites at times. This is true in the church community, and it is also true in our recovery groups. We have all found ourselves saying we believe in something, only to prove by our actions that we really don't!

James—the half brother of Jesus and one of the leaders of the Jerusalem church—wrote bluntly against this kind of hypocrisy. He recognized that being human means that we tend to hear God's Word without putting it into practice. His goal was simple: to get his audience, and all believers, to face their denial and start acting on what they claimed to believe.

James challenged his readers to be full of wisdom, faith, forgiveness, self-control, and generosity to others. And he did not encourage them to rely on mind games or tricks, but simply to do what they knew they needed to do. If their progress started anywhere, it started with an admission that they were responsible to obey God. Only then could they conquer denial and forge ahead with the activities and attitudes that reflected God's will for them.

It is easy to buy into a recovery program in principle, but never take the steps necessary for progress. James reminds us that just saying we believe God can help us is not enough. We need to show our faith and commitment by taking real steps of faith. If we don't take active steps toward recovery, we will never move forward in the process.

THE BOTTOM LINE

PURPOSE: To show God's people how to live. AUTHOR: James, the half brother of Jesus. AUDIENCE: Probably primarily the Jewish believers living in Gentile communities outside of Palestine. DATE WRITTEN: This short letter was probably written between A.D. 44 and A.D. 49, before the Jerusalem Council held in A.D. 50 (Acts 15:1-35). SETTING: James wrote to the persecuted believers who were once a part of the church in Jerusalem. He wanted to encourage them to live out their faith in everyday life. KEY VERSE: "Admit your faults to one another and pray for each other so that you may be healed" (5:16). KEY PEOPLE AND RELATIONSHIPS: James with his audience.

RECOVERY THEMES

The Importance of Action: If faith can be alive, it can also be dead. Dead faith is belief that does not prove itself in action. It claims to be something when it is not. Turning our life over to God always involves action. If we simply say that we have entrusted our life to God but do not make amends to others or confess our wrongs, then we are only fooling ourself. Effective recovery involves following through on our good intentions and professions of faith.

Gaining Strength from Hard Trials: Strength of character comes from patiently facing life's problems. Since most of us try to avoid our problems, how can we develop strength of character? We can learn to welcome trials and problems as opportunities to pray for wisdom, to ask God to give us patience, and to learn to depend on God. When we turn to God in times of trial, he can teach us the lessons necessary for us to grow spiritually and make progress in recovery.

True Recovery Leads to Wise Speech: One of the hardest things for us to control is a sharp tongue (1:26). James gives us very practical advice about how to handle our tongue. We are to ask God for wisdom, to be slow to speak in anger, and to listen more than we talk. Since our speech is a reflection of what is going on inside us, we can check it for clues to our strengths and weaknesses. As we take a personal inventory and admit our wrongs to God, he will begin to change us on the inside. Since what we say reveals what is happening inside us, we will find our inner changes reflected in our words.

CHAPTER 1

Greetings from James

From: James, a servant of God and of the Lord Jesus Christ.

To: Jewish Christians scattered everywhere. Greetings!

Enduring through Hard Times

2Dear brothers, is your life full of difficulties
and temptations? Then be happy, 3for when
the way is rough, your patience has a chance
to grow. 4So let it grow, and don't try to
squirm out of your problems. For when your patience is finally in full bloom, then you will be ready for anything, strong in character, full and complete.

5If you want to know what God wants you to do, ask him, and he will gladly tell you, for he is always ready to give a bountiful supply of wisdom to all who ask him; he
will not resent it. 6But when you ask him, be
sure that you really expect him to tell you, for a doubtful mind will be as unsettled as a wave of the sea that is driven and tossed by
the wind; 7,8and every decision you then
make will be uncertain, as you turn first this way and then that. If you don't ask with faith, don't expect the Lord to give you any solid answer.

9A Christian who doesn't amount to much in this world should be glad, for he is great in
the Lord's sight. 10,11But a rich man should be

1:2-4 Difficulties and temptations are facts of life for everyone, particularly those of us with backgrounds of addiction, abuse, or other dysfunctions. We may be tempted to fall back into our past behaviors and destructive patterns. As we face difficult times, though, our attitude can make all the difference. Here we are told to be happy as we face difficulties and temptations. This is hardly our natural reaction to painful situations in life. Seeing our trials as building blocks to God's work in our life, however, may help us change our negative attitude toward tough times. We can have joy during these trials because through them we learn patience, an essential ingredient for a successful recovery.

1:5 How many times have we scolded ourself for making an unwise decision? All of us have made wrong decisions that have led to frustration and depression, ultimately affecting our relationships with God and others. James reminds us that when we ask God for wisdom, he is more than willing to give it. Since God is the source of all wisdom, unwise decisions can be drastically reduced by turning to him for guidance. In recovery we are told to improve our conscious contact with God so we can better know his will for us. This can be achieved by studying God's Word, the Bible, and through regular times of prayer.

1:19-20 Who is in control of our life? Is it God? Is it another person? Is it a controlling dependency or compulsion? Is it an overpowering emotion? The issue of control is vital to our spiritual growth and recovery. For some of us, the emotion of anger is overpowering. James advises us to learn to listen, to have self-control, and to be patient, not letting anger control our actions in any situation. We may be angry over our past as well as over current events. To control our anger, we can give our life over to the care of God. Even when we feel out of control, he can help us maintain our composure. He can give us the strength and wisdom to think and listen before we speak or act.

glad that his riches mean nothing to the
Lord, for he will soon be gone, like a flower
that has lost its beauty and fades away, withered—killed by the scorching summer sun.
So it is with rich men. They will soon die and
leave behind all their busy activities.
12Happy is the man who doesn't give in
and do wrong when he is tempted, for afterwards he will get as his reward the crown of
life that God has promised those who love
him. 13And remember, when someone wants
to do wrong it is never God who is tempting
him, for God never wants to do wrong and
never tempts anyone else to do it. 14Tempta-
tion is the pull of man's own evil thoughts
and wishes. 15These evil thoughts lead to evil
actions and afterwards to the death penalty
from God. 16So don't be misled, dear brothers.
17But whatever is good and perfect comes to
us from God, the Creator of all light, and he
shines forever without change or shadow.
18And it was a happy day for him when he
gave us our new lives through the truth of his
Word, and we became, as it were, the first
children in his new family.

Listening and Doing

19Dear brothers, don't ever forget that it is best
to listen much, speak little, and not become
angry; 20for anger doesn't make us good, as
God demands that we must be.
21So get rid of all that is wrong in your life,
both inside and outside, and humbly be glad
for the wonderful message we have received,
for it is able to save our souls as it takes hold
of our hearts.
22And remember, it is a message to obey,
not just to listen to. So don't fool yourselves.
23For if a person just listens and doesn't obey,
he is like a man looking at his face in a mirror;
24as soon as he walks away, he can't see himself anymore or remember what he looks like.
25But if anyone keeps looking steadily into
God's law for free men, he will not only remember it but he will do what it says, and
God will greatly bless him in everything he
does.
26Anyone who says he is a Christian but
doesn't control his sharp tongue is just fooling himself, and his religion isn't worth
much. 27The Christian who is pure and without fault, from God the Father's point of view,
is the one who takes care of orphans and
widows, and who remains true to the Lord—
not soiled and dirtied by his contacts with the
world.

Looking in the Mirror

BIBLE READING: James 1:21-25

We continued to take personal inventory and when we were wrong promptly admitted it.

How many times do we look in the mirror each day? Suppose we saw someone looking in the mirror, and he found that he had mustard smeared around his mouth. We would find it very strange if he didn't immediately wash his face and clear up the problem. In the same way, we need to routinely look at ourself in a spiritual mirror. Then, if anything is wrong, we can make the proper adjustments.

James used a similar illustration to show how God's Word should be like a spiritual mirror in our life. He said, "And remember, it is a message to obey, not just to listen to. So don't fool yourselves. For if a person just listens and doesn't obey, he is like a man looking at his face in a mirror; as soon as he walks away, he can't see himself anymore or remember what he looks like. But if anyone keeps looking steadily into God's law for free men, he will not only remember it but he will do what it says, and God will greatly bless him in everything he does" (James 1:22-25).

We can use this illustration to support the sensibility of doing a routine personal inventory. As we examine our life, we need to respond with immediate action if something has changed since we last looked. If we put off taking care of a problem that we see, it may soon slip our mind. Just as we would think it foolish to go all day knowing there is mustard on our face, it is not logical to notice a problem that could lead to a fall and not correct it promptly. ***Turn to page 1431, 1 John 1.***

CHAPTER 2
A Warning against Prejudice
Dear brothers, how can you claim that you
belong to the Lord Jesus Christ, the Lord of
glory, if you show favoritism to rich people
and look down on poor people?
2If a man comes into your church dressed
in expensive clothes and with valuable gold
rings on his fingers, and at the same moment
another man comes in who is poor and
dressed in threadbare clothes, 3and you make
a lot of fuss over the rich man and give him
the best seat in the house and say to the poor
man, "You can stand over there if you like or
else sit on the floor"—well, 4judging a man by
his wealth shows that you are guided by
wrong motives.
5Listen to me, dear brothers: God has chosen poor people to be rich in faith, and the
Kingdom of Heaven is theirs, for that is the
gift God has promised to all those who love
him. 6And yet, of the two strangers, you have
despised the poor man. Don't you realize that
it is usually the rich men who pick on you and
drag you into court? 7And all too often they
are the ones who laugh at Jesus Christ, whose
noble name you bear.
8Yes indeed, it is good when you truly obey
our Lord's command, "You must love and
help your neighbors just as much as you love
and take care of yourself." 9But you are breaking this law of our Lord's when you favor the
rich and fawn over them; it is sin.
10And the person who keeps every law of
God but makes one little slip is just as guilty
as the person who has broken every law there
is. 11For the God who said you must not marry
a woman who already has a husband also said
you must not murder, so even though you
have not broken the marriage laws by committing adultery, but have murdered someone, you have entirely broken God's laws and
stand utterly guilty before him.
12You will be judged on whether or not you
are doing what Christ wants you to. So watch
what you do and what you think; 13for there
will be no mercy to those who have shown no
mercy. But if you have been merciful, then
God's mercy toward you will win out over his
judgment against you.

Faith Results in Good Works
14Dear brothers, what's the use of saying that
you have faith and are Christians if you aren't
proving it by helping others? Will *that* kind of
faith save anyone? 15If you have a friend who
is in need of food and clothing, 16and you say
to him, "Well, good-bye and God bless you;
stay warm and eat hearty," and then don't
give him clothes or food, what good does that
do?
17So you see, it isn't enough just to have
faith. You must also do good to prove that you
have it. Faith that doesn't show itself by good
works is no faith at all—it is dead and useless.
18But someone may well argue, "You say the
way to God is by faith alone, plus nothing;
well, I say that good works are important too,
for without good works you can't prove
whether you have faith or not; but anyone
can see that I have faith by the way I act."
19Are there still some among you who hold
that "only believing" is enough? Believing in
one God? Well, remember that the demons
believe this too—so strongly that they tremble in terror! 20Fool! When will you ever learn
that "believing" is useless without *doing* what
God wants you to? Faith that does not result
in good deeds is not real faith.
21Don't you remember that even our father
Abraham was declared good because of what
he *did* when he was willing to obey God, even

2:1-9 Since participation in recovery can lead to being rejected by others, the process can be a painful experience. Old friends reject us for trying to escape our bondage. Sometimes a Christian community or society at large may reject us, treating us like an unworthy outcast. All of us need to be accepted. And since we are in recovery, we probably have a special need in this area. Here James reminds us that Jesus intended the Christian community to graciously accept and love people whether they are wealthy and influential or poor and disenfranchised. Our Christian communities need to welcome outcasts who are honestly struggling with their problems. The essential truth here is captured by Jesus' call for us to treat others just as we want them to treat us (see Matthew 7:12).

2:14-26 Faith, the cornerstone of recovery, needs to be accompanied by action. Some of us may have found it easy to admit we needed God's help, but when called upon to take steps to prove our faith, we refused. We all have made commitments that we failed to back up with our actions. Because this is a prevalent problem, James left us this powerful reminder: "Faith that doesn't show itself by good works is no faith at all—it is dead and useless." If we believe in the principles of recovery but refuse to act upon them, we are not in recovery. If we believe God can help us but refuse to obey his will, we prove that our faith is dead. True faith in God expresses itself in committed action; our actions need to back up our words if we want to succeed in recovery.

JAMES & JUDE

It is difficult to live up to the high standards set by older brothers and sisters. It can be equally difficult, and sometimes more painful, to live down the reputation of a notorious or embarrassing older sibling. James and Jude had to deal with both challenges. Their older brother, Jesus, was both perfect and embarrassing.

It is probable that Mary, their mother, had always told James and Jude that Jesus was unique. But it is doubtful that they had any idea just how special Jesus was. One thing is certain: Jesus must have been a hard act to follow. It must have been difficult for James, Jude, and the rest of their siblings to feel close to their wonderful, though different, big brother. The situation probably became even worse after their father, Joseph, died. As the oldest child, Jesus probably had to take on the role of substitute dad.

After Jesus' public ministry began, James and Jude took a stand-back-and-watch attitude. One day Jesus would do great miracles and be acclaimed as a hero. The next he would present a convicting message and offend the powerful religious and political authorities. In the end, he went too far and was sentenced to death. He had claimed to be not only the promised Messiah, but also God himself! At this point, James and Jude probably suspected that their brother had gone off the deep end.

James and Jude had lost their father, Joseph, when they were young. Now they had lost their famous, though embarrassing, big brother. Could the family recover? The resurrection of Jesus brought the resounding answer: *yes!* After Jesus rose from the dead, he overcame the doubts of his younger brothers who became leaders in the early church. Their relationship with their big brother had been restored. James became one of the great leaders of the Christian community in Jerusalem. Both brothers are remembered for the books they wrote.

The transforming power of Christ's resurrection is still available for us today. As we read of the painful trial and death of Jesus, we see God's loving sacrifice on our behalf. As we discover his resurrection and experience its power in our life, we discover that the power that transformed James and Jude can transform us, too.

STRENGTHS AND ACCOMPLISHMENTS:
- James and Jude both apparently wanted to understand and know Jesus.
- Both grew beyond the relational problems that existed in their family.
- Both became effective leaders and writers.

WEAKNESSES AND MISTAKES:
- James and Jude did not really understand Jesus until after his resurrection.
- They became disillusioned with Jesus' claims when he faced opposition.

LESSONS FROM THEIR LIVES:
- Finding our identity when following a gifted sibling can be painful.
- Even the confused and disillusioned can regain trust and hope.
- Recovery offers hope for restoring broken relationships.

KEY VERSE:
"Then [Jesus] added, 'Anyone who obeys my Father in heaven is my brother, sister, and mother!'" (Matthew 12:50).

James and Jude are named or alluded to in the Gospels and Acts 1:14. James is mentioned in Acts 15; 21; Galatians 2; the book of James; and Jude 1:1. Jude's name is found in Jude 1:1.

---

if it meant offering his son Isaac to die on the
altar? 22You see, he was trusting God so much
that he was willing to do whatever God told
him to; his faith was made complete by what
he did—by his actions, his good deeds. 23And
so it happened just as the Scriptures say, that
Abraham trusted God, and the Lord declared
him good in God's sight, and he was even
called "the friend of God." 24So you see, a man
is saved by what he does, as well as by what
he believes.

25Rahab, the prostitute, is another example
of this. She was saved because of what she did
when she hid those messengers and sent

them safely away by a different road. 26Just as
the body is dead when there is no spirit in it,
so faith is dead if it is not the kind that results
in good deeds.

CHAPTER 3

Controlling the Tongue

Dear brothers, don't be too eager to tell others
their faults, for we all make many mistakes;
and when we teachers of religion, who should
know better, do wrong, our punishment will
be greater than it would be for others.

If anyone can control his tongue, it proves
that he has perfect control over himself in
every other way. 3We can make a large horse
turn around and go wherever we want by
means of a small bit in his mouth. 4And a tiny
rudder makes a huge ship turn wherever the
pilot wants it to go, even though the winds
are strong.

5So also the tongue is a small thing, but
what enormous damage it can do. A great
forest can be set on fire by one tiny spark.
6And the tongue is a flame of fire. It is full of
wickedness, and poisons every part of the
body. And the tongue is set on fire by hell
itself and can turn our whole lives into a
blazing flame of destruction and disaster.

7Men have trained, or can train, every kind
of animal or bird that lives and every kind of
reptile and fish, 8but no human being can
tame the tongue. It is always ready to pour out
its deadly poison. 9Sometimes it praises our
heavenly Father, and sometimes it breaks out
into curses against men who are made like
God. 10And so blessing and cursing come
pouring out of the same mouth. Dear brothers, surely this is not right! 11Does a spring of
water bubble out first with fresh water and
then with bitter water? 12Can you pick olives

3:1-2 We all are guilty of offending others by either our words or actions. When we have offended someone, we need to ask forgiveness and make amends for the wrongs we have committed. This is an essential part of the recovery process. Sometimes a quiet change of behavior can be the most effective way to make amends for our previous failures. By treating others with respect, we can slowly rebuild the trust we have destroyed and give back some of what we have taken. As we follow God's program for healthy living, we can learn to avoid offending others, instead encouraging them with our words and deeds.

3:3-12 The tongue is a difficult thing to control, but what it does is extremely important. Like a rudder that steers a ship or a bridle that directs a horse, our tongue does much to control and shape our life. Our speech may have been instrumental in destroying our relationships, causing a painful downward spiral in our life. It may be out of control, enslaved to the destructive dependencies in our life. If this is the case, our recovery will include yielding our tongue to God's control. Even when we feel powerless to control our destructive words, God can still tame our tongue. As he transforms us from the inside out, the words we speak will soon begin to reflect the changes. God will then be able to use our words to heal our relationships and encourage others in the recovery process.

3:13-18 Wisdom is essential to recovery. It must, however, be a godly wisdom, not one from an earthly perspective. Earthly wisdom leads to selfishness and pride and invariably causes confusion and strife. True wisdom is based on the knowledge of God and brings peace; it leads to selfless living and a faith that works; it never distinguishes between groups of people, but treats everyone with the same proper respect and love. This kind of wisdom allows us to admit our failures and rebuild our life from the ashes of defeat. It leads us to live for others, freeing us from our destructive dependencies and building relationships that will support our recovery on a permanent basis.

4:1-4 A right relationship with God is essential to the recovery process. Most of us would like to receive the freedom God offers, but we generally make one or two mistakes that hold us back. First, we try to gain our freedom by working hard for it. We forget to ask God for help and thus never receive the blessed life that God wants to give us. Second, if we do get around to asking God for help, we ask with the wrong motives. We ask for God's blessings just to satisfy our cravings for personal comfort, ignoring the fact that seeking our own selfish pleasure is allying ourself with God's enemies. God wants to give us an abundant life so we can pass it on to others. He blesses us so we can live according to his program. We can experience the freedom God offers by drawing close to God and asking for his guidance and help.

4:6-10 Most of us have a hard time modeling the attitudes of submission and humility. These attitudes are essential to the recovery process, however, as they show a willingness to be guided by God. Satan's pride—and our adoption of it—is opposed to God's program for healthy and godly living. And as many of us know from experience, the way of pride and selfishness only leads to confusion and strife. True contentment comes only when we submit our life to God and his program. As we admit our failures and humbly seek to do God's will, we find ourself drawing close to God. As we draw close to God, the grip of our dependencies will begin to weaken. He will help us rebuild our life according to his program.

from a fig tree, or figs from a grape vine? No,
and you can't draw fresh water from a salty
pool.

Real Wisdom Comes from God

13If you are wise, live a life of steady goodness
so that only good deeds will pour forth. And
if you don't brag about them, then you will be
truly wise! 14And by all means don't brag
about being wise and good if you are bitter
and jealous and selfish; that is the worst sort
of lie. 15For jealousy and selfishness are not
God's kind of wisdom. Such things are
earthly, unspiritual, inspired by the devil.
16For wherever there is jealousy or selfish ambition, there will be disorder and every other
kind of evil.

17But the wisdom that comes from heaven
is first of all pure and full of quiet gentleness.
Then it is peace-loving and courteous. It allows discussion and is willing to yield to
others; it is full of mercy and good deeds. It is
wholehearted and straightforward and sincere. 18And those who are peacemakers will
plant seeds of peace and reap a harvest of
goodness.

CHAPTER 4

Drawing Near to God

What is causing the quarrels and fights
among you? Isn't it because there is a whole
army of evil desires within you? 2You want
what you don't have, so you kill to get it. You
long for what others have, and can't afford it,
so you start a fight to take it away from them.
And yet the reason you don't have what you
want is that you don't ask God for it. 3And
even when you do ask you don't get it because
your whole aim is wrong—you want only
what will give *you* pleasure.

4You are like an unfaithful wife who loves
her husband's enemies. Don't you realize that
making friends with God's enemies—the evil
pleasures of this world—makes you an enemy
of God? I say it again, that if your aim is to
enjoy the evil pleasure of the unsaved world,
you cannot also be a friend of God. 5Or what
do you think the Scripture means when it says
that the Holy Spirit, whom God has placed
within us, watches over us with tender jealousy? 6But he gives us more and more
strength to stand against all such evil longings. As the Scripture says, God gives strength
to the humble but sets himself against the
proud and haughty.

7So give yourselves humbly to God. Resist
the devil and he will flee from you. 8And

Wisdom

READ JAMES 3:5-18

When we get caught up in catering to our addictions, it is almost like we are a different person. It is as if there are two of us tied up together. The Bible recognizes this dual nature in all of us. One part yearns for good, and the other part of us is drawn toward corrupt desires and animal passions. The Bible describes a kind of "worldly" wisdom that justifies destructive behavior and leads to disorder, instability, and confusion.

We need to beware of this type of wisdom, which is characterized by jealousy and selfishness. James wrote, "For jealousy and selfishness are not God's kind of wisdom. Such things are earthly, unspiritual, inspired by the devil. For wherever there is jealousy or selfish ambition, there will be disorder and every other kind of evil" (James 3:15-16).

This kind of thinking causes us to focus on what others are and have. It makes us want the same things so much that we are always dissatisfied. It is easy to become so consumed by our own desires that we become inconsiderate of others, often hurting the people we love. This type of wisdom is inspired by the devil and will lead to our ultimate destruction, since Satan's "purpose is to steal, kill and destroy" (John 10:10).

If our thoughts are still dominated by these characteristics, we need to ask God to replace our "wisdom" with his wisdom. We can trust him to change our mind and our life. ***Turn to page 1413, 1 Peter 1.***

when you draw close to God, God will draw
close to you. Wash your hands, you sinners,
and let your hearts be filled with God alone to
make them pure and true to him. 9Let there be
tears for the wrong things you have done. Let
there be sorrow and sincere grief. Let there be
sadness instead of laughter, and gloom instead of joy. 10Then when you realize your
worthlessness before the Lord, he will lift you
up, encourage and help you.
11Don't criticize and speak evil about each
other, dear brothers. If you do, you will be
fighting against God's law of loving one another, declaring it is wrong. But your job is
not to decide whether this law is right or
wrong, but to obey it. 12Only he who made
the law can rightly judge among us. He alone
decides to save us or destroy. So what right do
you have to judge or criticize others?

God Has a Plan for Us

13Look here, you people who say, "Today or
tomorrow we are going to such and such a
town, stay there a year, and open up a profitable business." 14How do you know what is
going to happen tomorrow? For the length of
your lives is as uncertain as the morning
fog—now you see it; soon it is gone. 15What
you ought to say is, "If the Lord wants us to,
we shall live and do this or that." 16Otherwise
you will be bragging about your own plans,
and such self-confidence never pleases God.
17Remember, too, that knowing what is
right to do and then not doing it is sin.

CHAPTER 5

A Warning to the Rich

Look here, you rich men, now is the time to
cry and groan with anguished grief because of
all the terrible troubles ahead of you. 2Your
wealth is even now rotting away, and your fine
clothes are becoming mere moth-eaten rags.
3The value of your gold and silver is dropping
fast, yet it will stand as evidence against you
and eat your flesh like fire. That is what you
have stored up for yourselves to receive on
that coming day of judgment. 4For listen! Hear
the cries of the field workers whom you have
cheated of their pay. Their cries have reached
the ears of the Lord of Hosts.
5You have spent your years here on earth
having fun, satisfying your every whim, and
now your fat hearts are ready for the slaughter. 6You have condemned and killed good
men who had no power to defend themselves
against you.

4:11-12 Many Christian communities are rendered ineffective by an attitude of self-righteous criticism. People become critical of anyone who doesn't measure up to their ideals of perfection. Some of us may have experienced this kind of destructive criticism as our addictions became public knowledge. Perhaps we left a church community for that very reason. Sadly, some of us are also guilty of criticizing others. We look down on people who make slower progress than we do in the recovery process. If this is a problem for us, we need to regain a healthy humility. No one is perfect except God; only he is in a position to judge others (see Romans 14:10-12). We need to focus on our own faults, including our tendency to criticize others. If we don't, our recovery is at risk.

5:1-5 Some of us may wonder why we have to give up our pursuit of pleasure. We see people living for wealth and pleasure who seem to be happier than we are. Here James reminds us that a selfish life-style inevitably leads to painful consequences. Some of us already have experienced the pain and emptiness brought on by the selfish pursuit of pleasure. A selfish life-style never yields lasting joy and peace; it always leads to one kind of bondage or another. When we make God's will our own and follow his program, we will experience freedom and become a blessing to the people around us.

5:7-11 We have all probably asked this question at one time or another: Why are these terrible things happening to us? This question might become especially urgent after we have entered the recovery process. We may recognize that God used our sufferings to get us started in our program, but why does he allow the pain to continue? Recovery is a painful, lifelong process. We need to get that straight at the outset. Just as our addictions didn't appear overnight, our recovery will also take some time. We need to learn patience as we take small steps forward, planting the seeds that will yield a harvest of healing and restoration. God will nurture the seeds we have planted, transforming our life from the inside out.

5:13-15 Since God has the power to heal us spiritually, emotionally, and physically, prayer is one of the most powerful tools available to us in recovery. When we pray to God, we display our faith that he can help us. Prayer is an essential part of the process of putting our broken life into God's caring and capable hands. He is more than able to help us and guide us into a life of blessing and peace. When our life seems out of control and we are in despair, we can begin the healing process by bringing our problems to God. He is listening, and he has the power to rebuild even the most shattered of lives.

Patience in Suffering
7Now as for you, dear brothers who are waiting
for the Lord's return, be patient, like a farmer
who waits until the autumn for his precious
harvest to ripen. 8Yes, be patient. And take
courage, for the coming of the Lord is near.
9Don't grumble about each other, brothers.
Are you yourselves above criticism? For see!
The great Judge is coming. He is almost here.
[Let him do whatever criticizing must be done.]
10For examples of patience in suffering,
look at the Lord's prophets. 11We know how
happy they are now because they stayed true
to him then, even though they suffered
greatly for it. Job is an example of a man who
continued to trust the Lord in sorrow; from
his experiences we can see how the Lord's
plan finally ended in good, for he is full of
tenderness and mercy.
12But most of all, dear brothers, do not
swear either by heaven or earth or anything
else; just say a simple yes or no so that you will
not sin and be condemned for it.

The Power of Prayer
13Is anyone among you suffering? He should
keep on praying about it. And those who have
reason to be thankful should continually be
singing praises to the Lord.
14Is anyone sick? He should call for the
elders of the church and they should pray
over him and pour a little oil upon him,
calling on the Lord to heal him. 15And their
prayer, if offered in faith, will heal him, for
the Lord will make him well; and if his sickness was caused by some sin, the Lord will
forgive him.
16Admit your faults to one another and pray
for each other so that you may be healed. The
earnest prayer of a righteous man has great
power and wonderful results. 17Elijah was as
completely human as we are, and yet when he
prayed earnestly that no rain would fall, none
fell for the next three and a half years! 18Then
he prayed again, this time that it *would* rain,
and down it poured, and the grass turned
green and the gardens began to grow again.

Restoring Wandering Believers
19Dear brothers, if anyone has slipped away
from God and no longer trusts the Lord and
someone helps him understand the Truth
again, 20that person who brings him back to
God will have saved a wandering soul from
death, bringing about the forgiveness of his
many sins.

Sincerely, James

Single-minded Devotion

BIBLE READING: James 4:7-10

We made a decision to turn our will and our life over to the care of God as we understood him.

We may already have chosen to follow God's way, letting his paths define the overall direction of our life. Even so, many of us still keep a part of our heart hidden away from God. We have devoted this part of ourself to gratifying our addictions, to doing things that are contrary to the will of God. This sets us up for living a double life, which can fill us with guilt, shame, and instability.

Even those of us who have made the decision to give our heart to God face new moments of decision every day. James was addressing believers when he wrote, "So give yourselves humbly to God. Resist the devil and he will flee from you. And when you draw close to God, God will draw close to you. Wash your hands, you sinners, and let your hearts be filled with God alone to make them pure and true to him" (James 4:7-8).

If we choose to live a double life, we will probably begin to doubt whether God hears us at all. As James wrote, "A doubtful mind will be as unsettled as a wave of the sea that is driven and tossed by the wind; and every decision you then make will be uncertain, as you turn first this way and then that" (James 1:6-8).

When we resist the devil at every turn and choose to draw close to God, he will draw close to us. When we open up our hidden heart and begin to make choices in favor of recovery, we will soon grow confident that God desires to help us. ***Turn to Step Four, page 7, Genesis 3.***

REFLECTIONS ON JAMES

***insights** ABOUT TRUE FAITH

We see in **James 1:6-8** that all truly wise decisions are rooted in a vital faith in God. Faith "is the confident assurance that something we want is going to happen. It is the certainty that what we hope for is waiting for us, even though we cannot see it up ahead" (Hebrews 11:1). God wants us to make progress in recovery. When we ask God to help us make a wise decision, we can make the request without a trace of doubt, fully believing that whatever we ask for in faith will be granted. God will supply the wisdom we need to make the right decisions for a successful recovery.

***insights** ABOUT HONEST CONFESSION

As we try to make an honest personal inventory, some of us may have nothing to measure our attitudes or actions against. We may never have had any good role models to follow. In **James 1:22-25** the apostle reminds us that God's Word functions like a mirror in our life. As we read it, we are given a clear picture of what God wants us to be like. It shows us where we don't measure up to God's intended program and provides a measuring stick for our personal inventory. But James also warns us not to stop after making a personal inventory. We cannot look into God's Word only to walk away and forget what we saw there. To make real progress in recovery we need to enlist God's help and take concrete steps to live according to the plan we find there.

Admitting our faults to God and a trustworthy person is an essential step in the recovery process. When we share our faults with others, we give them the opportunity to uphold us in prayer. James reminds us in **James 5:16-20** that confession is an important part of our personal prayer life. God invites us to admit our faults and failures to him through prayer. When we and others bring our defects of character before God, he starts the healing process in our life. Prayer is never a waste of time; it yields amazing results! God responds powerfully when we display our faith by sharing our problems with him.

THE BIG PICTURE

A. SUFFERING IS A VALUABLE PART OF LIFE (1:1-25)
B. LIVING HONESTLY AS WE WORK AT RELATIONSHIPS (2:1-10)
C. HOW TO LIVE WELL IN A DIFFICULT WORLD (2:11–4:6)
D. THE HOPE OF ULTIMATE RESTORATION (4:7–5:14)

Peter's audience was made up of hurting people. They were suffering persecution from unbelievers in the form of rejection and, in many cases, outright physical abuse. The price they paid for their beliefs included everything from broken relationships to physical pain and rejection.

Peter wrote to encourage them. The wonderful part of his message lay in the perspective he offered his audience. In response to their cries of anguish he did not say, "There must be something wrong with you" or "Pray harder and your problems will go away." Neither did he flippantly promise them an easy road ahead. Instead, he gave them this hope: they belonged to God. He offers this same hope to us.

Most of us would agree that suffering is one of the most difficult parts of life to accept, much less understand. Though we wish we were exempt or cushioned from life's harsh blows, pain is a reality. All of us suffer, and suffering is part of going through recovery. We must accept the fact that we will hurt from time to time.

God has equipped us with the means to live at peace in the midst of tough times. We obtain God's powerful help when we hold fast to Christ and live according to his will. This does not mean that our troubles will vanish because we believe in God. Rather, it means that God offers to surround us with his love when problems seem overwhelming. The way out of the storm is to take comfort in God's presence and persevere through it. As we do, God will use the trials to inspire our growth.

THE BOTTOM LINE

PURPOSE: To show us how to live well in a shattered and hopeless world. AUTHOR: The apostle Peter. AUDIENCE: Jewish Christians who were suffering persecution for their faith. DATE WRITTEN: Around A.D. 64, just prior to Nero's persecutions of the early Christians. SETTING: This letter was written during a period in which Peter and other Christians were being tortured and martyred for their faith. The believers faced opposition from both Jewish and secular authorities. KEY VERSE: "You are free from the law, but that doesn't mean you are free to do wrong. Live as those who are free to do only God's will at all times" (2:16). KEY PEOPLE AND RELATIONSHIPS: Peter with Silas and with John Mark.

RECOVERY THEMES

God's Way Can Be Painful: Part of the reason we can be afraid of recovery is that we know the changes God asks us to make will be painful. There was pain in our old way of life, but we usually found ways to escape it. When we decide to enter the recovery process, we also decide to face our pain head-on. Turning our life over to God, taking a moral inventory, making amends, and allowing God to remove our defects are all painful steps. But because they are part of God's plan, they will also lead to a life of joy and wholeness.

Nothing Is Hopeless with God: As we struggle in recovery, we may begin to feel helpless. We might be tempted to throw up our hands and say, "What's the use?" But *feeling* helpless is different from *being* helpless. We are never really helpless, for with God help is close at hand. We are not without hope, for God is the source of all hope. When we struggle with feelings of despair, this letter reminds us to turn our life over to God and to depend on his power. God will never leave us to face our trials alone.

The Importance of Relationships: Turning our life over to Jesus Christ makes us part of God's family. We enter into a community that has Jesus Christ as its founder and leader. Everyone in this community is related; no one stands alone. All healing and recovery takes place in the context of relationships with others, and Peter taught us how to manage those relationships: with loyalty, care, and humility, praying that we will become what God wants us to be.

CHAPTER 1

Greetings from Peter

From: Peter, Jesus Christ's missionary.

To: The Jewish Christians driven out of Jerusalem and scattered throughout Pontus, Galatia, Cappadocia, Asia Minor, and Bithynia.

The Hope of Eternal Life

2Dear friends, God the Father chose you
long ago and knew you would become his
children. And the Holy Spirit has been at
work in your hearts, cleansing you with the
blood of Jesus Christ and making you to
please him. May God bless you richly and
grant you increasing freedom from all anxiety and fear.
3All honor to God, the God and Father of
our Lord Jesus Christ; for it is his boundless
mercy that has given us the privilege of
being born again so that we are now members of God's own family. Now we live in the
hope of eternal life because Christ rose
again from the dead. 4And God has reserved
for his children the priceless gift of eternal
life; it is kept in heaven for you, pure and
undefiled, beyond the reach of change and
decay. 5And God, in his mighty power, will
make sure that you get there safely to receive it because you are trusting him. It will

---

1:7 The refiner would heat up the furnace and then put in the gold he had mined in order to separate the worthless and impure dross from the precious and beautiful gold. The dross would rise to the top and be skimmed off until the refiner could look into the crucible at the liquid gold and see his image. In like manner, God uses the fiery trials and tribulations in our life to purify and beautify our faith so that one day he will see clearly his image in us. This truth offers great comfort to those of us who struggle to make sense of a past marked by deep suffering. We can be confident that God will separate something priceless from the dross of our experiences.

1:8-9 Turning our will and our life over to God is a critical step in the recovery process. In the midst of our most painful trials, we may fail to see God with us. Yet Peter suggests that, strange as it may seem at the time, surrendering to God in difficult times can be a joyful experience. If we trust that God will use our trials to complete the process of healing in our life, even the tough times can become times of celebration.

1:10-13 The Good News of God's forgiveness in Christ flows from a plan that took God centuries to complete. Now that it is complete, we can count on God's continuing kindness as we trust in him until Jesus returns. We don't have to wonder if we are tricking ourself into believing something that isn't true: centuries of history and numerous promises stand behind the revelation of God in Jesus. As we turn our life and will over to him, we can be sure that he is the Power we need for a successful recovery.

1:17-20 The "impossible road to heaven" is that of trying to earn God's favor and acceptance. Many people misunderstand Peter's counsel to fear God's judgment; they think it means that God is looking to catch us in sin so he can punish us. Actually, if we perceive God and ourself rightly, we see that God knows we can't measure up on our own. He accepts our limitations, forgives our sin, seeks to help us learn from our mistakes, and helps us progress toward a healthier way of life.

be yours in that coming last day for all to
see. 6So be truly glad! There is wonderful joy
ahead, even though the going is rough for a
while down here.
7These trials are only to test your faith, to
see whether or not it is strong and pure. It
is being tested as fire tests gold and purifies
it—and your faith is far more precious to
God than mere gold; so if your faith remains strong after being tried in the test
tube of fiery trials, it will bring you much
praise and glory and honor on the day of his
return.
8You love him even though you have
never seen him; though not seeing him, you
trust him; and even now you are happy
with the inexpressible joy that comes from
heaven itself. 9And your further reward for
trusting him will be the salvation of your
souls.
10This salvation was something the
prophets did not fully understand. Though
they wrote about it, they had many questions as to what it all could mean. 11They
wondered what the Spirit of Christ within
them was talking about, for he told them to
write down the events which, since then,
have happened to Christ: his suffering, and
his great glory afterwards. And they wondered when and to whom all this would
happen.
12They were finally told that these things
would not occur during their lifetime, but
long years later, during yours. And now at last
this Good News has been plainly announced
to all of us. It was preached to us in the power
of the same heaven-sent Holy Spirit who
spoke to them; and it is all so strange and
wonderful that even the angels in heaven
would give a great deal to know more about
it.
13So now you can look forward soberly and
intelligently to more of God's kindness to you
when Jesus Christ returns.

A Call to Healthy Living
14Obey God because you are his children;
don't slip back into your old ways—doing evil
because you knew no better. 15But be holy
now in everything you do, just as the Lord is
holy, who invited you to be his child. 16He
himself has said, "You must be holy, for I am
holy."
17And remember that your heavenly Father
to whom you pray has no favorites when he
judges. He will judge you with perfect justice
for everything you do; so act in reverent fear

Hope

READ 1 PETER 1:3-7

Life is rough. We must constantly struggle against the sin inherent in our mortal bodies. We live with the realities of pain, sickness, and death. We live in a world that is constantly decaying. Even if we turn our life over to God, what is there to look forward to?

Peter tells us, "Now we live in the hope of eternal life because Christ rose again from the dead. And God has reserved for his children the priceless gift of eternal life; it is kept in heaven for you. . . . And God, in his mighty power, will make sure that you get there safely to receive it because you are trusting him. It will be yours in that coming last day for all to see. So be truly glad! There is wonderful joy ahead, even though the going is rough for a while down here" (1 Peter 1:3-6).

Paul encourages us with this, "Since we are his children, we will share his treasures—for all God gives to his Son Jesus is now ours too. But if we are to share his glory, we must also share his suffering. Yet what we suffer now is nothing compared to the glory he will give us later. For all creation is waiting patiently and hopefully for that future day when God will resurrect his children. For on that day thorns and thistles, sin, death, and decay—the things that overcame the world against its will at God's command—will all disappear, and the world around us will share in the glorious freedom from sin which God's children enjoy" (Romans 8:17-21). These promises are for us! ***Turn to page 1417, 1 Peter 3.***

of him from now on until you get to heaven. [18]God paid a ransom to save you from the impossible road to heaven which your fathers tried to take, and the ransom he paid was not mere gold or silver as you very well know. [19]But he paid for you with the precious lifeblood of Christ, the sinless, spotless Lamb of God. [20]God chose him for this purpose long before the world began, but only recently was he brought into public view, in these last days, as a blessing to you.

[21]Because of this, your trust can be in God who raised Christ from the dead and gave him great glory. Now your faith and hope can rest in him alone. [22]Now you can have real love for everyone because your souls have been cleansed from selfishness and hatred when you trusted Christ to save you; so see to it that you really do love each other warmly, with all your hearts.

[23]For you have a new life. It was not passed on to you from your parents, for the life they gave you will fade away. This new one will last forever, for it comes from Christ, God's ever-living Message to men. [24]Yes, our natural lives will fade as grass does when it becomes all brown and dry. All our greatness is like a flower that droops and falls; [25]but the Word of the Lord will last forever. And his message is the Good News that was preached to you.

CHAPTER 2

So get rid of your feelings of hatred. Don't just pretend to be good! Be done with dishonesty and jealousy and talking about others behind their backs. [2,3]Now that you realize how kind the Lord has been to you, put away all evil, deception, envy, and fraud. Long to grow up into the fullness of your salvation; cry for this as a baby cries for his milk.

Living Stones for God's House

[4]Come to Christ, who is the living Foundation of Rock upon which God builds; though men have spurned him, he is very precious to God who has chosen him above all others.

[5]And now you have become living building-stones for God's use in building his house. What's more, you are his holy priests; so come to him—[you who are acceptable to him because of Jesus Christ]—and offer to God those things that please him. [6]As the Scriptures express it, "See, I am sending Christ to be the carefully chosen, precious Cornerstone of my church, and I will never disappoint those who trust in him."

[7]Yes, he is very precious to you who believe; and to those who reject him, well—"The same Stone that was rejected by the builders has become the Cornerstone, the most honored and important part of the building." [8]And the Scriptures also say, "He is the Stone that some will stumble over, and the Rock that will make them fall." They will stumble because they will not listen to God's Word nor obey it, and so this punishment must follow—that they will fall.

[9]But you are not like that, for you have

2:2-3 Here Peter pinpointed an insight for helping us resist sin: We can live a godly life because we have tasted of God's kindness. To the extent that we experience God's love (which often comes through our relationships with other people), we won't want to sin because we will see that it isn't good for us and doesn't satisfy our longing for God's love. This puts the focus in recovery work not on improving outward behavior (which is more the result), but on seeking to experience more of God's kindness. We can come to him with all our needs, and he will fill our heart with the love we crave.

2:9-10 The Christian's true identity is no longer that of a sinner but that of a holy saint. We are no longer slaves, but chosen priests of the King. The priests of the King are those who receive God's healing love for themselves so they can share it with others who are hurting.

2:11 Sin is alluring because there is pleasure in sin. Many of us have struggled with the temptation to escape the painful realities of life by turning to the "pleasures" of alcohol, drugs, food, sex, work, money, or even religious activity. Yet sooner or later we realized that these pleasures, when used wrongly, fought against the welfare of our soul. By seeing ourself as a visitor on earth with our real home in heaven, we can learn to delay gratification, which leads to wisdom—and recovery.

2:15 The testimony of a changed life is a far better witness of God's grace than a lecture is. When hurting people who haven't yet started in recovery see how God has brought us through our life's challenges to a place of increased growth and contentment, they may want to know what God can do for them.

2:24 Not only did Jesus serve as our example for how to deal with suffering, but he also suffered for us. He received the punishment for our sin so we wouldn't have to. Instead of facing terrible punishment, we can receive his mercy. He desires to set us free from our bondage and heal us from the devastating effects of sin in our life.

been chosen by God himself—you are priests
of the King, you are holy and pure, you are
God's very own—all this so that you may
show to others how God called you out of the
darkness into his wonderful light. [10]Once you
were less than nothing; now you are God's
own. Once you knew very little of God's
kindness; now your very lives have been
changed by it.

Respecting People in Authority

[11]Dear brothers, you are only visitors here.
Since your real home is in heaven, I beg you
to keep away from the evil pleasures of this
world; they are not for you, for they fight
against your very souls.

[12]Be careful how you behave among your
unsaved neighbors; for then, even if they are
suspicious of you and talk against you, they
will end up praising God for your good works
when Christ returns.

[13]For the Lord's sake, obey every law of your
government: those of the king as head of the
state, [14]and those of the king's officers, for he
has sent them to punish all who do wrong,
and to honor those who do right.

[15]It is God's will that your good lives
should silence those who foolishly condemn
the Gospel without knowing what it can do
for them, having never experienced its
power. [16]You are free from the law, but that
doesn't mean you are free to do wrong. Live
as those who are free to do only God's will at
all times.

[17]Show respect for everyone. Love Christians everywhere. Fear God and honor the
government.

[18]Servants, you must respect your masters
and do whatever they tell you—not only if
they are kind and reasonable, but even if they
are tough and cruel. [19]Praise the Lord if you
are punished for doing right! [20]Of course, you
get no credit for being patient if you are
beaten for doing wrong; but if you do right
and suffer for it, and are patient beneath the
blows, God is well pleased.

[21]This suffering is all part of the work God
has given you. Christ, who suffered for you,
is your example. Follow in his steps: [22]He
never sinned, never told a lie, [23]never answered back when insulted; when he suffered he did not threaten to get even; he left
his case in the hands of God who always
judges fairly. [24]He personally carried the
load of our sins in his own body when he
died on the cross so that we can be finished
with sin and live a good life from now on.

A Servant's Heart

BIBLE READING: 1 Peter 2:18-25

We made direct amends to such people wherever possible, except when to do so would injure them or others.

At this point in recovery, most of us have experienced some major changes in our attitudes. At one time, we were so consumed by our addictions that we thought only of ourself, failing to show any consideration for others. In this step, the focus is on the interests and needs of others.

The apostle Paul taught, "Don't be selfish; don't live to make a good impression on others. Be humble, thinking of others as better than yourself. Don't just think about your own affairs, but be interested in others, too" (Philippians 2:3-4). Whether we make direct amends to others or choose not to because of the injury it would cause, we are concerned with protecting others from pain and suffering.

There may be situations in which we will suffer if we go back to make amends. This is part of the work of recovery, and the potential pain should not deter us. The apostle Peter wrote, "If you do right and suffer for it, and are patient beneath the blows, God is well pleased. . . . Christ, who suffered for you, is your example. Follow in his steps: He never sinned, never told a lie, never answered back when insulted; when he suffered he did not threaten to get even; he left his case in the hands of God who always judges fairly" (1 Peter 2:20-23).

This step can be very difficult as we face the painful consequences of past actions. During this time we need to turn our life over to the care of God, who always judges justly. *Turn to Step Ten, page 39, Genesis 31.*

For his wounds have healed ours! [25]Like sheep you wandered away from God, but now you have returned to your Shepherd, the Guardian of your souls who keeps you safe from all attacks.

CHAPTER 3

Advice for Wives and Husbands

Wives, fit in with your husbands' plans; for then if they refuse to listen when you talk to them about the Lord, they will be won by your respectful, pure behavior. Your godly lives will speak to them better than any words.

[3]Don't be concerned about the outward beauty that depends on jewelry, or beautiful clothes, or hair arrangement. [4]Be beautiful inside, in your hearts, with the lasting charm of a gentle and quiet spirit that is so precious to God. [5]That kind of deep beauty was seen in the saintly women of old, who trusted God and fitted in with their husbands' plans.

[6]Sarah, for instance, obeyed her husband Abraham, honoring him as head of the house. And if you do the same, you will be following in her steps like good daughters and doing what is right; then you will not need to fear [offending your husbands].

[7]You husbands must be careful of your wives, being thoughtful of their needs and honoring them as the weaker sex. Remember that you and your wife are partners in receiving God's blessings, and if you don't treat her as you should, your prayers will not get ready answers.

[8]And now this word to all of you: You should be like one big happy family, full of sympathy toward each other, loving one another with tender hearts and humble minds. [9]Don't repay evil for evil. Don't snap back at those who say unkind things about you. Instead, pray for God's help for them, for we are to be kind to others, and God will bless us for it.

[10]If you want a happy, good life, keep control of your tongue, and guard your lips from telling lies. [11]Turn away from evil and do good. Try to live in peace even if you must run after it to catch and hold it! [12]For the Lord is watching his children, listening to their prayers; but the Lord's face is hard against those who do evil.

[13]Usually no one will hurt you for wanting to do good. [14]But even if they should, you are to be envied, for God will reward you for it. [15]Quietly trust yourself to Christ your Lord, and if anybody asks why you believe as you do, be ready to tell him, and do it in a gentle and respectful way.

[16]Do what is right; then if men speak against you, calling you evil names, they will become ashamed of themselves for falsely accusing you when you have only done what is good. [17]Remember, if God wants you to suffer, it is better to suffer for doing good than for doing wrong!

3:1-7 God's design for marriage is for the wife to respect her husband and the husband to be sensitive and loving toward his wife. Husband and wife are to receive through each other the blessings of God's loving grace and guiding truth. This sounds wonderful, but, as anyone who is married knows, it is hard and painful! It requires being vulnerable, resolving conflicts, and being confronted with the truth even when it hurts. Working through such difficulties is part of God's plan for helping us grow to full maturity.

3:8-11 The Christian community is to be like a healthy and happy family. Some of us who come from a dysfunctional family may not know what this means, but Peter spelled it out: people share their hurts and find sympathy; they humbly express their needs and receive loving care; they forgive one another rather than plot revenge; they pray for each other; they are careful not to say things that will unnecessarily hurt others; they can be honest about who they are; they seek to do good for one another; and they try to live in peace by resolving conflicts with each other. The community Peter described is ideal for helping us with the recovery process.

3:13-17 We all know what it feels like to be hurt by someone we are trying to help, or to have someone falsely accuse us of wrongdoing. It is not uncommon in recovery for people to misunderstand us and resist the changes we are trying to make. The challenge in such situations is to be patient and maintain a quiet trust in God's promises. If we persevere, God will reward us with a mature faith and a deep experience of his love.

4:8 Real love for others requires that we face our own sinfulness and consider the well-being of those we have wronged in the past. In many cases this means humbly and sincerely asking the people we have offended for forgiveness; sometimes we may need to take the further step of making amends.

Hope for Those Who Suffer
18Christ also suffered. He died once for the
sins of all us guilty sinners although he
himself was innocent of any sin at any time,
that he might bring us safely home to God.
But though his body died, his spirit lived
on, 19and it was in the spirit that he visited
the spirits in prison and preached to them—
20spirits of those who, long before in the
days of Noah, had refused to listen to God,
though he waited patiently for them while
Noah was building the ark. Yet only eight
persons were saved from drowning in that
terrible flood. 21(That, by the way, is what
baptism pictures for us: In baptism we show
that we have been saved from death and
doom by the resurrection of Christ; not
because our bodies are washed clean by the
water but because in being baptized we are
turning to God and asking him to cleanse
our *hearts* from sin.) 22And now Christ is in
heaven, sitting in the place of honor next to
God the Father, with all the angels and
powers of heaven bowing before him and
obeying him.

CHAPTER 4
Since Christ suffered and underwent pain,
you must have the same attitude he did; you
must be ready to suffer, too. For remember,
when your body suffers, sin loses its power,
2and you won't be spending the rest of your
life chasing after evil desires but will be anxious to do the will of God. 3You have had
enough in the past of the evil things the
godless enjoy—sexual sin, lust, getting drunk,
wild parties, drinking bouts, and the worship
of idols, and other terrible sins.
4Of course, your former friends will be very
surprised when you don't eagerly join them
anymore in the wicked things they do, and
they will laugh at you in contempt and scorn.
5But just remember that they must face the
Judge of all, living and dead; they will be
punished for the way they have lived. 6That is
why the Good News was preached even to
those who were dead—killed by the flood—so
that although their bodies were punished
with death, they could still live in their spirits
as God lives.

A Call to Love Each Other
7The end of the world is coming soon. Therefore be earnest, thoughtful men of prayer.
8Most important of all, continue to show deep
love for each other, for love makes up for
many of your faults. 9Cheerfully share your

H*onesty*

READ 1 PETER 3:10-17

Lying can become a way of life. We may have even lied to ourself, pretending we don't have a problem with lying. We may have learned to cover up our problems by becoming excellent liars. But when we choose to face reality, we will see the unhappiness caused by our lies, how they have hurt us and our loved ones. Only when we stop lying can God begin to bring blessing and change into our life.

Think about these verses: "Do you want a long, good life? Then watch your tongue! Keep your lips from lying" (Psalm 34:12-13). "If you want a happy, good life, keep control of your tongue, and guard your lips from telling lies" (1 Peter 3:10). "Don't tell lies to each other; it was your old life with all its wickedness that did that sort of thing; now it is dead and gone. You are living a brand new kind of life that is continually learning more and more of what is right, and trying constantly to be more and more like Christ who created this new life within you" (Colossians 3:9-10).

There are great benefits to honesty. What other virtue is accompanied by such promises? Telling the truth is vital to recovery. Since lying may be second nature to us, it may be difficult to change. Part of any successful recovery involves guarding our lips and our thoughts from lies that will hurt us and others. Since this may have been a lifelong way of coping, we must accept that learning to tell the truth is also likely to be a gradual process. ***Turn to page 1425, 2 Peter 1.***

home with those who need a meal or a place
to stay for the night.
[10]God has given each of you some special
abilities; be sure to use them to help each
other, passing on to others God's many
kinds of blessings. [11]Are you called to
preach? Then preach as though God himself were speaking through you. Are you
called to help others? Do it with all the
strength and energy that God supplies so
that God will be glorified through Jesus
Christ—to him be glory and power forever
and ever. Amen.

Hard Times Bring Reward

[12]Dear friends, don't be bewildered or surprised when you go through the fiery trials
ahead, for this is no strange, unusual thing
that is going to happen to you. [13]Instead, be
really glad—because these trials will make you
partners with Christ in his suffering, and afterwards you will have the wonderful joy of
sharing his glory in that coming day when it
will be displayed.
[14]Be happy if you are cursed and insulted
for being a Christian, for when that happens
the Spirit of God will come upon you with
great glory. [15]Don't let me hear of your suffering for murdering or stealing or making
trouble or being a busybody and prying into
other people's affairs. [16]But it is no shame to
suffer for being a Christian. Praise God for
the privilege of being in Christ's family and
being called by his wonderful name! [17]For the
time has come for judgment, and it must
begin first among God's own children. And if
even we who are Christians must be judged,
what terrible fate awaits those who have
never believed in the Lord? [18]If the righteous
are barely saved, what chance will the godless
have?
[19]So if you are suffering according to God's
will, keep on doing what is right and trust
yourself to the God who made you, for he will
never fail you.

4:10-11 It is unfortunate that many of us don't realize that God has given us special and unique abilities. Discovering these is a part of recovery. It is a process of learning to esteem ourself and receive respect and encouragement from God and other people. Then we can pass on God's blessings to others, relying on his strength to enable us to use the gifts he has given us.

4:12-13 Here Peter returned to a central theme of his letter: we should not only expect to experience trials, but we should also rejoice in them. Through our difficult circumstances we receive an opportunity to share in Christ's sufferings as well as in his glory. This theme offers great hope for those of us in recovery because it affirms that our suffering has a purpose. Through it, God will draw us close and transform us into the people he intended for us to be.

4:14-16 We need wisdom to know the difference between suffering because of our own sin and suffering for doing what is right. If we ask for wisdom, God will grant it (see James 1:5). When we suffer because of our own sin, we naturally feel ashamed; it is then we need divine courage to change. When we are persecuted for our Christian conduct or godly character, we can rejoice in our sufferings; in this case, we need divine serenity to help us accept the things we cannot change.

5:1-4 Several qualities are necessary for a Christian leader: the willingness to care for others, a desire to serve others for their benefit, and the ability to lead by example rather than force. We may have grown up surrounded by leaders who embodied none of these principles, and now we find ourself in a position of leadership at work, at church, or as the head of a family. How do we avoid following in the footsteps of the negative models that have influenced us? Jesus has provided the best example for a leader to follow. To become the type of leader God wants, we can submit to Christ's leadership and allow his grace, peace, and wisdom to flow through us.

5:7 God cares about whatever troubles us. He is watching over us and is continually concerned for our welfare! To the extent that we truly believe this about God we will turn our worries over to him. However, many of us find it hard to trust God so fully. Because of our background, we may have trouble believing that anyone is that concerned about us. We may have found in the past that if we didn't worry about our problems, no one would. One way to increase our level of trust in God is to find another person further along in recovery and Christian maturity with whom we can begin to learn trust. As we are able to share our concerns with a caring person, we can consciously remind ourselves that God's concern is like our friend's, only much wider and deeper.

5:8-9 Satan is ultimately responsible for the evil that happens to us. Whether he tempts us to relapse in our recovery or kicks us when we are already down, Satan is there lurking and prowling about. We are commanded to stand firm and fight the battle, knowing that the war is already won. We are not alone; others are fighting the same battles. Meeting with others in recovery will help us see that victory over addictions is attainable and that we are not alone in the battle.

CHAPTER 5
Advice for Teachers and Students
And now, a word to you elders of the
church. I, too, am an elder; with my own
eyes I saw Christ dying on the cross; and I,
too, will share his glory and his honor when
he returns. Fellow elders, this is my plea to
you: 2Feed the flock of God; care for it willingly, not grudgingly; not for what you will
get out of it but because you are eager to
serve the Lord. 3Don't be tyrants, but lead
them by your good example, 4and when the
Head Shepherd comes, your reward will be
a never-ending share in his glory and
honor.
5You younger men, follow the leadership
of those who are older. And all of you serve
each other with humble spirits, for God gives
special blessings to those who are humble,
but sets himself against those who are proud.
6If you will humble yourselves under the
mighty hand of God, in his good time he will
lift you up.
7Let him have all your worries and cares,
for he is always thinking about you and
watching everything that concerns you.
8Be careful—watch out for attacks from
Satan, your great enemy. He prowls around
like a hungry, roaring lion, looking for some
victim to tear apart. 9Stand firm when he
attacks. Trust the Lord; and remember that
other Christians all around the world are
going through these sufferings too.
10After you have suffered a little while, our
God, who is full of kindness through Christ,
will give you his eternal glory. He personally
will come and pick you up, and set you firmly
in place, and make you stronger than ever.
11To him be all power over all things, forever
and ever. Amen.

Peter's Final Greetings
12I am sending this note to you through the
courtesy of Silvanus who is, in my opinion,
a very faithful brother. I hope I have encouraged you by this letter, for I have given you
a true statement of the way God blesses.
What I have told you here should help you
to stand firmly in his love.
13The church here in Rome—she is your
sister in the Lord—sends you her greetings; so
does my son Mark. 14Give each other the
handshake of Christian love. Peace be to all of
you who are in Christ.

The Narrow Road

BIBLE READING: 1 Peter 4:1-4

Having had a spiritual awakening as the result of these steps, we tried to carry this message to others and to practice these principles in all our affairs.

We probably came into recovery because we'd had enough! We'd had enough of the pain, the lies, and the destruction that result from addictive behaviors. One day at a time, we learned the principles on the road to recovery. Now we are at a place we weren't sure we could ever reach—Step Twelve. Now we are encouraged to share the message with others—even though not everyone will welcome the message.

Peter pointed out, "You have had enough in the past of the evil things the godless enjoy—sexual sin, lust, getting drunk, wild parties, drinking bouts. . . . Your former friends will be very surprised when you don't eagerly join them anymore in the wicked things they do, and they will laugh at you in contempt and scorn" (1 Peter 4:3-4).

Jesus said, "Heaven can be entered only through the narrow gate! The highway to hell is broad, and its gate is wide enough for all the multitudes who choose its easy way. But the Gateway to Life is small, and the road is narrow, and only a few ever find it" (Matthew 7:13-14).

Our message won't be accepted by the masses. The people on the "highway to hell" won't eagerly restrict themselves to the clearly defined steps on the road to recovery. But for those who do listen, our story could be the difference between life and death. ***End of the Twelve Step Reading Program.***

REFLECTIONS ON
FIRST
PETER

✲insights ABOUT THE PERSON OF GOD

As the apostle greeted his friends in **1 Peter 1:1-2,** he reminded them of how they were related to the triune God: they are chosen by God the Father, cleansed by the blood of Jesus Christ, and renewed by the Holy Spirit, who was at work in their hearts. On the basis of God's work in our life, we can be confident that he will bless us richly and grant us increasing freedom from anxiety and fear. This freedom from anxiety is a process that continues as we trust him (1:8).

In **1 Peter 1:3-6** the apostle praised our Father God for the free gift of his loving grace. All who receive God's gift become his children and belong together in his family. All who trust in him share the hope of eternal life with God. This hope gives us the strength to persevere in our recovery with joy, despite the difficult and painful circumstances we face.

1 Peter 2:4-6 leaves us with two wonderful promises upon which we can build our life and our recovery: We are acceptable to God because of Jesus, and God will never disappoint us if we trust in him. With these truths as the foundation, we can build a life that pleases God. As we join other believers in the context of Christ's Spirit of love, together we can create a place in which others feel safe and included.

✲insights ABOUT THE DANGER OF RELAPSE

In **1 Peter 1:14-17** the apostle warned his readers about the temptation to give up on their faith. Peter knew what it felt like to "slip back into old ways." Once he boldly proclaimed that he was willing to die in Jesus' defense. A few hours later he denied knowing Jesus just to save his reputation (see Matthew 26:31-35, 69-75). The only way to keep from slipping back into sinful and unhealthy patterns is to maintain a conscious and sober awareness of our identity: we are children of a holy God. Like children, we are weak and dependent, but the Father we depend on is strong, loving, just, and perfect.

✲insights ABOUT OUR NEW LIFE IN CHRIST

In **1 Peter 1:23-25** the apostle contrasted the new life we have in Christ with the natural life our parents gave us. Even the most positive legacy from our natural parents will fade and decay, for from them we inherit the dysfunctions of a sinful race. But the life God gives us increases in beauty and lasts forever. God's promises to save us will never fail.

In **1 Peter 2:1** the apostle tells us to avoid five destructive behaviors: hanging on to feelings of hatred; pretending to be good when there is unacknowledged sin in our heart; neglecting to be honest about how we are feeling; being jealous of others instead of making the best of our own situation; and talking about people behind their backs instead of talking directly with them. Peter knew that doing these things would hurt us and hinder the growth of loving and intimate relationships. These verses spur us to examine our heart and continue to work toward the recovery goals of forgiveness, honesty, contentment, and openness.

In **1 Peter 4:1-5** we are called to follow Christ's example of self-control, resisting the sinful pleasures that come our way, and instead focusing our energy on living according to God's will. The sins Peter listed here can exert incredible power over us when they become the central focus of our life. To break free of an addictive life-style, we have to cut ourself off from past practices and sometimes even adjust our relationships. To "just say no" alone won't set us free. We also need to say yes to God and redirect our energy into our recovery and, eventually, the recovery of others.

✲insights ABOUT PERSEVERING THROUGH TRIALS

In **1 Peter 2:21-23** the apostle made it clear that persevering through difficulty and pain is the

God-ordained path to maturity. God does not ask us to endure anything that he did not endure himself in Christ. Like us, Jesus felt temptations to give in to sinful pleasures, to lie his way out of a dilemma, to return insult for insult, and to seek revenge. Like Jesus, we can respond to injustice with a faith that entrusts matters into God's hands, knowing that ultimately he will bring about justice.

In **1 Peter 4:19** the apostle encourages us to rejoice in the persecution we face. We probably have been persecuted by old friends who want us to return to our old way of life. Perhaps family members are afraid of the changes we are making and are putting obstacles in the way of our progress. As we face these trials we can trust that God will be faithful to us and remember that he can use even our painful experiences for our good. God wants us to continue in recovery. So if we are suffering for our work in recovery, we need to keep on doing what we know to be right. No matter what obstacles may be placed in our way, God will never desert us once we have entrusted our life to him.

SECOND PETER

THE BIG PICTURE

A. A WORD OF BLESSING (1:1-2)
B. GOD HAS EVERYTHING WE NEED (1:3-21)
C. THE PERIL WITHIN: BEWARE! (2:1-22)
D. HOPE FOR TOMORROW; PURPOSE FOR TODAY (3:1-18)

Peter's audience had a problem. False teachers were moving into church fellowships and promoting wrong ideas about God. In many of these early churches a majority of the people were uneducated. They were easily swayed by the eloquence of traveling false teachers who intentionally deceived the people, using lies and half-truths to manipulate the believers for their own ends.

The apostle Peter sent a series of warnings to his readers: watch out for false teachers; remember that they will give account for their errors; recognize false teachers by their deeds; and remember the price they will pay for misleading people. Peter wanted his readers to experience the life-changing power of God in their lives, and that would mean avoiding manmade substitutes. How could Peter's audience follow Christ if they believed all kinds of false teachings about him?

The challenge Peter left them went beyond a mere warning, however. He included a plan of action: "Do you want more and more of God's kindness and peace?" he asked. "Then learn to know him better and better. For as you know him better, he will give you, through his great power, everything you need for living a truly good life" (1:2-3).

Why do the pains, disappointments, and sins of life bring us down? Why do we hurt those we love the most? Perhaps we will never learn the answer to those questions. But 2 Peter does tell us how to change: get to know God. The God of the universe has made himself available to us on a personal level. As we get to know him, he will help us overcome our shortcomings and replace them with self-control, kindness, love, forgiveness, perseverance, patience, and peace.

THE BOTTOM LINE

PURPOSE: To help his readers keep their focus on God's grace and truth. AUTHOR: The apostle Peter. AUDIENCE: All believers everywhere. DATE WRITTEN: Around A.D. 66–67, a few years after 1 Peter was written. SETTING: Peter was probably writing from Rome, giving words of encouragement and warning to people he did not expect to see again. He wanted them to watch out for false teachings and to be faithful to God and one another. KEY VERSE: "For as you know him better, he will give you, through his great power, everything you need for living a truly good life: he even shares his own glory and his own goodness with us!" (1:3). KEY PEOPLE AND RELATIONSHIPS: Peter with Paul and with the church at large.

RECOVERY THEMES

True Recovery Involves Surrender to God: In the area of recovery, some people say that we have the power to heal ourself. That false idea is fed by our own wishful thinking. We wish we had the power within ourself to overcome our problems. This idea also assumes that recovery is a simple process. But for recovery to be complete, it must involve our entire self—our heart, our mind, our spirit, and our will—being handed over to God's rule. Recovery is never an easy and painless process. It demands complete commitment and surrender to God. But if we are willing to entrust our life to God, we will discover the joy and peace that God intends for all of us.

God Is Our Help and Hope: Peter wrote to people who were facing severe opposition. The Roman emperor Nero had begun heavy persecution of Christians, and many would soon face death at his hands. At the same time, false ideas about God threatened their new faith. Peter helped them face these assaults on their faith by reminding them to keep their eyes on God, the only reliable source of help and hope. As we focus on God, we will find new hope no matter what circumstances we face. Then, as we persevere through tough times, our behavior will show that God is working powerfully in our life.

The Importance of Perseverance: God does not require that we suddenly become perfect. He knows we will slip and fall at times. But, as Peter warned his audience, we must be careful not to get tangled up in our sins to the point of becoming enslaved again. This only adds to our burden of guilt and makes our recovery that much more difficult. The secret to making progress is perseverance. With God's help we can get up quickly and get back on track as soon as possible, no matter what the circumstances. When we accept God's free gift of forgiveness, we will grow closer to God, who loves us and promises to be with us. In this way, God helps us to persevere through the tough times and experience his joy in the process.

CHAPTER 1

Greetings from Peter

From: Simon Peter, a servant and missionary of Jesus Christ.

To: All of you who have our kind of faith. The faith I speak of is the kind that Jesus Christ our God and Savior gives to us. How precious it is, and how just and good he is to give this same faith to each of us.

Steps toward Spiritual Growth

2Do you want more and more of God's kindness and peace? Then learn to know him
better and better.3For as you know him better,
he will give you, through his great power,
everything you need for living a truly good
life: he even shares his own glory and his own
goodness with us! 4And by that same mighty
power he has given us all the other rich and
wonderful blessings he promised; for instance, the promise to save us from the lust
and rottenness all around us, and to give us
his own character.
5But to obtain these gifts, you need more
than faith; you must also work hard to be
good, and even that is not enough. For then
you must learn to know God better and discover what he wants you to do. 6Next, learn
to put aside your own desires so that you will
become patient and godly, gladly letting God
have his way with you. 7This will make possible the next step, which is for you to enjoy
other people and to like them, and finally you
will grow to love them deeply. 8The more you
go on in this way, the more you will grow
strong spiritually and become fruitful and

1:1-2 Peter greeted his readers by reminding them of the gift of forgiveness and new life they had received through faith in Jesus Christ. It is a gift that no one deserves; no one can claim to be worthy of the salvation God offers in Christ (see Ephesians 2:8-9). Truly God is good! Experiencing God's kindness and peace depends on how well we know him. Sometimes we expect peace to come before we make healthy choices, but Peter reminds us that grace and peace come when we concentrate on getting to know God. We can take concrete steps to improve our conscious contact with God through prayer and meditation on his Word.

1:3-4 One of the most comforting by-products of faith is the simple awareness that we possess everything we need to live a full and meaningful life. How do we experience this provision? By participating in God's nature through faith and by growing through practice into all that he has designed us to be. The past is part of who we are, the future is securely in God's hands, and today is filled with the opportunity to grow in our understanding of love, forgiveness, truth, and grace! As a parent ought to provide for a child, so God supplies all that we need, including the ability to rise above our circumstances and temptations.

useful to our Lord Jesus Christ. 9But anyone
who fails to go after these additions to faith is
blind indeed, or at least very shortsighted and
has forgotten that God delivered him from
the old life of sin so that now he can live a
strong, good life for the Lord.
10So, dear brothers, work hard to prove that
you really are among those God has called
and chosen, and then you will never stumble
or fall away. 11And God will open wide the
gates of heaven for you to enter into the
eternal kingdom of our Lord and Savior Jesus
Christ.

Paying Attention to Scripture

12I plan to keep on reminding you of these
things even though you already know them
and are really getting along quite well! 13,14But
the Lord Jesus Christ has showed me that my
days here on earth are numbered, and I am
soon to die. As long as I am still here I intend
to keep sending these reminders to you,
15hoping to impress them so clearly upon you
that you will remember them long after I have
gone.
16For we have not been telling you fairy
tales when we explained to you the power of
our Lord Jesus Christ and his coming again.
My own eyes have seen his splendor and his
glory: 17,18I was there on the holy mountain
when he shone out with honor given him by
God his Father; I heard that glorious, majestic
voice calling down from heaven, saying,
"This is my much-loved Son; I am well
pleased with him."
19So we have seen and proved that what the
prophets said came true. You will do well to
pay close attention to everything they have
written, for, like lights shining into dark corners, their words help us to understand many
things that otherwise would be dark and difficult. But when you consider the wonderful
truth of the prophets' words, then the light
will dawn in your souls and Christ the Morning Star will shine in your hearts. 20,21For no
prophecy recorded in Scripture was ever
thought up by the prophet himself. It was the
Holy Spirit within these godly men who gave
them true messages from God.

CHAPTER 2

The Danger of False Teachers

But there were false prophets, too, in those
days, just as there will be false teachers among
you. They will cleverly tell their lies about
God, turning against even their Master who
bought them; but theirs will be a swift and

Self-control

READ 2 PETER 1:2-9

We would love to have self-control! But trying to find it within ourself can become as much of an obsession as our primary addiction. The more we try to get a hold on it, the more elusive it seems.

According to Peter, self-control is one step in the middle of a larger progression. He said, "Do you want more and more of God's kindness and peace? Then learn to know him better and better. For as you know him better, he will give you, through his great power, everything you need for living a truly good life: he even shares his own glory and his own goodness with us! And by that same mighty power he has given us all the other rich and wonderful blessings he promised; for instance, the promise to save us from the lust and rottenness all around us and to give us his own character. But to obtain these gifts, you need more than faith; you must also work hard to be good, and even that is not enough. For then you must learn to know God better and discover what he wants you to do. Next, learn to put aside your own desires [*self-control*] so that you will become patient and godly, gladly letting God have his way with you. This will make possible the next step, which is for you to enjoy other people and to like them, and finally you will grow to love them deeply" (2 Peter 1:2-7).

Self-control is something that comes as we grow progressively closer to God. Taking one step at a time, one day at a time, God will give us his own character, including self-control. ***Turn to page 1433, 1 John 2.***

terrible end. 2Many will follow their evil
teaching that there is nothing wrong with
sexual sin. And because of them Christ and
his way will be scoffed at.
3These teachers in their greed will tell you
anything to get hold of your money. But God
condemned them long ago and their destruction is on the way. 4For God did not spare
even the angels who sinned, but threw them
into hell, chained in gloomy caves and darkness until the judgment day. 5And he did not
spare any of the people who lived in ancient
times before the flood except Noah, the one
man who spoke up for God, and his family of
seven. At that time God completely destroyed
the whole world of ungodly men with the
vast flood. 6Later, he turned the cities of
Sodom and Gomorrah into heaps of ashes
and blotted them off the face of the earth,
making them an example for all the ungodly
in the future to look back upon and fear.
7,8But at the same time the Lord rescued Lot
out of Sodom because he was a good man,
sick of the terrible wickedness he saw everywhere around him day after day. 9So also the
Lord can rescue you and me from the temptations that surround us, and continue to punish the ungodly until the day of final
judgment comes. 10He is especially hard on
those who follow their own evil, lustful
thoughts, and those who are proud and willful, daring even to scoff at the Glorious Ones
without so much as trembling, 11although the
angels in heaven who stand in the very presence of the Lord, and are far greater in power
and strength than these false teachers, never
speak out disrespectfully against these evil
Mighty Ones.
12But false teachers are fools—no better
than animals. They do whatever they feel like;
born only to be caught and killed, they laugh
at the terrifying powers of the underworld
which they know so little about; and they will
be destroyed along with all the demons and
powers of hell.
13That is the pay these teachers will have for
their sin. For they live in evil pleasures day
after day. They are a disgrace and a stain
among you, deceiving you by living in foul
sin on the side while they join your love feasts
as though they were honest men. 14No
woman can escape their sinful stare, and of
adultery they never have enough. They make
a game of luring unstable women. They train
themselves to be greedy; and are doomed and
cursed. 15They have gone off the road and
become lost like Balaam, the son of Beor, who
fell in love with the money he could make by
doing wrong; 16but Balaam was stopped from
his mad course when his donkey spoke to him
with a human voice, scolding and rebuking
him.
17These men are as useless as dried-up
springs of water, promising much and delivering nothing; they are as unstable as clouds
driven by the storm winds. They are doomed
to the eternal pits of darkness. 18They proudly
boast about their sins and conquests, and,
using lust as their bait, they lure back into sin
those who have just escaped from such
wicked living.
19"You aren't saved by being good," they
say, "so you might as well be bad. Do what
you like; be free."
But these very teachers who offer this "freedom" from law are themselves slaves to sin
and destruction. For a man is a slave to whatever controls him. 20And when a person has
escaped from the wicked ways of the world by
learning about our Lord and Savior Jesus
Christ, and then gets tangled up with sin and
becomes its slave again, he is worse off than
he was before. 21It would be better if he had
never known about Christ at all than to learn
of him and then afterwards turn his back on
the holy commandments that were given to
him. 22There is an old saying that "A dog

2:1-12 Here we are reminded of the consequences to be faced by those who reject God's program and lead others away from the truth. Perhaps these verses describe the way we were before entering recovery. Thankfully, God has provided us with the help we need to start again and rebuild our life according to his will. The consequences of a self-centered pursuit of pleasure and power are terrible. It is good to be reminded every so often of what we have been delivered from: "a swift and terrible end."

2:13-22 An important part of most recovery work is the setting of appropriate boundaries. People who do not have our best interests at heart abound, even in the Christian community. Peter emphasized the need for discernment here. Apparently, the church in Peter's day was plagued by those who once professed faith in Christ but then "added to" the simple truth of the gospel. They advocated "freedom," but that freedom was really only a license to become enslaved once again by sin. Setting healthy boundaries for our behavior involves knowing God's truth and allowing neither the false teachings of others nor our own sinful inclinations to lead us astray.

comes back to what he has vomited, and a pig
is washed only to come back and wallow in
the mud again." That is the way it is with
those who turn again to their sin.

CHAPTER 3

Hope for Growing Christians

This is my second letter to you, dear brothers,
and in both of them I have tried to remind
you—if you will let me—about facts you already know: facts you learned from the holy
prophets and from us apostles who brought
you the words of our Lord and Savior.
3First, I want to remind you that in the last
days there will come scoffers who will do
every wrong they can think of and laugh at
the truth. 4This will be their line of argument:
"So Jesus promised to come back, did he?
Then where is he? He'll never come! Why, as
far back as anyone can remember, everything
has remained exactly as it was since the first
day of creation."
5,6They deliberately forget this fact: that
God did destroy the world with a mighty
flood long after he had made the heavens by
the word of his command and had used the
waters to form the earth and surround it. 7And
God has commanded that the earth and the
heavens be stored away for a great bonfire at
the judgment day, when all ungodly men will
perish.
8But don't forget this, dear friends, that a
day or a thousand years from now is like
tomorrow to the Lord. 9He isn't really being
slow about his promised return, even though
it sometimes seems that way. But he is waiting, for the good reason that he is not willing
that any should perish, and he is giving more
time for sinners to repent. 10The day of the
Lord is surely coming, as unexpectedly as a
thief, and then the heavens will pass away
with a terrible noise, and the heavenly bodies
will disappear in fire, and the earth and everything on it will be burned up.
11And so since everything around us is going to melt away, what holy, godly lives we
should be living! 12You should look forward to
that day and hurry it along—the day when
God will set the heavens on fire, and the
heavenly bodies will melt and disappear in
flames. 13But we are looking forward to God's
promise of new heavens and a new earth
afterwards, where there will be only goodness.
14Dear friends, while you are waiting for
these things to happen and for him to come,
try hard to live without sinning; and be at
peace with everyone so that he will be pleased
with you when he returns.
15,16And remember why he is waiting. He is
giving us time to get his message of salvation
out to others. Our wise and beloved brother
Paul has talked about these same things in
many of his letters. Some of his comments are
not easy to understand, and there are people
who are deliberately stupid, and always demand some unusual interpretation—they
have twisted his letters around to mean something quite different from what he meant,
just as they do the other parts of the Scripture—and the result is disaster for them.
17I am warning you ahead of time, dear
brothers, so that you can watch out and not
be carried away by the mistakes of these
wicked men, lest you yourselves become
mixed up too. 18But grow in spiritual strength
and become better acquainted with our Lord
and Savior Jesus Christ. To him be all glory
and splendid honor, both now and forevermore. Good-bye.

Peter

3:3-9 It is difficult to wait on God, particularly when he seems so slow in bringing about our healing. Why doesn't God return for us now? Why does he allow further suffering and frustration? The answer is simple yet profoundly full of love: God is patient! He wants all to come to him and discover the only true way of life. As we wait, we can trust that it is always for a good purpose.

3:10-16 We live in a world that encourages and rewards our active life-style. We are "doers" and "fixers," "arrangers" and "controllers." We seek to bolster our self-esteem by the things we do. When Christ returns, however, who we are will be far more important than what we do. Peter reminds us that as we wait for this day we are called to be God's people. It is good to take time to ask: Am I enjoying the privilege of being? In all my doing, have I lost sight of what's important—the kind of person I am, and am becoming?

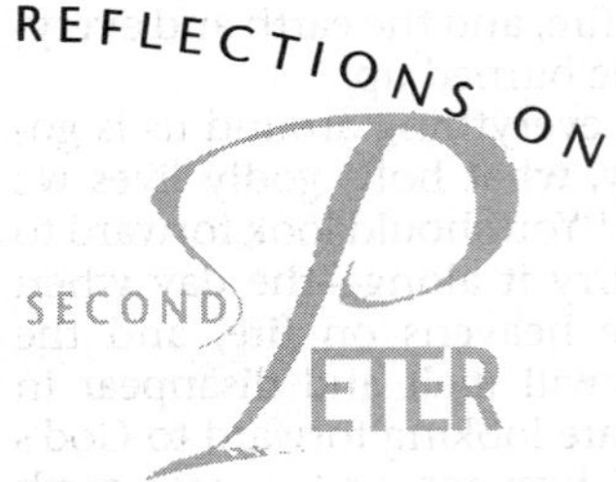
REFLECTIONS ON
SECOND
PETER

✲insights ABOUT OUR ROLE IN RECOVERY

When we entrust our life to God, we might wonder if there is any part for us to play. In **2 Peter 1:5-11** the apostle reminds us that God expects us to do our part in the recovery process. As we seek change in our life, we will share in God's nature and receive the ability to think new thoughts and formulate new behavior patterns. "Work hard to be good," Peter urges. But even more importantly, "Learn to know God better and discover what he wants you to do." The result? God "will open wide the gates of heaven" for us, and in this life we will experience healthier, stronger relationships.

It is easy to remember the painful moments of life—the disappointments and the people who disappointed us. It is sometimes harder to remember the many blessings we receive in small ways each day. In **2 Peter 1:12-18** the apostle reminded his readers that they could overcome the pain of past trials by focusing on the good things in life, like God's faithfulness. Peter wanted them to etch the truth of God's amazing love into their minds. We must work through our painful memories (they do not disappear on their own!), but as we do so, we can also take time to reflect on the amazing love of God. As we recall the good things God has done, the painful memories will begin to fade.

✲insights ABOUT GOD'S TRUTH

God's truth is dependable; our human perspective often is not. In **2 Peter 1:19-21** the apostle made this distinction clear. God's truth is not weak or questionable; it is not a theory waiting to be proven false. God's truth, instead, is certain and can be counted on. In recovery, a central question is: Are we ready to believe what God says? Or do we prefer the perspectives of fallible people, the messages ingrained in our mind from past events, the doubts instilled by friends not yet in recovery? As we take God's Word to heart, we come to understand more and more of the truth—about ourself, about God, and about our future in Christ.

FIRST JOHN

THE BIG PICTURE

A. INTRODUCTION (1:1–2:2)
B. RECOVERY FROM FALSE THINKING: OBEDIENCE (2:3-27)
C. RECOVERY FROM FALSE THINKING: THE WORK OF CHRIST (2:28–4:6)
D. RECOVERY FROM FALSE THINKING: THE GIFTS OF GOD (4:7–5:5)
E. CONCLUSION: ASSURANCE OF SPIRITUAL RECOVERY (5:6-21)

False spiritual teachers were a big problem in the early church. Because there was no New Testament that new believers could refer to, many churches fell prey to pretenders who taught their own ideas and advanced themselves as leaders. John wrote this letter to set the record straight on some important issues, particularly concerning the identity of Jesus Christ.

Because John's letter was about the basics of faith in Christ, it helped his readers take inventory of their faith. It helped them answer the question, Are we true believers? John told them that they could tell by looking at their actions: If they loved one another, that was evidence of God's presence in their lives. But if they bickered and fought all the time, or were selfish and did not look out for one another, they were betraying that they, in fact, did not know God.

That did not mean they had to be perfect. In fact, John also recognized that believing involved admitting our sins and seeking God's forgiveness. Depending on God for cleansing from guilt, along with admitting our wrongs against others and making amends, was another important part of getting to know God.

Our recovery program requires us to make amends because this is essential to a successful recovery. John's letter challenges us to treat others with respect and dignity as we grow spiritually. A person transformed by Christ will show it in how he or she treats others. In a similar way, our recovery will progress only as far as we right the wrongs we have committed against others. It takes humility and commitment to live at peace with others, but it is a price worth paying as we seek God's blessing.

THE BOTTOM LINE

PURPOSE: To set boundaries on the content of faith and to give believers assurance of their salvation. AUTHOR: The apostle John. AUDIENCE: An unnamed group of early churches. DATE WRITTEN: Probably between A.D. 85 and 96. SETTING: John was the only surviving apostle when he wrote this circular letter. He was living in Ephesus, supervising the churches of Asia Minor. KEY VERSE: "I have written this to you who believe in the Son of God so that you may know you have eternal life" (5:13). KEY PEOPLE AND RELATIONSHIPS: John, with the believers to whom he wrote.

RECOVERY THEMES

God's Desire for Our Recovery: One of the ways God cares for us is by listening to us. When Satan (called the "Accuser of our brothers" in Revelation 12:10) plants thoughts of hopelessness in our mind, telling us that we have gone too far for God to forgive us, John urges us not to give up hope. Jesus Christ, our advocate, has already paid the penalty for any and every wrong we have done or could do. We do not need to shy away from asking him to plead our case; he has already won it.

The Invitation to Love: One of the evidences of salvation in a person's life is love for others—shown in action, not just words. An important part of our recovery is the willingness to extend God's love to others as God showed his love toward us. He loved us while we were in the middle of our insanity—we did not have to clean up our act to get him to love us. And through us he wants to love others in the midst of their insanity, using us to carry the message of God's love and forgiveness to them. God loves us enough to free us from bondage and use us to show his love toward others in need of recovery.

The Importance of Boundaries: The false teachers whom John corrected said that they could throw off all moral restraints because what they did "in the body" did not matter. Those who listened to their message were becoming indifferent to sin and returning to old habits. They were relapsing into immoral ways of life and thinking it was all right. John pointed out that there are boundaries around what we believe, and that Jesus Christ is the focus. Anything that leads us away from Christ is outside the boundaries. Staying focused on Christ is an essential part of our spiritual growth and the only means for a continued recovery.

CHAPTER 1

Jesus Christ Is God's Son

Christ was alive when the world began, yet
I myself have seen him with my own eyes
and listened to him speak. I have touched
him with my own hands. He is God's message of life. [2]This one who is life from God
has been shown to us, and we guarantee
that we have seen him; I am speaking of
Christ, who is eternal Life. He was with the
Father and then was shown to us. [3]Again I
say, we are telling you about what we ourselves have actually seen and heard, so that
you may share the fellowship and the joys
we have with the Father and with Jesus
Christ his son. [4]And if you do as I say in this
letter, then you, too, will be full of joy, and
so will we.

Living in God's Light

[5]This is the message God has given us to pass
on to you: that God is Light and in him is no
darkness at all. [6]So if we say we are his friends
but go on living in spiritual darkness and sin,
we are lying. [7]But if we are living in the light
of God's presence, just as Christ does, then we
have wonderful fellowship and joy with each
other, and the blood of Jesus his Son cleanses
us from every sin.
[8]If we say that we have no sin, we are only

1:1-4 John wrote to assure those who were doubting the value of their Christian faith. He showed that faith in Christ is intellectually (1:1-2), socially (1:3), and emotionally (1:4) satisfying. Spiritual recovery takes place only where there is this healthy balance between the intellectual, social, and emotional aspects of life, all centered on genuine Christian faith. Dealing with our shortcomings and making amends where possible means facing all our shortcomings—in our thought life, our social life, and our emotional life.

1:5-7 There is a strong contrast between the light in the Christian life and the darkness in a life given to sin. If we live in sin while claiming to be a Christian, we will never successfully navigate the recovery process. Honest and accurate self-examination and personal inventory of our spiritual state is a crucial step. The results of choosing to live in the light—continually acknowledging our flaws as the light reveals them—are a cleansed conscience and fulfilling relationships.

2:3-6 How can we be sure that we belong to Christ? Our assurance is validated by our continuing desire to obey God's will for us. Those who claim to be saved but continually disobey God's revealed will are liars. We cannot make progress in recovery unless we are willing to submit to God's program for right and healthy living. That means continuing our personal inventory, promptly admitting our wrongs to others, and confessing our sins to God. As we learn to love God more and more, this will be more a joy than a burden.

2:7-11 Another distinctive mark of our faith is love. Hatred toward other Christians is a sure sign that recovery has not yet begun. Light and darkness cannot exist in the same heart. Notice that the absence of love will keep us in the dark and prove a severe hindrance to progress in recovery. Love is never weak or compromising; it is the insignia of emotional strength. The love God gives us provides the energy to approach those we have harmed and to make amends when possible.

fooling ourselves and refusing to accept the
truth. 9But if we confess our sins to him, he
can be depended on to forgive us and to
cleanse us from every wrong. [And it is perfectly proper for God to do this for us because
Christ died to wash away our sins.] 10If we
claim we have not sinned, we are lying and
calling God a liar, *for he says we have sinned.*

CHAPTER 2
My little children, I am telling you this so that
you will stay away from sin. But if you sin,
there is someone to plead for you before the
Father. His name is Jesus Christ, the one who
is all that is good and who pleases God completely. 2He is the one who took God's wrath
against our sins upon himself and brought us
into fellowship with God; and he is the forgiveness for our sins, and not only ours but all
the world's.
3And how can we be sure that we belong to
him? By looking within ourselves: are we
really trying to do what he wants us to?
4Someone may say, "I am a Christian; I am
on my way to heaven; I belong to Christ." But
if he doesn't do what Christ tells him to, he is
a liar. 5But those who do what Christ tells
them to will learn to love God more and
more. That is the way to know whether or not
you are a Christian. 6Anyone who says he is a
Christian should live as Christ did.
7Dear brothers, I am not writing out a new
rule for you to obey, for it is an old one you
have always had, right from the start. You
have heard it all before. 8Yet it is always new,
and works for you just as it did for Christ; and
as we obey this commandment, *to love one
another,* the darkness in our lives disappears
and the new light of life in Christ shines in.
9Anyone who says he is walking in the light
of Christ but dislikes his fellow man is still in
darkness. 10But whoever loves his fellow man
is "walking in the light" and can see his way
without stumbling around in darkness and
sin. 11For he who dislikes his brother is wandering in spiritual darkness and doesn't know
where he is going, for the darkness has made
him blind so that he cannot see the way.

A Call to Know and Love God

12I am writing these things to all of you, my
little children, because your sins have been
forgiven in the name of Jesus our Savior. 13I
am saying these things to you older men
because you really know Christ, the one who
has been alive from the beginning. And you
young men, I am talking to you because you

Recurrent Sins

BIBLE READING: 1 John 1:8-10

We continued to take personal inventory and when we were wrong promptly admitted it.

We may feel awkward about bringing our recurrent sins before God. We may be embarrassed by the number of times we have had to deal with the same issues—issues that stubbornly refuse to be washed away. We may imagine that God is collecting a long list to be used against us.

The apostle John wrote, "If we say that we have no sin, we are only fooling ourselves and refusing to accept the truth. But if we confess our sins to him, he can be depended on to forgive us and to cleanse us from every wrong. [And it is perfectly proper for God to do this for us because Christ died to wash away our sins.] If we claim we have not sinned, we are lying and calling God a liar" (1 John 1:8-10).

To confess means to agree with God that what he declares to be wrong really is wrong. This means we need to recognize our wrongs when they occur. Notice that he says he will forgive us and cleanse us of *every* wrong. Each time we confess a sin it is washed away. Our life is like a slate that has been wiped clean. Our sins are not recorded on some celestial list. They are gone forever! And each time we confess a sin we have dealt with before, it's forgiven all over again. Some areas of our life need more cleaning than others! God doesn't get angry when we come back to him again and again. This is the process he set up to cleanse the areas in our life that cause the most trouble. There is no need to feel awkward. God wants us to come every time we sin. ***Turn to Step Eleven, page 371, 2 Samuel 22.***

have won your battle with Satan. And I am writing to you younger boys and girls because you, too, have learned to know God our Father.

[14]And so I say to you fathers who know the eternal God, and to you young men who are strong with God's Word in your hearts, and have won your struggle against Satan: [15]Stop loving this evil world and all that it offers you, for when you love these things you show that you do not really love God; [16]for all these worldly things, these evil desires—the craze for sex, the ambition to buy everything that appeals to you, and the pride that comes from wealth and importance—these are not from God. They are from this evil world itself. [17]And this world is fading away, and these evil, forbidden things will go with it, but whoever keeps doing the will of God will live forever.

A Warning about God's Enemies

[18]Dear children, this world's last hour has come. You have heard about the Antichrist who is coming—the one who is against Christ—and already many such persons have appeared. This makes us all the more certain that the end of the world is near. [19]These "against-Christ" people used to be members of our churches, but they never really belonged with us or else they would have stayed. When they left us it proved that they were not of us at all.

[20]But you are not like that, for the Holy Spirit has come upon you, and you know the truth. [21]So I am not writing to you as to those who need to know the truth, but I warn you as those who can discern the difference between true and false.

[22]And who is the greatest liar? The one who says that Jesus is not Christ. Such a person is antichrist, for he does not believe in God the Father and in his Son. [23]For a person who doesn't believe in Christ, God's Son, can't have God the Father either. But he who has Christ, God's Son, has God the Father also.

[24]So keep on believing what you have been taught from the beginning. If you do, you will always be in close fellowship with both God the Father and his Son. [25]And he himself has promised us this: *eternal life.*

[26]These remarks of mine about the Antichrist are pointed at those who would dearly love to blindfold you and lead you astray. [27]But you have received the Holy Spirit, and he lives within you, in your hearts, so that you don't need anyone to teach you what is right. For he teaches you all things, and he is the Truth, and no liar; and so, just as he has said, you must live in Christ, never to depart from him.

[28]And now, my little children, stay in happy fellowship with the Lord so that when he comes you will be sure that all is well and will not have to be ashamed and shrink back from meeting him. [29]Since we know that God is always good and does only right, we may rightly assume that all those who do right are his children.

2:24-27 Belief in Jesus as the Son of God and reliance upon the Holy Spirit will guard us against being deceived by false doctrines. The quest for new, sophisticated solutions to the consequences of sin and despair only leads to new kinds of enslavement to cultic religions, substance abuse, and codependency. Historical Christianity gives us the only perspective of ourself and the world that leads to true freedom from the enslavement of sin because only the Christian faith asserts that Jesus took upon himself the penalty for our sin.

2:28–3:3 Many of us struggle with the issue of shame. John tells us that as we live in Christ, trusting him for forgiveness and walking with him consistently, we will have no reason to be ashamed at his return. We can rest assured that we are loved and acceptable because God himself has made us his children. As his children, we long to be with him and to be like him. The ultimate step in recovery is for this longing to be fulfilled. In the meantime, the knowledge that God is coming again provides powerful motivation to live a godly life and to seek to know God better through prayer and meditation on his Word.

3:4-9 As we take a moral inventory of our life, let's face the essence of sin honestly: it is breaking God's law, doing things our own way rather than God's way. Once we commit our life to God, he himself gives us a new nature that is no longer comfortable with sin. We still sin (1:8), but we no longer make it a practice. We know that our sin was the reason Jesus gave his life on the cross, and our desire is to please him, in accordance with our new nature. Whereas before—in our sin, codependency, and/or addiction—we continued with little sense of wrongdoing, now we know better. In our recovery work we constantly affirm that we have new power to break old patterns.

3:10-20 Using Cain and Abel as examples, John underscored the importance of love. Having true love means being willing to make sacrifices for the ones we love. In our recovery, the best way to express our love for God is to be willing to make amends for the wrongs we have done to others. Our actions toward others, not just our words, are what count.

CHAPTER 3

We Are God's Children

See how very much our heavenly Father loves
us, for he allows us to be called his children—
think of it—and we really *are!* But since most
people don't know God, naturally they don't
understand that we are his children. 2Yes, dear
friends, we are already God's children, right
now, and we can't even imagine what it is
going to be like later on. But we do know this,
that when he comes we will be like him, as a
result of seeing him as he really is. 3And everyone who really believes this will try to stay
pure because Christ is pure.

4But those who keep on sinning are against
God, for every sin is done against the will of
God. 5And you know that he became a man
so that he could take away our sins, and that
there is no sin in him, no missing of God's will
at any time in any way. 6So if we stay close to
him, obedient to him, we won't be sinning
either; but as for those who keep on sinning,
they should realize this: They sin because they
have never really known him or become his.

7Oh, dear children, don't let anyone deceive you about this: if you are constantly
doing what is good, it is because you *are* good,
even as he is. 8But if you keep on sinning, it
shows that you belong to Satan, who since he
first began to sin has kept steadily at it. But the
Son of God came to destroy these works of the
devil. 9The person who has been born into
God's family does not make a practice of
sinning because now God's life is in him; so
he can't keep on sinning, for this new life has
been born into him and controls him—he has
been *born again.*

10So now we can tell who is a child of God
and who belongs to Satan. Whoever is living
a life of sin and doesn't love his brother shows
that he is not in God's family;11for the message to us from the beginning has been that
we should love one another.

12We are not to be like Cain, who belonged
to Satan and killed his brother. Why did he
kill him? Because Cain had been doing wrong
and he knew very well that his brother's life
was better than his. 13So don't be surprised,
dear friends, if the world hates you.

Loving Fellow Believers

14If we love other Christians, it proves that we
have been delivered from hell and given eternal life. But a person who doesn't have love
for others is headed for eternal death. 15Any-
one who hates his Christian brother is really
a murderer at heart; and you know that no
one wanting to murder has eternal life within.

Forgiveness

READ 1 JOHN 2:1-6

At times we may feel like we are the worst sinner on earth. We just seem to keep doing the same things over and over again. We feel guilty! Can God just wink at our sin and pretend that it's all right? How can he repeatedly forgive us for committing the same wrongs?

The apostle John said, "My little children, I am telling you this so that you will stay away from sin. But if you sin, there is someone to plead for you before the Father. His name is Jesus Christ, the one who is all that is good and who pleases God completely. He is the one who took God's wrath against our sins upon himself and brought us into fellowship with God; and he is the forgiveness for our sins, and not only ours but all the world's" (1 John 2:1-2).

God takes sin very seriously. As a righteous Judge, he can't just ignore sin and act like it doesn't matter. But we can be forgiven completely and repeatedly. The words used here are legal terms. Jesus is our advocate, a defense attorney in a court of law, who intercedes for us, the lawbreakers. But he is not only the defense attorney; he is also "the one who took God's wrath against our sins upon himself." This means that his death has been accepted by the court as admissible payment for all of our sins. We are all guilty. The sentence is death! But our sentence has already been paid by Jesus. When we bring our sin to Jesus, he goes back to the Judge on our behalf, reminding him that the sentence has already been paid. ***Turn to page 1447, Jude 1.***

[16]We know what real love is from Christ's
example in dying for us. And so we also ought
to lay down our lives for our Christian brothers.
[17]But if someone who is supposed to be a
Christian has money enough to live well, and
sees a brother in need, and won't help him—
how can God's love be within *him?* [18]Little
children, let us stop just *saying* we love
people; let us *really* love them, and *show it* by
our *actions.* [19]Then we will know for sure, by
our actions, that we are on God's side, and our
consciences will be clear, even when we stand
before the Lord. [20]But if we have bad consciences and feel that we have done wrong,
the Lord will surely feel it even more, for he
knows everything we do.
[21]But, dearly loved friends, if our consciences are clear, we can come to the Lord
with perfect assurance and trust, [22]and get
whatever we ask for because we are obeying
him and doing the things that please him.
[23]And this is what God says we must do:
Believe on the name of his Son Jesus Christ,
and love one another. [24]Those who do what
God says—they are living with God and he
with them. We know this is true because the
Holy Spirit he has given us tells us so.

CHAPTER 4

Distinguishing Truth from Falsehood

Dearly loved friends, don't always believe
everything you hear just because someone
says it is a message from God: test it first to see
if it really is. For there are many false teachers
around, [2]and the way to find out if their
message is from the Holy Spirit is to ask: Does
it really agree that Jesus Christ, God's Son,
actually became man with a human body? If
so, then the message is from God. [3]If not, the
message is not from God but from one who is
against Christ, like the "Antichrist" you have
heard about who is going to come, and his
attitude of enmity against Christ is already
abroad in the world.
[4]Dear young friends, you belong to God
and have already won your fight with those
who are against Christ because there is someone in your hearts who is stronger than any
evil teacher in this wicked world. [5]These men
belong to this world, so, quite naturally, they
are concerned about worldly affairs and the
world pays attention to them. [6]But we are
children of God; that is why only those who
have walked and talked with God will listen
to us. Others won't. That is another way to
know whether a message is really from God;
for if it is, the world won't listen to it.

Love Comes from God

[7]Dear friends, let us practice loving each
other, for love comes from God and those
who are loving and kind show that they are
the children of God, and that they are getting
to know him better. [8]But if a person isn't
loving and kind, it shows that he doesn't
know God—for God is love.
[9]God showed how much he loved us by
sending his only Son into this wicked world
to bring to us eternal life through his death.
[10]In this act we see what real love is: it is not
our love for God but his love for us when he
sent his Son to satisfy God's anger against our
sins.
[11]Dear friends, since God loved us as much
as that, we surely ought to love each other

4:1-6 No religious system can be true if it denies that Jesus was God in a human body. A clear view of Jesus will help us develop a relationship with God through prayer, so we know what his will is and how to accomplish it in our life. Even if other people don't understand or accept our new way of life, as we walk with God we can know that he who lives in our heart is stronger than our past and our present struggles with sin.

4:7-12 Recovery depends upon God's gifts, and the most important among them is the provision of a Savior. The Father loves us enough to have sent his Son to save us; as we grow to be more like him, we also grow in our ability to love one another with a sacrificial love. Many of us feel our recovery would be greatly expedited if only we could see God. But no one has seen God, except as he is seen through his people when they love one another. That is why it is so important for us to restore relationships with the people we have harmed. That is also why we need the fellowship of believers—because we desperately need the love they have to offer.

4:16–5:3 John spoke again about the importance of love. True Christianity is characterized by loving relationships in which there is no fear. Experiencing such relationships—first with God, then with other believers—is at the heart of recovery. We can trust God wholly, without fear, because our punishment for sin has already taken place (with Christ). Where love reigns, we can be openly transparent with fellow believers, trusting that our honesty will not be used to hurt us. Mature Christian love delights in helping others, and it creates an environment in which we can develop accountability and a new sense of responsibility toward ourself and toward others.

too. 12For though we have never yet seen God,
when we love each other God lives in us, and
his love within us grows ever stronger. 13And
he has put his own Holy Spirit into our hearts
as a proof to us that we are living with him
and he with us. 14And furthermore, we have
seen with our own eyes and now tell all the
world that God sent his Son to be their Savior.
15Anyone who believes and says that Jesus is
the Son of God has God living in him, and he
is living with God.
16We know how much God loves us because
we have felt his love and because we believe
him when he tells us that he loves us dearly.
God is love, and anyone who lives in love is
living with God and God is living in him.
17And as we live with Christ, our love grows
more perfect and complete; so we will not be
ashamed and embarrassed at the day of judgment, but can face him with confidence and
joy because he loves us and we love him too.
18We need have no fear of someone who
loves us perfectly; his perfect love for us eliminates all dread of what he might do to us. If
we are afraid, it is for fear of what he might do
to us and shows that we are not fully convinced that he really loves us. 19So you see, our
love for him comes as a result of his loving us
first.
20If anyone says "I love God," but keeps on
hating his brother, he is a liar; for if he doesn't
love his brother who is right there in front of
him, how can he love God whom he has never
seen? 21And God himself has said that one
must love not only God but his brother too.

CHAPTER 5

Love Is Proven by Action

If you believe that Jesus is the Christ—that he
is God's Son and your Savior—then you are a
child of God. And all who love the Father love
his children too. 2So you can find out how
much you love God's children—your brothers
and sisters in the Lord—by how much you
love and obey God. 3Loving God means doing
what he tells us to do, and really, that isn't
hard at all; 4for every child of God can obey
him, defeating sin and evil pleasure by trusting Christ to help him.
5But who could possibly fight and win this
battle except by believing that Jesus is truly
the Son of God?6-8And we know he is, because
God said so with a voice from heaven when
Jesus was baptized, and again as he was facing
death—yes, not only at his baptism but also
as he faced death. And the Holy Spirit, forever
truthful, says it too. So we have these three

Eyes of Love

BIBLE READING: 1 John 5:11-15

We humbly asked him to remove our shortcomings.

Most of us probably aren't used to getting the things we ask for. How can we have confidence that God will hear our prayers? How do we know he will answer when we ask him to remove our shortcomings?

The apostle Paul wrote, "Long ago, even before he made the world, God chose us to be his very own through what Christ would do for us; he decided then to make us holy in his eyes, without a single fault—we who stand before him covered with his love" (Ephesians 1:4). God's primary goal is to make us holy—that is, to form his character in us. Looking through the eyes of love, he already sees us as we will look when his work is done. Then he works out his goals for us in the arena of everyday life. The Bible tells us: "God's correction is always right and for our best good, that we may share his holiness" (Hebrews 12:10). Our holiness—the removal of our shortcomings—is God's will.

The apostle John wrote, "And we are sure of this, that he will listen to us whenever we ask him for anything in line with his will. And if we really know he is listening when we talk to him and make our requests, then we can be sure that he will answer us" (1 John 5:14-15).

It is clearly God's will to have our shortcomings removed. And he has promised to give us anything we ask for within his will. Therefore, we can have full confidence that God will remove our shortcomings in his time. ***Turn to Step Eight, page 93, Exodus 22.***

witnesses: the voice of the Holy Spirit in our
hearts, the voice from heaven at Christ's baptism, and the voice before he died. And they
all say the same thing: that Jesus Christ is the
Son of God. [9]We believe men who witness in
our courts, and so surely we can believe whatever God declares. And God declares that
Jesus is his Son. [10]All who believe this know in
their hearts that it is true. If anyone doesn't
believe this, he is actually calling God a liar
because he doesn't believe what God has said
about his Son.

[11]And what is it that God has said? That he
has given us eternal life and that this life is in
his Son. [12]So whoever has God's Son has life;
whoever does not have his Son, does not have
life.

[13]I have written this to you who believe in
the Son of God so that you may know you
have eternal life. [14]And we are sure of this, that
he will listen to us whenever we ask him for
anything in line with his will. [15]And if we
really know he is listening when we talk to
him and make our requests, then we can be
sure that he will answer us.

[16]If you see a Christian sinning in a way that
does not end in death, you should ask God to
forgive him, and God will give him life unless
he has sinned that one fatal sin. But there is
that one sin which ends in death, and if he
has done that, there is no use praying for him.
[17]Every wrong is a sin, of course. I'm not
talking about these ordinary sins; I am speaking of that one that ends in death.

[18]No one who has become part of God's
family makes a practice of sinning, for Christ,
God's Son, holds him securely, and the devil
cannot get his hands on him. [19]We know that
we are children of God and that all the rest of
the world around us is under Satan's power
and control. [20]And we know that Christ, God's
Son, has come to help us understand and find
the true God. And now we are in God because
we are in Jesus Christ his Son, who is the only
true God; and he is eternal Life.

[21]Dear children, keep away from anything
that might take God's place in your hearts.
Amen.

Sincerely, John

5:6-13 How can we who are committed to a life of recovery know that we are actually achieving it in a way that pleases God? Scripture tells us that we can look for certain evidence. Belief that Jesus is the Son of God and a life committed to obeying him are two sources of assurance. Another is the witness of the Holy Spirit, who points to Christ in our life. God gives us a sense of rightness as we continue to maintain contact with him through prayer and study of his Word, and as we obey his revealed will.

5:16-19 Another evidence of spiritual recovery is godly discernment. Discernment means that we have the spiritual capacity to know right from wrong, wherever we may find it—in our own heart, in the lives of others, or in the world at large. This power of discernment is lost in codependent relationships; regaining it is at the heart of the recovery process. Until we are able to see ourself as God sees us, our moral inventory will be flawed and self-excusing.

5:20-21 John ends this letter by reminding us who the true God is and warning us not to let anything take God's place in our heart. He cautions against entertaining any false ideas about God, which are at the root of all false religious systems. Recovery involves elimination of not only all wrong ideas about God, but also any material substitutes for him and all controlling sins. Recovery means putting God back in his rightful place as the absolute Lord of our life. Someone has said, "Only Jesus Christ is able to control a person's life without destroying it." In a restored relationship with God, the submission of our life and will to his control is the way back to sanity.

REFLECTIONS ON FIRST JOHN

✲*insights* INTO CONFESSION AND FORGIVENESS

Accurate personal inventory normally leads to a consciousness of sin. We are assured in **1 John 1:8-10** that if we confess our sins, we will experience the forgiveness and cleansing God has provided through the blood shed by his Son, Jesus Christ. The lesson is simple: confession must precede cleansing. Confession should be followed by a willingness to make amends where possible.

In every recovery situation, whether the need is for cleansing from sin or for deliverance from the trauma of abuse or codependence, honest self-evaluation will usually lead to an admission of powerlessness. We see in **1 John 2:1-2** that at this point we can turn to the greatest resource and advocate of all: Jesus Christ. Because he received the full force of God's anger against sin, we in recovery need not live in fear of God's displeasure for past transgressions. Trusting that Christ suffered for our sin, we can now come to the Father freely, with complete trust that we will be accepted unconditionally.

✲*insights* ABOUT THE DANGER OF WORLDLY VALUES

In **1 John 2:15-17** we are reminded that the more we are wrapped up in this world and its attractions, the harder it will be to establish spiritual goals for our life. If we feed our desires for what the world offers, we starve ourself spiritually. The best way to avoid entanglement with worldly values is to "feed" our spirit by seeking God through prayer and meditation on his Word. Then we will discover his will and his help in redirecting our life.

✲*insights* ABOUT THE IMPORTANCE OF RIGHT BELIEFS

In **1 John 2:18-23** we find that an important secret to recovery is a commitment to right beliefs. As we rely on the Holy Spirit, we are able to recognize the spirit of Antichrist. The critical doctrinal issue for John was that of the deity of Jesus Christ. One cannot genuinely profess belief in God while denying his Son. Full spiritual recovery cannot take place unless we recognize Jesus as the higher Power who can restore us to sane living.

We are told in **1 John 5:4-5** that if we believe in Jesus and live by faith, we are equipped to triumph over the negative influences of our hostile world. For those of us who trust Christ with our life, recovery is not only possible but certain. Neither addictive behavior nor abusive people can dominate where God has promised the power to overcome.

✲*insights* ABOUT ASSURANCE IN SALVATION AND RECOVERY

In **1 John 4:13-15** we are told that assurance comes from believing that Jesus is the Son of God, because that ability to believe is proof that God himself, through the Holy Spirit, is living in us. Confession of Christ is both the evidence and the expression of a genuine faith. It is more than intellectual belief; our confession of Christ must lead us to a confession of sin and a commitment to live for God. We do this as we take responsibility for our life and deal with our past failures and broken relationships.

In **1 John 5:14-15** we are told that another encouraging sign of true recovery is answered prayer. It is gratifying to know that when we pray according to the will of God he has promised to hear and to answer. Our greatest resources for recovery are the Word of God, by which we learn God's will, and prayer, through which we can talk to God and present our needs to him.

SECOND JOHN

THE BIG PICTURE

A. SALUTATION (1:1-3)
B. RECOVERY WITH LOVE AND OBEDIENCE (1:4-6)
C. RECOVERY WITH TRUTH AND VIGILANCE (1:7-11)
D. FINAL GREETINGS (1:12-13)

Recovery is a fragile process. Without vigilance and encouragement from others, we live with the prospect of relapse. In the face of this, we need help from others who have courage and sensitivity toward our situation. Harsh "reprogramming" will not help us, but neither will friends who flatter us with falsely positive words. Diligence together with faithful support is what we need.

This letter is a highly personal one that dealt with the kinds of issues that are addressed in a broader way in 1 John. The tone is warm and pastoral, John even calling himself "the old Elder" (1:1). He wrote this letter with a twofold purpose: to commend and to encourage Cyria, his addressee. She had already demonstrated her faithfulness to God; she did not need to be corrected. But John did not want her to trip over the obstacles ahead that might threaten her continued service to God.

In balancing commendation and encouragement, John proved himself to be a wise counselor and a splendid example to all of us in recovery. We need to recognize each other's past successes, affirming one another. At the same time, we must be willing to point out the hazards ahead when we see them, sharing our hard-won wisdom as a warning for the unwary. Pointing out the obstacles ahead and encouraging one another to be careful are the loving things to do. Thus, this letter underscores the critical importance of carrying the message of recovery to others.

THE BOTTOM LINE

PURPOSE: To commend a faithful woman and to encourage her to continue teaching others about Christ. AUTHOR: The apostle John. AUDIENCE: A woman named Cyria and her children. DATE WRITTEN: Probably written before 1 John, sometime near A.D. 90. SETTING: The woman to whom John wrote was involved in one of the churches that John oversaw. KEY VERSE: "If anyone comes to teach you, and he doesn't believe what Christ taught, don't even invite him into your home. Don't encourage him in any way" (1:10). KEY PEOPLE AND RELATIONSHIPS: John, with Cyria and her children.

RECOVERY THEMES

The Importance of Boundaries: John urged this special lady to be careful about those whom she let into her life. Like David, who in Psalm 101 vowed not to allow deceitful people to stay in his house, she was not to allow false teachers into her home. In fact, she was not to encourage them in any way. Sometimes we think that out of fairness we need to listen to everyone, but there are dangers in such an attitude. We must set limits on whom we listen to if we are to protect our own recovery and growth.

The Challenge to Love: Loving one another is the most basic act of obedience to God. It is also an important ingredient in our recovery. As we recover, we may tend to focus inward or even become self-centered. Remembering to be loving toward others will not only please God, it will also heal our relationships.

CHAPTER 1

Greetings from John

From: John, the old Elder of the church.

To: That dear woman Cyria, one of God's very own, and to her children whom I love so much, as does everyone else in the church. 2 Since the Truth is in our hearts forever, 3 God the Father and Jesus Christ his Son will bless us with great mercy and much peace, and with truth and love.

A Warning about False Teachers

4 How happy I am to find some of your children here and to see that they are living as they should, following the Truth, obeying God's command.

5 And now I want to urgently remind you, dear friends, of the old rule God gave us right from the beginning, that Christians should love one another. 6 If we love God, we will do whatever he tells us to. And he has told us from the very first to love each other.

7 Watch out for the false leaders—and there are many of them around—who don't believe that Jesus Christ came to earth as a human being with a body like ours. Such people are against the truth and against Christ. 8 Beware of being like them and losing the prize that you and I have been working so hard to get. See to it that you win your full reward from the Lord. 9 For if you wander beyond the teaching of Christ, you will leave God behind; while if you are loyal to Christ's teachings, you will have God too. Then you will have both the Father and the Son.

10 If anyone comes to teach you, and he doesn't believe what Christ taught, don't even invite him into your home. Don't encourage him in any way. 11 If you do, you will be a partner with him in his wickedness.

Concluding Remarks

12 Well, I would like to say much more, but I don't want to say it in this letter, for I hope to come to see you soon, and then we can talk over these things together and have a joyous time.

13 Greetings from the children of your sister—another choice child of God.

Sincerely, John

1:4-6 Note the wise approach John used here: first he commended this woman and her fellow believers for their faithfulness; then he exhorted them to act according to Christian love; finally he followed his exhortation with an explanation. There is a pattern here for helping others: first encouragement, next exhortation, and then explanation. Even though we are communicating truths established by the authority of God's Word, sharing the Good News with others must still be done in a way that will communicate to people. An initial commendation will edify and build rapport; the exhortation will communicate the truth or confront a problem; and an explanation will establish the truth and build the relationship.

1:7-9 Clear boundaries for belief and practice are essential for an effective recovery. Many of us have been deceived and pulled into unhealthy relationships, damaging habits, or false religions. People may even have tried to convince us that such things will lead to our recovery. We need to be aware of the subtle lies and distortions of truth used by people who would like to deceive us. The best way to avoid being deceived is to anchor our faith in God's Word and seek his will for us through prayer. Faith in God through Jesus Christ is the only viable means for a successful recovery.

1:10-11 With heresy on the rise, John warned believers not to allow those with suspect doctrinal views to infiltrate the Christian community. He did not want new believers who had made a good beginning in the Christian faith to be led astray. We also need godly people in our life—people like John—who can warn us away from false teachings and dangerous activities. If we don't have relationships that hold us accountable, we need to take steps to develop them. All of us are susceptible to being deceived and led astray. Building healthy relationships with wise and godly people is a necessary part of any successful recovery program.

THIRD JOHN

THE BIG PICTURE

A. SALUTATION (1:1)
B. GAIUS: A CASE FOR COMMENDATION (1:2-8)
C. DIOTREPHES: A CASE FOR CONFRONTATION (1:9-10)
D. DEMETRIUS: A CASE FOR CONGRATULATION (1:11-12)
E. CONCLUDING REMARKS (1:13-15)

We know little about Gaius except that he was generous and hospitable, and that he was highly regarded by the apostle John. Apparently, Gaius took it upon himself to provide free room and board for traveling pastors and missionaries. In a day when most preachers had to travel from town to town with no regular means of support, the service Gaius provided was greatly needed. John wrote this letter to commend him and to warn him to watch out for a self-important spiritual teacher named Diotrephes. John challenged Gaius not to be influenced by Diotrephes' bad example and to warn others about him, too.

Aside from his warning about Diotrephes, John was primarily concerned with encouraging his friend Gaius. This reminds us that the simple act of including others in our life and sharing ourself with them is especially pleasing to God. One of the reasons God places people in our life is so we can support and encourage them. And as we reach out to help others, we will discover that we, too, are blessed and strengthened in a special way.

Hospitality doesn't have to be complicated. It can mean setting an extra place at the table, offering a ride, giving a hug or a handshake, or speaking a word of greeting. We all need a little support sometimes; it is part of the process of recovery to open up and support one another as we face our struggles. How affirming it is to be shown some hospitality or to be invited into someone else's life. Hospitality can be such a simple act, and yet it is a potent way to show love, appreciation, and support, and each of us has some of it to share.

THE BOTTOM LINE

PURPOSE: To commend Gaius for his hospitality and to encourage him in his faithfulness. AUTHOR: The apostle John. AUDIENCE: Gaius, a prominent believer, perhaps from Derbe in Asia Minor. DATE WRITTEN: Around A.D. 90. SETTING: Like 1 and 2 John, 3 John was probably written from Ephesus and circulated among the churches in Asia Minor. KEY VERSE: "Dear friend, don't let this bad example influence you. Follow only what is good. Remember that those who do what is right prove that they are God's children; and those who continue in evil prove that they are far from God" (1:11). KEY PEOPLE AND RELATIONSHIPS: John with Gaius, with Diotrephes, and with Demetrius.

RECOVERY THEMES

Pride Leads to Relapse: Diotrephes refused to humble himself before others and decided that he alone would be the boss. His arrogant attitude disqualified him from the leadership role he coveted. One of the vices we face in recovery is pride. As we experience success in our recovery, it is all too easy to feel as if we have arrived. We begin to think we are superior to others and self-sufficient at last. A word to the wise: pride and self-sufficiency often lead to relapse.

The Importance of Helping Others: In contrast to Diotrephes, Gaius and Demetrius were commended for their service to others. They had generously shared with others, both in hospitality and in their teaching of the truth, without complaint. In their own way they were carrying the message of God's transforming power to people who were still in bondage. John did not take them for granted; instead, he commended them for their service, and today they live on as examples to each of us.

CHAPTER 1

Greetings from John

From: John, the Elder.

To: Dear Gaius, whom I truly love.

2 Dear friend, I am praying that all is well with you and that your body is as healthy as I know your soul is. 3 Some of the brothers traveling by have made me very happy by telling me that your life stays clean and true and that you are living by the standards of the Gospel. 4 I could have no greater joy than to hear such things about my children.

John Commends Gaius's Hospitality

5 Dear friend, you are doing a good work for God in taking care of the traveling teachers and missionaries who are passing through. 6 They have told the church here of your friendship and your loving deeds. I am glad when you send them on their way with a generous gift. 7 For they are traveling for the Lord and take neither food, clothing, shelter, nor money from those who are not Christians, even though they have preached to them. 8 So we ourselves should take care of them in order that we may become partners with them in the Lord's work.

9 I sent a brief letter to the church about this, but proud Diotrephes, who loves to push himself forward as the leader of the Christians there, does not admit my authority over him and refuses to listen to me. 10 When I come I

1:1-4 Recovery is a process that involves our total being. Spiritual problems are often intimately tied to personal difficulties or physical disorders, and resolving these problems may be key to restoring spiritual health. Conversely, neglecting our spiritual needs may contribute to our physical and emotional problems. As we make an honest and fearless inventory of our life, we need to examine how our unhealthy spiritual condition contributes to our other problems.

1:5-8 Here John commended Gaius for the hospitality he had shown to the Christian teachers who periodically passed through town. Hospitality is a special gift that is often overlooked. Some of us may feel like we just aren't good at sharing our faith with others. We may wonder if there is any way we can encourage others in the recovery process. Hospitality may be one way we can show others what God has done in our life. By quietly serving others, we will show them that we have become a new person, and they will wonder how it happened. This may open the opportunity for us to share our faith in God in a more natural way. Opening our homes to others may also give needy people a context in which to relax and explore the truth about themselves.

1:9-10 Confrontation is a necessary part of the recovery process, but it scares many of us. Here John deals with an individual who is hurting people in the Christian community. He warns Gaius and his fellow believers about this man and gives them the tools they need to stand against him. There may be people in our life who are doing everything they can to stop our recovery. We may need to confront them about what they are doing. This may be difficult and can cause some pain, but it is a necessary part of our recovery. We need to be honest with other people and break free of them, especially if they are trying to make us reject God's will for our life. God wants us to make progress in recovery; he will help us deal wisely with the people who stand in our way.

1:11-12 Having a good role model is an important part of an effective recovery. John urged Gaius to follow good examples and to avoid imitating anyone who was doing evil. We need to develop relationships with people who will encourage our recovery. This means that we need to put relationships that lead us back into our dependencies on hold for a while. It also means that we need to take concrete steps toward building relationships with people who model a godly life-style. Since God desires our success in recovery, he will help us as we seek to build healthy relationships in our life.

will tell you some of the things he is doing and what wicked things he is saying about me and what insulting language he is using. He not only refuses to welcome the missionary travelers himself but tells others not to, and when they do he tries to put them out of the church.

11Dear friend, don't let this bad example influence you. Follow only what is good. Remember that those who do what is right prove that they are God's children; and those who continue in evil prove that they are far
from God. 12But everyone, including Truth itself, speaks highly of Demetrius. I myself can say the same for him, and you know I speak the truth.

Concluding Remarks

13I have much to say, but I don't want to write
it, 14for I hope to see you soon and then we
will have much to talk about together. 15So
good-bye for now. Friends here send their love, and please give each of the folks there a special greeting from me.

Sincerely, John

THE BIG PICTURE

A. A CAUTION TO BELIEVERS (1:1-16)
B. A CHALLENGE TO BELIEVERS (1:17-25)

Jude wrote this letter to young believers who had left their old life behind to follow Christ. They had made a spiritual and moral commitment to do what God wanted them to do. But it was not long before false teachers claimed that believers could live however they wanted because God had paid for their sins. Consequently, many new believers were tempted to go back to their destructive life-styles.

Jude called on his readers to stand up for the truth and not to fall back into their old ways as the false teachers counselled. He explained that the false teachers were wrong: it did matter how they lived, and their actions did have consequences. They could not just go back to their old ways without paying a terrible price.

Pressures to fall back into our addictions surround us, but perhaps at no time are they more difficult to resist than when they come from other people. There will always be people who make us feel like giving up on our recovery. Some try to get us to give in just a little. "Just take one drink," they say. Others discourage us by their contempt for us or lack of hope that we will ever change.

It pays to recognize and stand up for God's truth. Our addictions are like hungry lions, devouring whatever they touch. God has gone to great lengths to help us and wants us to succeed even more than we do. When we entrust our life to him and faithfully obey his will for our life, we will experience the freedom from bondage that he wants for us.

THE BOTTOM LINE

PURPOSE: To warn believers of the dangers of false teachings about God. AUTHOR: Jude, the brother of James and half brother of Jesus. AUDIENCE: All believers everywhere. DATE WRITTEN: Probably around A.D. 65–70. SETTING: From the beginning, the church had been threatened by false teachers. Jude wrote this letter to caution all believers not to accept just any teaching about God, but to defend the truth they had received from the apostles. KEY VERSES: "But you, dear friends, must build up your lives ever more strongly upon the foundation of our holy faith, learning to pray in the power and strength of the Holy Spirit. Stay always within the boundaries where God's love can reach and bless you" (1:20-21). KEY PEOPLE AND RELATIONSHIPS: Jude with his audience.

RECOVERY THEMES

The Importance of Action: This letter is a call to action, a call to "stoutly defend the truth" (1:3). Recovery, too, is an active process, not a passive one. Once we are over the crisis that led us into recovery, there is always the temptation to sit back and relax. But actively taking inventory, making amends, and asking God to remove our defects of character are all part of the recovery process. We need to persevere in the process of recovery, taking active steps toward wholeness.

Carrying the Message to Others: Because following Jesus is not a solitary activity, Jude urged his audience to intervene in one another's lives. He told them to be merciful and help each other by gently confronting one another, keeping others from falling prey to destructive beliefs and activities (1:22-23). Recovery is the same way: it always gets us involved with other people. Our recovery cannot stabilize unless we make carrying the message of hope to others an integral part of our life. We will discover that as we share our story of deliverance, we will gain new strength to persevere in the struggle.

CHAPTER 1

Greetings from Jude

From: Jude, a servant of Jesus Christ, and a brother of James.

To: Christians everywhere—beloved of God and chosen by him. [2]May you be given more and more of God's kindness, peace, and love.

The Danger of False Teachers

[3]Dearly loved friends, I had been planning to
write you some thoughts about the salvation God has given us, but now I find I must write of something else instead, urging you to stoutly defend the truth that God gave once for all to his people to keep without change
through the years. [4]I say this because some
godless teachers have wormed their way in among you, saying that after we become Christians we can do just as we like without fear of God's punishment. The fate of such people was written long ago, for they have turned against our only Master and Lord, Jesus Christ.

[5]My answer to them is: Remember this
fact—which you know already—that the Lord saved a whole nation of people out of the land of Egypt and then killed every one of them
who did not trust and obey him. [6]And I re-
mind you of those angels who were once pure and holy but turned to a life of sin. Now God has them chained up in prisons of darkness,
waiting for the judgment day. [7]And don't for-
get the cities of Sodom and Gomorrah and their neighboring towns, all full of lust of every kind, including lust of men for other men. Those cities were destroyed by fire and continue to be a warning to us that there is a hell in which sinners are punished.

[8]Yet these false teachers carelessly go right
on living their evil, immoral lives, degrading their bodies and laughing at those in authority over them, even scoffing at the Glorious
Ones. [9]Yet Michael, one of the mightiest of
the angels, when he was arguing with Satan about Moses' body, did not dare to accuse even Satan, or jeer at him, but simply said,
"The Lord rebuke you." [10]But these men mock
and curse at anything they do not understand, and like animals, they do whatever they feel like, thereby ruining their souls.

[11]Woe upon them! For they follow the ex-
ample of Cain who killed his brother; and like Balaam, they will do anything for money; and

1:3-7 Our problems don't usually attack us head-on; they often come when we least expect them. Sometimes we are completely unaware of the dangers that certain people, ideas, or activities pose to us. Jude warned his readers about people who would try to lead them away from a true faith in Jesus Christ. These false teachers claimed that God's grace set them free to do whatever they wanted. Our society often gives us a similar message, claiming that boundaries to behavior are limiting and destructive. Most of us have discovered firsthand, however, that this teaching leads to painful bondage. We should take Jude's warning seriously. We may need to avoid people and activities that are likely to lead us back into slavery. The only road to freedom is God's program for healthy living.

1:14-16 Jude reminded his readers that the false teachers among them would suffer terrible consequences for their selfish and sinful life-styles. We may be tempted to follow our old friends back into the "pleasures" of our old destructive habits. Jude's warning can help us to turn away from any such temptations. If we take part in destructive activities, we will be enslaved and then destroyed. If we plant seeds of righteousness by following God's will, we will receive God's blessings and help. True freedom can be found only through a vibrant relationship with God.

like Korah, they have disobeyed God and will
die under his curse.
12When these men join you at the love
feasts of the church, they are evil smears
among you, laughing and carrying on, gorg-
ing and stuffing themselves without a
thought for others. They are like clouds blowing over dry land without giving rain, promising much, but producing nothing. They are
like fruit trees without any fruit at picking
time. They are not only dead, but doubly
dead, for they have been pulled out, roots and
all, to be burned.
13All they leave behind them is shame and
disgrace like the dirty foam left along the
beach by the wild waves. They wander around
looking as bright as stars, but ahead of them
is the everlasting gloom and darkness that
God has prepared for them.
14Enoch, who lived seven generations after Adam, knew about these men and said
this about them: "See, the Lord is coming
with millions of his holy ones. 15He will
bring the people of the world before him in
judgment, to receive just punishment and
to prove the terrible things they have done
in rebellion against God, revealing all they
have said against him." 16These men are
constant gripers, never satisfied, doing
whatever evil they feel like; they are loud-
mouthed "show-offs," and when they show
respect for others, it is only to get something from them in return.

A Call to Defend God's Truth

17Dear friends, remember what the apostles of
our Lord Jesus Christ told you, 18that in the
last times there would come these scoffers
whose whole purpose in life is to enjoy themselves in every evil way imaginable. 19They stir
up arguments; they love the evil things of the
world; they do not have the Holy Spirit living
in them.
20But you, dear friends, must build up
your lives ever more strongly upon the
foundation of our holy faith, learning to
pray in the power and strength of the Holy
Spirit.
21Stay always within the boundaries
where God's love can reach and bless you.
Wait patiently for the eternal life that our
Lord Jesus Christ in his mercy is going to
give you. 22Try to help those who argue
against you. Be merciful to those who
doubt. 23Save some by snatching them as
from the very flames of hell itself. And as for
others, help them to find the Lord by being

Accountability

READ JUDE 1:20-23

As we grapple with our addictions we are likely to avoid honest communication with others about our problems. It is important, however, that we return to the relationships that will help us face the truth. Paul spoke of the value of honesty, saying, "Stop lying to each other; tell the truth, for we are parts of each other and when we lie to each other we are hurting ourselves" (Ephesians 4:25). Jude, the brother of Jesus, reminded his readers that they were to deal honestly and directly with those who were doing wrong. He wrote, "Try to help those who argue against you. . . . help them to find the Lord by being kind to them, but be careful that you yourselves aren't pulled along into their sins. Hate every trace of their sin while being merciful to them as sinners" (Jude 1:22-23).

Jesus even laid out specific instructions for dealing with people who have done wrong but are persisting in denial. He said, "If a brother sins against you, go to him privately and confront him with his fault. If he listens and confesses it, you have won back a brother. But if not, then take one or two others with you and go back to him again, proving everything you say by these witnesses. If he still refuses to listen, then take your case to the church, and if the church's verdict favors you, but he won't accept it, then the church should excommunicate him" (Matthew 18:15-17).

Accountability and honesty in our relationships are essential to successful recovery. When we make ourself accountable to others, the caring influence of friends can help keep us on the right track. They can provide us with an objective perspective, helping us to admit the truth. We often become isolated as a result of our shame or the fear that we will be rejected if we ever reveal who we really are. Admitting our wrongs to a trustworthy person helps break down the isolation. ***Turn to page 1453, Revelation 3.***

kind to them, but be careful that you yourselves aren't pulled along into their sins. Hate every trace of their sin while being merciful to them as sinners.

A Closing Doxology

24,25And now—all glory to him who alone is God, who saves us through Jesus Christ our Lord; yes, splendor and majesty, all power and authority are his from the beginning; his they are and his they evermore shall be. And he is able to keep you from slipping and falling away, and to bring you, sinless and perfect, into his glorious presence with mighty shouts of everlasting joy. Amen.

Jude

1:17-23 God's Word is reliable and true. It warns us about people who might try to hinder our spiritual growth. When we learn to expect to meet such people, we can prepare to stand up against the temptations they put before us. By learning to recognize our weaknesses and walk humbly, following the Holy Spirit's guidance, we will be able to shun the things that tear us and others down. When we seek to encourage others in recovery, the story we tell must be clear and consistent with our way of life. We can share God's message of hope by showing others the kind of selfless love that God has already shown to us. We cannot live this kind of life under our own power; we can do it only by receiving the power God offers through his Holy Spirit.

REVELATION

THE BIG PICTURE

A. JOHN'S PAIN AND GOD'S GLORY (1:1-20)
B. THE NEED FOR RECOVERY AMONG THE CHURCHES (2:1–3:22)
C. GOD'S GLORIOUS POWER—HOPE FOR RECOVERY (4:1–5:14)
D. GOD'S WRATH TOWARD UNBELIEF AND DENIAL (6:1–16:21)
E. BABYLON'S GRAND APPEARANCE AND FIERCE JUDGMENT (17:1–18:24)
F. CHRIST'S VICTORY, RULE, AND FINAL JUDGMENT (19:1–20:15)
G. THE NEW HEAVENS AND NEW EARTH (21:1–22:21)

From beginning to end, the book of Revelation is about struggle. In its opening chapters, John dictated seven letters from the resurrected Christ to seven churches. Each church had its own set of struggles, but some had deeper problems than others. In each letter, Jesus urged his people to cling to him and do what they knew to be right. The ones who listened he called overcomers.

The rest of the book contains the story of another dramatic struggle: God's plan to rid the world of sin and its destructive consequences. We are told of a time when Jesus will return in glory to conquer Satan and restore his broken world, vindicating God's people and judging the wicked. All people will get their due when Christ returns. Believers will receive eternal joy; unbelievers, unending separation from God. In the end, God will rebuild what has been broken by sin: he will introduce a new heaven and a new earth.

The book of Revelation ends with Christ as the victor. All that he said will come true; all that he taught will be proven right; all who followed him will be vindicated; and all who rejected him will be judged. God will have his way. And he wants nothing more than to have us stand beside him as a victor! What we face in recovery is a struggle; God knows that. Through this book he urges us not to give up, but to believe in him and to overcome. As he renews our broken world, he will make our broken life new and perfect as well.

THE BOTTOM LINE

PURPOSE: To give hope to believers and warn them not to compromise their loyalty to God. AUTHOR: The apostle John. AUDIENCE: Seven churches in Asia Minor. DATE WRITTEN: Probably about A.D. 95, during the Roman emperor Domitian's persecution of Christians. SETTING: John, who was in exile on the island of Patmos, wrote to the seven churches to urge them to devote themselves to Christ. KEY VERSE: "Look! I have been standing at the door, and I am constantly knocking. If anyone hears me calling him and opens the door, I will come in and fellowship with him and he with me" (3:20). KEY PLACES: Patmos, seven cities in Asia Minor, Babylon, and the New Jerusalem. KEY PEOPLE: John, the risen Christ, and members of the churches of Asia Minor.

RECOVERY THEMES

God Is Over All: God is sovereign. He is greater than any other power in the universe—including our dependencies. There is nothing that can compare to him. When we look at the abuse we may have suffered as a child or at the pain we have caused someone else, we may feel powerless to change things or make amends. But John wrote this book to assure us that though evil may seem to win today's battles, God is all-powerful and will assert his power for his people. In the end, all things will be made new in Christ. As we submit our life to God, he will begin that process of renewal in our life right away.

God Is the Source of Our Hope: We may feel helpless and be about to give up all hope, but the book of Revelation reveals to us the ultimate source of hope—Jesus Christ. He is coming again and will deal with the problems of our sin-tattered world, restoring what is broken and dealing with the injustices around us. Life is never hopeless, regardless of what has happened to us or what we have done. We can focus on God's love, grace, and forgiveness. He has made our restoration possible in Christ, and he will return to complete his task of cosmic renewal. If we are looking to Christ, we can hang on to our hope despite the difficult circumstances we may face.

The Pain of Consequences: There is something in every one of us that cries out for justice. When evil and injustice prosper, we may begin to feel angry and think that people ultimately get away with their selfish and wicked deeds. But in reality God will judge all wicked actions. Those who openly defy him will face the awful consequences in the end. Those who turn to him for forgiveness need not fear the future day of judgment. Judgment is an awful thing, but the pain of sin's consequences can motivate us to turn our life over to God and obediently follow his plan.

Justice Belongs to God: Being in recovery does not release us from our sense of justice. As we deal with the wrongs we have done, we may feel that others are not dealing with theirs and that we have a legitimate grudge to harbor. While these feelings are natural, they also endanger our recovery. The book of Revelation makes it clear that justice belongs to God; he alone has the right to avenge the wrongs of others. What's more, he alone has the power to change their lives. Anger and bitterness make recovery more difficult than it already is. Part of giving our life and our will over to God is releasing the bitterness we feel toward others.

CHAPTER 1

A Revelation of Jesus Christ

This book unveils some of the future activities soon to occur in the life of Jesus Christ. God permitted him to reveal these things to his servant John in a vision; and then an angel was sent from heaven to explain the vision's meaning. [2]John wrote it all down—the words of God and Jesus Christ and everything he heard and saw.

[3]If you read this prophecy aloud to the church, you will receive a special blessing from the Lord. Those who listen to it being read and do what it says will also be blessed. For the time is near when these things will all come true.

Greetings from John

[4]*From:* John

To: The seven churches in Turkey.

Dear Friends:

May you have grace and peace from God who is, and was, and is to come; and from the seven-fold Spirit before his throne; [5]and from

---

1:1-2 The book of Revelation tells us about things that will happen in the future. It looks forward to the time of Christ's return, when our new life in Christ will be perfected. It also tells about the hard battle God will fight to restore our world from the destructive consequences of sin. Many of the symbols of this book are difficult to interpret, but one message comes through loud and clear: no matter how bad things are right now, God has a solution! Jesus Christ will return to re-create our broken and polluted world. He will give us a new body and a healed heart. God has already started his healing in our life through a relationship with Christ; he will complete this task when he returns to rule.

1:4-6 The powerful work of Jesus Christ is the only valid foundation for recovery. Christ shed his redemptive blood on the cross in order to free us from our bondage to sin, past abuse, destructive habits, compulsions, and addictions. God loved us enough to send his Son to die on our behalf. But then Jesus rose from the dead, conquering death forever! Through him, we also can rise to new life. No matter who we are or what we have done, in Christ, God has a solution for our problems. Even death has been overcome! Through Christ, we have been made citizens of his eternal Kingdom (see Philippians 3:20), and we have an eternity of healthy living to look forward to.

Jesus Christ who faithfully reveals all truth to us. He was the first to rise from death, to die no more. He is far greater than any king in all the earth. All praise to him who always loves us and who set us free from our sins by pouring out his lifeblood for us. 6He has gathered us into his Kingdom and made us priests of God his Father. Give to him everlasting glory! He rules forever! Amen!

7See! He is arriving, surrounded by clouds; and every eye shall see him—yes, and those who pierced him. And the nations will weep in sorrow and in terror when he comes. Yes! Amen! Let it be so!

8"I am the A and the Z, the Beginning and the Ending of all things," says God, who is the Lord, the All Powerful One who is, and was, and is coming again!

John's Vision of Christ

9It is I, your brother John, a fellow sufferer for the Lord's sake, who am writing this letter to you. I, too, have shared the patience Jesus gives, and we shall share his Kingdom!

I was on the island of Patmos, exiled there for preaching the Word of God and for telling what I knew about Jesus Christ. 10It was the Lord's Day and I was worshiping, when suddenly I heard a loud voice behind me, a voice that sounded like a trumpet blast, 11saying, "I am A and Z, the First and Last!" And then I heard him say, "Write down everything you see, and send your letter to the seven churches in Turkey: to the church in Ephesus, the one in Smyrna, and those in Pergamos, Thyatira, Sardis, Philadelphia, and Laodicea."

12When I turned to see who was speaking, there behind me were seven candlesticks of gold. 13And standing among them was one who looked like Jesus, who called himself the Son of Man, wearing a long robe circled with a golden band across his chest. 14His hair was white as wool or snow, and his eyes penetrated like flames of fire. 15His feet gleamed like burnished bronze, and his voice thundered like the waves against the shore. 16He held seven stars in his right hand and a sharp, double-bladed sword in his mouth, and his face shone like the power of the sun in unclouded brilliance.

17,18When I saw him, I fell at his feet as dead; but he laid his right hand on me and said, "Don't be afraid! Though I am the First and Last, the Living One who died, who is now alive forevermore, who has the keys of hell and death—don't be afraid! 19Write down what you have just seen and what will soon be shown to you. 20This is the meaning of the seven stars you saw in my right hand and the seven golden candlesticks: The seven stars are the leaders of the seven churches, and the seven candlesticks are the churches themselves.

CHAPTER 2

The Loveless Church

"Write a letter to the leader of the church at Ephesus and tell him this:

"I write to inform you of a message from him who walks among the churches and holds their leaders in his right hand.

"He says to you: 2I know how many good things you are doing. I have watched your hard work and your patience; I know you

1:7-8 The future coming of Jesus Christ will be a desperately painful moment for those who refuse to believe and follow him. The terrifying consequences of their denial will be eternal judgment (see 20:11-15). On the other hand, if we pursue recovery by faith in Christ, we can rejoice in the new life his return will bring. God is "the Beginning and the Ending of all things." We can have hope because God is in control of our past, present, and future.

1:9-11 John had suffered a great deal for Christ and had persevered through it all. All the pain and exile had not embittered him toward God; in fact, the apostle still worshiped God faithfully. We are told he was worshiping when he received the visions recorded in this book. It is easy to become discouraged as we work our program. Some people reject us because we are trying to change, and others reject us for having a problem. We know what it's like to be looked down upon. John's example provides encouragement to persevere despite the difficulties we face. If we give up now, we face sure disaster in the future. If we stick with our recovery, God will help us to build a new life.

2:1-7 Christ addressed the church in Ephesus first, since it was the largest congregation. It was probably responsible for planting the other churches (see Acts 19:10). Initially, the apostle commended the Ephesian believers for their perseverance through hardship. John began his communication on a positive note, then he turned to confront the more painful realities. He moved beyond his "encouraging word" to challenge his readers to repent and rekindle their love, which had waned. Confrontations are best made in the context of love. We need to begin our conversations building others up and showing that we care. After laying the groundwork we will be better able to communicate the more painful message.

don't tolerate sin among your members, and
you have carefully examined the claims of
those who say they are apostles but aren't.
You have found out how they lie. 3You have
patiently suffered for me without quitting.
4"Yet there is one thing wrong; you don't
love me as at first! 5Think about those times
of your first love (how different now!) and
turn back to me again and work as you did
before; or else I will come and remove your
candlestick from its place among the
churches.
6"But there is this about you that is good:
You hate the deeds of the licentious
Nicolaitans, just as I do.
7"Let this message sink into the ears of
anyone who listens to what the Spirit is saying to the churches: To everyone who is victorious, I will give fruit from the Tree of Life
in the Paradise of God.

The Persecuted Church

8*"To the leader of the church in Smyrna write this
letter:*
"This message is from him who is the First
and Last, who was dead and then came back
to life.
9"I know how much you suffer for the Lord,
and I know all about your poverty (but you
have heavenly riches!). I know the slander of
those opposing you, who say that they are
Jews—the children of God—but they aren't,
for they support the cause of Satan. 10Stop
being afraid of what you are about to suffer—
for the devil will soon throw some of you into
prison to test you. You will be persecuted for
'ten days.' Remain faithful even when facing
death and I will give you the crown of life—an
unending, glorious future. 11Let everyone
who can hear listen to what the Spirit is saying to the churches: He who is victorious shall
not be hurt by the Second Death.

The Lenient Church

12*"Write this letter to the leader of the church in
Pergamos:*
"This message is from him who wields the
sharp and double-bladed sword. 13I am fully
aware that you live in the city where Satan's
throne is, at the center of satanic worship;
and yet you have remained loyal to me and
refused to deny me even when Antipas, my
faithful witness, was martyred among you by
Satan's devotees.
14"And yet I have a few things against you.
You tolerate some among you who do as
Balaam did when he taught Balak how to ruin
the people of Israel by involving them in
sexual sin and encouraging them to go to idol
feasts. 15Yes, you have some of these very same
followers of Balaam among you!
16"Change your mind and attitude, or else I
will come to you suddenly and fight against
them with the sword of my mouth.
17"Let everyone who can hear, listen to
what the Spirit is saying to the churches:
Everyone who is victorious shall eat of the
hidden manna, the secret nourishment from
heaven; and I will give to each a white stone,
and on the stone will be engraved a new name
that no one else knows except the one receiving it.

2:8-11 The church in Smyrna was the closest to Ephesus of the other six, and it was experiencing similar hardships. This small Christian community was suffering from unrelenting oppression by Satan and his evil spiritual forces. John's vision reminded the believers that their perseverance through dangerous times would be rewarded by God with new life in Jesus Christ. We also are called to persevere through the tough times. As we entrust our life to God and follow his will, he will slowly transform our life. At Christ's return, we will receive a new body and a cleansed heart—a completely new life!
2:12-17 The church in Pergamos had also been intensely loyal to Jesus Christ through a satanic onslaught. Yet, there were some in the church who had fallen prey to sexual misconduct. Such relational and spiritual dysfunctions threatened to undermine, or at least neutralize, the testimony of this Christian community. Sometimes great victories in recovery can be neutralized by small mistakes. We need to be consistent in our walk with God, making sure that all areas of our life are yielded to him. Ignoring even the smallest sin or bad habit might ultimately lead to our undoing.
2:18-29 The church in Thyatira was commended for its acts of faith, love, and patience, and it was encouraged to persevere in doing them. However, there was a serious spiritual cancer growing in their midst: a self-styled prophetess known as Jezebel was encouraging a totally profligate lifestyle. God's harsh punishment of this woman shows us how much he wanted to protect his people from her destructive influence. This gives us some idea of how dangerous it is to have relationships with people who might try to lead us astray. We need to choose carefully the people with whom we spend time. A dysfunctional relationship may lead us away from God and quickly destroy all our progress in recovery.

The Compromising Church
18"*Write this letter to the leader of the church in*
Thyatira:
"This is a message from the Son of God,
whose eyes penetrate like flames of fire,
whose feet are like glowing brass.
19"I am aware of all your good deeds—your
kindness to the poor, your gifts and service to
them; also I know your love and faith and
patience, and I can see your constant improvement in all these things.
20"Yet I have this against you: You are permitting that woman Jezebel, who calls herself
a prophetess, to teach my servants that sex sin
is not a serious matter; she urges them to
practice immorality and to eat meat that has
been sacrificed to idols. 21I gave her time to
change her mind and attitude, but she refused. 22Pay attention now to what I am saying: I will lay her upon a sickbed of intense
affliction, along with all her immoral followers, unless they turn again to me, repenting of
their sin with her; 23and I will strike her children dead. And all the churches shall know
that I am he who searches deep within men's
hearts, and minds; I will give to each of you
whatever you deserve.
24,25"As for the rest of you in Thyatira who
have not followed this false teaching ('deeper
truths,' as they call them—depths of Satan,
really), I will ask nothing further of you; only
hold tightly to what you have until I come.
26"To everyone who overcomes—who to
the very end keeps on doing things that
please me—I will give power over the nations.
27You will rule them with a rod of iron just as
my Father gave me the authority to rule them;
they will be shattered like a pot of clay that is
broken into tiny pieces. 28And I will give you
the Morning Star!
29"Let all who can hear listen to what the
Spirit says to the churches.

CHAPTER 3
The Lifeless Church
"*To the leader of the church in Sardis write this*
letter:
"This message is sent to you by the one
who has the seven-fold Spirit of God and the
seven stars.
"I know your reputation as a live and active
church, but you are dead. 2Now wake up!
Strengthen what little remains—for even
what is left is at the point of death. Your deeds
are far from right in the sight of God. 3Go back
to what you heard and believed at first; hold
to it firmly and turn to me again. Unless you

Love

READ REVELATION 3:14-22

We may feel like love just doesn't seem to work for us. We may wonder if we are doing something wrong. Perhaps we have problems loving because we are disconnected from the source of true love.

The apostle John wrote, "Dear friends, let us practice loving each other, for love comes from God. . . . But if a person isn't loving and kind, it shows that he doesn't know God—for God is love" (1 John 4:7-8).

Jesus said, "I am giving a new commandment to you now—love each other just as much as I love you" (John 13:34). Trying to love without first receiving God's love is like trying to water something with a hose that's disconnected from the faucet. When we receive God's unconditional love for us, we can begin to love ourself. We are then told to love others as we love ourself and as Jesus has loved us. There is a boundless reservoir of love available to us; but without receiving the love of God in Christ we will quickly run dry.

Jesus is waiting for us to open up and receive his love. He said, "Look! . . . I am constantly knocking. If anyone hears me calling him and opens the door, I will come in and fellowship with him and he with me" (Revelation 3:20). Love is waiting. We receive it when we open up to the love God offers us.
Turn to page 1471, Revelation 22.

do, I will come suddenly upon you, unexpected as a thief, and punish you.

4"Yet even there in Sardis some haven't soiled their garments with the world's filth; they shall walk with me in white, for they are worthy. 5Everyone who conquers will be clothed in white, and I will not erase his name from the Book of Life, but I will announce before my Father and his angels that he is mine.

6"Let all who can hear listen to what the Spirit is saying to the churches.

The Obedient Church

7"*Write this letter to the leader of the church in Philadelphia.*

"This message is sent to you by the one who is holy and true and has the key of David to open what no one can shut and to shut what no one can open.

8"I know you well; you aren't strong, but you have tried to obey and have not denied my Name. Therefore I have opened a door to you that no one can shut.

9"Note this: I will force those supporting the causes of Satan while claiming to be mine (but they aren't—they are lying) to fall at your feet and acknowledge that you are the ones I love.

10"Because you have patiently obeyed me despite the persecution, therefore I will protect you from the time of Great Tribulation and temptation, which will come upon the world to test everyone alive. 11Look, I am coming soon! Hold tightly to the little strength you have—so that no one will take away your crown.

12"As for the one who conquers, I will make him a pillar in the temple of my God; he will be secure and will go out no more; and I will write my God's Name on him, and he will be a citizen in the city of my God—the New Jerusalem, coming down from heaven from my God; and he will have my new Name inscribed upon him.

13"Let all who can hear listen to what the Spirit is saying to the churches.

The Lukewarm Church

14"*Write this letter to the leader of the church in Laodicea:*

"This message is from the one who stands firm, the faithful and true Witness [of all that is or was or evermore shall be], the primeval source of God's creation:

15"I know you well—you are neither hot nor cold; I wish you were one or the other! 16But since you are merely lukewarm, I will spit you out of my mouth!

17"You say, 'I am rich, with everything I want; I don't need a thing!' And you don't realize that spiritually you are wretched and miserable and poor and blind and naked.

18"My advice to you is to buy pure gold from me, gold purified by fire—only then will you truly be rich. And to purchase from me white garments, clean and pure, so you won't be naked and ashamed; and to get medicine from me to heal your eyes and give you back your sight. 19I continually discipline and pun-

---

3:1-6 The believers in Sardis were, for the most part, just going through the motions spiritually. They were warned that if they didn't make some immediate changes, they would suffer painful consequences. Fortunately, there were some believers in Sardis who stood firm in their faith, and they would be rewarded accordingly. It is possible, with God's help, to stand firm even when everyone around us is falling away. We don't have to follow the crowd; we can follow God instead. As we do, he will bless us and write our name in the Book of Life. We don't have to be victims of our environment or society at large.

3:7-13 The church in Philadelphia was not strong, but it had remained obedient to God and stood firm against satanic oppression. As a result, Christ promised the church protection from the greatest time of tribulation that would ever come upon the whole world. He encouraged them to persevere, promising that they would live forever with Christ in his New Jerusalem. This promise has been greatly delayed, but that doesn't make it any less secure (see 21:1–22:21). We have this same hope if we entrust our life to God through faith in Jesus Christ. Though the years of recovery can sometimes seem long, our hope in God's eternal deliverance is just as certain.

3:19-21 The believers in Laodicea were engaged in full-blown denial. Though they portrayed themselves as being self-sustaining and having no needs, Christ saw their situation quite differently. To him they were spiritually blind and destitute. But, worst of all, they were spiritually indifferent—lukewarm. Sometimes after making progress in recovery we grow indifferent to the new life we have found. We forget how desperate we were before entering recovery; we also forget that God is the one who set us free. We begin to long for things that will lead us back into bondage. We can avoid that long slide back toward destruction by taking an honest inventory and getting back on track.

ish everyone I love; so I must punish you unless you turn from your indifference and become enthusiastic about the things of God. 20“Look! I have been standing at the door, and I am constantly knocking. If anyone hears me calling him and opens the door, I will come in and fellowship with him and he with me. 21I will let everyone who conquers sit beside me on my throne, just as I took my place with my Father on his throne when I had conquered. 22Let those who can hear listen to what the Spirit is saying to the churches.”

CHAPTER 4

God’s Glorious Throne

Then as I looked, I saw a door standing open in heaven, and the same voice I had heard before, which sounded like a mighty trumpet blast, spoke to me and said, “Come up here and I will show you what must happen in the future!”

2And instantly I was in spirit there in heaven and saw—oh, the glory of it!—a throne and someone sitting on it! 3Great bursts of light flashed forth from him as from a glittering diamond or from a shining ruby, and a rainbow glowing like an emerald encircled his throne. 4Twenty-four smaller thrones surrounded his, with twenty-four Elders sitting on them; all were clothed in white, with golden crowns upon their heads. 5Lightning and thunder issued from the throne, and there were voices in the thunder. Directly in front of his throne were seven lighted lamps representing the seven-fold Spirit of God. 6Spread out before it was a shiny crystal sea. Four Living Beings, dotted front and back with eyes, stood at the throne’s four sides. 7The first of these Living Beings was in the form of a lion; the second looked like an ox; the third had the face of a man; and the fourth, the form of an eagle, with wings spread out as though in flight. 8Each of these Living Beings had six wings, and the central sections of their wings were covered with eyes. Day after day and night after night they kept on saying, “Holy, holy, holy, Lord God Almighty—the one who was, and is, and is to come.”

9And when the Living Beings gave glory and honor and thanks to the one sitting on the throne, who lives forever and ever, 10the twenty-four Elders fell down before him and worshiped him, the Eternal Living One, and cast their crowns before the throne, singing, 11“O Lord, you are worthy to receive the glory and the honor and the power, for you have created all things. They were created and called into being by your act of will.”

CHAPTER 5

The Scroll and the Lamb

And I saw a scroll in the right hand of the one who was sitting on the throne, a scroll with writing on the inside and on the back, and sealed with seven seals. 2A mighty angel with a loud voice was shouting out this question: “Who is worthy to break the seals on this scroll and to unroll it?” 3But no one in all heaven or earth or from among the dead was permitted to open and read it.

4Then I wept with disappointment because

4:1-3 The apostle John was allowed to view this spectacular scene in God’s heavenly throne room (4:1–5:14), but he did it as a prisoner on the island of Patmos. We also may be living in bondage, feeling hopelessly entrapped and distant from any kind of help or deliverance. But we, like John, can draw close to God even when the world around us is dark and foreboding. John’s vision of heaven gave him the hope he needed to face many lonely days ahead. And the record the apostle left us can give us hope during hard times, too. Even when we are alone and helpless, God is still with us. We can draw near to him, even when we are shunned by the people close to us. God’s grace and power are never limited by the circumstances we face.

4:4-8 Two principles from this passage can bring encouragement as we work toward recovery: First, the fact that the twenty-four elders represent the people of God shows that believers are honored significantly by God in heaven. Second, the diversity in appearance of the four living creatures implies that God wants all of us to be unique, utilizing our special characteristics for his glory. God values us because he created us; each of us has unique gifts to be used in his service and for his glory. These truths can encourage us as we deal with the problems and pressures of the recovery process.

4:8-11 God is worthy of our continual praise. Even the great spiritual beings in heaven make praising God their primary occupation. As we make God a daily focus in our life, choosing to offer him our gratitude and praise, we will discover a new freedom from our problems and dependencies. Our painful circumstances will fade away in the light of his glorious love and power. God is greater and more powerful than anything we have to face. We can entrust our life to him, take steps to follow his will, and then praise him for the amazing transformation that will happen in our life.

no one anywhere was worthy; no one could
tell us what it said.
5But one of the twenty-four Elders said to
me, "Stop crying, for look! The Lion of the
tribe of Judah, the Root of David, has conquered, and proved himself worthy to open
the scroll and to break its seven seals."
6I looked and saw a Lamb standing there
before the twenty-four Elders, in front of the
throne and the Living Beings, and on the
Lamb were wounds that once had caused his
death. He had seven horns and seven eyes,
which represent the seven-fold Spirit of God,
sent out into every part of the world. 7He
stepped forward and took the scroll from the
right hand of the one sitting upon the throne.
8And as he took the scroll, the twenty-four
Elders fell down before the Lamb, each with a
harp and golden vials filled with incense—the
prayers of God's people!
9They were singing him a new song with
these words: "You are worthy to take the scroll
and break its seals and open it; for you were
slain, and your blood has bought people from
every nation as gifts for God. 10And you have
gathered them into a kingdom and made
them priests of our God; they shall reign upon
the earth."
11Then in my vision I heard the singing of
millions of angels surrounding the throne
and the Living Beings and the Elders: 12"The
Lamb is worthy" (loudly they sang it!) "—the
Lamb who was slain. He is worthy to receive
the power, and the riches, and the wisdom,
and the strength, and the honor, and the
glory, and the blessing."
13And then I heard everyone in heaven and
earth, and from the dead beneath the earth
and in the sea, exclaiming, "The blessing and
the honor and the glory and the power belong to the one sitting on the throne, and to
the Lamb forever and ever." 14And the four
Living Beings kept saying, "Amen!" And the
twenty-four Elders fell down and worshiped
him.

CHAPTER 6
Breaking the Seven Seals
As I watched, the Lamb broke the first seal
and began to unroll the scroll. Then one of
the four Living Beings, with a voice that
sounded like thunder, said, "Come!"
2I looked, and there in front of me was a

5:1-7 Many of us know the tremendous pain of not being able to live up to our perfectionistic tendencies. Expecting absolute perfection in this life is unrealistic. In heaven, however, perfection will be the norm. Even there, though, initially there was no one worthy to open the scroll of revelation and judgment. The Lamb—Jesus Christ—is the only one worthy to open the scroll. He is perfect and has conquered sin and death through his death and resurrection. Because of him, we are able to overcome the sins and dependencies in our life. He will be called upon to open the scroll, beginning the process of recovery for our broken and sinful world. If we entrust our life to him, he will begin the same process of restoration in our life. Someday, by God's grace and power, even we will be made perfect.

5:9-10 By shedding his blood on the cross, Jesus Christ, the Lamb, made salvation possible for all of us (see Matthew 28:19; Acts 1:8). But God does far more than just deliver us from our destructive sins and dependencies. He promises to make us a part of his team for restoring and maintaining his world. We will be members of a kingdom of priests to our God. As soon as we entrust our life to God and seek to follow his will, we can begin our priestly duties. This involves sharing our story of deliverance and calling others to entrust their lives to God's care. We can play an important role in the restoration of people's lives by leading them to faith in Jesus Christ—the only Power available for true recovery.

5:11-14 In these final verses of John's description of the heavenly throne room, praise for the divine Lamb spills over from heaven to the rest of the created realm. No matter how much unbelief and denial apparently dominate the earthly scene today, there will come a time when all will honor God. Such praise will necessarily include the admission of guilt, responsibility, and unbelieving denial by many (see Philippians 2:9-11). We don't have to wait until Christ returns to acknowledge his lordship in our life. We can do it today and begin to enjoy the immediate benefits of a vital relationship with God through Jesus Christ.

6:1-8 Jesus Christ, the Lamb, begins the process of opening the scroll (see 5:1). This sets in motion the events leading to God's victory over sin and death. War, famine, and disease will be rampant during the period of the first four seals. Notice that the first steps toward God's cosmic restoration lead through painful times. Millions of people will die as God begins to deal with the sinful dysfunctions that dominate our world. God often leads us through a period of pain as we suffer the consequences for our behavior. But God does this for our ultimate good. Even though he allows us to suffer for a time, he has plans for our restoration and recovery. Sometimes the trials brought on by our dependencies are the only way God can teach us how helpless we are and how much we need him.

white horse. Its rider carried a bow, and a
crown was placed upon his head; he rode out
to conquer in many battles and win the war.
3Then he unrolled the scroll to the second
seal and broke it open, too. And I heard the
second Living Being say, "Come!"
4This time a red horse rode out. Its rider was
given a long sword and the authority to banish peace and bring anarchy to the earth; war
and killing broke out everywhere.
5When he had broken the third seal, I heard
the third Living Being say, "Come!" And I saw
a black horse, with its rider holding a pair of
balances in his hand. 6And a voice from
among the four Living Beings said, "A loaf of
bread for $20, or three pounds of barley flour,
but there is no olive oil or wine."
7And when the fourth seal was broken, I
heard the fourth Living Being say, "Come!"
8And now I saw a pale horse, and its rider's
name was Death. And there followed after
him another horse whose rider's name was
Hell. They were given control of one-fourth of
the earth, to kill with war and famine and disease and wild animals.
9And when he broke open the fifth seal, I
saw an altar, and underneath it all the souls of
those who had been martyred for preaching
the Word of God and for being faithful in
their witnessing. 10They called loudly to the
Lord and said, "O Sovereign Lord, holy and
true, how long will it be before you judge the
people of the earth for what they've done to
us? When will you avenge our blood against
those living on the earth?" 11White robes were
given to each of them, and they were told to
rest a little longer until their other brothers,
fellow servants of Jesus, had been martyred
on the earth and joined them.
12I watched as he broke the sixth seal, and
there was a vast earthquake; and the sun became dark like black cloth, and the moon was
blood-red. 13Then the stars of heaven appeared to be falling to earth—like green fruit
from fig trees buffeted by mighty winds.
14And the starry heavens disappeared as
though rolled up like a scroll and taken away;
and every mountain and island shook and
shifted. 15The kings of the earth, and world
leaders, and rich men, and high-ranking military officers, and all men great and small,
slave and free, hid themselves in the caves
and rocks of the mountains, 16and cried to the
mountains to crush them. "Fall on us," they
pleaded, "and hide us from the face of the one
sitting on the throne, and from the anger of
the Lamb, 17because the great day of their
anger has come, and who can survive it?"

CHAPTER 7

The 144,000 Marked by God

Then I saw four angels standing at the four
corners of the earth, holding back the four
winds from blowing so that not a leaf rustled
in the trees, and the ocean became as smooth
as glass. 2And I saw another angel coming
from the east, carrying the Great Seal of the
Living God. And he shouted out to those four
angels who had been given power to injure
earth and sea, 3"Wait! Don't do anything

6:9-11 The opening of the fifth seal reveals those who have died in God's service. They are waiting for God to avenge their unjust deaths. God tells them that they will have to wait because still other martyrs will join their number. This passage contains an important principle for us to follow. Many of us have suffered abuse in the past. Perhaps the abuse we suffered is at the root of our present problems and dependencies. We may desire to take revenge against people who have wronged us. Maybe we spend our time blaming others for our addictions. We, like the martyrs of Revelation, need to let God avenge the wrongs done to us. When we release our bitterness and forgive our abusers, we will make progress in recovery. Ultimately we are responsible for our addictions, whatever other factors may be involved.

6:12-17 The opening of the sixth seal is followed by a huge earthquake and amazing phenomena in the sky. Leaders and military commanders will want to die, mistakenly thinking they can escape God's terrible judgment in that way. Sadly, their hearts are so hard that though they recognize God, they will not repent and turn to him in faith (see 9:20-21). Their continued denial will lead to their eventual destruction. Continuing in denial about our destructive dependencies and compulsions will lead to similar consequences. If we refuse to recognize God's rule in our life, we will inevitably head toward deeper bondage and ultimate destruction. God wants to give us a meaningful and joyful life, but to receive it we need to accept his program for healthy living.

7:1-3 As difficult as things will be during the period of the seals, God's protection will also be present for those who belong to him. They will be "sealed" with God's sign of ownership and protection. Perhaps this seal is similar to the seal of the Holy Spirit now present in the lives of all who believe in Jesus Christ (see Ephesians 1:13-14; 4:30). In each case the seal signifies an eternal relationship with God. We can begin an eternal relationship with God right now if we accept God's loving forgiveness through Jesus Christ and submit our life to his good plan.

yet—hurt neither earth nor sea nor trees—until we have placed the Seal of God upon the
foreheads of his servants."
4-8How many were given this mark? I heard
the number—it was 144,000; out of all twelve
tribes of Israel, as listed here:

Judah	12,000	Simeon	12,000
Reuben	12,000	Levi	12,000
Gad	12,000	Issachar	12,000
Asher	12,000	Zebulun	12,000
Naphtali	12,000	Joseph	12,000
Manasseh	12,000	Benjamin	12,000

The Great Crowd

9After this I saw a vast crowd, too great to
count, from all nations and provinces and
languages, standing in front of the throne and
before the Lamb, clothed in white, with palm
branches in their hands. 10And they were
shouting with a mighty shout, "Salvation
comes from our God upon the throne, and
from the Lamb."
11And now all the angels were crowding
around the throne and around the Elders and
the four Living Beings, and falling face down
before the throne and worshiping God.
12"Amen!" they said. "Blessing, and glory, and
wisdom, and thanksgiving, and honor, and
power, and might, be to our God forever and
forever. Amen!"
13Then one of the twenty-four Elders asked
me, "Do you know who these are, who are
clothed in white, and where they come
from?"
14"No, sir," I replied. "Please tell me."
"These are the ones coming out of the
Great Tribulation," he said; "they washed
their robes and whitened them by the blood
of the Lamb. 15That is why they are here
before the throne of God, serving him day
and night in his temple. The one sitting on
the throne will shelter them; 16they will never
be hungry again, nor thirsty, and they will be
fully protected from the scorching noontime
heat. 17For the Lamb standing in front of the
throne will feed them and be their Shepherd
and lead them to the springs of the Water of
Life. And God will wipe their tears away."

CHAPTER 8

The Seventh Seal

When the Lamb had broken the seventh seal,
there was silence throughout all heaven for
what seemed like half an hour. 2And I saw the
seven angels that stand before God, and they
were given seven trumpets.
3Then another angel with a golden censer
came and stood at the altar; and a great quantity of incense was given to him to mix with
the prayers of God's people, to offer upon the
golden altar before the throne. 4And the perfume of the incense mixed with prayers ascended up to God from the altar where the
angel had poured them out.
5Then the angel filled the censer with fire
from the altar and threw it down upon the
earth; and thunder crashed and rumbled,
lightning flashed, and there was a terrible
earthquake.

The Seven Trumpets

6Then the seven angels with the seven trumpets prepared to blow their mighty blasts.
7The first angel blew his trumpet, and hail

7:9-14 This vast multitude from all races and nations is the harvest Christ envisioned from his great commission (see Matthew 28:19). They are truly thankful and worshipful toward God, appreciating greatly the salvation and recovery he has promised. The white garments worn by this innumerable crowd speak not only of the purity of their life-style, but also of their redemption through the blood of Christ. By entering recovery, admitting our failures, accepting God's forgiveness in Jesus Christ, and seeking to follow his will, we can join this joyful throng of people who have been saved by God's wonderful grace.

7:15-17 This majestic passage describes the heavenly relationship between Christ and his people. They will serve him constantly, but he will always protect them. All their other needs will be met by Christ, the Lamb who is also the Shepherd. In such a close and secure relationship, all the tears of painful oppression, loss, and misunderstanding will be done away with. What wonderful hope these verses offer! By trusting in Jesus Christ, we can hope for a future filled with joy and peace.

8:1-2 The opening of the seventh, and climactic, seal on the scroll of judgment brings a short period of silence. Before the sounding of the seven trumpets and their horrible judgments, the silence offers the opportunity for people to prepare for the incredibly difficult time ahead. Sometimes in recovery we get these "silence before the storm" kind of experiences. Things may be all right at the moment, but we can sense that difficult times lie ahead. We can use these quiet times to get ready for what is about to happen by continuing with our honest personal inventory and entrusting our life—problems and all—to God. If God is with us, no future trial or testing will be too great to overcome.

and fire mixed with blood were thrown down
upon the earth. One-third of the earth was set
on fire so that one-third of the trees were
burned, and all the green grass.
[8,9]Then the second angel blew his trumpet,
and what appeared to be a huge burning
mountain was thrown into the sea, destroying a third of all the ships; and a third of the
sea turned red as blood; and a third of the fish
were killed.
[10]The third angel blew, and a great flaming
star fell from heaven upon a third of the rivers
and springs. [11]The star was called "Bitterness"
because it poisoned a third of all the water on
the earth and many people died.
[12]The fourth angel blew his trumpet, and
immediately a third of the sun was blighted
and darkened, and a third of the moon and
the stars so that the daylight was dimmed by
a third, and the nighttime darkness deepened.
[13]As I watched, I saw a solitary eagle flying
through the heavens crying loudly, "Woe,
woe, woe to the people of the earth because
of the terrible things that will soon happen
when the three remaining angels blow their
trumpets."

CHAPTER 9

Then the fifth angel blew his trumpet, and I
saw one who was fallen to earth from heaven,
and to him was given the key to the bottomless pit. [2]When he opened it, smoke poured
out as though from some huge furnace, and
the sun and air were darkened by the smoke.
[3]Then locusts came from the smoke and
descended onto the earth and were given
power to sting like scorpions. [4]They were told
not to hurt the grass or plants or trees, but to
attack those people who did not have the
mark of God on their foreheads. [5]They were
not to kill them, but to torture them for five
months with agony like the pain of scorpion
stings. [6]In those days men will try to kill
themselves but won't be able to—death will
not come. They will long to die—but death
will flee away!
[7]The locusts looked like horses armored for
battle. They had what looked like golden
crowns on their heads, and their faces looked
like men's. [8]Their hair was long like women's,
and their teeth were those of lions. [9]They
wore breastplates that seemed to be of iron,
and their wings roared like an army of chariots rushing into battle. [10]They had stinging
tails like scorpions, and their power to hurt,
given to them for five months, was in their
tails. [11]Their king is the Prince of the bottomless pit whose name in Hebrew is Abaddon,
and in Greek, Apollyon [and in English, the
Destroyer].
[12]One terror now ends, but there are two
more coming!
[13]The sixth angel blew his trumpet, and I
heard a voice speaking from the four horns of
the golden altar that stands before the throne
of God, [14]saying to the sixth angel, "Release
the four mighty demons held bound at the
great River Euphrates." [15]They had been kept
in readiness for that year and month and day
and hour, and now they were turned loose to
kill a third of all mankind. [16]They led an army
of 200,000,000 warriors—I heard an announcement of how many there were.
[17,18]I saw their horses spread out before me

8:6-13 At the blowing of the trumpets, the people of our dysfunctional and sinful world will suffer the terrible consequences for their sin and the sins of their ancestors before them. There is a day of reckoning for all who reject God's program for living. Many of us have experienced a similar day of reckoning in our own life. Our attitudes and actions led us into a period of great suffering. When we shed our denial, however, Jesus Christ will deliver us from our powerful dependencies and help us escape the terrible judgments described in these verses.

9:1-4 As the fifth trumpet blows, a demonic locust plague will be unleashed. Unlike regular locusts, however, these creatures will attack people, not plants. Notice that God will not allow these creatures to harm everyone—just those not protected by God's seal. As we seek recovery with God's help, we can be secure in the fact that God is able and willing to protect us. He will allow hard times into our life to help us grow. If we continue to trust and obey him, he won't allow us to be destroyed by sin and its terrible consequences.

9:12-21 As the sixth trumpet blows, a demonically inspired army will slaughter one-third of the remaining population of the world (see 6:8). Certainly circumstances would seem completely hopeless to most inhabitants of the earth at this point. They could either humble themselves and begin recovery by faith, or sink into depressed denial. Sadly, we see that only a few will accept God's gracious offer of forgiveness at that late stage in history. We have a similar choice before us today as we face the painful consequences of our sins and destructive habits. We can either give up and fall into an even deeper bondage, or we can recognize how helpless we are and receive God's gift of deliverance and recovery. The choice is ours to make!

in my vision; their riders wore fiery-red
breastplates, though some were sky-blue and
others yellow. The horses' heads looked much
like lions', and smoke and fire and flaming
sulphur billowed from their mouths, killing
one-third of all mankind. 19Their power of
death was not only in their mouths, but in
their tails as well, for their tails were similar to
serpents' heads that struck and bit with fatal
wounds.
20But the men left alive after these plagues
still refused to worship God! They would not
renounce their demon-worship, nor their
idols made of gold and silver, brass, stone, and
wood—which neither see nor hear nor walk!
21Neither did they change their mind and
attitude about all their murders and witchcraft, their immorality and theft.

CHAPTER 10

The Angel with a Small Scroll

Then I saw another mighty angel coming
down from heaven, surrounded by a cloud,
with a rainbow over his head; his face shone
like the sun and his feet flashed with fire. 2And
he held open in his hand a small scroll. He set
his right foot on the sea and his left foot on
the earth 3and gave a great shout—it was
like the roar of a lion—and the seven thunders crashed their reply.
4I was about to write what the thunders said
when a voice from heaven called to me,
"Don't do it. Their words are not to be revealed."
5Then the mighty angel standing on the sea
and land lifted his right hand to heaven 6and
swore by him who lives forever and ever, who
created heaven and everything in it and the
earth and all that it contains and the sea and
its inhabitants, that there should be no more
delay, 7but that when the seventh angel blew
his trumpet, then God's veiled plan—mysterious through the ages ever since it was announced by his servants the prophets—would
be fulfilled.
8Then the voice from heaven spoke to me
again, "Go and get the unrolled scroll from
the mighty angel standing there upon the sea
and land."
9So I approached him and asked him to give
me the scroll. "Yes, take it and eat it," he said.
"At first it will taste like honey, but when you
swallow it, it will make your stomach sour!"
10So I took it from his hand, and ate it! And
just as he had said, it was sweet in my mouth,
but it gave me a stomachache when I swallowed it.
11Then he told me, "You must prophesy
further about many peoples, nations, tribes,
and kings."

CHAPTER 11

The Two Prophets of God

Now I was given a measuring stick and told to
go and measure the temple of God, including
the inner court where the altar stands, and to
count the number of worshipers. 2"But do not
measure the outer court," I was told, "for it
has been turned over to the nations. They will
trample the Holy City for forty-two months.

10:1-4 As the mighty angel begins to shout out the contents of the additional scroll, John assumes that he is to record all that he hears. But God intervenes, preventing him from doing so (see Daniel 12:9). This episode reminds us that along with honesty, we need God-directed discretion. In recovery we are told to make amends with those we have wronged, except when to do so would injure them or others. Sometimes we need to hold back and be discreet because telling the whole story or seeking restoration might do lasting damage to someone else. God can help us know when to be discreet, but the guiding principle is that of love. We need to do what is best for others, not just what is best for ourself.

10:8-10 The apostle John was told to eat the scroll, much as the prophet Ezekiel had been instructed to do (see Ezekiel 2:8; 3:1-3). The scroll would be sweet in his mouth, but bitter in his stomach. God's Word to us can sometimes work the same way. It contains a sweet message of deliverance for all who repent, but it also calls us to account for our selfish actions. If we are willing to abide by the wise boundaries that God has set out for us, his Word is filled with promises of joy and peace. If, on the other hand, we choose to reject God's program, his Word will be filled with predictions of judgment.

11:1-13 Like John, the two witnesses described here will serve as God's prophets. During their 1,260-day ministry, they will be protected by God. They will then be killed at the hands of the tyrant from the pit. Notice that God's two prophets are treated even more despicably than Christ, who, in similar circumstances, was at least given a decent burial (see Matthew 27:57-61). In three and a half days, however, God would raise them from the dead, showing that even death cannot thwart his plans. No obstacle is so great that God has to abandon the program he has laid out for the world and its people. We can be confident that God wants us to experience an effective recovery. So if we trust him and follow his plan, no obstacle will be too great for us to overcome.

3And I will give power to my two witnesses to
prophesy 1,260 days clothed in sackcloth."
4These two prophets are the two olive trees,
and two candlesticks standing before the God
of all the earth. 5Anyone trying to harm them
will be killed by bursts of fire shooting from
their mouths. 6They have power to shut the
skies so that no rain will fall during the three
and a half years they prophesy, and to turn
rivers and oceans to blood, and to send every
kind of plague upon the earth as often as they
wish.
7When they complete the three and a half
years of their solemn testimony, the tyrant
who comes out of the bottomless pit will declare war against them and conquer and kill
them; 8,9and for three and a half days their
bodies will be exposed in the streets of Jerusalem (the city fittingly described as "Sodom" or
"Egypt")—the very place where their Lord was
crucified. No one will be allowed to bury
them, and people from many nations will
crowd around to gaze at them. 10And there will
be a worldwide holiday—people everywhere
will rejoice and give presents to each other and
throw parties to celebrate the death of the two
prophets who had tormented them so much!
11But after three and a half days, the spirit
of life from God will enter them, and they will
stand up! And great fear will fall on everyone.
12Then a loud voice will shout from heaven,
"Come up!" And they will rise to heaven in a
cloud as their enemies watch.
13The same hour there will be a terrible
earthquake that levels a tenth of the city,
leaving 7,000 dead. Then everyone left will, in
their terror, give glory to the God of heaven.
14The second woe is past, but the third
quickly follows:

The Seventh Trumpet

15For just then the seventh angel blew his
trumpet, and there were loud voices shouting
down from heaven, "The Kingdom of this
world now belongs to our Lord, and to his
Christ; and he shall reign forever and ever."
16And the twenty-four Elders sitting on
their thrones before God threw themselves
down in worship, saying, 17"We give thanks,
Lord God Almighty, who is and was, for now
you have assumed your great power and have
begun to reign. 18The nations were angry with
you, but now it is your turn to be angry with
them. It is time to judge the dead and reward
your servants—prophets and people alike, all
who fear your Name, both great and small—
and to destroy those who have caused destruction upon the earth."
19Then, in heaven, the temple of God was
opened and the ark of his covenant could be
seen inside. Lightning flashed and thunder
crashed and roared, and there was a great
hailstorm, and the world was shaken by a
mighty earthquake.

CHAPTER 12

The Woman and the Dragon

Then a great pageant appeared in heaven,
portraying things to come. I saw a woman
clothed with the sun, with the moon beneath
her feet, and a crown of twelve stars on her
head. 2She was pregnant and screamed in the
pain of her labor, awaiting her delivery.
3Suddenly a red Dragon appeared, with
seven heads and ten horns, and seven crowns
on his heads. 4His tail drew along behind him
a third of the stars, which he plunged to the
earth. He stood before the woman as she was
about to give birth to her child, ready to eat
the baby as soon as it was born.
5She gave birth to a boy who was to rule all
nations with a heavy hand, and he was
caught up to God and to his throne. 6The
woman fled into the wilderness, where God

11:15-18 The sounding of the seventh trumpet accompanies a proclamation of God's control over his Kingdom. Many among the nations of the earth have been angry with God without just cause, but now it is time for God's righteous anger to be released. Those who have committed themselves to God will be rewarded, while those who have turned their back on him will be judged. The same principle holds true for us. If we reject God and his plan for us, we will have to face his terrible anger. If we commit our life to God, he will lovingly heal us.

12:1-14 The birth of Christ and its opposition by Satan are graphically depicted in this scene. Jesus the Messiah was born into this world to implement God's plan for the world's restoration. Satan had planted the destructive effects of sin into God's good creation by tempting Adam and Eve to sin. So as Jesus was born to reverse the effects of that sin, Satan did all he could to destroy the infant Savior. Thankfully, Satan was unsuccessful and the future Ruler of the world was able to complete his earthly mission. As much as Satan desires to thwart God's plan for the world's recovery, he will not be able to do it. Our personal recovery is an important part of God's plan for cosmic recovery. If we entrust our life to God and follow his program, he will certainly complete the task of recovery in our life.

had prepared a place for her, to take care of her for 1,260 days.

7Then there was war in heaven; Michael and the angels under his command fought the Dragon and his hosts of fallen angels. 8And the Dragon lost the battle and was forced from heaven. 9This great Dragon—the ancient serpent called the devil, or Satan, the one deceiving the whole world—was thrown down onto the earth with all his army.

10Then I heard a loud voice shouting across the heavens, "It has happened at last! God's salvation and the power and the rule, and the authority of his Christ are finally here; for the Accuser of our brothers has been thrown down from heaven onto earth—he accused them day and night before our God. 11They defeated him by the blood of the Lamb and by their testimony; for they did not love their lives but laid them down for him. 12Rejoice, O heavens! You citizens of heaven, rejoice! Be glad! But woe to you people of the world, for the devil has come down to you in great anger, knowing that he has little time."

13And when the Dragon found himself cast down to earth, he persecuted the woman who had given birth to the child. 14But she was given two wings like those of a great eagle, to fly into the wilderness to the place prepared for her, where she was cared for and protected from the Serpent, the Dragon, for three and a half years.

15And from the Serpent's mouth a vast flood of water gushed out and swept toward the woman in an effort to get rid of her; 16but the earth helped her by opening its mouth and swallowing the flood! 17Then the furious Dragon set out to attack the rest of her children—all who were keeping God's commandments and confessing that they belong to Jesus. He stood waiting on an ocean beach.

CHAPTER 13

The Two Strange Creatures

And now, in my vision, I saw a strange Creature rising up out of the sea. It had seven heads and ten horns, and ten crowns upon its horns. And written on each head were blasphemous names, each one defying and insulting God. 2This Creature looked like a leopard but had bear's feet and a lion's mouth! And the Dragon gave him his own power and throne and great authority.

3I saw that one of his heads seemed wounded beyond recovery—but the fatal wound was healed! All the world marveled at this miracle and followed the Creature in awe. 4They worshiped the Dragon for giving him such power, and they worshiped the strange Creature. "Where is there anyone as great as he?" they exclaimed. "Who is able to fight against him?"

5Then the Dragon encouraged the Creature to speak great blasphemies against the Lord; and gave him authority to control the earth for forty-two months. 6All that time he blasphemed God's Name and his temple and all those living in heaven. 7The Dragon gave him power to fight against God's people and to overcome them, and to rule over all nations and language groups throughout the world. 8And all mankind—whose names were not written down before the founding of the world in the slain Lamb's Book of Life —worshiped the evil Creature.

9Anyone who can hear, listen carefully: 10The people of God who are destined for prison will be arrested and taken away; those destined for death will be killed. But do not be dismayed, for here is your opportunity for endurance and confidence.

11Then I saw another strange animal, this one coming up out of the earth, with two little horns like those of a lamb but a fearsome voice like the Dragon's. 12He exercised all the authority of the Creature whose death-wound had been healed, whom he required all the world to worship. 13He did unbelievable miracles such as making fire flame down to earth from the skies while everyone was watching. 14By doing these miracles, he was deceiving people everywhere. He could do these marvelous things whenever the first Creature was there to watch him. And he ordered the people of the world to make a great statue of the first Creature, who was

13:1-10 Some of Satan's primary representatives are described in these verses. For a time, God will allow them free rein in the world, making life difficult for all who trust Christ for salvation. Ever since the days when Jesus Christ walked this earth, Satan has sought to lead people away from the delivering power God offers. The creatures mentioned here are an intensified form of the spirit of antichrist already active in our world. We will face opposition as we seek recovery from addiction and its powerful effects. Satan doesn't want us to succeed at recovery; he only wants to destroy us. Despite the power Satan wields in our world, he cannot remove us from God's loving care. When we trust in God to help us and cooperate with the program he lays out for us, our recovery is assured. Satan and his henchmen won't be able to stand in our way.

fatally wounded and then came back to life. 15He was permitted to give breath to this statue and even make it speak! Then the statue ordered that anyone refusing to worship it must die!

16He required everyone—great and small, rich and poor, slave and free—to be tattooed with a certain mark on the right hand or on the forehead. 17And no one could get a job or even buy in any store without the permit of that mark, which was either the name of the Creature or the code number of his name. 18Here is a puzzle that calls for careful thought to solve it. Let those who are able, interpret this code: the numerical values of the letters in his name add to 666!

CHAPTER 14

The Lamb and a Great Choir

Then I saw a Lamb standing on Mount Zion in Jerusalem, and with him were 144,000 who had his Name and his Father's Name written on their foreheads. 2And I heard a sound from heaven like the roaring of a great waterfall or the rolling of mighty thunder. It was the singing of a choir accompanied by harps.

3This tremendous choir—144,000 strong—sang a wonderful new song in front of the throne of God and before the four Living Beings and the twenty-four Elders; and no one could sing this song except those 144,000 who had been redeemed from the earth. 4For they are spiritually undefiled, pure as virgins, following the Lamb wherever he goes. They have been purchased from among the men on the earth as a consecrated offering to God and the Lamb. 5No falsehood can be charged against them; they are blameless.

Three Angels and Their Messages

6And I saw another angel flying through the heavens, carrying the everlasting Good News to preach to those on earth—to every nation, tribe, language, and people.

7"Fear God," he shouted, "and extol his greatness. For the time has come when he will sit as Judge. Worship him who made the heaven and the earth, the sea and all its sources."

8Then another angel followed him through the skies, saying, "Babylon is fallen, is fallen—that great city—because she seduced the nations of the world and made them share the wine of her intense impurity and sin."

9Then a third angel followed them shouting, "Anyone worshiping the Creature from the sea and his statue, and accepting his mark on the forehead or the hand 10must drink the wine of the anger of God; it is poured out undiluted into God's cup of wrath. And they will be tormented with fire and burning sulphur in the presence of the holy angels and the Lamb. 11The smoke of their torture rises forever and ever, and they will have no relief day or night, for they have worshiped the Creature and his statue, and have been tattooed with the code of his name. 12Let this encourage God's people to endure patiently every trial and persecution, for they are his saints who remain firm to the end in obedience to his commands and trust in Jesus."

A Time of Judgment

13And I heard a voice in the heavens above me saying, "Write this down: At last the time has come for his martyrs to enter into their full reward. Yes, says the Spirit, they are blessed indeed, for now they shall rest from all their toils and trials; for their good deeds follow them to heaven!" 14Then the scene changed, and I saw a white cloud and someone sitting on it who looked like Jesus, who was called

13:11-18 Another Creature representing Satan rises from the earth. Notice that it looks like a lamb, Satan's attempt to copy the appearance of Christ, the Lamb (see 5:6). Notice also that this Creature's miracles copy the amazing deeds that were performed by God's two witnesses (see 11:5-6). Satan is clearly trying to deceive people into thinking this lamb represents the true God. He is trying to sell a counterfeit in order to lead people away from the true deliverer—Jesus Christ. Satan is using this same strategy today. Numerous recovery plans claim to offer the power of deliverance, but only God can truly deliver. If we seek help from some other source, Satan has succeeded in leading us away from the only real Power that can save us. We need to be on guard against the counterfeit solutions that Satan puts before us.

14:1-20 In these verses we see some of the blessings enjoyed by those who trust in Christ (14:1-7, 13-14); then we are shown the terrible consequences of rejecting him (14:8-11, 15-20). The deliverance that God offers us through Jesus Christ is Good News. We are called to rejoice in God's infinite rule, praising him for his greatness and in return receiving eternal rest. If we refuse to acknowledge God's rule and do things our own way, we are headed toward complete destruction. But when we persevere in our faith in Jesus Christ, we will be rewarded by God.

"The Son of Man," with a crown of solid gold upon his head and a sharp sickle in his hand.

[15]Then an angel came from the temple and called out to him, "Begin to use the sickle, for the time has come for you to reap; the harvest is ripe on the earth." [16]So the one sitting on the cloud swung his sickle over the earth, and the harvest was gathered in. [17]After that another angel came from the temple in heaven, and he also had a sharp sickle.

[18]Just then the angel who has power to destroy the world with fire, shouted to the angel with the sickle, "Use your sickle now to cut off the clusters of grapes from the vines of the earth, for they are fully ripe for judgment." [19]So the angel swung his sickle on the earth and loaded the grapes into the great winepress of God's wrath. [20]And the grapes were trodden in the winepress outside the city, and blood flowed out in a stream 200 miles long and as high as a horse's bridle.

CHAPTER 15

And I saw in heaven another mighty pageant showing things to come: Seven angels were assigned to carry down to earth the seven last plagues—and then at last God's anger will be finished.

[2]Spread out before me was what seemed to be an ocean of fire and glass, and on it stood all those who had been victorious over the Evil Creature and his statue and his mark and number. All were holding harps of God, [3,4]and they were singing the song of Moses, the servant of God, and the song of the Lamb:

"Great and marvelous
Are your doings,
Lord God Almighty.
Just and true
Are your ways,
O King of Ages.
Who shall not fear,
O Lord,
And glorify your Name?
For you alone are holy.
All nations will come
And worship before you,
For your righteous deeds
Have been disclosed."

[5]Then I looked and saw that the Holy of Holies of the temple in heaven was thrown wide open!

[6]The seven angels who were assigned to pour out the seven plagues then came from the temple, clothed in spotlessly white linen, with golden belts across their chests. [7]And one of the four Living Beings handed each of them a golden flask filled with the terrible wrath of the Living God who lives forever and forever. [8]The temple was filled with smoke from his glory and power; and no one could enter until the seven angels had completed pouring out the seven plagues.

CHAPTER 16

The Flasks of God's Wrath

And I heard a mighty voice shouting from the temple to the seven angels, "Now go your ways and empty out the seven flasks of the wrath of God upon the earth."

[2]So the first angel left the temple and poured out his flask over the earth, and horrible, malignant sores broke out on everyone who had the mark of the Creature and was worshiping his statue.

[3]The second angel poured out his flask upon the oceans, and they became like the watery blood of a dead man; and everything in all the oceans died.

[4]The third angel poured out his flask upon the rivers and springs and they became blood. [5]And I heard this angel of the waters declaring, "You are just in sending this judgment, O Holy One, who is and was, [6]for your saints and prophets have been martyred and their blood poured out upon the earth; and now, in turn, you have poured out the blood of those who murdered them; it is their just reward."

[7]And I heard the angel of the altar say, "Yes, Lord God Almighty, your punishments are just and true."

[8]Then the fourth angel poured out his flask upon the sun, causing it to scorch all men with its fire. [9]Everyone was burned by this blast of heat, and they cursed the name of God who sent the plagues—they did not change their mind and attitude to give him glory.

15:1–16:21 The seven angels with the flasks of God's judgment are portrayed in these chapters. After their actions, the wrath of God directed against the unbelieving world will be complete (see 6:17; 11:18). As sure as the coming of dawn, the day of reckoning will arrive. Those in denial tend to live as though things will continue forever just the way they are. But there is always a day of reckoning. We cannot live forever under the control of sin or in bondage to powerful addictions. There will be a day when we have to face the truth about our life. We have the choice to submit our life to God and his good plan before the bottom drops out from under us.

10 Then the fifth angel poured out his flask upon the throne of the Creature from the sea, and his kingdom was plunged into darkness. And his subjects gnawed their tongues in anguish, 11 and cursed the God of heaven for their pains and sores, but they refused to repent of all their evil deeds.

12 The sixth angel poured out his flask upon the great River Euphrates and it dried up so that the kings from the east could march their armies westward without hindrance. 13 And I saw three evil spirits disguised as frogs leap from the mouth of the Dragon, the Creature, and his False Prophet. 14 These miracle-working demons conferred with all the rulers of the world to gather them for battle against the Lord on that great coming Judgment Day of God Almighty.

15 "Take note: I will come as unexpectedly as a thief! Blessed are all who are awaiting me, who keep their robes in readiness and will not need to walk naked and ashamed."

16 And they gathered all the armies of the world near a place called, in Hebrew, Armageddon—the Mountain of Megiddo.

17 Then the seventh angel poured out his flask into the air; and a mighty shout came from the throne of the temple in heaven, saying, "It is finished!" 18 Then the thunder crashed and rolled, and lightning flashed; and there was a great earthquake of a magnitude unprecedented in human history. 19 The great city of "Babylon" split into three sections, and cities around the world fell in heaps of rubble; and so all of "Babylon's" sins were remembered in God's thoughts, and she was punished to the last drop of anger in the cup of the wine of the fierceness of his wrath. 20 And islands vanished, and mountains flattened out, 21 and there was an incredible hailstorm from heaven; hailstones weighing a hundred pounds fell from the sky onto the people below, and they cursed God because of the terrible hail.

CHAPTER 17

A Prostitute on a Scarlet Animal

One of the seven angels who had poured out the plagues came over and talked with me. "Come with me," he said, "and I will show you what is going to happen to the Notorious Prostitute, who sits upon the many waters of the world. 2 The kings of the world have had immoral relations with her, and the people of the earth have been made drunk by the wine of her immorality."

3 So the angel took me in spirit into the wilderness. There I saw a woman sitting on a scarlet animal that had seven heads and ten horns, written all over with blasphemies against God. 4 The woman wore purple and scarlet clothing and beautiful jewelry made of gold and precious gems and pearls, and held in her hand a golden goblet full of obscenities:

5 A mysterious caption was written on her forehead: "Babylon the Great, Mother of Prostitutes and of Idol Worship Everywhere around the World."

6 I could see that she was drunk—drunk with the blood of the martyrs of Jesus she had killed. I stared at her in horror.

7 "Why are you so surprised?" the angel asked. "I'll tell you who she is and what the animal she is riding represents. 8 He was alive but isn't now. And yet, soon he will come up out of the bottomless pit and go to eternal destruction; and the people of earth, whose names have not been written in the Book of Life before the world began, will be dumbfounded at his reappearance after being dead.

9 "And now think hard: his seven heads represent a certain city built on seven hills where this woman has her residence. 10 They also represent seven kings. Five have already fallen, the sixth now reigns, and the seventh is yet to come, but his reign will be brief. 11 The scarlet animal that died is the eighth king, having reigned before as one of the seven; after his second reign, he too, will go to his doom. 12 His ten horns are ten kings who have not yet risen to power; they will be appointed to their kingdoms for one brief moment, to reign with him. 13 They will all sign a treaty giving their power and strength to him. 14 Together they will wage war against the Lamb, and the Lamb will conquer them; for he is Lord over all lords, and King of kings, and his

---

17:1–19:5 Just as the previous chapters portray God's judgment of those who refuse to believe in Christ, these chapters foretell God's conquest over Satan's henchmen. Even the power of Satan will be overthrown by God when the time is ripe. The devil's representatives will be called to account for the suffering they imposed on God's people. God's team will always win out in the end. To be on the winning side, we need to admit our need for God and trust him to deliver us from the power of sin. That way we won't weep when the evil powers in this world are destroyed; we will rejoice instead.

people are the called and chosen and faithful ones.

15"The oceans, lakes, and rivers that the woman is sitting on represent masses of people of every race and nation.

16"The scarlet animal and his ten horns—which represent ten kings who will reign with him—all hate the woman, and will attack her and leave her naked and ravaged by fire. 17For God will put a plan into their minds, a plan that will carry out his purposes: They will mutually agree to give their authority to the scarlet animal so that the words of God will be fulfilled. 18And this woman you saw in your vision represents the great city that rules over the kings of the earth."

CHAPTER 18

The Fall of Babylon

After all this I saw another angel come down from heaven with great authority, and the earth grew bright with his splendor.

2He gave a mighty shout, "Babylon the Great is fallen, is fallen; she has become a den of demons, a haunt of devils and every kind of evil spirit. 3For all the nations have drunk the fatal wine of her intense immorality. The rulers of earth have enjoyed themselves with her, and businessmen throughout the world have grown rich from all her luxurious living."

4Then I heard another voice calling from heaven, "Come away from her, my people; do not take part in her sins, or you will be punished with her. 5For her sins are piled as high as heaven, and God is ready to judge her for her crimes. 6Do to her as she has done to you, and more—give double penalty for all her evil deeds. She brewed many a cup of woe for others—give twice as much to her. 7She has lived in luxury and pleasure—match it now with torments and with sorrows. She boasts, 'I am queen upon my throne. I am no helpless widow. I will not experience sorrow.' 8Therefore the sorrows of death and mourning and famine shall overtake her in a single day, and she shall be utterly consumed by fire; for mighty is the Lord who judges her."

9And the world leaders who took part in her immoral acts and enjoyed her favors will mourn for her as they see the smoke rising from her charred remains. 10They will stand far off, trembling with fear and crying out, "Alas, Babylon, that mighty city! In one moment her judgment fell."

11The merchants of the earth will weep and mourn for her, for there is no one left to buy their goods. 12She was their biggest customer for gold and silver, precious stones, pearls, finest linens, purple silks, and scarlet; and every kind of perfumed wood, and ivory goods, and most expensive wooden carvings, and brass, and iron, and marble; 13and spices, and perfumes, and incense, ointment, and frankincense, wine, olive oil, and fine flour; wheat, cattle, sheep, horses, chariots, and slaves—and even the souls of men.

14"All the fancy things you loved so much are gone," they cry. "The dainty luxuries and splendor that you prized so much will never be yours again. They are gone forever."

15And so the merchants who have become wealthy by selling her these things shall stand at a distance, fearing danger to themselves, weeping and crying, 16"Alas, that great city, so beautiful—like a woman clothed in finest purple and scarlet linens, decked out with gold and precious stones and pearls! 17In one moment, all the wealth of the city is gone!"

And all the shipowners and captains of the merchant ships and crews will stand a long way off, 18crying as they watch the smoke ascend, and saying, "Where in all the world is there another city such as this?" 19And they will throw dust on their heads in their sorrow and say, "Alas, alas, for that great city! She made us all rich from her great wealth. And now in a single hour all is gone. . . ."

20But you, O heaven, rejoice over her fate; and you, O children of God and the prophets and the apostles! For at last God has given judgment against her for you.

21Then a mighty angel picked up a boulder shaped like a millstone and threw it into the ocean and shouted, "Babylon, that great city, shall be thrown away as I have thrown away this stone, and she shall disappear forever. 22Never again will the sound of music be there—no more pianos, saxophones, and trumpets. No industry of any kind will ever

19:6–20:10 In these verses we are given a glimpse of Christ, the conquering King. He will return to deliver all those who believe in him. Though great human armies led by Satan and his henchmen will gather to resist, there will be no contest. Jesus Christ will ride to an overwhelming victory. As Christ triumphs over Satan and his armies, he will vindicate our individual battles against sin and addiction. What a glorious day that will be! All our efforts to overcome our dependencies will be supported by Christ's final conquest over sin and evil. Satan and his helpers will be bound forever!

again exist there, and there will be no more
milling of the grain. 23Dark, dark will be her
nights; not even a lamp in a window will ever
be seen again. No more joyous wedding bells
and happy voices of the bridegrooms and the
brides. Her businessmen were known around
the world, and she deceived all nations with
her sorceries. 24And she was responsible for
the blood of all the martyred prophets and
the saints."

CHAPTER 19

The Lamb's Wedding Feast

After this I heard the shouting of a vast crowd
in heaven, "Hallelujah! Praise the Lord! Salvation is from our God. Honor and authority
belong to him alone; 2for his judgments are
just and true. He has punished the Great Prostitute who corrupted the earth with her sin;
and he has avenged the murder of his servants."
3Again and again their voices rang, "Praise
the Lord! The smoke from her burning ascends forever and forever!"
4Then the twenty-four Elders and four Living Beings fell down and worshiped God, who
was sitting upon the throne, and said, "Amen!
Hallelujah! Praise the Lord!"
5And out of the throne came a voice that
said, "Praise our God, all you his servants,
small and great, who fear him."
6Then I heard again what sounded like the
shouting of a huge crowd, or like the waves of
a hundred oceans crashing on the shore, or
like the mighty rolling of great thunder,
"Praise the Lord. For the Lord our God, the
Almighty, reigns. 7Let us be glad and rejoice
and honor him; for the time has come for the
wedding banquet of the Lamb, and his bride
has prepared herself. 8She is permitted to wear
the cleanest and whitest and finest of linens."
(Fine linen represents the good deeds done by
the people of God.)
9And the angel dictated this sentence to
me: "Blessed are those who are invited to the
wedding feast of the Lamb." And he added,
"God himself has stated this."
10Then I fell down at his feet to worship
him, but he said, "No! Don't! For I am a
servant of God just as you are, and as your
brother Christians are, who testify of their
faith in Jesus. Worship God. The purpose of
all prophecy and of all I have shown you is to
tell about Jesus."

The Rider on the White Horse

11Then I saw heaven opened and a white

God's Mercy

BIBLE READING: Revelation 20:11-15

We made a searching and fearless moral inventory of ourselves.

We may wish we could avoid making a moral inventory; it's normal to want to hide from personal examination. But in our heart we probably sense that a day will come when we will have to face the truth about our life.

The Bible tells us there is a day coming when an inventory will be made of every life. No one will be able to hide. In John's vision he saw "a great white throne and the one who sat upon it, from whose face the earth and sky fled away, but they found no place to hide. I saw the dead, great and small, standing before God; and The Books were opened, including the Book of Life. And the dead were judged according to the things written in The Books, each according to the deeds he had done. . . . And if anyone's name was not found recorded in the Book of Life, he was thrown into the Lake of Fire" (Revelation 20:11-12, 15).

It is best to do our own moral inventory now to make sure we are ready for the one to come. Anyone whose name is in the Book of Life will be saved. This includes all whose sins have been atoned for by the death of Jesus. Those who refuse God's offer of mercy are left to be judged on the basis of their own deeds recorded in "The Books." No one will pass that test! Perhaps now is a good time to make sure our name is in the right book. Knowing that our life is covered with God's forgiveness can help us examine it fearlessly. ***Turn to Step Five, page 51, Genesis 38.***

horse standing there; and the one sitting on
the horse was named Faithful and True—the
one who justly punishes and makes war.
12His eyes were like flames, and on his head
were many crowns. A name was written on
his forehead, and only he knew its meaning. 13He was clothed with garments dipped
in blood, and his title was "The Word of
God." 14The armies of heaven, dressed in
finest linen, white and clean, followed him
on white horses.
15In his mouth he held a sharp sword to
strike down the nations; he ruled them with
an iron grip; and he trod the winepress of the
fierceness of the wrath of Almighty God. 16On
his robe and thigh was written this title: "King
of Kings and Lord of Lords."
17Then I saw an angel standing in the sunshine, shouting loudly to the birds, "Come!
Gather together for the supper of the Great
God! 18Come and eat the flesh of kings, and
captains, and great generals; of horses and
riders; and of all humanity, both great and
small, slave and free."
19Then I saw the Evil Creature gathering the
governments of the earth and their armies to
fight against the one sitting on the horse and
his army. 20And the Evil Creature was captured, and with him the False Prophet, who
could do mighty miracles when the Evil Creature was present—miracles that deceived all
who had accepted the Evil Creature's mark,
and who worshiped his statue. Both of
them—the Evil Creature and his False
Prophet—were thrown alive into the Lake of
Fire that burns with sulphur. 21And their entire army was killed with the sharp sword in
the mouth of the one riding the white horse,
and all the birds of heaven were gorged with
their flesh.

CHAPTER 20

The Binding of Satan

Then I saw an angel come down from heaven
with the key to the bottomless pit and a
heavy chain in his hand. 2He seized the
Dragon—that old Serpent, the devil, Satan—
and bound him in chains for a thousand
years, 3and threw him into the bottomless pit,
which he then shut and locked so that he
could not fool the nations any more until the
thousand years were finished. Afterwards
he would be released again for a little while.
4Then I saw thrones, and sitting on them
were those who had been given the right to
judge. And I saw the souls of those who had
been beheaded for their testimony about
Jesus, for proclaiming the Word of God, and
who had not worshiped the Creature or his
statue, nor accepted his mark on their foreheads or their hands. They had come to life
again and now they reigned with Christ for a
thousand years.
5This is the First Resurrection. (The rest of
the dead did not come back to life until the
thousand years had ended.) 6Blessed and holy
are those who share in the First Resurrection.
For them the Second Death holds no terrors,
for they will be priests of God and of Christ,
and shall reign with him a thousand years.

Satan's Final Destruction

7When the thousand years end, Satan will be
let out of his prison. 8He will go out to deceive
the nations of the world and gather them
together, with Gog and Magog, for battle—a
mighty host, numberless as sand along the
shore. 9They will go up across the broad plain
of the earth and surround God's people and
the beloved city of Jerusalem on every side.

20:11-15 At the climactic "white throne judgment," those who reject God and his ways will have to face eternal consequences. All those who believe in Christ, however, will be shown amazing grace. Most of us expect our judgment to be based upon whether we are guilty or not. At this judgment, though, everyone is guilty. The people who believe in Christ will be forgiven; the people who choose to go their own way will be judged. No matter who we are or how terrible our past, we can have our name written in the Book of Life. We cannot earn a place in that book; we can only receive it as a gift. By admitting our failures, entrusting our life to God in Jesus Christ, and building a new life according to God's will, we are made a member of God's family. Those who look to other solutions to their problems, however, are headed to a place of eternal torment.

21:1-7 What hope this scene gives us! Ever since the first sin in the Garden of Eden, God has been working to restore his earth to its original perfection. He even sent his Son to suffer and die to overcome the power of sin and death and to begin the process of healing. It is God's program to make old things new! By following his will for our life, we become part of God's plan of restoration. Here we see that God will restore the earth and satisfy everyone who belongs to him. The Water of Life will spring forth, healing our soul from its bondage to sin. This passage shows us what it will be like when Christ returns. But by believing in Christ today, we can receive him into our life and begin this restoration process without delay.

READ REVELATION 21:3-6

GOD grant me the serenity
to accept the things I cannot change
the courage to change the things I can
and the wisdom to know the difference
AMEN

As we think about making changes in our life, we probably find ourself dwelling on the defects in our character.

Removing our defects may seem to be an overwhelming task, despite the fact that God has promised to do the work. Perhaps if we could just catch a glimpse of life beyond recovery, our hope would be revived. The apostle Paul wrote, "And I am sure that God who began the good work within you will keep right on helping you grow in his grace until his task within you is finally finished" (Philippians 1:6).

The apostle John wrote, "I heard a loud shout from the throne saying, 'Look, the home of God is now among men, and he will live with them and they will be his people; yes, God himself will be among them. He will wipe away all tears from their eyes, and there shall be no more death, nor sorrow, nor crying, nor pain. All of that has gone forever.' And the one sitting on the throne said, 'See, I am making all things new!' And then he said . . . 'Write this down, for what I tell you is trustworthy and true: It is finished! I am the A and the Z—the Beginning and the End. I will give to the thirsty the springs of the Water of Life—as a gift!'" (Revelation 21:3-6).

There is hope for all of us, no matter how terrible the problems we face. Someday all our defects will be gone; all things will be made new; the thirst of our soul will be quenched by the Water of Life. ***End of the Serenity Prayer reading plan.***

But fire from God in heaven will flash down
on the attacking armies and consume them.
[10]Then the devil who had betrayed them
will again be thrown into the Lake of Fire
burning with sulphur where the Creature and
False Prophet are, and they will be tormented
day and night forever and ever.

The Final Judgment
[11]And I saw a great white throne and the one
who sat upon it, from whose face the earth
and sky fled away, but they found no place to
hide. [12]I saw the dead, great and small, standing before God; and The Books were opened,
including the Book of Life. And the dead were
judged according to the things written in The
Books, each according to the deeds he had
done. [13]The oceans surrendered the bodies
buried in them; and the earth and the underworld gave up the dead in them. Each was
judged according to his deeds. [14]And Death
and Hell were thrown into the Lake of Fire.
This is the Second Death—the Lake of Fire.
[15]And if anyone's name was not found recorded in the Book of Life, he was thrown
into the Lake of Fire.

CHAPTER 21
The New Earth
Then I saw a new earth (with no oceans!) and
a new sky, for the present earth and sky had
disappeared. [2]And I, John, saw the Holy City,
the new Jerusalem, coming down from God
out of heaven. It was a glorious sight, beautiful as a bride at her wedding.
[3]I heard a loud shout from the throne saying, "Look, the home of God is now among
men, and he will live with them and they will
be his people; yes, God himself will be among
them. [4]He will wipe away all tears from their
eyes, and there shall be no more death, nor

sorrow, nor crying, nor pain. All of that has
gone forever."
[5]And the one sitting on the throne said,
"See, I am making all things new!" And then
he said to me, "Write this down, for what I tell
you is trustworthy and true: [6]It is finished! I
am the A and the Z—the Beginning and the
End. I will give to the thirsty the springs of the
Water of Life—as a gift! [7]Everyone who conquers will inherit all these blessings, and I will
be his God and he will be my son. [8]But cowards who turn back from following me, and
those who are unfaithful to me, and the corrupt, and murderers, and the immoral, and
those conversing with demons, and idol worshipers and all liars—their doom is in the Lake
that burns with fire and sulphur. This is the
Second Death."

The New Jerusalem

[9]Then one of the seven angels who had emptied the flasks containing the seven last
plagues came and said to me, "Come with me
and I will show you the bride, the Lamb's
wife."
[10]In a vision he took me to a towering
mountain peak, and from there I watched
that wondrous city, the holy Jerusalem, descending out of the skies from God. [11]It was
filled with the glory of God and flashed and
glowed like a precious gem, crystal clear like
jasper. [12]Its walls were broad and high, with
twelve gates guarded by twelve angels. And
the names of the twelve tribes of Israel were
written on the gates. [13]There were three gates
on each side—north, south, east, and west.
[14]The walls had twelve foundation stones, and
on them were written the names of the twelve
apostles of the Lamb.
[15]The angel held in his hand a golden measuring stick to measure the city and its gates
and walls. [16]When he measured it, he found it
was a square as wide as it was long; in fact it
was in the form of a cube, for its height was
exactly the same as its other dimensions—
1,500 miles each way. [17]Then he measured the
thickness of the walls and found them to be
216 feet across (the angel called out these
measurements to me, using standard units).
[18-20]The city itself was pure, transparent gold
like glass! The wall was made of jasper, and
was built on twelve layers of foundation
stones inlaid with gems: the first layer with
jasper; the second with sapphire; the third
with chalcedony; the fourth with emerald;
the fifth with sardonyx; the sixth layer with
sardus; the seventh with chrysolite; the
eighth with beryl; the ninth with topaz; the
tenth with chrysoprase; the eleventh with
jacinth; the twelfth with amethyst.
[21]The twelve gates were made of pearls—
each gate from a single pearl! And the main
street was pure, transparent gold, like glass.
[22]No temple could be seen in the city, for
the Lord God Almighty and the Lamb are
worshiped in it everywhere. [23]And the city has
no need of sun or moon to light it, for the
glory of God and of the Lamb illuminate it.
[24]Its light will light the nations of the earth,
and the rulers of the world will come and

21:7-8 At the conclusion of these wonderful promises of restoration, we are reminded that some will mourn at Christ's return. Those who have rejected God and opposed him by selfish and ungodly living will suffer the consequences for their actions. If we remain enslaved to our dependencies, we are headed for that terrible end. Rejecting God's offer of healing will lead to an eternity of suffering—the Second Death. But we can choose to stop being controlled by ungodly people and destructive substances and put our life into God's hands. Only he has the power to deliver us from the power of sin and addiction. If we rely on him, he can restore our life and make us a significant part of his plan for restoring his created world.

21:10-27 The New Jerusalem is portrayed here as the radiant bride of the Lamb (see 21:2). Notice that the eternal city has twelve gates, representing the twelve tribes of Israel (see 7:4-8), and twelve foundation stones, representing the twelve apostles of Christ. Thus, the city—the bride—represents the people of God. We as the community of faith are members of the church, the bride of Christ. What a wonderful picture of grace! No matter how many mistakes we have made in the past, God forgives us through Christ, and we are brought into an intimate relationship with God. We can begin a healing relationship with God today by entrusting our life to God in Jesus Christ.

22:1-5 These verses are a climax to the book of Revelation, portraying the eternal state as a new and better Garden of Eden (see Genesis 2–3). God has accomplished his desire to re-create his broken creation. God's healing power will be easily accessible, and an intimate, face-to-face relationship with God will be the norm. God's presence will bring light to every dark corner, making cruelty and deception impossibilities in his new world. What can only be a dream in our present sinful world will then be eternal reality. What a source of hope this picture can be for us! No matter how bad our life is now, there is hope for the future. If we accept the wonderful offer of salvation that God holds out to us in Jesus Christ, we will someday be a part of that blessed world.

bring their glory to it. [25]Its gates never close; they stay open all day long—and there is no night! [26]And the glory and honor of all the nations shall be brought into it. [27]Nothing evil will be permitted in it—no one immoral or dishonest—but only those whose names are written in the Lamb's Book of Life.

CHAPTER 22

The River of Life

And he pointed out to me a river of pure Water of Life, clear as crystal, flowing from the throne of God and the Lamb, [2]coursing down the center of the main street. On each side of the river grew Trees of Life, bearing twelve crops of fruit, with a fresh crop each month; the leaves were used for medicine to heal the nations.

[3]There shall be nothing in the city that is evil; for the throne of God and of the Lamb will be there, and his servants will worship him. [4]And they shall see his face; and his name shall be written on their foreheads.
[5]And there will be no night there—no need for lamps or sun—for the Lord God will be their light; and they shall reign forever and ever.

The Promise of Christ's Return

[6,7]Then the angel said to me, "These words are trustworthy and true: 'I am coming soon!' God, who tells his prophets what the future holds, has sent his angel to tell you this will happen soon. Blessed are those who believe it and all else written in the scroll."

[8]I, John, saw and heard all these things, and fell down to worship the angel who showed them to me; [9]but again he said, "No, don't do anything like that. I, too, am a servant of Jesus as you are, and as your brothers the prophets are, as well as all those who heed the truth stated in this book. Worship God alone."

[10]Then he instructed me, "Do not seal up what you have written, for the time of fulfillment is near. [11]And when that time comes, all doing wrong will do it more and more; the vile will become more vile; good men will be better; those who are holy will continue on in greater holiness."

[12]"See, I am coming soon, and my reward is with me, to repay everyone according to the deeds he has done. [13]I am the A and the Z, the Beginning and the End, the First and Last.
[14]Blessed forever are all who are washing their robes, to have the right to enter in through the gates of the city and to eat the fruit from the Tree of Life.

Forgiveness

READ REVELATION 22:1-5

We all suffer from brokenness in our life, in our relationship with God, and in our relationships with others. Brokenness tends to weigh us down and can easily lead us back into our addictions. Recovery isn't complete until all the areas of brokenness are mended.

God's ultimate plan for us and our world involves our complete healing. In Revelation, the apostle John saw a vision of a new heavens and new earth where this ultimate healing will take place: "And [the angel] pointed out to me a river of pure Water of Life, clear as crystal, flowing from the throne of God and the Lamb. . . . On each side of the river grew Trees of Life . . . the leaves were used for medicine to heal the nations" (Revelation 22:1-2).

Although we know that God will heal all things when he returns to rule, we still need to take steps toward mending the brokenness right now. Jesus taught, "So if you are standing before the altar in the Temple, offering a sacrifice to God, and suddenly remember that a friend has something against you, leave your sacrifice there beside the altar and go and apologize and be reconciled to him, and then come and offer your sacrifice to God" (Matthew 5:23-24).

Giving and receiving forgiveness is an essential part of our present healing. This requires that we make peace with God, within ourself, and with others whom we have alienated. Once we go through the process of making amends, we must keep our mind and heart open to anyone we may have overlooked. God will often remind us of relationships that need attention. When these come to mind, we should stop everything and go to those we have offended, seeking to repair the damage.
End of the Recovery Principle reading plan.

15"Outside the city are those who have
strayed away from God, and the sorcerers and
the immoral and murderers and idolaters,
and all who love to lie, and do so.
16"I, Jesus, have sent my angel to you to tell
the churches all these things. I am both
David's Root and his Descendant. I am the
bright Morning Star. 17The Spirit and the bride
say, 'Come.' Let each one who hears them say
the same, 'Come.' Let the thirsty one come—
anyone who wants to; let him come and drink
the Water of Life without charge. 18And I solemnly declare to everyone who reads this
book: If anyone adds anything to what is
written here, God shall add to him the
plagues described in this book. 19And if anyone subtracts any part of these prophecies,
God shall take away his share in the Tree of
Life, and in the Holy City just described.
20"He who has said all these things declares:
Yes, I am coming soon!"

Amen! Come, Lord Jesus!

21The grace of our Lord Jesus Christ be with
you all. Amen!

22:20-21 It is unhealthy to harbor unrealistic dreams, living in a future that will never come about. But it is very healthy for us to anchor our new life and recovery in the certainty that Christ is coming again. By trusting Christ with our future, we can better deal with our past and live a more productive present. We, like the apostle John, can pray for Christ to return soon, because we know for certain that he will come. This will not only give us hope to persevere during tough times; it will also enhance the growth of our personal relationship with him. As we trust in him, having the hope of meeting him face-to-face, we will grow closer to him. Christ's unconditional acceptance and power will then continually undergird our recovery process.

TOPICAL INDEX

This index locates the notes, profiles, devotionals, and recovery themes related to key issues in recovery. Page numbers are provided to make it easy to find all the features listed. Related issues are named in parentheses to make an expanded study on any topic a simple task. For additional information, see the other specialized indexes that follow this topical index: Index to Recovery Profiles, Index to Twelve Step Devotionals, Index to Recovery Principle Devotionals, Index to Serenity Prayer Devotionals, Index to Recovery Reflections.

CHOICES *(see also Freedom)*

CODEPENDENCY

COMFORT *(see also Holy Spirit, Peace)*

COMMITMENTS *(see also Promises, Relationships)*

CONFRONTATION

▶ NOTES

▶ PROFILES

▶ TWELVE STEP DEVOTIONALS

▶ RECOVERY PRINCIPLE DEVOTIONALS

▶ RECOVERY THEMES IN...

CONSCIENCE *(see also Guilt)*

▶ NOTES

▶ TWELVE STEP DEVOTIONALS

CONSEQUENCES *(see also Judgment)*

▶ NOTES

CONTENTMENT *(see also Peace)*

CONTROL *(see Self-Control)*

COUNSELORS *(see Mentors)*

COURAGE *(see also Fear)*

CRITICISM *(see also Blame, Communication)*

DECEPTION

DECISIONS *(see Choices)*

DELAYED GRATIFICATION *(see also Patience, Self-Control)*

DELIVERANCE *(see Salvation)*

DENIAL *(see also Blame, Honesty, Truth)*

DEPENDENCIES *(see also Drinking)*

DEPRESSION *(see Discouragement)*

DESCENDANTS *(see Inheritance)*

DESPAIR *(see Discouragement)*

DILIGENCE *(see Perseverance)*

DISCIPLINE *(see also Consequences, Self-Discipline)*

DISCOURAGEMENT *(see also Rejection, Sadness)*

DIVORCE *(see Marriage)*

DOUBT *(see also Faith)*

FAITH *(see also Doubt, Trust)*

FAVORITISM *(see Partiality)*

FEAR *(see also Worry)*

FELLOWSHIP *(see also Accountability, Mentors)*

FORGIVENESS *(see also Repentance, Restoration)*

FREEDOM *(see also Choices, Bondage)*

FRIENDSHIP *(see also Mentors, Peer Pressure)*

FUN *(see Enjoyment)*

GIVING *(see Service)*

GOD'S POWER

GOD'S SUFFICIENCY *(see God's Power)*

GOD'S WILL *(see also Guidance)*

GOD'S WORD *(see also Guidance, Wisdom)*

GOSSIP *(see also Communication, Lying)*

GRACE *(see also Legalism)*

HABITS *(see Dependencies)*

HAPPINESS *(see also Contentment, Enjoyment, Joy)*

HARDHEARTEDNESS *(see Denial)*

HATRED *(see also Anger, Bitterness, Revenge)*

HEALING *(see also Wholeness)*

HELPLESSNESS *(see Powerlessness)*

HITTING BOTTOM *(see also Consequences, Discouragement)*

HOLY SPIRIT

HOMOSEXUALITY *(see Sexuality)*

HONESTY *(see also Lying, Truth)*

HOPE

IDOLATRY

INADEQUACY *(see Powerlessness)*

INCEST *(see also Abuse)*

INFERIORITY *(see Self-Esteem)*

INHERITANCE *(see also Family, Parenting)*

INSECURITY *(see Fear)*

INTEGRITY *(see Honesty)*

INVENTORY *(see also Repentance)*

JEALOUSY

JOY *(see also Enjoyment, Happiness)*

JUDGMENT *(see also Consequences)*

JUSTICE *(see Fairness)*

KINDNESS

LAZINESS *(see Procrastination)*

LEGALISM *(see also Freedom, Grace)*

LIES *(see Lying)*

LONELINESS

LOVE

LOYALTY *(see Faithfulness, Friendship)*

LUST

LYING *(see also Denial, Honesty, Truth)*

MARRIAGE *(see also Friendship, Relationships)*

MATERIALISM *(see also Greed)*

MEDITATION *(see also Prayer)*

MENTORS *(see also Accountability, Friendship)*

MERCY

MIRACLES *(see also God's Power)*

OBEDIENCE *(see also Submission)*

OBSTACLES *(see also Trials)*

OCCULT

OPPRESSION

PARDON *(see Forgiveness)*

PARENTING *(see also Family, Inheritance)*

PEER PRESSURE *(see also Friendship, Temptation)*

PERFECTIONISM

PERSEVERANCE *(see also Patience, Self-Discipline)*

PERSISTENCE *(see Perseverance)*

POWERLESSNESS *(see also Hopelessness)*

PRAISE *(see also Celebration, Gratitude, Worship)*

PRAYER *(see also Praise, Worship)*

PREJUDICE *(see Partiality)*

PRIDE *(see also Humility, Self-Sufficiency)*

PROCRASTINATION *(see also Rationalization)*

PROMISES *(see also Commitments)*

PUNISHMENT *(see Consequences, Judgment)*

RELATIONSHIPS *(see also Marriage)*

REMEMBERING *(see also Inheritance)*

REPENTANCE *(see also Forgiveness, Inventory)*

REPUTATION

RESPONSIBILITY *(see also Accountability)*

REST *(see also Peace, Serenity)*

RESTITUTION

SADNESS *(see also Discouragement, Rejection)*

SALVATION *(see also Redemption, Transformation)*

SELF-EXAMINATION *(see Inventory)*

SELF-HATRED *(see also Self-Esteem, Suicide)*

SELF-IMAGE *(see Self-Esteem)*

SELFISHNESS *(see also Greed, Materialism)*

SELF-PERCEPTION *(see Self-Esteem)*

SELF-PROTECTION *(see also Boundaries)*

SELF-SUFFICIENCY *(see also Pride)*

SELF-WORTH *(see Self-Esteem)*

SERENITY *(see also Peace, Rest)*

SERVICE *(see also Witnessing)*

SEXUALITY *(see also Marriage)*

SHAME

SHARING *(see Witness)*

SIN *(see also Character Defects)*

SUFFICIENCY *(see Adequacy, Self-Sufficiency)*

SUICIDE *(see also Self-Hatred)*

TEMPTATION *(see also Trials)*

THANKFULNESS *(see Gratitude)*

TRANSFORMATION *(see also God's Power, Salvation)*

TRIALS *(see also Obstacles)*

TRUST *(see also Doubt, Faith)*

TRUTH *(see also Honesty, Wisdom)*

UNITY *(see Fellowship, Reconciliation)*

VICTIMIZATION *(see Abuse, Incest, Oppression)*

VOWS *(see Promises)*

WAITING *(see Patience, Perseverance)*

WHOLENESS *(see also Healing, Peace)*

WISDOM *(see also Truth)*

WITNESSING *(see also Communication)*

WORRY *(see also Fear)*

WORSHIP *(see also Celebration, Praise, Prayer)*

INDEX TO RECOVERY PROFILES

INDEX TO TWELVE STEP DEVOTIONALS

INDEX TO RECOVERY PRINCIPLE DEVOTIONALS

Serenity

INDEX TO SERENITY PRAYER DEVOTIONALS

INDEX TO RECOVERY REFLECTIONS